N

C000089469

AISNE — Aisne — Oise

Reims
Épernay
MARNE
Paris
SEINE-
ET-
MARNE
CHAMPAGNE
AUBE
Troyes
les Riceys
HAUTE-
MARNE
LOIRET
YONNE
Auxerre
Chablis
BOURGOGNE
CÔTE-D'OR
Dijon
Sancerre
NIÈVRE
Beaune
VALLÉE
CHER
BOURGOGNE
SAÔNE-ET-LOIRE
ALLIER
Mâcon
Saint-Pourçain-
sur-Sioule
AIN
Villefranche-
sur-Saône
Clermont-
Ferrand
Roanne
BEAUJOLAIS
CENTRE
RHÔNE
Lyon
PUY-DE-DÔME
LOIRE
Vienne
VALLÉE
Valence
ARDÈCHE
DU
DRÔME
Die
Montélimar
AVEYRON
RHÔNE
Orange
Avignon
GARD
VAUCLUSE
Nîmes
TARN
LANGUEDOC
BOUCHES-
DU-RHÔNE
Montpellier
HÉRAULT
Béziers
Aix-
en-Provence
Marseille
Narbonne
AUDE
Limoux
Toulon
ROUSSILLON
Perpignan
Banyuls
PYRÉNÉES-
ORIENTALES

MOSELLE
EST
BAS-RHIN
Strasbourg
Toul
MEURTHE-
ET-MOSELLE
ALSACE
Colmar
HAUT-
RHIN

Besançon
Arbois
JURA
JURA
HAUTE-
SAVOIE
Annecy
SAVOIE
Chambéry
SAVOIE

ALPES-
DE-HAUTE-
PROVENCE
ALPES-
MARITIMES
PROVENCE
Draguignan
Nice
VAR

Patrimonio
Bastia
HAUTE-
CORSE
CORSE
Ajaccio
CORSE-
DU-SUD

The

HACHETTE

Guide to

FRENCH

WINES

2004

THE HACHETTE GUIDE TO FRENCH WINES 2004

Copyright © 2003, Hachette Livre (Hachette Pratique), Paris
Copyright © English translation Octopus Publishing Group Ltd 2003

This edition published in 2003 by Mitchell Beazley, an imprint of Octopus Publishing Group Limited, 2–4 Heron Quays, London E14 4JP.

ISBN: 1 84000 908 X

Editorial director: Catherine Montalbetti

With the help of: Christian Asselin, INRA, Vigne et Vin research unit; Jean-François Bazin; Claude Bérenguer; Richard Bertin, oenologist; Pierre Bidan, lecturer at ENSA, Montpellier; Jean Bisson, former director of the INRA viticultural centre; Jean-Pierre Callède, oenologist; Pierre Casamayor, Conference Director at the Science Faculty, Toulouse; Béatrice de Chabert, oenologist; Robert Cordonnier, Research Director at INRA; Jean-Pierre Deroudille; Michel Dovaz; Michel Feuillat, lecturer at the Science Faculty, Dijon; Bernard Hébrard, oenologist; Pierre Huglin, Research Director at INRA; Robert Lala, oenologist; Antoine Lebègue; Jean-Pierre Martinez, Chamber of Agriculture, Loir-et-Cher; Marc Médevielle; Pierre Pérez; Mariska Pezzutto, oenologist; Jacques Puisais, Honorary President of the Union Française des Oenologues; Pascal Ribéreau-Gayon, former Dean of the Oenology Faculty, Bordeaux University II; André Roth, agricultural engineer; Alex Schaeffer, oenologist; Anne Seguin; Eric Stonestreet; Bernard Thévenet, agricultural engineer; Pierre Torrès, oenologist.

Assistant editors: Christine Cuperly, Anne Le Meur.
Computer processing: Marie-Line Gros-Desormeaux, Luc Audrain, Sylvie Clochez, Martine Lavergne.

We should like to express our very grateful thanks to the 900 members of wine-tasting committees who met specially to help produce this guide, and who, as is customary, remain anonymous, and also to the organizations who kindly gave their support to the book or took part in general research: the Institut National des Appellations d'Origine, INAO; the Institut National de la Recherche Agronomique, INRA; the board of Consumption and Fraud Prevention; the Office National Interprofessionel des Vins and its regional delegations, ONIVINS; the CFCE; the DGDDI; the various professional committees, councils, federations and unions; the Institut des Produits de la Vigne of Montpellier and ENSAM; the Paul Sabatier University, Toulouse; the wine-growing unions and wine-growers' associations; the unions and federations for the Grands Crus; the wine-merchants' unions; the chamber of agriculture; the departmental analytical laboratories; the agricultural colleges of Amboise, Avize, Blanquefort, Bommes, Montagne-Saint-Emilion, Montreuil-Bellay, Nîmes-Rodilhan and Orange, the hotelier's colleges of Bastia (Fred Scamaroni) and Tain l'Hermitage, the CFPPA at Hyères; the Institut Rhodanien; the Union Française des Oenologues and the Fédérations Régionale des Oenologues; the wine-brokers' unions; the Union de la Sommellerie Française and the Associations Régionales de Sommeliers.

Layout: François Huertas; Cartography: Fabrice Le Goff; Illustrations: Véronique Chappée; Photo credits: Charlus (p. 24, 40); Scope/C. Gesquière (p. 62); Scope/J. Guillard (pp. 9, 19, 25, 56, 59, 67, 70); Scope/M. Guillard (p.16); Scope/J.-L. Barde (pp. 28, 29, 32, 38, 44, 52, 55).

For the English-language edition:

English translation by Translate-A-Book, Oxford

Managing editor: Hilary Lumsden
Production: Gary Hayes
Phototypeset by WestKey Ltd, Falmouth Cornwall

Typeset in Times New Roman
Printed and bound in Italy by Rotolito Lombarda

The

HACHETTE

Guide to

FRENCH

WINES

2004

CONTENTS

CONTENTS

A selection of the best French wines

SYMBOLS

SYMBOLS USED IN THIS GUIDE

A photo of the label signifies that the wine is strongly recommended by the committee.

★★★	exceptional wine
★★	excellent wine
★	good wine
	cited wine (unstarred)

1999 vintage or year of wine tasted

▢	still white wine	◯	sparkling white wine
▪	still rosé wine	⬤	sparkling rosé wine
■	still red wine	⬤	sparkling red wine

50,000, 12,500 … average number of bottles on offer

4 ha (10 acres): area of vineyard for this wine (in hectares and acres)

Ī	aged in vat
❿	aged in cask
♨	temperature regulation
☛	address
☑	for sale on the premises
⟁	conditions of visit or tasting (if appropriate)
⟐	hotel
⌂	gîte
☚	name of owner, if different from that mentioned in address
n.c.	information not supplied

PRICES

Prices are shown in Euros and are for guidance only (average price of a bottle in France per case of 12).

– 3 €	3–5 €	5–8 €	8–11 €	11–15 €
15–23 €	23–30 €	30–38 €	38–46 €	46–76 €
+76 €	Prices shown in red indicate good value for money, e.g., 11–15 €

VINTAGES ⑧②)83 |85| |86| 89 |90| 91 |92| 93 95 96 |97| 98

83 91 the vintages marked in red are ready to drink

93 95 the vintages marked in black should be kept

|86| |92| the vintages marked in black between two vertical lines are ready to drink but can be kept

83 **95** the best vintages are in bold

⑨⓪ exceptional vintages are circled

The vintages mentioned are not necessarily for sale at the property but can be found at wine-merchants and restaurants.

CONVERSIONS

Length		Weight		Volume	
1mm	0.0394 in	1g	0.035 oz	1 cu cm	0.061 cu in
1cm	0.394 in	1kg	2.2 lb	1 cu m	35.3 cu ft
1m	39.4 in	1kg	0.001 ton	1 cu m	1.31 cu yd
1m	1.09 yd	1 tonne	2,200 lb		
1km	0.621 miles	1 tonne	0.984 ton		
Area		**Liquid Capacity**			
1sq cm	0.155 sq in	1ml	0.035 fl oz		
1sq m	10.76 sq ft	1l	0.53 pt (US pint = 16 fl oz)		
1sq m	1.2 sq yd	1hl (100 litre)	26.4 gal		
1ha	2.47 acre				
1sq km	247 acres				
1sq km	0.386 sq miles				
1a (are)	0.25 acre	Note: Conversions are into US measurements.			

HOW THE GUIDE WORKS

The selection of the year

This guide contains details of the 9,000 best wines from France, all tasted in the year 2003. This is an entirely new selection, focusing on the latest bottled vintage. These wines have been chosen for you by 900 experts during the course of blind tastings held by the *Hachette Guide to French Wine 2004* of more than 30,000 wines from every appellation. In addition, while not given a separate entry, some thousand wines are featured in bold type in the entries that review producers' most highly rated wines.

An objective guide

The absence of any financial or promotional involvement by the producers, wine-merchants or cooperatives mentioned ensures the impartiality of the book, the sole aim of which is to be a wine-buying guide for consumers. The tasting notes should be used only to draw comparisons within the same appellation; it is, in fact, impossible to judge different appellations according to exactly the same criteria.

The tasting process and classification

Each unlabelled wine is examined by a jury. The colour, aroma and taste are described, and it is given a mark between 0 and 5.

0   faulty wine: eliminated
1   poor or mediocre wine: eliminated
2   wine typical of the area: worth a mention but not starred
3   good wine: one star
4   excellent wine: two stars
5   exceptional wine and a perfect example of the appellation: three stars.

How to interpret an entry:

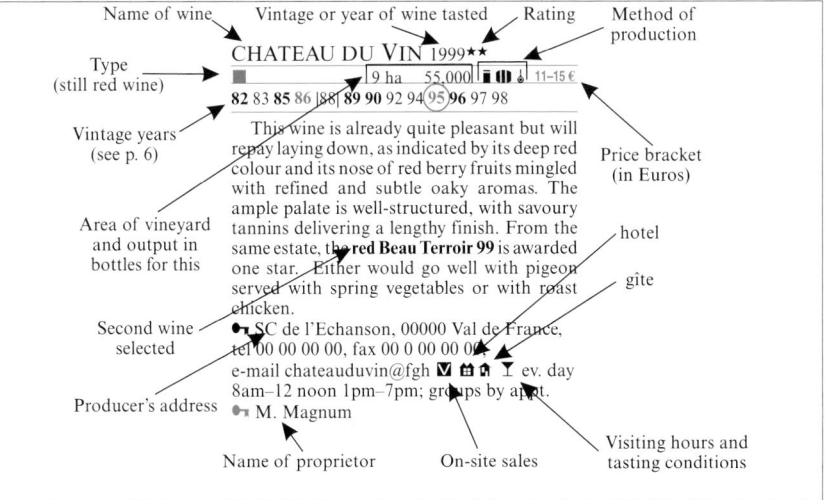

Of all the wines tasted only approximately 30% have been selected. Wines given one, two or three stars are described within their appellation. Of the 30% of wines selected, those worth a mention but not starred appear at the end of their particular appellation. They are not described but they include useful information (address, telephone, fax, visiting times and conditions of sale).

Our choice
The wines whose labels are reproduced in the guide represent the "coups de coeur". These are wines that inspired our tasters to "love at first sip", wines that are so good that they are particularly recommended to readers. References to wines being success-ful in previous years refer to previous editions of the French guide. References to a *Grappe d'or*, *Grappe d'argent* or *Grappe de bronze* refer to outstanding wines nominated as overall winners on publication of previous editions of the *Guide*.

How to use this guide

— The wines selected are listed:
  - By region, in alphabetic order, followed by three sections devoted to Vins Doux Naturels, Vins de Liqueur and Vins de Pays.
  - By appellation, presented geographically within each region.
  - Alphabetically within each appellation.
  - Four indices at the back list the appellations, communes, producers and wines featured.
  - 49 original maps show the geographical distribution of the vineyards.

Omissions
Some well-known and reputable wines are missing from this guide, either because the producers did not take part in, or were eliminated from, the tastings. Some wines were tasted and favourably assessed but additional information was not supplied; next to these wines you will see "nc" (information not supplied).

  Elsewhere, it is not surprising that there is no vintage or year for Vins d'Assemblage (mixed wines – for example, non-vintage champagnes), nor for liqueurs or sweet fortified wines, nor for those wines that are offered by different producers, supplied by wine-merchants or cooperatives.

Reader's guide

Because the object of this book is to advise the consumer on choosing wines, according to his or her individual taste, and to advise on the best value for money (where the price range is indicated in red), everything has been done to make this guide practical and easy to read.

  It is important to read the general introduction as well as the ones to the regions and the appellations, because information common to all the wines is not repeated in each section.

Prices
The price range (average price per bottle for a case of 12) is subject to market trends and is given as a guide only. All prices are given in Euros.

Telephone numbers
In France telephone numbers have ten digits. If you want to phone or fax a French producer from abroad you need to dial the international code (00 from the UK and 011 from the USA) followed by the country code, which is 33 for France, and then the number, omitting the first zero.

FROM VINE TO WINE

The vine belongs to the genus *Vitis*, in which there are many species. Traditionally, wine is produced from different varieties of *Vitis vinifera*, which originated on the European continent. There are however, other species that originated on the American continent. Some of these are infertile, others produce wines with very particular organoleptic qualities (known as *foxé* or foxy), and these are not very popular. However, these "American" varieties have a greater resistance to disease than *Vitis vinifera*. In the 1930s attempts were made to create hybrids that would be resistant to disease, like the American species, but would also produce wines of the same quality as *Vitis vinifera*. Unfortunately, these were a complete failure.

— *Vitis vinifera* is susceptible to phylloxera, an insect that attacks the roots of the vine and that caused terrible devastation at the end of the 19th century. The development of a graft onto an American rootstock that was resistant to phylloxera led to a vinestock that had the properties of its own grape family but roots that could not be infected by the insect. *Vitis vinifera* is also susceptible to the leaf hopper that spreads the disease *flavescence dorée*.

— The species *Vitis vinifera* includes many varieties, known as *cépages*. Each wine-growing region has chosen the most suitable variety for its area, but economic conditions and the tastes of consumers can also play a part in modifying what is planted. Some vineyards produce wine from a single variety (for example, Pinot Noir and Chardonnay in Burgundy and Riesling in Alsace). In other regions (for example, in Champagne and Bordeaux) the greatest wines are the result of blending several varieties with complementary characteristics. The varieties are themselves made up of "individuals" (clones), which do not have identical characteristics (of productivity, rate of ripening, resistance to disease). The search is always on for the best stock. At the moment, research is being carried out into creating disease-resistant vines by genetic modification.

— Growing conditions have a decisive effect on the quality of wine. It is possible to increase yields considerably by changing fertilization and pruning methods, choosing different stock and altering the density of the plants. It is not possible however to increase yields dramatically without affecting quality, except when nature intervenes; then quality is rarely compromised, and some of the greatest vintages have been produced from abundant harvests.

— In recent years the increase in yields has been linked to better growing conditions. The advisable limit depends on the style of the wine: for good red wines the maximum advisable yield is between 45 and 60 hl per ha and a little more for dry white wines. To produce very good wines, you also need vines that are ten years old or more, with a well-developed root system.

— The vine is susceptible to numerous diseases, various types of mildew and rot, which deplete the harvest and give the grapes a nasty taste, which is detectable in the wine. Wine-growers now have the means to treat these diseases effectively and this has certainly contributed to the general improvement in quality. In the past, a concern for security has probably led to an over-zealous use of chemical pesticides, but today they are used more prudently. In general, these chemical treatments are used only when absolutely necessary, and research within agricultural biology is now focusing on soil biodynamics, with the aim of creating natural conditions that will make the vine less susceptible to disease.

SOILS FOR WINE-GROWING:
THE ADAPTATION OF VARIETIES TO SOIL AND CLIMATE

Taken in its broadest sense, the notion of "soils for wine-growing", often referred to as terroir, brings together several different factors: biological (choice of variety), geographical, climatic, geological and pedological (types of soil). Added to these are the human, historical and commercial aspects: for example, the existence of the port at Bordeaux and its commerce with Scandinavian countries encouraged the wine-growers of the 18th century to improve the quality of their wines.

— In the northern hemisphere the vine is cultivated between the latitudes of 35° and 50°; it therefore has to adapt to very different climates. However, the most northerly vineyards usually cultivate only white varieties, which ripen slowly and whose grapes are resistant to early autumn frosts. In warmer climates, later fruiting varieties with high yields are grown. To make good wine you need well-ripened grapes, but the maturation process should not be too rapid nor too advanced because this leads to a loss in aroma; thus varieties are chosen with close attention paid to the maturation period. For the vineyards that are situated at the edges of climatic zones, the big problem is inconsistency of climatic conditions during the maturation period.

— Excessive dryness or humidity also play a part. The soil plays an essential role in the irrigation of the plant; in spring, during the growing period, it supplies the vines with water and allows any excess rain during maturation to drain away. Gravelly and chalky soils are particularly suited to this, but there are also highly reputable *crus* that are grown on sandy and even clayey soils. Artificial drainage is sometimes used, and this accounts for the existence of high-quality *crus* being grown on different types of soil, while neighbouring vineyards, with the same soil type, produce wine of varying quality.

— The different types of soil and subsoil can affect the colour, aroma and taste of wines from the same variety and growing in the same climatic conditions. Wines can vary depending on whether the soil is chalky, clayey, sandy or gravelly or a combination of any of these. An increase in the proportion of clay in Graves makes the wine more acidic, more tannic and full bodied and less refined; a white Sauvignon takes on more flowery notes when grown on chalky, gravelly or marly soils. In any case, the vine is not particular about the quality of the soil on which it grows. In fact, poor soil is often a contributory factor in good wines, as the yield is limited and characteristics, such as colour, aroma and taste, are subsequently advanced.

THE CYCLE OF WORK IN THE VINEYARD

Annual pruning, aimed at limiting excessive growth of the woody stem and giving a balanced yield, normally takes place between December and March. The potential number of buds is determined by the strength of the plant, and this has a direct effect on the size of the harvest. In spring the work consists of "unearthing" the vines – the soil is raked into the middle of the row, creating a loose layer that should stay relatively dry.

— The ground is tended throughout the whole growing cycle, according to need: self-propagating plants are destroyed, the loose topsoil is maintained and loss of moisture through evaporation is prevented. Sometimes chemical herbicides are used for weeding; if they are applied to the whole vineyard, this is usually done at the end of winter and all ploughing is halted. This is known as "non-cultivation" and represents a considerable saving. However, some environmentally aware producers prefer not to weed the rows, as the weeds act to limit the growth of the vines naturally.

— During the growing cycle, several different procedures are employed to limit excessive growth: *épamprage*, thinning out selected branches; *rognage*, trimming the tips; *effeuillage*, the removal of leaves, which allows the grapes to be more exposed to the sun; and *accolage*, training the shoots along wire espaliers. The wine-grower also has to protect the vines from disease, and to help him the Service for the Protection of Plants distributes information about various treatments, mainly sprays made from either natural or chemical products.

— Finally, in autumn, after the harvest, the earth is heaped up around the vines to protect them from the winter frosts; a furrow in the middle of the row allows rain water to run away, and fertilizer is sometimes dug in here as well.

GRAPES AND THE HARVEST

The degree of maturity of the grape is an essential factor in the quality of the wine. But even within the same region climatic conditions vary from one year to the next, leading to differences in the composition of the grapes, which in turn determines the characteristics of each vintage. Hot, dry weather is generally needed for the grapes to fully ripen, and the date to start picking must be fixed with great care, taking into account both the ripeness and the health of the grapes.

— Increasingly, manual harvesting is giving way to mechanical picking. The machines, fitted with "beaters", knock the grapes on to a conveyor belt, and a fan is used to remove most of the leaves. The shock effect on the grapes detracts somewhat from their quality, especially where white grapes are concerned; the most reputable crus will be the last ones to use this form of grape-picking, despite the considerable progress that has been made in the design and construction of the machines. When the grapes are overripe at harvest-time, the level of acidity can be increased by adding tartaric acid, and if the grapes are underripe the acidity can be decreased by adding calcium carbonate. A wine that is not rich enough may not have a sufficiently high alcohol content and can be improved by adding concentrated must. Finally, in certain well-defined conditions, legislation allows for the adding of sugar to the must – this is known as "chaptalization".

THE MAKING OF WINE

Wine is defined as "the product obtained exclusively from partial or total alcoholic fermentation of grape must or fresh grapes, which can be pressed or whole".

— All legal definitions require wine to have a minimum alcohol content of 8.5% vol or 9.5% vol, depending on the wine-growing area. The degree of alcohol is expressed in the percentage of the volume consisting of pure alcohol; 17 grams of sugar are needed for the must to produce 1% vol of alcohol by fermentation.

— The essential microbiological phenomenon that creates wine is alcoholic fermentation. The development of a type of yeast (*Saccharomyces cerevisae*), which is not exposed to the air, breaks down the sugar into alcohol and carbon dioxide; numerous by-products appear (glycerol, succinic acid, ethyl esters etc), and these enhance the aroma and taste of the wine. The process of fermentation produces heat, and the vat may need to be cooled down by refrigeration.

— In some cases, malolactic fermentation occurs after alcoholic fermentation; with the aid of certain bacteria, the malic acid is broken down into lactic acid and carbon dioxide. This results in a lowering of acidity, a smoothing out and refining of the aroma and a more stable wine. Red wines are always improved by this process, but it is not always so for white wines. Yeast and bacteria exist naturally on the grapes; they develop during the procedures carried out in the wineries, and often they are all that is needed to start fermentation. However, the use of dried commercial yeast is becoming more common because it allows more control of the fermentation process and avoids certain defects (odours caused by reduction or lack of aeration) associated with some naturally occurring yeast varieties. In some cases, a modified stock allows dormant aromas specific to a particular variety (Sauvignon) to be released from non-aromatic characteristics already existing in the grape. In any case, the quality and the character of the wine depend not wholly on the quality of the grape but also on natural factors, such as exposure and soil.

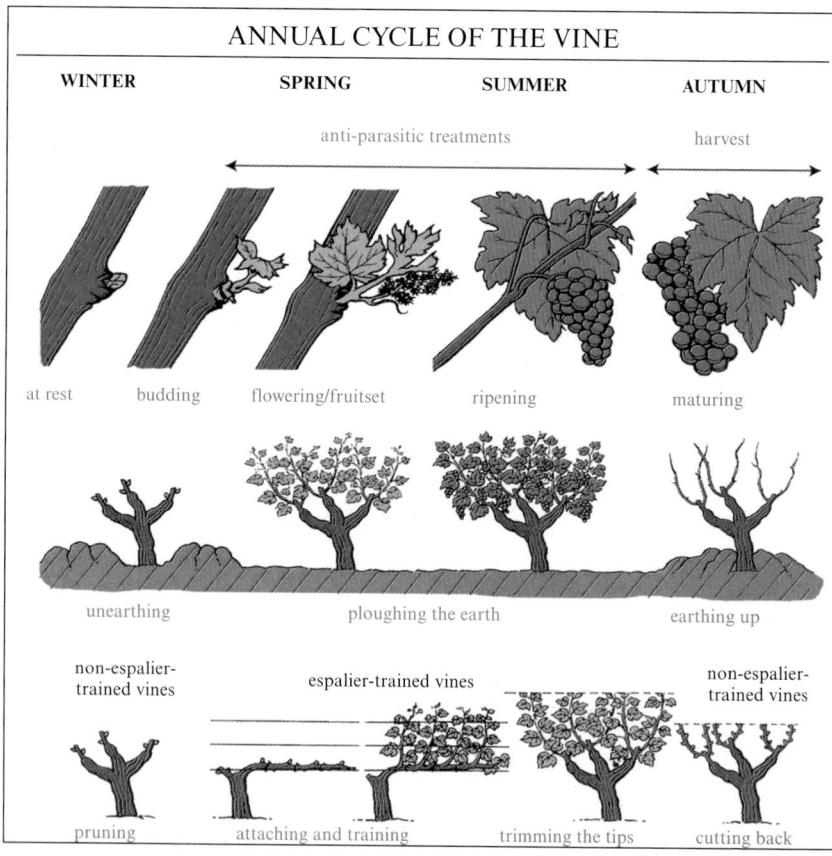

ANNUAL CYCLE OF THE VINE

WINTER	SPRING	SUMMER	AUTUMN

anti-parasitic treatments

harvest

at rest — budding — flowering/fruitset — ripening — maturing

unearthing — ploughing the earth — earthing up

non-espalier-trained vines — espalier-trained vines — non-espalier-trained vines

pruning — attaching and training — trimming the tips — cutting back

— Yeast always develops before the bacteria, which begin to grow only when the yeast has stopped fermenting. If the yeast stops fermenting before all the sugar has been transformed into alcohol, the residual sugar can be broken down by the bacteria, producing acetic acid (volatile acid); this is a serious setback, known as *piqûre*. A recently discovered procedure allows toxic substances formed from the yeast itself to be eliminated. During the ageing process, bacteria are still present in the wine and could lead to serious problems, such as the decomposition of fruit elements of the wine, oxidation and the formation of acetic acid (a process in the making of vinegar). Today, however, the precautions used in vinification can help to avoid these risks.

THE DIFFERENT TYPES OF WINE

European regulations, which incorporate French usage, distinguish between table wine and VQPRD. The Vins de Qualité Produits dans une Région Déterminée (VQPRD) are subject to certain controls. In France, they correspond to Appellations d'Origine Vins Délimités de Qualité Supérieure (AOVDQS) and to Vins d'Appellation d'Origine Contrôlée (AOC). It is worth noting that young vines (those under four years old) are excluded from appellations, because the wines they produce are too light to represent the appellation.

— Dry wines and sweet wines (*demi-secs, moelleux* and *doux*) are characterized by varying amounts of sugar. The production of sweet wine requires very ripe grapes, rich in sugar, of which only a part is transformed into alcohol by fermentation. Sauternes, for example, are particularly rich wines obtained from grapes whose sugar has been concentrated by *pourriture noble* (noble rot). They are often termed Grands Vins Liquoreux, not to be confused with Vins de Liqueurs, which are defined by European legislation (see below).

— Sparkling wines differ from still wines by the escape of carbon dioxide (the familiar "pop") on opening – this comes from a second fermentation known as *prise de mousse*. In the traditional method, which used to be known as *méthode champenoise*, this is achieved in the bottle; if it is carried out in the vat, it is called the *cuve close* (tank) method.

— Vins Mousseux Gazéifiés also give off carbon dioxide on opening, but with these wines it has been added, either partially or totally. Vins Pétillants (lightly sparkling wines) have a carbon dioxide pressure of between 1 and 2.5 bars and need contain only 7% of alcohol. Pétillant de Raisin is obtained from the partial fermentation of grape must, and its alcohol content is low, the minimum being 1% vol.

— *Vins de Liqueur* (sweet fortified wines) are obtained by adding – before, during and after fermentation – pure alcohol, *eau-de-vie de vin* (wine brandy), concentrated grape must or a mixture of these products. The term "mistelle" is not included in the European regulations, which refer to "fresh grape must mixed with alcohol", the result of alcohol or brandy being added to the grape must (without fermentation). Pineau des Charentes, Floc de Gascogne and Macvin du Jura belong in this category.

WINEMAKING PROCESSES

Making red wine

In most cases, the grapes are first detached from their stalks and then crushed; the mixture of pulp, pips and skins is put into the fermenting vat along with a small dose of sulphur dioxide, which helps to protect against bacteria and oxidation. Once fermentation has started, the carbon dioxide lifts all the solid particles to the top of the vat where they form a solid mass called *chapeau* or *marc*.

THE WINE-GROWER'S CALENDAR

JANUARY

St Vincent's Day is the feast day of the patron saint of wine growers.

JULY

Anti-parasitic treatments continue and the vines are studied carefully; this is a time when temperatures can vary enormously, and there is a risk of summer hail storms.

FEBRUARY

Wine contracts with the cold. Barrels need to be checked periodically and topped up if necessary. Malolactic fermentation should now be completed.

AUGUST

Disturbing the soil could be harmful to the vines, but a close look-out must be kept for parasites. In early ripening regions, the vats and casks are prepared.

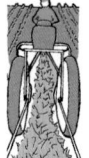
MARCH

Clear heaped-up earth away from the vines to let air circulate between them. Pruning should now be finished. Wines for early drinking should now be bottled.

SEPTEMBER

Grapes are picked and tested regularly for maturation in order to set a date for the harvest; harvest begins in Mediterranean areas.

APRIL

Before phylloxera, vines were trained on sticks. Nowadays, vines are trained along wire espaliers (except at l'Hermitage, Côte-Rôtie and Condrieu).

OCTOBER

In most vineyards, it is harvest-time and winemaking begins. Wines for laying down are put in casks to mature.

MAY

This is the time to watch out for and protect against spring frosts. The spaces between the rows are ploughed.

NOVEMBER

Young wines ready for drinking en primeur are bottled now. Progress of the nouveau wines is checked. The autumn cutback begins.

JUNE

Vines are trained and the stems are pruned. The way the fruits set, known as the flowering, will determine the volume of the harvest.

DECEMBER

The temperature in the winecellar is monitored to ensure alcoholic and malolactic fermentation.

— Alcoholic fermentation takes place in the vat at the same time as the maceration of the skins and pips in the juice. It usually takes a minimum of five to eight days for the sugar to ferment completely; this is helped by allowing air in to increase the growth of the yeast and by controlling the temperature (at around 30°C) to avoid killing off the yeast. The maceration gives red wine its colour and much of its tannic structure. Wines that are to be aged should be rich in tannin and need a long period of maceration (two or three weeks) at 25–30°C. On the other hand, wines that are to be drunk young, such as Vins Nouveaux, should be fruity and not very tannic; these need to be macerated for only a few days.

— The liquid part of the mixture is then separated from the residue or *marc*. The liquid part is known as *vin de goutte* (free-run wine) or *grand vin*. The *marc* is then pressed and this gives what is known as *vin de presse*. *Vin de presse* is sometimes blended with *vin de goutte*, depending on defined criteria for taste and analysis. The wines are put into separate vats for the final settling and for malolactic fermentation to take place. With expensive, hand-made wines it is becoming more and more common for the liquid to be run off directly into small oak barrels in which malolactic fermentation takes place. Red wines thus acquire a more consistently complex character.

— This is the basic method, but other vinification procedures are of special interest, including thermovinification, continuous vinification and carbonic maceration.

Making rosé wine

Rosé, *clairet* (deep rosé) or *gris* (light rosé) wines are obtained by macerating, for varying lengths of time, grapes that are either strongly coloured or very lightly coloured. More often than not, they are vinified by pressing black grapes or by a short maceration process. For the latter, the vat is filled, as it is for the vinification of a classic red wine, then after a few hours a certain amount of juice is run off to ferment separately. The vat is then refilled to make red wine, which is, in consequence, more concentrated.

Making white wine

There is a wide variety of types of white wine, each one with its own particular vinification technique and appropriate harvesting method. In most cases white wine results from the fermentation of grape juice, without the skins, which occurs after pressing. In some cases, however, the skins are macerated for a short time before fermentation in order to extract their aroma. To achieve this you need perfectly healthy and ripe grapes in order to avoid defects in taste and aroma, such as bitterness and unpleasant odours. The juice is extracted by crushing the grapes, running off the juice and pressing. The *jus de presse* is fermented separately because it is inferior in quality. The white must, which is very susceptible to oxidation, is protected by the addition of sulphur dioxide. After the juice has been extracted, it will be clarified by a process known as *débourbage* (settling the sediment from the wine). During the whole fermentation process the vat has to be maintained at a temperature of between 20° and 24°C to protect the aroma.

— The great white wines are vinified in barrels and consequently take on a succulent, woody character. This method also allows, among other things, an ageing on the yeast lees or sediments, which increases the richness and flavour of the wine. This development is accentuated by stirring the wine with a pole to keep the lees in suspension.

— In many cases malolactic fermentation is not required for white wines, which have a fresher more acid taste, and a second fermentation can often reduce the characteristic aromas of the variety. However, those white wines that have a fairly long ageing in casks (for example, white Burgundies) develop richness and volume during this second fermentation. They are also more stable biologically once bottled.

— Grapes very rich in sugar are needed for the vinification of sweet wines. Part of the sugar is transformed into alcohol, but the fermentation is stopped before it is completed by the addition of sulphur dioxide, and the yeast is eliminated by racking, by centrifuge or by pasteurization. Sauternes and Barsacs, which are particularly rich in both alcohol (13–15% vol) and in sugar (50–100 g per litre), need very ripe grapes, which cannot be obtained by the normal ripening process. This requires the action on the grape of a fungus, *Botrytis cinerea*, to produce noble rot; the grapes are also harvested in successive stages according to the development of the noble rot.

THE DIFFERENT STAGES OF MATURATION

New wine is rough, cloudy and full of carbon dioxide. It needs *élevage* (clarification, stabilization and refining) to prepare it for the next stage, that of bottling. The time this takes varies according to the type of wine: Vins Nouveaux are bottled a few weeks after vinification, whereas wines for laying down are aged for two or more years.

— If the wine is kept in small containers, such as 225-litre oak barrels, clarification can be obtained by racking the wine (*soutirage*) and removing the sediments. If the wine is kept in large vats, however, centrifugation or other methods of filtration have to be used.

— Because of its complexity, cloudiness and deposits can occur in the wine. These are totally natural phenomena of microbiological or chemical origin. When this happens in the bottle, it can be very serious, which is why stabilization should take place beforehand.

— Microbiological spoilage (acescency caused by bacteria or refermentation) can be avoided by preventing exposure to air and by keeping the container full. A topping-up process is carried out to prevent contact with air. Sulphur dioxide, which is both an antioxidant and an antiseptic, is often added, as is sorbic acid (an antiseptic) and ascorbic acid (an antioxidant).

— The treatment of wines is born from necessity; the products added are relatively few, they do not affect the quality of the wine, and they have been proved to be harmless. Laboratory tests help to predict risks of instability and to limit treatments to what is absolutely essential. However, the modern tendency is towards taking action immediately after vinification in order to limit the need for later treatments and the handling operations that these involve.

— Refrigeration can help to prevent deposits of tartar before bottling. Metatartaric acid, which inhibits crystallization, has an immediate but not a long-lasting effect. Fining consists of adding a protein, such as egg white or gelatine, to the wine. This has a coalescent action, taking out suspended particles that are liable to make the wine cloudy or to leave deposits at a later stage. The adding of substances (usually egg white) to red wine is an ancient practice, indispensable for getting rid of excess colouring matter that would otherwise line the inside of the bottle. Gum arabic has a similar effect and is used for table wines that are to be consumed soon after bottling. The coagulation of natural proteins in white wines is avoided by adding bentonite which is a protective colloid. An excess of certain metals such as iron or copper, can also lead to cloudiness; they can be eliminated by adding potassium ferrocyanide.

— *Elevage* also contains a refining stage. First of all there is the elimination of any excess carbon dioxide that has been produced during fermentation. How this is done depends on the type of wine, for while it gives freshness to dry white wines and young wines, it has a coarsening effect on wines to be laid down, especially good red wines. The carefully controlled introduction of oxygen acts on the tannins of young red wines and is indispensable for their later ageing in bottles. Controlled aeration happens naturally in oak casks, but it is possible to introduce precise amounts of oxygen; the technique is known as *microbullage*.

— When the wood is new, oak casks give wines tones of vanilla and toastiness, which harmonize perfectly with the aromas of the fruit. Allier oak (from the Tronçais forest) is more suitable than Limousin oak. The wood must be split and dried in the open air for three years before it is used. This is all part of the traditional method used for fine

VINIFICATION OF RED WINE

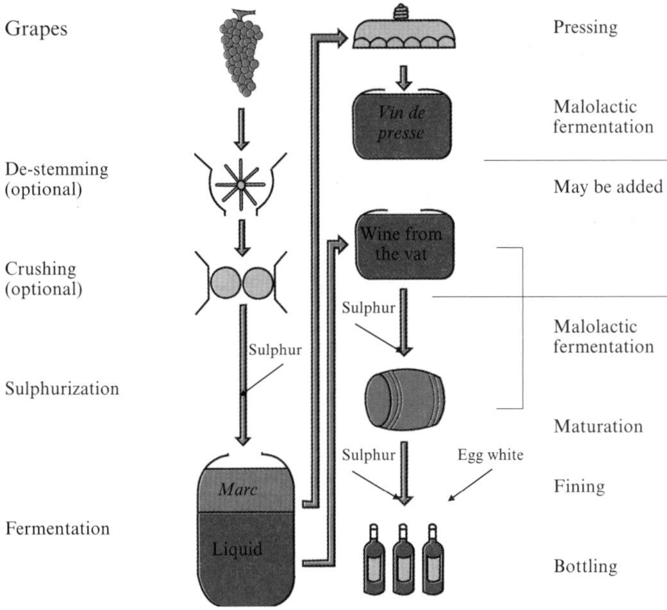

Grapes

Pressing

Vin de presse

Malolactic fermentation

De-stemming (optional)

May be added

Crushing (optional)

Wine from the vat

Sulphurization

Sulphur

Malolactic fermentation

Maturation

Sulphur

Egg white

Fining

Fermentation

Marc

Liquid

Bottling

VINIFICATION OF WHITE WINE

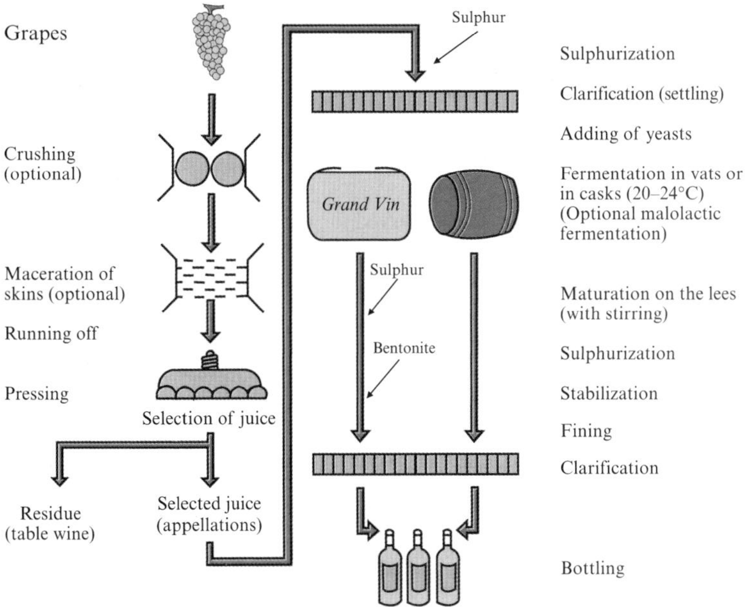

Grapes

Sulphur

Sulphurization

Clarification (settling)

Adding of yeasts

Crushing (optional)

Grand Vin

Fermentation in vats or in casks (20–24°C) (Optional malolactic fermentation)

Maceration of skins (optional)

Sulphur

Maturation on the lees (with stirring)

Running off

Bentonite

Sulphurization

Pressing

Selection of juice

Stabilization

Fining

Residue (table wine)

Selected juice (appellations)

Clarification

Bottling

wines, but it is very expensive in terms of the cost of the casks, the manual labour involved and the loss of wine through evaporation. In addition, when the casks are old they can be a source of microbiological contamination and can sometimes do more harm than good. This type of ageing should be reserved for wines that are sufficiently rich for the oakiness not to dominate the fruity aromas of the wine and mask its typical characteristics. The contribution that oak can make depends on the structure of the wines (taking into account the length of ageing and the proportion of new casks), and care must be taken that the wine does not become too dry. Attempts have been made to simplify the process by, for example, macerating the wine with oak shavings or wood chips, but this is forbidden in the production of AOC wines.

AGEING

The word "ageing" is specifically reserved for the slow transformation of wine in the bottle, with no exposure to the oxygen in the air. Bottling must be carried out with great care in very hygienic conditions. By this stage the wine has been thoroughly clarified and must not be contaminated. Care must also be taken to fill the bottles with the right quantity. Because of its elasticity and imperviousness to liquids, cork still remains the first choice for sealing bottles. However, it is advisable to re-cork bottles every 25 years or so, as cork is degradable. There are also two risks of contamination connected with corks: leaky bottles and a "corky" taste.

—   The changes that occur in the bottle are many and complex. There is, first of all, a change in colour, which is most evident in red wines. The bright red colour of young wines evolves into a more yellowy shade, resembling the colour of tiles or bricks. In very old wines the red is replaced by tones of brown and orange. This process of change is responsible for the deposits that are often present in very old wines. Bottle age also "softens" the general structure of the wine by reducing the tannic element.

— It is during the ageing process in the bottle that aromas and the individual "bouquets" of old wines develop. These developments are due to complex chemical changes that are still not fully understood but that do not involve esterification.

QUALITY CONTROL

Good wine is not necessarily great wine. A wine of quality can be anything from a table wine to a Grand Cru or any permutation in between. A distinction also has to be made between the human factors and natural factors that contribute to the quality of the wine. The first category is indispensable for a good wine, but a great wine requires very specific environmental conditions of soil and climate.

— Chemical analysis has helped to point out anomalies and defects, but it has its limitations when it comes to defining quality: in the final analysis, taste is the essential criterion. However, considerable progress has been made over the last 20 years in sensory analytical techniques, giving us a better understanding and knowledge of the physiology of odour and taste and of practical tasting conditions. Tasting expertise is playing an increasingly large part in gauging quality, in particular in the registration of AOC wines and in legal cases.

— In fact, quality control has been subject to regulation for some time. The first official text was the French wine law of 1 August 1905 concerning commercial transactions. Regulations have progressed in step with developments in the understanding of the composition of wine and the changes that occur. With the help of chemical analysis, regulations define a minimum level of quality, thus eliminating major defects; they also encourage ways of improving this minimum level. The Consumers and Fraud Association is responsible for checking the analytical standards that have been established.

— Added to this is the work carried out by the *National Institute of Appellations d'Origine* (INAO), which, in consultation with the *syndicats* concerned, lays down and controls production conditions, including production zones, varieties, planting and pruning methods, cultivation techniques, vinification, composition of musts and wines, and yields. This body is also responsible for representing AOC wines within France and abroad.

— Finally, in every region, wine-growing *syndicats* defend the interests of their members, especially when it comes to matters concerning appellations. This work is often coordinated by councils, bodies or inter-professional committees that bring together representatives from various unions and from groups of producers and wine-merchants, as well as people from the professional and administrative worlds.

Pascal Ribéreau-Gayon

A CONSUMER'S GUIDE

Buying wine is the easiest thing in the world; choosing wisely is the most difficult. If you were to consider everything that is on offer, you would find that there are several hundreds of thousands of different wines to choose from. France alone produces tens of thousands of wines, each of which has its own individuality and characteristics. What distinguishes them in appearance, apart from their colour, is their label, hence the importance and care that the public and professional authorities attach to controlling the use and presentation of labelling. It is also important for the buyer to understand a label's many "mysteries".

THE LABEL
The label fulfils several functions.
— The first is a legal one. It indicates who is responsible for the wine in case of any dispute. This could be a wine-merchant or the grower himself. In some cases this information is also indicated on the top of the cap or capsule.
— The second function of the label is very important, because it establishes the category to which the wine belongs: *vin de table*, *vin de pays*, AOVDQS or AOC; the last two of these have been assimilated into the European term *Vin de Qualité Produit dans des Régions Déterminées* (VQPRD).

AOC
This is the top class, the category for all the great wines. The label has to have "XXXX Appellation Contrôlée" or "Appellation XXXX Contrôlée" on it. This mentions the precise region, town or commune or even sometimes the cru (or *climat*, a part of a cru) where the vineyard is situated. To have the right to an AOC, a wine must have been produced according to "local, loyal and consistent usage" – that is, it is from approved "noble" varieties planted in specific vineyards and vinified according to regional traditions. The yield per hectare and alcoholic content (minimum and sometimes maximum) are also fixed by law. The wines are approved every year by a tasting committee.

— National regulations are supplemented by the institutionalized application of local customs. Thus, in Alsace the letters indicating the regional appellation are nearly always double the size of the name of the variety. In Burgundy on the other hand, only the Premiers Crus can be printed in letters that are the same size as those used for the appellation of the commune; the *climats* that are not in the highest classification can be mentioned only in small letters, half the size of the characters indicating the appellation. In addition, the communes of the Grands Crus do not appear on the labels, because these wines have their own individual appellations. These requirements are all given in detail in current French wine law.

Appellation d'Origine Vin Délimité de Qualité Supérieure (AOVDQS)

The "antechamber" of AOC, this category is sensibly subject to the same rules. AOVQDS wines are labelled after they have been tasted. The label must include the words "Appellation d'Origine Vin Délimité de Qualité Supérieure" and its corresponding stamp. These are not wines for laying down, but some of them improve after being kept in cellars for a while.

Vins de Pays

The labels for *vins de pays* indicate which region the wine comes from, so you will see "Vin de Pays de ..." followed by the name of the region.

— Wines in this category come from a legally defined list of more or less "noble" grape varieties grown in large regional areas that are nevertheless "limited". Their alcoholic content, acidity and acidic volatility are all subject to controls. These are fresh, fruity and lively wines, to be drunk young. They are not suitable for laying down, and they can, in fact, deteriorate if kept.

— Labels can contain other information that is not compulsory, unlike the above requirements, but is nevertheless subject to regulations. The terms *"clos"*, "Château" and *"cru classé"*, for example, can be used only in accordance with traditional usage and only if they refer to something that actually exists. What labels might lose in creativity they make up for in honesty, and the buyer should feel reassured that the information on labels is more credible nowadays than in times past.

Vintages and bottling

Two non-compulsory pieces of information on the bottle will interest the wine-lover: first, the vintage, which will either be on the label (which is the best option) or on another label attached to the neck of the bottle, and, second, the exact location of the bottling.

— A keen wine-lover will be satisfied only with a label that indicates that bottling has taken place at the estate, property or château. Any other indication that does not establish a direct link between the place where the wine was vinified and where it was bottled is not of any great interest. No matter how accurate such phrases as "bottled in the region of production", "bottled by ourselves", "bottled in our cellars", "bottled by X (X being an intermediary)" may be, they do not have the same guarantee of origin as "bottled at the property".

— The concern of the public authorities and of professional committees has always been twofold: first, to encourage producers to improve the quality of their wine and to check this by tasting before labelling and second to make sure that the wine described on the label is indeed the wine that is in the bottle, without any mixing, additions or substitutions. However, despite all sorts of precautions, including possible checks during transportation, the best guarantee of authenticity remains "bottled at the property" (*mis en bouteille à la propriété*). This is because a wine-grower does not have the right to purchase other wine to store in his commercial cellar, which can contain only wine that he has produced himself.

— Note that a cooperative that bottles its own wine can use the term "bottled at the property".

The label

HOW TO READ A LABEL

The label must identify the wine and indicate who is responsible for it. The last person in the production process is the bottler, and his name must also appear on the label. Each category of wine is subject to its own specific labelling regulations. The first duty of the label is to inform the consumer and to indicate which category the wine belongs to:

– *vin de table* (origin, alcohol content, volume, name and address of bottler must all be mentioned; vintages, or years, are forbidden).
– *vins de pays.*
– Appellation d'Origine Vin Délimité de Qualité Supérieure (AOVDQS).
– Appellation d'Origine Contrôlée (AOC).

Alsace AOC
   green fiscal stamp (on cap)
   1 wine category (compulsory)
   2 variety (only allowed if grapes are from one single variety)
   3 volume (compulsory)
   4 all other compulsory indications
   5 necessary for export to certain countries
   6 alcohol content in degrees (compulsory)
   7 lot number (compulsory)

Bordeaux AOC
   green fiscal stamp
   1 brand (optional)
   2 vintage (optional)
   3 class of category (optional)
   4 category (compulsory)
   5 name and address of bottler (compulsory)
   6 the word "owner" (optional) fixes the status of the vineyard optional
   7 volume (compulsory)
   8 necessary for export to certain countries
   9 alcohol content in degrees (compulsory)
   10 lot number (compulsory)

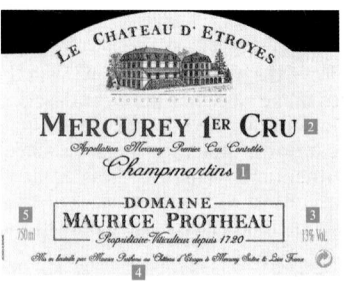

Burgundy AOC
   green fiscal stamp
   the vintage is often on a label around the neck of the bottle (optional)
   1 name of the cru (optional); if the letters are the same size as those of the appellation, it is a Premier Cru
   2 category (compulsory)
   3 alcohol content (compulsory)
   4 name and address of bottler (compulsory); also indicates that it is bottled at the property not by a wine-merchant
   5 volume (compulsory)

22

Champagne AOC

green fiscal stamp

1 compulsory
all Champagne is AOC, so this does not figure on the label; this is the only exception to the rule that requires a reference to the category of wine

2 brand and address (compulsory; it is taken as read that it is bottled at the same address)

3 volume (compulsory)

4 status of the vineyard and its professional identification number (optional)

5 type of wine (compulsory)

AOVDQS

green fiscal stamp

vintage (optional)

1 variety (optional, only allowed if grapes are from one single variety)

2 name of the appellation (compulsory)

3 category (compulsory)

4 alcohol content (compulsory)

5 name and address of bottler (compulsory)

6 indicates whether bottled on premises (optional)

7 stamp (compulsory)

8 volume (compulsory)

9 number (which indicates it has been checked),

10 compulsory in France

Vins de Pays

blue fiscal stamp

table wines are subject to the same regulations. The words "Vin de Pays" must be followed by the name of the region (compulsory)

1 "au domaine" optional

2 geographical area (compulsory)

3 name and address of bottler (compulsory)

4 alcohol content in degrees (compulsory)

5 volume (compulsory)

CAPS AND STAMPING CORKS

Most bottles are topped with a cap or capsule. Sometimes the cap bears a French government fiscal stamp, which is proof that all legal requirements have been fulfilled for its distribution. This clearance certificate is known colloquially as a *congé*, and that is why the caps are often referred to as *capsules congés*. When the bottles are not stamped, they have to be accompanied by a receipt or certificate issued by the nearest tax office (see the section on transporting wine).

— The stamp shows the status of the producer (owner or wine-merchant) and the region of production. The caps do not officially have to be stamped or personalized, but in general one or the other is usually done. The producers of quality wine have felt the need to confirm the information on their labels by marking the corks as well. A label can become unstuck but a cork cannot; that is why the vintage and the origin of the wine are stamped on the cork. It is also a way of discouraging potential fraudsters who can no longer just replace the labels. Note that the appellation of AOC sparkling wines, must be mentioned on the cork.

HOW TO BUY WINE

The ways in which wine is distributed are complex and vary from the very simple to the most convoluted, each method having its advantages and disadvantages. The ways in which wine is sold also take different forms according to the method of presentation (whether it is in containers or in bottles) and when it is bought, for example, if it is bought *en primeur* (before it is bottled).

Wines to drink and wines to keep

The procedures for buying wine to drink and buying wine for laying down are not the same: there are different methods for different purposes. Wines destined for immediate consumption are ready to drink as they are; these are "nouveau" wines or *vins de pays*, of "small" or "medium" origin and modest vintages, which do not require much ageing. Or they may be great wines that have reached their peak (but these are practically impossible to find on the market).

— In every case, but obviously more importantly for fine wines, it is essential that there is a rest period of two days to two weeks between purchasing (including transportation) and consumption. Old bottles should be transported with great care, in a vertical position and protected from knocks, to avoid any stirring up of sediments.

— Wines for keeping or laying down should be bought young with the aim of ageing them. Always choose the best possible wines from the finest vintages; these are not only less likely to deteriorate over time but will improve over the years.

Buying in containers

Wine that is not bought in bottles is bought *en vrac* (in bulk, i.e., in containers). The term *en cercle* is reserved for wines in barrels, whereas *vrac* means containers of any kind, from a 220 hl steel tank on a truck to a 5-litre plastic container or glass demijohn.

— Wine is sold in containers by cooperatives, by some wine-growers and wine-merchants, and even by some retailers. It is sometimes called wine sold *à la tireuse* or "drawn by hand". Usually, table wines or wines of medium quality are sold in this way; it is rare to find a good-quality wine sold in a container. In fact, in certain areas, it is forbidden – for example, Bordeaux *crus classés* cannot be sold in this way.

— The wine-lover should be aware that even when a wine-grower says that the wine he is selling in containers is the same as the one that he is selling in bottles, this is not strictly true. He will always choose the best batches for the wine that he bottles himself.

— Buying wine in containers can represent a saving of about 25%, as it is common practice to pay, at most, the same price for a litre as you would pay for a 75cl bottle.

— The purchaser can also save on transport costs, but will have to buy corks and bottles if he or she does not have any to hand. If the transaction is made by the barrel, the costs (not very high in France) of returning the cask have also to be taken into account.

These are the most commonly used containers:

Bordeaux barrique	225 litres
Burgundy pièce	228 litres
Mâconnais pièce	216 litres
Chablis pièce	132 litres
Champagne pièce	205 litres

— Bottling, which can be fun when it is done with a group of friends, does not pose too many problems, whatever anyone might say, provided that certain elementary rules (see below) are adhered to.

Buying by the bottle
In France bottles can be bought from the wine-grower, from a cooperative, at a wine-merchant or at any of many other outlets.

— Where should a wine-lover in France go to get the best deal? For wines that are not widely distributed the best option is to go to the wine-grower, and there are many of these. To avoid paying the ever-increasing costs of transport for small quantities of wine, cooperatives are a good choice. In other cases, such a strategy is not as simple as it seems. It should be borne in mind that wine-growers and wine-merchants are not in competition with their distributors, and they are not going to sell their bottles more cheaply. In fact, a number of Bordeaux châteaux that do very little direct selling sell their bottles at an even higher price than retailers to discourage buyers who, through ignorance or for whatever other reason, persist in buying directly from the owners. For wines of repute prices are bound to be lower at the retailers, which can obtain much better deals by placing large orders, than an individual can obtain by buying a single case.

— A general rule can be drawn from this: it is not worth buying widely distributed wines direct from famous domains and châteaux, except when it is a rare vintage or a special reserve.

Buying en primeur
This method of buying wine, practised for several years in the Bordeaux region, was very successful during the 1980s. Today, it is probably better to talk about buying or selling by subscription. The principle is simple: you buy a wine before it has been aged or bottled, at a lower price than it would be sold at when it is ready to be delivered.

— Subscriptions are available for a limited time and for specified quantities, usually in the spring or the beginning of the summer that follows the harvest. The purchaser pays a deposit of half the total cost when he or she orders and the rest on delivery, i.e., 15 months later. In this way, the producer has ready cash and the buyer can make a profit if prices increase. This was the case from 1974–5 to the end of the 1980s. This type of transaction is similar to what, on the Stock Exchange, is known as a forward-exchange transaction.

— If, because of overproduction or an economic crisis, the price goes down between subscription and delivery, the subscribers pay more for their bottles than those who did not subscribe. This has happened in the past and could well happen again. In fact, some leading wine-merchants have been ruined in the past by trying to guarantee their supplies with this type of speculation. It is true that such speculators run more risks if their contract spans several years.

— Under normal circumstances, buying wine *en primeur* is undoubtedly the only way to buy wine for less than its normal price (between 20% and 40% less). Opportunities to buy *en primeur* are organized by the wine-growers themselves, and also by wine-merchants and wine clubs.

Alsace   Muscadet   Anjou   Provence

Clavelin   Jura   Burgundy   Italian   Bordeaux   Champagne

Buying directly from the producer
Apart from the rather technical aspects described above, a visit to the producer, which is indispensable if the wine is not very widely distributed, gives the wine-lover a different kind of satisfaction from that of simply getting a bargain. Only by visiting the producers, the true "fathers" of their wines, can oenophiles fully understand the meaning of terroir and its characteristics, appreciate the art of vinification, which brings out the very essence of the grape, and, finally, see the strong links that exist between a wine-grower and his wine – between a creator and his creation. It is a stage that needs to be experienced in order to "drink well and drink better", as the French say. To truly appreciate a wine, nothing can replace a visit to the grower.

Buying from a cooperative

The quality of wines sold by cooperatives is improving all the time. They are well equipped for selling wines, either in containers or in bottles, at prices that are usually slightly lower than those of other sales outlets offering similar quality.

— The principle underlying cooperatives is well known. The members bring in their harvested grapes, and those responsible for the technical side (usually oenologists) take care of the pressing, vinification and, in some appellations, the ageing and selling.

— The fact that they usually produce several types of wine gives cooperatives an opportunity of either using the best grapes (by separating them out from the others) or of highlighting certain terroirs through separate vinifications. For the best cooperatives, the system of special payments for the ripest and noble grapes, coupled with the possibility of making and selling wines according to the quality of each individual delivery of grapes, opens up opportunities to produce quality wines or even wines for laying down. Other cooperatives remain suppliers of table wines and *vins de pays* that are not intended for ageing or laying down.

Buying from a wine-merchant

In France a wine-merchant, by definition, buys wines for resale. In addition, he or she may often be a vineyard owner. Such a merchant-owner may thus produce and sell his or her own wine, sell wine from independent producers without having to do anything other than arrange transportation (this is the case for Bordeaux wine-merchants who sell wines that have been château bottled) or may even have an exclusive contract with a single production unit. A merchant may be a *négociant-éleveur*, producing wines by assembling or mixing wines from the same appellation, but supplied by different growers; such a practice influences the final product twice: once by the choice of purchase and second by mixing the wines. Wine-merchants are usually located in the larger wine-growing areas, but there is, of course, nothing to stop a Burgundian wine-merchant from selling wine from Bordeaux or vice versa. The main purpose of a wine-merchant is to distribute and feed the retail network rather than to sell wines at much lower prices than retailers.

Buying from a cellarman (*caviste*) or a retailer

This is the easiest and quickest way of buying wine, and it is also the safest if the cellarman is sufficiently expert. Over the last few years, a number of shops specialising in the sale of quality wines have appeared. A good cellarman is someone who stores wines in good conditions but who also knows how to choose original wines from producers who love their work. In addition, a good retailer or cellarman should be able to advise clients, helping them to discover new wines and to choose appropriate wines to complement different types of food.

Supermarkets

In France buying quality wines in supermarkets has become a widespread practice, compared with the 1970s when it was rare. Whatever the location, the presentation in this type of shop is not always of the best, with problems such as too high a temperature, harsh neon lighting and the vertical storage of bottles. However, these oversights are becoming increasingly rare. Today in France, and elsewhere, many establishments possess specialized, well-equipped shelves where the bottles are stored horizontally and are classified by appellation. In France especially the wine-lover will find not only ordinary wines in supermarkets but also prestigious crus. The only wines not represented in supermarkets are appellations that are not widely distributed and wines from smaller vineyards. Contrary to common belief, it can be advantageous for the visitor to buy a prestigious bottle of French wine from a French supermarket.

Clubs

All over the world wine is delivered directly to wine-lovers, by the bottle or by the case, by so-called "wine clubs", which offer their members a certain number of advantages, including serious and informed critiques. Often, the wines on offer are chosen by wine experts and well-known and competent personalities. There is a wide choice, which sometimes includes little-known wines. However, it is worth noting that many such "clubs" are, in reality, wine-merchants.

Auction sales

In France, sales by auction, which are becoming increasingly fashionable and popular, are organized by auctioneers with the help of wine experts. Wherever the sale takes place, it is extremely important to know the origin of the bottles. If they have come from a good restaurant or from the cellar of a wine-lover who has had to relinquish some bottles for personal reasons, it is probable that they have been kept in very good condition. If they consist of smaller lots that have been brought together from various sources, there is nothing to guarantee that the wine has been kept properly.

— The appearance of the wine is the only indicator. The alert wine-lover will not bid for a bottle that is not filled to the correct level, nor for a white wine that is veering towards a darkish bronze colour, nor for red wine that looks "tired".

— It is rare to be able to buy great appellations that restaurateurs are interested in having on their lists at a bargain price; however, the lesser appellations, which are not so sought keenly after by professionals, are sometimes more affordable.

The Hospices de Beaune wine auction and similar auctions

Wines sold during these charity events are sold in casks and have to be aged for 12–14 months. They are therefore reserved for professionals.

Transporting wine

Once the problem of choosing wine has been resolved and you know that there is somewhere to store the bottles in good condition (*see* below), the next step is transporting them. The transportation of quality wines requires that several precautions be taken and in France it is also subject to strict regulations.

— Whether you transport the wine yourself by car or use the services of a shipper, the height of summer and the depths of winter are not the best times to undertake it. The wine must be protected from extremes of temperature, especially from high temperatures, which not only affect wine in the short term but also in the long term, no matter how long a rest period (even years) it may be given and no matter what its colour, type or origin may be.

— Once they are at their destination, the bottles should be stored in the cellar without delay. If the wine has been bought in containers, it should be stored where it is going to be bottled as soon as possible – in the cellar if space allows – in order to avoid having to move it again. Plastic containers should be placed 80 cm from the ground (at table height), and casks 30 cm from the ground, so that the wine can be drawn to the very last drop without changing its position, which is essential.

Regulations governing shipping wine in France

In France shipping alcoholic drinks is subject to a special regime and incurs taxes. These take the form of either a capsule (known as a *capsule fiscalisée* or a *capsule congé*), which is found on the top of each bottle, or an accompanying document issued by the tax office nearest to the sales point or by the wine-grower, if empowered to do so. Wine in containers must always be accompanied by the relevant permit.

— The name of the seller, the cru, the volume and number of containers, the recipient, the method of transport and length of journey must all appear on this document. If the journey takes longer than predicted, the length of the validity of the permit must be altered accordingly by the nearest tax office.

— In France shipping wine without clearance is considered to be fiscal fraud and is punishable as such. It is advisable to keep relevant fiscal documents in case the wine is moved again, because they can be used to establish a new *congé*.

— The taxes that are levied are in proportion to the volume of wine and are divided into one of two categories: table wine or appellation wine.

Exporting wine

Like all products made or manufactured in France, wine is subject to a certain number of taxes. When these products or objects are exported, it is possible to obtain tax exemptions or rebates. Wine is exempt from VAT and transport tax (but not from the *taxe parafiscale*, a special tax assigned to the national fund for the development of agriculture). When a visitor wishes to benefit from tax exemption on exports, the wine that he or she buys must be accompanied by its *titre de mouvement* (a green form No. 8102 for appellation wines, and a blue form No. 8101 for table wines), which will be accepted by the customs office that oversees the export of the merchandise. If the bottles have fiscal stamps the tax cannot be reclaimed. In order to benefit from a tax rebate, therefore, it is advisable to indicate to the seller that the wine is intended for export at the time of purchase. It is also advisable to find out about importing wines and other alcoholic drinks into the countries concerned, as each country has its own regulations, which can range from import taxes to quotas to a blanket ban. Potential exporters of French wines should always contact their own customs authorities to clarify relevant regulations.

KEEPING WINE

Building up a good wine cellar involves a lot more than simply accumulating bottles. In addition to the principles already described, there are a number of important factors. One useful approach is to try to acquire wines of similar character and style, which need different lengths of time to age, so that they do not all reach their peak at the same time. It is also best to select wines that stay at their peak for the maximum possible period and so do not all need to be consumed within a short space of time. Choose a wide variety of wines so that you do not always have to drink the same sort, even if they are of the best, and so that you can be sure that there is always something appropriate to every occasion and to accompany all sorts of different food. Finally, there are two constraints that condition all other requirements – your budget and the size of the cellar space itself.

— A good cellar space should be enclosed, dark, free from vibration, noise and smells, and protected from draughts. At the same time it should be airy, not too dry nor too damp (a humidity level of about 75%). Most importantly, it should have a constant temperature of about 11°C.

— Cellars in towns rarely have all these characteristics. It is, therefore, important to try to improve the cellar before storing the wine by increasing or decreasing the ventilation as required. For example, it is possible to adjust the humidity of a too-dry cellar by introducing a basin of water and charcoal. If a cellar is too damp, dry it out by putting a layer of gravel on the floor and increasing the ventilation. If necessary the temperature can be regulated with the help of insulating panels, and, if vibration is a problem, by placing the racks on rubber blocks. If there is a central heating boiler nearby giving off oil fumes, the future will be less than bright for your wine.

— It is possible that a cellar may not be available or even if there is, that it may not be fit for use. In this case, there are two options: either buy a specially made unit that can store between 50 and 500 bottles, whose temperature and humidity are automatically regulated, or build a unit from scratch, somewhere at the back of your house or apartment. You will need a store-room in which the temperature is fairly constant and, if possible, does not rise above 16°C. Bear in mind that the higher the temperature the more quickly a wine ages and that it is not true, as was once commonly thought, that a wine that reaches its peak quickly in bad conditions is of the same quality as one that has matured slowly in a good cool cellar. Thus, fine wines that need to mature slowly should not be aged in a cellar, or any other type of store, that is too warm. Wine-lovers should plan their purchases and storage according to the premises that they have at their disposal.

Establishing a good cellar

Experience has shown that a cellar is always too small. The storage of the bottles has to be organized logically. A wine-rack with one or two rows has several advantages: it is not expensive, it can be installed straight away, and it gives easy access to the bottles. Unfortunately, it takes up a lot of room for the number of bottles stored. To gain extra space, the only way is to store the bottles in piles. In order to separate the stacks and have access to different wines you need to build, or have built, "bins", which are made from breeze-blocks and which can contain 24, 36 or 48 bottles in stacks on two levels.

— If there is enough room it is possible to raise the bins on planks. However, these will need to be checked regularly for rot as well as for the presence of insects that might attack the corks.

— Two pieces of apparatus will complete the cellar: a maximum-and-minimum thermometer and a hygrometer to measure the humidity. Regular readings will help to correct any variations in temperature or humidity and to maintain the long-term requirements for ageing wines to best effect.

Storing wine in the cellar

As far as possible, the following rules should be observed: white wines should be stored close to the ground with the red wines on top; wines for long-term keeping should be stored on the less-accessible racks at the back, with bottles ready for drinking near the front.

— Bottles bought or delivered in cardboard boxes should not be left in this type of packaging, unlike those delivered in wooden crates. Buyers who envisage reselling

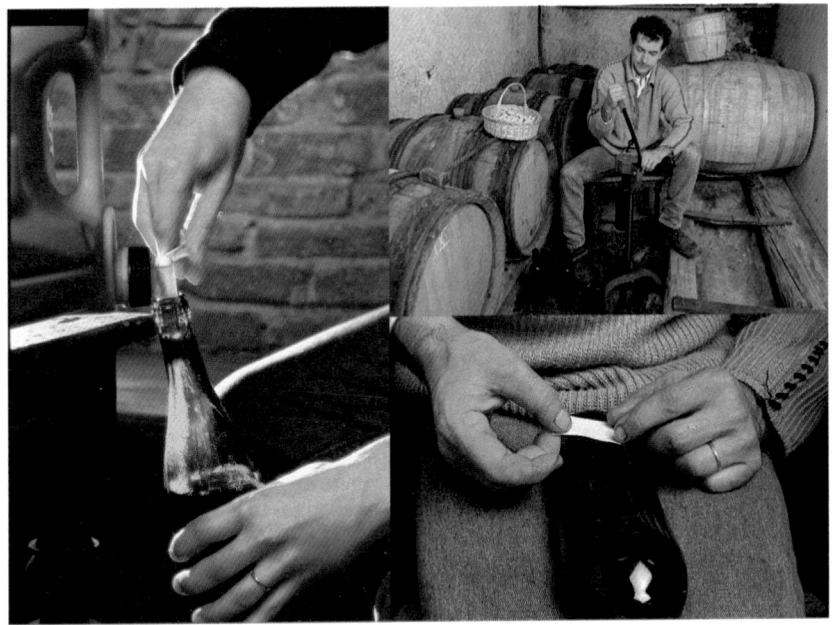

the wine should leave it in the crate, but others should not for two reasons: it takes up a lot of room, and it is a prime target for thieves. In any case, a cataloguing system (numerical, for example) will help to identify racks and bottles. This system can be logged in the most useful tool of the wine-cellar, the cellar book.

BOTTLING

If the wine has been transported in a container, it should be bottled as soon as possible; if it has been shipped by barrel, it is essential that it should rest for two weeks before bottling. This general advice needs to be tempered in light of the atmospheric conditions prevailing on the day chosen for bottling.

— Ideally, the weather should be mild, with high barometric pressure and no threat of rain or storms. In practice, the wine-lover will have to compromise between the ideal and the possible. However, no compromises should be made with the necessary equipment. First of all, the bottles should be the appropriate ones for the wine. As a rule, Bordeaux bottles should be used for all wines from the southwest and, possibly, from the Midi too, and Burgundy bottles for wines from the southeast, Beaujolais and Burgundy (always bearing in mind that there are other types of regional bottles for specific appellations).

— If the bottles are to be stored in stacks, it should be noted that, whether they are Bordeaux or Burgundy in style, bottles are of varying thickness (some bottles have flat, or nearly flat, bases). As well as weight, the height and diameter also vary.

— All bottles are suitable for keeping wine in, but the lighter bottles are less suitable for storing wine in stacks over a long period of time. In addition, if lighter gauge bottles are over-filled they can sometimes explode when the cork is forced into place. Generally, it is better to use the heavier gauge bottles. It is almost as incongruous to bottle a great wine in light glass as it would be to use a clear glass bottle for a red wine. Custom dictates that these bottles should be used only for certain white wines, so that the colour can be clearly seen. However, white wines are particularly sensitive to the light, and this custom should be ignored. Their sensitivity to light is so great that champagne houses that sell wine in clear bottles always protect them with opaque paper or with a box.

— Whichever type of bottle is chosen, it is essential that there are sufficient bottles and corks available before bottling is begun, because once under way this operation should be completed rapidly. If the cask or container is left open, the remaining wine may become oxidized and develop acescency, making the wine unfit to drink. Cleanliness is also essential, and the bottles should be scrupulously rinsed and dried before they are used.

Corks

Despite extensive research, cork remains the only material suitable for sealing bottles. Corks are not identical, differing in diameter, length and quality.

— The diameter of the cork is always 6 mm larger than the bottleneck. The better the wine, the longer the cork required. This is necessary for long-term ageing and is no more than due consideration for the wine and for those who will one day enjoy it.

— The quality of a cork is more difficult to assess. It needs to be about ten years old to have the necessary suppleness. Good corks should not have those little cracks that are sometimes blocked up with cork powder – these are known as "improved" corks. It is also possible to buy corks that have been stamped (or to have them stamped) with the vintage of the wine that is to be bottled.

— Today, it is possible to buy ready-to-use corks, which are available in ozone-sterilized packaging. They are no longer moistened, but inserted dry, as this has proved to be the most successful method.

Filling the bottles

The ideal apparatus for filling bottles is a pump. There are two types: a piston pump and a vane pump, both of which are available in DIY stores for a modest price.
— The bottle should be slightly tilted to let the wine run down the whole length of the side, to minimize the amount of oxidation and stirring up. This precaution is even more necessary for white wines. In no circumstances should a scum be allowed to appear on the surface of the liquid. The bottles should be filled as full as possible, so that the cork is in contact with the wine when the bottle is in an upright position. The cork should be inserted with the help of a special corking device that compresses the cork width-wise before insertion. There is a wide range of equipment available at varying prices for this purpose.

Labels

These can be attached with wallpaper paste or a mixture of flour and water. Simpler still, the labels can be moistened with milk and stuck on the bottles. The bottom edge of the label should be 3 cm from the base of the bottle. Perfectionists will add ready-made capsules to the top of the bottle with the aid of a little machine, or they will seal the tops with melted coloured wax, which can be bought from a cork merchant.

THREE SUGGESTIONS FOR YOUR CELLAR

Everyone stocks his or her own cellar according to personal taste. The collections described on the following page are only suggestions and the main theme is diversity. Vins Nouveaux, and wines that gain nothing from being aged in the cellar do not feature in these lists. The fewer the bottles, the greater the need to maintain stocks. The prices in brackets are, of course, applicable only to France and are given as a guide only.

A 50-bottle cellar (€880)

25 bottles of Bordeaux	17 red (Graves, Saint-Emilion, Médoc, Pomerol, Fronsac) 8 white: 5 dry (Graves), 3 sweet (Sauternes-Barsac)
20 bottles of Burgundy	12 red (Côte de Nuits crus, Côte de Beaune crus) 8 white (Chablis, Meursault, Puligny)
10 bottles of Vallée du Rhône	7 red (Côte-Rôtie, Hermitage, Châteauneuf-du-Pape) 3 white (Hermitage, Condrieu)

A 150-bottle cellar (about €2,700)

Region		Red	White
40 Bordeaux	30 red 10 white	Fronsac, Pomerol Saint-Emilion, Graves, Médoc (Crus Classés, Crus Bourgeois)	5 good, dry white wines 5 { Sainte-Croix-du-Mont Sauternes-Barsac
30 Burgundy	15 red 15 white	Côte de Nuits crus Côte de Beaune crus Côte Chalonnaise	Chablis Meursault Puligny-Montrachet
25 Vallée du Rhône	19 red 6 white	Côte-Rôtie Hermitage (red) Cornas Saint-Joseph Châteauneuf-du-Pape Gigondas Côtes-du-Rhône Villages	Condrieu Hermitage (white) Châteauneuf-du-Pape (white)

15	Vallée de la Loire	8 red 7 white	Bourgueil Chinon Saumur-Champigny	Pouilly-Fumé Vouvray Coteaux du Layon
10	Southwest	7 red 3 white	Madiran Cahors	Jurançon (sweet and dry)
8	Southeast	6 red 2 white	Bandol Palette (red)	Cassis Palette (white)
7	Alsace	(white)		Gewurtztraminer Riesling Tokay
5	Jura	(white)		Vins Jaunes (yellow wines) Côtes du Jura-Arbois
10	Champagne and sparkling wines (readily accessible, as these wines do not improve with age)			Crémant de { Loire Burgundy Alsace Various types of Champagne

A 300-bottle cellar

To create such a cellar an investment of about €6,500 is needed. You double the numbers required for the 150-bottle cellar but should bear in mind that the more bottles you have, the longer the life of the wine has to be. This usually means, unfortunately, that despite discounts the wine is going to be more expensive.

THE ART OF DRINKING

If drinking is a physiological necessity, drinking wine is a pleasure. This pleasure varies in intensity depending on the wine, the tasting conditions and the sensitivity of the taster.

TASTING

There are several types of winetasting, each suited to a particular end. The technical, analytical, comparative, triangular and so forth types of tasting are reserved for professionals. The wine-lover practises tasting purely for pleasure, to discover the quintessence of a wine, to learn how to put this into words and to improve the sensitivity of the nose and palate.

— Tasting and, more generally, consumption of wine, should not take place anywhere and in any fashion. The location should be pleasant, well lit natural light or "daylight" lighting, which does not alter colours, preferably with light-coloured walls and free from any stray odours, such as perfume, smoke (tobacco and fire), cooking smells or flowers. The temperature should be between 18 and 20°C.

— The choice of an appropriate glass is extremely important. It should be clear, so that the colour of the wine can be clearly seen, and if possible not too thick. It should have a tulip shape – that is it should not turn outwards at the top, which is often the case, but should in fact turn slightly inwards. The body of the glass should be separated from the foot by a stem. This prevents the glass from being warmed when it is held (by the stem) and makes it easier to swirl the wine; this is done in order to oxygenate the wine and to release its bouquet.

— The shape of the glass is so important and has such an influence on the olfactory appreciation of wine (both taste and smell) that the *Association Française de Normalisation* (AFNOR) and the *Instances Internationales de Normalisation* (ISO) have, as a result of a study, adopted a glass that is eminently suitable for both taster and

consumer. This type of glass, which is commonly referred to in France as "the INAO glass", is not just for professionals but can be found in France in specialist shops. Over the last few years, French, German and Austrian glassmakers have considerably extended the choice of wine glasses available.

Tasting techniques
Tasting involves sight, smell, taste and touch – not touching with the fingers, of course, but with the mouth, which is sensitive to "mechanical" effects of wine, such as temperature, consistency and fizz.

Sight
The first contact that a consumer has with wine is with the eye. Examining the visual appearance of the wine, which includes assessing its distinguishing colour, can reveal a lot of information. This is the first test. Whatever the colour and tint of the wine, it should be clear, not cloudy. Any trace of streaks or cloudiness is a sign of disease and the wine should be rejected. Only small insoluble tartaric crystals (*gravelle*), which occur when there is a sudden cold spell, should be accepted; the quality of the wine is not affected by them.

— The clarity of a wine can be tested by placing the glass between the eye and a source of light that should, if possible, be at the same height. The transparency of red wine can be determined by looking at it against a white background, such as a tablecloth or a piece of paper. The glass should be tilted and the surface, or "disc", should form an ellipse; the shape can say a lot about the age of the wine and how it has been kept. The next thing to examine is the actual shade of the colour. All young wines should be transparent, which is not the case with old, quality wines.

Wine	Shade of colour	Interpretation
White	Almost colourless	Very young, well protected from oxidization. Modern vinification in vat
	Very light yellow with hints of green	Young to very young. Vinified and aged in vat
	Straw yellow, golden yellow	Matured. Perhaps aged in wood
	Coppery gold, bronze gold	Already old
	Amber to black	Oxidized, too old
	Flecked white, partridge eye (soft corn colour) with hints of pink	Rosé obtained by pressing and light young rosés
Rosé	Very light, clear salmon-pink to red	Young, fruity rosé, ready to drink
	Pink with shades of yellow to onion skin	Beginning to be old for its type
Red	Purple	Very young. Good shade for nouveau Gamay and Beaujolais Nouveau (6 to 18 months)
	Pure red (cherry)	Neither young nor old. Peak period for wines which are neither nouveau nor for laying down (2–3 years)
	Red with bands of orange	Mature wine (short-term keeping). Beginning of ageing (3–7 years)
	Brownish red to brown	Only great wines have reached their peak when they are this colour. For others, it is too late.

— The brilliance or luminosity of a wine is also important. If a wine is luminous it is lively; a dull wine will be lifeless. The intensity of colour, which is not to be confused with shade or tone, should also be taken into account.

Wine	Shade of colour	Interpretation
Too light	Not pressed enough Rainy year Too large a yield Young vines Grapes not sufficiently ripe Rotten grapes Too short a time in vat Fermentation at low temperature	Light wines for short-term keeping Unexceptional vintages
Dark	Well pressed Low yield Old vines Successful vinification	Good or great wines Good future

— "Legs" or "tears", formed on the side of the glass when it is swirled around to breathe in the bouquet (see below) are also part of the visual aspect of wine. They are related to the alcoholic content: cognac always produces these, *vins de pays* rarely do so.

> Examples of vocabulary used when talking about the appearance of wine:
>
> *Shades:* purple, garnet, ruby, violet, cherry, peony
>
> *Intensity:* light, strong, dark, deep, intense
>
> *Brilliance:* matt, dull, sad, sparkling, brilliant
>
> *Clarity and transparency:* opaque, hazy, veiled, crystalline, flawless

Smell

Olfactory examination is the next test that wine has to undergo during tasting. Certain odours, such as volatile acidity (acescency, vinegar), and a corky smell discount wines straight away, but in most cases the bouquet – that is, the combination of odours released from the glass – is a new voyage of discovery each time.

— The aromatic components of the bouquet are expressed according to their volatility. What takes place is a kind of evaporation, and that is why the temperature at which wine is served is so important. If the wine is too cold, there will be no bouquet; too hot, and the result is too rapid evaporation, marked by aromas joining together, oxidation, the loss of highly volatile aromas and the release of abnormally heavy aromatic elements.

— The bouquet of a wine is like a kaleidoscope of scents that is forever changing; they emerge one after another depending on temperature and exposure to the air. This is why the way the glass is handled is important. First of all, the aromas released from a still glass are breathed in, then the glass is swirled around, and exposure to the air releases yet other scents.

— The quality of a wine is a function of the intensity and complexity of its bouquet. Mediocre wines have a small bouquet, if any; they usually have one note only and can be summed up very simply, in one word. On the other hand, great wines have full, deep bouquets, and their complexity is constantly changing.

— The vocabulary used to describe bouquets is almost infinite, because it uses analogy. Several classifications to describe them have been put forward, but to simplify matters we will use the following characteristics: floral, fruity, vegetable (or herbaceous), spicy, balsamic, gamey, woody, smoky or burnt and chemical.

Examples of vocabulary used to describe the bouquet:	
Flowers:	violets, linden flowers, jasmine, elderflower, acacia, iris, peony
Fruits:	raspberry, blackcurrant, cherry, Morello cherry, gooseberry, apricot, apple, banana, prune
Vegetable:	grassy, fern, moss, undergrowth, damp ground, chalky, various mushrooms
Balsamic:	resin, pine, terebinth (turpentine tree)
Gamey:	meat, well-hung meat, game, civet, musk
Burnt:	burnt, grilled, toasted, tobacco, dried hay, all roasted aromas (coffee etc).

Taste

Having triumphantly passed through the two examinations of sight and smell, a wine's final test is that of taste.

— A small amount of wine is taken into the mouth, where it is held, and a breath of air is also taken in and diffused throughout the oral cavity. If this is not possible, the wine is just swirled around the mouth. As the wine warms up in the mouth, it releases new aromas that are captured by the retronasal passage. The papillae (taste-buds) on the tongue can detect only the four basic flavours – bitter, acidic, sweet and salty – which is why a person with a cold cannot taste wine (or food) because the retronasal passage is blocked.

— In addition to the four flavours mentioned above, the mouth is also sensitive to the temperature of the wine, its viscosity, the presence or absence of carbon dioxide and astringency (the effect of astringency is the contraction of mucous membranes in response to tannin, which is felt as the absence of lubrication from the saliva glands).

— It is by tasting that the balance and harmony of a wine is revealed or, conversely, that the characteristics of a badly constructed wine, which is not to be bought, are discovered.

— White wines, light rosés and rosés are characterized by a good balance between acidity and sweetness.

Too much acidity:	the wine is aggressive; not acidic enough, it is flat
Too sweet:	the wine is heavy and thick; not sweet enough, it is thin and dull

In red wines there should be a balance between acidity, sweetness and tannin.

Excess acidity:	wine is too vigorous and often thin
Excess tannin:	wine is hard and astringent
Excess sweetness (rare):	heavy wine
Lack of acidity:	flabby wine
Lack of tannin:	unstructured, undefined wine
Lack of sweetness:	wine will dry out

A good wine balances the three components acidity, sweetness and tannin. These elements give it its richness of aroma. A great wine can be distinguished from a good wine by its rigorous, powerful but harmonious structure and the fullness of its aromatic complexity.

Examples of vocabulary used to describe the actual tasting of wine:	
Minus points:	unstructured, flabby, flat, thin, watery, limited, transparent, poor, heavy, massive, coarse, thick, unbalanced
Plus points:	structured, well-built, well-constructed, balanced, fleshy (or full-bodied), elegant, fine, good texture, rich

After this analysis in the mouth, the wine is swallowed. The wine-lover then concentrates on measuring the persistence of its aromas, known familiarly as "length on the palate". This estimation is expressed in caudals, one unit being equal quite simply, to one second. The "longer" a wine is, the better the quality. The "length on the palate" alone is the only method of grading wines from the poorest to the greatest.
— This measuring in seconds is very simple and at the same time very complicated. It concerns only the length of the aromas, not the structure of the wine (acidity, bitterness, sweetness or alcohol content), which cannot be measured in this way.

Identifying wine

Tasting, like consuming, is a way of appreciating wine. It involves tasting it fully and deciding whether it is of average, good or excellent quality. Often, it is a matter of deciding whether it conforms to its type, so its origin also needs to be identified.
— Tasting to identify – that is recognition – is a sport, a kind of parlour game, but it is an impossible game to play without a minimum of information. It is easy enough to identify a variety such as a Cabernet Sauvignon, but to know whether it comes from Italy, Languedoc, California, Chile, Argentina, Australia or South Africa is another matter. If the range is limited to France, it is possible to identify the larger regions, but being more precise presents serious problems. If there were six glasses representing six Médoc appellations (Listrac, Moulis, Margaux, Saint-Julien, Pauillac, Saint-Estèphe), how many people would be able to guess which was which without making any mistakes?
— A classic experiment that anyone can try proves how difficult tasting can be: the taster, blindfolded, tastes in random order red wines with very little tannin and non-aromatic white wines, preferably oak-aged. The taster has simply to distinguish between red and white (and vice versa); it is very rare not to make a mistake! Paradoxically, it is much easier to recognize a very characteristic wine whose memory and taste lingers on in your memory – but what are the chances of being offered the same wine?

REGIONS	VARIETIES	CHARACTERISTICS
All the red Burgundy AOCs	Pinot	Fine wines to lay down
All the white Burgundy AOCs	Chardonnay	Fine wines to lay down
Beaujolais	Gamay	"Nouveau" or "Primeur" wines or wines for rapid consumption
Northern Rhône (red)	Syrah	Fine wines to lay down
Northern Rhône (white)	Marsanne, Roussanne	Wines for medium to long-term maturing
Northern Rhône (white)	Viognier	Full-bodied wines to lay down
Southern Rhône, Languedoc, Côtes de Provence	Grenache, Cinsault Mourvèdre, Syrah	Full-bodied wines for medium to long-term maturing
Alsace (each variety, vinified separately, lends its name to the wine)	Riesling, Pinot Gris, Gewurztraminer, Sylvaner, Muscat . . .	Aromatic wines to be drunk quickly except for Grands Crus, Vendanges Tardives or Sélections de Grains Nobles
Champagne	Pinot, Chardonnay	Can be drunk on purchase

Loire (white)	Sauvignon	Aromatic wines to be drunk rapidly
Loire (white)	Muscadet	To be drunk quickly
Loire (white)	Chenin	Improve with age
Loire (red)	Cabernet Franc (Breton)	Short to long-term maturing
All the red Bordeaux, Bergerac and southwestern AOCs	Cabernet Sauvignon, Cabernet Franc, Merlot	Fine wines to lay down
Madiran	Tannat, Cabernets	Fine wines to lay down
Bordeaux (white), Bergerac, Montravel, Monbazillac, Duras	Sémillon, Sauvignon, Muscadelle	Dry: for short to long-term maturing; Sweet dessert wines: for laying down;
Jurançon	Petit Manseng	Dry: short-term maturation;
	Gros Manseng	Sweet: long-term maturation

Tasting with a view to purchasing

When you visit a vineyard with a view to purchasing wine, the first step towards choosing the wine is to taste it. Tasting is an act both of appreciation and of comparison. It is easy to compare two or three wines, but the situation becomes more complicated when price has to be taken into account. With a fixed budget – and budgets are invariably fixed – purchases are automatically eliminated. The tasting is further complicated when the purpose of the wine (for example, as an accompaniment to different kinds of food) is considered. To guess what you might be eating in ten years' time, and consequently to buy an appropriate wine for the occasion, has something of the magician's art about it. Comparative tasting, easy and simple in principle, becomes a delicate matter when the buyer has to guess the necessary length of ageing and peak periods of various wines. Wine-growers themselves sometimes make mistakes when they try to envisage the future of their wines and it is not unknown for wine-growers to buy back their own wine, originally sold at cut-price, because they had thought wrongly, that it would age badly.

— Nevertheless, some general principles can help in the appreciation of wine. To age well, wines must have a solid structure. They must have a sufficient degree of alcohol, and chaptalization (the adding of sugar, regulated by law) can be a contributory factor if necessary. It is also advisable to pay attention to the levels of acidity and tannin. A wine that is too supple because its acidity is low or very low (which can, nevertheless, taste very pleasant), will be fragile and its longevity uncertain. A wine that is low in tannin will also not have much of a future. In the first example, the grapes will have been over-exposed to the sun and heat; in the second, the grapes will not have ripened sufficiently, will have been attacked by rot or will have suffered an inappropriate vinification.

— These two components of wine, acidity and tannin, can be measured. Acidity can be calculated by its equivalence in sulphuric acid, in grams per litre or in pH, and tannin can be measured according to the Folain scale, but this needs to be carried out in a laboratory.

— A wine with less than three grams per litre of acidity does not have much of a future. It is more difficult to give an exact estimation of the level of tannin below which long-term keeping would be problematic, but it is useful to know what the scale is, as very ripe, smooth tannins are sometimes underestimated on tasting and are not always revealed.

— In any case, wine should be tasted in good conditions, without the ambience of the wine-cellar taking over. Avoid tasting immediately after a meal or after consuming a liqueur, coffee, chocolate or mints, or after smoking. Beware if a wine-grower offers nuts, because they make any wine taste better! Beware also of cheese, as this changes the sensitivity of the palate; if absolutely necessary, eat a piece of plain bread.

Practising tasting

Like any other technique, tasting can be learned. It can be practised at home following the guidelines above or, if you are very keen, you can enrol on one of the ever-increasing number of courses offered by various private organizations. The best of such courses cover a whole range of topics in addition to just tasting, including food and wines, the discovery of the larger wine-producing areas (not only French regions) through tasting, an analysis of the influence of grape varieties, vintages and soils, the effect of vinification techniques and organized visits to wine estates in the company of the vineyard owner.

SERVING WINE

In a restaurant serving wine is the responsibility of the wine waiter. At home no wine waiter will be available, and it pays to learn some of the tricks of the trade. There are many of these, starting with choosing the bottles that are best suited to the dishes making up the meal and those that have reached their peak.

— Individual taste does come into matching food and wine, but, centuries of experience have made it possible to establish some general principles, ideal combinations and major incompatibilities.

— The rate at which wines age varies tremendously. The wine-lover who wants nothing but the best will be interested only in the wine's peak period. Depending on the appellation, variety, soil and vinification, this could be any time between one and twenty years. Depending on the year on the label, the same wine could age two or three times more rapidly. However, it is possible to establish average times that can be used as a basis and that can be adapted to the cellar and the information on the vintage cards.

Peak (in years)

W = White; R = Red	
Alsace (W): within the year	Vallée du Rhône, Southern (W): 2; (R): 4–8
Alsace Grand Cru (W): 1–4	Loire (W): 1–5; (R): 3–10
Alsace (late harvest) (W): 8–12	Loire, sweet, rich (W): 10–15
Jura (W): 4; (R): 8	Périgord wines (W): 2–3; (R): 3–4
Jura, rosé: 6	Périgord wines, sweet (W): 6–8
Vin Jaune (W): 20	Bordeaux (W): 2–3; (R): 6–8
Savoie (W): 1–2; (R): 2–4	Bordeaux, fine (W): 4–10; (R): 10–15
Burgundy (W): 5 (R): 7	Bordeaux, sweet (W): 10–15
Burgundy, fine (W): 8–10; (R): 10–15	Jurançon, dry (W): 2–4
Mâcon (W): 2–3; (R): 1–2	Jurançon, sweet, rich (W): 6–10
Beaujolais (R): within the year	Madiran (R): 5–12
Beaujolais Crus (R): 1–4	Cahors (R): 3–10
Vallée du Rhône, Northern (W): 2–3; (R): 4–5	Gaillac (W): 1–3; (R): 2–4
Côte-Rôtie, Hermitage etc. (W):8; (R): 8–15	Languedoc (W): 1–2; (R): 2–4
	Côtes de Provence (W): 1–2; (R): 2–4
	Corsican (W): 1–2; (R): 2–4

NB: Do not confuse peak period with maximum longevity.
A warm cellar or one with a variable temperature accelerates the ageing process.

Methods of serving

Care must be taken with the wine from its selection in the cellar to its arrival in the glass. The older the wine, the more care should be taken. The bottle should be taken from its stack and gently returned to an upright position, ready to be taken to table, unless it is going to be put straight into a special pouring basket.

— Wines of average quality should be served simply. A very old and consequently very delicate wine should be poured from the basket, where it has been carefully placed in the same position as it was in the stack. Younger wines and robust wines should be decanted, either to oxygenate them because they still contain gas left over from

fermentation or to start oxidization, which improves the taste of the wine, or simply to separate clear wine from sediment at the bottom of the bottle. In the last case, the wine must be decanted with care and should be done in front of a light source, traditionally

Serving wine

a candle – a custom that predates the arrival of electric lighting and has no particular advantage – to allow the sediments and cloudy wine to stay in the bottle.

Opening the bottle and serving

Professor Peynaud, France's leading scientific authority on winetasting, maintains that it is not necessary to open a bottle a long time before drinking the wine, because the surface area of the wine that is exposed to the air (at the neck of the bottle) is too small to make a difference. However, the table on the following page summarizes traditional usage that, if it does not always improve the wine, never spoils it.

White aromatic wines Red or white nouveau wines Red and white young wines Rosé wines	Open, drink straight away Bottle vertical
White Loire wines Sweet white wines	Open, wait an hour Bottle vertical
Young red wines Red wines at their peak	Decant half an hour to two hours before drinking
Old delicate red wines	Open in pouring basket and serve immediately; in some cases, decant and drink immediately

Opening

The capsule should be cut below the ring or in the middle of it. The wine should never come into contact with the metal of the capsule. If the neck is sealed with wax, chip the wax away gently or, better still, remove the wax from the top part of the neck with a knife; this method is preferable because it does not disturb the wine or the bottle.
— To remove the cork, a traditional-style corkscrew (or one with arms, if handled gently) should be used. Theoretically, the cork should not be pierced all the way through. Once removed, it should be smelt to make sure that there are no bacterial odours present and that there is no corky smell. Afterwards, as a final test, the wine should be tasted before it is served.

The right temperature

A wine can be completely spoiled by serving it at the wrong temperature; conversely a wine can be improved by being served at the right temperature. It is rare to achieve this without the help of a wine thermometer – a pocket version is handy for taking to restaurants and for dipping in the wine when at home. The temperature for serving wine depends on its appellation (its type), its age and, in a few cases, the temperature of the room. It should be remembered that wine warms up in the glass.

Bordeaux, fine wines, red	16–17°C
Burgundy, fine wines, red	15–16°C
Quality red wines	14–16°C
White, dry fine wines	14–16°C
Light, fruity, young red wines	11–12°C
Rosé wines, nouveau wines	10–12°C
Dry white wines, red Vins de Pays	10–12°C
Average white wines, white Vins de Pays	8–10°C
Champagne, sparkling	7–8°C
Sweet	6°C

These temperatures should be increased by one or two degrees if the wine is old.
— There is a tendency to serve wines slightly more chilled when they are offered as an apéritif and warmer when they are to accompany a meal. Similarly, the climate of the area and the temperature of the room should be taken into account; in very hot weather a wine drunk at 11°C can seem icy and it is therefore advisable to serve it at 13° or even 14°C.

— Nevertheless, the 20°C mark should not be passed because physico-chemical phenomena, independent of the environment, can cause irreversible changes, altering the qualities of the wine and the pleasure that we expect from it.

| Burgundy | Alsace | Bordeaux | INAO | Champagne |

Glasses

Each region has its own particular glass. In practice, and to avoid being excessively purist, it is best to use either a universal-style glass (a tasting glass) or the two sorts most commonly used, the Bordeaux and the Burgundy. Whichever glass is used, it should be filled in moderation, nearer one-third full rather than half full.

In the restaurant

In the restaurant the wine waiter looks after the bottle and examines the cork but allows the person who ordered the wine to taste it. Before this, the wine waiter will have recommended wines to accompany the dishes.

— Reading the wine list is instructive, not only because it reveals the secrets of the cellar, which is its function, but because it is also indicative of the level of competence of the wine waiter, the cellar-master or the manager. A good wine list should definitely include the following information for each wine: appellation, vintage, place where it was bottled and the name of the wine-merchant or owner responsible for the wine. This last piece of information is often omitted – for no good reason.

— A good wine list should offer a wide range of appellations and a variety of vintages of different qualities (some restaurateurs have the annoying habit of offering only average quality vintages). An intelligent list should be adapted to the style or specialities of the cuisine and should offer a good selection of local wines.

— Sometimes, house wine is on offer. It is possible to buy a pleasant wine that does not benefit from an AOC, but these wines are never great wines.

Wine bistros and wine bars

In France there have always been wine bistros selling good-quality wine by the glass, often wines selected by the bistro owner on personal visits to vineyards. Selections of cold meat and cheese are usually on offer to customers in these establishments.

— In the 1970s a new generation of French wine bistros appeared, often referred to as "wine bars". The perfecting of an apparatus that protects wine in open bottles with a layer of nitrogen (*le cruover*) has allowed these establishments to offer customers very good wines with prestigious vintages. More sophisticated menus have been developed to accompany these wines.

VINTAGES

All quality wines have vintages. The only exceptions to this rule are a few particular wines and some Champagnes, whose own individual production involves the blending of several different years.

— Having said this, what should we make of a bottle that does not have a vintage? There are two possible reasons for the omission: either the year is inadmissible because its reputation is so tarnished within the appellation, or it cannot be given a year because it is a mixture of several years blended together (known among professionals as *vins de plusieurs années*). The quality of the product depends on the talent of the blender; generally, a blended wine is superior to each of its individual components, but it is not advisable to age this type of bottle. A wine from a great year is concentrated and balanced and is usually, but not always, the result of small yields, harvested early.

— In every case, great vintages come only from perfectly healthy grapes, untainted by rot. To obtain a great vintage, it does not matter what the weather is like at the beginning of the vegetative cycle. It can even be said that a few mishaps such as frost or *coulure* (the falling of young grapes before maturation) are a good thing, as they reduce the number of grapes per bunch, thus reducing the volume. On the other hand, the period between 15 August to harvest time (end of September) is crucial; a maximum of sun and heat are necessary. The year 1961, *the* year of the 20th century, was exemplary; everything happened as it should. On the other hand, 1963, 1965 and 1968 were disastrous years, because they suffered from a combination of cold and rain, which meant that the grapes did not mature properly. There was a glut and the grapes were swollen with water. The combination of rain and heat is not much better as warm water invites rot. This was the stumbling-block that tripped up the potentially great 1976 vintage in the south west. Progress in the development of treatments to protect grapes, in particular from the grape worm and from rot, have led to quality harvests that previously would have been spoiled. These treatments also make it possible to wait with equanimity for the grapes to ripen fully (which improves the quality) even if the immediate meteorological conditions are not encouraging. From 1978 onwards, there have been some excellent late-harvested vintages.

— It is customary to record and grade the quality of vintages in table form. These grades are averages only and do not take into account microclimates, or the heroic efforts of hand sorting the grapes at harvest time or the vagaries of the winemaking process. For example, a Graves, Domaine de Chevalier from 1965 – which elsewhere was a terrible year – proves that a great wine can be produced even during a year that is ranked at zero!

Vintage table (from 0–20)

	Bordeaux Red	Bordeaux White, Sweet	Bordeaux White, Dry	Burgundy Red	Burgundy White	Champagne	Loire	Rhône	Alsace
1900	19	19	17	13		17			
1901	11	14							
1902									
1903	14	7	11						
1904	15	17		16		19		18	
1905	14	12							
1906	16	16		19	18				
1907	12	10		15					
1908	13	16							

	Bordeaux Red	Bordeaux White, Sweet	Bordeaux White, Dry	Burgundy Red	Burgundy White	Champagne	Loire	Rhône	Alsace
1909	10	7							
1910									
1911	14	14		19	19	20	19	19	
1912	10	11							
1913	7	7							
1914	13	15				18			
1915		16		16	15	15	12	15	
1916	15	15		13	11	12	11	10	
1917	14	16		11	11	13	12	9	
1918	16	12		13	12	12	11	14	
1919	15	10		18	18	15	18	15	15
1920	17	16		13	14	14	11	13	10
1921	16	20		16	20	20	20	13	20
1922	9	11		9	16	4	7	6	4
1923	12	13		16	18	17	18	18	14
1924	15	16		13	14	11	14	17	11
1925	6	11		6	5	3	4	8	6
1926	16	17		16	16	15	13	13	14
1927	7	14		7	5	5	3	4	
1928	19	17		18	20	20	17	17	17
1929	20	20		20	19	19	18	19	18
1930							3	4	3
1931	2	2		2	3		3	5	3
1932				2	3	3	3	3	7
1933	11	9		16	18	16	17	17	15
1934	17	17		17	18	17	16	17	16
1935	7	12		13	16	10	15	5	14
1936	7	11		9	10	9	12	13	9
1937	16	20		18	18	18	16	17	17
1938	8	12		14	10	10	12	8	9
1939	11	16		9	9	9	10	8	3
1940	13	12		12	8	8	11	5	10
1941	12	10		9	12	10	7	5	5
1942	12	16		14	12	16	11	14	14
1943	15	17		17	16	17	13	17	16
1944	13	11	12	10	10		6	8	
1945	20	20	18	20	18	20	19	18	20
1946	14	9	10	10	13	10	12	17	9
1947	18	20	18	18	18	18	20	18	17
1948	16	16	16	10	14	11	12		15
1949	19	20	18	20	18	17	16	17	19
1950	13	18	16	11	19	16	14	15	14
1951	8	6	6	7	6	7	7	8	8
1952	16	16	16	16	18	16	15	16	14
1953	19	17	16	18	17	17	18	14	18
1954	10			14	11	15	9	13	9
1955	16	19	18	15	18	19	16	15	17
1956	5						9	12	9
1957	10	15		14	15		13	16	13
1958	11	14		10	9		12	14	12
1959	19	20	18	19	17	17	19	15	20
1960	11	10	10	10	7	14	9	12	12

	Bordeaux Red	Bordeaux White, Sweet	Bordeaux White, Dry	Burgundy Red	Burgundy White	Champagne	Loire	Rhône	Alsace
1961	20	15	16	18	17	16	16	18	19
1962	16	16	16	17	19	17	15	16	14
1963					10				
1964	16	9	13	16	17	18	16	14	18
1965			12				8		
1966	17	15	16	18	18	17	15	16	12
1967	14	18	16	15	16		13	15	14
1968									
1969	10	13	12	19	18	16	15	16	16
1970	17	17	18	15	15	17	15	15	14
1971	16	17	19	18	20	16	17	15	18
1972	10		9	11	13		9	14	9
1973	13	12		12	16	16	16	13	16
1974	11	14		12	13	8	11	12	13
1975	18	17	18		11	18	15	10	15
1976	15	19	16	18	15	15	18	16	19
1977	12	7	14	11	12	9	11	11	12
1978	17	14	17	19	17	16	17	19	15
1979	16	18	18	15	16	15	14	16	16
1980	13	17	18	12	12	14	13	15	10
1981	16	16	17	14	15	15	15	14	17
1982	18	14	16	14	16	16	14	13	15
1983	17	17	16	15	16	15	12	16	20
1984	13	13	12	13	14	5	10	11	15
1985	18	15	14	17	17	17	16	16	19
1986	17	17	12	12	15	9	13	10	10
1987	13	11	16	12	11	10	13	8	13
1988	16	19	18	16	14	18	16	18	17
1989	18	19	18	16	18	16	20	16	16
1990	18	20	17	18	16	18	17	17	18
1991	13	14	13	14	15	11	12	13	13
1992	12	10	14	15	17	12	14	12	13
1993	13	8	15	14	13	12	13	13	13
1994	14	14	17	14	16	12	14	14	12
1995	16	18	17	14	16	16	17	16	12
1996	15	18	16	17	18	19	17	14	12
1997	14	18	14	14	17	15	16	14	13
1998	15	16	14	15	15	13	14	18	13
1999	14	17	13	13	12	15	12	16	10
2000	18	10	16	11	15	15	16	17	12
2001	15	17	16	13	16	9	13	17	13
2002	15	16	18	17	17	17	14	8	10

The areas encircled with a thick line indicate wines that should be cellared.
Sweet wines from the Loire were given 20 for the year 1990.

Which vintages should be drunk now?

Wines evolve differently according to whether they are created during a gloomy year or a sunny year and also according to their appellation, their position in the hierarchy within the appellation, their vinification and their ageing, the latter stages of which depend also on the cellar in which they have been stored.

— The vintage table includes only good wines from recent years, which are therefore available, provided they have been looked after correctly. It does not include

THE ART OF DRINKING

exceptional wines or exceptional *cuvées*. Wines are graded at their peak, and the table does not include the current evolution of old vintages.

COOKING WITH WINE

Cooking with wine is not a recent phenomenon. The Roman gourmet Apicius gave us a recipe for suckling pig in wine sauce (it was a *vin de paille*, the grapes being ripened on a layer of straw). Wine is used in cooking for the flavour it brings to the dishes and for its digestive properties, which are due to the glycerine and tannin it contains. Even non-drinkers may approve, as alcohol all but disappears on cooking.

— The history of cooking can be traced through wine. Wine marinades were invented to preserve pieces of meat – today we use them for their taste – and the reduction of marinades that took place during cooking was the origin of sauces. Sometimes, meat was actually cooked in wine marinades, a method that gave rise to the development of such dishes as stews, casseroles, court-bouillons and *oeufs en meurette* (eggs in red wine sauce).

Recommendations
– Do not waste old vintages in cooking. It is expensive, ineffective and can be detrimental.
– Never use vins ordinaires or very light wines in cooking; their reduction only brings out their lack of presence.
– Drink the same wine that has been used in the preparation of the dish or one that has the same origin as an accompaniment.

WINE VINEGAR

Wine is man's friend, but vinegar is wine's enemy. However, it would be wrong to conclude that vinegar is man's enemy too – wines and vinegars each have their roles to play in the range of flavours that people enjoy. To throw away quality wines that are a little musty, corky or oxidized would be a shame as they can easily be turned into vinegar. A domestic vinegar-maker is a 3- to 5-litre receptacle, made of wood or, even better, glazed earthenware, with a tap. The acidity of vinegar acts as a counterbalance to other flavours. To keep its fieriness in check, gourmet-style aromatic vinegars have been developed. Many strong flavours blend harmoniously together, including garlic, shallots, pickled onions, mustard grains, peppercorns, cloves, elderflower, chicory, rose petals, bay leaves, thyme, parsley and so on.

Recommendations
– Never leave a vinegar-maker in a cellar.
– Whenever the so-called *mère du vinaigre* or "vinegar mother" (a viscous mass) develops in the vinegar, it should be quickly removed.
– Place the vinegar-maker in a warm room at 20°C.
– Never hermetically seal it because the acetic bacteria, which transform the alcohol in the wine into acetic acid, cannot live without air.
– Never put herbs or spices in the vinegar-maker. The vinegar needs to be extracted from the vinegar-maker and placed with the seasoning in another receptacle, this time preferably hermetically sealed.
– Never use wine that has no stated origin in the vinegar-maker.
– The vinegar-maker must be in constant use. Each time vinegar is withdrawn from the vinegar-maker, an equivalent volume of wine should be added.
– A vinegar that is left for more than two or three months will taste bitter. It will lose its wine flavour and will be of no use.

FOOD AND WINE

Nothing is more difficult than finding an ideal wine to accompany a dish. But should there be such a thing? The marrying of wine and food should not be a monogamous affair; the variety that French wines offer should be an opportunity to experiment, and a good cellar should allow us to experiment with different combinations in order to extend our range of eating and drinking pleasure.

HORS D'OEUVRE

ANCHOVY PUREE ON TOAST
- Côtes du Roussillon, rosé
- Coteaux d'Aix-en-Provence, rosé
- Alsace, Sylvaner

ASPARAGUS WITH CREAMY HOLLANDAISE SAUCE
- Alsace, Muscat

AVOCADO PEAR
- Champagne
- Bugey, white
- Bordeaux, dry

FOIE GRAS
- Barsac
- Corton-Charlemagne
- Listrac
- Banyuls Rimage

FOIE GRAS IN BRIOCHE
- Alsace Tokay, selection of quality wines
- Montrachet
- Pécharmant

FROGS' LEGS
- Corbières, white
- Entre-Deux-Mers
- Touraine Sauvignon

GRILLED FOIE GRAS
- Jurançon
- Graves, red
- Condrieu

GRILLED RED PEPPERS IN VINAIGRETTE
- Clairette de Bellegarde
- Muscadet
- Mâcon Lugny, white

PROVENÇALE ARTICHOKES
- Coteaux d'Aix-en-Provence, rosé
- Loire, rosé
- Bordeaux, rosé

SALADE NIÇOISE
- Alsace Sylvaner
- Côtes du Rhône, red
- Coteaux d'Aix-en-Provence, rosé

SNAILS À LA BOURGUIGNONNE
- Bourgogne Aligoté
- Alsace Riesling
- Touraine Sauvignon

SOYA BEAN SALAD
- Alsace Tokay
- Clairette du Languedoc
- Muscadet

COLD MEATS

BAYONNE HAM
- Côtes du Rhône-Villages
- Bordeaux, clairet
- Corbières, rosé

BRAISED HAM
- Alsace Tokay
- Côtes du Rhône, red
- Côtes du Roussillon, rosé

CHICKEN LIVER TERRINE
- Meursault-Charmes
- Saint-Nicolas de Bourgueil
- Morgon

COLD COOKED SAUSAGE
- Côtes du Rhône-Villages
- Beaujolais
- Côtes de Roussillon, rosé

HAM FLAVOURED WITH PARSLEY
- Chassagne Montrachet, white
- Coteaux de Tricastin, red
- Beaujolais, red

HARE PÂTE
- Côtes de Duras, red
- Saumur-Champigny
- Moulin à Vent

RILLETTES (POTTED PORK)
- Burgundy, red
- Alsace Pinot Noir
- Touraine Gamay

RILLONS (CUBES OF PORK)
- Touraine Cabernet
- Beaujolais-Villages
- Loire, rosé

SMOKED HAM (WILD BOAR)
- Côtes de Saint-Mont, red
- Bandol, red
- Sancerre, white

SHELLFISH

BROCHETTE OF SCALLOPS
- Graves, white
- Alsace Sylvaner
- Beaujolais-Villages, red

CHARENTAIS MUSSEL STEW
- Saint-Véran
- Bergerac, dry
- Haut-Poitou, Chardonnay

CLAMS WITH GRILLED CHEESE TOPPING
- Pacherenc du Vic-Bilh
- Rully, white
- Beaujolais, white

CRAB COCKTAIL
- Jurançon, dry
- Fiefs Vendéens, white
- Bordeaux Sauvignon, dry

CRAYFISH IN COURT-BOUILLON
- Sancerre, white
- Côtes du Rhône, white
- Gaillac, white

CRAYFISH WITH MAYONNAISE
- Patrimonio, white
- Alsace Riesling
- Savoie Apremont

DUBLIN BAY PRAWNS IN COGNAC
- Chablis, Premier Cru
- Graves, white
- Muscadet de Sèvres-et-Maine

FRESH RAW MUSSELS
- Coteaux du Languedoc, white
- Muscadet de Sèvre-et-Maine
- Coteaux d'Aix-en-Provence, white

GRILLED LOBSTER
- Hermitage, white
- Pouilly-Fuissé
- Savennières

LOBSTER IN TOMATO AND WHITE WINE SAUCE
- Arbois, jaune
- Juliénas

MOULES MARINIÈRES
- Burgundy, white
- Alsace Pinot
- Bordeaux Sauvignon, dry

MUSSELS WITH SPINACH
- Muscadet
- Bouzeron Bourgogne Aligoté
- Coteaux Champenois, white

OYSTERS
- Muscadet
- Bourgogne Aligoté
- Alsace Sylvaner
- Chablis
- Beaujolais Nouveau, red

OYSTERS IN CHAMPAGNE
- Burgundy, Hautes-Côtes de Nuit, white
- Coteaux Champenois, white
- Roussette de Savoie

PRAWNS WITH MAYONNAISE
- Burgundy, white
- Alsace Riesling
- Haut-Poitou Sauvignon

SEAFOOD PLATTER
- Chablis
- Muscadet
- Alsace Sylvaner

SHELLFISH SALAD WITH CUCUMBER
- Graves, white
- Muscadet, white
- Alsace Klevner

STUFFED CLAMS
- Graves, white
- Montagny
- Anjou, white

STUFFED SQUID
- Mâcon-Villages
- Good-quality Côtes de Bordeaux
- Gaillac, rosé

FISH

BARQUETTES GIRONDINES (PASTRY SHELLS FILLED WITH A SELECTION OF SEA-FOOD)
- Bâtard-Montrachet
- Good-quality Graves,
- Quincy

BOUILLABAISSE (FISH STEW)
- Côtes du Roussillon, white
- Coteaux d'Aix-en-Provence, white
- Muscadet des Coteaux de la Loire

BOURRIDE (CREAMY FISH SOUP WITH AÏOLI)
- Coteaux d'Aix-en-Provence, white
- Loire, rosé
- Bordeaux, rosé

BRILL WITH WHITE WINE AND SHELLFISH SAUCE
- Graves, white
- Puligny-Montrachet
- Coteaux de Languedoc, white

COD IN GARLIC SAUCE (AÏOLI)
- Coteaux d'Aix-en-Provence, rosé
- Bordeaux, rosé
- Haut-Poitou, rosé

COLD HAKE WITH MAYONNAISE
- Pouilly-Fuissé
- Savoie
- Chignin
- Bergeron
- Alsace Klevner

COQUILLES DE POISSON (SELECTION OF FISH SERVED IN SCALLOP SHELLS)
- Saint-Aubin, white
- Saumur, dry white
- Crozes-Hermitage, white

DEEP-FRIED WHITING
- Alsace Gutedel
- Entre-Deux-Mers
- Seyssel

FILLET OF SOLE BONNE FEMME
- Graves, white
- Chablis, Grand Cru
- Sancerre, white

FILLET OF TURBOT IN FLAKY PASTRY
- Chevalier-Montrachet
- Crozes-Hermitage, white

FISH STEW
- Chablis, Premier Cru
- Arbois, white
- Alsace Riesling

FRESHWATER FISH STEW WITH WHITE WINE
- Meursault
- L'Etoile
- Mâcon-Villages

GRILLED COD
- Gros Plant du Pays Nantais
- Loire, rosé
- Coteaux d'Aix-en-Provence, rosé

GRILLED RED MULLET
- Chassagne-Montrachet, white
- Hermitage, white
- Bergerac

GRILLED SALMON STEAK
- Chassagne-Montrachet, white
- Cahors
- Côtes du Rhône, rosé

GRILLED SARDINES
- Clairette de Bellegarde
- Jurançon, dry
- Bourgogne Aligoté

GRILLED SEA-BASS
- Auxey-Duresses, white
- Bellet, white
- Bergerac, dry

LAMPREY IN RED WINE SAUCE
- Graves, red
- Bergerac, red
- Bordeaux, rosé

MACKEREL IN WHITE WINE
- Alsace Sylvaner
- Haut-Poitou Sauvignon
- Quincy

MONKFISH
- Mâcon-Villages
- Châteauneuf-de-Papes, white
- Bandol, rosé

OYSTERS FROM ARCACHON IN WINE SAUCE
- Graves, white
- Bordeaux, dry
- Jurançon, dry

PAN-FRIED EEL WITH GARLIC AND PARSLEY
- Corbières, rosé
- Gros Plant du Pays Nantais
- Blaye, white

*PIKE QUENELLES
(DUMPLINGS) IN WINE
SAUCE*
- Montrachet
- Pouilly-Vinzelles
- Beaujolais-Villages, red

RED TUNA WITH ONIONS
- Coteaux d'Aix, white
- Coteaux du Languedoc, white
- Côtes de Duras
  Sauvignon

*ROUILLE SETOISE
(SELECTION OF SEAFOOD
IN SPICY GARLIC SAUCE)*
- Clairette du Languedoc
- Côtes du Roussillon, rosé
- Loire, rosé

SALMON IN PASTRY
- Pouilly-Vinzelles
- Graves, white
- Loire, rosé

SALMON ROE
- Haut-Poitou, rosé
- Graves, red
- Côtes du Rhône, red

SALT COD
- Haut-Poitou, rosé
- Bandol, rosé
- Corbières, rosé

SHAD WITH SORREL
- Anjou, white
- Loire, rosé
- Haut-Poitou,
  Chardonnay

*SMALL FRIED FISH
(WHITEBAIT)*
- Beaujolais, white
- Béarn, white
- Fiefs Vendéens, white

SMOKED SALMON
- Puligny-Montrachet, Premier
  Cru
- Pouilly-Fumé
- Bordeaux Sauvignon, dry

SOLE MEUNIÈRE
- Meursault, white
- Alsace Riesling
- Entre-Deux-Mers

*SOUFFLE WITH CRAYFISH
SAUCE*
- Bâtard-Montrachet
- Crozes-Hermitage, white
- Bergerac, dry

STUFFED CARP
- Montagny
- Touraine, Azay-le-Rideau,
  white
- Alsace, Pinot

STUFFED CRAB
- Premières Côtes de Bordeaux,
  white
- Burgundy, white
- Muscadet

TROUT WITH ALMONDS
- Chassagne-Montrachet,
  white
- Alsace Klevner
- Côtes du Roussillon

*TURBOT WITH
HOLLANDAISE SAUCE*
- Graves, white
- Saumur, white
- Hermitage, white

*WHITE TUNA IN BASQUE
SAUCE*
- Graves, white
- Pacherenc de Vic-Bilh
- Gaillac, white

*ZANDER (PIKE PERCH) IN
BUTTERY SAUCE*
- Muscadet
- Saumur, white
- Saint-Joseph,
  white

RED AND WHITE MEAT

Lamb

*COLD LAMB WITH
MAYONNAISE*
- Saint-Aubin, white
- Bordeaux, red
- Entre-Deux-Mers

*FILLET OF LAMB EN
CROÛTE*
- Pomerol
- Mercurey
- Coteaux du Tricastin

LAMB CARBONADE
- Graves de Vayres, red
- Fitou
- Crozes-Hermitage, red

LAMB CURRY
- Montagne Saint-Emilion
- Alsace Tokay
- Côtes du Rhône

LAMB STEW (DAUBE)
- Patrimonio, red
- Côtes du Rhône-Villages, red
- Morgon

LAMB STEW (NAVARIN)
- Anjou, red
- Bordeaux Côtes-de-Francs, red
- Bourgogne Marsannay, red

*LAMB STEW FLAVOURED
WITH THYME*
- Châteauneuf-du-Pape, red
- Saint-Chinian
- Fleurie

*MARLY LAMB CHOPS
(FROM BEST END OF NECK)*
- Saint-Julien
- Ajaccio
- Coteaux du Lyonnais

ROAST BARON OF LAMB
- Haut-Médoc
- Savoie-Mondeuse
- Minervois

ROAST LAMB
- Morey-Saint-Denis
- Saint-Emilion
- Côte de Provence, red

*SADDLE OF LAMB
FLAVOURED WITH HERBS*
- Vin de Corse, red
- Côtes du Rhône, red
- Coteaux de Giennois, red

*SAUTEED LAMB
PROVENÇALE STYLE*
- Gigondas
- Côtes de Provence, red
- Bourgogne Passetoutgrain, red

*SHOULDER OF LAMB IN
ONION SAUCE*
- Hermitage, red
- Côtes de Bourg, red
- Moulin à Vent

STUFFED BREAST OF LAMB
- Côtes de Jura, red
- Graves, red
- Haut-Poitou Gamay

Beef

*BEEF FONDUE
BURGUNDY-STYLE*
- Bordeaux, red
- Côtes du Ventoux, red
- Burgundy, rosé

BEEF STEW
- Buzet, red
- Côtes du Vivarais, red
- Arbois, red

BEEF STEW WITH RED WINE
- Lirac, red
- Côtes du Luberon, red
- Costières de Nîmes, red

BOEUF BOURGUIGNON
- Rully, red
- Saumur, red
- Côte du Marmandais, red

ENTRECOTE STEAK WITH BORDELAISE SAUCE
- Saint-Julien
- Saint-Joseph, red
- Côtes du Roussillon-Villages

FILLET OF BEEF DUCHESSE
- Côte-Rôtie
- Gigondas
- Graves, red

FILLET STEAK WITH BEARNAISE SAUCE
- Listrac
- Saint-Aubin, red
- Touraine Amboise, red

POT-AU-FEU
- Anjou, red
- Bordeaux, red
- Beaujolais, red

ROAST BEEF (COLD)
- Madiran
- Beaune, red
- Cahors

ROAST BEEF (HOT)
- Moulis
- Aloxe-Corton
- Côtes du Rhône, red

STEAK CHATEAUBRIAND
- Margaux
- Alsace Pinot
- Coteaux du Tricastin

STEAK MAITRE D'HOTEL (WITH PARSLEY AND LEMON SAUCE)
- Bergerac, red
- Arbois, rosé
- Chénas

Pork

ANDOUILLETTE (CHITTERLING SAUSAGE) WITH CREAM SAUCE
- Touraine, white
- Burgundy, white
- Saint-Joseph, white

CASSOULET (CASSEROLE OF WHITE BEANS AND PORK, GOOSE OR DUCK MEAT)
- Côtes du Frontonnais, red
- Minervois, red
- Bergerac, red

CHOUCROUTE
- Alsace Riesling
- Alsace Sylvaner

COLD ROAST PORK
- Burgundy, white
- Lirac, red
- Bordeaux, dry

CONFIT
- Tursan, red
- Corbières, red
- Cahors

COUNTRY-STYLE SOUP WITH CABBAGE
- Côtes du Luberon
- Côte de Brouilly
- Bourgogne Aligoté

GRILLED ANDOUILLETTE
- Coteaux Champenois, white
- Petit Chablis
- Beaujolais, red

GRILLED TOULOUSE SAUSAGE
- Saint-Joseph or Bergerac, red
- Côtes du Frontonnais, rosé

PORK CHOP WITH ONION AND WHITE WINE SAUCE
- Burgundy, white
- Côtes d'Auvergne, red
- Bordeaux, clairet

ROAST PORK FLAVOURED WITH SAGE
- Rully, white
- Côtes du Rhône, red
- Minervois, rosé

SHOULDER OF PORK WITH SAUVIGNON
- Bergerac, dry
- Menetou-Salon
- Bordeaux, rosé

STUFFED CABBAGE
- Côtes du Rhône, red
- Touraine Gamay
- Bordeaux Sauvignon, dry

SUCKLING PIG EN GELEE
- Graves de Vayres, white
- Costières du Gard, rosé
- Beaujolais-Villages, red

Veal

BRAISED TOPSIDE OF VEAL
- Mâcon-Villages, white
- Côtes de Duras, red
- Brouilly

CALVES LIVER À L'ANGLAISE
- Médoc
- Coteaux d'Aix-en-Provence, red
- Haut-Poitou, rosé

GRILLED VEAL CHOP
- Côtes du Rhône, red
- Anjou, white
- Burgundy, rosé

KIDNEY BROCHETTES
- Cornas
- Beaujolais-Villages
- Coteaux du Languedoc, rosé

SAUTEED KIDNEYS IN VIN JAUNE
- Arbois, white
- Gaillac, Vin de Voile
- Bourgogne Aligoté

VEAL ESCALOPE IN BREADCRUMBS
- Côtes du Jura, white
- Corbières, white
- Côtes du Ventoux, red

VEAL KIDNEYS WITH MARROW-BONE
- Saint-Emilion
- Saumur-Champigny
- Coteaux d'Aix-en-Provence, rosé

VEAL MARENGO (TOMATO AND WINE SAUCE)
- Côtes de Duras Merlot
- Alsace Klevner
- Coteaux du Tricastin, rosé
- Lirac, rosé

VEAL PARCELS
- Anjou Gamay
- Minervois, rosé
- Costières de Nîmes, white

VEAL STEW IN WHITE SAUCE À L'ANCIENNE
- Arbois, white
- Alsace Riesling, Grand Cru
- Côtes de Provence, rosé

VEAL SWEETBREADS WITH LANGOUSTINES
- Graves, white
- Alsace Tokay
- Bordeaux, rosé

POULTRY, RABBIT

BARBARY DUCK WITH OLIVES
- Savoie-Mondeuse, red
- Canon-Fronsac
- Anjou Cabernet, red

BREAST OF DUCK WITH GREEN PEPPER
- Saint-Joseph, red
- Bourgueil, red
- Bergerac, red

CHICKEN COOKED WITH SALT CRUST
- Listrac
- Mâcon-Villages, white
- Côtes du Rhône, red

CHICKEN CURRY
- Montagne Saint-Emilion
- Alsace Tokay
- Côtes du Rhône

CHICKEN WITH TRUFFLE SAUCE
- Chevalier-Montrachet
- Arbois, white
- Juliénas

COQ AU VIN
- Ladoix
- Côte de Beaune
- Châteauneuf-du-Pape, red
- Touraine Cabernet

DUCK HEART BROCHETTES
- Saint-Georges-Saint-Emilion
- Chinon
- Côtes du Rhône-Villages

DUCK WITH ORANGE
- Côtes du Jura, jaune
- Cahors
- Graves, red

DUCK WITH TURNIPS
- Puisseguin Saint-Emilion
- Saumur-Champigny
- Coteaux d'Aix-en-Provence, red

DUCKLING WITH PEACHES
- Banyuls
- Chinon, red
- Graves, red

GUINEA-FOWL WITH ARMAGNAC
- Saint-Estèphe
- Chassagne-Montrachet, red
- Fleurie

PIGEON WITH DICED VEGETABLES
- Crozes-Hermitage, red
- Bordeaux, red
- Touraine Gamay

POULET BASQUAISE
- Côtes de Duras, Sauvignon
- Bordeaux, dry
- Coteaux du Languedoc, rosé

RABBIT FRICASEE
- Touraine, rosé
- Côtes de Blaye, white
- Beaujolais-Villages, red

ROAST CAPON
- Burgundy, white
- Touraine-Mesland
- Côtes du Rhône, rosé

ROAST RABBIT WITH MUSTARD
- Sancerre, red
- Tavel
- Côtes de Provence, white

SAUTEED CHICKEN WITH MOREL MUSHROOMS
- Savigny-lès-Beaune, red
- Arbois, white
- Sancerre, white

SPIT-ROASTED TURKEY
- Monthélie
- Graves, white
- Châteaumeillant, rosé

STUFFED DUCK
- Saint-Emilion, Grand Cru
- Bandol, red
- Buzet, red

STUFFED GOOSE
- Anjou Cabernet, red
- Côtes du Marmandais, red
- Beaujolais-Villages

TURKEY WITH CHESTNUTS
- Saint-Joseph, red
- Sancerre, red
- Meursault, white

TURKEY ESCALOPES WITH ROQUEFORT
- Côtes du Jura, white
- Bourgogne Aligoté
- Coteaux
- d'Aix-en-Provence, rosé

GAME

BRAISED WILD BOAR
- Fronsac
- Châteauneuf-du-Pape, red
- Moulin à Vent

FILLET OF WILD BOAR WITH BORDELAISE SAUCE
- Pomerol
- Bandol
- Gigondas

FLAMBEED WOODCOCK
- Pauillac
- Musigny
- Hermitage

HARE À LA ROYALE
- Saint-Joseph, red
- Volnay
- Pécharmant

HAUNCH OF WILD BOAR WITH VENISON SAUCE
- Chambertin
- Montage Saint-Emilion
- Corbières, red

JUGGED HARE
- Canon-Fronsac
- Bonnes-Mares
- Minervois, red

PARTRIDGE À LA CATALANE
- Maury
- Côtes du Roussillon, red
- Beaujolais-Villages

PARTRIDGE WITH CABBAGE
- Burgundy, Irancy
- Arbois, rosé
- Cornas

PHEASANT IN CHARTREUSE
- Moulis
- Pommard
- Saint-Nicolas de Bourgueil

ROAST PARTRIDGE
- Haut-Médoc
- Vosne-Romanée
- Bourgueil

ROAST RABBIT
- Auxey-Duresses, red
- Puisseguin Saint-Emilion
- Crozes-Hermitage, red

ROAST WILD DUCK
- Saint-Emilion, Grand Cru
- Côte-Rotie
- Faugères

SADDLE OF HARE WITH JUNIPER
- Chambolle, Musigny
- Savoie-Mondeuse
- Saint-Chinian

VENISON CHOPS CONTI STYLE
- Lalande-de-Pomerol
- Côtes de Beaune, red
- Crozes-Hermitage, red

VENISON GRAND VENEUR
- Hermitage, red
- Corton, red
- Côtes de Roussillon, red

*WILD DUCK IN RED WINE
SAUCE*
- Côte-Rôtie
- Chinon, red
- Bordeaux, superior quality

*WOODCOCK IN RED WINE
SAUCE*
- Saint-Julien
- Côte de Nuits-Villages
- Patrimonio

VEGETABLES

BRAISED CELERY
- Côtes de Ventoux, red
- Alsace Pinot Noir
- Touraine Sauvignon

DAUPHINOIS POTATOES
- Bordeaux Côtes de Castillon
- Châteauneuf-du-Pape, white
- Alsace Riesling

FRIED AUBERGINES
- Burgundy, red
- Beaujolais, red
- Bordeaux, dry

GREEN BEANS
- Côte de Beaune, white
- Sancerre, white
- Entre-Deux-Mers

MANGETOUT PEAS
- Graves, white
- Côtes du Rhône, red
- Alsace Riesling

MUSHROOMS
- Beaune, white
- Alsace Tokay
- Coteaux de Giennois, red

PASTA
- Côtes du Rhône, red
- Coteaux d'Aix, rosé

PETITS POIS
- Saint-Romain, white
- Côtes du Jura, white
- Touraine Sauvignon

*SAUTEED MUSHROOMS
MARBLED WITH PARSLEY*
- Beaune, white
- Alsace Tokay
- Coteaux du Giennois, red

STUFFED PEPPERS
- Mâcon-Villages
- Côtes du Rhône, rosé
- Alsace Tokay

CHEESE

Made with cow's milk

BEAUFORT
- Arbois, jaune
- Meursault
- Vin de Savoie
- Chignin
- Bergeron

BLEU D'AUVERGNE
- Côtes de Bergerac, sweet
- Beaujolais
- Touraine Sauvignon

BLEU DE BRESSE
- Côtes du Jura, white
- Macon, red
- Côtes de Bergerac, white

BRIE
- Beaune, red
- Alsace Pinot Noir
- Coteaux du Languedoc, red

CAMEMBERT
- Bandol, red
- Côtes du Roussillon-Villages
- Beaujolais-Villages

CANTAL
- Coteaux du Vivarais, red
- Côtes de Provence, rosé
- Lirac, white

CARRE DE L'EST
- Saint-Joseph, red
- Coteaux d'Aix-en-Provence, red
- Brouilly

CARRE FRAIS
- Cahors
- Côtes du Roussillon, rosé
- Côtes du Rhône, white

CHAOURCE
- Montagne Saint-Emilion
- Cadillac
- Chénas

CITEAUX
- Aloxe-Corton
- Coteaux Champenois, red
- Fleurie

COMTE
- Graves, Château-Chalon, white
- Côtes du Luberon, white

EDAM DEMI-ETUVE
- Pauillac
- Fixin
- Costières de Nîmes, red

EPOISSES
- Savigny
- Côtes du Jura, red
- Côte de Brouilly

FOURME D'AMBERT
- L'Etoile, jaune
- Cérons
- Banyuls Rimage

GOUDA DEMI-ETUVE
- Saint-Estèphe
- Chinon
- Coteaux du Tricastin

LIVAROT
- Bonnezeaux
- Sainte-Croix-du-Mont
- Alsace Gewurztraminer

MAROILLES
- Jurançon
- Alsace, Gewurztraminer, late harvests

MIMOLETTE DEMI-ETUVE
- Graves, red
- Santenay
- Côtes du Rhône, red

MORBIER
- Gevrey-Chambertin
- Madiran
- Côtes du Ventoux, red

MUNSTER
- Coteaux du Layon-Villages
- Loupiac
- Alsace Gewurztraminer

CHEESE FONDUE
- Alsace Riesling
- Haut-Poitou Sauvignon
- Côtes du Rhône-Villages

PONT L'EVÊQUE
- Côtes de Saint-Mont
- Bourgueil
- Nuit Saint-Georges

RACLETTE
- Vin de Savoie
- Apremont
- Côtes de Duras Sauvignon
- Juliénas

REBLOCHON
- Mercurey
- Lirac, red
- Touraine Gamay

RIGOTTE
- Bourgogne Hautes-Côtes de Nuits, red
- Côte du Forez
- Saint-Amour

SAINT MARCELLIN
- Faugères
- Tursan, red
- Chiroubles

SAINT-NECTAIRE
- Fronsac
- Burgundy, red
- Mâcon-Villages, white

VACHERIN
- Corton
- Bordeaux, Premières Côtes
- Barsac

Made with goat's milk

CABEÇOU
- Burgundy, white
- Tavel
- Gaillac, white

CORSICAN GOAT'S CHEESE
- Patrimonio, white
- Cassis, white
- Costières de Nîmes, white

CROTTIN DE CHAVIGNOL
- Sancerre, white
- Bordeaux, dry
- Côte Roannaise

FRESH GOAT CHEESE
- Champagne
- Montlouis, medium dry
- Crémant d'Alsace

PELARDON
- Condrieu
- Roussette de Savoie
- Coteaux du Lyonnais, red

SAINTE-MAURE
- Rivesaltes, white
- Alsace Tokay
- Cheverny Gamay

SELLES-SUR-CHER
- Coteaux de l'Aubance
- Cheverny
- Romorantin
- Sancerre, rosé

VALENÇAY
- Vouvray, sweet
- Haut-Poitou, rosé
- Valençay, Gamay

Made with ewe's milk

CORSICAN EWE'S CHEESE
- Bourgogne, Irancy
- Ajaccio
- Côtes du Roussillon, red

EISBARECH
- Lalande-de-Pomerol
- Cornas
- Marcillac

ROQUEFORT
- Côtes du Jura, jaune
- Sauternes
- Muscat de Rivesaltes

LARUNS
- Bordeaux, Côtes de Castillon
- Gaillac, red
- Côtes de Provence, red

DESSERTS

ALMOND CAKE
- Maury
- Bonnezeaux
- Muscat de Lunel

BRIOCHE
- Rivesaltes, red
- Muscat de Beaumes-de-Venise
- Alsace, late harvest

CHOCOLATE CAKE
- Banyuls, Grand Cru
- Pineau des Charentes, rosé

CHRISTMAS LOG
- Champagne, medium dry
- Clairette de Die Tradition

CRÈME RENVERSEE
- Coteaux du Layon-Villages
- Sauternes
- Muscat de Saint-Jean de Minervois

ILE FLOTTANTE
- Loupiac
- Rivesaltes, white
- Muscat de Rivesaltes

KOUGLOF (CAKE FROM ALSACE)
- Quarts de Chaume
- Alsace, late harvests
- Muscat de Mireval

LEMON TART
- Alsace, various good quality wines
- Cérons
- Rivesaltes, white

ORANGE FRUIT SALAD
- Sainte-Croix-du-Mont
- Rivesaltes, white
- Muscat de Rivesaltes

PRUNE FLAN
- Pineau des Charentes
- Anjou, Coteaux de la Loire
- Cadillac

STRAWBERRIES
- Muscat de Rivesaltes
- Maury

TARTE TATIN
- Pineau des Charentes
- Arbois, Vin de Paille
- Jurançon

VANILLA ICE-CREAM WITH RASPBERRY SAUCE
- Loupiac
  Coteaux du Layon

NEWS FROM THE FRENCH WINE WORLD

There are two important events for the French wine industry, the harvest, of course, and every two years, Vinexpo in Bordeaux. This trade exhibition brings together everyone who counts in the world of wine, including experts and journalists from five continents. The exhibition, which took place for the 12th time in June 2003, is growing, something that underlines the emergence of the new wine producing countries in the Americas, Africa, Oceania and also in Eastern Europe. Wine is beginning to be treated by everyone as a major economic force.

Worldwide overproduction is provoking great concerns: in 2000 the world produced a surplus of 60 million hectolitres, more than the annual production of France. Alarmist reports on the crisis in the French wine industry have been multiplying since the beginning of the new century. While Europe is forced to curb production through a policy of massive uprooting of vineyards, the New World continues to plant more, following equally organized programmes.

The years 1999 and 2000 produced particularly excessive volumes, and experts say that overproduction cannot be maintained at this level. According to the CFCE (Centre Français du Commerce Exterieur or French foreign trade office), in 2002 France maintained its export position, registering a slight increase in volume sold (+1.1%), but a more noticeable one in value (+5.6%): 5.7 million Euros. However, what is generally emphasized is the stagnation, or even erosion of France's position and its loss of share of the market: it is France's competitors who have benefited from the world increase in wine consumption. Also worth noting is that above all Champagne and *vins de pays* have provided the significant increases; that Vins de Pays d'Oc exported more volume than Bordeaux; and that a number of still AOC wines are in a crisis situation. These facts fuel the critics of the European system of AOCs, based on terroir, which is judged by some to have too many constraints, to be against the concept of profitability and to be too complex for the new consumer. Streamlining the industry, simplifying the marketing approach, and putting emphasis on varietal wines are sometimes held up as the golden rules for the new economy. Yet recently, experts have stressed that "the growth area in consumption is occurring in premium wines", which cost more than 5 € a bottle, a tendency which provides every opportunity to appellation wines. Elsewhere, the crisis is not sparing the new wine producing countries. The news from the various wine regions of France, even if it often shows the realities of a downturn, requires more careful analysis. It reveals some real successes though these are breakthroughs that remain fragile in a market that is volatile due to an increasingly indulgent and occasional pattern of wine drinking. However, this Guide details some superb wines, so that once again the harvest can be celebrated for its diversity and its quality.

WHAT'S NEW IN ALSACE?

While in 2003, the *route des vins* (wine route) has been given a face-lift to celebrate its 50th anniversary, the 2002 vintage has resulted in some great Rieslings for ageing. Apart from the Muscats and some lesser Pinot Gris and Pinot Noir wines, the other varieties have performed quite well. However, everything depends on the producer, something that makes the Guide more necessary than ever.

A complicated year
It really was a complicated year. Contrary to the previous, mild winter, the 2001–2002 winter was harsh. The ground remained frozen throughout January. During spring, the sun played at hide-and-seek with the clouds and the rain: the vegetative cycle started slowly. The vines came into bud in April. The flowering went well in June, so well that the vintage promised

to be an early one, with abundant quantities of grapes. Summer saw alternate periods of very hot weather and rain. Local storms and drizzle followed: there was quite a lot of grey rot in September. The harvest, taking place occasionally in stormy weather, started on 16 September for *crémant*, 30 September for the normal appellations (each Grand Cru can fix a later date according to its own judgement), and on 14 October for Vendanges Tardives and Sélections de Grains Nobles. Often producers wanted to wait for the sun to return in October before harvesting, but sometimes rot forced them to rush things. Ripeness was often present however there was some concern about the presence of shrivelled grapes. The ideal was to produce little quantity but good quality, to select and to vinify carefully and correctly. It is difficult to name one particular terroir where marvellous wines were produced consistently everywhere. There are some stars here and there: the year is a little similar to 1996 with a sugar ripeness that was higher than the acidity level.

Riesling has the wind in its sails

The best Pinot Blanc, Auxerrois and Sylvaner wines are on the whole correct and quite tasty. Much Pinot Gris and Pinot Noir suffered from attacks of rot and seem generally to be of average quality. The Gewurztraminer is not exuberant, but seems fine and fruity. There are no real successes amongst the Muscats. However, the Rieslings will make excellent wines for ageing for between five and ten years, and the acidity will hold them in the long term. They have the style of 1995, straightforward and mineral with a suggestion of citrus fruits. The Vendanges Tardives and Sélections de Grains Nobles, can hardly be

described as spectacular, because they had to be harvested early in 2002. It is what one calls "a wine-grower's year": the quality depends above all on the know-how of the winemaker.

Volumes quite stable, but yields often excessive

The volume of the harvest reached 1,223,000 hl, very close to that of the previous year. Certain producers were wise enough to limit their yields to 40 hl per hectare, whereas the average over the whole vineyard area is 86 hl per hectare. The production is in the order of 1,013,000 hl for AOC Alsace (as in 2001), 44,000 hl for Alsace Grand Cru (47,300 hl in 2001) and 165,000 hl for Crémant d'Alsace. Vendanges Tardives: 10,000 hl. Sélections de Grains Nobles: 2,000 hl; these special wines have had a slight reduction in volume compared to 2001.

Contrasting developments of the market

Sales of Alsace wines amounted to 1,147,000 hl in 2002. The still wines have seen a slight drop in 2001 (–1.1%) but it has been more appreciable on export markets (–5.4% by volume, but +3.3% by value). Belgium and Luxembourg remain in first place ahead of Holland, Germany (a drop of 22% by volume, but an increase of 2.1% by value!), Denmark, the United States (a significant increase) and Great Britain (in strong decline). Crémant d'Alsace (162,000 hl) suffers problems on export markets (–10%) but remains the leading French sparkling wine apart from Champagne. However, the United States are becoming more and more interested in *crémant* even if their purchases are still modest (900 hl); Germany heads the list of client countries, but sales here have diminished by 16% in one year.

WHAT'S NEW IN BEAUJOLAIS?

The 2002 harvest registered a distinct drop in volume almost everywhere in France. The control of production yields is already bearing fruit in Beaujolais, but even so, the market is not very strong.

100,000 hl less than in 2001

Fairly good weather conditions gave an early start to the harvest: from the 7 September.

Quite frequent storms provoked some areas of rot. Alternate sun and rain followed. From then wine-growers did not always wait for complete ripeness being worried about the development of rot, especially if they registered sufficient natural potential alcohol and if the level of acidity appeared satisfactory.

The end result of the production in terms of volume bears witness to the positive effects of the new rulings on yields, applied here since the 2001 vintage: elsewhere it is gaining widespread acceptance, including in the 2002 Burgundy vintage. In 2002, Beaujolais produced 1.25 million hecto-litres, which is 100,000 hl less than in the previous year. In quality, the wines are mostly average, even weak. One third of this volume is destined for Beaujolais Nouveau.

A market in crisis

Beaujolais Nouveau may continue to be carried along on a wave and to provide a fast turn-around, but Beaujolais-Villages and the crus are going through difficult times. The quantity of unsold stocks in the cellars is high. Even Georges Dubœuf, the Beaujolais "pope", heading up his large company, finished his 2001–2002 year with a turnover down some 2%. Having decided therefore to no longer buy in wine, but grapes instead, he has embarked upon building a huge vinification cellar in Lancié (6.85 million Euros of investment, with a tank capacity of 18,000 hl). At the Hospice de Beaujeu, the 206th auction did not live up to its promise: of 50 lots sold, 26 were sold at their reserve prices. There was nothing spectacular, with only half the volume put on sale compared to 2001. The average price was 6.87% down on last year with Morgon dropping by 29%. Only Beaujolais-Villages was up by 5.65%. The Hospices are therefore planning to conduct future sales in a different manner. Another sign of market difficulties, the cooperative cellar at Lachassagne found itself with 9,000 hl of unsold wine on its hands, equal to two-thirds of its annual production.

Japan, the most important customer for Beaujolais Nouveau

Total exports from the region in 2002 reached 610,377 hl, a drop of 4.4% in volume and 5.7% in value compared to 2001. Since 1999, Beaujolais has seen a succession of falls on foreign markets. Switzerland, formerly the most important foreign outlet for Beaujolais, almost without competition, has dropped 19.2% in five years. Germany, Belgium and Holland are declining similarly. However, there is an increase in the United States, Canada, Sweden, and, with the opening of Eastern European markets, there are good results in Russia as well as in Poland. Japan now represents 43.6% of Beaujolais Nouveau export volumes, ahead of Germany. Italy is also a fan of Nouveau.

Recent average prices have dropped for the crus Côte de Brouilly, Moulin-à-Vent, Saint-Amour and Fleurie, but are rising for Beaujolais-Villages and the crus Régnié, Chénas and Chiroubles; they remain stable for the others.

WHAT'S NEW IN BORDEAUX?

News in brief from the vineyards

Through the Pellerin company that he has bought out, the Burgundian Jean-Claude Boisset has established Château de Pierreux in Odenas: some 90 ha with one owner in the AOC Brouilly. He wants to make Pierreux one of the leading lights of Beaujolais. The writer Patrice Dard has received the Victor-Peyret prize, whilst the Juliénas trophy has been awarded to Jean Beaudet. Georges Dubœuf's *Hameau du Vin* (Wine Village) celebrated its tenth birthday on 10 June 2003.

The 24th Fête des Crus will be hosted by Moulin-à-Vent at the beginning of May 2004.

A falling market, disorientated producers and négociants, but a correct vintage in 2002, especially for red wines based on Cabernet Sauvignon. Consumers will be able to find some excellent wines at prices that have become reasonable again.

Crisis sets in

After numerous warning signs, all ignored, a certainty finally reached the Bordeaux wine region by the end of Vinexpo, the international wine and spirit exhibition that finished on 26 June 2003 in the metropolis of the Gironde *département*: a crisis has absolutely and truly taken hold in the French wine regions, and Bordeaux will not be spared.

The rise of the Euro; ongoing economic slowdown in Europe; chronic overproduction on a world scale with determined competition from the New World (despite a small 2002 harvest throughout the old continent); quality levels too often uneven in the *appellation contrôlée* areas; with political uncertainty in the long term, the wine industry was disorientated, divided and uneasy.

These worries did not spoil the wonderful parties held in the great châteaux. Notably there was the Fête de la Fleur at Mouton Rothschild which, celebrated at the same time 150 years of ownership. At the one held at Château Margaux, Corinne Mentzelopoulos celebrated winning back control of the most fabulous wine estate in Bordeaux, bought by her father in 1979, and which she had to share with the Agnelli family for inheritance reasons in 1993. The death of Giovanni Agnelli, the captain of industry from Turin, gave her the chance to raise the capital for a company valued at some 350 million Euros, whilst relinquishing other financial interests to her partners.

Primeurs fall

It is going to take more effort to get the prices right. Even the primeur campaign for the Grands Crus and the Crus Bourgeois that are sold to négociants when they still have several months more in barrel, was hardly encouraging. Prices were low even compared to the disappointing 2002 campaign. After an average reduction of 10% on the offer price, the 2003 campaign saw château owners making even more reductions, still without generating any enthusiasm from the buyers. The négociants, watched closely by the banks who were tracking down the "bad risks", are reluctant to leave themselves exposed, whilst the consumers are reluctant to buy the top wines that are still being sold to them today on the basis of the primeur prices for 1999 or 2000. As at other times, especially at the beginning of the 1990s, the supermarket groups are waiting their turn to grab the many unsold wines which will soon be affordable. They will offer them to wine-lovers during their promotional wine fairs, playing once again their roles as ruthless regulators of the market.

Red Bordeaux at one Euro?

At the other extreme of the price scale, the rate for bulk red wine, which is used for making branded wines, remained stable until January 2003 despite some harbingers of doom. The year 2002 was excellent for the sales of Bordeaux. Exports increased again 4% by volume and 7% by value, while home sales remained stable. Red Bordeaux is therefore holding its position.

But, the warning signs are there. The sales from the château owners to the négociants might have increased by 15% during the 2001–2002 campaign, but the négociants withdrew 2% less, leaving wine-growers to carry the stock. The quantities that have been reserved but not withdrawn are still pushing down the market one year later in June 2003. The result is that prices have been pushed down.

The previous campaign finished with an average price of 1,112 Euros a 900-litre cask of red Bordeaux in bulk and at a price of only 1,069 Euros for the year up to the end of June 2003, the price for June being just 903 Euros, equivalent to just 1 Euro per litre. It will not take much more for the re-emergence of the spectre of Bordeaux at 1 Euro a bottle in the supermarket, something that Bergerac has just suffered. As Bordeaux plays a role in influencing the market for numerous South West appellations and beyond, it is understandable that these difficulties will be heard by others with anxiety but also with a certain spirit of revenge.

Recommendations

Faced with a new, but not a novel situation, worries are being expressed. Recommendations are numerous and varied. Firstly, the *appellations d'origine contrôlée* system could be tightened up: by following the recommendation to follow production rules more strictly (number of vines per hectare, number of bunches per vine) and to improve the procedures for the *agrément* (tasting test for AOC wines), with stricter tastings; there is the suggestion to rule out the "second-chance" that has become so systematic, leading to few wines being rejected, damaging the general image of Bordeaux. In 20 years, the vineyard area in Bordeaux has increased by more than a third, going from 90,000 to 120,000 ha. During the same period, *vin de table* has disappeared and the proportion of white wine fell to 12% in 2002. All this means that the production of AOC red wines has more than doubled. Is it time to admit that the market cannot absorb such an increase, especially if the quality of a significant proportion of the production leaves something to be desired?

Certain people believe this, notably the members of the strategic committee created by Jacques Berthomeau at the request of the minister for agriculture Jean Glavany. The same idea has been taken up by the president of the CIVB (*Comité Interprofessionnelle des Vins de Bordeaux*), Jean-Louis Trocard. They plead for the creation of a Vin de Pays d'Aquitaine designation which would serve as an outlet for production that was judged to be excessive for AOC wines. This denomination could be obtained from yields above 80 hl/ha and could mention the main grape variety that was used to make it: Merlot, Cabernet Sauvignon, Sauvignon etc. This would bring us back to the time when white *vin de table* from the Gironde, incapable of being sold as AOC, would serve as a base for making sparkling wines from the Charente, or would be distilled for "Bordeaux brandy". One of the South West vineyard areas, Gaillac, has managed a similar process very well with *vins de pays* des Côtes du Tarn. Bordeaux would therefore be reduced to imitating this on a grand scale, which is a prospect that does not thrill those who manage the "lesser appellations".

Vintage 2002: a drop in volume

Whilst awaiting such innovations, we can always examine the quality of the vintage

What's new in Bordeaux?

2002 and the weather conditions that were responsible for such a small harvest. Despite an absolute record of AOC vine plantings amounting to 119,817 ha in production, the harvest only ended up producing 4,976,441 hl of reds and 636,051 hl of whites, a drop of 15 and 9% respectively compared to 2001. Taking into account the situation of the market, this decline in production was quite a blessing. In effect, prices did not collapse at harvest time, because the harvest was so small: they only started to crumble in January 2003.

As every year, the following observations have been taken from the report of the vintage from Professors Pascal Ribéreau-Gayon and Guy Guimberteau, of the oenology faculty of Bordeaux (at Université Victor-Segalen).

After a mild and very dry winter, the start of the vegetative cycle was early. One has to go back to 1988–1989 to find lower rainfall than 2001–2002 during the period from 1 October to 31 March. With these conditions, bud break took place quickly during the last week of March. April remained hot and dry; allowing the emergence of ample bunches. May remained mild on average, but rainfall was frequent and abundant, preparing the ground for the *coulure* that was observed later on. June had very uneven weather, with showers and dry periods taking turns and very up-and-down temperatures. Flowering was affected by this. Slow and mixed, it was followed by *coulure* and *millerandage* suffered most of all by Merlot, which encountered difficulties at harvest time. The only advantage as a result of this weather pattern was that the yields were already largely reduced during the month of June.

Summer holiday-makers who were tempted to spend their time on the Médoc coast in July 2002, and even in August, do not need to read these lines to remember that the sun came very late to the Gironde during summer. Despite the early budding, *véraison* on the vine appeared four days later than the average of the last ten years. This is a relative delay, because the dates show an advance of eight days based on the average of the last 30 years (another piece of information to put in the file on global warming!)

Sauvignons and Cabernets are the winners

As often observed in Bordeaux, after a wet summer, the end of the season can be miraculous, and this was the case in 2002. From 9 to 20 September, the weather was hot during the day, cool at night with a dry wind from the northwest, and this reduced the areas of grey rot and rapidly accelerated the ripening of the grapes, which did however show slightly excessive acidity. Huge storms, sometimes accompanied by hail, hit the vineyard area on 20 September, rebalancing the sugar and acidity levels, but good weather set in again until 10 October, encouraging the craziest gambles to obtain Cabernets Sauvignons at perfect ripeness, yet still healthy. Merlot did not allow such positive results. On this subject the oenology professors are condemning the fashion for maximum extraction, which gives "wines that are excessively hard, with a slightly bitter finish and a tannic structure that may be difficult to integrate on ageing". This is a fault that we already noted in 1985, a year when the autumn had been particularly hot.

In the whites, the Sauvignons that were harvested before 20 September have played the game well and given fruity wines, whereas the Sémillons, which ripen later, suffered more. The sweet wines escaped grey rot thanks to a period of hot weather in September, which allowed good concentration; the abundant rainfall from 10 October, however, lead to a certain amount of dilution. There will be some good sweet wines, but success is not general.

News in brief from the vineyards

At Vinexpo, the revision of the classification of the *crus bourgeois* of the Médoc, which led to an elimination of almost half of them, constituted a greater controversy than the revision of the classification of Saint-Emilion in 1985. Obviously some rigour must be introduced into a list that has not been reviewed for more than 60 years, but its interest remains limited, because it only complicates the labels that are already difficult for the consumer to understand. Note that there are also "Crus Artisans" and other "Crus Paysans".

WHAT'S NEW IN BURGUNDY?

There was good news from the Côte d'Or and the Chablis districts in 2002. Occasionally an exceptional vintage occurs here. Their enthusiasm might appear a little exaggerated, but after two rather morose years, a smile has returned. Above all, concerns arise from the state of the market.

Climatic conditions:
Burgundy, the exception to the rule?

This was a real winter, harsh and long, the likes of which had not been seen for several years. At the beginning of June, the early spring gave rise to nice flowering, and a confident ripening period continued during the radiant and dry summer, continuing up to harvest. Little or no chaptalisation was necessary, because the natural alcohol level reached around 12–13%. Very concentrated in sugar, the 2002 grapes have plenty of drive. Is Burgundy the exception to the rule? Not completely, if one looks around here and there in the other vineyard areas. Even with some storms occurring on 19 September, they hardly provoked any problems, and both sunny and dry weather allowed good concentration and excellent healthy grapes, helped along by a North wind, which arrived at just the right time.

Chablis and Côte de Nuits favoured

There were however, some regional variations. In the northern part, ripening was often slowed down by the appearance of some *millerandage* (aborted berries, frequently a sign of quality), but in the end, producers experienced a very enjoyable harvest period, notably in the Yonne (especially Chablis) and in the Côte de Nuits. In the southern part of the Côte d'Or and from Côte Chalonnaise to the Mâconnais, results are more uneven. The 2002 harvest reached 940 million hectolitres for whites, as against 952.5 million in the previous year. For reds, 585 million hectolitres were produced compared to 583 millions in 2001. The wines have fruit, weight and notable acidity in both Chablis and the Côte de Nuits, the areas that came out best. Whereas the wines were correct in the Côte de Beaune and in Côte Chalonnaise, they were rather variable in the Mâconnais, where the Gamays were more uneven.

Back to basics

Burgundy has made "back to basics" its mantra, first of all with a Charter of quality. The Foire des Grands Vins de France (national wine fair) in Mâcon has adopted a new image. The moveable Saint-Vincent (wine festival) became unmanageable as the *Confrérie des Chevaliers du Tastevin* held everything up; so it did not take place at Vougeot contrary to previous announcements. In future, the organisation should be reviewed based more closely on the ideas of the founders. Will the Saint-Vincent festival die? No, because the village of Monthélie is taking up the gauntlet for January 2004.

The crisis gets whipped up

The great appellations may sail well on the international ocean, but their scarcity cannot meet the demand. The same cannot be said for the more modest appellations produced in greater volume. Hence there are lower figures, both by volume and by value: 685,000 hl, –3.1% compared to 2001 and 542 million Euros, –5.3%, according to the CFCE. The United Kingdom is the largest importer of Burgundy (28 million bottles), followed by the United States (the top market in terms of value) and Japan, then Germany, Belgium and Switzerland. The level of trade might have been acceptable in 2002, but négociants suffered greatly during the first six months of 2003: a downturn of 20–30%, something never seen before. At the Hospices de Nuits-Saint-Georges, the decline was 11.9% (and for the first time it included a Gevrey-Chambertin). At the Hospices de Beaune, the decline was 8.8% (average price for a barrel of 300 bottles: 7,050 Euros for whites, 4,651 Euros for reds.)

News in brief from the vineyards

There are no more VDQS wines in Burgundy: the AOC Saint-Bris was officially recognized on 10 January 2003 replacing the VDQS Sauvignon de Saint-Bris (wines made exclusively from Sauvignon, the only area in Burgundy where this variety is allowed). The vintages 2001 and 2002 were included in the new appellation, something that should be noted by label collectors! The Cave Henry de Vézelay has created the Caves du Pèlerin in association with the other cooperatives of the Yonne district. The former president of the BIVB (*Bureau Interprofessionnelle des Vins de Bourgogne* or Burgundy wine regional office), Louis Trébuchet has left Chartron et Trébuchet (in Puligny-Montrachet) which now becomes a Chartron family business. A wine-grower at Cary-Potet (in Buxy), Pierre du Besset who is also an architect receives the *Equerre d'argent* (silver square) 2002: the highest award in France for architecture. The Ballande group (who own Prieuré-Lichine along with nickel mines in New Caledonia) has bought La Reine Pédauque and part of the family estate (including 3.5 ha of Grand Cru vineyards), the remainder (43 ha in the Côte d'Or, 30 ha in the Rhône Valley) stays with the family.

The Beaune firm Louis Latour has made its first purchase outside the district: Simonnet-Febvre in Chablis. A merger has taken place between Leymarie-CECI in Vougeot and Bordeaux Grands Crus Diffusion in Libourne both within the same Franco-Belgian company.

Louis Max has bought Maison Misserey (including the brands Coron Père-et-Frères and Jules Belin) at Nuits-Saint-Georges along with its 36-ha estate, most notably in Clos de Vougeot. The J. Drouhin family have taken back control (60%) of its Beaune firm, recently disposed of to its Japanese importer Snow Brand Milk. The takeover project of the Domaine du Château de Pommard (owned by the Laplanche family) by the Cathiard family (of Château Smith Haut Lafitte) was announced and then withdrawn. Whilst Jean-Claude Boisset continues his foreign investments (in Canada and South America), Michel Picard has concluded a joint-venture agreement with the *Société des Alcools du Québec* to create a vineyard near Niagara Falls next door to that of Jean-Claude Boisset (a winery designed by the famous American architect Frank Gehry).

We have learnt of several deaths: the world renowned cooper Roger Rémond (based in Ladoix-Serrigny); Al Hotchkin, the well-known American who founded the Burgundy Wine Company in 1987; and Baronne Bertrand de Ladoucette (Domaine Comte Georges de Vogüé in Chambolle Musigny).

Note: les Grands Jours de Bourgogne tasting days take place from March 18–24 2004.

WHAT'S NEW IN CHAMPAGNE?

After a miserable vintage in 2001, the worst was feared. All things considered, the result is better than one could have ever imagined in August. That said, 2002 will definitely not go down in history as a great year. Atypical, it remains to be seen how it will develop …

September arrived to a sigh of relief

At the beginning of winter there was cold, dry and sunny weather, and then the thaw arrived around 15 January. A very rainy and windy, mild weather system set in until mid-March. There was some spring frost 14–15 April, but it had minimal effects. Bud break occurred between 7 and 15 April depending on grape variety. At the end of May and in early June, hail caused damage at Château-Thierry (with 15 ha affected) and especially around Verneuil and Passy Grigny (with 150 ha affected).

Warm and dry weather encouraged a fast flowering period in mid-June. July and August saw cool, rainy weather followed by hot and dry periods. These were hardly favourable conditions, especially when the storms of 27 August provoked areas of grey rot. Fortunately, from 10 September, dry and sunny weather favoured the harvest, helping both the sugar concentration and the health of the grapes. The Côte des Blancs started harvesting from 12 September, the Montagne de Reims at the end of September to early October.

Meunier vinous and extremely soft, and Chardonnay rich in all senses of the word, with an emphatic character. Predictions are difficult. One hopes for wines that are full of grace and liveliness to drink young, but the unusual level of concentration may allow some longer-term prospects.

A muted fizz of excitement
Stocks of Champagne reached 1,081 million bottles (including the *"réserve qualitative"*): the same figure as for the previous year. Turnover went from 2.9 billion Euros in 2001 to 3.3 billion Euros in 2002. Shipments reached 288 million bottles (262 million bottles in 2001), the proportion shipped by the growers and the cooperatives has fallen from 34.4% to 32.2% in one year. On the export market (nearly 40% of sales), Great Britain grew from 25 to 31 million bottles, the United States from 14 to 18 million bottles. Figures are falling in Germany and Switzerland, but rising in Belgium and Italy.

The international down-turn that appeared at the beginning of 2003 seems to have muted this fizz of excitement, with a slow-down on export markets. Suddenly, prices have calmed down...

After five nights of unusually hard frost, down to –11°C, from 7 to 11 April 2003, a loss of 50% was announced over the whole of the vineyard area. Even if certain areas effectively did suffer badly, the loss is not nearly as serious as the climatic disasters of 1956, 1951, 1936 and 1930.

Very attractive concentration
Fixed at 12,000 kg per hectare, the yield is quite generous (1,149,086 casks of 205 l, as against 1,042,730 in the previous year): 600 kg per hectare has been placed into *"réserve qualitative"* (quality reserves). This harvest is the equivalent of 314 million bottles.

Ripeness reached on average a natural potential alcohol of 10.5%, generally above the norm. One can weigh up good concentration and powerful flavours on the one hand, as against rather weak acidity levels on the other. The grape varieties behaved in quite different ways, with Pinot Noir appearing flamboyant,

News in brief from the vineyards
The Martin-Delbeck-Bricout group was to have been taken over by the American Schneider group via its subsidiary Opson but the purchase cannot now take place because the group has been put into receivership. Rémi Krug succeeds his brother Henri as president of Champagne Krug. Philippe Vidal replaces Aymeric de Montault (appointed to Château d'Yquem) as head of Canard-Duchêne.

A controversy seems to be brewing: the Champagne growers who produce their own wines deplore the fact that the rules allow the mention RM (*Récoltant Manipulant*) to be on the label of members of the cooperative who takes bottles back there for disgorgement: they should use RC (*Récoltant Coopérateur*).

WHAT'S NEW IN THE JURA?

The weather in 2002 hardly allowed any great hopes, yet a very decent vintage has been produced.

A year of ups and downs
Until the summer Jura did not have too many problems. It was often sunny and growth started off well. Then the rain set off various areas of rot. Luckily, September saw the return of hot, dry weather. The harvest lasted between 16 and 27 September in the Château-Chalon area. In volume, the big drop in 2001 continued: 82,070 hl, whereas in the recent past production has often overtaken 100,000 hl. This is the smallest harvest since 1998. Year on year, there has been a steady growth in the AOC Etoile. It is worth remembering that, for strict quality reasons, Château-Chalon was unable to produce the 2001 vintage under this AOC; in 2002 it returned with a volume of around 1,503 hl in this AOC. However, the harvest was down in the two larger appellations Arbois and Côtes du Jura. Macvin is doing well: it has been increasingly steadily for the past ten years (3,605 hl), and *crémant* shows similar growth, close to 14,500 hl (5,700 hl in its first year, 1995).

Amongst the numerous Jura grape varieties, Trousseau takes the lion's share in reds: perfumed and structured, it seems to like the limelight. Pinot Noir seems a little less expressive, but everything depends on the producer. For whites, the vintage has produced excellent Savagnins. These wines could be kept for several years without a problem.

The *fruitières* (cooperatives) link with Burgundy
A sign of the times: the five cooperative cellars (called "*fruitières*" in Jura) Arbois, Pupillin, Voiteur, Vernois (les Byards) et Poligny (Caveau des Jacobins) have joined the Fédération des Caves de Bourgogne in order to develop a more efficient and less isolated commercial approach. Cooperatives represent here 220 growers on 435 ha (about a quarter of the total area).
The now traditional Percée du Vin Jaune festival will take place on 7 and 8 February 2004 in Cramans, a village close to Arc-et-Senans in the Côtes du Jura.

WHAT'S NEW IN SAVOIE?

2001 was the year of false hopes. The year 2002 was doubly hit by a long frost and heavy rainfall in summer,. However, the grape varieties that are late-ripening, along with grapes harvested near the end of the harvest gave some good results. A winter sports accessory, Vin de Savoie would like to look for new horizons.

After a particularly harsh winter (six consecutive weeks of frost!), 2002 did, however, allow particularly good development for the vine. Its vegetative growth went well up to the end of the summer. On the other hand, the end of the season was particularly difficult due to unusual and heavy rainfall from mid-August to mid-September. The threat of rot forced wine-growers to bring in their early-ripening varieties very early, sometimes before they were perfectly ripe. Luckily a cold snap followed, blocking the advancement of the rot, but not damaging the ripening thanks to good sunshine levels. Sugar levels were satisfactory at the end of

the harvest, with high acidity. It was simply a case of strict selection, to avoid vinifying grapes spoilt by grey rot.

The best wines were harvested late
Harvest volumes (139,184 hl, of which 100,719 hl was white) were almost identical to those of 2001. Without pretending it reached great heights, the quality remained respectable. The wines are light, when rain and rot were predominant, but when the harvest was later, they were sufficiently concentrated and quite acidic to make them suitable for ageing. Ask your supplier for the harvest dates! Jacquère, Altesse and Mondeuse held up well in

general and are honest, sometimes outstanding. In whites, Roussette is rich, Jacquère perfumed and lively. In reds, Mondeuse plays on clean flavours and nice accompanying tannins. The other varieties (Gamay and Pinot noir) are often less exuberant. Apremont, Abymes, and Chignin gave excellent wines.

Expansion being restricted to 1%, the extent of the vineyard areas remains stable from one year to another from Lac Léman to Mont Blanc. This winter sports wine, consumed with fondue and raclette, is mainly sold in the area. The aim of the region is to "escape from the ski business"; it has succeeded gradually, even achieving some export sales. The efforts of the growers are also turning to sustainable agriculture: an approach which is progressing noticeably in Savoie.

WHAT'S NEW IN LANGUEDOC AND ROUSSILLON?

The year 2002 was very gloomy for the area, especially in the eastern sectors of the Gard *département* and the eastern part of the Hérault *département*, ravaged by storms and floods. Let the reader be reassured, the region has also produced some really good wines, even if they are rarely for ageing. The producers, however, could have done without these disruptions: to make things worse, the market is depressed for appellation wines, both in France and abroad. This is a situation that has fuelled debate on the hierarchy of the appellations in the region: should there be a new overall regional appellation or recognition of new *crus*?

Survivors and victims of the storms

The weather behaved like a yoyo during the whole of the 2001–2002 campaign in Languedoc and Roussillon. The vegetative

cycle started with a lack of water, noticeable from the west of the Hérault to the Roussillon area, not so extreme in the east of Hérault and the Gard. In spring, rains and above-average temperatures provoked a constant risk of mildew and botrytis attacks. Things came back to normal in June and July, thanks to normal rainfall levels. Despite certain signs of weakness in the grapes (early symptoms of water stress, thin skins and numerous small areas of botrytis and downy mildew), signs of a good vintage (very small berries and low yields) seemed to come together during the summer. The technical vineyard experts, however, found very mixed ripeness levels due to the staggered period of *véraison*.

The rains of early September will remain as the most notable event of the 2002 vintage. The violence of the storms in the Gard and the Vaucluse will remain in everyone's memories. The catastrophic and fatal floods that followed, submerged 8,000 ha of vines in the Gard and led to the loss of 600,000 hl.

In the west of the region – the Aude *département* and the Roussillon (with the exception of Aspres which was very wet) – were mainly spared the storms, and in the late-ripening areas where the rains only affected the vineyards at the start of ripening, very good vintage conditions came together. According to the managers of the *Institut Coopératif du Vin*, "looking beyond a very mixed situation, the 2002 vintage produced wines suiting the demands of the chief markets: refreshing, rounded and flavourful wines, which however, sometimes lack tannins and colour."

The Vins Doux Naturels of Languedoc and Roussillon together produced 379,364 hl. Banyuls (22,218 hl) and Rivesaltes (126,182 hl) lost volume, as well as the Muscats that only reached 171,455 hl.

A depressed situation

Have the AOC wines of Languedoc had it too easy? After a fairly euphoric period, 2002 seems to signal a halt in their advancement. Whilst their overall production has made a leap of 25%, surpassing two million hectolitres in 2001, it fell by 7.5% in 2002 (1.86 million hectolitres). Climatic conditions do not explain everything: the development of the markets has not kept up with that of production, leading to an appreciable increase in stocks. The AOC Corbières, the largest appellation, has had a reduction in sales of 18.5% during the 2001–2002 campaign.

Certain observers freely blame this reduction on a marked price increase in wines at the top of the range; the decline however penalizes mostly entry-level wines, which suffer from competition with low-priced Bordeaux, and more generally, from the reduction in French wine consumption and supermarket sales. The appellation wines of Languedoc and Roussillon have seen a reduction of 9% in volumes sold through supermarkets in 2001–2002. Corbières, which alone represents 44% of the Languedoc wines sold in supermarkets, has lost sales of a million litres, affecting in particular the lowest price wines and own-label wines.

Likewise on export markets, Languedoc appellation wines have seen a reduction of 10% in volume over the 12 months of 2002 (–4.6% in value), especially in the markets of Northern Europe, with the exception of Belgium.

Despite this down-turn, the bulk sales have seen generally stable prices over the 2001–2002 campaign, around 90 Euros per hectolitre. But the situation with AOC wines has got worse since the start of 2003. This is the opposite to *vins de table* that have increased almost by 20% during the first six months of the 2002–2003 campaign. *Vins de pays* have done even better, with a rise of nearly 23% in volume sold and more than 10% in price. This significant increase is greeted with caution by the trade who judge it to be closely linked to the present economic situation.

For the future, it remains to be seen if the regional *plan d'adaption viticole* (plan to restructure the vineyards), which is financed by the State, the regional council and the European Union, and includes a programme of uprooting and re-planting around 10,000 ha of vineyards annually over five years, will give a boost to the whole region.

New appellations

Whilst the debate concerning the creation of a new regional appellation in Languedoc is ongoing, the process of creating a hierarchy within the different appellations continues too. So after the AOC Coteaux du Languedoc–Grès de Montpellier was definitively recognized in March 2003, other sub-regional appellations are on the point of being established. This is the case with Terrasses du Larzac, within Coteaux du Languedoc, with Berlou and with Roquebrun in Saint-Chinian, and the area of Boutenac in Corbières.

Elsewhere, as from the 2003 vintage, the AOC Limoux, in the Aude, will now also be offered in a red version, Merlot having to make up at least half of the blend. The INAO has also agreed to modify the ruling for Crémant de Limoux, which from now will be much more clearly differentiated from the traditional Blanquette, due to a much greater proportion of Chardonnay and Chenin, and also 10% Pinot Noir in the blends.

Another new appellation in the region, AOC Collioure Blanc, is made mostly from the traditional varieties Grenache Blanc and Gris. The first vintage will be the 2002. Finally, in the south, Roussillon has recognized the appellation Côtes du Roussillon-Les Aspres; 2003 will see the first harvest of this wine, which will have to be matured for 12 months and is suitable for ageing.

Interest from Bordeaux investors

On the investment side, even if they are far from being the only investors in the region, it is the Bordeaux buyers who are in the news. There is négociant Bernard Magrez who, in partnership with Gérard Depardieu, has purchased 2.5 ha in the Aniane vineyard area, north of Montpellier. More discreetly, Bernard Magrez has bought around 20 hectares at Montner, in Roussillon, very close to the Maury area which, now that Jean-Luc Thunevin has formed partnership agreements with several local growers, seems more and more sought after by the châteaux owners of Saint-Emilion.

Elsewhere, Jacques and François Lurton, who are also in Maury, have purchased Château des Erles, the biggest single producer in AOC Fitou with 70 ha of vineyards, and where they have undertaken huge construction work on the winery, with the aim of making it the flagship estate in this Aude appellation. For his part, Jean-Michel Cazes, owner of Château Lynch-Bages in Pauillac, has opted for the AOC Minervois-la-Livinière, buying 25 ha of vineyards from Domaine de Vipur. Also in Hérault the Axa-Millésimes group has decided to invest at Caux, near Pézenas, where it has bought two estates in quick succession, with a total of 90 ha of vineyards.

Finally, note the creation of Château d'Angles, with 82 ha of vineyards in La Clape, in the Aude, by the former winery manager of Lafite-Rothschild, Eric Fabre, in partnership with Pierre Martineau.

WHAT'S NEW IN PROVENCE?

The year 2001 was notable for being very dry, but 2002 proved to be astonishingly wet and stormy from the end of spring. Showers and storms kept the producers on high alert. Luckily, the mistral blew from mid-September. The reds are refreshing, whereas the rosés, still much in demand, were the real stars.

An extremely wet summer

In winter, lower temperatures than the previous year favoured bud break, whilst spring delivered generally mild temperatures with good sunshine levels. However, the lack of water was notable at the start of the season. A destructive local frost during the last week of March affected the area around Saint-Maximin. From May onwards, it was the level of rainfall that

became a worry. The month proved changeable, with fluctuating temperatures; in some areas the amount of rain recorded was equivalent to three months of normal rainfall. The same wet trend was apparent in June, when rainfall was twice the normal level, but accompanied by above average temperatures, that were scorching from 19 June. The drought was no longer a problem: instead wine-growers were pre-occupied with the excess water and the violence of the July downpours. Hail damaged several vineyards around Cogolin and Grimaud. There were severe storms on 14 July and around mid-August. The particularly wet spring conditions encouraged the appearance of mildew, and, unusual for the region, many outbreaks of botrytis and of sour rot. The damage was made worse in some places by hail storms on 14 July.

Luckily, the arrival of the mistral in mid-September quickly cleaned up the vineyard. Nature behaved herself at harvest time, and selection of the grapes allowed a quality harvest to be brought in. Compared to the previous year, ripening was staggered over a period of time, with a gradual, steady accumulation of sugar in the berries. Finally, by the eve of harvest, it turned out to be fairly promising.

Provence produced 1,219,000 hl of wine, including just 4.1% of whites. Côtes de Provence represented 879,000 hl, a reduction in volume compared to the previous year (about 916,000 hl), with the proportion of reds dropping slightly (a little less than 12% as against roughly 14%). On the other hand, production remained steady in other appellations of the region (Cassis and Les Baux). In Bandol and Coteaux d'Aix en Provence, volumes were higher than those achieved in 2002.

Freshness and softness
Ripening early in Provence, the white grape varieties gave wines that are fresh and balanced with restrained richness and moderate alcohol levels, around 11.5%. As for reds, there are some structured wines for ageing, from long maceration of Syrah, Mourvèdre or Cabernet Sauvignon grapes and a period of time in oak. However, the general style of the year is more for refreshing wines with a light touch of acidity, soft, even lively on the palate, from a short period of maceration on the skins. These are wines with various red fruit flavours, ready to drink right away.

The rosés have good freshness and they too show a moderate level of alcohol. Best drunk with a meal, they benefit from having marked acidity which will also allow them to age.

WHAT'S NEW IN CORSICA?

The 2002 harvest took place in frequently rainy weather, especially on the east coast and at Patrimonio. The result was a "winemaker's year", where care and know-how made all the difference…whites and rosés are of quality, and the reds are not too bad, in a rounded style.

After a very typical start to the season and a scorching period in mid-June, the weather deteriorated from 14 July, with showers at regular intervals until the middle of the harvest. The ripeness levels were atypical for most grape varieties, with particular problems for the Muscats. Those wine-growers, who were attentive to grape quality right through the growing cycle, managed to get a good quality of green canopy at harvest time, controlled their yields perfectly and had the back-up of modern vinification equipment, will have succeeded in obtaining the best expression from their grapes.

A surprisingly good vintage
All the professionals agreed that the 2002 vintage would be better for whites and rosés than for reds. The first official appellation tastings tended to confirm these forecasts. However, from February, the reds presented for tasting showed well. They were quite rounded wines, with no great potential for very long ageing, but

distinguished by undeniably good quality flavours and silky tannins.

The production in 2002 was approximately the same as 2001, with a small increase in the proportion of rosés made (44%): their volume is similar to that of reds (42%). Whites represented 11% of volume and the Muscats du Cap Corse, 2.25%. The total production for 2003 is 94,650 hl.

Improvements for 2003

A grouping together of several sectors of AOC products is underway. This will improve the effectiveness of the trade professionals in Corsican agriculture. The wine sector is joining in this initiative so that, with all appellations working together, they can support Corsican wines even better, as much on the island, as on the continent.

WHAT'S NEW IN THE SOUTH WEST?

Structured red wines, flavourful white wines, lower volumes: this small, but high quality harvest has prevented the market from collapse, but overall there is a crisis of confidence.

Bergerac seeks a second wind

Producers from the greater Aquitaine area have always wanted to free themselves from the guardianship of their powerful Bordeaux cousins, but this wish for autonomy appears difficult to implement, especially in times of crisis, as in the delicate time at the start of the 2002–2003 campaign. This concerns Bergerac more than elsewhere, because its vineyard area is effectively an extension of Bordeaux and it uses the same grape varieties, giving wines which are inevitably compared with those of Bordeaux. Moreover, this is the appellation that caused a scandal in 2003, when a consignment of red Bergerac was found in a local supermarket selling for 1 Euro a bottle, giving rise to anger amongst the producers. It did not in any way concern a case of fraud; the wines were "saleable and true", if not of great quality. All the same, the producers were justifiably angry, as such commercial practices contribute to a devaluation of Bergerac,

and consequently, in the mind of the consumer, all appellation wines, as could be seen by higher prices not only for *vins de pays*, but also for *vins de table*.

However at the CIVRB (*Conseil Interprofessionnel des Vins de la Région de Bergerac* or Bergerac regional wine council), they estimate that the market is far from being damaged, and it is rather in Bordeaux that one should look at the surpluses and the huge quantities sold at knock-down prices.

Encouraging signs

That Bergerac sells for less than Bordeaux is effectively a historical constant and the price of being less famous. Yet, things have held up well in 2002–2003, without dramatic changes, with an average price for reds of 740 Euros per cask of 900 litres during the first 11 months of the campaign, hardly below that of red Bordeaux. Above all, they have managed to sell at least as much as the year's production, contrary to Bordeaux. Effectively, during the first ten months of the campaign, the CIVRB has recorded transactions for 256,832 hl of red Bergerac, for a 2002 harvest of 261,923 hl; it is therefore obvious that the stock at 31 July 2003 will be lower than that at the same date in 2002. Also worth noticing is that dry white Bergerac, at 706 Euros per cask, is evenly matched with its red counterpart, whilst Monbazillac continues to rise, although its production has only slightly increased (+5%) in 2002.

Vagaries of the weather welcomed

The 2002 harvest provided all the characteristics to stabilize the market without putting off the consumer, in fact quite the reverse. In Bordeaux they talked of a miracle, in Bergerac they wrote "saved by the rain!" which amounts to the same thing due to their very similar terroir. In Bergerac, there was a dry and mild spring, and then a wet May, followed by an uneven June leading to an erratic flowering period with *coulure* and *millerandage*. Summer had no torrential rainfall, but the weather was permanently wet and never really sunny, encouraging grey rot. Hence why September, which was hot during the day and cold at night (more so than in Bordeaux due to Bergerac's slightly more continental position), was such a blessing. The grapes were able to ripen perfectly, except for those already badly affected by rot; acidity maintained the flavours in the whites and the reds have good colour and structure. Production in Bergerac fell sharply, by 13.4% for the reds, giving a total of 323,497 hl and a yield of only 45 hl/ha. White wine production, with 217,869 hl, was virtually unchanged (−0.77%), with an even lower average yield of 40 hl/ha. It was therefore not surprising to find wines that were both structured and with good colour.

Volumes down from Madiran to Gaillac

The same reduction can be found in Madiran where production reached only 59,000 hl out of a potential 80,000 hl. Nevertheless, sales progressed 8% compared with 2001, and Pacherenc, which has decidedly become fashionable recently, saw its sales improve by 10%. These appellations sell at least as much as they produce. In Cahors, with areas designated as AOC rising by around 100 hectares year on year – from 4,375–4,445 ha – production has gone from 251,873 to 212,686 hl: a sharp reduction in volume as well as in yield, since that plummeted to 48 hl/ha as against 57.5 hl/ha the previous year! In Gaillac, the situation is always a little bit different, because the vineyard area is much further away from Bordeaux, escaping from its commercial influence, and because its dual purpose production of AOC wines and *vin de pays*, facilitates controlling stock and the market. The

differences can also be seen in the climate, which is marked by a strong Mediterranean influence. And yet, in 2002, the AOC red and rosé wines (including the *primeurs*) reached a harvest total of 132,039 hl compared to 149,372 hl the previous year, whilst the white AOC wines dropped from 34,747 to 26,837 hl and the *vins de pays* showed the same drop. These quantities seem to closely match the amounts that the market absorbs each year, something which reached its absolute peak of 168,547 hl (for reds and whites) during the 1999–2000 campaign and which has levelled out since at around 162,000 hl. It is also worth noting that price has remained stable, for whites at 67 Euros per hectolitre and for reds at 100 Euros, distinctly higher than Bergerac and very close to Bordeaux. From these figures it can be seen that a small appellation does not necessarily equate to a small price; especially when how it is sold is considered: in Gaillac, hardly more than 15% of the AOC production is sold in bulk by the tanker-load. That does not mean to say that they are unconcerned by the unsold wines of other appellations.

Contrasting economic situations

Things are fairly similar in the Garonne Valley, in Buzet, but on a different scale: the cooperative cellar, that "holds together' the appellation as well as the sales of wine, celebrates its 50th birthday in 2003 and represents a magnificent success in terms of organisation and sales for the benefit of quality wine production. A great achievement, but one which, even if it means encouraging imitation, undoubtedly can no longer be transposed to all the vineyard areas in a country where above all one enjoys diversity.

The other vineyards of the Lot-et-Garonne *département*, Côtes de Duras and Côtes du Marmandais were both rather downbeat, despite the small 2002 harvest. Red Côtes de Duras, at around 600 Euros per 900-litre cask, has definitely reached the bottom, despite wines of a quality that has not declined. The absence of a négociant, of press interest and a visible commercial outlet constitutes a dangerous situation in this vineyard area where there are, nevertheless, still some finds to be made...

The year 2003 in the South West region is best characterized by a disarray that is reminiscent of the period of great crisis 30 years ago when the organization of the common wine market put all the wines from the European Community, especially the *vins de table*, in competition with each other. In certain appellations, like in the Marmandais, they are considering creating a type of "Grand Cru" system or a *"villages"* appellation that would pull up the other wines to get them better recognized. In Madiran, they are increasing the density in the vineyards to at least 4,000 vines per hectare, which is visualized, in the same way as in the Médoc they are talking about the number of bunches per vine, as being a better measure than the yield per hectare. However, in general, there is the impression of a crisis of confidence in a world where competition is these days so universal that it has reached as far as the small vineyard areas of Aquitaine whose markets are rarely far away.

WHAT'S NEW IN THE LOIRE VALLEY?

Although the growing season was not at all in advance of the norm, except in the Central Vineyards, and summer was hardly encouraging, all the Loire Valley vineyards enjoyed a late season under the beneficial influence of a high pressure system giving sunny, dry and windy weather. The year 2002 is of very good quality for all three colours. The appellation wines of the Loire are amongst the few to maintain their export positions, both in terms of volume and of value. On the home market, results are more mixed: varying according to the grape variety, the type of wine and the appellation. Muscadets, sparkling wines and reds from Gamay are experiencing some difficulties, whilst wines from Sauvignon, the Cabernets, and sweet wines are doing well.

NANTES
Winter and spring were temperate, rather dry and typical, with bud break for Melon in early April, two days later than for the 2001 vintage, and flowering around 15 June, more or less at the same time as in 2001. The exceptional weather conditions during the harvest were notable this year. After some storms at the beginning of September, there were five weeks of fine weather, accompanied by easterly winds, lasting up to the beginning of October. The 2002 Vintage is therefore of very good quality, flavoursome and fruity, with, at the same time, good acidity. The quantity was also good: 792,000 bottles in Muscadet AOC (+20% compared to 2001).
The market is the concern: at the end of April 2003, volumes sold since 1 August 2002 for all Muscadets were down by 6% compared to the 2001–2002 campaign. Average prices remain low and the financial difficulties of wine-growing remain. With bulk prices lower than cost price, numerous producers are looking to develop direct sales. Fortunately, export sales have experienced a slight recovery. The 2002 vintage should allow the build-up of stocks, which are at their lowest level since the 1991 frost.

Recognition of communal crus in the Muscadet vineyards
The launch of an initiative to recognize communal crus took place in 2001. A number of Muscadet producers vinify wines for ageing, often from specific terroirs, and then put them on the market late. They want to allow these terroirs and appellation wines to gain more recognition. Currently, nearly 90 producers have become involved in this initiative and they are celebrating their third vintage.
The first step towards the recognition of communal appellations was the setting up of specifications for both the vineyard and the winery. Secondly, the *Syndicat de Défense des AOC Muscadet* defined how production conditions should be monitored. Checks are made on the potential yield in every plot, the quality of the terroir, the estate in general and the condition of the vines.
In 2002–2003, a steering committee considered the drawing up of a certification system for the wines. A jury of experts was

specially trained to taste these wines and the first tastings took place over the first four months of 2003. By the beginning of summer, 26 wines had obtained their certification for the vintage 2001. Now, a steering committee is working on defining the conditions for marketing the wines.

News in brief from the vineyards

A new organization, the Syndicat Général des Vignerons de Nantes has been formed by linking together several Nantes area syndicates. It has been given five objectives: to unite the region's wine industry; to tackle wine-related problems in a practical and non-populist way; to coordinate the policies of the trade organizations; to energize future projects; and to communicate.

ANJOU-SAUMUR

Late-season conditions are decisive in the Anjou wine district. The 2002 vintage was, as further down-river, strongly affected by the high pressure system in September and October. After a rather wet start to the year, with average sunshine levels and warmth, and bud break in early April, vine growth was slowed at the end of May by minimum temperatures often lower than 10°C, with averages lower than 15°C. From 10 June there was a dry and warm period

(above 20°C) which allowed the flowering period to finish quickly. A heat wave from 14–17 June (with a maximum of 34.9°) managed in some areas to shrivel the grapes.

In summer, frequent rain storms (134 mm in July-August as against the average of 83 mm); generally lower than average temperatures and sunshine levels; areas of rot; and *véraison* occurring later than during the past five years, conspired to leave more than one producer worried.

Everything changed dramatically in September, which was marked by exceptional sunshine levels (236 hours compared to an average of 184 hours); and dry, warm weather with drying winds from the north and northwest. There were plenty of factors favourable for good ripening and healthy grapes. The rain returned at the end of October and continued throughout November.

For all the grape varieties the harvest was later than for the past five years, with, as a result, slightly higher acidity levels than normal. Grolleau, the main variety for rosés, turned out very well, with a natural potential alcohol of 11%, particularly high for this variety.

Yields for Cabernet Franc were affected in places by the drought in June, but the variety was harvested with good potential sugar levels and phenolic content. The official start to the vintage was set at 7 October in Saumur and 10 October in Anjou, very slightly later than average but with very favourable vintage conditions. Chenin behaved equally well with a high potential alcohol level and high acidity. Harvest started between 2 and 9 October depending on the type of wine produced (sparkling, dry or sweet). For the early grape selections, overripeness was characterized by some drying on the vine due to the wind, whereas later selections in November could, conversely, be diluted.

A varied market

The market reinforced the tendencies of the last ten years: an improvement for reds and rosés, with a decline for whites. Amongst the first, the AOC Saumur-Champigny reinforced its position as leader with prices going above 2 Euros a litre, and low stocks. The good groundwork undertaken by the AOC syndicate on the methods of vine training and yield control has profoundly changed this vineyard area. In 2002, more than 600 ha of the 1,450 in the AOC were checked by officers of the INAO. The Anjou appellation continued its progress of the last few years and maintained both price and volumes of the 2001 campaign. The work done over the past ten years by the *Syndicat des Vins rouges d'Anjou* (the syndicate for the red wines of Anjou), continued to bear fruit. Notable was the style definitions for Anjou and Anjou-Villages, as, respectively, wines for early drinking and wines for a period of short ageing. The market is less favourable for red Saumur wines and the syndicate is trying to define a wine of a higher quality than required by the appellation.

Rosé wines were the nice surprise of 2002 with increased volumes and prices, and very low stocks. This good result may reflect good sales nationally, but it is equally due to the improvements in quality. For whites, the volumes are stuck at a very low level, notably for the Traditional method sparkling wines (with the exception of Crémant de Loire). Individual successes seem to show the way: hand harvesting with grape selection, and good ripeness levels, as with sweet wines.

Sélection de Grains Nobles and AOC Chaume

Two recognitions have been made to reward the producers of sweet wines in Anjou for all their hard work over several years.

The first is the legal recognition of the term "Sélection de Grains Nobles" for the AOC wines Coteaux du Layon and Coteaux de l'Aubance. This applies to wines offering a minimum 234 g/l equivalent to a potential alcohol of 17.5% with no chaptalisation allowed, and sold no earlier than 18 months after the harvest.

The second is the creation of the Chaume AOC, with the additional obligatory statement "Premier Cru des Coteaux du Layon". This puts the slope of the little hamlet of Chaume, in the *commune* of Rochefort-sur-Loire, amongst some of the greatest appellations of France.

TOURAINE

In 2002, the vine started its vegetative cycle on time, but not on the early date that we have become used to in the past few years. After a fairly dry and sunny April, May proved changeable, as did the first half of June. The fine weather that arrived in the half of the month returned the situation to normal. Slight *coulure* was the only concern. Over the first few days of summer, it seemed that to achieve a good harvest the vines only had to keep going for long enough to ripen their grapes.

According to the *Unité d'Analyses et de Recherches du Laboratoire de Touraine* (the Touraine research and analysis laboratory) run by Etienne Carre, and the technical service of the INAO at Tours, the summation of the temperatures and sunshine hours during July and August was lower than normal; rainfall, without being excessive, was marked by having a number of days with heavy downpours. On 5 September, the growth was late compared to previous years. Thereafter, an unexpected Indian summer reigned from 10 September to 21 October, letting a northeast wind through the rows of vines to clean up the grapes. At the same time, sugar and colouring matter were concentrated in the berries.

A storm warning on 23 September made producers fear the worst. However, in the end, this downpour was a blessing, re-starting the photosynthesis which allowed the breakdown of acids. For this reason, the late-ripening varieties (the Cabernets and Chenin), harvested from 5–20 October, were able to reach full ripeness in complete peace.

The wines of Bourgueil and Chinon acquired a phenolic concentration rarely equalled. The ripeness of the tannins gave the wines a silky finish, whilst maintaining the acidity that is so typical of Loire wines.

In Montlouis and Vouvray, the dry and medium dry wines, clean and straight-forward, show much richness and character. More unusually, the sweeter wines made from selective pickings appear elegant and ethereal, promising a good future.

In AOC Touraine where the vines ripen earlier, the harvest started on 20 September with Sauvignon, followed by Gamay. Marked by a citrus-fruit nose (blood oranges), the Sauvignons show a mouth-filling and warm palate with a refreshing finish, linked to the incomplete breakdown of acids at harvest time. The Gamay wines are more mixed, but show nice fruit.

The exceptional climatic conditions of autumn also benefited the outer appellations such as Jasnières, Coteaux du Loir, Cheverny, Coteaux du Vendômois and Valençay.

In terms of volume, the 2002 vintage is more or less the same as last year, for Chinon, Bourgueil and Saint-Nicolas-de-Bourgueil. In Vouvray, there is a slight reduction in volume, with a lower proportion of spar-kling wines (50% compared with 59%). In Montlouis sur Loire, there is a similar reduction in the sparkling wine proportions, but volumes are greater overall. The AOC wines Touraine, Touraine-Amboise, Touraine-Azay le Rideau, Touraine-Mesland, and Noble-Joué have slightly increased volumes. This year, they produced 132,200 hl of white wines and 165,700 hl of reds and rosés. Today, reds clearly dominate these appellations, because the decline in white grapes grown for sparkling wines has not been compensated for by the increase in Sauvignon plantings.

The situation is stable in Coteaux du Vendômois, for Coteaux du Loir and for Jasnières, whilst Cheverny increases. Touraine *primeur* has not found its second wind.

Winners and losers in the market

The current campaign (2002–2003) looks the same as last year. Red Touraine continues its slow decline in both volumes and price. The other red appellations, Chinon, Bourgueil and Saint-Nicolas-de-Bourgueil remain stable, with a con-tinuing difficulty for Saint-Nicolas in explaining its price premium. Vouvray is much in demand and prices have climbed slightly. There has been the same rise for white Touraine (from Sauvignon), which benefits from the high price of Sancerre. On the other hand, there has been a decline in demand and in price for sparkling Touraine.

The home market, with two principal areas of consumption, western France and the Paris region, absorbs almost all the production of Touraine and its neighbour-ing AOC wines. Exports play their role too, especially for Vouvray that sold one-third of its production abroad, notably to Great Britain and the United States. White Touraine finds a good outlet (20%) in Great Britain, Belgium, Germany and Holland. In terms of distribution, the supermarket groups provide the main supply source (60%) for consumers, followed by 'hard discount' outlets (16%). Finally, subject to much satisfaction on the part of those who work for the Loire Valley wine sector is their position of leader in restaurant sales (more than 23%), ahead of Bordeaux, the Rhône Valley and Alsace.

News in brief from the vineyards

An American financier Anthony Hwang, originally from the Philippines, has bought the majority share of Société Huet, one of the leading lights in Vouvray, but Noël Pinguet, son-in-law of Gaston Huet, who died last year, remains in charge of the estate.

The *Syndicat de Défense des AOC Jasnières et Coteaux du Loir* has decided to join Interloire (the overall Loire wine promo-tional body).

Annick Coucharrière, managing director of Etablissements Monmousseau in Montrichard, and Alain Chambaud, new general director of the firm Blanc Foussy will combine forces within the framework of Interloire to promote sparkling Touraine. These two companies alone represent almost half of the 3.5 million bottles of sparkling Touraine produced every year from the Chenin variety. This grape was the theme for the "Rendez-vous du Chenin" ("Chenin symposium"), organised within the general framework of "Paysages de Vignes et de Vins" ("Landcapes of vineyards and wines") run by Interloire which took place in l'Abbaye Royale de Fontevraud in July 2003. This event also established the enrolment of the Loire Valley as one of UNESCO's World Heritage sites.

CENTRAL VINEYARDS
With an average date for bud break of 5 April for Sauvignon, the vines started growth ten days ahead of the last decade's average. An extremely rapid flowering period took place mainly over the scorching weekend of 15–16 June. Very high temperatures encouraged *coulure* and *millerandage*, especially for the red varieties. The strong heat of the week of 15 August encouraged a quite even and rapid *véraison*.
Over all of the Central Vineyards, the harvest was spread from 16 September to 15 October, in dry and mild weather. The majority of the grapes were harvested between 25 September and 5 October. However, using increasingly detailed knowledge of grape physiology, many wine-growers harvested in several stages, picking each parcel as close as possible to its optimum ripeness. Generally, the reds were brought in first, then the whites from limestone and flint soils, and finally those from Kimmeridgean clay.

The health of the grapes was good. Fleshy and of a smaller size than normal, the berries released their juice more slowly than usual, so much so that the musts only contained light particles and were very clean.
The wines of the 2002 vintage show very good structure, made from grapes that were highly concentrated in sugars and with high total acidity levels.
The white wines combine power, firmness and finesse. The flavours are elegant and complex, showing all the diversity of their terroir; they appear to have a very good future. Rich on the palate, showing both weight and acidity, they will mostly reach their peak towards the end of this year, when the *Guide* appears. They should hold well over time.
For the reds, the colour is deep, often with a pronounced purple tinge. The tannins are dense and balanced. The aromas are revealed little by little, expressing particularly fruity notes. Depending on individual wines, the ageing potential is good to excellent.
The 2002 production reached 273,800 hl, lower than the previous vintage (–7%). White wines represented some 80% of these volumes, reds 16%. Sancerre represents 58% of the volume produced in the whole of the Central Vineyards.
Demand remains sustained, especially for exports. In decreasing order of volume, Great Britain, the United States, Belgium and Germany represent together around 80% of the wines exported.

WHAT'S NEW IN THE RHONE VALLEY?

A rainy summer with little sunshine, and delayed ripening: the 2002 vintage caused many worries to wine-growers, who often had to bring in the harvest as quickly as possible, before the vineyards were affected by floods. The result is a vintage of lower quantity than in previous years. On the flooded markets, the Rhône Valley is maintaining its position well.

Sun in winter, rain in summer
After a cold, dry and windy Autumn, December was harsh with below zero temperatures over several days, and lower and less frequent rainfall than average. Winter was fairly mild, sunny and dry apart from in February when the level of rainfall was 56% above average. A warm

and sunny spring allowed a rapid start to the vine's growth cycle. The only incident was a hail storm in May in the area of the Dentelles de Montmirail.
The highest temperatures of the year were recorded in June. Summer proved to be extremely wet, with a lack of sunshine, a big storm in mid-July and then a deluge at

the beginning of September, most fortunately followed by a more wind-blown period. Generally the year was windier than usual.

From the end of August, there were higher anthocyanins levels than normal in Grenache and Mourvèdre, but slightly lower levels in Syrah compared to the equivalent time over the last four years. For all three varieties, the total phenolic content was slightly lower.

The most notable point at the beginning of the study into ripeness levels was that the total acid levels were generally higher than over the past four years. The vintage was therefore about four days later than in 2001.

Pressures of the harvest

Rain at the end of August, and then the heavier falls from 8–9 September, really upset the vines: ripeness developed slowly; the sugar levels increased little and the acidity levels plummeted. The other notable fact was the rapid deterioration of the health of the grapes. There were widespread areas of grey rot, encouraged by warm and wet weather. Some sectors, especially late-ripening areas, benefited from the onset of the favourable mistral wind and by lower rainfall.

Therefore, this year the decision of when to harvest was more focused on the health of the grapes rather than on ripeness levels. In general, wine-growers acted quickly and did not hesitate to change their harvest programmes in order to make the best of the vintage. Effectively, harvest was less spread out than normal, taking a week less than in previous vintages.

Harvest started around 2 September in the early-ripening sectors of the Gard and the Vaucluse *départements*. It was carried out faster than in a normal year as can be seen from the fact that by the end of September, all the Southern Rhône areas were picked. In the North, the harvest started around 10 September and was equally fast.

In the same way, vinifications were quite short with few delays and very few stuck fermentations. The strict grape selection made in each plot was accompanied by a reduction in yield in certain sectors and allowed *cuvées* to be selected according to the quality of the base grape material. Production reached some 3,390,000 hl (186,000 hl of dry white wine). Côtes du

Rhône (2,054,000 hl) and Côtes du Rhône-Villages (288,000 hl) took the lion's share in volume; Côtes du Ventoux (311,000 hl) and Côtes du Luberon (170,000 hl) also accounted for large volumes.

Rosés, and likewise the whites offered good balance showing clean aromas, and for rosés, delicacy with a great range of red berry fruits. The whites showed more stone fruits, in particular *pêche de vigne*.

The range of reds was very great, going from soft fruity wines with a light character up to structured reds, with bright, deep colours and silky tannins.

Sales hold up reasonably well

Over five years, the average shelf-space allotted to the Rhône Valley by French supermarket groups has increased by 27%. This growth has been particularly notable for Côtes du Rhône-Villages, where the wines are now listed in 95% of French supermarkets.

On export markets, the CFCE notes a slight reduction in volumes compared to 2001: 770,000 hl (–0.6%), but the figures for value still grow: +6.1%. The only country in Europe to consume 75% red wine, Denmark enjoys Côtes du Rhône wines. In three years, sales there have progressed by 32% in volume and 36% in value to reach 540,000 €.

A study conducted by Inter Rhône (the Rhône Valley wine promotional body) into sales patterns of the wines of the Luberon over the last five years, showed the growth in distribution via high-value channels: export, direct sales and the traditional sector. The volumes sold in supermarkets declined (56% in 1998 compared to just 37% in 2001) to benefit all the other distribution channels. The total volume sold changed little (155,000–160,000 hl), but there is a real transformation. The number of *caves particulières* (independent producers) grew from 29 in 1998 to 42 today and corresponds to a growth in sales from the cellar-door (from 5 to 13% of volume). The rapid development of tourism in the Luberon and the emergence of a good reputation for the appellation have certainly contributed to this change. Export represents 35% of total sales, 55,500 hl. The so-called traditional sector (the hotel-restaurant trade and wine shops) is also experiencing an increase, having gone from 8% to 14%. One weakness of the appellation is in the wholesale sector (one of the key suppliers to restaurants), which only represents 1% of sales.

Ecological studies

Vast stretches of land, exclusively planted with vineyards, without any other vegetation can lead to a depletion in the amount of flora and fauna. The vineyard of Bois des Dames at Violès (owned by Hugues Meffre) is typical of the case. To compensate for this loss, a trial ecological zone has been established on the estate. The Vaucluse Chamber of Agriculture, in partnership with the *Conservatoire Botanique National de Porquerolles* (National Botanic Academy at Porquerolles), with assistance from the regional council is conducting a study on the feasibility and impact of such zones on the vineyards. Students from the Louis Giraud agricultural college in Carpentras undertook the task of planting shrubs and hedges, made up of 20 different Mediterranean species including rosemary, bay leaf, thyme, pistachio, cade, sage (tree) and many more obscure plants. At the same time a trial has been undertaken of mulching with the stalks from the previous vintage, which maintains both weed control and humidity. These studies will now allow observers to find out what type of wildlife will settle there. It is hoped that the plantings will shelter predators of vine pests. Other reserve zones are also being studied such as mixed hedges sited on the edge of vine plots and grassed-down areas on the edges or in between the vine rows. These can be seen notably in the experimental vineyards of the Chamber of Agriculture at Piolenc and in some estates at Violès, Cairanne, Caromb and Uchaux. Apart from their ecological interest in the search for more environmentally friendly viticulture, these zones should enrich the landscape and improve the image of the vineyard region.

In brief from the vineyards

Some anniversaries: on the occasion of the 75th Marché aux Vins (wine fair) in Ampuis, the Côte-Rôtie producers celebrated the ?th anniversary of their syndicate. In ?, the University at Suze la Rousse ?ted 25 years by getting together with the universities at Aix-en-Provence to organise a conference and a party. This is an organisation that has risen from two employees in 1978 (Patrick Galant and Jacques Avril) to 40 people in 2003.

Companies: Robert Skalli has raised his stake in the négociant company Bouachon in Châteauneuf du Pape to 100%. Henry Bouachon remains the general director.

The Marie Brizard group has confirmed its purchase of Chais Beaucairois (producing 120 million bottles) a subsidiary of the Casino Group. In 2001, Chais Beaucairois had a turnover of 154 million Euros with 20% exported.

The Grands Vins Gabriel Meffre group has just celebrated the fifth anniversary since the management buyout of the Meffre company. It was an occasion to take stock of a fairly positive situation. In 1997, with 47 employees, the company achieved a turnover of 17 million Euros. Today, it employs 100 people with a turnover of 37 million Euros (including Domaines du Soleil). Today, Gabriel Meffre has become the owner of Domaine de Longue Toque (with 18 ha in Gigondas) and owns two other estates. Continuing its concentration on vineyards, the company has just taken over the lease of the Château Grand Escalon (in Générac, near Nîmes). Finally, it has invested 5.24 million Euros into a new bottling hall. This allows their production capacity to increase from 10 to 25 million bottles per year.

La Société Provençale des Vins d'Origine (SPVO-Mathieu Carlier) in Vacqueyras until now included four shareholder cooperatives from Vaucluse. It has just welcomed seven new ones. Joining Caves de Bedoin, Puyméras, Sablet and Valréas are, in the Gard, those of Gaujac, Montfrin, Orsan, Saint-Gely-du-Cornillon and les Coteaux de Fournès, and in Vaucluse, le Cellier des Templiers de Richerenches and Les Vignerons Réunis de Sainte-Cécile-les-Vignes. The capital has been increased to allow the new shareholders to join, and with the four existing cooperatives this provides 50% of the stock requirements for this company that deals in bulk with all the AOC wines of the Rhône Valley and Côtes de Provence.

Les Caves Les Roches Blanches in Mormoiron and La Montagne Rouge in Villes sur Auzon merged in December 2002, forming Cave Terra Ventoux. This new organization is now positioned amongst the very large operators since they should handle about 55,000 hl of which 45,000 hl is Côtes du Ventoux.

Le Prieuré de Montezargues, the famous AOC Tavel estate, has already been sold to the Richard group who already own Château le Nerthe in Châteauneuf-du-Pape.

The interprofessional wine "Plaisir du Rhône" is taking a growing position on the market. With 12 million bottles sold in 1999, 13.5 in 2000, 14 in 2001 and 15 in 2002, it has great appeal to Rhône Valley sales outlets.

Le Syndicat des Vignerons de Vacqueyras and the syndicate of Lirac have each adopted a new bottle in the classic Burgundy shape. The colour is an antique brown and the bottle neck has been modified. The bottles are engraved with the words Appellation Contrôlée.

The study "Côtes du Rhône Génération Future" has reached its conclusion. Conducted by trade professionals to examine the future of the sector, it produced ten objectives and 45 proposals to meet the demands of tomorrow. The time has now arrived for consultation to make this plan, their project for the future.

ALSACE AND THE EAST

Alsace

Most of the Alsace wine region is on the hills that rise at the foot of the Vosges mountains and run eastward to the Rhine plain. The Vosges form a natural barrier between Alsace and the rest of France and help to create the region's individual climate. Because the moisture absorbed over the Atlantic falls as rain on the mountains, it leaves the eastern slopes only lightly watered. The average annual rainfall in the Colmar region is the lowest in France, less than 500 mm a year. In summer the mountains also provide some protection from the cool Atlantic winds. Most importantly, the undulating relief of the hills creates minute variations in microclimate, which ultimately contributes to the variety and quality of the vineyards.

The Alsace vineyards are also characterized by a great diversity in soil types. Some fifty million years ago, the recent past in geological terms, the Vosges and the Black Forest formed a single mass, created by a sequence of geological activity during the Tectonic era – floods, erosion and the folding of the earth's crust. From the Tertiary era, the central part of the mountains began to subside, creating, over time, a plain. As a result of this compression, nearly all the strata (layers of soil that had accumulated over different geological periods) were exposed along the line of the schism. This is the area where the vineyards are located. In most of the wine-growing communes there are at least four or five different geological structures to the terrain.

The origins of the Alsatian vineyards are lost in the mists of time, but it is thought that the early inhabitants of the region probably harvested grapes, although organized cultivation did not take place until after the Roman conquest. In the wake of Germanic invasions in the fifth century, vine-growing fell into decline for a period, although manuscripts show the vineyards soon began to flourish again under powerful centres of Christianity such as bishoprics, abbeys and convents. Documents from before AD 900 cite more than 160 places where vines were cultivated.

The development of the vineyards continued uninterrupted until the 16th century, the period when wine-growing in Alsace was at its peak. The magnificent Renaissance-style houses that can be seen in the wine villages bear witness to the undoubted prosperity of the times, when great quantities of Alsatian wines were exported to every country in Europe. But the Thirty Years' War was devastating: pillage, famine, plague and destruction had catastrophic consequences for wine-growing and were ruinous for economic activity in the region. When peace was restored, cultivating vines and wine production were gradually put back on a stable footing and began again to flourish and expand. The areas of vineyards increased, but they were mainly planted with ordinary grape varieties, which meant wine was produced in quantity but was not necessarily of high quality. In 1731 a royal edict attempted to put a stop to this situation, but without much success. The expansion of the vineyards continued unabated after the Revolutions and by 1808 more than 23,000 ha were under vines, an area that increased to 30,000 ha by 1828. There was significant over-production of wine and the situation was made worse when the export market collapsed and the consumption of wine dropped as beer-drinking increased. At the same time, wines from southern France offered stiff competition, and they could now easily be shipped to the rest of France on the new railways. In Alsace the vines suffered from a variety of diseases, vine worm and phylloxera, which compounded the difficulties. From 1902 the once-extensive vineyards gradually diminished, and by 1948 the area of vine cultivation had fallen to 9,500 ha, of which 7,500 ha was given the Alsace appellation.

The post-war economic boom and the increased professionalism of the wine-growers combined to drive the revival and redevelopment of the Alsace vineyards. They now cover an area of about 14,800 ha with an annual production that in 2002 amounted to 1,218,840 hl – 43,576 hl of Grands Crus and 165,768 hl of Crémant d'Alsace – and the wine is marketed throughout France and abroad. Exports represent about a quarter of total sales. The widespread improvements in the production and quality of Alsace wines were the collaborative work of the various professional groups which all agreed to limit the quantities of wine on the market. These groups included the winemaking wine-growers, cooperatives and négociants (local wine wholesalers), who were often also wine-growers themselves and who also bought large quantities of grapes from growers who did not vinify their own harvest.

The villages and towns along the Route des Vins hold wine festivals throughout the year. These are great tourist attractions and important cultural events for the region. The annual wine fair, held at Colmar in August, is undoubtedly the most important festival, and the ones held earlier in Guebwiller, Ammerschwihr, Ribeauvillé, Barr and Molsheim are also worth visiting. The most prestigious event is organized by the *Confrérie Saint-Etienne*, which was first established in the 14th century and revived in 1947.

Alsace

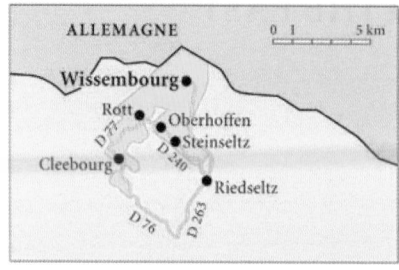

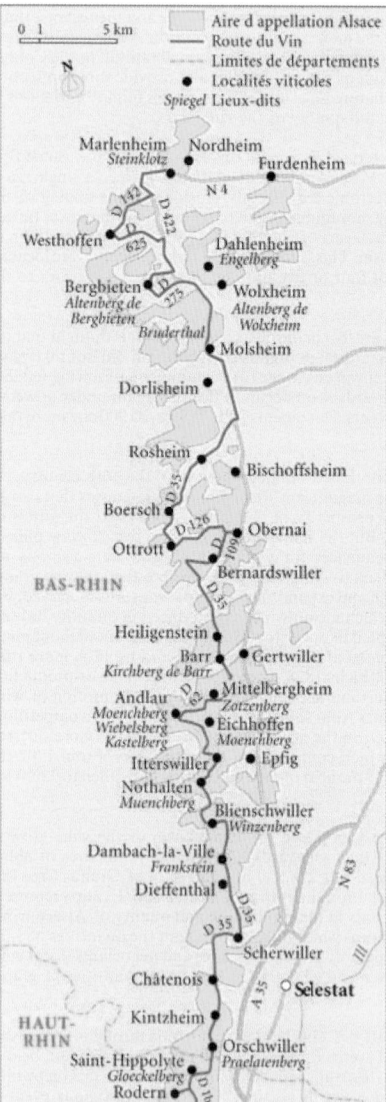

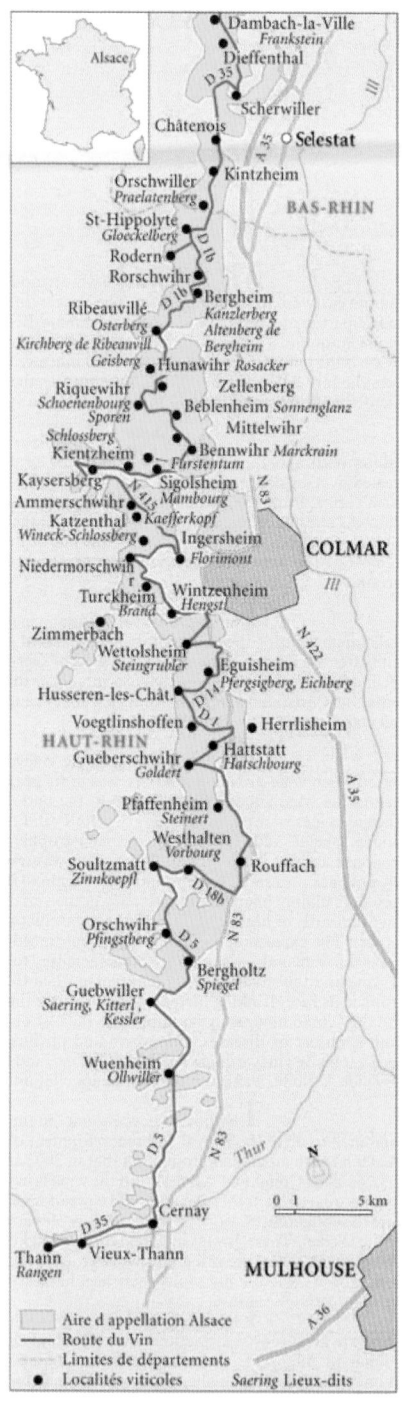

The most distinctive attribute of Alsace wines is their aromatic perfume, which is at its best from grapes grown in cool, temperate areas where they ripen slowly and over a long time. The particular flavours naturally depend on the grape variety, and in Alsace wines are almost always labelled and sold under their grape variety, as distinct from most other French AOC wines which, as a rule, are named after the region or particular geographical location where the grapes are grown.

The grapes are harvested in October and transported as quickly as possible to the wine store for first pressing. Sometimes the grapes are stripped from the stalks, then they undergo a second pressing. The must that flows from the press is full of residual particles from pressing, such as fragments of grape flesh, seeds, skins and stalks, which must be removed as quickly as possible by sedimentation or centrifugation. The clarified must then starts its fermentation. During this crucial phase enormous care has to be taken to avoid excessive temperatures. The young wine is often murky, and the winemaker can use a variety of methods to clarify it, including racking, adding sulphur dioxide, and fining. The developing wine is kept in vats or barrels until late spring when most of it is bottled. This method of production makes the dry white wines, which represent more than 90% of Alsace wine production.

The Alsace wines made from late-harvested grapes and the Sélection de Grains Nobles, (wines made from late-harvested grapes that are individually selected from the bunch for their ripeness and sweetness) have had their own official appellation only since 1984. These wines are made under strictly regulated production guidelines, the most rigorous concerning the amount of sugar in the grapes. These wines are in a class of their own and, in addition to being very expensive, cannot be produced every year. Only certain grape varieties qualify for late harvesting, mainly Gewurztraminer, Pinot Gris and Riesling, but also Muscat, though more rarely.

Alsace wines are generally considered to be better when drunk young, and this is mostly true for the Sylvaner, Chasselas, Pinot Blanc varieties and Edelzwicker, a blend of varieties. But their youthfulness can mature and Riesling, Gewurztraminer and Pinot Gris often benefit from being kept for at least two years. There is no hard and fast rule, but some Grands Vins, made in years when the grapes are very ripe, can keep longer, sometimes for decades.

The Alsace appellation applies to all of the 110 areas of communal production and is restricted to the use of 11 grape varieties: Gewurztraminer, Riesling Rhénan, Pinot Gris, Muscat Blanc à Petits Grains and Rosé à Petits Grains, Muscat Ottonel, Pinot Blanc, Auxerrois Blanc, Pinot Noir, Sylvaner and Chasselas Blanc and Rosé.

Alsace Klevener de Heiligenstein

Klevener de Heiligenstein is no different from Vieux Traminer (or Savagnin Rose), which have been known in Alsace for centuries.

Mostly it has given way over time to the spicy "Gewurztraminer" variant but has remained popular in Heiligenstein and five neighbouring communes.

Its rarity and elegance are what make it original. The wines are very well balanced and discreetly aromatic.

CAVE VINICOLE D'ANDLAU-BARR

2001★

	n.c.	20,000	▮ ⬥	8–11 €

Barr is not far from Heiligenstein, which explains why the Andlau-Barr cooperative has chosen to specialize in Heiligenstein Klevener, with one of their wines winning a *coup de coeur* in last year's *Guide*. This 2001 has a deep yellow colour with beautiful green glints, and immediately releases a rich variety of floral and spicy aromas. Although the residual sugar is still fairly evident on the palate, the wine is supple, powerful and very well balanced, with further spicy notes on a full and pleasant finish. This will be a good accompaniment to white meats. (Residual sugar: 10.8 g/l.)
➤ Cave vinicole d'Andlau et environs, 15, av. des Vosges, 67140 Barr, tel. 03.88.08.90.53, fax 03.88.47.60.22 ☑
☥ by appt.

CHARLES BOCH

Vieilles vignes L'Authentique Cuvée n° 1 2001★

	0.4 ha	n.c.	▮	5–8 €

This young Heiligenstein winemaker is very attached to the local grape variety, which is similar to Gewurztraminer but has a more restrained aromatic character. His 2001 has a strong yellow colour and a nose of great finesse combining intense, complex aromas of roses and overripe fruit. It has an excellent structure, and is a full, rich, supple wine with good length. The residual sugar on the palate is still quite pronounced, and although it will fade with time it suggests that this wine will be best served as an aperitif or with dessert. (Residual sugar: 16 g/l.)
➤ Charles Boch, 6, rue Principale, 67140 Heiligenstein, tel. 03.88.08.41.26, fax 03.88.08.58.25 ☑ ☥
☥ by appt.

ANDRE DOCK

Cuvée Tentation 2001★

	0.3 ha	1,000	▯▯	11–15 €

One of the mountains near Heiligenstein is Mont Sainte-Odile, named after the patron saint of Alsace. This provides an excellent hillside location for the commune's vineyard, where André and Christian Dock cultivate 10 ha. Once again we are featuring their Cuvée Tentation, which in 1999 won a *coup de coeur*. It has a golden yellow colour with brilliant green glints, and a highly concentrated nose of floral and almond aromas. This is a well-structured wine with a rich, fleshy, palate-filling body and a long finish on further notes of crushed almonds. With its high sugar content it will be a good accompaniment to foie gras. (Residual sugar: 47 g/l.)
➤ André et Christian Dock, 20, rue Principale, 67140 Heiligenstein, tel. 03.88.08.02.69, fax 03.88.08.19.72 ☑ ☥
☥ ev. day 8am–12 noon 2pm–6pm

PAUL DOCK

Cuvée Prestige 2001★★

| | 0.8 ha | 3,000 | | 8–11 € |

This wine producer is often featured for his Heiligenstein Klevener, which is not surprising since he grows just over 8 ha around the village that gives the grape its name. This Cuvée Prestige particularly appealed to the judges. It has a golden colour and an aromatic range of great finesse and unusual complexity, in which floral notes appear along with spices and liquorice. On the palate it is very full and sweet, with a distinctly overripe quality. The fresh, elegant finish is delightful. This is a high-class wine that will be good to serve as an aperitif or with foie gras. (Residual sugar: 40 g/l.)
⊶ GAEC Paul Dock et Fils, 55, rue Principale, 67140 Heiligenstein, tel. 03.88.08.02.49, fax 03.88.08.25.65 ☑
⏀ by appt.

Alsace Sylvaner

It is not clear where the Sylvaner originated, but it has customarily been grown only in vineyards in Germany and the Lower Rhine in France, to which it is eminently suited. In Alsace this variety, accounting for around 14% of the total vineyard, is particularly successful and regularly produces a large and reliable yield.

Sylvaner makes remarkably fresh, quite acid wines, which have a delicate fruitiness. There are two different types of Sylvaner on the market. The first, by far the better, comes from the well-exposed vineyards that do not produce over-large quantities of grapes. The second type is for those who like a particularly appealing, unpretentious, thirst-quenching wine. Sylvaner is an excellent accompaniment to sauerkraut, and is often drunk with shellfish and seafood. It goes particularly well with oysters.

AGATHE BURSIN 2001★★

| | 0.1 ha | 817 | ▮ | 5–8 € |

With an oenology diploma and a postgraduate qualification in vine and wine law under her belt, Agathe Bursin took over the family estate in 2001. Her parents used to supply grapes to other people, but now she is developing her own wines. This Sylvaner shows that she has made the right decision. It comes from vines that are over 50 years old, and has an intense yellow colour and a richly aromatic nose with a range of crystallized fruit notes and some lively touches of toast. The palate is very rich, round and concentrated, with flavours of overripe fruits and a perfect note of freshness on the finish. "A very great wine of a rather unusual type", noted one taster. It's true that this particular Sylvaner will not be ideal with seafood, but should be drunk as an aperitif or with white meats.
⊶ Agathe Bursin, 11, rue de Soultzmatt, 68250 Westhalten, tel. 03.89.47.04.15, fax 03.89.47.04.15 ☑
⏀ by appt.

JACQUES MAETZ

Mittlerer Altenberg 2001★

| | 0.1 ha | 1,000 | ▮ ⬗ | 8–11 € |

The Sylvaner grape produces wines that go very well with various dishes, and in particular with the main specialities of the region. Its reputation has not been helped by a certain amount of over-production and less than perfectionistic winemaking, and as a result the grape variety is beginning to lose ground. This is a pity, since when it is carefully developed, it yields high-quality wines. This 2001 is a good example; it

has a brilliant, light yellow colour and a powerful nose of slightly smoky vegetal aromas. It reveals all its freshness on the palate, which is quite round and has a long, pleasant finish. "A very fine wine, a bit round for a Sylvaner, but such a long finish," concludes one taster. This wine will be a good accompaniment to roast fatted chicken.
⊶ Jacques Maetz, 49, av. de la Gare, 67560 Rosheim, tel. 03.88.50.43.29, fax 03.88.49.20.57 ☑

SCHAEFFER-WOERLY 2001★

| | 0.35 ha | 2,860 | ⬤ | 5–8 € |

This old winemaking family is based in a half-timbered 16th century house right in the centre of Dambach-la-Ville, where visitors to the tasting room can see an 18th century wine press. They can also taste this light yellow Sylvaner with brilliant green glints and the grape variety's typically fresh nose of mown hay along with some delicate hints of lemon. The same notes persist during a clean attack which leads on to a well-balanced palate. "Just the right crispness," comments one taster. A fine, classic wine, which will go well with entrées and seafood.
⊶ Schaeffer-Woerly, 3, pl. du Marché, 67650 Dambach-la-Ville, tel. 03.88.92.40.81, fax 03.88.92.49.87, e-mail schaeffer-woerly@wanadoo.fr ☑
⏀ ev. day 9am–12 noon 2pm–6pm; Sun. and public holidays by appt.

Alsace Pinot or Klevner

Wine labelled with either of these names (the second is the old Alsace name) can be a blend of grape varieties, usually Pinot Blanc Vrai or Auxerrois Blanc. These two varieties are not too hard to cultivate and can produce excellent wines on mediocre soil. The wines are pleasantly fresh as well as having body and suppleness. In ten years the area given over to cultivating these two varieties has doubled, from 10% to 21% of the total vineyard.

In the range of Alsace wines, Pinot Blanc ranks just about in the middle, and it can outclass some Rieslings. When it comes to food, it goes well with a great range of dishes, although it is not especially good with cheese or desserts.

JEAN-PIERRE BECHTOLD 2001★

| | 0.8 ha | 6,000 | | 5–8 € |

Dahlenheim is part of Strasbourg's "Golden Crown," as the high-quality wine-growing area close to the European capital has come to be known. This commune expanded rapidly during the last decade, and includes 19 ha that are cultivated by Jean-Pierre Bechtold. He is now offering a Pinot Blanc which, as its pale yellow colour indicates, is still very young, but already has a strikingly pleasant nose of fine, elegant, fruity aromas (yellow fruits: peaches and mirabelles). The palate is fresh and supple, again with a mirabelle flavour and also some slight hints of vanilla. This is a well-balanced, characteristic wine.
⊶ Dom. Jean-Pierre Bechtold, 49, rue Principale, 67310 Dahlenheim, tel. 03.88.50.66.57, fax 03.88.50.67.34, e-mail bechtold@wanadoo.fr ☑
⏀ by appt.

BESTHEIM

Strangenberg 2001★

| | 3 ha | 30,000 | ▮ ⬗ | 8–11 € |

This wine is produced at Westhalten on terroirs where the flora and fauna are Mediterranean – clearly a hot, dry microclimate which will be good for wine-growing. First impressions of this wine indicate that it comes from good stock. It has a golden yellow colour, and intense aromas of crystallized fruits along with a few vegetal notes and hints of almond. After a fresh attack, there is a noticeable sweetness on the palate that needs to fade. Further almond notes return on a delightful finish.

↠ Bestheim, Cave de Westhalten, 52, rte de Soultzmatt, 68250 Westhalten, tel. 03.89.49.09.29, fax 03.89.49.09.20, e-mail bestheim@gofornet.com ☑
☿ ev. day 8am–12 noon 2pm–6pm; Sat. Sun. 10am–12 noon 3pm–6pm

DOM. EINHART

Westerberg 2001★

| 1.4 ha | 8,000 | ⦿ | 5–8 € |

The Rosenwiller vineyard is located about 20 kilometres south of Strasbourg. It has expanded considerably, largely thanks to winemakers such as Nicolas Einhart, whose Westerberg Pinot Blanc often wins high praise in the Guide. The 2001 has a pale yellow colour with green highlights, and a subtle nose of wild flower aromas. It becomes more fruity on the palate, which is quite powerful and well balanced. This is a very pleasant wine.

↠ Dom. Einhart, 15, rue Principale, 67560 Rosenwiller, tel. 03.88.50.41.90, fax 03.88.50.29.27, e-mail info@einhart.com ☑
☿ by appt.

FRANCOIS LICHTLE

Hohrain 2001★

| 0.2 ha | 1,200 | ▐ | 5–8 € |

This Pinot Blanc comes from one of the highest perched villages in Alsace, overlooked by three castles. The different grape varieties do wonderfully well here, especially when the vines are of a decent age; the ones that produced this 2001 are over 50 years old. The wine has a limpid yellow colour with green highlights, and a fully open, complex nose combining fresh fruits with crystallized fruits and honey. Although the overripe features are not characteristic of Pinot Blanc, the wine's richness, fullness and good length will ensure that it has fine prospects for the future.

↠ Dom. François Lichtlé, 17, rue des Vignerons, 68420 Husseren-les-Châteaux, tel. 03.89.49.31.34, fax 03.89.49.37.51, e-mail hlichtle@aol.com ☑ ☖
☿ by appt.

DOM. LOEW

Barrique 2001★

| 0.3 ha | 1,500 | ⦿ | 8–11 € |

Etienne Loew is based at Westhoffen, a fortified village on the Route des Vins, not far from Strasbourg. After gaining his diploma in oenology he left the cooperative, and has now developed a Pinot Blanc Cuvée that comes from 40-year-old vines and has been matured in oak for one year. This wine has a beautiful old gold colour, and releases a nose of aromas which although as yet restrained are very fine: exotic touches, a hint of citrus fruits, and a slight note of vanilla from the oak. The attack is quite lively, revealing oaky and fruity flavours (dried apricots, prunes). This oaky character continues on the palate, without in any way spoiling the wine's good balance.

↠ Etienne Loew, 28, rue Birris, 67310 Westhoffen, tel. 03.88.50.59.19, fax 03.88.50.59.19 ☑
☿ by appt.

CHARLES NOLL 2001★

| 0.2 ha | 2,000 | ⦿ | 5–8 € |

Representing the fourth generation on his family's estate, Charles Noll runs his business in the village of Mittelwihr, which is located a few kilometres northwest of Colmar, right at the heart of the Route des Vins region. His Pinot Blanc has a light yellow colour with green and gold highlights, and the nose is already well developed, first of all releasing scents of undergrowth with a touch of flint, then fruity aromas dominated by peach. With its fresh, fine, light palate, this is a very elegant wine that will go well with a hot entrée like chicken vol-au-vent, or with fillet mignon.

↠ EARL Charles Noll, 2, rue de l'Ecole, 68630 Mittelwihr, tel. 03.89.47.93.21, fax 03.89.47.86.23 ☑
☿ ev. day 9am–12 noon 1.30pm–8pm

RIEFFEL

Vieilles Vignes 2001★

| 0.45 ha | 4,000 | | 5–8 € |

This venerable 16th century cellar can be found on the main street in Mittelbergheim, amid the opulent old winemaker's houses. The wine comes from 50-year-old vines, and has a strong yellow colour with lighter glints (straw or even white gold). The nose is already very open, and releases some fragrances of honey and then white flowers that suggest a wine with a fine, mature body. These first impressions are confirmed on the palate, which is round, balanced, long, and brimming with ripe fruit flavours. This will be a good accompaniment to chicken à la crème.

↠ Lucas et André Rieffel, 11, rue Principale, 67140 Mittelbergheim, tel. 03.88.08.95.48, fax 03.88.08.28.94 ☑
☿ by appt.

WACKENTHALER 2001★

| 0.9 ha | 10,000 | ⦿ | 3–5 € |

This producer operates in Ammerschwihr, one of the largest wine towns in the Alsatian vineyard. It has been a very prosperous place since the Middle Ages, and has also been involved in winemaking from very early on. In the 1920s Ammerschwihr launched its Wine Fair, which is held every April, and after the Second World War and all the destruction it caused, the town took on the job of reviving the Confrérie Saint-Etienne. From his biodynamically cultivated estate, François Wackenthaler is now offering a wine with a strong, golden yellow colour and a very expressive nose combining ripe fruits with some slight vegetal notes. After a good attack, the palate has a rich, full body and overripe flavours, but not a great deal of freshness. This Pinot Blanc will go well with meat or fish in sauce.

↠ EARL François Wackenthaler, 8, rue du Kaefferkopf, 68770 Ammerschwihr, tel. 03.89.78.23.76, fax 03.89.47.15.48, e-mail wackenthal@wanadoo.fr ☑
☿ ev. day except Sun. 10am–12 noon 1pm–7pm

ZEYSSOLFF

Auxerrois 2001★

| 3 ha | 26,000 | ⦿ | 3–5 € |

Founded in 1778, this wine-merchants in the Barr area is probably one of the oldest in the region. Its Pinot Auxerrois has a golden yellow colour with green highlights, and a complex nose of fruit aromas (peaches and citrus fruits) and floral scents (white flowers and violets). On the palate there is a similar range of peach and white flower flavours, and also some hints of yeasty bread that add a great sense of distinction. This delightful, honest wine is supple, round and very well balanced, and can even be drunk on its own, "at teatime," as one taster suggests.

↠ G. Zeyssolff, 156, rte de Strasbourg, 67140 Gertwiller, tel. 03.88.08.90.08, fax 03.88.08.91.60, e-mail yvan.zeyssolff@wanadoo.fr ☑ ☖
☿ by appt.

Wines selected but not starred

HENRI KLEE

Auxerrois Cuvée Frédérique 2001

| n.c. | 8,000 | ▐ ♦ | 5–8 € |

↠ EARL Henri Klée et Fils, 11, Grand-Rue, 68230 Katzenthal, tel. 03.89.27.03.81, fax 03.89.27.28.17 ☑ ☖
☿ by appt.

MARC KREYDENWEISS

Kritt Les Charmes 2001

| | 3 ha | 15,000 | ◫ | 8–11 € |

↱ Dom. Marc Kreydenweiss, 12, rue Deharbe,
67140 Andlau, tel. 03.88.08.95.83, fax 03.88.08.41.16,
e-mail marc@kreydenweiss.com ☑ ☗
⚲ by appt.

JEAN RAPP

Auxerrois Muhlweg 2001

| | 0.43 ha | 3,300 | ◫ | 3–5 € |

↱ Jean Rapp, 1, fg des Vosges, 67120 Dorlisheim,
tel. 03.88.38.28.43, fax 03.88.38.28.43,
e-mail vins-rapp@wanadoo.fr ☑
⚲ by appt.

SPITZ ET FILS

Auxerrois Sélection 2001

| | 0.6 ha | 4,000 | ◫ | 5–8 € |

↱ EARL Spitz et Fils, 2–4, rte des Vins,
67650 Blienschwiller, tel. 03.88.92.61.20,
fax 03.88.92.61.26 ☑
⚲ ev. day 8.30–12 noon 1.30pm–7pm

Alsace Edelzwicker

Edelzwicker occupies a special place amongst the Alsace appellations. An extremely ancient designation, this denomination refers to wines made from a blend of grape varieties. We should not forget that a century ago, vineyard plots planted with just one single grape variety were rare. The grape varieties that are mainly used for the Edelzwicker blend are Pinot Blanc, Auxerrois, Sylvaner and Chasselas. Aside from a number of rather weak examples that lack any great quality and have a tendency to discredit this appellation, Edelzwicker wines are much appreciated by the Alsace locals, and most restaurants and cafés make a point of serving a very enjoyable one as carafe wine. This is an appellation that deserves to have its reputation re-assessed. It could even respond to one of the current claims of certain wine producers for whom the virtues of blends seem self-evident.

Wines selected but not starred

KUEHN

Kaefferkopf 2001

| | 2 ha | 10,000 | ◫ | 8–11 € |

↱ SA Kuehn, 3, Grand-Rue, 68770 Ammerschwihr,
tel. 03.89.78.23.16, fax 03.89.47.18.32,
e-mail vin@kuehn.fr ☑
⚲ ev. day except Sat. Sun. 8am–12 noon 1.30pm–5pm

Alsace Riesling

Riesling is the grape variety of the Rhineland, and the Rhine valley is where it originated and flourished. It matures later than other varieties in the region and can be relied on to produce both quality and quantity. About 23% of the Alsace vineyard is planted with Riesling.

The Alsace Riesling is made in a dry style compared with the sweeter German Rieslings. Typically, there is a harmonious balance between its delicately fruity bouquet, good body and finely pronounced acidity. To fulfil its promise it must come from a sunny, sheltered terroir.

Riesling is planted in many other wine-growing countries, and there are at least ten other varieties that carry the Riesling name. Unless you specify Riesling Rhénan, the wines can be disappointing. On the gastronomic front, Riesling is particularly good when it is drunk with fish dishes, seafood and, naturally enough, a good Alsace sauerkraut or, alternatively, *coq au Riesling*. When the late-harvested grapes do not contain sufficient sugar, they are used as blending wines for *vins blancs liquoreux*.

DOM. YVES AMBERG

Damgraben Vieilles Vignes 2001★

| | 0.3 ha | 3,000 | 🗎 ⬇ | 8–11 € |

This 10-hectare vineyard has been run by Yves Amberg since 1988. It is offering two Rieslings from different *lieux-dits*, both of which were awarded one star by the Jury. This one comes from 50-year-old vines, and has beautiful ripe fruit aromas with hints of quince. On the palate it has great depth, excellent balance, and a long, fresh finish. It will go better with dishes in sauce than with the traditional sauerkraut. (Residual sugar: 7 g/l.) You were delighted with the **Riesling Wolsgrube Vieilles Vignes 2001** because of its good balance, full body, and aromatic finesse (a nose of citronnella and exotic fruits, white peaches on the palate). (Residual sugar: 7 g/l.)
↱ Yves Amberg, 19, rue Fronholz, 67680 Epfig,
tel. 03.88.85.51.28, fax 03.88.85.52.71,
e-mail ambergyves@wanadoo.fr ☗
⚲ by appt.

JEAN-PIERRE BECHTOLD

Susenberg 2001★

| | 0.5 ha | 3,000 | | 8–11 € |

Dahlenheim is located in the north of the Route des Vins area, to the west of Strasbourg. The fact that several monasteries owned vineyards at "Dalaheim" as early as the ninth century shows just how good these terroirs are. These days Jean-Pierre Bechtold grows 19 ha of vines here, and he has now produced this lovely Riesling with hints of exotic fruits and slight notes of overripening. After a supple attack, the palate has an excellent structure based on a good, full body. The long, fresh finish is extremely pleasant. This wine will be a good accompaniment to pies and white meats. (Residual sugar: 6 g/l.)
↱ Dom. Jean-Pierre Bechtold, 49, rue Principale,
67310 Dahlenheim, tel. 03.88.50.66.57, fax 03.88.50.67.34,
e-mail bechtold@wanadoo.fr ☑
⚲ by appt.

FRANCIS BECK

Hertenstein 2001★

| | 0.52 ha | 4,500 | 🗎 ⬇ | 5–8 € |

Since leaving the cooperative in 1974, Francis Beck has been operating via direct selling and exports (30% of sales). He has produced a Riesling whose golden yellow colour is a typical feature of overripening. This is a balanced, not particularly

vigorous wine, which is very supple on the palate. (Residual sugar: 3.8 g/l.)
➤ Francis Beck, 79, rue Sainte-Marguerite, 67680 Epfig, tel. 03.88.85.54.84, fax 03.88.57.83.81 ☑ ✿
☐ by appt.

BECK DOMAINE DU REMPART Cuvée de l'Ours Prestige de Dambach-la-Ville 2001★

| | 0.5 ha | 4,000 | ◑ | 5–8 € |

Dambach-la-Ville still has its beautiful 14th century fortifications, and the ramparts provide a lovely, cool location for Gilbert Beck's cellar. This Riesling takes its name from the grape-loving bear that is the town's emblem. It has the typical white flower aromas and slight mineral note of a wine from a granite terroir, and is fresh and even somewhat lively on a well-balanced palate with quite a long finish. This wine will go well with sauerkraut and fish. (Residual sugar: 6 g/l.)
➤ Beck, Dom. du Rempart, 5, rue des Remparts, 67650 Dambach-la-Ville, tel. 03.88.92.62.03, fax 03.88.92.49.40,
e-mail beck.domaine@wanadoo.fr ☑ ✿ ✿
☐ ev. day except Sun. 9am–11.45am 2pm–6.30pm

DOM. BERNHARD-REIBEL

Meisenberg 2001★

| | 0.5 ha | 4,000 | ◑ | 8–11 € |

For many years this family business has been growing wine on the hillsides overlooking Châtenois, and in 2002 they were joined by the son of the family, Pierre. This Meisenberg wine has a nose of very ripe fruit aromas, then similar flavours on a pleasantly balanced palate with plenty of depth and a fresh finish. (Residual sugar: 7 g/l.)
➤ Dom. Bernhard-Reibel, 20, rue de Lorraine, 67730 Châtenois, tel. 03.88.82.04.21, fax 03.88.82.59.65, e-mail bernhard-reibel@wanadoo.fr ☑
☐ by appt.
➤ Cécile Bernhard

ALBERT BOHN

Sonnenberg 2000★

| | 0.36 ha | 2,300 | ◑ | 8–11 € |

This family concern was founded in 1956, and altogether has nearly 7 ha of vines. The granite terroir on the Sonnenberg has produced a Riesling with a delightful, complex range of aromas and flavours combining hints of fruit with mineral notes. The structure is equally pleasant, but owing to the high level of residual sugar it would be best to keep this wine for two or three years until it achieves a better balance. It should be served as an aperitif or with desserts such as *tarte au citron*. (Residual sugar: 38 g/l.)
➤ EARL Albert Bohn et Fils, 4, rue du Cerf, 68770 Ammerschwihr, tel. 03.89.78.25.77, fax 03.89.78.16.34, e-mail vins.bohn@wanadoo.fr ☑
☐ by appt.

PAUL DOCK 2001★

| | 0.83 ha | 5,000 | | 3–5 € |

Heiligenstein is overlooked on the western side by the fortified castle on the Landsberg. There are many old houses in the village, including one dating back 250 years where this estate has its offices. They are offering an excellent Riesling, with a nose which is restrained at first, then gradually opens out on to the essentially mineral notes which also characterize the palate. This is a clean, fresh wine, whose appeal lies in being very much a product of its terroir. (Residual sugar: 2.5 g/l.)
➤ GAEC Paul Dock et Fils, 5, rue Principale, 67140 Heiligenstein, tel. 03.88.08.02.49, fax 03.88.08.25.65 ☑
☐ by appt.

DOM. ANDRE DUSSOURT

Vendanges tardives 2000★

| | 0.26 ha | 1,789 | ◧ ↓ | 15–23 € |

This estate is based in the centre of Scherwiller, a charming village 3 km northeast of Sélestat. The oldest part of its premises dates back to 1695, and is built over the barrel cellar. The vineyard consists of 10 ha in all, divided over various terroirs. This Vendanges Tardives was grown on granitic sand,

and has a light straw colour and a very distinguished, beautifully fruity nose of passion-fruit aromas and subtle mineral notes. Everything about the palate is highly satisfying: the attack, the structure, the good balance between sugar, alcohol and acidity, and the long finish. This is a really delightful Riesling that can be drunk on its own.
➤ Dom. André Dussourt, 2, rue de Dambach, 67750 Scherwiller, tel. 03.88.92.10.27, fax 03.88.92.18.44, e-mail vins.dussourt@worldonline.fr ☑
☐ ev. day except Sun. 9am–12 noon 1.30pm–6pm

MARCEL EBELMANN ET FILS

Cuvée Fanny 2001★

| | 0.15 ha | 800 | ▮ | 5–8 € |

José Ebelmann has been running this 6.5-hectare family vineyard since 1992. His Cuvée Fanny comes from a small plot with a sand and sandstone soil, and has rich, intense aromas of overripening. There is the same richness on the palate, which is sweet and thoroughbred. This wine has a late-harvest feel about it, and should be kept for two years owing to the high residual sugar content. (Residual sugar: 35 g/l.)
➤ Marcel et José Ebelmann, 27, rue des Chèvres, 68570 Soultzmatt, tel. 03.89.47.00.09, fax 03.89.47.65.33 ☑
☐ ev. day except Sun. 9am–12 noon 2pm–6pm

JEAN-PAUL ECKLE

Hinterburg 2001★★

| | 0.45 ha | 5,000 | ◑ | 5–8 € |

The keep of the old castle at Wineck is part of the landscape around the ancient Katzenthal vineyard, which has been run by the Ecklé family for several generations. Their Hinterburg Riesling has a very ripe, fruity nose of citrus fruits and pineapples. It is rich and complex, with a good structure and a long finish. It will go very well with fish in sauce or a meat pie. (Residual sugar: 5 g/l.)
➤ Jean-Paul Ecklé et Fils, 29, Grand-Rue, 68230 Katzenthal, tel. 03.89.27.09.41, fax 03.89.80.86.18 ☑ ✿
☐ ev. day except Sun. 9am–12 noon 1.30pm–6.30pm

ANTOINE FONNE 2001★

| | 0.25 ha | 2,000 | ▮ | 5–8 € |

This young, 4.5-hectare vineyard was started in 1971, and since 1998 has been run by sustainable agriculture methods. It is offering a lovely Riesling with yellow fruit aromas, a supple attack, good balance on the palate, and a long, fine finish. (Residual sugar: 4 g/l.)
➤ Antoine Fonné, 14, Grand-Rue, 68770 Ammerschwihr, tel. 03.89.47.37.90, fax 03.89.47.18.83 ☑
☐ by appt.

CHARLES AND DOMINIQUE FREY

Vieilles Vignes 2001★

| | 1 ha | 8,000 | ◑ | 5–8 € |

This vineyard has been using biodynamic methods for several years, and is now offering a brilliant golden Riesling with a complex, expressive nose of very ripe fruit aromas. After a good attack, the palate is well balanced, with a certain degree of roundness and a pleasant note of freshness on the finish. (Residual sugar: 4 g/l.)
➤ EARL Charles et Dominique Frey, 4, rue des Ours, 67650 Dambach-la-Ville, tel. 03.88.92.41.04, fax 03.88.92.62.23, e-mail frey.dom.bio@wanadoo.fr ☑
☐ ev. day except Sun. 9.30am–12 noon 1.30pm–6pm

MARCEL FREYBURGER 2001★

| | 0.4 ha | 3,500 | ◑ | 5–8 € |

After being razed to the ground in 1944, the village of Ammerschwir was rebuilt in the regional style. Next to this estate, a section of the old *mairie* wall still stands as a reminder of the terrible damage done during the Second World War. Christophe Freyburger took over this 5-hectare vineyard from his father in 1994, and is now offering a pale yellow Riesling with green highlights and a nose of fruity aromas, along with a slight mineral note. Balanced, smooth,

fresh and elegant on the palate, this is a classic wine. (Residual sugar: 5 g/l.)
● EARL Marcel Freyburger, 13, Grand-Rue, 68770 Ammerschwihr, tel. 03.89.78.25.72, fax 03.89.78.15.50, e-mail marcel.freyburger@libertysurf.fr ▼
⊥ by appt.

FREY-SOHLER

Rittersberg 2001★

| | 1 ha | 8,000 | ⦿ | 8–11 € |

Overlooked by the medieval Château de l'Ortenbourg, the village of Scherwiller holds a Riesling festival every year on the weekend following 15 August. This 2001 brings out characteristics of the grape variety very well on a nose of fine, as yet somewhat restrained fruit aromas, accompanied by a slight mineral note. The wine becomes more assertive on the palate, where it is delightfully fine and elegant while at the same time giving an impression of richness. It has a beautiful freshness on the finish, and is very much a thoroughbred Riesling. (Residual sugar: 4.1 g/l.)
● Frey-Sohler, 72, rue de l'Ortenbourg, 67750 Scherwiller, tel. 03.88.92.10.13, fax 03.88.82.57.11, e-mail freysohl@wanadoo.fr ▼ ⬥
⊥ ev. day except Sun. 8am–12 noon 1.15pm–7pm

DOM. GUNTZ

Scherwiller Vieilles Vignes 2001★

| | 0.21 ha | 2,100 | ▮ | 5–8 € |

Every summer Scherwiller celebrates Arts, Crafts and Riesling, which is the village's leading grape variety. This 2001 is an exceptionally good example of what the grape can produce. It has an intense yellow colour with golden glints, and shows its maturity in a nose of floral and citrus fruit aromas. There are similar slightly overripe flavours on the palate, which is well structured, balanced and elegant, with a long finish.
● Dom. Guntz, 27, rue de Dambach, 67750 Scherwiller, tel. 03.88.58.30.30, fax 03.88.82.18.76 ▼ ⬥
⊥ by appt.

ANDRE HARTMANN

Armoirie Hartmann 2001★

| | 0.7 ha | 5,500 | ▮ ⬥ | 5–8 € |

André Hartmann aims to produce well-balanced, dense wines. His Armoirie Cuvée regularly receives high praise in the Guide, and this 2001 is no exception. It is characterized by powerful aromas of very ripe fruits, a fairly rich, round palate, and a long, beautifully fresh finish. This thoroughbred wine will go well with white meats and poultry in sauce. (Residual sugar: 10 g/l.)
● André Hartmann, 11, rue Roger-Frémeaux, 68420 Voegtlinshoffen, tel. 03.89.49.38.34, fax 03.89.49.26.18 ▼ ⬥
⊥ ev. day except Sun. 9am–12 noon 2pm–6pm; by appt. during the harvest

EMILE HERZOG

Herrenweg Vendanges tardives 2000★★★

| | 0.16 ha | 400 | ▮ ⬥ | 15–23 € |

Emile Herzog's ancestors were making wine in Turckheim as far back as 1686. Trained as an agricultural engineer, he took

over the family estate in 1974. Its vine plots are located on the best terroirs in the commune, and now the one on the Herrenweg has produced this little masterpiece. It has a straw yellow colour, and a well-developed nose of floral aromas enlivened by citrus fruit notes and hints of honey that suggest overripe fruits. The structure is perfect: all the lovely freshness of a thoroughbred wine, an elegant balance of real finesse, plenty of richness, and a full finish embellished by flavours of crystallized fruits and citrus fruit peel.
● Vins d'Alsace Emile Herzog, 28, rue du Florimont, 68230 Turckheim, tel. 03.89.27.08.79, fax 03.89.27.08.79, e-mail e.herzog@laposte.net ▼
⊥ by appt.
● Mme Herzog

KNELLWOLF-JEHL

Felsberg 2001★

| | 0.8 ha | 5,333 | ▮ | 8–11 € |

In 1997 Frédéric Jehl took over the family estate, which at the beginning of the 1980s was still a mixed-farming concern. He now sells his wines directly to private clients. Visitors to his 1772 cellar will discover this excellent terroir Riesling, which has lovely aromas of ripe fruits with a slight note of smoke, a clean, lively, thoroughbred attack, and a long, fresh finish on notes of citrus fruits. "This is a real Riesling, and I love it!" said its most enthusiastic judge. (Residual sugar: 5.7 g/l.)
● SA Knellwolf-Jehl, 34, rte du Vin, 68590 Saint-Hippolyte, tel. 03.89.71.81.54, fax 03.89.86.48.98, e-mail k.jehl@infonie.fr ▼
⊥ by appt.

LEIPP-LEININGER 2001★

| | 0.8 ha | 9,000 | ⦿ | 5–8 € |

Wine has been made in this 18th century house since 1760, and the Leipp-Leininger family has been there since 1911. Gilbert Leininger took over the estate in 1981, and now makes his debut in the Guide with this Riesling. The nose opens on white flower notes before moving on to citrus fruit aromas. There is a clean, fresh attack on the palate, which is pleasantly balanced and quite rich, with a long, full finish.
● Leipp-Leininger, 11, rue du Dr-Sultzer, 67140 Barr, tel. 03.88.08.95.98, fax 03.88.08.43.26, e-mail leipp-leininger@terre-net.fr ▼ ⬥
⊥ by appt.

JEAN-LOUIS AND FABIENNE MANN

Altengarten 2001★★

| | 0.37 ha | 2,100 | | 8–11 € |

This old winemaking family has been in Eguisheim since 1950, and now runs a vineyard of just over 7 ha by sustainable agriculture methods. They have a great talent for bringing out the characteristics of the terroir in wines such as this Riesling, which has a clean, fine nose of slightly overripe aromas and subtle, elegant mineral notes. After a fairly supple attack, the palate is well balanced and very characteristic, with a long, pleasant finish. (Residual sugar: 6 g/l.)
● EARL Jean-Louis Mann, 11, rue du Traminer, 68420 Eguisheim, tel. 03.89.24.26.47, fax 03.89.24.09.41, e-mail mann.jean.louis@wanadoo.fr ▼
⊥ by appt.

ALBERT MAURER

Lerchenberg 2001★

| | 0.8 ha | 6,200 | | 5–8 € |

Albert Maurer grows nearly 12 ha of vines at Eichhoffen, near Andlau, and now has almost 40 years' experience of wine-producing behind him. He practises sustainable agriculture, and gets the best out of terroirs such as the Lerchenberg on which this wine was grown. It has a fresh, lemony nose and a clean attack on the palate, which has a fine structure, quite a crisp balance, and a delightfully long finish. "A wine with a future," noted one taster. (Residual sugar: 6 g/l.)
● Albert Maurer, 11, rue du Vignoble, 67140 Eichhoffen, tel. 03.88.08.96.75, fax 03.88.08.59.98, e-mail info@vins-maurer.fr ▼ ⬥
⊥ ev. day except Sun. 9am–12 noon 1.30pm–6.30pm

ALFRED MEYER

Kaefferkopf 2001★★

| | 0.35 ha | 3,000 | | 8–11 € |

Long famous for its wines, the Kaefferkopf *lieu-dit* was classified in 1932, and is the jewel in Ammerschwihr's crown. Its granitic soils have yielded this remarkable Riesling, whose strong, fruity character on the nose becomes even more intense on the palate. The Jury was bowled over by its excellent balance, fullness and long finish, which although still fruity is also delightfully fresh. This is the perfect wine for fish in sauce. (Residual sugar: 4 g/l.)
• Alfred Meyer, 98, rue des Trois-Epis, 68230 Katzenthal, tel. 03.89.27.24.50, fax 03.89.27.55.40 ◪
☏ by appt.

MOELLINGER

Sélection 2001★★

| | 0.75 ha | 7,500 | ⦿ | 3–5 € |

Off in the distance stands the Château de Hohlandsbourg, built in the 13th century, destroyed and rebuilt several times since, and restored in recent years. This 14-hectare vineyard has been run since 1998 by Michel Moellinger, who has now produced a remarkable wine with a complex range of floral and fruit aromas. It is very fresh and full on the palate, and there is a delightfully long finish. (Residual sugar: 8.9 g/l.)
• SCEA Joseph Moellinger et Fils, 6, rue de la 5ᵉ-D.-B., 68920 Wettolsheim, tel. 03.89.80.62.02, fax 03.89.80.04.94 ◪
☏ ev. day 8am–12 noon 1.30pm–7pm; Sun. by appt.; cl. Oct.

JULES MULLER

Réserve 2001★★

| | 4 ha | 30,000 | | 8–11 € |

This very old wine concern is the sole owner of 32 ha of vines. It is run by G. Lorentz and M. Kempf, and exports 45% of its wines. The Riesling has a citrus fruit character with a fine mineral note both on the nose and on the palate. The attack is supple, the balance is good, and all in all this is an agreeable, very characteristic wine. (Residual sugar: 5 g/l.)
• Jules Muller, 91, rue des Vignerons, 68750 Bergheim, tel. 03.89.73.22.22, fax 03.89.73.30.49 ◪
☏ ev. day except Sun. 10am–12 noon 2pm–6.30pm
• Gustave Lorentz

FRANCIS MURE 2001★★

| | 0.4 ha | 2,500 | ▮ ♦ | 5–8 € |

Westhalten is surrounded by the limestone foothills of the Vosges, where the unusual flora includes the Pulsatilla anemones that appear on the label of this Riesling. Its thoroughbred character shows that this hilly ground is also an excellent vine-growing terroir. It has intense, unusually fine citrus fruit aromas (grapefruit), along with some floral fragrances. These powerful notes are sustained on the palate, which is balanced, complex and full-bodied, with a long, clean finish. This wine has good ageing potential. (Residual sugar: 3 g/l.)
• Francis Muré, 30, rue de Rouffach, 68250 Westhalten, tel. 03.89.47.64.20, fax 03.89.47.09.39, e-mail mure-francis@club-internet.fr ◪ ⌂
☏ by appt.

ERNEST PREISS

Cuvée particulière 2001★

| | n.c. | 23,000 | ▮ | 8–11 € |

Riquewihr probably attracts more visitors than any other wine-growing town in Alsace. They come for the lovely architecture, but also for the excellent terroirs, which produce wines such as this Riesling with its mixture of floral and fruity aromas. The white flower and grapefruit notes emerge more clearly on the palate, which is pleasantly fresh and has an excellent structure, good balance and a long finish. (Residual sugar: 5.5 g/l.)
• Ernest Preiss, BP 3, 68340 Riquewihr, tel. 03.89.47.91.21, fax 03.89.47.98.90 ◪
☏ by appt.

PREISS-ZIMMER

Réserve comte Jean de Beaumont 2001★★

| | 2.5 ha | 26,000 | | 5–8 € |

Founded in 1848, this excellent wine-merchants now operates in collaboration with the Turckheim cellar, and is offering a remarkable Réserve Cuvée. It has a golden yellow colour with green highlights and a fine, fruity nose of citrus aromas accompanied by some slight mineral notes. On the palate it has the same strikingly fruity character, with a delightful acidity and just a touch of residual sugar. This rich, concentrated Riesling has very good length, and can be drunk as an aperitif or served with shellfish. (Residual sugar: 3 g/l.)
• SARL Preiss-Zimmer, 40, rue du Gal-de-Gaulle, 68340 Riquewihr, tel. 03.89.47.86.91, fax 03.89.27.35.33, e-mail preiss-zimmer@calixo.net

DOM. RUNNER 2001★

| | 1.85 ha | 15,000 | ▮ ♦ | 5–8 € |

This wine estate is prestigiously located in a 17th century house right in the centre of Pfaffenheim. Founded in 1935, it now has 12 ha of vines. In 1997 Francis-Claude Runner took over here, representing the third generation of his family to be in charge of the vineyard. His Riesling has a nose of fine, subtle, rather fruity aromas, and is clean and dry on a well-balanced palate with an elegant finish. (Residual sugar: 6 g/l.)
• Dom. François Runner et Fils, 1, rue de la Liberté, 68250 Pfaffenheim, tel. 03.89.49.62.89, fax 03.89.49.73.69 ◪ ⌂
☏ ev. day 8am–12 noon 1pm–7pm; groups by appt.

SAULNIER 2001★

| | 0.3 ha | 2,400 | ▮ | 5–8 € |

From the wine trail that partly cuts across this estate there is a lovely panoramic view over the town of Gueberschwihr with its Romanesque church and vineyard. The estate here is recent, founded by Marco Saulnier in 1992. He has produced two Riesling *cuvées*, both of which won the Jury's approval. This one has a very open nose of fresh fruit aromas, a clean, full, crisp opening on the palate, and delightful exotic fruit flavours. (Residual sugar: 4.3 g/l.) The other, which received a special mention, is the **Riesling Cuvée Prestige 2001**. This is a young wine with a restrained nose, a supple, full, round attack, and a fruitier character on the palate. It needs to be kept for a while. (Residual sugar: 11 g/l.)
• Marco Saulnier, 43, rue Haute, 68420 Gueberschwihr, tel. 03.89.86.42.02, fax 03.89.49.34.82 ◪
☏ by appt.

Riesling

SCHAEFFER-WOERLY
Vieilles Vignes 2001★★★

	0.5 ha	3,770	(I)	5–8 €

The buildings on the market square in Dambach date back to the 16th and 17th centuries, and it is here that the Vincent Woerly estate has its head office, in a half-timbered house with an old cellar where the 18th century family wine-press is kept. The cellar also contains a superb Riesling that comes from vines that are over 40 years old, grown on a sandy granitic terroir. It has fine floral aromas with an elegant mineral note, and after a good attack opens out with great finesse on a palate that is fresh, almost lively, full and well balanced. "Wonderful! A model wine!" said the Jury members. (Residual sugar: 7 g/l.)
� Schaeffer-Woerly, 3, pl. du Marché, 67650 Dambach-la-Ville, tel. 03.88.92.40.81, fax 03.88.92.49.87, e-mail schaeffer-woerly@wanadoo.fr ☑
☒ ev. day 9am–12 noon 2pm–6pm; Sun. and public holidays by appt.

SCHOENHEITZ
Linsenberg 2001★

	1.6 ha	9,000	▮	5–8 €

This old winemaking family goes back to the 17th century. In recent decades it has concentrated on growing on the hillsides and the best *lieux-dits* around the village of Wihr-au-Val. One of these is the Linsenberg, a granite and two-mica terroir that has produced this Riesling. The judges were delighted by its intense floral and spicy aromas and supple, clean first impression on a palate that is rich and balanced, although the finish is still somewhat restrained. (Residual sugar: 10 g/l.)
↳ Henri Schoenheitz, 1, rue de Walbach, 68230 Wihr-au-Val, tel. 03.89.71.03.96, fax 03.89.71.14.33, e-mail vins.schoenheitz@calixo.net ☑
☒ by appt.

JEAN-VICTOR SCHUTZ
Vieilles Vignes 2001★

	1.5 ha	10,300	▮ ⚱	5–8 €

This wine-merchants was started in 1997, and is essentially concerned with exports and mass distribution. Its Vieilles Vignes Riesling comes from a limestone-clay soil, and from vines that are over 30 years old. Its delightful nose opens on fine citrus fruit aromas and then becomes fuller. On the palate there are more citrus fruit flavours, along with a slight mineral note. This is a fresh wine with plenty of promise. (Residual sugar: 10 g/l.)
↳ Jean-Victor Schutz, 34, rue du Mal-Foch, 67650 Dambach-la-Ville, tel. 03.88.92.41.86, fax 03.88.92.61.81

VINCENT SPANNAGEL
Cuvée réservée 2001★

	0.31 ha	n.c.		5–8 €

Vincent Spannagel has been running this 9.5-hectare estate for 20 years now. His Cuvée Réservée has a range of ripe fruit notes and is delightfully round and smooth, with a fine balance and good length. (Residual sugar: 10.5 g/l.)
↳ EARL Vincent Spannagel, 82, rue du Vignoble, 68230 Katzenthal, tel. 03.89.27.52.13, fax 03.89.27.56.48 ☑
☒ by appt.

PIERRE SPERRY
Pflintz 2001★

	0.52 ha	4,000	(I)	5–8 €

Blienschwiller is a little village between Sélestat and Barr. Here Pierre Sperry, who is descended from several generations of winemakers, runs his estate from a modern house built in the style of the region. His very light-coloured Pflintz Riesling has hints of white dead-nettles along with some mineral notes. This characteristic, lively wine has great promise and should have gained in refinement by 2004. It will go well with grilled fish and shellfish. (Residual sugar: 3.8 g/l.)
↳ Pierre Sperry Fils, 5, rte des Vins, 67650 Blienschwiller, tel. 03.88.92.41.29, fax 03.88.92.62.38 ☑
☒ by appt.

SPITZ ET FILS
Prestige 2001★

	0.97 ha	4,400	(I)	5–8 €

This winemaking family can be relied upon for high quality, as can be seen from the regular mentions it receives in the *Guide*, especially for its dry wines. As last year, one of its Riesling Cuvées has been selected by the judges. This 2001 opens on citrus and exotic fruit aromas. It makes a clean, honest first impression on the palate, which is balanced, fresh, and full of flavour. The finish is long and elegant. (Residual sugar: 5.8 g/l.)
↳ EARL Spitz et Fils, 2–4, rte des Vins, 67650 Blienschwiller, tel. 03.88.92.61.20, fax 03.88.92.61.26 ☑
☒ ev. day 8.30am–12 noon 1.30pm–7pm

BERNARD STAEHLE
Rotenberg 2001★

	0.36 ha	3,300	(I)	5–8 €

Bernard Staehlé is based at Wintzenheim near Colmar, and since 1974 has been running an estate of nearly 7 ha which is overlooked by the Château de Hohlandsbourg. His Rotenberg Riesling comes from a limestone-clay terroir, and has a nose of fine, fruity, crystallized aromas and a highly expressive palate. This fresh, vigorous wine is very typical of the grape variety. (Residual sugar: 5 g/l.)
↳ Bernard Staehlé, 15, rue Clemenceau, 68920 Wintzenheim, tel. 03.89.27.39.02, fax 03.89.27.59.37 ☑
☒ by appt.

ANDRE STENTZ
Rosenberg 2001★★

	0.75 ha	5,000	▮ ⚱	8–11 €

This family estate is over 30 years old. When André Stentz inherited it in 1976, he went over to organic methods, and now grows more than 9 ha of vines according to *Nature et Progrès* (Nature and Progress) specifications. His Rosenberg Riesling comes from a limestone-clay terroir, and is both rich and fresh. It has intense crystallized fruit aromas, and a thoroughbred balance that ensures high quality on the palate. There is still a small amount of residual sugar in evidence, but it is already well integrated. This is a delightful wine, which will be a good accompaniment to fish in sauce. (Residual sugar: 12 g/l.)
↳ André Stentz, 2, rue de la Batteuse, 68920 Wettolsheim, tel. 03.89.80.64.91, fax 03.89.79.59.75, e-mail andre.stentz@wanadoo.fr ☑
☒ by appt.

DOM. STOEFFLER
Kronenbourg 2001★★

	0.5 ha	3,500	(I)	5–8 €

The couple who run this 12-hectare estate are both oenologists, and every year they produce more than 30 different wines. One of their top performers is this Kronenbourg Riesling, which regularly features in the *Guide*. The 2001 opens on rich aromas of crystallized fruits and overripe grapes. Exotic fruit notes then emerge on the palate, which is both supple and well structured, and has a long, beautifully fresh finish. (Residual sugar: 4.3 g/l.)

● Dom. Martine et Vincent Stoeffler, 1, rue des Lièvres,
67140 Barr, tel. 03.88.08.52.50, fax 03.88.08.17.09,
e-mail info@vins-stoeffler.com ☑
⚐ by appt.

ANTOINE STOFFEL 2001★★

| | 1.11 ha | 8,000 | ▮ ♦ | 5–8 € |

The Antoine Stoffel estate was founded in 1962, and now has
just under 8 ha of vines. Its 2001 Riesling will provide an extra
attraction for visitors to the picturesque village of Eguisheim.
It makes a delightful first impression with its intense, fine nose
of fruity and slightly musky aromas. The same notes reappear
on the palate, which the judges unanimously applauded for its
balance, freshness, harmony and character. "A real pleasure,"
said one taster. This wine will go well with *coq au Riesling* or
fish in sauce. (Residual sugar: 5 g/l.)
● Antoine Stoffel, 21, rue de Colmar, 68420 Eguisheim,
tel. 03.89.41.32.03, fax 03.89.24.92.07 ☑ ☗
⚐ ev. day except Sun. 8am–12 noon 2pm–6pm

LAURENT VOGT

Wolxheim Rothstein 2001★

| | 0.5 ha | 4,500 | ◖◗ | 5–8 € |

Wolxheim is in the "Golden Crown", which consists of 19
famous wine-growing communes to the west of Strasbourg in
the northern part of the Route des Vins area. In 1998 Thomas
Vogt took over this family estate, where visitors are received in
a traditional cellar dating back to 1715. This 2001 Rothstein
Riesling comes from a red sandstone terroir, which seems to
have marked it with some very unusual, slightly unsubtle
aromas. It is dry, vigorous, balanced and well structured, and
although the finish lacks intensity the judges believe the wine
has promise and should become more expressive with time.
(Residual sugar: 7 g/l.)
● EARL Laurent Vogt, 4, rue des Vignerons,
67120 Wolxheim, tel. 03.88.38.50.41, fax 03.88.38.50.41,
e-mail thomas@domaine-vogt.com ☑
⚐ by appt.

WASSLER

Fruehmess 2001★

| | 0.26 ha | 1,300 | ◖◗ | 5–8 € |

The old Roman road at the foot of the Vosges runs through
the village of Itterswiller, where the Fruehmess *lieu-dit* is
especially well-suited to Riesling. This 2001 has a fine nose
with a typical range of citrus fruit, white flower and mineral
notes. There is a clean attack on the palate, which is agreeably
crisp and fresh. (Residual sugar: 4.5 g/l.)
● EARL Henri Wassler Successeurs, 71, rte du Vin,
67140 Itterswiller, tel. 03.88.57.82.19, fax 03.88.57.83.98,
e-mail vinswassler@libertysurf.fr ☑
⚐ by appt.
● Frédéric Sohler

GERARD WEINZORN 2001★★

| | 1 ha | 6,000 | | 8–11 € |

This estate has been run by Claude Weinzorn since 1995, and
sets great store by tradition. The house where it is based was
built in 1619, and has a delicately carved oriel window, which
is a fine example of the Rhenish Renaissance. This Riesling
comes from a granitic sand terroir, and opens with a fine
nose of fruity aromas that suggest high quality from the
start. It is well balanced and full of flavour on the palate,
and its long finish shows that it is a wine of great character. It
will go well with turbot, bass, or any other fish in sauce.
(Residual sugar: 2.5 g/l.)
● Gérard Weinzorn et Fils, 133, rue des Trois-Epis,
68230 Niedermorschwihr, tel. 03.89.27.40.55,
fax 03.89.27.04.23, e-mail contact@weinzorn.fr ☑
⚐ by appt.

WELTY ET FILS

Bollenberg 2001★★

| | 0.98 ha | 7,800 | ▮ | 8–11 € |

Since 1992, Guy Welty has represented the third generation of
his family in running this 7-hectare estate in the southern part
of the Route des Vins region. This Riesling comes from the limestone-clay soils of the Bollenberg, a hillside vineyard that is
shared between four communes. The nose opens on citrus
fruit aromas, then develops towards floral notes. There are
more fruit notes on the palate, which won unanimous praise
for its balance based on roundness, and also for its finesse and
elegance. This is a thoroughbred wine that will go well with
dishes such as crayfish. (Residual sugar: 5 g/l.)
● Welty et Fils, 15–17, Grand-Rue, 68500 Orschwihr,
tel. 03.89.76.95.21, fax 03.89.74.63.53 ☑
⚐ by appt.
● Guy Welty

W. WURTZ

Cuvée Maryline 2001★

| | 0.2 ha | 2,000 | | 5–8 € |

This Riesling comes from a small plot with a sandy soil. It has
a pale yellow colour with green highlights, and opens timidly
on notes of lime with some slight mineral notes. The wine is
crisp and agreeable on the palate, but it still has quite a high
level of residual sugar, and needs to be kept for one or two
years. (Residual sugar: 12 g/l.)
● GAEC Willy Wurtz et Fils, 6, rue du Bouxhof,
68630 Mittelwihr, tel. 03.89.47.93.16, fax 03.89.47.89.01 ☑
⚐ ev. day 9am–7pm

ALBERT ZIEGLER 2001★

| | 0.3 ha | 1,900 | ▮ | 5–8 € |

Taken over by a new generation in 1998, this estate grows
vines on the Bollenberg and Pfingstberg hills around
Orschwihr. It has a 17th century vaulted cellar in which you
will find this pale yellow Riesling with a very pleasant nose
that opens out on to overripe aromas. The palate has the same
overripe, fruity quality, along with a lovely freshness and a
very full structure. The finish is well balanced. (Residual
sugar: 9.8 g/l.)
● Albert Ziegler, 10, rue de l'Eglise, 68500 Orschwihr,
tel. 03.89.76.01.12, fax 03.89.74.91.32 ☑
⚐ ev. day 8am–12 noon 1.30pm–7pm

FERNAND ZIEGLER

Clos Saint-Ulrich 2001★

| | 0.8 ha | 9,600 | ◖◗ | 8–11 € |

The Clos Saint-Ulrich is located in the commune of
Ribeauvillé, and takes its name from the castle at the top of
the very steep hill whose granitic clay soils have produced this
Riesling. The wine has an exuberant, elegant complex nose of
white flower aromas with a slight mineral note. There is a
supple attack on the palate, which is rich and shows great
potential. (Residual sugar: 4 g/l.)
● EARL Fernand Ziegler, 7, rue des Vosges,
68150 Hunawihr, tel. 03.89.73.64.42,
fax 03.89.73.71.38 ☑ ☗
⚐ by appt.

Wines selected but not starred

JEAN-PHILIPPE AND JEAN-FRANCOIS BECKER Lerchenberg 2001

	0.6 ha	4,600	▌ ♦	8–11 €

♦┐ GAEC Jean-Philippe et François Becker, 2, rte d'Ostheim, 68340 Zellenberg, tel. 03.89.47.87.56, fax 03.89.47.99.57 ☑
☥ by appt.

LEON BEYER

Cuvée des Comtes d'Eguisheim 2001

2 ha	5,000	◖▌	15–23 €

♦┐ Léon Beyer, 2, rue de la 1ʳᵉ Armée, 68420 Eguisheim, tel. 03.89.21.62.30, fax 03.89.23.93.63, e-mail contact@leonbeyer.fr ☑
☥ ev. day except Wed. 10am–12 noon 2pm–6pm

DOM. CLAUDE BLEGER

Coteaux du Haut-Koenigsbourg 2001

0.35 ha	2,800	◖▌	5–8 €

♦┐ Dom. Claude Bléger, 23, Grand-Rue, 67600 Orschwiller, tel. 03.88.92.32.56, fax 03.88.82.59.95, e-mail vins.c.bleger@wanadoo.fr ☑ ▯ ▮
☥ ev. day 9am–12.15pm 1.15pm–7.30pm

HUBERT BLUMSTEIN

Riesling de Scherwiller 2001

0.38 ha	4,500	▌ ♦	5–8 €

♦┐ Hubert Blumstein, rte du Vin, 67730 Châtenois, tel. 03.88.82.13.65, fax 03.88.82.34.09, e-mail sylvie@vins-blumstein.com ☑ ▯ ▮
☥ ev. day 9am–12 noon 1pm–7pm

HENRI BRECHT 2001

0.4 ha	4,000		5–8 €

♦┐ Henri Brecht, 4, rue du Vignoble, 68420 Eguisheim, tel. 03.89.41.96.34, fax 03.89.24.45.29 ☑
☥ by appt.

PIERRE-HENRI GINGLINGER

Vieilles Vignes 2001

0.7 ha	5,500		5–8 €

♦┐ Pierre-Henri Ginglinger, 33, Grand-Rue, 68420 Eguisheim, tel. 03.89.41.32.55, fax 03.89.24.58.91, e-mail gingling@terre-net.fr ☑ ▯ ▮
☥ by appt.

MICHEL GOETTELMANN 2001

0.2 ha	2,000	▌	5–8 €

♦┐ Michel Goettelmann, 27, rue des Goumiers, 67730 Châtenois, tel. 03.88.82.12.40, fax 03.88.82.12.40, e-mail mgoettelmann@wanadoo.fr ☑
☥ ev. day 8am–12 noon 1pm–7pm

GERARD AND SERGE HARTMANN

Bildstoecklé 2001

0.5 ha	6,000		5–8 €

♦┐ Gérard et Serge Hartmann, 13, rue Frémeaux, 68420 Voegtlinshoffen, tel. 03.89.49.30.27, fax 03.89.49.29.78 ☑

LOUIS HAULLER

Tradition 2001

3.5 ha	10,000	▌	5–8 €

♦┐ Louis et Claude Hauller, La Cave du Tonnelier, 88, rue Foch, 67650 Dambach-la-Ville, tel. 03.88.92.41.19, fax 03.88.92.47.10, e-mail claude@louishauller.com ☑ ▯ ▮
☥ by appt.

VICTOR HERTZ 2001

0.65 ha	5,000	▌	5–8 €

♦┐ Dom. Victor Hertz, 8, rue Saint-Michel, 68420 Herrlisheim, tel. 03.89.49.31.67, fax 03.89.49.22.84 ☑
☥ by appt.

JEAN HIRTZ ET FILS

Weingarten 2001

n.c.	2,400	▌	5–8 €

♦┐ EARL du Rotland Jean Hirtz et Fils, 13, rue Rotland, 67140 Mittelbergheim, tel. 03.88.08.47.90, fax 03.88.08.47.90 ☑
☥ ev. day 9am–12 noon 2pm–7pm

HORCHER

Cuvée Sélection 2001

0.65 ha	5,600	▌ ♦	8–11 €

♦┐ Ernest Horcher et Fils, 6, rue du Vignoble, 68630 Mittelwihr, tel. 03.89.47.93.26, fax 03.89.49.04.92, e-mail info@horcher.fr ☑ ▮
☥ ev. day except Sun. 9am–12 noon 2pm–7pm

ROBERT KARCHER

Harth 2001

2.2 ha	6,000	◖▌	5–8 €

♦┐ Dom. Robert Karcher et Fils, 11, rue de l'Ours, 68000 Colmar, tel. 03.89.41.14.42, fax 03.89.24.45.05, e-mail info@vins-karcher.com ☑
☥ ev. day 8am–12 noon 2pm–7pm except Sun. pm; groups by appt.

METZ-GEIGER 2001

0.36 ha	3,000	◖▌	5–8 €

♦┐ Metz-Geiger, 9, rue Fronholz, 67680 Epfig, tel. 03.88.85.55.21, fax 03.88.85.55.21 ☑
☥ ev. day 8am–12 noon 1pm–7pm

GILBERT MEYER

Cuvée Saint-Michel 2001

0.65 ha	7,000	◖▌	5–8 €

♦┐ Gilbert Meyer, 5, rue du Schauenberg, 68420 Voegtlinshoffen, tel. 03.89.49.36.65, fax 03.89.86.42.45, e-mail info@vins-meyer.com ☑ ▮
☥ by appt.

DOM. DU MITTELBURG 2001

0.15 ha	1,700	◖▌	5–8 €

♦┐ EARL Henri Martischang, 15, rue du Fossé, 68250 Pfaffenheim, tel. 03.89.49.60.83, fax 03.89.49.76.61, e-mail vin.h.martischang@free.fr ☑ ▮
☥ by appt.

MUHLBERGER

Clos Philippe Grass 2001

2.4 ha	n.c.		5–8 €

♦┐ Vignobles François Muhlberger, 1, rue de Strasbourg, 67120 Wolxheim, tel. 03.88.38.10.33, fax 03.88.38.47.65, e-mail muhlberger@wanadoo.fr ☑
☥ ev. day 9am–12 noon 1pm–7pm

MICHEL NARTZ

Vieilles Vignes 2001

■	0.23 ha	1,200	❿	5–8 €

❧ Michel Nartz, 12, pl. du Marché,
67650 Dambach-la-Ville, tel. 03.88.92.41.11,
fax 03.88.92.63.01 ☎
☥ by appt.

GILBERT RUHLMANN FILS

Scherwiller 2001

■	1.5 ha	9,000	■	⚘	3–5 €

❧ Gilbert Ruhlmann Fils, 31, rue de l'Ortenbourg,
67750 Scherwiller, tel. 03.88.92.03.21, fax 03.88.82.30.19,
e-mail vin.ruhlmann@terre-net.fr ☑
☥ ev. day 8am–12 noon 1pm–7pm; Sun. by appt.

STEINER

Elsbourg 2001

■	0.24 ha	1,100	■	⚘	8–11 €

❧ GAEC Steiner, 11, rte du Vin,
68420 Herrlisheim-près-Colmar, tel. 03.89.49.30.70,
fax 03.89.49.29.67, e-mail steiner.vins@wanadoo.fr ☑ ☎
☥ by appt.

Alsace Muscat

Two varieties of Muscat are used to make this dry, aromatic white wine, which is reminiscent of the burst of flavour you get when biting into a fresh grape. One variety, traditionally called Muscat d'Alsace, is more accurately known as the Muscat de Frontignan. It is a late-maturing variety so it is planted on slopes with the best aspect. The second variety, which develops earlier and so is more widely grown, is the Muscat Ottonel. The two varieties are planted on 340 ha, 2.3% of the Alsace vineyard. The Muscat d'Alsace is a pleasing and sometimes surprising speciality. It makes a good aperitif and is a good wine to serve at drinks parties. It goes well with cakes or salty nibbles like pretzels.

FERNAND ENGEL

Sélection de grains nobles 2000★★★

■	0.6 ha	2,600	■	⚘	30–38 €

Located south of the Haut-Koenigsbourg, this is an unusually large estate of 40 ha, 15 of which are cultivated organically, and the other 25 by sustainable agriculture methods. This gem of a wine has been produced by M. Engel's son-in-law Xavier Baril, who is an oenologist. It has a gold colour with sparkling highlights and a very decent nose of Muscat aromas that are both intense and extremely delicate. As for the palate, one taster exclaimed: "Just remarkable!". It has a superb balance, a good level of acidity and a warming, heady quality, all of which reminds you of biting into a golden grape straight from the vine. The finish goes on for ever, ending with an explosion of flavour: ferns, dried fruits, and crystallized fruits. This is a great sweet wine, which can be drunk straightaway. (Half-litre bottles)

❧ GAEC Fernand Engel et Fils, 1, rte du Vin,
68590 Rorschwihr, tel. 03.89.73.77.27, fax 03.89.73.63.70,
e-mail f-engel@wanadoo.fr ☑
☥ ev. day 8am–12 noon 1pm–6pm
except Sun. 10am–12 noon

SYLVAIN HERTZOG 2001★★

■	0.26 ha	2,000	■	⚘	5–8 €

Located on a hillside to the southwest of Colmar, the village of Obermorschwihr produces Muscat wines of very high quality. This one has a brilliant yellow colour and an expressive, very pleasant nose of ripe, mainly citrus fruit aromas. The wine is supple from start to finish on the palate, which is also rich and mouth-filling and offers a wide range of flavours: musky, heady notes embellished by touches of wax and tea. There is an unctuous finish on a delicious variety of citrus fruit notes. (Residual sugar: 4 g/l.)

❧ EARL Sylvain Hertzog, 18, rte du Vin,
68420 Obermorschwihr, tel. 03.89.49.31.93,
fax 03.89.49.28.85 ☑
☥ ev. day 8am–7pm; Sun. by appt.

FREDERIC KUHLMANN

Réserve personnelle 2001★

■	0.5 ha	2,200	❿	8–11 €

With its fortified church (popularized by the illustrator Hansi) and its swan park, Hunawihr is the epitome of a traditional Alsace village. Wine-growing is part of the picture as well; there are some very good terroirs here, with rather heavy soils which tend to produce wines with good ageing potential. This one has a pale yellow colour with gold glints, and very fresh aromas of lime and pineapple. The palate starts cleanly, develops complex flavours of overripe fruits (peaches and apricots), and has a long, pleasant finish. This wine has good prospects for the future. (Residual sugar: 8.9 g/l.)

❧ SCEA Frédéric Kuhlmann et Fils, 8, rue de la Fontaine,
68150 Hunawihr, tel. 03.89.73.60.33, fax 03.89.47.81.92,
e-mail info@fkuhlmann.com ☑
☥ by appt.

JEAN-LOUIS SCHOEPFER 2001★

■	0.35 ha	2,000	■	3–5 €

In 1656 Louis Schoepfer bought some vines at Wettolsheim, west of Colmar, and 347 years later Jean-Louis Schoepfer, who was joined by his son Gilles in 1997, still has a ten-hectare vineyard in the same commune. Their Muscat has a pale, brilliant colour and a fine, intense nose combining ripe fruit aromas (oranges, mandarines) and floral notes (acacia, honeysuckle). It is very fresh on the palate, with a delicious grapey flavour. There are more citrus fruit notes on the middle palate, but they are more in the lemon and grapefruit range. This high-class wine has a light, delicate quality which makes it extremely pleasant. (Residual sugar: 3 g/l.)

❧ EARL Jean-Louis Schoepfer, 35, rue Herzog,
68920 Wettolsheim, tel. 03.89.80.71.29, fax 03.89.79.61.35,
e-mail jlschoepfer@libertysurf.fr ☑
☥ by appt.

DOM. SCHOFFIT 2001★

■	0.54 ha	3,000	■	⚘	8–11 €

This Colmar-based winemaker's reputation is established beyond question. He has a large, 17-hectare estate consisting of famous terroirs which he cultivates with talent, and he exports 50% of his output to a remarkable variety of countries, including New Zealand! His Muscat comes from the gravelly soil on the Hardt de Colmar, and has a pale colour with brilliant gold highlights. The nose opens quickly on to delightfully fine aromas of very ripe fruits mingled with spicy notes. This is an intense, balanced, elegant wine with a long finish, which can be drunk straightaway as an aperitif, or with salad. (Asparagus sugar: 9 g/l.)

❧ Dom. Schoffit, 66–68, Nonnenholz-Weg, 68000 Colmar,
tel. 03.89.24.41.14, fax 03.89.41.40.52 ☑
☥ by appt.

Wines selected but not starred

BROBECKER 2001

| | 0.3 ha | 2,000 | | 3–5 € |

◆┐ SCEA Vins Brobecker, 3, pl. de l'Eglise,
68420 Eguisheim, tel. 06.87.52.80.72, fax 03.89.41.55.93,
e-mail pascal.joblot@free.fr ☑
☥ ev. day except Sun. 8am–6pm
◆┐ Pascal Joblot

MARTIN SCHAETZEL
Réserve 2001

| | 0.4 ha | 3,000 | ⓪ | 5–8 € |

◆┐ Martin Schaetzel, 3, rue de la 5ᵉ-D.-B.,
68770 Ammerschwihr, tel. 03.89.47.11.39,
fax 03.89.78.29.77 ☑
☥ by appt.

Alsace Gewurztraminer

The grape variety used to make this wine is a particularly aromatic member of the Traminer family. In a treatise published in 1551 it was already being acknowledged as a variety that was typical of Alsace. Ideally suited to the Alsace terroir, it has been adapted over the centuries to create top-quality wines with a worldwide reputation.

It makes full-bodied, well-structured wines, which are basically dry but with some softness and have a marvellous, characteristic bouquet, which varies in power depending on the year and on where the grapes are grown. Gewurztraminer is an early-fruiting variety and has a limited and unreliable yield, but it produces very ripe grapes. About 2,500 ha are planted with Gewurztraminer, 17.6% of the Alsace wine region. It is often served as an aperitif or at drinks parties, and it is a good accompaniment to desserts, as well as being an excellent foil, particularly when full and rich in character, for strongly flavoured cheeses, such as Roquefort and Munster.

DOM. PIERRE ADAM
Kaefferkopf 2001★

| | 0.6 ha | 4,000 | ▮ ♦ | 11–15 € |

This estate is based in a beautiful half-timbered house in the middle of the vineyard. Today it has 11 ha of vines in all, including this plot on the famous Kaefferkopf, a clay-limestone terroir whose soils produce particularly intense, aromatically complex wines. This one is very fruity, with over-ripe flavours on the palate. It is an elegant, well-structured wine with a pleasant finish. (Residual sugar: 25 g/l.)
◆┐ Dom. Pierre Adam, 8, rue du Lt-Louis-Mourier,
68770 Ammerschwihr, tel. 03.89.78.23.07,
fax 03.89.47.39.68,
e-mail info@domaine-adam.com ☑ ▯ ▯
☥ ev. day 8am–12 noon 1pm–7pm

BARON DE HOEN
Vieilles Vignes 2001★

| | 1.4 ha | 5,400 | ▮ ♦ | 8–11 € |

The Beblenheim wine-producers' cooperative wisely extended its operations to include this company, which is based in a remarkable half-timbered building formerly owned by Baron de Hoen. This Vieilles Vignes *cuvée* comes from a marly clay terroir, and has a whole range of spice aromas (cinnamon, pepper, cloves). The palate is supple and very full, with further sweet, spicy notes that linger on to a long finish. (Residual sugar: 18 g/l.)
◆┐ SICA Baron de Hoen, 20, rue de Hoen,
68980 Beblenheim, tel. 03.89.47.89.93 ☑
☥ by appt.

CHARLES BAUR
Vendanges tardives 2000★

| | 0.4 ha | 1,630 | ⓪ | 15–23 € |

This estate dates back to the 18th century, and occupies a prominent position on the main road through Eguisheim. Since 1980 it has been run by the talented oenologist Armand Baur. This Vendanges Tardives has a very suitable label in radiant late-autumn colours, while the wine itself is a golden straw yellow. It has a nose of overripe fruit aromas, and is quite delightful on the palate, which is full and has a long finish on liquorice and vanilla flavours accompanied by very overripe notes of quince and lychee.
◆┐ Charles Baur, 29, Grand-Rue, 68420 Eguisheim,
tel. 03.89.41.32.49, fax 03.89.41.55.79,
e-mail cave@vinscharlesbaur.fr ☑
☥ ev. day except Sun. 9am–12 noon 2pm–6pm

FRANCIS BECK
Fronholz 2001★★

| | 0.45 ha | 3,500 | ▮ ♦ | 5–8 € |

This estate is opposite the Chapelle Sainte-Marguerite, a gem of Romanesque art which is the main attraction in the village of Epfig. The cellar here contains other treasures however, such as this 2001 Gewurztraminer. It has a pale gold colour, and opens on spicy notes and hints of dried fruits. The wine is powerful and quite full on the palate, leaving an excellent impression on a finish that has the same complexity as the nose. This wine will go very well with food, and should be served with exotic foods or blue cheese. (Residual sugar: 21.5 g/l.)
◆┐ Francis Beck, 79, rue Sainte-Marguerite, 67680 Epfig,
tel. 03.88.85.54.84, fax 03.88.57.83.81 ☑ ▯
☥ by appt.

LEON BEYER
Cuvée des Comtes d'Eguisheim 2001★

| | 1.5 ha | 3,000 | ⓪ | 15–23 € |

The Beyer family is based in Eguisheim, a town full of history whose streets run concentrically around its 13th century castle. The estate has been handed down from generation to generation since 1580, and spreads the renown of Alsace wines far and wide by exporting three-quarters of its output. This wine has quite a complex range of honey and toast aromas with some notes of *pain d'épice*. It has excellent balance on the palate, and also a subtle freshness that gives it great finesse. This is a thoroughbred wine with plenty of promise for the future. (Residual sugar: 8 g/l.)
◆┐ Léon Beyer, 2, rue de la 1ʳᵉ Armée, 68420 Eguisheim,
tel. 03.89.21.62.30, fax 03.89.23.93.63,
e-mail contact@leonbeyer.fr ☑
☥ ev. day except Wed. 10am–12 noon 2pm–6pm

JEAN BOESCH
Vallée Noble 2001★

| | 0.2 ha | 800 | ▮ | 8–11 € |

This family has been making wine since the 18th century, and now runs a seven-hectare vineyard. Named after the famous valley that opens out on to the plain at Soultzmatt, this wine has intense, fine aromas of overripening, along with a mineral note. The round, full palate reveals subtle touches of honey which linger on to a long finish on a slight note of bitterness.

This wine should be drunk as an aperitif, or with foie gras or dessert. (Residual sugar: 51 g/l.)
➶ EARL Jean Boesch et Petit-Fils, 1, rue Wagenbourg, 68570 Soultzmatt, tel. 03.89.47.00.87, fax 03.89.47.08.19 ☑ ☗
🍷 by appt.

BOTT FRERES

Réserve personnelle 2001★

	2.4 ha	12,000	🍶	11–15 €

The Bott family has been running its estate in the town of Ménétriers since 1835. The cellars are very old, and the oak barrels date back more than 100 years. This Réserve has a nose of spicy aromas accompanied by touches of flowers and honey. The same subtle notes appear on the palate, where the wine is well balanced, fine and very characteristic. The finish is sweet and full of flavour.
➶ Dom. Bott Frères, 13, av. du Gal-de-Gaulle, 68150 Ribeauvillé, tel. 03.89.73.22.50, fax 03.89.73.22.59, e-mail vins@bott-freres.fr ☑
🍷 by appt.

CAMILLE BRAUN

Cuvée Annabelle 2001★★

	0.6 ha	4,000	🍶 🥂	8–11 €

This 13-hectare vineyard in Orschwihr on the southern part of the Route des Vins was taken over in 1990 by Christophe Braun, whose family has been making wine here since the end of the 17th century. His wine is dedicated to Annabelle, and has a very feminine style about it. On the floral side it has some subtle rose fragrances, and its fruity aromas have a touch of exoticism. It is fresh, soft and even silky on the palate, and the finish is delightfully fine. (Residual sugar: 29 g/l.)
➶ Camille Braun, 16, Grand-Rue, 68500 Orschwihr, tel. 03.89.76.95.20, fax 03.89.74.35.03, e-mail cbraun@terre-net.fr ☑ ☗
🍷 ev. day except Sun. 8.30am–12 noon 1.30pm–6.30pm

BROBECKER

Cuvée spéciale 2001★★

	0.4 ha	2,500		5–8 €

Located just below the historic church tower in the picturesque village of Eguisheim, Pascal Joblot has been in charge of the family estate since 1998. He runs his 3.5-hectare vineyard by sustainable agriculture methods, and although the area is not particularly large, he certainly gets the very best out of it, judging by the quality of this 2001. It has a nose of rich oriental spice and exotic fruit aromas, a fresh attack, and a full-bodied, well-balanced palate on which fruit flavours open out to make for a very pleasant finish. This is a really delightful wine. (Residual sugar: 18 g/l.) One star is also awarded to this producer for his **Gewurztraminer Vendanges Tardives 2000**, which is well balanced and has a long finish. It will be at its best in a few years' time.
➶ SCEA Vins Brobecker, 3, pl. de l'Eglise, 68420 Eguisheim, tel. 06.87.52.80.72, fax 03.89.41.55.93, e-mail pascal.joblot@free.fr ☑
🍷 ev. day except Sun. 8am–6pm
➶ Pascal Joblot

DOMAINES DU CHATEAU DE RIQUEWIHR Les Sorcières 2001★★

	6 ha	38,000	🍶 🥂	8–11 €

Formerly owned by the Dukes of Württemberg, the vineyards at the Château de Riquewihr have helped build the reputation of Dopff et Irion, who occupies a prominent position in this historic Haut-Rhin town. This Sorcières Cuvée has an expressive nose of crystallized fruits, toast and roses. It is fresh, well structured, luscious and complex on the palate, finishing on a spicy note. This sorceress will certainly cast a spell. (Residual sugar: 13.2 g/l.)
➶ Dopff et Irion, Dom. du château de Riquewihr, 68340 Riquewihr, tel. 03.89.47.92.51, fax 03.89.47.98.90, e-mail post@dopff-irion.com ☑
🍷 by appt.

CLOS SAINTE-ODILE 2001★

	n.c.	14,000	🍶 🥂	8–11 €

Overlooking the town of Obernai are the terraces of the Clos Sainte-Odile, a very old vineyard that was first laid out in the 17th century. The upper part is planted with Gewurztraminer, which does very well there. This 2001 is closed at first, then opens out on to notes of white fruits and roses. On the palate it makes an extremely good impression with its balance, unusual finesse, and good length. (Residual sugar: 12.5 g/l.)
➶ Sté vinicole Sainte-Odile, 30, rue du Gal-Leclerc, 67210 Obernai, tel. 03.88.47.60.29, fax 03.88.47.60.22 ☑
🍷 by appt.

JEAN DIETRICH

Altenburg Vieilles Vignes 2001★

	0.37 ha	2,500	🍶 🥂	8–11 €

In Kaysersberg there is a 15th century fortified bridge with loopholes and an oratory, leading towards the picturesque, half-timbered Renaissance house from which this family vineyard is run. The estate is offering a Gewurztraminer with the subtle floral scents that are typical of the grape variety, along with some restrained notes of spices and pepper. The palate is full and rich, with a slight touch of freshness on the finish. This is quite a dry wine which will go well with food, for instance with exotic dishes. (Residual sugar: 7 g/l.)
➶ Jean Dietrich, 4, rue de l'Oberhof, 68240 Kaysersberg, tel. 03.89.78.25.24, fax 03.89.47.30.72 ☑
🍷 ev. day 10am–12 noon 2pm–6pm

CHRISTIAN DOLDER 2001★

	0.6 ha	4,200	🍶 🥂	8–11 €

Mittelbergheim is worth a visit for its opulent, flower-bedecked Renaissance houses with their pink sandstone porches and windows. Here in Christian Dolder's cellar you will discover this delightful, elegant wine, which has a nose of floral, slightly smoky aromas. It is fresh and well balanced on the palate, which is full-bodied and brimming with crystallized fruit flavours. This is a pleasant wine right up to the finish. (Residual sugar: 9 g/l.)
➶ Christian Dolder, 4, rue Neuve, 67140 Mittelbergheim, tel. 03.88.08.96.08, fax 03.88.08.50.23 ☑ ☗
🍷 by appt.

EBLIN-FUCHS

Vieilles Vignes 2001★

	0.6 ha	3,900	🍶	8–11 €

This estate came into being in the 1950s as a result of the union between two families who have been growing wine for centuries on the Zellenberg spur. The vineyard is run from a neo-classical building with a freestone cellar beneath it. All the wines here are matured in oak. This Gewurztraminer comes from 65-year-old vines, and has complex fruit and flower notes which continue on a full-bodied palate with sweet, fresh, fine flavours and a good finish. It should become even more aromatically expressive if kept for a year or two. (Residual sugar: 40 g/l.)
➶ Christian et Joseph Eblin, 19, rte des Vins, 68340 Zellenberg, tel. 03.89.47.91.14, fax 03.89.49.05.12 ☑ ☗
🍷 by appt.

DOM. DE L'ECOLE

Côte de Rouffach 2001★★

	n.c.	2,200	🍶 🥂	5–8 €

South of Colmar the viticultural college at Rouffach trains winemakers and technicians from all over the region. It has a 13-hectare vineyard, and the students are certainly learning a lot there if this Gewurztraminer is anything to go by. It has a pale, brilliant golden colour, and a lovely range of rose and white fruit aromas. With its fairly round structure and fresh notes, this is a delightfully well-balanced, fine, harmonious wine. (Residual sugar: 42 g/l.)
➶ Dom. de l'Ecole, Lycée agricole et viticole, 8, aux Remparts, 68250 Rouffach, tel. 03.89.78.73.16, fax 03.89.78.73.43, e-mail expl.legta.rouffach@educagri.fr ☑
🍷 ev. day except Sat. Sun. 9am–12 noon 1.30pm–5pm; groups by appt.

FERNAND ENGEL

Sélection de grains nobles Cuvée Amélie 2000★★

	0.57 ha	3,900	🍾 🥂	38–46 €

Sélection de Grains Nobles wines are one of the specialities of this estate. This Cuvée Amélie was produced by Xavier Baril, an oenologist who is also M. Engel's son-in-law, and it really shows what a good winemaker he is. It has a very deep amber yellow colour and a unusually complex nose of crystallized fruit (apricot and peach) aromas, and orange peel notes. Although rich, full and heady on the palate, it is also very fine and delicate, with the clearly dominant overripe fruit flavours being subtly nuanced by citrus peel and honey notes. The finish is extraordinarily long. Considering how young it still is, this wine is remarkably expressive. (Half-litre bottles)
☛ GAEC Fernand Engel et Fils, 1, rte du Vin, 68590 Rorschwihr, tel. 03.89.73.77.27, fax 03.89.73.63.70, e-mail f-engel@wanadoo.fr
🍷 ev. day 8am–12 noon 1pm–6pm except Sun. 10am–12 noon

FAHRER-ACKERMANN

Silbergrube 2001★

	0.4 ha	2,000	🍾 🥂	8–11 €

In 1999 Vincent Ackermann bought a 7.5-hectare estate from his former employer, and he is now working with motivation and talent there to produce very good results. His Silbergrube Gewurztraminer comes from a siliceous terroir, and has all the features to prove it. Its complex range of exotic fruit, over-ripe and violet notes is evident both on the nose and on the palate, which is round and full, with a warming touch on the finish. (Residual sugar: 41 g/l.)
☛ Fahrer-Ackermann, 15, rte du Vin, 67600 Orschwiller, tel. 03.88.92.90.23, fax 03.88.92.90.23 🗹 🏠
🍷 by appt.

ANDRE FALLER

Sélection de grains nobles Cuvée Mireille 2000★★

	0.3 ha	1,500	🍾 🥂	30–38 €

Itterswiller is located just south of Barr, on an escarpment that gives it an excellent, sunny aspect. The village is decked with flowers in the summer, and is home to numerous winemakers such as André Faller. His estate is offering a remarkable Sélection de Grains Nobles, with a deep gold colour and a rich, fragrant nose which opens on a rose scent, then moves on to crystallized fruits before opening out into some more spicy notes. On the palate it is rich, full and very pleasant, with flavours of Agen prunes and a long finish on the very fine hints of violets that characterize this terroir. (Half-litre bottles)
☛ André Faller, 2, rte du Vin, 67140 Itterswiller, tel. 03.88.85.53.55, fax 03.88.85.51.13, e-mail andre.faller@wanadoo.fr 🗹
🍷 by appt.

DOM. FLEISCHER

Brettling 2001★

	0.55 ha	4,000	🍾 🥂	8–11 €

This estate started bottling wines in 1990, and at the same time expanded its wine-growing area, going from 3.5 ha to the 9 ha of vines it has today. It is offering a wine with a powerful nose of spice and crystallized fruit aromas, and a palate that opens very pleasantly and has excellent balance. Its overripe flavours are in keeping with its very full structure, and the finish is long and agreeable. (Residual sugar: 17.5 g/l.)
☛ Dom. Fleischer, 28, rue du Moulin, 68250 Pfaffenheim, tel. 03.89.49.62.70, fax 03.89.49.50.74 🗹 🏠 🏠
🍷 by appt.

RENE FLEITH-ESCHARD ET FILS

Vendanges tardives 2000★★★

	0.3 ha	1,125		15–23 €

This family vineyard is located at Ingersheim, at the point where the Munster and Kaysersberg valleys meet. Since 2001 it has had a storage cellar that enables it to rationalize its methods of wine production. It is very often selected for its *liquoreux* or *moelleux* wines, but this year has presented a superb Vendanges Tardives from a limestone-clay terroir. It has a gold colour, and although the nose is still not fully open it is already showing a certain potential by releasing some slight notes of flowers, crystallized fruits and spices. The palate is perfectly balanced, powerful, rich and full, finishing on some very elegant peppery notes. This 2000 has the long finish of a really great wine, and is delightfully harmonious.
☛ René Fleith-Eschard et Fils, lieu-dit Lange Matten, 68040 Ingersheim, tel. 03.89.27.24.19, fax 03.89.27.56.79 🗹 🏠
🍷 by appt.

DOMINIQUE FREYBURGER

Vendanges tardives Cuvée Théo 2000★

	0.11 ha	1,400	🍶	15–23 €

This property was founded in 1945, and taken over in 1997 by Domnique Freyburger, who had been a wine waiter for 15 years. This pale yellow Cuvée Théo has an intense, fruity aroma on the nose, followed by a slight hint of toast and finally some exotic mango touches. Similar notes appear on the palate, which is powerful and full, with a very long, delightfully fine finish. This Gewurztraminer has all the characteristics one expects from a Vendanges Tardives. (Half-litre bottles)
☛ Dominique Freyburger, 11A–12, rue du Tir, 68770 Ammerschwihr, tel. 03.89.78.17.62, fax 03.89.78.17.62, e-mail vinsfreyb@aol.com 🗹
🍷 ev. day 9am–12 noon 2pm–6.30pm except Sun. 9am–12 noon; cl. 1–10 July

PAUL GINGLINGER

Sélection de grains nobles 2000★★

	0.4 ha	1,500		30–38 €

Although the Ginglingers have deep roots in the Alsatian vineyard and have been growing wine here since 1636, that hasn't prevented Michel, who is an oenologist, from seeking further experience in various regions of France, and even in the southern hemisphere. His Sélection de Grains Nobles has a deep yellow colour and a nose which opens on rose scents, then develops towards exotic fruit (lychee) aromas. On the palate it is very powerful yet balanced, rich and full. It has a long finish, and a remarkably complex range of citrus fruit, exotic fruit, quince and crystallized fruit flavours.
☛ Paul Ginglinger, 8, pl. Charles-de-Gaulle, 68420 Eguisheim, tel. 03.89.41.44.25, fax 03.89.24.94.88 🗹
🍷 by appt.

GOETZ

Réserve particulière 2001★★

	0.5 ha	3,100		5–8 €

This fresh, fruity Gewurztraminer releases some subtle mandarine aromas, which are a sign of slight overripening. The same notes continue rather strikingly on the palate, which is well balanced, rich and fresh, with a fine spicy note on the finish. This wine will be good to drink as an aperitif or at the end of a meal, especially with a chocolate dessert because of its slight citrus-fruit flavours. (Residual sugar: 18 g/l.)
☛ Mathieu Goetz, 2, rue Jeanne-d'Arc, 67120 Wolxheim, tel. 03.88.38.10.47, fax 03.88.38.67.61, e-mail mathieu.goetz@wanadoo.fr 🗹
🍷 by appt.

DOM. HENRI HAEFFELIN ET FILS

Cuvée Arnaud 2000★

	0.5 ha	4,000	🍶	8–11 €

Since 1989, Guy Haeffelin has been running a good-sized vineyard of over 16 ha. This Gewurztraminer is dedicated to his eldest son, and has a mixture of fruity and spicy aromas that give it the feel of a mature wine. It is powerful and rich on the palate, which finishes on a spicy note. All these features are typical of a Gewurztraminer in the 2000 vintage. (Residual sugar: 15 g/l.)
☛ Dom. Henri Haeffelin et Fils, 13, rue d'Eguisheim, 68920 Wettolsheim, tel. 03.89.80.76.81, fax 03.89.79.67.05, e-mail guyhaeffelin@wanadoo.fr 🗹
🍷 by appt.

BERNARD HANSMANN

Pfoeller 2001★★

| 0.2 ha | 1,200 | ◗◗ | 5–8 € |

Eight generations of winemakers have lived in this family house dating back to 1732, and in 2002, Frédéric Hansmann joined his father in running the vineyard. This 2001, produced by Bernard Hansmann, is a remarkable wine. It has an intense nose of fruit notes (lychee) and floral aromas, and a balanced, fresh palate where the flavours linger on to a very long finish. All in all this is a delightfully harmonious wine. (Residual sugar: 9 g/l.)
➦ Bernard et Frédéric Hansmann, 66, rue Principale, 67140 Mittelbergheim, tel. 03.88.08.07.44,
fax 03.88.08.07.44,
e-mail bernard.hansmann@libertysurf.fr ☑
☾ ev. day except Sun. 8am–6pm

JEAN-PAUL AND FRANK HARTWEG

Schloesselreben 2001★

| 0.35 ha | 4,000 | ▮ | 8–11 € |

Jean-Paul Hartweg is assisted by his son Franck, who studied oenology in Beaune before joining him in 1996. Together they have produced a Gewurztraminer whose aromas are highly characteristic but still restrained. On the palate it is fresh, round, and delightfully full-bodied. The finish is agreeably long, and marked by a warm note. This wine will gain from a year or two of ageing. (Residual sugar: 54 g/l.)
➦ Jean-Paul et Frank Hartweg, 39, rue Jean-Macé, 68980 Beblenheim, tel. 03.89.47.94.79, fax 03.89.49.00.83,
e-mail frank.hartweg@free.fr ☑ ☗
☾ ev. day except Sun. 8am–11.30am 1.30pm–6pm

LEON HEITZMANN

Kaefferkopf Vendanges tardives 2000★★

| 0.7 ha | 5,400 | ◗◗ | 15–23 € |

Ammerschwihr lies to the northwest of Colmar, and has a very extensive vinyard. The village is famous for its Wine Fair that takes place every year in April. One winemaker here who is well known to readers of the *Guide* is Léon Heitzmann. He grows 11 ha of vines, and his 2002 Vendanges Tardives comes from the famous Kaefferkopf *lieu-dit*. It has a most agreeable straw yellow colour and a very fruity, somewhat overripe nose with subtle hints of white flowers and honey. The palate is remarkably well balanced, fresh and elegant, with a very long finish on fruity and floral flavours.
➦ Léon Heitzmann, 2, Grand-Rue, 68770 Ammerschwihr, tel. 03.89.47.10.64, fax 03.89.78.27.76 ☑
☾ ev. day except Sun. 8am–12 noon 1pm–6pm

JEAN HIRTZ ET FILS

Vendanges tardives 2000★★

| n.c. | 1,400 | ▮ | 15–23 € |

Mittelbergheim has a rich architectural heritage, and is equally well known for the quality of its terroirs, the very best of which is the Zotzenberg Grand Cru. This Vendanges Tardives comes from its marly limestone soils, which are very good for growing Gewurztraminer. It has a magnificent, golden yellow colour, and a whole range of fruit aromas including notes of overripeness, dried fruits and quince. The palate is full, fleshy, rich and rather heady, with a beautifully long, fresh finish on spice and crystallized fruit flavours. (Half-litre bottles)
➦ EARL du Rotland Jean Hirtz et Fils, 13, rue Rotland, 67140 Mittelbergheim, tel. 03.88.08.47.90,
fax 03.88.08.47.90 ☑
☾ ev. day 9am–12 noon 2pm–7pm

JEAN HUTTARD

Burgreben 2001★★

| 0.4 ha | 3,200 | ▮ ♦ | 5–8 € |

Fortified in the 13th century, the village of Zellenberg stands on a hill and overlooks its vineyard, which has been in existence at least since the 11th century. The castle's vines or "Burgreben" have produced this remarkable Gewurztraminer with powerful fruit and spice fragrances. It is supple, robust and full on the palate, which has a delightfully long finish on some slightly exotic fruit flavours and a fine but unmistakeable touch of bitterness. (Residual sugar: 15 g/l.)
➦ Jean Huttard, 10, rte du Vin, 68340 Zellenberg, tel. 03.89.47.90.49, fax 03.89.47.90.32 ☑
☾ ev. day except Mon. 9am–12 noon 2pm–6pm

JEAN GEILER

Vendanges tardives 2000★

| 7.98 ha | 36,950 | ▮ ♦ | 11–15 € |

A few kilometres west of Colmar lies Ingersheim, where the wine-producers' cooperative is now finishing the building work for its expansion. Visitors are received in a tasting cellar on the Route des Vins, which runs through the little town. One unusual sight here is a giant barrel, the largest in the Rhine valley with a capacity of 35,400 litres. The cooperative is offering an excellent Vendanges Tardives with no limits to its production. It has a magnificently intense, golden yellow colour, and powerful aromas of honey, spices, roses and quince. In keeping with this first impression the palate is balanced and harmonious, with a long finish and flavours in the same aromatic register as the nose.
➦ Cave vinicole d'Ingersheim, 45, rue de la République, 68040 Ingersheim, tel. 03.89.27.90.27, fax 03.89.27.90.30,
e-mail vin@geiler.fr ☑
☾ by appt.

DOM. JUX

Prestige 2001★

| n.c. | n.c. | ▮ ♦ | 11–15 € |

Since 1989 this estate on the Hardt de Colmar has belonged to the Wolfmar group, which is the largest wine-marketing organisation in Alsace. This Cuvée Prestige does them proud, with a brilliant gold colour, powerful, fruity aromas, and a rich, full-bodied, spicy palate with a slight note of freshness on the finish. (Residual sugar: 36 g/l.)
➦ Dom. Jux, 5, chem. de la Fecht, 68000 Colmar, tel. 03.89.79.13.76, fax 03.89.79.62.93 ☑

KIEFFER 2001★★

| 0.15 ha | 1,500 | | 8–11 € |

Itterswiller is a charming village that is famous for its award-winning floral decorations. Now a hotel, the Maison Kieffer contributes to this summer explosion of colour with over 300 geraniums on its half-timbered façade that cannot fail to stop visitors in their tracks. The estate's Gewurztraminer is also full of rich floral scents that it releases along with a touch of honey and overripe fruit. The palate is well balanced, supple and fresh, with remarkably good length. It should be kept for a year or two, and as a good accompaniment to fruit desserts. (Residual sugar: 20 g/l.)
➦ Jean-Charles Kieffer, 7, rte des Vins, 67140 Itterswiller, tel. 03.88.85.59.80, fax 03.88.57.81.44,
e-mail jean-charles-kieffer@wanadoo.fr ☑
☾ by appt.

KIENTZLER

Vendanges tardives 2000★★

| 0.5 ha | 1,130 | | 23–30 € |

André Kientzler is based at Ribeauvillé, a pretty little town overlooked by three castles. He has gained a worldwide reputation for his wines, 40% of which he exports. This Vendanges Tardives Gewurztraminer comes from a limestone-clay terroir and has a golden yellow colour and a nose that, although still restrained, already shows signs of good aromatic potential. The wine is much more expressive on the palate; well structured, full and rich, with a certain degree of roundness which is counter-balanced by its power. The finish is marked by crystallized fruit notes and a subtle hint of lychees. This 2000 has a great deal to offer, and should achieve a better balance if kept for a while.
➦ André Kientzler, 50, rte de Bergheim, 68150 Ribeauvillé, tel. 03.89.73.67.10, fax 03.89.73.35.81 ☑
☾ by appt.

L. KIRMANN

Vieilles Vignes 2001★★

	2 ha	2,000	🍷 ♦	8–11 €

The winemaker in this huge half-timbered house is also a book-seller and restaurateur! And as well as that, the estate organizes folk evenings in summer. Visitors to Au Fou d'Epfig can buy second-hand books, eat Alsatian specialities, and of course try the estate's wines, such as this 2001 Gewurztraminer with a nose of powerful, overripe citrus fruit aromas, and a well-structured, full-bodied palate whose freshness, balance, finesse and elegance make it a real delight. (Residual sugar: 15 g/l.)
• Dom. Kirmann, 6, rue des Alliés, 67680 Epfig, tel. 03.88.85.59.07, fax 03.88.85.56.41, e-mail contact@kirmann.com 🅥
☿ by appt.

ANDRE KLEINKNECHT

Sélection de grains nobles 2000★★★

	0.15 ha	1,200	🍷	23–30 €

Based in an old inn in the picturesque village of Mittel-bergheim, 2 km south of Barr, the Kleinknechts have been growing wine for seven generations. Their Sélection de Grains Nobles Gewurztraminer won the highest acclaim from the Jury. It shows its quality from the start with a deep gold colour, then explodes on the nose, releasing overripe fruit fragrances and very fine, elegant spicy notes. The palate is remarkably well structured, brimful with pineapple and lychee flavours, impressively full-bodied and very powerful, with a long finish on pepper and spice notes softened by acacia honey. (Half-litre bottles)
• André Kleinknecht, 45, rue Principale, 67140 Mittelbergheim, tel. 03.88.08.49.46, fax 03.88.08.49.46, e-mail andre.kleinknecht@wanadoo.fr 🅥
☿ ev. day 10am–11.30am 2pm–6pm; Sun. by appt.

CLEMENT KLUR

Vendanges tardives 2000★★

	0.8 ha	3,000	🍷🍷	15–23 €

Clément Klur belonged to an Alsace cooperative until 1999. Since then he has gone his own way and created a new type of cave, not a cooperative this time, but a round cellar which is completely underground to provide natural temperature control. This is where his superb Vendanges Tardives has been developed. It has a brilliant gold colour and an intense, elegant nose dominated by lychees. The remarkably full, velvety palate is embellished by very fresh, slightly lemony flavours along with subtle notes of white flowers and dried or crystallized fruits. There is a powerful, unusually long finish. One taster remarked: "This wine stands out from the crowd for its balance, richness and finesse".
• Clément Klur, 105, rue des Trois-Epis, 68230 Katzenthal, tel. 03.89.80.94.29, fax 03.89.27.30.17, e-mail info@klur.net 🅥 🏠 🏠
☿ ev. day 8am–12 noon 2pm–7pm

CLEMENT KLUR

Sélection de grains nobles 2000★

	0.6 ha	1,500	🍷🍷	23–30 €

Clément Klur has certainly produced some remarkable fine sweet wines in the 2000 vintage, because this Sélection de

Grains Nobles has also been very well received. It has a golden colour with green highlights, and opens on the nose with floral fragrances (roses and violets) before developing towards some exotic fruit notes (papaya, guava). There are fruit flavours right from the start on the palate, still in the exotic fruit range, with hints of lychee. This is a rich, full wine, with a long, well-balanced finish which shows real potential.
• Clément Klur, 105, rue des Trois-Epis, 68230 Katzenthal, tel. 03.89.80.94.29, fax 03.89.27.30.17, e-mail info@klur.net 🅥 🏠 🏠
☿ ev. day 8am–12 noon 2pm–7pm

KROSSFELDER

Vendanges tardives 2000★★

	n.c.	n.c.	🍷 ♦	15–23 €

The Krossfelder cooperative in Dambach-la-Ville is part of the Wolfberger group. Founded early in the 20th century, this is one of the oldest wine cooperatives in Alsace, along with Eguisheim. It still has an oak barrel cellar that dates back to its beginnings. This Vendanges Tardives Gewurztraminer has an intense, very elegant nose of fruit and spice aromas. Its full-bodied palate is rich and ample, with similar flavours to the aromas on the nose, and a long finish on subtle notes of spice. This is a charming wine of great distinction.
• Cave vinicole Krossfelder, 39, rue de la Gare, 67650 Dambach-la-Ville, tel. 03.88.92.40.03, fax 03.88.92.42.89 🅥
☿ by appt.

KUEHN

Sélection de grains nobles 2000★

	0.3 ha	5,100	🍷🍷🍷	23–30 €

Based in Ammerschwihr, one of the meccas of the Alsatian vineyard, Kuehn is part of the Ingersheim wine-producers' cooperative. It mainly uses grapes from its own vines, and with sole ownership of 11 ha is able to develop some very original wines. This 2000 is pale gold with very brilliant glints, and has fairly heavy aromas of honey and very ripe fruits. It is fine, quite rich and very full on the palate, which is enlivened by spice flavours (pepper) and already seems well integrated. (Half-litre bottles)
• SA Kuehn, 3, Grand-Rue, 68770 Ammerschwihr, tel. 03.89.78.23.16, fax 03.89.47.18.32, e-mail vin@kuehn.fr 🅥
☿ ev. day except Sat. Sun. 8am–12 noon 1.30pm–5pm

FRANCOIS LICHTLE

Réserve personnelle 2001★

	0.32 ha	2,400	🍷	8–11 €

Perched at an altitude of 380 m, the village of Husseren is at the highest point in the Alsatian vineyard. It is overlooked by the keeps of Eguisheim's three castles, Weckmund, Wahlenbourg and Dagsbourg. François Lichtlé set up business here in 1992, and has now produced this Réserve Personnelle with a wide range of floral, exotic fruit and honey aromas. With its full body and fruity finish, this is a wine of character. (Residual sugar: 8 g/l.)
• Dom. François Lichtlé, 17, rue des Vignerons, 68420 Husseren-les-Châteaux, tel. 03.89.49.31.34, fax 03.89.49.37.51, e-mail hlichtle@aol.com 🅥 🏠
☿ by appt.

JEROME LORENTZ FILS

Cuvée des Templiers 2001★★

	4.3 ha	30,000		8–11 €

Lorentz is a long-established wine concern in Bergheim, a charming little fortified town where it is sole owner of a 32-hectare vineyard, and also operates as a winemerchants. Once again its Cuvée de Templiers has been singled out by the judges, who were extremely impressed by the 2001 vintage. It comes from a limestone-clay terroir, and has a strong golden yellow colour and very appealing rose fragrances. These floral notes reappear on the palate, which is powerful and well structured, with a long finish. (Residual sugar: 13 g/l.)
• Jérôme Lorentz, 1–3, rue des Vignerons, 68750 Bergheim, tel. 03.89.73.22.22, fax 03.89.73.30.49 🅥
☿ ev. day except Sun. 10am–12 noon 12pm–6.30pm

RENE MEYER Croix du Pfoeller Vieilles
Vignes Cuvée Martin 2001★

| | 0.6 ha | 4,500 | ⅏ | 8–11 € |

This 8.3-hectare estate has been run since 1999 by Jean-Paul Meyer. Produced from 45-year-old vines, this *cuvée* also comes from a limestone-clay terroir, which generally helps to produce well-structured wines. It has a delightful nose of somewhat exotic fresh fruit aromas. After a supple attack, the wine asserts itself richly and powerfully on the palate, which has a long, agreeable finish. (Residual sugar: 35 g/l.)
� EARL René Meyer et Fils, 14, Grand-Rue, 68230 Katzenthal, tel. 03.89.27.04.67, fax 03.89.27.50.59, e-mail domaine.renemeyer@wanadoo.fr ☑
☒ by appt.

DENIS MEYER
Vendanges tardives 2000★★

| | 0.25 ha | 1,800 | | 15–23 € |

Denis Meyer is descended from a long line of winemakers going back to 1761, and now cultivates just over 8 ha of vines. His two daughters, Patricia and Valérie, are due to join him in the near future. The property has often been singled out in the *Guide* for its sweet wines, and this one has been particularly well received. It is a very brilliant, golden yellow, and although the nose still seems closed, it is already releasing some overripe scents (acacia honey with a touch of liquorice) that show its aromatic potential. The palate is full, unctuous and very full-bodied, with a long finish on lychee and crystallized fruit notes.
� Denis Meyer, 2, rte du Vin, 68420 Voegtlinshoffen, tel. 03.89.49.38.00, fax 03.89.49.26.52, e-mail vins.denis.meyer@terre-net.fr ☑
☒ by appt.

MEYER-FONNE
Kaefferkopf 2001★

| | 0.3 ha | 1,900 | | 11–15 € |

François and Félix Meyer work as a father-and-son team in their traditional 17th century cellar, where the emphasis is on very long fermentation and maturation on fine lees. This 2001 from the famous Kaefferkopf has been matured for 11 months, and has a golden yellow colour and a very intense, fruity nose combining ripe fruit aromas with overripe and spicy notes. The palate is rich, unctuous and very full-bodied. (Residual sugar: 30 g/l.)
� Meyer-Fonné, 24, Grand-Rue, 68230 Katzenthal, tel. 03.89.27.16.50, fax 03.89.27.34.17 ☑
☒ by appt.

DOM. DU MOULIN DE DUSENBACH
Kaefferkopf 2001★★

| | 0.7 ha | 5,600 | ⅏ | 11–15 € |

This used to be an oil mill, but now Bernard Schwach makes wine here. It was in 1976 that he set up his estate, which consists of 25 ha of vines divided over several communes. This powerful Gewurztraminer comes from the famous Kaefferkopf terroir at Ammerschwihr. The judges were highly impressed by its strikingly fruity nose of subtle exotic fruit aromas and its rich, sweet, agreeable palate, which has a very full body and a long finish. It will go well with a Roquefort and fig *feuilleté* with honey sauce, or with créme brûlée. (Residual sugar: 40 g/l.)
� GAEC Bernard Schwach, 25, rte de Sainte-Marie-aux-Mines, 68150 Ribeauvillé, tel. 03.89.73.72.18, fax 03.89.73.30.34, e-mail bernard.schwach@wanadoo.fr ☑
☒ by appt.

ERNEST PREISS
Cuvée particulière 2001★

| | n.c. | 30,000 | | 11–15 € |

This wine has a somewhat restrained nose of floral notes with some fine hints of spice. Its delicate fruity character opens out on a more assertive palate that is well structured, full-bodied and powerful. The balance is excellent. (Residual sugar: 10.5 g/l.)

� Ernest Preiss, BP 3, 68340 Riquewihr, tel. 03.89.47.91.21, fax 03.89.47.98.90 ☑
☒ by appt.

A. REGIN 2001★

| | 0.8 ha | 4,400 | ⅃ ⅃ | 5–8 € |

Wolxheim is located on the northern part of the Route des Vins. In the Middle Ages, its vineyards were cultivated by many monasteries in Wissembourg and Strasbourg, and in the 19th century its wines were very popular with Napoleon Bonaparte and Napoleon III. This 2001 starts with floral aromas which indicate that it is a very typical, no-nonsense Gewurztraminer. The palate has good balance, an average structure, and a finish on fruit and spice flavours. This is an excellent, classic wine. (Residual sugar: 17.5 g/l.)
� André Regin, 2, rue Principale, 67120 Wolxheim, tel. 03.88.38.17.02, fax 03.88.38.17.02, e-mail regin.andre@free.fr ☑
☒ by appt.

LA CAVE DES RENARDS 2001★★

| | 1.24 ha | 1,000 | | 5–8 € |

Since her husband's death in 1992, Jacqueline Fuchs has been running the family estate, which all in all has 5.5 ha of vines. This wine comes from a marly limestone terroir, and starts with some fine, floral notes before opening out on intense, elegant, fruity aromas. Its structure and good length on the palate give it a sense of richness, and the balance is excellent. (Residual sugar: 10 g/l.)
� Dom. André Fuchs, 19, rue de la 1re-Armée, La Cave des Renards, 68240 Sigolsheim, tel. 03.89.47.12.21, fax 03.89.47.12.21 ☑
☒ by appt.

EDMOND RENTZ 2001★

| | 2 ha | 18,000 | ⅏ | 5–8 € |

Like a number of old Alsace properties, this one (dating back to 1785) still has 100-year-old barrels in its cellars. Nowadays the estate has 20 ha of vines. Its Gewurztraminer has the very fine fruit aromas that are typical of the grape variety, and a particularly elegant palate with very good balance and a finish on notes of honey. (Residual sugar: 30 g/l.)
� Dom. Edmond Rentz, 7, rte du Vin, 68340 Zellenberg, tel. 03.89.47.90.17, fax 03.89.47.97.27, e-mail edmond.rentz1@fnac.net ☑
☒ ev. day except Sun. 8am–12 noon 2pm–6pm

RIEFLE
Vendanges tardives 2000★

| | 1 ha | 5,000 | | 23–30 € |

Driving along the RN 83 between Pfaffenheim and Rouffach, you will see the Rieflé estate on your right. This very large property (22 ha) is very often singled out for high praise in the *Guide*. Its 2000 Vendanges Tardives has a very brilliant, golden straw yellow colour, and a nose that already seems remarkably expressive with its fragrances of honey and overripe or crystallized fruits. The palate is powerful, rich, very round, well balanced and harmonious, with a delightfully fine, unusually long finish on notes of dried fruits.
� Dom. Rieflé, 11, pl. de la Mairie, 68250 Pfaffenheim, tel. 03.89.78.52.21, fax 03.89.49.50.98, e-mail riefle@riefle.com ☑ ♨
☒ ev. day except Sun. 9am–12 noon 1pm–6.30pm

WILLY ROLLI-EDEL
Brandhurst de Bergheim 2001★

| | 0.53 ha | 2,100 | | 8–11 € |

Willy Rolli has been running this eleven-hectare family estate since 1981. His Brandhurst de Bergheim Gewurztraminer comes from overripe grapes grown on a limestone-clay terroir, and this has given it a complex nose of citrus fruit and spice aromas. It has plenty of intensity on the palate, which is round and warming, but at the same time enlivened by a slight touch of freshness. (Residual sugar: 41.6 g/l.)
� Willy Rolli-Edel, 5, rue de l'Eglise, 68590 Rorschwihr, tel. 03.89.73.63.26, fax 03.89.73.83.50 ☑
☒ by appt.

DOM. RUNNER 2001★

| | 1.12 ha | 9,000 | ◧ | 5–8 € |

Right at the centre of Pfaffenheim stands its church, which despite the damage inflicted on it in the Second World War still has its beautiful late Romanesque chancel. The architectural style is powerfully expressive, and so is this Gewurztraminer, whose intense, rather spicy aromas, strikingly fruity palate, good overall balance and agreeable finish make it altogether a highly satisfying wine. (Residual sugar: 10 g/l.)

➤ Dom. François Runner et Fils, 1, rue de la Liberté, 68250 Pfaffenheim, tel. 03.89.49.62.89, fax 03.89.49.73.69 ☑ ☗
☖ ev. day 8am–12 noon 1pm–7pm; groups by appt.

DOM. SAINT-REMY

Réserve 2001★

| | 0.49 ha | 4,800 | | 5–8 € |

This wine has a lovely range of fresh aromas, embellished by some spicy notes. It opens out fully on an ample, elegant palate whose pleasant, fruity flavours and slight hints of pepper linger on to a long finish. (Residual sugar: 22 g/l.)

➤ François et Philippe Ehrhart, 6, rue Saint-Rémy, 68920 Wettolsheim, tel. 03.89.80.60.57, fax 03.89.79.74.00, e-mail vins@domainesaintremy.com ☑ ☗
☖ ev. day except Sun. 8am–12 noon 1.30pm–6.30pm

SCHEIDECKER

Réserve 2001★

| | 0.2 ha | 2,000 | ▮ ♣ | 8–11 € |

Based in Mittelwihr near Riquewihr, this family vineyard (founded in 1954) has been run since 1990 by Philippe Scheidecker. He is now offering a lovely Gewurztraminer with a characteristic nose of fresh roses and acacia honey. The palate is round and full, with spicy flavours and an agreeably long finish. (Residual sugar: 20 g/l.)

➤ Philippe Scheidecker-Zimmerlin, 13, rue des Merles, 68630 Mittelwihr, tel. 03.89.49.01.29, fax 03.89.49.06.63 ☑
☖ by appt.

A. SCHERER

Holzweg 2001★★★

| | 0.4 ha | 2,000 | ◧ | 8–11 € |

Founded in 1780 and run since 1980 by Christophe Scherer, this estate is deeply rooted in Alsatian tradition, but at the same time shows that it is forward-looking by exporting 80% of its output. Its wines are very often singled out in the *Guide*, and have more than once been awarded a *coup de coeur*. This limestone-clay plot on the Holzweg has produced several well-received vintages in the past, but with this golden yellow 2001 it has soared to new heights. The Jury were bowled over by its fine, intense, floral notes both on the nose and one the palate, and by its extraordinarily long and aromatic finish. "Just the sort of Gewurztraminer everyone loves!" enthused one taster.

➤ Vignoble A. Scherer, 12, rte du Vin, BP 4, 68420 Husseren-les-Châteaux, tel. 03.89.49.30.33, fax 03.89.49.27.48,
e-mail contact@a-scherer.com ☑ ☗
☖ ev. day except Sun. 8am–12 noon 1pm–6pm

THIERRY SCHERRER

Cuvée de l'An 2001 2001★

| | 0.2 ha | 1,000 | | 11–15 € |

We have seen plenty of wines in the 2000 vintage, but not so many that are dedicated to the first year of the new millennium. This 2001 Gewurztraminer has been produced by Thierry Scherrer, an oenologist and winemaker who took over his family's estate at Ammerschwihr in 1993. The wine opens on floral notes that develop towards exotic fruit aromas. It is both fresh and warming on the palate, which does not have a particularly long finish but nevertheless makes a very pleasant impression. (Residual sugar: 50 g/l.)

➤ Thierry Scherrer, 1, rue de la Gare, 68770 Ammerschwihr, tel. 03.89.47.15.86, fax 03.89.47.15.86,
e-mail thierry.scherrer@wanadoo.fr ☑ ☗ ☗
☖ by appt.

DOM. PIERRE SCHILLE

Vogelgarten 2001★

| | 0.37 ha | 3,050 | ▮ ♣ | 8–11 € |

This estate was founded in 1954 by Pierre Schillé, who handed it on to his son Christophe in 1990. His wines are marketed largely in Ile-de-France. This Gewurztraminer has spicy aromas mingled with slight hints of exotic fruits (lychees), and a palate that is both powerful and elegant, with lovely fruit flavours and quite a long finish. (Residual sugar: 24 g/l.)

➤ Pierre Schillé et Fils, 14, rue du Stade, 68240 Sigolsheim, tel. 03.89.47.10.67, fax 03.89.47.39.12 ☑
☖ by appt.

SCHILLINGER

Cuvée Emilie 2001★★

| | 0.4 ha | 2,800 | | 11–15 € |

Gueberschwihr's tall, Romanesque church tower with windows on three levels has symbolic significance for a village once owned by the bishops of Basle and Strasbourg, who were very fond of the wines from its vineyard. This one is somewhat closed on the nose, but does release some elegant notes of peaches and exotic fruits. The palate is supple and round, with a very pleasant, long finish. (Residual sugar: 50 g/l.)

➤ EARL Emile Schillinger, 2, rue de la Chapelle, 68420 Gueberschwihr, tel. 03.89.47.91.59, fax 03.89.47.91.75 ☑
☖ ev. day 8am–12 noon 2pm–7pm

DOM. SCHIRMER

Weingarten Cuvée Antoine 2001★

| | 0.25 ha | 1,500 | ▮ | 8–11 € |

At the heart of the Vallée Noble lies Soultzmatt, a pretty little village known for its mineral water and very high-class wines. Coming from a clay and sandstone terroir, this Gewurztraminer opens timidly on some floral notes, then asserts itself fully on the palate, which is clean, ample, powerful and spicy, with a delightfully round finish. (Residual sugar: 25 g/l.)

➤ Dom. Lucien Schirmer et Fils, 22, rue de la Vallée, 68570 Soultzmatt, tel. 03.89.47.03.82, fax 03.89.47.02.33 ☑
☖ ev. day 8am–12 noon 1pm–7pm

DAMIEN SCHLEGEL

Sélection de grains nobles 2000★★★

| | 0.27 ha | 2,000 | ▮ | 38–46 € |

Damien Schlegel's estate is at Westhalten, at the foot of the Zinnkoepflé. This limestone hill has a dry microclimate, and is home to animal and plant species normally found near the Mediterranean. The label on this Gewurztraminer actually shows a type of wild orchid that can be found on this hilly ground – a rare plant to illustrate a precious wine. This golden yellow Sélection de Grains Nobles has a whole range of impressively intense, honey-coated crystallized citrus fruit and raisin aromas. The palate is complex, heady, rich and full, but even so gives an impression of lightness. There is a very long finish, enlivened by hints of fruit and in particular of crystallized oranges. This wine will have achieved its full balance in two or three years' time.

➤ Damien Schlegel, 28, rue de la Liberté, 68250 Westhalten, tel. 03.89.47.01.29, fax 03.89.47.01.29,
e-mail damienschlegel@aol.com ☑ ☗
☖ by appt.

DOM. MAURICE SCHOECH

Vendanges tardives 2000★★★

	0.5 ha	2,900	23–30 €

The Schoech estate is at Ammerschwihr, the largest wine-producing commune in the Haut-Rhin, and the one where the Confrérie Saint-Etienne was revived in 1947. This Vendanges Tardives will make an excellent ambassador for Alsatian wine. It has a very bright, golden yellow colour, and releases white flower scents, then some acacia honey notes, and finally some crystallized fruit aromas. There is perfect balance on the palate, which is powerful, full and unctuous, with just the right amount of richness, a great deal of finesse, and a very long, subtle finish on the same aromatic notes as the nose.
➤ Dom. Maurice Schoech, 4, rte de Kientzheim, 68770 Ammerschwihr, tel. 03.89.78.25.78, fax 03.89.78.13.66 ◪
Ⴠ ev. day except Sun. 9am–12 noon 1.30pm–6pm

EDMOND SCHUELLER 2001★

	0.4 ha	2,400	8–11 €

Damien Schueller's estate is at Husseren-les-Châteaux, a perched village whose history is undoubtedly linked to the construction of the three castles at Eguisheim that overlook the commune. This is only a four-hectare vineyard, but it produces good wines like this 2001. It has fine, fruity, fresh elegant aromas and a powerfully structured, very full-bodied palate with slight touches of spice on a long finish. (Residual sugar: 10 g/l.)
➤ Damien Schueller, 26, rte du Vin, 68420 Husseren-les-Châteaux, tel. 03.89.49.32.60, fax 03.89.49.32.60,
e-mail damienschueller@aol.com ◪ 🏠 🏠
Ⴠ by appt.

SEILLY

Schenkenberg Vieilles Vignes 2001★

	1.7 ha	7,000	11–15 €

This estate is at Obernai, a charming town with beautiful Renaissance architecture. Its 2001 Gewurztraminer comes from 50-year-old vines, and makes you dream of far-off places with its notes of fruits and crystallized fruits, spices, honey and roses: a very rich aromatic range indeed. These overripe flavours combine with a supple structure to make this a very well-balanced wine.
➤ Dom. Seilly, 18, rue du Gal-Gouraud, 67210 Obernai, tel. 03.88.95.55.80, fax 03.88.95.54.00,
e-mail info@seilly.fr ◪ 🏠
Ⴠ ev. day 8am–12 noon 1.30pm–6pm; Sat. Sun. by appt.

RENE SIMONIS

Kaefferkopf 2001★★

	0.3 ha	1,500	8–11 €

Descended from a long line of winemakers going back to the 17th century, Etienne Simonis took over from his father René in 1996. The vineyard is at Ammerschwihr, a wine commune famous for the Kaefferkopf lieu-dit which has produced this remarkable Gewurztraminer. This wine has the characteristic aromas of the grape variety, but is also marked by overripeness. The palate is full, rich and powerful, and has a range of spicy

flavours with some floral notes. It is a well-integrated wine with a good, long finish. (Residual sugar: 45 g/l.)
➤ René et Etienne Simonis, 2, rue des Moulins, 68770 Ammerschwihr, tel. 03.89.47.30.79, fax 03.89.78.24.10 ◪
Ⴠ by appt.

JEAN SIPP

Vieilles Vignes 2001★

	1 ha	5,000	11–15 €

This 20-hectare estate, run since 1973 by Jean Sipp, is based in a Renaissance house which was once the home of the lords of Ribeauvillé, the Ribeaupierres. Coming from vines that are 30–50 years old, this 2001 gradually opens on to complex aromas of slightly overripe fruit. The full, elegant palate is enlivened on the finish by some spicy notes. This wine should be served as an aperitif, or with foie gras or perhaps some Munster cheese. (Residual sugar: 40 g/l.)
➤ Dom. Jean Sipp, 60, rue de la Fraternité, 68150 Ribeauvillé, tel. 03.89.73.60.02, fax 03.89.73.82.38, e-mail domaine@jean-sipp.com ◪ 🏠
Ⴠ by appt.

PHILIPPE SOHLER

Vendanges tardives 2000★

	0.16 ha	1,000	15–23 €

The one-street village of Nothalten stretches out along the Route des Vins, and is overlooked by the hills whose granitic sand soils have produced this Vendanges Tardives. The wine clearly bears the stamp of its terroir; it has a deep golden colour, intense aromas of crystallized and exotic fruits, and more overripe mango notes on the middle palate, which is powerful and very full, leading on to a long, spicy finish. This wine needs to be kept for a while before it can be enjoyed to the full.
➤ Dom. Philippe Sohler, 80A, rte des Vins, 67680 Nothalten, tel. 03.88.92.49.89, fax 03.88.92.49.89 ◪
Ⴠ by appt.

PAUL SPANNAGEL

Vignoble de Katzenthal 2001★★

	0.7 ha	7,000	8–11 €

The square keep of the Wineck is surrounded by vines, and overlooks the little valley, at the bottom of which nestles the village of Katzenthal, highly reputed for its wines since the 13th century. This Gewurztraminer starts with a somewhat closed nose of restrained fruit aromas, then explodes on to a full palate with very pronounced fruit flavours and a delightful freshness which is well integrated with the sweetness of the wine. (Residual sugar: 38 g/l.)
➤ EARL Paul Spannagel et Fils, 1, Grand-Rue, 68230 Katzenthal, tel. 03.89.27.01.70, fax 03.89.27.45.93, e-mail paul.spannagel@wanadoo.fr ◪
Ⴠ ev. day except Sun. 8am–12 noon 2pm–7pm; groups by appt.

E. SPANNAGEL ET FILS

Altenbourg 2001★★

	0.15 ha	1,500	5–8 €

Since 1995, Rémy Spannagel has been cultivating a little hillside plot of just 1.5 ha, where all the work is carried out manually. This wine made an excellent impression on the judges, who saluted the complexity of its characteristic, fine, intensely fruity aromas, and its power on the palate, which brims with highly subtle flavours and has a very long finish. This is a thoroughbred wine. (Residual sugar: 12 g/l.)
➤ Eugène Spannagel et Fils, 11, rue de Cussac, 68240 Sigolsheim, tel. 03.89.78.25.90, fax 03.89.78.25.90, e-mail remy.spannagel@free.fr ◪
Ⴠ by appt.

MICHELE AND JEAN-LUC STOECKLE

Cuvée réservée 2001★

	0.96 ha	8,000	5–8 €

Michèle and Jean-Luc Stoeckle aim to produce wines which are characteristic, no-nonsense, and within most people's budget. Every year 3,000 customers come here to buy their

wines. This Cuvée Réservée has an expressive nose of fruit, toast and spice aromas, and a well-balanced palate combining power, freshness and flavour to ensure a delightfully long finish. (Residual sugar: 12 g/l.)
➥ Michèle et Jean-Luc Stoecklé, 9, Grand-Rue, 68230 Katzenthal, tel. 03.89.27.05.08, fax 03.89.27.33.61 ☑ ☎
Ⓨ ev. day 8am–12 noon 1pm–7pm

ANTOINE STOFFEL 2001★★

| | 0.8 ha | 4,800 | ⑪ | 5–8 € |

Built around its castle in this lush green mountain-foot wine-growing area, the "round town" of Eguisheim is one of the most picturesque in Alsace, with its narrow streets of little houses beautifully decorated with flowers. Many winemakers have chosen to live here, including Antoine Stoffel, who moved to the commune about 40 years ago. He has now produced an excellent 2001 Gewurztraminer with rich, intense floral notes that are enlivened by freshness on a well-balanced palate with a most agreeable finish. This is a very harmonious wine. (Residual sugar: 10.2 g/l.)
➥ Antoine Stoffel, 21, rue de Colmar, 68420 Eguisheim, tel. 03.89.41.32.03, fax 03.89.24.92.07 ☑ ☎
Ⓨ ev. day except Sun. 8am–12 noon 2pm–6pm

ANDRE THOMAS ET FILS

Sélection de grains nobles 2000★

| | 0.4 ha | 600 | | 23–30 € |

This six-hectare vineyard is often singled out in the *Guide*, and is now moving over to organic methods. It has produced an excellent Sélection de Grains Nobles with a brilliant straw yellow colour and an expressive nose dominated by crystallized fruit aromas with hints of toast. The palate is already well-balanced, and has a complex range of crystallized and dried fruit flavours.
➥ André Thomas et Fils, 3, rue des Seigneurs, 68770 Ammerschwihr, tel. 03.89.47.16.60, fax 03.89.47.37.22 ☑ ☎
Ⓨ by appt.

CH. WAGENBOURG

Sélection de grains nobles 2000★

| | 0.5 ha | 1,800 | ▮ | 23–30 € |

This family has been making wine at Soultzmatt for nearly four centuries now. Since 1905 the vineyard has been based in and around the Château Wagenbourg, an impressive building that visitors can admire while paying a visit to the Kleins. Their Sélection de Grains Nobles has a golden yellow colour with brilliant orange glints. It is still somewhat closed on the nose, which has a mixture of fig, date and walnut aromas. The same sort of notes reappear on the palate, along with a slight hint of caramel. This is a well-balanced wine, with plenty of good flavour on a long finish.
➥ Joseph et Jacky Klein, Ch. Wagenbourg, 25, rue de la Vallée, 68570 Soultzmatt, tel. 03.89.47.01.41, fax 03.89.47.65.61 ☑ ☎
Ⓨ ev. day except Sun. 8am–12 noon 1.30pm–7pm

DOM. WEINBACH

Altenbourg Cuvée Laurence 2001★★

| | 1 ha | 4,200 | ⑪ | 30–38 € |

Colette Faller and her daughters Catherine and Laurence run the Weinbach estate and its vineyard, the Clos des Capucins, which is a landmark in Alsace and is cultivated organically. The Cuvée Laurence is a Gewurztraminer grown on the marly limestone and sandstone terroir of the Altenbourg. This 2001 has an intense golden colour and a powerful nose with a wide range of aromas combining floral and spicy notes with fresh and dried fruits. Its roundness on the palate does not detract from its refined balance. With its excellent structure and high-quality, harmonious character, this is a great wine. (Residual sugar: 50 g/l.)
➥ Colette Faller et ses Filles, Dom. Weinbach, Clos des Capucins, 68240 Kaysersberg, tel. 03.89.47.13.21, fax 03.89.47.38.18, e-mail contact@domaineweinbach.com ☑
Ⓨ by appt.

WELTY

Cuvée Aurélie 2001★

| | 0.5 ha | 2,500 | ▮ ﹖ | 8–11 € |

Wine has been made here since 1738. Built in 1579, the historic cellar was once a tithe barn, and is worth visiting for its architecture as well as its wines. This 2001 has fruit aromas that are still somewhat restrained, and a supple, powerful, slightly overripe palate. This is a promising wine, which should open out over the months to come. (Residual sugar: 29 g/l.)
➥ Dom. Jean-Michel Welty, 22–24, Grand-Rue, 68500 Orschwihr, tel. 03.89.76.09.03, fax 03.89.76.16.80, e-mail jean-michel.welty@terre-net.fr ☑ ☎ ☎
Ⓨ ev. day 8.30am–11.30am 1.30pm–6.30pm; Sun. by appt.

W. WURTZ 2001★

| | 0.4 ha | 2,000 | | 8–11 € |

This pale yellow Gewurztraminer starts on the nose with a surprising little mineral note along with the floral aromas. On the palate it is fresh, fruity, well-balanced, full and easy to drink, finishing on a touch of spice. (Residual sugar: 15 g/l.)
➥ GAEC Willy Wurtz et Fils, 6, rue du Bouxhof, 68630 Mittelwihr, tel. 03.89.47.93.16, fax 03.89.47.89.01 ☑
Ⓨ ev. day 9am–7pm

WYMANN

Vieilles Vignes 2001★★★

| | 5.24 ha | 2,410 | ▮ | 8–11 € |

Founded in 1946, this property in the upper part of Ribeauvillé originally just grew grapes to sell, then sold its wine in bulk. That goes to show how far they have come. Xavier Wymann, who took over the estate in 1996, is interested in the relationship between the soil, the vine and the wine. His Vieilles Vignes Gewurztraminer comes from 40-year-old vines, and makes a delightful first impression with a whole range of citrus fruit, pineapple and crystallized fruit aromas. With its good balance between sweetness and freshness on a full palate with a long finish, this wine has clearly been produced from very high-quality grapes. It will go well with foie gras and some desserts, and can also be served as an aperitif. (Residual sugar: 52.6 g/l.)
➥ Dom. Xavier Wymann, 41, rue de la Fraternité, 68150 Ribeauvillé, tel. 03.89.73.66.83, fax 03.89.73.66.83 ☑
Ⓨ by appt.

Wines selected but not starred

CHARLES SCHLERET

Sélection de grains nobles 2000

| | 0.87 ha | 7,000 | ▮ ﹖ | 23–30 € |

➥ Charles Schleret, 1–3, rte d'Ingersheim, 68230 Turckheim, tel. 03.89.27.06.09, fax 03.89.27.06.09 ☑
Ⓨ ev. day 9am–7pm; Sun. 10am–12 noon

Alsace Tokay-Pinot Gris

Pinot Gris has been known locally as Tokay d'Alsace for over four centuries. This is quite astonishing, because it is a variety that has never been grown in eastern Hungary (famous for Tokay). Legend has it, however, that Tokay was brought back to Alsace by General L. de Schwendi, who was the owner of a substantial vineyard in Alsace. The original area in which it was grown belonged to the historic Duchy of Burgundy, as did all the areas where Pinot is grown.

Pinot Gris is planted on 10% of the vineyard and produces a full-bodied, heavy, fine wine, which can easily be substituted for red wine to accompany meat dishes. At its most sumptuous, as it was in 1983, 1989 and 1990, which were exceptional vintages, it is one of the best possible accompaniments for foie gras.

ANDRE ACKERMANN

Sélection de grains nobles 2000★

	0.8 ha	n.c.	🍶	15–23 €

Rorschwihr is a small wine-producing town between Bergheim and Saint-Hippolyte. There is a wealth of different terroirs here, most of which have limestone-clay or marly clay soils and a south-to-southeastern aspect, and are therefore particularly good for growing Pinot Gris. This Sélection de Grains Nobles has a limpid golden yellow colour and exotic mango aromas with a slight hint of smoke, followed by flavours of crystallized fruit (oranges) then lychees on the palate. The wine is still dominated by sweetness, which fortunately is counterbalanced by a very decent level of acidity. There is a delightfully fine finish on some more fruity, orange peel notes. If kept for a while this 2000 will become better integrated. (Half-litre bottles)
🍷 EARL André Ackermann, 25, rte du Vin, 68590 Rorschwihr, tel. 03.89.73.63.87, fax 03.89.73.38.16 ☑ 🏠 🏠
🍸 by appt.

DOM. PIERRE ADAM

Katzenstegel Cuvée Théo 2001★

	0.6 ha	4,000	🍶	11–15 €

Founded after the Second World War, this estate started with just 1 ha and has now increased its area more than tenfold to 11 ha. It has its offices in the middle of the vineyard heading in the Kaysersberg direction, and grows its vines by sustainable agriculture methods. This Cuvée Théo has a nose of honey and smoke aromas, and a very round, rich palate that tends towards sweetness but nonetheless shows great elegance and finesse. This wine has good ageing potential, and will be best served as an aperitif or with foie gras. (Residual sugar:18 g/l.)
🍷 Dom. Pierre Adam, 8, rue du Lt-Louis-Mourier, 68770 Ammerschwihr, tel. 03.89.78.23.07, fax 03.89.47.39.68, e-mail info@domaine-adam.com ☑ 🏠 🏠
🍸 ev. day 8am–12 noon 1pm–7pm

DOM. ALLIMANT-LAUGNER

Sélection de grains nobles 2000★

	0.68 ha	7,400	🍶	15–23 €

Orschwiller is the last Bas-Rhin commune you will come to as you head towards Haut-Koenigsbourg. It is surrounded by its vineyard, which is planted mainly on granitic soils but sometimes on gneiss. These rather light terroirs produce wines that open out quite quickly, as in the case of this sweet Pinot Gris. It has an intense, golden colour and a nose of crystallized fruit aromas with a slight hint of dried banana. The palate is particularly pleasant, offering very concentrated fruity flavours within a well-balanced acidic structure. There is a very long finish on dried and crystallized fruit notes. This wine is ready to be enjoyed straight away. (Half-litre bottles)
🍷 Allimant-Laugner, 10, Grand-Rue, 67600 Orschwiller, tel. 03.88.92.06.52, fax 03.88.82.76.38, e-mail alaugner@terre-net.fr ☑ 🏠
🍸 ev. day except Sun. 9am–7pm
🍷 Hubert Laugner

DOM. BARMES-BUECHER

Rosenberg de Wettolsheim Bas de Coteau 2001★

	0.7 ha	3,200	🍶🍶	15–23 €

This estate was formed by an alliance between two old wine-making families, and has now gone over to organic methods. It has a large, 16-hectare vineyard near Colmar, and can therefore use a variety of terroirs. This Pinot Gris comes from the limestone-clay slopes of the nearby Vosges foothills. It has a slightly amber yellow colour and leaves tears on the glass, showing from the start what a rich wine it is. The nose has fruit and pepper notes with a little touch of oak that fits like a glove, and the palate does indeed have exceptional richness, underlined by some overripe fruit and honey aromas. The finish is pleasantly fresh. This wine will be an ideal accompaniment to foie gras. (Residual sugar: 43 g/l.)
🍷 Dom. Barmès-Buecher, 30, rue Sainte-Gertrude, 68920 Wettolsheim, tel. 03.89.80.62.92, fax 03.89.79.30.80, e-mail barmes-buecher@terre-net.fr ☑
🍸 by appt.

DOM. BERNHARD-REIBEL

Rittersberg 2001★

	0.5 ha	2,700	🍶🍶	11–15 €

This estate was started at the beginning of the 1980s by Cécile Bernhard, who was joined by her son there in 2002. Located near Sélestat, it has a large vineyard (nearly 18 ha) planted on the granitic slopes of the nearby Vosges foothills, or on the gravelly alluvial cone of the Giessen. This Pinot Gris comes from a *lieu-dit* with a granitic soil and a very good due-south-facing aspect. It has a golden yellow colour with brilliant highlights, and leaves tears in the glass. The attack is both fresh and round, showing that this is a powerful wine made from top-quality grapes, and the finish is very long. This wine has good prospects for the future, and will soon have found its full balance. (Residual sugar: 28 g/l.)
🍷 Dom. Bernhard-Reibel, 20, rue de Lorraine, 67730 Châtenois, tel. 03.88.82.04.21, fax 03.88.82.59.65, e-mail bernhard-reibel@wanadoo.fr ☑
🍸 by appt.

LUCIEN BRAND

Kefferberg 2001★★

	1 ha	5,000		8–11 €

Lucien Brand is based at Ergersheim, one of the 19 communes in the "Golden Crown" near Strasbourg. He grows 9 ha of vines, and with this Tokay has produced a wine of exquisite sensitivity. Its colour is a pale yellow with green glints, and although the nose is not yet open, it is already releasing just a touch of the characteristic Pinot Gris smoky aroma, along with refined hints of crystallized fruits. The clean attack is supported by a pleasant freshness, after which exotic fruit notes assert themselves quickly on a full-bodied palate with a long, lingering finish. This is a highly promising wine that should be more fully open in a year or two from now. It will go well with many types of food, such as foie gras, exotic dishes and fish.
🍷 Dom. Lucien Brand, 71, rue de Wolxheim, 67120 Ergersheim, tel. 03.88.38.17.71, fax 03.88.38.72.85, e-mail fbrand7173@wanadoo.fr ☑
🍸 by appt.

EBLIN-FUCHS

Vieilles Vignes 2001★

	0.6 ha	3,500	🍶🍶	5–8 €

This estate came into being when two long-established families united here in Zellenberg, right at the heart of the Route des Vins region. They have a great passion for exploring their double family tree – the Eblins going back to 1294, the Fuchs to 1615 – but at the same time make sure to take very good care of their 8 ha of vines. This wine comes from a small Pinot Gris plot, and has a straw yellow colour and a nose that opens quickly on to intense notes of dried and crystallized fruit. It makes a clean first impression on the palate, whose delightful flavours grow increasingly powerful and carry on to a long finish. This is a well-balanced Tokay with very classic aromas. (Residual sugar: 15 g/l.)
🍷 Christian et Joseph Eblin, 19, rte des Vins, 68340 Zellenberg, tel. 03.89.47.91.14, fax 03.89.49.05.12 ☑ 🏠
🍸 by appt.

DOM. DE L'ECOLE
Côte de Rouffach 2001★

	n.c.	3,000	🍶 ♦	5–8 €

Many wine professionals in Alsace train at the viticultural college in Rouffach, which has a 13-hectare vineyard and a cellar where the students make their debut as winemakers. They have certainly put all their know-how into this Pinot Gris; it has a dense, gold colour and an intense, very smoky nose opening out on to mineral notes. The palate is full-bodied, deep and well balanced, finishing on flavours of dried fruit and honey. This wine has very good length, and can be served both as an aperitif and with food. (Residual sugar: 21 g/l.)

➽ Dom. de l'Ecole, Lycée agricole et viticole, 8, aux Remparts, 68250 Rouffach, tel. 03.89.78.73.16, fax 03.89.78.73.43,
e-mail expl.legta.rouffach@educagri.fr ☑
☎ ev. day except Sat. Sun. 9am–12 noon 1.30pm–5pm; groups by appt.

DOM. ANDRE EHRHART
Vendanges tardives 2000★

	0.35 ha	2,000	🍶 ♦	15–23 €

This estate at Wettolsheim near Colmar has been singled out more than once in the *Guide* for its Pinot Gris wines. Their 2000 Vendanges Tardives comes from limestone-clay terroirs, and although still very young shows real potential. It has a golden yellow colour with brilliant highlights, and a delightful range of elegant aromas combining fresh orange and lemon notes with some typically Pinot Gris hints of smoke. There are similar orange and lemon flavours on the palate, which has a thoroughbred freshness and very good length. This wine is already agreeable, but deserves to be kept for three years until it achieves a perfect balance. It will be a good accompaniment to pan-fried foie gras with apples.

➽ André Ehrhart et Fils, 68, rue Herzog, 68920 Wettolsheim, tel. 03.89.80.66.16, fax 03.89.79.44.20 ☑
☎ ev. day except Sun. 8am–12 noon 2pm–6pm

RENE FLECK 2001★

	0.68 ha	7,300	🍶 🍾	5–8 €

Soulzmatt lies at the point where the Vallée Noble opens out into the plain. The vines around the town are sheltered from damp sea air by the high peaks of the Vosges – a very good location which is reflected in this Tokay with an intense, golden yellow colour and powerful aromas of toast and roasted almonds. The palate is quite dry, extremely full-bodied, supple and very well balanced. This is a wine for food-lovers, and should be kept for the finest dishes. (Residual sugar: 17 g/l.)

➽ René Fleck et Fille, 27, rte d'Orschwihr, 68570 Soultzmatt, tel. 03.89.47.01.20, fax 03.89.47.09.24, e-mail renefleck@voila.fr ☑
☎ by appt.

FERNAND FROEHLICH ET FILS
Cuvée sélectionnée 2001★★

	0.36 ha	4,000	🍶	5–8 €

The Froehlich family lives in Ostheim, on the plain north of Colmar, but its vines are planted on the great terroirs of the Beblenheim commune. The estate has been run since 1992 by the third generation, and in ten years has doubled its area from 4 to 8 ha, and almost tripled its sales of bottled wines. In so doing it has reached its management targets, and has therefore been able to adapt its mix of grape varieties to the needs of the soil. This wine has a brilliant golden colour and a nose which is already releasing some very ripe fruit notes in addition to its intense, typically Pinot Gris smoke aromas. The palate is equally intense and very well balanced, with fruit flavours that linger on to a long, exquisite finish. This is a wine for fine food. (Residual sugar: 21 g/l.)

➽ EARL Fernand Froehlich et Fils, 29, rte de Colmar, 68150 Ostheim, tel. 03.89.86.01.46, fax 03.89.86.01.54 ☑ ⌂
☎ ev. day except Sun. 8am–12 noon 1.30pm–6.30pm; groups by appt.

HENRI GROSS
Cuvée Christine 2001★★

	0.39 ha	3,000		8–11 €

Henri Gross was a pioneer of wine production at Gueberschwihr, and has passed his passion on to his son Rémy, who since 1990 has proved a talented successor to his father. Named after the winemaker's wife, this wine has a very strong, golden yellow colour that is a sure sign of high quality. Its intense aromas of flowers, smoke and spices create an equally good first impression. After a fresh attack, the palate is supple and very classy, with fruit flavours in addition to the usual smoky notes. This very rich wine has a great future ahead of it, and is clearly destined to be drunk with fine foods such as pan-fried foie gras. (Residual sugar: 34 g/l.)

➽ EARL Henri Gross et Fils, 11, rue du Nord, 68420 Gueberschwihr, tel. 03.89.49.24.49, fax 03.89.49.33.58, e-mail vins.gross@wanadoo.fr ☑
☎ by appt.

DOM. HENRI HAEFFELIN ET FILS
Le Silex 2001★★

	0.51 ha	4,800		8–11 €

This estate near Colmar has given ample proof of its know-how over the years, as can be seen from the number of times it has been mentioned in the *Guide*. It does particularly well with Pinot Gris, and this is the fourth consecutive year that the Jury has singled out this Silex Cuvée, named after its gunflint aromas. The winemaker has shown great flair here in producing a wine that really does reflect the terroir it comes from. It has a deep gold colour with subtle shades of green, and an intense nose with a flavour of very ripe grapes and the characteristic Pinot Gris smoky flint aroma. Despite its youth it asserts itself on the palate, which deserves the highest praise for its elegance, freshness, high quality and exceptionally good flavour. This is a wine for lovers of fine food. (Residual sugar: 20 g/l.)

➽ Dom. Henri Haeffelin et Fils, 13, rue d'Eguisheim, 68920 Wettolsheim, tel. 03.89.80.76.81, fax 03.89.79.67.05, e-mail guyhaeffelin@wanadoo.fr ☑
☎ by appt.

HAULLER
Cuvée Saint-Sébastien 2001★

	1 ha	9,000	🍶 ♦	5–8 €

This wine is dedicated to Saint Sebastian, as is the Romanesque chapel that overlooks Dambach-la-Ville. It is worth standing beneath the little church and looking out at the panoramic view stretching away over Dambach and its vineyard, which is the most extensive in Alsace. This Pinot Gris comes from a granitic terroir, and has a dense, green-yellow colour and restrained yet elegant aromas. It has a very well-balanced, agreeable palate with a long finish, and the wine is not too sweet, which means that it will go well with food. (Residual sugar: 20 g/l.)

➽ J. Hauller et Fils, 3, rue de la Gare, 67650 Dambach-la-Ville, tel. 03.88.92.40.21, fax 03.88.92.45.41, e-mail j.hauller@wanadoo.fr ☑
☎ by appt.

MAISON JULG 2001★

	0.28 ha	3,460	🍶 ♦	5–8 €

This is a new name in the *Guide*: Peter Jülg, who runs an estate of some 7 ha at Seebach, in the northern part of the Alsatian vinyard, and exports about 40% of his output to nearby Germany. This Pinot Gris was grown on limestone-clay soils, and has an eye-catchingly intense, slightly amber yellow colour that is a sign of very high-quality grapes. The nose is fresh and intense, with some mineral-type notes that reappear later on the finish. The first impression on the palate is dry and fresh, and as one taster commented, the wine is "sober and elegant, surprising but very agreeable". These features will enable it to accompany a wide variety of dishes. (Residual sugar: 4 g/l.)

➽ Peter Jülg, 116, rue des Eglises, 67160 Seebach, tel. 03.88.94.79.98 ⌂
☎ by appt.

HENRI KLEE

Cuvée particulière 2001★★

| 1.2 ha | 4,000 | | 8–11 € |

Descended from a long line of winemakers who have been at Katzenthal since the beginning of the 17th century, Henri Klee and his son have produced a golden yellow wine with intense aromas of the smoky type that characterizes this grape variety. Its great presence on the palate was much appreciated by the tasters, one of whom commented that "everything about this wine is very strong". It should be kept for a year to achieve its full balance. (Residual sugar: 25 g/l.)
EARL Henri Klée et Fils, 11, Grand-Rue, 68230 Katzenthal, tel. 03.89.27.03.81, fax 03.89.27.28.17 ☑ ☖
☥ by appt.

CLEMENT KLUR

Vieilles Vignes 2001★

| 1 ha | 7,500 | | 8–11 € |

A very old winemaking family, but a new label in a contemporary style: until 1999, Clément Klur belonged to an Alsace wine cooperative, but now he has become independent and built a new cellar. This Pinot Gris comes from a limestone-clay terroir that suits the grape variety very well. It has a brilliant, light yellow colour, and opens on citrus fruit and white flower aromas with a slight hint of smoke. The palate makes a fresh impression at first, then becomes round and very elegant, with a whole range of remarkably well-balanced flavours. The tasters suggest serving it with scallops. (Residual sugar: 25 g/l.)
Clément Klur, 105, rue des Trois-Epis, 68230 Katzenthal, tel. 03.89.80.94.29, fax 03.89.27.30.17, e-mail info@klur.net ☑ ☷ ☖
☥ ev. day 8am–12 noon 2pm–7pm

KOEHLY

Vendanges tardives 2000★★★

| 1.1 ha | 3,100 | ☖ ☙ | 11–15 € |

Jean-Marie Koehly runs a large, 16-hectare estate based at Kintzheim, at the foot of the Haut-Koenigsbourg castle. He specializes in Vendanges Tardives (although that did not prevent him from winning a *coup de coeur* for a 2000 Pinot Noir in the last edition). He clearly got the very best out of that vintage, since this Vendanges Tardives is a 2000 as well. It has a fairly light, straw yellow colour, and impresses from the start by the extreme cleanness of its crystallized fruit and pineapple aromas, which are intense and highly appealing. What follows is exquisite: rich fruit flavours combined with a good level of acidity, on a palate that is full, fleshy, impressively unctuous and already perfectly balanced. There are crystallized or even jammy apricot flavours on a finish that seems to go on for ever.
Jean-Marie Koehly, 64, rue du Gal-de-Gaulle, 67600 Kintzheim, tel. 03.88.82.09.77, fax 03.88.82.70.49 ☑ ☖
☥ by appt.

LOBERGER

Vendanges tardives 2000★★

| 0.3 ha | 1,800 | ☖ ☙ | 15–23 € |

From year to year this vineyard presents wines which are very well received by the *Guide*'s Juries, and this Vendanges

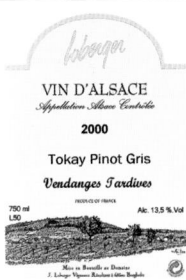

VIN D'ALSACE
Appellation Alsace Contrôlée

2000

Tokay Pinot Gris
Vendanges Tardives

750 ml
L50
Alc. 13,5 % Vol

Mise en Bouteille au Domaine
J. Loberger Vigneron Récoltant à Ottmar-Bergholtz

Tardives provides yet more proof of the winemaker's talent. Grown on a sandy clay terroir on the hillside that runs along the entrance to the Guebwiller valley, it has a brilliant, golden yellow colour, and starts with an elegant, powerful nose of undergrowth fragrances combined with very ripe, fruity peach aromas. There are more notes of undergrowth along with a smoky aroma on the palate, which is rich and full, finishing on some typically Pinot Gris flavours of honey and spice. The sweetness will need to become better integrated, but the wine has almost found its balance, and leaves an impression of perfect freshness and concentration.
EARL Joseph Loberger, 10, rue de Bergholtz-Zell, 68500 Bergholtz, tel. 03.89.76.88.03, fax 03.89.74.16.83, e-mail vin.loberger@worldonline.fr ☑
☥ by appt.

PREISS-ZIMMER

Vendanges tardives 2000★★

| 4 ha | 19,000 | | 30–38 € |

Preiss-Zimmer has a prestigious location in Riquewihr, and belongs to the Turckheim wine-producers' cooperative. The company's oenologist, Michel Lihrmann, has shown his skill by producing this perfectly characteristic Vendanges Tardives. It has a beautiful, golden straw colour, and makes an excellent first impression with the intensity, elegance and extreme complexity of its aromas: just a touch of iodine along with a whole range of subtle crystallized fruit fragrances which eventually open out on to a note of dried bananas. Similar flavours continue on the palate, which is stunningly rich and very well structured, with a remarkably long finish. "The perfect aperitif to offer special guests", said one taster.
SARL Preiss-Zimmer, 40, rue du Gal-de-Gaulle, 68340 Riquewihr, tel. 03.89.47.86.91, fax 03.89.27.35.33, e-mail preiss-zimmer@calixo.net

VIGNOBLES REINHART

Cuvée Charlotte 2001★

| 0.85 ha | 6,400 | ☖ | 5–8 € |

Located on the southern part of the Route des Vins, the commune of Orschwihr has a variety of terroirs, most of which have an east-southeast-facing aspect. This seven-hectare estate has diversified its activities by opening an inn where they sell their wines. This 2001 has a slightly amber colour, and releases notes of honey along with a slight floral touch. After a light attack, the palate shows good balance and has fine white flower flavours embellished by a hint of overripening. This is an elegant wine, which will be a good accompaniment to many different dishes. (Residual sugar: 5 g/l.)
Pierre Reinhart, 7, rue du Printemps, 68500 Orschwihr, tel. 03.89.76.95.12, fax 03.89.74.84.08, e-mail reinhart.pierre@wanadoo.fr ☑ ☖
☥ by appt.

WILLY ROLLI-EDEL 2001★

| 0.65 ha | 2,900 | ☖ | 8–11 € |

The Rolli-Edel family has a long-established reputation in Alsace, and the current generation continues to cultivate its 11 ha of vines with great skill, as can be seen from the numerous mentions this estate receives in the *Guide*. It is now offering a pale-yellow Tokay which is still closed on the nose but already releasing slight hints of the typical Pinot Gris aromas. This is a very young, fairly fresh wine, with lingering flavours of honey and crystallized fruits, but also a fair amount of dryness that means that it can be served with food. (Residual sugar: 21.7 g/l.)

🕿 Willy Rolli-Edel, 5, rue de l'Eglise, 68590 Rorschwihr, tel. 03.89.73.63.26, fax 03.89.73.83.50 ☑
☀ by appt.

ROLLY GASSMANN

Vendanges tardives 2000★★

	1.75 ha	6,000	⦀	23–30 €

Wines from this very famous estate appear on the tables of the best restaurants in France and elsewhere. It grows vines over a large area (33 ha), in a commune with no fewer than 21 types of subsoil and 12 *lieux-dits* that have existed since the 14th century, and is thus in a position to produce a very varied range of wines. This Vendanges Tardives has a strong, golden yellow colour and an exceptionally good nose of smoke and spice aromas that are both intense and unusually fine. The palate is remarkably rich and full, with a very long, fresh finish on overripe fruit flavours. This is a promising wine, which will soon have achieved its full balance.

🕿 Rolly Gassmann, 2, rue de l'Eglise, 68590 Rorschwihr, tel. 03.89.73.63.28, fax 03.89.73.33.06, e-mail rollygassmann@wanadoo.fr ☑
☀ by appt.

ALINE AND REMY SIMON

Vieilles Vignes 2001★★

	0.2 ha	2,000	⦀	8–11 €

These winemakers took over a small family estate here in 1996, and are working extremely hard to expand it. The vineyard may still only amount to 3 ha, but there is no shortage of skill on the part of its owners, who make their debut in the *Guide* with this Pinot Gris. It comes from a sandstone-clay terroir and vines that are nearly 40 years old, and has a deep, golden yellow colour and an agreeably toasty nose with notes of smoke and honey. The palate is a delight to the taste buds: rich, fleshy and round, but not over-sweet. This is a top-quality wine that can be served with the most refined dishes. (Residual sugar: 19 g/l.)

🕿 Dom. Aline et Rémy Simon, 12, rue Saint-Fulrade, 68590 Saint-Hippolyte, tel. 03.89.73.04.92, fax 03.89.73.04.92 ☑ ▥ ☗
☀ by appt.

JEAN SIPP

Clos Ribeaupierre 1999★★

	1 ha	2,500	⦀	23–30 €

This estate's very high reputation was built by the grandfather and has been carried on by the son and grandson. The Clos Ribeaupierre from which this 1999 comes is undoubtedly the jewel in the property's crown. Located on a very steep, terraced slope with a gradient of 1:38, it has a granitic soil that has certainly contributed to the remarkable development of this wine. The brilliant, golden yellow colours gleam with highlights, and there is a very open, complex nose of intense fruity aromas (mainly crystallized fruits), along with some honey and spice notes. After a supple opening the palate is impressively full-bodied, displaying both richness and elegance. This very well-balanced wine should be kept for special occasions and served as an aperitif or with foie gras or dessert. (Residual sugar: 40 g/l.)

🕿 Dom. Jean Sipp, 60, rue de la Fraternité, 68150 Ribeauvillé, tel. 03.89.73.60.02, fax 03.89.73.82.38, e-mail domaine@jean-sipp.com ☑ ▥
☀ by appt.

ANTOINE STOFFEL

Vendanges tardives 1997★

	0.29 ha	3,000	⦀	15–23 €

Eguisheim regards itself as the cradle of Alsatian wine. Built all around its castle, this picturesque village has lovingly restored its old houses for the enjoyment of the tourists who throng into the cellars of winemakers such as Antoine Stoffel. His 1997 Vendanges Tardives has a golden, slightly orangey-yellow colour and a very sweet, expressive nose of vanilla and oak. After five years of maturation this wine is well-integrated, pleasantly supple, rich and full on the palate,

with a long finish marked by concentrated or even overripe fruit flavours.

🕿 Antoine Stoffel, 21, rue de Colmar, 68420 Eguisheim, tel. 03.89.41.32.03, fax 03.89.24.92.07 ☑ ☗
☀ ev. day except Sun. 8am–12 noon 2pm–6pm

ACHILLE THIRION 2001★★

	0.6 ha	6,000	▮ ♦	5–8 €

Achille Thirion's ancestors were growing vines at the foot of the Haut-Koenigsbourg as early as 1760. Nowadays he has 17 ha of vines, which is no mean area in Alsace, and he also knows how to get the best out of them, as we can see from this Pinot Gris. Grown on a silty clay hillside terroir, it makes a very good first impression with a remarkably dense, golden yellow colour. It is particularly expressive and complex on the nose, which develops overripe fruit aromas and exquisite notes of honey. The rich, full-bodied palate has a good, long finish, and the Jury was also delighted by its finesse and elegance. (Residual sugar: 18 g/l.)

🕿 Dom. Achille Thirion, 69, rte du Vin, 68590 Saint-Hippolyte, tel. 03.89.73.00.23, fax 03.89.73.06.46 ☑ ▥ ☗
☀ by appt.

DOM. DE LA TOUR

Oberberg 2001★

	0.8 ha	4,000	▮ ⦀ ♦	8–11 €

Based in the wine-producing village of Blienschwiller, the Straubs are descended from a long line of winemakers dating back to 1510. They are especially proud of their house, which has turrets and flower-bedecked balconies, and their ancestral cellar with its Vosges sandstone pillars, cob ceiling and rows of oak barrels. Their Oberberg Pinot Gris is pale gold and has some delicate smoky aromas. Its rich, somewhat round palate is very pleasant indeed, and has an impressively long finish. (Residual sugar: 18 g/l.)

🕿 Jean-François Straub, Dom. de la Tour, 35, rte des Vins, 67650 Blienschwiller, tel. 03.88.92.48.72, fax 03.88.92.62.90 ☑ ▥ ☗
☀ ev. day 8am–12 noon 2pm–6pm; Sun. by appt.; cl. Feb. holiday

JEAN WACH 2001★★★

	0.8 ha	6,500		5–8 €

There are plenty of reasons for paying a visit to the little town of Andlau; it has a remarkable architectural heritage, notably a Romanesque abbey-church, is the starting-point for trips into the Vosges mountains (Champ du Feu, Hohwald), and finally has a wealth of famous wine-growing terroirs, including two Grands Crus. It is also well worth coming here for Jean Wach's Pinot Gris, which despite its rather light yellow colour has an expressive, extremely fine nose of floral aromas. It is equally delicate on the palate, which is very supple, rather dry, and ethereally light. This wine will go well with "cuisine from all over the world" as one taster emphatically put it. (Residual sugar: 7 g/l.)

🕿 GAEC Jean Wach et Fils, 16 a, rue du Mal-Foch, 67140 Andlau, tel. 03.88.08.09.73, fax 03.88.08.09.73 ☑
☀ ev. day except Sun. 9am–12 noon 2pm–6.30pm

BERNARD WEBER

Finkenberg 2001★★

	0.4 ha	3,000	▮ ♦	8–11 €

This vineyard is at Molsheim, which is located near Strasbourg at the point where the Bruche valley opens out into the plain. Although the town has prospered for centuries (it still has traces of its ramparts) it was in particular associated with Ettore Bugatti, who set up his factory here in 1909 and went on to produce some of the finest motorcars in the business. With this Tokay we are looking at one of the finest gems in the wine industry; coming from the Webers' small, 100-year-old vineyard, it has a golden yellow colour with brilliant green glints, and intense fruity and floral aromas along with a subtle mineral note. After a light opening the palate is remarkably elegant, combining freshness with an ethereal quality that is quite delightful and carries on to a very delicate finish on a mixture of white flower notes and the smoky flavours that characterize the grape variety. This well-balanced wine is

the type of dry Pinot Gris that will go well with a whole range of dishes. (Residual sugar: 5 g/l.)
☛ Bernard Weber, 49, rue de Saverne, 67120 Molsheim, tel. 03.88.38.52.67, fax 03.88.38.58.81,
e-mail info@bernard-weber.com ☑
☿ by appt.

DOM. DU WINDMUEHL 2001★

	1.2 ha	9,000	∎		5–8 €

Saint-Hippolyte is one of the wine-producing villages that lie at the foot of the Haut-Koenigsbourg. Claude Bléger has 7 ha of vines here, and is now offering a golden yellow Tokay with a nose that combines citrus fruit, citrus peel and raisin aromas. After a supple opening, the palate is delightfully elegant and has a very long finish. This is just the sort of Pinot Gris that everyone enjoys. (Residual sugar: 15 g/l.)
☛ EARL Claude Bléger, Dom. du Windmuehl, 92, rte du Vin, 68590 Saint-Hippolyte, tel. 03.89.73.00.21, fax 03.89.73.04.22,
e-mail vins.bleger.claude@wanadoo.fr ☑ ⌂ ⌂
☿ by appt.

Wines selected but not starred

LAURENT BANNWARTH

Sélection de grains nobles 2000

	0.3 ha	2,077	∎		15–23 €

☛ Laurent Bannwarth et Fils, 9, rte du Vin, 68420 Obermorschwihr, tel. 03.89.49.30.87, fax 03.89.49.29.02, e-mail bannwarth@calixo.net ☑ ⌂ ⌂
☿ by appt.

ROBERT BLANCK

Sélection de grains nobles 2000

	0.21 ha	300	⦚		38–46 €

☛ Robert Blanck, 167, rte d'Ottrott, 67210 Obernai, tel. 03.88.95.58.03, fax 03.88.95.04.03,
e-mail blanckobernai@tiscali.fr ☑
☿ ev. day 8am–12 noon 2pm–6pm

PAUL KUBLER

Sélection de grains nobles 2000

	0.2 ha	500	∎ ⌂		30–38 €

☛ EARL Paul Kubler, 103, rue de la Vallée, 68570 Soultzmatt, tel. 03.89.47.00.75, fax 03.89.47.65.45, e-mail kubler@lesvins.com ☑
☿ by appt.

CHARLES SCHLERET

Sélection de grains nobles 2000

	0.55 ha	4,100	∎ ⌂		23–30 €

☛ Charles Schleret, 1–3, rte d'Ingersheim, 68230 Turckheim, tel. 03.89.27.06.09, fax 03.89.27.06.09 ☑
☿ ev. day 9am–7pm; Sun. 10am–12 noon

Alsace Pinot Noir

Alsace is particularly renowned for its white wines, but it is not widely known that in the Middle Ages red grapes were widely grown. Pinot Noir virtually disappeared from the area but it is now the best red-wine grape variety in regions further south, and 85,000 hl were produced from 1,090 ha in 2002.

It is principally used to make a pleasant rosé that is dry and fruity, and, like other rosés, it can be drunk with a variety of different dishes. Increasing efforts are being made to produce red wines with Pinot Noir, and this is a welcome development.

J.-B. ADAM

Cuvée Jean-Baptiste 2001★★

	1 ha	3,600	⦚		15–23 €

The Jean-Baptiste Adam firm has been established since 1614 at Ammerschwihr, one of the cradles of the Alsatian vineyard. Its well-deserved reputation can only be enhanced by this oak-matured Pinot Noir, which has a highly elegant, deep red colour, a delicately oaky nose of leather and undergrowth aromas, and a powerful, warming, very full-bodied palate. It will go well with the most highly-seasoned game dishes.
☛ Jean-Baptiste Adam, 5, rue de l'Aigle, 68770 Ammerschwihr, tel. 03.89.78.23.21, fax 03.89.47.35.91, e-mail adam@jb-adam.com ☑
☿ ev. day except Sun. 8am–12 noon 2pm–6.30pm; groups by appt.

DOM. YVES AMBERG

Kappentanz 2001★

	0.35 ha	3,000	∎ ⌂		8–11 €

Located between Obernai and Sélestat, Epfig is a very large wine-producing commune, and is also one of the most progressive in Alsace. Yves Amberg now grows 10 ha of vines here organically, and his reputation has spread far and wide. This Pinot Noir has a fairly light, ruby colour and intense, elegant soft fruit flavours. It has a well-structured, full-bodied palate with a long finish.
☛ Yves Amberg, 19, rue Fronholz, 67680 Epfig, tel. 03.88.85.51.28, fax 03.88.85.52.71,
e-mail ambergyves@wanadoo.fr ☑ ⌂
☿ by appt.

DOM. DE L'ANCIEN MONASTERE

Rouge de Saint-Léonard Cuvée du Grand Chapitre 2001★★

	0.8 ha	6,400	⦚		5–8 €

Until the French Revolution, Saint-Léonard had a 12th century Benedictine monastery where it is said that the monks planted Pinot Noir vines from Burgundy. The Ancien Monastère estate here was taken over by Bernard Hummel in 1979, and he now runs it with his three daughters. This Cuvée du Grand Chapitre gives an impression of power with its very strong colour and oak and vanilla aromas, but most of all by its well-structured, warming palate. This is a wine for longer maturing, which has an ageing potential of five years and should certainly be kept for a while.
☛ Bernard Hummel et ses Filles, Dom. de l'Ancien Monastère de Saint-Léonard, 4, cour du Chapître, 67530 Boersch-Saint-Léonard, tel. 03.88.95.81.21, fax 03.88.48.11.21,
e-mail b.hummel@wanadoo.fr ☑ ⌂ ⌂
☿ by appt.

DOM. BARMES-BUECHER

Vieille Vigne 2000★★

	0.6 ha	1,800	⦚		23–30 €

The Barmès-Buecher estate came into being through an alliance between two long-established local wine-producing families, and now has 16 ha of vines in a good, sunny location. This Pinot Noir comes from 46-year-old vines and marly clay soils, and has been matured in oak for 24 months. It makes a delightful start with a very deep colour and complex aromas of soft fruits, vanilla and musk. With its exceptionally mouth-filling, powerful, warming palate, this

Pinot Noir

will be a good wine to serve with game once it has been kept for at least two years.
➴ Dom. Barmès-Buecher, 30, rue Sainte-Gertrude, 68920 Wettolsheim, tel. 03.89.80.62.92, fax 03.89.79.30.80, e-mail barmes-buecher@terre-net.fr ☑
☕ by appt.

ROBERT BLANCK
Affenberg Vieilli en barrique 2000★
| ■ | 0.8 ha | 6,000 | ◫ | 11–15 € |

The beautiful medieval town of Obernai is where the Blanck family has passed its know-how from generation to generation since the 15th century. Their cellar is more recent, and has a fine array of oak barrels which every year are filled with the harvest from their 18-hectare vineyard. This wine has been matured for two years, and has an elegant ruby colour and a nose of cherry and floral notes. The powerful, complex palate is very fruity, full-bodied, and not at all dominated by oak.
➴ Robert Blanck, 167, rte d'Ottrott, 67210 Obernai, tel. 03.88.95.58.03, fax 03.88.95.04.03, e-mail blanckobernai@tiscali.fr ☑
☕ ev. day 8am–12 noon 2pm–6pm

LEON BLEESZ
Elevé en barrique 2000★
| ■ | 0.4 ha | 2,200 | ◫ | 11–15 € |

Representing the fourth generation on this family estate, Christophe Bleesz has been growing 11 ha of vines since 1990. Every Whit Monday he opens his estate to the public for a picnic. His oak-matured Pinot Noir has an intense, elegant colour and a delightfully complex range of soft fruit and undergrowth aromas. After a robust opening, the palate is supported by tannins that are assertive but well integrated.
➴ Christophe Bleesz, 1, pl. de l'Eglise, 67140 Reichsfeld, tel. 03.88.85.53.57, fax 03.88.57.83.44, e-mail bleesz@terre-net.fr ☑ ⌂ ⌂
☕ by appt.

DOM. LEON BOESCH
Luss Vallée Noble 2001★
| ■ | 0.4 ha | 2,000 | ◫ | 15–23 € |

The Léon Boesch estate has a plaited straw cellar door which dates back to the 13th century, and serves as a reminder that this vineyard has age-old experience of making wines whose fame has long since spread far beyond this region. This Pinot Noir comes from a limestone soil and has been matured in oak for one year. It has a very strong colour and an aromatic range combining ripe fruits and musky notes. The ample, fleshy palate is very full-bodied and has good ageing potential. It should be kept for at least two years.
➴ Dom. Léon Boesch, 6, rue Saint-Blaise, 68250 Westhalten, tel. 03.89.47.01.83, fax 03.89.47.64.95 ☑ ⌂
☕ by appt.
➴ Gérard Boesch

CLOS SAINT-LANDELIN 2000★★
| ■ | 1.5 ha | 4,000 | ◫ | 30–38 € |

The Clos Saint-Landelin is a gem of Rouffach's wine-producing heritage. René Muré grows 22 ha of vines here, using organic methods. His 2000 Pinot Noir comes from a limestone-clay soil and has been matured in oak for 15 months. It has a beautifully deep, dark colour, remarkably intense aromas, and a full, very structured palate with a remarkably long finish, which will enable it to accompany the most highly-seasoned game dishes.
➴ René Muré, Dom. du Clos Saint-Landelin, rte du Vin, 68250 Rouffach, tel. 03.89.78.58.00, fax 03.89.78.58.01, e-mail rene@mure.com ☑
☕ by appt.

PIERRE FRICK
Rot-Murle 2001★
| ■ | 0.4 ha | 1,800 | ◫ | 11–15 € |

Pierre Frick was a pioneer of organic growing in Alsace, and in 1981 his son Jean-Pierre took this 12-hectare estate a step further by going over to biodynamic methods. This Pinot Noir comes from a limestone-clay soil, and has a very strong colour and an intense nose of soft fruit aromas. The palate is rich and perfectly structured, with delightfully well-integrated tannins. It would be best to keep this wine for a year or two.
➴ Pierre Frick, 5, rue de Baer, 68250 Pfaffenheim, tel. 03.89.49.62.99, fax 03.89.49.73.78, e-mail pierre.frick@wanadoo.fr ☑
☕ ev. day except Sun. 8.30am–11.30am 1.30pm–6.30pm

GINGLINGER-FIX 2001★
| ■ | 0.8 ha | 8,700 | ▮ | 5–8 € |

For nearly four centuries now, the lives of the Ginglinger family have revolved around vine-growing and wine production. Their Pinot Noir comes from a limestone-clay soil and has been matured according to the rule book. It makes a delightful first impression with its elegant colour and expressive, complex aromas. The palate opens very pleasantly, and is both structured and well-balanced. This wine can be drunk now with grilled meats, or even with dishes like game cooked with bilberries.
➴ Ginglinger-Fix, 38, rue Roger-Frémeaux, 68420 Voegtlinshoffen, tel. 03.89.49.30.75, fax 03.89.49.29.98, e-mail ginglinger-fix@wanadoo.fr ☑
☕ ev. day except Sun. 8.30am–12 noon 1.30pm–7pm
➴ André Ginglinger

HARTWEG
Elevé en fût de chêne 2001★★
| ■ | 0.25 ha | 2,600 | ◫ | 8–11 € |

Jean-Paul Hartweg took over this family vineyard in 1972, and was then joined in 1996 by his son Franck who had trained as an oenologist in Beaune and now produces Pinots Noirs. This 2001 has a very dark colour and an intense nose with an extremely good balance between fruit notes and subtle hints of very high-quality oak. This excellent first impression is confirmed on the palate, which is powerful, structured, and remarkably long. A Pinot Noir like this will go well with red meat and game.
➴ Jean-Paul et Frank Hartweg, 39, rue Jean-Macé, 68980 Beblenheim, tel. 03.89.47.94.79, fax 03.89.49.00.83, e-mail frank.hartweg@free.fr ☑ ⌂
☕ ev. day except Sun. 8am–11.30am 1.30pm–6pm

PH. HEITZ
Hahnenberg 2001★
| ■ | 0.25 ha | 1,200 | ▮ ◫ | 8–11 € |

In 1957, Fernand Heitz started this estate in the town of Molsheim, made famous by Ettore Bugatti. In 1986 he was joined by his son Philippe, and now the vineyard is cultivated organically. This Pinot Noir has a very strong colour and a nose of blackcurrant aromas. The palate is very full, and the fact that the tannins are already well integrated is an indication of very high-quality grapes. This wine will be a good accompaniment to red meat and game.
➴ Philippe Heitz, 4, rue Ettore-Bugatti, 67120 Molsheim, tel. 03.88.38.25.38, fax 03.88.38.82.53, e-mail philippe.heitz-vins@wanadoo.fr ☑
☕ ev. day 9am–12 noon 2pm–7pm; Sun. by appt.

EMILE HERZOG 2001★
| ■ | 0.21 ha | 1,800 | ▮ ◊ | 8–11 € |

With its ramparts, three towers and "guard-room," Turckheim is one of the most picturesque towns in Alsace. The Herzog family has owned vines here since 1686. This Pinot Noir comes from a gravelly soil, and has a very intense garnet colour and a nose of dark berry and bilberry aromas. The palate is well structured, with a long finish and well-integrated tannins which should enable it to be served with game and red meat.
➴ Vins d'Alsace Emile Herzog, 28, rue du Florimont, 68230 Turckheim, tel. 03.89.27.08.79, fax 03.89.27.08.79, e-mail e.herzog@laposte.net ☑
☕ by appt.

HUBER AND BLEGER

Rouge de Saint-Hippolyte Elevé en barrique 2001★

■	0.23 ha	1,800	■ Ⅲↈ		8–11 €

Marcel Huber and Robert Bleger are cousins who decided to work together in 1967. Since then the next generation has taken over the estate, which now has 18 ha of vines. For the first time it is offering an oak-matured Pinot Noir, which has a very strong colour and an exceptionally pleasant, complex nose on which fine oak notes mingle with aromas of undergrowth and soft fruits. It is powerful and warming on the palate, but at the same time the tannins are elegant and well integrated. This wine should be served with game or red meat.
⌕ Dom. Huber et Bléger, 6, rte du Vin, 68590 Saint-Hippolyte, tel. 03.89.73.01.12, fax 03.89.73.00.81, e-mail domaine@huber-bleger.fr ☑
Ⓣ ev. day except Sun. 9am–12 noon 2pm–5.30pm; cl. Sat. 1 Jan. to Easter

HUMBRECHT

Vieilli en fût de chêne 2001★

■	0.56 ha	2,000	Ⅲ		8–11 €

In 1992, Claude Humbert took over from his father on this family estate, thus continuing a tradition that dates back to 1620. His Pinot Noir has quite a brilliant ruby colour, a nose of floral and oak aromas, and a well-balanced palate with a flavour of soft fruits. This is a very typical red wine for the region.
⌕ EARL Claude et Georges Humbrecht, 33, rue de Pfaffenheim, 68420 Gueberschwihr, tel. 03.89.49.31.51 ☑ 🏠 🏠
Ⓣ by appt.

GEORGES KLEIN

Rouge de Saint-Hippolyte 2001★★

■	0.5 ha	3,000	■		5–8 €

Georges Klein started this vineyard in 1956, and was joined by his son in 1986. The estate originally had just 3 ha of vines, and now it has ten. This Pinot Noir has a very strong ruby colour, and intense, delicate aromas which show that it comes from a granitic soil. With its well-structured, full-bodied palate, it will give pleasure to wine-lovers for many years to come.
⌕ EARL Georges Klein, 10, rte du Vin, 68590 Saint-Hippolyte, tel. 03.89.73.00.28, fax 03.89.73.06.28, e-mail a.klein@calixe.net ☑ 🏠 🏠
Ⓣ by appt.

KLEIN-BRAND

Elevé en fût de chêne 2001★★

■	0.2 ha	1,800	Ⅲ		5–8 €

Founded in 1950, this estate now has 10 ha of vines. It has a very good location for wine-growing, right at the heart of the Vallée Noble. This Pinot Noir comes from a limestone terroir and has been matured in oak for one year. Its colour is very brilliant, and it wins high praise for its soft fruit aromas, tannic power and remarkably good balance.
⌕ Klein-Brand, 96, rue de la Vallée, 68570 Soultzmatt, tel. 03.89.47.00.08, fax 03.89.47.65.53, e-mail kleinbrand@free.fr ☑
Ⓣ ev. day except Sun. 8am–12 noon 1.30pm–6pm

JEAN-LUC MADER

Cuvée Théophile 2001★★

■	0.3 ha	2,000	Ⅲ		8–11 €

Since 1981 Jean-Luc Mader has been growing 7 ha of vines at Hunawihr, a wine-producing village which is famous for its fortified church. Regular readers of the *Guide* will be familiar with this estate's Cuvée Théophile, which won a *coup de coeur* in the 1999 vintage. This 2001 has a strong, very elegant garnet colour, and a complex nose on which the oak is well integrated with the fruit and spice aromas. The power and good structure on the palate are a sign of very high-quality grapes, and the flavours linger on to a particularly long finish.
⌕ Jean-Luc Mader, 13, Grand-Rue, 68150 Hunawihr, tel. 03.89.73.80.32, fax 03.89.73.31.22 ☑
Ⓣ by appt.

MARZOLF 2001★

■	0.41 ha	2,354	Ⅲ		5–8 €

The village of Gueberschwihr boasts a tall, Romanesque church tower, and is also home to numerous wine-growing estates including this one, which dates back to 1846. It is offering a Pinot Noir whose intense garnet colour is an indication of high-quality grapes. With its Morello cherry aromas, clean attack and well-integrated tannins, this wine will be a good accompaniment to game. It also has a fair amount of ageing potential.
⌕ GAEC Marzolf, 9, rte de Rouffach, 68420 Gueberschwihr, tel. 03.89.49.31.02, fax 03.89.49.20.84, e-mail vins@marzolf.fr ☑
Ⓣ by appt.

OTTER

Barriques 2001★★

■	0.39 ha	2,600	Ⅲ		15–23 €

In 1998 Jean-François Otter took over here from three previous generations of winemakers, and immediately achieved great things, especially with this Pinot Noir which won a *coup de coeur* in the two previous vintages. This 2001 carries on in the same vein, making a delightful first impression with its very deep purple colour and nose of boxwood, blackcurrants and liquorice. It is full-bodied and perfectly structured on the palate, which has a remarkably long finish. This wine will go very well with roast meat and game, and deserves to be kept for a while.
⌕ Dom. François Otter et Fils, 4, rue du Muscat, 68420 Hattstatt, tel. 03.89.49.33.00, fax 03.89.49.38.69, e-mail ottjef@newel.net ☑
Ⓣ by appt.

RUHLMANN-DIRRINGER

A Fleur de Roche 2001★★

■	0.5 ha	3,000	Ⅲ		5–8 €

The Ruhlmann-Dirringer family has been based for four generations in the former home of the Comtes de Mullenheim, where they are particularly proud of their vaulted cellar. The wines they produce fully live up to this delightful setting. The 2001 Pinot Noir has a very strong garnet colour, and a nose of very intense blackberry and Morello cherry aromas that are characteristic of the granitic soil this wine comes from. With its ample, full-bodied palate, it will be an ideal accompaniment to red meat and game.
⌕ Ruhlmann-Dirringer, 3, imp. de Mullenheim, 67650 Dambach-la-Ville, tel. 03.88.92.40.28, fax 03.88.92.48.05 ☑
Ⓣ by appt.

DOM. SAINT-REMY

Cuvée Florian 2001★

■	1.5 ha	13,600	■		5–8 €

Although very close to Colmar, Wettolsheim is still a peaceful village entirely given over to winemaking. The Saint-Rémy estate has a prestigious location here. This Cuvée Florian has a deep red colour that is a sign of excellent concentration. The nose combines cherry and prune aromas, and the palate is rich and full-bodied, with a very long finish. This wine will go well with red meat and game, and should be left to age for two years.
⌕ François et Philippe Ehrhart, 6, rue Saint-Rémy, 68920 Wettolsheim, tel. 03.89.80.60.57, fax 03.89.79.74.00, e-mail vins@domainesaintremy.com ☑ 🏠
Ⓣ ev. day except Sun. 8am–12 noon 1.30pm–6.30pm

DOM. CLAUDE SCHOETTEL

Cuvée Prestige 2001★

■	0.25 ha	1,300	◫	8–11 €

Following the example of the monks who brought Pinot Noir here from Burgundy in 1109, the winemakers of Ottrott use this variety to produce one of the most highly-prized wines in Alsace. There's no doubt what grape this wine is made from! It has a beautiful ruby colour, and a very intense nose combining soft fruit aromas with subtle hints of oak. The palate is long and well balanced, which is an indication of high-quality grapes. This Cuvée Prestige is ready to drink now. The family also has a restaurant, where you can try Ottrott red wine with wild-boar stew or ham, or with noisettes of hind.

☛ Claude Schoettel, 5 A, rue du Stade, 67530 Ottrott, tel. 03.88.48.13.13, fax 03.88.48.13.14 ☑
⚐ by appt.

DOM. MARIE-HELENE SCHOETTEL

Rouge d'Ottrott Cuvée Prestige 2001★

■	0.8 ha	4,500	◫	5–8 €

Ottrott has a long-estabished and very sound reputation for its red wines. This Pinot Noir has been produced by Marie-Hélène Schoettel, who is proud of being the only female winemaker in the village. The wine has a cherry colour with slight nuances, and a very complex nose of soft fruit aromas. It is full, well integrated and lingering on the palate, and should go well with stewed hind.

☛ Marie-Hélène Schoettel, 1, rue du Stade, 67530 Ottrott, tel. 03.88.95.80.05, fax 03.88.48.13.14 ☑
⚐ by appt.

EMILE SCHWARTZ

Cuvée Louis Elevé en fût de chêne 2001★

■	0.25 ha	1,500	◫	11–15 €

High above the Rhine plain stands the well-favoured village of Husseren, where one can't help feeling that the winemakers working away on hillsides almost 400 m high must almost feel that they are growing wings. Be that as it may, this is a very successful Pinot Noir. It has an intense, deep colour, and is made from high-quality grapes that are well up to the challenge of maturation in oak. There are very clear soft fruit notes on the nose and again on the palate, which is powerful and tannic. This is a wine with very good ageing potential.

☛ EARL Emile Schwartz et Fils, 3, rue Principale, 68420 Husseren-les-Châteaux, tel. 03.89.49.30.61, fax 03.89.49.27.27 ☑
⚐ ev. day except Sun. 8am–12 noon 2pm–7pm

STEINER

Elsbourg 2001★★

■	0.25 ha	1,000	◫	8–11 €

This estate to the south of Colmar has been passed on from father to son since 1895. It makes a notable debut in the *Guide* with this Pinot Noir, which comes from a limestone terroir at Elsbourg. It has a strong garnet colour and a nose combining fruity aromas with delicate notes of oak. The palate is very intense and well structured, with an exceptionally long finish. This wine should be drunk with red meat or game, and can be kept for at least five years.

☛ GAEC Steiner, 11, rte du Vin, 68420 Herrlisheim-près-Colmar, tel. 03.89.49.30.70, fax 03.89.49.29.67, e-mail steiner.vins@wanadoo.fr ☑ ☎
⚐ by appt.

STRUSS 2001★★

■	0.37 ha	3,500	▮	5–8 €

Obermorschwihr is a traditional village south of Colmar, and is well known not only for its half-timbered church, but also for its wine-producing estates, such as this one belonging to the Struss family. Their Pinot Noir has a very intense ruby colour, and is delightfully elegant. With its soft fruit flavours and excellent balance, this is a lingering, fully open wine that makes you feel like inviting some friends round to share it. It can be drunk straightaway.

☛ André Struss et Fils, 16, rue Principale, 68420 Obermorschwihr, tel. 03.89.49.36.71, fax 03.89.49.37.30 ☑ ☎
⚐ by appt.
☛ Philippe Struss

DOM. DE LA TOUR

Cuvée Xavière 2000★

■	0.6 ha	4,000	◫	8–11 €

The Straubs have passed this wine estate from father to son since 1510, and are proud of their ancestral cellar with its Vosges sandstone pillars. Their Cuvée Xavière is a Pinot Noir from a granitic terroir. It is very open on the nose, which has aromas of spice and cooked fruits. After a clean opening, the palate has very good balance and well-integrated tannins. This wine is ready to be enjoyed straight away.

☛ Jean-François Straub, Dom. de la Tour, 35, rte des Vins, 67650 Blienschwiller, tel. 03.88.92.48.72, fax 03.88.92.62.90 ☑ ☎
⚐ ev. day 8am–12 noon 2pm–6pm; Sun. by appt.; cl. Feb. holiday.

ULMER

Coteaux du Bruderberg 2001★

■	0.3 ha	3,000	◫	3–5 €

Overlooked by Mont Sainte-Odile, Rémy Ulmer's estate has existed for three generations, but has expanded over time to the 12 ha of vines it owns today. Its Pinot Noir has a highly elegant garnet colour and a very mature nose of wild berry aromas. It opens pleasantly on to a well-structured, full-bodied palate, and has good ageing potential (three years).

☛ Dom. Rémy Ulmer, 3, rue des Ciseaux, 67650 Rosheim, tel. 03.88.50.45.62, fax 03.88.50.45.62 ☑ ☎
⚐ by appt.

VORBURGER

Elevé en pièces 2001★★

■	n.c.	n.c.	◫	8–11 €

This estate is located at Voegtlinshoffen, a picturesque village which offers a wonderful view straight down on to the Rhine plain. The vineyard was founded in the 1950s, and then taken over by Jean-Pierre Vorburger, who was recently joined by his son. His Pinot Noir, matured in oak for one year, won unanimous praise from the judges. It has a strong colour, a nose of soft fruit and toast aromas, and a full, rich, exceptionally powerful palate that is delightfully well-balanced and harmonious. This wine can be drunk now or kept for five or six years.

☛ EARL Jean-Pierre Vorburger et Fils, 3, rue de la Source, 68420 Voegtlinshoffen, tel. 03.89.49.35.52, fax 03.89.86.40.56 ☑
⚐ by appt.

J.-P. WASSLER

Elevé en barrique 2000★★

■	0.3 ha	2,200	◫	8–11 €

This estate chose to leave the centre of the village and move into modern buildings with better facilities for making and storing wine. Judging by this Pinot Noir it was an excellent decision. Matured in oak for 14 months, it shows its power from the start by the strength of its colour. This first impression is confirmed by its forest fruit and vanilla aromas on the nose. The palate has plenty of fruit flavour, despite its oaky quality. This is very much a wine for longer maturing, which will keep for at least two or three years and be a good accompaniment to red wine in sauce.

☛ Jean-Paul Wassler Fils, 1, rte d'Epfig, 67650 Blienschwiller, tel. 03.88.92.41.53, fax 03.88.92.63.11 ☑
☒ by appt.
☛ Marc Wassler

DOM. DU WINDMUEHL
Rouge de Saint-Hippolyte 2001 ★

■	1 ha	8,000	▮	5–8 €

Overlooked by the majestic silhouette of Haut-Koenigsbourg, the Windmuehl has 7 ha of vines in all. It has produced this ruby-coloured Pinot Noir with an intense nose that reflects the granitic soil it comes from. It is full and well balanced on the palate, and is a typical Alsace red, which will go well with grilled or roasted red meats.

☛ EARL Claude Bléger, Dom. du Windmuehl, 92, rte du Vin, 68590 Saint-Hippolyte, tel. 03.89.73.00.21, fax 03.89.73.04.22,
e-mail vins.bleger.claude@wanadoo.fr ☑ 🏠 🏠
☒ by appt.

ZEYSSOLFF
Cuvée Z 2001 ★

■	0.15 ha	1000	⑪	11–15 €

Located very near Barr, the commune of Gertwiller is not without charm. The Zeyssolffs have a 1778 house, and grow 8 ha of vines here. This Pinot Noir makes a delightful start with a very intense colour and a nose of soft fruit aromas. With its full, tannic, powerful, lingering palate, it will be a good accompaniment to turkey with chestnuts. It would be best to keep it for a while before opening it.

☛ G. Zeyssolff, 156, rte de Strasbourg, 67140 Gertwiller, tel. 03.88.08.90.08, fax 03.88.08.91.60,
e-mail yvan.zeyssolff@wanadoo.fr ☑ 🏠
☒ by appt.

Wines selected but not starred

ANSTOTZ ET FILS 2001

■	0.65 ha	3,500	⑪	5–8 €

☛ Anstotz et Fils, 51, rue Balbach, 67310 Balbronn, tel. 03.88.50.30.55, fax 03.88.50.58.06 ☑ 🏠
☒ by appt.

PIERRE ARNOLD
Rouge d'Alsace 2001

■	0.3 ha	1,500	⑪	5–8 €

☛ Pierre Arnold, 16, rue de la Paix, 67650 Dambach-la-Ville, tel. 03.88.92.41.70, fax 03.88.92.62.95 ☑
☒ ev. day 9am–7pm; Sun. by appt.

DANIEL FRITZ ET FILS
Cuvée particulière 2001

■	0.35 ha	2,400		5–8 €

☛ Daniel Fritz, 3, rue du Vieux-Moulin, 68240 Sigolsheim, tel. 03.89.47.11.15, fax 03.89.78.17.07 ☑
☒ by appt.

JEAN-PAUL GERBER
Langenberg 2001

■	0.5 ha	4,500	▮	5–8 €

☛ EARL Jean-Paul et Dany Gerber, 16, rue Théophile-Bader, 67650 Dambach-la-Ville, tel. 03.88.92.41.84, fax 03.88.92.42.18 ☑
☒ by appt.

EUGENE KLIPFEL
Cuvée particulière 2001

■	2 ha	5,000	⑪	5–8 €

☛ Klipfel, 6, av. de la Gare, 67140 Barr, tel. 03.88.58.59.00, fax 03.88.08.53.18, e-mail alsacewine@klipfel.com ☑
☒ ev. day 10am–12 noon 2pm–6pm
☛ X. Lorentz

CAVE D'OBERNAI
Elevé en fût de chêne 2000

■	n.c.	15,000	⑪	8–11 €

☛ Cave vinicole d'Obernai, 30, rue du Gal-Leclerc, 67211 Obernai, tel. 03.88.47.60.20, fax 03.88.47.60.22 ☑
☒ by appt.

SCHLEGEL-BOEGLIN
V 2001

■	0.9 ha	4,100	⑪	8–11 €

☛ Dom. Jean-Luc Schlegel-Boeglin, 22 A, rue d'Orschwihr, 68250 Westhalten, tel. 03.89.47.00.93, fax 03.89.47.65.32, e-mail schlegel-boeglin@wanadoo.fr ☑
☒ by appt.

J.-M. SOHLER
Les Terrasses du Bubenberg 2001

■	0.2 ha	1,500	⑪	5–8 €

☛ Jean-Marie et Hervé Sohler, 16, rue du Winzenberg, 67650 Blienschwiller, tel. 03.88.92.42.93 ☑ 🏠 🏠
☒ by appt.

STRAUB
Elevé en barrique 2000

■	0.18 ha	1,200	⑪	8–11 €

☛ Jean-Marie Straub, 61, rte du Vin, 67650 Blienschwiller, tel. 03.88.92.40.42, fax 03.88.92.40.42 ☑
☒ by appt.

WINTER
Elevé en fût de chêne 2001

■	0.3 ha	2,000	⑪	8–11 €

☛ Albert Winter, 17, rue Sainte-Hune, 68150 Hunawihr, tel. 03.89.73.62.95, fax 03.89.73.62.95 ☑
☒ by appt.

Alsace Grand Cru

As a way of promoting the best-situated vineyards, a new appellation, Alsace Grand Cru, was established by decree in 1975. Strict limits were set on the quantity that the designated vineyards qualifying for this appellation could produce, and the sugar content of the wine was also limited. They were to be vineyards growing only Gewurztraminer, Pinot Gris, Riesling and Muscat. Along with wines labelled with the seal of the

Confrérie Saint-Étienne and some notable vintages, the vineyards that qualify produce the *non plus ultra* of Alsace wines.

In 1983 a decree identified a group of 25 vineyards that qualified for the appellation, but the decree was rescinded and superseded by a new one on 17 December 1992. There are 50 official Grands Crus from 47 communes, although the decree mentions only 46, Rouffach having been omitted in error. Each vineyard covers an area of between 3.23 ha and 80.28 ha, and each had to meet certain geological criteria appropriate to Grands Crus. The volume of wine produced by the Grands Crus is still modest: only 43,576 hl in 2002 from an area of 806 ha.

New regulations were put in place after the 1987 harvest. They increased the minimum alcoholic content from 11 to 12 in Gewurztraminers and Tokay-Pinot Gris. At the same time, there were new requirements for labels to show the specific vineyard alongside the grape variety and the year, and this information also had to be shown on all administrative and commercial documentation.

Alsace Grand Cru Altenberg-de-Bergbieten

CHARLES MULLER ET FILS
Gewurztraminer 2001★

	0.23 ha	2,000	🍷	11–15 €

The terroir of Altenberg-de-Bergbieten in the north of the Alsace delimited area has the advantage of facing southeast. The soil is a homogeneous pebbly limestone-clay that warms up well. It has produced this Gewurztraminer grown on 40-year-old vines. Pale yellow, with green highlights, this 2001 is still young. Nonetheless, behind its still very closed nose and masked fruit, the tasters discern real potential. The rounded attack and lovely body are full of promise. (Residual sugar: 35 g/l.)
☛ Charles Muller et Fils, 89c, rte du Vin, 67310 Traenheim, tel. 03.88.50.38.04, fax 03.88.50.58.54 🅥
✠ by appt.

Wines selected but not starred

LA CAVE DU ROI DAGOBERT
Riesling 2001

	2.36 ha	17,333	🍷 ♦	5–8 €

☛ La cave du Roi Dagobert, 1, rte de Scharrachbergheim, 67310 Traenheim, tel. 03.88.50.69.00, fax 03.88.50.69.09, e-mail dagobert@cave-dagobert.com 🅥
✠ by appt.

DOM. ROLAND SCHMITT
Riesling Vieilles Vignes 2001

	1.3 ha	4,500	ⅲ	8–11 €

☛ Anne-Marie Schmitt, 35, rue des Vosges, 67310 Bergbieten, tel. 03.88.38.20.72, fax 03.88.38.75.84 🅥
✠ by appt.

Alsace Grand Cru Altenberg-de-Bergheim

FERNAND ENGEL
Gewurztraminer Sélection de grains nobles 2000★

	0.71 ha	5,800	🍷 ♦	30–38 €

This 40-hectare estate has an important position in the Altenberg-de-Bergheim terroir. Some 220–320 m above sea-level, this Grand Cru is on limestone and clay. Gewurztraminer is one of the specially favoured varieties here, along with Riesling. This old-gold colour Sélection de Grains Nobles has a well-developed bouquet which confides notes of crystallized fruits with hints of honeyed walnut. Rich, well supported by good acidity, the palate will soon attain a perfect blend. The long finish marries lively citrus flavours (lemon and grapefruit) with crystallized-fruit style sweetness. (Half-litre bottles)
☛ GAEC Fernand Engel et Fils, 1, rte du Vin, 68590 Rorschwihr, tel. 03.89.73.77.27, fax 03.89.73.63.70, e-mail f-engel@wanadoo.fr 🅥
✠ ev. day 8am–12 noon 1pm–6pm except Sun. 10am–12 noon.

LORENTZ
Riesling 2001★

	5 ha	20,000		15–23 €

Founded in 1836, the firm of Lorentz is now a leading Alsatian wine-merchant, exporting some 45% of its production. It has not abandoned its wine-growing origins, as is shown by the care it bestows on its own 32-hectare vineyard, a large part of which is on the limestone-clay of the Altenberg-de-Bergheim terroir. This Riesling, characteristic of its origins, has a good future ahead of it. Its elegant, fruity nose is indicative of an excellent structure. This is a thoroughbred, well-blended wine that will be fully integrated in two or three years' time. Serve with a fish in sauce. (Residual sugar: 8 g/l)
The **Gewurztraminer Grand Cru Altenberg-de-Bergheim 2001 (23–30 €)** obtained a similar rating. It is a full, rich, unctuous wine, intensely aromatic and possessing good length. (Residual sugar: 29 g/l.)
☛ Gustave Lorentz, 91, rue des Vignerons, 68750 Bergheim, tel. 03.89.73.22.22, fax 03.89.73.30.49, e-mail info@gustavelorentz.com 🅥
✠ ev. day except Sun. 10am–12 noon 2pm–6.30pm
☛ Charles Lorentz

Alsace Grand Cru Altenberg-de-Wolxheim

DOM. JOSEPH SCHARSCH
Riesling 2001★

| 0.45 ha | 3,000 | 🍷 ⬇ | 8–11 € |

Joseph Scharsch, who took over in the early 1970s, resolved to make a go of wine-growing and marketed his first bottles in 1976. He managed to pass on his enthusiasm to his son Nicolas, who joined him in 1999. Their Riesling Grand Cru reflects the limestone-clay terroir, and is still very fruity. This rather supple wine is a thoroughbred that will attain good balance in several years' time. (Residual sugar: 7.6 g/l.)
↳ Dom. Joseph Scharsch, 12, rue de l'Eglise, 67120 Wolxheim, tel. 03.88.38.30.61, fax 03.88.38.01.13, e-mail domaine.scharsch@wanadoo.fr 📩 🏠
🍷 by appt.

MAISON ZOELLER
Riesling 2001★★

| 0.75 ha | 6,500 | 🍷 | 5–8 € |

Established in 1700, this estate has all the traditional attributes, including a half-timbered house (17th century) and a winepress dating from the same period. It was nevertheless a pioneer of selling in bottles, which it has practised since 1900. The new generation, represented by Mathieu, has built a cellar. Over the past four years, the concern has regularly been distinguished for its Rieslings. Its 99 obtained a *coup de coeur*. This 2001 has an intense bouquet with notes of lime and mint. The lively, full palate offers a highly exotic blend. "A fascinating wine" was the conclusion of one taster, who recommended it as an accompaniment to shrimps, scallops, or fish in sauce. (Residual sugar: 7 g/l.)
↳ EARL Maison Zoeller, 14, rue de l'Eglise, 67120 Wolxheim, tel. 03.88.38.15.90, fax 03.88.38.15.90, e-mail vins.zoeller@wanadoo.fr 📩
🍷 by appt.
↳ Mathieu Zoeller

Wines selected but not starred

MATHIEU GOETZ
Riesling 2001

| 0.6 ha | 3,400 | 5–8 € |

↳ Mathieu Goetz, 2, rue Jeanne-d'Arc, 67120 Wolxheim, tel. 03.88.38.10.47, fax 03.88.38.67.61, e-mail mathieu.goetz@wanadoo.fr 📩
🍷 by appt.

Alsace Grand Cru Brand

DOPFF AU MOULIN
Gewurztraminer 2001★

| 3.3 ha | 20,000 | 🍷 | 11–15 € |

A certain Jean-Daniel Dopff set up as a baker and innkeeper in 17th century Riquewihr. Since then the firm, which is still in

family hands, has built up a large estate of more than 70 ha. It exports some 30% of its production worldwide. Yellow with gold highlights, its Brand Grand Cru has a bouquet of fine yet strong toasty notes. Full, rich and round, this wine finishes on long-lasting notes of lychee. It has almost reached a perfectly integrated state. (Residual sugar: 21 g/l.)
↳ SA Dopff au Moulin, 2, av. Jacques-Preiss, 68340 Riquewihr, tel. 03.89.49.09.69, fax 03.89.47.83.61, e-mail domaines@dopff-au-moulin.fr 📩
🍷 ev. day 9am–12 noon 2pm–6pm; groups by appt.

ARMAND HURST
Riesling Sélection de grains nobles 2000★

| 0.3 ha | 1,400 | 🍷 | 15–23 € |

Armand Hurst tends 8.6 ha of vines and is one of the best-known wine-growers in Turckheim. A large proportion of his vines cover the granite terroir of the Brand, from which this Sélection de Grains Nobles comes. Bright yellow with golden highlights, it has a subtle nose of crystallized citrus fruits (lemon, grapefruit) with hints of dry grass and toast. First impressions of sweetness quickly yield to an acid freshness, and the middle palate experiences a revival of citrus aromas. The finish has length and great warmth. This wine has good ageing potential and will be at its best in three to four years. (Half-litre bottles) The same estate's **Muscat Grand Cru Brand Vendanges Tardives 2000** is commended for its complex aromas and powerful palate, which nevertheless leaves an impression of finesse and lightness.
↳ Armand Hurst, 8, rue de la Chapelle, BP 46, 68230 Turckheim, tel. 03.89.27.40.22, fax 03.89.27.47.67 📩
🍷 by appt.

PREISS-ZIMMER
Gewurztraminer 2001★★

| 3 ha | 23,100 | 🍷 ⬇ | 11–15 € |

The firm of Preiss-Zimmer, located at Riquewihr, grows some of its vines at Turckheim, in the Brand Grand Cru, a highly-privileged terroir owing to its exposure to the south-east and granite soils. It has produced this good-looking straw-yellow Gewurztraminer with green highlights. The nose is still reserved, but allows some floral notes through before developing a citrus-dominated fruitiness. The palate begins with suppleness and finesse, then discloses flavours that correspond to those of the bouquet. The finish is enhanced by a mineral note derived from the terroir. A young but promising wine that deserves to be kept for a few years. (Residual sugar: 24 g/l.)
↳ SARL Preiss-Zimmer, 40, rue du Gal-de-Gaulle, 68340 Riquewihr, tel. 03.89.47.86.91, fax 03.89.27.35.33, e-mail preiss-zimmer@calixo.net

Wines selected but not starred

PAUL BUECHER ET FILS
Riesling 2001

| 0.5 ha | 3,500 | 🍷 ⬇ | 11–15 € |

↳ Paul Buecher et Fils, 15, rue Sainte-Gertrude, 68920 Wettolsheim, tel. 03.89.80.64.73, fax 03.89.80.58.62, e-mail buecherp@aol.com 📩
🍷 ev. day except Sun. 8am–12 noon 2pm–6pm

Alsace Grand Cru Bruderthal

GERARD NEUMEYER

Tokay-pinot gris 2001★★

| | 0.93 ha | 4,600 | ⦙⦙⦙ | 15–23 € |

Near this estate is the Chartreuse museum, which exhibits, in particular, memorabilia of the Bugatti automobile firm. The Bruderthal terroir benefits from a southeastern exposure and a limestone-clay soil well-aerated by a pebbly structure that allows the vines to make the most of the sun's heat. Gérard Neumeyer is regularly commended for his Grand Crus. This year, no fewer than three varieties have made the grade. The greatest favourite is the Pinot Gris: the somewhat refined nose is developing aromas between crystallized fruits and lychee. The palate is where the wine's full force is demonstrated; it is full, rich, and well-integrated, finishing on exquisite, long-lasting notes of quince and apricot. Serve as an aperitif, with foie gras or as an accompaniment to duck with orange. (Residual sugar: 61 g/l.)

☛ Dom. Gérard Neumeyer, 29, rue Ettore-Bugatti, 67120 Molsheim, tel. 03.88.38.12.45, fax 03.88.38.11.27, e-mail domaine.neumeyer@wanadoo.fr ☑
☖ ev. day except Sun. 9am–12 noon 2pm–7pm

DOM. GERARD NEUMEYER

Gewurztraminer 2001★

| | 0.94 ha | 3,300 | ⦙⦙⦙ | 15–23 € |

This Gewurztraminer is a very intense gold with a beautiful glow. The discreet nose hints at perfumes of dried fruits. This very long, supple, full wine reveals all its power and richness, however, to the palate, which has flavours characteristic of crystallized fruits. (Residual sugar: 52 g/l.) Those who like drier wines will prefer the commended **Riesling 2001 (11–15 €)**, a supple wine with a lovely complex of aromas. (Residual sugar: 4.1 g/l.)

☛ Dom. Gérard Neumeyer, 29, rue Ettore-Bugatti, 67120 Molsheim, tel. 03.88.38.12.45, fax 03.88.38.11.27, e-mail domaine.neumeyer@wanadoo.fr ☑
☖ ev. day except Sun. 9am–12 noon 2pm–7pm

Alsace Grand Cru Eichberg

CHARLES BAUR

Riesling 2001★★

| | 0.4 ha | 3,300 | ⦙⦙⦙ | 11–15 € |

This family estate, dating from the 18th century, started its own bottling in 1946. With 13 ha of vines today, it has an envied place in the cradle of the Alsatian wine region. Following the *coup de coeur* awarded for its 99, it offers an elegant, fruity Riesling worthy of its reputation. This highly concentrated wine has a fairly supple attack, then goes on to reveal its crystallized fruit flavours to the palate. The finish is distinctively complex. (Residual sugar: 11.7 g/l.)

☛ Charles Baur, 29, Grand-Rue, 68420 Eguisheim, tel. 03.89.41.32.49, fax 03.89.41.55.79, e-mail cave@vinscharlesbaur.fr ☑
☖ ev. day except Sun. 9am–12 noon 2pm–6pm

ALBERT HERTZ

Riesling 2001★

| | 0.25 ha | 2,000 | ⦙⦙⦙ | 8–11 € |

In charge since 1976, Albert Hertz exports 40% of this estate's production. He has received numerous international distinctions that have taken the colours of his cherished town of Eguisheim to the heights. Selection by this *Guide* also has an impact abroad. The star awarded to this Riesling is for a wine whose nose is already very open despite its limestone-clay origins. Beginning with a lovely attack, it is dry, classy and long-lasting. Ideal for the most refined of fish dishes. (Residual sugar: 4 g/l.)

☛ Albert Hertz, 3, rue du Riesling, 68420 Eguisheim, tel. 03.89.41.30.32, fax 03.89.23.99.23, e-mail info@alberthertz.com ☑
☖ by appt.

Wines selected but not starred

EMILE BEYER

Riesling 2001

| | 0.85 ha | 3,200 | ⦙⦙⦙ | 11–15 € |

☛ Emile Beyer, 7, pl. du Château, BP 3, 68420 Eguisheim, tel. 03.89.41.40.45, fax 03.89.41.64.21, e-mail info@emile-beyer.fr ☑ ☖
☖ ev. day 9am–12 noon 2pm–6pm

HAEFFELIN

Riesling 2001

| | 0.42 ha | 3,000 | ▮ | 5–8 € |

☛ Vignoble Daniel Haeffelin, 8, rue des Merles, 68420 Eguisheim, tel. 03.89.41.77.85, fax 03.89.23.32.43 ☑
☖ ev. day 8am–12 noon 2pm–7pm

ODILE ET DANIELLE WEBER

Riesling 2001

| | 0.3 ha | 2,000 | ⦙⦙⦙ | 11–15 € |

☛ Odile et Danielle Weber, 14, rue de Colmar, 68420 Eguisheim, tel. 03.89.41.35.56, fax 03.89.41.35.56 ☑
☖ by appt.

Alsace Grand Cru Florimont

FRANCOIS BOHN

Riesling 2001★

| | 0.9 ha | 1,500 | ▮ | 8–11 € |

This wine-grower cultivates more than 6 ha across the boundaries of four civil parishes in the Colmar district. Most are planted on slopes. François Bohn had enough going for him to begin bottling his own in 1998. His success has been reflected by selections in this *Guide*. Here are two very different one-star Grand Cru wines. First, this Riesling: a complex bouquet of ripe fruit and a hint of minerals, a supple attack, a rich palate and a liveliness that emphasizes the lemony finish. (Residual sugar: 12 g/l.) Then the **Gewurztraminer 2001 (11–15 €)**: a bright golden yellow colour with orange tinges, notes of overripeness, toast and spices, and a palate that begins in freshness despite a very definite sweetness, and a long-lasting finish of dried fruit flavours. (Residual sugar: 24 g/l.)

☛ François Bohn, 35, rue des Trois-Épis, 68040 Ingersheim, tel. 03.89.27.31.27, fax 03.89.27.31.27 ☑
☖ by appt.

RENE MEYER

Tokay-pinot gris Vendanges tardives 2000★★

	0.28 ha	1,450	⬛	15–23 €

Jean-Paul Meyer works over 8 ha of vines planted mainly on limestone-clay terroirs that often yield wines with good structures and enduring aromas. This is true of the Florimont terroir, which previously produced a three-star 99 Pinot Gris and a *coup de coeur* Gewurztraminer 2000, and which now gives us this late harvest Pinot Gris wine. Bright gold in the glass, it has a complex and expressive nose of honey, crystallized fruits and citrus fruit. On the palate, it is full-bodied, rich, full and soundly structured, with liveliness and a finish of crystallized and dried fruits. It has everything. A classy wine and a wine to keep.

➻ EARL René Meyer et Fils, 14, Grand-Rue, 68230 Katzenthal, tel. 03.89.27.04.67, fax 03.89.27.50.59, e-mail domaine.renemeyer@wanadoo.fr ☑
🍷 by appt.
🍇 Jean-Paul Meyer

Alsace Grand Cru Frankstein

YVETTE ET MICHEL BECK-HARTWEG

Gewurztraminer 2001★

	0.31 ha	2,300	11–15 €

Dambach-la-Ville and its medieval walls, a 17th century half-timbered house, a cellar lined with oak casks, a vineyard passed down the generations: such is the background to the Frankstein Grand Cru. Yvette and Michel Beck-Hartweg grow some 5 ha of vines, several plots of which produce this Grand Cru. It is a granite terroir and has yielded two wines selected by the Jury, of which this Gewurztraminer is the finer. A fairly pale yellow with straw tinges, it is already expressive and complex, with notes of citrus fruits and spices that are evident to nose and palate alike. After pleasing first impressions, the palate goes on to demonstrate good balance, length and suppleness. (Residual sugar: 28 g/l.) The **Riesling 2001 (8–11 €)** is selected for its intense and complex bouquet of ripe fruits, almond and mint, as well as for its fairly honeyed palate. It will achieve final balance in two to three years' time. (Residual sugar: 8 g/l.)

➻ Yvette et Michel Beck-Hartweg, 5, rue Clemenceau, 67650 Dambach-la-Ville, tel. 03.88.92.40.20, fax 03.88.92.63.44, e-mail yvette.michel.beck.hartweg@wanadoo.fr ☑
🍷 by appt.

KROSSFELDER

Tokay-pinot gris 2001★

	n.c.	n.c.	11–15 €

The Frankstein terroir, at Dambach-la-Ville, consists of south-southeast-facing slopes of granitic sandy soils. Every spring, this Grand Cru is honoured by the *Pierres et Vins de Granite* demonstration organized by the *Confrérie des Bienheureux du Frankstein*. The Krossfelder cooperative has been in the village some hundred years and here offers a golden-yellow Tokay with bright glints. There is a bouquet of elegant perfumes of ripe fruits and honeyed notes. Balanced, not excessively sweet, the palate has a rich, long-lasting finish characterized by flavours of crystallized quince. A gastronomic wine. (Residual sugar: 30 g/l.)

➻ Cave vinicole Krossfelder, 39, rue de la Gare, 67650 Dambach-la-Ville, tel. 03.88.92.40.03, fax 03.88.92.42.89 ☑
🍷 by appt.

Alsace Grand Cru Furstentum

DOM. PAUL BLANCK

Riesling 2001★

	1.7 ha	9,000	⬛⬛	11–15 €

The Blanck family has been in viticulture since the 17th century. The estate of Paul Blanck et Fils, founded in 1947, has grown since, not only in area (36 ha) but also in reputation. It is very committed to promotion of the Grand Cru, and has plots in five of the delimited terroirs. This Riesling comes from the Furstentum terroir, with its limestone soil, and has aromas of dried fruits and overripeness. After a beautiful start, the palate goes on to reveal a rare richness and breadth. This is a wine to leave in the cellars for a few years. (Residual sugar: 18 g/l.)

➻ Dom. Paul Blanck, 32, Grand-Rue, 68240 Kientzheim, tel. 03.89.78.23.56, fax 03.89.47.16.45, e-mail info@blanck.com ☑
🍷 ev. day except Sun. 9am–12 noon 1.30pm–6pm; cl. Nov. until Mar.

DOM. BOTT-GEYL

Gewurztraminer 2001★★

	0.5 ha	3,200	⬛	15–23 €

At Beblenheim, established there by Jean-David Geyl in 1825, this estate is nowadays run on biodynamic lines. The owner gets the best out of his 12.5 ha of vines, as is proved by the number of wines that get into the *Guide*, including several *coups de coeur*. This Gewurztraminer, from the brown, limestone soil of the Furstentum Grand Cru, is a marvel: a gold colour with intense orange highlights, a nose of ripe fruits and citrus fruits (grapefruit), a perfect attack combining crystallized fruits with a lovely freshness, plus a rich, unctuous, heady palate of great length. A high-class wine. (Residual sugar: 55 g/l.)

➻ Dom. Bott-Geyl, 1, rue du Petit-Château, 68980 Beblenheim, tel. 03.89.47.90.04, fax 03.89.47.97.33, e-mail bottgeyl@libertysurf.fr ☑ ☎
🍷 by appt.
🍇 Bott

J. FRITSCH

Gewurztraminer 2001★

	0.37 ha	3,100	⬛	8–11 €

Kientzheim has hung onto its medieval walls and tower, and it is here that the *Confrérie Saint-Etienne* is based, in Baron de Schwendi's castle. The estate owns some vines locally in the Furstenheim Grand Cru, the source of Gewurztraminers often commended by the Hachette Juries, as is this 2001. Its pale yellow colour signals its youth. Though still discreet, it reveals its aromatic potential in the perfumes of rose and lychee already evident. It will be appreciated for its excellent substance, length, and fruity finish, which evokes half-stewed and exotic fruits (Residual sugars: 35 g/l.)

➻ EARL Joseph Fritsch, 31, Grand-Rue, 68240 Kientzheim, tel. 03.89.78.24.27, fax 03.89.78.16.53, e-mail vinsjosephfritsch@wanadoo.fr ☑
🍷 by appt.

Alsace Grand Cru Gloeckelberg

KOEBERLE KREYER

Tokay-pinot gris 2001★★

	0.11 ha	800	⬛	11–15 €

Dominated by the castle of Haut-Koenigsbourg, the village of Rodern is surrounded by vineyards whose most famous terroir is the Gloeckelberg, on sandy granitic soils. It is a

Grand Cru that has produced some very expressive Pinots Gris, like those of this estate, which often gain mention in the *Guide*. After the exceptional 99, which was a *coup de coeur*, here is a similar wine, with a shining golden colour, mingled scents of citrus fruit, quince and passion-fruit, and great concentration. These traits give it an almost late-harvest style. Here is beautiful complexity and fruity notes that underscore the long finish: remarkable. (Residual sugar: 35 g/l.)
↜ Koeberlé Kreyer, 28, rue du Pinot-Noir, 68590 Rodern, tel. 03.89.73.00.55, fax 03.89.73.00.55,
e-mail fkoeberle@free.fr ☑ 🏠
☂ by appt.

Alsace Grand Cru Goldert

HENRI GROSS
Gewurztraminer 2001★

	0.47 ha	3,000		8–11 €

The headquarters of this estate are in an 18th century house in Gueberschwihr, a pretty village famous for the tall Romanesque bell-tower of pink sandstone depicted on the wine-label. Within the village boundary is the Goldert Cru, a limestone-clay terroir particularly suited to Gewurztraminer. It has yielded this golden wine with occasional orange highlights. Though discreet at first, the nose of this 2001 opens to reveal notes of overripe fruit with hints of almond paste, honey and lychee. Potent, generous, and long-lasting, the palate is still a trifle over-sweet and needs time for further refinement. Sample on its own or with dessert – a cherry tart, perhaps. (Residual sugar: 31.1 g/l.)
↜ EARL Henri Gross et Fils, 11, rue du Nord, 68420 Gueberschwihr, tel. 03.89.49.24.49,
fax 03.89.49.33.58,
e-mail vins.gross@wanadoo.fr ☑
☂ by appt.

SAULNIER
Tokay-pinot gris Les Eboulis 2001★

	0.35 ha	2,400		8–11 €

Wine-growers' houses with cellars and courtyards, Renaissance dwellings, a former washhouse, a Romanesque house: Gueberschwihr reflects prosperity. This is old wealth, to which the Goldert Grand Cru has contributed. This Tokay shows the terroir's potential. Golden yellow in the glass, with a slightly discreet bouquet, this wine nevertheless is starting to waft notes of flowers and fruits. It also has a cleanness and freshness that is unhindered by an excess of sweetness. The fullness of the palate is underscored by a very authentic minerality. This wine has almost achieved perfect integration and will go very well with a fish or with poultry in sauce. (Residual sugar: 16 g/l.)
↜ Marco Saulnier, 43, rue Haute, 68420 Gueberschwihr, tel. 03.89.86.42.02, fax 03.89.49.34.82 ☑
☂ by appt.

Alsace Grand Cru Hatschbourg

BUECHER-FIX
Gewurztraminer 2001★★

	0.58 ha	4,900		11–15 €

The Hatschbourg is located in the district of Hattstatt and Voegtlinshoffen, south of Colmar. The vines are stepped on a regular slope between 200 and 230 m above sea-level. They gain from facing south and being planted in a well-aerated stony limestone-clay. In recent years this estate has produced some very fine Gewurztraminers. This golden-yellow 2001 has green highlights and an intensely expressive nose, with concentrated perfumes of exotic fruits (lychee, mango, passion-fruit). The balance is perfect, joining potency, fullness and length to finesse and elegance. Its fruity overripeness and superb spicy notes complete the portrait of a remarkable vintage. (Residual sugar: 26 g/l.)
↜ Buecher-Fix, 21, rue Sainte-Gertrude,
68920 Wettolsheim, tel. 03.89.30.12.80, fax 03.89.30.12.81,
e-mail buecher@terre-net.fr ☑
☂ by appt.

GINGLINGER-FIX
Gewurztraminer 2001★

n.c.	4,000		11–15 €

Heirs to a long line of wine-growers going back to 1610, André and Marie-Paule Ginglinger, recently joined by their daughter Eliane, an oenologist, run this estate. Part of their vineyard extends over the Hatschbourg Grand Cru, a limestone-clay terroir with a scattering of débris on which the Gewurztraminer grapes turn to gold in the midday sun. This variety has produced a bright golden-yellow wine with green highlights and a bouquet richly evocative of crystallized fruits. After hitting the palate with pleasing finesse, the wine reveals delicate flavours of airy elegance. (Residual sugar: 24 gl.)
↜ Ginglinger-Fix, 38, rue Roger-Frémeaux,
68420 Voegtlinshoffen, tel. 03.89.49.30.75,
fax 03.89.49.29.98,
e-mail ginglinger-fix@wanadoo.fr ☑
☂ ev. day except Sun. 8.30am–12 noon 1.30pm–7pm
↜ André Ginglinger

ANDRE HARTMANN
Gewurztraminer Armoirie Hartmann 2001★★

	0.8 ha	6,000		8–11 €

The Hartmann family have, since the 17th century, clung to the "balcony of Alsace" – the village of Voegtlinshoffen, south of Colmar, so-called because of the altitude of its position at the start of the Vosges and the panoramic views it affords. A sizeable number of its vines grow on the Hatschbourg, a clay-limestone Grand Cru suited to all the noble varieties of Alsace, starting with Gewurztraminer and Pinot Gris. This golden 2001 with orange highlights begins in a reserved manner, yet goes on to disclose intense aromas of exotic fruits (lychee and mango). First impressions on the palate are of a remarkable alliance of richness and freshness, leading to a very concentrated, lengthy, beautiful elegance, which finishes on notes of honey-wrapped crystallized fruits. Authentic to its terroir, this wine would go well with glazed duck or *tarte Tatin* (upside-down apple tart). (Residual sugar: 30 g/l.)
↜ André Hartmann, 11, rue Roger-Frémeaux, 68420 Voegtlinshoffen, tel. 03.89.49.38.34,
fax 03.89.49.26.18 ☑ 🏠
☂ ev. day except Sun. 9am–12 noon 2pm–6pm;
by appt. during the grape harvest

ANDRE HARTMANN
Tokay-pinot gris Armoirie Hartmann 2001★

	0.27 ha	2,000		8–11 €

The Hatschbourg is a favoured terroir for Pinot Gris. This Pinot is an intense yellow with golden highlights, and already has powerful aromas very typical of the cru, of very ripe, honey-coated fruit (especially kernel fruits). Full and powerful, the very authentic palate reveals a complex range of aromas including mirabelle (plum) and exotic fruits. The finish is very pleasantly long. This is a food-lover's wine and will go well with veal and mushrooms, spicy foie gras, poultry, or spicy dishes in general. (Residual sugar: 25 g/l.)
↜ André Hartmann, 11, rue Roger-Frémeaux,
68420 Voegtlinshoffen, tel. 03.89.49.38.34,
fax 03.89.49.26.18 ☑ 🏠
☂ ev. day except Sun. 9am–12 noon 2pm–6pm;
by appt. during the grape harvest

LUCIEN MEYER ET FILS

Gewurztraminer 2001★

| | 0.39 ha | 3,200 |  | 8–11 € |

This estate's headquarters are in an ancient (16th century) dwelling opposite Hattstatt town hall. Though in existence since 1890, it has grown over the generations to its present 10 ha. Part of the vineyard lies on the limestone-clay of the Hatschbourg Grand Cru, which greatly favours Gewurztraminer. This particular Gewurztraminer is a glinting golden yellow, with a nose already authentically perfumed and rich in notes of overripened fruits verging towards jamminess. It also has an acidity that gives the palate a great freshness. The long finish is underscored by peppery notes. "Superbly balanced and well-blended" was one taster's conclusion. (Residual sugar: 36 g/l.) Lovers of dry wines will want to try the **Riesling Grand Cru Hatschbourg 2001 (5–8 €)**, selected by the Jury. It has a bouquet of white flowers and acacia, and a palate that hints also at bergamot. Lively and well-balanced, it will suit fish and seafood. (Residual sugar: 35 g/l.)
☞ EARL Lucien Meyer et Fils, 57, rue du Mal-Leclerc, 68420 Hattstatt, tel. 03.89.49.31.74, fax 03.89.49.24.81 ▨ ⌂
⌐ by appt.

Alsace Grand Cru Hengst

DOM. ANDRE EHRHART

Gewurztraminer 2001★

| | 0.52 ha | 3,200 | | 8–11 € |

Founded in 1959, this estate is run from a traditional house dating from 1739. It works some 10 ha of vines planted on terroirs of varying sorts. The Hengst Grand Cru is probably the jewel in the crown. It has produced a Gewurztraminer with a deep golden colour and a most attractive bouquet redolent of lychee and hazelnut. The attack is full, with both richness and great finesse, heightened by an exotic fruitiness (mango). The palate has length, good balance, and sufficient freshness. This wine could be served with certain blue cheeses or a dessert. (Residual sugar: 45 g/l.)
☞ André Ehrhart et Fils, 68, rue Herzog, 68920 Wettolsheim, tel. 03.89.80.66.16, fax 03.89.79.44.20 ▨
⌐ ev. day except Sun. 8am–12 noon 2pm–6pm

HUBERT KRICK

Gewurztraminer 2000★

| | 0.49 ha | 3,600 | | 8–11 € |

Hubert Krick is based at Wintzenheim, several kilometres west of Colmar at the entrance to the Munster valley. Here we find the Hengst Grand Cru, a terroir composed of Oligocene conglomerates over limestone-clay. It has produced a Gewurztraminer with an attractive bright gold colour and a very rich nose that mingles a varied fruitiness (exotic fruits, fig, pear) with peppery notes. After initial impressions of finesse, one discovers a typical product of this terroir, classy and somewhat lively. A well-balanced, elegant whole, that would go well with spicy dishes. (Residual sugar: 18 g/l.)
☞ EARL Hubert Krick, 93–95, rue Clemenceau, 68920 Wintzenheim, tel. 03.89.27.00.01, fax 03.89.27.54.75 ▨
⌐ by appt.

ALBERT MANN

Tokay-pinot gris 2001★★★

| | 0.7 ha | 5,000 | | 11–15 € |

Developed since 1984 by Jacky and Maurice Barthelmé, the Mann estate runs to 19 ha of vines, which is no mean size for an Alsatian vineyard. Its other big advantage lies in having

plots in five Grands Crus, which explains why it often appears in the *Guide*. This year, it gets a top position for its superb Pinot Gris. Deep gold in colour, the wine exhales a rich mix of floral perfumes, which hint at pepper, assorted spices and crystallized fruits. After a firm attack, the palate has a distinctive freshness and finesse. It also has a very assertive aromatic character, with notes of flowers and fruits, and a highly elegant finish. "Plenty of energy," commented one Jury member. Overall, a classy example of what this terroir can produce. (Residual sugar: 48 g/l.)
☞ Dom. Albert Mann, 13, rue du Château, 68920 Wettolsheim, tel. 03.89.80.62.00, fax 03.89.80.34.23, e-mail vins@mann-albert.com ▨
⌐ by appt.
☞ Barthelmé

MOELLINGER

Gewurztraminer 2001★

| | 0.52 ha | 4,000 | | 5–8 € |

The Hengst is one of the great wine terroirs in Alsace. It faces southeast on a steep slope 270–360 m above sea-level. Its somewhat heavy limestone-clay soil suits Gewurztraminer. This is the case with the Moellinger estate, which has done well with this 2001. Pale gold with green highlights, it betrays relative youth, while nonetheless revealing a rich bouquet of well-defined aromas of honey and exotic fruits. The palate shows high elegance and has great length. The wine's considerable freshness contributes to its balance and makes it easy to drink despite its potency. It could be served with goose liver or a Munster cheese (not too ripe). (Residual sugar: 43.1 g/l.)
☞ SCEA Joseph Moellinger et Fils, 6, rue de la 5ᵉ-D.-B., 68920 Wettolsheim, tel. 03.89.80.62.02, fax 03.89.80.04.94 ▨
⌐ ev. day 8am–12 noon 1.30pm–7pm; Sun. by appt.; cl. Oct.

BERNARD STAEHLE

Gewurztraminer 2001★

| | 0.24 ha | 1,700 | | 11–15 € |

The limestone-clay and conglomerates of the Hengst can produce wines with solid, well-built characters, and they can be as spirited as the stallion Hengst that gave its name to this Grand Cru. This 2001 is a pleasing, well-balanced wine. The colour is a bright, clear gold, the nose fairly intense and typically Gewurztraminer, with an extra hint at crusty bread. After pleasing beginnings evocative of fruit and roses, the palate goes on to an extremely long finish on lychee. This Gewurztraminer may be drunk as an aperitif or served with all kinds of dishes – sweet or savoury. (Residual sugar: 17 g/l.)
☞ Bernard Staehlé, 15, rue Clemenceau, 68920 Wintzenheim, tel. 03.89.27.39.02, fax 03.89.27.59.37 ▨
⌐ by appt.

DOM. AIME STENTZ ET FILS Clos du

Vicus romain Muscat Vendanges tardives 2000★

| | 0.19 ha | 1,300 | | 15–23 € |

It is not easy to produce good late-harvest wine from a variety as delicate as Muscat. When successful, however, the result can have a rare elegance. Take this 2000. The colour is a very intense golden yellow, and the nose is rich and concentrated, evocative of dried or even crystallized Muscat grapes. On the palate the wine reveals its full power, sweet yet not heavy, with flavours recalling the bouquet, similar in quality and no less rich. The finish is firm, consistent and enjoyable. A lovely aperitif wine.

➤ Aimé Stentz, 37, rue Herzog, 68920 Wettolsheim, tel. 03.89.80.63.77, fax 03.89.79.78.68, e-mail stentz.e@calixo.net ☑
☿ ev. day except Sun. 8am–12 noon 2pm–6pm

Alsace Grand Cru Kanzlerberg

DOM. SYLVIE SPIELMANN
Gewurztraminer 2001★

	0.5 ha	3,500		11–15 €

Sylvie Spielmann is a very sensitive wine-grower. A proportion of her eight-hectare estate is situated on the Kanzlerberg, and she has made a speciality of this Grand Cru near Bergheim, the smallest delimitation in all Alsace. The terroir faces south and southwest, and is remarkable for the presence of gypsum, mixed with grey and black clay and limestone. It has produced this yellow Gewurztraminer with bright golden highlights and a bouquet that is already intensely spicy. Rich and solidly structured, the wine opens on complex flavours of crystallized fruits with hints of citrus fruits that contribute freshness. The palate finishes on spices that captivate the taste buds. A very pleasant whole that would go well with Alsatian cinnamon specialities. (Residual sugar: 36 g/l.)

➤ Dom. Sylvie Spielmann, 2, rte de Thannenkirch, 68750 Bergheim, tel. 03.89.73.35.95, fax 03.89.73.27.35, e-mail sylvie@sylviespielmann.com ☑
☿ ev. day except Sun. 9am–12 noon 2pm–6pm; Sat. by appt.

Alsace Grand Cru Kastelberg

GUY WACH
Riesling Cuvée Vieilles Vignes 2001★

	0.58 ha	3,600		11–15 €

The age-old town of Andlau has retained a fine church with a superb Romanesque porch, the remnant of an abbey whose Carolingian origins are lost in a legend about Saint Richardis, a mother bear and a wild valley. The land was soon given up to vines, and today favours several Grands Crus, including Kastelberg, the only delimited schist terroir in this AOC Grand Cru. It has provided Guy Wach with some extremely interesting wines (a 99 Riesling was a *coup de coeur*). This one has a bouquet marked by notes of brioche and dried fruits. The palate is round and rich, with noteworthy residual sugar. The structure is nonetheless powerful enough to provide balance. (Residual sugar: 22 g/l.)

➤ Guy Wach, Dom. des Marronniers, 5, rue de la Commanderie, 67140 Andlau, tel. 03.88.08.93.20, fax 03.88.08.45.59 ☑ 🏠 🏠
☿ by appt.

Alsace Grand Cru Kirchberg-de-Barr

DOM. STOEFFLER
Riesling 2001★★

	0.6 ha	4,000		8–11 €

Comprising some 12 ha of vines in Riquewihr and Barr, the Stoeffler estate has over the last twenty years earned a merited reputation for its wines, which are often selected for the *Guide*, especially the Rieslings. This vintage comes from a limestone-clay terroir and is characterized by aromas of citrus fruit and overripeness. After agreeable first impressions, the palate reveals fullness, balance, and length. The lovely acid structure gives it bearing. "A wine with a strong voice," said one taster. An excellent accompaniment to lobster or fish in sauce.

➤ Dom. Martine and Vincent Stoeffler, 1, rue des Lièvres, 67140 Barr, tel. 03.88.08.52.50, fax 03.88.08.17.09, e-mail info@vins-stoeffler.com ☑
☿ by appt.

Alsace Grand Cru Kirchberg-de-Ribeauvillé

JEAN SIPP
Riesling 2001★★★

	1.5 ha	6,000		11–15 €

Based in a Renaissance dwelling that used to belong to the powerful Ribeaupierre family, Jean Sipp currently works a large vineyard of 20 ha. Its reputation extends abroad, as half the estate's production is exported. The nose is extremely complex, with aromas of citrus fruit, honey and quince, showing that once again this Riesling deserves its top reputation for excellence. The palate is equally intense, well structured, concentrated, fresh and long-lasting. A unanimous rating for this wine. (Residual sugar: 8 g/l.)

➤ Dom. Jean Sipp, 60, rue de la Fraternité, 68150 Ribeauvillé, tel. 03.89.73.60.02, fax 03.89.73.82.38, e-mail domaine@jean-sipp.com ☑ 🏠
☿ by appt.

LOUIS SIPP
Riesling 2001★★

	1.29 ha	8,222		11–15 €

Although the firm of Louis Sipp has been in the wine trade since 1920, it has not entirely forgotten its wine-growing origins; it still works its own 32 ha of vines and prides itself on making successful vintages. This Riesling has a nose of fruits (citrus fruits, raisins and apricot) and white flowers, and a palate of great complexity. Lively, rich, and well-structured, this is a classy wine that is well-equipped to keep for a long time. (Residual sugar: 10 g/l.)

- Louis Sipp, 5, Grand-Rue, 68150 Ribeauvillé, tel. 03.89.73.60.01, fax 03.89.73.31.46, e-mail louis@sipp.com ☑
- by appt.
- Pierre Sipp

Alsace Grand Cru Kitterlé

DOMAINES SCHLUMBERGER
Gewurztraminer Vendanges tardives 2000★★★

				30–38 €
4.9 ha	12,764			

Established by Nicolas Schlumberger in 1810 and developed by Ernest Schlumberger after the First World War, this wine estate is today the largest in Alsace and runs to 145 ha. The vines are planted on steep slopes, with gradients that can reach 55%. Almost one half (70 ha) is delimited Grand Cru. The Kitterlé has yielded this glinting old-gold late-harvest Gewurztraminer, which has intense perfumes of honeysuckle and rose with aftertones of spice. Deep, powerful, rich, heady and well-structured, it finishes on extremely long-lasting notes of crystallized fruits and spices. Ready to drink now, but could wait.

- Domaines Schlumberger, 100, rue Théodore-Deck, 68501 Guebwiller Cedex, tel. 03.89.74.27.00, fax 03.89.74.85.75, e-mail dvschlum@aol.com ☑
- by appt.

Alsace Grand Cru Mambourg

DOM. JEAN-MARC BERNHARD
Gewurztraminer 2001★★

			11–15 €
0.27 ha	2,000		

This estate has been passed down from father to son since 1802 and is today run by Jean-Marc Bernhard and his son Frédéric, who is an oenologist. Of their 9 ha, two are cultivated organically, the remainder sustainably. They have plots in four Grands Crus, including the Mambourg, which often produces vintages selected for the *Guide*. Gold in colour with strong, yellow highlights, this Gewurztraminer mingles aromas of overripened quince and mirabelle (plum) within a bouquet that is already powerful and complex. It is very rounded on the palate, where it provides a sensation of enveloping mellowness. Notes of quince jam emphasize the fullness and richness. A wine with length, which will improve its integration over time. (Residual sugar: 25.6 g/l.)

- Domaine Jean-Marc Bernhard, 21, Grand-Rue, 68230 Katzenthal, tel. 03.89.27.05.34, fax 03.89.27.58.72, e-mail jeanmarcbernhard@online.fr ☑
- ev. day except Sun. 9am–12 noon 2pm–6.30pm; groups by appt.

DANIEL FRITZ ET FILS Gewurztraminer
Sélection de grains nobles 2000★★★

			23–30 €
0.26 ha	1,100		

Sigolsheim, at the entrance to the Kayserberg valley, is a village famous for its wine, particularly those of the Mambourg Grand Cru. This south-facing terroir with its limestone-clay soils benefits from a microclimate that stores heat from spring through to autumn. It is extremely favourable to Gewurztraminer. This particular vintage is dressed in sunlight, having a golden colour with deep-yellow glints. There are early perfumes of pineapple and fresh apricots, followed by an explosion of aromatic complexity and a fondant palate that is "smooth as velvet" and perfectly balanced. The full, extraordinarily long-lasting finish leaves the palate with peppery notes but above all impressions of crystallized fruits.

- Daniel Fritz, 3, rue du Vieux-Moulin, 68240 Sigolsheim, tel. 03.89.47.11.15, fax 03.89.78.17.07 ☑
- by appt.

Alsace Grand Cru Mandelberg

DOM. DU BOUXHOF
Gewurztraminer 2001★

			8–11 €
0.21 ha	1,300		

The history of the Bouxhof estate goes back eight centuries, as is attested by some 12th century parchments. It is the only wine estate in Alsace officially classified as an historical monument. Part of its vineyard lies in the Mandelberg Grand Cru, which has produced this white-gold Gewurztraminer. The bouquet is a spicy mix with hints of beeswax and linden blossom; this complexity is confirmed by a full palate that is extended by long notes of roasted hazelnuts. (Residual sugar: 14.5 g/l.)

- EARL François Edel et Fils, Dom. du Bouxhof, 68630 Mittelwihr, tel. 03.89.47.90.34, fax 03.89.47.84.82, e-mail edel.bouxhof@online.fr ☑
- ev. day 9am–7pm

HORCHER
Gewurztraminer 2001★

			11–15 €
0.27 ha	1,800		

The Mandelberg hillside protects the village of Mittelwihr from northerly winds. Because it has an ideal south-southeast exposure and a well aerated stony limestone-clay soil that heats up early in spring, it is particularly suitable for Gewurztraminer; 40% of it is planted with that variety. A deep gold colour enlivened by odd glints of orangey yellow, this wine exhales smoky scents associated with honey. The well-balanced palate assimilates the residual sugar well and finishes on hints of acacia-perfumed smoke with mineral notes. (Residual sugar: 29 g/l.)

- Ernest Horcher et Fils, 6, rue du Vignoble, 68630 Mittelwihr, tel. 03.89.47.93.26, fax 03.89.49.04.92, e-mail info@horcher.fr ☑
- ev. day except Sun. 9am–12 noon 2pm–7pm

Wines selected but not starred

BERNARD WURTZ
Riesling 2001

			15–23 €
0.24 ha	800		

- Bernard Wurtz, 12, rue du Château, 68630 Mittelwihr, tel. 03.89.47.93.24, fax 03.89.86.01.69 ☑
- by appt.

Alsace Grand Cru Moenchberg

ALBERT MAURER
Tokay-pinot gris 2001★

| | 0.5 ha | 3,200 | | 5–8 € |

Eichhoffen, near Barr, is crowned by the Moenchberg Grand Cru, on limestone-clay. Pinot Gris is the grape-variety of choice. It has produced this limpid yellow wine, redolent of flowers and raisins and with a slightly smoky character. Powerful and round, it is not excessively sweet; the finish is long and complex with a final mineral note. (Residual sugar: 20 g/l.)
☎ Albert Maurer, 11, rue du Vignoble, 67140 Eichhoffen, tel. 03.88.08.96.75, fax 03.88.08.59.98,
e-mail info@vins-maurer.fr ☑ ⌂
⏰ ev. day except Sun. 9am–12 noon 1.30pm–6.30pm

Alsace Grand Cru Muenchberg

J.-M. WASSLER
Riesling 2001★

| | 0.1 ha | 900 | ▌ | 5–8 € |

Jean-Marie Wassler, who first ventured into wine-growing in 1968, was joined by his son Fabrice in 2001 on their 8 ha of vines. Their Riesling, grown on granite soil, has an intense colour and already shows some evolution. The nose mingles crystallized fruits with a mineral note, while the palate is lively, well-balanced, and long-lasting. (Residual sugar: 7.8 g/l.)
☎ EARL Jean-Marie Wassler et Fils, 22, rte des Vins, 67680 Nothalten, tel. 03.88.92.43.51, fax 03.88.92.63.97,
e-mail jeanmarie.wassler@free.fr ☑ ⌂
⏰ by appt.

Alsace Grand Cru Osterberg

RENE JOGGERST ET FILS
Riesling 2001★

| | 0.3 ha | 2,200 | | 11–15 € |

Based in very old buildings of the 15th and 18th centuries, the Joggerst family tend 7 ha of vines. They enter the *Guide* with a deep-yellow gold Riesling strongly redolent of citrus fruits. Lively as it hits the palate, this dry Riesling is complex and long-lasting. It could be served straightaway with fish, but may get even better given time. (Residual sugar: 2.9 g/l.)
☎ Joggerst et Fils, 19, Grand-Rue, 68150 Ribeauvillé, tel. 03.89.73.66.32, fax 03.89.73.65.45,
e-mail vins.joggerst@ifrance.com ☑
⏰ ev. day except Sun. 9am–12 noon 2pm–6pm

LOUIS SIPP
Gewurztraminer Sélection de grains nobles 2000★

| | 0.33 ha | 1,072 | | 38–46 € |

These merchants have their own sizeable estate of 32 ha, part of which lies within the Osterberg Grand Cru. From the terroir's limestone-clay soil and Gewurztraminer grapes they have followed up the gorgeous late-harvest 97 mentioned last year with a highly successful golden-yellow sweet wine that has a complex bouquet dominated by crystallized fruits. Notes of crystallized fruit (orange especially) are similarly found alongside notes of overripened fruits on the palate, which is powerful, rich and full, supported by a lovely acidity. Ready to drink now.
☎ Louis Sipp, 5, Grand-Rue, 68150 Ribeauvillé, tel. 03.89.73.60.01, fax 03.89.73.31.46,
e-mail louis@sipp.com ☑
⏰ by appt.
☎ Pierre Sipp

SIPP-MACK
Riesling 2001★

| | 0.75 ha | 5,000 | ▌⏰♦ | 11–15 € |

This estate, formed from the linking of two families working two different terroirs in the villages of Hunawihr, Ribeauvillé and Bergheim, is sizeable (20 ha). It offers a Riesling grown in the Osterberg, a terroir with limestone-clay soil. Despite the soil-type, the nose of this wine is already well open and is evocative of citrus fruits. Full and complex, well structured and long-lasting, it will go well with fish in sauce, shrimps or scampi. (Residual sugar:11 g/l)
☎ Dom. Sipp-Mack, 1, rue des Vosges, 68150 Hunawihr, tel. 03.89.73.61.88, fax 03.89.73.36.70,
e-mail sippmack@sippmack.com ☑ ⌂
⏰ by appt.

Alsace Grand Cru Pfersigberg

CHARLES BAUR
Gewurztraminer 2001★★

| | 0.46 ha | 1,380 | ⏰ | 11–15 € |

Established in the 18th century, this estate is today run by Armand Baur, an oenologist who has stamped his own style on the wines. This Gewurztraminer comes from the Pfersigberg, a magnificent east-southeast-facing slope with soils made up of limestone pebbles over limestone-clay. A brilliant light yellow colour, it has an attractively intense nose, dominated by citrus fruits (orange zest) with a hint of lychee. After an honest attack, the palate reveals a lovely balance; despite real sweetness, it is not at all heavy. A pleasing freshness marks the finish, which leaves the taster with delicate, elegant impressions of citrus fruits. For aperitif or dessert. (Residual sugar: 29 g/l.)
☎ Charles Baur, 29, Grand-Rue, 68420 Eguisheim, tel. 03.89.41.32.49, fax 03.89.41.55.79,
e-mail cave@vinscharlesbaur.fr ☑
⏰ ev. day except Sun. 9am–12 noon 2pm–6pm

JOSEPH FREUDENREICH ET FILS
Gewurztraminer 2001★

| | 0.5 ha | 3,700 | ▌♦ | 8–11 € |

This estate originated in the 11th century, during the days of Pope Leo IX. It is based at Eguisheim, in a tithe court, ancient like nearly everything within the encircling ramparts of the Alsatian Pope's native city. This wine, in contrast, is youthful, as is clear from the light yellow colour with green highlights and the nose that discreetly evokes ripe fruits and citrus. The palate makes a lovely beginning, and continues with a freshness that underscores a citrus fruitiness. Length and elegance also commend it. May be enjoyed now. (Residual sugar: 15 g/l.)
☎ Joseph Freudenreich et Fils, 3, cour Unterlinden, 68420 Eguisheim, tel. 03.89.41.36.87, fax 03.89.41.67.12,
e-mail info@joseph-freudenreich.fr ☑
⏰ ev. day 8am–12 noon 1.30pm–7pm; groups by appt.; cl. Sun. in winter

PAUL GINGLINGER

Riesling 2001★

| | 0.49 ha | 4,000 | 〰 | 8–11 € |

Eguisheim, assumed to be the cradle of Alsatian wine-growing, has kept its reputation thanks to wine-growers like Paul Ginglinger, now recently joined by his son. Their 12 ha of vines are planted on a variety of terroirs, some of them Grands Crus. This Riesling comes from the Pfersigberg and has a nose of citrus fruits and mineral notes. Well structured, lively and long-lasting, this is a food-lover's wine, ideal as an accompaniment to fish. (Residual sugar: 4 g/l.). Just as successful, though in a very different style, is the **Gewurztraminer Grand Cru Pfersigberg 2001**, a golden-yellow wine that leaves tears when swirled in the glass, with an open and elegant nose of crystallized fruits, linden blossom and spices. First impressions on the palate are honest and fruity, followed by complexity, richness and unctuousness, supported by fine acidity and good substance. (Residual sugar: 35 g/l.)
🍷 Paul Ginglinger, 8, pl. Charles-de-Gaulle,
68420 Eguisheim, tel. 03.89.41.44.25, fax 03.89.24.94.88 ☑
🍴 by appt.

HENRI GSELL

Gewurztraminer 2001★

| | 0.3 ha | 2,200 | 〰 | 11–15 € |

Here we find a small estate (a little under 4 ha), a cellar tucked away under one of the famous little streets in Eguisheim, and high-quality production, as witnessed by the selections in the *Guide*. This bright straw-yellow Gewurztraminer initially exhales floral scents before developing spicy aromas. Spices are similarly found on the palate (which is extremely sweet but has a clean attack), accompanied by aromas of leather and tobacco – a complex and highly original mix. This rich wine finishes on a very pleasant freshness. May be drunk as an aperitif, or as an accompaniment to foie gras, particular cheeses, or desserts. (Residual sugar: 34 g/l.)
🍷 Henri Gsell, 22, rue du Rempart-Sud, 68420 Eguisheim,
tel. 03.89.41.96.40, fax 03.89.41.58.46 ☑
🍴 by appt.

ALBERT HERTZ

Riesling 2001★

| | 0.31 ha | 2,600 | 〰 | 8–11 € |

This estate, which goes back to 1843, has been run since 1976 by Albert Hertz with much energy and enthusiasm. Forty per cent of the production is exported. The Pfersigberg Grand Cru has produced this Riesling, which already has an active bouquet, with aromas of dried apricot mixed with mineral notes. With its no-nonsense freshness, this is a long, well-balanced wine made from first-rate ingredients. (Residual sugar: 4 g/l.)
🍷 Albert Hertz, 3, rue du Riesling, 68420 Eguisheim,
tel. 03.89.41.30.32, fax 03.89.23.99.23,
e-mail info@alberthertz.com ☑
🍴 by appt.

FRANCOIS LICHTLE

Riesling 2001★

| | 0.18 ha | 1,200 | ▮ | 11–15 € |

Husseren-les-Châteaux is worth a detour. From there, perched up in the foothills of the Vosges, the visitor has a view over the plain of Alsace as far as Colmar. The village contains some talented wine-growers, like the Lichtlé family, who have tended vines here for four generations. Their vineyard includes some Grand Cru plots. The clayey sandstone of the Pfersigberg has produced a Riesling with a distinctive nose of overripe quince. After a lively attack, the palate has a structure that is typical of the variety. (Residual sugar: 3 g/l.)
🍷 Dom. François Lichtlé, 17, rue des Vignerons,
68420 Husseren-les-Châteaux, tel. 03.89.49.31.34,
fax 03.89.49.37.51, e-mail hlichtle@aol.com ☑ 🏠
🍴 by appt.

MICHEL SCHOEPFER

Riesling 2001★

| | 0.13 ha | 1,000 | 〰 | 5–8 € |

Descended from a long line of wine-growers, Michel Schoepfer has established his headquarters in the former tithe

court (13th century) of the Augustinian canons of Marbach Abbey. Reflecting the clayey limestone of its origins, his Pfersigberg Riesling still has a very young bouquet, the main accent being on lemon. After a floral attack, the palate reveals length and a well-balanced structure. (Residual sugar: 8 g/l.)
🍷 Dom. Michel Schoepfer et Fils, 43, Grand-Rue,
68420 Eguisheim, tel. 03.89.41.09.06, fax 03.89.23.08.50 ☑
🍴 by appt.

Alsace Grand Cru Pfingstberg

FRANCOIS BRAUN ET SES FILS

Gewurztraminer 2001★★

| | 0.55 ha | 3,600 | ▮ ♦ | 11–15 € |

This family have been tending vines since the 16th century, but have specialized in viticulture only in the last 50 years. They have considerably increased the surface area cultivated down the years to today's 21 ha, some of which is Grand Cru terrain. Gewurztraminer occupies a substantial proportion of the Pfingstberg, a terroir composed of limestone or micaceous sandstone. It has yielded this pale yellow wine with aromas of fig and crystallized fruits, notes of which elegantly enhance the finish. This 2001 is heady, powerful, unctuous and rounded. It is ready to drink now, but has real potential to mature further. (Residual sugar: 30 g/l.)
🍷 François Braun et ses Fils, 19, Grand-Rue,
68500 Orschwihr, tel. 03.89.76.95.13, fax 03.89.76.10.97 ☑
🍴 ev. day except Sun. 9am–11.30am 2pm–6pm

FRANCOIS SCHMITT

Gewurztraminer 2001★★

| | 0.44 ha | 1,500 | ▮ | 5–8 € |

This vineyard was established in 1972, which is recent for Alsace, though it has made headway by increasing in size from 3 to 11 ha. Quality has not been left behind, judging by this Gewurztraminer. The intense gold colour augures well. Though the nose is still discreet, there is potential in the fine perfumes of very ripe or crystallized fruits. Similar notes accompany the long finish of a wine that is noteworthy for its harmonious roundness and unctuosity. It would, of course, go with foie gras, but also with certain Chinese dishes. (Residual sugar: 45 g/l.)
🍷 Cave François Schmitt, 19, rte de Soultzmatt,
68500 Orschwihr, tel. 03.89.76.08.45, fax 03.89.76.44.02 ☑
🍴 by appt.

ALBERT ZIEGLER

Gewurztraminer Cuvée Elodie 2001★★

| | n.c. | 2,800 | ▮ | 8–11 € |

A large part of this estate lies on the slopes of the Bollenberg, a terroir with a dry, almost Mediterranean microclimate. It has been cultivated since 1998 by Michel and Christine Voelklin-Ziegler. As in the two previous years, they have a Gewurztraminer from the Pfingstberg, a terroir with a sandy limestone soil. This golden-yellow 2001 has a fairly original nose that mixes vanilla with tones of dry or crystallized fruits. Though the attack is rather sweet, the wine has impressive power. It will need keeping to reveal its full potential. (Residual sugar: 36.7 g/l.)
+🍷 Albert Ziegler, 10, rue de l'Eglise, 68500 Orschwihr,
tel. 03.89.76.01.12, fax 03.89.74.91.32 ☑
🍴 ev. day 8am–12 noon 1.30pm–7pm

Wines selected but not starred

CAMILLE BRAUN
Riesling 2001

	0.35 ha	2,500	🍴 🍷	8–11 €

📞 Camille Braun, 16, Grand-Rue, 68500 Orschwihr, tel. 03.89.76.95.20, fax 03.89.74.35.03, e-mail cbraun@terre-net.fr ☑ ⌂
🍷 ev. day except Sun. 8.30am–12 noon 1.30pm–6.30pm
📞 Christophe Braun

Alsace Grand Cru Praelatenberg

JEAN BECKER
Gewurztraminer 2001★

	0.2 ha	850	🍴 🍷	11–15 €

These Zellenberg merchants have their own 15 ha of vines. They offer a Gewurztraminer grown in the Praelatenberg, a terroir with a granitic soil that benefits from facing south-southeast. An intense golden-yellow colour, this wine has a pleasing nose of citrus fruits and honey. After a supple start, the palate reveals an intense fruitiness of mirabelle (plum) and quince. Full, unctuous, rich, well-balanced and lingering, this wine recalls late grape harvests. (Residual sugar: 60 g/l.)
📞 SA Jean Becker, 4, rte d'Ostheim, 68340 Zellenberg, tel. 03.89.47.90.16, fax 03.89.47.99.57 ☑
🍷 by appt.

DOM. ENGEL
Gewurztraminer 2001★★★

	0.85 ha	7,300	🍴 🍷	8–11 €

A large vineyard (18 ha), three-quarters of it planted on slopes, this estate benefits from 7 ha being in the siliceous Praelatenberg Grand Cru. Following the sweet, rich Gewurztraminer that was a remarkable *coup de coeur* in the last *Guide*, this year's 2001 Grand Cru is made from the same variety. An impressive straw-yellow with lots of nuances, the wine has a very delicate bouquet of citrus fruits, while the palate has real complexity: ripe or crystallized fruits (mirabelle plums) and spices. Extremely full, rich, unctuous and long-lasting, this wine leaves an impression of superb balance. A good wine to store. (Residual sugar: 30 g/l.)
📞 Dom. Engel Frères, 1, rue des Vignes, Haut-Koenigsbourg, 67600 Orschwiller, tel. 03.88.92.01.83, fax 03.88.92.17.27, e-mail vins-engel@wanadoo.fr ☑ ⌂
🍷 ev. day 9am–11.30am 2pm–6pm

DOM. ENGEL
Riesling 2001★

	0.85 ha	7,300	🍴 🍷	8–11 €

Influenced by its granitic origins, this Riesling exhales intense perfumes of fruits. The palate is rich and powerful, the result of using first-rate grapes. A well-balanced wine full of promise. (Residual sugar: 5 g/l.)
📞 Dom. Engel Frères, 1, rue des Vignes, Haut-Koenigsbourg, 67600 Orschwiller, tel. 03.89.92.01.83, fax 03.89.92.17.27, e-mail vins-engel@wanadoo.fr ☑ ⌂
🍷 ev. day 9am–11.30am 2pm–6pm

LES VIGNERONS RECOLTANTS D'ORSCHWILLER-KINTZHEIM
Riesling 2001★

	2.1 ha	12,600	🍴 🍷	5–8 €

This cooperative, founded in 1957, today totals 130 ha of vines. Its vinification cellar was renovated in 2001. This Riesling, from the Praelatenberg, a granite-gneiss terroir, is extremely good. The terroir is reflected in the nose, which is already well open and fruity, while the palate is classy and crunchy. An authentic, well-balanced wine. (Residual sugar: 11 g/l.)
📞 Cave vinicole Les Faîtières, 4A, rte du Vin, 67600 Orschwiller, tel. 03.88.92.09.87, fax 03.88.82.30.92, e-mail cave@cave-orschwiller.fr ☑
🍷 by appt.

LES VIGNERONS RECOLTANTS D'ORSCHWILLER-KINTZHEIM
Gewurztraminer 2001★★

	1.5 ha	9,000	🍴 🍷	8–11 €

The Praelatenberg terroir tends to be courted by the Gewurztraminer variety, and it must be said that the union tends to be a happy one. Proof is given by this straw-coloured wine with golden glints. The nose is of citrus fruits and spices. After a supple start, the palate goes on to reveal a pleasurably intense, almost crystallized fruitiness. There is an excellent lingering finish. The Jury advise storing in order to achieve fuller integration. (Residual sugar: 39 g/l.)
📞 Cave vinicole Les Faîtières, 4A, rte du Vin, 67600 Orschwiller, tel. 03.88.92.09.87, fax 03.88.82.30.92, e-mail cave@cave-orschwiller.fr ☑
🍷 by appt.

Alsace Grand Cru Rangen

CLOS SAINT-THEOBALD
Tokay-Pinot gris 2000★★★

	1.8 ha	6,000	🍴 🍷	46–76 €

The Schoffit estate has long figured among Colmar's vineyards. Under Bernard Schoffit, who took over in 1981, it extended into the Rangen terroir, and now has 17 ha. This famous volcanic Grand Cru, which faces due south, produces memorable wines year after year, as is witnessed by the many stars it earns in the *Guide*. This Tokay, with its intense yellow-gold colour, has a bouquet of rare complexity and richness, crowded with jostling honey-coated and crystallized fruits. The same degree of overripeness, with crystallized quince, appears on the palate, which is extremely concentrated, with a comprehensiveness that is quite out of the ordinary. Full, rich, unctuous, heady and extremely long, this is precious stuff. A wine to keep, of course. (Residual sugar: 50 g/l.)
Dom. Schoffit, 66–68, Nonnenholz-Weg, 68000 Colmar, tel. 03.89.24.41.14, fax 03.89.41.40.52
by appt.

CLOS SAINT-THEOBALD

Riesling 2001★★

1 ha 3,000 23–30 €

This Riesling, too, cannot deny its terroir, and was not far from a *coup de coeur*. Amber in the glass, it is developing a nose of dried fruits and overripeness. The palate, which is a trifle mellow, is distinguished by its extraordinary structure. (Residual sugar: 8 g/l.)
Dom. Schoffit, 66–68, Nonnenholz-Weg, 68000 Colmar, tel. 03.89.24.41.14, fax 03.89.41.40.52
by appt.

WOLFBERGER

Tokay-pinot gris 2001★★

n.c. n.c. 23–30 €

Thann is located at the southern end of the Route des Vins. This does not mean that its vineyards are of marginal importance. Far from it. The village has some very sought-after terroirs, including the Rangen, a famous Grand Cru that has earned many *coups de coeurs* in the *Guide*. The 99 was one, and the 2001 another. This version, an intense golden-yellow Pinot Gris, has a strong, complex bouquet dominated for the time being by somewhat charred notes. There is definite potential for further aromatic development. Full, concentrated, potent, robust, rounded, with all the richness one could wish for, the palate finishes on notes of crystallized fruits. A remarkable wine, for keeping. (Residual sugar: 70 g/l.)
Wolfberger, 6, Grand-Rue, 68420 Eguisheim, tel. 03.89.22.20.20, fax 03.89.23.47.09, e-mail contact@wolfberger.com
by appt.

Alsace Grand Cru Rosacker

CAVE VINICOLE DE HUNAWIHR

Tokay-pinot gris 2001★★★

0.8 ha 5,000 8–11 €

Surrounded by vines, the fortified church of Hunawihr is an emblem in stone of the Alsatian wine region. Half-way along the Route des Vins, the village is rich in famous vineyards, including the precious Rosacker Grand Cru. When grown on this clay-limestone terroir, the Pinot Gris variety can be marvellously expressive. This wine is a good example. The yellow-gold colour with silvery highlights is a sign of its potential. The nose is remarkably aromatic and highly complex, with notes of smoke, toast, flowers, dried apricots, crystallized pear and a dash of spice. Powerful yet pleasurably silky, robust and spicy, the palate finishes beautifully on aromas of crystallized fruits and raisins. A wine to keep, needless to say. (Residual sugar: 25 g/l.)
Cave vinicole de Hunawihr, 48, rte de Ribeauvillé, 68150 Hunawihr, tel. 03.89.73.61.67, fax 03.89.73.33.95
ev. day 8am–12 noon 2pm–6pm

DOM. SIPP-MACK

Riesling 2001★

0.56 ha 4,000 11–15 €

Born of the alliance of two ancient wine-growing families, the Sipp-Mack estate has a welcome diversity of terroirs. This powerful Riesling comes from the Rosacker Grand Cru. The nose has notes of citrus fruits and overripeness, while the palate has a fairly unusual roundness. Overall a complex and potent wine that would go well with a white meat. (Residual sugar: 10 g/l.)
Dom. Sipp-Mack, 1, rue des Vosges, 68150 Hunawihr, tel. 03.89.73.61.88, fax 03.89.73.36.70, e-mail sippmack@sippmack.com
by appt.

ALBERT WINTER

Riesling 2001★

0.33 ha 1,700 8–11 €

Near Hunawihr's famous fortified church, Albert Winter has total control over his small wine-estate of 4 ha. He has created a Riesling of rare aromatic intensity, strongly redolent of citrus fruits and white flowers. After a good attack, the palate reveals power and complexity. This wine would go well with fish in sauce or lobster. (Residual sugar: 0.8 g/l.)
Albert Winter, 17, rue Sainte-Hune, 68150 Hunawihr, tel. 03.89.73.62.95, fax 03.89.73.62.95
by appt.

FERNAND ZIEGLER

Riesling 2001★

6 ha n.c. 8–11 €

Fernand Ziegler's ancestors were already cultivating vines at Hunawihr in 1634. He himself tends some 6 ha with his son. Strongly marked by aromas of white flowers and lemon, his Rosacker Riesling has a beautifully fresh palate. Overall, a classy and authentic wine that would go well with cooked fish. (Residual sugar: 5.3 g/l.)
EARL Fernand Ziegler, 7, rue des Vosges, 68150 Hunawihr, tel. 03.89.73.64.42, fax 03.89.73.71.38
by appt.

Alsace Grand Cru Saering

LOBERGER

Tokay-pinot gris Cuvée Florian 2001★★

0.05 ha 200 11–15 €

As you go up the Guebwiller valley, the Saering terroir is over to the right, on south-facing slopes. Its sandy clay produces some highly expressive wines. This one is golden yellow with silvery highlights and has a very complex nose of honeyed

acacia flowers, followed by crystallized fruits and then an effective mineral note. The palate is rich, with a suppleness linked to a sweetness that is still noteworthy. As it finishes, there is a revival of the scents perceived earlier. This lovely Pinot Gris will improve its blend over time. But will there still be any in two or three years' time? (Residual sugar: 34 g/l.)
➷ EARL Joseph Loberger, 10, rue de Bergholtz-Zell, 68500 Bergholtz, tel. 03.89.76.88.03, fax 03.89.74.16.83, e-mail vin.loberger@worldonline.fr ☑
⟁ by appt.

DOM. SCHLUMBERGER
Riesling 2001★

	4.2 ha	20,784	🝙 ⬗	11–15 €

The vineyard was established by Nicolas Schlumberger in 1810. It was developed further by Ernest between 1920 and 1935, and is now the biggest in Alsace (145 ha of vines), some of it on particularly steep terrain. Almost two-thirds of the production is exported. This Riesling has a very pleasant bouquet of citrus fruits and white flowers; the palate starts quite lively, then reveals an attractive complexity that is due to the concentration of the outstanding fruit used. It would go well with most seafood, not just shellfish, but fish, steamed, poached, or in a sauce. (Residual sugar: 12 g/l.)
➷ Domaines Schlumberger, 100, rue Théodore-Deck, 68501 Guebwiller Cedex, tel. 03.89.74.27.00, fax 03.89.74.85.75, e-mail dvschlum@aol.com ☑
⟁ by appt.

Alsace Grand Cru Schlossberg

DOM. PAUL BLANCK
Riesling 2001★

	3.34 ha	12,000	🝙 ⬗ ⬥	11–15 €

This estate of 36 ha scarcely needs an introduction, given its worldwide reputation – 60% of the production is exported. It played an important role in the creation of the AOC Alsace Grand Cru. This Schlossberg Grand Cru Riesling, grown on granitic soils, has scents of white flowers. The palate's range of flavours includes white fruits (peach). With its somewhat supple finish, this is a very well-balanced wine. (Residual sugar: 8 g/l.)
➷ Dom. Paul Blanck, 32, Grand-Rue, 68240 Kientzheim, tel. 03.89.78.23.56, fax 03.89.47.16.45, e-mail info@blanck.com ☑
⟁ ev. day except Sun. 9am–12 noon 1.30pm–6pm; cl. Nov. until Mar.

ANDRÉ BLANCK ET SES FILS
Riesling 2001★

	1.8 ha	3,000		11–15 €

This estate has its headquarters in an historic and symbolic place: the former cellar of the Knights of Malta, which belonged to Lazare de Schwendi, the promoter of Alsatian tokay in the 16th century. With a bouquet that links power and elegance, this Riesling is the result of using excellent grapes, whose presence comes through in the notes of raisins and the suppleness of the palate. It ought to reach its full and final balance after two or three years' storage. (Residual sugar: 9,8 g/l.)
➷ André Blanck et Fils, Ancienne Cour des Chevaliers de Malte, 68240 Kientzheim, tel. 03.89.78.24.72, fax 03.89.47.17.07, e-mail charlesblanck@free.fr ☑ ☗
⟁ ev. day except Sun. 8am–7pm

DOM. WEINBACH
Riesling 2001★★

	1 ha	5,000	⬗	15–23 €

Once the property of Capucin monks, the Weinbach estate is run with enthusiasm by Colette Faller and her daughters. Its size (26 ha), the time-honoured ancient renown of its terroirs (several of them Grand Cru), its owners' competence and dynamism, together with the use of organic cultivation have won it a great reputation. Everything here serves elegance: the house, the barrel stores, but above all this Riesling, with its intense nose of citrus and crystallized fruits. The palate contributes force and structure to a wine with balance and rare complexity, worth reserving for gastronomic occasions. (Residual sugar: 4.9 g/l.)
➷ Dom. Weinbach-Colette Faller et ses Filles, Clos des Capucins, 68240 Kaysersberg, tel. 03.89.47.13.21, fax 03.89.47.38.18, e-mail contact@domaineweinbach.com ☑
⟁ by appt.

DOM. WEINBACH
Riesling Cuvée Sainte-Catherine 2001★

	1 ha	4,400	⬗	30–38 €

Cuvée Sainte-Catherine comes from 50-year-old vines managed biodynamically. It is harvested late. The result is an intense fruitiness dominated by exotic and citrus fruits. After attacking cleanly, this Riesling reveals an attractive minerality that reflects its granitic origins. A well-balanced wine that will go well with the finest fish (turbot, sole, etc.), with scallops, or lobster. (Residual sugar: 5.5 g/l.)
➷ Dom. Weinbach-Colette Faller et ses Filles, Clos des Capucins, 68240 Kaysersberg, tel. 03.89.47.13.21, fax 03.89.47.38.18, e-mail contact@domaineweinbach.com ☑
⟁ by appt.

ZIEGLER-MAULER
Riesling Les Murets 2001★★

	0.27 ha	900	⬗	8–11 €

Established in the 1960s, this estate has 5 ha of vines. Philippe Ziegler has been in charge since 1996. The Les Murets Riesling, grown in the Schlossberg Grand Cru, is one of the vineyard's gems and often figures in the *Guide*. The fine, floral bouquet of this 2001 quickly signals its noble origin; complementary notes of citrus fruit (grapefruit) and minerals follow. Lively as it hits the palate, this is a fresh, complex, long, well-integrated wine, a thoroughbred, and a wine to keep. It would be a good accompaniment to lobster and fish in sauce. (Residual sugar: 10.6 g/l.)
➷ Jean-Jacques Ziegler-Mauler Fils, 2, rue des Merles, 68630 Mittelwihr, tel. 03.89.47.90.37, fax 03.89.47.98.27 ☑
⟁ by appt.
➷ Philippe Ziegler

Wines selected but not starred

VINCENT SPANNAGEL
Riesling 2001

	0.2 ha	1,600	⬗	8–11 €

➷ EARL Vincent Spannagel, 82, rue du Vignoble, 68230 Katzenthal, tel. 03.89.27.52.13, fax 03.89.27.56.48 ☑
⟁ by appt.

Alsace Grand Cru Schoenenbourg

♜ EARL Raymond Renck, 11, rue de Hoën,
68980 Beblenheim, tel. 03.89.47.91.59, fax 03.89.47.91.75 ☑
⟁ ev. day 8am–12 noon 2pm–7pm

JEAN-PHILIPPE ET FRANCOIS BECKER Gewurztraminer 2001★★

0.6 ha	n.c.	▮ ♨	11–15 €

The origins of this estate, one of the pioneers of wine-growing in Alsace, are lost in the mists of time. Today it is in the hands of two brothers and a sister: Jean-Philippe Becker, oenologist, François, who tends the vines, and Martine, who looks after the commercial side. Martine's knowledge of Japanese has helped the vineyard to attract Japanese customers. This lovely wine will have no shortage of takers. Brilliantly golden yellow and already aromatically quite open, it mingles roses and spices. The rich attack immediately reveals flavours of flowers and crystallized fruits that linger through a full, warming finish. True to type and powerful, this is a Gewurztraminer for aperitif, to serve with a dessert or Munster cheese. (Residual sugar: 30 g/l.)
♜ GAEC Jean-Philippe et François Becker, 2, rte d'Ostheim, 68340 Zellenberg, tel. 03.89.47.87.56, fax 03.89.47.99.57
⟁ by appt.

DOPFF AU MOULIN Riesling Vendanges tardives 2000★

8.8 ha	3,000	▥	23–30 €

Dopff au Moulin are established in Riquewihr, the prosperous little medieval town that represents Alsace to the whole world. These wine-merchants cultivate their own vineyard of 70 ha, a holding that puts it among the largest wine-growing properties in the region. It offers a late-harvest Riesling from selected grapes grown on almost 9 ha. It has a light straw colour and a nose that mixes passion-fruit with citrus. A lively attack counterbalances the wine's evident sugar content, making for a well-balanced and concentrated whole. The long finish evokes a revival of citrus fruit (grapefruit)
♜ SA Dopff au Moulin, 2, av. Jacques-Preiss, 68340 Riquewihr, tel. 03.89.49.09.69, fax 03.89.47.83.61, e-mail domaines@dopff-au-moulin.fr ☑
⟁ ev. day 9am–12 noon 2pm–6pm; groups by appt.

ROGER JUNG ET FILS Riesling Sélection de grains nobles 2000★

0.6 ha	300	▮ ♨	46–76 €

Rémy and Jacques Jung took over from their father Roger in 1989. Their cellar lies close to the ramparts of Riquewihr. Among their 15.5 ha of vines, they have several Grand Cru plots, particularly in the Schoenenbourg, a clay and gypsum terroir good for Riesling. Following on from their magnificent late-harvest 98, the Jungs have created a sweet, rich wine with a dark-golden-yellow shine. Already expressive, the wine mixes characteristic citrus aromas (grapefruit) with notes of undergrowth and mushrooms. Similar flavours, enriched with orange, inform the long-lasting palate. It begins with an attractive acidity that conveys great freshness. If kept several years, this wine will gain in complexity.
♜ SARL Roger Jung et Fils, 23, rue de la 1re-Armée, 68340 Riquewihr, tel. 03.89.47.92.17, fax 03.89.47.87.63, e-mail rjung@terre-net.fr ☑ ♞
⟁ ev. day 8am–12 noon 1.30pm–6pm

RAYMOND RENCK Riesling 2001★

0.08 ha	600		8–11 €

In 1996, Gérard Schillinger-Renck settled in Beblenheim, a village with a rich history of wine-growing. Once again he has shown his talent with a well-made Riesling from the Schoenenbourg. Despite the terroir's clayey nature, the nose of this 2001 is already open, with perfumes of citrus and dried fruits. After a lively attack, the palate is full and extremely well-structured, revealing the use of top-quality grapes. (Residual sugar: 6.6 g/l.)

CAVE VINICOLE DE RIBEAUVILLE Riesling 2001★

0.32 ha	1,900	▮ ♨	11–15 €

Founded in 1895, this is the oldest cooperative in France. These days it vinifies the harvests from some 265 ha of vines and offers wines from several Grands Crus, including the Schoenenbourg. Despite the clayey growing medium of its terroir, this Riesling already has a very expressive nose, with dominant notes of citrus and exotic fruits. The palate is typified by a clean, lively start and a structure that will develop further given time. A promising wine overall that should be stored at least one more year. (Residual sugar: 15 g/l.)
♜ Cave vinicole de Ribeauvillé, 2, rte de Colmar, 68150 Ribeauvillé, tel. 03.89.73.61.80, fax 03.89.73.31.21 ☑
⟁ by appt.

Wines selected but not starred

DOM. BAUMANN Riesling 2001

2.08 ha	4,400	▥	15–23 €

♜ Dom. Baumann-Woelfflé, 8, av. Méquillet, 68340 Riquewihr, tel. 03.89.47.92.14, fax 03.89.47.99.31, e-mail info@domaine-baumann.com ☑
⟁ by appt.

Alsace Grand Cru Sommerberg

DOM. AIME STENTZ Riesling 2001★

0.47 ha	4,000	▥	8–11 €

With 15 ha of vines divided among the different terroirs of Wettolsheim, this important estate exports more than a third of its production. Influenced by its granitic origins, this Sommerberg Riesling has an expressive nose that is both mineral and floral. After a lively start, the palate is well-balanced and lingering, with a lemony finish. This is a classy wine that will have a welcome place alongside any seafood and fish. (Residual sugar: 7 g/l.)
♜ Aimé Stentz, 37, rue Herzog, 68920 Wettolsheim, tel. 03.89.80.63.77, fax 03.89.79.78.68, e-mail stentz.e@calixo.net ☑
⟁ ev. day except Sun. 8am–12 noon 2pm–6pm

Wines selected but not starred

GERARD WEINZORN Riesling 2001

0.5 ha	2,500		11–15 €

♜ Gérard Weinzorn et Fils, 133, rue des Trois-Epis, 68230 Niedermorschwihr, tel. 03.89.27.40.55, fax 03.89.27.04.23, e-mail contact@weinzorn.fr ☑
⟁ by appt.

Alsace Grand Cru Sonnenglanz

DOM. STIRN

Gewurztraminer 2000★★

| 0.2 ha | 1,500 | 🍶 | 8–11 € |

Since 1999 this young oenologist has been in charge of an estate with a rich variety of terroirs; he vinifies on a plot-by-plot basis so as to get the most out of them. The Sonnenglanz terroir has attracted wine-growers since the 1930s. It faces southeast and has a rather heavy soil with a large scattering of limestone débris. From it, Fabien Stirn has derived this remarkable wine. An intense golden colour with lots of yellow highlights, this Gewurztraminer opens on perfumes of great finesse: crystallized fruits with hints of sweet spices, honey, and clove. The palate begins in a supple vein, then reveals flavours of overripeness (very ripe fruits, quince, honey). The finish is both rich and elegant. (Residual sugar: 43 g/l.)

☛ Fabien Stirn, Dom. Stirn, 3, rue du Château, 68240 Sigolsheim, tel. 03.89.47.30.58, fax 03.89.47.30.58, e-mail domainestirn@free.fr ☑
☕ ev. day 8.30am–7pm; Sun. by appt.

intense-yellow wine with a nose dominated by exotic fruits (lychee, mango). The palate is full, supple, and has finesse from the start, though there is definite power. This is a wine with a future. Though already pleasing, it should be kept so as to allow the very evident residual sugar to blend in. (Residual sugar: 20 g/l.)

☛ Cave vinicole de Hunawihr, 48, rte de Ribeauvillé, 68150 Hunawihr, tel. 03.89.73.61.67, fax 03.89.73.33.95 ☑
☕ ev. day 8am–12 noon 2pm–6pm

ROGER JUNG ET FILS

Gewurztraminer 2001★

| 0.67 ha | 5,100 | 🍶 | 11–15 € |

The many tourists who wander around Riquewihr, between the castle of the Dukes of Wurtenberg and the Dolder Tower, encounter the Alsace of tradition through its museums and its ancient and prosperous houses. The wines here are authentic and traditional, too, thanks to famous terroirs like the Sporen, which is one of the best. It has produced this bright golden-yellow wine whose nose is still closed but yields the odd buttery hint. Rich, full, and very supple, the attack opens on to notes of crystallized fruits. A final note of bitterness should fade in time, but this wine will soon be ready to drink. (Residual sugar: 50 g/l.)

☛ SARL Roger Jung et Fils, 23, rue de la 1ʳᵉ-Armée, 68340 Riquewihr, tel. 03.89.47.92.17, fax 03.89.47.87.63, e-mail rjung@terre-net.fr ☑ ☎
☕ ev. day 8am–12 noon 1.30pm–6pm

Alsace Grand Cru Spiegel

LOBERGER

Gewurztraminer 2001★

| 0.18 ha | 800 | 🍶 | 11–15 € |

The east-facing Spiegel is one of the great terroirs of the southern part of the region, near Guebwiller. The soil is sandstone pebbles over clay covered with débris and sandy colluvium. Gewurztraminer is the choicest variety here. This wine is yellow with gold highlights and it has a floral nose that is still discreet. The palate is more open, with dried fruit flavours and hints of roses. Balance is achieved thanks to good acidity, which contributes freshness and verve. "I just love it," concluded one taster. (Residual sugar: 35 g/l.)

☛ EARL Joseph Loberger, 10, rue de Bergholtz-Zell, 68500 Bergholtz, tel. 03.89.76.88.03, fax 03.89.74.16.83, e-mail vin.loberger@worldonline.fr ☑
☕ by appt.

Alsace Grand Cru Steinert

MEISTERMANN

Riesling Sélection de grains nobles 2000★

| 0.2 ha | 500 | 🍶 | 76 €+ |

The Steinart Grand Cru overlooks the village of Pfaffenheim. This limestone-clay terroir is lightened by limestone débris, which promotes the warming of the soil in spring. It has yielded this sweet, rich wine with a bright yellow gold colour and a nose that is well open. First in line are buttery scents, followed quickly by notes of very ripe fruits (fruits of the forest and pineapple). The same complex aromatic spectrum is experienced on the palate, where it is enriched by hints of new-mown grass. There is freshness and length here too. An unusually aromatic wine.

☛ EARL Robert Meistermann et Fils, 7, Grand-Rue, 68250 Pfaffenheim, tel. 03.89.49.62.88, e-mail francis.meistermann2@libertysurf.fr ☑ ☎
☕ by appt.

DOM. MOLTES

Tokay-pinot gris 2001★

| 0.31 ha | 2,300 | 🍶 | 8–11 € |

Some kilometres south of Colmar is Pfaffenheim and the south-southeast-facing slopes of its Steinert Grand Cru. The conditions favour the production of highly expressive wines. Golden yellow in the glass, this Pinot Gris mixes smoky aromas with those of dried fruits. The palate has beautiful body, supple and round, and the long finish on crystallized quince has a lovely freshness. Wait two or three years, then serve as an aperitif or with foie gras. (Residual sugar: 75 g/l.) The Steinert terroir also produces sweet, rich wines. Its **Sélection de Grains Nobles 2000 Pinot Gris (15–23 € per half-litre bottle)** is commended for its personality and potential. Be patient.

☛ Dom. Antoine Moltès et Fils, 8–10, rue du Fossé, 68250 Pfaffenheim, tel. 03.89.49.60.85, fax 03.89.49.50.43, e-mail domaine@vins-moltes.com ☑
☕ ev. day 8am–12 noon 2pm–7pm

Alsace Grand Cru Sporen

CAVE VINICOLE DE HUNAWIHR

Gewurztraminer 2001★

| 0.3 ha | 1,200 | 🍶 | 8–11 € |

The Hunawihr cellar receives the harvests from 200 ha of vines. It distinguishes its terroirs, and vinifies plots located in five Grands Crus. The southeast-facing Sporen is a circular terroir at Riquewihr, 275 m above sea-level. Deep, with a tendency not to dry out, the limestone-clay soil suits Gewurztraminer. Here that variety has produced a bright,

Wines selected but not starred

Riesling and there is a good supply of it. The nose is very expressive and is already characterized by mineral notes.
☛ Sté des Vins et Crémants d'Als Metz-Laugel, 102, rue du Gal-de-Gaulle, 67520 Marlenheim, tel. 03.88.59.28.60, fax 03.88.87.67.58 ☑
𝕿 by appt.

PIERRE FRICK

Muscat 2001

	0.2 ha	900	⅓	15–23 €

☛ Pierre Frick, 5, rue de Baer, 68250 Pfaffenheim, tel. 03.89.49.62.99, fax 03.89.49.73.78,
e-mail pierre.frick@wanadoo.fr ☑
𝕿 ev. day except Sun. 8.30am–11.30am 1.30pm–6.30pm

Alsace Grand Cru Steingrübler

MOELLINGER

Riesling 2001★

	0.3 ha	2,000	⅓	5–8 €

It is now (since 1998) the grandson of Joseph Moellinger who runs the 14 ha of this estate. His Riesling has a very expressive nose, with aromas of citrus and overripened fruits. Rich and complex on the palate, this wine will achieve perfect integration after several years' keeping, i.e., at least two years. (Residual sugar: 17.4 g/l.)
☛ SCEA Joseph Moellinger et Fils, 6, rue de la 5e-D.-B., 68920 Wettolsheim, tel. 03.89.80.62.02, fax 03.89.80.04.94 ☑
𝕿 ev. day 8am–12 noon 1.30pm–7pm; Sun. by appt.; cl. Oct.

DOM. AIME STENTZ

Gewurztraminer 2001★

	0.52 ha	4,500	⅓	8–11 €

The Steingrübler is a hillside noteworthy for its southeastern exposure and soil type. This goes from sandy clay at the top to clay-limestone at the bottom. The lower part is particularly favourable to the Gewurztraminer variety. An engaging golden yellow colour, this wine exhales intensely floral aromas suggestive of roses. The excellent attack introduces a palate of rare suppleness. The finish is accompanied by notes of crystallized fruits. Pleasantly well-blended. (Residual sugar: 22 g/l.)
☛ Aimé Stentz, 37, rue Herzog, 68920 Wettolsheim, tel. 03.89.80.63.77, fax 03.89.79.78.68,
e-mail stentz.e@calixo.net ☑
𝕿 ev. day except Sun. 8am–12 noon 2pm–6pm

Alsace Grand Cru Steinklotz

LAUGEL

Riesling 2001★

	2.8 ha	24,114	ⓘ ↓	8–11 €

Laugel, founded in 1889, is one of the chief businesses in the Alsace wine region. It has a general market presence and exports 45% of its production. This is an extremely good

Alsace Grand Cru Vorbourg

CLOS SAINT-LANDELIN

Riesling 2000★

	4.6 ha	12,000	ⓘ ⅓	23–30 €

René Muré has headed this well known and fairly large estate (25 ha) for the last 25 years. It exports 40% of its production. The estate is managed organically. Bottling is done quite late on, which explains why this 2000 Riesling is the latest wine to have been bottled. The nose is elegant, having notes of citrus fruits and quince with mineral hints. The wine is lively when it hits the palate, then reveals good structure and length. A well-balanced whole, ready to drink now, with shellfish perhaps. (Residual sugar: 6 g/l.)
☛ René Muré, Dom. du Clos Saint-Landelin, rte du Vin, 68250 Rouffach, tel. 03.89.78.58.00, fax 03.89.78.58.01, e-mail rene@mure.com ☑
𝕿 by appt.

Alsace Grand Cru Wineck-Schlossberg

JEAN-PAUL ECKLE

Riesling 2001★

	0.21 ha	1,500	⅓	8–11 €

This estate was established by Jean-Paul Ecklé in 1955. Today he works with his son Emmanuel. His Wineck-Schlossberg wines are often praised in the *Guide*. Last year he presented a superb Gewurztraminer, but his Rieslings are often mentioned. Marked by its granitic origins, this 2001 already has a well-developed nose, mingling floral scents and mineral notes. This fairly supple, classy wine would go well with *coq au Riesling* (poultry in a white wine sauce). (Residual sugar: 5 g/l.)
☛ Jean-Paul Ecklé et Fils, 29, Grand-Rue, 68230 Katzenthal, tel. 03.89.27.09.41,
fax 03.89.80.86.18 ☑ ⌂
𝕿 ev. day except Sun. 9am–12 noon 1.30pm–6.30pm

MEYER-FONNE

Riesling 2001★

	0.45 ha	2,800	⅓	11–15 €

This family, which has a long wine-growing tradition behind it, is based in a 17th century cellar. Its Wineck-Schlossberg Riesling is aromatically very expressive of its granitic origins, mixing notes of citrus fruits and overripeness. Lively, well-balanced and long-lasting, it is a very fine ambassador for Alsatian wines. The tasters advise keeping for at least two years before drinking. (Residual sugar: 5 g/l.)
☛ Meyer-Fonné, 24, Grand-Rue, 68230 Katzenthal, tel. 03.89.27.16.50, fax 03.89.27.34.17 ☑
𝕿 by appt.

ALBERT SCHOECH

Riesling 2001★

	2.36 ha	15,400	☷ ⸙	8–11 €

Although this wine-merchants started out in 1675, the firm nevertheless manages to reconcile tradition with modernity. Alongside modern plant (mechanized bottling, additions to the sales cellar, fitting-out of a wine museum) there is a commitment to defined terroir vinification. The granitic soil of the Wineck-Schlossberg has produced an expressive wine with a nose of ripe fruits and minerals. After a lively start, the palate is straightforward and fresh. This wine has all the finesse of an authentic, thoroughbred Riesling. (Residual sugar: 4.6 g/l.)

☛ Albert Schoech, pl. du Vieux-Marché,
68770 Ammerschwihr, tel. 03.89.78.23.17,
fax 03.89.27.90.30, e-mail vin@schoech.fr

Alsace Grand Cru Winzenberg

HUBERT METZ

Gewurztraminer 2001★★

	0.63 ha	4,900		11–15 €

This vineyard is based in the former tithe cellar of Blienschwiller, which dates from 1728. Under the cellar-vaulting are some magnificent large oak casks with sculpted bars, in which Hubert Metz creates his best wines. The Winzenberg terroir has yielded a straw-yellow wine with a nose of citrus fruit and a hint of spices. The initial liveliness on the palate quickly gives way to a pleasant suppleness. The range of flavours is unusually complex: fruity, spicy and liquorice in succession. The long finish leaves an impression of great finesse and remarkable balance. Drink as an aperitif, with cheese, or with dessert. (Residual sugar: 34 g/l.)

☛ Hubert Metz, 3, rue du Winzenberg,
67650 Blienschwiller, tel. 03.88.92.43.06, fax 03.88.92.62.08,
e-mail hubertmetz@aol.com ☑
🍷 ev. day except Sun. 8am–7pm

PIERRE SPERRY

Gewurztraminer 2001★

	0.13 ha	1,000	⬛	8–11 €

Not far from Dambach-la-Ville is Blienschwiller, which is overlooked by the Winzenberg Grand Cru. Its light soils of two-micas granite grow wines with attractive aromatic expression. Such is the case with this straw-yellow Gewurztraminer. It has golden highlights and an intensely fruity nose with a note of menthol. The same aromatic power is perceived on the palate, where fruit flavours mix with spices. Lively when it first touches the palate, full, well-balanced, this is a fairly dry wine, a style that will allow a host of tasty accompaniments. (Residual sugar: 16.6 g/l.)

☛ Pierre Sperry Fils, 5, rte des Vins, 67650 Blienschwiller,
tel. 03.88.92.41.29, fax 03.88.92.62.38 ☑
🍷 by appt.
☛ Jean-Pierre Sperry

Alsace Grand Cru Zinnkoepflé

DOM. LEON BOESCH

Gewurztraminer Vendanges tardives 2000★

	0.6 ha	2,000		30–38 €

Because it faces between southeast and south, the Zinnkoepflé benefits from a microclimate reminiscent of the Mediterranean – conditions that eminently favour the vine, as do its clay-limestone and sandy clay soils. This locality has produced a late-harvest wine that is truly golden. The nose is extremely fruity, dominated by crystallized quince; its intensity indicates potential. The palate has some quite exuberant crystallized fruit flavours, mixed with exotic hints (mango). The wine's substance is attractive and well-balanced, with a clean finish that is pleasurably long. A wine with potential that should be left to age several years more.

☛ Dom. Léon Boesch, 6, rue Saint-Blaise,
68250 Westhalten, tel. 03.89.47.01.83,
fax 03.89.47.64.95 ☑ 🏠
🍷 by appt.
☛ Gérard et Matthieu Boesch

RENE FLECK

Riesling 2001★

	0.23 ha	2,100	⬛	8–11 €

The Fleck family have been wine-growers at Soultzmatt, a charming little town in the Noble valley, for several generations. The vineyard was taken over by René Fleck's daughter in 1995. The nose of this Riesling has mineral and menthol notes and a beautiful complexity on the palate. The product of excellent quality grapes, it is still dominated by a touch of residual sugar, but should find a proper balance in time. (Residual sugar: 15 g/l.)

☛ René Fleck et Fille, 27, rte d'Orschwihr,
68570 Soultzmatt, tel. 03.89.47.01.20, fax 03.89.47.09.24,
e-mail renefleck@voila.fr ☑
🍷 by appt.

ERIC ROMINGER

Gewurztraminer Les Sinneles 2001★

	0.6 ha	n.c.	☷ ⸙	11–15 €

Eric Rominger has expertly run this estate since 1986. It has grown: it now runs to some 9 ha, of which 6.5 ha are in production. More than half of these (3.5 ha) are in a Grand Cru, either the Saering or the Zinnkoepflé. The last-named has produced this intense-yellow Gewurztraminer. It has a potent nose of overripeness. The palate is robust, spicy, full, well-blended and fresh: the excellent body is due to its sugar–alcohol balance. It is the style of Gewurztraminer that will go with Munster or some other cheese with character. (Residual sugar: 61 g/l.)

☛ Eric Rominger, 16, rue Saint-Blaise, 68250 Westhalten,
tel. 03.89.47.68.60, fax 03.89.47.68.67 ☑
🍷 by appt.

DOM. SCHIRMER

Gewurztraminer 2001★★★

	0.23 ha	1,900	☷	11–15 €

Overlooking the Noble valley, the majestic hillside of the Zinnkoepflé ends at 420 m altitude. Its steep slopes, with soils made of sandy limestone, face south-southeast. Protected from the damp oceanic air by the heights of the Vosges, the vines benefit from a hot, dry microclimate. Given the wine-grower's talent, they have here turned out a minor masterpiece. This bright greenish-yellow wine delivers strong aromas of crystallized fruits mixed with scents of white flowers and spicy notes. These last similarly characterize the excellent first sensations on the palate. This potent, rich, heady, extremely warming wine finishes on notes of stewed fruit. "Finesse and elegance throughout, a noble ambassador

for the Grand Cru," was one taster's summing up. A wine complete in itself. (Residual sugar: 45 g/l.)
🍴 Dom. Lucien Schirmer et Fils, 22, rue de la Vallée, 68570 Soultzmatt, tel. 03.89.47.03.82, fax 03.89.47.02.33 ☑
🍷 ev. day 8am–12 noon 1pm–7pm

A. WISCHLEN

Tokay-Pinot gris Vendanges tardives 2000★★

0.27 ha	900	◧	11–15 €

This family of wine-growers is settled at the foot of the Zinnkoepflé. This Grand Cru is characterized by a dry, Mediterranean-style climate, while the fossil-bearing limestone soils resemble the garrigue scrublands of southern France. It has already yielded a superb mellow 2000 Gewurztraminer, hailed by a *coup de coeur* last year. The same summer also produced this noteworthy late-harvest Pinot Gris. Golden yellow with bright glints, it has distinctively fresh aromas, notes of citrus fruits preceding those of crystallized fruits, then the smokiness typical of the variety. Its sweetness is balanced by an attractive acidity that emphasizes the wine's fruit. The long finish evokes the scents perceived earlier, together with smoky, spicy (somewhat peppery), lemony notes. (Half-litre bottles)
🍴 François Wischlen, 4, rue de Soultzmatt, 68250 Westhalten, tel. 03.89.47.01.24, fax 03.89.47.62.90, e-mail wischlen@wanadoo.fr ☑
🍷 by appt.

Alsace Grand Cru Zotzenberg

DOM. HAEGI

Riesling Sélection de grains nobles 2000★★★

0.2 ha	550	▮	30–38 €

In good years, clayey limestone terrains can deliver wines of rare quality. Such is true of this Sélection de Grains Nobles, which Bernard and Daniel Haegi have been able to bring to the heights of expression. A bright straw-yellow colour with occasional green highlights, this Riesling releases fragrances of fresh hay, followed by scents of very ripe fruits and of lemon. The palate is enhanced by an attractive acidity that emphasizes the fruity flavours (pineapple, apricot, and again lemon), then the smokiness continues after the taster has put down his or her glass, for it accompanies what is a lingering and harmonious finish. At once warming and fresh, this wine has uncommon storage-potential. (Half-litre bottles)
🍴 Bernard et Daniel Haegi, 33, rue de la Montagne, 67140 Mittelbergheim, tel. 03.88.08.95.80, fax 03.88.08.91.20 ☑ 🏠 🏠
🍷 ev. day except Sun. 8am–11.45am 1pm–6pm

PIERRE ET JEAN-PIERRE RIETSCH

Riesling 2001★

0.3 ha	2,000	▮◧♦	8–11 €

From their 1576 residence, Pierre and Jean-Pierre Rietsch together work 12 ha of vines. Their Zotzenberg Riesling has a very elegant nose of citrus fruits and pineapple and a palate that starts with verve. This is a well-balanced, well-bred wine with storage potential; a wait of two years is recommended. (Residual sugar: 9.4 g/l.)
🍴 EARL Pierre et Jean-Pierre Rietsch, 32, rue Principale, 67140 Mittelbergheim, tel. 03.88.08.00.64, fax 03.88.08.40.91, e-mail contact@alsace-rietsch.com ☑
🍷 by appt.

Wines selected but not starred

LUCAS ET ANDRE RIEFFEL

Riesling 2001

0.27 ha	2,000	8–11 €

🍴 Lucas et André Rieffel, 11, rue Principale, 67140 Mittelbergheim, tel. 03.88.08.95.48, fax 03.88.08.28.94 ☑
🍷 by appt.

Crémant d'Alsace

When this appellation was created in 1976, there was an immediate increase in production of sparkling wines made by the *méthode traditionelle*, or Champagne method. They had always been produced, but on a smaller scale. Crémant d'Alsace is made from a blend of various grape varieties: Pinot Blanc, Auxerrois, Pinot Gris, Pinot Noir, Riesling and Chardonnay. The production of this sparkling wine, steadily gaining in reputation, increased to 165,700 hl in 2002.

ANSTOTZ ET FILS 2000★

1.5 ha	13,200	▮	5–8 €

Located on the northern stretch of the Alsatian Wine Route, the village of Balbronn is part of Strasbourg's "Golden Crown". Based in a former 15th century farmstead, Marc Anstotz cultivates 13 ha of vines. His cellar contains some ancient carved barrels, the oldest of which date from 1807. Blending 80% Pinot Blanc with 20% Riesling, this Crémant is of immediate interest: good mousse, fine, long-lasting bubbles, an already intense nose of citrus fruits together with a tiny touch of menthol – all show potential. The palate, with its attractive complexity of flavours, is well-balanced and has a fresh finish.
🍴 Anstotz et Fils, 51, rue Balbach, 67310 Balbronn, tel. 03.88.50.30.55, fax 03.88.50.58.06 ☑ 🏠
🍷 by appt.
🍴 Marc Anstotz

RENE BARTH 2000★★

0.4 ha	4,000	▮♦	5–8 €

The label on this Crémant bears the name of Michel Fonné's uncle, who handed the estate on to him in 1989. Michel is a trained oenologist who runs the vineyard expertly and is investing heavily in it: in 2002 he constructed a harvester and a cellar for vinification and in-bottle ageing; these are enabling him to rationalize his work. This wine, an equal blend of Pinot Blanc and Riesling, has perfect effervescence: fine bubbles rise within a beautifully bright yellow liquid. Floral aromas and notes of fresh bread jostle in an honest nose of good complexity. Refreshing, well-balanced, intense, and finishing well, this wine is really nice.
🍴 Dom. Michel Fonné, 24, rue du Gal-de-Gaulle, 68630 Bennwihr, tel. 03.89.47.92.69, fax 03.89.49.04.86, e-mail michel@michelfonne.com ☑
🍷 by appt.

BERNARD BECHT 2000★★

1.4 ha	16,000		5–8 €

This estate is at Dorlisheim, 20 or so kilometres south of Strasbourg and not far from a number of tourist sites in the Vosges (Mont Sainte-Odile, the Valley of the Bruche,

Obernai, etc.). The vineyard offers a Crémant composed of 75% Pinot Blanc enhanced by 5% Pinot Gris and 20% Chardonnay. The fine, persistent mousse, the string of bubbles and the verve of the citrus fruit aromas are extremely engaging. A good attack and a fine, well-balanced, gluggable palate complete this excellent impression.
- EARL Bernard Becht, 84, Grand-Rue,
67120 Dorlisheim, tel. 03.88.38.20.37, fax 03.88.38.88.00,
e-mail becht.bernard@wanadoo.fr ☑
�?? by appt.

PIERRE BECHT 2001★

| | 2 ha | 20,000 | 🍶 🍷 | 5–8 € |

A large village at the bottom end of the valley of the Bruche, southwest of Strasbourg, Dorlisheim affirms its wine-growing vocation in the persons of talented growers like Pierre and Frédéric Becht. Golden with green highlights, their Crémant has a fine mousse and persistent bubbles. The nose's first impression is of brioche, which develops into more complex notes of honey and smokiness. The agreeable, lively attack is followed by a palate that is expressive and well balanced. A nice aperitif wine.
- Pierre et Frédéric Becht, 26, fbg des Vosges,
67120 Dorlisheim, tel. 03.88.38.18.22, fax 03.88.38.87.81,
e-mail pbecht@terre-net.fr ☑
�? ev. day 8am–11.30am 2pm–5pm; Sun. by appt.

BESTHEIM★

| | 18 ha | 200,000 | 🍶 🍷 | 8–11 € |

Bestheim comes from the joining together of the cellars of Bennwihr and Westhalten. Westhalten have made Crémant one of their specialities. This one is in the tradition of others that they have made over the past few decades. Bright yellow, with a fine, persistent mousse, it has complex aromas of great delicacy dominated by quince, which lingers on the palate, mixed with flavours of very ripe yellow fruit. A well-balanced, easy-drinking wine.
- Bestheim, Cave de Westhalten, 52, rte de Soultzmatt,
68250 Westhalten, tel. 03.89.49.09.29, fax 03.89.49.09.20,
e-mail bestheim@gofornet.com ☑
�? ev. day 8am–12 noon 2pm–6pm;
Sat. Sun. 10am–12 noon 3pm–6pm

LEON BLEESZ 2000★★

| | 0.84 ha | 6,000 | 🍶 | 5–8 € |

Some kilometres west of Itterswiller, Reichsfeld nestles among the vines a little way off the Alsace Wine Route. The village lies at the bottom of a small valley and is a starting-point for hill-walkers in the Vosges. Its location also suits vines. Since he settled here in 1990, Christophe Bleesz has worked 11 ha of vines in the area. A dazzling light yellow colour, his Crémant has an engaging effervescence, albeit somewhat discreet. What distinguishes it is what follows. This is a wine with fresh and elegant aromas dominated by white flowers and citrus fruits; it is lively, well-balanced and harmonious. All of which make for a high-class wine. An attractive aperitif, it could also accompany seafood.
- Christophe Bleesz, 1, pl. de l'Eglise, 67140 Reichsfeld,
tel. 03.88.85.53.57, fax 03.88.57.83.44,
e-mail bleesz@terre-net.fr ☑ 🏠 🏠
�? by appt.

J.-L. DIRRINGER 2000★

| | 0.42 ha | 4,600 | 🍶 | 5–8 € |

Dambach-la-Ville, with its enclosing walls, evokes the Middle Ages, just like J.-L. Dirringer's estate, where you can see the emblems of the different wine crafts, the growers, the coopers, and the rest. Here too you can discover this well-crafted Crémant, with its light and persistent mousse, its fine, elegant aromas of brioche. First impressions on the palate are frank and lively, followed by a well-blended richness. A very good wine.
- Dom. Jean-Louis Dirringer, 5, rue du Mal-Foch,
67650 Dambach-la-Ville, tel. 03.88.92.41.51,
fax 03.88.92.62.76, e-mail jl.dirringer@free.fr ☑
�? by appt.

G. DOLDER 2000★

| | 1.19 ha | 12,640 | | 8–11 € |

Gérard Dolder is based in Mittelbergheim, a village near Andlau where the tourist can admire ancient wine-growers' houses that are prosperous-looking and well-restored. His Crémant has a discreet, fine mousse with very persistent bubbles. It exhales perfumes of great elegance, including notes of fresh citrus fruit (lemon). The palate too is richly fruity and has most agreeable length.
- Gérard Dolder, 29, rue de la Montagne,
67140 Mittelbergheim, tel. 03.88.08.02.94,
fax 03.88.08.55.86 ☑
�? by appt.

ARMAND GILG 2000★

| | 2 ha | 13,550 | 🍶 🍷 | 8–11 € |

The Gilg family runs a wine-estate of some 22 ha, which allows it to offer a diverse range of quality wines. The immediate attraction of this light-yellow Crémant is the almost perfect effervescence of fine bubbles and the intense, rich nose. This begins with smoky tones, doubtless due to the Pinot Gris part of the blend (13%, with 77% Pinot Blanc and 10% Riesling), then develops fruity notes (grapefruit, quince). The same aromatic complexity informs the palate, which is lively and has particularly pleasant length.
- Dom. Armand Gilg et Fils, 2, rue Rotland,
67140 Mittelbergheim, tel. 03.88.08.92.76,
fax 03.88.08.25.91 ☑ 🏠
�? ev. day 8am–12 noon 1.30pm–6pm; Sat. 5pm;
Sun. 9am–11.30am; groups by appt.

JOSEPH GRUSS ET FILS
Prestige 2001★★

| | 1.5 ha | 12,000 | 💧 | 5–8 € |

The vineyard was created in 1947 by Joseph Gruss, the grandfather. Since 1997, the grandson, André, has assisted his father, Bernard, after working in the antipodes straight after graduating in oenology. They make a variety of Crémants from different varietal blends, much commented upon by the Jury. Take this Prestige, made from a majority of Auxerrois grapes (70%) with Riesling (20%), and given extra interest by 10% Pinot Gris. The formula seems to have worked: mousse with fine, persistent bubbles; an intense, rich mix of aromas evolving on a note of smokiness; a supple attack, roundness contributed by the Pinot Gris, great finesse and liveliness on the palate, and a lovely fruity finish. They also earn a star for their **Brut 2001**, a blend of Auxerrois (80%) and Riesling. It has a light yellow colour with green highlights, a light palate with pleasant fruit flavours, and a nose that is discreet but promising.
- Dom. Gruss et Fils, 25, Grand-Rue, 68420 Eguisheim,
tel. 03.89.41.28.78, fax 03.89.41.76.66,
e-mail domainegruss@hotmail.com ☑
�? by appt.

DOM. JUX★

| | n.c. | n.c. | 🍶 🍷 | 8–11 € |

On the northern periphery of Colmar, the Jux estate was taken over by Wolfberger about 20 years ago. It has now launched its own estate Crémant, benefiting from the expertise of a group that pioneered sparkling wines in Alsace. With a fine string of bubbles, this light yellow wine with dancing green highlights, has an engaging nose of fruits with notes of violets. Its balance, length and freshness make it very pleasant indeed.
- Dom. Jux, 5, chem. de la Fecht, 68000 Colmar,
tel. 03.89.79.13.76, fax 03.89.79.62.93 ☑

KLEIN-BRAND 1999★★

| | 2 ha | 21,000 | 🍶 🍷 | 5–8 € |

West of Rouffach, the Noble valley is a prime terrain for vine-growing owing to its favourable climatic conditions. Grown on limestone soils, the varieties from which this Crémant is made (60% Pinot Blanc; remainder Auxerrois) have acquired a magnificent expressiveness that comes through in the wine. Bubbles and a fine mousse come out of the light yellow liquid. The nose is already intense and exhales a breadth of citrus fruit aromas. White flowers, fruity and toasty notes mingle in a replete palate which is remarkable for its suppleness – due to the grapes' extreme ripeness. Remarkably well blended.

🍷 Klein-Brand, 96, rue de la Vallée, 68570 Soultzmatt, tel. 03.89.47.00.08, fax 03.89.47.65.53, e-mail kleinbrand@free.fr

🍴 ev. day except Sun. 8am–12 noon 1.30pm–6pm

Wines selected but not starred

LAURENT VOGT 2000★

	0.4 ha	4,700		8–11 €

Settled in a wine-grower's house dating from 1715, Thomas Vogt took over from his father, Laurent, in 1998. His Crémant, a single-variety Chardonnay, has attractive fine bubbles which we admired emerging out of the bright light-yellow liquid. Though still a trifle discreet, the aromas nonetheless had a delightful subtlety. On the palate there is lots of freshness, supported by fruit aromas with a slight touch of aniseed. A lovely balance.

🍷 EARL Laurent Vogt, 4, rue des Vignerons, 67120 Wolxheim, tel. 03.88.38.50.41, fax 03.88.38.50.41, e-mail thomas@domaine-vogt.com

🍴 by appt.

🍇 Thomas Vogt

ZINK 2000★★

	0.88 ha	10,000		5–8 €

Pfaffenheim is south of Colmar. The vineyard is ideally situated: it faces southeast and has gravelly clay soil particularly suited to Pinot Blanc and Auxerrois. These varieties have produced this top-quality Crémant. Light yellow, with a fine effervescence, this wine has a nose of exquisite delicacy, which exhales notes of fruits (citrus fruits, plum) before developing those of white flowers with hints of acacia. The somewhat lively attack leads on to an expressive palate mixing citrus fruits and apple, then brioche. A very good aperitif wine.

🍷 Pierre-Paul Zink, 27, rue de la Lauch, 68250 Pfaffenheim, tel. 03.89.49.60.87, fax 03.89.49.73.05, e-mail pierre-paul.zink@worldonline.fr

🍴 by appt.

ANDRE ANCEL 2000

	0.24 ha	2,330		5–8 €

🍷 EARL André Ancel, 3, rue du Collège, 68240 Kaysersberg, tel. 03.89.47.10.76, fax 03.89.78.13.78, e-mail ancelandre@free.fr

🍴 by appt.

JEAN-CLAUDE BUECHER 2001

	5.27 ha	32,000		5–8 €

🍷 Jean-Claude Buecher, 31, rue des Vignes, 68920 Wettolsheim, tel. 03.89.80.14.01, fax 03.89.80.17.78

🍴 by appt.

ANTOINE FONNE

Blanc de blancs

	0.4 ha	3,500		8–11 €

🍷 Antoine Fonné, 14, Grand-Rue, 68770 Ammerschwihr, tel. 03.89.47.37.90, fax 03.89.47.18.83

🍴 by appt.

DOM. JOSEPH SCHARSCH 2001

	0.75 ha	8,000		5–8 €

🍷 Dom. Joseph Scharsch, 12, rue de l'Eglise, 67120 Wolxheim, tel. 03.88.38.30.61, fax 03.88.38.01.13, e-mail domaine.scharsch@wanadoo.fr

🍴 by appt.

JEAN-VICTOR SCHUTZ

Blanc de blancs

	4 ha	30,000		5–8 €

🍷 Jean-Victor Schutz, 34, rue du Mal-Foch, 67650 Dambach-la-Ville, tel. 03.88.92.41.86, fax 03.88.92.61.81

ALBERT ZIEGLER 2000

	0.85 ha	10,000		5–8 €

🍷 Albert Ziegler, 10, rue de l'Eglise, 68500 Orschwihr, tel. 03.89.76.01.12, fax 03.89.74.91.32

🍴 ev. day 8am–12 noon 1.30pm–7pm

🍇 Michel Voelklin

The Wines of the East

The Côtes de Toul and the Moselle are the last remaining vineyards of the once flourishing wine-growing area of Lorraine. In their heyday, Lorraine wines were held in high esteem, and in 1890 the vineyards covered more than 30,000 ha. The reputation of these two areas was at its height in the late 19th century. After that, various disasters contributed to its decline: the vines were destroyed by phylloxera, and the hybrid stock planted to replace them was of inferior quality; there was a slump in the wine industry in 1907; the battlefields of the First World War covered much of this part of eastern France; and the industrialization of the region led to a massive exodus of workers from the country to the town to work in the factories. The local authorities ultimately acknowledged the originality of the wines produced in these vineyards, but it was not until 1951 that the Côtes de Toul and the Moselle wines were officially recognized, finally regaining their place among the old-established wines of France.

Côtes de Toul

Located just west of Toul and the elbow-bend of the Moselle, the Côtes de Toul vineyards cover eight communes along the hillside. Sedimentary layers from the eastern part of the Paris Basin have been eroded to expose geological structures from the Jurassic period, mainly Oxford clay with significant deposits of calcareous scree, which gives good drainage. The slopes face south or south-east, and the semi-continental climate means high summer temperatures, which help to ripen the grapes. However, there are often frosts in spring.

The majority of the vineyards are planted with Gamay, although much is being replaced by Pinot Noir. The blending of these two varieties makes characteristic Vin Gris, which is obtained by direct pressing. To qualify as Vin Gris, the decree stipulates that at least 10% of Pinot Noir grapes must be blended with Gamay, which gives the wine greater roundness. Some Pinot Noir is made into single-variety red wines that are pleasant and full-bodied, while the locally grown Auxerrois makes light white wines.

The vineyards cover some 87 ha, and produced 5,211 hl of wine in 2002.

As you leave Toul, there is a well signposted Route des Vins et de la Mirabelle, which takes you through the vineyard.

On 31 March 1998, the vineyard was officially recognized as an AOC.

DOM. VINCENT GORNY
Pinot noir 2002★

■	1.2 ha	8,000	■	5–8 €

Vincent Gorny began on this family estate of 8 ha in 1991. In 2000, he built a new winery of 1,000 square metres. Eight days of maceration after de-stalking have produced this wine with a very intense colour. The characteristic cherry aroma heralds a well-structured, lingering palate. Excellent with roast beef.
➥ Vincent Gorny, Z.A., 50, rue des Triboulottes, 54200 Bruley, tel. 03.83.63.80.41, fax 03.83.63.53.80, e-mail vincentgorny@yahoo.fr ☑
🍷 ev. day except Sun. 9am–12 noon 2pm–7pm

MARCEL ET MICHEL LAROPPE Pinot
noir Elevé en fût de chêne 2001★★

■	2 ha	8,000	⦀	5–8 €

This flagship Côtes-de-Toul estate offers some really delightful wines, as these three testify. The above-named, an intense

ruby red, was matured for 12 months in oak casks (20% of them new) and came from Pinot vines 25 years old. The nose is fruity, slightly vanilla, with notes of raspberry and black-currant. Though evident to the palate, the oak is agreeably discreet; the well-softened tannins provide excellent substance. The **Pinot Noir 2000**, which has not seen oak, is selected (unstarred), as is also the **Auxerrois 2002**, which has attractive finesse and notes of citrus fruits.
➥ Marcel et Michel Laroppe, 253, rue de la République, 54200 Bruley, tel. 03.83.43.11.04, fax 03.83.43.36.92, e-mail vignoble.laroppe@wanadoo.fr ☑
🍷 ev. day except Sun. 8am–12 noon 1.30pm–6.30pm

MARCEL ET MICHEL LAROPPE
Gris 2002★★

■	2 ha	18,000	■ ♦	3–5 €

This was the Jury's *coup de coeur* after the tasting which, this year, took place in the Meuse département. It is a *vin gris*, blended from 75% Gamay, 20% Pinot Noir and 5% Auxerrois. The colour is a ravishing salmon-pink and the nose exhales an intense fruitiness. The palate is also fruity, with a roundness that contributes to the wine's overall good integration. A lovely success.
➥ Marcel et Michel Laroppe, 253, rue de la République, 54200 Bruley, tel. 03.83.43.11.04, fax 03.83.43.36.92, e-mail vignoble.laroppe@wanadoo.fr ☑
🍷 ev. day except Sun. 8am–12 noon 1.30pm–6.30pm

DOM. DE LA LINOTTE
Gris 2002★

■	0.84 ha	8,000	■	3–5 €

On his return from Champagne in 1993, Marc Laroppe planted vines here using lyre training. His three wines are selected. The above-named, a beautiful intense pink, has a nose of berry fruits. Though a little closed, the palate has a very pleasing roundness and finesse. Also selected (unstarred) are his **Auxerrois 2002** and his **Pinot Noir 2002**. These two are similarly well-crafted wine.
➥ Marc Laroppe, 90, rue Victor-Hugo, 54200 Bruley, tel. 03.83.63.29.02, fax 03.83.63.00.39 ☑
🍷 ev. day 9am–7pm

ISABELLE ET JEAN-MICHEL MANGEOT Gris 2002★

	0.6 ha	3,400	🍷 🍇	3–5 €

Bruley is a pretty village typical of the wine-growing part of Lorraine. This estate offers a *vin gris* whose colour is a trifle pale but beautifully clear. The nose is interestingly fruity. The palate is rich and round, beautifully balanced despite a touch of residual sugar.

↘ SCEA Dom. Régina, 350, rue de la République, 54200 Bruley, tel. 03.83.64.49.52, fax 03.83.64.49.52, e-mail jmmangeot@compuserve.com ☑
☞ ev. day 5pm–8pm; Sat. Sun. 10am–7pm
↘ Jean-Michel Mangeot

LES VIGNERONS DU TOULOIS

Auxerrois 2002★

	0.4 ha	3,500	🍷 🍇	3–5 €

The label on this cooperative's wine shows the cathedral of Saint-Etienne, flamboyant Gothic in style, with twin towers 65 m tall watching over Toul and its vineyard. A fine image for this pale yellow Auxerrois whose nose has both finesse and an intensity of floral aromas. The palate is well-rounded, made all the better for a lingering finish.

↘ Les Vignerons du Toulois, 43, pl. de la Mairie, 54113 Mont-le-Vignoble, tel. 03.83.62.59.93, fax 03.83.62.59.93 ☑
☞ ev. day except Mon. 2pm–6pm

Wines selected but not starred

ANDRE ET ROLAND LELIEVRE

Gris 2002

	10 ha	13,300	🍷 🍇	3–5 €

↘ André et Roland Lelièvre, 3, rue de la Gare, 54200 Lucey, tel. 03.83.63.81.36, fax 03.83.63.84.45, e-mail info@vins-lelievre.com ☑
☞ by appt.

Moselle AOVDQS

The vineyards are planted on the hillsides of the Moselle valley, which were originally layers of sedimentary rock at the eastern limit of the Paris Basin. The vineyards are clustered in three main centres: the first is south and west of Metz; the second in the region of Sierck-les-Bains, and the third along the Seille valley, around Vic-sur-Seille. Winemaking in this AOVDQS is influenced by that in neighbouring Luxembourg; the vines grow tall and wide, producing dry, fruity white wines. In terms of quantity, the AOVDQS is still modest, producing 1,720 hl in 2002, but the wine-growing area cannot expand because the land is broken up into very small plots.

MICHEL MAURICE

Pinot gris 2002★★

	0.58 ha	5,000	🍷 🍇	5–8 €

Having received a *coup de coeur* for his 2000 and 2001, Michel Maurice has followed that success with a noteworthy 2002 Pinot Gris. Shining gold in the glass, it has an intense and powerful nose that is highly aromatic and authentic to the variety. The palate is beautifully fresh, with subtle flavours. The wine is ready to drink now, but could age another two to three years. Maurice's **Auxerrois 2002** and **Gris Pinot Gamay**

2002 are selected (unstarred). Both reveal how much the sun shone over Lorraine in 2002.
↘ Michel Maurice, 1–3, pl. Foch, 57130 Ancy-sur-Moselle, tel. 03.87.30.90.07, fax 03.87.30.91.48, e-mail mauricem@netcourrier.com ☑
☞ by appt.

OURY-SCHREIBER

Cuvée du maréchal Fabert 2002★★

	1 ha	5,200	🍷	5–8 €

This estate of 6.5 ha did brilliantly with its 2002. This vintage honours a Marshal of France who, born in Metz in 1599, was to distinguish himself in the Wars of Religion. The wine is bright gold, with intense rose perfumes. The palate is lively, complex and full of flavours; it carried the day at the tasting. Two stars were similarly awarded to the oak-matured **Cuvée de Pinot Noir 2002 Elevée en Fût**. It has potent aromas of soft fruits and blackcurrants. The palate's silky and elegant tannins will assure it good keeping-quality.
↘ Oury-Schreiber, 57420 Marieulles, tel. 03.87.52.09.02, fax 03.87.52.09.17 ☑
☞ by appt.

J. SIMON-HOLLERICH

Pinot noir 2002★

	n.c.	2,000	🍷	3–5 €

Two of this estate's wines impressed the Jury. One, styled Joseph on the label, is a **Pinot Blanc 2002**: a greenish yellow, it has an agreeable freshness with notes of citrus fruits and is an unstarred selection. The other, called Jeanne, is this Pinot Noir with its strong, bright rosé colour and elegant nose of soft fruits. The palate is light, fresh, agreeable, and very fruity.
↘ Jeanne Simon-Hollerich, 16, rue du Pressoir, 57480 Contz-les-Bains, tel. 03.82.83.74.81, fax 03.82.83.69.70 ☑
☞ ev. day 8am–8pm

CH. DE VAUX

Pinot noir Les Hautes Bassières 2002★★★

	2 ha	12,600	🍷🍇	5–8 €

The vaulted cellars date from the 13th century, though the château was radically rebuilt in 1870. Since 1999, Marie-Geneviève and Norbert Molozy have worked this vineyard located half a kilometre from the 13th century church of Saint-Rémi. This Hautes Bassières wine is quite simply exceptional. The colour is intense crimson, while the nose is elegance itself, supported by a discreet oaky aroma. The palate's excellent body is sustained by the superb tannins and well-integrated flavours, which mingle soft fruits and elegant oak.
↘ Marie-Geneviève et Norbert Molozay, Ch. de Vaux, 4, pl. Saint-Rémi, 57130 Vaux, tel. 03.87.60.20.64, fax 03.87.60.24.67, e-mail chateaudevaux.m@wanadoo.fr ☑
☞ by appt.

CH. DE VAUX Gryphées 2002★

	1.8 ha	14,000	🍷 🍇	5–8 €

Two white wines here equally attracted the Jury. First, the oaky **Septentrion 2002**, which is selected (unstarred). Second, the above-named, vat-matured vintage, which has a delightfully full and floral nose. The palate has beautiful acidity and a good future before it due to its excellent body. The **Les Boserés rosé 2002** is agreeable and elegant; it is an unstarred selection.

🔗 Marie-Geneviève et Norbert Molozay, Ch. de Vaux, 4, pl. Saint-Rémi, 57130 Vaux, tel. 03.87.60.20.64, fax 03.87.60.24.67,
e-mail chateaudevaux.m@wanadoo.fr **Ⓥ**
🍷 by appt.

Wines selected but not starred

GAUTHIER Réserve de la Porte des Evêques
Muller-Thurgau 2002

	0.2 ha	2,130	▮	3–5 €

🔗 Claude Gauthier, 4, pl. du Palais, 57630 Vic-sur-Seille, tel. 03.87.01.11.55, fax 03.87.01.11.55 **Ⓥ**
🍷 by appt.

BEAUJOLAIS AND COTEAUX DE LYONNAIS

Beaujolais

Officially, Beaujolais is part of the Burgundy wine-growing region, although it has become separately identified and through skilful promotion and marketing has become famous in its own right through the whole world. Who can be unaware of the much-trumpeted arrival of the Beaujolais Nouveau on the third Thursday of November? The soil and the topography of the Beaujolais differ significantly from the countryside of its celebrated neighbour, where the vineyard slopes form an almost straight north–south line. The steeper hills and deeper valleys of the Beaujolais mean that many vineyards are frequently bathed in sunshine. The houses are different, too; rather than the roofs being covered by the flatter tiles of Burgundy, they are covered with bowed, Roman tiles which convey a Mediterranean flavour.

The Beaujolais region lies south of Burgundy, and is a gateway to southern France. There are 96 communes covering 23,000 ha, stretching 50 km from north to south, through two departments, the Saône-et-Loire and the Rhône, and average 15 km wide, though narrower in the south. In the north, the Arlois is the border with the Mâconnais. In the east, on the other hand, the Saône plain, where the sparkling river meanders her slow majestic way south, makes a natural barrier. Julius Caesar remarked that the river moved so slowly that it was virtually impossible to judge in which direction it was flowing. To the west, the Beaujolais hills form the foothills of the Massif Central. The highest point, Mont Saint-Rigaux, 1,012 m, is a gigantic milestone marking the junction of the lands of the Saône and Loire rivers. In the south, the Lyon wine country takes over as far as the city of Lyon itself, irrigated, as the saying goes, by three great "rivers": the Rhône, the Saône and ... the Beaujolais.

The great renown of Beaujolais wines owes a massive debt to Lyon. The wines are still sold in the city's famous small wine bars or bouchons, where they had a ready market after the highly successful expansion of the vineyards in the 18th century. Two hundred years previously, Villefranche-sur-Saône had become the region's capital, in place of Beaujeu, which had given the area its name. The lords of Beaujeu were skilful and wise; they carefully planned the expansion of their wealth and their domains, stimulated not least by their concern to protect themselves from their powerful neighbours, the Counts of Mâcon and Forez, the Abbots of Cluny and the Bishops of Lyon. The rapid development of the vineyard came about when Beaujolais was added to the ranks of the five Royal "farms", areas which were exempted from certain taxes normally levied for transporting goods to Paris. For many years, Beaujolais produce was carried via the Briare canal.

Today, Beaujolais produces an average of 1,400,000 hl of red wines of a distinctive character (there is virtually no white). With only the rare exception, Beaujolais reds are made from a single variety, the Gamay, a black-skinned grape with white flesh. This is one of the fundamental differences with Burgundy, where several varieties are grown. The wines produced fall into three appellations: Beaujolais, Beaujolais Supérieur and Beaujolais-Villages, and there are also ten recognized crus: Brouilly, Côte de Brouilly, Chénas, Chiroubles, Fleurie, Morgon, Juliénas, Moulin-à-Vent, Saint-Amour and Régnié. The first three appellations may apply to reds, whites or rosés, while the ten others are exclusively reds which qualify legally as AOC Bourgogne. Geologically speaking, the Beaujolais region was affected by the folding of the earth's crust in the Hercynian period of the Primary era and again in the Tertiary era when the Alps were formed. This was the era that created the relief of the present-day Beaujolais; the sedimentary deposits from the Secondary era were fractured when outcrops of rocks formed in the Primary period were pushed up. More recently, in the Quaternary era, glaciers and rivers flowing from west to east gouged out numerous valleys and fashioned the landscape from which outcrops of hard rock that are resistant to erosion stand out like islands. This is when the relief of the present-day Beaujolais was created with its eastern-facing slopes that descend like a gigantic staircase to the Saône.

Northern and southern Beaujolais have distinctive features and Villefranche-sur-Saône stands on an invisible dividing line between the two parts of the vineyard. The hills in the north are softly rounded and the bottoms of the valleys are filled with sand. It is a region of ancient rocks such as granite, porphyry, shale and diorite. As the granite has decomposed slowly over time, it has left siliceous sands, known locally as gore, which can vary in depth from a few centimetres down to several metres and are areas of clay and sand. This poor, acid soil lacks organic matter and retains neither moisture nor nutrients, so it is prone to drying out though it is easy to work. This terrain, with other areas of shale, is where the local appellations and Beaujolais-Villages wines are grown. The southern area has a larger proportion of sedimentary soil, with clay and limestone being found on the more steeply sloping hills. The soils are richer in limestone and sandstone than in the north. This area is known for its "golden stones", which are coloured by ferrous oxide, giving a warm look to the buildings. The earth is richer and retains moisture better. This is where the AOC Beaujolais wines are grown. In both areas, vines prosper between altitudes of 190 and 550 m. A background to these two

Beaujolais

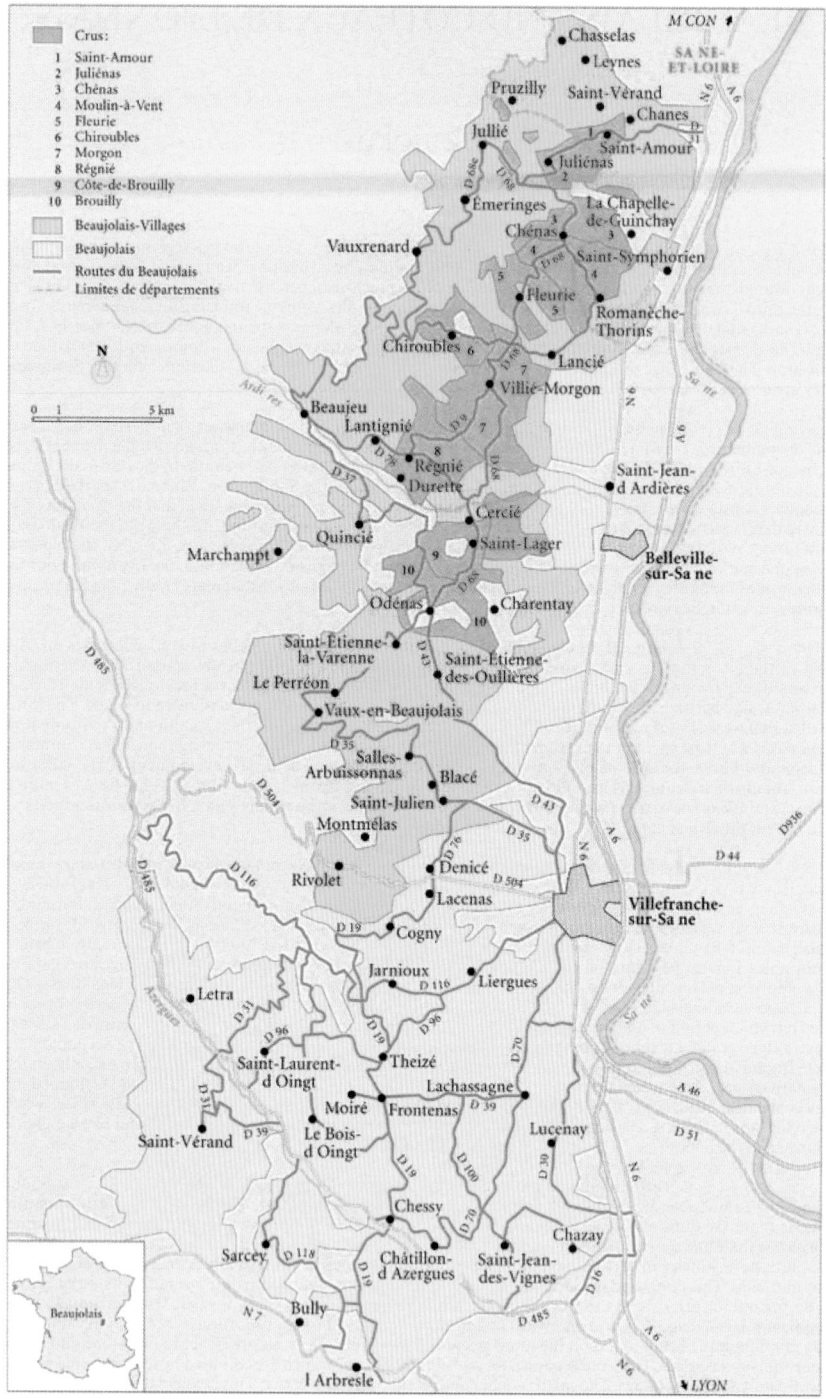

distinct areas is Haut Beaujolais, an area of harder metamorphic rock which at over 600 m is covered by pine and chestnut forests and ferns. The best wine-growing land has a south-south-easterly aspect and lies between 190 and 350 m.

The Beaujolais region is temperate though it has three competing prevailing climates: a continental influence, a maritime influence and another from the Mediterranean. Depending on the season, each of them can dominate and the change from one to another can be rapid and unexpected, making pressures and temperatures rise or plummet violently. Winters can be cold or wet; spring can be wet or dry; July and August are scorching when the desiccating wind blows up from the Midi, or drenched when there are rain and hail storms; autumn can be wet or hot. The average rainfall is 7.5 cm and the temperature ranges from −20°C to +38°C. Throughout the region, however, there are tiny micro-climates which do not follow the general rule and vines can flourish in situations which, on the face of it, should not be propitious. Generally speaking, the vineyards have good sunshine and enjoy good conditions for the grapes to ripen.

To describe the grape varieties planted in Beaujolais is particularly simple: 99% of the vineyards are planted with Gamay, often called "Gamay Beaujolais" locally. In 1395, Philip the Brave banished Gamay from the Côte d'Or, considering it a "disloyal plant", which it was, when compared with Pinot Noir. However, it is a very adaptable variety which can prosper in many different climates – some 33,000 ha are planted with Gamay in France and it is remarkably well suited to the soils of the Beaujolais. It has a trailing habit so has to be staked and supported for the first ten years of its life; in the north of the region you will see fields of vine props holding up the plants. It is susceptible to spring frosts and to the main parasites and vine diseases. The vines can bud early, at the end of March, but more usually in the second week of April. As the Beaujolais saying goes, "When the vines shine in Saint George's tide, they are not late". The flowering season is the first fortnight in June and the harvest starts in mid-September.

Varieties other than Gamay are also entitled to the appellation: Pinot Noir and Pinot Gris for red and rosé wines and Chardonnay and Aligoté for white wines. Until the year 2015, the expansion of Pinot Noir planting has been restricted to a total of 15% of the Beaujolais vineyard (currently very much less than that is planted); blends of red or rosé wines using up to a maximum of 15% of Pinot Noir or Pinot Gris, Chardonnay, Melon or Aligoté are also permitted. Vines are pruned in one of two ways: a hard prune, training the plant into the shape of a goblet or fan is used for all appellations, while for the Beaujolais appellation vines are pruned to one stem, known as a "baguette" (the French word for the typical French loaf shape). Vines can also be pruned as cordons in the AOC Beaujolais vineyards.

All the red Beaujolais wines are made according to the same precepts: the bunches are kept whole and there is a short maceration period of three to seven days, depending on the type of wine. The technique used is classic fermentation for the 10–20% of juice produced when the grape skins are broken as the clusters are loaded into the vat; meanwhile intracellular fermentation ensures a quite considerable breaking down of malic acid which releases particular aromas. This is what gives Beaujolais wines their structure and their aromatic characteristics, which are both enhanced and individually defined by the soil on which the vines are grown. Because so much of this technique depends on letting the grapes work by themselves, it is very difficult for the winemaker to control the wine's development reliably in this early stage, given the unpredictability of the reactions between the volume of must released in relation to the entire content of the vat. On the whole, Beaujolais wines are dry but not tannic, supple, fruity and very aromatic; they are usually 12–13% volume, with a total acidity of 3.5 g/l in terms of H_2SO_4.

One of the common peculiarities in the Beaujolais vineyards is métayage, a system from the past but one that has persisted and still lives on. This means that the harvest and certain costs are shared between the grower and the owner, who provides the vineyard, lodgings, a vat room equipped with all that is required to make the grapes into wine, any products required during winemaking as well as the plantations of vines. The grower, or métayer, provides all the machinery required for cultivation, engages any workers, pays the pickers at harvest-time and ensures that the vines are kept in perfect condition. These management contracts start on St Martin's Day, 11 November, and many growers find it attractive to use them; 46% of Beaujolais vineyards are managed in this way compared with 45% which are managed by the owner. The remaining 9% of vineyards are run by tenant farmers. It is not unusual for growers to be owners of certain parcels of vineyards and métayers as well. A typical Beaujolais vineyard covers 7–10 ha, and they tend to be smaller in the area of the recognized crus, where the system of métayage dominates, while in the south, where mixed farming is more common, the vineyards are larger. Nineteen cooperatives vinify 30% of the grapes produced, while 85% of the wine is sold by growers and local shippers. AOC Beaujolais is sold by the 216-litre barrel, and AOC Beaujolais-Villages and the crus are sold by the 215-litre barrel. The wine is sold throughout the year but local incomes rise most appreciably when the Vins de Primeur, or new season's wines, are released onto the market. Some 50% of the wine is exported to Switzerland, Germany, Belgium, Luxembourg, Britain, the United States, the Netherlands, Denmark, Canada, Japan, Sweden and Italy.

Beaujolais Nouveau is red or rosé wine that comes only from the non-cru appellations, usually from the Beaujolais or Beaujolais-Villages appellations. The wines, grown on sandy granite soil in certain parts of Beaujolais-Villages, are vinified after a short maceration which lasts only four days, creating soft, light wines with a mouthful of flavour. The colour is not particularly intense and the fruity perfumes sometimes have a hint of ripe banana. There are strict regulations which lay down the criteria the wine must meet and how it can be marketed. By mid-November, the Vins de Primeur are ready to be drunk around the world. In 1956 only 13,000 hl of this wine was sold; by 1970 the figure was 100,000 hl, 200,000 hl in 1976,

400,000 hl in 1982, 500,000 hl in 1985, rising to 600,000 hl in 1990, 655,000 hl in 1996 and 790,000 hl in 2002. From 15 December, the crus are tasted and judged, then marketed. The majority of sales of these are made after Easter. Beaujolais wines are not for keeping and most are consumed within two years. However, some particularly good bottles can be kept up to ten years and drink very well. The appeal of these wines lies in their freshness and the delicacy of their nose, reminiscent of flowers – peony, rose, violet, iris – and also certain fruits, including apricot, cherry, peach and summer fruits (berries).

Beaujolais and Beaujolais Supérieur

Nearly half of the wine produced is Appellation Beaujolais. Some 10,500 ha mainly south of Villefranche, produced 584,955 hl in 2002. Of this, 8,899 hl are white wines made from Chardonnay, 20% of the Chardonnay grapes being harvested in the small canton of La Chapelle-de-Guinchay, where the flinty soil of the crus changes to the limestone terrain of the Mâconnais. In the area of the "golden stones", east of Bois-d'Oingt and south of Villefranche, the red wines are aromatic with scents that are more fruity than flowery with even some traces of vegetation. These colourful wines are well structured, if sometimes a little rustic, and keep quite well. In the upper part of the Azergues valley, in the west of the region, the crystalline rocks give the wine a more flinty flavour which improves with age. The vineyards at the top of the slopes produce more sharply flavoured wines that are lighter in colour but also less heavy in hot years. The nine Caves Coopératives in this area have put a great deal of effort into developing their techniques and have significantly improved the economy of the area which produces about 75% of the "Vins de Primeur".

The Appellation Beaujolais Supérieur does not come from a specifically defined area. To qualify for this appellation, the wines must be identified each year and are required to meet certain criteria: the must, at harvest, should have an alcoholic content 0.5° higher than the Appellation Beaujolais wines. Altogether, 5,000 hl are declared as Appellation Beaujolais Supérieur each year, principally from the area of AOC Beaujolais.

Villages are scattered and the architecture of the wine-growers' houses is attractive; traditionally they have the cellar at ground level and an exterior staircase leads to a canopied balcony and the living quarters. At the end of the 18th century, large vat rooms were built separately from the proprietor's house. The one at Lacenas, 6 km from Villefranche, which is on the domain of the Château de Montauzan, is the headquarters of the Confrérie des Compagnons du Beaujolais, established in 1947 to regulate and promote Beaujolais wines. Today, it is recognized internationally. The Confrérie des Grappilleurs des Pierres Dorées was set up in 1968 with the task of organizing a whole range of festivals and fairs in the region. When it comes to downing a *pot* of Beaujolais, the heavy-bottomed bottle containing 46 cl of wine that is plonked on every bistro table, it goes perfectly with pork scratchings, tripe, black pudding, saucisson and charcuterie of all kinds, and also with quenelles topped with cheese. The fresh young wines are a good accompaniment for dishes such as cardoons with bone marrow or gratiné potatoes and onions.

Beaujolais

DOM. DES BALMES 2002★

| | 8.71 ha | 3,300 | | | 3–5 € |

This ruby wine with delicate aromas of soft fruits, chiefly raspberry, was made from 20-year-old vines planted on light granitic soil. Its very soft fullness was much enjoyed. This is a well-made, beautifully smooth Beaujolais, to be drunk within a year.

Serge Laville, 69220 Corcelles-en-Beaujolais, tel. 04.74.06.10.10, fax 04.74.66.13.77
by appt.

MICHEL CARRON
Coteaux de Terre noire 2001★

| | 0.8 ha | 5,000 | | | 3–5 € |

This pale-yellow wine comes from established vines on clay-limestone soil. Its rich aromas, a blend of exotic fruits and floral notes, continue on the well-rounded, substantial palate. Pleasant and of good length, this wine should be drunk within a year as an aperitif or with starters or fish. The **red Beaujolais Coteaux de Terre Noire 2002** from the same estate is also recommended.

EARL Michel Carron, Terre-Noire, 69620 Moiré, tel. 04.74.71.62.02, fax 04.74.71.62.02
by appt.

CH. DE CERCY 2001★

| | 1.2 ha | 5,000 | | | 5–8 € |

This deep-yellow 2001 was partly matured in cask, and opens with aromas of vanilla and acacia. Its richness is immediately apparent. Although there is a strong oaky taste, this is pleasantly integrated in the body. This attractive, well-balanced wine should be drunk within a year. It goes well with fish, and even some desserts.

Michel Picard, Ch. de Cercy, 69640 Denicé, tel. 04.74.67.34.44, fax 04.74.67.32.35, e-mail earl-michel.picard@wanadoo.fr
by appt.

DOM. CHATELUS
Cuvée Terroir 2002★

| | 3 ha | 120,000 | | | 5–8 € |

Pascal Chatelus's estate is in the Pierres Dorées area, but the 40-year-old vines for this *cuvée* grow on a granitic soil. The bright-red colour is streaked with violet glints. The intense aromas suggest raspberry and blackcurrant. A fruity first impression, soft body and integrated tannins give a balanced taste on the palate. The finish is long with a slightly acid touch. Keep an eye on this well-made Beaujolais for the first two years, and drink it with charcuterie or chicken livers.

Pascal Chatelus, La Roche, 69620 Saint-Laurent-d'Oingt, tel. 04.74.71.24.78, fax 04.74.71.28.36
by appt.

MICHEL CHATOUX 2001★

■   0.31 ha   3,400   3–5 €

The first harvest of this vineyard's young Chardonnay grapes has produced a white Beaujolais with a deep-golden colour and a lovely bouquet of very ripe fruits developing notes of toast and sweet almonds. Its fruity body is pleasantly rich and fresh, even if it is not very characteristic of the grape variety. The **red Beaujolais 2002 Cuvée des Roches Vieilles Vignes** from the same estate was also singled out; this is a wine to keep for a while.

↪ Michel Chatoux, Le Favrot, 69620 Sainte-Paule, tel. 04.74.71.20.50 ☑
🍷 ev. day 8am–8pm

DOMINIQUE CHERMETTE

Cuvée Vieilles Vignes 2002★

■   2 ha   15,000   ■   5–8 €

This wine from an exposed hillside vineyard in the south-southeast of the region has plenty of body. It has an intense red, almost purplish colour, and pleasant aromas of very ripe soft fruits, strawberry to the fore. The first impression is of a good structure, with integrated tannins and an agreeable fruitiness of good length. This is a well-balanced wine to be drunk within a year.

↪ Dominique Chermette, Le Barnigat, 69380 Saint-Laurent-d'Oingt, tel. 04.74.71.20.05, fax 04.74.71.20.05 ☑
🍷 by appt.

CLOS DU CHÂTEAU DE LACHASSAGNE 2002★

■   4 ha   13,300   ■ ♦   8–11 €

The château grounds are open for six weekends a year, between April and September, so that visitors can walk through the 25 ha of woodland next to the 21-ha vineyard overlooking the Saône. This wine is dark red in colour with some yellow glints, and exudes aromas of garrigue and spices with notes of leather, oak and smoke which continue on the palate. This is a rather unusual but well-made Beaujolais with rounded tannins and good length. Drink within two years.

↪ SARL ch. de Lachassagne, Le Bourg, 69480 Lachassagne, tel. 04.74.67.00.53, fax 04.74.67.00.53, e-mail info@lachassagne.com ☑
🍷 ev. day except Wed. 10am–12 noon 3pm–6pm; Sun. 10am–1pm
🍷 Greenland

CLOS DU CHÂTEAU LASSALLE 2001★★

■   0.65 ha   3,000   ■ ⅏   5–8 €

Frédéric Pérol practises sustainable agriculture by the Terra Vitis method, and has produced a wine with a lovely bright-gold colour and green glints, a sign of youth. The subtle but intense aromas combine floral and fruity shades with buttered notes. The flavour is full and charming. This is a well-balanced wine that can be enjoyed both as an aperitif and with shellfish or fish in butter.

↪ Frédéric Pérol, N447, La Colletière, 69380 Châtillon-d'Azergues, tel. 04.78.43.99.84, fax 04.78.43.99.84 ☑ 🏠
🍷 by appt.

CH. DES CORREAUX 2001★

■   2 ha   10,000   ■ ♦   5–8 €

Located on the borders of Beaujolais and the Mâconnais, this vineyard was formerly known as the Château de Leynes, then in 2002 became the Château des Correaux. That year, Jean Bernard redesigned the family estate of less than 30 ha. This white Beaujolais has a strong golden-yellow colour which is still developing, but its fine floral bouquet with a touch of vanilla is already delightful. On the palate it reveals a rich lively body and subtle fruitiness. This well-balanced wine is ready to drink now.

↪ Jean Bernard, Ch. Les Correaux, 71570 Leynes, tel. 03.85.35.11.59, fax 03.85.35.13.94, e-mail bernardleynes@yahoo.fr ☑
🍷 by appt.

DOM. DE CRUIX 2002★

■   2 ha   10,000   3–5 €

From his 17th century house, Jean-Claude Brossette cultivates a vineyard of nearly 12 ha. This year, he wins one star for this deep-ruby Beaujolais with delicate aromas of peony and violet combining with a touch of cherry. This attractive, well-balanced wine has a rich but fairly soft body and a light fruitiness. It will be ready to drink in spring 2004.

↪ Jean-Claude Brossette, Dom. de Cruix, 69620 Theizé, tel. 04.74.71.24.74, fax 04.74.71.29.16, e-mail jcbrossette@wanadoo.fr ☑
🍷 ev. day 9am–12 noon 2pm–6pm

CH. DE L'ECLAIR 2002★

■   0.6 ha   4,000   ■ ⅏ ♦   5–8 €

This estate was built by Victor Vermorel, the inventor of the "Eclair" portable crop spray designed to help research as vineyards were being replanted after the phylloxera disaster. It has partly retained its original function in that the winery is equipped for experimental winemaking. He also produces wines that have been much praised in recent years. This one is light yellow in colour with green glints, and has a fairly subtle floral bouquet. The first impression is smooth and pleasant, revealing a well-made wine with no sugar left in it. It is balanced and full of flavour, with notes of citrus fruits and honey, and is a good ambassador for its appellation. It should be drunk within a year.

↪ SICAREX Beaujolais, Ch. de l'Eclair, 69400 Liergues, tel. 04.74.68.76.27, fax 04.74.68.76.27 ☑
🍷 by appt.

DOM. GARLON 2002★

■   4 ha   80,000   ■ ♦   5–8 €

This vineyard dates back to 1750. Its present owner cultivates 15 ha, tends the soil keenly and grasses down between the rows when this is appropriate. His Beaujolais has a very strong morello cherry colour, and opens with shades of cherry, peony and iris. After a good start, it reveals excellent balance. This is a fine, soft, fruity and fresh wine, to be drunk in the two next years. It goes with all kinds of meats and grilled game, or more simply with a plate of charcuterie.

↪ Jean-François Garlon, Le Bourg, 69620 Theizé, tel. 04.74.71.11.97, fax 04.74.71.23.30, e-mail jf.garlon@wanadoo.fr ☑
🍷 by appt.

DOM. JEAN-FELIX GERMAIN 2002★★

■   0.7 ha   4,000   ■ ♦   3–5 €

This clear garnet wine with strong aromas of raspberry, blackcurrant and redcurrant was made from 35-year-old vines and a well-controlled winemaking process in terms of temperatures. From the start, the tannins are quite pronounced but already integrated with a pleasant fullness and flavours of fresh fruits (cherry), which open out at some length. Drink it this year with sausage from Lyon.

↪ Dom. Jean-Félix Germain, Les Crozettes, 69380 Charnay, tel. 04.78.43.94.52, fax 04.78.43.94.52 ☑
🍷 ev. day 8.30am–12 noon 2pm–7pm

HENRI ET BERNARD GIRIN

Cuvée Coteaux du Razet 2002★

■   1.5 ha   10,000   ■ ♦   5–8 €

This estate dates back to 1870, and its Cuvée Coteaux du Razet is made from 40-year-old vines. The 2002 vintage has a dark-ruby colour and a perfume of blackcurrant with a hint of cherry. This wine has an amylic fruitiness and good length, and the full-bodied impression and integrated tannins fill the mouth. This Beaujolais has made the best possible use of its ingredients and should be drunk within a year.

↪ Henri et Bernard Girin, Aucherand, 69620 Saint-Vérand, tel. 04.74.71.63.49, fax 04.74.71.85.61, e-mail beaujolais.girin@free.fr ☑
🍷 ev. day except Sun. 8am–7pm

VIGNOBLE GRANGE-NEUVE 2002★★

■   3.2 ha   18,000   ⅏   3–5 €

Denis Carron took over this estate from his parents in 1980 and enlarged the property in 1997; today he farms 18 ha. This

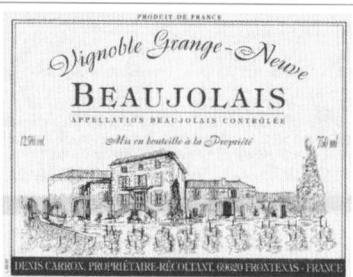

wine with its deep morello cherry colour and intense perfumes of very ripe cherry and blackcurrant was made from 45-year-old vines planted in a stony clay soil. The good first impression is rounded and powerful, and is followed by a rich and balanced palate. This well-structured, fresh and tasty Beaujolais should be drunk in two years. It goes with white meat, roast poultry or charcuterie.

➤ Denis Carron, chem. des Brosses, 69620 Frontenas, tel. 04.74.71.70.31, fax 04.74.71.86.30 ☑

⏳ by appt.

DOM. DU GUELET 2002★

	0.5 ha	3,600	🍶 👓	3–5 €

Didier Puillat and his wife Christine took over this estate of some 13 ha in 1994. They say it is a paradise for those who love nature. Their rosé Beaujolais has a strong pink colour inclining to red. Its perfumes suggest fresh grapes blended with hints of strawberry. This is a full-bodied wine, chewy like a grape seed, structured, balanced and long, and will be very pleasant to drink in the next year.

➤ Christine et Didier Puillat, Le Fournel, 69640 Rivolet, tel. 04.74.67.34.05,
e-mail puillat@beaujolais-domaine-du-guelet.com ☑

⏳ by appt.

DOM. DE JASSERON
Cuvée Spéciale 2002★★

	8 ha	5,000	🍶 👓	3–5 €

Most of the vines on this estate, created just 30 years ago, are planted on flinty clay soils. They have produced a deep-crimson wine developing fairly strong winey perfumes alongside spicy and fruity notes. The palate is dominated by flavours of spices and blackcurrant, has rounded tannins and good substance. This remarkable and well-structured wine will be ready in one to two years, to be drunk with meats in sauce or a Beaujolais andouillette.

➤ Georges Barjot, Grille-Midi,
69220 Saint-Jean-d'Ardières, tel. 04.74.66.47.34,
fax 04.74.66.47.34 ☑

⏳ ev. day 8am–8pm

CAVE DES VIGNERONS DE LIERGUES
2002★

	5 ha	12,000	🍶 👓	3–5 €

The Liergues cooperative established their business in 1929, and cultivate 550 ha including five of Chardonnay, which went to make this bright pale-yellow wine with the typically intense perfume of the grape variety plus a touch of lemon. The lively first impression recalls citrus fruits (grapefruit). This well-balanced, fresh and easy-to-drink wine is fairly long and slightly mentholated at the finish. It will go well either as an aperitif or served with cheese or charcuterie. The **red Beaujolais 2002** has also been singled out.

➤ Cave des Vignerons de Liergues, 69400 Liergues, tel. 04.74.65.86.00, fax 04.74.62.81.20,
e-mail jp.caveliergues@wanadoo.fr

⏳ ev. day except Sun. 8am–12 noon 2pm–7pm

DOM. LONGERE 2002★

	n.c.	4,200	🍶 👓	5–8 €

This highly subdivided estate contains at least fifty plots. Its granitic soil was responsible for this bright and clear

pale-golden wine with green glints. Its fruity and floral perfumes are typical and intense. The first impression is fresh and mineral, and combines with the fruity and rich flesh to fill the mouth. It is well balanced and expressive, and should be drunk in the next two years. The estate's **red Beaujolais-Villages 2002** was also singled out.

➤ Régine et Jean-Luc Longère, Le Duchamp, 69460 Le Perréon, tel. 04.74.03.27.63, fax 04.74.03.27.63,
e-mail jean-luc. longere@wanadoo.fr ☑ 🏠 🏠

⏳ by appt.

DOM. MONTERNOT 2002★★

	3 ha	2,000	🍶 👓	5–8 €

The vines for this rosé were grown on flinty clay soil and harvested from 7 September. The wine is beautifully bright, an excellent sign. It continues well with intense and fine perfumes of fresh fruit and a well-balanced, structured palate with good length. It is ready to drink now. Another recommended wine is the **red Beaujolais-Villages, la Réserve du Domaine Vieilles Vignes, Cuvée Brut du Cuve 2002.**

➤ GAEC J. et B. Monternot, Les Places, 69460 Blacé, tel. 04.74.67.56.48, fax 04.74.60.51.13 ☑

⏳ by appt.

DOM. DES NUGUES 2002★★

	2 ha	7,000	🍶 👓	5–8 €

This vineyard dates from 1968, and now has more than 21 ha. In 2000, the owner's son joined his father on the estate. Together they have produced a clear, intense crimson wine with a full and pleasant bouquet of soft fruits. It is full and rounded on the palate with silky tannins, and a lasting fruity flavour of strawberry and raspberry. This winey, well-made Beaujolais should be drunk in the next two years.

➤ EARL Gelin, Les Pasquiers, 69220 Lancié,
tel. 04.74.04.14.00, fax 04.74.04.16.73,
e-mail earl-gelin@wanadoo.fr ☑

⏳ by appt.

SEBASTIEN PARIAUD 2002★

	0,61 ha	740	🍶🍶	3–5 €

Although he is new here, this young winemaker has made an encouraging start with this deep-ruby wine with an intense and expressive bouquet of very ripe cherry and blackcurrant. The cherry re-emerges on a fine, well-balanced palate along with a full-bodied fruitiness and soft tannins of good length. This wine will go well with your charcuterie for one or two years.

➤ Sébastien Pariaud, La Merlatière, 69220 Lancié, tel. 04.74.04.10.16 ☑

⏳ ev. day 8am–12 noon 2pm–7pm

CH. DES PERTONNIERES
Cuvée Tonnelières 2002★

	10 ha	n.c.		5–8 €

On their estate of 30 ha, the Dupeubles continue the work of a winemaking family that goes back to 1512. They have produced a clear, bright-ruby wine with cherry glints and an aroma of blackcurrant on both the bouquet and the palate. A lovely first impression discloses a rich wine with fine tannins and a long and fresh finish. This is a very good ambassador for the appellation, to be drunk over the next two years with white meat, grills or charcuterie.

➤ Dom. Dupeuble Père et Fils, Ch. des Pertonnières, 69620 Le Breuil, tel. 04.74.71.68.40, fax 04.74.71.64.22,
e-mail beaujolais.dupeuble@horeis.com ☑

⏳ by appt.

DOM. DE ROTISSON
Cuvée Prestige Vieilles Vignes 2002★

	0.38 ha	2,000	🍶 👓	5–8 €

This vineyard dating from 1920 changed hands in 1998. The new owners put on many events such as: vintage car rallies, equestrian events and exhibitions. They also make good wines. This one has a lively-red colour and releases pleasant perfumes of very ripe fruits developing notes of kirsch. The well-balanced palate has a rich body with aromas of stewed

fruits and fills the mouth. Drink it within a year. The **white Beaujolais 2001** was also singled out.
📞 Dom. de Rotisson, rte de Conzy, 69210 Saint-Germain-sur-L'Arbresle, tel. 04.74.01.23.08, fax 04.74.01.55.41, e-mail domaine-de-rotisson@wanadoo.fr
🍽 ev. day except Sun. 9am–12.30pm 2pm–6.30pm
📞 Didier Pouget

ROUDON MERE ET FILS

Cuvée Prestige 2002★

2 ha	6,000	▮ ◆	3–5€

This ruby wine with bluish glints was made from 50-year-old vines and has delicate perfumes of peony and stone fruits, with a touch of fresh mint. The fresh palate is very pleasant with good length, despite a certain austerity which should disappear. The Jury called it "a chewy Beaujolais," to be drunk within a year.
📞 Roudon Mère et Fils, GAEC du Charverron, le Farginet, 69620 Létra, tel. 04.74.71.33.97, fax 04.74.71.33.97
🍽 by appt.

TERRES DOREES 2002★★

3 ha	20,000	▮	5–8€

These are Terres Dorées and the wines are golden too. The previous vintage won a *coup de coeur* for its white wine. The 2002 vintage is in the same tradition. It is clear, pale gold in colour and emits intense and elegant floral notes with shades of peony. The first impression is fresh, supple, full bodied and rounded, and the palate is well balanced. It should be drunk in the next two years.
📞 Jean-Paul Brun, Dom. des Terres Dorées, Crière, 69380 Charnay, tel. 04.78.47.93.45, fax 04.78.47.93.38
🍽 by appt.

DOM. DES TERRES MOREL 2002★★

1,3 ha	6,000		3–5€

This vineyard was founded in 1898, but mixed farming continued for another century. The vines are cultivated by sustainable agriculture, with grassing down over the clay-limestone soil. A *coup de coeur* goes to this strong-ruby wine with intense perfumes of strawberry and raspberry. It is full bodied, particularly fruity and fresh, and the palate reveals a range of flavours of soft fruits combining a hint of cinnamon and a note of menthol on the finish. This rich and refreshing Beaujolais will be good with a tarte Tatin.
📞 Dom. des Terres Morel, 587, rte de Morancé, 69480 Lucenay, tel. 04.74.67.17.00, fax 04.74.60.22.08
🍽 ev. day except Sun. 10.30am–12.30pm 4pm–7.30pm
📞 Antoine Riche

DOM. VIDONNEL 2001★

1.8 ha	3,000	▮ ◆	5–8€

This estate has more than once demonstrated its skill in making white wines (the 95 vintage won a *coup de coeur*). Like the previous vintage, the 2001 wine is awarded one star. It is clear and pale gold in colour, with a rich mineral bouquet developing shades of leather and exotic fruits. It is fresh, rounded and full on the palate with good length. This is a well-balanced and confident product, to be drunk within the year.
📞 Guy Vignat, 70, rte de Chazay, 69480 Morancé, tel. 04.78.43.64.34, fax 04.78.43.77.31
🍽 by appt.

Wines selected but not starred

DOM. DES AMPHORES 2002

1.07 ha	4,000	▮	3–5€

📞 Pascal Gonnachon, La Ville, 71570 Saint-Amour-Bellevue, tel. 03.85.37.42.44, fax 03.85.37.43.01, e-mail p.gonnachon@wanadoo.fr
🍽 by appt.

BEAUJOLAIS D' ARENA

Terroirs des Granits 2002

25 ha	150,000	▮ ◆	3–5€

📞 Grands Terroirs et Signatures, Cuvage de la Pierre-Bleue, 69460 Saint-Etienne-des-Oullières, tel. 04.74.03.52.72, fax 04.74.03.38.58, e-mail signe-vigneron1@wanadoo.fr
🍽 by appt.

DOM. DE BALUCE 2001

0.52 ha	3,000	▮ ◆	5–8€

📞 Jean-Yves et Annick Sonnery, Dom. de Baluce, 69620 Bagnols, tel. 04.74.71.71.43, fax 04.74.71.71.43, e-mail baluce@cario.fr
🍽 by appt.

DOM. PASCAL BERTHIER

Réserve des 7 Pièces Vieilles Vignes 2002

0.4 ha	2,000	▮	8–11€

📞 Pascal Berthier, chem. des Bruyères, 71680 Crèches-sur-Saône, tel. 03.85.37.41.64, fax 03.85.37.44.65, e-mail pascal.berthier4@wanadoo.fr

CAVE DU BOIS DE LA SALLE

Cuvée des Amis 2002

1.12 ha	8,700	▮ ◆	3–5€

📞 Cave coop. des grands vins du Bois de la Salle, Ch. du Bois de la Salle, 69840 Juliénas, tel. 04.74.04.42.61, fax 04.74.04 47.47
🍽 by appt.

DOM. DU BOIS DU JOUR 2001

0.35 ha	2,500	▮ ◆	3–5€

📞 Gilles Carreau, Lachanal, 69640 Cogny, tel. 04.74.67.41.40, fax 04.74.67.46.24
🍽 by appt.

DOM. BOURBON 2002

0.2 ha	1,000	▮ ◆	5–8€

📞 Jean-Luc Bourbon, Le Marquison, 69620 Theizé, tel. 04.74.71.14.13, fax 04.74.71.14.13
🍽 by appt.

PIERRE CHARMET

Cuvée La Ronze 2002

0.7 ha	5,000	▮ ◆	5–8€

📞 Pierre Charmet, Le Martin, 69620 Le Breuil, tel. 04.78.43.92.69, fax 04.78.43.90.31
🍽 ev. day except Sun. 8am–12 noon 2pm–6pm

DOM. CHASSELAY

Cuvée des Quatre Saisons 2002

2 ha	12,000		5–8€

📞 Dom. Jean-Gilles Chasselay, 123/157, chem. de la Roche, 69380 Châtillon-d'Azergues, tel. 04.78.47.93.73, fax 04.78.43.94.41, e-mail jgchasselay@aol.com 🏠
🍽 by appt.

CLOS DES VIEUX MARRONNIERS 2002

| | 5 ha | 4,000 | ▮ ♦ | 3–5 € |

•┑ Ghyslaine et Jean-Louis Large, 69380 Charnay,
tel. 04.78.47.95.28, fax 04.78.47.95.28,
e-mail jean-louis.large@wanadoo.fr ▼
⟁ by appt.

CAVE DES VIGNERONS DU DOURY
Cuvée Prestige 2002

| | 3 ha | 5,000 | ▮ ♦ | 5–8 € |

•┑ Cave des Vignerons du Doury, 69620 Létra,
tel. 04.74.71.30.52, fax 04.74.71.35.28 ▼
⟁ by appt.

AGNES ET MARCEL DURAND 2002

| | 3 ha | 5,000 | ▮ ♦ | 5–8 € |

•┑ Agnès et Marcel Durand, Les Trions, 69220 Lancié,
tel. 04.74.69.81.32, fax 04.74.69.86.70,
e-mail durand.lancie@free.fr ▼ 🏠
⟁ ev. day 9am–7pm

VINCENT FONTAINE
Cuvée des Vieilles Vignes 2002

| | 1 ha | 2,500 | ▮ ♦ | 3–5 € |

•┑ Vincent Fontaine, Les Gondoins, 69480 Pommiers,
tel. 04.74.68.33.08, fax 04.74.65.97.68 ▼
⟁ by appt.

DIDIER GERMAIN
Rosé d'une nuit 2002

| | 0.2 ha | 1,500 | ⑪ | 3–5 € |

•┑ Didier Germain, Bel-Air, 69380 Charnay,
tel. 04.78.43.96.59, fax 04.78.43.96.59,
e-mail germdid@wanadoo.fr ▼
⟁ by appt.

DOM. LES GRYPHEES
Cuvée Tradition 2002

| | 1 ha | 36,000 | ▮ ♦ | 5–8 € |

•┑ Pierre Durdilly, 2, rte de Saint-Laurent, 69620 Le
Bois-d'Oingt, tel. 04.74.72.49.93, fax 04.74.71.62.95 ▼
⟁ by appt.

DOM. DE LA MANTELLIERE 2002

| | 7.7 ha | 20,000 | ⑪ | 3–5 € |

•┑ Christophe Braymand, Le Bourg, 69620 Le Breuil,
tel. 04.74.71.85.72, fax 04.74.71.85 72 ▼
⟁ by appt.

DAVID MARCHAND 2002

| | 1.1 ha | 8,000 | ▮ ♦ | 5–8 € |

•┑ David Marchand, Les Meules, 69640 Cogny,
tel. 06.82.42.34.94,
fax 04.74.67.33.94 ▼
⟁ by appt.

DOM. DU MARQUISON 2002

| | 1 ha | 8,000 | | 3–5 € |

•┑ Christian Vivier-Merle, Dom. du Marquison, Verjouttes,
69620 Theizé, tel. 04.74.71.26.66, fax 04.74.71.10.32,
e-mail ncviviermerle@wanadoo.fr ▼ 🏠
⟁ by appt.

CEDRIC MARTIN 2001

| | 1 ha | 4,000 | ▮ ♦ | 5–8 € |

•┑ Cédric Martin, Les Verchères, 71570 Chanes,
tel. 03.85.37.46.32, fax 03.85.37.46.32 ▼
⟁ by appt.

DOM. DE PIERRE-FILANT 2002

| | 2 ha | 10,000 | ▮ | 3–5 € |

•┑ Emmanuel Fellot, Dom. de Pierre-Filant, 69640 Rivolet,
tel. 04.74.67.37.75, fax 04.74.67.39.06,
e-mail ne.fellot@wanadoo.fr ▼
⟁ by appt.

DOM. DE POUILLY-LE-CHATEL 2001

| | 1 ha | 5,000 | ▮ ♦ | 5–8 € |

•┑ Bruno Chevalier, Dom. de Pouilly-le-Chatel,
69640 Denicé, tel. 04.74.67.41.01, fax 04.74.67.37.86,
e-mail br.chevalier@free.fr ▼ 🏠
⟁ by appt.

DOM. DE ROCHEBONNE
Cuvée des Générations 2002

| | 2 ha | 8,000 | | 3–5 € |

•┑ Jean-François Pein, Dom. de Rochebonne, La Roche,
69620 Theizé, tel. 04.74.71.21.47, fax 04.74.71.21.47 ▼
⟁ by appt.

CAVE BEAUJOLAISE DE SAINT-LAURENT-D'OINGT 2001

| | 2 ha | 8,000 | ▮ ⑪ ♦ | 5–8 € |

•┑ Cave coop. beaujolaise de Saint-Laurent-d'Oingt, Le
Gonnet, 69620 Saint-Laurent-d'Oingt, tel. 04.74.71.20.51,
fax 04.74.71.23.46,
e-mail cave-saintlaurent@wanadoo.fr ▼
⟁ by appt.

GUY ET BERNARD SAPIN
Tradition Vieilles Vignes 2002

| | 2 ha | 4,000 | ▮ ♦ | 3–5 € |

•┑ GAEC Guy et Bernard Sapin, Le Barnigat,
69620 Saint-Laurent-d'Oingt, tel. 04.74.71.20.82,
fax 04.74.71.20.82 ▼
⟁ ev. day 8.30am–8pm; Sun. by appt.

SELECTION DU TERROIR 2002

| | 0.7 ha | 2,000 | ▮ ♦ | 3–5 € |

•┑ Pascal Desgranges, chem. du Saint-Pré, 69420 Pommiers,
tel. 04.74.09.06.12 ▼
⟁ by appt.

Beaujolais Supérieur

CAVE DU BEAU VALLON
Au Pays des Pierres Dorées 2002★

| | 4.31 ha | 30,000 | ▮ ♦ | 5–8 € |

For the second year running, the Beau Vallon cooperative
has distinguished itself in this "private" appellation, with a
crimson wine with bright-violet glints and a good bouquet
of very ripe fresh fruits. This is a well-made, balanced wine,
easy to drink, that will refresh you for two years. In the same
price range, the white Beaujolais 2002 was recommended by
the Jury.
•┑ Cave du Beau Vallon, 69620 Theizé, tel. 04.74.71.48.00,
fax 04.74.71.84.46, e-mail info@cave-beauvallon.com ▼
⟁ by appt.

LES VIGNERONS DE LA CAVE DE BULLY 2002★

| | 17 ha | 60,000 | ▮ ♦ | 5–8 € |

In this appellation, vines with a controlled yield are pre-
selected. They have produced a purplish-crimson wine with
fresh perfumes of ripe red berries. The velvety first impression

combines the richness and roundness of a fruity substance. This wine is easy to drink, so serve it within a year with white meats, even a carp. Also recommended is the **white Beaujolais 2002**, which was awarded the same mark.

☛ Cave des vignerons de Bully-en-Beaujolais, La Martinière, 69210 Bully, tel. 04.74.01.27.77, fax 04.74.01.22.30, e-mail cavedebully@wanadoo.fr ☑
⏳ by appt.

Beaujolais-Villages

The term "Villages" was adopted to replace a multitude of commune names that used to be attached to the Beaujolais appellation to identify wines that were considered superior. Nearly all the producers opted for the name Beaujolais-Villages.

Thirty-eight communes, including eight in the canton of La Chapelle-de-Guinchay, qualify for the appellation Beaujolais-Villages, but only 30 are entitled to add the name of the commune after it. Identifying wines as Beaujolais-Villages has been helpful in marketing them since 1950. In 2002, the 6,250 ha, located mostly between the Beaujolais and the crus vineyards, produced 347,980 hl of red wine and 2,856 hl of whites.

The wines of the appellation grown nearest the crus are cultivated under the same terms (pruned either in a goblet or fan shape; the alcoholic content of the must should be 0.5° higher than that required for Beaujolais). Grown on sandy granite soil, they are fruity, smooth wines with a beautiful, rich red colour, typical of the first pressings for the Vins de Primeur. The wines from granite soils on some upper slopes have enough character to develop, and drink well into the following year. Between these two extremes there is every shade of difference; some wines have finesse, a good nose and sufficient body to accompany dishes of all kinds, and gratify every taste; both pike with cream sauce and grilled Charolais steak will be well complemented by a good Beaujolais-Villages.

CH. DU BLUIZARD
Elevé en fût de chêne 2001★

	1,28 ha	9,000	🕮	5–8 €

Jean de Saint-Charles works 43 ha to the south of the Montagne de Brouilly. His white Beaujolais-Villages bears the signs of having matured for one year in an oak barrel. It is clear, bright and pale yellow in colour, combining perfumes of vanilla with notes of toast and herbs. The first impression is mineral, followed by expressive oaky notes which continue for a good while. This is a well-balanced and pleasant wine which suggested a variety of dishes to the tasters: oysters, carpaccio de Saint-Jacques, and fish in sauce, or it could be drunk as an aperitif. Also recommended from this estate was the **Côte de Brouilly Domaine de Conroy 2001 (5–8 €)**.

☛ SCE des Dom. Saint-Charles, Le Bluizard, 69460 Saint-Etienne-la-Varenne, tel. 04.74.03.30.90, fax 04.74.03.30.80, e-mail saintcharles@sofradi.com ☑
⏳ by appt.

DOM. DES BRILLATS
Cuvée Vieilles Vignes 2002★

	1,5 ha	10,000	☷ ♦	3–5 €

The village of Perréon is located in the middle of the Beaujolais-Villages region. The Paquet family work a vineyard of 13 ha there, on a property which has been handed

down since 1762. Its 2002 wine has an intense bright-garnet colour, and emits expressive and elegant perfumes of soft fruits and floral notes. These aromas recur on the palate, combining with a balanced fullness and integrated tannins. This clear-cut wine, with its lingering palate, is an agreeable representative of the appellation. To be drunk within a year.

☛ Jean-François Paquet, Les Loges, 69460 Le Perréon, tel. 04.74.03.26.16, fax 04.74.03.26.16, e-mail jfpaquet01@infonie.fr ☑
⏳ by appt.

DOM. BURNICHON
Sélection Vieilles Vignes 2002★

■	1 ha	4,000	☷ ♦	5–8 €

This bright-red wine with brick highlights was made from 45-year-old vines and vinified in the traditional way with a so-called "American" wine-press. The fine and slightly closed bouquet blends small, very ripe red berries and floral notes. The palate makes a sweet and pleasant impression, and has a good structure. This well-made wine is a fine example of the terroir. It is ready to drink now, but could also be kept for a year or two.

☛ Daniel Burnichon, Vitry, 69430 Quincié-en-Beaujolais, tel. 04.74.04.31.56, fax 04.74.04.31.56 ☑

CH. DU CHATELARD 2002★

■	2,9 ha	9,100	☷	3–5 €

This is a true château, descended from an 8th century feudal mound, the "Poype du Chatelard," which stood on the site. The vineyard was taken over in 2000 by Sylvain Rosier, a former radio director who has turned to winemaking. Although the hill at Chatelard consists of limestone, sandy and clay soils (good for Chardonnay), brought there in former times from the nearby Mâconnais, this bright-red wine was grown on a separate plot away from those Burgundian soils. It has expressive and elegant perfumes of very ripe fruits which open out on the palate. It is well structured, balanced and without sophistication. Drink it over the next two years.

☛ Sylvain Rosier, Ch. du Chatelard, 69220 Lancié, tel. 04.74.04.12.99, fax 04.74.69.86.17, e-mail vinduchato@aol.com ☑
⏳ ev. day 9am–12 noon 2pm–6pm

RECOLTE CHERMIEUX 2002★

■	2,8 ha	5,000	☷ ♦	5–8 €

This fairly pale plum-coloured wine comes from 40-year-old vines. It has pleasant perfumes of soft fruits, particularly raspberry. The straightforward opening continues with fresh and fruity notes. This well-structured, finely-made wine can be drunk over the next two years.

☛ Gérard Genty, Vaugervan, 69430 Lantignié, tel. 04.74.69.23.56, fax 04.74.69.23.56 ☑
⏳ by appt.

CLOCHEMERLE 2002★

■	20 ha	150,000	☷ ♦	3–5 €

The name of this wine refers to Gabriel Chevalier's very successful novel about life in a village in the Beaujolais. This wine is just as good. The 2001 vintage won a *coup de coeur*. The 2002 wine is clear, bright ruby in colour and opens with perfumes combining very ripe soft fruits (wild strawberries) with blackcurrant and a hint of mineral. Although the palate is not particularly long, it is full bodied and pleasantly rounded, with well-integrated tannins. Drink this in the next two years with hot sausages and boiled potatoes.

☛ Maison François Paquet, 435, rte du Beaujolais, 69830 Saint-George-de-Reneins, tel. 04.74.09.77.27, fax 04.74.09.60.17, e-mail coquard.c@fpaquet.fr

DOM. DU CLOS DU FIEF 2002★★

■	5 ha	30,000	☷ ♦	3–5 €

Michel Tête took over in 1980, representing the fourth generation on the estate. He cultivates 13 ha of vines. His Beaujolais-Villages has an intense-ruby colour and a bouquet combining notes of black fruits and flowers with a hint of undergrowth. It is well structured on the palate, fleshy, very fruity, soft, fresh and of good length. Although already well balanced, this wine should improve still further. Drink it in the next two years with white meat or charcuterie.

🕿 Michel Tête, Les Gonnards, 69840 Juliénas, tel. 04.74.04.41.62, fax 04.74.04.47.09 ▼

🍷 by appt.

PHILIPPE DESCHAMPS

Sélection Cuvée Vieilles Vignes 2002★★

	2 ha	12,000	▮ ♦		5–8 €

This wine made from 60-year-old vines was matured in an underground cellar. Its ruby colour has lovely violet highlights. The rather intense, fine perfumes recall very ripe fruits, with nuances of blackcurrant and blackberry. After a straight-forward attack, the palate is quite seductive: full bodied, winey, well structured, balanced and fruity. The length is good, the finish fresh with a hint of grapefruit. This remarkable *Villages* will be good with an entrecôte over the next two years.

🕿 Philippe Deschamps, Morne, 69430 Beaujeu, tel. 04.74.04.82.54, fax 04.74.69.51.04 ▼

🍷 by appt.

YVAN DUFOUR

Cuvée Vieilles Vignes 2002★

	0.4 ha	3,040	▮		3–5 €

The story of this property began in 1999 with the purchase of 3.34 ha of vines. There should be accommodation for motor homes from Easter 2003. The vineyard makes its first appearance here with this deep-red wine made from 60-year-old vines. Its aromas are charming and fruity, suggesting blackcurrant and stone fruits, and linger on the rather intense, rounded palate which hovers nicely between acidity and tannins. This well-made, harmonious wine is still developing. Drink it within a year.

🕿 Yvan Dufour, La Roche, 69430 Quincié-en-Beaujolais, tel. 04.74.04.33.59, fax 04.74.04.33.59, e-mail beaujol@club-internet.fr ▼

🍷 ev. day 8am–8pm

STEPHANE GARDETTE 2002★★

	3.09 ha	1,800	▮ ♦		3–5 €

A new name in the *Guide* and an estate to look out for. It was bought in 1996 by the parents of Stéphane Gardette and taken over by him in 1998. This vivid-crimson Beaujolais-Villages was made from 40-year-old vines and opens with most attractive perfumes of cherry and other soft fruits. After a good first impression, its rounded tannins develop with great finesse. It is fruity and fresh in the finish, which is typical of the Gamay grape variety, and well balanced. It should be drunk in the next two years with white meat. The Jury also singled out a pleasant **Régnié 2002**.

🕿 Stéphane Gardette, La Haute-Ronze, 69430 Régnié-Durette, tel. 04.74.69.50.05, fax 04.74.69.50.05 ▼

🍷 by appt.

DOM. DU GRANIT BLEU

Le Perréon 2002★

	4.61 ha	13,000	▮ ♦		3–5 €

Jean Favre's ancestors were already established in Perréon in 1580. The vineyard stands on south-facing hillsides and is worked by sustainable agriculture. This bright-garnet wine was grown on a granitic sandy soil on a blue granite and porphyry subsoil. It has perfumes of soft fruits and blackcurrant with spicy vanilla nuances (cinnamon). The soft fruits continue on the palate, which has good length and a balanced, elegant structure. It can be drunk now or kept for a year or two.

🕿 Jocelyne et Jean Favre, Dom. du Granit Bleu, Brouilly-Le Perrin, 69460 Le Perréon, tel. 04.74.03.20.90, fax 04.74.03.20.90 ▼

🍷 by appt.

DOM. DES HAYES 2002★

	18 ha	30,000			5–8 €

This clear ruby wine with an attractive bouquet of redcurrant and spices comes from 40-year-old vines. After a lovely first impression full of finesse, the palate reveals a good smooth structure. This fruity and full-bodied wine is a typical Beaujolais-Villages and should be drunk in the next two years.

🕿 Pierre Deshayes, Les Grandes-Vignes, 69460 Le Perréon, tel. 04.74.03.25.47, fax 04.74.03.23.90 ▼

🍷 by appt.

MICHEL JUILLARD 2002★

	2.2 ha	7,500	▮ ♦		3–5 €

Chânes is located in the north of the Beaujolais region, not far from the Mâconnais. Michel Juillard took over there in 1978. In 1998, he joined up with Alexandre Wolkowicki, whose daughter Muriel will take charge in 2003. The estate offers a very well-made wine grown from 50-year-old vines. It has a lovely garnet-red colour, and opens on intense perfumes of soft fruits with a touch of herbs. The clear-cut palate has good structure with integrated tannins, fruity, spicy flavours, good length and a hint of the terroir. Drink it within two years.

🕿 EARL Juillard Wolkowicki, Le Chapitre, 71570 Chânes, tel. 03.85.36.51.38 ▼

🍷 by appt.

CH. DE LAVERNETTE 2002★

	1.5 ha	7,000	⦀		5–8 €

This property dating from 1596 stands on flinty clay soils and has produced a bright-garnet wine with deep-purple glints. Fairly strong oaky perfumes admit notes of very ripe soft fruits. The palate reveals a surprisingly rich body blending the fullness of the grape to the oaky tannins. This is not a typical Beaujolais-Villages but is a high-quality wine. Keep it for two or three years for serving with small game, lamb, roast dark poultry or in a salmi, or even with a Reblochon cheese from Savoie. The estate's **white Beaujolais 2002** is full and rounded and also received one star.

🕿 Bertrand de Boissieu, Ch. de Lavernette, 71570 Leynes, tel. 03.85.35.63.21, fax 03.85.35.67.32, e-mail ba.de-boissieu@tiscali.fr ▼ 🏠

🍷 ev. day 11am–12 noon 2pm–5.30pm

DOM. DE LA MAISON GERMAIN 2002★

	6 ha	6,000	▮ ♦		5–8 €

Patrick Bossan, from the third generation, took over here in 1993 and has developed a camping and *chambres d'hôte* business on the farm. His Beaujolais-Villages has a strong ruby colour and a confident bouquet of soft fruits. Its aromatic flesh completely fills the mouth. This well-structured and expressive wine is ready to drink now.

🕿 Patrick et Marie-Paule Bossan, Hameau de Blaceret, D 20, 69460 Blacé, tel. 04.74.67.56.36, fax 04.74.60.55.23, e-mail patrick.bossan@wanadoo.fr ▼ 🏠

🍷 by appt.

DOM. DES MAISONS NEUVES 2002★

	12.5 ha	5,000			3–5 €

This other Maisons Neuves estate has produced a ruby wine with an intense grapey perfume. The palate is delicate and fruity, well-structured and full bodied. This well-balanced and lively wine should be drunk in the next two years.

🕿 Emmanuel Jambon, Le Gonnu, 69460 Blacé, tel. 04.74.60.56.36, fax 04.74.66.70.00 ▼

🍷 by appt.

CELLIER DE LA MERLATIERE LANCIÉ 2002★★

	n.c.	4,000	⦀		3–5 €

Beaujolais-Villages

A judicious blend of differently vinified wines went into the making of this Beaujolais, awarded a *coup de coeur* by the Grand Jury. It has a very strong ruby colour with lovely bluish highlights, and an elegantly assertive bouquet of soft fruits and peony. Its flesh is well structured and balanced, and full of lovely flavours of stone fruits. This full, supple, persistent wine is a Beaujolais "as we like them to be," concluded one of the tasters. It can be drunk for the next two years.
➦ Paul Pariaud, La Merlatière, 69220 Lancié,
tel. 04.74.04.10.16, fax 04.74.69.83.64 ☑
☰ ev. day 8am–12 noon 2pm–7pm

DOM. MIOLANE 2002★
| ■ | 10.5 ha | 20,000 | ▮ | 3–5€ |

This family estate expanded rapidly in 1975. Since 1995, the son, Christian Miolane, has further developed it, building a *gîte* and laying out reception facilities. His Beaujolais-Villages has a lovely garnet colour and expressive perfumes of blackcurrant, blackcurrant leaf and redcurrant. The soft and fruity palate reveals a touch of pear-drops and develops aromas of chocolate. This well-structured wine should be drunk within a year. It will go well with red meat or charcuterie or, as its maker suggests, with a Beaujolais sausage cooked with a fondue of leeks.
➦ EARL Dom. Christian Miolane, La Folie,
69460 Salles-Arbuissonnas, tel. 04.74.67.52.67,
fax 04.74.67.59.95 ☑ ☖
☰ by appt.

CH. DE MONTMELAS 2002★
| ■ | 10 ha | 80,000 | ▮ ☖ | 5–8€ |

The Princesse de Clèves is said to have stayed at this château, built in the 14th century and restored in the 16th and 19th centuries. In 1565, it was bought by the Harcourt family, and still dominates the Beaujolais landscape. Its Beaujolais-Villages is distributed by the Mommessin company. It has a clear and lively red colour, and releases perfumes of soft fruits and fresh grapes together with strong spicy notes. It is full bodied and fine on the palate, and pleasantly fresh. This is a well-balanced wine which only needed a little more flesh to win two stars. Drink it in the next two years with charcuterie.
➦ Famille d' Harcourt, Ch. de Montmelas,
69640 Montmelas, tel. 04.74.67.32.94, fax 04.74.67.30.54,
e-mail chateau.de.montmelas@wanadoo.fr ☑
☰ by appt.

DOM. DE L'OISILLON 2002★
| ■ | 4 ha | 2,000 | ▮ | 3–5€ |

This 12-ha estate produced a very good **red Beaujolais 2002**, but this Beaujolais-Villages was preferred. It has a deep-red colour and releases perfumes of strawberry and rose with spicy notes. It is fruity, fresh and soft on the palate, with smooth tannins and reveals a harmonious balance of fruitiness and structure. This fine 2002 is for drinking in the next two years, perhaps with chicken in a cream sauce.
➦ Michel et Béatrix Canard, Le Bourg, 69820 Vauxrenard,
tel. 04.74.69.90.51, fax 04.74.69.90.51,
e-mail beatrix-michel.canard@wanadoo.fr ☑
☰ by appt.

DOM. DE L'OREE DU BOIS
Le Perréon 2002★
| ■ | 3.5 ha | 15,000 | ▮ ☖ | 5–8€ |

Curiously, this wine is 99% Gamay. The remaining 1% is probably Pinot Noir, this grape variety being authorized in the Beaujolais. This clear, bright-garnet 2002 releases intense perfumes of very ripe, almost jammy soft fruits with nuances of *pêche de vigne* and pepper. The full-bodied palate is still dominated by tannins which are a little austere in the finish. Although its aromas are unusual, it is well made and ready to drink now with côte de veau.
➦ Olivier Bererd, Le Bourg, 69460 Le Perréon,
tel. 04.74.03.21.85, fax 04.74.03.27.19 ☑
☰ by appt.

DOM. DES PLAISANCES
Tradition Cuvée Vieilles Vignes 2002★
| ■ | 1 ha | 2,000 | ▥ | 5–8€ |

In 1991, Daniel Bouchacourt took over this estate established by his parents in 1960. His dark-red wine has a fresh bouquet of soft fruits and spices. Its tannic structure is initially impressive but softens as the wine's more full-bodied flavours come through, notably raspberry and fresh grapes. It is fine and well balanced and should be drunk in the next two years.
➦ Daniel Bouchacourt, Lieu-dit Espagne,
69640 Saint-Julien, tel. 04.74.60.52.81,
fax 04.74.60.52.81 ☑
☰ by appt.

DOM. SAINT SORLIN
Montmelas Cuvée Tradition 2002★
| ■ | 4 ha | 20,000 | ▥ | 5–8€ |

This estate of 16 ha is partly cultivated biodynamically. This red wine has delicate perfumes of soft fruits, is well balanced, full of flavour and shows good length. Ready to drink now, it has enough structure to be kept for a year.
➦ Bernard et Eric Jacquet, EARL Dom. Saint-Sorlin, le Bourg, 69640 Montmelas-Saint-Sorlin, tel. 04.74.67.37.60,
fax 04.74.67.41.47, e-mail domaine-saint-sorlin@free.fr ☑
☰ by appt.

DOM. DE SERMEZY 2002★★
| ■ | 5 ha | 12,000 | ▮ ☖ | 3–5€ |

Patrice Chevrier continues the work of several generations on this family estate of 12 ha. This clear, bright-ruby wine was made from 70-year-old vines and almost won a *coup de coeur*. Intense perfumes of soft fruits (raspberry and blackcurrant) reveal a superb balance between fruitiness and the compact, well-integrated tannins which lingers on a clean and rounded palate. To be drunk in the next two years.
➦ Patrice Chevrier, Dom. de Sermezy, 69220 Charentay,
tel. 04.74.66.86.55, fax 04.74.66.86.55,
e-mail pchevrier@free.fr ☑
☰ by appt.

DOM. DE LA SORBIERE 2002★
| ■ | 6.2 ha | 5,000 | ▮ | 3–5€ |

Jacques Juillard acquired this old property from the Pivot family in 2000. All its vines are devoted to Beaujolais-Villages. This 2002 wine opens with a perfume of soft fruits. The lovely first impression discloses good finesse, a blend of rounded tannins and a pleasant blackberry fruitiness. This velvety wine should be drunk in the next two years. Serve it with white meat.
➦ Jacques Juillard, La Roche, 69430 Quincié-en-Beaujolais,
tel. 04.74.69.06.82, fax 04.74.66.53.68 ☑
☰ by appt.

DOM. LE TRACOT
Cuvée d'Appagnié et des Pins 2002★
| ■ | n.c. | 60,000 | ▮ ☖ | 5–8€ |

This estate of 16 ha has specialized in winegrowing for two generations. It has a museum of old winemaking equipment and has just renovated its winery. This garnet-coloured wine with deep-purple glints releases fairly fine perfumes of pear-drops and spices. The fresh first impression is consistent with the perfume and is followed by a palate with compact tannins and a concentrated fruitiness suggesting prunes. This is a well-balanced wine with a beautiful finish, and will go well with an andouillette.
➦ Jean-Paul Dubost, Le Tracot, 69430 Lantignié,
tel. 04.74.04.87.51, fax 04.74.69.27.33,
e-mail j.pdubost@wanadoo.fr ☑ ☖
☰ ev. day except Sun. 8am–12 noon 2pm–7pm

CH. DES VERGERS 2002★
| ■ | 6.3 ha | 15,000 | ▮ ▥ | 3–5€ |

This 18th century château has an original roof in the shape of an upturned boat. Receptions are held in the park, which has a pool. This deep-garnet Beaujolais-Villages has a very ripe grapey bouquet of strawberry and blackcurrant. Its fine full body and substance blends with the compact tannins. This

145

BEAUJOLAIS

balanced but still young wine should be kept for a few months. Drink it with a selection of cold pork or ham.
☛ Bassouls, EURL Ch. des Vergers, 69430 Lantignié, tel. 06.08.47.49.90, fax 04.74.04.83.50 ☑ ☷
🍷 by appt.

Wines selected but not starred

CH. DU BASTY
Lantignié 2002

■	12 ha	50,000	▮⦀		5–8 €

☛ Gilles Perroud, Ch. du Basty, 69430 Lantignié, tel. 04.74.04.85.98, fax 04.74.69.26.63 ☑
🍷 by appt.

DOM. FRANCOIS BEROUJON 2002

■	6 ha	12,700	▮ ♦	3–5 €

☛ François Béroujon, La Laveuse, 69460 Salles-Arbuissonnas, tel. 04.74.67.52.47, fax 04.74.67.52.47 ☑
🍷 by appt.

FRANCK BESSON 2002

■	6 ha	4,500	▮	3–5 €

☛ Franck Besson, Les Chanoriers, 69840 Jullié, tel. 04.74.04.46.12, fax 04.74.04.46.12 ☑ ♙
🍷 by appt.

DOM. DU BREUIL 2002

■	1 ha	6,400	▮ ♦	5–8 €

☛ Franck Large, rue du Breuil, 69460 Salles-Arbuissonnas, tel. 04.74.60.51.00, fax 04.74.67.59.15, e-mail franck.large@libertysurf.fr ☑
🍷 by appt.

DOM. DE LA CHAPELLE DE VATRE
2002

■	3 ha	7,000	▮ ♦	3–5 €

☛ Dom. de la Chapelle de Vâtre, Le Bourbon, 69840 Jullié, tel. 04.74.04.43.57, fax 04.74.04.40.27, e-mail dominique.capart@libertysurf.fr ☑ ☷ ♙
🍷 by appt.
☛ Dominique Capart

DOM. CHASSAGNE
Lantignié 2002

■	2.5 ha	16,000	▮ ♦	5–8 €

☛ SCEA Chassagne-Bertoldo, Les Bruyères, 69430 Lantignié, tel. 04.74.04 82.11, fax 04.74.69.25.53 ☑

DOM. DES COMBIERS 2002

■	5 ha	4,000		3–5 €

☛ Yves Savoye, Les Combiers, 69820 Vauxrenard, tel. 04.74.69.92.69, fax 04.74.69.92.69 ☑
🍷 by appt.

DOM. DES GAROCHES 2002

■	n.c.	5,000	▮ ♦	3–5 €

☛ Pierre-Louis Dufaitre, Garanches, 69460 Odenas, tel. 04.74.03 40.16, fax 04.74.03.40.16 ☑
🍷 ev. day 8am–8pm

DOM. GOUILLON 2001

■	0.4 ha	3,500	⦀	5–8 €

☛ Dominique Gouillon, Les Vayvolets, 69430 Quincié-en-Beaujolais, tel. 04.74.04.38.50, fax 04.74.69.00.67, e-mail gouillon.dominique@club-internet.fr ☑
🍷 by appt.

DOM. DE LA GRANGE MENARD
Coteau des Pierres rouges Cuvée d'Eve 2002

■	2 ha	6,000	▮ ♦	5–8 €

☛ Evelyne et Guy Pignard, Dom. de la Grange Ménard, 69400 Arnas, tel. 04.74.62.87.60, fax 04.74.62.87.60, e-mail evelyne-pignard@bonjour.fr ☑
🍷 by appt.

JEROME LACONDEMINE
Cuvée Vieilles Vignes 2002

■	1 ha	4,000	▮ ♦	5–8 €

☛ Jérôme Lacondemine, Dom. Croix-Charnay, 69430 Beaujeu, tel. 04.74.69.29.80, fax 04.74.69.29.80 ☑
🍷 by appt.
☛ Maillot

DOM. DES MAISONS NEUVES 2002

■	6 ha	20,000	▮⦀♦	3–5 €

☛ Jean-Pierre Merle, Dom. des Maisons-Neuves, 69460 Blacé, tel. 04.74.67.53.10, fax 04.74.60.51.87, e-mail j-p-merle@wanadoo.fr ☑ ☖
🍷 by appt.

DOM. DU MARRONNIER ROSE 2002

■	5 ha	8,000	▮ ♦	3–5 €

☛ Nathalie Dory, Le Bourg, 69820 Vauxrenard, tel. 04.74.69.90.80, fax 04.74.69.97.15, e-mail natalie-dory@wanadoo.fr ☑
🍷 by appt.

DOM. DE MONSEPEYS 2002

■	5.5 ha	2,500		5–8 €

☛ Jean-Luc Canard, Les Benons, 69840 Emeringes, tel. 04.74.04.45.11, fax 04.74.04.45.19 ☑ ☷
🍷 by appt.

CH. DE MONVALLON
Elevé en fût de chêne 2002

■	2.03 ha	7,000	▮ ♦	5–8 €

☛ Françoise et Benoît Chastel, La Grange-Bourbon, 69220 Charentay, tel. 04.74.66.86.60, fax 04.74.66.73.23 ☑
🍷 by appt.

DOM. DU QUESNEL 2002

■	7.5 ha	2,500	▮ ♦	3–5 €

☛ Sandrin, Le Quesnel, 69640 Rivolet, tel. 04.74.67.43.32, e-mail isabelle.sandrin@free.fr ☑ ☷
🍷 by appt.

DOM. DE LA ROCHE 2002

■	5 ha	3,760	▮ ♦	3–5 €

☛ Alain Démule, La Roche, 69430 Quincié-en-Beaujolais, tel. 04.74.04.31.37, fax 04.74.04.31.37 ☑
🍷 by appt.

DOM. DE ROCHEBRUNE 2002

■	1 ha	4,000	▮ ♦	3–5 €

☛ EARL Dom. de Rochebrune, Le Pont-Mathivet, 69460 Saint-Etienne-des-Oullières, tel. 04.74.03.46.41, fax 04.74.03.46.41 ☑
🍷 by appt.
☛ Xavier Dumont

CHRISTIAN ET MICHELE SAVOYE
Cuvée Prestige Sélection de Vieilles Vignes 2002

| ■ | 0.5 ha | 2,328 | | 5–8 € |

• Christian Savoye, 69820 Vauxrenard, tel. 04.74.69.91.60, fax 04.74.69.91.60 ☑
Ⴑ by appt.

DOM. DE LA TOUR DES BOURRONS
2002

| ■ | 3 ha | 3,000 | ■ ♦ | 3–5 € |

• Monique et Bernard Guignier, Les Bourrons, 69820 Vauxrenard, tel. 04.74.69.92.05, fax 04.74.69.92.05 ☑
Ⴑ by appt.

DOM. LES VILLIERS 2002

| ■ | 0.18 ha | 1,500 | | 5–8 € |

• Lucien Chemarin, Les Villiers, 69430 Marchampt, tel. 04.74.04.37.11 ☑
Ⴑ ev. day 8am–8pm

Brouilly and Côte de Brouilly

On the last Saturday in August, the vineyards ring with song and music. Even though the harvest has not begun, crowds of walkers carrying baskets clamber 484 m up Mont Brouilly to the top where, near the chapel, bread, wine and salt are given away. From the summit there is a panoramic view over the Beaujolais, the Mâconnais, the Dombes and the Mont d'Or. There are two sister appellations next to each other, Brouilly and Côte de Brouilly, which have had many disputes about the precise limits of their territories.

Côte de Brouilly is an AOC, on the slopes of the mount which is hard granite and greenish-blue shale, nick-named "green horn", or diorite. The mount is the remains of ancient volcanic activity or, according to legend, where the giant who dug out the Saône emptied his hod. Production, 18,770 hl from 331 ha, covers four communes: Odenas, Saint-Lager, Cercié and Quincié. The Brouilly appellation runs around the foot of the mount, covering 1,315 ha and producing 75,223 hl in 2002. Other neighbouring communes are Saint-Étienne-la-Varenne and Charentay while the famous "Pisse Vieille" vineyard is in the Cercié commune.

Brouilly

MURIEL ET YVAN CHAVRIER Cuvée
Vieilles Vignes Vieilli en fût de chêne 2001★

| ■ | 1.5 ha | 2,000 | ⓤ | 5–8 € |

The Chavriers have been tenant farmers at the château de La Chaize since 1992. Their ruby Vieilles Vignes was matured in oak, which is reflected in the bouquet by pleasant notes of

vanilla blended with perfumes of soft fruits. The clear-cut first impression reveals a good combination of oak and fruity flesh. This agreeable and persistent wine is well worth keeping for two years. The same estate's **Brouilly Cuvée Tradition 2002** was also specially commended.
• Muriel et Yvan Chavrier, Les Caboches, 69460 Odenas, tel. 04.74.03.30.15, fax 04.74.03.30.15 ☑
Ⴑ by appt.
• de Roussy de Salles

FLORENCE ET DIDIER CONDEMINE
Pisse-Vieille 2002★

| ■ | 7 ha | 14,000 | ■ ♦ | 5–8 € |

The third generation has been running this estate belonging to the Hospices de Beaujeu since 2001. They have produced a Brouilly from the famous *lieu-dit* of Pisse-Vieille. It has a superb red colour, an elegant bouquet with notes of tobacco and nougat. The palate is well structured and balanced, and the aromas of soft fruits combined with herbs have good length. This is a distinguished wine to drink within a year. Also recommended is the estate's **Régnié 2002 (3–5 €)**.
• EARL Florence et Didier Condemine, La Martingale, 69220 Cercié, tel. 04.74.66.72.24, fax 04.74.66.72.24 ☑
Ⴑ ev. day 8am–12 noon 2pm–7pm

DOM. DE LA FULLY 2001★

| ■ | 2.2 ha | 15,000 | ⓤ | 5–8 € |

They have been making wine here from father to son for six generations. The latest generation has been in charge since 1975 and cultivates the vines by sustainable agriculture. This Brouilly 2001 was made from 50-year-old vines and has an elegant dark-red colour with brick-red glints. Notes of roasting and chocolate combine with nuances of very ripe fruits on a rich and full-bodied palate with a balanced tannic structure. This very pleasant wine is ready to drink now.
• Martine Vermorel, Chambon, 69460 Blacé, tel. 04.74.67.56.37, fax 04.74.67.51.08 ☑
Ⴑ by appt.

GRAND CLOS DE BRIANTE 2002★

| ■ | 15 ha | 60,000 | | 5–8 € |

This dark-red Brouilly comes from 40-year-old vines and opens with subtle perfumes of black berries. The rounded attack gives way to tannins which blend harmoniously with the aromatic flesh. This wine should open out still more and should be left for at least a year until it is fully ready.
• GFA des Beillard, Briante, 69220 Saint-Lager, tel. 04.74.09.60.00, fax 04.74.09.60.17

DANIEL GUILLET 2002★★

| ■ | 1.5 ha | 4,000 | ■ ♦ | 5–8 € |

This tenanted farm at the château de la Chaize has made a dark-red wine with concentrated perfumes of very ripe blackberry and floral notes. The rounded first impression is followed by fairly pronounced tannins which give the wine good length. This rich wine should be kept for two or three years to allow its finish to become even smoother.
• Daniel Guillet, Les Lions, 69460 Odenas, tel. 04.74.03.48.06, fax 04.74.03.48.06 ☑

ANNE-MARIE JUILLARD 2002★

| ■ | 1.3 ha | 4,000 | ■ | 5–8 € |

This family estate has produced two Beaujolais winning one star each: the **Régnié 2002 (3–5 €)**, and this Brouilly with a clear, bright-red colour and a fine, expressive bouquet of soft fruits. The clear-cut first impression yields to fairly strong but balanced tannins. The ripe fruit flavours and excellent structure are evidence of a successful product. Drink it within a year.
• Anne-Marie Juillard, Bergeron, rte de Beaujeu, 69220 Saint-Lager, tel. 04.74.66.82.28, fax 04.74.66.53.68 ☑
Ⴑ by appt.

JEAN-MARC LAFOREST 2002★

| ■ | 5.8 ha | 34,000 | ■ ♦ | 5–8 € |

Jean-Marc Laforest's **Régnié 2002** wins one star, as does this Brouilly with its lovely red colour and intense perfumes of soft fruits. Its full and elegant flavours of peony and iris, and

its balanced structure make it a seductive wine. It is ready to drink now but can still be kept for a while.
◆ Jean-Marc Laforest, Chez le Bois, 69430 Régnié-Durette, tel. 04.74.04.35.03, fax 04.74.69.01.67 ☑
♁ by appt.

DOM. DES MAISONS NEUVES
Fût de chêne 2001★

	0.6 ha	5,000	■ ⅲ ♦		5–8 €

This 2001 vintage was made from 30-year-old vines grown on silty clay soil and matured in barrel for nine months. It has an intense garnet-red colour with brick-red glints, a well-developed bouquet of soft fruits with lightly smoky notes and a tang of vanilla. The palate is full and long, with rounded, well-integrated tannins. This is a typical balanced wine with good prospects for laying down, and will appeal to wine-lovers who like wines steeped in oak. It is ready to drink now but can be kept.
◆ Robert Jambon, Bergiron, 69220 Saint-Lager, tel. 04.74.66.81.24, fax 04.74.66.70.00 ☑
♁ by appt.

DOM. DE LA MOTTE 2002★★

	6.5 ha	40,000	■ ♦	5–8 €

This purple-ruby wine releases pleasant perfumes of pear-drops veering rapidly towards *pêche de vigne* and notes of chocolate, with raspberry and cherry completing the aromatic range. It is rich, elegant and very fresh on the palate and has an attractive lingering fruitiness and a beautiful balance that can be enjoyed for two or three years. Drink it with roast poultry. The same firm's **Fleurie Domaine de la Chapelle des Bois 2002 (8–11 €)** was also awarded one star.
◆ Paul Beaudet, rue Paul-Beaudet, 71570 Pontanevaux, tel. 03.85.36.72.76, fax 03.85.36.72.02,
e-mail contact@paulbeaudet.com ☑
♁ ev. day except Sat. Sun. 8am–12 noon 1.30pm–5pm; cl. Aug.

DOM. DU MOULIN FAVRE
Cuvée Vieilles Vignes 2002★★

	8.5 ha	30,000	■ ♦	5–8 €

Armand Vernus has been the head of the family estate since 1994. His 45-year-old vines have produced this Brouilly Vieilles Vignes, made after a long period of maceration. It has a bright-red colour and gradually reveals subtle mineral perfumes. The opening features clear-cut notes of ripe fruits blending with the original notes in a good structure. This full and rounded wine is ready to drink now, but could be kept for a year.
◆ Armand Vernus, Le Vieux-Bourg, 69460 Odenas, tel. 04.74.03.40.63, fax 04.74.03.40.76 ☑
♁ by appt.

JOSEPH PELLERIN 2002★★

	16 ha	80,000	■ ♦	5–8 €

This fresh red Brouilly has a lot going for it: an expressive bouquet of soft fruits, a full, supple, balanced and persistent palate featuring the soft fruits again, and harmonious tannins. It could be kept for a year. The Pellerin firm has two other recommended wines: a **Fleurie 2002 (3–5 €)**, one star, and its **Beaujolais Père La Grolle 2002**.
◆ Joseph Pellerin, 435, rue du Beaujolais, 69830 Saint-Georges-de-Reneins, tel. 04.74.09.60.00, fax 04.74.09.60.17, e-mail coquard.c@jpellerin.fr

CAVE BEAUJOLAISE DU PERRÉON 2002★

	4.91 ha	10,000		5–8 €

This Brouilly has a wonderful bright-red colour. Its perfumes of soft fruits blend with notes of mixed nuts (almond and hazelnut). It is well balanced with a beautiful tannic structure and is ready to drink now.
◆ Cave Beaujolaise du Perréon, 69460 Le Perréon, tel. 04.74.03.22.83, fax 04.74.03.27.60 ☑

CH. DE PIERREUX 2002★

	6 ha	40,000		5–8 €

The château de Pierreux was a fortified manor house in the 13th century and two towers survive from that time. Most of

the buildings date from the beginning of the 19th century. The lord of the manor has produced a clear dark-red Brouilly with pleasant perfumes of small soft fruits and fresh grapes. It opens on the palate with intense fruitiness joined by more tannic flavours. This full, rich and rounded wine is ready to drink now but could be kept for a year or two more.
◆ Comte de Toulgoët, Pierreux, 69460 Odenas, tel. 04.74.03.46.17, fax 04.74.06.60.17

DOM. DE LA ROCHE SAINT MARTIN
2002★

	6.5 ha	20,000	■ ♦	5–8 €

This 10-ha estate has been run since 1979 by Jean-Jacques Béréziat. It has distinguished itself with a **Côte de Brouilly 2002**, which the Jury singled out, and particularly with this deep-red wine made from 45-year-old vines. It opens with fairly strong perfumes of very ripe soft fruits. These continue on the palate, and with the expressive tannins make a pleasant wine which has yet to mature. It will be at its peak in one year.
◆ SCEA Jean-Jacques Béréziat, Briante, 69220 Saint-Lager, tel. 04.74.66.85.39, fax 04.74.66.70.54 ☑
♁ by appt.

DOM. DES TERRES BLEUES 2002★

	7 ha	50,000	■ ♦	5–8 €

The Collin-Bourisset firm was founded 182 years ago. Two of its wines were singled out by the Jury: a **Beaujolais-Villages red 2002 Domaine des Hospices Civils de Lyon**, and a **Morgon 2002 Les Trois Porches**. In addition, they produced this deep-red Brouilly with mauve glints. It has fairly intense perfumes of soft fruits, blackberry and blackcurrant which continue with good length on the palate together with notes of walnut. This fleshy, balanced wine has a good tannic structure, and is ready to drink now or can be kept for one or two years.
◆ Collin-Bourisset Vins Fins, rue de la Gare, 71680 Crèches-sur-Saône, tel. 03.85.36.57.25, fax 03.85.37.15.38, e-mail cbourisset@gofornet.com ☑
♁ by appt.

CH. DES TOURS 2002★

	20 ha	400,000	■ ♦	8–11 €

This is a real château, going back to feudal times with two towers, one square and the other round. This beautiful property was bought in 1987 by the Richard family. It has 70 ha, of which 20 ha has been devoted to this very successful Brouilly. There is also a short-stay *gîte*. The wine has a clear crimson colour and releases fairly delicate perfumes of raspberry and cherry, with nuances of very ripe fruits and a hint of peony. The palate is well bred, elegant and long with a good tannic structure. This well-made Brouilly is ready now, but could be kept for a year.
◆ SCI Dom. des Tours, Ch. des Tours, 69460 Saint-Etienne-la-Varenne, tel. 04.74.03.40.86, fax 04.74.03.50.22 ☑
♁ by appt.

BERNARD TRICHARD
Sélection 2001★

	2.56 ha	8,000	■ ⅲ	5–8 €

This clear ruby wine was made from 55-year-old vines. It has an expressive and complex bouquet of fruits (redcurrant, blackberry and cherry) and flowers (hawthorn) with notes of vanilla. Its tannins are starting to become more supple, contributing to the wine's pleasant, balanced and fairly long palate. This is an original product to be drunk now or laid down for a year or two.
◆ Jeanine et Bernard Trichard, Les Nazins, 69220 Saint-Lager, tel. 04.74.66.80.48, fax 04.74.66.81.60 ☑
♁ ev. day 8am–7.30pm; Sun. by appt.

GEORGES VIORNERY 2002★

	5.15 ha	12,000	■	5–8 €

This vineyard was set up by George Viornery in 1972. It occupies a little more than 7 ha and extends over the two wine-growing areas on Mont Brouilly. While its **Côte de Brouilly 2002** receives a special mention, all the estate's wines deserve praise. This purplish-crimson 2002 releases intense perfumes of black-cherry and blackcurrant, enhanced by

notes of *pain d'épice*. Its elegant, fruity and rich fullness fills the mouth pleasantly. The tannins seem fine and rounded and the length is good. This wine will be ready in one to two years.
☛ Georges Viornery, Brouilly, 69460 Odenas,
tel. 04.74.03.41.44, fax 04.74.03.41.44 ☑
🍷 by appt.

Wines selected but not starred

DOM. BALLOQUET 2001

■	n.c.	n.c.	■	8–11€

☛ Maison Louis Jadot, 21, rue Eugène-Spuller,
21200 Beaune, tel. 03.80.22.10.57, fax 03.80.22.56.03,
e-mail contact@louisjadot.com
🍷 by appt.

JEAN BARONNAT 2002

■	n.c.	n.c.	5–8€

☛ Maison Baronnat, 491, rte de Lacenas, Les Bruyères,
69400 Gleizé, tel. 04.74.68.59.20, fax 04.74.62.19.21,
e-mail info@baronnat.com ☑
🍷 by appt.

DOM. DE BEAUVOIR 2002

■	7 ha	47,000	5–8€

☛ Maison Thorin, Le Pont des Samsons,
69430 Quincié-en-Beaujolais, tel. 04.74.69.09.10,
fax 04.74.69.09.28,
e-mail information@maisonthorin.com
☛ SCEA Monette

CH. BEILLARD 2002

■	6 ha	40,000	■ ♦	5–8€

☛ GFA des Beillard, Briante, 69220 Saint-Lager,
tel. 04.74.09.60.00, fax 04.74.09.60.17

DOM. LIONEL BERTRAND

Bonnège 2002

■	1.7 ha	13,300	■ ♦	5–8€

☛ Lionel Bertrand, 69220 Charentay, tel. 04.74.06.10.10,
fax 04.74.66.13.77 ☑
🍷 by appt.

DOM. DU CHÂTEAU DE LA VALETTE
2002

■	4.74 ha	14,000	■	5–8€

☛ Jean-Pierre Crespin, Le Bourg, 69220 Charentay,
tel. 04.74.66.81.96, fax 04.74.66.71.72,
e-mail jp.crespin@wanadoo.fr ☑
🍷 by appt.

DOM. PAUL CINQUIN 2002

■	n.c.	2,000	■ ♦	5–8€

☛ Paul Cinquin, Les Nazins, 69220 Saint-Lager,
tel. 04.74.66.80.00, fax 04.74.66.70.78 ☑
🍷 by appt.

LE JARDIN DES RAVATYS 2001

■	7 ha	10,000	■ ⑪ ♦	5–8€

☛ Institut Pasteur, Ch. des Ravatys, 69220 Saint-Lager,
tel. 04.74.66.80.35, fax 04.74.66.88.95 ☑
🍷 by appt.

DOM. LENOIR ET FILS

La Saigne 2001

■	1.4 ha	10,000	■	5–8€

☛ Lenoir Fils, Cimes de Cherves,
69430 Quincié-en-Beaujolais, tel. 04.74.69.02.03,
fax 04.74.69.01.45 ☑
🍷 by appt.

AGNÈS ET PIERRE-ANTHELME
PEGAZ Vieilles Vignes 2001

■	2.6 ha	4,500	⑪	5–8€

☛ Pierre-Anthelme et Agnès Pegaz, 69220 Charentay,
tel. 04.74.66.82.34, fax 04.74.66.82.34,
e-mail vinspegaz@wanadoo.fr ☑
🍷 ev. day 9am–6pm

DOM. DE PIERREFAIT 2002

■	7 ha	28,000	■ ♦	5–8€

☛ Claude Echallier, Creigne, 69460 Odenas,
tel. 04.74.06.10.10, fax 04.74.66.13.77 ☑
🍷 by appt.

DOM. DE PONCHON 2002

■	3 ha	5,000	■ ♦	5–8€

☛ Yves Durand, Ponchon, 69430 Régnié-Durette,
tel. 04.74.04.34.78, fax 04.74.04.34.78 ☑
🍷 ev. day 8am–12 noon 2pm–7pm

LES ROCHES BLEUES 2002

■	4.65 ha	20,000	⑪	5–8€

☛ Dominique Lacondemine, Dom. les Roches Bleues, Côte
de Brouilly, 69460 Odenas, tel. 04.74.03.43.11,
fax 04.74.03.50.06,
e-mail lacondemine. dominique@wanadoo.fr ☑ 🏠
🍷 ev. day 8.30am–8pm; Sun. by appt.

DOM. RUET

Voujon 2002

■	3 ha	22,000	■ ♦	5–8€

☛ Dom. Jean-Paul Ruet, Voujon, 69220 Cercié,
tel. 04.74.66.85.00, fax 04.74.66.89.64,
e-mail ruet.beaujolais@wanadoo.fr ☑ 🏠
🍷 by appt.

DOM. DE SAINT-ENNEMOND 2002

■	5 ha	30,000	■ ♦	5–8€

☛ Christian et Marie Béréziat, Saint-Ennemond,
69220 Cercié, tel. 04.74.69.67.17, fax 04.74.69.67.29,
e-mail christian.bereziat@wanadoo.fr ☑ 🏠
🍷 ev. day 8am–8pm

CH. DE SAINT-LAGER 2002

■	n.c.	n.c.	5–8€

☛ SCEA Ch. de Pizay, 69220 Saint-Jean-d'Ardières,
tel. 04.74.66.26.10, fax 04.74.69.60.66,
e-mail chateau-de-pizay@chateau-de-pizay. com ☑ 🏠
🍷 by appt.

DOM. DU SANCILLON 2001

■	4 ha	5,000	■	5–8€

☛ Mme Charles Champier, Dom. du Sancillon, Le Moulin
Favre, 69460 Odenas, tel. 04.74.03.42.18,
fax 04.74.03.30.62 ☑
🍷 by appt.

DOM. DE TANTE ALICE 2002

■	1.2 ha	5,000	■ ♦	5–8€

☛ SCEA Dom. de Tante Alice, La Pilonnière,
69220 Saint-Lager, tel. 04.74.66.89.33, fax 04.74.66.86.20 ☑
🍷 by appt.

CH. DE LA TERRIERE 2002
■ 10.1 ha 20,000 8–11 €
➤ SCEV du Ch. de La Terrière, La Terrière, 69220 Cercié,
tel. 04.74.66.73.19,
fax 04.74.66.73.07 ☑
⌁ by appt.
➤ Barbet

DOM. DE VURIL 2001
■ 8.5 ha 18,000 5–8 €
➤ Gabriel Jambon, Chapoly, 69220 Charentay,
tel. 04.74.66.84.98, fax 04.74.66.80.58 ☑
⌁ by appt.

Côte de Brouilly

structure, full of flavour and length. This is flavoursome,
balanced *vin de terroir* that will be ready in two or three years
to drink with an entrecôte charolaise. Another good prospect
is the **white Beaujolais 2001 (3–5 €)**, also commended.
➤ Agnès et Franck Tavian, Les Gilets, 69220 Saint-Lager,
tel. 04.74.69.02.26, fax 04.74.69.02.26 ☑
⌁ by appt.

DOM. DU BARVY 2001★
■ n.c. n.c. ▮ 5–8 €
Dominique and Pascal Bouillard farm 8 ha of vines; they
have also built a three-star *gîte*. Although their **Brouilly 2001**
was singled out, the Jury preferred this Côte de Brouilly. It is
purplish-red in colour and releases complex perfumes of soft
fruits, blackcurrant leaf and peony which incline towards
pêche-de-vigne. On the palate are flavours of liquorice and
soft fruits, which blend with still lively tannins. This wine is
ready to drink now and will go well with dry sausage.
➤ Dom. du Barvy, La Commune, 69460 Odenas,
tel. 04.74.03.40.30, fax 04.74.03.49.27,
e-mail pbouillard@wanadoo.fr ☑ ⌂
⌁ by appt.
➤ Bouillard

DOM. DU CHEMIN RONDE 2002★
■ 3 ha 12,000 8–11 €
This clear bright-garnet 2002 has an attractively intense
and complex bouquet of raspberry and blackcurrant with
notes of pepper and mineral, peony and rose. The pleasure
continues on the palate: the first impression reveals rounded
tannins which assert themselves at the finish. This well-
made, balanced and promising wine will open out fully in
one or two years.
➤ Gérard Monteil, 70, Grande-Rue, 69220 Cercié,
tel. 04.74.66.80.50, fax 04.74.66.70.91,
e-mail gerardmonteil@terre.net.fr ☑
⌁ by appt.

VALERIE DALAIS 2002★
■ 0.5 ha 2,000 ▮ 5–8 €
This clear bright-ruby wine releases pleasant perfumes of
cherry, blackberry and blackcurrant. Its substantial structure
reflects the thoroughness of the winemaking process. This is a
sturdy wine, not over-sophisticated despite a touch of
minerality. It will become more refined. Drink it in one or two
years with an entrecôte charolaise. Also recommended is the
estate's **Brouilly 2002**.
➤ Valérie Dalais, La Grand-Raie, 69220 Saint-Lager,
tel. 04.74.66.75.37, fax 04.74.66.75.77 ☑
⌁ by appt.

DOM. FRANCHET 2001★★
■ 4.1 ha 4,500 ▮ ♦ 5–8 €
Franck Tavian took over in 1995, representing the fifth generation to run this estate. Its exceptional Côte de Brouilly is
made from 60-year-old vines planted on the hillside and
vinified in a wine cellar which was renovated in 2002. The
winemaking process has not used either sulphur dioxide or
exogenic yeast. The result is a purplish-carmine wine with rich
perfumes of wild strawberry and peony evolving towards the
granitic minerality so characteristic of the appellation. It
is fleshy on the palate with compact tannins and a superb

DOM. DES GRANDES VIGNES 2002★
■ 6.13 ha 40,000 ▮ ♦ 5–8 €
This family estate has a Côte de Brouilly made from old vines
which is entirely satisfying, with a clear garnet-red colour and
pleasant flavours evolving from floral perfumes (peony and
rose) towards notes of moist granite, a balanced palate with
compact and elegant tannins, and a good future potential. It
can be drunk over the next two years.
➤ Jean-Claude and Jacky Nesme, Dom. des Grandes Vignes,
Chavanne, 69430 Quincié-en-Beaujolais, tel. 04.74.04.31.02,
fax 04.74.04.33.97 ☑
⌁ ev. day 9am–12 noon 1.30pm–7pm

DOM. DE LA GRAND RAIE 2001★
■ 1.6 ha 6,000 ▮ 5–8 €
The previous vintage won a *coup de coeur*. This clear ruby
2001 makes an excellent impression with its intense bouquet
of liquorice, toast and soft fruits with notes of peony and
violet. The palate is not to be outdone, offering not only the
soft fruits but also gunflint with evident but supple tannins.
This rich and well-balanced wine can be drunk over the next
two years. The estate's **Moulin-à-Vent 2001** was also awarded
one star.
➤ EARL Laurent Charrion, La Grand-Raie,
69220 Saint-Lager, tel. 04.74.66.81.69, fax 04.74.66.71.32 ☑
⌁ by appt.

DOM. DU GRIFFON 2002★★
■ 6 ha 20,000 ▮ ♦ 5–8 €
This family property built in 1978 has 12 ha of vines. This
year its garnet-coloured Côte de Brouilly has had nothing but
praise. It opens on intense fresh perfumes of soft fruits and
spices characteristic of the appellation. On the palate the soft
tannins blend with flavours of soft fruits and nuances of
prune. It is balanced with good length, and combines finesse
and character. It can be drunk in the next two years.
➤ Jean-Paul Vincent, Le Bourg, 69220 Saint-Lager,
tel. 04.74.66.85.06, fax 04.74.66.73.18 ☑ ⌂
⌁ by appt.

DOM. LAFOND 2002★
■ n.c. n.c. 5–8 €
This estate has often come to our Juries' notice. The vat room
was renovated and enlarged in 2002. The **Brouilly 2002**
received a special mention, but preference was given to this
ruby Côte de Brouilly with purple highlights. The bouquet
opens on complex notes of soft fruits. These fruity flavours
are even more clean-tasting on the palate. This well-structured, chewy wine should be drunk in the next two years.
➤ Dom. Lafond, Bel-Air, 69220 Saint-Lager,
tel. 04.74.66.04.46, fax 04.74.66.37.91 ☑
⌁ ev. day 8am–12 noon 2pm–6pm

DOM. DE LA MERLETTE

Cuvée Tradition 2001★

■	0.77 ha	6,000	▥▥	5–8 €

This Côte du Brouilly was made in Vaux-en-Beaujolais, a village which provided certain features of the famous rural novel by Gabriel Chevallier, *Clochemerle*. It was vinified by the current president of the *Confrérie du Gosier Sec*, and is well up to par. It has a bright-garnet colour with paler glints and releases fairly fine perfumes of vanilla and notes of soft fruits. The palate is rather tannic, firm and showing good length and balance. Keep it for one or two years.
↬ René et Marie-Claire Tachon, Le Sottizon, 69460 Vaux-en-Beaujolais, tel. 04.74.03.24.80, fax 04.74.03.24.80, e-mail tachon@tiscali.fr ▣
☿ by appt.

JEAN-FRANCOIS MORIN

Cuvée Tradition Elevé en fût de chêne 2001★

■	0.33 ha	1,600	▥▥	5–8 €

This ruby wine has some brick-red highlights. It was matured for seven months in barrel but still bears all the signs of its origins. "Nose in the glass, eyes shut, and we're on the famous mountain," wrote one of the tasters. The palate reveals a blend of vanilla notes, mineral impressions and nuances of stewed fruits: a very fine olfactory experience. This is a full-bodied wine with good tannic support. Drink it over the next two years with red meat.
↬ Jean-François Morin, Chateland, 69220 Saint-Lager, tel. 04.74.66.83.12, fax 04.74.66.83.12 ▣
☿ by appt.

DOM. ROBERT PERROUD

La Fournaise du Pérou Vieilles Vignes 2002★

■	0.45 ha	3,000		8–11 €

The furnace in the name refers to 45 ares of old established vines on a granite and andesite soil. It has produced a bright-ruby wine with purple glints. Its pleasant perfumes suggest a black fruit jam (blackcurrant and blackberry) and toast, with aniseed and pepper notes. The first impression is soft, with rounded tannins. The soft fruits continue, along with hints of mineral. This well-balanced wine should be drunk in the next two years with meat in sauce, or with a game-bird.
↬ Robert Perroud, Les Balloquets, 69460 Odenas, tel. 04.74.04.35.63, fax 04.74.04.32.46, e-mail robertperroud@wanadoo.fr ▣
☿ by appt.

DOM. DU PETIT PRESSOIR 2002★

■	4 ha	10,000	▤	8–11 €

This deep-red, almost purplish wine was made from 35-year-old vines. It opens with complex perfumes of cherry, raspberry and blackcurrant, with some amylic nuances. The aromas of the bouquet reappear in more lively form on the palate, which is very tannic. This rich wine will keep well and needs to mature for one or two years to allow the tannins time to soften.
↬ Daniel Mathon, Chardignon, 69220 Saint-Lager, tel. 04.74.66.86.48, fax 04.74.66.70.42 ▣ ⌂
☿ by appt.

JACKY PIRET

Vieilles Vignes 2001★

■	1.6 ha	11,000	▤▥▥	5–8 €

Jacky Piret runs a vineyard of 10 ha. The estate also has four three-star *chambres d'hôte*. This Côte de Brouilly is deep red and clear with some brick-red glints. It releases intense perfumes of violet and fruit with notes of liquorice and oak. The pleasant, full-bodied attack soon gives way to aromas from the maturation process: oak and nuances of toast and caramel. It is well structured with a strong but integrated oakiness, and should be drunk in the next two or three years.
↬ Jacky Piret, La Combe, 69220 Belleville, tel. 04.74.66.30.13, fax 04.74.66.08.94 ▣ ⌘
☿ by appt.

DOM. ROLLAND 2002★

■	6 ha	8,700		5–8 €

This deep-garnet wine comes from 40-year-old vines and has concentrated perfumes of very ripe soft fruits (wild strawberry, raspberry and blackberry) with spicy notes. After the powerful and rounded first impression, the soft fruits fill the mouth with good persistence. The fruitiness and structure are well balanced, and although this wine is ready now it could still be kept for one or two years.
↬ Pierre Ferraud et Fils, 31, rue du Mal-Foch, 69220 Belleville, tel. 04.74.06.47.60, fax 04.74.66.05.50, e-mail ferraud@ferraud.com ▣
☿ ev. day except Sun. 8am–12 noon 2.15pm–6.15pm

BERNADETTE ET GILLES VINCENT 2002★★

■	1 ha	3,000	▥▥	5–8 €

Gilles Vincent has farmed 9 ha as a tenant since 1989. Production of Côte de Brouilly started in 1990 with the purchase of these 55-year-old vines. His 2002 vintage has a bright-ruby colour and garnet glints, and releases pleasant perfumes of redcurrant, blackberry and *pêche de vigne* which evolves towards mineral notes. The full-bodied attack is followed by compact tannins accompanied by fruity and spicy flavours. This wine is well balanced and full of charm, and almost won a *coup de coeur*. It can be enjoyed for two or three years with red meat.
↬ Bernadette et Gilles Vincent, Les Grands-Croix, 69220 Saint-Lager, tel. 04.74.66.82.05, fax 04.74.66.82.05 ▣
☿ ev. day 9am–7pm; cl. Sep.

Wines selected but not starred

CAVE DES VIGNERONS DE BEL-AIR 2002

■	30 ha	55,000	▤ ⚲	5–8 €

↬ Cave des Vignerons de Bel-Air, rte de Beaujeu, 69220 Saint-Jean-d'Ardières, tel. 04.74.06.16.05, fax 04.74.06.16.09, e-mail cvba@wanadoo.fr ▣
☿ by appt.

JEAN-CHARLES PIVOT 2001

■	3 ha	22,000		5–8 €

↬ Jean-Charles Pivot, Montmay, 69430 Quincié-en-Beaujolais, tel. 04.74.04.30.32, fax 04.74.69.00.70 ▣
☿ ev. day except Sun. 8am–6pm; Sat. by appt.

Chénas

According to legend, a vast oak forest once covered this land. A woodcutter noticed that a wild vine had grown from a grape pip, apparently dropped by a bird. Convinced of divine intervention, the man set about making a clearing in the forest to cultivate the plant – which proved to be none other than the great Gamay, the black-skinned grape with white flesh.

Chénas is one of the smallest appellations in the Beaujolais, covering only 285 ha on the borders of the departments of Rhône and Saône-et-Loire. In 2002 it produced 15,170 hl harvested from the communes of Chénas and La Chapelle-de-Guinchay. The wines produced on the steep granite slopes to the west are intensely coloured, strongly flavoured but not aggressively so, and release scents of rose and violet; they are not dissimilar to the perfumes of the wines from Moulin-à-Vent, which occupies most of the land in the commune. Chénas, which is produced on the boggier and less hilly eastern part of the vineyard, is usually less full bodied. This wine tends to be regarded as the poor relation of the crus and, because of the size of the vineyard, is also limited to producing small quantities. The 17th century cellar of the Coopérative du Château vinifies 45% of the appellation and is an impressive sight when it is full of large oak barrels, or foudres, filled with wine.

HUBERT LAPIERRE
Cuvée Vieilles Vignes 2002★★

| | 4.2 ha | 25,000 | ∎ ♦ | 5–8 € |

You can find this Chénas in a tasting cellar built in 2001. It was made from 45-year-old vines, has a deep-ruby colour and releases perfumes of very ripe bilberry and blackcurrant. It is full bodied, rich and full of flavour with a very good structure and pleasant tannins, which suggest it will keep well. This remarkable, well-made wine can be laid down for two or three years. The same estate's **Moulin-à-Vent Vieilles Vignes 2002 (8–11 €)** received one star.
☛ Hubert Lapierre, Les Gandelins, 71570 La Chapelle-de-Guinchay, tel. 03.85.36.74.89, fax 03.85.36.79.69, e-mail hubert.lapierre@terre-net.fr ☑
⬗ by appt.

DOM. JACQUES ET ANNIE LORON 2002★

| | 0.5 ha | 3,000 | ∎ ⬗ | 5–8 € |

This deep-ruby wine with intense perfumes of red stone fruits was made from 45-year-old vines. On the palate, a fruity attack is followed by oaky notes with hints of mocha coffee. This full-bodied, well-balanced wine with a very good structure will be at its best in two or three years. Also recommended was the **Moulin-à-Vent La Rochelle 2002**.
☛ EARL Jacques et Annie Loron, Les Blancs, 69840 Chénas, tel. 04.74.04.48.76, fax 04.74.04.42.14, e-mail jacques.loron@wanadoo.fr ☑
⬗ by appt.

DOM. DU P'TIT PARADIS 2002★

| | 0.52 ha | 3,800 | ∎ | 5–8 € |

This estate, open seven days a week, stands on a hillside filled with vines. Its dark-crimson wine has a bouquet of black fruits with mineral and musky nuances. The palate reveals a rich substance, still dominated by tannins which need to become more rounded, and fruity flavours with notes of rose. This chewy wine will improve after keeping for a year or two. Also commended was the estate's **Moulin-à-Vent 2002**.
☛ Denise et Francis Margerand, Les Pinchons, 69840 Chénas, tel. 04.74.04.48.71, fax 04.74.04.46.29 ☑
⬗ by appt.

DOM. DES ROSIERS 2002★

| | 1.8 ha | 11,000 | ∎ ⬗ | 5–8 € |

Gérard Charvet has been running this estate since 1975, and has kept the name "Les Rosiers", which the former owners gave it. His deep-ruby Chénas has a rather delicate bouquet of soft fruits, peony and iris. The soft, floral attack is followed by a pleasant oakiness. This well-made, balanced wine with integrated tannins can be drunk over the next three years. Also recommended was the **Moulin-à-Vent 2002**.
☛ Gérard Charvet, Les Rosiers, 69840 Chénas, tel. 04.74.04.48.62, fax 04.74.04.49.80 ☑
⬗ ev. day 8am–8pm

LE VIEUX DOMAINE 2001★

| | 1 ha | 3,000 | ⬗ | 5–8 € |

Vieux Domaine was started by the great-great-grandfather of the present occupants of Vieux Bourg, on the site of the original church at Chénas that was demolished after it had become dilapidated. The property is regularly mentioned in the *Guide*, and has won more than one *coup de cœur* (Moulin-à-Vent 92 and 97). This year, all its 2001 wines were selected by the Jury, who preferred the Chénas: a ruby wine with amber highlights, and perfumes of ripe soft fruits with oaky notes. Rich and well structured, the palate offers a harmonious blend of fruitiness and well-integrated oak. It is ready now but could be kept for two years. Serve it with game or roast guineafowl. Look out also for the **Moulin-à-Vent 2001**.
☛ EARL M.-C. et D. Joseph, Le Vieux-Bourg, 69840 Chénas, tel. 04.74.04.48.08, fax 04.74.04.47.36, e-mail le.vieux.domaine@wanadoo.fr ☑
⬗ by appt.

Wines selected but not starred

DOM. PASCAL AUFRANC
Vieilles vignes de 1939 2002

| | 4.5 ha | 9,000 | ∎ ⬗ | 5–8 € |

☛ Pascal Aufranc, En Rémont, 69840 Chénas, tel. 04.74.04.47.95, fax 04.74.04.47.95, e-mail aufranc.pascal@proveis.com ☑
⬗ by appt.

CAVE DU CHATEAU DE CHENAS
Sélection de La Hante 2002

| | 3.75 ha | 28,600 | ∎ ⬗ | 5–8 € |

☛ Cave du Ch. de Chénas, Les Michauds, 69840 Chénas, tel. 04.74.04.48.19, fax 04.74.04.48.19, e-mail cave.chenas@wanadoo.fr ☑
⬗ ev. day 8am–12 noon 2pm–6pm

DOM. DES DARROUX 2002

| | 5 ha | 20,000 | ∎ | 5–8 € |

☛ Pascal Colvray, Les Darroux, 71570 La Chapelle-de-Guinchay, tel. 03.85.36.73.97, fax 03.85.36.79.37 ☑
⬗ ev. day 9.30am–12 noon 2pm–7pm

DOM. DES DUC 2001

| | 9.2 ha | 20,000 | ∎ ⬗ ⬗ | 5–8 € |

☛ Dom. des Duc, La Piat, 71570 Saint-Amour-Bellevue, tel. 03.85.37.10.08, fax 03.85.36.55.75, e-mail duc@vins-du-beaujolais.com ☑
⬗ by appt.

GEORGES ROSSI
Vignoble en Guinchay 2002

| | 2.5 ha | 9,300 | ∎ ⬗ | 5–8 € |

☛ Georges Rossi, 71570 La Chapelle-de-Guinchay, tel. 04.74.06.10.10, fax 04.74.66.13.77 ☑
⬗ by appt.

PATRICK THEVENET 2002

| | 4.2 ha | 10,000 | ∎ | 5–8 € |

☛ Patrick Thévenet, Les Gandelins, Cidex 324, 71570 La Chapelle-de-Guinchay, tel. 03.85.36.72.68, fax 03.85.33.89.51, e-mail patrick-thevenet@wanadoo.fr ☑
⬗ ev. day 9am–7pm

Chiroubles

Perched at 400 m, Chiroubles is the highest of the cru vineyards in Beaujolais. It covers 376 ha of light, impoverished granite sand, in a single commune, and in 2002 produced 20,663 hl of red wine from the Gamay grape. Chiroubles is an elegant, delicate, charming and smooth wine, containing little tannin and with traces of violet perfumes. The Confrérie des Demoiselles de Chiroubles, supported by their Chevaliers, was created in 1996 to assist in the marketing of this wine which is sometimes referred to as "the ladies' Beaujolais". It is a wine for early drinking and is sometimes reminiscent of Fleurie or Morgon, which are neighbouring vineyards. Chiroubles is the perfect wine to drink with charcuterie. On the route to Fût d'Avenas, which leads out of the village towards the top of the mount, there is a chalet de dégustation where the wine can be tasted.

Chiroubles holds a festival every April to celebrate the memory of Victor Pulliat, born there in 1827. His considerable research into the pace of growth of different vine varieties and their comparative grafting qualities is world famous. He made his observations in his domaine at Tempéré and gathered a collection of over 2,000 vine varieties. Chiroubles has a cooperative cellar which vinifies 3,000 hl of the cru.

LA MAISON DES VIGNERONS DE CHIROUBLES Cuvée Vidame de Rocsain 2001★★

3.34 ha	26,200		5–8 €

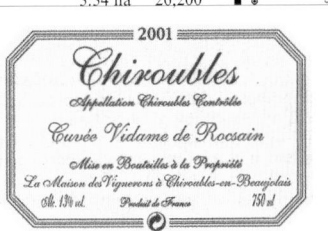

This year, one of the *coups de coeur* goes to La Maison des Vignerons at Chiroubles, a cooperative established in 1928. This 2001 wine has a lovely garnet colour, and opens on notes of quince, redcurrant jam and a touch of violet. On the palate, the Jury were won over by its good tannic structure, aromatic flesh with a touch of roasting, and by its length. This is a full, well-balanced wine to drink over the next two years with grilled meat or poultry. The cooperative's **Morgon Cuvée de la Chenevière 2001** was also recommended.
☛ La Maison des Vignerons de Chiroubles, Le Bourg, 69115 Chiroubles, tel. 04.74.69.14.94, fax 04.74.69.10.59 ☑
☖ by appt.

DOM. DE LA COMBE AU LOUP 2001★

5 ha	n.c.		8–11 €

This estate has appeared many times in the *Guide*, particularly in this appellation. The 2001 vintage has a garnet colour with brick-red highlights and well-developed perfumes of stone fruits, soft red fruits and blackcurrant, with additional notes of peony and toast. The palate is well structured and fresh, with attractive flavours of very ripe fruits, though a harsh touch slightly mars the finish. Drink it within a year.
☛ Méziat Père et Fils, Dom. de la Combe au Loup, Le Bourg, 69115 Chiroubles, tel. 04.74.04.24.02, fax 04.74.69.14.07 ☑
☖ by appt.

DOM. DE LA COUR PROFONDE 2002★

3 ha	12,000		5–8 €

Cyril Revollat occupied this property in 1999 and has 9 ha. He takes great care during the harvest, the grapes are sorted by hand on a table. This has stood him in good stead, as two of his wines have been awarded one star: the **Fleurie 2002 (8–11 €)** and this deep-red Chiroubles with fairly strong perfumes of raspberry, strawberry and blackcurrant with a buttery touch. After a clear-cut attack, the palate is fleshy and full with recurring flavours of strawberry and blackcurrant and a tannic structure which is fairly evident at the finish. This is a well-balanced and promising wine which is ready to drink but can be kept.
☛ Cyril Revollat, La Cour Profonde, 69115 Chiroubles, tel. 04.74.69.13.72, fax 04.74.04.22.84 ☑
☖ ev. day 8am–7pm

DOM. DES GATILLES 2001★

5 ha	25,000		8–11 €

This estate has been in the Fourneau family since 1917, and has 13 ha of vines. The winery was renovated in 2001. The 2001 vintage is better than the 2000, and receives one star. It has a deep-garnet colour with brick-red highlights, and releases complex perfumes of very ripe fruits, spices and peony; these aromas continue on a palate featuring integrated tannins and a fruity fullness. This wine is full and round, and can be drunk in the next two years.
☛ SCE de Javernand, 69115 Chiroubles, tel. 04.74.69.16.04, fax 04.74.69.16.04, e-mail pfourneau@libertysurf.fr ☑
☖ by appt.
☛ Pierre Fourneau

JEAN-MARC MATHIEU 2002★

0.4 ha	2,500		5–8 €

This clear garnet wine was matured in vaulted 17th century cellars. It has intense perfumes of stone fruits, blackcurrant and wild strawberry. The fresh and fruity palate has excellent length. The fine tannins which appear at the finish do not impair this wine's good balance. Drink it within a year.
☛ Jean-Marc Mathieu, Les Bourrons, 69820 Vauxrenard, tel. 04.74.69.92.84, fax 04.74.69.91.64, e-mail mathieu-madru@wanadoo.fr ☑
☖ by appt.

BERNARD METRAT 2002★★

n.c.	7,200		5–8 €

This deep-ruby wine was made from 50-year-old vines. It has complex perfumes of soft red fruits and blackcurrant with spicy and smoky notes. Its rich aromatic flesh and good tannic structure fill the mouth completely. This balanced 2002 wine has good length and can be kept for two years.
☛ EARL Bernard Métrat, Le Brie, 69820 Fleurie, tel. 04.74.69.84.26, fax 04.74.69.84.49 ☑
☖ by appt.

DOM. DU PETIT PUITS 2002★★

5.5 ha	20,000		5–8 €

This estate's Chiroubles are often mentioned in the *Guide*, and this year it has surpassed itself with an outstanding 2002 vintage. It was made from 50-year-old vines planted in granitic sands, has a bright deep-ruby colour, and expressive and rich perfumes of blackcurrant, bilberry and fresh strawberry, with a buttery touch. It is very concentrated, and the silky flesh and well-balanced, velvety tannins are very

promising. The Jury greatly enjoyed its long fruity palate. This wine will be an excellent companion for two years.
➼ Gilles Méziat, Le Verdy, 69115 Chiroubles,
tel. 04.74.69.15.90, fax 04.74.04.27.71,
e-mail domainedupetitpuitschiroubles@wanadoo.fr ☑
☖ by appt.

DOM. DE PRE-NESME

Cuvée Vieilles Vignes 2001★

| ■ | 6.68 ha | 7,000 | ▮ | 5–8 € |

The oldest vine is 107 years old, but this garnet-coloured wine came from 80-year-old vines. It has a bouquet of blackberry with shades of chocolate, leather and coffee. A good tannic structure is accompanied by a slightly alcoholic vinous flavour with a touch of coffee. It is balanced and fairly long on the palate, and should be drunk within a year.
➼ André Dépré, Le Moulin, 69115 Chiroubles,
tel. 04.74.69.11.18, fax 04.74.69.12.84,
e-mail andre.depre@wanadoo.fr ☑
☖ ev. day 9am–12 noon 2pm–7.30pm

DOM. DU PRESSOIR FLEURI

Vieilles Vignes 2001★

| ■ | n.c. | n.c. | ▮ | 8–11 € |

This family estate dating from 1789 was taken over in June 2001 by the daughter and son-in-law. Their first harvest has produced a deep-red wine which opens with rich and very pleasant perfumes of stewed fruits and cherry in brandy. The generous palate continues the flavours of the bouquet accompanied by a good tannic structure. This is a balanced wine with good length which is ready to drink now but could be kept for up to a year.
➼ Dom. du Pressoir Fleuri, Le Bourg, 69115 Chiroubles,
tel. 04.74.04.23.12, fax 04.74.69.12.65,
e-mail dom.pressoir.fleuri@terre-net.fr
☖ by appt.

CH. DE RAOUSSET 2001★★

| ■ | 5.63 ha | 15,000 | ▮ ♦ | 5–8 € |

This wine's red colour has just a few brick-red highlights. The perfumes suggest notes of soft fruits with nuances of pepper and coffee. The honest attack is followed by a full-bodied, well-structured palate with integrated tannins and aromas of morello cherry, prune, tobacco and spices. Well balanced and with good length, this is a wine to drink over the next two years.
➼ SCEA héritiers de Raousset, Les Prés, 69115 Chiroubles,
tel. 04.74.69.16.19, fax 04.74.04.21.93,
e-mail remy@scea-de-raousset.fr ☑
☖ by appt.

Wines selected but not starred

DOM. CHEYSSON 2002

| ■ | 3.2 ha | 24,000 | ▮ ♦ | 5–8 € |

➼ Dom. Emile Cheysson, Clos Les Farges,
69115 Chiroubles, tel. 04.74.04.22.02, fax 04.74.69.14.16 ☑
☖ ev. day 8am–12 noon 2pm–7pm

DOM. DE FONTRIANTE 2002

| ■ | 3.1 ha | 8,000 | ▮ ♦ | 5–8 € |

➼ Jacky Passot, Fontriante, 69910 Villié-Morgon,
tel. 04.74.69.10.03, fax 04.74.69.14.29,
e-mail jacky.passot@wanadoo.fr ☑
☖ by appt.

ALAIN ET GEORGES GAUTHIER 2001

| ■ | 0.56 ha | 4,250 | ▮ | 5–8 € |

➼ Alain Gauthier, La Roche Pilée, 69910 Villié-Morgon,
tel. 04.74.69.15.87, fax 04.74.69.15.87 ☑
☖ by appt.

DOM. DES GLYCINES 2001

| ■ | 0.7 ha | 5,800 | ▥ | 5–8 € |

➼ Eric Morin, Javernand, 69115 Chiroubles,
tel. 04.74.69.11.70, fax 04.74.04.22.28 ☑
☖ by appt.

DOM. MORIN 2002

| ■ | 3 ha | 20,000 | | 5–8 € |

➼ SNJP, 435, rue du Moulin,
69830 Saint-Georges-de-Reneins, tel. 04.74.09.60.00,
fax 04.74.09.60.17

CH. DE RAOUSSET 2001

| ■ | 15 ha | 50,000 | ▮ ▥ ♦ | 5–8 € |

➼ Ch. de Raousset, Les Prés, 69115 Chiroubles,
tel. 04.74.69.17.28, fax 04.74.69.61.38,
e-mail chateau-de-raousset@wanadoo.fr ☑
☖ ev. day 8am–12 noon 2pm–6pm; Sat. Sun. by appt.

DOM. CHRISTOPHE SAVOYE 2002

| ■ | 5.4 ha | 17,000 | ▮ ♦ | 5–8 € |

➼ Christophe Savoye, Le Bourg, 69115 Chiroubles,
tel. 04.74.69.11.24, fax 04.74.04.22.11 ☑
☖ ev. day except Sun. 8am–7pm

Fleurie

A chapel surmounts the rounded hillock of the Fleurie and appears to keep a watchful eye over the vineyard that is planted entirely with Gamay. This is the Madonna of Fleurie and it marks the physical location of the third most important cru after Brouilly and Morgon. The 879 ha of the vineyard are inside the commune boundaries and produced 50,697 hl in 2002. The terrain is similar throughout the vineyard and made up of crystalline granite which contributes to the wine's finesse and charm. The wine can be drunk cool or at room temperature and, either way, it is the perfect accompaniment for andouillette beaujolaise made with Fleurie. It has the promise of the countryside in spring: light, bright and with a bouquet of iris and violets.

There are two wine-tasting cellars in the centre of the village, one near the town hall and the other in the Cave Coopérative which vinifies 30% of the cru. They offer a full range of local wines with evocative names: La Rochette, La Chapelle des Bois, Les Roches, Grille-Midi and La Joie-du-Palais.

DOM. BERROD

Les Roches du Vivier 2002★★

| ■ | 8 ha | 30,000 | ▮ | 8–11 € |

This estate, established in 1954, has produced a dark-ruby wine shading to purple from its 40-year-old vines. It has expressive perfumes of violet which combine on the palate with clear but elegant tannins. This full and rich young wine has good length and is already pleasant to drink now, but

could be kept for up to three years. The property's **Moulin-à-Vent 2001** was also recommended.
🐦 Dom. Berrod, Le Vivier, 69820 Fleurie,
tel. 04.74.69.83.83, fax 04.74.69.86.19,
e-mail domaine.berrod@libertysurf.fr 🔣
👅 by appt.

DOM. DU CALVAIRE DE ROCHE-GRES

2002★★

■	2.24 ha	17,000		5–8 €

This estate takes its name from a calvary of 13 standing stones like menhirs, erected nearby in 1934. Its Fleurie is remarkable: bright-garnet in colour, its fine bouquet blends the scents of fresh flowers (iris and peony) and spicy nuances. After an excellent attack, full-bodied and rich impressions fill the aromatic and lingering palate. This characteristic wine is ready to drink now and can also be laid down to mature further. The estate's **Morgon Les Charmes 2002** was awarded one star.
🐦 Didier Desvignes, Saint-Joseph, 69910 Villié-Morgon, tel. 04.74.69.92.29, fax 04.74.69.97.54 🔣
👅 by appt.

DOM. ANDRE COLONGE ET FILS 2002★

■	7.3 ha	55,000	■ 👍	5–8 €

They have made wine here from father to son since 1789. The estate of André Colonge merged with that of his son in 1988. Their Fleurie has a deep-ruby colour with purple highlights, and fairly concentrated perfumes of spices, iris and faded rose. It has a good tannic structure and length. It could be drunk now but would benefit from keeping for some time.
🐦 Dom. André Colonge et Fils, Les Terres-Dessus, 69220 Lancié, tel. 04.74.04.11.73, fax 04.74.04.12.68, e-mail andrecolonge6@aol.com 🔣
👅 ev. day 8am–7pm

DOM. DE LA COTE DE CHEVENAL

2002★

■	0.5 ha	3,500	■ 👍	5–8 €

This estate has been worked by father and son for several generations, expanding rapidly from from 5.10 ha in 1975 to its present 24 ha. This deep-garnet Fleurie with indigo highlights releases intense perfumes of soft fruits, blackcurrant and peony. These aromas continue on a pleasant, very rounded and full-bodied palate which has good balance and structure and is still evolving. This characteristic, attractive wine is ready to drink now, but could be kept for two to three years. It will go well with an andouillette in sauce or a salmi of guineafowl. Look out too for the estate's **Juliénas 2002**, which the Jury recommended.
🐦 Jean-François et Pierre Bergeron, Emeringes, 69840 Juliénas, tel. 04.74.04.41.19, fax 04.74.04.40.72, e-mail domaine-bergeron@wanadoo.fr 🔣
👅 ev. day 8.30am–12.30pm 1.30pm–7pm

DOM. DES DEUX LYS 2001★

■	2.16 ha	2,800	■	5–8 €

This farm is located just beneath the chapel of the Madonna, 500 m from the village of Fleurie. It was created by a young couple who moved there in 1994. The vines are much older, and produced this bright-ruby wine with very good aromas of fruits with notes of liquorice and charring. The palate is fleshy with integrated tannins, well balanced and long with a finish containing notes of kirsch. Drink it in the next two years.
🐦 Franck Mathray, La Chapelle des Bois, 69820 Fleurie, tel. 04.74.69.89.93, fax 04.74.69.89.93 🔣
👅 by appt.

DOM. DE HAUTE MOLIERE 2002★★

■	1.9 ha	1,500	■ 👍	5–8 €

This old family property has kept its traditional bread oven which is used five or six times a year. The estate has been run by the sixth generation since 1998. Its deep-garnet Fleurie was made from 40-year-old vines, and releases beautiful spicy perfumes of nutmeg evolving towards more floral notes. After a good attack, which brings out the suppleness of the flesh, more tannic impressions appear. The structure is a little firm but this very pleasant wine will certainly improve. It will be

ready in two years. The same estate's **Morgon 2002** received a special mention.
🐦 Jean-François Patissier, Le Bourg, 69820 Vauxrenard, tel. 04.74.69.92.58, fax 04.74.69.92.58 🔣
👅 by appt.

MOMMESSIN

Réserve 2002★★

■	2 ha	12,000	■	8–11 €

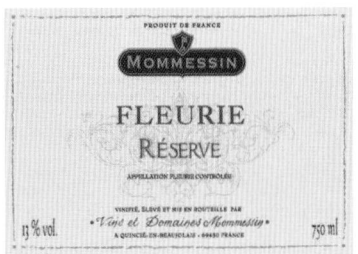

This bright-garnet wine opens with intense perfumes of very ripe, almost stewed fruits and spices. After a good attack, its richness continues on a full-bodied palate with a balanced structure. This remarkable wine could be kept for two years. The Mommessin firm's **Moulin-à-Vent Domaine de Champ de Cour Réserve 2001** was also singled out.
🐦 Mommessin, Le Pont-des-Samsons, 69430 Quincié-en-Beaujolais, tel. 04.74.69.09.30, fax 04.74.69.09.28, e-mail information@mommessin.fr 🔣
👅 by appt.

OLIVIER RAVIER

La Madone 2002★★

■	1 ha	n.c.	■ 🍶 👍	5–8 €

This dark-ruby wine comes from a plot surrounding the chapel of the Madonna, and opens with strong and clear-cut fruity perfumes. This good start continues with a charming, soft and full-bodied palate with excellent tannins; all of which indicates a light, characteristic Fleurie of good length. Although pleasant enough to drink now, it could also be kept for two or three years. It will go well with poultry or a selection of cheeses.
🐦 SARL Olivier Ravier, Descours, 69220 Belleville, tel. 04.74.66.12.66, fax 04.74.66.57.50, e-mail olivier.ravier@wanadoo.fr
👅 by appt.

DOM. LES ROCHES DES GARANTS

Les Moriers 2001★

■	3 ha	11,000	■ 👍	5–8 €

This estate dates from 1870, and today has 10 ha of vines producing Fleurie. This bright deep-ruby wine comes from 60-year-old vines. It opens slowly with floral notes. The attack is good and fresh, and is followed by full-bodied, fruity

impressions and fine, elegant tannins. This very pleasant wine has good length and is ready to drink now, but could be kept for two or three years.
☛ Jean-Paul Champagnon, La Treille, 69820 Fleurie, tel. 04.74.04.15.62, fax 04.74.69.82.60, e-mail j-paul.champagnon@wanadoo.fr ☑
☗ ev. day 8am–8pm

DOM. DE LA TREILLE 2002★

| ■ | 5 ha | 16,500 | 🍶 | 5–8 € |

Three generations have succeeded each other since 1955. The estate now has 14.30 ha of vines, and offers a purplish-red wine which opens quickly with perfumes of soft fruits and a floral note. The palate is full and rounded, with fine and elegant tannins and a blackcurrant flavour. This is a very well-balanced Fleurie to be drunk in the next two years.
☛ EARL Jean-Paul et Hervé Gauthier, Les Frébouches, 69220 Lancié, tel. 04.74.04.11.03, fax 04.74.69.84.13, e-mail jean-paul.gauthier2@wanadoo.fr ☑
☗ by appt.

Wines selected but not starred

PIERRE ANDRE

La Treille 2001

| ■ | 1.5 ha | 9,000 | 🍶 ⚬ | 15–23 € |

☛ Pierre André, Ch. de Corton-André, 21420 Aloxe-Corton, tel. 03.80.26.44.25, fax 03.80.26.43.57, e-mail pandre@axnet.fr

DOM. DES CHAFFANGEONS

La Madone Cuvée Michel et Martine 2002

| ■ | 2.5 ha | 18,000 | 🍶 ⚬ | 5–8 € |

☛ Michel Perrier, 69820 Fleurie, tel. 04.74.69.83.05, fax 04.74.69.84.92 ☑
☗ by appt.

DOM. DE LA CHAPELLE DES BOIS 2001

| ■ | 1.3 ha | 10,000 | 🍶 ⚬ | 5–8 € |

☛ Eric et Chantal Coudert-Appert, Le Colombier, 69820 Fleurie, tel. 04.74.69.86.07, fax 04.74.04.12.66 ☑
☗ ev. day 8am–8pm
☛ Michel Appert

DOM. CHIGNARD

Les Moriers 2001

| ■ | n.c. | 25,000 | 🍶 | 5–8 € |

☛ Michel Chignard, Le Point du Jour, 69820 Fleurie, tel. 04.74.04.11.87, fax 04.74.69.81.97 ☑
☗ ev. day except Sun. 8am–12 noon 1.30pm–7pm

DOM. COTEAU DE BEL AIR

Cuvée Tradition 2001

| ■ | 1 ha | 3,000 | ⚌ | 5–8 € |

☛ Jean-Marie Appert, Bel-Air, 69115 Chiroubles, tel. 04.74.04.23.77, fax 04.74.69.17.13 ☑
☗ by appt.

DOM. DES GRANDS FERS 2001

| ■ | 10 ha | 50,000 | 🍶 ⚬ | 5–8 € |

☛ SARL Christian Bernard, Les Grands Fers, 69820 Fleurie, tel. 04.74.04.11.27, fax 04.74.69.86.64, e-mail vins@christianbernard.fr ☑
☗ by appt.

DOM. LUCIEN LARDY

Le Vivier Vieilles Vignes 2001

| ■ | 1.8 ha | 10,000 | 🍶 ⚌ | 8–11 € |

☛ Lucien Lardy, Le Vivier, 69820 Fleurie, tel. 04.74.69.81.74, fax 04.74.04.12.30 ☑
☗ by appt.

DOM. DES MARRANS 2001

| ■ | 10 ha | 13,500 | 🍶 | 8–11 € |

☛ Jean-Jacques et Liliane Melinand, Les Marrans, 69820 Fleurie, tel. 04.74.04.13.21, fax 04.74.69.82.45, e-mail melinand.m@wanadoo.fr ☑ 🏠
☗ by appt.

DOM. MATHRAY 2001

| ■ | 2.51 ha | 4,000 | 🍶 | 5–8 € |

☛ Jean-Paul Mathray, Montgenas, 69820 Fleurie, tel. 04.74.04.13.84, fax 04.74.69.85.69 ☑
☗ by appt.

DOM. MICHEL PERRIER

Les Marrants 2002

| ■ | 1.4 ha | 3,300 | 🍶 ⚬ | 5–8 € |

☛ Michel Perrier, 69820 Fleurie, tel. 04.74.69.83.05, fax 04.74.69.84.92 ☑
☗ by appt.

DOM. DE ROCHE-GUILLON 2002

| ■ | 4 ha | 20,000 | 🍶 ⚬ | 5–8 € |

☛ Bruno Coperet, Roche-Guillon, 69820 Fleurie, tel. 04.74.69.85.34, fax 04.74.04.10.25, e-mail roche-guillon.coperet@wanadoo.fr ☑ 🏠
☗ by appt.

DOM. DES TROIS TERROIRS 2002

| ■ | 4 ha | 2,000 | 🍶 | 5–8 € |

☛ Hubert Perraud, le Bourg, rte du Thyl, 69820 Fleurie, tel. 04.74.69.93.53, fax 04.74.69.90.92 ☑
☗ by appt.

Juliénas

A wine with an imperial heritage, Juliénas does indeed owe its name to Julius Caesar, as does Jullié, another of the four communes which make up the vineyard (the others are Emeringes and Pruzilly, which is just over the border in Saône-et-Loire). The soil in the western part of the vineyard is granite while in the east the soil is sedimentary with ancient alluvial deposits. Its 609 ha are planted exclusively with Gamay, and produced 31,814 hl of well-structured wine in 2002. The richly-coloured wines drink well in the spring, after being kept only a few months. They are as vigorous and spirited as the characters on the frescoes in the Caveau de l'Église, the wine-tasting cellar in the centre of the town where, in November of each year, the Victor Peyrat prize ceremony is held. The prize is awarded to the artist, painter, writer or journalist who has celebrated the crus with the most distinction. The actual prize consists of 104 bottles of wine, two for each weekend in the year. The Cave Coopérative, situated in the old priory of the Château du Bois de la Salle, vinifies 30% of the appellation.

CH. BONNET
Vieilles Vignes 2002★

■	1.8 ha	12,000	■ ♦	5–8 €

This château was built in 1630 by Claude Bonnet, and remained in the same family until 1973, when it was bought by Pierre Perrachon. Since 2000, his son has been in charge. His Vieilles Vignes, made from 50-year-old vines, has a dark-ruby colour and releases perfumes of cherry and redcurrant with musky notes. The straightforward attack continues on a balanced palate with good length. Although it is ready now, it would be better if kept for two years.

➤ Pierre-Yves Perrachon, Ch. Bonnet, 71570 La Chapelle-de-Guinchay, tel. 03.85.36.70.41, fax 03.85.36.77.27, e-mail chbonnet@terre-net.fr ☑
☙ by appt.

DOM. LE CHAPON 2002★

■	4.92 ha	13,000	■ ⏍	5–8 €

This wine was made from 45-year-old vines grown on a soil of granite and clay and was matured for ten months. It has a ruby colour with purple highlights and releases scents of under-growth accompanied by pronounced and very pleasant shades of vanilla and soft fruits. An honest attack reveals excellent tannins which are still young but balanced, along with very pleasant flavours of soft fruits and a slight taste of oak. This wine should be laid down for two years.

➤ Jean Buiron, Le Chapon, 69840 Juliénas, tel. 04.74.04.40.39, fax 04.74.04.47.52 ☑
☙ by appt.

DOM. DE LA CROIX ROUGE 2002★★

■	2 ha	13,000	■ ♦	5–8 €

This brilliant deep-red wine was made from 35-year-old vines. It has very pleasant perfumes of soft fruits (cranberry) and blackcurrant with peppery notes. Its richness on the palate underlines the balance between the fruitiness of the flesh and the fine tannins. This Juliénas is full and rounded, elegant with good length of flavour, and is ready now but could be kept for one or two years.

➤ Pascal Granger, Les Poupets, 69840 Juliénas, tel. 04.74.03.52.72, fax 04.74.03.38.58 ☑

DOM. DAVID-BEAUPÈRE
Le Saint-Antoine Elevé en fût de chêne 2001★

■	1.8 ha	6,800	⏍	8–11 €

This special vintage takes its name from the Clos Saint-Antoine, a wine-growing estate in the high plateaux of Algeria which was owned by five generations of the David family up to 1962. This pure-red 2001 releases fruity and floral perfumes, which have not aged, and a fine oakiness from its eight-month maturation in barrel. The palate shows good signs of development in the still youthful tannins, the fruity flavours and the oak. This is a very well-made and balanced wine.

➤ Dom. David-Beaupère, La Bottière, 69840 Juliénas, tel. 03.85.33.86.67, fax 03.85.36.70.35 ☑
☙ by appt.
➤ GFA Saint-Antoine

THIERRY DESCOMBES
Coteau des Vignes 2002★

■	3.3 ha	10,000	■ ♦	5–8 €

Thierry Descombes belongs to the fourth generation to farm these hillside vines. His wine has a very clear, deep-garnet colour and releases perfumes of peony evolving towards a mineral scent, and nuances of *pêche de vigne* and pear. The palate is fairly full bodied, combining roundness with compact tannins, and shows excellent balance. A member of the Jury described this fruity wine as "well born and well brought up." It is ready to drink now or can be kept for two years. Serve it with red meat.

➤ Thierry Descombes, Les Vignes, 69840 Jullié, tel. 04.74.04.42.03, fax 04.74.04.42.03 ☑
☙ ev. day 8am–8pm

CH. D'ENVAUX 2002★★

■	5 ha	10,000	⏍	5–8 €

In the west of the Juliénas region, the château d'Envaux was built in the 16th century. It has belonged to the same family for nearly four hundred years. This ruby 2002 with sparkling purple highlights was matured in enormous cellars. It has very expressive and unusually long perfumes of kirsch, raspberry, peony and cherry jam. There is an impressive structure with firm tannins and a complex aromatic range of flavours in which the raspberry reappears, along with wild strawberry and mineral touches. This is a well-balanced, sound, traditional and high-class Juliénas which could be laid down for at least two or three years.

➤ Yves de Coligny, Vaux, 69840 Juliénas, tel. 04.74.04.45.48, fax 04.74.04.45.48 ☑ ⌂
☙ by appt.

P. GRANGER
Cuvée spéciale 2002★

■	1.5 ha	10,000	■ ⏍ ♦	5–8 €

This purplish-red wine was made in the former village church (open to the public outside the harvest period). It has intense and very elegant nuances of soft fruits and flowers. The rich, vinous palate with its supple, fruity tannins shows great finesse. This remarkable Juliénas, combining length, good structure and delicacy, is ready to drink now but could be kept for another year. Also recommended was the estate's **Moulin-à-Vent 2002**.

➤ Pascal Granger, Les Poupets, 69840 Juliénas, tel. 04.74.04.44.79, fax 04.74.04.41.24 ☑
☙ by appt.

DOM. DU GREFFEUR 2001★

■	2 ha	2,600	■ ⏍	5–8 €

This clear and brilliant-red wine was matured for six months, first in tank and then in barrel. It opens with an intense bouquet of soft fruits, flowers, spicy notes and good vinosity. A sustained and clear-cut attack is followed by aromas of ripe fruits and spices in a palate marked by soft tannins. This is an attractive, fresh wine with good length that is ready to drink now.

➤ Jean-Claude Lespinasse, Les Marmets, 71570 La Chapelle-de-Guinchay, tel. 03.85.36.70.42, fax 03.85.33.85.49 ☑
☙ by appt.

DOM. JANIN BOIS DE LA SALLE 2002★

■	3.5 ha	15,000	■	5–8 €

In 2001, Michel Janin changed the name of his estate. His dark-red Juliénas was made from 60-year-old vines and opens with perfumes of cherry and flowers, with delicate notes of small soft fruits. The first impression is rounded and continues on a palate with fine tannins and aromas of fruits (cranberry). This wine is ready now, but could be kept for one or two years.

➤ Michel Janin, Bois de la Salle, 69840 Juliénas, tel. 04.74.04.44.74, fax 04.74.04.44.45 ☑ ⌂
☙ by appt.

DOM. MAISON DE LA DIME 2002★★

■	6 ha	20,000	■ ♦	5–8 €

The Maison de la Dîme de Juliénas (the tithe house) has fine architecture with two galleries of superimposed arcades, and has been listed as a historic monument since 1927. It has a wine-growing estate of 6.5 ha. Its 2002 vintage has a clear and brilliant-purple colour with garnet glints, and releases floral perfumes (iris, peony and wallflower) with nuances of spices and blackcurrant. The palate is pleasant, full bodied, fresh and long, with a very beautiful structure of sweet and spicy tannins. This promising wine is already good to drink, but can be kept for two years. Serve it with an entrecôte.

➤ François Mignot, 435, rue du Beaujolais, 69830 Saint-Georges-de-Reneins, tel. 04.74.09.60.00, fax 04.74.09.60.17 ☑

DOM. JEAN-PIERRE MARGERAND
2002★★

| ■ | 5 ha | 10,000 | | 5–8 € |

This family of winemakers has been established in the Beaujolais for many generations. Their crimson wine with lovely garnet highlights releases sumptuous perfumes of iris and soft fruits. The full-bodied palate reveals a tannic structure of excellent balance and attractive and long-lasting aromas of flowers and wild strawberry. This remarkable Juliénas has not yet opened out fully but is already characteristic of the appellation. Keep it for one or two years.
☛ Jean-Pierre Margerand, Les Crots, 69840 Juliénas, tel. 04.74.04.40.86, fax 04.74.04.46.54, e-mail contact@dom-jp-margerand.com ☑
𝕀 by appt.

DOM. MATRAY
Vieilles Vignes Elevé en fût de chêne 2001★

| ■ | 1.3 ha | 8,000 | �**III** | 5–8 € |

In 1988, Lilian Matray took over the work of four generations of winemakers. Her Juliénas Vieilles Vignes is made from vines more than 60 years old and was matured in oak for ten months. It has a clear garnet colour and releases pleasant scents of spice and vanilla. Its richness is immediately apparent in the aromas of raspberry and an elegant oakiness. This clean, soft and balanced Juliénas is ready to drink now but can be kept for one or two years. Also recommended is the **Juliénas 2002** which was not matured in oak.
☛ EARL Lilian et Sandrine Matray, Les Paquelets, 69840 Juliénas, tel. 04.74.04.45.57, fax 04.74.04.47.63, e-mail domaine.matray@wanadoo.fr ☑
𝕀 ev. day 8am–8pm

DOM. DE LA MILLERANCHE 2001★

| ■ | 4 ha | 11,000 | ▮ | 5–8 € |

This clear ruby wine was made from 45-year-old vines grown by the Terra Vitis method of sustainable agriculture. It has pure and persistent perfumes of soft fruits, and notes of undergrowth and iris. The slightly feminine aromas of this Juliénas are counterbalanced by a rich structure with dense tannins. It is already beautifully developed but could be kept for one or two years to mature further.
☛ Jérôme Corsin, Le Bourg, 69840 Jullié, tel. 04.74.04.40.64, fax 04.74.04.49.36, e-mail milleranche.corsin@wanadoo.fr ☑
𝕀 by appt.

DOM. J.-M. MONNET 2002★

| ■ | 4.6 ha | 4,000 | ▮ ♦ | 5–8 € |

This tenancy of château Juliénas has produced a fresh and brilliant red wine with delicate fruity perfumes. A good attack is followed by aromas of soft fruits, blackcurrant and blackberry, well supported by young and fairly fine tannins. Long and well structured, this Juliénas needs two years to mature.
☛ Jean-Marc Monnet, 69840 Juliénas, tel. 04.74.06.10.10, fax 04.74.66.13.77 ☑
𝕀 by appt.

DOM. MARIUS SANGOUARD 2001★

| ■ | n.c. | 16,500 | ▮ | 5–8 € |

The firm of Trénel Fils was set up in 1928. Its clear, light-ruby and slightly brick-red Juliénas has lovely perfumes of soft fruits with floral notes (peony and iris) with a touch of mint. After a fruity attack, the tasting continues on a more supple note. This 2001 wine is full of flavour and well balanced, and is ready to drink now. The estate's **Morgon Trénel Fils Côte de Py 2001** was also singled out.
☛ Trénel et Fils, 33, chem. du Buéry, 71850 Charmay-lès-Mâcon, tel. 03.85.34.48.20, fax 03.85.20.55.01, e-mail info@trenel.com ☑
𝕀 ev. day except Sun. 8am–6pm;
Mon. 2pm–6pm and Sat. 8am–12noon; Feb. by appt.

CELLIER DE LA VIELLE ÉGLISE
Cuvée fût de chêne 2001★★

| ■ | n.c. | 1,000 | �**III** | 8–11 € |

In the centre of Juliénas, the old church which had been unused since 1868 became, on the initiative of Victor Peyret, the Cellier de la Vieille Eglise and is managed by the association of Juliénas producers. It holds tastings and various events, including the award of the V. Peyret prize for the best eulogists of the appellation, covering journalists, writers and artists. There is also a permanent photographic exhibition on wines and winemaking. After the *coup de coeur* won by their 2000 vintage, the **2001 (5–8 €)** has to be content with two stars, but did receive high praise. It was matured for eight months in oak, and has a lovely ruby colour with shades of garnet. Its excellent and complex perfumes reflect its origins, a blend of stewed fruits, undergrowth and vanilla. The structure with rounded tannins gives it good balance. This is a well-made, full and natural Juliénas, ready to drink now, but it can be kept for one or two years.
☛ Cellier de la Vieille Eglise, le Bourg, 69840 Juliénas, tel. 04.74.04.42.98, fax 04.74.04.42.98 ☑
𝕀 ev. day 9.45am–12 noon 2.30pm–6.30pm

Wines selected but not starred

LES CAPITANS 2002

| ■ | 3 ha | 20,000 | | 5–8 € |

☛ Louis Tête, 69430 Saint-Didier-sur-Beaujeu, tel. 04.74.04.82.27, fax 04.74.69.28.61

CH. DE JULIENAS 2001

| ■ | n.c. | 10,000 | ▮ ♦ | 5–8 € |

☛ François et Thierry Condemine, Ch. de Juliénas, 69840 Juliénas, tel. 04.74.04.41.43, fax 04.74.04.42.38 ☑

PATRICE MARTIN 2002

| ■ | 0.85 ha | 2,000 | ▮ | 5–8 € |

☛ Patrice Martin, Le Village, 71570 Chânes, tel. 03.85.36.53.58 ☑
𝕀 by appt.

DOM. DU MATINAL
Les Capitans 2002

| ■ | 0.68 ha | 3,900 | ▮ | 5–8 € |

☛ Noël Musy, Le Bourg, 69840 Chénas, tel. 04.74.04.48.31, fax 04.74.04.47.64 ☑
𝕀 ev. day 8am–7pm; groups by appt.

DOM. DES MOUILLES 2002

| ■ | 4.5 ha | 34,000 | ▮ �**III** ♦ | 5–8 € |

☛ Laurent Perrachon, Dom. des Mouilles, 69840 Juliénas, tel. 04.74.04.40.44, fax 04.74.04.40.44, e-mail laurent.perrachon@wanadoo.fr ☑
𝕀 by appt.

DOM. M. PELLETIER
Les Envaux 2002

| ■ | 3.28 ha | 10,600 | �**III** | 5–8 € |

☛ Pelletier, 69840 Juliénas, tel. 04.74.06.10.10, fax 04.74.66.13.77 ☑
𝕀 by appt.

DOM. DU PENLOIS 2002

■	1.92 ha	13,000	■ ♦	5–8 €

🍷 SCEA Besson Père et Fils, Dom. du Penlois,
69220 Lancié, tel. 04.74.04.13.35, fax 04.74.69.82.07,
e-mail domaine-du-penlois@wanadoo.fr ☑
🍴 by appt.

MICHEL REY
Les Paquelets Vieilles Vignes 2001

■	1.11 ha	3,500	◀▮▶	5–8 €

🍷 Michel Rey, Le Repostère, 71960 Vergisson,
tel. 03.85.35.85.78, fax 03.85.35.87.91,
e-mail michel.rey19@wanadoo.fr ☑
🍴 by appt.

DOM. SANCY 2002

■	7.5 ha	7,000	◀▮▶	3–5 €

🍷 Bernard Broyer, Les Bucherats, 69840 Juliénas,
tel. 04.74.04.46.75, fax 04.74.04.45.18 ☑
🍴 by appt.

BERNARD SANTE 2002

■	2.5 ha	15,000	■ ♦	5–8 €

🍷 Bernard Santé, rte de Juliénas, 71570 La
Chapelle-de-Guinchay, tel. 03.85.33.82.81,
fax 03.85.33.84.46, e-mail bernardsante@terre-net.fr ☑
🍴 by appt.

DOM. GUY VOLUET 2002

■	n.c.	20,000	■ ♦	5–8 €

🍷 Jean-Marc Aujoux, Les Chers, 69840 Juliénas,
tel. 04.74.06.78.00, fax 04.74.06.78.71, e-mail avf@free.fr ☑

Morgon

Morgon is the second largest
cru after Brouilly, its vineyards located in a single
commune. The 1,132 ha of AOC produced 63,966 hl
of robust, generous, fruity wine with flavours of
cherry, bitter cherry and apricot. It is often the most
robust of the crus and many of its characteristics
come from the soil which is made from weathered,
mainly alkaline shale with deposits of ferrous oxide
and manganese, described by the local winemakers
as terre pourrie or rotten land. It is said of the
Morgon wines that they morgonne, *i.e.* that they
develop in their own unique way. The situation of the
vineyard is particularly propitious for Gamay and
makes a wine that is for keeping and which, with age,
can take on some of the qualities of a red Burgundy.
It is a robust enough wine to drink with coq au vin.
The soil of the Py hill, which rises 300 m in a perfectly
shaped rump near the old Roman road between Lyon
and Autun, is typical of the area.

The commune of Villié-Morgon
is justifiably proud to have been the first to promote
their wines, encouraging wine-drinkers who appreciate Beaujolais to visit the wine-tasting cellars in the
Château de Fontcrenne which can cater for several
hundred visitors. The cellar has a welcoming atmosphere which is very popular with the visitors and
associations who visit.

DOM. AUCOEUR
Tradition Vieilles Vignes 2001★★★

■	4 ha	20,000	■ ♦	5–8 €

This estate dating from 1825 has been regularly mentioned in
the *Guide*, sometimes as a top producer. It is now run by the
ninth generation. It offers walks and tastings of old wines
going back more than 20 years. This very deep-garnet 2001
has a bouquet of cherry and plum with shades of chocolate, is
chewy and fills the mouth. This pleasant, fresh-tasting and
full wine with soft tannins has good length and can be drunk
over the next five years.
🍷 Dom. Aucoeur, Le Rochaud, 69910 Villié-Morgon,
tel. 04.74.04.22.10, fax 04.74.69.16.82 ☑
🍴 ev. day 9.30am–12 noon 2pm–7pm

CH. DE BELLEVUE 2001★★

■	n.c.	n.c.	■	11–15 €

The two châteaux in the Beaujolais region which belong to
this company from Beaune are in the honours list: in this
edition of the *Guide*, this clear garnet Morgon has won the
coup de coeur. Its very intense perfumes blend coffee and
vanilla with fruity nuances. The palate is very pleasant, based
on a fruity and long flesh. This wine has remarkable balance
and is already excellent, but can be kept for one or two years.
Meanwhile the **Moulin-à-Vent Château des Jacques 2001** was
awarded one star.
🍷 Maison Louis Jadot, 21, rue Eugène-Spuller,
21200 Beaune, tel. 03.80.22.10.57, fax 03.80.22.56.03,
e-mail contact@louisjadot.com
🍴 by appt.

DOM. PATRICK BOULAND 2002★★

■	6 ha	8,000	■ ◀▮▶	5–8 €

Patrick Bouland has been in business for 20 years and has
appeared more than once in the *Guide*. One of his Morgons
won two stars in the last edition, and this 2002 follows suit. It
was made from 40-year-old vines in a traditional manner. It
has a deep-garnet colour and pleasant perfumes of soft fruits
with peppery nuances. The consistent and mouth-filling
palate has a balanced tannic structure and fruity flavours.
This remarkable Morgon is still young but already rich and
long, though not excessively so. Keep it for one year, and serve
with red meat and charcuterie.
🍷 Patrick Bouland, 77, montée des Rochauds,
69910 Villié-Morgon, tel. 04.74.69.16.20,
fax 04.74.69.13.55, e-mail patrick.bouland@free.fr ☑
🍴 by appt.

Morgon

CH. DE LA BOURDONNIERE 2001★

■	5.2 ha	18,750	🍷 ◖◗ ♦		5–8 €

This fiefdom of the château de Thulon has had a vineyard since 1669. The buildings were partly reconstructed at the end of the 18th century. The Witrant family have worked the estate for five generations, the latest one taking over in 2001. Its Morgon was matured for more than a year, and has a slightly brick-red colour and complex perfumes of soft fruits and oak with some musky notes. On the palate, it is balanced, long and shows good finesse, like some of its neighbours to the north. This is a full, rounded wine which is ready to drink now but can be kept this year with game.
☛ Jérôme Witrant, 69430 Lantignié, tel. 04.74.04.82.58, fax 04.74.69.52.63,
e-mail jerome.witrant@wanadoo.fr ☑ 🏛
✲ by appt.

DOM. NOEL BULLIAT

Cuvée Vieilles Vignes 2001★

■	0.7 ha	4,000	◖◗	5–8 €

Noël Bulliat cultivates 10 ha in three Beaujolais appellations. His Morgon Vieilles Vignes is regularly selected in the *Guide*. It is made from vines about 80 years old, and has a dark-red, almost purple colour with a slight oakiness. The persistent and well-integrated tannins fill the mouth pleasantly, but the oaky taste is still predominant. It would be best to keep it for a few months.
☛ Noël Bulliat, Le Colombier, 69910 Villié-Morgon, tel. 04.74.69.13.51, fax 04.74.69.14.09,
e-mail noel.bulliat@wanadoo.fr ☑
✲ by appt.

MAISON CHANDESAIS 2001★

■	n.c.	n.c.	8–11 €

This purple Morgon with garnet highlights releases intense perfumes of morello cherry and stewed fruits, along with mineral notes suggesting moist granite. The palate reveals soft tannins and finishes on a note of liquorice. This long and fresh *vin de terroir* is ready to drink now. It will go well with a grilled côte de mouton. The same estate's **red Beaujolais-Villages Château de Néty 2002 (5–8 €)** also receives one star.
☛ Maison Chandesais, Château Saint-Nicolas, 71150 Fontaines, tel. 03.85.87.51.17, fax 03.85.87.51.12

ARMAND ET RICHARD CHATELET

Cuvée du P'tit Moustachu Elevé en fût de chêne 2001★★

■	1 ha	7,000	◖◗	5–8 €

Richard Chatelet is a graduate in oenology and joined up with his father, Armand, in 1998. They have made a remarkable dark-ruby Morgon which releases intense perfumes of very ripe soft fruits, roasted coffee and fresh grapes. It was matured for six months in oak and has a very good oaky flavour, blending with strong fruity and spicy notes. This is a complex wine which can be drunk now but could be kept for two or three years.
☛ EARL Armand et Richard Chatelet, Les Marcellins, 69910 Villié-Morgon, tel. 04.74.04.21.08, fax 04.74.69.16.48,
e-mail armand-richard-chatelet@tiscali.fr ☑
✲ ev. day except Sun. 8am–12 noon 2pm–7pm

DOM. DU CHAZELAY 2001★★

■	2 ha	10,000	🍷 ♦	5–8 €

Henri Chavy and his two sons work this estate which the grandfather occupied as a tenant. They are a talented trio, to judge from their **Régnié 2002**, and from this crimson Morgon which opens quickly on clean and expressive perfumes of ripe cherry with pleasant nuances of herbs and peony. It is both fleshy and full bodied with rich flavours of fruits and peach stone, and has remained remarkably fresh. This high-class 2001 has kept its youthfulness. Drink it over the next three years with, for example, poultry.
☛ Henri Chavy, Le Chazelet, 69430 Régnié, tel. 04.74.69.24.34, fax 04.74.69.20.00 ☑
✲ by appt.

CAVE JEAN-ERNEST DESCOMBES
2002★

■	1 ha	7,500	🍷	8–11 €

This family property's wines have been distributed by the G. Duboeuf company since 1967. This Morgon has an intense red colour and complex perfumes blending violet and musky notes. The palate is balanced, fine and long. This well-made wine could be drunk this year with game.
☛ Nicole Descombes, Les Micouds, 69910 Villié-Morgon, tel. 04.74.04.21.92, fax 04.74.04.26.04 ☑
✲ by appt.

DOM. DONZEL

Cuvée Prestige 2001★★★

■	1.3 ha	10,000	◖◗	5–8 €

This vineyard was set up in 1948 and is run by the second generation. The 2001 vintage has produced their best wine, winning the Grand Jury's *coup de coeur*. This dark-crimson Prestige has intense perfumes of very ripe soft fruits and nuances of grilling, coffee and spices which develop with great finesse. The superb, balanced palate continues the first impressions pleasantly. A broad range of flavours enfold the rich body which is not unlike that of a Burgundy. This high-quality Morgon can be drunk now with côte de boeuf, gigot or cheeses, but could also be kept for two to five years. The **Morgon Tradition 2001**, matured in tank, has also been singled out.
☛ Bernard Donzel, Fondlong, 69910 Villié-Morgon, tel. 04.74.04.20.56, fax 04.74.69.14.52 ☑
✲ by appt.

GAEC DES GAUDETS 2002★

■	1.8 ha	13,000	🍷	5–8 €

The son joined up with his father in 1993. Their Morgon 2000 won a *coup de coeur*. This one has an intense, clear bright-ruby colour and opens on elegant notes of soft fruits. Its tannic structure is well developed, and with the flavours of very ripe fruits forms a concentrated, characteristic wine with good balance. This complex Morgon is ready to drink now but can be kept for three years. The same estate's **Régnié 2002 (3–5 €)** also received one star. It is fleshy, full of red fruit and long. Serve it with poultry.
☛ Noël et Christophe Sornay, GAEC des Gaudets, Le Brye, 69910 Villié-Morgon, tel. 04.74.04.21.69, fax 04.74.69.10.70 ☑
✲ by appt.

J. GONARD ET FILS 2001★★★

■	1.5 ha	4,000	◖◗	5–8 €

The wines selected by this négociant specializing in the wines of the Beaujolais and the Mâconnais were very well received. The well-balanced **Moulin-à-Vent 2001** was awarded one star, while this Morgon was one of the best the Jury tasted. It has a clear deep-garnet colour and releases intense perfumes of morello cherry and nuances of caramel and almond. In line with the bouquet, the palate opens out strongly and at length, disclosing a beautiful balance and structure and characteristic Morgon flavours. This well-made wine gave real pleasure. It is ready to drink now but will keep for five years.
☛ SARL J. Gonard et Fils, La Varenne, Jullie, 69840 Juliénas, tel. 04.74.04.45.20, fax 04.74.04.45.69 ☑
✲ ev. day 9am–12 noon 2pm–7pm

DOM. DE GRY-SABLON 2002★

	2.37 ha	18,000	■ ◫ ♦		5–8 €

This 13.5-ha estate is well known to readers of the *Guide*, and produces four versions of Beaujolais. The wine cellar was renovated in 2001. The **Juliénas 2002** was singled out, but the Jury preferred this ruby Morgon with beautiful garnet highlights. Its very expressive perfumes of blackcurrant and redcurrant reflect a modern winemaking method based on maximum extraction from the grapes. The palate is full, chewy and well balanced with high-class tannins. This enjoyable wine is ready now.
↰ Dominique Morel, Les Chavannes, 69840 Emeringes, tel. 04.74.04.45.35, fax 04.74.04.42.66, e-mail gry-sablon@wanadoo.fr ☑
Ⅰ by appt.

DOM. JENNY

Côte-du-Py 2002★

	n.c.	40,000	■ ♦		5–8 €

The purplish colour indicates the strength of this wine. On the palate, flavours of ripe fruit and leather jostle with a lively fullness and tannins. This promising Morgon has a beautiful richness and good potential, but needs a year to mature. Then it will undoubtedly give pleasure for several years.
↰ Chanut Joannès, Les Chers, 69840 Juliénas, tel. 04.74.06.78.00, fax 04.74.06.78.71
Ⅰ by appt.

DOM. DE LEYRE-LOUP

Corcelette 2001★

	6.24 ha	24,000	■		5–8 €

This family estate was started ten years ago, and devotes its 6 ha of vines entirely to Morgon. The bright-ruby 2001 has pretty highlights and opens on intense perfumes of roasting, spices and undergrowth. Its beautiful tannic structure combines well with flavours of kirsch. This wine could be drunk now and over the next three years.
↰ Christophe Lanson, 20, rue de l'Oratoire, 69300 Caluire, tel. 04.78.29.24.10, fax 04.78.28.00.57, e-mail cclanson@wanadoo.fr
Ⅰ by appt.

DOM. DES PILLETS

Les Charmes Cuvée Vieilles Vignes 2001★

	1.5 ha	6,000	◫	8–11 €

The Pillets have a 35-ha estate mainly given over to Morgon. One of the principal buildings dates from the 18th century and has vaulted cellars, and the winery buildings are 19th century. This Vieilles Vignes was made from 60-year-old vines and the previous vintage won a *coup de coeur*. The clear dark-ruby 2001 releases characteristic perfumes of morello cherry and very ripe strawberry. It was matured for 18 months in barrel, has rounded tannins and is both fruity and balanced. This well-made wine is ready to drink, but could be kept for two or three years. The **Morgon Les Charmes 2001**, made from 45-year-old vines and aged in tank, was also singled out – and there are 40,000 bottles of it!
↰ Gérard Brisson, chem. des Romains, Les Pillets, 69910 Villié-Morgon, tel. 04.74.04.21.60, fax 04.74.69.15.28 ☑
Ⅰ ev. day except Sun. 9am–12 noon 1.30pm–7pm; cl. 15–31 Aug., 20–31 Dec.

DOM. DU PUITS BENI 2002★

	2.3 ha	15,000	■		5–8 €

Since it was established in 1927, the Fleurie cooperative has made many improvements. Following changes to the winery and its temperature regulation, a new sales room was built in 2003. Their bright-ruby Morgon opens with complex notes of fruits and mineral. On the palate, redcurrant, cherry and spices combine with a good tannic structure. This balanced and well-made Morgon can be drunk over the next two years.
↰ Cave Prod. des Grands Vins de Fleurie, BP 2, 69820 Fleurie, tel. 04.74.04.11.70, fax 04.74.69.84.73, e-mail cave-de-fleurie@wanadoo.fr ☑
Ⅰ by appt.

DOM. DE LA ROCHE PILEE 2001★★

	2.5 ha	16,000		5–8 €

This clear ruby wine was made from 40-year-old vines grown on a sandy and stony soil. It releases rich and long-lasting perfumes of cherry, kirsch and spices. These aromas combine with the full-bodied substance to give a pleasant and well-balanced wine. Drink it over the next two years with white meat.
↰ Bernard Botteron, Bellevue, 69910 Villié-Morgon, tel. 04.74.04.25.98, fax 04.74.69.11.97 ☑

DOM. DE ROCHE SAINT JEAN

Côte-du-Py 2001★★

	1 ha	5,000	■ ◫		5–8 €

Bernard Mathon produces just over 13 ha of Morgon. His Côte-du-Py was matured for 16 months, eight of these in barrel. It has a very fresh bright-crimson colour and characteristic perfumes of kirsch and with damson, peppery nuances which blend nicely with oaky notes and a hint of fresh hay. It is very well balanced with supple, rounded tannins and a rich body with lasting toasty notes. This harmonious wine can be drunk now or kept for three years.
↰ SCEA Bernard Mathon, Bellevue, dom. de Roche-Saint-Jean, 69910 Villié-Morgon, tel. 04.74.04.23.92, fax 04.74.04.23.92 ☑
Ⅰ by appt.

HENRI SERVAGE 2001★

	1.19 ha	9,000	■		5–8 €

This clear garnet wine with lovely purple glints was made from 50-year-old vines grown on a shale and clay soil. Strong palatal aromas combine with a structured palate with rather pronounced but pleasant tannins. This balanced, rich and characteristic Morgon can be drunk now or laid down for two or three years.
↰ Henri Servage, Les Marcellins, 69910 Villié-Morgon, tel. 04.74.69.14.80, fax 04.74.04.20.31, e-mail henri.servage-morgon.beaujolais@wanadoo.fr ☑ ⌂
Ⅰ by appt.

DOM. DES SOUCHONS

Cuvée Tradition 2002★

	10 ha	60,000	■	8–11 €

This estate dates from 1752. It has been gradually expanded and today grows 14 ha of Morgon. Its clear garnet wine was made from 50-year-old vines and releases perfumes of very ripe soft fruits and notes of undergrowth. The palate is rich and full bodied, and also well balanced despite the youthful tannins which appear at the finish. This is a good representative of the appellation, and is worth waiting for.
↰ Serge Condemine-Pillet, Morgon-le-Bas, 69910 Villié-Morgon, tel. 04.74.69.14.45, fax 04.74.69.15.43, e-mail domainesouchons@free.fr ☑
Ⅰ ev. day 8.30am–12 noon 2pm–7pm

Wines selected but not starred

DOM. DU BOIS DE LYS 2001

	0.85 ha	7,000	■ ♦		5–8 €

↰ Georges Boulon, le Bourg, 69115 Chiroubles, tel. 04.74.04.27.27, fax 04.74.69.13.16, e-mail georges-boulon@wanadoo.fr ☑
Ⅰ ev. day 8am–12noon 2pm–6pm

RAYMOND BOULAND

Corcelette 2001

| ■ | 6 ha | 10,000 | ▮ | 5–8 € |

➶ Raymond Bouland, Corcelette, 69910 Villié-Morgon,
tel. 04.74.04.22.25, fax 04.74.04.22.25 ☑
☖ by appt.

DOM. JEAN-LOUIS BRUN

Côte-du-Py 2002

| ■ | 4.41 ha | 8,000 | ◫ | 5–8 € |

➶ Jean-Louis Brun, 69910 Villié-Morgon,
tel. 04.74.06.10.10, fax 04.74.66.13.77 ☑
☖ by appt.

JEAN-MARC BURGAUD

Côte-du-Py 2001

| ■ | 7 ha | 20,000 | ▮ | 5–8 € |

➶ Jean-Marc Burgaud, 69910 Villié-Morgon,
tel. 04.74.69.16.10, fax 04.74.69.16.10,
e-mail jeanmarcburgaud@libertysurf.fr ☑
☖ by appt.

CYRILLE CHAVY

Cuvée Vieilles Vignes 2002

| ■ | 2 ha | 5,000 | ▮◫☖ | 5–8 € |

➶ Cyrille Chavy, Les Versauds, 69910 Villié-Morgon,
tel. 04.74.04.20.47, fax 04.74.69.20.00 ☑
☖ by appt.

DOM. DE LA CROIX MULINS 2002

| ■ | 4.5 ha | 17,800 | ▮☖ | 5–8 € |

➶ Pierre Depardon, Les Raisses, 69910 Villié-Morgon,
tel. 04.74.69.10.15, fax 04.74.09.60.17
☖ by appt.

JEAN-MARC LAFONT

Côte-du-Py 2002

| ■ | 4.32 ha | 30,000 | ▮☖ | 5–8 € |

➶ SARL Bel Air, 69430 Lantignié, tel. 04.74.04.82.08,
fax 04.74.04.89.33, e-mail lafont-jean-marc@wanadoo.fr ☑
☖ ev. day 8am–6pm

ANDRÉ LAISSUS 2002

| ■ | n.c. | 5,000 | ▮ | 3–5 € |

➶ André Laissus, La Grange Charton,
69430 Régnié-Durette, tel. 04.74.04.38.06,
fax 04.74.04.37.75 ☑ ⌂
☖ ev. day 9am–8pm

DOM. CEDRIC LATHUILIERE 2001

| ■ | 1.5 ha | 6,000 | ▮ | 5–8 € |

➶ Dom. Cédric Lathuilière, Vermont,
69910 Villié-Morgon, tel. 04.74.69.17.81,
fax 04.74.04.27.76, e-mail c.lathuiliere@libertysurf.fr ☑
☖ ev. day 8am–12 noon 2pm–7pm

DOM. DE LA LEVRATIERE 2001

| ■ | 7.3 ha | 20,000 | ▮☖ | 5–8 € |

➶ André et Marylenn Meyran, Dom. de La Levratière, Les
Presles, 69910 Villié-Morgon, tel. 04.74.69.11.80,
fax 04.74.69.16.51, e-mail domlalevratiere@aol.com ☑
☖ by appt.

DOM. DES MULINS 2001

| ■ | 1 ha | 5,000 | | 5–8 € |

➶ Alain Aufranc, Dom. Les Mulins, 69910 Villié-Morgon,
tel. 04.74.69.13.02, fax 04.74.69.13.02 ☑
☖ by appt.

DOM. PASSOT-COLLONGE

Les Charmes 2001

| ■ | 2.5 ha | 7,750 | ▮☖ | 5–8 € |

➶ Bernard et Monique Passot, Le Colombier,
69910 Villié-Morgon, tel. 04.74.69.10.77,
fax 04.74.69.13.59, e-mail mbpassot@infonie.fr ☑ ⌂
☖ by appt.

DOM. DES ROCHES DU PY

Côte-du-Py 2001

| ■ | 5 ha | 20,000 | ▮ | 5–8 € |

➶ Marcel Jonchet, Côte du Py, 69910 Villié-Morgon,
tel. 04.74.04.23.03, fax 04.74.69.10.35 ☑
☖ by appt.

DOM. DES RONZE

Les Charmes 2001

| ■ | 1 ha | 5,000 | ◫ | 5–8 € |

➶ Mariane et Frédéric Sornin, 69430 Régnié,
tel. 04.74.04.87.46, fax 04.74.04.89.73,
e-mail mariane.sornin@domaine-des-ronze.com ☑
☖ by appt.

DOM. SAVOYE

Sur Côte-du-Py Cuvée Vieilles Vignes 2001

| ■ | 1.35 ha | 12,000 | ▮☖ | 8–11 € |

➶ Pierre Savoye, Les Micouds, 69910 Villié-Morgon,
tel. 04.74.04.21.92, fax 04.74.04.26.04,
e-mail pierre.savoye@wanadoo.fr ☑
☖ ev. day 8.30am–11.30am 1.30pm–6.30pm;
Sat. Sun. by appt.

Moulin-à-Vent

The domain of the "lord" of the Beaujolais crus is 681 ha of vineyard stretching over the communes of Chénas in the Rhône and Romanèche-Thorins in Saône-et-Loire. The emblem of the appellation is an ancient windmill at Les Thorins, standing proudly on the top of a gently rounded hillock, 240 m high, consisting of pure granite sand. In 2002 the vineyard produced 35,212 hl of wine made from Gamay grapes. The thin topsoil is rich in manganese and other minerals which give the wines their strong, deep colour and scent of iris. These are full-bodied wines, sometimes reminiscent of their sturdier Burgundy cousins in the Côte d'Or. Each year, in a traditional rite, the vintage is carried to the baptismal fonts in the local villages, starting at Romanèche-Thorins at the end of October and finishing at the "capital" in early December.

Moulin-à-Vent can readily be drunk young, in its first few months, but also keeps well for a number of years. This "prince" of wines was one of the first crus recognized as an Appellation d'Origine Contrôlée in 1936, after its borders were legally defined by the Civil Tribunal in Mâcon. There are two wine-cellars where you can taste the wine: one at the foot of the windmill and the other at the edge of the main road. Moulin-à-Vent will accompany any dish and hold its own against many other reds.

Moulin-à-Vent

DOM. BENOIT RACLET 2002★

| | 10 ha | 37,000 | | 5–8 € |

Benoît Raclet started up in the Beaujolais region at the beginning of the 19th century, and discovered a simple process for fighting the meal moth, which were destroying the vines, by scalding the grapes. He gave his name to this estate whose wines are distributed by the Thorin company. Its Moulin-à-Vent has a bright-garnet colour and opens with perfumes of blackberry and cherry. A fairly lively attack combines a rounded flesh and integrated tannins. It has good length and finishes with an alcoholic note. It should keep well and needs to be laid down for two years in the cellar before serving with game or red meat in sauce.
➤ Dom. Benoît Raclet, 71570 Romanèche-Thorins, tel. 04.74.69.09.10, fax 04.74.69.09.28, e-mail information@maisonthorin.com
➤ Frédérique Coste

DOM. DES CAVES

Cuvée Etalon 2001★★

| | 2 ha | 12,000 | | 5–8 € |

Laurent Gauthier is a young winemaker who started here in 1993. His estate takes its name from the small vaulted wine cellar dating from 1620. This is where he matured his Etalon, the jewel among the estate's wines which was awarded two stars last year. His 2001 vintage wins the Grand Jury's *coup de coeur*. The brilliant deep-ruby colour indicates the wine's youth. Its strong winey perfumes combine notes of roasted coffee, oak and spices. The palate has a powerful structure, the tannins still a little firm with nuances of undergrowth and oak, and a rich, harmonious and concentrated body which has great keeping potential. This wine is already remarkable, but should be laid down for a year or two. Serve it with game or meat in sauce. Look out too for the **Chénas Le Fief 2001** from the same estate (recommended).
➤ Laurent Gauthier, Les Caves, 69840 Chénas, tel. 04.74.69.86.59, fax 04.74.69.83.15 ✉
Ⴤ by appt.

DOM. MICHEL CROZET 2001★★

| | n.c. | 4,500 | | 8–11 € |

In 1976, Michel Crozet took over the estate founded by his grandfather in 1922 and expanded by his father. He cultivates just over 7 ha, a modest property in terms of area but one worth following; his Moulin-à-Vent, made from 50-year-old vines, was unanimously praised by the Grand Jury. It has a bright garnet colour and releases rich fruity perfumes with vanilla notes. The flesh is full, rounded and fairly long, and supports the clean, fresh attack. Integrated tannins give it great finesse. This well-balanced wine is ready to drink now, but could be kept for three or four years. It will go well with red meat and game.
➤ Michel Crozet, Les Fargets, 71570 Romanèche-Thorins, tel. 03.85.35.53.61, fax 03.85.35.20.16, e-mail michel.crozet@wanadoo.fr ✉
Ⴤ ev. day except Sun. 9am–12 noon 2pm-6.30pm

AMEDEE DEGRANGE 2001★

| | 2 ha | 10,000 | | 5–8 € |

Vines averaging 50 years of age went to make this clear garnet 2001. It opens with floral notes (peony), then fruity notes come to the fore. The clean and rounded attack is followed by impressions of freshness. This Moulin-à-Vent is well balanced and full of flavour, and is ready to drink now but could be kept for two years. Serve it with red meats and also white (côtes de veau).
➤ Dom. Amédée Degrange, Les Vérillats, 69840 Chénas, tel. 04.74.04.48.48, fax 04.74.04.46.35, e-mail domaine.a.degrange@free.fr ✉
Ⴤ ev. day 8am–12 noon 2pm–7pm

GEORGES DUBOEUF

Prestige 2001★

| | n.c. | 26,000 | | 5–8 € |

The firm of George Duboe has its headquarters in the Moulin-à-Vent region. Since it was set up in 1964, this company of négociants has always been innovative. At present it is forming service partnerships with wine producers from the growing stage until the wine is bottled. This Prestige wine is an example of the process. It has a bright-garnet colour and intense perfumes of spices and coffee with notes of roasting which continue on a balanced palate. The successful blending of wine and oak are the result of controlled maturation. This very fine 2001 is ready to drink now, but can be kept for two or three years. The **Beaujolais-Villages red 2002 (3–5 €)** wins one star and the **Beaujolais white 2001 (3–5 €)** is specially commended.
➤ SA Les Vins Georges Duboeuf, La Gare, BP 12, 71570 Romanèche-Thorins, tel. 03.85.35.34.20, fax 03.85.35.34.25, e-mail gduboeuf@duboeuf.com ✉
Ⴤ ev. day 9am–6pm at the Hameau-en-Beaujolais; cl. 1–15 Jan.

DOM. LES FINES GRAVES 2001★

| | 2 ha | 6,000 | | 5–8 € |

This estate's Moulin-à-Vent was thought remarkable last year, and the 2001 has also turned out very well. It is made from 50-year-old vines and was matured for six months in barrel. Its has a deep-ruby colour with clear-cut brick-red highlights. Its perfumes of vanilla and oak, combined with notes of stewed fruits, spices and undergrowth, are intense and elegant. The same flavours reappear on the palate, which has a fairly light structure. Its best points are its delicacy and attractive bouquet. Drink it in the next two years.
➤ Jacky Janodet, Les Garniers, 71570 Romanèche-Thorins, tel. 03.85.35.57.17, fax 03.85.35.21.69 ✉
Ⴤ by appt.

DOM. DE FORETAL 2002★

| | 1.25 ha | 4,000 | | 5–8 € |

This purplish-red wine was made from 40-year-old vines planted on clay-silicious soils. It has complex perfumes of plum and stone fruits with notes of vanilla, chocolate and aniseed. It is full bodied and elegant on the palate, the fruits more prominent than in the bouquet, with fairly fine tannins, and remains fresh-tasting. Drink it over the next three years with meat in sauce, game or cheese.
➤ Jacques et Marie-Thérèse Perraud, Forétal, 69820 Vauxrenard, tel. 04.74.69.90.45, fax 04.74.69.90.45, e-mail domaine.foretal@laposte.net ✉ 🏠
Ⴤ ev. day 8am–12 noon 1pm–7pm; cl. Sept.

DOM. GAY-COPERET

Cuvée Réserve Vieilles Vignes 2002★

| ■ | 6 ha | 8,000 | | 8–11 € |

This dark-garnet wine was made from 55-year-old vines, and opens on notes of very ripe soft fruits. The strength of the tannins is evident from the attack. This 2002 vintage is well structured and balanced, the nose more attractive than the palate. Keep it for a year to allow it to reach its best.
☛ Catherine et Maurice Gay, Les Vérillats, 69840 Chénas, tel. 04.74.04.48.86, fax 04.74.04.42.74,
e-mail gay.m-c@wanadoo.fr ✔
☎ by appt.

DOM. DU GROSEILLER 2002★★

| ■ | 3 ha | 13,000 | ◗▮ | 5–8 € |

The vines here grow on soils rich in manganese, and the colour of this dark-red, almost black, wine indicates plenty of extraction. The bouquet is dominated by rich perfumes of blackberry with notes of stewed fruits and fine touches of spices and soft fruits. The attack is very good with plenty of fruitiness which sweeps on to the palate to accompany silky and balanced tannins. This is a complex, lingering wine, full of youth and harmony throughout the tasting, and only just missed the *coup de coeur*. It is ready now, but can be served for at least five years with a wild boar cooked in Moulin-à-Vent.
☛ SNJP, 435, rue du Moulin,
69830 Saint-Georges-de-Reneins, tel. 04.74.09.60.00,
fax 04.74.09.60.17

DOM. DU MOULIN D'EOLE

Les Champs de Cour Tradition 2001★

| ■ | 0.42 ha | 3,100 | ◗▮ | 8–11 € |

Philippe Guérin has run this 9-ha estate since 1984. His wines matured in oak have been very well received in recent years. This one was kept for 11 months in barrel. It has a bright dark-red colour, and releases strong and complex notes of oak and toast with nuances of undergrowth. The clean attack is prolonged by fruitiness, well integrated in the oak. This is a balanced wine with sweet tannins, in which the oakiness remains prominent. It is ready to drink now or can be kept for one or two years.
☛ Philippe Guérin, le Bourg, 69840 Chénas,
tel. 04.74.04.46.88, fax 04.74.04.47.29 ✔
☎ ev. day except Sun. 9am–12 noon 2pm–7pm

DOM. DES PERELLES

Cuvée spéciale Elevé en fût de chêne 2001★

| ■ | 2 ha | 10,000 | ◗▮ | 5–8 € |

Everything here is old. The family was established in the Juliénas region in 1601; the wine tradition started in 1877, when the Perrachons starting making wine, and the vines responsible for this Cuvée Spéciale are 60 years old. This purplish-coloured wine is youthfully attractive and releases perfumes of soft fruits with notes of charring and carnation, and a hint of smokiness The good structure of the tannins and the frankness of the attack were much appreciated. This is a fruity, fresh and straightforward 2001 that can be enjoyed now and for the next three years.
☛ Jacques Perrachon, La Bottière, 69840 Juliénas,
tel. 03.85.36.75.42, fax 03.85.33.86.36 ✔
☎ by appt.

DOM. DE LA PIERRE

Clos Raclet 2001★

| ■ | 0.1 ha | 780 | ◗▮ | 5–8 € |

This typical 18th century winegrower's house was the residence of Benoît Raclet, who discovered an effective cure for meal moth by scalding, and a small museum recalls the life of this "saviour of the vines". This clean and brilliant carmine-red 2001 has a fruity bouquet of musky notes and a shade of leather. On the palate, it opens with curious shades of Pinot Noir, along with elegant spicy tannins. This intensely aromatic and very well-structured wine would be better in one or two years' time. Serve it with game or poultry.
☛ Dom. de la Pierre, La Pierre, 71570 Romanèche-Thorins, tel. 03.85.35.51.37, fax 03.85.35.51.37,
e-mail benoit_raclet@hotmail.com ✔
☎ by appt.
☛ Pierre Brault

DOM. DU POURPRE 2002★★

| ■ | 11 ha | 15,000 | ▮ ◗▮ | 5–8 € |

Of the 12 ha cultivated by Bernard Méziat, 11 are devoted to this Moulin-à-Vent which is matured for 16 months in barrel. It has a brilliant-crimson colour and opens with intense notes of very ripe soft fruits. On the palate, the tannins are for the time being more evident than the fresh fruitiness, and will need to become more rounded. The tasters were nonetheless pleased with the length, complexity and potential of this promising 2002. It will open out fully in a few months.
☛ EARL Dom. du Pourpre, Les Pinchons, 69840 Chénas, tel. 04.74.04.48.81, fax 04.74.04.49.22 ✔ ⌂
☎ ev. day 8am–8pm

DOM. DU PRIEURE SAINT ROMAIN

2002★

| ■ | 5 ha | 35,000 | ▮ ⚜ | 5–8 € |

This clear deep-ruby wine releases fairly complex perfumes combining soft fruits, cherry and vanilla notes. After a clean attack, its rounded flesh has lingering aromas of very ripe blackcurrant. This 2002 wine has a good structure which still needs one or two years before it is served with meat in sauce or poultry à la crème. Also distributed by the Thorin company is this **Chiroubles Domaine des Rocassières 2002**, which was specially commended.
☛ Dom. du Prieuré Saint Romain,
71570 Romanèche-Thorins, tel. 04.74.69.09.10,
fax 04.74.69.09.28, e-mail information@maisonthorin.com

DOM. DE LA ROCHE MERE 2002★★

| ■ | 1.66 ha | 7,000 | ▮ ◗▮ | 8–11 € |

The estate's evocative name refers to the substratum responsible for the soils here which shows through the surface in two places. This terroir has produced a wine opening with a complex range of clean and elegant perfumes: rose, violet, blackberry and black-cherry with shades of oak and aniseed. The very rich palate has supple tannins coated by aromas of oak and chocolate and a lovely long and balanced substance. This distinguished, well-made wine almost won the *coup de coeur*. It is ready now but could be kept for at least three years.
☛ Robert Bridet, le Bourg, 69840 Jullié, tel. 04.74.04.42.32, fax 04.74.04.42.32, e-mail robertbridet@wanadoo.fr ✔
☎ by appt.

DOM. DE LA TEPPE 2001★

| ■ | 3 ha | 10,000 | ◗▮ | 5–8 € |

This estate has been farmed for five generations, and took its name in 1976. This Moulin-à-Vent 2001 has a deep-garnet colour with brick-red highlights. The perfumes are very delicate and suggest fig with musky notes. Its good, winey flesh reveals a fairly firm tannic structure and aromas of soft fruits. This well-balanced, straightforward wine can be kept for two or three years. The same estate produced another Moulin-à-Vent under the label **Les Graves 2002**, bottled for the Thorin company (commended).
☛ EARL Robert et Pierre Bouzereau, Dom. de La Teppe, 71570 Romanèche-Thorins, tel. 03.85.35.52.47,
fax 03.85.35.59.40,
e-mail domainedelateppe@wanadoo.fr ✔
☎ by appt.

DOM. BENOIT TRICHARD

Mortperay 2002★

| ■ | 6 ha | 30,000 | ◗▮ | 8–11 € |

This brilliant dark-red wine was matured for one year in a large barrel and for part of the time in new oak. It releases rich and intense perfumes of fruits and flowers. Very structured and lingering, a little austere at the finish, this Moulin-à-Vent has good keeping potential. Leave it for one or two years.
☛ Dom. Benoît Trichard, Le Vieux-Bourg, 69460 Odenas, tel. 04.74.03.40.87, fax 04.74.03.52.02,
e-mail dbtricha@club-internet.fr ✔
☎ by appt.

Wines selected but not starred

ANTOINE BARRIER 2002

■	15 ha	110,000	▮ ♦	5–8 €

☛ Antoine Barrier, 52, rue Camille-Desmoulins,
92135 Issy-les-Moulineaux, tel. 01.46.62.76.00,
fax 01.46.44.34.08

BERNARD ET JOSIANE CANARD 2002

■	0.4 ha	3,000		5–8 €

☛ Bernard et Josiane Canard, Les Grandes Vignes,
69840 Emeringes, tel. 04.74.04.44.49, fax 04.74.04.45.16,
e-mail bernard.canard@wanadoo.fr ☑ 🏠
☚ ev. day except Sun. 10am–6pm

PIERRE CHANAU 2002

■	7.75 ha	70,000		5–8 €

☛ Auchan, 200, rue de la Recherche,
59650 Villeneuve-d'Ascq, tel. 04.74.69.09.10,
fax 04.74.69.09.28

CH. DU MOULIN-A-VENT

Cuvée exceptionnelle 2001

■	29.62 ha	14,000	⑪	8–11 €

☛ Ch. du Moulin-à-Vent, 71570 Romanèche-Thorins,
tel. 03.85.35.50.68, fax 03.85.35.20.06,
e-mail chateau-du-mav@noos.fr ☑
☚ ev. day 9am–12 noon 2pm–6pm; cl. 20 Jul. to 15 Aug.
☛ Flornoy-Bloud

DOM. DE LA ROCHELLE 2001

■	8 ha	10,000	⑪	5–8 €

☛ GFA des domaines Sparre, La Tour du Bief,
69840 Chénas, tel. 04.74.66.62.05, fax 04.74.69.61.38 ☑
☚ by appt.

DOM. ROMANESCA 2002

■	7 ha	15,000	▮ ♦	5–8 €

☛ Guy Chastel, Les Thorins, 71570 Romanèche-Thorins,
tel. 03.85.35.57.31, fax 03.85.35.20.50 ☑
☚ by appt.

DOM. DES VIGNES DU TREMBLAY 2002

■	4 ha	24,000	⑪	8–11 €

☛ Paul et Eric Janin, La Chanillière,
71570 Romanèche-Thorins, tel. 03.85.35.52.80,
fax 03.85.35.21.77 ☑
☚ by appt.

Régnié

Régnié was officially recognized in 1988. This recent cru closes the breach between Morgon to the north and Brouilly to the south, extending the limits of the ten Beaujolais appellations.

Apart from a tiny parcel of 5.93 ha on the neighbouring commune of Lantignié, the 746 ha of the appellation are all in the area of Régnié-Durette. As is the case with Morgon, its older sibling, the single village name Régnié designates the wine. Only 525 ha were declared as AOC Régnié in 2002 with an output of 29,676 hl.

The aspect of the commune is northwest and southeast, so the vineyards get sun most of the day, and they may be planted on the hillsides from 300 m to as high as 500 m.

The hillsides are part of the granite Fleurie range, and the mainly sandy and stony soil is exclusively planted to Gamay. There are, however, some areas which also contain some clay.

The vines are cultivated like all the other local appellations and the wines are made in the same way. However, an exception in the local regulations means that the winemakers of Régnié are unable to request an AOC Bourgogne for their wines.

In the Caveau des Deux Clochers – the church it is next to has unusual architecture, symbolizing wine – you can taste examples of local wines. They are fruitily aromatic with scents of redcurrant, strawberries and flowers. Overall, they are fleshy and supple, well balanced and elegant, sometimes described as "frivolous", "fun" or "feminine" wines.

DOM. DES BRAVES 2002★

■	6 ha	30,000	▮ ♦	5–8 €

This clear garnet wine was made from 40-year-old vines grown on sandy and stony soils. After the glass has been swirled, the wine releases rich and very pleasant perfumes of fresh soft fruits. The clean and lively attack continues with fruity aromas over fine tannins. Balanced and of good length, this youthful 2002 will go well with crudités or ham; it will be just as good in a year or two. Also recommended was this **Domaine des Celliers, a Beaujolais-Villages red 2002 (3–5 €)**, vinified by Franck Cinquin.
☛ Franck Cinquin, Les Braves, 69430 Régnié-Durette, tel. 04.74.69.05.32, fax 04.74.69.97.31 ☑
☚ by appt.

DOM. DES BRAVES 2002★★

■	7 ha	40,000	▮ ♦	5–8 €

In charge of this other Domaine des Braves is Paul Cinquin, the father of Franck and a cycling enthusiast. He has very skilfully made this clear garnet Régnié from 40-year-old vines. It has clean and fresh perfumes of raspberry and redcurrant with notes of pear-drops and flowers. These continue pleasantly on the palate which is slightly acid with fine tannins. This 2002 wine is balanced and shows good length, and can be drunk over the next two years with charcuterie and white meats.
☛ Paul Cinquin, Les Braves, 69430 Régnié-Durette, tel. 04.74.04.31.11 ☑
☚ by appt.

CLAUDINE ET CLAUDE CINQUIN 2002★

■	4 ha	8,000		5–8 €

The Cinquins have run an estate of 4 ha since 1974, and have now followed the modern trend by creating a logo: a drawing showing two vines, a pun on their surname. The Cinquins renovated their wine cellar recently, so the star they have won was certainly not a matter of luck. This deep-red Régnié releases rich perfumes of blackcurrants and cherry which continue on the palate after a lively and clean attack. This is a full, well-structured and promising wine which can be drunk now or kept for two or three years.
☛ Claudine et Claude Cinquin, Les Forchets, 69430 Régnié-Durette, tel. 04.74.69.01.28, fax 04.74.69.01.28, e-mail cc51regnie@free.fr ☑ 🏠
☚ by appt.

Régnié

DOM. DE COLETTE

Coteaux de Colette 2002★

| | 1 ha | 5,000 | | 5–8 € |

Jacky Gauthier's estate stands on the slopes of a southeast facing hill, and here he produced two Régnié wines which each received one star: the **Sélection Vallière 2002** and this intense-red Coteaux de Colette which opens with very ripe perfumes of soft fruits. After a good attack, youthful tannins integrate well in a pleasant fruity flesh. This well-balanced wine is ready now and can be drunk for the next two or three years.
☛ EARL Jacky Gauthier, Colette, 69430 Lantignié, tel. 04.74.69.25.73, fax 04.74.69.25.14
⚑ by appt.

DOM. DU COTEAU DE VALLIERES

2002★★

| | 4.96 ha | 10,000 | 🍷 🍸 | 3–5 € |

From this isolated estate on a hillside, you have a vast panorama reaching as far as Mont Blanc. Here they have made a superb dark-red Régnié with blueish highlights. It releases lovely complex perfume with blackcurrant to the fore and floral and spicy notes. Its aromatic flesh completely fills the mouth around a powerful and balanced tannic structure. This well-made 2002 is ready now but could be kept for at least three years. Serve it with meats or cheeses.
☛ Lucien et Lydie Grandjean, Vallières, 69430 Régnié-Durette, tel. 04.74.69.24.92, fax 04.74.69.23.36 ☑
⚑ by appt.

DOM. GAUDET 2001★

| | 2.6 ha | 3,500 | 🍷 | 5–8 € |

This wine was made from 40-year-old vines and matured for seven months in tank. It has a clear burlat cherry colour, which shows some signs of evolution, and releases winey and concentrated perfumes with notes of soft fruits and flowers. This is a full-bodied, fresh wine to drink over the next two years with game or cheese.
☛ Jean-Michel Gaudet, La Haute-Plaigne, 69430 Régnié-Durette, tel. 04.74.69.21.66, fax 04.74.69.21.66 ☑
⚑ by appt.

DOM. DOMINIQUE JAMBON 2002★

| | 4 ha | 5,000 | 🍷 🍸 | 5–8 € |

Dominique Jambon took over the family estate in 1995 after working on another estate between 1982 and 1995. He thus has more than 20 years' experience of winemaking. This very dark-ruby Régnié was made from 45-year-old vines and releases very pleasant, complex and fairly intense perfumes of blackcurrant and redcurrant. Its full-bodied substance and still youthful tannins, which for the time being prevail over the fruitiness, fill the mouth well. This powerful 2002 needs time to mature, then will go well for two or three years with an entrecôte in wine or meat à la bourguignonne.
☛ Dominique Jambon, Arnas, 69430 Lantignié, tel. 04.74.04.80.59, fax 04.74.04.80.59 ☑
⚑ by appt.

DIDIER LAGNEAU 2002★

| | 5.2 ha | 600 | 🍷 | 5–8 € |

This young winemaker made his first harvest in 1999, on his 20th birthday. The estate was created in 1999 with the purchase of 1.8 ha and now has 5.2 ha, the others taken over from his grandfather. The wine cellar was renovated in 2001. This dark-ruby Régnié opens with notes of black fruits, flowers and liquorice. The palate is full bodied and powerful – but not hard – and improves if the glass is swirled. This is a balanced and characteristic wine which is ready now and can be drunk for two years.
☛ Didier Lagneau, Huire, 69430 Quincié-en-Beaujolais, tel. 06.07.05.97.66, fax 04.74.04.89.44, e-mail didier.lagneau@mail.com ☑
⚑ ev. day 9am–7pm

DOM. LES PETITES PIERRES 2002★★

| | 5 ha | 17,000 | 🍷 🍸 | 5–8 € |

This dark-red Régnié with purple highlights releases intense and complex perfumes of blackcurrant and bilberry with very pleasant nuances of undergrowth and violet. These very fresh flavours continue on the soft and most attractive palate with raspberry joining the blackcurrant. This 2002 Régnié combines finesse and strong tannins, and is ready now but can be kept for two to three years. Serve it with a selection of local cold pork or ham.
☛ Grands Terroirs et Signatures, Cuvage de la Pierre-Bleue, 69460 Saint-Etienne-des-Oullières, tel. 04.74.03.52.72, fax 04.74.03.38.58, e-mail signe-vigneron1@awanadoo.fr
⚑ by appt.

CH. DE PIZAY 2002★★

| | n.c. | n.c. | 🍷 | 5–8 € |

This former château of the lords of Beaujeu dates from the 10th century. The 14th century keep and the Renaissance wing have been converted into a high-class hotel-restaurant. This estate has produced an excellent ambassador for the Beaujolais region, an intense bright-red Régnié with a fine and elegant bouquet of raspberry, violet and blackcurrant. The palate is well structured, rich and lingering with flavours of soft fruits. This wine is already very pleasant and will keep for a good while. Also selected, and winning one star, was the **Morgon 2001 Château de Pizay**; this will be excellent with a tarte Tatin.
☛ SCEA Ch. de Pizay, 69220 Saint-Jean-d'Ardières, tel. 04.74.66.26.10, fax 04.74.69.60.66, e-mail chateau-de-pizay@chateau-de-pizay.com ☑ 🏠
⚑ by appt.

JEAN-PAUL RAMPON

Les Larmes du Granit 2002★

| | 2 ha | 8,000 | 🍷 | 5–8 € |

This very attractive purplish-red wine was made from 50-year-old vines and has perfumes of raspberry and violet. A rather fresh and lingering fruitiness fills the mouth and balances harmoniously with the clean body. This 2002 wine can be drunk over the next two years.
☛ EARL Jean-Paul Rampon, Les Rampeaux, chem. de la Place, 69430 Régnié-Durette, tel. 04.74.04.36.32, fax 04.74.69.00.04, e-mail jp@rampon.fr ☑
⚑ by appt.

MICHEL RAMPON ET FILS 2002★★

| ■ | 6.7 ha | 10,000 | ■ | 5–8 € |

This purplish-red Régnié was made from 40-year-old vines planted on a pink granite soil. It has pleasant perfumes of blackcurrant, blackberry and other soft fruits. The pleasant and promising palate is developing a lovely rounded structure with aromas of cherry and blackcurrant. There is good balance between the structure and fruitiness, which makes this wine enjoyable now, but it could be kept for two or three years.
↠ GAEC Michel Rampon et Fils, La Tour Bourdon, 69430 Régnié-Durette, tel. 04.74.04.32.15, fax 04.74.69.00.81
↧ ev. day 8am–7pm

DOM. JOEL ROCHETTE 2002★

| ■ | 4.4 ha | 20,000 | ■ ↓ | 3–5 € |

The stone house dates from the 19th century. The wine cellar is equipped with large oak barrels where a **Beaujolais-Villages 2002**, which receives one star, and this Régnié with a dark-purple colour, which releases intense notes of black-cherry and blackcurrant, were matured. Despite the youthful tannins, the palate remains pleasant and of good length. The lovely balance between bouquet and taste suggest it is worth laying this wine down for one or two years to let it mature further.
↠ Joël Rochette, Le Chalet, 69430 Régnié-Durette, tel. 04.74.04.35.78, fax 04.74.04.31.62 Ⓥ
↧ by appt.

DOM. DE LA RONZE Grande Sélection

Cuvée vieillie en fût de chêne 2001★

| ■ | 1.5 ha | 8,000 | ⑪ | 5–8 € |

This estate has produced a deep-ruby wine with rich perfumes of fruits and an oaky note heightened by shades of butter. The happy marriage of the oak and the fruitiness opens out powerfully on the long palate which finishes on a note of liquorice and is well balanced. This Régnié is for lovers of oak and is ready now, but can be kept for two or three years.
↠ Séraphin Bernardo et Fils, La Haute-Ronze, 69430 Régnié-Durette, tel. 04.74.69.20.06, fax 04.74.69.21.69 Ⓥ
↧ by appt.

DOM. DE THULON 2002★

| ■ | 4 ha | 20,000 | ■ ↓ | 5–8 € |

Laurent and Carine joined their parents in 2002 at this former tenancy of the château de Thulon (13th and 15th century), and have produced an attractive garnet-red wine with intense and elegant notes of very ripe fruits. The full-bodied attack on the soft fruits is consistent with the bouquet. The palate is rounded and soft, with some youthful tannins which make up a very pleasant, rich and charming wine. It is ready to drink now but can be kept for two years. The **red Beaujolais-Villages, Domaine des Souzons 2002**, presented by Laurent Jambon, also received one star.
↠ EARL A. et R., C., L. Jambon, Thulon, 69430 Lantignié, tel. 04.74.04.80.29, fax 04.74.69.29.50 Ⓥ
↧ by appt.

Wines selected but not starred

MAISON DES BULLIATS

Réserve Terroir 2001

| ■ | 9 ha | 15,000 | ■ | 3–5 € |

↠ Jean-Max Lambinon, Les Bulliats, 69430 Régnié-Durette, tel. 04.74.69.03.38, fax 04.74.69.03.39, e-mail maison.bulliats@wanadoo.fr Ⓥ
↧ by appt.
↠ SCI Maison des Bulliats

CLOS DE PONCHON 2001

| ■ | 8.5 ha | 10,000 | ■ ↓ | 5–8 € |

↠ Dufour Père et Fils, Ponchon, 69430 Régnié-Durette, tel. 04.74.04.35.46, fax 04.74.69.03.89, e-mail florent.dufour@free.fr Ⓥ
↧ by appt.

DOM. GILLES COPERET 2001

| ■ | 2.7 ha | 12,000 | ■ ⑪ | 5–8 € |

↠ Coperet, Les Chastys, 69430 Régnié-Durette, tel. 04.74.04.38.08, fax 04.74.69.01.33, e-mail gilles-coperet@wanadoo.fr Ⓥ
↧ by appt.

REGINE ET DIDIER COSTE-LAPALUS 2002

| ■ | 1.7 ha | 4,000 | ■ | 5–8 € |

↠ Coste-Lapalus, chem. des Bruyères, 69430 Régnié-Durette, tel. 04.74.04.38.04 Ⓥ
↧ by appt.

DOM. DU CRET DES BRUYERES

Cuvée réservée 2002

| ■ | 6.5 ha | 15,000 | ■ | 5–8 € |

↠ EARL René et Gilles Desplace, Aux Bruyères, 69430 Régnié-Durette, tel. 04.74.04.37.13, fax 04.74.04.30.55, e-mail gillesdesplace@wanadoo.fr Ⓥ ⌂
↧ by appt.

DOM. DU CRET D'ŒILLAT 2002

| ■ | 9.3 ha | 5,000 | ■ | 3–5 € |

↠ EARL du Crêt d'Œillat, Le Bourg, 69430 Régnié-Durette, tel. 04.74.04.38.75, fax 04.74.04.38.75 Ⓥ
↧ by appt.
↠ J.-F. Matray

REMY CROZIER 2002

| ■ | 2.5 ha | 14,000 | ■ ↓ | 3–5 € |

↠ Rémy Crozier, Les Maisons Neuves, 69430 Régnié-Durette, tel. 04.74.04.39.59, fax 04.74.04.39.59 Ⓥ
↧ by appt.

DOM. DES FORCHETS 2001

| ■ | 1.5 ha | 8,000 | ■ ↓ | 5–8 € |

↠ Jean-Charles Braillon, Les Forchets, 69430 Régnié-Durette, tel. 04.74.04.30.48, fax 04.74.04.36.72, e-mail jean-charles.braillon@wanadoo.fr Ⓥ
↧ by appt.

DAVID GOBET 2002

| ■ | 0.5 ha | 2,000 | | 3–5 € |

↠ David Gobet, L'Ermitage, 69430 Régnié-Durette, tel. 04.74.69.22.10, fax 04.74.69.22.10, e-mail sanybonn@wanadoo.fr Ⓥ
↧ by appt.

GERARD ET JEANNINE LAGNEAU 2002

| ■ | 3 ha | 20,000 | ■ | 5–8 € |

↠ Gérard et Jeannine Lagneau, Huire, 69430 Quincié-en-Beaujolais, tel. 04.74.69.20.70, fax 04.74.04.89.44, e-mail lagneau-gerard@wanadoo.fr Ⓥ ⊞
↧ by appt.

MARCELLE ET JEAN-LOUIS LAPUTE
2001

■	6 ha	6,000		5–8 €

•┐ Marcelle et Jean-Louis Lapute, La Roche,
69430 Régnié-Durette, tel. 04.74.04.31.79,
fax 04.74.04.31.79
☙ by appt.

CAVE BEAUJOLAISE DE QUINCIE 2001

■	4 ha	9,000	■ ♦	3–5 €

•┐ Cave Beaujolaise de Quincié, Le Ribouillon,
69430 Quincié-en-Beaujolais, tel. 04.74.04.32.54,
fax 04.74.69.01.30, e-mail cavedequincie@terre-net.fr
☙ by appt.

THIERRY ET CECILE ROBIN 2002

■	5.8 ha	12,000	■	5–8 €

•┐ Thierry Robin, Le Bourg, 69430 Régnié-Durette,
tel. 04.74.04.37.71, fax 04.74.04.37.71
☙ by appt.

LA TOUR BOURDON 2002

■	1 ha	3,300	■ ♦	5–8 €

•┐ Alain Crozier, 69430 Régnié, tel. 04.74.06.10.10,
fax 04.74.66.13.77
☙ by appt.

Saint-Amour

All 317 ha of the Appellation Saint-Amour are in the department of Saône-et-Loire, producing some 17,172 hl of wine. The soil is decalcified sandstone and clay and granite pebbles, and forms the boundary between the primary rock of the south and the limestone soils of neighbouring Mâcon and Saint-Véran in the north. Two different approaches are taken to bringing out the qualities of the Gamay grape: the first, using grapes grown on the granite rocks, favours the traditional method of long fermentation in vats, creating wines with body and strong colour that are made to keep; the second is better adapted to Primeur wines, which can be drunk early and so assuage the curiosity of wine-lovers. Saint-Amour goes well with snails, fried fish, frogs' legs, mushrooms and chicken with cream sauces.

The appellation has become a great favourite with wine-drinkers outside France and a large proportion of the wine is exported. Visitors to Plâtre-Durant can taste Saint-Amour in a cellar which was established in 1965, before continuing to the church and the town hall which, standing on a hill 309 m high, dominates the region. On the corner by the church there is a statue commemorating the conversion of the Roman soldier after whom the commune is named.

DOM. DU MOULIN BERGER 2002★

■	3.5 ha	10,000	▥	5–8 €

This 10-ha estate was worked under a tenancy agreement from 1976 to 1985, then was bought by Michel Laplace. This clear light-red releases good perfume of very ripe soft fruits. The cherry and redcurrant continue into the fresh attack which is more expressive than the bouquet. On the palate, these flavours accompany integrated tannins and a rich and balanced flesh. It is ready to drink now. The same estate's **Juliénas Valoyette 2002** was singled out by the Jury.
•┐ Michel Laplace, Le Moulin Berger,
71570 Saint-Amour-Bellevue, tel. 03.85.37.41.57,
fax 03.85.37.44.75
☙ by appt.

Wines selected but not starred

CELINE ET CYRILLE MIDEY
Vieilles Vignes 2002

■	0.37 ha	2,700	▥	5–8 €

•┐ Céline Midey, Les Capitans,
71570 Saint-Amour-Bellevue, tel. 04.74.04.41.17
☙ by appt.

MICHEL PICARD 2001

■	n.c.	n.c.		11–15 €

•┐ Michel Picard, Ch. de Chassagne-Montrachet,
21190 Chassagne-Montrachet, tel. 03.85.87.51.01,
fax 03.85.87.51.12

DOM. DES RAVINETS
Cuvée Vieilles Vignes 2002

■	2 ha	10,000	■ ▥	5–8 €

•┐ Georges Spay, Les Ravinets,
71570 Saint-Amour-Bellevue, tel. 03.85.37.14.58,
fax 03.85.37.41.20
☙ ev. day except Sun. 9am–6pm

RAYMOND TRICHARD 2002

■	1.2 ha	4,000		5–8 €

•┐ Raymond Trichard, Les Blémonts, 71570 La
Chapelle-de-Guinchay, tel. 03.85.36.79.41,
fax 03.85.36.79.41 🍶
☙ ev. day 8am–8pm

Coteaux du Lyonnais

The vineyards that produce wines under the Coteaux du Lyonnais appellation are situated on the eastern slopes of the Massif Central. In the east they are bordered by the Rhône and the Saône, in the west by the Monts du Lyonnais. Their northern limit is the Beaujolais vineyards, and they go south as far as the Rhône valley. The historic vineyards of Lyon have been cultivated since Roman times and wine growing reached its zenith at the end of the 16th century when religious institutions and wealthy merchants favoured and protected the cultivation of the vine. A land survey dating from 1836 identified 13,500 ha of vineyards. Phylloxera decimated them and the city of Lyon expanded significantly, thus reducing the area under vines. Nowadays it is down to only 350 ha, divided among 49 communes which form a semi-circle to the west of the city, from Mont d'Or in the north to the Gier valley in the south.

The area is 40 km long and 30 km wide and is marked by a succession of valleys at about 250 m, running southwest to northeast with hills reaching some 500 m. The ground is varied, being made from granite, metamorphic and sedimentary rocks with alluvial or loess deposits. The soil is light with good drainage and is very shallow, as is common in wine-growing areas where the underlying geological structure is ancient rock.

Coteaux du Lyonnais

The three prevailing climates of Beaujolais are also found in this region, though there is a greater influence from Mediterranean weather. However, the topology of the area is particularly susceptible to the influences of the oceanic and continental climates which means the vines can be planted only up to 500 m and not on exposed, north-facing slopes. The best areas are on the plateau. The vine varieties planted are essentially Gamay, vinified according to the Beaujolais method to give appealing red wines which are the favourites of the local Lyonnais clientele. Chardonnay and Aligoté also qualify under the appellation and are used for making white wines. Vineyards must be planted at a density of 6,000 plants per hectare and are pruned either in the shape of a goblet, as in the Beaujolais, cordoned or reduced to a single stem. Production bases start at 60 hl/ha. Red wine has a minimum strength of 10° and a maximum strength of 13° while white wine goes from 9.5° to 12.5°. In 2002 20,696 hl of red and rosé and 1,868 hl of white were produced. The Cave Coopérative de Sain-Bel vinifies three-quarters of the harvest and is a significant force in the region where there is a good deal of mixed farming with large tracts of land being given over to cultivating fruit trees.

The Coteaux du Lyonnais became an AOC in 1984. They are fruity, fresh, well-scented wines which go perfectly with all sorts of Lyonnais pork dishes, including sausages, savelovs, pig's tails, salted pork, pigs' trotters, knuckles of ham, together with goats' cheeses of the region.

DOM. DU CLOS SAINT-MARC

Les Doyennes 2002★

	5 ha	26,000	▮ ⚘	3–5 €

This estate was created just 20 years ago, inheriting much older vines such as the "Doyennes" that are more than 50 years old. They produced this clear deep-ruby wine with its bouquet of very ripe fruits and floral notes. This is a well-balanced wine, both rounded and long, with supple tannins and aromas of almond. Drink it in the next two years.
☛ GAEC du Clos Saint-Marc, 60, rte des Fontaines, 69440 Taluyers, tel. 04.78.48.26.78, fax 04.78.48.77.91 ☑
☖ Mon. until Thu. 5pm–6.30pm; Fri. until Sun. 3pm–6.30pm

REGIS DESCOTES

Les Chênes 2001★★

	1 ha	5,000	▥	5–8 €

"The best Lyonnais are born on the hillsides," proclaims the brochure of this estate located to the south of Lyon. Also relevant here was the fact that the vinification and maturation were carried out in an oak room – certainly a daring form of originality. Perhaps, but what a great success the wine is! It has a clear golden colour, and perfumes of citrus fruit and exotic fruits, vanilla and vervain along with notes of brioche and butter that recur on the palate. The clean and fruity attack gives way to a balanced but still very evident oakiness. Leave it for a few months and then serve it with shellfish or a white meat in sauce.
☛ Régis Descotes, 16, av. du Sentier, 69390 Millery, tel. 04.78.46.18.77, fax 04.78.46.16.22, e-mail vinsdescotes@wanadoo.fr ☑
☖ by appt.

ANNE MAZILLE 2001★

	0.3 ha	2,000	▮ ⚘	3–5 €

This lovely golden wine made from Chardonnay planted on granitic soils releases very fresh lemon perfumes with a touch of vegetation. After a supple attack, one senses the rich and generous flesh, and mineral and fruity notes. This wine is still young, and could be served as an aperitif or with frogs' legs.
☛ Anne Mazille, 10, rue du 8-Mai, 69390 Millery, tel. 04.78.46.20.61, fax 04.72.30.16.65 ☑
☖ by appt.

DOM. DE PRAPIN 2002★★

	1.5 ha	8,000	▮ ⚘	3–5 €

Taluyers, southwest of Lyon, has two beautiful Romanesque monuments, a church and a priory. Henri Jullian has been farming 19 ha there since 1989. The silt and granite soils, where the vines grow, are worked all year round. He matured this pale-golden wine in a wine cellar renovated in 2001. It has fairly intense perfumes of white flowers and citrus fruits with a hint of toast. A very fresh attack is followed by a series of well-balanced, rich and tasty impressions. This promising wine will be at its peak in one year.
☛ Henri Jullian, Prapin, 69440 Taluyers, tel. 04.78.48.24.84, fax 04.78.48.24.84, e-mail domainedeprapin@free.fr ☑ ⌂
☖ by appt.

Wines selected but not starred

PIERRE ET JEAN-MICHEL JOMARD 2002

| ■ | 0.93 ha | 8,000 | ■ ♦ | 3–5 € |

🔸 Pierre et Jean-Michel Jomard, Le Morillon,
69210 Fleurieux-sur-l'Arbresle, tel. 04.74.01.02.27,
fax 04.74.01.24.04 ✅
🍷 by appt.

DOM. DE CHAMP GUICHARD 2002

| ■ | 11 ha | 50,000 | ■ ♦ | 5–8 € |

🔸 Cave de Vignerons réunis de Sain-Bel, RN 89,
69210 Sain-Bel, tel. 04.74.01.11.33, fax 04.74.01.10.27,
e-mail cave.vignerons.reunis@wanadoo.fr ✅
🍷 by appt.

DOM. DE PETIT FROMENTIN

Vieilles Vignes 2002

| ■ | 3 ha | 15,000 | ■ ♦ | 3–5 € |

🔸 André et Franck Decrenisse, Le Petit-Fromentin,
69380 Chasselay, tel. 04.78.47.35.11, fax 04.78.47.35.11 ✅
🍷 ev. day except Sun. 6pm–7.30pm

BORDEAUX

Bordeaux is the ultimate symbol of wine, everywhere in the world, but visitors seeking an old wine town with beautiful rows of hogsheads stretching along the port near the inviting wine stores of the shippers will be disappointed: the shippers have long since relocated to the industrial zones on the outskirts of the town, and the small cellar bars, where you could down a glass of sweet wine in the early morning, have practically disappeared. Echoes of another time, another way of life.

The history of wine in Bordeaux stretches back to ancient times. A wine trade was recorded in the area even before vines were cultivated there. In the first half of the 1st century BC, some years before Roman legions invaded Aquitaine, merchants from Campania in Italy came to sell their wine to the Bordelais. Thus, in some ways, wine was the medium through which the people of Aquitaine first experienced Roman life. Vine-growing was under way during the 1st century AD, but it seems that more serious cultivation began in the area even before vines were cultivated there. The marriage of Eleanor of Aquitaine to Henry Plantagenet, the future King Henry II of England, encouraged the export of "clarets" (as the English called them) to Britain. The wines of the year were shipped to England before Christmas. In those days no one knew how to preserve wine, and it would deteriorate after a year as a result of natural chemical changes.

At the end of the 17th century claret encountered stiff competition from the introduction of new beverages – tea, coffee and chocolate – and also from other, more robust wines from the Iberian peninsula. In addition, the foreign wars waged by Louis XIV led importing countries to levy punitive taxes on French wines. In spite of this, high society in England remained devoted to the flavour of claret. In the early 18th century some London shippers sought to create a new style of more refined wines, "the new French clarets," which they bought young to lay down. In an inspired marketing initiative, shippers started to sell the wine in bottles that were corked and sealed to guarantee their origin, and could thus be sold at a premium. Almost imperceptibly, the connection between the terroir, the château and Grands Vins (fine wines) evolved, bringing about wines of a more reliable standard. Wines began to be judged, appreciated and priced according to their quality. As a consequence, wine-growers began to select land for cultivating the vines more carefully, limiting the amount of wine produced and improving the conditions for maturing the wines in casks. At the same time, they introduced new methods, protecting their wines during ageing through the use of sulphur dioxide and clarifying wine by fining or racking. The first ranking of the Bordeaux Crus was established at the end of the 18th century. In spite of the French Revolution and the Napoleonic Wars, which closed the English market for a period, the prestige of the Grands Vins of Bordeaux increased through the 19th century, as illustrated by the classification of the Crus du Médoc in 1855. This system, although not without its critics, is still in use today.

Following this period of growth, the Bordeaux vineyards were devastated by two major vine diseases, phylloxera and mildew, and suffered further from economic slumps and two world wars. Between 1960 and the end of the 1980s, however, Bordeaux recovered its prosperity by virtue of a remarkable improvement in the quality of its wines and a significantly increased worldwide demand for fine wines in general. The hierarchy of Bordeaux's terroirs and crus regained some international respect, although the red wines benefited more than the whites. At the beginning of the 1990s the market suffered from a variety of economic factors affecting the structure of all the Bordeaux vineyards.

The Bordeaux vineyards are situated along three major waterways: the Garonne, the Dordogne and the estuary they both feed into, the Gironde. The environment they create – sunny, sheltered slopes and steady temperatures – is ideal for growing vines. These waterways have historically also played an important economic role as the means for transporting the wines to market. The climate in the Bordelais region is temperate, with average annual temperatures of 7.5°C minimum and 17°C maximum, and the vineyards are sheltered from ocean storms by pine forests. Winter frosts are rare (1956, 1958, 1985), but if the temperature drops to –2°C or below in April and May the young shoots can be severely damaged or destroyed. The vines flower in June, and cool, rainy weather during this period can wash away the pollen: as a result the flowers do not pollinate and the grapes do not form. Spring frosts and summer rains alike can have a critical impact on the amount of grapes harvested and thus explain the great year-to-year variations in the quantity of wine produced. The final quality of the harvest depends on having hot, dry weather from July to October, particularly in the four weeks just before picking begins (in all, grapes need 2,008 hours of sun each year to ripen properly). The local climate is in fact fairly wet, 900 mm of rain per year falling mainly in the spring, when the weather can be very poor. Autumns, on the other hand, are famously warm, and exceptional late-season weather has often saved many vintages. The reputation of the Grands Vins de Bordeaux depends entirely on this fortuitous combination of location and climate.

Along the Gironde the vine is cultivated on a variety of different soils; and no particular soil type determines the quality of the wine. Most of the Grands Crus red wines are from alluvial, sandy and gravelly soils, other reputable wines come from clay on limy subsoil, sandstone or even sedimentary clay. The vines for dry white wines grow equally well on soil with layers of sand or gravel, chalky soils, on alluvium or sandstone. Vines for sweet wines are usually grown on gravelly sand or clay. In every case, natural or mechanical methods of drainage and control over how much water the vines receive are essential factors in the

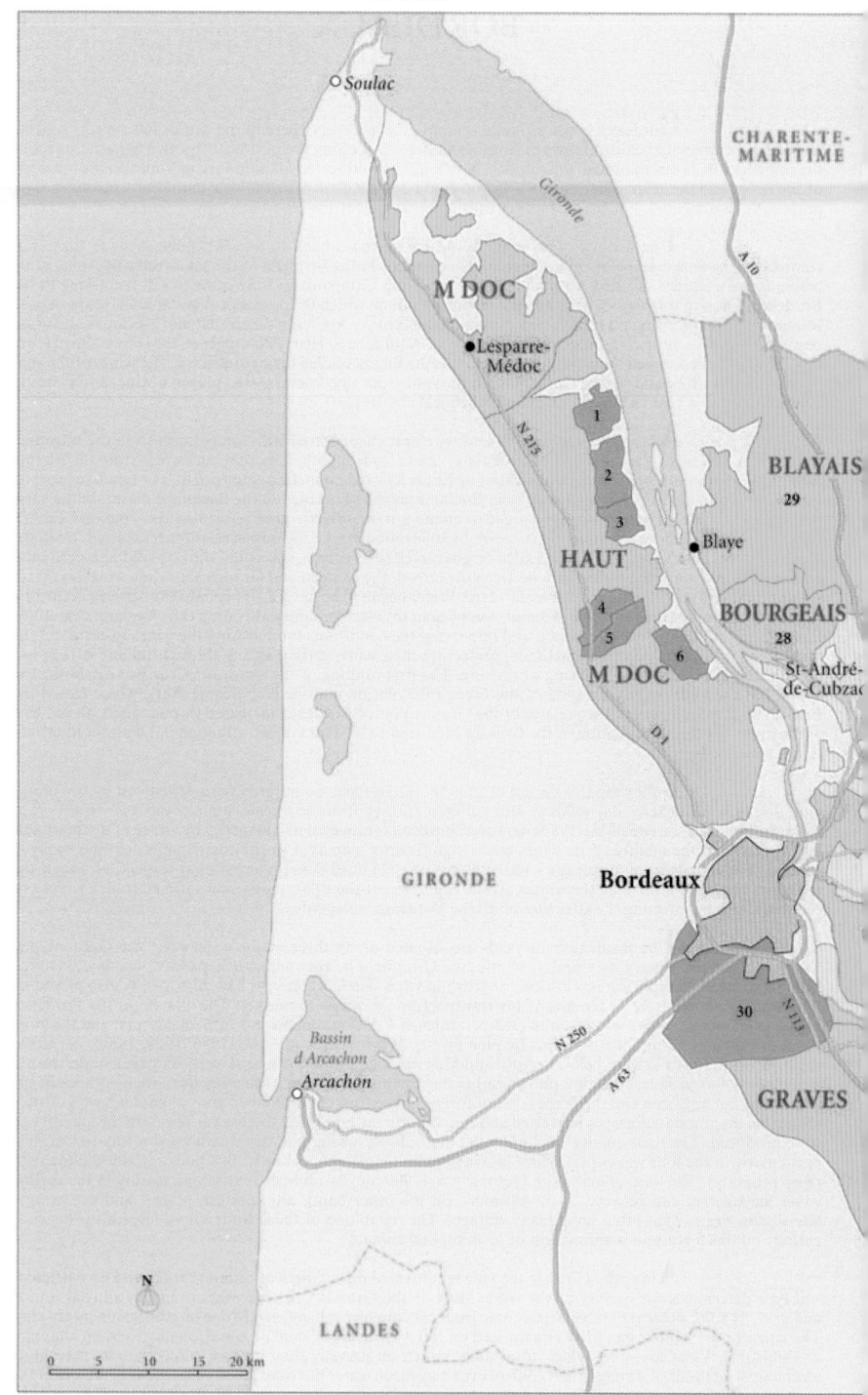

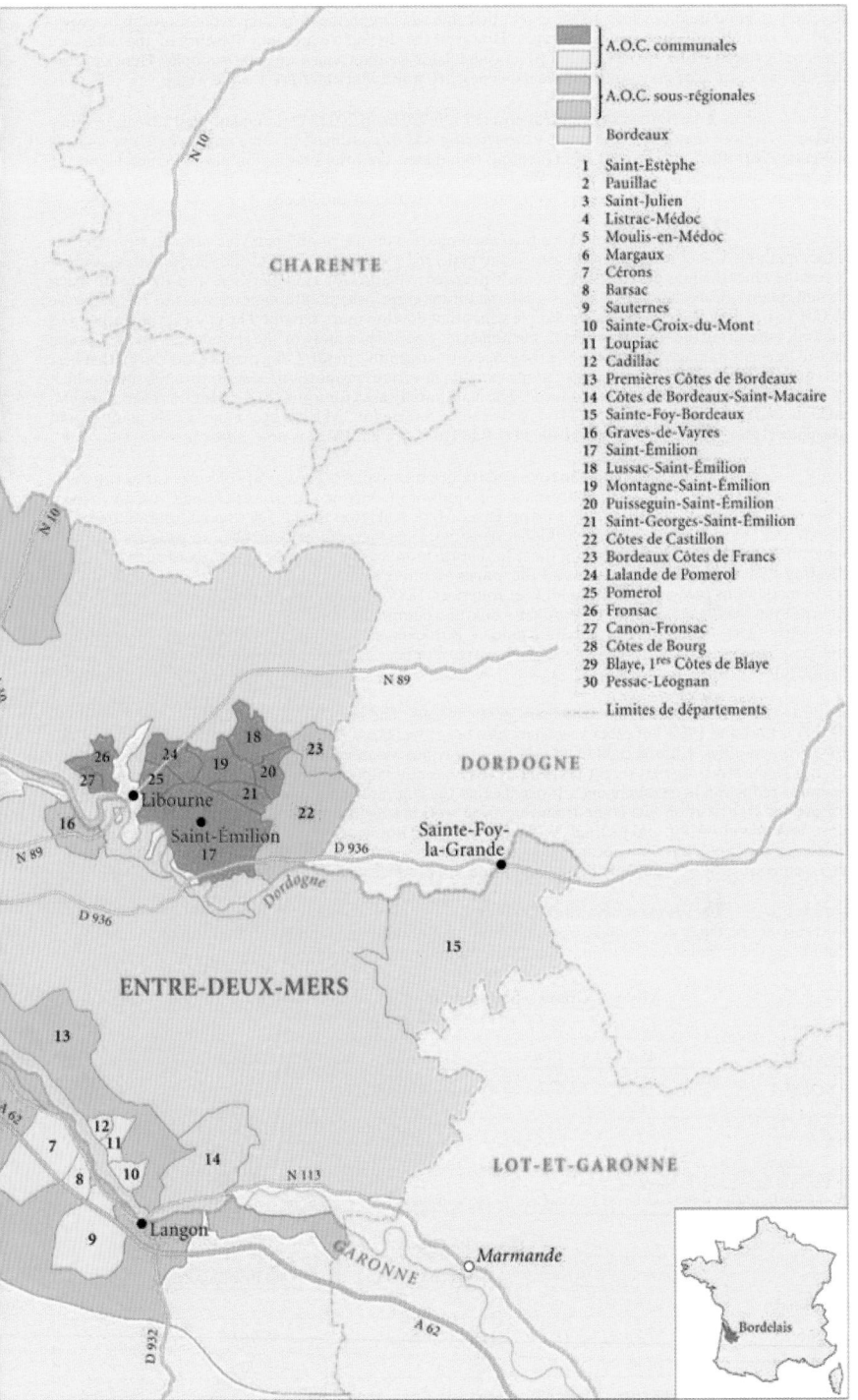

A.O.C. communales

A.O.C. sous-régionales

Bordeaux

1   Saint-Estèphe
2   Pauillac
3   Saint-Julien
4   Listrac-Médoc
5   Moulis-en-Médoc
6   Margaux
7   Cérons
8   Barsac
9   Sauternes
10 Sainte-Croix-du-Mont
11 Loupiac
12 Cadillac
13 Premières Côtes de Bordeaux
14 Côtes de Bordeaux-Saint-Macaire
15 Sainte-Foy-Bordeaux
16 Graves-de-Vayres
17 Saint-Émilion
18 Lussac-Saint-Émilion
19 Montagne-Saint-Émilion
20 Puisseguin-Saint-Émilion
21 Saint-Georges-Saint-Émilion
22 Côtes de Castillon
23 Bordeaux Côtes de Francs
24 Lalande de Pomerol
25 Pomerol
26 Fronsac
27 Canon-Fronsac
28 Côtes de Bourg
29 Blaye, 1res Côtes de Blaye
30 Pessac-Léognan

- - - - Limites de départements

CHARENTE

DORDOGNE

Libourne

Saint-Émilion

Sainte-Foy-
la-Grande

ENTRE-DEUX-MERS

LOT-ET-GARONNE

Langon

Marmande

Bordelais

production of good-quality wines, to the extent that fine wines with the same high reputation can be grown on soils of entirely different geological types. However, the distinctive aromatic flavours of the wines are influenced by the structure of the soils: the Médoc and Saint-Emilion wines are good examples. Here and elsewhere, the same soil type may well produce red wines, dry white wines and sweet white wines.

The Bordeaux vineyards covered 120,720 ha in 2002. At the end of the 19th century they extended over more than 150,000 ha, but wine-growing was discontinued in some areas where the soil was inadequate. With the improvement of cultivating techniques, the total production has remained about the same, currently approaching 7 million hl. While the average size of a vineyard is still about 7 ha, changes in ownership have resulted in a progressive reduction in the number of producers.

Bordeaux wines have always encompassed the use of different vine varieties with complementary qualities. Cabernet and Merlot are used to make red wines (about 90% of the vineyard area). Cabernet gives the wines their tannic structure, but the wines need to mature for a number of years if they are to reach optimum quality; Cabernet Sauvignon is a late-maturing grape, which, although resistant to rot, can have difficulty in ripening. Merlot makes for supple wines that develop more rapidly. The grapes fruit earlier and ripen well, but during the flowering season the pollen may be washed away by the spring rains and the young vines can be easily damaged by frost, while the grapes are susceptible to rot. Long practice has shown that best results are achieved by blending these two grape varieties in various proportions according to the soil in which they are grown and to the wine to be produced. The main variety used for white wine is Sémillon (52%), supplemented in some areas by Colombard (11%), above all by Sauvignon, which is ever more widely planted, and Muscadelle (15%), which has characteristic, very fine aromas. Ugni Blanc is now more rarely grown.

Vines are planted in rows and trained on espaliers. The density of vines varies considerably: as many as 10,000 plants per hectare in the vineyards of the Médoc and Graves Grand Crus, down to an average of 4,000 in the classified areas of Entre-Deux-Mers, and fewer than 2,500 when the plants are left to grow tall and are widely spaced out. At higher densities, each vine can be controlled to produce a limited number of bunches of grapes, allowing them to mature more easily. However, the costs of managing and cultivating such vineyards are greater and the grapes are more susceptible to rot. Cultivation of the vines requires meticulous care and attention all year round. In 1885, the science faculty of Bordeaux University discovered the *bouillie bordelaise*, or Bordeaux mixture, compounded of copper sulphate and lime, which proved particularly successful in combating mildew. Bordeaux mixture is still in use throughout the world, although modern wine-growers can now look to a large number of more ecologically friendly products to do the same job.

Bordeaux can boast many great vintages. The years for great reds were 2000, 1995, 1990, 1982, 1975, 1961 and 1959, but other years have also been excellent: 1989, 1988, 1985, 1983, 1981, 1979, 1978, 1976, 1970 and 1966. Unforgettable vintages from previous years were 1955, 1949, 1947, 1945, 1929 and 1928. It is worth stressing that recent years have seen a general improvement in the quality of vintages and a consequent reduction in mediocre ones. It may be that the vineyards have enjoyed better climatic conditions, but a greater contribution has come from improved working methods and the incorporation of research discoveries into cultivation and methods of vinification. The Bordeaux vineyards are situated on exceptional land for wine-growing, but sophisticated modern technologies now help to make the most of what nature has to offer; consequently, it is unlikely that the Gironde will produce any very poor vintages in the future.

Bordeaux's dry white wines may not feature prominently among the great vintages but sweet wines certainly do. To make a good sweet wine, the conditions for the development of noble rot are essential (see the introductory section, "Wine" and the individual entries for the wines concerned).

Médoc – Graves – Saint-Emilion – Pomerol – Fronsac

vintages	to drink	to keep	to drink or keep
exceptional	45 47 61 70 75 85		82
very good	49 53 55 59 62 64 66 67 71* 76 78 79	90 95 96 98	81 83 86 88 89
good	50 73 74 77 80 84 87 91 92 93 94	99 2001	

* For Pomerol this vintage is exceptional.
– Appellation Bordeaux wines and the red Vins de Côte should be drunk in 5 or 6 years. Some can be kept for as long as 10 years.

Dry white Graves

vintages	to drink	to keep	to drink or keep
exceptional	78 81 82 83		
very good	76 85 87 88 92 93 94	99 2000 2002	95 96 98
good	79 80 84 86 97	2001	89 90

– It is preferable to drink the other dry white Bordeaux wines very young, within 2 years.

Sweet white wines

vintages	to drink	to keep	to drink or keep
exceptional	47 67 70 71 75 76	95 97 2002	83 88 89 90
very good	49 59 62 81 82	96 2001	86
good	50 55 77 78 79 80 84 91	98	85 87 94 2000

– Sweet wines can be drunk young (as an aperitif their fruitiness can be particularly enjoyed), but they acquire their classic qualities only after long ageing.

Bordeaux Grands Crus wines have long been bottled at the property, but it is only in the last ten or fifteen years that the whole task, from vinification to bottling, has been carried out there. For other wines (generic appellations or regional wines), the wine-grower was traditionally primarily responsible for cultivating the vines and making the grapes into wine. In this system, négociants (local wholesale wine-buyers and shippers) not only undertook the sales of the wines but also oversaw their production right up to the time of bottling in order to ensure their quality. The situation is gradually changing, and nowadays, on the whole, the great majority of AOC wines are grown, aged and warehoused by the producers. Progress in wine technology makes it possible to produce reliable wines on a regular basis and, naturally enough, the winemakers wish to make the most profit by bottling the wine themselves. The Caves Coopératives have played a significant role in this change by creating organizations that take care of the ageing and marketing of the wines on behalf of their members. The négociant still has an important role in distributing the wines, particularly for export, exploiting long-established sales networks. On the other hand, it is possible to envisage a time in the future when it will be more profitable for producers to sell their wines directly to the consumer.

Marketing the significant quantities of wine produced in Bordeaux is subject to the vagaries of economic conditions as well as to the volume and quality of the harvest. In recent years, the Conseil Interprofessionel des Vins de Bordeaux has played an important role in sales and marketing by establishing benchmark levels of stockholding and production, by stipulating certain conditions of quality and by implementing financial measures relating to the organization of the market.

The regional syndicats or wine unions also protect the different Appellations d'Origine Contrôlées by defining criteria for quality. Under the management and control of INAO, they organize tastings at which all the wines produced each year are judged; they have the power to take away the appellation rights of a wine if its quality is deemed inadequate.

The various wine Confréries (Jurade in Saint-Emilion, Commanderie du Bontemps in Médoc and Graves, Connétablie in Guyenne and so on) organize regular festivals and popular events to promote Bordeaux wines. Their activities are co-ordinated by the Grand Conseil du Vin de Bordeaux.

All these promotional and marketing activities and production controls demonstrate that Bordeaux wines make up a major industry that is rigorously managed. The AOC wines produced in Bordeaux represent more than a quarter of the all wines produced in France, with a volume of 5,743,291 hl in 2002, worth billions of Euros in total, of which 1,265 billion Euro is earned through exports. The industry plays an important role in the life of the region, since it is estimated that one Girondin in six is directly or indirectly dependent on the activities of the wine industry. But for Gascony, the region of the Bordeaux wines, wine is more than simply a product of the economy. It is also, and above all, part of the culture. Behind the labels may lie châteaux with stunning architecture or simple peasant houses, but also the vineyards and the wine cellars where people work, applying their know-how and contributing their traditions and their memories to the production of great wine.

BORDEAUX: THE REGIONAL APPELLATIONS

While it is relatively straightforward to identify the Appellation Communale wines, it is not so easy to understand what the Appellation Bordeaux means. In fact, the definition is quite simple: it applies to all good-quality wines produced within the boundaries of the department of the Gironde, excluding any that come from the sandy area to the west and south (namely La Lande, which has been set aside as a pine forest since the 19th century). Put more simply, the appellation applies to all wines from the designated wine-growing areas of the Gironde. All the wines produced there have the right to use it subject to meeting the fairly strict regulations concerning the selection of grape varieties, limits on quantities produced and so on. However, this simple provision conceals great variations. Indeed, rather than talking about a single Bordeaux appellation, it is more correct to talk about the Bordeaux appellations, which include red wine, rosé, clairets, both dry and sweet white wines, and white or rosé sparkling wines. The variety of geographical origins for Bordeaux appellation wines gives rise to several types of wines that can claim the appellation. In some cases it means wines that are produced in parts of the Gironde that have the right to use only the Bordeaux appellation, such as the marshy districts (made up of alluvial soils) near the rivers or in parts of the Libournais (communes such as

Saint-André-de-Cubzac, Guîtres, Coutras, for example). In other cases, the wines come from regions that also have the right to a specific appellation (Médoc, Saint-Emilion, Pomerol, and so on). Alternatively, a regional appellation can be used by a local appellation that may be less well known commercially (such as the Bordeaux-Côtes de Francs, Bordeaux Haut-Benauge, Bordeaux Sainte-Foy or Bordeaux Saint-Macaire); the specific appellation is, in real terms, no more than an adjunct to the Appellation Régionale and, in fact, adds nothing to the intrinsic value of the product. In such cases, winemakers are happier to rely on the image of the Bordeaux "brand name". Occasionally, Bordeaux wines may come from a property located in the \ production area of a particular, sometimes prestigious, appellation, an occurrence that can provoke a good deal of curiosity among inquisitive wine-lovers. But here, too, the explanation is not difficult to find: traditionally, many properties in the Gironde produced several types of wine (more usually both reds and whites); now, in numerous cases (Médoc, Saint-Emilion, Entre-Deux-Mers and Sauternes), the specific appellation applies to only one type. Consequently, the other wines produced are marketed as Bordeaux or Bordeaux Supérieur.

Though these wines may be less celebrated than the Grands Crus, in a quantitative sense all these Bordeaux constitute the largest appellation of the Gironde with, in 2002 2,842,520 hl of red, 400,730 hl of white and 9,184 hl of sparkling Crémant de Bordeaux.

Taken at face value, the quantity of wine produced and the impressive area of the vineyards could lead one to suppose that there are few similarities among Bordeaux wines. The wines do indeed have distinctions in character, but they, also have qualities in common that give an overall identity to the Appellations Régionales. Thus Bordeaux red wines are well-balanced, and delicate; generally they should be fruity but not too full-bodied, so they can be drunk young. The Bordeaux Supérieur reds tend to be more full-bodied; they are made from the best grapes and vinified by a method that will ensure they can keep for some time. They form a select group among Bordeaux wines.

Bordeaux clairets and rosés are made by allowing red-grape varieties to macerate for a short time; the clairets have a slightly more intense colour. They are fresh, fruity wines, but only a limited quantity is produced.

White Bordeaux are dry, lively, fruity wines. In recent years their quality has been improved by new techniques of vinification, but it should be said that this appellation does not yet enjoy the popularity it deserves. Some of these wines are "demoted" to table wines, not least because the difference in profit is slight and it is sometimes easier to sell them as table wine than as Bordeaux Blanc. As a group, white Bordeaux Supérieur wines are luscious and rich; production, though, is small.

There is also an Appellation Crémant de Bordeaux. To qualify, all the grapes used must come from the designated Bordeaux appellation region. The second fermentation (the prise de mousse), must occur in bottle at wine cellars in the Bordeaux region.

CH. LES ANGUILLERES

Cuvée Gabriel 2000★

| | 1.1 ha | 5,000 | ■ ❶ ↓ | 5–8 € |

Jean-François Ossard has made a good start to his career as an independent wine-maker with this vintage. Aromas of black-cherry and vanilla combine happily with nuances of leather and smoke. The dark-garnet colour is in tune with the full, structured, almost robust palate, which will soon find a good balance. A Bordeaux fit for good home-cooking.
↪ EARL Ossard, 3, La Lambertine, 33220 Pineuilh, tel. 05.57.46.12.04, fax 05.57.46.31.28 ▣
� by appt.

CH. LES ARROMANS 2001★

| | 6 ha | 50,000 | ■ | 3–5 € |

Joël Duffau, one of the region's excellent producers, has kept the traditions handed down over nine generations on this family estate of 34 ha, located just outside Libourne. His 2001 wine has a lovely scent of grapes and summer soft fruits. Blackcurrant and prune are to the fore, foreshadowing the aromatic harmony of a palate structured by the tannins. This well-made wine is still developing at the moment, but will be very good with a meal in two years. Also very successful is the **Château Les Arromans Cuvée Prestige Elevé en Fût de Chêne 2001 (5–8 €)**, with its fruity and velvety substance. Although the tannins and the oak are evident and suggest the wine should be laid down for a good while, they take nothing away from the pleasure of drinking it right now.
↪ Joël Duffau, Les Arromans no. 2, 33420 Moulon, tel. 05.57.74.93.98, fax 05.57.84.66.10, e-mail lamothed@club-internet.fr ▣
� ev. day except Sun. 9am–12.30pm 2pm–7pm; cl. 15–31 Aug.

CH. DE BALAN 2001★

| | n.c. | 8,000 | ■ ↓ | 3–5 € |

This Bordeaux was made chiefly from Cabernet Sauvignon (75%) planted on a clay-limestone terroir, and has a fresh carmine colour with aromas of ripe fruits and sweet spices. The fairly full-bodied palate finishes on a pleasant note of slightly peppery violet. Keep this wine until 2005.
↪ GAEC ch. de Balan, 5, Balan, 33490 Sainte-Foy-la-Longue, tel. 05.56.76.43.41, fax 05.56.76.47.34 ▣
� by appt.
↝ Jeans

BEAU-RIVAGE 2001★

| | n.c. | 2,500,000 | ■ ↓ | –3 € |

The regular quality of Beau-Rivage accounts for its huge worldwide sales figures. The colour of this 2001 wine is definitely pale but attractive, and the bouquet is intense with floral aromas and stronger ones of spices (nutmeg). The round and smooth structure will apeal especially to lovers of supple characteristic wines. It is ready to drink now.
↪ Borie Manoux, 86, cours Balguerie-Stuttenberg, 33082 Bordeaux Cedex, tel. 05.56.00.00.70, fax 05.57.87.48.61, e-mail borie-manoux@dial.oleane.com

CH. BEL AIR 2001★

| | 10 ha | 80,000 | ■ ↓ | 5–8 € |

Anyone who claims to know the Gironde will be aware of Blasimon and its abbey, famous for its magnificent portal with six arches, its capitals and its abacuses with their friezes. The charterhouse of Bel Air (17th–18th century) is also worth a visit; it offers, moreover, an interesting Bordeaux. Its 2001 wine is dark red with carmine highlights and an attractive complex bouquet of spring flowers and nuts. The supple and charming palate has a good structure which supports the fruity finish. This wine could already be enjoyed with a meal.
↪ Philippe Moysson, Ch. Bel Air, 33540 Blasimon, tel. 05.57.84.10.74, fax 05.57.84.00.51, e-mail scea.moysson@wanadoo.fr ▣
� by appt.

CH. BEL AIR MOULARD 2001★

| | 4 ha | 27,000 | | | 3–5 € |

This pleasant and cheerful Bordeaux will make every day seem special. Its colour and coppery highlights reveal the influence of the Merlot (80%) in the blend and herald a rich aromatic bouquet. Fine flavours of soft fruit are enhanced by strong tannins on the consistent and firm palate, which is already showing good balance. Keep this until 2005. The **Château Le Prieur Cuvée Passion 2000 (5–8 €)**, matured in barrel, is commended. It will be ready to drink next year.
♠ EARL Vignobles Garzaro, Ch. Le Prieur, 33750 Baron, tel. 05.56.30.16.16, fax 05.56.30.12.63, e-mail garzaro@vingarzaro.com ☑ ☷ ☗
✠ by appt.

CH. BELLE-GARDE
Elevé en fût de chêne 2001★★

| | 14 ha | 90,000 | | | 5–8 € |

Eric Duffau offers the dazzling spectacle of a combination of rich fruit and the smooth vanilla-flavoured perfumes of a high-quality oak. The full, powerful and complex bouquet releases opulent aromas of grape, blackcurrant, coffee and cinnamon. The wine is wonderfully impressive on the palate, revealing opulent tannins and a round and tasty structure. This 2001 wine is full of delightful vigour and wins a unanimous *coup de coeur*. This is a great Bordeaux which will become even greater.
♠ Eric Duffau, Monplaisir, 33420 Génissac, tel. 05.57.24.49.12, fax 05.57.24.41.28, e-mail duffau.eric@wanadoo.fr ☑
✠ by appt.

BLAISSAC 2001★

| | n.c. | n.c. | | | 3–5 € |

The oenologists of the Castel company know their business, and offer a wine that responds in every respect to the consumer's demands for a characteristic wine: a fresh, clear and brilliant colour and a fresh range of aromas of small summer fruits (strawberry, raspberry and bigaroon cherry). This Blaissac hits the mark with its soft and silky palate which is instantly enjoyable. However, it will improve further if you lay it down for a little while.
♠ Castel Frères, 21–24, rue Georges-Guynemer, 33290 Blanquefort, tel. 05.56.95.54.04, fax 05.56.95.54.20

CH. BONNET
Divinus 2000★★

| | 5 ha | 20,000 | | | 15–23 € |

This great Bordeaux winemaker, a very sturdy character of great experience, has produced one of the flagships of the appellation. Everything has been carefully controlled, right up to the maturation *en barrique*. It has an intense garnet colour and a subtle bouquet of very ripe soft fruits, spices and cocoa. The palate rests on integrated, velvety tannins. This Bordeaux will improve still further in a cool cellar. The **Château Guibon 2001 (5–8 €)**, matured in barrel, is commended: its lively tannins suggest it be kept until 2006.
♠ André Lurton, Ch. Bonnet, 33420 Grézillac, tel. 05.57.25.58.58, fax 05.57.74.98.59, e-mail andrelurton@andrelurton.com ☑
✠ by appt.

DOM. DE BOUILLEROT 2000★★

| | 2 ha | 9,000 | | | 3–5 € |

Thierry Bos is a perfectionist – he was noticed last year for his Côtes de Bordeaux Saint Macaire – and here offers an attractive Bordeaux with a surprisingly intense bouquet of bilberry and blackberry. This elegant fruitiness reappears on the powerful but balanced palate, whose freshness is a good match for the muffled tannins. This remarkable wine is already balanced, and ready to be enjoyed now and in the future.
♠ Thierry Bos, Lacombe, 33190 Gironde-sur-Dropt, tel. 05.56.71.46.04, fax 05.56.71.46.04, e-mail thierry.bos@wanadoo.fr ☑
✠ by appt.

CH. BOURDICOTTE 2001★

| | 10 ha | 76,000 | | | 3–5 € |

This owner has made the most of his estate to produce this wine: a Merlot grown in a well-exposed position on the foothills of the Butte de Launay, the highest point in the Gironde, with maceration for 30 days followed by rigorous maturation. It is therefore not surprising to find a bouquet of such warm intensity: ripe grape, fruit stone, quince and fig. The round, powerful substance has good balance and character and lingers with finesse. Also very successful is the **Château Moulin de Pillardot 2001**, matured in barrel, a happy combination of fruits and tannins. These two wines can be drunk from 2004 onwards.
♠ Dom. de Bourdicotte, Le Bourg, 33790 Cazaugitat, tel. 05.56.61.32.55, fax 05.56.61.38.26
♠ Rolet Jarbin

CH. DE BRUSSAC 2001★

| | n.c. | 100,000 | | | 5–8 € |

The crimson colour, fringed with garnet, shows that this wine is beginning to develop. This is confirmed by the well-integrated bouquet which still releases a few menthol- and liquorice-flavoured notes. The pleasant palate is rich in jammy nuances, and rises to a smooth finish. This wine is ready now
♠ M. Roussarie, BP 100, 33330 Saint-Emilion, tel. 05.57.55.58.00, fax 05.57.74.18.47, e-mail contact@noueix-lebegue.com

CH. DU BUISSON
Elevé en fût de chêne 2001★

| | 8 ha | 40,000 | | | 3–5 € |

This wine was produced according to the quality code of the Ginestet company. It has a strong colour and aromas of crystallized fruits and plum in brandy. Clean-tasting from the attack, it soon unveils its rich flesh and flavours of blackberry and grape jelly. Some of the tannins are still firm, suggesting that it should be kept until 2005. The **La Chapelle Saint-Vincent Elevé en Fût de Chêne 2001** also wins one star for its tasty tannic structure and range of flavours: tobacco, cocoa, ripe fruits and spices. This brand, issued by Ginestet, is distributed by the Carrefour chain.
♠ Ginestet, 19, av. de Fontenille, 33360 Carignan-de-Bordeaux, tel. 05.56.68.81.82, fax 05.56.20.94.47, e-mail contact@ginestet.fr ☑
✠ by appt.
♠ François Zaros

CALVET
Réserve Elevé en fût de chêne 2001★

| | n.c. | 2,100,000 | | | 3–5 € |

The Réserve de Calvet is a regular in the *Guide*, offering a dependable level of quality which guarantees its success in the export market. The 2001 wine has a deep-red, brilliant colour and a bouquet releasing soft fruits with fine spicy nuances and a slightly vanilla-flavoured base. The well-extracted tannins reveal flavours of cocoa, then merge into a praline-flavoured, balsamic finish. This wine can be drunk now or left in the cellar to achieve perfect harmony.
♠ Calvet, 75, cours du Médoc, BP 11, 33028 Bordeaux Cedex, tel. 05.56.43.59.00, fax 05.56.43.17.78, e-mail calvet@calvet.com

CH. CAMERAC 2001★

| ■ | 3,5 ha | 26,000 | ▮ ♦ | 5–8 € |

Anyone wishing to get away from the main tourist roads should visit the little commune of Puy, near Monségur, the chapel with its square chevet and the old mills on the edge of the River Dropt. The Château Camerac will also welcome visitors and show them this 2001 wine with its bouquet of iris and Morello cherry. The attack is supple, then a velvety substance is revealed with fine, ripe tannins. It is ready to drink now.

☙ SCEA Regaud, La Tuilerie du Puy, 33580 Le Puy, tel. 05.56.61.61.92, fax 05.56.61.86.90, e-mail regaud@free.fr ☑
☙ ev. day 8.30am–12 noon 1pm–6pm

CARAYON-LA-ROSE

Cuvée d'Excellence 2001★

| ■ | 13 ha | 100,000 | ▮ ♦ | 3–5 € |

This Bordeaux from the Dulong company, an old Bordeaux firm, is a safe bet with plenty of happy customers. The bouquet is complex and powerful, and when the glass is swirled reveals floral notes (iris) and aromas of ripe grapes, while the consistent but supple palate develops crystallized nuances and flavours of plum in brandy. The velvety tannins form a background to show off the lingering aromas.

☙ Dulong Frères et Fils, 29, rue Jules-Guesde, 33270 Floirac, tel. 05.56.86.51.15, fax 05.56.40.66.41, e-mail dulong@dulong.com ☑
☙ by appt.

CH. CHANTELOISEAU 2000★

| ■ | 25,03 ha | 70,000 | ▮ ♦ | 5–8 € |

This wine was grown on the slopes of a hill visited both by François Mauriac and Toulouse-Lautrec, and which stands under the protection of the Virgin and Child (at Verdelais). It has already developed well, as can be seen from the garnet colour with brick-red nuances and the skilful blending of the aromas of blackcurrant syrup and bilberry. The tannic framework is still a little austere, but harmony will soon come after a spell in the cellar. Quite soon, this 2001 wine will be ready to serve with a meal.

☙ EARL Dulac Séraphon, 2, Pantoc, 33490 Verdelais, tel. 05.56.62.02.08, fax 05.56.76.71.49 ☑
☙ by appt.

CH. LA CHAPELLE-MAILLARD

Elevé en fût de chêne 2001★

| ■ | 9.45 ha | 51,000 | ❰❱ | 5–8 € |

In the middle of this 15-ha estate is a mythical umbrella pine (featured on the label), which used to be a secret recognition sign for Protestants scattered about the countryside. This is now the logo of Chapelle-Maillard, the source of this deep-garnet Bordeaux 2001. The bouquet has musky and peppery nuances, enhanced by light touches of toast and roasting. The palate is full and fairly soft, with good-quality tannins that support its gently vanilla-flavoured finish. Keep it in a prime spot in the cellar until 2005.

☙ Jean-Christophe Mauro, SCEA Ch. La Chapelle-Maillard, Bérard, 33220 Saint-Quentin-de-Caplong, tel. 05.57.41.26.92, fax 05.57.41.27.87, e-mail jean-christophe.mauro@wanadoo.fr ☑
☙ by appt.

CLOS DE PELIGON

Elevé en fût de chêne 2001★

| ■ | 6 ha | 30,000 | ▮❰❱ | 3–5 € |

The Reynaud estate is cultivated in the traditional manner. They always harvest by hand, and plough the land in the old style. The vines are mostly Merlot, planted on sand, clay and gravel; this 2001 wine has a brilliant, clear red colour, and releases various notes of ripe grape, vanilla and toasted almond. The firm tannins give the palate good shape and a lingering finish. This Bordeaux should be kept for two to three years.

☙ EARL Vignobles Reynaud, 13, rte de Libourne, 33450 Saint-Loubès, tel. 05.56.20.47.52, fax 05.56.68.65.21 ☑
☙ by appt.

DOM. DE LA COLOMBINE 2001★

| ■ | n.c. | 10,000 | ▮ ♦ | 3–5 € |

This wine is an almost equal blend of Merlot, which gives it its softness, and a Cabernet Franc rich in delicately peppery notes. The aromas of soft fruits (Morello cherry) spread through the rounded, vigorous flesh, which is also well supported by tannins. This is a cheerful wine, just right for a Sunday feast in the near future.

☙ Les producteurs réunis de Puisseguin et Lussac-Saint-Emilion, Durand, 33570 Puisseguin, tel. 05.57.55.50.40, fax 05.57.74.57.43, e-mail vignoble@producteurs-reunis.com ☑
☙ by appt.
☙ Jean-Louis Rabiller

CH. LA COMMANDERIE DE QUEYRET 2001★

| ■ | 30 ha | 180,000 | ▮ ♦ | 5–8 € |

This former property of the Templars is now a family business with some 30 ha devoted to this wine (Merlot and Cabernet on a clay-limestone soil). It has a crimson colour and the bouquet releases aromas of cherry and fig combined with overripe black grape. The palate immediately reveals its full and generous substance, with no trace of harshness. This wine has a very good, impressive flavour, and will go well with a dish of roast pork.

☙ Claude Comin, Ch. La Commanderie, 33790 Saint-Antoine-du-Queyret, tel. 05.56.61.31.98, fax 05.56.61.34.22, e-mail vignoblecomin@wanadoo.fr ☑
☙ by appt.

CH. LA CROIX DES DUCS 2000★

| ■ | 3 ha | 18,000 | ▮ ♦ | 5–8 € |

The first attraction of this wine with crimson highlights, made from 90% Merlot, is a fairly intense spicy bouquet with gamey nuances (meat). The second comes from its forthcoming, full structure, which develops silkily towards a complex fruity finish. This is a balanced wine, ready to be enjoyed.

☙ Bruno Marchand, 4, Bonneau, 33570 Montagne, tel. 05.57.74.69.23, fax 05.57.74.54.21, e-mail chateauhaut.bonneau-contact@wanadoo.fr ☑
☙ ev. day 9am–12 noon 2pm–6pm

CH. DES DEUX RIVES 2001★★

| ■ | 20 ha | 62,000 | ▮ ♦ | 5–8 € |

The commune of Saint-Avit-Saint-Nazaire still has traces of Roman occupation. The main quality of this wine-growing terroir is its richness, or so one would think after tasting this intensely coloured Bordeaux with its powerful perfumes of ripe soft fruit (cherry and strawberry). The dense, velvety structure develops towards a smooth finish. It is ready to drink now. Also distributed by Delong is the Château Les Bruges 2001, matured in tank, which is commended.

☙ Dulong Frères et Fils, 29, rue Jules-Guesde, 33270 Floirac, tel. 05.56.86.51.15, fax 05.56.40.66.41, e-mail dulong@dulong.com
☙ by appt.

ESSENCE DE DOURTHE 2001★★

| ■ | 8 ha | 6,400 | ❰❱ | 46–76 € |

2001

e∫∫eŋce
DE DOURTHE
BORDEAUX

This vintage of Essence de Dourthe is worthy of its predecessor, which also won the *coup de coeur* last year. The art of blending is here brought to perfection, an admirable synthesis of rigorously selected components. The wine has a deep colour and a complex nose combining notes of roasting with cherry, prune and cocoa butter. The soft tannins are very

expressive, but rounded and coated in a rich substance, and contribute to the balance of the finely toasted palate. Lay this remarkable wine down for two to three years. Another to try is the Bordeaux **Beau Mayne 2001 (3–5 €)** matured in barrel, which the Jury commended for its fruitiness and supple nature.
- Dourthe, 35, rue de Bordeaux, 33290 Parempuyre, tel. 05.56.35.53.00, fax 05.56.35.53.29, e-mail contact@cvbg.com ☑
☥ by appt.

EPICURE
Elevé en fût de chêne 2000★
| ■ | 35 ha | 46,200 | ⅲ | 5–8 € |

Once more, Epicure wins its one star for the qualities which have made it such a success. The crimson colour is very elegant, as is the integrated bouquet, where the oak ("French oak," says the label) is redolent of Merlot, the main variety in its composition. The Cabernet Sauvignon lends qualities of cinnamon and nutmeg, while the tasty tannins guarantee that it will keep well.
- SARL Bordeaux Vins Sélection, 27, rue Roullet, 33800 Bordeaux, tel. 05.57.35.12.35, fax 05.57.35.12.36, e-mail bvs.grands.crus@wanadoo.fr
- B. Pujol

L'ESPRIT DE BRANDEY
Elevé en fût de chêne 2001★
| ■ | 2 ha | 13,500 | ⅲ | 5–8 € |

This wine was made to fulfill a desire to draw the essence from this very fertile terroir, excellent for growing Merlot, whose limited area justifies harvesting by hand. It has a strong garnet colour, offering what Merlot does best, that is, a very soft bouquet where prune, truffles and leather combine harmoniously. The palate is just as impressive, prolonging the gentle aromas thanks to a successful balance between the fruit of the grape and a fairly smooth toasty note. Drink this wine while it is still lovely and fresh.
- SCEA Vignobles Chevillard, Ch. de Brandey, 33350 Ruch, tel. 05.57.40.54.18, fax 05.57.40.58.82 ☑
☥ by appt.

VIGNES ET PASSION D'EXCELLOR
Elevé en fût de chêne 2001★★
| ■ | n.c. | 72,000 | ⅲ | 5–8 € |

Excellor has won much praise, on a par with the enthusiasm demonstrated by its producer on the label. The deep-violet colour, with purplish highlights, heralds aromas of raspberry enriched by notes of vanilla and warm oak. The consistent and stimulating body is full, round and tannic. This long and tasty wine will be ready in 2005 to serve with roast beef and strong cheeses. Also distributed by Prodiffu is the **Château Talmont 2001 (3–5 €)**, matured in tank, which wins one star: its tasty but still youthful tannins mean it should be kept for two to three years. Another star goes to the **Château Cèdre Latache 2001 (3–5 €)**, matured in tank: this one is smooth enough to be ready in 2004.
- Prodiffu, 17–19, rte des Vignerons, 33790 Landerrouat, tel. 05.56.61.33.73, fax 05.56.61.40.57, e-mail prodiffu@prodiffu.com

CH. FLEUR SAINT-ESPERIT
Elevé en fût de chêne 2001★
| ■ | 0.88 ha | 7,000 | ⅲ | 3–5 € |

This wine was made from equal parts of Cabernet Franc and Cabernet Sauvignon grown on a sandy soil. It has a brilliant crimson colour, and reveals fine notes of pepper, liquorice and menthol derived from the Cabernet. Its full palate has well-integrated robust tannins and offers a touch of violet. The slight bitterness at the finish does no harm to the general balance.
- GFA V. et P. Fourreau, Chevrol, 33500 Néac, tel. 05.57.25.13.34, fax 05.57.51.91.79 ☑

DOM. FLORIMOND-LA-BREDE 2001★
| ■ | 15 ha | 20,527 | ▮ ♦ | 3–5 € |

This authentic Bordeaux commemorates Louis Marinier, the former owner of the château and a great upholder of wine-making in the Gironde. It is made solely from Merlot, has a great array of vermillion highlights, and a fruity bouquet (blackberry and bigaroon cherry), enhanced by perfumes of praliné. The palate is round, full-bodied and well supported by tasty tannins. This wine will open out in two to three years.
- Vignobles Louis Marinier, Dom. Florimond-La-Brède, 33390 Berson, tel. 05.57.64.34.63, fax 05.57.64.23.27, e-mail vignobleslouismarinier@wanadoo.fr ☑
☥ ev. day 8am–12 noon 2pm–5pm; Sat. Sun. by appt.; cl. Aug.

CH. DE GADRAS 2001★★
| ■ | 14 ha | 40,000 | ⅲ | 5–8 € |

Once more, experience has paid off: Claude Delpech, estate owner and highly skilled wine-grower who was trained in the Grands Crus of the Médoc, has done his best ... and it wins him the *coup de coeur*. This wine is fringed with youthful highlights, leading to a bouquet of jammy soft fruits, vanilla and coconut. On the palate it is soft and round, revealing a fine tannic structure supporting an elegant oak, and a tasty freshness which indicates that it will soon be ready to drink. However, it will reach its full potential if kept for several years.
- Claude et Michèle Delpech, 4, Gadras, 33580 Saint-Vivien-de-Monségur, tel. 05.56.61.82.69, fax 05.56.61.82.69 ☑
☥ by appt.

GINESTET 2001★
| ■ | n.c. | 2,000,000 | ▮ ♦ | 3–5 € |

This firm of négociants aims to sell two million bottles of its reliable brand. The 2001 vintage has an attractive brilliant colour with brick-red highlights; there are plenty of scents of ripe grapes and macerated fruits in both the elegant bouquet and the supple palate, which is well structured and fairly long. Two other wines win one star: the **Mascaron par Ginestet 2000 (5–8 €)**, matured in barrel, and the **Grande Lice 2001 (3–5 €)**, distributed by Système U.
- Ginestet, 19, av. de Fontenille, 33360 Carignan-de-Bordeaux, tel. 05.56.68.81.82, fax 05.56.20.94.47, e-mail contact@ginestet.fr ☑
☥ by appt.

DOM. DES GRANDS ORMES 2001★
| ■ | 10 ha | 60,000 | ⅲ | 5–8 € |

Saint-Sulpice-de-Faleyrens has the impressive Pierrefitte menhir and a Romanesque church dating from the 11th and 12th centuries. Do not miss the grotesque crows in the cornice, representing the Seven Deadly Sins. It would be difficult not to want to drink this brilliant violet Bordeaux with its complex perfumes combining mushroom, truffles and hyacinth. The well-integrated oak lingers on the soft, balanced palate. Fine-grained tannins join in the long, warm finish. Also very successful is the **Château Rambaud Sélection Vieilles Vignes 2001**, matured in barrel. This is a chewy wine, its high-grade tannins needing to settle for three years in the cellar.
- SCEA Daniel Mouty, Ch. du Barry, 33350 Sainte-Terre, tel. 05.57.84.55.88, fax 05.57.74.92.99, e-mail daniel.mouty@wanadoo.fr ☑
☥ ev. day except Sun. 8am–12.30pm 2pm–6pm; cl. week of 15 Aug., 20 Dec.–5 Jan.

CH. LA GUILLAUMETTE

Cuvée Prestige Elevé en fût de chêne 2000★

| ■ | 35 ha | 100,000 | ◧ | 3–5 € |

Bernard Artigue is a regular in the *Guide* because of the way he cultivates his vines: double Guyot pruning, leaf-thinning and bunch-thinning. Nothing has been spared to produce this garnet-coloured wine with a bouquet releasing fine scents of nutmeg and resin. Its fruity and rounded flesh (70% Merlot) will make it ready to drink in 2004.

➤ Bernard Artigue, Ch. Beaule, 33370 Pompignac, tel. 05.56.72.48.93, fax 05.56.72.92.97

CH. HAUT-MEDOU 2001★★

| ■ | 24 ha | 180,000 | ▮ ♦ | 5–8 € |

The Château Haut-Medou has made an outstanding deep-red wine with a developing bouquet of spices and ripe fruits. From the attack, the tannic shape appears and is soon coated by a fruity flesh recalling quince and blackberry. A mouth-filling Bordeaux which will slowly improve in the shadows of a cool cellar.

➤ Grands Vins de Gironde, Dom. du Ribet, BP 59, 33451 Saint-Loubès Cedex, tel. 05.57.97.07.20, fax 05.57.97.07.27, e-mail gvg@gvg.fr
➤ SCEA CSA

CH. HAUT-MEYREAU

Entre ciel... et terre... 2000★

| ■ | 1 ha | 6,000 | ◧ | 23–30 € |

This family of wine-growers, using the skills passed on by six generations, have made a prestige wine for the first time with an output per hectare worthy of a communal appellation. And at a very steep price! Although the colour has only developed to a slight extent, the intense bouquet bears signs of the barrel in its roasted notes of cinnamon and Virginia tobacco, as well as a note of soft fruits. The palate reveals good-quality oak, combining length with a vanilla-flavoured softness.

➤ SCEA Ch. Haut-Meyreau, Goumin, 33420 Dardenac, tel. 05.56.23.91.90, fax 05.56.23.49.57
Ⅰ ev. day except Sat. Sun. 9am–7pm
➤ Bernard

CH. HAUT PEYRUGUET 2001★

| ■ | 63 ha | 450,000 | ▮ ♦ | –3 € |

The intense-red colour heralds a winey and powerfully fruity bouquet. This wine's very pleasant opening is not let down by the round and full first impression on the palate, which develops towards a structured shape and a fruity finish. This 2001 wine is still youthful, but will improve if kept for two years. The **Château Saint-Florin 2001**, matured in tank, also wins one star: it has already achieved good balance and will be ready to drink in 2004.

➤ Jean-Marc Jolivet, Ch. Saint-Florin, 33790 Soussac, tel. 05.56.61.31.61, fax 05.56.61.34.87
Ⅰ by appt.

CH. HAUT-PRADOT 2001★★

| ■ | 5.8 ha | 32,766 | ▮ ♦ | 3–5 € |

This Bordeaux has been most carefully made: maceration of the Merlot and the Cabernet Sauvignon within the "cup," that is, by a series of daily tastings. The result is a happy marriage of aromas of ripe grapes and fine notes of blackcurrant and redcurrant. A fruity and tender flesh fills the palate, enhanced by balsamic flavours. This 2001 wine is already pleasant, and will improve further in the course of the next two years. The **B de Bertiac 2001**, matured in tank, wins one star, as does the Cheval-Quancard **Château Belle Cure 2000**, matured in tank.

➤ André Quancard, chem. de La Cabeyre, 33240 Saint-André-de-Cubzac, tel. 05.57.33.42.42, fax 05.57.33.42.05, e-mail aqa@andrequancard.com
➤ Fazenbat

CH. LAGRAVE-PARAN 2001★

| ■ | 5 ha | 6,500 | ◧ | 3–5 € |

Merlot and Cabernet Sauvignon were harvested by hand on a clay-gravel terroir. The wine was carefully vinified, then was kept in a French oak barrel for one year. It has a brilliant red colour, its toasty and smoky aromas revealing a certain maturity on the round palate, underlined by toasted notes of good-quality oak. It will achieve perfect balance in two or three years.

➤ EARL Lafon, Ch. Lagrave-Paran, 33490 Saint-André-du-Bois, tel. 06.89.33.20.20, fax 05.56.76.49.78, e-mail pierre-lafon@wanadoo.fr
Ⅰ by appt.

CH. LAUDUC

Classic 2001★★

| ■ | 28 ha | 150,000 | ▮ ♦ | 3–5 € |

The saga of the Grandeau family at the Château Lauduc is typical of the troubled history of agriculture in the 20th century. Nowadays, the wines from this estate are rewarded by being selected in this *Guide*. This ruby Classic with deep-purple highlights reveals a delicate and well-extracted substance. The developing bouquet recalls soft spices, *rancio* and hyacinth. This is a very charming Bordeaux with a palate of great finesse, which means it can be drunk now. The **D:vin 2001 (15–23 €)**, matured in barrel, also wins two stars: its aromas of small ripe soft fruits combined with a vigorous and structured flesh which will become more rounded between now and 2005.

➤ GAEC Grandeau, Ch. Lauduc, 33370 Tresses, tel. 05.57.34.43.56, fax 05.57.34.43.58, e-mail m.grandeau@lauduc.fr
Ⅰ by appt.

CH. MAISON NOBLE

Cuvée Prestige Vieilli en fût de chêne 2001★★

| ■ | 2.5 ha | 15,000 | ◧ | 5–8 € |

The tasters praised the power and sturdy character of this brilliant, strong-coloured Cuvée Prestige with its intense perfumes of stewed fruits, leather and soft vanilla. Subtle oaky nuances mingle with spices on the complex palate, whose impressive tannic framework means it will keep remarkably well. Let time do its work to bring out the best in this wine.

➤ Bernard Sartron, Maison Noble, 33230 Maransin, tel. 05.57.69.19.36, fax 05.57.69.17.78
Ⅰ by appt.

CH. MEZAIN 2001★

| ■ | 17 ha | 130,000 | ▮ ♦ | 5–8 € |

The bell of the Church of Saint-Laurent-du-Bois, dedicated to Sainte Pétronille, summons the visitor to this commune, where the Château Mezain has produced this garnet-coloured 2001 wine with a bouquet of game, truffles and leather. The mouth is round and full, releasing notes of ripe, almost crystallized, grapes while Morello cherry makes an appearance in the smooth finish. This wine will be ready by the New Year. The **Château de Cathalogne 2001**, matured in tank, is commended.

➤ Dulong Frères et Fils, 29, rue Jules-Guesde, 33270 Floirac, tel. 05.56.86.51.15, fax 05.56.40.66.41, e-mail dulong@dulong.com
Ⅰ by appt.
➤ Despagne

CH. MOTTE MAUCOURT

Vieilli en fût de chêne 2001★★

| ■ | 10 ha | 10,000 | ◧ | 5–8 € |

The Villeneuve family have expanded their vineyard since 1984 and now have 46 ha. This wine demonstrates their skill. It is already so pleasant and yet its brilliant colour is still full of youthful freshness, as are the mentholated and floral aromas (rose and violet). The palate is initially honest and winey, soon revealing powerful tannins and concentration, enhanced by a sound oakiness. The lingering finish combines notes of pepper, undergrowth and agaric. Open a bottle from time to time and see how the wine develops in the longer term. The **Château Motte Maucourt 2001 Elevé en Cuve**, is commended: it should be kept for two years to allow it to soften.

➤ Villeneuve, EARL Ch. Motte Maucourt, 2, au Canton, 33760 Saint-Genis-du-Bois, tel. 05.56.71.54.77, fax 05.56.71.64.23
Ⅰ ev. day except Sun. 9am–12 noon 2pm–7pm

CH. MOULIN DE GALLINEAU 2001★

| | n.c. | 100,000 | 🔲 🍴 | 5–8 € |

This garnet-coloured Bordeaux with bronze highlights was made from equal parts of Cabernet and Merlot, and releases rather rough scents of undergrowth, leather and venison. Its solid palate is characterized by rather austere tannins, but releases interesting woodland notes which are part of the wine's personality. This is an unconventional wine, to be drunk around 2005.

↬ SCEA Vignobles Salagnac, BP 100,
33330 Saint-Emilion, tel. 05.57.55.58.00, fax 05.57.74.18.47,
e-mail contact@moueix-lebegue.com

CH. POUCHAUD-LARQUEY 2001★★

| | 14 ha | 50,000 | 🔲 🍴 | 5–8 € |

The 20 ha of vines on this estate are grown organically, and enjoy a south-facing clay-siliceous terroir. The Cabernets (60%) slightly dominate the Merlot in this brilliant purple wine which releases copious aromas of ripe soft fruits and cherry jam. A remarkable structure of settled tannins supports its rich, soft vigour. This is a strong party wine, to be drunk in two years with a roast leg of lamb. The **Château des Seigneurs de Pommyers 2001**, matured in tank, wins one star for its fullness and fruity length.

↬ Piva Père et Fils, Ch. Pouchaud-Larquey, 33190 Morizès,
tel. 05.56.71.44.97, fax 05.56.71.61.82 ☑
⚡ by appt.

PREMIUS

Elevé en fût de chêne 2001★

| | n.c. | 1,000,000 | 🍷 | 5–8 € |

The Yvon Mau company belongs to the Freixenet group, and distributes an interesting range of wines: three Bordeaux were given one star by the Jury. The **Comte de Maignac 2001 (3–5 €)**, matured in barrel, and the **Château Tuquet de Gaillard 2001 (3–5 €)**, matured in tank, are already pleasant and velvety and will be ready to drink in 2004. This Premius has an elegant colour with brick-red highlights, and toasty and gamey aromas (leather and venison). Fine notes of pepper are apparent on the palate, which is still marked by the tannins but will improve in time. Drink this with friends in 2005.

↬ SA Yvon Mau, 33190 Gironde-sur-Dropt,
tel. 05.56.61.54.54, fax 05.56.61.54.61,
e-mail info@ymau.com

PRIMO PALATUM 2001★

| | 3 ha | 2,100 | 🍷 | 11–15 € |

This Bordeaux was made in a tiny vineyard from a blend of three great grape varieties from the Gironde. Its crimson colour catches the eye. The harmonious palate has roundness and good length with toasty notes and the fruity scents of an attractive bouquet. The balance can be felt right up to the finish. This wine could improve further if kept for two to three years.

↬ Primo Palatum, 1, Cirette, 33190 Morizès,
tel. 05.56.71.39.39, fax 05.56.71.39.40,
e-mail xavier-copel@primo-palatum.com ☑
⚡ by appt.
↬ Xavier Copel

CH. RELEOU

Cuvée Prestige 2001★

| | 10 ha | 60,000 | 🔲 🍴 | 5–8 € |

This Cuvée Prestige from the Château Reléou has a lively red colour with shades of deep purple, and releases a subtle but already fruity and fine bouquet (almond). A supple attack gives way to a vigorous, robust body, reinforced by lively tannins which keep their elegance. This wine is still young and full of promise. From the same producer, the **Château Grand Bireau 2000**, matured in tank, is commended.

↬ SCEA Michel Barthe, 18, Girolatte,
33420 Naujan-et-Postiac, tel. 05.57.84.55.23,
fax 05.57.84.57.37,
e-mail scea.barthemichel@wanadoo.fr ☑
⚡ by appt.

CH. REYNIER

Cuvée Héritage 2000★★

| | 2 ha | 2,000 | 🍷 | 8–11 € |

This Bordeaux by Marc Lurton was made from a blend of Cabernet Sauvignon (60%) and 40% Merlot; the grapes were harvested on a high-quality clay-limestone plot. It has an intense garnet-red colour and combines fruit, roasting, pepper and balsamic notes. The solid but harmonious palate has a lingering softness. This 2000 wine is already very attractive, and will lose nothing from being kept for four or five years. In the same appellation, the **Château de Bouchet La Rentière 2001 (5–8 €)**, matured in tank, is commended: it has very concentrated aromas but is still lively and needs to be kept for a long time.

↬ SCEA Vignobles Marc Lurton, Ch. Reynier,
33420 Grézillac, tel. 05.57.84.52.02, fax 05.57.84.56.93,
e-mail marc.lurton@wanadoo.fr ☑
⚡ by appt.

CH. LA ROCHE SAINT JEAN 2001★

| | 3,5 ha | 25,000 | 🔲 🍴 | 3–5 € |

This pale-garnet Bordeaux has a summery feel with its notes of jammy fruits and prune, underlined by a hint of capsicum. The full mouth, with well-structured, compact tannins, reveals a rich, very mature substance. It will achieve good balance in three or four years.

↬ Jean-Pierre Pauquet, RN 23, Le Bourg, 33190 Camiran,
tel. 05.56.71.44.95, fax 05.56.71.49.02 ☑
⚡ by appt.

CH. ROQUEFORT

Roquefortissime 2001★★

| | 3 ha | 9,000 | 🍷 | 8–11 € |

The label of Roquefortissime is a familiar feature in the *Guide*. This one illustrates the *coup de cœur* given last year to the 2000 vintage. The 2001 version is rewa   :d with two stars for its multiple scents of dried fruits and spices. This wine is impressively concentrated and needs to be decanted to let it open out. Try it in 2005 or 2006. While you are waiting, you could drink the estate's main wine, the **Château Roquefort 2001 (5–8 €)**, matured in oak, which wins one star. The **Château Cabaron 2001 (11–15 €)** was also matured in oak and needs time to age; it is commended.

↬ Ch. Roquefort, 33760 Lugasson, tel. 05.56.23.97.48,
fax 05.56.23.50.60,
e-mail chateau-roquefort@vignobles-bellanger.com ☑
⚡ by appt.
↬ F. Bellanger

CH. LA ROSE DU PIN 2001★

| | 31 ha | n.c. | 🔲 🍴 | 5–8 € |

Lovers of old buildings will want to visit Romagne, in the Entre-Deux-Mers region, and the 12th century church surmounted by a gabled bell-tower; the bell itself is 450 years old. The Château La Rose du Pin is not far away, and offers a Bordeaux full of aromas of soft fruits. Its full and nicely structured substance is coated with spicy flavours. The tannins are still lively, and need time to soften. Keep it until 2005.

↬ Cordier-Mestrezat et Domaines, 109, rue Achard, BP
154, 33042 Bordeaux Cedex, tel. 05.56.11.29.00,
fax 05.56.11.29.01, e-mail mestrezat-domaines@wanadoo.fr
⚡ by appt.
↬ Vignobles Ducourt

CH. SEGONZAC LA FORET 2001★

	10 ha	67,000	▪ ♦	5–8 €

The two Cabernets were blended with Merlot to make this velvety violet-coloured Bordeaux which releases promising notes of spices and musk (leather). The straightforward, mouth-filling palate has good balance, the tannic framework derived from the Cabernets combining with the flavours. This wine is both invigorating and tasty, and the finish is good. Serve this from 2004.

☛ A. de Luze et Fils, Dom. du Ribet, BP 59, 33450 Saint-Loubès, tel. 05.57.97.07.20, fax 05.57.97.07.27, e-mail jm.alige@gvg.fr
☛ Jeanine Segonzac

CH. TIRE PE 2001★★

	2 ha	10,000	▪ ♦	5–8 €

With its violet colour and auburn highlights, this Bordeaux won over all the tasters with its rich aromas of ripe fruits. The wine's roundness comes from the predominance of Merlot in the blend (90%). The wine-grower has taken good advantage of his clay-limestone terroir on rocks, vinifying the wine in small batches per plot. The wine's body leaves a lasting silky impression, resting on robust tannins with peppery tones. This is a *coup de coeur* wine, complex and full of vigour, and should be kept for a long time.

☛ David Barrault, Ch. Tire Pé, 33190 Gironde-sur-Dropt, tel. 05.56.71.10.09, fax 05.56.71.10.09, e-mail tirepe@aol.com ☑
☎ by appt.

DOM. DE VALMENGAUX 2001★★

	0.9 ha	4,800	⦀	11–15 €

Vincent Rapin, a jazz musician, and his wife, an architect, embarked on a fantastic adventure when they bought this 1 ha of vines near Fronsac, located on a high-quality clay-limestone terroir. His wine is sold by a négociant on the Bordeaux market, and captivated the Grand Jury. Its deep-violet colour with purple highlights immediately reveals its remarkable concentration. The aromatic range combines soft fruits and spices: cinnamon, vanilla and pepper as well as roasted and cocoa-flavoured notes. There is good substance in the mouth-filling palate, velvety tannins and a long, soft finish. "Oh, it's so good!" exclaimed one delighted taster.

☛ Vincent Rapin, Dom. de Valmengaux, 7, Godineau, 33240 Vérac, tel. 05.57.74.48.92, fax 05.57.74.48.92, e-mail vincent.rapin@libertysurf.fr 🖂

LE VIEUX MOULIN 2001★

	n.c.	300,000	▪ ♦	3–5 €

This famous brand was officially registered in 1914 in the Dutch East Indies, in Batavia. Since then, generations have admired the scarlet colour of its wine and inhaled the spicy bouquet with delight. This 2001 wine is very much in the same spirit, elegantly combining clove and nutmeg all the way to the supple and concentrated substance. This is a promising wine, to be laid down for two years. The brand's Cuvée de Prestige, **Le Vieux Moulin Arte 2001 (5–8 €)**, matured in barrel, also wins one star: it is full, rich and delicately oaky (cinnamon, vanilla and roasting).

☛ SA Mähler-Besse, 49, rue Camille-Godard, 33000 Bordeaux, tel. 05.56.56.04.30, fax 05.56.56.04.59, e-mail france@mahler-besse.com ☑
☎ by appt.

Wines selected but not starred

CH. DE L'AUBRADE 2000

	34 ha	n.c.	▪	8–11 €

☛ GAEC Jean-Pierre et Paulette Lobre, 33580 Rimons, tel. 05.56.71.55.10, fax 05.56.71.61.94 ☑
☎ by appt.

CH. BASTIAN 2001

	6 ha	40,000	▪ ♦	3–5 €

☛ Stéphane Savigneux, Ch. Bastian, 33124 Auros, tel. 05.56.65.51.59, fax 05.56.65.43.78, e-mail stephane.savigneux@wanadoo.fr ☑
☎ by appt.

CH. DE BEAUREGARD-DUCOURT

Le Bois du Fanet 2001

	41 ha	n.c.	⦀	5–8 €

☛ SCEA Vignobles Ducourt, 18, rte de Montignac, 33760 Ladaux, tel. 05.57.34.54.00, fax 05.56.23.48.78, e-mail vignobles-ducourt@wanadoo.fr ☑
☎ by appt.

CH. BELLEVUE 2001

	2.5 ha	17,000	▪	3–5 €

☛ Françoise Alvergne, Ch. Bellevue, 33240 Lugon, tel. 05.57.84.42.66, fax 05.57.24.95.06, e-mail alvergne@oreka.com ☑
☎ by appt.

CH. BELLEVUE LA MONGIE 2001

	9 ha	65,000	▪ ♦	3–5 €

☛ Michel Boyer, Ch. Bellevue La Mongie, 33420 Génissac, tel. 05.57.24.48.43, fax 05.57.24.48.63, e-mail boyer.michel@worldonline.fr ☑
☎ by appt.

CH. BELLEVUE-LA-RANDEE 2000

	1.2 ha	8,300	▪ ♦	3–5 €

☛ GAEC Bourseau et Fils, 9, Boutin-Arnaud, 33133 Galgon, tel. 05.57.84.32.46, fax 05.57.84.32.46 ☑

CARREFOUR 2001

■	n.c.	3,500,000	▮ ◊	3–5 €

➤ Ginestet, 19, av. de Fontenille,
33360 Carignan-de-Bordeaux, tel. 05.56.68.81.82,
fax 05.56.20.94.47, e-mail contact@ginestet.fr
🍷 by appt.

CH. CAZEAU 2001

■	240 ha	1,200,000	▮ ◊	3–5 €

➤ SCI Domaines Cazeau et Perey,
33540 Sauveterre-de-Guyenne, tel. 05.56.71.50.76,
fax 05.56.71.87.70, e-mail cfontaniol@laguyennoise.com
➤ Anne-Marie and Michel Martin

CH. CLOS DU BOURG 2000

■	4.75 ha	38,500	▮ ◐ ◊	5–8 €

➤ Ch. Manieu, La Rivière, 33126 Fronsac,
tel. 05.57.24.92.79, fax 05.57.24.92.78,
e-mail chateaumanieu@wanadoo.fr ☑
🍷 ev. day 10am–12 noon 2pm–6pm; Sat. Sun. by appt.
➤ Léon

CH. CLUZAN 2001

■	25 ha	133,333	▮ ◊	5–8 €

➤ Maison Sichel, 8, rue de la Poste, 33210 Langon,
tel. 05.56.63.50.52, fax 05.56.63.42.28,
e-mail maison-sichel@sichel.fr

CH. FONCROZE 2001

■	10 ha	53,000	▮ ◊	3–5 €

➤ A. Lançon et Fils, GAEC de Foncroze,
33540 Sauveterre-de-Guyenne, tel. 05.56.71.59.74,
fax 05.56.71.59.74 ☑
🍷 by appt.

FONT-DESTIAC 2001

■	10 ha	66,000	▮ ◊	3–5 €

➤ Closerie Destiac, Les Lèves,
33220 Sainte-Foy-la-Grande, tel. 05.57.56.02.02,
fax 05.57.56.02.22, e-mail oeno@univitis.fr ☑
🍷 ev. day except Sun. and Mon. 9.30am–12.30pm
3.30pm–6.30pm

CH. GROSSOMBRE

Elevé en fût de chêne 2001

■	7 ha	50,000	▮ ◐ ◊	5–8 €

➤ Béatrice Lurton, BP 10, 33420 Grézillac,
tel. 05.57.25.58.58, fax 05.57.74.98.59,
e-mail andrelurton@andrelurton.com ☑

CH. HAUT GUILLEBOT 2001

■	n.c.	20,000	▮ ◊	5–8 €

➤ Eveline Rénier, Ch. Haut Guillebot, 33420 Lugaignac,
tel. 05.57.84.53.92, fax 05.57.84.62.73,
e-mail chateauhautguillebot@wanadoo.fr ☑
🍷 ev. day 9am–12 noon 2pm–5pm; Sat. Sun. by appt.;
cl. 15–31 Aug.

CH. HAUT PELLETAN 2001

■	25 ha	120,000	▮ ◊	3–5 €

➤ EARL Charrut, 33220 Saint-Quentin-de-Caplong,
tel. 05.57.41.22.51 ☑
🍷 by appt.

CH. LALANDE-LABATUT

Cuvée Prestige Elevé en fût de chêne 2001

■	18 ha	120,000	◐	5–8 €

➤ SCEA Vignobles Falxa, 38, ch. de Labatut,
33370 Salleboeuf, tel. 05.56.21.23.18, fax 05.56.21.20.98,
e-mail chateau.lalande-labatut@wanadoo.fr ☑
🍷 by appt.

CH. DE LIGNAC 2001

■	14 ha	109,000	▮ ◊	3–5 €

➤ Dulong Frères et Fils, 29, rue Jules-Guesde,
33270 Floirac, tel. 05.56.86.51.15, fax 05.56.40.66.41,
e-mail dulong@dulong.com
🍷 by appt.

MICHEL LYNCH 2000

■	n.c.	n.c.	▮ ◊	5–8 €

➤ Jean-Michel Cazes Sélection, Route de Bordeaux,
33460 Macau, tel. 05.57.88.56.73, fax 05.57.88.03.84,
e-mail contact@jmcazes-selection.com

DE LYNE 2001

■	6 ha	29,000	▮ ◐	5–8 €

➤ SCEA des Vignobles Denis Barraud, Haut-Renaissance,
33330 Saint-Sulpice-de-Faleyrens, tel. 05.57.84.54.73,
fax 05.57.84.52.07, e-mail denis-barraud@wanadoo.fr ☑
🍷 by appt.

CH. MAHON-LAVILLE

Elevé en fût de chêne 2001

■	1.3 ha	10,000	◐	3–5 €

➤ Jean-Christophe Barbe, Ch. Laville, 33210 Preignac,
tel. 05.56.63.59.45, fax 05.56.63.16.28 ☑
🍷 by appt.

MONTESQUIEU

Réserve du philosophe 2001

■	n.c.	150,000	◐	3–5 €

➤ Vins et Domaines H. de Montesquieu, Aux Fougères, BP
53, 33650 La Brède, tel. 05.56.78.45.45, fax 05.56.20.25.07,
e-mail montesquieu@bordeaux-montesquieu.com ☑

MOULIN DE GASSIOT 2000

■	4 ha	33,000	▮ ◊	5–8 €

➤ Vignerons de Guyenne, Union des producteurs de
Blasimon, 33540 Blasimon, tel. 05.56.71.55.28,
fax 05.56.71.59.32,
e-mail vigneronsdeguyenne@worldonline.fr ☑
🍷 by appt.

CH. MOULIN DE ROULET 2000

■	6 ha	18,000	▮ ◊	3–5 €

➤ Catherine Bonnamy, Moulin de Roulet,
33350 Sainte-Radegonde, tel. 05.57.40.50.51,
fax 05.57.40.58.51 ☑
🍷 by appt.

CH. DE SOURS 2000

■	12.14 ha	60,000	▮ ◐ ◊	8–11 €

➤ SCEA Ch. de Sours, 33750 Saint-Quentin-de-Baron,
tel. 05.57.24.10.81, fax 05.57.24.10.83 ☑
🍷 by appt.
➤ Johnstone

CH. TREYTINS DU GRAND PLANTIER 2001

■	2 ha	16,000	▮ ◊	3–5 €

➤ SCEA Vignobles Condou, quartier Laffitte,
33490 Saint-Pierre-d'Aurillac, tel. 05.56.76.41.70,
fax 05.56.76.49.68 ☑
🍷 by appt.

VIEUX CHATEAU RENAISSANCE

Vieilli en fût de chêne 2000

■	6 ha	12,000	◐	3–5 €

➤ Patrice Turtaut, 33220 Saint-Sulpice-Pommiers,
tel. 05.56.71.59.54, fax 05.56.71.63.81,
e-mail pturtaut@wanadoo.fr ☑
🍷 by appt.

Bordeaux Clairet

CH. BONNANGE 2002★

| | 0.5 ha | 2,000 | ▮ | | 3–5 € |

Claude Bonnange never intended to be a wine-grower, but when he retired with his wife, Julia, he acquired a passion for wine. Now, from his little 19th century mansion, which resembles Trianon, he surveys his vineyard. This enticing and charming Clairet, made from pure Merlot in a limited quantity, is full of scents of flowers and soft fruits (blackcurrent and cherry), and has a very attractive, tasty palate.
➼ Claude et Julia Bonnange, 10, chem. des Roberts, Mazerolles, 33390 Saint-Martin-Lacaussade, tel. 05.57.42.37.70 ☑
Ⓨ ev. day except Sun. 10am–6pm

CH. LESTRILLE-CAPMARTIN
Cuvée Tradition 2002★

| | 1.35 ha | 10,400 | ▮ ⚲ | | 5–8 € |

This pleasant Merlot-based Clairet was made by running the juice off the skins for 30 hours, then fermenting at a low temperature for a long time to protect the aromas. The bouquet is very expressive, full of wild strawberry and raspberry. The first impression is supple, the palate soon enlivened by a slight sparkle which titillates it and opens up its long fruity aromas. This wine has good harmony and is tastily refreshing. Serve it today with a grill.
➼ Jean-Louis Roumage, Lestrille, 33750 Saint-Germain-du-Puch, tel. 05.57.24.51.02, fax 05.57.24.04.58, e-mail jlroumage@lestrille.com ☑
Ⓨ by appt.

CH. MELIN 2002★

| | 1.55 ha | 6,000 | ▮ ⚲ | | 5–8 € |

This vineyard stands on lovely clay-gravel hilltops with a limestone bed beneath. It has excellent exposure, overlooking the Garonne, and is planted with several selected grape varieties. This wine was made with enormous care. When the glass is swirled, the wine releases aromas of flowers and fruits. It is balanced with good length, and would go well with a dish of fine charcuterie.
➼ EARL Vignobles Claude Modet et Fils, Constantin, 33880 Baurech, tel. 05.56.21.34.71, fax 05.56.21.37.72, e-mail vmodet@wanadoo.fr ☑
Ⓨ by appt.

CH. PENIN 2002★★

| | 4.2 ha | 33,000 | ▮ ⚲ | | 5–8 € |

Clairet has been Patrick Carteyron's passion for 20 years. His wine is one of the real originals in the region. The secret lies in the way it is fermented at a low temperature, and vinified on fine lees with yeast stirring. It is well supplied with fine substances which influence its quality, and its especially attractive, lightly fruity aromas suggest all manner of dishes to serve it with: Mediterranean sardines, or Basque-style snails in a piperade with peppers.
➼ SCEA Patrick Carteyron, Ch. Penin, 33420 Génissac, tel. 05.57.24.46.98, fax 05.57.24.41.99, e-mail vignoblescarteyron@wanadoo.fr ☑
Ⓨ by appt.

CH. PIOTE-AUBRION 2002★

| | 1 ha | 5,000 | ▮ | | 5–8 € |

The Aubrion family took over this property in 1998, and now the latest heiress is fiercely keen on preserving the old traditions of grape picking and vinification. This Clairet has a range of scents with elegant shades of intense fruitiness. The cherry colour and the fairly tannic palate contribute to a substantial, harmoniously shaped wine.
➼ Virginie Aubrion, Dom. de Piote, 33240 Aubie-Espessas, tel. 05.57.43.96.10, fax 05.57.43.96.10 ☑

CH. SAINT-OURENS 2002★

| | 0.5 ha | 3,300 | ▮ | | 3–5 € |

This committed countryman, from the cereal-growing lands of the North, came late to winemaking (1990). This year he is offering a wine in very small quantities, made from Merlot (70%) and Cabernet Sauvignon. It has an elegant bouquet of red berries, and a good balance between liveliness, softness and roundness. The technique of making Clairet, by maintaining long contact with the solid parts of the grapes, then running the juice off the skins, gives this wine a pleasant and refreshing character. Serve it with a casserole of poultry liver in a mushroom sauce or pork in caramel.
➼ Michel Maës, 57, rte de Capian, Ch. Saint-Ourens, 33550 Langoiran, tel. 05.56.67.39.45, fax 05.56.67.61.14 ☑
Ⓨ ev. day 9am–12 noon 1pm–6pm

CH. TOUR DE BIOT 2002★

| | 1.6 ha | 12,000 | ▮ ⚲ | | 3–5 € |

This terroir stands on clayey-silty soils planted chiefly with Merlot and Cabernet Franc, and is located in the canton of Sainte-Foy-la-Grande, an old French walled town founded in 1255 by Alphonse de Poitiers, brother of Saint Louis. This wine has surprisingly fine aromas which awaken our senses with floral and fruity notes, citrus fruits and blackcurrant bud to the fore. The richness and vinosity of this Clairet make us admire not only its taste but also the skill of the winemaker.
➼ Gilles Gremen, EARL La Tour Rouge, 33220 La Roquille, tel. 05.57.41.26.49, fax 05.57.41.29.84 ☑
Ⓨ by appt.

Wines selected but not starred

CH. DEGAS 2002

| | 0.8 ha | 4,000 | ▮ ⚲ | | 3–5 € |

➼ Marie-José Degas, La Souloire, 33750 Saint-Germain-du-Puch, tel. 05.57.24.52.32, fax 05.57.24.03.72 ☑
Ⓨ ev. day except Sat. Sun. 8am–5.30pm

JOLY RIVAGE 2002

| | 0.45 ha | 1,000 | ⦿ | | 3–5 € |

➼ SCEA Ch. Beau Rivage, 7, chem. du Bord-de-l'Eau, 33460 Macau, tel. 05.57.10.03.70, fax 05.57.10.02.00, e-mail beau-rivage@aol.com ☑
Ⓨ by appt.
➼ Christine Nadalié

LES VIGNERONS DE SAINT-MARTIN 2002

| | 1.61 ha | 13,150 | ▮ ⚲ | | 3–5 € |

➼ Les Vignerons de Génissac, 54, le Bourg, 33420 Génissac, tel. 05.57.55.55.65, fax 05.57.55.11.61, e-mail cave.genissac@wanadoo.fr ☑ 🏠 🏠
Ⓨ ev. day except Sun. 9am–12 noon 2pm–6pm; Sat. 9am–12 noon

Bordeaux Sec

CH. BOIS-MALOT
Cuvée marine 2002★

| | 0.6 ha | 3,600 | ▮ ⚲ | | 5–8 € |

This wine is packaged in blue bottles, perhaps to remind us of the sea as we serve it with a dish of sea foods. The Jury were surprised by its complex floral and fruity aromas (citrus fruits and banana) topped with honey. Its liveliness and freshness, as well as its flesh, added to its attractions. We should explain that this wine was tasted in a classic green Bordeaux bottle to preserve its anonymity.

➳ SCA Meynard, 133, rte des Valentons, 33450 Saint-Loubès, tel. 05.56.38.94.18, fax 05.56.38.92.47 ☑
☒ by appt.

CH. DE BONHOSTE

Elevé en fût de chêne 2002★★

	n.c.	1,500	🍶	8–11 €

This wine has an unusually transparent appearance, its colours more white than yellow, indicating its youthfulness. The first scents are floral, then a small exotic element appears with passion fruit, guava, mango and an apricot-flavoured sequel. The full and round texture bears the stamp of fermentation in new barrels and a substance provided by the alchemy of maturation on fine lees. It has a very balanced set of aromas, enriched by a skilfully controlled oak.

➳ SCEA des Vignobles Fournier, Ch. de Bonhoste, 33420 Saint-Jean-de-Blaignac, tel. 05.57.84.12.18, fax 05.57.84.15.36 ☑
☒ by appt.

CALVET RESERVE

Vinifié en barrique 2002★

	n.c.	300,000	🍶🍶🍶	3–5 €

Here a major négociant laid down quality standards for this wine, made from a selection of Sémillon (80%) and Sauvignon grown on 40-year-old vines on low-yielding plots. It was vinified with meticulous care, and the result is a wine with an intense bouquet of soft fruits and a fine oak. It is lively on the palate, revealing good body, breeding and vigour, with an elegant oakiness which adds spice to its exotic fruitiness; it remains excellent right up to the long fruity finish. Serve it with fish or white meat.

➳ Calvet, 75, cours du Médoc, BP 11, 33028 Bordeaux Cedex, tel. 05.56.43.59.00, fax 05.56.43.17.78, e-mail calvet@calvet.com

LA CHAPELLE D'ALIENOR 2002★

	n.c.	13,500	🍶	8–11 €

This vineyard is located on admirable gravelly clay-limestone soils in a sunny position, ideal for making *grands vins*. The grapes were picked by hand. The fine bouquet needs a little time to open out. When swirled in the glass, the wine releases primary aromas of the grape variety. It is very successful, with a good structure combining fruitiness, finesse and elegance, and mouth-filling qualities. The finish is harmoniously softened by notes of toasty oak. The **Château Chapelle Maracan Bordeaux Sec 2001 (3–5 €)** is commended.

➳ Alexandre de Malet Roquefort, Ch. Armens, BP 12, 33330 Saint-Emilion, tel. 05.57.56.40.80, fax 05.57.56.40.89, e-mail sales@malet-roquefort.com ☑
☒ by appt.

DOM. CHEVAL-BLANC SIGNE 2002★

	3 ha	25,000		3–5 €

Full of youth, joy and winning ways, this wine offers rich floral aromas enhanced by subtle notes of Sauvignon. The supple palate is good and rich. This 2002 wine is a nice combination of freshness and softness. It will go well with a bass with morels and green asparagus. The **Château Petit Moulin Bordeaux Sec 2002** is commended.

➳ SCEA Vignobles Signé, 505, Petit Moulin Sud, 33760 Arbis, tel. 05.56.23.93.22, fax 05.56.23.45.75, e-mail signevignobles@wanadoo.fr ☑
☒ by appt.

CH. DOISY-DAENE 2001★

	6 ha	30,000	🍶	11–15 €

This dry white Bordeaux comes from an estate which is among the elite of Barsac, made from pure low-yielding Sauvignon which was picked by hand. Its pale colour with pastel-green highlights and its bouquet echo the ripe musky Sauvignon, exotic fruits and a muffled vanilla flavour. Its

engaging, lively and fresh flavours combine with a round and vinous flesh up to the long and elegant finish.

➳ EARL Vignobles Pierre et Denis Dubourdieu, Ch. Doisy-Daëne, quartier Gravas, 33720 Barsac, tel. 05.56.27.15.84, fax 05.56.27.18.99, e-mail doisy-daene@terre-net.fr ☑
☒ by appt.

CH. DE L'ESPERANCE 2002★

	2.59 ha	16,000	🍶 🍶	3–5 €

This wine was made from 100% Sauvignon grown on a clay-limestone soil. It has a very pure, bright colour with silvery highlights. The scents of Sauvignon are full and powerful, accompanied by blackcurrant berries and grapefruit. Its rich and dense substance exudes fresh, lemony flavours. The finish is very pleasant.

➳ SCEA Dom. de Cazalis, 33350 Pujols, tel. 05.57.40.72.72, fax 05.57.56.19.19, e-mail chateau-cazalis@wanadoo.fr ☑
☒ by appt.
➳ Claude Billot

CH. FONREAUD

Le Cygne 2001★

	1.8 ha	12,000	🍶	8–11 €

About a dozen years ago, the Château Fonréaud, standing on a soil of Pyrenean gravels, revived one of its four white Listrac wines created at the beginning of the century and named after birds. The 'Swan' has a transparent colour with pale-gold and bright-green highlights. The elegant and romantic bouquet is redolent of exotic fruits, and blackcurrant sweetened by vanilla and sugared almond. The tasty Sauvignon flavour has good length (as usual, the grapes were picked by hand), while the supple and full-bodied Sémillon is enhanced by white flowers and the softly aromatic Muscadelle. An excellent wine for pure enjoyment.

➳ Ch. Fonréaud, 33480 Listrac-Médoc, tel. 05.56.58.02.43, fax 05.56.58.04.33 ☑
☒ ev. day except Sat. Sun. 9am–12 noon 2pm–5pm

DOM. DE LA GRAVE

Cuvée Prestige 2002★

	0.07 ha	600	🍶	5–8 €

This wine made from 100% Sauvignon will go perfectly with scallops served with slices of artichoke heart and a lightly peppered tomato fondant. The bouquet reveals a delicate selection of nutmeg-flavoured fruits coated with a slightly roasted and vanilla-flavoured oak. On the palate, this is a lively wine with notes of roasting.

➳ SCEA Roche, Perriche, 33750 Beychac-et-Caillau, tel. 05.56.72.41.28, fax 05.56.72.41.28, e-mail vignobleroche@wanadoo.fr ☑
☒ ev. day 9am–7pm

CH. GREYSAC 2002★

	2.01 ha	5,800	🍶	8–11 €

The Château Greysac is a large Médoc cru bourgeois which also produces a dry Bordeaux at Bégadan, made in a vineyard planted in 1989. The transparency and liveliness of this wine's pale-golden colour with green highlights catch the eye. The bouquet releases complex and powerful scents of flowery Sauvignon and a soft dormant toastiness. The palate is balanced. An attractive flavour of roasted vanilla combines gently with the fruit.

➳ SA Domaines Codem, Ch. Greysac, 18, rte de By, 33340 Bégadan, tel. 05.56.73.26.56, fax 05.56.73.26.58 ☑
☒ by appt.

CH. HAUT RIAN 2002★

	11 ha	90,000	🍶 🍶	3–5 €

Rions is a former Gallo-Roman citadel which became a fortified town around the 12th century. The medieval village adjoins this estate, owned by Michel Dietrich, an Alsatian oenologist and wine-maker who settled in the region with his family in 1988. He made this wine with its slowly emergent bouquet harmoniously combining acacia flowers, privet and citrus fruits. The tasty palate has an attractive structure recalling exotic fruits (mango).

☛ Michel Dietrich, La Bastide, 33410 Rions,
tel. 05.56.76.95.01, fax 05.56.76.93.51 ✅
🍷 ev. day except Sun. 9am–12 noon 2pm–5.30pm

CH. DU JUGE

Cru Quinette 2001★

1 ha	3,000	🍶	8–11 €

This wine's brilliant colour is sprinkled with golden highlights. The full and harmonious bouquet forms quickly with nuances of citrus fruits, bitter orange and crystallized fruits combining with lively scents from exotic lands. The palate is delicately toned with round forms which are opening out. The finish is particularly marked by the wine's maturation (vanilla and smoke).

☛ Pierre Dupleich, Ch. du Juge, rte de Branne,
33410 Cadillac, tel. 05.56.62.17.77, fax 05.56.62.17.59,
e-mail chateau-du-juge@wanadoo.fr ✅
🍷 by appt.
☛ David-Dupleich

CH. LAMOTHE VINCENT

Fleur de Cuvée 2002★

9.5 ha	86,000	🍶 🍷	3–5 €

This wine with its youthful light-yellow, almost white colour was made from 90% Sauvignon and a touch of Sémillon. The bouquet releases scents of very ripe yellow fruits, topped with a blackcurrant coulis, broom and citrus fruits. The smooth, full-bodied palate brings the best out of the Sauvignon, combining liveliness and fullness. Serve this wine with a pan of gambas or a fillet of grilled scorpion fish in fresh ginger.

☛ Vignobles Vincent, 3, chem. Laurenceau,
33760 Montignac, tel. 05.56.23.96.55, fax 05.56.23.97.72,
e-mail info@lamothe-vincent.com ✅
🍷 by appt.

CH. LESTRILLE CAPMARTIN

Vinifié et élevé en fût de chêne 2002★

0.42 ha	3,700	🍶	5–8 €

This wine is a blend of Sauvignon (61%), Sémillon (23%) and Muscadelle. It was picked by hand, macerated for a short time on the skins, fermented in new barrels and matured on fine lees with regular stirring of the yeast. The bouquet releases floral nuances and very evocative of citrus fruits (mango, passion fruit and pear). Its texture is silky and fine, and its freshness and clean taste make it suitable for drinking now.

☛ Jean-Louis Roumage, Lestrille,
33750 Saint-Germain-du-Puch, tel. 05.57.24.51.02,
fax 05.57.24.04.58, e-mail jlroumage@lestrille.com ✅
🍷 by appt.

JACQUES ET FRANCOIS LURTON

Sauvignon 2002★

16 ha	140,000	🍶 🍷	5–8 €

This Sauvignon with brilliant green and yellow highlights offers a grapey scent combining the softness of lychee with perfumes of rose, ripe yellow peach and grapefruit. The maceration for a short time on the skins has not made it at all heavy. This refreshing and pleasant, mouth-filling wine will go well with a fillet of turbot with asparagus and shrimps.

☛ SA Jacques et François Lurton, Dom. de Poumeyrade,
33870 Vayres, tel. 05.57.55.12.12, fax 05.57.55.12.13,
e-mail jflurton@jflurton.com

BARON DE LUZE

Cuvée spéciale 2002★

n.c.	30,000	🍶 🍶 🍷	3–5 €

For this wine, equal parts of Sauvignon and Sémillon from three vineyards were carefully vinified after a short maceration on the skins and maturation on fine lees in tank and barrel. The pale-golden colour, enlivened by green highlights, is appropriate. The rich perfumes suggest fresh grapes (Sauvignon) and yellow fruits with exotic aromas and an oaky scent. Its body is smooth but reinforced by a sparkle which makes it lively and fresh. The aromatic and oaky finish indicates that it will go well with a gratin of sea food.

☛ A. de Luze et Fils, Dom. du Ribet, BP 59,
33450 Saint-Loubès, tel. 05.57.97.07.20, fax 05.57.97.07.27,
e-mail jm.alige@gvg.fr ✅

CH. MARAC 2002★

3.25 ha	22,000	🍶 🍶 🍷	5–8 €

From 1975, when Alain and Martine Bonville took over this estate, a vast programme was launched to renovate this business, creating Château Marac. Nowadays, the plans include harvesting by hand and careful sorting of the grapes. This year it has produced a wine with a fresh bouquet and an attractive range of floral and fruity aromas with a hint of vanilla. It exudes roundness, delicacy and harmony throughout the tasting.

☛ Alain Bonville, Ch. Marac, 33350 Pujols,
tel. 05.57.40.53.21, fax 05.57.40.71.36,
e-mail vignoble-alain.bonville@wanadoo.fr ✅
🍷 by appt.

MAYNE D'OLIVET 2001★★

2 ha	12,000	🍶	11–15 €

It is very unusual to make white wine in the Saint-Emilion region. We should salute the courage of Jean-Noël Boidron and the success of this lovely wine with a golden-yellow colour. The complex, bewitching bouquet of exotic fruits and notes of soft spices and vanilla is already releasing a fine, integrated oakiness. The palate opens on a similar note. This white wine is sweet, very balanced, rich in nuances of crystallized fruits (pineapple and orange) and has a praline-flavoured finish. It has great potential and can be kept for a long time.

☛ Jean-Noël Boidron, Ch. Corbin Michotte,
33330 Saint-Emilion, tel. 05.57.51.64.88, fax 05.57.51.56.30,
e-mail vignoblesjnboidron@wanadoo.fr ✅
🍷 by appt.

CH. MOTTE MAUCOURT 2002★

6 ha	20,000	🍶 🍷	5–8 €

Saint-Genis-du-Bois, in the canton of Targon, and its little 12th century Templars' church with mural paintings is well worth a visit. So is the tumulus, 15 m high and 35 m in diameter. Here too the white wines have withstood the difficult weather. This wine was made by short maceration on the skins and maturation on fine lees. It reveals aromas of the Sauvignon and citrus fruits on a base of scented glycines. The tasters liked its fullness and richness. The finish on the palate is subdued. This 2002 wine is made for drinking with sea food.

☛ Villeneuve, EARL Ch. Motte Maucourt, 2, au Canton,
33760 Saint-Genis-du-Bois, tel. 05.56.71.54.77,
fax 05.56.71.64.23 ✅
🍷 ev. day except Sun. 9am–12 noon 2pm–7pm

CH. MOULIN DE PONCET 2002★

4.5 ha	40,000	🍶 🍷	5–8 €

This vineyard has been in the Barthe family since 1789, and today uses impressive technical equipment. This wine has the pastel-yellow colour of muslin, floral scents of rose petals, yellow and exotic fruits and citrus fruits. On the palate, its harmony is fruity and round. This is a refined and delightful wine.

☛ Vignobles Philippe Barthe, Peyrefus, 33420 Daignac,
tel. 05.57.84.55.90, fax 05.57.74.96.57,
e-mail vbarthe@club-internet.fr ✅
🍷 by appt.

CH. MYLORD 2002★

1 ha	9,000	🍶 🍷	3–5 €

For a long time this charterhouse was owned by an English family before it was taken over by the Large family more than a century ago. This wine is a blend of the three grape varieties of the AOC, and its bouquet releases a subtle combination of acacia flowers, white peach, mandarin and scents of honey. It has good presence and firmness, and light flavours. It has warmth, with a rounded body coated with dried fruits (almond and walnut).

☛ Michel et Alain Large, Ch. Mylord, 33420 Grézillac,
tel. 05.57.84.52.19, fax 05.57.74.93.95,
e-mail large@chateau-mylord.com ✅
🍷 by appt.

ORIGIN 2002★

n.c.	44,000	🍾 🔧	5–8 €

This pleasant dry Bordeaux comes from a very old firm of négociants from the region, founded in 1873. It has a pale colour with green highlights and releases good aromas of flowers sweetened with lime blossom, vine flowers and white peach. On the palate it is round, tasty and tender, and pleasant in every way. Another brand, the **Marquis d'Alban 2002** (3–5 €), made from 100% Sauvignon, also wins one star.
❧ Dulong Frères et Fils, 29, rue Jules-Guesde, 33270 Floirac, tel. 05.56.86.51.15, fax 05.56.40.66.41, e-mail dulong@dulong.com
🍷 by appt.

PAVILLON BLANC 2001★★★

n.c.	n.c.	🍾	46–76 €

This wine was grown on gravelly soils to the west of Margaux, and was made from three small pickings (25 hl/ha). It was vinified for four months in new oak, and demonstrates its good origins. The colour is a brilliant, almost lemon yellow, and is reflected in the bouquet of fresh notes of citrus fruits which combine with those of broom, menthol, aniseed and ripe grapes. The palate is chewy, round and rich, with delightful flavours of ginger, crystallized mandarin and white fruits on a slight oakiness. This is an outstanding dry Bordeaux with remarkable length which should be kept for three to four years.
❧ SC du Ch. Margaux, 33460 Margaux, tel. 05.57.88.83.83, fax 05.57.88.83.32
🍷 by appt.

CH. PEYRUCHET 2002★

n.c.	n.c.	🍾	5–8 €

This wine has a delightful bouquet with rich aromas of flowers and fruits and mineral notes. The first impression on the palate is supple and fresh, its full body balancing the richness and liveliness. This is a wine to serve with grilled lobster (a blue one from Brittany) and fennel butter.
❧ Bernard Queyrens, Ch. Peyruchet, 33410 Loupiac, tel. 05.56.62.62.71, fax 05.56.76.92.09 ☑
🍷 by appt.

CH. PIERRAIL 2002★

10 ha	50,000	🍾 🔧	5–8 €

The very beautiful 17th century Château Pierrail was bought in 1971 by the Demonchaux family. It has a large tasting room for visitors. This elegant wine, made from Sauvignon Blanc (70%) and Sauvignon Gris (30%), has tender green highlights and a clean and full-bodied palate, perfectly balanced and fresh.
❧ EARL Ch. Pierrail, 33220 Margueron, tel. 05.57.41.21.75, fax 05.57.41.23.77, e-mail alice@chateaupierrail.com ☑
🍷 by appt.

CH. POURQUEY-GAZEAU 2002★

n.c.	8,300	🍾	5–8 €

The Church of Notre-Dame de Castelvieil is a beautiful Romanesque building restored in 1867. The south portal is one of the finest sculptural creations in the Gironde. On the top of the hill is the old village and several very interesting houses. This wine has a springlike daffodil-yellow colour and a blooming bouquet mingling fruits and flowers. Its body is firm. The palate has a pleasing Sauvignon taste and lingering notes of white flowers.
❧ EARL de Pourquey-Gazeau, 1 A, Pourquey, 33540 Castelvieil, tel. 05.56.61.95.55, fax 05.56.61.99.48 ☑
🍷 ev. day 8am–8pm
❧ Fouilhac Père et Fils

QUINTET 2002★

20 ha	200,000	🍾 🔧	3–5 €

This wine comes from the cooperative of the Hauts de Gironde. It is very characteristic, displaying the merits of Bordeaux. It has a pale-yellow colour with green highlights. The bouquet has the musky, Sauvignon aromas of broom, white flowers and boxwood. On the palate it is both lively and supple, with a firm flesh, good length and fruity flavours (yellow peach and mirabelle plum). This 2002 wine will go well with a sea-bream in crystallized lemons.

❧ Cave des Hauts de Gironde, La Cafourche, 33860 Marcillac, tel. 05.57.32.46.33, fax 05.57.32.49.63 ☑
🍷 by appt.

CH. RAUZAN DESPAGNE

Grande Réserve 2001★

n.c.	n.c.	🍾	11–15 €

The Despagne family have a great deal going for them, including the quality of their terroir, the selection of grape varieties, the sorting after picking by hand, and the care taken during vinification. These have all helped them to win many *coups de coeur* in the *Guide*. While the **Cuvée de Landeron 2002 du Château Rauzan Despagne (5–8 €)**, matured in tank for three months, wins one star for its elegance, this Grande Réserve is not to be outdone. It reveals perfectly controlled vinification, producing scents of lilies, broom, boxwood and citrus fruits with a touch of vanilla. Part of the Sémillon had its malolactic fermentation *en barrique*, which gives it an elegant roundness that contrasts subtly with its freshness. This is a well-bred Bordeaux to be drunk with crayfish and *gambas à l'armoricaine*.
❧ GFA de Landeron, 33420 Naujan-et-Postiac, tel. 05.57.84.55.08, fax 05.57.55.57.31, e-mail contact@despagne.fr
🍷 by appt.
❧ J.-L. Despagne

CH. RECOUGNE

Terra Recognita 2002★

n.c.	20,000	🍾	5–8 €

"This is a wine out of the ordinary," noted one member of the Jury. This Terra Recognita has plenty of character and personality. Its colour is exquisite: a strong yellow with russet highlights. The bouquet opens with an intense aromatic symphony of ripe fruits (Sauvignon) and flowery, lemony notes. The palate has good body and is developing steadily and with freshness. The fine oak is lively and well-bred, sustained by the *barriques* made of oak from the South West.
❧ SEV Vignobles Jean Milhade, lieu-dit Peycher, 33133 Galgon, tel. 05.57.55.48.90, fax 05.57.84.31.27, e-mail milhade@milhade.fr ☑

CH. SAINT-FLORIN 2002★

15 ha	125,000	🍾 🔧	3–5 €

In the beginning, this vineyard in the Entre-Deux-Mers had 25 ha, and these have now swelled to 80 ha today. This wine has an opulent and brilliant straw-gold colour and a bouquet of yellow peach in crème de cassis. The delightful palate then reveals notes of chewy grapes. The short maceration on the skins has smoothed the rough corners off the Sauvignon and given the wine body. All it needs is a plate of gambas.
❧ Jean-Marc Jolivet, Ch. Saint-Florin, 33790 Soussac, tel. 05.56.61.31.61, fax 05.56.61.34.87 ☑
🍷 by appt.

CH. SUAU 2002★

3.12 ha	12,000		3–5 €

This vast estate standing on a clay-gravel subsoil is almost entirely devoted to cultivating vines. The very rich bouquet of this vintage has notes of white flowers (lime blossom) and exotic fruits (mango and passion fruit). Its balance on the palate is rich, round and full, supported by good flavours. The finish is lively, fresh and warm.
❧ Monique Bonnet, Ch. Suau, 33550 Capian, tel. 05.56.72.19.06, fax 05.56.72.12.43, e-mail bonnet.suau@wanadoo.fr ☑
🍷 by appt.

CH. TOUR DE MIRAMBEAU

Cuvée Passion 2001★

n.c.	n.c.	🍾	11–15 €

There is great finesse in this famous Cuvée Passion, which won a *coup de coeur* last year. Vinified *en barrique*, it is a blend of 70% Sauvignon and 30% Sémillon. The bouquet reveals a range of exotic fruits, with grapefruit to the fore, and floral perfumes combining with fine toasty notes from the oak. This rich, tasty structure has nuances of crystallized fruits with lemon peel and a hint of oak, indicating that it will develop

BORDEAUX

later. The **white Cuvée Principale du Château Tour de Mirambeau 2002 (5–8 €)** wins one star: it was matured in tank and tastes like chewy grapes. Three other wines by J.-L. Despagne were selected by the Jury in this appellation: the **Château Franc-Pérat 2002 (5–8 €)** wins one star; the **Château Bel Air Perponcher 2002 (5–8 €)** and the **Château Lion Beaulieu 2002 (5–8 €)** are commended.
⚡ SCEA Vignobles Despagne, 33420 Naujan-et-Postiac, tel. 05.57.84.55.08, fax 05.57.84.57.31,
e-mail contact@despagne.fr ☑

CH. TURCAUD 2001★

	n.c.	10,000	⊞		5–8 €

This wine has a very expressive and complex bouquet, dominated by scents of ripe Sauvignon combined with notes of white and yellow flowers and vanilla- and menthol-flavoured touches. On the palate there is a delightful encounter between the tasty flavours, a full texture, rounded and softened contours, and a return of the aromas noted in the bouquet. The wine's freshness lasts into the long finish.
⚡ EARL Vignobles Maurice Robert, Ch. Turcaud, 33670 La Sauve, tel. 05.56.23.04.41, fax 05.56.23.35.85,
e-mail chateau-turcaud@wanadoo.fr ☑
Ⓣ by appt.

Wines selected but not starred

L'AME DU TERROIR 2002

	22 ha	80,000	▮	◆	–3 €

⚡ Les Caves de la Brèche, ZAE de L'Arbalestrier, 33220 Pineuilh, tel. 05.57.41.91.50, fax 05.57.46.42.76,
e-mail negoce.grm@infonie.fr

CH. BELLE-GARDE 2002

	3 ha	20,000	▮	◆	3–5 €

⚡ Eric Duffau, Monplaisir, 33420 Génissac, tel. 05.57.24.49.12, fax 05.57.24.41.28,
e-mail duffau.eric@wanadoo.fr ☑
Ⓣ by appt.

BLASON TIMBERLAY 2002

	n.c.	n.c.	▮	◆	3–5 €

⚡ SA Robert Giraud, Dom. de Loiseau, BP 31, 33240 Saint-André-de-Cubzac, tel. 05.57.43.01.44, fax 05.57.43.08.75,
e-mail france@robertgiraud.com

CH. CRABITAN-BELLEVUE 2002

	1 ha	6,500	▮	◆	3–5 €

⚡ GFA Bernard Solane et Fils, 33410 Sainte-Croix-du-Mont, tel. 05.56.62.01.53, fax 05.56.76.72.09 ☑
Ⓣ ev. day 8am–12 noon 2pm–6pm; Sun. by appt.

CH. DU CROS 2002

	12 ha	60,000	▮		5–8 €

⚡ SA Vignobles M. Boyer, Ch. du Cros, 33410 Loupiac, tel. 05.56.62.99.31, fax 05.56.62.12.59,
e-mail contact@chateauducros.com ☑
Ⓣ ev. day except Sat. Sun. 8am–12 noon 2pm–6pm

CH. DESON 2002

	14.8 ha	134,000	▮	◆	–3 €

⚡ Prodiffu, 17–19, rte des Vignerons, 33790 Landerrouat, tel. 05.56.61.33.73, fax 05.56.61.40.57,
e-mail prodiffu@prodiffu.com
⚡ GFA Chauffepied

NUMERO 1 DE DOURTHE 2002

	n.c.	500,000	▮		5–8 €

⚡ Vignobles Dourthe, 35, rue de Bordeaux, 33290 Parempuyre, tel. 05.56.35.53.00, fax 05.56.35.53.29,
e-mail contact@cvbg.com ☑
Ⓣ by appt.

CH. LES EYMERIES

Cuvée Prestige 2002

	14.5 ha	113,000	▮	◆	–3 €

⚡ SCEA Les Eymeries, 33220 Margueron, tel. 05.57.41.21.97, fax 05.57.41.26.24
⚡ M. Charles

CH. DU GRAND PLANTIER 2002

	4 ha	25,000	▮	◆	5–8 €

⚡ GAEC des Vignobles Albucher, Ch. du Grand Plantier, 33410 Monprimblanc, tel. 05.56.62.99.03, fax 05.56.76.91.35 ☑ ⌂
Ⓣ by appt.

CUVEE JEAN

Elevé en fût de chêne 2001

	0.8 ha	2,700	⊞		5–8 €

⚡ SCEA Courtey, 2 bis, Courtey-Nord, 33490 Saint-Martial, tel. 05.56.76.42.56, fax 05.56.76.42.56 ☑ ⌂
Ⓣ by appt.

LABOTTIERE 2002

	n.c.	10,000	▮ ⊞		–3 €

⚡ Cordier-Mestrezat et Domaines, 109, rue Achard, BP 154, 33042 Bordeaux Cedex, tel. 05.56.11.29.00, fax 05.56.11.29.01,
e-mail mestrezat-domaines@wanadoo.fr
Ⓣ by appt.

CH. LESCURE 2002

	1.09 ha	4,966	▮	◆	5–8 €

⚡ CAT Ch. Lescure, 33490 Verdelais, tel. 05.57.98.04.68, fax 05.57.98.04.64, e-mail chateau.lescure@free.fr ☑
Ⓣ by appt.

CH. LOUDENNE 2001

	12 ha	40,000	⊞		8–11 €

⚡ SCS Ch. Loudenne, 33340 Saint-Yzans-de-Médoc, tel. 05.56.73.17.80, fax 05.56.09.02.87,
e-mail chateau-loudenne@wanadoo.fr ☑ ⌂
Ⓣ by appt.
⚡ Lafragette

CH. MEMOIRES

Fleur d'Opale Elevé en fût de chêne 2001

	n.c.	n.c.	⊞		5–8 €

⚡ Jean-François Ménard, Ch. Mémoires, 33490 Saint-Maixant, tel. 05.56.62.06.43, fax 05.56.62.04.32, e-mail memoires1@aol.com ☑
Ⓣ ev. day 8am–12 noon 1.30pm–6.30pm; Sat. Sun. by appt.

MOUTON CADET 2001

	n.c.	n.c.	▮		5–8 €

⚡ SA Baron Philippe de Rothschild, BP 117, 33250 Pauillac, tel. 05.56.73.20.20, fax 05.56.73.20.44, e-mail webmaster@bpdr.com

Bordeaux Rosé

CH. BELLEVUE LA MONGIE 2002★

0.5 ha	5,000	🍾 🍷	3–5 €

Vinification was carried out at a low temperature to bring out the Merlot (80%) and the Cabernet Sauvignon, producing intense aromas of blackcurrant bud, grapefruit, apricot and a pale colour with salmony highlights. Its roundness and fullness are enlived by a slight sparkle. The fine texture keeps its freshness and aromas for a long time.
↴ Michel Boyer, Ch. Bellevue La Mongie, 33420 Génissac, tel. 05.57.24.48.43, fax 05.57.24.48.63, e-mail boyer.michel@worldonline.fr ☑
🍷 by appt.

CH. BONNET 2002★★

11 ha	55,000	🍾 🍷	5–8 €

The Château Bonnet is located in the north of the Entre-Deux-Mers, on an undulating plateau standing on clay-limestone sediments. The reputation of this estate's wines need not be repeated. Its red and white wines make a great impression on the best tables and in the great restaurants of France and abroad. The intense floral notes of this rosé suggest acacia flowers and broom along with delicious fruity perfumes. After a round and clean attack, the palate reveals a fresh and aromatic texture which gives the delightful sensation of chewing grapes.
↴ André Lurton, Ch. Bonnet, 33420 Grézillac, tel. 05.57.25.58.58, fax 05.57.74.98.59, e-mail andrelurton@andrelurton.com ☑
🍷 by appt.

CHAI DE BORDES 2002★

n.c.	40,000	🍾	3–5 €

This wine from the négociants Quancard will undoubtedly arouse dulled appetites with its spirited temperament. It has a strong pinkish colour with salmony highlights and opens with powerful aromas of ripe grapes. The balanced palate is full-bodied and needs a little more time. The **rosé Cellier de Bordes 2002** also wins one star.
↴ Cheval-Quancard, La Mouline, 4 rue du Carbouney, BP 36, 33560 Carbon-Blanc, tel. 05.57.77.88.88, fax 05.57.77.88.99, e-mail chevalquancard@chevalquancard.com
🍷 by appt.

CARAYON LA ROSE 2002★

10 ha	80,000	🍾 🍷	3–5 €

This lovely pink Carayon radiates brilliance. The bouquet has captured all the magic of summer and offers a range of fruity aromas: wild strawberry, raspberry and redcurrant enhanced by a lemony verbena. The tasty palate is both round and firm. Drink it now with Béarnais broth and conserve of duck.
↴ Dulong Frères et Fils, 29, rue Jules-Guesde, 33270 Floirac, tel. 05.56.86.51.15, fax 05.56.40.66.41, e-mail dulong@dulong.com
🍷 by appt.

EXCELLOR 2002★

n.c.	40,000	🍾 🍷	3–5 €

The winemakers of this cooperative are trying to become established in markets abroad, and put all their skill into making quality products vinified by the most modern processes. Here they offer a wine with a pale vermilion colour and an expansive, mainly fruity bouquet underlined by a pleasant touch of fresh herbs. The tasters liked its harmonious, nicely rounded shape, its great fullness and the fruitiness of the finish.
↴ Prodiffu, 17–19, rue des Vignerons, 33790 Landerrouat, tel. 05.56.61.33.73, fax 05.56.61.40.57, e-mail prodiffu@prodiffu.com

ROSE DE GENIBON 2002★

0.5 ha	2,680	🍾 🍷	3–5 €

Next to the winery is a well with sculpted stones dating from the 16th century. This small family estate has produced a wine

in limited quantities made from 100% Cabernet Franc. A slow, steady fermentation at a low temperature has produced a strong, fruity bouquet enhanced by notes of raspberry pleasantly combined with white flowers. The body is full and round. This rosé has good length and an overerall balance, and will be popular served with salmon in dill.
↴ EARL Eynard-Sudre, Genibon, 33710 Bourg-sur-Gironde, tel. 05.57.68.25.34, fax 05.57.68.27.58, e-mail eynard.sudre@wanadoo.fr ☑
🍷 by appt.

CH. HAUT-GARRIGA 2002★

5 ha	30,000	🍾 🍷	3–5 €

This estate has a special terroir which produces refined wines with a particular cachet. The owners have vinified this wine well: it has a delightfully subtle bouquet of soft fruits and citrus fruits. The full and balanced palate tastes of black grapes refreshed by a very pleasant sparkle. This is a rich rosé, softly velvety and long. Drink it now.
↴ EARL Vignobles C. Barreau et Fils, Garriga, 33420 Grézillac, tel. 05.57.74.90.06, fax 05.57.74.96.63 ☑
🍷 by appt.

CH. HAUT GUILLEBOT 2002★

2 ha	10,000	🍾 🍷	3–5 €

This property has been handed down from mother to daughter for seven generations. Today, Eveline Rénier runs the estate. Flowery aromas and lively soft fruits emerge from this salmony pink wine. The first impression is velvety, then the wine reveals itself to be full-bodied, round, balanced and aromatic. It will go well with calf's liver in balsamic vinegar.
↴ Eveline Rénier, Ch. Haut Guillebot, 33420 Lugaignac, tel. 05.57.84.53.92, fax 05.57.84.62.73, e-mail chateauhautguillebot@wanadoo.fr ☑
🍷 ev. day 9am–12 noon 2pm–5pm; Sat. Sun. by appt.; cl. 15–31 Aug.

CH. LAMOTHE VINCENT

Cuvée Passion 2002★

5 ha	40,000	🍾 🍷	3–5 €

The Vincents cultivate 70 ha continuing the family tradition which started in 1920. The vineyard has been put through a large programme of renovation, and advanced technical equipment installed. Legend also has it that each year the voice of Saint Vincent, patron saint of wine-growers, inspires the alchemy of its blending process. This well-made wine has a strong vermilion colour, closer to a Clairet than a rosé, and releases heady, not excessively so but certainly unusual, scents of soft fruits. It is very pleasant with a full and round body.
↴ Vignobles Vincent, 3, chem. Laurenceau, 33760 Montignac, tel. 05.56.23.96.55, fax 05.56.23.97.72, e-mail info@lamothe-vincent.com ☑
🍷 by appt.

CH. PASSE CRABY 2002★

1.6 ha	7,300	🍾 🍷	3–5 €

Standing next to this property are the ruins of Notre-Dame de Queynac, a Romanesque church of the Knights Hospitallers which was sacked in the 15th century and then fortified. The beautiful statue of the Virgin now stands in the church at Galgon. This wine has a delightful lively pink colour with ruby nuances. The fresh bouquet releases perfumes mainly of soft fruits (wild strawberry and redcurrant), closely allied to white flowers, with a final impression of roses. The attack on the palate is soft and warm. Richness and good balance develop alongside the very fruity flavours. This is an enjoyable wine to be drunk while still young.
↴ Vincent Boyé, Lieu-dit Chiquet, 33133 Galgon, tel. 05.57.55.05.38, fax 05.57.55.49.81, e-mail v.boye@wanadoo.fr ☑
🍷 ev. day except Sun. 8am–12 noon 1.30pm–6pm; cl. Aug.

CH. LA RIVALERIE 2002★★

1 ha	6,500	🍾 🍷	5–8 €

Two vine-growing nurserymen, aware of the high-quality potential of this terroir, partly restored the property of the Château La Rivalerie from 1973 after it was left to run wild following the frosts of 1956. The colour of this wine is very fresh, a pretty shade of raspberry-pink. The powerful

bouquet combines blackberry and blackcurrant with a nice touch of fruit drops. The palate is soft and supple with a range of tasty flavours suggesting notes of macerated small soft fruit. A very successful wine.
🕿 SCEA La Rivalerie, 1, La Rivalerie, 33390 Saint-Paul-de-Blaye, tel. 05.57.42.18.84, fax 05.57.42.14.27, e-mail larivalerie@wanadoo.fr ☑
🍷 by appt.

CH. SAINT-FLORIN 2002★

| 7 ha | 50,000 | 🍶 ♦ | 5–8 € |

The visitor to the region's vineyards will find Launay hill, a stopping place for pilgrims to Santiago de Compostela, at the end of the Gironde. This is a fine blend of Merlot and the Cabernets, with 60% of the must extracted by running the juice off the skins and 40% by direct pressing. It has a pink colour with salmony glints. The grapey bouquet recalls wild strawberry and blackcurrant, heralding a full-bodied palate. The refreshing, round finish is spiced with a touch of carbonic gas.
🕿 Jean-Marc Jolivet, Ch. Saint-Florin, 33790 Soussac, tel. 05.56.61.31.61, fax 05.56.61.34.87 ☑
🍷 by appt.

CH. VIEUX CARREFOUR 2002★★

| 0.8 ha | 4,000 | 🍶 ♦ | 3–5 € |

This wine won two stars in 2001, and its 2002 vintage does even better, winning a *coup de cœur*. The vineyard occupies a particularly favourable position. The pale-vermilion colour with mauve highlights foreshadows the enjoyable bouquet releasing notes of blackberry, wild berries and blackcurrant enhanced by soft red peppers. The tasty palate grows in fruitiness and is supple and fresh. This is an attractive, typical and complex wine made from equal parts of Merlot and Cabernet Sauvignon.
🕿 EARL François Gabard, Le Carrefour, 33133 Galgon, tel. 05.57.74.30.77, fax 05.57.84.35.73 ☑
🍷 by appt.

Wines selected but not starred

FONT-D'ESTIAC 2002

| n.c. | n.c. | 🍶 ♦ | 3–5 € |

🕿 Closerie d'Estiac, Les Lèves, 33220 Sainte-Foy-la-Grande, tel. 05.57.56.02.02, fax 05.57.56.02.22, e-mail oeno@univitis.fr ☑
🍷 ev. day except Sun. Mon. 9.30am–12.30pm 3.30pm–6pm

CH. LES GUES RIVIERES 2002

| 3.5 ha | 3,000 | 🍶 ♦ | 3–5 € |

🕿 EARL Vignobles Siozard, Au Claouset, 33420 Lugaignac, tel. 05.57.74.90.05, fax 05.57.84.67.10, e-mail vignobles-siozard@wanadoo.fr
🍷 by appt.

CH. DE LUGAGNAC 2002

| 7.5 ha | 56,000 | 🍶 ♦ | 3–5 € |

🕿 Famille Bon, SCEA du Ch. de Lugagnac, 33790 Pellegrue, tel. 05.56.61.30.60, fax 05.56.61.38.48, e-mail clugagnac@aol.com ☑
🍷 ev. day 9am–12 noon 2pm–6pm

CH. MONTGAILLARD 2002

| 0.3 ha | 2,000 | 🍶 ♦ | 3–5 € |

🕿 SCEA Vignobles Chollet, 227, CD 10, 33490 Saint-Maixant, tel. 05.56.63.17.02, fax 05.56.63.32.69, e-mail francois.chollet@wanadoo.fr ☑
🍷 by appt.

DOM. DE LA NOUZILLETTE 2002

| 1.5 ha | 12,000 | 🍶 ♦ | 3–5 € |

🕿 GAEC du Moulin Borgne, 5, le Moulin Borgne, 33620 Marcenais, tel. 05.57.68.70.25, fax 05.57.68.09.12 ☑ ⌂
🍷 ev. day 9am–8pm
🕿 Catherinaud

Bordeaux Supérieur

CH. BEAULIEU
Comtes de Tastes 2001★

| 22 ha | 60,000 | 🍾 | 8–11 € |

The Château Beaulieu has not forgotten the old adage that good jam is made in small pans. They vinify their wines in small, thermoregulated vats, the grape yields are low and they pick them by hand. This has enabled them to extract the essence from the concentrated grapes to make a Bordeaux Supérieur which has an intense dark colour and equally intense aromas. The tannins are evident but not harsh on the rather charming full-bodied palate with its flavours of vanilla and coconut. Drink this wine in 2004.
🕿 Guillaume de Tastes, Haut Gay, Ch. Beaulieu, 33240 Salignac, tel. 06.23.17.19.88, fax 05.56.81.73.85
🍷 by appt.

BEAURILEGE
Elevé en fût de chêne 2001★

| 5 ha | 330,000 | 🍾 | 5–8 € |

This Beaurilège was made from a selection of Merlot grown on clay-limestone plots and harvested when they had reached perfect maturity. This wine was vinified in the classical manner, and placed in barrel in January 2002 (80% French and 20% American barrels). At first the bouquet is fruity (plum, blackberry and blackcurrant), then develops notes of roasting and cocoa, while the dense, full palate has well-integrated tannins and an elegant oakiness. A nice return of toasty and chocolatey flavours brings a final note of balance. This wine need not be kept for very long.
🕿 Domaine de Sansac, Les Lèves, 33220 Sainte-Foy-la-Grande, tel. 05.57.56.02.02, fax 05.57.56.02.22, e-mail oeno@univitis.fr ☑
🍷 by appt.

CH. BEAU RIVAGE
Cuvée Phare 2001★

| 0.8 ha | 4,000 | 🍾 | 15–23 € |

This wine demonstrates that well-controlled maturation can benefit a wine with a good constitution. It is made from old vines of Merlot (60%) and – unusually – Petit Verdot (40%) harvested with scissors. Cocoa, liquorice and toasted almond accentuate the velvety impression, and combine with the developing oak. This powerful 2001 will be at its best in two

to three years. The main wine, the **Château Beau Rivage 2001 (8–11 €)**, was also matured in barrel and is commended.
SCEA Ch. Beau Rivage, 7, chem. du Bord-de-l'Eau, 33460 Macau, tel. 05.57.10.03.70, fax 05.57.10.02.00, e-mail beau-rivage@aol.com
by appt.
Christine Nadalié

CH. BEL-AIR 2000★★

0.8 ha | 6,000 | 5–8 €

This remarkably concentrated wine is a classic blend (60% Merlot and 40% Cabernet Sauvignon), and releases nuances of undergrowth and venison, and intense flavours of vanilla and roasting. The palate is still firm but full and shows a good winey development. This is a characteristic wine that will show its quality in time.
Thierry Burnereau, 1, Baron, 33420 Saint-Jean-de-Blaignac, tel. 05.57.84.62.58
by appt.

CH. BELLEVUE-PEYCHARNEAU

Vieilli en fût de chêne 2001★

14 ha | 95,000 | 5–8 €

The Laulans made this wine from the three great Bordeaux grape varieties in a brand-new cellar which opened in 2001. When the glass is swirled, garnet-coloured glints appear, then it opens out with a rich and harmonious bouquet of soft fruits, cinnamon and vanilla. The structure is still a little firm but the wine's clean substance indicates a bright future.
SCEA Pécharnaud, Les Bouchets, 33220 Pineuilh, tel. 05.57.46.04.46, fax 05.57.46.47.56
by appt.

CH. BOIS-MALOT

Tradition Elevé en fût de chêne neuf 2000★

8 ha | 55,000 | 8–11 €

The Tradition wine was grown in a clay-limestone terroir, largely planted with Cabernet Sauvignon. Its bouquet is as intense as its velvety colour; an elegant toasty oak combines with aromas of dried fruits and slight praline-flavoured nuances, while the ripe fruit fills the rich, winey palate. This wine can be drunk immediately, but will also improve with keeping.
SCA Meynard, 133, rte des Valentons, 33450 Saint-Loubès, tel. 05.56.38.94.18, fax 05.56.38.92.47
by appt.

DOM. DU BOUSCAT

Cuvée la Gargone 2000★★

2.5 ha | 8,400 | 8–11 €

A significant proportion of Malbec (20%) was blended with the three main Bordeaux varieties to make this original wine which was vinified with great care. It is vigorous and characteristic, exploding with perfumes of Morello cherry and fruits in brandy on a base of roasting (coffee). Although it is still marked by the oak, it will become more harmonious in two to three years' time.
Dom. du Bouscat, 2, Le Bouscat, 33240 Saint-Romain-la-Virvée, tel. 05.57.58.20.82, fax 05.57.58.23.59, e-mail francois.dubernard@wanadoo.fr
by appt.
Dubernard

CH. BRESSAC DE LEZIN

Elevé en fût de Chêne 2000★★

5 ha | 20,000 | 5–8 €

Nearly 50 years ago, this estate only produced fruit juice. To judge from this wine, the changeover was a good idea. It has an intense crimson colour with deep-purplish highlights and develops from floral scents (violet) to spicy ones (liquorice and vanilla). On the palate it reveals a substance rich in tasty tannins. Keep it for two to three years.
Arnaud Giraud, Sté viticole du Domaine de Lézin, 33750 Saint-Germain-du-Puch, tel. 05.57.24.00.00, fax 05.57.24.00.98, e-mail domaine-de-lezin@wanadoo.fr
by appt.
Huillier

BRION DE LAGASSE 2000★★

5 ha | 17,000 | 5–8 €

This estate exports 56% of its production, from Ireland to Thailand. This wine has a dark-red, almost black colour and powerful musky, grapey aromas and leathery nuances. The fruits of its 35-year-old Merlot and 10% Cabernet, harvested by hand, are charmingly evident in its full and well-structured body, revealing flavours of blackcurrant through to the long finish which extends the taster's pleasure.
Roux, Brion de Lagasse, 33460 Baron, tel. 06.09.71.65.84, fax 05.56.95.06.37
by appt.

CH. LA CADERIE 2000★

8 ha | 37,000 | 5–8 €

This 18.5-ha vineyard takes its name from the old word "cade" meaning a barrel of 1,000 l. François Landais employs manual harvesting and vinifies his grapes by modern methods. The significance of this becomes clear when one tastes the wine, with its aromas of grape, prune, liquorice and vanilla. The oak asserts itself on the palate, but remains elegant up to the slightly praline-flavoured finish.
François Landais, Ch. La Caderie, 33910 Saint-Martin-du-Bois, tel. 05.57.49.41.32, fax 05.57.49.43.02, e-mail chateau-la-caderie@wanadoo.fr
by appt.

CH. CANEVAULT 2001★

4.5 ha | 25,000 | 5–8 €

Gallo-Roman grain silos were discovered beneath this 19th century château. Nowadays, there are no more pale crops of rye and oats gleaming in the sun on the hillsides of Lugon, but lovely Merlots and Cabernets which are harvested by hand. This Bordeaux Supérieur reveals its intensity as the bouquet opens with its rich spicy notes (cinnamon and black pepper). The full and silky palate has flavours of soft fruits, then pleasant rather vegetal tannins recalling capsicum.
SCEA Jean-Pierre Chaudet, Caneveau, 33240 Lugon, tel. 05.57.84.49.10, fax 05.57.84.42.07, e-mail scea-chaudet-j.p@wanadoo.fr
ev. day except Sat. Sun. 9am–12 noon 1.30pm–5.30pm
Sylvie Chaudet

DOM. DE COURTEILLAC 2001★★

22 ha | 87,000 | 8–11 €

This wine made from two-thirds Merlot was macerated cold for three days, then carefully fermented at a controlled temperature. The maturity of the grapes comes through in the dark-garnet colour and a concentrated bouquet of spices and fruits, while the elegant tannins are accompanied by a slight oakiness. This Bordeaux Supérieur will go well with a *sauté d'agneau à la provençale* in 2004.
SCA Dom. de Courteillac, 2, Courteillac, 33350 Ruch, tel. 05.57.40.79.48, fax 05.57.40.57.05, e-mail domainedecourteillac@free.fr
Dominique Meneret

BORDEAUX

CH. COURTEY

Cuvée Margo 2000★

| | 1.3 ha | 7,800 | ◫ | 5–8 € |

At the Château Courtey they know how to present their wines, especially on the open days they hold in June and July. There you can taste this brilliant garnet wine, releasing very mature aromas of stewed fruits and toasty notes. Beneath its framework of firm tannins, it is full-bodied and should age well.
♠ SCEA Courtey, 2 bis, Courtey-Nord, 33490 Saint-Martial, tel. 05.56.76.42.56, fax 05.56.76.42.56 ☑ ☗
☿ by appt.
♠ Norbert Depaire

CH. DE CUGAT

Cuvée Francis Meyer 2001★

| | 5 ha | 17,000 | ◫ | 8–11 € |

This estate has not only a high-quality vineyard but also an old château built at the end of the Middle Ages, near which there is a fortified watermill that is even older. The vines are more recent, but grown in a traditional way and harvested by hand. This wine has aromas of ripe grape with shades of soft spices and vanilla. Its framework of subtle tannins brings out the full and winey flesh which continues over toasty notes. Drink this in 2004.
♠ Benoît Meyer, Ch. de Cugat, 33540 Blasimon, tel. 05.56.71.52.08, fax 05.56.71.60.29 ☑
☿ by appt.

CH. DAVID 2001★

| | 16 ha | 130,000 | ▮ ♦ | 3–5 € |

This wine with its garnet colour and bluish highlights and attractive bouquet of soft fruits and violet is immediately delightful, even before it has revealed its pleasant roundness. Its pulpy and fresh body adapts to tannins that are still young but have a lovely texture. Crystallized cherry and vanilla notes make up the balanced, soft finish. This is a nice wine, ready for serving with a meal. Promocom also distributes the **Château Fleur de Rigaud 2001**, matured in tank, from the Cholet vineyards; this wins one star.
♠ SA Promocom, rte du Petit-Conseiller, 33750 Beychac-et-Cailleau, tel. 05.57.97.39.73, fax 05.57.97.39.74 ☑
♠ S.C.E.A Jalousie Beaulieu

CH. L'ESCART

Omar Khayam 2001★

| | 1.8 ha | 10,700 | ◫ | 11–15 € |

This wine is dedicated to the Persian poet and philosopher Omar Khayam, and has been made with great care: weeding with a plough, hand-picking a plot with a high density of vines, cold maceration before fermentation, and malolactic fermentation in barrel. This wine was woven together like an oriental carpet. The toasty, praline-scented bouquet with gentle perfumes of old rum heralds a full-bodied and rich palate. You can lay it down if you wish, but remember the words of the poet: "Make haste, my son, for life is short." The **Cuvée Prestige Manon 2001 (8–11 €)**, matured in barrel, is commended.
♠ Ch. L'Escart, 70, chem. Couvertaire, BP 8, 33450 Saint-Loubès, tel. 05.56.77.53.19, fax 05.56.77.68.59, e-mail lescart@wanadoo.fr ☑
☿ by appt.
♠ Gérard Laurent

CH.D'ESTHER 2001★

| | 4.2 ha | 17,000 | ◫ | 5–8 € |

This harmonious Bordeaux Supérieur offers notes of praline and a refined oak. The dark colour, with deep-purplish nuances, shows it is well concentrated. The tannins are prominent on the palate, but do not spoil the general impression of roundness. The wine opens out at the finish with vegetal and fine peppery notes, which suggest it should be drunk with roast meat.
♠ Thomas Fabian, 37, chem. de Caderot, 33450 Saint-Loubès, tel. 05.56.68.69.35, fax 05.56.68.69.35, e-mail thomasfabian@wanadoo.fr ☑
☿ by appt.

CH. DE FAISE 2000★★

| | 16 ha | n.c. | ▮ ◫ ♦ | 3–5 € |

In the Middle Ages, this vineyard was attached to the 12th century Cistercian abbey of Faise, of which some traces still remain in the village. Thirty-five-year-old vines of Merlot and Cabernet Franc went into this attractive-looking wine with its musky and spicy bouquet. The powerful and long palate mingles flavours of violet, and spicy faded rose. It will become more balanced, and reach its best around 2005–2006.
♠ EARL Vignobles Devaud, Faise, 33570 Les Artigues-de-Lussac, tel. 05.57.24.31.39, fax 05.57.24.34.17, e-mail devaud@vignobles-devaud.com ☑
☿ by appt.

CH. FLORIMOND 2000★

| | 5 ha | 13,654 | ▮ ♦ | 5–8 € |

This year's wines chosen by the *Guide* again prove that the estate of that great professional Louis Marinier is in safe hands: this Bordeaux Supérieur is the work of passionately keen women. The fruity aromas are very light, and the palate is richly vigorous, supported by silky tannins up to a lasting finish. A lovely Merlot wine.
♠ Vignobles Louis Marinier, Dom. Florimond-La-Brède, 33390 Berson, tel. 05.57.64.34.63, fax 05.57.64.23.27, e-mail vignobleslouismarinier@wanadoo.fr ☑
☿ ev. day 8am–12 noon 2pm–5pm; Sat. Sun. by appt.; cl. Aug.

CH. FREYNEAU 2000★

| | 6 ha | 30,000 | ▮ ♦ | 3–5 € |

With the help of his son Eric, J.-P. Maulin has continually modernized this estate for 20 years, and this year's results are worthy of their efforts. This is a strong, almost dark, garnet-coloured 2000 which reveals a spicy bouquet with musky nuances. Notes of game combine with the still rather lively tannins in a good-quality structure. Lay this down for two years so that the flavours can mature fully.
♠ EARL Maulin et Fils, Ch. Freyneau, 33450 Montussan, tel. 05.56.72.95.46, fax 05.56.72.84.29, e-mail accueil@chateau-freyneau.com ☑
☿ by appt.

CH. DE FUSSIGNAC 2001★

| | 16 ha | 85,000 | ▮ ◫ ♦ | 8–11 € |

On the day of your visit, you could also give your spirits an uplift by going to see the Romanesque church of Saint-Palais, before yielding to the pleasures of this world by tasting this Bordeaux Supérieur at the Château de Fussignac. It elegantly combines aromas of tobacco, truffles and dead leaves both in its bouquet and on the palate. Although the oak seems subdued, the tannins are still fierce and need two years to soften.
♠ Jean-François Carrille, pl. du Marcadieu, 33330 Saint-Emilion, tel. 05.57.24.74.46, fax 05.57.24.64.40, e-mail paulcarrille@worldonline.fr ☑
☿ by appt.

CH. DE LA GARDE

Elevé en fût de chêne 2000★★

| | 11 ha | 50,000 | ◫ | 5–8 € |

What is left of the old Château de la Garde? The name, certainly, but above all a wine of which the former lords of this place would have approved. Cherry is both the colour and principal aroma in the intense bouquet of ripe fruit. The palate is more subtle, leading the taster towards undergrowth and other flavours of mushroom, truffles and dead leaves. A good-quality oak is also integrated in this vegetal setting. The wine will reach its best in two or three years.
♠ SCEA Ch. de la Garde, 33240 Saint-Romain-la-Virvée, tel. 05.57.58.17.31, fax 05.57.58.17.31 ☑
☿ by appt.
♠ Ilja Gort

CH. LE GRAND VERDUS

Grande Réserve 2001★★

| | 7 ha | 16,000 | ◫ | 11–15 € |

The Grand Verdus, a superb 16th century fortified manor house, overlooks an impressive 88-ha vineyard farmed by

sustainable agriculture. In its vast winery they use the most up-to-date vinification techniques. The Grande Réserve 2001 has a brilliant garnet colour and a complex bouquet rich in aromas of soft fruits, nutmeg and spices. The round and tasty palate has oaky notes and is supported by good-quality tannins. Lay this wine down to let it become more balanced.
❦ Ph. et A. Legrix de La Salle, Ch. le Grand Verdus, 33670 Sadirac, tel. 05.56.30.50.90, fax 05.56.30.50.98, e-mail le.grand.verdus@wanadoo.fr ☑
⊤ by appt.

CH. LA GRAVETTE DES LUCQUES
Elevé en fût de chêne 2001★

■	4.62 ha	30,000	▮ ⑪ ♦	5–8 €

This château keeps its place in the *Guide*, winning another star. Its 2001 wine has a delightful bouquet of blackcurrant and cherry in brandy and a good balance between the fruit and the oak: nuances of cinnamon seem to have come about as a result of the wine being stored in oak. The palate is well structured and long, with the requisite balance for drinking immediately.
❦ EARL Patrice Haverlan, 11, rue de l'Hospital, 33640 Portets, tel. 05.56.67.11.32, fax 05.56.67.11.32, e-mail patrice.haverlan@worldonline.fr ☑
⊤ by appt.

CH. HAUT JEANGUILLON 2001★

■	13 ha	100,000	▮ ♦	5–8 €

This velvety red wine releases fresh perfumes of violet and a touch of pepper. Although the tannins are immediately apparent, their robust character does not conceal the quality of the round and well-extracted substance. This promising wine will be ready to drink in 2006. The **Château Vrai Caillou 2001**, matured in tank, also wins one star for its concentrated flesh and flavours of ripe fruits.
❦ Michel Pommier, Vrai Caillou, 33790 Soussac, tel. 05.56.61.31.56, fax 05.56.61.33.50, e-mail vignoblespommier@aol.com
⊤ by appt.

CH. HAUT-MONGEAT
Isabelle 2000★

■	0.56 ha	3,000	⑪	5–8 €

Bernard Bouchon and his daughter have worked together to produce this velvet Isabelle wine full of fruity perfumes and fine toasty notes. The substance is warm, round and supple, coating the rich tannins before continuing with fruity flavours and a subtle, good-quality oak. Drink it from 2004 and for a few years after that.
❦ Bernard Bouchon, Le Mongeat, 33420 Génissac, tel. 05.57.24.47.55, fax 05.57.24.41.21, e-mail info@mongeat.com ☑
⊤ by appt.

CH. HAUT NADEAU
Cuvée Prestige 2001★

■	1.4 ha	6,500	⑪	8–11 €

This wine has a strong colour and a balanced range of fruity aromas of blackcurrant and crushed strawberry allied to delicate liquorice-flavoured scents from the good-quality oak. It is full with a nice structure, revealing its complex personality up to the final nuances of coffee and spices. It could be served now, but will be very drinkable for many years.
❦ SCEA Ch. Haut Nadeau, 3, chem. d'Estévenadeau, 33760 Targon, tel. 05.56.20.44.07, fax 05.56.20.44.07, e-mail hautnadeaupa@wanadoo.fr ☑
❦⤙ Audouit

CH. HAUT SAINT MARTIN
Elevé en fût de chêne 2001★★

■	8 ha	45,000	⑪	5–8 €

The Château Saint-Martin can face the future with confidence: its Bordeaux Supérieur 2001 has the potential to be in demand for many years. It has an intense crimson colour fringed with deep purple – a sign of youthfulness – and releases a smooth and long bouquet of raspberry and plum in brandy. "Adorable," wrote one taster. It combines subtlety

and power with a full-bodied fresh character, showing too that it will age very well.
❦ Jean-Louis Lafon, ch. Haut Saint-Martin, Lieu dit la Garrigue, 33910 Saint-Martin-de-Laye, tel. 05.57.55.48.90, fax 05.57.84.31.27, e-mail milhade@milhade.fr

CH. HAUT-SORILLON
Cuvée Prestige 2001★★

■	3 ha	30,000	⑪	8–11 €

This Cuvée Prestige certainly deserves its name. The tasters were impressed by its concentration, a precise reflection of its deep-crimson colour. They were also surprised by the power of the bouquet with its nuances of musk and venison. This musky character combines on the palate with a well-integrated and lingering oak. Keep this one in your cellar until 2005. The main wine, the **Château Haut-Sorillon 2001 (5–8 €)**, matured in tank, also wins two stars; it reveals an impressively chewy character and flavours of currants. This wine will be good to drink for many years.
❦ SCE Vignobles Rousseau, 1, Petit-Sorillon, 33230 Abzac, tel. 05.57.49.06.10, fax 05.57.49.38.96, e-mail laurent@vignoblesrousseau.com ☑
⊤ by appt.

CH. L'ILE VERTE 2001★

■	40 ha	200,000	▮ ♦	5–8 €

The Ile Verte stands opposite the Margaux appellation, its vines extending as far as the silty waters of the Gironde estuary. It produces good-quality wines such as this brilliant crimson 2001. Merlot has the largest share of the blend, and this shows itself in the smooth bouquet of soft fruits and liquorice, while the supple and tasty, fairly winey palate leaves an impression of currants. This wine will be good to drink for many years. The **Château La Terrasse de l'Ile Verte Cuvée Michel Gonet 2001 (8–11 €)** also wins one star, as does the **Château Durand-Bayle 2001 (3–5 €)**, both of which were matured in tank.
❦ SCEV Michel Gonet et Fils, Ch. Lesparre, 33750 Beychac-et-Caillau, tel. 05.57.24.51.23, fax 05.57.24.03.99, e-mail vins.gonet@wanadoo.fr ☑
⊤ by appt.

CH. DES JOUALLES 2000★

■	30 ha	n.c.	▮ ♦	5–8 €

The owner of this château will certainly not be sorry he completely changed over to growing black grape varieties. This crimson-coloured wine offers the taster a range of spicy and balsamic oriental perfumes. Its rich and smooth, liquorice-flavoured substance unfurls soft tannins up to a charming finish. This wine is ready to drink now. From the same producer, the **Clos Grangeotte-Freylon 2000**, matured in tank, is commended.
❦ SCEA des Vignobles Freylon, 33350 Ruch, tel. 05.57.72.83, fax 05.57.74.48.88 ☑
⊤ by appt.

CH. LAFLEUR-NAUJAN
Cuvée des Chevaliers 2001★

■	3.5 ha	23,000	⑪	8–11 €

This estate, laid out round a 14th century castle, was still a mixed farm until the end of the 1990s. In 1999 the winery was built, and the use of modern vinification techniques has produced this good-quality wine whose well-advanced development is already apparent both visibly and in the bouquet. Soft fruits and oak combine happily together on the long palate with its lovely tannins. It will achieve harmony by 2004.
❦ SARL les Grands Châteaux de Naujan, 33240 Saint-Vincent-de-Pertignas, tel. 05.57.55.22.07, fax 05.57.84.04.98, e-mail info@direct-chateaux.com ☑
⊤ by appt.

CRU LAGAILLARDE 2000★★

■	2 ha	8,000	⑪	11–15 €

Balance is the word to describe this crimson wine made from almost equal shares of Merlot, Cabernet Sauvignon and Cabernet Franc. It has perfumes of crushed soft fruits accentuated with toasty nuances and soft chocolatey flavours. The body is round and full, and the elegant flesh is combined with lively but tasty tannins. The Grand Jury had no hesitation in

awarding the *coup de coeur* to this 2000 wine. It can be drunk in 2005.

☞ Vignobles Landeau, Dom. Grange-Brûlée, Mondion, 33440 Saint-Vincent-de-Paul, tel. 05.56.77.03.64, fax 05.56.77.11.17, e-mail xavier.landeau@wanadoo.fr ☑

☺ by appt.

CH. DE LAGARDE

Grand Millésime Vieilli en fût de chêne 2000★

■	5 ha	15,000	⦙⦙⦙	8–11 €

The buildings on this estate probably date from the same period as the Romanesque church of Saint-Laurent-du-Bois, but this Grand Millésime benefited from the advances of modern oenology. The Cabernets are the main grapes used (75%), and leave their vegetal and balsamic freshness on the bouquet (green pepper, cedar and resin). The body is shaped by evident tannins then softens in the finish of cinnamon and nutmeg. Keep this for a while, then serve it with a roast lamb.

☞ SCEA Raymond, Ch. de Lagarde, 33540 Saint-Laurent-du-Bois, tel. 05.56.76.43.63, fax 05.56.76.46.26, e-mail scea.raymond@libertysurf.fr ☑

☺ by appt.

CH. LAUDUC

Cuvée Prestige Elevé en fût de chêne 2001★

■	4.5 ha	33,000	⦙⦙⦙	5–8 €

Nothing is more typically Bordeaux than this Château Lauduc, located just a few kilometres from the regional capital. The Cuvée Prestige is characteristic of the appellation, and so is its Bordeaux red colour. The bouquet reflects the Merlot (75%) with its notes of leather, truffles and game. The fine palate has ripe tannins to give it an attractive structure. The finish reveals a nice combination of fruit (raspberry) and oak. Leave this wine for two or three years before opening it.

☞ GAEC Grandeau, Ch. Lauduc, 33370 Tresses, tel. 05.57.34.43.56, fax 05.57.34.43.58, e-mail m.grandeau@lauduc.fr ☑

☺ by appt.

CH. LORIENT

Elevé en fût de chêne 2000★

■	9.52 ha	26,000	⦙⦙⦙	5–8 €

This crimson wine has exuberant scents of stewed fruits and dried grapes. Notes of burning and roasting accompany the round and consistent palate. The wine's harmony suggests it should be drunk soon.

☞ Hervé de Domingo, 11, rue de Comet, 33450 Saint-Loubès, tel. 05.56.20.41.12, fax 05.56.20.41.12 ☑

☺ by appt.

CH. DE LUGAGNAC 2000★

■	25 ha	160,000	▌↓	5–8 €

Lugagnac is an autentic château of character which dates back to the Middle Ages, and still provides an attractive image of that period. However, its present owners are all for making wines by modern methods, like this amaranth-coloured 2000 with spicy and liquorice-flavoured tones. The rich substance

rests on a tasty tannic framework which supports a long finish of violet and lily of the valley.

☞ Famille Bon, SCEA du Ch. de Lugagnac, 33790 Pellegrue, tel. 05.56.61.30.60, fax 05.56.61.38.48, e-mail clugagnac@aol.com ☑

☺ ev. day 9am–12 noon 2pm–6pm

EXIGENCE D'YVON MAU 2001★

■	n.c.	15,000	⦙⦙⦙	11–15 €

This Exigence wine has only to be tasted to reveal the care that went into its making. It has a deep colour with purplish highlights, and reveals a complex range of fruity and spicy aromas: prune, almond and fruit stone are rounded off by vanilla and toasted flavours. The velvety substance bears the mark of a well-made oak, accompanied by intense flavours of smoke and leather. Serve this with game and stews. The **Château D'Auzanet 2001 (3–5 €)**, matured in tank, also wins one star, while the **Château Petit Martinot 2001 Elevé en Fût de Chêne (3–5 €)** is commended.

☞ SA Yvon Mau, 33190 Gironde-sur-Dropt, tel. 05.56.61.54.54, fax 05.56.61.54.61, e-mail info@ymau.com

CH. LA MOTHE DU BARRY

Cuvée Design Elevé en fût de chêne 2001★

■	3 ha	20,000	⦙⦙⦙	5–8 €

Joël Duffau has produced an elegant crimson wine with purplish glints from his 3 ha of clay-limestone soils planted wholly with Merlot. It is like a summer fruit salad accentuated with fairly intense notes of roasting. The rich and concentrated substance reveals tannins and long toasty flavours. This wine will become increasingly better balanced up to 2005. Also matured in barrel was the **Le Barry 2001 (8–11 €)**, which is commended. Its sister wine, Le Barry 2000, won the bronze grapes award in the 2003 *Guide* for AOC Bordeaux.

☞ Joël Duffau, Les Arromans no. 2, 33420 Moulon, tel. 05.57.74.93.98, fax 05.57.84.66.10, e-mail lamothed@club-internet.fr ☑

☺ ev. day except Sun. 9am–12.30pm 2pm–7pm; cl. 15–31 Aug.

CH. NAUDONNET PLAISANCE

Elevé en fût de chêne 2000★★

■	20 ha	70,000	⦙⦙⦙	5–8 €

The Château Naudonnet Plaisance is a regular in the *Guide*. Here it offers a strong crimson 2000. After the glass is swirled, the bouquet reveals aromas of stone fruits and nuances of port. The round, rich flesh has finely textured tannins and displays lingering flavours of cocoa butter, chocolate and roasting.

☞ Laurent Mallard, Ch. Naudonnet Plaisance, 33760 Escoussans, tel. 05.56.23.93.04, fax 05.57.34.40.78, e-mail l.mallard@wanadoo.fr ☑

☺ by appt.

CH. NOULET 2000★

■	28 ha	12,000	▌↓	3–5 €

This feudal château could tell you about the Hundred Years' War, and its wineries about the time Montesquieu often stayed at Baron. Today, it invites you to taste a characteristic wine with warm notes of soft fruits in brandy. It quite openly demonstrates its clean and direct nature. Its winey flavour suggests it will be good with red meats in 2004 and 2005.

☞ SCA de Crain, Ch. de Crain, 33750 Baron, tel. 05.57.24.50.66, fax 05.45.25.03.73 ☑

☺ by appt.

☞ Fougère

CH. PANCHILLE

Cuvée Alix 2001★

■	3 ha	n.c.	⦙⦙⦙	5–8 €

The Cuvée Alix appeared in the *Guide* in 1999, 2000 and 2001, each time winning one star. This latest vintage has a crimson colour and reveals a fresh fruitiness as well as a touch of clove and liquorice. Its dense and silky substance unfurls up to the soft toasty finish. This is a wine for the future, but it is already tasty. The main wine, the **Château Panchille 2001**, was matured in tank and also wins one star for its suave fruitiness and velvety substance.

☞ Pascal Sirat, Panchille, 33500 Arveyres, tel. 05.57.51.57.39, fax 05.57.51.57.39 ☑
☒ by appt.

CH. PASCAUD

Réserve élevé en fût de chêne 2001★★

| ■ | 2 ha | 120,000 | ⑪ | 8–11 € |

The Château Pascaud chose hand-picked grapes from its oldest vines for its Bordeaux Supérieur. This 2001 wine has a deep-red colour with light purple highlights and is developing a fairly intense vanilla-flavoured oak made more complex by the underlying fruitiness. The structured but already supple body has lovely aromas of prune in brandy, and tasters can sense the onset of harmony. This is a wine to enjoy for many years.

☞ SCEA Vignobles Avril, BP 12, 33133 Galgon, tel. 05.57.84.32.11, fax 05.57.74.38.62, e-mail ch.pascaud@aol.com ☑
☒ by appt.

CH. PENIN

Grande Sélection 2001★

| ■ | 9 ha | 6,200 | ⑪ | 8–11 € |

This Grande Sélection from the Château Penin reflects a well-defined gravelly terroir consisting of red sands and pebbles rolled along the Dordogne from the Massif Central. It was made from Merlot vines more than 30 years old and planted at a high density (90% of the blend), which helps the grapes to mature well. The 2001 wine has a brilliant colour and reveals the overripeness sought during the harvest in its light aromas of bilberry and cherry. It shows itself to be dense mouth-filling and robust, with good tannins. This is a complete wine, ready to drink now or keep for a while. Also very successful was the Les Cailloux 2001 (11–15 €), matured in barrel, which is already round with floral aromas.

☞ SCEA Patrick Carteyron, Ch. Penin, 33420 Génissac, tel. 05.57.24.46.98, fax 05.57.24.41.99, e-mail vignoblescarteyron@wanadoo.fr ☑
☒ by appt.

CH. PICON

Le Vin du Roi 2000★

| ■ | 2 ha | 10,000 | ⑪ | 11–15 € |

This wine is a selection of Merlot and Cabernet Sauvignon, and follows the Bordeaux tradition: hand-picked grapes and maturation in barrel for two years. It is full and smooth, with a ripe fruitiness (raspberry) and floral aromas (violet) which the gentle oak allows to come through. It will be at its best in 2005.

☞ Audry, Ch. Picon, 33220 Eynesse, tel. 05.57.41.01.91 ☑
☒ by appt.

CH. PIERRAIL

Elevé en fût de chêne 2001★★

| ■ | 33 ha | 175,000 | ⑪ | 8–11 € |

There is no need to introduce the lovely welcoming residence of the Château Pierrail, with its opulent salons rich in historic memories. Its vineyards, planted on a clay-limestone soil, have produced this Bordeaux Supérieur with fruity and peppery aromas which won over the whole of the Grand Jury.

Its concentrated, balanced palate lingers silkily thanks to the remarkably well-integrated tannins. This wine will give constant pleasure for many years.

☞ EARL Ch. Pierrail, 33220 Margueron, tel. 05.57.41.21.75, fax 05.57.41.23.77, e-mail alice@chateaupierrail.com ☑
☒ by appt.
☞ J.-M. Demonchaux

CH. PIOTE-AUBRION

Cuvée Prestige Vieilli en fût de chêne 2000★

| ■ | 2 ha | 10,000 | ⑪ | 5–8 € |

This is a small (10 ha) but very ambitious vineyard where Virginie Aubrion exercises her talents. The lovely constitution of this 2000 wine is apparent at first sight of the garnet colour, then in the light floral bouquet (rose and peony). It is confirmed on the full, round palate supported by mature and well-behaved tannins. Its balance guarantees it a long life.

☞ Virginie Aubrion, Dom. de Piote, 33240 Aubie-Espessas, tel. 05.57.43.96.10, fax 05.57.43.96.10 ☑

CH. RAUZAN DESPAGNE 2001★

| ■ | n.c. | n.c. | ⬛ ♦ | 5–8 € |

This vineyard is mainly planted with Merlot, and uses only vines more than 30 years old, grown on a clay-limestone soil and harvested by hand. This Bordeaux Supérieur, which was not matured in barrel, reveals a very charming bouquet of Morello cherry and redcurrant. The same fine fruitiness accompanies the framework of integrated tannins: you can scent the healthy, ripe grapes. Drink it from 2004 for its freshness, served with a gigot d'agneau aux fines herbes. Also very pleasant is the Château Lion Beaulieu 2001, matured in tank, which wins one star.

☞ GFA de Landeron, 33420 Naujan-et-Postiac, tel. 05.57.84.55.08, fax 05.57.55.57.31, e-mail contact@despagne.fr ☑
☒ by appt.
☞ J.-L. Despagne

LA ROSE BOISSIERE 2000★

| ■ | n.c. | 31,500 | ⬛ ⑪ ♦ | 5–8 € |

The négociants Aurélien Grenouilleau have been active since 1820 in the Gironde. This wine is an example of their work. Beneath its crimson colour, it has a lovely developing bouquet of almond and ripe fruits. Its clean palate is certainly still firm, but shows vigour and good vinosity. This is a wine to lay down for two years to let it develop fully.

☞ Aurélien Grenouilleau, 5, av. Foch, 33220 Pineuilh, tel. 05.57.46.00.01, fax 05.57.46.35.90, e-mail m.bauce@grenouilleau.com ☑
☒ by appt.
☞ Michel Baucé

CH. LA ROSE RENEVE 2000★

| ■ | 4 ha | 31,000 | ⬛ ♦ | 5–8 € |

Thirty-five-year-old vines, grown just outside Libourne, have produced this brilliant red-coloured 2000 which owes its power and concentration to limited grape yields. Stone fruits, then blackberry flavour the palate with its integrated tannins. It seems unnecessary to keep this wine for long, as it is already so pleasant.

☞ SCEA vignobles André Bertin, 1, chem. de Tire-Merle, 33500 Arveyres, tel. 05.57.24.81.72, fax 05.57.24.81.72, e-mail la-rose-reneve@wanadoo.fr ☑
☒ by appt.

CH. SEGONZAC

Héritage 2001★★

| ■ | 2.97 ha | 21,000 | ⑪ | 11–15 € |

Located 3 km from Blaye, the Château Segonzac is a magnificent estate whose vines stretch across a sunny hillside overlooking the Gironde. The Cuvée Héritage was made from a selection of the best plots in the vineyard, and majestically demonstrates the qualities of this terroir: it is a velvety, full wine, as dense as its crimson colour. The impression of balance

is clear, accentuated by the gradually developing aromas of blackcurrant, bilberry and violet. Drink this wine soon.
☛ SCEA Ch. Segonzac, 39, Segonzac, 33390 Saint-Genès-de-Blaye, tel. 05.57.42.18.16, fax 05.57.42.24.80, e-mail chateau.segonzac@wanadoo.fr ☒
☝ by appt.
☛ Charlotte Herter-Marmet

CH. DE SEGUIN

Cuvée Prestige Vieilli en barrique neuve 2000★

■	20 ha	150,000	⑪	8–11 €

This wine is charming both in colour (a lively red shot with garnet highlights) and in its bouquet of vanilla-flavoured fruits (cherry and strawberry). The firm body reveals musky notes and an elegant oak, indicating that the wine will improve with age, even if it can already be enjoyed today.
☛ Michael et Gert Carl, Ch. de Seguin, 33360 Lignan-de-Bordeaux, tel. 05.57.97.19.75, fax 05.57.97.19.72, e-mail info@chateau-seguin.fr ☒
☝ by appt.

CH. DU SIRON

Cuvée réservée 2001★

■	3 ha	20,000	🍾	5–8 €

This wine was made in enchanting surroundings, a real cinema set, for this is where Claude Miller made Le Sourire in 1993. Its amaranth colour glints in the glass with crimson highlights and its delightful bouquet is very summery: redcurrant, soft spices and cinnamon. The tannins dissolve in the folds of its silky substance flavoured by stewed fruits, nutmeg and dried grape, indicating that it is almost ready to drink.
☛ Pierre Ginelli, EARL Ch. du Siron, Le Siron, 33490 Saint-Martin-de-Sescas, tel. 05.56.76.44.79, fax 05.56.76.43.10, e-mail pierre.ginelli@wanadoo.fr ☒
☝ by appt.

CH. TARREYROTS 2001★

■	11 ha	60,000	🍾⑪♨	5–8 €

The beautiful old Château Tarreyrots is surrounded by a vineyard of 11 ha, mostly Merlot, grown on a clay-limestone soil. Its modern winery has created this crimson wine with slight brick-red nuances, which releases a soft and pleasantly vanilla-flavoured fruitiness. The round palate continues these aromas and leaves a lasting impression of harmony. This wine will go well with a fondue bourguignonne.
☛ Alain Vironneau, SCEA Ch. Tarreyrots, Le Majureau, 33240 Salignac, tel. 05.57.43.00.25, fax 05.57.43.91.34 ☒
☝ by appt.

CH. THIEULEY

Réserve Francis Courselle 2001★

■	12.5 ha	100,000	⑪	11–15 €

Francis Courselle is a master of maturation in barrel, and this wine lives up to his reputation. Its crimson colour reveals signs of good development, while the powerful bouquet of soft fruits and nutmeg are part of its attractive personality. The palate is mouth-filling and long with toasty notes, resting on still lively tannins which are, however, so tasty that they can be forgiven their youthfulness. Keep this wine until 2005.
☛ Sté des Vignobles Francis Courselle, Ch. Thieuley, 33670 La Sauve, tel. 05.56.23.00.01, fax 05.56.23.34.37 ☒
☝ by appt.

CH. THURON

Cuvée Martin de Monphélix 2000★

■	4.3 ha	20,000	⑪	8–11 €

In Occitan, the "thuron" is a property set on a hill. Here it reaches almost spiritual heights, because this 18th century mansion is on the route to Santiago de Compostela, and is still much used. This wine was made from hand-picked grapes that were macerated for a long time. Its fine bouquet of ripe grapes is enriched by smoky and oaky notes. Roasted nuances flavour the round palate, which has subdued tannins and a developing harmony which establishes itself in the pleasant finish.
☛ Jean-Pierre Lallement, SCEA du Ch. Turon, 33190 Pondaurat, tel. 05.56.71.23.92, fax 05.56.71.01.89, e-mail chateauthuron@wanadoo.fr ☒
☝ by appt.

CH. TIMBERLAY

Cuvée Prestige 2000★

■	10 ha	33,000	⑪	8–11 €

This wine has a crimson colour and fuchsia highlights, and its scents are first of all vegetal (humus and mushroom) but soon it releases subtle aromas of fruits, soft spices and toast. The well-shaped body has a round flesh with light balsamic flavours at the finish.
☛ EARL Vignobles Robert Giraud, Dom. de Loiseau, BP 31, 33240 Saint-André-de-Cubzac, tel. 05.57.43.01.44, fax 04.57.43.08.75, e-mail france@robertgiraud.com

CH. TOUR D'AURON 2001★★

■	8 ha	n.c.	⑪	5–8 €

Gérard Milhade offers a Bordeaux Supérieur which makes no false promises with its intense colour of bigaroon cherry. The bouquet reveals soft fruits (bilberry, blackberry and plum), while the full and long palate has harmonious flavours of grape and coconut with moderate tannins. This balanced wine can be drunk now, but will improve if you give it time.
☛ Gérard Milhade, Lieu-dit Peychez, 33144 Saillans, tel. 05.57.55.48.90, fax 05.57.84.31.27, e-mail milhade@milhade.fr

CH. TOUR DE GILET

L'Expression du petit verdot 2001★

■	5 ha	9,000	⑪	8–11 €

As its subtitle reveals, this wine is supposed to show off its Petit Verdot, an old Médoc variety which plays a major part in this blend (60%). The wine has an intense crimson colour and an attractive bouquet of undergrowth, dead leaves and crystallized grapes. Its tasty chewiness is memorable for its ripe grapes. This is a wine with plenty of personality which makes a good case for a renaissance of Petit Verdot in the Gironde.
☛ SC Ch. Tour de Gilet, BP 11, 33460 Macau, tel. 05.57.88.07.64, fax 05.57.88.07.00 ☒
☝ by appt.

CH. TOUR DE MIRAMBEAU

Cuvée Passion 2001★

■	n.c.	n.c.	⑪	11–15 €

The Château Tour de Mirambeau always does well in the Guide. Its Cuvée Passion 2001, is clothed as it should be in a brilliant crimson colour and, when the glass is swirled, releases intense scents of blackcurrant and violet with vanilla nuances. On the palate, the fruit and the oak combine well together, though favouring the latter as this wine is still developing and will benefit from being laid down until 2006. The main wine, the Château Tour de Mirambeau 2001 (5–8 €), matured in tank, also wins one star; its round substance will make it ready to drink next year.
☛ SCEA Vignobles Despagne, 33420 Naujan-et-Postiac, tel. 05.57.84.55.08, fax 05.57.84.57.31, e-mail contact@despagne.fr ☒
☛ J.-L. Despagne

CH. LA TUILERIE DU PUY

Elevé en barrique 2000★

■	3.5 ha	25,000	🍾⑪♨	5–8 €

This family property is more than 400 years old, though the château did not turn wholly to making wine until the 1930s. It offers a deep-red wine with some highlights indicating development, and a mature bouquet of prune, vanilla and roasting. On the clean palate, still marked by the tannins, the oak is evident alongside flavours of resin and leather. This is a wine of character; keep it for two years.
☛ SCEA Regaud, La Tuilerie du Puy, 33580 Le Puy, tel. 05.56.61.61.92, fax 05.56.61.86.90, e-mail regaud@free.fr ☒
☝ ev. day 8.30am–12 noon 1pm–6pm

CH. LA VERRIERE 2001★★

■	4 ha	26,000	🍾	3–5 €

This wine was made from a selection of 4 ha of vines planted with the three main Bordeaux varieties (60% Merlot) on clay hillsides. The Jury particularly liked its rich aromas of

prune and bilberry combined with musky notes (fur and venison). The opulent flesh coats a tasty tannic support. Serve this with a ragoût d'agneau in thyme.
- EARL André Bessette, 8, La Verrière, 33790 Landerrouat, tel. 05.56.61.33.21, fax 05.56.61.44.25
- by appt.
- André et Alain Bessette

CH. VIGNOL 2000★

■	4,5 ha	32,000	■ ↓	5–8 €

If, in landscapes where a single crop is grown, you like the scene to be more balanced, with vines mixed in with woods and rabbit warrens, then Château Vignol is the place for you. There you can try this Bordeaux Supérieur with delightful aromas of cherry and blackcurrant. Its finely vanilla-flavoured framework will flow like grape pulp over your palate, and its lasting roundness will fill you with joy.
- SCEA Bernard et Dominique Doublet, Ch. Vignol, 33750 Saint-Quentin-de-Baron, tel. 05.57.24.12.93, fax 05.57.24.12.83, e-mail d.doublet@free.fr
- by appt.

CH. VIRECOURT

Pillebourse 2001★

■	6 ha	26,000	■ ↓	8–11 €

The Chassagnoux family farms its vineyard in a traditional manner. It stands on a clay-limestone terroir, and is almost entirely given over to Merlot. The latter was probably responsible for this wine's crimson colour and scents of undergrowth, truffles and game on a lightly oaky base. The palate is still a little biting in the attack, but becomes rounder as it moves towards leathery and musky flavours. It has an attractive substance full of promise, and will improve between now and 2005.
- Xavier Chassagnoux, Renard, 33126 La Rivière, tel. 05.57.24.96.37, fax 05.57.24.90.18, e-mail chateau.renard.mondesir@wanadoo.fr
- by appt.

Wines selected but not starred

CH. BEL AIR

Cuvée Maxime 2001

■	2,78 ha	20,000	■ ↓	5–8 €

- Philippe Moysson, Ch. Bel Air, 33540 Blasimon, tel. 05.57.84.10.74, fax 05.57.84.00.51, e-mail scea.moysson@wanadoo.fr
- by appt.

CH. DE BLASSAN

Cuvée fût de chêne 2001

■	6.5 ha	42,000	⑪	5–8 €

- Guy Cenni, SCEA Ch. de Blassan, Blassan, 33240 Lugon, tel. 05.57.84.40.91, fax 05.57.84.82.93
- by appt.

CH. BOIS NOIR

Elevé en fût de Chêne 2000

■	22 ha	53,000	⑪	5–8 €

- Cyrille Grégoire, SARL Ch. Bois Noir, Le Bois Noir, 33230 Maransin, tel. 05.57.49.41.09, fax 05.57.49.41.09
- by appt.

DOM. DE CANTEMERLE

Grains du Terroir 2001

■	3.5 ha	20,000	■⑪↓	8–11 €

- Vignobles Mabille, Dom. de Cantemerle, 33540 Saint-Gervais, tel. 05.57.43.11.39, fax 05.57.43.42.28, e-mail cantemerle@wanadoo.fr
- by appt.

CH. CAZAT-BEAUCHENE

Elevé en fût de chêne 2001

■	38.61 ha	160,000	⑪	3–5 €

- SCEA des domaines Cazat-Beauchêne, 33570 Petit-Palais, tel. 05.57.69.86.92, fax 05.57.69.87.00, e-mail cazalio@wanadoo.fr
- by appt.
- J.-F. Carrère

COMTE AUGUSTE 2000

■	2 ha	10,000	⑪	5–8 €

- Bernard Yon, Ch. Gaury Balette, 33540 Mauriac, tel. 05.57.40.52.82, fax 05.57.40.51.71, e-mail bernard-yon@wanadoo.fr
- by appt.

CH. LA GALANTE

Le Grand Vin 2001

■	2 ha	6,500	⑪	8–11 €

- SC du Ch. la Galante, rte de la Joncasse, 33750 Beychac-et-Caillau, tel. 05.56.72.86.77, fax 05.56.68.34.31, e-mail chateau.lagalante@wanadoo.fr
- by appt.
- Christophe Pinard

GRAND LAVERGNE 2001

■	11 ha	80,000		5–8 €

- Jean Boireau, Les Grands Jays, 33570 Les Artigues-de-Lussac, tel. 05.57.24.32.08, fax 05.57.24.33.24, e-mail earl-vignoblesboireau@wanadoo.fr
- by appt.

L'HERITIER DE CLOS NORMANDIN

Cuvée Prestige 2001

■	n.c.	9,000	⑪	5–8 €

- EARL R. et fils Alicandri, 12, le bourg, 33750 Saint-Quentin-de-Baron, tel. 05.57.24.26.03, fax 05.57.24.26.03
- by appt.

CH. DE L'HERMITAGE

Elevé en fût de chêne 2000

■	2 ha	10,000	⑪	5–8 €

- EARL Gérard Lopez, L'Hermitage, 33540 Saint-Martin-du-Puy, tel. 05.56.71.57.58, fax 05.56.71.65.00, e-mail earl.lopez@wanadoo.fr
- by appt.

CH. JEAN MATHIEU 2000

■	1.5 ha	6,000	⑪	5–8 €

- EARL Vignobles Brasseur, Ch. La Paillette, 33500 Libourne, tel. 05.57.51.17.31, fax 05.57.51.33.75
- ev. day except Sun. 9am–12 noon 2pm–6pm

CH. LAMOTHE

Vieilli en fût de chêne 2000

■	8 ha	26,666	⑪	3–5 €

- Cheval-Quancard, La Mouline, 4 rue du Carbouney, BP 36, 33560 Carbon-Blanc, tel. 05.57.77.88.88, fax 05.57.77.88.99, e-mail chevalquancard@chevalquancard.com
- by appt.
- J.B.C. Vincent

CH. LASCAUX

Elevé en fût de chêne 2000

| | 3.5 ha | 18,500 | ◫ | 5–8 € |

🖢 Fabrice Lascaux, Ch. Lascaux, La Caillebosse, 33910 Saint-Martin-du-Bois, tel. 05.57.84.72.16, fax 05.57.84.72.17, e-mail chateau-lascaux@wanadoo.fr ☑

🍷 by appt.

CH. LESTRILLE 2001

| | 9 ha | 70,000 | ▮ ⬥ | 5–8 € |

🖢 Jean-Louis Roumage, Lestrille, 33750 Saint-Germain-du-Puch, tel. 05.57.24.51.02, fax 05.57.24.04.58, e-mail jlroumage@lestrille.com ☑

🍷 by appt.

CH. LEZIN 2001

| | 104 ha | 76,650 | ▮ ◫ ⬥ | 3–5 € |

🖢 SC du Ch. de la Tour, 35, rue de Bordeaux, 33290 Parempuyre, tel. 05.56.35.53.00, fax 05.56.35.53.29, e-mail contact@cvbg.com

🍷 by appt.

🖢 CVBG

CH. MARAC 2001

| | 10.86 ha | 75,000 | ▮ ⬥ | 5–8 € |

🖢 Alain Bonville, Ch. Marac, 33350 Pujols, tel. 05.57.40.53.21, fax 05.57.40.71.36, e-mail vignoble-alain.bonville@wanadoo.fr ☑

🍷 by appt.

CH. MARTOURET 2001

| | 10 ha | 70,000 | ◫ | 5–8 € |

🖢 SARL les vins Dominique Lurton, Martouret, 33750 Nérigean, tel. 05.57.24.50.02, fax 05.57.24.03.30, e-mail d.lurton@martouret.com ☑

🍷 by appt.

CH. MASSEREAU 2001

| | 5.5 ha | 12,000 | ▮ ⬥ | 5–8 € |

🖢 Jean-François Chaigneau, Ch. Massereau, 33720 Barsac, tel. 05.56.27.46.62, fax 05.56.27.02.18, e-mail chateau.massereau@wanadoo.fr ☑

🍷 ev. day 9am–12.30pm 2pm–8pm

CH. LE MAYNE 2000

| | 30 ha | 200,000 | ▮ ⬥ | 5–8 € |

🖢 SCEA Ch. le Mayne, 33220 Saint-Quentin-de-Caplong, tel. 05.57.41.00.05, e-mail chateaulemayne@wanadoo.fr ☑

🍷 by appt.

CH. PEUY-SAINCRIT

Montalon 2001

| | 3 ha | 20,000 | ▮ ◫ ⬥ | 8–11 € |

🖢 Vignobles Germain et Associés, Ch. Peyredoulle, 33390 Berson, tel. 05.57.42.66.66, fax 05.57.64.36.20, e-mail bordeaux@vgas.com

🍷 by appt.

CH. PEYAU 2001

| | 7 ha | 39,000 | ◫ | 5–8 € |

🖢 Dulong Frères et Fils, 29, rue Jules-Guesde, 33270 Floirac, tel. 05.56.86.51.15, fax 05.56.40.66.41, e-mail dulong@dulong.com

🍷 by appt.

CH. PUY-FAVEREAU 2001

| | 14 ha | 50,000 | ▮ ⬥ | 3–5 € |

🖢 SCEA les Ducs d'Aquitaine, Favereau, 33660 Saint-Sauveur-de-Puynormand, tel. 05.57.69.69.69, fax 05.57.69.62.84, e-mail vignobles@lepottier.com ☑

🍷 by appt.

🖢 Le Pottier

CH. ROZIER JOUBERT 2001

| | 10 ha | 60,000 | ▮ | 3–5 € |

🖢 Ginestet, 19, av. de Fontenille, 33360 Carignan-de-Bordeaux, tel. 05.56.68.81.82, fax 05.56.20.94.47, e-mail contact@ginestet.fr

🍷 by appt.

CH. SAINTE-MARIE

Vieilles Vignes 2001

| | 15 ha | 45,000 | ▮ ⬥ | 11–15 € |

🖢 Gilles et Stéphane Dupuch, 51, rte de Bordeaux, 33760 Targon, tel. 05.56.23.64.30, fax 05.56.23.66.80, e-mail ch.ste.marie@wanadoo.fr ☑

🍷 by appt.

SEIGNEUR DES ORMES

Cuvée réservée Elevé en fût de chêne 2000

| | 1.84 ha | 14,000 | | 5–8 € |

🖢 Union de producteurs Baron d'Espiet, Lieu-dit Fourcade, 33420 Espiet, tel. 05.57.24.24.08, fax 05.57.24.18.21, e-mail baron-espiet@dial.oleane.com ☑

🍷 by appt.

CH. TOUR CAILLET

Cuvée Prestige Elevé en barrique 2001

| | 8 ha | 50,000 | ◫ | 5–8 € |

🖢 Denis Lecourt, 8, Caillet, 33420 Génissac, tel. 05.57.24.46.04, fax 05.57.24.40.18 ☑

🍷 by appt.

VIEUX VAURE 2000

| | n.c. | 50,000 | ▮ ⬥ | 3–5 € |

🖢 Les Chais de Vaure, 33350 Ruch, tel. 05.57.40.54.09, e-mail chais-de-vaure@wanadoo.fr ☑

🍷 ev. day except Sun. 8.30am–12.30pm 2pm–6pm

🖢 P. de Larrard

Crémant de Bordeaux

The sparkling Crémant de Bordeaux was created in 1990. It is made according to the same strict fermentation and ageing rules as all other Appellations Crémants, using traditional Bordelais grape varieties. Generally speaking, Crémants are white (8,854 hl in 2002) but they can also be rosé (330 hl).

CLOS DE PELIGON

Demi-sec 2001 ★★

| ⬤ | 0.73 ha | 1,900 | ▮ | 5–8 € |

This wine comes from gravelly soils and is made entirely from fairly old Sémillon vines (30 years). It has a whitish-yellow colour and green highlights, with tiny bubbles dancing in a necklace beneath the slight effervescence. It has a light bouquet with a soft musky note to the fore of white peach and peppery menthol. This is followed by a scent of honeysuckle. The palate is soft, smooth and balanced.

🖢 EARL Vignobles Reynaud, 13, rte de Libourne, 33450 Saint-Loubès, tel. 05.56.20.47.52, fax 05.56.68.65.21 ☑

🍷 by appt.

LATEYRON 2000 ★

| ⬤ | n.c. | 12,411 | ◫ | 5–8 € |

This family business has been firmly rooted in the Libourne region since 1897. It stands immediately next to the prestigious appellations of Pomerol and Saint-Emilion. This

Crémant with good bubbles was made chiefly from Sémillon (90%) with 10% of Cabernet Franc, and has a delightful golden-yellow colour. The bouquet is very expressive and rich in ripe grapes, and heralds a palate which is silky and soft, tasty and honeyed. The finish is coated in notes of almond and white flowers.
🐟 SA Lateyron, Ch. Tour Calon, BP 1, 33570 Montagne, tel. 05.57.74.62.05, fax 05.57.74.58.58, e-mail lateyron@wanadoo.fr ☑
🍷 by appt.

MARINIER 2001★

	3 ha	5,941	🍶 🍷	5–8 €

This family property was enlarged and restructured by Louis Marinier, and today is passionately managed by his daughter and granddaughter. This Crémant has a swirl of attractive, fine and regular bubbles; a brilliant yellow colour with shades of creamy yellow. The delightful bouquet reveals brioche with toasted nut butter, joining together freshness, vivacity and tenderness in a pleasant roundness. It will make a perfect aperitif served with canapés of foie gras, rillette and salmon.
🐟 Vignobles Louis Marinier, Dom. Florimond-La-Brède, 33390 Berson, tel. 05.57.64.34.63, fax 05.57.64.23.27, e-mail vignobleslouismarinier@wanadoo.fr ☑
🍷 ev. day 8am–12 noon 2pm–5pm; Sat. Sun. by appt.; cl. Aug.

REMY-BREQUE

Cuvée Prestige★

	n.c.	10,000		5–8 €

This firm has made sparkling wines by the traditional method for four generations, and now offers its Crémant Prestige made from equal parts of Sémillon and Muscadelle. It has a good-looking mousse with fine bubbles which rapidly fade away, and a lovely pale yellow-white iridescence with green nuances. The bouquet is withdrawn at first, then opens out with scents of iris, buttered cream and menthol. Roundness and freshness make a successful balance. Try this with dishes combining salt and sugar such as a whole foie gras with *pain d'épice* or *magret de canard* in peaches and pears.
🐟 Maison Rémy-Brèque, 8, rue du Cdt-Cousteau, 33240 Saint-Gervais, tel. 05.57.43.10.42, fax 05.57.43.91.61 ☑
🍷 by appt.
🐟 Bonnefis

Wines selected but not starred

BALLARIN

Milady

	n.c.	n.c.		8–11 €

🐟 Jean-Louis Ballarin, 33550 Haux, tel. 05.56.67.11.30, fax 05.56.67.54.60, e-mail ballarin@wanadoo.fr ☑
🍷 by appt.

CRISTAL DE MELIN 2000

	1 ha	n.c.	🍶	8–11 €

🐟 EARL Vignobles Claude Modet et Fils, Constantin, 33880 Baurech, tel. 05.56.21.34.71, fax 05.56.21.37.72, e-mail vmodet@wanadoo.fr ☑
🍷 by appt.

DOM. DE LAUBERTRIE

	5 ha	3,200	🍶 🍷	5–8 €

🐟 Bernard Pontallier, Laubertrie, 33240 Salignac, tel. 05.57.43.24.73, fax 05.57.43.49.25 ☑
🍷 by appt.

LE TREBUCHET 2001

	0.5 ha	5,000		5–8 €

🐟 Bernard Berger, Ch. Le Trébuchet, 33190 Les Esseintes, tel. 05.56.71.42.28, fax 05.56.71.30.16 ☑
🍷 ev. day except Sun. 8am–12 noon 2pm–6pm

Blaye and Bourg

Blaye and Bourg are two small regions on the border between the Charente department and the Gironde. They are delightful to come upon for the first time, since both contain historic sites: the prehistoric paintings in the Pair-Non-Pair caves are almost as splendid as the ones at Lascaux. Both Blaye and Bourg are fortified towns, and there are several small châteaux and old hunting lodges. The landscape of hills and valleys creates an intimate atmosphere, which is in sharp contrast to the almost maritime horizons of the banks of the estuary. This is the only place outside Russia and Iran where sturgeon have been caught; it has also been wine country since Gallo-Roman times, which gives this historic landscape a special charm. Up to the beginning of the 20th century there was a considerable production of white wines, used in the distillation of Cognac. Nowadays, white wine production has significantly declined against the much more economically viable reds.

Blaye, Premières Côtes de Blaye, Côtes de Blaye, Bourg, Bourgeais, Côtes de Bourg, reds and whites ... there are so many slight differences in the names that it is not always easy to be clear about the different appellations of the region. Nonetheless, it is possible to identify two main groups: the wines from Blaye, where the soil types are varied, and the ones from Bourg, which is geologically more uniform.

BLAYE, CÔTES DE BLAYE AND PREMIÈRES CÔTES DE BLAYE

The fortress of Blaye was built by the great military engineer Vauban and is still completely intact. Today, the vineyards cover about 6,000 ha and are planted with both red and white grape varieties. The appellations Blaye and Blayais are used less and less frequently because the wine-growers prefer to produce wines using more noble vine varieties, which are entitled to the appellations Côtes de Blaye and Premières Côtes de Blaye. Nevertheless, 5,072 hl of Blaye was produced in 2002. The red wines of Premières Côtes de Blaye (265,798 hl in 2002) are intensely coloured and have an authentic simplicity, and are strong and fruity. The whites (10,837 hl) are aromatic. They are generally dry and light-coloured and best served at the beginning of a meal, while the red Premières Côtes go better with meat dishes and cheeses.

The new quality chart for AOC Blaye assumes bottling after an 18-month maturation period.

Blaye

CH. CANTELOUP 2000★

| ■ | 1 ha | 6,000 | ◗◗ | 8–11 € |

This 24 ha vineyard won a *coup de cœur* for its Premières Côtes de Blaye 99. Now it is offering a Blaye 2000, made from old vines. In the glass, the intense garnet colour reveals some highlights indicating development. The bouquet is already powerful, releasing very ripe grape, nut, roasted oak and mocha. The palate is dense and full-bodied as well as harmonious with good-quality tannins which guarantee it will age well. This is an interesting wine to lay down for five or six years.
🍷 Eric Vezain, Canteloup, 33390 Fours, tel. 05.57.42.13.16, fax 05.57.42.26.28 ☑
𝕐 by appt.

CH. MONDESIR-GAZIN 2000★

| ■ | 4.75 ha | 24,000 | ◗◗ | 11–15 € |

Marc Pasquet is a photographer and wine-lover who decided to become a wine-grower in 1990 after doing a course at Haut-Marbuzet. Now he is active in the regions of Saint-Emilion, the Côtes de Bourg and Blaye. This wine has a lively and intense garnet colour with fine and complex perfumes of flowers (violet), very ripe fruits and a well-integrated toasty oak. The dense and powerful structure rests on elegant tannins which should make this wine ready to drink in two to four years.
🍷 Marc Pasquet, Mondesir-Gazin, BP 7, 33390 Plassac, tel. 05.57.42.29.80, fax 05.57.42.84.86, e-mail mondesirgazin@aol.com ☑ 🏠
𝕐 by appt.

Blaye and Bourg

CH. PETIT BOYER 2000★

■ 1 ha 6,000 ⊞ 11–15€

This wine was made in a small quantity from old vines planted near the unusual 11th and 12th century church of Cars, which has a polychrome bell-tower. The bouquet explodes with numerous scents: ripe fruits, wax, *pain d'épice*, menthol, eucalyptus, roasted oak and mocha. The rich and well-structured palate finishes on ripe, lingering tannins. In three to five years this wine will go well with strong-tasting dishes such as game.
➤ EARL Vignobles Bideau, 5, Les Bonnets, 33390 Cars, tel. 05.57.42.19.40, fax 05.57.42.33.49, e-mail bideau.jv@wanadoo.fr ☑
☿ ev. day except Sat. Sun. 8.15am–12 noon 2pm–6.30pm; cl. Sept.

Wines selected but not starred

CH. HAUT-COLOMBIER 2000

■ 1 ha 6,500 ■⊞♦ 11–15€
➤ EARL Vignobles Jean Chéty et Fils, 2, La Maisonnette, 33390 Cars, tel. 05.57.42.10.28, fax 05.57.42.17.65 ☑
☿ by appt.

CH. MONCONSEIL GAZIN 2000

■ 2.5 ha 12,000 ■⊞♦ 11–15€
➤ Vignobles Michel Baudet, Ch. Monconseil Gazin, 33390 Plassac, tel. 05.57.42.16.63, fax 05.57.42.31.22, e-mail mbaudet@terre-net.fr ☑
☿ by appt.

CH. MOULIN DE CHASSERAT 2000

■ 2 ha 9,000 ⊞ 11–15€
➤ EARL Boyer-Fourcade, 11, Moulin de Chasserat, 33390 Cartelègue, tel. 05.57.64.63.14, fax 05.57.64.50.14, e-mail contact@chateauchasserat.fr ☑
☿ by appt.

Premières Côtes de Blaye

CH. L'ABBAYE

Vieilli en fût de chêne 2000★

■ 1.7 ha 13,300 ■⊞♦ 8–11€

Guy Rossignol and his son-in-law Stéphane Boinard cultivate 21 ha of vines, in the middle of which stand the remains of the abbey of Pleine-Selve, built between 1145 and 1150 on the borders of Aquitaine and Saintonge. It had its moments of glory up to the beginning of the 15th century when French troops sacked it after taking Bourg and Blaye. This estate, so full of history, also does well with its modern-style wines. Although the colour of this 2000 vintage is that of a classic Bordeaux, the bouquet reveals white oak and the flesh seems rich and robust with nuances of oak. Keep this wine for two to three years to let the oak soften, then serve it with red meat or a lamprey à la bordelaise.
➤ GAEC Rossignol et Gendre, L'Abbaye, 33820 Pleine-Selve, tel. 05.57.32.64.63, fax 05.57.32.74.35 ☑
☿ by appt.
➤ Guy Rossignol

CH. ANGLADE-BELLEVUE

Cuvée Prestige Elevé en fût de chêne 2000★★

■ 4 ha 33,000 ⊞ 5–8€

This large estate of 33 ha devoted 4 ha to this wine made almost entirely from Merlot (90%) which wins a *coup de coeur*. Beneath its dark Bordeaux colour a powerful and elegant bouquet emerges, with a succession of fruits (blackcurrant), mineral notes of spices (vanilla) and roasted nuances (cocoa). The wine has a nice framework of tasty tannins which support its full substance well. This is a wine to keep for drinking from 2006 and until 2013.
➤ SCEA Mège Frères, Aux Lamberts, 33920 Générac, tel. 05.57.64.73.28, fax 05.57.64.53.90, e-mail scea-mege@mege-freres.fr ☑
☿ by appt.

CH. BERTINERIE 2001★★

■ 16 ha 120,000 ⊞ 5–8€
The Bantégnies inherited their skills from five generations of wine-growers; today they ally tradition and innovation both to their vines (60 ha) and their winery, whose buildings were renovated and enlarged in 2001. In their reception room you will find this black-cherry wine, which already has tasty and balanced aromas of soft fruits, spices, coffee and toast. The complex palate is round and structured, resting on tannins which are still firm but guarantee good ageing potential. In two to ten years, you can drink this wine with a *magret de canard* or an entrecôte. The **Château Bertinerie white 2002** is commended.
➤ SCEA Bantégnies et Fils, Ch. Bertinerie, 33620 Cubnezais, tel. 05.57.68.70.74, fax 05.57.68.01.03, e-mail contact@chateaubertinerie.com ☑
☿ by appt.

NECTAR DES BERTRANDS 2001★

■ 3 ha 18,000 ⊞ 15–23€
The Dubois family farm a large group of vineyards extending over 87 ha. The Nectar des Bertrands 99 won a *coup de coeur* in the 2002 edition of the *Guide*; this new vintage, which wins one star, is no less interesting. It has an intense garnet colour and a bouquet with toasty oak and leather, then a tasty palate still dominated by the oak but which will soon reveal ripe cherry flavours. Keep it for two to four years to let the tannins soften, then serve it in a carafe with red meat and cheese.
➤ EARL Vignobles Dubois et Fils, Les Bertrands, 33860 Reignac, tel. 05.57.32.40.27, fax 05.57.32.41.36, e-mail chateau.les.bertrands@wanadoo.fr ☑
☿ ev. day except Sun. 9am–12.30pm 2pm–6.30pm

CH. LES BILLAUDS 2001★

■ 1.5 ha 11,000 ⊞ 8–11€
This 2001 wine has a dark colour with garnet and black highlights, and reveals a spicy range of aromas which are still subdued. On the other hand, the palate is powerful and structured, rich in flavours of soft fruits, spices and chocolate. The tannins are evident but pleasant, and will enable the wine to improve if kept for two or three years. The **2002 white (5–8 €)** is commended.
➤ SCEA Vignobles Plisson, 5, Les Billauds, 33860 Marcillac, tel. 05.57.32.77.57, fax 05.57.32.95.27 ☑
☿ by appt.
➤ J.-C. Plisson

CH. BOIS-VERT

Cuvée Prestige Elevé en fût de chêne 2001★

■	2 ha	11,600	〰	8–11 €

Patrick Penaud, who took over these 25 ha of vines from his parents in 1986, offers an intensely coloured wine showing the first signs of evolution. The oak is dominant, but a pleasant fruitiness is revealed when the glass is swirled. After a supple attack, good tannins keep the flavours going up to the finish. Drink this 2001 wine with red meat or game after laying it down for two to six years. The **2002 white (5–8 €)** is commended.

☛ Patrick Penaud, 12, Bois-Vert,
33820 Saint-Caprais-de-Blaye, tel. 05.57.32.98.10,
fax 05.57.32.98.10, e-mail p.penaud.boisvert@cario.fr ☑
☖ by appt.

CH. LA BRETONNIERE

Elevé en fût de chêne 2001★

■	1 ha	5,000	〰	8–11 €

To the northeast of Blaye, Stéphane Heurlier cultivates 11 ha on clayey-sandy gravels. He matured this deep-red young wine for 12 months in barrel. The aromas are characteristic, recalling fruit, leather and musk, while the balanced palate has notes of burning: burnt wood and coffee. Keep this wine for three to five years to let the tannins soften.

☛ Stéphane Heurlier, EARL Ch. La Bretonnière,
33390 Mazion, tel. 05.57.64.59.23, fax 05.57.64.67.41,
e-mail sheurlier@wanadoo.fr ☑
☖ by appt.

CH. CAILLETEAU BERGERON

Vieilli en fût de chêne 2001★

■	10 ha	50,000	〰	5–8 €

Mazion is a small village in the Blaye with four hundred inhabitants which is worth finding on the map, for a visit to the Dartiers will enable you to taste this lively ruby wine with its powerful bouquet of vanilla and roasting. The tannins from the oak are still very evident, combining with the concentrated body and promising to soften during the next four to five years. While you wait to drink this wine, you could the **2002 white Vinifié en Fût de Chêne** with fish or shellfish. This also wins one star.

☛ EARL Dartier et Fils, 24, Bergeron, 33390 Mazion,
tel. 05.57.42.11.10, fax 05.57.42.37.72,
e-mail chateau.cailleteau.bergeron@wanadoo.fr ☑
☖ by appt.

CH. CANTELOUP 2001★

■	4,3 ha	20,000	〰	5–8 €

The name Canteloup will not be unknown to faithful readers of the *Guide*, since the estate's 99 vintage won the *coup de coeur*. Its clay-limestone terroir has now created this dark and intense 2001 wine with some glints showing that evolution is under way. The oak is nicely stated in the toasty and vanilla-flavoured aromas, then by very evident but good tannins which should soften in the next two to four years.

☛ Eric Vezain, Canteloup, 33390 Fours, tel. 05.57.42.13.16,
fax 05.57.42.26.28 ☑
☖ by appt.

CH. CAP SAINT-MARTIN

Cuvée Prestige 2001★★

■	2 ha	12,000	〰	8–11 €

To the east of the citadel of Blaye, this large 19th century house overlooks a vineyard of 17 ha. The estate takes its name from the *lieu-dit* Gratte Cap and the patron saint of the parish, Saint Martin. This is an open wine with aromas of ripe fruits, spices and toasty oak which emerge from beneath its dark Bordeaux-red colour. The palate is full and round, unfurling flavours of fruits, vanilla and roasting alongside an elegant tannic structure. It should fully live up to its potential in three to six years' time. It will go well with red meat, game and cheese. The **Cuvée Principale Château Cap Saint-Martin red 2001 (5–8 €)**, matured in barrel for six months, is commended.

☛ SCEA des Vignobles Ardoin, 11, rte de Mazerolles,
33390 Saint-Martin-Lacaussade, tel. 05.57.42.91.73,
fax 05.57.42.91.73, e-mail vignobles.ardoin@wanadoo.fr ☑
☖ by appt.

CH. CHARRON

Les Gruppes 2001★

■	6 ha	40,000	▮〰 ♦	8–11 €

This clay terroir with a large element of Saint-Martin-Lacaussade chalk produced the Merlot grapes (90%) making up this intense wine. Fruity aromas (ripe grape and cherry), with nuances of spices lead to a warm, full and round palate. The oaky tannins are still very evident but will guarantee the wine will age well in the next five years. Serve this with a woodcock.

☛ SCEA Ch. Charron, Vignobles Germain et Associés,
33390 Berson, tel. 05.57.42.66.66, fax 05.57.64.36.20,
e-mail bordeaux@vjas.com
☖ by appt.

CH. CHASSERAT

Cuvée André Bouyé Elevé en fût de chêne 2000★

■	3 ha	20,000	〰	8–11 €

This wine has a pretty label showing a wine-grower working his vines with a horse, as though to remind us that sustainable agriculture is employed on this 20-ha vineyard. This clean and clear ruby 2000 reveals delicate aromas of dried fruits then continues, supple and balanced, over a framework of fine tannins. Drink this wine now or keep it for up to eight years. It should be served with fine cooking.

☛ EARL Boyer-Fourcade, 11, Moulin de Chasserat,
33390 Cartelègue, tel. 05.57.64.63.14, fax 05.57.64.50.14,
e-mail contact@chateauchasserat.fr ☑
☖ by appt.

CH. LE CHAY

Vieilli en fût de chêne 2000★

■	2 ha	12,000	〰	5–8 €

In 2003, Didier and Sylvie Raboutet celebrated their 20th anniversary in charge of this 36-ha estate. Their 2000 vintage wins one star to watch over it as it evolves in the next few years. At the moment, this brilliant ruby wine has an elegant bouquet with oaky and toasty notes taking over from its good-quality fruits. The palate is full and structured, leaving a memory of spicy and peppery flavours and promising tannins.

☛ Didier et Sylvie Raboutet, Ch. Le Chay, 33390 Berson,
tel. 05.57.64.39.50, fax 05.57.64.25.08,
e-mail lechay@wanadoo.fr ☑
☖ by appt.

CH. CRUSQUET DE LAGARCIE 2001★★

■	20 ha	80,000	〰	8–11 €

This family business, started in 1863 opposite the astonishing 11th and 12th century church of Cars, famous for its polychrome bell-tower, has become a flagship for the appellation. The 50 ha planted on a clay-limestone soil surround impressive buildings, including a two-storey winery where this wine was matured. It has an elegant appearance, releasing an intense, mentholated and toasty bouquet, then fills the palate with its warm and round flesh, underlined by vanilla flavours and well-integrated oaky tannins. This lovely wine can be drunk from 2004 or kept for a while to serve with small game, and white and red meats.

☛ SAS Vignobles Ph. de Lagarcie, Le Crusquet,
33390 Cars, tel. 05.57.42.15.21, fax 05.57.42.90.87,
e-mail vignobles.delagarcie@free.fr ☑
☖ by appt.

CH. DU GRAND BARRAIL

Révélation 2001★★

■	4.5 ha	22,000	〰	8–11 €

Denis Lafon is the latest in several generations of wine-makers, cultivating four vineyards in the Blaye with a total area of 35 ha. The 2001 wine is a remarkable Grand Barrail, which will be ready in two to seven years. For the time being, the "revelation" is in the deep Bordeaux colour with ruby highlights, in the fine bouquet of soft fruits (blackberry), and a well-integrated oak, and in the supple and fruity palate

BORDEAUX

which grows in power. The **Cuvée Prestige red Elevée en Fût de Chêne 2001 (5–8 €)** wins one star.
☛ Vignobles Denis Lafon, Bracaille 1, 33390 Cars, tel. 05.57.42.33.04, fax 05.57.42.08.92, e-mail denis-lafon@wanadoo.fr ☑
Ⴤ by appt.

CH. LES GRAVES
Elevé en fût de chêne 2001★

| ■ | 5 ha | 18,000 | ⅢⅡ | 5–8 € |

Last year the 2000 vintage won the *coup de coeur*. This time Jean-Pierre Pauvif offers a well-made dark-ruby 2001 with powerful aromas and oak. Its round and full substance is supported by still young but good tannins which should allow it to mature well in the next two or three years. Also look out for the **2002 white (3–5 €)**, commended for its pleasant floral and fruity character.
☛ SCEA Pauvif, 15, rue Favereau, 33920 Saint-Vivien-de-Blaye, tel. 05.57.42.47.37, fax 05.57.42.55.89, e-mail chateau.les.graves@wanadoo.fr ☑
Ⴤ by appt.

DOM. DES GRAVES D'ARDONNEAU
Cuvée Prestige Vieilli en fût de chêne 2001★

| ■ | 5 ha | 30,000 | ⅢⅡ | 5–8 € |

This estate of 28 ha stands on clay gravels, and one of its plots has produced this elegant wine with a well-balanced oak. Still in its early stages, the bouquet is at first oaky, but it only requires a slight swirling of the glass to release aromas of fruits, spices and some musky notes. This black-cherry 2001 should be kept for two years to reach its best, ready to be served with meats in sauce, game, or cheese.
☛ Simon Rey et Fils, Ardonneau, 33620 Saint-Mariens, tel. 05.57.68.66.98, fax 05.57.68.19.30, e-mail gravesdardonneau@wanadoo.fr ☑
Ⴤ ev. day except Sun. 8am–12.30pm 2.30pm–7pm
☛ Christian Rey

CH. HAUT-BOURCIER
Elevé en fût de chêne 2001★

| ■ | 24 ha | 150,000 | ⅢⅡ | 3–5 € |

This winemaker is in charge of 30 ha of vines, and up to the 99 harvest took his grapes to the cooperative. A few months later, he built his winery and set up his own brand. Here he offers a wine with a characteristic colour and an elegant bouquet of finely oaky soft fruits. It is supple but enriched by good tannins with a long flavour of roasting, and will need to be kept for two to five years. The red **2000 Elevé en Fût de Chêne (5–8 €)** is ready to drink now, and it is commended.
☛ SCEA des Vignerons Bourcier, 33390 Saint-Androny, tel. 05.57.64.43.74, fax 05.57.64.40.52, e-mail philippebourcier@cario.fr ☑
Ⴤ ev. day except Sun. 8am–7pm

CH. HAUT-CANTELOUP
Cuvée spéciale Elevé en fût de chêne 2001★

| ■ | 4 ha | 18,000 | ⅢⅡ | 5–8 € |

Sylvain Bordenave and his son Alexandre run a vineyard of 35 ha. Their dark-crimson 2001 has some highlights indicating evolution and a very oaky bouquet with vegetal notes. Then it reveals its full and balanced structure, coated by a good flesh. Keep this wine for three or four years to allow the tannins to soften. You could then serve this wine with meats in sauce or grills.
☛ Sylvain Bordenave, 1, Salvert, 33390 Fours, tel. 05.57.42.36.69, fax 05.57.42.36.69 ☑
Ⴤ ev. day except Sun. 8am–12 noon 2pm–7pm

CH. HAUT-COLOMBIER 2001★

| ■ | 16.5 ha | n.c. | ⅢⅡ | 3–5 € |

The Chétys' large 54-ha estate is located near the original church at Cars. This mouth-filling dark-coloured wine with crimson and black-cherry highlights was made from a blend of Merlot (75%) and Cabernet and a touch of Malbec. Although the attack seems supple, the tannins are quick to reveal their elegant character. When the glass is swirled,

aromas are released of a subtle oak and crystallized fruits. This vintage should be at its best in three or four years.
☛ EARL Vignobles Jean Chéty et Fils, 2, La Maisonnette, 33390 Cars, tel. 05.57.42.10.28, fax 05.57.42.17.65 ☑
Ⴤ by appt.

CH. HAUT DU PEYRAT 2001★★

| ■ | 10 ha | n.c. | ⅠⅢⅡ♨ | 5–8 € |

Muriel and Patrick Revaire offer their main wine from this old vineyard, located on a southeast facing clay-limestone hillside. Their 2001 wine gleams with dark glints in the glass, a mixture of ruby and garnet. After a supple and fruity attack, the flavours increase in power, supported by a good tannic structure. This is a well-made wine in which the oak does not overwhelm the grape. In two to five years, it will go well with lamprey, grills, game or cheese.
☛ Muriel and Patrick Revaire, Gardut, 33390 Cars, tel. 05.57.42.20.35, fax 05.57.42.12.84 ☑
Ⴤ by appt.

CH. HAUT MONGUILLON
Vieilli en fût de chêne 2000★

| ■ | 2 ha | 17,362 | ⅢⅡ | 5–8 € |

This property dates back to 1642, and now covers 18.3 ha. Beneath the label is a clean ruby wine. It has an intense bouquet rich in notes of fruit stone and almond, matched by a robust and vigorous palate shaped by good tannins from the grape and the oak. This solid Premières Côtes de Blaye will be ready between 2005 and 2010. Serve it with an entrecôte à la bordelaise, a wild-boar stew or a *magret de canard*.
☛ Vignobles Jean Bonnet, Ch. Fouché, 14, rue de la Gravette, 33620 Cubnezais, tel. 05.57.68.07.71, fax 05.57.68.06.08 ☑
Ⴤ by appt.

CH. LES HAUTS DE FONTARABIE 2001★

| ■ | 15 ha | 110,000 | ⅠⅢⅡ | 5–8 € |

The two daughters of Alain Faure represent the fifth generation of wine-growers in this family. They bought this property in 1995 to complete their range of Vins de Côtes. Here they offer a dark-ruby 2001 with delightful aromas of soft fruit and fine oak, as well as a well-structured palate, at first supple then slender and powerful. The oak tannins tend to dominate the fruity flavours at the moment, but will soften with two or three years of keeping.
☛ Vignobles Alain Faure, 33710 Saint-Ciers-de-Canesse, tel. 05.57.42.68.80, fax 05.57.42.68.81, e-mail belair-coubet@wanadoo.fr
Ⴤ by appt.

CH. LACAUSSADE SAINT-MARTIN
Trois Moulins 2001★

| ■ | 6 ha | 40,000 | ⅠⅢⅡ♨ | 8–11 € |

Jacques Chardat is an oenologist and cultivates 24 ha at Saint-Martin-Lacaussade. In the glass, his wine reveals a dark-ruby heart and a slightly brick-red disk – an invitation to inhale the fine and complex bouquet: fruits, spices, roasted oak, even old leather. It is round and full on the palate with harmonious flavours. On the palate the barrel has not overwhelmed the grape, the tannins are not excessive. This is a well-made wine to keep for two to five years and serve with a salad of duck. The **Château Lacaussade Saint-Martin Trois Moulins white 2002** wins one star.
☛ SCEA Ch. Labrousse, Vignobles Germain et Associés, 33390 Berson, tel. 05.57.42.66.66, fax 05.57.64.36.20, e-mail bordeaux@vgas.com
Ⴤ by appt.
☛ Jacques Chardat

CH. LAFON-LAMARTINE
Colère de Bruno Lafon 2001★

| ■ | 1 ha | n.c. | ⅢⅡ | 23–30 € |

This pure Merlot wine was harvested on a sandy soil. It has a dark colour and very expressive, open aromas revealing a spicy and liquorice-flavoured oak then, after swirling in the glass, perfumes of fruits. The round palate is supported on a solid tannic framework supplied by the oak. After laying

Premières Côtes de Blaye

down for two to eight years, this 2001 wine will be more supple and ready to serve with a *confit de canard*.
🍷 Vignobles Bruno Lafon, 7, pl. de La Libération, 33710 Bourg-sur-Gironde, tel. 06.73.37.63.91 ☑
🍴 ev. day except Sun. 8am–12 noon 2pm–8pm

CH. LARDIERE
Elevé en fût de chêne 2000★

| ■ | 13.86 ha | 10,900 | ⬛ | 5–8 € |

This 2000 wine has a classic Bordeaux colour and aromas of leather, tobacco and game. Its full and solid body is supported by grape tannins, which will enable it to mature well over time.
🍷 GAEC Lardière, 3, Lardière, 33860 Marcillac, tel. 05.57.32.50.11, fax 05.57.32.50.12, e-mail lardiere@chateaulardiere.com ☑
🍴 by appt.

CH. LOUMEDE
Elevé en fût de chêne 2000★

| ■ | 6 ha | 44,400 | ⬛ | 5–8 € |

Plassac is an old sailors' village a few kilometres north of the boundary between the Côtes de Blaye and the Côtes de Bourg, marked by the little river Brouillon, which flows into the Gironde. The Raynaud family cultivate nearly 18 ha of vines on a clay-limestone terroir. Their ruby wine is fringed with light glints revealing its evolution. It releases complex aromas of soft fruits, fresh mint, vanilla and spices. The silky, coffee-flavoured tannins convey an impression of elegance. In two to five years it will be ready to serve with poultry, game, an entrecôte or cheese.
🍷 SCE Loumède, Ch. Loumède, BP 4, 33390 Blaye, tel. 05.57.42.16.39, fax 05.57.42.25.30, e-mail chateauloumede@wanadoo.fr ☑
🍴 by appt.

CH. MALLARD
Elevé en fût de chêne 2000★

| ■ | 6 ha | 9,000 | ⬛ | 5–8 € |

This wine has a very youthful clear Bordeaux colour and aromas marked by good oak. After swirling in the glass, it releases aromas of very ripe fruit, caramel, tobacco and leather. Fine and compact tannins give shape to the warm and velvety substance, whose oaky character should soften in two years. This is a wine to serve with strongly flavoured dishes and hard cheeses over the following ten years.
🍷 Sté coopérative vinicole de Générac, 1, Bois-de-Girau, 33920 Générac, tel. 05.57.64.73.03, fax 05.57.64.57.30, e-mail coop-generac@wanadoo.fr ☑
🍴 ev. day except Sun. Mon. 8.30am–12.30pm 2pm–6pm
🍷 Bruno Cochon-Villier

CH. MAYNE-GUYON
Cuvée Héribert 2001★

| ■ | 12 ha | 70,000 | ⬛ | 8–11 € |

If you go to this château, the owners will give you the recipe for calves' liver à la Mayne-Guyon, which is pan-fried in butter with shallots and cooked in red wine. Back in front of your stove, you will prepare it easily, then serve it with a simple purée and, of course, this black-cherry coloured wine. It has a slightly oaky bouquet of soft fruits, and a supple and round palate supported by silky tannins. It seems almost ready now, but wait two years longer and it will be at its best.
🍷 Cazeneuve, Mayne-Guyon, Mazerolles, 33390 Cars, tel. 05.57.42.09.59, fax 05.57.42.27.93, e-mail mayneguyon@wanadoo.fr ☑
🍴 by appt.
🍷 Courjeaud

CH. MAZEROLLES 2000★

| ■ | 10 ha | 30,000 | ⬛ | 5–8 € |

This wine's ruby colour is enlivened by highlights indicating its evolution. The aromas are fresh, mentholated, a little vegetal, then recall game and leather. This is a balanced wine which can be drunk as it is, but its tannins are still firm and suggest it should be kept a while before it is served with red or white meat or cheese.

🍷 Guy Valleau, 11, chem. du Haut-Gradecap, 33390 Saint-Martin-Lacaussade, tel. 05.57.42.18.61, fax 05.57.42.18.61 ☑
🍴 by appt.

CH. MONCONSEIL GAZIN 2001★

| ■ | 17 ha | 110,000 | ⬛ | 5–8 € |

This beautiful wine estate surrounds a house with crenellated walls located near the little Gallo-Roman museum in Plassac. Its ruby-coloured wine releases engaging aromas of soft fruits, spices and oak. A similar aromatic balance occurs on the palate, where good-quality tannins show that the ripe grapes and the oak have combined well. Drink this wine in the next two years. The **Château Ricaud Elevé en Fût de Chêne 2001 red (8–11 €)** is commended.
🍷 Vignobles Michel Baudet, Ch. Monconseil Gazin, 33390 Plassac, tel. 05.57.42.16.63, fax 05.57.42.31.22, e-mail mbaudet@terre-net.fr ☑
🍴 by appt.
🍷 Jean-Michel Baudet

CH. PETIT LA GAROSSE 2000★

| ■ | n.c. | 13,500 | ⬛ | 5–8 € |

This vineyard, standing on the borders between the Blaye and the Libourne regions, was entirely created by Jean-Paul Clavé in 1990. The vineyard of 18.5 ha surrounds the residential buildings, which were recently extended. This wine's colour is somewhere between crimson and ruby. It has an intense and fine bouquet of soft fruits (Morello cherry) and roasted oak. Its young, vigorous body has compact tannins which guarantee it will age well. It will be at its best in two to four years.
🍷 Jean-Paul Clavé, Ch. Petit La Garosse, 7, la Garosse, 33620 Laruscade, tel. 05.57.68.67.20, fax 05.57.68.17.04, e-mail info@vignobles-clave.com ☑
🍴 by appt.

CH. PEYMELON 2001★

| ■ | 1 ha | 9,366 | ⬛ | 5–8 € |

The same family has worked this ground for three centuries. Not all the successive generations were active wine-makers. There were négociants, coopers, propagators... Today the vineyard covers 25 ha. The 2001 wine has an intense, still young colour and scents of wild strawberry and vanilla. The tannins are very evident, showing the wine's keeping potential. It should be laid down for five to eight years before serving with red meat, game or cheese.
🍷 SCE Chapard-Tuffreau, Les Petits, 33390 Cars, tel. 05.57.42.19.09, fax 05.57.42.00.73 ☑
🍴 by appt.

CH. LA RAZ CAMAN 2001★

| ■ | n.c. | 35,000 | ⬛ | 8–11 € |

This dark Bordeaux wine is made from Merlot, Cabernet Sauvignon, Malbec and Cabernet Franc. The bouquet is fresh and mentholated to start with, then reveals a lovely balance between the fruit and the oak. This is a tasty wine which will improve over the next four to ten years thanks to its solid tannic framework.
🍷 Jean-François Pommeraud, Ch. La Raz Caman, 33390 Anglade, tel. 05.57.64.41.82, fax 05.57.64.41.77, e-mail jean-francois.pommeraud@wanadoo.fr ☑
🍴 by appt.

CH. LES RICARD 2000★★

| ■ | 5 ha | 25,000 | ⬛ | 11–15 € |

This vineyard is on a human scale: 13 ha distributed among various terroirs of clay, limestone, sand and gravel. Corinne and Xavier Loriaud have succeeded very well with their 2000 wine, blending Merlot with 20% Malbec and 10% Cabernet Sauvignon. The colour is a very deep Bordeaux red, and the powerful bouquet releases a succession of soft fruit (blackcurrant), crystallized fruits, oak, undergrowth and leather. The full, robust palate rests on clean and civilized tannins which will support the wine's evolution for ten years to come. This wine can be drunk from 2005, and will go well with all meats.
🍷 Corinne et Xavier Loriaud, Ch. Bel Air La Royère, 1, Les Ricards, 33390 Cars, tel. 05.57.42.91.34, fax 05.57.42.32.87, e-mail chateau.belair.la.royere@wanadoo.fr ☑
🍴 by appt.

CH. LE RIMENSAC Cuvée Saint-Christophe

Elevé en fût de chêne 2000★★

■ 1,3 ha 8,000 🛢 5–8 €

Since 1905, five generations have helped to expand the family property which now covers 30 ha. The two little angels on the label represent both the appellation and the vintage perfectly. Beneath its Bordeaux-red colour, the bouquet seems deep, with a range of ripe fruits, nuts, undergrowth, ferns and leather. The full and vigorous palate grows in power, well shaped by the tanins of the grape and the oak. This is a wine to lay down and serve between 2005 and 2010 with traditional dishes.

🔑 SCE Vignobles Sigogneaud-Voyer, Chante-Alouette, 33390 Cars, tel. 05.57.64.36.09, fax 05.57.64.22.82, e-mail sigovoy@wanadoo.fr [V]
🍷 by appt.

CH. LA RIVALERIE

Cuvée Majoral Elevé en fût de chêne 2000★

■ 2.5 ha 12,000 🛢 8–11 €

François I is said to have ennobled the owners of this ancient property, which today is overlooked by a 19th century mansion. Equal shares of Merlot and Cabernet Sauvignon bring a noble character to this 2000 with a ruby-crimson colour. The oak and coconut come through first in the bouquet, soon joined by the fruit and a note of capsicum. The tasty palate, combining macerated fruits and oaky nuances, has quite evident but round tannins which will make it keep well for six years. Drink it with a duck, a stew of hare or young wild boar, or a *pavé de boeuf*.

🔑 SCEA La Rivalerie, 1, La Rivalerie, 33390 Saint-Paul-de-Blaye, tel. 05.57.42.18.84, fax 05.57.42.14.27, e-mail larivalerie@wanadoo.fr [V]
🍷 by appt.

CH. ROLAND LA GARDE

Prestige 2001★★

■ 10 ha 40,000 ▮ 🛢 🌡 8–11 €

Although this wine bears the name of the leader of the rear-guard of Charlemagne's army which passed through Blaye, it was far from last in the tastings. It regularly wins a star in the *Guide* and even a *coup de coeur*, and this year it wins the highest distinction. The Jury liked its Bordeaux colour with black highlights, its intense bouquet of soft fruits (Morello cherry) and mocha. The flavours on the palate perfectly reflect those of the bouquet, and are accompanied by a rich substance and powerful but pleasant tannins. This is a wine to lay down which will go well with many different dishes. The **red Grand Vin 2000 (15–23 €)**, matured for 18 months in barrel, is commended.

🔑 Ch. Roland La Garde, 8, La Garde, 33390 Saint-Seurin-de-Cursac, tel. 05.57.42.32.29, fax 05.57.42.01.86, e-mail contact@chateau-roland-la-garde.com [V]
🍷 ev. day except Sun. 8am–12 noon 2pm–7pm
🔑 Bruno Martin

CH. ROMFORT

Excellence 2001★

■ 3 ha 20,000 🛢 11–15 €

A contemporary label bearing the new logo of the Vins de Bordeaux adorns this very modern, intense ruby wine. After the bouquet with its scents of overripe fruits, the tasters enjoyed the full, well-structured palate. Certainly, the tannins still seem firm, but they will enable the wine to age well in the next four to ten years. It will go well with meat in sauce or a Reblochon (soft cheese from Savoy).

🔑 EARL La Bretonnière, 33390 Mazion, tel. 05.57.64.59.23, fax 05.57.64.67.41
🍷 by appt.

DOM. DES ROSIERS

Confidence 2001★★

■ 2.5 ha 12,000 ▮ 🛢 🌡 8–11 €

Near the estuary and the marshes in the north of Blaye, this 15.5-ha estate has made a delightful pure Merlot wine with a black-cherry colour. Its developing bouquet releases scents of crystallized fruits and toasted oak, while its full and fleshy palate seems harmoniously structured by fine and lingering tannins. This is an ideal wine for red meat, game and cheese.

🔑 Christian Blanchet, 12, La Borderie, 33820 Saint-Ciers-sur-Gironde, tel. 05.57.32.75.97, fax 05.57.32.78.37, e-mail cblanchet@wanadoo.fr [V]
🍷 by appt.

CH. SAINT-AULAYE

Harmonie Elevé en fût de chêne 2001★

■ 2.5 ha 13,000 🛢 8–11 €

This property has been in the same family since 1732, and is today run by Christèle Berneaud and Julien Bec, who comes from the Aveyron. They have made an intense crimson wine which opens after the glass is swirled with scents of soft fruits and spices. The body is fleshy and mouth-filling, but not heavy, for the tannins from the oak, which give it its frame-work, are elegant. In three to five years this Premières Côtes de Blaye will be at its best. The **red Cuvée Principale Château Saint-Aulaye 2001 (5–8 €)**, matured in tank, is commended.

🔑 SCEA Vignoble J. et H. Berneaud, 4, Saint-Aulaye, 33390 Mazion, tel. 05.57.42.11.14, fax 05.57.42.11.14, e-mail cberneaud@aol.com [V]
🍷 by appt.

CH. DE LA SALLE 2002★

□ 1 ha 7,000 🛢 8–11 €

The 99 vintage of this wine won a *coup de coeur*. It is made from pure Sauvignon harvested on a clay-limestone soil. The green-gold 2002 releases aromas that are still restrained, but fine, of white fruits (peach) and hot oak. The fruitiness lasts well in the supple, fresh and tasty palate. This wine will soon be ready to serve with a fish in black butter, a pan-fried foie gras or a lamb's cheese. But there is no reason not to keep it for a few years.

🔑 SCEA Ch. de La Salle, 33390 Saint-Genès-de-Blaye, tel. 05.57.42.12.15, fax 05.57.42.87.11, e-mail marc.bonnin19@voila.fr [V]
🍷 by appt.
🔑 Bonnin

CH. SEGONZAC 2001★★

■ 10 ha 70,000 ▮ 🌡 8–11 €

If you remember, the Héritage 2000 won a *coup de coeur* last year. This main wine is again amongst the stars with its almost black colour and complex aromas of very ripe soft fruits, spices, vanilla-flavoured and integrated oak. Its powerful body has lingering tannins and offers well-combined flavours of soft fruits and roasted oak. This is a very charming wine that could be served with a wild-boar stew in a few years. The **red Château Segonzac Vieilles Vignes 2001 (11–15 €)**, matured in barrel, wins one star for its good substance..

🔑 SCEA Ch. Segonzac, 39, Segonzac, 33390 Saint-Genès-de-Blaye, tel. 05.57.42.18.16, fax 05.57.42.24.80, e-mail chateau.segonzac@wanadoo.fr [V]
🍷 by appt.
🔑 Charlotte Herter-Marmet

CH. TOUR GALINEAU
Elevé en fût de chêne 2001★

| ■ | 4.75 ha | 30,000 | ⑪ | 3–5 € |

This wine won one star in 2000, and another in 2001, so it is certainly a regular performer. It was made by the Vignobles Chéty et Fils, and distributed by the André Quancard firm. It has a lively ruby colour and at first seems fresh, mentholated and finely oaked, then reveals a full and powerful substance. The oaky tannins will enable it to mature over the next two to five years. The **red Château Maine Blanc Elevé en Fût de Chêne 2001** is commended.
✦┑ André Quancard-André, chem. de La Cabeyre, 33240 Saint-André-de-Cubzac, tel. 05.57.33.42.53, fax 05.57.43.22.22, e-mail aqa@andrequancard.com
✦┑ Chéty et Fils

EXCELLENCE DE TUTIAC
Elevé en fût de chêne 2000★★

| ■ | 7 ha | 30,000 | ⑪ | 5–8 € |

This cooperative is very large for the region. Its president is James Espiot and the director is Olivier Bourdet-Pees. It is reputed for its white wines and also produces excellent red wines such as this one. Beneath its dark-ruby colour is a complex bouquet consisting of notes of grape, a musky touch and roasted nuances. The harmonious and well-constructed palate follows these aromas, and rests on civilized tannins. Once this wine has been kept for three years, and up to 2010, it will go well with a large range of dishes. Also look out for this white wine, the **Duchesse de Tutiac 2002 (3–5 €)**, which is commended.
✦┑ Cave des Hauts de Gironde, La Cafourche, 33860 Marcillac, tel. 05.57.32.46.33, fax 05.57.32.49.63 ☑
🍷 by appt.

Wines selected but not starred

CH. LA BRAULTERIE 2002

| ░ | 1.5 ha | 10,000 | ■ ♦ | 3–5 € |

✦┑ SARL La Braulterie Morisset, Les Graves, 33390 Berson, tel. 05.57.64.39.51, fax 05.57.64.23.60, e-mail braulterie@wanadoo.fr ☑
🍷 by appt.

CH. CORPS DE LOUP
Vieilli en fût de chêne 2001

| ■ | 6.59 ha | 25,750 | ⑪ | 5–8 € |

✦┑ Françoise Vidal-Le Guénédal, Ch. Corps de Loup, 33390 Anglade, tel. 05.57.64.45.10, fax 05.57.64.45.10, e-mail chateau-corps-de-loup@wanadoo.fr ☑
🍷 ev. day 10am–12 noon 3pm–6.30pm; Sat. Sun. by appt.

CH. FOMBRION
Elévé en fût de chêne 2000

| ■ | 1 ha | 5,000 | ⑪ | 5–8 € |

✦┑ SCEA des Vignobles Sicaud, Ch. Fombrion, no. 20, Le Bourg, 33390 Mazion, tel. 05.57.42.18.64, fax 05.57.42.18.62, e-mail chateaufombrion@wanadoo.fr ☑
🍷 by appt.
✦┑ Eric Sicaud

CH. GAUTHIER
Elévé en fût de chêne 2000

| ■ | 11.63 ha | 70,600 | ⑪ | 3–5 € |

✦┑ Union de producteurs de Pugnac, Bellevue, 33710 Pugnac, tel. 05.57.68.81.01, fax 05.57.68.83.17, e-mail udep.pugnac@wanadoo.fr
🍷 by appt.

CH. LE GRAND TRIE 2002

| | 2 ha | 10,700 | ■ ♦ | 3–5 € |

✦┑ Jany Haure, Les Augirons, 33820 Saint-Ciers-sur-Gironde, tel. 05.57.32.63.10, fax 05.57.32.95.34 ☑
🍷 by appt.

CH. DU HAUT GUERIN
Vieilli en fût de chêne 2001

| ■ | 3.3 ha | 24,000 | ⑪ | 5–8 € |

✦┑ Alain Coureau, Ch. du Haut Guérin, 1, Guérin, 33920 Saint-Savin, tel. 05.57.58.40.47, fax 05.57.58.93.09, e-mail j.coureau@cgmvins.com ☑
🍷 by appt.

CH. HAUT-TERRIER
Vieilli en barrique neuve 2001

| ■ | 20 ha | 80,000 | ⑪ | 8–11 € |

✦┑ Bernard Denéchaud, Ch. Haut-Terrier, 46, Le Bourg, 33620 Saint-Mariens, tel. 05.57.68.53.54, fax 05.57.68.16.87, e-mail chateau-haut-terrier@wanadoo.fr ☑
🍷 by appt.

CH. MAINE-GAZIN
Livenne Vieilles Vignes 2001

| ■ | 5 ha | 30,000 | ■ ⑪ | 8–11 € |

✦┑ Sylvie Germain, Ch. Maine-Gazin, 33390 Plassac, tel. 05.57.42.66.66, fax 05.57.64.36.20, e-mail bordeaux@vgas.com ☑
🍷 by appt.

CH. DES MATARDS
Cuvée Nathan Elevé en fût de chêne 2001

| ■ | 5 ha | 40,000 | ■ ⑪ ♦ | 8–11 € |

✦┑ GAEC Terrigeol et Fils, le Pas d'Ozelle, 33820 Saint-Ciers-sur-Gironde, tel. 05.57.32.61.96, fax 05.57.32.79.21 ☑
🍷 by appt.

CH. MOULIN DE LA GACHE
Cuvée Saint-Pierre 2001

| ■ | 3 ha | 13,000 | ⑪ | 5–8 € |

✦┑ SCEV Ch. Moulin de La Gache, La Gache, 33920 Saint-Christoly-de-Blaye, tel. 05.57.42.51.47, fax 05.57.42.40.27 ☑
🍷 ev. day 9am–6pm
✦┑ Lacuisse

CH. MOULIN NEUF
Elevé en fût de chêne 2001

| ■ | 1 ha | 5,000 | ■ ⑪ ♦ | 5–8 € |

✦┑ Laurent Glemet, Le Moulin Neuf, 33920 Saint-Christoly-de-Blaye, tel. 05.57.42.55.38, fax 05.57.42.55.08 ☑
🍷 by appt.

CH. PATY CLAUNE 2002

| | 1.15 ha | 5,000 | ■ ♦ | 3–5 € |

✦┑ Jean-Michel Bertrand, 1, Les Renauds, 33820 Saint-Ciers-Sur-Gironde, tel. 05.57.32.65.45, fax 05.57.32.65.45 ☑
🍷 by appt.

CH. PETIT-BOYER 2000

| | 2 ha | 11,900 | ⑪ | 8–11 € |

✦┑ EARL Vignobles Bideau, 5, Les Bonnets, 33390 Cars, tel. 05.57.42.19.40, fax 05.57.42.33.49, e-mail bideau.jv@wanadoo.fr ☑
🍷 ev. day except Sat. Sun. 8.15am–12 noon 2pm–6.30pm; cl. Sept.

CH. LES PETITS ARNAUDS 2002

n.c.	n.c.	■ ♦	5–8 €

☛ SCEV G. Carreau et Fils, Ch. Les Petits Arnauds, 33390 Cars, tel. 05.57.42.36.57, fax 05.57.42.14.02, e-mail scevcarreau@wanadoo.fr ☑
☗ by appt.

CH. PEYBONHOMME LES TOURS 2001

■			
58.4 ha	306,866	⑪	5–8 €

☛ SCEA Vignobles Bossuet-Hubert, Ch. Peybonhomme les Tours, 33390 Cars, tel. 05.57.42.11.95, fax 05.57.42.38.15 ☑ ☗
☗ ev. day 9am–12 noon 1pm–6pm
☛ J.-L. Hubert

CH. PRIEURE MALESAN

Elevé en fût de chêne 2001

■			
25 ha	160,000	⑪	5–8 €

☛ SCEA Ch. Prieuré Malesan, 1, Perenne, 33390 Saint-Genès-de-Blaye, tel. 05.57.42.18.25, fax 05.57.42.15.86
☗ by appt.
☛ Bernard Magrez

CH. LA ROSE BELLEVUE

Cuvée Prestige Elevé en fût de chêne 2002

2 ha	10,000	⑪	5–8 €

☛ EARL Vignobles Eymas et Fils, 5, Les Mouriers, 33820 Saint-Palais, tel. 05.57.32.66.54, fax 05.57.32.78.78, e-mail service-commercial@chateau-larosebellevue.com ☑
☗ ev. day 9am–7pm

CH. TAYAT 2002

3 ha	12,000	■ ♦	5–8 €

☛ SCEA Favereaud, 2, Tayat, 33620 Cézac, tel. 05.57.68.62.10, fax 05.57.68.15.07 ☑
☗ ev. day 8am–1pm 3pm–7pm

CH. DE TERRE TAILLYSE 2002

3.5 ha	3,600	■ ♦	3–5 €

☛ EARL Ragot et Fils, 81, Millepied, 33920 Saint-Vivien-de-Blaye, tel. 05.57.42.53.37, fax 05.57.42.53.37 ☑
☗ by appt.

CH. LE VIROU

Les Vieilles Vignes 2001

■			
8 ha	69,546	⑪	5–8 €

☛ SC du Ch. Le Virou, 33920 Saint-Girons-d'Aiguevives, tel. 05.57.43.43.82, fax 05.57.43.01.89
☛ B. Bessède

Côtes de Bourg

The AOC covers about 3,973 ha. The Merlot grape variety dominates and the reds (183,582 hl in 2002) often have a distinctively beautiful colour and a marked aroma of soft fruits. They are quite tannic when young so in many cases may need to be kept. There are only a few whites (960 hl), which are generally dry and have a distinctive nose.

CH. BEGOT

Cuvée Prestige Elevé en fût de chêne 2001★★

2 ha	12,700	⑪	5–8 €

The lovely house, covered in slate, is surrounded by 16 ha of vines. Here members of the same family have lived for several generations. The grape selection must have been done well for this Cuvée Prestige; the result is remarkable. The heart of the glass is red-black, the fringe more developed. The very expressive bouquet releases notes of violet, iris, blackberry, coffee and cocoa. The palate has an impressive structure and fruity flavours (cherry and prune) elegantly supported by a vanilla-flavoured oak. This wine could be served in three or four years with *magrets*, red meats and cheeses.
☛ Alain Gracia, 5, Bégot, 33710 Lansac, tel. 05.57.68.42.14, fax 05.57.68.20.99, e-mail chateau.begot@libertysurf.fr ☑
☗ by appt.

CH. BELAIR-COUBET 2001★

■			
25 ha	150,000	■ ⑪ ♦	5–8 €

The garden of the estate has a panoramic view over the Gironde. The vines have been tended by sustainable agriculture since 1995, and once again have produced a very pretty wine with a deep, youthful colour. The bouquet is fine: subtly oaky soft fruits. The fresh and fruity palate is supported by well-integrated and lingering tannins from the fruit and the oak. It will be at its best in two to three years.
☛ Vignobles Alain Faure, 33710 Saint-Ciers-de-Canesse, tel. 05.57.42.68.80, fax 05.57.42.68.81, e-mail belair-coubet@wanadoo.fr ☑
☗ by appt.

CH. DU BOIS DE TAU 2001★★

■			
14 ha	100,000	■ ⑪ ♦	5–8 €

Alain Faure's two daughters have come to join their father in the "magic" work that produces a *grand vin*. Together, they have succeeded with this remarkable 2001 wine. It has everything. The intense crimson colour; the bouquet with scents of vanilla and roasting; the full and balanced palate in which the good fruit is supported by a high-quality oak. This wine has excellent potential and in two years will go well with shad or lamprey in red wine.
☛ Vignobles Alain Faure, 33710 Saint-Ciers-de-Canesse, tel. 05.57.42.68.80, fax 05.57.42.68.81, e-mail belair-coubet@wanadoo.fr
☗ by appt.

CH. BRULESECAILLE 2001★★

■			
20 ha	80,000	⑪	8–11 €

A long time ago, Jacques Rodet brought this estate to a level of excellence. As proof of the care he takes, this main wine, produced from 20 ha cultivated by sustainable agriculture and harvested by hand, was matured for 12 months in barrel. In the glass, it has an attractive colour, mingling crimson and garnet highlights. The bouquet is already powerful and expressive, combining the fresh fruits (blackcurrant) and the fine oak which recur in the velvety, very long palate. This harmonious wine will be perfect in two to four years. Drink it with a roasted pigeon or a baron of lamb *aux fines herbes*.
☛ Jacques Rodet, Brulesécaille, 33710 Tauriac, tel. 05.57.68.40.31, fax 05.57.68.21.27, e-mail cht.brulesecaille@freesbee.fr ☑ ☗
☗ by appt.

CH. BRULESECAILLE 2002★

■			
0.75 ha	4,000	⑪	5–8 €

At his large 28.5-ha vineyard, Jacques Rodet sets aside 0.75 ha for the production of a dry white Côtes de Bourg (for a limited market). His 2002 is very pleasant. The still very pale gold colour has a slight sparkle, making rich tears on the glass. The bouquet opens on toasty oak, along with white flowers (acacia) and ripe Sauvignon. The palate is fresh but full, with a flavour of fruits with white flesh which leaves a lovely impression. Serve this with a pike in white butter.
☛ Jacques Rodet, Brulesécaille, 33710 Tauriac, tel. 05.57.68.40.31, fax 05.57.68.21.27, e-mail cht.brulesecaille@freesbee.fr ☑ ☗
☗ by appt.

Côtes de Bourg

CH. BUJAN 2001★

| | 8 ha | 53,000 | ▣ ⅲ ♦ | 8–11 € |

This wine makes up half the production of Pascal Méli. It comes from a clay-limestone terroir planted with 70% Merlot, 25% Cabernet Sauvignon and 5% Cabernet Franc, and is a good representative of its appellation and the vintage. The dark crimson colour has garnet and black highlights. The bouquet of crystallized fruits, blackcurrant and oak with a note of coffee heralds a round, full-bodied and robust palate with solid, clean tannins which will enable this wine to improve over the next two to ten years. Drink it with fairly traditional dishes.

↰ Pascal Méli, Ch. Bujan, 33710 Gauriac,
tel. 05.57.64.86.56, fax 05.57.64.93.96,
e-mail pmeli@alienor.fr ☑ ♘
🍷 ev. day except Sun. 9am–12 noon 2pm–7pm

CH. CASTEL LA ROSE
Cuvée Sélection Vieilli en fût de chêne 2001★

| | 7 ha | 40,000 | | 5–8 € |

You may be surprised by the orange label with the motto "Do well and let others have their say." The growers here are people of character. This year they are offering a wine grown on a clay-limestone soil, and produced in a fairly large quantity. Its appearance features several glints demonstrating its evolution. The bouquet is already expressive, open and well-bred, with pleasant notes of vanilla and coffee. The palate is warm with a very long chocolatey and balsamic flavour supported by well-integrated tannins. This wine will soon be ready to serve with roast chicken or lamb.

↰ GAEC Rémy Castel et Fils, 3, Laforêt, 33710 Villeneuve,
tel. 05.57.64.86.61, fax 05.57.64.90.07 ☑ ♘
🍷 by appt.

CH. LE CLOS DU NOTAIRE
Cuvée sélectionnée 2001★

| | 15 ha | 36,000 | ▣ ⅲ ♦ | 5–8 € |

Bourg-sur-Gironde in fact stands on the Dordogne. It was a citadel in the Roman period and is well worth a visit. This estate's main wine was made from 15 ha of its 22-ha vines, planted with the classic grape varieties on a lovely terroir of gravels on limestone with starfish. This 2001 wine has an intense youthful colour. When the glass is swirled, the bouquet reveals spicy fruit and toasty oak. The harmonious palate has a restrained oak, and tannins which need two to four years to soften.

↰ Ch. le Clos du Notaire, 33710 Bourg-sur-Gironde,
tel. 05.57.68.44.36, fax 05.57.68.32.87,
e-mail closnot@club-internet.fr ☑
🍷 by appt.
↰ Roland Charbonnier

CH. DE COTS
Cuvée Prestige Elevé en fût de chêne 2001★★

| | 2 ha | 6,000 | | 8–11 € |

A beautiful Romanesque church is the most charming building in the village of Bayon. About 1 km away is this family estate, cultivated by sustainable agriculture. The grape selection for this wine was well done, as can be seen in the dark-ruby glints reflected in the glass. The bouquet is already notably rich, releasing jammy soft fruits and spicy oak. The palate is very forthcoming, conveying both the terroir and the grapes used (70% Merlot), and shaped by tannins that are still firm but liquorice-flavoured and long, and will enable the wine to age well. In a few years it will go well with game and red meat.

↰ Gilles et Anne-Marie Bergon, 3, Cots,
33710 Bayon-sur-Gironde, tel. 05.57.64.82.79,
fax 05.57.64.95.82 ☑
🍷 ev. day 10am–12 noon 2pm–7pm

LA COULEE DE BAYON 2001★

| | 0.5 ha | 1,600 | | 8–11 € |

This newcomer to wine-growing started in 1995. He cultivates a tiny vineyard opposite a 13th century Romanesque church. For all its small size, the grape varieties and the terroir itself are quite varied. He has planted 55% Merlot, 20% Cot

(Malbec), 13% Cabernet Franc and 12% Cabernet Sauvignon on clays, sands and limestone. The wine he obtains is certainly full of ingredients. The colour of this one is intense and fresh. The bouquet is attractive, at first releasing ripe fruits (cherry), then a liquorice-flavoured oak. The palate is powerful and balanced: the oaky flavour is supported by evident but integrated tannins. This is a very promising wine, and will be ready to drink in two to four years.

↰ Jean-Marc Delhaye, 2, Le Bourg,
33710 Bayon-sur-Gironde, tel. 05.57.64.81.74,
e-mail jm.delhaye@planetis.com ☑
🍷 by appt.

CH. LA CROIX-DAVIDS
Tradition 2001★

| | 15 ha | 50,000 | ▣ ⅲ ♦ | 5–8 € |

The Croix-Davids stands on land which in the Middle Ages belonged to a monastery, a stopping place for pilgrims going to Santiago de Compostela. Some remains of the building can still be seen on the estate. This wine was produced in a large quantity from 15 ha out of the 39 ha owned by the château. Its colour is still young and lively. The developing bouquet releases floral notes (lime blossom), nuances of small soft fruits and spices. A flavour of dried fruits is accompanied by ripe, liquorice-flavoured tannins. This is a fine product, and should be ready fairly soon. Drink it with an entrecôte à la bordelaise. The **Prestige 2000 (8–11 €)**, matured for 18 months in barrel, is commended. It needs to be laid down for a few years to let the oak mature.

↰ SCE Birot Meneuvrier, 57, rue Valentin-Bernard,
33710 Bourg-sur-Gironde, tel. 05.57.94.03.94,
fax 05.57.94.03.90,
e-mail chateau.la-croix-davids@wanadoo.fr ☑
🍷 by appt.

CH. FOUGAS
Maldoror 2001★★

| | 8 ha | 45,000 | | 15–23 € |

This is Jean-Yves Béchet's main wine, taking up two-thirds of his production. This has not impaired its quality at all. The Grand Jury chose this 2001 wine by an overwhelming majority. It has a sumptuous black colour with ruby highlights, and an extremely expressive bouquet: overripe grapes, prune, toasted almond, vanilla and roasted oak. The powerful and full-bodied palate is structured on silky tannins. In four to five years, this wine will be perfect for serving with a haunch of venison. The **Prestige 2001 (8–11 €)** just missed the *coup de coeur*. This is a very great wine, subtle and elegant, and wins two stars.

↰ Jean-Yves Béchet, Ch. Fougas, 33710 Lansac,
tel. 05.57.68.42.15, fax 05.57.68.28.59,
e-mail jean-yves.bechet@wanadoo.fr ☑
🍷 ev. day except Sat. Sun. 9am–12 noon 2pm–6pm

CH. GALAU
Elevé en fût de chêne 2001★★

| | 4.5 ha | 20,000 | | 5–8 € |

This excellent winemaker from Tauriac has produced a remarkable dark-ruby wine from a clay-limestone terroir with a blend of 75% Merlot and 25% Cabernet Sauvignon. The bouquet is still very oaky and vanilla-flavoured, with notes of coffee and coconut. It is mouth-filling and powerful on the

208

palate, with a long smooth finish of fruit and oak. In two to three years it will be perfect to serve with game.
- Jean-Louis Magdeleine, Ch. Nodoz, 33710 Tauriac, tel. 05.57.68.41.03, fax 05.57.68.37.34 ☑
- by appt.

CH. GARREAU 2001★★

| ■ | 2.76 ha | 16,000 | ⑪ | 11–15€ |

This wine won a *coup de coeur* for its 2000 vintage. The 2001 version is also remarkable. It was matured entirely in new barrels, and has a dark colour with youthful ruby glints. The bouquet is still dominated by a balsamic oak, but the fruit appears once the glass is swirled. The palate is powerful and dynamic, enlivened by long liquorice-flavoured tannins. This is an excellent wine for keeping. Leave it for a year so the oak can settle down.
- SCEA Ch. Garreau, Lafosse, 33710 Pugnac, tel. 05.57.68.90.75, fax 05.57.68.90.84 ☑
- ev. day except Sat. Sun. 9am–12 noon 2pm–4.30pm
- Mme Guez

CH. GENIBON-BLANCHEREAU

Améthyste de Genibon Elevé en fût de chêne 2001★

| ■ | 0.8 ha | 6,000 | ⑪ | 5–8€ |

This tiny vintage was made from selected grapes on 0.8 ha of the vineyard of Château Genibon-Blanchereau, whose **2001**, matured in tank, is commended. The terroir and the grape varieties are the same, but this Améthyste was matured for 12 months in oak barrels. The colour is intense and dark. The open and powerful bouquet is marked by a fine toasty oak, with a touch of musk. This forthcoming wine coats the palate well with elegant and lingering tannins. In two to three years, you could begin to drink it with duck or other game.
- EARL Eynard-Sudre, Genibon, 33710 Bourg-sur-Gironde, tel. 05.57.68.25.34, fax 05.57.68.27.58, e-mail eynard.sudre@wanadoo.fr ☑
- by appt.

CH. DE LA GRAVE

Nectar 2001★

| ■ | 4 ha | 18,000 | ⑪ | 11–15€ |

This wine comes from a large vineyard (45 ha) surrounding a magnificent château with a feudal air. In the glass, the brilliant dark colour is fringed with light glints indicating its evolution. The glass needs to be swirled to release the complex nuances of the bouquet. The balanced palate is structured by oak tannins which are still a little austere. In two to three years, this wine will be ready to pour into a carafe and serve with a strong-tasting dish such as game.
- Philippe Bassereau, Ch. de La Grave, 33710 Bourg-sur-Gironde, tel. 05.57.68.41.49, fax 05.57.68.49.26, e-mail chateaudelagrave@chateaudelagrave.com ☑ ⌂
- by appt.

CH. LES GRAVES DE VIAUD

Elevé en fût de chêne 2001★

| ■ | 12 ha | 84,000 | ⑪ | 5–8€ |

This vineyard is all in one piece. It stands on a south-facing clay-gravel hillside and in 1994 was taken over by P. Derouineau. This vintage has a lovely garnet colour with black highlights. The bouquet is still dominated by roasted oak, but releases notes of soft fruits when the glass is swirled. The palate is full-bodied and the tannins are charming. This wine was made from very ripe grapes and is pleasant to drink now, but it can also be laid down. Serve it with white or red meats.
- Dom. de Viaud, 33710 Pugnac, tel. 05.57.68.94.37, fax 05.57.68.94.49 ☑
- by appt.
- P. Derouineau

CH. GROLEAU

Vieilli en fût de chêne 2000★

| ■ | 2 ha | 12,000 | ⑪ | 5–8€ |

Sylvie and Didier Raboutet run a large vineyard of 36 ha, essentially in Blaye, but they also produce a Côtes de Bourg on

2 ha of clay-limestone soil planted with 80% Merlot and 20% Cabernet Sauvignon. This 2000 wine has a dark-ruby colour and an interesting, finely oaked bouquet and a tasty palate that is still very fruity and balanced. This wine is already supple and harmonious and could be drunk now and over the next five years.
- Didier et Sylvie Raboutet, Ch. Le Chay, 33390 Berson, tel. 05.57.64.39.50, fax 05.57.64.25.08, e-mail lechay@wanadoo.fr ☑
- by appt.

CH. GUERRY 2000★

| ■ | 22 ha | 150,000 | 🍷⑪ | 8–11€ |

In 1972, Bertrand de Rivoyre, a well-known Bordeaux négociant (buyer for the firm of Nicolas), bought a magnificent stone house on the top of a hill in the Côtes de Bourg, surrounded by vines. His recent death greatly saddened his colleagues. He liked to take part in our tasting sessions. Now Claudie de Rivoyre has taken charge of the estate, and offers one wine from the whole of the harvest of her 22 ha (and not a micro-wine or a micro-selection, like many). The result is an excellent tribute to the work put in. The colour is still youthful, with brilliant ruby and black highlights. The developing bouquet releases mainly flowers and fruits (cherry and blackcurrant). On the palate, it is chewy and full-bodied, enlivened by silky tannins. This is a very good Côtes de Bourg which can be drunk in two or three years with lamprey à la bordelaise, game and all kinds of meats.
- SC du Ch. Guerry, 26, rte du Guérit, 33710 Tauriac, tel. 05.57.68.20.78, fax 05.57.68.41.31 ☑
- by appt.
- Claudie de Rivoyre

CH. GUIONNE

Elevé en fût de chêne 2001★

| ■ | 2.5 ha | 13,000 | ⑪ | 5–8€ |

The new owners of this beautiful wine-growing estate of about 20 ha selected 2.5 ha to make this wine. The south-facing clay-limestone terroir is divided almost in thirds among Merlot, Cot (Malbec) and Cabernet Sauvignon. The wine has a dark-crimson colour. The developing bouquet is still restrained but fine. On the palate it is round and fruity, supported by a good tannic chewiness. This young, powerful and structured wine will improve with keeping for a while, then can be served with red meats and cheeses.
- Alain Fabre, Ch. Guionne, 33710 Lansac, tel. 05.57.68.42.17, fax 05.57.68.29.61, e-mail chateauguionne@aol.com ☑
- by appt.

CH. HAUT-BAJAC

Elevé en fût de chêne 2001★

| ■ | 11 ha | n.c. | 🍷⑪♦ | 5–8€ |

Jacques Pautrizel, an oenologist, took over this estate, 1 km from Bourg, in 1996. He offers an intense and youthful ruby wine. The developing bouquet at first reveals a spicy and toasty oak, then opens out with a range of fruits (pear, blackberry and redcurrant). The palate is full of finesse and delight; the fruit is supported by a spicy oak that leaves a satisfying impression. This wine will be ready to enjoy in two or three years.
- Jacques Pautrizel, Ch. Haut-Bajac, 33710 Bourg-sur-Gironde, tel. 05.57.68.35.99, fax 05.57.68.32.15 ☑
- by appt.

CH. HAUT-GUIRAUD

Péché du Roy 2001★★★

| ■ | 10 ha | 20,000 | ⑪ | 8–11€ |

This wine won a *coup de coeur* for the 2000 vintage, and quite often wins two or three stars. This year, this "royal" wine wins three. They say that when the young Louis XIV stayed in Bourg, he was particularly fond of the Guiraud peaches (*pêches*), whence the pun calling this wine the "Péché du Roy" (The King's Weakness). It has a magnificent Bordeaux colour with black highlights. The powerful bouquet reveals good grapes, good oak, vanilla, clove, leather and liquorice. The warm, full-bodied palate finishes with noble tannins which

will enable this wine to be served for a good ten years with noble dishes: game or duckling in mushrooms, for example.
★⊐ EARL Bonnet et Fils, Ch. Haut-Guiraud,
33710 Saint-Ciers-de-Canesse, tel. 05.57.64.91.39,
fax 05.57.64.88.05 ☑
☗ by appt.

CH. HAUT-MACO
Cuvée Jean Bernard 2000★

		6 ha	47,718	▮ ⑪ ⬗		5–8 €

The Mallet brothers farm about 50 ha of vines planted on clay-limestone and washed silts in the east of the appellation. Their main wine, the **Château Haut-Macô 2000**, is very characteristic and is commended. This wine, which adopts the brothers' first names, has brilliant and lively highlights. The bouquet is very expresive, a succession of ripe fruits and scents of oak, spices, meat, minerals, honey and chocolate. The palate is equally tasty and harmonious, finishing on already silky tannins which will enable this wine to be drunk in the next two to five years.
★⊐ Jean et Bernard Mallet, Ch. Haut-Macô, 33710 Tauriac, tel. 05.57.68.81.26, fax 05.57.68.91.97,
e-mail hautmaco@wanadoo.fr ☑
☗ ev. day except Sat. Sun. 8am–12 noon 2pm–6pm

HAUT-MONDESIR 2000★★

		1.8 ha	12,000	⑪		11–15 €

Marc Pasquet is a former photographer who successfully made the changeover to wine-growing. He is based in the Blaye, but also makes Saint Emilion as well as this Côtes du Bourg. It is a remarkable, almost black wine with ruby glints. The bouquet is both distinguished and intense, at first fruity (woodland fruits, blackcurrant and prune), moving towards a finely oaky scent. The palate is very concentrated, mingling aromas of cherry, prune, oak and coffee. The evident tannins will ensure it keeps well and it should grow in finesse over the next three to ten years.
★⊐ Marc Pasquet, Mondesir-Gazin, BP 7, 33390 Plassac, tel. 05.57.42.29.80, fax 05.57.42.84.86,
e-mail mondesirgazin@aol.com ☑ ☖
☗ by appt.

CH. HAUT-MOUSSEAU
Cuvée Prestige 2001★

		9.3 ha	20,000	⑪		5–8 €

The Briolais family farm 33 ha of vines in the Bordelais. The terroir consists of gravels and clays, and the grapes grown are Merlot and the Cabernets, in equal proportions. The very dark colour of this wine reflects numerous black-cherry, ruby and garnet glints. The bouquet is already intense and elegant, combining very ripe grapes and toasty- and vanilla-flavoured oak. The palate is supple and full-bodied at first, then appears full and structured by tannins which are still a little firm but which should soften in the next two years and ensure that the wine will keep well after that. Dominique Briolais also offers a **red Château Terrefort-Bellegrave 2001 (8–11 €)** which also wins one star.
★⊐ Dominique Briolais, 1, Ch. Haut-Mousseau,
33710 Teuillac, tel. 05.57.64.34.38, fax 05.57.64.31.73 ☑ ☖
☗ by appt.

CH. JANSENANT 2001★

		15 ha	100,000	▮		5–8 €

This is one of the vineyards of the wine-growers A. Faure, wine-makers and négociants. Here we are on the clay-limestone soils of Villeneuve. This brilliant and intense-looking wine is fruity and well balanced. Its already pleasant character means it can be drunk fairly soon with white meats or poultry. The **Château Tour-Neuve 2001** was equally appreciated but is more suited to serving with game.
★⊐ Belair Sélection, Coubet, 33710 Villeneuve,
tel. 05.57.42.68.84, fax 05.57.42.68.80

CH. MACAY 2001★

		15 ha	80,000	▮ ⑪ ⬗		8–11 €

The main wine of this large wine-growing estate takes its name from the Scotsman who lived there at the time when Aquitaine was English. As well as its wine, this vineyard is known for its large reception facilities, particularly for groups.

There you can taste this very successful 2001 wine with a pretty, clean ruby colour. The fresh and fruity bouquet opens on notes of toasty oak and coconut. The palate is still a little dominated by the oak, but is rich and forthcoming. The tannins are long but already supple and will enable this wine to be served in the near future.
★⊐ Eric et Bernard Latouche, Ch. Macay, 33710 Samonac, tel. 05.57.68.41.50, fax 05.57.68.35.23,
e-mail chateaumacay@wanadoo.fr ☑
☗ by appt.

CH. MARTINAT 2001★★

	10 ha	52,000	⑪		8–11 €

The 2000 vintage came very close to the *coup de coeur*. The 2001 wine wins it. This is very deserved, partly because this year was more difficult and partly because its producers are among the rare ones to offer a wine representing the whole of their harvest (and not a mini-selection). This wine has a magnificent black-cherry colour and a bouquet, combining fresh grapes and an excellent oak. The flavours are quite charming (vanilla, coffee, and fruity and floral notes) and in perfect balance. This remarkable wine has a great potential for keeping (two to ten years) and will go well with traditional or modern dishes.
★⊐ SCEV Marsaux-Donze, Ch. Martinat, 33710 Lansac, tel. 05.57.68.34.98, fax 05.57.68.35.39,
e-mail chateaumartinat@aol.com ☑
☗ by appt.

CH. DE MENDOCE
Grande Réserve Vieilli en fût de chêne 2001★

		3 ha	16,800	⑪		5–8 €

Fifteen hectares of vines surround this château, including the original ones which date from the 7th century. The two hill-sides of Mendoce are separated by a stream which runs into the dense chalk of the subsoil. This wine has a dark, youthful colour. The bouquet is still very oaky, with vanilla- and biscuit-flavoured notes, but the palate is already round and balanced by silky tannins which will enable the wine to be drunk in two to three years.
★⊐ Philippe Darricarrère, Ch. de Mendoce,
33710 Villeneuve, tel. 05.57.68.34.95, fax 05.57.68.34.91,
e-mail info@mendoce.com ☑
☗ ev. day except Sun. 9am–12 noon 2pm–6pm;
Sat. by appt.; cl. Aug.

CH. MONTAIGUT
Vieilli et élevé en fût de chêne 2001★

		4 ha	18,000	⑪		5–8 €

François de Pardieu bought this property in 1975. Extending over 34 ha, the estate has a wonderful view over the estuary and the Médoc. Here the terroir is made of clay-limestone and red gravel. This 2001 wine is full of power. It is dark crimson with ruby highlights, and releases aromas of finely oaked soft fruits. The full and structured palate is flavoured by small soft fruits. The tannins are still a little firm but guarantee perfect maturation in time. This wine could be served with red meats (entrecôte) or game.
★⊐ SCEA vignobles de Pardieu, 2, Nodeau,
33710 Saint-Ciers-de-Canesse, tel. 05.57.64.92.49,
fax 05.57.64.94.20,
e-mail françois-de-pardieu@wanadoo.fr ☑
☗ ev. day 1.30pm–5.30pm; Sat. Sun. by appt.

CH. MOULIN DES GRAVES

Cuvée particulière 2001★

■	3 ha	2,000 ❚❙❚	5–8 €

At his 10-ha vineyard, Jean Bost keeps 3 ha of silicious gravels planted with Sauvignon to make this white Côtes de Bourg, which is for a limited market. This fruity wine is very pleasant from the first glance. Its green-gold colour is very brilliant and the aromas reveal delicious notes of honeyed white flowers and peach in syrup. The first impression on the palate is supple, with a recurring touch of honey. As a whole it is well balanced and will be ready to drink next summer.
☛ Jean Bost, L'Ombrière, 33710 Teuillac,
tel. 05.57.64.30.58, fax 05.57.64.20.59,
e-mail jean-bost@wanadoo.fr ☑
⊤ by appt.

CH. DU MOULIN VIEUX

Sélection Elevé et vieilli en fût de chêne 2000★★

■	6 ha	n.c. ❚❙❚	8–11 €

From the 24 ha that he farms, Jean-Pierre Gorphe keeps 6 ha of old vines for this wine which is matured for 24 months in barrel. Its superb colour, a ruby not marked by age, heralds a rich bouquet: a succession of crystallized fruits and very fine toasty oak. The structure is particularly concentrated, but well balanced between the fruit and the oak, and leads to a tasty lingering finish. This is a perfectly matured wine which will be ready to drink between three and ten years from now. The **Cuvée Tradition 2001 (5–8 €)** is simple and much more constructed. It is commended.
☛ Jean-Pierre Gorphe, Moulin-Vieux, 33710 Tauriac,
tel. 06.07.04.44.12 ☑
⊤ by appt.

CH. NODOZ

Elevé en barrique de chêne 2001★★

■	6 ha	30,000 ❚❙❚	8–11 €

This is not the first *coup de coeur* for Nodoz. And Jean-Louis Magdeleine is incontestably one of the best wine-growers in Bourg. This wine was made from 6 ha of gravels, and is a blend of 60% Merlot and 40% Cabernet. It has an impressive intensity and depth in its Bordeaux colour, and is impressive too in the power, complexity and finesse of its bouquet which combines fruits, spices and oak. The richness, harmony and length of its flavours of very ripe grape and well-controlled oaky tannins make it a great wine for laying down. It will be ready in two to three years and will go well with large game.
☛ Jean-Louis Magdeleine, Ch. Nodoz, 33710 Tauriac,
tel. 05.57.68.41.03, fax 05.57.68.37.34 ☑
⊤ by appt.

LA PETITE CHARDONNE

Elevé en fût de chêne 2001★★

■	6 ha	14,660 ❚❙❚	8–11 €

Marie-Hélène and Monique Marinier took over from their father Louis Marinier who played a great rôle in Bordeaux wine-growing in the 1980s. The family farm 48 ha to the north of the Gironde. In the Bourg, they offer this wine made from Merlot grown on a clay-limestone terroir at Teuillac. This 2001 wine has a magnificent, particularly dark Bordeaux colour. The emerging bouquet is very elegant, both floral, fruity (very ripe Merlot), oaky and vanilla-flavoured. The body is powerful, shaped by compact tannins and enhanced by intense notes of vanilla, liquorice and toasted bread. Its very "Bordeaux" character makes it well suited to traditional dishes.
☛ Vignobles Louis Marinier, Dom. Florimond, La Brède, 33390 Berson, tel. 05.57.64.34.63, fax 05.57.64.23.27, e-mail vignobleslouismarinier@wanadoo.fr ☑
⊤ ev. day 8am–12 noon 2pm–5pm; Sat. Sun. by appt.; cl. Aug.
☛ Marie-Hélène et Monique Marinier

CH. PEYCHAUD

Maisonneuve Vieilles Vignes 2001★

■	5 ha	40,000 ❚❙❚ ♦	8–11 €

At his 29-ha property at Teuillac, Bernard Germain offers a wine including 10% Petit Verdot, a traditional Médoc grape variety. It has produced an original wine with a very dense garnet colour. The well-bred and complex bouquet releases aromas of very ripe soft fruit, leather and toasted bread. This 2001 vintage is supple in the attack, then reveals mouth-filling qualities and good length, as well as supple and lingering tannins. The flavour remains fruity, and the oak is restrained. A taster noted: "The oak serves the wine, not the reverse, and it's all the better for that." In two or three years, this wine will be ready to serve with unusual meat dishes.
☛ SCEA Ch. Peychaud, Vignobles Germain et Associés, 33390 Berson, tel. 05.57.42.66.66, fax 05.57.64.36.20, e-mail bordeaux@vgas.com 🏠 🏠
⊤ by appt.

CH. REPIMPLET

Cuvée Amélie Julien 2001★

■	3 ha	20,000 ❚❙❚	8–11 €

This wine was made from 3 ha of the 14.5 ha farmed by Michèle and Patrick Touret. The 98 vintage won a *coup de coeur*. The 2001 wine is less ambitious but nonetheless very successful. It has a very dense garnet colour. Its well-bred bouquet releases aromas of soft fruits, crystallized fruits, prune, leather and a restrained oak. After a clean and fruity attack on the palate, the tannins soon appear and remain for a long time. They will need time, between three and ten years, to soften. The main wine, the **Repimplet red 2001 (5–8 €)**, is commended. Drink it in three years from now.
☛ Michèle et Patrick Touret, 4, Repimplet, 33710 Saint-Ciers-de-Canesse, tel. 05.57.64.31.31, fax 05.57.64.31.78,
e-mail chateau.repimplet@wanadoo.fr ☑
⊤ by appt.

CH. LES ROCQUES

Cuvée Elégance Elevé en fût de chêne 2000★★

■	1.2 ha	6,000 ❚❙❚ ♦	8–11 €

This wine was made from low-yielding old vines harvested by hand and matured in new barrels for 12 months. It would have been surprising if that had not produced remarkable results for this 2000 vintage. What we have is a very powerful wine for laying down. Its almost black colour is still youthful. The very complex bouquet mingles notes of fruits (soft fruits and crystallized fruits), minerals, spices and oak, forming an elegant combination. The palate is mouth-filling and structured by oaky tannins, but the returning aromas are fruity. This wine will be ready to drink in two to ten years from now with red meats, game, stews and cheese.
☛ Feillon Frères et Fils, Ch. Les Rocques, 33710 Saint-Seurin-de-Bourg, tel. 05.57.68.42.82, fax 05.57.68.36.25,
e-mail feillon.vins.de.bordeaux@wanadoo.fr ☑
⊤ ev. day 9am–12 noon 2pm–6pm; Sat. Sun. by appt.

CH. LE SABLARD

Cuvée Prestige Vieillie en fût de chêne 2001★

■	1.5 ha	8,500 ❚❙❚	5–8 €

Of the 12 ha of vines they farm, the Buratti family keep 1.5 for this Cuvée Prestige matured in new barrels and made from old vines planted in Lansac on a clay-limestone terroir and harvested by hand. The youthful dark-garnet colour heralds a bouquet which opens with fruit then with powerful balsamic notes. The palate is full and fresh, structured by integrated, vanilla-flavoured tannins and offering a particularly tasty

finish. In two to four years, this wine will go well with an entrecôte or smoked *magrets de canard*.
�↑ SCEA Jacques Buratti, 7, Le Rioucreux, 33920 Saint-Christoly-de-Blaye, tel. 05.57.42.57.67, fax 05.57.42.43.06 ☑
🍴 ev. day 9am–12 noon 2.30pm–6pm
↥ Catherine et Thomas Berlinger

CH. LE TERTRE DE LEYLE
Cuvée Réserve Elevé en fût de chêne 2001★★

■	1.5 ha	7,500	⦿	5–8 €

This large family property of 18.79 ha offers a wine made on clay-limestone soil. The remarkable crimson colour is deep and youthful. The bouquet is already intense and complex with aromas of ripe grapes, and hot, spicy and peppery oak. The palate is heady and well bred; the mature fruit returns, also the elegant oak and silky, liquorice- and vanilla-flavoured tannins. This very promising and harmonious wine will be ideal in two to four years for drinking with game and strong cheeses.
↥ SC Vignobles Grandillon, Au Bourg, 33710 Teuillac, tel. 05.57.64.23.81, fax 05.57.64.24.18 ☑
🍴 by appt.

CH. TOUR DE GUIET
Elevé en fût de chêne 2001★

■	1.5 ha	9,000	⦿	8–11 €

Stéphane Heurlier produces Blaye wines, but also makes successful Côtes de Bourg: The Jury selected two of them. The **Tour de Guiet 2001 (5–8 €)**, matured in tank, is fresh and fruity and is commended. The other is this Cuvée Spéciale matured in barrel, its colour shot with crimson and garnet highlights. It has an already complex, very fruity bouquet with oaky notes and nuances of cinnamon. The palate is mouth-filling, structured by long coated tannins, giving a fine wine characteristic of both the appellation and the year.
↥ Stéphane Heurlier, EARL Ch. La Bretonnière, 33390 Mazion, tel. 05.57.64.59.23, fax 05.57.64.67.41, e-mail sheurlier@wanadoo.fr ☑
🍴 by appt.

CH. LA TUILIERE
Les Armoiries 2001★

■	3 ha	15,000	⦿	11–15 €

This vineyard of 13.5 ha is all in one piece, and its main wine, **La Tuilière 2001 (5–8 €)**, is commended. This selection consists of 60% black Merlot and 40% Cabernet Sauvignon grown on a clay-limestone terroir and has produced a wine that was matured in barrel for a long time. This is noticeable, and gives it a classic Bordeaux character combining good, very ripe grapes and oak. Its aromas include crystallized fruit, coconut, vanilla and coffee. The palate is robust, enriched by long tannins. In two to ten years from now, this wine can be served with a wide range of dishes.
↥ Les Vignobles Philippe Estournet, Ch. La Tuilière, 33710 Saint-Ciers-de-Canesse, tel. 05.57.64.80.90, fax 05.57.64.89.97, e-mail chateau.la.tuiliere@wanadoo.fr ☑ ⊞
🍴 by appt.

Wines selected but not starred

CH. DE BARBE
Pourpre 2001

■	6 ha	13,000	▬⦿⚬	5–8 €

↥ SC Villeneuvoise, Ch. de Barbe, 33710 Villeneuve, tel. 05.57.42.64.00, fax 05.57.64.94.10 ☑
🍴 ev. day except Sat. Sun. 9am–12 noon 2pm–5pm
↥ Richard

CH. DU BOUSQUET 2001

■	62 ha	450,000	▬ ⚬	5–8 €

↥ Castel Frères, 21–24, rue Georges-Guynemer, 33290 Blanquefort, tel. 05.56.95.54.04, fax 05.56.95.54.20

CH. COLBERT
Cuvée Prestige 2001

■	3 ha	15,000	⦿	5–8 €

↥ Duwer, Ch. Colbert, 33710 Comps, tel. 05.57.64.95.04, fax 05.57.64.88.41 ☑
🍴 ev. day 9am–12 noon 2pm–7pm

CH. COUBET 2000

■	2 ha	10,000	▬⦿⚬	5–8 €

↥ Michel Migné, Ch. Coubet, 33710 Villeneuve, tel. 05.57.64.91.04 ☑
🍴 by appt.

CH. LE GALION 2001

■	6 ha	30,000	⦿	8–11 €

↥ SCEA Ch. de La Salle, 33390 Saint-Genès-de-Blaye, tel. 05.57.42.12.15, fax 05.57.42.87.11, e-mail marc.bonnin19@voila.fr
🍴 by appt.
↥ Bonnin

CH. LES GRANDS THIBAUDS
Réserve du Château Elevé en fût de chêne 2001

■	1.5 ha	9,300	⦿	5–8 €

↥ Daniel Plantey et Fils, Les Grands-Thibauds, 33240 Saint-Laurent-d'Arce, tel. 05.57.43.08.37, fax 05.57.43.08.37 ☑
🍴 ev. day 9am–7pm

CH. GRAVETTES-SAMONAC
Elevé et vieilli en fût de chêne 2001

■	5 ha	20,000	⦿	8–11 €

↥ Gérard Giresse, Ch. Gravettes-Samonac, 33710 Samonac, tel. 05.57.68.21.16, fax 05.57.68.36.43 ☑
🍴 by appt.

CH. LA GROLET
Tête de cuvée 2001

■	2.81 ha	21,500	⦿	8–11 €

↥ SCEA Vignobles Bossuet-Hubert, Ch. La Grolet, 33710 Saint-Ciers-de-Canesse, tel. 05.57.42.11.95, fax 05.57.42.38.15 ☑
🍴 by appt.

CH. L'HOSPITAL
Elevé en fût de chêne 2001

■	3 ha	15,000	⦿	8–11 €

↥ Christine et Bruno Duhamel, Ch. L'Hospital, 33710 Saint-Trojan, tel. 05.57.64.33.60, fax 05.57.64.33.60, e-mail alvitis@wanadoo.fr ☑
🍴 by appt.

CH. LABADIE
Vieilli en fût de chêne 2001

■	13 ha	95,000	▬⦿⚬	8–11 €

↥ SCEA Vignobles Joël Dupuy, 1, Cagna, 33710 Mombrier, tel. 05.57.64.23.84, fax 05.57.64.23.85, e-mail vignoblesjdupuy@aol.com ☑
🍴 by appt.

CH. LAMOTHE
Grande Réserve 2001

■	n.c.	15,000	⦿	5–8 €

↥ Anne Pousse et Michel Pessonnier, Ch. Lamothe, 33710 Lansac, tel. 05.57.68.41.07, fax 05.57.68.46.68, e-mail chateaulamothe@yahoo.fr ☑
🍴 by appt.

CH. LANGUIREAU

Elevé en fût 2001

■	0.75 ha	5,290	■ ❶❶	5–8 €

☛ Fabien Vitu et Hervé Cwiklinski, 147, av. du
Gal-de-Gaulle, 33450 Izon, tel. 05.57.74.86.52 ☑
⟐ by appt.

CH. LAROCHE

Elevé en fût de chêne 2001

■	16 ha	115,000	❶❶	5–8 €

☛ Baron Roland de Onffroy, Ch. Laroche, 33710 Tauriac,
tel. 05.57.68.20.72, fax 05.57.68.20.72 ☑
⟐ by appt.

CH. MERCIER 2001

■	10 ha	30,000	■ ❶❶ ♦	5–8 €

☛ SCEA Famille Chéty, Ch. Mercier, 33710 Saint-Trojan,
tel. 05.57.42.66.99, fax 05.57.42.66.96,
e-mail vin@chateaumercier.fr ☑
⟐ ev. day except Sat. Sun. 8am–12 noon 2pm–6pm

CH. MOULIN DE GUIET

Elevé en fût de chêne 2000

■	9.01 ha	70,500	❶❶	3–5 €

☛ Union de producteurs de Pugnac, Bellevue,
33710 Pugnac, tel. 05.57.68.81.01, fax 05.57.68.83.17,
e-mail udep.pugnac@wanadoo.fr
⟐ by appt.
☛ Philippe Blanchard

CH. MOULIN EYQUEM 2000

■	19.32 ha	80,000	❶❶	5–8 €

☛ Mostermans-Mercherz, Ch. Moulin Eyquem, Les
Justices, 33710 Bourg-sur-Gironde, tel. 05.56.52.53.06 ☑
⟐ by appt.

CH. PONT DE LA TONNELLE

Cuvée Prestige Elevé en fût de chêne 2001

■	1 ha	6,000	❶❶	8–11 €

☛ André Quancard-André, chem. de La Cabeyre,
33240 Saint-André-de-Cubzac, tel. 05.57.33.42.53,
fax 05.57.43.22.22, e-mail aqa@andrequancard.com
☛ Pauvif

CH. PUY D'AMOUR

Cuvée Grain de Folie Elevé en fût de chêne 2001

■	n.c.	1,200	❶❶	11–15 €

☛ Johann et Murielle Demel, Marchais no. 5,
33710 Saint-Seurin-de-Bourg, tel. 05.57.68.38.01,
fax 05.57.68.38.01 ☑
⟐ by appt.

CH. PUY DESCAZEAU

Vieilli en fût de chêne 2001

■	0.57 ha	1,800	❶❶	5–8 €

☛ Jean-Marc Médio, Ch. Puy Descazeau, 33710 Gauriac,
tel. 06.12.47.75.75, fax 01.48.71.39.33,
e-mail jmmedio@club-internet.fr ☑
⟐ by appt.

CH. DE RIVEREAU

Cuvée Prestige 2001

■	3 ha	14,500	■ ♦	5–8 €

☛ Sabine Drode, Ch. de Rivereau, 33710 Pugnac,
tel. 05.57.68.92.02, fax 05.57.68.92.02 ☑
⟐ ev. day except Sun. 10am–12 noon 1pm–6pm

CH. ROC PLANTIER

Cuvée Prestige Elevé en fût de chêne 2001

■	1.5 ha	8,000	❶❶	5–8 €

☛ Eric Eymas, 104, av. des Côtes-de-Bourg,
33710 Prignac-et-Marcamps, tel. 06.12.63.68.90,
fax 05.57.43.82.85 ☑ ⚘
⟐ by appt.

CH. DE ROUSSELET

Elevé en fût de chêne 2000

■	3.5 ha	24,000	❶❶	5–8 €

☛ Emmanuel Sou, EARL du Ch. de Rousselet,
33710 Saint-Trojan, tel. 05.57.64.32.18, fax 05.57.64.26.10,
e-mail chateau.de.rousselet@wanadoo.fr ☑
⟐ by appt.

CH. ROUSSELLE

Prestige 2001

■	4.5 ha	25,000	❶❶	11–15 €

☛ Vincent et Nathalie Lemaitre, Ch. Rousselle,
33710 Saint-Ciers-de-Canesse, tel. 05.57.42.16.62,
fax 05.57.42.19.51,
e-mail chateau@chateaurousselle.com ☑ ▥
⟐ by appt.

CH. DE THAU 2001

■	n.c.	n.c.	■ ❶❶ ♦	5–8 €

☛ SCEA Vignobles Schweitzer et Fils, Ch. de Thau,
33710 Gauriac, tel. 05.57.64.80.79, fax 05.57.64.83.72,
e-mail schweitzer.vignoble@free.fr ☑
⟐ by appt.

CH. TOUR DES GRAVES 2002

	1.5 ha	12,000	■ ♦	3–5 €

☛ GAEC Arnaud Frères, Le Poteau, 33710 Teuillac,
tel. 05.57.64.32.02, fax 05.57.64.23.94 ☑
⟐ ev. day except Sun. 9am–12 noon 2pm–7pm

Libournais

Although there is no "Appella-
tion Libourne", the Libournais district exists in its
own right. While Bordeaux is the major town and
the Dordogne is the major waterway, Libourne has a
distinct individuality in the Gironde and is not as
dependent as other areas on the regional metropolis.
It is not unusual for the Libournais to be distinguished from the Bordelais itself, with its less
ostentatious architecture, its wine châteaux and
wine-merchant quarter. But what sets the Libournais
apart most of all is undoubtedly the concentration of
the vineyards, which start right on the edge of the
town and cover nearly the whole countryside in
several communes, producing famous appellations,
such as Fronsac, Pomerol and Saint-Emilion, on
land that is parcelled up into small or medium-sized
properties. Large properties, like those of the Médoc,

or the wide expanses characteristic of Aquitaine, are practically unknown here.

T he vineyard's individuality also comes from the varieties of grape grown: Merlot predominates, giving fruitiness and finesse to the wines, which are able to age well, even if they keep for less time than the appellations made mainly from Cabernet-Sauvignon. On the other hand, they can be drunk a little sooner and accompany a variety of foods (red and white meat, cheeses and even certain fish, such as lamprey).

CANON-FRONSAC
AND FRONSAC

T he Fronsadais is bounded by the Dordogne and Isle rivers. The beautiful country-side is rugged with two mounds of 60 and 75 metres, which offer magnificent views over the area. The region is a strategic point and under Charlemagne a sturdy fortress was built there; during the following centuries the area continued to play an important role in the history of France. Nowadays there is no trace of the original fortress, but the Fronsadais has some beautiful churches and numerous châteaux. Wine-growing is an ancient activity, and the vine-yards, which cover six communes, produce individual wines that are balanced and full-bodied, while also being fine and distinguished. All the communes are entitled to use the Appellation Fronsac (32,578 hl in 2002), but of the wines produced on the limestone and clay slopes on a footing of opaline lime, only Fronsac and Saint-Michel-de-Fronsac are entitled to use the Appellation Canon-Fronsac (12,961 hl).

Canon-Fronsac

CH. BARRABAQUE
Prestige 2000★★

| ■ | 5.5 ha | 26,000 | ◫ | 15–23 € |

88 |89| |90| 91 92 |94|(95)(96) 97 98 99 00

This wine wins its fourth *coup de coeur* in five years (a real feat!) and once more puts itself at the top of its appellation. The 2000 wine has a crimson colour shining with superb garnet highlights. The expressive and complex bouquet has aromas of blackcurrant, pepper, coffee and raspberry. On the attack, the rich and velvety tannins grow in power and balance, and develop great aromatic length. This is a *grand vin* to drink three to eight years from now.
↳ SCEA Noël Père et Fils, Ch. Barrabaque, 33126 Fronsac, tel. 05.57.55.09.09, fax 05.57.55.09.00, e-mail chateaubarrabaque@yahoo.fr ☑
☖ by appt.

CH. CANON DE BREM 2000★★

| ■ | 4.57 ha | 31,000 | ◫ | 11–15 € |

Jean-Pierre Moueix, who built up the quality of wines in the Libourne, died this year. His descendants share his standards and have worked for a long time in the business. This magnificent Petit Cru is regularly one of the leaders of the appellation, blending 68% Cabernet Franc and 32%

The Libournais Appelation

The Libournais map showing appellations: Fronsac, Canon-Fronsac, Lalande-de-Pomerol, Pomerol, with châteaux labelled including St-Germain-de-la-Rivière, Ch. Rouet, Saillans, St-Aignan, St-Michel-de-Fronsac, Ch. Canon, Ch. Toumalin, Ch. Junayme, Ch. Canon-de-Brem, Ch. la Dauphine, Fronsac, Libourne, Ch. Laborde, Ch. de Musset, Ch. de la Commanderie, Ch. Bourseau, Lalande-de-Pomerol, Ch. du Grand-Ormeau, Ch. Bel-Air, Ch. Cheval-Bel-Air, Ch. Lavinot-la-Chapelle, Ch. Moulin-à-Vent, Ch. Siaurac, Ch. la Croix, Pomerol, Néac, Ch. Haut-Ballet, Ch. Nénin.

1 Vieux-Château-Certan	6 Ch. le Gay	12 Ch. la Conseillante
2 Ch. Certan de May de Certan	7 Ch. la Fleur	13 Ch. Petit-Village
3 Ch. Trotanoy	8 Ch. Petrus	14 Ch. Beauregard
4 Ch. Latour à Pomerol	9 Ch. la Fleur-Petrus	15 Ch. la Rose-Figeac
5 Ch. l'Église-Clinet	10 Ch. Gazin	16 Ch. Taillefer
	11 Ch. le Bon Pasteur	17 Ch. Ferrand
		18 Ch. Nénin
Fronsac		19 Ch. la Pointe
Canon-Fronsac		20 Ch. Bonalgue
Lalande-de-Pomerol		21 Clos René
Pomerol		22 Ch. de Sales
		23 Ch. Tournefeuille
		24 Ch. Belles-Graves

Merlot matured for 18 months in barrel. Its strong ruby colour is brilliant. The complex aromas mingle ripe fruit, liquorice and an elegant oak. The well-extracted tannins are full-bodied and tasty and have plenty of power at the finish. It is essential to keep this wine for four to eight years. The **Château Canon-Moueix 2000** is commended for its very pleasant fruitiness (redcurrant) and its balance. It blends 10% Cabernet Franc with the Merlot. The **Château Canon 2000** is 100% Merlot and wins one star. All these wines benefit from a very fine clay-limestone terroir and the work of Jean-Claude Berrouet.

🍷 Ets Jean-Pierre Moueix, 54, quai du Priourat, 33500 Libourne, tel. 05.57.51.78.96

CH. CANON SAINT-MICHEL 2000★

| ■ | 4.2 ha | 18,000 | ⊞ | 8–11 € |

This vineyard was taken over in 1998, and improves with every year. This 2000 wine is very successful, both in its intense ruby colour and its delightful aromas of soft stone fruit and fine oak. Its supple structure makes it mouth-filling, rich and long. This is a tasty wine to enjoy in three to six years with small game.

🍷 Jean-Yves Millaire, Lamarche, 33126 Fronsac, tel. 06.08.33.81.11, fax 05.57.24.94.99 Ⓥ
🍷 ev. day 8am–1pm 2pm–8pm

CH. CAPET-BEGAUD 2000★★

| ■ | 4 ha | 30,000 | ⊞ | 11–15 € |

The Merlot (80%) and Cabernet Sauvignon (20%) vines occupy an ideal position, planted on on a sandy soil over limestone. The intense colour of this 2000 wine is almost black and the perfumes of very ripe crystallized fruit and liquorice combine well with elegant oaky notes. The attack is supple, the palate has good vinosity and shows itself to be powerful and balanced with a long finish. Leave this wine to mature for five to eight years. The **Cuvée Saint-Jacques du Château Coustolle 2000 (15–23 €)**, from the same producers, wins one star.

🍷 Denis et Xavier Roux, Ch. Coustolle, 33126 Fronsac, tel. 05.57.51.31.25, fax 05.57.74.00.32 Ⓥ
🍷 by appt.

CH. LA CHAPELLE-LARIVEAU 2000★

| ■ | 3.8 ha | 30,000 | ⊞ | 5–8 € |

This traditional property offers a very well-made wine of pure Merlot. The perfumes of soft fruit (blackberry) are enhanced by spicy and musky notes; the balanced palate rests on round and tasty tannins. This wine can be drunk now and for the next three years.

🍷 Serge Ravat, 13, Lariveaux, 33126 Saint-Michel-de-Fronsac, tel. 05.57.24.97.27, fax 05.57.24.92.00 Ⓥ
🍷 by appt.

CH. LA CROIX CANON 2000★★

| ■ | 14 ha | 75,000 | ⊞ | 11–15 € |

This vineyard enjoys an excellent terroir. This wine, matured for 18 months in barrel, is a blend of 81% Merlot and Cabernet Franc. It has a superb intense ruby colour with pretty purple highlights and an elegant bouquet revealing ripe fruit and quince. The lovely tannic structure grows in power and elegance at the same time. The balance will be perfect after keeping for two to five years.

🍷 SCEA Ch. Bodet, 33126 Fronsac

CH. DU GABY 2000★★

| ■ | 5 ha | 20,260 | ⊞ | 11–15 € |

This château dating from 1780 occupies a remarkable position, and is planted with 85% Merlot and 15% Cabernets. The intense crimson colour of this 2000 has brilliant garnet highlights; the bouquet of cinnamon, cherry, toasted bread and coffee is very charming and complex. The tannins are both velvety and concentrated and reveal a touch of liveliness which is good for the wine's development. The finish is particularly long and aromatic, which means the wine should be laid down for at least four to six years.

🍷 SCEA Vignobles famille Khayat, Ch. du Gaby, 33126 Fronsac, tel. 05.57.51.24.97, fax 05.57.25.18.99, e-mail chateau.du.gaby@wanadoo.fr
🍷 by appt.

CH. GRAND RENOUIL 2000★

| ■ | 3 ha | 14,000 | ⊞ | 15–23 € |

This 2000 wine was made from 100% Merlot, and deserves your attention not only because of its brilliant garnet colour and particularly elegant aromas of soft fruits and pepper, but also for its suave and forthcoming tannins, enhanced by a very evident oak which needs ageing for three to five years to let it soften. From the same proprietor, the **Château du Pavillon 2000 (11–15 €)** also wins one star; it is like the previous wine in terms of balance and typicity. However, it can be drunk sooner, in one to two years.

🍷 Michel Ponty, Les Chais du Port, 33126 Fronsac, tel. 05.57.51.29.57, fax 05.57.74.08.47, e-mail michel.ponty@wanadoo.fr Ⓥ
🍷 by appt.

CH. HAUT-MAZERIS 2000★

| ■ | 4.01 ha | 30,400 | ■ ⊞ ♦ | 11–15 € |

This château offered two 2000 Canon Fronsac wines, and this time the Jury preferred the Cuvée Classique for its expressive bouquet of fruits (strawberry, raspberry and blackcurrant) and liquorice, and for its intense, supple and balanced structure on the palate. Drink this in two to three years' time. The **Cuvée Spéciale 2000** is commended: it is made from older vines (50 years), and is not very different from its "big sister" except that its tannins have more flavour at the finish. This wine will grow in balance with time.

🍷 SCEA Ch. Haut-Mazeris, 33126 Saint-Michel-de-Fronsac, tel. 05.57.24.98.14, fax 05.57.24.91.07
🍷 by appt.

CH. LAMARCHE CANON

Candelaire 2000★

| ■ | 5 ha | 25,000 | ■ ⊞ ♦ | 11–15 € |

This wine was made from old vines (95% Merlot) planted on a southeast facing chalk hillside. It has a dark-crimson colour, and powerful aromas still dominated by oaky and burnt notes, while the soft and rich, concentrated tannins are good and long. This wine should mature in four to eight years when the oak will be more integrated. Serve it with woodcock.

🍷 Eric Julien, Ch. Lamarche-Canon, 33126 Fronsac, tel. 05.57.51.20.13, fax 05.57.51.28.13, e-mail bordeaux@vgas.com Ⓥ
🍷 ev. day except Sun. 8am–12 noon 2pm–6pm

CH. MAZERIS 2000★

| ■ | 17 ha | 80,000 | ■ ⊞ ♦ | 11–15 € |

This estate has been in the same family since 1769, and this time it offers two wines from the same year. The Cuvée Classique (80% Merlot), of which 30% was matured in barrel, was liked for its emerging bouquet of soft fruits and spices and its powerful but also elegant structure on the palate. Drink it in two to five years. The Cuvée Spéciale, **La Part des Anges 2000 (15–23 €)**, 100% Merlot, is more oaky: it spent 14 months in barrel and the tannins are very evident. It needs time (three to five years) to reach its best; it is commended.

🍷 EARL de Cournuaud, Ch. Mazeris, 33126 Saint-Michel-de-Fronsac, tel. 05.57.24.96.93, fax 05.57.24.98.25, e-mail mazeris@free.fr Ⓥ
🍷 ev. day except Sun. 8am–12 noon 2pm–6pm; cl. Aug.

CH. MONTCANON 2000★★

| ■ | 4 ha | 24,000 | ⊞ | 8–11 € |

Here the vines consist of 90% Merlot and 10% Cabernet Franc, planted on a clay-limestone terroir. They have produced a remarkable 2000 wine with an intense, almost black, crimson colour and elegant perfumes redolent of ripe crystallized fruits, vanilla and light leather. The palate is both elegant and silky, developing harmoniously with the help of ripe and balanced tannins, and a successful period of maturation in oak. This wine will be mature in three to eight years.

🍷 Palais du Fronsadais, BP 12, 33126 Fronsac, tel. 06.08.32.26.59, fax 05.57.25.98.67, e-mail a.rouxoulie@free.fr Ⓥ
🍷 by appt.
🍷 Marcel Durant

CH. ROULLET 2000★

■ 2.8 ha 11,500 ◫ 8–11 €

This estate has been farmed for four generations by the Dorneau family, who have improved it with regular investments as well as their own skills. The wineries used to belong to the Master of Toulouse-Lautrec, Princeteau. This vintage appears in a strong and brilliant ruby colour; its perfumes of blackcurrant, blackberry and menthol are in tune with its good vanilla-flavoured oak. On the palate it is round, full-bodied and powerful, and needs to open out. Let it age for three to six years.

☛ SCEA Dorneau et Fils, Ch. La Croix, 33126 Fronsac, tel. 05.57.51.31.28, fax 05.57.74.08.88, e-mail scea-dorneau@wanadoo.fr ☑
☏ by appt.

CH. SAINT-BERNARD

Elevé en fût de chêne 2000★★

■ 0.26 ha 2,000 ◫ 8–11 €

This wine was made from 100% Merlot. Its garnet colour is very strong, and the elegant and toasty oak is in harmony with the spices, the very ripe soft fruit (blackcurrant) and the notes of burning. The first impression on the palate is soft and rich, then come powerful and tasty tannins, perfectly balanced at the finish. This limited-edition wine was vinified remarkably well by the owner.

☛ Sébastien Gaucher, 1, Nardon, 33126 Saint-Michel-de-Fronsac, tel. 05.57.24.90.24, fax 05.57.24.90.24, e-mail s.gaucher@free.fr ☑
☏ by appt.

CH. VRAI CANON BOUCHE 2000★

■ 8 ha 48,000 ◫ 11–15 €

|90| 91 |94| |95| |96| 97 98 99 00

Located on the hillock at Canon, from which it takes its name, this vineyard stands directly over vast limestone quarries. This 2000 wine has a garnet colour with ruby highlights, perfumes of very ripe soft fruits and caramel with an elegant floral note and a very long, emphatic tannic structure, which is a little austere at the moment. It is essential to wait two to five years before opening this wine. From the same producer, the **Château Comte 2000** also wins one star.

☛ Françoise Roux, Ch. Lagüe, 33126 Fronsac, tel. 05.57.51.24.68, fax 05.57.25.98.67 ☑
☏ by appt.

Wines selected but not starred

CH. BELLOY

Cuvée Prestige 2000

■ 3 ha 13,500 ▌◫ ♨ 11–15 €

☛ SA Travers, BP 1, 33126 Fronsac, tel. 05.57.24.98.05, fax 05.57.24.97.79 ☑
☏ by appt.
☛ GAF Bardibel

CH. LARCHEVESQUE 2000

■ 3.63 ha 11,400 ▌♨ 8–11 €

☛ Cave de Larchevesque, 1, rue Guadet, 33330 Saint-Emilion, tel. 05.57.24.67.78, fax 05.57.24.71.31 ☑
☏ ev. day 10am–12.30pm 1.30pm–7pm
☛ Viaud

CH. MOULIN PEY-LABRIE 2000

■ 6.5 ha 20,000 ◫ 23–30 €

88 |89| |90| 91 92 93 94 95 |96| |97| 99 00

☛ B. et G. Hubau, Ch. Moulin Pey-Labrie, 33126 Fronsac, tel. 05.57.51.14.37, fax 05.57.51.53.45, e-mail moulinpeylabrie@wanadoo.fr ☑
☏ by appt.

CH. BARBEY

Esprit des Caudalies 2000★

■ 4.5 ha 5,000 ▌◫ 11–15 €

This vineyard stands on a molasse terroir on the hillsides of Saillans, and has belonged to the Trocard family since 1628! This 2000 wine has a strong crimson colour. Its has aromas of leather and blackberry with toasty notes. The velvety and rich tannins move towards finesse, fruit and great elegance at the finish. This is an enjoyable wine to be drunk in three to five years.

☛ Benoit Trocard, Ch. Barbey, 33141 Saillans, tel. 05.57.84.37.35, fax 05.57.74.39.86, e-mail winemaker@chateau-barbey.com ☑
☏ by appt.

CH. DE CAROLUS 2000★

■ 2.26 ha 8,400 ◫ 15–23 €

The name Carolus reminds us that Charlemagne (Carolus Magnus) once passed through Fronsac and may even have stayed there. This 2000 wine, made from 100% Merlot, has powerful and complex aromas of soft fruits, caramel, liquorice and vanilla. It is supple and elegant, and somewhat robust, and should be drunk in three to six years. Also from this estate, but made by Stéphane Roux, the **Château La Fleur Vincent 2000 (8–11 €)** also wins one star. It will be ready earlier (two to three years).

☛ Arnaud Roux-Oulié, Palais du Fronsadais, BP 12, 33126 Fronsac, tel. 05.57.51.24.68, fax 05.57.25.98.67, e-mail a.rouxoulie@free.fr ☑
☏ by appt.

CH. CHADENNE 2000★

■ 4 ha 15,000 ▌◫ ♨ 15–23 €

This vineyard changed hands in 1999, and has benefited from considerable investment both in the vineyard and in the wineries. This 2000 wine is the first of the new vintages. It was made with the oenologist Christian Veyry acting as a consultant, and is very successful. This can be seen in the ruby colour with garnet highlights, and the intense bouquet of vanilla combining well with fruity notes such as blackberry and raspberry. On the palate, this is a powerful, full-bodied and long wine, with a very good keeping potential (five to eight years).

☛ SCEA Ph. et V. Jean, Ch. Chadenne, 33126 Saint-Aignan, tel. 05.57.24.93.10, fax 05.57.24.95.98, e-mail chateau.chadenne@wanadoo.fr ☑
☏ by appt.

CLOS DU ROY

Cuvée Arthur 2000★

■ n.c. 20,000 ◫ 11–15 €

The Cuvée Arthur is made from old vines of Merlot (90%) and Cabernet Franc (10%). It is a cherry-red wine with a youthful dark-purple fringe. The bouquet is also young, with aromas of coffee and vanilla which rather hide the fruit. It is rich and still tannic, and should stay in the cellar for three to four years.

☛ Hermouet, Clos du Roy, 33141 Saillans, tel. 05.57.55.07.41, fax 05.57.55.07.45, e-mail hermouetclosduroy@wanadoo.fr ☑
☏ by appt.

CH. DALEM 2000★

| ■ | 10.6 ha | 55,800 | ◫ | 15–23 € |

88 89 90 92 **93** 94 |95| |96| |97| 98 **99** 00

This excellent vineyard is regularly mentioned as one of the big names of the appellation, and once more offers a very successful vintage whose ink-black colour shines with beautiful raspberry highlights. It has aromas of *pain d'épice* and cinnamon alongside toasty notes. On the palate, the fruitiness surrounds a supple and silky structure which is developing with good density. It should be kept for three to five years to let the oak become better integrated. This also applies to the **Château de la Huste 2000 (11–15 €)** which also wins one star.
➥ Michel Rullier, SCEA Ch. Dalem, 1, Dalem, 33141 Saillans, tel. 05.57.84.34.18, fax 05.57.74.39.85, e-mail château-dalem@wanadoo.fr ☑
☈ by appt.

CH. L'ESCARDERIE

Elevé en fût de chêne 2000★

| ■ | 2.5 ha | 8,600 | ◫ | 11–15 € |

This wine is a blend of Merlot (65%) and 35% Cabernets grown on a silty clay-limestone terroir. It has an intense and brilliant garnet-red colour and a bouquet of leather, crystallized fruits and roasted and vanilla-flavoured oak. The tannins are supple and rich in the attack, then develop with finesse and charm. This is a real characteristic Fronsac, to be drunk after laying down for two to five years with a roast guinea-fowl.
➥ Patrice de Taffin, Ch. L'Escarderie, 33240 Saint-Germain-la-Rivière, tel. 05.57.84.35.25, fax 05.57.84.35.25, e-mail lescarderiedt@wanadoo.fr ☑
☈ by appt.

CH. FONTENIL 2000★

| ■ | 10 ha | 45,000 | ◫ | 23–30 € |

|88| |89| (90) 92 |93| 94 **95** 96 |97| 98 **99** 00

This château has belonged since 1985 to Dany and Michel Rolland, oenologists of international renown. It stands on an excellent Saillans terroir and naturally benefits from all the latest technological advances. Here they use micro-oxygenation. The 2000 wine has a deep-garnet colour with dark-purple highlights and heady perfumes of ripe fruits and toasted vanilla. Its silky and powerful structure means it should be kept for two to three years.
➥ Michel et Dany Rolland, Catusseau, 33500 Pomerol, tel. 05.57.51.23.05, fax 05.57.51.66.08 ☑

CH. LA GRAVE 2000★

| ■ | 3.7 ha | 20,000 | ◫ | 8–11 € |

This estate has been farmed biodynamically since 1990, and since then has become a research leader in this area. This crimson-coloured wine is quite delightful. Its perfumes of stewed fruits, spices and tobacco herald a mouth-filling tannic structure. This wine will be perfectly balanced in two to five years; drinking it should be a real pleasure.
➥ Paul et Pascale Barre, La Grave, 33126 Fronsac, tel. 05.57.51.31.11, fax 05.57.25.08.61, e-mail p.p.barre@wanadoo.fr ☑
☈ by appt.

CH. HAUCHAT 2000★

| ■ | 2.5 ha | 12,000 | ◫ | 5–8 € |

This 100% Merlot comes from a clay-limestone plateau. In 2003, the estate offered two wines from the 2000 vintage which each won one star. The Cuvée Classique releases notes of spicy ripe fruits with a harmonious touch of toast, and velvety and ripe tannins that are already charming. This wine is ready to drink now and for the next three years. The **Cuvée La Rose 2000 (11–15 €)** is much more oaky and powerful on the palate, so needs more time (at least four to eight years) to mature properly.
➥ Vignobles J.-B. Saby et Fils, Ch. Rozier, 33330 Saint-Laurent-des-Combes, tel. 05.57.24.73.03, fax 05.57.24.67.77, e-mail info@vignobles-saby.com ☑
☈ by appt.

HAUT-CARLES 2000★★★

| ■ | 8,4 ha | 23,500 | ◫ | 23–30 € |

GRAND VIN DE BORDEAUX

FRONSAC

HAUT-CARLES

2000

Mis en bouteille à la propriété
APPELLATION FRONSAC CONTRÔLÉE
G.F.A. Château de Carles, 33141 Saillans, Gironde, France - A. Chastenet, S. Droulers, gérants

The château de Carles has figured in the history of France for six centuries, and since the end of the 19th century has belonged to the Chastenet family, one of whom is the historian Jacques Chastenet, a member of the Académie Française. It is also one of the most famous vineyards in Fronsac, this wine having won many *coups de coeur*. It is made from plots of old vines, basically Merlot, and gets the best out of its magnificent terroir. Once again, it is superb: the intense colour is almost black. The powerful aromas of spices, liquorice and soft fruits combine well with oaky notes. It has very concentrated but elegant tannins. This is an exceptional wine that should be laid down for five to ten years. The **Cuvée Principale du Château de Carles 2000 (5–8 €)** is commended: it is almost ready to drink, and will help you wait for its big sister.
➥ SCEV Ch. de Carles, Ch. de Carles, 33141 Saillans, tel. 05.57.84.32.03, fax 05.57.84.31.91 ☑
☈ by appt.

CH. JEANDEMAN 2000★

| ■ | n.c. | n.c. | ▮ ⚭ | 8–11 € |

This estate of 30 ha is all in one piece, and stands at the edge of the appellation. It offers two wines from the same vintage which each win one star. The main wine has complex aromas with floral, mineral and spicy touches, and a full and forthcoming tannic structure which is growing in power. Keep this wine for two to three years. The **Chêneraie 2000 (8–11 €)** is the Cuvée Spéciale and was matured in barrel; it has intense oaky aromas and a very interesting complexity on the palate. It could be kept for longer, at least four to six years.
➥ M. Roy-Trocard, Ch. Jeandeman, 33126 Fronsac, tel. 05.57.74.30.52, fax 05.57.74.39.96 ☑
☈ by appt.

CH. MAGONDEAU BEAUSITE 2000★

| ■ | n.c. | 22,204 | ◫ | 8–11 € |

This wine was grown on a classic clay-limestone terroir with 85% Merlot and 15% Cabernets. It has a deep, clear colour and a pleasant bouquet, very ripe but still rather dominated by the oak, and powerful, well-balanced tannins. Drink this in two to five years. The **Cuvée Passion 2000 (15–23 €)** also wins one star; it is very oaky and powerful but not unbalanced, and will please lovers of rather virile wines.
➥ Ch. Magondeau, SCEV Vignobles Goujon et Fils, 1, le Port-de-Saillans, 33141 Saillans, tel. 05.57.84.32.02, fax 05.57.84.39.51, e-mail p.goujon@free.fr ☑
☈ ev. day 9am–12 noon 2pm–6pm

CH. MAYNE-VIEIL 2000★★

| ■ | 28 ha | 170,000 | ▮ ◫ ⚭ | 5–8 € |

This very large 45-ha estate stands on a silty clay soil, and and has produced a remarkable wine made solely from Merlot. It has a strong crimson colour and very fruity aromas with a toasty note. The tannins are round, expressive and elegant as they develop on the palate, with good fruity length. This is a wine of character to drink in three to six years. The **Cuvée Aliénor 2000 (8–11 €)** is more oaky; it wins one star and will gratify lovers of more modern wines, but its ageing potential is shorter.
➥ SCEA du Mayne-Vieil, 33133 Galgon, tel. 05.57.74.30.06, fax 05.57.84.39.33, e-mail maynevieil@aol.com ☑
☈ ev. day except Sat. Sun. 9am–12.30 2pm–6.30pm

CH. MOULIN HAUT-LAROQUE 2000★

| | 14 ha | 60,000 | 🔲 📖 ♦ | 15–23 € |

86 88 (89) |90| 91 95 |96| |97| 98 **99** 00

This château stands on a very steep hillside with a terroir of limestone with starfish. Its excellent 2000 has a crimson colour and a powerful and fine bouquet of ripe fruit (blackcurrant), spices and toasted bread. The suave and full-bodied tannins are very evident, so the wine needs to age for two to three years.

♦¬ Jean-Noël Hervé, Le Moulin, 33141 Saillans, tel. 05.57.84.32.07, fax 05.57.84.31.84, e-mail hervejnoel@aol.com ☑
ℐ by appt.

CH. PLAIN-POINT 2000★

| | 17 ha | 105,000 | 🔲 | 11–15 € |

This 16th century château is located at the highest point in the appellation, overlooking a magnificent vineyard of Merlot (75%) and Cabernets (25%). This wine has an intense dark-purple colour, revealing elegant and fruity perfumes which need to open out. Its tannic structure is full and balanced, and is developing length which will give it a good keeping potential of at least four to eight years.

♦ SA Ch. Plain-Point, 33126 Saint-Aignan, tel. 05.57.24.96.55, fax 05.57.24.91.64, e-mail chateau.plain-point@libertysurf.fr ☑
ℐ ev. day except Sat. Sun. 8am–12.30pm 2pm–6.30pm

CH. PUY GUILHEM 2000★★★

| | 8 ha | 50,000 | 🔲 📖 ♦ | 11–15 € |

This château, built in the Empire style in 1868, overlooks the vallée de l'Isle; it was bought in 1995 by the present owner who has spared no effort to restore its glory. The result is amazing: three stars for this 2000 vintage, which is extremely rare. In the glass it sparkles with a thousand fiery glints, and the powerful bouquet of very ripe soft fruit is marked by vanilla-flavoured and toasty notes. The structure on the palate is fleshy, rich and very mouth filling. The finish is very long and notably well bred, showing that it should be kept for five to ten years.

♦ GFA Ch. Puy Guilhem, 33141 Saillans, tel. 05.57.84.32.08, fax 05.57.74.36.45, e-mail puy.guilhem@infonie.fr ☑
ℐ by appt.

CH. DE LA RIVIERE 2000★★

| | 59 ha | 260,000 | 🔲 📖 ♦ | 11–15 € |

This estate is a flagship for the appellation. The view sweeps across the vallée de la Dordogne. After its last vintages had shown an increase in power, this one wins a unanimous *coup de cœur* from the Grand Jury. Its black colour has pretty dark-purple highlights, and the powerful and complex aromas recall very ripe soft fruits and roasted toast. The velvety and very evident tannins are well balanced as a result of good maturation, but still rather dominate the finish. This is a great wine which will be at its best in three to eight years. Serve it with game.

♦ SA Ch. de la Rivière, 33126 La Rivière, tel. 05.57.55.56.56, fax 05.57.24.94.39, e-mail info@chateau-de-la-riviere.com ☑
ℐ by appt.
♦¬ Jeanne Leprince

CH. LES ROCHES DE FERRAND

Elevé en fût de chêne 2000★

| | 4 ha | 23,000 | 🔲 📖 ♦ | 11–15 € |

Since 1986, Rémy Rousselot has run these vineyards, passed down through many generations. Two wines were selected in this AOC. This one is made from 85% Merlot, and has a deep-crimson colour and intense aromas of spices, leather and soft fruit. It has power and a silky balance which will enable it to be drunk in two to five years. From the same owner, the **Château Vray Houchat 2000 (8–11 €)** is commended for its harmony and elegant aromatic character. Drink it in the next three years.

♦¬ Rémy Rousselot, Ch. Les Roches de Ferrand, 33126 Saint-Aignan, tel. 05.57.24.95.16, fax 05.57.24.91.44, e-mail vignobles.remy.rousselot@wanadoo.fr ☑
ℐ by appt.

CH. TESSENDEY 2000★

| | 5,51 ha | 36,000 | 🔲 🔲 | 5–8 € |

This traditional property is continually seeking to get the best out of its terroir. This fine, well-bred 2000 is a good example. It has a brilliant crimson colour, and the well-advanced bouquet recalls soft fruits and toast. The tannins are full and round, making the palate balanced and harmonious. This is a wine of character to be drunk in two to five years.

♦¬ P. Bernard d'Arfeuille, Ch. Tessendey, 33141 Saillans, tel. 05.57.84.32.26, fax 05.57.84.33.84, e-mail p.b.darfeuille@wanadoo.fr ☑
ℐ by appt.

CH. LA VIEILLE CROIX

Cuvée DM 2000★★

| | 7 ha | 26,000 | 🔲 🔲 ♦ | 8–11 € |

This château has been run by eight generations of two daughters, and is regularly featured in the *Guide*. The 2000 wine is also successful, both in its intense and clean ruby colour and its remarkable aromas of soft fruit, toasted bread and vanilla with a pleasant touch of freshness. The tannins are rich and complex and grow in power, the oak is evident but integrated with plenty of elegance at the finish. Keep this wine for two to six years.

♦ SCEA de la Vieille Croix, La Croix, 33141 Saillans, tel. 05.57.74.30.50 ☑
ℐ ev. day except Sun. 9am–12 noon 2pm–7pm

CH. LA VIEILLE CURE 2000★

| | 17 ha | 80,000 | 🔲 | 15–23 € |

88 89 90 91 92 93 **94** |95| |96| |**97**| **98** |99| 00

This château offers a well-made 2000 wine with a bouquet rich in expressive notes of fruits and pepper, with roasted and vanilla-flavoured nuances. On the palate, a velvety attack is followed by a mature and balanced development. The finish is still very oaky; it will become better integrated after keeping for two to five years.

♦¬ SNC Ch. la Vieille Cure, 1, Coutreau, 33141 Saillans, tel. 05.57.84.32.05, fax 05.57.74.39.83, e-mail vieillecur@aol.com
ℐ by appt.

CH. VILLARS 2000★★

| | 20 ha | 101,000 | 🔲 | 11–15 € |

93 |94| **95** 96 98 99 **00**

Once again, this château has produced a remarkable vintage that demonstrates its great skills in both the vineyard and the winery. The dark-ruby colour is intense, matched by a bouquet of very ripe soft fruits, toast and spices. The palate is supple and round in the attack, revealing a fine, well-bred and balanced tannic structure. This is a characteristic Fronsac which needs two to five more years to mature fully.

♦¬ Jean-Claude Gaudrie, Villars, 33141 Saillans, tel. 05.57.84.32.17, fax 05.57.84.31.25, e-mail chateau.villars@wanadoo.fr ☑
ℐ by appt.

Wines selected but not starred

CH. ARNAUTON 2000

| | 19 ha | n.c. | ■ ❶ ♦ | 8–11 € |

☛ SC du Ch. Arnauton, rte de Saillans, 33126 Fronsac, tel. 05.57.55.06.00, fax 05.57.55.06.01, e-mail arnauton.chateau@free.fr ☑
🍷 ev. day except Sat. Sun. 8am–12 noon 2pm–6pm
☛ Hérail

CH. BOURDIEU LA VALADE 2000

| | 13 ha | 30,000 | ❶ | 8–11 € |

☛ Denis et Xavier Roux, Ch. Coustolle, 33126 Fronsac, tel. 05.57.51.31.25, fax 05.57.74.00.32 ☑
🍷 by appt.

CH. LA BRANDE 2000

| | 5 ha | 35,000 | ■ ❶ ♦ | 8–11 € |

☛ Vignoble Pierre Béraud, La Brande, 33141 Saillans, tel. 05.57.74.36.38, fax 05.57.74.38.46, e-mail labrande.saillans@wanadoo.fr ☑
🍷 ev. day 8.30am–12.30pm 2pm–7pm; Sat. Sun. and groups by appt.

CH. CANEVAULT 2000

| | 1.4 ha | 8,500 | ■ ♦ | 5–8 € |

☛ SCEA Jean-Pierre Chaudet, Canevau, 33240 Lugon, tel. 05.57.84.49.10, fax 05.57.84.42.07, e-mail scea-chaudet-j.p@wanadoo.fr ☑
🍷 ev. day except Sat. Sun. 9am–12 noon 1.30pm–5.30pm

CH. DE LA DAUPHINE 2000

| | 9 ha | 54,000 | ❶ | 11–15 € |

☛ Ets Jean-Pierre Moueix, 54, quai du Priourat, 33500 Libourne, tel. 05.57.55.05.80, fax 05.57.25.73.30

CH. LAROCHE-PIPEAU 2000

| | 3.5 ha | 23,000 | ❶ | 11–15 € |

☛ EARL Jocelyne et Jean Grima, Ch. Laroche-Pipeau, 33126 Fronsac, tel. 05.57.24.90.69, fax 05.57.24.90.61, e-mail jean.grima@wanadoo.fr ☑
🍷 by appt.

CH. RENARD MONDESIR 2000

| | 7 ha | 18,000 | ■ ❶ ♦ | 11–15 € |

|93| 94 |95| 96 |97| 98 |99| 00

☛ Xavier Chassagnoux, Renard, 33126 La Rivière, tel. 05.57.24.96.37, fax 05.57.24.90.18, e-mail chateau.renard.mondesir@wanadoo.fr ☑
🍷 by appt.

CH. LA ROUSSELLE 2000

| | 4.5 ha | 18,000 | ❶ | 11–15 € |

☛ Jacques et Viviane Davau, Ch. La Rousselle, 33126 La Rivière, tel. 05.57.24.96.73, fax 05.57.24.91.05 ☑
🍷 by appt.

CH. LES TONNELLES

Cuvée Prestige 2000

| | 2.7 ha | 16,000 | ❶ | 11–15 € |

☛ SCEA les Tonnelles, 90, av. Foch, BP 132, 33502 Libourne Cedex, tel. 05.57.51.07.83, fax 05.57.51.99.94, e-mail leymarie@ch-leymarie.com ☑
🍷 by appt.
☛ D. Leymarie

CH. TOUR DU MOULIN 2000

| | 7 ha | 15,000 | ■ ❶ ♦ | 8–11 € |

☛ SCEA Ch. Tour du Moulin, Le Moulin, 33141 Saillans, tel. 05.57.74.34.26, fax 05.57.74.34.26, e-mail chttourdumoulin@aol.com ☑
🍷 by appt.

CH. VIEUX MOULEYRE 2000

| | 2 ha | 6,400 | ❶ | 11–15 € |

☛ SCEA Anna et Jacques Favier, Ch. Vieux Mouleyre, 33126 Fronsac, tel. 06.80.58.42.10, fax 01.47.58.08.92, e-mail jacques-favier@vieux-mouleyre.com ☑
🍷 by appt.

Pomerol

Pomerol covers only about 800 ha. It is one of the smallest appellations in the Gironde and one of the least interesting from an architectural point of view.

The 19th-century fashion for building wine châteaux in an eclectic architectural style appears not to have impressed the Pomerolais, who were happier with their rural or bourgeois houses. All the same, the appellation does boast the Château de Sales, built in the 17th century, which is undoubtedly the model for many of the charterhouses in the Gironde, and the Château Beauregard, which is one of the most beautiful houses built in the 18th century. A copy was built by the Guggenheims on their Long Island estate in New York.

The simplicity of the architecture is in harmony with this AOC, whose originality is staunchly defended by each individual, and where each inhabitant has his or her own vision, while seeking to maintain the harmony and cohesion of the community. This may explain why the wine-producers have been more than reticent in defining the guidelines for classifying the Crus.

The quality and specific nature of the terroirs alone should justify official recognition of the merit of the wines in this appellation. As with all the great terroirs, Pomerol is the result of the action of a river, in this case the Isle, which began by breaking down the limestone substratum and strewing it with layers of stones that assisted further erosion. The result is a complicated muddle of gravel and smoothed stones which originated in the Massif Central. The soils are particularly complex and hard to identify separately. However, four general types can be identified: in the south, towards Libourne there is a sandy area; near Saint-Emilion gravel lies on sand or clay (the soil is similar to that found on the Plateau de Figeac); in the middle of the AOC the soil is gravel, sometimes on top of clay and sometimes underneath it (Pétrus); finally, in the northeast and northwest the gravel is finer and more sandy.

This variety of soils does not prevent Pomerol wines from having a basically common structure. They are very fragrant, round and supple with a real strength which allows them to keep for a long time although they can be drunk quite young. Their character means they go well with a range of different dishes and are just as good with sophisticated dishes as they are with simpler ones. In 2002, the appellation produced 27,300 hl.

CH. BEAUREGARD 2000★★

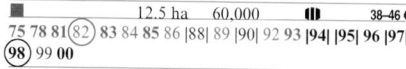

| | 12.5 ha | 60,000 | 🍾 | 38–46 € |

75 78 81(82) 83 84 85 86 |88| 89 |90| 92 93 |94| |95| 96 |97| (98) 99 00

MIS EN BOUTEILLE AU CHATEAU

Château Beauregard

POMEROL

APPELLATION POMEROL CONTRÔLÉE

2000

S.C.E.A. CHATEAU BEAUREGARD EXPLOITANT A POMEROL GIRONDE FRANCE

13% vol.   PRODUCE OF FRANCE   750 ml ℮

This is a very fine wine estate: a real 18th century Gironde charterhouse with a broad stone terrace surrounded by a moat. Such were its attractions, in the 1930s the Guggenheim family had a copy of it built on Long Island for their summer residence, which they called "Mille Fleurs." The original was bought in 1991 by the Foncier-Vignoble group, which has interests in the Bordelais and Bourgogne. Since then, the vineyard has produced many very high-quality wines such as this 2000 vintage. It has a deep colour, a bouquet of Virginia tobacco, blackcurrant, toast and violet in the finish. The flavours and the ripe tannins are intense, superbly made and very promising for the future. This wine's potential is enormous: it will last for many years and go well with a wide range of dishes. The second wine, **Le Benjamin de Beauregard 2000 (15–23 €)**, wins one star. Serve it with a magret de canard in two or three years.

☛ SCEA Ch. Beauregard, 33500 Pomerol,
tel. 05.57.51.13.36, fax 05.57.25.09.55,
e-mail pomerol@chateau-beauregard.com ▮
𝍅 by appt.

CH. BEAU SOLEIL 2000★

| ■ | 3.52 ha | 20,000 | 🍾 | 38–46 € |

This little 3.5-ha vineyard stands on fine sands and gravels and is planted with Merlot and 5% Cabernet Sauvignon. The 2000 wine was vinified and matured with care, and has a crimson colour with dark-purple highlights. The elegant and complex bouquet combines fruity and spicy aromas, good toasty oak and floral notes. The palate is charming, round and full-bodied with velvety and powerful tannins that are still firm at the finish. This wine needs laying down for a long time.

☛ Anne-Marie Audy-Arcaute, Ch. Jonqueyres,
33750 Saint-Germain-du-Puch, tel. 05.56.68.55.88,
fax 05.56.30.17.23 ▮

CH. BELLEGRAVE 2000★

| ■ | 7 ha | 45,000 | 🍾 | 23–30 € |

88 89 91 **92** 93 94 |95| |96| |**97**| **98** 99 00

This vineyard was bought in 1951 by the father of Jean-Marie Bouldy, who took over 30 years later. It offers a wine made from 75% Merlot. It has a lovely black colour with dark-purple highlights, and is already revealing its youthfulness and power. The intense and elegant bouquet combines soft fruits, notes of pepper and a floral touch. At first the palate is supple, round and full-bodied, developing rich and dense tannins, very long in the finish, which show that it will keep well.

☛ Jean-Marie Bouldy, Lieu-dit René, 33500 Pomerol,
tel. 05.57.51.20.47, fax 05.57.51.23.14 ▮
𝍅 by appt.

CH. LE BON PASTEUR 2000★★

| | 7 ha | 33,000 | 🍾 | +76 € |

78 79 81(82) 83 |85| |86| |88| |89| |90| |92| |93| 94(95)96|97| (98) **99 00**

This vineyard is a benchmark for Pomerol. It is one of the Libourne estates farmed by Michel and Dany Rolland, well-known Bordeaux oenologists. It is located at Maillet, in the east of the appellation, on a terroir combining clays, gravels and sands. The 2000 vintage is remarkably successful, and has a very intense crimson colour. Its powerful and complex bouquet releases aromas of stewed fruits, liquorice-flavoured oak, cachou and coffee. The flavour is dense, full-bodied, harmonious and perfectly balanced between the ripe grapes and the good-quality oak. This top-of-the-range wine could be served with the finest dishes.

☛ SCEA Fermière des domaines Rolland, Maillet,
33500 Pomerol, tel. 05.57.51.23.05, fax 05.57.51.66.08,
e-mail rolland.vignobles@wanadoo.fr ▮
𝍅 by appt.

CH. BOURGNEUF-VAYRON 2000★

| ■ | 9 ha | 40,000 | 🍾 | 30–38 € |

89 |90| 91 93 94 **95** |96| |97| 98 99 00

This family vineyard stands on a clay-gravel terroir and grows 90% Merlot. Xavier Vayron represents the fourth generation on the estate. This new 2000 vintage has a good intense colour. The bouquet is very expressive and long, combining fruit, oak, resin, menthol and roasted coffee. The palate is round, full-bodied, and balanced by the toasty oak. Serve this in two or three years with a terrine of young rabbit.

☛ Xavier Vayron, Ch. Bourgneuf-Vayron, 1, le Bourgneuf,
33500 Pomerol, tel. 05.57.51.42.03, fax 05.57.25.01.40 ▮
𝍅 by appt.

CH. CERTAN DE MAY DE CERTAN 2000★

| ■ | 5 ha | 24,000 | 🍾 | 46–76 € |

85 86 88 |89| (90)|94| |95| |96| |97| 98 99 00

We know that Scotland was often an ally of France. As a reward for services rendered, the May family was granted the stronghold of Certan in the 16th century, and planted vines on it. Today, the vineyard's 5 ha produce respected and elegant wines such as this 2000 vintage with its intense and dark garnet colour. The bouquet is rich and pleasant with aromas of ripe cherry, chocolate and liquorice, with a touch of cinnamon. The full-bodied palate is rich and silky, not very powerful but fine and delicate. This wine will be ready to be enjoyed from 2005.

☛ Mme Barreau-Badar, Ch. Certan de May de Certan,
33500 Pomerol, tel. 05.57.51.41.53, fax 05.57.51.88.51 ▮
𝍅 by appt.

CH. CLINET 2000★

| | 8.34 ha | 30,000 | 🍾 | 46–76 € |

It is a pleasure to return to this vineyard. In the 17th century, it was already called a château. It belonged to M. Georges Audy until 1985, then to GAN-Assurances until 1998, and is now owned by M. Jean-Louis Laborde. This 2000 wine has a lovely intense garnet colour, and notes of burning, toast and leather, with a good structure resting on solid and long tannins. This is a good wine for laying down (two to three years).

☛ Vignobles Georges Audy, 3, rue Fénelon,
33000 Bordeaux, tel. 05.56.79.12.12, fax 05.56.79.01.11,
e-mail contact@wines-uponatime.com
☛ J.-L. Laborde

CLOS DE LA VIEILLE EGLISE 2000★★

| | 1.5 ha | 9,000 | 🍾 | 30–38 € |

92 93 94 |95| |96| (98) 99 **00**

This little 1.5-ha vineyard belongs to Jean-Louis Trocard, a senior official in Bordeaux winemaking. It stands on clay gravels and is mainly planted with Merlot, with 10% Cabernet Franc. This has produced a remarkable 2000 wine with a superb, dark, deep and dense colour. The complex and elegant bouquet mingles aromas of very ripe soft fruits and a nice oak

with flavours of vanilla, spice and a slight toast. The full and powerful palate has well-bred, full-bodied tannins which are tasty and long. This wine has very good keeping potential.
🕭 Jean-Louis Trocard, Clos de la Vieille Eglise, BP 3, 33570 Artigues-de-Lussac, tel. 05.57.55.57.90,
fax 05.57.55.57.98, e-mail trocard@wanadoo.fr ☑
🍷 ev. day 8am–12 noon 2pm–5pm; Sat. Sun. by appt.

CLOS DU CLOCHER 2000★★

■	4.3 ha	18,900	⑪	38–46 €

82 83 85⟨86⟩|88| |89| |90| |93| |94| 95 |97| 98 99 00

This wine is a blend of 80% Merlot and 20% Cabernet Franc grown on clay-gravel soils. This has produced a remarkable 2000 vintage with a superb ruby colour. The bouquet is very rich: crystallized soft fruit and notes of burning and smoke. The forthcoming palate is full and winey, with magnificent long and elegant tannins. Serve this in five to eight years with game in sauce. The **Château Monregard La Croix 2000 (23–30 €)** wins one star.
🕭 SC Clos du Clocher, BP 79, 33500 Libourne, tel. 05.57.51.62.17, fax 05.57.51.28.28,
e-mail jeanbaptiste.audy@wanadoo.fr
🍷 by appt.

CLOS RENE 2000★

■	12 ha	65,000	⑪	23–30 €

86 88 |89| |90| 91 92 93 |95| |96| |97| 98 99 00

This lovely 12-ha property was already listed in 1764 under the name of "Reney" on the map drawn up by the geographical engineer Pierre de Belleyme. It has beloged to the family of Jean-Marie Garde for several generations. This 2000 wine incorporates 10% of Malbec (red Cot) alongside the traditional Merlot (70%) and Cabernet Franc (20%). It has a beautiful intense, deep ruby colour and reveals a distinguished bouquet rich in very ripe soft fruit, and a good toasty oak which is fine and elegant. The palate is supple, round and well balanced with silky, integrated tannins and long fruity flavours in the finish. Serve it in three to five years with a plump capon.
🕭 SCEA Garde-Lasserre, Clos René, 33500 Pomerol, tel. 05.57.51.10.41, fax 05.57.57.16.28 ☑
🍷 by appt.
🕭 J.-M. Garde

CH. LA COMMANDERIE DE MAZEYRES 2000★★

■	8.9 ha	16,000	⑪	38–46 €

This pretty vineyard was taken over in 2000 by Clément Fayat, and has changed its name; the Clos Mazeyres has been transformed into a Commanderie! The wine is mainly made from Merlot with 10% Cabernet Franc, and has a crimson colour with black highlights. The bouquet is rich and in full bloom, revealing crystallized soft fruits, spices and vanilla, with toasty notes and a touch of game. The winey and full-bodied palate is powerful and rich with tasty, harmonious tannins that are very long on the finish. In five to six years this 2000 should be ideal with a roast goose. The second wine, **Closerie Mazeyres 2000 (15–23 €)**, is commended. Keep it for two or three years.
🕭 Clément Fayat, SCEA Clos Mazeyres, Ch. La Dominique, 33330 Saint-Emilion, tel. 05.57.51.31.36, fax 05.57.51.63.04,
e-mail info@vignobles.fayat-group.com ☑
🍷 by appt.

CH. LA CONSEILLANTE 2000★★

■	12 ha	60,000	⑪	+76 €

82 85 88 |89| |90| 91 92 |93| |95| |96| |97| 98 99 00

In the 17th century, this vineyard belonged to Catherine Conseillan, after whom it is named. In 1871 it was bought by Louis Nicolas. Today his descendants keep up the tradition. The vineyard is an archetype for Pomerol: 80% Merlot and 20% Cabernet Franc grown on a clay-gravel terroir. This wine is also a classic for the appellation: very dark to look at, very deep in the bouquet (combining very ripe Merlot with toasted oak), and very forthcoming on the palate with a charming roundness supported by silky tannins. This wine has great sensual appeal. The skills revealed are admirable, as is the fact that it does not yield to fashion, but was made from the whole crop of the vineyard.
🕭 SC Héritiers Nicolas, Ch. La Conseillante, 33500 Pomerol, tel. 05.57.51.15.32, fax 05.57.51.42.39, e-mail chateau.la.conseillante@wanadoo.fr
🍷 by appt.

CH. LA CROIX 2000★

■	9.5 ha	50,600	⑪	38–46 €

86 |89| |90| 92 94 |95| ⟨96⟩|97| 98 00

In the 18th century, this vineyard belonged to Jean de Sèze, Louis XVI's lawyer, who took great care of his vines. This vintage has a pretty dark-garnet colour, and a bouquet which opens on fruits in brandy combined with an elegant oak on notes of vanilla, caramel and resin. The round and full-bodied palate is fairly tasty in the finish. This wine needs to be laid down for two to three years.
🕭 SC Ch. La Croix, 37, rue Pline-Parmentier, BP 192, 33506 Libourne Cedex, tel. 05.57.51.41.86, fax 05.57.51.53.16,
e-mail info@j-janoueix-bordeaux.com ☑
🍷 by appt.

CH. LA CROIX DE GAY 2000★★

■	10 ha	34,125	⑪	30–38 €

⟨85⟩86 88 89 91 92 |93| |95| |99| 00

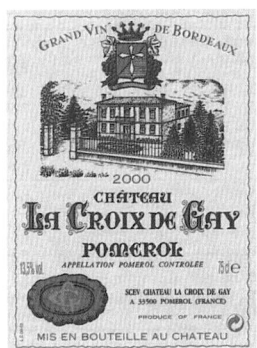

This estate has been handed down through the same family since the 15th century. Its clay and sandy gravels are planted with 90% Merlot. Chantal Lebreton has been in charge since 1998, and his great efforts have been rewarded by this very charming and distinguished wine with a magnificent classic Bordeaux colour. The mineral bouquet has scents of warm earth, caramel, cocoa and mocha which are matched on the vigorous, spicy palate, supported by powerful but elegant tannins which will enable it to age well and be served with a wide range of dishes.
🕭 SCEV Ch. La Croix de Gay, 33500 Pomerol, tel. 05.57.51.19.05, fax 05.57.51.81.81,
e-mail contact@chateau-lacroixdegay.com ☑
🍷 by appt.
🕭 C. Lebreton et A. Raynaud

CH. LA CROIX DU CASSE 2000★

■	9 ha	n.c.	⑪	46–76 €

|96| |97| |98| 00

This vineyard stands on ancient gravels and sands and is planted with 70% Merlot and 30% Cabernet. This very interesting wine was matured for 24 months in new barrels. Its garnet colour shimmers with dark highlights. Its fine and elegant bouquet reveals fresh and mentholated oak. The palate is pleasant and mouth-filling, and still fruity, finishing on very toasty oak tannins. Keep this wine for about three years.
🕭 GAM Audy-Ch. Jonqueyres, 33750 Saint-Germain-du-Puch, tel. 05.57.34.51.66, fax 05.56.30.11.45, e-mail info@gamaudy.com

CH. LA CROIX SAINT GEORGES 2000★★

■ 3.15 ha   12,600   ❙❙❙   46–76 €
(82) 83 85 86 |88| |89| 90 93 |96| 97 98 **99 00**

This 2000 wine was made from 95% Merlot with alcoholic fermentation in oak barrel, malolactic fermentation in barrel then maturation in barrel in a new winery which opened in 1999. After such prodigious efforts, the wine charmed the Jury with its very dense colour and black and crimson highlights. The bouquet is expressive, rich and delightful, releasing aromas of very ripe soft fruits and a vanilla-flavoured, toasty oak that is well bred and elegant. The palate is concentrated and full-bodied, combining power, vinosity and finesse, and a remarkable length in the finish. This is a very distinguished wine to be kept for five to six years before serving with a haunch of venison.
➤ SC Ch. La Croix, 37, rue Pline-Parmentier, BP 192, 33506 Libourne Cedex, tel. 05.57.51.41.86, fax 05.57.51.53.16, e-mail info@j-janoueix-bordeaux.com ▼
☓ by appt.

CH. LA CROIX-TOULIFAUT 2000★

■ 1.62 ha   8,600   ❙❙❙   46–76 €
85 86 88 89 90 93 94 |95|(96)|97| 99 00

The name of this Petit Cru from the Joseph Janoueix firm comes from the Romance language: "tot li falt" means "everything falls to it" or "everyone succumbs to it". The vineyard stands on sandy soils with a ferruginous base including large quantities of clinker which gives it a special character. This wine has a lively and brilliant cherry-red colour and a delicate bouquet with aromas of small soft fruits and floral notes of violet, harmoniously linked to an integrated oak. The palate is robust and solid, a little lively, well equipped for a good period in the cellar thanks to its firm and long tannins.
➤ Jean-François Janoueix, 37, rue Pline-Parmentier, BP 192, 33506 Libourne Cedex, tel. 05.57.51.41.86, fax 05.57.51.53.16, e-mail info@j-janoueix-bordeaux.com ▼
☓ by appt.

CH. ELISEE 2000★

■ 1 ha   6,000   ❚❙❙❘ ⬥   15–23 €
This Petit Cru of 1 ha, standing on sandy-gravel soils, has 10% of Cabernet Franc in addition to the Merlot. It was bought by the Garzaro family in 1987, who named it after a grandparent. This 2000 wine has an intense and dark ruby colour with dark-purple highlights and a charming bouquet revealing crystallized soft fruits and a toasty and vanilla-flavoured oak. The palate is full-bodied and velvety, developing on a tannic structure which is still firm in the finish. This is a good Pomerol to lay down, and the price is also reasonable.
➤ EARL Vignobles Garzaro, Ch. Le Prieur, 33750 Baron, tel. 05.56.30.16.16, fax 05.56.30.12.63, e-mail garzaro@vingarzaro.com ▣ ⬗
☓ by appt.

CH. L'EVANGILE 2000★★★

■ n.c.   31,000   ❙❙❙   +76 €
The Evangile is one of the most famous vineyards in Pomerol, and belongs to the prestigious collection of Grands Crus of the Rothschild estates. Tasting this vintage makes it clear why. There is a perfect classicism about its deep-red colour with dark-garnet highlights, and the aromas of roasting, vanilla and very ripe grapes are delightful. The attack on the palate is soft and charming, followed by a velvety structure formed on very fine tannins. It is both youthful and tasty with lovely crystallized notes, and finishes with the bravura of a wine that will keep for a long time. The second wine, the **Blason de l'Evangile 2000 (23–30 €)**, is also very elegant and wins one star.
➤ SC Ch. l'Evangile, 33500 Pomerol, tel. 01.53.89.78.00, fax 01.53.89.78.01

CH. FEYTIT-CLINET 2000★

■ 6.34 ha   25,000   ❙❙❙   30–38 €
This beautiful 7-ha estate was cultivated as a tenant farm by the Libourne firm of J.-P. Moueix until 2000, when the owners, the Chasseuil family, decided to run it directly. They offer a wine with a lively ruby colour. The bouquet combines soft fruits with vanilla and liquorice, and notes of tobacco. The palate is supple, round and full-bodied, balanced by rich tnnins with a long finish. It will go very well with a dish of small game.
➤ Jérémy Chasseuil, Ch. Feytit-Clinet, 33500 Pomerol, tel. 05.57.25.51.27, fax 05.57.25.93.97 ▼
☓ by appt.

CH. FRANC-MAILLET 2000★

■ 5.1 ha   32,000   ❙❙❙   15–23 €
Since Jean-Baptiste Arpin acquired his first plot of vines in 1919, on his return from the Great War, three generations have followed him at this vineyard, which now occupies 5 ha. The 2000 wine is made from 80% Merlot matured for 11 months in barrel. It has a deep-garnet colour, and a winey and complex bouquet combining aromas of soft fruit with a lovely toasted and smoked oak. The full-bodied rich palate reveals rich, ripe tannins in a fresh and spicy finish. The **Cuvée Jean-Baptiste 2000 (38–46 €)** of 3,600 bottles is a blend of 90% Merlot and Cabernet Franc, and was matured for 15 months in barrel. It is still a little marked by the oak and also wins one star.
➤ EARL Vignobles G. Arpin, Maillet, 33500 Pomerol, tel. 06.22.08.70.56, fax 05.57.51.96.75, e-mail vignobles.g.arpin@cario.fr ▼
☓ by appt.

CH. LE GAY 2000★

■ 6.1 ha   24,000   ❙❙❙   +76 €
This beautiful 6-ha estate, bought in 2002 by the SCEA des Vignobles Péré-Vergé, belongs to the Mesdemoiselles Robin. This 2000 has a very lovely dark and brilliant ruby colour. The bouquet calls to mind very ripe, even stewed soft fruits along with an attractive oak with vanilla flavours and notes of cocoa and liquorice. The palate is full-bodied and velvety, with a powerful and balanced tannic structure which has a long finish.
➤ SCEA Vignobles Péré-Vergé, Le Gay, 33500 Pomerol, tel. 05.57.51.87.92, fax 03.21.93.21.03

CH. GAZIN 2000★★

■ 24.24 ha   67,427   ❙❙❙   46–76 €
70 75 76 78 79 80 81 82 **83** 84 **85 86 87** |88| |89| (90) 91 92
93 |94|(95)(96)|97| **98 99 00**

This Pomerol vineyard always appears among the best of the AOC. This applies once again to the 2000 wine. It comes from a clay-gravel soil and is a blend of 85% Merlot, 12% Cabernet Sauvignon and 3% Cabernet Franc. This has produced a wine with a very dense Bordeaux colour with black highlights, a delicately intense bouquet featuring overripe grapes (prune) and a vanilla-flavoured oak. The palate is very pleasant, warm and round, and has a tannic chewiness which should ensure it keeps well. Drink it in three to five years from now with a wide range of dishes, such as hare, pigeon and venison.
➤ GFA Ch. Gazin, 33500 Pomerol, tel. 05.57.51.07.05, fax 05.57.51.69.96, e-mail contact@gazin.com ▼
☓ by appt.

CH. GRAND BEAUSEJOUR 2000★

	0.6 ha	4,000	⑪	38–46 €

98 99 00

This plot of old Merlot vines, located on the border with Saint Emilion, was bought by Daniel Mouty in 1998. The château stands beside the RN 89, away from the vines, and dates from the Louis XV period; it was restored in 2001; it can now receive visitors. This 2000 made from 100% Merlot has a lovely dark and deep ruby colour. The bouquet is suave and warm, dominated by a very elegant vanilla and toasty oak. The palate is concentrated and structured, but the oak is a little too evident at the moment. Wait several years for this wine's great potential to be fulfilled harmoniously.
➦ SCEA Daniel Mouty, Ch. du Barry, 33350 Sainte-Terre, tel. 05.57.84.55.88, fax 05.57.74.92.99, e-mail daniel.mouty@wanadoo.fr ☑
🍷 ev. day except Sun. 8am–12.30pm 2pm–6pm; cl. week of 15 Aug., 20 Dec.–5 Jan.

CH. GRAND MOULINET 2000★

	1.5 ha	10,000	⑪	15–23 €

94 |96| |97| 98 99 00

This small vineyard is a very steady performer. It contains 90% Merlot planted on gravelly sands, and has been part of the château Haut Surget, in Lalande de Pomerol, for five generations. The wine has a deep garnet colour. The bouquet is still closed but opens when the glass is swirled, revealing musky notes and a pleasant oak. The palate is full-bodied and concentrated, and finishes on tannins that are still a little firm and will need three to four years to soften. Serve it with red meats.
➦ GFA Ch. Haut-Surget, Chevrol, 33500 Néac, tel. 05.57.51.28.68, fax 05.57.51.91.79 ☑
🍷 ev. day 8am–12 noon 2pm–6pm; Sat. Sun. by appt.
➦ Fourreau

CH. GRANGE-NEUVE 2000★

	6 ha	39,000	⑪	15–23 €

This pure Merlot wine comes from old vines planted on clay-silicious soils between the Bordeaux-Lyon *route nationale* and the church of Pomerol. It has a lovely dark and intense garnet colour and, when the glass is swirled, reveals notes of fruits (cherry, blackcurrant and soft fruits) and a toasty oak. The palate is full and warm. The integrated oak combines well with the ripe grapes. The good consistency between the bouquet and the palate makes this seem a very pleasant wine.
➦ Gros et Fils, SCE Ch. Grange-Neuve, 33500 Pomerol, tel. 05.57.51.23.03, fax 05.57.25.36.14
🍷 by appt.

CH. LA GRAVE A POMEROL TRIGANT DE BOISSET 2000★★

	8.68 ha	41,000	⑪	38–46 €

82 83 85 86 |88| |89| (90) 92 |94| |95| 98 99 00

This attractive vineyard of just over 8 ha is still relatively new (the vines are on average 15 years old). Merlot (89%) and Cabernet Franc (11%) grow on clay-gravel soils. This 2000 wine has a superb, dark, intense and deep garnet colour and a fine and complex bouquet combining ripe soft fruit, liquorice and leather. The full-bodied and powerful palate has a remarkable substance, both rich and balanced, which continues pleasantly in the finish on fruity and spicy flavours. This is a great wine for laying dowm; serve it in five to six years with red meat or game.
➦ Ets Jean-Pierre Moueix, 54, quai du Priourat, 33500 Libourne, tel. 05.57.55.05.80, fax 05.57.25.73.30

CH. LAFLEUR 2000★★

	3 ha	12,000	⑪	+76 €

|85| |86| |88| |89| |90| 92 (93) |94| |95| 96 |97| 98 99 00

Sylvie and Jacques Guinaudeau farmed here for their aunt, Marie Robin, since 1985. Now they have bought all the vineyard's plots after the latter died in 2001. Lafleur has a vineyard of 4.5 ha planted on variable soils combining sands, gravels and clay. This wine of character is a blend of Merlot

(60%) and Cabernet Franc (40%), and is likely to keep for a long while. Its colour is deep in the middle of the glass and lively on the surface. The rich and warm bouquet releases crystallized soft fruits, cinnamon and vanilla. The powerful, winey and full-bodied palate has a superb, firm and well-bred tannic structure which promises a long life for the wine. The second wine, **Pensées de Lafleur (46–76 €)**, wins one star.
➦ Sylvie et Jacques Guinaudeau, Grand Village, 33240 Mouillac, tel. 05.57.84.44.03, fax 05.57.84.83.31

CH. LATOUR A POMEROL 2000★

	7.93 ha	45,200	⑪	38–46 €

61 64 66 67 70 71 75 (76) 80 81 82 83 85 86 87 |88| |89| |90| 92 (93) |94| 95 |96| 97 98 99 00

This vineyard is farmed by the négociants Jean-Pierre Moueix under the leadership of Jean-Claude Berrouet. It has 8 ha of vines planted on sandy-gravel soils covering a layer of clay. This vintage is a blend of 91% Merlot and 9% Cabernet Franc, and has a very dark and deep garnet colour. The concentrated bouquet is still a little closed, for now revealing only aromas of soft fruits and a good oak. The palate is powerful, rich and winey, with a superb, well-bred and elegant substance. This is a very nce wine which should open out in five to six years.
➦ Ets Jean-Pierre Moueix, 54, quai du Priourat, 33500 Libourne, tel. 05.57.51.78.96
➦ Lily Lacoste

CH. MAZEYRES 2000★

	21.12 ha	70,000	▌⑪ ♦	15–23 €

92 93 94 |95| |96| |97| 00

This is a large vineyard planted on clay-silicious soils. The main variety grown is Merlot with 90%. Great efforts have been made both on the production and selection sides to make this very fine 2000 wine. Its ruby colour is intense and youthful. The bouquet is original, offering notes of fresh fruits and toasty oak. It opens out on the palate on very ripe grapes and silky but very evident tannins, which will ensure it keeps well. In a few years, this wine will be perfect with a tournedos Rossini.
➦ SC Ch. Mazeyres, 56, av. Georges-Pompidou, 33500 Libourne, tel. 05.57.51.00.48, fax 05.57.25.22.56, e-mail mazeyres@wanadoo.fr ☑
🍷 by appt.

CH. MONTVIEL 2000★★

	3.5 ha	16,600	⑪	23–30 €

88 89 |90| 91 |93| 94 |95| |96| |97| 98 **99 00**

This vineyard was bought by the Péré-Vergé family in 1986, and for this remarkable wine they blended 80% Merlot and 20% Cabernet Franc. It has a sumptuous dark-ruby colour. The bouquet is very elegant, combining a roasted and toasty oak with aromas of stewed soft fruits and a slight spicy note. The palate is pleasant and full-bodied, supported by rich and velvety tannins which show good length in the finish. This is a superb wine, to be kept for at least five years in the cellar.
➦ SCEA Vignobles Péré-Vergé, Grand Moulinet, 33500 Pomerol, tel. 05.57.51.87.92, fax 03.21.93.21.03 ☑
🍷 by appt.

CH. MOULINET 2000★

	14.04 ha	80,000	⑪	23–30 €

93 94 95 96 98 99 00

Marie-José and Nathalie Moueix took over the running of this large vineyard after the death of Armand Moueix, a great personality in the worlds of wine-making and sport in the Libourne region. The charterhouse and the park are next to the Bordeaux-Paris railway line. The terroir is gravelly and silicious, and 80% of the vines are Merlot. This wine has an intense, still very youthful colour. The bouquet is closed, so the glass has to be swirled to release the fresh fruit, Virginia tobacco, vanilla and spices. The palate is structured by oaky tannins which are still rather prominent. This is a wine for laying down and should be kept for three or four years before serving with classic dishes.
➦ Nathalie et Marie-José Moueix, Ch. Fonplégade, 33330 Saint-Emilion, tel. 05.57.74.43.11, fax 05.57.74.44.67, e-mail domaines-armand-moueix@wanadoo.fr ☑
🍷 by appt.

CH. MOULINET-LASSERRE 2000★

■	5 ha	25,000	⑪	23–30 €

|89| |90| 91 92 93 94 |95| |96| |97| 98 99 00

This vineyard is connected with Clos René, its neighbour. This 2000 wine has a deep and dense cherry-red colour. The very open bouquet reveals aromas of very ripe soft fruits, spices and a toasty oak. The pleasant, robust and full-bodied palate has an excellent substance, both well bred and powerful, which entertains the taste buds for a long time with fruity, liquorice and toasty flavours. This is a lovely wine to drink in three to five years with a tournedos Rossini.

• SCEA Garde-Lasserre, Clos René, 33500 Pomerol, tel. 05.57.51.10.41, fax 05.57.57.16.28 ☑
Ⲻ by appt.
• J.-M. Garde

CH. LA PATACHE 2000★

■	3 ha	17,000	⑪	15–23 €

The name of this small vineyard and the company that runs it means the same thing: a horse-drawn coach which worked on the Bordeaux-Lyon route. Here we are just northeast of Libourne on a sandy-gravel soil planted with 70% Merlot and 30% Cabernet Franc. This 2000 wine is very successful. The crimson colour is dense and youthful. When the glass is swirled, the bouquet reveals a succession of aromas of violet, blackcurrant, laurel, toasty oak and a musky touch. The very warm palate indicates that the wine will mature very well. The tannins are still a little firm and should be left for two to three years. Serve this wine with a monkfish in wine sauce or grilled meats.

• SARL de la Diligence, La Patache, 33500 Pomerol, tel. 05.57.55.38.03, fax 05.57.55.38.01 ☑
Ⲻ by appt.

PETRUS 2000★★★

■	11.42 ha	34,500	⑪	+76 €

61 67 71 74 75 76 78 |79| |81| (82) |83| |85| |86| |87| (88) |89| 90 |92| |93| |94| (95) (96) |97| 98 99 00

It is stunning how regularly this wine manages to be exceptional. What more is there to say about this vineyard, which does not even have a château on its name, and which, when asked about their methods of production and vinification, always give this one answer: tradition, which means leaving the clay and the Merlot to express themselves. Saint Peter, who appears on the label, holds the key to the mystery firmly in his hand, but when we taste the wine we realize that it is also the key to paradise. We could fill pages with descriptive eulogies, like our expert tasters. It is tempting just to use their unanimous conclusion: MAGNIFICENT. But the reader would be frustrated, because this adjective applies to everything: the dark-garnet colour with black highlights, the elegant bouquet with its aromas of fruit, the remarkable oak, the sumptuous and silky tannins, and the flavour combining fruit, truffles, spices and oak. This wine is a perfect example of completeness.

• SC du Ch. Petrus, 33500 Pomerol

CH. PLINCE 2000★

■	8.66 ha	41,500	⑪	15–23 €

86 |89| |90| 91 92 |95| |96| |98| 00

This is an attractive family estate. The Gironde-style house is surrounded by a park of chestnut trees and a vineyard of 10 ha on a terroir of sand and iron slag. The 2000 wine has a lovely dark-garnet colour with an amber fringe and reveals an already intense, powerful bouquet which is dominated by notes of roasted oak (melba toast and mocha). The attack is clean and warm. The very evident oaky flavour finishes on fairly velvety tannins which will enable this wine to be enjoyed in two to three years with red meat, or later with white meat.

• SCEV Moreau, Ch. Plince, 33500 Libourne, tel. 05.57.51.68.77, fax 05.57.51.43.39, e-mail plince@tiscali.fr ☑
Ⲻ by appt.

CH. POMEAUX 2000★★

■	3.78 ha	11,000	⑪	38–46 €

|98| |99| 00

This little vineyard in the Toulifaut district was selected for the first time with its 98 wine. It is made solely from Merlot planted on ferruginous sands, and quickly acquires a rare distinction. The almost black colour glints with crimson and garnet highlights. The bouquet explodes with a series of aromas: violet, blackcurrant, vanilla, tobacco and toasty oak. The palate is full but elegant, the tannins powerful but without asperity. In a few years this 2000 wine will be ready to serve with tournedos Rossini in truffles and game. Nor should we forget the *coup de coeur* won by the 99 vintage.

• Ch. Pomeaux, 6, Lieu-dit Toulifaut, 33500 Pomerol, tel. 05.57.51.98.88, fax 05.57.51.88.99, e-mail info@pomeaux.com ☑
Ⲻ by appt.
• A.T. Powers

CH. PONT-CLOQUET 2000★

■	0.53 ha	3,600	🍾⑪	30–38 €

This limited-edition vineyard was bought in 1996 by Stéphanie Rousseau, and has produced a very successful wine thanks to its old Merlot vines growing on a gravelly soil. The colour is dark and deep, stll glinting with dark-purple highlights. The bouquet is intense and powerful, mingling aromas of ripe soft fruits and an elegant oak, with a touch of cinnamon. After a smooth attack, the palate develops on a lovely tannic structure which is rich and full-bodied and has a good, pleasant length in the finish.

• Stéphanie Rousseau, 1, Petit Sorillon, 33230 Abzac, tel. 05.57.49.06.10, fax 05.57.49.38.96, e-mail chateau@vignoblesrousseau.com ☑
Ⲻ by appt.

CH. PRIEURS DE LA COMMANDERIE 2000★

■	2.8 ha	16,000	⑪	23–30 €

86 88 |89| |90| 91 (93) 94 |96| 97 98 99 00

Since 1984, Clément Fayat, an entrepreneur in the Libourne region, has put together several plots of Pomerol to make this vineyard. This gives the wine its great complexity. The dark and dense colour combines Bordeaux-red and black highlights. The very intense bouquet opens on vanilla- and liquorice-flavoured oak and then, after the glass is swirled, releases crystallized fruit. The palate is full-bodied and structured by plenty of oaky tannins but the ripe grape is still very much there too. This is a great wine for keeping that will go well with white meat.

• Clément Fayat, Ch. Prieurs de La Commanderie, La Dominique, 33330 Saint-Emilion, tel. 05.57.51.31.36, fax 05.57.51.63.04, e-mail info@vignobles.fayat-group.com
Ⲻ by appt.

DOM. DU REMPART

Elevé en fût de chêne 2000★

■	1.98 ha	11,500	⑪	15–23 €

This small 2-ha vineyard has belonged to the Estager family since 1848. It stands on sandy-clay soils over a bed of iron

slag, and is planted with 85% Merlot and 15% Cabernet Franc. It has produced a very successful wine with an attractive, lively and brilliant ruby colour. The bouquet releases aromas of crystallized soft fruits, blackberry, blackcurrant and grape jelly. The palate is robust and full-bodied, winey and pulpy, with rich firm tannins which last well at the finish but need two or three years to soften.

Propriété P. Estager, 55, rue des Quatre-Frères-Robert, 33500 Libourne, tel. 05.57.51.06.97, fax 05.57.25.90.01 ☑
by appt.

CH. ROUGET 2000★

■	n.c.	n.c.	⑪	30–38 €

94 |95| |96| 97 98 **99** 00

This large estate was known for more than two centuries by its old name, "Rougier". Today it belongs to a family who come from the Beaujolais. This very successful 2000 wine has a dark-garnet colour and a still lively fringe. The bouquet is both intense and fine, revealing Morello cherry and toasty oak. The palate is already balanced, the aroma still resting on the warm oak. In two to three years this wine will be ready to enjoy with a hare à la royale.

SGVP Ch. Rouget, 33500 Pomerol, tel. 05.57.51.05.85, fax 05.57.55.22.45, e-mail chateau.rouget@wanadoo.fr ☑
by appt.
Labruyère

CH. SAINT-PIERRE 2000★

■	2.7 ha	14,000	⑪	11–15 €

This Petit Cru is produced close the church of Pomerol on clay-silicious gravels. The grapes are two-thirds Merlot and one-third Cabernets. The colour is both dark and youthful, heralding a still emerging bouquet which needs the glass to be swirled a little to release its perfumes of ripe fruits and roasted oak. The palate's elegant structure comes from a good combination of fruit and barrel. This wine will be ready fairly soon to drink with white meat. It will reach its best in five to six years.

SCEA de Lavaux, Ch. Martinet, 64 av. du Gal-de-Gaulle, 33500 Libourne, tel. 05.57.51.06.07, fax 05.57.51.59.61 ☑
by appt.

CH. TAILLEFER 2000★★

■	11.45 ha	60,000	⑪	30–38 €

This estate can be seen from the Libourne bypass. The vineyard surrounds a lovely slate-roofed château just after the Saint-Emilion exit. It has a sandy-gravel terroir planted with 75% Merlot and 25% Cabernet Franc. The dark-ruby colour of this 2000 wine shimmers with black glints. The charming and elegant bouquet offers notes of flowers, fruits, spices and oak. The palate is both smooth and robust. The flavour is still fruity, finishing on spicy tannins which will enable this wine to be enjoyed in a few years with a gigot d'agneau in mushrooms or a fatted chicken with truffles.

SC Bernard Moueix, Ch. Taillefer, BP 9, 33501 Libourne Cedex, tel. 05.57.25.50.45, fax 05.57.25.50.45

CH. TOUR MAILLET 2000★★

■	2.22 ha	12,000	⑪	15–23 €

The Lagardère family are at Montagne-Saint-Emilion, and cultivate this small vineyard on a sandy-gravel terroir. Here they offer a 100% Merlot wine. The colour is very dark, almost black. the extremely powerful bouquet is very fine, combining crystallized fruits and warm oak. The palate is concentrated and dense, but not aggressive, and has a great potential, with good power and length. This wine will be at its best in five to seven years.

Lagardère, Négrit, 33570 Montagne, tel. 05.57.74.61.63, fax 05.57.74.59.62 ☑
by appt.

CH. TROTANOY 2000★★

■	7.16 ha	35,400	⑪	+76 €

75 79 80(82) 85 86 87 |88| |89| (90) 92 94(95)(96) |97| **98 99 00**

Trotanoy belongs to the galaxy of wines vinified by Jean-Claude Berrouet for Christian Moueix. Its clay-gravel terroir is very troublesome to work but is very good for Merlot

vines, producing wines of character like this superb 2000 with a sumptuous, very dark-garmet colour. It only missed the *coup de coeur* by one vote. The elegant and complex perfumes combine aromas of stewed fruits, liquorice and spices, with a few notes of burning. The palate is pleasant and full-bodied, resting on lovely rich, velvety tannins which have very good length in the finish and fruity and spicy flavours. This is a great wine for laying down. It has class and vigour.

SC du Ch. Trotanoy, 33500 Pomerol

CH. DE VALOIS 2000★

■	7.66 ha	36,000	⫼ ⑪ ♦	15–23 €

This property has been in the same family since 1862. It is in the Figeac district on eolian sands, gravels and iron slag. More than three-quarters of the vineyard is planted with Merlot. This wine's colour is an engaging dark garnet with a vermilion fringe. The aromas of the bouquet are very intense, mingling soft fruits and spicy and toasty oak. The palate is both full and elegant, with a pleasant flavour of cherry, accompanied by silky and long tannins which will enable this wine to age for six to ten years before serving with grilled red meat and dishes in sauce.

EARL Vignobles Leydet, Ch. de Valois, Rouilledimat, 33500 Libourne, tel. 05.57.51.19.77, fax 05.57.51.00.62, e-mail frederic.leydet@wanadoo.fr ☑
by appt.

VIEUX CHATEAU CERTAN 2000★★

■	14 ha	n.c.	⑪	+76 €

81 82 83 85 86(88) |89| |90| 92 |93| |94| |95| 96 |97| (98) **99 00**

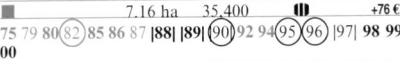

This estate has been known by its present name since 1745. It has an elegant charterhouse surrounded by hundred-year-old trees and 14 ha of vines all in one piece. It was bought in 1924 by the Thienpont family and is a great classic of the AOC as, once again, this remarkable vintage demonstrates. It has a dense and youthful crimson colour. The bouquet is already extremely complex with aromas of violet, truffles, mocha, vanilla and leather. The palate is full-bodied but elegant, with a lovely combination of very ripe grapes and fine oak. It lacks for nothing. Nothing overwhelms anything else. Its maturation was excellent, giving it perfect balance. The second wine, **La Gravette de Certan 2000**, is commended: it will be delicious with roast veal.

SC du Vieux Château Certan, 33500 Pomerol, tel. 05.57.17.33, fax 05.57.25.35.08, e-mail info@vieuxchateaucertan.com
by appt.
Thienpont

CH. VIEUX MAILLET 2000★

■	2.62 ha	12,000	⑪	30–38 €

95 |96| |97| 98 **99** |00|

This property was taken over in 1994 by Isabelle Motte, and since then has featured regularly in the *Guide*. The grapes are mostly Merlot with 20% of Cabernets. The soils are sandy clay or gravelly clay. This 2000 wine is very successful. It was matured in 70% new oak and has a lovely strong ruby colour. The bouquet recalls ripe fruits and crystallized prunes, combined with an attractive vanilla-flavoured oak. The palate is silky and full-bodied, revealing good balance with ripe, integrated tannins which are delightfully tasty in the finish. Drink this wine between 2005 and 2010.

🠒 Isabelle Motte, 8, rte de Maillet, 33500 Pomerol, tel. 05.57.51.04.67, fax 05.57.51.04.67, e-mail chateau.vieux.maillet@wanadoo.fr ☑
☿ by appt.

Wines selected but not starred

CH. LA BASSONNERIE 2000

■	3.07 ha	18,000	ⅅ	15–23 €

96 97 98 99 00

🠒 Dominique Leymarie et J.-P. Compin, SCEA La Bassonnerie, "René", 33500 Pomerol, tel. 06.09.73.12.78, fax 05.57.51.99.94, e-mail leymarie@ch-leymarie.com ☑
☿ by appt.

CH. LA CABANNE 2000

■	10 ha	50,000	ⅅ	30–38 €

🠒 Vignobles Jean-Pierre Estager, 33–41, rue de Montaudon, 33500 Libourne, tel. 05.57.51.04.09, fax 05.57.25.13.38, e-mail estager@estager.com ☑
☿ by appt.

CH. CLOS DE SALLES 2000

■	1.3 ha	6,900	ⅅ	30–38 €

🠒 EARL du Ch. Clos de Salles, Ch. du Pintey, 33500 Libourne, tel. 05.57.51.03.04, fax 05.57.51.03.04, e-mail merlet@club-internet.fr ☑
☿ by appt.

CLOS SAINT-ANDRE 2000

■	0.65 ha	3,500	ⅅ	23–30 €

🠒 SCEA Daniel Mouty, Ch. du Barry, 33350 Sainte-Terre, tel. 05.57.84.55.88, fax 05.57.74.92.99, e-mail daniel.mouty@wanadoo.fr ☑
☿ ev. day except Sun. 8am–12.30pm 2pm–6pm; cl. week of 15 Aug., 20 Dec.–5 Jan.

CH. DU DOMAINE DE L'EGLISE 2000

■	n.c.	29,000	ⅅ	30–38 €

🠒 Indivision Castéja-Preben-Hansen, 33500 Pomerol, tel. 05.56.00.00.70, fax 05.57.87.48.61
☿ by appt.

CH. L'ENCLOS 2000

■	9.45 ha	52,044	▮ⅅ⚬	30–38 €

|85| 86 |88| |89| |95| |96| 98 99 00

🠒 SCEA du Ch. L'Enclos, 20, rue du Grand-Moulinet, 33500 Pomerol, tel. 05.57.51.04.62, fax 05.57.51.43.15, e-mail chateaulenclos@wanadoo.fr ☑
☿ by appt.

DOM. LA GANNE 2000

■	n.c.	16,000	ⅅ	15–23 €

86 88 |90| 93 94 |96| 97 98 99 00

🠒 Michel Dubois, 224, av. Foch, 33500 Libourne, tel. 05.57.51.18.24, fax 05.57.51.62.20, e-mail laganne@aol.com ☑
☿ by appt.

CH. GOMBAUDE-GUILLOT 2000

■	8 ha	32,300	ⅅ	30–38 €

86 |89| |90| 91 93 |94| |95| |96| 98 99 00

🠒 SCEA Famille Laval, 4, chem. des Grands-Vignes, 33500 Pomerol, tel. 05.57.51.17.40, fax 05.57.51.16.89, e-mail chateaugombaude-guillot@wanadoo.fr ☑
☿ by appt.
🠒 Claire Laval

CH. GOUPRIE 2000

■	4.57 ha	12,020	ⅅ	15–23 €

🠒 SCEA Patrick et Sylvie Moze-Berthon, Bertin, 33570 Montagne, tel. 05.57.74.66.84, fax 05.57.74.58.70 ☑
☿ by appt.

CH. GUILLOT 2000

■	4.3 ha	26,000	ⅅ	23–30 €

82 83 85 86 88 |89| 93 94 |95| 96 97 98 99 00

🠒 SCEA Vignobles Luquot, 152, av. de l'Epinette, 33500 Libourne, tel. 05.57.51.18.95, fax 05.57.25.10.59 ☑
☿ by appt.

CH. LA POINTE 2000

■	22 ha	1,100,000	ⅅ	23–30 €

82 83 85 86 88 |89| |93| |94| |95| |96| |97| (98) 00

🠒 SCE Ch. La Pointe, 33500 Pomerol, tel. 05.57.51.02.11, fax 05.57.51.42.33, e-mail chateau.lapointe@wanadoo.fr ☑
☿ by appt.

CH. ROCHER-BONREGARD 2000

■	2.58 ha	16,000	▮ⅅ⚬	8–11 €

🠒 Jean-Pierre Tournier, Tailhas, 194, rte de Saint-Emilion, 33500 Libourne, tel. 05.57.51.36.49, fax 05.57.51.98.70 ☑
☿ by appt.

CH. LA ROSE FIGEAC 2000

■	3 ha	18,000	ⅅ	46–76 €

82 86 |88| |89| |90| 92 93 |94| |95| |96| |97| 98 00

🠒 Vignobles Despagne-Rapin, Maison Blanche, 33570 Montagne, tel. 05.57.74.62.18, fax 05.57.74.58.98 ☑
☿ by appt.

CH. DE SALES 2000

■	47.5 ha	130,000	▮ⅅ⚬	23–30 €

86 88 89 90 97 98 00

🠒 Bruno de Lambert, Ch. de Sales, 33500 Libourne, tel. 05.57.51.04.92, fax 05.57.25.23.91, e-mail chdesales@chateaudesales.fr ☑
☿ by appt.

CH. DU TAILHAS 2000

■	11 ha	60,000	▮ⅅ⚬	23–30 €

🠒 Nebout et Fils, SC Ch. du Tailhas, 33500 Pomerol, tel. 05.57.51.26.02, fax 05.57.25.17.70 ☑
☿ by appt.

CH. TOUR ROBERT 2000

■	1.2 ha	6,000	ⅅ	15–23 €

🠒 Dominique Leymarie, Ch. Tour Robert, BP 132, 33502 Libourne Cedex, tel. 06.09.73.12.78, fax 05.57.51.99.94, e-mail leymarie@ch-leymarie.com ☑
☿ by appt.

CH. VRAY CROIX DE GAY 2000

■ 3.7 ha 22,000 ⑪ 23–30 €

85 86 88 |89| |90| |93| |94| |95| |97| 98 99 00

☛ SCE Baronne Guichard, Ch. Siaurac, 33500 Néac,
tel. 05.57.51.64.58,
fax 05.57.51.41.56 ☑
Ⓨ by appt.
☛ Olivier Guichard

Lalande-de-Pomerol

The Hospitallers of the Knights of Saint John created this vineyard and its neighbour Pomerol; indeed, they also built the beautiful church in Lalande that dates from the 12th century. The vineyard covers about 1,120 ha, growing classic Bordeaux grape varieties to make well-coloured red wines, which are powerful and have a good bouquet. They enjoy a good reputation and the best wines can rival Pomerols and Saint-Emilions. In 2002, 47,251 hl were declared.

CH. BECHEREAU

Cuvée spéciale Elevé en fût de chêne 2000★

■ n.c. 22,000 ▤⑪♦ 8–11 €

This very successful Cuvée Spéciale is good and mouth-filling. Its strong garnet colour and aromas of soft fruits (raspberry), enhanced by elegant spicy nuances, are immediately delightful. The balanced tannins are very ripe, matching the well-dosed maturation in oak. The finish is full of finesse, indicating good keeping potential (at least three to six years).
☛ SCE Jean-Michel Bertrand, Béchereau, 33570 Les Artigues-de-Lussac, tel. 05.57.24.31.22, fax 05.57.24.34.69, e-mail contact@chateaubechereau.com ☑
Ⓨ by appt.

CH. BERTINEAU-SAINT-VINCENT 2000★

■ 5.6 ha 21,000 ⑪ 15–23 €

This vineyard belongs to the well-known oenologists Dany and Michel Rolland, and benefits from all the latest techniques for creating *grands vins*. This 2000 wine has a sumptuous colour and an intense bouquet of raspberry jam, cherry, coffee and vanilla. The rich tannins are still firm and the very oaky finish needs time to soften. Keep this wine for three to five years.
☛ SCEA Fermière des domaines Rolland, Maillet, 33500 Pomerol, tel. 05.57.51.23.05, fax 05.57.51.66.08, e-mail rolland.vignobles@wanadoo.fr ☑
Ⓨ by appt.

CH. BOIS DE LABORDE 2000★

■ 2 ha 13,000 ⑪ 11–15 €

This small traditional vineyard standing on good gravels offers a 2000 wine with a very attractive crimson colour and rich perfumes of violet, truffles, menthol and soft fruits. On the palate, the balance is excellent thanks to the ripe tannins, matured well in good oak. This wine will be a real pleasure to drink in three to five years. Try it with stuffed roast veal.
☛ Bruno Vedelago, Ch. Bois de Laborde, 33500 Lalande-de-Pomerol, tel. 06.07.13.95.49, fax 05.56.27.47.01 ☑
Ⓨ by appt.

CH. BOUQUET DE VIOLETTES 2000★★

■ n.c. 9,374 ⑪ 23–30 €

This vineyard grows a lot of Cabernets (50%), which is unusual for the region. Its 2000 is nonetheless remarkable, both in its deep ruby colour and its intense bouquet of black-cherry, liquorice and toasted bread. The velvety and winey tannic structure is also very good, developing with plenty of concentration towards perfect balance. This is an excellent wine to drink in eight years from now. From the same owner, the **Vieux Clos Chambrun 2000 (30–38 €)**, 100% Merlot, is commended. It will delight lovers of very concentrated, oaky wines.
☛ Jean-Jacques Chollet, La Chapelle, 50210 Camprond, tel. 02.33.45.19.61, fax 02.33.45.35.54 ☑
Ⓨ by appt.

CH. LES CHAGNASSES 2000★

■ 0.65 ha 4,400 ▤⑪♦ 8–11 €

This property is now run by Isabelle Fort, an oenologist, and has been making steady progress for several years. This 2000 wine has a strong, almost black, cherry colour and a powerful and spicy bouquet with well-integrated fruity and toasty nuances. On the palate, the tannins are rich, concentrated and perfectly ripe, and pleasantly full-bodied in the finish. This is a very well-made wine which needs to be kept for two to five years to come out fully.
☛ EARL Vignobles Carrère, 9, rte de Lyon, Lamarche, 33910 Saint-Denis-de-Pile, tel. 05.57.24.31.75, fax 05.57.24.30.17 ☑
Ⓨ by appt.
☛ Isabelle Fort

CLOS DES TEMPLIERS 2000★

■ 10 ha 60,000 ⑪♦ 8–11 €

This very well-bred 2000 wine with a deep-crimson colour contains only 35% Merlot as against 55% Cabernet Franc and 10% Cabernet Sauvignon. Its pleasant bouquet has aromas of spicy and roasted notes. Round, balanced and aromatic tannins accompany a long and very elegant palate. Drink this wine while it is fairly young, between 2005 and 2008.
☛ Vignobles Meyer, SCEA Ch. de Bourgueneuf, 7, chem. de la Cabanne, 33500 Pomerol, tel. 05.57.51.16.73, fax 05.57.25.16.89 ☑
Ⓨ ev. day except Sat. Sun. 8am–12 noon 2pm–6pm

CH. LA CROIX BELLEVUE 2000★

■ 4 ha 26,000 ⑪ 11–15 €

Here the blend consists of Merlot (50%) and equal shares of the two Cabernets, producing a 2000 wine with a deep colour and cherry highlights and a bouquet which is still restrained of sloe and blackcurrant combined with notes of integrated oak. The rich and balanced tannins are developing firmly; they will soften after the wine is laid down for three to five years. The Cuvée Spéciale **l'Ambroisie du Château la Croix des Moines 2000 (46–76 €)** also wins one star. It was made solely from Merlot, and is marked by an intense toasty oak that needs a long ageing period.
☛ SCEA Vignobles Jean-Louis Trocard, Ch. La Croix Bellevue, BP 3, 33570 Artigues-de-Lussac, tel. 05.57.55.57.90, fax 05.57.55.57.98, e-mail trocard@wanadoo.fr ☑
Ⓨ ev. day 8am–12 noon 2pm–5pm; Sat. Sun. by appt.

LA FLEUR DE BOUARD 2000★★

■ 13.5 ha 63,000 ⑪ 30–38 €

After winning a *coup de coeur* last year, this vineyard offers a remarkable 2000 wine made from early harvests begun under licence one week before the official time. After 20 months in oak and a blend dominated by Merlot (80%), the wine has a brilliant, almost black, crimson colour with deep-purple highlights. The bouquet is full of notes of spices, soft fruits and toasty and vanilla-flavoured oak. In the attack, the forthcoming and rich tannins develop with great aromatic finesse and a welcome firmness. The lovely finish promises that this will be a great wine to drink after five to ten years of ageing.
☛ Hubert de Boüard de Laforest, BP 7, 33500 Pomerol, tel. 05.57.25.25.13, fax 05.57.51.65.14, e-mail contact@lafleurdebouard.com ☑
Ⓨ by appt.

BORDEAUX

CH. GRAND ORMEAU

Cuvée Madeleine 2000★★

	2.5 ha	7,000		30–38 €

Currently at the top of its appellation, this vineyard belongs to Jean-Claude Beton, founder of the Orangina group. For 15 years now, he has done everything to modernize the wineries and get the best out of his excellent gravel terroir. This 2000 wine is quite simply sumptuous. Its colour is attractively deep, as is the intense bouquet of ripe fruits, liquorice and delicately toasted oak. The tasty, rich and very ripe tannins are perfectly coated as a result of their maturation. This is a high-class wine to drink in five to ten years. The **Cuvée Principale 2000 (15–23 €)** wins one star: it has an intense and harmonious fruity character and a rather more supple structure; you can drink it a little earlier than the other, in two to five years from now.

☞ Jean-Claude Beton, Ch. Grand Ormeau, 33500 Lalande-de-Pomerol, tel. 05.57.25.30.20, fax 05.57.25.22.80, e-mail grand.ormeau@wanadoo.fr ☑
☊ by appt.

CH. LA GRAVIERE 2000★★

	1 ha	4,800		15–23 €

Only 1 ha was given over to this wine belonging to M. Péré, owner of the châteaux Montviel and Le Gay in Pomerol. The technique and quality revealed in this 2000 wine are full of promise. The dark-garnet colour matches the pleasant, almost exotic perfumes of toast, liquorice and coffee. On the palate, the structure is powerful, fruity (blackberry and cherry) and very marked by a toasty oak which fortunately does not mask the wine. This is a charming, rather modern wine which should be drunk in three to ten years.
☞ SCEA Vignobles Péré-Vergé, Grand Moulinet, 33500 Pomerol, tel. 05.57.51.87.92, fax 03.21.93.21.03 ☑
☊ by appt.

CH. LE GRAVILLOT 2000★

	1.1 ha	7,000		11–15 €

This little vineyard is entirely planted with Merlot, and its wine was matured for 18 months in oak. It is very characteristic, revealing intense aromas of raspberry, vanilla and liquorice. In the attack, the tannins are elegant and then grow in power but are well balanced, indicating the wine's good ageing potential (at least three to eight years). Serve this with a lamprey à la bordelaise.
☞ SCEA J.-B. Brunot et Fils, 1, Jean-Melin, 33330 Saint-Emilion, tel. 05.57.55.09.99, fax 05.57.55.09.95, e-mail vignobles.brunot@wanadoo.fr ☑
☊ by appt.

CH. HAUT-CHAIGNEAU

Cuvée Prestige Elevé en fût de chêne 2000★★

	20 ha	80,000		15–23 €

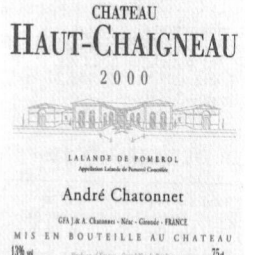

This château is regularly one of the leaders of the appellation. It benefits from the most modern techniques and knowledge, Pascal Chatonnet being one of the best-known oenologists in the Bordelais. This unanimous *coup de coeur* was won for a very dark-garnet colour, an intense bouquet in which black-cherry jam mingles with notes of smoke and vanilla. The tannins are full-bodied, powerful and warm up to the very elegant and long finish. This wine will keep for a long

time; drink it in five to ten years. From the same owner, the **Château La Sergue 2000 (23–30 €)** wins one star; this wine too is a benchmark for the appellation, and will appeal to lovers of very powerful and oaky wines.
☞ GFA J. et A. Chatonnet, Haut-Chaigneau, 33500 Néac, tel. 05.57.51.31.31, fax 05.57.25.08.93 ☑
☊ by appt.

CH. HAUT-CHATAIN

Cuvée Prestige 2000★

	1.8 ha	10,000		11–15 €

This wine deserves all the reader's attention. It was made from a selection of old vines of Merlot (90%) and Cabernet Sauvignon (10%) planted on a gravelly soil. The deep colour has brilliant garnet highlights; the perfumes of ripe fruits harmonize with the oaky nuances. On the palate, the tannins are full-bodied, rich and concentrated in the finish. This wine is very representative of the appellation; it should be drunk in two to five years with white meats.
☞ Vignobles Rivière-Junquas, Ch. Haut-Chatain, 33500 Néac, tel. 05.57.25.98.48, fax 05.57.25.95.45 ☑
☊ by appt.

CH. HAUT-GOUJON 2000★★

	8.5 ha	28,000		11–15 €

This château standing on a clay-gravel soil wins a unanimous *coup de coeur* for its authentic, well-bred 2000 wine. The crimson colour has brilliant blueish highlights. The elegant bouquet recalls ripe fruits, violet, camphor and toasted vanilla. On the palate, it is rich and full, developing fruity notes. It is well structured and has remarkable length. This is unquestionably a classy wine, to be drunk in five years, or even longer, with noisettes of venison or a chicken in foie gras The second wine, the **Château La Rose Saint-Vincent 2000 (8–11 €)**, is commended for the finesse of its fruit and harmonious structure; this can be drunk sooner.
☞ SCEA Garde et Fils, Goujon, 33570 Montagne, tel. 05.57.51.50.05, fax 05.57.25.33.93 ☑
☊ by appt.

CH. HAUT-SURGET 2000★

	17 ha	100,000		11–15 €

This property has been in the same family for five generations. It stands on a gravel and clay terroir suitable for making high-quality wines, such as this very good vintage. The strong garnet colour is delightful. The intense fruity perfumes (cherry) combine well with spicy (clove) and oaky notes. In the attack, the tasty tannins are supple, then develop towards a harmonious finish. Keep this wine for two to six years. From the same owner, the **Château Lafleur-Vauzelle 2000 (8–11 €)** is commended for its good typicity: it can be drunk soon.
☞ GFA Ch. Haut-Surget, Chevrol, 33500 Néac, tel. 05.57.51.28.68, fax 05.57.51.91.79 ☑
☊ ev. day 8am–12 noon 2pm–6pm; Sat. Sun. by appt.
☞ Fourreau

CH. JEAN DE GUE

Cuvée Prestige 2000★★

	6 ha	40,000		15–23 €

Jean-Claude Aubert has a vast number of vines in several AOCs. Here, he is concerned with Lalande and has made a very successful wine. The dark and shimmering ruby colour is at one with the complex perfumes of ripe soft fruit, roasting and vanilla. The tannic structure is full and forthcoming, and very harmonious despite a pronounced toasty oak. The long finish indicates a wine that will keep well (five to ten years) before serving with game or roasts.

📧 SCE Vignobles Aubert, Ch. La Couspaude, 33330 Saint-Emilion, tel. 05.57.40.15.76, fax 05.57.40.10.14, e-mail vignobles.aubert@wanadoo.fr

CH. LABORDE

Mil six cent vingt-huit 2000★

■	5 ha	19,000	◖◗	11–15 €

According to the date on the first document recording their presence, the family of Jean-Marie Trocard were established here by 1628. This Cuvée Spéciale is named after the family. It was matured in barrel and grown on a gravel soil planted with 90% Merlot. This is a very pleasing 2000 wine: it has a strong crimson colour with garnet highlights, and an emerging bouquet of humus, soft spices and vanilla. Its fine and balanced tannins are developing firmly and there is a very pleasant and long flavour of violet. It will be perfectly harmonious after laying down for three to six years.

📧 Jean-Marie Trocard, Ch. Laborde, 33500 Lalande-de-Pomerol, tel. 05.57.74.30.52, fax 05.57.74.39.96 ☑

🍷 by appt.

CH. MONCETS 2000★

■	18.6 ha	100,000	🍾◖◗♨	11–15 €

This lovely 19th century house has been in the same family for 130 years. It is surrounded by an attractive park and a vineyard planted on clayey sands. This dark-ruby wine releases aromas of crystallized cherry, violet and musk, and an oaky nuance. The intense and very concentrated palate is delightfully velvety. This is a well-made wine, to be drunk in two to five years.

📧 SCEA MM de Jerphanion, Moncets, 33500 Néac, tel. 05.57.51.19.33, fax 05.57.51.56.24, e-mail moncets@moncets.com ☑

🍷 by appt.

CH. PERRON

La Fleur 2000★

■	6 ha	70,000	◖◗	23–30 €

This Cuvée Spéciale made from 100% Merlot has an intense cherry-red colour, and pleasant aromas of notes of leather and soft fruits with a delicate oaky nuance. On the palate, the tannins are silky, full-bodied and rich. This wine has a satisfying length and will be ready to drink in two to three years.

📧 SCEA Vignobles Michel-Pierre Massonie, Ch. Perron, BP 88, 33503 Lalande-de-Pomerol Cedex, tel. 05.57.51.40.29, fax 05.57.51.13.37, e-mail b_massonie@libertysurf.fr

DOM. PONT DE GUESTRES

Elevé en fût de chêne 2000★

■	2 ha	12,000	🍾◖◗♨	15–23 €

This estate appears regularly in the *Guide*, and this year offers a selection of Merlot planted on sandy gravels. It has an intense crimson colour, and a bouquet of toasty oak which combines well with fruity nuances. The powerful tannic structure is a little lively at the moment, but the balance in the finish promises a good future for this wine in four to five years. The **Château au Pont de Guitres Elevé en Fût de Chêne (11–15 €)** is commended; it is fruity and round, and will be ready to drink in two to three years.

📧 Rémy Rousselot, Ch. Les Roches de Ferrand, 33126 Saint-Aignan, tel. 05.57.24.95.16, fax 05.57.24.91.44, e-mail vignobles.remy.rousselot@wanadoo.fr ☑

🍷 by appt.

CH. DES TOURELLES 2000★

■	4.44 ha	18,500	◖◗	11–15 €

This little vineyard has an interesting view of four of the bell-towers marking the AOCs of the Libournais. It is planted solely with Merlot on an excellent gravel soil. This wine has a ruby colour with garnet highlights, and a still restrained bouquet of blackcurrant, pepper and menthol. It is supple

and velvety, very ripe and tasty, and very well balanced. Drink this wine in three to five years with a nice entrecôte bordelaise.

📧 François Janoueix, Château Clos-du-Roy, 33570 Montagne, tel. 05.57.25.54.44, fax 05.57.25.26.07, e-mail phbb@janoueixfrancois.com ☑

🍷 by appt.

CH. TOURNEFEUILLE 2000★

■	10 ha	50,000	◖◗	15–23 €

A young pigeon in cream would be ideal for this wine from a lovely hillside terroir overlooking the Pomerol plateau. The owners here have made use of the most modern techniques in both the vineyard and the wineries to produce this very successful wine. Its powerful aromas mingle soft fruits and leather, both in the bouquet and on the palate where the general balance is perfect. Drink this wine in three to six years.

📧 Emeric Petit, 24, rue de l'Eglise, 33500 Néac, tel. 05.57.51.18.61, fax 05.57.51.00.04, e-mail fpetit@terre-net.fr ☑

🍷 by appt.

VIEUX CHATEAU GACHET 2000★★

■	4.8 ha	33,000	◖◗	11–15 €

The old vines of Merlot (70%) and Cabernets (30%), planted on a silicious-clay soil, are farmed here by sustainable agriculture. The oenological consultant Gilles Pauquet supervised the vinification of two of the AOC's three *coups de coeur*! The producer naturally also deserves credit. This 2000 wine has a very dark cherry colour and develops fragrances of raspberry, iris, leather and spices. The dense and full tannins grow in power and volume; they were carefully extracted and in five to ten years should produce a remarkable wine in every respect. Serve it with a good gigot d'agneau.

📧 EARL Vignobles G. Arpin, Maillet, 33500 Pomerol, tel. 06.22.08.70.56, fax 05.57.51.96.75, e-mail vignobles.g.arpin@cario.fr ☑

🍷 by appt.

Wines selected but not starred

CH. BELLES-GRAVES 2000

■	15.5 ha	80,000	◖◗	11–15 €

📧 GFA Theallet-Piton, SC du Ch. Belles-Graves, 33500 Néac, tel. 05.57.51.09.61, fax 05.57.51.01.41, e-mail x.piton@belles.graves.com ☑ 📧

🍷 ev. day 9am–6pm; Sat. Sun. by appt.

CH. CANON CHAIGNEAU 2000

■	5 ha	25,000	🍾◖◗♨	15–23 €

📧 SCEA Marin Audra, 3 bis, rue Porte-Brunet, 33330 Saint-Emilion, tel. 05.57.24.69.13, fax 05.57.24.69.11, e-mail suzanne.marin@wanadoo.fr ☑

🍷 by appt.

CLOS DES GALEVESSES 2000

■ 3 ha n.c. ⓘ ⑪ 11–15 €
⬥ SCEA de Lavaux, Ch. Martinet, 64 av. du
Gal-de-Gaulle, 33500 Libourne, tel. 05.57.51.06.07,
fax 05.57.51.59.61
Ⓨ by appt.

CH. LA CROIX 2000

■ 7 ha 45,000 ⑪ 11–15 €
⬥ SARL Roc de Boissac, 33570 Puisseguin,
tel. 05.57.74.61.22, fax 05.57.74.59.54 Ⓜ
Ⓨ by appt.

CH. LA CROIX SAINT ANDRE 2000

■ 16.2 ha 70,000 ⑪ 11–15 €
⬥ GFA Chabiran, 1, av. de la Mairie, 33500 Néac,
tel. 05.57.84.36.67, fax 05.57.74.32.58 Ⓜ
Ⓨ by appt.

CH. LES HAUTS-CONSEILLANTS 2000

■ 9 ha 47,200 ⑪ 15–23 €
⬥ SA Pierre Bourotte, 62, quai du Priourat,
33500 Libourne, tel. 05.57.51.62.17, fax 05.57.51.28.28,
e-mail jeanbaptiste.audy@wanadoo.fr
Ⓨ by appt.

CH. MOULIN A VENT 2000

■ 11.35 ha 82,000 ⑪ 8–11 €
⬥ SARL Moulin à Vent, 17, av. Julien-Ducourt,
33610 Cestas, tel. 05.57.26.26.66, fax 05.56.07.60.73
⬥ François M. Marret

CH. REAL-CAILLOU 2000

■ 4.3 ha 25,000 ⑪ 11–15 €
⬥ Lycée viticole de Libourne-Montagne, 7, le Grand
Barail, Goujon, 33570 Montagne, tel. 05.57.55.21.22,
fax 05.57.55.13.53,
e-mail expl.legta.libourne@educagri.fr Ⓜ
Ⓨ by appt.

CH. SERGANT 2000

■ n.c. 80,000 ⑪ 11–15 €
⬥ SEV Vignobles Jean Milhade, lieu-dit Peycher,
33133 Galgon, tel. 05.57.55.48.90, fax 05.57.84.31.27,
e-mail milhade@milhade.fr Ⓜ

CH. DE VIAUD 2000

■ 19.3 ha 66,400 ⑪ 15–23 €
⬥ SAS du Ch. de Viaud, 33500 Lalande-de-Pomerol,
tel. 05.57.51.17.86, fax 05.57.51.79.77,
e-mail sophie.lafargue@free.fr ▤
Ⓨ by appt.

CH. VIEUX CARDINAL LAFAURIE 2000

■ n.c. 27,800 ⑪ 8–11 €
⬥ Cheval-Quancard, La Mouline, 4 rue du Carbouney, BP
36, 33560 Carbon-Blanc, tel. 05.57.77.88.88,
fax 05.57.77.88.99,
e-mail chevalquancard@chevalquancard.com
Ⓨ by appt.
⬥ SCE de Bertineau

CH. VIEUX CHEVROL 2000

■ 21 ha 120,000 ⑪ 11–15 €
⬥ Jean-Pierre Champseix, Vieux Chevrol, 33500 Néac,
tel. 05.57.51.09.80, fax 05.57.51.31.05 Ⓜ
Ⓨ by appt.

CH. VIEUX RIVIERE 2000

■ 4.8 ha 30,000 ⑪ 8–11 €
⬥ SARL La Croix Taillefer, BP 4, 33500 Pomerol,
tel. 05.57.25.08.65, fax 05.57.25.08.65,
e-mail romain.riviere@voila.fr Ⓜ
Ⓨ by appt.
⬥ Marie-Claude Rivière

Saint-Emilion and Saint-Emilion Grand Cru

SAINT-EMILION

Covering the slopes of a hill that looks down on the valley of the Dordogne, Saint-Emilion (3,300 inhabitants) is a peaceful and charming little wine village. But it is also a place full of history. It was once a stopping point on the pilgrims' route to Santiago de Compostela, a fortified town in the Hundred Years' War and the refuge of the Girondin deputies who were proscribed by the Convention during the Revolution, and there are a good number of historic ruins to see. Local legend has it that the vineyard was originally planted by Roman legionaries. It is more likely that its beginnings, at least part of them, were in the 13th century. However that may be, Saint-Emilion today is the centre of one of the most famous vineyards in the world. It extends over nine communes and is planted on a rich range of soils. A number of classic growths come from the lime plateau and clay on the limey subsoil around the village. They make wines of good colour, which are well structured and full bodied. The vineyards bordering Pomerol have a more gravelly soil and produce wines noted for their great finesse (this region also produces many Grands Crus). But the majority of the Saint-Emilion appellation is on sandy alluvial soil, sloping down to the Dordogne, which produces very pleasant wines. With regard to the vine varieties, Merlot predominates but there is also Cabernet Franc, called "Bouchet" in the region, and, in much lesser quantities, Cabernet Sauvignon.

One of the things that differentiates Saint-Emilion is the classification of the wines. It was only established recently, in 1955, and it is regularly and systematically reviewed (the first revision took place in 1958 and the most recent in 1996). The Saint-Emilion appellation can be used by all the wines produced in the commune itself and in the eight other communes surrounding it. The second appellation, Saint-Emilion Grand Cru, does not correspond to a defined terroir, but to particular wines that must satisfy the most rigorous criteria of quality and that are selected by expert tastings. The wines must be submitted to a second tasting before they are bottled. The châteaux are selected from the Saint-Emilion Grands Crus and the wines are then classified. In 1986 74 were classified, of which 11 were Premiers Grands Crus. In the 1996 classification 68 were classified and 13 were Premiers Grands Crus. They divide into two groups: A for two of them (Ausone and Cheval Blanc) and B for the other eleven. It is worth pointing out that the Union des Producteurs de Saint-Emilion is without question the largest Cave Coopérative in France to be located in a top AOC. In 2002 Saint-Emilion produced 82,754 hl and Saint-Emilion Grand Cru produced 134,850 hl.

Lalande-de-Pomerol

The Hachette tastings were in two parts in the Appellation Saint-Emilion Grand Cru. One team tasted the Saint-Emilion Grands Crus Classés (without separating out the Premiers Crus), while a different team tasted the Saint-Emilion Grands Crus. The stars printed correspond to these two sets of criteria.

CH. L'ARCHANGE 2000★★

■ 1.21 ha 6,500 **�** 46–76 €

This limited-quantity wine, made solely from Merlot planted on silicious soils with a clay subsoil containing iron slag, was vinified in a wooden vat and matured in new barrels by the oenologist Pascal Chatonnet. The dark, deep and dense ruby colour, then the intense bouquet of soft fruits and *pain d'épice* prefigure the degree of concentration on the palate revealed by this lovely *vin de garde*. The attack is full bodied and rich, then the tannic structure rises in power, and the fruity, oaky finish is both long and harmonious. The price is above average.
🍷 GFA J. et A. Chatonnet, Haut-Chaigneau, 33500 Néac, tel. 05.57.51.31.31, fax 05.57.25.08.93 ✔
🍷 by appt.

CH. BARBEROUSSE 2000★

■ 6 ha 40,000 **III** 8–11 €

This family property stands on silicious gravel soils planted mainly with Merlot plus 10% Cabernets. It offers a lovely 2000 wine with a dark and deep ruby colour. The bouquet is fairly complex and at present dominated by oaky scents of toasted bread and vanilla- and liquorice-flavoured notes. The palate is pleasant and full bodied, with a good structure which will enable the wine to be kept while the oak softens a little. From the same producer, the **Château Montremblant 2000** wins one star.
🍷 GAEC Jean Puyol et Fils, Ch. Barberousse, 33330 Saint-Emilion, tel. 05.57.24.74.24, fax 05.57.24.62.77 ✔
🍷 by appt.

CH. BARRAIL-DESTIEU

Elevé en fût de chêne 2000★

■ 1.17 ha 6,000 **IIII** 8–11 €

Barrail-Destieu is a small vineyard bought in 1995 by a winemaker from the neighbouring appellation of Côtes de Castillon. It is planted on clay soils at the foot of a hillside with 75% Merlot and 25% Cabernet Franc. This 2000 wine has a dark and intense garnet colour, and a burnt bouquet with toasty and burnt notes mingling with spices and floral scents. The palate is pleasant and harmonious, providing a good balance and length in the finish. Keep this wine for three to four years, then enjoy it with a dish of small game.
🍷 Bernard et Gilles Verger, 4, chem. de Beauséjour, 33350 Saint-Magne-de-Castillon, tel. 05.57.40.13.14, fax 05.57.40.34.06 ✔
🍷 by appt.

CH. BELLECOMBE 2000★

■ 0.8 ha 4,000 **III** 5–8 €

Bellecombe comes from a mixture of sandy soils and iron slag. This wine contains 90% Merlot plus Cabernet Franc and has a dark, clear ruby colour. The bouquet is powerful and elegant, combining aromas of ripe soft fruit and oaky, spicy notes with nuances of game. The palate is full and structured and very mouth-filling, revealing good general balance and a long firm finish which will need laying down for a few years to mature properly.
🍷 Jean-Marc Carteyron, 43, rue de Vincennes, 33000 Bordeaux, tel. 06.82.84.84.63, fax 05.56.96.49.56 ✔
🍷 by appt.

CH. BEZINEAU 2000★

■ 0.8 ha 5,300 **III** 8–11 €

This micro-wine comes from a selection from less than 1 ha of vines out of the ten or so grown for more than six generations by the Faure family in Saint-Emilion. The vines are mostly Merlot, completed by 15% Cabernet Franc, and are planted on a sandy terroir with iron slag in the subsoil. The garnet colour has attractive crimson highlights, and the bouquet is very expressive: cocoa, spices and tobacco mingle with fruity aromas. The palate is robust, supple and round, with well-integrated tannins. This is a very charming wine that can be drunk throughout a meal.
🍷 SCEA Vignobles Faure, Ch. Bézineau, 33330 Saint-Emilion, tel. 05.57.24.72.50, fax 05.57.24.72.50 ✔
🍷 by appt.

CH. BOIS GROULEY 2000★

■ 6 ha 10,000 **IIII** 8–11 €

This property stands on sandy-gravel soils and devoted 6 ha to making this Saint-Emilion consisting of 70% Merlot, 20% Cabernet Franc and 10% Cabernet Sauvignon. The lively and intense ruby colour is a delight to look at. The bouquet is powerful and a little dominated by an attractive vanilla-flavoured and roasted oak, but is very charming. The palate is robust and vigorous supported by a firm structure that is rather austere at the moment but very promising.
🍷 SCEA Vignobles Lusseau, 276, Bois Grouley, 33330 Saint-Sulpice-de-Faleyrens, tel. 05.57.24.74.03, fax 05.57.74.46.09 ✔
🍷 by appt.

The Saint-Emilion Region

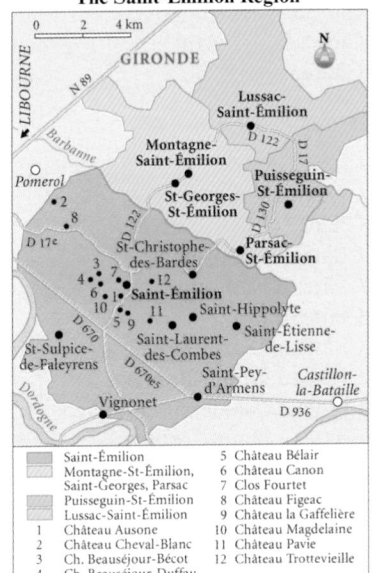

1996 CLASSIFICATION OF SAINT-EMILION GRANDS CRUS

SAINT-EMILION, PREMIERS GRANDS CRUS CLASSES

A   Château Ausone
     Château Cheval Blanc

Château Belair
Château Canon
Clos Fourtet
Château Figeac

B   Château Angelus
     Château Beau-Séjour (Bécot)
     Château Beauséjour
       (Duffau-Lagarrosse)

Château La Gaffelière
Château Magdelaine
Château Pavie
Château Trottevieille

SAINT-EMILION, GRANDS CRUS CLASSES

Château Balestard La Tonnelle
Château Bellevue
Château Bergat
Château Berliquet
Château Cadet-Bon
Château Cadet-Piolat
Château Canon-La Gaffelière
Château Cap de Mourlin
Château Chauvin
Clos des Jacobins
Clos de L'Oratoire
Clos Saint-Martin
Château Corbin
Château Corbin-Michotte
Couvent des Jacobins
Château Curé Bon La Madeleine
Château Dassault
Château Faurie de Souchard
Château Fonplégade
Château Fonroque
Château Franc-Mayne
Château Grand Mayne
Château Grand-Pontet
Château Guadet Saint-Julien
Château Haut-Corbin
Château Haut-Sarpe
Château La Clotte
Château La Clusière
Château La Couspaude

Château La Dominique
Château La Marzelle
Château Laniote
Château Larcis-Ducasse
Château Larmande
Château Laroque
Château Laroze
Château L'Arrosée
Château La Serre
Château La Tour du Pin-Figeac
   (Giraud-Belivier)
Château La Tour du Pin-Figeac
   (Moueix)
Château La Tour-Figeac
Château Le Prieuré
Château Les Grandes Murailles
Château Matras
Château Moulin du Cadet
Château Pavie-Decesse
Château Pavie-Macquin
Château Petit-Faurie-de-Soutard
Château Ripeau
Château Saint-Georges Côte
Pavie
Château Soutard
Château Tertre Daugay
Château Troplong-Mondot
Château Villemaurine
Château Yon-Figeac

CH. BRUN 2000★

■	n.c.	45,000	▮ ⑪ ⬦		8–11 €

The Brun family, who are descended from the famous Decazes family, gave their name to this vineyard which they have been farming for several centuries at Saint-Christophe-des-Bardes. This wine has a very pretty, lively and intense ruby colour, and a bouquet of stewed and crystallized fruits (cherry, black-currant and morello cherry). The powerful and full-bodied palate is structured on a lovely balanced tannic substance which is very winey. The finish is still firm and the wine needs to be kept for three to five years.

➼ SCEA du Ch. Brun, 33330 Saint-Christophe-des-Bardes, tel. 05.57.24.77.06, fax 05.57.24.78.19 ✅

CH. LES CABANNES 2000★

■	2 ha	10,000	▮ ⑪		11–15 €

This vineyard was bought in 1997 and is run by a Canadian oenologist who trained in Bordeaux. It now has 7 ha of vines. This Saint-Emilion is made from 80% young Merlot and 20% old Cabernet Franc vines planted on gravelly soils. This has produced a wine with a good colour, a lively shade of ruby, and a bouquet revealing pleasant aromas of small and fresh soft fruits. The palate is harmonious, supple, round and balanced, with a superb fruitiness and fine, restrained oaky notes. This is a wine to enjoy, ready to drink now or in three to four years.

➼ EARL Vignobles Kjellberg-Cuzange, Les Cabannes, 33330 Saint-Sulpice-de-Faleyrens, tel. 05.57.24.62.86, fax 05.57.24.66.08, e-mail kjellberg.cuzange@wanadoo.fr ✅
♈ by appt.

LE "D" DE DASSAULT 2000★

■	9.09 ha	47,700	⑪	15–23 €

This brand was launched in 1997, and is the second wine of the Château Dassault, a Saint-Emilion Grand Cru Classé. The youngest vines of the vineyard were employed: 75% Merlot and 25% Cabernet Franc planted on ancient sandy glacis. This has produced a 2000 wine with a lovely deep and intense garnet colour. The bouquet is elegant and expressive, mingling notes of soft fruits with an attractive toasty and vanilla-flavoured oak. The palate is robust, pleasant, round and full bodied with plenty of harmony and a long finish, which will enable it to be kept for a long time.

➼ SARL Ch. Dassault, 33330 Saint-Emilion, tel. 05.57.55.10.00, fax 05.57.55.10.01, e-mail lbv@chateaudassault.com
♈ by appt.

DOURTHE

La Grande Cuvée 2000★

■	n.c.	60,000	⑪	8–11 €

Beside the 350 ha farmed by this négociant, their branded wines have joined the great Bordeaux. This intense and clear, garnet-coloured wine was matured in new barrels and has a prominent and very attractive toasty oak. The palate is full and structured by good grape and oak tannins, and needs several years to mature.

➼ Dourthe, 35, rue de Bordeaux, 33290 Parempuyre, tel. 05.56.35.53.00, fax 05.56.35.53.29, e-mail contact@cvbg.com ✅
♈ by appt.

EPICURE

Elevé en fût de chêne français 2000★★

■	n.c.	9,000	⑪	8–11 €

This wine is offered by Bordeaux Vins Sélection, a brand created in 1996 by Hubert de Bouard and Bernard Pujol. It is made from Merlot grapes selected from clay-limestone terroirs and vinified and matured by the hand of the master. This 2000 wine has a magnificent dark and dense crimson colour and an elegant and complex bouquet mingling aromas of soft fruits and a well-developed, spicy and mentholated oak. The palate is full and tasty, resting on full-bodied, velvety tannins that have good length in the finish. This is a very successful wine at a reasonable price, and will go well with a pheasant or a salmi of woodpigeon.

➼ SARL Bordeaux Vins Sélection, 27, rue Roullet, 33800 Bordeaux, tel. 05.57.35.12.35, fax 05.57.35.12.36, e-mail bvs.grands.crus@wanadoo.fr
➼ B. Pujol

CH. LA FLEUR CHANTECAILLE 2000★

■	3.6 ha	26,000	▮ ⬦	5–8 €

This 3.6 ha vineyard has belonged to the family of Guy Arpin for four generations, and its wines are distributed exclusively by the Compagnie Médocaine des Grands Crus. It is planted with 70% Merlot and 30% Cabernet Franc growing on silty sandy soils. This wine has a bright ruby colour. The bouquet is very promising, mingling aromas of stewed fruits, pepper and vanilla. The palate is powerful and balanced; the tannins are still firm and need keeping for three to five years to soften.

➼ Vignobles G. Arpin, Chantecaille, 33500 Saint-Emilion, tel. 06.09.73.69.47, fax 05.57.51.96.75, e-mail vignobles.g.arpin@cario.fr
♈ by appt.

CH. LA FLEUR GUEYROSSE 2000★

■	n.c.	16,000	⑪	8–11 €

This Saint-Emilion is bottled by the Sichel company. It is grown on sandy-gravel soils and consists of two-thirds Merlot, a quarter Cabernet Franc and a touch of Cabernet Sauvignon. It has a dark and deep ruby colour and is developing a complex and elegant bouquet with aromas of fresh soft fruits and a subtle hint of oak. The robust, full-bodied and harmonious palate reveals a well-balanced structure that will enable it to keep well. This is a very characteristic wine.

➼ Maison Sichel, 8, rue de la Poste, 33210 Langon, tel. 05.56.63.50.52, fax 05.56.63.42.28, e-mail maison-sichel@sichel.fr

CH. GRAVIER-FIGEAC 2000★

■	5 ha	16,794	▮ ⑪ ⬦	3–5 €

Distributed by the négociants André Quancard-André, this wine comes from clay-limestone terroirs and consists of 85% Merlot and 15% Cabernet Franc. This very attractive 2000 wine has a strong ruby colour. The bouquet is intense and very pleasant with aromas of ripe and crystalized fruits (cherry, blackcurrant and prune) and a touch of liquorice. The palate is full bodied and pleasant with a good tannic structure. This wine can be kept for several years.

➼ André Quancard-André, chem. de La Cabeyre, 33240 Saint-André-de-Cubzac, tel. 05.57.33.42.53, fax 05.57.43.22.22, e-mail aqa@andrequancard.com
➼ Despagne

CH. HAUT GROS CAILLOU 2000★

■	4.93 ha	36,000	⑪	11–15 €

Located in the south of Saint-Emilion on clay-gravel soils, this estate grows 45% Cabernet and 55% Merlot. Here it offers a very successful 2000 wine with a very pretty, lively and brilliant ruby colour. The powerful bouquet reveals soft fruits that combine well with a good vanilla-flavoured, toasty oak. The round and full-bodied palate has a good balance between the grapes and the oak. This is a very powerful but charming and elegant wine, which should be a joy to drink in two to three years.

➼ SCEA Haut Gros Caillou, 33330 Saint-Sulpice-de-Faleyrens, tel. 05.56.62.66.16, fax 05.56.76.93.30 ✅
♈ by appt.
➼ Alain Thiénot

HAUT-RENAISSANCE 2000★

■	1 ha	6,700	⑪	8–11 €

Denis Barraud's small vineyard is a very steady performer. He cultivates old Merlot vines on clay-limestone soils. The wine benefits from maturation in barrel in a superb barrel store dating from the 17th century, located beside the Dordogne on the quais de Brame. This 2000 wine has a lovely ruby colour and pleasant oaky bouquet with fruity and spicy aromas. On the palate it is well balanced, rich and vinous, with a good tannic structure suitable for keeping. Drink this with meats and cheeses.

➼ SCEA des Vignobles Denis Barraud, Haut-Renaissance, 33330 Saint-Sulpice-de-Faleyrens, tel. 05.57.84.54.73, fax 05.57.84.52.07, e-mail denis-barraud@wanadoo.fr
♈ by appt.

CH. JUPILLE CARILLON

Cuvée sélectionnée Elevé en fût de chêne 2000★

| | 6.1 ha | 9,500 | 🍷 | 8–11 € |

An 18th century charterhouse overlooks these 6 ha of vines (85% Merlot, 15% Cabernet Franc), which are grown on brown sand and gravel soils. This Cuvée Sélectionnée is matured in oak for 12 months, which in 2000 has produced a very good wine with a strong, deep ruby colour and an intense bouquet of ripe soft fruit aromas combined with smoky oak and some slight hints of musk. The palate is balanced and well structured, which means that this wine will keep for three to six years.

➦ SCEA des Vignobles Visage, Jupille,
33330 Saint-Sulpice-de-Faleyrens, tel. 05.57.24.62.92,
fax 05.57.24.69.40,
e-mail vignobles.visage@wanadoo.fr 🅥
🍷 by appt
➦ Isabelle Visage

CH. PAILHAS 2000★

| | 12.2 ha | 14,400 | 🍷 | 8–11 € |

Located at Saint-Hippolyte, this family property is on sandy and sandy-clay soils, and grows 80% Merlot and 20% Cabernet Franc. This Saint-Emilion has been aged exclusively in tank, and has a beautifully fresh, intense colour and a nose of fresh soft fruit aromas. The palate is robust, supple and full bodied, and has a well-balanced structure and fruity flavours which are ready to be enjoyed straight away.

➦ SCEA Robin-Lafugie, Ch. Pailhas,
33330 Saint-Hippolyte, tel. 05.57.74.46.02,
fax 05.57.74.46.02, e-mail ch.pailhas@wanadoo.fr 🅥
🍷 by appt

CH. PAS DE L'ANE 2000★

| | 2.25 ha | 8,493 | 🍷 🍷 | 23–30 € |

Founded in 1999, this small vineyard grows 50% Merlot and 50% Cabernet Franc on the limestone-clay soils of Saint-Christophe-des-Bardes. This has produced a wine with a beautiful, dense, deep purple colour and a rich, complex bouquet of red and black berries, spices, liquorice and some lovely notes of toast. The powerful, well-structured palate has very good tannic concentration and a long finish. This is a classic wine with good ageing potential.

➦ SCE Pas de l'Ane, Jean Guillot,
33330 Saint-Christophe-des-Bardes, tel. 05.57.74.62.55,
fax 05.57.74.57.33 🅥
🍷 by appt

PAVILLON DU HAUT ROCHER 2000★

| | 2 ha | 12,185 | 🍷 🍷 | 8–11 € |

This brand was taken over in 1991 by Jean de Monteil, whose great-grandfather created it in 1874. It represents the second wine on this beautiful property, which has belonged to the family since the 17th century. The 2000 has a gleaming ruby colour, and an expressive bouquet of very ripe soft fruits, mingled with some spicy notes. On the palate it has a well-balanced structure and a delightfully long finish on flavours of fruit and liquorice. This is a good wine which should be kept for three or four years until it opens out more.

➦ Jean de Monteil, Ch. Haut-Rocher,
33330 Saint-Etienne-de-Lisse, tel. 05.57.40.18.09,
fax 05.57.40.08.23,
e-mail ht-rocher@vins-jean-de-monteil.com 🅥
🍷 by appt

CH. PEREY-GROULEY 2000★

| | 4.35 ha | 32,000 | 🍷 | 8–11 € |

The Xans family has been on this property since 1880, and now has more than 13 ha of vines. This wine is made from 80% Merlot, 10% Cabernet Franc and 10% Cabernet Sauvignon, and has a very dark, strong ruby colour and a full-bodied, warming palate. Its good tannic structure and very long finish will guarantee that it ages well.

➦ Vignobles Florence et Alain Xans, Ch. la Fleur-Perey,
33330 Saint-Sulpice-de-Faleyrens, tel. 06.80.72.84.87,
fax 05.50.24.63.61 🅥
🍷 by appt

CUVÉE ROSARIO 2000★

| | 1 ha | 6,500 | 🍷 🍷 | 15–23 € |

This wine comes from old vines (85% Merlot and 15% Cabernet Franc) grown on a gravelly soil, and makes an admirable first impression with its dark, dense ruby colour and purple glints. Its powerful, rich, highly concentrated bouquet is embellished by a lovely oak aroma. The palate is well balanced and harmonious, with mature, silky tannins which linger on to a long finish on flavours of fruit and spices.

➦ Michel Rosario Tabbacchiera, 13, Bourret,
33330 Saint-Pey-d'Armens, tel. 05.57.47.16.73,
fax 05.57.47.16.73 🅥
🍷 by appt

DOM. DU SEME 2000★★

| | 1.44 ha | 5,000 | 🍷 🍷 | 8–11 € |

Made exclusively from Merlot, this wine is produced with greatest care, as can be seen from this 2000 vintage. The colour is dark and deep with highlights which are still purple. The bouquet is already powerfully expressive, releasing ripe soft fruit aromas along with an elegant note of well-integrated oak. The very good structure on the palate is based on high-quality tannins and plenty of fullness. The finish is still firm, so this wine will need to be kept for a few years.

➦ SCEA du Moulin Blanc, Le Moulin Blanc,
33570 Lussac, tel. 05.57.74.50.27, fax 05.57.74.58.88,
e-mail lemoulinblanc@wanadoo.fr 🅥
🍷 by appt
➦ Brigitte Mérias

CH. TOINET-FOMBRAUGE 2000★

| | 5.4 ha | 6,000 | 🍷 | 8–11 € |

Located 2 km from the 11th century church in Parsac, this vineyard grows the appellation's classic mix of grape varieties and is offering a 2000 vintage with a dark, deep garnet colour and an intense bouquet of jammy soft fruit aromas and delightful oaky notes of grilling and toast. The palate is full bodied and fleshy, and has a good tannic structure which will enable the wine to keep for three to five years.

➦ Bernard Sierra, Toinet-Fombrauge,
33330 Saint-Christophe-des-Bardes, tel. 05.57.24.77.70,
fax 05.57.24.76.49 🅥 🏠
🍷 ev.day 10am–12 noon 3pm–7pm

CH. VIEUX CHANTECAILLE 2000★

| | 1.25 ha | 2,533 | 🍷 | 8–11 € |

This tiny vineyard has a sandy soil and grows 60% Merlot and 40% Cabernets. In the 2000 vintage it is offering a wine with a dark, strong garnet colour and a rich bouquet of soft fruit aromas combined with vanilla and other spices. The well-balanced, harmonious palate is delightfully mouth-filling and has a good tannic structure which will enable this wine to keep for at least three to five years.

➦ SCEA Patrick et Sylvie Moze-Berthon, Bertin,
33570 Montagne, tel. 05.57.74.66.84, fax 05.57.74.58.70 🅥
🍷 by appt

CH. LES VIEUX MAURINS

Cuvée Prestige Vieilli en fût de chêne 2000★★

| | 2 ha | 8,000 | 🍷 | 11–15 € |

Created in 1998 by Michel Goudal, this Cuvée Prestige is a selection of old Merlot matured in new oak for 15 months; it won a *coup de coeur* for the 1998 vintage. The 2000 has a sumptuously dark, dense Bordeaux colour, and a rich, powerful bouquet combining stewed red berry notes with a superb note of vanilla oak and slight hints of dried apricots and orange blossom. The palate is robust, full bodied and fleshy, with high-quality, velvety tannins which linger on to a long finish. "A great wine for longer maturing which will be a worthy accompaniment to a haunch of venison cooked with pears and bilberries," notes one gourmet taster.

➦ Michel et Jocelyne Goudal, 187, Les Maurins,
33330 Saint-Sulpice-de-Faleyrens, tel. 05.57.24.62.96,
fax 05.57.24.65.03,
e-mail les-vieux-maurins@wanadoo.fr 🅥
🍷 by appt

BORDEAUX

Wines selected but not starred

CH. BARADOL 2000
■ 2.13 ha 8,000 ▮ ⚬ 11–15 €
☛ Françoise de Wilde, Ch. Ripeau, 33330 Saint-Emilion, tel. 05.57.74.41.41, fax 05.57.74.41.57, e-mail chat.ripeau@wanadoo.fr ☑
☍ by appt

CASSINI 2000
■ 2 ha 10,000 ▮⦿⚬ 8–11 €
☛ Arnaud Daudier de Cassini, Lartigue, 33330 Saint-Emilion, tel. 05.57.24.73.83, fax 05.57.74.46.93, e-mail chcassini@aol.com ☑
☍ by appt

LA CLEF DE VOUTE 2000
■ 0.25 ha 1000 ▮⦿⚬ 5–8 €
☛ EARL Moreau, Ch. d'Arvouet, 33570 Montagne, tel. 05.57.74.56.60, fax 05.57.74.58.33, e-mail moreaulavoute@aol.com ☑
☍ by appt

CH. CLOS JEAN VOISIN 2000
■ 3.05 ha 12,000 ▮⦿⚬ 8–11 €
☛ Jacques Sautarel, Ch. Clos Jean Voisin, 33330 Saint-Emilion, tel. 05.57.24.67.10, fax 05.57.24.67.12, e-mail jacques-sautarel@wanadoo.fr ☑
☍ by appt

CLOS LE BREGNET 2000
■ n.c. 20,000 ▮ 8–11 €
☛ EARL vignobles Coureau, Le Brégnet, 33330 Saint-Sulpice-de-Faleyrens, tel. 05.57.24.76.43, fax 05.57.24.76.43, e-mail clos-le-bregnet@wanadoo.fr ☑
☍ ev.day except Sun. 8.30am–12 noon 1.30pm–6.30pm

CH. COTE PUYBLANQUET 2000
■ 6.5 ha 43,000 ▮ ⚬ 5–8 €
☛ Christian Bertoni, 11, Puyblanquet, 33330 Saint-Etienne-de-Lisse, tel. 05.57.40.18.35, fax 05.57.40.19.04 ☑
☍ by appt

CH. COTES DU GROS CAILLOU
Vieilli et élevé en fût de chêne 2000
■ 5.8 ha 11,500 ▮⦿ 5–8 €
☛ SCEA vignoble Tourenne, Gros-Caillou, 33330 Saint-Sulpice-de-Faleyrens, tel. 05.57.24.75.17, fax 05.57.24.76.50 ☑
☍ by appt

CH. DE LA COUR 2000
■ 4.7 ha 24,800 ▮⦿⚬ 8–11 €
☛ EARL du Châtel Delacour, Ch. de La Cour, 33330 Vignonet, tel. 05.57.84.64.95, fax 05.57.84.65.00 ☑ ⌂
☍ by appt

CH. FLEUR DE LISSE 2000
■ 7.55 ha 7,500 ▮⦿⚬ 8–11 €
☛ Xavier Minvielle, 1, Giraud, Ch. Fleur de Lisse, 33330 Saint-Etienne-de-Lisse, tel. 05.57.40.18.46, fax 05.57.40.35.74 ☑
☍ by appt

CH. LAGARDE BELLEVUE
Vieilli en fût de chêne 2000
■ 1.1 ha 8,400 ⦿ 8–11 €
☛ SARL SOVIFA, 36 A, rue de la Dordogne, 33330 Saint-Sulpice-de-Faleyrens, tel. 05.57.24.68.83, fax 05.57.24.63.12 ☑
☍ by appt
☛ Richard Bouvier

CH. LOUVIE 2000
■ 3 ha 8,000 ▮⦿⚬ 11–15 €
☛ Christian Veyry, Paupin, 33330 Saint-Laurent-des-Combes, tel. 06.07.28.53.80, fax 05.57.74.09.56, e-mail veyry@wanadoo.fr ☑
☍ by appt

CH. LE MAINE 2000
■ 1.16 ha 6,600 ▮ ⚬ 8–11 €
☛ Chantal Veyry-Seguillon, Ch. Maine-Reynaud, 33330 Saint-Pey-d'Armens, tel. 05.57.24.74.09, fax 05.57.24.64.81 ☑ ⌂
☍ by appt

CH. MONT BELAIR 2000
■ 11 ha 13,000 8–11 €
☛ Jean-Pierre Denamiel, 1, Bréat, 33330 Saint-Etienne-de-Lisse, tel. 05.57.40.14.09, fax 05.57.40.42.90 ☑
☍ by appt

CH. MOULIN DES GRAVES 2000
■ 3.7 ha 28,000 ▮⦿ 8–11 €
☛ EARL des Vignobles J.-CL. Musset, 20, d'Arthus, 33330 Vignonet, tel. 05.57.84.53.15, fax 05.57.84.53.15 ☑
☍ by appt

CH. PAGNAC 2000
■ 12.42 ha 86,008 ▮ ⚬ 11–15 €
☛ Union de producteurs de Saint-Emilion, Haut-Gravet, BP 27, 33330 Saint-Emilion, tel. 05.57.24.70.71, fax 05.57.24.65.18, e-mail contact@udpse.com
☍ ev.day except Sun. 8am–12 noon 2pm–6pm
☛ Jean Pagnac

CH. PETIT BOUQUEY 2000
■ 8.06 ha 45,200 ▮ ⚬ 11–15 €
☛ Union de producteurs de Saint-Emilion, Haut-Gravet, BP 27, 33330 Saint-Emilion, tel. 05.57.24.70.71, fax 05.57.24.65.18, e-mail contact@udpse.com
☍ ev.day except Sun. 8am–12 noon 2pm–6pm
☛ Eric Bordron

CH. LA POINTE CHANTECAILLE
Elevé en fût de chêne 2000
■ 1.2 ha 7,200 ⦿ 11–15 €
☛ Propriété P. Estager, 55, rue des Quatre-Frères-Robert, 33500 Libourne, tel. 05.57.51.06.97, fax 05.57.25.90.01 ☑
☍ by appt

DOM. DU SABLE 2000
■ 1.1 ha 6,000 ▮⦿ 5–8 €
☛ Joël Appollot, Troquart, 33570 Montagne, tel. 05.57.74.61.62, fax 05.57.74.61.33 ☑
☍ by appt

CH. LE SABLE 2000
■ 3.2 ha 16,000 ▮ ⚬ 8–11 €
☛ Cave de Larchevesque, 1, rue Guadet, 33330 Saint-Emilion, tel. 05.57.24.67.78, fax 05.57.24.71.31 ☑
☍ ev.day 10am–12.30pm 1.30pm–7pm
☛ Viaud

CH. SAINT-VALERY 2000

	2 ha	13,000	🍾	5–8 €

🍾 GFA Perey-Chevreuil, Ch. Saint-Valéry, 283, Perey, 33330 Saint-Sulpice-de-Faleyrens, tel. 05.57.74.41.14, fax 05.57.74.41.14, e-mail cl.moquet@wanadoo.fr ✓
🍷 ev.day 8am–12 noon 2pm–6pm; cl. 24 Dec.–3 Jan.

CH. DE SARPE 2000

	2.26 ha	15,000	🍷	15–23 €

🍾 Jean-François Janoueix, 37, rue Pline-Parmentier, BP 192, 33506 Libourne Cedex, tel. 05.57.51.41.86, fax 05.57.51.53.16,
e-mail info@j-janoueix-bordeaux.com ✓
🍷 by appt

CH. TARREYRE 2000

	3 ha	10,000	🍷	5–8 €

🍾 Jean-Paul Brissaud, Ch. Tarreyre, 33330 Saint-Emilion, tel. 05.57.24.74.30 ✓
🍷 by appt

CH. YON 2000

	4.05 ha	23,866	🍾 ♦	11–15 €

🍾 Union de producteurs de Saint-Emilion, Haut-Gravet, BP 27, 33330 Saint-Emilion, tel. 05.57.24.70.71, fax 05.57.24.65.18, e-mail contact@udpse.com
🍷 ev.day except Sun. 8am–12 noon 2pm–6pm
🍾 C. Quenouille

Saint-Emilion Grand Cru

CH. L'APOLLINE 2000★★

	2.8 ha	16,000	🍷	15–23 €

Previously known as Château Le Brégnet, this vineyard changed its name when it was bought by a new owner in 1996. It is located on the sandy-clay gravel soils in the south of the appellation, on the road leading to Branne. The 2000 has a superb Bordeaux colour with purple and ruby glints. When the wine is swirled in the glass, the developing bouquet releases an impressive succession of aromas: blackcurrants, blackberries, jammy fruits, chocolate, and oaky toast. The palate is both fine and powerful, with complex tannins (both grape and oak) which give the wine a very long finish and excellent ageing potential (six to ten years or more).
🍾 EARL Ch. L'Apolline, Le Brégnet, 33330 Saint-Sulpice-de-Faleyrens, tel. 05.57.51.26.80, fax 05.57.51.26.80, e-mail chateaul-apolline@wanadoo.fr ✓
🍷 by appt
🍾 P. et P. Genevey

CH. ARMENS 2000★★

	10 ha	40,000	🍷	23–30 €

Alexandre de Malet Roquefort has been running this vineyard since 1999, so this is the first time that he is presenting his own wine. The vineyard is at Saint-Pey-d'Armens, in the southeast of the appellation area. This wine is both modern and very full and round. It has an intense, complex bouquet of dark berry, jammy fruit, fine oak and toast aromas. The palate is well balanced, powerful and velvety, and the tannins and oak are well integrated. This Saint-Emilion Grand Cru will achieve its full expression between 2006 and 2013.
🍾 Alexandre de Malet Roquefort, Ch. Armens, BP 12, 33330 Saint-Emilion, tel. 05.57.56.40.80, fax 05.57.56.40.89, e-mail sales@malet-roquefort.com ✓
🍷 by appt

AURELIUS 2000★★

	20 ha	55,450	🍾 🍷 ♦	30–38 €

This branded wine is developed by the Union of Saint-Emilion Producers, and is made from 85% Merlot and 15% Cabernet Franc selected from various terroirs. It has been matured in oak for 15 months. The Jury was delighted from the start by its superbly dense, deep garnet colour. The vigorous, concentrated bouquet offers a harmonious combination of very ripe red and dark berry aromas and a highly thoroughbred note of oaky toast. The palate is full bodied, rich and substantial, with a long, supple finish.
🍾 Union de Producteurs de Saint-Emilion, Haut-Gravet, BP 27, 33330 Saint-Emilion, tel. 05.57.24.70.71, fax 05.57.24.65.18, e-mail contact@udpse.com ✓
🍷 ev.day except Sun. 8am–12 noon 2pm–6pm

CH. AUSONE 2000★★★

	1er gd cru clas. A	7 ha	22,000	🍷	+76 €

61 64 75 76 78 79 80 81 (82) 83 85 86 88 (89) |90| 92 93 |94| (96) (97)(98) (99)(00)

Ausone is a legendary Bordelais cru named after the Roman poet who lived in Saint-Emilion in the fourth century, and seems to have been created in the 14th century on vineyards that had existed since the vine arrived in Aquitaine. This wine is made from equal shares of Merlot and Cabernet Franc, and is matured in a very classic way. The 2000 fully lives up to its reputation by once again carrying off a *coup de coeur*. The colour gleams with ruby and Bordeaux highlights, while the bouquet seems very elegant despite its youth, because although the oak is evident it does not dominate the grape and the characteristic aromas of the terroir. The palate is dense, vigorous, well-balanced, and structured by fine tannins, with flavours of liquorice, cinnamon, and arabica coffee. This wine has an exceptional ageing potential of five to 15 years, and is a truly great example of the art of winemaking.
🍾 Catherine et Alain Vauthier, Ch. Ausone, 33330 Saint-Emilion, tel. 05.57.24.70.26, fax 05.57.74.47.39

CH. BADETTE 2000★

	7.63 ha	38,000	🍾 🍷 ♦	11–15 €

Dominique Leymarie has other vineyards in the Libournais in addition to this one, which is in the northeast of Saint-Emilion on a limestone-clay terroir with a relatively large number of Cabernet Franc vines (30%). This has produced a thoroughbred wine with an intense ruby colour and a spicy bouquet of liquorice, nutmeg and mint aromas. Although the palate is still somewhat dominated by oak, the flavour has an invigorating quality and is both supple and fresh. With the tannins still very much in evidence, this is a good wine for longer maturing.

➡ Dominique Leymarie, SCEA Ch. Badette, 33330 Saint-Christophe-des-Bardes, tel. 06.09.73.12.78, fax 05.57.51.99.94, e-mail leymarie@ch-leymarie.com ☑
🍷 by appt

CH. DU BARRY 2000★★

■	8 ha	45,000	🍾	15–23 €

89 |90| 93 **95** |**98**| |99| **00**

Daniel Mouty has six wine-estates in the Bordelais. This one was purchased in 1920 by his grandfather, Donat Mouty, who had come here from the Auvergne. Located on deep gravel soils in the south of the appellation, it has produced a remarkably good 2000 which exudes a sense of harmony from start to finish. It has a delightfully sumptuous, dark Bordeaux colour, and a nose of ripe grapes and other fruity aromas (prunes, blackcurrants), along with an elegant note of oak. In three to ten years this vintage will be the perfect accompaniment to guinea-fowl. The second wine here is the **Comte du Barry 2000 (11–15 €)** which wins one star. Its strong point is not so much its power as its finesse.

➡ SCEA Daniel Mouty, Ch. du Barry, 33350 Sainte-Terre, tel. 05.57.84.55.88, fax 05.57.74.92.99, e-mail daniel.mouty@wanadoo.fr ☑
🍷 ev.day except Sun. 8am–12.30pm 2pm–6pm; cl. week of 15 Aug. and 20 Dec.–5 Jan.

CH. BEAU-SEJOUR BECOT 2000★

■ 1er gd cru clas. B	16.52 ha	70,500	🍾	+76 €

75 78 79 81 **82** 83 85 (86) 87 |**88**| |**89**| |90| 91 |**92**| |93| |**94**| 95 96 |97| **98 99 00**

There are two Châteaux Beau Séjour (just as there are two called La Tour du Pin Figeac). This one is run by the Bécot family, who have worked hard in the last few decades and are now reaping the rewards – last year their 1999 won a *coup de coeur*. This year they are offering a 2000 which is still young and has a black-cherry colour. The intense bouquet is marked by warm oak, but has a pleasant background aroma of stewed fruits. As yet the palate is a little too rich with its tannins and flavours of oak, stewed fruits and cocoa. Once this wine has been kept for two to 12 years, it will become more refined and be a good accompaniment to a wide range of dishes.

➡ SCEA Beau-Séjour Bécot, 33330 Saint-Emilion, tel. 05.57.74.46.87, fax 05.57.24.66.88, e-mail contact@beausejour-becot.com
🍷 by appt
➡ G. et D. Bécot

CH. BELLEFONT-BELCIER 2000★

■	12.85 ha	42,000	🍾	23–30 €

|95| 96 |97| 98 99 00

This vineyard belongs to a group of investors, and is located in the east of the appellation on limestone-clay soils where the vines are two-thirds Merlot and one-third Cabernet Franc. The wine makes a pleasant, inviting first impression with a brilliant colour which has a few highlights to show that it is developing. It has a very intense nose of fresh fruit notes (strawberries) and oak aromas (vanilla, liquorice, chocolate) which although perhaps slightly dominant are very pleasant. The palate is warming, and has a ripe fruit flavour combined with toasty and peppery tannins. This is a modern type of wine, and needs to be kept for three to ten years.

➡ SCI Bellefont-Belcier, Belcier, 33330 Saint-Laurent-des-Combes, tel. 05.57.24.72.16, fax 05.57.74.45.06, e-mail bellefontbelcier@aol.com ☑
🍷 by appt

CH. BELLISLE MONDOTTE 2000★

■	4.5 ha	21,000	🍾	15–23 €

This vineyard to the east of Saint-Laurent-des-Combes has an excellent limestone-clay terroir in an ideal hillside and plateau location which regularly enables it to produce wines of very high quality. The 2000 has a deep colour which still contains youthful highlights, and delightful, warm aromas of summer fruits and vanilla oak. The palate is well balanced,

powerful but not heavy, and warming but not excessively so. The flavours are both oaky and fruity (ripe red berries). This elegant wine shows all the potential of this terroir and vintage, and will keep for three to eight years. The **Cuvée Prestige du Château Grand Pey Lescours 2000 (11–15 €)** receives a special mention.

➡ SCEA Héritiers Escure, 54, rue Jean-Jaurès, 33500 Libourne, tel. 05.57.74.41.17, fax 05.57.24.67.81 ☑
🍷 by appt

CH. BERLIQUET 2000★★

■ Gd cru clas.	8.52 ha	29,000	🍾	38–46 €

88 89 93 94 |95| |96| 97 **98 99 00**

After several years of good performances winning one or two stars, Château Berliquet now goes right to the top by winning a *coup de coeur*. This is yet another honour for a vineyard which was classified in 1986, and as early as 1768 was shown on the maps of Belleyme, the king's geographer. It is ideally situated on the La Magdeleine plateau, a few hundred metres south of the town. This 2000 has a sumptuous Bordeaux colour with shimmering black highlights, a very young bouquet of dark berry and oaky toast aromas, and a warming, powerful palate with a fine flavour of oak. The wine's structure is based on fresh tannins which will ensure that it develops well over a long ageing period. For maximum pleasure, serve in a carafe.

➡ Vicomte Patrick de Lesquen, Ch. Berliquet, 33330 Saint-Emilion, tel. 05.57.24.70.48, fax 05.57.24.70.24
🍷 by appt

CH. LA BIENFAISANCE 2000★

■	12 ha	60,000	🍾	11–15 €

This vineyard was created by regrouping a number of plots located on the limestone-clay plateau between Saint-Emilion and Saint-Christophe, in the northeast of the appellation. Although still somewhat marked by oak, this wine wins a star for its structure and good ageing potential. It has a fairly complex bouquet of ripe fruit and musk aromas combined with oaky vanilla and empyreumatic notes. The palate is elegant but tannic, and needs to become rounder over four to six years of ageing. The **Cuvée Sanctus 2000 (38–46 €)** wins one star. This very fashionable wine has been matured in oak for 20 months, but despite its oakiness, a flavour of very ripe grapes is already coming through which just needs time to become more expressive. It will be pleasant to drink in 2006, and for a long time after that.

➡ SA Ch. La Bienfaisance, 39, le Bourg, 33330 Saint-Christophe-des-Bardes, tel. 05.57.24.65.83, fax 05.57.24.78.26 ☑
🍷 by appt

CH. BOUTISSE 2000★★

■	23 ha	80,000	🍾	23–30 €

|97| 98 99 **00**

This property was purchased in 1996 by the Milhade family, who are based in the Libournais and own more than 200 ha of vines there. This 2000 has a dark, deep colour and a powerful bouquet in which oaky toast and vanilla notes combine harmoniously with vinous aromas of soft fruits and jammy dark berries. The palate is substantial and well structured, with a very rich body which will ensure excellent ageing

MIS EN BOUTEILLE AU CHATEAU

CHATEAU BOUTISSE

SAINT-EMILION GRAND CRU
Appellation Saint-Emilion Grand Cru Contrôlée

2000

potential. The judges were unanimous in awarding this wine a *coup de coeur*.
★ SCE des Domaines du Ch. Boutisse,
33330 Saint-Christophe-des-Bardes, tel. 05.57.55.48.90,
fax 05.57.84.31.27, e-mail milhade@milhade.fr ☑
⚑ by appt
★ Milhade

CH. LES CABANNES 2000★

| ■ | 1 ha | 4,800 | ⦿ | 15–23 € |

This small property is run by Peter Kjellberg, a Canadian oenologist who trained at the Oenological Institute in Bordeaux. For his Grand Cru wine, he selects 1 ha of old Merlot vines grown on deep gravelly soils. This vintage has a dense, young colour and a delightfully fine nose of dark berry aromas (blackberries) and high-quality oak, along with a touch of spices. The palate is full, rich and very supple, with more fruit flavours (greengages) and elegant, thoroughbred tannins on the finish.
★ EARL Vignobles Kjellberg-Cuzange, Les Cabannes,
33330 Saint-Sulpice-de-Faleyrens, tel. 05.57.24.62.86,
fax 05.57.24.66.08, e-mail kjellberg.cuzange@wanadoo.fr ☑
⚑ by appt

CH. CADET-BON 2000★

| ■ | Gd cru clas. 4.46 ha | 8,000 | ⦿ | 38–46 € |

|90| 93 |94| 95 |96||97| 98 99 00

Visitors will enjoy the view from the Butte de Cadet, north of the medieval town, and will also be charmed by the appearance of this wine, which already has a subtle bouquet of floral aromas along with copious dark berry notes, and a powerful palate based on elegant grape tannins. This is a well-made wine which should be excellent in five to six years' time.
★ SCEV Ch. Cadet-Bon, 1, Le Cadet,
33330 Saint-Emilion, tel. 05.57.74.43.20, fax 05.57.24.66.41,
e-mail chateau-cadet-bon@terre-net.fr ☑
⚑ by appt

CH. CANON 2000★★

| ■ | 1er gd cru clas. B | n.c. | 40,000 | ⦿ | 46–76 € |

|89| |90| 96 |97| 98 99 00

This is a Saint-Emilion Premier First Growth Classé, in other words a highly-coveted luxury product. Having been taken over by the Wertheimers, who already own Rauzan-Ségla in Margaux, Canon is now managed by John Kolasa, and with this vintage has achieved a superb level of quality. The vineyard was originally called the Saint-Martin estate, and is located next to the rampart of the medieval town. It is named after Lieutenant Kanon, who bought it in 1760 and really created the modern-day château with its buildings and magnificent vineyard planted over underground quarries and surrounded by rubble-stone walls. This is a highly appealing wine, with a dark colour and a bouquet of over-ripe grapes, fine oak, cedar and tobacco. The delicious palate is based on silky tannins and opens out like a peacock fanning its tail: very elegant indeed.
★ SC Ch. Canon, 33330 Saint-Emilion, tel. 05.57.55.23.45,
fax 05.57.24.68.00, e-mail contact@chateau-canon.com
⚑ by appt
★ Wertheimer

CH. CANON-LA-GAFFELIERE 2000★

| ■ | Gd cru clas. 19.5 ha | 65,000 | ⦿ | +76 € |

At the beginning of the 19th century this vineyard was called La Gaffelière Boitard after its owner, Boitard de La Poterie. It was purchased in 1953 by Pierre Meyrat, the mayor of Saint-Emilion, then in 1971 by the Comtes von Neipperg, who own several other vineyards in the region. This wine is still young, and has a dense, intense colour and a very rich bouquet of fruit and oak aromas along with a touch of musk. With its mouth-filling palate and velvety, well-balanced, vanilla tannins it is already pleasant to drink, but it can become even better if kept for four to five years.
★ SCEV des Comtes von Neipperg, Ch.
Canon-La-Gaffelière, BP 34, 33330 Saint-Emilion,
tel. 05.57.24.71.33, fax 05.57.24.67.95,
e-mail info@neipperg.com ☑
⚑ by appt

CH. CAP DE MOURLIN 2000★

| ■ | Gd cru clas. 13.81 ha | 49,000 | ⦿ | 23–30 € |

(82) 83 85 86 88 |89| |90| 92 93 |94| |96| 98 99 00

This is one of the emblematic vineyards of the appellation. It bears the name of the family which created it nearly five centuries ago, and which is still in evidence here today – very much so. Jean relaunched Saint-Emilion wines after the Second World War, and Jacques is First Magistrate. These are real local people, and their wine is also the genuine article: nothing pretentious, but full, round and satisfying. Its dark Bordeaux colour has shimmering black bigaroon highlights. The nose is still restrained, but is beginning to open out on to jammy fruit and prune aromas, along with a note of warm oak. The palate is very concentrated and structured, but also well-balanced. The tannins are still young, and will take two to three years to become more refined, after which they will enable the wine to keep for a long time (ten years or more).
★ SCEA Capdemourlin, Ch. Roudier, 33570 Montagne,
tel. 05.57.74.62.06, fax 05.57.74.59.34,
e-mail info@vignoblescapdemourlin.com ☑
⚑ by appt

CH. CARTEAU-MATRAS

Côte Daugay Cuvée Prestige 2000★

| ■ | 1 ha | 3,000 | ⦿ | 15–23 € |

This limited-production Cuvée Prestige is made from 75% Merlot and 25% Cabernet Franc. It makes a good first impression with a dark, deep garnet colour, and has a bouquet of red and dark berry aromas along with sweet spice and pleasant oaky toast notes. The palate is ample, full bodied and elegant, with a highly agreeable finish.
★ Jean-Marie Bion, Ch. Carteau-Matras,
33330 Saint-Emilion, tel. 05.57.74.49.78,
fax 05.57.74.45.97 ☑
⚑ by appt

CH. CHAMPION 2000★

| ■ | 6 ha | 30,600 | ⦿ | 11–15 € |

93 |95| |96| |98| 99 00

This property is 1 km north of Saint-Emilion, and is offering a particularly good 2000 with a shimmering, dark Bordeaux colour and a bouquet which is already intense and has a succession of soft fruit, liquorice, blackcurrant and brioche aromas, along with some musky and oaky notes. The palate is round, warming, and cloaked by silky tannins. A delightful bouquet, high-quality tannins…what more could you ask for? In two to four years' time this wine will be perfect.
★ SCEA Bourrigaud et Fils, Ch. Champion,
33330 Saint-Emilion, tel. 05.57.74.43.98, fax 05.57.74.43.98,
e-mail info@chateau-champion.com ☑
⚑ by appt

CH. CHANTE ALOUETTE 2000★

| ■ | 5 ha | 27,000 | ⦿ | 11–15 € |

This is a lovely little family vineyard where the grapes are vinified by the owner's son, Benoît d'Arfeuille. Although the terroir is mainly sandy, he has managed to produce a Saint-Emilion Grand Cru for longer maturing. It has an intense colour with ruby and purple highlights, and a fine, clean bouquet of soft fruit, dried fruit (almond) and oaky toast aromas, which develop on to notes of leather and mushrooms. The flavour on the palate gradually opens out, with the support of toasty tannins. This wine will be very good in two to five years' time.

➼ Guy d'Arfeuille, Ch. Chante Alouette, 33330 Saint-Emilion, tel. 05.57.24.71.81, fax 05.57.24.74.82, e-mail contact@chateau-chante-alouette.com ☑

� ev.day 9am–12 noon 2pm–7pm

DOM. CHANTE ALOUETTE CORMEIL
2000★

	8 ha	40,000	▢ ⊞ ♦	15–23 €

(82) 83 85 86 88 89 90 93 |95| 98 00

Yves Delol has two vineyards on the sandy soils of Saint-Emilion. This wine comes from the larger of the two, where he grows two-thirds Merlot and one-third Cabernets. It has a dark garnet colour with black highlights, and a nose which is already expressive and releases aromas of violets, prunes, cooked fruits, *pain d'épice* and leather, all of these against a subtle background of oak. After a supple, silky attack on the palate, the flavour is fruity and supported by intense, well-integrated tannins. This wine will be ready to drink in about four years from now.

➼ EARL Vignobles Yves Delol, Ch. Gueyrosse, 33500 Libourne, tel. 05.57.51.02.63, fax 05.57.51.93.39 ☑

� by appt

CH. LA CHAPELLE-LESCOURS 2000★

	3 ha	20,000	⊞	11–15 €

François Quentin studied oenology at Bordeaux University, and now represents the seventh generation of his family on this little vineyard, where vines are said to have been specially reserved by the De Lescours chaplains and also served to Henri IV. This 2000 has the typical features of a wine grown on gravel soil: a garnet colour, and a bouquet of ripe grape, port and roasted almond aromas. The palate also has a jammy flavour of ripe grapes, along with a touch of spices and an oaky note which does not dominate the fruit. In three to eight years' time this Saint-Emilion Grand Cru will go well with roast woodcock.

➼ CL. Quentin, Ch. La Chapelle-Lescours, 33330 Saint-Sulpice-de-Faleyrens, tel. 05.57.74.41.22, fax 05.57.24.65.37, e-mail f.quentin@free.fr ☑

� by appt

CH. CHAUVIN 2000★

	Gd cru clas. 13.5 ha	55,000	⊞	30–38 €

82 85 86 88 89 90 93 94 |96| |98| 99 00

This family-owned *cru classé* was purchased in 1891 by Victor Ondet, and is now run by his great-granddaughters, Béatrice and Marie-France. The vineyard is near Pomerol, and has a sand and gravel soil on iron dross. This has produced an excellent 2000; the colour is almost black with shimmering purple and garnet glints, and the bouquet is already intense, releasing dark berry, prune and coffee aromas and some empyreumatic notes. The palate has a concentrated, powerful flavour, along with an elegant note of liquorice. In three to seven years' time when the oak tannins are a little more subdued, this wine will go well with any sort of meat, either grilled or in a sauce, and with dry cheeses which are not too strong.

➼ SCEA Ch. Chauvin, BP 67, 33330 Saint-Emilion, tel. 05.57.24.76.25, fax 05.57.74.41.34, e-mail chateauchauvinge@aol.com ☑

� by appt
➼ Mmes Ondet et Février

CH. CHEVAL BLANC 2000★★

	1er gd cru clas. A	37 ha	n.c.	⊞	+76 €

61 64 66 69 70 71 72 73 74 |75| 76 77 78 79 80 |81| |82| |83| |85| |86| 87 88 89 (90) |92| |93| |94| 95 (96) |97| 98 99 00

This is one of the most famous vineyards in France, chosen by Vladimir Putin for a visit at the end of his official visit in 2003. He may have needed some respite from his cares as a world leader, but in any case he certainly proved that he is a connoisseur! This 2000 is still in its very early youth, but shows great promise with a magnificent dark Bordeaux and

black-cherry colour, an open bouquet of very ripe soft fruits and vanilla oak, and a delightful palate with delicate, balanced tannins, a youthful flavour, and a full finish. This is a wine of real elegance.

➼ SC du Cheval Blanc, 33330 Saint-Emilion, tel. 05.57.55.55.55, fax 05.57.55.55.50

� by appt

LE PETIT CHEVAL 2000★

	n.c.	n.c.	⊞	46–76 €

The second wine at Cheval Blanc has a lovely ruby colour and a developing bouquet which suggests Cabernet Franc with its delicate, thoroughbred notes of red berries and fine oak. The palate is also fruity, with a warming flavour supported by good-quality oak tannins. Once this wine has been kept for a while it will be a good accompaniment to woodcock flambéd in armagnac.

➼ SC du Cheval Blanc, 33330 Saint-Emilion, tel. 05.57.55.55.55, fax 05.57.55.55.50

� by appt

CH. CHEVALIER BLANC 2000★

	0.8 ha	4,300	⊞	11–15 €

The Bouvier family has been here since 1994, and reserves about 1 ha for the production of this wine which is made mainly from Merlot with just 10% Cabernet Franc, and is matured in oak for 14 months. This 2000 releases a vinous bouquet with an elegant combination of jammy fruit and oaky toast aromas. The palate is supple, round and full bodied to begin with, then opens out on to a tannic structure which is slightly firm on the finish, and needs a few years of ageing to become more subdued.

➼ SARL SOVIFA, 36 A, rue de la Dordogne, 33330 Saint-Sulpice-de-Faleyrens, tel. 05.57.24.68.83, fax 05.57.24.63.12 ☑

� by appt
➼ Richard Bouvier

CLOS DE L'ORATOIRE 2000★

	Gd cru clas. 10.32 ha	50,000	⊞	46–76 €

The von Neipperg family has several vineyards in Saint-Emilion and Côtes de Castillon, including this *cru classé* which they purchased in 1971. It is believed to be made up of the best plots at Château Peyreau, which were split up when Saint-Emilion was first classified. This vintage has a dark, intense, young colour and a nose which is not yet open and needs aeration to release the aromas of blackberries, bilberries and empyreumatic oak. The palate starts with plenty of roundness but then becomes very tannic, which means that the wine will need to be kept for two or three years.

➼ SC du Ch. Peyreau, BP 34, 33330 Saint-Emilion, tel. 05.57.24.71.33, fax 05.57.24.67.95, e-mail info@neipperg.com ☑

� by appt
➼ Comtes von Neipperg

CLOS DES JACOBINS 2000★

	Gd cru clas. 8.5 ha	20,000	⊞	23–30 €

The 2000 is the last vintage of this *cru classé* to be produced by the Cordier estates, who sold it to Gérald Frydman in January 2001. The terroir has a sandy clay soil, and the vines are 75% Merlot and 25% Cabernet Franc. This wine has a fresh purple colour fringed with crimson glints, and a developing bouquet of fruity aromas (blackcurrants, cherries), finishing on a note of tobacco. The palate is full bodied and vigorous, with ripe grape flavours accompanied by a subtle note of oaky liquorice and good-quality tannins. This is a good example both of the appellation and of the vintage.

➼ Gérald Frydman, SAS Clos des Jacobins, La Gomerie, 33330 Saint-Emilion, tel. 05.57.24.70.14, fax 05.57.24.68.08

� by appt

CH. CLOS DES PRINCE 2000★

	2 ha	8,400	⊞	23–30 €

No, there is no "s" missing from the name of this little vineyard; Gilles Prince the wine-broker simply named it after himself and his family (always left in the singular in French) when he set it up in 2000 around a house in Saint-Laurent-des-Combes on the main road from Libourne to Castillon.

His first attempt has produced excellent results; the wine has an intense, young purple colour, and its developing bouquet releases aromas of jammy fruits, Morello cherries and oaky smoke when it is swirled in the glass. The palate is warming and powerful, with a dark berry flavour (blackcurrants) and supple tannins. This wine will keep for five to ten years with no problem at all, and will go well with lamprey *à la bordelaise* or sirloin of beef with ceps.

🍷 SCA des Vignobles Prince, 68, rue E.-Roy, 33420 Branne, tel. 06.76.81.04.11, fax 05.57.84.64.54, e-mail prince.g@wanadoo.fr ☑
⌷ by appt

CLOS FOURTET 2000★★

		1er gd cru clas. B	n.c.	58,000	🍾	46–76 €

71 73 74 75 76 78 79 81 82 83 85 86 87 |88| |89| |90| 91 92 93 |94| (95) 96 |97| 98 99 00

The 2000 is the last vintage that was produced here by the brothers André and Lucien Lurton before they sold this Premier Grand Cru Classé to Philippe Cuvelier. Back in the Roman era, the Fourtet camp just to the west of the collegiate church was there to defend the weak side of the city. These days it is the reputation of Saint-Emilion wines that is being stoutly defended by this remarkable Clos Fourtet 2000. It has a very classic Bordeaux colour, an impressive range of fruit, oak and spice aromas, and a full, warming palate based on dense tannins. This great wine is both powerful and elegant, and deserves to accompany refined dishes such as veal Orloff or filet mignon with ceps. The second wine here is **La Closerie de Fourtet 2000 (15–23 €)**, which receives a special mention.

🍷 SC Clos Fourtet, 33330 Saint-Emilion,
tel. 05.57.24.70.90, fax 05.57.74.46.52
⌷ by appt
🍷 M. Cuvelier

CLOS LA MADELEINE 2000★

		2 ha	9,000	🍾	30–38 €

This *clos* is the sister vineyard of Magnan La Gaffelière, and is located south of the town on a limestone-clay terroir. The wine is made from 60% Merlot and 40% Cabernet Franc, and has a dark purple colour and a bouquet of jammy red and dark berry aromas, elegantly combined with a delicate note of oaky toast. The palate is full bodied, vinous and rich, with tannins that linger on to a long finish.

🍷 SA du Clos La Madeleine, La Gaffelière Ouest, BP 78, 33330 Saint-Emilion, tel. 05.57.55.38.03, fax 05.57.55.38.01 ☑
⌷ by appt

CLOS SAINT-JULIEN 2000★★

		1.2 ha	4,200	🍾	23–30 €

Catherine Papon Nouvel is a Bordelais oenologist who has followed on from her father as manager of the family estates. She wins a *coup de cœur* with the wine from this vineyard, which is a genuine *clos* surrounded by stone walls and located just outside the town. It used to be under the protection of a statue of Pomona (the Roman goddess of fruits and gardens), but unfortunately this was stolen a few years ago. The main grape variety here is Cabernet Franc (60%). The judges were delighted by the wine's intense, young ruby colour, the power and complexity of its bouquet of prune and coffee notes, and

the perfect balance on the palate between fruit and oak, concentration and finesse. This is a great example of the art of winemaking. What a pity they are so few and far between!

🍷 SCEA Vignobles J.-J. Nouvel, Clos Saint-Julien, BP 84, 33330 Saint-Emilion, tel. 05.57.24.72.44, fax 05.57.24.74.84
⌷ by appt

CH. LA CLOTTE 2000★

		Gd cru clas.	n.c.	n.c.	🍾	30–38 €

This vineyard is located along the ramparts of the medieval town. In times gone by it belonged to the de Grailly family, but these days it is run by the descendants of M. Chailleau, who bought it in 1913. The wine has a dark, bigaroon cherry colour, and a bouquet which opens on fresh menthol and fruit stone aromas and develops on to soft fruit fragrances with a fine note of oak. The palate has a warming flavour of very ripe grapes, supported by well-integrated tannins and subtle oak. Drink this wine between 2005 and 2018.

🍷 SCEA du Ch. La Clotte, 33330 Saint-Emilion,
tel. 05.57.24.66.85, fax 05.57.24.79.67,
e-mail chateau-la-clotte@wanadoo.fr ☑
⌷ by appt

CH. CORBIN 2000★

		Gd cru clas.	12.67 ha	60,000	🍾	23–30 €

64 75 79 81 (82) 83 85 86 88 |89| |90| 93 94 |95| |96| 98 |99| 00

This *cru classé* is located in the northwest of the commune, near Pomerol, on a sand and limestone terroir. There is no second wine or "extra-special cuvée" here; just one homogeneous product is on offer. The results are encouraging. The wine's ruby colour with garnet highlights is intense, as are its powerful, concentrated ripe fruit aromas. The flavour is also very fruity (raspberries), and supported by dense yet elegant tannins. This is a delightful wine which will be ready to drink in four to ten years' time.

🍷 SC Ch. Corbin, 33330 Saint-Emilion, tel. 05.57.25.20.30, fax 05.57.25.22.00, e-mail chateau.corbin@wanadoo.fr ☑
⌷ by appt

CH. COTE DE BALEAU 2000★★

		8 ha	38,000	🍾	11–15 €

88 |95| |96| |98| 00

This champagne has belonged to the Reiffers family since 1643. Made from 70% Merlot, 20% Cabernet Franc and 10% Cabernet Sauvignon, all grown on a limestone-clay terroir, this is a powerful wine with a dark, fine, distinguished colour and a bouquet of very ripe red and dark berry aromas, combined with an elegant note of oak. The palate is very rich and mouth-filling, and has an exceptionally long finish. This is a remarkable wine for longer maturing, and the price is affordable too.

🍷 SA Les Grandes Murailles, Ch. Côte de Baleau, 33330 Saint-Emilion, tel. 05.57.24.71.09, fax 05.57.24.69.72, e-mail lesgrandesmurailles@wanadoo.fr

COTES ROCHEUSES 2000★★

		n.c.	173,500	🍾	11–15 €

This Union de Producteurs is a highly-renowned cooperative which has lived through the whole history of winemaking in the 20th century, and been a driving force in Saint-Emilion. It is offering a 2000 with a deep, fresh ruby colour, and a pleasant bouquet of dried fruits and vanilla along with a few musky notes. The palate is robust, full bodied, and delightfully invigorating, but the finish is still slightly severe and will need a few years to soften.

🍷 Union de producteurs de Saint-Emilion, Haut-Gravet, BP 27, 33330 Saint-Emilion, tel. 05.57.24.70.71, fax 05.57.24.65.18, e-mail contact@udpse.com ☑
⌷ ev.day except Sun. 8am–12 noon 2pm–6pm

CH. LA COURONNE 2000★

		10 ha	60,000	🍾	11–15 €

The Mühler-Besse *maison de négoce* owns prestigious vineyards in the Médoc, such as Palmer in Margaux. For a decade now they have been growing vines in Saint-Emilion on the sandy-clay soils in the southeast of the appellation. With a 40% Cabernet component, the grape blend is not unlike those in the Médoc. No surprise therefore that the 2000 here is more fine than powerful. It has an intense, but not dark, garnet colour and a delightful nose of floral (violet), fruity (cherry), musky and very spicy aromas. The palate is well structured but still somewhat austere and marked by oak. It should become more supple in three to four years' time, however. A special mention goes to the **Le Fer 2000 (30–38 €)** brand; this is a micro-*cuvée* which is firm, toasty and very modern.

↝ SA Mühler-Besse, 49, rue Camille-Godard,
33000 Bordeaux, tel. 05.56.56.04.30, fax 05.56.56.04.59,
e-mail france@mahler-besse.com **▼**
⚒ by appt

COUVENT DES JACOBINS 2000★

▮ Gd cru clas. 9.5 ha	38,000	🍷	46–76 €

This Grand Cru Classé is bottled not in a château but in a former monastery, which has its own classification as a historic monument. In 2002 this family celebrated the centenary of their arrival on this vineyard, which was bought in 1902 by their forebear Jean Jean. This 2000 has a lovely, strong, fresh colour, and a nose still dominated by a dark berry aroma, along with a restrained note of oak. The palate is full and structured by well-balanced tannins which just need some time to soften. In the next five to ten years this wine will be a good accompaniment to roast meat and game birds.

↝ SCEV Joinaud-Borde, 10, rue Guadet,
33330 Saint-Emilion, tel. 05.57.24.70.66, fax 05.57.24.62.51
⚒ by appt
↝ M. et Mme Borde

CH. LA CROIX DE TOURANS

Elevé en fût de chêne Cuvée Prestige 2000★

▮	4.5 ha	22,720	🍷	5–8 €

This cru is made from 90% Merlot and 10% Cabernet Franc grown on limestone-clay soils, and has been matured in oak for a year. It has a beautiful garnet colour, and a nose of soft fruit aromas and very elegant toast notes. The palate is well balanced, with round, supple tannins which make up for a slight lack of power by providing a great deal of finesse. This is a good, classic Saint-Emilion.

↝ André Quancard-André, chem. de La Cabeyre,
33240 Saint-André-de-Cubzac, tel. 05.57.33.42.53,
fax 05.57.43.22.22,
e-mail aqa@andrequancard.com

CH. LA CROIX DE VIGNOT 2000★

▮ n.c.	10,000	🍷	8–11 €

This very reasonably-priced 2000 comes from a hillfoot Merlot plot with a limestone-clay soil. The wine makes a rather restrained first impression, but then really comes into its own. It needs to be swirled in the glass a little before it releases pleasant grape aromas along with a slight mineral note. The palate is clean, agreeable and elegant, with tannins which are still slightly austere but very promising, and will enable the wine to be kept for three to ten years.

↝ René Micheau-Maillou, la Vieille Eglise,
33330 Saint-Hippolyte, tel. 05.57.24.61.99,
fax 05.57.74.45.37 **▼**
⚒ by appt

LES CHARMILLES DE CROQUE MICHOTTE 2000★

▮ n.c.	6,000	🍷 🍶	11–15 €

This Charmilles is Croque Michotte's second wine. It has an intense ruby colour, and a fresh, spicy bouquet of menthol and liquorice aromas combined with elegant notes of undergrowth. The palate is robust and full-bodied, with flavours in the same register as the bouquet. This highly appealing wine will be ready to drink in two years' time.

↝ GFA Geoffrion, Ch. Croque Michotte,
33330 Saint-Emilion, tel. 05.57.51.13.67, fax 05.57.51.07.81,
e-mail croque-michotte@monaoc.com **▼**
⚒ by appt

CH. DARIUS 2000★

▮ 6.9 ha	40,000	🍷	15–23 €

This vineyard was started in 1990 by the Pommiers, a wine-growing family from Entre-Deux-Mers. They grow 60% Merlot and 40% Cabernet Franc here on a sandy-clay soil which contains iron dross. Their 2000 has been matured in

oak for 18 months, and has a bouquet still marked by an oaky toast note which masks the ripe fruit aromas. The palate is powerful and firm, with tannins which are still a little severe at the moment, but hold great promise for the future.

↝ GFA des Pommiers, Ch. Darius,
33330 Saint-Laurent-des-Combes, tel. 05.56.61.31.56,
fax 05.56.61.33.52, e-mail vignoblespommier@aol.com **▼**
⚒ by appt
↝ Michel Pommier

CH. DASSAULT 2000★

▮ Gd cru clas. 13.86 ha	59,000	🍷	38–46 €

83 86 88 89 **|90|** 92 94 **|95|** |96| 98 99 00

In 1995, Marcel Dassault bought Château Couprie and gave it his own family name. It is now run by his grandson Laurent, who practises sustainable agriculture methods. The wine comes from the *cru classé* on the old glacis in the north of the commune, and has been matured in new French oak for 18 months. It has a very strong colour, and a bouquet which is still dominated by oak, but releases a multitude of aromas when the wine is swirled in the glass: jammy fruits, violets, sloes, liquorice, musk, cocoa and cachous. The Jury was impressed by its round palate with plenty of tannins, which although still slightly oaky are of high quality and should become more refined once the wine has been kept for three to eight years.

↝ SARL Ch. Dassault, 33330 Saint-Emilion,
tel. 05.57.55.10.00, fax 05.57.55.10.01,
e-mail lbv@chateaudassault.com
⚒ by appt

CH. L'EGLISE D'ARMENS 2000★

▮ 4.37 ha	29,000	📖 🍷	8–11 €

This cru was started in 1988, and is made up of several plots spread over the communes of Saint-Sulpice-de-Faleyrens and Saint-Pey-d'Armens. The buildings where the wine is made are opposite the church, whose porch is listed as an historic monument. This 2000 has a lovely ruby colour, and a nose which although still somewhat closed is already releasing some fruit and spice notes. The palate is well structured, vinous, and supported by tannins which are still firm but well cloaked, and will make sure that the wine keeps well. "An authentic wine," notes one taster: "Just as much oak as it takes, and no more!"

↝ Bertrand et Jocelyne Martigne, Le Bourg,
33330 Saint-Pey-d'Armens, tel. 05.57.47.16.45,
fax 05.57.47.16.54, e-mail bmartigne@hotmail.com **▼**
⚒ by appt

CH. FAUGERES 2000★★

▮ 22 ha	92,000	🍷	23–30 €

|93| |94| |95| |96| |97| 98 99 **00**

Corinne Guisez is having great success in running this family estate which was inherited by her film-maker husband. With the help of Alain Dourthe she has produced a great wine which delighted the Jury with a deep, dark colour with purple highlights, and a vinous bouquet elegantly combining red and dark berry aromas with oaky vanilla and toast notes. The palate is just as good: admirably concentrated and mouth-filling, with mature tannins which will ensure good ageing potential. This is a wine which deserves to be drunk with game.

↝ C. Guisez, Ch. Faugères, 33330 Saint-Etienne-de-Lisse,
tel. 05.57.40.34.99, fax 05.57.40.36.14,
e-mail faugeres@chateau-faugeres.com **▼**
⚒ by appt

CH. FERRAND LARTIGUE 2000★★

■ 5.8 ha 24,000 ⬭ 30–38 €
|95| |96| 97 98 99 00

Since his first harvest in 1994, this producer has regularly been selected by our Juries. They were impressed this year by the 2000's purple-red colour, complex bouquet of ripe soft fruits and vanilla oak, and "Merlot" character on the palate. The wine is warming, rich, agreeable, unctuous and very elegant despite still being slightly dominated by oak. In four to eight years' time it will be perfect with game and soft cheeses. The **Château Grand Faurie La Rose 2000 (11–15 €)** is full of flavour and highly distinguished. It will be ready to drink in 2006, and will keep for eight to ten years.
🍷 Pierre Ferrand, Lartigue, 33330 Saint-Emilion, tel. 05.57.74.46.19, fax 05.57.74.46.19, e-mail vincent.rapin@libertysurf.fr

CH. FIGEAC 2000★

■ 1er gd cru clas. B 37.5 ha 130,000 ⬭ +76 €
62 64 66 (70) 71 74 75 76 77 78 79 80 |81| |82| |83| |85| |86| 87 |88| |89| 90 92 |93| |94| (95) 96 97 **98** 99 00

This cru gives its name to the area halfway between Saint-Emilion and Libourne. It once belonged to the Duc de Cazes, then to the Marquis de Carles, and since 1892 has been owned by the Manoncourt family. Thierry Manoncourt has been running it since 1945, and is now assisted by his son-in-law, Eric d'Aramon. The grape blend here is two-thirds Cabernets, and this has produced a rather unusual type of wine with a very young, dark Bordeaux colour. The bouquet is reserved, as indeed it should be at such a young age, and the wine needs to be swirled in the glass before it comes forth in all its complexity and richness. The palate is warming and has a dense tannic structure which will need a few years of ageing to become more refined. Serve this wine in a carafe.
🍷 SCEA Famille Manoncourt, Ch. de Figeac, 33330 Saint-Emilion, tel. 05.57.24.72.26, fax 05.57.74.45.74, e-mail chateau-figeac@chateau-figeac.com
🍷 by appt

CH. FLEUR DE LISSE

Elevé en fût de chêne 2000★

■ 1.4 ha 8,000 🍶⬭♦ 11–15 €
This vineyard grows two-thirds Merlot and one-third Cabernet Franc on a limestone-clay, southeast-facing, hillfoot terroir a few kilometres to the east of Saint-Emilion. This 2000 has a ruby colour with some crimson glints, and a rich bouquet of stewed fruits (prunes) and fine oaky toast. The very well-balanced palate is both round and fine, fruity and oaky, and structured by firm yet elegant tannins. With such good balance already, it should keep for eight to ten years and be a good accompaniment to red meat or lamprey.
🍷 Xavier Minvielle, 1, Giraud, Ch. Fleur de Lisse, 33330 Saint-Etienne-de-Lisse, tel. 05.57.40.18.46, fax 05.57.40.35.74
🍷 by appt

CH. LA FLEUR DU CASSE 2000★

■ 1.2 ha 7,080 🍶⬭♦ 15–23 €
This tiny cru was bought in 1996 by the Garzaro family to complement its vineyards in Entre-Deux-Mers and Pomerol. The dominant grape variety here is Merlot, with just an additional 5% Cabernet Franc, and the soils are limestone-clay. From this terroir comes a wine with a ruby colour, and an elegant bouquet with a combination of ripe soft fruit aromas and high-quality oaky toast notes. The palate makes a supple impression at first, then develops on to mature, full-bodied tannins which linger on a long finish.
🍷 EARL Vignobles Garzaro, Ch. Le Prieur, 33750 Baron, tel. 05.56.30.16.16, fax 05.56.30.12.63, e-mail garzaro@vingarzaro.com 📧 📠
🍷 by appt

CH. LA FLEUR PICON 2000★

■ 5.6 ha 32,800 🍶⬭♦ 11–15 €
Anita Lassègues and her daughter courageously took over the running of this vineyard when the head of the family died. Located northeast of Saint-Emilion on a siliceous-clay terroir with an iron dross subsoil, it has produced a wine with a slightly-developed colour and a bouquet of jammy fruit and

prune aromas combined with some spice notes and a touch of menthol. The well-balanced, supple, round palate is supported by mature, silky tannins which give it a very classy finish.
🍷 Anita Lassègues, La Fleur Picon, 33330 Saint-Emilion, tel. 05.57.24.70.60, fax 05.57.24.68.67
🍷 by appt

CH. FOMBRAUGE 2000★

■ 30 ha 160,000 ⬭ 15–23 €
88 |90| 91 92 93 (95) (96) |97| 98 99 00

Built in 1679, this charterhouse overlooks a property of 75 ha which was purchased in 1999 by Bernard Magrez. It took 30 ha of vines to produce this 2000, which has an intense ruby colour and a developing bouquet of jammy fruit aromas combined with a fine, elegant note of oak. The palate is very well-balanced, supple and round, with a long finish. This wine should keep for a decent length of time and will be a good accompaniment to leg of lamb. A special mention goes to the second wine, **Le Cadran de Fombrauge 2000 (11–15 €)**, which although less complex is very silky.
🍷 SA Ch. Fombrauge, 33330 Saint-Christophe-des-Bardes, tel. 05.57.24.77.12, fax 05.57.24.66.95, e-mail chateau@fombrauge.com
🍷 B. Magrez

CH. FONPLEGADE 2000★

■ Gd cru clas. 10.4 ha 50,000 ⬭ 23–30 €
82 83 85 86 88 90 92 93 94 |95| |96| |97| 98 99 00

This cru classé takes its name from a fountain which can still be seen on the estate today. The property once belonged to the Duc de Morny, Napoleon III's half-brother, and was purchased in 1953 by a branch of the Moueix family. The last few decades were very much influenced by Armand Moueix, a strong Libournais personality who unfortunately has now died. The estate is now run by his wife and daughter, who are offering a 2000 with great charm and finesse. It has a shimmering ruby and garnet colour, an entirely fruity bouquet, and a round, velvety palate with a finish on vanilla and liquorice tannins. In four or five years' time this wine will be perfect with leg of lamb.
🍷 Nathalie and Marie-José Moueix, Ch. Fonplégade, 33330 Saint-Emilion, tel. 05.57.74.43.11, fax 05.57.74.44.67, e-mail domaines-armand-moueix@wanadoo.fr
🍷 by appt

CH. FONRAZADE 2000★

■ 10.8 ha 70,000 🍶⬭♦ 15–23 €
86 88 |90| |95| |96| **98** 00

This cru is a very beautiful property on the way out of Libourne. It has brown, sandy soils, grows 75% Merlot and 25% Cabernet Sauvignon, and is run in masterly fashion by Fabienne Balotte and his father Guy. This 2000 has a ruby colour with vermilion highlights, and an open bouquet with a wealth of ripe red and dark berry aromas and spicy notes, along with an elegant note of oaky toast. The palate is ample and full bodied, with powerful tannins and an agreeable finish. This is a well-balanced wine which should be kept for three years before drinking.
🍷 Fabienne Balotte, Ch. Fonrazade, 33330 Saint-Emilion, tel. 05.57.24.71.58, fax 05.57.74.40.87, e-mail chateau-fonrazade@wanadoo.fr
🍷 ev.day except Sat. Sun. 8am–12 noon 2pm–6pm
🍷 Guy Balotte

CH. FRANC GRACE-DIEU 2000★

■ 6.13 ha 30,000 🍶⬭♦ 15–23 €
This property is located between Libourne and Saint-Emilion on a brown sand and blue clay soil. This wine is made from 60% Merlot and 40% Cabernet, and has been matured in oak for a year. It has a gleaming, very dark purple colour, and an intense bouquet of jammy dark berries along with a note of high-quality, slightly spicy oak. The ripe, vinous flavour on the palate is supported by a very good tannic structure and lingers on to a very long finish. This wine has good ageing potential.
🍷 Domaines Daniel Fournier, Ch. Franc Grace-Dieu, 33330 Saint-Emilion, tel. 05.57.24.66.18, fax 05.57.24.67.86, e-mail fournier.daniel.domaine@wanadoo.fr
🍷 by appt

CH. FRANC LA ROSE 2000★

■ 1.11 ha 40,000 ⑪ 15–23 €

The Trocard family runs several vineyards in the Libournais. This one was bought in 1995, and is located on the limestone-clay soils of the La Rose area to the north of the town, on the road to Montagne. This 2000 has a beautiful, brilliant garnet colour with crimson highlights, and a fine, elegant bouquet which is already open and combines soft fruit aromas with sweet spice, toast and oaky toast notes. The palate has a very Merlot, well-balanced, jammy flavour and is supported by well-integrated, lingering tannins. This wine will be a good accompaniment to game birds in two or three years' time and for a long time after that.

☛ Jean-Louis Trocard, Ch. Franc La Rose, BP 3, 33570 Artigues-de-Lussac, tel. 05.57.55.57.90, fax 05.57.55.57.98, e-mail trocard@wanadoo.fr ☑

CH. FRANC LARTIGUE 2000★

■ 7 ha 25,000 ⑪ 11–15 €

This 2000 is a blend of 70% Merlot, 15% Cabernet Franc, and 15% Cabernet Sauvignon. It has an intense garnet colour and an expressive bouquet of ripe red berry aromas and high-quality oak notes of toast and vanilla. The palate is embellished by round, velvety tannins which are slightly hardened by oak on the finish. This is a very good wine which should open out fully in three to four years' time.

☛ Vignobles Marcel Petit, 6, chem. de Pillebois, 33350 Saint-Magne-de-Castillon, tel. 05.57.40.33.03, fax 05.57.40.06.05, e-mail vignobles.marcel.petit@wanadoo.fr ☑
🍷 by appt

LES CEDRES DE FRANC-MAYNE 2000★

■ 2 ha 10,000 ⑪ 15–23 €

It is unusual for a second wine to receive a higher rating than the top wine, and it is true that the *cru classé* here is heavily marked by oak, whereas this has had a shorter period of oak maturation. Its purple colour is dense, deep, and gleaming with darker purple highlights. The fruit aromas on the nose (blackcurrants and prunes) are combined with an elegant note of oaky toast and vanilla. The palate is well-structured, powerful, and more full bodied than that of the Château Franc-Mayne.

☛ Georgy Fourcroy, SCEA Ch. Franc-Mayne, 14, La Gomerie, 33330 Saint-Emilion, tel. 05.57.24.62.61, fax 05.57.24.68.25, e-mail contact@chateau-francmayne.com ☑ 🏠
🍷 by appt

CH. GAILLARD 2000★

■ 11 ha 70,000 ⑪ 11–15 €

This family vineyard is located on the sand and clay soils of Saint-Hippolyte, in the southeast of the AOC area. At 80%, Merlot is the dominant grape variety here. The 2000 has a bouquet of fruit aromas (blackcurrants) and spice notes (pepper), along with subtle hints of truffles and musk, and a fine touch of oak. The palate is warming and full, the tannins are still young, and the fruity grape flavour is not overwhelmed by oak. This is a thoroughbred, mouthwatering wine which should be ready to drink in two to five years' time. Catherine Papon-Nouvel also produces the **Château Petit Gravet Aîné 2000 (23–30 €)**, which comes down from her grandmother. Made from 80% Cabernet Franc and 20% Merlot, it wins one star and will be a worthy accompaniment to a haunch of venison any time between 2006 and 2013.

☛ SCEA Vignobles J.-J. Nouvel, Ch. Gaillard, BP 84, 33330 Saint-Emilion, tel. 05.57.24.72.44, fax 05.57.24.74.84, e-mail chateau.gaillard@wanadoo.fr ☑
🍷 by appt

CH. GONTEY 2000★

■ 2.4 ha 12,000 ⑪ 15–23 €

Laurence and Marc Pasquet produce Côtes de Bourg, Premières Côtes de Blaye and Blaye wines. They have been cultivating this little Saint-Emilion vineyard on an old sand soil since 1997, and clearly they have been successful, since their first few wines have been selected by the Jury. The 2000 has a dark purple colour with ruby highlights, and a bouquet with a well-balanced combination of jammy fruit aromas and oak notes of vanilla and liquorice. The palate is supple, long

and well structured, opening out on to flavours of soft fruits and oaky toast. This wine should be just right three to six years from now.

☛ Laurence et Marc Pasquet, Grand Gontey, 33330 Saint-Emilion, tel. 05.57.42.29.80, fax 05.57.42.84.86, e-mail mondesirgazin@aol.com ☑

CH. GRANDBARRAIL LAMARZELLE FIGEAC 2000★

■ 19.12 ha 100,000 ⑪ 15–23 €

This cru is easy to find; it is halfway between Libourne and Saint-Emilion, and surrounds a magnificent château which is now a four-star hotel. The estate has just built a circular barrel store, and has a siliceous gravel and ferruginous soil which tends to produce a thoroughbred type of wine. That is certainly true of this 2000, which has an intense, fresh colour and young aromas of very ripe fruits, finely marked by a spice oak note. Although still somewhat closed, the palate is fresh, and opens out gently when the wine is swirled in the glass. Keep this wine for two to ten years, then decant it before serving with red meats grilled on vine shoots.

☛ SCEA Ch. Grand Barrail Lamarzelle Figeac, 33330 Saint-Emilion, tel. 05.57.24.71.43, fax 05.57.24.63.44, e-mail grandbarrail2@wanadoo.fr ☑
🍷 by appt
☛ BCN

CH. GRAND CORBIN-DESPAGNE 2000★

■ 26.54 ha 102,000 ⑪ 23–30 €

|89| **|90|** 93 |94| |95| |96| |97| 98 |99| 00

This very large vineyard is the flagship of the Despagne family and is built around a 17th century Girondin house which since 1812 has been handed down through seven generations. Just like the family, the wine here is entirely reliable. This one has an intense, brilliant colour and is beginning to release a warming bouquet of very ripe grape and undergrowth aromas. The full-bodied, robust palate has fine tannins, and is developing flavours of soft fruits and oak. This is a vintage for longer maturing which will gain from being served in a carafe, and will go well with dishes such as an entrecôte steak *à la bordelaise*.

☛ Famille Despagne, Ch. Grand Corbin-Despagne, 33330 Saint-Emilion, tel. 05.57.51.08.38, fax 05.57.51.29.18, e-mail f-despagne@grand-corbin-despagne.com ☑
🍷 by appt

CH. GRAND MAYNE 2000★

■ Gd cru clas. 17 ha 60,000 ⑪ 46–76 €

75 78 81 82 83 85 86 88 |89| **|90|** 91 92 93 |94| 95 **96** |97| **99** 00

This *cru classé* always does exceptionally well in the trickier vintages, such as 1996 and 1999, for both of which it won a *coup de coeur*. As Professor Emile Peynaud said: "It is the difficult vintages that show who are the good winemakers." When everything is going well it is harder to stand out from the crowd, and this has meant that many vineyards have not been selected this time by our experts. The wine we are looking at here is a very interesting 2000, with an intense purple colour and an elegant, fruity bouquet with a strong note of oak. After a warming and powerful yet velvety attack, the palate is structured by flavourful tannins and shows great potential. Keep this wine in a safe place for four to five years.

☛ SCEV J.-P. Nony, Ch. Grand Mayne, 33330 Saint-Emilion, tel. 05.57.74.42.50, fax 05.57.74.41.89, e-mail grand-mayne@grand-mayne.com ☑
🍷 by appt

CH. GRAND-PONTET 2000★★

■ Gd cru clas. 14 ha 46,000 ⑪ 30–38 €

85 86 88 |89| **|90|** 93 94 95 96 |97| 98 **00**

This *cru classé* is located on the limestone plateau to the west of the town, a few hundred metres from the old church of Saint-Martin de Mazerat. Our judges were so impressed by the 2000 here that, strict though they are, they were unable to deny it a *coup de coeur*. It delights the eye with a splendid black colour shimmering with Bordeaux highlights. The bouquet explodes with floral, fruity, spicy and oak aromas which are still young. The palate is a perfect example of harmony, balance, finesse and elegance: all the qualities that go to make

2000

CHATEAU
GRAND-PONTET
GRAND CRU CLASSÉ
SAINT-ÉMILION GRAND CRU

APPELLATION SAINT-ÉMILION GRAND CRU CONTRÔLÉE

CHATEAU GRAND PONTET S.A.
PROPRIÉTAIRE A SAINT-ÉMILION - GIRONDE - FRANCE

MIS EN BOUTEILLE AU CHATEAU

a real Grand Cru Classé. In three to eight years' time this wine will be able to accompany a wide range of dishes.
☛ Ch. Grand-Pontet, 33330 Saint-Emilion,
tel. 05.57.74.46.88, fax 05.57.74.45.31
🍷 by appt
☛ Pourquet Bécot

CH. LA GRANGERE 2000★

| | 6.85 ha | 15,000 | 〓 | 15–23 € |

This cru was purchased in 2001 by Olympic horse-riding champion Pierre Durand and his wife Nadia Devilder, who is an auctioneer. The new label shows a horse's head crowned by a laurel wreath: winning horse Jappeloup perhaps? Moving on to the wine, this one comes from vines grown on limestone-clay hillside and hillfoot soils. It has a deep ruby colour, and a bouquet of jammy fruit, fine oaky toast and mocca aromas. The palate is full but at the same time fine and delicate. This 2000 is a modern type of wine, but it also represents the terroir and the vintage. It will be ready to drink in two to five years' time.
☛ SCEA Ch. La Grangère, 3, Tauzinat
Est-Saint-Christophe, BP 56, 33330 Saint-Emilion,
tel. 05.57.76.43.07, fax 05.57.24.60.94,
e-mail devilder.durand@free.fr ☑
🍷 by appt

CH. HAUT-GRAVET 2000★★

| | 9.01 ha | 58,000 | 〓 | 23–30 € |

Since storming into the *Guide* with a *coup de coeur* for the 1998 vintage, this cru has made a regular habit of winning two stars, and now does so again with this remarkable 2000. It comes from the gravelly soils at Saint-Sulpice, where the grape mix is an equal share of Cabernets and Merlot. The wine has a magnificent Bordeaux colour with black glints, and is extraordinarily intense both on the nose and on the palate, offering a multitude of aromas and flavours: very ripe grapes, figs, jammy fruits, empyreumatic smoke, toast, charred oak and coffee. The palate is round and deliciously soft, with long, lingering tannins. This is a very well-balanced wine which should reach its peak two to five years from now.
☛ Alain Aubert, 57 bis, av. de l'Europe,
33350 Saint-Magne-de-Castillon, tel. 05.57.40.04.30,
fax 05.57.56.07.10, e-mail domaines.a.aubert@wanadoo.fr

CH. HAUT LA GRACE DIEU 2000★★

| | 2.05 ha | 7,000 | 〓 | 15–23 € |

On the Saby family's very large wine-estate, 2 ha are given over to this Saint-Emilion, which is made from old Merlot grapes grown on a plateau and hillside terroir with limestone-clay soils. The first of these gives this 2000 its finesse and good length, the other makes it well-structured and mouth-filling; some of the judges could sense this from a blind tasting. The wine delights the eye, nose and palate with its character, elegance, power and fine tannins, in short with all the characteristics that go to make a great Saint-Emilion. This one should be excellent in three to six years' time. From the same owner, the **Château Rozier 2000** receives a special mention.
☛ Vignobles J.-B. Saby et Fils, Ch. Rozier,
33330 Saint-Laurent-des-Combes, tel. 05.57.24.73.03,
fax 05.57.24.67.77, e-mail info@vignobles-saby.com ☑
🍷 by appt

CH. HAUT LAVALLADE 2000★

| | 7.56 ha | 51,000 | 〓 〓 | 15–23 € |

Jean-Marc Chagneau carries on the family tradition on this 11-hectare vineyard in the north-east of the appellation, where the Cabernets represent 30% of the grape blend. He is offering a wine with a bouquet which is still young and fresh, with notes of roasted almonds and liquorice. The palate is developing in a gradual, balanced way, which suggests that this will be a pleasant wine in two to three years' time. The **Audace Haut Lavallade 2000 (30–38 €)** cuvée was created to celebrate the new millennium. It impressed the Jury, but needs to be kept until the oak is integrated.
☛ SARL J.P.M.D. Chagneau, Ch. Haut-Lavallade,
33330 Saint-Christophe-des-Bardes, tel. 05.57.24.77.47,
fax 05.57.74.43.25, e-mail chagneau.sarl@wanadoo.fr ☑
🍷 by appt

CH. HAUT-POURRET 2000★

| | 3 ha | 12,000 | 〓 〓 | 11–15 € |

This small vineyard is located 1 km to the west of the town, along the road to Libourne. The terroir has a limestone clay soil and has a grape mix of 70% Merlot and 30% Cabernets. The wine has a black cherry colour and an intense, complex bouquet of overripe, macerated fruit aromas and fine, vanilla oak. The palate has the same warming flavour of macerated fruits, and is supported by dense, thoroughbred tannins. Keep this wine for two to seven years, then decant it and serve with game or red meat.
☛ Serge Lepoutre, Ch. Haut-Pourret, 33330 Saint-Emilion,
tel. 05.57.74.46.76, fax 05.57.74.45.17,
e-mail serge.lepoutre@worldonline.fr ☑
🍷 by appt

CH. HAUT-SARPE 2000★

| | Gd cru clas. | 12.04 ha | 68,000 | 〓 | 23–30 € |

85 86 88 89 |90| 92 |93| |94| |95| |96| 98 |99| 00

This is a good-sized wine-estate which surrounds a large neo-classical house near the road from Saint-Emilion to Saint-Christophe, to the northeast of the town on the edge of the limestone plateau. It belongs to the Joseph Janoueix family who are originally from the Corrèze. Their 2000 is a great wine for longer maturing, with a dark, almost black colour and a powerfully fruity nose with an elegant oak note which does not mask the blackcurrant and blackberry aromas. The round, liquoricy palate is supported by dense tannins. This wine will be ready to enjoy in three to nine years' time.
☛ SCE du Ch. Haut-Sarpe, BP 192, 33506 Libourne Cedex,
tel. 05.57.51.41.86, fax 05.57.51.53.16,
e-mail info@j-janoueix-bordeaux.com ☑
🍷 by appt

CH. JUCALIS 2000★

| | 3 ha | 6,900 | 〓 | 15–23 € |

This cru comes from old Merlot grapes grown on brown gravel and sand soils. Matured in new oak for 14 months, it has only been entitled to the Saint-Emilion Grand Cru appellation since the 1999 vintage. This delightful 2000 has a dark, deep colour, and an elegant bouquet of dark berry aromas combined with a high-quality oaky toast note. The palate is well-balanced, supple, round and full-bodied, with a long, lingering finish on fruit and vanilla flavours.
☛ SCEA des Vignobles Visage, Jupille,
33330 Saint-Sulpice-de-Faleyrens, tel. 05.57.24.62.92,
fax 05.57.24.69.40,
e-mail vignobles.visage@wanadoo.fr ☑
🍷 by appt
☛ Isabelle Visage

CH. LAFLEUR VACHON 2000★★

| | 4 ha | 22,700 | 〓 〓 | 15–23 € |

The Tapon family owns about 30 ha in the Libournais, four of which are given over to this cru produced by Nicole Tapon, whose father Raymond still takes care of the vines. This remarkable, very expressive 2000 has an intense purple colour, and a fresh, elegant bouquet of blackcurrant, blackberry and raspberry aromas. The palate also has a range of fruit flavours, but develops on to spicy and oaky notes, finishing on high-quality tannins. In two years' time and for ten years in

all, this wine will be an ideal accompaniment to roast lamb with beans and various other dishes.
☙ Vignobles Raymond Tapon, Ch. Lafleur Vachon,
33330 Saint-Emilion, tel. 05.57.74.61.20, fax 05.57.74.61.19,
e-mail information@tapon.net ✓
�by appt

CH. LANIOTE 2000★

■ Gd cru clas. 5 ha	28,000	🍶	15–23 €

89 93 |94| |95| |96| 98 99 00

Having taken over this *cru classé* a few kilometres west of the town, these young producers also have the benefit of the architectural gems in this village, which is listed by Unesco as a World Heritage Site: the Chapelle de la Trinité, the Saint-Emilion hermitage, and the catacombs on the Place du Tertre, to the left of the monolithic church. Moving on to the wine, this very successful 2000 was produced by Florence Ribereau-Gayon, and although still a young wine, it is already showing its richness at every stage. It is both powerful and elegant, with just the right amount of oak, and will keep for three to eight years. Serve in a carafe. .
☙ De La Filolie, Ch. Laniote, 33330 Saint-Emilion,
tel. 05.57.24.70.80, fax 05.57.24.60.11,
e-mail laniote@wanadoo.fr ✓
☙ by appt

CH. LARMANDE 2000★★

■ Gd cru clas. 22.4 ha	70,000	🍶	+76 €

85 86 (88) |89| |90| 92 |93| |94| 96 |97| 98 99 00

This 25-hectare *cru classé* was purchased in 1990 by the La Mondiale insurance group, and has produced a remarkably good 2000 made from a blend of both Cabernets and 65% Merlot. It is a full, round wine with a magnificent colour and an equally delightful bouquet in which the dark berry aromas are not masked by a strong note of charred oak. The palate is round and velvety to start with, then gains in power thanks to dense grape and oak tannins. This Grand Cru is both elegant and powerful, and has the potential to become quite sublime in a few years' time (three to eight years or more).
☙ Ch. Larmande, BP 26, 33330 Saint-Emilion,
tel. 05.57.24.71.41, fax 05.57.74.42.80 ✓
☙ by appt
☙ Groupe La Mondiale

CH. LAROZE 2000★

■ Gd cru clas. 25 ha	95,000	🍶	23–30 €

85 86 88 89 90 93 95 |96| |97| 98 99 00

This large, 27-hectare *cru classé* vineyard is run by Guy Meslin, a descendant of the Gurchy family who were making wine at Saint-Emilion in 1610, on the Mazerat *lieu-dit*. Built in 1812, this château has produced an attractive 2000 with a subtle ruby and garnet colour, and exceptional finesse both on the nose and on the palate. Soft fruit aromas, a touch of musk, a restrained oak note, velvety tannins: none of these are in excess, the whole wine is very elegant and will be ready to be enjoyed to the full in two to four years' time. The second wine is **Lafleur Laroze 2000 (11–15 €)**, which deserves a special mention for the pleasure it can afford you straight away.
☙ Famille Meslin, SCE Ch. Laroze, 33330 Saint-Emilion,
tel. 05.57.24.79.79, fax 05.57.24.79.80,
e-mail info@laroze.com ✓
☙ by appt

CH. DES LAUDES 2000★★

■	2.5 ha	13,000	🍶	15–23 €

Started in 1997, this small vineyard grows 35-year-old vines (70% Merlot and 30% Cabernets) on the sandy-gravel and sandy-clay soils of Vignonet. They have produced a remarkable 2000 with an intense, dark garnet colour and a very expressive nose on which the fruit aromas are perfectly combined with high-quality oak notes of roast hazelnuts and sweet spices. After a supple, round attack, the palate is well balanced, with rich velvety tannins which linger on to a long finish and will give the wine excellent ageing potential.
☙ GFA du Haut-Saint-Georges, Vignonet,
33330 Saint-Emilion, tel. 05.57.55.38.03,
fax 05.57.55.38.01 ✓
☙ by appt

CH. LAVALLADE

Carpe Diem 2000★

■	4.02 ha	24,500	🍶	11–15 €

The Gaudry family has been running this delightful wine-estate since 1946. Carpe Diem is a *cuvée* with purple highlights, and a bouquet which opens on to fine notes of very ripe grapes and oaky toast when the wine is swirled in the glass. The palate is full bodied, concentrated, fruity (Morello cherries), and structured by tannins which are still slightly firm and will enable the wine to keep without any problems for three to ten years.
☙ SCEA Gaury et Fils, Ch. Lavallade,
33330 Saint-Christophe-des-Bardes, tel. 05.57.24.77.49,
fax 05.57.24.64.83, e-mail chateau.lavallade@wanadoo.fr ✓
☙ by appt

CH. MAGNAN LA GAFFELIERE 2000★

■	8.33 ha	51,000	■ 🍶 ♦	11–15 €

This attractive property is located on a sandy glacis at the foot of a hill. The grape blend here is 65% Merlot, 25% Cabernet Franc and 10% Cabernet Sauvignon; a third of the wine is aged in tank, and the remainder is matured in oak for 15 months. The result is a fresh, brilliant 2000 with dark and red berry aromas, with a touch of vanilla and some hints of spice. The palate is well balanced, vinous, rich, and supported by elegant tannins which carry it on to a long finish on fruity flavours and a well-integrated note of oak.
☙ SA du Clos La Madeleine, La Gaffelière Ouest, BP 78, 33330 Saint-Emilion, tel. 05.57.55.38.03,
fax 05.57.55.38.01 ✓
☙ by appt

CH. MANGOT

Cuvée Quintessence 2000★

■	5.2 ha	24,000	🍶	23–30 €

96 97 |98| 99 00

Mangot is a very large wine-estate whose vineyard (34 ha) is planted on a marine-based limestone terroir. The **Cuvée Principale Château Mangot 2000 (11–15 €)** receives a special mention. This Cuvée Quintessence is made from a selection of pure Merlot, and is a wine for longer maturing. It has an intense, young colour and a bouquet of spice, vanilla and toast aromas. Its full-bodied, elegant structure and powerful tannins suggest that it should be kept for at least three years.
☙ Vignobles Jean Petit, Ch. Mangot,
33330 Saint-Etienne-de-Lisse, tel. 05.57.40.18.23,
fax 05.57.56.43.97,
e-mail todeschini@chateaumangot.fr ✓
☙ ev.day 8.30am–12 noon 1.45pm–5pm; Sat. Sun. by appt
☙ GFA Ch. Mangot

CH. MARQUEY 2000★

■	3 ha	18,000	🍶	15–23 €

This is one of Georgy Fourcroy's three Saint-Emilion properties. It was bought in 1998, and is located at the foot of the Pavie hill. This 2000 is one of the first wines he has produced here. It has a brilliant ruby colour, shot through by some glints that show it is developing. The nose has aromas of fresh fruits and fine oak, while the palate is full, supple and well balanced. This is a wine which brings out the characteristics of the terroir very clearly, and has great promise for the next four to six years.
☙ Georgy Fourcroy, SCEA Ch. Franc-Mayne, 14, La Gomerie, 33330 Saint-Emilion, tel. 05.57.24.62.61,
fax 05.57.24.68.25,
e-mail contact@chateau-francmayne.com ✓ ☙
☙ by appt

CH. MATRAS 2000★

■ Gd cru clas. 9 ha	n.c.	■ 🍶 ♦	23–30 €

83 85 86 |90| 92 93 94 97 98 99 00

This *cru classé* has its cellar in the 12th century Mazerat chapel to the west of the town. The grape mix here is an equal blend of Merlot and Cabernet Franc. This 2000 has intense ruby and garnet glints, and a bouquet which is already attractive, with aromas of jammy fruit, cherries and spices, along with a touch of musk and leather. The palate is rich and

flavourful, although still somewhat dominated by tannins which should settle down over the next two to four years.
🔑 Vignobles Véronique Gaboriaud-Bernard, Ch. Matras, 33330 Saint-Emilion, tel. 05.57.51.52.39, fax 05.57.51.70.19, e-mail chateau.bourseau@wanadoo.fr ☑
Y by appt

LES PLANTES DU MAYNE 2000★★

■ 4 ha 12,000 ⬮ 15–23 €

This brand was started in 1986, and is the second wine to the Château Grand Mayne *cru classé*. It comes from younger vines, and in the 2000 vintage has a remarkably dark, deep purple colour, and a magnificent nose of Morello cherry and jammy fruit aromas along with a note of very toasty oak. The palate is just as delightful, with a full-bodied, round attack, a well-balanced structure with velvety tannins, and a rich, long, charming finish on dark berries. This is a superb wine which should be kept for a while before drinking.
🔑 SCEV J.-P. Nony, Ch. Grand Mayne, 33330 Saint-Emilion, tel. 05.57.74.42.50, fax 05.57.74.41.89, e-mail grand-mayne@grand-mayne.com ☑
Y by appt

CH. MONDOU 2000★

■ 5.18 ha 31,236 ▮⬮♁ 11–15 €

This cru is planted with 80% Merlot and 20% Cabernets on the sandy and siliceous-gravel soils at Saint-Sulpice-de-Faleyrans. It has produced a 2000 with an intense, deep ruby colour and a nose which, although still reticent, is releasing some aromas of sloes and small, slightly acid red berries. The palate is well balanced, with somewhat firm tannins which need to age for three to four years.
🔑 Union de producteurs de Saint-Emilion, Haut-Gravet, BP 27, 33330 Saint-Emilion, tel. 05.57.24.70.71, fax 05.57.24.65.18, e-mail contact@udpse.com
Y ev.day except Sun. 8am–12 noon 2pm–6pm
🔑 EARL Vignobles Naulet

CH. MONTLABERT 2000★

■ 13 ha 70,000 ⬮ 11–15 €

This property has a beautiful Girondin house surrounded by 15 ha of vines, 2 km from the medieval town. The adjoining building has three large bedrooms to accommodate B & B visitors. They will be able to taste this 2000, which has a purple colour with ruby glints, and a nose of fresh dark berries (blackcurrants) along with fine oaky vanilla and spice notes. The palate is supple and very agreeable, with a combination of fresh fruit flavours and smooth, liquoricy oak. This is a very good example of the vintage, which will keep for ten years and be a good accompaniment to game birds or tournedos Rossini.
🔑 G. Fourcroy, SCA du Ch. Montlabert, 33330 Saint-Emilion, tel. 05.57.24.62.61, fax 05.57.24.68.25, e-mail contacts@chateau-francmayne.com ☑ 🏠
Y by appt

CH. LA MOULEYRE 2000★

■ 6 ha 36,600 ⬮ 11–15 €

This delightful vineyard comprises just six of the 106 ha that Philippe Bardet cultivates in Saint-Emilion and Côtes de Castillon. The terroir here is on a south-facing limestone-clay hillside, planted with 88% Merlot and 12% Cabernet Franc. It has produced a very classic Saint-Emilion Grand Cru with a dense colour and a bouquet which starts on very ripe fruit notes (prunes and currants), then develops on to more oaky aromas of toast. The palate is still fruity and full of flavour, with a good balance between a rich body and well-integrated tannins. In three to seven years' time this wine will be the perfect accompaniment to red meat and game.
🔑 SCEA des Vignobles Bardet, 17, La Cale, 33330 Vignonet, tel. 05.57.84.53.16, fax 05.57.74.93.47, e-mail vignobles@vignobles-bardet.fr ☑
Y by appt

CH. MOULIN DU CADET 2000★★

■ Gd cru clas. 4.62 ha 22,000 ⬮ 23–30 €

82 85 86 88 89 |90| 94 96 **00**

We do not often have the opportunity to taste this very exclusive Grand Cru Classé which is being offered by the Jean-Pierre Moueix company, and having experienced this beautifully made, very classic 2000, we know what we are missing. It has a dark, delightfully subtle colour and a bouquet which is reticent at first but then releases its fruit aromas free from any masking by oak. The palate is dense and well balanced, with the oak offering subtle support to the characteristic flavours of very ripe grapes and a genuine terroir. Lovers of classic Saint-Emilion will be able to enjoy this wine is three to six years' time. (Price not guaranteed as stated).
🔑 SC du Ch. Moulin du Cadet, 33330 Saint-Emilion

CH. MOULIN GALHAUD 2000★

■ 2 ha 6,000 ⬮ 15–23 €

97 |98| 99 00

Since this cru was started in 1997 by the Galhaud family on the gravel soils in the south of the appellation, it has made regular appearances in the *Guide*. This vintage has plenty of character and no shortage of attractive features, even though its intense colour only shows very slight signs of development. The bouquet has lovely fragrances of very ripe grapes, along with leather notes and a powerful note of oaky toast. The palate is full and powerful, with warming flavours and fine, agreeable tannins which will enable the wine to keep for two to eight years. One star goes to the **Château La Rose Brisson (8–11 €)**, which is from the same producer.
🔑 SCEA Martine Galhaud, La Rouchonne, 33330 Vignonet, tel. 06.63.77.39.75, fax 05.57.74.48.93 ☑
Y by appt

CH. ORME BRUN 2000★

■ 4 ha 22,000 ⬮ 11–15 €

This wine is made from 80% Merlot and 20% Cabernet Sauvignon. It has a dark, intense Bordeaux colour, and a pleasant bouquet of ripe red berry, blackcurrant and cherry stone aromas, combined with very appealing notes of oaky vanilla and toast. The palate is supple, round and full bodied, with a very good structure which is still firm on the finish. This wine will be ready to drink in 2004 and will keep for ten years.
🔑 SCEA Vignobles Yvan Brun, 271, Belle-Assise, 33330 Saint-Sulpice-de-Faleyrens, tel. 05.57.24.61.62, fax 05.57.24.68.82 ☑
Y ev.day except Sun. 9.30am–12.30pm 2pm–5.30pm

CH. PATRIS 2000★★

■ 6 ha 24,000 ⬮ 30–38 €

88 **|90|** 92 93 95 |96| |97| **98 99 00**

This wine is made almost entirely from Merlot, with just 5% Cabernet Franc. It has a sumptuous, dense, dark purple colour and a thoroughbred bouquet of dark berry aromas (blackberries, blackcurrants), combined with rich oaky toast. The palate has a very rich body, an excellent balance between the oak and grape tannins, and an admirable finish on fruit and liquorice flavours.
🔑 Michel Querre, SCEA Ch. Patris, Hospices de la Madeleine, 33330 Saint-Emilion, tel. 05.57.55.51.60, fax 05.57.55.51.61 ☑
Y by appt

CH. PAVIE 2000★★

■ 1er gd cru clas. B 37 ha 90,000 ⬮ +76 €

70 71 75 76 **78** 79 80 **81 82 83** |85| |86| 87 **|88| |89|** (90) **91 92 |93| |94| 95 |96|** 98 99 **00**

This Premier Grand Cru Classé vineyard is superbly lit by the sun at midday, and at night by the lights from the buildings rising in tiers up the hillside which one can admire from the road between Bordeaux and Bergerac. This is the flagship of Gérard Perse, and he has made it a major investment. The 2000 has a magnificent Bordeaux colour with black cherry glints, and a bouquet of powerful, complex aromas: flowers, vanilla, blackcurrants, leather, cocoa, and so on. The palate warming, with fruity, exotic flavours accompanied by tannins with a silky yet persistent texture. This Grand Cru will be ready to drink quite soon, but will also keep for a long time.
🔑 Gérard Perse, SCA Ch. Pavie, 33330 Saint-Emilion, tel. 05.57.55.43.43, fax 05.57.24.63.99, e-mail vignobles.perse@wanadoo.fr

CH. PAVIE MACQUIN 2000★★

■ Gd cru clas. 11.85 ha 52,000 ◫ 46–76 €

83 85 86 88 |89| |90| |93| |94| |96| (97) 98 99 00

This *cru classé* won a *coup de coeur* with its 1997 (a difficult vintage), and always maintains a very high standard thanks to its exceptionally good terroir and situation at the top of the Pavie hill. This 2000 has a magnificent, dark garnet colour with a few glints which show it is developing. The bouquet is already fine and delicate, combining red berry aromas with a soft oak note. The palate is extremely well balanced, elegant and silky, with a remarkably long, well-cloaked finish. This great wine is a already very pleasant to drink and should open out further in two to five years' time.

➤ SCEA Ch. Pavie Macquin, 33330 Saint-Emilion,
tel. 05.57.24.74.23, fax 05.57.24.63.78,
e-mail pavie.macquin@wanadoo.fr ☑
⟁ by appt
➤ Famille Corre-Macquin

CH. PETIT-FIGEAC 2000★

■ 1.6 ha 11,000 ◫ 15–23 €

This small vineyard is located right on the border with the Pomerol appellation, and has a fine gravel soil planted with 60% Merlot and 40% Cabernet Sauvignon. This gives the wine a very eclectic style: a combination of Saint-Emilion, Pomerol and even Médoc. Once the judges had got over their initial surprise, they awarded one star to this 2000 for its complexity, intensity, freshness and elegance. It should have achieved its full expression in four to six years' time, when it will be a good accompaniment to a wide range of dishes.

➤ Christian Seely, Ch. Petit Figeac, SNCEPV,
33330 Saint-Emilion
➤ Axa Millésimes

CH. PEYMOUTON 2000★

■ 31 ha 125,000 ▮ ◫ ⚬ +11–15 €

The 31 ha of this cru comprise the non-classified plots of the wine-estate which produces Château Laroque (a Saint-Emilion *cru classé*. These are located on the limestone-clay terroirs of Saint-Christophe-des-Bardes, and have produced a 2000 with an intense ruby colour and a developing bouquet of pleasant fresh fruit aromas along with some pepper and menthol notes. The palate is supple and balanced, with fine, fleshy, lingering tannins. This is a well-made wine which should be ready to drink before too long (in two to three years' time).

➤ SCA Famille Beaumartin, Ch. Laroque,
33330 Saint-Christophe-des-Bardes, tel. 05.57.24.77.28,
fax 05.57.24.63.65, e-mail contact@chateau-laroque.com ☑
⟁ by appt

LA PLAGNOTTE 2000★

■ 1 ha 3,800 ◫ 23–30 €

This cru is attached to Laplagnotte Bellevue, and, like it, is run by descendants of the Fourcaud-Laussac family which used to own Cheval Blanc. It is located in the eastern part of the appellation, on a siliceous-clay soil. This wine is very representative of its vintage, with a dark, dense Bordeaux colour and a complex bouquet of very ripe fruit aromas (cherries, blackcurrants, prunes) and caramelized vanilla oak. The palate is really delightful, with a perfect balance between fruit, spice and oak flavours, and also between the body and the structure, which is based on silky tannins. In a year's time and for ten more years after that this 2000 will be a magnificent accompaniment to game and dry cheeses.

➤ Claude de Labarre, Ch. Laplagnotte-Bellevue,
33330 Saint-Christophe-des-Bardes, tel. 05.57.24.78.67,
fax 05.57.24.63.62, e-mail arnauddl@aol.com ☑
⟁ by appt

CH. PLAISANCE 2000★

■ 17 ha n.c. ◫ 15–23 €

Along the road to Branne, in the south of the appellation, Château Plaisance has a sandy-clay terroir which has produced this 2000 with an intense ruby colour and a nose still dominated by oak and releasing aromas of vanilla, toast, grilling and roasting. The palate is powerful and concentrated, with very ripe grape flavours supported by

excellent-quality oak. This is a rich wine which will take five to six years or more to open out fully.

➤ SCEA Ch. Plaisance, 33330 Saint-Sulpice-de-Faleyrens,
tel. 05.57.24.78.85, fax 05.57.74.44.94 ☑
⟁ by appt
➤ Xavier Mareschal

CH. DE PRESSAC 2000★

■ 25.5 ha 58,000 ◫ 23–30 €

|96| 97 |98| |99| 00

This large wine-estate surrounds the château where, on 20 July 1453, the treaty was signed which brought an end to the Hundred Years' War, after the battle of Castillon. The new owners here are doing everything possible to restore the vineyard, which is on an ideally situated terroir. Their 2000 delights the eye, the nose and the palate, and will continue to do so for many years (three to ten or more). The second wine, **Tour de Pressac 2000 (15–23 €)**, receives a special mention.

➤ GFA Ch. de Pressac, 33330 Saint-Etienne-de-Lisse,
tel. 05.57.40.18.02, fax 05.57.40.10.07,
e-mail jfetdquenin@libertysurf.fr ☑
⟁ by appt
➤ J.-CL. et D. Quenin

CH. PUY-RAZAC 2000★

■ 3 ha 19,000 ▮ ◫ ⚬ 11–15 €

The Thoilliez family selects 3 ha of vines planted on a sand and iron dross soil. This 2000 is made from 60% Merlot and 40% Cabernet Franc, and has a ruby colour and a bouquet which needs a little aeration before it opens on to ripe fruit aromas with a slight touch of musk. The palate is delicious and well structured, with no sense of artificiality, since the grape flavour is not masked by oak. This wine should develop well over the three to eight years to come.

➤ SC Thoilliez, Ch. Puy Razac, 33330 Saint-Emilion,
tel. 05.57.24.73.32, fax 05.57.24.75.99,
e-mail puy-razac@wanadoo.fr ☑
⟁ by appt

CH. ROLLAND-MAILLET 2000★

■ 3.35 ha 16,600 ▮ ◫ ⚬ 15–23 €

(82) 85 86 |89| |90| |93| |94| |95| |97| 98 00

It is possible to be a great oenologist and travel the world, while still looking after your own vines, as is proved by Michel and Dany Rolland, who carry out rigorous grape selections and have produced this 2000 from 75% Merlot and 25% Cabernet Franc grown on siliceous-gravel-clay soils. It has a strong ruby colour with dark purple glints, and a fruity, spicy, vinous bouquet with subtle hints of liquorice and eucalyptus. The palate is well structured and full bodied, with mature tannins which are still very firm on the finish and will ensure that this wine has a great future.

➤ SCEA Fermière des domaines Rolland, Maillet,
33500 Pomerol, tel. 05.57.51.23.05, fax 05.57.51.66.08,
e-mail rolland.vignobles@wanadoo.fr ☑
⟁ by appt

CH. ROL VALENTIN 2000★★

■ 4.6 ha 15,000 ◫ +76 €

95 (98) 00

The label here shows a little golden heart borne by two cherubs, which is very symbolic; Eric Prisette, an ex-professional footballer from Lille, and his wife Virginie, fell in love first with Saint-Emilion and then with the vines. They started to produce their own wine in 1994, and were very soon rewarded by Hachette with two *coups de coeur* for the 1995 and 1998 vintages. Hardly surprising then that the heart (also the symbol of Saint Valentine) should be in evidence all around them. It should be added that their remarkably robust 2000 will be excellent for the hearts of those who get the chance to drink it. It has extremely good tannins which will enable it to keep for the next five to ten years.

➤ Eric Prissette, Ch. Rol Valentin, 33330 Saint-Emilion,
tel. 05.57.74.43.51, fax 05.57.74.45.13,
e-mail info@rolvalentin.com

BORDEAUX

Saint-Emilion Grand Cru

CH. LA ROSE PRESSAC 2000★★

11 ha	41,994	🔳🍶	8–11 €

The Lafaye family owns vineyards at Saint-Etienne-de-Lisse to the east of the town, and reserves this cru exclusively for the Cordier-Mestrezat company, acting through the Club Cordier which maintains a close partnership between production and marketing. The 2000 here is remarkable. It has a gleaming colour with ruby and purple glints which are still young. The complex, distinguished bouquet releases a wide range of aromas (sloes, cherry plums, truffles, spices and charred oak), and the palate is both flavourful and well structured. This expressive, substantial wine should develop elegantly over the next two to five years, and will be a particularly good accompaniment to roasted white meats. And let's not forget that it is also excellent value for money.
🍷 Cordier-Mestrezat et Domaines, 109, rue Achard, BP 154, 33042 Bordeaux Cedex, tel. 05.56.11.29.00, fax 05.56.11.29.01, e-mail mestrezat-domaines@wanadoo.fr
⚓ by appt

ROYAL 2000★

12 ha	81,333	🔳🍶	11–15 €

The cooperative's leading brand was given an equal rating for their **Galius 2000** and **Haut-Quercus 2000**, brands, both priced at 15–23 €. In all that makes 248,000 bottles of wine which can be served with complete confidence as an accompaniment to either red meat or poultry. This 2000 makes a good first impression with a fresh, ruby colour. The nose is still reticent, but is releasing aromas of dried fruits and pepper with a few notes of musk. After a round, supple attack, the palate has a firm, powerful tannic structure and a long, lingering finish.
🍷 Union de producteurs de Saint-Emilion, Haut-Gravet, BP 27, 33330 Saint-Emilion, tel. 05.57.24.70.71, fax 05.57.24.65.18, e-mail contact@udpse.com ▓
⚓ ev.day except Sun. 8am–12 noon 2pm–6pm

CH. SAINT GEORGES COTE PAVIE 2000★

Gd cru clas. 5.5 ha	25,000	🔳	15–23 €

82 83 (85) 86 88 89 |90| 92 |95| 97 98 00

This family cru classé is very well situated on the Pavie hillside, just facing Ausone, which means that it is in very good company. The terroir shows in the colour of the wine, which has numerous ruby and garnet glints. The bouquet has dark berry aromas, and the palate is dense and full bodied, with slight flavour of cloves. The tannins are heavy and dense, and will take three to seven years to become more refined, after which this wine will go very well with an entrecôte steak.
🍷 Jacques Masson, 33330 Saint-Emilion, tel. 05.57.74.44.23 ▓
🍷 Gabriel Masson

CH. SAINT-HUBERT 2000★

3 ha	20,000	🔳	15–23 €

St Hubert is the patron saint of hunting, and hunters will no doubt appreciate not only the name of this cru but also its intense purple colour and complex, powerful bouquet of jammy fruit aromas and notes of undergrowth and toast. The dense, velvety palate is supported by a good tannic structure. Over the next four to five years this wine can be served with game (of course!) or with any red meat.
🍷 SCE Vignobles Aubert, Ch. La Couspaude, 33330 Saint-Emilion, tel. 05.57.40.15.76, fax 05.57.40.10.14, e-mail vignobles.aubert@wanadoo.fr ▓

CH. SANSONNET 2000★

6.5 ha	20,000	🔳	30–38 €

In the 19th century this cru belonged to Duc Decazes, who was Louis XVIII's prime minister. The estate was bought in 1999 by the Marquis d'Aulan, the former owner of Piper-Heidsieck champagne: another example of the special relationship between Champagne and Bordeaux. This 2000 has a dark colour and a powerful, expressive nose with a perfect combination of fruit and oak aromas. It is very clean on the palate, with flavours of toast and roasting, and tannins which are still slightly firm and will take three to six years to become more refined.

🍷 Patrick d'Aulan, GAM-AUDY, Château Jonqueyres, 33750 Saint-Germain-du-Puch, tel. 05.57.34.51.66, fax 05.56.30.11.45, e-mail info@gamaudy.com
⚓ by appt

CH. LA SERRE 2000★

Gd cru clas. 7 ha	24,000	🔳	23–30 €

|90| 92 93 |95| |96| |98| 99 00

This family vineyard is located 200 metres to the east of the town's ramparts, and surrounds a house built over the ruins of an ancient monastery which was destroyed at the end of the 16th century. The wine here is of a traditional type; it has a dark colour fringed with crimson, and an attractive bouquet of very ripe soft fruit aromas combined with well-balanced oak. The palate is delicious, full bodied, and supported by well-cloaked tannins. This 2000 is already pleasant to drink, but its structure also gives it the potential to develop further over the next four or five years.
🍷 SCE Luc d'Arfeuille, Ch. La Serre, 33330 Saint-Emilion, tel. 05.57.24.71.38, fax 05.57.24.63.01, e-mail darfeuille.luc@wanadoo.fr
⚓ by appt

CH. TAUZINAT L'HERMITAGE 2000★★

9.28 ha	53,000	🔳	11–15 €

88 89 93 94 95 96 |97| 00

This cru once belonged to the Comte de Carles, who was lieutenant-general of the king's armies. Today it is run by the descendants of Marcel Moueix, who like many Libournais wine professionals originally came from the Corrèze. They certainly know how to make great wines in this area, and even very great ones, as is proved by this 2000, to which the Jury has awarded a coup de cœur. This wine has it all: a dense Bordeaux colour with black glints, an intense, complex bouquet with a succession of aromas (dark berries, truffles, spicy oak...), and a full palate with a high-quality tannic structure and a perfect balance between power and finesse. In four to ten years' time it will be the perfect accompaniment to a leg of lamb.
🍷 SC Bernard Moueix, Ch. Taillefer, BP 9, 33501 Libourne Cedex, tel. 05.57.25.50.45, fax 05.57.25.50.45
🍷 Héritiers Marcel Moueix

CH. TERTRE DAUGAY 2000★

Gd cru clas. 13 ha	65,000	🔳	23–30 €

82 83 86 88 |89| |90| 93 94 96 98 99 00

Overlooking the Dordogne valley, this cru classé is a classic limestone-clay terroir in a wonderfully sunny location. This 2000 is made from 60% Merlot and 40% Cabernet Franc, and has a dark, young colour and a somewhat reticent nose which opens on to oaky toast, blackcurrant and liquorice aromas when the wine is swirled in the glass. The palate is very concentrated, with a robust texture, dense tannins, and a new oak flavour which is present right up to the finish on a note of liquorice. Lovers of rich wines will be able to enjoy this wine in five to ten years' time.
🍷 SARL Ch. Tertre daugay, 33330 Saint-Emilion, tel. 05.57.24.72.15, fax 05.57.24.69.06 ▓
⚓ by appt

CH. TOINET FOMBRAUGE 2000★

■ 1.9 ha 12,000 ▐ ⦀ 11–15 €

93 94 |95| |96| |97| 98 99 00

Of the 7.3 ha that he cultivates on a limestone-clay soil in the north east of the appellation, Bernard Sierra selects 1.9 ha of old vines to produce this Grand Cru, which is regularly featured in the *Guide*. This year the 2000 is highly impressive. Its strong colour is still young, and it has a developing bouquet of fresh fruit and ripe fruit aromas. The elegant palate is based on high-quality tannins, and the restrained oak note does not mask the flavour of very ripe grapes and the characteristics of the terroir. This wine will be ready to drink in two years' time, and will keep for a decade.

➡ Bernard Sierra, Toinet-Fombrauge,
33330 Saint-Christophe-des-Bardes, tel. 05.57.24.77.70,
fax 05.57.24.76.49 ▐ ⓐ
⏱ ev.day 10am–12 noon 3pm–7pm

CH. TOUR BALADOZ 2000★

■ 10 ha 50,000 ▐ ⦀ ♦ 15–23 €

|93| |94| |95| |96| |97| 98 99 00

This cru is the flagship of the Schepper de Moor vineyards, which are located on limestone-clay soils in the east of the appellation. Merlot is the main grape variety here, complemented by 30% Cabernet Franc. This 2000 has a beautiful, brilliant ruby colour and a bouquet which releases powerful aromas of stewed fruits and oaky vanilla and toast when the wine is swirled in the glass. After a round attack, the palate has a balanced structure and well-integrated, lingering tannins which will enable the wine to keep for three to five years. The **Château La Croizille 2000 (46–76 €)** is a similar type of wine, but with a stronger note of oak. It needs to be kept for five to eight years before drinking.

➡ SCEA Ch. Tour Baladoz, Baladoz,
33330 Saint-Laurent-des-Combes, tel. 05.57.88.94.17,
fax 05.57.88.39.14, e-mail gdemour@aol.com ▐
⏱ by appt
➡ de Schepper

CH. LA TOUR DU PIN FIGEAC 2000★

■ Gd cru clas. 8 ha 36,000 ⦀ 30–38 €

There are two La Tour du Pin Figeac *crus classées*, (just as there are two Beau-séjours). This 2000 is made by Jean-Michel Moueix, and comes from old vines (70% Merlot and 30% Cabernet Franc) grown on a sand and gravel terroir. It has a great deal of appeal, with a young, fresh, fruity character and a gleaming colour. The nose is dominated by fruit, and is beginning to open on to elegant oak and chocolate notes. The palate is also very young and dominated by fruit and tannins, but in two to three years' time all these features will be rounder and will make this a very attractive wine.

➡ Jean-Michel Moueix, Ch. La Tour du Pin Figeac,
33330 Saint-Emilion, tel. 05.57.74.18.44,
fax 05.57.51.52.87 ▐
⏱ by appt

CH. TRIMOULET 2000★

■ 10 ha 50,000 ⦀ 11–15 €

This good-sized wine-estate has been in the same family for two centuries. Its wine is marketed by the Mau company (Freixenet). This 2000 has a deep colour with ruby and garnet highlights, and a complex nose with a succession of fruit, oak and above all spice aromas. The structure is based on tannins which are still fresh and will need to settle down over the next two to six years.

➡ SA Yvon Mau, 33190 Gironde-sur-Dropt,
tel. 05.56.61.54.54, fax 05.56.61.54.61,
e-mail info@ymau.com
➡ Michel Jean

CH. TROTTEVIEILLE 2000★★

■ 1er gd cru clas n.c. 33,000 ⦀ 46–76 €

82 85 86 88 90 93 94 |95| |96| |97| 98 99 **00**

This Premier Grand Classé comes from a wonderful location above the medieval town, with a view on one side over the Dordogne valley, and on the other over Pomerol and

Fronsac. This 2000 has scaled the heights as well (thanks to Denis Dubourdieu's advice, perhaps?) by winning a *coup de coeur*. The wine makes a very strong impression with its complexity and elegance. It has a sumptuous Bordeaux colour with black glints, and a bouquet which, although still young, already has very expressive aromas of cherries, stewed fruits, hazelnuts and almonds, along with some mineral and oak notes. The palate is fresh, fruity, and supported by fine, spicy tannins. In a few years' time this wine will be a worthy accompaniment to fine dishes such as saddle of venison or *gigot à la ficelle*.

➡ Indivision Castéja-Preben-Hansen, Ch. Trottevieille,
33330 Saint-Emilion, tel. 05.56.00.00.70, fax 05.57.87.48.61,
e-mail domaines boriemanoux@dial.oleane.com ▐
⏱ by appt

CH. DU VAL D'OR 2000★

■ 5 ha 30,000 ⦀ 11–15 €

94 |95| |96| 97 98 **99** 00

This cru is one of a large group run by Philippe Bardet. The wine here won a *coup de coeur* last year, but despite that it still remains very reasonably priced, which is a godsend for the wine-buyer. This winemaker uses the very latest machinery to select his grapes, and has now produced a 2000 whose young purple and strong garnet colour shimmers in the glass. The nose opens on to very ripe grape and oaky toast aromas, and the palate is well structured but still slightly dominated by an oak flavour which should become more integrated within two to five years.

➡ SCEA des Vignobles Bardet, 17, La Cale,
33330 Vignonet, tel. 05.57.84.53.16, fax 05.57.74.93.47,
e-mail vignobles@vignobles-bardet.fr ▐
⏱ by appt

CH. VIEILLE TOUR LA ROSE 2000★

■ 5.06 ha 39,000 ▐ ⦀ 8–11 €

This cru is located on the sandy ferruginous soils in the north of Saint-Emilion, and is offering a 2000 made from 80% Merlot and 20% Cabernet Franc. It has a very strong, inviting ruby colour and a bouquet of agreeable soft fruit aromas combined with a slightly spicy oak note and some lovely, fresh hints of resin and menthol. The palate is well balanced, with delicate tannins and a fruity finish.

➡ SCEA Vignobles Daniel Ybert, La Rose,
33330 Saint-Emilion, tel. 05.57.24.73.41, fax 05.57.74.44.83,
e-mail commercial@vignoblesybert.fr ▐
⏱ by appt

VIEUX CHATEAU HAUT BEARD 2000★★

■ 2.5 ha 13,000 ▐ ⦀ ♦ 11–15 €

This property has 7 ha of vines (mainly Merlot), planted on the well-exposed limestone-clay slopes in the southeast of the appellation. The work there has been done by traditional methods for four generations, and in the 2000 vintage this has produced remarkable results: a Bordeaux colour with ruby highlights, an explosive bouquet of fresh fruit aromas (cherries and blackcurrants) and fine spice notes (nutmeg and curry), and a supple palate with a delicate oak flavour and silky tannins. This wine is already pleasant to drink, and in two to five years' time will be the perfect accompaniment to entrecôte steak *à la bordelaise* or game in sauce.

➡ SCEA Vignoble Riboulet, 2, Grandes-Plantes,
33330 Saint-Laurent-des-Combes, tel. 05.57.24.62.71,
fax 05.57.24.63.92, e-mail gmaye@aol.com ▐
⏱ by appt

CH. VIEUX FORTIN 2000★

■ 5.39 ha · 32,000 ◫ 38–46 €

Vieux Fortin is right next to Pomerol, and has produced a 2000 made from 60% Merlot and 40% Cabernet Franc, and matured in new oak. The result is a deep, intense garnet colour, a bouquet of toast and roasted coffee aromas along with some dark berry notes, and a full, dense, powerful palate with firm yet elegant tannins which linger on to a long finish.
🕿 Claude Sellan, Ch. Vieux Fortin, 33330 Saint-Emilion, tel. 05.57.24.69.97, fax 05.57.24.69.97,
e-mail vieuxfortin@hotmail.com ☑
☘ by appt

CH. VIEUX GRAND FAURIE 2000★★

■ 4.8 ha 17,500 ▮◫⬩ 11–15 €

Planted on old sand soils to the north of Saint-Emilion, this cru is offering a classic wine with an intense purple colour and a nose which although still restrained is very elegant, with aromas of jammy fruits, cherries and soft, well-balanced oak. The palate is velvety and has a long finish on mature, well-cloaked tannins. This is an excellent, thoroughbred wine.
🕿 SCEA Bourrigaud et Fils, Ch. Vieux Grand Faurie, 33330 Saint-Emilion, tel. 05.57.74.43.98, fax 05.57.74.41.07, e-mail info@chateau-champion.com ☑

CH. VIRAMON

Réserve Prestige 2000★

■ 3 ha 12,000 ◫ 15–23 €

This 2000 comes from a selection of 3 ha of old vines grown on limestone-clay soils in the eastern part of the appellation. It is made from 80% Merlot and 20% Cabernet Sauvignon, and has cherry and dark berry aromas combined with notes of good-quality oaky toast. The palate is smooth, with firm yet mature tannins and very good length. This is a very characteristic Saint-Emilion for longer maturing.
🕿 Vignobles Lafaye Père et Fils, Ch. Viramon, 33330 Saint-Etienne-de-Lisse, tel. 05.57.40.18.28, fax 05.57.40.02.70 ☑
☘ by appt

CH. LA VOUTE 2000★

■ 1.14 ha 6,000 ◫ 11–15 €

This estate was only started in 1993, but even so it has the benefit of 20-year-old Merlot vines. This 2000 has a garnet colour and a powerful, elegant bouquet of red and dark berry aromas, along with vanilla and liquorice notes. The supple, full palate has mouthwatering, well-integrated tannins which linger pleasantly on to the finish. This will keep for four to six years, and will go well with dishes such as a *civet* of goose.
🕿 EARL Moreau, Ch. d'Arvouet, 33570 Montagne, tel. 05.57.74.56.60, fax 05.57.74.58.33,
e-mail moreaulavoute@aol.com ☑
☘ by appt

CH. YON-FIGEAC 2000★★

■ Gd cru clas. 22 ha 120,000 ▮◫⬩ 23–30 €

|88| |89| 92 1993 94 |95| |96| 99 00

Bernard Germain bought this large vineyard fifteen years ago, and has worked extremely hard on it. This is a great wine for longer maturing which is very characteristic of the Figeac area. It has a gleaming, deep garnet colour, and a bouquet

which is already rich, with aromas of blackberries, blackcurrants and oaky liquorice, combined with some spicy and musky notes. The full-bodied, rich palate is structured by very high-quality tannins. Within the next two to eight years this vintage will be perfect.
🕿 SA Ch. Yon-Figeac, 33330 Saint-Emilion, tel. 05.57.42.66.66, fax 05.57.64.36.20,
e-mail bordeaux@vgas.com ☑
☘ by appt
🕿 B. Germain

Wines selected but not starred

CH. L'ARROSEE 2000

■ Gd cru clas. 9.18 ha 38,000 ◫ 38–46 €

🕿 EARL Famille Caille, Ch. L'Arrosée, 33330 Saint-Emilion, tel. 05.57.24.69.44, fax 05.57.24.66.46, e-mail chateau.larrosee@wanadoo.fr

CH. BALESTARD LA TONNELLE 2000

■ Gd cru clas. 10.6 ha 45,000 ▮◫⬩ 23–30 €

(83) 85 86 88 |89| |90| |94| |95| |96| 99 00

🕿 SCEA Capdemourlin, Ch. Roudier, 33570 Montagne, tel. 05.57.74.62.06, fax 05.57.74.59.34,
e-mail info@vignoblescapdemourlin.com ☑
☘ by appt

CH. BERGAT 2000

■ Gd cru clas. n.c. 13,000 ◫ 30–38 €

88 89 93 94 |95| |96| 97 **98** 99 00

🕿 Indivision Castéja-Preben-Hansen, Ch. Bergat, 33330 Saint-Emilion, tel. 05.56.00.00.70, fax 05.57.87.48.61, e-mail domainesborimanoux@dialoleane.com ☑
☘ by appt

CH. LA BONNELLE 2000

■ 12.6 ha 60,000 ◫ 11–15 €

93 94 |95| |96| 97 98 |99| |00|

🕿 Vignobles Sulzer, La Bonnelle, 33330 Saint-Pey-d'Armens, tel. 05.57.47.15.12, fax 05.57.47.16.83 ☑
☘ by appt

CH. CADET-PIOLA 2000

■ Gd cru clas. 6.81 ha 28,000 ◫ 30–38 €

86 |89| |90| 93 |95| |96| 99 00

🕿 Alain Jabiol, SCEA du Ch. Cadet-Piola, BP 24, 33330 Saint-Emilion, tel. 05.57.74.47.69, fax 05.57.24.68.28, e-mail infos@chateaucadetpiola.com ☑
☘ by appt

CH. CANTENAC 2000

■ n.c. 55,000 ▮◫⬩ 15–23 €

🕿 Nicole Roskam-Brunot, Ch. Cantenac, Cantenac 2, 33330 Saint-Emilion, tel. 05.57.51.35.22, fax 05.57.25.19.15, e-mail roskam@club-internet.fr ☑
☘ ev.day 9am–12 noon 2pm–6pm

CH. DU CAUZE 2000

■ 20 ha 120,000 ◫ 15–23 €

85 88 89 90 92 93 |94| |95| |97| 98 00

🕿 Ch. du Cauze, 33330 Saint-Christophe-des-Bardes, tel. 05.57.74.62.47 ☑
☘ by appt
🕿 Bruno Laporte

CH. CLOS SAINT-EMILION PHILIPPE

2000

| ■ | 4.6 ha | 29,000 | ⑪ | 15–23 € |

☛ Jean-Claude Philippe, 101, av. Gallieni, 33500 Libourne, tel. 05.57.51.05.93, fax 05.57.25.96.39, e-mail vignobles.philippe@libertysurf.fr ☑
☷ by appt

CLOS SAINT-MARTIN 2000

| ■ | Gd cru clas. 1.33 ha | 5,000 | ▮⑪⚬ | 38–46 € |

88 89 90 92 93 |95| |96| |97| 98 99 00

☛ SA Les Grandes Murailles, Ch. Côte de Baleau, 33330 Saint-Emilion, tel. 05.57.24.71.09, fax 05.57.24.69.72, e-mail lesgrandesmurailles@wanadoo.fr

CLOS SAINT-VINCENT 2000

| ■ | 4.64 ha | 24,000 | ⑪ | 11–15 € |

☛ SC Clos Saint-Vincent, 236, Lanseman, 33330 Saint-Sulpice-de-Faleyrens, tel. 05.57.74.44.80, fax 05.57.74.44.80, e-mail lionellatorse@aol.com ☑
☷ by appt
☛ Latorse

CH. LA COMMANDERIE 2000

| ■ | 6 ha | 11,000 | ⑪ | 15–23 € |

82 85 88 |89| (90) 95 |96| 98 99 00

☛ M. Frydman, SC Ch. La Commanderie, Fortin, 33330 Saint-Emilion, tel. 05.57.24.70.14, fax 05.57.24.68.08
☷ by appt

CH. CORBIN MICHOTTE 2000

| ■ | Gd cru clas. 6.8 ha | 30,000 | ▮⑪⚬ | 30–38 € |

☛ Jean-Noël Boidron, Ch. Corbin Michotte, 33330 Saint-Emilion, tel. 05.57.51.64.88, fax 05.57.51.56.30, e-mail vignoblesjnboidron@wanadoo.fr ☑
☷ by appt

CH. CORMEIL-FIGEAC 2000

| ■ | 10 ha | 50,000 | ⑪ | 15–23 € |

82 83 86 88 89 90 |94| |95| |96| 98 00

☛ SCEA Cormeil-Figeac, BP 49, 33330 Saint-Emilion, tel. 05.57.24.70.53, fax 05.57.24.68.20, e-mail moreaud@cormeil-figeac.com ☑
☷ by appt
☛ Richard Moreaud

CH. CROS FIGEAC 2000

| ■ | 1.8 ha | 7,500 | ⑪ | 30–38 € |

☛ SCEA Ch. Cros Figeac, Les Hospices de La Madeleine, BP 51, 33330 Saint-Emilion, tel. 05.57.55.51.60, fax 05.57.55.51.61 ☑

CH. LA DOMINIQUE 2000

| ■ | Gd cru clas. 18.5 ha | 57,600 | ⑪ | 46–76 € |

(82) 86 87 88 |89| |90| 91 92 93 |94| |95| |96| |97| |98| 99 00

☛ Vignobles Clément Fayat, Ch. La Dominique, 33330 Saint-Emilion, tel. 05.57.51.31.36, fax 05.57.51.63.04, e-mail info@vignobles.fayat-group.com ☑
☷ by appt

CH. L'EVECHE

Sonia Rykiel 2000

| ■ | 1.2 ha | 6,000 | ⑪ | +76 € |

☛ CL. Quentin, La Chapelle Lescours, 33330 Saint-Sulpice-de-Faleyrens, tel. 01.44.51.96.40, fax 05.57.24.65.37, e-mail info@chateau-eveche.com ☑

CH. FONROQUE 2000

| ■ | Gd cru clas. n.c. | 80,000 | ⑪ | 38–46 € |

81 82 83 85 86 88 89 |90| 95 |97| 98 00

☛ Ets Jean-Pierre Moueix, 54, quai du Priourat, 33500 Libourne, tel. 05.57.55.05.80, fax 05.57.25.73.30
☛ GFA Ch. Fonroque

CH. FRANC-MAYNE 2000

| ■ | Gd cru clas. 5 ha | 25,000 | ⑪ | 46–76 € |

85 86 |88| |89| |90| 92 |95| |96| 97 98 99 00

☛ Georgy Fourcroy, SCEA Ch. Franc-Mayne, 14, La Gomerie, 33330 Saint-Emilion, tel. 05.57.24.62.61, fax 05.57.24.68.25, e-mail contact@chateau-francmayne.com ☑ ⌂
☷ by appt

CH. GODEAU 2000

| ■ | 5 ha | 30,000 | ⑪ | 11–15 € |

☛ Grégoire Bonte, Ch. Godeau, 33330 Saint-Laurent-des-Combes, tel. 05.57.24.72.64, fax 05.57.24.65.89, e-mail chateau.godeau@free.fr ☑ ⌂
☷ by appt

CH. LA GOMERIE 2000

| ■ | 2.52 ha | 11,500 | ⑪ | +76 € |

95 96 97 98 99 00

☛ G. et D. Bécot, GFA La Gomerie, 33330 Saint-Emilion, tel. 05.57.74.46.87, fax 05.57.24.66.88

CH. LA GRACE DIEU 2000

| ■ | 11.73 ha | 70,500 | ▮⑪⚬ | 11–15 € |

☛ SCEA Pauty, Ch. La Grâce Dieu, 33330 Saint-Emilion, tel. 05.57.24.71.10, fax 05.57.24.67.24 ☑

CH. LA GRACE DIEU DES PRIEURS

Fortin 2000

| ■ | 2.8 ha | 15,000 | ⑪ | 15–23 € |

☛ SCEA Laubie-Prach, Fortin, 33330 Saint-Emilion, tel. 05.57.74.42.97, fax 05.57.24.69.59 ☑ ⌂
☷ by appt

CH. LA GRACE DIEU LES MENUTS

2000

| ■ | 13.35 ha | 100,000 | ⑪ | 15–23 € |

☛ EARL Vignobles Pilotte-Audier, Ch. La Grâce-Dieu-les-Menuts, 33330 Saint-Emilion, tel. 05.57.24.73.10, fax 05.57.74.40.44 ☑
☷ by appt

CH. GRAND BERT 2000

| ■ | 7 ha | 42,000 | ▮⑪ | 8–11 € |

☛ SCEA Lavigne, Tuillac, 33350 Saint-Philippe-d'Aiguilhe, tel. 05.57.40.60.09, fax 05.57.40.66.67, e-mail scea.lavigne@wanadoo.fr ☑
☷ by appt

CH. GRAND CORBIN 2000

| ■ | 15.45 ha | 100,000 | ▮⚬ | 15–23 € |

☛ Sté Familiale Alain Giraud, 5, Grand Corbin, 33330 Saint-Emilion, tel. 05.57.24.70.62, fax 05.57.74.47.18, e-mail grand-corbin@wanadoo.fr ☑
☷ by appt

CH. LES GRANDES MURAILLES 2000

| ■ | Gd cru clas. 1.6 ha | 6,500 | ▮⑪⚬ | 38–46 € |

88 (89) 94 |95| |96| |97| 98 99 00

☛ SA Les Grandes Murailles, Ch. Côte de Baleau, 33330 Saint-Emilion, tel. 05.57.24.71.09, fax 05.57.24.69.72, e-mail lesgrandesmurailles@wanadoo.fr

CH. LA GRAVE FIGEAC 2000

■ 6.4 ha 40,000 🍾▯♿ 15–23 €
☛ Jean-Pierre Clauzel, Ch. La Grave Figeac, 1,
Cheval-Blanc-Ouest, 33330 Saint-Emilion,
tel. 05.57.74.11.74, fax 05.57.74.17.18 ☑
☖ ev.day except Sun. 9am–12.30pm 2pm–7pm

CH. GRAVET 2000

■ 3.5 ha 23,000 ▯ 11–15 €
☛ Vignobles Philippe Faure, 7, rue de la Cité,
33330 Saint-Sulpice-de-Faleyrens, tel. 05.57.74.41.85,
fax 05.57.74.42.39,
e-mail vignobles.philippe.faure@wanadoo.fr ☑
☖ by appt

CH. GUADET-SAINT JULIEN 2000

■ Gd cru clas. 5.7 ha n.c. ▯ 23–30 €
☛ Guy-Petrus Lignac, Ch. Guadet-Saint-Julien,
33330 Saint-Emilion, tel. 05.57.74.40.04, fax 05.57.24.63.50,
e-mail guadet@aol.com ☑
☖ by appt
☛ Robert Lignac

CH. GUEYROSSE 2000

■ 4.6 ha 20,000 🍾▯♿ 15–23 €
86 90 |96| 97 98 |99| |00|

☛ EARL Vignobles Yves Delol, Ch. Gueyrosse,
33500 Libourne, tel. 05.57.51.02.63, fax 05.57.51.93.39 ☑
☖ by appt

CH. HAUT-CORBIN 2000

■ Gd cru clas. 6.01 ha 42,700 ▯ 23–30 €
81 (82) 83 85 86 88 90 |93| |94| (97) |98| 99 00

☛ SC Ch. Haut-Corbin, 33330 Saint-Emilion,
tel. 05.57.51.95.54, fax 05.57.51.90.93 ☑
☖ by appt

CH. HAUTE-NAUVE 2000

■ n.c. 49,573 🍾▯♿ 11–15 €
☛ Union de producteurs de Saint-Emilion, Haut-Gravet,
BP 27, 33330 Saint-Emilion, tel. 05.57.24.70.71,
fax 05.57.24.65.18, e-mail contact@udpse.com ☑
☖ ev.day except Sun. 8am–12 noon 2pm–6pm
☛ SCEA Ch. Haute-Nauve

CH. HAUT-PLANTEY 2000

■ 9 ha 50,000 🍾▯♿ 15–23 €
☛ Vignobles Michel Boutet, Ch. Haut-Plantey,
33330 Saint-Emilion, tel. 05.57.24.70.86,
fax 05.57.24.68.30 ☑
☖ by appt

CH. HAUT ROCHER 2000

■ 6 ha 36,395 🍾▯♿ 11–15 €
☛ Jean de Monteil, Ch. Haut-Rocher,
33330 Saint-Etienne-de-Lisse, tel. 05.57.40.18.09,
fax 05.57.40.08.23,
e-mail ht-rocher@vins-jean-de-monteil.com ☑
☖ by appt

CH. HAUT-SEGOTTES 2000

■ 8.82 ha 40,000 🍾▯ 11–15 €
88 89 90 93 94 |96| 98 99 00

☛ Vignobles André-Meunier, Ch. Haut-Segottes,
33330 Saint-Emilion, tel. 05.57.24.60.98,
fax 05.57.74.47.29 ☑
☖ by appt

CH. HAUT TROQUART LA GRACE DIEU Cuvée Passion 2000

■ 1.5 ha 8,500 ▯ 15–23 €
☛ Odile Audier, Ch. Haut Troquart La Grâce Dieu,
33330 Saint-Emilion, tel. 05.57.24.73.10,
fax 05.57.74.40.44 ☑
☖ by appt

CH. HAUT VEYRAC 2000

■ 6 ha 40,000 🍾▯♿ 11–15 €
☛ SCA Ch. Haut Veyrac, 33330 Saint-Etienne-de-Lisse,
tel. 05.57.40.02.26, fax 05.57.40.37.09 ☑
☖ by appt
☛ Claverie-Castaing

CH. HAUT-VILLET 2000

■ 6.1 ha 31,000 ▯ 15–23 €
88 |89| |90| |95| 98 99 00

☛ Eric Lenormand, Ch. Haut-Villet, BP 17,
33330 Saint-Etienne-de-Lisse, tel. 05.57.47.97.60,
fax 05.57.47.92.94, e-mail haut.villet@free.fr ☑
☖ ev.day except Sun. 10am–12 noon 2pm–6pm,
cl. 1 Dec.–28 Feb.

CH. JEAN VOISIN 2000

■ 13.3 ha 34,000 ▯ 15–23 €
☛ SCEA du Ch. Jean Voisin, 33330 Saint-Emilion,
tel. 05.57.24.70.40, fax 05.57.24.79.57 ☑
☖ by appt

CH. JUGUET Révélation 2000

■ 2 ha 10,000 ▯ 15–23 €
☛ SCEA Landrodie Père et Fille,
33330 Saint-Pey-d'Armens, tel. 05.57.24.74.10,
fax 05.57.24.66.33, e-mail chateau.juguet@wanadoo.fr ☑
☖ ev.day 8am–12 noon 2pm–7pm

CH. LE JURAT 2000

■ 7.58 ha 50,200 ▯ 15–23 €
☛ Ch. le Jurat, 33330 Saint-Emilion, tel. 05.57.51.95.54,
fax 05.57.51.90.93 ☑
☖ by appt

CH. LARCIS DUCASSE 2000

■ Gd cru clas. 10.98 ha 50,000 ▯ 38–46 €
82 83 85 86 88 93 94 |96| 00

☛ SCEA Gratiot, Ch. Larcis Ducasse,
33330 Saint-Laurent-des-Combes, tel. 05.57.24.70.84,
fax 05.57.24.64.00, e-mail larcis-ducasse@wanadoo.fr ☑
☖ by appt

CH. LAROQUE 2000

■ Gd cru clas. 27 ha 148,000 ▯ 23–30 €
☛ SCA Famille Beaumartin, Ch. Laroque,
33330 Saint-Christophe-des-Bardes, tel. 05.57.24.77.28,
fax 05.57.24.63.65, e-mail contact@chateau-laroque.com ☑
☖ by appt

CH. LE LOUP 2000

■ 6.37 ha 4.173 🍾▯♿ 11–15 €
☛ Union de producteurs de Saint-Emilion, Haut-Gravet,
BP 27, 33330 Saint-Emilion, tel. 05.57.24.70.71,
fax 05.57.24.65.18, e-mail contact@udpse.com
☖ ev.day except Sun. 8am–12 noon 2pm–6pm
☛ Patrick Garrigue

CH. MAGDELAINE 2000

■ 1er gd cru clas 10.37 ha 26,000 ❙❙❙ 46–76 €
70 75 78 79 80 82 (83) 85 |86| |87| |88| |89| |90| 92 93 |94| 95 |96| |97| 98 99 00

🍷 Ets Jean-Pierre Moueix, 54, quai du Priourat,
33500 Libourne, tel. 05.57.55.05.80, fax 05.57.25.73.30

CH. MARQUEY LA GARELLE

Elevé en fût de chêne 2000
■ 6 ha 14,394 ❙❙❙ 5–8 €
🍷 André Quancard-André, chem. de La Cabeyre,
33240 Saint-André-de-Cubzac, tel. 05.57.33.42.53,
fax 05.57.43.22.22, e-mail aqa@andrequancard.com
🍷 Bouquey

CH. LA MARZELLE 2000

■ Gd cru clas. 13 ha 80,000 ❙❙❙ 23–30 €
🍷 SCEA Ch. La Marzelle, 33330 Saint-Emilion,
tel. 05.57.55.10.55, fax 05.57.55.10.56,
e-mail chateau.lamarzelle@wanadoo.fr
🍷 J.-J. Sioen

CH. MAUVEZIN 2000

■ 3 ha 12,000 ❙❙❙ 23–30 €
90 94 |95| 96 97 98 99 00

🍷 GFA Cassat et Fils, BP 44, 33330 Saint-Emilion,
tel. 05.57.24.72.36, fax 05.57.74.48.54 ☑
🍷 by appt

CH. MOINE VIEUX 2000

■ 1 ha 6,000 ❙❙❙ 15–23 €
|95| |98| 99 00

🍷 P. Dentraygues, Lanseman,
33330 Saint-Sulpice-de-Faleyrens, tel. 05.57.74.40.54 ☑
🍷 by appt

CH. MONBOUSQUET 2000

■ 33 ha 80,000 ❙❙❙ +76 €
93 94 |95| |96| |97| 98 99 00

🍷 SA Ch. Monbousquet, 33330 Saint-Sulpice-de-Faleyrens,
tel. 05.57.55.43.43, fax 05.57.24.63.99,
e-mail vignobles.perse@wanadoo.fr
🍷 Gérard Perse

CH. MONT BELAIR

Cuvée Jean Denamiel 2000
■ 3 ha 5,700 ❙❙❙ 11–15 €
🍷 Jean-Pierre Denamiel, 1, Bréat,
33330 Saint-Etienne-de-Lisse, tel. 05.57.40.14.09,
fax 05.57.40.42.90 ☑
🍷 by appt

CH. DE LA NAUVE

Elevé en fût de chêne 2000
■ 4 ha 20,000 ❙❙❙ 15–23 €
🍷 SCEA Ch. de La Nauve, 9, Nauve-Sud,
33330 Saint-Laurent-des-Combes, tel. 05.57.24.71.89,
fax 05.57.74.46.61, e-mail la-nauve@wanadoo.fr
🍷 by appt
🍷 Richard Veyry

CH. PAILHAS 2000

■ 6 ha 20,000 ❙❙❙ 15–23 €
🍷 SCEA Robin-Lafugie, Ch. Pailhas,
33330 Saint-Hippolyte, tel. 05.57.74.46.02,
fax 05.57.74.46.02, e-mail ch.pailhas@wanadoo.fr ☑
🍷 by appt

CH. DE PASQUETTE 2000

■ 3.2 ha 18,000 ▮❙❙❙ ⚬ 11–15 €
🍷 Alain Jabiol, SCEA du Ch. Cadet-Piola, BP 24,
33330 Saint-Emilion, tel. 05.57.74.47.69, fax 05.57.24.68.28,
e-mail infos@chateaucadetpiola.com ☑

CH. PETIT-FAURIE-DE-SOUTARD 2000

■ Gd cru clas. 7.57 ha 37,000 ▮❙❙❙ 23–30 €
🍷 SCEV Aberlen, Ch. Petit-Faurie-de-Soutard,
33330 Saint-Emilion, tel. 05.57.74.62.06, fax 05.57.74.59.34,
e-mail info@vignolescapdemourlin.com ☑
🍷 by appt
🍷 Mme Capdemourlin

CH. PETIT FOMBRAUGE 2000

■ 2.5 ha 12,000 ❙❙❙ 23–30 €
🍷 Pierre Lavau, Ch. Petit Fombrauge,
33330 Saint-Christophe-des-Bardes, tel. 06.11.08.62.40,
fax 05.57.24.66.24, e-mail petitfombrauge@terre-net.fr ☑
🍷 by appt

CH. PIERRE DE LUNE 2000

■ 0.95 ha 2,500 ❙❙❙ 38–46 €
🍷 Véronique et Tony Ballu, 1, Châtelet-Sud,
33330 Saint-Emilion, tel. 05.57.74.49.72,
fax 05.57.74.49.72 ☑
🍷 by appt

CH. PIPEAU 2000

■ 35 ha 190,000 ❙❙❙ 15–23 €
86 88 89 92 93 94 |95| |96| |97| 98 99 00

🍷 Mestreguilhem, Ch. Pipeau,
33330 Saint-Laurent-des-Combes, tel. 05.57.24.72.95,
fax 05.57.24.71.25, e-mail chateau.pipeau@wanadoo.fr ☑
🍷 by appt

CH. PONTET-FUMET 2000

■ 15 ha 103,200 ❙❙❙ 11–15 €
86 88 |89| 92 |93| |94| |95| |96| |97| 99 00

🍷 SCEA des Vignobles Bardet, 17, La Cale,
33330 Vignonet, tel. 05.57.84.53.16, fax 05.57.74.93.47,
e-mail vignobles@vignobles-bardet.fr ☑
🍷 by appt

CH. QUERCY 2000

■ 6 ha 23,000 ❙❙❙ 15–23 €
88 89 90 92 93 94 |95| |96| 98 99 |00|

🍷 GFA du Ch. Quercy, 3, Grave, 33330 Vignonet,
tel. 05.57.84.56.07, fax 05.57.84.54.82,
e-mail chateauquercy@wanadoo.fr ☑
🍷 by appt

CH. RABY-JEAN VOISIN

Cuvée Prestige 2000
■ 8.5 ha 54,000 ❙❙❙ 15–23 €
🍷 Vignobles Raby-Saugeon, Ch. du Paradis,
33330 Saint-Emilion, tel. 05.57.55.07.20, fax 05.57.55.07.21,
e-mail chateau.du.paradis@wanadoo.fr ☑
🍷 by appt

CH. LES RELIGIEUSES 2000

■ 4 ha 40,000 ❙❙❙ 8–11 €
🍷 SCEA Les Religieuses, Jaumat,
33330 Saint-Christophe-des-Bardes, tel. 05.57.40.09.34,
fax 05.57.40.09.34
🍷 Dumas

CH. ROC DE BOISSEAUX 2000

■ 6.2 ha 37,000 ▮⦶⦿ 11–15 €
92 93 94 97 98 99 00

☙ SCEA du Ch. Roc de Boisseaux, Trapeau,
33330 Saint-Laurent-de-Faleyrens, tel. 05.57.74.45.40,
fax 05.57.88.07.00 ☑
⦿ by appt
☙ GFA Mme Clowez

CH. ROCHEBELLE 2000

■ 3 ha 18,000 ⦿ 23–30 €
88 |89| 93 |96| |97| 98 99 00

☙ SCEA Faniest, Ch. Rochebelle, BP 73,
33330 Saint-Laurent-des-Combes, tel. 05.57.51.30.71,
fax 05.57.51.01.99, e-mail faniest@archimedia.fr ☑
⦿ by appt

CH. LA ROSE COTES ROL 2000

■ 7.3 ha 49,000 ▮⦶⦿ 11–15 €
☙ SCEA Vignobles Mirande, La Rose Côtes Rol,
33330 Saint-Emilion, tel. 05.57.24.71.28, fax 05.57.74.40.42,
e-mail pierremirande@aol.com ☑
⦿ by appt

CH. LA ROSE-TRIMOULET 2000

■ 5 ha 30,000 ⦿ 11–15 €
☙ Jean-Claude Brisson, Ch. La Rose Trimoulet,
33330 Saint-Emilion, tel. 05.57.24.73.24, fax 05.57.24.67.08,
e-mail cl.brisson@libertysurf.fr ☑
⦿ by appt

CH. TOUR DES COMBES 2000

■ 13 ha 58,500 ▮⦿ 11–15 €
☙ SCE des Vignobles Darribéhaude, 1, Au Sable,
33330 Saint-Laurent-des-Combes, tel. 05.57.24.70.04,
fax 05.57.74.46.14 ☑
⦿ by appt

CH. LA TOUR DU PIN FIGEAC 2000

■ Gd cru clas. 11 ha 70,000 ▮⦶⦿ 15–23 €
|88| |89| |90| 95 98 00

☙ SARL André Giraud, Ch. Le Caillou, 33500 Pomerol,
tel. 05.57.51.06.10, fax 05.57.51.74.95 ☑
⦿ by appt
☙ Giraud-Belivier

CH. TOUR RENAISSANCE 2000

■ 3 ha 15,000 ⦿ 11–15 €
89 90 91 92 93 94 96 97 |98| 99 |00|

☙ SCEA Daniel Mouty, Ch. du Barry, 33350 Sainte-Terre,
tel. 05.57.84.55.88, fax 05.57.74.92.99,
e-mail daniel.mouty@wanadoo.fr ☑
⦿ ev.day except Sun. 8am–12.30pm 2pm–6pm;
cl. week of 15 Aug., 20 Dec.–5 Jan.

CH. TOUR VACHON
Elevé en fût de chêne 2000

■ 5 ha 13,200 ▮⦶⦿ 5–8 €
☙ André Quancard-André, chem. de La Cabeyre,
33240 Saint-André-de-Cubzac, tel. 05.57.33.42.53,
fax 05.57.43.22.22, e-mail aqa@andrequancard.com
☙ Soucaze et Fils

VIEUX CHATEAU DES COMBES 2000

■ 18 ha 112,000 ▮⦶⦿ 11–15 €
☙ Vignobles J. Leprince, Ch. Cantin,
33330 Saint-Christophe-des-Bardes, tel. 05.57.24.65.73,
fax 05.57.24.65.82, e-mail contact@chateau-cantin.fr ☑

VIEUX CHATEAU L'ABBAYE 2000

■ 1.73 ha 10,000 ⦿ 15–23 €
95 96 |97| 98 99 00

☙ Françoise Lladères, Le Bourg,
33330 Saint-Christophe-des-Bardes, tel. 05.57.47.98.76,
fax 05.57.47.93.03 ☑
⦿ by appt

CH. DU VIEUX-GUINOT 2000

■ 12.5 ha 73,800 ▮⦶⦿ 15–23 €
☙ Vignobles Rollet S.A., Ch. Fourney, BP 23,
33330 Saint-Emilion, tel. 05.57.56.10.20, fax 05.57.47.10.50,
e-mail contact@vignoblesrollet.com ☑
⦿ by appt

CH. VIEUX LARTIGUE 2000

■ 6.14 ha 33,500 ⦿ 11–15 €
☙ SC du Ch. Vieux Lartigue,
33330 Saint-Sulpice-de-Faleyrens, tel. 05.57.55.38.03,
fax 05.57.55.38.01
⦿ by appt

CH. VIEUX SARPE 2000

■ 3.41 ha 20,000 ⦿ 23–30 €
☙ SCE du Ch. Haut-Sarpe, BP 192, 33506 Libourne Cedex,
tel. 05.57.51.41.86, fax 05.57.51.53.16,
e-mail info@j-janoueix-bordeaux.com ☑
⦿ by appt
☙ J.-CL. Janoueix

Other appellations in the Saint-Emilion region

LUSSAC-SAINT-EMILION

Several communes bordering Saint-Emilion that used to be under its jurisdiction are permitted to put their name on their wine labels along with that of their famous neighbour. These are the Appellations Lussac-Saint-Emilion (1,447 ha producing 65,156 hl), Montagne-Saint-Emilion (1,595 ha producing 70,315 hl), Puisseguin-Saint-Emilion (745 ha producing 33,784 hl) and Saint-Georges-Saint-Emilion (185 ha producing 7,812 hl). In fact, the last two correspond to two communes that have now joined Montagne. They are all located northeast of the small town, in a charming, topographically mixed region where a number of grand historic houses top the hills. The soils are very varied and the vine varieties are the same as Saint-Emilion; consequently, the quality of the wines is also much the same.

CH. DE BARBE BLANCHE
Réserve 2000★★

■ 10 ha 40,000 ▮⦶⦿ 11–15 €
This cru was purchased by André Lurton in 1999. It is ideally located on a limestone-clay hilltop, and is now offering an excellent wine which has a deep colour with brilliant ruby glints, and a developing bouquet of vanilla and toast notes.

The palate is structured on supple, full-bodied tannins which are well integrated with high-quality oak. This is a very well-made wine, and will be ready to drink in three to six years' time. From the same estate, the **Château Tour de Ségur 2000 (8–11 €)** wins a star for the finesse of its aromas (Morello cherries) and the elegance of its tannins; it will be ready sooner, within the next three years.

➽ André Lurton, Ch. Bonnet, 33420 Grézillac, tel. 05.57.25.58.58, fax 05.57.74.98.59, e-mail andrelurton@andrelurton.com ☑

☦ by appt

CH. BEL-AIR

Cuvée Jean-Gabriel 2000★★

■	2 ha	12,000	⏱	11–15 €

This château is located on a very good clay terroir with a subsoil of iron dross. The Cuvée Spéciale here is matured in oak for 18 months. It has a deep, brilliant colour and an elegant bouquet of dark berry and clove aromas which are harmoniously combined with the oak. The structure on the palate is complex, powerful and well balanced. This superb wine will be ready to drink in three to six years' time. The Cuvée Classique is the **Bel-Air 2000 (8–11 €)**. It receives a special mention for its fruity flavour and supple tannins, which mean that it is ready to drink straight away.

➽ Jean-Noël Roi, EARL Ch. Bel-Air, 33570 Lussac, tel. 05.57.74.60.40, fax 05.57.74.52.11, e-mail jean.roi@wanadoo.fr ☑

☦ by appt

CH. DE BELLEVUE 2000★★

■	12 ha	80,000	▮⏱⚲	11–15 €

Run from an elegant 18th century charterhouse, this property is tended with the greatest of care, and is currently going over to organic methods. This 2000 has a ruby colour with purplish glints, and a bouquet brimful with complex aromas of ripe berries, undergrowth and vanilla. The palate starts with concentrated, very fresh tannins which then develop towards greater elegance and perfect balance, whilst remaining very powerful right up to the finish. This wine needs three to five years of ageing to open out fully.

➽ Ch. Chatenoud et Fils, Ch. de Bellevue, 33570 Lussac, tel. 06.72.83.18.04, fax 05.57.74.53.69, e-mail andrechatenoud@wanadoo.fr ☑

☦ by appt

CH. BONNIN 2000★

■	2 ha	8,000	⏱	8–11 €

This wine comes from a limestone-clay soil, and is an equal blend of Merlot and Cabernet Sauvignon, which is rather unusual for this region. The result is very good indeed: intense aromas of red berries and oaky vanilla, followed by tannins which are supple and mature at the start, then develop with finesse and good balance on to a very pleasant, long, fruity finish. Leave this wine to mature for two to four years.

➽ Philippe Bonnin, Pichon, 33570 Lussac, tel. 05.57.74.53.12, fax 05.57.74.58.26 ☑

☦ by appt

CH. DE BORDES

B de B 2000★

■	0.25 ha	2,100	⏱	11–15 €

This *cuvée spéciale* comes in an old-style bottle, and is made from pure Merlot. It has a deep cherry colour and an intense bouquet of jammy fruit aromas combined with a pronounced note of oaky toast. The palate is full bodied, ample and well balanced, but even so has a very evident oak flavour which will need time to become better integrated (at least two to five years).

➽ Vignobles Paul Bordes, Faize, 33570 Les Artigues-de-Lussac, tel. 05.57.24.33.66, fax 05.57.24.30.42, e-mail vignobles.bordes.paul@wanadoo.fr ☑

☦ by appt

CH. DU COURLAT 2000★

■	12 ha	66,000	▮⏱⚲	8–11 €

This château is located on a limestone-clay terroir, and is offering two different wines in the 2000 vintage, both of which have won a star. The main wine is made from 70% Merlot, 20% Cabernet Franc and 10% Cabernet Sauvignon. It has a dark ruby colour with purplish glints, a bouquet of fruit and spice aromas, and a supple, very well-balanced tannic structure. It should be kept for two to five years before drinking. The **Cuvée Jean-Baptiste (11–15 €)** is 90% Merlot, and has been matured more lavishly in new oak. This wine is a little more powerful and heady than the other. It is still closed, however, and will improve over an ageing period of five to six years.

➽ SA Pierre Bourotte, 62, quai du Priourat, 33500 Libourne, tel. 05.57.51.62.17, fax 05.57.51.28.28, e-mail jeanbaptiste.audy@wanadoo.fr

☦ by appt

CH. CROIX DE RAMBEAU 2000★

■	6 ha	50,000	⏱	8–11 €

Currently president of the CIVB, Jean-Louis Trocard gets the very best out of this attractive property, and regularly offers good wines here. This 2000 is a blend of 80% Merlot, 15% Cabernet Sauvignon and 5% Cabernet Franc. It has an elegant bouquet of jammy ripe fruits and vanilla, and a structure on the palate which is supple yet concentrated at the start, then develops on to an attractive oaky flavour with a toast note on the finish. Drink this wine in two to three years' time.

➽ Jean-Louis Trocard, Ch. Croix de Rambeau, BP 3, 33570 Les Artigues-de-Lussac, tel. 05.57.55.57.90, fax 05.57.55.57.98, e-mail trocard@wanadoo.fr ☑

☦ ev.day 8am–11.30am 2pm–5.30pm; Sat. Sun. by appt

CH. LE GRAND BOIS 2000★★

■	3.3 ha	18,600	⏱	8–11 €

This cru is located on an excellent limestone-clay terroir planted with 50% Merlot and 50% Cabernet Franc. The 2000 here makes a remarkably good first impression; it has an intense, deep red colour with near-black highlights, and a powerful nose of dark berry, undergrowth and oaky toast aromas. The palate is both round and well structured, and gains in silkiness and finesse as it develops. The very well-balanced finish on a delicate oak note shows that this wine has excellent ageing potential.

➽ SARL Roc de Boissac, 33570 Puisseguin, tel. 05.57.74.61.22, fax 05.57.74.59.54 ☑

☦ by appt

CH. DE LA GRENIERE Cuvée de la Chartreuse Elevé en barrique de chêne 2000★★

■	3 ha	15.000	▮⏱	11–15 €

This remarkable wine takes its name from the elegant 17th century charterhouse here, which is surrounded by 40 ha of vines. It has a purple colour gleaming with lovely ruby glints, and a bouquet of fruit, pepper, prune and vanilla aromas. The tannins are powerful, rich, complex and well cloaked by high-quality oak, which means that the wine will keep for three to eight years. From the same owner, the **Château Haut La Grenière (8–11 €)** wins one star; it is a well-constructed, balanced, harmonious wine, which is already pleasant to drink but will keep without any problem for two to five years.

➽ EARL Vignobles Dubreuil, 14, La Grenière, 33570 Lussac, tel. 05.57.74.64.96, fax 05.57.74.56.28, e-mail earl.dubreuil@wanadoo.fr ☑

☦ by appt

CH. JAMARD BELCOUR 2000★

■	5.34 ha	12,000	▮⚲	5–8 €

This 2000 has been aged exclusively in tank, and is a blend of 80% Merlot, 15% Cabernet Franc, and 5% Cabernet Sauvignon. It has an intense, fresh ruby colour and a powerful bouquet of red berry and leather aromas. The tannins are velvety and well-balanced on the attack, then develop with finesse and characteristic flavour on to a long finish. This is a "true" Lussac, and will be ready to drink in two to six years' time.

➽ SCEV Despagne et Fils, 3, Bonneau, 33570 Montagne, tel. 05.57.74.60.72, fax 05.57.74.58.22, e-mail despagne@tiscali.fr ☑

☦ ev.day except. Sun. 8.30–12 noon 2pm–7pm

BORDEAUX

CH. LA JORINE 2000★

| 3.53 ha | 25,000 | | 5–8 € |

This small estate grows 85% Merlot and 15% Cabernet Franc on a limestone-clay soil. It has produced a very good 2000 with a deep garnet colour, delicate, vinous, slightly smoky aromas, and a full, rich structure on the palate with delightfully characteristic flavours. Keep this wine for two or three years before drinking.

☛ EARL Vignobles Fagard, Cornemps, 33570 Petit-Palais, tel. 05.57.69.73.19, fax 05.57.69.73.75,
e-mail vignobles.fagard@wanadoo.fr ☑
☡ by appt

CH. LUCAS
L'Esprit de Lucas 2000★★

| 2.5 ha | 12,500 | | 15–23 € |

This *cuvée spéciale* is made from a blend of Merlot and Cabernet Franc, grown by methods which respect both tradition and the environment. In the 2000 vintage this wine is remarkable; it has a deep purple colour, an elegant, intense bouquet of spice and ripe fruit aromas with some balsamic notes, and full-bodied, powerful, velvety tannins enlivened by a perfect note of oak. The **Grand de Lucas (8–11 €)** receives a special mention for its supple, smooth character; it is ready to drink now.

☛ Frédéric Vauthier, Ch. Lucas, 33570 Lussac, tel. 05.57.74.60.21, fax 05.57.74.62.46,
e-mail chateau.lucas.fred.vauthier@wanadoo.fr ☑
☡ by appt

CH. LYONNAT 2000★★

| 47 ha | 200,000 | | 11–15 € |

The Milhade et Fils company was founded in 1938, and developed a wine-merchant's business while at the same time purchasing a number of châteaux in the Libournais. This cru is offering a remarkable wine which has the advantage of unlimited production. It has an intense, near-black colour, fine, complex aromas of fruit, roasting and undergrowth, and an elegant, fruity, well-structured palate. The finish is perfectly balanced, with very long, lingering flavours. Drink this wine in two to six years' time.

☛ SEV Vignobles Jean Milhade, lieu-dit Peycher, 33133 Galgon, tel. 05.57.55.48.90, fax 05.57.84.31.27,
e-mail milhade@milhade.fr ☑

CH. MAYNE-BLANC
Cuvée Saint-Vincent 2000★

| 4 ha | 28,000 | | 8–11 € |

This wine is frequently singled out as one of the best in the appellation, and once again has been very successful in the 2000 vintage. It has an intense ruby colour, an elegant bouquet with a slight touch of vanilla, and a structure which is supple but also develops powerfully on a well-balanced, pleasantly oaky palate. This excellent wine will be ready to drink in two to five years' time. The **Cuvée Tradition (5–8 €)** receives a special mention: it is a simpler, less oaky wine, whose fruity character and supple palate already make it pleasant to drink.

☛ EARL Jean Boncheau, Ch. Mayne-Blanc, 33570 Lussac, tel. 05.57.74.60.56, fax 05.57.74.51.77,
e-mail mayne.blanc@wanadoo.fr ☑
☡ ev.day except Sun. 8am–12 noon 2pm–7pm

CH. MOULIN DE GRENET 2000★

| 5 ha | 22,500 | | 8–11 € |

This vineyard is planted on a very good limestone-clay terroir around an old mill built in 1711. The 2000 here has an elegant bouquet of fruit aromas, along with a balsamic touch. Its full-bodied, concentrated tannic structure is full of flavour (jammy fruits, vanilla), and the perfectly balanced finish bodes well for the future of this wine, which will keep for at least five or six years.

☛ SCEA Ch. 333, 33330 Saint-Emilion, tel. 05.57.51.35.22, fax 05.57.25.19.15, e-mail roskam@club-internet.fr ☑
☡ by appt
☛ Nicole Roskam-Brunot

CH. DU MOULIN NOIR 2000★

| 6.1 ha | 46,000 | | 11–15 € |

This Tessandier property is managed by Vitigestion using modern methods such as malolactic fermentation partly in new oak. This 2000 has a deep colour and ripe fruit aromas, with a slight touch of elegant oak. The silky, harmonious tannins are well balanced right up to the very flavourful finish. Drink this bottle in four to six years' time.

☛ SC Ch. du Moulin Noir, Lescalle, 33460 Macau, tel. 05.57.88.07.64, fax 05.57.88.07.00 ☑
☡ by appt
☛ Tessandier

CH. DES ROCHERS 2000★★★

| 2.77 ha | 22,000 | | 8–11 € |

This cru is ideally located on a clay terroir, and the wine produced here is made from pure Merlot. In this vintage it is quite simply splendid. It has an intense, near-black colour and powerful aromas of stewed ripe fruits, vanilla and toast. With its very concentrated, rich attack on the palate and great finesse on the finish, this is a wine which is not only full of charm but also has extremely good ageing potential. This is a truly delightful wine which should be drunk in four to six years' time.

☛ SCE Vignobles Rousseau, 1, Petit-Sorillon, 33230 Abzac, tel. 05.57.49.06.10, fax 05.57.49.38.96,
e-mail laurent@vignoblesrousseau.com ☑
☡ by appt

Wines selected but not starred

CH. CAILLOU LES MARTINS 2000

| 8 ha | 45,000 | | 8–11 € |

☛ Jean-François Carrille, pl. du Marcadieu, 33330 Saint-Emilion, tel. 05.57.24.74.46, fax 05.57.24.64.40,
e-mail paulcarrille@worldonline.fr ☑
☡ by appt

CH. LA CLAYMORE 2000

| n.c. | 80,000 | | 8–11 € |

☛ SCEA Claymore, La Claymore, 33570 Lussac-Saint-Emilion, tel. 05.57.74.67.48, fax 05.57.74.52.05, e-mail sovramfl@aol.com ☑
☡ by appt
☛ Linard

CH. LES COUZINS
Cuvée Prestige 2000

| 2 ha | 12,000 | | 8–11 € |

☛ Robert Seize, Ch. Les Couzins, 33570 Lussac, tel. 05.57.74.60.67, fax 05.57.74.60.67 ☑
☡ ev.day 9am–12 noon 2pm–7pm, cl. Jan.

CH. LA HAUTE CLAYMORE 2000

| ■ | 3 ha | n.c. | ■ ⬛ ⚱ | 5–8 € |

☛ EARL Vignobles Devaud, Faise, 33570 Les
Artigues-de-Lussac, tel. 05.57.24.31.39, fax 05.57.24.34.17,
e-mail devaud@vignobles-devaud.com ☑
♈ by appt

CH. HAUT-PIQUAT 2000

| ■ | 22 ha | 150,000 | ■ ⬛ ⚱ | 11–15 € |

☛ Jean-Pierre Rivière, Ch. Haut-Piquat, 33570 Lussac,
tel. 05.57.55.59.59, fax 05.57.55.59.51 ☑
♈ ev.day 9am–12 noon 2pm–6pm

CH. DES LANDES

Cuvée Prestige 2000

| ■ | 1.2 ha | 10,000 | ⬛ | 8–11 € |

☛ Daniel Lassagne, EARL Vignobles des Landes, 5,
Lagrenière, 33570 Lussac, tel. 05.57.74.68.05,
fax 05.57.74.68.05, e-mail chateaudeslandes@yahoo.fr ☑
♈ ev.day 8am–12 noon 1.30pm–8pm

CH. DE LUSSAC 2000

| ■ | 14.5 ha | 60,000 | ⬛ | 15–23 € |

☛ Mme Griet Laviale Van Malderen, 15, rue de Lincent,
33570 Lussac, tel. 05.57.74.56.58, fax 05.57.74.56.59,
e-mail chateaudelussac@terre-net.fr ☑
♈ ev.day 8.30am–12 noon 2pm–6pm

CUVEE RENAISSANCE

Vieilli en fût de chêne 2000

| ■ | n.c. | 15,000 | ⬛ | 5–8 € |

☛ Les producteurs réunis de Puisseguin et
Lussac-Saint-Emilion, Durand, 33570 Puisseguin,
tel. 05.57.55.50.40, fax 05.57.74.57.43,
e-mail vignoble@producteurs-reunis.com ☑
♈ by appt

VIEUX CHATEAU FOURNAY

Cuvée réservée en fût de chêne 2000

| ■ | 2 ha | 12,000 | ■ ⬛ | 8–11 € |

☛ EARL Albert et Vergnaud, Ch. Vieux Fournay, lieu-dit
Poitou, 33570 Lussac, tel. 05.57.74.57.09,
fax 05.57.74.57.17, e-mail vieux-fournay@wanadoo.fr ☑
♈ by appt

Montagne-Saint-Emilion

CH. DE BEAULIEU 2000★

| ■ | 3.5 ha | 26,000 | ■ ⬛ ⚱ | 11–15 € |

This 2000 is made from 70% Cabernets with just 30% Merlot,
which is quite unusual in the Libournais. It has aromas of
cherry stones, spices and red berries. The full, rich palate
develops on to fresher notes with a certain austerity which is
typical of this grape blend, and means that the wine should be
kept for three to six years before drinking.
☛ Jean-Pierre Rivière, Ch. Haut-Piquat, 33570 Lussac,
tel. 05.57.55.59.59, fax 05.57.55.59.51 ☑
♈ ev.day 9am–12 noon 2pm–6pm

CH. CARDINAL 2000★

| ■ | 9 ha | n.c. | ■ ⬛ | 5–8 € |

The label on this bottle shows the remarkable Romanesque
church in Montagne, while the wine itself is very much in the
tradition of its predecessors. It has an intense ruby colour,
elegant aromas of dark berries and spices, and tannins which
are round and velvety but still develop with character on to a

long finish. This is a highly characteristic wine which can be
drunk now or kept for two to five years.
☛ SCEA Bertin et Fils, Dallau, 8, rte de Lamarche,
33910 Saint-Denis-de-Pile, tel. 05.57.84.21.17,
fax 05.57.84.29.44, e-mail vignoblebertin@wanadoo.fr

CH. LA CHAPELLE 2000★

| ■ | 9.39 ha | 65,000 | ■ | 5–8 € |

This small family property is offering a very pleasant 2000
which has been aged exclusively in tank and makes a delightful impression with its range of red berry and spice aromas,
supple, well-balanced structure on the palate, and deliciously
fruity finish. Drink this wine in one to three years' time.
☛ SCEA du Ch. La Chapelle, Berlière, Parsac,
33570 Montagne, tel. 05.57.24.78.33, fax 05.57.24.78.33 ☑
♈ by appt
☛ Th. Demar

CLOS LA CROIX D'ARRIAILH 2000★★

| ■ | 1 ha | 5,400 | ■ ⬛ ⚱ | 8–11 € |

This Clos is a brand, representing a wine which since 1997 has
come exclusively from the 50-year-old vines on the property.
In the 2000 vintage the results are remarkable: a garnet colour
with dark purple fringes, and powerful, complex aromas of
dark berries and oaky toast and vanilla. The tannins are rich
and fleshy, and also have very good balance and length which
show great potential. This wine will be ready to drink in three
to six years' time. **Le Château Croix-Beauséjour 2000 Elevé en
Fût de Chêne (5–8 €)**, wins one star for its complex range of
fruit aromas and delightfully fine, elegant structure; keep for
two to five years.
☛ Olivier Laporte, Ch. Croix-Beauséjour, Arriailh,
33570 Montagne, tel. 05.57.74.69.62,
fax 05.57.74.59.21 ☑ 🏠
♈ by appt

CH. COUCY 2000★

| ■ | 19.7 ha | 150,000 | ■ ⬛ ⚱ | 8–11 € |

Located on the Montagne plateau, this very beautiful family
property dates back to the 19th century, and is offering
wine-lovers a 2000 which has the advantage of not being a
cuvée spéciale! It has a fresh, luminous red colour, and a
bouquet which is still restrained, with aromas of red berries
and liquorice. The palate is concentrated, complex, and
highly characteristic. The tannins are still heavy, but should
soften after two to five years of ageing.
☛ GFA Vignobles Maurèze, Ch. Coucy, 33570 Montagne,
tel. 05.57.55.09.13, fax 05.57.55.09.12,
e-mail ccatala@aol.com ☑
♈ by appt

CH. LA COUROLLE

Elevé en fût de chêne 2000★

| ■ | 8 ha | 50,000 | ■ ⬛ ⚱ | 5–8 € |

This château is located 300 m from Montagne's ecomuseum,
and is regularly featured in the *Guide*. Once again it has been
selected for this thoroughbred 2000, which has expressive
aromas of red berries, mocca, smoke and leather. The tannins
on the palate are rich and fresh right up to a flavourful and
very well-balanced finish. This wine should keep for three to
five years without any problem.
☛ SARL Vignobles Claude Guimberteau, Arriailh,
33570 Montagne, tel. 05.57.74.62.38, fax 05.57.74.50.78 ☑
♈ by appt

CH. LA COURONNE 2000★★

| ■ | n.c. | 50,000 | ⬛ | 11–15 € |

This château is located right at the heart of the appellation on
a classic hillside limestone-clay terroir planted with 100%
Merlot. The wine has a strong, brilliant purplish colour, a
delightfully fine, expressive bouquet of prune, smoke, spice
and liquorice aromas, and a well-structured, full-bodied,
ample, elegant palate. Its richness, good balance and very
harmonious finish mean that it can be drunk very soon, but in
this vintage it will also keep for four to eight years.
☛ EARL Thomas Thiou, Ch. La Couronne, BP 10,
33570 Montagne, tel. 05.57.74.66.62, fax 05.57.74.51.65,
e-mail lacouronne@aol.com ☑
♈ by appt

Montagne-Saint-Emilion

L'ENVIE 2000★

| | 2 ha | 10,000 | ⊞ | 11–15 € |

Alain and Franck Despagne have created a *cuvée spéciale* made mainly from Merlot with 10% Cabernet Sauvignon. This 2000 has a strong colour and a complex bouquet of red berry aromas which are still dominated by notes of oaky toast. The tannins are fine and well balanced with the oak, which is very evident on the finish. Drink this wine in two to five years' time. From the same owner, the **Château Vieux Bonneau 2000** (5–8 €) receives a special mention for its authentic, fruity character and supple palate; it can be drunk straight away.
↗ SCEV Despagne et Fils, 3, Bonneau, 33570 Montagne, tel. 05.57.74.60.72, fax 05.57.74.58.22,
e-mail despagne@tiscali.fr ☑
☏ ev.day except Sat. Sun. 8.30am–12 noon2pm–7pm

CH. FAIZEAU
Sélection Vieilles vignes 2000★★

| | 10 ha | 34,252 | ▮⊞⚭ | 15–23 € |

This château was the priory for the Abbaye de Faize until the French Revolution, and since then has become well known for the quality and reliability of its wines. Once again it has produced an excellent wine in the 2000 vintage. Made exclusively from Merlot, it has a delightful bouquet of vanilla oak notes, and supple, very rich tannins on a velvety palate with a very good balance between fruit and oak. With its unusually long, flavourful finish, this wine will keep for three to four years if not more.
↗ SCE du Ch. Faizeau, 33570 Montagne, tel. 05.57.24.68.94, fax 05.57.24.60.37,
e-mail contact@chateau.faizeau.com ☑
☏ by appt
↗ Chantal Lebreton

CH. LA FAUCONNERIE 2000★

| | 0.88 ha | 7,000 | ▮⊞⚭ | 5–8 € |

This 2000 has 25% Cabernets in its blend, which gives it a very elegant bouquet. The tannins are fresh and fruity on the attack, and have plenty of power on the palate even though at this stage they are still slightly dominated by oak. The balance should be just right in two to four years' time. From the same owner, the **Château Tricot 2000** also wins a star.
↗ Bernadette Paret, 3, Château Tricot, 33570 Montagne, tel. 05.57.74.65.47, fax 05.57.74.65.47 ☑
☏ by appt

CH. LA FLEUR GRANDS LANDES
2000★★

| | 8 ha | 11,771 | ▮⊞ | 8–11 € |

This cru has a gravelly soil, and is now run by the owner's daughter Isabelle Fort, an oenologist who taught viticulture for ten years but has now moved from theory into practice. She has produced a magnificent 2000 with a purple colour and lighter purple glints, complex, intense aromas of vanilla and oak, and rich, lingering tannins which are powerful but also well balanced. This is a highly characteristic wine which will need to be kept for two to ten years before being opened.
↗ EARL Vignobles Carrère, 9, rte de Lyon, Lamarche, 33910 Saint-Denis-de-Pile, tel. 05.57.24.31.75, fax 05.57.24.30.17 ☑
☏ by appt
↗ Isabelle Fort

CH. FORLOUIS 2000★★

| | 10 ha | 40,000 | ▮⊞⚭ | 11–15 € |

This château is owned by the Janoueix family, who are very influential in the Libournais, and have invested in numerous new projects here, especially in the winery. This 2000 has reaped the benefit; it is a sumptuous wine with a brilliant purple colour, elegant aromas of prunes, spices and very ripe fruits, and a round, full-bodied palate built on well-balanced tannins which provide a truly wonderful finish. This is a classic yet modern wine which is intelligently constructed and should be drunk within the next five years. From the same family, the **Château Petit Clos du Roy 2000** (8–11 €) wins one star.
↗ SCEA des Vignobles François Janoueix, 20, quai du Priourat, 33500 Libourne, tel. 05.57.55.55.44, fax 05.57.51.83.70 ☑
☏ by appt

CH. GRAND BARAIL 2000★

| | 6 ha | n.c. | ▮⊞⚭ | 5–8 € |

This wine comes from old vines grown on a good, typically Saint-Emilion limestone-clay terroir. It has a dark garnet colour and an intense bouquet in which the Morello cherry and blackberry aromas are well balanced with the elegant oak notes. The tannins are vinous and well-extracted, but give a slight sense of firmness on the finish, which makes it absolutely essential to leave this wine to age for three to six years.
↗ EARL Vignobles Devaud, Faise, 33570 Les Artigues-de-Lussac, tel. 05.57.24.31.39, fax 05.57.24.34.17, e-mail devaud@vignobles-devaud.com ☑
☏ by appt

CH. GRAND BARIL
Elevé en fût de chêne 2000★

| | 28 ha | 13,000 | ▮⊞⚭ | 8–11 € |

This cru belongs to the viticultural college in Montagne, but it is not just there for teaching purposes; it also needs to market its own wines, and for that reason has just installed some very good facilities for visitors. The wine provides the perfect opportunity to go and have a look. It has a delightful purple colour and an equally pleasant bouquet of dark berry aromas combined with notes of smoke. Although the tannins are concentrated on the attack, they then develop elegantly on to a pleasantly long and fruity finish. Drink this wine in one to three years' time.
↗ Lycée viticole de Libourne-Montagne, 7, le Grand Baril, Goujon, 33570 Montagne, tel. 05.57.55.21.22, fax 05.57.55.13.53,
e-mail expl.legta.libourne@educagri.fr ☑
☏ by appt

CH. LA GRANDE BARDE 2000★★

| | 9 ha | 60,000 | ▮⊞⚭ | 8–11 € |

This cru is located on a sandy-clay plateau and a limestone hilltop with excellent exposure to sunlight. It has produced a remarkable 2000 with an unusually fresh crimson colour, a developing bouquet of floral notes (peonies) and fruit aromas (with touches of prunes), and very young tannins which are supple and well balanced. This delicious wine should be drunk in three to six years' time.
↗ SCE de La Grande Barde, Ch. La Grande Barde, 33570 Montagne, tel. 05.57.74.64.98, fax 05.57.74.64.98, e-mail dominiquemaureze@wanadoo.fr ☑
☏ by appt

CH. HAUT-BONNEAU 2000★

| | 10 ha | 42,000 | ⊞ | 8–11 € |

This cru was founded in 1822, and has a very Libournais grape blend which is dominated by Merlot (80%). The 2000 has a lovely purple colour and a bouquet of ripe fruit and liquorice aromas along with some toast notes. The tannins are concentrated but also well integrated, thanks to the high quality of the oak. This is a wine with a very considerable ageing potential of at least four to six years.
↗ Héritiers Marchand, 4, Bonneau, 33570 Montagne, tel. 05.57.74.69.23, fax 05.57.74.54.21,
e-mail chateauhaut.bonneau-contact@wanadoo.fr ☑
☏ ev.day 9am–12 noon 2pm–6pm

CH. HAUT-GOUJON 2000★★

| | 7.2 ha | 18,000 | ▮⊞⚭ | 8–11 € |

This 16-ha property has a very good gravelly-clay terroir, and is offering a remarkable 2000 with a deep purple colour, a nose strongly marked by oak, and concentrated tannins which become both powerful and smooth as they develop. It is essential to keep this wine for three to eight years before drinking. The second wine from this château is **La Fleur du Barril 2000** (5–8 €), which wins a star for its expressive aromas of spices and menthol, and for its supple, well-balanced structure. It is ready to drink now, but will keep for three to five years.
↗ SCEA Garde et Fils, Goujon, 33570 Montagne, tel. 05.57.51.50.05, fax 05.57.25.33.93 ☑
☏ by appt

CH. MAISON BLANCHE 2000★

| | 15 ha | 97,200 | | 11–15 € |

This estate has a magnificent 19th century house, surrounded by a park and overlooking a large, uninterrupted vineyard which is cultivated by traditional methods. The result is clear to see in this 2000; it has elegant aromas of fruits, spices and leather, and a structured palate which is also round, fruity, and very mature. This well-balanced wine should be drunk in one to five years' time.
☛ Vignobles Despagne-Rapin, Maison Blanche, 33570 Montagne, tel. 05.57.74.62.18, fax 05.57.74.58.98 ☑
☖ by appt

CH. DE MAISON NEUVE 2000★

| | 62 ha | 400,000 | | 8–11 € |

This very large 78-ha property is ideally situated at the heart of the appellation, and is well worth a visit. You will be able to taste this 2000, which has an attractive colour, a bouquet of spice, cherry and menthol aromas, and a structure which is both powerful and well balanced. The unusually fruity, well-balanced finish indicates good ageing potential (two to five years).
☛ Michel Coudroy, Maison-Neuve, 33570 Montagne, tel. 05.57.74.62.23, fax 05.57.74.64.18 ☑
☖ by appt

CH. MONTAIGUILLON 2000★

| | 26 ha | 140,000 | | 8–11 € |

This château has an exceptionally good hillside location, and has produced a 2000 with an intense cherry colour and a bouquet of jammy fruit, prune, toast and vanilla aromas. The well-balanced, powerful tannic structure has a very pleasant acidity which indicates that the wine has considerable ageing potential (three to six years).
☛ Amart, Ch. Montaiguillon, 33570 Montagne, tel. 05.57.74.62.34, fax 05.57.74.59.07, e-mail chantalamart@montaiguillon.com ☑
☖ by appt

CH. DE MONTURON 2000★

| | 1.2 ha | 9,000 | | 11–15 € |

This cru is located on a lovely limestone-clay hillside planted exclusively with Merlot. It is now offering an very good 2000 with a brilliant colour and purplish glints, and a bouquet dominated by oaky toast but also with some black cherry and ripe raspberry notes. This is an appealing, well-balanced wine which can be drunk now or kept for two to five years.
☛ Vignobles J.-B. Saby et Fils, Ch. Rozier, 33330 Saint-Laurent-des-Combes, tel. 05.57.24.73.03, fax 05.57.24.67.77, e-mail info@vignobles-saby.com ☑
☖ by appt

CH. PALON GRAND SEIGNEUR 2000★

| | 6.14 ha | 40,000 | | 5–8 € |

Founded in 1935, this cooperative offered two wines for selection. This one has an intense, brilliant garnet colour and fresh, fruit aromas. The supple, elegant tannins are unusually balanced and well integrated. Drink this wine in two or three years' time. One star is also awarded to **La Tour Mont d'Or 2000 Vieillie en Fût**. It has been matured in oak for one year, and is a rich, vinous wine with notes of dark berries and spices.
☛ Groupe de Producteurs de Montagne, La Tour Mont d'Or, 33570 Montagne, tel. 05.57.74.62.15, fax 05.57.74.50.51, e-mail la.tour.mont.dor@wanadoo.fr ☑
☖ ev.day except Sat. Sun. 8am–12 noon 2pm–6pm
☛ Fellonneau

CH. LA PAPETERIE 2000★

| | 10 ha | 44,000 | | 11–15 € |

This cru is located along the Barbanne, a famous little river which once separated the *langue d'Oc* (southern) and *langue d'Oïl* (northern) regions. It is offering a very good 2000 with a brilliant garnet colour and a bouquet of ripe fruit aromas (strawberries) enlivened by some slight hints of freshness and vanilla. The tannins are dense, silky and very full. This is undoubtedly a wine with ageing potential (three to five years).

☛ Vignobles Jean-Pierre Estager, 33–41, rue de Montaudon, 33500 Libourne, tel. 05.57.51.04.09, fax 05.57.25.13.38, e-mail estager@estager.com ☑
☖ by appt

CH. LA PICHERIE

Cuvée Privilège 2000★★

| | 1.4 ha | 5,200 | | 11–15 € |

This Cuvée Privilège comes from a selection of Merlot (80%) and Cabernet Franc (20%) vines which are 103 years old (no, your eyes are not deceiving you!) This great rarity has brought its rewards with this 2000, which was unanimously selected by the Jury for a *coup de coeur*. It has a purple, near-black colour and an elegant, complex bouquet of ripe grape and spice aromas, along with a distinguished note of oak. The tannins are thoroughbred and also powerful, while maintaining a great deal of freshness on the finish. This is a great wine in a contemporary style, which will keep for five to six years without any problem.
☛ Rodolphe Guimberteau, 2, Champ Tricot, 33570 Montagne, tel. 05.57.74.57.66, fax 05.57.74.50.78 ☑
☖ by appt

CH. PUYNORMOND

Sélection 2000★

| | 1.8 ha | 10,000 | | 8–11 € |

The founder of this estate was a soldier in the First World War who came home and took out a loan to buy a few vines. The property now amounts to over 10 ha and belongs to his grand-children. This Sélection is a blend of 90% Merlot and 10% Cabernet Sauvignon. It has a clear colour with violet glints, and powerful aromas of toast mingled with touches of fruit (raspberries and black cherries). The palate is supple, full-bodied and very silky. This is a well-made wine which is ready to drink now but can also be left to age for a while.
☛ EARL Vignobles Lamarque, BP 4, 33570 Puisseguin, tel. 05.57.74.66.69, fax 05.57.74.52.62, e-mail lamarque.philippe@wanadoo.fr ☑
☖ ev.day except Sun. 9am–12.30pm 2pm–7pm

CH. ROC DE CALON

Cuvée Prestige 2000★★

| | 4.5 ha | 28,000 | | 11–15 € |

Château Roc de Calon has produced two wines in the 2000 vintage. This Cuvée Prestige (95% Merlot) wins two stars and missed a *coup de coeur* by only one vote. It has a powerful, elegant nose of toast notes and ripe fruit aromas (raspberries), and an equally elegant palate on which the tannins are full-bodied, rich, powerful, well balanced and very long. This is a thoroughbred wine with excellent ageing potential (three to eight years). The **Cuvée Classique (5–8 €)** wins one star; it is very fruity and well balanced, and will be ready to drink after two to three years of ageing.
☛ Bernard Laydis, 2, Barreau, 33570 Montagne, tel. 05.57.74.63.99, fax 05.57.74.51.47, e-mail rocdecalon@wanadoo.fr ☑
☖ by appt

CH. ROCHER CORBIN 2000★★

| | 9 ha | 59,000 | | 11–15 € |

This château is located on the western side of the Tertre de Calon, a limestone promontory overlooking the Dordogne.

Every effort is made here, both on the vineyard and in the winery, to get the very best out of this high-quality terroir. The results are remarkable. The wine has a dark, almost black colour and complex aromas of cherries, almonds, undergrowth, and oaky vanilla and toast. As the warming, rich tannins develop on the palate, they become mouth-filling and unctuous. The finish is still firm, which means that the wine will need to be kept for four to eight years.
↬ SCE Ch. Rocher Corbin, 33570 Montagne, tel. 05.57.74.55.92, fax 05.57.74.53.15 ☑
⊥ by appt

CH. ROUDIER 2000★

	27.5 ha	95,000	▮ ▯	11–15 €

This 2000 has a dense colour with some subtle shades of violet. The aromas of strawberries, blackcurrants and leather in the nose reappear along with a slight hint of musk on the palate, which is fine and well cloaked by a balanced oak flavour, with a long finish which will ensure that the wine has very good ageing potential (at least three to six years).
↬ SCEA Capdemourlin, Ch. Roudier, 33570 Montagne, tel. 05.57.74.62.06, fax 05.57.74.59.34, e-mail info@vignolescapdemourlin.com ☑
⊥ by appt

CH. SAINT-JACQUES CALON

Grande Réserve Elevé en fût de chêne neuf 2000★

	8.88 ha	4,500	▮ ▯ ▯	15–23 €

The Butte des Moulins de Calon is 114 m high, and really does look down over some mills, which have now been restored. This property is offering an excellent Grande Réserve with a dark, brilliant colour, an open bouquet of toast, vanilla and smoke aromas, and full, rich tannins which at present are somewhat dominated by oaky vanilla. Keep this wine for three to five years before serving.
↬ SCEA Ch. Saint-Jacques Calon, La Maçonne, BP 9, 33570 Montagne, tel. 05.57.74.62.43, fax 05.57.74.53.13, e-mail stjacquescalon@wanadoo.fr ☑
⊥ by appt
↬ Frédéric Maule

CH. TEYSSIER 2000★

	22 ha	69,340	▯ ▯	11–15 €

This estate is managed by the Dourthe *maison de négoce*, which is developing modern techniques here, both on the vineyard and in the winery. Their brilliant purple 2000 is a highly characteristic wine, even though its bouquet is still quite strongly marked by 15 months of maturation in oak. It has a clean, fruity, fairly full-bodied palate with a long finish, and deserves to be kept for two to four years.
↬ Ch. Teyssier, 35, rue de Bordeaux, 33290 Parempuyre, tel. 05.56.35.53.00, fax 05.56.35.53.29, e-mail contact@cvbg.com ☑
⊥ by appt
↬ Famille Durand-Teyssier

CH. TREYTINS 2000★

	2.5 ha	18,900	▯ ▯	8–11 €

This is a small cru with a high-quality terroir and a very careful approach to winemaking, both of which are essential factors in producing a wine as good as this 2000. It has an intense, garnet colour, and a lovely bouquet of red berry and menthol aromas along with some notes of smoke. With its well-balanced, harmonious tannic structure, this is a wine which should open out fully after two to five years of ageing.
↬ Vignobles Léon Nony, Ch. Garraud, 33500 Néac, tel. 05.57.55.58.58, fax 05.57.25.13.43, e-mail info@vln.fr ☑
⊥ by appt

VIEUX CHATEAU CALON 2000★

	3 ha	15,000	▯ ▯	8–11 €

This cru grows mainly Merlot (90%) on a clay-limestone terroir which is typical of the appellation. The 2000 has a purple colour with ruby glints, and a developing bouquet of clove and vanilla aromas. The palate has harsh tannins which need to become better integrated, but it also has very good balance, and this will ensure that in two to three years' time this is a delightful wine.

↬ Gros et Fils, SCE Ch. Grange-Neuve, 33500 Pomerol, tel. 05.57.51.23.03, fax 05.57.25.36.14 ☑
⊥ by appt

VIEUX CHATEAU SAINT-ANDRE 2000★

	10 ha	50,000	▮ ▯ ▯	8–11 €

This estate is owned by Jean-Claude Berrouet, who makes wine on the most highly-reputed crus in Pomerol (notably Petrus). This wine has the benefit not only of his experience, but also of his philosophy of winemaking: respect the grape and the terroir, and do not use technology when it isn't necessary. Coming from a limestone-clay soil, this is a subtle wine with aromas of undergrowth and spices, and a well-balanced, flavourful palate based on delicately extracted tannins which are well integrated and mature. It can be drunk now, but will also keep for four to five years.
↬ SCEA Vieux Château Saint-André, 1, Samion, 33570 Montagne, tel. 05.57.74.59.80 ☑

Wines selected but not starred

CH. DU MOULIN NOIR 2000

	6.2 ha	46,000	▮ ▯ ▯	11–15 €

↬ SC Ch. du Moulin Noir, Lescalle, 33460 Macau, tel. 05.57.88.07.64, fax 05.57.88.07.00 ☑
⊥ by appt

CH. NOTRE-DAME 2000

	4 ha	30,000	▮ ▯ ▯	5–8 €

↬ J.-M. Leynier, GAEC Clos des Religieuses, 33570 Puisseguin, tel. 05.57.74.67.52, fax 05.57.74.64.12, e-mail clos.des.religieuses@wanadoo.fr ☑
⊥ ev.day 8am–12.30pm 2pm–8pm; Sat. Sun. by appt

VIEUX CHATEAU PALON 2000

	3 ha	16,000	▯ ▯	15–23 €

↬ EARL Vignobles Naulet, Mondou, 33330 Saint-Sulpice-de-Faleyrens, tel. 06.89.10.90.01, fax 05.57.51.23.79, e-mail vignobles.naulet@wanadoo.fr ☑
⊥ by appt

Puisseguin-Saint-Emilion

CH. BEL-AIR

Cuvée de Bacchus Vieilli en fût de chêne 2000★

	4 ha	20,000	▮ ▯ ▯	8–11 €

This *cuvée* comes from a selction of very old vines (45 years old) grown on a good limestone-clay soil. It has a brilliant ruby colour, well-integrated bouquet of toast, hazelnut and Morello cherry aromas, and an equally harmonious palate where the tannins are mature, supple and very well balanced. This is a very characteristic wine which will be ready to drink in one to three years' time. The main wine here is the **Château Bel-Air 2000 (5–8 €)**, which receives a special mention.
↬ SCEA Adoue Bel-Air, Bel-Air, 33570 Puisseguin, tel. 05.57.74.51.82, fax 05.57.74.59.94 ☑
⊥ ev.day 9am–1pm 2pm–7pm

Puisseguin-Saint-Emilion

CH. BRANDA 2000★★

| 8 ha | 35,800 | ◫ | 15–23 € |

Mis en bouteille au château

2000

CHATEAU BRANDA
PUISSEGUIN-St-EMILION
Appellation Puisseguin-Saint-Emilion Contrôlée

ALC 13% BY VOL.   Produce of France   750 ML
SC Château du Branda propriétaire à Puisseguin France

Eighteen months of maturation in new oak with malolactic fermentation, rigorous grape selection, green harvesting, thinning out of leaves: every effort is made here to ensure that Branda stays at the top of the appellation. This year it won another *coup de cœur* for this magnificent 2000 which has an intense purple colour with lighter purple glints, and an elegant, expressive bouquet of dark berries (blackcurrants), cherries, liquorice and vanilla. On the palate the tannins are silky and fruity at the start, then reveal all their potential for ageing by their great maturity and harmony and their perfect balance on the finish. This is a very great wine which should be left to age in a cool, safe place for three to eight years.
☛ SC Ch. du Branda, Roques, 33570 Puisseguin, tel. 05.57.74.62.55, fax 05.57.74.57.33, e-mail chateau.branda@wanadoo.fr ☑
☀ by appt

CH. DURAND-LAPLAGNE
Cuvée Sélecion Elevée en barriques 2000★

| 3.5 ha | 20,000 | ◫ | 8–11 € |

This cru practises grassing down between their rows of old Merlot vines (80%) and Cabernet Franc. It is offering a wine which has a delightful ruby colour with orangey glints, and an equally pleasant intense bouquet of red berry and vanilla aromas. Its tannic structure remains firm and full of flavour, whilst also developing plenty of power. This a highly agreeable wine which will be ready to drink in two to five years' time.
☛ Vignobles Bessou, Ch. Durand-Laplagne, 33570 Puisseguin, tel. 05.57.74.63.07, fax 05.57.74.59.58 ☑
☀ by appt
☛ Bertrand et Sylvie Bessou

CH. FONGABAN 2000★★

| 7 ha | 35,000 | ◫ | 8–11 € |

This is a classic château with a 17th century Girondin house. Once again it receives an excellent rating for its 2000, which has an intense garnet colour with gleaming purple glints, and a powerful bouquet of Morello cherry, pepper, clove and violet aromas. The palate is soft, rich and very mouth-filling to start with, then develops on to an elegant oaky flavour. The fresh, well-balanced finish bodes well for this wine's ageing potential (three to eight years). It will be a worthy accompaniment to guinea-fowl cooked with morels.
☛ SARL de Fongaban, Monbadon, 33570 Puisseguin, tel. 05.57.74.54.07, fax 05.57.74.50.97, e-mail fongaban@vignobles-taix.com ☑
☀ ev.day except Sat. Sun. 9am–12 noon 2pm–6pm
☛ Georges Taïx

CH. GONTET 2000★

| 5 ha | 25,000 | ◫ | 8–11 € |

This 2000 is made from a blend of 80% Merlot and 20% Cabernet Franc. It has a lovely, intense garnet colour, and aromas of vanilla, cachous, jammy fruits and spices. After a rich, round attack, the tannins reveal their very good structure. The finish needs two to three years of careful ageing before this wine is ready to serve with magret of duck and caramelized apples.
☛ Jean-Loup Robin, Ch. Gontet, 33570 Puisseguin, tel. 06.84.54.78.40, fax 05.57.74.63.28, e-mail chateau.gontet@wanadoo.fr ☑
☀ by appt

CH. GUIBEAU
Sélection Henri Bourlon Elevée en fût 2000★★

| 20 ha | 60,000 | ◫ | 11–15 € |

One of the current owner's ancestors went with Maximilian to conquer Mexico and started a family there. These days visitors to this very interesting estate will have the chance to taste this magnificent 2000, which has a brilliant garnet colour and a complex bouquet of jammy fruit, blackberry, pepper and violet aromas. The tannins are rich, velvety and very powerful, and the wine should be allowed to age for five to eight years until they settle down a little. This will be a good accompaniment to roast guinea-fowl.
☛ Henri Bourlon, Ch. Guibeau, 33570 Puisseguin, tel. 05.57.55.22.75, fax 05.57.74.58.52, e-mail vignobles.henri.bourlon@wanadoo.fr ☑
☀ by appt

CH. HAUT-BERNAT
Elevé en fût de chêne 2000★

| 5.65 ha | 32,000 | ◫ | 11–15 € |

The year 2000 saw the opening here of a very attractive new winery made from brick and wood. It also produced this wine, which has a deep, brilliant colour and elegant aromas of oaky vanilla, smoke and menthol. Its tannic structure is supple and well balanced, but still somewhat dominated by oak. It will be ready to drink in one to five years' time, and will go well with small game birds.
☛ SA Vignobles Bessineau, 8, Brousse, BP 42, 33330 Belvès-de-Castillon, tel. 05.57.56.05.55, fax 05.57.56.05.56, e-mail bessineau@cote-montpezat.com ☑
☀ by appt

CH. HAUT-LAPLAGNE 2000★★

| 4 ha | 18,666 | ◫ | 11–15 € |

This property changed hands in 2000, and since then has re-organized the winery and vineyard, and introduced rigorous selection. This wine has a garnet colour with dark purple glints, and aromas of red berries and well-integrated oak (toast with a touch of resin). The mature tannins are rich and velvety to start with, then develop very charmingly and with good balance on to a long finish. This thoroughbred wine is highly characteristic of the appellation, and will be ready to drink in two to six years' time, when it will be a good accompaniment to a tournedos of young wild boar with spring vegetables.
☛ Anne Godet, Haut-Laplagne, 33570 Puisseguin, tel. 05.49.43.26.33 ☑
☀ by appt

CH. LACABANNE-DUVIGNEAU 2000★

| 3 ha | 20,000 | ◫ | 5–8 € |

This vineyard has been handed down from generation to generation since 1870. The 2000 has a lovely, strong purple colour and aromas of very ripe red and dark berries, smoke and fine oak. The tannins have a strong vanilla flavour on the attack, then reveal all their potential on a concentrated palate with a well-balanced finish. Drink this wine in two to five years' time.
☛ Vignobles Celerier, Moulin Courrech, 33570 Puisseguin, tel. 05.57.74.61.75, fax 05.57.74.52.79, e-mail vignobles.celerier@terre-net.fr ☑ ☎
☀ ev.day 8am–12 noon 2pm–7pm

CH. LAFAURIE 2000★

| 5 ha | 30,000 | ◫ | 8–11 € |

Made from 60% Merlot and 40% Cabernets, this wine has a deep, cherry-red colour and a powerful bouquet of spice aromas (cloves), menthol and toast. The tannins are both velvety and powerful, and develop with finesse on the palate which needs an ageing period of three to five years.
☛ Vignobles Paul Bordes, Faize, 33570 Les Artigues-de-Lussac, tel. 05.57.24.33.66, fax 05.57.24.30.42, e-mail vignobles.bordes.paul@wanadoo.fr ☑
☀ by appt

CH. DES LAURETS 2000★

| | 5.5 ha | 30,000 | | 8–11 € |

Château des Laurets is a very large property (88 ha), ideally located on a limestone-clay terroir. It has produced a very well-made wine with an intense garnet colour and a complex nose of fruit and undergrowth aromas, along with a restrained note of toast. The palate is well-balanced, round and long. Serve this wine with game in two to five years' time.
- SAS Château des Laurets, BP 12, 33570 Puisseguin, tel. 05.57.74.63.40, fax 05.57.74.65.34, e-mail chateau-des-laurets@wanadoo.fr
- by appt

CH. DE MOLE
Cuvée Prestige élevée en fût de chêne 2000★★

| | 1 ha | 6,000 | | 5–8 € |

This *cuvée spéciale* comes from a selection of Merlot vines grown on a limestone-clay soil. It has been matured in oak for 14 months, and wins very high praise for its intense garnet colour with purplish glints, and delightful aromas of jammy fruit, spices, fresh oak and vanilla. The rich, noble tannins develop on the palate with finesse and plenty of flavour. Drink this wine in three to five years' time with *coq au vin*. From the same owner, this wine-merchant is offering the **Château Saint-Jacques 2000 Elevé en Fût (3–5 €)**, which receives a special mention. You will need to go to the estate in Puisseguin however in order to buy its main wine, the **Château de Mole 2000 (8–11 €)** (40,000 bottles), which wins one star.
- André Quancard-André, chem. de La Cabeyre, 33240 Saint-André-de-Cubzac, tel. 05.57.33.42.53, fax 05.57.43.22.22, e-mail aqa@andrequancard.com
- Ginette Lenier

CH. MOUCHET 2000★

| | 6 ha | 13,800 | | 8–11 € |

This cru grows mainly Merlot (90%), and is now offering an excellent wine with a brilliant garnet colour and characteristic aromas of cherries, prunes, liquorice and vanilla. The tannins are full bodied, and develop a firmness on the palate which indicates that the wine will need to age for two to six years in order to achieve its balance.
- SCEA Ch. Croix de Mouchet, Mouchet, 33570 Montagne, tel. 05.57.74.62.83, fax 05.57.74.59.61, e-mail lacroixdemouchet@wanadoo.fr
- by appt

CH. RIGAUD 2000★★

| | 8.08 ha | 30,000 | | 8–11 € |

This property is ideally located on a limestone-clay terroir, and was run throughout the 20th century by female owners. The 21st century starts triumphantly here with this unanimous *coup de coeur* for a wine with a deep purple colour and complex aromas of ripe fruits, spices and bay, along with a note of fine vanilla oak. The wine is rich, round and full-bodied on the palate, which develops with elegance and good balance on to a really long finish. It will be a wonderful accompaniment to a *civet* of goose in three to eight years' time.
- Josette Taïx, Rigaud, 33570 Puisseguin, tel. 05.57.74.54.07, fax 05.57.74.50.97, e-mail rigaud@vignoble-taix.com
- by appt

CH. ROC DE BOISSAC 2000★

| | n.c. | n.c. | | 8–11 € |

This wine has a fresh, intense colour, an elegant bouquet of red berry and toast aromas, and a full, silky structure on the palate, which is mouth-filling and has plenty of acidity. It should be drunk within the next two to three years.
- SARL Roc de Boissac, 33570 Puisseguin, tel. 05.57.74.61.22, fax 05.57.74.59.54
- by appt

CH. SEIGLA-LAPLAGNE 2000★★

| | 5 ha | 30,000 | | 8–11 € |

The new owners here have made an excellent start in the appellation with this 2000, which is their first vintage. Made from 95% Merlot, it has an intense garnet colour and a bouquet of spice, toast and ripe fruit aromas, accompanied by some notes of resin. It is well structured on the palate, which is rich and very mouth-filling, with a slightly robust finish. The balance will be perfect once the wine has aged for two or three years.
- Anne Godet, Haut-Laplagne, 33570 Puisseguin, tel. 05.49.43.26.33
- by appt

Wines selected but not starred

CH. LE BERNAT 2000

| | 6 ha | 13,000 | | 11–15 € |

- SARL Ch. Le Bernat, 1, Champs-des-Boys, 33570 Puisseguin, tel. 05.57.74.58.54, fax 05.57.74.59.02
- ev.day 10am–12 noon 2pm–6pm

CH. DU MOULIN 2000

| | 8 ha | 50,000 | | 8–11 € |

- SCEA Chanet et Fils, n° 1 Jacques, 33570 Puisseguin, tel. 05.57.74.60.85, fax 05.57.74.59.90
- ev.day 8am–12 noon 2pm–6pm

CH. MOULINS-LISTRAC 2000

| | 10.3 ha | 70,000 | | 5–8 € |

- GAEC Lalande Fils, 1, Aux Moulins, 33570 Puisseguin, tel. 05.57.74.61.90, fax 05.57.74.59.04, e-mail moulinslis@aol.com
- by appt

CUVEE RENAISSANCE 2000

| | n.c. | 5,000 | | 5–8 € |

- Les producteurs réunis de Puisseguin et Lussac-Saint-Emilion, Durand, 33570 Puisseguin, tel. 05.57.55.50.40, fax 05.57.74.57.43, e-mail vignoble@producteurs-reunis.com
- by appt

Saint-Georges-Saint-Emilion

CH. DIVON 2000★

| | 4.75 ha | 13,000 | | 8–11 € |

This family property is located on a limestone-clay terroir planted with 70% Merlot and 30% Cabernet Sauvignon. This very good 2000 has a dark purple colour with ruby glints, intense, very warming aromas of ripe fruits, and a tannic

structure whose combination of suppleness and power indicates that the wine has excellent ageing potential (at least three to six years).
☛ Christian Andrieu, SCEA Ch. Divon, 33570 Montagne, tel. 05.57.74.66.07, fax 05.57.74.53.79 ☑
☖ by appt

CH. HAUT-SAINT-GEORGES 2000★

| ■ | 3.5 ha | 20,000 | ▮ ⅏ ⌁ | 11–15 € |

This château is ideally located on an excellent terroir, and having won a *coup de coeur* for its 1999 vintage is now offering a 2000 which is also excellent, but much oakier than the 1999. It has an intense purple colour and a bouquet in which aromas of cocoa and oaky toast dominate the more elegant fruity notes. The very mature tannins are rich on the attack, then develop powerfully on to a long finish. Keep this wine carefully for two to five years to give it time to become better integrated.
☛ SCE De La Grande Barde, Ch. La Grande Barde, 33570 Montagne, tel. 05.57.74.64.98, fax 05.57.74.64.98, e-mail dominiquemaureze@wanadoo.fr ☑
☖ by appt

CH. SAINT-ANDRE CORBIN 2000★

| ■ | 17.5 ha | 74,000 | ⅏ | 8–11 € |

The wine here is made by Jean-Claude Berrouet and Alain Moueix, who are two major figures in the Bordelais area, and in this vintage have brought out all the characteristics of the château's ideally located limestone-clay terroir. It has a deep cherry colour and very elegant aromas of ripe fruits, violets and menthol. The tannins are fresh and firm at the start, then develop powerfully on to an especially long finish. This 2000 has all that it takes to become a great thoroughbred wine in two to five years' time.
☛ SAS Alain Moueix, 56, av. Georges-Pompidou, 33500 Libourne, tel. 05.57.51.00.48, fax 05.57.25.22.56 ☑

CH. SAINT-GEORGES 2000★

| ■ | 40 ha | 300,000 | ⅏ | 15–23 € |

92 93 94 |95| 96 97 (98) 99 00

This magnificent château is at the top of its appellation in terms of both fame and geology. It is worth visiting for its own sake, but you will also discover an excellent wine here made from 80% Merlot with 10% each of the Cabernets. It makes a delightful first impression with its deep bigaroon colour, and has a complex bouquet of cocoa notes and aromas of toast and ripe fruits. The powerful but well-balanced tannins are still very oaky; the balance should be perfect in two to five years' time.
☛ Desbois, Ch. Saint-Georges, 33570 Montagne, tel. 05.57.74.62.11, fax 05.57.74.58.62, e-mail g.desbois@chateau-saint-georges.com
☖ by appt

Wines selected but not starred

CH. LA CROIX DE SAINT-GEORGES 2000

| ■ | 6.58 ha | 33,000 | ▮ ⅏ ⌁ | 8–11 € |

|96| 97 98 |99| 00

☛ Jean de Coninck, Ch. du Pintey, 33500 Libourne, tel. 05.57.51.03.04, fax 05.57.51.03.04 ☑
☖ by appt

CH. MOULIN LA BERGERE

Elevé en fût de chêne 2000

| ■ | 3.3 ha | 17,630 | ⅏ | 8–11 € |

☛ André-Camille Benoist, Ch. Moulin La Bergère, 33570 Montagne, tel. 05.57.74.61.61, fax 05.57.74.64.86, e-mail ablaunay@wanadoo.fr ☑
☖ ev.day 8am–8pm

Côtes de Castillon

In 1989 a new appellation was created: Côtes de Castillon. It applies to an area of 3,019 ha, which was extracted from the Appellation Bordeaux Côtes de Castillon, that is, the nine communes of Belvès-de-Castillon, Castillon-la-Bataille, Saint-Magne-de-Castillon, Gardegan-et-Tourtirac, Sainte-Colombe, Saint-Genès-de-Castillon, Saint-Philippe-d'Aiguilhe, Les Salles-de-Castillon and Monbadon. Nonetheless, to leave the "Bordeaux" group, the wine-growers are obliged to follow particularly strict rules of production, especially those that apply to density of plantation, which is limited to 5,000 plants per ha. Compliance has been set for the year 2010 to take account of the vines that are already planted. In 2002, 132,250 hl of wine were produced.

CH. D'AIGUILHE QUERRE 2000★★

| ■ | 1.12 ha | 5,000 | ⅏ | 15–23 € |

Located on the way into the village of Saint-Philippe-d'Aiguilhe, at the highest point in the appellation, this little cru of barely more than 1 ha has clearly found the way to excel, as can be seen from its first vintage, for which the Grand Jury awarded it a unanimous *coup de coeur*. It makes a delightful start with a dense, near-black colour and an open bouquet of cherry, pepper and toast aromas. The tannins are powerful, velvety and very mature, and maintain their great freshness right up to a very long finish which indicates an ageing potential of five to ten years.
☛ Emmanuel Querre, Moulin de Lavaud, 33500 Pomerol, tel. 05.57.25.22.52, fax 05.57.25.22.53, e-mail e-querre@fiducie-conseil.com ☑

CH. BEL-AIR

Collection Charles Grand-Champs 2000★

| ■ | 13.5 ha | 60,000 | ⅏ | 8–11 € |

The current owner of this estate will tell you that the druids used to come together here to perform ritual sacrifices on animals. He will also offer you a tasting of this 2000 with a bouquet of smoke, cocoa and toast aromas and a palate with rich, fruity tannins which are well integrated with the oak. The wine will be ready to drink in two to five years' time. In the meantime you can enjoy the second wine here, which is the **Château La Chapelle Monrepos (5–8 €)**, and receives a special mention for its fruity flavours and good overall tannic balance.
☛ SCEA du Dom. de Bellair, 33350 Belvès-de-Castillon, tel. 06.80.13.02.12, fax 05.56.42.44.47, e-mail patrick.david.cgc@wanadoo.fr ☑
☖ by appt
☛ Patrick David

LE PIN DE BELCIER 2000★

| ■ | 3 ha | 4,820 | ⅏ | 23–30 € |

This *cuvée spéciale* from the Château de Belcier makes a very good first impression in the 2000 vintage; the colour is very intense with mauve highlights, and the bouquet has aromas of dark berries, spices and toast. It is full, silky and very mouth-filling on the palate, which has a long, flavourful finish. Serve this wine in two to five years' time.
☛ SCA Ch. de Belcier, 33350 Les Salles-de-Castillon, tel. 05.57.40.67.58, fax 05.57.40.67.58 ☑
☖ by appt

CH. BELLEVUE

Cuvée Tradition 2000★

| ■ | 7 ha | 18,000 | ▮ | 3–5 € |

This 2000 is made from a blend of 90% Merlot and 10% Cabernet Franc. It has a deep garnet colour, aromas of coffee, red berries and pepper, and a palate cloaked by supple, velvety tannins which have great finesse and very good length. This highly characteristic wine should be left to age for two to five years.

✆ Michel Lydoire, "05" Rouye, 33350 Belvès-de-Castillon, tel. 05.57.47.94.29, fax 05.57.47.94.29 **Ⓥ**
🍷 by appt

CH. BEYNAT
Cuvée Léonard 2000★★

| ■ | 2 ha | 10,000 | ▮ ⑪ | 8–11 € |

This Cuvée Léonard is made from a rigorous selection from old Merlot vines (50%) and Cabernet Sauvigon (50%). It has a purple colour with crimson glints, and a powerful nose of toast and especially coffee aromas, along with some raspberry jam and prune notes. Its supple, silky, very full tannic structure develops with time and a really good balance between fruit and oak. This wine should open out fully after two to five years of ageing.

✆ Xavier Borliachon, 27, rue de Beynat, 33350 Saint-Magne-de-Castillon, tel. 05.57.40.01.14, fax 05.57.40.18.51,
e-mail chateau.beynat@wanadoo.fr **Ⓥ** 🏠
🍷 ev.day 9am–7pm

CH. BLANZAC
Cuvée Prestige 2000★

| ■ | 8 ha | 35,000 | ⑪ | 8–11 € |

Run from an 18th century Bordelais charterhouse, this cru is well known both for its equestrian centre and for the quality of its wines. This really delightful 2000 makes a superb first impression with its aromas of mocca, smoky notes, and slight hints of *pain d'épice*. It has an ample, full-bodied tannic structure which will enable it to keep for at least three to six years.

✆ Bernard Depons, Ch. Blanzac, 22, rte de Coutras, 33350 Saint-Magne-de-Castillon, tel. 05.57.40.11.89, fax 05.57.40.49.69, e-mail chateaublanzac@wanadoo.fr **Ⓥ**
🍷 by appt

CH. LA BRANDE 2001★

| ■ | 15 ha | 72,000 | ▮ ⑪ ♦ | 5–8 € |

This property grows 30-year-old vines on a delightful, due-south-facing hillside terroir. This wine is a blend of 70% Merlot, 22% Cabernet Franc and 8% Cabernet Sauvignon, and has an intense garnet colour and elegant aromas of dark berries, spices and Morello cherries. Its supple, mature tannins are powerful and well balanced on the finish, and will make this an elegant wine to serve in two to five years' time.

✆ Vignobles Jean Petit, Ch. Mangot, 33330 Saint-Etienne-de-Lisse, tel. 05.57.40.18.23, fax 05.57.56.43.97,
e-mail todeschini@chateaumangot.fr **Ⓥ**
🍷 ev.day 8.30am–12 noon 1.45pm–5pm;
Sat. Sun. by appt

CH. CANTEGRIVE 2000★

| ■ | 17 ha | 54,000 | ⑪ | 8–11 € |

This property was purchased in 1990 by a firm from Champagne who invested in the vineyard and winery with the aim of producing very good wines. They have certainly succeeded with this 2000, which has a deep cherry colour and elegant aromas of dark berries and oaky vanilla. The palate is full, long, and structured around powerful tannins which are very mature and well balanced. This wine should be drunk in three to six years' time.

✆ SC Ch. Cantegrive, Terrasson, 33570 Monbadon-Puisseguin, tel. 03.26.52.14.74, fax 03.26.52.24.02 **Ⓥ**
🍷 by appt
✆ Doyard Frères

CH. CAP DE FAUGERES 2000★★

| ■ | 27 ha | 87,000 | ⑪ | 11–15 € |

This very fine property has been one of the jewels of the appellation for some years now, thanks to major renovations and the rigorous care taken here both with the vines and in the winery. This 2000 has a deep, intense colour and a superb nose of dark berry, leather and menthol aromas. The tannins are rich and velvety on the attack, then develop with finesse and good balance on to a long, flavourful finish. This is a

thoroughbred wine which can be drunk two to eight years from now.

✆ Corinne Guisez, Ch. Cap de Faugères, 33350 Sainte-Colombe, tel. 05.57.40.34.99, fax 05.57.40.36.14,
e-mail faugeres@chateau-faugeres.com **Ⓥ**
🍷 by appt

CH. LA CLARIERE LAITHWAITE 2000★

| ■ | 4.6 ha | 26,100 | ⑪ | 8–11 € |

This château belongs to an Englishman who built a business in England has set up a mail-order wine-marketing company which is currently the world leader in its field. Every effort is made here to produce wines of excellent quality such as this 2000, which has a powerful nose of raspberry, cherry and blackcurrant aromas, and an equally powerful palate where the tannins are well extracted, mature, and delightful on the finish. The wine is already fully open, and can be drunk now or kept for a few years.

✆ SARL Direct Wines, Les Confrères de la Clarière, 33350 Sainte-Colombe, tel. 05.57.47.95.14, fax 05.57.47.94.47
🍷 by appt

CH. LA CROIX LARTIGUE 2000★

| ■ | 7.18 ha | 40,000 | ▮ ⑪ ♦ | 5–8 € |

Recently purchased by the Fourcaud-Laussac family which used to own the Château Cheval Blanc at Saint-Emilion, this cru has all it takes to make a fine reputation for itself in the years to come. Clearly it has made progress already with this second vintage, which wins a star. Its complex bouquet of spice aromas (nutmeg) is enlivened by some fruity and floral notes, and the well-balanced structure on the palate has plenty of fruity flavour and a guaranteed ageing potential of at least five years. A special mention goes to **Les Cimes de Lartigue 2000 (11–15 €)**, which needs to be kept until the oak is better integrated.

✆ SCEA Fourcaud-Laussac, Laplagnotte-Bellevue, 33330 Saint-Christophe-des-Bardes, tel. 05.57.24.78.67, fax 05.57.24.63.62, e-mail arnauddl@aol.com **Ⓥ**
🍷 by appt

CH. FONTBAUDE Sélection de vieilles vignes
Elevé en fût de chêne 2001★★

| ■ | 4 ha | 20,000 | ⑪ | 8–11 € |

This château is frequently singled out in the *Guide* as one of the best in the appellation, and is now offering a remarkable 2001 which comes from a selection of 60% old Merlot vines and 40% Cabernets. It has a clear, strong colour and intense, complex aromas of cocoa, smoke and vanilla. The palate has fruit flavours, supple tannins and a very concentrated finish which is characteristic and well balanced. This wine will reach its peak after three to five years of careful ageing. **L'Ame de Fontbaude 2000 (11–15 €)** (2,000 bottles) won a *coup de coeur* last year for the 1999 vintage. The reader will not be disappointed with this one either; it wins one more star.

✆ GAEC Sabaté-Zavan, 34, rue de l'Eglise, 33350 Saint-Magne-de-Castillon, tel. 05.57.40.06.58, fax 05.57.40.26.54,
e-mail chateau.fontbaude@wanadoo.fr **Ⓥ**
🍷 by appt

CH. GRAND BARRAIL
Elevé en fût de chêne 2000★

| ■ | 3 ha | 18,000 | ▮ ⑪ ♦ | 5–8 € |

This 15.3 ha property has been in the same family for eight generations, and devotes all its efforts to its vines and to this wine, which is matured in oak for 12 months. It has a fresh, red colour and a delightfully fine bouquet of red berries and vanilla. The palate has very pleasant tannins which are rich and fleshy but also fresh and fruity. This very characteristic wine can be drunk straight away or left to age for a few years.

✆ Vignobles Jean Coste, Ch. Grand Barrail, 11, rte Bourrée, 33350 Saint-Magne-de-Castillon, tel. 05.57.40.07.83, fax 05.57.40.08.56,
e-mail vignoblesjean.coste@wanadoo.fr **Ⓥ**
🍷 by appt

CH. GRAND PEYROU 2000★★

| | 2.3 ha | 15,000 | ▮ | 5–8 € |

There are two excellent wines in the 2000 vintage here, both of which have been awarded two stars. The *cuvée classique* will delight those who like very fruity, spicy wines with full, powerful, very round tannins. Drink this wine within two to five years. The **Château Grand Peyrou Elevé en Fût de Chêne 2000 (8–11 €)** has been matured in oak for 12 months, and is characterized by its remarkably deep, complex aromas, and very substantial, well-balanced structure on the palate, which has an unusually flavourful finish. It is essential to keep this wine for four to eight years.
➕ EARL Vignobles Laguillon, 2, rte de Liamet, 33330 Saint-Étienne-de-Lisse, tel. 05.57.40.16.08, fax 05.57.40.43.79 ▩
☷ by appt

CH. GRAND TERTRE 2000★

| | 6.2 ha | 27,000 | ▮ ▥ ♦ | 8–11 € |

This wine has a dense, garnet colour with near-black glints, and delicate aromas of red berries, oaky smoke and vanilla. After a round, well-balanced attack, it becomes powerful, mouth-filling and assertive. The well-integrated, harmonious, lingering palate indicates an ageing potential of two to five years.
➕ Vignobles Rollet S.A., Ch. Fourney, BP 23, 33330 Saint-Emilion, tel. 05.57.56.10.20, fax 05.57.47.10.50, e-mail contact@vignoblesrollet.com ▩
☷ by appt

CH. GRIMON 2000★★

| | 5 ha | 40,000 | ▥ | 3–5 € |

Château Grimon is a small, 7 ha property which is run with a great deal of rigour. The Jury has awarded a *coup de coeur* to this remarkable 2000, which is a blend of 70% Merlot and 30% Cabernet. It has a very young, garnet colour with mauve highlights, and elegant aromas of ripe fruits, coffee and well integrated oak, along with a floral note. The palate has an excellent structure based on tannins which are both dense and velvety. This wine will give great pleasure in three to six years' time. The *cuvée spéciale* here is the **Château Dubois-Grimon 2000 (15–23 €)**, which wins one star for its powerful, oaky aromas and well-balanced tannic structure. Drink this wine within one to three years.
➕ Gilbert Dubois, Ch. Grimon, 33350 Saint-Philippe-d'Aiguilhe, tel. 05.57.40.67.58, fax 05.57.40.67.58 ▩

EXCELLENCE DE LAMARTINE 2000★★

| | 1 ha | 7,000 | ▥ | 11–15 € |

This château has been selected for two wines in the 2000 vintage. The *cuvée spéciale* has a superb, brilliant garnet colour, and very pleasant aromas of menthol, smoke, vanilla and dark berries. Its velvety, powerful, very long tannins will enable it to keep for three to eight years. The *cuvée classique* is the **Château Lamartine 2000 (5–8 €)** which is awarded one star; although the nose is reticent, the palate is more expressive thanks to its tannins, which are supple, well balanced and also quite long. This wine should be drunk within one to three years.
➕ EARL Gourraud, 1, la Nauze, 33350 Saint-Philippe-d'Aiguilhe, tel. 05.57.40.60.46, fax 05.57.40.66.01 ▩ ▩
☷ by appt

CH. LAPEYRONIE 2000★★

| | 4 ha | 5,000 | ▥ | 11–15 € |

Once again this cru shows all its potential and good qualities in this excellent 2000. Coming from a rigorous selection of old vines, it has a magnificent garnet colour and an elegant bouquet of ripe berry aromas and oaky toast and vanilla notes. After a round, fruity attack, it develops remarkable power and balance on the palate thanks to the perfect ripeness of the grapes. The long, thoroughbred finish shows that the wine has a very good ageing potential of at least five to ten years.
➕ Jean-Frédéric Lapeyronie, 4, Castelmerle, 33350 Sainte-Colombe, tel. 05.57.40.19.27, fax 05.57.40.14.38, e-mail lapeyroniefred@wanadoo.fr ▩
☷ by appt

CH. MONBADON
Cuvée Jeanne de l'Isle 2000★

| | 25 ha | 30,000 | ▥ | 8–11 € |

Built in the 14th century, this château is listed as a historic monument and has four turrets overlooking the vineyard, which is planted with 75% Merlot and 25% Cabernet Sauvignon. The wine has a dark garnet colour and a pleasant, restrained bouquet of ripe fruit, menthol and elegant oak aromas. The silky, well-integrated tannic structure will guarantee that the wine has good ageing potential; it will most certainly be very pleasant in two to five years' time.
➕ Antoine Moueix et Lebègue, BP 100, 33350 Saint-Emilion, tel. 05.57.55.58.00, fax 05.57.74.18.47, e-mail contact@moueix-lebegue.com
➕ Montfort

CH. MOULIN DE CLOTTE
Cuvée Dominique Vieilli en fût de chêne 2000★

| | 0.45 ha | 3,000 | ▥ | 8–11 € |

Visitors to this château will find that, as its name suggests, there is a mill here complete with millstone. They will also discover this Cuvée Dominique; it has a garnet colour with black glints and a bouquet which is still restrained but releases some notes of smoke, leather and fruits in brandy. This is a mature, well-balanced wine which will open out fully after two to five years of ageing.
➕ SCEV Françoise et Philippe Lannoye, Ch. Moulin de Clotte, 33350 Les Salles-de-Castillon, tel. 05.57.55.23.28, fax 05.57.55.23.29, e-mail lannoye@vignoble.fr.st ▩
☷ by appt

CH. LA NAUZE
Emotion Elevé en fût de chêne 2001★

| | 2 ha | 13,300 | ▥ | 8–11 € |

This wine is made exclusively from Merlot, and has a garnet colour with ruby glints, and well-integrated aromas of dark berries and oaky vanilla and toast. The full-bodied palate is based on rich, powerful tannins which are delightfully fine and well extracted. This wine will open out fully when it has been kept for two to five years.
➕ SARL Le Vignoble C. et L. Jamet, Le Bourg, 24610 Carsac-de-Gurson, tel. 05.53.80.71.34, e-mail li.jamet@wanadoo.fr ▩
☷ by appt

CH. PERVENCHE-PUY ARNAUD 2000★★

| | n.c. | 7,000 | ▥ | 11–15 € |

Château Puy-Arnaud is ideally located at Belvès-de-Castillon, and has two different wines in this vintage, both of which are awarded two stars. This Cuvée Pervenche also wins a unanimous *coup de coeur*; its garnet colour is quite simply sumptuous, and the bouquet is equally good, with an elegant combination of truffle, raspberry, tobacco aromas and some notes of oaky toast. Its mature, velvety, powerful tannins will enable it to keep for five to ten years. The **Clos Puy Arnaud (23–30 €)** is also very powerful, and even oakier (perhaps a little too oaky?) but remarkably well made. Like the other wine it should have a long, harmonious ageing period ahead.

🍷 EARL Thierry Valette, 7, Puy-Arnaud, 33350 Belvès-de-Castillon, tel. 05.57.47.90.33, fax 05.57.47.90.53 ☑
👤 by appt

CH. PEYROU 2000★★

	5 ha	25,000	🍷	8–11 €

Catherine Papon-Nouvel is regularly saluted in the *Guide* – note her *coup de coeur* in another appellation – and here again has achieved a real feat with this remarkable 2000. It is made from 80% Merlot and 20% Cabernets, and has a shimmering dark purple colour and complex aromas of spices, very ripe red berries, and elegant oak. The palate has very fresh, high-quality tannins which are delightfully full and lively on the finish. The overall balance is that of a great wine with excellent prospects for an ageing period of at least five to ten years.

🍷 Catherine Papon-Nouvel, Peyrou, 33350 Saint-Magne-de-Castillon, tel. 05.57.24.72.44, fax 05.57.24.74.84 ☑
👤 by appt

CH. PILLEBOIS

Vieilles Vignes Vieilli en fût de chêne 2000★

	2 ha	15,000	🍷	5–8 €

Located on a sand and gravel terroir planted with 80% Merlot and 20% Cabernet Franc, this château has produced an excellent 2000 with a cherry colour and a developing bouquet of elegant blackcurrant, blond tobacco and very ripe raspberry aromas. The tannins are ample, silky and full bodied, and will not need more than two or three years of ageing.

🍷 Vignobles Marcel Petit, 6, chem. de Pillebois, 33350 Saint-Magne-de-Castillon, tel. 05.57.40.33.03, fax 05.57.40.06.05, e-mail vignobles.marcel.petit@wanadoo.fr ☑
👤 by appt

CH. DE PITRAY 2000★

	31 ha	210,000	🍷🍷	8–11 €

This very fine 16th century manor house once belonged to Ségur, and has a large, 100 ha vineyard in an ideal location. This 2000 has a dark ruby colour and aromas of ripe fruit (cherries), liquorice and vanilla. On the palate the tannins are still somewhat vigorous and remain very fresh on the finish. This wine will be highly agreeable in two or three years' time.

🍷 SC de la Frérie, Ch. de Pitray, 33350 Gardegan, tel. 05.57.40.63.38, fax 05.57.40.66.24, e-mail pitray@pitray.com ☑
👤 by appt
🍷 Comtesse de Boigne

CH. PUY GALLAND 2001★

	0.2 ha	1,200	🍷	5–8 €

This property has been in the same family for three generations and is now offering a very successful 2000. It has a garnet colour with black glints, a bouquet of leather, soft fruit (cherry) and blackcurrant aromas, and a full, rich tannic structure which develops on the palate with plenty of fruity flavour and good length. This highly characteristic wine should be drunk in two to five years' time.

🍷 Bernard Labatut, 12, Le Bourg, 33570 Saint-Cibard, tel. 05.57.40.63.50, fax 05.57.40.63.50 ☑
👤 by appt

CH. ROBIN 2000★

	11 ha	45,000	🍷	11–15 €

Regularly featured in the *Guide* as one of the bench-marks of the appellation, this cru grows 80% Merlot and 20% Cabernets on a well-exposed hillside with a limestone-clay soil. This wine has a deep colour with brilliant garnet glints, and notes of cherry liqueur and oaky toast which continue on

the palate along with supple tannins, lingering on to a long, velvety finish. Drink now or leave to age for two to five years according to taste.

🍷 SCEA Ch. Robin, 33350 Belvès-de-Castillon, tel. 05.57.47.92.47, fax 05.57.47.94.45, e-mail chateau.robin@wanadoo.fr ☑
👤 by appt
🍷 Sté Lurckroft

AMAVINUM DU CH. LA ROCHE BEAULIEU Elevé en fût de chêne 2001★★

	8 ha	32,400	🍷	15–23 €

2001 was the first vintage for the new owners here – Serge Tchekhov, a painter and winemaker, and some his Libournais wine-growing friends – and they decided for this Amavinum (lover of wine) *cuvée* to select the oldest vines on the estate. The wine's purple colour with lighter purple glints is very young, as are its complex aromas of very ripe dark berries, spices, cocoa and toast. The tannins are powerful and rich but also soft, and well cloaked by oak on a palate with a very long finish. This is a very great wine for this appellation, and should be drunk in three to eight years' time. The **Cuvée Prestige du Château La Roche Beaulieu 2000 (8–11 €)** receives a special mention.

🍷 SCEA Tchekhov et Associés, Ch. la Roche Beaulieu 1, Peyrelebade, 33350 Les-Salles-de-Castillon, tel. 05.57.40.64.37, fax 05.57.40.65.05, e-mail larochebeaulieu@wanadoo.fr
👤 by appt

CH. LA ROCHE-PRESSAC 2001★

	2 ha	7,500	🍷	11–15 €

Made from 80% Merlot and 20% Cabernet Franc, this wine has a deep, garnet colour and a powerful bouquet of prune and undergrowth aromas which are well integrated with the oaky toast and vanilla notes. The tannins are powerful and very round, with a welcome note of freshness on the finish. This well-balanced wine should be drunk in two to five years' time.

🍷 SCEA Ch. La Roche-Pressac, Clos Puylazat, 33350 Saint-Magne-de-Castillon, tel. 05.57.40.48.24, fax 05.57.40.48.24, e-mail contact@laroche-pressac.com ☑
👤 by appt

CH. DES ROCHERS 2000★

	7.5 ha	20,000	🍷	3–5 €

Located on a classic limestone-clay terroir, this château is offering a wine with an intense, near-black colour and a fruity bouquet enlivened by notes of liquorice and menthol. There are Morello cherry flavours on the palate, which is rich, velvety and well balanced. The wine is already elegant, but will give real delight to the wine-lover in two or three years time.

🍷 Jacques Aroldi, Le Bourg, 33350 Belvès-de-Castillon, tel. 05.57.47.96.20, fax 05.57.47.93.02, e-mail ch.des.rochers@wanadoo.fr ☑
👤 by appt

DOM. ROCHES BLANCHES

L'Extrême 2000★

	1.7 ha	6,300	🍷	11–15 €

This château is located on a red clay soil over limestone rock, and planted with 80% Merlot and 20% Cabernet Franc. The wine has a deep purplish colour and intense aromas of red berries and spices (cinnamon and vanilla). The dense, well-balanced, long tannins will enable this wine to keep for three to six years.

🍷 SCEA Vignobles Patrice Roux, 90, av. du Gal-de-Gaulle, 33350 Saint-Magne-de-Castillon, tel. 05.57.40.21.30, fax 05.57.40.21.87, e-mail scea-roux@wanadoo.fr ☑
👤 ev.day 8am–8.30pm

CH. ROQUE LE MAYNE

Elevé en fût de chêne 2001★★

	10 ha	51,000	🍷	8–11 €

The vineyard is located on two different *lieux-dits*, Roque and Le Mayne, which have given their names to this wine, created in 1997 when the vineyard was purchased. Since then the

Wines selected but not starred

owners have made major investments which have clearly been beneficial, as can be seen from this remarkable 2001. It has a very young, almost black colour and a bouquet which is still reticent but has complex aromas of undergrowth, red berries and oaky toast. The palate is powerful, rich, and well-balanced right up to the finish. Serve this wine in four to six years' time.

�'• SCEA des vignobles Meynard, 10, av. de Labourrée, 33330 Saint-Magne-de-Castillon, tel. 05.57.40.17.32, fax 05.57.40.38.93,
e-mail vignobles-meynard@wanadoo.fr ☑
🍷 by appt

DOM. DU ROUX
Cuvée Sélection 2001★
| | 0.7 ha | 3,000 | 🍷 | 8–11€ |

This small family property is offering a wine made from 60% Merlot and 40% Cabernet Franc, and fermented malolactically in new oak. It has a strong colour and aromas of fruits in brandy combined with some musky and toasty notes. The supple, rich tannins develop on a palate which is essentially fruity. This is a delightfully delicate wine, which will give of its best in two to three years' time.
�'• EARL Gilles Teyssier, 50, av. de Saint-Emilion, 33330 Saint-Sulpice-de-Faleyrens, tel. 05.57.24.64.77, fax 05.57.24.64.77, e-mail gilles.teyssier@free.fr ☑
🍷 by appt

CH. LA SENTINELLE 2000★
| | 3.8 ha | 20,000 | 🍷 | 5–8€ |

The owners of this cru arrived here in 1997 as novices, and decided to take advice from Michel Rolland. In their third vintage they have produced a wine with a dark colour streaked with purplish highlights, and an intense nose of pepper and sweet spice aromas which are well integrated with notes of oaky toast. The tannins are both firm and silky, and keep their freshness and good, fruity balance right up to the finish. Open this wine in one to two years' time.
�ّ• Sté viticole du Dom. de Lézin, 11, Giraud-Arnaud, 33750 Saint-Germain-du-Puch, tel. 05.57.24.00.00, fax 05.57.24.00.98, e-mail domaine-de-lezin@wanadoo.fr ☑
🍷 by appt

CH. TERRASSON
Cuvée Prévenche 2000★★
| | 3 ha | 15,000 | 🍷 | 5–8€ |

Château Terrasson is offering three wines in this very good 2000 vintage. The Cuvée Prévenche has remarkably intense aromas of vanilla, cocoa and liquorice, and exceptionally high-quality tannins which are powerful, thoroughbred and very long. This is a great wine which will make a good accompaniment to grilled meats in three to eight years' time. One star is awarded to the **Cuvée Classique**, which is well balanced, with fruity flavours of blackberries and raspberries and a complex finish; it will be ready to drink sooner than the first wine, and will also keep for at least three to five years. Finally, the **Château Damas de Montdespic 2000** receives a special mention. It can be drunk straight away.
➑• EARL Christophe et Marie-Jo Lavau, Ch. Terrasson, BP 9, 33570 Puisseguin, tel. 05.57.56.06.65, fax 05.57.56.06.76, e-mail contact@chateau-terrasson.com ☑ 🏠 🏠
🍷 by appt

JOHANNA DE VIEUX CHATEAU CHAMPS DE MARS 2000★★
| | 4 ha | 15,000 | 🍷 | 15–23€ |

Over the last few years this property has modernized to achieve a higher level of quality: very rigorous grape selection, wooden vats, malolactic fermentation in oak. This remarkable vintage has a deep, brilliant colour and a complex, powerful bouquet of oaky toast, cherry, strawberry and vanilla notes. The round, rich, mature tannins are a sign of very good maturation in oak. The balance on the finish is perfect, indicating that the wine will open out fully in three to five years' time.
➑• GFA Régis et Sébastien Moro, Le Pin, 33350 Les-Salles-de-Castillon, tel. 05.57.40.63.49, fax 05.57.40.61.41 ☑
🍷 by appt

AETOS 2001
| | n.c. | 15,500 | 🍷 | 11–15€ |

➑• Calvet, 75, cours du Médoc, BP 11, 33028 Bordeaux Cedex, tel. 05.56.43.59.00, fax 05.56.43.17.78, e-mail calvet@calvet.com

CH. BREHAT 2000
| | 8 ha | 41,300 | 🍷 | 5–8€ |

➑• Jean de Monteil, Ch. Haut-Rocher, 33330 Saint-Etienne-de-Lisse, tel. 05.57.40.18.09, fax 05.57.40.08.23, e-mail ht-rocher@vins-jean-de-monteil.com ☑
🍷 by appt

CH. COTE MONTPEZAT
Elevé en fût de chêne 2001
| | n.c. | 150,000 | 🍷 | 8–11€ |

➑• SA Vignobles Bessineau, 8, Brousse, BP 42, 33350 Belvès-de-Castillon, tel. 05.57.56.05.55, fax 05.57.56.05.56, e-mail bessineau@cote-montpezat.com ☑
🍷 by appt

CH. FONGABAN 2000
| | 32 ha | 190,000 | 🍷 | 5–8€ |

➑• SARL de Fongaban, Monbadon, 33570 Puisseguin, tel. 05.57.74.54.07, fax 05.57.74.50.97, e-mail fongaban@vignobles-taix.com ☑
🍷 ev.day except Sat. Sun. 9am–12 noon 2pm–6pm

CH. GERBAY
Elevé en fût de chêne 2000
| | 12.23 ha | 15,000 | 🍷 | 5–8€ |

➑• Consorts Yerles, SCEA Ch. Gerbaÿ, 33350 Gardegan, tel. 05.57.40.63.87, fax 05.57.40.66.39, e-mail gerbay@wanadoo.fr ☑
🍷 by appt

CH. GRAND TUILLAC
Cuvée Elégance Elevé en fût de chêne 2000
| | 6 ha | 40,000 | 🍷 | 5–8€ |

➑• SCEA Lavigne, Tuillac, 33350 Saint-Philippe-d'Aiguilhe, tel. 05.57.40.60.09, fax 05.57.40.66.67, e-mail scea.lavigne@wanadoo.fr ☑
🍷 by appt

CH. HAUTE TERRASSE 2001
| | n.c. | 8,900 | 🍷 | 5–8€ |

➑• Pascal Bourrigaud, Ch. Haute Terrasse, 33350 Saint-Magne-de-Castillon, tel. 05.57.74.43.98, fax 05.57.74.41.07 ☑

CH. PUY GARANCE 2001
| | 2 ha | 6,000 | 🍷 | 5–8€ |

➑• Frédéric Burriel, 3 bis, Le Caufour, 33350 Sainte-Colombe, tel. 05.57.47.99.23, fax 05.57.47.99.23 ☑
🍷 by appt

CH. ROC DE JOANIN 2000
| | 1.3 ha | 9,600 | 🍷 | 5–8€ |

➑• SCEA Vignobles Mirande, La Rose Côtes Rol, 33330 Saint-Emilion, tel. 05.57.24.71.28, fax 05.57.74.40.42, e-mail pierremirande@aol.com ☑
🍷 by appt

CH. ROC DE TIFAYNE

Elevé en fût de chêne 2000

| ■ | 2.3 ha | 16,000 | ▮ ▥ ▲ | 8–11 € |

➦ SCEA des Vignobles Limbosch-Zavagli, Tifayne, 33570 Puisseguin, tel. 05.57.40.61.29, fax 05.57.40.60.98, e-mail info@tifayne.com ☑
🍷 by appt
➦ CFA Côtes à Côtes

CH. DE SAINT-PHILIPPE

Séduction 2000

| ■ | n.c. | 9,000 | ▥ | 8–11 € |

➦ EARL Vignobles Bécheau, Ch. de Saint-Philippe, 33350 Saint-Philippe-d'Aiguilhe, tel. 05.57.40.60.21, fax 05.57.40.62.28, e-mail pbecheau@terre-net.fr ☑
🍷 by appt

Bordeaux-Côtes de Francs

The vineyard of Bordeaux-Côtes de Francs (536 ha producing a volume of 22,781 hl of red wine and 284 hl of white) is 12 km east of Saint-Emilion and encompasses the communes of Francs, Saint-Cibard and Tayac. The vines are planted on an excellent site, on the lime, clay and marly slopes of some of the highest hills in the Gironde. They almost all produce red wines, except for about 20 ha, and are cultivated by some dynamic wine-growers and a Cave Coopérative. Between them, they produce some very attractive wines, which are rich, with a good bouquet.

CH. LES CHARMES-GODARD 2001★★★

| ▨ | 1.65 ha | 11,400 | ▥ | 15–23 € |

Château
Les Charmes-Godard
2001

13% Vol.   BORDEAUX CÔTES DE FRANCS
APPELLATION BORDEAUX CÔTES DE FRANCS CONTRÔLÉE
G.F.A. LES CHARMES-GODARD PROPRIÉTAIRE A SAINT-CIBARD FRANCE
NICOLAS THIENPONT VITICULTEUR   750 Ml
MIS EN BOUTEILLES AU CHÂTEAU

Michel Thienpont's château maintains its position at the top of the appellation; his white wine is masterly, and once again he wins a unanimous *coup de cœur* for the 2001, which has had nine months of oak maturation on lees with stirring. Everything about this wine is enchanting: the brilliant colour with pale gold glints, the fine, expressive bouquet of honey and very ripe Sauvignon aromas and elegant oak notes, the flavourful attack, and the very full-bodied palate with a perfect balance between acidity and roundness. This is a very ample, round, well-balanced white wine which can be drunk now or left to age for a few years.
➦ GFA Les Charmes-Godard, Lauriol, 33570 Saint-Cibard, tel. 05.57.56.07.47, fax 05.57.56.07.48, e-mail ch.puygueraud@wanadoo.fr ☑
🍷 by appt

CH. CRU GODARD

Moelleux Elevé en fût de chêne 2001★★

| ■ | 0.2 ha | 1,200 | ▥ | 8–11 € |

This small cru is located on a silty-clay soil, and is offering a sweet white wine which is remarkable in every respect. It has a golden yellow colour with some green glints, a delicate bouquet of lime-blossom, honey, raisin and orange peel aromas, and a very rich, complex palate which develops with perfect balance and agreeable flavours of honey and toast. This wine is ready to drink now.
➦ Corinne et Franck Richard, Godard, 33570 Francs, tel. 05.57.40.65.94, fax 05.57.40.65.94, e-mail franck.richard@libertysurf.fr ☑
🍷 by appt

CH. DE FRANCS

Les Cerisiers Vieilli en fût de chêne 2000★★

| ■ | 8 ha | 23,500 | ▥ | 8–11 € |

This château shares the name of the appellation, and last year won a *coup de cœur*. Once again the 2000 vintage is remarkable. It has a cherry colour with crimson glints, and elegant, appealing aromas of stewed fruits, prunes and well-integrated oaky toast. After a clean, spicy attack, the tannins become assertive, but they are already becoming better integrated, as is apparent on the very long finish, which has as good a balance as the very great wines. After two to five years of ageing this will be a very pleasant wine.
➦ SCEA Ch. de Francs, 33570 Francs, tel. 05.57.40.65.91, fax 05.57.40.63.04 ☑
🍷 by appt
➦ D. Hébrard et H. de Bouärd

CH. GODARD BELLEVUE

Elevé en fût de chêne 2000★

| ■ | 6 ha | 23,500 | ▥ | 5–8 € |

This cru grows equal shares of Merlot and the Cabernets, and is well worth a visit for its 2000. It has a deep, near-black colour and flavours of fruit and undergrowth which are well balanced with the oaky toast notes and rich, unctuous, flavourful tannins. This wine can be drunk now or kept for a few years.
➦ EARL Arbo, Godard, 33570 Francs, tel. 05.57.40.65.77, fax 05.57.40.65.77 ☑
🍷 by appt

L'EDEN DE LAPEYRONIE 2000★★★

| ■ | 2 ha | 5,000 | ▥ | 15–23 € |

This small, 2 ha cru is currently going over to organic growing, and has installed 10-hl tanks to vinify the Cabernet Sauvignon (50%) and Merlot (40%) grapes separately. Once again it has produced an astonishingly good wine, which has been unanimously awarded a *coup de cœur* by the Grand Jury. It has an intense, garnet colour and a fine, expressive bouquet of very ripe red berries, truffles, smoke and elegant oak aromas. The tannins are clean and very rich to start with, then become round, well balanced and elegant. After three to six years of ageing this will be the perfect wine for a very special occasion.
➦ Jean-Frédéric Lapeyronie, 4, Castelmerle, 33350 Sainte-Colombe, tel. 05.57.40.19.27, fax 05.57.40.14.38, e-mail lapeyroniefred@wanadoo.fr ☑
🍷 by appt
➦ A. Charrier

CH. MARSAU 2000★

■ 9 ha 34,300 🍷 11–15 €

This château is at one of the highest points in the Côtes de Francs terroir, and grows only Merlot vines. The 2000 has an intense, purple colour and a bouquet which is still reticent but releases some slight notes of musk and toast. The tannins are full-bodied, mature and mentholy, but still firm on the finish. This wine will be perfect in two to five years' time.

☞ Ch. Marsau, Bernaderie, 33570 Francs,
tel. 05.56.44.30.49, e-mail contact@cobg.com ✉
🍷 by appt
☞ S. et J.-M. Chadronnier

CH. LA PRADE 2000★

■ 3.5 ha 12,900 🍷 23–30 €

This small vineyard has a silty-limestone-clay soil, and has now produced an excellent 2001. It has a garnet colour with brilliant mauve glints, a very pleasant nose of leather, jammy fruit and coffee aromas, and an equally agreeable palate with rich, fine tannins which linger on to a finish on notes of liquorice and vanilla. Keep this wine carefully for two to five years.

☞ Nicolas Thienpont, 33570 Saint-Cibard,
tel. 05.57.56.07.47, fax 05.57.56.07.48,
e-mail ch.puygueraud@wanadoo.fr ✉
🍷 by appt

CH. PUYANCHE

Elevé en fût de chêne 2001★

■ 1 ha 3,800 🍷 5–8 €

This excellent white wine is a blend of 65% Sauvignon and 35% Semillon, and has been fermented and matured in oak. The rich, powerful bouquet is still marked by the dominant Sauvignon grape, and the palate is fresh, vigorous and quite substantial, with a slightly austere note on the finish. The balance will be perfect in one or two years' time. A special mention goes to the **Puyanché red 2000 (3–5 €)**, which has been aged in tank, and is fruity, almost a little acid, and supple. It should be drunk very soon.

☞ EARL Arbo, Godard, 33570 Francs, tel. 05.57.40.65.77, fax 05.57.40.65.77 ✉
🍷 by appt

FLEURON DU CH. DU PUY GALLAND

2001★★

■ n.c. 2,000 🍷 11–15 €

This château has belonged to the same family for three generations, and has a good limestone-clay terroir which has produced this very high-quality Le Fleuron *cuvée spéciale*. It has an intense cherry colour and aromas of fruit (cherries) and spices, enlivened by some oaky toast notes. The mature, full, velvety tannins develop on the palate with balance and elegance. This remarkable wine will be even better in two to five years' time. The **Cuvée Classique 2001 (5–8 €)** receives a special mention for its overall balance, which is fruity and supple; it can be drunk very soon.

☞ Bernard Labatut, 12, Le Bourg, 33570 Saint-Cibard, tel. 05.57.40.63.50, fax 05.57.40.63.50 ✉
🍷 by appt

CH. PUYGUERAUD 2000★

■ 35 ha 85,000 🍷 15–23 €

This very beautiful 14th century manor house overlooks a vineyard planted with 50% Merlot, 45% Cabernets and 5% Malbec. The 2000 vintage has a deep, dark colour, and very fine aromas of red berries, cocoa and coffee. The tannins are powerful and also very harmonious and well balanced by high-quality oak. This wine will be really delightful in two to five years' time.

☞ SCEA Ch. Puygueraud, 33570 Saint-Cibard,
tel. 05.57.56.07.47, fax 05.57.56.07.48,
e-mail ch.puygueraud@wanadoo.fr ✉
🍷 by appt
☞ Héritiers George Thienpont

Wines selected but not starred

CLOS LA CABANE

Moelleux 2001

■ 0.99 ha 2,040 🍷 3–5 €

☞ Didier et Cédric Gaillardou, Larthomas,
24610 Saint-Méard-de-Gurson, tel. 05.53.82.49.18,
fax 05.53.82.49.18 ✉
🍷 by appt

CH. NARDOU 2001

■ 8 ha 50,000 🍷 5–8 €

☞ EARL Vignobles Dubard, Nardou, 33570 Tayac,
tel. 05.57.40.69.60, fax 05.57.40.69.20,
e-mail f.dubard@aol.fr ✉ 🏠 🏠
🍷 by appt

CH. VIEUX SAULE 2001

■ 4 ha 12,000 🍷 5–8 €

☞ Thierry Moro, La Vergnasse, 33570 Saint-Cibard,
tel. 05.57.40.65.75, fax 05.57.40.65.75,
e-mail thierry.moro@tiscali.fr ✉
🍷 by appt

BETWEEN THE GARONNE AND THE DORDOGNE

The geographical region of Entre-Deux-Mers is the large triangular area bounded by the Garonne and Dordogne rivers and the southeast border of the department of the Gironde. Here, in one of the sunniest and most pleasant parts of Bordeaux, the vines occupy 23,000 ha, about a quarter of the region's vineyard. The hilly terrain offers sweeping views as well as quiet corners adorned with fine examples of the traditional regional architecture (fortified manor houses, small châteaux in green estates and larger numbers of fortified mills). Entre-Deux-Mers also lies at the heart of the Gironde's mythical past, with a rich heritage of beliefs and traditions dating from time immemorial.

Entre-Deux-Mers

The appellation Entre-Deux-Mers does not correspond exactly to the geographical area of Entre-Deux-Mers, excluding as it does some communes with their own appellations. It applies specifically to dry white wines produced under a set of regulations almost as rigorous as those for Appellation Bordeaux. As a matter of practice, the wine-growers try to keep their best white wines for this appellation. As a result, production is voluntarily limited to (1,448 ha planted, producing

Between Garonne and the Dordogne

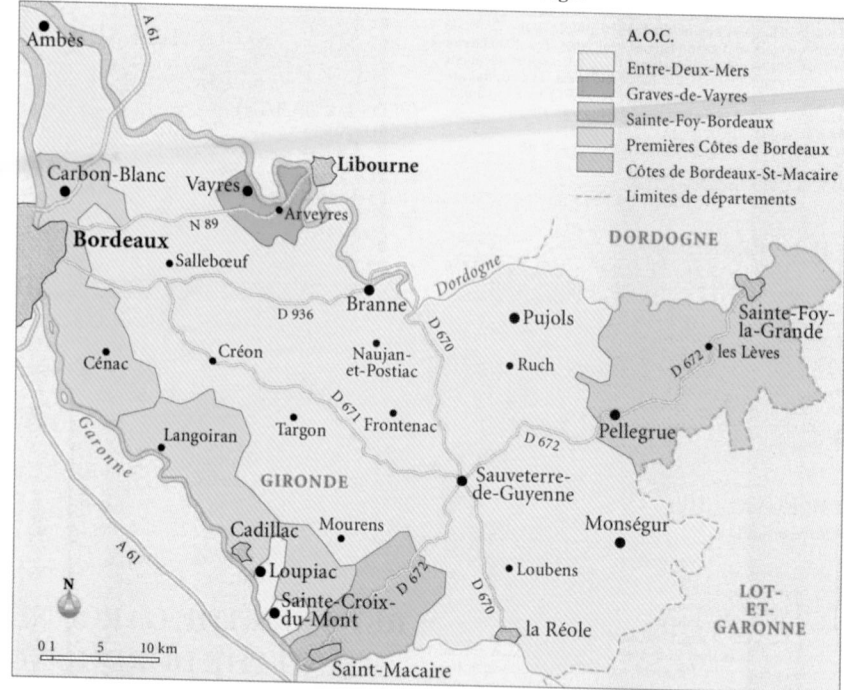

A.O.C.

Entre-Deux-Mers
Graves-de-Vayres
Sainte-Foy-Bordeaux
Premières Côtes de Bordeaux
Côtes de Bordeaux-St-Macaire
--- Limites de départements

84,373 hl in 2002), and the annual tastings approving the wines are particularly demanding. The major grape variety is Sauvignon, giving the Entre-Deux-Mers whites their singular bouquet, to be appreciated particularly when the wine is young.

CH. BEL AIR PERPONCHER 2002★

	n.c.	n.c.	🍷 🍸	5–8 €

As ever, this Château Bel Air Perponcher is delightful. It starts a little reticently with subtle aromas of pineapple and mango heightened by some mineral notes, then becomes more assertive on the palate, which was praised by the tasters for its round attack, very rich body, and open finish enlivened by a slight touch of freshness. This is a bench-mark wine.
🍷 SCEA Vignobles Despagne, 33420 Naujan-et-Postiac,
tel. 05.57.84.55.08, fax 05.57.84.57.31,
e-mail contact@despagne.fr

CH. BONNET 2002★

	124 ha	900,000	🍷 🍸	5–8 €

It is a pleasure to see this château featured yet again in the Guide, this time for a wine with an most unusual bouquet of rich, delicate fragrances: intense floral notes (roses) and aromas of Reunion lychees and citrus fruits, all with shades of Muscat... "Surprising," noted one taster. The body on the palate is fresh and elegantly round. A special mention goes to the Château Guibon 2002 which although certainly more restrained is a well-made wine.
🍷 André Lurton, Ch. Bonnet, 33420 Grézillac,
tel. 05.57.25.58.58, fax 05.57.74.98.59,
e-mail andrelurton@andrelurton.com ☑
🍸 by appt

COMTE DE RUDEL 2002★★

	10.5 ha	80,000	🍷 🍸	3–5 €

Visitors here will enjoy looking around the feudal château where Rauzan took refuge, and by contrast will admire the modernity of this large Producers' Union, represented here by two branded wines and a château wine. This Comte de Rudel has lovely fragrances of broom and white peaches, and a very fresh palate which is carried by a teasing touch of sparkle and a slight, well-integrated herbaceous touch. This wine will be a perfect accompaniment to oysters. Fleur 2002 has spring flower aromas and a well-balanced freshness which wins it a star. A special mention goes to the Château Canteloudette 2002, an aromatic wine which is unusually sweet for this appellation.
🍷 Caves de Rauzan, L'Aiguilley, 33420 Rauzan,
tel. 05.57.84.13.22, fax 05.57.84.12.67,
e-mail magasin@cavesderauzan.com ☑
🍸 by appt

CH. DE CRAIN 2002★

	11 ha	32,000	🍷 🍸	3–5 €

Château de Crain was built in the 13th century for Edward IV of England, while the winery dates back to the 18th century. As for the wine, it is a classic composition with a classic appearance and excellent performance. The bouquet includes Sauvignon grapes, along with mineral and toast aromas and touches of hazelnut which add complexity to the ripe fruit notes both on the nose and on the long, supple palate. This is an Entre-Deux-Mers which wine-lovers will take their time to savour.
🍷 SCA de Crain, Ch. de Crain, 33750 Baron,
tel. 05.57.24.50.66, fax 05.45.25.03.73 ☑
🍸 by appt
🍷 Fougère

CH. LA GRANDE METAIRIE 2002★

	4.5 ha	40,000	🍷 🍸	3–5 €

Sustainable agriculture means having the wisdom to act sensibly and make intelligent use of modern techniques in matters such as the balance of grape varieties, good ways of running the vineyard, specialized wineries, maceration at low temperatures, controlled fermentation and maturation on fine lees. It is a difficult art to learn, but it has been well mastered at this château. The wine has a fairly intense bouquet which opens on floral aromas, then develops on to jammy fruit notes against a background of buttery toast. The first impression on the palate is fresh, but it soon becomes richer, and the flavours are enriched by notes of orchard fruits (pears and ripe apples). The finish is long, well balanced and delicious. This wine is guaranteed to succeed as an aperitif or the accompaniment to a first course.

➺ SCEA Vignobles Buffeteau, lieu-dit Dambert, 33540 Gornac, tel. 05.56.61.97.59, fax 05.56.61.97.65 ☑

CH. L'HOSTE-BLANC

Elevé en fût de chêne 2002★

	1 ha	3,000	🍶	5–8 €

This château selection includes 15% Sauvignon Gris, which is known to give the wine roundness and elegant aromas. The unusual structure of this 2002 is also partly due to the vinification methods used here, and to the fact that it has been matured in new oak and on lees. It has a brilliant, crystal-clear yellow colour, aromas of citrus fruits, peaches and vine-blossom, and lingering flavours of dried apricots, hazelnuts, brioche and buttery toast. The body on the palate is round, supple, fresh throughout, and supported to perfection by the oak. This wine will be a delightful accompaniment to white meats and cheese once it has been kept for a while.

➺ SC Vignobles Baylet, Ch. Landereau, 33670 Sadirac, tel. 05.56.30.64.28, fax 05.56.30.63.90, e-mail vignoblesbaylet@free.fr ☑
🍷 ev.day except Sat. Sun. 8am–12 noon 1.30pm–5.30pm
➺ Michel Baylet

CH. LALANDE-LABATUT 2002★

	n.c.	n.c.	🍶 🍷	5–8 €

This wine's bouquet opens straight on to intense, fresh white flower aromas, which give way on the palate to fruit flavours (apples, quince, ripe citrus fruits), heightened by some notes of smoke. After a fresh attack, the palate is both rich and slightly acid, with a slight note of toast on the finish. A wine as rich as this deserves to be served with shellfish or white meat. The **Cuvée Prestige Elevé en Fût de Chêne 2002** also wins a star for its very good balance between a full body with flavours of white vine-blossom and an oak note which is already well integrated.

➺ SCEA Vignobles Falxa, 38, ch. de Labatut, 33370 Salleboeuf, tel. 05.56.21.23.18, fax 05.56.21.20.98, e-mail chateau.lalande-labatut@wanadoo.fr ☑
🍷 by appt

CH. LESTRILLE 2002★

	1.38 ha	11,600	🍶 🍷	5–8 €

Made from Semillon (46%). Muscadelle (32%) and Sauvignon (22%), this wine makes the mouth water with its unrestrained yet very delicate range of aromas and flavours, in which floral notes with shades of Muscat and slight hints of menthol are well balanced with an overall sense of ripe fruits. "Taste it slowly," advised one taster, as an aperitif or an accompaniment to a special entrée.

➺ Jean-Louis Roumage, Lestrille, 33750 Saint-Germain-du-Puch, tel. 05.57.24.51.02, fax 05.57.24.04.58, e-mail jlroumage@lestrille.com ☑
🍷 by appt

CH. MYLORD 2002★

	18 ha	130,000	🍶 🍷	3–5 €

This château is run by a well-known winemaker from a beautiful 18th century charterhouse. He has produced a very good wine made from the three grape varieties (40% Muscadelle). It has a hugely varied bouquet ranging from vine-blossom to exotic fruit aromas, and a rich palate with a slight note of freshness, both of which are the result of truly masterly wine-making; before being fermented the ripe grapes were macerated, then stabilized at a low temperature. This Entre-Deux-Mers will go well with oven-baked fish, white meat, or even cheese.

➺ Michel et Alain Large, Ch. Mylord, 33420 Grézillac, tel. 05.57.84.52.19, fax 05.57.74.93.95, e-mail large@chateau-mylord.com ☑
🍷 by appt

CH. NARDIQUE LA GRAVIERE 2002★

	17 ha	80,000	🍶 🍷	5–8 €

The little church at Saint-Genès can be found between the Abbaye de la Sauve-Majeure and the ruins of the Château de Langoiran, amid a landscape where there are still woods as well as vines. This château has blended a very small amount of Muscadelle with Sauvignon and Semillon to produce a fresh wine with elegantly assertive citrus fruit flavours (orange peel and ripe grapefruit), and a slight hint of bitterness on the finish. This Entre-Deux-Mers will be a mouthwatering accompaniment to oysters and shellfish.

➺ Vignobles Thérèse, Ch. Nardique La Gravière, 33670 Saint-Genès-de-Lombaud, tel. 05.56.23.01.37, fax 05.56.23.25.89 ☑
🍷 by appt

CH. POLIN

Cuvée Prestige 2001★

	1 ha	6,000	🍶	5–8 €

This wine has a clean, gleaming yellow colour and aromas of acacia honey, bergamot orange, crystallized fruits, white peaches and vine-blossom. The palate is supple, well balanced and round, with a lively, fresh menthol note on the finish. The oak flavour from a year's fermentation and maturation in barrels is pleasantly restrained. This wine will be a good accompaniment to white meats and cheese, and will keep for several years.

➺ GAEC La Lande de Taleyran, Ch. Polin, 33750 Beychac-et-Caillau, tel. 05.56.72.98.93, fax 05.56.72.81.94, e-mail chateau.lalandedetaleyran@wanadoo.fr ☑
🍷 by appt
➺ Jacques Burliga

DOM. DE RICAUD 2002★

	1.5 ha	10,000	🍶 🍷	5–8 €

Two generations share the work on this family estate located at Cantois, a hamlet in a lovely part of Entre-Deux-Mers where forests still co-exist peacefully with vineyards...This wine's bouquet seems rather reticent at the start, but then develops with plenty of complexity on to aromas of white flowers (eglantine), peaches, citrus fruits and lychees. The same flavours reappear on a rich, round palate, where they open out and continue right to the finish. This wine is the result of a very successful blend of grape varieties slightly dominated by Sauvignon (50%), and perfectly controlled by modern techniques of vinification.

➺ Vignobles Chaigne et Fils, Ch. Ballan-Larquette, 33540 Saint-Laurent-du-Bois, tel. 05.56.76.46.02, fax 05.56.76.40.90, e-mail regis@chaigne.fr ☑
🍷 by appt
➺ Régis Chaigne

CH. TURCAUD 2002★★

	13.18 ha	105,000	🍶 🍷	5–8 €

This property is close to the famous Abbaye de La Sauve-Majeure, just beneath which you will find the syndicate of the Entre-Deux-Mers appellation. Made from equal shares of Sauvignon and Semillon, this is an aromatic wine with a well-balanced bouquet of broom, menthol, exotic fruits (lychees, grapefruit, orange peel) and white flowers (acacia). The dense, full palate is lifted by a slight sparkle, and has a long, fresh finish. This wine has plenty of character, and will go well with white meat, cheese, or even chocolate desserts. A special mention goes to the **Château Moulin de la Grave 2002**; it is less complex, but has a very slight note of acidity which is both characteristic and delightful.

🍷 EARL Vignobles Maurice Robert, Ch. Turcaud, 33670 La Sauve, tel. 05.56.23.04.41, fax 05.56.23.35.85, e-mail chateau-turcaud@wanadoo.fr ☑

🍸 by appt

CH. DE VAURE 2002★

	4.5 ha	15,000	🍾 ⚬	3–5€

This Château de Vaure was very successful last year as well, and is a fine example of a really good Entre-Deux-Mers. It has a bouquet of exotic fruit aromas (citrus fruits and lychees) combined with fragrant notes of crystallized or dried fruits against a mineral background which is characteristic of the appellation. The palate has plenty of vigour, and is complex, fresh, elegant and long. The **Château Jandille 2002** is vinified by the Union des Producteurs, and also wins a star. It is made from 70% Sauvignon, and has a rich range of flavours (acacia honey, peaches, mandarines and kugelhopf) and a long, fresh, floral finish.

🍷 Les Chais de Vaure, 33350 Ruch, tel. 05.57.40.54.09, e-mail chais-de-vaure@wanadoo.fr ☑

🍸 ev.day except Sun. 8.30am–12.30pm 2pm–6pm

🍷 P. de Larrard

CH. VIGNOL 2002★

	5.5 ha	40,000	🍾 ⚬	5–8€

The name of this château is a clear sign that it has a tradition of winemaking, and the quality of its wines is confirmed by the numerous times it has appeared in the *Guide*. Its Entre-Deux-Mers won a *coup de coeur* last year, and this 2002 vintage is another brilliant success. It has a very fine, light straw colour, and open aromas of very ripe citrus fruits with shades of lime-blossom, dried apricots and exotic fruits. The palate has a round, flavourful, caressing body, and some fresh notes on the finish.

🍷 SCEA Bernard et Dominique Doublet, Ch. Vignol, 33750 Saint-Quentin-de-Baron, tel. 05.57.24.12.93, fax 05.57.24.12.83, e-mail d.doublet@free.fr ☑

🍸 by appt

Wines selected but not starred

CH. DE L'AUBRADE 2002

	2.45 ha	n.c.	🍾 ⚬	5–8€

🍷 GAEC Jean-Pierre et Paulette Lobre, 33580 Rimons, tel. 05.56.71.55.10, fax 05.56.71.61.94 ☑

🍸 by appt

BARON D'ESPIET

Cuvée Pinasse 2002

	0.57 ha	5,000	🍾 ⚬	3–5€

🍷 Union de producteurs Baron d'Espiet, Lieu-dit Fourcade, 33420 Espiet, tel. 05.57.24.24.08, fax 05.57.24.18.21, e-mail baron-espiet@dial.oleane.com ☑

🍸 by appt

CH. BELLEVUE 2002

	10 ha	2,400	🍾 📖 ⚬	3–5€

🍷 SCEA Ch. Bellevue, 33540 Sauveterre-de-Guyenne, tel. 05.56.71.54.56, fax 05.56.71.83.95 ☑

🍸 by appt

🍷 D'Amécourt

CH. CHANTELOUVE 2002

	3.7 ha	26,000		3–5€

🍷 EARL J.C. Lescoutras et Fils, Le Bourg, 33760 Faleyras, tel. 05.56.23.90.87, fax 05.56.23.61.37 ☑

🍸 by appt

CH. LA COMMANDERIE DE QUEYRET 2002

	12 ha	50,000	🍾 ⚬	3–5€

🍷 Claude Comin, Ch. La Commanderie, 33790 Saint-Antoine-du-Queyret, tel. 05.56.61.31.98, fax 05.56.61.34.22, e-mail vignoblecomin@wanadoo.fr ☑

🍸 by appt

CH. DE FONTENILLE 2002

	6 ha	42,000	🍾	5–8€

🍷 SC Ch. de Fontenille, 33670 La Sauve, tel. 05.56.23.03.26, fax 05.56.23.30.03, e-mail defraine@chateau-fontenille.com ☑

🍸 by appt

🍷 Stéphane Defraine

CH. LA FREYNELLE 2002

	4 ha	30,000	🍾 ⚬	5–8€

🍷 Vignobles Philippe Barthe, Peyrefus, 33420 Daignac, tel. 05.57.84.55.90, fax 05.57.74.96.57, e-mail vbarthe@club-internet.fr ☑

🍸 by appt

CH. GRAND BIREAU 2002

	1.1 ha	8,300	🍾 ⚬	3–5€

🍷 SCEA Michel Barthe, 18, Girolatte, 33420 Naujan-et-Postiac, tel. 05.57.84.55.23, fax 05.57.84.57.37, e-mail scea.barthemichel@wanadoo.fr ☑

🍸 by appt

CH. DU GRAND FERRAND 2002

	1 ha	8,000	🍾 ⚬	3–5€

🍷 SCEA n° 2 Vignobles Rocher Cap de Rive, Ch. du Grand Ferrand, 33540 Sauveterre-de-Guyenne, tel. 05.56.71.60.42, fax 05.56.71.69.08 ☑

🍷 ,

FRANCOIS GREFFIER 2002

	3.1 ha	22,000	🍾 ⚬	3–5€

🍷 Greffier, Castenet, 33790 Auriolles, tel. 05.56.61.40.67, fax 05.56.61.38.82, e-mail ch.castenet@wanadoo.fr ☑

🍸 by appt

CH. GROSSOMBRE 2002

	n.c.	n.c.	🍾 ⚬	5–8€

🍷 André Lurton, Ch. Bonnet, 33420 Grézillac, tel. 05.57.25.58.58, fax 05.57.74.98.59, e-mail andrelurton@andrelurton.com ☑

🍸 by appt

CH. HAUT RIAN 2002

	13.79 ha	110,000	🍾 ⚬	3–5€

🍷 Michel Dietrich, La Bastide, 33410 Rions, tel. 05.56.76.95.01, fax 05.56.76.93.51 ☑

🍸 ev.day except Sun. 9am–12 noon 2pm–5.30pm

CH. RAUZAN DESPAGNE

Cuvée de Landeron 2002

	n.c.	n.c.	🍾 ⚬	5–8€

🍷 SCEA Vignobles Despagne, 33420 Naujan-et-Postiac, tel. 05.57.84.55.08, fax 05.57.84.57.31, e-mail contact@despagne.fr

🍷 J.-L. Despagne

CH. REYNIER 2002

	4 ha	n.c.	🃏 ♦	5–8 €

♠ SCEA Vignobles Marc Lurton, Ch. Reynier,
33420 Grézillac, tel. 05.57.84.52.02, fax 05.57.84.56.93,
e-mail marc.lurton@wanadoo.fr ☑
� by appt

CH. TOUR DE MIRAMBEAU 2002

	n.c.	n.c.	🃏 ♦	5–8 €

♠ SCEA Vignobles Despagne, 33420 Naujan-et-Postiac,
tel. 05.57.84.55.08, fax 05.57.84.57.31,
e-mail contact@despagne.fr ☑

CH. VALADE 2002

	4 ha	30,000	🃏 ♦	3–5 €

♠ Greffier, Castenet, 33790 Auriolles, tel. 05.56.61.40.67,
fax 05.56.61.38.82, e-mail ch.castenet@wanadoo.fr ☑
☍ by appt

Entre-Deux-Mers Haut-Benauge

CH. PEYRINES 2002★★

	12 ha	3,000	🃏 ♦	5–8 €

This is essentially a blend of Sauvignon (50%) and Semillon (40%), with just 10% Muscadelle. The result is very successful both on the nose and on the palate, which has plenty of freshness and open aromas of white flowers, citrus fruits (oranges) and citronnella. This delightful vigour continues in sprightly fashion on to a long finish, and is highly characteristic of the appellation. This wine should be drunk as an aperitif, or with cold entrées and oysters.
♠ Behaghel, Ch. Peyrines, 33410 Mourens,
tel. 05.56.61.98.05, fax 05.56.61.98.23 ☑
☍ by appt

Graves de Vayres

Despite the similarity of the name, this wine-growing district on the left bank of the Dordogne, not far from Libourne, is not to be confused with the Graves wine-growing area. Graves de Vayres is a relatively small, well-defined enclave of gravelly soil of a different type to that of Entre-Deux-Mers. The appellation has been used since the 19th century, though it was not officially recognized until 1931. Initially, it was used for dry or medium white wines, but currently there is an increase in the proportion of red wines which qualify for the appellation.

The total area of the vineyards is divided into 490 ha of red grape varieties and 110 ha of whites. A significant quantity of the reds is also sold as Appellation Régionale Bordeaux. In 2002 the production of AOC Graves de Vayres reached some 30,815 hl, of which 5,224 hl were white wines.

CH. DE BARRE GENTILLOT

Cuvée Jean Julien 2000★

	2 ha	13,000	🍷	5–8 €

This *cuvée spéciale* comes from a selection of old Merlot vines grown on a silt and gravel soil. It has a brilliant ruby colour, and a developing bouquet marked by subtle hints of undergrowth and smoke. The tannins are full bodied, mature and balanced. This is a very good, characteristic wine, which should be left to age for two to five years until it achieves a better balance.
♠ SCEA Yvette Cazenave-Mahé, Ch. de Barre,
33500 Arveyres, tel. 05.57.24.80.26, fax 05.57.24.84.54,
e-mail chateau.de.barre@online.fr ☑
☍ by appt

CH. CANTELAUDETTE 2002★★

	10 ha	60,000	🃏	–3 €

This dry white *cuvée classique* is made mainly from Semillon (95%), with just 5% Muscadelle. It is a remarkable wine, with a pale, brilliant colour gleaming with straw glints, and a bouquet of ripe grape and hazelnut aromas along with a mineral touch. After a fresh attack, the palate develops with plenty of freshness and elegance, and a good overall balance. This is an excellent wine which came close to winning a *coup de coeur*. It can be drunk now or left to age for three to five years.
♠ Jean-Michel Chatelier, Ch. Cantelaudette,
33500 Arveyres, tel. 05.57.24.84.71, fax 05.57.24.83.41,
e-mail jm.chatelier@wanadoo.fr ☑
☍ by appt

CH. DURAND-BAYLE

Elevé en fût de chêne 2001★

	10 ha	10,667	🃏 🍷 ♦	8–11 €

Michel Gonet and his children are now in charge of a huge Bordelais *vignoble* stretching over several appellations. They also keep a foothold in Champagne, and here in Vayres as elsewhere, their policy for the last 15 years has been to pursue high quality. This 2001 has a dark purple colour and a bouquet of red berries, fresh mushrooms and elegant oak. With its complex, powerful, long tannic structure, this is an excellent wine for longer maturing which will be ready to drink in two to three years' time. The Gonets' leading property also wins a star for the **red Château Lesparre 2001, Elevé en Fût de Chêne**.
♠ SCEV Michel Gonet et Fils, Ch. Lesparre,
33750 Beychac-et-Caillau, tel. 05.57.24.51.23,
fax 05.57.24.03.99, e-mail vins.gonet@wanadoo.fr ☑
☍ by appt

CH. FAGE

First 2001★

	2 ha	3,200	🍷	8–11 €

This wine is made from a rigorous selection of 65% Semillon and 35% Sauvignon Gris. It makes a very good first impression with a lovely golden colour gleaming with straw glints. The developing bouquet has aromas of honey, roses and crystallized fruits, while the tender, delicate palate still has a fair amount of sparkle and continues pleasantly right up to the finish. This rather unusual wine should be drunk within the next three years with fine fish dishes.
♠ SA Ch. Fage, 33500 Arveyres, tel. 04.67.39.10.51,
fax 04.67.39.15.33,
e-mail maxcazottes@domainecaton.com ☑
☍ by appt

CH. HAUT-GAYAT 2001★

	n.c.	n.c.	🍷	5–8 €

This large property has been in the same family for at least eight generations, and is now offering a wine made from an exactly equal blend of Merlot and Cabernet Sauvignon. It has a brilliant ruby colour with violet glints, but the bouquet is restrained, with red berry, toast and smoke aromas. The tannins are round, complex, and well balanced on the finish. Drink this wine while it is still young to get the full benefit of its fruitiness.
♠ Marie-José Degas, La Souloire,
33750 Saint-Germain-du-Puch, tel. 05.57.24.52.32,
fax 05.57.24.03.72 ☑
☍ ev.day except Sat. Sun. 8am–5.30pm

MAISON NOBLE DU PETIT PUCH 2001★

| | 11 ha | n.c. | 🍷 | 8–11 € |

After more than two centuries in this noble house dating back to the 14th century, the Meaudre de Lapouyade family handed the buildings and 11 ha vineyard over in 1998 to the Chalands, who since then have carried out major restoration work. This vintage is made from 80% Merlot and 20% Cabernet Sauvignon, and has a brilliant ruby colour and a delightful developing bouquet of dark berry and toast aromas which show that it has been matured in oak. The palate is still very oaky, with aggressive tannins which need to become better integrated. Keep this wine carefully for three to four years.
➼ Isabelle et Patrice Chaland, GFA du Petit Puch, 33750 Saint-Germain-du-Puch, tel. 05.57.24.52.36, fax 05.57.24.01.82, e-mail ipchaland@libertysurf.fr ☑
�ይ by appt

CH. PICHON-BELLEVUE 2002★

| | 8 ha | 27,000 | 🍶 ⚫ | 3–5 € |

This very successful dry white 2002 is a blend of 70% Sauvignon and 30% Semillon. It has a pale gold colour with green, slightly golden highlights, and a clean bouquet of gunflint and boxwood aromas. The palate is dominated by Sauvignon flavours, whose vigour is due to a good level of acidity. This vintage can be drunk straight away, but will also keep for three to five years. The red Château Pichon-Bellevue 2001 (5–8 €) receives a special mention; its silky tannins are fruity and well balanced. Drink this wine within the next three or four years.
➼ Ch. Pichon-Bellevue, 33870 Vayres, tel. 05.57.74.84.08, fax 05.57.84.95.04 ☑
☕ by appt
➼ Reclus

CH. LES TUILERIES DU DEROC 2001★

| | 11 ha | 32,000 | 🍶 | 5–8 € |

This cru is so near to the Dordogne that when there is a tidal bore you can hear the sound of the waves rushing in. Made from 70% Merlot, this is an agreeable wine with a delicate bouquet of red berry and floral aromas, a dense tannic structure and plenty of acidity. Don't be afraid to keep to keep this very good 2001 for two or three years until it achieves its full balance.
➼ Vignobles Colombier, 14, lieu-dit Montifaut, 33870 Vayres, tel. 05.57.74.71.59, e-mail vignobles-colombier@wanadoo.fr ☑
☕ by appt

Wines selected but not starred

CH. LA CAUSSADE
Vieilli en fût de chêne 2001

| | 10 ha | 14,000 | 🍶🍷⚫ | 5–8 € |

➼ GFA Jean-Claude et Nathalie Ballet, Ch. La Caussade, 33870 Vayres, tel. 05.57.74.83.17, fax 05.57.84.94.53 ☑
☕ by appt

CH. LA PONTETE 2002

| | 3.5 ha | 4,000 | 🍶 | 3–5 € |

➼ SCEA Ch. et S. Lacombe, Ch. La Pontête, 33870 Vayres, tel. 05.57.74.76.99, fax 05.57.74.79.88, e-mail christianlacombe2@wanadoo.fr ☑ ⛪
☕ by appt

CH. LE TERTRE 2002

| | 1.6 ha | 8,000 | 🍶 ⚫ | 3–5 € |

➼ Pierrette et Christian Labeille, Vignobles Labeille, Ch. Le Tertre, 33870 Vayres, tel. 05.57.74.76.91, fax 05.57.74.87.40, e-mail vignobles.labeille.le.tertre@wanadoo.fr ☑
☕ ev.day except Sat. Sun. 9am–12 noon 2pm–7pm

Sainte-Foy-Bordeaux

Saint-Foy, a medieval city of great tourist interest, is also a wine town, situated between Lot-en-Garonne and the Dordogne. Its 387 ha of vines produced 1,841 hl of white wine and 14,584 hl of red wine in 2002.

CH. LES BAS-MONTS 2001★

| | 4.65 ha | 33,000 | | 5–8 € |

Made from 60% Cabernet Sauvignon and 40% Merlot grown on a limestone-clay soil, this vintage is somewhat atypical of the region, but good nonetheless. In keeping with this grape blend, it has a dark ruby colour, a fruity and slightly spicy nose with a hint of pepper, and powerful, very long tannins which are still a little harsh on the finish. This wine will need to be kept for two to five years before it is ready to drink. The same cru also produces a **Château Les Bas-Monts Moelleux 2001 (8–11 €)**, which receives a special mention for its delightful, concentrated flavour on the palate, and very well-balanced finish. Drink this wine now, or keep for two to three years.
➼ GAEC Basso Frères, Le Raymond, 33220 Margueron, tel. 05.57.41.29.16, fax 05.57.41.29.16 ☑
☕ by appt

CH. DU CHAMP DES TREILLES 2001★★

| | 1.5 ha | 7,500 | 🍷 | 8–11 € |

As technical director of Château Pontet-Canet, a Pauillac *cru classé*, Jean-Michel Comme came here in 1998 with his wife to take over this family property. Since then they have begun work on modernizing both the vineyard and the winery. This remarkable 2001 has an intense, near-black colour, a bouquet of fruit, toast and delicate oak aromas, and a powerful, elegant tannic structure. This perfectly-balanced wine should be drunk in two to five years' time. The **Vieilles Vignes Moelleux 2001 (15–23 €)** receives a special mention for its range of crystallized fruit, honey and caramel flavours; it is ready to drink now.
➼ Corinne et Jean-Michel Comme, Pibran, 33250 Pauillac, tel. 05.56.59.15.88, fax 05.56.59.15.88 ☑
☕ by appt

CH. DES CHAPELAINS
Cuvée La Découverte 2001★★

| | 2 ha | 14,000 | 🍷 | 8–11 € |

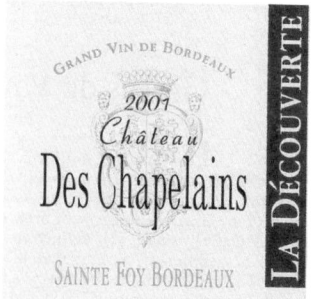

This is not the first *coup de cœur* to be awarded to this family vineyard dating back to the 13th century. This dry white wine makes an enchanting first impression with a straw-gold colour and fine, elegant aromas of hazelnuts, delicate oak and roasted almonds. It is supple and warming on the palate, with a remarkably good balance provided by well-controlled maturation in oak which gives it complexity and very good length. A touch of acidity on the finish adds a welcome note of freshness. In one to three years' time this 2001 will be the perfect accompaniment to an avocado mousse with crayfish tails. The **red Cuvée Momus 2001 (5–8 €)** is a well-made,

mature wine with well-balanced tannins. Drink it in two to three years' time.
�753 Pierre Charlot, Les Chapelains,
33220 Saint-André-et-Appelles, tel. 05.57.41.21.74,
fax 05.57.41.21.74,
e-mail chateaudeschapelains@wanadoo.fr ☑
☖ ev.day 8.30–12 noon 2pm–5.30pm; Sat. Sun. by appt

CH. CLAIRE ABBAYE
Cuvée Prestige 2001★

■	n.c.	5,000	▮▮▯ ⬥	15–23 €

The owners of this cru have been here for nine years now, and last year won a *coup de coeur* for this same wine in the 2000 vintage. The 2001 is made from pure Merlot grown on a limestone-clay soil, and has a brilliant ruby colour and aromas of very ripe fruit which are somewhat overwhelmed by the oaky toast notes. The tannins are supple and also very fruity, however, and will enable this wine to be drunk between 2004 and 2007.
�753 Bruno Sellier de Brugière, Ch. Claire Abbaye, 33890 Gensac, tel. 05.57.47.42.04, fax 05.57.47.48.16, e-mail bruno.sellier@free.fr ☑
☖ by appt

CH. HOSTENS-PICANT
Sec Cuvée des Demoiselles 2002★

■	6.81 ha	20,000	▮▮▯	11–15 €

This property along with some others started the revival of the appellation, and is now offering a dry white wine which has been macerated on the skins with stirring on lees. It has a clear, straw colour and elegant aromas of honey, apricots and crystallized fruits. Its freshness and good balance make it pleasant to drink already, but also give it good ageing potential. The red Cuvée d'Exception Lucullus 2001 (23–30 €) also wins a star. It has a good balance on the palate between powerful, well-integrated tannins and an agreeable range of flavours. This wine will need to be kept for three to five years.
�753 Ch. Hostens-Picant, Grangeneuve Nord, 33220 Les Lèves-et-Thoumeyragues, tel. 05.57.46.38.11, fax 05.57.46.26.23, e-mail chateauhp@aol.com ☑ ⌂
☖ by appt

DOM. DE KARLIAC
Elevé en fût de chêne 2001★

■	0.9 ha	6,900	▮▮▯	5–8 €

This 22 ha property is offering a wine which has been matured in oak for 14 months, and is a blend of 55% Sauvignon and 45% Merlot. It has a deep ruby colour and an elegant, restrained bouquet of red berries and spices. The round, velvety tannins are well balanced and long. This wine will keep for two to three years without any problem.
�753 Dom. de Karliac, Le Petit Roc, 33220 Les Lèves-et-Thoumeyragues, tel. 06.80.61.01.15, fax 05.57.41.28.93, e-mail site@karliac.com ☑
☖ by appt
�753 Eric Gaulhiac

CH. MARTET
Réserve de Famille 2001★★

■	8 ha	32,000	▮▮▯	15–23 €

This used to be a resting-place for pilgrims on their way to Compostella, but today it has been turned over to wine-growing. This wine is made exclusively from Merlot grapes which have been picked by hand, put into crates, and carefully sorted. It has a strong garnet colour and an intense bouquet of spices, dark berries and high-quality oak. The velvety, powerful, mouthwatering tannins develop on to a fresh flavour (cedar) and a very agreeable final note of oak. This is a great, complex, thoroughbred wine, which should be drunk in five to ten years' time.
�753 SCEA Ch. Martet, 33220 Eynesse, tel. 05.57.41.00.49, fax 05.57.41.09.36, e-mail pde@conickwien.com ☑
☖ by appt
�753 Patrick de Coninck

CH. PICHAUD SOLIGNAC 2001★

■	9 ha	37,000		8–11 €

This château is offering two different wines, both of which have won one star. The *cuvée classique* is still closed on the nose, but the tannic structure on the palate is full, mature and very fruity. This well-balanced 2001 should be left to age for two to five years. The red Cuvée des Danaïdes 2001, is limited to 1,800 bottles, and is a very concentrated, oaky wine with some notes of musk. The tannins on the palate are powerful and vanilla-flavoured, but they keep their good balance on the finish. This is another wine which will age very well, for three to eight years in this case.
�753 EARL Pichaud Solignac, La Niolaise, 33790 Pellegrue, tel. 05.56.61.43.55, fax 05.56.61.43.55, e-mail ch-pic-sol@terre-net.fr ☑
☖ ev.day 9am–12 noon 2pm–7pm
�753 Delbeuf

CH. ROBERPEROTS 2001★

■	10 ha	28,000	▮▮▯	3–5 €

This 2001 is a blend of 70% Cabernets and 30% Merlot, with a brilliant purple colour and a bouquet of spice, toast and leather aromas. The palate is well structured, full and very balanced, with an elegant finish on flavours of cedar and dark berries. Another wine from Prodiffu is the red Saint-Angel Cuvée Prestige 2000 (5–8 €) (50,000 bottles) which is also awarded a star. It is ready to drink now.
�753 Prodiffu, 17–19, rte des Vignerons, 33790 Landerrouat, tel. 05.56.61.33.73, fax 05.56.61.40.57, e-mail prodiffu@prodiffu.com
�753 Odile et Jean-François Bruère

CH. DE VACQUES
Cuvée Prestige 2001★

■	1.8 ha	10,000	▮▮▯ ⬥	5–8 €

This 12 ha estate is located on a due-south-facing limestone-clay hillside with gravel outcrops which are very good for producing great wines. Its *cuvée spéciale* is still closed on the nose but opens out fully on the palate, where the mature, rich, well-balanced tannins develop on to a very agreeable finish on blackcurrant and redcurrant notes. This wine should be drunk in two to three years' time.
�753 Christian Birac, Ch. de Vacques, 33220 Pineuilh, tel. 05.57.46.15.01, fax 05.57.46.16.12, e-mail christian-birac@club-internet.fr ☑ ⌂
☖ ev.day 11am–12.30pm 5pm–6.30pm; cl. 15–30 Aug.

CH. VERRIERE BELLEVUE
Moelleux 2001★

■	1 ha	4,000	▮▮▯	5–8 €

This sweet white wine comes from Semillon (70%) and Sauvignon (30%) grapes grown on a clay hillside whose south-southwest-facing aspect gives it very good exposure to the sun. It has a brilliant golden colour, an intense bouquet of crystallized fruit and lemon notes, and a powerfully sweet palate which is very round and has a caramel flavour on the finish. This well-balanced 2001 should be drunk in a few years' time. (Half-litre bottles)
�753 EARL Alice et Jean-Paul Bessette, 5, La Verrière, 33790 Landerrouat, tel. 05.56.61.36.91, fax 05.56.61.41.12, e-mail jeanpaul.bessette@wanadoo.fr ☑ ⌂
☖ by appt

Wines selected but not starred

long-established reputation for their colour, body and strength, while those produced on the slopes above add a certain finesse to these qualities. The white wines, of which 10,593 hl are soft and increasingly tend towards the sweet.

CH. L'ENCLOS
Réserve de la Marquise 2001

	5.18 ha	38,000	▪ ▥ ◊	5–8 €

◆⊤ SCEA Ch. L'Enclos, 33220 Pineuilh, tel. 05.57.46.55.97, e-mail info@chateaulenclos.fr ☑
⊤ by appt

CH. LES MANGONS 2001

	8.6 ha	25,000	▥	8–11 €

◆⊤ EARL Ch. Les Mangons, Les Mangons 3–4, 33220 Pineuilh, tel. 05.57.46.17.27, fax 05.57.46.17.67, e-mail michel.comps@chateaulesmangons.com ☑
⊤ by appt
◆⊤ Comps

CH. LES PARIS 2001

▪	5 ha	33,000	▪ ▥ ◊	5–8 €

◆⊤ Domanie de Sansac, Les Lèves, 33220 Sainte-Foy-la-Grande, tel. 05.57.56.02.02, fax 05.57.56.02.22, e-mail oeno@univitis.fr
⊤ by appt
◆⊤ Huguette Comme

CH. DES THIBEAUD
Cuvée Thibeaud 2001

	2.15 ha	15,600	▪ ▥ ◊	5–8 €

◆⊤ EARL Dom. Le Canton, Ch. des Thibeaud, 33220 Caplong, tel. 05.57.41.25.65, fax 05.57.41.27.84, e-mail thibeaud@libertysurf.fr ☑
⊤ by appt
◆⊤ Delaplace

CH. TROIS FONDS 2002

▪	0.5 ha	2,700	▪ ◊	3–5 €

◆⊤ EARL Jacques Deffarge, 23, La Beysse, 33220 Eynesse, tel. 05.57.41.02.65, fax 05.57.41.01.42 ☑
⊤ by appt

Premières Côtes de Bordeaux

The region of the Premières Côtes de Bordeaux stretches some 60 km along the right bank of the Garonne, from the gates of the city of Bordeaux to Cadillac. The vines are grown on slopes facing the river, which offer magnificent views. Soils here are very varied: along the Garonne it is a recent alluvial soil, producing some excellent red wines. On the slopes, gravelly and limey soils predominate, the amount of clay in the soil increasing further away from the river. The vines, the conditions of cultivation and methods of vinification are all in the classic Bordeaux mould. In all, this appellation consists of 3,525 ha planted for reds, with 310 ha planted for sweet whites; a significant proportion of the wines, mainly whites, are also sold under the Appellation Régionale Bordeaux. The red wines, of which 155,488 hl were produced in 2002, have a

CH. BALOT
Tradition d'Excellence 2000★

	19 ha	31,000	▥	5–8 €

Product of a predominantly Merlot (85%) vineyard, this Cuvée Prestige has the characteristic fruity bouquet and supple, rounded structure, based on well-integrated tannins. It will be a very pleasant wine in three to four years. The **Cuvée Principale** attracted a special mention.
◆⊤ SCEA Vignobles Yvan Réglat, Ch. Balot, 33410 Monprimblanc, tel. 05.56.62.98.96, fax 05.56.62.19.48, e-mail vins.yvanreglat@wanadoo.fr ☑
⊤ by appt.

CH. DU BIAC
Elevé en barrique 2001★

	55 ha	20,000	▥	5–8 €

A small estate which for generations has dominated the Garonne valley. A reliable company, as this wine demonstrates. Well made and expressive, it has sufficient structure and aromatic character to be laid down for two to three years, giving time for the oak to blend in.
◆⊤ Ch. du Biac, 19, rte de la Ruasse, 33550 Langoiran, tel. 05.56.67.19.98, fax 05.56.67.32.63, e-mail palas@quaternet.fr ☑ ☗
⊤ by appt.
◆⊤ Rossini

CH. BRETHOUS
Cuvée Prestige 2000★

	12.7 ha	50,000	▥	8–11 €

The extent of the vineyards, the size of the house and vinery at Brethous are all deliberately kept to a human scale, though this has not prevented it from bringing its equipment and methods right up to date. An attractive, intense garnet-red, this 2000 vintage bears witness to its effectiveness, both for its ripe fruit bouquet and its supple and clean structure.
◆⊤ Denise and Cécile Verdier, Ch. Brethous, 33360 Camblanes, tel. 05.56.20.77.76, fax 05.56.20.08.45, e-mail brethous@libertysurf.fr ☑
⊤ ev. day 8.30am–12noon 2pm–6pm; Sat. Sun. by appt.

CH. CAMAIL 2001★

▪	8 ha	60,000	▪	5–8 €

The 40-year-old vines undoubtedly contributed to the quality of this wine, which is not limited to its superb colour. Agreeably fruity, with notes of game, the bouquet opens the way to a solid structure, still tannic but without harshness, justifying a period of three to five years in the cellar.
◆⊤ François Masson-Regnault, Ch. Camail, 33550 Tabanac, tel. 05.56.67.07.51, fax 05.56.67.21.22, e-mail planet-fmr@terre-net.fr ☑
⊤ by appt.

CH. CARSIN 2001★

	19.53 ha	50,344	▥	8–11 €

A fine 50 ha holding, of which 20 are taken up with vineyards, Carsin is one of the most reliable among the Premières Côtes. Attractive to look at, the 2001 vintage stands out for its balance, which is evident in the complexity of the bouquet, ranging from spices to floral, and on the rich, but already very pleasant palate. The **Cuvée Noire (11–15 €)** received a special mention.
◆⊤ Juha Berglund, GFA Ch. Carsin, 33410 Rions, tel. 05.56.76.93.06, fax 05.56.62.64.80, e-mail chateau@carsin.com ☑
⊤ by appt.

CH. DES CEDRES

Cuvée Cédric Elevé en fût de chêne 2001★

■	0.4 ha	2,000	⊞	8–11 €

Belonging to the Special Cuvée of this cru created in 1970, this wine, made from 90% Merlot with 10% Cabernet Sauvignon, was produced in a limited amount, but it is nevertheless interesting for its fine, delicate bouquet and its structure, which is well supported by the oak.

↘ SCEA Vignobles Larroque, 15, allée de Gageot, 33550 Paillet, tel. 05.56.72.16.02, fax 05.56.72.34.44, e-mail vignobles.larroque@wanadoo.fr ✔
⌇ by appt.

CH. LA CHEZE

Elevé en fût de chêne 2001★

■	10 ha	40,000	⊞	8–11 €

The oldest building in Capian, the 16th century château overlooks the Garonne from the top of the slope; a very favorable situation for the vines, as is immediately evident when tasting this wine, with its attractive dark-red colour and its full, rich and intense palate, supported by good tannins. It needs to be laid down for some time.

↘ SCEA Ch. La Chèze, La Chèze, 33550 Capian, tel. 05.56.72.11.77, fax 05.56.72.11.77 ✔
⌇ by appt.
↘ Priou-Rontein

CLOS BOURBON

Vieilli en fût de chêne 2001★

■	3.36 ha	26,000	⊞	5–8 €

Enclosed by more than a kilometre of walls and run from a 18th century house, this cru is not lacking in style. While still a little severe, this wine is also good to look at. Starting with appealing aromas of toast, it develops a palate that is both supple and flavoursome, and which calls for three to four years in the cellar.

↘ Clos Bourbon, 33550 Paillet, tel. 05.56.72.11.58, fax 05.56.72.13.76 ✔
⌇ by appt.
↘ d'Halluin

CH. CLOS CHAUMONT 2000★

■	9 ha	24,500	⊞	11–15 €

Of a regular quality, this cru, awarded a *coup de coeur* for the 99 vintage, maintains its reputation with this wine. A fine, brilliant, intense garnet-red, it develops a bouquet with marked perfumes of red fruits before a supple opening on the palate followed by a show of fine tannins that, while very much present, are never aggressive.

↘ EARL Ch. Clos Chaumont, 8, Chomar, 33550 Haux, tel. 05.56.23.37.23, fax 05.56.23.30.54 ✔
⌇ by appt.

CH. LA CLYDE Cuvée Garde de la Clyde Elevé

en fût de chêne 2000★

■	2 ha	13,333	⊞	8–11 €

Situated on the picturesque slopes of Tabanac, this cru offers a 2000 vintage that already has a pleasant aromatic complexity (fruits, leather, mild tobacco) but whose silky tannins will allow it to improve further over one to two years.

↘ EARL Philippe Cathala, Ch. La Clyde, 33550 Tabanac, tel. 05.56.67.56.84, fax 05.56.67.12.06 ✔
⌇ by appt.

CH. LE DOYENNE 2000★

■	6.8 ha	32,000	⊞	8–11 €

Dating from at least the 17th century, this château is a handsome example of a charterhouse of the Bordeaux region. A characteristic garnet-red colour, this wine offers an agreeable combination of floral notes (violet and peony) and oakiness (vanilla). Full and rounded, the structure reveals a good tannic presence which supports the oak. An attractive wine, to lay down for three to four years.

↘ SCEA du Doyenné, 27, chem. de Loupes, 33880 Saint-Caprais-de-Bordeaux, tel. 05.56.78.75.75, fax 05.56.21.30.09, e-mail doyenne@francom.fr ✔
⌇ by appt.

CH. FRANC-PERAT 2001★

■	n.c.	150,000	■ ⊞ ⚭	8–11 €

At the head of a vast group of estates, the Despagnes have never sacrificed quality to economic efficiency. Produced in a quantity that is far from limited, this wine is also extremely well made. Intense-red in colour, with a pleasingly complex bouquet (redcurrants, toast, butter) and a supple opening, with ripe tannins and excellent length, everything indicates good potential for laying down.

↘ SCEA de Mont-Pérat, 33550 Capian, tel. 05.57.84.55.08, fax 05.57.84.57.31, e-mail contact@despagne.fr ✔

CH. GOURRAN 2000★

■	6.5 ha	40,000	■ ⊞ ⚭	5–8 €

With vines of an already respectable age (30 years), this cru is also noted for sticking to Bordeaux traditions of blending grape varieties, with even a touch of Petit Verdot. The result is a well-constructed wine. Fresh and complex in its aromatic expression and upheld by a good tannic presence, it is suitable for laying down for three to four years.

↘ SCA Ch. de Haux, 33550 Haux, tel. 05.57.34.51.11, fax 05.57.34.51.15 ✔ ⚭
⌇ by appt.
↘ Kaare Thal-Jantzen

CH. DU GRAND MOUEYS 2000★

■	18 ha	100,000	⊞	8–11 €

This vast estate (170 ha, 76 of them given over to vineyards) spans three hills. It produces quality wines. This wine? Its smoky, musky bouquet is still a touch oaky. Its substance being supported by a solid, tannic structure, one should not hesitate to lay it down for two or three years. The **Château du Piras red 2000 (5–8 €)**, a cru from another part of the Les Trois Collines estate, was also awarded a star.

↘ SCA Les Trois Collines, Ch. du Grand Mouëys, 33550 Capian, tel. 05.57.97.04.44, fax 05.57.97.04.60, e-mail cavif.gm@ifrance.com ✔
⌇ by appt.

CH. DE HAUX 2000★

■	60 ha	300,000	■ ⊞ ⚭	5–8 €

Belonging to a huge entity (more than 110 ha in all), this cru offers a wine with a personality that is evident from the first glance at its profoundly intense colour. One finds real complexity on the bouquet, where the oak reveals itself with notes of vanilla. But it is on the palate that its fine potential comes to the fore, with a solid structure and a powerful finish. The **Château Carmel de Mingot red 2000** was also awarded one star.

↘ SCA Ch. de Haux, 33550 Haux, tel. 05.57.34.51.11, fax 05.57.34.51.15 ✔ ⚭
⌇ by appt.
↘ Peter Jorgensen

CH. JORDY D'ORIENT

Vieilli en fût de chêne 2001★

■	7 ha	20,000	■ ⊞ ⚭	5–8 €

The major quantity of Merlot in the blend of varieties (80%) is scarcely noticeable on the nose, which is still dominated by maturation in cask, but the roundness on the palate is an unmistakable sign of the Merlot grape. A most seductive wine.

↘ Laurent Descorps, Ch. Haut-Liloie, 33760 Escoussans, tel. 05.56.23.94.23, fax 05.57.34.40.09 ✔
⌇ by appt.

CH. JOURDAN

Elevé en fût de chêne 2001★

■	20 ha	109,000	⊞	5–8 €

The distant heir of an ancient Benedictine Priory, this cru is a fine production unit. Pale-ruby in colour, this wine is definitely not hidden under a monk's cowl. And its bouquet has real intensity. Supple, rounded, well balanced and

agreeably fruity, the palate indicates, even demands, a period of three to four years in the cellar.
🕿 Grands Vins de Gironde, Dom. du Ribet, BP 59, 33451 Saint-Loubès Cedex, tel. 05.57.97.07.20, fax 05.57.97.07.27, e-mail gvg@gvg.fr

CH. LAGAROSSE
Les Comtes 2001★★

| | 3,5 ha | 15,000 | 🍾 | 15–23 € |

Product of 38-year-old vines, carefully selected for their situation at the top of the slope, this *cuvée* has no difficulty in displaying its fine origins; they show in its intense-crimson colour and in the good aromas of red fruit, brought out by spicy notes that make no attempt to dominate. Its tannic strength, its balance, its body and length are all utterly convincing. A very good wine to drink with a joint of beef for a memorable meal to record in your cellar-book, but not for another four or five years.
🕿 SAS Ch. Lagarosse, Lagarosse, 33550 Tabanac, tel. 05.56.67.00.05, fax 05.56.67.58.90, e-mail lagarosse@wanadoo.fr 🆅
🍷 by appt.

CH. LANGOIRAN
Cuvée La Gravière 2001★

| | 0,6 ha | 4,500 | 🍾 | 8–11 € |

Not many crus can boast of owning a medieval castle, but Langoiran is one which can. When you visit it you can discover this attractive selection. Both easy and well made, it links a bouquet intensely reminiscent of vanilla and leather to a well-balanced structure. Rounded, soft and rich, the whole leaves an agreeable sense of liquorice on the palate. The **Cuvée Prestige 2000 (5–8 €)** (40,000 bottles) was specially mentioned.
🕿 SC Ch. Langoiran, Le Pied du Château, 33550 Langoiran, tel. 05.56.67.08.55, fax 05.56.67.32.87, e-mail chateaulangoiran@wanadoo.fr 🆅
🍷 ev. day 9am–12noon 2pm–5pm; Sat. Sun. and groups by appt.
🕿 Nicolas Filou

CH. LEZONGARS 2000★★

| | 8,5 ha | 49,000 | 🎏🍾 | 8–11 € |

Two years after buying this cru, British national Philip Iles offers proof that this acquisition was indeed driven by a passion. The very colour of this wine, dark and intense, proclaims its power. Add to that an agreeable roundness and length and one finds a very good wine, which needs laying down for two to four years. Equally well structured, the **L'Enclos du Château Lezongars red 2001** was awarded a star.
🕿 SC du Ch. Lezongars, 323, Roques-Nord, 33550 Villenave-de-Rions, tel. 05.56.72.18.06, fax 05.56.72.31.44, e-mail info@chateau-lezongars.com 🆅
🍷 by appt.

CH. MACALAN 2001★★

| | 3 ha | 22,000 | 🎏🍾🥄 | 3–5 € |

Coming from a small cru situated in the north of the appellation, this wine presents itself well beneath a good, deep-red colour with purple highlights. The keeping qualities implicit in this are confirmed by the structure on the palate. Tannic

and fine at the same time, fruity and spiced, this prolongs the elegance found on the nose, signalling the perfect union of wine (fruit) and barrel.
🕿 Jean-Jacques Hias, Ch. Macalan, 20, rue des Vignerons, 33560 Sainte-Eulalie, tel. 05.56.38.92.41, fax 05.56.38.81.82 🆅
🍷 by appt.

PRESTIGE DU CHATEAU DE MALHERBES Elevé en fût de chêne 2000★

| | 1,5 ha | 10,000 | 🍾 | 5–8 € |

Strangely, there is no sign on the bouquet of the finesse of the Merlot grape variety, even though this is the major element in the blend. Happily, the wine softens and increases in strength, leaving the taster with the memory of a well-constructed whole.
🕿 Ch. de Malherbes, 33360 Latresne, tel. 05.56.20.02.90, fax 05.56.20.03.85, e-mail sancier@chateau-de-malherbes.com 🆅 🏠
🍷 by appt.

CH. MESTREPEYROT 2001★★

| | 4 ha | 15,000 | 🍾 | 3–5 € |

While essentially dedicated to the making of red wines, this cru is far from lacking when it comes to whites. The appeal of the intense, limpid colour joins with that of the bouquet, and everyone will appreciate the concentration, the roasted aromas and the many nuances (honey, linden blossom, oak). Just as complex, with apricot and orange flavours, the palate ends on the memory of a rich, full-bodied wine, which will be perfect as an aperitif, or with foie gras or white meat. The **red Cuvée Prestige Elevée en Fût de Chêne 2001 (5–8 €)** was specially mentioned.
🕿 GAEC des Vignobles Chassagnol, Bern, 33410 Gabarnac, tel. 05.56.62.98.00, fax 05.56.62.93.23 🆅
🍷 by appt.

CH. DES MILLE ANGES 2000★

| | 16.11 ha | 81,394 | 🍾 | 5–8 € |

The year 2000 was notable for this cru because of the renovation of the winery. It also left behind the memory of a very successful vintage. An intense colour, as rich on the bouquet as on the palate, this wine shows by its fleshiness, its substance and its complexity that it is well worth laying down for a while before being served with a roast shoulder of lamb.
🕿 Mme Heather Van Ekris, SARL Mille Anges, Lieu-dit Millanges, 33490 Saint-Germain-de-Graves, tel. 05.56.76.41.04, fax 05.56.76.46.72
🍷 by appt.

CH. OGIER DE GOURGUE 2001★

| | 5,7 ha | n.c. | | 5–8 € |

Managed by Jacques Fourès, oenologist and inventor of the "cruover", this cru attaches as much importance to the vines as to the winery. Still a little firm in aromatic expression, its toasty, vanilla and red fruit notes show promise, as does the rounded, powerful structure. A well-extracted wine, which needs one to three years in the cellar.
🕿 Josette Fourès, 41, av. de Gourgues, 33880 Saint-Caprais-de-Bordeaux, tel. 05.56.78.70.99, fax 05.56.20.18.72, e-mail foures@quaternet.fr 🆅
🍷 by appt.

CH. DE PIC
Cuvée Tradition 2000★★

| | 6 ha | 40,000 | 🍾 | 5–8 € |

This wine models its personality on the superb château from whence it comes. A beautiful colour, it develops a rich and powerful bouquet. Upheld by a good tannic presence, the palate harmoniously mingles the fruit and the oak. A truly pleasure-giving wine, to lay down for several years.
🕿 François Masson-Regnault, Ch. de Pic, 33550 Le Tourne, tel. 05.56.67.07.51, fax 05.56.67.21.22, e-mail planet-fmr@terre-net.fr 🆅
🍷 by appt.

CH. PLAISANCE

Cuvée Tradition 2001★

| ■ | n.c. | n.c. | ⅡⅠ | 8–11 € |

Managed from a beautiful 18th century charterhouse, this estate once belonged to the Duberns, a famous family of restaurateurs in the Bordeaux area. Still a little reserved in its aromatic expression, this rich and full wine will be excellent in one to three years' time, served with poultry.

☛ Patrick Bayle, SCEA Ch. Plaisance, 33550 Capian, tel. 05.56.72.15.06, fax 05.56.72.13.40, e-mail contact@chateauplaisance.fr ▼
🍷 by appt.

CH. DE PLASSAN

Elevé en fût de chêne 2000★

| ■ | 15 ha | 60,000 | ∎ ⅡⅠ ⌀ | 8–11 € |

A splendid Paladian villa, Plassan is one of the most beautiful châteaux on the Premières Côtes. This wine's bouquet, with its finesse and richness, seems to be attempting to emulate the architecture. On the palate it increases in power to reveal the strength of its tannins and its fleshiness. Since the oak in no way detracts from the fruit, the result is a wine well balanced by an excellent constitution that will allow it to be laid down for three to four years.

☛ SCEA Ch. de Plassan, 33550 Tabanac, tel. 05.56.67.53.16, fax 05.56.67.26.28, e-mail contact@chateauplassan.fr ▼
🍷 by appt.
☛ J. Brianceau

CH. PRIEURE CANTELOUP

Cuvée Quentin Elevé en fût de chêne 2000★

| ■ | 10 ha | 70,000 | ⅡⅠ | 5–8 € |

A *cuvée* matured in cask, this wine fulfils the promise made by its intense-red colour. A fine bouquet with nice notes of red fruits, it develops harmoniously on the palate where its body, balance and mouth-filling qualities invite one to lay it down for two to four years.

☛ SE Xavier et Valérie Germe, 63, chem. du Loup, 33370 Yvrac, tel. 05.56.31.58.61 ▼

CH. PUY BARDENS

Cuvée Alphine 2000★★

| ■ | 2 ha | 10,000 | ⅡⅠ | 8–11 € |

It is worth noting the diverse grape varieties, which even include Malbec. For this reason, the complexity of the bouquet, which goes from fruit to flowers, by way of notes of game, is hardly surprising. The palate is similarly complex; supple and strong, this selection will be perfect with a meat dish in a sauce, in three to four years' time.

☛ Yves Lamiable, Ch. Puy Bardens, 33880 Cambes, tel. 05.56.21.31.14, fax 05.56.21.86.40, e-mail chateau-puybardens@wanadoo.fr ▼
🍷 by appt.

CH. LA RAME

La Charmille 2001★

| ■ | 7 ha | 33,000 | ⅡⅠ | 8–11 € |

Without wishing to compete with the Sainte-Croix from the same cru, this red Premières Côtes is agreeable and interesting in its aromatic complexity and its structure, which is both tannic and well balanced. It will be at its peak in 18 to 24 months.

☛ Yves Armand, GFA du Ch. La Rame, 33410 Sainte-Croix-du-Mont, tel. 05.56.62.01.50, fax 05.56.62.01.94, e-mail dgm@wanadoo.fr ▼
🍷 by appt.

CH. REYNON 2001★★

| ■ | 19.23 ha | 70,000 | ⅡⅠ | 11–15 € |

While the château dates only from 1848, its classic style gives it a nobility found in the wine itself, sprung from the chalky soil of this choice terroir. You can discern it in the colour and in the finesse of the bouquet, with its liquorice notes. Supported by well-dosed oak, the palate is no mere afterthought. Balanced, long and utterly elegant, this 2001 vintage

may be drunk right away, or laid down for four to five years in the cellar.

☛ Denis et Florence Dubourdieu, Ch. Reynon, 33410 Béguey, tel. 05.56.62.96.51, fax 05.56.62.14.89, e-mail reynon@gofornet.com ▼
🍷 by appt.

CH. ROQUEBERT

Cuvée spéciale Elevé en fût de chêne 2001★★

| ■ | 3 ha | 30,000 | ⅡⅠ | 5–8 € |

Overlooking Quinsac, this cru has a very fortunate exposure. It was particularly favourable in 2001, as this Cuvée Spéciale demonstrates. To the intense vanilla notes of the bouquet is added a well-constructed palate, with solid tannins. Rounded and fleshy, well balanced and long, it offers an excellent illustration of wine from the Premières Côtes. The Cuvée **Tradition 2001 (3–5 €)** received a special mention.

☛ Christian Neys, Ch. Roquebert, 33360 Quinsac, tel. 05.56.20.84.14, fax 05.56.20.84.14, e-mail roquebert.neys@ciscali.fr ▼
🍷 ev. day 9am–12noon 1.30pm–7pm; cl. 1–16 Aug.

CH. SISSAN

Grande Réserve Vieilli en fût de chêne 2001★★

| ■ | 6 ha | 40,000 | ⅡⅠ | 5–8 € |

Astride the two villages of Camblanes and Quinsac, this fine estate, now in the hands of the Yung family, was built by the animal painter Rosa-Bonheur. There is no doubt that the beautiful red-purple colour of this wine from the *cuvée prestige* would have pleased him. At any rate, the complexity of its bouquet, with notes of red fruit, leather, tobacco and roasted coffee, and the strength of its structure give it good keeping potential. Fresh, tannic and well balanced, this attractive 2001 vintage is worthy of a five-year stay in the cellar. From the same estate, the **Cuvée Prestige du Château Grimont 2001** received one star. While well made and with good ageing potential, it could nevertheless be drunk young (now to three years from now).

☛ SCEA Pierre Yung et Fils, 33360 Quinsac, tel. 05.56.20.86.18, fax 05.56.20.82.50 ▼
☛ Jean Yung

CH. SUAU

Elevé en fût de chêne 2001★

| ■ | 10.38 ha | 72,000 | ⅡⅠ | 8–11 € |

A charming country house behind a screen of 100-year-old oak trees, this château maintains its tradition for quality with this wine. Its colour has attractive purplish highlights; the toasty, spiced notes of the bouquet are a touch austere at the start, as is its structure, but they show great promise (it needs to be laid down for three to four years).

☛ Monique Bonnet, Ch. Suau, 33550 Capian, tel. 05.56.72.19.06, fax 05.56.72.12.43, e-mail bonnet.suau@wanadoo.fr ▼
🍷 by appt.

EXTRAVAGANCE DU CH. VIEILLE

TOUR Elevé en fût de chêne 2000★

| ■ | 0.5 ha | 1,805 | ⅡⅠ | 8–11 € |

While the estate is quite large (33 ha), this *cuvée* comes from small lots that are tended like gardens. The result is a very pleasant wine, with delicate aromas of red fruit; its roundness, suppleness and its fine tannins all suggest a wait of two to four years.

☛ SCEA des vignobles Gouin, 1, Lapradiasse, 33410 Laroque, tel. 05.56.62.61.21, fax 05.56.76.94.18, e-mail chateau.vieille.tour@wanadoo.fr ▼
🍷 by appt.

Wines selected but not starred

DUCHESSE DE GRAMAN 2001

| | n.c. | 60,000 | ▉ ♦ | 3–5 € |

✚ Cellier de Graman, rte de Créon, 33550 Langoiran, tel. 05.56.67.09.06, fax 05.56.67.13.34, e-mail cellierdegraman@wanadoo.fr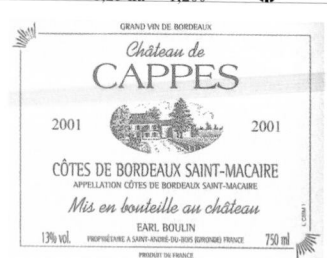
☙ ev. day 9am–12noon 2pm–6pm

CH. DU GRAND PLANTIER

Elevé en fût de chêne 2000

| | 14 ha | 16,000 | Ⅲ | 5–8 € |

✚ GAEC des Vignobles Albucher, Ch. du Grand Plantier, 33410 Monprimblanc, tel. 05.56.62.99.03, fax 05.56.76.91.35 ▉ ▉
☙ by appt.

CH. DE L'HOSTE 2000

| | 24.6 ha | 27,000 | Ⅲ | 5–8 € |

✚ SCEA vignobles F. and J. Arjeau, chem. Chapelle-Sainte-Catherine, 33550 Paillet, tel. 05.56.72.11.64, fax 05.56.72.13.62 ▉
☙ by appt.

CH. LIGASSONNE

Vieilli en fût de chêne 2000

| | n.c. | 2,000 | Ⅲ | 5–8 € |

✚ SCA Bordenave-Dauriac, Ch. Ligassonne, 33550 Langoiran, tel. 05.56.67.36.01 ▉
☙ by appt.

CH. MATHEREAU 2000

| | 11 ha | 50,000 | Ⅲ | 8–11 € |

✚ Philippe Boulière, Ch. Mathereau, 33560 Sainte-Eulalie, tel. 05.56.06.05.56, fax 05.56.38.02.01 ▉
☙ by appt.

CH. NAUJAN LAPEREYRE

Cuvée Tradition Elevé en fût de chêne 2001

| | 8.9 ha | 40,000 | Ⅲ | 5–8 € |

✚ Grands Châteaux de Naujan, 33420 Saint-Vincent-de-Pertignas, tel. 05.57.55.22.07, fax 05.57.84.04.98, e-mail info@direct-chateaux.com
☙ by appt.

CH. SAINT-HUBERT

Vieilli en fût de chêne 2001

| | 5.5 ha | 18,000 | Ⅲ | 5–8 € |

✚ EARL Vignobles Laurent Réglat, Ch. de Teste, 33410 Monprimblanc, tel. 05.56.62.92.76, fax 05.56.62.98.80, e-mail vignobles.l-reglat@wanadoo.fr ▉
☙ by appt.

Côtes de Bordeaux Saint-Macaire

The Appellation Côtes de Bordeaux Saint-Macaire is a southeasterly extension of the Premières Côtes de Bordeaux. The area makes supple, sweet white wines, producing 1,469 hl of wine in 2002 on an area of 48 ha given over to AOC wines.

CH. DE CAPPES
Moelleux 2001★★

| | 0,25 ha | 1,200 | Ⅲ | 5–8 € |

The Château de Cappes has selected a small lot of just 0.25 ha of Semillon to make this excellent, *moelleux* wine which was unanimously awarded a *coup de coeur* by the Grand Jury. The yellow-gold colour sparkles with green highlights. The elegant bouquet of honey, crystallized fruits and white blossom is in harmony with touches of charred oak. The balance of flavours is perfect. Of great and elegant complexity, with good aromatic length, this is a wine of distinction that should be left to age for three to eight years.
✚ EARL Boulin, Ch. de Cappes, 33490 Saint-André-du-Bois, tel. 05.56.76.40.88, fax 05.56.76.46.15 ▉
☙ by appt.

CH. DE DAMIS
Moelleux 2001★

| | 1.3 ha | 6,400 | ▉ ♦ | 5–8 € |

This vast, 40-ha estate offers a 2001 vintage made solely from the Semillon grape. The pale-golden colour has green and gold highlights; the peach, apricot and floral bouquet is elegant, well on the level of the rounded, balanced palate, with its welcome dose of acidic freshness. The harmonious finish is interesting. A wine that is ready to be served as an aperitif now.
✚ SCEA Vignobles Michel Bergey, Ch. de Damis, 33490 Sainte-Foy-la-Longue, tel. 05.56.76.41.42, fax 05.56.76.46.42, e-mail contact@vignoblesbergey.com ▉
☙ by appt.

CH. MAJOUREAU
Moelleux 2001★

| | 7 ha | 3,000 | ▉ | 3–5 € |

This estate, established at the start of the 20th century as a mixed farm, went over completely to wine-growing in 1978. Its 2001 vintage is made from 100% Sémillon. Pale yellow, with tinges of gold, it offers aromas of honey, enhanced by notes of crystallized fruit. The balance on the palate is elegant and fruity (apricot, peach) and its length is by no means the least part of its appeal. Try it with a roast chicken in the next two or three years.
✚ Bernard Delong, Ch. Majoureau, 33490 Caudrot, tel. 05.56.62.81.94, fax 05.56.62.75.87 ▉
☙ by appt.

Wines selected but not starred

CH. FAYARD 2001

| | 2.7 ha | 13,000 | Ⅲ | 11–15 € |

✚ Jacques-Charles de Musset, Ch. Fayard, 33490 Le Pian-sur-Garonne, tel. 05.56.63.33.81, fax 05.56.63.60.20, e-mail chateau.fayard@wanadoo.fr
☙ by appt.
✚ Saint-Michel SA

CH. DE FLORES

Moelleux 2001

| | 5.92 ha | 26,000 | ▮ | | 8–11 € |

📞 EARL Joël Richard, Ch. des Ruats, 33490 Le Pian-sur-Garonne, tel. 06.10.34.81.59, fax 05.56.62.04.17 ☑
🍷 by appt.

CH. DE JAYLE

Moelleux Elevé en fût de chêne 2001

| | 1 ha | 1,600 | ⑪ | | 5–8 € |

📞 EARL des Vignobles Denis Pellé, 1–2, Jayle, 33490 Saint-Martin-de-Sescas, tel. 05.56.63.60.90, fax 05.56.62.71.60, e-mail vignobles.pelle@worldonline.fr ☑ 🏠
🍷 by appt.

CH. TOUR DU MOULIN DU BRIC

Moelleux 2001

| | n.c. | 20,000 | ⑪ | | 5–8 € |

📞 SCEA Vignobles Faure, Le Moulin du Bric, 33490 Saint-André-du-Bois, tel. 05.56.76.40.20, fax 05.56.76.45.29, e-mail vignoblesfaure@wanadoo.fr ☑
🍷 by appt.
📞 P. Faure and S. Thomasson

The Graves Region

The excellent Graves vineyards of Bordeaux no longer need to prove their past: from Roman times, their vines have encircled the capital of Aquitaine and, according to Columelle, began to produce "a wine with good keeping qualities and potential for ageing." The name "Graves" first appeared in the Middle Ages. At that time it covered all the land above Bordeaux, between the left bank of the Garonne and the Plateau Landais. Eventually, Sauternes became more individual and formed an enclave devoted to sweet wines within the Graves region.

GRAVES AND GRAVES SUPERIEURES

Graves

The Graves vineyards extend for some 50 km and owe their name to the structure of the soil, principally made up of terraces deposited by the Garonne or its predecessors, which left behind a great variety of stony débris (pebbles and gravels originating in the Pyrenees and the Massif Central).

Since 1987 not all the wines produced there have been sold as Graves. Pessac-Léognan is now identified by a specific appellation, even though "Vin de Graves", "Grand Vin de Graves"

or "Cru Classé de Graves" may be printed on its labels. In precise terms, the description Appellation Graves applies to qualifying vineyards from the south of the region.

One of the peculiarities of Graves is the balance established between the areas devoted to red wines (2,568 ha, excluding Pessac-Léognan) and those growing dry whites wines (1,140 ha). The red Graves (122,667 hl in 2002) have a delicately smoky bouquet and an elegant, full-bodied structure that allows them to keep well. The dry white wines (48,063 hl), are elegant and plump, and rank amongst the best in the Gironde. The finest of them, many of which are now vinified and matured in barrels, develop in richness and complexity after several years. There are also some softer wines sold under the appellation Graves Supérieures which still claim their admirers.

CH. D'ARCHAMBEAU 2001★

| ▮ | 28 ha | 120,000 | ⑪ | | 8–11 € |

Situated not far from the town of Illats, where the church, founded in the 12th century, contains a fine 17th century polychrome wood reredos, this cru blends equal parts of Merlot and Cabernet. The result is most seductive in its harmony, clearly evident in its bright-red colour and its fruity bouquet. The gentle opening is quite intense, as is the mouth-filling, tannin-rich palate. Lay it down for two or three years. Also very expressive, with a touch of Sauvignon (grapefruit, passion fruit and broom), the white 2001 (5–8 €) was also awarded one star.
📞 SARL Vignobles Famille Dubourdieu, Ch. d'Archambeau, 33720 Illats, tel. 05.56.62.51.46, fax 05.56.62.47.98 ☑
🍷 by appt.

CH. D'ARDENNES 2001★

| ▮ | 20 ha | 120,000 | ▮ ⑪ ♦ | | 11–15 € |

88 ⑧⑨ 90 92 93 94 |96| 97 |98| |99| 00 01

Established in the 17th century, this cru is one of the most consistent of the appellation. Graves and clay-limestone, Cabernets (both), Merlot and Petit Verdot: the conditions in the vineyard prepare the way for the good work of the winery and this wine provides the proof. The colour: sparkling ruby red; the bouquet: a mixture of red fruits, violets and toast; on the palate: fine, well-blended tannins and fleshiness. An attractive finish completes a wine that is as elegant as it is promising.
📞 SCEA Ch. d'Ardennes, 33720 Illats, tel. 05.56.62.53.66, fax 05.56.62.43.67 ☑
🍷 by appt.
📞 Cyril Dubrey

CH. D'ARGUIN

Vieilli en fût de chêne 2000★

| ▮ | 6.12 ha | 32,077 | ⑪ | | 8–11 € |

The predominant grape variety (70%), Merlot also dominates the bouquet, with a touch of leather reinforcing agreeable perfumes of cocoa and coffee. Like the limpid, clear colour, with its garnet highlights, the suppleness and fine, elegant tannins of the palate are pleasing. The structure gives a good indication of the time needed for the oak to integrate (two or three years).
📞 SA Pouey International, chem. de Gaillardas, Jeansotte, 33650 Saint-Selve, tel. 05.56.78.49.10, fax 05.56.78.49.11, e-mail bertrand.lacampagne@pouey-international.fr ☑
🍷 by appt.

CH. D'ARRICAUD

Cuvée Prestige 2000★

| | n.c. | 15,000 | ▮ ⑪ ♦ | | 11–15 € |

⑧⑤ 88 89 90 91 93 |96| |98| 99 00

The Château d'Arricaud, begun in the 18th century, contains an 19th century oil-painting of Bacchus keeping company

The Graves Region

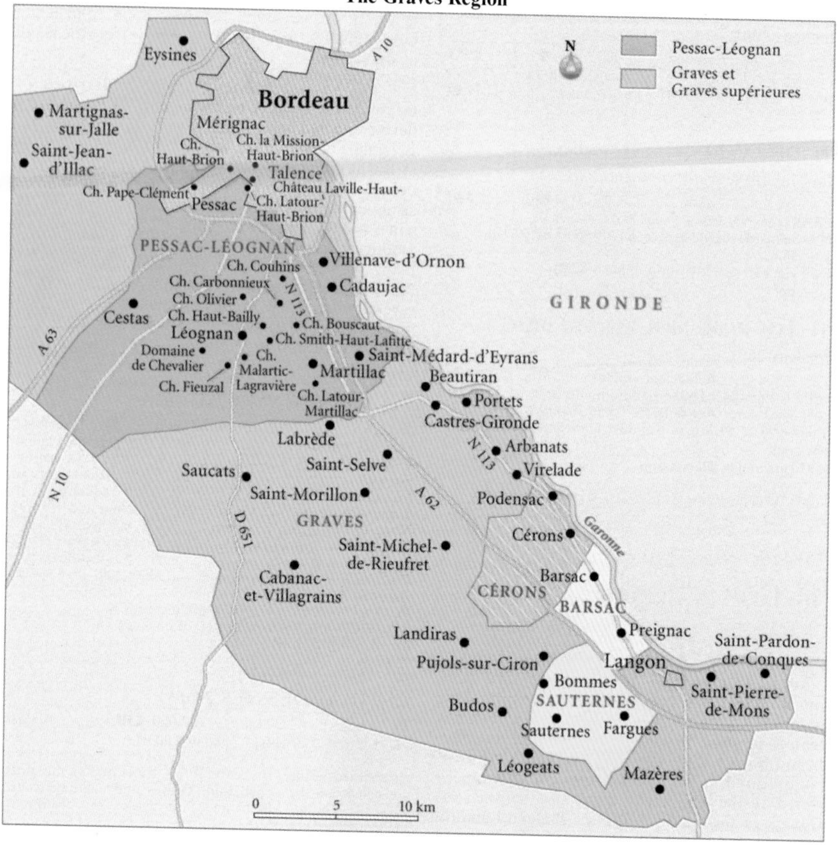

Eysines

Bordeau

Martignas-
sur-Jalle

Mérignac

Saint-Jean-
d'Illac

Ch.
Haut-Brion

Ch. la Mission-
Haut-Brion

Talence

Ch. Pape-Clément

Pessac

Château Laville-Haut-
Ch. Latour-
Haut-Brion

PESSAC-LÉOGNAN

Ch. Couhins

Villenave-d'Ornon

Cadaujac

GIRONDE

Ch. Carbonnieux

Ch. Olivier

Cestas

Ch. Haut-Bailly

Ch. Bouscaut

Léognan

Ch. Smith-Haut-Lafitte

Domaine
de Chevalier

Ch.
Malartic-
Lagravière

Saint-Médard-d'Eyrans

Ch. Fieuzal

Martillac

Beautiran

Ch. Latour-
Martillac

Portets

Castres-Gironde

Labrède

Saint-Selve

Arbanats

Saucats

Virelade

Saint-Morillon

Podensac

GRAVES

Cérons

Saint-Michel-
de-Rieufret

Barsac

Cabanac-
et-Villagrains

CÉRONS

BARSAC

Landiras

Preignac

Saint-Pardon-
de-Conques

Pujols-sur-Ciron

Langon

Budos

Bommes

SAUTERNES

Saint-Pierre-
de-Mons

Sauternes

Fargues

Léogeats

Mazères

N

Pessac-Léognan

Graves et
Graves supérieures

0   5   10 km

CRUS CLASSES OF THE GRAVES REGION

NAME OF CRU CLASSE	TYPE OF WINE	NAME OF CRU CLASSE	TYPE OF WINE
Château Bouscaut	red and white	Château Laville-Haut-Brion	white
Château Carbonnieux	red and white	Château Malartic-Lagravière	red and white
Domaine de Chevalier	red and white	Château La Mission-Haut-Brion	red
Château Couhins	white	Château Olivier	red and white
Château Couhins-Lurton	white	Château Pape-Clément	red
Château de Fieuzal	red	Château Smith-Haut-Lafitte	red
Château Haut-Bailly	red	Château Latour-Haut-Brion	red
Château Haut-Brion	red	Château La Tour-Martillac	red and white

with one of his priestesses. This wine, from a *cuvée spéciale* of the cru, is a fine ruby-red colour. While the bouquet that follows is less flamboyant, with its delicate notes of truffle and damp undergrowth and hints of vanilla and cinnamon, it shows good substance and balance, and the maturation in cask has been brought well under control.

➛ EARL Bouyx, Ch. d'Arricaud, 33720 Landiras, tel. 05.56.62.51.29, fax 05.56.62.41.47, e-mail chateaudarricaud@wanadoo.fr ☑
☕ by appt.

CH. BEAUREGARD DUCASSE
Albert Duran Elevé en fût de chêne 2000★

| ■ | 10 ha | 40,000 | ⬗ | 8–11 € |

Whilst it is a *cuvée prestige*, matured in cask, there is nothing limited about the quantity of this wine produced, which makes its true qualities the more interesting: the beautiful red colour; its aromatic expression (crystallized red fruits, raspberries, a hint of musk); its vinous initial impression; its tannins; its flavours of vanilla and Merlot grape; its soaring finish. One would not hesitate to lay it down for about two years. The **Cuvée Principale 2000 (5–8 €)** received a special mention, and the **Albertine Peyri white 2001** was awarded one star for its freshness and fruitiness.

➛ Jacques Perromat, Ducasse, 33210 Mazères, tel. 05.56.76.18.97, fax 05.56.76.17.73 ☑
☕ by appt.
➛ GFA de Gaillote

LA PART DES ANGES DU CH. DE BEAU-SITE 2000★★

| ■ | 0,77 ha | 3,500 | ⬗ | 15–23 € |

Despite its name, this *cuvée spéciale* does not come from the banks of the Charente. It would be easy to convince oneself otherwise, looking at the deep ruby-red colour with its purple highlights, and inhaling that fine, subtle and nicely complex bouquet, made up of red and black fruit, spices, liquorice and cedarwood. On the palate, which lacks none of the elements present on the bouquet, one finds silky tannins, fleshiness, richness and a good fruit–oak balance on the finish. A classic replay of its aromas is the crowning touch; don't hesitate to lay this wine down for four or five years.

➛ SA du Ch. de Beau-Site, 33640 Portets, tel. 05.56.67.18.15, fax 05.56.67.38.12, e-mail chateaudebeausite@dial.oleane.com ☑ ☖
☕ by appt.
➛ Mme Dumergue

CH. BELON 2000★

| ■ | 10 ha | 53,000 | ⬗⬗ | 5–8 € |

This is one of the rare estates that still boasts a working baker's oven. A fine crimson colour with tinges of ruby, its 2000 vintage combines a fruity, straightforward (blackcurrant, raspberry, pomegranate) bouquet with a supple, fleshy and rounded structure. The strongly-extracted tannins appearing on the finish dictate a need for three or four years patient waiting.

➛ Laurent and Anne-Marie Dépiot, Ch. Belon, 33650 Saint-Morillon, tel. 05.56.20.30.35 ☑
☕ by appt.

CH. BICHON CASSIGNOLS
Grande Réserve 2000★

| ■ | 1 ha | 5,160 | ⬗⬗ | 11–15 € |

Grown on a lot containing equal quantities of Merlot and Cabernet, this wine shows its excellent substance in the near-black ruby of its colour. Musky at first, after agitation in the glass the bouquet reveals notes of spice, oak, toast and smoke. On the palate one senses a real tannic richness. Still sharp, the tannins need to soften. The **Petit Bichon 2000 (5–8 €)** not matured in cask, is fruity and pleasant and was also awarded one star.

➛ Jean-François Lespinasse, 50, av. Edouard-Capdeville, 33650 La Brède, tel. 05.56.20.28.20, fax 05.56.20.20.08 ☑
☕ by appt.

CH. LA BLANCHERIE 2001★

| | 10,52 ha | 42,600 | ▮ ⬗ | 5–8 € |

Françoise Coussié's father published a book about the famous man from Graves: *Montesquieu. Une pensée politique étonnamment moderne* (An astonishingly modern political thinker). Here we congratulate this winemaker who, for this vintage, chose to blend equal quantities of Sémillon and Sauvignon grape varieties. The result is a wine of a fine colour with intense highlights, of which the floral and citrus fruit aromas are delicately expressed. Everything goes to enhance its finesse and freshness, with notes of lemon and white peaches. Lively and delicate, this Graves would be a happy choice with oysters.

➛ Françoise Coussié, La Blancherie, 33650 La Brède, tel. 05.56.20.20.39, fax 05.56.20.35.01, e-mail chateau-la-blancherie@atlantic-line.fr ☑
☕ by appt.

TENTATION DU CH. LE BOURDILLOT 2001★

| | 7 ha | 35,000 | ▮ ⬗ | 8–11 € |

Awarded a *coup de coeur* last year for the Cuvée Prestige 2000, Le Bourdillot presented this same **Cuvée Prestige red 2001 (11–15 €)** which, like its second wine, Tentation, was awarded one star. The latter shows its good origins. Its intense-ruby colour inspires confidence, as does the bouquet, of which the Jury particularly appreciated the originality and the floral perfumes combined with those of cherries and prunes. Supple, silky and tender, the palate rests on soft tannins and a delicate oakiness, and shows good potential for ageing. Lay it down for three or four years. The **white 2001 of the same cru (11–15 €)** also received one star.

➛ EARL Patrice Haverlan, 11, rue de l'Hospital, 33640 Portets, tel. 05.56.67.11.32, fax 05.56.67.11.32, e-mail patrice.haverlan@worldonline.fr ☑
☕ by appt.

CAPRICE DE BOURGELAT 2001★

| | 1,6 ha | 12,000 | ⬗ | 8–11 € |

Originally this cru was a hunting lodge belonging to the Ch. d'Epernon. Product of long maceration on the skins, this wine displays its marque in its fine aromatic development, predominantly citrus fruit (mandarin oranges). Well supported by the maturation factor, the result is rich and lively.

➛ Dominique Lafosse, Clos Bourgelat, 33720 Cérons, tel. 05.56.27.01.73, fax 05.56.27.13.72 ☑
☕ ev. day ex. Sun. 9am–2noon 2pm–7pm; groups by appt.

CH. BRONDELLE 2000★

| | 15 ha | 100,000 | ⬗ | 8–11 € |

94 |96| **|98|** 99 |00|

The first vintage to come from new tanks installed in 1999, this wine represents a happy inauguration of the new installations. A fine crimson, with darker tinges, the colour immediately inspires confidence. The bouquet, still rather closed, is more delicate, but has real complexity: red fruits, raspberries, redcurrants and oak. The latter component is well dosed and doesn't spoil the suppleness of the palate. Very complex flavours, dense tannins, appealing liquorice finish, this wine is both traditional and modern at the same time. The **white Brondelle Cuvée Anaïs 2001(11–15 €)** also received one star. Still very marked by the maturation in cask, it needs to wait for the end of 2004 before being served with cooked dishes.

➛ Vignobles Belloc-Rochet, Ch. Brondelle, 33210 Langon, tel. 05.56.62.38.14, fax 05.56.62.23.14, e-mail chateau.brondelle@wanadoo.fr ☑
☕ ev. day ex. Sat. Sun. 8.30am–12noon 2pm–6pm

CH. DE CALLAC 2000★

| | 3 ha | n.c. | ⬗ | 8–11 € |

Coming from Illats, in the south of Graves, this is a wine that presents well: a rich, deep garnet-red, its bouquet is open and complex. Notes of undergrowth, charred wood and roasting mingle with those of ripe fruit and prunes. After a clean attack, the palate is full and generous in its aromatic expression. An attractive wine that will give real pleasure without needing to wait too long. Well balanced and with a good bouquet (grapefruit and vanilla), the **white 2002** was also awarded one star.

🍷 SCEA Philippe Rivière, Ch. de Cellac, 33720 Illats, tel. 05.57.55.59.59, fax 05.57.55.59.51, e-mail priviere@riviere-stemilion.com **Ⓜ**
♈ by appt.

CH. CAMARSET 2001★

| | 1.5 ha | 3,000 | 🍶 | 5–8 € |

A small estate (barely 3 ha) but heir to an old domain that belonged to the Montesquieu family. A nice yellow colour with green and grey nuances, this white 2001 vintage shows appealing and delicate qualities on its bouquet. Its suppleness brings out the aromas of exotic fruits, which go to make up an agreeably complex finish.

🍷 SCEA Ch. Camarset, 33650 La Brède, tel. 05.56.20.31.94, fax 05.56.20.31.94 **Ⓜ** 🐓
♈ by appt.

CH. DE CASTRES 2001★

| | 2 ha | 4,500 | 🍶 | 11–15 € |

The château is a fine, 18th century charterhouse; the park is filled with century-old trees; the wine is a fleshy 2001 vintage, lively and vigorous, which holds the attention with its lovely pale-yellow colour tinged with green and fine aromas of citrus fruit, pears and caramel that make up its bouquet. The long finish was sufficient to convince the taster that this wine will be just as pleasant in two years' time as it is now. The **red Château de Castres 2001** received a special mention, as did the **Tour de Castres red 2000 (8–11 €)**.

🍷 Rodrigues-Lalande, Ch. de Castres, 33640 Castres-sur-Gironde, tel. 05.56.67.51.51, fax 05.56.67.52.22, e-mail chateaudecastres@free.fr **Ⓜ**
♈ ev. day 8am–1pm 2pm–8pm

CH. DE CHANTEGRIVE 2000★

| | 35 ha | 200,000 | 🍶 | 11–15 € |

82 83⟨85⟩86 88 89 |90| 91 92 93 |95| |96| 99 00

The absence of a real château, in the architectural sense, has not prevented Chantegrive from becoming a prestigious wine producer over the last 35 years. Its cellars are equipped with the most modern technical advances and the barrels in its winery are very impressive. Straightforward, fleshy and rounded, the 2000 vintage demonstrates the expertise of its team. Its bouquet is still delicate but promising, with fine notes of blackcurrant, and its good tannic structure invites a period of four to five years laying-down in the cellar. The **white La Cuvée Caroline 2001** was specially mentioned for its balance and charm.

🍷 GFA des vignobles Lévêque, Ch. de Chantegrive, 33720 Podensac, tel. 05.56.27.17.38, fax 05.56.27.29.42 **Ⓜ**
♈ ev. day ex. Sun. 8.30am–6pm
🍷 Henri and Françoise Lévêque

CH. LE CHEC 2001★★

| | 3 ha | 8,500 | 🍶 | 5–8 € |

The Moors occupied this region in the 8th century, hence the origin of the name of the estate. Sémillon, Sauvignon, Muscadelle, we see here that the great Bordeaux wines are made from blends of grape varieties. And they know just how to do it, as this attractive wine shows. Its delicate floral notes harmonize with the perfume of exotic fruits to create a sensation of freshness in the run-up to an attack that reveals the powerful evolution of the palate. Rich, as well as supported by acidity, this wine has sufficient balance to be ready to drink now, while still showing potential for development.

🍷 Christian Auney, La Girotte, 33650 La Brède, tel. 05.56.20.31.94, fax 05.56.20.31.94 **Ⓜ**
♈ by appt.

CH. CHERCHY-DESQUEYROUX 2000★

| | 3,6 ha | 9,000 | 🍶🍶 | 5–8 € |

Coming from Pujols-sur-Ciron, this wine is a deep, limpid colour, with a delicate, still rather closed first bouquet. When agitated in the glass, however, it opens up on lightly toasted notes and agreeable aromas of red fruits. On the palate, the oak respects the wine. Well balanced, the whole culminates in a prolonged finish.

🍷 SCEA Vignobles Francis Desqueyroux et Fils, 1, rue Pourière, 33720 Budos, tel. 05.56.76.62.67, fax 05.56.76.66.92, e-mail vign.fdesqueyroux@wanadoo.fr **Ⓜ**
♈ by appt.

CLOS FLORIDENE 2001★

| | 5.13 ha | 30,430 | 🍶 | 11–15 € |

85 86 88 89⟨90⟩92 93 94 95 96 **98 99 00** 01

Red sand on fissured limestone, the terroir of Pujols recalls that of Barsac, none of which prevents it from making some fine red wines. Take this 2001 vintage, of which the ruby colour is entirely true to type in the Bordeaux spirit. On the bouquet, the aromas of toast hark back to the maturation, but without altering the fine and distinctive characteristics of the whole. Soft and progressive, the attack introduces a classy note to the palate, which is vigorous, well balanced and harmonious. The finish stays within the same tonality and suggests that the wine should be laid down for three or four years. Denis Dubourdieu presented the **white 2001** which also received one star. Choose it to accompany pike in a butter and shallot sauce, or frogs legs.

🍷 Denis and Florence Dubourdieu, Ch. Reynon, 33410 Béguey, tel. 05.56.62.96.51, fax 05.56.62.14.89, e-mail reynon@gofornet.com **Ⓜ**
♈ by appt.

CLOS LES MAJUREAUX 2000★

| | 10 ha | 18,000 | 🍶🍶 | 5–8 € |

From the same producer as the Château Ludeman, this beautiful bright red wine opens up after a period of aeration on toasted notes mixed with stewed red fruit, then goes on to show greater freshness. After a gentle opening, the palate reveals all its complexity and fleshiness. Resting on solid tannins, this vintage has a good potential for ageing.

🍷 Vignobles Chaloupin-Lambrot, Ch. Ludeman-La-Côte, 33210 Langon, tel. 05.56.63.07.15, fax 05.56.63.48.17 **Ⓜ**
♈ by appt.

CLOS MOLEON

Vieilli en fût de chêne 2000★

| | 4 ha | 15,000 | 🍶 | 8–11 € |

Simultaneously producing wines at Langon and on the right bank of the Garonne, Laurent Réglat presented this wine with its attractive bouquet combining notes of tobacco, roasting, camphor and vanilla. While it is essential to decant this wine, to rid it of a tiny touch of musk, it will leave you with a pleasant memory of its harmonious structure.

🍷 EARL Vignobles Laurent Réglat, Ch. de Teste, 33410 Monprimblanc, tel. 05.56.62.92.76, fax 05.56.62.98.80, e-mail vignobles.l-reglat@wanadoo.fr **Ⓜ**
♈ by appt.

CH. COUSTAUT 2002★

| | 5 ha | 20,000 | 🍶🍶 | 5–8 € |

From the same producer as the Château Magneau, but from a different cru, this attractive yellow wine with green highlights has a resolutely complex bouquet mingling notes of oranges, pineapple and grapefruit. Lively and light on the palate, one is left with the impression of a very pleasant whole which will be an admirable accompaniment for seafood or white meat.

🍷 Henri Ardurats et Fils, EARL Les Cabanasses, 12, chem. Maxime-Ardurats, 33650 La Brède, tel. 05.56.20.20.57, fax 05.56.20.39.95, e-mail ardurats@chateau-magneau.com
♈ ev. day 8.30am–12noon 2pm–6pm; Sat. Sun. by appt.

GRAND VIN DE CH. CRABITEY 2001★★

| | 10 ha | 60,000 | 🍶 | 11–15 € |

For some years now this cru has entertained a voluntarist policy towards renovation, but this has not stopped it from obtaining some fine results, such as this entirely successful 2001 vintage. The concentration of the colour is echoed in the intensity of the bouquet. Its ripe, black fruit aromas are set off by elegant oak. Supple in attack, the palate rests on dense, velvety tannins with a good balance between wine and cask. As classic as it is chic, this pleasure-giving wine has a rich and

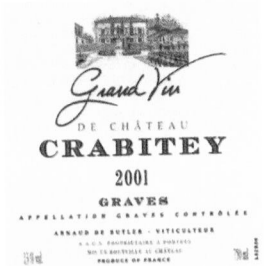

satisfying finish. The red **Château Trebiac 2001 (5–8 €)** from the same producer received one star.
🕿 Ass. Les Amis de la Chartreuse de Seillon, 63, rte du Courneau, 33640 Portets, tel. 05.56.67.18.64,
fax 05.56.67.14.73,
e-mail chateau.crabitey@libertysurf.fr ☑
🍷 by appt.

LA GRANDE CUVÉE DE DOURTHE

2000★

■	n.c.	50,000	⦿	8–11 €

A highly respected Bordeaux wine-merchant, this wine from the Dourthe company is once again fully representative of its excellent reputation. A pleasant, strong ruby-red colour, the wine develops a fresh bouquet of fruit enclosed within notes of toast and spices. Warm and rounded, the palate is sustained by silky tannins that contrive to make their presence felt, while in no way detracting from the elegance of this beautiful wine.
🕿 Dourthe, 35, rue de Bordeaux, 33290 Parempuyre,
tel. 05.56.35.53.00, fax 05.56.35.53.29,
e-mail contact@cvbg.com ☑
🍷 by appt.

CH. L'ETOILE 2002★

■	15 ha	77,000	▮ ◇	5–8 €

Very classic in concept, this wine charms the taster with its aromatic expression, which ranges from peach to acacia blossom. Fine and well balanced, it is already a very pleasant wine.
🕿 Maison Sichel, 8, rue de la Poste, 33210 Langon,
tel. 05.56.63.50.52, fax 05.56.63.42.28,
e-mail maison-sichel@sichel.fr

CH. FERRANDE 2002★

■	5 ha	29,300	⦿	5–8 €

Although smaller than the area planted with red varieties, this white vineyard receives just the same care and attention. The 2002 vintage is clear proof of this, with its straw-yellow colour and a bouquet that is restrained initially but becomes much more expressive, with appealing floral notes and aromas of apples and pears. Citrus fruit aromas take over at the opening on the palate. Supple and light, this wine would be excellent with oysters or grilled fish.
🕿 Castel Frères, 21–24, rue Georges-Guynemer, 33290 Blanquefort, tel. 05.56.95.54.04, fax 05.56.95.54.20

CH. LA FLEUR CLEMENCE 2001★

■	3 ha	16,000	⦿	8–11 €

Even though it is right next-door to the Sauterne area, this cru does not neglect its red wine production, as this well-made, quite complex wine shows. Starting from its garnet-red colour, it reveals its personality through its bouquet, with its early notes of menthol, liquorice and fruit, becoming gradually more warming. Its rich tannic matter is supported by completely integrated oak. It needs to be laid down for two or three years.
🕿 Ch. Carbon d'Artigues, 33720 Landiras,
tel. 05.56.62.53.24, fax 05.56.62.44.32 ☑
🍷 by appt.

CH. LA FLEUR JONQUET 2001★

■	1 ha	7,000	⦿	11–15 €

Member of the association *Les Aliénor de Bordeaux*, this cru presented a wine that accurately reflects the spirit of the brotherhood, both in the elegance of its bouquet, with its floral and apple and pear aromas, and in the flavoursome aspect of its palate. Supple, tender and fine, this 2001 vintage is already very pleasant, but could be kept for two or three years. In either case, it would be an ideal accompaniment for fish (sole à la normande or pike *au beurre blanc*). The **red 2000** received a special mention.
🕿 Laurence Lataste, 5, rue Amélie, 33200 Bordeaux,
tel. 05.56.17.08.18, fax 05.57.22.12.54,
e-mail l.lataste@wanadoo.fr ☑
🍷 by appt.

CH. DU GRAND BOS 2000★★

■	6 ha	32,051	⦿	15–23 €

Of reliable quality, this cru, awarded a *coup de coeur* for the 98, could not miss its 2000 vintage. From the start, the deep-garnet colour shows that the triple zero date seems to have been particularly auspicious. The spiced, toasted notes, with just a hint of prunes, give a hoped-for complexity to this intense wine, with its many nuances. Apart from a noticeable chewiness, it shows strength and a good balance of flavours. A spicy, fruity finish completes the picture. A wine that should be laid down for four or five years. Also with good keeping potential is the **Cadet du Grand Bos red 2000 (11–15 €)** which received one star.
🕿 SCEA du Ch. du Grand Bos, chem. de l'Hermitage, 33640 Castres-Gironde, tel. 05.56.67.39.20,
fax 05.56.67.16.77, e-mail chateau.du.grand.bos@free.fr ☑
🍷 by appt.
🕿 GFA de Gravesaltes

GRAND ENCLOS DU CHATEAU DE CERONS 2001★★

■	8.23 ha	28,000	⦿	8–11 €

Tuscan wine-grower, Giorgio Cavanna acquired this cru in 2000 with the avowed purpose of producing exceptional wines. And he has not wasted time reaching his objective, as this 2001 vintage, with its beautiful colour tinged with grey-gold, valliantly demonstrates. As delicate as they are fresh, its perfumes lead you off on a journey: starting with vanilla notes they evolve towards the scent of exotic fruit, almonds and coconut. On the palate it gives a fresh, delicious aspect, with great finesse and softness. Very well balanced, the fruit and oak flavours create a real sensation of elegance. A true, pleasure-giving wine that will go well with a number of different dishes and which can be served young or kept for several years.
🕿 SCEA du Grand Enclos de Cérons, 33720 Cérons,
tel. 05.56.27.01.53, fax 05.56.27.08.86,
e-mail grand.enclos.cerons@wanadoo.fr ☑
🍷 by appt.
🕿 Giorgio Cavanna

CH. HAUT-GRAMONS

Vieilli en fût de chêne 2001★

■	12 ha	78,000	⦿	8–11 €

Though the Boudat Cigana family have only owned this cru since 1997, their winemaking history goes back through five generations. This wine, with its attractive bouquet linking slightly overripe red crystallized fruit with Morello cherries, bears witness to their expertise. The colour indicates a good concentration of anthocyanins. On the palate the young and fresh flavours are added to aromas of spice, oak and fruit, forming a warm accompaniment for flavoursome tannins. The crowning touch is a long finish. This wine is well worth a wait of two or three years. The **white Haut-Gramons Vieilli en Fût 2001 (5–8 €)** was specially mentioned. Its Sauvignon and oak flavours are of a notable freshness.

↘ F. Boudat Cigana, Ch. de Viaut, 33410 Mourens, tel. 05.56.61.98.13, fax 05.56.61.99.46 ☑
♟ by appt.

CH. HAUT-MAYNE
Prestige Elevé en fût de chêne 2000★★

	5 ha	26,000	⊕	8–11 €

The *cuvée prestige* of the cru, this wine received great care and attention in the making, with excellent results, as the purple colour and the bouquet show. As lively as it is complex, it reveals subtle notes of coconut and smoke, happily allied to cherries. On first acquaintance the palate seems easy, and indeed it is, but that doesn't stop the substance from being very much present, based on fleshy, well-integrated tannins. Thanks to the successful marrying of oak and wine, the pleasant whole leaves behind agreeable flavours and is worth waiting three years for. The fine and aromatic **Cuvée Haut-Mayne Prestige white 2001** was awarded one star. Generous and finely toasted and marked by exotic fruits, it will make an excellent aperitif wine.

↘ SC Haut-Mayne-Gravaillas, 10, Cambillon, 33720 Cérons, tel. 05.56.27.08.53, fax 05.56.27.08.53

CH. DE L'HOSPITAL 2000★★

	10.65 ha	10,500	⊕	11–15 €

From its vineyards enclosed within a wall and run from a lovely 18th century house, this cru, of parliamentary origin, presented a wine whose nobility is clearly discernible in its ruby-red colour and its harmonious aromas, born out of a successful alliance of ripe and crystallized fruit with charred and toasted notes. On the palate the finesse and roundness make a perfect balance with the fine, elegant tannins, resulting in a wine with a solid potential. The **white 2001 from the same château** received a special mention: well balanced, it has good length.

↘ SCS Vignobles Lafragette, Darrouban, 33640 Portets, tel. 05.56.73.17.80, fax 05.56.09.02.87, e-mail chateau-loudenne@wanadoo.fr ☑
♟ by appt.

CH. HOUNADE 2001★

	10 ha	50,000	▊⊕↧	8–11 €

Though it may not appear in the "Who's Who" of Bordeaux wines, this cru definitely knows what it is doing. A fine ruby-red with garnet highlights, this 2001 vintage develops a bouquet that is already expressive (fruit and spices). Its softness and roundness, its body and silky tannins all ensure a robust and well-balanced structure which will allow it to be laid down for three or four years.

↘ Héritiers Pascaud, Ch. de Carles, 33720 Barsac, tel. 05.57.27.07.19 ☑
♟ by appt.

CH. DE LANDIRAS 2000★

	14.17 ha	20,000	⊕	11–15 €

In all its aspects, hectareage, buildings and terroir, this is a fine estate. And its wine is well up to the same standard: agreeable to the eye, with its purple highlights, it unreservedly deploys the fruity notes of its powerful bouquet. Supple in its first impression, it allows the oak to make its presence felt, but there is no doubt that after three or four years in the cellar everything will blend in to give a very nice wine to drink with red meat.

↘ SCA Dom. La Grave, Ch. de Landiras, 33720 Landiras, tel. 05.56.62.40.75, fax 05.56.62.43.78, e-mail mail@chateau-de-landiras.com ☑
♟ by appt.

CH. LANGLET 2001★

	0,6 ha	4,000	⊕	5–8 €

Product of a small vineyard entirely planted with Sauvignon, this wine with its yellow highlights is very marked by the grape variety in its aromas with notes of holly and exotic fruit. Devoid of any aggression, it culminates in a flavoursome finish of citrus fruit and roses. A very nice Graves.

↘ Sté fermière Domaines Kressmann, 33650 Martillac, tel. 05.57.97.71.11, fax 05.57.97.71.17, e-mail langlet@domaines-kressmann.com

CH. LEHOUL
Plénitude 2000★★

	2,2 ha	11,800	⊕	15–23 €

This cru has carved out a solid reputation for itself, thanks to its Graves Supérieures. But its expertise doesn't end there. Perfectly made, this Cuvée Plénitude shows that the team understands red wines too. Showing its youth in its crimson colour, its bouquet seduces with its notes of toasted bread, spices, cocoa and ripe red berries. The initial impact is balanced, preparing the ground for roundness on the palate supported by well-blended tannins and well-integrated oak. Very concentrated, this wine is one that will leave fond memories in the cellar record-book, but not until five or six years hence. Equally full and harmonious, the **white Lehoul Sec 2002 Elevé en Fût (8–11 €)**, which is very well-balanced and lively, received one star.

↘ EARL Fonta et Fils, rte d'Auros, 33210 Langon, tel. 05.56.63.17.74, fax 05.56.63.06.06 ☑
♟ by appt.
↘ Eric Fonta

CH. LUDEMAN LA COTE
Alix de Ludeman 2001★

	3 ha	15,000	⊕	8–11 €

Operating sustainable culture, this cru offers a *cuvée* that admirably keeps the promise made by its bright red colour, tinged with dark glints. While the first bouquet is a touch shy the second opens after aeration on toasty, fruity (red fruit) and jammy notes. After that the wine becomes rather fresher, on a blackcurrant theme, followed by warm oak making its entrance. Soft, complex and fleshy, the attack goes before a palate and a finish that together guarantee good potential for development by their solid tannins. Elsewhere, the **white Ludeman La Côte 2002 (5–8 €)** was awarded a star. The freshness of its citrus fruit notes will awaken the appetite.

↘ Vignobles Chaloupin-Lambrot, Ch. Ludeman-La-Côte, 33210 Langon, tel. 05.56.63.07.15, fax 05.56.63.48.17 ☑
♟ by appt.

CH. MAGENCE 2001★

	9.14 ha	27,000	▊↧	5–8 €

Family tradition is strong here because an ancestor of the Comte and Comtesse d'Antras already lived in the charterhouse before establishing their steamship company on the Garonne, more than two centuries ago. This straw-coloured wine, with green highlights, product of a vineyard of 55 ha belonging to a single holding, shows that the decades have not diminished the passion: the finesse of its fruity, floral aromas harmonize with the balance, the weight and the liveliness of the palate, making up a flavoursome whole.

�'t SCEA Ch. Magence, 33210 Saint-Pierre-de-Mons, tel. 05.56.63.07.05, fax 05.56.63.41.42, e-mail magence@magence.com ✅

✖ by appt.

➟ Guillot de Suduirat-d'Antras

M. DE MALLE 2001★

■	3 ha	6,800	❒❒	8–11 €

A dry white wine from the Château de Malle (one of the gems of Bordeaux architecture and a Sauternes Cru Classé), this attractive pale lemon wine with golden highlights is shown in an appealing light by its floral and fruity aromas (grapefruit). Rounded and upright, the palate reveals a good balance between richness and acidity. The red 2000, labelled **Château de Cardaillan** received a special mention.

➟ Comtesse de Bournazel, GFA des Comtes de Bournazel, Ch. de Malle, 33210 Preignac, tel. 05.56.62.36.86, fax 05.56.76.82.40, e-mail chateaudemalle@wanadoo.fr ✅

✖ by appt.

CH. DE L'ORDONNANCE

Elevé en fût de chêne 2000★

■	1 ha	n.c.	❒❒	5–8 €

Deliberately conceived by lovers of oaked wines, this wine, with its very young colour, has hit the mark, notably with its toasted aromas. But the balance of the product has been maintained, as the red berry presence indicates. Its structure and its luscious softness will give it the two to three years it needs for problem-free integration of the oak.

➟ GAEC Bélis et Fils, Tourmilotte, 33210 Langon, tel. 05.56.62.22.11, fax 05.56.62.22.11 ✅

✖ by appt.

CH. LE PAVILLON DE BOYREIN 2001★

■	32 ha	40,000	▮	5–8 €

Product of a vineyard with a notable majority presence of Merlot, this wine carries the mark on its bouquet, with its delicate red berry notes enhanced by a touch of leather, and its straightforward, young structure. Still a little harsh, it will need to spend three to four years in the cellar.

➟ Vignobles Bonnet, Le Pavillon de Boyrein, 33210 Roaillan, tel. 05.56.63.24.24, fax 05.56.62.31.59, e-mail vignobles-bonnet@wanadoo.fr ✅

✖ by appt.

➟ Franck Bonnet

CH. PEYRAGUE

Elevé en fût de chêne 2001★

■	12 ha	30,000	❒❒	5–8 €

Presented by Ginestet, this wine was vinified with the technical assistance of the celebrated wine-merchant. One is not, therefore, surprised by its quality. The highly-flavoured, vigorous attack, with aromas of coconut, truffles and a mineral touch, progressively increases in richness; this wine lacks neither originality nor character.

➟ Ginestet, 19, av. de Fontenille, 33360 Carignan-de-Bordeaux, tel. 05.56.68.81.82, fax 05.56.20.94.47, e-mail contact@ginestet.fr ✅

✖ by appt.

➟ M. Pargade

CH. PEYREBLANQUE 2001★

■	1 ha	6,000	❒❒	5–8 €

Installed at Cadillac (at the Château Fayau), the Médeville family is also present on the left bank, with this cru offering this beautiful gold-yellow wine. The oak still plays a strong part in the bouquet, but the evolution on the palate, rich, weighty and full of magnificent substance is a clear indication that this wine has good ageing potential. This is confirmed by the nice return of the well-blended oak, together with floral aromas. The **Peyreblanque red 2000 (8–11 €)** was awarded one star.

➟ SCEA Jean Médeville et Fils, Ch. Fayau, 33410 Cadillac, tel. 05.57.98.08.08, fax 05.56.62.18.22, e-mail medeville-jeanetfils@wanadoo.fr ✅

✖ ev. day ex. Sat. Sun. 8.30am–12noon 2pm–6pm

CH. DES PLACES

Cuvée Prestige Vieilli en fût de chêne 2001★

■	4.2 ha	25,000	❒❒	5–8 €

Established in 1900 by a cooper and enlarged since 1960, this estate spanned the 20th century. The 21st century seems to have got off to a good start if one is to judge by this wine, with its good aromatic complexity and dense, balanced structure. The fairly rounded tannins indicate a well-managed extraction and will allow this wine to be laid down until the oak has integrated with the wine.

➟ EARL Vignobles Reynaud, 46, av. Maurice-La-Chatre, 33640 Arbanats, tel. 05.56.67.20.13, fax 05.56.67.17.05, e-mail vignobles.reynaud@wanadoo.fr ✅

✖ by appt.

CH. PONT DE BRION 2001★★

■	7 ha	40,000	❒❒	8–11 €

Wine-lovers will note with interest that this cru practises sustainable culture. This step, taken in the joint interests of ecology and quality, shows here what it can achieve. The colour is a strong cardinal purple, the bouquet contains elegant oaky notes of cocoa and liquorice. *Moelleux*, rich and harmonious, the palate derives the maximum from its fruity aromas. The long, warm and flavoursome finish brings the demonstration to a simple conclusion: lay this wine down for five years, even though it is already very pleasant. The **white Pont de Brion 2001** and the **red Ludeman Les Cèdres 2001 (5–8 €)** each received a special mention.

➟ SCEA Molinari, Ludeman, 33210 Langon, tel. 05.56.63.09.52, fax 05.56.63.13.47 ✅

✖ by appt.

PRIMO PALATUM 2000★★

■	2 ha	1,800	❒❒	15–23 €

Part of the range put together by Xavier Copel, *de l'Atlantique à la Méditerranée* (from Atlantic to Mediterranean). While the quantity of this *cuvée* is limited there are no limits to its character. Intense ruby-red, it develops a very aromatic bouquet, with charred and fruity notes. Rich and ambitious, the palate is marked by the cask and structured by the soft tannins. A superb finish of black fruit and prunes adds the final touch. This wine can definitely be left in the cellar for four or five years, before opening it to accompany an entrecote or a game dish.

➟ Primo Palatum, 1, Cirette, 33190 Morizès, tel. 05.56.71.39.39, fax 05.56.71.39.40, e-mail xavier-copel@primo-palatum.com ✅

✖ by appt.

➟ Xavier Copel

CH. RAHOUL 2000★

■	20 ha	113,000	❒❒	15–23 €

Regular clients of this cru will find all the fruitiness they have come to expect in this vintage. They will also appreciate its limpid, dark colour and its bouquet, with intense notes of crystallized fruits and a touch of roasting wood. On the palate they will notice a certain youthfulness in the flavours, resulting more from the grape variety than the maturation. An elegant finish concludes on a happy note. All these are good reasons for laying this wine down for two or three years. The **white 2001 (11–15 €)** received a special mention.

➟ SA Ch. Rahoul, 4, rte du Courneau, 33640 Portets, tel. 05.56.67.01.12, fax 05.56.67.02.88, e-mail chateau-rahoul@alain-thienot.fr ✅

✖ by appt.

CH. DE RESPIDE

Cuvée Callipyge 2000★

■	30 ha	40,000	▮❒❒	11–15 €

Largely matured in cask, this wine presents extremely well: a good, intense colour; a rich bouquet that is still a touch dominated by the oak. On the palate the influence of the cask is much more restrained and red berries prevail. From attack to finish the general balance demonstrates that both vinification and maturation have been well managed. A simpler wine, but also well made, is the **Cuvée Principale**

Graves

2001 (8–11 €), which received a special mention, as did the **Cuvée Orpale white 2002 (5–8 €)**.
🕊 Vignobles Pierre Bonnet, Le Pavillon de Boyrein, 33210 Roaillan, tel. 05.56.63.24.24, fax 05.56.62.31.59, e-mail vignobles-bonnet@wanadoo.fr ☑
☂ by appt.

CH. RESPIDE-MEDEVILLE 2000★★

| ■ | 7,7 ha | 30,000 | ◫ | 15–23 € |

"The antiques expert of Sauternes," Christian Médeville is equally knowledgeable about red wines. And who could possibly doubt it having tasted his superb 2000 vintage? The quite dark purplish-red colour is not without appeal, and the complex and rich bouquet is well up to standard. Almost the whole aromatic range is present, with roasted aromas of caramel, cocoa and liquorice and, of course, fruit. On the palate, the good oakiness of the attack is followed by prune notes. As elegant as it is promising, this wine will be an excellent accompaniment for *Magrets de Canard* (duck breasts) in four or five years' time, or perhaps even longer. Rounded and pleasant, the **red Dame de Respide 2000 (8–11 €)** received a special mention, as did the **white Château Respide Médeville 2001 (11–15 €)**.
🕊 Christian Médeville, Ch. Gilette, 33210 Preignac, tel. 05.56.76.28.44, fax 05.56.76.28.43, e-mail christian.medeville@wanadoo.fr ☑
☂ by appt.

CH. ROQUETAILLADE LA GRANGE 2000★

| ■ | 23 ha | 150,000 | ◫ | 8–11 € |

Only a hundred or so metres from the famous Château Fort de Roquetaillade, this estate is one of the most highly regarded of the appellation. The location appears to be a successful one, if judged by the colour, the fruity aromatic expression with nuances of oak, and the tannic structure and balance of this wine, all of which indicate that it should be laid down for two or more years. From the same producer, the **red Château de Carolle 2001 Elevé en Fût (5–8 €)** was awarded one star.
🕊 GAEC Guignard Frères, 33210 Mazères, tel. 05.56.76.14.23, fax 05.56.62.30.62, e-mail contact@vignobles-guignard.com ☑
☂ by appt.

CH. SAINT-AGREVES
Vieilli en fût de chêne 2000★

| ■ | 11 ha | 75,000 | ◫ | 5–8 € |

A medium-sized estate, this cru has produced a wine which, on the nose, successfully and delicately combines balsamic notes with fruit (raspberries) and spices. All these aromas mingle with the full, rich, rounded palate. Well made and balanced, this wine can be drunk now or kept for a while.
🕊 EARL Landry, Ch. Saint-Agrèves, 17, rue Joachim-de-Chalup, 33720 Landiras, tel. 05.56.62.50.85, fax 05.56.62.42.49, e-mail saint.agreves@free.fr ☑
☂ by appt.

CH. SAINT-ROBERT
Poncet-Deville 2001★★

| ■ | 6 ha | 25,000 | ◫ | 11–15 € |
| 89 90 92 93 94 95 96 97 98 |99| 00 01 |

A known quantity, the Cuvée Poncet-Deville du Château Saint-Robert is once again remarkable. From its brilliant

ruby-red colour, this 2001 vintage develops an extraordinarily complex bouquet. The roasted notes rest on a basis of fruit (stewed strawberries) and spices. The tannins are just as soft as the aromas. Round and flavoursome, the palate reveals the great skill that went into the choice of the well-ripened grape, the extraction of the tannins and the maturation. A superb wine to lay down for three or four years. Pleasant and silky, the **Cuvée Principale 2001** was awarded one star, as was the **white 2001 la Cuvée Poncet-Deville**, which has a particularly interesting bouquet.
🕊 SCEA Vignobles Bastor et Saint-Robert, Dom. de Lamontagne, 33210 Preignac, tel. 05.56.63.27.66, fax 05.56.76.87.03, e-mail bastor-lamontagne@dial.oleane.com ☑
☂ by appt.
🕊 Foncier-Vignobles

CH. DE SANSARIC 2000★★

| ■ | 8 ha | 13,000 | ◫ | 5–8 € |

Once an 18th century hunting lodge, this cru presented a wine of a brilliant, most seductive colour in perfect harmony with the restrained elegance of the bouquet, where fruit and oak are in complete agreement. After a clean opening, the supple, long palate also finds good balance, right up to the finish on red berries and damp woodland. A charming wine.
🕊 D. Abadie, 6, Impasse des Domaines, 33640 Castres-Gironde, tel. 05.56.67.03.17, fax 05.56.67.59.53 ☑
☂ by appt.

T DU TEIGNEY
Vieilli en fût de chêne 2000★

| ■ | 1 ha | 6,600 | ◫ | 11–15 € |

Product of a 30 ha estate, this *cuvée spéciale* was not made in any great quantity, but its deep colour, the aromas of coffee, tobacco, chocolate, red berries and blackcurrant leaf-buds on its bouquet, the smooth attack and rounded, well-balanced palate will be much appreciated by those wine-lovers who manage to procure a few bottles. The **Cuvée Principale 2001 (3–5 €)** also received one star, with its very expressive, generous range of aromas.
🕊 EARL Buytet et Fils, Ch. Teigney, 33210 Langon, tel. 05.56.63.17.15, fax 05.56.76.20.19 ☑
☂ by appt.

CH. DU TOURTE 2001★

| ■ | 6 ha | 20,000 | ◫ | 11–15 € |

Deriving its name from a mound once used for hunting turtledoves, this deep-red wine possesses a good substance that will allow it to age. Its red fruit and spice aromas, and its pleasant, rounded tannins make it an appropriate wine to serve with game dishes.
🕊 Ch. du Tourte, 33210 Toulenne, tel. 01.46.88.40.08, fax 01.46.88.01.45, e-mail hubert.arnaud@c2a.fr ☑
☂ by appt.
🕊 Arnaud

CH. LE TUQUET
Vinifié et élevé en fût de chêne 2001★★

| ■ | 13.5 ha | 30,000 | ◫ | 8–11 € |

A fine example of Bordeaux architecture, this charterhouse, belonging to the Pontacs in the 17th century, was modified in the 18th century. The cru offers a white Graves, pleasantly yellow in colour with amber highlights. Its bouquet seeks out finesse and freshness rather than strength, with perfumes of lemon, citrus fruits and flowers. The supple, rounded and fleshy palate is well balanced, with touches of lemon and toast. In addition it has considerable length. This is a wine that will reach its harmonious peak two or three years from now, but that is already worthy of serving with a fine fish dish. The **red Tuquet 2000**, very elegant, true to type and with great potential, was awarded one star.
🕊 Paul Ragon, GFA Ch. Le Tuquet, 33640 Beautiran, tel. 05.56.20.21.23, fax 05.56.20.21.83 ☑
☂ by appt.

288

CH. LA VIEILLE FRANCE

Cuvée Marie 2001★

| | 1.5 ha | 5,000 | ◫ | 11–15€ |

A *cuvée prestige*, this wine carries the fleur de lys on its label. Pale-yellow tinged with gold, it develops a bouquet mingling exotic fruits and pineapple with vanilla and cinnamon. Rounded, quite rich and fleshy, the palate is well balanced. The **La Vieille France red 2000** received a special mention. Concentrated, but with velvety aromas, this wine should be laid down for two to three years.
☛ Michel Dugoua, EARL Ch. La Vieille France, 1, chem. du Malbec, BP 8, 33640 Portets, tel. 05.56.67.19.11, fax 05.56.67.17.54, e-mail courrier@chateau-la-vieille-france.fr ☑
⌇ by appt.

CH. VILLA BEL-AIR 2001★★

| | 33 ha | 220,000 | ◫ | 8–11€ |

While the superb 18th century charterhouse is still in need of restoration, the estate has rediscovered its vitality over the last few years. It has even become one of the appellation's most well-regarded producers. And don't expect this wine to detract anything from the cru's reputation. The deep colour and the distinguished bouquet, maintaining a judicious balance between ripe black fruit and oak, and the palate all bear witness to its potential. The full structure, supported by silky tannins, and the spiced, toasted flavours invest it with an impression of harmony. Keep a prominent place for it in the cellar. Rich in sensations and aromas (exotic fruits, toast), the **white 2002** was awarded one star.
☛ Jean-Michel Cazes, Ch. Villa Bel-Air, 33650 Saint-Morillon, tel. 05.56.20.29.35, fax 05.56.78.44.80
⌇ by appt.

Wines selected but not starred

BARON PHILIPPE 2000

| | n.c. | n.c. | | 8–11€ |

☛ SA Baron Philippe de Rothschild, BP 117, 33250 Pauillac, tel. 05.56.73.20.20, fax 05.56.73.20.44, e-mail webmaster@bpdr.com

CH. BARTHE

Elevé en fût de chêne 2002

| | 3 ha | 15,000 | ◫ | 5–8€ |

☛ SA Yvon Mau, 33190 Gironde-sur-Dropt, tel. 05.56.61.54.54, fax 05.56.61.54.61, e-mail info@ymau.com
☛ D. Lafosse

CH. LE BONNAT 2000

| | 25 ha | 150,000 | ◫ | 8–11€ |

☛ SCA Ch. Branda and Cadillac, 9, Ch. de Cadillac, 33240 Cadillac-en-Fronsadais, tel. 05.57.94.09.20, fax 05.57.94.09.30, e-mail haut-selve@wanadoo.fr ☑
⌇ by appt.

CH. CABANNIEUX

Réserve du château Elevé en barrique 2000

| | 13.42 ha | 54,800 | ◫ | 5–8€ |

☛ SCEA du Ch. Cabannieux, 44, rte du Courneau, 33640 Portets, tel. 05.56.67.22.01, fax 05.56.67.32.54, e-mail dudignacbarrière@free.fr ☑ ☎
⌇ ev. day 9am–12noon 3pm–7pm
☛ Mme Régine Dudignac

CH. CAMUS

Cuvée Zoé 2002

| | 3 ha | 1,200 | ◫ | 5–8€ |

☛ Jean-Luc Larriaut, SCEA Vignobles de Bordeaux, 33212 Saint-Pierre-de-Mons, tel. 05.56.63.19.34, fax 05.56.63.21.60, e-mail lvb.sica@libertysurf.fr ☑
⌇ by appt.

CH. CLARON 2000

| | 6 ha | 7,000 | ▮◫♦ | 5–8€ |

☛ GAEC Bertrand Ardurats, 575, Le Claron, 33650 Saint-Morillon, tel. 05.56.20.25.75, fax 05.56.78.42.29 ☑
⌇ by appt.

CLOS D'UZA 2001

| | 29 ha | 63,000 | ◫ | 3–5€ |

☛ GAF Ch. Les Queyrats, 33210 Saint-Pierre-de-Mons, tel. 05.56.63.07.02, fax 05.61.54.41.73, e-mail dulac.queyrats@wanadoo.fr ☑
⌇ by appt.

CH. DES FOUGERES 2001

| | 4 ha | 8,000 | ◫ | 8–11€ |

☛ Vins et Domaines H. de Montesquieu, Aux Fougères, BP 53, 33650 La Brède, tel. 05.56.78.45.45, fax 05.56.20.25.07, e-mail montesquieu@bordeaux-montesquieu.com ☑

CH. GRAND MOUTA

Elevé en fût de chêne 2000

| | 3 ha | 23,000 | ◫ | 5–8€ |

☛ SCEA Domaines Latrille-Bonnin, Petit-Mouta, 33210 Mazères, tel. 05.56.63.41.70, fax 05.56.76.83.25 ☑
⌇ by appt.
☛ GFA du Brion

CH. GRAVEYRON

Cuvée Tradition 2000

| | 6 ha | 8,000 | ▮◫♦ | 5–8€ |

☛ EARL Vignobles Pierre Cante, 67, rte des Graves, 33640 Portets, tel. 05.56.67.23.69, fax 05.56.67.58.19 ☑
⌇ ev. day ex. Sun. 9am–12noon 2pm–7pm

CH. HAUT-CALENS

Elevé en fût de chêne 2001

| | 3 ha | 12,000 | ◫ | 5–8€ |

☛ EARL Vignobles Albert Yung, Ch. Haut-Calens, 33640 Beautiran, tel. 05.56.67.05.25, fax 05.56.67.24.91 ☑
⌇ ev. day 9am–11.30am 3pm–5.30pm; cl. Aug.

CH. HAUT REYS

Réserve 2002

| | 2 ha | 10,000 | ▮ | 5–8€ |

☛ EARL Gabin, 18, allée Perrucade, 33650 La Brède, tel. 05.56.20.38.29, fax 05.56.78.47.78 ☑
⌇ by appt.

CH. LASSALLE 2000

| | 4 ha | 25,000 | ◫ | 5–8€ |

☛ Louis-Michel Labbé, 7, allée Lassalle, 33650 La Brède, tel. 05.56.20.20.19, fax 05.56.78.42.75 ☑
⌇ by appt.

CH. LUGAUD 2000

| | 6 ha | 10,000 | ◫ | 5–8€ |

☛ Didier May, 3, pl. de Jeansotte, 33650 Saint-Selve, tel. 05.56.78.41.85, fax 05.56.78.48.39 ☑

CH. MAGNEAU 2000

| | 15 ha | 60,000 | ❸ | 8–11 € |

➽ Henri Ardurats et Fils, EARL Les Cabanasses, 12, chem. Maxime-Ardurats, 33650 La Brède, tel. 05.56.20.20.57, fax 05.56.20.39.95,
e-mail ardurats@chateau-magneau.com ✅
🍷 ev. day 8.30am–12noon 2pm–6pm; Sat. Sun. by appt.

CH. MARQUIS DE RUAT 2000

| | 5 ha | 30,000 | ❸ ❸ ⬥ | 8–11 € |

➽ Les Vignobles Dumon, Ch. Béchereau de Ruat, 33210 Bommes, tel. 05.56.76.61.73, fax 05.56.76.67.84 ✅
🍷 ev. day 9am–12noon 2pm–5pm;
Sat. Sun. and groups by appt.

CH. MOURAS 2001

| | 3 ha | 10,000 | ❸ | 5–8 € |

➽ Ch. Laville, 33210 Preignac, tel. 05.56.63.59.45, fax 05.56.63.16.28 ✅
🍷 ev. day ex. Sat. Sun. 8.30am–12.30pm
1.30pm–6.30pm

CH. MOUTIN 2001

| | 1 ha | 3,000 | ❸ | 8–11 € |

➽ Jean Darriet, Ch. Dauphiné-Rondillon, 33410 Loupiac, tel. 05.56.62.61.75, fax 05.56.62.63.73,
e-mail vignoblesdarriet@wanadoo.fr ✅
🍷 ev. day 8am–12.30pm 2pm–7pm; Sat. Sun. by appt.; cl. 10–20 Aug.

CH. DU SEUIL 2000

| | 4.13 ha | 32,000 | ❸ | 11–15 € |

➽ SCEA Ch. du Seuil, 33720 Cérons, tel. 05.56.27.11.56, fax 05.56.27.28.79, e-mail chateau-du-seuil@wanadoo.fr ✅
🍷 by appt.

CH. TOUR DE CALENS

Elevé en fût de chêne 2000

| | 6.4 ha | 30,000 | ❸ ❸ ⬥ | 8–11 € |

➽ Bernard and Dominique Doublet, 33750 Saint-Quentin-de-Baron, tel. 05.57.24.12.93, fax 05.57.24.12.83, e-mail d.doublet@free.fr ✅
🍷 by appt.

CH. TOURTEAU-CHOLLET 2000

| | 50 ha | 238,000 | | 3–5 € |

➽ SC du Ch. Tourteau Chollet, 3, chem. de Chollet, 33640 Arbanats, tel. 05.56.67.40.09, fax 05.56.67.47.78
🍷 by appt.
➽ M. Bontoux

VIEUX CHATEAU GAUBERT 2001

| | 25 ha | 60,000 | ❸ | 11–15 € |
| 89 90 93 94 95 |96| 97 |98| |99| 00 01 | | | |

➽ Dominique Haverlan, Vieux Château Gaubert, 33640 Portets, tel. 05.56.67.18.63, fax 05.56.67.52.76, e-mail dominique.haverlan@libertysurf.fr ✅
🍷 by appt.

Graves Supérieures

CH. BRONDELLE 2000★

| | 1 ha | 6,000 | ❸ ❸ ⬥ | 8–11 € |

From the same producer as the Graves of the same name, this wine presents itself with a flourish. The eye is held by its brilliant gold-yellow colour. Following initial citrus fruit perfumes the bouquet tends towards notes of crystallized fruits. The palate, imposing in its attack, goes on to reveal a touch of roasted flavours and a good balance between sugar and acidity.
➽ Vignobles Belloc-Rochet, Ch. Brondelle, 33210 Langon, tel. 05.56.62.38.14, fax 05.56.62.23.14,
e-mail chateau.brondelle@wanadoo.fr ✅
🍷 ev. day ex. Sat. Sun.. 8.30am–12noon 2pm–6pm

CH. LEHOUL
Elevé en fût de chêne 2001★★

| | 1 ha | 2,000 | ❸ | 8–11 € |

As always, this cru presented a Graves Supérieures which is a model of its kind. It delivers on all the promises made by its bronze-yellow, amber-tinged colour: generous bouquet with dried fruit, apricot and toasted almond notes, not forgetting the orange peel; and a rich and full palate, with just the right touch of acidity. It is already very pleasant but promises an attractive evolution over the next three or four years. Even if it is the label of its red equivalent in Graves that is shown, this wine nevertheless drew many compliments from the Grand Jury.
➽ EARL Fonta et Fils, rte d'Auros, 33210 Langon, tel. 05.56.63.17.74, fax 05.56.63.06.06 ✅
🍷 by appt.

Pessac-Léognan

Corresponding to the northern part of Graves (formerly called Hautes-Graves), the region of Pessac and Léognan is today an Appellation Communale similar to those of the Médoc. Its creation, historically justifiable, (medieval clarets were produced from the ancient vines that surrounded the towns) is supported by the originality of its soil. The terracing further south gives way to a much more irregular landscape. The area between Martillac and Mérignac consists of an archipelago of gravelly hilltops whose steep slopes guarantee good drainage and whose soil, composed of a variety of different types of pebble, are excellent for wine-growing. Pessac-Léognan wines have great originality – a fact which specialists noticed long before the creation of the appellation, so much so that in 1855, at the time of the imperial classification, Haut-Brion became the only non-Médoc château to be classed (Premier Cru). Eventually in 1959, when the 16 Graves crus were classed, we find that all were in the present Appellation Communale.

The red wines (45,444 hl in 2002) possess all the general characteristics of Graves wines, yet their bouquet, velvetiness and structure sets them apart. The white wines (9,721 hl) are particularly suited to barrel maturation and cellaring, allowing them to acquire great richness of flavour with fine notes of broom and lime blossom.

CH. BAHANS HAUT-BRION 2000★

| | n.c. | n.c. | ❸ | 38–46 € |

With its deep Bordeaux colour, Bahans, the second Haut-Brion, is far from banal with its bouquet tending towards leather, prunes, stewed fruit and intense oak. It exudes great finesse. It is there again on the opening, as silky as one could wish for, then the structure asserts itself. On the finish there is a certain harshness in the tannins, but they will have integrated in four to five years' time.
➽ Dom. Clarence Dillon, Ch. Haut-Brion, 33608 Pessac Cedex, tel. 05.56.00.29.30, fax 05.56.98.75.14,
e-mail info@haut-brion.com
🍷 by appt.

CH. BARET 2000★

| ■ | n.c. | n.c. | ⊞ | 11–15 € |

This cru, completely renovated over the last 20 years both in the winery and the vineyards, has not yielded to fashion and Cabernet remains the main grape variety. Happily this wine's bouquet has all the characteristics of Cabernet, as does the palate. After an almost timid first impression, the palate opens out to reveal nice tannins and ends on a long finish. A fine wine that needs five years in the cellar.
☛ Héritiers André Ballande, Ch. Baret, 33140 Villenave-d'Ornon, tel. 05.56.87.87.71
☿ by appt.

CH. BOUSCAUT 2000★

| ■ | Cru clas. | 17 ha | 90,000 | ⊞ | 15–23 € |

76 79 **80 81** 82 83 84 85(86)87 88 **89 90** 93 94|95| |96| 97 98 **99** 00

Established in the 17th century, Bouscaut was burned down in 1962 – when the singer, Gilbert Bécaud lived there. Rebuilt in its original form, it was bought in 1979 by Lucien Lurton, whose daughter, Sophie, now manages the cru. The lovely purple colour is just as elegant as that of its white equivalent, and marvellously in harmony with the finesse of the bouquet, enhanced by notes of tobacco and spices. The full and flattering palate indicates a period of five or six years in the cellar, prior to enjoying it with a dish of ceps and chanterelles in a cream sauce. The red **Lamothe Bouscaut 2000 (11–15 €)** received a special mention.
☛ SA Ch. Bouscaut, rte de Toulouse, 33140 Cadaujac, tel. 05.57.83.12.20, fax 05.57.83.12.21,
e-mail cb@chateau-bouscaut.com ☑
☿ by appt.
☛ S. and L. Cogombles

CH. BOUSCAUT 2001★★

| ■ | Cru clas. | 3,2 ha | 21,000 | ⊞ | 15–23 € |

82 83 85 86 88 89 90 93 |95| 96 97 |98| **99** |00| 01

In an out-of-the-way part of the appellation, far from the main highways, Bouscaut's beautiful, classic facade is something of an exception, overlooking the route nationale, as it does. Its elegance is echoed in the pale-yellow, golden-tinged colour of this wine. The intense and complex bouquet mingles notes of roasted coffee and toast with perfumes of fresh fruits. The palate has a seductive vigour and richness, but the still-marked imprint of the oak justifies laying this wine down for two or three years. The **Lamothe Bouscaut white 2001 (11–15 €)** was awarded one star for its balance, freshness and distinction.
☛ SA Ch. Bouscaut, rte de Toulouse, 33140 Cadaujac, tel. 05.57.83.12.20, fax 05.57.83.12.21,
e-mail cb@chateau-bouscaut.com ☑
☿ by appt.

CH. LE BRUILLEAU 2000★

| ■ | | 2 ha | 10,650 | ⊞ | 8–11 € |

It is reassuring to find small family concerns among the great AOCs, especially when they offer wines like this 2000 vintage. A fine, brilliant ruby-red in colour, it is initially somewhat reserved before opening up on aromas of ripe fruit and mild spices. The rounded first impression on the palate goes on to develop ample fullness, with a good tannic presence which will enable this wine to be laid down for five or six years.
☛ Nadine Bédicheau, 12, chem. de Bruilleau, 33650 Saint-Médard-d'Eyrans, tel. 05.56.72.70.45, fax 05.56.72.70.45,
e-mail chateau.lebruilleau@wanadoo.fr ☑
☿ by appt.

CH. CANTELYS 2000★

| ■ | | 25 ha | 30,000 | ⊞ | 11–15 € |

From the same producer as the Smith Haut Lafitte, this wine's pedigree is displayed in its expressive, silky tannins but its interest goes further than that: its colour is rich in nuances, while its bouquet combines intensity and balance, in which the oak does not detract from the fruit. On the palate one finds attractive aromatic expression with notes of clove. Its mouth-filling qualities suggest that it should be laid down for

three or four years. The **white 2001 (11–15 €)** was also awarded one star. It could be drunk now or kept for a year or two.
☛ SARL Daniel Cathiard, Ch. Cantelys, 33650 Martillac, tel. 05.57.83.11.22, fax 05.57.83.11.21,
e-mail f.cathiard@smith-haut-lafitte.com ☑
☿ by appt.

CH. CARBONNIEUX 2000★★

| ■ | Cru clas. | 45 ha | 300,000 | ⊞ | 15–23 € |

75 81 82 83 85(86)87 |88| |89| |90| 91 92 93 |94| |95| **96** |97| 98 |99| **00**

For the visitor this is a manor house among the vineyards, for the historian it is an ancient ecclesiastical seat and for the wine-lover it is a fine wine. Its attractions do not stem solely from its brilliant-purple colour. The bouquet unfolds on fine, very ripe fruit perfumes and delicate toasted notes, indicating carefully judged maturation. After a gentle opening, the palate demonstrates good tannic structure and shows its mouth-filling qualities and potential for ageing. This wine should be laid down for five or six years before being opened.
☛ SC des Grandes Graves, Ch. Carbonnieux, 33850 Léognan, tel. 05.57.96.56.20, fax 05.57.96.59.19,
e-mail chateau.carbonnieux@wanadoo.fr ☑
☿ by appt.
☛ Antony Perrin

CH. CARBONNIEUX 2001★

| ■ | Cru clas. | 42 ha | 220,000 | ⊞ | 15–23 € |

81 82 83 85 86 87 **88 89** |90| 91 92 |93| **|94|** |95| **|96| |97|** |98| 99 (00)|01|

The white variety vines, at Carbonnieux, are almost as extensive as the red, as the terroir is well suited to producing white wine. The elegance of this authentic Pessac-Léognan is a good example. Its perfumes are of flowers and lime, while the silky palate is highly expressive of the terroir. This vintage may be served now or kept another year or two.
☛ SC des Grandes Graves, Ch. Carbonnieux, 33850 Léognan, tel. 05.57.96.56.20, fax 05.57.96.59.19,
e-mail chateau.carbonnieux@wanadoo.fr ☑
☿ by appt.

CH. LES CARMES HAUT-BRION 2000★

| ■ | | 4.66 ha | 26,000 | ⊞ | 46–76 € |

80 82 83 85 **88** |89| 90 91 92 93 94 |95| **96** |97| |98| **99** 00

Just a few hundred metres from the Haut-Brion archipelago, this wine-growing island in the suburbs is managing to hold on because of the quality of its production, as revealed by this wine. The intense bouquet ranges between notes of crystallized black berry-fruits and oak. The palate is full, with leathery, crystallized fruit flavours supported by silky tannins that provide a delightful finish. Wait two to four years.
☛ SCEA du Ch. les Carmes Haut-Brion, 197, av. Jean-Cordier, 33600 Pessac, tel. 05.56.93.23.40, fax 05.56.93.10.71,
e-mail chateau@les-carmes-haut-brion.com
☿ by appt.
☛ Didier Furt

DOM. DE CHEVALIER 2000★★

| ■ | Cru clas. | n.c. | n.c. | ⊞ | 46–76 € |

64 66 70 73 75 78 79 83 84 |85| |86| 87 88 (89)|90| 91 92 |93| |94| **96** |97| 98 99 00

Low yields, rigorous selection of grapes, and perfect blending of 65% Cabernet Sauvignon with Merlot are all aspects of the great care that Chevalier take to ensure their wines fully express the terroir's personality. Such is the case with this 2000, which has all the elegance that gives this appellation its charm. Supported by silky tannins, it reveals the richness of its body and flavours (fruit, roses, sweet spices). A real laying-down wine (up to eight to ten years). Their **red Esprit de Chevalier 2000 (15–23 €)** is also well-made, and is rated one-star for its very ripe fruitiness and liquorice, chocolaty roundness. A classic of the appellation.
☛ SC Dom. de Chevalier, 33850 Léognan, tel. 05.56.64.16.16, fax 05.56.64.18.18,
e-mail domainedechevalier@domainedechevalier.com
☿ by appt.
☛ Famille Bernard

DOM. DE CHEVALIER 2000★★

| | Cru clas. | n.c. | n.c. | ⑪ | 46–76 € |

82 83 85 86 |89| (90) 91 92 93 94 |95| |96| |97| |98| (99) 00

In line with its reputation, Chevalier offer a wine of real elegance here. It has a strong yellow colour and a bouquet of beeswax and crystallized orange. The palate is rounded, full and rich. The somewhat oakier **white Esprit de Chevalier 2001 (15–23 €)** was also commended by the Jury.
🍷 SC Dom. de Chevalier, 33850 Léognan,
tel. 05.56.64.16.16, fax 05.56.64.18.18,
e-mail domainedechevalier@domainedechevalier.com
☿ by appt.

CH. COUHINS-LURTON 2001★★

| | Cru clas. | 5.5 ha | 15,000 | ⑪ | 23–30 € |

82 83 85 86 87 88 89 |90| 91 |92| 93 |94| |95| (96) 97 98 |99| 00 01

This cru, entirely given over to white grapevines (Sauvignon), has just acquired a new winery and a fine tasting hall. Its 2001 is certainly worthy of the new surroundings. It has an elegant lemon-yellow colour and a character that evolves throughout the tasting. Citrus fruits, rose, honey, grapefruit all contribute to the bouquet's richness. The attack is oaky, but grape flavours quickly show their presence, and the palate is round, lively and intense. The finish is particularly expressive (dried fruits and nuts, honey, wax). Already an extremely enjoyable wine.
🍷 André Lurton, Ch. Bonnet, 33420 Grézillac,
tel. 05.57.25.58.58, fax 05.57.74.98.59,
e-mail andrelurton@andrelurton.com ☑
☿ by appt.

CH. DE CRUZEAU 2000★★★

| | | 40 ha | 180,000 | ⑪ | 11–15 € |

81 82 83 85 86 88 89 90 |93| |94| |95| |96| |97| 98 99 (00)

The fact that André Lurton has better-known crus, like Couhins or La Louvière, does not mean that this estate is neglected. It is hard to judge whether the colour of this wine should be described as very deep garnet or simply black: the tasters had long debates on the subject. They were unanimous about its other characteristics, however. The bouquet is fine, elegant and classy, with a profusion of scents ranging from soft fruits to leather. The palate is full and supple, with remarkable balance and very considerable keeping potential. Leave at least three to five years, or even longer, before drinking; ten to fifteen years is entirely conceivable. Nominated for a *coup de coeur*, this Cruzeau was only beaten by a short head by La Louvière.
🍷 André Lurton, Ch. Bonnet, 33420 Grézillac,
tel. 05.57.25.58.58, fax 05.57.74.98.59,
e-mail andrelurton@andrelurton.com ☑
☿ by appt.

CH. DE CRUZEAU 2001★★★

| | | 10 ha | 50,000 | ⑪ | 8–11 € |

88 89 90 92 93 94 95 |96| |97| |98| |99| (01)

Like the red (above), nothing would have stopped this wine gaining a *coup de coeur* but for competition from the La Louvière. Notes of yellow fruits, peach, mandarin, vanilla, dried fruits and nuts, and toast make for a gorgeous bouquet. The palate is well-structured, round, rich and well-balanced, with a superb finish. A magnificent, elegant and complex wine, which the Jury applauded.
🍷 André Lurton, Ch. Bonnet, 33420 Grézillac,
tel. 05.57.25.58.58, fax 05.57.74.98.59,
e-mail andrelurton@andrelurton.com ☑
☿ by appt.

CH. FERRAN 2000★★

| | | 10 ha | 65,000 | ⑪ | 8–11 € |

83 85 88 89 |90| 94 |95| |97| 98 99 00

Robert Ferran, onetime advocate to the Bordeaux parliament, gave his name in the 17th century to this property; in the 18th century it belonged to Montesquieu, the author of *L'Esprit des Lois*. The present château was built in 1885. The

50% Merlot-variety grapes have marked this wine with their personality, especially the attack, which is particularly unctuous. The bouquet is rich and complex, with an aromatic expression that strikes a good balance between fruit and oak. The structure has a very Cabernet Sauvignon tannic weave. The finish is long, indicating good keeping potential. It could be laid down for five or six years, or indeed much longer.
🍷 Ch. Ferran, 33650 Martillac, tel. 06.07.41.86.00,
fax 05.56.72.62.73 ☑
☿ by appt.
🍷 Hervé Béraud-Sudreau

CH. DE FIEUZAL 2000★

| | Cru clas. | 35 ha | 88,000 | ⑪ | 30–38 € |

70 75 76 77 78 79 80 81 82 83 84 |85| |86| |88| |89| (90) 91 92 93 94 (95) (96) |97| 98 99 00

Under Irish ownership since 1999, Fieuzal offers this 2000 grown on a nice soil of white gravel. A confidence-inspiring deep-garnet colour, it is as full in its aromatic development as in its well-ripened tannic structure. Self-evidently, this wine has all it needs to keep five or six years.
🍷 SC Ch. de Fieuzal, 124, av. de Mont-de-Marsan,
33850 Léognan, tel. 05.56.64.77.86, fax 05.56.64.18.88 ☑
☿ by appt.
🍷 Lochlann Quinn

CH. DE FIEUZAL 2001★★

| | | 18 ha | 27,000 | ⑪ | 30–38 € |

83 84 85 86 87 |88| |89| (90) 91 92 |93| |94| |95| |96| |97| |98| (99) 00 01

Though not classified for white wine, this Fieuzal nonetheless does credit to its appellation in the quality of its production. The wine is a half-and-half Sémillon–Sauvignon blend, in which the Sauvignon dominates by virtue of its notes of boxwood. After a well-balanced attack, the palate develops a dialogue between finesse and potency which delivers a host of flavours, mingling citrus fruits, vanilla and exotic fruits.
🍷 SC Ch. de Fieuzal, 124, av. de Mont-de-Marsan,
33850 Léognan, tel. 05.56.64.77.86, fax 05.56.64.18.88 ☑
☿ by appt.

CH. DE FRANCE 2001★★

| | | 2.33 ha | 5,700 | ⑪ | 15–23 € |

88 89 **90** 95 96 97 99 00 **01**

Bernard Thomassin acquired this estate in 1971. Today, assisted by his son Arnaud, he offers this 2001 grown on deep gravels and blending 30% Sémillon with Sauvignon. Skilful tending of this particularly well-orientated terroir has produced this rich, full, generous white wine. From bouquet to finish it has an extremely attractive and expressive development of mouth-watering aromas and flavours of vanilla, very ripe citrus fruits, pineapple and dried apricot.
🍷 SA Bernard Thomassin, Ch. de France, 98, av. de
Mont-de-Marsan, 33850 Léognan, tel. 05.56.64.75.39,
fax 05.56.64.72.13,
e-mail chateau-de-france@chateau-de-france.com ☑
☿ by appt.

BORDEAUX

CH. DE FRANCE 2000★

	20 ha	80,000		15–23 €

81 82 83 85 86 88 89 |90| 92 93 95 |96| 97 98 99 |00|

This wine is a classic garnet colour, but less classic in its other aspects. Pleasingly full and generous, it provides a developing bouquet and body of black fruits sustained by sufficiently mature tannins to allow it to be drunk now. However, it has good potential to develop further, and could be stored (three to seven years).

☞ SA Bernard Thomassin, Ch. de France, 98, av. de Mont-de-Marsan, 33850 Léognan, tel. 05.56.64.75.39, fax 05.56.64.72.13,
e-mail chateau-de-france@chateau-de-france.com ☑
☗ by appt.

DOM. DE GRANDMAISON 2000★

	12.5 ha	90,000		11–15 €

This half-and-half 2000 blend of Cabernet and Merlot has an extremely individual bouquet with notes of cherry brandy, *rancio* and chocolate, mingled with oak, to provide a characterful synthesis. The tannins are still a little over-strong and indicate long keeping potential.

☞ J. Bouquier, Dom. de Grandmaison, 33850 Léognan, tel. 05.56.64.75.37, fax 05.56.64.55.24,
e-mail courrier@domaine-de-grandmaison.fr ☑
☗ by appt.

CH. HAUT-BAILLY 2000★

	Cru clas.	26 ha	75,000		38–46 €

78 79 80 81 82 83 85 |86| 87 88(89) |90| 92 |93| |94|(95)9 6 |97| 98 99 00

One of the rare estates whose surface-area is unchanged since 1630. Still quite tannic in character, this wine, which nonetheless has considerable finesse, does not seem to have found its definitive expression. The attack is powerful and promising, followed by flavours of berry fruits which are quickly dominated by the oak. The Jury cannot say how long the wine should be stored before drinking: something between three and ten years perhaps.

☞ SCA du Ch. Haut-Bailly, 103, rte de Cadaujac, 33850 Léognan, tel. 05.56.64.75.11, fax 05.56.64.53.60,
e-mail mail@chateau-haut-bailly.com
☗ by appt.
☞ Robert G. Wilmers

CH. HAUT-BERGEY 2000★

	22 ha	40,000		46–76 €

91 92 93 94 96 97 **98** 99 00

Using fermentation in small vats, malolactic fermentation and maturation in new oak, this cru spares no effort to produce a good-looking wine. This 2000 proves that the care was worth it. The colour is almost black, and the bouquet has mouth-watering scents of red berries, exotic wood (sandalwood) and cigar-boxes. Rich and fleshy, sustained by well-extracted tannins, the palate has a texture that will call for substantial keeping, after which it will go well with chargrilled entrecôte of beef. The **red L'Etoile de Bergey 2000 (8–15 €)** is also commended, and is a very good second wine indeed.

☞ Ch. Haut-Bergey, 69, cours Gambetta, 33850 Léognan, tel. 05.56.64.05.22, fax 05.56.64.06.98,
e-mail haut.bergey@wanadoo.fr ☑ ☷
☗ by appt.
☞ Sylviane Garcin

CH. HAUT-BERGEY 2001★

	2 ha	5,000		30–38 €

Grown in a vineyard of mainly Sauvignon vines, the variety has left its mark on this wine's aromatic expression. It is nonetheless well-balanced. The palate has an elegance that goes to make this a wine highly suitable for drinking with delicate fish, for example *Sole à la Normande* (sole with a mushroom and seafood sauce).

☞ Ch. Haut-Bergey, 69, cours Gambetta, 33850 Léognan, tel. 05.56.64.05.22, fax 05.56.64.06.98,
e-mail haut.bergey@wanadoo.fr ☑ ☷
☗ by appt.

CH. HAUT-BRION 2001★★★

	2.7 ha	n.c.		+76 €

(82)83 85 87 88 |89| |90| 94 95 |96| |97| 98 (99)(00)(01)

Haut-Brion belongs to the fine-wine aristocracy. Originating in the 16th century under the aegis of Jean de Pontac, it quickly became the influential model of the "New French Clarets" so prized by the English in the 17th century and glorified by Thomas Jefferson in the 18th. Its illustrious proprietors have included Talleyrand. In 1935, it was acquired by an important New York banker, Clarence Dillon. Today, his granddaughter watches over its future, together with her son, Prince Robert of Luxemburg. This 2000 white is unquestionably one of the best the cru has produced. The density of the golden colour and its highlights are very appealing. The bouquet is elegantly oaky and sufficiently discreet to allow aromas of flowers and lemons to come through. The palate has notes of well-ripened citrus fruits, together with a continuation of lemony freshness. The body has fullness, with all the richness one would expect, yet is never heavy. The supreme distinction lies in the finish, which is informed by a hint of ginger that gives it great originality. Already very good to drink now, this Haut-Brion will wait (five years or more). It was much mentioned as a possible *coup de coeur*.

☞ Dom. Clarence Dillon, Ch. Haut-Brion, 33608 Pessac Cedex, tel. 05.56.00.29.30, fax 05.56.98.75.14,
e-mail info@haut-brion.com
☗ by appt.

CH. HAUT-BRION 2000★★★

	1er cru clas.	43.2 ha	n.c.		+76 €

73 74 |75| 76 77 78 |79| 81 (82)|83| 84 |85| |86| 87 88 89(90) |91| |92| |93| 94(95)(96)(97)(98)99(00)

This wine marries power and distinction. The bouquet is of a rare subtlety, with melting tones of fruits and oak that create more an emotion than a sensation. Perfection to the very end, this full, round, dense wine has an elegance that is as superb as the long-lingering character of the finish. This truly great wine will require patience (seven to ten years), but will be well worth the wait.

☞ Dom. Clarence Dillon, Ch. Haut-Brion, 33608 Pessac Cedex, tel. 05.56.00.29.30, fax 05.56.98.75.14,
e-mail info@haut-brion.com
☗ by appt.

LES PLANTIERS DU HAUT-BRION 2001★

	n.c.	n.c.		15–23 €

Another Haut-Brion label mainly of Sémillon (98%, with 2% Muscadelle), worthy of its origins. A beautiful pale yellow colour, it has a developing bouquet in which the evident presence of oak nevertheless allows fine notes of acacia flowers and beeswax to filter through. The grapey, charming palate is no less rich: notes of linden blossom and vine flowers mix with those of citrus fruits to create an overall elegance.

☞ Dom. Clarence Dillon, Ch. Haut-Brion, 33608 Pessac Cedex, tel. 05.56.00.29.30, fax 05.56.98.75.14,
e-mail info@haut-brion.com
☗ by appt.

CH. HAUT-NOUCHET 2000★

	27 ha	71,900		15–23 €

This cru, from the vast hectarage assembled by Lucien Lurton, is now in the hands of his son, Louis Lurton, who has chosen to cultivate organically. This 2000 has a garnet colour that marks out a powerful wine, but it is still a little closed: the finely oaky bouquet includes some early notes of berry fruits. The richness and good balance on the palate indicate that the wine will open further in time. Wait four or five years.
➤ SCEA Louis Lurton, Ch. Haut-Nouchet, 33650 Martillac, tel. 05.56.72.69.74, fax 05.56.72.56.11, e-mail chateau.haut-nouchet@libertysurf.fr

CH. LAFARGUE 2000★★

	18.17 ha	120,000		11–15 €

This cru, a family property, remains faithful to the spirit of Bordeaux by virtue of its varietal diversity. The complexity of the bouquet reveals the success of that approach. Notes of chocolate and spices mix with scents of noble wood (sandalwood, cask wood) to produce a superb nose. The palate is equally expressive. The structure and body are full and rich in tannins which indicate good keeping potential.
➤ Jean-Pierre Leymarie, 5, imp. de Domy, 33650 Martillac, tel. 05.56.72.72.30, fax 05.56.72.64.61, e-mail chateau.lafargue@wanadoo.fr 🅥
🍷 by appt.

CH. LAFONT MENAUT 2001★

	3 ha	20,000		8–11 €

Made by the Carbonnieux team, this wine has a lovely crystal-clear appearance and an evolving fresh bouquet which mixes notes of menthol, lemon and liquorice. After an uncomplicated attack, the palate reveals great fruitiness and is expressive of great finesse, finishing on a floral, rich, silken note. Though ready to drink now, this 2001 will keep. The Jury also commended the **red 2000**.
➤ SCEA Philibert Perrin, Ch. Lafont Menaut, 33850 Léognan, tel. 05.57.96.56.20, fax 05.57.96.59.19, e-mail chateau.carbonnieux@wanadoo.fr 🅥
🍷 by appt.

CH. LATOUR-MARTILLAC 2000★★

Cru clas.	30 ha	150,000		23–30 €

79 81(82)83 84 85 86 87 88 |89| |90| 91 92 |93| |94| 95 96 |97| 98 99 **00**

The terroir, grape varieties and methods of work on this cru are all in the Bordeaux spirit, and have given rise to some great laying-down wines, like this 2000. Its deep red colour and youthful highlights, the bouquet of well-blended, complex aromas of spicy vanilla and crystallized fruits, the potent yet unctuous attack, the well-ripened tannins and remarkable length all mark this out as a wine destined for a long time in the cellar. A good representative of a second wine and of the appellation by dint of its elegance is the **red Château Lagrave-Martillac 2000 (11–15 €)** (one star), while the **red Lespault 2000 (11–15 €)** is commended.
➤ Domaines Kressmann, Ch. Latour-Martillac, 33650 Martillac, tel. 05.57.97.71.11, fax 05.57.97.71.17, e-mail latour-martillac@latour-martillac.com
🍷 by appt.
➤ Famille Jean Kressmann

CH. LATOUR-MARTILLAC 2001★

Cru clas.	10 ha	30,000		23–30 €

81 82 83 84 85 86 87(88)89 90 91 92 93 |94| 95 96 97 |98| |99| (00)(01)

Here is a 12th century tower and a vineyard that belonged to the Baroness de Montesquieu; it was acquired in 1929 by Alfred Kressmann, son of the founder of the great firm of wine-merchants established in 1871. One rare feature is that the cru possesses a plot of Sémillon dating from 1884 and still in production. This wine, though it would have benefited from a trifle more acidity, has an agreeably full palate and aromas of citrus fruits and vanilla. Also commended is the **white Lespault 2001 (11–15 €)**. Last year, this estate's Latour-Martillac white 2000 gained a *coup de coeur*.
➤ Domaines Kressmann, Ch. Latour-Martillac, 33650 Martillac, tel. 05.57.97.71.11, fax 05.57.97.71.17, e-mail latour-martillac@latour-martillac.com
🍷 by appt.

CH. LAVILLE HAUT-BRION 2001★★★

Cru clas.	3.7 ha	n.c.		+76 €

81 82 83 |85| 87 88 (89)|90| 92 |93| |94| |95| |96| |97| (98) 99 **00**(01)

Although, compared to the other crus belonging to the Haut-Brion group, this cru is not very sizeable, it cannot, however, be described as unimportant. Never was that truer than in relation to this marvellously classic vintage. The colour is a remarkable straw yellow with lemon highlights, and the bouquet is of citrus fruits to which notes of brioche and butter bring a sweetness of their own. After a superb attack, the palate reveals a breadth of fullness and richness that is sustained by a charmingly fine, elegant, supple structure. It offers a crunchy grapeyness before finishing on fresh notes of white peaches and lemon. Keep this wine in reserve for ten to twelve years and drink with high-class fish dishes (turbot or sole) or seafood (lobster, crayfish, scallops).
➤ Dom. Clarence Dillon, Ch. Haut-Brion, 33608 Pessac Cedex, tel. 05.56.00.29.30, fax 05.56.98.75.14, e-mail info@haut-brion.com
🍷 by appt.

CH. LA LOUVIERE 2000★★★

	30 ha	150,000		23–30 €

75 80 81 82 83 85 86 |88| |89| (90)91 92 |93| |94| 95 96 97 98 99(00)

All the refinement of the château, a superb 18th century building designed by François Lhote, is to be found in this wine whose colour is rich with promise. The bouquet has finesse and subtlety, with notes of chocolate, vanilla and small black berry fruits, while the palate contains all the corresponding flavours. Notes of chocolate and blackcurrant, well-extracted tannins, a full, silky body, and a perfectly constructed finish all provide a sure sign of good, durable keeping quality. The supremely elegant second wine, the **red L de La Louvière 2000 (11–15 €)**, which obtained two stars, is almost as good as the first. Its tannic concentration promises it a good future.
➤ André Lurton, Ch. Bonnet, 33420 Grézillac, tel. 05.57.25.58.58, fax 05.57.74.98.59, e-mail andrelurton@andrelurton.com 🅥
🍷 by appt.

CH. LA LOUVIERE 2001★

	8 ha	40,000	▥	23–30 €

86 88 89(90) 91 92 93 |94| |95| |96| |97| **98 99** |00| |01|

Without rivalling its red counterpart, this wine (15% Sémillon, 85% Sauvignon) has all the finesse and delicacy which one associates with the appellation, and which inform the tasting throughout from bouquet to finish.

🐓 André Lurton, Ch. Bonnet, 33420 Grézillac, tel. 05.57.25.58.58, fax 05.57.74.98.59, e-mail andrelurton@ andrelurton.com ☑
🍷 by appt.

CH. MALARTIC-LAGRAVIERE 2001★★★

	Cru clas.	4 ha	8,000	▥	23–30 €

97 |98| |99| |00| (01)

The handsome white classical-style château and its wine-making facilities in recent years undergone thorough renovation. Working methods, too, have been updated, as the quality of this wine demonstrates. The pale, limpid, shining appearance is as irresistible as the attractively deep, Sauvignon-style bouquet. Nor does the palate disappoint: rich, full, and extremely well-balanced, it has a delicious finish of toast and fruity flavours. This rich, complex wine will gain from three years' storage. The second label, the **white Le Sillage de Malartic 2001 (11–15 €)**, has a one-star rating for its delightful structure and freshness.

🐓 Ch. Malartic-Lagravière, 33 av. de Mont-de-Marsan, 33850 Léognan, tel. 05.56.64.75.08, fax 05.56.64.99.66, e-mail malartic-lagravière@malartic-lagravière.
🍷 by appt.
🐓 A.-A. Bonnie

CH. MALARTIC-LAGRAVIERE 2000★

	Cru clas.	23 ha	61,000	▥	30–38 €

64 66(70) 71 75 76 79 81 82 83 |85| |86| |88| |89| |90| |91| 92 |93| 95 96 |97| 98 99 00

Methods of vinification adapted to the terroir (a superb outcrop of Graves) mean that Malartic are able to offer wines suitable for long storage. This vintage is no exception. The complexity of the bouquet and the tannic structure, very evident at the tasting, confirm the impression given by the very youthful garnet colour: five to six years in the cellar will be fully necessary before drinking.

🐓 Ch. Malartic-Lagravière, 43, av. de Mont-de-Marsan, 33850 Léognan, tel. 05.56.64.75.08, fax 05.56.64.99.66, e-mail malartic-lagravière@malartic-lagravière.
🍷 by appt.

CH. MANCEDRE 2000★

	5 ha	7,000	▥	15–23 €

Produced on a small estate, this wine has a very beautiful appearance, but the nose is somewhat reticent. This is but a passing phenomenon. As soon as the wine hits the palate, its qualities all declare themselves unambiguously. Unctuous and well-structured, the body is sustained by silky tannins to create an elegant synthesis which will keep well.

🐓 SCEV Héritiers Dubos, Ch. Mancèdre, 33850 Léognan, tel. 05.57.74.30.52, fax 05.57.74.39.96
🍷 by appt.
🐓 J. Trocard

DOM. DE MERLET 2000★

	4.2 ha	19,000	▤ ▥	8–11 €

Replanted in 1989 after a century's absence caused by phylloxera, this cru's vines are still rather young. Nevertheless they are already yielding some attractive wines, like this 2000, with its promising garnet colour. Full, well-balanced, and rich in aromas of fruit, leather, tobacco and musk, it has a long peppery, chocolaty finish that is a guarantee of good keeping quality.

🐓 Indivision Tauzin, 35, cours du Mal-Leclerc, 33850 Léognan, tel. 05.56.64.77.74, fax 05.56.64.77.74 ☑
🍷 by appt.

CH. MIREBEAU 2000★

	4.28 ha	26,000	▥	15–23 €

This cru, which belonged to Alexandre Dumas's family, is a small wine-growing enclave surrounded by development. That has not prevented this wine having a real richness of structure and aroma. The robust tannic structure could have done with a trifle more fleshiness, but this is a wine that will have no problems in being laid down. Do not open for at least five years.

🐓 Cyril Dubrey, SCEA Ch. d'Ardennes, rte de Mirebeau, 33650 Martillac, tel. 05.56.72.61.76, fax 05.56.62.43.67 ☑
🍷 by appt.

CH. LA MISSION HAUT-BRION 2000★★★

	Cru clas.	n.c.	n.c.	▥	+76 €

78 80 81 |82| |83| 84 |85| |86| 87 |88| 89 (90) 92 |93| |94| 95 (96) **97 98 99** (00)

Like Haut-Brion, which acquired the 20 ha of the cru in November 1983, the La Mission vintage belongs to the world of the legendary fine wines that wine-lovers' dreams are made of. The colour is so intense it is almost black, while the bouquet of well-ripened grapes and palate of cherry, blackberry and bilberry flavours give an impression of finesse. There is plenty of substance here; dense, well-structured and tannic (but not excessively so), with extreme generosity, the body is superb, leaving no doubt that this wine will keep well. The cru's second label, **La Chapelle de La Mission Haut-Brion red 2000 (30–38 €)**, gained a one-star rating. Like the first wine, it has a distinctive elegance.

🐓 Dom. Clarence Dillon, Ch. Haut-Brion, 33608 Pessac Cedex, tel. 05.56.00.29.30, fax 05.56.98.75.14, e-mail info@haut-brion.com
🍷 by appt.

CH. OLIVIER 2000★

	Cru clas.	31.82 ha	126,000	▥	15–23 €

82 83 |85| |86| 87 |88| |89| |90| 91 92 |93| |94| 95 96 |97| 98 99 00

Here there are genuine medieval towers and a moat that goes round the 12th century château. It is said that the Black Prince imprisoned Du Guesclin here in 1382. Now entirely given over to wine, this cru offers a vintage of a deep and intense colour in harmony with the bouquet, which exhales powerful notes of red berry fruits, spices and leather. Rounded and full, supported by sturdy tannins, the palate has a well-blended elegance. This wine would be the perfect accompaniment to game or meats served with a wine sauce. Less powerful, yet nonetheless distinguished is the second wine, **Olivier red 2000 (8–10 €)**, which is commended.

🐓 Jean-Jacques de Bethmann, Ch. Olivier, 175, av. de Bordeaux, 33850 Léognan, tel. 05.56.64.73.31, fax 05.56.64.54.23, e-mail chateau-olivier@wanadoo.fr ☑
🍷 by appt.

CH. LE PAPE

L'Excellence 2000★

	5 ha	30,000	▥	11–15 €

The finesse and fruitiness of the bouquet comes from the large proportion of Merlot (70%) grapes used to make this wine. The aromatic range is further enhanced by notes of spices and roses. The attack is powerful and, though the palate is still a little harsh, the fleshiness and richness of the body will gradually efface the tannins' austerity. Given its strong construction, this wine will gain from some keeping.

🐓 Patrick Monjanel, Ch. Le Pape, 33850 Léognan, tel. 05.56.64.10.90, fax 05.56.64.17.78, e-mail pmonjanel@chateaulepape.com ☑
🍷 by appt.

CH. PAPE CLEMENT 2000★

	Cru clas.	30 ha	88,000	▥	+76 €

75 78 79 80 (81) 82 83 85 |86| 87 |88| 89 |90| |91| 92 |93| |94| **95 96 97 98 99** 00

Though the château is neo-Gothic (19th century), the estate is medieval in origin and belonged to an Avignon pope who was previously a bishop of Bordeaux, Bertrand de Got. The 28 months of maturing in oak casks have left their mark, which is still noticeable, but the grapes are nonetheless able to express themselves. Rich, deep, and classy, the grapey body appeals to both nose and palate. The long, complex finish enhances the whole tasting and confirms that this wine really needs a few more years' storage in order to attain its definitive character.

↝ Bernard Magrez, Ch. Pape Clément, 216, av. du Dr-Nancel-Penard, 33600 Pessac, tel. 05.57.26.38.38, fax 05.57.26.38.39, e-mail chateau@pape-clement.com 🖂
℞ by appt.

CH. PAPE CLEMENT 2001★★

| | 2 ha | 4,500 | 📖 | 46–76 € |

92(93)94 96 |97| 98 99 |00| 01

While no novice to the art of communication, Bernard Magrez is also an expert creator of fine wines. It is impossible to think otherwise, when one is faced with the fresh look of this wine, which blends Muscadelle (3%) with Sémillon (48%) and Sauvignon. The bouquet clearly reveals the way in which the wine has been matured, but it nonetheless has a complexity of white fruits. The palate has a richness and power which are self-evident guarantors of this superb wine's future.

↝ Bernard Magrez, Ch. Pape Clément, 216, av. du Dr-Nancel-Penard, 33600 Pessac, tel. 05.57.26.38.38, fax 05.57.26.38.39, e-mail chateau@pape-clement.com
℞ by appt.

CH. PICQUE CAILLOU 2000★★

| ■ | 14 ha | 80,000 | 📖 | 15–23 € |

81 86 |88| |89| |90| 93 94 95 |96| 98 99 00

This is the last remaining vineyard in Mérignac, the AOC's northernmost village. It is valiantly holding out against urbanization despite the presence of Chaban-Delmas airport. The colour is dark and plain but promising; the nose is complex and appetizing, exhaling aromas of fruit and toast, with hints of smoke and spice (sweet spices). The palate is no less rich, thanks to its winey, concentrated body sustained by rounded tannins. It is a wine that will keep for a long time: six or seven years, or even longer. The white 2001 (11–15 €) was singled out.

↝ GFA Ch. Picque Caillou, av. Pierre-Mendès-France, 33700 Mérignac, tel. 05.56.47.37.98, fax 05.56.97.99.37, e-mail chateaupicquecaillou@wanadoo.fr ☑
℞ by appt.
↝ Paulin et Isabelle Calvet

CH. PONTAC MONPLAISIR 2000★★

| ■ | 11 ha | 55,000 | 📖 | 11–15 € |

92 94 95 (96)|97 |98| 00

While several châteaux have been encircled by the town, Pontac is surrounded by bypasses. It nonetheless offers a really lovely 2000. The dark glints of the colour are indicators of power. The bouquet is an expressive marriage of very ripe fruit and musky, woodland notes. After a supple attack, the palate reveals its ample, fleshy character, sustained by silky, sappy tannins to create a voluptuous effect. Imposing and lingering, the finish has gorgeous hints of coffee and spices. The white 2001 was singled out.

↝ Jean et Alain Maufras, Ch. Pontac Monplaisir, 33140 Villenave-d'Ornon, tel. 05.56.87.08.21, fax 05.56.87.35.10 ☑
℞ by appt.

CH. DE ROCHEMORIN 2000★★

| ■ | 40 ha | 180,000 | 📖 | 11–15 € |

85 86 88 89 90 91 92 93 94 |95| |96| |97| 98 99 00

Before long this cru's white will see the light of day in a brand new winery. Even if this vintage had to make do with the old, it nonetheless shows fine qualities. The colour is intense, almost black, and the complex bouquet hints at leather and toast as well as redcurrant. The attack is full and ripe, while the tannins are not over-heavy. Here is a wine that will keep very well, three to five years, perhaps much longer. The white 2001 is highly aromatic with notes of vanilla, dried fruits and nuts, and honey; it is rated one-star for its well rounded, generous body.

↝ André Lurton, Ch. Bonnet, 33420 Grézillac, tel. 05.57.25.58.58, fax 05.57.74.98.59, e-mail andrelurton@andrelurton.com ☑
℞ by appt.

CH. DE ROUILLAC 2000★★

| ■ | 7.5 ha | 35,000 | 📖 ♦ | 15–23 € |

98 99 00

The famous urban planner having once owned this cru, nobody will be surprised to discover a château corresponding to Haussmann's architectural canons. With its lovely plum colour and a bouquet that allies finesse, richness and complexity, this 2000 has a strong personality. Sustained by powerful tannins and a well-judged oakiness, the fleshiness, richness and balance of the palate point to a wine that may be enjoyed young, yet also has good ageing potential.

↝ Vignobles Lafragette, Ch. de Rouillac, 33610 Canéjan, tel. 05.56.73.17.82, fax 05.56.09.02.87 ☑
℞ by appt.

CH. SEGUIN 2000★★

| ■ | 17 ha | 30,000 | 📖 | 11–15 € |

This estate combines traditional and modern methods to produce wines of quality. The 2000 has a very handsome youthful dark colour that charms all the more in view of the finesse of the bouquet, which mixes notes of very ripe fruits, sweet spices and blond tobacco. The palate has an oaky presence that respects the fruit and does not impair its elegance. The rich grapeyness, warm tannic texture of the palate and the long-lingering flavours on which it finishes leave no doubt about the ageing potential of this wine.

↝ SC Dom. de Seguin, chem. de la House, 33610 Canéjan, tel. 05.56.75.02.43, fax 05.56.89.35.41, e-mail chateau-seguin@wanadoo.fr ☑
℞ ev. day 8am–12 noon 1pm–7pm; Sat. Sun. by appt.

CH. SMITH HAUT LAFITTE 2000★★

| ■ Cru clas. | 44 ha | 90,000 | 📖 | 46–76 € |

61 62 70 71 72 73(75)80 82 83 85 86 87 |88| |89| |90| |91| 92 93 94 95 |96| 97 98 99 00

When they bought Smith 12 years ago, the Cathiard family aimed to bring the red Pessac-Léognan up to the standard of the white. They can congratulate themselves on achieving their aim with this vintage grown in the year with the magic number. With its red lamé appearance, the wine has a developing bouquet of complexity and finesse which plays on notes of well-ripened black fruits and roasting coffee. The powerful palate is remarkably well balanced between fruit and oak. Throughout the tasting, ripe Cabernet Sauvignon aromas express the personality of this wine, which is very authentic to its terroir. Cellaring for three to four years will be necessary for it to reach its optimum. More supple, yet perfectly put together, with richness and well-extracted tannins, the second wine, Les Hauts de Smith 2000 (15–23 €) obtained a one-star rating.

↝ SARL Daniel Cathiard, Ch. Smith Haut Lafitte, 33650 Martillac, tel. 05.57.83.11.22, fax 05.57.83.11.21, e-mail f.cathiard@smith-haut-lafitte.com ☑
℞ by appt.

CH. SMITH HAUT LAFITTE 2001★★

| | 11 ha | 40,000 | 📖 | 30–38 € |

88 89 90 91 92 93 94 95 96 97(98)99 |00| 01

With their Vinothérapie and Sources de Caudalies, the Cathiards have not stopped developing the activities of this cru which goes back to the 14th century. With its 5% Sauvignon Gris grapes, this wine is one of the great whites of the AOC. Its very limpid appearance and really lovely Sauvignon-style bouquet of citrus fruits give an impression of great freshness. Rich, complex, and silky, with an overtone of exotic fruits, the palate has excellent balance which confirms the initial impression.

↝ SARL Daniel Cathiard, Ch. Smith Haut Lafitte, 33650 Martillac, tel. 05.57.83.11.22, fax 05.57.83.11.21, e-mail f.cathiard@smith-haut-lafitte.com ☑
℞ by appt.

BORDEAUX

DOM. DE LA SOLITUDE 2000★

| | n.c. | n.c. | ❚❚❚ | 15–23 € |

This cru still belongs to the nuns of the Congregation of the Holy Family, and is managed by the Chevalier team. This 2000 has a dark colour which contrasts with the finesse of the bouquet of ripened fruits and flowers (peony) with overtones of vanilla. The palatal tannins are still on the young side, but guarantee the wine's potential for further development. The estate's **Solitude white 2001** is commended.
➤ SC Dom. de Chevalier, Dom. de La Solitude, 33650 Martillac, tel. 05.56.72.74.74, fax 05.56.72.52.00, e-mail olivierbernard@domainedelasolitude.com ☑
✝ by appt.
➤ Com. religieuse de Ste Famille

CH. LE THIL COMTE CLARY 2000★

| | 8.5 ha | 50,000 | ❚❚❚ | 15–23 € |

In 1990, Jean de Laitre, a medical student, chose to establish a vineyard on the family's property: the vines are 70% Merlot because the soil is mainly limestone-clay. The result is this dark ruby wine, which is still very young. The nose is elegant, with smoky notes of red fruits. The palate has a rich, mouth-filling vinosity, with an attractive evolution of flavours that continue through an agreeably long finish. Wait three or four years before drinking this high-quality wine.
➤ Ch. le Thil Comte Clary, Le Thil, 33850 Léognan, tel. 05.56.30.01.02, fax 05.56.30.04.32, e-mail jean-de-laitre@chateau-le-thil.com ☑
✝ by appt.
➤ Barons de Laitre

CH. LA TOUR HAUT-BRION 2000★

| | Cru clas. | 4.9 ha | n.c. | ❚❚❚ | 38–46 € |

78 79 80 81 (82) |83| 84 |85| |86| 87 |88| |89| |90| 92 |93| |94| 95 96 |97| 98 99 00

This *cru classé* benefits from a fine terroir. Once again, it has produced an attractive wine. The colour of this 2000 is a promising dark garnet, and the bouquet mixes red fruits and sandalwood. The palate is a powerful synthesis of fullness, fleshiness and delicacy. The oak structure calls for further cellaring of five to seven years.
➤ Dom. Clarence Dillon, Ch. Haut-Brion, 33608 Pessac Cedex, tel. 05.56.00.29.30, fax 05.56.98.75.14, e-mail info@haut-brion.com
✝ by appt.

CH. TOUR LEOGNAN 2001★★

| | 10 ha | 40,000 | ❚❚❚ | 8–11 € |

96 97 99 00 01

For this vintage the Carbonnieux team, who own this cru, have chosen to increase the proportion of Sauvignon to 65% (with 35% Sémillon). The bouquet noticeably reflects the change, and the palate seems none the worse for it. Full and long-lasting as well as fine and fresh, this wine is already very attractive, though it has good keeping potential. The **red 2000** is rated one star. It will need to be laid down for three or four years before drinking.
➤ SC des Grandes Graves, Ch. Carbonnieux, 33850 Léognan, tel. 05.57.96.56.20, fax 05.57.96.59.19, e-mail chateau.carbonnieux@wanadoo.fr ☑
✝ by appt.
➤ Antony Perrin

Wines selected but not starred

CH. BROWN 2000

| | 14.21 ha | 98,200 | ❚❚❚ | 23–30 € |

➤ SA Ch. Brown, allée John-Lewis-Brown, 33850 Léognan, tel. 05.56.87.08.10, fax 05.56.87.87.34, e-mail chateau.brown@wanadoo.fr ☑
➤ Bernard Barthe

CLOS MARSALETTE 2001

| | 0.6 ha | 3,000 | ❚ ⚱ | 11–15 € |

➤ SCEA Marsalette, 31, rte de Loustalade, 33850 Léognan, tel. 05.56.64.09.93, fax 05.56.64.10.08 ☑
✝ by appt.
➤ Boutemy-Von Nepperg-Sarpoulet

CH. D'EYRAN 2000

| | 10 ha | 55,000 | ❚❚❚ | 11–15 € |

➤ SCEA Ch. d'Eyran, 33650 Saint-Médard-d'Eyrans, tel. 05.56.65.51.59, fax 05.56.65.43.78, e-mail stephane.savigneux@wanadoo.fr ☑
✝ by appt.
➤ de Sèze

CH. LA GARDE 2000

| | 44 ha | 138,000 | ❚❚❚ | 15–23 € |

(90) 91 93 94 (95) 96 |97| 98 99 00

➤ Vignobles Dourthe, 35, rue de Bordeaux, 33290 Parempuyre, tel. 05.56.35.53.00, fax 05.56.35.53.29, e-mail contact@cvbg.com ☑
✝ by appt.

CH. HAUT LAGRANGE 2000

| | 11.5 ha | 60,000 | ❚❚❚ ⚱ | 11–15 € |

➤ Francis Boutemy, SA Ch. Haut-Lagrange, 31, rte de Loustalade, 33850 Léognan, tel. 05.56.64.09.93, fax 05.56.64.10.08, e-mail chateau-haut-lagrange@wanadoo.fr ☑
✝ by appt.

CH. HAUT-PLANTADE 2000

| | 6 ha | 30,000 | ❚❚❚ | 15–23 € |

➤ GAEC Plantade Père et Fils, Ch. Haut-Plantade, 33850 Léognan, tel. 05.56.64.07.09, fax 05.56.64.02.24, e-mail hautplantade@wanadoo.fr ☑
✝ by appt.

CH. LARRIVET-HAUT-BRION 2000

| | 45 ha | 110,000 | ❚❚❚ | 30–38 € |

➤ Ch. Larrivet-Haut-Brion, rue Haut-Brion, 33850 Léognan, tel. 05.56.64.75.51, fax 05.56.64.53.47 ☑
✝ by appt.
➤ Ph. Gervoson

CH. LE SARTRE 2001

| | 7 ha | 30,000 | ❚❚❚ | 8–11 € |

92 93 94 95 96 97 |98| |99| |00| |01|

➤ Ch. Le Sartre, 33850 Léognan, tel. 05.57.96.56.20, fax 05.57.96.59.19, e-mail chateau.carbonnieux@wanadoo.fr ☑
✝ by appt.
➤ Antony Perrin

Médoc

Médoc occupies a place apart from the rest of the Gironde region, being virtually contained within the peninsula from which it gazes across the waters of the deep Gironde estuary. The Médoc and the Médocains may thus be seen as perfect illustrations of the Aquitaine temperament: they are both self-contained yet outward-looking. It is not unusual to find small family-run vineyards alongside grand, prestigious domains belonging to powerful French or foreign companies.

The Médoc vineyards (representing only a part of the historically- and geographically-defined Médoc) occupy a strip more than 80 km long and 10 km wide. As a result, visitors can admire the great wine châteaux of the 19th century with their splendid, monumental wine stores and also make discoveries deep in the surrounding countryside. The terrain is very varied, offering flat, uniform landscapes around Margaux, hilly ridges towards Pauillac, and the entirely original world of the northern part of the Médoc, an unusual combination of terrestrial and maritime features. The area of the Médoc AOC covers about 15,400 ha.

For those who enjoy investigating places off the beaten track, the Médoc is full of unexpected surprises. But its real riches lie in the gravelly terrain that slopes gently down towards the Gironde estuary. The soil is thin and poor in natural fertilizers, an excellent medium for the production of fine wines. In addition, the topography allows perfect drainage.

The Médoc and Haute Médoc Appelations

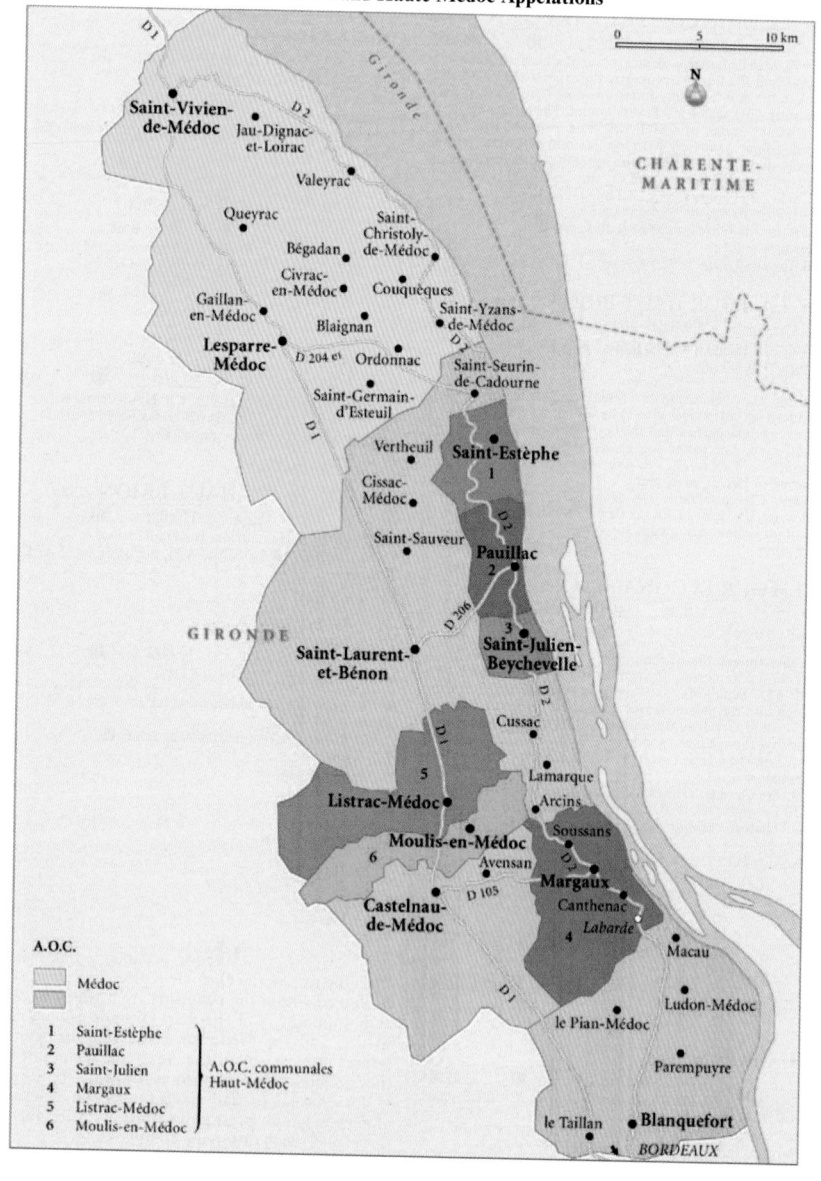

A.O.C.

Médoc

1 Saint-Estèphe
2 Pauillac
3 Saint-Julien
4 Margaux
5 Listrac-Médoc
6 Moulis-en-Médoc

A.O.C. communales
Haut-Médoc

It has become usual to divide the Médoc into the Haut Médoc, from Blanquefort to Saint-Seurin-de-Cadourne, and the Bas Médoc, from Saint-Germain-d'Esteuil to Saint-Vivien. In the first area, six Appellations Communales produce the most famous wines. Virtually all of the 60 Crus Classés are from these appellations; however, five of them are labelled only as Appellation Haut-Médoc. The Crus Classés represent approximately 25% of the vineyard area, producing 20% of the wines and more than 40% of the income. In addition to the Crus Classés, the Médoc also produces a number of château-bottled Crus Bourgeois, which enjoy an excellent reputation. There are many Caves Coopératives in the Appellation Médoc and Appellation Haut-Médoc and also in three of the Appellations Communales.

The Médoc vineyard is spread among eight AOCs, from north to south. There are two sub-regional appellations, Médoc and Haut-Médoc, comprising some 60% of the Médoc vineyards, and six Appellations Communales: Saint-Estephe, Pauillac, Saint-Julien, Listrac-Médoc, Moulis en Médoc and Margaux (totalling 40% of the Médoc vineyards). The regional appellation is Bordeaux, as in the rest of the Bordeaux wine-growing area.

Cabernet Sauvignon was the traditional Médoc grape but is now grown less than it was formerly; even so, it still accounts for 52% of the whole vineyard area. At 34%, Merlot is the second most important grape; its supple wines are of excellent quality and develop quickly so they can be drunk when still young. Cabernet Franc, which gives wine finesse, is planted on 10% of the area. The Petit Verdot and Malbec varieties are also planted, although they do not play a big role.

Médoc wines enjoy an exceptional reputation; they are among the most prestigious red wines produced either in France or in the rest of the world. They are noted for their beautiful ruby colour that takes on a tile-red hue with age, and by their fruity aromas blending the spicy notes of Cabernet with hints of vanilla from the new oak barrels. Their tannic structure is dense and full, although the wines remain elegant and soft, and their perfect balance means they age remarkably well, softening without becoming thin and gaining in bouquet and flavour.

Médoc

The whole of the Médoc vineyard (15,995 ha) has the right to the Appellation Médoc, although in practice it is used only in Bas Médoc (the northern sector of the peninsula, around Lesparre); the communes located between Blanquefort and Saint-Seurin-de-Cadourne may apply for the Appellation Haut-Médoc or for a communal appellation within the area of their specific delimited territory. Nevertheless, Appellation Médoc remains the most significant, with an area of 5,358 ha and an output of 278,474 hl in 2002.

Noted for their intense colour, Médoc wines are made using a higher percentage of Merlot than those of Haut-Médoc and the Appellations Communales. The Merlot character makes itself felt in the fruity nose and round, mouth-filling flavour of these wines, some of which, grown on isolated, gravelly ridges, can develop great finesse and tannic depth.

CH. BELLERIVE 2000★

| ■ | Cru bourg. | 13 ha | 15,000 | ▮ ⑴ | 5–8 € |

This is Annie Perrin's second vintage, and she has definitely gone up a gear. Suppleness has moved over now to make room for power, richness and chewiness. This more "masculine" character still allows for great delicacy in the bouquet, with its fine grilled notes. There is every indication of perfect maturity and good keeping potential.

➻ SCEA Ch. Bellerive-Perrin, 1, rte des Tourterelles, 33340 Valeyrac, tel. 05.56.41.52.13, fax 05.56.41.52.13 ☑
⟁ by appt.
➻ Annie Perrin

CH. BESSAN SEGUR 2000★

| ■ | Cru bourg. | 41.5 ha | 303,000 | ▮ ⑴ ♦ | 5–8 € |

Having modernized the vat and barrel-store at great expense in 1998, this cru shows with this 2000 that it has both the will and skill to succeed. The bouquet is still excessively oaky, but this does not swamp the warm notes of red stewed fruits and prune. The palate is full and straightforward, sustained by a structure of good tannins that call for three or four years' further ageing.

➻ Rémi Lacombe, Bessan Ségur, 33340 Civrac-en-Médoc, tel. 05.56.41.56.91, fax 05.56.41.59.06, e-mail scflacombe@free.fr ☑
⟁ by appt.

CH. LE BOSCQ

Vieilles Vignes 2000★

| ■ | Cru bourg. | 27 ha | 50,000 | ▮ ⑴ ♦ | 11–15 € |

Quietly but surely, Jean-Michel Lapalu and his friends are building a veritable wine-growing empire. This cru, vinified in the wineries of Patache d'Aux since 1972, reveals their professionalism. Though the tannins are still austere, the wine's fullness and growing strength on the palate indicate good keeping potential.

➻ SA Patache d'Aux, 1, rue du 19-Mars, 33340 Bégadan, tel. 05.56.41.50.18, fax 05.56.41.54.65, e-mail info@adomaines-lapalu.com ☑
⟁ by appt.
➻ Jean-Michel Lapalu

CH. BOURNAC 2000★

| ■ | Cru bourg. | 8 ha | 42,000 | ▮ ⑴ ♦ | 11–15 € |

93 94 |95| |96| 98 99 00

This cru, a mainstay of the appellation, offers a 2000 very typical of its AOC and year. A blend of equal proportions of Merlot and Cabernet Sauvignon, the wine is partly (10%) vat-matured, with the remaining majority spending 12 months in oak. The aromas are beautifully complex, with a range dominated by black fruits and liquorice. The palate is supple, round, full, and well-constructed, with silky tannins. Good for keeping from four to six years.

➻ SA Bruno Secret, 11, rte des Petites-Granges, 33340 Civrac-en-Médoc, tel. 06.07.30.68.03, fax 05.56.73.59.23, e-mail bournac@terre-net.fr ☑
⟁ by appt.

CH. LE BREUIL RENAISSANCE 2000★

| ■ | | 13 ha | 85,000 | ⑴ | 5–8 € |

This year's vintage sees an increase in the percentage of Merlot (now in the majority at 60%). Even so, the Cabernet makes its presence felt with a characteristic note of green pepper and powerful, attractive tannins. Four or five years' storage is definitely recommended. Also rated one star is **Le**

Breuil Excellence 2000 (8–11 €), which is very obviously a new-cask wine.
☛ SCA Philippe Bérard,
6, rte du Bana, 33340 Bégadan, tel. 05.56.41.50.67,
fax 05.56.41.36.77, e-mail phil.berard@wanadoo.fr ☑
☖ ev. day 9am–5pm; Sat. Sun. by appt.

CH. DES BROUSTERAS
Vieilli en fût de chêne 2000★

■ Cru bourg.	25 ha	190,000	■ ⑪ ♦	8–11 €

This sizeable estate is divided equally between Merlot and Cabernet vines. Merlot appears to dominate the bouquet with its softer, fruitier character. But the palate, with its robust yet excellent tannins, reveals the strong presence of Cabernet grapes. Three to four years' cellaring is advisable to allow the oak to blend.
☛ SCF Ch. des Brousteras, 2, rue de l'Ancienne-Douane, 33340 Saint-Yzans-de-Médoc, tel. 05.56.09.05.44, fax 05.56.09.04.21,
e-mail chateaudesbrousteras@terre-net.fr ☑
☖ by appt.
☛ Renouil

CH. LA CARDONNE 2000★★

■ Cru bourg.	87 ha	421,000	■ ⑪ ♦	11–15 €

88 89 90 **94 |95| |96|** 97 |98| **99 00**

This *cru*, which belongs to one of the appellation's biggest estates (125 ha), is also one of its mainstays. Nobody could doubt it after tasting this wine. Engagingly purple in colour, it has an attractive bouquet of toast followed by black fruits (blackberry) and red berry fruits. Mellow, full, and substantial, the palate has excellent tannic presence, rich and soft. Wait three to five years. In the meantime, in a year's time you could open a bottle of their **Château Cardus 2000 (8–11 €)**, which is singled out for its toothsome body and well-trained tannins.
☛ Les Domaines CGR, rte de la Cardonne, 33340 Blaignan, tel. 05.56.73.31.51, fax 05.56.73.31.52, e-mail cgr@domaines-cgr.com ☑
☖ ev. day except Sat. Sun. 8.30am–12 noon 1.30pm–5pm; groups by appt.

CH. CHANTEMERLE
Vieilli en fût de chêne 2000★

■	7.1 ha	56,799	■ ⑪	5–8 €

Located on the road from Vendays-Montalivet at Gaillan, this cru is only 15 or so kilometres from the Atlantic beaches. A classic Médoc, this wine is sustained by pleasant tannins, which are lively yet soft and which contribute to a well-structured synthesis. Three to four years' cellaring would be helpful.
☛ SCEA Vignoble Cruchon et Fils, 2, rte de Vendays, 33340 Gaillan-Médoc, tel. 05.56.41.69.71, fax 05.56.41.69.71 ☑
☖ ev. day 8am–8pm

CH. DAVID 2000★★

■ Cru bourg.	11 ha	40,000	⑪	8–11 €

This cru, overlooked by a pretty 18th century house, regularly produces good wines and has a real success with this 2000. Beautifully dark, it has a powerful bouquet of oak, stewed fruits and vanilla. After a sumptuous attack, the palate is round, spacious, dense and full, with a host of different flavours ranging from grapes to spices. A remarkable wine, ideal for laying down.
☛ EARL Coutreau, Ch. David, 40, Grande-Rue, 33590 Vensac, tel. 05.56.09.44.62, fax 05.56.09.59.09, e-mail chateaudavid@online.fr ☑
☖ ev. day except Sun. 9am–12.30pm 2pm–6.30pm; cl. Oct.

EPICURE
Elevé en fût de chêne 2000★

■	n.c.	28,500	⑪	8–11 €

The flagship of the firm established by Bernard Pujol in 1996, this brand covers several appellations. The Médoc is still strongly imprinted by the oak both in the bouquet and on the palate. It has not yet attained its final character. On the other hand, the tannins indicate that it has good potential to change further. It will be essential to leave this wine in the cellar for some considerable time so that it can achieve harmony and balance.
☛ SARL Bordeaux Vins Sélection, 27, rue Roullet, 33800 Bordeaux, tel. 05.57.35.12.35, fax 05.57.35.12.36, e-mail bvs.grands.crus@wanadoo.fr
☛ Bernard Pujol

CH. D'ESCURAC 2000★★

■ Cru bourg.	12 ha	60,000	⑪	11–15 €

This vintage has put Cabernet Sauvignon in the ascendancy (60% as opposed to 40% Merlot). It was a good decision, as the dense tannins reveal. A lovely ruby colour with purple glints, it has a complex range of aromas: notes of blackberry and blackcurrant are clothed in an oakiness of quality. A well-balanced, classy, genuine Médoc, which will be ready in seven to ten years' time. In the meantime, drink their **Château Haut-Myles 2000 (5–8 €)**, which is commended and is ready to drink now.
☛ Jean-Marc Landureau, Ch. d'Escurac, 33340 Civrac-en-Médoc, tel. 05.56.41.50.81, fax 05.56.41.36.48 ☑
☖ by appt.

CH. FONTIS 2000★

■ Cru bourg.	10 ha	50,000	⑪	11–15 €

Thirty-eight metres up, with a good view over the Gironde estuary, this cru has an attractive terroir that has produced this classy 2000 with its character of ripe fruits, vanilla, cocoa, caramel and spices, sustained by well-blended tannins. The finish is long and fresh, indicating that three years' storage will improve the wine still further.
☛ Vincent Boivert, Ch. Fontis, 33340 Ordonnac, tel. 05.56.73.30.30, fax 05.56.73.30.31 ☑
☖ by appt.

CH. GARANCE HAUT GRENAT 2000★

■	4.1 ha	15,000	⑪	8–11 €

Made in a winery fewer than 300 m from the Gironde, from grapes grown on the Butte de By, this wine is unquestionably of fine origin. Its worth is evident throughout the tasting: very intense colour; a powerful and complex bouquet mixing all the fruits of the forest; a palate sustained by good tannins; fresh flavours of ripe grapes. Open in two to four years' time.
☛ Laurent Rebes, 14, rte de la Reille, 33340 Bégadan, tel. 05.56.41.37.61, fax 05.56.41.37.61, e-mail l.rebes@free.fr ☑
☖ by appt.

CH. GRAND BERTIN DE SAINT CLAIR 2000★★

■ Cru bourg.	2.57 ha	19,900	⑪	5–8 €

A tiny property established in 1998 by the partnership of a wine-grower and a law specialist. Their joint enthusiasm for vines and wines has borne fruit in this highly successful 2000. A real fun wine, its youth is evident from its purplish-blue colour and the truly delightful bouquet in which aromas of violets mingle with well-judged oakiness. The palate is rich in flavours and well constructed, ending in a lovely blackcurrant finish. Leave in the cellar for four or five years before drinking.
☛ SCEA Ch. Grand Bertin de Saint Clair, 10, rte de l'Esparre, 33340 Bégadan, tel. 05.56.41.57.75, fax 05.56.41.53.22, e-mail compagnetvins@wanadoo.fr ☑
☖ ev. day except Sat. Sun. 8am–12 noon 2pm–6pm

CH. LE GRAND SIGOGNAC
Elevé en fût de chêne 2000★

■	5 ha	32,400	■ ⑪	5–8 €

Following its quest for improvements in quality, this little cru offers a 2000 with the millennial year's characteristic garnet colour. Though the bouquet is still a little discreet and discernibly oaky, it has a strong palate with plenty of sappiness and well-clothed tannins. A true Médoc.
☛ Philippe Olivier, Le Grand Sigognac, 33340 Saint-Yzans-de-Médoc, tel. 05.56.09.06.38, fax 05.56.09.06.38

CH. GRIVIERE 2000★★★

■ Cru bourg. 18 ha 50,000 🍾▯▮↧ 11–15 €
93 94 **95** 96 |97| 98 **99**⟨00⟩

MIS EN BOUTEILLE AU CHÂTEAU
2000

CHÂTEAU GRIVIÈRE
MÉDOC
APPELLATION MÉDOC CONTRÔLÉE

750 ML Les Bourgeois ALC. 13% by VOL.
C.G.R. PROPRIETAIRE À BLAIGNAN (GIRONDE) FRANCE
RED BORDEAUX WINE · PRODUCE OF FRANCE

With Cardonne, this *cru* is at the core of the large collection of Médoc crus owned by the Domaines CGR. It is also its finest ambassador, as this superb 2000 testifies. Its attractive dark colour is full of promises that the bouquet and palate go on to keep. The bouquet is beautifully complex and of great finesse (soft fruits that are ever so slightly chocolaty and toasted). The palate is rounded, fleshy, full, and opulent, with a richness of high-quality tannic sensations. Its energy and classiness would suit a celebration meal a few years hence with special dishes like braised quails on a bed of spring vegetables. Equally, it may be possible to begin to enjoy the charms of this wine in just a few months' time. The estate's second wine, **Château Barbaran 2000 (8–11 €)** gains a one-star rating.
➦ Les Domaines CGR, rte de la Cardonne,
33340 Blaignan, tel. 05.56.73.31.51, fax 05.56.73.31.52,
e-mail cgr@domaines-cgr.com ☑
⏳ ev. day except Sat. Sun. 8.30am–12 noon 1.30pm–5pm;
groups by appt.

CH. HAUT BARRAIL 2000★★

■ Cru bourg. 6 ha 20,000 ▯▮ 8–11 €

PRODUIT DE FRANCE - BORDEAUX
CRU BOURGEOIS
2000 2000
CHATEAU HAUT BARRAIL
MÉDOC
Appellation Médoc Contrôlée
E.A.R.L. CYRIL GILLET,
12.5% vol PROPRIETAIRE À BÉGADAN GIRONDE - FRANCE 75cl
Mis en bouteilles au Château

This very ancient estate has 17th century buildings which replaced a medieval construction evidenced now only by a mill. The classic Bordeaux colour of this Médoc therefore befits the historic surroundings. The wine's aromatic complexity is already perceptible in the burgeoning bouquet of ripe fruits mixing deliciously with scents of roasted almonds derived from the oak. Full-bodied, robust, fleshy and warm, the palate reveals an excellent concentration of fine tannins which augur a fine wine with a long future. Leave for at least three or four years, if not seven or eight, or even longer.
➦ EARL Cyril Gillet, 6, rte du Château-Landon,
33340 Bégadan, tel. 05.56.41.50.42, fax 05.56.41.57.10,
e-mail chateau.landon@wanadoo.fr ☑
⏳ ev. day 8am–12 noon 2pm–6pm; Sat. Sun. by appt.

CH. HAUT BLAIGNAN 2000★

■ Cru artisan 16 ha 14,285 ▯▮ 5–8 €
As its name indicates, this wine comes from the village of Blaignan. A lovely bright colour, it honours its origins with a

powerful bouquet of stewed red berry fruits and liquorice. Soft and smooth as it hits the palate, it goes on to develop an attractive fruitiness, which makes it already very drinkable, even if it will also keep well.
➦ EARL Brochard-Cahier, 19, rue de Verdun,
33340 Blaignan, tel. 05.56.09.04.70, fax 05.56.09.00.08 ☑
⏳ ev. day 9am–12 noon 2pm–7pm

CH. HAUT CONDISSAS
Cuvée Prestige 2000★

■ 3 ha 13,000 ▯▮ 46–76 €
This wine, made by the same producer as Rollan de By, has spent 24 months maturing in new oak, and is a blend of 50% Merlot, 25% Cabernet Sauvignon, and 25% Petit Verdot. The colour is a majestic dark red. Though still somewhat dominated by warm oak notes, the bouquet allows some liquorice hints and notes of high-quality fruit to come through. There is a revival of corresponding fruity flavours in the finish, together with some evident tannins which mark this out as a wine for storage.
➦ Jean Guyon, 7, rte Rollan-de-By, 33340 Bégadan,
tel. 05.56.41.58.59, fax 05.56.41.37.82,
e-mail rollan-de-by@wanadoo.fr
⏳ by appt.

CH. HAUT-GRAVAT 2000★

■ 8.68 ha 18,000 🍾▯▮↧ 5–8 €
Ten or so kilometres from the Atlantic, this cru cannot argue with the year 2000, for its smile produced this wine. The colour is intense, and the oak-maturing has left its mark on both bouquet and palate. Ripe, toasted fruits and Morello cherry make discreet appearances, and the structure indicates that this wine has good potential for future development.
➦ Sté Alain Lanneau, Ch. Haut-Gravat, 5, chem. du Clou, 33590 Jau-Dignac-et-Loirac, tel. 05.56.09.41.20,
fax 05.56.73.98.06 ☑
⏳ by appt.

CH. HAUT-MAURAC 2000★

■ Cru bourg. 15 ha n.c. ▯▮ 8–11 €
An outcrop of Graves overlooking the estuary, a varietal mix with the accent on Cabernet Sauvignon, and twelve months in oak so as not to flatten the fruit: this wine shows that the old recipes are still successful. A lovely bright ruby colour, a bouquet that opens on fruity, discreetly oaky notes, and a rich, well-made body, with good flavour and well-blended tannins – in three to four years' time, this wine will be a pleasurable accompaniment to braised pigeon with apples.
➦ Ch. Haut-Maurac, 3, rue de Mazails,
33340 Saint-Yzans-de-Médoc, tel. 05.56.09.05.37,
fax 05.56.09.00.90, e-mail haut-maurac@wanadoo.fr ☑
⏳ by appt.
➦ O. Decelle

CH. HOURBANON 2000★

■ Cru bourg. 1.5 ha n.c. ▯▮ 8–11 €
In line with its own traditions, this cru has produced a wine in which Cabernet Sauvignon reigns (70%, with 8% Cabernet Franc and 22% Merlot). This 2000 has good structure, sustained by good-quality tannins. The attractive bouquet has fresh notes of autumn undergrowth, and there is a straightforward, long-lingering finish that plumbs again the wine's depth of flavour.
➦ SCEA Delayat et Fils, Ch. Hourbanon,
33340 Prignac-en-Médoc, tel. 05.56.41.02.88,
fax 05.56.41.24.33,
e-mail hourbanon@chateauhourbanon.com ☑
⏳ by appt.

CH. LABADIE 2000★

■ Cru bourg. 20 ha 120,000 ▯▮ 8–11 €
⟨90⟩ 94 |95| 96 |97| 98 99 00

The regularity with which this cru recurs in the *Guide* is a testimony to its quality. The garnet colour, the bouquet of lovely aromas of red berries, spices and vanilla, and the development on the palate make it very much a Médoc. Supple and round, sustained by silky tannins, this 2000 is a well-balanced whole

Médoc

that really needs three or four years' storage before it accompanies sirloin of beef with mushrooms.
☛ GFA Bibey, 1, rte de Chassereau, 33340 Bégadan, tel. 05.56.41.55.58, fax 05.56.41.39.47 **V**
Y by appt.

CH. LAFON 2000★★

■ Cru bourg. 9 ha 60,000 **◫** 11–15 €
93 (95)|96| |97| 98 99 00

Representing the fourth generation on this estate, Rémy Fauchey knows the terroir by heart. He understands how much care and patience it asks of him to produce a real Médoc like this one, with its promise-laden, sumptuous colour. From behind the oakiness appear aromas of redcurrants and blackcurrants, while the palate is mouth-fillingly full-bodied, with a structure of well-matured tannins. A rich, dense synthesis that calls for good storage. Worthy of a leg of lamb with haricots.
☛ Rémy Fauchey, 4, chem. des Vignes, 33340 Prignac-en-Médoc, tel. 05.56.09.02.17, fax 05.56.09.04.96 **V**
Y ev. day 9.30am–6pm

CH. LASSUS 2000★★

■ Cru bourg. 2.5 ha 13,000 **◫** 5–8 €

A fine terroir, rows of vines with grass between, a half-and-half blend of Merlot and Cabernet Sauvignon, and 14 months of cask-maturing: nothing has been left to chance to create this successful wine with its rich colour. It combines great aromatic elegance (toasty notes on a background of concentrated grapes) with an attractively firm tannic structure that is rounded and rich. Wait five to six years and it will be fabulous with strong game like hare, boar or venison.
☛ SCEA Vignobles Chaumont, 7, rte du Port-de-By, 33340 Bégadan, tel. 05.56.41.50.79, fax 05.56.41.51.36, e-mail vignobles.chaumont@wanadoo.fr **V**
Y by appt.

CH. LAULAN DUCOS 2000★★

■ 21 ha 26,000 **◫** 5–8 €

Given that it was to inaugurate the cru's new label, this vintage needed to be a distinguished one. And so it is. The 67% Cabernet blend has a lovely rich garnet colour that promises great things. The bouquet is a happy marriage of red berries, crystallized fruits and plums, all lightly toasted. The attack is

full, round, fleshy, elegant, followed by the appearance of fine tannins and welcoming notes of well-ripened grapes with a hint of liquorice. This wine will be a fabulous accompaniment to traditional fine food, but not until it has aged a further four to six years.
☛ SCEA Ch. Laulan Ducos, 4, rte de Vertamont, 33590 Jau-Dignac-et-Loirac, tel. 05.56.09.42.37, fax 05.56.09.48.40, e-mail chateau@laulanducos.com **V**
Y ev. day except Sat. Sun. 9am–12 noon 2pm–5pm

CH. LOIRAC

Elevé en fût de chêne 2000★
■ 8.5 ha 16,000 **▮◫▬** 5–8 €
Grown on a well-rated terroir, this wine has a surprisingly discreet bouquet. When swirled in the glass, however, it releases its true personality of musk, caramel and spices. It is rounded and warm, is well supported by the oak, and has a long, smooth finish.
☛ J.-L. Camelot, 1, rte Queyrac, 33590 Jau-Dignac-et-Loirac, tel. 06.08.46.68.21, fax 05.56.73.98.22, e-mail jlcchtloirac@aol.com **V**
Y by appt.

CH. LOUDENNE 2000★

■ Cru bourg. 42 ha 260,000 **◫** 11–15 €
(82)|83 85 86 88 89 90 93 94 |95| (96)|97| 98 99 00

One of the very few châteaux in the Médoc to have its own private harbour, perhaps because it has been in British hands for the past 125 years. Yet again it offers an excellent wine. The deep purple colour is a sign of youth, but the developing bouquet shows class and power with its slightly jammy notes of toast, spices and cinnamon. The rich, mellow attack is followed by beautifully evolving tannins that make it good drinking already, though they do equally confer good keeping potential.
☛ SCS Ch. Loudenne, 33340 Saint-Yzans-de-Médoc, tel. 05.56.73.17.80, fax 05.56.09.02.87, e-mail chateau-loudenne@wanadoo.fr **V** **▥**
Y by appt.
☛ Lafragette

CH. LOUSTEAUNEUF

Art et Tradition Elevé en fût de chêne 2000★★
■ Cru bourg. n.c. 70,000 **◫** 8–11 €
93 94 (95)|96| 97 98 99 00

Grown on 40-year-old vines cultivated in grassed rows, this wine is neither fined nor filtered. The result is worthy of the vineyard and the care it devotes to its vinification. A beautifully frank, limpid ruby, it has a confidence-inspiring bouquet of oaky aromas followed by black fruits, black pepper and cinnamon. After a supple attack, the palate is supported by fine, silky tannins which contribute to a well-balanced synthesis offering a host of flavours and tactile impressions. The entire experience is sustained by well-blended oak and has a clear, clean finish. Wait six or seven years, or even longer; this is a model to follow within its AOC.
☛ Bruno Segond, EARL Ch. Lousteauneuf, 2, rte de Lousteauneuf, 33340 Valeyrac, tel. 05.56.41.52.11, fax 05.56.41.38.52, e-mail chateau.lousteauneuf@wanadoo.fr **V** **▥**
Y by appt.

CH. LES MOINES

Prestige 2000★
■ Cru bourg. 16.5 ha 132,000 **▮◫▬** 8–11 €
86 88 89 90 91 92 |93| 94 (95)|96| |97| 98 99 00

Although this year's version cannot rival the coups de coeur of earlier years, this Prestige 2000 nonetheless shows what a mainstay this cru is. A blend of Cabernet Sauvignon (70%) and Merlot grown on limestone-clay, this wine is still a bit dominated by the oak (grilled notes). The bouquet nonetheless reveals considerable complexity. The attack is fleshy and round, and the fairly full-bodied palate has a long-lasting finish which reveals that the wine will be ready to drink in three to four years' time.
☛ SCEA Vignobles Pourreau, 9, rue Château-Plumeau, 33340 Couquèques, tel. 05.56.41.38.06, fax 05.56.41.37.81 **V**
Y by appt.

CH. LA MOTHE 2000★

◼ Cru bourg. 10 ha   40,000   ◫   8–11 €

This time, the cru has put the accent on Cabernet Sauvignon, which was a good idea, judging by this vintage. It has a very pleasing character, in terms both of its aromatic development, where blackcurrant is joined by spices, and its structure, which will enable it to be stored.

☛ Thierry Berrouet, 4, rue de l'Etoile, 33340 Saint-Yzans-de-Médoc, tel. 05.56.09.05.29, fax 05.56.09.04.51, e-mail chateau-la-mothe@wanadoo.fr ☑

☕ by appt.

CH. NOAILLAC 2000★

◼ Cru bourg. 31 ha   200,000   ◫   8–11 €

86 88 91 92 93 94 |95| |96| 97 98 99 00

Well known and well thought of, Noaillac is another of the appellation's mainstays. The 2000 has a pleasingly deep, glossy colour and a delightfully complex bouquet of fruits (redcurrant and raspberry) and sweet spices. The palate combines a fleshy body with rich tannic sensations, all of which make this an attractive Médoc that should be aged for a further three to five years.

☛ Ch. Noaillac, 33590 Jau-Dignac-et-Loirac, tel. 05.56.09.52.20, fax 05.56.09.58.75, e-mail noaillac@noaillac.com ☑

☕ ev. day except Sat. Sun. 8am–12 noon 1.30pm–5pm

☛ Xavier Pagès

CH. LES ORMES SORBET 2000★★

◼ Cru bourg. 21 ha   100,000   ◫   15–23 €

78 81 83 85 86 88 89 (90) 91 92 93 94 95 96 |97| 98 99 00

Typical of the current tendency to give Merlot pride of place (here 65%), the cru offers a wine characterized by the Merlot variety's roundness. Attractive to the eye because of its shimmering highlights, it has a bouquet of fine perfumes, mainly floral with hints of wild cherry, port wine and chocolate, not to mention impressions of ripe fruits. The palate reveals the success with which an attractive grape body has here allied itself with the oak. Though already very nice to drink, this wine could also be kept.

☛ Jean Boivert, Ch. Les Ormes-Sorbet, 33340 Couquèques, tel. 05.56.73.30.30, fax 05.56.73.30.31, e-mail ormes.sorbet@wanadoo.fr ☑

☕ ev. day except Sun. 9am–12 noon 2pm–6pm; Sat. by appt.

PAVILLON DE BELLEVUE 2000★

◼ n.c.   100,000   ◫   8–11 €

Vinified by the cooperative at Ordonnac, this wine has an eye-catching rich ruby colour. Though at first discreet, even shy, the bouquet goes on to express perfumes of fresh red berries and spices. The palate is full-bodied right from the start, and is sustained by silky tannins and a well-judged oakiness. Finishing with echoes of the bouquet, it leaves pleasurable sensations that will be perfect in three years' time.

☛ SCAV Pavillon de Bellevue, 1, rte de Peyressan, 33340 Ordonnac, tel. 05.56.09.04.13, fax 05.56.09.03.29, e-mail pavillon.bellevue@wanadoo.fr ☑

☕ by appt.

CH. LE PEY 2000★★

◼ Cru bourg. 14.94 ha   107,338   ◫   5–8 €

After last year's *coup de coeur* for a 99, this family cru has also done well with its 2000. It would be hard not to appreciate the lovely blood-red colour or the complex bouquet of fine, enduring notes of chocolate and berry fruits. They are well supported by the oak, which is making its own contribution to the wine's fine, smooth and flavoursome tannins. This well-structured wine has a long-lingering, elegant and classy finish. An authentic Médoc needing three or four years' storage.

☛ SCEA Compagnet, Ch. Le Pey, 10, rte de Lesparre, 33340 Bégadan, tel. 05.56.41.57.75, fax 05.56.41.53.22, e-mail compagnetvins@wanadoo.fr ☑

☕ ev. day except Sat. Sun. 8am–12 noon 2pm–6pm

CH. LA PIROUETTE 2000★

◼ Cru bourg. 7 ha   35,000   ◫   5–8 €

As the label reminds us, this is a place where horses have been bred for several generations past. The Roux also breed fine wines, like this lovely 2000. Rich, full and well-balanced, it has a particularly attractive bouquet and mouthwatering flavours that range from warm fruit-filled brioche to chocolate.

☛ SCEA Yvan Roux, Semensan, 33590 Jau-Dignac-et-Loirac, tel. 05.56.09.42.02, fax 05.56.09.42.02, e-mail lapirouette@wanadoo.fr ☑

☕ by appt.

CH. PLAGNAC 2000★

◼ Cru bourg. 30 ha   164,400 ▌◫ ♠   5–8 €

On this cru, Cordier have allied the produce of old and young wines (average age 26 years) and have blended 65% Cabernet Sauvignon with Merlot. An intelligent choice, judging by this wine. Though still a bit overwhelmed by its two years in oak, it is beginning to let the fruit through to the nose, which will be complex, and to the palate, which is sustained by well-extracted, well-clothed tannins.

☛ Cordier-Mestrezat et Domaines, 109, rue Achard, BP 154, 33042 Bordeaux Cedex, tel. 05.56.11.29.00, fax 05.56.11.29.01, e-mail mestrezat-domaines@wanadoo.fr ☑

☕ by appt.

CH. POITEVIN

Elevé en barrique de chêne 2000★

◼ 15 ha   110,000   ◫   8–11 €

This cru, part of the fine collection assembled by Poitevin, offers a wine that is still a bit rustic but whose excellent texture is of great promise for the future. The same can be said of the intensity of its deep-purple colour and developed bouquet. The cru's second wine, **Château Lamothe Pontac 2000 (5–8 €)** was singled out by the Jury.

☛ Guillaume Poitevin, 14, rue du 19-Mars–1962, 33590 Jau-Dignac-et-Loirac, tel. 05.56.09.45.32, fax 05.56.09.45.32, e-mail chateau.poitevin@voila.fr ☑

CH. PONTAC GADET 2000★★

◼ 10 ha   40,000   ▌◫   5–8 €

Despite the Blaye to Lamarque ferry, not many wine-growers have crossed the Gironde's vast estuary to practise their art on both banks. The Briolais are among the few to have done so, and nobody drinking this wine will be sorry that they did. A beautiful Médoc with black glints, it has an attractive bouquet of cocoa, coffee and black fruits. Its keeping potential is evident in the well-extracted tannins and flavours, as well as in the long, elegant finish.

☛ Dominique Briolais, Vignobles Briolais, 33590 Jau-Dignac-Loirac, tel. 05.56.09.56.86 ☑

☕ by appt.

CH. PONTEY 2000★★

◼ Cru bourg. 13.31 ha 34,564   ◫   8–11 €

This cru's "triple-zero" vintage is a particular success. It is confidence-inspiring from the very start. The eye-catching purplish ruby colour is very Médoc. The bouquet has toasty notes that nonetheless respect the wine's red fruitiness, a sign of well-crafted maturation. The structure is sound, well-balanced and integrated, with a finish that indicates at least three or four years' cellaring.

☛ GFA du Ch. Pontey, 33340 Blaignan, tel. 05.56.20.71.03, fax 05.56.20.11.30 ☑

☕ by appt.

CH. PREUILLAC 2000★

◼ Cru bourg. 20 ha   120,000 ▌◫ ♠   8–11 €

This cru, on a fine estate of some 40 uninterrupted hectares, has produced an authentic Médoc 2000 with a structure whose richness and tannic presence make for long keeping quality – evidenced here all the more by the wine's youthful violet highlights. The bouquet is of the same character: generous, with aromas of wild fruits and good, supportive oakiness.

☛ Yvon Mau, Ch. Preuillac, 33340 Lesparre-Médoc, tel. 05.56.09.00.29, fax 05.56.09.00.34, e-mail chateau.preuillac@wanadoo.fr ☑

☕ by appt.

CH. LE PRIVERA

Elevé en fût de chêne 2000★

■	Cru bourg.	4.56 ha	12,000	ⅠⅠⅠ	15–23 €

Coming from the same producer as Château d'Escot, this wine is well made. It has a bouquet of red berries, blackcurrant and oak. The palate is round, fleshy, and well-structured, amply confirming first impressions that this is a well-crafted wine.

➱ SCEA du Ch. d'Escot, 33340 Lesparre-Médoc, tel. 05.56.41.06.92, fax 05.56.41.82.42 ☑
Ⓧ ev. day except Sat. Sun. 8.30am–12.30pm 1.30pm–5.30pm; Fri. cl. 4.30pm

LES FILS DE MARCEL QUANCARD

Grande Tradition Gourmet 2000★

■		n.c.	30,000	ⅠⅠⅠ	5–8 €

This wine, which bears the name of one of the main family wine-merchants in the Bordeaux region, begins with a bouquet of finesse that evokes a happy marriage of fruit and oak, before showing its power on the palate. The firm, ripe tannins will justify cellaring for two or three years.

➱ Cheval-Quancard, La Mouline, 4 rue du Carbouney, BP 36, 33560 Carbon-Blanc, tel. 05.57.77.88.88, fax 05.57.77.88.99, e-mail chevalquancard@chevalquancard.com
Ⓧ by appt.

ANDRE QUANCARD

Elevé en fût de chêne 2000★

■		n.c.	28,340	ⅠⅠⅠ	3–5 €

A creation of the firm of André Quancard, this serial-numbered wine has eye-catching violet glints and a bouquet of cherries sustained by oaky notes of vanilla and spices. The palate is supple, with good structure and balance, and displays a well-integrated character that is extended by a lingering finish. Several cru from different producers and distributed by this merchant gained a star. They are all oak-matured and priced at 5–8 €: **Château du Courneau Elevé en Fût de Chêne**; **Château Bois Cardon Elevé en Fût de Chêne**; **Château Bellegrave Elevé en Fût de Chêne** from M. Chauvin (Valeyrac).

➱ André Quancard-André, chem. de La Cabeyre, 33340 Saint-André-de-Cubzac, tel. 05.57.33.42.53, fax 05.57.43.22.22, e-mail aqa@andrequancard.com

CH. RAMAFORT 2000★

■	Cru bourg.	20 ha	139,000	▮ ⅠⅠⅠ ⬦	11–15 €

Produced on a cru neighbouring La Cardonne and belonging to the same owner, this wine is less full-bodied but nonetheless well put together, with fine, round tannins that integrate well with the bouquet. The latter is beginning to come alive, with a mix of fruity, floral notes and vanilla. Overall, the wine is pleasantly soft. Other labels from the same cru are the **Château Ribeiron 2000** and the **Le Vivier 2000**, both priced at 8–11 €, and both rated at one star.

➱ Les Domaines CGR, rte de la Cardonne, 33340 Blaignan, tel. 05.56.73.31.51, fax 05.56.73.31.52, e-mail cgr@domaines-cgr.com ☑
Ⓧ ev. day except Sat. Sun. 8.30am–12 noon 1.30pm–5pm; groups by appt.

CH. LE REYSSE 2000★★

■		n.c.	25,000	ⅠⅠⅠ	5–8 €

With its 2000, this cru was only one vote away from a *coup de coeur*. The rich crimson colour and the bouquet of toast, preceded by notes of red berries and spices, combine to make it a real charmer. Similar notes are found on the palate, which also has lots of roundness and flavours of finesse. This wine is so nice that one is almost tempted to drink it now, but the excellence of the tannins shows that it is really a wine to keep: enjoy it in six or seven years' time with a sophisticated dish, something like aiguillettes of foie gras with citrus fruits.

➱ SCEA Vignobles Chaumont, 7, rte du Port-de-By, 33340 Bégadan, tel. 05.56.41.50.79, fax 05.56.41.51.36, e-mail vignobles.chaumont@wanadoo.fr ☑
Ⓧ by appt.

CH. ROLLAN DE BY 2000★★

■	Cru bourg.	30 ha	195,000	ⅠⅠⅠ	15–23 €

|89| **91 92 93 94** ⦿**96**⦿ **97 98 00**

This is one of the most famous crus in the appellation, and the estate has grown from 2 ha in 1990 to today's 30 ha. Overlooked by a 19th century charterhouse surrounded by French-style parkland, the estate grows a majority of Merlot vines (70%). The colour of this wine is attractively dark, and the bouquet is of an oaky vanilla that respects the finesse of the other aromas (liquorice with a hint of meat). The palate reveals a remarkable tannic structure with lots of mellow cushioning, and the finish is long. Overall, this is a both charming and serious wine. It will keep in the cellar for seven or eight years, maybe longer.

➱ Jean Guyon, 7, rte Rollan-de-By, 33340 Bégadan, tel. 05.56.41.58.59, fax 05.56.41.37.82, e-mail rollan-de-by@wanadoo.fr ☑ 🏠
Ⓧ by appt.

CH. ROUSSEAU DE SIPIAN

Elevé en barrique 2000★

■	Cru bourg.	4.5 ha	10,000	ⅠⅠⅠ	8–11 €

The year 2000 was a major turning-point in the history of this cru, since it was acquired by the Racey family, of British origins. It is also the date of this wine, whose gorgeous youthfulness is evident in the colour. A trifle more discreet is the bouquet, which notes of green pepper and spices are just beginning to make interesting. The rich tannic structure shows that this wine will keep for the three or four years it will need for its aromas and flavours to reach optimum expression.

➱ Ch. Rousseau de Sipian LTD, 26, rte du Port-de-Goulée, 33340 Valeyrac, tel. 05.56.41.54.92, fax 05.56.41.53.26, e-mail rousseaudesipian@aol.fr ☑
Ⓧ ev. day except Sat. Sun. 9am–12 noon 2pm–5pm

CH. SAINT-AUBIN 2000★

■	Cru bourg.	15 ha	100,000	ⅠⅠⅠ	8–11 €

Two kilometres from the Phare de Richard lighthouse on the Gironde estuary, this cru is part of maritime Médoc. It is nonetheless a very true-to-type Médoc by virtue of the purplish red colour with dark glints and the well-constructed palate, which has a full range of flavours: the vanilla leaves plenty of room for raspberry fruitiness, green pepper and spices (pepper). Wait three or four years before drinking.

➱ Charles Fernandez de Castro, Ch. Saint-Aubin, 27, chem. de Dignac, 33590 Jau-Dignac-et-Loirac, tel. 05.56.58.08.57, fax 05.56.58.08.59, e-mail chateau.st-aubin@wanadoo.fr ☑
Ⓧ by appt.

SAINT-BRICE 2000★

■		72.69 ha	1,000,000	▮ ⬦	5–8 €

The cooperative at Saint-Yzans can always be relied upon for good products. Although their 2000 is not imposingly full-bodied, it honours their traditions with its round, winey, well-balanced, well-constructed character. The fine aromas of red berry fruits add a friendly dimension. Their **Grand Saint-Brice 2000**, matured for 12 months in oak, was selected (unstarred), as was also another of their labels, the **La Colonne 2000 (11–15 €)**, similarly matured for 12 months in oak.

➱ SCV Cave Saint-Brice, 33340 Saint-Yzans-de-Médoc, tel. 05.56.09.05.05, fax 05.56.09.01.92 ☑
Ⓧ ev. day except Sun. 8am–12 noon 2pm–6pm

CH. SAINT-HILAIRE

Vieilli en fût de chêne 2000★

■		10 ha	60,000	ⅠⅠⅠ	5–8 €

Owned since 1983 by a Dutchman with a passion for wine, three-fifths of this cru is located on Quartenary soils overlooking the estuary; the varietal emphasis (55% Cabernet Sauvignon) is typical of the appellation. No less truly Médoc in character is this luminously red wine, with its clean, potent bouquet. The palate is classically structured, with a full, vigorous body, and tannins that are powerful yet elegant. A nice wine to forget a while in the cellar.

➱ A. et F. Uijttewaal, Ch. Saint-Hilaire, 13, chem. de La Rivière, 33340 Queyrac, tel. 05.56.59.80.88, fax 05.56.59.87.68, e-mail chateau.st.hilaire@wanadoo.fr ☑
Ⓧ ev. day except Sun. 9am–12 noon 2pm–6pm

CAVE SAINT-JEAN
Le Grand Art 2000★

| | 7.1 ha | 40,000 | ▮❶♦ | 5–8 € |

The 2000 vintage of this prestige label belonging to the cellar at Bégadan does not simply catch the eye with its attractive purple colour; it has a complex, expressive bouquet of toasty, chocolaty aromas which prepares the way for a rich, full, well-equipped palate. The aromatic concentration of this wine, its flavours, and powerful tannins call for some storage, after which it will be a graceful accompaniment to a goose roasted with dried fruits.
☛ Les Vignerons d'Uni-Médoc, Cave Saint-Jean, 2, rte de Canissac, 33340 Bégadan, tel. 05.56.41.50.13, fax 05.56.41.50.78, e-mail saintjean@uni-medoc.com ☑
☕ ev. day except Sat. Sun. 8.30am–12.30pm 2pm–5.30pm

CH. SIPIAN
Quintessence 2000★

| | Cru bourg. | 3 ha | 14,000 | ❶ | 15–23 € |

This estate of 25 ha is still in the hands of a genuine Médoc family, a fact that risks becoming increasingly rare as time progresses. It offers this red wine which is almost black in colour with deep-purple glints. The well-defined, powerful bouquet is full of subtle notes ranging from roasting coffee to plum, via Morello cherry, cinnamon, and sugared chestnut. The suppleness of the attack accords with the round, well-blended tannins on the palate. Enhanced by jammy hints, the wine shows all-round that the grapes received the skilful treatment after harvest that they deserved. The same estate's **Cuvée Principale du Château Sipian 2000 (8–11 €)** was commended.
☛ Bernard Méhaye, 28, rte du Port-de-Goulée, 33340 Valeyrac, tel. 05.56.41.56.05, fax 05.56.41.35.36, e-mail chateausipian@net-up.com ☑
☕ ev. day except Sat. Sun. 9am–12 noon 2pm–5pm

CH. LE TEMPLE 2000★

| | Cru bourg. | 14.5 ha | 80,000 | ▮❶♦ | 8–11 € |

This cru regularly produces quality wines, and has remained true to its traditions with this well-crafted, typical Médoc blend of 60% Cabernet Sauvignon, 5% Petit Verdot, and 35% Merlot. The bouquet has lots of personality, with jammy notes of ripe grapes and liquorice. Though the palate is delicate and charming, its ripe, smooth tannins mark it out as a wine for the cellar.
☛ Denis Bergey, Ch. Le Temple, 33340 Valeyrac, tel. 05.56.41.53.62, fax 05.56.41.57.35, e-mail letemple@terre-net.fr ☑
☕ ev. day except Sun. 8.30am–12.30pm 1.30pm–7.30pm

CH. LA TILLE CAMELON
Elevé en fût de chêne 2000★

| | | 15.39 ha | 30,600 | ❶ | 5–8 € |

Grown in a vineyard of mainly Merlot vines, this wine has the character of that variety, which is most noticeable in the blackberry aroma. The palate is on the powerful side. The tannins are still a little severe, and call for a short time in the cellar.
☛ SCV Cave Saint-Brice, 33340 Saint-Yzans-de-Médoc, tel. 05.56.09.05.05, fax 05.56.09.01.92 ☑
☕ ev. day except Sun. 8am–12 noon 2pm–6pm
☛ G. Courrian

CH. TOUR BLANCHE 2000★

| | Cru bourg. | 32 ha | 170,000 | ▮❶♦ | 8–11 € |

This cru, which overlooks the Gironde from its hilltop of Graves, will not disappoint its devotees with this vintage, whose fine constitution is evident from the lovely purple colour. The bouquet is richly complex, with a balance of fruity and oaky aromas. On the palate, the smooth, fine, high-quality tannins strike a good balance between power and suppleness. This will be a very nice wine in three to four years' time.
☛ SVA Ch. Tour Blanche, 15, rte du Breuil, 33340 Saint-Christoly-Médoc, tel. 05.56.58.15.79, fax 05.56.58.39.89, e-mail hessel@moulin-a-vent.com ☑
☕ by appt.

CH. LA TOUR DE BY 2000★★

| | Cru bourg. | 64 ha | 450,000 | ▮❶♦ | 11–15 € |

82 83 85 86 |88| |89| |90| 91 |93| |94| 95 **96** |97| 98 **99** 00

With its fire-tower proudly sitting on a hilltop of Graves overlooking the estuary, this cru has become an essential place to visit on any tourist jaunt to the Médoc's furthest point. The 2000 is an eye-catchingly beautiful garnet colour, and its bouquet mixes notes of leather and black fruits. After a frank, round attack, the palate reveals a full, all-round, thoroughbred character. Its flavours of red berries, chewy grapeyness and silky tannins all bear witness to the high standard of the maturing and call for patience in the waiting – four to five years, perhaps longer. The **Château La Roque de By 2000 (8–11 €)** is rated one star for the quality of its bouquet of fresh fruits and for its tannins, which are already supple.
☛ Marc Pagès, Ch. La Tour de By, 33340 Bégadan, tel. 05.56.41.50.03, fax 05.56.41.36.10, e-mail la.tour.de.by@wanadoo.fr ☑
☕ ev. day except Sat. Sun. 8am–12 noon 1.30pm–4.30pm; groups by appt.

CH. TOUR HAUT-CAUSSAN 2000★★

| | Cru bourg. | 15 ha | 88,080 | ❶ | 11–15 € |

82 83 85 86 |89| ⟨90⟩ 91 92 93 94 |95| ⟨96⟩ 97 **98 99** 00

With his enthusiasm for the Médoc and its viticulture, Philippe Courrian has even written a book about his occupation. He is aware, however, that the best ambassador for the Médoc wine-growing region could have is the wine itself. His 2000 is a perfect diplomat in this respect: the colour is a rich ruby with violet highlights, the bouquet is truly complex, and the palate is full-bodied, with good tannic support. The tannins have a ripeness which is often a characteristic of this cru. With its combination of jammy notes and hints of toast, this great wine will be an excellent accompaniment to elaborate, fine dishes in five to six years' time. The second wine, **Château la Landotte 2000 (5–8 €)**, was selected (unstarred) by the Jury. Its 70% Cabernet Sauvignon variety gives it an old-fashioned profile. A wine-lovers' wine.
☛ Philippe Courrian, 33340 Blaignan, tel. 05.56.09.00.77, fax 05.56.09.06.24 ☑
☕ by appt.

TRADITION DES COLOMBIERS
Elevé en fût de chêne 2000★

| | | 7 ha | 39,200 | ▮❶♦ | 5–8 € |

The Prignac cooperative having long appeared in the *Guide* with several of its labels, it offers a 2000 of unabashed charm. The bouquet is oaky yet not overpoweringly so. The palate is full and well-structured. Overall, a charming wine that will make for very pleasant drinking over the next two years.
☛ Les Vignerons d'Uni-Médoc, Cave Les Vieux Colombiers, 23, rue des Colombiers, 33340 Prignac-en-Médoc, tel. 05.56.09.01.02, fax 05.56.09.03.67, e-mail vieuxcolombiers@uni-medoc.com ☑
☕ ev. day except Sun. 8.30am–12.30pm 2pm–5.30pm

CH. LES TUILERIES 2000★

| | Cru bourg. | 12 ha | 66,600 | ❶ | 8–11 € |

90 91 92 93 |94| **96** 98 **99** 00

Descendants of a long line of coopers, the owners of this cru have made a half-and-half blend of Merlot and Cabernet grapes. The keynote is elegance rather than power, as much in the texture as in the freshness and liveliness of the wine's aromatic expression. Drink young with grilled beef.
☛ Jean-Luc Dartiguenave, Ch. Les Tuileries, 33340 Saint-Yzans-de-Médoc, tel. 05.56.09.05.31, fax 05.56.09.02.43 ☑
☕ ev. day except Sat. Sun. 9am–12 noon 2pm–6pm

CH. VERNOUS
Elevé en fût de chêne 2000★★

| | Cru bourg. | 22.3 ha | 110,000 | ❶ | 8–11 € |

Grown on a terroir of Graves and blended from 60% Cabernet Sauvignon, 7% Cabernet Franc and 33% Merlot, this wine is extremely good. The fresh colours are a delight to the eye, and

the bouquet is pleasantly rich in fruity, toasted notes. Round, fleshy and mellow, this is the palate of a real Médoc, full of breeding and vigour. A powerful wine: open in five to six years' time to accompany a guinea-fowl.
🕿 SCA Ch. Vernous, Saint-Trélody, 33340 Lesparre-Médoc, tel. 05.56.41.13.57, fax 05.56.41.21.12

CH. VIEUX ROBIN
Bois de Lunier 2000★

■ Cru bourg.	12 ha	63,000	■ ⦿ ᵇ	11–15 €

|82| 83 |85| |86| 87 |88| |89| |90| 91 |93| 94 95 96 97 98 99 00

This is a modern enterprise that has long been good at public relations while not forgetting the main point, the quest for quality. Quality is to be found in this 2000, whose garnet colour gives an indication of its well-built character. It has delicate aromas of red fruits, and a frank, soft palate with a long-lasting finish. A promising wine to keep.
🕿 SCE Ch. Vieux Robin, 3, rte des Anguilleys, 33340 Bégadan, tel. 05.56.41.50.64, fax 05.56.41.37.85, e-mail contact@chateau-vieux-robin.com ⦿
🍷 by appt.
🕿 Maryse et Didier Roba

Wines selected but not starred

CH. L'ARGENTEYRE
Vieilles vignes Elevé en barrique 2000

■	8.5 ha	50,000	■ ⦿	5–8 €

🕿 GAEC des vignobles Reich, rte de Courbian, 33340 Bégadan, tel. 05.56.41.52.34, fax 05.56.41.52.34 ⦿
🍷 ev. day 9am–12 noon 2pm–6pm

CH. LES GRAVES DE BALIRAC
Elevé en fût de chêne 2000

■	n.c.	34,000	⦿	8–11 €

🕿 Maison Sichel, 8, rue de la Poste, 33210 Langon, tel. 05.56.63.50.52, fax 05.56.63.42.28, e-mail maison-sichel@sichel.fr

CH. BEJAC ROMELYS
Elevé en fût de chêne 2000

■ Cru artisan	14.88 ha	14,000	■ ⦿ ᵇ	5–8 €

🕿 Xavier et Sylvie Berrouet, 4, rue de Rigon, 33340 Saint-Yzans-de-Médoc, tel. 05.56.09.08.21, fax 05.56.09.06.68, e-mail romelys@aol.com ⦿
🍷 by appt.

CH. BELLEGRAVE 2000

■ Cru bourg.	16 ha	120,000	■ ⦿	5–8 €

🕿 EARL des Vignobles Caussèque, Janton, 33340 Valeyrac, tel. 05.56.41.53.82, fax 05.56.41.50.10 ⦿
🍷 ev. day 9am–12 noon 2pm–7pm; cl. 15 Sep.–30 Apr.

CH. BELLEVUE 2000

■ Cru bourg.	15 ha	110,000	⦿	8–11 €

🕿 EARL Lassalle et Fils, 10, rue du 8-Mai–1945, 33340 Valeyrac, tel. 05.56.41.52.17, fax 05.56.41.36.64 ⦿
🍷 ev. day except Sun. 9.30am–12 noon 2pm–6pm

CH. BOIS CARRE 2000

■	5.1 ha	36,000	■ ⦿	8–11 €

🕿 David Renouil, 1, rue de Mazails, 33340 Saint-Yzans-de-Médoc, tel. 05.56.09.08.12, fax 05.56.09.04.21 ⦿
🍷 ev. day except Sun. 8am–12 noon 1.30pm–7pm

CH. LA BRANNE
Elevé en fût de chêne 2000

■	2 ha	8,300	⦿	5–8 €

🕿 GAEC de Peyressac-Videau, 1, rte de la Hargue, 33340 Bégadan, tel. 05.56.41.55.24, fax 05.56.41.55.24 ⦿ ☗
🍷 by appt.
🕿 Philippe Videau

CH. BREUILH 2000

■	4.5 ha	20,000	■ ⦿	8–11 €

🕿 Denis Bergey, 14, rte de Breuilh, 33340 Bégadan, tel. 05.56.41.56.45, fax 05.56.41.57.35 ⦿

CH. CASTERA 2000

■ Cru bourg.	n.c.	200,000	⦿	15–23 €

🕿 SNC Ch. Castéra, 33340 Saint-Germain-d'Esteuil, tel. 05.56.73.20.60, fax 05.56.73.20.61, e-mail chateau@castera.fr ⦿
🍷 ev. day except Sat. Sun. 10am–12 noon 2pm–5pm

ELITE SAINT-ROCH
Vieilli en fût de chêne 2000

■	4.15 ha	27,000	■ ⦿ ᵇ	5–8 €

🕿 Les Vignerons d'Uni-Médoc, cave Saint-Roch, rte de Lacave, 33340 Queyrac, tel. 05.56.59.83.36, fax 05.56.59.86.57, e-mail saintroch@uni-medoc.com ⦿
🍷 ev. day except Sun. 8.30am–12.30pm 2pm–5.30pm

CH. D'ESCOT 2000

■ Cru bourg.	12.8 ha	90,000	■ ⦿ ᵇ	8–11 €

🕿 SCEA du Ch. d'Escot, 33340 Lesparre-Médoc, tel. 05.56.41.06.92, fax 05.56.41.82.42 ⦿
🍷 ev. day except Sat. Sun. 8.30am–12.30pm 1.30pm–5.30pm; Fri. cl. 4.30pm

CH. GREYSAC 2000

■ Cru bourg.	70 ha	500,000	⦿	15–23 €

85 86 |88| |89| 91 93 94 |95| |96| 97 98 99 00

🕿 SA Domaines Codem, Ch. Greysac, 18, rte de By, 33340 Bégadan, tel. 05.56.73.26.56, fax 05.56.73.26.58 ⦿
🍷 by appt.

CH. HAUT BRISEY 2000

■ Cru bourg.	n.c.	70,000	⦿	5–8 €

(86) 87 88 89 90 91 93 94 95 |96| 97 98 |99| 00

🕿 SCEA Ch. Haut Brisey, 4, chem. de Sestignan, 33590 Jau-Dignac-et-Loirac, tel. 05.56.09.56.77, fax 05.56.73.98.36 ⦿
🍷 ev. day except Sat. Sun. 9am–12 noon 2pm–5pm

CH. HAUT-GRIGNON 2000

■	5 ha	25,000	⦿	8–11 €

🕿 Léa Ducos, Ch. Haut-Grignon, 33340 Valeyrac, tel. 05.56.41.58.76, fax 05.56.41.35.12, e-mail dmarelf@aol.com ⦿
🍷 by appt.

CH. LACOMBE NOAILLAC 2000

■ Cru bourg.	15 ha	100,000	■ ⦿ ᵇ	8–11 €

🕿 SC Ch. Lacombe Noaillac, Le Broustéra, 33590 Jau-Dignac-et-Loirac, tel. 05.56.41.50.18, fax 05.56.41.54.65, e-mail info@domaines-lapalu.com
🍷 by appt.
🕿 Jean-Michel Lapalu

CH. MAREIL 2000

	16 ha	13,000	■ ♦	8–11 €

�581 EARL du Ch. Mareil, 4, chem. de Mareil,
33340 Ordonnac, tel. 05.56.09.00.32, fax 05.56.09.07.33,
e-mail chateau.mareil@terre-net.fr ☑
♈ by appt.
�581 M. et Mme Brun

CH. MAZAILS

Vieilli en fût de chêne 2000

■	Cru bourg. 15.51 ha	41,400	❙❙❙	8–11 €

�581 Philippe Chacun, Ch. Mazails,
33340 Saint-Yzans-de-Médoc, tel. 05.56.09.00.62,
fax 05.56.09.06.02 ☑
♈ by appt.

CH. MERIC 2000

■	Cru bourg. 10.32 ha	70,000	❙❙❙	11–15 €

�581 SCEA Ch. Méric, 19, rte de Vensac,
33590 Jau-Dignac-et-Loirac, tel. 05.57.75.01.55,
fax 05.57.75.01.57, e-mail denis.hecquet1@libertysurf.fr ☑
♈ by appt.

LA PATACHE 2000

■	n.c.	80,000	■❙❙❙♦	5–8 €

�581 SARL Dom. Lapalu, 1, rue du 19-Mars, 33340 Bégadan,
tel. 05.56.41.50.18, fax 05.56.41.54.65,
e-mail info@domaines-lapalu.com ☑
♈ by appt.

CH. DU PERIER 2000

■	Cru bourg. 7 ha	35,000	❙❙❙	8–11 €

90 91 92 **93** 94 95 96 |97| **98** 99 00

�581 Bruno Saintout, Dom. de Cartujac,
33112 Saint-Laurent-Médoc, tel. 05.56.59.91.70,
fax 05.56.59.46.13 ☑
♈ by appt.

CH. PEY DE PONT 2000

■	Cru bourg. 3.5 ha	13,000	■❙❙❙♦	5–8 €

�581 EARL Henri Reich et Fils, 3, rte du Port-de-Goulée,
Trembleaux, 33340 Civrac-en-Médoc, tel. 05.56.41.52.80,
fax 05.56.41.52.80, e-mail cht.pey-de-pont@wanadoo.fr ☑
♈ ev. day except Sun. 8am–12 noon 1.30pm–6pm

CH. SAINT-CHRISTOLY 2000

■	Cru bourg. 26 ha	150,000	■ ♦	5–8 €

�581 Hervé Héraud, 9, rue du 19-Mars-1962,
33340 Saint-Christoly-Médoc, tel. 05.56.41.38.17,
fax 05.56.41.59.34 ☑
♈ ev. day except Sat. Sun. 9am–12 noon 2pm–5pm;
cl. Nov. to Apr.

CH. TOUR CASTILLON 2000

■	Cru bourg. 13 ha	16,000	❙❙❙	8–11 €

�581 EARL Vignobles Peyruse, 3, rte du Fort-Castillon,
33340 Saint-Christoly-Médoc, tel. 05.56.41.54.98,
fax 05.56.41.39.19 ☑
♈ ev. day except Sun. 9am–12 noon 2pm–6pm;
15–31 Aug. by appt.

VIEUX CHATEAU LANDON 2000

■	Cru bourg. 20 ha	100,000	❙❙❙	8–11 €

�581 EARL Cyril Gillet, 6, rte du Château-Landon,
33340 Bégadan, tel. 05.56.41.50.42, fax 05.56.41.57.10,
e-mail chateau.landon@wanadoo.fr ☑
♈ ev. day 8am–12 noon 2pm–6pm; Sat. Sun. by appt.

Haut-Médoc

Producing almost as much as the Appellation Médoc, with 210,567 hl in 2002 from 4,591 ha, the Haut-Médoc wines have the edge on reputation, due in part to the presence of five Crus Classés grown within the AOC boundaries. Others are found in the six Appellations Communales contained within the Haut-Médoc area.

The first truly authoritative classification of Bordeaux wines was that of the Médoc in 1855 – that is, nearly a century before the other regions. This recognition arose directly from advances made in wine-growing in the Médoc area from the 18th century onwards. It was here in particular that the concept of quality came into being, along with new thinking about terroirs and crus, and an understanding that there was a relationship between the terroir, or specific vineyard, and the quality of a wine. Haut-Médoc wines are generous in character, although not excessively powerful, with real finesse on the nose and in, general, good ageing qualities. They are best drunk at cool room temperature, and go as well with white meat and poultry as with the lighter sorts of game. Drunk young and served chilled, they can also accompany some fish dishes.

CH. D'AGASSAC 2000★★

■	Cru bourg. 26.8 ha	152,102	❙❙❙	15–23 €

95 96 |97| **98** 99 **00**

The Médoc's golden age was during the 19th century, when there was a rage for new building. Hence the relative rarity of medieval châteaux in the region. All the same, there remain a few lovely medieval examples, like this 12th century edifice, altered during the Renaissance. Grown on a terroir of deep Graves, this 2000 has a fashionably oaky bouquet. Balance is restored, however, on the palate, where there is an evolving overall richness of well-assembled flavours sustained by smooth tannins which will enable the wine to be kept over several years. Another true-to-type Médoc is the same château's **Château Pomiès-Agassac (11–15 €)**, which receives a one-star rating.
�581 SCA du Ch. d'Agassac, 15, rue du Château-d'Agassac,
33290 Ludon-Médoc, tel. 05.57.88.15.47,
fax 05.57.88.17.61, e-mail contact@agassac.com ☑
♈ by appt.
�581 Groupama

CH. D'ARCHE 2000★★

■	Cru bourg. 9 ha	55,000	❙❙❙	15–23 €

|94| |95| **|96|** |97| |98| **99 00**

Grown in an uninterrupted vineyard on a fine outcrop of Graves, this wine comes from a high-quality terroir whose products are typically well-integrated, as indeed this one is. A lovely violet colour, this 2000 has a developing bouquet of real complexity (cedar, ripe fruits and leather). There is a sensation of mouth-filling fullness on the palate where the ripe, well-clothed tannins predict that this wine will be truly delicious in four to five, or even ten years' time.
�581 SA Mähler-Besse, 49, rue Camille-Godard,
33000 Bordeaux, tel. 05.56.56.04.30, fax 05.56.56.04.59,
e-mail france@mahler-besse.com ☑
♈ by appt.

CH. ARNAULD 2000★

■	Cru bourg. 35 ha	200,000	❙❙❙	11–15 €

Once a priory, this cru is a good unit whose production is high-quality, as is witnessed by this fine, powerful wine. The successful alliance of fruit and oak gives complexity to both bouquet and palate. Both fulfil all the promises implicit in the

dark rich garnet colour. Three years' storage will be essential before drinking.
☛ SCEA Theil-Roggy, Ch. Arnauld, Arcins, 33460 Margaux, tel. 05.57.88.89.10, fax 05.57.88.89.20 ☑
🍷 by appt.

CH. D'AURILHAC 2000★★
■ Cru bourg. 12.5 ha 93,000 ⑪ 8–11 €
96 |97| 98 99 00

Wines grown at Saint-Seurin-de-Cadourne are privileged, as this wine proves throughout its tasting. The dark colour with its black glossy highlights creates a confidence which is justified by the finesse and elegance of the bouquet's aromas of leather, musk and well-measured oak. The long, smooth, well-balanced palate reveals the perfect mastery with which the vinification was carried out, and shows that the wine will keep for four or five years.
☛ SCEA Ch. d'Aurilhac et La Fagotte, Sénilhac, 33180 Saint-Seurin-de-Cadourne, tel. 05.56.59.35.32, fax 05.56.59.35.32 ☑
🍷 by appt.
☛ Erik Nieuwaal

CH. BALAC
Cuvée Prestige 2000★
■ Cru bourg. 15 ha 105,000 ▮⑪⚬ 11–15 €
88 89 90 92 93 94 |95| |96| |97| 99 00

An 18th century château with a wine-estate on a good-quality outcrop of Graves: how very Médoc this property is. It was restored by the Touchais, who came here from Anjou in 1964. The wine is a lovely crimson colour and its highest card is its finesse. It has a bouquet of spices against a backdrop of roasted coffee, and a palate of richness and fleshiness with complex flavours of cooked fruits (fig jam). The finish is rich in sensations and warm.
☛ Luc Touchais, Ch. Balac, 33112 Saint-Laurent-Médoc, tel. 05.56.59.41.76, fax 05.56.59.93.90, e-mail chateau.balac@wanadoo.fr ☑
🍷 ev. day 10am–12.30pm 2pm–6pm

CH. BARATEAU 2000★★
■ Cru bourg. 15 ha 90,000 ⑪ 8–11 €
85 86 **88** |89| |90| 93 94 95 96 **|97|** |98| 99 **00**

Curiously, the name of the château is not derived from the name of the family that built it, but from that of the priest who blessed the laying of the first stone. The vinification has been geared towards producing a wine for laying down, and the rich colour of this wine amply proves that. The palate is long-lasting and full, well-equipped to give the fruit, given time, the opportunity to assimilate the oak.
☛ Sté Fermière du Ch. Barateau, 33112 Saint-Laurent-Médoc, tel. 05.56.59.42.07, fax 05.56.59.49.91, e-mail cb@leroy.com ☑
🍷 by appt.
☛ Famille Leroy

CH. BELGRAVE 2000★★
■ 5e cru clas. 54.38 ha 245,000 ⑪ 23–30 €
82 **83 84 85 86** 87 88 89(90)91 92 93 |94| |95| |96| |97| 98 99 00

Classified in 1855 under the name of Coutanceau, this cru derives its current name from an owner who came from Belgravia in London. Grown on a characteristically Médoc terroir of deep Graves over clay, this vintage has a very authentic character shown on the palate by the robust tannins that are good ageing indicators. The wine's liquorice perfumes blend well with notes of roasted coffee to create a high-quality product that will be excellent drinking in three to five years' time and even after that.
☛ Dourthe, Ch. Belgrave, 35, rue de Bordeaux, 33290 Parempuyre, tel. 05.56.35.53.00, fax 05.56.35.53.29, e-mail contact@cvbg.com ☑
🍷 by appt.

CH. BELLE-VUE 2000★
■ Cru bourg. 9.73 ha 36,000 ⑪ 15–23 €
Having long been simply an appendage to the château of Gironville, this vineyard recently gained its autonomy. A

particular feature is the one-eighth of the estate given over to the Petit Verdot variety. The result is a good-looking wine with a fine garnet colour and an interesting bouquet of blackcurrant flowers, caramel, prune, and chocolate. The palate is supple and round, and has good body. Very pleasant drinking now, but may be kept a short time.
☛ SC de la Gironville, 69, rte de Louens, 33460 Macau, tel. 05.57.88.19.79, fax 05.57.88.41.79, e-mail contact@scgironville.com ☑
🍷 by appt.

CH. BERNADOTTE 2000★★
■ Cru bourg. 35 ha n.c. ⑪ 11–15 €
Château Bernadotte in the past belonged to the family of Napoleon's famous marshal, who went on to become king of Sweden. This 2000 vintage is no less regal in the richness and concentration of its body and dense tannins. The bouquet and finish are of a piece with the palate and offer superb notes of toast and spices. A gorgeous wine to open in seven or eight years' time as an accompaniment to game.
☛ SC Ch. Le Fournas, Le Fournas-Nord, 33250 Saint-Sauveur, tel. 05.56.59.57.04, fax 05.56.59.54.84, e-mail bernadotte@chateau-bernadotte.com ☑
🍷 by appt.
☛ de Lencquesaing

CH. DE BRAUDE 2000★
■ 6.2 ha 24,000 ⑪ 8–11 €
This small estate on the edge of Bordeaux offers a 2000 whose complexity is very evident from the bouquet. Though dominated by fruits, it includes notes of cinnamon, liquorice, caramel and spices, to create a variety of sensations. The palate is a happy marriage of finesse and power, supported by tasty tannins. It will be worth waiting for this wine, four or five years, maybe longer. Still marked by the oak but no less aromatically expressive and well-structured is the same estate's **Château Braude-Fellonneau 2000 (15–23 €)**, similarly one-star rated.
☛ Régis Bernaleau, 8, av. Jean-Luc-Vonderheyden, 33460 Arsac, tel. 05.56.58.84.51, fax 05.56.58.83.39, e-mail chateau.mongravey@wanadoo.fr ☑
🍷 by appt.

CH. CAMBON LA PELOUSE 2000★★
■ Cru bourg. 35 ha 220,000 ⑪ 11–15 €
Since its purchase by the current owner in 1996 and the renewal of its wineries and methods of cultivation, Cambon has seen a spectacular improvement in quality. This dark wine with ruby highlights has an emerging bouquet of authentic tannic aromas (undergrowth, venison, roasting), a complex palate and a lingering finish. It will keep well. Leave it in the cellar and forget about it for five to seven years before drinking.
☛ Jean-Pierre Marie, SCEA Cambon La Pelouse, 5, chem. de Canteloup, 33460 Macau, tel. 05.57.88.40.32, fax 05.57.88.19.12, e-mail contact@cambon-la-pelouse.com ☑
🍷 by appt.

CH. CAMENSAC 2000★★
■ 5e cru clas. 70 ha 265,000 ⑪ 30–38 €
85 86 88 89 90 92 94 (95)(96) |97| 98 99 00

This cru, watched over by a beautiful charterhouse, is one of the five AOC Haut-Médocs classified in 1855. The estate repays the honour by the regularity with which it produces fine wines. This 2000 will be remembered a long time for its elegant colour, between purple and garnet, its powerful bouquet of red and black berries, and its promising palate. The latter is fine, sappy and fleshy, with gorgeous tannic support. Though already excellent drinking, it will gain from four or five years' more storage. The estate's second wine, **La Closerie de Camensac 2000 (11–15 €)**, is commended.
☛ Ch. Camensac, rte de Saint-Julien, BP 9, 33112 Saint-Laurent-Médoc, tel. 05.56.59.41.69, fax 05.56.59.41.73, e-mail chateaucamensac@wanadoo.fr ☑
🍷 by appt.

THE 1855 CLASSIFICATION REVIEWED IN 1973

PREMIERS CRUS (FIRST GROWTHS)
Château Lafite-Rothschild (Pauillac)
Château Latour (Pauillac)
Château Margaux (Margaux)
Château Mouton-Rothschild (Pauillac)
Château Haut-Brion (Pessac-Léognan)

SECONDS CRUS (SECOND GROWTHS)
Château Brane-Cantenac (Margaux)
Château Cos-d'Estournel (Saint-Estèphe)
Château Ducru-Beaucaillou (Saint-Julien)
Château Durfort-Vivens (Margaux)
Château Gruaud-Larose (Saint-Julien)
Château Lascombes (Margaux)
Château Léoville-Barton (Saint-Julien)
Château Léoville-Las-Cases (Saint-Julien)
Château Léoville-Poyferré (Saint-Julien)
Château Montrose (Saint-Estèphe)
Château Pichon-Longueville-Baron (Pauillac)
Château Pichon-Longueville
Comtesse-de-Lalande (Pauillac)
Château Rauzan-Ségla (Margaux)
Château Rauzan-Gassies (Margaux)

TROISIEMES CRUS (THIRD GROWTHS)
Château Boyd-Cantenac (Margaux)
Château Cantenac-Brown (Margaux)
Château Calon-Ségur (Saint-Estèphe)
Château Desmirail (Margaux)
Château Ferrière (Margaux)
Château Giscours (Margaux)
Château d'Issan (Margaux)
Château Kirwan (Margaux)
Château Lagrange (Saint-Julien)
Château La Lagune (Haut-Médoc)
Château Langoa (Saint-Julien)

Château Malescot-Saint-Exupéry (Margaux)
Château Marquis d'Alesme-Becker (Margaux)
Château Palmer (Margaux)

QUATRIEMES CRUS (FOURTH GROWTHS)
Château Beychevelle (Saint-Julien)
Château Branaire-Ducru (Saint-Julien)
Château Duhart-Milon-Rothschild (Pauillac)
Château Lafon-Rochet (Saint-Estèphe)
Château Marquis-de-Terme (Margaux)
Château Pouget (Margaux)
Château Prieuré-Lichine (Margaux)
Château Saint-Pierre (Saint-Julien)
Château Talbot (Saint-Julien)
Château La Tour-Carnet (Haut-Médoc)

CINQUIEMES CRUS (FIFTH GROWTHS)
Château d'Armailhac (Pauillac)
Château Batailley (Pauillac)
Château Belgrave (Haut-Médoc)
Château Camensac (Haut-Médoc)
Château Cantemerle (Haut-Médoc)
Château Clerc-Milon (Pauillac)
Château Cos-Labory (Saint-Estèphe)
Château Croizet-Bages (Pauillac)
Château Dauzac (Margaux)
Château Grand-Puy-Ducasse (Pauillac)
Château Grand-Puy-Lacoste (Pauillac)
Château Haut-Bages-Libéral (Pauillac)
Château Haut-Batailley (Pauillac)
Château Lynch-Bages (Pauillac)
Château Lynch-Moussas (Pauillac)
Château Pédesclaux (Pauillac)
Château Pontet-Canet (Pauillac)
Château du Tertre (Margaux)

THE SAUTERNES CRUS CLASSES OF 1855

PREMIER CRU SUPERIEUR
(SUPERIOR FIRST GROWTH)
Château d'Yquem

PREMIERS CRUS (FIRST GROWTHS)
Château Climens
Château Coutet
Château Guiraud
Château Lafaurie-Peyraguey
Château La Tour-Blanche
Clos Haut-Peyraguey
Château Rabaud-Promis
Château Rayne-Vigneau
Château Rieussec
Château Sigalas-Rabaud
Château Suduiraut

SECONDS CRUS (SECOND GROWTHS)
Château d'Arche
Château Brousset
Château Caillou
Château Doisy-Daëne
Château Doisy-Dubroca
Château Doisy-Védrines
Château Filhot
Château Lamothe (Despujols)
Château Lamothe (Guignard)
Château de Malle
Château Myrat
Château Nairac
Château Romer
Château Romer-du-Hayot
Château Suau

Haut-Médoc

CH. DE CANDALE 2000★

| ■ | n.c. | n.c. | ◧ | 8–11 € |

Grown in the Haut-Médoc dependencies of the ancient feudal estate of Issan, the name of this wine honours the memory of the former lords of the locality, the Foix-Candale family. This wine has something of the warrior character of that ancient dynasty, for its colour is deep ruby and the bouquet is quite leathery. The palate, on the other hand, leaves the taster with an overwhelming impression of elegance and balance.

☛ SFV de Cantenac, Ch. d'Issan, 33460 Cantenac,
tel. 05.57.88.35.91, fax 05.57.88.74.24,
e-mail issan@chateau-issan.com ☑
☕ by appt.
☛ Famille Cruse

CH. CANTEMERLE 2000★

| ■ | 5e cru clas. | 87 ha | 504,000 | ◧ | 23–30 € |

81 82 83 (85) 86 87 |88| (89) |90| 91 92 93 94 |95| 96 97 98 99 00

Grown on a vast estate of 190 ha, of which 87 ha are planted with vines, this cru is something of a rarity in the Gironde, being located in parkland with small forest areas crossed by a river. This 2000 reveals that the team making it have given pride of place to the use of high-quality oak. Its mark is still quite strong. The purple colour, the tannins, and the bouquet (aromas of very ripe fruit, roasting and spices) all indicate that the wine should be stored for three to four years before opening.

☛ Ch. Cantemerle, 33460 Macau, tel. 05.57.97.02.82,
fax 05.57.97.02.84, e-mail cantemerle@cantemerle.com ☑
☛ groupe SMABTP

CH. CARONNE SAINTE-GEMME 2000★★

| ■ | Cru bourg. | 40 ha | 270,000 | ◧ | 11–15 € |

It is not surprising that this wine is so good. It is a typical Médoc varietal blend grown on a fine terroir of Gunzian gravel; the family have invested heavily in quality. The intensity of the colour is on a par with that of the bouquet (stewed berry fruits, truffles, leather, prune). The palate is silky, full and well-blended, with good tannic support that calls for storage. Wait four or five years before opening this bottle. Made in another area of the estate is their **Château Labat 2000 (8–11 €)**, which was commended.

☛ Vignobles Nony-Borie, Caronne,
33112 Saint-Laurent-Médoc, tel. 05.57.87.56.81,
fax 05.56.51.71.51, e-mail fnony@aol.com ☑
☕ by appt.

DOM. DE CARTUJAC 2000★

| ■ | Cru paysan | 7 ha | 30,000 | ◧ | 5–8 € |

Saintout are producers in other appellations on the Médoc peninsula, and here offer a Haut-Médoc with an expressive and highly original bouquet. Its notes range from crystallized fruits to bergamot and from cherry to blond tobacco, via redcurrant and blackcurrant, all sustained by an elegant oakiness. A nice wine to open in three years' time.

☛ Bruno Saintout, Dom. de Cartujac,
33112 Saint-Laurent-Médoc, tel. 05.56.59.91.70,
fax 05.56.59.46.13 ☑
☕ by appt.

CH. CHARMAIL 2000★

| ■ | Cru bourg. | 22.5 ha | 120,000 | ▮◧♦ | 15–23 € |

88 89 90 91 92 93 |94| |95| (96) |97| 98 99 00

Though not up to the remarkable standard of certain earlier years, this 2000 still has plenty going for it. The richness of the colour says it all. The bouquet is powerful, with toasty notes, and the well-structured palate is rich, generous, and long-lasting. A wine with potential, that deserves to be laid down for five years before drinking.

☛ Olivier Sèze, Ch. Charmail,
33180 Saint-Seurin-de-Cadourne, tel. 05.56.59.70.63,
fax 05.56.59.39.20 ☑
☕ by appt.

CH. CITRAN 2000★★★

| ■ | Cru bourg. | 57 ha | n.c. | ◧ | 15–23 € |

88 |89| (90) 91 92 93 |94| (95) |96| |97| 98 99 (00)

Hidden away in the depths of Avensan, Citran is a fine estate whose products have become benchmarks in Haut-Médoc. This 2000 will only enhance its reputation. The colour oscillates between deep-purple, violet, and mauve, and is majestically impressive. The bouquet is no less sumptuous, with notes of mint and roasted coffee. The fleshy body is unveiled by a charming attack, which contrasts with the current austerity of the tannins. These are both potent and of high quality; they guarantee the future of this great wine, which in three years' time will go well with fillet of beef and chanterelle mushrooms.

☛ Ch. Citran, chem. de Citran, 33480 Avensan,
tel. 05.56.58.21.01, fax 05.57.88.84.60,
e-mail info@citran.com ☑
☕ by appt.

MOULINS DE CITRAN 2000★★

| ■ | n.c. | n.c. | ◧ | 8–11 € |

Another wine from the Citran team, who have had the good sense not to sacrifice everything to their first wine. The consequence is this second, very classy wine, whose keeping potential is so very characteristic of Médoc wines. Full, fleshy, and flavoursome, it is a successful alliance of power and charm.

☛ Ch. Citran, chem. de Citran, 33480 Avensan,
tel. 05.56.58.21.01, fax 05.57.88.84.60,
e-mail info@citran.com ☑
☕ by appt.

CH. COUFRAN 2000★

| ■ | Cru bourg. | 76 ha | 530,000 | ◧ | 15–23 € |

82 83 85 86 88 89 90 93 94 |95| |96| |97| 98 99 00

Whilst no longer planted entirely with Merlot, as it was until 1990, this cru is still highly unusual in the Médoc for the primacy accorded to that variety, currently 85%. This 2000, a beautiful garnet wine, is still hesitant to reveal its aromas: a few notes of vanilla and leather are all that filters through. However, the structure of the palate makes abundantly clear, through its strong-willed tannins, that this wine has a lot in store for the future. If kept for four or five years, it will then be fully expressive.

☛ SCA Ch. Coufran, 33180 Saint-Seurin-de-Cadourne,
tel. 05.56.59.31.02, fax 05.56.81.32.35
☕ by appt.
☛ Groupe Jean Miailhe

CH. DEVISE D'ARDILLEY 2000★

| ■ | 7.84 ha | 32,000 | ◧ | 8–11 € |

Although this cru cultivates some 20 ares of dessert grapes, the wine-lover will be more interested in their Merlot (53%) and Cabernet Sauvignon (47%), which have yielded this rather nice 2000. A lovely violet colour, it is developing complex perfumes of red berries, blackcurrant and prune, which are complemented by a high-quality oakiness. The palate's body and the elegance of the finish pleasantly extend the first impressions, whilst equally indicating good keeping

potential. Open in three to five years' time to accompany poultry or game birds.
🕊 Vignoble Vimes-Philippe SAS, Ch. Devise d'Ardilley, 33112 Saint-Laurent-Médoc, tel. 05.57.75.14.26, fax 05.57.75.14.26 ☑
�☖ by appt.

CH. DILLON 2000★

■ Cru bourg.	30 ha	200,000 ■ ⑪ ♨	11–15 €

82 83 85⟨86⟩88 |89| |90| 91 93 |95| |96| |97| |98| |99| 00

Cabernets, Merlot, Petit Verdot and even the aimiable Carménère variety have all contributed to this wine. No-one will be critical of that, if they inhale its bouquet of fresh red berry fruits (redcurrant) and blackcurrant, or savour its rich, intense, flavoursome and well-balanced palate. Sustained by well-judged oakiness, this well-rounded wine will be ready to drink in two years' time.
🕊 Lycée agricole de Blanquefort, Ch. Dillon, rue Arlot de Saint-Saud, 33290 Blanquefort, tel. 05.56.95.39.94, fax 05.56.95.36.75,
e-mail chateau-dillon@chateau-dillon.com ☑
☖ by appt.

CH. LA FAGOTTE 2000★★

■ Cru bourg.	4 ha	30,000	⑪	8–11 €

Made by the same producer as Château d'Aurilhac, this wine is just as well made. The dark colour, the bouquet of leather and crystallized fruit, and the sturdy tannic structure make for good keeping potential (wait four or five years before drinking) and a most enjoyable pure fruitiness.
🕊 SCEA Ch. d'Aurilhac et La Fagotte, Sénilhac, 33180 Saint-Seurin-de-Cadourne, tel. 05.56.59.35.32, fax 05.56.59.35.32 ☑
☖ by appt.
🕊 Erik Nieuwaal

LE FERRE DU CH. FERRE 2000★★

■	8 ha	25,000	⑪	11–15 €

With a demanding approach to maceration and fermentation, this cru at Vertheuil has left no stone unturned to produce this characterful wine, which marks the château's entry into the *Guide*. The colour is rich and the bouquet has a well-bred softness of stewed cherries and toast; the palate is rich, flavoursome and warm. Overall, this is an unctuous, silky wine. Keep in the cellar for four or five years.
🕊 EARL Châteaux Ferré et Haut Brignaïs, 3, rue des Aubépines, 33180 Vertheuil, tel. 05.56.41.96.39, fax 05.56.41.95.52, e-mail fer33c@wanadoo.fr ☑
☖ ev. day 9.30am–12.30pm 2.30pm–7.30pm

FORT DU ROY

Grand Art 2000★

■	5 ha	29,000	⑪	5–8 €

"Grand Art": the label of the cooperative cellar at Cussac is a declaration of the cooperators' quest for quality. Rich ruby in colour, with garnet highlights, subtly perfumed, and supported by a sturdy tannic presence, this wine reveals that they have given themselves the means to achieve their ambitions.
🕊 SCA les Viticulteurs du Fort-Médoc, 105, av. du Haut-Médoc, 33460 Cussac-Fort-Médoc, tel. 05.56.58.92.85, fax 05.56.58.92.86, e-mail cave-fort-medoc@wanadoo.fr ☑
☖ ev. day except Sun. 9.30am–12.30pm 2pm–6pm

CH. GASTON-RENA 2000★

■	2.43 ha	12,000 ■ ⑪ ♨	8–11 €

This is one of the newest wine-growing estates in the Reynats district of Cissac, established in 1991 by the oenologist Daniel Gaston. Nice-looking and with an elegant range of aromas, in which blackcurrant is joined by notes of leather, black fruits and spices, his 2000 is enhanced by an oakiness that is respectful of the grapes. A good wine to lay down, best left for four or five years.
🕊 Catherine et Daniel Gaston, 1, chem. de la Grave, Le Reynats, 33250 Cissac-Médoc, tel. 06.85.20.51.91, fax 05.56.47.84.78, e-mail gastonrena@wanadoo.fr ☑
☖ by appt.

LE GRAND PAROISSIEN

Elevé et vieilli en fût de chêne 2000★

■	4 ha	18,000	⑪	5–8 €

The cellar at Saint-Seurin-de-Cadourne has a tradition of quality that is well known to the people of the Médoc and Bordeaux. The colour of this wine is ruby, and the bouquet marries vanilla to dried fruits: it is a wine with an elegance of presentation. Honest, well-balanced, and solidly constructed on well-softened tannins, the palate has a long, lingering finish.
🕊 Sté coop. de vinification la Paroisse, 33180 Saint-Seurin-de-Cadourne, tel. 05.56.59.31.28, fax 05.56.59.39.01 ☑
☖ ev. day except Sun. 8.30am–12.30pm 2pm–6pm; Sat. 8.30am–12.30pm

CH. HANTEILLAN 2000★

■ Cru bourg.	33.29 ha	248,000 ■ ⑪ ♨	8–11 €

This vineyard claims to be medieval, having been a dependency of the abbey of Vertheuil in its heyday. It now offers this quality 2000. Beautifully black, it is developing an expressive bouquet (cinnamon on oaky notes) and a powerful attack. The palatal structure is good, with dense tannins and an attractive fruitiness, guarantors of the wine's future. Wait three years before enjoying its personality.
🕊 SA Ch. Hanteillan, 12, rte d'Hanteillan, 33250 Cissac-Médoc, tel. 05.56.59.35.31, fax 05.56.59.31.51, e-mail chateau.hanteillan@wanadoo.fr ☑
☖ ev. day except Sat. Sun. 9am–12 noon 2pm–5.30pm
🕊 Catherine Blasco

CH. HAUT BELLEVUE

Cuvée Océane 2000★

■	3 ha	6,700	⑪	15–23 €

A pretty name for a wine grown on an estate that has been patiently put together by one family over more than 100 years of its history. The ruby colour and purple highlights say straight away that this wine has ambitions and the means to realize them. The intense, subtle bouquet mixes cinnamon, clove and green pepper. The palate is developing agreeable tannins. A nice wine to open in three or four years' time. The same estate's **Cuvée Principale 2000 (8–11 €)** has also achieved a one-star rating.
🕊 Alain Roses, 10, chem. des Calinottes, 33460 Lamarque, tel. 05.56.58.91.64, fax 05.57.88.50.64, e-mail haut-bellevue@worldonline.fr ☑
☖ by appt.

CH. HAUT-BREGA 2000★

■ Cru artisan 7.9 ha	40,000	⑪	8–11 €

Charmingly termed an artisan wine, this wine shows that at Haut-Bréga they believe things should be done properly. The colour is darkly attractive, and the bouquet, although it has not yet attained its final character, already has seductive notes of toast. The palate is fresh and well-integrated.
🕊 Joseph Ambach, 16, rue des Frères-Razeau, 33180 Saint-Seurin-de-Cadourne, tel. 05.56.59.70.77, fax 05.56.59.62.50, e-mail cht.haut.brega@wanadoo.fr ☑
☖ ev. day 10am–8pm; winter by appt.

KAROLUS 2000★★

■	3 ha	10,000	⑪	23–30 €

Though the name of this wine is original, not to say strange, this special vintage of Château Sénéjac is distinguished for its excellence. The colour, with its black highlights, suggests as much, and the bouquet confirms it. Although the oak is still dominant, it is of good quality, and one detects the beginnings of a well-balanced complexity (ripe fruits, blackcurrant, rose, spices). The palate has corresponding flavours, plus some chocolaty notes. The whole creation is sustained by the tannins, which are rich, ripe, not over-dry, and which promise and require good storage. Leave in the cellar and open in five or six years' time.

↰ M. et Mme Thierry Rustmann, Ch. Sénéjac, 33290 Le Pian-Médoc, tel. 05.56.70.20.11, fax 05.56.70.23.91, e-mail chateausenejac@free.fr
🍷 by appt.

CH. LABARDE 2000★

| ■ | 4.82 ha | 26,000 | ⦙⦙⦙ | 8–11 € |

A fine unit of more than 40 ha, Château Dauzac (Margaux AOC) has a few hectares in the Haut-Médoc appellation. These vines have produced a nice blend (60% Cabernet Sauvignon, 40% Merlot), matured 12 months in oak casks. Supple and fleshy, this 2000 opens up fully in the finish to leave the memory of some very attractive fruit flavours. The fine tannic presence will permit drinking in two to three years from now.

↰ SE du Ch. Dauzac, 33460 Labarde, tel. 05.57.88.32.10, fax 05.57.88.96.00, e-mail andrelurton@andrelurton.com ☑
🍷 by appt.
↰ MAIF

CH. LACHESNAYE 2000★

| ■ | Cru bourg. | n.c. | n.c. | ⦙⦙⦙ | 11–15 € |

Though adjacent to Lanessan and belonging to the same owner, Lachesnaye is nonetheless a separate cru with a wine that has a personality of it own, as you will discover if you sample it. The deep-purple colour is a sign of youth, and the fine, well-extracted tannins leave no doubt that this is a wine with a decent future before it.

↰ SCEA Delbos-Bouteiller, Ch. Lachesnaye, 33460 Cussac-Fort-Médoc, tel. 05.56.58.94.80, fax 05.57.88.89.92, e-mail bouteiller@bouteiller.com
🍷 ev. day 9.15am–12 noon 2pm–6pm; groups by appt.

CH. LACOUR JACQUET 2000★★

| ■ | 10 ha | 30,000 | 🗓⦙⦙⦙ | 8–11 € |
89 90 94 |95| |96| 97 98 99 **00**

The year 2000 was a good one on this family estate at Cussac. This 2000 is an authentic classic of the genre. A beautiful violet with purple highlights, it has a bouquet of delicate notes of cinnamon and clove, a silky attack, and a full, firm, lingering body. This beautifully made wine will need, and deserves, five years' patience, after which it will be a fine accompaniment to red meat.

↰ GAEC Lartigue, 70, av. du Haut-Médoc, 33460 Cussac-Fort-Médoc, tel. 05.56.58.91.55, fax 05.56.58.94.82 ☑
🍷 ev. day 8am–12.30pm 1.30pm–7pm

CH. LAGRAVE

Cuvée Héritage 2000★

| ■ | Cru bourg. | 13 ha | 30,000 | 🗓⦙⦙⦙♨ | 8–11 € |

Created only in 1999, this Cuvée Héritage makes a welcome entry into the Guide with this 2000, which allies simplicity with charm, no less in the bouquet, with its notes of blackcurrant buds, than on the palate, where it betrays roundness, fullness and good balance. This amiable, expressive wine may be drunk in its youth or kept for just a year or two.

↰ SCEA Garri du Gai, 1, rte de la Chatole, 33250 Saint-Sauveur-Médoc, tel. 05.56.41.50.18, fax 05.56.41.54.65, e-mail info@domaines-lapalu.com
🍷 by appt.

CH. LA LAGUNE 2000★★

| ■ | 3e cru clas. | 71.23 ha | n.c. | ⦙⦙⦙ | 23–30 € |
75 78 81 |82| 83 85 |86| 87 88⦿89⦀90 91 92 |93| 94 **95 96** |97|98 99⦿00

This fair-sized unit of 75 ha, overlooked by a pretty charterhouse raised in the 18th century, is the traditional start of the famous Médoc Route des Châteaux (the Médoc Wine Route). It has long been one of the mainstays of the appellation, with a traditional varietal mix that admits only 25% Merlot and grows 10% Petit Verdot. Once again it shows its class in a wine whose noble origins are immediately apparent from the classic Bordeaux colour. The bouquet allies a well-judged oakiness with notes of ripe fruits and liquorice and develops with great elegance before yielding to the palate's powerful flavours. After a round attack, the solid tannic structure reveals itself and sustains a lingering finish. These are characteristics that underscore the wine's real potential for storage. Indeed, it would be a shame to open the bottle in less than three years from now.

↰ Ch. La Lagune, 81, av. de l'Europe, 33290 Ludon-Médoc, tel. 05.57.88.82.77, fax 05.57.88.82.70, e-mail lalagune@club-internet.fr
🍷 by appt.

CH. DE LAMARQUE 2000★

| ■ | Cru bourg. | 35 ha | 160,000 | ⦙⦙⦙ | 11–15 € |
83 86 88 89 90 **91** 92 93 94 |95| 96 97 98 99 **00**

The château at Lamarque still belongs to the descendants of the count of Fumel, who acquired the estate in 1841. The château itself is a genuine medieval castle. Its wine has a shimmering appearance that when viewed here almost evokes life in the courts of lords of long ago. The bouquet is of ripe fruits, brioche and spices, the palate has presence, and there is an elegant, silky finish. The wine will cope with several years' storage.

↰ SC Gromand d'Evry, Ch. de Lamarque, 33460 Lamarque, tel. 05.56.58.90.03, fax 05.56.58.93.43, e-mail chdelamarq@aol.com ☑
🍷 by appt.

CH. LAMOTHE BERGERON 2000★

| ■ | Cru bourg. | 67.04 ha | 266,500 | ⦙⦙⦙ | 11–15 € |
95 96 97 |99| 00

To bear the name of an ancien régime parliamentary enthusiast for agronomy is an honour of which this cru has made itself worthy by the quality of its 2000 vintage. Although the bouquet may somewhat astound at first, its youthfulness and scents of flint and cinnamon will finally captivate. The palate is all subtlety and finesse, and owes its good constitution to the Cabernet grapes, which will enable it to benefit from a time in the cellar.

↰ SC du Ch. Grand-Puy Ducasse, La Croix Bacalan, 109, rue Achard, BP 154, 33042 Bordeaux Cedex, tel. 05.56.11.29.00, fax 05.56.11.29.01

CH. LANESSAN 2000★

| ■ | Cru bourg. | n.c. | 280,000 | ⦙⦙⦙ | 15–23 € |
86 88 **90** 91 92 93 |94| 95 |96| |97| 98 **99** 00

This cru has belonged to the Bouteiller family, a leading Médoc wine family, since their wine-merchant ancestor Jean

Delbos acquired it in 1793. In line with their traditions, they offer a sturdy, well-structured wine. Dark in appearance with bluish tinges, the bouquet of Morello cherry and spicy, minty hints, is already agreeable. But the rich body, tannic support and long, classy finish say clearly that this very true-to-type wine deserves the honours of the cellar.
⌐ SCEA Delbos-Bouteiller, Ch. Lanessan,
33460 Cussac-Fort-Médoc, tel. 05.56.58.94.80,
fax 05.57.88.89.92, e-mail bouteiller@bouteiller.com ☑
Ⓨ ev. day 9.15am–12 noon 2pm–6pm

CH. LAROSE PERGANSON 2000★★

■ Cru bourg.	33 ha	130,000	⑪	11–15 €

This is an old label that disappeared in 1900 and reappeared in 1996. The wine comes from the oldest vines that Larose-Trintaudon possess. The care devoted to its creation has been crowned with success. With its glossy black appearance, this 2000 has a lovely complex bouquet: cherry, roasted coffee, vanilla – nothing is wanting to create a seductive, mouth-watering synthesis. The palate is no less tempting, with its alliance of oaky, fruity, spicy notes set off by a hint of liquorice. A very fine wine.
⌐ SA Ch. Larose Trintaudon, rte de Pauillac,
33112 Saint-Laurent-Médoc, tel. 05.56.59.41.72,
fax 05.56.59.93.22, e-mail info@trintaudon.com ☑
Ⓨ by appt.
⌐ AGF

CH. LAROSE-TRINTAUDON 2000★

■ Cru bourg.	139 ha	945,000	⑪	8–11 €

81 82 83 85 86 87 88 89 |90| 91 92 93 |94| 95 |96| |97| 98 99 00

This vast estate of more than 170 ha belonging to the AGF group is very much in the Bordeaux tradition by dint of its varietal balance, the age of its vines, and its production potential. With its appetizing and potent bouquet of high-quality fruity, oaky, spicy notes, this 2000 has a good tannic presence on the palate that does not exclude roundness.
⌐ SA Ch. Larose Trintaudon, rte de Pauillac,
33112 Saint-Laurent-Médoc, tel. 05.56.59.41.72,
fax 05.56.59.93.22, e-mail info@trintaudon.com ☑
Ⓨ by appt.
⌐ AGF

CH. DE LAUGA 2000★

■ Cru artisan n.c.	30,000	⑪	5–8 €

This is a small property very much in line with Médoc tradition by reason of its diverse varietal mix, which even includes a plot of Petit Verdot. The result is a wine that is full of charm and attractions: the bouquet has fresh notes of red berries and vanilla, and the palate is well-constructed and resolute. The finish is enhanced by a lovely revival of fruity aromas. This wine left a good impression and has the potential to develop.
⌐ Christian Brun, 4, rue des Capérans,
33460 Cussac-Fort-Médoc, tel. 05.56.58.92.83,
fax 05.56.58.97.88, e-mail chateau@lauga.com ☑
Ⓨ ev. day 8am–7pm

CH. MALESCASSE 2000★★★

■ Cru bourg.	37 ha	160,000	⑪	11–15 €

82 83 |88| |89| |90| 91 93 |94| |95| |96| 97 98 99 00

A regular producer of good wine over the last few years, this cru has taken a spectacular leap forward with this 2000, thanks to the care with which the grapes were harvested and vinified. The richness of the garnet colour and its velvety highlights immediately create confidence, and the bouquet simply confirms that, with its joyful and expressive alliance of red berries, caramel and chocolate. The smooth attack and concentrated generosity of the body convince that this wonderful wine is one for the cellar. Leave it there for six or seven years, before opening as an accompaniment to beef or some other tasty meal. Simpler but well made is the second wine, **La Closerie de Malescasse 2000 (8–11 €)**, which was commended by the Jury.
⌐ Ch. Malescasse, 6, rte du Moulin-Rose, 33460 Lamarque, tel. 05.56.58.90.09, fax 05.57.38.07.00,
e-mail malescasse@free.fr ☑
Ⓨ by appt.
⌐ Alcatel

CH. MAUCAMPS 2000★★

■ Cru bourg.	18 ha	100,000	⑪	11–15 €

82 83 85 86 88 |89| |90| 93 94 |95| |96| |97| 98 99 00

This conscientious, well-situated cru well deserves attention. Its 2000 has plenty going for it: a fine garnet appearance, a complex bouquet of crystallized fruits and coffee, a round, fleshy attack, an elegant, well-built palatal structure, and a spicy finish. It looks as if it will keep well.
⌐ SARL Ch. Maucamps, BP 11, 33460 Macau,
tel. 05.57.88.07.64, fax 05.57.88.07.00 ☑
Ⓨ ev. day except Sat. Sun. 9am–12 noon 2pm–6pm

CH. MEYRE

Optima 2000★

■ Cru bourg.	15.5 ha	15,000	⑪	8–11 €

88 89 90 91 93 94 |95| |96| 97 98 99 |00|

This wine, produced by Château Meyre – part of the Châteaux et Hôtels de France chain – has been carefully made. The bouquet is highly expressive (minty and spicy), and the developing palate is as well-balanced as it is elegant, with attractive tannins and a nice hint of cinnamon as it finishes.
⌐ SA Ch. Meyre, 16, rte de Castelnau, 33480 Avensan,
tel. 05.56.58.10.77, fax 05.56.58.13.20,
e-mail chateau.meyre@wanadoo.fr ☑
Ⓨ ev. day 2pm–6pm; Sat. Sun. by appt.; cl. 1 Nov.–30 Mar.

CH. MICALET

Réserve Elevé en fût de chêne 2000★

■ Cru artisan 0.7 ha	4,800	⑪	11–15 €

Being a "special", this wine follows current trends: it is a 50% Merlot. The oak-maturing is very noticeable both in the bouquet and on the palate, but does not overpower the wine's other characteristics. The structure promises good keeping, and the finish has some agreeable roasted notes.
⌐ EARL Denis Fédieu, Ch. Micalet, 10, rue Jeanne-d'Arc,
33460 Cussac-Fort-Médoc, tel. 05.56.58.95.48,
fax 05.56.58.96.85, e-mail earl.fedieu@wanadoo.fr ☑
Ⓨ ev. day except Sun. 9am–12 noon 3pm–7pm;
groups by appt.

CH. MILLE ROSES 2000★

■	n.c.	9,500	⑪	11–15 €

This small estate entered the *Guide* last year, and confirms its ambitions with this wine, whose bouquet shows that it is an authentic Haut-Médoc. The same finesse informs the palate to create an overall impression of charm and quality. This wine will deserve its place in the cellar over the next four to five years. It is a 65% Cabernet Sauvignon (remainder Merlot), has undergone malolactic fermentation in the cask, and has spent 18 months in oak.
⌐ David Faure, Ch. Mille Roses, 16, chem. de Canteloup,
33460 Macau, tel. 05.57.88.42.16, fax 05.57.88.42.16,
e-mail davidfaure@mageos.com ☑
Ⓨ by appt.

CH. MOULIN DE BLANCHON 2000★

■   12 ha   50,000   ◫   5–8 €

This quiet estate is not without interest in view of this current wine, which is a successor to many others. Ruby, with black glints, it is a pleasing toasty bouquet in which notes of thyme mingle with those of ripe fruits to conjure up a pretty picture. All very confidence-inspiring. Fleshy, rich, powerful, and well-balanced, the palate indicates good keeping potential.
↝ Henri Négrier, Ch. Moulin de Blanchon,
33180 Saint-Seurin-de-Cadourne, tel. 05.56.59.38.66,
fax 05.56.59.32.31 ☑
ℐ ev. day 8.30am–7pm

CH. DU MOULIN ROUGE 2000★

■ Cru bourg.   16.48 ha   100,000   ▮ ◫   8–11 €

Don't expect to see a saucy wink behind the name of this cru – just an old mill built of reddish-pink bricks! The wine is none the worse for it, and it certainly has a strong accent. Extremely well put together, it is supported by sturdy tannins which call for storage-time in order to soften, and it has an expressive bouquet (roasting, fruits in alcohol, and crystallized fruits) that shows its generosity and undoubted keeping potential.
↝ Pelon-Ribeiro, 18, rue de Costes,
33460 Cussac-Fort-Médoc, tel. 05.56.58.91.13,
fax 05.56.58.93.68 ☑
ℐ by appt.

CH. MOUTTE BLANC

Marguerite Déjean 2000★★

■ Cru artisan   0.37 ha   2,200   ◫   11–15 €

A somewhat atypical Haut-Médoc by virtue of being a 100% Merlot, this very limited-edition wine has been the object of meticulous attention, first on the vine, where it was effectively gardened, and then in the vat and barrel-store. The result is a wine with an extremely expressive bouquet and a well-judged oakiness. Full, round, tender, well-balanced, it is already pleasing, but will also keep. You will be able to serve it happily in one or two years' time, in four or five, or even after.
↝ Patrice de Bortoli-Dejean, 6, imp. de la Libération,
33460 Macau, tel. 05.57.88.40.39, fax 05.57.88.40.39 ☑
ℐ by appt.

CH. PEYRABON 2000★

■ Cru bourg.   41.16 ha   233,900   ▮ ◫   15–23 €
86 88 |89| 90 91 92 93 94 |96| 97 98 |99| 00

Since 1998, when it last changed hands, this cru has undergone large investment. This 2000 shows that the money was not spent in vain. Even though there is a strong presence of oak, there is a sturdy tannic structure and an attractively fine and complex bouquet, which will allow it to develop favourably in the cellar over the next three to four years (at least).
↝ SARL Ch. Peyrabon, Vignes de Peyrabon,
33250 Saint-Sauveur, tel. 05.56.59.57.10, fax 05.56.59.59.45,
e-mail chateau.peyrabon@wanadoo.fr ☑
ℐ ev. day except Sat. Sun. 9am–12 noon 2pm–5pm

CH. LA PEYRE 2000★

■ Cru artisan   1.2 ha   8,500   ◫   8–11 €
|95| 96 |97| 98 99 00

This tiny cru at Cissac belonging to the Vignobles Rabiller (Saint-Estèphe) offers this rather nice wine to lay down, which turns out to be as good as its garnet colour suggests. It has a pleasant bouquet of toast and spices, and a good structure. Its fruity, rich, concentrated body shows that it has what is needed to develop well over several years. Some time in the cellar will help to polish up the finish.
↝ EARL Vignobles Rabiller, Le Cendrayre, Leyssac,
33180 Saint-Estèphe. tel. 05.56.59.32.51,
fax 05.56.59.70.09 ☑
ℐ ev. day 10am–12 noon 2.30pm–7pm; Sun. by appt.

CH. PEYRE-LEBADE 2000★

■ Cru bourg.   55 ha   200,000   ◫   11–15 €

Taking its name from the wide plain situated in the heart of the Médoc peninsula, this wine, signed by Benjamin de Rothschild, is pre-eminently one of finesse, both in the bouquet of fruity, floral notes and on the palate, where there is a roundness and fleshiness that will make it very pleasant drinking in a year or two from now.
↝ CV Edmond et Benjamin de Rothschild,
33480 Listrac-Médoc, tel. 05.56.58.38.00,
fax 05.56.58.26.46, e-mail chateau.clarke@wanadoo.fr

CH. PRIBAN 2000★

■   0.47 ha   3,500   ◫   11–15 €

Once a larger unit, this cru in the Macau district is one of the smallest in the Médoc, being slightly under half a hectare. Nevertheless, it contains a diversity of varieties and offers a formidable wine with a complex bouquet (red and black berries, mint, roasting, jamminess, and more) and a well-blended palate sustained by nicely softened tannins.
↝ C. et J.-F. Denis, 33, rue Tourat, 33000 Bordeaux,
tel. 06.80.07.72.59, fax 05.56.51.69.17 ☑
ℐ by appt.
↝ Lestelle

CH. RAMAGE LA BATISSE 2000★

■ Cru bourg.   32.24 ha   253,000   ▮ ◫ ⚭   11–15 €
85 86 88 89 |90| 91 92 94 |95| |96| |97| 98 99 00

This vast estate of nearly 65 ha belongs to the French civil servants' friendly society. Their members might like to invest in this 2000 wine, which has a lovely ruby colour and a very fruity bouquet. Round and fresh, characterized by both finesse and openness, this is a very authentic Médoc, as is revealed by the hint of fruit-kernel on which it finishes. The estate's second wine, **Clos de Ramage 2000 (8–11 €)**, is commended; it should be kept in the cellar for a year before drinking, like its fellow.
↝ Ch. Ramage La Batisse, Tourteran, 33250 Saint-Sauveur,
tel. 05.56.59.57.24, fax 05.56.59.54.14 ☑
ℐ by appt.
↝ MACIF

CH. DU RAUX 2000★

■ Cru bourg.   19 ha   83,000   ◫   8–11 €

Located at Cussac, this cru is made from a majority of Merlot grapes, as is revealed by the fruity bouquet and the supple structure. Round, fine, and elegant, it nonetheless has sufficient structure to allow it to keep for two to three years.
↝ SCI du Raux, 33460 Cussac-Fort-Médoc,
tel. 05.56.58.91.07, fax 05.56.58.91.07 ☑
ℐ by appt.

CH. DU RETOUT 2000★

■ Cru bourg.   15 ha   90,000   ▮ ◫ ⚭   8–11 €

Typical of the Bordeaux region with its large bourgeois house flanked by a tower in one corner, this château will provide a conversation piece with its 2000. The tannins are still very young and may astound some wine-lovers, but others will see them as a guarantee of long life, especially as the bouquet begins discreetly, then opens wide to disclose notes of red and black fruits. Supported by a well-judged oakiness, this is a wine with personality.
↝ Gérard Kopp, Ch. du Retout,
33460 Cussac-Fort-Médoc, tel. 05.56.58.91.08,
fax 05.56.58.91.08, e-mail chateauduretout@wanadoo.fr ☑
ℐ ev. day 8am–12 noon 2pm–6pm; Sat. Sun. by appt.

CH. REYSSON

Réserve du Château 2000★

■ Cru bourg.   39.18 ha   60,000   ◫   11–15 €

Made by a cru which changed its managing organization in 2001 in favour of Douthe, this 2000 vintage is a product (so to speak) of transition. It was evidently made under good conditions, as its development throughout the tasting showed. The bouquet is a successful marriage of fruity aromas (jammy notes of red berries and prune) and oakiness, and the palate has a good structure which is tannic and sturdy as well as fleshy. It will need two to three years' storage before drinking in order to achieve full integration.
↝ Vignobles Dourthe, 35, rue de Bordeaux,
33290 Parempuyre, tel. 05.56.35.53.00, fax 05.56.35.53.29,
e-mail contact@cvbg.com
ℐ by appt.

Haut-Médoc

CH. SAINT-PAUL 2000★

■ Cru bourg. 20 ha 120,000 ▌❚▶ ↓ 11–15 €

This cru respects tradition with its varietal diversity, even if Merlot does make up a full half of the blend. The result is a pleasant wine: a deep colour, full of subtlety, a bouquet with warm, sunny notes, a gradual, fleshy development, and a long finish. It has the air of a good laying-down wine.
➥ SC du Ch. Saint-Paul, 33180 Saint-Seurin-de-Cadourne, tel. 05.56.59.34.72, fax 05.56.59.38.35 ✓
🍷 by appt.

BEL AIR DE SIRAN 2000★

■ 0.93 ha 6,400 ❚▶ 8–11 €

Although this wine (grown on Haut-Médoc AOC land) plays something of a second fiddle to Margaux, its origins are nonetheless excellent and it does them credit. The colour is a beautiful deep garnet, and the bouquet is a fine compromise between red berry fruit and oak, where both can express themselves. The palate is supple and rich, sustained by well-honed tannins. This wine deserves to be left alone for four or five years, after which it will go very well with red meat or roast capon with a panful of ceps.
➥ SC du Ch. Siran, Ch. Siran, 33460 Labarde, tel. 05.57.88.34.04, fax 05.57.88.70.05, e-mail chateau.siran@wanadoo.fr ✓
🍷 ev. day 10.15am–12.45pm 1.30pm–6pm
➥ Alain Miailhe

CH. SOCIANDO-MALLET 2000★★★

■ Cru bourg. 46 ha 312,000 ❚▶ 46–76 €

75 76 78 80 81 (82) 83 84 85 86 87 |88| |89| |90| 91 92 93 94 (95) (96) |97| (98) (99) (00)

Sociando, created in the 17th century, really flies the flag for the village of Saint-Seurin-de-Cadourne, and once again proclaims the special qualities of its terroir. The colour of this 2000 is a deep, rich purple. The bouquet is almost shy at first, but the aromas quickly gather and gain in complexity: spices and black fruits, smokiness, nothing is left out. After a round, velvety attack, the palate reveals the full measure of its power, sustained by silky, well-clothed tannins. An ideal wine to lay down. Leave it in the cellar for six, eight, or even ten years. "An example to follow," the Jury said unanimously.
➥ SCEA Jean Gautreau, Ch. Sociando-Mallet, 33180 Saint-Seurin-de-Cadourne, tel. 05.56.73.38.80, fax 05.56.73.38.88, e-mail scea-jean-gautreau@wanadoo.fr ✓
🍷 by appt.

CH. SOUDARS 2000★★

■ Cru bourg. 22.25 ha 160,000 ❚▶ 15–23 €

82 83 85 86 |89| |90| 93 94 95 |96| |97| |98| |99| 00

Located near the archaeological site at Brion and the mysterious Reysson marshes, this cru has the benefit of a rather original terroir on a finely filtering limestone-clay soil full of marine fossils. This 2000 is an elegant wine both by virtue of its noteworthy dark colour and because of its bouquet of red berries and spices. The palate is well balanced with an oaky toastiness that nicely accompanies yet never overwhelms the fruit.
➥ Ch. Soudars, 33180 Saint-Seurin-de-Cadourne, tel. 05.56.59.36.09, fax 05.56.59.72.39
🍷 by appt.
➥ Vignobles E. F. Miailhe SAS

CH. DU TAILLAN

Cuvée des Dames 2000★

■ Cru bourg. 2.5 ha 15,000 ❚▶ 11–15 €

This cru, famous for its legend of the White Lady and its wineries, which are listed historic monuments, is located at the gates of Bordeaux. It belongs to five sisters, hence the name of this particular wine. Dark in colour, it has a bouquet in which cherry and blackcurrant manage to find expression in a miscellany still dominated by the oak. The palate reveals sufficient body to allow the different elements to blend together in time.
➥ SCEA Ch. du Taillan, 56, av. de La Croix, 33320 Le Taillan-Médoc, tel. 05.56.57.47.00, fax 05.56.57.47.01, e-mail chateaudutaillan@wanadoo.fr ✓
🍷 ev. day 9am–6pm; Sat. Sun. by appt.

CH. LA TOUR CARNET 2000★★

■ 4e cru clas. 48 ha 180,000 ❚▶ 15–23 €

79 81 82 83 85 86 (88) |89| |90| 93 94 (96) |97| 98 99 00

Since 2000, La Tour Carnet has belonged to Bernard Magrez's vast wine-growing empire and is now one of the jewels in that crown, having a château that comprises elements from the 18th century and the Middle Ages. This vintage, which is dark garnet with deep-purple tinges, is still marked by the oak, though the latter respects the overall balance. There is great aromatic intensity here (dominated by notes of grills and roasted coffee), and an excellent tannic presence, which makes this a genuine laying-down wine. Wait four or five years.
➥ Ch. La Tour Carnet, 33112 Saint-Laurent-Médoc, tel. 05.56.73.30.90, fax 05.56.59.48.54, e-mail la-tour-carnet@tiscali.fr
🍷 by appt.
➥ Bernard Magrez

CH. TOUR DU HAUT-MOULIN 2000★★

■ Cru bourg. n.c. n.c. ❚▶ 11–15 €

78 79 81 82 (83) 84 85 86 87 88 |89| |90| 91 92 93 94 |95| 96 |97| 98 99 00

Pay a visit to Fort-Médoc, built by Vauban, then go 500 m to find one of the recognized mainstays of the appellation, this cru on Garonne gravels, comprising 51% Cabernet Sauvignon, 47% Merlot, and 2% Petit Verdot. The wine is every bit as good as its bright, rich ruby colour suggests. The bouquet is still rather on the oaky side, with good quality roasted notes, but these do not eclipse the notes of ripe red fruits. The palate, which is powerful, tannic and rich, calls for laying down. Wait three or four years.
➥ Lionel Poitou, 24, av. du Fort-Médoc, 33460 Cussac-Fort-Médoc, tel. 05.56.58.91.10, fax 05.57.88.83.13, e-mail contact@tour-du-haut-moulin.com ✓
🍷 by appt.

CH. TOUR DU ROC 2000★

■ Cru bourg. 12 ha 48,000 ▌ ↓ 3–5 €

This wine's identity as a Médoc is evidenced by the Cabernet Sauvignon bouquet of green pepper and spices. It is still somewhat restive, and will need to be left for two or three years in order to give of its best. It does, however, have the necessary tannic structure and aromatic reserve to age well.
➥ Cheval-Quancard, La Mouline, 4 rue du Carbouney, BP 36, 33560 Carbon-Blanc, tel. 05.57.77.88.88, fax 05.57.77.98.99, e-mail chevalquancard@chevalquancard.com
🍷 by appt.

CH. TOUR MARCILLANET 2000★

■ Cru bourg. 15.2 ha n.c. ▌ ↓ 11–15 €

As you leave Saint-Laurent on the road to Hourtin, you come across this part-14th century château, which is the appellation's easternmost estate. The location is good for wine-growing, as this 2000 reveals. Its aromatic character is elegant, with notes of oak and wild fruits; the palate has a silky, rich, supple, velvety structure. A charming synthesis, which will improve over four or five years.
➥ SCEV Ponsar-Mahieu, Ch. Tour Marcillanet, 33112 Saint-Laurent-Médoc, tel. 05.56.59.92.94, fax 01.43.20.14.75 ✓
🍷 by appt.

315

BORDEAUX

BORDEAUX

CH. VERDIGNAN 2000★★

■ Cru bourg. 59 ha 390,000 ⬛ 15–23 €
(86) 88 89 90 93 94 |95| |96| 98 99 **00**

This cru does not simply have a superb view over the estuary, it also benefits from a choice terroir of Graves (80%) and limestone-clay. Yet again, Eric Miailhe has got the best out of it for this vintage. The bouquet is full of subtlety, being a fine mix of ripe fruits (prune) against an oaky background. The palate is elegant; the fresh, well-blended tannins will ensure good keeping over a long time and will never be overbearing.
•➤ Ch. Verdignan, 33180 Saint-Seurin-de-Cadourne, tel. 05.56.59.31.02, fax 05.56.81.32.35
⬛ by appt.
•➤ Groupe Jean Miailhe

CH. VIALLET NOUHANT
Vieilli en fût de chêne 2000★

■ Cru artisan 2.6 ha 16,000 ⬛⬛ 5–8 €
The year 2000 was important for this cru. The winery was renovated then, and this wine, the first to enjoy its benefits, reveals that the work was a success. The garnet colour has lovely highlights, and the rich bouquet has notes of crystallized stewed fruits with a hint of spices. The elegance of this wine also includes the palate, with its smooth tannins; it has a rich-ness and unctuousness that persists right through the finish.
•➤ Alain Nouhant, 5, rue Jeanne-d'Arc, 33460 Cussac-Fort-Médoc, tel. 05.57.88.51.43, fax 05.57.88.51.43, e-mail alain.nouhant@libertysurf.fr ⬛
⬛ by appt.

CH. VIEUX LANDAT 2000★

■ 13 ha 20,000 ⬛ 8–11 €
This wine was grown on sandy gravel and is a 50:50 blend of Merlot and Cabernet Sauvignon. The bouquet is on the powerful side, with notes of ripe fruits and spices creating a mouth-watering mix. Robust and fleshy, with rather firm tannic support, the palate reveals good storage potential. Two or three years' patience will be needed for the structure to become sufficiently rounded.
•➤ Ch. Vieux Landat, 42, rte du Landat, 33250 Cissac-Médoc, tel. 05.56.59.56.30, fax 05.56.59.56.30 ⬛ ⬛
⬛ ev. day 8am–12 noon 1.30pm–5.30pm; Sat. Sun. by appt.
•➤ Signolle

Wines selected but not starred

CH. ANEY 2000

■ 22 ha 163,000 ⬛ 8–11 €
•➤ SCF Ch. Aney, 6, av. du Haut-Médoc, 33460 Cussac-Fort-Médoc, tel. 05.56.58.94.89, fax 05.56.58.98.15 ⬛
⬛ ev. day 9am–12 noon 2pm–6pm

CH. BEL AIR 2000

■ Cru bourg. 37 ha 235,000 ⬛ 8–11 €
•➤ Domaines Martin, Ch. Gloria, 33250 Saint-Julien-Beychevelle, tel. 05.56.59.08.18, fax 05.56.59.16.18, e-mail domainemartin@wanadoo.fr ⬛
⬛ by appt.
•➤ Françoise Triaud

CH. BEL ORME
Tronquoy de Lalande 2000

■ Cru bourg. 26 ha 160,000 ⬛⬛⬛ 11–15 €
|95| |96| 97 98 99 00

•➤ Jean-Michel Quié, Ch. Bel Orme, 33180 Saint-Seurin-de-Cadourne, tel. 05.56.59.38.29, fax 05.56.59.72.83 ⬛
⬛ by appt.

CH. LE BOURDIEU VERTHEUIL 2000

■ Cru bourg. 20 ha 140,000 ⬛ 8–11 €
•➤ SC Ch. Le Bourdieu-Vertheuil, 33180 Vertheuil, tel. 05.56.41.98.01, fax 05.56.41.99.32 ⬛
⬛ by appt.

CH. DU CARTILLON 2000

■ Cru bourg. 35 ha 120,000 ⬛ 8–11 €
•➤ EARL Vignobles Robert Giraud, Ch. du Cartillon, 33460 Lamarque, tel. 05.57.43.01.44, fax 05.57.43.08.75, e-mail direction@robertgiraud.com
⬛ by appt.

L'ERMITAGE DE CHASSE-SPLEEN 2000

■ 40 ha 250,000 ⬛ 8–11 €
•➤ SA Ch. Chasse-Spleen, 2558, Grand-Poujeaux Sud, 33480 Moulis-en-Médoc, tel. 05.56.58.02.37, fax 05.56.88.84.40, e-mail info@chasse-spleen.com
⬛ by appt.

CH. CLEMENT-PICHON 2000

■ Cru bourg. 25 ha 141,333 ⬛ 15–23 €
85 86 88 89 90 94 |95| 97 **98 99** 00

•➤ Vignobles Clément Fayat, Ch. Clément-Pichon, 33290 Parempuyre, tel. 05.56.35.23.79, fax 05.56.35.85.23, e-mail info@vignobles.fayat-group.com ⬛
⬛ by appt.

CLOS DU CHATEAU LE COTEAU 2000

■ 0.9 ha 6,500 ⬛ 5–8 €
•➤ Eric Léglise, Ch. Le Coteau, 39, av. J.-L.-Vonderheyden, 33460 Arsac, tel. 05.56.58.82.30, fax 05.56.58.82.30 ⬛
⬛ by appt.

CH. DOYAC 2000

■ 12 ha 90,000 ⬛⬛⬛ 5–8 €
•➤ EARL Max de Pourtalès, Ch. Doyac, 33180 Saint-Seurin-de-Cadourne, tel. 05.56.59.34.49, fax 05.56.59.74.82 ⬛
⬛ by appt.
•➤ Mme du Vivier

CH. DUTHIL 2000

■ 7 ha 50,000 ⬛ 8–11 €
•➤ SAE Ch. Giscours, 10, rte de Giscours, Labarde, 33460 Margaux, tel. 05.57.97.09.09, fax 05.57.97.09.00, e-mail giscours@chateau-giscours.fr ⬛
⬛ by appt.

CH. GRANDIS 2000

■ Cru bourg. 9.6 ha 24,637 ⬛ 11–15 €
88 |89| |90| 91 92 93 |95| 96 |97| 98 99 00

•➤ François-Joseph Vergez, Ch. Grandis, 33180 Saint-Seurin-de-Cadourne, tel. 05.56.59.31.16, fax 05.56.59.39.85 ⬛ ⬛
⬛ by appt.

CH. HAUT-MADRAC 2000

■ Cru bourg. n.c. 145,000 ⬛ 8–11 €
•➤ Héritiers Castéja, 33250 Pauillac, tel. 05.56.00.00.70, fax 05.57.87.48.61, e-mail domaines.borimanoux.@dial.oleane.com

CH. LAMOTHE-CISSAC 2000

■ Cru bourg. 35.92 ha 200,000 ∎ ⊞ ⸸	11–15 €

85 86 89 |90| 94 |95| |96| |98| 99 00

🡒 SC Ch. Lamothe, BP 3, 33250 Cissac-Médoc,
tel. 05.56.59.58.16, fax 05.56.59.57.97,
e-mail domaines.fabre@enfrance.com ☑
🍷 by appt.

CH. LESTAGE SIMON 2000

■ Cru bourg. 26 ha 188,761 ⊞	11–15 €

🡒 SCEA Ch. Lestage Simon,
33180 Saint-Seurin-de-Cadourne, tel. 05.56.59.31.83,
fax 05.56.59.70.56 ☑
🍷 by appt.

CH. LIVERSAN 2000

■ Cru bourg. n.c. 160,000 ∎ ⊞ ⸸	11–15 €

🡒 SCEA Ch. Liversan, 1, rte de Fonpiqueyre,
33250 Saint-Sauveur-Médoc, tel. 05.56.41.50.18,
fax 05.56.41.54.65, e-mail info@domaines-lapalu.com ☑
🍷 by appt.

CH. DE MALLERET 2000

■ Cru bourg. 37 ha n.c. ⊞	11–15 €

🡒 SCEA du Ch. de Malleret, Dom. du Ribet,
33450 Saint-Loubès, tel. 05.57.97.07.20,
fax 05.57.97.07.27 ☑
🍷 by appt.
🡒 Olivier Fargeot

CH. MAURAC

Les Vignes de Cabaleyran 2000

■ 5 ha 32,000 ⊞	11–15 €

🡒 SCEA Ch. Maurac, Le Trale,
33180 Saint-Seurin-de-Cadourne, tel. 05.57.88.07.64,
fax 05.57.88.07.00 ☑
🍷 by appt.

CH. MILOUCA 2000

■ 1.98 ha 8,000 ∎ ⊞	5–8 €

🡒 Ind. Lartigue-Coulary, 6, chem. des Sallies,
33460 Cussac-Fort-Médoc, tel. 05.56.58.93.23 ☑
🍷 by appt.

CH. MURET 2000

■ Cru bourg. 12 ha 94,500 ∎ ⊞ ⸸	8–11 €

91 93 94 95 |96| |97| 98 99 00

🡒 SCA de Muret, Ch. Muret,
33180 Saint-Seurin-de-Cadourne, tel. 05.56.59.38.11,
fax 05.56.59.37.03, e-mail chateau.muret@wanadoo.fr ☑
🍷 by appt.
🡒 Boufflerd

CH. D'OSMOND 2000

■ Cru artisan 4 ha 24,000 ∎ ⊞ ⸸	8–11 €

🡒 Philippe Tressol, 36, rte des Gûnes, 33250 Cissac,
tel. 05.56.59.59.17, fax 05.56.59.59.17,
e-mail chateaudosmond@wanadoo.fr ☑
🍷 by appt.

CH. PUY CASTERA 2000

■ 28 ha 140,000 ⊞	8–11 €

🡒 SCE Ch. Puy Castéra, 8, rte du Castéra,
33250 Cissac-Médoc, tel. 05.56.59.58.80,
fax 05.56.59.54.57 ☑
🍷 by appt.
🡒 Marès

CH. DE SAINTE-GEMME 2000

■ Cru bourg. n.c. 80,000 ⊞	15–23 €

🡒 SCEA Delbos-Bouteiller, Ch. de Sainte-Gemme,
33460 Cussac-Fort-Médoc, tel. 05.56.58.94.80,
fax 05.57.88.89.92,
e-mail bouteiller@bouteiller.com ☑
🍷 by appt.

CH. DE VILLAMBIS 2000

■ Cru bourg. 12.44 ha 62,000 ⊞	8–11 €

🡒 Adapei de la Gironde, CAT Villambis, 3, all. de
Villambis, 33350 Cissac-Médoc, tel. 05.56.73.90.90,
fax 05.56.73.90.99, e-mail deroeck.vlb@free.fr ☑
🍷 by appt.

CH. DE VILLEGEORGE 2000

■ Cru bourg. 18.58 ha 54,400 ∎ ⊞ ⸸	15–23 €

83 85 |86| 87 |89| 90 93 |94| |95| 96 |97| 98 |99| |00|

🡒 SC Les Grands Crus Réunis, 2036, Chalet,
33480 Moulis-en-Médoc, tel. 05.56.58.22.01,
fax 05.56.58.15.10,
e-mail marie-laure.lurton.lgcr@wanadoo.fr
🡒 Marie-Laure Lurton

Listrac-Médoc

This appellation corresponds exactly to the boundaries of the Listrac commune itself. The Appellation Communale is the furthest away from the Gironde estuary, and one of the few on the tourist routes to Soulac or from the Pointe-de-Grave. The terroir is most original, best described in geological terms as a hollowed-out dome in an anticlinal valley where erosion has created an inverse relief. To the west, along the edge of the forest, three ridges of Pyrenean gravel rise, their limestone slopes and subsoil giving good natural drainage. The centre of the AOC, the hollowed dome, is occupied by the Peyrelebade plain, which is composed of clay and lime soils. Finally, the ridges of the Graves by the Garonne rise to the east.

Listrac is a vigorous, robust wine, which has outgrown its former reputation for a somewhat crude quality. While some Listracs may be a little hard when young, the majority balance tannic strength with roundness. They all have a good capacity for keeping: 7 to 18 years, depending on the vintage. In 2002, the 664 ha produced 29,154 hl.

Moulis and Listrac

CH. BIBIAN 2000★

■ Cru bourg.　24 ha　110,000　⑪　11–15 €

This very old estate, acquired by Alain Meyre in 1999, has some respectably-aged wines (40 years old on average and some more than 70 years old). With tannins that are still evidently youthful and a bouquet that is still emerging, his 2000 is already achieving a degree of integration, and it will gain in grace given a few more years in the cellar.
➽ Alain Meyre, SARL Ch. Bibian, 33480 Listrac-Médoc, tel. 05.56.58.07.28, fax 05.56.58.07.50 ☑
☖ by appt.

CH. CAP LEON VEYRIN 2000★

■ Cru bourg.　15 ha　50,000　⑪　11–15 €

This estate, with its fine and welcoming bourgeois residence, deserves a visit. Well balanced and with well-behaved tannins, it has good overall integration which two or three years of laying down will only improve.
➽ SCEA Vignobles Alain Meyre, Donissan, 33480 Listrac-Médoc, tel. 05.56.58.07.28, fax 05.56.58.07.50, e-mail capleonveyrin@aol.com ☑ 🏠🏠
☖ ev. day except Sat. Sun. 9am–12 noon 2pm–6pm

CH. CLARKE 2000★★

■ Cru bourg.　54 ha　300,000　⑪　15–23 €
(86) 88 89 90 93 |95| |96| 97 98 99 00

The varietal choice here gives pride of place to Merlot (70%), but this has nothing to do with fashion. As in many of the Listrac terroirs, it is the nature of the soil, limestone-clay, that has motivated this choice, and this 2000 appears to vindicate it. The colour is a flawless ruby red, and the bouquet is intense and subtle, with delicate toasty notes and powerful aromas of red berries. The round attack is followed by a release of well-clothed tannins, which create a strong impression. The finish is characterized by a revival of fruitiness, which nonetheless does not detract from the wine's keeping potential.
➽ CV Edmond et Benjamin de Rothschild, 33480 Listrac-Médoc, tel. 05.56.58.38.00, fax 05.56.58.26.46, e-mail chateau.clarke@wanadoo.fr ☑

CH. DUCLUZEAU 2000★

■ Cru bourg.　5 ha　38,000　⑪　8–11 €
81 (82) 83 85 86 |88| |89| |90| 91 92 |94| 96 |97| 98 99 00

This wine bears testimony to this cru's professionalism and commitment to quality. Its elegance is apparent in the bouquet of fine notes of red berries and spices. The palate is full: it is sustained by well-clothed tannins and has a well-extracted grapeyness that is due to skilful vinification.
➽ Mme Jean-Eugène Borie, Ch. Ducluzeau, 33480 Listrac-Médoc, tel. 05.56.73.16.73, fax 05.56.59.27.37

CH. FOURCAS-DUMONT 2000★

■　8 ha　53,000　⑪　11–15 €

While some producers do not have deep roots in wine-growing, the same could not be said of the owners of this cru, since one of them is descended from Ernest David, who experimented on the *Bouillie Bordelaise* fungicide with Alexis Millardet. This wine shows their professionalism. A lovely rich garnet colour, it has a developing bouquet of attractive complexity (blackcurrant, spices, and toast) and a well-provided palate. Fleshy and unctuous, sustained by dense tannins, it deserves to be laid down for four or five years.
➽ SCA Ch. Fourcas-Dumont, 12, rue Odilon-Redon, 33480 Listrac-Médoc, tel. 05.56.58.03.84, fax 05.56.58.01.20, e-mail info@chateau-fourcas-dumont.com ☑
☖ ev. day except Sat. Sun. 9am–12 noon 2pm–5pm
➽ Lescoutra et Miquau

CH. FOURCAS DUPRE 2000★

■ Cru bourg.　44.08 ha　262,000　⑪　11–15 €
(78) 79 81 82 83 |85| |86| |88| |89| |90| 91 92 93 94 |95| |96| |97| 98 99 00

The buildings on this fair-sized estate were entirely renovated in 1999. The 2000 offered here is a well-constructed wine with

a pleasant bouquet of toast and ripe red berries, which surges back as the wine finishes. Though the youth of the finish indicates that a little keeping may be possible, this 2000 will be best drunk young.
➽ Ch. Fourcas Dupré, Le Fourcas, 33480 Listrac-Médoc, tel. 05.56.58.01.07, fax 05.56.58.02.27, e-mail chateau-fourcas-dupre@wanadoo.fr ☑
☖ ev. day except Sat. Sun. 8am–12 noon 2pm–5pm

CH. FOURCAS HOSTEN 2000★

■ Cru bourg.　46.67 ha　265,000　⑪　11–15 €
75 78 81 (82) 83 |85| |86| 88 |89| |90| 91 92 93 94 95 96 97 98 99 00

This charterhouse is in the heart of Listrac itself, surrounded by a beautiful landscaped park. Its charm comes through in this wine, whose pretty ruby colour suits the finesse of the bouquet, which is both fruity and oaky, and the well-balanced, supple, well-structured palate. This pleasant wine could be drunk now or within the next two to three years. Having chosen this wine, make sure to visit the 12th century church opposite. Though much altered down the centuries, it is of interest.
➽ SC du Ch. Fourcas-Hosten, rue de l'Eglise, 33480 Listrac-Médoc, tel. 05.56.58.01.15, fax 05.56.58.06.73, e-mail fourcas@club-internet.fr ☑
☖ by appt.

CH. FOURCAS LOUBANEY 2000★

■ Cru bourg.　19 ha　92,000　⑪　11–15 €
Produced by a cru known for consistent quality, this wine has a youthful dark colour with bluish highlights. The bouquet begins with notes of small red berries, then gathers in complexity, while the palate shows the fullness and balance one would expect from the presentation. Open in two to three years from now. The same producer's **Château Moulin de Laborde (8–11 €)** is singled out.
➽ SEA Fourcas-Loubaney, 17, av. Julien-Ducourt, 33610 Cestas, tel. 05.57.26.26.66, fax 05.56.07.60.73, e-mail divin@divin-sa.fr
➽ F.-M. Marret

CH. JANDER 2000★

■　4 ha　20,000　⑪　11–15 €
A 50:50 blend of Cabernet Sauvignon and Merlot given 18 months of oak maturing, this dark, glossy wine is extremely pleasant. The bouquet is a happy marriage of fruit and oak, while the palate is tannic, but not excessively so. Open in two to three years' time.
➽ SCE Les Vignobles Jander, 41, av. de Soulac, 33480 Listrac-Médoc, tel. 05.56.58.01.12, fax 05.56.58.01.57, e-mail vignobles.jander@wanadoo.fr ☑
☖ ev. day except Sat. Sun. 9am–12 noon 2pm–6pm

CH. MAYNE LALANDE 2000★★

■ Cru bourg.　15 ha　60,000　⑪　11–15 €
85 86 88 89 |90| 91 92 94 |95| |96| 97 98 99 00

This cru appeared in the first edition of the *Guide* nearly 20 years ago, and is now regarded as one of the mainstays of the appellation. Bernard Lartigue, a real man of the Médoc, has created this wine for laying down: the colour is dark purple, and the bouquet an elegant marriage of well-ripened red fruits and oaky vanilla. The palate is solidly constructed, with silky tannins which supply both a mouth-filling quality and richness. A lovely synthesis, but forget about it for four to five years.
➽ Bernard Lartigue, Ch. Mayne Lalande, 33480 Listrac-Médoc, tel. 05.56.58.27.63, fax 05.56.58.22.41, e-mail b.lartigue@terre-net.fr ☑
☖ by appt.

CH. DES MERLES 2000★

■　5 ha　20,000　⑪　8–11 €
A rounded wine is what the cooperative were after here. Although this 2000 still seems far from that, given the firm tannins with which it finishes, they will no doubt achieve their object in two or three years' time. The suppleness of the structure and the complexity of its aromatic character (toast,

mint, vanilla) mean that it will give real pleasure at table in the fairly near future.

☛ Cave de vinification de Listrac, 21, av. de Soulac, 33480 Listrac-Médoc, tel. 05.56.58.03.19, fax 05.56.58.07.22, e-mail grandlistrac@cave-listrac-medoc.com ☑
Ⴤ by appt.

CH. PEYREDON LAGRAVETTE 2000★

■ Cru bourg.	5.03 ha	35,000	⑪	11–15 €

81 (82) 83 85 86 88 |89| |90| 94 |95| |96| 97 98 99 00

In an appellation where Merlot is gaining the upper hand (now 60–65% of the average blend), Paul Hostein has kept to tradition with this 60% Cabernet Sauvignon. A judicious choice, if this lovely 2000 is anything to go by. Powerful, well built and possessed of an aromatic character that is as intense as it is complex (tobacco, red fruits, green pepper, leather), this wine has all it needs in order to profit from five to six years' cellaring.

☛ Paul Hostein, 2062, Médrac, 33480 Listrac-Médoc, tel. 05.56.58.05.55, fax 05.56.58.05.50 ☑
Ⴤ ev. day 9am–12.30pm 2pm–7pm; cl. 20 Sep.–10 Oct.

CH. SAINT-MARTIN 2000★

■	10 ha	30,000	⑪	8–11 €

This cru is vinified by the cooperative cellar, and this 2000 is a wine with a promising dark appearance. Neither the bouquet nor the palate disappoints. They have beautifully expressive notes of red fruits, vanilla, and lightly-toasted cedar, all sustained by silky tannins. Lay down for three to five years.

☛ Cave de vinification de Listrac, 21, av. de Soulac, 33480 Listrac-Médoc, tel. 05.56.58.03.19, fax 05.56.58.07.22, e-mail grandlistrac@cave-listrac-medoc.com ☑
Ⴤ by appt.
☛ Michel Chevalier

CH. SARANSOT-DUPRE 2000★

■ Cru bourg.	14 ha	60,000	⑪	11–15 €

70 71 75 78 81 82 83 85 86 88 |89| |90| 91 93 |94| |95| 96 97 |98| 99 00

This fine *maison de maître* with its small pediment looks like something from the Directory period, the 1790s. In fact it dates from 1868 and belongs very much to the Bordeaux region. No less does this ruby 2000 wine, with its thousand glints; it has an elegant discretion that may be appreciated in its mature tannins and fruity aromas enhanced by a spicy note.

☛ Yves Raymond, Ch. Saransot-Dupré, 33480 Listrac-Médoc, tel. 05.56.58.03.02, fax 05.56.58.07.64, e-mail yraymond@wanadoo.fr ☑
Ⴤ by appt.

CH. VIEUX MOULIN 2000★

■	7 ha	30,000	⑪	8–11 €

Grown in a vineyard that practises sustainable agricultural methods, this wine has a robust tannic character that is not unpleasant. It calls for two to three years' patience; this is confirmed by the fruity dominance of the bouquet, which includes a touch of cinnamon and good oakiness.

☛ Cave de vinification de Listrac, 21, av. de Soulac, 33480 Listrac-Médoc, tel. 05.56.58.03.19, fax 05.56.58.07.22, e-mail grandlistrac@cave-listrac-medoc.com ☑
Ⴤ by appt.
☛ SCE Fort-Boscq

Wines selected but not starred

CH. BAUDAN 2000

■	4.35 ha	26,600	⑪	23–30 €

☛ Alain Blasquez, Ch. Baudan, 33480 Listrac-Médoc, tel. 05.56.58.07.40, fax 05.56.58.04.72, e-mail chateau.baudan@wanadoo.fr ☑
Ⴤ ev. day 9am–7.30pm

LA CARAVELLE

Cuvée Prestige 2000

■	4 ha	27,000	⑪	11–15 €

☛ Cave de vinification de Listrac, 21, av. de Soulac, 33480 Listrac-Médoc, tel. 05.56.58.03.19, fax 05.56.58.07.22, e-mail grandlistrac@cave-listrac-medoc.com ☑
Ⴤ by appt.

CH. LALANDE

Cuvée spéciale 2000

■ Cru bourg.	11.07 ha	70,000	▮⑪ ♦	8–11 €

☛ EARL Darriet-Lescoutra, Ch. Lalande, 33480 Listrac-Médoc, tel. 05.56.58.19.45, fax 05.56.58.15.62 ☑
Ⴤ ev. day 9am–12 noon 2pm–7pm; Sun. by appt.

CH. LESTAGE 2000

■ Cru bourg.	42 ha	190,000	⑪	8–11 €

☛ SC Ch. Lestage, 33480 Listrac-Médoc, tel. 05.56.58.02.43, fax 05.56.58.04.33, e-mail vignobles.chanfreau@wanadoo.fr ☑
Ⴤ ev. day except Sat. Sun. 9am–12 noon 2pm–5pm; cl. 22 Dec.–2 Jan.

CH. MOULIN D'ULYSSE 2000

■	10 ha	6,000	⑪	11–15 €

☛ Jean-Claude Castel, Donissan, 33480 Listrac-Médoc, tel. 05.56.58.04.18, fax 05.56.58.00.15 ☑
Ⴤ by appt.

CH. REVERDI 2000

■ Cru bourg.	18 ha	135,000	⑪	11–15 €

☛ SCEA Vignobles Thomas, Donissan, 33480 Listrac-Médoc, tel. 05.56.58.02.25, fax 05.56.58.06.56 ☑
Ⴤ ev. day except Sun. 9am–12 noon 2pm–6pm; cl. 20 Sep.–20 Oct.

Margaux

Margaux is the only appellation name that is also a feminine first name. This is unlikely to have happened by chance. You have only to taste a glass of Margaux to savour the subtle relationship between wine and terroir.

Margaux wines are famous for keeping well, but they are equally distinguished for their suppleness and delicacy and for the elegance of their wonderfully fruity perfumes. They are the finest examples of generously tannic, soft wines to be proudly registered in the cellar book as wines for the long term.

The originality of Margaux comes from several different factors. Human input should not be underestimated. For example, Margaux growers have historically given less predominance to Cabernet Sauvignon than have the other great Médoc communes. Here, while still the minority variety, Merlot plays a more significant part. In addition, although the appellation stretches through five communes, namely Margaux and Cantenac, Soussans, Labarde and Arsac, only the soils that are best suited to growing vines for wine-making have been retained for the AOC. The result is a strikingly homogenous terroir, featuring a series of gravel ridges.

The ridges fall into two groups: on the periphery is a string of "islands" separated by valleys, streams and boggy marsh; at the heart of the appellation, in the Margaux and Cantenac communes, what was formerly a plateau of white gravel measuring some 6 km by 2 km is now worn away into ridges by erosion. This is where the 18 Grand Crus Classés of the appellation are grown.

The Margaux wines are remarkably elegant and should be drunk only with the finest-quality dishes such as Chateaubriand, duck, partridge or, in the local tradition, steak à la Bordelaise. In 2002, 53,342 hl were produced from 1,403 ha.

ALTER EGO DE PALMER 2000★

| ■ | 51 ha | 105,000 | ⅠⅠⅠ | 46–76 € |

Palmer's "alter ego" differs from Palmer by virtue of its varietal make-up, being 67% Merlot. The aim, which the wine achieves, is finesse and the possibility of somewhat earlier consumption. Although it has ripe, silky tannins not unlike those of Palmer, it developed with a great deal of elegance and mellowness throughout the tasting. Wait several years before drinking.
☛ Ch. Palmer, Cantenac, 33460 Margaux, tel. 05.57.88.72.72, fax 05.57.88.37.16, e-mail chateau-palmer@chateau-palmer.com
🍷 by appt.

CH. D'ANGLUDET 2000★

| ■ | 30 ha | 130,000 | ▌ⅠⅠⅠ ♦ | 23–30 € |

Few estates are as charming as Angludet, with its Girondin house and lawn going down to a small stream. The wine, too, is not lacking in charm, with its pretty red colour and bluish tinges. The bouquet has intense perfumes of ripe fruits spiced by notes of new oak. The palate is delicately concentrated, and its tannins are smooth, showing what a true Margaux this is, classic right through to the finish. Keep for three or four years before drinking. The second wine, **La Ferme d'Angludet 2000 (11–15 €)**, was singled out.
☛ Ch. d'Angludet, 33460 Cantenac, tel. 05.57.88.71.41, fax 05.57.88.72.52, e-mail contact@chateau-angludet.fr ☑
🍷 by appt.
☛ Sichel

LA BERLANDE 2000★

| ■ | 3 ha | 20,000 | ⅠⅠⅠ | 11–15 € |
| 94 | **95** |96| 97 | **98** 99 00 | | |

The owner of Château Haut Marbuzet (Saint-Estèphe), Henri Duboscq, is also a wine-merchant, and it is in that capacity that he offers this wine whose pleasing perfumes of stewed fruits and blackcurrent are nicely integrated with oakiness. This 2000 is very true-to-type, spacious, and mouth-filling; it is sustained by refined tannins, and deserves to be kept a decent while before drinking. It will go well with game birds (e.g., woodcock).
☛ Brusina-Brandler, 3, quai de Bacalan, 33300 Bordeaux, tel. 05.56.39.26.77, fax 05.56.69.16.84 ☑
🍷 by appt.

Margaux

Map legend:
- A.O.C. Margaux
- ● Cru classé
- ● Cru bourgeois
- – – – Limites de communes

CH. LA BESSANE 2000★★

| ■ | 3 ha | 12,000 | ⑪ | 30–38 € |

The 60% Petit Verdot variety makes this cru atypical. Such audaciousness, however, has paid off, given this highly successful wine. The colour is a lovely ruby with tinges of purple, and there is a fine, deep bouquet of ripe fruit aromas, toast and spices. The palate has finesse and warmth, a concentrated, well-balanced structure, and well-blended oakiness. The finish is warm and spacious. In several years' time this promises to be a very good wine indeed.
☛ Ch. Paloumey, 50, rue Pouge-de-Beau,
33290 Ludon-Médoc, tel. 05.57.88.00.66,
fax 05.57.88.00.67, e-mail info@chateaupaloumey.com ☑
☥ by appt.

CH. BOYD-CANTENAC 2000★★

| ■ | 3e cru clas. | 15.3 ha | 78,000 | ▮⑪♦ | 23–30 € |

70 75 79 80 81 ⑧②83 |85| 86 88 |89| |90| 91 92 94 |95| |96| |97| 98 99 00

Though somewhat off the beaten track, this cru is a reliable and authentic pillar of the appellation. Once again, its Margaux is very true-to-type, especially given the tannins, which are powerful, smooth, and well-covered. Its aromatic character is superbly complex, with notes of liquorice, black fruits, bigaroon cherry, and roasted coffee and chicory, all of which indicate what a radiant future this wine is likely to have after a period in the cellar. The same producer's small Cru Bourgeois, the **Château La Tour Massac 2000 (11–15 €)** is commended.
☛ SCE Ch. Boyd-Cantenac, 33460 Cantenac,
tel. 05.57.88.90.82, fax 05.57.88.33.27,
e-mail contact@boyd-cantenac.fr ☑
☥ by appt.

CH. BRANE-CANTENAC 2000★★

| ■ | 2e cru clas. | n.c. | 136,000 | ⑪ | 46–76 € |

70 71 75 76 78 79 81 82 83 84 85 ⑧⑥ 87 |88| |89| |90| 91 92 93 94 95 ⑨⑥ |97| 98 99 00

Henri Lurton modestly acknowledges what he owes to his team. But the fact that his wine is such an ideal and authentic Margaux is due to his determination. Such deliberation is evident in the perfectly judged maturation. The oak respects the rich personality of the very concentrated bouquet, and confers balance on the palate, whose tannins will ensure long keeping (you could wait six to eight years) yet are not at all overbearing. The Jury was unanimous in electing this wine as their *coup de coeur*. The second label, **Baron de Brane 2000 (23–30 €)**, was rated one star. This is equally a good keeping wine and shows great elegance in both its aromas and its tannins. It needs to be left to breathe before serving.
☛ Henri Lurton, SCEA Ch. Brane-Cantenac,
33460 Margaux, tel. 05.57.88.83.33, fax 05.57.88.72.51,
e-mail hlurton@brane-cantenac.com ☑
☥ by appt.

CH. CANTENAC-BROWN 2000★

| ■ | 3e cru clas. | 42 ha | 144,000 | ⑪ | 30–38 € |

75 76 79 80 81 82 |83| 85 |86| |88| |89| ⑨⓪ 91 92 93 94 |95| |96| 97 98 99 00

This vast neo-Tudor château, built during the first part of the 19th century by the painter John Lewis Brown, the son of an English wine-merchant, possesses a vineyard of some 42 ha. The wine, a bright ruby colour with violet highlights, has a superbly complex aromatic character with notes of pepper, meat, coffee, wild strawberries and even port. Round, supple and full-bodied, it will need two to three years' storage before drinking. The second wine, **Château Canuet 2000 (11–15 €)**, is commended.
☛ Christian Seely, Ch. Cantenac-Brown, 33460 Margaux,
tel. 05.57.88.81.81, fax 05.57.88.81.90,
e-mail infochato@cantenacbrown.com
☥ by appt.
☛ Axa Millésimes

CH. LE COTEAU 2000★

| ■ | Cru bourg. | 9.6 ha | 50,000 | ⑪ | 11–15 € |

The plain dark colour of this wine, grown at Arsac, is very confidence-inspiring, as is the bouquet with its dominance of liquorice, an oaky liquorice to be precise. The dense palate is supported by ripe, supple tannins and finishes on a spicy note which admirably sets off this wine and confirms that it will keep well.
☛ Eric Léglise, Ch. Le Coteau, 39, av. J.-L.-Vonderheyden, 33460 Arsac, tel. 05.56.58.82.30, fax 05.56.58.82.30 ☑
☥ by appt.

CH. DAUZAC 2000★★

| ■ | 5e cru clas. | 25 ha | 120,000 | ⑪ | 30–38 € |

78 79 80 81 82 83 84 85 |86| 87 |88| |89| ⑨⓪ 91 92 |93| 95 96 |97| 98 99 00

Famous once as one of the places where *Bouillie Bordelaise* was perfected, this cru is famous these days for the quality of its wine. This 2000 is black with bluish tinges and is more than just promising. The bouquet has a freshness enhanced by notes of oak, crystallized fruits, mint and sweet spices; the palate has a round, well-balanced beginning, then goes on to reveal a good structure, which is extended by a lingering finish on a revival of fruity aromas. This very well-integrated wine has solid keeping potential.
☛ SE du Ch. Dauzac, 33460 Labarde, tel. 05.57.88.32.10, fax 05.57.88.96.00, e-mail andrelurton@andrelurton.com ☑
☥ by appt.
☛ MAIF

CH. DEYREM VALENTIN 2000★★

| ■ | Cru bourg. | 11 ha | 65,000 | ⑪ | 15–23 € |

75 76 81 82 83 85 86 |88| |89| |90| 91 92 93 94 95 97 98 99 00

Discretion has not prevented this Cru Bourgeois from possessing a pretty dwelling that is typically Bordelais or from offering an extremely interesting wine. This deep-red 2000 revealed its authentic Margaux traits throughout the tasting with a smoothness and velvetiness that make it very agreeable. The bouquet delivers fine, delicate notes of blackcurrant. After a superbly supple attack, the palate displays sufficient tannic development to ensure good keeping (four to five years or more), though the tannins are already quite well-covered and flavoursome.
☛ EARL des Vignobles Jean Sorge, 1, rue Valentin-Deyrem, 33460 Soussans, tel. 05.57.88.35.70, fax 05.57.88.36.84, e-mail deyremvalentin@aol.com ☑

CH. DURFORT-VIVENS 2000★

| ■ | 2e cru clas. | 27.6 ha | 70,000 | ⑪ | 38–46 € |

75 76 81 82 83 85 ⑧⑥ |88| |89| |90| 91 92 93 94 |95| ⑨⑥ |97| 99 00

This vintage has not had the advantage of the new wooden vat first used in 2002. Nonetheless, this is an extremely attractive wine with a purplish ruby colour and an enticing bouquet of coffee, roasting, and jammy red fruits. The same delicacy informs the palate, and it finishes in similar vein, with a final freshness and soft oakiness that confers a really well-blended feel. This wine will be at its best in four to five years. Before then (in two to three years' time), it will be possible to enjoy the same producer's **Segond de Durfort 2000 (15–23 €)**, which was singled out by the Jury.
☛ Gonzague Lurton, Ch. Durfort-Vivens, 33460 Margaux, tel. 05.57.88.31.02, fax 05.57.88.60.60
☥ by appt.

L'ENCLOS GALLEN 2000★

■	1.58 ha	7,500	▐ ❚▮❚ ♨	23–30 €

This cru belongs to the friendly "Aliénor" group, an association of leading female wine-growers. They are honoured by this wine, whose complex bouquet of red fruits and grilled, spicy notes is on a par with the rising power of the palate, which closes on an extremely well-balanced finish. An attractive wine that will deserve some time in the cellar.
❦ SA Ch. Meyre, 16, rte de Castelnau, 33480 Avensan, tel. 05.56.58.10.77, fax 05.56.58.13.20, e-mail chateau.meyre@wanadoo.fr � 🏠
ℐ ev. day 2pm–6pm; Sat. Sun. by appt.; cl. 1 Nov.–30 Mar.

CH. FERRIERE 2000★★

■	3e cru clas.	8 ha	30,000	❚▮❚	23–30 €

70 75 78 81 83 84 ⟨85⟩ |86| 87 |88| 89 92 **93** |**94**| **95 96** |97| **98 99 00**

The name Ferrière is that of an officer of the royal hunts who owned the estate in the 17th century. The varietal proportions are very characteristic of the Médoc: 80% Cabernet Sauvignon, 15% Merlot, 5% Petit Verdot. This 2000 has a rich purple colour with garnet highlights, and a pleasant, well-balanced bouquet, which includes smoky, roasting notes. The palate has an excellent balance between grape and oak. Its richness, concentration and long finish indicate remarkable laying-down potential. The same owner's **Château La Gurgue 2000 (11–15 €)** was commended. A fruity, well-made wine, with soft tannins.
❦ Claire Villars-Lurton, Ch. Ferrière, 33 bis, rue de la Trémoille, 33460 Margaux, tel. 05.57.88.76.65, fax 05.57.88.98.33
ℐ by appt.

CH. LA GALIANE 2000★

■	5.71 ha	33,400	❚▮❚	15–23 €

Here is no Sleeping Beauty-style towered château, but an authentic Girondin house. The wine is in the spirit of the appellation, having an expressive bouquet (blackberry, raspberry, and prune with a touch of cocoa) and a body possessing roundness and finesse.
❦ SCEA René Renon, Ch. La Galiane, 33460 Soussans, tel. 05.57.88.35.27, fax 05.57.88.70.59, e-mail scea.rene.renon@wanadoo.fr ▮
ℐ by appt.

CH. GISCOURS 2000★★

■	3e cru clas.	80 ha	300,000	❚▮❚	30–38 €

75 78 81 82 83 85 ⟨86⟩ |88| |89| 90 91 93 94 |97| 98 **99 00**

Built by the banker Pescatore to receive Empress Eugenie, Château Giscours commands an enormous estate. The appearance of this 2000 is dark and deep, and the bouquet is not surprisingly dominated by notes of toasted oak, though these are elegant enough not to cause distortion. The palate, with its long finish, reveals considerable power, while nonetheless demonstrating real smoothness and plenty of mellowness. In sum, this is a remarkable wine with an assured future of five, ten, or even fifteen years, though it is already extremely tempting to drink. Another well-constructed wine with tannins that are a bit coarse is **Sirène de Giscours 2000 (15–23 €)**, which received special mention.
❦ SAE Ch. Giscours, 10, rte de Giscours, Labarde, 33460 Margaux, tel. 05.57.97.09.09, fax 05.57.97.09.00, e-mail giscours@chateau-giscours.fr ▮ 🏠
ℐ by appt.
❦ Albada Jelgersma

CH. HAUT BRETON LARIGAUDIERE
Le Créateur 2000★

■	Cru bourg.	1 ha	2,628	❚▮❚	46–76 €

This small specialist cru, named after its Flemish creator, De Schepper, is very oaky, with a rather original note of graphite. The rich, concentrated palate calls for four or five years' storage, perhaps more, which will enable the wine to become better integrated overall. Much bigger in terms of production (63,000 bottles) is the same estate's **Cuvée Principale Château Haut Breton Larigaudière 2000 (15–23 €)**, which was singled out by the Jury.

❦ Ch. Haut Breton Larigaudière, 33460 Soussans, tel. 05.57.88.94.17, fax 05.57.88.39.14 ▮
ℐ by appt.
❦ de Schepper

CH. D'ISSAN 2000★★

■	3e cru clas.	30 ha	97,000	❚▮❚	46–76 €

82 83 85 86 87 |**88**| |89| |90| 92 93 **94** 95 96 |97| 98 99 **00**

Issan is a special place in the Médoc owing to its architecture (a fine 17th century manorhouse) and its environment, one of moats and, on either side of the château, a different world: vines in the east, meadows in the west. Its 2000 has a very dense appearance and a mouthwatering bouquet of red fruits (strawberries) and toasty vanilla. The palate is complex, deep and rich, revealing a structure and long finish which are good keeping indicators. Similarly well-constructed, balanced and complex is the cru's second wine, **Blason d'Issan 2000 (23–30 €)**, which has a one-star rating.
❦ SFV de Cantenac, Ch. d'Issan, 33460 Cantenac, tel. 05.57.88.35.91, fax 05.57.88.74.24, e-mail issan@chateau-issan.com
ℐ by appt.
❦ Famille Cruse

CH. KIRWAN 2000★★

■	3e cru clas.	35 ha	120,000	❚▮❚	46–76 €

75 79 81 82 83 85 ⟨86⟩ |88| 89 93 94 **95 96** |97| 98 **99 00**

Though they came together only in 1925, the tradition of the Schÿlers, wine-merchants who came to the Chartrons in Bordeaux in 1739, and that of Kirwan, established in 1780, both go back a long way. The result is wines that are very much in the Bordeaux spirit yet take advantage of today's oenological know-how. This vintage is a remarkable example in which the grilled notes of the oak-maturing skilfully fade behind the fruit. Clean, long, welcoming, fine, well-built upon the support of silky tannins, it merits cellaring for five or six years, after which it will be delicious with lamb and herbs. The cru's second label, **Les Charmes de Kirwan 2000 (15–23 €)**, was commended.
❦ Famille Schÿler, Ch. Kirwan, 33460 Cantenac, tel. 05.57.88.71.00, fax 05.57.88.77.62, e-mail mail@chateau-kirwan.com ▮
ℐ ev. day 9.30am–12.30pm 2pm–5.30pm; Sat. Sun. by appt.
❦ J. H. Schÿler

CH. LABEGORCE 2000★

■	36 ha	n.c.	❚▮❚	15–23 €

Overlooked by a beautiful classical residence on the outskirts of Margaux towards Pauillac, this cru has a diverse varietal mix that is typical of the Médoc (Cabernets and Petit Verdot, with 40% Merlot). The result is a wine whose bouquet elegantly marries fruit and oak, while the palate reveals an excellent tannic structure that calls for the wine to be laid down for three to five years.
❦ Ch. Labégorce, 33460 Margaux, tel. 05.57.88.71.32, fax 05.57.88.35.01, e-mail labegorce@chateau-labegorce.fr ▮
ℐ by appt.
❦ H. Perrodo

CH. LABEGORCE-ZEDE 2000★

■	Cru bourg.	27 ha	n.c.	❚▮❚	30–38 €

82 ⟨83⟩ 85 86 |88| 89 90 91 92 |93| |94| |**95**| 96 |97| 98 99 00

Although they have many other crus in the Bordeaux region, including Vieux Château Certan at Pomerol, the Thienponts do not neglect this estate, as this wine shows. It is a blend of 8% Petit Verdot, 67% Cabernets and 25% Merlot grapes expertly processed to yield a wine with deep purple colour and a powerful bouquet of grilling, smoke, stewed fruit (strawberry) and toast. The palate is spacious and well-balanced, harmoniously tannic and oaky. This vintage will be ready to drink in four to six years' time to accompany strong-tasting, up-market dishes like lamprey Bordeaux-style or hare royale.
❦ SCEA du Ch. Labégorce-Zédé, 33460 Soussans, tel. 05.57.88.71.31, fax 05.57.88.72.54 ▮
ℐ ev. day except Sat. Sun. 8am–12 noon 1pm–5pm
❦ Luc Thienpont

CH. LARRUAU 2000★

| ■ Cru bourg. | 11.5 ha | 70,000 | ⦀ | 11–15 € |

86 |88| |89| 90 93 |94| |95| |96| 97 |98| |99| 00

This cru is all finesse and elegance, though not at the expense of a good structure: the body and its balance will enable this wine to keep for five years. Deep purple in colour, it has a nose which develops from musk towards grilling and spices, and a palate where equivalent flavours combine with fruitiness.
🕿 Bernard Château, 4, rue de La Trémoille, 33460 Margaux, tel. 05.57.88.35.50, fax 05.57.88.76.69 ✓
🍷 by appt.

CH. LASCOMBES 2000★★

| ■ 2e cru clas. | 65 ha | 217,000 | ⦀ | 38–46 € |

76 81 82 83 85 (86) |88| |89| |90| 95 |96| 97 |98| 00

Since its purchase by the American group Colony Capital, Lascombes, a huge estate of 84 ha, has benefited from a big investment programme. This vintage missed out, but all the same greatly impressed the Jury. The colour is a deep and dense ruby-red, and the bouquet is rich in sensations of toast, vanilla and blackcurrant. The concentrated, rich palate has rounded tannins which give clear indication that this wine will keep for five to ten years, and there is a development of fresh notes of fruits and spicy hints that leave an impression of great elegance.
🕿 Ch. Lascombes, 1, cours Verdun, 33460 Margaux, tel. 05.57.88.70.66, fax 05.57.88.72.17, e-mail chateaulascombes@chateau.lascombes.fr ✓ 🏠
🍷 by appt.

CH. MALESCOT SAINT-EXUPERY 2000★★

| ■ 3e cru clas. | 23.5 ha | 103,200 | ⦀ | 46–76 € |

81 82 83 85 86 |88| |89| |90| 91 92 93 |94| 95 96 98 99 00

Malescot is a modest 16th century estate, which has sufficiently ennobled itself down the centuries to become one of the most reliable in the Bordeaux region. The vines, planted on a terroir of Pyrenean gravels, have yielded a wine with a very dense colour. After a bouquet, in which strong notes of toast and grilling still somewhat mask the fruit, first impressions on the palate are superb. There follows a disclosure of round, well-balanced tannins; these create an impression of a lovely synthesis and a remarkable structure, and sustain a long finish. So many indicators of a great wine, whose life is bound to exceed five years.
🕿 SCEA Ch. Malescot Saint-Exupéry, 33460 Margaux, tel. 05.57.88.97.20, fax 05.57.88.97.21 ✓
🍷 by appt.
🕿 Roger Zuger

CH. MARGAUX 2000★★★

| ■ 1er cru clas. | 78 ha | n.c. | ⦀ | +76 € |

59 |61| 66 70 71 |75| 78 |79| 80 |81| (82) |83| 84 |85| |86| |87| 88 89 90 91 |92| 93 94 (95) (96) 97 (98) (99) (00)

If ever there was a mythical château with a legendary cru, it is surely Margaux, with its Palladian-inspired neo-classical architecture, its history going back to the Middle Ages, and its terroir. How could the wine be anything but exceptional? In the glass, the colour is sumptuously intense and bright. The nose is extravagant: coffee, black chocolate at first, followed by cherry, then a mouth-watering grapeyness. The palate is no less rich, with a perfect balance between power and subtlety. The tannins are fleshy and flavoursome, long and elegant. They promise long life.
🕿 SC du Ch. Margaux, 33460 Margaux, tel. 05.57.88.83.83, fax 05.57.88.83.32
🍷 by appt.

CH. MARQUIS DE TERME 2000★★★

| ■ 4e cru clas. | 38 ha | 160,000 | ⦀ | 30–38 € |

75 81 82 (83) 85 |86| 89 90 |93| |94| 95 96 97 98 99 (00)

This cru, within Margaux itself, is overlooked by an elegant château and is both discreet and efficient. Its know-how is utterly confirmed by this 2000. The bouquet is fine and complex, with lovely revivals of aromas, and there is an alliance between fruit and oak that creates a well-integrated whole. Full, rich, powerful and well-blended, the palate similarly reveals an excellent balance and real keeping potential (seven to eight years, even longer). A Margaux perfectly true to type.
🕿 Ch. Marquis de Terme, 3, rte de Rauzan, 33460 Margaux, tel. 05.57.88.30.01, fax 05.57.88.32.51, e-mail marquisterme@terre-net.fr ✓
🍷 by appt.
🕿 Sénéclauze

CH. MONBRISON 2000★

| ■ Cru bourg. | 13.2 ha | 48,000 | ⦀ | 30–38 € |

82 83 |85| (86) |88| |89| |90| 91 |95| |96| |97| 98 00

If it is difficult not to succumb to the charm of this estate at Arsac, it not easy either to resist the beautifully intense ruby red colour of this Margaux. The bouquet is similarly intense, with its mix of grilling, coffee and black fruits. The tannins still need time to soften, but they do not impede the impression of suppleness and good integration that appears as soon as the wine touches the palate. These aspects are enhanced by a lingering finish with a note of eucalyptus.
🕿 E.M. Davis et Fils, Ch. Monbrison, 33460 Arsac, tel. 05.56.58.80.04, fax 05.56.58.85.33, e-mail lvdh33@wanadoo.fr ✓
🍷 by appt.

CH. MONGRAVEY

Cuvée de Tradition 2000★★

| ■ | 9.7 ha | 32,000 | ⦀ | 15–23 € |

This cru produces several different wines, among which this Cuvée de Tradition particularly impressed the Jury. Ink-like in appearance, it has a bouquet of toast, coffee, black fruits and dried fruits. Throughout the tasting its power and concentration were as imposing as its complexity. Well-softened tannins support every aspect, and mean that the wine will keep seven or eight years, and perhaps much longer still. The very similar **Microcuvée Château Mongravey 2000 (30–38 €)** (3,500 bottles) was equally proposed for a *coup de coeur*, whilst the **Cuvée Prestige Château Mongravey 2000 (15–23 €)** received one star.
🕿 Régis Bernaleau, 8, av. Jean-Luc-Vonderheyden, 33460 Arsac, tel. 05.56.58.84.51, fax 05.56.58.83.39, e-mail chateau.mongravey@wanadoo.fr ✓
🍷 by appt.

Margaux

CH. PALMER 2000★★

3e cru clas.	51 ha	135,000	▯ +76 €

78 79 80 **81 82 83** 84 |85| (86) |88| |89| 90 91 92 |93| 94 |95| |96| |97| **98 99 00**

The eclectic architecture of this château, beside the D2, the famous Wine Road, will ensure that it does not escape notice. This wine, too, has a strong personality, witnessed throughout the tasting, which makes it a good ambassador for the Margaux appellation. The colour is a lovely dark red, and the attractive bouquet mixes jammy fruit notes with oak. The palate gathers in strength to disclose a spacious, full, rich, round character. The support of silky tannins will enable this wine to gain from storage of five to ten years.

➽ Ch. Palmer, Cantenac, 33460 Margaux,
tel. 05.57.88.72.72, fax 05.57.88.37.16,
e-mail chateau-palmer@chateau-palmer.com
⟁ by appt.

PAVILLON ROUGE 2000★★

	n.c.	n.c.	▯ 38–46 €

78 81 |82| |83| 84 |85| |86| |88| |89| |90| 92 |93| |94| |95| |96| |97| **98 99 00**

Pavillon is Château Margaux's second label, and its elegance similarly captures the spirit of the appellation. This wine is as expressive in its aromas of delicate floral, spices notes, as it is in its structure of fine, rounded, friendly tannins. The finish is extremely well balanced and leaves an impression of a well-integrated synthesis that will develop well in the future.

➽ SC du Ch. Margaux, 33460 Margaux, tel. 05.57.88.83.83,
fax 05.57.88.83.32
⟁ by appt.

CH. POUGET 2000★

4e cru clas.	7.5 ha	44,000	▮ ▯ ⚘ 15–23 €

75 85 86 88 |89| |90| 92 |94| |95| |96| |97| 98 99 00

Tradition has it that the Duc de Richelieu discovered that the wine of Château Pouget had dietetic powers. Health considerations are not necessary in order to be tempted by the lovely deep-purple hue of this 2000 and the bouquet of delicate flowers (rose), vanilla and toast. Supple and welcoming, sustained by round, soft tannins, the palate plays on strawberry and prune flavours, with a pleasing finish that invites one to lay this wine down for two to eight years.

➽ SCE Ch. Boyd-Cantenac, 33460 Cantenac,
tel. 05.57.88.90.82, fax 05.57.88.33.27,
e-mail contact@boyd-cantenac.fr ☑
⟁ by appt.

CH. PRIEURE-LICHINE 2000★

4e cru clas.	40 ha	220,000	▯ 38–46 €

82 83 86 |88| |89| |90| 91 92 93 96 97 (98) 99 00

This is the first vintage entirely seen through by the Ballandes and it is undoubtedly destined for the cellar. Such is already clear from the intense colour, a gorgeous dark ruby, and confirmed by the strength and complexity of the bouquet, which is nonetheless not overwhelmed by the strong oakiness. On the palate, the tannins are almost excessive in their concentration, indicating that at least five years' cellaring will be necessary before drinking. The estate's second wine, **Le Cloître du Château Prieuré Lichine 2000 (15–23 €)**, received special mention from the Jury.

➽ Ch. Prieuré-Lichine, 34, av. de la 5ᵉ-République,
33460 Cantenac, tel. 05.57.88.36.28, fax 05.57.88.78.93,
e-mail prieure.lichine@wanadoo.fr ☑
⟁ ev. day except Sun. 9am–12 noon 2pm–5pm
➽ GPE Ballande

CH. RAUZAN-GASSIES 2000★★

2e cru clas.	27 ha	120,000	▮ ▯ ⚘ 30–38 €

|93| |94| 96 **97** 98 99 00

The classically-styled label is the only thing not to have changed here; progress has been spectacular over the past few years. This vintage confirms that Rauzan-Gassies has returned completely to the reality of its classification. The appearance, with its purplish tinges, has a sumptuous finesse which is shared by the bouquet of red fruits and flowers, with its notes of prune, cocoa, blackcurrant and juniper. No less complex in its flavours is the rich, well-constructed palate, which reveals a perfect marriage of fruit and oak. A very fine wine. Open in four or five years' time.

➽ SCI du Ch. Rauzan-Gassies, rue Alexis-Millardet,
33460 Margaux, tel. 05.57.88.71.88, fax 05.57.88.37.49 ☑
⟁ ev. day except Sat. Sun. 8am–11.30am 2pm–5.30pm
➽ J.-M. Quié

CH. RAUZAN-SEGLA 2000★★★

2e cru clas.	51 ha	100,000	▯ +76 €

81 82 |83| |85| |88| |89| 90 91 92 |93| 94 95 (96) |97| (98) (99) 00

The château is a pretty 17th century manor-house and the wine is of a rare magnificence. 20 months in oak, this wine is a blend of 61% Cabernet Sauvignon, 36% Merlot and 3% Petit Verdot. The presentation is perfect, a bouquet of great aromatic complexity (ripe black fruits, elegant toastiness and warm brioche). After a straightforward attack, the palate reveals velvety, silky tannins, a structure of excellent balance and a charming revival of the bouquet. This wine has taste and is of good taste; it will deserve a place in the cellar for the next ten years.

➽ SA Ch. Rauzan-Ségla, BP 56, 33460 Margaux,
tel. 05.57.88.82.10, fax 05.57.88.34.54
⟁ by appt.

SEGLA 2000★★

	51 ha	95,000	▯ 23–30 €

This is Château Rauzan-Ségla's second wine, with 47% Merlot in the blend. It is quite simply remarkable: a lovely ruby colour, a bouquet that gains in harmony when swirled in the glass, and a frank, fresh palate underpinned by dense tannins and a full, fondant, silky finish. Keep for five to ten years.

➽ SA Ch. Rauzan-Ségla, BP 56, 33460 Margaux,
tel. 05.57.88.82.10, fax 05.57.88.34.54
⟁ by appt.

CH. SIRAN 2000★★

Cru bourg.	22.2 ha	90,000	▯ 30–38 €

66 78 79 80 **81 82 83** 85 86 87 88 |89| |90| 91 92 |93| |94| |95| 96 |97| 98 99 **00**

The Miailhe, a very ancient family of the Bordeaux brokerage, bought this property from the count of Toulouse-Lautrec, the famous painter's grandfather. Wines like this show that they remain worthy of the cru's past. Although Merlot occupies the dominant place with 57%, this 2000 is still very much a Margaux, by virtue of the complex bouquet, which is elegant and well-balanced, and the palate, which has silky tannins and is supported by quality oak. The spacious finish points to a radiant future for this wine (over five years). An astonishing wine, classically constructed but crowned by a drawing by Ben. The second wine, **S. de Siran 2000 (15–23 €)**, is awarded a one-star rating.

➽ SC du Ch. Siran, Ch. Siran, 33460 Labarde,
tel. 05.57.88.34.04, fax 05.57.88.70.05,
e-mail chateau.siran@wanadoo.fr ☑
⟁ ev. day 10.15am–12.45pm 1.30pm–6pm
➽ Alain Miailhe

CH. DU TERTRE 2000★

5e cru clas.	50.4 ha	200,000	▯ 23–30 €

90 91 92 93 95 96 **98** 99 00

This wine is privileged: it is aged in handsome vaulted cellars. It seems to have benefited from that, given the lovely dark-purple colour, the bouquet with intense oaky notes that marry well with those of crystallized fruits, and the rich, concentrated body. A slightly hot note appears on the finish, but this should disappear in three or four years.

➽ SEV Ch. du Tertre, 33460 Arsac, tel. 05.57.97.09.09,
fax 05.57.97.09.00 ☑
⟁ by appt.
➽ Eric Albada Jelgersma

CH. LA TOUR DE MONS 2000★

■ Cru bourg. 24.4 ha 190,000 ▥ 15–23 €

Although this is a very ancient estate that goes back to the Middle Ages, it is nonetheless open to modern methods, namely those of sustainable agriculture. They have certainly helped production, as is shown by this wine's complex bouquet of black fruits, chocolate, liquorice and vanilla, its well-structured palate supported by ripe, well-covered tannins, and the long, spicy finish.

☛ SAS Ch. La Tour de Mons, 20, rte de Marsac, 33460 Soussans, tel. 05.57.88.33.03, fax 05.57.88.32.46, e-mail chateau-latourdemons@wanadoo.fr

🍷 by appt.

CH. VINCENT 2000★

■ Cru bourg. 2 ha 8,500 ▥ 15–23 €

Here is an aspect of increasing rarity: the cru still belongs to the estate's founder's descendants. This 2000 is a very youthful Bordeaux colour and has an attractively somewhat fashionable character: round, fine tannins still influenced by the oak (vanilla and coffee extract), and a floral bouquet with gamey and fruity overtones. Drink in two to three years' time. Remember: the 99 was a *coup de coeur*.

☛ Domec-Barrault, Ch. Vincent, Issan, 33460 Cantenac, tel. 05.57.88.90.56, fax 05.57.88.90.56 ☑

Wines selected but not starred

CH. CHARMANT 2000

■ 4.7 ha 30,900 ▥ 15–23 €

☛ SCEA René Renon, Ch. Charmant, 33460 Margaux, tel. 05.57.88.35.27, fax 05.57.88.70.59, e-mail scea.rene.renon@wanadoo.fr ☑

🍷 by appt.

CH. DESMIRAIL 2000

■ 3e cru clas. 30 ha n.c. ▥ 23–30 €
81 82 (83) |85| |86| 87 |88| |89| |90| 91 92 93 94 95 96 |97| 99 00

☛ SCEA du Ch. Desmirail, 33460 Cantenac, tel. 05.57.88.34.33, fax 05.57.88.96.27

🍷 by appt.

CH. MARQUIS D'ALESME

Becker 2000

■ 3e cru clas. 16 ha 100,000 ▥ 23–30 €

☛ Jean-Claude Zuger, Ch. Marquis d'Alesme, 33460 Margaux, tel. 05.57.88.70.27, fax 05.57.88.73.78, e-mail marquisdalesme@wanadoo.fr ☑

🍷 ev. day 10am–12 noon 2pm–5pm

CH. MARTINENS 2000

■ Cru bourg. 25 ha n.c. ▤▥ 15–23 €

☛ Jean-Pierre Seynat-Dulos, Ch. Martinens, 33460 Cantenac, tel. 05.57.88.71.37, fax 05.57.88.38.35, e-mail chateau-martinens@wanadoo.fr ☑

🍷 by appt.

CH. PONTAC-LYNCH 2000

■ Cru bourg. 8.05 ha 45,000 ▥ 15–23 €

☛ Ch. Pontac-Lynch, Issan-Cantenac, 33460 Margaux, tel. 05.57.88.30.04, fax 05.57.88.32.63 ☑

🍷 by appt.

☛ Bondon

Moulis-en-Médoc

An area consisting of a narrow ribbon 12 km long and only 300–400 m wide, Moulis is the least extensive of the Appellations Communales in the Médoc. However, it offers a range of different terroirs.

As with Listrac, it falls into three main areas. The Bouqueyran area, to the west near the road from Bordeaux to Soulac, has a varied topography with limestone crests and a slope of ancient, Pyrenean gravel. In the centre, a plain of clay and limestone forms an extension of the Peyrelebade plain (see Listrac-Médoc). Finally, to the east and northeast, near the railway line, there rises a series of fine ridges of Garonne gravel forming a first-class terroir within which the famous hillocks of Grand-Poujeaux, Maucaillou and Médrac are clustered.

Moulis wines are soft and full, with a supple, delicate character. Even though they can be kept for some time (seven or eight years), they can develop more rapidly than wines from other communes in the area. The 2002 vintage produced 27,133 hl from 607 ha.

CH. ANTHONIC 2000★

■ Cru bourg. 22.5 ha 150,000 ▮▥♦ 11–15 €
85 (86) 88 89 |90| 91 92 93 94 |95| |96| 97 |98| 99 00

The château was named around 1920 after a former owner, but with an added "h", perhaps an anglophile gesture. Its wine will certainly suit English tastes, thanks to its fullness and its soft yet evident tannins. Their character is presaged by the plain, rather dark-red colour. Nevertheless, this wine does have finesse; it appears in the notes of ripe fruits. Given the unaggressive way in which it hits the palate and the fullness of the finish, this wine is already pleasant, but deserves to be laid down for three years.

☛ SCEA Pierre Cordonnier, Ch. Anthonic, 33480 Moulis-en-Médoc, tel. 05.56.58.34.60, fax 05.56.58.72.76, e-mail chateau.anthonic@terre-net.fr ☑

🍷 by appt.

CH. BEL-AIR LAGRAVE 2000★

■ Cru bourg. 9 ha 50,000 ▥ 11–15 €

Made by the same producer as Château La Closerie de Grand Poujeaux, this wine is of as fine a quality. Though the tannins are still a bit lively on the finish, the finesse of the wine's fruity (cherry) and floral aromas, enhanced by a tiny note of grilling, makes it most agreeable, as do also the freshness and good balance of the palate.

☛ SARL Seguin-Bacquey, Grand-Poujeaux, 33480 Moulis-en-Médoc, tel. 05.56.58.01.89, fax 05.56.58.05.21 ☑

🍷 ev. day 9am–12 noon 2pm–8pm

CH. BISTON-BRILLETTE 2000★★

■ Cru bourg. 22 ha 130,000 ▥ 11–15 €
86 88 89 (90) 91 93 94 |95| |96| 97 98 99 00

Both the traditional sobriety of the buildings and the authenticity of the wine made in them are in the spirit of the appellation. With its very pleasing attack, this 2000 has a flavoursome fleshiness that is provided by its gorgeous tannins. The bouquet is very intense, with an elegance and finesse that one expects in a Médoc. The flavoursome finish is confirmation of the wine's potential. Wait three or four years before drinking.

☛ EARL Ch. Biston-Brillette, Petit-Poujeaux, 33480 Moulis-en-Médoc, tel. 05.56.58.22.86, fax 05.56.58.13.16, e-mail contact@châteaubistonbrillette.com ☑

🍷 ev. day except Sun. 10am–12 noon 2pm–6pm; Sat. 10am–12 noon

☛ Michel Barbarin

CH. BRILLETTE 2000★★

■ Cru bourg. 22.5 ha 115,000 🔲 🍾 15–23 €
94 95 |96| 98 99 00

The château, a fine dwelling surrounded by vines, adjoins the winery as if to show that here everything focuses on wine. This particular vintage shows itself worthy of such attention. It has a superbly promising colour between Bordeaux and black cherry, and the taster's expectation is realized by the bouquet, whose empyreumatic and floral notes mix happily with hints of crystallized fruits, flowers and caramel. After an oaky attack, the palate evolves towards a lovely balance of fruit, tannins and oak. The fullness of the perfectly constructed palate makes this wine already very good drinking, though it may also be kept.
🍾 SA Ch. Brillette, 33480 Moulis-en-Médoc,
tel. 05.56.58.22.09, fax 05.56.58.12.26 ☑
🍷 by appt.
🍾 J.-L. Flageul

CH. CHASSE-SPLEEN 2000★★

■ Cru bourg. 45 ha 346,000 🍾 15–23 €
75 76 78 79 80 81 82 (83) 85 86 |88| 89 |90| 91 92 93 94 |95|
|96| |97| 98 99 00

Some say that this château, in perfect harmony with the vines that surround it, owes its name to Baudelaire; others say Byron. At all events, the name is well chosen, for its wine does indeed chase away melancholy. The colour is a cheering ruby, and the bouquet a happy mix of delicate vanilla notes and spices. After a faultless attack, the palate develops a fruity elegance sustained by well-judged oak and silky tannins. Overall, the wine is already well-blended, but it will be at its best in five years' time.
🍾 SA Ch. Chasse-Spleen, 2558, Grand-Poujeaux Sud, 33480 Moulis-en-Médoc, tel. 05.56.58.02.37, fax 05.57.88.84.40, e-mail info@chasse-spleen.com
🍷 by appt.

CH. LA CLOSERIE DU GRAND-POUJEAUX 2000★★

■ Cru bourg. 7 ha 35,000 🍾 11–15 €
This cru believes in sustainable cultivation methods and seeks to preserve the ecosystem without damaging the wine's quality. The object is realized with this 2000, whose colour is an intense ruby and whose bouquet is attractively complex. The nose first exhales perfumes of very ripe fruits, pepper and cinnamon, then, when swirled in the glass, releases jammy notes. The palate is charming, smooth, well-covered, with a lovely balance of fine, elegant tannins and ripe fruits which come back strongly in the fresh, spacious finish. The same producer's **Château Haut-Franquet 2000 (8–11 €)** is commended.
🍾 SARL Seguin-Bacquey, Grand-Poujeaux, 33480 Moulis-en-Médoc, tel. 05.56.58.01.89, fax 05.56.58.05.21 ☑
🍷 ev. day 9am–12 noon 2pm–8pm

CH. DUPLESSIS FABRE 2000★

■ Cru bourg. 2.5 ha 17,000 🍾 11–15 €
90 91 92 93 94 |95| |96| 98 |99| 00

Produced by the same estate as Château Maucaillou, this ruby wine is marked by typical varietal notes of Cabernet Sauvignon, even though Merlot is the majority variety. Round, fleshy and rich, the palate has a long finish which is still a trifle severe, calling for three or four years' cellaring.
🍾 Ch. Maucaillou, quartier de la Gare, 33480 Moulis-en-Médoc, tel. 05.56.58.01.23, fax 05.56.58.00.88 ☑
🍷 by appt.
🍾 Philippe Dourthe

CH. GUITIGNAN 2000★★

■ Cru bourg. 8 ha 40,000 🍾 8–11 €
Graves and small pebbles over limestone-clay: this cru has the advantage of a real Médoc terroir. Vinification is undertaken by the cellar at Listrac and, being up to the quality of the grapes, has produced a wine of character. The dark colour suggests power. The bouquet demonstrates a fairly tenacious oakiness with underlying fruit. When the wine touches the palate, the fruit gets the upper hand and there is lots of fleshy body, even if it is somewhat rugged. This is a sturdy, serious wine, destined for the cellar. Open in three or four years' time and serve with game.
🍾 Cave de vinification de Listrac, 21, av. de Soulac, 33480 Listrac-Médoc, tel. 05.56.58.03.19, fax 05.56.58.07.22, e-mail grandlistrac@cave-listrac-medoc.com ☑
🍷 by appt.
🍾 Annie Vidaller

CH. LALAUDEY 2000★

■ 6.5 ha 45,000 🍾 11–15 €
This rich ruby wine complements the range of fine wines from the Margaux château of Mongravey. It has a charming aroma of toast over deeper notes of blackcurrant and blackberry. The tannins are well-covered but powerful, and call for four or five years' storage.
🍾 Régis Bernaleau, 8, av. Jean-Luc-Vonderheyden, 33480 Arsac, tel. 05.56.58.84.51, fax 05.56.58.83.39, e-mail chateau.mongravey@wanadoo.fr ☑
🍷 by appt.

CH. MALMAISON 2000★

■ Cru bourg. 24 ha n.c. 🍾 11–15 €
88 89 90 91 92 93 94 |95| |96| 97 98 99 00

This somewhat original varietal blend (80% Merlot) is a Moulis extension to the Clarke estate. The variety has left its imprint on the fruity bouquet of this 2000, whose deep ruby colour and complex aromas make a very good impression. The fine, delicate structure has an elegance which is enhanced by a finish in which the fruit aromas return strongly. Despite appearances, this wine is sufficiently strongly constructed to be kept for four or five years.
🍾 CV Edmond et Benjamin de Rothschild, 33480 Listrac-Médoc, tel. 05.56.58.38.00, fax 05.56.58.26.46, e-mail chateau.clarke@wanadoo.fr ☑

CH. MAUCAILLOU 2000★

■ Cru bourg. 60 ha 430,000 🍾 15–23 €
81 82 83 85 86 87 |88| |89| |90| 91 92 93 94 |95| (96) |97| 98
99 00

This château, built in 1875 in the somewhat surprising style of an Arcachon villa, houses a rich museum of vines and wines. This bright rich-red 2000, made of 58% Cabernets, 7% Petit Verdot and 35% Merlot, is still somewhat rebellious. Its bouquet and palate are, however, true to type and it has good potential to age well.
🍾 Ch. Maucaillou, quartier de la Gare, 33480 Moulis-en-Médoc, tel. 05.56.58.01.23, fax 05.56.58.00.88 ☑
🍷 by appt.
🍾 Philippe Dourthe

CH. POUJEAUX 2000★★

⬛ Cru bourg. 53 ha n.c. 🍶 ⬛⬛ ♨ 23–30€
81 82 83 85 (86) 87 |88| |89| |90| 93 94 |95| |96| |97| 98 **99 00**

All the tasters agreed that the promotion of Poujeaux to classification as a Cru Bourgeois Exceptionnel last June was a just recognition of the patient and efficient work that Theil have done here. This 2000 says as much. It has a superb bright red colour with ruby highlights and a bouquet that reveals maturation of quality. The oak respects the notes of red and black fruits, as well as the hint of lily that lends a certain originality to the wine's aromatic character. After a good attack, the wine's oakiness is impressive, but the tannins are nonetheless silky, round and well-blended. The long finish confirms, if confirmation were needed, that this 2000 will be a remarkable wine when the oak has become totally integrated, say in five years' time.
🍷 Jean Theil SA, Ch. Poujeaux, 33480 Moulis-en-Médoc, tel. 05.56.58.02.96, fax 05.56.58.01.25, e-mail poujeaux@chateaupoujeaux.com ☑
🍷 by appt.

Wines selected but not starred

CH. DUPLESSIS 2000

⬛ Cru bourg. 19.25 ha 88,368 11–15€
🍷 SC Les Grands Crus Réunis, 2036, Chalet, 33480 Moulis-en-Médoc, tel. 05.56.58.22.01, fax 05.56.58.15.10, e-mail marie-laure.lurton.lgcr@wanadoo.fr
🍷 M.-L. Lurton

CH. DUTRUCH GRAND POUJEAUX 2000

⬛ Cru bourg. 26 ha 120,000 🍶 ⬛⬛ ♨ 11–15€
81 82 (83) 85 86 |88| 89 90 93 94 |95| |96| 97 |98| 99 00

🍷 EARL François Cordonnier, Ch. Dutruch Grand Poujeaux, 33480 Moulis-en-Médoc, tel. 05.56.58.02.55, fax 05.56.58.06.22, e-mail chateau.dutruch@aquinet.net ☑
🍷 by appt.

GRESSIER GRAND POUJEAUX 2000

⬛ Cru bourg. 18 ha 130,000 🍶 ⬛⬛ ♨ 11–15€
🍷 Bertrand de Marcellus, Ch. Gressier Grand Poujeaux, 33480 Moulis-en-Médoc, tel. 05.56.58.05.48, fax 05.56.58.05.48 ☑
🍷 by appt.
🍷 de Saint-Affrique

CH. MOULIN A VENT 2000

⬛ Cru bourg. 25 ha 150,000 🍶 ⬛⬛ ♨ 11–15€
🍷 Dominique Hessel, Ch. Moulin à Vent, Bouqueyran, 33480 Moulis-en-Médoc, tel. 05.56.58.15.79, fax 05.56.58.39.89, e-mail hessel@moulin-a-vent.com ☑
🍷 ev. day except Sat. Sun. 9am–12 noon 1.30pm–5.30pm

CH. MYON DE L'ENCLOS 2000

⬛ 5 ha 25,000 ⬛⬛ 8–11€
|95| |96| |97| 98 99 00

🍷 Bernard Lartigue, Ch. Mayne Lalande, 33480 Listrac-Médoc, tel. 05.56.58.27.63, fax 05.56.58.22.41, e-mail b.lartigue@terre-net.fr ☑
🍷 by appt.

CH. PEY BERLAND 2000

⬛ 0.85 ha 5,200 ⬛⬛ 11–15€
🍷 Jean Charpentier, Ch. Pey Berland, 33480 Moulis-en-Médoc, tel. 06.16.12.52.53, fax 05.56.58.38.84 ☑ 🏛
🍷 by appt.

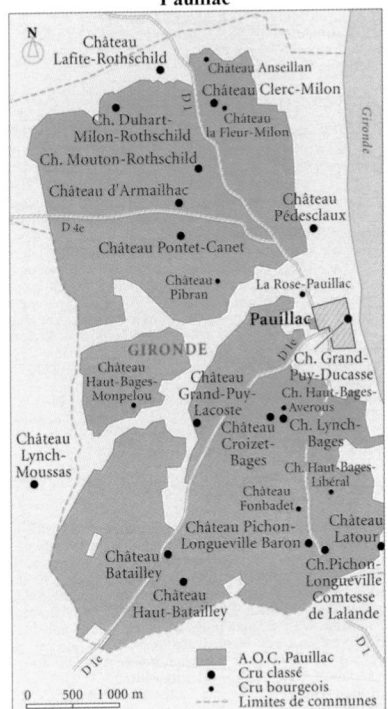

Pauillac

With a population hardly greater than that of a large market town, Pauillac has a real urban feel, enhanced by a pleasure-boat harbour on the route of the Canal du Midi. The café terraces on the quay are the place to enjoy a plate of freshly caught shrimps from the estuary. But Pauillac is also, and above all, the capital of the Médoc wine-growing region, both by virtue of its geographical location in the middle of the vineyard and by the presence of three of the Premiers Crus Classés (Lafite, Latour and Mouton), which complete a really impressive tally of 18 Crus Classés. The cooperative produces a large quantity of wines. The appellation as a whole produced 48,999 hl from 1,209 ha in 2002.

The appellation is cut in two by the Chenal du Gahet, a small stream running through the middle of the two plateaux where the vines are grown. The area to the north, which takes its name

Pauillac

Château Lafite-Rothschild
Château Anseillan
Château Clerc-Milon
Ch. Duhart-Milon-Rothschild
Château la Fleur-Milon
Ch. Mouton-Rothschild
Château d'Armailhac
Château Pédesclaux
D 4e
Château Pontet-Canet
Château Pibran
La Rose-Pauillac
Pauillac
GIRONDE
Château Haut-Bages-Monpelou
Château Grand-Puy-Lacoste
Ch. Grand-Puy-Ducasse
Ch. Haut-Bages-Averous
Château Lynch-Moussas
Château Croizet-Bages
Ch. Lynch-Bages
Ch. Haut-Bages-Libéral
Château Fonbadet
Château Pichon-Longueville Baron
Château Latour
Château Batailley
Ch. Pichon-Longueville Comtesse de Lalande
Château Haut-Batailley
D 1e

A.O.C. Pauillac
● Cru classé
● Cru bourgeois
---- Limites de communes

0 500 1 000 m

Pauillac

from the hamlet of Pouyalet, is slightly higher, by about 30 m, and has steeper slopes. It is the home of two of the Premiers Crus Classés (Lafite and Mouton) and enjoys an outstandingly fine balance between soil and subsoil, an attribute shared by the plateau of Saint-Lambert to the south. This second area stretches south from the Gahet to the Juillac Valley, where a small stream runs along the southern border of the commune and gives excellent drainage. The area's gravels, which are formed from large stones, are particularly distinctive on the terroir of its Premier Cru, Château Latour.

Pauillacs from pure gravel ridges are very full-bodied wines, powerful and well-structured, but also fine and elegant, with a delicate bouquet. They develop very well as they age, and are worth waiting for. When mature, they can be served with confidence to accompany strongly flavoured dishes prepared with mushrooms, for instance, or to complement red meat, dark game meat or foie gras.

CH. D'ARMAILHAC 2000★

| ■ | 5e cru clas. | 49 ha | 185,200 | ⦿ | 38–46 € |

72 73 74 75 78 **79 80 81 82 83 84 |85|** (86) 87 **|88| |89| |90|** 92 **|93|** 94 **95** |96| 97 **98** 99 00

A small Bacchus in enamelled glass dating from the 17th century adorns the label of this cru, which has changed name several times and was classified in 1855 under the name Mouton d'Armailhac. Grown in a vineyard where the 58% Cabernet vines dominate, yet do not overwhelm, their Merlot counterparts, this wine has a charming balance between suppleness and tannic richness. The tannins guarantee real potential for ageing, and this will enable the oak, which is still very evident in the bouquet with its lovely toasty, roasted notes, to blend in with the rest.
🍷 SA Baron Philippe de Rothschild, BP 117, 33250 Pauillac, tel. 05.56.73.20.20, fax 05.56.73.20.44, e-mail webmaster@bpdr.com
🍷 Baronne Ph. de Rothschild

CH. BATAILLEY 2000★

| ■ | 5e cru clas. | 55 ha | 70,000 | ⦿ | 30–38 € |

70 75 76 78 79 80 81 82 83 **|85| |86| |88|** |89| |90| 91 92 **|93|** **|95|** (96) **|97|** **98** 99 00

The Castéja family, which owns this cru, is one of the oldest in Pauillac. Their deep roots in the region doubtless explain their adherence to the spirit of the appellation, which is evidenced by the high proportion of Cabernet Sauvignon (70%) in this blend. The variety's character comes through in the bouquet, which has a hint of green pepper associated with subtle notes of red fruits (redcurrant and cherry). After a supple attack, the palate is sustained by fine tannins and frank, uncomplicated flavours enhanced by a well-judged oakiness. Wait two to four years before drinking.
🍷 Héritiers Castéja, 33250 Pauillac, tel. 05.56.00.00.70, fax 05.57.87.48.61, e-mail domaines.boriemanoux.@dial.oleane.com ▪
🍷 Emile Castéja

CH. LA BÉCASSE 2000★★

| ■ | | 4 ha | 28,000 | ⦿ | 23–30 € |

91 92 93 94 **|95|** 96 97 98 **00**

This small cru, established in 1966, is proud of its authentic Médoc credentials which come through in the quality of its production. This 2000 is an archetypal Pauillac: powerful, built for laying down, yet full of style and class. The deep colour speaks of power, which is confirmed by the palate's dense tannic structure. Even so, there is a pulpy fleshiness which allies with elegant notes of blackcurrant and blackberry to create a well-blended synthesis. This wine will pass long years in the calm of the cellar, before it can go down in the annals of great mouth-watering wines.
🍷 Roland Fonteneau, 21, rue Edouard-de-Pontet, 33250 Pauillac, tel. 05.56.59.07.14, fax 05.56.59.18.44 ▪

CH. BELLEGRAVE 2000★★

| ■ | Cru bourg. | 7.02 ha | 35,000 | ⦿ | 15–23 € |

97 98 **99 00**

The unoriginal name of this cru will not do much to promote it among the great estates of Pauillac. Not so the quality of its production. This 2000 testifies to the potentiality of its soil, the predominance of the Cabernets (72%) and the labours of the new owner since 1997. Though sombre and full of tears, the appearance ought not to depress. On the contrary, the connoisseur will see it as an encouraging sign, like the complexity of the bouquet, with its notes of smoke, ripe fruits and spices. First impressions on the palate are of ampleness, and indeed this is a well-built, full-bodied, rich, thick, fleshy wine with fine, well-coated tannins. In a few years time, when it leaves the cellar, it will do credit to venison with caramelized vegetables.
🍷 Ch. Bellegrave, 22, rte des Châteaux, 33250 Pauillac, tel. 05.56.59.06.47, fax 04.90.65.03.73 ▪
🍸 by appt.
🍷 Meffre

CH. CLERC MILON 2000★★

| ■ | 5e cru clas. | 31 ha | 132,000 | ⦿ | 46–76 € |

|75| 76 78 79 **|82| |83| |85| |86|** 87 **|88| 89 |90| |92| |93|** 94 (95) **96 |97| 98 99 00**

Clerc Milon has a reputation for strong, good-keeping wines. It will not be tarnished by this 2000, an archetypal Pauillac, made from 67% Cabernet Sauvignon and 33% Merlot. The finer and more delicate aromas of red fruits are somewhat over-dominated by the oak at present. But on the palate the flavours of black fruit get the upper hand, while the structure, which is dense, tannic and fleshy, confirms the promise afforded by the intense garnet colour. The excellence of the finish urges that the wine be left for several years in the cellar, in order to allow the oak to soften.
🍷 SA Baron Philippe de Rothschild, BP 117, 33250 Pauillac, tel. 05.56.73.20.20, fax 05.56.73.20.44, e-mail webmaster@bpdr.com
🍷 Baronne Ph. de Rothschild

CH. CROIZET BAGES 2000★★

| ■ | 5e cru clas. | 27 ha | 160,000 | ▮⦿♦ | 23–30 € |

93 94 **|95| |96| |97| |98| 99 00**

All who think that Grand Cru quality can be improved only through the purchase of estates by financial groups with huge resources will be made to think again by the Quiés and their 2000 vintage. Croizet Bages' continuing comeback does credit to its producer by reason both of its presentation and its development on the palate. The colour is a bright, rich garnet, and the bouquet has undeniable class, with a successful marriage of quality oak and well-ripened grapes. Wine-lovers will appreciate the chewiness and strength of the palate, as well as the finish, which leaves an impression of a flavoursome synthesis with a fine future before it.
🍷 Jean-Michel Quié, Ch. Croizet-Bages, 9, rue du Port-de-la-Verrerie, 33250 Pauillac, tel. 05.56.59.01.62, fax 05.56.59.23.39 ▪
🍸 ev. day except Sun. 9am–12.30pm 1.30pm–5.30pm

328

BORDEAUX

CH. DUHART-MILON 2000★

■ 4e cru clas. 66 ha 310,000 🍷🍷 46–76 €
61 70 75 76 79 80 81 |82| |83| |85| |86| 87 |88| |89| 90 |91| |92| |93| |94| 95 96 97 98 99 00

As usual, this cru offers a wine that responds to the criteria governing the great classics of the appellation. Thus its tannins, somewhat austere in their youth, will need time to evolve, as the structure is currently extremely forceful. The bouquet has musky, leathery notes, which recur on the palate in association with red fruit flavours. The attack on the palate is fresh, and the finish is long-lasting and tannic. In sum, this 2000 will need six or seven years in the cellar before drinking. The same cru's **Moulin de Duhart 2000 (11–15 €)** will also need cellaring, and is singled out by the Jury.
☛ Ch. Duhart-Milon, 33250 Pauillac, tel. 01.53.89.78.00, fax 01.53.89.78.01 ☑

CH. LA FLEUR MILON 2000★★

■ Cru bourg. 12.5 ha 85,000 🍷🍷 15–23 €
94 (95) 96 97 98 00

Created in 1958 by the acquisition of plots, La Fleur Milon is a traditional Médoc blend. This 2000 is beautifully presented, having an appearance of great depth and a fine, delicate bouquet composed of floral and fruity notes. The oak shows its presence, but without devouring the other aromas, and there is a sense of Cabernet fullness. The palate also reveals a lovely complexity born of a remarkable association of power and freshness. The strong revival of aromas on the finish convinces that this wine will have a long life. The same producer's **Château Chantecler Milon 2000 (5–8 €)**, marketed by the wine-merchants André Quancard André, is commended.
☛ SCE Ch. La Fleur Milon, Le Pouyalet, 33250 Pauillac, tel. 05.56.59.29.01, fax 05.56.59.23.22, e-mail contact@lafleurmilon.com ☑
🍴 ev. day except Sat. Sun. 8.30am–12 noon 2pm–5pm; cl. 24–31 Aug., during the grape-harvest
☛ Héritiers Gimenez

CH. LA FLEUR PEYRABON 2000★★

■ Cru bourg. 4.87 ha 32,410 🍷 23–30 €
Although most of Château Peyrabon's vines are at Saint-Sauveur, in the AOC Haut-Médoc, Patrick Bernard and his team are mindful of the small Pauillac unit they have had since 1998. This wine is a testimony to their care: the colour is a lovely garnet, and the bouquet is dense and complex, with fine notes of fruits and vanilla. The well-balanced palate has great integration and much elegance, which will make it a suitable accompaniment to high-class food.
☛ SARL Ch. Peyrabon, Vignes de Peyrabon, 33250 Saint-Sauveur, tel. 05.56.59.57.10, fax 05.56.59.59.45, e-mail chateau.peyrabon@wanadoo.fr ☑
🍴 ev. day except Sat. Sun. 9am–12 noon 2pm–5pm

CH. GRAND-PUY DUCASSE 2000★★

■ 5e cru clas. 38.66 ha 122,800 🍷 38–46 €
82 83 84 85 86 88 89 |90| 91 92 93 94 |95| 96 97 98 99 00

This cru, which belongs via Cordier to the Val d'Orbieu group presided over by Yves Barsalou, was established in the 18th century, and has the particularity of possessing an urban château, on the quays at Pauillac. This 2000 does not simply have an eye-catching appearance, between purple and garnet. The nose is very expressive, being rich in a thousand fruity notes with hints of toast. The palate is fondant, rich and fleshy, with a rich, sturdy structure sustained by elegant, rounded tannins. This will be a lovely wine to drink in four to five years' time. Characterized by more delicate tannins is the same producer's **Prélude à Grand-Puy Ducasse 2000 (15–23 €)**, which gains one star. It will be ready to drink sooner.
☛ SC du Ch. Grand-Puy Ducasse, La Croix Bacalan, 109, rue Achard, BP 154, 33042 Bordeaux Cedex, tel. 05.56.11.29.00, fax 05.56.11.29.01

CH. GRAND-PUY-LACOSTE 2000★★

■ 5e cru clas. 53 ha 190,000 🍷 46–76 €
61 66 70 71 75 76 78 81 82 |83| |85| (86) 87 88 89 90 |91| |92| |93| |94| 95 96 |97| 98 99 00

This Grand Cru, whose buildings date from 1750, produces wines of great character and quality. This 2000 is a very true-to-type example, whose authenticity is plain from the rich garnet colour. The bouquet has a broad range of fine aromas of red fruits enhanced by notes of vanilla and spices. The same generosity characterizes the palate, where ripe, elegant tannins contribute to the wine's complexity and balance of flavours. Rich, full and silky, the liquorice finish emphasizes the superb potential of this wine, which should be left in the cellar for six years. More supple, but also very true-to-type is the one-starred **Lacoste Borie 2000 (11–15 €)**.
☛ Ch. Grand-Puy-Lacoste, 33250 Pauillac, tel. 05.56.73.16.73, fax 05.56.59.27.37
🍴 by appt.

CH. HAUT BAGES LIBERAL 2000★★★

■ 5e cru clas. 28 ha 120,000 🍷 15–23 €
75 76 78 79 80 81 (82) |83| 84 |85| |86| 87 88 89 90 91 92 |93| |94| 95 96 |97| (98) 99 (00)

With its deep Garonne gravels and varietal composition of 80% Cabernet Sauvignon, this cru definitely has an authentic Pauillac profile. The wine has an attractively youthful colour with deep-purple tinges. Powerful and rich in fruity, floral aromas, the bouquet is similarly youthful, as indeed is the full, well-integrated structure, which is supported by fine, silky tannins. This wine, in the finest traditions of the appellation, may be left in the cellar for eight to twelve years. Destined for a shorter life is the same estate's **La Chapelle de Bages 2000 (8–11 €)** and **La Fleur de Haut Bages Libéral 2000 (8–11 €)**, both of which are one-star wines.
☛ Claire Villars Lurton, Ch. Haut-Bages Libéral, 33250 Pauillac, tel. 05.57.88.76.65, fax 05.57.88.98.33
🍴 by appt.

CH. HAUT BAGES MONPELOU 2000★

■ Cru bourg. n.c. 50,000 🍷 15–23 €
Detached from Duhart-Milon in 1948, this cru benefits from an excellent terroir, as is demonstrated by this wine's bouquet. Though still somewhat dominated by the oak, a hint of green

pepper is nevertheless discernible from the Cabernet grapes. First impressions on the palate are round and rich, preceding a lovely tannic weave and a clean surge as it finishes.

� Héritiers Castéja, 33250 Pauillac, tel. 05.56.00.00.70, fax 05.57.87.48.61, e-mail domaines.boriemanoux.@dial.oleane.com

CH. HAUT-BATAILLEY 2000★★

■ 5e cru clas.	20 ha	115,000	❙❚❙	30–38 €

66 71 75 78 81 82 83 84 |85| |86| 87 88 89 90 91 |92| |93| 94 95 96 |97| 98 99 00

The varietal mix, with its majority of Cabernet Sauvignon grapes, is one of the reasons for this wine's success. The ebony colour is full of promise. From behind a welcoming charred note the bouquet quickly unveils fine notes of blackberry and vanilla. It comes as no surprise that the attack is pure class, being elegant and powerful, with hints of blackcurrant and oaky flavours. The structure of powerful, dense tannins provides a lingering finish. A very stylish Pauillac, which calls for a good period in the cellar. Haut-Batailley's second wine, the one-star **Latour l'Aspic 2000 (8–11 €)**, has great delicacy, which reflects a quality harvest and well-managed extraction.

� SA Jean-Eugène Borie, 33250 Saint-Julien-Beychevelle, tel. 05.56.73.16.73, fax 05.56.59.27.37, e-mail je-borie@je-borie-sa.com
➠ Mme des Brest-Borie

CH. LAFITE ROTHSCHILD 2000★★★

■ 1er cru clas.	100 ha	280,000	❙❚❙	+76 €

59 (61) 64 |66| 69 |70| 73 |75| 76 77 |78| |79| |80| |81| |82| |83| |84| 85 86 |87| 88 89 90 92 93 94 (95) (96) 97 (98) 99 (00)

Great wines are rare, and those that become legendary rarer still. Lafite is one of those. Once the property of the Ségurs, it was bought by Baron James de Rothschild in 1868. The elegant château has the benefit of a winery designed by Ricardo Bofill. The dark, dense appearance of this 2000 is immediately seductive. The bouquet increases the wine's magic, the distinguished marrying of vanilla, small red berries, blackcurrant, liquorice, and cedarwood. The attack is sumptuous, an extraordinary combination of power and freshness. The palate is rich, unctuous, silky, with never a suspicion of dullness. There is a last, fleeting tannic note, then a beautiful finish that is spacious and lingering. The finish prescribes storage of this prestigious wine for a minimum of five years; it could even be kept for 20 or 30 years. Drink only on exceptional gastronomic occasions.

� Ch. Lafite Rothschild, 33250 Pauillac, tel. 01.53.89.78.00, fax 01.53.89.78.01
♁ by appt.

CARRUADES DE LAFITE 2000★

■		n.c.	340,000	❙❚❙	46–76 €

|85| |86| 87 88 89 90 91 92 |93| |94| 95 96 97 98 99 00

As its name indicates, this cru comes from the prestigious plateau of the Carruades, which is shared by Lafite and Mouton. In accordance with the spirit of the terroir, this a wine for the cellar. Its relative youth is obvious from the colour, the palate, and the bouquet, which is both fresh and elegant.

➠ Ch. Lafite Rothschild, 33250 Pauillac, tel. 01.53.89.78.00, fax 01.53.89.78.01
♁ by appt.

CH. LATOUR 2000★★★

■ 1er cru clas.	30 ha	n.c.	❙❚❙	+76 €

(61) 67 71 73 74 75 |76| 77 |78| 79 |80| 81 |82| |83| 84 |85| |86| |87| 88 89 90 |91| |92| 93 |94| (95) 96 97 (98) 99 (00)

The old wineries have been replaced by an ultramodern building, reminding us that Latour has always been a laboratory of innovation. Though the cru's décor may change, one thing does not: the deep, dark, almost black-cherry colour of the wine. The bouquet is equally dense, and has great complexity. The range of aromas is remarkable: blackcurrant, bilberry, and small ripe fruits, with a delicate note of toast. The attack is extremely full and paves the way for richness of body sustained by dense, extremely well-extracted tannins. Not that the tannic power of the wine in any way inhibits its thorough friendliness. The finish is not simply long and fresh, but holds a surprise in store with a superb aromatic return that centres on ripe strawberries. There is just one uncertainty: it is impossible to know how many decades this wine will last.

➠ SCV du Ch. Latour, Saint-Lambert, 33250 Pauillac, tel. 05.56.73.19.80, fax 05.56.73.19.81
♁ by appt.
➠ M. Pinault

LES FORTS DE LATOUR 2000★★

■	23 ha	n.c.	❙❚❙	38–46 €

80 81 82 83 85 86 87 |88| 89 90 |92| |94| 95 96 |97| 98 99 00

Even if this is Latour's "little brother", it nonetheless has a strong personality of its own. The appearance is dark, with black glints. The bouquet is an original mix of bilberry, cocoa and cedar. After an initial freshness, the palate is full of tactile sensations thanks to the soft, dense tannins, which join flavours of tobacco and leather to bear witness to fine maturing.

➠ SCV du Ch. Latour, Saint-Lambert, 33250 Pauillac, tel. 05.56.73.19.80, fax 05.56.73.19.81
♁ by appt.

CH. LYNCH-BAGES 2000★★★

■ 5e cru clas.	90 ha	420,000	❙❚❙	+76 €

70 71 |75| 76 78 |79| 80 |81| (82) |83| 84 |85| |86| |87| |88| |89| 90 |91| |92| |93| 94 95 96 |97| (98) 99 (00)

Lynch-Bages is the Cazes's flagship estate, and indeed it is one of the leading vineyards in the whole Bordeaux wine region. Its 2000 is worthy of the greatest of Pauillacs. The depth of the appearance is a first indicator. The bouquet is a composition of power and finesse, a marriage of fruit-flowers and oak (toast). The palate rests on sturdy tannic pillars, while retaining a mellowness and a fleshiness that make it particularly flavoursome. This elegant wine merits a wait of five to six years. The second wine, **Château Haut-Bages Averoux 2000 (23–30 €)**, is expressive, full and fleshy, and obtains a star for its structure of easy tannins, the product of quality grapes.

➠ Jean-Michel Cazes, Ch. Lynch-Bages, 33250 Pauillac, tel. 05.56.73.24.00, fax 05.56.59.26.42, e-mail infochato@lynchbages.com ❱
♁ by appt.

CH. LYNCH-MOUSSAS 2000★★

■ 5e cru clas.	n.c.	100,000	🍾	30–38 €

81 82 83 85 86 88 |89| |90| |93| 95 |96| |97| 98 00

From Lynch to Castéja, this cru has had some renowned owners. The wine is worthy of the place: dense and dark, with bright highlights, the appearance is very attractive. The bouquet is an intense, profound mix of roast coffee and black fruits. The palate is flavoursome and powerful, sustained by dense, silky tannins, whose quality assures this wine a long life (but ten years' patience will be required). The tannic power does not detract from the wine's elegance; it is a true Pauillac.
☛ Emile Castéja, 33250 Pauillac, tel. 05.56.00.00.70, fax 05.57.87.48.61,
e-mail domaines.boriemanoux.@dial.oleane.com ▥

CH. MOUTON ROTHSCHILD 2000★★★

■ 1er cru clas.	78 ha	254,600	🍾	+76 €

71 72 73 74 |75| 76 77 |78| 79 80 |81| |82| |83| |84| 85(86)|87|
88 89 90 |91| |92| |93| |94| (95) 96 97(98)|99(00)

In 2003, Mouton celebrates the 150th anniversary of the estate's acquisition by Baron Nathaniel de Rothschild. Collectors will wonder which artist will design the label for the 2003 vintage. In the meantime, the legendary 2000 vintage has a bottle engraved with a golden sheep. A blend of 86% Cabernet Sauvignon with 14% Merlot, this luminous deep-red wine reveals its character by its delicate, intense bouquet. The complexity ranges from coffee and vanilla to gorgeous aromas of red fruits, plum and prune. The attack is surprisingly round and frank. The palate has a structure of great freshness, while still dominated by the elegant oak to which it owes its spicy flavours. The tannins have great finesse, but are still dense, indicating that this truly great Mouton has a splendid future ahead of it.
☛ SA Baron Philippe de Rothschild, BP 117,
33250 Pauillac, tel. 05.56.73.20.20, fax 05.56.73.20.44,
e-mail webmaster@bpdr.com
⚲ by appt.
☛ Baronne Ph. de Rothschild

CH. PIBRAN 2000★

■ Cru bourg.	10 ha	50,000	🍾	15–23 €

The quality of this cru enabled it to be promoted from Cru Bourgeois to Cru Bourgeois Supérieur last July. This 2000 will need time to integrate. As indicated by the dark appearance, it has a sufficiently strong tannic structure to allow it to develop over the next four to five years to a stage where it can give of its best. The bouquet similarly holds a great deal of complexity in store, ranging from fresh floral notes to warm aromas of roasting coffee. The second wine is equally tannic and is rated at one star: **Château Tour Pibran 2000**.
☛ Ch. Pibran, 33250 Pauillac, tel. 05.56.73.17.17,
fax 05.56.73.17.28
☛ Axa Millésimes

CH. PICHON-LONGUEVILLE BARON 2000★★

■ 2e cru clas.	70 ha	n.c.	🍾	+76 €

78 81 |82| |83| 84 |85| |86| 87 |88| |89| (90) 91 92 93 94 95(96)
|97| 98 99 00

The daring architecture of this château comes from the collaboration of two Franco-American architects engaged to restore the château in 1988, when it was bought by the AXA insurance group. The year 2000, the year of ISO 14001 certification and the last of the 20th century, is marked by this very attractive wine. Bright and young in appearance, it has a developing bouquet of intensity: although the blackcurrant fruitiness is somewhat masked by the oaky vanilla, the result is nonetheless elegant and charming. First impressions on the palate are of homogeneity, after which the wine gradually reveals its fleshiness, its flavours of crème and fine toast. This very well-crafted wine will need five or six years' cellaring to achieve its full character. The same producer's one-star **Les Tourelles de Longueville 2000 (15–23 €)** is an elegant, tannic wine with a good chewy body.
☛ Christian Seely, Ch. Pichon-Longueville, 33250 Pauillac, tel. 05.56.73.17.17, fax 05.56.73.17.28,
e-mail infochato@pichonlongueville.com
⚲ by appt.
☛ Axa Millésimes

CH. PICHON-LONGUEVILLE COMTESSE DE LALANDE 2000★★

■ 2e cru clas.	75 ha	180,000	🍾	+76 €

66 70 71 75 76 78 79 80 81 82 83 84 |85| (86) 87 (88) |89|
|90| |91| 92 |93| |94| 95 96 |97| 98 99 00

The year 2000 might have proved difficult for this cru, where in general Merlot is accorded an important place. However, wisdom prevailed, and Cabernet is the great winner in the blending, as the Cabernet-style bouquet of this wine proves, even if the aromas are actually far more complex than just that. After a rich and powerful attack, the palate goes on to encounter the silky tannins that contribute to its well-integrated development. This wine merits keeping for several years before drinking. Pleasantly fruity, the second wine, **Réserve de la Comtesse 2000 (23–30 €)**, gains a star for its refined oakiness, subtle fruit, and overall attractiveness.
☛ SCI Ch. Pichon-Longueville Comtesse de Lalande, 33250 Pauillac, tel. 05.56.59.19.40, fax 05.56.59.26.56,
e-mail pichon@pichon-lalande.com ▥
⚲ by appt.
☛ May-Eliane de Lencquesaing

CH. PONTET-CANET 2000★★

■ 5e cru clas.	80 ha	250,000	🍾	38–46 €

(61) 70 75 76 77 78 79 81 82 83 84 85 86 87 |88| |89| |90| 91 92
93 |94| 95 96 97 98 99 00

This admirably situated, fair-sized cru benefits from a choice terroir. The work in the vineyard and in the winery is correspondingly good and the result is great quality. The colour of this 2000 is seductively deep. The bouquet is still dominated by the oak, but its good balance and aromas of prune and blackcurrant make it very agreeable. It gives an impression of maturity which is similarly discovered on the palate, where the well-bred tannins and first-class grape body give assurance of long life. "Just the sort of Pauillac I love," said one taster, who is a well-known dealer. Still rather severe but possessed of a robust weave of tannins is the second wine, **Les Hauts de Pontet-Canet 2000 (15–23 €)**, which was singled out by the Jury.
☛ Alfred Tesseron, Ch. Pontet-Canet, 33250 Pauillac, tel. 05.56.59.04.04, fax 05.56.59.26.63,
e-mail pontet-canet@wanadoo.fr ▥
⚲ by appt.

CH. PUY LA ROSE 2000★

■ Cru bourg.	8 ha	40,000	🍾	15–23 €

Vinified from plots in the sectors of Artigues and the Carruades, this wine is of good origin. The wine has a appearance of youthful promise, which is confirmed by the typical Pauillac bouquet of quality oak-coated blackcurrant notes. Fresh and well-balanced, the palate has a mellow attack, a

BORDEAUX

powerful structure of flavoursome tannins, and an elegant finish. A real Pauillac, which needs six or seven years in the cellar before drinking. This cru is also marketed by Maison Schröder et Schÿler. Less rounded, but equally well-equipped for long keeping is **Château Colombier Monpelou 2000**, which is an unstarred selection.

➤ Sté des Vignobles Jugla, Ch. Colombier-Monpelou, 33250 Pauillac, tel. 05.56.59.01.48, fax 05.56.59.12.01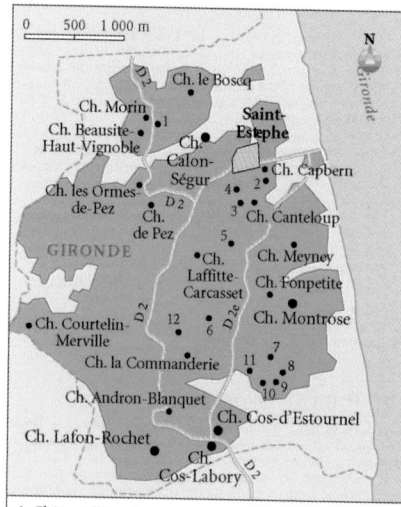
☥ by appt.

LA ROSE PAUILLAC 2000★

| ■ | n.c. | 100,000 | ◫ | 15–23 € |

This label belongs to the cooperative cellar at Pauillac, established in the early 1930s. This 2000 vintage has a dark appearance and a fruity, spicy bouquet that combines freshness with finesse. After a supple attack, the palate reveals good tannic presence, which will enable this wine to blossom in four to five years' time.

➤ Sté coopérative La Rose Pauillac, 44, rue du Mal-Joffre, BP 14, 33250 Pauillac, tel. 05.56.59.26.00, fax 05.56.59.63.58 ☑
☥ by appt.

Wines selected but not starred

CH. ARTIGUES ARNAUD 2000

| ■ | 38.66 ha | 103,600 | ▯ ♦ | 11–15 € |

➤ SC du Ch. Grand-Puy Ducasse, La Croix Bacalan, 109, rue Achard, BP 154, 33042 Bordeaux Cedex, tel. 05.56.11.29.00, fax 05.56.11.29.01

CH. FONBADET 2000

| ■ | Cru bourg. | 20 ha | 60,000 | ◫ | 15–23 € |

75 76 78 79 81 82 83 85 86 87 |88| |89| |90| 91 93 95 |96| |97| 98 99 00

➤ SCEA Domaines Peyronie, Ch. Fonbadet, 33250 Pauillac, tel. 05.56.59.02.11, fax 05.56.59.22.61, e-mail pascale@chateaufonbadet.com ☑
☥ by appt.

CH. HAUT MILON 2000

| ■ | 10.49 ha | 6,000 | ◫ | 15–23 € |

➤ Sté coopérative La Rose Pauillac, 44, rue du Mal-Joffre, BP 14, 33250 Pauillac, tel. 05.56.59.26.00, fax 05.56.59.63.58 ☑
☥ by appt.

CH. PEDESCLAUX 2000

| ■ | 5e cru clas. | 12.5 ha | 96,500 | ◫ | 15–23 € |

➤ SCEA Ch. Pédesclaux, Padarnac, 33250 Pauillac, tel. 05.56.59.22.59, fax 05.56.59.63.19, e-mail contact@chateau-pedesclaux.com ☑
☥ by appt.

CH. LA TOURETTE 2000

| ■ | 3 ha | 20,000 | ◫ | 15–23 € |

➤ SA Ch. Larose Trintaudon, rte de Pauillac, 33112 Saint-Laurent-Médoc, tel. 05.56.59.41.72, fax 05.56.59.93.22, e-mail info@trintaudon.com ☑
☥ by appt.
➤ AGF

Saint-Estèphe

Not very far up the Garonne from Pauillac and its port lies Saint-Estèphe. Its charming rustic hamlets fittingly suggest a locale closely bound to the soil. Apart from a few acres that are part of the Appellation Pauillac, the Appellation Saint-Estèphe, which declared 1,254 ha, producing 52,872 hl in 2002, encompasses the whole commune. As the most northerly of the six Médoc Appellations Communales, it has a fairly well-identified character, lying as it does at an average altitude of 40 m on gravelly soils that have a little more clay than the more southerly appellations. The Saint-Estèphe appellation includes five Crus Classés and the wines produced there have a noticeable tang of the terroir. Compared with other Médocs, the Saint-Estèphe wines have a higher degree of acidity in the grapes, a greater depth of colour and a more significant richness of tannin. They are very robust, and are excellent wines for laying down.

CH. L'ARGILUS DU ROI 2000★

| ■ | 3 ha | 15,000 | ◫ | 11–15 € |

This small cru was created only recently (1996) by a former Mouton master cellarer, but has tripled in size now to 3 ha. The colour is discreet, but the bouquet is explosive, being an expressive marriage of violets, red fruits, and delicate oak. The palate has a strong, rich, tannic character. A promising wine that will require at least three years' patience.

➤ José Bueno, 6, rue du Luc, 33250 Cissac-Médoc, tel. 05.56.59.53.74, fax 05.56.59.53.74 ☑
☥ by appt.

Sainte Estephe

1 Château Beausite
2 Château Phélan-Ségur
3 Château Picard
4 Château Beauséjour
5 Ch. Tronquoy-Lalande
6 Château Houissant
7 Château Haut-Marbuzet
8 Ch. la Tour-de-Marbuzet

9 Ch. de Marbuzet
10 Ch. Mac Carthy
11 Château le Crock
12 Château Pomys

A.O.C. Saint-Estèphe
● Cru classé
● Cru bourgeois
--- Limites de communes

332

Saint-Estèphe

BORDEAUX

CH. BEAU-SITE 2000★

■	Cru bourg. n.c.	180,000	〘〙	11–15 €

Here is no château in the architectural sense, just a very pleasant terrace that blends in with the bourgeois character of the buildings and the view over the vineyard and the estuary. A situation that explains why this wine has the character it has. The finish is a bit on the short side, but the colour is a lovely garnet, and the bouquet has elegant notes of fruits and toast. The palate makes it own round and unctuous contribution to what is simply a wine to enjoy.

➥ Héritiers Castéja, 33250 Pauillac, tel. 05.56.00.00.70, fax 05.57.87.48.61,
e-mail domaines.boriemanoux.@dial.oleane.com ☑

CH. BEL-AIR 2000★★

■	4.93 ha	24,000	〘〙	15–23 €

|96| 97 |98| **99 00**

After the superb 99, which was a *coup de coeur*, this cru again reveals what mastery it has in vinification. This fine, well-assembled 2000 reflects the personality of its Graves terroir. A lovely colour with bright tinges, with a complex bouquet of red fruits, violets and caramel. After a supple, harmonious attack, the palate is flavoursome, tannic, and well-blended, indicating that this wine will keep well. Wait five to seven years.

➥ SCEA du Ch. Bel Air, 4, chem. de Fontauge, 33180 Avensan, tel. 05.56.58.21.03, fax 05.56.58.17.20, e-mail jfbraq@aol.com ☑
❦ by appt.
➥ J.-F. Braquessac

CH. LE BOSCQ 2000★★

■	Cru bourg.	16.62 ha	60,600	〘〙	15–23 €

82 83 85⑧⑥88 89 90 95 96 97 |98| **99 00**

An 18th century building and a cru whose reputation is being strengthened by the association with Dourthe. The eloquent result is a wine whose bouquet combines power with complexity. Although the oak betrays its presence in spicy, vanilla notes, these do not mask the other constituent aromas, some of them floral (violets), some fruity (red berries). Good first impressions prepare the palate to discover a round, fine body, which is not lacking in tannic support. A nice wine that will be very pleasing to drink in about five years' time.

➥ Ch. Le Boscq - Vignobles Dourthe, 35, rue de Bordeaux, 33290 Parempuyre, tel. 05.56.35.53.00, fax 05.56.35.53.29, e-mail contact@cvbg.com ☑
❦ by appt.

CH. CHAMBERT-MARBUZET 2000★

■	Cru bourg.	7 ha	50,000	〘〙	15–23 €

66 76 79 81 82 83 |85| |86| |88| |89| |90| **93 94 95** 96 |97| 98 99 00

Acquired by Henri Duboscq in 1962 (Château Haut Marbuzet). The strong personality of this typical Médoc blend does its maker credit. The bouquet has great subtlety: notes of leather, cinnamon, grilling, against a mineral background. The full, spacious, elegant palate has a lingering finish. Though already good to drink, this wine could be laid down for four years or so.

➥ Henri Duboscq et Fils, Ch. Chambert-Marbuzet, 33180 Saint-Estèphe, tel. 05.56.59.30.54, fax 05.56.59.70.87 ☑
❦ by appt.

CH. CLAUZET 2000★★★

■	Cru bourg.	13.7 ha	75,000	〘〙	15–23 €

Though its wines are usually good, this cru's 2000 is exceptional. The bouquet is stunningly complex: delicate floral perfumes (violets), mouth-watering notes of chocolate, pepper, and wild strawberry – the range of aromas is a wide one. The palate is rich, fleshy, sappy, and tannic: an elegant and extremely flavoursome synthesis. It would not make any sense to open this truly great wine for at least five years.

➥ SA Baron Velge, Leyssac, 33180 Saint-Estèphe, tel. 05.56.59.34.16, fax 05.56.59.37.11 ☑
❦ by appt.

CH. DE COME 2000★

■	Cru bourg. n.c.	45,000	〘〙	11–15 €

Though not all that well known, this cru actually goes back to a certain Mademoiselle De Côme, who founded it in 1838. Some might infer a certain femininity about the wine, and they would not necessarily be wrong. All wine-lovers will be attracted by its charming finesse, its unctuousness and sappiness. Its qualities will be best appreciated if it is laid down for a short period (two years).

➥ SA Baron Velge, Leyssac, 33180 Saint-Estèphe, tel. 05.56.59.34.16, fax 05.56.59.37.11 ☑
❦ by appt.

COS D'ESTOURNEL 2000★★★

■	2e cru clas.	64 ha	260,000	〘〙	46–76 €

75 76 78 79 80 81 |82| 83 |85| 86 88 |89| ⑨⓪|91| |92| |93| |94| 95 96 97 98⓪⓪

A harvest of uniformly ripe and healthy grapes with thick skins, followed by a long maceration in small vats, and the result is this wine, whose power is implicit in the quality of the garnet colour. Delicately sustained by oakiness, the bouquet is truly complex, with black fruits, especially bilberry, in the forefront. The dense tannins, richness and length of the palate leave no doubt as to the potential of this powerful, elegant and complex wine. Wait six to twelve years.

➥ SA Domaines Reybier, Cos d'Estournel, 33180 Saint-Estèphe, tel. 05.56.73.15.50, fax 05.56.59.72.59, e-mail estournel@estournel.com
❦ by appt.

CH. COS LABORY 2000★

■	5e cru clas.	19 ha	80,000	〘〙	23–30 €

64 70 75 78 79 80 81 82 83 84 85 86 87 88 |89| ⑨⓪91 92 93 |94| 95 **96** |97| 98 99 00

The château is typically Bordelais and the cru has an equally typical terroir as its name indicates; "cos" means "hillock of pebbles" This 2000 is pleasantly fruity and spicy, with a supple attack, which introduces a developing tannic structure that will need laying down for three to four years. The second wine, **Le Charme Labory 2000** (11–15 €), is singled out by the Jury.

➥ SCE Domaines Audoy, Ch. Cos Labory, 33180 Saint-Estèphe, tel. 05.56.59.30.22, fax 05.56.59.73.52, e-mail cos-labory@wanadoo.fr ☑
❦ by appt.

CH. COUTELIN-MERVILLE 2000★

■	Cru bourg.	23.5 ha	170,000	〘〙	11–15 €

This cru does not create a lot of noise; it just gets on with making wines of regular quality, of which this 2000 is a further example. Its youth is evident from the excellent colour, and from the fine, elegant bouquet of oaky notes mixed with notes of red berries. After a supple, round start, the palate's dense, well-blended tannins confirm the initial impression of

youthful good quality. A well-balanced whole that will need five or six years' storage before drinking.
☛ G. Estager et Fils, Ch. Coutelin-Merville, Blanquet, 33180 Saint-Estèphe, tel. 05.56.59.32.10, fax 05.56.59.32.10 ☑
☕ by appt.

CH. LE CROCK 2000★

■ Cru bourg.	32.17 ha	150,000	▊ ⑪ ♨	15–23 €

90 |95| 96 97 98 **99** 00

Crock is a remarkable château dating from the late 18th century, and is surrounded by parkland. Its 2000 is another very attractive wine. Being a quality Saint-Estèphe, it has good keeping qualities. The colour is a traditional dark ruby, the bouquet is a marriage of fruit and vanilla oak, and the palate has a sturdy structure that does not drive out elegance.
☛ Sté fermière Cuvelier, Ch. Le Crock, Marbuzet, 33180 Saint-Estèphe, tel. 05.56.59.08.30, fax 05.56.59.60.09
☕ by appt.
☛ Domaines Cuvelier

CH. HAUT-BEAUSEJOUR 2000★

■ Cru bourg.	20 ha	130,000	⑪	15–23 €

Grown in a vineyard where a majority of the vines are Merlot, this wine reflects that variety's roundness and suppleness. The colour is delicate, and the bouquet plunges the taster into a soft world of vanilla and cinnamon, with an underlying note of citrus fruit. This well-balanced wine will be best enjoyed drunk young or after short keeping.
☛ Ch. Haut-Beauséjour, rue de la Mairie, 33180 Saint-Estèphe, tel. 05.56.59.30.26, fax 05.56.59.39.25, e-mail philippe.moureau@champagne-roederer.com ☑
☕ by appt.
☛ Roederer

CH. HAUT-COUTELIN 2000★★

■	3.5 ha	26,000	⑪	11–15 €

From the same producer as Château Tour de Pez, this wine is in the same vein. The dense red colour has nothing deceptive about it. It heralds an intense bouquet of fruity, spicy, coffee notes, and a palate of gathering force. The balanced combination of oak, fruit, and finesse leaves an impression of elegant synthesis.
☛ SA Ch. Tour de Pez, L'Hereteyre, 33180 Saint-Estèphe, tel. 05.56.59.31.60, fax 05.56.59.71.12, e-mail chtrpez@terre-net.fr ☑
☕ by appt.
☛ Ph. Bouchara

CH. HAUT-MARBUZET 2000★★

■ Cru bourg.	58 ha	350,000	⑪	23–30 €

61 62 64 66 **67** 70 71 73 **75** 76 77 78 79 80 81 (82) 83 85 86 |88| |89| 90 |92| |93| |94| 95 |96| |97| (98) **99** 00

Within the Girondin landscape, this cru is a place apart owing to the strong personality of the boss. The terroir is exceptional, being an outcrop of Gunzian gravel over a limestone-clay substrate. This bright-ruby wine (60% Cabernets) has undergone a remarkable maturation process. The bouquet has soft notes of blackcurrant, toast and clove. The palate is fresh and round, without bitterness; the structure is powerful, yet does not sacrifice the wine's grapeyness and good balance. A pleasure to drink.
☛ Henri Duboscq et Fils, Ch. Haut-Marbuzet, 33180 Saint-Estèphe, tel. 05.56.59.30.54, fax 05.56.59.70.87, e-mail henridubourg@hotmail.com ☑
☕ ev. day except Sun. 9am–12 noon 2pm–6pm

CH. LA HAYE 2000★

■ Cru bourg.	6 ha	46,863	⑪	11–15 €

89 90 91 92 93 94 |95| |96| |97| 99 00

Certain parts of the château remind one how old this estate is. The wine also has an old-fashioned elegance, both in its appearance and its bouquet. The latter is rather original, with notes of spices and ripe fruit, but strongest of all is the aroma of violets. The complexity and quality of the tannic structure on the palate reveal good ageing potential.

☛ Georges Lecallier, Ch. la Haye, Leyssac, 33180 Saint-Estèphe, tel. 05.56.59.32.18, e-mail chateau.lahaye@free.fr ☑
☕ by appt.

CH. LAFON-ROCHET 2000★★

■ 4e cru clas.	40 ha	134,000	▊ ⑪ ♨	30–38 €

(64) 75 76 77 78 79 81 82 |83| 85 86 |88| |89| |90| 91 92 93 |94| (95) 96 97 98 **99** 00

Having once been a part of Pontet-Canet (Pauillac), Lafon-Rochet is now autonomous. It has not suffered through the separation. Last year was a *coup de cœur*, and this 2000 is also of very high quality. The rich dark-ruby colour is a sign of youth; the bouquet is developing aromas of spices, mint, and thyme, with plenty of touches of black fruits macerating in alcohol. The attack is firm, indicating a dense structure. This nippy, powerful, well-bred wine is still a little on the reserved side, but holds plenty of surprises in store for the future. The second wine, the amiable and generous **Les Pèlerins de Lafon-Rochet 2000 (11–15 €)**, is awarded one star.
☛ SCF Ch. Lafon-Rochet, 33180 Saint-Estèphe, tel. 05.56.59.32.06, fax 05.56.59.72.43, e-mail lafon@lafon-rochet.com ☑
☕ by appt.
☛ Tesseron

CH. MEYNEY 2000★

■ Cru bourg.	50 ha	237,733	▊ ⑪ ♨	23–30 €

81 82 83 85 (86) 88 |89| 90 92 93 94 |95| |96| |97| 99 00

Many of the cru in the Médoc evoke the parliamentary beginnings of Bordeaux wine-growing, but this one recalls the ancient role of the monks. This 2000 in fact finishes on a somewhat monastic note. The appearance is quite intense, as is the structure of dense tannins, which demonstrates the wine's potential for being laid down. The bouquet is agreeably fruity, and the general good balance reveals the wine's well-crafted vinification.
☛ SAS Ch. Prieuré de Meyney, 109, rue Achard, BP 154, 33042 Bordeaux Cedex, tel. 05.56.11.29.30, fax 05.56.11.29.31, e-mail fdobbels@listel.fr
☕ by appt.

CH. MONTROSE 2000★★

■ 2e cru clas.	68.39 ha	155,000	⑪	46–76 €

64 66 67 |70| |75| 76 78 |79| 81 (82) 83 |85| 86 87 **88 89 90** |91| |92| |93| 94 95 96 |97| 98 **99** 00

Founded on the dominant side of the estuary, Montrose benefits from a choice terroir on which vines of a very Médoc mix grow (69% Cabernets). This vintage shows the quality of care given to the harvest. The colour is a beautiful red, and there is a complex and expressive bouquet of fruity aromas combined with slightly burnt notes derived from the maturation in oak. The powerful palate, sustained by well-rounded tannins, is rich, unctuous and well balanced. This is a classic wine of its appellation, and calls for some four or five years' further ageing. The estate's second wine, **La Dame de Montrose 2000 (23–30 €)**, gains a star. Rich, aromatic and complex, this is also a wine to lay down. Serve the main wine with roast leg of lamb, and the second with *confit de canard*.
☛ Jean-Louis Charmolüe, SCEA du Ch. Montrose, 33180 Saint-Estèphe, tel. 05.56.59.30.12, fax 05.56.59.38.48 ☑
☕ by appt.

CH. LES ORMES DE PEZ 2000★★

■ Cru bourg.	35 ha	204,000	⑪	23–30 €

81 82 83 |85| |86| |88| |89| 90 |91| 92 93 |94| |95| |96| 97 |98| **99** 00

Made by Jean-Michel Cazes and his team, this powerful all-round wine is testimony to their know-how and commitment to the spirit of the Médoc. A successful blend of 70% Cabernet grapes, it has an intense colour with plenty of pigment. The bouquet is attractively fruity, spicy and floral.

Spacious, fleshy, rich and no less complex is the palate, which, together with the bouquet, points to good ageing potential.
☛ Jean-Michel Cazes, Ch. Les Ormes de Pez, 33250 Pauillac, tel. 05.56.73.24.00, fax 05.56.59.26.42,
e-mail infochato@ormesdepez.com ☑
☛ Famille Cazes

CH. PETIT BOCQ 2000★★

■	14 ha	90,000	ⅲ	15–23 €

94 |95| 96 97 |98| 99 **00**

The regular improvement of this cru, which has been noted over preceding editions of the *Guide*, is confirmed again this year with this 2000. Ruby with garnet highlights, it has a bouquet with a complex range of aromas going from the floral to blackcurrant. The palate has superb balance due to its rich, well-covered tannins. Fine and powerful, it calls for six to eight years' storage, after which it will go well with gamebirds (woodcock).
☛ SCEA Lagneaux-Blaton, 3, rue de la Croix-de-Pez, BP 33, 33180 Saint-Estèphe, tel. 05.56.59.35.69,
fax 05.56.59.32.11,
e-mail petitbocq@hotmail.com ☑
✠ by appt.

CH. LA PEYRE 2000★

■	Cru artisan	6.5 ha	32,000	ⅲ	15–23 €

95 (96) 97 |98| 99 00

The Rabiller family have no regrets about leaving the world of industry to return to the family vineyard. Wine-lovers will approve of this reconversion if they sample this wine with its characterful bouquet, which mixes notes of truffles and humus. The palate has silkiness and elegance right from the start. Long and tannic, this Saint-Estèphe calls for more than four years in the cellar.
☛ EARL Vignobles Rabiller, Le Cendrayre, Leyssac, 33180 Saint-Estèphe, tel. 05.56.59.32.51,
fax 05.56.59.70.09 ☑
✠ ev. day 10am–12 noon 2.30pm–7pm; Sun. by appt.

CH. DE PEZ 2000★★★

■	Cru bourg.	24 ha	120,000	ⅲ	23–30 €

This cru, owned by Champagnes Roëderer, does not hide its ambitions and has given itself the means to realize its objectives. This wine is the proof. Dark ruby, with deep purple highlights, one still young. The bouquet, with its grilled notes, explodes with sensations: jammy notes (bramble jelly), prune, crystallized fruits, blackcurrant, etc. Rich, robust, full-bodied, yet smooth and generous, the palate rests on elegant, dense tannins which give the whole a classiness that is already delightful to knowledgeable amateurs, but which really ought to be cellared for four or five years, or indeed longer still.
☛ Ch. de Pez, 33180 Saint-Estèphe, tel. 05.56.59.30.26, fax 05.56.59.39.25,
e-mail philippe-moureau@champagne-roederer.com ☑
✠ by appt.
☛ J.-C. Rouzaud

CH. PHELAN SEGUR 2000★★

■	64 ha	155,000	ⅲ	30–38 €

81 82 86 88 |89| |90| 91 92 93 94 |95| 96 97 98 99 00

Though plenty of Saint-Estèphe crus have succumbed to the appeal of Merlot, Phélan has retained a majority share (62%) of Cabernet Sauvignon for its 2000 blend. The result is an authentic Médoc whose suitability for laying down (here five to ten years) is, like the strong dark colour, typical of the appellation. Finesse and charm are by no means absent. The bouquet is elegant and complex, with attractive aromas of red and black fruits which are respected by the grilled notes contributed by the oak. The full, round palate rests on silky tannins and a fine fleshiness which would go well with leg of wild boar. Also for laying down is the second wine, **Franck Phélan 2000 (15–23 €)**, which gains one star, while the **La Croix Bonis 2000 (11–15 €)** receives special mention from the Jury.
☛ Ch. Phélan Ségur, 33180 Saint-Estèphe,
tel. 05.56.59.74.00, fax 05.56.59.74.10,
e-mail phelan.segur@wanadoo.fr
✠ by appt.
☛ X. Gardinier

CH. SAINT ESTEPHE 2000★

■	Cru bourg.	11 ha	54,000	ⅲ	15–23 €

The terroir's diversity (gravel and clay-limestone) is reflected by diversity in the blend (55% Cabernet Sauvignon, 35% Merlot, 5% Cabernet Franc, 5% Petit Verdot). The quality of the blend translates into the wine, which has a well-balanced structure and a complex bouquet of black fruits, liquorice and spices. Wait two or three years before drinking. Another wine from the same producer, **Château Pomys 2000** (a three-star hotel), is singled out by the Jury.
☛ SA Arnaud, Ch. Saint-Estèphe et Pomys, 33180 Saint-Estèphe, tel. 05.56.59.32.26,
fax 05.56.59.35.24 ☑
✠ by appt.

CH. SEGUR DE CABANAC 2000★★

■	Cru bourg.	7.07 ha	45,000	ⅲ	15–23 €

86 88 89 90 |93| 94 |95| |96| 97 98 99 00

This cru, reconstituted in 1986, once belonged to the Ségur family. Certain boundary stones in the vineyard actually bear the name "Prince des Vignes". This 2000 will not disappoint. The dark-ruby colour with deep-purple highlights assures a radiant future. The dense, mellow structure, sustained by ripe tannins, confirms this potential, and calls for five to seven years' cellaring, if not longer, especially as the bouquet is also extremely complex. Its range includes black crystallized fruits with hints of mint and cedar.
☛ SCEA Guy Delon et Fils, Ch. Ségur de Cabanac, 33180 Saint-Estèphe, tel. 05.56.59.70.10,
fax 05.56.59.73.94 ☑
✠ by appt.

CH. TOUR DE PEZ 2000★★

■	Cru bourg.	16.4 ha	80,000	ⅲ	15–23 €

89 90 91 93 |94| (95) 96 |97| 98 99 00

Having been a *coup de coeur* last year, the cru's 2000 is also a very good wine. The bouquet has life and finesse, being a good combination of oakiness (grilled and smoky notes) with small black, well-ripened fruits; it is of even quality with the dense, deep colour, which has dark glints and forms a lovely red ring. The same density characterizes the tannic structure, which is powerful without being aggressive. This rich, elegant, well-balanced wine deserves long cellaring. The cru's other labels, the **Tour de Pez 2000 (11–15 €)** and the **Château Les Hauts de Pez 2000 (8–11 €)**, distributed by merchants (Cheval-Quancard at Carbon-Blanc), were commended.
🍷 SA Ch. Tour de Pez, L'Hereteyre, 33180 Saint-Estèphe, tel. 05.56.59.31.60, fax 05.56.59.71.12, e-mail chtrpez@terre-net.fr ☑
🍸 by appt.

CH. TOUR DES TERMES 2000★

| ■ | Cru bourg. | 15 ha | 80,000 | ⅲ | 15–23 € |

The remains of a medieval tower on a plot called Les Termes explain the name of this cru, whose 2000 is characterized above all by finesse. The wine's colour is intense, but the bouquet has an elegance that reveals itself in delicate notes of oak, undergrowth, moss and liquorice. The palate is similarly elegant from start to finish. A charming wine that needs three to four years in the cellar before drinking.
🍷 SCEA Vignobles Jean Anney, Ch. Tour des Termes, 33180 Saint-Estèphe, tel. 05.56.59.32.89, fax 05.56.59.73.74 ☑
🍸 ev. day except Sat. Sun. 8.30am–12 noon 2pm–4.30pm

CH. TRONQUOY-LALANDE 2000★

| ■ | Cru bourg. | 17 ha | 128,000 | ⅲ | 15–23 € |

(82) 83 **85 86** 87 88 |89| 90 |93| |94| |95| |96| 98 99 00

The year 2000 saw important works here to modernize the estate, and the wine from that year is actually very good. The oak is still a little over-dominant, but there is a sturdy construction in the background which is signalled by the wine's dense appearance. The lovely fruity bouquet, the classy attack and the well-ripened tannins call for two or three years' storage. Distributed by Dourthe.
🍷 Ch. Tronquoy-Lalande, 33180 Saint-Estèphe, tel. 05.56.35.53.00, fax 05.56.35.53.29, e-mail contact@cvbg.com
🍸 by appt.
🍷 Mme Castéja-Texier

CH. VALROSE

Cuvée Aliénor 2000★

| ■ | | 5.04 ha | 26,600 | ⅲ | 23–30 € |

Following on from last year's encouraging beginnings, the 2000 version of this particular wine is a definite success. Its quality is evident from the strong colour, the bouquet, which has hints of mint, and the attack, whose breadth prefigures that of the palate. The whole effect is supported by the well-judged, well-coated tannins. Enjoy with beef or other roast meat in six or seven years' time.
🍷 Gérard Neraudau, GAM Audy-Ch. Jonqueyres, 33750 Saint-Germain-du-Puch, tel. 05.57.34.51.51, fax 05.56.30.11.45, e-mail info@gamaudy.com

Wines selected but not starred

CH. ANDRON BLANQUET 2000

| ■ | Cru bourg. | 16 ha | 92,000 | ⅲ | 11–15 € |

75 76 79 **81** 82 83 **85 86** 87 88 89 |90| 91 92 93 |94| |95| |96| 97 98 99 00

🍷 SCE Domaines Audoy, Ch. Andron Blanquet, 33180 Saint-Estèphe, tel. 05.56.59.30.22, fax 05.56.59.73.52, e-mail cos-labory@wanadoo.fr ☑
🍸 by appt.

CH. COSSIEU-COUTELIN 2000

| ■ | | 2.76 ha | 23,500 | ⅲ | 8–11 € |

🍷 Cheval-Quancard, La Mouline, 4 rue du Carbouney, BP 36, 33560 Carbon-Blanc, tel. 05.57.77.88.88, e-mail chevalquancard@chevalquancard.com
🍸 by appt.

CH. L'ENCLOS BONIS 2000

| ■ | | n.c. | 9,000 | ⅲ | 11–15 € |

🍷 Maison Sichel, 8, rue de la Poste, 33210 Langon, tel. 05.56.63.50.52, fax 05.56.63.42.28, e-mail maison-sichel@sichel.fr

CH. LAVILLOTTE 2000

| ■ | Cru bourg. | 10 ha | 50,000 | ■ⅲ♦ | 11–15 € |

🍷 SCEA des Dom. Pedro, Ch. Le Meynieu, 33180 Vertheuil, tel. 05.56.73.32.10, fax 05.56.41.98.89, e-mail ddompedro@aol.com ☑
🍸 ev. day except Sat. Sun. 9am–12 noon 2pm–6pm; groups by appt.; cl. 9–18 Aug.

CH. LILIAN LADOUYS 2000

| ■ | Cru bourg. | 30 ha | 220,000 | ⅲ | 15–23 € |

|89| (90) 91 92 93 94 |95| 96 97 |98| |99| 00

🍷 SA Ch. Lilian Ladouys, Blanquet, 33180 Saint-Estèphe, tel. 05.56.59.71.96, fax 05.56.59.35.97, e-mail chateau-lilian-ladouys@wanadoo.fr
🍸 by appt.

CH. MOUTINOT 2000

| ■ | | 3 ha | 18,000 | ⅲ | 8–11 € |

🍷 M. Marcelis, Ch. Moutinot, 33250 Saint-Estèphe, tel. 05.57.43.01.44, fax 05.57.43.08.75
🍸 by appt.

CH. PICARD 2000

| ■ | Cru bourg. | 8 ha | n.c. | ⅲ | 11–15 € |

🍷 SA Mähler-Besse, 49, rue Camille-Godard, 33000 Bordeaux, tel. 05.56.56.04.30, fax 05.56.56.04.59, e-mail france@mahler-besse.com ☑
🍸 by appt.

CH. TOUR HAUT VIGNOBLE 2000

| ■ | Cru bourg. | 15 ha | 40,000 | ⅲ | 11–15 € |

🍷 Maison Schröder and Schÿler, 55, quai des Chartrons, 33000 Bordeaux, tel. 05.57.87.64.55, fax 05.57.87.57.20, e-mail m@schroder-schyler.com
🍷 J.-L. Braquessac

CH. TOUR SAINT-FORT 2000

| ■ | Cru bourg. | 5.8 ha | 38,595 | ⅲ | 15–23 € |

🍷 SCA ch. Tour Saint-Fort, 5, rue du Golf, 33700 Mérignac, tel. 05.56.34.16.16, fax 05.56.13.05.54, e-mail chris48@aol.com ☑
🍸 ev. day 10am–12 noon 2pm–5pm; Sat. Sun. by appt.; cl. 15–31 Aug.
🍷 Jean-Louis Laffort

Saint-Julien

The wine is Saint-Julien but the town is Saint-Julien-Beychevelle, making Saint-Julien the only Appellation Communale in the Haut-Médoc not to follow the standard practice of using the same name for both. The second name, it is true, has the drawback of being rather long. Both commune and appellation cover the same area, straddling two plateaus of pebbly and gravelly soil.

The vineyard of Saint-Julien is fairly small at 909 ha and producing 35,978 hl in 2002, and is located in the exact centre of the Haut-Médoc. Its wine can be thought of as a harmonious synthesis of Margaux and Pauillac, and so it is hardly surprising that Saint-Julien produces 11 Crus Classés (five of which are second growths). The wines reflect their terroir, offering a good balance between the qualities of Margaux (particularly their finesse) and the body of Pauillac wines. Generally speaking, Saint-Julien wines have a good colour, a fine, characteristic bouquet, good body, great richness and a beautifully aromatic flavour. It goes without saying that the wines in the 6.6 million bottles produced on average each year in Saint-Julien are far from all alike. Tasters with fine palates will distinguish between the crus from the south (nearer to Margaux) and those from the north (which are closer to Pauillac), as well as between wines that come from nearer the estuary and those from further inland (near Saint-Laurent).

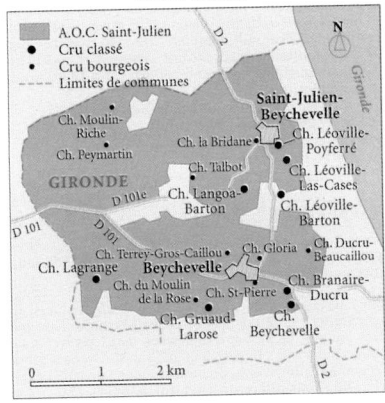

Saint-Julien

CH. BEYCHEVELLE 2000★★

4e cru clas.   75 ha   250,000   46–76 €

70 76 79 81 82 83 85 |86| 88 (89) 90 91 92 93 94 95 96 |97| 98 99 00

Few châteaux in the Bordeaux region have as much charm and elegance as this palatial charterhouse. Established in the 17th century, it has belonged to some powerful local families. The delicacy of its architecture is mirrored by the deep colour and ruby glints of this wine, as also by the bouquet, which contains notes of toast and spices. The attack is pleasantly round, leading to a palate of good structure, with softened tannins. The finish is full, warming and long, indicating that this wine will keep for three to four years, or even longer. The same estate's **Amiral de Beychevelle 2000 (11–15 €)**, singled out by the Jury, is also sustained by good tannins and will keep for at least two to three years.

➥ SC Ch. Beychevelle, 33250 Saint-Julien-Beychevelle, tel. 05.56.73.20.70, fax 05.56.73.20.71, e-mail beychevelle@beychevelle.com ✓

☏ by appt.

CH. BRANAIRE

Duluc-Ducru 2000★★

4e cru clas.   n.c.   n.c.   30–38 €

81 82 83 85 86 88 |89| 90 93 94 |95| |96| 97 98 99 00

Branaire is a lovely Directory-period château which helps to give Saint-Julien an aristocratic image. The colour of this 2000 is a purplish-ruby, and the finely oaky bouquet has a large range of aromas that especially includes notes of crystallized black fruits. Although the palate seems full and round, the grape and oak tannins have not yet completely consummated their marriage. At least five years in the cellar will be needed to achieve a well-rounded blend. The same estate's second wine, **Château Duluc 2000 (11–15 €)**, was commended.

➥ SAE du Ch. Branaire-Ducru, 33250 Saint-Julien-Beychevelle, tel. 05.56.59.25.86, fax 05.56.59.16.26

☏ by appt.

CH. LA BRIDANE 2000★

Cru bourg.   15 ha   60,000   15–23 €

Bruno Saintout is a conscientious wine-grower whose wines are consistently good, witness this wine whose quality can immediately be gauged from the lovely garnet colour and mauve and deep-purple highlights. The nose is intense, with attractive notes of jammy fruits, and the palate is equally good, having a full attack, rounded tannins and a liquorice finish. Leave in the cellar for four to six years, then enjoy with game, *e.g.*, woodcock. Simpler but also well made is the merchant-distributed **Moulin de la Bridane 2000 (8–11 €)**, which was commended.

➥ Bruno Saintout, Dom. de Cartujac, 33112 Saint-Laurent-Médoc, tel. 05.56.59.91.70, fax 05.56.59.46.13 ✓

☏ by appt.

CH. DUCRU-BEAUCAILLOU 2000★★★

2e cru clas.   50 ha   210,000   +76 €

|61| 64 66 |70| 71 |75| 76 |78| 79 81 (82) 83 84 |85| |86| 87 88 89 90 91 92 |93| 94 (95) (96) |97| 98 99 (00)

Ducru has a very rigorous approach to its blends. This 2000 assembles all the varieties: Petit Verdot, Cabernet Franc, Merlot and Cabernet Sauvignon, with the last-named dominant (65%). The result is a powerful, elegant wine, whose balance is apparent from the deep-red (yet not black) appearance. The bouquet is no less magnificent; it has distinction and power: aromas of small red berry fruits are respected by well-judged oakiness. The attack is high-class, as is the palate as a whole; it is sustained by tannins whose extreme silkiness is due to excellent extraction. The long finish is enhanced by a revival of the wine's aromas and crowned by spiciness. This wine has as much flavour as anyone could wish for, and will be memorably impressive in five to ten years' time. The estate's elegant second wine, **La Croix de Beaucaillou 2000 (15–23 €)**, a one-starred selection, will also keep well. Its velvety tannins and notes of leather and truffles mingling with blackcurrant and oak mark it out as a wine of quality.

➥ SA Jean-Eugène Borie, Ch. Ducru-Beaucaillou, 33250 Saint-Julien-Beychevelle, tel. 05.56.73.16.73, fax 05.56.59.27.37, e-mail je-borie@je-borie-sa.com

☏ by appt.

CH. DU GLANA 2000★

Cru bourg.   43.67 ha   150,000   15–23 €

94 |95| |96| 97 00

In 40 years this estate has gone from five hectares to 40, thereby providing an encouraging commentary on the history of wine-growing in the Bordeaux region over the last few decades. The wine is a most attractive deep-ruby colour, and the bouquet, after a slightly hesitant start, opens up to release a fine oakiness that still dominates (though does not overwhelm) the notes of blackcurrant. The palate has a fine, elegant, mouth-filling body, and confirms that this wine will have a good future.

☛ Ch. du Glana, 33250 Saint-Julien-Beychevelle,
tel. 05.56.59.06.47, fax 04.90.65.03.73,
e-mail contact@cvbg.com ☑
☖ by appt.
☛ J.-P. Meffre

CH. GLORIA 2000★

	44 ha	250,000	⑾	23–30 €

64 66 70 71 75 76 78 |79| 81 82 83 84 85 86 87 |88| |89| |90| 93 94 |95| |96| 97 |98| |99| 00

It must have required a degree of clearsightedness and much enthusiasm on the part of Henri Martin to have built up this cru plot by plot at a time when meadows were more lucrative than vines. His daughter and son-in-law have proved yet again that after several decades his efforts are still bearing fruit. This 2000 offers a delightful bouquet and a well-balanced palate, which is supported by a sufficiently rich (yet not over-rich) body.

☛ Domaines Martin, Ch. Gloria,
33250 Saint-Julien-Beychevelle, tel. 05.56.59.08.18,
fax 05.56.59.16.18, e-mail domainemartin@wanadoo.fr ☑
☖ by appt.
☛ Françoise Triaud

CH. GRUAUD LAROSE 2000★★★

	2e cru clas.	82 ha	267,000	⑾	38–46 €

70 71 75 76 77 78 79 80 81 82 83 84 |85| (86) 87 |88| |89| 90 |91| 92 |93| |94| (95) 96 |97| 98 99 (00)

In 1757, Abbé Gruaud established an estate which he granted to his nephew Sébastien Larose. Such is the origin of this cru, which was reconstituted in its entirety by Désiré Cordier in 1934. Cabernets, Malbec and Petit Verdot grapes share with 31% Merlot in this 2000 blend. The firm tannins derive from excellent extraction, as does also the deep rich colour. The bouquet has potent aromas of vanilla, toast and grilling, which are reinforced by musk. The palate is no less satisfying, having a complexity of flavours which is further enhanced by fine notes of liquorice. A very great wine, which should be left in the cellar untouched for ten or fifteen years.

☛ SA Ch. Gruaud-Larose, BP 6,
33250 Saint-Julien-Beychevelle, tel. 05.56.73.15.20,
fax 05.56.59.64.72,
e-mail contact@chateau-gruaud-larose.com
☖ by appt.

CH. LAGRANGE 2000★★

	3e cru clas.	113 ha	300,000	⑾	23–30 €

79 81 82 83 85 |86| 87 88 |89| (90) 91 92 |93| 94 |95| 96 97 98 99 00

This charming château, with its park and lake, is home to an equally impressive vineyard. Like its place of origin, this wine has a dual character, which shows itself in a remarkable combination of elegance and power. The wine's power is clear

from the deep and intense garnet colour, and its elegance comes through in the fine, distinguished bouquet, whose great richness and complexity includes high-quality oak and oriental spices. After an attack which is no less sumptuous than the bouquet, the palate's distinguished expressiveness is sustained by a tannic weave that provides a well-integrated finish. It would be a mistake to drink this wine too soon, however, as it really needs a wait of five to ten years. Not so the estate's one-star second label, **Les Fiefs de Lagrange (11–15 €)**, which is very pleasant drinking now.

☛ SAS Ch. Lagrange, 33250 Saint-Julien-Beychevelle,
tel. 05.56.73.38.38, fax 05.56.59.26.09,
e-mail chateau-lagrange@chateau-lagrange.com
☖ by appt.

CH. LALANDE-BORIE 2000★

	Cru bourg.	23 ha	140,000	⑾	11–15 €

From the same producer as Château Ducru-Beaucaillou, this wine makes clear its good origins. The complex bouquet includes notes of well-ripened grapes, coffee, and smoke; the breadth of the attack and good constitution of the tannins make this wine very acceptable drinking now to lovers of young wines. Others may wish to wait four or five years longer, as this is also possible.

☛ SA Jean-Eugène Borie, 33250 Saint-Julien-Beychevelle,
tel. 05.56.73.16.73, fax 05.56.59.27.37,
e-mail je-borie@je-borie-sa.com

CH. LANGOA BARTON 2000★★

	3e cru clas.	19 ha	90,000	▮⑾♨	38–46 €

70 75 76 78 80 81 |82| 83 |85| 86 |88| (89) 90 92 |93| |94| 95 96 |97| 98 99 00

Between the Bartons and this lovely old noble dwelling, a long, steady relationship has grown up since its purchase in 1821. This has proved a fruitful partnership, as is shown by this 2000, an 80% Cabernet blend grown on gravel overlying a clay substrate. This charming wine is remarkable not only for its deep colour but because of its bouquet of grilled, smoky notes and fruit aromas (blackcurrant). The palatal tannins are still very young, but the structure is well balanced. Concentrated and powerful. Wait five to ten years.

☛ Anthony Barton, Ch. Langoa Barton,
33250 Saint-Julien-Beychevelle, tel. 05.56.59.06.05,
fax 05.56.59.14.29, e-mail chateau@leoville-barton.com
☖ by appt.

CH. LEOVILLE-BARTON 2000★★★

	2e cru clas.	46 ha	250,000	▮⑾	+76 €

64 67 70 71 75 76 78 79 80 81 |82| 83 |85| 86 |88| 89 (90) 91 92 |93| 94 95 96 |97| 98 99 00

The large Léoville vineyard was broken up in 1826, and Hugh Barton gave his name to the portion he acquired. Since then, the wine has been vinified and matured at the beautiful charterhouse of Langoa-Barton. Known for its powerful character, this particular Léoville-Barton will take its faithful admirers by storm. The colour is a beautiful dark red, almost an intense garnet, an indicator of a strong tannic stucture. The bouquet has attractive notes of vanilla, toast, and well ripened fruits. The palate is a succession of mouth-filling sensations, the flavoursome, elegant tannins leaving an impression of balance and integration. This wine is very seductive and will be gorgeous in five or ten years' time.

☛ Anthony Barton, Ch. Léoville-Barton,
33250 Saint-Julien-Beychevelle, tel. 05.56.59.06.05,
fax 05.56.59.14.29, e-mail chateau@leoville-barton.com
☖ by appt.

CH. LEOVILLE LAS CASES 1999★★★

	n.c.	n.c.		+76 €

Léoville Las Cases certainly has ambiance, being a superb terroir beside the estuary, enclosed by a wall with an emblematic gateway. As for its wine, to taste this 99 is to fall under its charm. Its dark colour, a rich garnet, is instantly seductive. The nose allies finesse and power, combining oaky notes with black berries and aromas of very ripe grapes. The attack is full, rich, generous, with soft-centred flavours; indeed, the palate as a whole is somewhat surprising: one might have expected tannic violence from so dark a wine. Instead, it is generally characterized by elegance, and the tannins are

associated with a host of liquorice, smoky sensations of great freshness, culminating in a magnificent finish. This wine will keep a very long time.
☛ SC. du Ch. Léoville-Las-Cases, 33250 Saint-Julien-Beychevelle

CH. LEOVILLE POYFERRE 2000★★

■	2e cru clas.	60 ha	240,000	🍷	46–76 €

76 78 79 80 81 |82| (83) 84 85 |86| 87 88 89 |90| 91 |93| |94| 95 96 |97| 98 99 00

Like the other two crus derived from the vast seigneurial domain that existed under the *ancien régime*, Léoville Poyferré benefits from a high-quality terroir with naturally good drainage that encourages the vines to send down deep roots. That partly explains the excellence of this beautiful ruby wine; the rest is down to human factors. The bouquet is complex and powerful, mixing notes of toast, vanilla, liquorice and well-ripened grapes. The palate contains supple, silky tannins, which testify to well-crafted extraction and talent on the part of the vinifiers. This elegant wine, which has a long life ahead of it, will be a good accompaniment to fine-fleshed game. Rich, but less complex, is the estate's second wine, the one-starred **Château Moulin Riche 2000 (15–23 €)**.
☛ Sté fermière du Ch. Léoville Poyferré, 33250 Saint-Julien-Beychevelle, tel. 05.56.59.08.30, fax 05.56.59.60.09, e-mail lp@leoville-poyferre.fr
🍷 by appt.
☛ GFA Domaines Saint-Julien

CH. MOULIN DE LA ROSE 2000★★

■	Cru bourg.	4.7 ha	32,000	🍷	15–23 €

|93| |94| 95 **96** 97 98 |99| **00**

Moulin de la Rose is made up of a host of plots scattered among several *crus classés*. The work of one of the leading personalities in Médoc wine-growing, Guy Delon, this wine does not lack character. Its bouquet is powerful, with musky notes, hints of prune and crystallized fruits, and the palate has a sturdy tannic structure. Right through to the long, unctuous finish, the whole tasting reveals a handsome constitution which promises a superb wine in four to five years' time.
☛ SCEA Guy Delon et Fils, Ch. Moulin de la Rose, 33250 Saint-Julien-Beychevelle, tel. 05.56.59.08.45, fax 05.56.59.73.94 ✅
🍷 by appt.

PORT CAILLAVET 2000★

■	4 ha	25,000	🍷	11–15 €

The name of this wine pays homage to Henri Duboscq's mother, née Caillavet, and this in itself is a demand on the merchant for quality. It is also a guarantee to the wine-lover, who will delight in the bouquet of this 2000, in which notes of fruit, musk and leather gracefully mingle. The palate is powerful and full, yet elegant, and promises good things in four to five years from now.
☛ Brusina-Brandler, 3, quai de Bacalan, 33300 Bordeaux, tel. 05.56.39.26.77, fax 05.56.69.16.84 ✅
🍷 by appt.

CH. TALBOT 2000★★

■	4e cru clas.	102 ha	300,000	🍷	38–46 €

78 79 80 81 82 83 84 (85) |86| 87 |88| 89 90 93 |94| 95 96 |97| 98 99 **00**

By virtue of its large size (102 ha for the estate as a whole) and its terroir of gravel overlooking the estuary, Talbot is perfectly representative of the Saint-Julien Grand Cru. The wine is also very true-to-type. A bright rich ruby colour, it has a bouquet whose evolving complexity ranges from truffles to roasting via various spices. The palate has a round start, then reveals tannins that still need to soften, a fact which actually underlines the wine's serious ageing potential. Wait at least five years or even longer.
☛ Ch. Talbot, 33250 Saint-Julien-Beychevelle, tel. 05.56.73.21.50, fax 05.56.73.21.51, e-mail chateau-talbot@chateau-talbot.com
🍷 by appt.
☛ Mmes Rustmann et Bignon

CH. TERREY GROS CAILLOUX 2000★

■	Cru bourg.	n.c.	100,000	🍷	11–15 €

94 96 |97| 98 99 00

There is little ostentation here, just a very simple barrel-store and a wine in harmony with its surroundings. An attractive colour somewhere between Bordeaux and garnet, this 2000 has a developing bouquet balanced between delicate oaky aromas and delightful scents of ripe fruit. The palate already has a good integration of flavours. All the same, some patience will be required in order fully to enjoy this wine's qualities (four to five years).
☛ SCEA Ch. Terrey Gros Cailloux, 33250 Saint-Julien-Beychevelle, tel. 05.56.59.06.27, fax 05.56.59.29.32 ✅
🍷 by appt.
☛ Henri Pradère

CH. TEYNAC 2000★

■	9 ha	50,000	🍷	15–23 €

93 94 |95| 96 97 98 99 00

This cru remains faithful to its tradition of consistent good quality with this very nice 60:40 blend of Cabernet Sauvignon and Merlot, matured 14 months in oak. Supple and well constituted, it has resolutely chosen its guiding characteristics: elegance and finesse. Wait three or four years in order to enjoy it fully. Simpler and lighter is the **Eléonore de Teynac 2000 (8–11 €)**, commended by the Jury.
☛ Ch. Teynac, Grand-rue, Beychevelle, 33250 Saint-Julien-Beychevelle, tel. 05.56.59.93.04, fax 05.56.59.46.12, e-mail chateau.teynac@wanadoo.fr ✅
🍷 by appt.
☛ F. et Ph. Pairault

Wines selected but not starred

CH. LALANDE 2000

■	31 ha	158,000	🍷	11–15 €

☛ SCEA Ch. Lalande, 2, Grand-Rue, 33250 Saint-Julien-Beychevelle, tel. 05.56.59.06.47, fax 04.90.65.03.73
🍷 by appt.
☛ J.-Paul Meffre

Sweet White Wines

When you consult a wine map of the Gironde, you immediately notice that the appellations for the sweet wines (Vins Liquoreux) are clustered in a small region that straddles the Garonne, around its confluence with the River Ciron. Is this just a coincidence? Certainly not: the chill waters of this little river, whose entire course is shaded by leafy trees, contribute to a very particular micro-climate, encouraging *Botrytis cinerea*, the fungus that causes noble rot. In autumn, damp mornings and warm, sunny afternoons create ideal conditions for the fungus to develop on the perfectly ripe grapes, but without causing them to burst; the pips behave exactly like a sponge and, as the grapes shrivel, the juice evaporates and becomes concentrated. This makes for musts that are very rich in sugar.

Many problems have to be overcome to achieve this sweet must. The development of noble rot varies from grape to grape, so the vines must be picked several times, each time harvesting only individual grapes that are in their optimum state. The quantities produced per hectare are tiny, with a maximum amount permitted in Sauternes and Barsac of 25 hl per ha. The way the grapes reach over-ripeness is very unpredictable and depends entirely on climatic conditions, so it is an extremely risky time for the growers.

Cadillac

This village with its fine 17th century château, known as the Fontainebleau of the Gironde, is often thought of as the capital of the Premières Côtes. But, since 1980, it is also an appellation for sweet wines and produced 5,536 hl on 218 ha in 2002.

CH. CARSIN 2001★

	6.68 ha	n.c.	❶❶	11–15 €

With a presence also in Premières Côtes, this cru, which belongs to a Finn, has a solid reputation that this 2001 will do nothing to dent. Although the colour, pale yellow with golden glints, and the burgeoning bouquet, which includes notes of honey and toast, are somewhat reticent, the palate is pleasantly mouth-filling and well balanced, with crystallized fruit flavours and a friendly spring-like quality. (Half-litre bottles)
↪ Juha Berglund, GFA Ch. Carsin, 33410 Rions, tel. 05.56.76.93.06, fax 05.56.62.64.80, e-mail chateau@carsin.com ☑
⟟ by appt.

DELICE D'EXCEPTION

Cuvée Julien Elevé en fût de chêne 2001★★

	1 ha	1,200	❶❶	15–23 €

This special vintage by the Château des Cèdres (see the Premières Côtes) has been the object of attentive and efficient care. The superb gold colour is immediately impressive. The bouquet, too, impresses by virtue of its association of lemony aromas with those of crystallized and exotic fruits. After a supple and straightforward attack, the palate marries breadth, richness and finesse to create a synthesis that is already very pleasing, especially as an aperitif, though it does also have sound keeping potential (five to ten years, perhaps longer).
↪ SCEA Vignobles Larroque, 15, allée de Gageot, 33550 Paillet, tel. 05.56.72.16.02, fax 05.56.72.34.44, e-mail vignobles.larroque@wanadoo.fr ☑
⟟ by appt.

CH. FAYAU 2001★

	6 ha	15,000	▮	5–8 €

This cru, headquarters of the Cadillac wine-merchants Médeville, once again confirms its reputation for consistent quality with this successful 2001. It has a pleasant bouquet, developing an attractive mix of aromas of honey, crystallized and exotic fruits. The supple, well-balanced palate has a finish which reveals its structured character. May be enjoyed now. Equally successful but requiring three to five years cellaring is the one-starred **Château Boisson 2000**.
↪ SCEA Jean Médeville et Fils, Ch. Fayau, 33410 Cadillac, tel. 05.57.98.08.08, fax 05.56.62.18.22, e-mail medeville-jeanetfils@wanadoo.fr ☑
⟟ ev. day except Sat. Sun. 8.30am–12 noon 2pm–6pm

CH. HAUT-VALENTIN

Prestige 2001★

	4 ha	6,000	❶❶	8–11 €

The Mérics, who also produce other appellations, acquired this estate in 1997. Their beautiful golden wine is entirely made from Sémillon grapes and is characterized by the presence of botrytis, which comes through in the bouquet's notes of crystallized fruits and alcohol. The palate confirms the sweet, rich character of this full, well-structured wine, which will be a good aperitif or go well with white meat and poultry.
↪ Vignobles M. Méric et Fils, 33410 Sainte-Croix-du-Mont, tel. 05.56.62.01.19, fax 05.56.62.09.33, e-mail jeanguy.meric@tiscali.fr ☑
⟟ by appt.

CH. MANOS 2001★★

	4 ha	13,000	❶❶	8–11 €

This wine, which marks the tenth anniversary of the passing of the torch from Pierre Niotout to the Néels, shows that the flame is far from extinct. The limpid golden-yellow colour announces the personality which is confirmed by the bouquet of crystallized fruits, honey, and beeswax. Robust and sappy, this sweet, rich wine will be an excellent aperitif over the next ten years.
↪ Les Caves du Ch. Lamothe, 33550 Haux, tel. 05.57.34.53.00, fax 05.56.23.24.49, e-mail neel-chombart@chateau-lamothe.com ☑
⟟ by appt.

CH. MARGOTON 2000★

	3.3 ha	5,100	▮❶❶	8–11 €

True to their own traditions, the Courrèges again stress the importance of the varietal blend with a wine made from 40% Muscadelle grapes. Although it has used overripened rather than noble-rotted grapes, it is extremely attractive, with a golden colour, a strong bouquet of lemon and honey, and a supple, rich palate.
↪ F. Courrèges, 31, chem. des Vignes, 33880 Saint-Caprais-de-Bordeaux, tel. 05.56.21.32.87, fax 05.56.21.37.18, e-mail f.courreges@gt-sa.com ☑
⟟ ev. day except Sun. 9am–12 noon 2pm–7pm

CH. MEMOIRES 2001★

	9 ha	13,000	❶❶	8–11 €

Richness is the keynote of this utterly reliable cru's 2001. The bouquet is a generous combination of floral (acacia) and fruity (peach and white peach) aromas, while the palate is powerful and the finish long. A well-balanced wine that merits a time in the cellar before drinking.
↪ Jean-François Ménard, Ch. Mémoires, 33490 Saint-Maixant, tel. 05.56.62.06.43, fax 05.56.62.04.32, e-mail memoires1@aol.com ☑
⟟ ev. day 8am–12 noon 1.30pm–6.30pm; Sat. Sun. by appt.

CH. DE TESTE 2001★★

	5 ha	7,000	❶❶	8–11 €

From the same producer as Château Saint-Hubert (Premières Côtes de Bordeaux), this Cadillac comes from respectably aged vines (65 years old). The clear, bright colour inspires confidence, but the bouquet is where the wine fully reveals

its personality: supported by grilled and toasted notes, powerful aromas of crystallized fruits and beeswax affirm the wine's authentic character. The same style is repeated on the palate, which is supple, rich and well balanced.
🔹 EARL Vignobles Laurent Réglat, Ch. de Teste, 33410 Monprimblanc, tel. 05.56.62.92.76, fax 05.56.62.98.80, e-mail vignobles.l-reglat@wanadoo.fr ☑
🍷 by appt.

CH. VIEILLE TOUR 2001★

▨	0.74 ha 1,200	⅏	11–15 €

This cru, which also appears in the *Guide* for its Premières Côtes de Bordeaux red, offers a mellow Cadillac with a limpid appearance and a fresh bouquet of attractive floral perfumes (acacia), enhanced by several notes of crystallized fruits. Supple, delicate and full, the palate leaves an impression of flavoursome synthesis.
🔹 SCEA des vignobles Gouin, 1, Lapradiasse, 33410 Laroque, tel. 05.56.62.61.21, fax 05.56.76.94.18, e-mail chateau.vieille.tour@wanadoo.fr ☑
🍷 by appt.

Wines selected but not starred

CH. LABATUT BOUCHARD 2001

▨	3 ha 6,000	⅏	8–11 €

🔹 Ch. Labatut-Bouchard, 2, des Arnauds, 33490 Saint-Maixant, tel. 05.56.41.56.05, fax 05.56.41.35.36, e-mail vignoblesbouchard@net-up.com ☑
🍷 by appt.

LES LARMES DE SAINTE-CATHERINE 2001

▨	2.95 ha 9,000	⅏	3–5 €

🔹 SCEA vignobles F. et J. Arjeau, chem. Chapelle-Sainte-Catherine, 33550 Paillet, tel. 05.56.72.11.64, fax 05.56.72.13.62 ☑
🍷 by appt.

CH. SALINS 2000

▨	0.52 ha 800	⅏	11–15 €

🔹 Marie-Claude et Bernard Gay, Dom. des Salins, 33410 Rions, tel. 05.56.62.92.09, fax 05.56.76.90.75 ☑
🍷 by appt.

Loupiac

The Loupiac vineyard, which declared (13,167 hl from 404 ha in 2002), is very ancient, its existence first recorded in the 13th century. In aspect, terroirs and the vines grown there, this appellation is very similar to the Appellation Sainte-Croix-du-Mont (see below). Yet, as one travels north, one can detect a subtle development in the flavour of the sweet wines, which become rounder, more in the style of the left bank.

CH. DU CROS 2000★

▨	37 ha 11,000	⅏	11–15 €

This estate owes its fame not simply to the beautiful medieval remains of its château; it has forged a reputation for the

Sweet white wines

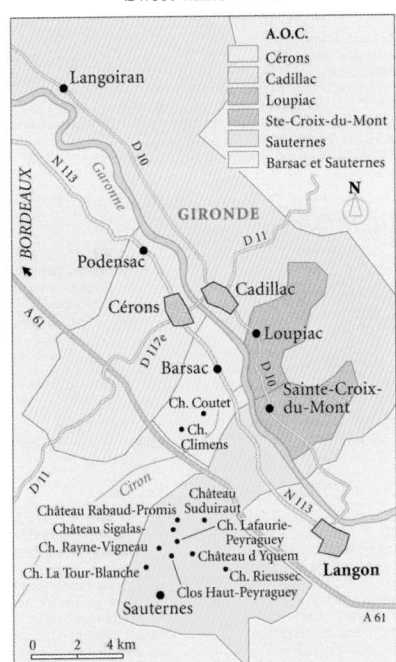

A.O.C.	
☐	Cérons
☐	Cadillac
▨	Loupiac
▨	Ste-Croix-du-Mont
▨	Sauternes
▨	Barsac et Sauternes

quality of its production. This 2000 has a strong colour that speaks of its richness. The bouquet confirms this in the form of roast and crystallized notes, while the rich, unctuous structure of the palate makes this a wine suitable both for aperitif and as an accompaniment to food. Drink now and over the next three years.
🔹 SA Vignobles M. Boyer, Ch. du Cros, 33410 Loupiac, tel. 05.56.62.99.31, fax 05.56.62.12.59, e-mail contact@chateauducros.com ☑
🍷 ev. day except Sat. Sun. 8am–12 noon 2pm–6pm

CH. DU GRAND PLANTIER

Elevé en fût de chêne 2000★

▨	14 ha 4,000	⅏	8–11 €

From a producer of Premières Côtes, this vintage has a golden-yellow colour. Though not intense, the bouquet releases notes of crystallized fruits that similarly inform the palate. Characterized by good sucrosity, this wine has real balance and a solid structure that will enable it to be served either with foie gras or with roast poultry.
🔹 GAEC des Vignobles Albucher, Ch. du Grand Plantier, 33410 Monprimblanc, tel. 05.56.62.99.03, fax 05.56.76.91.35 ☑ 🏠
🍷 by appt.

CH. DE LOUPIAC 2001★★

▨	2 ha 6,000	⅏	15–23 €

Just 100 m from the Romanesque church, this château is a lovely charterhouse flanked by pavilions. The wine, too, has plenty of ambiance with its golden appearance and bright straw-coloured highlights. The bouquet is quite oaky, but this does not detract from the freshness of the aromas, which include notes of citrus fruits and mint. The supple, elegant, well-balanced palate is sweet and full. A nice wine which calls for three or four years' cellaring, perhaps longer. (Half-litre bottles)
🔹 SCEA Marc Ducau, Ch. Loupiac-Gaudiet, 33410 Loupiac, tel. 05.56.62.99.88, fax 05.56.62.60.13, e-mail loupiac-gaudiet@atlantic-line.fr ☑
🍷 by appt.

CH. MAZARIN 2001★

10 ha	20,000	�	5–8 €

This well-known mainstay of the appellation has stayed true to its reputation with this 2001. Though still oaky, with vanilla notes, the bouquet is seductively evocative of flowers, apples and pears, and dried figs. The palate is supple and round, with plenty of oak support which will soften during storage so that the whole palate will come to resemble today's unctuous finish.

� SCEA Vignobles Jean-Yves Arnaud, La Croix,
33410 Cadillac, tel. 05.56.20.23.52, fax 05.56.20.23.52 ☑
ℐ by appt.

CH. MEMOIRES 2001★★

5 ha	12,000	ⅲ	8–11 €

This cru, which also makes Cadillac, reminds us here that Loupiac is its preferred appellation. The colour is a superb gold, shining with a thousand highlights. The bouquet is a complex association of dried fruits (apricots, raisins, figs) with spices and notes of caramel. Rich and powerful, yet delicate, the palate is already pleasing, but it also has sufficient structure to be laid down.

� Jean-François Ménard, Ch. Mémoires,
33490 Saint-Maixant, tel. 05.56.62.06.43,
fax 05.56.62.04.32, e-mail memoires1@aol.com ☑
ℐ ev. day 8am–12 noon 1.30pm–6.30pm; Sat. Sun. by appt.

CH. PEYROT-MARGES 2000★★

1.6 ha	n.c.	ⅲ	5–8 €

This vineyard, which is entirely planted with Sémillon vines, may be small, but it is only one of the crus that belong to the Vignobles Chassagnol, who are present in a number of appellations. Far from the small size being an excuse not to bother with quality, it is here a stimulus to performing good work. Both the bouquet and the palate through to the finish are characterized by great aromatic complexity, and the palatal structure is rich and well constituted. Though already pleasant drinking, this wine will be just as good in four or five years' time.

�' GAEC des Vignobles Chassagnol, Bern,
33410 Gabarnac, tel. 05.56.62.98.00, fax 05.56.62.93.23 ☑
ℐ by appt.

CH. LES ROQUES

Cuvée Frantz 2001★

4 ha	1,500	ⅲ	15–23 €

Whilst last year's version was a *coup de cœur*, this 2001 is still a very good wine. A strong, bright gold colour, it is somewhat hesitant at first to release its aromas, which are of fruit and grills. The palate is very round, and is strongly structured in order to provide a deliciously sweet, rich sensation, which promises to be even better in four to five years' time.

� SCEA Ch. du Pavillon, 33410 Sainte-Croix-du-Mont,
tel. 05.56.62.01.04, fax 05.56.62.00.92,
e-mail a.v.fertal@wanadoo.fr ☑
ℐ by appt.

Wines selected but
not starred

DOM. DU CHAY

Cuvée Charlotte 2001

2 ha	5,000		8–11 €

�'Ϯ SCEA Tourré-Delmas, Le Chaÿ, 33410 Loupiac,
tel. 05.56.62.99.45, fax 05.56.62.19.44 ☑
ℐ by appt.
�'Ϯ Pierre Tourré

DOM. DU NOBLE 2001

10 ha	30,000	🍾 ♦	15–23 €

↑Ϯ EARL Déjean, Dom. du Noble, 33410 Loupiac,
tel. 05.56.62.98.30, fax 05.56.62.15.90,
e-mail pdejean@cario.fr ☑
ℐ by appt.

Sainte-Croix-du-Mont

This area of steep hills overlooking the Garonne is comparatively little known, despite its considerable charm. The wines have long suffered from a reputation of being favourites at weddings and banquets, as have other Vins Liquoreux appellations from the right bank.

However, this appellation, which faces the Sauternes vineyards and which produced 13,191 hl from 399 ha in 2002, deserves better. The soil is good, mainly limestone with deposits of gravel, the micro-climate favouring the growth of noble rot. The grape varieties are similar to those grown in Sauternes, as are the methods of vinification. The wines are more rounded and soft rather than intensely sweet, with a pleasantly fruity taste. They can be served with the same dishes as their grander neighbours from the left bank, but their prices are more affordable, sufficiently so to serve them as a sumptuous extra at drinks parties.

CH. DES ARROUCATS 2001★

23 ha	40,000	🍾 ♦	5–8 €

For those who like fine views, this cru offers one over the valley of the Garonne and Yquem. Fruity and floral, the bouquet of this vintage is in keeping with the well-balanced palate, which will enable this wine to keep well without any problem.

↑Ϯ Annie Lapouge, Les Arroucats,
33410 Sainte-Croix-du-Mont, tel. 05.56.62.07.37,
fax 05.57.98.06.29 ☑
ℐ ev. day except Sun. 8.30am–12.30pm 1.30pm–7pm

CH. LA CAUSSADE 2000★★

20 ha	26,000	🍾 ♦	8–11 €

It may seem a tough bet for any second wine to exist alongside the famous Château La Rame, but this Château La Caussade, which is equally signed by Yves Armand, has managed it. Its noble-rotted, complex character is immediately evident from the bouquet. Rich, full and elegant, this wine ought to be cellared for five years before it accompanies foie gras or small gamebirds.

↑Ϯ Yves Armand, GFA du Ch. La Rame,
33410 Sainte-Croix-du-Mont, tel. 05.56.62.01.50,
fax 05.56.62.01.94, e-mail dgm@wanadoo.fr ☑
ℐ by appt.

CH. CRABITAN-BELLEVUE

Cuvée spéciale 2001★

20 ha	10,000	ⅲ	8–11 €

The Solane estate is a fair size and produces a wide number of appellations. This Cuvée Spéciale is a good ambassador for them. The bouquet is discreet but elegant, and the palate has a fresh start and continues with gathering power. This well-balanced wine may be drunk now or kept for a short time.

↑Ϯ GFA Bernard Solane et Fils,
33410 Sainte-Croix-du-Mont, tel. 05.56.62.01.53,
fax 05.56.76.72.09 ☑
ℐ ev. day 8am–12 noon 2pm–6pm; Sun. by appt.

CH. LA GRAVE 2000★

| | 11 ha | 24,000 | ∎ ♦ | | 8–11 € |

This cru, a regular for good quality, offers a very attractive 2000. The colour is strong and bright, and the bouquet is complex, with notes of honey mixed with fruit. The palate is rich and full, clearly noble-rotted. The structure appears adequate for keeping for up to four to five years. The **Sentiers d'Automne 2000** is commended and **Château Grand Peyrot 2000** gains one star. The latter is a rich wine with an expressive crystallized fruit character; it will keep well.
♦┐ EARL Vignoble Tinon, Ch. La Grave,
33410 Sainte-Croix-du-Mont, tel. 05.56.62.01.65,
fax 05.56.62.00.04, e-mail tinon@terre-net.fr ◪
☨ by appt.

CH. LOUSTEAU-VIEIL 2001★

| | 20 ha | 50,000 | ∎ ◫ | | 11–15 € |

From this estate, one of the high spots in the locality, you can see the Pyrenees on a clear day. This noble-rotted wine is similarly a lovely sight, with its bright golden-yellow colour and golden-brown fringe. The citrus perfumes of the bouquet include a hint of roasts, and corresponding flavours appear on the palate, sustained by oakiness to constitute a fresh, well-balanced whole.
♦┐ Vignobles R. Sessacq, Ch. Lousteau-Vieil,
33410 Sainte-Croix-du-Mont, tel. 05.56.62.01.15,
fax 05.56.62.01.68, e-mail m.sessacq@wanadoo.fr ◪
☨ ev. day 9am–8pm
♦┐ Martine Sessacq

CH. DES MAILLES

Cuvée Laurence 2000★

| | 19 ha | 11,000 | ∎ ◫ ♦ | | 11–15 € |

The colour of this special wine seems to fluctuate between pale and strong gold before expressing its personality in its bouquet, where botrytized notes of overripened fruits are assisted by fine touches of honey, pine and white flowers. The well-balanced palate will be ready to offer its charms in two to three years' time.
♦┐ Daniel Larrieu, SCEA des Mailles,
33410 Sainte-Croix-du-Mont, tel. 05.56.62.01.20,
fax 05.56.76.71.99 ◪
☨ by appt.

CH. DU MONT

Cuvée Pierre 2001★★

| | 16 ha | 10,000 | ◫ | | 11–15 € |

96 |97| |98| 99 00 01

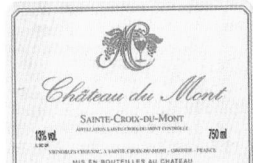

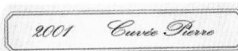

This special wine, the product of densely-planted vines and maturation in new barrels, has had the best of care. Once again the Chouvacs have met with success in the form of a wine whose golden colour is an encouragement for the taster. The bouquet is all one would expect from the colour: rich and complex (violets, crystallized fruits, citrus and exotic fruits). The palate is rich and concentrated, powerful and long-lasting. This is a real *liquoreux* and will need some time in the cellar.
♦┐ Hervé Chouvac, Ch. du Mont,
33410 Sainte-Croix-du-Mont, tel. 05.56.62.07.65,
fax 05.56.62.07.58 ◪
☨ by appt.
♦┐ Paul Chouvac

CH. LA RAME

Réserve du Château 2001★★

| | 20 ha | 20,000 | ◫ | | 15–23 € |

96 **97** |98| 99 **00 01**

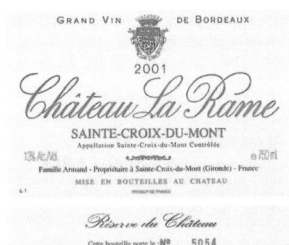

As the house, which dates from 1766, testifies, the estate is heir to a long history. It is, however, the patient and determined work of Yves Armand that has made La Rame one of the stars of the *vins liquoreux* of the right bank. This 2001 is in the best tradition of the cru and can only enhance its reputation. A beautiful golden-yellow colour with eye-catching glints, the wine has a developing bouquet of seductive notes of honey and vanilla happily marrying aromas of crystallized orange and apricot. Rich, well-balanced and complex, the palate bears witness to a rigorously selected overripe harvest. A remarkably successful wine. Wait five, six, seven years, or even longer.
♦┐ Yves Armand, GFA du Ch. La Rame,
33410 Sainte-Croix-du-Mont, tel. 05.56.62.01.50,
fax 05.56.62.01.94, e-mail dgm@wanadoo.fr ◪
☨ by appt.

Wines selected but not starred

CH. BEL AIR

Cuvée Prestige 2001

| | 20 ha | 10,000 | ◫ | | 11–15 € |

♦┐ Vignobles M. Méric et Fils,
33410 Sainte-Croix-du-Mont, tel. 05.56.62.01.19,
fax 05.56.62.09.33, e-mail jeanguy.meric@tiscali.fr ◪
☨ by appt.

CH. LAMARQUE 2001

| | 15 ha | 45,000 | ◫ | | 11–15 € |

♦┐ Bernard Darroman, Ch. Lamarque,
33410 Sainte-Croix-du-Mont, tel. 05.56.62.01.21,
fax 05.56.76.72.10 ◪ ☖
☨ by appt.

CH. LESCURE 2001

| | 4.86 ha | 14,000 | ∎ ◫ | | 8–11 € |

♦┐ CAT Ch. Lescure, 33490 Verdelais, tel. 05.57.98.04.68,
fax 05.57.98.04.64, e-mail chateau.lescure@free.fr ◪
☨ by appt.

Cérons

Enclosed by the Graves region (an appellation that they can also claim, unlike the Sauternes and Barsac), the wines of Cérons offer a link between Barsac and the sweet Graves Supérieures. Production was 1,622 hl from 63 ha in 2002. These are, nonetheless, original wines, with a characteristic vigour and great finesse.

CLOS BOURGELAT 2000★

1.53 ha	5,000			8–11 €

This cru, which also makes Graves, offers a Cérons which will doubtless not keep very long, but which will be very attractive in its youth for its well-balanced palate and crystallized orange character.

➼ Dominique Lafosse, Clos Bourgelat, 33720 Cérons, tel. 05.56.27.01.73, fax 05.56.27.13.72 ☑
Ⴜ ev. day except Sun. 9am–12 noon 2pm–7pm; groups by appt.

CH. HURADIN 2000★

2.55 ha	6,500		8–11 €

This cru, which often appears in the *Guide*, reveals its quality yet again with this 2000, which is a trifle light but nonetheless pleasing for its fresh almond aromas. It is sufficiently well-constructed to be laid down for a short while.

➼ SCEA Vignobles Ricaud-Lafosse, Ch. Huradin, 33720 Cérons, tel. 05.56.27.09.97, fax 05.56.27.09.97 ☑
Ⴜ by appt.
➼ Catherine Lafosse

Barsac

All the wines carrying the Appellation Barsac can also be Appellation Sauternes. Barsac (605 ha and producing 12,570 hl in 2002) differs from the communes of the Sauternais proper by virtue of a less hilly terrain and by the stone walls that enclose many of the vineyards. The wines themselves differ from those of Sauternes, being slightly sweeter in character. However, like Sauternes, they may be served with desserts or, as is more and more popular, to accompany a starter of foie gras or strongly flavoured cheeses, such as Roquefort.

CYPRES DE CLIMENS 2000★★

n.c.	n.c.		30–38 €

Climens, whose vineyard was built up from the 16th century, is overlooked by a château built in the 17th century and altered in the 18th. Acquired by Lucien Lurton in 1971, it is one of the jewels of Barsac. The wine is worthy of its origins, even if its tone is very different from the austerity of the charterhouse. The lovely golden-yellow colour is immediately suggestive of the power that is contained in the intense, complex bouquet of *pain d'épice* (a sweet spiced loaf), exotic fruits or ripe fruits. Full and rich, the palate demonstrates the influence of noble rot, yet without losing freshness.

➼ S. F. du Ch. Climens, 33720 Barsac, tel. 05.56.27.15.33, fax 05.56.27.21.04, e-mail contact@chateau-climens.fr
Ⴜ by appt.

CH. FARLURET 2001★

9 ha	23,000		15–23 €

Made by the same producers as Haut Bergeron, but from a vineyard at Barsac. An attractive pale colour with golden glints, this 2001 opens on a bouquet of wax and citrus fruits. The palate has a most pleasant roast flavour, with plenty of

richness and sweetness. The finish is long-lingering, with notes of crystallized fruits and oak. The wine promises to age well and to maintain its quality over several years to come.

➼ Hervé et Patrick Lamothe, quartier du Haire, 33210 Preignac, tel. 05.56.63.24.76, fax 05.56.63.23.31, e-mail haut-bergeron@wanadoo.fr ☑
Ⴜ by appt.

CH. GRAVAS 2001★

15 ha	28,000		15–23 €

If the passing of Pierre Bernard a year ago was a blow to Barsac and the whole of the Sauternes district, in which he cut such a prominent figure, things continue as before at Gravas, where Pierre's son Michel took over several years back. This wine's elegant perfumes of acacia flowers, peaches and apricots are sufficient proof. The palate is sweet and rich without excess and has excellent balance. With its agreeable finesse, this wine may be enjoyed young or kept a few years.

➼ Michel Bernard, Ch. Gravas, 33720 Barsac, tel. 05.56.27.06.91, fax 05.56.27.29.83, e-mail graves.chateau@libertysurf.fr ☑
Ⴜ by appt.

CH. PIOT-DAVID 2001★

7 ha	19,000		15–23 €

Boundaried by the forest, this Barsac vineyard has charm. Like this wine. It is still dominated by the oak. But its personality is far more complex than that. A bright, honest golden-yellow colour, it has a bouquet of dried apricots, roasted almonds and noble rot. The powerful, unctuous palate is a real complexity of flavours. Scents of a thousand wild flowers mingle with notes of grilling, dried fig and overripe bilberries, a real joy to the taster. Wait three or four years.

➼ Jean-Luc David, Ch. Poncet, 33410 Omet, tel. 05.56.62.97.30, fax 05.56.62.66.76 ☑
Ⴜ by appt.

Wines selected but not starred

CH. LATREZOTTE 2001

4 ha	10,000		15–23 €

➼ Jan de Kok, Ch. Latrezotte, 33720 Barsac, tel. 05.56.27.16.50, fax 05.56.27.08.89 ☑
Ⴜ by appt.

CH. ROUMIEU LACOSTE 2001

8 ha	11,000		30–38 €

➼ Hervé Dubourdieu, Ch. Roûmieu-Lacoste, 33720 Barsac, tel. 05.56.27.16.29, fax 05.56.27.02.65, e-mail hervedubourdieu@aol.com ☑
Ⴜ by appt.

Sauternes

If you visit any of the châteaux in Sauternes, you will hear the story of the grower who one day had the brilliant, but perverse, idea of bringing in his harvest late, even though the grapes were overripe. However, if you go to five châteaux you will find that each grower has his own version of the story, which, naturally enough, took place on his property. The truth is, no one knows who "invented" Sauternes, nor when it was invented, nor where.

BORDEAUX

While history in the Sauternais insists on hiding behind legend, there is no confusion about the geography of the area. Every pebble in the five communes making up the appellation (including Barsac, which has its own appellation) is counted and every constituent recorded. The variety of soils and subsoils (limestone or chalk and clay under gravel) give a special character to each cru, with the most famous vineyards being planted on gravelly hillocks. The Sauternes wines are made from three grape varieties – Sémillon (70–80%), Sauvignon (20–30%) and Muscadelle; these are golden and luscious but also fine and delicate. Their "toasted" bouquet develops very well with age, becoming rich and complex with notes of honey, hazelnut and crystallized orange. It is worth noting that Sauternes and Barsac were the only white wines to be classified in 1855. The AOC covered an area of 1,669 ha in 2002. It produced 32,375 hl of wine.

CH. ANDOYSE DU HAYOT 1999★

	20 ha	36,000		11–15 €

|90| 91 93 94 |95| |96| |97| 98 99

This cru, which regularly produces good quality, again offers its one-star 99. Light-yellow, with golden glints, it now has a complex bouquet (crystallized fruit, acacia flowers, angelica, citrus fruits and light oakiness), which accords with the delicate, well-balanced palate. The finish has a grace and charm contributed by the oak. A characterful synthesis that will benefit from service in a carafe.
SCE Vignobles du Hayot, Ch. Andoyse, 33720 Barsac, tel. 05.56.27.15.37, fax 05.56.27.04.24, e-mail vignoblesduhayot@aol.com
by appt.

CH. D'ARCHE 2000★★

2e cru clas. 23 ha	n.c.		30–38 €

This fine unit, in terms both of its terroir and of its size, offers a true cellar-wine that may also be enjoyed young (from two to twelve years). An attractive bright gold colour, with an amber fringe, the 2000 has a developing bouquet of deep crystallized fruit aromas, prune and acacia, on a hint of noble rot. Warm, round, fleshy and concentrated, this is a thorough Sauternes that will suit a wide range of food: chicken, veal, foie gras, herb cheeses.
SA Ch. d'Arche, 33210 Sauternes, tel. 05.56.76.66.55, fax 05.56.76.64.38, e-mail chateau-arche@terre-net.fr
by appt. except summer ev. day 9am–5pm

CH. D'ARMAJAN DES ORMES 2000★

	6 ha	12,000		15–23 €

|95| |96| |97| |98| |99| 00

The château was rebuilt in the 18th century by Montesquieu's son-in-law, Vincent d'Armajan, but the cru goes back considerably further. This millennial 2000 has a very clear amber-gold appearance and a bouquet still so discreet that it releases only the odd note of grilling and *rancio*. The palate is well balanced between sweetness and acidity, finishing on an elegant revival of the aromas.
EARL Jacques et Guillaume Perromat, Ch. d'Armajan, 33210 Preignac, tel. 05.56.63.22.17, fax 05.56.63.21.55, e-mail guillaume.perromat@wanadoo.fr
by appt.

CH. BARBIER 1998★

7 ha	20,000		11–15 €

The label has an original shape, and the contents, signed by Médeville of Cadillac, are similarly eye-catching: a lovely bright gold. Both bouquet and palate are sweet and rich; they have a lot of charm. The structure is supple and round, well sustained by very evident vanilla oak. A wine to enjoy in two years' time – or in ten.

SCEA Jean Médeville et Fils, Ch. Fayau, 33410 Cadillac, tel. 05.57.98.08.08, fax 05.56.62.18.22, e-mail medeville-jeanetfils@wanadoo.fr
ev. day except Sat. Sun. 8.30am–12 noon 2pm–6pm

CRU BARREJATS 1998★

	3.88 ha	6,500		46–76 €

|90| 91 92 |94| |95| |96| 97 98 00

This beautiful golden wine is very true to type, with a honeyed bouquet enriched by notes of crystallized fruit, *pain d'épices* (spice loaf) and dried fruits, with discreet oak support. The round, full, rich palate is well balanced, with good acidity. A very fresh finish concluded the tasting of this wine, which will need two years' storage before it can accompany the sort of gourmet menus advocated by the Sapros association, which campaigns for noble-rotted wines.
SCEA Barréjats, Clos de Gensac, Mareuil, 33310 Pujols-sur-Ciron, tel. 05.56.27.01.15, fax 05.56.27.01.15, e-mail mireille.daret@free.fr
by appt.

CH. BASTOR-LAMONTAGNE 2000★★

	58 ha	40,000		23–30 €

82 83 84 85 86 |88| |89| (90) 94 95 |96| |97| 98 99 00

This cru, based in an 18th century château surrounded by fine parkland, has a choice terroir whose quality comes through in this 2000. Bright gold in colour, with the odd straw-coloured highlight, the wine has an evolving bouquet that illustrates the finesse and elegance that are characteristic of Sauternes: well-ripened apricot, crystallized lemon, then more complex notes that appear when the wine has had time to breathe. The palate is rich, round and elegant, with a beautiful fresh, mellow body, finishing on a friendly note of crystallized lemon. A really great Sauternes. Wait between five and fifteen years.
SCEA Vignobles Bastor et Saint-Robert, Dom. de Lamontagne, 33210 Preignac, tel. 05.56.63.27.66, fax 05.56.76.87.03, e-mail bastor-lamontagne@dial.oleane.com
by appt.
Foncier-Vignobles

CH. BECHEREAU 2001★

	10.63 ha	11,500		15–23 €

A rarity in Sauternes: this cru has fine cellars underground, in which this characterful amber-yellow wine was aged. The nose is of ripe fruits and spices, and the palate is full and powerful. Though still a trifle rustic, the wine will soften if cellared for three to five years.
Les Vignobles Dumon, Ch. Béchereau de Ruat, 33210 Bommes, tel. 05.56.76.61.73, fax 05.56.76.67.84
ev. day 9am–12 noon 2pm–5pm; Sat. Sun. & groups by appt.

CRU BORDENAVE 2000★

	2.5 ha	3,600		38–46 €

This vineyard has come from a small cru rented until 1999 by the team of Bastor-Lamontagne; it is now managed on an autonomous basis, having been bought by Foncier-Vignobles. The bouquet of this 100% Sémillon has an unusual note of mead. Supple and unctuous, with caramelized notes of roasting, the palate is marked by a good presence of noble rot. An attractive wine that is already nice to drink, but can wait.
SCEA Vignobles Bastor et Saint-Robert, Dom. de Lamontagne, 33210 Preignac, tel. 05.56.63.27.66, fax 05.56.76.87.03, e-mail bastor-lamontagne@dial.oleane.com
by appt.
Foncier-Vignobles

CH. CAILLOU 1998★

2e cru clas. 13 ha	10,000		30–38 €

Located in upper Barsac, this estate is near the remains of the ancient Peybale-Peyrebidanne Roman road. It shows how far back wine-growing in this district goes. Although it cannot compete with the superb 97 that was a *coup de coeur* last year, this wine's finesse, suppleness and sweetness constitutes a fresh, elegant, almost airy synthesis, from which the roasted

notes of noble rot are not absent. Its floral perfumes may be enjoyed now in its youth or in three or four years' time.
☛ M. et Mme Pierre, Ch. Caillou, 33720 Barsac, tel. 05.56.27.16.38, fax 05.56.27.09.60, e-mail chateaucaillou@aol.com
✠ by appt.

CH. CAPLANE 2001★

| | 3.5 ha | 6,000 | 🍷 📖 | | 11–15 € |

A small cru, but a quality terroir with black sands and gravel. Its viticultural worth is proved by this light yellow wine. The fresh, subtle bouquet reveals lovely aromas of honey, currants and linden blossom. Supple and soft-bodied, the palate has a sweet, rich elegance. Two to five years' cellaring will enable this Sauternes to achieve full expression.
☛ Guy David, 6, Moulin de Laubes, 33410 Laroque, tel. 05.56.62.93.76 ✅
✠ by appt.
☛ Mme Garbay

DOM. DE CARBONNIEU

Sélection prestige 2001★★

| | n.c. | 12,000 | 📖 | 15–23 € |

The overwhelming proportion of Sémillon here (93%) is complemented by Sauvignon and Muscadelle. The limpid, very transparent gold appearance inspires confidence and prepares the taster for the important development of the bouquet (exotic fruits and currants). The richness of sugar and body sustain a lovely evolution of flavours through to a highly successful finish. A wine to enjoy in five years' time with a herb cheese.
☛ Alain Charrier, SCEA Charrier et Fils, Dom. de Carbonnieu, 33210 Bommes, tel. 05.56.76.64.48, fax 05.56.76.69.95, e-mail vignobles.charrier@wanadoo.fr ✅
✠ ev. day 9am–12 noon 2pm–7pm

CLOS DADY

Sélection vieilles vignes 2001★

| | 3.5 ha | 5,000 | 📖 | 15–23 € |

A small vineyard full of charm by the Ciron, this cru offers an attractive wine. Elegant and well balanced, this 2001 has an agreeable freshness thanks to its citrus-fruit aromas; these make it good to drink now, even if it can be left for three to five years. The second wine, **Château de Bastard 2001 (8–11 €)**, is commended. Its nose of wax and multi-floral honey will appeal to many wine-lovers.
☛ Chrisophe et Catherine Gachet, Ch. Bastard, 33720 Barsac, tel. 05.56.62.20.01, fax 05.56.62.33.11, e-mail clos.dady@wanadoo.fr ✅

CH. CLOSIOT 2000★

| | 4 ha | 5,200 | 📖 | 15–23 € |

Cultivated by a friendly Franco-Belgian couple, this cru offers a wine with a pretty straw-gold colour. The nose has an appealing freshness that comes through on delicate notes of acacia flowers. The palate is round, rich, and well-blended, finishing on a light touch of noble rot that leaves an impression of fine, elegant synthesis.
☛ Françoise Soizeau, Ch. Closiot, 33720 Barsac, tel. 05.56.27.05.92, fax 05.56.27.11.06, e-mail closiot@vins-sauternes.com ✅ 🏠
✠ ev. day except Sat. Sun. 9am–12 noon 2pm–6pm

CH. DOISY DAENE 2001★★

| | 2e cru clas. | n.c. | 35,000 | 📖 | 30–38 € |

50 71 |75| |76| 78 79 80 |81| |82| (83) 84 85 |86| |88| |89| |90| |91| |94| |95| |96| |97| |98| |00| 01

Although Denis Dubourdieu is best known for his research into dry white wines, he never forgets that his roots are in Barsac. This lovely golden-yellow 2001 has a developing bouquet of remarkable complexity in which mineral notes mix with honey and yellow fruits. The perfectly well-balanced palate has lots of mellow richness and concentration, while nonetheless retaining great freshness. The whole is crowned by a long, well-integrated finish. A generous wine that will keep well.

☛ EARL Vignobles Pierre et Denis Dubourdieu, Ch. Doisy-Daëne, quartier Gravas, 33720 Barsac, tel. 05.56.27.15.84, fax 05.56.27.18.99, e-mail doisy-daene@terre-net.fr ✅
✠ by appt.

CH. L'ERMITAGE 2001★

| | 7 ha | 20,000 | 📖 | 15–23 € |

This single-variety Sémillon is a golden-yellow colour. Although still a little closed, the nose releases fresh perfumes of citrus fruits mixed with almonds and resin. On the palate, after a round, full start, the wine steadily increases in body and richness until it finishes. It calls for two to four years' cellaring.
☛ SCEA Ch. l'Ermitage, 9, V.C., M. Lacoste, 33210 Preignac, tel. 05.56.76.24.13, fax 05.56.76.12.75, e-mail chateau.lermitage@free.fr ✅
✠ ev. day 8am–6pm
☛ Fontan-Chambers

CH. DE FARGUES 1997★★

| | 14 ha | 15,000 | 📖 | +76 € |

|47| |49| |53| |59| 62 (67) 71 |75| |76| |83| 84 85 |86| 87 |88| |89| |90| |91| |94| |95| 96 97

Although the grounds are vast (170 ha), the vineyard is of modest size; the wine is worthy of the château's great age and of the prestige of the Lur-Saluces, who have owned it since time immemorial. Slighty lemony gold in colour, the 97 is aromatically quite complex. Notes of crystallized fruit mix with notes of overripeness (apricot jam, quince jelly). The palate is rich, full and round, with a distinguished balance between the sugar and the alcohol. Remarkable for its fullness and freshness, this wine has a long finish on almonds and crystallized lemon. A great *vin liquoreux*. Wait six to ten years.
☛ Comte Alexandre de Lur-Saluces, Ch. de Fargues, 33210 Fargues-de-Langon, tel. 05.57.98.04.20, fax 05.57.98.04.21, e-mail fargues@chateau-de-fargues.com ✅
✠ by appt.

CH. GRILLON 2001★★

| | 11.5 ha | 25,000 | 📖 | 11–15 € |

Grown in Barsac, this wine illustrates the quality of that locality's terroir. It is a quite strong yellow colour with a developing bouquet that is both rich and complex (honey and dried fruits, with a finesse derived from well-measured noble-rotting). The palate is subtle and full, enhanced by very attractive notes of crystallized orange and pleasurably sustained by oak right through the finish. A lovely, successful wine. Leave in the cellar for a while.
☛ Odile Roumazeilles-Cameleyre, Ch. Grillon, 33720 Barsac, tel. 05.56.27.16.45, fax 05.56.27.12.18 ✅
✠ ev. day 9am–12.30pm 2pm–7pm

CH. GUIRAUD 2000★★

| | 1er cru clas. 85 ha | n.c. | 📖 | 38–46 € |

83 85 86 88 |89| (90) 92 |95| 96 (97) 98 99 00

Overlooked by a vast and beautiful residence, this estate is the only Premier Cru in the village of Sauternes itself. When it produces wines like this 2000, it repays the honour. It has an engaging pale-yellow colour and an attractive bouquet that is both floral (wild rose) and fruity (apples, pears and lemons). The attack is full and oaky. The palate is rich and long-lasting, characterized by excellent balance and a robust finish that is well supported by the oak. A remarkable wine for the year. Wait a few years.

➤ SCA du Ch. Guiraud, 33210 Sauternes,
tel. 05.56.76.61.01, fax 05.56.76.67.52,
e-mail x.planty@club-internet.fr ☑
🍷 by appt.

CH. HAUT-BERGERON 2001★★

	17 ha	43,000	〇〇	15–23 €

83 85 86 88 |89| |90| 91 94 95 |96| 97 |98| 99 00 **01**

This pillar of the appellation is once again up in the realm of *coups de cœur* with this superbly classic Sauternes. Its quality is evident from the old-gold colour, as well as from the bouquet with its hints of beeswax, crystallized and dried fruits, and elegant note of roasting. The palate is supple, rich, and full, with a sucrosity, a richness of flavour and a mellowness which all contribute to its complexity and guarantee its future. Just as well put together and possessing a well-integrated bouquet is the one-starred **Fontebride 2001**.

➤ Hervé et Patrick Lamothe, quartier du Haire, 33210 Preignac, tel. 05.56.63.24.76, fax 05.56.63.23.31, e-mail haut-bergeron@wanadoo.fr ☑
🍷 by appt.

CH. HAUT-MAYNE 2001★

	5.01 ha	10,000	〇〇	11–15 €

A small traditional cru and a bright golden-yellow wine that knows how to make a good impression. The bouquet is developed and expressive; it combines flowery notes of hawthorn with aromas of dried fruits (apricot). After a full, unctuous attack, the palate has a pleasing development of flavours.

➤ EARL Roumazeilles, Ch. Haut-Mayne, 33210 Preignac, tel. 05.56.76.88.41, fax 05.56.27.12.18 ☑
🍷 by appt.

CH. LAFAURIE-PEYRAGUEY 2001★★

	1er cru clas. 41 ha	90,000	〇〇	38–46 €

75 |76| 79 80 |81| 82 83 84 85 86 |87| (88) |89| |90| 91 92 93 |94| |95| |96| 97 |98| **99 01**

Built in the 16th century and altered in the 19th, this château is one of the most unusual in the Sauternes district, with its quasi-medieval enclosure. The wine has a friendlier appearance with its lovely, if shy, pale colour and green tinges. The freshness of the bouquet combines notes of citrus fruits with jammy notes of apricot. On the palate, the well-measured oak marks its presence by an attractive toasty note which respects the balance and very great complexity of this characterful wine. The finish is classy and long-lasting. It calls for cellaring of five to fifteen years.

➤ Ch. Lafaurie-Peyraguey, 160, cours du Médoc, 33300 Bordeaux, tel. 05.57.19.57.77, fax 05.57.19.57.87
🍷 by appt.

CH. LAMOTHE GUIGNARD 2000★

	2e cru clas. 18 ha	20,000	〇〇	15–23 €

81 82 (83) 84 |85| |86| 87 |88| 89 **90** 92 93 |94| |95| |96| 97 98 |99| 00

Grown on an estate above the Ciron, this 2000 is a typical product of this cru by virtue of the finesse of its bouquet of springtime white flowers and ferns with a hint of autumnal undergrowth. Sustained by well-judged oak, the round, mellow palate is developing agreeable flavours of apples and pears. In two years' time it will be even more seductive.

➤ GAEC Philippe et Jacques Guignard, Ch. Lamothe Guignard, 33210 Sauternes, tel. 05.56.76.60.28, fax 05.56.76.69.05 ☑
🍷 ev. day 8am-12 noon 2pm–6pm; Sat. Sun. by appt.

CH. LARIBOTTE 2000★

	15.46 ha	10,000	▮〇〇♦	11–15 €

Those familiar with this cru will be able to reacquaint themselves with its characteristic floral aromas, if they try this wine. But its personality goes beyond the scents of acacia flowers and broom: let's not ignore its good balance, its honeyed flavours and lingering finish. This fresh, classic-tasting Sauternes will be ready to drink in two to three years' time.

➤ Jean-Pierre Lahiteau, Ch. Laribotte, 33210 Preignac, tel. 05.56.63.27.88, fax 05.56.62.24.80 ☑
🍷 by appt.

CH. LAVILLE 2001★

	13 ha	20,000	〇〇	15–23 €

92 94 |95| |96| 97 98 99 00

Without being gigantic, this is still a decent-sized unit. It probably helps when creating quality wines like this good-looking straw-yellow 2001 with green highlights. Very ripe yellow fruits, apricots and lemony beeswax: such finesse on the part of the bouquet anticipates the elegance of the palate, where notes of liquorice mingle with blond tobacco. The finish is most agreeably fresh. The same producer's **Château de Rochefort 2001** is commended.

➤ Ch. Laville, 33210 Preignac, tel. 05.56.63.59.45, fax 05.56.63.16.28 ☑
🍷 ev. day except Sat. Sun. 8.30am–12.30pm 1.30pm–6.30pm

CH. DE MALLE 2000★

	2e cru clas. 27 ha	20,000	〇〇	30–38 €

71 (75) 76 81 83 85 86 87 88 89 90 91 |94| |95| |96| 97 98 |99| 00

Here are monumental wrought-iron gates, a 17th century château, a chapel decked with paintings, an Italianate park with statues, and a history of eminent owners, from the Lur-Saluces to the Bournazels. Malle is indeed one of the finest properties in the Sauternes district. This wine is a resplendent straw colour with gold highlights. Though the floral, lemony bouquet remains a little closed, the palate has breadth, sweetness, richness, and long flavours that it will not hurt to wait four or five years. The cru's second wine, **Château de Sainte-Hélène 2000 (15–23 €)**, which is also one-star rated, is a full, rich, fine wine.

➤ Comtesse de Bournazel, GFA des Comtes de Bournazel, Ch. de Malle, 33210 Preignac, tel. 05.56.62.36.86, fax 05.56.76.82.40, e-mail chateaudemalle@wanadoo.fr ☑
🍷 by appt.

DOM. DE MONTEILS
Cuvée Sélection 2000★★

	8 ha	5,960	▮〇〇♦	15–23 €

Grown on a small family cru established in 1861 in the village of Preignac, which has many such, this wine shows that modest-sized vineyards can rival the larger ones where quality is concerned. Old gold in colour, this 2000 is a generous bouquet of linden blossom and broom-flower tisane enhanced by a hint of beeswax and a slightly toasty note. Round and warming, the palate bears the mark of noble rot;

BORDEAUX

the finish is velvety and intense. Keep three to fifteen years. Try with a Roquefort cheese.

☛ SCEA Dom. de Monteils, 3, rte de Fargues, 33210 Preignac, tel. 05.56.62.24.05, fax 05.56.62.22.30, e-mail vins.sauternes@wanadoo.fr ☑
🍷 by appt.

DOM. DE PAVILLON-BOUYOT 2000★

	4.3 ha	4,500	🎗	11–15 €

With its varietal mix of Sémillon, Muscadelle and Sauvignon, this cru is very much in the Bordeaux spirit. The wine is a strong colour with dark glints, and the bouquet evokes notes of stewed fruit similar to those of overripened grapes. The powerful development on the palate leaves an impression of a very sweet, rich wine, which really needs to be cellared for four to five years before it can fully express itself alongside a blue cheese or foie gras.

☛ Lardeau, 25, chem. de Rouquette, 33210 Preignac, tel. 05.56.76.11.81, e-mail yvan.lardeau@laposte.com ☑
🍷 by appt.

CH. RAYMOND-LAFON 1999★★

	15.2 ha	21,000	🎗	38–46 €

This estate, surrounded by vineyards belonging to various *crus classés*, possesses a fine terroir. Its quality is proved by this wine, whose elegance is visible in the pale gold colour and perceptible in the bouquet's notes of roasting and flowers (acacia). The palate gets off to a supple start, with round, sweet flavours, before moving on to richer flavours of melon jam and crystallized lemon. The long grilled finish reveals a strong oakiness, but it is of excellent quality and needs only time to blend in. A lovely wine to come, for those with patience.

☛ Famille Meslier, Ch. Raymond-Lafon, 33210 Sauternes, tel. 05.56.63.21.02, fax 05.56.63.19.58, e-mail famille.meslier@chateau-raymond-lafon.fr ☑
🍷 by appt.

CH. RAYNE VIGNEAU 2000★

	1er cru clas. 76 ha	96,300	🎗	23–30 €

85 86 |88| |89| |90| |91| 92 94 |95| |96| 97 98 99 00

Did the onyx and agates found on this estate come from Atlantis, as some authors have suggested? One can always dream. Imagination is not required to discover the charm of this wine which, even if it cannot compete with last year's 99, a *coup de coeur*, is nonetheless a lovely fresh, tender wine. Although the effects of noble rot are fairly discernible, more especially noticeable are the notes of cinnamon and mandarin orange. Reserve this wine to drink with poultry.

☛ SC du Ch. de Rayne Vigneau, La Croix Bacalan, 109, rue Achard, BP 154, 33042 Bordeaux Cedex, tel. 05.56.11.29.00, fax 05.56.11.29.01
🍷 by appt.

CH. RIEUSSEC 2000★★

	1er cru clas. n.c.	35,000	🎗	46–76 €

62 67 70 71 |75| |76| |78| 79 80 81 82 83 84 85 |86| 87 |88| 89 90 92 |94| |95| 96 97 98 99 00

The entire team of Château Rieussec, which also looks after the destiny of the superb Lafite-Rothschild at Pauillac, is very attentive to the quality of its terroir and applies the strictest rules in regard to the environment. That does the wine no harm at all, as this 2000 readily shows. It is an opulent, generous wine, certainly powerful, rich and mellow. It is also unctuous and truly elegant, as the bouquet's fine notes of beeswax and fresh fruits demonstrate. The palate is lively, rich and sweet. It is a real cellar wine, but, as one taster pointed out, it can be drunk over an entire lifetime and one can start quite young! Delicate yet also powerful is the same producer's **Clos Labère 2000 (15–23 €)**, which is one-star rated.

☛ Ch. Rieussec, 33210 Fargues-de-Langon, tel. 01.53.89.78.00, fax 01.53.89.78.01 ☑
🍷 by appt.

CH. LA RIVIÈRE 2001★

	3 ha	8,000	🎗	15–23 €

Guillaume Réglat also produces other appellations on both banks of the Garonne. His 2001 Sauternes has a relatively discreet bouquet, but it has finesse and freshness (citrus fruit

and roasted notes). The attack is similar in vein, as is the very well-balanced palate, whose body is rich without being heavy and is elegantly accompanied by lemony notes.

☛ Guillaume Réglat, Ch. Cousteau, 33410 Monprimblanc, tel. 05.56.62.98.63, fax 05.56.62.17.98 ☑
🍷 by appt.

CH. ROMER DU HAYOT 1999★

	2e cru clas. 16 ha	23,600	🍾🎗♨	15–23 €

75 76 79 81 82 |83| |85| |86| 88 89 90 91 93 |95| |96| |97| 98 99

This wine, grown on a fine outcrop of gravelly clay, is a blend of 5% Muscadelle, with 25% Sauvignon and 70% Sémillon. Discreetly botrytized and rich, its personality comes through in delightful honey and multi-floral perfumes, as well as in crystallized fruit flavours of orange, apricot and angelica.

☛ SCE Vignobles du Hayot, Ch. Andoyse, 33720 Barsac, tel. 05.56.27.15.37, fax 05.56.27.04.24, e-mail vignoblesduhayot@aol.com ☑
🍷 by appt.
☛ A. du Hayot

CH. SAINT-VINCENT 2001★★

	8.03 ha	3,600	🎗	23–30 €

This cru, which overlaps the Barsac–Sauternes boundary, has produced a wine with a beautiful copper colour. The bouquet is as smooth as one could wish, with notes of broom-flowers, honey and *pain d'épice* (spice loaf); the palate has excellent body and a well-judged oakiness (vanilla and grilling). At once lively and rich, it develops well through to a very well-blended finish.

☛ SCEA Vignobles Francis Desqueyroux et Fils, 1, rue Pourière, 33720 Budos, tel. 05.56.76.62.67, fax 05.56.76.66.92, e-mail vign.fdesqueyroux@wanadoo.fr ☑
🍷 by appt.

CH. SIGALAS RABAUD 2001★★

	1er cru clas. 13.37 ha	n.c.	🎗	15–23 €

66 75 76 81 82 83 85 |86| 87 |88| |89| 90 91 92 94 (95) |9 6| 97 98 |99| 00 01

This cru, in the heart of the appellation, was established in the 17th century. It is worked by the team at Lafaurie-Peyraguey, and has yielded this wine which fulfils all the promises implied by its straw-yellow appearance. The bouquet is a cross between apricot purée and whole-apricot conserve, while the body has been perfectly respected and worked so as to give generously yet without sacrificing the freshness of the whole. This well-integrated, characterful wine will age well.

☛ Ch. Sigalas-Rabaud, 33210 Bommes, tel. 05.56.11.29.00, fax 05.56.11.29.01
☛ de Lambert des Granges

CH. SUDUIRAUT 1999★★

	1er cru clas. 90 ha	n.c.	🎗	38–46 €

(67) 75 82 |83| 85 86 |88| |89| (90) |96| (97) 99

The 17th century charterhouse, flanked by high pavilions, is certainly not without interest. The essential is, however, elsewhere, in the French-style gardens designed by Le Nôtre. Already tasted last year, this 99 has undergone major evolution since. The relative shyness which it displayed because of its youth has now completely disappeared, and from behind its finesse and good breeding it is revealing superb potential. Supported by its beautifully rich, sweet structure, it calls for 15 years' cellaring or even longer, even if its freshness and aromatic complexity (toast, dried apricot, crystallized fruits) make it already tempting.

☛ Ch. Suduiraut, 33210 Preignac, tel. 05.56.63.61.90, fax 05.56.63.61.93, e-mail infochato@suduiraut.com
🍷 by appt.
☛ Axa Millésimes

LES CHARMILLES DE TOUR BLANCHE 2000★

	37.92 ha	31,457	🎗	15–23 €

Made up of outcrops of gravel surrounded by damp areas (the forest and the Ciron), the terroir of La Tour Blanche is one of fine quality. This *cru classé* chose not to produce a first wine from the 2000 harvest. All the same, its second is very good. The bouquet has delicate scents of acacia and apple; the palate is round and rich. The balance between a degree of sucrosity on the one hand and acidity on the other makes it a classic Sauternes that will suit foie gras.

➤ Ch. La Tour Blanche, 33210 Bommes,
tel. 05.57.98.02.73, fax 05.57.98.02.78,
e-mail tour-blanche@tour-blanche.com ☑
𝗬 by appt.
➤ Ministère de l'Agriculture

CH. LES TUILERIES 1996★

	3 ha	2,400	🍷	11–15 €

Made by the same producer as Château Brondelle (Graves), this wine deploys a complex bouquet (preserves, under-growth, spices, quince jelly with a zest of honey). After a soft start, the palate broadens out and develops delightful flavours of crystallized fruits, while retaining a good balance between sweetness and acidity.

➤ Vignobles Belloc-Rochet, Ch. Brondelle, 33210 Langon,
tel. 05.56.62.38.14, fax 05.56.62.23.14,
e-mail chateau.brondelle@wanadoo.fr ☑
𝗬 ev. day except Sat. Sun. 8.30am–12 noon 2pm–6pm

CH. VALGUY 2001★

	4.16 ha	6,000	🍷	15–23 €

The house is old and possesses a 16th century fireplace. The wine combines power with finesse and complexity. After a well-structured attack, the palate reveals its richness of con-struction and verve. It will become better integrated after three or four years' cellaring.

➤ SCEA Grands vignobles Loubrie, 4, chem. de Couitte, 33210 Preignac, tel. 05.56.63.58.25, fax 05.56.63.58.25 ☑
𝗬 ev. day 8am–8pm

CH. D'YQUEM 1998★★★

	1er cru sup. n.c.	n.c.	🍷	+76 €

21 29 37 42 |45| 53 55 59⟨67⟩70 71 |75| |76| 80 |82| |83| |84| |85| |86| |87| |88| 89 |90| |91| 93 |94|⟨95⟩⟨96⟩⟨97⟩98

Having entered the patrimony of the Lur-Saluces family by marriage in 1785, this superb fortified manor-house remained a family property until it was bought by the LVMH group in April 1999. Alexandre de Lur-Saluces has remained the man in charge. This year, 1998, is worthy of the lineage of the "King of Wines". Its bright-golden colour heralds the bouquet, which begins with delicate notes of linden blossom, cinnamon and verbena, passes to scents of citrus fruits, lemon zest, and fruit jelly, before the entry on the scene of aromas more in a roasted style. As soon as the wine hits the palate, it shows its seductiveness, then goes on to reveal all its harmony. All this has great elegance, but finesse is not the only card that this great wine can play. Fullness, generosity, richness of structure come to complete the picture. The finish does not finish; one leaves the tasting with the tongue impregnated with multiple flavours (vanilla, flowers, very ripe fruits). Even so, this superb Sauternes still needs a few more years in the cellar before it reaches its full potential. Though it deserves to be drunk on its own, it may also accompany a gourmet course of fish in sauce.

➤ Comte Alexandre de Lur-Saluces, Ch. d'Yquem,
33210 Sauternes, tel. 05.57.98.07.07, fax 05.57.98.07.08,
e-mail info@yquem.fr
𝗬 by appt.
➤ LVMH

Wines selected but not starred

CH. L'AGNET LA CARRIERE 2001

	5 ha	3,300	🍷	23–30 €

➤ Laurent Mallard, Ch. Naudonnet Plaisance, 33760 Escoussans, tel. 05.56.23.93.04, fax 05.57.34.40.78, e-mail l.mallard@wanadoo.fr ☑
𝗬 by appt.

CLOS L'ABEILLEY 2001

	76.24 ha	37,742	🍶	15–23 €

➤ SC du Ch. de Rayne Vigneau, La Croix Bacalan, 109, rue Achard, BP 154, 33042 Bordeaux Cedex, tel. 05.56.11.29.00, fax 05.56.11.29.01
𝗬 by appt.

CH. DOISY-VEDRINES 2000

	2e cru clas.	27 ha	18,000	🍷	30–38 €

70 75 76 81⟨83⟩85 |86| |88| 90 92 94 |95| 97 98 00

➤ SC Doisy-Védrines, 33720 Barsac, tel. 05.56.27.15.13, fax 05.56.27.26.76
𝗬 by appt.

RESERVE DULONG 2001

	50 ha	100,000	🍶 ⚭	11–15 €

➤ Dulong Frères et Fils, 29, rue Jules-Guesde, 33270 Floirac, tel. 05.56.86.51.15, fax 05.56.40.66.41, e-mail dulong@dulong.com
𝗬 by appt.

CH. FILHOT 2000

	2e cru clas.	22 ha	33,000	🍶🍷	15–23 €

81 82 83 85 86 88 89 91 92 |95| |96| 97 98 99 |00|

➤ SCEA du Ch. Filhot, 33210 Sauternes, tel. 05.56.76.61.09, fax 05.56.76.67.91, e-mail filhot@filhot.com
𝗬 by appt.
➤ Famille de Vaucelles

CH. LAFON 2001

	12 ha	5,000	🍷	15–23 €

➤ Fauthoux, Ch. Lafon, 33210 Sauternes, tel. 05.56.63.30.82, fax 05.56.63.30.82 ☑
𝗬 by appt.

CH. LAMOURETTE 2000

	10 ha	4,300	🍶	15–23 €

➤ Anne-Marie Léglise, Ch. Lamourette, 33210 Bommes, tel. 05.56.76.63.58, fax 05.56.76.60.85, e-mail leglise@terre-net.fr ☑
𝗬 by appt.

CH. LANGE-REGLAT

Cuvée spéciale 2001

	12 ha	40,000	❶❶		15–23 €

✦┐ Bernard Réglat, Ch. de La Mazerolle,
33410 Monprimblanc, tel. 05.56.62.98.63,
fax 05.56.62.17.98,
e-mail reglat.bernard@wanadoo.fr ✅
🍷 by appt.

CH. MAYNE DU HAYOT 2000

	8 ha	12,300	❚❶❶⚲		11–15 €

✦┐ Ch. Le Mayne, 33720 Barsac, tel. 05.56.27.15.37,
fax 05.56.27.04.24,
e-mail vignoblesduhayot@aol.com ✅

CH. DU MONT

Cuvée Jeanne 2001

	0.54 ha	1,600	❶❶		11–15 €

✦┐ Vignobles Chouvac, Ch. du Mont,
33410 Sainte-Croix-du-Mont, tel. 05.56.62.07.65,
fax 05.56.62.07.58 ✅
🍷 by appt.

CH. LA PELOUE 2001

	4 ha	10,000	❚❶❶		11–15 €

✦┐ Vincent Labouille, Ch. de Crabitan,
33410 Sainte-Croix-du-Mont, tel. 05.56.62.01.78,
fax 05.56.76.71.17, e-mail mlabouille@aol.fr ✅
🍷 by appt.
✦┐ D. Elichondo

CH. SIMON 2001

	17 ha	24,000	❚❶❶⚲		15–23 €

✦┐ EARL Dufour, Ch. Simon, 33720 Barsac,
tel. 05.56.27.15.35, fax 05.56.27.24.79,
e-mail chateau.simon@worldonline.fr ✅
🍷 by appt.

CH. VILLEFRANCHE 2001

	12 ha	20,000	❚❶❶⚲		11–15 €

✦┐ Benoît Guinabert, Ch. Villefranche, 33720 Barsac,
tel. 05.56.27.05.77, fax 05.56.27.33.02 ✅
🍷 by appt.

BURGUNDY

"**A**miable and vinous Burgundy," wrote the historian Michelet, and no wine-lover could fail to subscribe to his view. Around the world, Bordeaux, Champagne and Burgundy epitomize everything that's best in French fine wine, just as all are associated with the best in French gastronomy. The sheer variety of the wines from these three regions can satisfy every taste and complement the finest food.

In Burgundy the world of wine is more intricately involved with daily life than in any other wine-growing region: the culture and character of Burgundy and the Burgundians have been forged by the unchanging rhythms of the winemaking year. From the edge of the Auxerrois to the hills of Beaujolais, throughout the length and breadth of a province that connects the two great cities of Paris and Lyon, vines and wines have been a way of life, and a good life at that, since antiquity. Gaston Roupnel was a Burgundian author who wrote a history of the French countryside. He was also a winemaker in Gevrey-Chambertin and, according to him, the vine was introduced into Gaul in the 6th century BC "through Switzerland and the mountain passes of the Jura," ultimately being successfully cultivated on the slopes of the Saône and Rhône valleys. Other writers believe that Greek colonists in the Midi were responsible for introducing the cultivation of grapes to southern Gaul and thereafter bringing the knowledge north with trade. However, no-one can challenge the fact that vine cultivation quickly became very important in the Burgundy region, as some of the early reliefs exhibited in the archaeological museum in Dijon bear witness. And when, in the 4th century AD, the orator Eumenus addressed the Emperor Constantine at Autun, he eulogized the vines cultivated around Beaune as already "admirable and ancient".

In the Middle Ages the now long-established Burgundy wine trade was further re-shaped by a revolution in agricultural methods, in which the monks and the monastic movements of Cluny and Cîteaux played a vital role. Burgundy's vineyards gradually developed their mosaic of *climats*, or plots of ground, and their crus, while growers constantly aimed to improve the quality and individuality of their incomparable wines. During the reigns of the four dukes of Burgundy (1342–1477), rules were laid down to ensure that the high quality of the wines was maintained. Throughout the turbulent centuries that followed, Burgundian wines consistently remained at the forefront of reputation and quality, a position continued into modern times.

It is worth noting that not all wines produced today in the administrative region of Burgundy are, in fact, Burgundies. In the Nièvre department (administratively part of Burgundy, as are the departments of the Côte d'Or, the Yonne and the Saône-et-Loire) the vineyards of Pouilly-sur-Loire belong to the vineyards of central France and the Loire valley. In addition, the Rhône department, which in terms of judicial and administrative authority belongs to Burgundy, is home to the Beaujolais area. The Beaujolais wine region is usually treated as an autonomous entity – except in commercial terms – because it grows a specific grape variety, the Gamay (see below). This is the approach followed by this guide (see the section on Beaujolais). So Burgundy is understood to mean the vineyards of the Yonne (lower Burgundy), the Côte d'Or and the Saône-et-Loire, even though some wines produced in Beaujolais can also be sold under the Appellation Régionale Bourgogne.

Disregarding Beaujolais, which is planted with Gamay, a variety with black skin and white flesh, Burgundy's character as a wine-growing area is dominated by two grape varieties: Chardonnay, which produces white wines, and Pinot Noir, which produces red wines. In addition there are some other minor varieties, either throwbacks to earlier winemaking practices or specific varieties to suit particular terroirs: Aligoté, for example, is a white grape producing the famous Bourgogne Aligoté, which is frequently used to make kir, a mixture of white wine and cassis (blackcurrant liqueur). The best quality Aligoté wines are produced in the small village of Bouzeron, very close to Chagny (Saône-et-Loire). The César, a red variety cultivated mainly in the region of Auxerre, is gradually falling from use. The Sacy produces Bourgogne Grand Ordinaire in the Yonne but is increasingly being replaced by Chardonnay. Gamay is used in Bourgogne Grand Ordinaire and is also mixed with Pinot Noir to make Bourgogne Passetoutgrain. Finally, Sauvignon, the famous aromatic grape variety planted in the vineyards of Sancerre and Pouilly-sur-Loire, is also grown in the region of Saint-Bris-le-Vineux in the Yonne. Currently bottled as AOVDQS Sauvignon de Saint-Bris, this wine is likely to become a recognized AOC in the near future.

Burgundy has a relatively uniform climate. It is mainly semi-continental (hot summers, cold winters) but is also affected by the Atlantic maritime climate, which reaches as far east as the edge of the Paris Basin. Thus it is the soil rather than climatic variations that gives the large number of wines grown in Burgundy their individual characteristics. As a rule, the vineyards are small plots of land mainly sited on a variety of outcrops of quite different geological origins, which can occur virtually side by side; these are the source of the rich palette of scents and flavours of the Burgundy crus. According to the specific chemical structure of the rock formation in each *climat*, or individual part of a vineyard, different wines with highly individual characteristics may be produced within a single appellation, thus complicating the overall classification and presentation of the Grands Vins de Bourgogne…These *climats*, which often have particularly evocative names (La Renarde, Les Cailles, Genevrières, Clos de la Maréchale, Clos des Ormes, Montrecul), have existed since at least the 18th century. They are only a few hectares in size, and sometimes only several *ouvrées* (1 ouvrée = 428 m2) and correspond to a "natural entity which can be identified because of the specific character of the wine it produces" (A. Vedel). You can, in fact, see that there is sometimes less difference between two vines several hundred metres apart but in the same *climat* than there is between two neighbouring vines in two different *climats*.

There are four levels of appellation in the hierarchy of Burgundy wines: Appellation Régionale (56% of the production), Villages (or Appellation Communale) de Bourgogne, Premier Cru (12%) and Grand Cru (2%, consisting of 33 Grand Crus listed in the Côte d'Or and Chablis). The number of legally defined terroirs or *climats* is very high; for example, 27 different denominations for the Premiers Crus are harvested in the commune of Nuits-Saint-Georges, all from barely a hundred hectares!

Recent scientific studies have confirmed earlier empirical observations about the relationship between the soils and the *lieux-dits* (names in common usage that identify a place) that gave rise to the appellations, the crus and the *climats*. Thus, for example, 59 different soil types can be identified by their external structure and physical chemistry (slope, stoniness, amount of clay and so on), all of which happen to match up with the boundaries between Grand Cru, Premier Cru, Villages and Régionale appellations.

Put more simply, and taking a more general geographical approach, it is usual to divide Burgundy's wine-growing area into four distinct zones: going from north to south these are the vineyards of the Yonne (or Basse Bourgogne), the Côte d'Or (Côte de Nuits and Côte de Beaune), the Côte Chalonnaise and the Mâconnais.

The Chablis vineyards are the best-known vineyards of the Yonne. Chablis wines were held in high esteem by the Parisian court in medieval times, when river transport made it easy to sell the wines in the capital. Indeed, for a long time the wines of the Yonne were thought of as the wines of Burgundy. Nestling in the charming valley of the River Serein, the town of Noyers its medieval jewel, the Chablis vineyard is like a remote satellite 100 km northwest of the heart of the main Burgundy vineyard. The Chablis AOC area is quite spread out, covering more than 4,500 ha of hilly slopes of varied aspect, where a "constellation of hamlets and a scattering of farms share the harvest of this dry, light, lively, delicately perfumed wine whose astonishing limpidity, lightly flecked with gold and green, delights the eye" (P. Poupon). Ten communes stretch south from Auxerre in the Auxerrois; in the vineyards of Irancy there are still a few hectares planted with César, a variety that gives very tannic wines. Along with Coulanges-la-Vineuse, Irancy is undergoing rapid expansion. Saint-Bris-les-Vineux is Sauvignon country and shares the production of white wines with Chitry.

Three other vineyards in the Yonne were almost completely destroyed by phylloxera, although efforts are currently being made to revive them. Joigny, in the extreme northwest of Burgundy, covers an area of barely ten hectares, but the vineyards are laid out on the hills surrounding the town and overlooking the River Yonne. A *vin gris*, which is an Appellation Bourgogne, is produced mainly for local consumption in addition to red and white wines. The vineyard of Tonnerre, on the approach to Epineuil, was once as famous as that of Auxerre; custom allows an Appellation Bourgogne-Epineuil. Finally, a small vineyard on the slopes of the celebrated hill at Vézelay, where the grand dukes of Burgundy themselves once owned a vineyard, has been back in production since 1979. These wines, sold as Appellation Bourgogne, should continue to benefit from the crowds of visitors to Vézelay's famous Romanesque basilica, which was once a place of pilgrimage.

The arid eroded limestone of the Langres plateau is the traditional invasion route from the northeast, both in the past and for today's tourists. It separates the Chablisien, the Auxerrois and the Tonnerrois from the Côte d'Or, the so-called "hillside of purple and gold," more simply referred to as "La Côte," which is the product of complex geological events in the remote past. During the Tertiary era, following the formation of the Alps, the Bresse Sea covered the region, pounding the ancient Hercynian mountains of the Morvan. This ancient sea drained away over the millennia, depositing a variety of sedimentary limestone soils. There are also numerous parallel north-south faults dating from the birth of the Alps; the great Tertiary glaciations flowed from north to south, while combes were later hollowed out by powerful torrents. The result has given us an extraordinary variety of quite different subsoils lying cheek by jowl beneath a shallow uniform layer of arable topsoil. From this underlying geology flows the abundance of appellations, which are largely determined by their soils, and the even larger number of *climats*, which define the mosaic more minutely.

From the geographical point of view, the Côte runs for about 50 km from Dijon to Dezize-lès-Maranges in the north of the Saône-et-Loire. For the most part, the hillside faces the rising sun, essential for Grands Crus in a semi-continental climate, then slopes down from the higher plateau, indented by the vineyards of the Hautes Côtes, and continues as far as the agricultural land of the Saône plain.

The Côte is a long, narrow feature with an excellent east-southeasterly aspect. It is traditionally divided into several sectors. The first, in the north, has been overwhelmed by the encroaching suburbs of Dijon (this is the Chenôve commune). Ever faithful to tradition, the town council of Dijon has replanted a parcel of land in the very heart of town. The next sector, the Côte de Nuits, starts at Marsannay and goes down to Clos des Langres in the commune of Corgoloin. It is a narrow hill, only a matter of a few hundred metres wide, interrupted by alpine woods and outcrops of rock weathered by cold, dry winds. This hillside produces 29 appellations, each with its own place in the hierarchy of crus, and the village names form a roll of honour: Gevrey-Chambertin, Chambolle-Musigny, Vosne-Romanée, Nuits-Saint-Georges and so on. The Premiers Crus and the Grands Crus (the highest class) include Chambertin, Clos de la Roche, Musigny and Clos de

Vougeot; these are to be found higher up the hillside, between 240 and 320 m. The largest number of outcrops of marly limestone is to be found here among the various different types of scree, producing the best structured of the red Burgundies, which can be kept for a long time.

Next comes the more temperate Côte de Beaune, which broadens to a depth of one or two kms. It receives moist winds, which encourage the grapes to mature more quickly. The Côte de Beaune is geologically more homogeneous than the Côte de Nuits; the lower part of the plateau is nearly horizontal, formed from layers of soft limestone, clay or shale covered by vividly coloured earth. These are the fairly deep soils in which the great red wines are grown (Beaune Grèves, Pommard Epenots and so forth). To the south of the Côte de Beaune, banks of oolitic limestone under hard limestone marl, covered with débris and scree and overlaid with limestone, give pebbly, gravelly soils, which produce the most prestigious Burgundy whites, the Premiers and Grands Crus from the communes of Meursault, Puligny-Montrachet and Chassagne-Montrachet. If people here talk of a "côte des rouges" (red wine area) and a "côte des blancs" (white wine area), between the two is the Volnay vineyard, which must be given special mention. It is planted on stony, clay and limestone soils that produce red wines of great finesse.

In the Côte de Beaune the vines are planted higher up than in the Côte de Nuits, to 400 m and sometimes higher still. The hillside is sliced through by wide combes, particularly at Pernand-Vergelesses, where the combe seems to cut the famous Corton mountain off from the rest of the Côte.

In the last 30 years sections of the Hautes Côtes have been gradually replanted to produce Appellations Régionales Bourgognes Hautes Côtes de Nuits and Bourgogne Hautes Côtes de Beaune. The Aligoté grows at its best here, and the terroir shows off the wine's freshness to advantage. Other terroirs make excellent red wines from Pinot Noir, and these are characterized by scents of soft fruits such as raspberry and blackcurrant, which are also locally grown Burgundy specialities.

The countryside opens out somewhat in the Côte Chalonnaise, which covers 4,500 ha. The linear structure of the basic relief softens into low-rising hills, which extend further to the west of the Saône valley. The geological structure differs again from the vineyards of the Côte d'Or; the soil rests on Jurassic limestone, on marl from the same period or even earlier or on sedimentary terrain made up of sandstone, limestone and marl. Red wines are produced from Pinot Noir in Mercurey, Givry and Rully, but the same communes also make white wines from Chardonnay, as does Montagny. Bouzeron, home of a highly reputable Aligoté, is also to be found here. There is a noteworthy vineyard on the way to Couches, which is dominated by its medieval château. The Romanesque churches and ancient estates of the region are worth a visit and any tourist itinerary can easily be combined with a route through the vineyards.

The range of hills in the Mâconnais, with 5,700 ha of vineyards, opens up wide horizons where white Charolais cattle speckle the green meadows. The countryside was dear to the poet Lamartine – he came from Milly, a wine-producing village where he owned vineyards – and it is geologically simpler than the Chalonnais. The sedimentary soils from the Triassic and Jurassic periods are scored by east-west faults. Some 20% of the wines are Appellations Communales and 80% are Appellations Régionales (Mâcon white and Mâcon red). The highest quality white wines are made from Chardonnay grapes, planted on dark lime-rich soil on the slopes at Pouilly, Solutré and Vergisson, which have a particularly good, sunny aspect; the wines are remarkable for their appearance and their capacity to keep a long time. Appellation Bourgogne reds and rosés are made from Pinot Noir, while the black-skinned Gamay with white juice produces the Mâcons that are harvested lower down the hills or on less well-exposed, flinty, alluvial soils with good drainage.

No matter how essential the local geology and climatic conditions may be, no picture of wine-growing in Burgundy would be complete without recognizing the contribution that human effort makes to the vineyards and wines. The winemakers have a deep attachment to their land, and in some villages the family names of many owners can be traced back for five hundred years. By the same token, some of the shipping companies were founded as long ago as the 18th century.

The Burgundy vineyard is divided into family-owned plots (domains), which cover very small areas. So a domain of four or five ha in, say, Nuits-Saint-Georges, can provide an adequate living for a worker and his family. It is rare to find producers who own and cultivate more than about ten ha: for example, the illustrious Clos-Vougeot covers 50 ha and is divided among 70 owners. This parcelling up of the ownership of *climats* results in a greater diversity of wines and leads to a healthy rivalry among producers. In Burgundy a tasting will often consist of comparing two wines made from the same grape variety and from the same appellation but coming from different *climats*, or two wines made from the same grape and the same *climat* but from different years. Thus, in Burgundy, two basic elements must constantly be kept in mind when tasting the wines: the cru, or *climat*, and the year of the vintage; you must also allow for the personal touch of the wine-grower who makes them. From the technical point of view, Burgundian winemakers are keen to maintain traditional methods, although this does not mean they are resistant to modernization. As a result, the mechanization of viticulture has developed, and many winemakers have benefited greatly from new equipment and techniques. However, some traditions remain unchallenged by wine-growers and shippers alike, and one of the best examples is the maturing of wines in oak barrels.

There are 3,500 domaines registered as dedicated solely to vines. They represent two-thirds of the 24,000 ha making Appellation d'Origine wines. Nineteen cooperatives are listed: the cooperative movement is very active in Chablis and the Côte Chalonnaise, and particularly so in the Mâconnais (13

Burgundy

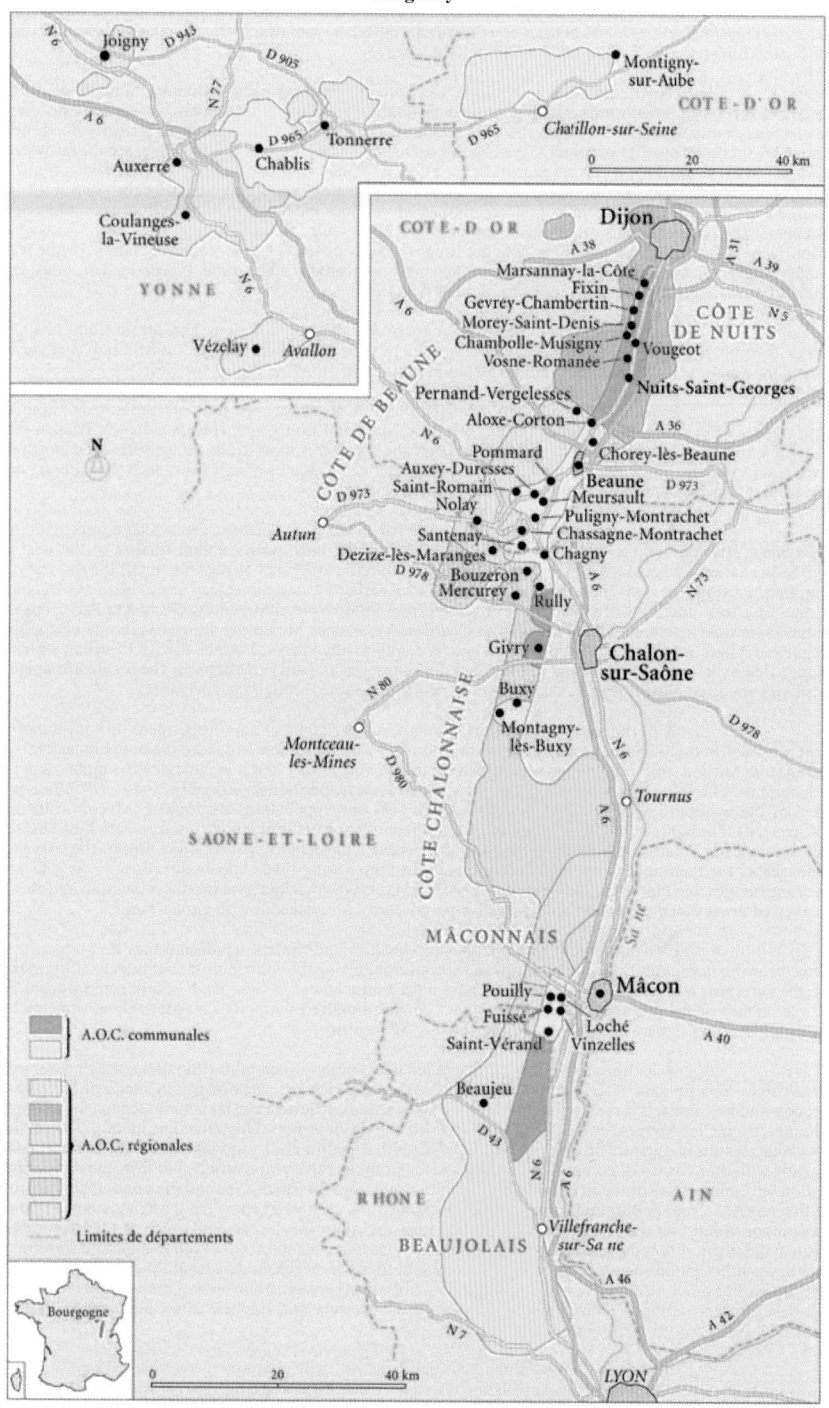

Joigny D 943
D 905
Montigny-sur-Aube
N 77
CÔTE-D'OR
A 6
Tonnerre
D 965
D 965
Châtillon-sur-Seine
Auxerre
Chablis
Coulanges-la-Vineuse
YONNE
N 6
Vézelay Avallon

N

CÔTE-D'OR
Dijon
A 38
A 31
A 39
Marsannay-la-Côte
Fixin
CÔTE
N 5
Gevrey-Chambertin
DE NUITS
Morey-Saint-Denis
Chambolle-Musigny
Vougeot
Vosne-Romanée
A 6
Pernand-Vergelesses
Nuits-Saint-Georges
Aloxe-Corton
A 36
CÔTE DE BEAUNE
Pommard
Chorey-lès-Beaune
Auxey-Duresses
Beaune D 973
D 973
Saint-Romain
Meursault
Nolay
Puligny-Montrachet
Autun
Santenay
Chassagne-Montrachet
Dezize-lès-Maranges
Chagny
D 978
Bouzeron
Mercurey
Rully
A 6
N 73
Givry
Chalon-sur-Saône
N 80
Buxy
CÔTE CHALONNAISE
Montagny-lès-Buxy
N 6
D 978
Montceau-les-Mines
D 980
SAÔNE-ET-LOIRE
Tournus
A 6
Saône
MÂCONNAIS
Pouilly
Mâcon
Fuissé
Loché A 40
Saint-Vérand
Vinzelles
A.O.C. communales
Beaujeu
D 43
A.O.C. régionales
N 6
A 6
RHÔNE
AIN
Limites de départements
BEAUJOLAIS
Villefranche-sur-Saône
A 46
A 42
Bourgogne
N 7
LYON
0   20   40 km

354

cellars). They produce about 25% of the wines. Since the 18th century an important role has been played by the *négociants-éleveurs*, the merchants who buy wine from the grower and bring it on to bottling age in their own cellars. They sell more than 60% of the wine produced and own 35% of the total area of the Grands Crus of the Côte de Beaune. On their domains the merchants produce 8% of all the wine produced in Burgundy. This represents an average of 180 million bottles (105 million white and 75 million red) and generates a turnover of two million euros. Total exports approximate 3,000,000 hl.

The importance of bringing on a wine (how it develops from its early youth to its optimum quality before it is bottled) demonstrates the significance of the *négociant-éleveur* to the system; in addition to being responsible for the sale of the wine, he also takes on a technical role. This technical and marketing knowledge lies at the heart of the harmonious professional relationship that has developed between wine-growers and merchants.

The Bureau Interprofessionnel des Vins de Bourgogne (BIVB), which initiates developments in the technical, economic and promotional fields, has three "listening posts" at Mâcon, Beaune and Chablis. In 1934 the University of Burgundy was the first establishment in France, at least at university level, to set up and run courses in oenology and to offer a technical diploma. At the same time, the Confrérie des Chevaliers du Tastevin was founded to promote the reputation of Burgundy wines around the world. Its headquarters are at the Château du Clos-Vougeot and, with other local confréries, it makes a great contribution to keeping regional traditions alive. Without question, one of the most brilliant events is the auction sales in the Hospices de Beaune, first held in 1851. This is the meeting place of the international wine élite and the exchange for establishing the value of the Grands Crus. Together with the assembly of the Confrérie and the "Paulée" in Meursault, the sale is one of the "three glorious days of wine". But the whole of Burgundy knows how to celebrate wine joyously, be it from a 228-litre hogshead or from a bottle. It does not take much to love Burgundy and its wines; it is simply a "region that you can take away in your glass".

Appellations Régionales Bourgogne

The Appellation Régionale Bourgogne and the Appellation Bourgogne Grand Ordinaire, together with their related off-shoots or equivalents, account for the largest area of Burgundy's vineyards. They can be produced in the traditional wine communes of the department of the Yonne, the Côte d'Or, the Saône-et-Loire and the canton of Villefranche-sur-Saône in the Rhône. The average production amounts to 500,000 hl.

The registration of land use and, more specifically, the definition of the terroirs by establishing the borders of the parcels of land within the vineyards, created a hierarchy of appellations régionales. The Appellation Bourgogne Grand Ordinaire is the most common and the most productive in the areas defined. Using specified vines, Bourgogne Aligoté, Bourgogne Passetoutgrain and Crémant de Bourgogne are also produced in the same areas.

BOURGOGNE

The production area of this appellation is vast if you take into account the names of the different sub-regions (Hautes Côtes, Côte Chalonnaise) or of the villages (Irancy, Chitry and Epineuil) that can be added, each of which is a separate entity and is listed here as such. Given the extent of this appellation, it is not surprising that producers should have sought to personalize their wines and to persuade the regulator that the area of origin should be individually identified. In the Châtillon area, which is in the Côte d'Or, the name of

Massingy has been used in this way, even though the original vineyard has practically disappeared. More recently (and now as a matter of course) the winemakers on the banks of the Yonne use the name of the village and add it after the words "Appellation Bourgogne". This is the case in Saint-Bris, the Côtes d'Auxerre on the right bank of the river and in Coulanges-la-Vineuse on the left bank.

The white-wine producers make wine from Chardonnay vines, which are still known as Beaunois in the Yonne region. The Pinot Blanc, although referred to in the official texts and formerly grown more widely in the Hautes Côtes de Bourgogne, has now practically disappeared. In the past it was often confused with Chardonnay

The Pinot Noir is king amongst the reds and rosés. Unfortunately, the Pinot Beurot grape has largely fallen from favour because it contained insufficient colour; it used to add remarkable finesse to red wines. In some years the volumes of wine declared can be augmented by wines that are downgraded from the Beaujolais Appellations Communales: Brouilly, Côte de Brouilly, Chénas, Chiroubles, Fleurie, Juliénas, Morgon, Moulin-à-Vent and Saint-Amour. These wines are made from the black Gamay grape only and have different characteristics. The production of rosé wines can increase in cool years when the grapes do not ripen well or when there is a great deal of grey rot, and they can be declared as Appellation Bourgogne Rosé or Bourgogne Clairet.

To make things more difficult, some labels have the name of the *lieu-dit* (a name in common usage that identifies a place) where the wine was produced, in addition to the Appellation Bourgogne. Some old and reputable vineyards are examples justifing this practice: Chapitre à Chenôve and Des Montreculs keep alive names from the Dijon vineyards that are now smothered by the growth of the suburbs; another example is La Chapelle-Notre-Dame in Serrigny. As for the rest, some may be

Bourgogne

too easily confused with the Premiers Crus and may not always deserve the comparison.

DOM. DE L'ABBAYE DU PETIT QUINCY Epineuil 2001★

| | 13 ha | n.c. | ▪ ⑪ ♦ | | 5–8 € |

Built up by the Gruhier family since 1990, Petit Quincy is an old Cistercian abbey founded in 1212. This 2001 fully merits a place in your wine cellar where it will easily uphold the honour of the Tonnerrois: its deep colour precedes a still immature nose but some floral notes are perceptible. Pleasant, balanced, this is a wine which has successfully overcome this vintage's difficulties.
➧ Dominique Gruhier, rue du Clos-de-Quincy, 89700 Epineuil, tel. 03.86.55.32.51, fax 03.86.55.32.50, e-mail gruhier@domaine-abbaye.com ☑
☒ ev. day. 10am–6pm; Sun., Jan.–Mar. by appt.

BERTRAND AMBROISE
Cuvée Vieilles Vignes 2001★

| | n.c. | n.c. | | 8–11 € |

Cuvée Vieilles Vignes does not mean a great deal because there is no recognized definition of a "vielle vigne" (old vine), and cuttings are frequently planted out. That being so, this ruby-red wine is not the ordinary stuff one picks up on a Saturday morning at the Nuits market. The aroma is of red fruits. Firm attack, long on the palate, tannins and acidity complementing each other, all good indications that it will keep one to two years.
➧ Bertrand Ambroise, rue de l'Eglise, 21700 Premeaux-Prissey, tel. 03.80.62.30.19, fax 03.80.62.38.69, e-mail bertrand.ambroise@wanadoo.fr ☑
☒ by appt.

BAILLY-LAPIERRE
Côtes d'Auxerre 2002★★★

| | n.c. | 22,000 | ▪ ♦ | 5–8 € |

The Bailly Cooperative does not only produce sparkling wines. This Chardonnay is by far the best of the Côtes d'Auxerre. Pale yellow with green highlights, its nose contains notes of fresh butter and it is progressing well on the palate. Rich, aromatic, very smooth, one could keep it for a while or give oneself the early pleasure of its honest quality to price ratio. This is a 2002 that has put its best foot forward. Excellent to drink with hot entrées. **white Bourgogne Chitry 2002 Bailly-Lapierre** awarded one star.
➧ Caves de Bailly, BP 3, 89530 Saint-Bris-le-Vieux, tel. 03.86.53.77.77, fax 03.86.53.80.94, e-mail home@caves-bailly.com ☑
☒ ev. day. 8am–12noon 2pm–6pm; Apr. to Oct. from 2.30pm–6pm

JEAN-BAPTISTE BEJOT 2001★★

| | n.c. | 20,000 | | 5–8 € |

Concentrated and radiant, this is a great Burgundy. Brilliant in colour, its aroma is pure honey. Its richness delights the palate. Does it come from Meursault, where this wine-merchant is established? Nothing is known, but it could well be. It has the kind of typical, pervasive Chardonnay opulence that is hard to resist.
➧ SA Jean-Baptiste Béjot, 21190 Meursault, tel. 03.80.21.22.45, fax 03.80.21.28.05

BERSAN ET FILS
Côtes d'Auxerre 2001★

| | n.c. | 6,000 | ▪ ⑪ ♦ | 5–8 € |

Family-owned for centuries, this estate is right in the centre of Saint-Bris and reflects the rich wine-producing history of the area. To drink once it has had time to mature, this 2001 is lively and vigorous with notes of citrus fruits. Yellow with gold highlights and perfectly limpid, it leaves a pleasant hint of minerality on the palate and a floral touch. It could well keep for two to three years
➧ SARL Bersan et Fils, 20, rue du Dr-Tardieux, 89530 Saint-Bris-le-Vieux, tel. 03.86.53.33.73, fax 03.86.53.38.45, e-mail bourgognes-bersan@wanadoo.fr ☑
☒ by appt.

DOM. GABRIEL BILLARD
Milliane 2000★

| | 0,7 ha | 2,000 | ⑪ | 8–11 € |

Milliane is the name of the grandmother of Laurence Jobord (oenologist to the Joseph Drouhin Company) and Mireille Desmonet, who own this estate. Made from the old vines located "at the foot of Pommard," this wine is true to type: brilliant cherry-red in colour, the nose is complex, and while not full on the palate it has a marked flavour of ripe fruit and a note of oak. Drink with grilled meat.
➧ SCEA Dom. Gabriel Billard, imp. de la Commaraine, 21630 Pommard, tel. 03.80.22.27.82, fax 03.85.49.49.02, e-mail domaine-gabriel.billard@wanadoo.fr ☑
☒ by appt.

DOM. BORGNAT
Coulanges-la-Vineuse Tête de cuvée 2000★★

| | 4 ha | 8,000 | ⑪ | 5–8 € |

Escolives is one of the most interesting archaeological sites in Burgundy: already in the time of the Gallo-Romans its vines and wines were highly regarded. The château is more recent, but the "fortified cellar" is worth a visit and an inn with guestrooms awaits your pleasure! An intense colour, this Coulanges needs to develop, but already it is soft and rounded on the palate, fresh, with a good complexity, showing plenty of potential. The oakiness is quite restrained.
➧ EARL Dom. Benjamin Borgnat, 1, rue de l'Eglise, 89290 Escolives-Sainte-Camille, tel. 03.86.53.35.28, fax 03.86.53.65.00, e-mail domaineborgnat@wanadoo.fr ☑ 🏠 🏠
☒ ev. day. 8am–8pm; Sun. by appt.

REGIS BOUVIER
Montre-Cul 2001★

| | 1.2 ha | 8,000 | ⑪ | 5–8 € |

Montre-Cul (literally, "show-backside") is the ancient name of a sloping *climat* located between Dijon and Chenôve, given to jokey labels, and this one is no exception. It is one of the rare burgundies to have official permission to use a geographical name (many do so without authorization). The ruby colour and fruitiness of this 2001, its robustness and texture represent much more than an animal curiosity: this Pinot Noir is among the best of the 2001 vintage.
➧ Régis Bouvier, 52, rue de Mazy, 21160 Marsannay-la-Côte, tel. 03.80.51.33.93, fax 03.80.58.75.07 ☑
☒ by appt.

JEAN-MARC BROCARD
Jurassique 2002★

| | n.c. | 40,000 | ▪ ♦ | 5–8 € |

Imaginative Jean-Marc Brocard borrows from geology names for his *cuvées*. Here we have the Jurassique Chablisien. The sentiment on the label is: "My wine draws its aroma from the earth." The wine is pleasing, limpid pale yellow, with aromas of citrus fruit (lemon, grapefruit). The natural, supple palate tends towards apples and pears. Ready to drink from now on.
➧ SARL Jean-Marc Brocard, 3, rte de Chablis, 89800 Préhy, tel. 03.86.41.49.00, fax 03.86.41.49.09, e-mail info@brocard.fr ☑
☒ ev. day. 9am–12.30pm 2pm–7pm

PASCAL BRULE
Vézelay Le Clos 2001★

| | 0.45 ha | 2,500 | ▪ ♦ | 5–8 € |

Jacques Lacarrière is a writer living at Sacy, and Pascal Brulé is a wine producer in the same village. Not to mention Rétif de La Breton who was the bad boy of the village! This wine has no defects, no weaknesses. Pale gold with green highlights, it has the look of a Chablis. Its bouquet is a skilful combination of newly-baked bread and green apples. Lively but well-balanced, it is like a Bach *suite for cello* recorded by Rostropovitch in the Basilica of the Madeleine at Vézelay.
➧ Pascal Brulé, 2, rue de Vézelay, 89270 Sacy, tel. 03.86.81.66.13, fax 03.86.81.66.13, e-mail brulepascal@wanadoo.fr ☑ 🏠
☒ by appt.

DOM. CARRE-COURBIN 2001★★

| | 3 ha | 5,000 | 🍷 | 5–8 € |

Wine-growers who are not also négociants are rare in Beaune. In 1996, Philippe and Maëlle had the good fortune to reacquire this family property, with its beautiful house, 500 m from the Hospices. For a burgundy, this wine has great keeping potential. A classic ruby colour, its bouquet presents quite ripe red berries against a background of vanilla. Still a little harsh, but with amazing structure and concentration. One can imagine how beautiful the grapes were.
↝ Dom. Carré-Courbin, 9, rue Celer, 21200 Beaune, tel. 03.80.24.67.62, fax 03.80.24.66.93, e-mail carre.courbin@wanadoo.fr
⚘ by appt.

PATRICK ET CHRISTINE CHALMEAU

Chitry 2001★★

| | 2.5 ha | 16,000 | 🍶 | 5–8 € |

This wine is among the best in its class. A splendid appearance. A very open, lemony aroma leads up to a sustained attack, vigorous and filled with fruit. The final touch of freshness is not in the least aggressive. An excellent white Chitry, to drink now or keep for one to two years.
↝ Patrick et Christine Chalmeau, 76, rue du Ruisseau, 89530 Chitry, tel. 03.86.41.43.71, fax 03.86.41.47.51, e-mail chalmeau.patrick@wanadoo.fr ☑
⚘ by appt.

CHAMPY

Signature 2001★

| | n.c. | n.c. | 🍷 | 8–11 € |

Dimitri Bazas (the oenologist at the Champy estate) offers this pale yellow burgundy made from the Chardonnay grape. On the nose it wavers between mirabelle plums and vanilla, before veering towards buttery aromas. While not very pronounced, the body is very well presented and of good account. Clean, lively, fresh and altogether quite rounded. Also worth noting is the **Signature 2001** red burgundy: it was put in the same category.
↝ Maison Champy, 5, rue du Grenier-à-Sel, 21200 Beaune, tel. 03.80.25.09.99, fax 03.80.25.09.95 ☑
⚘ by appt.
↝ Pierre Meurgey-Pierre Beuchet

PHILIPPE CHARLOPIN

Cuvée Prestige 2000★★

| | 2 ha | 10,000 | | 11–15 € |

Only one of the tasters did not want to give a *coup de coeur* to this bottle which could receive the *Mérite agricole* (agricultural merit), the greatly coveted "*poireau*." In the viticultural sense, naturally! And it is not the first time that Philippe Charlopin, pupil of Henri Jayer, has lurked in the vicinity of the *coup de coeur*, or been awarded it. This 2000 is a deep purple colour, with a superb appearance. Its bouquet is still closed (blackcurrant) but on the palate it is remarkable, rich and lingering: this is the Côte de Nuits and the tannins of the Pinot Noir are not to be taken lightly. Perfect from start to finish and clearly on a level with a cru.
↝ Dom. Philippe Charlopin, 18, rte de Dijon, 21220 Gevrey-Chambertin, tel. 03.80.51.81.18, fax 03.80.51.81.27, e-mail charlopin.philippe@wanadoo.fr

DOM. DU CHATEAU DE MEURSAULT

Clos du Château 2000★

| | 8 ha | 58,000 | 🍶🍷♦ | 11–15 € |

The Clos du Château is the work of André Boisseaux who has saved it from urbanization which had begun to creep in. This regional appellation is in the immediate vicinity of AOC Meursault, and is matured in these fabulous wine cellars. A very limpid 2000 vintage, with aromas of fern and fruit and a little balsamic note. Firm and well-structured, it is rich in secondary aromas. One will have to wait until 2004 to find out how it turns out.
↝ Dom. du Château de Meursault, 21190 Meursault, tel. 03.80.26.22.75, fax 03.80.26.22.76 ☑
⚘ by appt.

DOM. CHRISTIAN CLERGET 2000★★

| | 0.69 ha | 3,900 | 🍶🍷 | 5–8 € |

Coming from a 6-ha estate at Vougeot, this burgundy is not like the Compte d'Artois during the Restoration (of the Bourbons) who offered two fingers, for fear of wearing out the others…no, it offers you a whole hand. Fine, deep cherry-red in colour, it ranks among the best. Already integrated, it conveys an impression of youth and freshness while still being full of flavour. *Des oeufs en meurette* (eggs poached in red wine) will go admirably with it.
↝ SCEV Dom. Christian Clerget, 21640 Vougeot, tel. 03.80.62.87.37, fax 03.80.62.84.37 ☑
⚘ by appt.

BERNARD COILLOT PERE ET FILS 2001★

| | 0.8 ha | 2,400 | 🍷 | 8–11 € |

At Marsannay, the Coillots are the pillars that hold up the building, the winemaker's soul. Their wine will be ready next spring in time for the opening of the pike-fishing season. Apart from its yellow gold colour and orange-peel nose (with well-integrated oakiness), its richness and length on the palate are pleasing. A fine wine.
↝ Bernard Coillot Père et Fils, 31, rue du Château, 21160 Marsannay-la-Côte, tel. 03.80.52.17.59, fax 03.80.52.12.75, e-mail domaine.coillot@wanadoo.fr ☑
⚘ by appt.

DOM. DE LA COMBE

Tradition Vieilli en fût de chêne 1999★★

| | 6 ha | 13,000 | 🍷 | 8–11 € |

Here we are in the Cluny area and one naturally expects a burgundy that is all Roman architecture and rounded vaults. And this is what we have. Note the vintage (1999). Deep red, fruity and a little jammy, on account of its age, it shows power and concentration. And what fruit! Just like the market. Plenty of keeping quality but, in our opinion, one should seize the opportunity when it comes along, especially when it comes from a place close to Cluny and Taizé.
↝ Henri Lafarge, Dom. de La Combe, le Bourg, 71250 Bray, tel. 03.85.50.02.18, fax 03.85.50.05.37, e-mail henri.lafarge@wanadoo.fr ☑
⚘ by appt.

DOM. COSTE-CAUMARTIN 2001★★

| | 0.54 ha | 3,450 | 🍷 | 5–8 € |

This estate has been in the same family since 1793: the Coste-Caumartins are very known in the area not only for their wines but also for their contribution to gastronomy: they were manufacturers of cookers. As for this 2001 vintage, it seems to lack nothing. Delicate gold in colour with green highlights, honey, butter and hazelnut aromas mingle. On the palate it has what is known as a "good fleshiness". The fine, fruity and lively finish suggests waiting until Easter 2004 before drinking this wine.
↝ Dom. Coste-Caumartin, rue du Parc, 21630 Pommard, tel. 03.80.22.45.04, fax 03.80.22.65.22, e-mail coste.caumartin@wanadoo.fr ☑
⚘ ev. day 9am–12 noon 2pm–7pm; Sun. by appt.
↝ Jérôme Sordet

MARIA CUNY 2001★

| | 0.8 ha | 2,000 | 🍶♦ | 8–11 € |

Maria Cuny enjoys a view of the basilica at Vézelay, an architectural jewel and classed as a World Heritage site by UNESCO. Its wine labels are very attractive and stay within conventional usage: the basilica of Vézelay appears on the one star **Vézelay white Bourgogne 2001**, but not on this label of similar design because the Vézelay denomination is reserved for white wines. Ruby purple, with a spicy nose, still fairly closed, this particularly successful wine, product of a difficult year, is based on good tannins. Clean and structured, it will keep for one to two years, and will become more rounded.
↝ Maria Cuny, 16, rte de Saint-Père, 89450 Saint-Père, tel. 03.86.33.27.95, fax 03.86.33.27.95 ☑
⚘ by appt.

DOM. JEAN-MICHEL DAULNE

Côtes d'Auxerre Elevé en fût de chêne 2000★

	3 ha	6,000	🍶	5–8 €

Jean-Michel Daulne is a first generation wine-grower; after studying at the *Lycée Viticole* (college of viticulture) at Beaune, set up here fifteen years ago. Marilyn, who shares his name on the label, certainly inspires him. Their Chardonnay is excellent in all its aspects: Chablis colour, fresh aroma, charming roundness. *L'andouillette au Chablis* (an offal sausage cooked in Chablis) would accompany it perfectly.
☛ Jean-Michel and Marilyn Daulne, RN 6, Le Bouchet, 89460 Bazarnes, tel. 03.86.42.20.97, fax 03.86.42.33.91 ☑
�***I*** by appt.

DOUDET-NAUDIN

Vicomté 2001★★

	4 ha	21,200	🍶 ⅰⅱ ⅰ	5–8 €

A first impression can be clear-cut without being massive. A fresh wine, full of finesse that leaves just the right amount of room for the tannins and acidity and watches over the follow-on. Deep ruby, it combines wild-strawberries with charred hints. Matured half in tank and half in barrel, it has not suffered over-extraction; the reader will appreciate the sensitivity of this wine.
☛ Doudet-Naudin, 3, rue Henri-Cyrot, 21420 Savigny-lès-Beaune, tel. 03.80.21.51.74, fax 03.80.21.50.69, e-mail doudet-naudin@wanadoo.fr ☑
�***I*** by appt.
☛ Yves Doudet

CH. DE DRACY

Côtes du Couchois 2001★

	n.c.	3,900	ⅰⅱ	8–11 €

Founded in the 13th century, the Château de Dracy has often undergone alteration, but it retains its proud bearing, as the label shows. This estate belongs to the Baron de Charette, a director of the A. Bichot company: Colin Ware is their oenologist. An intense ruby colour, fresh and fruit-filled, this wine is elegance personnified, as the writer of one of the tasting cards put it. Its touch of acidity ensures that it will keep for two or three years. Its delightful structure is accompanied by aromas of *cerises eau-de-vie* (cherries in alcohol), cinnamon and nutmeg.
☛ SCA Ch. de Dracy, 71490 Dracy-lès-Couches, tel. 03.85.49.62.13, fax 03.80.24.37.38
�***I*** by appt.
☛ Benoît de Charette

JOSEPH DROUHIN 2001★★

	n.c.	n.c.	ⅰⅱ	5–8 €

The J. Drouhin house, founded in 1880, is one of the best burgundy marques. Pale yellow with lime-blossom highlights, this 2001 vintage is a typical Chardonnay. Butter, toasted almonds and a hint of vanilla touch, this is an extremely viable wine. On the palate it has a mineral character, perfect acidity and ample richness. If all the burgundies were like this, one would celebrate Saint Vincent every day of the year.
☛ Maison Joseph Drouhin, 7, rue d'Enfer, 21200 Beaune, tel. 03.80.24.68.88, fax 03.80.22.43.14, e-mail maisondrouhin@drouhin.com
�***I*** by appt.

DUPONT-FAHN

Chaumes des Perrières 2001★★

	1.35 ha	8,000	ⅰⅱ	8–11 €

A very small rented domaine of about 4 ha. This vineyard was planted in 1975. A Burgundy plot that was "de-classified" in 1976 by a decision of the wine-growers after extra land was acquired. The superb wine produced by this vineyard is "worthy of cru", a taster told us. Yes indeed…Initially light, rich on the middle palate, a complex finish, it is not merely interesting: it is enthralling.
☛ Raymond Dupont-Fahn, Les Toisières, 21190 Monthélie, tel. 03.80.21.29.21, fax 03.80.21.21.22 ☑
�***I*** by appt.

SYLVAIN DUSSORT

Cuvée des Ormes Vieilles Vignes 2001★★

	1 ha	6,000	ⅰⅱ	8–11 €

One of our jurors saw this as a *coup de coeur*, unaware that its big brothers had already received four *coups de coeur*. Beneath its clear and brilliant colour, this 2001 vintage is not exactly generous with its aromas, which need aerating to bring them out. With its vivacious finish it is the opposite of aggressive. A balance of finesse and charm, this wine is delicious on the palate. It is the equal of a cru. Of course, these plots of old vines are located at Meursault.
☛ Sylvain Dussort, 12, rue Charles-Giraud, 21190 Meursault, tel. 03.80.21.27.50, fax 03.80.21.27.50, e-mail dussvins@aol.com ☑
�***I*** by appt.

FICHET

Le Vignot Elevé en fût de chêne 2000★★

	2 ha	10,000	ⅰⅱ	5–8 €

It came close to obtaining a *coup de coeur*. this is a great success for the Mâconnais. While its garnet-red colour is not very pronounced, its bouquet is much more developed, bordering on musky (with hints of game). On the palate, it has real quality. Its body? That of a Greek statue. Perhaps lacking the richness required for a third star, but almost perfectly harmonious. It will easily keep for two to three years.
☛ Dom. Fichet, Le Martoret, 71960 Igé, tel. 03.85.33.30.46, fax 03.85.33.44.55, e-mail contact@domaine-fichet.com ☑
�***I*** by appt.

DENIS GABRIELLE

Vieilles Vignes 2001★

	0.5 ha	2,400	🍶 ⅰ	3–5 €

This family estate of 5 ha is at Venoy, not far from the motorway service station, near Auxerre; but only a short distance away, one finds the tranquility of the vineyard and this yellow gold wine from the 2001 vintage, with a fine, delicate nose bordering on minerality. This elegant simplicity follows through in the impressions of citrus fruits (lemons, grapefruit) lingering on the palate.
☛ Denis Gabrielle, 43, rue des Trois-Soleines, 89290 Venoy, tel. 03.86.40.33.88, fax 03.86.40.38.65, e-mail denis.gabrielle@wanadoo.fr ☑
�***I*** by appt.

PAUL GARAUDET 2001★

	1 ha	7,000	ⅰⅱ	5–8 €

This 2001 vintage? Liquid gold if its colour is anything to go by. The bouquet? Clean and open, floral, with a hint of oak from the cask. On the palate, fruit makes a perfect union with hazelnut. A wine to drink rather that keep in the cellar.
☛ Paul Garaudet, imp. de l'Eglise, 21190 Monthélie, tel. 03.80.21.28.78, fax 03.80.21.66.04 ☑
�***I*** by appt.

XAVIER GIRARDIN

Aux Rouanchottes Elevé en fût de chêne 2001★

	0.45 ha	2,000	ⅰⅱ	5–8 €

A new conqueror in the Hautes Côtes de Nuits. This vineyard was established in 2000 on less than 1 ha. Today its 2.5 ha of rented land are an invaluable foothold in the Vosne. This 2001 vintage has the perfect mauvish purple colour. The oakiness is clearly discernable, but there is a powerful blackcurrant element. A pulpy first impression developing into tannin: it has plenty of keeping potential and offers a spicy finish; this full-bodied wine is the product of a Master's hand.
☛ Xavier Girardin, SCEA Les Ormes, rue des Magniens, 21700 Arcenant, tel. 03.80.62.11.80, fax 03.80.61.22.72 ☑
�***I*** by appt.

GHISLAINE ET JEAN-HUGUES GOISOT

Côtes d'Auxerre Corps de Garde 2001★★

	3 ha	18,000	🍷	5–8 €

A *cuvée* destined to accompany freshwater fish. Gently floral, honeyed and warm on the palate, this wine from 2001 can be drunk right away or kept for one to two years. Ideally, drink it in the not-too-far distant future. The *Corps de Garde* (Guard) drawn from cellars almost 1,000 years old, has not yet finished raising its glass to this vintage. The superb, generous **2001 red** should be decanted a good hour before serving: it was also awarded two stars.
↣ Ghislaine et Jean-Hugues Goisot, 30, rue Bienvenu-Martin, 89530 Saint-Bris-le-Vineux, tel. 03.86.53.35.15, fax 03.86.53.62.03, e-mail jhetg.goisot@cerb.cernet.fr 🖥
👤 by appt.

DOM. GRAND ROCHE

Côtes d'Auxerre 2001★

	4 ha	13,000	🍶🍷🥄	5–8 €

A fine, big wine which, considering the vintage, makes no mistake when it comes to colour and sticks to it as closely as possible. The nose is unmistakably Pinot but doesn't dwell on it, but it does bring out the fruitiness. It is well structured on the palate. A delicious, harmonious wine to drink in 2004, ideally with white meats.
↣ Erick Lavallée, Dom. Grand Roche, 6, rte de Chitry, 89530 Saint-Bris-le-Vineux, tel. 03.86.53.84.07, fax 03.86.53.88.36 🖥
👤 by appt.

GRIFFE

Chitry 2001★

	0.81 ha	4,000	🍶	5–8 €

David Griffe has taken over this family-run *Groupment Agricole d'Exploitation en Commun* (Group running agricultural enterprises in common) which has been in existence for three centuries. Its white Chitry has the appropriate colour and brightness. There is a hint of Muscat on the nose, with a very fruity finish. Typical of the vintage is its good acidity, its adequate structure and length. A wine that will not suffer if kept for a while.
↣ EARL Griffe, 15, rue du Beugnon, 89530 Chitry, tel. 03.86.41.41.06, fax 03.86.41.47.36 🖥
👤 by appt.

DOM. GUEUGNON-REMOND

Cuvée de l'Aurore 2001★

	0.5 ha	3,500	🍷	5–8 €

A small family estate taken over in 1997 by the son-in-law and daughter of the original owners. Called Aurore, this *cuvée* from the Mâcon, with its shining golden yellow colour, is as complex on the nose as on the palate, where one finds aromas of Viennese pastry, yellow fruits, carefully mingled. Good opening, satisfactory length, successful balance, what more could one ask? A wine to cherish for a while in the cellar or to drink as of now. The **red Bourgogne 2001** also obtained one star. Cherry, a well-integrated basis of oak, it will be ready to drink in 2004.
↣ Dom. Gueugnon-Remond, chem. de la Cave, 71850 Charnay-lès-Mâcon, tel. 03.85.29.23.88, fax 03.85.20.20.72 🖥
👤 by appt.
↣ V. and J.-C. Remond

JEAN-LUC HOUBLIN

Coulanges-la-Vineuse Cuvée Prestige 2001★★

	3.03 ha	4,600		5–8 €

The label depicting the famous windmill of Migné, restored a few years ago, adorns a Coulanges which came very close to taking the *coup de coeur*. It is really out of the ordinary for a wine of the 2001 vintage. Not too much colour, notes of vanilla-cinnamon, an oakiness which doesn't dry the palate, rich and supple, a fine wine! Smooth but structured, this is a wine that will keep for a while but is ready for drinking now.
↣ Jean-Luc Houblin, 1, passage des Ruats, 89580 Coulanges-la-Vineuse, tel. 03.86.41.69.87, fax 03.86.41.71.95, e-mail houblin.fr@wanadoo.fr 🖥
👤 by appt.

JOEL HUDELOT-BAILLET 2001★

	1.19 ha	4,500	🍷	5–8 €

Coming from Chambolle-Musigny, top-class wine area, this burgundy has a fine pedigree. Ruby-red with purplish highlights, its potential is clear from the start and the intense, generous and fruity nose in no way detracts from it. On the palate it is structured, with just the right amount of tannin, and the promises it holds out will be kept in one to two years' time. Drink it with white meats.
↣ Dom. Joël Hudelot-Baillet, 21, rue Basse, 21220 Chambolle-Musigny, tel. 03.80.62.85.88, fax 03.80.62.49.83 🖥
👤 by appt.

REMI JOBARD 2000★

	0.25 ha	1,500	🍶🍷🥄	5–8 €

A burgundy from Meursault is rather like a National Premier Division club fielding a third division or an honorary team. As Guy Roux often says, a great club must be successful at all championship levels. In this case the score is definitely favorable. A superb colour and an expressive, if slightly aggressive nose; integrated, fruity and lingering on the palate, with a recurring freshness on the palate. The **Bourgogne white 2000 (8–11 €)** was also placed in the same category: full of charm, floral, it demonstrates the happy combination of six months in tank and twelve months in cask.
↣ Rémi Jobard, 12, rue Sudot, 21190 Meursault, tel. 03.80.21.20.23, fax 03.80.21.67.69, e-mail remi.jobard@libertysurf.fr 🖥
👤 by appt.

GILLES JOURDAN

Vieilles Vignes 2001★

	1.5 ha	3,000	🍷	5–8 €

The ancient vineyard of the Marey-Monge family, south of the Côte de Nuits, was formerly illustrious but has faded since 1976. Beneath its very limpid, garnet-red, moderately intense colour, this wine offers a distinct oakiness on the nose developing towards fruits in *eau-de-vie*. Velvety and full-bodied, it merits a wait of one to two years. Ideal with small game birds or white meat.
↣ Gilles Jourdan, 114, Grande-Rue, 21700 Corgoloin, tel. 03.80.62.76.31, fax 03.80.62.98.55 🖥
👤 by appt.

PIERRE LABET

Vieilles Vignes 2001★★

	1 ha	n.c.	🍷	8–11 €

Château de la Tour to the Clos de Vougeot, a Beaune vineyard, this estate comes under the category of: *Rara avis*. This wine from 2001 is perhaps not such a rare bird but it undoubtedly is first-rate; oaky, certainly, but with a studied approach. Purplish ruby-red with a tendency to cling to the glass (let us stress, this is not a defect), its attack is carefully combined with red berry aromas. With its silky tannins, this is a high-class wine, but it needs time to finish taming the influence of the oak cask.
↣ Dom. Pierre Labet, Clos de Vougeot, 21640 Vougeot, tel. 03.80.62.86.13, fax 03.80.62.87.72, e-mail contact@françoislabet.com 🖥
👤 ev. day. except Tue. 10am–7pm; cl. 15 Nov.–Easter
↣ François Labet

DOM. MICHEL LAHAYE 2000★

	0.51 ha	1,200	🍶🍷	5–8 €

A wine to dream about, to make the mouth water. Tasters suggested serving it with a truffled fowl or a pike-perch from the river Saône. They probably saw themselves already in the kitchen pestering the mistress of house. Made in the Côte de Beaune, the colour of this Chardonnay swings between gold and green-gold. A slightly oakiness on a mineral background, it manages to be an excellent compromise between texture and structure: Fred Astaire in the arms of Ginger Rogers. Will keep for one to two years.
↣ Michel Lahaye, pl. de l'Eglise, 21630 Pommard, tel. 03.80.22.52.22 🖥
👤 by appt.

MARIE-HELENE LAUGEROTTE 2001★★

| | 0.32 ha | 2,500 | ∎ | 5–8 € |

Proposed for the *coup de cœur*, this burgundy rosé, from the Côte Chalonnaise, stands head and shoulders above the wines one generally finds under this name. Its colour is very light, even making all possible allowances; Light but limpid, pleasingly restrained. The nose, however, is expressive; one can discern buttery notes well as red berries, notably redcurrants. On the palate none of the elements predominates: acidity, robustness, alcohol, all have their allotted place.
✷┐ Marie-Hélène Laugerotte, 71640 Saint-Denis-de-Vaux, tel. 03.85.44.36.35, fax 03.85.44.42.70 ☑
☨ by appt.

SERGE LEPAGE

Côte Saint-Jacques 2001★

| | 0.77 ha | 4,500 | ∎ | 5–8 € |

If you would like to know the result of combining 75% Pinot Gris (a favourite grape variety now sadly rare in Burgundy) and 25% Pinot Noir, taste this good "thirst-quenching rosé." Its colour is a pale grey-pink, its aromas fruity fresh, and on the palate it is light, fresh and very pleasant.
✷┐ Serge Lepage, 9, rue Principale, Grand Longueron, 89300 Champlay, tel. 03.86.62.05.58, fax 03.86.62.20.08 ☑
☨ by appt.

LOUIS DE BEAUMONT

Tonnerre 2001★

| | 2.81 ha | 18,700 | ∎ ♦ | 5–8 € |

Louis de Beaumont was the real name of the Chevalier d'Eon, whose memory is honoured in Tonnerre. If the gentleman was somewhat equivocal, this wine is completely straightforward. Gold in colour, with green highlights, it benefits from various floral perfumes. Underlain by an acidity that is effective without being aggressive, it is representative of its vintage with a slightly apricot finish.
✷┐ EARL Hervé Dampt, 1, rue de Fleys, 89700 Collan, tel. 03.86.55.29.55, fax 03.86.54.49.89 ☑
☨ by appt.

CATHERINE ET CLAUDE MARECHAL

Cuvée Gravel 2001★

| | 3,42 ha | 19,000 | ⫿⫿ | 8–11 € |

This *cuvée*, known as Gravel, was not named after a friend but refers to the gravelly terroir found to the east of Beaune. The gravelly Burgundian soil! This wine from the 2001 vintage could be worn as a charm. Its deep ruby-red colour reflects back a beautiful light. On the nose, the maturity of the grape shows in the concentrated notes of ripe red fruit. On the palate, the texture is fine and dense, effective and long-lasting.
✷┐ EARL Catherine et Claude Maréchal, 6, rte de Chalon, 21200 Bligny-lès-Beaune, tel. 03.80.21.44.37, fax 03.80.26.85.01, e-mail marechalcc@wanadoo.fr ☑
☨ by appt.

GHISLAINE ET BERNARD MARECHAL-CAILLOT 2001★★

| | 3,1 ha | 8,000 | ⫿⫿ | 5–8 € |

A deep, ruby-red colour with hints of mauve sets the tone. The fruitiness that follows is the result of a perfectly-judged 12 months in cask. Blackcurrant predominates in a harmonious and rounded whole, even though there is a hint of copper on the finish. The tannins need two more years in the cellar to integrate.
✷┐ Bernard Maréchal, 10, rte de Chalon, 21200 Bligny-lès-Beaune, tel. 03.80.21.44.55, fax 03.80.26.88.21 ☑
☨ by appt.

DOM. MATHIAS 2001★★

| | 0.5 ha | 3,000 | ∎ ♦ | 5–8 € |

Yellow with gold highlights, this wine is strong on nuances. Opening on peach and citrus fruits, the nose is seductive, which is a good start. The fruity character of the bouquet is confirmed on the structurally balanced palate. Its expression is elegantly long.This burgundy comes from the southern region of Burgundy.

✷┐ Béatrice and Gilles Mathias, rue Saint-Vincent, 71570 Chaintré, tel. 03.85.27.00.50, fax 03.85.27.00.52, e-mail domaine-mathias@wanadoo.fr ☑ ⌂
☨ by appt.

DOM. DU MERLE 2001★★

| | 2.5 ha | 2,000 | ⫿⫿ | 5–8 € |

A strong yellow in colour with hints of green, this wine knows its classics. The nose speaks with a rich, lemony accent. Full of charm, it is long on the palate. A taster called it "durable," a magic term from the year 2000. Produced near Chalon-sur-Saône, this wine is at the top of the appellation.
✷┐ Dom. du Merle, Sens, 71240 Sennecey-le-Grand, tel. 03.85.44.75.38, fax 03.85.44.73.63 ☑
☨ ev. day. 8am–7pm
✷┐ Michel Morin

JEAN-MICHEL MOREAU 2002★

| | 1.65 ha | 6,000 | ∎ ♦ | 5–8 € |

This 5-ha estate is a fine example of the revival of a vineyard that had almost disappeared at the beginning of th 20th century! *Coup de cœur* for his 2000 vintage white burgundy last year, Jean-Michel Moreau also offered a **Bourgogne rosé 2001**, a fresh wine with blackcurrant notes which received a special mention. Already a dark ruby-red colour, this red burgundy with raspberry firmly imprinted on the nose, is coherent and quite tannic on the palate.
✷┐ Jean-Michel Moreau, EARL Grange Aubert, 89700 Tonnerre, tel. 03.86.55.23.37, fax 03.86.55.23.37 ☑
☨ ev. day. 6pm–8pm; Sat. 2pm–8pm

LUCIEN MUZARD ET FILS 2001★★★

| | 0.8 ha | 4,500 | ⫿⫿ | 5–8 € |

For the *coup de cœur*, there was some hesitation. In his definition of God, Saint Bernard said: "He is length, width, height and depth." So, within the same parameters, is this superb, very big wine. It flies over the subject literally. There is no point in going into further details: this one holds all the aces in his hand.
✷┐ Lucien Muzard et Fils, 11 bis, rue de la Cour-Verreuil, BP 25, 21590 Santenay, tel. 03.80.20.61.85, fax 03.80.20.66.02, e-mail lucien-muzard-et-fils@wanadoo.fr ☑
☨ by appt.

FRANCOIS PARENT 2001★

| | n.c. | 7,000 | ∎ ⫿⫿ | 8–11 € |

Internet site on the label conjures up a lyrical picture of the Burgundy truffle, which is not black but brown…It is not often one reads a dictionary definition on a wine label! This is a burgundy that is as easy as can be, very classic, rounded and integrated, with no acidity or tannins in the foreground. We want to drink it here and now.
✷┐ François Parent, La Garelle, Grande-Rue, 21630 Pommard, tel. 03.80.22.61.85, fax 03.80.24.03.16, e-mail francois@parent-pommard.com ☑
☨ by appt.

DOM. ALAIN PATRIARCHE

La Monatine 2001★

| | 4 ha | 10,000 | ⫿⫿ | 5–8 € |

This is a wine which will continue to mature. Let us say for drinking in 2005 or the end of 2004. Its quite intense golden yellow is very much the local colour. The nose is a trifle herbaceous and connoisseurs will detect a hint of nettle-flowers. Its aroma is well-known and studied. Coming from Meursault, this wine has character, with a touch of greenness and a flinty side.
✷┐ Dom. Alain Patriarche, 12, rue des Forges, 21190 Meursault, tel. 03.80.21.24.48, fax 03.80.21.63.37 ☑
☨ by appt.

DOM. DES PERDRIX 2000★★

| | 1.89 ha | 12,026 | ⫿⫿ | 11–15 € |

This estate in the Côte de Nuits (Mugneret-Gouachon) was taken over in 1996 by the Devillard family (Antonin Rodet). The wine sleeps safely in the Jobert de Chambertin cellar, which was excavated at Gevrey in 1755. A simple burgundy can be a great burgundy – a statement of which this wine offers ample proof! Voluptuous and dense, its colour is that of a ball-gown: one could lose oneself among its sparkling highlights. Spices and crystallized fruits indicate excellent maturation. Without too many secondary aromas (clove, mild spices), its tannins are admirably polished, smooth to the touch, and the body has suppleness and length.

☛ B. et C. Devillard, Dom. des Perdrix, Ch. de Champ Renard, 71640 Mercurey, tel. 03.85.98.12.12, fax 03.85.45.25.49, e-mail rodet@rodet.com

LES PIERRES BLANCHES

Côtes d'Auxerre 2000★

	n.c.	n.c.	🍷 ❚ ↓	5–8 €

Very dynamic, this wine displays great potential. Floral, quite expressive, it is vigorous enough to remain in the cellar for two or three years. It was produced by a good wine-merchant in the Chablis.

☛ Pascal Bouchard, parc des Lys, 89800 Chablis, tel. 03.86.42.18.64, fax 03.86.42.48.11, e-mail info@pascalbouchard.com ☑
🍴 by appt.

DOM. DES PITOUX 2001★★

	1 ha	3,000	❚ ↓	5–8 €

Go and visit this Master-winemaker's house, with its Mâconnais gallery, vaulted 18th century cellar, in an area favoured by poet and politician, Alphonse de Lamartine, who was born in the Mâcon. The wine will be worth the journey. Fiery red in colour, this is a Pinot Noir with aromas of fruit containing stones (cherries), clearly recognizable in the rounded and supple initial impression. Small liquorice notes overlay a comfortable structure. And its elegance! An excellent 2001 vintage that could well be drunk as of now. Very much a "Sunday" wine.

☛ Jean-Yves Guyard, rue du Grand-Bussières, 71960 Bussières, tel. 03.85.37.74.74, fax 03.85.37.74.74 ☑
🍴 by appt.

POULEAU-PONAVOY

Cuvée Alexis 2000★

	1 ha	1,200	🍷	5–8 €

While the nose needs a little coaxing, it is based on floral and mineral aromas. The colour is agreeably golden. Lively without being too acid, intense without losing its mineral quality, it is a good-looking wine that leaves a light touch of dried fruits on the palate. Drink it now or wait a year or two "A worthy accompaniment to the classical dishes," said one taster.

☛ GAEC Pouleau-Ponavoy, rue Saint-Georges, 21340 La Rochepot, tel. 03.80.21.84.36, e-mail r.pouleau@aol.com ☑
🍴 ev. day. 8am–12 noon 2pm–7pm

SERGE PROST ET FILS

Côtes du Couchois 2000★

	35 ha	2,000	❚	5–8 €

This estate of almost 20 ha was established by the owner's grandfather on his return from the First World War. If you are unfamiliar with the nature of a Côtes du Couchois Burgundy (a recent denomination), take this wine and you will find out in the glass: it has colour, a concentrated bouquet (spices and small black berries). On the palate, the flavours are all in agreement and don't be surprised if you find the wine somewhat rustic. That is precisely what Couchois is and one would not wish to change it.

☛ EARL Serge Prost et Fils, Les Foisons, 71490 Couches, tel. 03.85.49.64.00, fax 03.85.49.64.00 ☑
🍴 by appt.

ROGER ET JOËL REMY 2001★

	0.5 ha	2,400	🍷	5–8 €

An attractive wine to look at with strong perfumes of honey and honeysuckle. From the moment it makes contact with the palate, right through to the finish, it remains fresh, slightly mineral with good length. You could well keep it for two years if you wish. A freshwater fish terrine would delight a Jury.

☛ SCEA Roger et Joël Rémy, 4, rue du Paradis, 21200 Sainte-Marie-la-Blanche, tel. 03.80.26.60.80, fax 03.80.26.53.03, e-mail domaine.remy@wanadoo.fr ☑
🍴 by appt.

JACKY RENARD

Côtes d'Auxerre 2001★

	45 ha	3,500	❚ ↓	5–8 €

Cadet-Rousselle was a historical figure from Auxerre where he was a much-taunted bailiff at the time of the Révolution (1792). This wine conforms to the criteria of the AOC: honey, bitterness, acidity, pronounced terroir, creditable length…Its present bitterness is merely a guarantee of keeping qualities. In two years' time it will be very pleasant with grilled fish.

☛ Dom. Jacky Renard, La Côte-de-Chaussan, 89530 Saint-Bris-le-Vineux, tel. 03.86.53.38.58, fax 03.86.53.33.50 ☑
🍴 by appt.

DOM. RIGOUTAT Coulanges-la-Vineuse

Cuvée Prestige Elevé en fût de chêne 2001★

	4 ha	6,000	🍷	5–8 €

Out of the 12 ha which comprise this estate, 4 ha are dedicated to this Cuvée Prestige which has plenty of keeping potential (approximately three years). It has quite a bit of colour for the vintage and the aroma of wild-strawberries on the nose that turns the thoughts to spring. Above average for the 2001 vintage, its firm tannins prevent its true qualities from emerging. This wine needs to stay in the cellar for two to three years.

☛ Dom. Rigoutat, 2, rue du Midi, 89290 Jussy, tel. 03.86.53.33.79, fax 03.86.53.66.89, e-mail domainerigoutat@wanadoo.fr ☑
🍴 by appt.

ARMELLE ET BERNARD RION 2001★

	1 ha	7,000	🍷	5–8 €

The colour is universally appreciated, as is the vanilla surrounding the blackcurrants and blackberries, but will the oakiness ever manage to soften? Will the structure win out over the tannic finish? A wine worthy of this name will find the answers after two or three years in the cellar.

☛ Dom. Armelle et Bernard Rion, 8, rte Nationale, 21700 Vosne-Romanée, tel. 03.80.61.05.31, fax 03.80.61.34.60, e-mail rionab@wanadoo.fr ☑
🍴 by appt.

DOM. MICHELE ET PATRICE RION

Les Bons Bâtons 2001★

	0.62 ha	5,000	🍷	8–11 €

This small domaine of 2,5 ha, established in 1990, is situated 80 m from Premeaux church. With the charming name of *climat* in the Côte, these *Bons Bâtons* are good company. Ruby-red in colour, reminiscent of red fruit, the eye attunes itself to what comes next: a light, oak-wood nose; an honest attack with tannins that are substantial but completely unaggressive; a body that needs to age and a deep finish.

☛ SCE Michèle et Patrice Rion, 1, rue de la Maladière, 21700 Premeaux-Prissey, tel. 03.80.62.32.63, fax 03.80.62.49.63, e-mail patrice.rion@wanadoo.fr ☑
🍴 by appt.

DOM. NICOLAS ROSSIGNOL 2001★★

	1.54 ha	3,000	🍷	8–11 €

Made at Volnay with grapes from 50-year-old vines, this is a burgundy that is "worthy of the appellation *village*," wrote one oenologist taster. The intense colour is that of black-cherries. The oak cask is clearly present on the nose, but doesn't swamp the ripe fruit aromas. The extraction was quite considerable but this wine, with its fine volume, can support it. When the liquorice and vanilla have integrated with the fruit, in about two years' time, this will be a great wine.

☛ Nicolas Rossignol, rue de Mont, 21190 Volnay, tel. 03.80.21.62.43, fax 03.80.21.27.61 ☑
🍴 by appt.

DOM. ROSSIGNOL-FEVRIER
PERE ET FILS 2001★★

| ■ | 1.65 ha | 9,000 | ■ ◗ ◖ | 5–8 € |

The name burgundy carries certain obligations. This wine fulfills them all amply. Of course, the Pinot Noir is completely at home in Volnay. The blackcurrant colour, tender, raspberry nose, a slightly harsh first impression but good tannins and a solid construction on the palate. Small game birds, or even a pigeon come to mind. A perfect combination.
☛ EARL Rossignol-Février, rue du Mont, 21190 Volnay, tel. 03.80.21.64.23, fax 03.80.21.67.74 ☑
☖ ev. day ex. Sun. 8am–12 noon 2pm–6pm

CH. DE SASSANGY
Clos du Prieuré-Monopole 2000★

| ■ | 1.74 ha | 13,000 | ◗ ◖ | 5–8 € |

Since 1980, Jean and Geno Musso have been reviving the vine-yards, devastated by phylloxera, of a very old family property and also the vines belonging to this beautiful, classically elegant château, in the Chalon-sur-Saône hinterland, which they subsequently acquired. Committed to organic farming methods (Nature and Progress – Ecocert [Organization for organic farming]) since the beginning, they were among its early pioneers. The product is a deep red Pinot Noir, aromatically complex and glorious on the palate. With a spicy style, rich, lingering, bursting with energy. Two to three years in the cellar will not intimidated it in the least. Ideal wine for a Boeuf à la Bourguignonne.
☛ Ch. de Sassangy, Le Château, 71390 Sassangy, tel. 03.85.96.18.61, fax 03.85.96.18.62 ☑
☖ by appt.
☛ Jean and Geno Musso

SORIN-COQUARD
Côtes d'Auxerre 2001★

| ■ | 2.72 ha | 12,000 | ■ | 5–8 € |

A truly controlled Côte d'Auxerre. Limpid straw in colour, it has an attractive nose which says all it needs to without over-doing it. Pleasing to the palate: its acidity enlivens a fresh and fruity initial impression. It is not a particularly complex wine but it is entirely in keeping with the classic profile of the appellation. The **red 2001** has quality and potential: serve it in 2004 with game (obtained a special mention).
☛ EARL Sorin-Coquard, 25, rue de Grisy, 89530 Saint-Bris-le-Vineux, tel. 03.86.53.37.76, fax 03.86.53.37.76 ☑
☖ by appt.
☛ Pascal and Christine Sorin

JEAN-CLAUDE THEVENET ET FILS
2000★

| ■ | 3 ha | 10,000 | ■ ◖ | 5–8 € |

A sign of the times: the Mâconnais relies more and more on the AOC Burgundy and puts its money on the Pinot Noir. Like this straightforward, quite intense wine, which concentrates on raw red fruit and leaves the taste of tannins on toast on the palate. There is also a tail-end of black-cherry. The finish on the palate is very pleasant.
☛ Jean-Claude Thévenet et Fils, Le Bourg, 71960 Pierreclos, tel. 03.85.35.72.21, fax 03.85.35.72.03, e-mail vignoblethevenet.jeanclaude@wanadoo.fr ☑
☖ ev. day ex. Sun. 7.30am–12 noon 1.30pm–6pm

DIDIER TRIPOZ 2002★

| ■ | 0.8 ha | 2,600 | ◗ ◖ | 5–8 € |

A chicken…of Bresse, not less. There is an understanding between AOCs. This Pinot Noir from the Mâconnais plays its game well right in the heart of Gamay country. Garnet-red in colour with a lively bouquet, these are the first impressions. The structure fears nothing. Red fruits accompany moderately powerful tannins. And it has a touch of elegance for good measure.
☛ Didier Tripoz, 450, chem. des Tournons, 71850 Charnay-lès-Mâcon, tel. 03.85.34.14.52, fax 03.85.20.24.99, e-mail didier.tripoz@wanadoo.fr ☑
☖ by appt.

DOM. DES TROIS MONTS
Côtes du Couchois 2001★

| ■ | 0.41 ha | 3,000 | ◗ ◖ | 5–8 € |

A sixth generation Pichard is at the helm of this 17 ha estate. A good foot, a good eye, this bordeau-coloured wine shows that here in Burgundy they are broad-minded! Its bouquet is distinctly drawn to leather and spices: the nose needs a wide screen to do it justice. On the palate it is well-balanced and, while robust, it is upright and possesses a certain complexity. In short, a beautiful wine-discovery from the Côtes du Couchois.
☛ EARL Dom. des Trois Monts, 8, rue des Grandes-Plantes, 71510 Saint-Sernin-du-Plain, tel. 03.85.45.58.10, fax 03.85.49.50.17 ☑
☖ by appt.
☛ Daniel Pichard

CH. DU VAL DE MERCY
Chitry 2001★

| ■ | 3,5 ha | 20,000 | ■ ◖ | 5–8 € |

This is the estate that Daniel Colbois repurchased in 1990, ten years after it was extended: the Vieux-Fort domaine. This beautiful yellow-gold Chitry conjures up very ripe fruit against a vanilla background. Its attack is supple but then it widens and takes on breadth, with an almond note on the middle palate. Drink it within the year if possible, with a terrine of Chitry rabbit.
☛ Dom. du Ch. du Val de Mercy, 8, promenade du Tertre, 89530 Chitry, tel. 03.86.41.48.00, fax 03.86.41.45.80, e-mail chateauduval@aol.com ☑
☖ by appt.
☛ Meroni

ROMUALD VALOT 2001★

| ■ | n.c. | n.c. | ■ | 5–8 € |

"Wine of the proprietor," it says on the label from this relatively new wine-merchant. The formula is a little surprising. The wine itself, however, doesn't ask any such question. The colour of cherries left to ripen on the tree, tending towards raspberry and redcurrant on the nose each time one inhales. It passes the palate test with flying colours, with its roundness, its progressive development that comes to a climax on the finish, its concentration and balance; an excellent wine, and ready to drink as of now.
☛ SARL Bourgogne Romuald Valot, 14, rue des Tonneliers, BP 213, 21206 Beaune, tel. 03.80.25.91.30

DOM. DE VAUROUX 2001★

| ■ | 2 ha | 15,000 | ◗ ◖ | 5–8 € |

Slightly gilded pale yellow in colour, this wine from the 2001 vintage was matured in oak barrels and has a striking aromatic complexity. "Minerally oaky," one might call it. Its constitution gives no cause for criticism. Supple, rounded, its body shows no unnecessary modesty when approached. The right measure of acidity ensures the balance of this wine from a vast, 43-ha estate in the Chablis. AOC; also offered a **Domaine des Héritières 2001** from the same AOC; though not matured in cask, this one was marked by fine mineral notes and the flavour of dried fruits. It was awarded one star.
☛ SCEA Dom. de Vauroux, rte d'Avallon, BP 56, 89800 Chablis, tel. 03.86.42.10.37, fax 03.86.42.49.13, e-mail domaine-de-vauroux@domaine-de-vauroux.com ☑
☖ by appt.
☛ Tricon

DOM. VERRET
Côtes d'Auxerre 2001★

| ■ | 3.6 ha | 20,000 | ■ ◗ ◖ | 5–8 € |

Product of a vast, 52-ha estate, this is a burgundy from the Auxerrois with a very direct approach in which one finds the characteristics of a Chardonnay: intensity, good balance between the fruit and vanilla, pale yellow colour with green highlights and a spicy, floral nose. A classic combination of which the acidity is dominant on the palate. Try it with a terrine of young rabbit with mixed fresh herbs.
☛ Dom. Verret, 7, rte de Champs, BP 4, 89530 Saint-Bris-le-Vineux, tel. 03.86.53.31.81, fax 03.86.53.89.61, e-mail dverret@domaineverret.com ☑
☖ by appt.

Wines selected but not starred

FRANCOIS D'ALLAINES
Tête de cuvée 2000

| | n.c. | 1,500 | ⅢD | 11–15 € |

➻ François d'Allaines, La Corvée du Paquier, 71150 Demigny, tel. 03.85.49.90.16, fax 03.85.49.90.19, e-mail francois@dallaines.com
⟡ by appt.

CH. DE LA BRUYERE
Elevé en fût de chêne 2000

| | 0.36 ha | 2,400 | ⅢD | 5–8 € |

➻ Paul-Henry Borie, Ch. de La Bruyère, 71960 Igé, tel. 03.85.33.30.72, fax 03.85.33.40.65, e-mail mph.borie@wanadoo.fr
⟡ ev. day. 8am–12 noon 2 pm–5pm

BENOIT CANTIN 2001

| | 1 ha | 7,000 | ■ ⧫ | 5–8 € |

➻ Benoît Cantin, 35, chem. des Fossés, 89290 Irancy, tel. 03.86.42.21.96, fax 03.86.42.21.96
⟡ ev. day ex. Sun. 8am–12 noon 2pm–6pm

FRANCK CHALMEAU 2001

| | 0.4 ha | 2,000 | ■ ⧫ | 3–5 € |

➻ Franck Chalmeau, 2, pl. de l'Eglise, 89530 Chitry-le-Fort, tel. 03.86.41.43.99, fax 03.86.41.46.84
⟡ by appt.

DOM. DU CHATEAU-GRIS
Clos de Lupé 2000

| | 1.89 ha | 14,000 | ⅢD | 8–11 € |

➻ Dom. du Château-Gris, 17, av. du Gal-de-Gaulle, 21700 Nuits-Saint-Georges, tel. 03.80.61.25.02, fax 03.80.24.37.38

DOM. DE LA CRAS
Coteaux de Dijon 2001

| | 2.45 ha | 8,000 | ⅢD | 5–8 € |

➻ EARL Jean Dubois, Dom. de La Cras, 21370 Plombières-lès-Dijon, tel. 03.80.41.70.95, fax 03.80.59.13.96, e-mail j-dubois@cerb.cernet.fr
⟡ by appt.

DOM. DE LA CREA
Clos de La Perrière Monopole 2001

| | 1.15 ha | 9,500 | ⅢD | 5–8 € |

➻ Dom. de la Créa, Cave de Pommard, 3, rte de Beaune, 21630 Pommard, tel. 03.80.24.99.00, fax 03.80.24.62.42, e-mail cavedepommard@wanadoo.fr
⟡ ev. day. 10am–7pm
➻ Cécile Chenu

ERIC DAMPT
Epineuil 2001

| | 0.39 ha | 2,600 | ■ⅢD | 5–8 € |

➻ Eric Dampt, 16, rue de l'Ancien-Presbytère, 89700 Collan, tel. 03.86.55.36.28, fax 03.86.54.49.89
⟡ by appt.

HENRI DARNAT
La Jumalie 2001

| | 1.25 ha | 6,000 | ⅢD | 8–11 € |

➻ Dom. Darnat, 20, rue des Forges, 21190 Meursault, tel. 03.80.21.23.30, fax 03.80.21.64.62, e-mail domaine.darnat@libertysurf.fr
⟡ by appt.

JOCELYNE ET PHILIPPE DEFRANCE
2001

| | 0.5 ha | 4,000 | ■ ⧫ | 5–8 € |

➻ Philippe Defrance, 5, rue du Four, 89530 Saint-Bris-le-Vineux, tel. 03.86.53.39.04, fax 03.86.53.66.46
⟡ by appt.

DEMESSEY 2001

| | n.c. | 3,000 | ⅢD | 5–8 € |

➻ Marc Dumont, Ch. de Messey, 71700 Ozenay, tel. 03.85.51.33.83, fax 03.85.51.33.82, e-mail vin@demessey.com
⟡ by appt.

LES FAVERELLES 2001

| | 0.1 ha | 720 | ⅢD | 8–11 € |

➻ Les Faverelles, 15, rue du Four, 89450 Asquins, tel. 03.86.32.30.04, fax 03.86.32.30.04, e-mail faverelles@lesfaverelles.com
⟡ by appt.
➻ Georgelin

CAVE DE GENOUILLY
Les Champs Perdrix 2001

| | 1 ha | 8,000 | ■ ⧫ | 3–5 € |

➻ Cave des vignerons de Genouilly, 71460 Genouilly, tel. 03.85.49.23.72, fax 03.85.49.23.58
⟡ ev. day. ex. Sun. 8am–12 noon 2pm–6pm

CHRISTIAN GROS 2000

| | 0.5 ha | 1,800 | ⅢD | 5–8 € |

➻ Christian Gros, rue de la Chaume, 21700 Premeaux-Prissey, tel. 03.80.61.29.74, fax 03.80.61.39.77
⟡ by appt.

HENRY DE VEZELAY
Vézelay Les Coeuriots 2001

| | 7 ha | 26,000 | ■ ⧫ | 8–11 € |

➻ Cave Henry de Vézelay, rte de Nanchèvres, 89450 Saint-Père, tel. 03.86.33.29.62, fax 03.86.33.35.03, e-mail henrydevezelay@wanadoo.fr
⟡ ev. day. 8am–12 noon 2pm–6pm

PIERRE JANNY 2001

| | 8 ha | 50,000 | | 5–8 € |

➻ Sté Janny, La Condemine, Cidex 1556, 71260 Péronne, tel. 03.85.23.96.20, fax 03.85.36.96.58, e-mail pierre-janny@wanadoo.fr

DOM. DE MAUPERTHUIS
Les Truffières 2001

| | 1 ha | 4,600 | ■ | 5–8 € |

➻ Laurent Ternynck, Dom. de Mauperthuis, Civry, 89440 Massangis, tel. 03.86.33.86.24, e-mail ternynck@hotmail.com
⟡ ev. day. 9am–7.30pm

OLIVIER MORIN
Chitry Olympe 2001

■	2 ha	10,000	■ ⑪	8–11 €

➤ Olivier Morin, 2, chem. de Vaudu, 89530 Chitry,
tel. 03.86.41.47.20, fax 03.86.41.47.20 ☑
✶ by appt.

MORIN PERE ET FILS 2000

■	n.c.	220,000	5–8 €

➤ Morin Père et Fils, 9, quai Fleury,
21700 Nuits-Saint-Georges, tel. 03.80.61.19.51,
fax 03.80.61.05.10, e-mail caves@morinpere-fils.com ☑
✶ ev. day. 9am–12 noon 2pm–6pm; summer 9am–7pm

SYLVIE NUGUES
Clos Saint-Pierre 2001

■	0.85 ha	2,500	■ ⑪	3–5 €

➤ Sylvie Nugues, rue de la Pompe, 71390 Saint-Désert,
tel. 03.85.47.94.40, fax 03.85.47.94.40 ☑
✶ by appt.

DOM. GEORGES ET THIERRY PINTE
2000

■	n.c.	3,600	■ ⑪	3–5 €

➤ GAEC Georges et Thierry Pinte, 11, rue du Jarron,
21420 Savigny-lès-Beaune, tel. 03.80.21.57.59,
fax 03.80.21.51.59 ☑
✶ ev. day. 9.15am–11.30am 2pm–7pm

DOM. DU PUITS FLEURI
Côtes du Couchois 2001

■	0.9 ha	6,000	■	5–8 €

➤ Picard Père et Fils, GAEC du Puits Fleuri,
71490 Saint-Maurice-les-Couches, tel. 03.85.49.68.44,
fax 03.85.45.55.61 ☑
✶ by appt.

SIMONNET-FEBVRE
Côte de Palotte 2000

■	n.c.	2,000	11–15 €

➤ Simonnet-Febvre et Fils, La Maladière, BP 12, 9, av.
d'Oberwesel, 89800 Chablis, tel. 03.86.98.99.00,
fax 03.86.98.99.01, e-mail simonnet@chablis.net ☑
✶ ev. day. 8.30am–12 noon 2pm–5.30pm; Sat. Sun. by appt.
➤ Laurent Simonnet

DOM. JEAN-PIERRE TRUCHETET
Vieilles Vignes 2001

■	0.4 ha	4,400	⑪	5–8 €

➤ Jean-Pierre Truchetet, RN 74, 21700 Premeaux-Prissey,
tel. 03.80.61.07.22, fax 03.80.61.34.35 ☑
✶ by appt.

VAUDOISEY-CREUSEFOND 2001

■	1.87 ha	12,000	⑪	5–8 €

➤ Vaudoisey-Creusefond, rte d'Autun, 21630 Pommard,
tel. 03.80.22.48.63, fax 03.80.24.16.81 ☑
✶ by appt.

DOM. ELISE VILLIERS
Vézelay La Chevalière 2001

■	1.5 ha	8,000	■ ⚬	5–8 €

➤ Elise Villiers, Précy-le-Moult, 89450 Pierre-Perthuis,
tel. 03.86.33.27.62, fax 03.86.33.27.62 ☑ ⌂
✶ ev. day. 9am–12.30pm 1.30pm–7pm; groups by appt.

Bourgogne Grand Ordinaire

In real terms, the Appellations Bourgogne Ordinaire and Bourgogne Grand Ordinaire are used very rarely. When they are, the one that is less frequently used is Bourgogne Grand Ordinaire. This name may appear a little dull, but some terroirs on the margins of great vineyards can, nonetheless, produce some excellent wines that sell at very affordable prices. Almost all the Burgundy vine varieties can be used to produce white, red, rosé or clairet wines for this appellation.

The grapes used for white wine are Chardonnay or Melon. Although only a very few Melon vines remain, this variety reaches the heights of quality further west in France, where it is used to produce a reputable Muscadet in the Nantes region. The Aligoté is almost always declared as Appellation Bourgogne Aligoté. The Sacy grape, now grown exclusively in the Yonne, was once grown in the whole Chablis area and in the Yonne river valley to produce sparkling wines for export; it is now used for Crémant de Bourgogne.

The principal varieties for red and rosé, are the traditional Burgundy grapes, Gamay Noir and Pinot Noir. In the Yonne the César variety, reserved exclusively for Burgundy wines, can still be used, particularly in Irancy, while the Tressot makes an appearance in the annals but never in the vineyards. The best wines made from Gamay are found in the Yonne, especially in Coulanges-la-Vineuse, where they are bottled under that appellation. The production of wines from this AOC averages 9,500 hl.

POULEAU-PONAVOY 2001★

■	0.5 ha	1,500	⑪	3–5 €

Burgundy Grand Ordinaire rosé, from the pure Gamay grape, comes to us from Hautes Côtes de Beaune. Light, of course, but with an interesting finesse not often encountered in this appellation which is rarely made any more. Lively, as it should be, with no aggressiveness, and true to type; an ideal wine to accompany brochettes. Fire up the barbecue…
➤ GAEC Pouleau-Ponavoy, rue Saint-Georges, 21340 La Rochepot, tel. 03.80.21.84.36, e-mail r.pouleau@aol.com ☑
✶ ev. day. 8am–12 noon 2pm–7pm

Bourgogne Aligoté

This has been described as the "Muscadet of Burgundy". It is an excellent carafe wine to be drunk young, when it shows off the aromas of the variety at their best. Burgundians drink it for its freshness while they wait for the Chardonnay to mature. On the Côte Aligoté has been replaced by Chardonnay and has rather "gone downhill," literally, in terms of the areas allotted to it; it was grown previously on the slopes. But the soils influence it just as much as any other variety and there are as many types of Aligoté as there are regions producing it. The Aligotés of Pernand were renowned for their suppleness and their fruity nose (before the vines were replaced with Chardonnay); the Aligotés of the Hautes Côtes are sought after for their freshness and liveliness; those from Saint-Bris in the Yonne are light and pleasant to drink and seem to have borrowed traces of the elderflower scents found in Sauvignon. Production in 2002 reached 106,540 hl.

BERSAN ET FILS 2001★★

	n.c.	n.c.		5–8 €

One can simultaneously attack with trumpet, fife and drum, occupy the ground and still remain the balanced Master of the situation. This is precisely the case of this 2001 vintage, with its grey-green highlights. Its bouquet, which is not all-pervading, is essentially mineral, with citrus fruits and yellow fruits. It opens as already described, then it goes on to combine the freshness of the grape variety with a richness that fills the palate. An attractive wine.
➽ SARL Bersan et Fils, 20, rue du Dr-Tardieux, 89530 Saint-Bris-le-Vineux, tel. 03.86.53.33.73, fax 03.86.53.38.45, e-mail bourgognes-bersan@wanadoo.fr ✓
☖ by appt.

PASCAL BOUCHARD 2002★

	n.c.	150,000	■ ♦	5–8 €

Pascal Bouchard combines the roles of négociant and wine-grower on 32 ha. Imagine a golden-brown *gougère* (a savory made with cheese and choux pastry), well rounded and crisp, light and yielding, and warm, of course. Then marry it with this Aligoté 2004. They will make a happy couple. A beautiful straw colour with a delicate bouquet (hawthorn, acacia blossom), this wine has exactly the amount of liveliness needed and a sensation of lemon for a better effect.
➽ Pascal Bouchard, parc des Lys, 89800 Chablis, tel. 03.86.42.18.64, fax 03.86.42.48.11, e-mail info@pascalbouchard.com ✓
☖ by appt.

JEAN-CLAUDE BOUHEY ET FILS 2001★★

	13 ha	13,000	■ ♦	3–5 €

Sharp as flint, fresh as a breeze in May, good-natured and a touch impertinent, fruity and charming, this is a wine that will wake up the taste-buds. The Aligoté for the Hautes Côtes de Nuits sometimes reaches the heights. It is apparent again this time, on agreeable, perfumed notes of pear. No blackcurrant; drink it by itself, or perhaps with snails.
➽ Dom. Jean-Claude Bouhey et Fils, 7, rte de Magny, 21700 Villers-la-Faye, tel. 03.80.62.92.62, fax 03.80.62.74.07 ✓
☖ by appt.

CAVE DE BUXY 2002★

	100 ha	120,000	■ ♦	3–5 €

While the Buxy label speaks to us in Latin (*vivere in amore vini*), its Aligoté speak good French. Its colour is finely shaded and delicate. Vanilla, lemon, exotic fruits, the nose follows predictable tendencies. The attack is enthusiastic, the freshness and length are all there. It is a successful wine, and also the product of some 100 ha. There will be plenty for everybody!
➽ Sica des Vignerons réunis de Buxy, BP 6, 71390 Buxy, tel. 03.85.92.03.03, fax 03.85.92.08.06, e-mail labuxynoise@cave-buxy.fr ✓
☖ ev. day. ex.Sun. 9am–12 noon 2pm–6.30pm; groups by appt.

DOM. CARRE-COURBIN 2001★★

	0.29 ha	1,400	■ ♦	5–8 €

Estates that stick strictly to wine production are becoming rare in Beaune. This is one of the few, and its Aligoté plays the role of arbiter of elegances among the wines tasted. A delicious colour. And on the nose? One could be crunching an apple. On the palate, the purity of the variety is admirably discernible. It will not remain in the cellar for long; the temptation to drink it right away will be too great.
➽ Dom. Carré-Courbin, 9, rue Celer, 21200 Beaune, tel. 03.80.24.67.62, fax 03.80.24.66.93, e-mail carre.courbin@wanadoo.fr
☖ by appt.

DOM. DES CHAMBRIS 2001★

	0.45 ha	2,500	■	5–8 €

We are at Chevannes, a village some distance from the Hautes Côtes de Nuits. Going there is not exactly an adventure but one should make the effort. It produces a wine with a clear, light, almost floral colour. Fresh and fruity, it plays a recital on a lemon theme which gives enduring pleasure. A wine to drink now, and perfect as an aperitif.
➽ SCEV du Dom. des Chambris, 7, rue du Lavoir, 21220 Chevannes, tel. 03.80.61.44.77, fax 03.80.61.48.87, e-mail leschambris@wanadoo.fr ✓
☖ by appt.

PHILIPPE CHAVY 2001★

	0.53 ha	4,966	■ ♦	5–8 €

When a wine-grower from Puligny produces an Aligoté, one wonders about its acidity. This wine is a good colour and a powerful nose that combines apricot, honey and florals notes. A touch of liquorice, a mineral link and a fortunate, long-lasting lively temperament.
➽ Philippe Chavy, 22, Grande-Rue, 21190 Puligny-Montrachet, tel. 03.80.21.92.41, fax 03.80.21.93.15, e-mail chavyp@aol.com ✓
☖ by appt.
➽ Pierre Thomas

DOM. CHEVROT
Cuvée des Quatre Terroirs 2001★

	1.3 ha	10,000	■ ♦	5–8 €

Aligoté from Maranges, that agreeable area between Côte de Beaune and Côte Châlonnaise. Cuvée de Quatre Terroirs, we are told. Which four terroirs? That being said, we are dealing here with a very mature wine. It presents well, from its colour right through to its finish on the middle palate. Floral and elegant, it has no difficulty solving the problem of combining its acidity and its richness. Quite supple, always within the constraints of the grape variety.
➽ Catherine and Fernand Chevrot, Dom. Chevrot, 19, rte de Couches, 71150 Cheilly-lès-Maranges, tel. 03.85.91.10.55, fax 03.85.91.13.24, e-mail domaine.chevrot@wanadoo.fr ✓ ⌂
☖ ev. day. 9am–12 noon 1.30pm–6pm; Sun. 9am–12 noon

BERNARD COLIN ET FILS 2000★

	0.92 ha	n.c.	■ ♦	3–5 €

Coup de cœur for the 97 vintage of this wine, this Chassagne producer could devote himself body and soul to Chardonnay. He tried his luck with an Aligoté and offered a thoroughbred wine, white gold in colour, with all the characteristic highlights. Boxwood and acacia flowers on the nose confirm its identity and its vigorous freshness is smooth on the palate.
➽ Bernard Colin et Fils, 22, rue Charles-Paquelin, 21190 Chassagne-Montrachet, tel. 03.80.21.92.40, fax 03.80.21.93.23 ✓
☖ ev. day. 9am–12 noon 2pm–7pm; Sun. by appt.

DOM. JEAN FOURNIER
En Champforey Vieilles Vignes 2001★★

	2 ha	2,600	■ ▥ ♦	5–8 €

Now under the management of his son Laurent, Jean Fournier has produced a golden Aligoté (a variety from Bouzeron), 95% with 5% Melon. This is a rare combination for a burgundy; a white Gamay, it used to be called. This wine is something of a rare bird, a curiosity but a successful one. It is light, fresh, true to type and above all very fruity. The kind of wine that is not lost on the palate. It won't be intimidated by a dozen snails.
➽ Dom. Jean Fournier, 34, rue du Château, 21160 Marsannay-la-Côte, tel. 03.80.52.24.38, fax 03.80.52.77.40, e-mail domaine.jean.fournier@wanadoo.fr ✓
☖ by appt.

DOM. MARCEL ET BERNARD FRIBOURG 2001★

| | 2.9 ha | 6,000 | | | 3–5 € |

A champion of the Aligoté in the Hautes Côtes de Nuits, Marcel Freiburg is a well-known figure. The pale, light colour of his Aligoté is characteristic of that wine. On the nose, ripe pears open another chapter. Not a great deal of fruit on the palate, but strength and acidity are well in place. This is a true, turbulent Aligoté from the Hautes Côtes.

☛ SCE Dom. Marcel et Bernard Fribourg, 8, rue de l'Ancienne-Cure, 21700 Villers-la-Faye, tel. 03.80.62.91.74, fax 03.80.62.71.17 ✓
☕ by appt.

GERMAIN PERE ET FILS 2001★

| | 1.43 ha | 1,400 | | | 3–5 € |

Must one use this beautiful Aligoté to make a *kir* (white wine with blackcurrant liqueur)? One could aim a little higher and try it with an *andouillette* (offal sausage). Colour: brilliant. Bouquet: unsophisticated and lemony. As nice as can be. It is pure, sincere, and exactly what one expects.

☛ EARL Dom. Germain Père et Fils, rue de la Pierre-Ronde, 21190 Saint-Romain, tel. 03.80.21.60.15, fax 03.80.21.67.87,
e-mail patrick.germain8@wanadoo.fr ✓ ☗
☕ by appt.

GHISLAINE ET JEAN-HUGUES GOISOT 2001★★

| | 7 ha | 41,000 | | | 3–5 € |

The whole of this 28-ha estate is farmed organically and Ghislaine and Jean-Hugues Goisot have dedicated a large part of it to their Aligoté. And the result really is good! One of best, when we tasted it at Yonne. White gold in colour, the nose is delicate nose, but straight-forward and honest. The rounded and supple body produces a degree of vigour on the middle palate, but this does not surprise. A wine with all the characteristics of its kind. Ideal to drink with a cheese soufflé...

☛ Ghislaine et Jean-Hugues Goisot, 30, rue Bienvenu-Martin, 89530 Saint-Bris-le-Vineux, tel. 03.86.53.35.15, fax 03.86.53.62.03,
e-mail jhetg.goisot@cerb.cernet.fr ✓
☕ by appt.

DOM. GRAND ROCHE 2001★

| | 1.8 ha | 8,000 | | | 5–8 € |

Erick Lavallée has charge of this 21.5-ha estate. Pale yellow and limpid, this Aligoté has a seductive quality, with its remarkable delicate mineral bouquet. On the palate it is lively, with, as the nose leads one to expect, floral notes, a slight butteriness and the classic touch of bitterness on the finish.

☛ Erick Lavallée, Dom. Grand Roche, 6, rte de Chitry, 89530 Saint-Bris-le-Vineux, tel. 03.86.53.84.07, fax 03.86.53.88.36 ✓
☕ by appt.

REMI JOBARD 2001★

| | 1 ha | 5,000 | | | 5–8 € |

Producing an Aligoté at Meursault is rather like wearing clogs at Versailles! The colour is classic, the bouquet very pure, combining flint and green apples. On the palate is lingering, powerful and vigorous at the same time, exactly what one expects of this grape variety. In the Meursault area, the Aligoté tends towards Chardonnay, but not in this case.

☛ Rémi Jobard, 12, rue Sudot, 21190 Meursault, tel. 03.80.21.20.23, fax 03.80.21.67.69,
e-mail remi.jobard@libertysurf.fr ✓
☕ by appt.

GILLES JOURDAN 2001★

| | n.c. | 2,400 | | | 5–8 € |

This grape variety was already recognized in 1667 under the name of *beaunié*. It was described as *plant gris, griset, alligotay, blanc de Troyes* (old French, meaning "grey plant, greyish, Aligoté, white from Troyes") etc. In fact, *Aligoté* fits it like a glove: a lively name that equates with its nature. Brilliant straw in colour, this wine from the 2001 vintage, with its floral bouquet is completely typical of the appellation: good acidity and a piquancy that is not the least bit aggressive.

☛ Gilles Jourdan, 114, Grande-Rue, 21700 Corgoloin, tel. 03.80.62.76.31, fax 03.80.62.98.55 ✓
☕ by appt.

DOM. DES MOIROTS 2001★

| | 0.5 ha | 2,400 | | | 5–8 € |

Coming from the charming village of Bissey-sous-Cruchaud in the Côte Chalonnaise, this fine example of the cru is sound and true to type; of a rich colour and filled with flower aromas, it follows a well-trodden path. A platter of *charcuterie du pays* (assorted cold meats from the area) will perk it up.

☛ Lucien and Christophe Denizot, Dom. des Moirots, 14, rue des Moirots, 71390 Bissey-sous-Cruchaud, tel. 06.83.41.55.24, fax 03.85.92.09.42,
e-mail domainedesmoirots@free.fr ✓
☕ by appt.

LUCIEN MUZARD ET FILS 2001★★

| | 0.08 ha | 615 | | | 5–8 € |

Produced on barely two *ouvrées* (a traditional Burgundian measurement), or 8 ares (about 800 square metres), this Aligoté positively exudes fascinating fruit aromas. It delights the palate; the taste-buds are bowled over by it. Not a wine to keep hanging about. Drink it at its best. Sadly there is so little of it...

☛ Lucien Muzard et Fils, 11 bis, rue de la Cour-Verreuil, BP 25, 21590 Santenay, tel. 03.80.20.61.85, fax 03.80.20.66.02,
e-mail lucien-muzard-et-fils@wanadoo.fr ✓
☕ by appt.

DOM. HENRI NAUDIN-FERRAND 2001★

| | 2.38 ha | 22,037 | | | 3–5 € |

What should one serve with this wine? A home-made *jambon persillée* (ham with parsley set in aspic). The colour shows good highlights, the nose was not revealing its full range in March 2003 but should eventually be more forthcoming. Richness and acidity are nicely balanced on the palate and the length shows promise.

☛ Dom. Henri Naudin-Ferrand, rue du Meix-Grenot, 21700 Magny-lès-Villers, tel. 03.80.62.91.50, fax 03.80.62.91.77, e-mail dnaudin@ipac.fr ✓
☕ by appt.

OLIVIER-GARD

Vieilles Vignes 2001★

| | 0.5 ha | 4,000 | | | 5–8 € |

Corboin is a hamlet in the Hautes Côtes joined to Nuits-Saint-Georges. Soft fruits grow well in the area and this estate makes them into liqueurs, syrups and jams. The Aligoté also thrives in this environment. Brilliant without too much colour, centered around floral notes, this one demonstrates an uncompromising liveliness from its first contact with the palate right through to the finish. It has every right to its name. The 2000 vintage was *coup de coeur* last year.

☛ Dom. Olivier-Gard, Concoeur-et-Corboin, 21700 Nuits-Saint-Georges, tel. 03.80.62.39.33, fax 03.80.62.10.47 ✓ ☗
☕ by appt.
☛ Manuel Olivier

DOM. GERARD PERSENOT 2001★★

| | 6 ha | 40,000 | | | 5–8 € |

This pale yellow wine, tending towards the exotic on the nose, is elegant and fruity. An Aligoté in the modern style, it doesn't rub you up the wrong way. It even allows itself the luxury of a touch of complexity which is not at all unpleasant.

☛ EARL Gérard Persenot, 20, rue de Gouaix, 89530 Saint-Bris-le-Vineux, tel. 03.86.53.61.46, fax 03.86.53.61.52 ✓
☕ by appt.

DOM. MICHELE ET PATRICE RION

2001 ★

	0.15 ha	1,200	🍷	5–8 €

A new estate created in 1990 some 80 m from the church of Premeaux. Brilliant light yellow in colour, possessing fairly original aromas for an Aligoté, this wine is from the Côte de Nuits. The terroir is discernible but the cask has added a vanilla note. It is a pleasant wine of undoubted character. Should be drunk in the months to come.

☛ SCE Michèle et Patrice Rion, 1, rue de la Maladière, 21700 Premeaux-Prissey, tel. 03.80.62.32.63, fax 03.80.62.49.63, e-mail patrice.rion@wanadoo.fr ☑
🍴 by appt.

DOM. SORIN DE FRANCE 2001 ★★★

	11,63 ha	100,000	🍾 🍷	3–5 €

"*Et buvez frais si faire se peut* (And drink it cool if one can do so)." Writer François Rabelais made this suggestion in the 16th century. Take his advice when serving this pale straw-yellow wine, with a nose that puts one in mind of a bunch of wild-roses. On the palate there is hint of acid-drops, of grapefruit. Fresh and rounded, this is an exceptionally smooth wine from 2001 (a difficult vintage) which really stands out from the rest. Proposed for the *coup de coeur*. the only one from the Yonne to be so.

☛ Dom. Sorin-Defrance, 11 *bis*, rue de Paris, 89530 Saint-Bris-le-Vineux, tel. 03.86.53.32.99, fax 03.86.53.34.44 ☑
🍴 by appt.

TABIT ET FILS 2001 ★★

	10 ha	11,000	🍾 🍷	3–5 €

This cellar, dating from the 16th century, is one of the delights of the wine-producing town of Saint-Bris. The wine, which needs to be decanted before serving, represents good value for money, which is rare in an Aligoté, but why not? Its quality destines it to accompany fish, or a cooked dish. As mineral as one could wish, without harshness or bitterness; a classic wine.

☛ Cave Tabit et Fils, 2, rue Dorée, 89530 Saint-Bris-le-Vineux, tel. 03.86.53.33.83, fax 03.86.53.67.97, e-mail tabit@wanadoo.fr ☑
🍴 by appt.

Wines selected but not starred

DOM. YVES BAZIN 2001

	1.88 ha	3,000	🍾	3–5 €

☛ Yves Bazin, 21700 Villars-Fontaine, tel. 03.80.61.35.25, fax 03.80.61.21.46 ☑
🍴 ev. day. 9am–12 noon 2pm–6pm;
Sun. and groups by appt.

DOM. CHENE

Vieilles Vignes 2000

	0.3 ha	2,200	🍾	5–8 €

☛ Dom. Chêne, Ch. Chardon, 71960 Berzé-la-Ville, tel. 03.85.37.65.30, fax 03.85.37.75.39, e-mail gaecchene@aol.com ☑
🍴 by appt.

LA CAVE DU CONNAISSEUR 2001

	1 ha	6,000	🍾 🍷	5–8 €

☛ La Cave du Connaisseur, rue des Moulins, BP 78, 89800 Chablis, tel. 03.86.42.87.15, fax 03.86.42.49.84, e-mail connaisseur@chablis.net ☑
🍴 ev. day. 10am–6pm

DOM. LES DAVIGNOLLES 2001

	0.4 ha	700	🍾	3–5 €

☛ Denis Vessot, Le Bourg, 71640 Barizey, tel. 03.85.44.59.79, fax 03.85.44.59.79
🍴 by appt.

DOM. ANNE ET ARNAUD GOISOT

Coteaux de Saint-Bris 2001

	7 ha	30,000	🍾 🍷	3–5 €

☛ Dom. Anne et Arnaud Goisot, 4 bis, rte de Champs, 89530 Saint-Bris-le-Vineux, tel. 03.86.53.32.15, fax 03.86.53.64.22 ☑
🍴 ev. day. ex. Sun. 8am–12 noon 1.30pm–7pm

DOM. HUBER-VERDEREAU 2001

	0.85 ha	6,500	🍾 🍷	3–5 €

☛ Dom. Huber-Verdereau, rue de la Cave, 21190 Volnay, tel. 03.80.22.51.50, fax 03.80.22.48.32 ☑
🍴 by appt.

PASCAL MELLENOTTE 2001

	1 ha	2,000	🍷	3–5 €

☛ Pascal Mellenotte, Le Martray, 71640 Mellecey, tel. 03.85.45.15.64, fax 03.85.45.15.64, e-mail pascal.mellenotte@wanadoo.fr ☑
🍴 ev. day. ex. Sun. 10am–7pm

MORIN PERE ET FILS 2001

	n.c.	25,000		5–8 €

☛ Morin Père et Fils, 9, quai Fleury, 21700 Nuits-Saint-Georges, tel. 03.80.61.19.51, fax 03.80.61.05.10, e-mail caves@morinpere-fils.com ☑
🍴 ev. day. 9am–12 noon 2pm–6pm; summer 9am–7pm

DOM. ROYET ET FILS 2001

	2 ha	5,000	🍾 🍷	3–5 €

☛ GAEC Royet et Fils, Combereau, 71490 Couches, tel. 03.85.49.64.01, fax 03.85.49.61.77 ☑
🍴 by appt.

SORIN-COQUARD 2001

	5.5 ha	15,000	🍷	5–8 €

☛ EARL Sorin-Coquard, 25, rue de Grisy, 89530 Saint-Bris-le-Vineux, tel. 03.86.53.37.76, fax 03.86.53.37.76 ☑
🍴 by appt.
☛ Pascal and Christine Sorin

DOM. VERRET 2002

	12.74 ha	80,000	🍷	5–8 €

☛ Dom. Verret, 7, rte de Champs, BP 4, 89530 Saint-Bris-le-Vineux, tel. 03.86.53.31.81, fax 03.86.53.89.61, e-mail dverret@domaineverret.com ☑
🍴 by appt.

Bourgogne Passetoutgrain

This appellation applies exclusively to red and rosé wines produced in the inner part of the Bourgogne Grand Ordinaire area, and it requires the wines to be made from a blend of Pinot Noir and Gamay Noir grapes. The blend must contain a minimum of one-third of Pinot Noir. Current thinking holds that the best wines

Bourgogne Passetoutgrain

are made of roughly equal quantities of grapes from the two varieties, with a slight preponderance of Pinot Noir.

The rosé wines are obtained by the *saignée* method, a technical process distinct from the *vins gris*, which are obtained by the direct pressing of black grapes and vinifying them like white wines. In the *saignée* process the grapes are left to macerate, and the juice is extracted (or "bled") only when the winemaker has obtained the desired colour – which can very well occur in the middle of the night! Very little Passetoutgrain Rosé is made, and in general this appellation is regarded as a red wine. It is produced mainly in the Saône-et-Loire (about two-thirds), the remainder being made in the Côte d'Or or the Yonne valley. In 2002 production amounted to 43,456 hl. The wines are light, deliciously flavoured and should be drunk young.

DOM. BOUZERAND-DUJARDIN 2000★

| ■ | 0,3 ha | 2,300 | ◫ | 5–8 € |

A Passetoutgrain that knows how to spell its name! A light brick-red colour but its aromas tell us quite a lot about it. The initial impression is true to type. Two-thirds Gamay, this wine from Côte de Beaune has all the characteristics of the appellation.
☛ Dom. Bouzerand-Dujardin, pl. de l'Eglise,
21190 Monthélie, tel. 03.80.21.20.08, fax 03.80.21.28.16 ▨
⚇ by appt.

DOM. DES CHAMBRIS 2001★★

| ■ | 0,5 ha | 580 | ◫ | 5–8 € |

Coups de cœur are rarely awarded for a Passetoutgrain, so we offer our warmest congratulations to this fairly new estate, nestled in a top corner Hautes Côtes de Nuits. Made with 30% Gamay, the result tends towards the Pinot side. Of an intense red colour, the wine evokes an aroma of prunes right across both nose and palate. A quite light and soft, full and rounded wine. Perhaps not representative of the appellation's rather rugged image, but who would complain about that?
☛ SCEV du Dom. des Chambris, 7, rue du Lavoir,
21220 Chevannes, tel. 03.80.61.44.77, fax 03.80.61.48.87,
e-mail leschambris@wanadoo.fr ▨
⚇ by appt.

CH. DE CHAMILLY 2000★

| ■ | 1.74 ha | 11,000 | ■ ☙ | 3–5 € |

Made in the Côte Chalonnaise, from half Gamay and half Pinot, this is a very good wine considering it is from the 2000 vintage. A good, intense red in colour, the nose is herbaceous and the palate pleasant and quite original, giving it an attractive personality. And its length? Satisfactory.
☛ Véronique Desfontaine, Le Château, 71510 Chamilly,
tel. 03.85.87.22.24, fax 03.85.91.23.91,
e-mail chateau.chamilly@wanadoo.fr ▨
⚇ by appt.

FRANCOISE CHAUVENET
Millefleurs 2001★

| ■ | n.c. | 35,000 | | 5–8 € |

Françoise Chauvenet was one of those women with a vibrant personality who contributed to the development of burgundy wines in the 19th century. "She tastes like a man," they said respectfully, at a time when the feminine cause still had a long way to go. Two-thirds Gamay, and it shows. Red fruit and tannins go arm-in-arm to a splendid finish. This is what one expects of a Passetoutgrain.
☛ Françoise Chauvenet, 9, quai Fleury,
21700 Nuits-Saint-Georges, tel. 03.80.61.39.83,
fax 03.80.61.32.72, e-mail chauvenet@chauvenet.com

GUY FONTAINE ET JACKY VION 2000★★

| ■ | 0,3 ha | 3,500 | ■ ☙ | 3–5 € |

60% Gamay, this Passetoutgrain from Côte de Beaune (Remigny is in the Saône-et-Loire but is close to Santenay) is up near the head of the column. Both its colour and its bouquet are straightforward, clean and true to type. At base it is a good wine and a Boeuf Bourguignon will bring out the best in it.
☛ GAEC des Vignerons, rue du Bourg, 71150 Remigny,
tel. 03.85.87.03.35, fax 03.85.87.03.35 ▨
⚇ by appt.
☛ Fontaine-Vion

DOM. GUEUGNON-REMOND 2001★★

| ■ | 0.2 ha | 1,000 | ◫ | 5–8 € |

This small estate, established in 1981, has produced a remarkable wine. Of an intense garnet colour, it positively exhales kirsch and Morello cherries (it is two-thirds Gamay). Already last year we were impressed with the quality of the Passetoutgrain produced by this Mâconnais wine-grower.
☛ Dom. Gueugnon-Remond, chem. de la Cave,
71850 Charnay-lès-Mâcon, tel. 03.85.29.23.88,
fax 03.85.20.20.72 ▨
⚇ by appt.

DOM. SYLVAIN PATAILLE
Vieilles Vignes 2001★

| ■ | 0.32 ha | 1,500 | ◫ | 5–8 € |

Two-thirds Gamay went into the making of this Marsannay, produced by Sylvain Pataille who divides his time between the vines on his tenant holding and his position as a consultant-oenologist. Garnet-red with purplish highlights, his 2001 vintage brings out the perfume of the Gamay grape and is reminiscent of a real Beaujolais made with grapes from old vines. In addition to the irreproachably mature nose, it is fleshy and well-structured and of a good length. Rustic? No doubt, but at one time Passetoutgrain was just that.
☛ Dom. Sylvain Pataille, 14, rue Neuve,
21160 Marsannay-la-Côte, tel. 06.70.11.62.15,
fax 03.80.52.49.49 ▨
⚇ by appt.

VIGNOBLE DE SOMMERE 2001★

| ■ | 0.6 ha | 2,600 | | 3–5 € |

This is the sixth generation of the family to work the Sommère vineyard in the Mâconnais (La Roche-Vineuse). A light ruby-red Passetoutgrain, 50% Pinot and the same of Gamay, quite soft, more rounded than tannic and beautifully balanced.
☛ Hervé Santé, Sommeré, 71960 La Roche-Vineuse,
tel. 03.85.37.80.57, fax 03.85.37.64.13,
e-mail domaine.sante@wanadoo.fr ▨
⚇ by appt.

Wines selected but not starred

DOM. FOREY PERE ET FILS 2001

| ■ | 1.16 ha | 9,000 | ▮ | 3–5 € |

☛ Dom. Forey Père et Fils, 2, rue Derrière-le-Four,
21700 Vosne-Romanée, tel. 03.80.61.09.68,
fax 03.80.61.12.63 ☑
☖ by appt.

PASCAL 2001

| ■ | n.c. | 10,000 | ▮ ♦ | 5–8 € |

☛ Pascal, Clos des Noirets, 21220 Gevrey-Chambertin,
tel. 03.80.34.37.82, fax 03.80.51.88.05 ☑
☖ by appt.

Bourgogne Hautes Côtes de Nuit

The appellation Bourgogne Hautes Côtes de Nuits is most often used for red, rosé and white wines produced in the 16 communes that lie in the hinterland of the Côte, together with parts of the communes above the appellations communales and the crus of the Côte de Nuit. In 2002 these vineyards produced 30,998 hl, of which 5,636 hl were white. The amount produced has increased significantly since 1970 when the vineyards used to produce more regional wines, essentially Bourgogne Aligoté. Extensive replanting has taken place since that time, and plants infected with phylloxera have been replanted.

In some years, the best exposed slopes produce wines that can rival some of the vineyards on the Côte; the best of them tend to be white, and it is a pity that more of the vineyards have not been planted with Chardonnay, which would undoubtedly give more reliable results more often. Along with the commitment to recreating the vineyard an equal effort has been put into encour- aging tourism. In particular, a Maison des Hautes Côtes gives visitors the chance to learn about the area and to taste the wines along with good local cuisine.

DOM. BARBIER ET FILS

Corvée de Villy 2000★★

| ■ | 1.88 ha | 9,200 | ⑪ | 8–11 € |

Corvée de Villy

**BOURGOGNE
HAUTES-CÔTES DE NUITS**

Appellation
Bourgogne Hautes-Côtes de Nuits
Contrôlée

Mis en bouteille à la propriété
Domaine Barbier et Fils
Propriétaire à Nuits-Saint-Georges, Côte-d'Or

It is often said, *de mère en mère* (from mother to mother). Here we have to say: mayor to mayor, since Bernard Barbier's family have put his successor at the Town Hall in charge of the vineyard. The new mayor of Nuits could have ambitions at cantonal level, if this wine, which gained an overwhelming majority among the upper villages, is anything to go by. More crimson than is strictly permissible, this 2000 vintage retains its fruitiness without rejecting the effect of the cask. Roundness on top of structure, power: it is a perfect illustration of the new style of Pinot Noir from the Hautes Côtes. It is good and effective. And pleasing. And it will keep.
☛ Dom. Barbier et Fils, 17, rue Thurot,
21700 Nuits-Saint-Georges, tel. 03.80.61.21.21,
fax 03.80.61.10.65, e-mail domaine.barbier@wanadoo.fr ☑
☖ ev. day. 9am–7pm

DOM. YVES BAZIN

Elevé en fût de chêne 2000★

| ■ | 4.75 ha | 3,200 | ⑪ | 8–11 € |

Matured in oak barrels, this wine is testimony to the quality obtained by this estate in the space of 20 years. Deep crimson, with good length and keeping potential, it has a good tannin support and the right amount of acidity. How, on one's return from military service, does one progress from hopeless mixed-farming to the vineyards which sustain the life of these villages? That is a thumbnail sketch of the career of Yves Bazin.
☛ Yves Bazin, 21700 Villars-Fontaine, tel. 03.80.61.35.25,
fax 03.80.61.21.46 ☑
☖ ev. day. 9am–12 noon 2pm–6pm;
Sun. and groups by appt.

JEAN-BAPTISTE BEJOT 2001★

| ■ | n.c. | 18,000 | | 5–8 € |

An old Burgundian house recently taken over by Protheau, another négociant. Its wine is an intense colour, still young and lively, with purplish tinges. The delicate, Pinot nose is far from banal. The velvety palate is all-enveloping, like an election campaign by a candidate for the Senate. A touch of acidity on the finish mingles with fairly pronounced tannins. Drink it now, or postpone the pleasure until a little later.
☛ SA Jean-Baptiste Béjot, 21190 Meursault,
tel. 03.80.21.22.45, fax 03.80.21.28.05

JEAN-CLAUDE BOUHEY ET FILS

Les Dames Huguettes 2000★

| ■ | 1.3 ha | 8,000 | ⑪ | 5–8 € |

This *climat*, probably the best known in the Hautes Côtes, is situated above Nuits, around the television pylon. A wine which has all the channels at its disposition but, far from sitting back, offers you a charming serial of its own starring damp woodlands and crystallized cherries, whose episodes run from nose to palate and on into the memory. There is no point in keeping this ready and welcoming wine for too long.
☛ Dom. Jean-Claude Bouhey et Fils, 7, rte de Magny,
21700 Villers-la-Faye, tel. 03.80.62.92.62,
fax 03.80.62.74.07 ☑
☖ by appt.

DOM. DES CHAMBRIS 2001★

| ■ | 5 ha | 7,500 | ⑪ | 5–8 € |

Perfumed with liquorice and spices, this robust and very young wine is powerful and tannic. Its red colour is very effective. The maturation in cask has not overwhelmed its essential aromas. The **white Cuvée des Chambris 2001 (8–11 €)** was placed in the same category. Well-chosen label.
☛ SCEV du Dom. des Chambris, 7, rue du Lavoir,
21220 Chevannes, tel. 03.80.61.44.77, fax 03.80.61.48.87,
e-mail leschambris@wanadoo.fr ☑
☖ by appt.

DOM. MARCEL ET BERNARD FRIBOURG 2000★

| ■ | 10 ha | 6,800 | ⑪ | 5–8 € |

"*Bon Pied bon oeil* (Good foot, good eye)," this estate was the first to be awarded a *coup de coeur* in this appellation for the 1984 vintage. From year to year, it remains among the best. It has also contributed a great deal (one thinks of

Marcel) to the development of the Hautes Côtes. A limpid cherry-red colour, with a predominantly blackcurrant bouquet, this wine from the 2000 vintage has strength when it is needed and flexibility for the rest of the time. A perfect example of the appellation.

🍷 SCE Dom. Marcel et Bernard Fribourg, 8, rue de l'Ancienne-Cure, 21700 Villers-la-Faye, tel. 03.80.62.91.74, fax 03.80.62.71.17 ☑
🍷 by appt.

XAVIER GIRARDIN

La Croix Basse 2001★

■	0.27 ha	1,700	🍶	5–8 €

Little by little the bird builds its nest. Not even 1 ha in 2000 when this estate was established, today it covers 2.5 ha. This newcomer has made great strides and its 2001 vintage seems true to type and representative of its appellation. Brilliant garnet-ruby-red, it tends towards almost jammy red fruit; its attack is straightforward, and thereafter it is well- balanced. Some slight astringency, but that is in the nature of the things and will disappear after it has been kept for one or two years.

🍷 Xavier Girardin, SCEA Les Ormes, rue des Magniens, 21700 Arcenant, tel. 03.80.62.11.80, fax 03.80.61.22.72 ☑
🍷 by appt.

DOM. GLANTENET PERE ET FILS 2001★

■	9.44 ha	13,600	🍶	8–11 €

Magny-lès-Villers is the link between the Hautes Côtes de Nuits and Beaune. A threshold. Here it leans towards the Hautes Côtes de Nuits side, with a 2001 vintage red that has the roundness and bouquet of a plump ripe cherry. A touch of oak signals results from 12 months maturing in cask. In the depth of its soul it is tannic; this is a well-structured, fine wine that simply needs time to soften. In this same AOC, the **2001 white** was given a special mention: it also needs time for the oak to integrate.

🍷 Dom. Glantenet Père et Fils, rue de l'Aye, 21700 Magny-lès-Villers, tel. 03.80.62.91.61, fax 03.80.62.74.79, e-mail domaine.glantenet@wanadoo.fr ☑
🍷 ev. day. ex. Sun. 9am–12 noon 2pm–6.30pm

DOM. HENRI GROS

Cuvée Prestige 2001★★

■	2.5 ha	13,000	🍶	8–11 €

This is not a wine that should be taken lightly. It hovered around the *coup de coeur* and so one can choose it without hesitation. "Congratulations, an excellent wine," reads one of the tasters' cards. Sombre, purplish, almost black, the colour evokes the sun setting behind the Côte. And heaven knows it's beautiful. The bouquet has maturity without too much freshness. On the palate there is concentration and finesse. The **Hautes Côtes de Nuits white2001 (5–8 €)** was awarded one star.

🍷 Henri Gros, rue de la Grande-Fontaine, 21220 Chamboeuf, tel. 03.80.51.81.20, fax 03.80.49.71.75, e-mail henrigros.fr ☑
🍷 by appt.

DOM. MICHEL GROS 2001★

■	8 ha	40,000	🍶	5–8 €

Holder of a *coup de coeur* for the 1999 and 1993 vintages, this estate knows what it is talking about. The cherry-red colour of this vintage is dense and intense. The nose starts on a musky note which quite quickly turns to ripe red fruit. The musky note lingers, within a concentration that is very strong, structured and powerful. For the moment, elegance takes second place. A strong, lasting keeping potential. Note that it will improve with the aeration, which will bring out the ripe fruit aromas.

🍷 Dom. Michel Gros, 7, rue des Communes, 21700 Vosne-Romanée, tel. 03.80.61.04.69, fax 03.80.61.22.29 ☑
🍷 by appt.

DOM. ROBERT ET RAYMOND JACOB

2001★★

■	0.7 ha	5,800	🍶	5–8 €

Pale, barely golden, with an aroma of almonds, white-fleshed fruit and crushed grapes, this wine, whose balance is sure though not easy, offers a refreshing fruitiness that lingers on. A really good wine from one of the most reliable estates of the Côte.

🍷 Dom. Robert et Raymond Jacob, hameau de Buisson, 21550 Ladoix-Serrigny, tel. 03.80.26.40.42, fax 03.80.26.49.34 ☑
🍷 by appt.

JEAN LECELLIER

Les Genévrières 2001★

■	3 ha	2,100	🍶	23–30 €

An austere, concentrated wine which is still very young. Its tannins and its acidity cover the fruitiness but it will be worth the wait. An intense red colour, its aromas are of toast (it spent 15 months in cask) also raspberry. Jean Lecellier is part of the Clavelier Company.

🍷 Jean Lecellier, 49, N 74, 21700 Comblanchien, tel. 03.80.62.98.99, fax 03.80.62.95.20

OLIVIER JOUAN 2001★★

■	3.5 ha	3,000	🍶	8–11 €

While the colour is a deep cherry-red, the bouquet is all blackberries and vanilla (14 months in cask).These 3.5 ha (half of the Morey-Saint-Denis estate) produce a wine which fulfils all your hopes: tannic, complex, generous, lingering and with good keeping potential.

🍷 Olivier Jouan, 21, Grande-Rue, 21220 Morey-Saint-Denis, tel. 03.80.58.59.36, fax 03.80.58.59.36 ☑
🍷 by appt.

DOM. JEAN-PHILIPPE MARCHAND

2001★★

■	n.c.	24,000	🍶	8–11 €

A *coup de coeur* for its 1998 vintage and again this time a very rich wine and one that will develop in the cellar. This enterprising and dynamic family from Gevrey were quick to spot the development of the Hautes Côtes. This product of from wine-grower-négociant is remarkable; vanilla undoubtedly, but it is so substantial it urgently needs a few years in the cellar. Crimson-carmine, there is no argument about the colour. As for the nose, it is crafty. On the whole, a perfect specimen of this type of wine.

🍷 Jean-Philippe Marchand, 4, rue Souvert, BP 41, 21220 Gevrey-Chambertin, tel. 03.80.34.33.60, fax 03.80.34.12.77, e-mail marchand@axnet.fr ☑ 🏠🏠
🍷 by appt.

DOM. MAREY

Les Jamées 2000★★

■	3.8 ha	4,800	⬛🍶	11–15 €

Selected for the final of the *coup de coeur*, this wine is on that level and it is tremendous; a 2000 vintage from a relatively recent estate which is really trying hard. Crimson, it fills the nose with the aroma of Morello cherry and the palate remains lost in admiration. One of the last examples of mixed-farming – combined here with 16 ha of vineyards for this latest wine, which is very, very good. Meuilley was formerly famous for its strawberries. There remains a hint of berries in this wine. The **white Cuvée Les Monbourgeons 2000 (8–11 €)** which was awarded one star.

↝ Dom. Marey, rue Bachot, 21700 Meuilley,
tel. 03.80.61.12.44, fax 03.80.61.11.31,
e-mail dommarey@aol.com �
☿ by appt.

DOM. MOILLARD 2001★★

| | 6.32 ha | 36,000 | ⑪ | 5–8 € |

There is no doubt that the lady of the manor of Vergy, heroine of a courtly love poem set in the Hautes Côtes area, must have tasted this type of Chardonnay in the course of her amorous encounters…The finest gold colour, with quite exotic perfumes of mango and grapefruit, this wine positively rebounds on the palate thanks to its impulsive liveliness. Don't hesitate to drink it young.

↝ Dom. Moillard, chem. rural, 29,
21700 Nuits-Saint-Georges, tel. 03.80.62.42.00,
fax 03.80.61.28.13, e-mail nuicave@wanadoo.fr ▪
☿ ev. day. 10am–6pm; 10am–7pm in summer; cl. Jan.

OLIVIER-GARD

Cuvée Tradition 2001★

| | 1.5 ha | 7,000 | ▪ ♦ | 5–8 € |

The **Cuvée de Garde en Hautes Côtes de Nuit red 2000 (8–11 €)** matured in cask for ten months, that received a special mention, or this Cuvée Tradition 2001, which was not matured in cask? It is sincere and spontaneous beneath a light ruby-red colour. With its raspberry notes, it is a wine to drink young to enjoy its suppleness, its easy-drinking quality and its delightful finish. A true, unpretentious Pinot from the Hautes Côtes.

↝ Dom. Olivier-Gard, Concoeur-et-Corboin,
21700 Nuits-Saint-Georges, tel. 03.80.62.39.33,
fax 03.80.62.10.47 ▪ ☖
☿ by appt.
↝ Manuel Olivier

PIERRE LAMOTTE 2001★★

| | n.c. | n.c. | ▪ | 5–8 € |

A game terrine for this Pinot from the Hautes Côtes with such delicate tannins they might be made out of silk from Lyons. There's nothing surprising about that: the Cottin family who are jointly responsible for this great *coup de coeur* wine, gained their first coat of arms among the silks of Lyons. And one of the brothers is at Mouton-Rothschild. This wine, therefore, has something to emulate. Its colour and richness show through the moment it enters the glass. The structure is well based on a good, lively acidity where the red fruit is by no means the last to arrive. Keep it for three or four years.

↝ Pierre Lamotte, rue Lavoisier,
21700 Nuits-Saint-Georges, tel. 03.80.62.64.00,
fax 03.80.62.64.00
☿ by appt.

CH. DE PREMEAUX 2001★

| | 2.1 ha | 8,000 | ⑪ | 8–11 € |

Awarded a *coup de coeur* last year for its 2000, the Premeaux estate knows how to climb the Hautes Côtes in search of

something special. The 16 months this purplish ruby-red 2001 vintage spent in cask is evident on the nose from the very first, distinguishable by its interesting notes of charring, muskiness and damp woodlands. This rich and powerful wine, with its well-constituted structure, should benefit greatly from two to three years in the cellar, after which it will be irresistible with a sauced meat dish.

↝ Dom. du Ch. de Premeaux, 21700 Premeaux-Prissey,
tel. 03.80.62.30.64, fax 03.80.62.39.28,
e-mail chateau.de.premeaux@wanadoo.fr ▪
☿ by appt.
↝ Pelletier

HENRI ET GILLES REMORIQUET 2001★★

| | 1.8 ha | 10,000 | ⑪ | 8–11 € |

Our *coup de coeur* in 98 for a 95 vintage does you the honour of offering this fine wine, the colour and richness of which is dazzling. Yes, indeed, it has richness to give away: blackcurrant, mushrooms, damp woodlands, the nose takes a stroll through familiar territory. Tannins, liquorice, then the symphony brings in the brasses. The colour is impeccable and more certain, as Giraudoux said, than a vessel on a wild sea. A wine that will last.

↝ Henri et Gilles Remoriquet, 25, rue de Charmois,
21700 Nuits-Saint-Georges, tel. 03.80.61.24.84,
fax 03.80.61.36.63,
e-mail domaine.remoriquet@wanadoo.fr ▪
☿ by appt.

LAURENT ROUMIER 2000★★

| | 2 ha | 6,000 | ⑪ | 8–11 € |

When one is called Laurent Roumier and one is wine-grower at Chambolle-Musigny who has worked hard for his place with the sun, after creating this estate in 1991, one is entitled to sincere congratulations on this brilliant and deep-coloured wine. The bouquet opens on blackberries and damp woodland. The black fruit predominates on the palate and adds a few extra points to a match won by the harmonious, balanced and long structure.

↝ Dom. Laurent Roumier, rue de Vergy,
21220 Chambolle-Musigny, tel. 03.80.62.83.60,
fax 03.80.62.84.10 ▪
☿ by appt.

GUY SIMON ET FILS 2000★

| | 2 ha | 6,000 | ⑪ | 8–11 € |

A success and a future! Produced by one of the best architects of the reconstruction of this vineyard, this ruby-red bordering on crimson wine from the 2000 vintage, which shows notes of leather connected with its age, and an oakiness, is harmonious and balanced on the palate. A touch of acidity and some young tannins, but a taste of Morello cherry that is not easily forgotten and a length that goes well beyond the norm. The **white 2000** in the same appellation was also awarded one star: fruity and a charmer, without the least false note.

↝ Guy Simon et Fils, 21700 Marey-lès-Fussey,
tel. 03.80.62.91.85, fax 03.80.62.71.82 ▪
☿ by appt.

DOM. THEVENOT-LE BRUN ET FILS 2000★★

| | 3.79 ha | 8,500 | ▪ ⑪ ♦ | 8–11 € |

The Thévenot family knows how to mount a presentation of this white Hautes Côtes de Nuits, a Chardonnay which has the aroma of a Chablis field mushroom. A small hint of cask (six months), merely a touch. The substance is generous and full-bodied; this is a wine that bends over backwards to give satisfaction. From the first mouthful to the back of the palate, all the Hautes Côtes characteristics are present.

↝ Dom. Thévenot-Le Brun et Fils,
21700 Marey-lès-Fussey, tel. 03.80.62.91.64,
fax 03.80.62.99.81,
e-mail thevenot-le-brun@wanadoo.fr ▪
☿ by appt.

DOM. DU VAL DE VERGY

Cuvée de la Tour Saint-Denis 2001★★

■	5 ha	30,000	⊞	11–15 €

After entertaining Prince Charles of England for a week, when he visited Val de Vergy to do some watercolour painting, one could hardly ruin one's *cuvée*. And indeed, Yves Chaley has not done so. The first glance is cherry-red, the nose opens on toasted, raspberry notes. Rounded, elegant, complex even, this *cuvée* could grace the buffet at the Cheltenham Gold Cup. Nothing could clear the jumps better. Perhaps Prince Charles, who often attends this event, would find a touch of watercolour in his eye remembering this small corner of Burgundy, where he spent a few happy days at Chaley, which has 12 guest-rooms.
☛ Yves Chaley, Curtil-Vergy, 21220 Gevrey-Chambertin, tel. 03.80.61.43.81, fax 03.80.61.42.79 ☑ ▦
↧ by appt.

DOM. DE LA VIGNE AU ROY

Haute Gêne 2001★

■	1 ha	4,500	⊞	5–8 €

The old Geisweiler domaine was originally created by Maurice Eisenchteter, then acquired by a family from Champagne (Gonnet) and subsequently by Eric Piffaut (Veuve Ambal). The Jury liked the **Cuvée Pertuis de Rousseau white 2001**, and equally this yellow-gold wine with its agreeable fruitiness and the good length of its exotic notes. A touch of liveliness on the finish. Only moderately characteristic but with real charm.
☛ Dom. de la Vigne au Roy, rue de la Vigne-au-Roy, 21220 Bévy, tel. 03.80.61.44.87, fax 03.80.61.44.87 ☑
↧ by appt.
↧ Eric Piffaut

CH. DE VILLARS FONTAINE

Les Genévrières 2000★

■	6 ha	42,000	⊞	15–23 €

Bernard Hudelot is a notable player in the contemporary Hautes Côtes saga. Capable, he teaches at Dijon. Imaginative, he produced wine for friends while living in Tahiti. Curious, he settled in the area of Vergy, where his family originated, at the time of its renaissance. He bought Clavelier, the house in the Hautes Côtes and, last but not least, the Château de Villars Fontaine. A splendid path trodden by this impassioned and conquering spirit. His Genévrières under a new label spent, according to the house litany, some 30 months in cask. We are dealing, therefore, with a wine marked by its maturation: intense and fruity, with an elusive nose but demonstrative and long on the palate.
☛ Dom. de Montmain, 21700 Villars-Fontaine, tel. 03.80.62.31.94, fax 03.80.61.02.31, e-mail bernard.hudelot@wanadoo.fr ☑ ▦
↧ ev. day. ex. Sat. Sun. 9am–12 noon 2pm–6pm
↧ Hudelot

Wines selected but not starred

BERTRAND AMBROISE 2001

■	1.18 ha	6,000		11–15 €

☛ Bertrand Ambroise, rue de l'Eglise, 21700 Premeaux-Prissey, tel. 03.80.62.30.19, fax 03.80.62.38.69, e-mail bertrand.ambroise@wanadoo.fr ☑
↧ by appt.

JEAN BROCARD-GRIVOT 2000

■	3.36 ha	3,590	▮⊞	5–8 €

☛ Jean Brocard-Grivot, rue Basse, 21220 Reulle-Vergy, tel. 03.80.61.42.14, fax 03.80.61.42.14 ☑
↧ by appt.

DOM. YVAN DUFOULEUR

Les Dames Huguettes 2000

■	1.3 ha	9,000	⊞	11–15 €

☛ Dom. Yvan Dufouleur, 1, rue de l'Eglise, 21700 Quincey, tel. 03.80.62.31.00, fax 03.80.62.31.00, e-mail gaelle.dufouleur@21700–nuits.com ☑
↧ by appt.

JEAN-YVES GUYARD

Pièce Dame-Marie 2001

■	2.3 ha	5,000	▮	5–8 €

☛ Jean-Yves Guyard, 21, rue de Chaux, 21700 Villers-la-Faye, tel. 03.80.62.91.14, fax 03.80.62.75.72, e-mail jeanyvesguyard@wanadoo.fr ☑
↧ by appt.

FREDERIC JACOB 2001

■	1 ha	6,000	▮	5–8 €

☛ Frédéric Jacob, 50, Grande-Rue, 21420 Changey-Echevronne, tel. 03.80.21.55.58, fax 03.80.62.75.36 ☑
↧ by appt.

DOM. JEAN-PIERRE TRUCHETET 2001

■	0.53 ha	3,300	⊞	5–8 €

☛ Jean-Pierre Truchetet, RN 74, 21700 Premeaux-Prissey, tel. 03.80.61.07.22, fax 03.80.61.34.35 ☑
↧ by appt.

ROMUALD VALOT 2001

■	n.c.	8,000	▮⊞	5–8 €

☛ SARL Bourgogne Romuald Valot, 14, rue des Tonneliers, BP 213, 21206 Beaune, tel. 03.80.25.91.30

Bourgogne Hautes Côtes de Beaune

The Appellation Bourgogne Hautes Côtes de Beaune applies to about 20 communes, extending in the north into the Saône-et-Loire. In 2002 the quantity of wines produced under the appellation totalled 42,658 hl, including 7,216 hl of white, rather more than the Hautes Côtes de Nuits production. In situation, the two areas are quite similar, and a considerable area is given over to growing Aligoté and Gamay.

The Coopérative des Hautes Côtes, which started life in Orches, a hamlet near Baubigny, is now based under the "banner" of Pommard, at the intersection of the D973 and the main RN74, just south of Beaune. A significant amount of Bourgogne Hautes Côtes de Beaune is vinified there. The vineyards have greatly developed since the years 1970–75, as in the north.

The countryside is more picturesque than that of the Hautes Côtes de Nuits, and there are many places to visit, including Orches, La Rochepot and its château and Nolay, a little Burgundian village. It is worth adding that the Hautes Côtes formerly grew a variety of crops and is still an area where soft fruits are grown to supply the liqueur-makers of Nuits-Saint-Georges and Dijon. The fruit liqueurs and brandies made from these blackcurrants and raspberries are of excellent quality. There is a single appellation for the pear brandy of Monts-de-Côte d'Or, which is also made here.

DOM. BOISSON

Elevé en fût de chêne 2000★

	6 ha	11,000	⅏	5–8 €

Near to Nolay, Cormot-le-Grand is famous for its cliffs and its rock-climbing. As for this Pinot Noir, it needs no crampons or cords to help it rise to the heights. Perfectly limpid, the grape variety is evident both on the nose and the palate. Light, oaky notes, but the fruit predominates. Already very pleasant to drink because of its balance, acidity and alcohol content, but it also has great potential. Invite it to your table in two or three years time.
↪ Dom. Boisson, 21340 Cormot-le-Grand, tel. 03.80.21.71.92, fax 03.80.21.71.92 ✔ ⌂
☥ by appt.

DOM. JEAN-FRANCOIS BOUTHENET

Au Paradis Elevé en fût de chêne 2001★

	1.25 ha	1,700	⅏	5–8 €

Here we find ourselves in Paradis. What an attractive name for a *climat* and so easy to live with. Ruby-red of medium intensity, this wine, which has a slight oakiness but doesn't allow the cask to monopolize the bouquet, is clean from beginning to end. A little light, undoubtedly, while still showing good intentions (balance and length in particular). The grape variety is well represented.
↪ Jean-François Bouthenet, Mercey, 4, rue du Four, 71150 Cheilly-lès-Maranges, tel. 03.85.91.14.29, fax 03.85.91.18.24 ✔
☥ by appt.

DOM. DENIS CARRE 2001★

	3,5 ha	n.c.	▮⅏♦	5–8 €

Twelve months in cask for this wine with the sparkling garnet-red colour. The nose has fruit, but also oakiness. All that is found on the palate where the fine and rounded tannins guarantee an excellent balance and a two to three year life.
↪ Denis Carré, rue du Puits-Bouret, 21190 Meloisey, tel. 03.80.26.02.21, fax 03.80.26.04.64 ✔
☥ by appt.

DOM. CHARACHE-BERGERET

Les Bignons 2001★

	2 ha	5,000	⅏	5–8 €

This estate was founded in 1976 by Rene Charache and his wife Jacqueline. The initial 3 ha have extended to 19 ha. On the nose, this crimson-red wine from 2001 has a very pleasant, raspberry-tinged strawberry aroma. Its tannins are not inactive, but the richness and power on the palate are what one would expect.
↪ René Charache-Bergeret, 21200 Bouze-lès-Beaune, tel. 03.80.26.00.86, fax 03.80.26.00.86, e-mail bourgogne-charache.bergeret@wanadoo.fr ✔
☥ by appt.

DOM. FRANCOIS CHARLES ET FILS

2000★

	0.15 ha	3,000	⅏	8–11 €

One still builds wine cellars in Burgundy. One was constructed on this estate, recently. Pale yellow, gently toasted, this Chardonnay is balance incarnate. After an exotic passage (pineapple, grapefruit), it ends on a mineral, iodized note that conjures up seaweed and shellfish. With average structure but representative of the appellation. The 94 vintage was *coup de coeur* in the 1997 edition.
↪ EARL François Charles et Fils, rue de Pichot, 21190 Nantoux, tel. 03.80.26.01.20, fax 03.80.26.04.84, e-mail charles.francois@terre-net.fr ✔ ⌂
☥ by appt.

DOM. CHEVROT 2001★★

	1 ha	5,000	▮⅏♦	5–8 €

A wine with confident, pleasing elegance, it readily displays its Chardonnay characteristics, lending himself to hot entrées, a tart, perhaps. A clean golden yellow colour, it opts for acacia blossom and hawthorn, but it has still to develop its aromatic potential. Greater in length than depth, but very harmonious, it give an excellent performance. From the Domaine des Maranges, where the two sons are both oenologists.
↪ Catherine et Fernand Chevrot, Dom. Chevrot, 19, rte de Couches, 71150 Cheilly-lès-Maranges, tel. 03.85.91.10.55, fax 03.85.91.13.24,
e-mail domaine.chevrot@wanadoo.fr ✔ ⌂
☥ ev. day. 9am–12 noon 1.30pm–6pm; Sun. 9am–12 noon

FRANCOISE ET DENIS CLAIR 2001★

	1.5 ha	7,000	▮♦	5–8 €

Very sombre ruby-garnet-red, this 2001 vintage opens little by little on cherries in *eau-de-vie* and jam. With a rounded attack, it then shows a lively side because its tannins are still much in evidence. But they are quite silky. This will be a wine to serve in 2004 with a sauced meat, a Boeuf Bourguinon, perhaps.
↪ Françoise et Denis Clair, 14, rue de la Chapelle, 21590 Santenay, tel. 03.80.20.61.96, fax 03.80.20.65.19 ✔
☥ by appt.

DOM. DERATS-DUMAY 2000★

	8 ha	40,000		5–8 €

A weak colour and a good nose supported by a tripod: cherry, leather and toasted hazelnut. Harmonious on the palate, this is a well-balanced wine which is not miserly with its gifts, right up to the spicy finish. Its potential, too, is not uninteresting; this wine will keep for another two to four years. The Domaine des Maranges is now established in the Château de Melin near Auxey-Duresses.
↪ Dom. Dumay, Ch. de Melin, 21190 Auxey-Duresses, tel. 03.80.21.21.19, fax 03.80.21.21.72,
e-mail derats@chateaudemelin.com ✔ ⌂
☥ ev. day. 9am–7pm

DOUDET-NAUDIN

Château d'Antigny 2001★★

	25 ha	8,900	▮⅏♦	5–8 €

The Château d'Antigny is one of oldest baronnies in Burgundy, though it belongs to the Arnay area, but this is not very far from the Hautes Côtes de Beaune. An intense red colour, this wine, with its slightly-cooked red berries aromas, accompanied by vanilla, is good-natured, with an interesting structure: its acidity will allow it to age a little. It will go well with a fairly mild cheese.
↪ Doudet-Naudin, 3, rue Henri-Cyrot, 21420 Savigny-lès-Beaune, tel. 03.80.21.51.74, fax 03.80.21.50.69, e-mail doudet-naudin@wanadoo.fr ✔
☥ by appt.
↪ Yves Doudet

CH. DE DRACY 2000★

	1 ha	3,400	⅏	8–11 €

The Château de Dracy is located in Couchois. Built in 1728, its cellar is testimony to its ancient and fine connection with wine-growing. One of the 17 tanks holds 57 hl! The estate is part of the A. Bichot Company and is managed by Colin Ware. A limpid garnet colour with a few highlights, this Pinot Noir has a foxy nose against a background of red berries. On the palate, one finds fruit on an oakwood basis and notes of leather. A wine to drink with red meats.
↪ SCA Ch. de Dracy, 71490 Dracy-lès-Couches, tel. 03.85.49.62.13, fax 03.80.24.37.38
☥ by appt.
↪ Benoît de Charette

HUBERT JACOB MAUCLAIR 2000★

	5.2 ha	13,000	▮⅏	5–8 €

On this estate, inherited from his parents and enlarged by new purchases, Hubert Jacob Mauclair's daughter is training to take it over. This Hautes Côtes de Beaune has all the characteristics of the appellation: good colour, classic nose. On the palate it is not very lively, but it is fruity and really very pleasant. Rabbit with rosemary? Why not, but you must make up your mind because this is a wine that should be drunk in two years' time.

☛ Hubert Jacob Mauclair, 56, Grande-Rue, Changey, 21420 Echevronne, tel. 03.80.21.57.07, fax 03.80.21.57.07 ☑
☖ by appt.

JEAN-HERVE JONNIER 2000★

■	0.85 ha	10,000	▮ ▥	5–8 €

A sombre but limpid and brilliant garnet-red, this wine is characterized by a violet perfume that is most effective. The first impression gets off to a good start, clean and – on a sustained aromatic note combined with ripe red berries– one finds good quality tannins, a touch of acidity, not too much warmth. All these parameters combined give it the potential to keep for several years. One could, however, enjoy it as of now.

☛ Jean-Hervé Jonnier, BerCully, 71150 Chassey-le-Camp, tel. 03.85.87.21.90, fax 03.85.87.23.63 ☑
☖ ev. day. 9am–7pm

LABOURE-ROI
Vieilli en fût de chêne 2001★

■	n.c.	n.c.	▥	5–8 €

One could drink this wine with the festive turkey: a crimson-red colour, the nose is still very redolent of the cask, but on the palate, rounded and fresh, with musky notes and nuances of damp woodlands, it is balanced and long.

☛ Labouré-Roi, rue Lavoisier, 21700 Nuits-Saint-Georges, tel. 03.80.62.64.00, fax 03.80.62.64.10
☖ by appt.

HENRI LATOUR ET FILS 2000★★

■	5.14 ha	11,800	▥	5–8 €

An estate of 16 ha, five of them are dedicated to this appellation. One of our tasters would willingly have awarded the *coup de coeur* for this wine from the 2000 vintage. Opinions were divided, but this is a well-made, sucessful Pinot. Intense red in colour, it is based on a certain aromatic complexity (wild berries, leather) and a quite well-formed structure in which the tannins are beginning to integrate. A slightly monastic herbaceous side does not detract from the enjoyment of this wine, since the finish is successful.

☛ Henri Latour et Fils, rte de Beaune, 21190 Auxey-Duresses, tel. 03.80.21.65.49, fax 03.80.21.63.08, e-mail h.latour.fils@wanadoo.fr ☑
☖ by appt.

DOM. MAZILLY PERE ET FILS
La Perrière 2001★★

■	0.3 ha	2,400	▥	5–8 €

Did they really drink Meloisey at the consecration of Philippe-Auguste in 1180? Dr Morelot maintains that they did. At all events, it is a mantra that is repeated religiously, and this wine in no way diminishes the honour. It positively shines. Its bouquet, based on apricot, is well-favoured. Warm and structured, on the palate is modestly palatial. Exotic nuances and sufficient acidity to hold out until the next anniversary of the sacrament. Powerful finish.

☛ Dom. Mazilly Père et Fils, rte de Pommard, 21190 Meloisey, tel. 03.80.26.02.00, fax 03.80.26.03.67 ☑
☖ by appt.

CHRISTIAN MENAUT 2001★

■	0.25 ha	1,900	▮ ▥	5–8 €

This wine, with its long, slim legs sheathed in golden silk (Cyd Charisse on the silver screen) alternates floral and mineral with great aptness. Freshness and acidity will ensure its successful development right up to 2005 to 2006. A characteristic wine, and one which, as we say here, "pleases us". What more can one say? To also note is the **Jolivode red 2001** also judged to be very pleasant. *Coup de coeur* in the 2000 edition for its 1997 vintage.

☛ Christian Menaut, rue Chaude, 21190 Nantoux, tel. 03.80.26.07.72, fax 03.80.26.01.53 ☑
☖ by appt.

CH. DE MERCEY
Vignes en lyres 2000★

■	7 ha	49,000	▮ ▥ ▤	8–11 €

The Antonin Rodet Company, which owns this estate, increased it in 2002 by taking back the 4 ha estate dedicated to producing Maranges Premier Cru Clos Roussots. As for the lyre system of training vines, it was authorized (by the decree of 1982) for only two Hautes Côtes appellations. Elsewhere, it is under discussion…Straw-gold in colour, this Chardonnay lurks beneath aromas of yellow peach and slightly toasted orange peel. On the palate, richness takes over the baton from the fresh, mentholated first impression. The glasses will not remain empty for long! The **red 2000** is of comparable quality.

☛ Ch. de Mercey, 71150 Cheilly-lès-Maranges, tel. 03.85.91.13.19, fax 03.85.91.16.28 ☑
☖ ev. day. ex. Sat. Sun. 8am–12 noon 1.30pm–5pm; cl. Aug.

DOM. HENRI NAUDIN-FERRAND
Elevé en fût de chêne 2001★

■	1.5 ha	10,469	▮ ▥ ▤	5–8 €

This is a fantastic wine. Golden, limpid, fruity, with length, and so on. But why this oakiness? Without this vanilla, this grilled aroma, this toastiness, this wine could have been a candidate for a *coup de coeur*. The **Cuvée Fût de Chêne red 2000** was also awarded one star but – strangely – appears to be less oaked and more evocative of grape variety.

☛ Dom. Henri Naudin-Ferrand, rue du Meix-Grenot, 21700 Magny-lès-Villers, tel. 03.80.62.91.50, fax 03.80.62.91.77, e-mail dnaudin@ipac.fr ☑
☖ by appt.

DOM. PARIGOT PERE ET FILS
Clos de la Perrière 2001★

■	n.c.	n.c.	▥	8–11 €

Coup de coeur in the 1996 edition for the white from the 93 vintage, this Meloisey estate offered us another good wine to taste. Its colour is very intense. In spite of the fact that red berries come insistently to the fore, the cask manages to capture the nose. Moderate strength, but body that is equal to the task. Its slight astringency indicates the need for one to two years in the cellar.

☛ Dom. Parigot Père et Fils, rte de Pommard, 21190 Meloisey, tel. 03.80.26.01.70, fax 03.80.26.04.32, e-mail parigot-pere-et-fils@wanadoo.fr ☑
☖ by appt.

RIJCKAERT
Les Perrières 2001★

■	0,53 ha	2,800	▥	11–15 €

This company, created in 1998, produces wine two sites, one in Burgundy and the other in the Jura. For this limpid, pale-yellow burgundy, enveloped in aromas of boxwood and lime blossom, the ten months spent in cask refuse to be ignored. A slight roughness on the palate, but acidity and richness are exactly right. Medium term prospects. Drink with poultry.

☛ Rijckaert, En Correaux, 71570 Leynes, tel. 03.85.35.15.09, fax 03.85.35.15.09, e-mail jeanrijckaert@infonie.fr ☑
☖ by appt.

DOM. DES VIGNES DES DEMOISELLES
Cuvée Delphine Saint-Eve 2001★

■	0.8 ha	5,400	▥	11–15 €

Cuvée Delphine Saint-Eve was named in memory of this wine producer's grandmother. Why jasmine flowers on the label? It was her favourite perfume, Chanel N° 5. This wine displays considerable youth. Jasmine on the nose? Not really, but its basis is flowery. The development on the palate is correct with acidity, and therefore balance, strength and good length. This Hautes Côtes has a great deal of character.

☛ SCE du Dom. Gabriel Demangeot et Fils, rue de Santenay, 21340 Change, tel. 03.85.91.11.10, fax 03.85.91.16.83 ☑
☖ by appt.

DOM. JEAN-LOUIS ZECCHINI 2001★

	n.c.	6,000	🍷🍷	5–8 €

We know that Magny-lès-Villers is the border post between Hautes Côtes de Nuits and Hautes Côtes de Beaune, so here we are dealing with a diplomatic and consiliatory wine, dressed in delicate gold. Mushrooms invest it with a Chablis note, but butter and vanilla also play their part. Still fresh and oaky, in two years it will be at its height. "A capon with mushrooms would go well with it," said one taster.
🍷 Dom. Zecchini, chemin-rural n°29,
21700 Magny-lès-Villers, tel. 03.80.62.42.00,
fax 03.80.61.28.13, e-mail nuicave@wanadoo.fr ☑
🍽 by appt.

Wines selected but not starred

DOM. LE BOUT DU MONDE

Le Cul de Fussey Elevé en fût de chêne 2001

	1 ha	2,400	🍷	15–23 €

🍷 Dom. le Bout du Monde, rte de Bourguignon,
21200 Combertault, tel. 03.80.26.67.05,
fax 03.80.26.67.05 ☑
🍽 by appt.

DOM. DE LA CONFRERIE 2001

	0.5 ha	2,000	🍾	8–11 €

🍷 Jean Pauchard et Fils, Dom. de La Confrérie, rue Perraudin, Cirey, 21340 Nolay, tel. 03.80.21.89.23,
fax 03.80.21.70.27, e-mail domj.pauchard@wanadoo.fr ☑
🍽 by appt.

R. DUBOIS ET FILS

Les Monts Battois 2001

	0.8 ha	8,000		5–8 €

🍷 Dom. R. Dubois et Fils, rte de Nuits-Saint-Georges,
21700 Premeaux-Prissey, tel. 03.80.62.30.61,
fax 03.80.24.07, e-mail rdubois@wanadoo.fr ☑
🍽 ev. day. 8am–11.30am 2pm–6pm; Sat. Sun. by appt.

GILBERT ET PHILIPPE GERMAIN 2001

	1.2 ha	7,000	🍷🍷	5–8 €

🍷 Gilbert et Philippe Germain, 21190 Nantoux,
tel. 03.80.26.05.63, fax 03.80.26.05.12,
e-mail germain.vins@wanadoo.fr ☑ 🏠
🍽 by appt.

JACOB-FREREBEAU 2001

	3.5 ha	10,000	🍾	5–8 €

🍷 Jacob-Frèrebeau, 50, Grande-Rue,
21420 Changey-Echevronne, tel. 03.80.21.55.58,
fax 03.80.62.75.36 ☑
🍽 by appt.

Crémant de Bourgogne

Like nearly all other French wine regions, Burgundy had its own appellation, the Bourgogne Mousseux, for the sparkling wines produced and made throughout the whole of the vineyard. Without being unnecessarily critical of the wine produced, it must be said that the quality was not consistent and nor, for the most part, did it compare with the reputation of the other wines of the region, undoubtedly because the base wines used were too heavy. A working group, established in 1974, laid down the rules for Crémant, setting out conditions for its production that were as strict as the ones in the Champagne region on which they were based.

A decree instituted in 1975 gave official approval to the enterprise, and eventually all the makers supported it, whether they really wanted to or not, because the Appellation Bourgogne Mousseux was terminated in 1984. After difficult beginnings, the Crémant de Bourgogne appellation is developing well and produced 78,051 hl in 2002.

BAILLY-LAPIERRE

Pinot noir 2001★★

	n.c.	40,000	🍾 ♦	5–8 €

The Bailly cellars at Saint-Bris-le-Vineux (Yonne) were installed in an old quarry, stone from which was for centuries used in the building of Paris. Four underground hectares for a single tenant: he can even park his car there! *Coup de coeur* last year, this year the Cooperative's pure Pinot Noir was placed among the best. Full, long and fruity, it is a very well-made and carefully developed wine. The lighter **Blanc de Noirs 2001** (Pinot and a small amount of Gamay), was awarded one star.
🍷 Caves de Bailly, BP 3, 89530 Saint-Bris-le-Vineux,
tel. 03.86.53.77.77, fax 03.86.53.80.94,
e-mail home@caves-bailly.com ☑
🍽 ev. day. 8am–12 noon 2pm–6pm;
from Apr. to Oct. from 2.30pm–6pm

JEAN BARONNAT

Blanc de blancs★

	n.c.	n.c.		8–11 €

Situated in Beaujolais, this family business, now run by the third generation, offered this *crémant*; "It will satisfy everyone," one taster wrote on his card. Fine bubbles that form light strings, this *crémant* made with Chardonnay from Southern Burgundy has a quite smooth perfume of brioche. This aroma is repeated on the palate together with a spoonful of honey. Facile perhaps, but straightforward and reliable
🍷 Maison Baronnat, 491, rte de Lacenas, Les Bruyères,
69400 Gleizé, tel. 04.74.68.59.20, fax 04.74.62.19.21,
e-mail info@baronnat.com ☑
🍽 by appt.

DOM. DU BICHERON

Blanc de blancs 1999★★

	1 ha	5,000	🍾 ♦	5–8 €

Superior quality, as one used to say. The generous bubbles, the pale-gold colour, the bouquet of fresh butter with a touch of crystallized fruits, this *crémant* is soft and rounded, pleasant and seductive; and easy to drink. From the Mâconnais, it is an interesting wine for its vintage and well representative of its grape variety.
🍷 Daniel Rousset, Dom. du Bicheron,
Saint-Pierre-de-Lanques, 71260 Péronne,
tel. 03.85.36.94.53, fax 03.85.36.99.80 ☑
🍽 by appt.

DOM. DE LA BOFFELINE 2000★★

	0.7 ha	6,500	🍾	5–8 €

A newcomer among our sparkling wine *coups de coeur*. A fairly recent vineyard and estate (15 or so years since the first planting) they send their Chardonnay to Loron to be processed. The area is the Mâconnais. Coming second out of the 107 *crémants* presented, this one stands out as a fine wine; a quite intense lemon colour, with a superb floral nose, it is a model of balance and presence. It all comes down to nuances

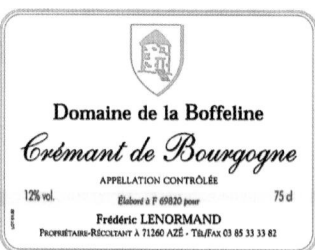

Domaine de la Boffeline

Crémant de Bourgogne

APPELLATION CONTRÔLÉE

12% vol.   Élaboré à F 69820 pour   75 cl

Frédéric LENORMAND
PROPRIÉTAIRE-RÉCOLTANT À 71260 AZÉ · Tél/Fax 03 85 33 33 82

and being true to form. Make a note: it is perfect on its own; don't be tempted to make it into a kir royale.
☛ Frédéric Lenormand, En Fourgeau, 71260 Azé, tel. 03.85.33.33.82, fax 03.85.33.33.82 ☑
☒ ev. day. 9am–12 noon 2pm–7pm

DOM. ALBERT BOILLOT

Blanc de noirs 2001★

| | 0.27 ha | 2,500 | | 5–8 € |

This family estate, established at Volnay in the 17th century, offered a pale-gold *crémant* with an attractive mousse. The nose is all fresh fruits. The wine keeps its liveliness right to the end. Elegant, very pleasant, it is among the ones that really appealed to us.
☛ SCE du Dom. Albert Boillot, ruelle Saint-Etienne, 21190 Volnay, tel. 03.80.21.61.21, fax 03.80.21.61.21, e-mail dom.albert.boillot@wanadoo.fr ☑
☒ by appt.

LOUIS BOUILLOT

Perle d'Aurore★

| | n.c. | 45,000 | | 8–11 € |

Louis Bouillot, a very venerable company from the Nuits specializing in sparkling wines, was taken over by J-Cl. Boisset. It offered this *rosé de saignée* Perle d'Aurore. The bubbles are Montgolfier-sized, the colour, that of a nymph's thigh, its responsiveness is delicate and supple from start to finish. The fruit takes up the whole of the last act. Charming in a word. Also, don't neglect the **Perle d' Ivoire**; this 100% Chardonnay, one star, is exactly what one expects.
☛ Louis Bouillot, 5, quai Dumorey, 21700 Nuits-Saint-Georges, tel. 03.80.62.61.44, fax 03.80.62.61.61, e-mail gauthier.r@attglobal.net

DOM. JEAN CHARTRON

Blanc de blancs★

| | n.c. | 1,200 | | 8–11 € |

One hundred per cent Chardonnay, from Chartron at Puligny-Montrachet. Excellent wine, exuberant bubbles and a bouquet hovering between white bread and citrus fruits. Reasonable potential for laying down, with good vinosity, pleasing structure, and a harmoniousness that will last. An aperitif or a dessert wine.
☛ Jean Chartron, 13, Grande-Rue, 21190 Puligny-Montrachet, tel. 03.80.21.32.85, fax 03.80.21.36.35 ☑
☒ ev. day. 10am–12 noon 2pm–6pm; Sat. and Sun. from end Nov. to mid-Mar. by appt.

DOM. CORNU 2000★★

| | 0.25 ha | n.c. | | 5–8 € |

Here we are in the Hautes Côtes de Nuits: 100% Pinot Noir, made by J-F. Delorme at Rully. This 2000 vintage is successful for the year: one senses the Pinot, even without prior knowledge. It shows intensity right from the start and goes fervently into the attack. Its length has good vinosity and this is where one recognizes whether a *crémant* is simply an accumulation of bubbles, or a wine. This one is a wine. Why not prepare a pikeperch with *crémant*? One of Bernard Loiseau's recipes; in his memory.

☛ Dom. Claude Cornu, rue du Meix-Grenot, 21700 Magny-lès-Villers, tel. 03.80.62.92.05, fax 03.80.62.72.22 ☑
☒ by appt.

DELIANCE PERE ET FILS

Ruban mauve★

| | 2 ha | 12,000 | | 8–11 € |

Coming from the Côte Chalonnaise, this mauve Ruban is made from Pinot Noir (85%) and the rest Chardonnay. Marked by light bubbles forming fine strings, the nose is all freshness and floral notes, this straight-forward wine has character. Wine-lovers will find it pleasing because it fills the mouth: this is a real wine. Two other *cuvées* received a special mention: the **Ruban Vert** and the **Ruban Or**.
☛ Dom. Deliance, le Buet, 71640 Dracy-le-Fort, tel. 03.85.44.40.59, fax 03.85.44.36.13 ☑
☒ ev. day. ex. Sun. 9am–12 noon 2pm–7pm

ANDRE DELORME

Blanc de noirs★

| | n.c. | 25,700 | 5–8 € |

Jean-François Delorme plays an important role in the wine-making world of Burgundy. He could not fail to offer his *crémants*, given that his company has been dedicated to the production of sparkling wines for more than half a century. Lemon-gold, with fine, elegant bubbles, this blanc de noirs has a citrus fruit bouquet. The length is remarkable. It would be ideal with a blackcurrant vacherin. It is the 274 Cuvée. The **Cuvée rosé 293** is also worthy of your attention: it received a special mention.
☛ André Delorme, 2, rue de la République, BP 15, 71150 Rully, tel. 03.85.87.10.12, fax 03.85.87.04.60, e-mail andre-delorme@wanadoo.fr ☑
☒ ev. day. ex. Sun. 9am–12 noon 2pm–6pm; groups by appt.

DOM. GILLON FRERES★

| | 0.26 ha | 2,666 | | 5–8 € |

A remarkable result for this agricultural concern at Châtillonnais, which only started wine-growing in 1995, and this year gains its first entry in the Guide. This is a *crémant* made with 60% Pinot Noir and 40% Chardonnay. A taster said: "This *cuvée* has all the qualities." Its generous colours and its strings of rising bubbles, its rich mousse, its really complex nose (a rare adjunct for *crémant*), its lively freshness deserve a whole rosary of praises.
☛ Dom. Gillon Frères, rue du Moulin, 21400 Pothières, tel. 03.80.81.95.20, fax 03.80.81.92.96 ☑
☒ ev. day. 7am–11pm

DOM. GIROUX

Blanc de blancs 2000★

| | 0,5 ha | 3,500 | | 8–11 € |

This *crémant*, made from pure Chardonnay grown opposite the Roche de Solutré, has a light, almost ethereal side. From its colour and its floral aromas and notes of hazelnut it could almost be a still white wine. Fresh, fruity impression overlaying lemon at the heart of a delicate palate. Well made and elegant.
☛ Yves Giroux, Les Molards, 71960 Fuissé, tel. 03.85.35.63.64, fax 03.85.32.90.08 ☑
☒ by appt.

LES CAVES DES HAUTES-COTES

Blanc de noirs★

| | 25 ha | 139,700 | | 5–8 € |

The fantastic cellar at Côte d'Or (*coup de coeur* in the 2001 Guide) will hold your attention with a specially mentioned **Blanc de Blancs**, and also with this blanc de noirs which starts and finishes well. Pleasant throughout the tasting, it's a wine for a family celebration.
☛ Les Caves des Hautes Côtes, rte de Pommard, 21200 Beaune, tel. 03.80.25.01.00, fax 03.80.22.87.05, e-mail vinchc@wanadoo.fr ☑
☒ by appt.

Crémant de Bourgogne

LES VIGNERONS D'IGE★★

15 ha   150,000   🍾   5–8 €

Close to 1,000 ha, the Igé Cooperative in the Mâconnais does not lack grapes. Nor does it lack the skills needed for making sparkling wines because this combination of 80% Chardonnay and 20% Pinot Noir was a finalist for the *coup de coeur*. This *crémant*, with its strong personality can easily face up to a pikeperch or a dish of coquilles St. Jacques gratinées. Don't drink it as an aperitif. Fine bubbles, a touch of brioche and dried fruit on the nose, and breath-taking charm from the very first that one goes on tasting right to the end.
🍷 Cave des vignerons d'Igé, rue du Tacot, 71960 Igé, tel. 03.85.33.33.56, fax 03.85.33.41.85, e-mail lesvigneronsdige@lesvigneronsdige.com 🅥 🏠
Ⓨ ev. day. ex. Sun. 8am–12 noon 2pm–6pm

PIERRE JANNY★

n.c.   30,000   5–8 €

Limpid white-gold, a *crémant* with fine strings of bubbles. Intense, well-evolved nose tending towards dried fruits and honey. Harmonious on the palate, it repeats the aromas and adds *pain d'épice* on the middle palate. On a good level, this wine looks beyond the aperitif stage and aspires to the fish course.
🍷 Sté Janny, La Condemine, Cidex 1556, 71260 Péronne, tel. 03.85.23.96.20, fax 03.85.36.96.58, e-mail pierre-janny@wanadoo.fr

ANDRE ET BERNARD LABRY★

1 ha   3,000   8–11 €

Côte de Beaune, Pinot Noir (60%) and Aligoté (40%): an astonishing combination. And they get along admirably. The colour is almost overripe, the nose welcomes both butter and hazelnut. Vinified by Delorme at Rully, this is a well-made *crémant*, product of good workmanship, ready to pop its cork on the slenderest of excuses. The touch of bitterness comes from major grape variety but this is no cause for reproach.
🍷 Dom. André et Bernard Labry, Melin, 21190 Auxey-Duresses, tel. 03.80.21.21.60, fax 03.80.21.64.15, e-mail domaine-labry@wanadoo.fr 🅥 🏠
Ⓨ by appt.

LA CAVE DES VIGNERONS DE LIERGUES 2001★

5 ha   30,000   🍾   5–8 €

Chardonnay (60%) and Pinot Noir make this a very prestigious *crémant* from the Beaujolais Cooperative which has been producing *crémant* since 1990, after the cellar-master studied at Epernay. The colour is light and the mousse dense and long-lasting; the fruity nose leans towards the Pinot grape. On the palate it is soft and clean. This aperitif wine is good enough to serve with an entrée of fish terrine. Try it. As an aperitif it is best served without any additions.
🍷 Cave des Vignerons de Liergues, 69400 Liergues, tel. 04.74.65.86.00, fax 04.74.62.81.20, e-mail jp.caveliergues@wanadoo.fr 🅥
Ⓨ ev. day. ex. Sun. 8am–12 noon 2pm–7pm

DOM. MOISSENET-BONNARD

Pinot noir 2000★★

0.5 ha   2,200   5–8 €

Finalist for the *coup de coeur.* here we are at the top. Pinot Noir from Pommard, and Delorme of Rully to process it. The result? Love at first sight! Delicate mousse, intense-gold colour, fabulous palate. What presence! A guaranteed pleasure, particularly as the finish is so velvety. This very small property (4.5 ha) works wonders and will excite great interest among the critics.
🍷 Dom. Moissenet-Bonnard, rte d'Autun, 21630 Pommard, tel. 03.80.24.62.34, fax 03.80.22.30.04 🅥
Ⓨ by appt.

PICAMELOT 2001★★

n.c.   50,065   🍾   8–11 €

Joseph and Louis Picamelot, who founded the company in 1926, left their descendants with a taste for sparking wines and a job well done. The *coup de coeur* (the first judged) was the reward for this skilful blend of Chardonnay (60%), Aligoté (10%) and Pinot Noir (30%). Pure art: a dense mousse that sensibly refrains from being too insistent, a lemon-gold

colour, a floral bouquet and a lively and vinous character: this perfectly true to type wine would be wasted as an aperitif. With smoked salmon? Worth a try.
🍷 Louis Picamelot, 12, pl. de la Croix-Blanche, BP 2, 71150 Rully, tel. 03.85.87.13.60, fax 03.85.87.63.81, e-mail louispicamelot@wanadoo.fr 🅥
Ⓨ ev. day. 8am–12 noon 1.30pm–6.30pm; Sat. Sun. by appt.

DOM. PIGNERET FILS★

1 ha   9,000   5–8 €

Estate established jointly in 2001 by Eric and Joseph Pigneret. This wine departs from the beaten track. It doesn't fit the standard specifications (it shows a touch of nutmeg), but as the Jury said: "What a strange phenomenon, and what a pleasure on the palate!" Completely atypical right from the first impression on the nose. But so enjoyable. Pinot Noir (40%) and 20% Gamay, the rest is Aligoté and Chardonnay. One to surprise your guests.
🍷 EARL Dom. Pigneret Fils, Vingelles, 71390 Moroges, tel. 03.85.47.15.10, fax 03.85.47.15.12, e-mail pigneret.joseph@wanadoo.fr 🅥
Ⓨ ev. day. 9am–12 noon 2pm–9pm

PRIEURE DU BOIS DE LEYNES 2001★

0.25 ha   2,600   5–8 €

One hundred per cent Chardonnay, Mâconnais to the tips of its fingers, this *crémant* is pale gold with greenish tinges, and has fine, delicate bubbles. The nose awakens the appetite with its notes of flowers and pastries. Acidity and alcohol complement each other; the length on the palate is absolutely appropriate as the freshness develops. The very essence of a sparkling aperitif wine.
🍷 Bruno Jeandeau, Prieuré du Bois de Leynes, Le Bois de Leynes, 71570 Leynes, tel. 03.85.35.11.56, fax 03.85.35.15.15 🅥 🏠
Ⓨ by appt.

CAVES DE PRISSE-SOLOGNY-VERZE

Blanc de blancs★

23.5 ha   240,000   🍾   5–8 €

Fine, long-lasting bubbles grace this *crémant* with its fresh, understated colour. A significant bouquet, along citrus fruit lines. Once the bubbles have subsided one notices the acidity but within a good general balance. A little Crème de Cassis from Dijon will make it even more imaginative.
🍷 Caves de Prissé-Sologny-Verzé, Les Grandes-Vignes, 71960 Prissé, tel. 03.85.37.88.06, fax 03.85.37.61.76, e-mail caves.prisse@wanadoo.fr 🅥 🏠
Ⓨ by appt.

DOM. DE ROTISSON

Cuvée Prestige 1999★

0.77 ha   8,000   🍾   5–8 €

Didier Pouget bought this domaine in 1998 after completing a course in viticulture and oenology. This vintage *crémant* will be ready to drink from now until 2005. Made from the Chardonnay, it comes from the Department of the Rhône; it has an attractive mousse, fine bubbles and a gold colour with straw highlights. Butter, hazelnut, plenty of richness right from the first impression and a particularly studied finish. A substantial and effective wine.
🍷 Dom. de Rotisson, rte de Conzy, 69210 Saint-Germain-sur-l'Arbresle, tel. 04.74.01.23.08, fax 04.74.01.55.41, e-mail domaine-de-rotisson@wanadoo.fr 🅥
Ⓨ ev. day. ex. Sun. 9am–12.30pm 2pm–6.30pm
🍷 Didier Pouget

BURGUNDY

SIMONNET-FEBVRE★

	n.c.	n.c.	5–8 €

The only Chablis house to vinify its *crémant* as well as producing it for wine-growers. Vastly experienced: 100 years ago the sparkling Chablis Simonnet-Febvre graced all the best tables on the planet. Seventy-five per cent Pinot Noir, 25% Chardonnay: this is a Champagne-type wine with regular strings of bubbles, a fervent *mousse*, and a white-gold colour. Lively and fresh, balanced. Ready and waiting to pop its cork!
↬ Simonnet-Febvre et Fils, La Maladière, BP 12, 9, av. d'Oberwesel, 89800 Chablis, tel. 03.86.98.99.00, fax 03.86.98.99.01, e-mail simonnet@chablis.net ☑
Ⴤ ev. day. 8.30am–12 noon 2pm–5.30pm; Sat. Sun. by appt.
↬ Laurent Simonnet

ALBERT SOUNIT

Cuvée Prestige 105 2000★

	n.c.	30,000	5–8 €

The company is now Danish but remains Burgundian. Go and visit its wine cellar, with the amazingly high vaults, located in an old quarry. Sixty per cent Pinot Noir and the rest Chardonnay, this pale-yellow *crémant* has all the mousse you could wish for. Supple, basic, it is thoroughly appealing, with a hint of masculinity, as one says! It has body. Also recommended: the **Cuvée Chardonnay 99** and the **Cuvée Prestige, known as 52** (black label), Pinot and Chardonnay.
↬ Albert Sounit, 5, pl. du Champ-de-Foire, 71150 Rully, tel. 03.85.87.20.71, fax 03.85.87.09.71, e-mail albert.sounit@wanadoo.fr ☑
Ⴤ ev. day. 9am–12 noon 2pm–6pm; Sat. Sun. by appt.

VEUVE AMBAL

Carte noire★★

	n.c.	150,000	5–8 €

Company founded in 1898, specialist in sparkling wines, as is shown by this remarkable pale-gold *crémant* with green highlights. The nose touches on ripe fruits (quince) and other fruits with stones (white peaches). These are confirmed on the palate against a harmoniously rounded and fresh structure. The **La Tête de Cuvée** was awarded one star.
↬ Veuve Ambal, rue des Bordes, 71150 Rully, tel. 03.85.87.15.05, fax 03.85.87.30.15, e-mail vve.ambal@aol.com ☑
Ⴤ by appt.
↬ Eric Piffaut

DOM. DE LA VIGNE AU ROY

La Grande Chaume Cuvée Prestige★

	16 ha	29,000	5–8 €

What a history! Maurice Eisenchteter was the architect of the revival of the vineyard at Bévy in the Hautes Côtes de Nuits about 30 years ago, when he was in charge of Geisweiler. He amalgamated hundreds of plots of land. These were first taken over by the Champagne company Gonet then by Veuve Ambal. This *crémant* is made from 60% Chardonnay, 30% Aligoté and 10% Pinot Noir. The bubbles are perfect, the colour entirely suitable, the nose fresh and undeveloped and it is very lively on the palate, but on a peach theme: let it mature for a year or two.
↬ Dom. de la Vigne au Roy, rue de la Vigne-au-Roy, 21220 Bévy, tel. 03.80.61.44.87, fax 03.80.61.44.87 ☑
Ⴤ by appt.
↬ Eric Piffaut

CAVE DE VIRE 2000★★

	50 ha	200,000	5–8 €

One hundred per cent Chardonnay from Southern Burgundy, a perfectly made *crémant* produced by the Viré Cooperative, created in 1928. Green-gold in colour it produces a good *mousse*. Aromas of hawthorn and acacia flowers, it swings between lively and velvety. It is ready to serve now but will keep for a while.
↬ Cave de Viré, En Vercheron, 71260 Viré, tel. 03.85.32.25.50, fax 03.85.32.25.55, e-mail cavedevire@wanadoo.fr ☑
Ⴤ by appt.

L. VITTEAU-ALBERTI

Blanc de blancs 2001★

	4 ha	30,000	8–11 €

A *coup de cœur* last year and already mentioned in the 1995 Guide, the Rully company is very successful with its blanc de blancs. One recognizes the grape variety (Chardonnay and Aligoté 80/20%). Freshness and lightness, and an aromatic finesse which is the Ariadne's thread of wine-tasting. This pleasing wine would grace any happy occasion.
↬ Vitteau-Alberti, 20, rue du Pont-d'Arrot, BP 8, 71150 Rully, tel. 03.85.87.23.97, fax 03.85.87.16.24, e-mail vitteau-alberti@lesvinsfrancais.com ☑
Ⴤ by appt.

Wines selected but not starred

CAVE D'AZE

Blanc de noirs 2001

	1.5 ha	12,500	5–8 €

↬ Cave coop. d'Azé, En Tarroux, 71260 Azé, tel. 03.85.33.30.92, fax 03.85.33.37.21 ☑
Ⴤ by appt.

BERNARD DURY

Blanc de blancs

	0.5 ha	2,000	5–8 €

↬ Bernard Dury, 27, rue du Château, hameau de Cissey, 21190 Merceuil, tel. 03.80.21.48.44, fax 03.80.21.48.44 ☑ ☖
Ⴤ by appt.

LES VIGNERONS DE HAUTE-BOURGOGNE Chardonnay 2000

	10 ha	50,000	8–11 €

↬ SICA les Vignerons de Haute-Bourgogne, Les caves du Bois de Langres, 21400 Prusly-sur-Ource, tel. 03.80.91.07.60, fax 03.80.91.24.76, e-mail lesvignerons.htbourgogne@wanadoo.fr

DOM. MICHEL ISAIE

Blanc de blancs 1999

	2 ha	10,400	5–8 €

↬ Michel Isaïe, chem. de l'Ouche, 71640 Saint-Jean-de-Vaux, tel. 03.85.45.23.32, fax 03.85.45.29.38 ☑
Ⴤ by appt.

CELINE ET LAURENT TRIPOZ

	0.5 ha	6,000	8–11 €

↬ Céline et Laurent Tripoz, pl. de la Mairie, 71000 Loché-Mâcon, tel. 03.85.35.66.09, fax 03.85.35.64.23, e-mail celine_laurent.tripoz@libertysurf.fr ☑
Ⴤ by appt.

Chablis

Despite having a reputation that has seen it imitated to a fantastic degree all around the world, the Chablis vineyard once nearly

Chablis

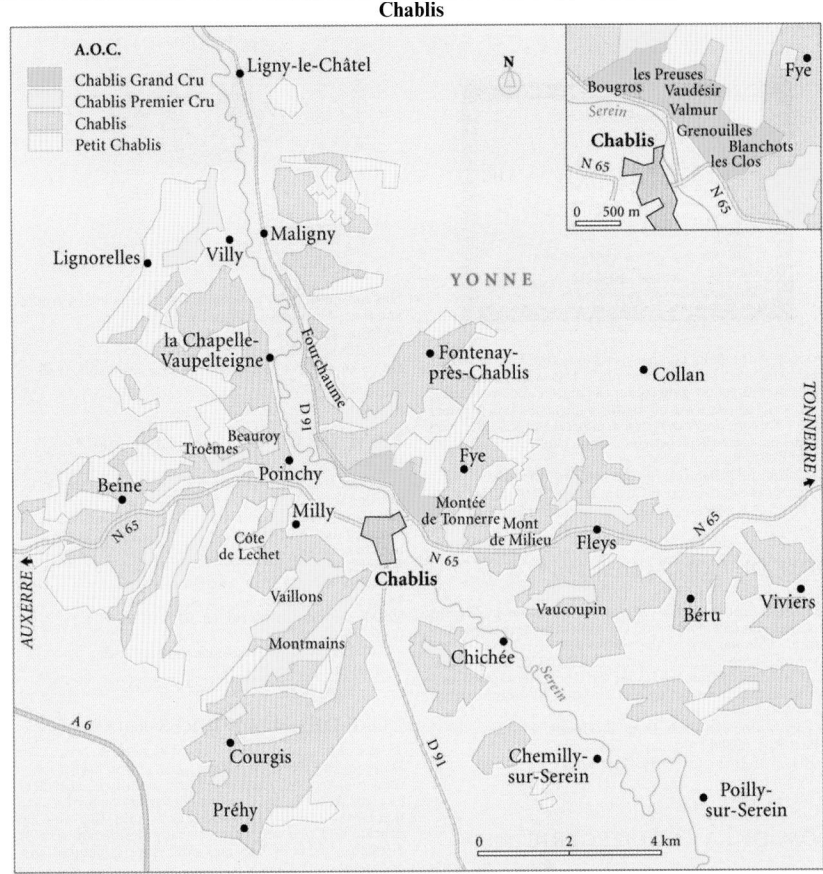

disappeared altogether. Catastrophic late frosts in 1957 and 1961 added to the difficulties of cultivating the vines on very steep hills with stony soils led to vine-growing being progressively abandoned; the value of land in the Grands Crus fell to laughably low prices and the people who bought then were very well advised. New systems of protection against frost and the development of mechanisation brought the vineyards back from the brink.

The appellation covers territories in the commune of Chablis and 19 of its neighbours; 4,274 ha are presently planted with vines. Production was 264,175 hl in 2002. The vines cover the steeply sloping hills on both sides of the Serein, a small tributary flowing into the Yonne. At this latitude, a south-southeasterly aspect is best for the grapes to ripen well, but in some of the more favoured locations vines may be planted on slopes facing away from the sun as well as towards it. The soil is made up of Jurassic marl or Kimmeridge clay (the other end of the rim of this geological basin is in Dorset, England, which is why it has this name) or Portland stone, which is limestone. These are the perfect soils for growing white wines, and in the 12th century the Cistercian monks of the Abbey of Pontigny realized this, most likely planting Chardonnay, known locally

as Beaunois. Here, more than anywhere else, Chardonnay shows off the finesse and elegance that make it a superlative accompaniment to seafood, snails or charcuterie. The Premiers and Grands Crus will complement the choicest foods: chicken, fine charcuterie, fowl or white meat dishes, especially those prepared with wine.

Petit Chablis

This appellation is at the bottom of the hierarchy of wines in the Chablis area. In 2002 almost 36,195 hl of wine were produced over 623 ha. The Petit Chablis is less aromatically complex than Chablis, with a greater degree of acidity, which gives its flavour a quality of greenness. It used to be served by the carafe, in the year of harvest, but it is now bottled. Held back by its name, it initially had great difficulty in getting established in its own right, but today the consumer seems to take less and less account of the diminutive adjective "Petit".

JULES BELIN 2001★★

	n.c.	2,400	🍶 ⚲	8–11 €

Product of the Belin company of Nuits (the Lanvin family, the Coron and Misserey marques), this wine shines with all the fires its yellow-gold colour can muster and overwhelms the nostrils before going on to satisfy the taste-buds. Number one for the *coup de coeur*, it is rich, mineral and has a finish on the palate somewhere between lemon and spices that one would like to hold on to for ever.
🍷 Maison Jules Belin, 3, rue des Seuillets, BP 143, 21704 Nuits-Saint-Georges Cedex, tel. 03.80.61.07.74, fax 03.80.61.31.40, e-mail lanvin-sa@worldonline.fr ▼
☕ by appt.

DOM. DU COLOMBIER 2001★

	1.65 ha	12,000	🍶 ⚲	5–8 €

The three brothers who run this 40-ha estate in Chablis produced this pale-gold, floral and mineral wine in close association. This was one of the most true to type noses in the tasting. Is it too rich on the palate for a Petit Chablis? Could it be a Chardonnay from the Côte d'Or? The tasters appreciated its remarkable construction and said that "it sat in the glass like a pasha on his throne."
🍷 Guy Mothe et ses Fils, Dom. du Colombier, 42, Grand-Rue, 89800 Fontenay-près-Chablis, tel. 03.86.42.15.04, fax 03.86.42.49.67 ▼
☕ by appt.
🍷 Mothe Frères

DOM. DE LA CONCIERGERIE 2001★

	1 ha	7,000	🍶 ⚲	5–8 €

If one believes Henry Clos Jouve, the cradle of the snail is right here. The hibernating snail that sleeps behind drawn curtains throughout the dead season and that one eats with a sprinkling of salt…This wine could team up with these Burgundy emblems. Delicate gold, with green highlights, it has plenty of bouquet, and freshness in a structure dominated by fruit.
🍷 EARL Christian Adine, 2, allée du Château, 89800 Courgis, tel. 03.86.41.40.28, fax 03.86.41.45.75, e-mail nicole.adine@free.fr ▼

DOM. BERNARD DEFAIX 2001★★

	1,5 ha	12,000	🍶 ⚲	5–8 €

A photograph of Doisneau or Janine Niépce could not offer a better picture of the Petit Chablis than this marvellous wine. Finesse and freshness characterize this clear and limpid wine. The nose is a little introverted but clean, elegant, reminiscent of flint. Balanced and harmonious on the palate.
🍷 Dom. Bernard Defaix, 17, rue du Château, Milly, 89800 Chablis, tel. 03.86.42.40.75, fax 03.86.42.40.28, e-mail didier@bernard-defaix.com ▼
☕ by appt.

DOM. PHILIPPE GOULLEY 2001★★

	2.5 ha	20,000	🍶 ⚲	8–11 €

At the second stage, an almost unanimous *coup de coeur*. Philippe Goulley created this estate in 1991. It is certified organic and a member of the Biobourgogne Group, one of most active in France. It is not known if the fish terrine is also guaranteed organic, but try it to accompany this wine from 2001 – a beautiful example of success in a complicated year.

Not too much yellow, its beautiful aromas are of fruitiness and flint. A wine that will give great pleasure.
🍷 Dom. Philippe Goulley, 89800 La Chapelle-Vaupelteigne, tel. 03.86.42.40.85, fax 03.86.42.81.06, e-mail phil.goulley@wanadoo.fr ▼
☕ by appt.

DOM. DE GUETTE-SOLEIL 2001★

	2.81 ha	4,000	🍶 ⚲	5–8 €

The three Vilain brothers started a venture together in 1974. Starting from nothing, they planted 30 ha, one-third on their own land, two-thirds on a tenancy holding. Then they acquired the Château de Chemilly. Their Petit Chablis doesn't need to seek out the sun, it is golden already in the bottle. The bouquet is a little surprising but not in any pejorative sense; the attack and the lively, lengthy body vouch for it.
🍷 Dom. de Guette-Soleil, 20, rue du Pont, 89800 Chemilly-sur-Serein, tel. 03.86.42.16.91, fax 03.86.42.12.79, e-mail domainedeguettesoleil@wanadoo.fr ▼
☕ by appt.

DOM. DES HERITIERES 2001★★

	1.5 ha	12,000	🍶 ⚲	5–8 €

Domaine des Héritières (Heiresses)…If you have a son you want to marry off, telephone them urgently in case there is one left! Actually, the wedding Olivier Tricon invites us to is that of the vine and the terroir. Grey-gold, this wine has a delicate and pleasant nose basically floral. Soft and very drinkable, its body becomes ever more structured and it opens out on the finish.
🍷 Olivier Tricon, 15, rue de Chichée, 89800 Chablis, tel. 03.86.42.10.37, fax 03.86.42.49.13

DOM. DES MALANDES 2001★

	1,9 ha	15,000	🍶 ⚲	5–8 €

No doubt it is not as long as from here to Dijon, but it cuts a good figure in the series. A clear, rather brilliant yellow it has an aroma of mushrooms, as does any Chablis that knows its classics. One finds the mushrooms again on the palate while the body is amply clothed in richness. A classsic example of a robust and powerful Petit Chablis. Not for serving as an aperitif but rather with an entrée.
🍷 Dom. des Malandes, 63, rue Auxerroise, 89800 Chablis, tel. 03.86.42.41.37, fax 03.86.42.41.97, e-mail contact@domainedesmalandes.com ▼
☕ by appt.
🍷 Jean-Bernard Marchive

DOM. DES ORMES 2001★

	8.5 ha	870	🍶 ⚲	5–8 €

There is a Domaine de l'Orme and a Domaine des Ormes. Both of them appear in this chapter. This one maintains a certain reserve but upholds the honour of its name and will improve with time. Pale colour, mineral notes in prospect and sufficient liveliness to get it going.
🍷 Dom. des Ormes, 4, rte de Lignorelles, 89800 Beine, tel. 03.86.42.40.91, fax 03.86.42.48.58 ▼
☕ ev. day. 8am–12 noon 2pm–8pm
🍷 GFA Cota-Château

DOM. DE PERDRYCOURT 2001★

| | 4 ha | 9,000 | 🍾 ♦ | 5–8 € |

Arlette Courty and her daughter Virginie are at the helm of this domain and opened a new cellar at Beines a few months ago. Their 2000 vintage was awarded a *coup de coeur* in last year's edition. This wine lacks a certain liveliness, though it is very smooth. Characteristically floral on the nose, mineral on the palate, well constructed, clear proof of its successful vinification.
➤ EARL Arlette et Virginie Courty, Dom. de Perdrycourt, 9, voie Romaine, 89230 Montigny-la-Resle, tel. 03.86.41.82.07, fax 03.86.41.87.89, e-mail domainecourty@wanadoo.fr ☑
✆ ev. day. 9am–7pm; Sun. 9am–12 noon

REGNARD 2001★

| | 3 ha | 25,000 | 🍾 ♦ | 8–11 € |

A venerable Chablis company, taken over in 1984 by Baron Patrick de Ladoucette, who transferred from one valley (the Loire) to another. The colour is light, the nose expressive (needs a little aeration) and the palate full and rich, already most agreeable. An attractive wine.
➤ Régnard, 26, bd Tacussel, 89800 Chablis, tel. 03.86.42.10.45, fax 03.86.42.48.67 ☑
✆ by appt.

DOM. ROY 2001★

| | 0.86 ha | 6,400 | 🍾 ♦ | 5–8 € |

Pale gold, this is a Petit Chablis that is not at all small…It has a touch of freshness and acidity, but, above all, a strength that is unusual in an AOC. A distinctive style.
➤ Dom. Roy, 71, Grand-Rue, 89800 Fontenay-près-Chablis, tel. 03.86.42.10.36 ☑

FRANCINE ET OLIVIER SAVARY 2001★

| | 2.5 ha | 20,000 | 🍾 ♦ | 5–8 € |

Established in 1984 on a one-hectare estate, today Francine and Olivier Savary are at the head of a 17-ha property. Grey-gold in colour, this delicate wine has mineral aromas, freshness and undoubted structure.
➤ Francine and Olivier Savary, 4, chem. des Hâtes, 89800 Maligny, tel. 03.86.47.42.09, fax 03.86.47.55.80, e-mail f.o.savary@wanadoo.fr ☑
✆ by appt.

DOM. DE LA TOUR 2001★

| | 0.55 ha | 4,000 | | 3–5 € |

A limpid, intense gold colour, with plenty of highlights, this is a good-looking wine. Its ripe-fruit bouquet seems somewhat uncharacteristic. After an agreeable attack, the impression on the palate is of honey and grapefruit chastened together. Tender and relatively lingering, it is ready for drinking now.
➤ SCEA Dom. de la Tour, 3, rte de Montfort, 89800 Lignorelles, tel. 03.86.47.55.68, fax 03.86.47.55.86 ☑
✆ by appt.
➤ Fabrici

DOM. YVON VOCORET 2001★

| | 3 ha | 7,900 | 🍾 | 5–8 € |

An intense and original colour, and a nose that shows great promise without neglecting a few mineral notes. On the palate, too, it needs to open out in order to reveal its terroir, but it is already balanced and harmonious. Another year in the cellar will give it time to express its character.
➤ Dom. Yvon Vocoret, 9, chem. de Beaune, 89800 Maligny, tel. 03.86.47.51.60, fax 03.86.47.57.47 ☑
✆ by appt.

Wines selected but not starred

LA CAVE DU CONNAISSEUR 2001

| | 3 ha | 20,000 | 🍾 ♦ | 5–8 € |

➤ La Cave du Connaisseur, rue des Moulins, BP 78, 89800 Chablis, tel. 03.86.42.87.15, fax 03.86.42.49.84, e-mail connaisseur@chablis.net ☑
✆ ev. day. 10am–6pm

DOM. ERIC DAMPT

Vieilles Vignes 2001

| | 2.9 ha | 19,200 | 🍾 ♦ | 5–8 € |

➤ Eric Dampt, 16, rue de l'Ancien-Presbytère, 89700 Collan, tel. 03.86.55.36.28, fax 03.86.54.49.89 ☑
✆ by appt.

AGNES ET DENIS DAUVISSAT 2001

| | n.c. | 1,500 | 🍾 | 5–8 € |

➤ Agnès et Didier Dauvissat, chem. de Beauroy, 89800 Beine, tel. 03.86.42.46.40, fax 03.86.42.80.82 ☑
✆ ev. day. 9am–12 noon 2pm–7pm

DOM. D'ELISE 2001

| | 7.02 ha | 14,000 | 🍾 ♦ | 5–8 € |

➤ Frédéric Prain, Côte de Léchet, 89800 Milly, tel. 03.86.42.40.82, fax 03.86.42.44.76 ☑
✆ by appt.

DOM. DE L'ORME 2002

| | 10 ha | 35,000 | 🍾 ♦ | 5–8 € |

➤ Dom. de l'Orme, 16, rue de Chablis, 89800 Lignorelles, tel. 03.86.47.41.60, fax 03.86.47.56.66 ☑
✆ by appt.

DENIS POMMIER 2001

| | 4 ha | 20,000 | 🍾 ♦ | 5–8 € |

➤ EARL Denis Pommier, 31, rue de Poinchy, Poinchy, 89800 Chablis, tel. 03.86.42.83.04, fax 03.86.42.17.80, e-mail denis.pommier@libertysurf.fr ☑
✆ ev. day. 9am–12 noon 2pm–7pm; Sun. by appt.

MICHELE ET CLAUDE POULLET 2001

| | 1.4 ha | 3,100 | 🍾 ♦ | 5–8 € |

➤ Claude Poullet, 6, rue du Temple, 89800 Maligny, tel. 03.86.47.51.37, fax 03.86.47.51.37 ☑
✆ by appt.

Chablis

In 2002 178,483 hl of Chablis were produced over 3,014 ha. This wine owes its inimitable qualities of freshness and lightness to the soils from which it springs. Ill-suited to cold and rainy years, when it acquires too much acidity, in warm years it gains a refreshing quality lacking in the Côte d'Or Chardonnays. It should be drunk young (in one to three years) but can be left to age for up to ten years or more, when it gains in complexity and in the richness of its bouquet.

DOM. BEGUE-MATHIOT 2001★

	8.6 ha	1,150			5–8 €

Here Joel and Maryse Bègue-Mathiot take us into their secret garden with this Chablis, which is full of potential, and more dynamic than it has the right to be. Serve it between 2004 and 2006 to get the full benefit of its aromas (flint, honey and a lemony note) and of its substance on the palate which is above average.
• Dom. Joël et Maryse Bègue-Mathiot, Les Epinottes, 89800 Chablis, tel. 03.86.42.16.65, fax 03.86.42.81.54
Ⅰ by appt.

DOM. BESSON 2001★

	7.59 ha	9,000			5–8 €

It has vigour and appeal, this brilliant Chablis! Limpid, bright, it is right there on cue. The continuation is mineral, but includes moss, damp woodlands – highly individual. What youth on the palate! One has the impression of a wine that is pleased with itself. The terroir clearly confirms all that the body and the décor have to say.
• EARL Alain Besson, rue de Valvan, 89800 Chablis, tel. 03.86.42.19.53, fax 03.86.42.49.46, e-mail domaine-besson@wanadoo.fr
Ⅰ by appt.

DOM. BILLAUD-SIMON

Tête d'or 2001★

	3 ha	23,000			8–11 €

Golden head: is this a literary reference to Claudel who had a weakness for the Yonne wines? Elegant and with astonishing concentration, this light-gold Chablis shows impeccable balance right from start. Fullness on the palate, length and complexity combine to give a wine that is at the top of its form and well able to face two or three more years in the cellar.
• Dom. Billaud-Simon, 1, quai de Reugny, BP 46, 89800 Chablis, tel. 03.86.42.10.33, fax 03.86.42.48.77
Ⅰ ev. day. ex. Sun. 9am–12 noon 2pm–6pm; Sat. by appt., cl. 15–30 Aug.

LA CHABLISIENNE

Les Vieilles Vignes 2000★

	25 ha	150,000			11–15 €

La Chablisienne is a cooperative that manages 700 ha and which has an excellent reputation. This is a wine from 2000 which spent 16 months in tank and six months in cask. The verdict of our tasters, who were aware of this double maturation and the softening effect of the oak on the white-gold colour, was "original". Its aromas are delicate without being secretive: though initially secondary, they develop on the palate: russet apples, particularly. Leave it for one to two years.
• La Chablisienne, 8, bd Pasteur, BP 14, 89800 Chablis, tel. 03.86.42.89.89, fax 03.86.42.89.90, e-mail chab@chablisienne.fr
Ⅰ by appt.

CHANSON PERE ET FILS 2001★★

	n.c.	8,300			11–15 €

Dry, limpid, scented, lively and light: a thumbnail definition of the sort of Chablis one dreams of drinking. In reality it applies to this very attractive, oaky-tasting wine with the full range of characteristic qualities. Light-gold in colour, this 2001 vintage has a lively, well-ripened-fruit nose. Hints of lemons, spices, appropriate minerality; it is all going in the right direction, without hurrying.
• Dom. Chanson Père et Fils, 10, rue Paul-Chanson, BP 232, 21206 Beaune Cedex, tel. 03.80.25.97.97, fax 03.80.24.17.42, e-mail tmarion@vins-chanson.com

DOM. DE CHANTEMERLE 2001★

	10 ha	73,000			5–8 €

Chantemerle is a vast, 5-ha vineyard where one hears the blackbird (merle) sing (chanter). Domain famous for its Homme Mort (dead man) climat that Adhémar Boudin praised to the skies, a little like La Forest de Dauvissat. True to type, this is a straw-yellow, slightly floral Chablis which, under its reserved manner, is putting together a well-balanced, lively harmonious palate.

• SCEA de Chantemerle, 3, pl. des Cotats, 89800 La Chapelle-Vaupelteigne, tel. 03.86.42.18.95, fax 03.86.42.81.60
Ⅰ by appt.
• Francis Boudin

DOM. J. CHATELAIN 2002★

	27.47 ha	80,000			5–8 €

An 11th century church will attract you to the village where this estate was established in 1955. In the beneficial air of Chablis, Lucien de Oliveira and Jacky Chatelain have not wasted their time. This 2002 vintage spent four months in tank: menthol; grapefruit; it is quite modern and expressive. Its fruitiness is maturing correctly and its well-balanced acidity should back it up in time, but it is already pleasant.
• GAEC De Oliveira Lecestre, J. Chatelain, 11, Grand-Rue, 89800 Fontenay-près-Chablis, tel. 03.86.42.40.78, fax 03.86.42.83.72
Ⅰ by appt.

DOM. DES CHAUMES

Elevé en fût de chêne 2001★★

	1 ha	2,500			8–11 €

"When one is depressed, one needs to get far away from Paris. And to see life through rose-coloured glasses, go straight to Chablis"; so sang Aristide Bruand, almost a native of the area. This wine could perhaps sing the chorus to that verse; life seen through emerald-yellow glasses rather than rose-coloured? A clean and fruity bouquet; a fine example of the 2001 vintage, soft and of quite remarkable length and just the right amount of acidity. In short, a unanimous coup de coeur. This one is the Cuvée en Fût de Chêne, which would be ideal with white meat in a cream sauce or cheese (Epoisses). The other, Chablis 2001 (5–8 €) without any other name, was awarded one star. Choose it to drink as an aperitif with a Gougère.
• Romain Poullet, EARL des Chaumes, 6, rue du Temple, 89800 Maligny, tel. 03.86.98.21.83, fax 03.86.98.21.84
Ⅰ by appt.

DOM. CHEVALLIER 2001★

	12 ha	6,000			5–8 €

The vaulted wine cellars on this estate are not all medieval, but wine has been made there since that era...A limpid pale-yellow, this is a Chablis perfumed with citronella, lively without exaggeration, nicely balanced, that the Jury "liked very much," and thought should be accompanied by a fillet of pikeperch in a chaud-froid sauce.
• Dom. Claude and Jean-Louis Chevallier, 6, rue de l'Ecole, 89290 Montallery-Venoy, tel. 03.86.40.27.04, fax 03.86.40.27.05
Ⅰ by appt.

DOM. CHRISTOPHE ET FILS 2001★

	0.5 ha	4,000			5–8 €

Coup de coeur last year: you already know your way about its cellars. Readers who would like to visit the estate, though, will need a good map and some advice on where to find it. The wine itself doesn't even think of hiding, even if it does need to be swirled in the glass to show itself to best advantage. Green highlights, fruity notes, all the characteristics of the

appellation. A touch spicy and capable of being firm-handed. Meticulously true to type, it would accompany a seafood platter or a *truite au bleu*.
↪ Dom. Christophe et Fils, Ferme des Carrières à Fyé, 89800 Chablis, tel. 03.86.55.23.10, fax 03.86.55.23.10
Ⲗ by appt.

DOM. JEAN COLLET ET FILS 2001★

| | 4 ha | 31,000 | ▮ ♦ | 5–8 € |

An amiable estate with a history of inventing and implementing progressive techniques, and patenting them. This wine? Harmony and charm in a lively and ethereal context. Acacia wood. It is substantial on the palate with a fresh, long finish. It would go well with smoked ham.
↪ Dom. Jean Collet et Fils, 15, av. de la Liberté, 89800 Chablis, tel. 03.86.42.11.93, fax 03.86.42.47.43, e-mail collet.chablis@wanadoo.fr
Ⲗ by appt.
↪ Gilles Collet

DOM. DU COLOMBIER 2001★

| | 35 ha | 150,000 | ▮ ♦ | 5–8 € |

There are the four Aymon sons and three Mothe brothers: Jean-Louis, Thierry and Vincent; a typical winemaking family. Their Chablis, light gold in colour, is positively crunchy. Its fruity aromas are already toasting each other in the glass. A strong fleshiness, a mouth-filling sensation with just a touch of greenness to remind us of the true Chablis characteristics. Ready to go to table with a Pâté de Campagne, for example.
↪ Guy Mothe et ses Fils, Dom. du Colombier, 42, Grand-Rue, 89800 Fontenay-près-Chablis, tel. 03.86.42.15.04, fax 03.86.42.49.67
Ⲗ by appt.

DOM. DE LA CONCIERGERIE

Vieilles Vignes 2001★★★

| | 1.2 ha | 8,000 | ▮ ♦ | 8–11 € |

Classed first in the *coups de cœur* by the Grand Jury, this Chablis is extraordinarily accomplished; it really takes you where you want to be; a journey that is well worth-while. A very light silver-gold, it has settled on a pleasant and distinguished colour. An attractive, subtle nose, delicate and lightly floral. A mineral body goes with the characteristic attributes of a wine which "has love to give," as they used to say about the sort of particularly successful Chablis that was a shining example of its kind. At one time the entry to the Château de Courgis was through the Conciergerie.
↪ EARL Christian Adine, 2, allée du Château, 89800 Courgis, tel. 03.86.41.40.28, fax 03.86.41.45.75, e-mail nicole.adine@free.fr

DOM. DANIEL DAMPT 2001★

| | 15 ha | 80,000 | ▮ ♦ | 8–11 € |

A ham cooked in Chablis if you are a traditionalist. A more trendy accompaniment would be a salmon carpaccio…Let us look at the wine more closely. Its small green highlights show it to be true to type. Citrus fruits meet on the bouquet. The follow-on stays with this aromatic length of flavour, adding a very characteristic mineral effect, known here as "*le caillou*" (the stone).

↪ Dom. Daniel Dampt et Fils, 1, rue des Violettes, 89800 Milly, tel. 03.86.42.47.23, fax 03.86.42.46.41, e-mail domaine.dampt.defaix@wanadoo.fr
Ⲗ by appt.

EMMANUEL DAMPT

Cuvée Prestige 2000★

| | n.c. | 6,000 | ▮ ♦ | 5–8 € |

Birthplace of the Cistercian order, the hermitage at Collan – on the D 35 between Chablis and Tonnerre – was visited by Saint Robert at the beginning of the 11th century. Powerful and rich, a heady Chablis that one could imagine gracing the cellars of a sultan. Light-gold in colour, the nose gradually opens up to reveal mineral notes. The alcohol is well-sustained and the impression on the palate is excellent. A wine like this would go well with a dish prepared *à la crème*.
↪ Emmanuel Dampt, 3, rte de Tonnerre, 89700 Collan, tel. 03.86.54.49.52, fax 03.86.54.49.89
Ⲗ by appt.

ERIC DAMPT

Vieilles Vignes 2001★

| | 2.6 ha | 16,800 | ▮ ♦ | 5–8 € |

Eric Dampt has been at the head of this estate of less than 13 ha since 1988. Brilliant gold in colour, this Chablis, matured on the lees, opens after aeration on nuances of exotic fruits. On the palate it conforms precisely to the characteristics of the AOC; mineral and lively, a worthy wine to drink with a dozen oysters.
↪ Eric Dampt, 16, rue de l'Ancien-Presbytère, 89700 Collan, tel. 03.86.55.36.28, fax 03.86.54.49.89
Ⲗ by appt.

DOM. DE L'EGLANTIERE 2001★

| | 35 ha | 275,000 | ▮ ♦ | 8–11 € |

Jean Durup, who created this 176-ha estate, has two spheres of activity: chartered accountant in Paris and wine-growing at Maligny. He is one of the major success-stories of the area. His Chablis is tasting well. A slightly golden straw colour, opening on honey and dried fruits, it continues on its way across the palate: lively, then pleasant, then fresh. It has a slight mushroom aroma, and we know how attached this area is to its mushrooms. This is a wine that will fill out as it ages.
↪ SA Jean Durup Père et Fils, 4, Grande-Rue, 89800 Maligny, tel. 03.86.47.44.49, fax 03.86.47.55.49, e-mail cdurup@club-internet.fr
Ⲗ by appt.

ALAIN GAUTHERON 2001★

| | 13.11 ha | n.c. | ▮ ♦ | 5–8 € |

Not so long as the road from Chablis to Compostella but one would readily drink it with *coquilles St. Jacques* (scallops): this 2001 leaves a pleasant trace, dominantly of citrus fruits, on both nose and palate. A slightly golden pale-yellow, it is not too mineral and constitutes a different, but by no means unpleasing, category. A small touch of acidity, without going overboard.
↪ Alain et Cyril Gautheron, 18, rue des Prégirots, 89800 Fleys, tel. 03.86.42.44.34, fax 03.86.42.44.50
Ⲗ by appt.

DOM. DES GENEVES

Vieilles Vignes 2001★

| | 0,6 ha | 3,000 | ▮ ♦ | 5–8 € |

Fleys can be proud of its fortified church dating from the 13th and 16th centuries, and also of its Mont de Milieu Premier Cru and its famous *climat* which is Kimmeridgian to the tips of its fingers. They say this is snail country. This rich and powerful wine from the 2001 vintage moves rather faster than that. Green-gold, with "legs," its nose is natural, mineral and iodized. A well-balanced, harmonious wine
↪ Dom. des Genèves, 3, rue des Fourneaux, 89800 Fleys, tel. 03.86.42.10.15, fax 03.86.42.47.34
Ⲗ by appt.
↪ Dominique Aufrère et Fils

DOM. GRAND ROCHE 2001★

| 6,5 ha | 22,000 | | | 8–11 € |

Founded in 1987 by one who was totally smitten and starting from nothing, this estate of more than 20 ha offered a 2001 vintage which, at first sight, is full of energy. On the nose it is fruity and fresh, almost green, as in green apples. It is straightforward and successful, without much in the background, but with enough length to stand up to a dozen snails.
➥ Erick Lavallée, Dom. Grand Roche, 6, rte de Chitry, 89530 Saint-Bris-le-Vineux, tel. 03.86.53.84.07, fax 03.86.53.88.36 ☑
⌶ by appt.

DOM. DE GRILLOT 2001★

| 2.9 ha | 4,000 | | | 5–8 € |

A little-known estate of just over 4 ha; a Winery Boutique, as one says in California. Against a pale-gold background, with aeration the bouquet develops notes of honey, flowers and iodine. The rather light palate is developing rapidly. Quite characteristic already and getting more so, a wine to drink in two or three years' time.
➥ James Haigre, 16, rue de l'Ancien-Presbytère, 89700 Collan, tel. 06.07.62.64.08, fax 03.86.54.49.89 ☑
⌶ by appt.

DOM. HAMELIN 2001★★

| 10.18 ha | n.c. | | | 5–8 € |

This beautiful Chablis has come well out of a complex year. Limpid, brilliant, it is very representative of the AOC colour, and its bouquet is rich, distinguished, and well developed. Not much fleshiness on the palate but it has freshness and the length appears generous. Needs keeping for another year.
➥ EARL Hamelin, 1, rue des Carillons, 89800 Lignorelles, tel. 03.86.47.54.60, fax 03.86.47.53.34 ☑
⌶ ev. day. ex. Wed.Sun. 8.30am–12 noon 1.30pm–6pm; cl. Aug.

HENRY FRERES 2001★

| 0.98 ha | 7,000 | | | 5–8 € |

This one has chosen its side. Silver rather that yellow, it does have nuances however. Slightly mineral, delicately spring-like, it goes little further than that on the nose. On the other hand, its opening is forceful and the first impressions on the palate are quickly swept away by its aromatic momentum, predominantly mineral with an undercurrent of flint. Fully representative of its AOC.
➥ GAEC Henry Frères, 30, chem. des Fossés, 89800 Saint-Cyr-les-Colons, tel. 03.86.41.44.87, fax 03.86.41.41.48 ☑
⌶ by appt.

PIERRE JANNY 2001★

| 5 ha | 34,000 | | | 8–11 € |

This négociant from Péronne in Mâconnais is a long way from his base but he knows how to choose his terrain. Do not wait any longer to enjoy this clean, straightforward Chablis. Floral notes, flint, it has all the characteristics, like the pale-gold colour. Fresh and lively, all the aromas are present on the palate.
➥ Sté Janny, La Condemine, Cidex 1556, 71260 Péronne, tel. 03.85.23.96.20, fax 03.85.36.96.58, e-mail pierre-janny@wanadoo.fr

DOM. LAROCHE

Saint-Martin 2001★★

| 61.57 ha | n.c. | | | 11–15 € |

The very first large Chablis barrels were undoubtedly rolled in the cellars at l'Obédiencerie, in the heart of the Laroche company's estates. We know that the remains of this famous bishop of Tours were once buried at Chablis. It is delightful, this Chardonnay dressed in the green-gold of the area. Its mineral and fruity bouquet will fill the most exigent of noses. Intense and rounded, and substantial nevertheless, the palate is admirably constituted. The Jury recommended waiting until 2005 before enjoying it with a poached salmon.

➥ Michel Laroche, L'Obédiencerie, 22, rue Louis-Bro, 89800 Chablis, tel. 03.86.42.89.00, fax 03.86.42.89.29, e-mail info@michellaroche.com ☑
⌶ by appt.

DOM. DES MALANDES

Cuvée Tour du Roy Vieilles Vignes 2001★★

| 1.3 ha | 10,000 | | | 8–11 € |

Placed fourth by the Grand Jury, this remarkable *cuvée* has aromas of flint cut to sharp angles and a fresh springtime breeze. Its minerality and its freshness fill both the nose and the palate with wonder. Its balance is perfect. This wine could be drunk right away but is worth waiting a year or two then serving it with a fish dish.
➥ Dom. des Malandes, 63, rue Auxerroise, 89800 Chablis, tel. 03.86.42.41.37, fax 03.86.42.41.97, e-mail contact@domainedesmalandes.com ☑
⌶ by appt.

CHRISTIAN MORIN 2001★★

| 1.9 ha | 3,000 | | | 5–8 € |

Selected for the final of the *coup de coeur* and already *coup de coeur* last year, is this *vin jaune*, gold with green highlights and limpid and intense as it should be. Reminiscent of honey and *pain d'épice*, the bouquet is slightly alcohol-tainted but still within the normal bounds. Extremely sensitive on the palate, it brings out the finesse of grape variety, its rich fruitiness, its character. And luck had nothing to do with it: this wine-grower from Auxerre takes his wines very seriously.
➥ Christian Morin, 17, rue du Ruisseau, 89530 Chitry-le-Fort, tel. 03.86.41.44.10, fax 03.86.41.48.21 ☑
⌶ by appt.

DOM. DE LA MOTTE 2001★

| 6 ha | 48,000 | | | 5–8 € |

Old property family which grew grapes in the Chablis area until 1990; since then it has been making and marketing wine from the product of its 16 ha. Small golden highlights herald a Chablis with the slightly truffled perfumes that are typical of the terroir. Mineral, lemony, it is one hundred percent Chablis right to the finish on the palate. A guaranteed pleasure with seafood.
➥ Michaut-Robin, SCEA Dom. de La Motte, 35, Grande-Rue, 89800 Beines, tel. 03.86.42.43.71, fax 03.86.42.43.43, e-mail domainedelamotte@wanadoo.fr ☑
⌶ ev. day. ex. Wed. 8am–12 noon 2pm–6pm

DOM. JEAN-MARIE NAULIN 2001★

| 9 ha | 10,000 | | | 5–8 € |

Goat's milk cheese, all right. But let us take a wider view, since we are in Burgundy, and insist that the cheese merchant supplies us with a *chèvreton*, a "trouser button" from the Mâconnais. Brilliant gold, this 2001 vintage offers aromas of field-mushrooms that couldn't be more orthodox. Fruity and mineral on the palate, it is very well balanced and ready to drink.
➥ Dom. Jean-Marie Naulin, 30, rue de la Voie-Neuve, 89800 Beines, tel. 03.86.42.46.71, fax 03.86.42.12.74 ☑
⌶ by appt.

DOM. DE L'ORME 2002★

| | 20 ha | 65,000 | 🍷 🍶 | 5–8 € |

A 2002 wine matured six months in tank. The colour is charming, the aromas are of fresh fruit and flowers. There is grapefruit on the palate, where acidity play its part. Excellent wine to drink with oysters.
☛ Dom. de l'Orme, 16, rue de Chablis, 89800 Lignorelles, tel. 03.86.47.41.60, fax 03.86.47.56.66 ☑
⚘ by appt.

DOM. DE PISSE-LOUP 2001★

| | 1.5 ha | 8,000 | 🍷 🍶 | 5–8 € |

The team at Pisse-Loup (what a strange name!) elsewhere produced the Château Lagarde-Rouffiac, a Cahors AOC. Its Chablis starts off voluble, then closes up again on the palate; it will undoubtedly need keeping for a year or two. The colour is superb and the nose quite communicative, but in essence this is an elegant and balanced wine.
☛ Romuald Hugot, 30, rte Nationale, 89800 Beines, tel. 03.86.42.85.11, fax 03.86.42.85.11 ☑
⚘ by appt.

DOM. ROY 2001★

| | 8 ha | 9,000 | 🍷 🍶 | 5–8 € |

Limpid and clear with green tinges, a frank and fruity nose, this is a Chablis with dense, intense body, to drink with goat's milk cheeses.
☛ Dom. Roy, 71, Grand-Rue, 89800 Fontenay-près-Chablis, tel. 03.86.42.10.36 ☑

VAUCHER PERE ET FILS 2001★

| | n.c. | n.c. | | 8–11 € |

Vaucher Père et Fils is an old company from the Dijon area with a foot in the Côte de Nuits, today part of Labouré-Roi. This is a Chablis with a good colour and an Atlantic-style, iodized nose. Honest structure and good length for the vintage, it is all roundness and suppleness; it could well accompany an *andouillette* (offal sausage) in the months to come.
☛ Vaucher Père et Fils, rue Lavoisier, 21700 Nuits-Saint-Georges, tel. 03.80.62.64.00, fax 03.80.62.64.10, e-mail vaucher@axnet.fr

DOM. DU VIEUX LOUP 2001★

| | 2.26 ha | 1,300 | 🍷 🍶 | 8–11 € |

A small wine-producing village, Beines has a 13th century church. This 18th century cellar was used as the location for a Japanese film, and the grapes here stood in for cereals. This Chablis expounds its subject well: starting with pale gold with grey highlights, developing on apples, it finishes on the palate with delicate, floral accents that offer the prospect of ripe fruits. An interesting wine, to drink in the near future with a cheese of the Epoisses type.
☛ Goublot Longhi, 1, Grande-Rue, 89800 Beines, tel. 03.86.42.43.34, fax 03.86.42.43.34 ☑
⚘ by appt.

Wines selected but not starred

PIERRE ANDRE
Le Grand Pré 2001

| | 1.5 ha | 8,000 | 🍷 🍶 | 15–23 € |

☛ Pierre André, Ch. de Corton-André, 21420 Aloxe-Corton, tel. 03.80.26.44.25, fax 03.80.26.43.57, e-mail pandre@axnet.fr

DOM. JEAN-CLAUDE COURTAULT 2001

| | 8.7 ha | 36,000 | 🍷 🍶 | 5–8 € |

☛ Dom. Jean-Claude Courtault, 1, rte de Montfort, 89800 Lignorelles, tel. 03.86.47.50.59, fax 03.86.47.50.74 ☑
⚘ by appt.

JEAN DAUVISSAT
Saint-Pierre 2001

| | 2.35 ha | 18,000 | 🍷 🍶 | 8–11 € |

☛ Jean et Sébastien Dauvissat, 3, rue de Chichée, 89800 Chablis, tel. 03.86.42.14.62, fax 03.86.42.45.54, e-mail jean.dauvissat@terre-net.fr ☑
⚘ by appt.

DOM. BERNARD DEFAIX
Cuvée Vieilles Vignes 2001

| | 1.5 ha | 9,000 | 🍷 🍾 🍶 | 8–11 € |

☛ Dom. Bernard Defaix, 17, rue du Château, Milly, 89800 Chablis, tel. 03.86.42.40.75, fax 03.86.42.40.28, e-mail didier@bernard-defaix.com ☑
⚘ by appt.

DOM. PHILIPPE GOULLEY 2001

| | 1 ha | 7,500 | 🍷 🍶 | 11–15 € |

☛ Dom. Philippe Goulley, 89800 La Chapelle-Vaupelteigne, tel. 03.86.42.40.85, fax 03.86.42.81.06, e-mail phil.goulley@wanadoo.fr ☑
⚘ by appt.

DOM. JEAN GOULLEY ET FILS 2001

| | 7 ha | 50,000 | 🍷 🍶 | 8–11 € |

☛ Dom. Jean Goulley et Fils, 11 bis, vallée des Rosiers, 89800 La Chapelle-Vaupelteigne, tel. 03.86.42.40.85, fax 03.86.42.81.06, e-mail phil.goulley@wanadoo.fr ☑
⚘ by appt.
☛ Philippe Goulley

DOM. GUITTON-MICHEL
Prestige Vieilles Vignes 2001

| | 6 ha | 15,000 | 🍷 🍾 🍶 | 8–11 € |

☛ Guitton-Michel, 2, rue de Poinchy, Poinchy, 89800 Chablis, tel. 03.86.42.43.14, fax 03.86.42.17.64 ☑
⚘ by appt.

DOM. DE VAUROUX
Vieilles Vignes 2001

| | 3 ha | 25,000 | 🍷 🍶 | 8–11 € |

☛ SCEA Dom. de Vauroux, rte d'Avallon, BP 56, 89800 Chablis, tel. 03.86.42.10.37, fax 03.86.42.49.13, e-mail domaine-de-vauroux@domaine-de-vauroux.com ☑
⚘ by appt.

Chablis Premier Cru

Chablis Premier Cru comes from around 30 locations selected for their situation and the quality of their wines. They produced 44,164 hl in 2002 over 766 ha. The comparison with Chablis lies chiefly in the Premier Cru's complex and lingering bouquet, the aromas offering a mixture of acacia honey, a touch of iodine and hints of vegetation. The amount produced per hectare is limited to 50 hl. All the winemakers agree that Chablis Premier Cru reaches a peak in its fifth year when it takes on a distinctive "hazelnut" note. The most substantial examples are produced by the *climats* of La Montée de Tonnerre, Fourchaume, Mont de Milieu, Forêt, Butteaux and Côte de Léchet.

DOM. BACHELIER

Les Fourneaux 2001★

	0.23 ha	1,800	🍶 ◊	11–15 €

Several tasters raised this wine to the two-star level. It is, therefore, very successful from head to toe. A limpid pale-yellow, it has a promising delicacy. The bouquet bears its name well and to this floral charm one can add a clear-cut initial impression. Still closed, it is a solidly-constructed wine and has great keeping potential.

🍷 Dom. Bachelier, 14, rue Genillotte, 89800 Villy, tel. 03.86.47.49.56, fax 03.86.47.57.96 ☑
⚲ by appt.

DOM. BARAT

Vaillons 2001★

3 ha	10,000	🍶 ◊	8–11 €

"Fleshy, full-bodied, incisive, it fills the mouth," is often said about a Vaillons. This one doesn't give lie to the axiom: it shares its aromas equally between floral and flinty. The follow-on is definitely more mineral. The vinification was reliable and truly successful. Serve it with a roast of veal with cream and mushrooms. Receiving a special mention: the **Monts de Milieu 2000 (11–15 €)**, which is coming along nicely and will keep a year or two in the cellar.

🍷 EARL Dom. Barat, 6, rue de Léchet, Milly, 89800 Chablis, tel. 03.86.42.40.07, fax 03.86.42.47.88, e-mail domaine.barat@wanadoo.fr ☑
⚲ by appt.

JULES BELIN

Fourchaumes 2001★★

	n.c.	1,500	🍶 ◊	15–23 €

This old Premeaux company (now Arlot) was revived as a marque by the Lanvin family at Nuits (Misserey and Coron). This wine has the fine, well-balanced mineral and lively side that goes to make a great Fourchaume.

🍷 Maison Jules Belin, 3, rue des Seuillets, BP 143, 21704 Nuits-Saint-Georges Cedex, tel. 03.80.61.07.74, fax 03.80.61.31.40, e-mail lanvin-sa@worldonline.fr ☑
⚲ by appt.

DOM. BESSON

Vaillon 2001★

2.44 ha	5,000	🍶 ⦿ ◊	8–11 €

Grandson of cooper, son of wine-grower, Alain Besson presented this Vaillon which justifies its reputation as a Grand Premier Cru. Gold-yellow, this wine from 2001 evokes a touch of honey, dried apricots, then the "maritime" aromas that are typical of the AOC (call them iodized). Quite fruity on the middle palate, quite intense, this wine turns mineral again on the finish. Very true to type.

🍷 EARL Alain Besson, rue de Valvan, 89800 Chablis, tel. 03.86.42.19.53, fax 03.86.42.49.46, e-mail domaine-besson@wanadoo.fr ☑
⚲ by appt.

DOM. BILLAUD-SIMON

Montée de Tonnerre 2001★★

2.5 ha	18,000	🍶 ◊	15–23 €

Between the **Mont de Milieu 2001** and Montée de Tonnerre of same vintage, obtained the same marks and one can put them down as a tie. Opening with fresh fruits, first is full-bodied and powerful: the second is all honey and hazelnuts, and delicate nuances. It has breadth and richness and a real but regular liveliness. Perfectly true to type. The **Vaillons** and **Fourchaume 2001** were each awarded one star. You will also find this well-regarded estate elsewhere in this Chablis chapter.

🍷 Dom. Billaud-Simon, 1, quai de Reugny, BP 46, 89800 Chablis, tel. 03.86.42.10.33, fax 03.86.42.48.77 ☑
⚲ ev. day. ex. Sun. 9am–12 noon 2pm–6pm; Sat. by appt., cl. 15–30 Aug.

PASCAL BOUCHARD Montmains Grande Réserve du domaine Vieilles Vignes 2000★★

	0.55 ha	4,000	🍶 ⦿ ◊	11–15 €

This Montmains from the year 2000, with its clear, youthful colour, was considered by several tasters for the *coup de coeur*. Well made, a characteristic Chablis, mineral, lively and fresh, everything about this wine is pleasing. Its structure, however, means it will not keep beyond two to three years. Drink it with a ham cooked in Chablis, for example. Another attractive wine from this cellar is the **Beauroy 2001**, a fine example of winemaking which was awarded one star.

🍷 Pascal Bouchard, parc des Lys, 89800 Chablis, tel. 03.86.42.18.64, fax 03.86.42.48.11, e-mail info@pascalbouchard.com ☑
⚲ by appt.

LA CHABLISIENNE

Mont de Milieu 2001★★★

6 ha	40,000	🍶 ⦿ ◊	15–23 €

Founder of this cooperative in 1923, the abbot Balitran would have been happy to invite this wine to his table. *Coup de coeur*, it was given first place in the tasting by the Grand Jury. This Mont de Milieu has a lot of Mount Blanc about it. A minerality still closed in the shell of its fossilized oyster, the sharp finesse of white cherries, a touch of mentholated oakiness (nine months in vat and two in cask). It is tender, energetic, in the purest classic style. *coup de coeur* already last year (for a Fourchaume). The **Montmain** and the **Beauroy 2001 (11–15 €)** were each awarded one star. Buy them without hesitation.

🍷 La Chablisienne, 8, bd Pasteur, BP 14, 89800 Chablis, tel. 03.86.42.89.89, fax 03.86.42.89.90, e-mail chab@chablisienne.fr ☑
⚲ by appt.

DOM. DE CHANTEMERLE

L'Homme mort 2001★

	0.22 ha	1,700	🍶 ◊	11–15 €

To say *l'Homme mort (the dead man) d'Adhémar Boudin*, is like saying the *Cros Parantoux of Henri Jayer*. Wine cults, and mythical in both cases. Citrus fruits dominate the tastings of this vintage, which also offers notes of acacia-flowers and lychees. Balanced, fine and of good length, it will keep for one to two years. The **Fourchaume 2001 (8–11 €)**, *coup de coeur* in the 98 vintage, was given a special mention; this is another.

🍷 SCEA de Chantemerle, 3, pl. des Cotats, 89800 La Chapelle-Vaupelteigne, tel. 03.86.42.18.95, fax 03.86.42.81.60 ☑
⚲ by appt.
🍷 A. et F. Boudin

DOM. DU CHARDONNAY

Mont de Milieu 2001★

	0.69 ha	4,600	🍶 ◊	8–11 €

Here we have a joint effort by Christian Simon, William Nahan and Etienne Boileau on their 36 ha. To be called Domaine du Chardonnay is already an achievement. And this is another: four wines picked out from this vintage: the **Vaugiraut** and the **Montée de Tonnerre 2001** are in the same category as this one, a **Montmains**. This Mont de Milieu swells and grows on the palate, tender initially then full and with good acidity. A wine to drink with a meal.

🍷 Dom. du Chardonnay, Moulin du Patis, 89800 Chablis, tel. 03.86.42.48.03, fax 03.86.42.16.49, e-mail chardonnay@ipoint.fr ☑
⚲ ev. day. 9am–11.45am 2pm–4.45pm; Sat. Sun. by appt.; cl. 12 Aug–2 Sep. 20 Dec.–6 Jan.

CHARDONNIER
Vaillons 2001★

	4.56 ha	26,763	🍶 ⚱	11–15 €

A Vaillons from D. Wilmotte (Vosne-Romanée). The light colour with green highlights sets the tone. The bouquet, initially light becoming more voluble, is based on the iodine bequeathed by the ancient sea that deposited the millions of fossil oysters from which we make such good wine. The finish is still a little severe. Concentration and terroir are both in this wine, which shouldn't leave the cellar before its fifth or sixth birthday.
🍷 Chardonnier, 44, RN 74, 21700 Vosne-Romanée, tel. 03.80.61.26.76, fax 03.80.62.11.52, e-mail chardonnier@wanadoo.fr
🍷 D. Wilmotte

DOM. DE CHAUDE ECUELLE
Montmains 2001★

	0,76 ha	5,949	🍶 ⚱	8–11 €

Coup de coeur last year for a Montée de Tonnerre, these two winemakers from Chemilly-sur-Serein were jointly responsible for this white-gold, clean young wine from 2001 with quite complex aromas of flowers and elderberries. Well-made for this vintage, this Premier Cru is charming and pleasant to the taste. Some lemony notes on the finish.
🍷 Dom. de Chaude Ecuelle, 35, Grande-Rue, 89800 Chemilly-sur-Serein, tel. 03.86.42.40.44, fax 03.86.42.85.13 ✅
🍷 by appt.
🍷 Gabriel and Gérald Vilain

DOM. JEAN COLLET ET FILS
Montée de Tonnerre 2001★

	2.25 ha	17,500	🍷	11–15 €

All the morels and the cream need is the capon from Bresse AOC and this Montée de Tonnerre. Lemon-yellow, with a slight oakiness (eleven months in cask), it is a wine that needs a while to mature; structured, powerful enough, of a good length; the finish, with its touch of bitterness, exudes pure Chardonnay.
🍷 Dom. Jean Collet et Fils, 15, av. de la Liberté, 89800 Chablis, tel. 03.86.42.11.93, fax 03.86.42.47.43, e-mail collet.chablis@wanadoo.fr ✅
🍷 by appt.
🍷 Gilles Collet

DOM. DANIEL DAMPT
Les Lys 2001★★

	0.8 ha	6,000	🍶 ⚱	11–15 €

This *climat* is regarded with some reverence in Chablis. Does not the city's coat of arms carry the fleur de lys? Pale yellow with sustained nuances, this is a wine with iodized and mineral aromas. You can smell the kelp, the seaweed. The fleshiness adds to its finesse because the terroir is clearly perceptible. A fruity charm evokes the ripeness of the grape and the care taken with the vinification. See also the **Fourchaume 2001** which was awarded one star.
🍷 Dom. Daniel Dampt et Fils, 1, rue des Violettes, 89800 Milly, tel. 03.86.42.47.23, fax 03.86.42.46.41, e-mail domaine.dampt.defaix@wanadoo.fr ✅
🍷 by appt.

VINCENT DAUVISSAT
Séchet 2001★★

	0.8 ha	6,200	🍷	11–15 €

Mineral and iodized, this handsome, one-star **Vaillons 2001** is like a sea breeze. The bouquet of this brilliant pale-yellow Séchet is flawless: not too intense but delicate and complex. Beneath the initial slight oakiness there is a clean, still somewhat austere structure that will improve with age. A wine that has been well matured – to lay down for three to four years.
🍷 EARL Vincent Dauvissat, 8, rue Emile-Zola, 89800 Chablis, tel. 03.86.42.11.58, fax 03.86.42.85.32

DOM. BERNARD DEFAIX
Les Lys 2001★★

	1 ha	6,000	🍶 🍷 ⚱	11–15 €

This historic Premier Cru forms part of the "Crown Jewels". Needless to say, gold and emeralds conspire joyously together to bring out the colour of this delicately-oaked warm-hearted wine that hovers between flint and honey, with a touch of ginger on the finish. A worthy accompaniment for a large fish *en papillote*. For a dish of scallops choose the **Côte de Léchet Réserve Cuvée Vieille Vigne 2001** which was awarded one star.
🍷 Dom. Bernard Defaix, 17, rue du Château, Milly, 89800 Chablis, tel. 03.86.42.40.75, fax 03.86.42.40.28, e-mail didier@bernard-defaix.com ✅
🍷 by appt.

JEAN-PAUL DROIN
Montmains 2001★

	2.15 ha	16,000	🍶 🍷	11–15 €

A little tour of Montmains with Jean-Paul Droin as guide. Without forgetting Benoît, newly-arrived at the estate. Here is a 2001which has not yet revealed all its qualities. But it will; "hidden harmony is better than visible harmony," said Heraclitus. Quite oaked, perfumed with vanilla, butter-cup-yellow; it is on a par with the **Vosgros 2001**, of much the same type. Both need to wait for the oak to integrate.
🍷 Dom. Jean-Paul Droin, 14 bis, rue Jean-Jaurès, BP 19, 89800 Chablis, tel. 03.86.42.16.78, fax 03.86.42.42.09, e-mail benoit@jeanpaul-droin.fr ✅
🍷 ev. day. ex. Sat. Sun. 8.30am–12 noon 1.30pm–5pm; cl. 1–15 Aug.

DOM. DE L'EGLANTIERE
Montmain 2001★★

	0,5 ha	3,500	🍶 ⚱	11–15 €

The Durup estates (one of the principal architects of the modern Chablis vineyard) extend over 176 ha. The Durup family offered a **Homme Mort 2001** (literally, dead man), which was a long way from needing a tomb stone (excellent, characteristic wine), also this Montmain on top form. An adequately highlighted colour, a very mineral character, a tender style and sustained balance. Great finesse.
🍷 SA Jean Durup Père et Fils, 4, Grande-Rue, 89800 Maligny, tel. 03.86.47.44.49, fax 03.86.47.55.49, e-mail cdurup@club-internet.fr ✅
🍷 by appt.

WILLIAM FEVRE
Montmains 2001★★

	2.21 ha	n.c.	🍶 🍷 ⚱	15–23 €

William Fèvre came close to the *coup de coeur* with this Montmains: it's a great pleasure to see all its gold tinges, to inhale its mineral bouquet which is straight out of the ground and devilishly Kimmeridgian. On the palate it is well-balanced, full of strength, utterly praiseworthy. Other successes: a **Montée de Tonnerre 2001**, a **Fourchaume Vignoble de Vaulorent 2001** and a **Vaillons 2001**. One star for each of these.
🍷 Dom. William Fèvre, 21, av. d'Oberwesel, 89800 Chablis, tel. 03.86.98.98.98, fax 03.86.98.98.99, e-mail france@williamfevre.com ✅
🍷 ev. day. ex. Sun. 9am–12 noon 2pm–6pm; groups by appt.

RAOUL GAUTHERIN ET FILS
Vaillons 2001★

	n.c.	n.c.	🍶 🍷	8–11 €

The pleasant first impression has a *pain d'épice* side. The second reveals the general constitution, balance, length on the palate. There, too, everything is positive. The nose is quite spicy, the colour as it should be for the area. A certain auster-ity but harmonious and well made: a wine to keep for one to two years.
🍷 Dom. Raoul Gautherin et Fils, 6, bd Lamarque, 89800 Chablis, tel. 03.86.42.11.86, fax 03.86.42.42.87, e-mail domainegautherin@wanadoo.fr ✅
🍷 by appt.

ALAIN GAUTHERON

Les Fourneaux Vieilles Vignes 2001★★

	1 ha	8,000	🍴 🍷	8–11 €

Made from genuine, 60-year-old *vieilles vignes*, a fresh and limpid, lively wine. The nose is delicate, on the floral side. The body is not small but very fine, embellished with mineral notes and nuances of citrus fruits, which confer all the freshness typical of the AOC. The **Mont de Milieu 2001** received one star.

☛ Alain and Cyril Gautheron, 18, rue des Prégirots, 89800 Fleys, tel. 03.86.42.44.34, fax 03.86.42.44.50 ☑
🍷 by appt.

DOM. ALAIN GEOFFROY

Beauroy 2001★

	8.5 ha	68,000	🍴 🍷	11–15 €

Two closely similar wines, both marked in the same way by the Jury: **Vau-Ligneau 2001** with aromas that go from strength to strength and which answers all the criteria, and this Beauroy in court dress, exuding the perfume of mushroom as if it had read all the classic authors. Quite fleshy, balanced, in two to three years' time this could become a great wine. Don't be tempted to open it too soon.

☛ SARL Alain Geoffroy, 4, rue de l'Equerre, 89800 Beine, tel. 03.86.42.43.76, fax 03.86.42.13.30,
e-mail info@chablis-geoffroy.com ☑
🍷 by appt.

DOM. PHILIPPE GOULLEY

Montmains 2001★

	1.25 ha	10,000	🍴 🍷	11–15 €

This organic producer's **Fourchaume 2001** needs to develop and has everything it needs to do so: it received a special mention. As for the Montmains, with its seductive highlights, its bouquet is still delicate and just beginning to show the characteristic mineral aroma. Well-balanced and supple, a Chablis of average length.

☛ Dom. Philippe Goulley, 89800
La Chapelle-Vaupelteigne, tel. 03.86.42.40.85,
fax 03.86.42.81.06, e-mail phil.goulley@wanadoo.fr ☑
🍷 by appt.

CORINNE ET JEAN-PIERRE GROSSOT

Les Fourneaux 2001★★

	1.6 ha	7,000	🍴 🍶 🍷	11–15 €

One of the three Premiers Crus in the Fleys area. It produces excellent wines and fully deserves, as here, three rousing Burgundian cheers. From the green highlights in this 2001 vintage one expects to find gold and emeralds in the bottle. Its slight oakiness (nine months in tank, six in cask) is tempered by flowers and citrus fruits. Marvellously rounded and lively on the palate. Also worth tasting is the **Côte de Troême 2001**, one of the best Premiers Crus from the left bank, which received one star.

☛ Corinne et Jean-Pierre Grossot, 4, rte de Mont-de-Milieu, 89800 Fleys, tel. 03.86.42.44.64, fax 03.86.42.13.31 ☑
🍷 by appt.

DOM. DES HERITIERES

Montmains 2001★

	1.5 ha	10,000	🍴 🍷	11–15 €

Delicate yellow, this Montmains gives the impression on the nose of maturity and richness, with the buttery nuances one also finds in a Côte de Beaune. The palate echoes the same theme: fleshy and *moelleux* beneath the fruitiness. Quite complex on the middle palate, with the right amount of concentration.

☛ Olivier Tricon, 15, rue de Chichée, 89800 Chablis, tel. 03.86.42.10.37, fax 03.86.42.49.13

LAMBLIN ET FILS

Mont de Milieu 2000★

	0.8 ha	4,600	🍴 🍷	11–15 €

There have been Lamblins on this terroir since 1690. This Mont de Milieu is enchanting. Nothing clashes. One is cradled against a pale green background by the exquisite finesse of the slightly mentholated bouquet, with its fresh and rounded notes. This wine, with its fine breadth, would be ideal with white meats.

☛ Lamblin et Fils, Maligny, 89800 Chablis,
tel. 03.86.98.22.00, fax 03.86.47.50.12,
e-mail infovin@lamblin.com ☑
🍷 ev. day. ex. Sun. 8am–12.30pm 2pm–5pm;
Sat. 8am–12.30pm

DOM. LAROCHE

Les Fourchaumes Vieilles Vignes 2001★★

	6.8 ha	n.c.	🍴 🍶 🍷	23–30 €

The Laroche estate offered a **Vaillons 2001 Vieilles Vignes (15–23 €)** which was awarded one star. This pale-yellow, silvery grey-gold Fourchaumes has an aromatic complexity that in itself is a worthy subject for discussion. Butter, liquorice, hawthorn blossom, apples and pears, are all characteristic of a Chablis with a slight oakiness that is in no way detrimental. Fine and structured, straightforward and lingering, it will open further. This wine, listed fourth by the Grand Jury, has a great future.

☛ Michel Laroche, L'Obédiencerie, 22, rue Louis-Bro, 89800 Chablis, tel. 03.86.42.89.00, fax 03.86.42.89.29,
e-mail info@michellaroche.com ☑
🍷 by appt.

OLIVIER LEFLAIVE

Les Fourchaumes 2001★★

	n.c.	14,000		15–23 €

Olivier Leflaive offered a sumptuous Fourchaumes; one to keep for a special occasion and a worthy wine to drink with lobster. Hawthorn, apricot, the bouquet proceeds step by step but all in the right direction. The Jury liked its strong and well-presented structure. Needs at least five years in the cellar! As for the **Beauroy 2001**, lordly product of a harvest ripened to the full, it was awarded one star.

☛ Olivier Leflaive Frères, pl. du Monument, 21190 Puligny-Montrachet, tel. 03.80.21.37.65,
fax 03.80.21.33.94,
e-mail olivier-leflaive@dial.oleane.com ☑
🍷 by appt.

DOM. DES MALANDES

Montmains Vieilles Vignes 2001★

	1.18 ha	9,400	🍴 🍷	11–15 €

Coup de coeur for their Fourchaume 98, this year Lyne and Jean-Bernard Marchive offered this Montmains as their visiting card. Their estate consists of 26 ha, of which more than 1 ha is dedicated to this Premier Cru. This allows them to give special care to the vinification of a true *cuvée*. Yellow, with buttery perfumes, the wine fulfils its promise. Perhaps the finish is not interminable, as is often the case with the 2001 vintage, but after a year in the cellar, it will find a welcome beside a dish of shellfish for the next three or four years.

☛ Dom. des Malandes, 63, rue Auxerroise, 89800 Chablis, tel. 03.86.42.41.37, fax 03.86.42.41.97,
e-mail contact@domainedesmalandes.com ☑
🍷 by appt.
☛ Lyne and Jean-Bernard Marchive

DOM. DES MARRONNIERS

Montmains Vieilles Vignes 2001★

	4 ha	20,000	🍴 🍷	8–11 €

Les Marronniers belongs to the rather exclusive club of our old *coups de coeur* (for a 93 vintage). It was a quite fantastic Côte de Jouan. Estate created in 1976 (a drought year) it is approaching its thirtieth anniversary and extends over 19 ha. This is a Montmains, known as *de vieilles vignes*, elegant gold in colour and singing the praises of the *exogyravirgula* (an extinct mollusc) that made up the layer of Kimmeridgian clay beneath the soil. The palate is classic and very present. A miniature Pontigny (a 12th century Roman and Gothic church in the Yonne) sitting on the tongue and arching the tastebuds.

☛ Bernard Légland, 1 et 3, Grande-Rue-de-Chablis, 89800 Préhy, tel. 03.86.41.42.70, fax 03.86.41.45.82 ☑
🍷 ev. day. 9am–8pm; groups by appt.

DOM. DE LA MEULIERE
Monts de Milieu 2001★★

2.8 ha	15,000	🍾 ♦	8–11 €

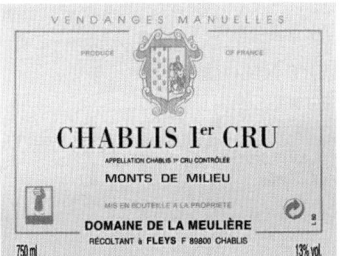

One can no longer count the generations that have been involved with wine-growing here: Henri, Ulysses, Roger, Claude and the present-day young ones on a Laroche estate. The 93 vintage was awarded an earlier *coup de coeur*. The colour of this 2001 is gold; the bouquet is oranges and dill, brioche, mineral, and very open. The palate is opulent and fresh at the same time. Its remarkable length contributes to its success. The **Fourchaume 2001** was given a special mention.
➽ Dom. de la Meulière, 18, rte de Mont-de-Milieu, BP 25, 89800 Fleys, tel. 03.86.42.13.56, fax 03.86.42.19.32, e-mail domainedelameuliere@caramail.com ☑
🍷 ev. day. 9am–7pm
➽ Laroche

LOUIS MICHEL ET FILS
Montmain 2001★

n.c.	35,000	🍾 ♦	15–23 €

The **Montée de Tonnerre 2001** or this Montmain? You could take both, since they are of equal quality. The first will reach its peak around 2006. This one is a little more precocious. Nice colour, lightly floral, a little short, like most of the 2001 wines, but harmonious, polished and balanced.
➽ Louis Michel et Fils, 9, bd de Ferrières, 89800 Chablis, tel. 03.86.42.88.55, fax 03.86.42.88.56, e-mail louis.michel.et.fils@wanadoo.fr ☑
🍷 by appt.

SYLVAIN MOSNIER
Beauroy 2001★

0.99 ha	7,700	🍾 ♦	11–15 €

"*Le style est l'homme même*" (The style is the essence of the man), said Buffon (18th century French historian). A formula one could also apply to wine. This Beauroy, with its pale-yellow colour, has that little something that interests. Fresh, mentholated aromas lead on to a supple first impression of green fruits. It is still a little closed and deserves to be allowed to mature because its good balance indicates that the grape was probably well-ripened when harvested.
➽ Sylvain Mosnier, 4, rue Derrière-les-Murs, 89800 Beine, tel. 03.86.42.43.96, fax 03.86.42.42.88 ☑
🍷 by appt.

DOM. PINSON
Vaugiraut 2001★

0.35 ha	2,600	🍾 ⅰ	11–15 €

Coup de coeur for the 98 and 2000 vintages, this estate seldom goes unnoticed. We tasted the **Vaillons 2001** which has powerful and generous breadth, just as successful as this pale-gold Vaugiraut, with its subtle and fine aromas of nose of mignonette and honeysuckle. Already pleasant but with good keeping potential (one to three years), the first impression is full, with a good, Chablis roundness, the right amount of acidity and essential minerality. An attractive comparability between bouquet and palate.
➽ Dom. Pinson, 5, quai Voltaire, 89800 Chablis, tel. 03.86.42.10.26, fax 03.86.42.49.94, e-mail contact@domaine-pinson.com ☑
🍷 by appt.

DENIS POMMIER
Fourchaume 2001★

0.25 ha	2,000	🍾 ⅰ ♦	11–15 €

The **Côte de Léchet 2001** has a robust roundness but a slightly overweening oakiness that needs to integrate. Equal to it is this Fourchaume, also predominantly vanilla (ten months in cask) with notes of flowers and apples and pears. A fleshy wine with somewhat concentrated body, spicy, and quite original within the batch tasted.
➽ EARL Denis Pommier, 31, rue de Poinchy, Poinchy, 89800 Chablis, tel. 03.86.42.83.04, fax 03.86.42.17.80, e-mail denis.pommier@libertysurf.fr ☑
🍷 ev. day. 9am–12 noon 2pm–7pm; Sun. by appt.

DANIEL SEGUINOT
Fourchaume 2001★

3.9 ha	10,000	🍾 ♦	8–11 €

Fourchaume is undoubtedly the best known of the Premiers Crus, and is widely unifying. This one is very well-made. Pleasing to the eye and satisfying to the nose, it offers the palate minerality together with freshness and roundness.
➽ SCEA Daniel Seguinot, rte de Tonnerre, 89800 Maligny, tel. 03.86.47.51.40, fax 03.86.47.43.37 ☑
🍷 by appt.

DOM. DE VAUROUX
Montée de Tonnerre 2001★

1.2 ha	9,000	🍾 ♦	11–15 €

This estate was established just over 40 years ago by the Tricon family and possesses one of the last remaining 17th century vigneron's huts. No false modesty about this fresh and lively wine; a Montée de Tonnerre which runs up the stairs four at a time. Its green side is a good sign for the future. More herbaceous than fruity, this Premier Cru, with its notes of iodine, cries out for a seafood platter.
➽ SCEA Dom. de Vauroux, rte d'Avallon, BP 56, 89800 Chablis, tel. 03.86.42.10.37, fax 03.86.42.49.13, e-mail domaine-de-vauroux@domaine-de-vauroux.com ☑
🍷 by appt.
➽ O. Tricon

CH. DE VIVIERS
Vaillons 2001★★

0.55 ha	4,200	🍾 ⅰ ♦	11–15 €

Second in the *coup de coeur* and all honour to the Albert Bichot Company (Lupé-Cholet), this Vaillons reminds us that it was a Burgundian, Bernard Courtois, who discovered iodine. This is indeed what we call here a "maritime wine": a wine with an iodized attack, due to the Kimmeridgian influence. Its aromatic concentration is superb, based on flint. A good, intense colour. A very lively but well-structured wine, that will appeal to the enlightened wine-lover; the Jury did not know the name of the cru and tried to guess it: what a good idea for a parlour game! The **Vaucopins 2001** received one star.
➽ Lupé-Cholet, SCEA Ch. de Viviers, 89700 Viviers, tel. 03.80.61.25.02, fax 03.80.24.37.38, e-mail bourgogne@lupe-cholet.com

DOM. VOCORET ET FILS
Vaillon 2001★★

	5 ha	35,000	▉ ⬛ ♦	8–11 €

Generally very demonstrative and masterful, Vaillon (that should really be Vaillons) is represented here as golden-yellow and appetizing. A delicate honeyed fruitiness is slowly brought out. Acidity makes its mark from the start and catches up with the unctuousness. But the fruitiness remains in evidence right to the end. All the characteristics of a true Premier Cru are here, and a good poultry dish will be perfectly at ease in its company.
✆ Dom. Vocoret et Fils, 40, rte d'Auxerre, 89800 Chablis, tel. 03.86.42.12.53, fax 03.86.42.10.39,
e-mail domainevocoret@wanadoo.fr �(V)
Ⓨ ev. day. ex. Sun. 8am–12 noon 1.30pm–5.30pm

DOM. VRIGNAUD
Fourchaume 2001★

	4,23 ha	5,500	▉ ♦	8–11 €

This estate, covering a dozen hectares, was an ancient Templers' farm. A tender and fruity **Mont de Milieu 2001** and this yellow Fourchaume with its green highlights were judged to be of equal quality. With a good bouquet, the latter tends towards apples and pears. It has little acidity but the body is very lively and pleasant. Ready to serve now but could be left to age a little.
✆ Dom. Vrignaud, 10, rue de Beauvoir, 89800 Fontenay-près-Chablis, tel. 03.86.42.15.69, fax 03.86.42.40.06,
e-mail guillaume.vrignaud@wanadoo.fr ▇(V)
Ⓨ by appt.

Wines selected but not starred

DOM. DES AIRELLES
Vaugiraut 2001

	1 ha	2,500	▉ ⬛	8–11 €

✆ Robin, Grande-Rue du Gain, 89800 Chichée, tel. 03.86.42.80.49, fax 03.86.42.85.40,
e-mail didirobin@aol.com ▇
Ⓨ by appt.

DOM. DU COLOMBIER
Vaucoupin 2001

	1.1 ha	8,000	▉ ♦	8–11 €

✆ Guy Mothe et ses Fils, Dom. du Colombier, 42, Grand-Rue, 89800 Fontenay-près-Chablis, tel. 03.86.42.15.04, fax 03.86.42.49.67 ▇
Ⓨ by appt.

DOM. HAMELIN
Beauroy 2001

	3.89 ha	n.c.	▉ ♦	8–11 €

✆ EARL Hamelin, 1, rue des Carillons, 89800 Lignorelles, tel. 03.86.47.54.60, fax 03.86.47.53.34 ▇
Ⓨ ev. day. ex. Wed. Sun. 8.30am–12 noon 1.30pm–6pm; cl. Aug.

DOM. DES ILES
Côte de Léchet 2001

	3 ha	22,000	▉ ⬛ ♦	11–15 €

✆ Gérard Tremblay, 12, rue de Poinchy, 89800 Chablis, tel. 03.86.42.40.98, fax 03.86.42.40.41 ▇
Ⓨ by appt.

MOREAU-NAUDET
Montée de Tonnerre 2001

	0,86 ha	6,500	▉ ⬛ ♦	11–15 €

✆ GAEC Moreau-Naudet, 5, rue des Fossés, 89800 Chablis, tel. 03.86.42.14.83, fax 03.86.42.85.04 ▇
Ⓨ ev. day. 10am–12noon 2pm–7pm

ROBERT NICOLLE
Les Fourneaux 2001

	3.7 ha	15,000	▉ ♦	8–11 €

✆ Robert Nicolle, 55, rte de Mont-de-Milieu, 89800 Fleys, tel. 03.86.42.19.30, fax 03.86.42.80.07 ▇
Ⓨ by appt.

DOM. OUDIN
Vaugiraut 2000

	0.5 ha	4,000	▉ ♦	8–11 €

✆ Dom. Oudin, 5, rue du Pont, 89800 Chichée, tel. 03.86.42.44.29, fax 03.86.42.10.59,
e-mail domaine.oudin@wanadoo.fr ▇
Ⓨ by appt.

DOM. DE PERDRYCOURT
Vauligneau 2000

	n.c.	2,000		11–15 €

✆ Dom. de Perdrycourt, 9, voie Romaine, 89230 Montigny-la-Resle, tel. 03.86.41.82.07, fax 03.86.41.87.89,
e-mail domainecourty@wanadoo.fr ▇
Ⓨ ev. day. 9am–7pm; Sun. 9am–12 noon
✆ EARL Courty

DOM. ROY
Fourchaume 2000

	2.93 ha	8,600	▉ ♦	8–11 €

✆ Dom. Roy, 71, Grand-Rue, 89800 Fontenay-près-Chablis, tel. 03.86.42.10.36 ▇

Chablis Grand Cru

Grown on the best exposed hills on the right bank of the Yonne and divided into seven *lieux-dits* (Blanchot: 680 hl); Bougros: 775 hl; les Clos: 1,393 hl; Grenouilles: 506 hl; Preuses: 540 hl; Valmur: 553 hl, and Vaudésir: 737 hl), Chablis Grand Cru is a clear cut above its juniors. Chablis Grand Cru is, at its peak, a most complete wine with a lingering aroma and a certain bite from the terroir (a sedimentary layer of stones and clay) that distinguishes it from its rivals further to the south. It has an astonishing capacity for ageing, requiring between eight and 15 years to develop harmoniously and to acquire its unforgettable gunflint bouquet (in the best Clos, it even has traces of gunpowder!).

DOM. BILLAUD-SIMON
Les Blanchots Vieilles Vignes 2001★★★

	0.2 ha	1000	⬛	38–46 €

The outright winner of the tasting and also in the opinion of the Grand Jury. Already *coup de coeur* in the 2001 edition for Vaudésir 98 and in the 1996 Guide for a Les Preuses 92, this estate is clearly top-of-the-range and the appellation's paradise. Freshness and liveliness, a texture which is tight for these Blanchots, with power well under control, the sense of detail is on both nose and palate. "Kimmeridgian purity," one Juror

called it. Hurry; it's expensive but very good. Worthy of a lobster or a sea-bass.

🔴 Dom. Billaud-Simon, 1, quai de Reugny, BP 46, 89800 Chablis, tel. 03.86.42.10.33, fax 03.86.42.48.77 ☑
🍷 ev. day. ex. Sun. 9am–12 noon 2pm–6pm;
Sat. by appt., cl. 15–30 Aug.

DOM. PASCAL BOUCHARD
Les Clos 2001★

	0.7 ha	4,500	🔳 ⅏ ⚭	30–38 €

Founder-member of *L'Union des Grands Cru de Chablis* (the reader, of course, knows that at Chablis there is only one Grand Cru divided into *climats*), Pascal Bouchard is a true son of Chablis, holding 32 ha. This *clos* is dressed for the ball, the fruit is the highest bidder in the barrel. This wine doesn't take you for a ride in a hot-air balloon, but for a serious tour around the vineyard, on foot in all its ripeness. A generous, fleshy style, of fine extraction.

🔴 Pascal Bouchard, parc des Lys, 89800 Chablis, tel. 03.86.42.18.64, fax 03.86.42.48.11,
e-mail info@pascalbouchard.com ☑
🍷 by appt.

DOM. CAMU
Les Clos 2001★

	0.4 ha	300	⅏	23–30 €

Establishing his estate when he finished at the Viticultural college at Beaune in 1990, Christophe Camu bought, rented, took on a tenancy; today he has 8 ha of which just a few *ares* (1 are = 100 sq.m.) are dedicated to the *clos* but his wine is up to the standard of a Grand Cru. Gold-green in colour, conditioned by aromas of flint and blackcurrant leaf-buds, the opening is well in line with the nose. An enveloping liveliness and a perfect performance. It will be a pleasure to serve in a year's time, and for several years after that.

🔴 Christophe Camu, 1, av. de la Liberté, 89800 Chablis, tel. 03.86.42.12.50, fax 03.86.42.14.40 ☑
🍷 ev. day. 9am–7pm

LA CHABLISIENNE
Blanchot 2001★★

	1.5 ha	10,000	🔳 ⅏ ⚭	23–30 €

The southeastern extremity of Côte du Grand Cru. The cooperative holds 1.5 ha and offered here this pale straw-yellow 2001 with a fresh and citrous nose. Its stay in cask (three months) was no mere formality. After a sober initial impression, the aromas take off together with an increase in strength that offers hope of things to come. Its vinosity is a little marked by alcohol but as vigorous as you could possibly wish for.

🔴 La Chablisienne, 8, bd Pasteur, BP 14, 89800 Chablis, tel. 03.86.42.89.89, fax 03.86.42.89.90,
e-mail chab@chablisienne.fr ☑
🍷 by appt.

JEAN DAUVISSAT
Les Preuses 2000★

	0.7 ha	5,000	🔳 ⅏ ⚭	23–30 €

An attractive little Chablis estate created at the end of the 19th century. The Les Preuses has its set character and refuses to be rushed. This one will have to wait for two or three years before it is ready to drink with a lobster. The very characteristic colour is a delight. Fresh, floral, delicately

oaked, this straightforward, balanced wine is logical from beginning to end.

🔴 Jean et Sébastien Dauvissat, 3, rue de Chichée, 89800 Chablis, tel. 03.86.42.14.62, fax 03.86.42.45.54,
e-mail jean.dauvissat@terre-net.fr ☑
🍷 by appt.

VINCENT DAUVISSAT
Les Clos 2001★★

	1.7 ha	12,000	⅏	15–23 €

Vincent Dauvissat shows himself a true "vigneron," intent on expressing his terroir. Brilliant straw-yellow, this 2001 vintage is initially closed on its cask, then opens on a mineral note. Restrained, the nuances of menthol and mineral on the palate are accompanied by oakiness. One feels it is capable of better. A wine that must at all costs be left in the cellar for four or five years. It will last a long time.

🔴 EARL Vincent Dauvissat, 8, rue Emile-Zola, 89800 Chablis, tel. 03.86.42.11.58, fax 03.86.42.85.32

JEAN-PAUL DROIN
Les Clos 2001★★

	1 ha	7,000	🔳 ⅏	15–23 €

Coup de coeur in the 1987 Guide (Vaudésir), 1990 (Grenouille), 1991 (Vaudésir), 1996 (*Les Clos*), 2001 (Vaudésir) and 2003 (*Les Clos*), this estate is almost an honorary member of the Guide. The more so because this *cuvée* was one of the five wines selected for the *coup de coeur*. It didn't win but it is among the best of the Grand Cru wines. A 2001 vintage that speaks of ripe fruit and well-integrated oak, dazzling on the palate. There's little point in listing its prizes on the roll of honour. It has taken most of them. See also the one-star **Blanchot 2001**, a wine that promises much.

🔴 Dom. Jean-Paul Droin, 14 bis, rue Jean-Jaurès, BP 19, 89800 Chablis, tel. 03.86.42.16.78, fax 03.86.42.42.09,
e-mail benoit@jeanpaul-droin.fr ☑
🍷 ev. day. ex. Sat. Sun. 8.30am–12 noon 1.30pm–5pm; cl. 1–15 Aug.

JOSEPH DROUHIN
Vaudésir 2000★★

	n.c.	n.c.	⅏	30–38 €

Between Preuses and Valmur, Vaudésir wears its name well. This famous estate of the Beaune area took root a long time ago in Chablis and this wine is made from its grapes. The wine is well up to the challenge: pale-gold with green highlights, right from the start it shows a complexity that marks it out from the others. It is agreeably fleshy, with a slight oakiness that doesn't detract from the elegant aromas of citrus fruits and the apples and pears. Richness, maturity and length indicate a magnificent wine. We should also mention the **Les Clos 2000**, which has a stronger vanilla aroma; an interesting wine, it received one star.

🔴 Maison Joseph Drouhin, 7, rue d'Enfer, 21200 Beaune, tel. 03.80.24.68.88, fax 03.80.22.43.14,
e-mail maisondrouhin@drouhin.com
🍷 by appt.

DOM. WILLIAM FEVRE
Vaudésir 2001★★

	n.c.	n.c.	⅏	30–38 €

CHABLIS GRAND CRU
VAUDÉSIR
APPELLATION CHABLIS GRAND CRU CONTRÔLÉE

Domaine

WILLIAM FEVRE
2001

CE VIN A ÉTÉ RÉCOLTÉ, ÉLEVÉ ET MIS EN BOUTEILLE PAR
WILLIAM FEVRE
CHABLIS - FRANCE

13% alc. vol. PRODUIT DE FRANCE - PRODUCT OF FRANCE 750 ml

BURGUNDY

It's difficult to know where to point one's tastebuds first; William Fèvre, already honoured in the 2002 and 2001 editions for his Preuses, enjoys the luxury of a third *coup de coeur* in the space of four years among the Chablis Grands Crus. In addition, the Jury was full of praise for the **Clos 2001** and **Valmur 2001**, both also two stars. The winner, however, was this divine Vaudésir. A true Grand Cru, it will improve with age. Despite its maturation in cask, it exudes delicious notes of hawthorn blossom and fresh almonds. Its white-gold colour with silvery highlights is perfect. On the palate it is a happy combination of minerality and richness, finishing on a remarkable complexity in which the wine is supported by the oakiness.

🠒 Dom. William Fèvre, 21, av. d'Oberwesel, 89800 Chablis, tel. 03.86.98.98.98, fax 03.86.98.98.99, e-mail france@williamfevre.com ☑
☖ ev. day. ex. Sun. 9am–12 noon 2pm–6pm; groups by appt.

DOM. ALAIN GEOFFROY

Les Clos 2000★

| | n.c. | n.c. | 🍶 ⚏ | 23–30 € |

No one knows why the *clos* are scooping so many of the honours this year…It must be their turn for the crown. There is no doubt about this wine from the 2000 vintage, with its light-yellow nuances. Its aromatic freshness, where white blossom and minerality come together, is full of tact. Sparkling in its initial impression and in its balance. It is not the Colossus of Rhodes, but an undoubted Grand Cru.

🠒 SARL Alain Geoffroy, 4, rue de l'Equerre, 89800 Beine, tel. 03.86.42.43.76, fax 03.86.42.13.30, e-mail info@chablis-geoffroy.com ☑
☖ by appt.

DOM. DES ILES

Vaudésir 2001★

| | 0.6 ha | 3,000 | 🍶 🍷 | 23–30 € |

Gerard Tremblay has been managing his 34 ha since 1973. The Jury complimented him on a "well-made" Grand Cru. With delicate minerality and a gold colour strewn with green highlights, supple, fleshy, of a good length, this wine offers a honeyed sensation which makes it full of flavour.

🠒 Gérard Tremblay, 12, rue de Poinchy, 89800 Chablis, tel. 03.86.42.40.98, fax 03.86.42.40.41 ☑
☖ by appt.

DOM. LAROCHE

Les Blanchots 2000★★

| | 4,5 ha | n.c. | 🍶 🍷 ⚏ | 38–46 € |

Primus inter pares (first among equals), the Laroche estate takes up its bow, aims at the familiar target and scores a bulls-eye: the *coup de coeur*. Already *coup de coeur* with a Blanchots 98, Laroche almost always succeeds with its Blanchots, as if they were the children of the house. Absolute perfection! Mineral, and dominating the oak, this is a Grand Cru that concentrates on what it's doing and does it in an impeccable manner. You could be drinking essence of Kimmeridge.

🠒 Michel Laroche, L'Obédiencerie, 22, rue Louis-Bro, 89800 Chablis, tel. 03.86.42.89.00, fax 03.86.42.89.29, e-mail info@michellaroche.com ☑
☖ by appt.

DOM. LONG-DEPAQUIT

Les Clos 2000★

| | 1.54 ha | 10,500 | 🍶 🍷 ⚏ | 23–30 € |

A historical estate of which the jewel is Moutonne, a true principality; nowadays part of the Albert Bichot Company and under the excellent management of Gerard Vullien. Pale yellow, a Chablis that is very characteristic of its vintage. Twelve months in tank, nine in cask for 40% of the harvest, a judicious maturation which has resulted in a light oakiness that doesn't run over onto the mineral. A style made up more of roundness than breadth; a pleasant, fleshy finish.

🠒 Dom. Long-Depaquit, 45, rue Auxerroise, 89800 Chablis, tel. 03.86.42.11.13, fax 03.86.42.81.89, e-mail chateau-long-depaquit@wanadoo.fr ☑
☖ by appt.
🠒 Albert Bichot

LOUIS MICHEL ET FILS

Grenouilles 2000★

| | 0.5 ha | 3,000 | 🍶 ⚏ | 30–38 € |

One often feels that a Grenouilles sums up the qualities of a Grand Cru, and this 2000 confirms it. White gold with silvery highlights and so not a very strong colour (let's not forget that the Chablis was always admired for its rare paleness), a balanced wine, rich in the traditional aromas (mineral and floral). Its maturity, its character, its finesse are all typical of a Grand Cru. Ready to drink towards 2005 to 2006 with a capon from Bresse.

🠒 Louis Michel et Fils, 9, bd de Ferrières, 89800 Chablis, tel. 03.86.42.88.55, fax 03.86.42.88.56, e-mail louis.michel.et.fils@wanadoo.fr ☑
☖ by appt.

J. MOREAU ET FILS

Les Clos 2001★★

| | 6.11 ha | 48,900 | 🍶 🍷 ⚏ | 23–30 € |

A structured, elegant *clos* whose brilliant colour, already complex bouquet, and presence and charm on the palate, were admired by the Jury. It is said that this *climat* was the original Chablis vineyard. This ancient company was taken over by Jean-Claude Boisset who wisely gave it its head.

🠒 J. Moreau et Fils, La Croix Saint-Joseph, rte d'Auxerre, BP 5, 89800 Chablis, tel. 03.86.42.88.00, fax 03.86.42.88.08, e-mail moreau@jmoreau-fils.com ☑
☖ ev. day. ex. Sun. Mon. 8am–12 noon 2pm–6pm from May to Sep.

DOM. SERVIN

Les Clos 2001★

| | 0.88 ha | 5,500 | 🍷 | 23–30 € |

Less than 1 ha dedicated to this Grand Cru *climat* out of 30 ha in production. Enough to make a golden, honeyed wine, very much a 2001 on the aromatic side. The obvious richness overwhelms the finesse but nevertheless it has depth. The Jury, as a whole, found it smooth and complex. In other words, we are in good company. Keep it for a year in the cellar then enjoy it in the three that follow.

🠒 Dom. Servin, 20, av. d'Oberwesel, 89800 Chablis, tel. 03.86.18.90.00, fax 03.86.18.90.01, e-mail servin@domaine-servin.fr ☑
☖ by appt.

Wines selected but not starred

DOM. JEAN COLLET ET FILS

Valmur 2001

■	0.5 ha	3,500	◖◗	23–30 €

☛ Dom. Jean Collet et Fils, 15, av. de la Liberté,
89800 Chablis, tel. 03.86.42.11.93, fax 03.86.42.47.43,
e-mail collet.chablis@wanadoo.fr ☑
⏳ by appt.
☛ Gilles Collet

SYLVAIN ET DIDIER DEFAIX

Bougros 2001

■	n.c.	n.c.	▮◖◗ ⚲	23–30 €

☛ Sylvain et Didier Defaix, 17, rue du Château, Milly,
89800 Chablis, tel. 03.86.42.40.75, fax 03.86.42.40.28,
e-mail didier@bernard-defaix.com ☑
⏳ by appt.

DOM. PINSON

Les Clos 2001

■	2.57 ha	13,700	▮◖◗	15–23 €

☛ Dom. Pinson, 5, quai Voltaire, 89800 Chablis,
tel. 03.86.42.10.26, fax 03.86.42.49.94,
e-mail contact@domaine-pinson.com ☑
⏳ by appt.

REGNARD

Les Preuses 2000

■	0.35 ha	2,500	▮	30–38 €

☛ Régnard, 26, bd Taussel, 89800 Chablis,
tel. 03.86.42.10.45, fax 03.86.42.48.67 ☑
⏳ by appt.

DOM. VOCORET ET FILS

Valmur 2001

■	0.3 ha	2,000	▮◖◗ ⚲	15–23 €

☛ Dom. Vocoret et Fils, 40, rte d'Auxerre, 89800 Chablis,
tel. 03.86.42.12.53, fax 03.86.42.10.39,
e-mail domainevocoret@wanadoo.fr ☑
⏳ ev. day. ex. Sun. 8am–12 noon 1.30pm–5.30pm

Irancy

The fame of this small vineyard, located about 15 km south of Auxerre, was acknowledged when it became an AOC commune.

The red wines of Irancy have acquired something of a reputation thanks to the César or Romain, a local grape variety which may go back as far as Gallic times. It is a rather temperamental variety, capable of giving the best and the worst of results. When production is low to average, it stamps a particularly tannic character on the wine that makes for very long-term keeping. On the other hand, when the volume of production is high, the César does not easily lend itself to good winemaking, and this is why it is not a compulsory ingredient for the appellation.

The Pinot Noir variety is the main one used, and on the slopes of Irancy it makes a high-quality, very fruity and ruddy-coloured wine. The terroir takes its character mainly from the topographical situation of the vineyard, essentially laid out on slopes forming a bowl with the village standing in the hollow. This terroir also borders on the two neighbouring communes of Vincelotte and Cravant, whose Côte de Palotte wines were once very highly thought of. Production was 7,450 hl in 2002.

BERSAN ET FILS

Cuvée Louis Bersan 2001★

■	1 ha	4,000	▮◖◗ ⚲	8–11 €

Drink it with a pigeon or with a pie? It's the kind of question one asks. Pigeon for preference because here we are in the presence of the attractive Irancy "new look," 100% Pinot Noir, rounded and open. The colour is not entirely stable. The nose is herbaceous. A wine to be left to mature until autumn 2004.
☛ SARL Bersan et Fils, 20, rue du Dr-Tardieux,
89530 Saint-Bris-le-Vineux, tel. 03.86.53.33.73,
fax 03.86.53.38.45,
e-mail bourgognes-bersan@wanadoo.fr ☑
⏳ by appt.

BENOIT CANTIN

Cuvée Emeline Elevé en fût de chêne 2001★

■	1 ha	7,000	▮◖◗ ⚲	8–11 €

A still very young Irancy which has this rubicond and tannic side that is described on its indentity card. Delightful on the palate, it needs one to two years in the cellar.
☛ Benoît Cantin, 35, chem. des Fossés, 89290 Irancy,
tel. 03.86.42.21.96, fax 03.86.42.21.96 ☑
⏳ ev. day. ex. Sun. 8am–12 noon 2pm–6pm

ROGER DELALOGE 2001★

■	5.2 ha	19,000	▮◖◗	5–8 €

Coup de coeur in the 99, 96 and even the 88 editions, it holds a subscription to the podium of which the 18th century estate possesses a maze of vaulted cellars. With 1% of César, a dying grape variety which was very much at home here, this wine, with its herbaceous aromas, should be rounded and well structured by this autumn.
☛ Roger Delaloge, 1, ruelle du Milieu, 89290 Irancy,
tel. 03.86.42.20.94, fax 03.86.42.33.40 ☑
⏳ by appt.

FRANCK GIVAUDIN 2001★

■	n.c.	5,000	▮	5–8 €

Winemaking here is an old family business. This Irancy is testimony to the resistance of a last patch of César (5%) within a large army of Pinot. Little colour but a fruity, pleasing bouquet. Slightly tannic, a wine of a certain breadth but not much length, which would last one to two years in the cellar.
☛ Franck Givaudin, sentier de la Bergère, 89290 Irancy,
tel. 03.86.42.20.67, fax 03.86.42.54.33 ☑
⏳ by appt.

ANNICK NAVARRE 2000★★

■	2 ha	6,000	▮	5–8 €

This wine hovered around the *coup de coeur* and just missed being awarded it. We can put our trust in Annick Navarre who took over in May 2000 after the death of her husband. This vintage is a beautiful homage to Yves: superb in one word or in a thousand. A very concentrated colour, a ripe-cherry nose, tannins held well in check and an honourable structure. Drink it with the Sunday roast of beef.
☛ Annick Navarre, 10, rue des Morts, 89290 Irancy,
tel. 03.86.42.31.00 ☑
⏳ ev. day. 10am–12 noon 2pm–6pm

BURGUNDY

DOM. SAINT-GERMAIN
La Bergère 2001★★

■ 0,75 ha	5,000	⅏	8–11 €

An estate created in 1987 by combining two small vineyards. It is a real success, and honoured by a *coup de coeur*. This crowns a light-red wine, with the terroir and some vanilla notes on the bouquet. Not very tannic, this Irancy excels in its roundness and fleshiness, demonstrating the qualities of a fairly recent village appellation. Drink it within two years.
☛ Christophe Ferrari, 7, chem. des Fossés, 89290 Irancy, tel. 03.86.42.33.43, fax 03.86.42.39.30 ☑ ⌂
⫿ by appt.

CAVE TABIT ET FILS
Haut-Champreux 2000★

■ 1 ha	3,500	▮⅏	8–11 €

A slightly orange brilliance on a crimson basis, this is an Irancy with musky, spicy notes. There is plenty of well-coated body and the woodiness is balanced. Beneath the slightly kitsch parchment label with folded edges is a wine in the spirit of the appellation and a Pinot boasting about its grape variety. as is the way in the Yonne.
☛ Cave Tabit et Fils, 2, rue Dorée, 89530 Saint-Bris-le-Vineux, tel. 03.86.53.33.83, fax 03.86.53.67.97, e-mail tabit@wanadoo.fr ☑
⫿ by appt.

Wines selected but not starred

ANITA ET JEAN-PIERRE COLINOT
Palotte 2001

■ 0.25 ha	n.c.	▮	8–11 €

☛ Anita, Stéphanie et Jean-Pierre Colinot, 1, rue des Chariats, 89290 Irancy, tel. 03.86.42.33.25, fax 03.86.42.33.25 ☑
⫿ by appt.

LUCIEN JOUDELAT
Les Mazelots Elevé en fût de chêne 2000

■ 1.5 ha	9,000	▮⅏	8–11 €

☛ Lucien Joudelat, 10, chem. des Fossés, 89290 Irancy, tel. 03.86.42.31.46, fax 03.86.42.31.46 ☑
⫿ by appt.

DOM. DES REMPARTS 2000

■ 3 ha	20,000	⅏	8–11 €

☛ GAEC Dom. des Remparts, 6, rte de Champs, 89530 Saint-Bris-le-Vineux, tel. 03.86.53.33.59, fax 03.86.53.62.12 ☑
⫿ by appt.
☛ Patrick and Jean-Marc Sorin

DOM. JACKY RENARD 2000

■ 1.5 ha	7,000	▮⅏♣		5–8 €

☛ Dom. Jacky Renard, La Côte-de-Chaussan, 89530 Saint-Bris-le-Vineux, tel. 03.86.53.38.58, fax 03.86.53.33.50 ☑
⫿ by appt.

THIERRY RICHOUX 2001

12 ha	40,000	▮⅏♣	5–8 €

☛ Thierry Richoux, 73, rue Soufflot, 89290 Irancy, tel. 03.86.42.21.60, fax 03.86.42.34.95 ☑
⫿ ev. day. ex. Sun. 9am–12 noon 2pm–7pm

DOM. VERRET
Elevé en fût de chêne 2001

4 ha	16,000	⅏	8–11 €

☛ Dom. Verret, rte de Champs, BP 4, 89530 Saint-Bris-le-Vineux, tel. 03.86.53.31.81, fax 03.86.53.89.61, e-mail dverret@domaineverret.com ☑
⫿ by appt.

Saint-Bris

Having only been VDQS Burgundy since 1974, Saint-Bris received AOC status for the 2001 vintage. This wine is made from the Sauvignon grape from an area of around 895 ha, largely in the commune of Saint-Bris. It is grown mainly on areas of limestone plateaux from which it draws a certain aromatic intensity. In contrast to wines made from the same grape variety in the Loire Valley and the Sancerre, the Sauvignon de Saint-Bris generally goes through a malolactic fermentation, though this does not affect its perfumed, supple character.

BERSAN ET FILS 2001★

■ n.c.	n.c.	▮♣	5–8 €

Producers and negociants at Saint-Bris-le-Vineux, Jean-Louis and Jean-François Bersan offered a wine of a pale, watercolour-yellow and a bouquet that is pure Sauvignon. Very vigorous, it outlines a certain complexity based on citrus fruits. A little sharp, like all the 2001 vintage, but refreshing and destined to accompany seafood. From the same estate, the **Cuvée Louis Bersan 2001 (8–11 €)**, of which 20% spent time in cask, was awarded one star.
☛ SARL Bersan et Fils, 20, rue du Dr-Tardieux, 89530 Saint-Bris-le-Vineux, tel. 03.86.53.33.73, fax 03.86.53.38.45, e-mail bourgognes-bersan@wanadoo.fr ☑
⫿ by appt.

JOCELYNE ET PHILIPPE DEFRANCE
2001★

■ 3.8 ha	6,000	▮♣	5–8 €

In the heart of the old village of Saint-Bris are wine cellars dating from the Middle Ages. Limpid and brilliant, the colour of this wine is not too accentuated. An identikit picture of the Sauvignon as soon as it meets the nose: one finds mineral stone there, blackcurrant leaf-buds, and a pronounced herbaceousness is very much present. This wine knows its classics. Quite a bit of character shows next. The trial on the palate is equally conclusive, in the context of well-controlled acidity.
☛ Philippe Defrance, 5, rue du Four, 89530 Saint-Bris-le-Vineux, tel. 03.86.53.39.04, fax 03.86.53.66.46 ☑
⫿ by appt.

DOM. FELIX 2001★

| | 0.86 ha | 8,000 | 🍶 🥄 | 5–8 € |

This 2001 can call itself a Saint-Bris because, while the official date was January 2003, the 2001 and 2002 vintages are entitled to the *village* appellation as of the time they obtained an analytical and organoleptic certificate of approval. Which was the case in this instance. An attractive, pale-gold wine, with an original and interesting bouquet (fruit in white alcohol, then more oxydized on a basis of crusty bread). This wine is still very energetic. Nuances of mirabelle plums on the palate and a slightly iodized finish. Drink it now, with fish.

➼ Dom. Félix, 17, rue de Paris, 89530 Saint-Bris-le-Vineux, tel. 03.86.53.33.87, fax 03.86.53.61.64, e-mail scea.felix@wanadoo.fr 🔟
🍷 ev. day, except Sun. 9am–11.30am 2pm–6.30pm
➼ Hervé Félix

WILLIAM FEVRE 2002★

| | n.c. | n.c. | 🍶 🥄 | 5–8 € |

Slightly golden in colour, this is one wine from 2002 that didn't want to miss this historical meeting: it is called Saint-Bris! The bouquet is holding on to some of its secrets, from a citrus point of view. The first impression is supple, the wine fills the mouth, the acidity is there but measured. It's almost like crunching fruit...Homogeneous from beginning to end and faithful to the grape variety. William Fèvre, here is Bouchard Père et Fils, the Champagne family Henriot.

➼ Dom. William Fèvre, 21, av. d'Oberwesel, 89800 Chablis, tel. 03.86.98.98.98, fax 03.86.98.98.99, e-mail france@williamfevre.com 🔟
🍷 ev. day. ex. Sun. 9am–12 noon 2pm–6pm; groups by appt.

GHISLAINE ET JEAN-HUGUES GOISOT 2001★★

| | 7 ha | 40,000 | 🍶 🥄 | 5–8 € |

Coup de coeur! What a beautiful way to leave the VDQS and join the appellation of the village. Delicate pale-yellow in colour, this Sauvignon has a very open bouquet, relatively fine and complex (more focussed on peach and mineral that on the herbaceous side). On the palate, the grape variety too is not pronounced (no blackcurrant leaf-bud) but it is there, nevertheless, beneath the surface. And always this fruity sensation, peach especially. Definitely a wine to have in the cellar.
➼ Ghislaine et Jean-Hugues Goisot, 30, rue Bienvenu-Martin, 89530 Saint-Bris-le-Vineux, tel. 03.86.53.35.15, fax 03.86.53.62.03, e-mail jhetg.goisot@cerb.cernet.fr 🔟
🍷 by appt.

Wines selected but not starred

DOM. JEAN-MICHEL DAULNE 2001

| | 1.5 ha | 4,000 | 🍶 | 5–8 € |

➼ Jean-Michel et Marilyn Daulne, RN 6, Le Bouchet, 89460 Bazarnes, tel. 03.86.42.20.97, fax 03.86.42.33.91 🔟
🍷 by appt.

GRIFFE 2001

| | 0.56 ha | 1,900 | 🍶 | 3–5 € |

➼ EARL Griffe, 15, rue du Beugnon, 89530 Chitry, tel. 03.86.41.41.06, fax 03.86.41.47.36 🔟
🍷 by appt.

DOM. GERARD PERSENOT 2001

| | 2 ha | 13,000 | 🍶 🥄 | 5–8 € |

➼ EARL Gérard Persenot, 20, rue de Gouaix, 89530 Saint-Bris-le-Vineux, tel. 03.86.53.61.46, fax 03.86.53.61.52 🔟
🍷 by appt.

Côte de Nuits

Marsannay

Geographers are still discussing where the northern limits of the Côte de Nuits should be drawn. During the 19th century, flourishing vineyards in communes around Dijon made up the Côte Dijonnaise. Today, apart from a few remaining vines like Marcs d'Or and Montreculs, Dijon's urban sprawl has forced the vineyards to the south of the city, and even Chenôve has difficulty in keeping its pretty hillside planted with vines.

At one time, Marsannay, then Couchey, supplied the town with Grands Ordinaires, but failed to obtain recognition as AOC Communales in 1935. Little by little, the winegrowers replanted the terroirs with Pinot, starting the tradition of making rosé which is identified as a local appellation: "Bourgogne Rosé de Marsannay". Then red and white wines of the pre-phylloxera era were rediscovered and, after more than 25 years of effort and research, the AOC Marsannay was registered in 1987 for all three colours. There is also a local Burgundy peculiarity, the "Marsannay Rosé," which is produced on the lower slopes on gravelly soil. This vineyard occupies a larger area than those given to the red and white wines, which can be grown only on the slopes of the three communes of Chenôve, Marsannay-la-Côte and Couchey.

These sturdy red wines are a little harsh in their youth and must wait a few years to mature. It is most unusual to find white wines in the Côte de Nuits, but the Chardonnay and the Pinot Blanc find the marly soils particularly well adapted to their needs and these whites are particularly sought after for their finesse and solid body.

The vineyards produced 5,809 hl of red wine, 1,535 hl of rosé and 1,446 hl of white in 2002. The hillsides are currently being replanted.

DOM. CHARLES AUDOIN

Les Favières 2000★★★

| ■ | 0.85 ha | 5,000 | ◫ | 8–11 € |

It is perfect: very deep red, Morello cherry aromas, good body, length, a peacock tail finish. Balanced from A to Z And it's ready to drink now. The **white Marsannay 2000 (11–15 €)** deserves one star and the **Marsannay rosé 2001 (5–8 €)**, which made us think of the classics, was specially mentioned by the tasters.
• Dom. Charles Audoin, 7, rue de la Boulotte, 21160 Marsannay-la-Côte, tel. 03.80.52.34.24, fax 03.80.58.74.34, e-mail domaine-audoin@wanadoo.fr ☑
☎ by appt.

MARC BROCOT

Les Echézeaux 2001★

| ■ | 0.99 ha | 4,400 | ◫ | 8–11 € |

Les Echézeaux is a Grand Cru a little further down the Côte, but a number of *climats* bear that name. Here, for example. A beautiful colour and an excellent bouquet: cinnamon, red berries, this wine is overwhelming from the very first. On the palate, elegance dominates everything else. The already frank, robust body is embraced by roundness. The tannins remain delicate. It needs to stay in the cellar for a year or two.
• Marc Brocot, 34, rue du Carré, 21160 Marsannay-la-Côte, tel. 03.80.52.19.99, fax 03.80.59.84.39 ☑
☎ by appt.

DOM. BRUNO CLAIR

Les Longeroies 2000★

| ■ | 1.55 ha | 9,000 | ◫ | 11–15 € |

This family has links with the history of Marsannay and in particular of its rosé (The father was Joseph Clair-Daÿ). *Coup de coeur* for its white 88, it was one of the very first of this appellation to receive such a distinction. Deep and intense, the colour of this 2000 vintage characterizes the aims of this Longeroies (on the way to Marsannay after leaving Chenôve); this wine has a subtle, restrained nose and is soft and rounded. It is unlikely to go on developing over a long period, but it is a nice wine.
• SCEA Dom. Bruno Clair, 5, rue du Vieux-Collège, BP 22, 21160 Marsannay-la-Côte, tel. 03.80.52.28.95, fax 03.80.52.18.14, e-mail brunoclair@wanadoo.fr ☑
☎ by appt.

CLOS SAINT-LOUIS 2001★

| ■ | 1.5 ha | 7,500 | ▮◫ | 8–11 € |

The vineyard is situated mainly in the territory of Couchey, one of the three villages of the Marsannay AOC. As for the wine, its delicacy and fruitiness are most pleasing. Flawless right to its enthusiastic finish. Aromatic and complex, it seems to have dedicated itself to the Morello cherry. Elegant, a wine to drink with white meat.
• Dom. du Clos Saint-Louis, 4, rue des Rosiers, 21220 Fixin, tel. 03.80.52.45.51, fax 03.80.58.88.76, e-mail clos.st.louis@wanadoo.fr ☑
☎ by appt.
• Ph. Bernard

BERNARD COILLOT PERE ET FILS

Les Boivins 2000★★★

| ■ | 1 ha | 6,000 | ◫ | 11–15 € |

Dédé Coillot, this wine-grower's uncle, was considered by many to be the leading light of Marsannay rosé. This wine is red, so "let's go and take a look," as one says in the Côte. Well, that seems to be going smoothly. It is a Pinot Noir, fleshy, rounded, lingering, and exceptionally mouth-filling and satisfying. To be drunk within the next ten years, it conforms absolutely with the appellation at its best. The **white Marsannay 2001 (8–11 €)**, with a subtle bouquet of grilled hazelnuts and white blossom, and the **red Les Longeroies 2000** were both awarded one star.

• Bernard Coillot Père et Fils, 31, rue du Château, 21160 Marsannay-la-Côte, tel. 03.80.52.17.59, fax 03.80.52.12.75, e-mail domaine.coillot@wanadoo.fr ☑
☎ by appt.

DEREY FRERES 2001★

| ■ | 1.8 ha | 12,000 | ◫ | 8–11 € |

Albert and Maurice Derey established this estate in the 1950s, and played an active role in the regeneration of the vineyards of Couchey, between Marsannay and Fixin. The next generation now invites us to share in the pleasure of a true Chardonnay from Burgundy, full of life under its brilliant colour. A citrus fruit and white blossom bouquet for an elegant, velvety wine, to drink over the coming five years.
• Derey Frères, 1, rue Jules-Ferry, 21160 Couchey, tel. 03.80.52.15.04, fax 03.80.58.76.70, e-mail derey-freres@wanadoo.fr ☑
☎ ev. day except Sun. 10am–6pm

HUGUENOT PERE ET FILS 2000★★

| ■ | 2.2 ha | 12,000 | ◫ | 11–15 € |

There are countless numbers of Huguenots in the village records at Marsannay. And when it comes to winemaking they are, for the most part, traditionalist. Straw-yellow, this is a beautiful wine which is not too marked by the cask and which generates aromas of grapefruit and mineral notes. Its flexibility and fleshiness make it ready to drink as of now. With a seafood platter? Of course. *Coup de coeur* in our 2000 edition for its 97 white, and already in Guide 1994 for its 91. Another strongly recommended wine: the **red Champs Perdrix 2000**, which received two stars.
• Dom. Huguenot Père et Fils, 7, ruelle du Carron, 21160 Marsannay-la-Côte, tel. 03.80.52.11.56, fax 03.80.52.60.47, e-mail domaine.huguenot@wanadoo.fr ☑
☎ by appt.

DOM. SYLVAIN PATAILLE

L'Ancestrale 2001★★

| ■ | 0.23 ha | 600 | ◫ | 23–30 € |

This Cuvee Ancestrale refers to those who went before and to the age of the vines. "It will be marketed wrapped in tissue paper and in wooden cases," said this perfectionist, only established since 1999. Its Marsannay is more than up to the challenge, very well marked by the Jury who appreciated its fleshiness, its generosity and, even more, the qualities that go into its make-up. An opaque black colour and a bouquet which shows great promise. Body and elegance: what more could one wish for?
• Dom. Sylvain Pataille, 14, rue Neuve, 21160 Marsannay-la-Côte, tel. 06.70.11.62.15, fax 03.80.52.49.49 ☑
☎ by appt.

DOM. DU VIEUX COLLEGE

Les Vignes-Marie 2001★

| ■ | 0.5 ha | 3,500 | ◫ | 11–15 € |

The Jury was unanimous about this one. Under its pure and limpid appearance the bouquet is all finesse: menthol, newly-cut grass, hazelnut…aromas which are prolonged on the palate. Its character is not phenomenal, but the well-balanced palate clearly indicates a successful wine. This *climat* is located at the same level on the hillside as the village of Marsannay. Note that the **red Les Favières 2000** also received one star.
• Jean-Pierre et Eric Guyard, Dom. du Vieux Collège, 4, rue du Vieux-Collège, 21160 Marsannay-la-Côte, tel. 03.80.52.12.43, fax 03.80.52.95.85 ☑
☎ by appt.

Wines selected but not starred

DOM. RENE BOUVIER
En Ouzeloy 2000

| ■ | 1 ha | 2,500 | ⑪ | 11–15 € |

•┑ Dom. René Bouvier, 29 bis, rte de Dijon,
21220 Gevrey-Chambertin, tel. 03.80.34.36.12,
fax 03.80.59.95.96, e-mail rene-bouvier@wanadoo.fr ☑
☓ by appt.
•┑ Bernard Bouvier

DOM. COLLOTTE
Les Boivins 2000

| ■ | 1 ha | 4,000 | ⑪ | 8–11 € |

•┑ Dom. Collotte, 44, rue de Mazy,
21160 Marsannay-la-Côte, tel. 03.80.52.24.34,
fax 03.80.58.74.40 ☑
☓ by appt.

DOM. FOUGERAY DE BEAUCLAIR
Saint-Jacques 2000

| ■ | 1.17 ha | 5,000 | ■⑪♦ | 15–23 € |

•┑ Dom. Fougeray de Beauclair, 44, rue de Mazy, BP 36,
21160 Marsannay-la-Côte, tel. 03.80.52.21.12,
fax 03.80.58.73.83,
e-mail fougeraydebeauclair@wanadoo.fr ☑
☓ ev. day 8am–12 noon 2pm–6pm;
Sun. 10am–12 noon 3.30pm–5.30pm
•┑ J.L. Fougeray

DOM. JEAN FOURNIER
Clos du Roy 2000

| ■ | 1.6 ha | 6,500 | ⑪ | 8–11 € |

•┑ Dom. Jean Fournier, 34, rue du Château,
21160 Marsannay-la-Côte, tel. 03.80.52.24.38,
fax 03.80.52.77.40,
e-mail domaine.jean.fournier@wanadoo.fr ☑
☓ by appt.

ALAIN GUYARD
Les Etales 2000

| ■ | 1 ha | 5,000 | ⑪ | 8–11 € |

•┑ Alain Guyard, 10, rue du Puits-de-Têt,
21160 Marsannay-la-Côte, tel. 03.80.52.14.46,
fax 03.80.52.67.36 ☑
☓ by appt.

OLIVIER GUYOT
La Montagne 2001

| ■ | 1 ha | 4,000 | ⑪ | 23–30 € |

•┑ Dom. Olivier Guyot, 39, rue de Mazy,
21160 Marsannay-la-Côte, tel. 03.80.52.39.71,
fax 03.80.51.17.58, e-mail domaine.guyot@libertysurf.fr ☑
☓ by appt.

CH. DE MARSANNAY
Les Echézeaux 2000

| ■ | 1.74 ha | 10,355 | ■⑪♦ | 11–15 € |

•┑ Dom. du Ch. de Marsannay, rte des Grands-Crus, BP 78,
21160 Marsannay-la-Côte, tel. 03.80.51.71.11,
fax 03.80.51.71.12,
e-mail chateau.marsannay@kriter.com ☑
☓ ev. day 10am–12 noon 2pm–6.30pm; groups by appt.;
cl. Sun. from Nov. to Mars

Fixin

After visiting the wine presses of the Dukes of Burgundy in Chenôve and tasting some Marsannay, the wine tourist arrives at Fixin, the first in a series of communes that give their names to various Appellations d'Origine Contrôlée. Here growers produce mainly red wines – 4,210 hl of red wine and 178 hl of white – which are sturdy, well-structured, often tannic, and keep well. They can also request the Appellation Côte de Nuits-Villages at the time of the harvest.

The *climats* Hervelets, Arvelets, Clos du Chapitre and Clos Napoléon, all classed as Premiers Crus, are among the best known, though the best of all is Clos de la Perrière, which has been described by eminent Burgundian writers as a "Cuvée Hors Classe" (a wine beyond class) and has been compared to Chambertin; the vineyard extends a little into the commune of Brochon and neighbouring Meix-Bas.

DOM. BART
Hervelets 2000★★

| ■ | 1er cru | 1.3 ha | 6,000 | ⑪ | 15–23 € |

The family has provided a pillar of the *Cadets de Bourgogne* and a Professor of Legal History at the university. As for this Premier Cru, its colour is dark and quite intense. The liquorice bouquet tends towards ripe red berries. Pure pleasure on the palate, this elegant and fruity wine lacks neither robustness nor power. Typical of the "natural" wines of the 2000 vintage.
•┑ Dom. Bart, 23, rue Moreau, 21160 Marsannay-la-Côte,
tel. 03.80.51.49.76, fax 03.80.51.23.43 ☑
☓ by appt.

VINCENT ET DENIS BERTHAUT
Les Arvelets 2001★

| ■ | 1er cru | 1 ha | 5,000 | ⑪ | 15–23 € |

It is so young that the nose offers only charred notes. But it is soft and quite fresh on the palate with a fruity and powerful finish. Well-made, balanced, this is a wine that must stay in the cellar for three to four years.
•┑ Vincent et Denis Berthaut, 9, rue Noisot, 21220 Fixin,
tel. 03.80.52.45.48, fax 03.80.51.31.05,
e-mail denis.berthaut@wanadoo.fr ☑
☓ ev. day 10am–12 noon 2pm–6pm; cl. Jan.

DOM. RENE BOUVIER
Crais de chêne Vieilles Vignes 2000★

| ■ | 1.09 ha | 4,000 | ⑪ | 11–15 € |

This *village* 2000, produced in Crais de Chêne (a *climat* situated on the edge of Couchey), is an impeccable, brilliant, very noticeable colour. Still a little restrained, the bouquet can't wait to burst forth (cherry). The body is generous and powerful, fairly tannic, in the classic Fixin tradition. This estate is established at Gevrey-Chambertin (RN 74) on the old Goillot-Bernollin property.
•┑ Dom. René Bouvier, 29 bis, rte de Dijon,
21220 Gevrey-Chambertin, tel. 03.80.34.36.12,
fax 03.80.59.95.96, e-mail rene-bouvier@wanadoo.fr ☑
☓ by appt.
•┑ Bernard Bouvier

DEREY FRERES
Vieilles Vignes 2001★

| ■ | 2.2 ha | 7,000 | ⑪ | 11–15 € |

Tenant farmers in the town of Dijon aux Marcs-d'Or, the members of this family can call themselves the successors of the Ducs de Bourgogne! This is a fairly dark ruby-red Fixin, matching the cherry and prune aromas. If you want a chewey wine, try this characteristic 2001, with its attractive fruitiness. The oak is well-integrated. A strictly old-style wine with enough substance to age well.

➤ Derey Frères, 1, rue Jules-Ferry, 21160 Couchey, tel. 03.80.52.15.04, fax 03.80.58.76.70,
e-mail derey-freres@wanadoo.fr ▼
☼ ev. day except Sun. 10am–6pm

DOM. DURAND PERE ET FILLE

2000★

| ■ | 3.88 ha | 29,000 | ⬡ | 11–15 € |

Oenologist Marie-Pierre Durand took over from her father in 2001. She offered this *village* with a deep, intense colour, and clean, frank, slightly toasty bouquet. Right up to its tannic finish, it has all the richness it needs on the palate and is

properly balanced. You would be well-advised to leave it in the cellar for two to three years.

➤ Durand Père et Fille, 5, rue du Professeur-Jules-Violle, 21220 Fixin, tel. 03.80.52.45.28, fax 03.80.58.74.61,
e-mail dom.durandfixin@waika9.com ▼
☼ by appt.

DOM. FOUGERAY DE BEAUCLAIR

Clos Marion 2000★

| ■ | 3.16 ha | 12,000 | ⬡ | 23–30 € |

This estate (originally Jean-Louis Fougeray, Evelyne Beauvais and Bernard Clair) spread over into Languedoc in 1999, when Patrice Ollivier, the son-in-law of Jean-Louis, took over the management of the Burgundy vineyards. This wine is fully representative of the vintage: supple and elegant. The substance is not extensive, but one can taste it clearly. A

Côte de Nuits (North 1)

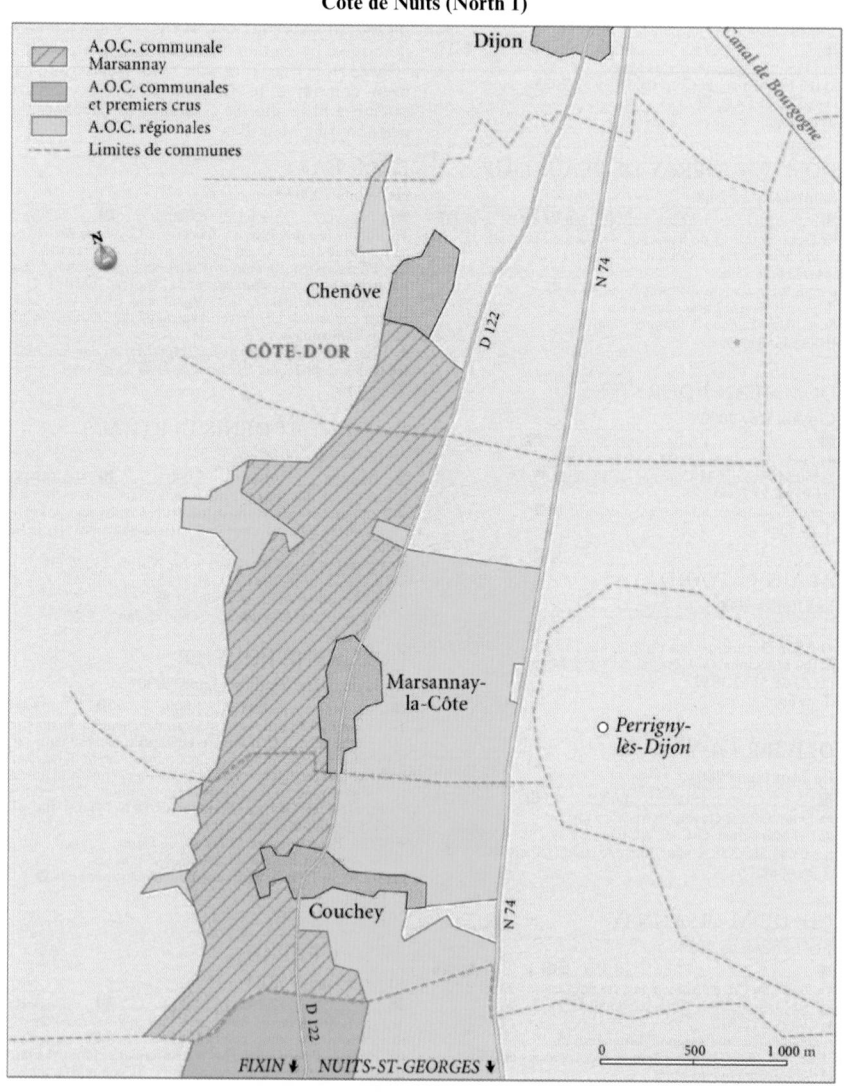

dark, ruby-garnet colour, it concentrates on black fruits, without completely the traces of its maturation in cask. No point in keeping it too long.

☛ Dom. Fougeray de Beauclair, 44, rue de Mazy, BP 36, 21160 Marsannay-la-Côte, tel. 03.80.52.21.12, fax 03.80.58.73.83,
e-mail fougeraydebeauclair@wanadoo.fr ☑
⌚ ev. day 8am–12 noon 2pm–6pm;
Sun. 10am–12 noon 3.30pm–5.30pm
☛ J.-L. Fougeray

DOM. OLIVIER GUYOT
Les Chenevrières 2001★

■	0.45 ha	2,500	◖◗	23–30 €

One can tour the estate in the barouche drawn by Indigo, the estate's horse that also helps with the ploughing in the vineyards. If you want to know what a burlat cherry Fixin resembles, these are the indications. Fine aromas of fresh fruitiness and a touch of oakiness. This wine should be kept for a while, if only to attenuate the influence of the cask and to allow the flavours to develop. It appears to have the capacity.
☛ Dom. Olivier Guyot, 39, rue de Mazy, 21160 Marsannay-la-Côte, tel. 03.80.52.39.71, fax 03.80.51.17.58, e-mail domaine.guyot@libertysurf.fr ☑
⌚ by appt.

JOLIET PERE ET FILS
Clos de la Perrière Monopole 2000★

■	1er cru	4.5 ha	22,000	■ ◖◗ ⚬	15–23 €

An estate worth visiting for its cellar (formerly part of the abbey of Cîteaux) which is classified as a Historic Monument, and for its ancient wine-press. Perrière has been an authentic *tête de cuvée* since the 19th century, equal to the greatest and the family has had a monopoly on it for almost two centuries. Red and some white. The colour of this Pinot is near-black with garnet-red highlights. Liquorice, blackcurrant, the bouquet opens gradually, without forcing the pace. Freshness, fruit, balance, are all there in this pleasant wine. The **white Clos de la Perrière 2001** received a special mention.
☛ EARL Joliet Père et fils, manoir de La Perrière, 21220 Fixin, tel. 03.80.52.47.85, fax 03.80.51.99.90, e-mail benigne@wanadoo.fr ☑
⌚ ev. day 8am–6pm; cl. during the harvest

ARMELLE ET JEAN-MICHEL MOLIN
2001★

■	2.5 ha	6,000	◖◗	8–11 €

Fixin (pronounced fissang) has many treasures, among them a 10th and 12th century church. with the glazed-tile roof. Here we have an old-fashioned Pinot Noir, like those of 20 years ago. The colour of a burlat cherry, a slightly-cooked cherry bouquet, it has effective and by no means astringent tannins. Supple and one could say rustic on account of its recurring raspberry notes. One used to think of Fixin as a winter wine, one to drink with game, rabbit, even a hot-pot. And that is the case with this one.
☛ EARL Armelle et Jean-Michel Molin, 54, rte des Grands-Crus, 21220 Fixin, tel. 03.80.52.21.28, fax 03.80.59.96.99 ☑
⌚ by appt.

CHARLES VIENOT
Cuvée de l'Empereur 2000★

■	n.c.	7,000	◖◗	11–15 €

This Cuvée de l'Empereur has a long history: a forebear of Charles Viénot was married at Fixin to Noisot, an old soldier of Napoleon's Guard, and financed the "Réveil de Napoleon," the statue by François Rude that is situated on the high ground above the village. As red as the Légion d'honneur, this is a wine with a typically Pinot bouquet (liquorice, stewed fruits), soft and fine, without too much acidity. It needs keeping for a year or two. Under the marque **Bouchard Aîné, Cuvée Signature 2001 Fixin Mazière** (received a special mention) needs to age.

☛ Charles Viénot, 5, quai Dumorey, 21703 Nuits-Saint-Georges, tel. 03.80.62.61.41, fax 03.80.62.61.60
☛ SA Boisset

Wines selected but not starred

REGIS BOUVIER 2001

■	0.3 ha	n.c.	◖◗	11–15 €

☛ Régis Bouvier, 52, rue de Mazy, 21160 Marsannay-la-Côte, tel. 03.80.51.33.93, fax 03.80.58.75.07 ☑
⌚ by appt.

CLOS SAINT-LOUIS 2001

■	3.5 ha	18,000	◖◗	11–15 €

☛ Dom. du Clos Saint-Louis, 4, rue des Rosiers, 21220 Fixin, tel. 03.80.52.45.51, fax 03.80.58.88.76, e-mail clos.st.louis@wanadoo.fr ☑
⌚ by appt.
☛ Philippe Bernard

DOM. GUY DUFOULEUR
Clos du Chapitre Monopole 2000

■	1er cru	4.78 ha	28,000	◖◗	30–38 €

☛ Dom. Guy Dufouleur, 19, pl. Monge, 21700 Nuits-Saint-Georges, tel. 03.80.62.31.00, fax 03.80.62.31.00 ☑ 🏠
⌚ by appt.
☛ Guy and Xavier Dufouleur

DOM. PIERRE GELIN
Clos Napoléon 2000

■	1er cru	1.8 ha	9,000	◖◗	15–23 €

☛ Dom. Pierre Gelin, 2, rue du Chapitre, 21220 Fixin, tel. 03.80.52.45.24, fax 03.80.51.47.80 ☑
⌚ by appt.
☛ Stéphen Gelin

ALAIN GUYARD
Les Chenevières 2000

■	1.5 ha	4,000	◖◗	8–11 €

☛ Alain Guyard, 10, rue du Puits-de-Têt, 21160 Marsannay-la-Côte, tel. 03.80.52.14.46, fax 03.80.52.67.36 ☑
⌚ by appt.

DOM. HUGUENOT PERE ET FILS 2000

■	5 ha	25,000	◖◗	11–15 €

☛ Dom. Huguenot Père et Fils, 7, ruelle du Carron, 21160 Marsannay-la-Côte, tel. 03.80.52.11.56, fax 03.80.52.60.47,
e-mail domaine.huguenot@wanadoo.fr ☑
⌚ by appt.

DOM. DU VIEUX COLLEGE 2000

■	1.2 ha	6,000	◖◗	11–15 €

☛ Jean-Pierre et Eric Guyard, Dom. du Vieux Collège, 4, rue du Vieux-Collège, 21160 Marsannay-la-Côte, tel. 03.80.52.12.43, fax 03.80.52.95.85 ☑
⌚ by appt.

Gevrey-Chambertin

North of Gevrey, three appellations communales are produced in the commune of Brochon: Fixin on a small part of the Clos de la Perrière, Côtes de Nuits-Villages on the northern part (at Préau and Queue-de-Hareng) and Gevrey-Chambertin in the south.

Of these, the Appellation Communale Gevrey-Chambertin is not only the biggest producer by volume – 14,524 hl in 2002 but also the home of a number of world-famous Grands Crus producing in total less than 3,644 hl. The combe of Lavaux divides the commune in two. To the north we find, among other climats, Les Evocelles (which borders on Brochon), Les Champeaux, La Combe Aux Moines (once the walk of Cluny Abbey, where the monks were the first important growers of

Gevrey), Les Cazetiers, Le Clos Saint-Jacques, Les Varoilles, etc. South of the village, the crus are less numerous because nearly the whole of the slope produces Grand Cru wines, for example the *climats* of Fonteny, Petite-Chapelle, Clos-Prieur, etc.

The wines of this appellation are robust and powerful when grown on the hillside, elegant and subtle when grown at the foot of the hill. With regard to the lower vineyard, some have taken the inaccurate view that the part running down to the Dijon-Beaune railway line should not qualify as Appellation Gevrey-Chambertin. This view makes a mockery of what Gevrey's winemakers know as fact, but it gives us the opportunity to explain the background. At various times in the past, the hill has been the site of a great deal of different geological activity, some of which was the result of glacial action in the Quaternary era; a base of Bajocian limestone is overlaid by different layers of chalky soil with clay particles and pebbles. The combe of Lavaux was a

Côte de Nuits (North 2)

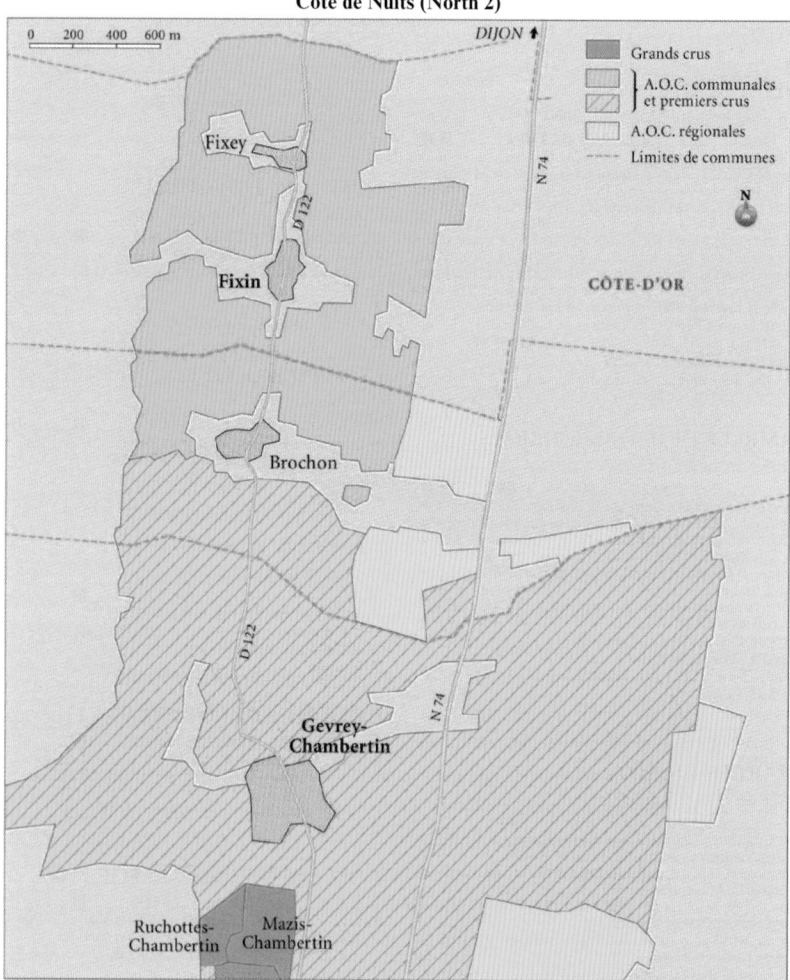

sort of channel down which deposits ran, causing a huge plug of waste to be deposited at its foot, made of identical or similar minerals to those found at the top of the hillside. In some places, the soils are simply deeper, so further away from the substratum. But they form essentially the same base, with its layers of limestone pebbles, giving rise to the elegant, subtle wines mentioned above.

DOM. ARLAUD 2001★

| ■ | | 0,79 ha | 4,100 | ⑪ | | 23–30 € |

The estate has redesigned its label in a classic format which appears on this well-presented wine. One of our tasters described the colour as garnet-red with crimson highlights (the other way round is more usual). After aeration, the bouquet starts on an oaky note, followed by fruitiness. Acidity contributes freshness and the indication of good keeping qualities. Balanced, subtly woody on the palate, a silky wine which still needs to open out (three to five years).
☛ SCEA Dom. Arlaud Père et Fils, 41, rue d'Epernay, 21220 Morey-Saint-Denis, tel. 03.80.34.32.65, fax 03.80.34.10.11,
e-mail cyprien.arlaud@wanadoo.fr ☑
☧ by appt.

DOM. RENE BOUVIER

Jeunes Rois 2000★★

| ■ | n.c. | n.c. | ⑪ | | 15–23 € |

When he arrived at Gevrey (the former Goillot-Bernollin company), Bernard Bouvier, from Marsannay, mounted the steps of the palace, in every sense. For it is the Jeunes Rois (sur Brochon) that brings him distinction here. A spruce colour, intense burlat cherry. The bouquet is fruit compote, on an elegant oakiness. Full, fleshy and exuberantly fruity on the palate. Concentration and finesse combine to bring out the terroir.
☛ Dom. René Bouvier, 29 bis, rte de Dijon, 21220 Gevrey-Chambertin, tel. 03.80.34.36.12, fax 03.80.59.95.96,
e-mail rene-bouvier@wanadoo.fr ☑
☧ by appt.
☛ Bernard Bouvier

DOM. DES CHAMBRIS 2001★

| ■ | n.c. | 900 | ⑪ | | 15–23 € |

The néo-classic style is well known when applied to buildings, but in oenology? "This wine is an example of it," said one of the Jurors. Dense, purplish-red, it doesn't joke about intensity. The woodiness argues every inch of the way with the candied fruits. The opening on the palate is clean and rounded. Liquorice on the finish, on a basis of integrated tannins. Behind all this is a real wine, which will keep for two to three years.
☛ SCEV du Dom. des Chambris, 7, rue du Lavoir, 21220 Chevannes, tel. 03.80.61.44.77, fax 03.80.61.48.87,
e-mail leschambris@wanadoo.fr ☑
☧ by appt.

DOM. PHILIPPE CHARLOPIN

Cuvée Vieilles Vignes 2000★★

| ■ | 3 ha | 10,000 | ⑪ | | 30–38 € |

The 99 vintage of this wine received the *coup de coeur* last year, as did the 98 in the preceding year. This, therefore, is a known value. Sombre ruby-red with purple highlights, the bouquet offered by this 2000 vintage is true to type and very fresh, and the oak does nothing to modify the blackcurrant aromas. The initial impact is young, fruity and generous, opening onto a balanced structure whose tannins will need three or four years to integrate. A wine with great potential. The **La Justice 2000 Village (23–30 €)**, one star, is a Gevrey with the seductive richness of a Vosne. Of course, Philippe Charlopin was taught by Henri Jayer.
☛ Dom. Philippe Charlopin, 18, rte de Dijon, 21220 Gevrey-Chambertin, tel. 03.80.51.81.18, fax 03.80.51.81.27,
e-mail charlopin.philippe@wanadoo.fr

DOM. DROUHIN-LAROZE

Lavaux Saint Jacques 2001★

| ■ | 1er cru | 0.29 ha | 1,800 | ⑪ | 15–23 € |

Excellent Premier Cru from one of the most prestigious Gevrey estates. Bernard Drouhin left us after the 2001 harvest: the last grapes he saw ripen. The already quite open bouquet is reminiscent of blackcurrant and chocolate. No hard or rustic tannins, but a nice ripe fruitiness. Very rich on the palate, elegant and of a good length, it should age well (two or four years). The **Gevrey-Village 2001** received a special mention.
☛ Dom. Drouhin-Laroze, 20, rue du Gaizot, 21220 Gevrey-Chambertin, tel. 03.80.34.31.49, fax 03.80.51.83.70, e-mail drouhin-laroze@aol.com ☑
☧ by appt.

DOM. DUJAC

Aux Combottes 2000★★

| ■ | 1er cru | 1.15 ha | 6,000 | ⑪ | 38–46 € |

"All the Grand Bourgogne you could possibly want," a taster took up Gaston Roupnel's refrain. Neighbours of the Latricières-Chambertin, Combottes could have been classified as a Grand Cru under the name of Combottes-Chambertin. A deep, purplish-red colour, this 2000 has an open, straightforward, bouquet with plenty of warmth: cherry-stone, spices, well-tempered oak. Full and rich on the palate, it needs no coaxing. Remarkable for a wine of this vintage.
☛ Dom. Dujac, 7, rue de la Bussière, 21220 Morey-Saint-Denis, tel. 03.80.34.01.00, fax 03.80.34.01.09, e-mail dujac@dujac.com ☑
☧ by appt.
☛ Seysses

DOM. DUPONT-TISSERANDOT

Les Cazetiers 2001★★

| ■ | 1er cru | 2.11 ha | n.c. | ⑪ | 23–30 € |

The two Dupont daughters (Mmes Guillard and Chevillon) took over this estate in 1990; it has developed considerably since 1960, going from three to 24 ha in that time. Dark red, this very attractive Cazetiers was one of the leaders at this tasting. You have to wait for the second bouquet to distinguish the intense aromas of humus, undergrowth and leather. A hint of warmth and a touch tannic, but good flavours of soft red berries. A noble wine that needs to be laid down for four or five years. The **Premier Cru Lavaux Saint-Jacques 2001** was given a special mention. This one will not keep as long.
☛ Dupont-Tisserandot, 2, pl. des Marronniers, 21220 Gevrey-Chambertin, tel. 03.80.34.10.50, fax 03.80.58.50.71 ☑
☧ ev. day 9am–12 noon 2pm–6pm; Sat. Sun. by appt.; cl. 2–20 Aug. and 24 Dec.–3 Jan.

FERY-MEUNIER 2000★

| ■ | 1.3 ha | 7,000 | ⑪ | | 15–23 € |

This small business, created in 1995, vinifies grapes which it buys in. Its Gevrey 2000 offers amber highlights on a good red background of Pinot Noir. Its maturation in cask is detectable on the nose. On the palate it is rounded with a finish that is both fruity and tannic. The secondary aromas are simple but delicious. To drink within the next two years.
☛ Maison Fery-Meunier, Les Vignottes, 21700 Premeaux-Prissey, tel. 03.80.62.31.08, fax 03.80.61.34.21,
e-mail jj.confuron@wanadoo.fr ☑ ☖
☧ by appt.

DOM. DOMINIQUE GALLOIS

La Combe aux Moines 2001★★

| ■ | 1er cru | n.c. | n.c. | ⑪ | 23–30 € |

Related to Gaston Roupnel, the Gallois family carefully kept all their files and manuscripts which has allowed American researcher, Philip Whalen, to publish a recent study on the writer. As for this Combe en Moines, it would have inspired the author of *Nono*. Generous tears on a brilliant, limpid colour; aromas of spice and blueberry. On the palate, the fresh fruitiness leads to a feeling of solidity which ensures that it will keep well. But don't forget **Les Petits Cazetiers 2001**, one star.

☛ Dom. Dominique Gallois, 9, rue du Mal-de-Lattre-de-Tassigny, 21220 Gevrey-Chambertin, tel. 03.80.34.11.99, fax 03.80.34.38.62, e-mail d.gallois@tiscali.fr ☑
☈ by appt.

DOM. PIERRE GELIN
Clos de Meixvelles 2000★

■	1.83 ha	9,000	◫	15–23 €

The colour of this 2000 is a fresh, light ruby-red. The bouquet, however, is more assertive (cherries in *eau-de-vie*, chocolate cream). Its softness and fruitiness balance a tannic presence which, of course, is not surprising considering the terroir. A very characteristic *village* wine. Meixvelles (or Mévelles au Cadastre) is at the centre of the village.
☛ Dom. Pierre Gelin, 2, rue du Chapitre, 21220 Fixin, tel. 03.80.52.45.24, fax 03.80.51.47.80 ☑
☈ by appt.

DOM. ROBERT ET SERGE GROFFIER
2001★

■	n.c.	5,000	◫	15–23 €

The grandfather Jules (1898–1974) did his Tour de France, not as a journeyman cooper, but as a racing cyclist. The analogy is apt for this wine, which was well-placed in its group. A light but flawless colour; on the nose it tends towards muskiness and blackberries. Freshness on the palate and very evident tannins. It then goes on to liquorice and and oakiness that should integrate with the wine in the coming three years.
☛ Dom. Robert et Serge Groffier, 3–5, rte des Grands-Crus, 21220 Morey-Saint-Denis, tel. 03.80.34.31.53, fax 03.80.34.15.48 ☑
☈ by appt.

JEAN-MICHEL GUILLON
Les Champonnets 2001★

■ 1er cru	0.9 ha	4,600	◫	15–23 €

Two wines of equal quality: the **Cuvée Vieilles Vignes Village 2001 (11–15 €)**, which has structure and a certain maturity already, and this magnificently coloured Premier Cru. It would be a good wine to find in your cellar one day, five to ten years from now. The concentration inspired our tasters to make some flattering comments, but they underlined the current influence of the cask on the underlying nature of the wine. Nuances of spices, stewed fruits. And where does this Les Champonnets hide itself? At the junction of the Combe de Lavaux and the Côte.
☛ Jean-Michel Guillon, 33, rte de Beaune, 21220 Gevrey-Chambertin, tel. 03.80.51.83.98, fax 03.80.51.85.59, e-mail eurlguillon@aol.com ☑
☈ by appt.

DOM. ANTONIN GUYON 2000★

■	2.4 ha	12,000	◫	15–23 €

This huge family estate has been in existence for decades; a string of vineyards and crus the whole length of the Côte and the Hautes Côtes. The colour of this Gevrey is between mauve and black. The bouquet takes shape little by little, on notes of eucalyptus and menthol. A great deal of character on the palate following the entry on firm and fruity substance. Hard but concentrated, it could take out a lease for three, six or even nine years in your cellar.
☛ Dom. Antonin Guyon, 21420 Savigny-lès-Beaune, tel. 03.80.67.13.24, fax 03.80.66.85.87, e-mail vins@guyon-bourgogne.com ☑
☈ by appt.

OLIVIER GUYOT
Les Champs 2001★★

■	0.45 ha	3,000	◫	23–30 €

Two equal wines: **Les Champeaux Premier Cru 2001 (30–38 €)** and this Les Champs from Brochon, on the Gevrey side. And both are fine, true Gevrey-Chambertins. Olivier Guyot was one of the first wine-growers in the Côte to start using horses again for ploughing. Deep crimson, this is a 2001 remarkable

for its classic aromas (blackcurrant, blackberry) which already gives an impression of roundness. The silky tannins and a more than adequate length are confirmed on the palate. This wine should be ready in 2005.
☛ Dom. Olivier Guyot, 39, rue de Mazy, 21160 Marsannay-la-Côte, tel. 03.80.52.39.71, fax 03.80.51.17.58, e-mail domaine.guyot@libertysurf.fr ☑
☈ by appt.

DOM. HARMAND-GEOFFROY
Les Champeaux 2000★

■ 1er cru	0.21 ha	1,300	◫	23–30 €

Gerard Harmand and his wife took over the Lucien Geoffroy et Fils family estate in 1989. A lively red with purplish highlights, this Les Champeaux – a *climat* occupying an elevated site in the middle of the Saint-Jacques hillside – does honour to its name. Still somewhat reserved, the wine is rich, quite tannic and tends toward musky and liquorice aromas (with leather nuances). A perfect wine to drink in the next three to four years.
☛ Dom. Harmand-Geoffroy, 1, pl. des Lois, 21220 Gevrey-Chambertin, tel. 03.80.34.10.65, fax 03.80.34.13.72, e-mail harmand-geoffroy@wanadoo.fr ☑
☈ by appt.

DOM. HERESZTYN
Les Corbeaux 2001★

■ 1er cru	0.19 ha	900	◫	23–30 €

Having been awarded a *coup de coeur* for its Perrière 96 a few years ago, this estate represents an excellent marriage of Burgundian and Polish. What a lot of water under the bridge since then! In addition to this Corbeaux, with its superb nose (spices, saffron) and its velvety body (richness, a little warmth), the **La Perrière Premier Cru 2001** received a special mention. Both are wines to lay down for two to three years.
☛ Dom. Heresztyn, 27, rue Richebourg, 21220 Gevrey-Chambertin, tel. 03.80.34.30.86, fax 03.80.34.13.99, e-mail domaine.heresztyn@wanadoo.fr ☑
☈ by appt.

DOM. HUMBERT FRERES
Petite Chapelle 2001★★

■ 1er cru	0.1 ha	600	◫	30–38 €

If the **Estournelles Saint-Jacques Premier Cru 2001** is worth the detour by way of the Combe de Lavaux, and was awarded one star – as was the **Le Poissenot Premier Cru 2001** – this Petite Chapelle makes one feel like kneeling in prayer. Its colour is like the sun shining through a stained glass window. The cask doesn't hold back the fruit (blackcurrant and blackberry). A successful wine in the modern style, starting from a carefully-gathered harvest: *moelleux* and full-bodied.
☛ Dom. Humbert Frères, rue de Planteligone, 21220 Gevrey-Chambertin, tel. 03.80.51.80.14 ☑
☈ by appt.

DOM. LEYMARIE
La Justice 2000★

■	0.67 ha	2,700	◫	15–23 €

The Leymarie family, which succeeded in flying the Belgian flag on Burgundy soil, does not count a French Consul among its members for nothing: its sense of diplomacy has given it one foot in Burgundy and the other in Bordeaux. This is a wine which recalls crystallized cherries and cherries in alcohol. While the initial impression is severe and tannic, it shows its power in its fruit and its well-balanced acidity. With a tight texture and substantial backbone, it will be excellent with venison, but not for a while yet.
☛ Dom. Leymarie-CECI, Clos du Village, 24, rue du Vieux-Château, 21640 Vougeot, tel. 03.80.62.86.06, fax 03.80.62.88.53, e-mail leymarie@skynet.be ☑
☈ by appt.

DOM. LIGNIER-MICHELOT 2001★

| | 0.5 ha | 2,800 | 🍷 🥂 ♦ | 15–23 € |

A constantly evolving palate – one of the nice comments on a tasting card! This family estate began making wine a little more than ten years ago and recently set up a tasting-room in one of the classified houses. An intense garnet-red, this *village* has a quite fascinating and aromatic complexity: nutmeg, pepper and cocoa. A supple and straightforward opening, a pronounced acidity, length, fine tannins and – to complete an ideal picture – a note of bitterness without which one would be utterly lost. Will keep for two to three years.
🍷 Dom. Lignier-Michelot, 11, rue Haute, 21220 Morey-Saint-Denis, tel. 03.80.34.31.13, fax 03.80.58.52.16 ✅
🍷 by appt.

FREDERIC MAGNIEN

La Perrière 2001★★

| | 1er cru | 0.3 ha | 1,800 | 🍷 🥂 ♦ | 30–38 € |

A *climat* situated by the side of the road that runs through the Grands Crus between Gevrey and Morey. Here it gives of its best, and the Jury would like to see this one again in a few years' time! Black-cherry, its nose is not that of a Cyrano de Bergerac, but one detects ferns and cut flowers. Rich, full, rounded and balanced, it has an agreeable aroma of the Pinot grape and keeps its oakiness in check. If you prefer finesse to strength of character, the **Cuvée Vieilles Vignes 2001 Village (11–15 €)** was awarded one star. To lay down for four years.
🍷 Frédéric Magnien, 26, rte Nationale, 21220 Morey-Saint-Denis, tel. 03.80.58.54.20, fax 03.80.51.84.34, e-mail fredericmagnien.grandsvinsdebourgogne@wanadoo.fr ✅
🍷 by appt.

DOM. MICHEL MAGNIEN ET FILS

Les Cazetiers 2001★

| | 1er cru | 0.25 ha | 1,500 | 🍷 🥂 | 23–30 € |

A Cazetiers is always acceptable. This is a Gevrey from over by Saint-Jacques, Lavaux. The terroir and the distinctive style are very strongly expressed here. One can sense leather, muskiness and blackcurrant, too. Undoubtedly this is 2001 with a still austere aspect, but it will keep well (five years). With its very dedicated structure it will go well with a roast of wild boar once it has been decanted. **Les Seuvrées Vielles Vignes 2001 (15–23 €)** was awarded one star: a very attractive wine to lay down for three to five years.
🍷 Dom. Michel Magnien et Fils, 4, rue Ribordot, 21220 Morey-Saint-Denis, tel. 03.80.51.82.98, fax 03.80.58.51.76 ✅
🍷 by appt.

DOM. MARCHAND FRERES

Les Combottes 2001★★

| | 1er cru | 0.05 ha | 300 | 🥂 | 23–30 € |

Here we have two family estates grouped around a 17th century winepress. Intense carmine-red with a touch of deep purple, this is a fine Gevrey des Combottes, a *climat* superbly situated between Latricières, Charms and Mazoyères. One is in very good company here and, while initially the nose is a trifle immature, it opens when swirled around in the glass. It is still a young wine and a touch withdrawn, but it is full and well structured, and its soft, red-berry notes embrace a remarkable oakiness. Will need keeping until the tannins have sheathed their claws. Buy it with confidence for the years 2006 and 2007.
🍷 EARL Dom. Marchand Frères, 1, pl. du Monument, 21220 Gevrey-Chambertin, tel. 03.80.62.10.97, fax 03.80.62.11.01, e-mail dmarc2000@aol.com ✅ 📅
🍷 by appt.

DOM. THIERRY MORTET 2001★

| | 3.5 ha | 12,000 | 🥂 | 15–23 € |

Denis, the elder brother and Thierry, the younger took over in 1992 from Charles Mortet, their father, and each created his own domaine. Almost black in colour, this wine with the voluptuous nose goes through sequences by turn toasty and blackcurrant. The woodiness stays on the palate, together with the well-balanced tannins. True to type, balanced, this will be a very attractive wine in three years' time.
🍷 Dom. Thierry Mortet, 16, pl. des Marronniers, 21220 Gevrey-Chambertin, tel. 03.80.51.85.07, fax 03.80.34.16.80 ✅
🍷 by appt.

PHILIPPE ROSSIGNOL

Les Corbeaux 2000★

| | 1er cru | 0.67 ha | 2,500 | 🥂 | 15–23 € |

Wine-grower established since 1976 on some 6 ha in the Côte de Nuits, Philippe Rossignol practises controlled natural grassing down. Of a not very deep but very clear-red colour, this wine exudes the aromas of cherries, liquorice, and perhaps a touch of menthol. The structure and length are irreproachable. However, only the first few notes of the symphony have been played, and one will have to wait to see how it develops.
🍷 Philippe Rossignol, 61, av. de la Gare, 21220 Gevrey-Chambertin, tel. 03.80.51.81.17, fax 03.80.51.81.17 ✅
🍷 by appt.

GERARD SEGUIN

Les Crais 2001★

| | | 0.6 ha | 3,100 | 🥂 | 11–15 € |

Deep garnet-red in colour, this wine from 2001 has an intense, slightly oaked bouquet of red berries. Rounded, fleshy and soft, it has hardly a care in the world. It has a little something in reserve and a very pleasant finish. The **Craipillot Premier Cru 2001 (15–23 €)**, a *climat* situated between Ruchottes and Cazetiers, also received one star.
🍷 Gérard Seguin, 11–15, rue de l'Aumônerie, 21220 Gevrey-Chambertin, tel. 03.80.34.38.72, fax 03.80.34.17.41 ✅
🍷 by appt.

CHARLES THOMAS

La Croix des Champs 2000★

| | | n.c. | 5,500 | 🥂 | 15–23 € |

Charles Thomas is one of the marques of Maison Moillard (Thomas family). It presents itself here as a Gevrey 2000, which would have been better named Croix des Vignes, since there are hardly fields (*champs*) in this area. An intense carmine-red, the rim is very fresh. Spices and cherries in *eau-de-vie* essentially make up a bouquet which still has to reach a balance. On the palate it is massive and full of richness. Serve this wine with a coq-au-vin in two to five years.
🍷 Charles Thomas, BP 6, 21701 Nuits-Saint-Georges Cedex, tel. 03.80.62.42.00, fax 03.80.61.28.13, e-mail info@thomasfreres.com ✅
🍷 ev. day 10am–6pm; cl. Jan.

DOM. TORTOCHOT

Les Corvées 2000★

| | | 0.86 ha | 5,000 | 🥂 | 11–15 € |

At Tortochot (and Gaby, Chantal's father already took several *coups de coeur* with his Chambertin), they offer almost the whole range. And so we have seen all the estate's wines. The Jury noted this Les Corvées located between the Croix des Champs and the centre of the village; burlat cherry in colour, the aromas combine raspberry, currant and oakwood from the cask. The entry on the palate is rich (fleshy and good concentration of tannins) and the follow-on progresses as it should. Opulent, "this Les Corvées belongs to the nobility," said one taster. Also worth noting is the **Lavaux Saint-Jacques Premier Cru 2000 (23–30 €)**, which received a special mention.
🍷 Dom. Tortochot, 12, rue de l'Eglise, 21220 Gevrey-Chambertin, tel. 03.80.34.30.68, fax 03.80.34.18.80, e-mail chantam@aol.com ✅
🍷 by appt.
🍷 Chantal and Michel Tortochot

DOM. DES VAROILLES

Clos des Varoilles 2000★★

■ 1er cru	6 ha	32,335	❶❶	23–30 €

A 100% authentic Varoilles *clos* and judged the best of the series of the 2000 vintage. An intense ruby-red, it has all three cardinal virtues: it is mouth-filling, with length and fruitiness. Admittedly, the nose doesn't rush to open, but the black-currant is right there, just behind the door. The harvest has produced a wine which offers a fresh and delightful initial impression. Elegance, power, nothing is lacking. The owners fought for a long time to call their estate Domaine des Varoilles, because a marque cannot, in theory, take the name of a Premier Cru of an AOC, even as a monopoly. The precedent set by La Romanée-Conti in its time tipped the balance.
❧ Dom. des Varoilles, rue de l'Ancien-Hôpital, 21220 Gevrey-Chambertin, tel. 03.80.34.30.30, fax 03.80.51.88.99,
e-mail contact@domaine-varoilles.com ☑
♈ by appt.

Wines selected but not starred

DOM. DES BEAUMONT

Aux Combottes 2001

■ 1er cru	0.24 ha	1,200	❶❶	23–30 €

❧ EARL Dom. des Beaumont, 9, rue Ribordot, 21220 Morey-Saint-Denis, tel. 03.80.51.87.89, fax 03.80.51.87.89,
e-mail thierry.beaumont1@libertysurf.fr ☑ 🏚
♈ by appt.

VINCENT ET DENIS BERTHAUT

Clos des Chezeaux 2001

■	0.3 ha	2,000	❶❶	15–23 €

❧ Vincent et Denis Berthaut, 9, rue Noisot, 21220 Fixin, tel. 03.80.52.45.48, fax 03.80.51.31.05,
e-mail denis.berthaut@wanadoo.fr ☑
♈ ev. day 10am–12 noon 2pm–6pm; cl. Jan.

PIERRE BOUREE FILS

Les Cazetiers 2000

■ 1er cru	0.19 ha	1,194	❶❶	23–30 €

❧ Maison Pierre Bourée Fils, 13, rte de Beaune, BP 32, 21220 Gevrey-Chambertin, tel. 03.80.34.30.25, fax 03.80.51.85.64, e-mail pierre.bouree@wanadoo.fr ☑
♈ by appt.
❧ Louis Vallet

DOM. BRUNO CLAVELIER

Les Corbeaux 2000

■ 1er cru	0.25 ha	1,250	❶❶	23–30 €

❧ Dom. Bruno Clavelier, 6, RN 74, 21700 Vosne-Romanée, tel. 03.80.61.10.81, fax 03.80.61.04.25 ☑
♈ by appt.

FORGEOT PERE ET FILS 2001

■	n.c.	n.c.	❙❶❶⬇ 23–30 €

❧ Grands Vins Forgeot, 15, rue du Château, 21200 Beaune, tel. 03.80.24.80.50, fax 03.80.22.55.88

S.C. GUILLARD

Les Corbeaux 2000

■ 1er cru	0.48 ha	3,000	❶❶	15–23 €

❧ SCEA Guillard, 3, rue des Halles, 21220 Gevrey-Chambertin, tel. 03.80.34.32.44 ☑
♈ by appt.

DOM. HUGUENOT PERE ET FILS

Les Fontenys 2000

■ 1er cru	n.c.	2,400	❶❶	23–30 €

❧ Dom. Huguenot Père et Fils, 7, ruelle du Carron, 21160 Marsannay-la-Côte, tel. 03.80.52.11.56, fax 03.80.52.60.47,
e-mail domaine.huguenot@wanadoo.fr ☑
♈ by appt.

JABOULET-VERCHERRE

Les Grimoises 2000

■	n.c.	8,000	❶❶	30–38 €

❧ Jaboulet-Vercherre, 6, rue de Chaux, 21700 Nuits-Saint-Georges, tel. 03.80.62.43.27, fax 03.80.62.68.02

JEAN-PHILIPPE MARCHAND

Lavaux Saint-Jacques 2001

■ 1er cru	n.c.	2,400	❶❶	23–30 €

❧ Jean-Philippe Marchand, 4, rue Souvert, BP 41, 21220 Gevrey-Chambertin, tel. 03.80.34.33.60, fax 03.80.34.12.77, e-mail marchand@axnet.fr ☑ 🏚 🏚
♈ by appt.

CH. DE MARSANNAY 2000

■	2.09 ha	11,800	❙❶❶⬇ 23–30 €

❧ Dom. du Ch. de Marsannay, rte des Grands-Crus, BP 78, 21160 Marsannay-la-Côte, tel. 03.80.51.71.11, fax 03.80.51.71.12,
e-mail chateau.Marsannay@kriter.com ☑
♈ ev. day 10am–12 noon 2pm–6.30pm; groups by appt.; cl. Sun. from Nov. to Mars

DOM. MAZILLY PERE ET FILS

Vieilles Vignes 2001

■	0.89 ha	4,500	❶❶	15–23 €

❧ Dom. Mazilly Père et Fils, rte de Pommard, 21190 Meloisey, tel. 03.80.26.02.00, fax 03.80.26.03.67 ☑
♈ by appt.

PIERRE NAIGEON

Les Fontenys 2001

■ 1er cru	0.06 ha	300	❶❶	30–38 €

❧ Pierre Naigeon, 4, rue du Chambertin, 21220 Gevrey-Chambertin, tel. 03.80.34.14.87, fax 03.80.58.51.18,
e-mail pierre.naigeon@wanadoo.fr ☑
♈ ev. day 10am–1pm 2pm–6pm; cl. Dec.–Mars

DOM. HENRI REBOURSEAU 2000

■	7.02 ha	32,000	❙❶❶⬇ 15–23 €

❧ NSE Dom. Henri Rebourseau, 10, pl. du Monument, 21220 Gevrey-Chambertin, tel. 03.80.51.88.94, fax 03.80.34.12.82, e-mail rebourseau1@aol.com ☑
♈ by appt.

DOM. HENRI RICHARD 2001

■	2.07 ha	12,000	❶❶ 15–23 €

❧ SCE Dom. Henri Richard, 75, rte de Beaune, 21220 Gevrey-Chambertin, tel. 03.80.34.35.81, fax 03.80.34.35.81, e-mail scehenririchard@aol.com ☑
♈ ev. day 9am–6pm; cl. 15–31 Aug.

DOM. TAUPENOT-MERME

Bel Air 2000

| | 1er cru | n.c. | 2,700 | 🍶 | 30–38 € |

➻ Taupenot-Merme, 33, rte des Grands-Crus,
21220 Morey-Saint-Denis, tel. 03.80.34.35.24,
fax 03.80.51.83.41,
e-mail domaine.taupenot-merme@wanadoo.fr ☑
⟂ by appt.

Chambertin

Bertin, who was a winemaker in Gevrey, owned a parcel of vineyard neighbouring the Clos de Bèze and, noting the quality of the wines the monks made there, planted the same vines and produced a similar wine. This was the "Champ de Bertin," or Bertin's field, from which evolved the name Chambertin. In 2002 the AOC produced 478 hl from 13.29 ha.

CH. DE MARSANNAY 2000★★

| | Gd cru | 0.1 ha | 522 | 🍶 | 46–76 € |

The Grand Jury tasted this wine in the course of the final of the *coup de cœur*. It is, therefore, a Chambertin that bears its name proudly. Its still young colour is intense. Its bouquet is complex: liquorice, vanilla, blackcurrant. Forthright in its attack, the palate is just as complex as the nose with plenty of freshness and a substantial structure. As to the tannins, they are kept in check. The Château de Marsannay belongs to the Boisseaux Company. These are two products from the Jouanny family, tenant farmers at Quillardet.
➻ Dom. du Ch. de Marsannay, rte des Grands-Crus, BP 78, 21160 Marsannay-la-Côte, tel. 03.80.51.71.11, fax 03.80.51.71.12,
e-mail chateau.marsannay@kriter.com ☑
⟂ ev. day 10am–12 noon 2pm–6.30pm; groups by appt.; cl. Sun. from Nov. to Mar.

DOM. HENRI REBOURSEAU 2000★

| | Gd cru | 0.79 ha | 2,700 | 🍶 | +76 € |

92 94 **96** 98 ⟨99⟩ 00

In the 20th century this family played an active role in the creation and promotion of the Gevrey-Chambertin Grands Crus. Well-balanced, the colour is ruby-red but a hint of development is perceptible to the eye. Its aromas? A touch of Viennese pastry and some black small fruit. Its tannins are fine and lively. Seventeen months spent in cask have left their impression on the palate, but this is not unpleasant since the Pinot Noir is allowed its say. Needs to be laid down for three to four years.
➻ NSE Dom. Henri Rebourseau, 10, pl. du Monument, 21220 Gevrey-Chambertin, tel. 03.80.51.88.94, fax 03.80.34.12.82, e-mail rebourseau1@aol.com ☑
⟂ by appt.

DOM. A. ROUSSEAU PERE ET FILS 2001★

| | Gd cru | 2.15 ha | 9,800 | 🍶 | 46–76 € |

|97| 98 **99 00** 01

One of the founding fathers of the Gevrey AOCs. For the rest, the Chambertin label has not changed since the 1930s, a beautiful example of the Art Déco of the era. As for the wine, it is perfectly presented (the density and intensity of the colour are excellent for a wine of the 2001 vintage), a trifle vanilla-flavoured at the start then a blackcurrant finish on the nose. The tannins quickly go on the attack. But don't forget, this is a Chambertin, and still in the cradle. Everything is in place for a wine that will satisfy your guests five to ten years hence.

➻ Dom. Armand Rousseau, 1, rue de l'Aumônerie, 21220 Gevrey-Chambertin, tel. 03.80.34.30.55, fax 03.80.58.50.25, e-mail contact@domaine-rousseau.com
➻ C. Rousseau

DOM. TRAPET PERE ET FILS 2001★★

| | Gd cru | 2 ha | n.c. | 🍶 | 46–76 € |

|96| **98** 99 ⟨00⟩ 01

All it lacks is the sceptre and the crown: this wine is well and truly the king of the Chambertins. Above all, do His Majesty the courtesy of waiting for him because all your hopes will be fulfilled. A true miracle of nature, was how Gaston Roupnel put it. Tannins of course, but not the least bit harsh, rather they are beneficial and are careful not to mask the fruit. Full and round, this wine still bears the mark of its maturation (another reason to lay it down) against a bilberry background. *Grappe d'or* in the 2003 Guide for a 2000 vintage, *coup de cœur* in the old Marey-AOC.
➻ Dom. Trapet Père et Fils, 53, rte de Beaune, 21220 Gevrey-Chambertin, tel. 03.80.34.30.40, fax 03.80.51.86.34, e-mail message@domaine-trapet.com ☑
⟂ by appt.

Chambertin-Clos de Bèze

In 630 the monks from the Abbey at Bèze planted a vineyard on a small parcel of land which produced a particularly highly rated wine; today the appellation bearing the abbey's name covers about 15 ha; the wines can also be called Chambertin. In 2002, 461 hl of wine were produced from 14.62 ha.

DOM. DROUHIN-LAROZE 2001★

| | Gd cru | 1.5 ha | 4,300 | 🍶 | 46–76 € |

95 96 97 |00| |01|

A Clos de Bèze! When one thinks that this vineyard was founded in the seventh century and remained in the hands of the Canons of Langres until the Revolution. Five hundred and fifty years! The ruby-garnet-red colour of this 2001, while not very deep, is worth looking at. Expressive and well-balanced the bouquet combines the cask and the fruit. On the palate it is still tannic, of course, and needs to open but it promises much: in four to five years it will be fully developed. Three plots, forming an area of almost 1.5 ha, part of which is from the old Marey-Monge estate.
➻ Dom. Drouhin-Laroze, 20, rue du Gaizot, 21220 Gevrey-Chambertin, tel. 03.80.34.31.49, fax 03.80.51.83.70, e-mail drouhin-laroze@aol.com ☑
⟂ by appt.

FREDERIC MAGNIEN 2001★★

| | Gd cru | 0.6 ha | 3,000 | 🍶🍶 ☙ | 46–76 € |

This is the ouverture to the *Symphonie Bourgogne*. Not that of Edgard Varese, now sadly deceased, but that of the Grands Crus! This dazzling Clos de Bèze has all the vigour of the Côte de Nuits Pinot Noir, a single theme with infinite variations. More deep than brilliant, the colour is superb. A bouquet of vanilla and blackcurrant, fleshy on the palate with rounded, pleasant tannins. A marvellous, thoroughbred wine, utterly true to type and with an immense future.
➻ Frédéric Magnien, 26, rte Nationale, 21220 Morey-Saint-Denis, tel. 03.80.58.54.20, fax 03.80.51.84.34, e-mail fredericmagnien.grandsvinsdebourgogne@wanadoo.fr ☑
⟂ by appt.

BURGUNDY

Wines selected but not starred

DOM. BRUNO CLAIR 2000

| ■ | Gd cru | 0.98 ha | n.c. | ⅠⅠⅠ | 46–76 € |

●⊓ SCEA Dom. Bruno Clair, 5, rue du Vieux-Collège,
BP 22, 21160 Marsannay-la-Côte, tel. 03.80.52.28.95,
fax 03.80.52.18.14, e-mail brunoclair@wanadoo.fr ☑
⅄ by appt.

DOM. ROBERT ET SERGE GROFFIER 2001

| ■ | Gd cru | 0.41 ha | 1,800 | ⅠⅠⅠ | 46–76 € |

●⊓ Dom. Robert et Serge Groffier, 3–5, rte des Grands-Crus,
21220 Morey-Saint-Denis, tel. 03.80.34.31.53,
fax 03.80.34.15.48 ☑
⅄ by appt.

OTHER GRANDS CRUS FROM GEVREY-CHAMBERTIN

Surrounding the two previous vineyards is a huddle of others which, while not quite their equal, nonetheless bear a family resemblance. The regulations for producing these wines are slightly less demanding, but the wines share the sturdiness, strength and fullness, with a hint of liquorice, that generally distinguish Gevrey wines. These are Les Latricières (about 7 ha); Les Charmes (31.6 ha); Les Mazoyères, which can also be called Charmes (the reverse is not allowed); Les Mazis, including Les Mazis-Haut (about 8 ha) and Les Mazis-Bas (4.6 ha); Les Ruchottes, which comes from the word *roichot* meaning a rocky place, and which covers a tiny area comprising Les Ruchottes-du-Dessus (1.92 ha) and Les Ruchottes-du-Bas (1.27 ha); Les Griottes, where wild cherries are supposed to have grown (5.48 ha); and finally, Les Chapelles (5.39 ha), its name deriving from the chapel built in 1155 by monks from the Abbey at Bèze, but destroyed during the French Revolution.

Latricières-Chambertin

DOM. DROUHIN-LAROZE 2001★

| ■ | Gd cru | 0.68 ha | 2,200 | ⅠⅠⅠ | 30–38 € |

Fuschia, mauve; purple, it would seem, is the fashion world's colour for 2003–2004. This dense-textured Latricières is, therefore, very much in the trend. After aeration it opens on grilled hazelnut aromas and fine, expressive oakiness, finishing with strawberry jam. On the palate it is all fruit, rounded and satisfying. The extraction is well controlled and *caudalies* (French term for the seconds the impact of the wine remains on the palate after it is swallowed or spat out) on the finish are too numerous to count. It will certainly need four to five years in the cellar.
●⊓ Dom. Drouhin-Laroze, 20, rue du Gaizot,
21220 Gevrey-Chambertin, tel. 03.80.34.31.49,
fax 03.80.51.83.70, e-mail drouhin-laroze@aol.com ☑
⅄ by appt.

FAIVELEY 1999★

| ■ | Gd cru | 1,2 ha | 7,000 | ⅠⅠⅠ | 46–76 € |

François Faiveley, the grandson of the founder of *tastevin*, offered us some older vintages than those we usually taste. This Latricières 99, a leader in its class, is redolent of the hunt. An intense ruby-red, it takes us through aromas of damp woodlands, of leather and game. More full than lingering, it is a wine with muscular tone that has not yet said its final word. Still a little rasping and astringent, it should remain undisturbed in the cellar until 2006 at least.
●⊓ Bourgognes Faiveley, 8, rue du Tribourg,
21700 Nuits-Saint-Georges, tel. 03.80.61.04.55,
fax 03.80.62.33.37,
e-mail bourgognes.faiveley@wanadoo.fr ☑

DOM. TRAPET PERE ET FILS 2001★★

| ■ | Gd cru | 0,8 ha | n.c. | ⅠⅠⅠ | 46–76 € |

98 99 **00 01**

Coup de coeur and *Grappe d'or* in the 2003 edition, Jean-Louis Trapet offered a Latricières which has the stuff of a Grand Cru and figures among the fore-runners. This vineyard has been in the family exactly 100 years! Intense garnet-red in colour, well-integrated cask effect, strong fruitiness with liquorice notes, tannins there but harmonious, it is a very "Trapet" wine (made in the modern manner, but "Trapet" just the same), the result of rigorous organic farming methods. Restrained, it should keep its freshness for a long time.
●⊓ Dom. Trapet Père et Fils, 53, rte de Beaune,
21220 Gevrey-Chambertin, tel. 03.80.34.30.40,
fax 03.80.51.86.34, e-mail message@domaine-trapet.com ☑
⅄ by appt.

Chapelle-Chambertin

Wines selected but not starred

DOM. TRAPET PERE ET FILS 2001

| ■ | Gd cru | 0.6 ha | n.c. | ⅠⅠⅠ | 46–76 € |

91 |94| 95 96 **98** 99 00 01

●⊓ Dom. Trapet Père et Fils, 53, rte de Beaune,
21220 Gevrey-Chambertin, tel. 03.80.34.30.40,
fax 03.80.51.86.34, e-mail message@domaine-trapet.com ☑
⅄ by appt.

Charmes-Chambertin

DOM. ARLAUD 2001★

| | Gd cru | 1.2 ha | 4,500 | ⑪ | 30–38 € |

With 1.2 ha in Les Charmes, this 12.6 ha estate is totally at ease here. Deep ruby, purplish at the rim, the first impact of this 2001 is coffee, then, after aeration, liquorice, Morello cherry, damp woodlands, and blackberries evolve in the glass. The cask and the tannins take the stand next. This characteristic wine needs five to six years in the cellar to develop into a truly excellent product.
➥ SCEA Dom. Arlaud Père et Fils, 41, rue d'Epernay, 21220 Morey-Saint-Denis, tel. 03.80.34.32.65, fax 03.80.34.10.11, e-mail cyprien.arlaud@wanadoo.fr ☑
⊺ by appt.

DOM. DOMINIQUE GALLOIS 2001★

| | Gd cru | 0,3 ha | 1,600 | ⑪ | 38–46 € |

96 |97| 98 **99** 01

The family of Gaston Roupnel, the writer from Gevrey who did so much for its wines! It has contributed a great deal to local history and this Charmes-Chambertin also illustrates, in its own way, the bounty of the Côte. Dark crimson-red, this is a 2001 which doubles the stakes of the game. The aromas have not yet shaken off the influence of the cask but are not imprisoned by it. Substance, roundness and fleshiness; the body is full and flavoursome. For drinking in two or three years.
➥ Dom. Dominique Gallois, 9, rue du Mal-de-Lattre-de-Tassigny, 21220 Gevrey-Chambertin, tel. 03.80.34.11.99, fax 03.80.34.38.62, e-mail d.gallois@tiscali.fr ☑
⊺ by appt.

DOM. HUMBERT FRERES 2001★★

| | Gd cru | 0.2 ha | 1,050 | ⑪ | 46–76 € |

|96| 98 99 **01**

Frédéric and Emmanuel Humbert worked as a team to achieve a fine result. Their Charmes has a great deal of panache under its deep, intense garnet-red colour. With scents of mild tobacco and cocoa beans, the bouquet is out-of-the-ordinary. The tannins are still rough, but the nobility shines through their armour and such a wine is destined for a splendid future. A good reserve of fruit and strength, with nothing that detracts from its elegance.
➥ Dom. Humbert Frères, rue de Planteligone, 21220 Gevrey-Chambertin, tel. 03.80.51.80.14
⊺ by appt.

FREDERIC MAGNIEN 2001★★

| | Gd cru | 0,6 ha | 3,000 | ▮⑪⬇ | 38–46 € |

CHARMES-CHAMBERTIN

GRAND CRU

APPELLATION CHARMES-CHAMBERTIN CONTRÔLÉE

VIN NON FILTRÉ   **2004**   DÉCANTATION RECOMMANDÉE

Mis en bouteille par Frédéric Magnien à Morey-St-Denis F.21220

ALC. 13% BY VOL.   RED BURGUNDY WINE · PRODUCE OF FRANCE   750 ML

All the beauty of movement is in this firm and powerful elegance which could never flag. The *coup de coeur* was awarded to this wine, judged the best of all the Gevrey Grands Crus. An almost black, slightly purplish red, it is like the sun going down over the Combe de Lavaux. The nose needs to open, but blackberry jam is already bubbling in the cauldron. Quite soft at first, this wine soon reveals itself as rich, even opulent. A Charmes fully worth of its name and with a great future!

➥ Frédéric Magnien, 26, rte Nationale, 21220 Morey-Saint-Denis, tel. 03.80.58.54.20, fax 03.80.51.84.34, e-mail fredericmagnien.grandsvinsdebourgogne@ wanadoo.fr ☑
⊺ by appt.

DOM. MICHEL MAGNIEN ET FILS 2001★★

| | Gd cru | 0,3 ha | 1,500 | ▮⑪ | 38–46 € |

Pluck the cockerel! But not for another three or four years. This wine's opening seems a little rustic, its clogs firmly planted in the vineyard. More like a Mazoyères than a Charmes. But the prospects are far from morose! Its colour, due to strong extraction, is pure Technicolor. A fine, precise, black-cherry bouquet; the body dense, slightly woody, lingering and powerful. A very good impression overall.
➥ Dom. Michel Magnien et Fils, 4, rue Ribordot, 21220 Morey-Saint-Denis, tel. 03.80.51.82.98, fax 03.80.58.51.76 ☑
⊺ by appt.

DOM. HENRI PERROT-MINOT 2000★

| | Gd cru | 0.7 ha | 4,000 | ⑪ | 46–76 € |

Les Charmes and Mazoyères are both near to Morey and the wine-growers of this village often have vineyards there. This one, for example, which offers you the pleasure of a Grand Cru that is remarkably true-to-type. There are tannins, certainly, but they have been civilized and, after all, here in Chambertin we are not choirboys…Very strong red, a musky, cherry-stone bouquet. It will need aerating or decanting before serving in three to five years' time.
➥ Henri Perrot-Minot, 54, rte des Grands-Crus, 21220 Morey-Saint-Denis, tel. 03.80.34.32.51, fax 03.80.34.13.57
⊺ by appt.

DOM. HENRI RICHARD 2001★

| | Gd cru | n.c. | n.c. | ⑪ | 30–38 € |

Until 1938 this vineyard belonged to Gaston Roupnel (the author of *l'Histoire de la Campagne Française* and was acquired by this family more than half a century ago. The wine offered here is a true Grand Cru bearing the colours of its grape variety. Its bouquet of small red berries is quite intense on a background of oakwood. Fleshy and robust, distinguished, a genuine wine that doesn't need to show its indentity card as proof of its Gevrey roots.
➥ SCE Dom. Henri Richard, 75, rte de Beaune, 21220 Gevrey-Chambertin, tel. 03.80.34.35.81, fax 03.80.34.35.81, e-mail scehenririchard@aol.com ☑
⊺ ev. day 9am–6pm; cl. 15–31 Aug.

DOM. TAUPENOT-MERME 2000★★

| | Gd cru | n.c. | 7,300 | ⑪ | 46–76 € |

96 97 98 99 **00**

This wine was considered for the *coup de coeur*. Ready to drink now but it will keep for a while; long enough, in fact, for you to visit this estate, established in the 18th century, and ask Virginia and Romain, the young Taupenot-Mermes, whether the best thing to drink it with would be a game stew. Nice colour and a good aromatic intensity bringing out the humus and rose aromas (both classic Chambertin perfumes). Lively and vigorous, it begins on the palate with a satisfying note of Morello cherry, then follows with a flavoursome fleshiness. An attractive wine.
➥ Taupenot-Merme, 33, rte des Grands-Crus, 21220 Morey-Saint-Denis, tel. 03.80.34.35.24, fax 03.80.51.83.41, e-mail domaine.taupenot-merme@wanadoo.fr ☑
⊺ by appt.

DOM. TORTOCHOT 2001★

| | Gd cru | 0,57 ha | 2,200 | ⑪ | 30–38 € |

91 92 93 94 95 96 98 01

The colour of this wine is deeper than the famous well of Gevrey (27 m); brilliant, deep-ruby red. Charred notes followed by red berries; the aromatic path is a well-trodden one. Balanced, the

palate shows itself to be nicely-balanced with tannins that are already coated. Everything finishes on a spicy note. This wine will be ready to serve in two years' time with game.
☙ Dom. Tortochot, 12, rue de l'Eglise,
21220 Gevrey-Chambertin, tel. 03.80.34.30.68,
fax 03.80.34.18.80, e-mail chantam@aol.com ☑
✲ by appt.
☙ Chantal and Michel Tortochot

Wines selected but not starred

DOM. DES BEAUMONT 2001

■ Gd cru	0.5 ha	2,500	◖▮◗	38–46 €	

☙ EARL Dom. des Beaumont, 9, rue Ribordot,
21220 Morey-Saint-Denis, tel. 03.80.51.87.89,
fax 03.80.51.87.89,
e-mail thierry.beaumont1@libertysurf.fr ☑ ▣
✲ by appt.

ALBERT BICHOT 2000

■ Gd cru	n.c.	900	◖▮◗	38–46 €	

☙ Maison Albert Bichot, 6 bis, bd Jacques-Copeau,
21200 Beaune, tel. 03.80.24.37.37, fax 03.80.24.37.38

JEAN-CLAUDE BOISSET 2000

■ Gd cru	n.c.	900	◖▮◗	30–38 €	

☙ Jean-Claude Boisset, 5, quai Dumorey,
21700 Nuits-Saint-Georges, tel. 03.80.62.61.61,
fax 03.80.62.61.59, e-mail patriat.g@jcboisset.fr
✲ by appt.

DOM. DUPONT-TISSERANDOT 2001

■ Gd cru	0.8 ha	4,000	◖▮◗	38–46 €	

☙ Dupont-Tisserandot, 2, pl. des Marronniers,
21220 Gevrey-Chambertin, tel. 03.80.34.10.50,
fax 03.80.58.50.71 ☑
✲ ev. day 9am–12 noon 2pm–6pm; Sat. Sun. by appt.;
cl. 2–20 Aug. et 24 Dec.–3 Jan.

JEAN-PAUL MAGNIEN 2001

■ Gd cru	0.2 ha	1000	◖▮◗	30–38 €	

☙ Jean-Paul Magnien, 5, ruelle de l'Eglise,
21220 Morey-Saint-Denis, tel. 03.80.51.83.10,
fax 03.80.58.53.27, e-mail dommagnien@aol.com ☑
✲ by appt.

PIERRE NAIGEON 2001

■ Gd cru	n.c.	n.c.	◖▮◗	38–46 €	

☙ Pierre Naigeon, 4, rue du Chambertin,
21220 Gevrey-Chambertin, tel. 03.80.34.14.87,
fax 03.80.58.51.18, e-mail pierre.naigeon@wanadoo.fr ☑
✲ ev. day 10am–1pm 2pm–6pm; cl. Dec.–Mar.

DOM. DES VAROILLES 2000

■ Gd cru	0.75 ha	1,800	◖▮◗	30–38 €	

☙ Dom. des Varoilles, rue de l'Ancien-Hôpital,
21220 Gevrey-Chambertin, tel. 03.80.34.30.30,
fax 03.80.51.88.99, e-mail contact@domaine-varoilles.com
✲ by appt.

Griotte-Chambertin

DOM. MARCHAND FRERES 2001★

■ Gd cru	0,13 ha	750	◖▮◗	30–38 €

98 99 00 01

The origin of the word *griotte* has nothing to do with sour cherries, it is a deformation of the words *criot, crai*: stony ground. That said, this wine is a little jewel. It sometimes strives, as it does here, to live up to its name with flavours of Morello cherries and cherry jam. A nice colour and rather restrained palate, this wine is sustained more by its tannins than by its acidity, a characteristic often found in a Griotte-Chambertin. Give it time to finish its work (five years?).
☙ EARL Dom. Marchand Frères, 1, pl. du Monument,
21220 Gevrey-Chambertin, tel. 03.80.62.10.97,
fax 03.80.62.11.01, e-mail dmarc2000@aol.com ☑ ▣
✲ by appt.

Mazis-Chambertin

DOM. CHARLOPIN-PARIZOT 2000★

■ Gd cru	n.c.	n.c.	◖▮◗	46–76 €

|97| 99 00

If Napoleon had had the support of such a wine at Waterloo (he is known to have drunk this wine throughout his imperial life), no doubt things would have turned out differently! Soft and velvety, a refined and elegant Mazis 2000. Great presence and sensitivity, both on the eye and on the nose. Its charming, mouth-filling fruitiness is also very pleasing. Good, good, and good again. Leave it in the cellar for between three and five years.
☙ Dom. Philippe Charlopin, 18, rte de Dijon,
21220 Gevrey-Chambertin, tel. 03.80.51.81.18,
fax 03.80.51.81.27, e-mail charlopin.philippe@wanadoo.fr

DOM. DUPONT-TISSERANDOT 2001★

■ Gd cru	0.35 ha	1,600	◖▮◗	38–46 €

A colour extraction which could serve as an example at the *Lycée Viticole de Beaune*. Deep but sincere and capable, like Stendhal, of combining red with black. The end however is less dramatic than in the novel. Notes of spices and crystallized fruit are followed by fullness on the palate. Complexity, length, here we are in the Grand Cru Chambertin where Pinot Noir achieves its peak of excellence. It will need rich food to do it justice.
☙ Dupont-Tisserandot, 2, pl. des Marronniers,
21220 Gevrey-Chambertin, tel. 03.80.34.10.50,
fax 03.80.58.50.71 ☑
✲ ev. day 9am–12 noon 2pm–6pm; Sat. Sun. by appt.;
cl. 2–20 Aug. and 24 Dec.–3 Jan.

JEAN-MICHEL GUILLON 2001★★

■ Gd cru	0.17 ha	1,050	▮◖▮◗♦	30–38 €

If all the Mazis wines were like this one, the church-bells at Gevrey would never stop ringing. Selected for the final of the *coup de coeur*, this is a strong, well-balanced wine. It is not as long as the road to Curley, but it gives off perfumes of blackcurrant and blackberries that are very enticing: a beautifully aromatic palate ranging over cocoa and spices. Velvety on the palate, it nevertheless takes its work very seriously: structure and complexity are both in evidence. Open it in 2007, and see what it does for a roast of beef; other the sundiest dishes bring out the best in these Burgundy Grands Crus!
☙ Jean-Michel Guillon, 33, rte de Beaune,
21220 Gevrey-Chambertin, tel. 03.80.51.83.98,
fax 03.80.51.85.59, e-mail eurlguillon@aol.com ☑
✲ by appt.

DOM. HENRI REBOURSEAU 2000★

	Gd cru	0.96 ha	3,600		38–46 €

|97| 98 99 00

Black-cherry highlights. The tone then becomes aromatic as leather mixes with *pain d'épice* (ginger-bread). There is oakiness present but it is delicate and not overstated. This leather nose is typical of the Mazis wines, a cru first noted in history in 1420 and which looks the Clos de Bèze straight in the eye. This faithful representation of the terroir was indeed noted on the tasting cards. Suitably mouth-filling and fine length on the finish.
☛ NSE Dom. Henri Rebourseau, 10, pl. du Monument, 21220 Gevrey-Chambertin, tel. 03.80.51.88.94, fax 03.80.34.12.82, e-mail reboursea1@aol.com ☑
☗ by appt.

DOM. TORTOCHOT 2001★

	Gd cru	0.42 ha	2,100		30–38 €

Of a quite pronounced colour with mauve highlights, this is a rather vanilla-flavoured Mazis which brings red berries to the feast. Quite rounded right from the first impression, its length is acceptable and its balance just right. On the palate it is aromatic and complex, with dense but fine tannins and a frank, straightforward finish. A wine which will give great pleasure after a few years in bottle.
☛ Dom. Tortochot, 12, rue de l'Eglise, 21220 Gevrey-Chambertin, tel. 03.80.34.30.68, fax 03.80.34.18.80, e-mail chantam@aol.com ☑
☗ by appt.
☛ Chantal and Michel Tortochot

Mazoyères-Chambertin

Wines selected but not starred

DOM. HENRI PERROT-MINOT 2000

	Gd cru	0.7 ha	4,000		38–46 €

☛ Henri Perrot-Minot, 54, rte des Grands-Crus, 21220 Morey-Saint-Denis, tel. 03.80.34.32.51, fax 03.80.34.13.57
☗ by appt.

Ruchottes-Chambertin

DOM. ARMAND ROUSSEAU

Clos des Ruchottes Monopole 2001★

	Gd cru	1,06 ha	4,800		46–76 €

A monopoly of this estate, the walls of the Clos des Ruchottes, bought in 1977 from the heirs of Thomas-Bassot, enclose a good hectare of vineyard, which is quite unusual in Burgundy. The colour of this wine is in keeping with the vintage, lively and fresh. The bouquet is initially closed before opting for blackcurrant, blackberries and other small black fruit. The tannins are of course very dense, coming after an honest opening; the concentration is attractive. Time and patience could be the watchword of every Grand Cru: don't serve it until five years have elapsed.
☛ Dom. Armand Rousseau, 1, rue de l'Aumônerie, 21220 Gevrey-Chambertin, tel. 03.80.34.30.55, fax 03.80.58.50.25, e-mail contact@domaine-rousseau.com
☛ Ch. Rousseau

Wines selected but not starred

DOM. DU CHATEAU DE MARSANNAY 2000

	Gd cru	0.1 ha	521		46–76 €

☛ Dom. du Ch. de Marsannay, rte des Grands-Crus, BP 78, 21160 Marsannay-la-Côte, tel. 03.80.51.71.11, fax 03.80.51.71.12, e-mail chateau.Marsannay@kriter.com ☑
☗ ev. day 10am–12 noon 2pm–6.30pm; groups by appt.; cl. Sun. from Nov. to Mar.

Morey Saint-Denis

Covering a little more than 100 ha, of which 93.73 was used in 2002, Morey-Saint-Denis is one of the smallest appellations communales in the Côte de Nuits. You can find some excellent Premier Crus and five Grands Crus which qualify for the Appellation d'Origine Contrôlée: Clos de Tart, Clos Saint-Denis, Bonnes-Mares (only a part), Clos de la Roche and Clos des Lambrays.

The appellation, which produced 4,016 hl of red wine and 206 of white in 2002, is squeezed between Gevrey and Chambolle and could be said to be halfway between the strength of the first and the finesse of the second. On the Friday before the sale at the Hospices de Nuits (which takes place in the third week in March) the winemakers put Morey Saint-Denis, and only this wine, on sale to the public at the festival of the "Carrefour de Dionysos," held in the village hall.

DOM. ARLAUD

Aux Cheseaux 2001★★

	1er cru	0.71 ha	4,000		30–38 €

The **Village 2001 (23–30 €)** was very much appreciated and was awarded one star. This Premier Cru Cheseaux is quite similar to the Mazoyères or the Charmes-Chambertin. It is a wine with heart to spare: an almost black colour with a garnet border, the bouquet is still reluctant to deal its cards, but it is deep and will eventually reveal itself. With weight and a mouth-filling quality, vinosity and a good tannic load, this is a wine in which the Pinot flavours are enhanced by an elegant oakiness. Have faith in the influence of time: lay it down for five to ten years and don't give in to temptation.
☛ SCEA Dom. Arlaud Père et Fils, 41, rue d'Epernay, 21220 Morey-Saint-Denis, tel. 03.80.34.32.65, fax 03.80.34.10.11, e-mail cyprien.arlaud@wanadoo.fr ☑
☗ by appt.

REGIS BOUVIER

En la Rue de Vergy 2001★

		0.53 ha	3,000		15–23 €

Deep, limpid black-cherry with a certain fluidity, this Rue de Vergy starts with grilled, fruity aromas, delicate and nicely combined. Supple and long, the wine slides over the palate on a little note of spice which is not unpleasant. To drink now, with a fine cheese, if possible, one bathed with Marc de Bourgogne.
☛ Régis Bouvier, 52, rue de Mazy, 21160 Marsannay-la-Côte, tel. 03.80.51.33.93, fax 03.80.58.75.07 ☑
☗ by appt.

BURGUNDY

JOSEPH DROUHIN

Clos Sorbé 2000★

■ 1er cru	n.c.	n.c.	◫	23–30 €

Did you know that Gaspard Monge, now buried in the Pantheon, had a vineyard in this *climat* when, towards the end of his life, he settled at Morey (there is not even a commemorative plaque on his house)? This wine is a Clos Sorbé with a clean, lively colour and an quite open bouquet that is still influenced by the cask. It does, however, have an aroma of Pinot which does not play a part. On the palate, the impression is quite weighty and vinous. Integrated tannins and a quite long finish are not the least among its trump cards.
☛ Maison Joseph Drouhin, 7, rue d'Enfer, 21200 Beaune, tel. 03.80.24.68.88, fax 03.80.22.43.14, e-mail maisondrouhin@drouhin.com
Ⅼ by appt.

DUFOULEUR PERE ET FILS

Monts-Luisants 2000★

■ 1er cru	n.c.	3,100	◫	23–30 €

A pleasing ruby-crimson colour, this wine is most appealing. Based on blackcurrant, spices and slight caramelization, the bouquet is going the right way. Seductive from the start and never wavering, this is a most pleasing wine that will be ready to drink in 2004. The Company Chairman is the mayor of Nuits-Saint-Georges, but Morey is not in his district…
☛ Dufouleur Père et Fils, 17, rue Thurot, 21700 Nuits-Saint-Georges, tel. 03.80.61.21.21, fax 03.80.61.10.65, e-mail dufouleur@dufouleur.com ⊻
Ⅼ ev. day 9am–7pm

DOM. DUJAC 2000★

■	2,92 ha	15,000	◫	15–23 €

The inhabitants of Morey are not known as the wolves for no reason! Just taste this wine with its spicy, musky, liquorice notes – pure local colour. At base it is red berries and damp woodlands with hints of vanilla. A quite light, bright colour. Why is the estate called Domaine Dujac? When Jacques Seysses established himself at Morey, in 1968, he felt the name Seysses was not very suitable so, since the whole village referred to it as "Le domaine du Jacques," he called it just that – Domaine Dujac!
☛ Dom. Dujac, 7, rue de la Bussière, 21220 Morey-Saint-Denis, tel. 03.80.34.01.00, fax 03.80.34.01.09, e-mail dujac@dujac.com ⊻
Ⅼ by appt.
☛ Seysses

DOM. FOREY PERE ET FILS 2000★★

■	1.19 ha	6,000	◫	15–23 €

This family of tenant-farmers at La Romanée du Chanoine Liger-Belair knows how to make wine, as is shown by this beautiful, deep ruby-red Morey with its magnificent perfumes of cherry-stones and pepper. A robust and for the moment astringent wine to lay down. Plenty of structure and concentration, this wine will be perfect by 2010…and don't say you can't wait that long.
☛ Dom. Forey Père et Fils, 2, rue Derrière-le-Four, 21700 Vosne-Romanée, tel. 03.80.61.09.68, fax 03.80.61.12.63 ⊻
Ⅼ by appt.

JEAN-MICHEL GUILLON

La Riotte 2001★

■ 1er cru	0,19 ha	1,400	◫	15–23 €

Like Aznavour, this wine sings "Je m'voyais déjà" (I've been here before). One Juror judged it a candidate for the *coup de coeur*. Under its brilliant, sombre homogeneous garnet-red colour (strong colour extraction), it develops pure fruit aromas (black- cherry, blackcurrant) which one finds again on the palate where the structure foreshadows good keeping potential. An opulent style and already excellent; but it I were you I'd keep it for two or three years, perhaps even longer.
☛ Jean-Michel Guillon, 33, rte de Beaune, 21220 Gevrey-Chambertin, tel. 03.80.51.83.98, fax 03.80.51.85.59, e-mail eurlguillon@aol.com ⊻
Ⅼ by appt.

DOM. HERESZTYN

Les Millandes 2001★

■ 1er cru	0.37 ha	1,800	◫	30–38 €

This Les Millandes still carries the *coup de coeur* it was awarded in the 1996 edition in its buttonhole. The colour beautiful, garnet-red velvet, with good aromas of blackberries and vanilla, the body is coated with fruits. The outline is positive, fine and precise. The tannins have an integrated feel that creates a sense of balance with the alcohol. The vinosity and the Pinot Noir are quite evident
☛ Dom. Heresztyn, 27, rue Richebourg, 21220 Gevrey-Chambertin, tel. 03.80.34.30.86, fax 03.80.34.13.99, e-mail domaine.heresztyn@wanadoo.fr ⊻
Ⅼ by appt.

DOM. DES LAMBRAYS

Les Loups 2000★

■ 1er cru	1 ha	6,300	◫	30–38 €

Of good intensity and an incipient crimson colour, this 2000 vintage, where the woodiness rubs shoulders with blackcurrant and red berries, holds a number of trump cards. The fruit is there. Elegance is written all over the quite integrated tannins, carefully brought out by the Cellar Master, Thierry Brouin.
☛ Dom. des Lambrays, 31, rue Basse, 21220 Morey-Saint-Denis, tel. 03.80.51.84.33, fax 03.80.51.81.97 ⊻
Ⅼ by appt.
☛ Freund

LEYMARIE 2000★

■	0,4 ha	1,300	◫	15–23 €

More structured than rounded, this Morey corresponds closely to the general idea one has of the appellation. There is nothing more to say about its colour. The ripe fruitiness, jammy, takes over the bouquet after its peppery opening. Richness on the palate: there is body and a good base, which is unsurprising and calls for a solid meatiness. This wine is neither soprano nor baritone, but a tenor.
☛ Dom. Leymarie-CECI, Clos du Village, 24, rue du Vieux-Château, 21640 Vougeot, tel. 03.80.62.86.06, fax 03.80.62.88.53, e-mail leymarie@skynet.be ⊻
Ⅼ by appt.

LIGNIER-MICHELOT

En la Rue de Vergy 2001★

■	1,9 ha	5,000	▮◫⬗	15–23 €

This estate went over completely to direct selling in 1999. In the Rue de Vergy (*climat* located above the Clos-de-Tart) this is justified in some way because a wine as balanced as this one easily makes a name for itself and finds customers. The purplish colour indicates a dense texture. A slight grilled note accompanies very ripe cherry. The initial impression is supple, fruity, and the somewhat unctuous mouth produces an advantageous length and pleasant fruit sensation on the middle palate. Drink it with a soft-paste cheese (a Cîteaux).
☛ Dom. Lignier-Michelot, 11, rue Haute, 21220 Morey-Saint-Denis, tel. 03.80.34.31.13, fax 03.80.58.52.16 ⊻
Ⅼ by appt.

FREDERIC MAGNIEN

Les Ruchots 2001★★

■ 1er cru	0,28 ha	1,700	▮◫⬗	23–30 €

This *climat* is situated just below the Clos-de-Tart and les Bonnes-Mares, on the other side of the Route des Grands Crus. The Jury unanimously awarded the *coup de coeur* to this wine which is absolutely worthy of a Premier Cru, with its satiny, intense garnet-red colour and very young highlights. The cask combines well but delicately with the fruit. As for the rich, nicely-balanced body, it is charmingly rounded. Robust, with a tannic support, it is right within the parameters of the appellation.

☙ Frédéric Magnien, 26, rte Nationale,
21220 Morey-Saint-Denis, tel. 03.80.58.54.20,
fax 03.80.51.84.34,
e-mail fredericmagnien.grandsvinsdebourgogne@
wanadoo.fr ☑
☖ by appt.

JEAN-PAUL MAGNIEN

Les Faconnières 2000★

■	1er cru	0.57 ha	3,000	🍾 🍷	15–23 €

The fourth generation has arrived! Stéphane has created an Internet site for the estate but he does also know what a vine is. His sister, Christine, has just published a passionate book about a century of wine-growing in Gevrey-Chambertin. Of good, dark-red colour, this fragrant wine (blackberries, black-cherry) is pulpy and well balanced, with fairly good length. More spirit and complexity required? Patience! Drink in two or three years with venison.

☙ Jean-Paul Magnien, 5, ruelle de l'Eglise,
21220 Morey-Saint-Denis, tel. 03.80.51.83.10,
fax 03.80.58.53.27, e-mail dommagnien@aol.com ☑
☖ by appt.

DOM. MICHEL MAGNIEN ET FILS

Le Très Girard 2001★★

■		0.6 ha	3,000	🍾 🍷	15–23 €

The **Premier Cru Les Chaffots 2001 (23–30 €)** is not bad at all and received a special mention. On the next floor up, though it is a *village*, is this Très Girard, a *climat* well known because of a famous restaurant of the same name. Filled with colour, its welcoming bouquet is of cherry and redcurrant. Its fine opening is supported by a good acidity and greedy tannins. Concentrated but balanced, it allows the cask to have its say. Its length is appreciable and laden with spices. Not very fruity but on an excellent level.

☙ Dom. Michel Magnien et Fils, 4, rue Ribordot,
21220 Morey-Saint-Denis, tel. 03.80.51.82.98,
fax 03.80.58.51.76 ☑
☖ by appt.

DOM. DES MONTS LUISANTS 2000★

■		1.06 ha	3,290	🍾 🍷 ♦	23–30 €

This 2000 vintage is the first vinification by Jean-Marc Dufouleur, son of Bernard Dufouleur, since he took on the tenancy. An assertive ruby-garnet-red, this wine has an acidity which will ensure it keeps well. There is nothing aggressive about it. The elegant bouquet swings between oakiness and damp woodlands. A rounded and balanced prospect in two to five years' time.

☙ Dom. des Monts Luisants, 51, rue du
Faubourg-Madeleine, 21200 Beaune, tel. 03.80.24.00.96,
fax 03.80.22.78.87,
e-mail jeanmarc.dufouleur@club-internet.fr ☑
☖ by appt.

DOM. PALISSES-BEAUMONT 2001★

■		n.c.	285	🍷	15–23 €

On a mini-property (1.5 ha) inherited from his father, George Beaumont, Thierry Beaumont vinified this very dark *village*. Well built, clean and precise, this 2001 doesn't spin you a yarn but is content to play on its elegance. Damp woodlands and toast, presence and firmness: not a wine to let itself be forgotten. Needs laying down for three to four years. If you want to stay a while in the area, the estate has four guestrooms.

☙ Dom. Palisses-Beaumont, 17 b, rue Haute,
21220 Morey-Saint-Denis, tel. 03.80.58.51.83,
fax 03.80.58.56.48, e-mail stnicolas21@aol.com ☑ 🏠
☖ by appt.

Wines selected but not starred

DOM. DES BEAUMONT 2001

■	1er cru	0.35 ha	2,000	🍷	23–30 €

☙ EARL Dom. des Beaumont, 9, rue Ribordot,
21220 Morey-Saint-Denis, tel. 03.80.51.87.89,
fax 03.80.51.87.89,
e-mail thierry.beaumont1@libertysurf.fr ☑ 🏠
☖ by appt.

DOM. ALAIN JEANNIARD 2001

■		0.33 ha	2,000	🍾 🍷	11–15 €

☙ Dom. Alain Jeanniard, 4, rue aux Loups,
21220 Morey-Saint-Denis, tel. 06.11.85.74.93,
fax 03.80.58.53.49,
e-mail domaine.ajeanniard@wanadoo.fr ☑
☖ by appt.

MOILLARD 2000

■		n.c.	10,000	🍷	15–23 €

☙ Moillard, 2, rue François-Mignotte,
21700 Nuits-Saint-Georges, tel. 03.80.62.42.22,
fax 03.80.61.28.13, e-mail nuicave@wanadoo.fr ☑
☖ ev. day 10am–6pm; cl. Jan.

MORIN PERE ET FILS 2000

■		n.c.	350		15–23 €

☙ Morin Père et Fils, 9, quai Fleury,
21700 Nuits-Saint-Georges, tel. 03.80.61.19.51,
fax 03.80.61.05.10, e-mail caves@morinpere-fils.com ☑
☖ ev. day 9am–12 noon 2pm–6pm; summer 9am–7pm

DOM. HENRI PERROT-MINOT

La Riotte Vieilles Vignes 2000

■	1er cru	0.57 ha	3,000	🍷	38–46 €

☙ Henri Perrot-Minot, 54, rte des Grands-Crus,
21220 Morey-Saint-Denis, tel. 03.80.34.32.51,
fax 03.80.34.13.57
☖ by appt.

REMI SEGUIN 2000

■		0.51 ha	n.c.	🍷	11–15 €

☙ Rémi Seguin, 19, rue de Cîteaux,
21640 Gilly-lès-Cîteaux, tel. 03.80.62.89.61,
fax 03.80.62.80.92 ☑
☖ by appt.

DOM. J. ET M. SIMON 2000

■		1.09 ha	1000	🍷	11–15 €

☙ Dom. J. et M. Simon, 6, Grande-Rue,
21220 Morey-Saint-Denis, tel. 03.80.34.33.59,
fax 03.80.34.19.27, e-mail domainesimon@tiscali.fr ☑
☖ by appt.

CLOS DE LA ROCHE, DE TART, SAINT-DENIS, DES LAMBRAYS

The Clos de la Roche – which despite its name is not a walled vineyard – covers the biggest surface area (about 16 ha), and includes various *lieux-dits* or named locations; it produced 643 hl in 2002. Clos Saint-Denis, about 6.5 ha, is also unwalled, and it too incorporates a group of *lieux-dits* (233 hl). These two Crus are parcelled into small plots and cultivated by numerous growers. The Clos de Tart is entirely enclosed by stone walls and cultivated by one grower. It is just over 7 ha and the wines are vinified and matured on the property; the cellar on two levels is well worth a visit. The Clos des Lambrays has one main grower, but it is a group of several plots and *lieux-dits*: Les Bouchots, Les Larrêts or Clos de Lambrays and Le Meix-Rentier. It covers just under 9 ha, 8.5 of which are cultivated by the same grower. It produced almost 311.89 hl in 2002.

on black crown, the bouquet is still forming (bigaroon cherry, well-constructed oakiness) and a very fruity richness comes to the fore on the almost perfect palate. All quite unctuous and certainly a wine to lay down for several years.
☛ Dom. Michel Magnien et Fils, 4, rue Ribordot, 21220 Morey-Saint-Denis, tel. 03.80.51.82.98, fax 03.80.58.51.76 ☑
☚ by appt.

Wines selected but not starred

Clos de la Roche

DOM. PIERRE AMIOT ET FILS 2001★

| ■ | Gd cru | 1,2 ha | 3,000 | ⦿ | | 30–38 € |

The great courtesy shown by the Amiot family gives the lie to the village coat of arms which depicts…wolves. Their wine is distinguished, with its bluish highlights. Vanilla at first on the nose, the bouquet then adopts a Morello cherry tone. Young and dense, fruity and long, this impression of amiability is confirmed on the palate. You must, however, resign yourself to leaving this wine in the cellar for three or four years. This wine merits it.
☛ Dom. Pierre Amiot et Fils, 27, Grande-Rue, 21220 Morey-Saint-Denis, tel. 03.80.34.34.28, fax 03.80.58.51.17 ☑
☚ by appt.

DOM. ARLAUD 2001★

| ■ | Gd cru | 0.43 ha | 2,200 | ⦿ | | 30–38 € |

Ruby-red with bluish highlights, this wine is beautifully tailored. The nose remains subtle even when agitated in the glass. A little later, one finds the two usual characteristics: Morello cherry and vanilla. The attack evokes a war between lace-clad warriors: fought with hats rather than muskets. The whole is robust and well worth re-discovering in five years' time. By the same reckoning, the estate has modified its label. Its wine merits it.
☛ SCEA Dom. Arlaud Père et Fils, 41, rue d'Epernay, 21220 Morey-Saint-Denis, tel. 03.80.34.32.65, fax 03.80.34.10.11, e-mail cyprien.arlaud@wanadoo.fr ☑
☚ by appt.

DOM. DUJAC 2000★

| ■ | Gd cru | 1.95 ha | 9,000 | ⦿ | | 46–76 € |

Almost 2 ha for this Grand Cru and a *coup de cœur* a few years ago. The colour of this 2000 vintage is deep, very limpid ruby-red with a bright rim. Its bouquet takes its cue from Morello cherries and has not yet said its last word. On the palate it is rich and full, giving the impression of crunching a crisp fruit. A very nice wine, despite the difficulties of the vintage. For drinking in two or three years' time. *Success story* of the Côte de Nuits, the Dujac estate has lost none of its energy.
☛ Dom. Dujac, 7, rue de la Bussière, 21220 Morey-Saint-Denis, tel. 03.80.34.01.00, fax 03.80.34.01.09, e-mail dujac@dujac.com ☑
☚ by appt.
☛ Seysses

DOM. MICHEL MAGNIEN ET FILS 2001★★

| ■ | Gd cru | 0.4 ha | n.c. | ⦿⦿ | | 38–46 € |

Coup de cœur in the 2003 *Guide* for its 2000 vintage, *coup de cœur* this year in Clos Saint-Denis, this estate is on a roll. The Clos de la Roche, with its strong extraction, attempts, however, to maintain the elegance of the Pinot. Deep ruby-red

DOM. MARCHAND FRERES 2001

| ■ | Gd cru | 0.07 ha | 300 | ⦿ | | 30–38 € |

☛ EARL Dom. Marchand Frères, 1, pl. du Monument, 21220 Gevrey-Chambertin, tel. 03.80.62.10.97, fax 03.80.62.11.01, e-mail dmarc2000@aol.com ☑ ⛬
☚ by appt.

DOM. LOUIS REMY 2000

| ■ | Gd cru | 0.7 ha | n.c. | ⦿⦿ | | 46–76 € |

☛ Dom. Louis Remy, 1, pl. du Monument, 21220 Morey-Saint-Denis, tel. 03.80.34.32.59, fax 03.80.34.32.59, e-mail domaine.louis.remy@wanadoo.fr ☑
☚ by appt.

Clos Saint-Denis

DOM. PIERRE AMIOT ET FILS 2001★

| ■ | Gd cru | 0.17 ha | 900 | ⦿ | | 30–38 € |

Intense ruby-red with purplish highlights, this wine is produced on a scant four *ouvrées* (about one seventh of a hectare; *ouvrée* is an old Burgundian measurement of area). A little jewel, for its fresh colour. A fine, fairly severe 2001, but beautifully matured in a classic way. The bouquet swings between the peony and a mild spiciness from the cask. Its structure is warm, consistent, right to the chewy finish that is typical of Morey. This tannicity is marked but coated. You feel as if your are drinking the earth, if not eating it, in the Cistercian sense. "Clay," in quotes. Strict, right and, in a word, genuine.
☛ Dom. Pierre Amiot et Fils, 27, Grande-Rue, 21220 Morey-Saint-Denis, tel. 03.80.34.34.28, fax 03.80.58.51.17 ☑
☚ by appt.

DOM. HERESZTYN 2001★★

| ■ | Gd cru | 0.23 ha | n.c. | ⦿ | | 46–76 € |

Its colour could appear in *People*, the journal with the princely columns. Purity, softness, finesse all form part of the bouquet, which grabs your attention with bilberry then flies off at a tangent towards *pain d'épice* (spiced loaf) and liquorice. Purity again on the palate, which one could describe as crystalline, so concentrated is it on the essence while still attending to the detail. *Coup de cœur* for its 97 vintage, this Gevrey estate's Clos Saint-Denis is always successful. The finish evolves around firm but matured tannins. A wine that should be left in peace until around 2010.
☛ Dom. Heresztyn, 27, rue Richebourg, 21220 Gevrey-Chambertin, tel. 03.80.34.30.86, fax 03.80.34.13.99, e-mail domaine.heresztyn@wanadoo.fr ☑
☚ by appt.

DOM. MICHEL MAGNIEN ET FILS

2001★★★

■ Gd cru	n.c.	600	▮◫	46–76 €

The *coup de coeur* acclaimed best of the Morey Grands Crus tasted this year. It aims high and far into the future. With great class, exceptional class! To its deep, intense colour and its smoky bouquet of black-cherry, moving on to tobacco notes, add a rich and satisfying, velvety palate of disconcerting subtlety. This Clos Saint-Denis is really the Mozart of the Côte de Nuits under the baton of a great conductor. A single word sums it up: admirable.

☛ Dom. Michel Magnien et Fils, 4, rue Ribordot,
21220 Morey-Saint-Denis, tel. 03.80.51.82.98,
fax 03.80.58.51.76 ☑
⚲ by appt.

Clos des Lambrays

DOM. DES LAMBRAYS 2000★

■ Gd cru	8.66 ha	32,000	◫	46–76 €

79 81 **82** 83 **85** 88 **89** |90| 92 |93| 94 |95| |96| |97| **98 99** 00

Acquired a few years ago by the Freund family and remaining under the management of Thierry Brouin, the Clos des Lambrays (a quasi-monopoly) offered in this vintage a cherry-red in colour. Its bouquet gives preference first to vanilla, cinnamon, then cloves. This series of spices is repeated on the palate. The very harmonious tannins are soft right to the finish, when cherry and blackcurrant put in an appearance. It is not tremendously structured but its delicacy is seductive. Leave it for two or three years before opening.

☛ Dom. des Lambrays, 31, rue Basse,
21220 Morey-Saint-Denis, tel. 03.80.51.84.33,
fax 03.80.51.81.97 ☑
⚲ by appt.
☛ Freund

Chambolle Musigny

The Musigny name alone sets the pitch in the orchestral sweep of wines in this region. This is a commune of enormous reputation despite its tiny area, founded on the quality of its wines and the fame of its Premiers Crus, the most celebrated of which is the *climat* of Les Amoureuses. But Chambolle also has Charmes, Chabiots, Cras, Fousselottes, Groseilles and Lavrottes as well. The small village, with its narrow streets shaded by trees, has magnificent cellars (Domaine des Musigny). In 2002, the vineyard produced 6,637 hl, of which 2,432 were Premier Cru.

The Chambolle wines are elegant, subtle and soft, combining the strength of Bonne-Mares and the finesse of Musigny; within the Côte de Nuits this area represents a transition from one type of terroir to another.

DOM. AMIOT-SERVELLE

Les Charmes 2000★

■ 1er cru	1.2 ha	5,700	◫	23–30 €

The rules of engagement applied here are sensible. This Premier Cru was matured for 16 months in cask. Its deep purple colour is intense and young. The bouquet begins on musky notes, nuances of blackcurrant and black-cherry, with a touch of liquorice. The style is substantial, the oakiness high quality. Several of our Jurors said it would achieve beautiful balance in the future.

☛ Dom. Amiot-Servelle, rue du Lavoir,
21220 Chambolle-Musigny, tel. 03.80.62.80.39,
fax 03.80.62.84.16, e-mail domaine@amiot-servelle.com ☑
⚲ by appt.

JEAN-CLAUDE BOISSET

Les Charmes 2000★

■ 1er cru	n.c.	600	◫	15–23 €

This Les Charmes has…a great many charms: the brilliance of its beautiful, purplish-red colour; the black-cherry bouquet full of finesse and complexity; its excellent structure. The slight nuance of charring, particularly on the palate, is pleasant. This is a Chambolle that is robust rather than rounded and needs to stay in the cellar a year or two longer.

☛ Jean-Claude Boisset, 5, quai Dumorey,
21700 Nuits-Saint-Georges, tel. 03.80.62.61.61,
fax 03.80.62.61.59, e-mail patriat.g@jcboisset.fr
⚲ by appt.

SYLVAIN CATHIARD

Les Clos de l'Orme 2001★★

■	0.43 ha	2,500	◫	23–30 €

Generally well graded, this Vosne wine-grower took the *coup de coeur* in the 2000 *Guide* for the 97 vintage of this same Clos de l'Orme. Intense, brilliant colour; aromas centred on some profound convictions – strawberry or raspberry if one is obliged to specify the content. Fine, already-integrated attack, linked on the continuation with the characteristics of the terroir. With its delicate tannins, this is a very well-made, elegant wine, already pleasant but well able to last another ten years.

☛ Sylvain Cathiard, 20, rue de la Goillotte,
21700 Vosne-Romanée, tel. 03.80.62.36.01,
fax 03.80.61.18.21 ☑
⚲ by appt.

GUY COQUARD 2001★

■ 1er cru	0.5 ha	3,000	◫	23–30 €

While this wine is still enveloped by the cask, it will evolve, and it has all the ingredients for success. Limpid ruby-red, the bouquet evokes fruits in *eau-de-vie* against a grilled, toasty background. The delicacy of its tannins give it a perfect, classic Chambolle character: "Of silk and lace," as Gaston Roupnel put it. A charming wine that would be perfect with a leg of lamb.

☛ Guy Coquard, 55, rte des Grands-Crus,
21220 Morey-Saint-Denis, tel. 03.80.34.38.88,
fax 03.80.58.51.66 ☑

DOM. DIGIOIA-ROYER 2001★★

■	1.3 ha	7,000	◫	11–15 €

Estate created in 1930 by Mr. Moretti, taken over in 1982 by his daughter and managed since 1999 by that lady's son-in-law. This *village* is a beautiful colour and opens a little at a time on light aromas. On the palate, it seems quite floral and the finish is elegant on soft, spicy notes. The increase in

Côte de Nuits (Centre).

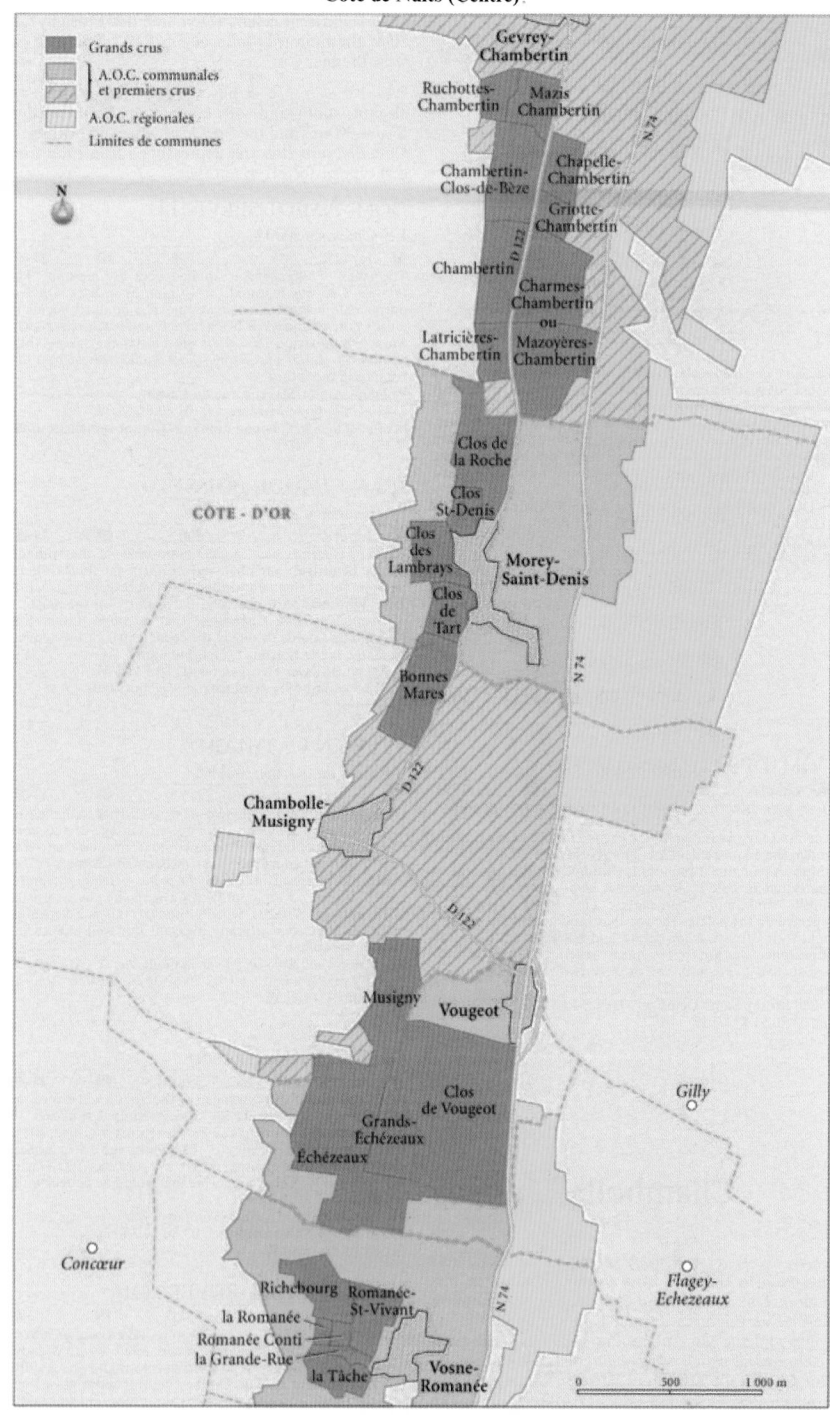

Grands crus

A.O.C. communales
et premiers crus

A.O.C. régionales

Limites de communes

N

Gevrey-
Chambertin

Ruchottes-
Chambertin

Mazis
Chambertin

Chapelle-
Chambertin

Chambertin-
Clos-de-Bèze

Griotte-
Chambertin

Chambertin

Charmes-
Chambertin
ou
Mazoyères-
Chambertin

Latricières-
Chambertin

Clos de
la Roche

Clos
St-Denis

CÔTE - D'OR

Clos
des
Lambrays

Morey-
Saint-Denis

Clos
de
Tart

Bonnes
Mares

Chambolle-
Musigny

Musigny

Vougeot

Gilly

Clos
de Vougeot

Grands-
Échézeaux

Échézeaux

Concœur

Richebourg

Romanée-
St-Vivant

Flagey-
Echezeaux

la Romanée

Romanée Conti
la Grande-Rue

la Tâche

Vosne-
Romanée

0   500   1 000 m

strength is regular and completely smooth. It could be served now, perhaps with guineafowl or pheasant, but it will certainly continue ageing for five to eight years.
☛ Dom. Digioia-Royer, rue du Carré, 21220 Chambolle-Musigny, tel. 03.80.61.49.58, fax 03.80.61.49.58 ☑
☖ by appt.

JOSEPH DROUHIN
Amoureuses 2000★

	1er cru	0.41 ha	n.c.	⑪	46–76 €

A Les Amoureuses of an attractive, deep garnet-red colour with perfumes of blackcurrant and violets on an elegant oakiness: Grasse could not do better. Pleasant and full of charm, very well balanced, this wine is a worthy Chambolle. The finesse of its tannins and its length will make it ready to drink in 2004.
☛ Maison Joseph Drouhin, 7, rue d'Enfer, 21200 Beaune, tel. 03.80.24.68.88, fax 03.80.22.43.14, e-mail maisondrouhin@drouhin.com
☖ by appt.

DUFOULEUR PERE ET FILS 2000★

		n.c.	2,700	⑪	23–30 €

A ruby-red of medium intensity, this is a Chambolle from the 2000 vintage that is well within its rank. Toasty notes surround a fruitiness that is beginning to come through. The opening is rather firm, and satisfactorily mouth-filling. The structure is flawless. Acidity and alcohol are admirably balanced. For drinking in the future, but don't wait more than two years.
☛ Dufouleur Père et Fils, 17, rue Thurot, 21700 Nuits-Saint-Georges, tel. 03.80.61.21.21, fax 03.80.61.10.65, e-mail dufouleur@dufouleur.com ☑
☖ ev. day 9am–7pm

FAIVELEY
Les Fuées 2000★

	1er cru	0.19 ha	1,200	⑪	46–76 €

A pillar of the *Confrérie des Chevaliers du Tastevin* (the Brotherhood of Knights of the Tastevin) which was founded by his grandfather, François Faiveley presented an excellent Chambolle. Limpid and brilliant, this 2000 is particularly aromatic (fruit and toast). The first impression is soft, the tannins dense, the substance consistent; this is a wine that must remain in the cellar for some time. Did you know that this Premier Cru adjoins Les Bonnes-Mares?
☛ Bourgognes Faiveley, 8, rue du Tribourg, 21700 Nuits-Saint-Georges, tel. 03.80.61.04.55, fax 03.80.62.33.37, e-mail bourgognes.faiveley@wanadoo.fr ☑

HENRI FELETTIG
Les Carrières 2001★

	1er cru	0.38 ha	2,300	⑪	15–23 €

Established in 1969, this estate is run by its creator and his two children, Christine and Gilbert. It represented this *climat* which is not, as its name implies, situated on the high ground of Chambolle, near the Roche de Grognot, but in the middle of the surrounding area. We are not dealing here with a powerful or very demonstrative wine, but it has a fruity finesse (strawberry) that passes pleasantly from nose to palate.
☛ GAEC Henri Felettig, rue du Tilleul, 21220 Chambolle-Musigny, tel. 03.80.62.85.09, fax 03.80.62.86.41 ☑
☖ by appt.

DOM. ANNE-MARIE GILLE 2000★

	1er cru	0.31 ha	1,500	⑪	23–30 €

We have here a taste from the past and a faithful memory, the more so because this is one of oldest winemaking families of the Côte de Nuits, with a domaine that goes back to 1570. Beneath its black cherry colour, the 2000 vintage has a bouquet that divides itself between red berries and roasted coffee. On the palate, it is *moelleux*, velvety and smooth. A true Chambolle.
☛ Dom. Anne-Marie Gille, 34, RN 74, 21700 Comblanchien, tel. 03.80.62.94.13,

fax 03.80.62.99.88, e-mail domaine.gille@wanadoo.fr ☑
☖ by appt.

DOM. ROBERT GROFFIER PERE ET FILS Les Sentiers 2001★★

	1er cru	1.07 ha	5,100	⑪	30–38 €

Awarded a *Coup de coeur* in previous editions, this estate again impressed the Jury. With its very deep colour, this 2001 offers a bouquet where controlled woodiness accompanies fruit. Quite well structured but without any aggressive astringency, it is very pleasant from start to finish. Already remarkable and capable of improving even further.
☛ Dom. Robert et Serge Groffier, 3–5, rte des Grands-Crus, 21220 Morey-Saint-Denis, tel. 03.80.34.31.53, fax 03.80.34.15.48 ☑
☖ by appt.

DOM. A.-F. GROS 2001★

		0.39 ha	2,400	⑪	15–23 €

The pretty girl pictured on the label is an original work by a true artist, reminding us that this wine is the work of a woman, Anne-Francoise Parent, née Gros. This is her Chambolle, fleshy and distinguished beneath its lively, brilliant appearance. We were delighted by the bouquet of slightly spiced ripe fruit, the fine way it is expressed on the palate and the lingering finish, prolonging the nose by rich, spiced, slightly chocolatey notes. It will need to be laid down for a few years to open out fully.
☛ Dom. A.-F. Gros, La Garelle, Grande-Rue, 21630 Pommard, tel. 03.80.22.61.85, fax 03.80.24.03.16, e-mail af-gros@wanadoo.fr ☑
☖ by appt.

DOM. HERESZTYN 2001★

		0.37 ha	2,100	⑪	23–30 €

A sombre colour with black tinges, an initially floral bouquet (peony), which then turns towards notes of liquorice. The first impression on the palate is a little sharp because the wine is very young but the balance is good and the finish supported by structured tannins: "a masculine sort of Chambolle," was the way one taster described it. The 99 vintage received the *coup de coeur* in the 2002 edition.
☛ Dom. Heresztyn, 27, rue Richebourg, 21220 Gevrey-Chambertin, tel. 03.80.34.30.86, fax 03.80.34.13.99, e-mail domaine.heresztyn@wanadoo.fr ☑
☖ by appt.

DOM. LEYMARIE
Aux Echanges 2000★

	1er cru	n.c.	2,900	⑪	15–23 €

Semper ad altum is the estate's motto, written on the label. Ever higher! And indeed this intense peony-red wine echoes the sentiment. Its aromas of fresh fruit lead on to a fine and silky opening. Its tannins are dense and svelte at the same time. Its warm finish does nothing to eradicate the pleasant sensation on a palate that is both fleshy and supple.
☛ Dom. Leymarie-CECI, Clos du Village, 24, rue du Vieux-Château, 21640 Vougeot, tel. 03.80.62.86.06, fax 03.80.62.88.53, e-mail leymarie@skynet.be ☑
☖ by appt.

DOM. LIGNIER-MICHELOT
Vieilles Vignes 2001★

		0,49 ha	3,000	▮⑪	15–23 €

A rather pale colour, but limpid and brilliant. It has very characteristic, fruity aromas. It starts at the quarter turn and its tannins show themselves to be quite fine and well integrated. Its length is appreciable. Tasting facilities have recently been set up on this family estate, which has been producing wine for ten years.
☛ Dom. Lignier-Michelot, 11, rue Haute, 21220 Morey-Saint-Denis, tel. 03.80.34.31.13, fax 03.80.58.52.16 ☑
☖ by appt.

FREDERIC MAGNIEN

Les Charmes Vieille Vigne 2001★

| ■ | 1er cru | 0.75 ha | 4,500 | ■ ❚❚❚ ♦ | | 30–38 € |

This Premier Cru, made from *vieilles vignes* is of a pronounced colour. Its perfumes mix Morello cherry and vanilla. On the palate, its vinosity is breathtaking and very pleasing. Richness and power exist side by side. It would be perfectly at home with a roast of veal "forestier". The **Chambolle Vieilles Vignes Village 2001 (15–23 €)**, received a special mention. It will keep for a long time.
❧ Frédéric Magnien, 26, rte Nationale,
21220 Morey-Saint-Denis, tel. 03.80.58.54.20,
fax 03.80.51.84.34,
e-mail fredericmagnien.grandsvinsdebourgogne@
wanadoo.fr ☑
☒ by appt.

DOM. MICHEL MAGNIEN ET FILS

Les Fremières 2001★

| ■ | | 0.25 ha | n.c. | ■ ❚❚❚ | | 23–30 € |

This is not a watercolour but a gouache: the result of strong colour extraction. The bouquet is still somewhat indecisive, with herbaceous notes (elder) and fruit (strawberry). Its tannins have their say but don't dominate the conversation. It has firm structure and body. This is a wine with sufficient acidity to lay down. Serve it in three years' time with small game birds.
❧ Dom. Michel Magnien et Fils, 4, rue Ribordot,
21220 Morey-Saint-Denis, tel. 03.80.51.82.98,
fax 03.80.58.51.76 ☑
☒ by appt.

DOM. THIERRY MORTET

Les Beaux Bruns 2001★

| ■ | 1er cru | 0.25 ha | 1,200 | ■ ❚❚❚ | | 23–30 € |

This Chambolle-Musigny has what one might call a powerful colour. It adds small fruity sensations to the usual characteristics of the bouquet, while its richness explodes on the palate, where one finds a great deal of body and robustness. In three or four years' time it will make a lot of people very happy.
❧ Dom. Thierry Mortet, 16, pl. des Marronniers,
21220 Gevrey-Chambertin, tel. 03.80.51.85.07,
fax 03.80.34.16.80 ☑
☒ by appt.

PIERRE NAIGEON

Les Feussellottes 2001★

| ■ | 1er cru | 0.1 ha | 900 | ❚❚❚ | | 30–38 € |

In 1850, Fernand Naigeon was a cooper with Gevrey-Chambertin; then he bought a small vineyard and founded his dynasty. Crimson-red with quite rich legs and a sustained intensity, this Chambolle evokes first thyme then red berries on the nose. After a velvety opening, one finds a range of fine, dense tannins and a sensation of richness. Its vinosity and its aromatic character suggest it should be laid down for a few years. It will undoubtedly need decanting.
❧ Pierre Naigeon, 4, rue du Chambertin,
21220 Gevrey-Chambertin, tel. 03.80.34.14.87,
fax 03.80.58.51.18, e-mail pierre.naigeon@wanadoo.fr ☑
☒ ev. day 10am–1pm 2pm–6pm; cl. Dec.–Mar.

DOM. MICHEL NOELLAT ET FILS

Les Feusselottes 2001★★

| ■ | 1er cru | 0.4 ha | 1000 | ❚❚❚ | | 23–30 € |

Does a feminine Chambolle still exist? Well, yes, and here it is, that rare bird. Deep crimson, redcurrant and vanilla-pod, this 2001 vintage, with a delicacy based on an exemplary acidity-tannin balance, is an absolute charmer. Truly a wine that makes no attempt to use force but prefers to seduce. A pleasant fleshiness to enjoy during the next five years.
❧ SCEA Dom. Michel Noëllat et Fils, 5, rue de la Fontaine, 21700 Vosne-Romanée, tel. 03.80.61.36.87,
fax 03.80.61.18.10 ☑
☒ by appt.

ARMELLE ET BERNARD RION

Les Gruenchers 2000★

| ■ | 1er cru | 0,4 ha | 2,000 | ❚❚❚ | | 15–23 € |

Les Gruenchers is in the centre of the area and perhaps that explains the balance and harmony of this Pinot Noir which, if without much length, is nevertheless full of grace. Its finesse is its trump card. Light cherry-red, it has a well-opened bouquet of brioche and black berries. Serve it if you can with Burgundy truffles, which this family propagate with passion.
❧ Dom. Armelle et Bernard Rion, 8, rte Nationale,
21700 Vosne-Romanée, tel. 03.80.61.05.31,
fax 03.80.61.34.60, e-mail rionab@wanadoo.fr ☑
☒ by appt.

REMI SEGUIN 2000★

| ■ | 1er cru | 0,26 ha | n.c. | ❚❚❚ | | 15–23 € |

If one has the good fortune to be born at Clos de Tart, like the son of the estate manager, one finds good fairies around one's cradle…An intense, deep black-cherry colour, this Chambolle is proof of profound winemaking know-how. The bouquet gradually reveals crystallized fruits. Fully rounded, the palate is heady, warming and concentrated. This wine will certainly please because of its ability to communicate effectively. To drink in 2005.
❧ Rémi Seguin, 19, rue de Cîteaux,
21640 Gilly-lès-Cîteaux, tel. 03.80.62.89.61,
fax 03.80.62.80.92 ☑
☒ by appt.

DOM. HERVE SIGAUT

Les Chatelots 2000★

| ■ | 1er cru | 0.51 ha | 3,200 | ❚❚❚ | | 15–23 € |

Where can one find Les Chatelots? Between Feusselottes and Gruenchers. You must taste this 2000 vintage, with its fine, fruity flavour that would be perfect with a Reblochon cheese. Its deep, sombre colour betrays its youth. It is still under the influence of the cask, but not excessively. The bouquet combines muskiness, damp woodlands and strawberry jam.
❧ Hervé Sigaut, 12, rue des Champs,
21220 Chambolle-Musigny, tel. 03.80.62.80.28,
fax 03.80.62.84.40, e-mail herve.sigaut@wanadoo.fr ☑
☒ by appt.

DOM. TAUPENOT-MERME

La Combe d'Orveau 2000★

| ■ | 1er cru | n.c. | 2,800 | ❚❚❚ | | 30–38 € |

Combe d'Orveau is a prolongation of Musigny in the direction of Les Echézeaux. Admirably placed, it produced this high quality Premier Cru whose aims are well based, It has a great deal of colour with most effective cherry tinges. The aromas, tending towards blackcurrant and mocha coffee, are quite accentuated. Against a background of truffle, the powerful, demonstrative and quite dense palate is well balanced. Lay it down for two to five years then arrange a marriage with a *filet mignon*.
❧ Taupenot-Merme, 33, rte des Grands-Crus,
21220 Morey-Saint-Denis. tel. 03.80.34.35.24,
fax 03.80.51.83.41,
e-mail domaine.taupenot-merme@wanadoo.fr ☑
☒ by appt.

Wines selected but not starred

DOUDET-NAUDIN

Les Condemennes 2001

| ■ | 1er cru | 0.5 ha | 2,100 | ❚❚❚ | | 15–23 € |

❧ Doudet-Naudin, 3, rue Henri-Cyrot,
21420 Savigny-lès-Beaune, tel. 03.80.21.51.74,
fax 03.80.21.50.69, e-mail doudet-naudin@wanadoo.fr ☑
☒ by appt.

DOM. JOEL HUDELOT-BAILLET

Les Cras 2000

■ 1er cru	0.37 ha	1,200	⑪	23–30 €

☛ Dom. Joël Hudelot-Baillet, 21, rue Basse,
21220 Chambolle-Musigny, tel. 03.80.62.85.88,
fax 03.80.62.49.83 ☑
⍀ by appt.

ALAIN HUDELOT-NOELLAT 2001

■	1.9 ha	11,000	⑪	15–23 €

☛ Alain Hudelot-Noëllat, ancienne rte Nationale,
21220 Chambolle-Musigny, tel. 03.80.62.85.17,
fax 03.80.62.83.13 ☑
⍀ by appt.

JACQUES-FREDERIC MUGNIER

Les Amoureuses 2000

■ 1er cru	0.51 ha	2,500	⑪	46–76 €

☛ Jacques-Frédéric Mugnier, Ch. de Chambolle-Musigny,
21220 Chambolle-Musigny, tel. 03.80.62.85.39,
fax 03.80.62.87.36, e-mail fm@mugnier.fr

DOM. HENRI PERROT-MINOT

La Combe d'Orveau Vieilles Vignes 2000

■ 1er cru	0.47 ha	2,500	⑪	38–46 €

☛ Henri Perrot-Minot, 54, rte des Grands-Crus,
21220 Morey-Saint-Denis, tel. 03.80.34.32.51,
fax 03.80.34.13.57
⍀ by appt.

PATRICE RION 2001

■	0.85 ha	5,200	⑪	15–23 €

☛ SCE Michèle and Patrice Rion, 1, rue de la Maladière,
21700 Premeaux-Prissey, tel. 03.80.62.32.63,
fax 03.80.62.49.63, e-mail patrice.rion@wanadoo.fr ☑
⍀ by appt.

LAURENT ROUMIER 2000

■	1.4 ha	6,000	⑪	15–23 €

☛ Dom. Laurent Roumier, rue de Vergy,
21220 Chambolle-Musigny, tel. 03.80.62.83.60,
fax 03.80.62.84.10 ☑
⍀ by appt.

Musigny

With its prominent position in the Clos de Vougeot, Musigny is set on limestone soil mixed with red clay. This Grand Cru has a surface area of nearly 11 ha and produced 123,81 hl in 2002.

JOSEPH DROUHIN 2000★

■ Gd cru	n.c.	n.c.	⑪	+76 €

Here we have 67.2 ares, result of the sale of Adrien (1961) and an exchange with the Leroy estate (1972), whose replantation spread over the period from 1960 to1976. Would the Pinot Noir be jealous of the green-gold of the Chardonnay? This wine is red with deep-purple, even bluish, highlights. A touch of wild rose brings not a single thorn to the bouquet; well-opened, it makes room for a hint of roasting coffee, born of its 18 months in cask. A substantial and structured wine. Its tannins are quite rounded, but it has the feel of a block of marble that the sculptor has marked out but still has to carve. It needs four to five years in the cellar before you can admire this work of art
☛ Maison Joseph Drouhin, 7, rue d'Enfer, 21200 Beaune, tel. 03.80.24.68.88, fax 03.80.22.43.14,
e-mail maisondrouhin@drouhin.com
⍀ by appt.

DOM. JACQUES PRIEUR 2000★

■ Gd cru	0.76 ha	2,680	⑪	+76 €

These 76.6 ares are dedicated to one of the jewels of the Côte de Nuits, situated beside Les Petits Musigny over towards Flagey and Vosne. They presented a 2000 vintage which exactly matches Roupnel's definition of the perfect Musigny: "A wine of silk and lace of supreme delicacy, utterly without violence and able to hide its strength behind a veil". There could be no better description of this ruby-red wine, tinged with garnet, with a bouquet based on violets and pepper, a theme which follows on to the next stage and rewards you with a charming, slightly acid finish. Ethereal! Awarded a *coup de coeur* twice in the past.
☛ Dom. Jacques Prieur, 6, rue des Santenots,
21190 Meursault, tel. 03.80.21.23.85, fax 03.80.21.29.19 ☑
⍀ by appt.

Bonnes-Mares

This appellation, which produced 497.96 hl in 2002, spreads into the commune of Morey along the wall of the Clos de Tart, but most of it is located in Chambolle. This is a Grand Cru par excellence. The wines of Bonnes-Mares are full, vinous and rich and have the capacity to keep for a long time. After a few years of ageing, they make excellent accompaniments to rich stews or game birds.

DOM. CHARLOPIN-PARIZOT 2000★

■ Gd cru	0,15 ha	600	⑪	46–76 €

Some four *ouvrées* (about one seventh of an hectare: *ouvrée* is an ancient Burgundian measurement of area) for the Grand Cru. A wine-grower who has certainly taken off! The 2000 vintage is a very sustained, intense colour, which is hardly surprising. Undergrowth, game (under-belly of hare) on the nose, on a background of black fruits which remains moderate. A fine initial impression followed by a muted replay of what went before; after which the body asserts itself. On the finish, some sensations of toast, due to the maturation. Could make the acquaintance of the corkscrew in three to five years' time.
☛ Dom. Philippe Charlopin, 18, rte de Dijon,
21220 Gevrey-Chambertin, tel. 03.80.51.81.18,
fax 03.80.51.81.27,
e-mail charlopin.philippe@wanadoo.fr ☑

DOM. FOUGERAY DE BEAUCLAIR 2001★

■ Gd cru	1.6 ha	3,000	⑪	46–76 €
88 89 90 92 93 94	95	96	97	98 99 00 01			

Jean-Louis Fougeray, Evelyne Beauvais, his wife, and Bernard Clair – one must do the honours – are the ones who make up Fougeray de Beauclair. A beautiful wine from Bonnes-Mares, near Morey, which gives the opportunity to check whether there is any basis to the legend of the Morey side and the Chambolle side…Not very brilliant, the colour is very deep. The legs are tenacious. The nose hovers between vanilla and stewed fruit. Then the rounded, soft opening with its delightful tannins, gives way to nuances of liquorice and toast, especially on the middle palate. We will know more about it in three or four years.
☛ Dom. Fougeray de Beauclair, 44, rue de Mazy, BP 36,
21160 Marsannay-la-Côte, tel. 03.80.52.21.12,
fax 03.80.58.73.83,
e-mail fougeraydebeauclair@wanadoo.fr ☑
⍀ ev. day 8am–12 noon 2pm–6pm;
Sun. 10am–12 noon 3.30pm–5.30pm
☛ J.-L. Fougeray

DOM. ROBERT GROFFIER PERE ET FILS 2001★

■ Gd cru	n.c.	4,500	◫	46–76 €
(93) 94 96 **97 98 99** 00 01				

The colour of the red velvet curtains in the theatre, clean and straightforward, this is a Bonne-Mares produced on just under 1 ha (a happy acquisition in 1933 from the Peloux company, by Jules, the grandfather, boxer, champion cycle-racer and attentive wine-grower). It lies next to Morey. In this vintage, the nose lingers on musky notes, humus, with a little flowering of peonies. Elegant, offering a real unctuousness and well constructed, this 2001 vintage has plenty of length. An investment that will bear fruit in four to ten years' time.

☛ Dom. Robert et Serge Groffier, 3–5, rte des Grands-Crus, 21220 Morey-Saint-Denis, tel. 03.80.34.31.53, fax 03.80.34.15.48 ☑
⊥ by appt.

FREDERIC MAGNIEN 2001★★

■ Gd cru	0.2 ha	1,100	▤ ◫ ♦	46–76 €

It was not awarded the *coup de coeur*, but it was the only Chambolle-Musigny Grand Cru to have been chosen for the last Wine Circle, which puts it at the head of the line. It is a full, rounded wine but not yet matured, and should go on the long-term rack of your cellar (lay it down for five to ten years – a normal length of time for this appellation). The crimson colour and jammy palate, supported by a well-integrated oakiness, are appealing. The link between a spirited impetuous body and secondary aromas of the blackcurrant type promise a fine future for this wine.

☛ Frédéric Magnien, 26, rte Nationale, 21220 Morey-Saint-Denis, tel. 03.80.58.54.20, fax 03.80.51.84.34, e-mail fredericmagnien.grandsvinsdebourgogne@wanadoo.fr ☑
⊥ by appt.

Wines selected but not starred

DOM. BART 2000

■ Gd cru	1 ha	1,800	◫	38–46 €

☛ Dom. Bart, 23, rue Moreau, 21160 Marsannay-la-Côte, tel. 03.80.51.49.76, fax 03.80.51.23.43 ☑
⊥ by appt.

DOM. DROUHIN-LAROZE 2001

■ Gd cru	1.5 ha	5,200	◫	38–46 €
95 96 98 **99** 00 01				

☛ Dom. Drouhin-Laroze, 20, rue du Gaizot, 21220 Gevrey-Chambertin, tel. 03.80.34.31.49, fax 03.80.51.83.70, e-mail drouhin-laroze@aol.com ☑
⊥ by appt.
☛ Philippe Drouhin

PIERRE NAIGEON 2001

■ Gd cru	0.54 ha	1,800	◫	38–46 €

☛ Pierre Naigeon, 4, rue du Chambertin, 21220 Gevrey-Chambertin, tel. 03.80.34.14.87, fax 03.80.58.51.18, e-mail pierre.naigeon@wanadoo.fr ☑
⊥ ev. day 10am–1pm 2pm–6pm; cl. Dec.–Mar.

LAURENT ROUMIER 2000

■ Gd cru	0.15 ha	750	◫	46–76 €

☛ Dom. Laurent Roumier, rue de Vergy, 21220 Chambolle-Musigny, tel. 03.80.62.83.60, fax 03.80.62.84.10 ☑
⊥ by appt.

Vougeot

This is the smallest commune of the Côte, only 80 ha in area. Of these, the famous Clos occupies 50 ha. Here you can find several Premiers Crus, the best-known being the Clos Blanc (white wines) and the Clos de la Perrière. Production rose to 463 hl of red wine and 171 hl of white in 2002.

DOM. BERTAGNA
Clos de la Perrière Monopole 2000★★

■ 1er cru	2.25 ha	10,000	◫	38–46 €

The Bertagna estate (property of the Reh family originally from the Rhineland-Palatinate) received a *coup de coeur* thanks to this intense-red Perrière that produces impressive tears in the glass. The purity of the fine oak and liquorice is followed by substantial tannins on a glorious body. Undoubtedly the woodiness still needs to be wrapped further, but this 2000 vintage deserves congratulations. It is a monopoly.

☛ Dom. Bertagna, 16, rue du Vieux-Château, 21640 Vougeot, tel. 03.80.62.86.04, fax 03.80.62.82.58 ☑ ⊞
⊥ by appt.
☛ Reh

DOM. DE LA VOUGERAIE
Clos du Prieuré Monopole 2000★★

■ 1er cru	0.82 ha	4,310	◫	30–38 €

Of astonishing finesse and weight, this Vougeot, produced as a monopoly on 82 a, comes from the Vougeraie estate (the Boisset family). It forms part of an island of Chardonnay in an ocean of Pinot Noir. This award honours a wine of a fresh, young colour, a mineral bouquet with buttered notes and cleverly-controlled woodiness. Its body is also noticeable for its length and density. The **Clos white Monopole Premier Cru 2000** (46–76 €), another Chardonnay but one to set aside, was specially mentioned.

☛ Dom. de La Vougeraie, rue de l'Eglise, 21700 Premeaux-Prissey, tel. 03.80.62.48.25, fax 03.80.61.25.44, e-mail vougeraie@domainedelavougeraie.com
⊥ by appt.
☛ Famille Boisset

Wines selected but not starred

ALAIN HUDELOT-NOELLAT
Les Petits Vougeot 2001

■ 1er cru	0.55 ha	3,500	⑪	15–23 €

➤ Alain Hudelot-Noëllat, ancienne rte Nationale,
21220 Chambolle-Musigny, tel. 03.80.62.85.17,
fax 03.80.62.83.13 ☑
ᵀ by appt.

DOM. ROUX PERE ET FILS
Les Petits Vougeot 2000

■ 1er cru	1.21 ha	4,800	⑪	30–38 €

➤ Dom. Roux Père et Fils, 21190 Saint-Aubin,
tel. 03.80.21.32.92, fax 03.80.21.35.00 ☑
ᵀ by appt.

Clos de Vougeot

Much has already been written about the Clos de Vougeot and the 70 plus growers who share its 50 ha and production of 1,752 hl as declared in 2002. Its great appeal is not just a matter of chance, but because it is good and consequently everyone in the world wants some. Of course, distinctions must be made between the wines at the top of the vineyard, those in the middle and those in the lower part, but nevertheless, when the monks of the medieval Abbey of Cîteaux built their high enclosing wall, they had chosen their site very well.

Founded at the beginning of the 12th century, the Clos rapidly grew to its present size; the surrounding wall predates the 15th century. The real appeal of the Clos itself can be tasted in the quality of the wines a few years after they have been bottled. In addition, the château itself, built in the 12th century and extended in the 16th century, is worth taking time to visit. The oldest parts are the cellar, nowadays used for meetings of the *Confrérie des Chevaliers du Tastevin*, its present owners, and the vat room, with its four magnificent 12th century wine presses, one in each corner.

DOM. DU CLOS FRANTIN 2001★

■ Gd cru	0,6 ha	3,000	⑪	46–76 €

Garnet-tinged on a ruby-red colour, this Clos de Vougeot offers up peppery notes and vanilla, with a tough of liquorice. Slightly astringent, the palate rests on real substance and follows pleasantly along the same aromatic path already trodden. A wine to entrust to the good offices of your cellar.
➤ Dom. du Clos Frantin, 6 bis, bd Jacques-Copeau, 21200 Beaune, tel. 03.80.24.37.37, fax 03.80.24.37.38
➤ Albert Bichot

FAIVELEY 2000★

■ Gd cru	1.28 ha	6,700	⑪	46–76 €

Three plots acquired at different times in three different places to make up 1.28 ha. Of the garnet-ruby-red colour that is well in keeping with the 2000 vintage, this oaky wine exudes fruity and liquorice notes. It then offers up a palate that is charming, shimmering, delicate and not excessively concentrated. Noble

undoubtedly, its tannins are members of the landed gentry. A touch of finesse is taking shape and will be its major asset, over and above the balanced structure, in five to ten years' time. Another pleasant prospect, equally well marked, is the **Clos de Vougeot Grand Cru 99**, with excellent ageing potential, of which some 7,000 bottles are available.
➤ Bourgognes Faiveley, 8, rue du Tribourg,
21700 Nuits-Saint-Georges, tel. 03.80.61.04.55,
fax 03.80.62.33.37,
e-mail bourgognes.faiveley@wanadoo.fr ☑

CH. GENOT-BOULANGER 2000★

■ Gd cru	0.43 ha	1,800	⑪	38–46 €

Beneath its strong, intense colour this wine, fermented in oak casks (25% of them new) and matured for 12 months, appears to have the potential for laying down for a long period. This is all the more so because of its pronounced acidity, its substantial tannins and the quite evident oak-barrel influence; it will age well. Almost a half-hectare for a 2000 wine that still needs to open but whose suave, firm vinosity inspires confidence.
➤ SCEV Ch. Génot-Boulanger, 25, rue de Cîteaux, 21190 Meursault, tel. 03.80.21.49.20, fax 03.80.21.49.21,
e-mail genot-boulanger@wanadoo.fr ☑
ᵀ by appt.
➤ Delaby

DOM. FRANCOIS GERBET 2001★

■ Gd cru	0.33 ha	1,600	⑪	38–46 €

Marie-Andrée and Chantal Gerbet manage this family estate of 12 ha. Their deep-crimson Grand Cru reveals a bouquet of stewed black fruits powdered with vanilla. Structured, rich and still severe, the rather elegant palate echoes the fruity theme. Its tannins still need to be tamed but they already underline the return of the fruit on the finish. One could taste it again in three years' time, then again, probably much later.
➤ Dom. François Gerbet, Caveau La Maison des Vins, pl. de l'Eglise, 21700 Vosne-Romanée, tel. 03.80.61.07.85, fax 03.80.61.01.65, e-mail vins.gerbet@wanadoo.fr ☑
ᵀ by appt.

DOM. GROS FRERE ET SOEUR
Musigni 2001★

■ Gd cru	0.75 ha	3,778	⑪	38–46 €

A *coup de coeur* last year for the 2000 vintage, this cru comes from the Musigni *climat* known by that name for centuries, high up in the *clos*. Under cover of its black-cherry colour – product of a strong extraction – the bouquet is of prunes, muskiness and leather and slots easily into the classic picture. It is rich and of excellent length. It doesn't shine too much at the moment because, at this age, it is the power that comes to the fore, on a liquorice theme. This distinguished wine merits five to ten years in your cellar.
➤ Dom. Gros Frère et Soeur, 6, rue des Grands-Crus, 21700 Vosne-Romanée, tel. 03.80.61.12.43, fax 03.80.61.34.05 ☑
ᵀ by appt.
➤ Bernard Gros

JEAN-MICHEL GUILLON
Cuvée Prestige 2001★

■ Gd cru	0.17 ha	1,060	▮⑪♦	30–38 €

Established since 1980 at Gevrey-Chambertin, this estate now covers more than 10 ha. This small *cuvée* reveals its youth from the start with its almost black colour. The nose is unified, musky and spiced (leather, liquorice, vanilla). The rich, dense substance is based on tannins that still need to integrate. A wine to put in the wine cellar for five to eight years.
➤ Jean-Michel Guillon, 33, rte de Beaune, 21220 Gevrey-Chambertin, tel. 03.80.51.83.98, fax 03.80.51.85.59, e-mail curlguillon@aol.com ☑
ᵀ by appt.

DOM. MONGEARD-MUGNERET 2001★

■ Gd cru	0.62 ha	3,000	⑪	46–76 €

Plots at the top of the *clos*. The colour is clean and limpid, a little light but still within a reasonable range. After an initial woodiness on the nose, natural fruit aromas quickly come to the fore, whereas the palate concentrates on spicy, liquorice notes, based on evident tannins that need time to integrate

(three years). This wine has personality but strictly within the style of the vintage, which produced few wonders.
☛ Dom. Mongeard-Mugneret, 14, rue de la Fontaine, 21700 Vosne-Romanée, tel. 03.80.61.11.95, fax 03.80.62.35.75, e-mail mongeard@reseauconcept.net

DENIS MUGNERET ET FILS 2001★

| ■ | Gd cru | 0.72 ha | 1,800 | ❶ | 30–38 € |
90 93 |94| 95 |97| 98 99 00 01

A plot of 72 ares, made up of acquisitions made by Liger-Belair in 1889, and located near Vosne-Romanée and Flagey, along the southern wall; it has been managed by tenant-farmers Denis Mugneret and his son since 1969. Beneath its carmine colour, the nose opens on damp wood-lands, fruit and the grilled notes from the cask. A straight-forward wine to leave in the cellar for at least five years because its structure is substantial and tannic, and the oak needs to integrate.
☛ Denis et Dominique Mugneret, 9, rue de la Fontaine, 21700 Vosne-Romanée, tel. 03.80.61.00.97, fax 03.80.61.24.54 ☑
☗ by appt.

DOM. MICHEL NOËLLAT ET FILS 2001★

| ■ | Gd cru | 0.46 ha | 1,500 | ❶ | 38–46 € |
Some 46 ares in Clos de Vougeot, on part of the old Charles Noëllat estate. Equal to a Grand Cru, this medium ruby-coloured wine opens on cherry-stones and the cask. The first impression is clean with a good amount of acidity, which guarantees its balance in the long term. The palate shows robustness, substance, on notes of blackcurrant and a good length of vanilla. Leave it in the cellar for the next five years and serve it with a young pigeon.
☛ SCEA Dom. Michel Noëllat et Fils, 5, rue de la Fontaine, 21700 Vosne-Romanée, tel. 03.80.61.36.87, fax 03.80.61.18.10 ☑
☗ by appt.

DOM. HENRI REBOURSEAU 2000★

| ■ | Gd cru | 2.21 ha | 7,961 | ❶ | 46–76 € |
89 90 92 |93| 94 95 96 97 98 |99| 00

These 2.21 ha came from the family's share of a sale in 1889, situated right in the heart of the *clos* and a perfect example of it. Grandson of Pierre Rebourseau – historical figure of the Clos-de-Vougeot, the syndicate which he chaired for a long time – Jean de Surrel presented an impressive deep and limpid ruby-red 2000. A classic bouquet, between mineral and incense, myrtle; with notes of Aleppo pine resin and rather austere notes of game, the palate prepares with its future role. A wine to lay down.
☛ NSE Dom. Henri Rebourseau, 10, pl. du Monument, 21220 Gevrey-Chambertin, tel. 03.80.51.88.94, fax 03.80.34.12.82, e-mail rebourseau1@aol.com ☑
☗ by appt.

ANTONIN RODET

Cave privée 2000★

| ■ | Gd cru | n.c. | 608 | | +76 € |
This, in all probability, is the Prieur plot. It has not changed owner since 1889. Six owners since the 12th century! Limpid bigaroon cherry-red with aromas of sweet cherry, touching on violets and spices, a still young and rather closed wine, notice-ably oaky at the time of the tasting. It nevertheless convinced us that it is a fleshy and worldly Clos de Vougeot. A wine to drink in four or five years' time with a partridge.
☛ Antonin Rodet, 71640 Mercurey, tel. 03.85.98.12.12, fax 03.85.45.25.49, e-mail rodet@rodet.com ☑
☗ ev. day except Sat. Sun. 9am–12 noon 2pm–6pm

CH. DE LA TOUR 2001★

| ■ | Gd cru | 5.4 ha | n.c. | ❶ | 46–76 € |
85 86 87 |88| |89| 90 91 93 94 95 96 97 (98) 99 01

In Pierre Labet's family since 1870 and enjoying 50-year-old vines, this estate received a *coup de coeur* for its 98 vintage. Purplish-garnet and nicely scented (black fruits), the 2001 vintage, matured in 75% new casks, opens on oaky, dense tannins, then the palate reveals a balance of vigour and fruit.

Severe at the moment, as it should be, it will have to wait three to five years before being served with a fillet of venison.
☛ Ch. de la Tour, Clos de Vougeot, 21640 Vougeot, tel. 03.80.62.86.13, fax 03.80.62.82.72, e-mail contact@chateaudelatour.com ☑
☗ ev. day except Tue. 10am–6pm; cl. 15 Nov.–31 Mar.
☛ François Labet

Wines selected but not starred

BERTRAND AMBROISE 2001

| ■ | Gd cru | 0.18 ha | 900 | ❶ | 46–76 € |
☛ Bertrand Ambroise, rue de l'Eglise, 21700 Premeaux-Prissey, tel. 03.80.62.30.19, fax 03.80.62.38.69, e-mail bertrand.ambroise@wanadoo.fr ☑
☗ by appt.

LABOURE-ROI 2001

| ■ | Gd cru | n.c. | n.c. | ❶ | 46–76 € |
☛ Labouré-Roi, rue Lavoisier, 21700 Nuits-Saint-Georges, tel. 03.80.62.64.00, fax 03.80.62.64.10
☗ by appt.

DOM. MOILLARD 2000

| ■ | Gd cru | 0.6 ha | 1,500 | ❶ | 46–76 € |
☛ Dom. Moillard, chem. rural, 29, 21700 Nuits-Saint-Georges, tel. 03.80.62.42.00, fax 03.80.61.28.13, e-mail nuicave@wanadoo.fr ☑
☗ ev. day 10am–6pm; 10am–7pm in summer; cl. Jan.

ARMELLE ET BERNARD RION 2001

| ■ | Gd cru | 0.91 ha | 2,400 | ❶ | 38–46 € |
☛ Dom. Armelle et Bernard Rion, 8, rte Nationale, 21700 Vosne-Romanée, tel. 03.80.61.05.31, fax 03.80.61.34.60, e-mail rionab@wanadoo.fr ☑
☗ by appt.

DOM. DE LA VOUGERAIE 2000

| ■ | Gd cru | 1.41 ha | 3,490 | ❶ | +76 € |
☛ Dom. de La Vougeraie, rue de l'Eglise, 21700 Premeaux-Prissey, tel. 03.80.62.48.25, fax 03.80.61.25.44, e-mail vougeraie@domainedelavougeraie.com
☗ by appt.
☛ Famille Boisset

ECHEZEAUX AND GRANDS-ECHEZEAUX

To the south of Clos de Vougeot lies the commune of Flagey-Echézeaux, with its village to the east on the flatter land, like Gilly-lès-Cîteaux (see map). Its border runs along the wall of the Clos de Vougeot, to the top of the upper slopes, taking in some of the vineyard. The vineyard on the lower slopes falls under the Appellation Vosne-Romanée. On the hills there are two Grands Crus next to each other: Le Grands-Echézeaux and L'Echézeaux. The first covers about 9 ha on several *lieux-dits* and produced only 321.6 hl in 2002, while the second covers more than 30 ha, producing 1,246.78 hl.

The wines of these two Crus, the most prestigious of which is the Grands-Echézeaux, are very "Burgundian": sturdy, well-structured, intensely aromatic and very expensive. They are mostly cultivated by wine-growers from Vosne and Flagey.

Echézeaux

DOM. DU CLOS FRANTIN 2001★

	Gd cru	0.99 ha	3,300		46–76 €

Part of the Albert Bichot company, this estate is located here at Champs Traversins: at 9,974 m² it is just 26 m² short of 1 ha. Deep red, this is a wine to lay down and its bouquet reveals a good concentration of red berries. A touch of freshness, tannins still a little severe, but warmed by the high alcohol content, it resembles the marshal of Camp Legrand which has created by the Clos Frantin after having lived though all wars of the Empire. It needs four years in the cellar to give of its best.

☛ Dom. du Clos Frantin, 6 bis, bd Jacques-Copeau, 21200 Beaune, tel. 03.80.24.37.37, fax 03.80.24.37.38
☛ Albert Bichot

DOM. A.-F. GROS 2001★★

	Gd cru	n.c.	1,200		38–46 €

89 90 94 96 |97| 98 **99** 00 **01**

The label is attractive, the wine is splendid. It will go far... Deep crimson-red, it is not yet ready to reveal its aromas but one can detect a touch of class, wrapped in very ripe black berries. After a brilliant opening, a substantial structure asserts itself, rich and mouth-filling with pleasant tannins. The compliments are added to heartfelt cries on the tasters' cards. The touch of Morello cherry on the finish, clinches the *coup de coeur*. Bravo the winemaker, François Parent, fortunate husband of Anne-Francoise, the daughter of Jeanine and Jean Gros. Elsewhere, under the label **François Parent, 2001** (600 bottles) was awarded two stars. A beef Wellington would be an appropriate dish to accompany it.

☛ Dom. A.-F. Gros, La Garelle, Grande-Rue, 21630 Pommard, tel. 03.80.22.61.85, fax 03.80.24.03.16, e-mail af-gros@wanadoo.fr
☿ by appt.

DOM. GUYON 2001★

	Gd cru	0.2 ha	1,115		46–76 €

85 86 |88| |89| |90| 92 94 95 99 **00** 01

A plot of 20 a 40 ca in Orveaux, the higher part of this Grand Cru. Barley for brewing was produced here as well as wine until 1993, when this family abandoned mixed-farming to devote itself entirely to wine-production. Beautiful blackcurrant aromas, deep, very pronounced, precede and equally fruity palate on the same notes. Its concentration does not

overwhelm its finesse. A wine that is still restrained, with that touch of rather classic bitterness that, far from being a defect, is exactly what it needs. In three to five years it will be perfect.
☛ EARL Dom. Guyon, 11–16, RN 74, 21700 Vosne-Romanée, tel. 03.80.61.02.46, fax 03.80.62.36.56
☿ by appt.

DOM. HENRI NAUDIN-FERRAND

2000★★

	Gd cru	0.34 ha	1,773		46–76 €

Claire Naudin does nothing by half: her 2000 vintage is one of the best Echézeaux tasted this time. Its colour is very pure, the nose is beginning to open on notes of cherry and cherry-stones. It slides easily across the palate, a combination of finesse and freshness that does not detract from the temperament and vigour of the wine. A really good wine to lay down but could equally be served young. You could even go as far as to match it with a roast of wild boar in a *Grand veneur* sauce, or a jugged hare: this is a wine that deserves something special.
☛ Dom. Henri Naudin-Ferrand, rue du Meix-Grenot, 21700 Magny-lès-Villers, tel. 03.80.62.91.50, fax 03.80.62.91.77, e-mail dnaudin@ipac.fr
☿ by appt.

DOM. DES PERDRIX 2000★★

	Gd cru	1.14 ha	4,312		+76 €

This 1.14 ha is divided into two roughly equal plots: Echézeaux du Dessus and Quartiers de Nuits. Formerly Mugneret-Gouachon, the Domaine des Perdrix is now worked by the Devillard family. This 2000 vintage is altogether remarkable. The colour is very strong with all the depth possible. The bouquet? Truffle, blackberries, spices, a well-judged touch of woodiness: it is positively gluttonous and hard to let go of. On the palate, it offers up sensations of musk and liquorice on a very smooth substance. Fine extraction that does not mask the terroir.
☛ B. et C. Devillard, Dom. des Perdrix, Ch. de Champ Renard, 71640 Mercurey, tel. 03.85.98.12.12, fax 03.85.45.25.49, e-mail rodet@rodet.com

DOM. JACQUES PRIEUR 2000★

	Gd cru	0.36 ha	1,300		46–76 €

The Domaine Jacques Prieur is co-managed by Bertrand Devillard (Antonin Rodet). Here we are dealing with an Echézeaux that is structured, concentrated, supported by a good acidity and which will hold marvellously for three to five years. A little note of faded flowers on the bouquet makes it quite original and romantic...
☛ Dom. Jacques Prieur, 6, rue des Santenots, 21190 Meursault, tel. 03.80.21.23.85, fax 03.80.21.29.19
☿ by appt.

DOM. DE LA ROMANEE-CONTI

2001★★★

	Gd cru	4.67 ha	n.c.		+76 €

SOCIÉTÉ CIVILE DU DOMAINE DE LA ROMANÉE-CONTI
PROPRIÉTAIRE À VOSNE-ROMANÉE (CÔTE-D'OR) FRANCE

ÉCHÉZEAUX
APPELLATION ÉCHÉZEAUX CONTRÔLÉE
16.444 Bouteilles Récoltées
LES ASSOCIÉS-GÉRANTS
BOUTEILLE N°
ANNÉE 2001
Mise en bouteille au domaine

Dynamic, almost exuberant, the superb energy of this Echézeaux is seductive. But the concentration of its deep substance (the 4.67 ha of this estate are in the *climat* of Poulaillères, just above Les Grands-Echézeaux), and the complexity of its bouquet and body are anything but impulsive.

On the contrary, this is a wine that plays simultaneously in several keys; and surely the only one among all the grape varieties capable of expressing such nuances is the Pinot Noir... the mighty organ of the Vosne-Romanée!
☛ SC du Dom. de la Romanée-Conti, 1, rue Derrière-le-Four, 21700 Vosne-Romanée, tel. 03.80.62.48.80, fax 03.80.61.05.72

Wines selected but not starred

BOUCHARD AINE ET FILS
Cuvée Signature 2001

■ Gd cru	n.c.	600	◗	+76 €

☛ Bouchard Aîné et Fils, hôtel du Conseiller-du-Roy, 4, bd Mal-Foch, 21200 Beaune, tel. 03.80.24.24.00, fax 03.80.24.64.12, e-mail bouchard@bouchard-aine.fr ☑
☒ ev. day 9.30am–12 noon 2pm–6pm

DOM. J. CONFURON-COTETIDOT 2000

■ Gd cru	n.c.	n.c.	◗	30–38 €

☛ EARL J. Confuron-Cotetidot, 10, rue de la Fontaine, 21700 Vosne-Romanée, tel. 03.80.61.03.39, fax 03.80.61.17.85 ☑
☒ by appt.

FAIVELEY 2000

■ Gd cru	0.86 ha	4,424	◗	46–76 €

☛ Bourgognes Faiveley, 8, rue du Tribourg, 21700 Nuits-Saint-Georges, tel. 03.80.61.04.55, fax 03.80.62.33.37, e-mail bourgognes.faiveley@wanadoo.fr ☑

ALEX GAMBAL 2000

■ Gd cru	n.c.	884	◗	46–76 €

☛ Maison Alex Gambal, 4, rue Jacques-Vincent, 21200 Beaune, tel. 03.80.22.75.81, fax 03.80.22.21.66, e-mail alexgambal@wanadoo.fr ☑
☒ by appt.

DOM. MONGEARD-MUGNERET 2001

■ Gd cru	2.16 ha	8,000	◗	30–38 €

☛ Dom. Mongeard-Mugneret, 14, rue de la Fontaine, 21700 Vosne-Romanée, tel. 03.80.61.11.95, fax 03.80.62.35.75, e-mail mongeard@reseauconcept.net ☑

MICHEL NOELLAT ET FILS 2001

■ Gd cru	0.46 ha	1,500	◗	30–38 €

☛ SCEA Dom. Michel Noëllat et Fils, 5, rue de la Fontaine, 21700 Vosne-Romanée, tel. 03.80.61.36.87, fax 03.80.61.18.10 ☑
☒ by appt.

Grands-Echézeaux

JOSEPH DROUHIN 2000★

■ Gd cru	n.c.	n.c.	◗	46–76 €

Half a hectare, acquired in 1970 by the J. Drouhin house (now 100% Burgundian again since the repurchase of shares sold not long ago to a Japanese group), for a wine with a shimmering colour. Its bouquet evokes blackberries and eucalyptus. The initial impression is delicate, opening on a pleasant texture, a substance that is fine and elegant, if still a little

blocked by the tannins. But what could be more normal at this age? It must be left in the cellar for two or three years.
☛ Maison Joseph Drouhin, 7, rue d'Enfer, 21200 Beaune, tel. 03.80.24.68.88, fax 03.80.22.43.14, e-mail maisondrouhin@drouhin.com
☒ by appt.

DOM. GROS FRERE ET SOEUR 2001★★★

■ Gd cru	0.37 ha	1,914	◗	46–76 €

A 36.62-are vineyard located along the wall of the Clos de Vougeot which has no complaints about the neighbourhood. It produced this *coup de cœur*. Its sumptuous red, bordering on black, colour is an experience in itself. A marvellous perfume, where one seems to find truffles, damp woodlands, mushrooms, evolving on mentholated notes. Dense and rich, warming and deep, this is a very *grand* Grands-Echézeaux, product of the exceptional maturity of the grape. Already full of flavour, if you haven't got the patience to wait ten years for it.
☛ Dom. Gros Frère et Soeur, 6, rue des Grands-Crus, 21700 Vosne-Romanée, tel. 03.80.61.12.43, fax 03.80.61.34.05 ☑
☒ by appt.
☛ Bernard Gros

DOM. DE LA ROMANEE-CONTI 2002★★★

■ Gd cru	n.c.	n.c.	◗	+76 €

In the same lineage as 90 and 99 vintages, this is a tender, charmingly delicate wine with little acidity. An instant wine, so to speak. Instantly pleasing. The fruit positively explodes out of it: cherry, fruit-stones, flavour long on the palate. On reflexion there is a kind of serenity in it, the expression of a more mature wine than it seems to be, a wine already dressed for summer in the last days of winter. But one will wait a long time for it.
☛ SC du Dom. de la Romanée-Conti, 1, rue Derrière-le-Four, 21700 Vosne-Romanée, tel. 03.80.62.48.80, fax 03.80.61.05.72

Vosne-Romanée

Here again, the Burgundian customs are well respected; the name of the vineyard is better known than that of the village. Like Gevrey-Chambertin, this commune is the site of many Grands Crus and next to them are a number of famous *climats* such as Les Suchots, Les Beaux-Monts, Les Malconsorts and many others. The appellation Vosne-Romanée produced 6,614 hl in 2002.

DOM. ROBERT ARNOUX

Les Suchots 2000★★★

| ■ | 1er cru | 0.43 ha | 1,500 | 🍷 | 46–76 € |

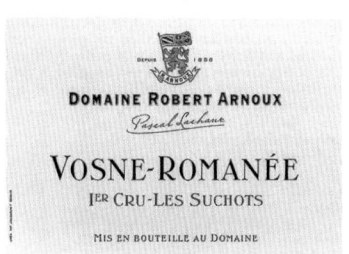

Coup de coeur last year for its Chaumes 99, this estate is again very well-placed on the podium for its Suchots. A very fine wine, where the Pinot Noir plays its part in every aspect: the colour and highlights, nose evoking a fruit salad of soft, red berries, the palate generous and refined. Velvety tannins, recurring aromas of stewed fruit, flexibility and richness; "*on y aime*" as one says in Burgundy. See also the **Village Les Hautes Maizières 2000 (30–38 €)**, a more robust and "chewy" wine which was awarded one star, as was the **Les Chaumes 2000 (30–38 €)**.
🖰 Dom. Robert Arnoux, 3, RN 74, 21700 Vosne-Romanée, tel. 03.80.61.08.41, fax 03.80.61.36.02 ☑
🍷 by appt.

SYLVAIN CATHIARD

Aux Reignots 2001★★

| ■ | 1er cru | 0.24 ha | 1,400 | 🍷 | 30–38 € |

Les Reignots is located just above Romanée, two paces away from Romanée-Conti. Deep garnet-red, this 2001 becomes complex after aeration but makes no clear choice between flowers and fruit. Fresh and young at the start, it has attractive tannins and is very characteristic of Vosne-Romanée. A robust vinification but no over-extraction. In four or five years' time, this wine will be very well-balanced. The **Premier Cru Aux Malconsorts 2001** received a star and half! It needs to age quietly in a good cellar.
🖰 Sylvain Cathiard, 20, rue de la Goillotte, 21700 Vosne-Romanée, tel. 03.80.62.36.01, fax 03.80.61.18.21 ☑
🍷 by appt.

DOM. DU CLOS FRANTIN

Les Malconsorts 2000★

| ■ | 1er cru | 1.76 ha | 5,000 | 🍷 | 38–46 € |

Bought by Albert Bichot, the Clos Frantin is one of the historic estates of Vosne. Founded by an officer of Napoleon, a Chevalier of the Empire, it belonged subsequently to Frantin, an eminent printing firm at Dijon. This 2000 vintage, with its deep purple colour, has a great deal of substance, of "chewiness," with notes of spices and liquorice. Bilberries and blackcurrants mingle with some quite musky notes. Well worked, the tannins are silky, dense and matured. One taster gave it two stars. Don't forget that Les Malconsorts is a neighbour of La Tâche.
🖰 Dom. du Clos Frantin, 6 bis, bd Jacques-Copeau, 21200 Beaune, tel. 03.80.24.37.37, fax 03.80.24.37.38
🖰 Albert Bichot

FRANCOIS CONFURON-GINDRE 2001★

| ■ | | 1.97 ha | 6,000 | 🍷 | 11–15 € |

The firm which printed the labels for this wine should be asked to change the direction of the diagonal bands on the Burgundy coat of arms – they go the wrong way. However, label collectors like these peculiarities. As to the object of the exercise – the wine – it is very successful. An intense ruby-red with purple highlights, with black fruits (blackcurrant, blackberries) lying in wait. Harmonious, a good balance has been achieved between tannin, fruits and acidity. It has plenty of potential. To confirm this, drink it in 2005.

🖰 François Confuron-Gindre, 2, rue de la Tâche, 21700 Vosne-Romanée, tel. 03.80.61.20.84, fax 03.80.62.31.29 ☑
🍷 by appt.

DOM. FRANCOIS GERBET

Les Suchots 2001★

| ■ | 1er cru | n.c. | 1,300 | 🍷 | 23–30 € |

The colour of this wine indicates an excellent Pinot Noir, with notes of violet and raspberry mixed with an elegant grilled oakiness, both on the nose and the palate. With its rich, rounded opening, this latter is well-constructed, revealing its youth in its most worthy finish. It needs keeping for two or three years. Also worth noting are the **Village Aux Réas 2001 (15–23 €)**, and the **Premier Cru Les Petits Monts 2001**, both of which received a special mention.
🖰 Dom. François Gerbet, Caveau La Maison des Vins, pl. de l'Eglise, 21700 Vosne-Romanée, tel. 03.80.61.07.85, fax 03.80.61.01.65, e-mail vins.gerbet@wanadoo.fr ☑
🍷 by appt.

DOM. A.-F. GROS

Clos de la Fontaine Monopole 2001★★

| ■ | | 0.35 ha | 2,200 | 🍷 | 15–23 € |

Wife of François Parent, Anne-Francoise Gros divides herself between Pommard and Vosne-Romanée. Her Clos de la Fontaine brought her this Grand Jury's *coup de coeur*. Beneath its intense, rich-velvet colour is a bouquet of very ripe blackcurrants and a fine, imposing structure. Its fruit is very pleasant on the palate and the finish is marked by its roundness and fleshy quality. To lay down for five years. Also worthy of attention is the **Maizières 2001** awarded one star.
🖰 Dom. A.-F. Gros, La Garelle, Grande-Rue, 21630 Pommard, tel. 03.80.22.61.85, fax 03.80.24.03.16, e-mail af-gros@wanadoo.fr ☑
🍷 by appt.
🖰 Anne-Françoise Parent-Gros

DOM. MICHEL GROS

Clos des Réas Monopole 2001★

| ■ | 1er cru | 2.12 ha | 12,000 | 🍷 | 30–38 € |

The son of Jean and Jeanine Gros, Michel created the fifth Domaine Gros at Vosne-Romanée. The wine he offered here is a wine with a future. Garnet-red with purple highlights, this 2001 has a deep, cheerful colour, a fine, grilled woodiness and a very fresh bouquet. Still rather closed on the palate but its prospects are discernible. A little warmth and tannin on the finish. A monopoly, the Clos des Réas has been in the family for a long time. In 1867 it earned Louis-Gustave Gros-Guénaud a gold medal at the Universal Exhibition!
🖰 Dom. Michel Gros, 7, rue des Communes, 21700 Vosne-Romanée, tel. 03.80.61.04.69, fax 03.80.61.22.29 ☑
🍷 by appt.

DOM. GUYON

En Orveaux 2001★

| ■ | 1er cru | 0.34 ha | 1,400 | 🍷 | 30–38 € |

The Guyon estate has been awarded so many *coups de coeur* that they have stopped counting. Last year's was for this Premier Cru. The 2001 vintage, purplish-black in colour, evokes blackcurrants and soft fruits on the nose. Its opening is rounded and full, with well-seated, robust balance and a pleasant length based on fruit and quite evident tannins. Everything is in place but, as St. Bernard said: "One must make time for time."

� EARL Dom. Guyon, 11–16, RN 74, 21700 Vosne-Romanée, tel. 03.80.61.02.46, fax 03.80.62.36.56 **Ⅴ**
☂ by appt.

ALAIN HUDELOT-NOELLAT

Les Suchots 2001★★★

| ■ 1er cru | 0.5 ha | 3,000 | ⅠⅠⅠ | 23–30 € |

This is not this estate's first *coup de coeur*: in the 2002 edition one was awarded for its Les Malconsorts. When a large terroir meets excellent winemaker, the result is a wine that is both complex and rich, as is this one. Beautiful colour, slightly chocolatey bouquet, full of nuances; on the palate, the opening is a touch severe, then it becomes "greedy" and full-bodied. The tannins seem exceptional. Note also that the **Les Beaumonts Premier Cru 2001** received one star. Two wines to lay down for three to five years.

➕ Alain Hudelot-Noëllat, ancienne rte Nationale, 21220 Chambolle-Musigny, tel. 03.80.62.85.17, fax 03.80.62.83.13 **Ⅴ**
☂ by appt.

S. JAVOUHEY

Vieilles Vignes 2000★★

| ■ 1er cru | n.c. | n.c. | ⅠⅠⅠ | 23–30 € |

This wine was mentioned during the discussions about the *coup de coeur* "Bottled on the estate by D at F 21640," it says on the label. This wine by a *négociant-éleveur* (merchant who also matures wine) is of an excellent level. Intense colour, elegant, understated taste of oak, beautiful balance: it is very upright. Well constructed, it combines acidity, tannins, fruit: this merchant can congratulate his winemaker. Not to be opened for five years! The **Les Suchots 2000 (38–46 €)** received one star; a Premier Cru to lay down for three to four years.

➕ S. Javouhey, 50, rue du Gal-de-Gaulle, BP 63, 21702 Nuits-Saint-Georges, tel. 03.80.61.10.30, fax 03.80.61.35.76, e-mail domaine@javouhey.com **Ⅴ**
☂ ev. day 9am–12 noon 1pm–7pm; cl. Jan.

DOM. DU VICOMTE LIGER-BELAIR

Les Chaumes 2000★

| ■ 1er cru | 0.12 ha | 600 | ⅠⅠⅠ | 46–76 € |

Louis-Michel Liger-Belair is slowly taking over his parents' estate; while barely more than 3 ha, this vineyard has the monopoly of the Grand Cru la Romanée. Two centuries of history. Here we have a Les Chaumes, garnet-red with crimson tinges, with a ripe fruit bouquet that is still restrained. The body appears to be concentrated and complex, with real length. The tannins are quite matured and fine. Note too the **Le Clos du Château (Monopole) 2000 (30–38 €)**, also worthy of interest (one star), and the **La Colombière 2000 (30–38 €)**, which was specially mentioned.

➕ Dom. du Vicomte Liger-Belair, Ch. de Vosne-Romanée, 21700 Vosne-Romanée, tel. 03.80.12.13.70, fax 03.80.62.13.70 **Ⅴ**

FREDERIC MAGNIEN

Au-dessus de la Rivière 2001★

| ■ | 0.5 ha | 3,000 | ⅠⅠⅠ ♣ | 15–23 € |

A little-known *climat* but one which certainly appears in the land register, near to the village and the fountain of Vosne. It has produced a wine which is rounded and pleasant on the palate, young, and developing on a humus note. A touch of acidity, raspberry aromas, the whole is coming along well and leaves a pleasant sensation. The oakiness is in the process of integrating with the flavour of blackberries.

➕ Frédéric Magnien, 26, rte Nationale, 21220 Morey-Saint-Denis, tel. 03.80.58.54.20, fax 03.80.51.84.34, e-mail fredericmagnien.grandsvinsdebourgogne@wanadoo.fr **Ⅴ**
☂ by appt.

DOM. MONGEARD-MUGNERET

Les Orveaux 2001★

| ■ 1er cru | 1.08 ha | 5,700 | ⅠⅠⅠ | 30–38 € |

This family's roots go deep in the Burgundian vineyards. Here we are dealing with a Les Orveaux (one part is classified as a Grand Cru among the Echézeaux) of an intense and brilliant red colour. Aromas of blackcurrant, bilberry and blackberries, a touch musky and spicy, introduce a structure that is quite "chewy" and textured, in a context that is dense, ripe and still tannic. To lay down for three to eight years.

➕ Dom. Mongeard-Mugneret, 14, rue de la Fontaine, 21700 Vosne-Romanée, tel. 03.80.61.11.95, fax 03.80.62.35.75, e-mail mongeard@reseauconcept.net **Ⅴ**

DENIS MUGNERET ET FILS 2001★

| ■ | 1.4 ha | 9,000 | ⅠⅠⅠ | 15–23 € |

The GAEC Denis Mugneret et Fils was created in 1982 as a tenant-farming enterprise on beautiful vineyards in Clos de Vougeot and Richebourg. "There is no ordinary wine in the Vosne," said the Abbé de Courtépée in the 18th century. Deep cherry-red, this slightly vanilla-flavoured 2001 brings out the full value of ripe red berries. The body is still quite tannic, but balanced and well-constructed, with a ripe and promising fleshiness.

➕ Denis et Dominique Mugneret, 9, rue de la Fontaine, 21700 Vosne-Romanée, tel. 03.80.61.00.97, fax 03.80.61.24.54 **Ⅴ**
☂ by appt.

DOM. MICHEL NOELLAT ET FILS

Les Beaux Monts 2001★

| ■ 1er cru | 1.6 ha | 4,000 | ⅠⅠⅠ | 23–30 € |

A very beautiful 20-ha estate, much appreciated by our readers and run by two brothers, Alain and Jean-Marc Noëllat. Deep crimson, this Les Beaux Monts is full and fleshy, tannic without excess; a wine made from a well-ripened harvest, with fairly strong but balanced extraction. In three to five years' time, its finesse and elegance will be fully developed.

➕ SCEA Dom. Michel Noëllat et Fils, 5, rue de la Fontaine, 21700 Vosne-Romanée, tel. 03.80.61.36.87, fax 03.80.61.18.10 **Ⅴ**
☂ by appt.

DOM. DES PERDRIX 2000★

| ■ | 1.05 ha | 5,472 | ⅠⅠⅠ | 46–76 € |

The family estate of the Devillards (Antonin Rodet), whose wine is matured in cask in the wine cellar excavated at Gevrey-Chambertin in 1755, by Claude Jobert de Chambertin. Respectful of its grape variety and the terroir, this deep ruby-red wine offers up an expressive bouquet of red fruits and a touch of vanilla. A well-balanced and genuine structure. For a *village* it is perfect and, in three to ten years' time it will have developed heart as well. To buy it, speak to Antonin Rodet.

➕ B. et C. Devillard, Dom. des Perdrix, Ch. de Champ Renard, 71640 Mercurey, tel. 03.85.98.12.12, fax 03.85.45.25.49, e-mail rodet@rodet.com

DOM. DE LA POULETTE

Les Suchots 2000★★

■ 1er cru	0.25 ha	1,400	◫	38–46 €

An estate handed down the female line and associated with the memory of Lucien Audidier, who was a great wine and vineyard personality at the Ministry of Agriculture. This Les Suchots is an undoubted success, very strongly coloured, oaky but not toasted, warming and full-bodied certainly, offering length and richness. To drink at the end of the meal, but not until three to five years have passed.
➦ Françoise Michaut-Audidier, Dom. de la Poulette, 103, Grande-Rue, 21700 Corgoloin, tel. 03.80.62.98.02, fax 01.45.25.43.23, e-mail f.michaut@wanadoo.fr ☑
⏰ by appt.

DOM. DANIEL RION ET FILS

Les Beaux-Monts 2001★

■ 1er cru	1.07 ha	5,800	■◫♨	23–30 €

This family estate was created in 1955 when Daniel Rion returned from doing his military service. "A Japanese once said to me that my wines have good legibility," said Patrice, one of Daniel's sons. "I remembered the expression!" This Les Beaux-Monts does indeed have an interesting legibility. A sombre deep-red colour, somewhat inclined towards the cask, a rounded and fleshy, smooth wine, which should should speak for itself in a few years, when the oak has integrated.
➦ Dom. Daniel Rion et Fils, RN 74, 21700 Premeaux, tel. 03.80.62.31.28, fax 03.80.61.13.41, e-mail contact@domaine-daniel-rion.com ☑
⏰ ev. day except Sun. 8.30am–12 noon 1.30pm–6pm; Sat. by appt.

DOM. ROBERT SIRUGUE ET SES ENFANTS 2001★

■	4.65 ha	14,000	◫	11–15 €

"A wine can sometimes divide the Gaulois," Henri Vincenot would have said. This one, for example. The marks ranged between the enthusiastic (two stars) and the more reserved. Everyone agreed on the colour: black-cherry with purplish highlights; and on the nose: not too lively but already surounding the subject with classic aromas. More roundness than length. At the moment the very young tannins are some-what vocal and will need two to four years in the cellar. The **Les Petits Monts 2001 (15–23 €)**, powerful and hard, has the stamina to age well and was unanimously awarded a star.
➦ Robert Sirugue et ses Enfants, 3, rue du Monument, 21700 Vosne-Romanée, tel. 03.80.61.00.64, fax 03.80.61.27.57 ☑
⏰ by appt.

MME ROLAND VIGOT 2001★

■	0.16 ha	900	◫	15–23 €

Fabrice and Thierry Vigot took over from their mother. Fabrice takes care of the vinification and marketing. This Vosne shows a good extraction of colour: very dark red. Black fruits, spices, vanilla all contribute their aromas. Good substance and integrated palate in a 2001 vintage that needs to stay in the cellar for four to five years.
➦ Mme Roland Vigot, 60, RN 74, 21700 Vosne-Romanée, tel. 03.80.61.17.70 ☑
⏰ by appt.

Wines selected but not starred

ALEX GAMBAL 2000

■	n.c.	1,311	◫	23–30 €

➦ Maison Alex Gambal, 4, rue Jacques-Vincent, 21200 Beaune, tel. 03.80.22.75.81, fax 03.80.22.21.66, e-mail alexgambal@wanadoo.fr ☑
⏰ by appt.

LA ROMANEE, RICHEBOURG, ROMANEE SAINT-VIVANT, GRANDE RUE, LA TACHE

La Romanée

These crus are all equally prestigious and it would be difficult to pick out the greatest. Romanée Conti undoubtedly enjoys the greatest fame, and through history there have been numerous references to the "exquisite quality" of the wine. The famous vineyard of Romanée was eyed covetously by the great and the good of the ancien régime, though Madame de Pompadour failed to win it when she was pitted against the Prince of Conti who acquired it in 1760. Until the Second World War, the vines were not grafted and were treated with sulphur carbonate to protect them against phylloxera. These had later to be grubbed up and the first harvest of the new vines took place in 1952. Romanée Conti, cultivated by a single grower on 1.8 ha, is one of the most famous and expensive wines in the world.

The Romanée vineyards cover 0.83 ha, Richebourg 8 ha, Romanée Saint-Vivant 9.5 ha, La Tâche covers a little more than 6 ha and the Grande Rue 1.65 ha. As with all the Grands Crus, the volumes produced are in the region of 20 to 30 hl per ha, depending on the year. Together, these Grands Crus produced no more than 946 hl in 2002, of which 307 hl were Richebourg, 57 hl were Romanée Conti and 289 hl Romanée Saint-Vivant. Grande Rue became an accredited Grand Cru on 2 July 1992.

Richebourg

DOM. A.-F. GROS 2001★

■ Gd cru	0.6 ha	3,000	◫	+76 €

89 90 **91** 92 |93| |94| (96) |97| **98 99** 00 |01|

This Richebourg with its dense, purplish colour, goes straight on to the attack from the very first contact with the nose. It aims at game, embellished by blackberries and bilberries. Soft and velvety on the palate, it in no way resembles the picture that Richard Olnay painted of it: "The most violent and intense of all the crus ". No, this one is velvety, tender. Its final bow is straight out of the court of Louis XIV. This famous estate received several *coups de cœur* (for the 98 and 96 vintages).
➦ Dom. A.-F. Gros, La Garelle, Grande-Rue, 21630 Pommard, tel. 03.80.22.61.85, fax 03.80.24.03.16, e-mail af-gros@wanadoo.fr
⏰ by appt.

DOM. GROS FRERE ET SOEUR 2001★

■ Gd cru	0,69 ha	3,521	〰	+76 €

89 90 91 92 93 94 (96) |97| **98 99** 00 01

Pleasant and lingering right through the tasting, it is obviously one to lay down. Absolutely not to be touched for four to five years. Black-cherry, it divides its bouquet between two sensations: red fruit jam and the violets that the classic authors (Rodier, Roupnel) readily recognized in the Grands Crus of the Côte de Nuits. On the palate, the power expresses itself gracefully. A well-made wine, whose maturation was not unduly disturbed by the (appreciable) cask.

☛ Dom. Gros Frère et Soeur, 6, rue des Grands-Crus, 21700 Vosne-Romanée, tel. 03.80.61.12.43, fax 03.80.61.34.05 ☑
✒ by appt.
☛ Bernard Gros

DENIS MUGNERET ET FILS 2001★

■ Gd cru	0.5 ha	1,200	〰	+76 €

(93) 94 |95| |96| |97| 98 99 (00) 01

Tenant farmers in Richebourg (the Xavier Liger-Belair family) on 52 ares. A *coup de coeur* for the 92 vintage and another for the 2000. Rich, fleshy, complex, this one shows strong extraction. Its tannins, too, will have to age; the cask dominates at the moment but everything is in place for the delivery of its promises: the deep colour, with its purplish highlights, the nose which lets through a hint of black fruits from beneath the woodiness, the well-filled structure.

☛ Denis et Dominique Mugneret, 9, rue de la Fontaine, 21700 Vosne-Romanée, tel. 03.80.61.00.97, fax 03.80.61.24.54 ☑
✒ by appt.

Romanée Saint-Vivant

DOM. ROBERT ARNOUX 2000★★

■ Gd cru	n.c.	1,700	〰	+76 €

Built more on elegance and finesse than on power and strength, this Romanée Saint-Vivant is a very successful wine, typical of its vintage. Deep cherry, dark garnet, the bouquet opens on a balsamic note on a background of small, very ripe black fruits. On the palate? Its balance centres on the elegant tannins, favouring finesse over power and the unctuousness of quality.

☛ Dom. Robert Arnoux, 3, RN 74, 21700 Vosne-Romanée, tel. 03.80.61.08.41, fax 03.80.61.36.02 ☑
✒ by appt.

DOM. FOLLIN-ARBELET 2001★★★

■ Gd cru	n.c.	1,100	〰	+76 €

The Poisot heirs are a branch of the Latour family. The estate was handed down to Marie Poisot, sister of Louis II Latour, then to Pierre Poisot, then to his three children at the time of his death in 1938, remaining intact until 1990. This vineyard is located in the famous, historic "Quatre Journaux." A great deal of colour and a *coup de coeur* for this wine with its aromas of blackcurrant leaf-buds and spices. Fleshy, fruity, complex, long, it fits perfectly with our ideal of a Grand Bourgogne.

☛ Dom. Follin-Arbelet, Les Vercots, 21420 Aloxe-Corton, tel. 03.80.26.46.73, fax 03.80.26.43.32 ☑
✒ by appt.

FRANCOIS PARENT 2001★★

■ Gd cru	n.c.	600	〰	+76 €

Does this Romanée Saint-Vivant, with its black-cherry colour, have the truffle bouquet advertised on its label? To tell truth, this 2001 vintage is not saying a great deal; it lets a little touch of kirsch escape in subtle, but peceptible homage to the good cooper who supplies the estate. A balance of acidity and tannins is well-maintained from start to finish. The wine is still young and will only improve with time, but its unctuous body is very pleasant – a tribute to both the terroir and the winemaker.

☛ François Parent, La Garelle, Grande-Rue, 21630 Pommard, tel. 03.80.22.61.85, fax 03.80.24.03.16, e-mail francois@parent-pommard.com ☑
✒ by appt.

DOM. DE LA ROMANEE-CONTI 2000★★

■ Gd cru	5,28 ha	n.c.	〰	+76 €

67 72 73 75 76 78 (79) 80 81 |82| |87| |89| |91| |92| 95 |97| 98 99 00 01

The La Romanée-Conti estate has been engaged for several years on the restoration of the old monastery at Saint-Vivant in the Hautes Côtes de Vergy, which was the origin of this vineyard one thousand years ago. A truly filial gesture, because Romanée Saint-Vivant is one of those marvels that make us believe in Eternity. This wine, in some ways, is like the 82. This is a vintage that has not sought power, makes no attempt to impose itself by shouldering its way to the fore. No, it is simply amiable, pleasant. The very essence of a delicate wine but not the least bit fragile...

☛ SC du Dom. de la Romanée-Conti, 1, rue Derrière-le-Four, 21700 Vosne-Romanée, tel. 03.80.62.48.80, fax 03.80.61.05.72

Grande Rue

DOM. FRANCOIS LAMARCHE 2001★

■ Gd cru	1,65 ha	6,600	▮〰🍷	+76 €

|89| (90) 91 92 93 94 |95| 98 99 **00** 01

A Grande Rue is closely-woven, longer than it is broad, but which could turn into the Champs-Elysées in a few years' time. In the course of maturing, it will need five to ten years in order to open out. Lively garnet-red, it offers a delicate, but frank and precise, fruity bouquet. The opening is fresh and cheerful, the follow-on more tannic on the middle palate. Enough acidity to indicate long-term keeping quality, and a classic finish.

☛ Dom. François Lamarche, 9, rue des Communes, 21700 Vosne-Romanée, tel. 03.80.61.07.94, fax 03.80.61.24.31, e-mail domainelamarche@wanadoo.fr ☑
✒ by appt.

La Tâche

DOM. DE LA ROMANEE-CONTI

2002★★★

	Gd cru	6.06 ha	n.c.	🍷	+76 €

72 73 75 78 ⟨79⟩ |80| |81| |82| |87| |89| |91| |92| ⟨97⟩⟨98⟩⟨99⟩ 00 02

How shall we put it? It is enterprising, this La Tâche, which has not stolen its name. There is a touch of William Tell's arrow about it: nothing impedes its line of fire. In its radiant youthfulness, it has marvellous appeal. The taste of liquorice is irresistible; liquorice that fills the middle-palate with an extraordinarily precise flavour.This vintage should be quite precocious, but it is obvious that the verdict will only be returned in some ten to fifteen years's time. May you have the good fortune to be present when the court delivers its verdict!

➤ SC du Dom. de la Romanée-Conti, 1, rue Derrière-le-Four, 21700 Vosne-Romanée, tel. 03.80.62.48.80, fax 03.80.61.05.72

Nuits-Saint-Georges

Nuits-Saint-Georges, a little town of 5,500 inhabitants, does not produce the Grands Crus of its northerly neighbour; the appellation spreads into the commune of Premeaux which borders it to the south. However, the many Premiers Crus to be found here have a deserved reputation and in this, the most northerly Appellation Communale of the Côte de Nuits, we find a very different type of wine being made in the *climats*. The wines here generally have a higher tannin content, which means they can keep a long time.

The best-known Premier Cru vineyards are: Nuits-Saint-Georges, which is reputed to have been a vineyard as early as the year 1000; Les Vaucrains which produces robust wines; Les Cailles; Les Champs-Perdrix (the "partridge fields"); Les Porets, in the commune of Nuits, the name of which comes from poirets or little pears, and indeed produces a pronounced flavour of wild pears; the various *clos* named la Maréchale: des Argillières, des Forêts-Saint-Georges, des Corvées, de l'Arlot and sur Prémeaux. The vineyards produced 13,080 hl in 2002, of which 222 hl were white wines.

Nuits-Saint-Georges is the little wine capital of Burgundy. It also has a Hospices vineyard, which holds the annual wine auction on the Sunday before Palm Sunday. Many of the wine-shippers have their head offices in the town as do the liqueur-makers who produce Cassis de Bourgogne, and the makers of sparkling wines that have evolved today as Crémant de Bourgogne. The administrative headquarters of the *Confrérie des Chevaliers du Tastevin* is also to be found here.

JEAN-LUC AEGERTER

Récolte du Domaine 2001★

		1.07 ha	5,700	🍷	23–30 €

A delightful wine with a perfume that will remind you of something: blackcurrant leaf-buds from the Hautes Côtes are frequently used by the perfumers of Grasse. The palate is never-ending. Quite open, a Nuits that is supple and rounded.

➤ Jean-Luc Aegerter, 49, rue Henri-Challand, 21700 Nuits-Saint-Georges, tel. 03.80.61.02.88, fax 03.80.62.37.99, e-mail jean-luc.aegerter@wanadoo.fr ☑

🍷 by appt.

DOM. DE L'ARLOT

Clos des Forêts Saint-Georges Monopole 2000★

	1er cru	7 ha	21,000	🕓	30–38 €

This estate was founded by AXA Millésimes in 1986 and put under the management of Jean-Pierre de Smet who dedicated his life to it. This is a wine from the same Premier Cru discovered by Bernard Loiseau who set this graduate of ESSEC (College of Economic and Commercial Sciences) on the road to wine-growing. A **Clos de l'Arlot Premier Cru white 2000 (38–46 €)**, floral and a Côtes de Nuits that is quite true to type, received the same mark as the red. Strong in colour, the latter, with an appealing bouquet of "a rosebud opening at dawn," as Roupnel said, with a touch of oak. Supple on the palate, it shows more finesse than robustness. One could drink it in the year to come; the same applies to the previous wine.

➤ Dom. de L' Arlot, Premeaux, 21700 Nuits-Saint-Georges, tel. 03.80.61.01.92, fax 03.80.61.04.22 ☑

🍷 by appt.
➤ Axa Millésimes

JEAN-CLAUDE BOISSET

Aux Boudots 2000★

	1er cru	n.c.	n.c.	🍷	15–23 €

Made by the parent company of the Jean-Claude Boisset group, this wine, with its deep, limpid colour has a delicate bouquet of damp woodlands, crushed fresh fruit, and a touch of spice. It is, no doubt, a Cistercian wine, austere, as is normal for a Nuits of this age; it will open out in two to three years' time.

➤ Jean-Claude Boisset, 5, quai Dumorey, 21700 Nuits-Saint-Georges, tel. 03.80.62.61.61, fax 03.80.62.61.59, e-mail patriat.g@jcboisset.fr

🍷 by appt.

SYLVAIN CATHIARD

Aux Murgers 2001★

	1er cru	0.47 ha	2,700	🍷	30–38 €

Murgers are heaps of stones collected in the vineyards over the centuries and often seen in the Côte. This is the origin of the name of this Premier Cru, dark red in colour with a purplish rim. The bouquet is made up of notes of under-growth, spices and roasted almonds. The still astringent palate does not lack elegance.

➤ Sylvain Cathiard, 20, rue de la Goillotte, 21700 Vosne-Romanée, tel. 03.80.62.36.01, fax 03.80.61.18.21 ☑

🍷 by appt.

DOM. JEAN CHAUVENET

Les Perrières 2001★★★

	1er cru	0.23 ha	1,200	🍷	23–30 €

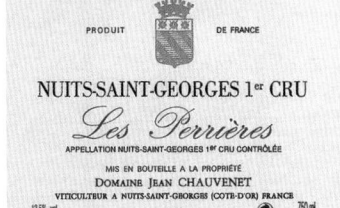

When you can recognize a Nuits wine on the taste-buds, you will also know that a Les Perrières will spoil you like a doting mother. *Coup de coeur*, this one cries out for a ham on the bone cooked in wine from the Nuits (which you will, of course, beg

BURGUNDY

from this estate!) A sumptuous wine, so deep-red it is quite black, with a bouquet of strawberries and liquorice; velvety on the palate but still full of character and concentration. The length is average, but it is fantastically good, this Grand Bourgogne! The **Les Vaucrains Premier Cru 2001 (30–38 €)** also at the top of its form, was awarded two stars, whereas the **Les Bousselots Premier Cru 2001 (23–30 €)** received one star.

•ↄ SCE Dom. Jean Chauvenet, 3, rue de Gilly,
21700 Nuits-Saint-Georges, tel. 03.80.61.00.72,
fax 03.80.61.12.87 **V**
I by appt.
•ↄ Ch. Drag

CHAUVENET-CHOPIN 2001★

■	1.5 ha	8,000	❙❙❙	11–15 €

A *coup de coeur* for their 98 and 91 vintages, this domaine seems to have a feeling for detail. Its *village*, with its an intense colour, and nose opening well on stewed fruit, has just the right amount of tannins on the palate, whose aromatic notes confirm the aromas of the bouquet. It has prospects for four to five years of life.

•ↄ Chauvenet-Chopin, 97, rue Félix-Tisserand,
21700 Nuits-Saint-Georges, tel. 03.80.61.28.11,
fax 03.80.61.20.02 **V**
I by appt. (without tasting)

A. CHOPIN ET FILS

Les Bas de Combes 2001★

■	2 ha	10,000	❙❙❙	11–15 €

Les Bas de Combes, a *climat* located below Les Boudots and right up against Vosne-Romanée. Still a little woody, this limpid garnet-red wine nevertheless expresses the qualities that will develop after it has spent two years in the cellar. The entry on the palate is pleasant with sufficient richness to give flavour to this quite pleasant 2001 vintage. Beside it one can also see the **Murgers Premier Cru 2001 (15–23 €)** which received a special mention.

•ↄ A. Chopin et Fils, RN 74, 21700 Comblanchien,
tel. 03.80.62.92.60, fax 03.80.62.70.78 **V**
I by appt.

DOM. DU CLOS SAINT-MARC

Clos Saint-Marc 2001★

■	1er cru	1 ha	n.c.	❙❙❙ ▮	30–38 €

At one time rented out to tenant farmers and used to grow grapes for Bouchard Père et Fils, this *clos* belonged to the director of the *Librairie Générale de Droit et Jurisprudence* (Library of Law and Jurisprudence), who also edited *Aventures de Bécassine* (a famous French children's book). The Clos Saint-Marc owes its name to the parish festival and a local fountain. More precisely, it refers to the Corvées Pagets and the Argillières. It is a beautiful wine, tightly woven with an impeccable texture. In appearance, a purplish rim surrounds the strongly extracted colour. Full of finesse, the bouquet is of spices and roasted almonds. On the palate, it is the Lion of Saint-Marc, showing a certain amount of its claws, but that will be tamed if it is laid down for two or three years.

•ↄ Bouchard Père et Fils, Ch. de Beaune, 21200 Beaune,
tel. 03.80.24.80.24, fax 03.80.22.55.88,
e-mail france@bouchard-pereetfils.com
I by appt.
•ↄ Henriot

R. DUBOIS ET FILS

Les Porêts Saint-Georges 2000★

■	1er cru	0.58 ha	3,500	❙❙❙	15–23 €

Open wide your *oreilles* (ears), as they say in Burgundy because there is a Porêts Saint-Georges and a Forêts Saint-Georges. In charge for the last ten years, Raphaël Dubois delivered a Premier Cru which the Jury found a pleasure to taste. Deep garnet-red, this wine swims in red berries and *pain d'épice* (gingerbread). The first impression is flint. Power, richness: the balance is excellent.

•ↄ Dom. R. Dubois et Fils, rte de Nuits-Saint-Georges,
21700 Premeaux-Prissey, tel. 03.80.62.30.61,
fax 03.80.61.24.07, e-mail rdubois@wanadoo.fr **V**
I ev. day 8am–11.30am 2pm–6pm; Sat. Sun. by appt.

DOM. GUY DUFOULEUR

Clos des Perrières 2000★

■	1er cru	0.78 ha	4,900	❙❙❙	30–38 €

On the site of an old quarry, close to the limestone cliff at Premeaux, this *climat* produced a wine with a good potential for laying down, considering the vintage. Beneath the very strong colour, the nose hesitates between blackcurrant and raspberry. No need for repeated ringing of the doorbell to gain entry on the palate: it is both velvety and powerful at the same time, spicy but without exaggeration, without excessive aromatic complexity. A wine vinified by Yvan Dufouleur.

•ↄ Dom. Guy Dufouleur, 19, pl. Monge,
21700 Nuits-Saint-Georges, tel. 03.80.62.31.00,
fax 03.80.62.31.00 **V** ▦
I by appt.

VINCENT DUREUIL-JANTHIAL

Clos des Argillières 2000★

■	1er cru	0.71 ha	3,400	❙❙❙	23–30 €

One foot in the Nuits and the other in Rully: the result is interesting. Intense colour, the finesse of the raspberry bouquet, the wine opens on a surfeit of fruit then holds back to achieve an honourable balance (in keeping with the vintage). Its structure is acceptable, and this Clos des Argillières (it was called Clos Labaume in the 19th century) appears to conform to the values of the appellation.

•ↄ Vincent Dureuil-Janthial, rue de la Buisserolle,
71150 Rully, tel. 03.85.87.26.32, fax 03.85.87.15.01,
e-mail vincent.dureuil@wanadoo.fr **V**
I by appt.

HENRI FELETTIG 2001★

■	0.3 ha	1,800	❙❙❙	15–23 €

A plot bought in the spring of 2001, harvested and vinified here a few months later. Interesting, structured: these are the strong points of this wine constructed on silky, quite lingering tannins; very Burgundian in type, it positively sings crystallized fruits, and a basket of soft fruits is the inspiration for its bouquet. It is a wine to drink in 12 to 16 months' time.

•ↄ GAEC Henri Felettig, rue du Tilleul,
21220 Chambolle-Musigny, tel. 03.80.62.85.09,
fax 03.80.62.86.41 **V**
I by appt.

DOM. JEAN FERY ET FILS 2000★★

■	0.3 ha	2,100	❙❙❙	11–15 €

A very special wine! Clean, upright, with no flourishes, a characteristic Côte de Nuits, a 2000 vintage of the contemporary Pinot colour. The second nose surpasses promises of the first: fruit and oak are both present in a perfect balance and show clear signs of linking up. Very fine presence on the palate on silky tannins. It is good, and that says it all. Drink it with confidence over the next five years.

•ↄ Dom. Jean Fery et Fils, 21420 Echevronne,
tel. 03.80.21.59.60, fax 03.80.21.59.59 **V** ▮
I by appt.

PHILIPPE GAVIGNET

Les Bousselots 2001★

■	1er cru	0.43 ha	2,700	❙❙❙	15–23 €

Philippe Gavignet has produced some good wines in this vintage. The **Pruliers Premier Cru**, one star, and a **Chaboeufs Premier Cru** which received a special mention. Still in red, with attractive coloured highlights, the deep-coloured Les Bousselots mingles oaky notes and clean, pure Morello cherry. The balance on the palate is sure; its structure and roundness are well matched. A wine to lay down for five to ten years; ideal with marinated meats.

•ↄ Dom. Philippe Gavignet, 36, rue Dr-Louis-Legrand,
21700 Nuits-Saint-Georges, tel. 03.80.61.09.41,
fax 03.80.61.03.56,
e-mail contact@domaine-gavignet.fr **V**
I ev. day 8am–12 noon 2pm–6pm; Sat. Sun. by appt.

LOUIS JADOT

Les Boudots 1999★★

◼ 1er cru	n.c.	n.c.	◐	38–46 €

Sloping and stony, this *climat* is near Malconsorts in Vosne-Romanée. Here it is shown off to best advantage. Note the vintage: 1999. Its colour, however, is a very young, deep garnet-red. Undergrowth, woodland fruits, the bouquet is a distinguished one. The first impression is of liquorice notes. The tannins are quite integrated. Powerful and full-bodied. Let it age for a year or two. It will keep quite a bit longer.
➥ Maison Louis Jadot, 21, rue Eugène-Spuller, 21200 Beaune, tel. 03.80.22.10.57, fax 03.80.22.56.03, e-mail contact@louisjadot.com
� by appt.

S. JAVOUHEY

Les Boudots 2000★

◼ 1er cru	n.c.	n.c.	◐	38–46 €

The **Village Vieilles Vignes 2000 (23–30 €)** received one star, as did this Les Boudots. All that "est bon, et bon, et bon," as the song goes. And this spirited, balanced wine from the 2000 vintage, which does its job conscientiously, does indeed make a good impression. Limpid, intense and already open on damp woodlands, ripe fruit, it inspired one of the Jurors to make the comment: "Finesse and roundness in the purest Burgundian style".
➥ S. Javouhey, 50, rue du Gal-de-Gaulle, BP 63, 21702 Nuits-Saint-Georges, tel. 03.80.61.10.30, fax 03.80.61.35.76, e-mail domaine@javouhey.com ☑
� ev. day 9am–12 noon 1pm–7pm; cl. Jan.

BERTRAND MACHARD DE GRAMONT Aux Allots 2000★★

◼	0.9 ha	4,500	◐	15–23 €

This Les Allots is in great form. Dark red with purplish highlights, a mixture of kirsch, Morello cherry and vanilla on the nose. This wine opens with a flourish and continues on firm, well-constructed tannins. Controlled structure; perfectly true to type, combining momentum, character and finesse. Drink it with a beef Wellington, or any kind of game. **Les Hauts Pruliers 2000 (11–15 €)** received one star.
➥ Bertrand Machard de Gramont, 13, rue de Vergy, 21700 Nuits-Saint-Georges, tel. 03.80.61.16.96, fax 03.80.61.16.96 ☑
� by appt.

FREDERIC MAGNIEN

Les Saint-Georges Vieilles Vignes 2001★★★

◼ 1er cru	0.5 ha	3,000	◐	30–38 €

No-one is a prophet in his own country: it was a *négociant-éleveur* from Morey who took first place in the Nuits tasting with this remarkably vinified wine, which would appear to represent an excellent job of work at the vineyard. Its concentration and roundness speak the same a language. A good note of terroir. The colour is dense, dark red, the nose predominantly blackcurrant. One could hardly do better.
➥ Frédéric Magnien, 26, rte Nationale, 21220 Morey-Saint-Denis, tel. 03.80.58.54.20, fax 03.80.51.84.34, e-mail fredericmagnien.grandsvinsdebourgogne@ wanadoo.fr ☑
� by appt.

DOM. ALAIN MICHELOT

Vieilles Vignes 2000★★

◼	1.3 ha	7,500	◐	15–23 €

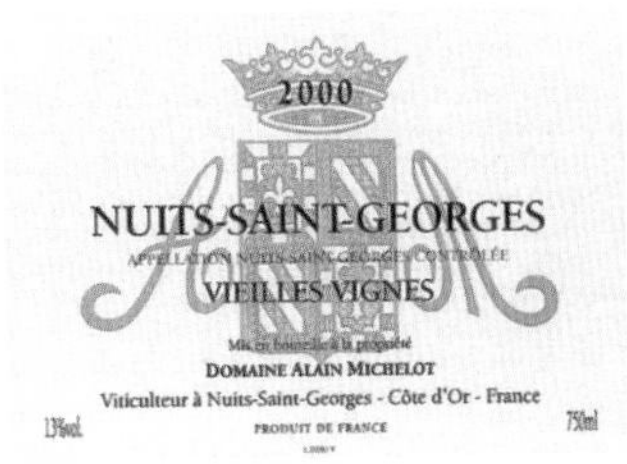

Deep ruby with hints of purple, this wine is a classic colour. Aeration brings out its perfumes on notes of vanilla and blackcurrant. The first impression is elegantly oaky with a very attractive, balanced fruitiness. Supple and elegant, very lingering tannins make up a delicious, aromatic palate. To lay down for two to five years. The **Les Porêts Saint-Georges Premier Cru 1999 (23–30 €)** was awarded one star; the **Les Vaucrains Premier Cru 2000 (23–30 €)** received a special mention.
➥ Dom. Alain Michelot, 6, rue Camille-Rodier, 21700 Nuits-Saint-Georges, tel. 03.80.61.14.46, fax 03.80.61.35.08, e-mail domaine.alainmichelot@wanadoo.fr ☑
� by appt.

P. MISSEREY

Les Cailles 2000★

◼ 1er cru	n.c.	3,500	◐	30–38 €

The sight of this label (our Jurors don't get to see it) always reminds one of Marc Misserey, who for many years was one of the pillars of the Tastevin. The Lanvin family took over this company; they have produced this Les Cailles, with its good, intense ruby-red colour. A wild raspberry bouquet and typically Pinot Noir on the palate: this wine needs to be laid down for two years.
➥ Maison P. Misserey, 3, rue des Seuillets, BP 10, 21701 Nuits-Saint-Georges Cedex, tel. 03.80.61.07.74, fax 03.80.61.31.40, e-mail lanvin-sa@worldonline.fr ☑
� by appt.

DENIS MUGNERET ET FILS

Les Saint-Georges 2001★★

◼ 1er cru	1.14 ha	3,600	◐	23–30 €

A pleasant and valorous **Boudots Premier Cru 2001** was awarded one star. The Les Saint-Georges with its arresting colour, offers up a typically Burgundian bouquet, not in the least complicated, but of a complex simplicity – essentially of liquorice and vanilla. The structure is substantial, enveloping rounded and fine tannins; the alternation of freshness at the start and the warmth that follows leaves a taste of crystallized fruit glowing on the final palate. Definitely a wine up on the heights.
➥ Denis et Dominique Mugneret, 9, rue de la Fontaine, 21700 Vosne-Romanée, tel. 03.80.61.00.97, fax 03.80.61.24.54 ☑
� by appt.

DOM. DES PERDRIX
Les Terres blanches 2000★★

	1er cru	0,13 ha	830	⊞	46–76 €

The old Mugneret-Gouachon estate is now in the hands of the Devillard family, who are winegrowers at Gevrey-Chambertin. This is one of the rare whites of this AOC, all decked out in gold. Its perfumes are elegant, combining fine notes of citrus fruits, hazelnuts and toast. Balanced, rich and lingering, it will be excellent served with a sauced fish dish sometime between 2004 and 2009. In red, **Les Terres Blanches Premier Cru 2000** also the **Nuits-Saint-George Village 2000** each received one star.
☛ B. et C. Devillard, Dom. des Perdrix, Ch. de Champ Renard, 71640 Mercurey, tel. 03.85.98.12.12, fax 03.85.45.25.49, e-mail rodet@rodet.com ☑

DOM. JEAN PETITOT ET FILS
Les Poisets 2000★

		1 ha	6,000	⊞	11–15 €

Les Poisets is located just below Cailles and not very far from Les Saint-Georges. It is a kind of Neuilly of the Nuits. Limpid and bright ruby-red, this wine starts off on a delicate fruitiness then goes to a spicy muskiness: an identikit picture of the appellation. The palate stays with this theme, quite spicy, almost meaty, while displaying a "greedy" temperament. It will open out in a year or two.
☛ EARL Dom. Jean Petitot et Fils, 26, pl. de la Mairie, 21700 Corgoloin, tel. 03.80.62.98.21, fax 03.80.62.71.64, e-mail domaine.petitot@wanadoo.fr ☑
☡ by appt.

CH. DE PREMEAUX 2001★

		2 ha	10,000	⊞	11–15 €

Alain Pelletier heads this estate, founded by his grandfather in 1933. The original Château de Premeaux was demolished at the beginning of the 19th century. This one is a pleasant manor house. This crimson-red *village* with a vinous nose on which vanilla and raspberry have an equal say, came close to a second star. Fine velvety tannins go hand in hand with a whole basketful of fruit on the palate, with both flavour and secondary aromas. The structure is substantial, so that one can lay this wine down for two to three years.
☛ Dom. du Ch. de Premeaux, 21700 Premeaux-Prissey, tel. 03.80.62.30.64, fax 03.80.62.39.28, e-mail chateau.de.premeaux@wanadoo.fr ☑
☡ by appt.
☛ Pelletier

HENRI ET GILLES REMORIQUET
Les Bousselots 2001★

	1er cru	0.55 ha	3,000	⊞	15–23 €

Gilles Remoriquet became a major player in the *Interprofession Bourguignonne* (Burgundian interprofessional organization). He speaks at the very illustrious press conference at the Hospices sale. His Les Bousselots is quite up to the level of his other responsibilities. The colour is brilliant, the oak well-balanced, the richness subservient to the quite significant structure, but it is down for two to five years. The still very young **Premier Cru Les Allots 2001** received a special mention.
☛ Henri et Gilles Remoriquet, 25, rue de Charmois, 21700 Nuits-Saint-Georges, tel. 03.80.61.24.84, fax 03.80.61.36.63, e-mail domaine.remoriquet@wanadoo.fr ☑
☡ by appt.

DOM. DANIEL RION ET FILS
Les Lavières 2001★

		0.8 ha	4,500	▮⊞♦	15–23 €

Les Lavières is right beside Vosne, below Les Murgers. Of an intense and deep colour, this 2001 vintage tends towards aromas of well-ripened cherries but which still need to be confirmed; the woodiness, while certainly integrated, also needs time. The acidity is as it should be, the tannins are quite imposing but tamed. A wine which should develop well, if patience is one of your virtues.
☛ Dom. Daniel Rion et Fils, RN 74, 21700 Premeaux, tel. 03.80.62.31.28, fax 03.80.61.13.41, e-mail contact@domaine-daniel-rion.com ☑
☡ ev. day except Sun. 8.30am–12 noon 1.30pm–6pm; Sat. by appt.

ANTONIN RODET
Les Porêts Cave privée 2000★★

	1er cru	n.c.	852	▮⊞♦	46–76 €

A private wine cellar, the marque of Antonin Rodet and vinified by Nadine Gublin. Its ceremonial colour is very youthful, its bouquet complex and rich: truffle, red berries and vanilla from the cask. Rounded and concentrated, the palate is balanced. A good result. A **Les Damodes Premier Cru 2000** was specially mentioned.
☛ Antonin Rodet, 71640 Mercurey, tel. 03.85.98.12.12, fax 03.85.45.25.49, e-mail rodet@rodet.com ☑
☡ ev. day except Sat. Sun. 9am–12 noon 2pm–6pm

DOM. VINCENT SAUVESTRE
Les Saint-Georges 2001★

	1er cru	0.6 ha	3,500	⊞	15–23 €

Standard bearer of the appellation, the Les Saint-Georges frequently overcomes the dragon. And it happens again this time. Limpid, lively ruby-red in colour, this 2001 vintage exudes a perfume of cherries. After a clear and frank opening the perfume remains and while the tannins are still rather upright, age will calm them down. The structure is stable and lasting.
☛ Dom. Vincent Sauvestre, rte de Monthélie, 21190 Meursault, tel. 03.80.21.22.45, fax 03.80.21.28.05

DOM. TAUPENOT-MERME
Les Pruliers 2000★

	1er cru	n.c.	3,300	⊞	30–38 €

Some of the stone used in the building of this cellar, in the 18th century, came from the cloister of the Carmes de Dijon. Les Pruliers probably owes its name to the wild plum trees which at one time brightened up the vineyard. According to the ancient authors they gave rise to wines with a copper, metallic flavour which diminished with age…Today's wines do not bear this out. This one is a 2000 which is characteristic of its vintage: intense ruby-red colour and concentrated bouquet of red berries and muted charred aromas; a very creditable and lengthy palate; a wine to lay down for three to five years.
☛ Taupenot-Merme, 33, rte des Grands-Crus, 21220 Morey-Saint-Denis, tel. 03.80.34.35.24, fax 03.80.51.83.41, e-mail domaine.taupenot-merme@wanadoo.fr ☑
☡ by appt.

DOM. FABRICE VIGOT 2001★

		0.37 ha	2,500	⊞	15–23 €

A new, elegant label for Fabrice Vigot who, having changed address, also changed his image. His Nuits *village* is well-worthy of this improved image because it has all the colour it could need and half-opens the door of its bouquet on kirsch and raspberry – an amiable gesture. The presence of tannins augurs well for the future. If you remember, its 89 vintage was *coup de coeur* in the 92 edition.
☛ Dom. Fabrice Vigot, 20, rue de la Fontaine, 21700 Vosne-Romanée, tel. 03.80.61.13.01, fax 03.80.61.13.01, e-mail fabrice.vigot@wanadoo.fr ☑
☡ by appt.

Wines selected but not starred

DOM. ROBERT ARNOUX
Clos des Corvées Pagets 2000

	1er cru	0.55 ha	2,200	⊞	30–38 €

☛ Dom. Robert Arnoux, 3, RN 74, 21700 Vosne-Romanée, tel. 03.80.61.08.41, fax 03.80.61.36.02 ☑
☡ by appt.

DOM. BARBIER ET FILS

Belle Croix 2000

◼	0.21 ha	1,300	🍶	15–23 €

📍 Dom. Barbier et Fils, 17, rue Thurot,
21700 Nuits-Saint-Georges, tel. 03.80.61.21.21,
fax 03.80.61.10.65, e-mail domaine.barbier@wanadoo.fr ☑
🍷 ev. day 9am–7pm
📍 Guy and Xavier Dufouleur

DOM. DES CHAMBRIS 2001

	n.c.	600	🍶	15–23 €

📍 SCEV du Dom. des Chambris, 7, rue du Lavoir,
21220 Chevannes, tel. 03.80.61.44.77, fax 03.80.61.48.87,
e-mail leschambris@wanadoo.fr ☑
🍷 by appt.

DOM. DU CHATEAU-GRIS

Château Gris Monopole 2000

◼ 1er cru	2.47 ha	14,000	🍶	30–38 €

📍 Dom. du Château-Gris, 17, av. du Gal-de-Gaulle,
21700 Nuits-Saint-Georges, tel. 03.80.61.25.02,
fax 03.80.24.37.38

DOM. GEORGES CHICOTOT

Les Rues de Chaux 2000

◼ 1er cru	0.29 ha	1,100	🍶	15–23 €

📍 Dom. Georges Chicotot, 15, rue du Gal-de-Gaulle,
21700 Nuits-Saint-Georges, tel. 03.80.61.19.33,
fax 03.80.61.38.94, e-mail chicotot@aol.com ☑
🍷 by appt.

JEAN-PIERRE DUFOUR

Les Allots 2000

◼	0.29 ha	1,466	🍶	11–15 €

📍 Gilberte et Jean-Pierre Dufour, 11, rue de Ley,
21200 Chorey-lès-Beaune, tel. 03.80.22.10.93,
fax 03.80.22.10.93, e-mail gilberte.dufour@terre-net.fr ☑
🍷 by appt.

FAIVELEY

Les Saint-Georges 2000

◼ 1er cru	0.29 ha	1,900	🍶	46–76 €

📍 Bourgognes Faiveley, 8, rue du Tribourg,
21700 Nuits-Saint-Georges, tel. 03.80.61.04.55,
fax 03.80.62.33.37,
e-mail bourgognes.faiveley@wanadoo.fr ☑

DOM. ANNE-MARIE GILLE 2000

◼	1.21 ha	7,000	🍶	15–23 €

📍 Dom. Anne-Marie Gille, 34, RN 74,
21700 Comblanchien, tel. 03.80.62.94.13,
fax 03.80.62.99.88, e-mail domaine.gille@wanadoo.fr ☑
🍷 by appt.

DOM. HENRI GOUGES

Clos des Porrets Saint-Georges 2000

◼ 1er cru	3.5 ha	15,000	🍶	23–30 €

📍 Dom. Henri Gouges, 7, rue du Moulin,
21700 Nuits-Saint-Georges, tel. 03.80.61.04.40,
fax 03.80.61.32.84

LABOURE-ROI 2001

◼	n.c.	n.c.	🍶	15–23 €

📍 Labouré-Roi, rue Lavoisier, 21700 Nuits-Saint-Georges,
tel. 03.80.62.64.00, fax 03.80.62.64.10
🍷 by appt.

JEAN-PIERRE TRUCHETET 2000

◼	1.63 ha	4,700	🍶	15–23 €

📍 Jean-Pierre Truchetet, RN 74, 21700 Premeaux-Prissey,
tel. 03.80.61.07.22, fax 03.80.61.34.35 ☑
🍷 by appt.

Côte de Nuits-Villages

After the village of Premeaux, the vineyard dwindles to only about 200 m at Corgoloin, the narrowest point on the Côte. Here, the "mountain" is not so high and the administrative jurisdiction of the Appellation Côte de Nuits-Villages, once known as "Vins Fins de la Côte de Nuits," stops at the level of the Clos des Langres above Corgoloin. Between them are two communes: Prissey, associated with Prémeaux, and Comblanchien, famous for a particular kind of limestone (incorrectly called marble) which is extracted from the quarries in the hills. They both have terroirs that are entitled to be called Appellation Communale. But the areas of these three communes are too limited to have their own appellation, so Brochon and Fixin became associated with them to share the unique Appellation Côte de Nuits-Villages, which in 2002 produced 6,502 hl of wine, of which 319 hl were whites. You can find excellent wines at affordable prices here.

VINCENT ET DENIS BERTHAUT 2001 ★

◼	0,4 ha	3,000	🍶	8–11 €

A Côte de Nuits-Village from near Fixin. Garnet-red, its aromas are equally divided between the cask (roasted, toast, liquorice) and the wine (ripe fruits). Its constitution is structured, both robust and fruity at same time: the tannins don't ring any alarm bells; on the contrary, they are smooth and benevolent. A wine that needs to age for two to four years.
📍 Vincent et Denis Berthaut, 9, rue Noisot, 21220 Fixin,
tel. 03.80.52.45.48, fax 03.80.51.31.05,
e-mail denis.berthaut@wanadoo.fr ☑
🍷 ev. day 10am–12noon 2pm–6pm; cl. Jan.

CLOS SAINT-LOUIS 2001 ★

	2.5 ha	13,500	🍷 🍶	8–11 €

The estate is only 300 m from a 12th century church which you must be sure to visit. From near Fixin, the deep-red colour of this 2001 vintage retains some of its youthful nuances. Its complex aromas make it a satisfying wine in which fruity and floral notes are joined by liquorice and cinnamon aromas. The tannins, long on the palate, denote an elegant wine.
📍 Dom. du Clos Saint-Louis, 4, rue des Rosiers,
21220 Fixin, tel. 03.80.52.45.51, fax 03.80.58.88.76,
e-mail clos.st.louis@wanadoo.fr ☑
🍷 by appt.
📍 Philippe Bernard

DOM. DESERTAUX-FERRAND 2001 ★

	n.c.	5,100	🍶	8–11 €

This AOC at one time produced mostly red wines but the whites are steadily catching up. This is a full, fleshy wine, straw-gold in colour and with quite open, characteristic aromas. Christine and Vincent Désertaux, brother and sister, established themselves there in 1995 and 1999 (the family estate goes back to 1899). Worth noting is the accepted, but rare combination of 70% Chardonnay and 30% Pinot Blanc, a grape variety which is not very widespread.
📍 Dom. Désertaux-Ferrand, 135, Grande-Rue,
21700 Corgoloin, tel. 03.80.62.98.40, fax 03.80.62.70.32,
e-mail contact@desertaux-ferrand.com ☑
🍷 by appt.

DOM. GACHOT-MONOT 2000 ★★

	9 ha	15,000	🍶	8–11 €

Coup de coeur in 2000 and 2001 editions of the *Guide*, this domaine stands out in the appellation. Once again, it has scored. The deep, purplish red colour is the customary one. The very attractive bouquet is fresh, integrated and expressive, tending towards blackcurrants. The well-seated palate offers up a fairly substantial finish in which blackcurrant still predominates. A wine with a good medium term future. A fillet of beef is waiting for it somewhere in the Charolais.

☙ GAEC Dom. Gachot-Monot, 13, rue Humbert-de-Gillens, 21700 Gerland, tel. 03.80.62.50.95, fax 03.80.62.53.85, e-mail gachot-monot@wanadoo.fr ☑
☿ by appt.

DOM. LALEURE-PIOT

Les Bellevues 2001★

■	0.85 ha	4,800	◗◗◗	8–11 €

The appellation is beginning to make the most of its *climats*. Les Bellevues is located on the heights at Comblanchien, not very far from the Clos de la Maréchale. Silky and charming, this is a wine with body, a quite rich tannic touch and a

certain chewiness. Perfumes of blackcurrant and a deep, garnet-red colour complete the picture. Open the bottle one hour before serving.

☙ Dom. Laleure-Piot, rue de Pralot, 21420 Pernand-Vergelesses, tel. 03.80.21.52.37, fax 03.80.21.59.48, e-mail infos@laleure-piot.com ☑
☿ ev. day 8am–12 noon 2pm–6pm; Sat. Sun. by appt.
☙ Frédéric Laleure

DOM. HENRI NAUDIN-FERRAND

Vieilles Vignes 2000★★

■	1.55 ha	9,266	◗◗◗	11–15 €

One of these days we will have to make this estate an honorary member or put it into a class of its own...*Coup de coeur* in

Côte de Nuits (South)

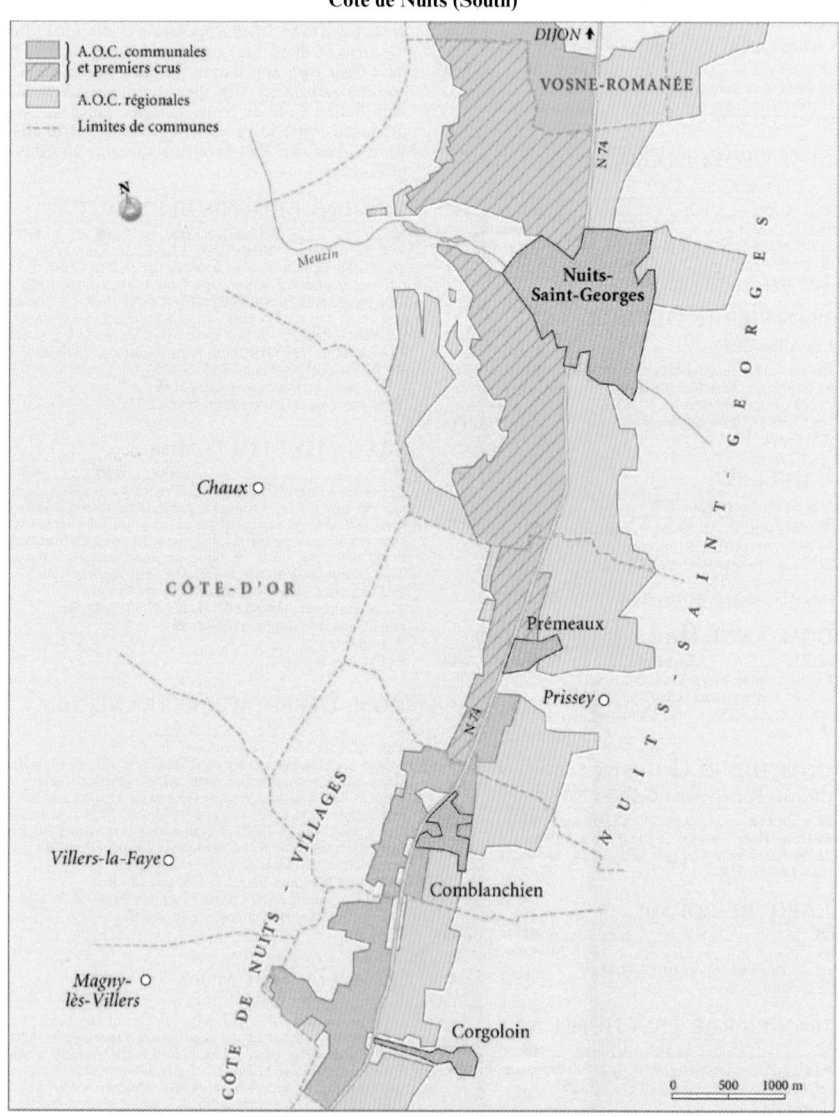

A.O.C. communales et premiers crus

A.O.C. régionales

Limites de communes

DIJON ↟

VOSNE-ROMANÉE

N 74

Meuzin

Nuits-Saint-Georges

N U I T S - S A I N T - G E O R G E S

Chaux ○

CÔTE-D'OR

Prémeaux

N 74

Prissey ○

Villers-la-Faye ○

C Ô T E   D E   N U I T S - V I L L A G E S

Comblanchien

Magny-lès-Villers ○

Corgoloin

0   500   1000 m

Wines selected but not starred

the 1995, 1999 and 2001 editions, and again this year. This is exceptional in a single appellation. This is what a Côtes de Nuits-Villages does best, thanks to the immense talent of Claire Naudin. The colour shows some signs of evolving, but the bouquet is made up of touches of pepper and ginger, red berries, blackcurrant. On the palate it is particularly full-flavoured with the delicate taste of cherries and blackcurrants, mild spices, integrated oak and delicious, well-made substance. Drink it for preference with poultry or a leg of lamb.
🔁 Dom. Henri Naudin-Ferrand, rue du Meix-Grenot, 21700 Magny-lès-Villers, tel. 03.80.62.91.50, fax 03.80.62.91.77, e-mail dnaudin@ipac.fr ☑
🍷 by appt.

DOM. DE LA POULETTE 2000★

| | 5.34 ha | 30,000 | 🍷 | 11–15 € |

This well-reputed estate is situated within 200 m of the beautiful 13th century church of Corgoloin. This is a fine wine from the Côte de Nuits. Intense ruby-red, its perfumes are of game, tending towards leather. On the palate, the fruit is well-integrated and the whole shows great coherence with a spicy note on the finish. A wine to lay down for two to three years: it doesn't lack potential.
🔁 Dom. de la Poulette, 103, Grande-Rue, 21700 Corgoloin, tel. 03.80.62.98.02, fax 01.45.25.43.23, e-mail f.michaut@wanadoo.fr ☑
🍷 by appt.
🔁 F. Michaut-Audidier

DOM. DANIEL RION ET FILS

Le Vaucrain 2001★★

| | 2.24 ha | 12,000 | 🍷 | 8–11 € |

This appellation makes wines that are excellent value for money. This Vaucrain, for example, a *climat* close to Premeaux and the Premier Cru Clos de la Maréchale: only a few dozen metres separate them. Deep, brilliant red, the wine is very appealing. Very true to type, it is all red berries enhanced by a violet note and spice; its elegant tannins and its length give it great elegance.
🔁 Dom. Daniel Rion et Fils, RN 74, 21700 Premeaux, tel. 03.80.62.31.28, fax 03.80.61.13.41, e-mail contact@domaine-daniel-rion.com ☑
🍷 ev. day except Sun. 8.30am–12 noon 1.30pm–6pm; Sat. by appt.

DOM. VINCENT SAUVESTRE 2001★

| | 2.25 ha | 11,800 | 🍷 | 8–11 € |

A wine to drink with fruit, a 2001 vintage of a deep ruby-red colour that couldn't be more classic. The raspberry perfume indicates a fine, extraction full of fruit aromas. Perhaps one could wish for a little more substance, but the richness and roundness are very satisfying. Nuances of musk and cooked fruit are present on the lingering finish. The winemaker effaced himself and let the terroir have its say.
🔁 Dom. Vincent Sauvestre, rte de Monthélie, 21190 Meursault, tel. 03.80.21.22.45, fax 03.80.21.28.05

A. CHOPIN ET FILS

Vieilles Vignes 2001

| | 2 ha | 4,000 | 🍷 | 8–11 € |

🔁 A. Chopin et Fils, RN 74, 21700 Comblanchien, tel. 03.80.62.92.60, fax 03.80.62.70.78 ☑
🍷 by appt.

DOM. CORNU

Le Clos de Magny 2000

| | 1.31 ha | 8,000 | 🍷 | 11–15 € |

🔁 Dom. Claude Cornu, rue du Meix-Grenot, 21700 Magny-lès-Villers, tel. 03.80.62.92.05, fax 03.80.62.72.22 ☑
🍷 by appt.

R. DUBOIS ET FILS

Les Monts de Boncourt 2001

| | 0.8 ha | 6,500 | | 8–11 € |

🔁 Dom. R. Dubois et Fils, rte de Nuits-Saint-Georges, 21700 Premeaux-Prissey, tel. 03.80.62.30.61, fax 03.80.61.24.07, e-mail rdubois@wanadoo.fr ☑
🍷 ev. day 8am–11.30am 2pm–6pm; Sat. Sun. by appt.

JEAN-YVES GUYARD

Le Clos de Magny 2001

| | 1.5 ha | 7,000 | 🍷 | 8–11 € |

🔁 Jean-Yves Guyard, 21, rue de Chaux, 21700 Villers-la-Faye, tel. 03.80.62.91.14, fax 03.80.62.75.72, e-mail jeanyvesguyard@wanadoo.fr ☑
🍷 by appt.

JEAN-MARC MILLOT 2000

| | 2.8 ha | 3,000 | | 8–11 € |

🔁 Jean-Marc Millot, Grande-Rue, 21700 Comblanchien, tel. 03.80.61.34.81, fax 03.80.61.34.81 ☑
🍷 by appt.

THIBAULT DE PLANIOL

Clos des Langres 2000

| | 1.5 ha | 7,000 | 🍷 | 11–15 € |

🔁 SC La Juvinière, Clos des Langres, 21700 Corgoloin, tel. 03.80.62.98.73, fax 03.80.62.95.15, e-mail domaine.ardhuy@wanadoo.fr
🔁 Liogier

DOM. JEAN-PIERRE TRUCHETET 2001

| | n.c. | 3,300 | 🍷 | 8–11 € |

🔁 Jean-Pierre Truchetet, RN 74, 21700 Premeaux-Prissey, tel. 03.80.61.07.22, fax 03.80.61.34.35 ☑
🍷 by appt.

Côte de Beaune

Ladoix

Three small villages – Serrigny near the railway line, Ladoix on the RN74, and Buisson at the end of the Côte de Nuits – make up the commune of Ladoix-Serrigny. The Appellation Communale is Ladoix. The hamlet of Buisson is located exactly at the geographical conjunction of the Côtes de Nuits and the Côtes de Beaune. The administrative border stops at the commune of Corgoloin, but the hill itself continues further as do the vineyards and the wine. The Corton "mountain" rises beyond the combe of Magny, which marks the physical separation. The steep inclines made up of layers of marl have many south- and west-facing slopes, making this one of the best wine-growing areas on the Côte.

The various aspects give the Appellation Ladoix a variety of different types of wine, added to which its white wines are exceptionally well adapted to growing on the Argovian marlstone soils. This is the case with Les Gréchons, for example, which is grown on the same geological soils as Corton-Charlemagne further south, though it has a less favourable aspect. The wines from this location have distinctive characteristics. Having produced 3,479 hl of red wine and 836 hl of white in 2002, the Appellation Ladoix is little known, but deserves better.

Another oddity: even though Ladoix was given a favourable classification by the Comité de Viticulture de Beaune in 1860, it was not awarded any Premiers Crus. This was put right by the INAO in 1978. The main Premiers Crus are La Macaude, La Corvée and Le Clou d'Orge, which produce wines with the same characteristics as those from the Côte de Nuits; Les Mourottes (Basses and Hautes) which have a wild appeal, and the Bois-Roussot, planted on "lava."

BERTRAND AMBROISE
Les Gréchons 2001★

| | 1er cru | 0.68 ha | 4,700 | | 15–23 € |

Ladoix, *la Douä*: a spring in the Vaucluse which travels a long way underground. In the same way this wine will disappear down into your cellar to emerge only in three or four years' time. A white that is as golden as you could wish for. Floral, very original, it is reminiscent of lilies, the hazelnut too. Still lively, it has plenty of fleshiness and an excellent structure.
☛ Bertrand Ambroise, rue de l'Eglise,
21700 Premeaux-Prissey, tel. 03.80.62.30.19,
fax 03.80.62.38.69,
e-mail bertrand.ambroise@wanadoo.fr ▼
⏱ by appt.

DOM. CACHAT-OCQUIDANT ET FILS
Les Madonnes Vieilles Vignes 2001★

| | 1.21 ha | 5,500 | | 8–11 € |

Les Madonnes is a very pretty name. A real *climat* name and much better than the neighbouring one which is called…Death! Not something to see on a label. While this wine does not hold the secret of eternal life, it should evolve well. Nice colour and a flattering nose: this Ladoix is upstanding and of an obvious frankness. Don't open it too soon because the tannins need to soften.

☛ Dom. Cachat-Ocquidant et Fils, 3, pl. du Souvenir,
21550 Ladoix-Serrigny, tel. 03.80.26.45.30,
fax 03.80.26.48.16 ▼
⏱ by appt.

CAPITAIN-GAGNEROT
Les Gréchons et Foutrières 2001★

| | 1er cru | 0.84 ha | 7,000 | | 11–15 € |

Coup de coeur in the 1990 and 1996 editions, this estate presented a white Premier Cru produced high up on the hillside. Still young, very pleasant, this 2001 vintage deserves to be allowed to age a little. Its colour is pale-gold, its bouquet concentrates on roasted almonds and acacia. It doesn't have exceptional length, but is fleshy and perfectly constructed. This estate celebrated its 200th anniversary two years ago under the fine motto that appears on the label: "*Loyauté fait ma force*" (Honesty is my strength).
☛ Capitain-Gagnerot, 38, rte de Dijon,
21550 Ladoix-Serrigny, tel. 03.80.26.41.36,
fax 03.80.26.46.29,
e-mail contact@capitain-gagnerot.com ▼
⏱ by appt.

CHEVALIER PERE ET FILS
Les Corvées 2000★

| | 1er cru | 1.44 ha | 7,500 | | 15–23 € |

One can list the **Ladoix 2001 white (11–15 €)** and the **Les Gréchons Premier Cru white 2001**, one star, among the wines produced by George Chevalier and Claude, his son, successors of Emile Dubois who founded this domaine (10 ha today) in 1885. This 2000 vintage (a Premier Cru, admittedly) is heady, full and rounded; a wine to decant and appreciate its balance. Don't leave it in the cellar for more than a few months. *Coup de coeur* last year for a Les Gréchons 2000 white.
☛ SCE Chevalier Père et Fils, Buisson,
21550 Ladoix-Serrigny, tel. 03.80.26.46.30,
fax 03.80.26.41.47, e-mail ladoixch@club-internet.fr ▼
⏱ by appt.

FRANCOIS GAY ET FILS 2000★

| | | 0.49 ha | 3,000 | | 11–15 € |

The 95, 96 and 99 vintages were awarded *coups de coeur*. That's impressive! This wine holds your attention with a colour that hovers between cherry and blackcurrant; its nose is not very exuberant but does offer a certain complexity. Tannins and body give to this Ladoix a substantial platform. Full of flavour and lingering, it could be served with a roast beef, but a pigeon would suit it better.
☛ EARL François Gay, 9, rue des Fiètres,
21200 Chorey-lès-Beaune, tel. 03.80.22.69.58,
fax 03.80.24.71.42 ▼
⏱ by appt.

DOM. JEAN GUITON
La Corvée 2000★

| | 1er cru | 0.79 ha | 3,000 | | 11–15 € |

A rounded wine, attractive, with a good scent of wild strawberries, tender and smooth. It nevertheless leaves one with the memory of the most delightful freshness on the finish. A success in its vintage.
☛ Dom. Jean Guiton, 4, rte de Pommard,
21200 Bligny-lès-Beaune, tel. 03.80.26.82.88,
fax 03.80.26.85.05, e-mail domaine.guiton@libertysurf.fr ▼
⏱ by appt.

DOM. ROBERT AND RAYMOND JACOB
2001★

| | | 0.7 ha | 4,860 | | 8–11 € |

This family gave up mixed-farming in 1950 to devote itself entirely to wine production. Its white Ladoix has a touch of oakiness but it is a wine that will give pleasure: its richness and length justify its presence in Guide. Pale-gold and crystalline, this is a brilliant 2001 vintage. Its acidity is absolutely right. A good representative of a *village* white.
☛ Dom. Robert and Raymond Jacob, hameau de Buisson,
21550 Ladoix-Serrigny, tel. 03.80.26.40.42,
fax 03.80.26.49.34 ▼
⏱ by appt.

S. JAVOUHEY
Les Gréchons 2000★

	1er cru	n.c.	n.c.	⑪	15–23 €

Pleasant, full and rounded, balanced: these comments from the tasting cards are sufficient in themselves. This pale-gold wine from the 2000 vintage is very attractive and sits well on the palate. The predominant theme is fine and floral. It is not perhaps very imaginative but offers a faithful picture of its terroir. Which is basically what is asked of it.
↜ S. Javouhey, 50, rue du Gal-de-Gaulle, BP 63, 21702 Nuits-Saint-Georges, tel. 03.80.61.10.30, fax 03.80.61.35.76, e-mail domaine@javouhey.com ☑
♈ ev. day 9am–12 noon 1pm–7pm; cl. Jan.

DOM. MICHEL MALLARD ET FILS
Le Clos Royer 2000★

		n.c.	3,000	⑪	11–15 €

Michel Mallard was one of the first wine-growers of the cru to "make it in the bottle" – to find links for selling his wine, and to create a cellar (Saint-Bacchus). His Clos Royer is grown right in the middle of the village. It is very dense and dark in appearance; blackberries mingled with vanilla make a harmonious mix. Very consistent, the body is of a satisfactory length: freshness at the start, a touch astringent on the finish. It still has to open.
↜ Dom. Michel Mallard et Fils, 43, rte de Dijon, 21550 Ladoix-Serrigny, tel. 03.80.26.40.64, fax 03.80.26.47.49 ☑
♈ by appt.

CATHERINE ET CLAUDE MARECHAL
Les Chaillots 2001★

0.63 ha	3,260	⑪	11–15 €

This 10-ha estate has produced a good wine to lay down carefully with no thought of drinking it until two to three years have elapsed. This *climat*, close to Les Petites Lolières, here offers a wine which is very intense, both in colour and in bouquet (red berries, liquorice). The first impression is supple, balanced and even if this 2001 is not not yet completely opened nor at the peak of its fullness, the first draft hold the promise of a beautiful picture to come.
↜ EARL Catherine et Claude Maréchal, 6, rte de Chalon, 21200 Bligny-lès-Beaune, tel. 03.80.21.44.37, fax 03.80.26.85.01, e-mail marechalcc@wanadoo.fr ☑
♈ by appt.

DOM. NUDANT
Les Gréchons 2001★

	1er cru	0.6 ha	3,000	⑪	15–23 €

When André Nudant was born in 1929, his grandfather soaked the baby's feet in a vat of year's new wine. If that doesn't set one on the road to becoming a good winemaker, what could? *Coup de coeur* last year for this same Premier Cru of the previous vintage, the estate offered the tasters a wine of pronounced, brilliant-yellow colour. There is nothing artificial about its bouquet, with its aromas of butter and hazelnut: it is distinguished and speaks of the Chardonnay grape. All these olfactive nuances are repeated on the palate, enhanced by a welcome acidity. A wine to keep in the depths of the cellar for a while for a pleasant future occasion.
↜ Dom. Nudant, BP 15, 21550 Ladoix-Serrigny, tel. 03.80.26.40.48, fax 03.80.26.47.13, e-mail domaine.nudant@wanadoo.fr ☑
♈ by appt.

DOM. CHRISTIAN PERRIN
Les Joyeuses 2001★

	1er cru	0.18 ha	900	⑪	11–15 €

The deep colour of the wine, the promise offered by its bouquet and its fleshy, full-bodied character, rich in alcohol, long on the palate, quickly marked this out as a quality wine, which is what one seeks.
↜ Christian Perrin, 14, av. de Corton, 21550 Ladoix-Serrigny, tel. 03.80.26.40.93, fax 03.80.26.48.40 ☑
♈ by appt.

Wines selected but not starred

DOM. MARGUERITE CARILLON 2001

	2.6 ha	13,500	⑪	5–8 €

↜ Dom. Marguerite Carillon, 7, rte de Monthélie, 21190 Meursault, tel. 03.80.21.22.45, fax 03.80.21.28.05

CHRISTIAN GROS 2001

	0.46 ha	1,500	▮ ♦	8–11 €

↜ Christian Gros, rue de la Chaume, 21700 Premeaux-Prissey, tel. 03.80.61.39.74, fax 03.80.61.39.77 ☑
♈ by appt.

DOM. MARATRAY-DUBREUIL
Les Gréchons 2001

	1er cru	0.4 ha	3,000	⑪	11–15 €

↜ Dom. Maratray-Dubreuil, 5, pl. du Souvenir, 21550 Ladoix-Serrigny, tel. 03.80.26.41.09, fax 03.80.26.49.07, e-mail maratray.dubreuil@club-internet.fr ☑
♈ by appt.

DOM. PRIN 2000

	0.97 ha	6,000	▮ ⑪	11–15 €

↜ Dom. Prin, 12, rue de Serrigny, Cidex 10, 21550 Ladoix-Serrigny, tel. 03.80.26.40.63, fax 03.80.26.46.16 ☑
♈ by appt.

Aloxe-Corton

Of the total classified as Corton and Corton-Charlemagne, the Appellation Aloxe-Corton applies only to a very small part of the smallest commune of the Côte de Beaune; it produced 5,505 hl of red wine and 55 hl of white in 2002. The Premiers Crus from here have a fine reputation: Les Maréchaudes, Les Valozières and Les Lolières (Grandes and Petites) are the best-known.

The commune is an important shipping centre and there are several châteaux, resplendent with magnificent glazed tiles, that are worth a visit. The Latour family owns a magnificent domaine where the 19th century vat room is a model of its type for making Burgundy wines.

ARNOUX PERE ET FILS 2001★

	1.25 ha	4,000	⑪	15–23 €

This wine will give the wine-lover full satisfaction in two or three years' time. The colour is a deep garnet-red. The delicate aromas go from blackcurrant to raspberry and develop with aeration. If the entry on the palate is rather lively, marked by the tannins, this is because the wine is young; it is evolving on a fine structure and needs to be laid down for two of three years, perhaps even more.
↜ Arnoux Père et Fils, rue des Brenôts, 21200 Chorey-lès-Beaune, tel. 03.80.22.57.98, fax 03.80.22.16.85 ☑
♈ by appt.

Côte de Beaune (North)

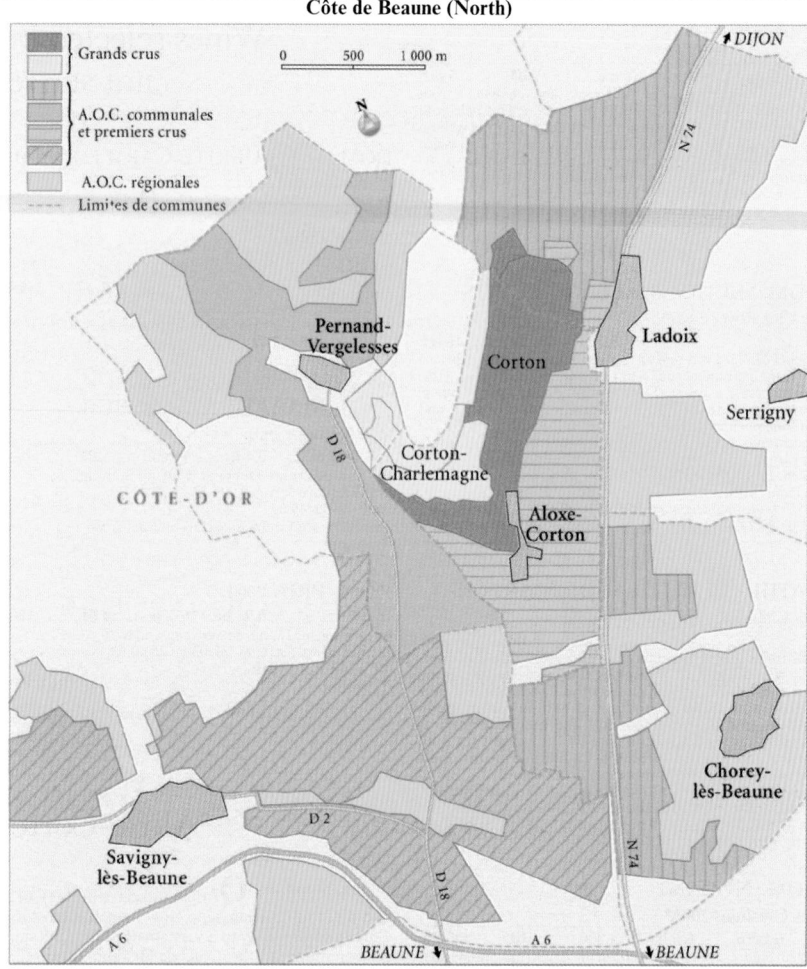

Grands crus

A.O.C. communales et premiers crus

A.O.C. régionales

Limites de communes

DIJON

Pernand-Vergelesses

Corton

Ladoix

Serrigny

Corton-Charlemagne

Aloxe-Corton

CÔTE-D'OR

Chorey-lès-Beaune

Savigny-lès-Beaune

BEAUNE

BEAUNE

DOM. CACHAT-OCQUIDANT ET FILS

Les Maréchaudes 2001★★

■ 1er cru	6 ha	900	▥	15–23 €

A beautiful wine, .y characteristic of an Aloxe-Corton, which should evolve well. Let us also recall the *coup de coeur* in the 2000 edition for a 97. This Les Maréchaudes has the red colour of Légion d'Honneur in its cheeks. A complex, blackcurrant nose. An infinite amount of substance and body, the tannin, good oak and length all combine to give a wine that is always well-balanced.

☛ Dom. Cachat-Ocquidant et Fils, 3, pl. du Souvenir,
21550 Ladoix-Serrigny, tel. 03.80.26.45.30,
fax 03.80.26.48.16 ☑
🍷 by appt.

CAPITAIN-GAGNEROT

Les Moutottes Elevé en fût 2000★

■ 1er cru	1.48 ha	6,000	▥	15–23 €

Patrice and Michel Capitain celebrated the bicentenary of the company in 2002, under the motto that appears on the label : "Loyauté fait ma force" (Honesty is my strength). This Les Moutottes is decked out for the parade in an impeccable colour. The bouquet, a hint oaky, evokes vanilla. The palate is initially delicate but opens little by little, concentrated,

slightly astringent. This attractive wine should develop well given three to four years in the cellar.

☛ Capitain-Gagnerot, 38, rte de Dijon,
21550 Ladoix-Serrigny, tel. 03.80.26.41.36,
fax 03.80.26.46.29,
e-mail contact@capitain-gagnerot.com ☑
🍷 by appt.

DOM. MARGUERITE CARILLON

Les Maréchaudes 2001★

■ 1er cru	0.4 ha	2,800	▥	15–23 €

A delicious wine that has matured quickly. Its palate is expressive, almost garrulous. The fruitiness is still fresh and the body velevety. The richness, weight, the beautiful, intense colour, the rather herbaceous nose with a hint of bilberry, all collect positive marks.

☛ Dom. Marguerite Carillon, 7, rte de Monthélie,
21190 Meursault, tel. 03.80.21.22.45, fax 03.80.21.28.05

DOM. DU CHATEAU-GRIS

Les Fournières 2000★

■ 1er cru	0.52 ha	2,100	▥	23–30 €

Built by the Compte Mayol de Lupé, in 1796, this Château Gris owes its name to the colour of its tiles. The colour of this wine is brilliant and precedes an attractive, very elegant jammy bouquet (fruit, vanilla and cedar). After a straightforward opening the palate is interesting, well-constructed along the same lines as the nose. Open in December 2003.

☛ Dom. du Château-Gris, 17, av. du Gal-de-Gaulle, 21700 Nuits-Saint-Georges, tel. 03.80.61.25.02, fax 03.80.24.37.38

EDMOND CORNU ET FILS

Les Valozières 2000★

	1er cru	0.45 ha	2,700		23–30 €

A beautiful bright colour with the right amount of intensity and bluish highlights. The bouquet is that of well-made, but still restrained wine (Morello cherry, coffee). This is because of its youth. Characteristic, and more than correctly vinified for a Premier Cru and a 2000 vintage. All is well on the palate. The great-great-grandfather founded the estate in 1870. In 1959, the tractor replaced the horse. And don't forget that, on the first Sunday in July, one can visit Ladoix and take a "gluttonous stroll" around the area.

☛ EARL Edmond Cornu et Fils, Le Meix Gobillon, 21550 Ladoix-Serrigny, tel. 03.80.26.40.79, fax 03.80.26.48.34 ☑
☕ by appt.

DOM. DUBOIS D'ORGEVAL 2000★

		0.47 ha	1,970		15–23 €

This 13-ha estate already goes back four generations. Very brilliant, light ruby-red tinged with purple, the Pinot Noir tells a story in which strawberry-jam plays the leading role.The first impression is soft, reinforced by richness, and followed by a progressive increase in the power of the tannins and secondary aromas, while the red berries linger and make their mark. A wine to lay down for at least two years, and, if you are fond of goulasch (Hungarian beef stew), this is the wine to drink with it.

☛ Dom. Dubois d'Orgeval, 3, rue Joseph-Bard, 21200 Chorey-lès-Beaune, tel. 03.80.24.70.89, fax 03.80.22.45.02 ☑
☕ by appt.

DOM. P. DUBREUIL-FONTAINE PERE ET FILS 2001★

		1 ha	6,000		15–23 €

One cannot open a bottle of Dubreuil-Fontaine wine without giving a thought to Piârre, inexhaustible storyteller and exemplary winemaker, friend of Jacques Copeau and his "Copiaus" (a pun on *copains* – chums. Here we are at the Vieux-Colombier theatre. The stage curtain is a bright cherry-red of a rare intensity. The first act starts gently, with intriguing complexity. Hints of red berries, leather…The following acts are exhilarating, balanced, with little emphasis on the oak. One Juror noted: "I would say this is a wine for a cultivated man." One couldn't put it better.

☛ Dom. Dubreuil-Fontaine, rue Rameau-Lamarosse, 21420 Pernand-Vergelesses, tel. 03.80.21.55.43, fax 03.80.21.51.69,
e-mail dubreuil.fontaine@wanadoo.fr ☑
☕ by appt.

DOM. LIONEL DUFOUR

Les Valozières Elevé en fût de chêne 2001★

	1er cru	0.34 ha	2,500		46–76 €

A brilliant, deep garnet-red colour; an elegant nose allowing glimpses of red berries and a note of vanilla. On the first palate one finds a touch of oak, but after thirteen months in cask, this is integrating well and rests on a rounded fleshiness with the silky tannins, the whole as "greedy" as can be. Balanced, harmonious, this is a very interesting wine.

☛ SCI Lionel Dufour, imp. des Amandiers, 21190 Marsault, tel. 03.80.21.67.02, fax 03.87.69.78.88

CHRISTIAN GROS

Les Petites Lolières 2000★

	1er cru	0.16 ha	900		11–15 €

Only 30 m from the 13th century village church, this estate covers 12 ha. This Ladoix *climat* is not far from Grand Cru,

and the Les Lolières is far from small. A good red colour, this 2000 vintage wine, with a nose that is charming but takes a while to appear (roasted almonds, blackcurrant), reveals itself on the palate as very fruity, with a remarkable length of flavour. Very characteristic of its vintage. A 1990 vintage in *village* received the *coup de coeur* in our 1993 edition.

☛ Christian Gros, rue de la Chaume, 21700 Premeaux-Prissey, tel. 03.80.61.29.74, fax 03.80.61.39.77 ☑
☕ by appt.

DOM. LES GUETTOTTES 2001★

		0.38 ha	2,300		11–15 €

Jean-Baptiste Lebreuil took over the management of the family estate in 1999. Under the manor house, the product of the 8.5 ha of vineyards is matured in vaulted, two centuries-old cellars. Beneath its intense ruby-red colour, this Aloxe hides a restrained nose that speaks in muted tones of spices and Morello cherry. On the other hand, it has plenty to say on the palate where acidity is the trump card that will allow it to age. Its tannins are very fine, almost melodious. The finish is all lightness. This is a wine worth making a detour for.

☛ Pierre and Jean-Baptiste Lebreuil, Dom. Les Guettottes, 17, rue Chanson-Maldant, 21420 Savigny-lès-Beaune, tel. 03.80.21.52.95, fax 03.80.26.10.82,
e-mail jean-baptiste.lebreuil@wanadoo.fr ☑
☕ ev. day except Sun. 9am–11.30am 2pm–6.30pm

DOM. NUDANT

Clos de la Boulotte Monopole 2000★

		1.12 ha	6,700		15–23 €

This estate was not established yesterday: there was already an André Nudant producing wine in Buisson in 1748. This Boulotte slips in between Brunette and Boulmeau, just below the village. A deep, shining red, this 2000 opens on woody aromas and nuances of black fruits. Well-constructed, it has richness, constructive tannins, without least aggression and shows proof of appreciable length. A true Aloxe-Corton. The **Premier Cru Coutière 2000** was also awarded one star.

☛ Dom. Nudant, 11, RN 74, 21550 Ladoix-Serrigny, tel. 03.80.26.40.48, fax 03.80.26.47.13,
e-mail domaine.nudant@wanadoo.fr ☑
☕ by appt.

DOM. PRIN 2000★

		95.4 ha	5,800		15–23 €

This estate uses long vatting periods (twenty-eight days in this case); it offered a delightful *village*. The nose has touches of liquorice, a small, toasted notes but especially ripe red berries. On the first palate this wine is elegant and fruity; on the finish, the tannins are still present, which is normal with this age: a wine to lay down for two or three years.

☛ Dom. Prin, 12, rue de Serrigny, Cidex 10, 21550 Ladoix-Serrigny, tel. 03.80.26.40.63, fax 03.80.26.46.16 ☑
☕ by appt.

COMTE SENARD

Les Valozières 2001★★

	1er cru	0.7 ha	n.c.		15–23 €

One would think that a great painter had mixed the colour for this wine, which is wondrous to behold. The bouquet opens with aeration on mature and slightly wild notes, with a small toasted touch. A fine example of a Premier Cru, young, with a splendid future, perfectly structured and pleasantly fleshy. The cask respects the wine to a remarkable degree. The **Village 2001** received one star. Daniel Senard who was a Grand-Master of the *Tastevin* can look down from on high and be proud of his descendants.

☛ Dom. Comte Senard, 7, rempart Saint-Jean, 21200 Beaune, tel. 03.80.24.21.65, fax 03.80.24.21.44 ☑
☕ ev. day except Sun. 10am–6pm; cl. From Dec. to Mar.

BURGUNDY

Wines selected but not starred

DOM. JEAN-CLAUDE BELLAND 2001

| ■ | 0.59 ha | 3,000 | ⦿ | 11–15 € |

➔ Jean-Claude Belland, 21590 Santenay,
tel. 03.80.20.61.90, fax 03.80.20.65.60 ☑

PHILIPPE BOUCHARD 2001

| ■ | n.c. | 6,000 | ⦿ | 15–23 € |

➔ Philippe Bouchard, 21420 Aloxe-Corton,
tel. 03.80.25.00.00, fax 03.80.26.42.00,
e-mail vinibeaune@bourgogne.net
Ⴤ by appt.

C. CHARTON FILS 2000

| ■ | n.c. | 2,000 | ⦿ | 23–30 € |

➔ C. Charton Fils, 38, fg Saint-Nicolas, 21200 Beaune,
tel. 03.80.22.53.33, fax 03.80.24.19.73

DOM. DOUDET

Les Boutières 2001

| ■ | 0.5 ha | 2,220 | ⦿ | 15–23 € |

➔ Dom. Doudet, 50, rue de Bourgogne,
21420 Savigny-lès-Beaune, tel. 03.80.21.51.74,
fax 03.80.21.50.69, e-mail doudet.naudin@wanadoo.fr ☑
Ⴤ by appt.

DUFOULEUR PERE ET FILS 2001

| ■ | n.c. | 4,200 | ⯅⦿ | 15–23 € |

➔ Dufouleur Père et Fils, 17, rue Thurot,
21700 Nuits-Saint-Georges, tel. 03.80.61.21.21,
fax 03.80.61.10.65, e-mail dufouleur@dufouleur.com ☑
Ⴤ ev. day 9am–7pm

DOM. FOLLIN-ARBELET

Les Vercots 2000

| ■ 1er cru | 1 ha | 4,000 | ⦿ | 15–23 € |

➔ Dom. Follin-Arbelet, Les Vercots, 21420 Aloxe-Corton,
tel. 03.80.26.46.73, fax 03.80.26.43.32 ☑
Ⴤ by appt.

DOM. MICHEL GAY ET FILS 2000

| ■ | 1.23 ha | 6,500 | ⯅⦿ | 11–15 € |

➔ EARL Dom. Michel Gay et Fils, 1b, rue des Brenôts,
21200 Chorey-lès-Beaune, tel. 03.80.22.22.73,
fax 03.80.22.95.78 ☑
Ⴤ by appt.

DOM. ANTONIN GUYON

Les Fournières 2000

| ■ 1er cru | 1.35 ha | 7,500 | ⦿ | 23–30 € |

➔ Dom. Antonin Guyon, 21420 Savigny-lès-Beaune,
tel. 03.80.67.13.24, fax 03.80.66.85.87,
e-mail vins@guyon-bourgogne.com ☑
Ⴤ by appt.

DOM. ROBERT ET RAYMOND JACOB 2001

| ■ | 1 ha | 5,900 | ⦿ | 11–15 € |

➔ Dom. Robert et Raymond Jacob, hameau de Buisson,
21550 Ladoix-Serrigny, tel. 03.80.26.40.42,
fax 03.80.26.49.34 ☑
Ⴤ by appt.

DANIEL LARGEOT 2001

| ■ | 0.6 ha | 3,600 | ⦿ | 11–15 € |

➔ Daniel Largeot, 5, rue des Brenôts,
21200 Chorey-lès-Beaune, tel. 03.80.22.15.10,
fax 03.80.22.60.62 ☑
Ⴤ by appt.

DOM. MICHEL MALLARD ET FILS

Les Valozières 2000

| ■ 1er cru | n.c. | 2,490 | ⦿ | 15–23 € |

➔ Dom. Michel Mallard et Fils, 43, rte de Dijon,
21550 Ladoix-Serrigny, tel. 03.80.26.40.64,
fax 03.80.26.47.49 ☑

D. MEUNEVEAUX 2001

| ■ 1er cru | 0.84 ha | 5,000 | ⦿ | 15–23 € |

➔ Didier Meuneveaux, 9, rue Boulmeau,
21420 Aloxe-Corton, tel. 03.80.26.42.33,
fax 03.80.26.48.60 ☑
Ⴤ by appt.

LA MAISON PAULANDS 2000

| ■ | n.c. | n.c. | ⦿ | 15–23 € |

➔ Caves des Paulands, RN 74, BP 12, 21420 Aloxe-Corton,
tel. 03.80.26.41.05, fax 03.80.26.47.56,
e-mail paulands@wanadoo.fr ☑
Ⴤ ev. day 8am–12 noon 2pm–6pm; cl. 22 Dec.–3 Jan.
➔ C. Fasquel

DOM. CHRISTIAN PERRIN

Les Boutières 2001

| ■ | 0.94 ha | 6,000 | ⦿ | 11–15 € |

➔ Christian Perrin, 14, av. de Corton,
21550 Ladoix-Serrigny, tel. 03.80.26.40.93,
fax 03.80.26.48.40 ☑
Ⴤ by appt.

CHARLES VIENOT 2000

| ■ | n.c. | 8,000 | ⦿ | 15–23 € |

➔ Charles Viénot, 5, quai Dumorey,
21703 Nuits-Saint-Georges, tel. 03.80.62.61.41,
fax 03.80.62.61.60
➔ Boisset SA

DOM. MICHEL VOARICK 2000

| ■ | 2.42 ha | 10,000 | ⦿ | 15–23 € |

➔ Jean-Marc Voarick, 2, pl. du Chapitre,
21420 Aloxe-Corton, tel. 03.80.26.40.44, fax 03.80.26.41.22,
e-mail voarickmichel@aol.com ☑
Ⴤ by appt.

Pernand-Vergelesses

The village of Pernand is situated where two valleys meet, facing due south, and it is, beyond the slightest doubt, the most typical wine village on the Côte. Narrow streets, deep cellars, vine-clothed hillsides, enthusiastic growers and subtle wines have built the village a solid reputation, and of course the old Burgundian families have made a significant contribution, too. In 2002, 4,051 hl of red wines were produced; the most famous Premier Cru here is L'Ile des Vergelesses, which has great finesse and fully deserves its reputation. Some excellent white wines are also made – 2,059 hl in 2002.

DOM. CHANSON PERE ET FILS

Les Vergelesses 2001★

| ■ 1er cru | 5.31 ha | 13,000 | ⦿ | 15–23 € |

Paul Chanson was a flamboyant figure in the world of Burgundy wines, its ambassador. The company was taken over by Bollinger, the great family Champagne company. This

Les Vergelesses has plenty of colour. The nose still tight, subtle, hovering around the freshness of the fruit. Tannic, this wine is like a block of marble that time will sculpt; it needs to age for three to four years.

➽ Dom. Chanson Père et Fils, 10, rue Paul-Chanson, BP 232, 21206 Beaune Cedex, tel. 03.80.25.97.97, fax 03.80.24.17.42, e-mail tmarion@vins-chanson.com

DOM. DU CHATEAU DE CHOREY

Les Combottes 2001★★

| | 2.75 ha | 16,000 | ◫ | 11–15 € |

There is no Combottes in the land register, but there is a *climat* called Plantes des Grands Champs et Combottes. This wine? In the colour and on the bouquet, the Chardonnay dwells amicably with the terroir. The attack is sparkling, the richness sumptuous and the finish pure Cinemascope. A *village* which could easily call itself a Premier Cru. The château, built in the 13th century and added to in the 17th century, has guest-rooms.

➽ Dom. du Château de Chorey, 21200 Chorey-lès-Beaune, tel. 03.80.24.06.39, fax 03.80.24.77.72 ✓ ⌂
⌁ by appt.
➽ Germain

DOM. DENIS PERE ET FILS

Sous Frétille 2001★

| 1er cru | 0.6 ha | 2,700 | ◫ | 11–15 € |

A recently promoted Premier Cru. On the edge of a second star, this recently promoted 2001, limpid and golden-yellow, goes straight to its destination. Its aromas are of pears and ripe apples. On the palate it is powerful, frank, rich, floral and the finish is well-balanced. Its perfect firmness is its guarantee for the future.

➽ Dom. Denis Père et Fils, chem. des Vignes-Blanches, 21420 Pernand-Vergelesses, tel. 03.80.21.50.91, fax 03.80.26.10.32, e-mail denis-pere-et-fils@wanadoo.fr ✓
⌁ by appt.

DOM. JEAN-JACQUES GIRARD

Les Belles Filles 2001★

| | 0.35 ha | 2,400 | ◫ | 11–15 € |

If you're worried that the conversation may flag after the entrée, serve a fish dish – a trout with almonds for example – and this wine. Show you guests the bottle, the label. Explain that it comes from *climat* that could not be more authentic and watch the conversation pick up again. Limpid with charming highlights, this 2001 vintage is redolent of brioche, of vanilla initially then floral and rounded.

➽ Dom. Jean-Jacques Girard, 16, rue de Cîteaux, BP 17, 21420 Savigny-lès-Beaune, tel. 03.80.21.56.15, fax 03.80.26.10.08 ✓
⌁ by appt.

DOM. JAFFELIN PERE ET FILS

Creux de la Net 2000★★

| ◼ 1er cru | 0.58 ha | 3,000 | ◫ | 11–15 € |

This year the Jaffelin estate is the one that mounts the podium and receives the *coup de coeur*. A little less than 10 ha, with solid winegrowing credentials: here they know what is meant by *aller aux vignes* (going to the vineyards)! This Premier Cru spent its formative years not far from Les Hauts

de Vergelesses. An intense, ruby-red Pinot, with its raspberry aromas, it evokes a delicious kirsch flavour on the palate. Very fine, smooth, it is pleasure incarnate and can only continue to evolve well.

➽ Roger Jaffelin et Fils, 21420 Pernand-Vergelesses, tel. 03.80.21.52.43, fax 03.80.26.10.39 ✓
⌁ ev. day 9am–12 noon 2pm–6.30pm; Sun. by appt.

DOM. LALEURE-PIOT

Les Vergelesses 2001★

| ◼ 1er cru | 1.7 ha | 8,000 | ◫ | 15–23 € |

Not for nothing did Pernand choose to place itself under the colours of Les Vergelesses. This wine-grower flies the flag high and with pride. Moreover, it was *coup de coeur* in the 1999 Guide for its red 96 vintage. Here we have a colour which holds the light and a bouquet full of prospects, that hides its treasures. Velvety, this is a rich and powerful, deep and concentrated 2000 vintage which needs to be laid down for three years. The **red Ile des Vergelesses 2001** is a warmhearted Premier Cru; it received the same assessment. As for the **white Village 2001 (11–15 €)**, it owes its star to its very characteristic aromatic richness and its long and well-made palate.

➽ Dom. Laleure-Piot, rue de Pralot, 21420 Pernand-Vergelesses, tel. 03.80.21.52.37, fax 03.80.21.59.48, e-mail infos@laleure-piot.com ✓
⌁ ev. day 8am–12noon 2pm–6pm; Sat. Sun. by appt.

DOM. MARATRAY-DUBREUIL 2000★★

| ◼ | 0.9 ha | 4,500 | ◫ | 11–15 € |

This has a deep, clean appearance. The strawberry aromas on the nose are not overpowered by vanilla. In short, one expects something good from this and indeed, this premier cru is one of the best of its kind. Its substantial constitution augurs well; it is a powerful wine with a background of cherry flavours. Keep for three to four years, or even more.

➽ Dom. Maratray-Dubreuil, 5, pl. du Souvenir, 21550 Ladoix-Serrigny, tel. 03.80.26.41.09, fax 03.80.26.49.07, e-mail maratray.dubreuil@club-internet.fr ✓
⌁ by appt.

DOM. PIERRE MAREY ET FILS

Les Belles Filles 2001★

| | 1.62 ha | 8,000 | ◫ | 8–11 € |

You can order the **red Fichots Premier Cru 2001 (11–15 €)**, one star. "It's a Caradeux," notes one taster who is completely unaware of the name of this Premier Cru. Not a bad guess: Fichots and Caradeux are next to each other! These Belles Filles are wearing their ball gowns: their aromatic complexity is comprised of oak notes and nuances of black cherry picked at the end of the season. It is a youthful and very spontaneous Pinot. Its structure dominates the fruit but that is normal at this age. "I believe in it!" wrote another juror.

➽ EARL Pierre Marey et Fils, rue Jacques-Copeau, 21420 Pernand-Vergelesses, tel. 03.80.21.51.71, fax 03.80.26.10.48 ✓
⌁ by appt.

LA MAISON PAULANDS

Les Fichots 2001★

| ◼ 1er cru | n.c. | n.c. | ◫ | 15–23 € |

Clear ruby in appearance, this wine is testament to the vitality of a human adventure: an owner turned négociant, then hotelier and restaurateur. This is La Maison Paulands, situated at the edge of the RN 74. This fruity-nosed wine is supported by integrated tannins within a framework of terroir. It has plenty of body and needs another three years.

➽ Caves des Paulands, RN 74, BP 12, 21420 Aloxe-Corton, tel. 03.80.26.41.05, fax 03.80.26.47.56, e-mail paulands@wanadoo.fr ✓
⌁ ev. day 8am–12noon 2pm–6pm; cl Dec 22–Jan 3.

DOM. PAVELOT

Sous Frétille 2001★★

| 1er cru | 0.75 ha | 4,800 | ◫ | 15–23 € |

To some, Pavelot is Pernand and has been since the 1700s. So we should question the old readers of *La Burgundy republican*! This new 1er cru has a fresh nose and a beautiful clear and

bright appearance. Rich and fruity on the palate with a beautiful finish. It would be wise to keep it for two to three years. Have it with lobster…or more simply with white meat. The **red Pernand-Vergelesses Village 2001 (8–11 €)** gets one star.
🍴 EARL Dom. Régis et Luc Pavelot, rue du Paulant, 21420 Pernand-Vergelesses, tel. 03.80.26.13.65, fax 03.80.26.13.65, e-mail earl.pavelot@cerb.cernet.fr ☑
🍷 by appt.

RAPET PERE ET FILS
Ile des Vergelesses 2001★

▨ 1er cru	0.65 ha	3,000	⅏	15–23 €

This ancestral domaine enjoys an unbroken view of Pernand. In Burgundy, l'Ile des Vergelesses is considered a little *Treasure Island*. It has an intense red colour. With initial raspberry notes, the nose becomes appreciably fuller, with vanilla notes and liquorice. Acidity, tannins, alcohol – the combination is complex but precise. It will all come together sooner than one would think.
🍴 Dom. Rapet Père et Fils, 21420 Pernand-Vergelesses, tel. 03.80.21.59.94, fax 03.80.21.54.01 ☑
🍷 by appt.

DOM. ROLLIN PERE ET FILS
Sous Frétille 2001★

▨ 1er cru	0.4 ha	2,200	⅏	15–23 €

This domaine achieved a *coup de coeur* as AOC Pernand in the 1996 edition. The Jury awarded a citation this year in the **2001 white Village (11–15 €)**. It is simple, quite rich and straightforward. This premier cru has a beautiful bright yellow appearance; there is vanilla and fruit on the nose; the palate is quite lively without being nervy and it has a good length. One for laying down.
🍴 Rollin Père et Fils, rte des Vergelesses, 21420 Pernand-Vergelesses, tel. 03.80.21.57.31, fax 03.80.26.10.38 ☑
🍷 by appt.

DOM. MICHEL VOARICK 2000★

▨	2.48 ha	10,000	⅏	8–11 €

Coming from a wine-growing family in the Côte Chalonnaise, the grandfather Pierre Voarick planted vines in Aloxe-Corton in 1924. Well done to him! First Michel, then Jean-Marc, the vines were handed down through the generations. With its notes of violet, this wine seduces from the start but also has some character. There is enough in this wine to merit a place in your cellar. Drink in two or three years' time.
🍴 Jean-Marc Voarick, 2, pl. du Chapitre, 21420 Aloxe-Corton, tel. 03.80.26.40.44, fax 03.80.26.41.22, e-mail voarickmichel@aol.com ☑
🍷 by appt.
🍷 Michel Voarick

Wines selected but not starred

ARNOUX PERE ET FILS 2001

▨	0.5 ha	2,500	⅏	11–15 €

🍴 Arnoux Père et Fils, rue des Brenôts, 21200 Chorey-lès-Beaune, tel. 03.80.22.57.98, fax 03.80.22.16.85 ☑
🍷 by appt.

DOM. BELIN-RAPET
Sous Frétille 2001

▨ 1er cru	0.24 ha	600	⅏	11–15 €

🍴 Dom. Belin-Rapet, Les Combottes, 21420 Pernand-Vergelesses, tel. 03.80.22.77.51, fax 03.80.22.76.59, e-mail ludovic.belin@wanadoo.fr ☑
🍷 by appt.

DOM. CHANDON DE BRIAILLES
Ile des Vergelesses 2000

▨ 1er cru	3 ha	12,000	⅏	23–30 €

🍴 Dom. Chandon de Briailles, 1, rue Soeur-Goby, 21420 Savigny-lès-Beaune, tel. 03.80.21.52.31, fax 03.80.21.59.15 ☑
🍷 by appt.
🍷 de Nicolay

CHARLES THOMAS 2001

▨	n.c.	12,000	⅏	8–11 €

🍴 Charles Thomas, BP 6, 21701 Nuits-Saint-Georges Cedex, tel. 03.80.62.42.00, fax 03.80.61.28.13, e-mail info@thomasfreres.com ☑
🍷 ev. day 10am–6pm; cl. Jan.

DOM. CORNU 2000

▨	0.39 ha	2,400	⅏	11–15 €

🍴 Dom. Claude Cornu, rue du Meix-Grenot, 21700 Magny-lès-Villers, tel. 03.80.62.92.05, fax 03.80.62.72.22 ☑
🍷 by appt.

DOM. P. DUBREUIL-FONTAINE PERE ET FILS 2001

▨	2.05 ha	11,000	⅏	8–11 €

🍴 Dom. Dubreuil-Fontaine, rue Rameau-Lamarosse, 21420 Pernand-Vergelesses, tel. 03.80.21.55.43, fax 03.80.21.51.69, e-mail dubreuil.fontaine@wanadoo.fr ☑
🍷 by appt.
🍷 Bernard Dubreuil

DUFOULEUR PERE ET FILS
Sous Frétille 2001

▨ 1er cru	n.c.	760	⅏	15–23 €

🍴 Dufouleur Père et Fils, 17, rue Thurot, 21700 Nuits-Saint-Georges, tel. 03.80.61.21.21, fax 03.80.61.10.65, e-mail dufouleur@dufouleur.com ☑
🍷 ev. day 9am–7pm

MARC DUMONT
Sous le Bois de Noël et les Belles Filles 2001

▨	n.c.	2,900	▨ ♠	11–15 €

🍴 Marc Dumont, 4, rue du Clos-de-Mazeray, 21190 Meursault, tel. 03.80.21.21.83, fax 03.80.21.66.48, e-mail vin@demessey.com ☑
🍷 by appt.

DOM. ANTONIN GUYON
Sous Frétille 2000

▨ 1er cru	1.13 ha	3,000	⅏	15–23 €

🍴 Dom. Antonin Guyon, 21420 Savigny-lès-Beaune, tel. 03.80.67.13.24, fax 03.80.66.85.87, e-mail vins@guyon-bourgogne.com ☑
🍷 by appt.

JACOB-FREREBEAU 2001

▨	0.6 ha	3,500	⅏	5–8 €

🍴 Jacob-Frèrebeau, 50, Grande-Rue, 21420 Changey-Echevronne, tel. 03.80.21.55.58, fax 03.80.62.75.36 ☑
🍷 by appt.

Corton

The "Corton Mountain" is made up of different types of soil and produces different wines at different levels of the slope. Topped with woods that grow on hard limestone from the Rauracian period (Superior Oxfordian), the Argovian marlstone emerges as white soil for several score metres, and is particularly good for white wines. These soils also cover shelves of pearly limestone incorporating numerous large oyster shells, overlaid by brown soil favourable for producing red wines.

The name of the *lieu-dit* appears under the Appellation Corton, and can be used for white wines but is mainly known for reds. Les Bressandes is produced on the red soils, which give the wine power and finesse. On the other hand, on the higher slopes of Les Renards, Les Languettes and the Clos du Roy, the white soils produce well-structured red wines which, as they age, take on the gamey, "sauvage" scents that can be found in the Mourottes de Ladoix. Corton is the biggest producer of the Grand Crus – 3,559 hl of red and 271 hl of white wine in 2002.

DOM. D' ARDHUY

Renardes 2001★

■ Gd cru 1.2 ha 5,000 🛢 23–30 €

This is a wine which develops the longer you keep it on the palate. Fairly clear red, it shows convincingly the fruity aromas of Pinot Noir. It has a touch of tobacco and the roasted notes that come with a well-managed oak maturation. The acidity and the tannins are the cornerstone of this wine, but there is much more to the palate than this. It reflects the vintage and has been well made. Under the label **Thibauld de Planiol 2001, Les Corton-Renardes** gets one star.

🔑 SARL Les Terres Vineuses, Clos des Langres, 21700 Corgoloin, tel. 03.80.62.98.73, fax 03.80.62.95.15, e-mail domaine.ardhuy@wanadoo.fr ☒

🍷 ev. day except Sun. 10am–12 noon 2pm–6pm

ARNOUX PERE ET FILS

Rognet 2001★

■ Gd cru 0.33 ha 1,500 🛢 30–38 €

82 83 |89| |90| **|91|** 92 **|97|** 98 99 00 01

This plot was bought in 1984 by the house Charles Viénot. Everything about this wine invites one to keep it for a family celebration meal. The palate is youthful, but full of character and ageing potential. Tannins are present and the attack is lively, but this impression gives way to the aromas perceived on the nose: burlat cherry, especially. There is a profusion of fruits you would find at the market. The appearance is faultless: superb, intense, violet.

🔑 Arnoux Père et Fils, rue des Brenôts, 21200 Chorey-lès-Beaune, tel. 03.80.22.57.98, fax 03.80.22.16.85 ☒

🍷 by appt.

DOM. REGINE BAILLY

Maréchaudes 2000★★

■ Gd cru 0.14 ha 450 🛢 23–30 €

This wine has a stylish appearance of a remarkable intensity and a lively bouquet (blackcurrant and cherry) forms a happy introduction. On the palate, the wine expresses a true presence. Fresh and supple, it suggests a high quality wine with some ageing potential. It can however be enjoyed within the next year. Structured, powerful, and charming, with an impressively long finish, it is produced by the Caves des Hautes Côtes.

🔑 Les Caves des Hautes Côtes, rte de Pommard, 21200 Beaune, tel. 03.80.25.01.00, fax 03.80.22.87.05, e-mail vinchc@wanadoo.fr ☒

🍷 by appt.

DOM. VINCENT BOUZEREAU

Clos des Fiètres 1999★

■ Gd cru 0.3 ha 1,800 🛢 30–38 €

Les Fiètres is an ignored *climat* without a Grand Cru. Just above the *village* lies the border with Aloxe. This wine seems to be a simple soul under a guise of finery. There is ripe cherry or *eau-de-vie* on the nose, which also suggests barrel maturation but the oak is supplementary to the fruit, which is good. The palate is a little less eloquent but has all the essentials and its silky tannins are promising. It has power behind its elegance.

🔑 Vincent Bouzereau, 7, rue Labbé, 21190 Meursault, tel. 03.80.21.61.08, fax 03.80.21.65.97, e-mail vincent.bouzereau@wanadoo.fr ☒

🍷 by appt.

DOM. CACHAT-OCQUIDANT ET FILS

Clos des Vergennes Monopole 2001★

■ Gd cru 1.42 ha 6,000 🛢 23–30 €

86 87 88 **|90|** 91 |95| |96| |97| 98 99 00 **01**

Vergennes is a well-known *climat*; as for the Clos des Vergennes (a single vineyard of 1.42 ha), it was acquired by this family in 1937. The wine has an impressionist appearance with the colour of the rim not yet very developed. On the nose there are wild animal notes as well as vivid fruit. The nose brings to mind red fruits in *eau-de-vie*. On the palate, there are noticeable tannins with a good overall structure: this is a wine to keep a few years.

🔑 Dom. Cachat-Ocquidant et Fils, 3, pl. du Souvenir, 21550 Ladoix-Serrigny, tel. 03.80.26.45.30, fax 03.80.26.48.16 ☒

🍷 by appt.

CHANSON PERE ET FILS

Vergennes 2001★

□ Gd cru 0.32 ha 1,100 🛢 46–76 €

This wine, while not unheard of, is unusual: a white Corton Vergennes. Not a Charlemagne, a Vergennes! This is not the Emperor, but the Minister for Foreign Affairs of Louis XVI. The appearance is attractive and the nose is powerful, with immediate fruit that is already complex. These qualities persist on the palate. The wine is balanced, and full of flavour, which only reveals itself at on the finish. Keep for at least two or three years.

🔑 Dom. Chanson Père et Fils, 10, rue Paul-Chanson, BP 232, 21206 Beaune Cedex, tel. 03.80.25.97.97, fax 03.80.24.17.42, e-mail tmarion@vins-chanson.com

CHEVALIER PERE ET FILS

Rognet 2000★★

■ Gd cru 1.16 ha 3,000 🛢 30–38 €

This wine reached the final of the *coup de coeur*. This Rognet makes it possible to understand why General de Gaulle placed Corton above all wines. What concentration and what sap! Intense purplish, crimson, in appearance, this wine combines notes of toast, game and cassis on the nose. One wants really to drink it when it is held on the palate: there are violet, lilac, and delicious secondary flavours associated with well-integrated oak, together with the slight bitterness of tannins which are still young. The wine has the body of a Grand Cru. And what length!

🔑 SCE Chevalier Père et Fils, Buisson, 21550 Ladoix-Serrigny, tel. 03.80.26.46.30, fax 03.80.26.41.47, e-mail ladoixch@club-internet.fr ☒

🍷 by appt.

DOM. DUPONT-TISSERANDOT

Le Rognet 2001★

■ Gd cru 0.32 ha 1,600 🛢 30–38 €

Marie-Francoise Guillard and Patricia Chevillon are the daughters of M. Dupont. In a few decades, this domaine has reached 24 ha (including these 32 ares in Corton-Rognet) on a

BURGUNDY

sub-soil of gibriacoises. Dark purple in appearance, this 2001 starts brightly and continues to please. Three nuances on the nose reveal gradually the wine's mystery: vanilla, raspberry, and undergrowth notes. The palate is full of flavour with noticeable tannins and liquorice notes, making for a respectable Corton. This wine will benefit from two to five years further cellaring.

☛ Dupont-Tisserandot, 2, pl. des Marronniers, 21220 Gevrey-Chambertin, tel. 03.80.34.10.50, fax 03.80.58.50.71 ☑
☲ ev. day 9am–12 noon 2pm–6pm; Sat. Sun. by appt.; cl. 2–20 Aug and 24 Dec.–3 Jan.

DOM. ESCOFFIER

Clos du Roi 2000★

■	Gd cru	0.57 ha	n.c.	◫	23–30 €

This Clos du Roi will go well with pigeon, but only in three or four years time, because it needs time for the tannins to integrate and become rounder. It has real potential and a bouquet which is characteristic of its appellation.

☛ Franck Escoffier, 16, rue du Parc, 71350 Géanges, tel. 06.11.55.80.67, fax 06.85.49.98.22, e-mail domaine.escoffier@wanadoo.fr ☑
☲ by appt.

DOM. FOLLIN-ARBELET

Bressandes 2001★★

■	Gd cru	0.45 ha	1,200	◫	30–38 €

This is a generous, full-bodied Corton. It is a traditional wine but that does not detract from its excellent potential. It is a wine that will become, for wine lovers, a powerful Grand Cru red. It has a classic ruby appearance. The nose is still oaky, but leaves a perfume of blackcurrent buds and flower borders. In the mouth it is straightforward and dominates the palate, and it is already round and full-bodied. If its acidity is anything to go by, it has good ageing potential as it is still a little fresh and lively, especially on the finish. Another excellent bottle, the **Corton 2001 (23–30 €)**, is in a similar style, and obtains one star.

☛ Dom. Follin-Arbelet, Les Vercots, 21420 Aloxe-Corton, tel. 03.80.26.46.73, fax 03.80.26.43.32 ☑
☲ by appt.

DOM. ANTONIN GUYON

Clos du Roi 2000★★

■	Gd cru	0.55 ha	3,000	◫	30–38 €

Antonin Guyon disappeared ten years ago from the wine scene, but he belonged to that group of men of great culture, who are passionate about wine. His sons continue his work with a sure taste for quality and the ability to follow in their father's footsteps. Generous and showing the characteristics of the apppellation, this Clos du Roi has an adorable liquorice note on the finish and oak flavours which are present but do not dominate. From the first taste this wine has body and concentration. On the nose, aromas of undergrowth, prune, leather, seem almost out of a novel by Henri Vincenot. Warming and heady, this 2000 is a wine lacking any roughness, and seemingly unaware even of how aggressive a wine can be.

☛ Dom. Antonin Guyon, 21420 Savigny-lès-Beaune, tel. 03.80.67.13.24, fax 03.80.66.85.87, e-mail vins@guyon-bourgogne.com ☑
☲ by appt.

DOM. ANTONIN GUYON

Bressandes 2000★★★

■	Gd cru	0.86 ha	3,900	◫	30–38 €

Reaching the final of the *coup de coeur*, this wine did not get more than its two rivals but it is a rising star. This Bressandes is magnificent for a 2000 and is ripe, rich and complex. It is in the Corton style, being round and fleshy on the palate, and having good concentration. It has aromas of elegant cherry and, to cap it all, is full of finesse and charm. The fruit remains a long time on the finish.

☛ Dom. Antonin Guyon, 21420 Savigny-lès-Beaune, tel. 03.80.67.13.24, fax 03.80.66.85.87, e-mail vins@guyon-bourgogne.com ☑
☲ by appt.

DOM. ROBERT ET RAYMOND JACOB

Les Carrières 2001★

■	Gd cru	0.24 ha	1,280	◫	15–23 €

This *climat* is located beside Ladoix, near Rognet and Corton of which only one part (this one) is classified as Grand Cru. This wine has not yet broken the mooring rope that connects it with its youthful tannins nor left its home port with a hint of nostalgia; the navigation along the course of this wine is not like the America's Cup. Dark and purplish, it has very good nose with raspberry and cherry aromas. Its flavour is equally fruity with a spicy note. Cellar for another three years.

☛ Dom. Robert et Raymond Jacob, hameau de Buisson, 21550 Ladoix-Serrigny, tel. 03.80.26.40.42, fax 03.80.26.49.34 ☑
☲ by appt.

LUPE-CHOLET 2000★

■	Gd cru	n.c.	3,000	◫	38–46 €

This is undoubtedly a Grand Cru. "Fire of God", if the Viscount of Cholet and the Count of Mayol de Lupé can forgive us this blasphemy from beyond the grave (it is nowadays only one part (this one) is the house of A. Bichot, also very honourable and traditional). Dark ruby, this Corton is subtly oaked and evokes blueberry fruit and spices, mingled with a character all of its own. It is chewy and its tannins make it substantial. This is a very successful wine in this vintage, concentrated enough to keep four to five years.

☛ Lupé-Cholet, 17, av. du Gal-de-Gaulle, 21700 Nuits-Saint-Georges, tel. 03.80.61.25.02, fax 03.80.24.37.38

DOM. MAILLARD PERE ET FILS

Renardes 2001★

■	Gd cru	1.1 ha	n.c.	◫	30–38 €

Established in 1952 by Daniel Maillard, this domaine has 18 ha spread over seven villages. This Grand Cru has an absolutely classic appearance, and reveals a bouquet full of nuances: vegetal and gamey notes, tending towards leather. The palate is fruity and full of vigour, with average length; the astringency of the tannins is still fighting with the fruit suggesting it is wise to cellar this wine for longer, as is normal for a young Grand Cru.

☛ Dom. Maillard Père et Fils, 2, rue Joseph-Bard, 21200 Chorey-lès-Beaune, tel. 03.80.22.10.67, fax 03.80.24.00.42 ☑
☲ by appt.

MAISON MALLARD-GAULIN

Renardes 2001★

■	Gd cru	0.6 ha	1,900	◫	46–76 €

This Renardes has something on the nose like a garden after rain. It lives up to its name and, as in the medieval story, it is wily and crafty and without too many scruples. The colour is violet: this wine disguises itself as a bishop. It continues the aromas of fresh and flowery violet on the nose. The oak is well managed and to achieve a balance on the palate one should wait three or four years.

☛ Maison Mallard-Gaulin, 21420 Aloxe-Corton, tel. 03.80.26.46.10

DOM. PRINCE FLORENT DE MERODE

Les Bressandes 2001★

■	Gd cru	1.19 ha	2,400	◫	23–30 €

The château and the land of Serrigny are past Clermont-Tonnerre in Merode. The wine has a dark red appearance and is a very deep, black-cherry colour. The nose begins almost in the manner of the Marquis de Foudras recounting the exploits of the gentlemen hunters in *Veillées de Saint-Hubert* (gamey). It then reveals more morello cherry notes. Initially very fruity on the palate, the tannins are still markedly oaky and need time to integrate. This wine will give you the impression of lunching in the *Jockey Club*. **Maréchauds 2001**, also very good, gets one star. Well structured and intended for long ageing, it will go well with roast lamb. These are both very much grand cru wines.

☛ Prince Florent de Merode, Ch. de Serrigny, 21550 Ladoix-Serrigny, tel. 03.80.26.40.80, fax 03.80.26.49.37

MESTRE PERE ET FILS

Les Languettes 2000★★

■ Gd cru	0.4 ha	1,500	❶	23–30 €

Made from vines grown on marl, this is a wine to drink with jugged hare, or more modestly, rabbit. This will compliment the earthy, fern, truffle, cinnamon and laurel flavours of the wine; try it later (three or four years) with some *époisses* cheese. It has a deep and brilliant colour and a very aromatic nose. It is a fleshy wine with silky tannins, vinosity and a good length. It is a real Grand Cru.

☛ Mestre Père et Fils, 12, pl. du Jet-d'Eau, BP 24, 21590 Santenay, tel. 03.80.20.60.11, fax 03.80.20.60.97, e-mail gilbert-mestre@wanadoo.fr ☑
🍷 ev. day 9am–12 noon 2pm–5.30pm; Sun. by appt.; cl. 20 Dec.–8 Jan.

LUCIEN MUZARD ET FILS

Grèves 2001★

■ Gd cru	n.c.	300	❶	30–38 €

Les Grèves in Corton is perhaps less known than its namesake in AOC Beaune, but it has its own attractions. Dark-red and very deeply coloured with bright glints, the wine has a nose full of finesse and nuances: vanilla and crushed red berries. The palate has everything you could want: fruit, richness and length. The elegant tannins, still quite evident, need two or three years of laying down.

☛ Lucien Muzard et Fils, 11 bis, rue de la Cour-Verreuil, BP 25, 21590 Santenay, tel. 03.80.20.61.85, fax 03.80.20.66.02,
e-mail lucien-muzard-et-fils@wanadoo.fr ☑
🍷 by appt.

DOM. NUDANT

Bressandes 2001★★

■ Gd cru	0.6 ha	3,300	❶❶	30–38 €

Red, bordering on mauve and bright in appearance, this wine seduces the eye before the nose reveals an almost incredible concentration of ripe fruit. Spices make up the picture. Its six months in vat and twelve months in barrel have resulted in gentle oak notes, without being over the top. The extraction is moreover well matched, combining pretty fruit flavours with fine tannins. This Bressandes is already flattering to drink, but it is a wine that can be kept for five to ten years.

☛ Dom. Nudant, 11, RN 74, 21550 Ladoix-Serrigny, tel. 03.80.26.40.48, fax 03.80.26.47.13,
e-mail domaine.nudant@wanadoo.fr ☑
🍷 by appt.

DOM. PARENT

Renardes 2000★

■ Gd cru	0.28 ha	800	❶	30–38 €

Anne and Catherine Parent have just blown out the candles on a *vacherin au cassis* for the bicentenary of this domaine. This Renardes is deep ruby, almost black, with a correct bouquet, and reveals on the palate the ampleness of the cru. With plenty of substance, this is a wine that will become even bigger and better in five to ten year's time.

☛ SAE Dom. Parent, pl. de l'Eglise, 21630 Pommard, tel. 03.80.22.15.08, fax 03.80.24.19.33,
e-mail parent-pommard@axnet.fr ☑
🍷 by appt.

PAULANDS 2001★

■ Gd cru	n.c.	n.c.	❶	23–30 €

Founded in 1898, the Pauland's winery also has an hotel – restaurant. 80% of the wines are sold at the cellar door, which is rare in the Côte. This 2001 has a limpid colour and on the nose it is slightly peppery and fine, with a vanilla note. It has a full and pleasant body to support its maturation in oak. It undoubtedly lacks some structure, but it is very typical and correct for this vintage in that it is not one-dimensional.

☛ Caves des Paulands, RN 74, BP 12, 21420 Aloxe-Corton, tel. 03.80.26.41.05, fax 03.80.26.47.56,
e-mail paulands@wanadoo.fr ☑
🍷 ev. day 8am–12 noon 2pm–6pm; cl. 22 Dec.–3 Jan.
☛ C. Fasquel

DOM. RAPET PERE ET FILS 2001★

■ Gd cru	0.75 ha	3,000	❶	23–30 €

If quality is sought, one must wait a number of years, Cid de Corneille is quoted as saying. This is true of this 2001. It still quite young but with a promising future. In the meantime, this wine is generous and appetizing. It is well made and perfectly representative of the appellation and the vintage, showing well-integrated oak. The appearance is deep and clear, with noticeable legs. The bouquet has crushed blueberry, elegant vanilla and roasted notes. This wine is full, balanced, and blessed with good tannins; it is complex and needs keeping for two to four years.

☛ Dom. Rapet Père et Fils, 21420 Pernand-Vergelesses, tel. 03.80.21.59.94, fax 03.80.21.54.01 ☑
🍷 by appt.

DOM. CHARLES THOMAS

Clos du Roi 2001★

■ Gd cru	0.84 ha	4,500	❶	30–38 €

"The most representative of the Cortons, is Le Roi," wrote Claude Chapuis: He is talking of course about Clos du Roi! One can understand why the king kept these *cuvées* for himself. The wine is purple-ruby, with blackcurrant and leather on the nose. It is a wine where the heart of the palate is already well married. The texture, acidity, tannins, and alcohol, in fact all the essential components are there. But where is the fruit? It will be better in three or four years. This is the family estate of Thomas (Moillard).

☛ Dom. Charles Thomas, chem. rural 59, 21700 Nuits-Saint-Georges, tel. 03.80.62.42.10, fax 03.80.61.28.13,
e-mail domainecharlesthomas@wanadoo.fr ☑
🍷 ev. day 10am–6pm; 7pm Summer; cl. Jan.

Wines selected but not starred

CLOS DES CORTONS FAIVELEY 2000

■ Gd cru	2.97 ha	13,350	❶	46–76 €

85 86 88 89 |90| 91 92 |94| (95) 96 97 98 99 00

☛ Bourgognes Faiveley, 8, rue du Tribourg, 21700 Nuits-Saint-Georges, tel. 03.80.61.04.55, fax 03.80.62.33.37,
e-mail bourgognes.faiveley@wanadoo.fr ☑

DOM. ANNE-MARIE GILLE

Les Renardes 2001

■ Gd cru	0.16 ha	800	❶❶	30–38 €

☛ Dom. Anne-Marie Gille, 34, RN 74, 21700 Comblanchien, tel. 03.80.62.94.13, fax 03.80.62.99.88, e-mail domaine.gille@wanadoo.fr ☑
🍷 by appt.

Corton-Charlemagne

The Appellation Charlemagne, which until 1948 could have Aligoté grapes added to it, is no longer used. In 2002, Appellation Corton-Charlemagne produced 1,979 hl, most of it grown in the communes of Pernand-Vergelesses and

Aloxe-Corton. The wines of this appellation – which owe their name to the Emperor Charles the Great who apparently ordered white grapes to be planted so the wines would not stain his beard – are a lovely greenish-gold and reach their peak after five or ten years.

BERTRAND AMBROISE 2001★★

	Gd cru	0.25 ha	2,000	🍶	46–76 €

Brilliant golden yellow, this is a wine where the nose is very young. It has lemon notes with a subtle vanilla. On the palate, it is really a pleasure. Cinnamon, fresh walnut, and pineapple contribute to the persistent flavours. A small touch of acidity on the finish suggests keeping potential. This négociant is a specialist of this style. (It won a *coup de coeur* for its 98 in this appellation).
☛ Bertrand Ambroise, rue de l'Eglise,
21700 Premeaux-Prissey, tel. 03.80.62.30.19,
fax 03.80.62.38.69,
e-mail bertrand.ambroise@wanadoo.fr ☑
⌷ by appt.

DOM. BOUCHARD PERE ET FILS 2000★★

	Gd cru	3,25 ha	n.c.	🍶	46–76 €

98 **99 00**

Founded in 1731, this house belonging to Henriot (Champagne) has a vineyard of 130 ha. The Grand Jury awarded unanimously a *coup de coeur* for this 2000 with its delicate and very pure colour. On the nose, the initial impression is closed, then notes of fresh hazelnut, sweet almond and the vine flowers appear. On the palate it is a little fleshy, with remarkable finesse. It is lightly oaked, with apricot nuances which will develop well for up to ten years. A racy wine, it is already enjoyable to taste. Eminent members of the Jury suggest it will go well with scallops.
☛ Bouchard Père et Fils, Ch. de Beaune, 21200 Beaune,
tel. 03.80.24.80.24, fax 03.80.22.55.88,
e-mail france@bouchard-pereetfils.com
⌷ by appt.

CAPITAIN-GAGNEROT 2001★

	Gd cru	0.42 ha	2,400	🍶	38–46 €

This producer has just celebrated a 200 year anniversary. As for this Corton-Charlemagne, it lives up to the motto on the label: "honesty is my strength". Clear gold in appearance, on the nose it blossoms with distinctive aromas of acacia honey, and wild mint. The palate is lively but structured, austere but dense, and mouthfilling. "It would be a pity not to get to know this wine." wrote one taster. It needs to be left to mature in peace.
☛ Capitain-Gagnerot, 38, rte de Dijon,
21550 Ladoix-Serrigny, tel. 03.80.26.41.36,
fax 03.80.26.46.29,
e-mail contact@capitain-gagnerot.com ☑
⌷ by appt.

MAURICE ET ANNE-MARIE CHAPUIS 2001★

	Gd cru	1 ha	4,500	🍶	30–38 €

This wine has the only label, with our knowledge, to show the emperor Charlemagne, his beard with his sceptre. For a 2001 imperial is rich, with a good body and length, and ripe fruit balanced by a fresh acidity. A fine oak flavour appears on the

end of the palate. Green-gold, this wine is perfect to the eye and although the first impression on the nose is a little closed, honey and nutmeg notes follow.
☛ Maurice Chapuis, 3, rue Boulmeau,
21420 Aloxe-Corton, tel. 03.80.26.40.99, fax 03.80.26.40.89,
e-mail info@domainechapuis.com ☑
⌷ by appt.

CHARTRON ET TREBUCHET 2001★

	Gd cru	n.c.	1,800	🍶	46–76 €

"It is necessary that the eye is seduced and flattered," an old handbook teaches about tasting. The eye can have no complaints about this Corton-Charlemagne which is a reflection of the appellation. There are honey and floral aromas on the nose, with a touch of oak, evolving towards notes of apples and pears. After a good first attack, fresh and lively, the palate still remains closed, but one senses potential. Keep for a long time…The Chartron family is no longer associated directly with Louis Trébuchet, the former president of the BIVB.
☛ Chartron et Trébuchet, 13, Grande-Rue,
21190 Puligny-Montrachet, tel. 03.80.21.32.85,
fax 03.80.21.36.35 ☑

DOM. DENIS PERE ET FILS 2000★

	Gd cru	0.5 ha	1,200	🍶	30–38 €

It is understood why the sons of Charlemagne disputed the heritage European. This bottle ushers in a beautiful classic wine, balanced, a little reserved, but evolving to perfection. It is quite pale and clear in appearance. Initially intense, the bouquet is dominated by nuances of dried fruit, honey and a note of oak. Gentle and minerally on the palate, it develops very similar flavours to the aromas on the nose with the addition of fig and almond qualities. Its complexity is not yet at its full potential because it has not yet opened up entirely. Have another look at it in five to ten years time.
☛ Dom. Denis Père et Fils, chem. des Vignes-Blanches,
21420 Pernand-Vergelesses, tel. 03.80.21.50.91,
fax 03.80.26.10.32, e-mail denis-pere-et-fils@wanadoo.fr ☑
⌷ by appt.

CH. GENOT-BOULANGER 2000★★

	Gd cru	0.29 ha	1,300	🍶	46–76 €

|97| 98 **00**

This was a finalist in the *coup de coeur* and classified number two. It is a wine which demands to be paired with dishes such as chicken with cream, truffles and morels. It is light in colour but an attractive natural appearance is preferable. The bouquet has Muscat notes, becoming more peachy and with exotic fruit nuances. Although powerful and persistent in style, this doesn't mask a very attractive vivacious mineral quality, a fact that will satisfy wine lovers.
☛ SCEV Ch. Génot-Boulanger, 25, rue de Cîteaux,
21190 Meursault, tel. 03.80.21.49.20, fax 03.80.21.49.21,
e-mail genot-boulanger@wanadoo.fr ☑
⌷ by appt.
☛ Delaby

DOM. ROBERT ET RAYMOND JACOB 2001★

	Gd cru	1.07 ha	n.c.	🍶	23–30 €

Clear and natural gold in appearance, this Corton-Charlemagne has a fruity bouquet with floral notes, pear and minerals. The palate has good concentration, underpinned by a lemon and mineral flavour and firm acidity, the latter suggesting further cellaring is necessary. The finish is as buttery as one would wish. A real Grand Cru which aims to please. Ideal with scallops.
☛ Dom. Robert et Raymond Jacob, hameau de Buisson,
21550 Ladoix-Serrigny, tel. 03.80.26.40.42,
fax 03.80.26.49.34 ☑
⌷ by appt.

DOM. MICHEL JUILLOT 2001★

	Gd cru	0.65 ha	n.c.	🍶	46–76 €

This wine, with a clear gold colour has come from a plot planted in 1965. The nose has notes of angelica which needs a little aeration to express itself: there are also nuances of dried fruits. On the palate it is luscious, robust and concentrated.

This 2001 is the cream of the crop – a very beautiful wine combining a fruity finish encased in oak. To achieve its potential, one should keep it for four to six years.
🔑 Dom. Michel Juillot, 59, Grande-Rue, BP 10, 71640 Mercurey, tel. 03.85.98.99.89, fax 03.85.98.99.88, e-mail infos@domaine-michel-juillot.fr ☑
🍷 ev. day except Sun. 9am–12 noon 2pm–6.30pm; groups by appt.

PIERRE MAREY ET FILS 2001★

	Gd cru	0.9 ha	3,500	🍾	30–38 €

Although this wine should be kept for another five years, a taster wanted to award it a *coup de coeur*! Its colour is yellow with green tones suggesting a good concentration. The nose playfully combines angelica and almond on a vanilla base (this wine has seen ten months oak ageing in Allier). Rich and ripe on the palate, this wine possesses an attractive acidity which gives great balance. Good length.
🔑 EARL Pierre Marey et Fils, rue Jacques-Copeau, 21420 Pernand-Vergelesses, tel. 03.80.21.51.71, fax 03.80.26.10.48 ☑
🍷 by appt.

DOM. NUDANT 2001★

	Gd cru	0.15 ha	900	🍾	38–46 €

This wine is a pretty straw colour in appearance but this yellowness suggests maturity. On the nose there are notes of fern, lemon and even marzipan. Initially mouth-filling and rich and powerful, this wine is quite characteristic of the appellation and is, without doubt, a wine to keep. It needs at least four to six years to integrate the acidity and the oak.
🔑 Dom. Nudant, 11, RN 74, 21550 Ladoix-Serrigny, tel. 03.80.26.40.48, fax 03.80.26.47.13, e-mail domaine.nudant@wanadoo.fr ☑
🍷 by appt.

DOM. DU PAVILLON 2001★

	Gd cru	1.09 ha	3,600	🍾	46–76 €

A *coup de coeur* in 2002 distinguished the 1999 vintage. This historical domaine was purchased, like many others (Frantin, Lupé – Cholet, Long – Depaquit), by Albert Bichot. Very successful in its appellation, this wine merits the title of Grand Cru. It is balanced perfectly between richness and acidity. Drinking now and for another four or five years, this 2001 will be splendid. Its colour is faultless with a bouquet of almond and eucalyptus.
🔑 Maison Albert Bichot, 6 bis, bd Jacques-Copeau, 21200 Beaune, tel. 03.80.24.37.37, fax 03.80.24.37.38

DOM. RAPET PERE ET FILS 2001★★

	Gd cru	2.5 ha	4,500	🍾	30–38 €

|90| |95| |98| 99 00 01

The new winery of this very old domaine has just entered service. If you go to visit it you could perhaps taste this Charlemagne whose appearance augurs well. Ethereal and feminine, the nose needs aeration for the aromas to develop. It has notes of almonds, fern, exotic fruits, cinnamon and pepper. The palate is round, floral and a little lemony, revealing a subtle use of oak which is very appealing. Pull the cork an hour before drinking…but not for another three or four years!
🔑 Dom. Rapet Père et Fils, 21420 Pernand-Vergelesses, tel. 03.80.21.59.94, fax 03.80.21.54.01 ☑
🍷 by appt.

Wines selected but not starred

FERY-MEUNIER 2000

	Gd cru	0.3 ha	1,800	🍾	38–46 €

🔑 Maison Fery-Meunier, 21420 Echevronne, tel. 03.80.21.59.60, fax 03.80.21.59.59, e-mail fery.meunier@wanadoo.fr ☑
🍷 by appt.

DOM. FOLLIN-ARBELET 2001

	Gd cru	0.25 ha	1,200	🍾	38–46 €

🔑 Dom. Follin-Arbelet, Les Vercots, 21420 Aloxe-Corton, tel. 03.80.26.46.73, fax 03.80.26.43.32 ☑
🍷 by appt.

DOM. MICHEL VOARICK 2001

	Gd cru	1.43 ha	6,300	🍾	30–38 €

🔑 Jean-Marc Voarick, 2, pl. du Chapitre, 21420 Aloxe-Corton, tel. 03.80.26.40.44, fax 03.80.26.41.22, e-mail voarickmichel@aol.com ☑
🍷 by appt.

Savigny-lès-Beaune

Savigny is another typical wine village. The spirit of the terroir is well in evidence here, and the Confrérie de la Cousinerie de Bourgogne is the symbol of Burgundian hospitality. The "Cousins" swear to welcome their guests "with bottles on the table and their hearts in their hands".

Savigny wines are reputedly "nourishing, prove the existence of God and stave off death"; they are fruity, supple and elegant, and are pleasant to drink young though they also age well. In 2002, the AOC produced 13,030 hl of red wine and 1,847 hl of white.

ARNOUX PERE ET FILS 2001★

	1er cru	4 ha	15,000	🍾	11–15 €

This wine appears with all the gentle purple tones that suggest a wine born to accompany roast duck. The bouquet is very closed with cherry notes. The acidity is still lively but the structure and the body provide a ray of sunshine under a sky of gentle spices and mild tobacco. The tannins do not dominate but are quite present. On the finish it retains richness and freshness. Drink in two years time.
🔑 Arnoux Père et Fils, rue des Brenôts, 21200 Chorey-lès-Beaune, tel. 03.80.22.57.98, fax 03.80.22.16.85 ☑
🍷 by appt.

BOUCHARD AINE ET FILS
Les Peuillets Cuvée Signature 2001★★

	1er cru	n.c.	2,985	🍾	23–30 €

This respected Beaune name was taken over some years ago by the J.-Cl. Boisset family who have preserved its character (in particular the beautiful hôtel of Conseiller du Roy on the boulevards of Beaune). One of their wines stands out every vintage in one village. This wine is crimson-garnet in appearance and the nose is already complex, with subtle oak nuances. It leaves a dazzling impression on the palate: grip, richness, tannins, body, roundness, length, balance – all contribute to its remarkable harmony.

☛ Bouchard Aîné et Fils, hôtel du Conseiller-du-Roy, 4, bd Mal-Foch, 21200 Beaune, tel. 03.80.24.24.00, fax 03.80.24.64.12, e-mail bouchard@bouchard-aine.fr **☑**
🍷 ev. day 9.30am–12 noon 2pm–6pm
☛ J.-Cl. Boisset

DOM. DENIS BOUSSEY 2001★

| ■ | 0.45 ha | 2,000 | ⦿ | 8–11 € |

Dark ruby with purple tones on the rim, this is a Savigny which combines effectively fruits in alcohol with spice. It has a full and pleasant structure. This wine should be left in peace for some years to allow everything to integrate. The fruit is already appetizing, and will be fully developed in four or five years. It will go well with game or strong cheese.

☛ Dom. Denis Boussey, 1, rue du Pied-de-la-Vallée, 21190 Monthélie, tel. 03.80.21.21.23, fax 03.80.21.62.46 **☑**
🍷 ev. day except Sun. 8am–12 noon 1.30pm–6.30pm; cl. 5–23 Aug

LUCIEN CAMUS-BRUCHON

Narbantons 2001★

| ■ | 1er cru | 0.45 ha | 2,500 | ⦿ | 11–15 € |

Sun-coloured highlights animate the cherry red colour of this wine: our Jury described with pleasure the wonderful appearance of this wine. It has a perfume of fine and elegant red fruits accompanied by a fleshy roundness on the palate and balanced with a respectful use of oak. This wine may certainly be kept for three or four years. **Aux Grands Liards 2001** gets a recommendation.

☛ Dom. Lucien Camus-Bruchon, Les Cruottes, 16, rue de Chorey, 21420 Savigny-lès-Beaune, tel. 03.80.21.51.08, fax 03.80.26.10.21 **☑**
🍷 by appt.

MAISON CHAMPY

Bas Liards 2000★

| ■ | 1.1 ha | 4,500 | ⦿ | 15–23 € |

Awarded a *coup de coeur* in our 1998 and 2000 Guides, Champy has an understanding of Savigny at the tip of his fingers. Brilliant-red in appearance, with an elegant and rather complex bouquet (reminiscent of blackcurrant), this Pinot Noir has made a good impression. There is nothing excessive about this wine; everything is very measured and with subtle nuances. Keep this wine for two years to allow it to fully integrate.

☛ Maison Champy, 5, rue du Grenier-à-Sel, 21200 Beaune, tel. 03.80.25.09.99, fax 03.80.25.09.95 **☑**
🍷 by appt.
☛ Pierre Meurgey Pierre Beuchet

DOM. CHARACHE-BERGERET

Les Godeaux 2001★

| ■ | 0.28 ha | 4,000 | ⦿ | 11–15 € |

This domaine was established in 1976 by Rene and Jacqueline Charache. Their two sons now work on the estate. Clearly from the Côte Pernand, the wines from this vineyard site fit the following definition: "Supple, with light tannins and a delicate structure which gives a feminine impression". Red-garnet in colour, it expresses on the nose a purée of small red fruits. This wine lives up to the reputation of the cru and is very enjoyable to taste now.

☛ René Charache-Bergeret, 21200 Bouze-lès-Beaune, tel. 03.80.26.00.86, fax 03.80.26.00.86, e-mail bourgogne-charache.bergeret@wanadoo.fr **☑**
🍷 by appt.

DOM. BRUNO CLAIR

La Dominode 2000★

| ■ | 1er cru | 1.71 ha | 8,000 | ▮⦿🍂 | 23–30 € |

When one is the grandson of Joseph Clair-Daÿ – a historical figure on the Côte, one has to put forth into the world great bottles of wine. This one is brilliantly intense in appearance. The nose is still rather closed, but opens up with red berries and coffee notes. The tannins are present, and the complexity is that of a Premier Cru. It is a warming and full-bodied wine which will go well with game dishes.

☛ SCEA Dom. Bruno Clair, 5, rue du Vieux-Collège, BP 22, 21160 Marsannay-la-Côte, tel. 03.80.52.28.95, fax 03.80.52.18.14, e-mail brunoclair@wanadoo.fr **☑**
🍷 by appt.

MAISON CLAVELIER 2000★★

| ■ | 1er cru | n.c. | 3,000 | ⦿ | 23–30 € |

The Clavelier house has remained faithful to its label of parchment with rolled edges, for more than its 50 years. The owner has changed several times however and today it is owned by the Thomas family, in Nuits. Just short of attaining the podium, this deep crimson Savigny is a great Premier Cru. Its has oak tones but these do not dominate the wine, and the palate has all the virtues of Pinot Noir portrayed with an even more beautiful expression.

☛ Maison Clavelier et Fils, 49, rte de Beaune, 21700 Comblanchien, tel. 03.80.62.94.11, fax 03.80.62.95.20, e-mail vins.clavelier@wanadoo.fr **☑**
🍷 ev. day 10am–6pm; cl. 25–31 Dec.

DOM. PHILIPPE DELAGRANGE 2001★★

| ■ | 0.48 ha | 3,249 | ⦿ | 11–15 € |

Pale-gold in colour, this is a Chardonnay with a particularly flattering perfume of honey and dried fruits. It wins its *coup de coeur* hands down. A casserole of seafood should honour this beautifully produced cru which evolves on the palate into very ripe peach notes in the warming style of country white wines. Elegant and powerful, it can be enjoyed now or kept for a little longer in the cellar (not longer than five years). Do not miss visiting a curiosity: a wine cellar with two floors.

☛ Philippe Delagrange, 10, rue du 11–Novembre, 21190 Meursault, tel. 03.80.21.22.72, fax 03.80.21.68.70 **☑**
🍷 ev. day 9am–7pm

DOUDET-NAUDIN

Récolte des Vermots 2001★

| ■ | 1 ha | 5,100 | ⦿ | 8–11 € |

This Savigny is a not bad, original white wine where a beeswax note forms part of the Oriental aroma which, at the same time, is fresh. On the mid-palate we retrace the range of fruit flavours with figs, dates, and a warming finish. It is certainly not a wine to leave a long time in the cellar, but it expresses real personality and will surprise your guests. The excellent **red Savigny 2001 (11–15 €)**, awarded a *coup de coeur* last year for the 2000, receives one star this year.

☛ Doudet-Naudin, 3, rue Henri-Cyrot, 21420 Savigny-lès-Beaune, tel. 03.80.21.51.74, fax 03.80.21.50.69, e-mail doudet-naudin@wanadoo.fr **☑**
🍷 by appt.
☛ Yves Doudet

PHILIPPE DUBREUIL-CORDIER 2000★

| ■ | 0.72 ha | 5,000 | ⦿ | 8–11 € |

The grapes were picked here on September 22, 2000, if you want to know all the details. They must have been healthy and of good quality, because this Chardonnay has a beautiful intensity and it doesn't stop showing us that. On the nose it has hazelnut and toasted almond aromas at first and even after standing a while. What of the palate? It is full and complete, with a little lively freshness calming the richness, and a peppery flavour with good length. Wine lovers know what is meant when one talks about the style of the wine as being like

a French *patisserie*. Also recommended, the **red Premier Cru Les Serpentières 2000 (11–15 €)** gets one star.
📧 Philippe Dubreuil, 4, rue Péjot,
21420 Savigny-lès-Beaune, tel. 03.80.21.53.73,
fax 03.80.26.11.46 ☑
👅 by appt.

DOM. LIONEL DUFOUR
Les Lavières Elevé en fût de chêne 2001★

■ 1er cru	0.4 ha	2,900	🍾	46–76 €

This vineyard is located at the bottom of Vergelesses, beside Pernand. This 2001 is showing well. Between mauve and garnet this wine has a classy appearance. The cassis notes come through subtly on the nose. The attack is direct and aromatic and suggests lasting qualities. This is a wine to lay down. It is rich, long on the palate and distinguished, showing an honourable complexity.
📧 SCI Lionel Dufour, imp. des Amandiers,
21190 Meursault, tel. 03.80.21.67.02, fax 03.87.69.78.88

LOU DUMONT 2001★

■	n.c.	n.c.	🍾	11–15 €

France, Korea and Japan. What does that produce? Tea? Not at all! Three partners from these countries have produced this Savigny. The colour is of an average intensity garnet-red. The oak does not obscure the blueberry notes which occur on the nose. After the soft initial attack there appears to be a substantial but silky structure, which is balanced by juicy fruit. What does this wine lack? A little length perhaps, but on the whole, nothing worth complaining about.
📧 Lou Dumont, 1, rue de Paris, 21220 Gevrey-Chambertin, tel. 03.80.51.82.82, fax 03.80.51.82.84,
e-mail sales@loudumont.com ☑
👅 by appt.

FRANCOIS GAY ET FILS
Les Serpentières 2000★

■ 1er cru	0.47 ha	2,900	🍾	11–15 €

Brilliant-crimson with violet tones, this wine is still a little closed: notes of crystallized fruit appear under the vanilla nuances of oak maturation. Closed initially, the first impression is of a well-structured palate where the aromas on the nose reassert themselves as flavours. This wine needs two or three years further cellaring for its beautifully firm structure to integrate and mature. The **red Savigny Village 2000 (8–11 €)** is singled out. It is balanced and fruity, full and silky. It will be ready in two years.
📧 EARL François Gay, 9, rue des Fiètres,
21200 Chorey-lès-Beaune, tel. 03.80.22.69.58,
fax 03.80.24.71.42 ☑
👅 by appt.

DOM. MICHEL GAY ET FILS
Les Serpentières 2000★

■ 1er cru	0.46 ha	2,700	🍾	11–15 €

Sebastien Gay represents the fourth generation of this domaine which shows here a Savigny with a brilliant crimson appearance and a particularly expressive nose: ripe fruit with musky, animal notes. The first impression is as it should be and shows roundness and power. Its complexity will make it a good wine with roasts, as has been said before. **Vergelesses Premier Cru red 2000**: a quite representative wine that gets a special mention.
📧 EARL Dom. Michel Gay et Fils, 1b, rue des Brenôts,
21200 Chorey-lès-Beaune, tel. 03.80.22.22.73,
fax 03.80.22.95.78 ☑
👅 by appt.

JEAN-MICHEL GIBOULOT
Aux Gravains 2001★

■ 1er cru	0.59 ha	3,200	🍾	15–23 €

"A wine for a young girl in the bloom of youth," writes one of our most distinguished tasters. Representative of its origin, it has a lively cherry colour, and the fruit on the nose is similar to the fruit on the palate. It has a touch of earthiness and well-balanced oak. Keep until 2004 or 2005. The **red Les Peuillets Premier Cru 2001** is singled out for a mention.
📧 Jean-Michel Giboulot, 27, rue du Général-Leclerc,
21420 Savigny-lès-Beaune, tel. 03.80.21.52.30,
fax 03.80.26.10.06 ☑
👅 by appt.

DOM. PHILIPPE GIRARD
Les Lavières Vieilles Vignes 2001★

■ 1er cru	0.34 ha	2,000	🍾	15–23 €

This is certainly closed, but it is often the case that a wine with a reserved temperament will wait a little before giving its best. Such is the case here. Purplish ruby in colour, this 2001 is gamey and spicy on the nose and will, in time, develop character and elegance. Its tannins should be more refined in two with five years. It has a richness ideally suited to the dinner table.
📧 Dom. Philippe Girard, 37, rue du Général-Leclerc,
21420 Savigny-lès-Beaune, tel. 03.80.21.57.97,
fax 03.80.26.14.84 ☑
👅 by appt.

DOM. A.-F. GROS
Clos des Guettes 2001★★

■ 1er cru	0.67 ha	4,000	🍾	15–23 €

This is a noble wine. It has the appearance of a fine painting. On the nose, the oak is not fully integrated but already raspberry, strawberry are becoming dominant…This *climat* near Pernand is showing superbly and one of our jurors rates it as a *coup de coeur*. Long, powerful and tannic, this is, if truth be told, a wine which one would never tire of drinking. The previous vintage won a *coup de coeur* and this remains at the top of its appellation. It is for laying down, of course.
📧 Dom. A.-F. Gros, La Garelle, Grande-Rue,
21630 Pommard, tel. 03.80.22.61.85, fax 03.80.24.03.16,
e-mail af-gros@wanadoo.fr ☑
👅 by appt.
📧 Anne-Françoise Parent-Gros

DOM. PIERRE GUILLEMOT
Serpentières 2001★

■ 1er cru	1.7 ha	6,000	🍾	11–15 €

Pierre Guillemot is a character. He has won the *coup de coeur* more often than one can say (1992, 1995, 2000, and we have probably forgotten some) and his wines should be tasted over more than one vintage. Make a note of: **Les Grands Picotins 2001, red Les Jarrons 2001** and the **white Dessus de Golardes 2001**, as they all have been cited by the Jury. These Serpentières will not snake along like their name-sake but will go straight to triumph in five to ten years. A Grand Premier Cru, which you could buy with your eyes closed.
📧 SCE du Dom. Pierre Guillemot, 1, rue
Boulanger-et-Vallée, 21420 Savigny-lès-Beaune,
tel. 03.80.21.50.40, fax 03.80.21.59.98 ☑
👅 by appt.

PIERRE JANNY 2000★★

■	n.c.	2,000	🍾	11–15 €

This wine-grower from Saône-et-Loire has now extended his activities to that of négociant. And he has been lucky enough to choose a quite remarkable wine, whose length of flavour is astonishing. Intense red in colour, this 2000 has a fairly characteristic, fruity nose with a touch of oak. It is supple on the attack with superb concentration. Harvested, vinified and bottled at the producers domaine. Ah! one would like to know which…
📧 Sté Janny, La Condemine, Cidex 1556, 71260 Péronne, tel. 03.85.23.96.20, fax 03.85.36.96.58,
e-mail pierre-janny@wanadoo.fr

DANIEL LARGEOT 2001★

■	0.6 ha	3,600	🍾	11–15 €

This wine is true to type, and has character and finesse. This summarizes the feelings inspired by this pretty bottle of beautiful, gleaming ruby wine. The bouquet is subtle, the oak having been well integrated with cassis. The fruit asserts itself from the initial attack until the end of the palate. It is still a little austere now, but that will lessen and it will harmonise over time. The 1999 received the *coup de coeur* in the 2002 *Guide*.
📧 Daniel Largeot, 5, rue des Brenôts,
21200 Chorey-lès-Beaune, tel. 03.80.22.15.10,
fax 03.80.22.60.62 ☑
👅 by appt.

PIERRE ET JEAN-BAPTISTE LEBREUIL

Aux Clous 2001★

| | 1er cru | 0.2 ha | 1,300 | ◻◻ | 11–15 € |

This vineyard is located along the length of this long village, and it produces a Chardonnay with a delicate but very golden colour. With vanilla, almond, and honeysuckle, there is nothing lacking here. There are excellent flavours on the palate where the alcohol and acidity are perfectly in balance with everything else. All the tasters were of the same mind so this wine is recommended to you with confidence. The **Premier Cru Aux Clous 2001 red** is a good investment for the future. It also gets a star.

☛ Pierre et Jean-Baptiste Lebreuil, Dom. Les Guettottes, 17, rue Chanson-Maldant, 21420 Savigny-lès-Beaune, tel. 03.80.21.52.95, fax 03.80.26.10.82, e-mail jean-baptiste.lebreuil@wanadoo.fr ☑
☳ ev. day except Sun. 9am–11h30 2pm–6.30pm

JEAN-LUC MALDANT 2001★

| | | 1.8 ha | 4,500 | ◻◻ | 15–23 € |

This wine has a good colour and lots of legs. The nose is immediate with cooked fruit and vanilla notes. This wine still lively, spontaneous, and pleasant to taste. The fruit forms an active part on the palate and the finish is positive. Do not uncork it too early; it will be ready about 2005. It is undoubtedly representative of its appellation.

☛ Jean-Luc Maldant, 26, Grande-Rue, 21200 Chorey-lès-Beaune, tel. 03.80.24.14.15, fax 03.80.24.14.50, e-mail domaine.maldant@wanadoo.fr ☑
☳ by appt.

CATHERINE ET CLAUDE MARECHAL

Vieilles Vignes 2001★

| | | 1.49 ha | 8,400 | ◻◻ | 11–15 € |

Savigny wines can sometimes prevent death. Indeed this proves capable of overcoming some maladies. Dark garnet in colour, it has a velvety appearance. On the nose ripe, blackcurrant provides a generous bouquet with an alluring intensity. The body has a lusciousness and fruitiness. Acidity and alcohol are a little present on the end of the palate, but without compromising the overall balance. It would be best to leave this bottle for three or four years in the cellar; it will then provide great pleasure.

☛ EARL Catherine et Claude Maréchal, 6, rte de Chalon, 21200 Bligny-lès-Beaune, tel. 03.80.21.44.37, fax 03.80.26.85.01, e-mail marechalcc@wanadoo.fr ☑
☳ by appt.

GHISLAINE ET BERNARD MARECHAL-CAILLOT 2001★★

| | | 2.22 ha | 6,600 | ◻◻ | 11–15 € |

If ever a wine just missed winning a *coup de cœur* from the Grand Jury, it is this one. Crimson with purple highlights, on the nose it marries notes of vanilla and cooked fruits in a reasonable way. It is still lively but superbly balanced. Substantial, and powerful, this wine is very complete and lasts a long time on the palate, leaving an impression of crunchy fruit. You are not likely to be disappointed.

☛ Bernard Maréchal, 10, rte de Chalon, 21200 Bligny-lès-Beaune, tel. 03.80.21.44.55, fax 03.80.26.88.21 ☑
☳ by appt.

MARINOT-VERDUN 2001★★

| | 1er cru | n.c. | 3,000 | ◻◻ | 8–11 € |

This firm of négociants, established in Saône-et-Loire has submitted a very convincing Premier Cru Savigny. "One licks one's lips three times and says 'good'", so the local saying goes. The colour is pleasant and the nose is quite wild and spicy. The chewiness, the graininess and the firmness are well mastered; the qualities that give this wine ageing potential remind one more of the hills of the Beaune area than those bordering Pernand. What we have here is a 2001 that is solid and serious.

☛ Marinot-Verdun, Cave de Mazenay, 71510 Saint-Sernin-du-Plain, tel. 03.85.49.67.19, fax 03.85.45.57.21
☳ ev. day except Sun. 8am–12 noon 2pm–6pm

DOM. MONGEARD-MUGNERET 2001★

| | | 0.59 ha | 3,300 | ◻◻ | 11–15 € |

This domaine has a foot in Languedoc-Roussillon, and has been run for a long time by one of the figureheads of Burgundian wine. Still fresh and lively, this wine is nevertheless sufficiently balanced on a serious basis. On the palate, oak is present and the tannins are not too aggressive but show a good persistence. Elegance compensates a little for the lack of structure, but in end there is nothing to complain about. It will give as much pleasure if matched with poultry as much as with roast meat.

☛ Dom. Mongeard-Mugneret, 14, rue de la Fontaine, 21700 Vosne-Romanée, tel. 03.80.61.11.95, fax 03.80.62.35.75, e-mail mongeard@reseauconcept.net ☑

ANDRE MONTESSUY 2000★

| | | n.c. | 5,985 | | 11–15 € |

It should be noted that this wine is from the stable of Antonin Rodet. It has a dark, vibrant red colour, a Savigny with liquorice and fruit. The tannins are still young, but there is richness to support this. Its finish is pleasant and fruity. In two or three years, it will be ideal to accompany game dishes.

☛ André Montessuy, 71640 Mercurey, tel. 03.85.98.12.12, fax 03.85.45.25.49, e-mail rodet@rodet.com ☑
☳ by appt.

ALBERT MOROT

La Bataillère aux Vergelesses 2000★★

| | 1er cru | 1.81 ha | 10,000 | ◻◻ | 15–23 € |

In his book on the wines of Burgundy (1831), Dr Morelot especially mentions this vineyard (Bataillère) among the most illustrious special vat selections, putting it on the level of a Romanée or Chambertin. It is therefore a great wine within Vergelesses and one which perhaps deserves to reinstate the name *clos*. It has a very deep colour, with a thoroughbred bouquet. This vintage unites vinosity and warmth with many other beautiful qualities, including complexity.

☛ Albert Morot, Ch. de la Creusotte, 20, av. Charles-Jaffelin, 21200 Beaune, tel. 03.80.22.35.39, fax 03.80.22.47.50, e-mail albertmorot@aol.com ☑
☳ by appt.

PIERRE OLIVIER 2001★

| | | n.c. | 10,000 | ◻◻ | 11–15 € |

This is the wine of the Moillard family in Nuits-Saint-Georges. It is a beautiful gold colour for a white Savigny, and on the nose it sings in the glass with almond and hazelnut notes. The oak is light, and not over-the-top. There is not too much acidity either, after a supple initial attack. On the mid-palate it reveals a buttery sensation. In fact, this wine is not at all disagreeable! It is best enjoyed next year, paired with grilled fish.

☛ Pierre Olivier, 2, rue François-Mignotte, 21700 Nuits-Saint-Georges, tel. 03.80.62.42.08, fax 03.80.61.28.13, e-mail nuicave@wanadoo.fr ☑
☳ ev. day 10am–6pm; cl. Jan.

OLIVIER PERE ET FILS

Les Peuillets 2001★★

| | 1er cru | 0.52 ha | 3,000 | ◻◻ | 11–15 € |

Established in 1960, this 9-ha domaine was taken over in 2003 by Antoine and Rachel Olivier. This wine is sumptuous. It was examined in the final of the *coup de cœur*. This is a dark garnet and brilliant coloured wine. On the nose initially there is liquorice, then fresh red fruits, punctuated by spice notes, all of which suggests successful wine worthy of a premier cru. It is produced here on a half-hectare of land.

☛ Olivier Père et Fils, 5, rue Gaudin, 21590 Santenay, tel. 03.80.20.61.35, fax 03.80.20.64.82, e-mail antoine.olivier2@wanadoo.fr ☑
☳ by appt.

JEAN-MARC ET HUGUES PAVELOT

La Dominode 2001★

| | 1er cru | 2.21 ha | 12,000 | ◻◻ | 15–23 € |

Here are three wines, each awarded a star: one is left with the choice between a **red Savigny 2001 (8–11 €)**, or the cru **red Aux**

Guettes 2001 (11–15 €) and this Dominode which, if it needs ageing, is already seductive. It is very deep garnet in appearance, and the nose begins on an animal note and opens into violet nuances. There are also well-integrated vanilla notes. The violet characteristics reappear on the palate. The tannins are firm, almost dominating at present but with time they will learn their place. This wine should not be broached before 2008. Wine-lovers will be willing to wait.

☞ Jean-Marc et Hugues Pavelot, 1, chem. des Guettottes, 21420 Savigny-lès-Beaune, tel. 03.80.21.55.21, fax 03.80.21.59.73 ⊠

☇ by appt.

DOM. DU PRIEURE

Moutier Amet 2000★

■	0.8 ha	4,000	〗	8–11 €

This was one of our *coups de coeur* last year. The son, Stéphan, returned from Australia and, with his BTS in his pocket, will maintain the honour of the domaine. Moutier Amet is a small vineyard which one encounters on the way to Savigny, on the right. Clear and bright ruby, this 2000 reveals fruit and has a good mouth feel. The acidity provides freshness and allows secondary raspberry flavours to arise. The tannins are subtle with spicy notes, which makes this a wine to drink in the next two years. **Les Gollardes 2000 red** receives a citation.

☞ Jean-Michel Maurice, Dom. du Prieuré, 23, rte de Beaune, 21420 Savigny-lès-Beaune, tel. 03.80.21.54.27, fax 03.80.21.59.77, e-mail maurice.jean-michel@wanadoo.fr ⊠

☇ by appt.

DOM. GEORGES ROY ET FILS

Les Picotins 2000★

■	1.85 ha	2,200	〗	8–11 €

Large or small according to the land register, Les Picotins is at the entrance to the village. Vincent Roy took his responsibilities seriously with the domaine (8,5 ha) in 1998. He has produced an intensely-ruby 2000. The nose seems quite subdued, reminiscent somewhat of crushed red fruit. On the palate, this wine is well-structured and robust. If kept for a year or two it will achieve its potential.

☞ Dom. Georges Roy et Fils, 20, rue des Moutots, 21200 Chorey-lès-Beaune, tel. 03.80.22.16.28, fax 03.80.24.76.38 ⊠

☇ by appt.

DOM. SEGUIN-MANUEL

Les Goudelettes 2000★

■	0.5 ha	2,400	〗	15–23 €

This vineyard is fine and long, at the exit of the village when one goes up towards Bouilland. This domaine is dedicated only to Savigny. The vineyard was bought in 1958 by Pierre Seguin whose wine cellar dates from the time of the Cistercians. Here we have a wine of character, clear straw in appearance with a bouquet between toasted almond and freshly baked pastries, such as brioche. On the palate the initial impression is of fruit, peach for example, but it doesn't reveal everything at once. It has an appreciably long finish.

☞ Dom. Seguin-Manuel, 15, rue Paul-Maldant, 21420 Savigny-lès-Beaune, tel. 03.80.21.50.42, fax 03.80.21.59.38, e-mail seguin-manuel@worldonline.fr ⊠

☇ ev. day 8am–12 noon 2pm–7pm; cl. Aug

☞ Pierre Seguin

DOM. DE TERREGELESSES

Les Vergelesses 2001★★

▢	1er cru	0.5 ha	n.c.	〗	15–23 €

This domaine is directed by Philippe Senard, of the *Grand Conseil du Tastevin*. The vineyard location draws obviously on Pernand. This wine has been the *coup de coeur* of our *coups de coeur* in Savigny, since it first arrived in front of the Grand Jury. It is the very image of a *vin de terroir* and has a straightforward yellow appearance, with a fresh and floral nose. On the palate it offers an impression of brioche while expressing a lively vivacity. It is perfectly true to type and one taster thinks it would go well with poached scallops.

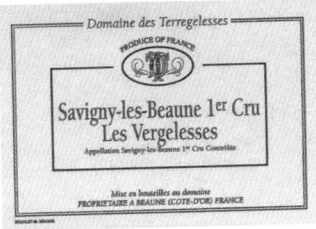

☞ Dom. des Terregelesses, 7, rempart Saint-Jean, 21200 Beaune, tel. 03.80.24.21.65, fax 03.80.24.21.44 ⊠

☇ ev. day except Sun. 10am–6pm; cl. Dec.–Mar

Wines selected but not starred

CAPITAIN-GAGNEROT

Les Charnières 2000

■	1er cru	0.63 ha	3,000	〗	11–15 €

☞ Capitain-Gagnerot, 38, rte de Dijon, 21550 Ladoix-Serrigny, tel. 03.80.26.41.36, fax 03.80.26.46.29, e-mail contact@capitain-gagnerot.com ⊠

☇ by appt.

DOM. DENIS CARRE 2001

■	1.1 ha	n.c.	〗	8–11 €

☞ Denis Carré, rue du Puits-Bouret, 21190 Meloisey, tel. 03.80.26.02.21, fax 03.80.26.04.64 ⊠

☇ by appt.

DOM. CHANSON PERE ET FILS

Hauts Marconnets 2001

■	1er cru	2.18 ha	8,600	〗	15–23 €

☞ Dom. Chanson Père et Fils, 10, rue Paul-Chanson, BP 232, 21206 Beaune Cedex, tel. 03.80.25.97.97, fax 03.80.24.17.42, e-mail tmarion@vins-chanson.com

C. CHARTON FILS

Les Dentellières 2000

■	n.c.	3,000	■〗⚕	23–30 €

☞ C. Charton Fils, 38, fg Saint-Nicolas, 21200 Beaune, tel. 03.80.22.53.33, fax 03.80.24.19.73

RODOLPHE DEMOUGEOT

Les Bourgeots 2001

■	0.75 ha	4,000	〗	11–15 €

☞ Dom. Rodolphe Demougeot, 2, rue du Clos-de-Mazeray, 21190 Meursault, tel. 03.80.21.28.99, fax 03.80.21.29.18 ⊠

☇ by appt.

DOM. P. DUBREUIL-FONTAINE PERE ET FILS Les Vergelesses 2001

■	1er cru	2.1 ha	10,000	〗	11–15 €

☞ Dom. Dubreuil-Fontaine, rue Rameau-Lamarosse, 21420 Pernand-Vergelesses, tel. 03.80.21.55.43, fax 03.80.21.51.69, e-mail dubreuil.fontaine@wanadoo.fr ⊠

☇ by appt.

☞ Bernard Dubreuil

MAISON FORGEOT PERE ET FILS 2001

| | n.c. | n.c. | ▮ ⑪ ♦ | 11–15 € |

↟ Grands Vins Forgeot, 15, rue du Château, 21200 Beaune, tel. 03.80.24.80.50, fax 03.80.22.55.88

CHRISTIAN GROS

Clos des Vermots 2001

| | 0.39 ha | 2,000 | ▮ ♦ | 8–11 € |

↟ Christian Gros, rue de la Chaume, 21700 Premeaux-Prissey, tel. 03.80.61.29.74, fax 03.80.61.39.77 ▼
☟ by appt.

JEAN-MARC MILLOT 2001

| | 0.83 ha | 3,000 | ⑪ | 8–11 € |

↟ Jean-Marc Millot, Grande-Rue, 21700 Comblanchien, tel. 03.80.61.34.81, fax 03.80.61.34.81 ▼
☟ by appt.

Chorey-lès-Beaune

Chorey-lès-Beaune is situated on flat land, opposite the pile of scree at the foot of the Combe de Bouilland, and some of the village's *lieux-dits* are neighbours to Savigny. In 2002, the Appellation Communale produced 6,179 hl of red wine and 213 hl of white.

BERNARD DUBOIS ET FILS

Les Beaumonts 2000★

| | 2.08 ha | 4,000 | ⑪ | 8–11 € |

This wine has black cherry notes and a nose poised between strawberries and oak, reinforced unsur- prisingly with vanilla. The first impression is of firm tannins, which leave you in no doubt that they know their role well: to produce a wine that is able to age. This feeling of austerity is normal with a wine of this age and at this stage of maturity. Four with five years' maturation in cellar will allow it to achieve its excellent potential.
↟ Dom. Bernard Dubois et Fils, 8, rue des Chobins, 21200 Chorey-lès-Beaune, tel. 03.80.22.13.56, fax 03.80.24.61.43 ▼
☟ by appt.

FRANCOIS GAY ET FILS 2000★

| | 2.75 ha | 15,000 | ⑪ | 8–11 € |

The beautiful ruby colour of this wine, darker than usual for this vintage (2000) and tending to purple, harbours intense aromas of strawberry and vanilla. The aromatic persistence of this wine helps to define its personality. It also has a good level of acidity, tannins that are not too bitter or too firm to dominate the richness of the wine.
↟ EARL François Gay, 9, rue des Fiêtres, 21200 Chorey-lès-Beaune, tel. 03.80.22.69.58, fax 03.80.24.71.42 ▼
☟ by appt.

DOM. MICHEL GAY ET FILS 2000★

| | 3,6 ha | 11,000 | ⑪ | 8–11 € |

Sebastien Gay continues the fourth generation of this family of winemakers. Their domaine consists of 8,5 ha divided evenly between Savigny, Beaune and the hill of Corton. Garnet in appearance, this is a Pinot Noir initially reminiscent on the nose of red fruits and oak. The first impression on the palate confirms the nose and these flavours persist to the finish. Mouthfilling and persistent, this is a 2000 which still has time ahead of it.
↟ EARL Dom. Michel Gay et Fils, 1b, rue des Brenôts, 21200 Chorey-lès-Beaune, tel. 03.80.22.22.73, fax 03.80.22.95.78 ▼
☟ by appt.

DANIEL LARGEOT

Les Beaumonts 2001★

| | 2 ha | 12,000 | ⑪ | 8–11 € |

Les Beaumonts is a vineyard located above the RN 74 on the way to Savigny. Lively ruby in appearance, this 2001 has round, fine tannins. Well-balanced and persistent, this wine has a youthful bouquet without being excessively oaky. The palate is already quite accessible and one can taste the vibrancy of the vintage. This is always an enjoyable type of wine to taste.
↟ Daniel Largeot, 5, rue des Brenôts, 21200 Chorey-lès-Beaune, tel. 03.80.22.15.10, fax 03.80.22.60.62 ▼
☟ by appt.

GHISLAINE ET BERNARD MARECHAL-CAILLOT 2001★

| | 0.8 ha | 4,800 | ⑪ | 11–15 € |

Wines from the Chorey appellation were formerly known as "tonic wine," because they served the purpose of reviving the pale colour and the meagre body of some of the neighbouring *cuvées*. This one could fulfill that role if this practice were still authorized today. This is a robust and powerful wine with a good colour and aromas tending towards raspberries in *eau-de-vie*. The tannins are still lively, but time will round out their angularity.
↟ Bernard Maréchal, 10, rte de Chalon, 21200 Bligny-lès-Beaune, tel. 03.80.21.44.55, fax 03.80.26.88.21 ▼
☟ by appt.

DOM. POULLEAU PERE ET FILS 2001★

| | 0.45 ha | 2,700 | ⑪ | 11–15 € |

This family domaine spans several generations; nowadays it covers little more than 8 ha. This is small enough to know each individual vine by name. This 2001 could be at its optimum in two years time. Limpid and ruby-garnet, with just enough intensity, it reveals delicate aromas of vanilla with perfumes of currants and cherries. On the palate the tannins have been refined a little by oak. On the finish, interesting flavours of red fruits return to haunt.
↟ Dom. Poulleau Père et Fils, rue du Pied-de-la-Vallée, 21190 Volnay, tel. 03.80.21.26.52, fax 03.80.21.64.03 ▼
☟ by appt.

ROGER ET JOEL REMY

Les Beaumonts 2001★

| | 1.5 ha | 11,000 | ⑪ | 8–11 € |

This domaine was taken over 1995 and therefore the head-quarters (as well as the visitors' centre) are in Sainte-Marie-la-Blanche, on the Beaune plain. The cherubs on the label gently escort this 2001 to us. It has a cherry-red colour and a perfume of cherries in *eau-de-vie*; cherries from start to finish. It sets a high standard, the more so as cherries excite the tastebuds. The initial attack is lively with a noticeable length. There are small nuances of alcohol but it suits the style of the wine.
↟ SCEA Roger et Joël Rémy, 4, rue du Paradis, 21200 Sainte-Marie-la-Blanche, tel. 03.80.26.60.80, fax 03.80.26.53.03, e-mail domaine.remy@wanadoo.fr ▼
☟ by appt.

Wines selected but not starred

DOM. CACHAT-OCQUIDANT ET FILS 2001

| | 1.7 ha | 4,500 | ⑪ | 8–11 € |

↟ Dom. Cachat-Ocquidant et Fils, 3, pl. du Souvenir, 21550 Ladoix-Serrigny, tel. 03.80.26.45.30, fax 03.80.26.48.16 ▼
☟ by appt.

MAURICE ET ANNE-MARIE CHAPUIS

2001

| | 0.9 ha | 5,500 | 🍷 | 8–11 € |

🔸 Maurice Chapuis, 3, rue Boulmeau,
21420 Aloxe-Corton, tel. 03.80.26.40.99, fax 03.80.26.40.89,
e-mail info@domainechapuis.com ☑
🍷 by appt.

CH. DE CHOREY 2000

| ■ | 6 ha | 20,000 | 🍷 | 11–15 € |

🔸 Dom. du Château de Chorey, 21200 Chorey-lès-Beaune,
tel. 03.80.24.06.39, fax 03.80.24.77.72 ☑ 🏠
🍷 by appt.
🔸 Germain

DOM. DUBOIS D'ORGEVAL 2000

| ■ | 2.15 ha | 4,500 | 🍷 | 11–15 € |

🔸 Dom. Dubois d'Orgeval, 3, rue Joseph-Bard,
21200 Chorey-lès-Beaune, tel. 03.80.24.70.89,
fax 03.80.22.45.02 ☑
🍷 by appt.

DOM. LALEURE-PIOT

Les Champs longs 2001

| ■ | 1.9 ha | 11,000 | 🍷 | 8–11 € |

🔸 Dom. Laleure-Piot, rue de Pralot,
21420 Pernand-Vergelesses, tel. 03.80.21.52.37,
fax 03.80.21.59.48, e-mail infos@laleure-piot.com ☑
🍷 ev. day 8am–12 noon 2pm–6pm; Sat. Sun. by appt.
🔸 Frédéric Laleure

DOM. MAILLARD PERE ET FILS 2001

| | n.c. | n.c. | 🍷 | 8–11 € |

🔸 Dom. Maillard Père et Fils, 2, rue Joseph-Bard,
21200 Chorey-lès-Beaune, tel. 03.80.22.10.67,
fax 03.80.24.00.42 ☑
🍷 by appt.

DOM. GEORGES ROY ET FILS 2000

| ■ | 3.1 ha | 2,000 | 🍷 | 5–8 € |

🔸 Dom. Georges Roy et Fils, 20, rue des Moutots,
21200 Chorey-lès-Beaune, tel. 03.80.22.16.28,
fax 03.80.24.76.38 ☑
🍷 by appt.

DOM. DES TERREGELESSES 2000

| | 0.22 ha | n.c. | 🍷 | 8–11 € |

🔸 Dom. des Terregelesses, 7, rempart Saint-Jean,
21200 Beaune, tel. 03.80.24.21.65, fax 03.80.24.21.44 ☑
🍷 ev. day except Sun. 10am–6pm; cl. Dec.–Mar

Beaune

The Appellation Beaune is one of the biggest on the Côte in terms of area. But Beaune, a town of some 20,000 inhabitants, is also and above all the wine capital of Burgundy, the headquarters of many wine shippers, and one of the most attractive tourist towns in France. The Hospices de Beaune wine sales have become an event with a world-wide reputation and are certainly one of the most celebrated of all the Burgundy charity sales. Situated at the hub of a motorway network, Beaune will undoubtedly continue to develop its appeal as a tourist destination.

Beaune is best known for its powerful and distinctive red wines. Its geographical advantages mean that a large part of the vineyard has been classified as Premiers Crus: amongst the most prestigious we should list Les Bressandes, Le Clos du Roi, Les Grèves, Les Teurons and Les Champimonts. In 2002, the AOC produced 15,644 hl of red wine and 2,266 hl of white.

FRANCOIS D' ALLAINES

Les Reversées 2001★

| ■ 1er cru | n.c. | 900 | 🍷 | 23–30 € |

Scallops with *beurre blanc*? That's what the Jury suggested to go with this wine, which comes from one of the vineyards closest to the town. It is white gold, not very intense, but brilliant in appearance. With aromas of butter and nuances of acacia, it reveals its power little by little upon aeration. Well made, it has the necessary attributes of acidity and body. It is consistent and elegant from beginning to end.
🔸 François d' Allaines, La Corvée du Paquier,
71150 Demigny, tel. 03.85.49.90.16, fax 03.85.49.90.19,
e-mail francois@dallaines.com
🍷 by appt.

DOM. CHARLES ALLEXANT ET FILS

Bressandes 2001★

| ■ 1er cru | n.c. | 4,500 | 🍷 | 15–23 € |

Charles Allexant bought his first vines in Volnay in 1957 then in 1958 he purchased the Bressandes vineyard in Beaune. Today, the domaine comprises 13 ha. Matured for 12 months in oak, this 2001 is essentially a fruit-driven wine (cherries and blackcurrants); oak is not far away, adding notes of spice. It is balanced and will keep for three or four years.
🔸 Charles Allexant et Fils, 3, rue du Château, Cissey,
21190 Merceuil, tel. 03.80.26.83.27, fax 03.80.26.84.04,
e-mail domaine-allexant@wanadoo.fr ☑
🍷 by appt.

ARNOUX PERE ET FILS

Les Cent Vignes 2001★

| ■ 1er cru | n.c. | n.c. | 🍷 | 15–23 € |

This is a dark-red Pinot Noir. The nose has ripe fruit and lightly toasted notes. The oak does not dominate the palate. The result is classic Beaune: there is a touch of bitterness to the tannins, but, having said that, they are not too hard. It lives up to its AOC, in that it is already pleasant but will keep for about two years. It will go well with a leg of lamb but not with *coq au vin*.
🔸 Arnoux Père et Fils, rue des Brenôts,
21200 Chorey-lès-Beaune, tel. 03.80.22.57.98,
fax 03.80.22.16.85 ☑
🍷 by appt.

LYCEE VITICOLE DE BEAUNE 2000★

| | 2.68 ha | 15,000 | 🍷 | 11–15 € |

The headmaster should be satisfied; three wines are judged worthy to appear here: the **red Montée 2000** gets a special mention. the **red Les Bressandes Premier Cru 2000** receives one star, as does this *village* wine. Its colour, its aromas are resolutely fruity; its tannins are quite fine; its balance and harmony suggest it will keep for two or three years without disappointing.
🔸 Dom. du Lycée viticole de Beaune, 16, av.
Charles-Jaffelin, 21200 Beaune, tel. 03.80.26.35.85,
fax 03.80.22.76.69 ☑
🍷 ev. day except Sun. 8am–12 noon 2pm–6pm;
Sat. 8am–12 noon

BOISSEAUX-ESTIVANT

Clos du Roi 2000★

| ■ 1er cru | n.c. | 2,500 | 🍷 | 23–30 € |

This house was founded in Beaune in 1878 by Gaston Boisseaux and Mlle Estivant. This **Clos du Roi** has an impressive appearance. It has been just sufficiently oaked to allow the soft fruit to show its advantage and make it a pleasure to nose. The attack is vivacious and the oak lasts to the finish.

The acidity is not overpowering but is present and its firm structure suggests future cellaring for three to five years.
🕎 Boisseaux-Estivant, Clos Saint-Nicolas, BP 107, 21203 Beaune, tel. 03.80.22.26.84, fax 03.80.24.19.73

BOUCHARD AINE ET FILS
Clos du Roi Cuvée Signature 2001★★

	1er cru	n.c.	3,550		23–30 €

This Clos du Roi is a remarkable wine. It is quite substantial for the vintage and has an appearance that is worthy of its prestige. On the nose, restrained use of oak allows the currant and raspberry fruits to come forward. It has firm tannins, and a tight texture and tasting it today, it seems to be both robust and firmly-structured, but with a transparent finesse. Keep this wine for three to four years and it will be sumptuous. This is an authentic wine from Beaune with ageing potential. Bouchard Aîné is part of the stable of wines from J.-Cl. Boisset. Under the label Charles Vienot, **Beaune Marconnets red 2001 (15–23 €)** receives a special mention.
🕎 Bouchard Aîné et Fils, hôtel du Conseiller-du-Roy, 4, bd Mal-Foch, 21200 Beaune, tel. 03.80.24.24.00, fax 03.80.24.64.12, e-mail bouchard@bouchard-aine.fr
☩ ev. day 9.30am–12 noon 2pm–6pm

BOUCHARD PERE ET FILS
Clos Saint-Landry 2001★

	1er cru	1.98 ha	n.c.		23–30 €

At the firm of Bouchard Father and Sons, this year, the Jury selected two white wines from Beaune: this *clos* Saint-Landry and a **Beaune Premier Cru 2001 (15–23 €)** choosing without any other special mention, this marriage of several different *climats*. What was formerly called a *cuvée ronde* receives one star here. The *clos* Saint-Landry is very bright, white-gold in appearance, and offers a flowery bouquet with notes of acacia, and hawthorn, followed by notes of white peach and butter. Vanilla does not overpower the rest of the bouquet and it has a subtle and elegant nose. The first impression is quite mouth-filling and there is a fleshiness on the mid-palate, together with a well-integrated use of oak. A thread of acidity remains persistent throughout the wine. "It is pleasant today and it will still be tomorrow", commented one Juror. Drink within the next five years with asparagus au gratin in May or June, or pair with fish in season.
🕎 Bouchard Père et Fils, Ch. de Beaune, 21200 Beaune, tel. 03.80.24.80.24, fax 03.80.22.55.88, e-mail france@bouchard-pereetfils.com
☩ by appt.

DOM. JEAN-MARC BOULEY
Les Reversées 2001★

	1er cru	0.6 ha	3,200		11–15 €

Jean-Marc Bouley is almost a descendent of the vine! His two grandfathers were winemakers in Volnay. His Beaune Premier Cru is quite intense in colour and also on the nose with blackcurrant buds being the dominant characteristic. It has an appetising palate which is full of fruit and finesse combined with elegant tannins.
🕎 Jean-Marc Bouley, chem. de la Cave, 21190 Volnay, tel. 03.80.21.62.33, fax 03.80.21.64.78, e-mail jeanmarc.bouley@wanadoo.fr
☩ by appt.

DOM. VINCENT BOUZEREAU
Les Pertuizots 2000★

	1er cru	0.25 ha	1,200		15–23 €

Les Pertuizots comes from a vineyard almost on the hillsides of Pommard. Typical Burgundian ruby in colour (described as a pretty plume of feathers by one of our tasters), this 2000 foxes us a little on the nose with cherries steeped in alcohol. On the finish it is lively and fruity and shows the distinctive qualities typical of its appellation and premier cru status. It is supple, silky, soft and full of fruit.

🕎 Vincent Bouzereau, 7, rue Labbé, 21190 Meursault, tel. 03.80.21.61.08, fax 03.80.21.65.97, e-mail vincent.bouzereau@wanadoo.fr
☩ by appt.

PIERRE BOUZEREAU-EMONIN
Pertuizots 2000★

	1er cru	0.75 ha	4,000		15–23 €

Ruby with purple highlights, this premier cru has a fine and complex nose which combines morello cherry fruit with signs of maturation, such as toasted oak, smoke, and spice qualities. The palate continues the interplay, alternately showing toasted oak and fruit flavours supported by a pretty structure of silky, long tannins.
🕎 Pierre Bouzereau-Emonin et Fils, 7, rue Labbé, 21190 Meursault, tel. 03.80.21.23.74, fax 03.80.21.24.39
☩ by appt.

DOM. CAMUS-BRUCHON
Clos du Roi 2001★

	1er cru	0.19 ha	1,100		15–23 €

This gives an excellent initial impression, thanks to a quite firm intensity which lasts on the palate. The seriousness of this wine is apparent straightaway because its flavours are already quite integrated; the fact that it will keep increases its promise. Its fresh, strong colour, without too much extraction, is borne out on the palate. A success!
🕎 Lucien Camus-Bruchon, Les Cruottes, 16, rue de Chorey, 21420 Savigny-lès-Beaune, tel. 03.80.21.51.08, fax 03.80.26.10.21
☩ by appt.

MAISON CHAMPY
Vieilles Vignes 2000★

		1.36 ha	7,800		11–15 €

Under its centenary label, the doyenne of all Beaune houses retains its ardour and breath. This 2000 must be complimented on its attractive, lively red colour. The nose offers good jammy fruit and strawberries. On the palate, the concert starts with a solo of morello cherry followed by a fortifying chewiness: this is the brass section giving voice. "This is Pinot!" noted one Juror on his card. This is a wine to keep, of course, but it is already accessible.
🕎 Maison Champy, 5, rue du Grenier-à-Sel, 21200 Beaune, tel. 03.80.25.09.99, fax 03.80.25.09.95
🕎 P. Meurgey et P. Beuchet

DOM. CHANSON PERE ET FILS
Clos des Mouches 2001★★

	1er cru	2.54 ha	5,400		23–30 €

This is the best, just beating the **red Clos des Fèves Premier Cru 2001 (30–38 €)**, also superb. Chanson Père et Fils return with another success. It has good legs and is red, very red, so red that it is almost black. There is a superb fruitiness on the nose, accompanied by smoky notes, which expresses the intense complexity of Pinot Noirs from the Côte de Beaune. A little richer and it would have attained a third star; but the Grand Jury adored it because of its body, its fruit and its power.
🕎 Dom. Chanson Père et Fils, 10, rue Paul-Chanson, BP 232, 21206 Beaune Cedex, tel. 03.80.25.97.97, fax 03.80.24.17.42, e-mail tmarion@vins-chanson.com

CH. DE LA CHARRIERE

Cuvée Vieilles Vignes 2001★

| ■ | 0.34 ha | 2,000 | ▥ | 11–15 € |

The concentration is apparent from the appearance. It has a certain complexity on the nose and notes of undergrowth develop with aeration. It has a delicate character, rather peppery, always complex but definitely well composed. Acidity animates the palate without hardening it. The fruit stands out like Beaune market on a Saturday. This is an elegant and very spirited wine which has not yet reached its full potential.

☛ Yves Girardin, Ch. de La Charrière, 1, rte des Maranges, 21590 Santenay, tel. 03.80.20.64.36, fax 03.80.20.66.32 ▨
☛ by appt.

DOM. DU CHATEAU DE CHOREY

Vignes-Franches 2000★

| ■ | 1er cru | 1 ha | 4,866 | ▥ | 30–38 € |

These producers are past owners of the firm Poulet Père et Fils, formerly of Nuits (Chauvenet, Louis Max). A special mention is given to the **red Les Teurons Premier Cru 2000**. The Jury has a liking for this Vignes Franches, grown near Clos des Mouches. Dark and brilliant red in appearance, this is a Beaune with raspberry flavours overlaying fine and balanced tannins. The finish has a touch of spice, the acidity is just right to give longevity, and the fruity flavours on the palate persist to the finish. It will go with all poultry dishes.

☛ Dom. du Château de Chorey, 21200 Chorey-lès-Beaune, tel. 03.80.24.06.39, fax 03.80.24.77.72 ▨ ▦
☛ by appt.
☛ Germain

DOM. DES CLOS

Champs Pimont 2000★★

| ■ | 1er cru | 0.65 ha | 2,800 | ▥ | 15–23 € |

This wine represents the work of Gregoire Bichot and this domaine was founded in 1996 in the old convent of Bernardins. The colour of this wine is very accentuated, as is often the case with high quality Pinot Noirs. The bouquet allows the fruit to hold its own. One taster wrote: "Surprisingly good, a Beaune that promises an almost exceptional future". Let's raise the stakes a little and say this is a wine with a longer life than even the candles of Beaune! It is very much a terroir wine, with flavours of prune and a classic structure.

☛ SCEA Dom. des Clos, Tailly, 21190 Meursault, tel. 03.80.21.42.66, fax 03.80.21.42.91 ▨
☛ by appt.
☛ M. Grégoire Bichot

RODOLPHE DEMOUGEOT

Clos Saint-Désiré 2001★

| ■ | 0.46 ha | 2,500 | ▥ | 11–15 € |

This first-generation wine-grower left Meloisey and les Hautes Côtes to set up in Meursault, a move which has proved successful. His Clos Saint-Désiré is a credit to its name. Brilliant gold in appearance, this wine has all the carats one could wish for and a floral bouquet that is already accessible. While it has hardly any acidity, and therefore does not have considerable ageing potential, it is fleshy, rounded, peaceful, and it should be enjoyable with dishes that have a creamy sauce.

☛ Dom. Rodolphe Demougeot, 2, rue du Clos-de-Mazeray, 21190 Meursault, tel. 03.80.21.28.99, fax 03.80.21.29.18 ▨
☛ by appt.

DOM. DOUDET

Clos du Roy 2001★

| ■ | 1er cru | 0.45 ha | 2,100 | ▥ | 15–23 € |

While this domaine has the monopoly of the rascal Redrescul in Savigny, it has other plots and its *Clos du Roy* resembles the ruby of the Crown Jewels. Black cherry with violet notes, the bouquet reveals a perfect compliment. The balance between the grape variety and the vineyard site is in a delicate filigree harmony. The palate is straightforwardly pleasant, balanced and rich suggesting genuine promise in three to four years' time.

☛ Dom. Doudet, 50, rue de Bourgogne, 21420 Savigny-lès-Beaune, tel. 03.80.21.51.74, fax 03.80.21.50.69, e-mail doudet.naudin@wanadoo.fr ▨
☛ by appt.

JOSEPH DROUHIN

Clos des Mouches 2000★

| ■ | 1er cru | 15 ha | n.c. | ▥ | 30–38 € |

Founded in 1880, this remarkable Beaune firm is presided over by Robert Drouhin. This wine, emblematic of its appellation, is full of jammy fruits. The tannins bring a harmonious balance to this elegant wine. Keep for two or three years.

☛ Maison Joseph Drouhin, 7, rue d'Enfer, 21200 Beaune, tel. 03.80.24.68.88, fax 03.80.22.43.14, e-mail maisondrouhin@drouhin.com
☛ by appt.

DOM. LOIS DUFOULEUR

Les Cent-Vignes 2001★★

| ■ | 1er cru | 0.87 ha | 5,400 | ▥ | 15–23 € |

Matured in cellars next to the Hotel-Dieu, these are two very enjoyable bottles of wine: one, a **red Clos du Roi Premier Cru 2001** gets one star. The other, with a brilliant appearance, has a flattering bouquet of toasted oak moderated by cherry. The palate plays with the same themes. It is fleshy in substance but is balanced and long. Almost ready now, this Cent-Vignes will be even better in two or three years. It will go equally well with red meat in sauce and with a *brillat-savarin affiné*.

☛ Dom. Loïs Dufouleur, 8, bd Bretonnière, 21200 Beaune, tel. 03.80.22.04.62, fax 03.80.24.25.60, e-mail domloisdufouleur@aol.com ▨
☛ by appt.

DOM. A.-F. GROS

Les Montrevenots 2001★

| ■ | 1er cru | 0.26 ha | 1,600 | ▥ | 15–23 € |

Les Montrevenots borders Pommard. It is not therefore so surprising to find a domaine in this *village* which has a 2001 where the colour is so successful. The nose opens progressively with vanilla and raspberry notes, but it still has some way to go. Lively and supple, it is more a young marquis rather than an old duke. What follows on the palate is less long, less concentrated, but it makes for a pleasant wine that one would want to spend time with.

☛ Dom. A.-F. Gros, La Garelle, Grande-Rue, 21630 Pommard, tel. 03.80.22.61.85, fax 03.80.24.03.16, e-mail af-gros@wanadoo.fr ▨
☛ by appt.

DOM. PIERRE LABET

Clos du Dessus des Marconnets 2001★

| ■ | 0.75 ha | n.c. | ▥ | 15–23 € |

This domaine has links to that of Château de la Tour in Clos de Vougeot. This Dessus des Marconnets is a round white wine, supple and dry and is very typical of its appellation. Green-gold in appearance, it is as if it has newly graduated from a Beaune winemaking college, it is so correct. The nose is a combination of citrus fruits and oak. The overall impression is of a nicely balanced wine that is ready to drink. It is not essential to match this wine with lobster, a nice trout would go as well. One star also goes to **Clos des Monsnières white and red 2001**: both rival each other for charm and quality.]

☛ Dom. Pierre Labet, Clos de Vougeot, 21640 Vougeot, tel. 03.80.62.86.13, fax 03.80.62.87.72, e-mail contact@françoislabet.com ▨
☛ ev. day except Tue. 10am–7pm; cl. 15 Nov.–Easter
☛ François Labet

CHRISTIAN MENAUT 2001★

| ■ | 0.82 ha | 4,200 | ▥ | 8–11 € |

Purple-crimson in appearance, this 2001 has a rather substantial colour. On the nose it has cherry aromas accompanied by notes of toasted oak. On the palate the tannins and fruit are balanced, giving an overall impression of a wine that

BURGUNDY

is rounded, fleshy, and rests on fine tannins. Open in two years' time served with a leg of lamb.

↩ Christian Menaut, rue Chaude, 21190 Nantoux, tel. 03.80.26.07.72, fax 03.80.26.01.53 ☑
☞ by appt.

ALBERT MOROT

Les Bressandes 2000★

■ 1er cru	1.27 ha	7,500	⑪	15–23 €

The **red Les Teurons Premier Cru 2000** will give you as much pleasure as the **red Les Toussaints 2000** and as this wine. They form a beautiful group of wines from this distinguished négociant firm which is now an 8-ha family estate (Choppin de Janvry). These red Bressandes are Morello-cherry coloured with mauve tones and have a perfectly harmonious appearance. The bouquet is still reserved with spices and blackcurrant in the background. As for the palate, it is full-bodied, silky, fruity, and it reminds one of being at the Hôtel-Dieu one Sunday at a wine sale.

↩ Albert Morot, Ch. de la Creusotte, 20, av. Charles-Jaffelin, 21200 Beaune, tel. 03.80.22.35.39, fax 03.80.22.47.50, e-mail albertmorot@aol.com ☑
☞ by appt.

DOM. JACQUES PRIEUR

Champs Pimont 2000★★

■ 1er cru	1.2 ha	7,800	⑪	23–30 €

Jacques Prieur entrusted this domaine in Meursault to Antonin Rodet with the authority to manage it as he sees fit. Charming, flattering, this **Champs Pimont** makes heads turn. Yellow-gold in appearance, it beguiles you with a concert of aromas such as grilled almonds, honey, and ripe fruits. On the palate, it combines a direct first impression with a subtle use of oak. It has richness, length, and acidity, indeed there is not really anything to criticize. One could call it a generous wine. The Jury thinks it would be best appreciated with lobster *navarin*!

↩ Dom. Jacques Prieur, 6, rue des Santenots, 21190 Meursault, tel. 03.80.21.23.85, fax 03.80.21.29.19 ☑
☞ by appt.

PASCAL PRUNIER-BONHEUR

Les Sizies 2000★

■ 1er cru	0.32 ha	1,800	⑪	11–15 €

This vineyard is an old property of the Hospices de Beaune and in 2000 it produced this beautiful wine, worth laying down and best drunk in three to five years' time. The appearance is elegant. On the nose the nuances of blackcurrant together with smoky notes are still reticent. On the palate, there are enjoyable raspberry flavours. It has a rather long length indicating good structure.

↩ Pascal Prunier-Bonheur, 23, rue des Plantes, 21190 Meursault, tel. 03.80.21.66.56, fax 03.80.21.67.33, e-mail pascal.prunier-bonheur@wanadoo.fr ☑
☞ by appt.

DOM. RAPET PERE ET FILS

Clos du Roi 2001★★

■ 1er cru	0.5 ha	2,000	⑪	11–15 €

In his will, Master Pathelin demands to be buried in a wine cellar "below a hogshead of Beaune wine". He would have perhaps chosen this deep, intense, garnet-ruby Clos du Roi, with its aromas of kirsch married with gentle oak. On the palate it is very balanced, in a warming and full manner. The finish is beautiful, savoury and long. This is one of the top wines. Let's not forget this domaine has existed at least since 1792.

↩ Dom. Rapet Père et Fils, 21420 Pernand-Vergelesses, tel. 03.80.21.59.94, fax 03.80.21.54.01 ☑
☞ by appt.

ROGER ET JOEL REMY

Les Cent Vignes 2001★

■ 1er cru	0.3 ha	2,500	⑪	11–15 €

Matured on lees and unfiltered, this 2001, with an insistent ruby appearance, has a fairly powerful nose with some noticeable alcohol. It is lightly oaked, very fruity and firmly

structured. It has been vinified as a wine intended for ageing. It is a straightforward wine that inspires confidence and will be ready in three to five years' time.

↩ SCEA Roger et Joël Rémy, 4, rue du Paradis, 21200 Sainte-Marie-la-Blanche, tel. 03.80.26.60.80, fax 03.80.26.53.03, e-mail domaine.remy@wanadoo.fr ☑
☞ by appt.

CH. DE LA VELLE

Les Cent Vignes 2000★★

■ 1er cru	0.14 ha	600	⑪	15–23 €

There is an annual medieval event with costumes and music that takes place every year at this domaine, nestled in a 15th century residence. Highly regarded, the **Clos des Monsnières white 2001 (11–15 €)** gets one star. It would be wise to cellar this wine for two years before cracking open the bottle. This Cent-Vignes has a very bright future and it will go well with venison. It is powerful and concentrated, but also elegant. It seduces the taster with its aromas of small forest fruits, blackcurrant, and ripe fruit, which is accompanied by gentle oak notes.

↩ Bertrand Darviot, 17, rue de la Velle, 21190 Meursault, tel. 03.80.21.22.83, fax 03.80.21.65.60, e-mail chateaudelavelle@darviot.com ☑ ⌂ ⌂
☞ by appt.

VIOLOT-GUILLEMARD

Clos des Mouches 2000★

■ 1er cru	n.c.	1,100	⑪	15–23 €

We came to a full stop, last year, with a Montagne Saint-Désiré. This time, we end on a Clos des Mouches with an engaging appearance. On the palate, the oak and the fruit are quite well married. Typical of its appellation and its vintage, this wine is lively, supple, and well balanced. It will be at its best in 2004.

↩ Christophe Violot-Guillemard, rue de la Refene, 21630 Pommard, tel. 03.80.22.03.49, fax 03.80.22.03.49 ☑
☞ by appt.

Wines selected but not starred

DOM. D' ARDHUY

Petit Clos des Theurons 2001

■ 1er cru	0.5 ha	1,200	⑪	15–23 €

↩ SC La Juvinière, Clos des Langres, 21700 Corgoloin, tel. 03.80.62.98.73, fax 03.80.62.95.15, e-mail domaine.ardhuy@wanadoo.fr ☑
↩ Liogier

PIERRE BOUREE FILS

Epenottes 2000

■ 1er cru	1.2 ha	7,500	⑪	15–23 €

↩ Maison Pierre Bourée Fils, 13, rte de Beaune, BP 32, 21220 Gevrey-Chambertin, tel. 03.80.34.30.25, fax 03.80.51.85.64, e-mail pierre.bouree@wanadoo.fr ☑
☞ by appt.

DOM. CARRE-COURBIN

Les Reversées 2000

■ 1er cru	0.17 ha	1,200	⑪	15–23 €

↩ Dom. Carré-Courbin, 9, rue Celer, 21200 Beaune, tel. 03.80.24.67.62, fax 03.80.24.66.93, e-mail carre.courbin@wanadoo.fr
☞ by appt.

DOM. DE LA CONFRERIE 2001

| | 0.7 ha | 1,040 | ▮ ⑪ | 11–15 € |

☛ Jean Pauchard et Fils, Dom. de La Confrérie, rue Perraudin, Cirey, 21340 Nolay, tel. 03.80.21.89.23, fax 03.80.21.70.27, e-mail domj.pauchard@wanadoo.fr ☑
♟ by appt.

YVES DARVIOT

Clos des Mouches 2001

| 1er cru | 0.26 ha | 1,600 | ⑪ | 23–30 € |

☛ Dom. Yves Darviot, 2, pl. Morimont, 21200 Beaune, tel. 03.80.24.74.87, fax 03.80.22.02.89, e-mail ydarviot@club-internet.fr ☑ 🏠
♟ by appt.

DOM. DUBOIS D'ORGEVAL

Les Marconnets 2000

| 1er cru | 0.68 ha | 1,342 | ⑪ | 15–23 € |

☛ Dom. Dubois d'Orgeval, 3, rue Joseph-Bard, 21200 Chorey-lès-Beaune, tel. 03.80.24.70.89, fax 03.80.22.45.02 ☑
♟ by appt.

DUFOULEUR PERE ET FILS

Les Cent Vignes 2000

| 1er cru | n.c. | 3,500 | ⑪ | 15–23 € |

☛ Dufouleur Père et Fils, 17, rue Thurot, 21700 Nuits-Saint-Georges, tel. 03.80.61.21.21, fax 03.80.61.10.65, e-mail dufouleur@dufouleur.com ☑
♟ ev. day 9am–7pm

DOM. DU GRAND CONTOUR

Les Grèves 2001

| 1er cru | n.c. | 10,000 | ⑪ | 15–23 € |

☛ Dom. du Grand Contour, chem. rural 29, 21700 Nuits-Saint-Georges, tel. 03.80.61.08.92, fax 03.80.61.30.26

GUILLEMARD-POTHIER

Les Perrières 2000

| 1er cru | 0.63 ha | 3,800 | ⑪ | 8–11 € |

☛ EARL Guillemard-Pothier, chem. de Mauilly, 21190 Meloisey, tel. 03.80.26.01.11, fax 03.80.26.03.72 ☑
♟ by appt.

DOM. BERNARD MILLOT

Les Sizies 2001

| 1er cru | n.c. | n.c. | ⑪ | 11–15 € |

☛ EARL Bernard Millot, 27, rue de Mazeray, 21190 Meursault, tel. 03.80.21.20.91, fax 03.80.21.62.50 ☑
♟ by appt.

NAUDIN TIERCIN

Les Bressandes 2000

| 1er cru | n.c. | 2,600 | ⑪ | 15–23 € |

☛ Naudin Tiercin, av. Charles-de-Gaulle, 21200 Beaune, tel. 03.80.25.91.30, fax 03.80.25.91.29
♟ ev. day except Sat. Sun. 9am–12 noon 2pm–6pm; cl. Aug

DOM. PARIGOT PERE ET FILS

Grèves 2001

| 1er cru | n.c. | n.c. | ⑪ | 15–23 € |

☛ Dom. Parigot Père et Fils, rte de Pommard, 21190 Meloisey, tel. 03.80.26.01.70, fax 03.80.26.04.32, e-mail parigot-pere-et-fils@wanadoo.fr ☑
♟ by appt.

DOM. DE LA SALLE

Champimonts 2000

| 1er cru | 2 ha | 10,000 | ⑪ | 15–23 € |

☛ Jean Bouchard, BP 47, 21202 Beaune Cedex, tel. 03.80.24.37.37, fax 03.80.24.37.38

DOM. VIRELY-ROUGEOT

Clos de l'Ermitage Saint Désiré Monopole 2001

| | 0.78 ha | 3,060 | ⑪ | 11–15 € |

☛ Dom. Virely-Rougeot, pl. de l'Europe, 21630 Pommard, tel. 03.80.22.34.34, fax 03.80.22.38.07 ☑
♟ by appt.

Côte de Beaune

The Appellation Côte de Beaune is not to be confused with Côte de Beaune-Villages, and can be produced only on a few specified places on the Beaune slopes. The appellation declared 1,114 hl of red wine and 537 hl of white in 2002.

DOM. DUBOIS D'ORGEVAL 2000★

| | 0.66 ha | 3,500 | ⑪ | 11–15 € |

White-gold in appearance, this is a Côte de Beaune with a modern taste, having lemon, grapefruit, and vanilla flavours. It is supple and unctuous with liquorice notes on the finish, and has the skill to associate some traditional mineral qualities with the aromas and flavours of Chardonnay. Overall it is more lively than dense having minty freshness and a good finish. The wine is ready to drink; it only needs to be uncorked.
☛ Dom. Dubois d'Orgeval, 3, rue Joseph-Bard, 21200 Chorey-lès-Beaune, tel. 03.80.24.70.89, fax 03.80.22.45.02 ☑
♟ by appt.

DOM. EMMANUEL GIBOULOT

Les Pierres Blanches 2001★

| | 2.65 ha | 5,800 | ⑪ | 11–15 € |

This producer makes wine using biodynamic methods (controlled by Ecocert, as stated on the label). The wine comes from one *climat* in the Montagne de Beaune, not very far from Bressandes. It has a typical golden colour, with floral and white peach aromas and a touch of the exotic (pineapple). The richness on the palate is silky and pleasant. This is one to uncork in the future, just like the **Grande Châtelaine white 2001 (8–11 €)** emanating from a *climat* close to the Hauteurs Beaunoises.
☛ Emmanuel Giboulot, 4, rue de Seurre, 21200 Beaune, tel. 03.80.22.90.07, fax 03.80.22.89.53 ☑
♟ by appt.

Wines selected but not starred

JOSEPH DROUHIN 2001

| | 0.5 ha | n.c. | ⑪ | 11–15 € |

☛ Maison Joseph Drouhin, 7, rue d'Enfer, 21200 Beaune, tel. 03.80.24.68.88, fax 03.80.22.43.14, e-mail maisondrouhin@drouhin.com
♟ by appt.

PIERRE JANNY 2001

3 ha	9,000	◫	8–11 €

☛ Sté Janny, La Condemine, Cidex 1556, 71260 Péronne,
tel. 03.85.23.96.20, fax 03.85.36.96.58,
e-mail pierre-janny@wanadoo.fr

DOM. POULLEAU PERE ET FILS

Les Mondes Rondes 2001

3,2 ha	6,400	◫	8–11 €

☛ Dom. Poulleau Père et Fils, rue du Pied-de-la-Vallée,
21190 Volnay, tel. 03.80.21.26.52, fax 03.80.21.64.03 ☑
☒ by appt.

Pommard

This appellation is the best-known Burgundy outside France. The vineyard produced 13,875 hl in 2002. Argovian marlstone is here replaced by soft limestone, and the vines it produces are sturdy, tannic and good for keeping. The best climats are classified as Premier Crus, of which the most celebrated are Les Rugiens and Les Épenots.

BALLOT-MILLOT ET FILS

Pézerolles 2000★★

1er cru	0.6 ha	3,000	◫	23–30 €

"The wines of Pommard are the flower of the wines of Beaune," wrote Guillaume Paradin in the Middle Ages. He was referring to the whole Côte de Beaune, and this wine confirms his judgement perfectly. It is crimson in appearance with pink tinges and the nose has initially mushroom and undergrowth notes. On the palate, where both structure and richness meet, it is still lively and very rounded at the same time.

☛ Ballot-Millot et Fils, 9, rue de la Goutte-d'Or,
21190 Meursault, tel. 03.80.21.21.39, fax 03.80.21.65.92 ☑
☒ by appt.

JEAN-CLAUDE BOISSET 2000★

n.c.	3,000	◫	11–15 €

Camille Rodier saw Pommard as a "Rabelaisian" wine, the king of *bons vivants*. This wine shows what he meant; it is very pleasurable, deprived of any austerity or severity. On the contrary, it addresses the taste buds with affection. The balance between alcohol, acidity and tannins gives a pleasant robustness. The colour, and the nose with its raspberry and vanilla aromas seduces us.

☛ Jean-Claude Boisset, 5, quai Dumorey,
21700 Nuits-Saint-Georges, tel. 03.80.62.61.61,
fax 03.80.62.61.59, e-mail patriat.g@jcboisset.fr
☒ by appt.

DOM. JEAN-MARC BOULEY

Les Fremiers 2000★

1er cru	0.5 ha	2,900	◫	15–23 €

Holder of a *Grappe d'or* in our *Guide* ten years ago, Jean-Marc Bouley does not only harvest grapes, but he harvests compliments as well. A case in point is this Fremiers from a vineyard close to Volnay. This wine's black-cherry appearance is quite limpid. Animal, undergrowth and game notes make up the nose. The initial attack is silky, then the tone becomes more severe; the tannins are firm, but are of a high quality. The oak is very subtle and well-integrated. This is, of course, a wine to keep and open in two years' time.

☛ Jean-Marc Bouley, chem. de la Cave, 21190 Volnay,
tel. 03.80.21.62.33, fax 03.80.21.64.78,
e-mail jeanmarc.bouley@wanadoo.fr ☑
☒ by appt.

DOM. HENRI ET GILLES BUISSON

Les Petits Noizons 2000★

0.15 ha	900	◫	15–23 €

With a beautiful, strong and clear appearance, this is a wine whose aromas are dominated by refined toasted notes which seem only to enhance the aroma of small fruits mixed together in a basket. The palate confirms this impression. Already pleasant to drink, this Petits Noizons is worth ageing a little to fully integrate the oak. It has weight and roundness and will go well with grilled poultry, without sauce.

☛ Dom. Henri et Gilles Buisson, imp. du Clou,
21190 Saint-Romain, tel. 03.80.21.27.91,
fax 03.80.21.64.87 ☑ ☒
☒ by appt.

DOM. CAILLOT 2000★

1.58 ha	5,000	▮◫	11–15 €

It is no good hurrying this wine, one must absolutely wait two to five years for the green light to go ahead. Its tannins are of the old-school Pommard style and are still austere. On the nose, blackcurrants and sloe nuances share the bouquet. Direct and full of flavour, this 2000 is a credit to the glass it is in

☛ Dom. Caillot, 14, rue du Cromin, 21190 Meursault,
tel. 03.80.21.21.70, fax 03.80.21.69.58 ☑
☒ by appt.

DOM. CAPUANO-JOHN

La Chanière 2001★★

n.c.	n.c.	◫	11–15 €

One can see why Alfred Hitchcock, who had one of the most impressive cellars of Burgundy wine in Hollywood, gave considerable importance, almost a rôle, to a bottle of Pommard in his film *Notorious (Les Enchaînés)*. Just taste this bottle! Its garnet-crimson colour is sumptuous. The bouquet has pepper notes. Vinified by the hand of a master, this 2001 lets cassis express itself fully on the palate. Rich and long, this is a great Pommard.

☛ Dom. Capuano-John, 14, rue Chauchien,
21590 Santenay, tel. 03.80.20.68.80, fax 03.80.20.65.75,
e-mail john.capuano@wanadoo.fr ☑
☒ by appt.

DOM. DENIS CARRE

Les Charmots 2001★

1er cru	n.c.	n.c.	◫	15–23 €

Awarded a *coup de cœur* in the 2002 *Guide* for the 1999 vintage, this producer is very consistent. This time, we have the excellent **Noizons 2001** which you should choose without hesitation, but by the same token it is necessary to allow this Premier Cru time to achieve suppleness and integration. Intense garnet-ruby in colour and endowed with a nose of wild fruits and fruits steeped in alcohol, this is a clean and complete wine. Decant before serving.

☛ Denis Carré, rue du Puits-Bouret, 21190 Meloisey,
tel. 03.80.26.02.21, fax 03.80.26.04.64 ☑
☒ by appt.

DOM. DE COURCEL

Les Vaumuriens 2000★★

0.7 ha	1,200	◫	23–30 €

DOMAINE DE COURCEL
POMMARD · CÔTE-D'OR · FRANCE
POMMARD
APPELLATION POMMARD CONTRÔLÉE
LES VAUMURIENS
2000
MIS EN BOUTEILLE AU DOMAINE
PRODUCT OF FRANCE · RED BURGUNDY WINE

One does not forget easily the past performance of this historical domaine. Our Grand Jury judged two of its wines

Côte de Beaune (North Central Region)

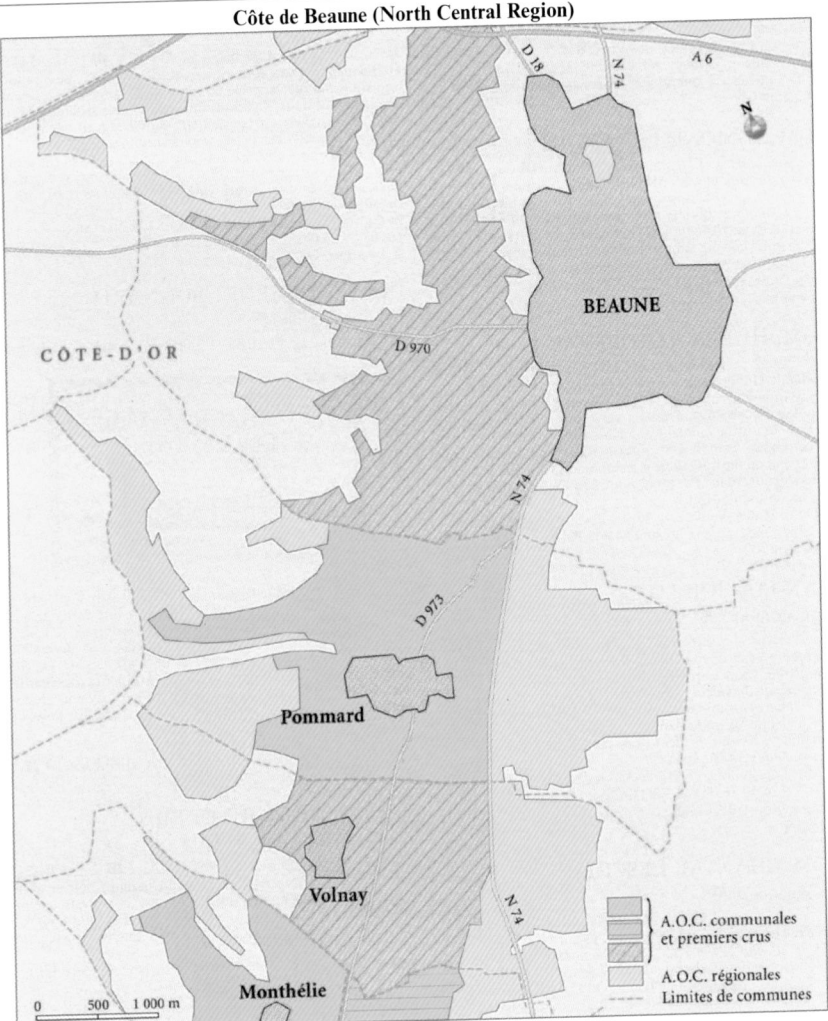

worthy of the *coup de coeur* in the final. The **Premier Cru Grand Clos des Epenots 2000** is therefore fabulous, but it obtained one vote less than this simple Vaumuriens, (if one can say simple, because they are all great wines). This 2000 is very accessible, but nevertheless a thoroughbred. It is undoubtedly a little oaky but overall, its palate sets an example. On the eye, it is straightforward; on the nose, it is complex, with a mixture of red berry, undergrowth and oaky notes. The palate reflects the same themes, with a more intense oakiness and a powerful tannic structure, which requires two to five years of further maturation. This wine has already won several *coups de coeur* in previous years.

↬ Dom. de Courcel, rue Notre-Dame, 21630 Pommard, tel. 03.80.22.10.64, fax 03.80.24.98.73 ☑

☖ by appt.

VINCENT DANCER

Les Pézerolles 2001★★

■	1er cru	0.33 ha	1,200	⦙⦙	23–30 €

This wine was spoken about during the final for the *coups de coeur*. In the end, this domaine obtained a distinction in the

Guide for the Pézerolles 1999. "Good balance!" wrote an English-speaking judge. The colour is brilliant velvet with a superb appearance. The nose has aromas of flowers, such as one gets in a good vintage. On the palate, there is nothing lacking other than time, which will allow the wine to harmonise. **Les Perrières 2001 Village (15–23 €)** has an equal claim on your attention: this very beautiful wine, substantial, genuine, and well-made, gets one star.

↬ Vincent Dancer, 23, rte de Santenay, 21190 Chassagne-Montrachet, tel. 03.80.21.94.48, fax 03.80.21.39.48, e-mail vincentdancer@aol.com ☑

☖ by appt.

FERY-MEUNIER 2000★

■		2 ha	8,000	⦙⦙	15–23 €

This producer has a small négociant and cellaring business founded in 1995, which only buys in grapes. The colour of this Pommard is of a burlat cherry. On the nose it is half fruit, half oak and it has subtle aromas. The charming palate is founded upon a rich but balanced substance, richly endowed for this vintage. It is fine-textured and the general impression is positive.

➻ Maison Fery-Meunier, Les Vignottes, 21700 Premeaux-Prissey, tel. 03.80.62.31.08, fax 03.80.61.34.21, e-mail jj.confuron@wanadoo.fr ☑ ☖
☕ by appt.

DOM. EDMOND GIRARDIN 2000★

| ■ | 1 ha | 2,746 | ⑪ | 15–23 € |

Pleasant to look at with purplish highlights this *village* 2000 has a quite spicy, almost gamey nose, yet it is already quite open, with more subtlety than intensity. Rich to a fault, this wine is fresh with the typical characteristics of its appellation and terroir, showing substantial and firm tannins.

➻ Dom. Edmond Girardin, ancienne rte d'Autun, BP 14, 21630 Pommard, tel. 03.80.22.61.21, fax 03.80.24.29.23 ☑
☕ by appt.

DOM. HUBER-VERDEREAU 2001★

| ■ | 0.4 ha | 2,100 | ⑪ | 15–23 € |

Thiébault Huber took over this family estate in 1994 after having trained as a *sommelier* (he gained a diploma from the school in Strasbourg). This is a very good wine intended for ageing, but for the moment it is at an unrewarding stage in its development. It has a straightforward and intense ruby colour and on the nose there is a combination of ripe fruit and well-integrated oak. The tannins are firmly structured leading to a very muscular finish.

➻ Dom. Huber-Verdereau, rue de la Cave, 21190 Volnay, tel. 03.80.22.51.50, fax 03.80.22.48.32 ☑
☕ by appt.

JEAN-LUC JOILLOT

Les Charmots 2001★★

| ■ 1er cru | 0.52 ha | 2,400 | ⑪ | 23–30 € |

Awarded a *coup de coeur* in the 2002 and 2003 *Guides*, this wine grower's wines are never far off the mark. "Good work," noted one of the tasters on his card. The colour is so brilliant and raspberry aromas dazzle on the nose. It is long and fruity with a palate of remarkable concentration and length. It is definitely a wine to keep. **Les Noizons 2001**, excellently constructed, gets one star.

➻ Jean-Luc Joillot, rue Marey-Monge, 21630 Pommard, tel. 03.80.24.20.26, fax 03.80.24.67.54, e-mail joillot@aol.com ☑
☕ by appt.

DOM. CHANTAL LESCURE

Les Vignots 2000★

| ■ | 1 ha | 3,300 | ⑪ | 15–23 € |

While the label evokes stag hunting, this garnet-crimson wine will go well with game. The oak on the nose gives the impression of a modern wine but it doesn't hide aromas of raspberry. "Enchanting," confided one taster. On the palate, red fruits find expression together with quite fine tannins. Characteristic of its appellation, it is still young and needs keeping a while. They have made a great success of this vintage. **Les Vaumuriens 2000** has similar qualities.

➻ Dom. Chantal Lescure, 34 A, rue Thurot, 21700 Nuits-Saint-Georges, tel. 03.80.61.16.79, fax 03.80.61.36.64, e-mail contact@domaine-lescure.com ☑
☕ by appt.

CATHERINE ET CLAUDE MARECHAL

La Chanière 2001★

| ■ | 0.87 ha | 4,800 | ⑪ | 15–23 € |

This Chanière will gain fullness after some years in bottle. In effect the austerity of youth is masking some of the richness that one perceives is underlying. The colour is very rich and bright. The nose is not forthcoming and evolves slowly with some notes of blackcurrant fruit. On the palate, the oak is still noticeable. Have patience for two to four years and then serve it with a saddle of hare.

➻ EARL Catherine et Claude Maréchal, 6, rte de Chalon, 21200 Bligny-lès-Beaune, tel. 03.80.21.44.37, fax 03.80.26.85.01, e-mail marechalcc@wanadoo.fr ☑
☕ by appt.

CHRISTIAN MENAUT 2001★

| ■ | 1.06 ha | 5,500 | ⑪ | 11–15 € |

On the palate, the texture of this well-balanced wine is round and silky and the very fine tannins emphasize the flavours of blackcurrant buds. The concentration and persistence of this Pommard suggest a wine that will only begin to open up in three four years' time, perhaps for a special celebration. It has a beautiful and classic garnet-ruby appearance. On the nose, notes of liquorice and currants are in harmony. A fillet of duck will go best with this wine, much more so than with a *cuissot* of young wild boar.

➻ Christian Menaut, rue Chaude, 21190 Nantoux, tel. 03.80.26.07.72, fax 03.80.26.01.53 ☑
☕ by appt.

DOM. MOISSENET-BONNARD

Les Epenots 2001★★★

| ■ 1er cru | 0.91 ha | 3,000 | ⑪ | 30–38 € |

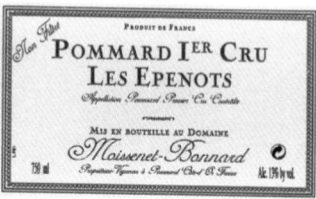

This was classified the best in the final. Already holder of a *coup de coeur* last time for Pézerolles 2000, this domaine has done it again with **Les Epenots 2001** which is deemed to have a great future. It has a violet appearance and a very accessible nose where blueberry and raspberry both play a part. On the palate, it is a "quiet force". It is a pure wonder in all regards. The vineyard plot was received as a dowry by the grand-mother Aline Demur-Lamarche in 1933. In paradise, how she must be proud of her descendants!

➻ Dom. Moissenet-Bonnard, rte d'Autun, 21630 Pommard, tel. 03.80.24.62.34, fax 03.80.22.30.04 ☑
☕ by appt.

LUCIEN MUZARD ET FILS

Les Cras Vieilles Vignes 2001★

| ■ | 0.31 ha | 690 | ⑪ | 15–23 € |

This bottle will keep its promises and perhaps deliver even more: deep crimson, in colour, the nose is reminiscent of blackcurrant buds and as one knows, this is a good base for the development of a bouquet. Already seductive, it will hold for three years or more.

➻ Lucien Muzard et Fils, 11 bis, rue de la Cour-Verreuil, BP 25, 21590 Santenay, tel. 03.80.20.61.85, fax 03.80.20.66.02, e-mail lucien-muzard-et-fils@wanadoo.fr ☑
☕ by appt.

DOM. PARENT

Les Chaponnières 2000★

| ■ 1er cru | n.c. | 3,600 | ⑪ | 23–30 € |

This really historic domaine celebrated its bicentenary in 2003. The vineyard producing **Les Chaponnières** is wedged up against Rugiens; one could have worse neighbours. The appearance is like a beautiful drawing and the nose is pure and intense and evokes morello cherries and vanilla. On the palate, the initial impression is fruity, then it evolves into mineral qualities with subtle oak characteristics.

➻ SAE Dom. Parent, pl. de l'Eglise, 21630 Pommard, tel. 03.80.22.15.08, fax 03.80.24.19.33, e-mail parent-pommard@axnet.fr ☑
☕ by appt.

FRANCOIS PARENT

Les Pézerolles 2001★★

| ■ 1er cru | 0.32 ha | 1,100 | ⑪ | 30–38 € |

Let us say from the start, that this domaine represents a remarkable consistency of quality. The **Premier Cru Arvelets**

2001 and **Epenots 2001**, one star each, are strongly recommended by the Jury, which however, places Les Pézerolles above them. This Pommard has a garnet colour which is pleasing to the eye. The nose has notes of undergrowth and blackcurrant. The initial impression is straightforward and full of youthful fruit. What follows is very consistent, with a lot of potential. This is a wine which could keep for five to ten years. Some advice for label collectors: this one is a curiosity because it has a picture of a truffle on it.
↝ François Parent, La Garelle, Grande-Rue,
21630 Pommard, tel. 03.80.22.61.85, fax 03.80.24.03.16,
e-mail francois@parent-pommard.com
☕ by appt.

DOM. PARIGOT PERE ET FILS

Clos de la Chanière 2001★

■ 1er cru	n.c.	n.c.	🍷	15–23 €

This Pommard is very true-to-type: with its richness and very good structure, it quickly overcomes the initial impression of firm tannins. It becomes almost heady. Rich in secondary flavours, it reveals a convincing persistence on the palate. It has a clean bouquet with initial vanilla notes developing into liquorice, leather and black fruit.
↝ Dom. Parigot Père et Fils, rue de Pommard,
21190 Meloisey, tel. 03.80.26.01.70, fax 03.80.26.04.32,
e-mail parigot-pere-et-fils@wanadoo.fr
☕ by appt.

CH. DE POMMARD 2000★

■	19 ha	40,000	🍷	30–38 €

Established by the Marey-Monge family, a favorite resting place of Gaspard Monge, this *clos* currently belongs to Professor Jean-Louis Laplanche, an important figure in Burgundy and at the Sorbonne. Only the best *cuvées* (40% of the 20 ha single holding) are marketed under the label of Château of Pommard. The resulting wine is limpid, lively and fruity. Very successful for the vintage, this wine at this age, like all good Pommards, is tannic and the oak is still very noticeable. Leave it for three or four years.
↝ Jean-Louis Laplanche, Ch. de Pommard,
21630 Pommard, tel. 03.80.22.12.59, fax 03.80.24.65.88
☕ ev. day 9am–6pm; cl. Dec.–Mar

LA POUSSE D'OR

Les Jarollières 2000★

■ 1er cru	1.44 ha	n.c.	🍷	30–38 €

This domaine divides its 15 ha between *premiers* and *grands crus*. The colour of this wine is like a mantle: deep with purplish and carmine tones. The nose has the same characteristics: subtle, the notes evolve from blackcurrant to very ripe red fruits with a little vanilla and coconut (it has spent 15 months in barrel) but the oak is well-integrated on the palate and envelops the finish. Approachable in three years' time, it will keep for eight to ten years.
↝ La Pousse d'Or, rue de la Chapelle, 21190 Volnay,
tel. 03.80.21.61.33, fax 03.80.21.29.97,
e-mail patrick@lapoussedor.fr
☕ by appt.
↝ Landanger

MICHEL REBOURGEON

Rugiens 2000★

■ 1er cru	0.17 ha	900	🍷	15–23 €

This Rugiens is really very fine. Under an intense colour, the fruit is concentrated and the vanilla is not too dominant. The body is typical Pommard: straightforward, rich, full-bodied, with good vinosity but at the same time, fine. Very classic, it will go well with game. This 2000 should be kept for two or three years.
↝ Dom. Michel Rebourgeon, pl. de l'Europe,
21630 Pommard, tel. 03.80.22.22.83, fax 03.80.22.90.64,
e-mail michel.rebourgeon@wanadoo.fr
☕ by appt.

DOM. REBOURGEON-MURE

Clos des Arvelets 2001★

■ 1er cru	0.61 ha	3,500	🍷	15–23 €

Victor Hugo saw in Pommard "the battle between day and night". The appearance of this wine is indeed like twilight. On the nose, light aromas of undergrowth are expressed against a background of half fruit, half oak. The structure is not too powerful, but is well wrapped in fleshiness. Overall it is a little warming with a promising finish. The **Premier Cru Grands Epenots 2001** is singled out. Both these bottles could age for two to three years.
↝ Dom. Rebourgeon-Mure, Grande-Rue, 21630 Pommard,
tel. 03.80.22.75.39, fax 03.80.22.71.00
☕ by appt.

DOM. REGIS ROSSIGNOL-CHANGARNIER 2000★

■	0.51 ha	2,400	🍷	15–23 €

The grapes for this wine were picked by several selective pickings then de-stemmed, and the wine aged for 13 months in barrel. This wine shows its youth by its appearance and purple tinges, and the presence on the palate of firm, but high quality tannins. The fruit character is a combination of black fruits, blackcurrant, ripe fruit and cherry, a fruit basket quite typical of Burgundy. Equipped with substantial potential, this Pommard is perfectly characteristic of its appellation.
↝ Régis Rossignol, rue d'Amour, 21190 Volnay,
tel. 03.80.21.61.59, fax 03.80.21.61.59
☕ by appt.

CH. ROSSIGNOL-JEANNIARD 2001★

■	0.6 ha	3,000	🍷	30–38 €

The colour of this wine is impressive, suggesting a good concentration. The nose is in fact quite full, and pivots on peony and violet aromas. The palate is full and round. Blackcurrant or cherry? One could argue either way but the tannins still need time to integrate and it has a firm backbone, undoubtedly because the wine has had a prolonged maceration. It should be put side until 2007 or 2008.
↝ Ch. Rossignol-Jeanniard, rue de Mont, 21190 Volnay,
tel. 03.80.21.62.43, fax 03.80.21.27.61
☕ by appt.

VAUDOISEY-CREUSEFOND

Croix Blanche 2001★★

■	0.53 ha	2,350	🍷	11–15 €

The White Cross in the name of this wine stands for a village at the bottom of Grands Epenots. This wine is awarded a *coup de coeur* justified by its balance, affability, the quality and mastery of the tannins, its structure and its length. One can feel the grapes for this wine have been picked at an excellent level of maturity. Happy moments. There is no sign of development in its deep colour. It has a concentrated bouquet with red fruit aromas. It is this frankness and directness, especially, which distinguishes this wine. This is a new style Pommard, less abrupt than in the past, more convivial and approachable from the first.
↝ Vaudoisey-Creusefond, rte d'Autun, 21630 Pommard,
tel. 03.80.22.48.63, fax 03.80.24.16.81
☕ by appt.

CHRISTOPHE VIOLOT-GUILLEMARD
Clos Orgelot 2000★

■ 1er cru	1.1 ha	4,000	ⅲ	15–23 €

Clos Orgelot is a small locality very near the village. This 2000 has a very intense colour, which is known as a good sign. On the nose, it has immediate spices and coffee, then it evolves into cooked fruit aromas. On the palate, it has an elegant roundness and is integrated in a promising way, unctuous to the finish. This is a Premier Cru where the acidity will support the wine during its long cellaring.
☛ Christophe Violot-Guillemard, rue de la Refene, 21630 Pommard, tel. 03.80.22.03.49, fax 03.80.22.03.49 ☑
☒ by appt.

Wines selected but not starred

ALBERT BICHOT
Le Clos Micault 2000

■ 1er cru	n.c.	4,500	ⅲ	15–23 €

☛ Maison Albert Bichot, 6 bis, bd Jacques-Copeau, 21200 Beaune, tel. 03.80.24.37.37, fax 03.80.24.37.38

HENRI DELAGRANGE ET FILS
Les Bertins 2001

■ 1er cru	0.45 ha	2,800	ⅲ	15–23 €

☛ Dom. Henri Delagrange et Fils, Dom. des Echards, 21190 Volnay, tel. 03.80.21.61.88, fax 03.80.21.67.09 ☑
☒ by appt.

GILBERT ET PHILIPPE GERMAIN 2001

■	1 ha	3,000	ⅲ	11–15 €

☛ Gilbert et Philippe Germain, 21190 Nantoux, tel. 03.80.26.05.63, fax 03.80.26.05.12, e-mail germain.vins@wanadoo.fr ☑ ☖
☒ by appt.

ALBERT GRIVAULT
Clos blanc 2001

■ 1er cru	0.88 ha	4,000	ⅲ	15–23 €

☛ SC du Dom. Albert Grivault, 7, pl. du Murger, 21190 Meursault, tel. 03.80.21.23.12, fax 03.80.21.24.70 ☑
☒ by appt.

DOM. JEAN GUITON 2000

■	0.64 ha	3,000	ⅲ	15–23 €

☛ Dom. Jean Guiton, 4, rte de Pommard, 21200 Bligny-lès-Beaune, tel. 03.80.26.82.88, fax 03.80.26.85.05, e-mail domaine.guiton@libertysurf.fr ☑
☒ by appt.

DOM. RAYMOND LAUNAY
Les Perrières 2000

■	2.2 ha	12,000	ⅲ	15–23 €

☛ Dom. Raymond Launay, rue des Charmots, 21630 Pommard, tel. 03.80.24.08.03, fax 03.80.24.12.87, e-mail domaine.launay@wanadoo.fr ☑
☒ ev. day 9am–6.30pm; groups by appt.

OLIVIER LEFLAIVE
Charmots 2000

■	0.7 ha	2,400	ⅲ	23–30 €

☛ Olivier Leflaive Frères, pl. du Monument, 21190 Puligny-Montrachet, tel. 03.80.21.37.65, fax 03.80.21.33.94, e-mail olivier-leflaive@dial.oleane.com ☑
☒ by appt.

DOM. MAILLARD PERE ET FILS
La Chanière 2001

■	n.c.	n.c.	ⅲ	15–23 €

☛ Dom. Maillard Père et Fils, 2, rue Joseph-Bard, 21200 Chorey-lès-Beaune, tel. 03.80.22.10.67, fax 03.80.24.00.42 ☑
☒ by appt.

DOM. MAZILLY PERE ET FILS 2001

■	1.2 ha	4,800	ⅲ	15–23 €

☛ Dom. Mazilly Père et Fils, rte de Pommard, 21190 Meloisey, tel. 03.80.26.02.00, fax 03.80.26.03.67 ☑
☒ by appt.

VINCENT ET MARIE-CHRISTINE PERRIN Chanlain 2000

■	0.57 ha	3,000	ⅲ	15–23 €

☛ Vincent Perrin, 21190 Volnay, tel. 03.80.21.62.18, fax 03.80.21.68.09 ☑
☒ by appt.

PIGUET-GIRARDIN 2001

■	0.8 ha	2,500	ⅲ	11–15 €

☛ Dom. Piguet-Girardin, rue du Meix, 21190 Auxey-Duresses, tel. 03.80.21.60.26, fax 03.80.21.66.61 ☑
☒ ev. day 9am–12.30 2pm–8pm; cl. 15–30 Aug

NICOLAS ROSSIGNOL
Chanlins 2001

■ 1er cru	0.12 ha	300	ⅲ	46–76 €

☛ Nicolas Rossignol, rue de Mont, 21190 Volnay, tel. 03.80.21.62.43, fax 03.80.21.27.61 ☑
☒ by appt.

DOM. VINCENT SAUVESTRE
Clos de La Platière 2001

■	n.c.	13,500	ⅲ	23–30 €

☛ Dom. Vincent Sauvestre, rte de Monthélie, 21190 Meursault, tel. 03.80.21.22.45, fax 03.80.21.28.05

DOM. VIRELY-ROUGEOT
Les Chanlins 2001

■ 1er cru	0.52 ha	2,700	ⅲ	15–23 €

☛ Dom. Virely-Rougeot, pl. de l'Europe, 21630 Pommard, tel. 03.80.22.34.34, fax 03.80.22.38.07 ☑
☒ by appt.

Volnay

Snuggling in the hollow of the hill, the village of Volnay is as pretty as a postcard. Though less well known than Pommard to the north, the appellation yields nothing to its neighbour and the wines have all the finesse you could hope for. They vary from the lightness of Les Santenots, situated on the neighbouring commune of Meursault, to the robustness and vigour of the Clos des Chênes or the Clos des Champans. We shall not list all of them here for fear of omitting some. The Clos des Soixante Ouvrées is another very well-known wine, and provides the opportunity to explain the origin of the word: an *ouvrée* dates from the Middle Ages and measures four ares and twenty-eight centiares, representing a basic unit of vineyard soil that a worker could break up in a day, using a pick. This area corresponds to 428 m².

Many 19th century writers have referred to Volnay wines. When the Viscount de Vergnette addressed the Congrès des Vignerons Français in 1845, he finished his erudite report with the following words: "The wines of Volnay will continue for a long time into the future to be the best wines in the world, as they were in the 16th century under our Dukes who owned the de Caille-du-Roy vineyards there." "Caille-du-Roy" became "Cailleray" then "Caillerets". In 2002, 9,221 hl of Volnay were produced.

BITOUZET-PRIEUR

Clos des Chênes 2000★

■ 1er cru	0.35 ha	2,100	❚❚❙	15–23 €

Well known on the English and American markets, this 12-ha domaine has submitted a Clos des Chênes with very ripe tannins. It is well balanced with a combination of oak and fruit flavours and it has a good length. Open in two years' time.
❦ Vincent Bitouzet-Prieur, rue de la Combe, 21190 Volnay, tel. 03.80.21.62.13, fax 03.80.21.63.39
Ⴠ by appt.

PHILIPPE BOUCHARD

Santenots 2001★★

■ 1er cru	n.c.	6,000	❚❚❙	23–30 €

Here is the phoenix of the hosts of these vines! This bottle shows character and a superb harmony in a difficult vintage. Purplish, black-cherry in appearance this Santenots evokes cherry-stone flavours and seems dedicated to this fruit. It is still a little tannic, which is normal with wines of this age. It has potential. Keep for two or three years. This house is part of Reine Pédauque.
❦ Philippe Bouchard, 21420 Aloxe-Corton, tel. 03.80.25.00.00, fax 03.80.26.42.00, e-mail vinibeaune@bourgogne.net
Ⴠ by appt.

BOUCHARD PERE ET FILS

Caillerets Ancienne Cuvée Carnot 2001★

■ 1er cru	4 ha	n.c.	❚❙❚❙ ❚❚❙ ⚭	23–30 €

Lazare Carnot, "l'organisateur de la victoire", was born at Nolay, not very far from here, and it is his family who rebuilt the Château de la Rochepot where this wine comes from. This cuvée is a pretty carmine-red colour, where vanilla and cinnamon notes combine on the nose. The palate is harmonious, built on excellent tannins and accompanied by a feeling of very ripe fruit.
❦ Bouchard Père et Fils, Ch. de Beaune, 21200 Beaune, tel. 03.80.24.80.24, fax 03.80.22.55.88, e-mail france@bouchard-pereetfils.com
Ⴠ by appt.

DOM. JEAN-MARC BOULEY

Les Carelles 2000★★★

■ 1er cru	0.38 ha	2,300	❚❚❙ ⚭	15–23 €

This is the best of the series. It has a glossy colour of shiny crimson, and a very expressive nose where leather and fruit aromas announce an undeniable success. The wine's vinosity,

its richness, its unctuousness envelop its affable tannins, and it all contributes to make this bottle of Carelles (the *climat* is situated near the chapel), a happy event. This wine-grower won "*Grappe d'or*" in the 1994 Guide thanks to a Caillerets 1990 *coup de coeur*. The interesting **Les Caillerets 2000** is singled out.
❦ Jean-Marc Bouley, chem. de la Cave, 21190 Volnay, tel. 03.80.21.62.33, fax 03.80.21.64.78, e-mail jeanmarc.bouley@wanadoo.fr ☑
Ⴠ by appt.

DOM. FRANCOIS BUFFET

Clos de la Rougeotte Monopole 2000★

■ 1er cru	0.5 ha	2,500	❚❚❙	23–30 €

Awarded a *coup de coeur* for a Clos des Chêne 1994, this domaine has a beautiful wine cellar dating back to the 1800s. and run by Jacques Buffet. The **Carelles Dessous Premier Cru 2000** has been singled out. This Clos de la Rougeotte, a monopoly of a half-hectare Premier Cru site, is our preference. Intense ruby in colour, this wine has a lightly oaked and flowery nose. The initial attack on the palate is direct and without any rough edges. The body is well structured, with fruit and character.
❦ Dom. François Buffet, petite place de l'Eglise, 21190 Volnay, tel. 03.80.21.62.74, fax 03.80.21.65.82, e-mail dfbuffet@aol.com ☑
Ⴠ by appt.

DOM. CARRE-COURBIN

Robardelles 2000★★

■ 1er cru	0.26 ha	1,200	❚❚❙	23–30 €

One of the best Premiers Cru of the tasting, this wine will meet all your expectations of what a Volnay should be. One lingers willingly on the nose, which has as much black cherry as one could wish for. The first impression is good and straightforward, then the fruit brings joy to the heart. "Well made from A to Z," notes one taster. The **Taillepieds 2000** gets one star for its elegance and its femininity.
❦ Dom. Carré-Courbin, 9, rue Celer, 21200 Beaune, tel. 03.80.24.67.62, fax 03.80.24.66.93, e-mail carre.courbin@wanadoo.fr ☑
Ⴠ by appt.

DOM. CYROT-BUTHIAU 2001★

■	0.45 ha	2,280	❚❚❙	15–23 €

This burlat cherry-coloured wine is brilliant and deep. The nose has aromas of blackcurrant buds and fern notes. The flavour is persistent with more raspberry notes this time. It is balanced and is a real Volnay from head to toe, showing freshness and suppleness. It is already enjoyable but is worth keeping in the medium term.
❦ Dom. Cyrot-Buthiau, rte d'Autun, 21630 Pommard, tel. 03.80.22.06.56, fax 03.80.24.00.86, e-mail cyrot.buthiau@wanadoo.fr ☑
Ⴠ by appt.

HENRI DELAGRANGE ET FILS 2001★

■	2 ha	10,000	❚❚❙	11–15 €

Henri Delagrange et Fils, or Domaine des Echards: both names are used. Bright carmine in appearance, this wine marries a hint of violet with a touch of toasted oak. Its tannins are still not very integrated. Fruity nuances follow on the palate. This wine, although rather rounded, is elegant. It will obviously go well with white meat dishes.
❦ Dom. Henri Delagrange et Fils, Dom. des Echards, 21190 Volnay, tel. 03.80.21.61.88, fax 03.80.21.67.09 ☑
Ⴠ by appt.

CH. GENOT-BOULANGER 2000★

■	1.28 ha	6,400	❚❚❙	15–23 €

This wine is considered representative, and that is really saying something coming from our judges. It is typical of the vintage, its appellation and its terroir. This 2000 has a fresh and fruity nose with a subtle note of oak. On the palate, the flavours are charming and it is particularly well-structured. It also has a notable length.
❦ SCEV Ch. Génot-Boulanger, 25, rue de Cîteaux, 21190 Meursault, tel. 03.80.21.49.20, fax 03.80.21.49.21, e-mail genot-boulanger@wanadoo.fr ☑
Ⴠ by appt.

BURGUNDY

Volnay

DOM. GEORGES GLANTENAY ET FILS
Santenots 2000★

1er cru	0.51 ha	3,000		15–23 €

There is no point telling you that this Volnay-Santenots is picked in Meursault. This is from the middle, the lower part or the *clos*? This is an important question in understanding Burgundy...This wine is an intense and brilliant crimson colour, circled with a pink rim. It is also quite open on the nose, with floral notes and measured oak nuances. The initial attack shows pleasant substance. The tannins are still a little firm, but that is a good thing in this vintage. Keep for two or three years and drink with *filet mignon*.
☛ Dom. Georges Glantenay et Fils, chem. de la Cave, 21190 Volnay, tel. 03.80.21.61.82, fax 03.80.21.68.66 ☑
⚭ ev. day except Sun. 10am–7pm

DOM. ANTONIN GUYON
Clos des Chênes 2000★

1er cru	0.87 ha	4,800		23–30 €

This wine is ruby in appearance with purple highlights: it is difficult not to notice it because of the intensity of its colour. The nose is sumptuous and very complex. There is obvious vanilla, but it is enhanced with raspberry. The first impression is supple and well-balanced; the aromas on the nose are repeated in flavours on the palate and it has a medium finish. It comes from a vast family domaine of 48 ha, comprised of many great vineyards.
☛ Dom. Antonin Guyon, 21420 Savigny-lès-Beaune, tel. 03.80.67.13.24, fax 03.80.66.85.87, e-mail vins@guyon-bourgogne.com ☑
⚭ by appt.

OLIVIER LEFLAIVE
Santenots 2000★

1er cru	n.c.	1,200		23–30 €

Former joint manager of domaine Leflaive, Olivier has founded his own firm. That was in 1984, and this year it celebrates its 20th anniversary. Classic in appearance and quite deep, dark ruby in colour, this 2000 has a nose that is still a little closed, with subtle light oak and fruit notes. The palate has more cherry fruit and is very enjoyable. There are no harsh tannins on the finish, and that is not surprising considering its age. This is a promising wine to be tasted in two or three years' time.
☛ Olivier Leflaive Frères, pl. du Monument, 21190 Puligny-Montrachet, tel. 03.80.21.37.65, fax 03.80.21.33.94,
e-mail olivier-leflaive@dial.oleane.com ☑
⚭ by appt.

DOM. DE MONTILLE
Les Mitans 1999★

1er cru	0.73 ha	3,000		38–46 €

This domaine is very famous and – what is rare in Burgundy – it existed before the French Revolution. The baton has been handed over to the younger generation, but the older generation of Montille keeps a keen eye on things. This wine, garnet-crimson in colour, with a youthful tone, has a nose of black cherry with pleasant notes of undergrowth. It is dense and tightly structured; the tannins still need to integrate, but they are of a high quality. One of the tasters suggested it would go well with a fillet of ostrich. However, in three to five years' time it will be better with white meat and make a more classic combination.
☛ SCE Dom. de Montille, 12, rue du Pied-de-la-Vallée, 21190 Volnay, tel. 03.80.21.62.67, fax 03.80.21.67.14 ☑
⚭ by appt.

PIERRE OLIVIER 2000★

	n.c.	8,000		15–23 €

This is a fleshy, tannic, aromatic Volnay, but there is no trace of astringency. What follows on the palate is very good and full of flavour. The nose tends towards almond and cherry stones. The colour is limpid ruby. It is not very long on the finish and it needs a little coaxing. Drink from next year. This house is part of Moillard.

☛ Pierre Olivier, 2, rue François-Mignotte, 21700 Nuits-Saint-Georges, tel. 03.80.62.42.08, fax 03.80.61.28.13, e-mail nuicave@wanadoo.fr ☑
⚭ ev. day 10am–6pm; cl. Jan.

DOM. JEAN PARENT
Clos des Chênes 2000★

1er cru		500		15–23 €

The Parents have never left their *goluches* since the end of the 19th century, and one of them was even the supplier to Thomas Jefferson. *Goluches*? Yes, their vines (if we translate). Intense ruby in colour, this Clos des Chênes has a delicate, floral nose that is fully open. It is not very complex, but it is balanced and classy. It got a *coup de coeur* in our 1996 edition as well as last year under the Annick label.
☛ Chantal Parent, rue du Château-Gaillard, 21190 Monthélie, tel. 03.80.21.22.05, fax 03.80.21.22.05, e-mail annick.parent@wanadoo.fr ☑
☛ Jean Parent

VINCENT ET MARIE-CHRISTINE PERRIN Les Mitans 2000★★

1er cru	0.3 ha	1,800		15–23 €

We can recommended this **Volnay Village 2000 (11–15 €)**, which received a special mention from the Jury, and this wine, Les Mitans, is even more marvellous. The name of this *climat* was mentioned as long ago as 1236! In spite of their name, they are not content to be just middle-of-the-road. It is mouth-filling and voluptuous and like a beautiful drawing! It is fleshy and fruity, with a vivacity which lasts to the finish. Behind an initial toasted oak impression, the nose reveals elegant notes of blackcurrant. A *charolais en croûte* is the Jury's suggested accompaniment. The neck label is decorated with a golden fleece: this wine carries it well. Let us not forget that the *Grands Ducs de Bourgogne* owned a *clos* in Volnay.
☛ Vincent Perrin, 21190 Volnay, tel. 03.80.21.62.18, fax 03.80.21.68.09 ☑
⚭ by appt.

DOM. PRIEUR-BRUNET
Santenots 2000★

1er cru	0.36 ha	n.c.		23–30 €

This was one of the last vintages made by Claude Uny-Prieur. Crimson coloured with jammy fruit and vanilla notes on the nose. It has a lovely opulence on the palate and the tannins have finesse: this wine is persistent with a fresh initial attack and will go well with chicken *chaud-froid*.
☛ Dom. Prieur-Brunet, rue de Narosse, 21590 Santenay, tel. 03.80.20.60.56, fax 03.80.20.64.31, e-mail uny-prieur@prieur-santenay.com ☑
⚭ by appt.

REINE PEDAUQUE
En Chevret 2001★

1er cru	n.c.	9,000		15–23 €

A historic name, Reine Pédauque is a *négociant-éleveur* in the pure Burgundian tradition. Half of its production is sold abroad. Stuffed quails will go well with this intense ruby coloured and elegant Premier Cru. The nose is also quite intense, with red fruits (cherry), a vegetal note and a touch of vanilla. The palate is well structured and reflects the same qualities as the nose; it has more black cherry flavours with pepper notes and an oaky finish. Keep for two years.
☛ Reine Pédauque, Le Village, 21420 Aloxe-Corton, tel. 03.80.25.00.00, fax 03.80.26.42.00, e-mail rpedauque@axnet.fr
⚭ by appt.

DOM. ROSSIGNOL-FEVRIER PERE ET FILS 2001★

	0.7 ha	3,300		11–15 €

The image of *Notre Dame des Vignes* on the label (a statue raised to the Virgin Mary, after the village had been saved during the 1870 war) seems to bless this bottle with a beautiful wine. The colour shows good extraction. With aromas of raspberry and blackcurrant buds, this wine has a perfectly classic nose. It fits the description given to Volnay by D. Morelot in 1831: "a finesse, a bouquet, a delicacy, a supple taste which is not found in any other type of wine". Drink cool and young while it is still fruity.

☛ EARL Rossignol-Février, rue du Mont, 21190 Volnay, tel. 03.80.21.64.23, fax 03.80.21.67.74 ☑
🍷 ev. day except Sun. 8am–12 noon 2pm–6pm

DOM. VINCENT SAUVESTRE

Les Santenots 2001★

	1er cru	0.35 ha	2,200	🍶	15–23 €

This Santenots is the colour of bigaroon cherries or crimson. The nose is a little subdued at present, but this happens sometimes at this age. The impressions on the palate are more about finesse and subtlety than power, in spite of an attractive tannic presence. That again is common. This is a bottle to keep for two or three years.

☛ Dom. Vincent Sauvestre, rte de Monthélie, 21190 Meursault, tel. 03.80.21.22.45, fax 03.80.21.28.05

CHRISTOPHE VAUDOISEY

Les Mitans 2001★

	1er cru	0.2 ha	n.c.	🍶	15–23 €

It is said that, when Bossuet prepared his sermons, he sought inspiration in a bottle of Volnay. In any case, he was good customer of the appellation. This wine, with its rather dense colour could inspire today the priest charged with writing a homily for the *Saint Vincent Tournante*. It has delicious aromas of blue plums and of fresh grapes. On the palate the attack is direct and becomes mouth-filling. It has excellent length and it will go well with quail with grapes.

☛ Christophe Vaudoisey, pl. de l'Eglise, 21190 Volnay, tel. 03.80.21.20.14, fax 03.80.21.27.80 ☑
🍷 by appt.

Wines selected but not starred

REYANE ET PASCAL BOULEY

Robardelle 2001

	1er cru	0.4 ha	1,600	🍶	15–23 €

☛ Pascal Bouley, pl. de l'Eglise, 21190 Volnay, tel. 03.80.21.61.69, fax 03.80.21.66.44 ☑
🍷 by appt.

DOM. JEAN-MARIE BOUZEREAU 2000

		0.3 ha	1,200	🍶	11–15 €

☛ Jean-Marie Bouzereau, 5, rue de la Planche-Meunière, 21190 Meursault, tel. 03.80.21.62.41, fax 03.80.21.24.39 ☑
🍷 by appt.

DOM. VINCENT BOUZEREAU

Les Champans 2000

	1er cru	0.25 ha	1,200	🍶	15–23 €

☛ Vincent Bouzereau, 7, rue Labbé, 21190 Meursault, tel. 03.80.21.61.08, fax 03.80.21.65.97, e-mail vincent.bouzereau@wanadoo.fr ☑
🍷 by appt.

DOM. JEAN CHARTRON 2000

		0.12 ha	780	🍶	23–30 €

☛ Jean Chartron, 13, Grande-Rue, 21190 Puligny-Montrachet, tel. 03.80.21.32.85, fax 03.80.21.36.35 ☑
🍷 ev. day 10am–12 noon 2pm–6pm; Sat. and Sun. End Nov. to mid-Mar by appt.

JAFFELIN

Clos des Chênes 2000

	1er cru	n.c.	n.c.	🍶	23–30 €

☛ Maison Jaffelin, 2, rue Paradis, 21200 Beaune, tel. 03.80.22.12.49, fax 03.80.24.91.87, e-mail jaffelin@maisonjaffelin.com

DOM. DU CHATEAU DE MEURSAULT

Clos des Chênes 2000

	1er cru	2.63 ha	10,300	🍶	30–38 €

☛ Dom. du Château de Meursault, 21190 Meursault, tel. 03.80.26.22.75, fax 03.80.26.22.76 ☑
🍷 by appt.

DOM. RENE MONNIER

Clos des Chênes 2001

	1er cru	n.c.	4,000	🍶	11–15 €

☛ Dom. René Monnier, 6, rue du Dr-Rolland, 21190 Meursault, tel. 03.80.21.29.32, fax 03.80.21.61.79 ☑
🍷 ev. day 8.30am–12 noon 2pm–6pm

MICHEL PICARD 2000

		n.c.	12,000	🍶	15–23 €

☛ Dom. Michel Picard, Ch. de Chassagne-Montrachet, BP 49, 71150 Chagny, tel. 03.85.87.51.01, fax 03.85.87.51.12 ☑
🍷 by appt.

MICHEL REBOURGEON 2000

	1er cru	0.31 ha	1,750	🍶	15–23 €

☛ Dom. Michel Rebourgeon, pl. de l'Europe, 21630 Pommard, tel. 03.80.22.22.83, fax 03.80.22.90.64, e-mail michel.rebourgeon@wanadoo.fr ☑
🍷 by appt.

DOM. REBOURGEON-MURE

Caillerets 2001

	1er cru	0.32 ha	1,500	🍶	15–23 €

☛ Rebourgeon-Mure, Grande-Rue, 21630 Pommard, tel. 03.80.22.75.39, fax 03.80.22.71.00 ☑
🍷 by appt.

CH. ROSSIGNOL-JEANNIARD 2001

		0.4 ha	1,800	🍶	30–38 €

☛ Ch. Rossignol-Jeanniard, rue de Mont, 21190 Volnay, tel. 03.80.21.62.43, fax 03.80.21.27.61 ☑
🍷 by appt.

Monthélie

The combe of Saint-Romain separates the terroirs producing red wines from those producing whites. Monthélie is on the south-facing slope of the combe. This little village is somewhat overshadowed by its more famous neighbours but produces wines of excellent quality. In 2002 production totalled 5,096 hl of red wine and 564 hl of white.

BOUCHARD AINE ET FILS

Le Meix Bataille Cuvée Signature 2001★

	1er cru	n.c.	3,942	🍶	15–23 €

Bouchard Aîné has kept important archives since the 19th century, and one study must come out. Hence the invaluable contribution of Jean-Claude Boisset to the history of the wine of Burgundy. This wine is another interesting contribution, this time to the appellation of Monthélie. It has an impeccable colour and a diplomatic nose which matches oak and fruit in harmony. It has an accessible palate which is full but benefits by having enough acidity to allow it to age in peace.

🍷 Bouchard Aîné et Fils, hôtel du Conseiller-du-Roy, 4, bd Mal-Foch, 21200 Beaune, tel. 03.80.24.24.00, fax 03.80.24.64.12, e-mail bouchard@bouchard-aine.fr ☑

🍷 ev. day 9.30am–12 noon 2pm–6pm

DOM. BOULARD 2001★

| | 0.15 ha | 900 | 🍷 | 11–15 € |

The domaine of Philippe Bouzereau et Fils (the beautiful Château de Cîteaux in Meursault) also runs the Boulard domaine, from the vineyard to the finished wine. They therefore have full and complete responsibility for the product: the result is very good. Dark-red in colour, it is a wine with quite fine aromas, composed of fruitiness with a touch of undergrowth. It is a little firm to drink at present but with an exceptional richness and good tannins, this 2001 should be kept for two to three years.

🍷 Philippe Bouzereau et Fils, 15, rue de Mazeray, BP 25, 21190 Meursault, tel. 03.80.21.20.32, fax 03.80.21.64.34, e-mail info@domaine-bouzereau.fr

DOM. DENIS BOUSSEY

Les Champs Fulliots 2001★★

| 1er cru | 0.58 ha | 3,000 | 🍷 | 11–15 € |

Awarded the *coup de cœur* in the 1996 *Guide* for the 1993, Denis Boussey just misses repeating the achievement. This *climat*, near Meursault, produces wines with good ageing potential. It has good vinosity and is a 2001 whose tannins, after the initial attack, are shown to be quite integrated. The **red Les Hauts Brins 2001 (8–11 €)** is not bad at all and impresses the Jury.

🍷 Dom. Denis Boussey, 1, rue du Pied-de-la-Vallée, 21190 Monthélie, tel. 03.80.21.21.23, fax 03.80.21.62.46 ☑

🍷 ev. day except Sun. 8am–12 noon 1.30pm–6.30pm; cl. 5–23 Aug

ERIC BOUSSEY 2000★

| | 0.5 ha | 3,000 | 🍷 | 8–11 € |

Production of white Monthélie was tiny for a long time: hardly more than 10,000 bottles per annum against 500,000 for red. It has developed a little because of the attraction exerted by Chardonnay. It should be admitted that these are often very enjoyable bottles and this bottle is proof of this. Bright gold in colour, the wine needs aeration in the glass to allow the aromas to come out (citrus fruits). Supple and well balanced, this 2000 succeeds in taking its first steps into the new century.

🍷 EARL du Dom. Eric Boussey, Grande-Rue, 21190 Monthélie, tel. 03.80.21.60.70, fax 03.80.21.26.12 ☑

🍷 by appt.

DOM. BOUZERAND-DUJARDIN 2000★

| | 0.8 ha | 2,500 | 🍷 | 11–15 € |

The 19th-century château is close to this domaine. If the **Village red 2001** is singled out, the 2000 white, already yellow-gold in colour, is interesting and complex. Rounded, well-balanced and harmonious, it is a good expression of its terroir. Drink in the next two or three years.

🍷 Dom. Bouzerand-Dujardin, pl. de l'Eglise, 21190 Monthélie, tel. 03.80.21.20.08, fax 03.80.21.28.16 ☑

🍷 by appt.

DOM. CHANGARNIER 2001★

| | 0.5 ha | 3,000 | 🍷 | 11–15 € |

Honest and with good ageing potential, this 2001 can either go immediately to the table or be cellared for two years. Yellow gold in appearance, the aromas on the nose combine fresh fruits with a little roasted note. The palate is pleasant and warming and this lasts until the finish. Try it with a lobster salad.

🍷 Dom. Changarnier, pl. du Puits, 21190 Monthélie, tel. 03.80.21.22.18, fax 03.80.21.68.21, e-mail changarnier@aol.com ☑

🍷 ev. day except Sun. 9am–12 noon 2pm–7pm

ALAIN COCHE-BIZOUARD

Les Duresses 2001★★

| 1er cru | 0.3 ha | 2,000 | 🍷 | 11–15 € |

Our Jury liked this Duresses very much, with its very deep colour and a nose which is already complex. It is slightly earthy on the nose, with undergrowth nuances, which will become pleasingly gamey later. There are also notes of coffee which has come from the oak. The tannins are a little young, but the palate is full and will become more rounded. This wine will be at its best in two or three years.

🍷 EARL Alain Coche-Bizouard, 5, rue de Mazeray, 21190 Meursault, tel. 03.80.21.28.41, fax 03.80.21.22.38 ☑

🍷 by appt.

🍷 Aain Coche

RODOLPHE DEMOUGEOT

La Combe Danay 2001★

| | n.c. | n.c. | 🍷 | 11–15 € |

This *climat* is located on the side of the hill of Auxey-Duresses when one takes the Nantoux road. As for the wine-grower, he obtained a *coup de cœur* in the 2001 edition for his 98 red. This one is also red but in a powerful *gouache* style. This 2001 is half-fruity, half-vegetal on the nose and shows finesse. Structured but still full-bodied, it demands to be aged for another two to three years. There will be no need to take out an insurance policy: it will be at its peak.

🍷 Dom. Rodolphe Demougeot, 2, rue du Clos-de-Mazeray, 21190 Meursault, tel. 03.80.21.28.99, fax 03.80.21.29.18 ☑

🍷 by appt.

M. DESCHAMPS 2000★

| | 0.7 ha | 5,000 | 🍷 | 8–11 € |

Within 150 m of this 13th century romance style Clunisian church, this wine-grower has set up in a large wine cellar dating from the 1900s. This wine is rich, with good acidity, and shows a good mastery of the parameters of quality. It is perhaps a little closed in terms of aroma (toasty then fresh flower notes) but it is engaging. It is a classic, faultless gold-green colour with a bright rim.

🍷 Michel Deschamps, rue du Château-Gaillard, 21190 Monthélie, tel. 03.80.21.28.60, fax 03.80.21.65.77 ☑

🍷 by appt.

CH. DE DRACY 2000★

| | 0.5 ha | 3,000 | 🍷 | 11–15 € |

Benoît de Charette shares his time between Albert Bichot and his own domaine around the family fortress of Dracy, close to Couches in Saône-et-Loire. His Monthélie has a very Burgundian style. It has a beautiful appearance, and has delicate oak and a touch of liquorice on the nose. The initial impression on the palate is excellent. It has a delicate structure but finesse and richness. The finish is quite lively and tends towards fruitiness.

🍷 SCA Ch. de Dracy, 71490 Dracy-lès-Couches, tel. 03.85.49.62.13, fax 03.80.24.37.38

🍷 by appt.

🍷 Benoît de Charette

GILBERT ET PHILIPPE GERMAIN 2001★

| | 2.7 ha | 8,000 | 🍷 | 8–11 € |

This is an example of a small domaine whose wine producer cleared and planted (1962 to 1975) a vineyard and bought some vines. In 1995, with the arrival of Philippe Germain, he developed the winery and acquired some vineyards in new appellations. This is a red wine with crimson highlights. On the nose, the aromas remain fruity, with undergrowth and oaky notes. It is very mouth-filling and supporting the tannins there is a good fleshy consistency. It is simple, but it will fulfill its promise. This wine will go well with poultry.

🍷 Gilbert et Philippe Germain, 21190 Nantoux, tel. 03.80.26.05.63, fax 03.80.26.05.12, e-mail germain.vins@wanadoo.fr ☑ 🏠

🍷 by appt.

DOM. RENE MONNIER 2001★

| | 0.47 ha | 2,000 | 🍷 | 11–15 € |

This Murisaltien domaine has made this green-gold Monthélie. The first impression on the nose is of toast. Upon

aeration, the bouquet is refined with an attractive personality: vine blossom. Is there a more beautiful aroma for a wine? It has a richness without being heavy and the first impression on the palate is minerally, with a lively and mouth-filling quality. It would go well with sole or monkfish.
➤ Dom. René Monnier, 6, rue du Dr-Rolland, 21190 Meursault, tel. 03.80.21.29.32, fax 03.80.21.61.79 ☑
Ⓣ ev. day 8.30am–12 noon 2pm–6pm

CH. DE MONTHELIE
Sur la Velle 2000★

| ■ 1er cru | 3 ha | 16,450 | ⬛ | 11–15 € |

Château de Monthélie expresses the bourgeois charm of the landed gentry. One feels that the wines are part of the house and that the old vintages count as much as the members of the family tree. Eric de Suremain has produced this 2000 which has firm tannins that are still quite noticeable. It has vinosity and richness behind this apparent harshness. The bouquet is particularly expressive and is dominated by red fruits. Keep for one or two years before opening.
➤ Eric de Suremain, Ch. de Monthélie, 21190 Monthélie, tel. 03.80.21.23.32, fax 03.80.21.66.37 ☑ ⌂
Ⓣ by appt.

PIERRE MOREY 2000★

| ■ | 0.82 ha | 4,500 | ⬛ | 11–15 € |

Pierre Morey is one of the craftsmen responsible for the admirable durability of the Domaine Leflaive wines in Puligny. He is also the owner of his own vineyard. He has applied biodynamic techniques rigorously since 1997. This is a seductive Monthélie with an intense colour and a powerful nose tending towards raspberry aromas. It is full and rich and one could call it a "true wine". It will still be drinking in two to five years: it has a firm backbone.
➤ Dom. Pierre Morey, 9, rue du Comte-Lafon, 21190 Meursault, tel. 03.80.21.21.03, fax 03.80.21.66.38, e-mail morey-blanc@wanadoo.fr ☑
Ⓣ by appt.

DOM. JEAN PARENT
Clos Gauthey 2000★★

| ■ 1er cru | 1.13 ha | 2,100 | ⬛ | 11–15 € |

The Parent family have been making wine in Volnay, then in Pommard since the 18th century. Nowadays in Monthélie, the Parents have never left their vines. This wine has a purplish red colour with youthful tones. On the nose, this Clos Gauthey (the *climat* is situated near to the village itself) is reminiscent of undergrowth intermingled with liquorice notes. It is very noteworthy for a 2000, as it is rich and round with an admirable length and a charming vinosity. This **white Premier Cru Monopole 2001**, under the Annick Parent label also gets the same note. "I like wines where the terroir is firmly underlined," wrote a member of the Jury, who regretted the fact that the tasting was not accompanied by a large plate of foie gras!
➤ Chantal Parent, rue du Château-Gaillard, 21190 Monthélie, tel. 03.80.21.22.05, fax 03.80.21.22.05, e-mail annick.parent@wanadoo.fr ☑
Ⓣ by appt.
➤ Jean Parent

VINCENT ET MARIE-CHRISTINE PERRIN 2000★

| ■ | 0.2 ha | 1,200 | ⬛ | 11–15 € |

The neck label has a golden fleece, a heraldic privilege owing more to Charles Quint than Philippe Le Bon. This *village* 2000 is a brilliant black-cherry colour and has a subtle and flattering nose of red berries. The attack has the surprise elements of the Swiss at Morat against Charles the Bold. It has acidity, richness and power. One has the impression that this wine is under an effective and firm command.
➤ Vincent Perrin, 21190 Volnay, tel. 03.80.21.62.18, fax 03.80.21.68.09 ☑
Ⓣ by appt.

VINCENT PONT 2001★

| ■ | 0.22 ha | 1,500 | ⬛ | 8–11 € |

Were these the first Burgundian vines to be planted in Celtic times? We cannot be sure. These vines are young but already

produce a pretty, clear green wine. It has a fruity nose which is still reticent. The palate is noticeable for its mineral notes (the terroir) and a certain austerity that will soften with two more years of cellaring. Match it with white fish.
➤ Vincent Pont, rue des Etoiles, 21190 Auxey-Duresses, tel. 03.80.21.27.00, fax 03.80.21.24.49 ☑
Ⓣ by appt.

CH. DE SAVIGNY-LES-BEAUNE
Les Duresses 2000★

| ■ | 2 ha | 10,000 | ⬛ | 11–15 € |

"The fruit, the terroir, the generosity: these are the things that speak to our senses," writes one of our experts. The entire Jury shared these impressions. One cannot criticize this wine for lacking a little acidity and for not being intended for long ageing. It is a brilliant gold colour in the glass.
➤ Michel Pont, Ch. de Savigny-lès-Beaune, 21420 Savigny-lès-Beaune, tel. 03.80.21.55.03, fax 03.80.21.54.84, e-mail chateau-savigny@wanadoo.fr ☑
Ⓣ by appt.

Wines selected but not starred

BOUCHARD PERE ET FILS 2001

| ■ | n.c. | n.c. | ⬛ | 11–15 € |

➤ Bouchard Père et Fils, Ch. de Beaune, 21200 Beaune, tel. 03.80.24.80.24, fax 03.80.22.55.88, e-mail france@bouchard-pereetfils.com ☑
Ⓣ by appt.
➤ Henriot

DOM. DARNAT
Les Meix Batailles 2001

| ■ 1er cru | 0.12 ha | 600 | ⬛ | 11–15 € |

➤ SARL Jacquinet-Marion, 20, rue des Forges, 21190 Meursault, tel. 03.80.21.23.30, fax 03.80.21.64.62 ☑
Ⓣ by appt.
➤ Marion Darnat

GUY DUBUET 2001

| ■ | 0.4 ha | 2,000 | ⬛ | 8–11 € |

➤ Guy Dubuet, rue Bonne-Femme, 21190 Monthélie, tel. 03.80.21.26.22, fax 03.80.21.29.79 ☑
Ⓣ by appt.

PIERRE LAMOTTE 2001

| ■ | n.c. | n.c. | ⬛ | 8–11 € |

➤ Pierre Lamotte, rue Lavoisier, 21700 Nuits-Saint-Georges, tel. 03.80.62.64.00, fax 03.80.62.64.00
Ⓣ by appt.

DOM. PINQUIER-BROVELLI 2001

| ■ | 1.3 ha | 7,600 | ⬛ | 8–11 € |

➤ Dom. Pinquier-Brovelli, 5, rue Pierre-Mouchoux, 21190 Meursault, tel. 03.80.21.24.87, fax 03.80.21.61.09 ☑ ⌂
Ⓣ Mon.–Sat. 9am–12 noon 1.30pm–7pm; Sun. 9am–12 noon
➤ Pinquier Père et Fils

PASCAL PRUNIER-BONHEUR

Les Vignes Rondes 2001

■ 1er cru	0.49 ha	3,000	◧	11–15 €

🍷 Pascal Prunier-Bonheur, 23, rue des Plantes,
21190 Meursault, tel. 03.80.21.66.56, fax 03.80.21.67.33,
e-mail pascal.prunier-bonheur@wanadoo.fr ☑
🍷 by appt.

PRUNIER-DAMY

Clos de Ressi Monopole 2001

■	0.6 ha	3,500	◧	8–11 €

🍷 Philippe Prunier-Damy, rue du Pont-Boillot,
21190 Auxey-Duresses, tel. 03.80.21.60.38,
fax 03.80.21.26.64 ☑
🍷 by appt.

Auxey-Duresses

Two wine slopes are to be found at Auxey-Duresses. The red Premier Crus of Duresses and Le Val are highly regarded. The "Meursault" slope produces excellent white wines that, although they lack the reputation of the great appellations, are very affordable. This appellation produced 2,017 hl of white wine in 2002, and 4,573 hl of red.

CHRISTOPHE BUISSON

Les Grandes Vignes 2001★★

■	n.c.	n.c.	◧	8–11 €

This wine was born of a passion which "started from nothing" in 1990 and has succeeded in taking its place among the domaines that count. Les Grandes Vignes is a *climat* very close to the village. On the nose, this 2001 is earthy with undergrowth notes and gamey qualities but still retains aromas of small red berries. The palate is very concentrated but elegant, intermingling liquorice and fresh fruits. It has great class.
🍷 Christophe Buisson, rue de la Tartebouille,
21190 Saint-Romain, tel. 03.80.21.63.92,
fax 03.80.21.67.03 ☑
🍷 by appt.

JEAN-PIERRE DICONNE 2001★

■	1.4 ha	3,500	◧	8–11 €

This is an excellent *village* wine. It has a velvet-red appearance, like curtains opening on a first scene of a play featuring blackcurrants and fresh walnuts. On the palate, the tannins are integrated and the flavours are mature; it is full and round and before long lets us know its appellation, in a very appetising way. It would go well with roast lamb with thyme. The **red Premier Cru Les Duresses 2001 (11–15 €)** is a firmly-structured wine which is not ready to drink immediately.
🍷 Jean-Pierre Diconne, rue de la Velle,
21190 Auxey-Duresses, tel. 03.80.21.25.60,
fax 03.80.21.26.80 ☑
🍷 by appt.

JEAN ET GILLES LAFOUGE 2001★★

■	2 ha	4,000	◧	8–11 €

This wine comes from a *climat* located at the boundary of Meursault. The **white Les Hautes 2000** is a wine with a full and generous initial impression. Its finesse, its richness and its minerality (especially apparent on the nose) are good assets. It gets one star. It will go well with poultry, such as *Poulet de Bresse* with apples and bacon. It has an intense colour and a nose where jammy fruit, undergrowth notes and evidence of oak maturation are elegantly combined. The palate is also charming. Keep for five to eight years.

🍷 Dom. Jean et Gilles Lafouge, 21190 Auxey-Duresses,
tel. 03.80.21.68.17, fax 03.80.21.60.43 ☑
🍷 by appt.

HENRI LATOUR ET FILS 2001★

■ 1er cru	0.99 ha	5,200	◧	11–15 €

Auxey was formerly a village of windmills. Their song brightened the countryside. It has been replaced nowadays by the sound of wine presses and vats. Produced on a 16-ha domaine, this *village* wine has a deep and brilliant colour. It has mineral notes on the nose and black fruit flavour on the palate. Firm and well structured, this wine is a good representative of its appellation. It could be served in three or four years with spicy meat. The **white 2001** has been singled out. Finely oaked and lemony, it plays its own song.
🍷 Henri Latour et Fils, rte de Beaune,
21190 Auxey-Duresses, tel. 03.80.21.65.49,
fax 03.80.21.63.08, e-mail h.latour.fils@wanadoo.fr ☑
🍷 by appt.

DOM. MAROSLAVAC-LEGER

Les Bretterins 2000★

■ 1er cru	0.27 ha	1,500	◧	11–15 €

Ruby with slightly purple tones, it has a nose where leather combines with black fruits. The initial impression on the palate is of fruitiness, the attack is direct and the tannins accommodating. This wine has structure and has a good balance of acidity and alcohol.
🍷 Dom. Maroslavac-Léger, 43, Grande-Rue,
21190 Puligny-Montrachet, tel. 03.80.21.31.23,
fax 03.80.21.91.39, e-mail maroslavac-leger@wanadoo.fr ☑
🍷 by appt.

AGNES ET SEBASTIEN PAQUET 2001★

■	3 ha	6,000	◧	11–15 €

This is a very new domaine, only established in 2000 and on a 8-ha site. The label has original graphics and works well but this Auxey does not only have a beautiful calling card. Clear white-gold in colour, the nose is flinty, and this minerality is retained on the palate. What follows is faultless but, even though it is drinking now, it will be at its best if you leave it a little longer. It will be at its peak in three or four years.
🍷 Agnès et Sébastien Paquet, rue du Puits-Bourret,
21190 Meloisey, tel. 03.80.26.07.41, fax 03.80.26.06.41,
e-mail sebpaquet@club-internet.fr ☑
🍷 by appt.

MICHEL PRUNIER 2000★

■ 1er cru	0.74 ha	3,000	◧	11–15 €

Michel Prunier created his domaine with 1 ha of inherited vineyard and another one he rented. This was in 1968. He now has 12 ha, and has recently purchased the village restaurant where you can taste his wines. His Premier Cru has a typical Pinot Noir appearance and a nose of jammy fruit and gentle spice (it has had 15 months in barrel). The palate is full-bodied, round and silky. Keep for two years, but it is already very well-balanced.
🍷 Michel Prunier, rte de Beaune, 21190 Auxey-Duresses,
tel. 03.80.21.21.05, fax 03.80.21.64.73 ☑
🍷 by appt.

PASCAL PRUNIER-BONHEUR

Les Duresses 2000★

■ 1er cru	0.47 ha	3,000	◧	11–15 €

This Duresses is a shiny crimson colour. The nose is still closed, but its reserve is more a sign of elegance. The body is enveloping and made up of a rather pulpy fruit which has absorbed the oak well. This wine has a good extraction and needs time to round out the edges. However, the finish is promising. It was awarded a *coup de cœur* for the 99 in the preceding edition. The **red Auxey-Duresses Village 2000 (8–11 €)** is singled out.
🍷 Pascal Prunier-Bonheur, 23, rue des Plantes,
21190 Meursault, tel. 03.80.21.66.56, fax 03.80.21.67.33,
e-mail pascal.prunier-bonheur@wanadoo.fr ☑
🍷 by appt.

DOM. DE LA ROCHE AIGUE 2000★

| | 1.5 ha | 2,300 | 〔ⅠⅠ〕 | 8–11€ |

Melin is a hamlet of Auxey-Duresses, on the road to Autun. Here, the vines sunbathe on the well-exposed hillside. Hence this wine has a beautiful gold colour with mineral and floral nuances on the nose. Flinty characteristics are a speciality of this area. The structure of this 2000 is quite firm. With light oak and a touch of vivacity, the overall effect is fresh and characteristic of the terroir.

🕯 Eric et Florence Guillemard, EARL La Roche Aigüe, Melin, 21190 Auxey-Duresses, tel. 03.80.21.28.33, fax 03.80.21.63.55

🍷 by appt.

HENRI DE VILLAMONT 1999★★

| | n.c. | 3,900 | 〔ⅠⅠ〕 | 15–23€ |

Henri de Villamont (subsidiary company of the Swiss group Schenk) presented some bottles of this 99. He had reason to keep them and they are now at their utmost peak. Green-gold without signs of development, the wine has a fruity nose and opens more and more in the glass. Its length and its richness are more reminiscent of a Meursault.

🕯 SA Henri de Villamont, 2, rue du Dr-Guyot, 21420 Savigny-lès-Beaune, tel. 03.80.24.70.07, e-mail hdv@planetb.fr

🍷 ev. day except Mon. 9.30am–7pm; Thurs. 2pm–6.30pm; cl. 15 Nov.–30 Mar

JEAN-MARC VINCENT

Les Hautes 2001★★★

| | 0.9 ha | 5,000 | 〔ⅠⅠ〕 | 11–15€ |

In 1997, Anne-Marie and Jean-Marc Vincent took over the family domaine of Bardollet-Bravard (less than 5 ha). They have made a wine which fills our Jury with enthusiasm. They gave it a *coup de coeur* without any changes of heart. White-gold with a green rim and many legs, the colour is splendid. Notes of mocha, coffee, hazelnut, citrus fruits and *patisserie*…And then, the explosion: an extremely well-managed use of oak, along with wild rose form the basis of the secondary flavours. Superb!

🕯 Jean-Marc et Anne-Marie Vincent, 3, rue Sainte-Agathe, 21590 Santenay, tel. 03.80.20.67.37, fax 03.80.20.67.37, e-mail vincent.j-m@wanadoo.fr

🍷 by appt.

Wines selected but not starred

PHILIPPE BOUCHARD 2001

| | n.c. | 6,000 | 〔ⅠⅠ〕 | 11–15€ |

🕯 Philippe Bouchard, 21420 Aloxe-Corton, tel. 03.80.25.00.00, fax 03.80.26.42.00, e-mail vinibeaune@bourgogne.net

🍷 by appt.

CHRISTIAN CHOLET-PELLETIER 2001

| | n.c. | 900 | 〔ⅠⅠ〕 | 5–8€ |

🕯 Christian Cholet, 21190 Corcelles-les-Arts, tel. 03.80.21.47.76

🍷 ev. day 8am–12 noon 2pm–6pm

ALAIN COCHE-BIZOUARD

Les Fosses 2000

| | 0.2 ha | 1,400 | 〔ⅠⅠ〕 | 11–15€ |

🕯 EARL Alain Coche-Bizouard, 5, rue de Mazeray, 21190 Meursault, tel. 03.80.21.28.41, fax 03.80.21.22.38

🍷 by appt.

PIERRE OLIVIER 2001

| | n.c. | 12,000 | 〔ⅠⅠ〕 | 8–11€ |

🕯 Pierre Olivier, 2, rue François-Mignotte, 21700 Nuits-Saint-Georges, tel. 03.80.62.42.08, fax 03.80.61.28.13, e-mail nuicave@wanadoo.fr

🍷 ev. day 10am–6pm; cl. Jan.

MAX ET ANNE-MARYE PIGUET-CHOUET Les Boutonniers 2001

| | 0.38 ha | 1,200 | 〔ⅠⅠ〕 | 8–11€ |

🕯 Max et Anne-Marye Piguet-Chouet, rte de Beaune, 21190 Auxey-Duresses, tel. 03.80.21.25.78, fax 03.80.21.68.31, e-mail piguet.chouet@wanadoo.fr

🍷 by appt.

DOM. JEAN-PIERRE ET LAURENT PRUNIER 2001

| | 0.99 ha | 5,800 | 〔ⅠⅠ〕 | 8–11€ |

🕯 Dom. Jean-Pierre et Laurent Prunier, rue Traversière, 21190 Auxey-Duresses, tel. 03.80.21.23.91, fax 03.80.21.27.51

🍷 by appt.

DOM. VINCENT PRUNIER

Les Grands Champs 2001

| 1er cru | 0.35 ha | 1,650 | 〔ⅠⅠ〕 | 11–15€ |

🕯 EARL Dom. Vincent Prunier, rte de Beaune, 21190 Auxey-Duresses, tel. 03.80.21.27.77, fax 03.80.21.68.87

🍷 by appt.

PRUNIER-DAMY

Clos du Val 2001

| 1er cru | 0.5 ha | 2,500 | 〔ⅠⅠ〕 | 11–15€ |

🕯 Philippe Prunier-Damy, rue du Pont-Boillot, 21190 Auxey-Duresses, tel. 03.80.21.60.38, fax 03.80.21.26.64

🍷 by appt.

PIERRE TAUPENOT 2001

| | 1.9 ha | 5,333 | 🍾〔ⅠⅠ〕 | 8–11€ |

🕯 Dom. Pierre Taupenot, rue du Chevrotin, 21190 Saint-Romain, tel. 03.80.21.24.37, fax 03.80.21.68.42

🍷 by appt.

Saint-Romain

This vineyard is situated midway between the Côte and the Hautes Côtes. The wines of Saint-Romain – 2,594 hl of red wine and 1,810 of white – are fruity, fresh-flavoured and, according to the winemakers, always ready to give more than they promise when young. The location itself is magnificent and very much worth a special trip to see.

DOM. HENRI ET GILLES BUISSON

Sous Roche 2000★

| | 3,14 ha | 10,000 | | 8–11 € |

This wine is dark red, transparent and bright, with a full and complex bouquet tending towards black fruit and toasted notes. On the palate, it is well structured and balanced by integrated tannins. One has two choices: you can enjoy this wine at present, benefiting from its generosity, and serving it with a young guinea-fowl; or you can wait to drink it in 2005 or 2006.
↬ Dom. Henri et Gilles Buisson, imp. du Clou, 21190 Saint-Romain, tel. 03.80.21.27.91, fax 03.80.21.64.87 ☑ 🏠
Ⲧ by appt.

DOM. DENIS CARRE

Le Jarron 2001★★

| | 0,44 ha | n.c. | | 8–11 € |

Awarded a *coup de coeur* for the 94 and 99 vintage of this same *climat*, Denis Carré is still considered one of the producers who count in this appellation. This wine will delight wine lovers. The 2001 is very dark red in colour. It has freshly-picked raspberry aromas on the nose and the oak is not overdone. It has excellent potential, balanced towards fruitiness. One could keep this wine a little longer.
↬ Denis Carré, rue du Puits-Bouret, 21190 Meloisey, tel. 03.80.26.02.21, fax 03.80.26.04.64 ☑
Ⲧ by appt.

DOM. DES MARGOTIERES 2001★

| | n.c. | n.c. | | 8–11 € |

With a youthful gold, shiny appearance, this wine has delicate floral aromas on the nose. The oak is well-integrated. On the palate, the initial impression is one of freshness where fruit and richness combine. It is lightly acidic on the finish but overall the wine is well balanced. This is an excellent bottle of wine. The **red 2000** will need to be kept for some time. It receives a citation.
↬ Dom. des Margotières, 21190 Saint-Romain, tel. 03.80.21.24.40, fax 03.80.21.27.91

JEAN POULET

Les Poillanges 2001★

| | 0,34 ha | 2,100 | | 8–11 € |

This is another Poulet, but this time he is a wine-grower in the village. The vines were abandoned with the death of the twins Henri and Robert Poulet, who were killed in the Battle of Verdun in 1915; they were later replanted by their grandson at the end of the 1940s. Try matching poached trout with the red Saint-Roman or roast young wild boar. Let us know how you get on. Not immediately however, because this very powerful wine needs to be cellared for another two or three years. Its black-cherry colour, beautiful legs and its vegetal aromas fit well within the profile of the appellation.
↬ Jean Poulet, Le Clos Sainte-Marie, 21190 Saint-Romain, tel. 03.80.21.21.63, fax 03.80.21.66.93 ☑ 🏠
Ⲧ by appt.

POULET PERE ET FILS

Clos de la Barière 2000★

| | n.c. | 1,300 | | 23–30 € |

This venerable Poulet house (in Beaune since the middle of the 19th century) became *nuitonne* under the auspices of Laurent Max who purchased Jaboulet-Vercherre recently. The colour of this wine is golden, without being showy. The nose, quite open and intense, suggests flint. The attack is gentle at the beginning, opening on an assembly of attractive flavours and nuances, such as hazelnut. This wine can age for three years and more.
↬ Poulet Père et Fils, 6, rue de Chaux, 21700 Nuits-Saint-Georges, tel. 03.80.62.43.02, fax 03.80.61.28.08

HENRI DE VILLAMONT 2000★

| | n.c. | 11,000 | | 15–23 € |

Henri de Villamont is one of the Burgundian calling cards of the Schenk group in Rolle (Switzerland). The firm is established in the historic and superb cellars of Léonce Bocquet in Savigny. This Saint-Romain is not very intense but bright in colour. The nose is a little subdued, but it ends up revealing notes of pear. The body is well-defined, a little slender and still reserved, but the potential is there. Leave this wine for some time to integrate and become more rounded.
↬ SA Henri de Villamont, 2, rue du Dr-Guyot, 21420 Savigny-lès-Beaune, tel. 03.80.24.70.07, e-mail hdv@planetb.fr ☑
Ⲧ ev. day except Mon. 9.30am–7pm; Thurs. 2pm–6.30pm; cl. 15 Nov.–30 Mar

Wines selected but not starred

DOM. GABRIEL BOUCHARD

Perrière 2001

| | 0,39 ha | 2,000 | | 8–11 € |

↬ Dom. Gabriel Bouchard, 4, rue du Tribunal, 21200 Beaune, tel. 03.80.22.68.63 ☑
Ⲧ by appt.
↬ Alain Bouchard

CHRISTOPHE BUISSON

Sous le Château 2001

| | n.c. | n.c. | | 8–11 € |

↬ Christophe Buisson, rue de la Tartebouille, 21190 Saint-Romain, tel. 03.80.21.63.92, fax 03.80.21.67.03 ☑
Ⲧ by appt.

BERNARD DELAGRANGE

Les Poyanges 2001

| | 0,58 ha | 3,898 | | 11–15 € |

↬ Bernard Delagrange, 10, rue du 11–Novembre, 21190 Meursault, tel. 03.80.21.22.72, fax 03.80.21.28.70 ☑
Ⲧ ev. day 9am–7pm

GERMAIN PERE ET FILS

Sous le Château 2001

| | 1,45 ha | 3,500 | | 8–11 € |

↬ EARL Dom. Germain Père et Fils, rue de la Pierre-Ronde, 21190 Saint-Romain, tel. 03.80.21.60.15, fax 03.80.21.67.87, e-mail patrick.germain8@wanadoo.fr ☑ 🏠
Ⲧ by appt.

ALAIN GRAS 2001

| | 2 ha | 10,000 | | 8–11 € |

↬ Alain Gras, rue Sous-la-Velle, 21190 Saint-Romain, tel. 03.80.21.27.83, fax 03.80.21.65.56 ☑
Ⲧ by appt.

DOM. GUY-PIERRE JEAN ET FILS

Clos de la Barière 2001

| | 1 ha | 1,500 | | 11–15 € |

↬ Dom. Guy-Pierre Jean et Fils, rue des Caillettes, 21420 Aloxe-Corton, tel. 03.80.26.44.72, fax 03.80.26.45.36, e-mail domaine.guypierrejeanetfils@wanadoo.fr ☑
Ⲧ by appt.

FRANCOIS RAPET ET FILS 2001

4 ha	8,000	▌▐▋	8–11 €

➤ EARL François Rapet et Fils, rue Sous-le-Château,
21190 Saint-Romain, tel. 03.80.21.22.08,
fax 03.80.21.60.19 ☑
♈ ev. day 9.30am–12 noon 2pm–7pm

DOM. DE LA ROCHE AIGUE 2001

0.5 ha	1,100	▐▋	8–11 €

➤ Eric et Florence Guillemard, EARL La Roche Aigüe,
Melin, 21190 Auxey-Duresses, tel. 03.80.21.28.33,
fax 03.80.21.63.55 ☑
♈ by appt.

CHRISTOPHE VIOLOT-GUILLEMARD

Clos des Ducs 2001

0.83 ha	6,000	▐▋	8–11 €

➤ Christophe Violot-Guillemard, rue de la Refene,
21630 Pommard, tel. 03.80.22.03.49, fax 03.80.22.03.49 ☑
♈ by appt.

Meursault

The area producing great white burgundies really begins at Meursault. In 2002, 20,150 hl were produced, and the Premiers Crus are famous world-wide: Les Perrières, Les Charmes, Les Poruzots, Les Genevrières, Les Gouttes d'Or, etc. They combine subtlety and strength, flavours of bracken and grilled almond, the appeal to be drunk young and the quality to keep. Meursault is undoubtedly the "capital of white burgundy wines". A small amount of red wine – 534 hl in 2002 – is also produced.

The "little châteaux" which still exist in Meursault are relics of a former opulence, and bear witness to a long tradition of famous wines from the area. The festival known as La Paulée began here as a communal banquet that everyone enjoyed at the end of the harvest. It became a traditional event marking the third of the "Trois Glorieuses", the annual three-day Burgundy wine festival.

DOM. BACHELET

Les Narvaux 2001★

0.8 ha	4,000	▌▐▋▖	15–23 €

Were they given the word? We have come across Narvaux wines frequently this year. Characteristic of Chardonnay, tending towards citrus fruit and a slight exotic note, this wine has a pure appearance. It is balanced and has good weight and length.
➤ Dom. Bernard Bachelet et Fils, rue Maranges,
71150 Dezize-lès-Maranges, tel. 03.85.91.16.11,
fax 03.85.91.16.48 ☑
♈ by appt.

BALLOT-MILLOT ET FILS

Charmes 2001★

1er cru	0.35 ha	2,000	▐▋	23–30 €

This old family from the Côte de Beaune has 12 ha spread out from Beaune to Chassagne. They make both white and red wine. Specially mentioned is their **Meursault 2000 (15–23 €)**, a good representative of its appellation. One should try to get some bottles of these Charmes, light straw-gold in colour with buttery, oaky and fruity aromas. The palate is quite full-bodied and the oak is subtle with a length which seems just right. This is a well-made wine.
➤ Ballot-Millot et Fils, 9, rue de la Goutte-d'Or,
21190 Meursault, tel. 03.80.21.21.39, fax 03.80.21.65.92 ☑
♈ by appt.

CHRISTIAN BELLANG ET FILS

Les Tillets 2000★

0.5 ha	2,000	▌▐▋	15–23 €

Christian Bellang set up this domaine in 1974. With golden tones, this wine is flattering on the nose and buttery like a slice of bread. On the palate it is fresh, full and honeyed. Isn't this a contradiction? Not at all, because it is balanced; it has a good supporting acidity, some complexity and a richly coated texture. A *poulet de Bresse* with morels and cream will go well with this wine.
➤ Dom. Christian Bellang et Fils, 2, rue de Mazeray,
21190 Meursault, tel. 03.80.21.22.61, fax 03.80.21.68.50,
e-mail christophe.bellang@wanadoo.fr ☑
♈ by appt.

DOM. GUY BOCARD

Charmes 2000★

1er cru	0.67 ha	4,000	▌▐▋▖	23–30 €

Let the procession pass! Guy Bocard (with a domaine of 8.5 ha and several times winner of the *coup de coeur*) has entered these very attractive wines. This Charmes is full of finesse, having just the right amount of oak and a very floral style. It evolves beautifully on the palate to a long and elegant finish. **Les Grands Charrons 2000 (15–23 €)** and the **Limozin (15–23 €)** were singled out, whereas **Les Narvaux 2000 (15–23 €)** received one star.
➤ Guy Bocard, 4, rue de Mazeray, 21190 Meursault,
tel. 03.80.21.26.06, fax 03.80.21.64.92 ☑
♈ by appt.

DOM. ERIC BOUSSEY

Limozin 2000★

0.69 ha	3,500	▐▋	11–15 €

Would this wine go best with a pikeperch or a *bec* (the local name for pike)? This is the kind of question which the Jury get passionate about. This Limozin is ready to drink but it can be done in a variety of ways. It is pale yellow-gold in colour and has fruity menthol notes floral nuances on the nose. It is silky and opulent on the palate at the same time. The oak brings a touch of vanilla to the flavour.
➤ EARL du Dom. Eric Boussey, Grande-Rue,
21190 Monthélie, tel. 03.80.21.60.70, fax 03.80.21.26.12 ☑
♈ by appt.

DOM. JEAN-MARIE BOUZEREAU

2001★★

1.5 ha	6,000	▐▋	15–23 €

La Goutte d'Or Premier Cru 2001 (23–30 €) does not disappoint and is singled out whereas this *village* wine has seduced the Jurors with its highlighted colour. It is everything one could dream of, from the clear and precise notes of almond and dried fruits on the nose to the lemony freshness and hazelnut flavours which are balanced on the palate. It would be advisable to age this wine in order to develop the complexity which at present is only outlined, but still evident.
➤ Jean-Marie Bouzereau, 5, rue de la Planche-Meunière,
21190 Meursault, tel. 03.80.21.62.41, fax 03.80.21.24.39 ☑
♈ by appt.

MICHEL BOUZEREAU ET FILS

Les Tessons 2001★

0.5 ha	n.c.	▐▋	15–23 €

With Michel Bouzereau, one is rarely disappointed! **Les Charmes-Dessus Premier Cru 2001 (23–30 €)** and **Les Grands Charrons 2001 (15–23 €)** should be in your shopping basket because they are as good as this Les Tessons. This wine has a winning limpid yellow-gold colour. With floral and dried fruits aromas, this Meursault lacks neither depth nor delicacy and the oak maturation has been well managed. It is both fleshy and fresh at the same time, with a touch of mineral complexity. It is well-made and long on the finish and will be really something in a year or two's time.
➤ Michel Bouzereau et Fils, 3, rue de la Planche-Meunière,
21190 Meursault, tel. 03.80.21.20.74, fax 03.80.21.66.41,
e-mail michel-bouzereau.et-fils@wanadoo.fr ☑
♈ by appt.

BURGUNDY

Côte de Beaune (South Central Region)

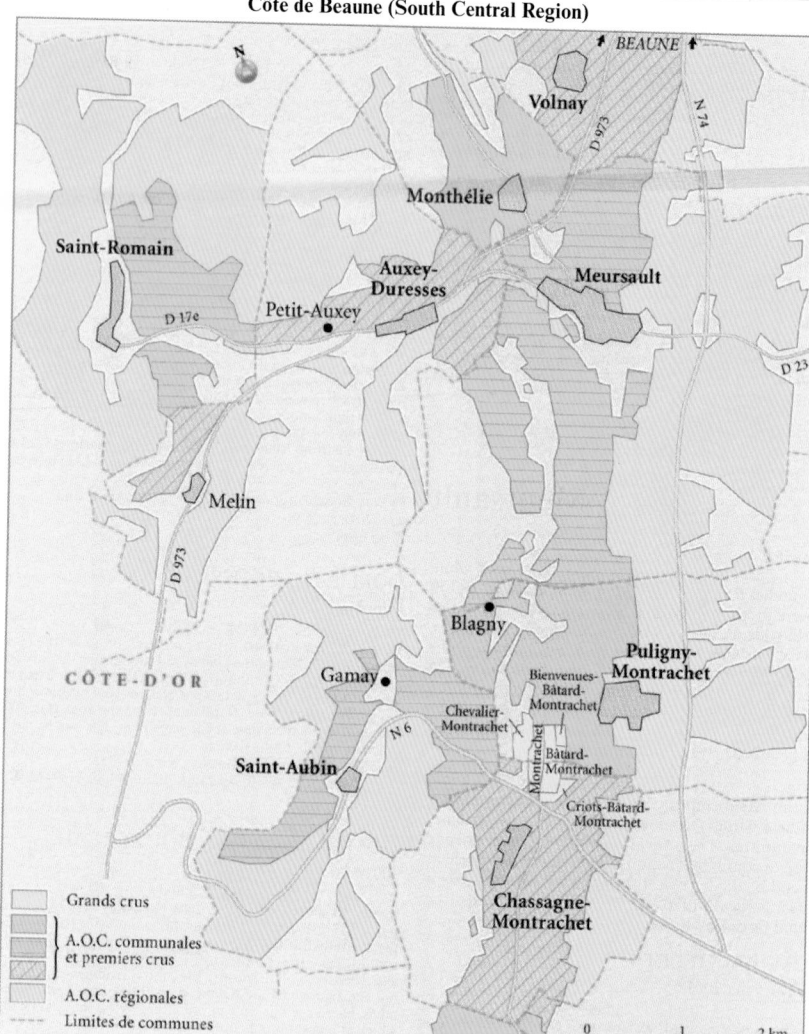

Grands crus

A.O.C. communales et premiers crus

A.O.C. régionales

Limites de communes

0   1   2 km

HUBERT BOUZEREAU-GRUERE ET FILLES Les Tillets 2001★

| | 0.8 ha | 2,000 | | 15–23 € |

Hubert Bouzereau-Gruère, is the father. Marie-Anne and Marie-Laure are the daughters. This wine is vinified by the former, sold by the daughters and the reception is manned by the latter. It is a real family-run company. The **Les Charmes Premier Cru 2001 (23–30 €)** is equally as good as this Les Tillets which will make you forget all your troubles. Pale yellow with golden tones, this Meursault is dedicated to citrus peel and floral qualities, yet everything is expressed in moderation. Fresh and well structured, the palate finishes on a candied orange peel note.

☛ Hubert Bouzereau-Gruère et Filles, 22 a, rue de la Velle, 21190 Meursault, tel. 03.80.21.20.05, fax 03.80.21.68.16, e-mail hubert.bouzereau.gruere@libertysurf.fr ☑ 🏛 ♈ by appt.

DOM. CAILLOT

La Barre Dessus Clos Marguerite 2000★

| | 0.59 ha | 4,000 | | 15–23 € |

A **Village 2000 (11–15)** without designation is equally as good as this wine which is white-gold in colour with buttery and brioche characteristics. This Clos Marguerite is not perhaps typically radiant, but it combines power and length with body and freshness. "I like it very much," wrote a taster quite simply.
☛ Dom. Caillot, 14, rue du Cromin, 21190 Meursault, tel. 03.80.21.21.70, fax 03.80.21.69.58 ☑ ♈ by appt.

MAISON CHAMPY

Les Grands Charrons 2001★

| | n.c. | 2,100 | | 30–38 € |

The Meurgey family took over in 1995 the venerable Maison Champy and contributed effectively to the blooming of

Burgundy's cultural inheritance. Its **Meursault 2000 (23–30 €)** inspires warmth and gets one star. Its Grands Charrons are very classy. They have potential but are already very pleasant and one should get the *pauchouse* ready. It has a ravishing appearance and a fresh floral nose with yellow fruits aromas. It is elegant on the palate and the oak is well integrated.

🍷 Maison Champy, 5, rue du Grenier-à-Sel, 21200 Beaune, tel. 03.80.25.09.99, fax 03.80.25.09.95 ☑

🍷 by appt.

🍷 Pierre Meurgey, Pierre Beuchet

DOM. CHANGARNIER 2001★

| | 0.25 ha | 1,700 | ⑪ | 15–23 € |

The Changarnier family have given France a famous general and Burgundy an excellent wine. It has a high quality appearance. The first impression on the nose is of a very fresh and intense wine, the aromas becoming, little by little, that of ripe fruit. Bravo this 2001: it wasn't so easy to produce this beautiful floral complexity which is both fruity and minerally at the same time and accompanied by the vanilla notes of its maturation. Open in 2005.

🍷 Dom. Changarnier, pl. du Puits, 21190 Monthélie, tel. 03.80.21.22.18, fax 03.80.21.68.21, e-mail changarnier@aol.com ☑

🍷 ev. day except Sun. 9am–12 noon 2pm–7pm

DOM. DU CHATEAU DE PULIGNY-MONTRACHET Les Poruzots 2000★★

| 1er cru | 0.71 ha | 4,000 | ⑪ | 15–23 € |

The domaine of Château de Puligny-Montrachet has taken the bull by the horns since it was bought and extended by Crédit Foncier of France. Here we have a superb Poruzots with a marvellous colour (white-gold with classic highlights) and with a floral bouquet. It is, quite simply, angelic. It has citrus fruit and floral nuances and the oak is not too dominant. It is a lovely wine, both powerful and rich. It is the epitome of Meursault.

🍷 SCEA Dom. du Château de Puligny-Montrachet, 21190 Puligny-Montrachet, tel. 03.80.21.39.14, fax 03.80.21.39.07

VINCENT DANCER

Perrières 2001★

| 1er cru | 0.29 ha | 1,800 | ⑪ | 30–38 € |

"This is a beautiful wine which I would have loved to have made," wrote one of our Jurors. A Premier Cru that lives up to its level, which can be drunk or kept as you wish. Shining gold in appearance, it has the finesse of the hawthorn: neither too much nor too little, according to the oracle of Delphi. Acidity and freshness confirm on the palate the harmony imagined at the start.

🍷 Vincent Dancer, 23, rte de Santenay, 21190 Chassagne-Montrachet, tel. 03.80.21.94.48, fax 03.80.21.39.48, e-mail vincentdancer@aol.com ☑

🍷 by appt.

JOSEPH DROUHIN

En Luraule 2000★

| | 0.46 ha | n.c. | ⑪ | 30–38 € |

One can produce excellent wines in Oregon and remain faithful to the essence of Burgundy. This Meursault, En Luraule (the *climat* neighbours that of 'Goutte d' Or') is representative of the vintage and its terroir. This wine is quite rich, with texture and grain and is delicate in colour. It has elegant oaky qualities. It received the *coup de coeur* for its 99 vintage.

🍷 Maison Joseph Drouhin, 7, rue d'Enfer, 21200 Beaune, tel. 03.80.24.68.88, fax 03.80.22.43.14, e-mail maisondrouhin@drouhin.com ☑

🍷 by appt.

ALBERT GRIVAULT

Clos des Perrières Monopole 2001★★

| 1er cru | 0.95 ha | 5,000 | ⑪ | 38–46 € |

This domaine has already received a *coup de coeur* for its Clos de Perrières 96. Michel Bardet has done it again. It is number one amongst the 143 samples tasted: top of the class. Property of the Marquis de La Troche until 1879, this *clos*, surrounded by its original walls, was acquired by Albert Grivault when he

was only 23 years old; it has remained in the family since then. On the nose, this *clos* 2001 is very Meursault, straightforward and intense. On the palate, lily of the valley and lime blossom flavours counteract each other in a perfect equilibrium: an excellent concentration will allow the elegant oak to become integrated. It is absolutely essential to cellar this wine for a while: to drink it too soon would be a pity. The **Meursault Village 2001 (15–23 €)** gets one star.

🍷 SC du Dom. Albert Grivault, 7, pl. du Murger, 21190 Meursault, tel. 03.80.21.23.12, fax 03.80.21.24.70 ☑

🍷 by appt.

DOM. JOBARD-MOREY

Les Narvaux 2001★

| | 0.66 ha | 2,000 | ⑪ ⑪ | 15–23 € |

Jobard and Morey are two of the famous names in Burgundy. One is astonished that they have united to create this distinguished wine. Substantial gold in colour, this 2001 has an already successful bouquet, where honey and the apricot give voice. Balanced to the last, the body lacks neither consistency nor finesse. **Les Tillets 2000 (11–15 €)** inspires the same feelings and gets the same note.

🍷 Dom. Jobard-Morey, 1, rue de la Barre, 21190 Meursault, tel. 03.80.21.26.43, fax 03.80.21.60.91 ☑

🍷 by appt.

DOM. MAZILLY PERE ET FILS

Les Meurgers 2001★★

| | 0.8 ha | 5,000 | ⑪ | 15–23 € |

A *coup de coeur* is awarded for this *village* wine which is held up a model to others. Meurgers? In Burgundy that means heaps of stones that have been piled up for centuries. The colour of this Meursault is worthy of a fashion show. The nose is a little toasty evoking also dried fruits, apricots, honey and menthol, with a note of well-integrated oak. The palate returns to the flavours of eucalyptus and *pain d'épice* and the structure defies criticism. Today it is still a long way from being at its peak.

🍷 Dom. Mazilly Père et Fils, rte de Pommard, 21190 Meloisey, tel. 03.80.26.02.00, fax 03.80.26.03.67 ☑

🍷 by appt.

DOM. MICHELOT MERE ET FILLE

Sous la Velle 2000★

| | 0.59 ha | 1000 | | 23–30 € |

Domaine Michelot Mère et Fille has a photograph of the mother as the queen of Meursault. And what a family: Bernard has given his inheritance to his three daughters, in this case, Véronique and her mother Geneviève. All this for a Meursault without fining or filtration which only needs to be matched with a pike in mayonnaise. Rich but still lively, this wine is not yet at its best "Silent like a Cistercian monk," wrote one Juror. Keep for two or three years for everything to be at its best.

🕯 Dom. Michelot Mère et Fille, 24, rue de la Velle, 21190 Meursault, tel. 03.80.21.68.99, fax 03.80.21.27.65 ☑
Ⴧ by appt.

MOILLARD

Clos du Cromin 2001★

	n.c.	4,800	🍷	23–30 €

This wine is pale gold in colour with green highlights and it wears, with imposing presence, the uniform of the cru. It has classic buttery and hazelnut aromas combined with a hint of minerality and an aroma similar to coconut. Its balance does not prevent it from showing its vivacity, particularly perceptible with a slight acidity shown on the finish. This is a good wine made by Maison Moillard, who have been one of the pillars of the *négociants-éleveurs* in Nuiton for more than 150 years.

🕯 Moillard, 2, rue François-Mignotte, 21700 Nuits-Saint-Georges, tel. 03.80.62.42.22, fax 03.80.61.28.13, e-mail nuicave@wanadoo.fr ☑
Ⴧ ev. day 10am–6pm; cl. Jan.

DOM. RENE MONNIER

Les Chevalières 2001★

	2.45 ha	14,000	🍷	11–15 €

This *climat* is located in the high country and the wine is worthy of its name because it is full of pleasure and liveliness. It is the sort of wine that Cardinal de Bernis would have liked to keep for his monthly mass. It is fresh and shows finesse while being rich and mouth-filling. All the qualities are here: initial toasty aromas are kept within reasonable limits. This wine is delicate and subtle. It should be tasted with a pâté made by the mother of Daugier, a mythical figure in Meursault. This domaine claims to have her recipe! It was thought that she had carried the secret to her grave.

🕯 Dom. René Monnier, 6, rue du Dr-Rolland, 21190 Meursault, tel. 03.80.21.29.32, fax 03.80.21.61.79 ☑
Ⴧ ev. day 8.30am–12 noon 2pm–6pm
🕯 M. et Mme J.-L. Bouillot

DOM. ALAIN PATRIARCHE

Les Grands Charrons 2000★★

	0.5 ha	2,000	🍷	23–30 €

At the *Paulée* in Meursault, try to sit near to this wine-grower. His Grands Charrons 2000 almost got the *coup de coeur*. with three votes, it is a rare bird. The colour corresponds to the criteria of the AOC, just as the nose has aromas of fresh grapes and hazelnuts. Suppleness, richness, finesse, the rhymes trip off the tongue. This wine is the expression of terroir.

🕯 Dom. Alain Patriarche, 12, rue des Forges, 21190 Meursault, tel. 03.80.21.24.48, fax 03.80.21.63.37 ☑
Ⴧ by appt.

DE SOUSA-BOULEY

Les Millerans 2001★

	0.51 ha	1,800	🍷	11–15 €

It all started in 1981 with the acquisition of the grandparents' vines. This *climat* is located between the road to Puligny and the RN 74. After receiving two stars for the 2000, Albert de Sousa-Bouley has made this wine, which flowers on the palate with a touch of complexity. The nose is smoky, minerally and murisaltien with a menthol note. It has a beautifully clear, crystalline colour. This full-bodied wine will keep its freshness for quite a long time. This is its best asset.

🕯 Albert de Sousa-Bouley, 7, RN 74, 21190 Meursault, tel. 03.80.21.22.79, fax 03.80.21.66.76 ☑
Ⴧ by appt.

CH. DE LA VELLE

Clos de la Velle 2001★★

	0.6 ha	2,500	🍷	15–23 €

This domaine has a strong house dating from the 16th century. and is a monument registered in *l'Inventaire des Sites*. It provides a warming reception…Back to the wine. The visual impression is largely favorable. The nose is complex, expressing terroir and very ripe fruit. The palate is harmonious and intense, well-balanced and showing a great purity. The overall impression is of precision and persistence and it will last from now until four or five years' time.

🕯 Bertrand Darviot, 17, rue de la Velle, 21190 Meursault, tel. 03.80.21.22.83, fax 03.80.21.65.60, e-mail chateaudelavelle@darviot.com ☑ 🏠
Ⴧ by appt.

HENRI DE VILLAMONT 2000★

	1.18 ha	6,247	🍷	23–30 €

The imaginary character in the history of the wine of Burgundy, Henri de Villamont, is made incarnate by the Swiss company Schenk. They are the *négociants-éleveur* who own this vineyard. Their Meursault acquitted itself very well in all regards. With fresh fruit and vanilla aromas, the nose is very expressive. As for the palate, "A good job," is noted by one taster on his card. It is not very fleshy, but on the other hand, its supple minerality and the acidity do not allow us to lose sight of the essence of the subject. The wine under the name of **François Martenot le Village 2001 (15–23 €)** gets the same mark.

🕯 SA Henri de Villamont, 2, rue du Dr-Guyot, 21420 Savigny-lès-Beaune, tel. 03.80.24.70.07, e-mail hdv@planetb.fr ☑
Ⴧ ev. day except Mon. 9.30am–7pm; Thurs. 2pm–6.30pm; cl. 15 Nov.–30 Mar

Wines selected but not starred

DOM. VINCENT BOUZEREAU

Les Narvaux 2001

	0.25 ha	1000	🍷	15–23 €

🕯 Vincent Bouzereau, 7, rue Labbé, 21190 Meursault, tel. 03.80.21.61.08, fax 03.80.21.65.97, e-mail vincent.bouzereau@wanadoo.fr ☑
Ⴧ by appt.

DOM. HENRI ET GILLES BUISSON

Les Chevalières 2000

	0.32 ha	1000	🍷	15–23 €

🕯 Dom. Henri et Gilles Buisson, imp. du Clou, 21190 Saint-Romain, tel. 03.80.21.27.91, fax 03.80.21.64.87 ☑ 🏠
Ⴧ by appt.

BUISSON-BATTAULT ET FILS

Limosin 2000

	0.55 ha	3,500	🍷	11–15 €

🕯 Buisson-Battault et Fils, 18, rue de Mazeray, 21190 Meursault, tel. 03.80.21.21.99, fax 03.80.21.63.23, e-mail buisson-battault@club-internet.fr ☑
Ⴧ by appt.

CH. DE CITEAUX

Les Narvaux 2001

	0.65 ha	3,000	🍷	15–23 €

🕯 Philippe Bouzereau, Ch. de Cîteaux, 18–20, rue de Cîteaux, BP 25, 21190 Meursault, tel. 03.80.21.20.32, fax 03.80.21.64.34, e-mail info@domaine.bouzereau.fr ☑
Ⴧ by appt.

ALAIN COCHE-BIZOUARD 2001

■ 1er cru	0.42 ha	2,800	❚❙	11–15 €

❧ EARL Alain Coche-Bizouard, 5, rue de Mazeray,
21190 Meursault, tel. 03.80.21.28.41, fax 03.80.21.22.38 ☑
☾ by appt.

DEMESSEY 2001

■	n.c.	3,600	❚❙	15–23 €

❧ Marc Dumont, Ch. de Messey, 71700 Ozenay,
tel. 03.85.51.33.83, fax 03.85.51.33.82,
e-mail vin@demessey.com ☑ ⛺ ⛩
☾ by appt.

DOM. DUPONT-FAHN

Cuvée Vieilles Vignes 2001

■	n.c.	n.c.	❚❙	11–15 €

❧ Michel Dupont-Fahn, 21190 Monthélie,
tel. 03.80.21.26.78, fax 03.80.21.21.22 ☑
☾ by appt.

DOM. VINCENT GIRARDIN

Les Narvaux 2000

■	0.7 ha	5,040	❚❙	15–23 €

❧ Caveau des Grands Crus, pl. de la Bascule,
21190 Chassagne-Montrachet, tel. 03.80.21.96.06,
fax 03.80.21.96.06 ☑
☾ ev. day 10am–1pm 2pm–7pm
❧ Vincent Girardin

CH. DE MEURSAULT 2000

■ 1er cru	5 ha	26,900	❚❙	38–46 €

❧ Dom. du Château de Meursault, 21190 Meursault,
tel. 03.80.26.22.75, fax 03.80.26.22.76 ☑
☾ by appt.

DOM. DU PAVILLON

Charmes 2000

■ 1er cru	1.17 ha	6,000	❚❙	30–38 €

❧ Dom. du Pavillon, 6 bis, bd Jacques-Copeau,
21200 Beaune, tel. 03.80.24.37.37, fax 03.80.24.37.38
❧ A. Bichot

MAX ET ANNE-MARYE PIGUET-CHOUET Les Narvaux 2001

■	1.33 ha	1,200	❚❙	15–23 €

❧ Max et Anne-Marye Piguet-Chouet, rte de Beaune,
21190 Auxey-Duresses, tel. 03.80.21.25.78,
fax 03.80.21.68.31, e-mail piguet.chouet@wanadoo.fr ☑
☾ by appt.

DOM. PINQUIER-BROVELLI 2001

■	0.1 ha	700	❚❙	11–15 €

❧ Dom. Pinquier-Brovelli, 5, rue Pierre-Mouchoux,
21190 Meursault, tel. 03.80.21.24.87,
fax 03.80.21.61.09 ☑ ⛺
☾ Mon.–Sat. 9am–12 noon 1.30pm–7pm;
Sun. 9am–12 noon

POULET PERE ET FILS 2001

■	n.c.	1,300	❚❙	30–38 €

❧ Poulet Père et Fils, 6, rue de Chaux,
21700 Nuits-Saint-Georges, tel. 03.80.62.43.02,
fax 03.80.61.28.08

G. PRIEUR

Chevalières 2000

■	0.55 ha	3,700	❚❙	15–23 €

❧ G. Prieur, Santenay-le-haut, 21590 Santenay,
tel. 03.80.21.23.92

Blagny

The Blagny vineyard, straddling the communes of Meursault and Puligny-Montrachet, is a self-contained vineyard that grew up around the village. Remarkable red wines are produced under the Appellation Blagny – 250 hl in 2002 – but the majority of the area is planted with Chardonnay, producing Meursault Premier Cru or Puligny-Montrachet Premier Cru, depending on the commune.

DOM. LARUE

Sous le Puits 2000★★

■ 1er cru	0.2 ha	1,200	❚❙	15–23 €

Situated at the edge of the vines, the oratory of Saint-Charles, going back to 1740, is reproduced on the label. This bottle shows that the 2000 can be superb. The colour is enticing and very bright. Red fruits are integrated with minerals to give some joy to the heart. This is what is called a feminine wine on the palate: it is charming, tender and affectionate. The acidity is noticeable but discreet and the secondary flavours bring good news.

❧ Dom. Larue, 32, rue de la Chatenière,
21190 Saint-Aubin, tel. 03.80.21.30.74, fax 03.80.21.91.36,
e-mail larue.gaec@wanadoo.fr ☑
☾ by appt.

DOM. MATROT-WITTERSHEIM

La Pièce sous le Bois 2000★

■ 1er cru	0.85 ha	5,000	❚❙	15–23 €

This domaine has a beautiful house situated in the heart of the village, with a *clos* contiguous with the AOC Meursault. The vines were planted here in 1961 and 1987. This is an attractive wine, typical of 2000, which reveals itself on the palate without hiding anything. It is well made and should be kept for four to six years because of its tannins, which are firm without being aggressive. The wine has a promising finish which confirms the excellent impression given by its brilliant ruby appearance.

❧ SCE Dom. Matrot-Wittersheim, 2, pl. de l'Europe,
21190 Meursault, tel. 03.80.21.21.13, fax 03.80.21.21.14,
e-mail matrot.wittersheim@wanadoo.fr ☑
☾ ev. day except Sun. 8.30am–12 noon 1.30pm–5.30pm

Meursault-Blagny

Wines selected but not starred

SYLVAIN LANGOUREAU

La Pièce sous le bois 2001

■ 1er cru	0.45 ha	3,300	❚❙	15–23 €

❧ Sylvain Langoureau, hameau de Gamay, 20, rue de la Fontenotte, 21190 Saint-Aubin, tel. 03.80.21.39.99,
fax 03.80.21.39.99 ☑
☾ by appt.

Puligny-Montrachet

Puligny-Montrachet is the fulcrum of the Côte d'Or white wines, situated between its two neighbours, Meursault to the north and Chassagne to the south. The vineyards of this small, peaceful commune occupy half the area of those in Meursault and are two-thirds the size of those in Chassagne, but despite their apparently modest extent they produce the greatest Grand Cru white wines in Burgundy, sharing the Montrachet name with Chassagne.

The geologists of the University of Dijon have discovered that the Grands Crus are located on an outcrop of Bathonian limestone, giving them greater finesse, harmony and aromatic subtlety than the wines harvested on the neighbouring marlstone. The AOC produced 11,318 hl of white wines and 130 hl of red in 2002.

The other climats and Premier Crus of the commune have a notably expressive bouquet smelling of vegetation with hints of essential oils and vegetal resins.

BOUCHARD AINE ET FILS
Champ Gain Cuvée Signature 2001★

1er cru	n.c.	900	◫	38–46 €

The vines for this Champ Gain are grown on very limestone soil. This *cuvée* Signature de Bouchard Aîné et Fils has an intense gold colour. With light vanilla and ripe fruit aromas and flavours, it gives joy to the heart. The first impression is a little lively but is compensated by the roundness, fleshiness and firm structure of Chardonnay when its at its best: all the secrets of a true Puligny are here. This is a bottle to uncork in 2004 or 2005.

☛ Bouchard Aîné et Fils, hôtel du Conseiller-du-Roy, 4, bd Mal-Foch, 21200 Beaune, tel. 03.80.24.24.00, fax 03.80.24.64.12, e-mail bouchard@bouchard-aine.fr ◩
♈ ev. day 9.30am–12 noon 2pm–6pm

GILLES BOUTON
La Garenne 2001★

1er cru	0.74 ha	3,900	◫	15–23 €

This *climat* is situated in the at the top of the *Coteau de Blagny*. This wine is very well made for mass consumption and is reasonably priced. It is a deep straw-coloured Puligny and has an intense nose with citrus fruit aromas. The outline is there but it is not yet fully developed. The first impression is silky and what follows is round and fruity. Serve in two to four years time with bass in pastry.

☛ Gilles Bouton, 24, rue de la Fontenotte, Gamay, 21190 Saint-Aubin, tel. 03.80.21.32.63, fax 03.80.21.90.74 ◩
♈ by appt.

MICHEL BOUZEREAU ET FILS
Les Champs Gains 2001★★

1er cru	0.4 ha	n.c.	◫	23–30 €

Awarded a *coup de coeur* last year and again this year for this same Champs Gains! It would be difficult to do better. Just looking at it, what an intensity of colour! Gold buttons. The opening aromas of rather ripe fruit are followed by spices, in particular pepper. The oak gives a subtle impression on the palate and is perfect. It is relieved by floral notes and fresh honey flavours. Splendid, in a word, thanks to its richness, power and a finish with a subtle quince note. It is rich indeed and original in its range of flavours.

☛ Michel Bouzereau et Fils, 3, rue de la Planche-Meunière, 21190 Meursault, tel. 03.80.21.20.74, fax 03.80.21.66.41, e-mail michel-bouzereau.et-fils@wanadoo.fr ◩
♈ by appt.

PHILIPPE BRENOT
Les Enseignères 2001★

	0.4 ha	2,000	◫	15–23 €

When you know that this *climat* is next to Bâtard-Montrachet, you will look at this bottle in a somewhat different light. Pale straw in appearance, this is a wine with a light but precise nose, with aromas between brioche and hazelnut. As for the initial attack on the palate, the freshness is apparent. It is accompanied by a rather minerally persistence: a correct wine, with a tight structure, showing character. Advice for collectors: this very old domaine stays faithful to a type of label which formerly caused a furore: it shows a map of the Côte.

☛ Dom. Brenot, SCE Dom. Brenot, 17, rue de Lavau, 21590 Santenay, tel. 03.80.20.61.27, fax 03.80.20.65.36 ◩
♈ by appt.

CHANSON PERE ET FILS
Hameau de Blagny 2001★

1er cru	n.c.	1,200	◫	38–46 €

Now owned by Bollinger, this label has made a Premier Cru which has been matured in oak on the lees and has undergone *bâtonnage*; the pale colour with green reflections is classic. On the nose it is powerful, with toasted notes of vanilla but also of quince, honey and acacia flowers. Well balanced (the richness and acidity have married) and of a good length, it is an attractive wine which should be opened in two or three years' time.

☛ Dom. Chanson Père et Fils, 10, rue Paul-Chanson, BP 232, 21206 Beaune Cedex, tel. 03.80.25.97.97, fax 03.80.24.17.42, e-mail tmarion@vins-chanson.com

DOM. DU CHATEAU DE PULIGNY-MONTRACHET
Les Folatières 2000★★

1er cru	0.52 ha	3,000	◫	23–30 €

"Truth above all," such is the motto of the Château de Puligny, acquired of late and developed by Crédit Foncier of France, and whose direction is from now on entrusted to E. de Montille. This Folatières resembles fine gold. It has chosen an exotic perfume of pineapple on the nose before returning to its natural minerality. The overall impression is rather flattering. We will talk about it again towards 2008 or 2010: this 2000 will be superb then.

☛ SCEA Dom. du Château de Puligny-Montrachet, 21190 Puligny-Montrachet, tel. 03.80.21.39.14, fax 03.80.21.39.07

DEMESSEY
Les Referts 2000★

1er cru	n.c.	2,000	◫	15–23 €

This *climat* lies contiguous to Meursault and close to Combettes. Impassioned by the wines of Burgundy, Marc Dumont came from Switzerland to get a foothold in Meursault and another in Ozenay in the Côte Chalonnaise (Château Demessey has found in J.-L. Daudon a manager attentive to quality). Pale clear gold, this is a 2000 that needs

aeration on the nose. The acidity is correct and the weight, the concentration and the length all appear satisfactory.
- Marc Dumont, Ch. de Messey, 71700 Ozenay, tel. 03.85.51.33.83, fax 03.85.51.33.82, e-mail vin@demessey.com ◨ ⛫ ⛨
☉ by appt.

RAYMOND DUREUIL-JANTHIAL

Les Champs Gains 2001★

1er cru	0.19 ha	1,300	⬚	23–30 €

This Puligny wine-grower married the only daughter of a Rully family, where they had established themselves by keeping an eye on their native land. Very golden in appearance, this wine has aromas of ripe grapes and honey. It honours the nose with a little vegetal note and is rather warming. Very typical but without a lot of length, it is well balanced and needs to be kept for three to five years. Serve with poached scallops.
- Raymond Dureuil-Janthial, rue de la Buisserolle, 71150 Rully, tel. 03.85.87.02.37, fax 03.85.87.00.24 ◨
☉ ev. day 9am–12 noon 3pm–7pm; Sun. by appt.

DOM. JEAN FERY ET FILS

Les Nosroyes 2001★

	0.7 ha	3,000	⬚	15–23 €

With an imposing presence, this wine will complement poultry and cream dishes. Its light yellow-gold colour incites curiosity. Acacia notes enliven the nose which is otherwise quite oaky. This sensation follows along the length of the palate which is clean and has good acidity, structure and is relatively persistent. Above average.
- Dom. Jean Fery et Fils, 21420 Echevronne, tel. 03.80.21.59.60, fax 03.80.21.59.59 ◨ ⛨
☉ by appt.

MAISON LOUIS JADOT

La Garenne 1999★★

1er cru	n.c.	n.c.	⬚	46–76 €

Jadot's handiwork is lively and deep: this is a sumptuous Garenne, golden, with a bouquet which is without doubt oaky but has floral and minerally qualities. On the palate it stays in this style with just a note of eucalyptus in its richness and generosity. Anyone can see it's a Puligny. When the grapes are very ripe, what more is there to add?
- Maison Louis Jadot, 21, rue Eugène-Spuller, 21200 Beaune, tel. 03.80.22.10.57, fax 03.80.22.56.03, e-mail contact@louisjadot.com ◨
☉ by appt.

SYLVAIN LANGOUREAU

La Garenne 2001★

1er cru	n.c.	3,900	⬚	15–23 €

If you haven't visited the vaulted cellars that Sylvain Langoureau has had built these last few years by a bricklayer's mate, do not fail to make a detour. At the same time you can perhaps taste this Garenne (the *climat* is close to Blagny). Clear gold in colour, the bouquet suggests kiwi, mango and almonds. Fleshy, the body is seductive. This wine is high in alcohol, powerful and a fine Premier Cru.
- Sylvain Langoureau, hameau de Gamay, 20, rue de la Fontenotte, 21190 Saint-Aubin, tel. 03.80.21.39.99, fax 03.80.21.39.99 ◨
☉ by appt.

DOM. LARUE

Sous le Puits 2001★

1er cru	2 ha	2,000	⬚	23–30 €

Sous le Puits is found above the hamlet of Blagny. Guy Larue took over his parents' small domaine in 1946. Denis and Didier today manage the 15 ha which they established in 2000. Very bright straw coloured, this bottle is showing well. The nose is more fruity than flowery and the oak is discreet. The wine is slightly nervy and the palate is smooth.
- Dom. Larue, 32, rue de la Chatenière, 21190 Saint-Aubin, tel. 03.80.21.30.74, fax 03.80.21.91.36, e-mail larue.gaec@wanadoo.fr ◨
☉ by appt.

DOM. MAROSLAVAC-LEGER

Les Folatières 2000★

1er cru	0.23 ha	1,200	⬚	23–30 €

Les Folatières wines often have the sensuality of wild flowers. For example the *Eve Couchée* in the Autun museum. This wine has a limpid colour with beautiful highlights and reveals an intense and complex nose with well-integrated vanilla and floral aromas. Being young, it bites back a little, but one rediscovers the aromas on the nose as flavours on the palate. It is well balanced. Leave to mature its fruit (two to five years).
- Dom. Maroslavac-Léger, 43, Grande-Rue, 21190 Puligny-Montrachet, tel. 03.80.21.31.23, fax 03.80.21.91.39, e-mail maroslavac-leger@wanadoo.fr ◨
☉ by appt.

DOM. DE MONTILLE

Le Cailleret 2000★

1er cru	1.02 ha	5,000	⬚	46–76 €

Le Cailleret: a soil made up of fine stones, close to Montrachet. That is to say it is one of the best areas, the Saint-Honoré suburb of the Côte. Made by one of the oldest family domaines in Burgundy (they were around before the Révolution), this is a green-gold wine, as it should be, with a floral bouquet that is slightly balsamic. Elegant and long, it yields itself to the demands of oak but still shows its vivacity.
- SCE Dom. de Montille, 12, rue du Pied-de-la-Vallée, 21190 Volnay, tel. 03.80.21.62.67, fax 03.80.21.67.14 ◨
☉ by appt.

DOM. MOREY-COFFINET

Les Pucelles 2001★

1er cru	0.2 ha	1,300	⬚	23–30 €

If you fear a little lull in the conversation, say for example if you did not invite a bishop, serve this Pucelles: it will always enliven the atmosphere. You can't help but say that it has lost its virginity as it is donkey's years since the assault of Bâtard-Montrachet. Bright yellow gold with an attractive richness on the sides of the glass, this 2001 has very evocative aromas on the nose. It is straightforward, elegant and well-made for this vintage.
- Dom. Michel Morey-Coffinet, 6, pl. du Grand-Four, 21190 Chassagne-Montrachet, tel. 03.80.21.31.71, fax 03.80.21.90.81 ◨
☉ by appt.

DOM. JACQUES PRIEUR

Les Combettes 2000★

1er cru	1.5 ha	7,500	⬚	38–46 €

Some people are crazy about Combettes in the same way as some people are crazy about black chocolate or asparagus. They are so impassioned that they dream about it. On these outcrops of rocks with deep pits of good soil, the ground gives wines of finesse and remarkable consistency. Such is the case here, and our Combettes fanatic will not regret the purchase of this bottle, expensive, certainly, but so tasty. Its bouquet is open with lightly toasty notes and the palate is impeccable and full of promise. Antonin Rodet joined the Prieur family to manage this domaine.
- Dom. Jacques Prieur, 6, rue des Santenots, 21190 Meursault, tel. 03.80.21.23.85, fax 03.80.21.29.19 ◨
☉ by appt.

DOM. ROUX PERE ET FILS

Les Enseignères 2001★

	0.33 ha	2,500	⬚	23–30 €

Awarded a *coup de coeur* in the 2000 *Guide* for its Enseignères 97, Roux Père et Fils (sons in the plural) have made a 2001 that is rich, velvety and well balanced. It still lacks a little maturity, but we should make an appointment with it in two years' time. Crystalline and light coloured in appearance it has toasty notes on the nose and then more subtle nuances of lemon and eucalyptus.
- Dom. Roux Père et Fils, 21190 Saint-Aubin, tel. 03.80.21.32.92, fax 03.80.21.35.00 ◨
☉ by appt.

Wines selected but not starred

having to guess how they may develop in the future. The amount of wine is very small: all the Montrachet Grands Crus accounted for only 1,470 hl in 2002.

DOM. HUBERT BOUZEREAU-GRUERE ET FILLES 2001

	0.5 ha	600	🍶	15–23 €

☛ Hubert Bouzereau-Gruère et Filles, 22 a, rue de la Velle, 21190 Meursault, tel. 03.80.21.20.05, fax 03.80.21.68.16, e-mail hubert.bouzereau.gruere@libertysurf.fr ☑ 🏛
Ⴑ by appt.

AURELIE ET CHRISTOPHE MARY 2001

	0.12 ha	150	🍶	11–15 €

☛ Christophe Mary, rue de la Garenne, 21190 Corcelles-les-Arts, tel. 03.80.21.48.98, fax 03.80.21.48.98 ☑
Ⴑ by appt.

DOM. PATRICK MIOLANE 2001

	0.74 ha	2,000	🍶	11–15 €

☛ Dom. Patrick Miolane, Derrière chez Edouard, 21190 Saint-Aubin, tel. 03.80.21.31.94, fax 03.80.21.30.62, e-mail domainepatrick.miolane@wanadoo.fr ☑
Ⴑ by appt.

JEAN-MARC PILLOT

Les Noyers Brets 2001

	0.46 ha	3,000	🍶	15–23 €

☛ Dom. Jean Pillot et Fils, 1, rue Combard, 21190 Chassagne-Montrachet, tel. 03.80.21.92.96, fax 03.80.21.92.57, e-mail jeanmarc.pillot@wanadoo.fr ☑
Ⴑ by appt.

VEUVE HENRI MORONI

Les Combettes 2001

1er cru	0.41 ha	1,032	🍶	23–30 €

☛ Veuve Henri Moroni, 1, rue de l'Abreuvoir, 21190 Puligny-Montrachet, tel. 03.80.21.30.48, fax 03.80.21.33.08, e-mail veuve.moroni@wanadoo.fr ☑
Ⴑ by appt.

MONTRACHET, CHEVALIER, BATARD, BIENVENUES-BATARD, CRIOTS-BATARD

In the recent past, the most astonishing characteristic of the Grands Crus was that they took quite some time before fully revealing the exceptional quality expected of them. It could mean waiting ten years for a "great" Montrachet to reach maturity or five years for the Bâtard and its cohorts; the Chevalier-Montrachet alone seemed to be more expressive much earlier.

However, in the last few years some of the Montrachet pressings show a bouquet of exceptional power and complex flavours whose quality can be appreciated immediately, without

Montrachet

CHARTRON ET TREBUCHET 2001★★

Gd cru	n.c.	450	🍶	+76 €

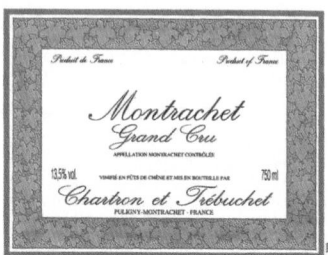

"This is not a wine, it is an event," said Frank M. Schoonmaker of Montrachet. This one is indeed a very great wine. It captures the eye. A light oakiness appears among aromas of fine flowers, honey and hawthorn. The body is in perfect proportions and the flavours are similar to the aromas on the nose so much so that it is dry and unctuous, firm yet caressing, enveloping and deep. Chartron and Trébuchet had already received the *coup de cœur* last year for the Bienvenues-Bâtard-Montrachet 2000. *bis repetita…*
☛ Chartron et Trébuchet, 13, Grande-Rue, 21190 Puligny-Montrachet, tel. 03.80.21.32.85, fax 03.80.21.36.35

OLIVIER LEFLAIVE 2001★

Gd cru	0.17 ha	900	🍶	+76 €

Dr Lavalle saw in Montrachet "one of these rare wonders whose perfection only a small number of the elite are able to appreciate." Alas! It is worth the trouble, however, to break the bank for such a bottle! It look like a *Faubourg Saint-Honoré* and the bouquet has the imprint of oak, liquorice and dried fruit. On the palate, citrus and very ripe fruits take turns until a touch of warm honey flavour takes over. It got a *coup de cœur* in the 2002 edition for the 99 vintage.
☛ Olivier Leflaive Frères, pl. du Monument, 21190 Puligny-Montrachet, tel. 03.80.21.37.65, fax 03.80.21.33.94, e-mail olivier-leflaive@dial.oleane.com ☑
Ⴑ by appt.

DOM. DE LA ROMANEE-CONTI 2001★★★

Gd cru	0.67 ha	n.c.	🍶	+76 €

|83| |86| |90||91| |93| 97|98| |99||00 01

In this bottle there is all the saga of a beehive. Clear gold in appearance, the wine tasted of old flowers which had already proclaimed their ambitions. The nose evokes beeswax and light honey. The grapes are ultra-ripe with a degree of natural alcohol between 13.5 and 14° which however produces an exquisite grace. It is opulent of course but enlivened by a discreet lively touch which gives relief to the tasting. A little touch of botrytis is found on exploring the palate. Is it feminine? Masculine? It is rather of the sex of angels.
☛ SC du Dom. de la Romanée-Conti, 1 rue Derrière-le-Four, 21700 Vosne-Romanée, tel. 03.80.62.48.80, fax 03.80.61.05.72

Wines selected but not starred

DOM. JACQUES PRIEUR 2000

| | Gd cru | 0.59 ha | 2,100 | ⅏ | +76 € |

➼ Dom. Jacques Prieur, 6, rue des Santenots,
21190 Meursault, tel. 03.80.21.23.85, fax 03.80.21.29.19 ☑
☗ by appt.

Chevalier-Montrachet

BOUCHARD PERE ET FILS 2000★

| | Gd cru | 2.54 ha | n.c. | ⅏ | +76 € |

Limpid, brilliant, this wine fits perfectly into Gaston Roupel's description: "the magic greenish highlights in this golden liquid". Its concentrated and complex bouquet tends towards floral against a liquorice-tinged whole. This is a wine to serve sometime during the next decade with a capon from Bresse stuffed with morels and foie gras, suggested one taster.
➼ Bouchard Père et Fils, Ch. de Beaune, 21200 Beaune, tel. 03.80.24.80.24, fax 03.80.22.55.88,
e-mail france@bouchard-pereetfils.com
☗ by appt.

DOM. JEAN CHARTRON

Clos des Chevaliers 2001★

| | Gd cru | 0.47 ha | 2,400 | ⅏ | +76 € |

91 92 93 94 |95| 96 |97| 98 |99| 00 01

This knight in shining armour, wearing the family gold and emerald colours, was matured in 39% new oak. Vanilla, lemon, the bouquet is not excessive but quite intense. A trifle austere on the palate, as it should be at this age, this wine is not yet very explicit but its rich substance shows honourable intentions. A worthy wine to drink with lobster.
➼ Jean Chartron, 13, Grande-Rue,
21190 Puligny-Montrachet, tel. 03.80.21.32.85,
fax 03.80.21.36.35 ☑
☗ ev.day. 10am–12noon 2pm–6pm;
Sat. and Sun. from end Nov. to mid-Mar. by appt.

Bâtard-Montrachet

DOM. CAILLOT 2000★

| | Gd cru | 0.48 ha | 1000 | ⅏ | 46–76 € |

This brilliant gold Bâtard needs to be laid down for several years as its structure and balance have not fully developed. Vanilla, cinnamon and toast on the bouquet are all evidence of 15 months maturation in cask. A few mineral notes are also discernible. On the palate? Angelic, "confectionery" style smoothness that is entirely in keeping with this Grand Cru. It will be delicious with foie gras, or seafood in a sauce.
➼ Dom. Caillot, 14, rue du Cromin, 21190 Meursault, tel. 03.80.21.21.70, fax 03.80.21.69.58 ☑
☗ by appt.

LOUIS LEQUIN 2001★

| | Gd cru | 0.12 ha | 750 | ⅏ | +76 € |

(94) (96) |98| 99 00 01

Coup de coeur in our 1999 edition for a 96 vintage, this golden-yellow Bâtard, with its lively highlights, is very open on currants, crystallized citrus fruit and especially honey. Full, quite fleshy, it has no great depth but is, nevertheless, a very nice wine. Recommended for serving with a creamy fish dish in two years' time.
➼ Louis Lequin, 1, rue du Pasquier-du-Pont,
21590 Santenay, tel. 03.80.20.63.82, fax 03.80.20.67.14,
e-mail louis.lequin@wanadoo.fr ☑
☗ by appt.

RENE LEQUIN-COLIN 2001★

| | Gd cru | 0.12 ha | 700 | ⅏ | 46–76 € |

(96)(98) 99 00 01

This estate, established a decade or so ago following a long family association, was *coup de coeur* for a 98 vintage. A "bastard" (*bâtard*) its father can be proud of! Rich in cask aromas, honey and acacia. In keeping with modern trends. The construction on the palate is perfect: richness, unctuousness, a powerful and concentrated structure… indeed a Grand Cru.
➼ René Lequin-Colin, 10, rue de Lavau, 21590 Santenay, tel. 03.80.20.66.71, fax 03.80.20.66.70,
e-mail renelequin@aol.com ☑
☗ by appt.

Bienvenues-Bâtard-Montrachet

DOM. BACHELET-RAMONET PERE ET FILS 2001★

| | Gd cru | 0.13 ha | 500 | ⅏ | 46–76 € |

A lot of 13.2 ha, Bachelet, Ramonet, famous names in the cru. Two stars last year for the 2000 vintage. Clear and luminous, with pleasant highlights, this 2001 vintage was tasted very young and so could not show itself to best advantage. The nose opens on the generous Puligny constitution which, at full maturity, often gives an impression of overripeness. After a full first impression, there follows a good acidity in a vanilla, brioche and exotic fruit context, then the oak comes to the fore, giving a harsh finish. Lay it down for three to five years.
➼ Dom. Bachelet-Ramonet Père et Fils, 11, rue du Parterre, 21190 Chassagne-Montrachet, tel. 03.80.21.32.49, fax 03.21.32.91.41 ☑
☗ by appt.

Criots-Bâtard-Montrachet

ROGER BELLAND 2001★

| | Gd cru | 0.61 ha | 300 | ⅏ | 46–76 € |

89 94 |95| |96| 98 |99| 00 01

A good overview of the Criots, since this vineyard covers more than one third of the entire acreage of this Grand Cru. This ancient Marcilly estate was taken over by the Belland family in 1982. A lively pale-gold, the Chardonnay grape shows up here in the distinctive floral features. The opening on the palate is very pleasant. Elegance and finesse are present throughout the tasting of this wine, whose balance promises great longevity.
➼ Dom. Roger Belland, 3, rue de la Chapelle,
21590 Santenay, tel. 03.80.20.60.95, fax 03.80.20.63.93,
e-mail belland-roger@wanadoo.fr ☑
☗ by appt.

BURGUNDY

Chassagne-Montrachet

A new combe rises at Saint-Aubin, running alongside the RN6, and more or less marks the southern limit of white wine production before red wines begin; Les Ruchottes vineyard is at the dividing line. Clos Saint-Jean and Clos Morgeot, both sturdy, vigorous wines, are the most famous of the Chassagnes. In 2002, the whites produced 9,136 hl and the reds 6,073 hl.

DOM. BACHELET
Les Benoîtes 2000★★★

■	4 ha	12,000	❶❶	8–11 €

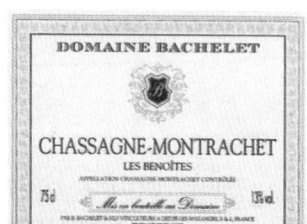

Les Benoîtes comes from just below Le Morgeot. Beauty itself. The estate is most impressive. Deep ruby-red in colour, on aeration this vintage develops spicy notes and a touch of mineral quality. Powerful and robust, balanced, full of agreeable tannins, its aromas are of small black fruit and cherries. Make a note, too, of the **Chassagne white 2001 Village (11–15 €)**. Light, admittedly, but very pleasing. It received a special mention.
❧ Dom. Bernard Bachelet et Fils, rue Maranges, 71150 Dezize-lès-Maranges, tel. 03.85.91.16.11, fax 03.85.91.16.48 ☑
☿ by appt.

DOM. BACHELET-RAMONET PERE ET FILS La Romanée 2001★

▣ 1er cru	0.26 ha	1,500	❶❶	15–23 €

The **Clos de la Boudriotte red 2000 (11–15 €)**, given a special mention by the Jury, is a classic Chassagne Premier Cru which represents the very soul of the area. The **Morgeot Premier Cru white 2001** is on the same level. As to this brilliant pale-gold Romanée, its floral and honeyed notes, combined with an elegant oakiness, are very seductive. On the very rich, aromatic palate one finds honey and lime-blossom enveloped in a balanced, frank and lingering whole. Keep it for one year and serve it over the ten that follow.
❧ Dom. Bachelet-Ramonet Père et Fils, 11, rue du Parterre, 21190 Chassagne-Montrachet, tel. 03.80.21.32.49, fax 03.21.32.91.41 ☑
☿ by appt.

DOM. BACHEY-LEGROS ET FILS 2001★★

■	1.41 ha	3,180	❶❶	11–15 €

An ancient grape-variety producing black grapes, is called le Bachet, name probably chosen long ago by a wine-grower from this family, as often happened in the past. As to this Pinot, it combines all the hoped-for qualities. Only the bouquet is still a touch closed and in need of coaxing. Excellent, rich robust structure on fine tannins; it is robust, with plenty of body and an interesting keeping-potential.
❧ Dom. Bachey-Legros, 12, rue de la Charrière, 21590 Santenay-le-Haut, tel. 03.80.20.64.14, fax 03.80.20.64.14, e-mail christiane.bachey-legros@wanadoo.fr ☑
☿ by appt.

ROGER BELLAND
Morgeot Clos Pitois Monopole 2001★★

▣ 1er cru	1.45 ha	7,600	❶❶	23–30 €

Together with the Clos Saint-Jean, this was once the most renowned *climat* in Chassagne. A monopoly in which the **red Premier Cru 2001 (15–23 €)** was specially mentioned. With aromas of acacia and lime-blossom, the white is a powerful wine, rich in body, if without great length, which will go on improving and reach its peak in two to three years' time. The texture is already silky, the substance richly satisfying. *Coup de cœur* in the 2001 edition for the 98 vintage of this same wine
❧ Dom. Roger Belland, 3, rue de la Chapelle, 21590 Santenay, tel. 03.80.20.60.95, fax 03.80.20.63.93, e-mail belland-roger@wanadoo.fr ☑
☿ by appt.

DOM. BORGEOT
Champs de Morgeot 2001★

■	0.3 ha	n.c.	❶❶	11–15 €

The two brothers have been running this 19 ha estate since 1989. Their **white Morgeot Premier Cru 2001 (23–30 €)** received a special mention. This *village* is of a classic, ruby-red colour. Its perfumes are equally divided between vanilla and blackcurrant, which fruit explodes on the palate amid evidence of a solid structure with a smooth, silky texture. It has all the red Chassagne distinctiveness without any excess extraction, all softness and in character.
❧ Dom. Borgeot, rte de Chassagne, 71150 Remigny, tel. 03.85.87.19.92, fax 03.85.87.19.95 ☑
☿ by appt.

BOUCHARD PERE ET FILS 2001★

■	n.c.	n.c.	❶❶	23–30 €

Proprietor of 130 ha of vineyards, Joseph Henriot has owned Bouchard Père et Fils since 1995. His clear straw-coloured *village* offers simple, tasteful floral features. By the same token, this is a rounded, agreeable 2001 vintage with a structure that does not claim to be poetry in motion. A good aperitif wine to drink with *gougères* (cheese-flavoured choux pastries).
❧ Bouchard Père et Fils, Ch. de Beaune, 21200 Beaune, tel. 03.80.24.80.24, fax 03.80.22.55.88, e-mail france@bouchard-pereetfils.com ☑
☿ by appt.
❧ Henriot

DOM. CAPUANO-FERRERI ET FILS
Morgeot 2001★

▣ 1er cru	n.c.	n.c.	❶❶	15–23 €

The bouquet and the palate both speak the same language. Under its sparklingly highlighted colour, this lively and fresh wine flirts with the floral but has still to capture it. On the palate it is a trifle closed as yet, but fine, polished, showing signs of hidden treasures. A wine to lay down for three or four years.
❧ Dom. Capuano-Ferreri et Fils, 1, rue de la Croix-Sorine, 21590 Santenay, tel. 03.80.20.64.12, fax 03.80.20.65.75, e-mail john.capuano@wanadoo.fr ☑
☿ by appt.

CHARTRON ET TREBUCHET
Les Morgeots 2001★

▣ 1er cru	n.c.	5,400	❶❶	38–46 €

Louis Trébuchet has now stepped back into the heart of the association formed with Jean Chartron. This Les Morgeots is well-constructed but needs time. Like most of the 2001 vintage, and particularly in this part of the Côte, they are flawless to look at, aromatic (acacia-honey or honey and acacia flowers) with a touch of oak from the cask and a fern on the finish. Ideal wine to serve with a vol-au-vent entrée.
❧ Chartron et Trébuchet, 13, Grande-Rue, 21190 Puligny-Montrachet, tel. 03.80.21.32.85, fax 03.80.21.36.35

CH. DE CHASSAGNE-MONTRACHET

2000★

■	1.28 ha	9,000	◫	15–23 €

Situated right at the top of the village, this *climat* is feeling its wings. A limpid gold colour, it offers a very pleasant bouquet of almonds and honey with floral notes, Round, full and classy, the palate echoes the aromas. The still-lively finish suggests one to two years in the cellar. Bader-Mimeur has been running the Clos du Château de Chassagne vineyards since 1919: first Elise Mimeur (70 years on the estate) then her granddaughter, Marie-Pierre.

➤ Bader-Mimeur, 1, chem. du Château, 21190 Chassagne-Montrachet, tel. 03.80.21.30.22, fax 03.80.21.33.29 ☑

☖ by appt.

➤ M.-P. Fossier

BERNARD COLIN ET FILS 2000★

■	1.12 ha	n.c.	▮◫♦	11–15 €

Sixteen stars in the *Guide* in the past years: a positive Milky Way! And three *coups de coeur*, including one in the 2002 edition for a white Le Cailleret 1998. It would be nice to follow the progress of this 2000 vintage as it should go on increasing in power until the end of the century. The colour is already agreeable, the floral bouquet is accompanied by small, woody notes. Plenty of flavour on the palate and a well-integrated oakiness on a touch of acidity to liven it up. Ideal wine to accompany a salmon cooked with sorrel.

➤ Bernard Colin et Fils, 22, rue Charles-Paquelin, 21190 Chassagne-Montrachet, tel. 03.80.21.92.40, fax 03.80.21.93.23 ☑

☖ ev.day. 9am–12noon 2pm–7pm; Sun. by appt.

GUY FONTAINE AND JACKY VION

Clos Saint-Jean 2000★

■	1er cru	0.3 ha	1,200	▮◫♦	15–23 €

Oldest of all the Chassagne crus, the Clos Saint-Jean took its name from a convent at Autun. One thousand years of history. The unusual red earth found in this vineyard is more commonly planted with red grape-varieties. How redolent of Chardonnay is this wine! Superb colour, pronounced mineral quality together with the usual vanilla; it is not yet markedly complex, but the Jury found it to have certain internal qualities and above all an admirable freshness. *Coup de coeur* in the 1999 *Guide* for a 95 vintage.

➤ GAEC des Vignerons, rue du Bourg, 71150 Remigny, tel. 03.85.87.03.35, fax 03.85.87.03.35 ☑

☖ by appt.

➤ Fontaine-Vion

JEAN GAGNEROT 2001★★

■	n.c.	1,500	◫	23–30 €

The label, with its picture of an 18th century *vigneron*, is evocative of Dijon generally; the estate is now under the patronage of La Reine Pédauque. Clear and agreeable to the eye, this is a wine with honeysuckle aromas, as luscious as a Chassagne can be when it sheaths its claws. The flavours are intense, the length significant.

➤ Jean Gagnerot, 21420 Aloxe-Corton, tel. 03.80.25.00.00, fax 03.80.26.42.00, e-mail vinibeaune@bourgogne.net ☑

☖ by appt.

VINCENT GIRARDIN

La Boudriotte 2001★

■	1er cru	0,8 ha	5,000	◫	11–15 €

A wine to drink with a rich rabbit stew or a coq au vin, its colour is a very intense garnet-crimson, the result of strong extraction. The bouquet confirms what the colour suggests: blackcurrant leaf-buds, leather, game. A good attack carried by the cask, a few liquorice nuances, then the fruit takes over on the average strength and structure which indicate the need to lay the wine down for one to two years. "A polished wine, very pleasant in all its aspects," was what one taster wrote.

➤ Caveau des Grands Crus, pl. de la Bascule, 21190 Chassagne-Montrachet, tel. 03.80.21.96.06, fax 03.80.21.96.06 ☑

☖ ev.day. 10am–1pm 2pm–7pm

➤ Vincent Girardin

GABRIEL AND PAUL JOUARD

Les Vides-Bourses 2001★★

■	1er cru	0.4 ha	1,500	◫	15–23 €

Four wines retained by the Jury! Within the **11–15 € price range, a red Cuvée Vieilles Vignes Village 2000** one star, and the **white Village 2001**, a sumptuous two star wine, pure and satisfying. The **white Premier Cru Morgeot 2001** received one star. Don't hesitate to come here to buy your wines! The prize goes to this Vides-Bourses. This *climat* is joined to the Bâtard-Montrachet. Maturity, sensations of honey and ripe fruit, solidity but balanced between power, acidity and suppleness; it's a great wine. It was, by the way, *coup de coeur* last year with a 99 vintage.

➤ Dom. Gabriel and Paul Jouard, 3, rue du Petit-Puits, 21190 Chassagne-Montrachet, tel. 03.80.21.94.73, fax 03.80.21.31.94, e-mail domgetpauljouard@club-internet.fr ☑

☖ by appt.

DOM. LARUE 2001★

■	0.25 ha	1,800	◫	11–15 €

Didier and Denis Larue head a 15 ha estate in the AOC Chassagne, Puligny and Saint-Aubin. They had the happy idea of depicting the 18th century Saint-Charles oratorio on their label. Their Chardonnay is all one expects of it: slightly green pale-gold, quite open on citrus and exotic fruits (pineapple), it show promise. Its liveliness does not detract from is delicate elegance. Not a huge amount of body, but well-matured and fruity.

➤ Dom. Larue, 32, rue de la Chatenière, 21190 Saint-Aubin, tel. 03.80.21.30.74, fax 03.80.21.91.36, e-mail larue.gaec@wanadoo.fr ☑

☖ by appt.

CH. DE LA MALTROYE

Morgeot Vigne Blanche 2001★★

■	1er cru	1.06 ha	6,500	◫	23–30 €

The **white Clos du Château de la Maltroye Premier Cru 2001**, fleshy, buttery, opulent, was awarded one star. This golden and brilliant Morgeot Vigne Blanche, in which one seems to recognize crystallized lemon and vanilla, is instantly elegant. The oak from the cask is well tempered, the wine perfectly balanced. Clean and full of finesse, this 2001 vintage should have become a fine wine around 2007. To accompany a chicken cooked with morels, or any fish dish.

➤ SCE Ch. de la Maltroye, 16, rue de la Murée, 21190 Chassagne-Montrachet, tel. 03.80.21.32.45, fax 03.80.21.34.54, e-mail chateau.maltroye@wanadoo.fr ☑

➤ Cournut

DOM. PATRICK MIOLANE

La Canière 2001★

■	1.1 ha	2,000	◫	11–15 €

This winegrower offered a **red Canière 2001 (8–11 €)** which received a special mention, as did the same *climat* in white in this 2001 vintage, which is a rare occurrence. Pale gold, with a delicately oaked, floral and very pleasant bouquet. One taster suggested serving it with frogs' legs. This *climat* is situated just below the Maltroye, the Champs Gains. The estate was *coup de coeur* in the 2003 *Guide* for a 99 vintage.

➤ Dom. Patrick Miolane, Derrière chez Edouard, 21190 Saint-Aubin, tel. 03.80.21.31.94, fax 03.80.21.30.62, e-mail domainepatrick.miolane@wanadoo.fr ☑

☖ by appt.

DOM. BERNARD MOREAU ET FILS

La Maltroie 2001★★

	1er cru	n.c.	4,500	23–30 €

This estate is in luck, since the Jury retained three of its wines: two Premiers Crus, the **Morgeot white 2001**, one star, and the **Grandes Ruchottes white 2001**, with a special mention; then this Maltroie which shows all the signs of a great wine for laying down. Pale gold in colour, the bouquet shows fine maturity, hovering around honeysuckle and lemon. Still rather closed on the palate and a certain liveliness, but a convincing advertisement for the Chassagne-Montrachet. It set one taster dreaming of Dublin Bay prawns cooked in the shell and served with lemon butter.

✦ Dom. Bernard Moreau et Fils, 3, rte de Chagny, 21190 Chassagne-Montrachet, tel. 03.80.21.33.70, fax 03.80.21.30.05 ☑
✇ by appt.

DOM. MOREY-COFFINET

Les Caillerets 2001★

	1er cru	0.65 ha	4,400	23–30 €

The Les Caillerets de Chassagne is different from the Les Caillerets de Puligny. They are easily distinguishable on tasting. Pale-yellow with green-gold highlights, this wine is moderately oaky, leaving room for some very complex aromas combining apricot, kiwi fruit and floral notes. No heaviness on the end palate, which is full and has length: durably pleasant on the end palate. One fine gourmet suggested serving it with scallops poached in a leek bouillon, with black truffles.

✦ Dom. Michel Morey-Coffinet, 6, pl. du Grand-Four, 21190 Chassagne-Montrachet, tel. 03.80.21.31.71, fax 03.80.21.90.81 ☑
✇ by appt.

LUCIEN MUZARD ET FILS

Vieilles Vignes 2001★★

		0.1 ha	840	15–23 €

Burgundian ruby-red with purple highlights, this 2001 vintage presents its aromas to best effect. The vanilla notes are undoubtedly evident but ripe fruit is also delicately sought. A charming, attractive, velvety wine, rounded and fleshy. Still rather closed, it is keeping this chest close to its chest with a view to several years (two or three) in the cellar, which will complete the development so well begun and give it depth.

✦ Lucien Muzard et Fils, 11 bis, rue de la Cour-Verreuil, BP 25, 21590 Santenay, tel. 03.80.20.61.85, fax 03.80.20.66.02, e-mail lucien-muzard-et-fils@wanadoo.fr ☑
✇ by appt.

PIERRE LAMOTTE 2001★

		n.c.	n.c.	11–15 €

Maximum colour extraction, which means that the colour is very deep, little animated by highlights. Aromas of charring on the bouquet and concentrated composition: a very robust and warm wine, rich in substance, successful in this style, the more so because of a touch of liquorice on its remarkable length. Pierre Lamotte is one of the Cottin family (Labouré-Roi) brands.

✦ Pierre Lamotte, rue Lavoisier, 21700 Nuits-Saint-Georges, tel. 03.80.62.64.00, fax 03.80.62.64.00
✇ by appt.

JEAN-MARC PILLOT

Les Champs-Gain 2001★

	1er cru	0.25 ha	1,500	23–30 €

While the oak of this Champs-Gain is already well-integrated on a background of brioche, the nose goes even further. Complete, powerful, it makes itself at home and doesn't leave you. A slight over-maturation? Undoubtedly, but it is not noticeable on the palate. On the contrary, that is marked by liveliness, and freshness, in complete accordance with its satisfying length. Could accompany any sauced fish dish.

✦ Dom. Jean Pillot et Fils, 1, rue Combard, 21190 Chassagne-Montrachet, tel. 03.80.21.92.96, fax 03.80.21.92.57, e-mail jeanmarc.pillot@wanadoo.fr ☑
✇ by appt.

DOM. VINCENT PRUNIER 2001★

		0.25 ha	1,510	11–15 €

Little by little the estate has grown, going from the 2.5 ha inherited from the parents to 11 ha today. This is a deep red 2001 vintage, with a very dark colour. One has to stand back a little to appreciate the impressive depth of the finely oaked bouquet. The vanilla is there again on the palate. A fine fermentation-period for a wine to lay down. The tannins are enveloped in blackberries and blackcurrants, and should integrate in three to five years.

✦ EARL Dom. Vincent Prunier, rte de Beaune, 21190 Auxey-Duresses, tel. 03.80.21.27.77, fax 03.80.21.68.87 ☑
✇ by appt.

DOM. ROUX PERE ET FILS

Les Chaumes 2001★

		0.65 ha	4,000	23–30 €

The estate received a *coup de coeur* in the 1998 edition for a white from the 95 vintage. Les Chaumes (more precisely, Les Chaumées) lies at the top of the slope going up towards Saint-Aubin. A brilliant straw-yellow colour, this wine needs aerating a little. It extols apples and pears and shows itself to be generally quite balanced. Simple and effective for a *village*. Serve it with Burgundy snails or a trout meunière.

✦ Dom. Roux Père et Fils, 21190 Saint-Aubin, tel. 03.80.21.32.92, fax 03.80.21.35.00 ☑
✇ by appt.

SORINE ET FILS

Vieilles Vignes 2001★

		0.42 ha	2,500	8–11 €

These *vieilles vignes* of which the average age is 46 years, have produced a red Chassagne of an intense colour and a quite expansive mineral bouquet. It doesn't give by halves, this one! The mineral quality is repeated on the palate in a velvet demonstration: tender and rounded, it stays supple to the very last note, where the tannins decide to show just the tips of their noses. Leave it in the cellar for two to three years.

✦ Dom. Sorine et Fils, 4, rue Petit, Le Haut-Village, 21590 Santenay, tel. 03.80.20.66.27, fax 03.80.20.61.65 ☑
✇ by appt.

Wines selected but not starred

FRANCOIS D' ALLAINES 2000

		n.c.	1,500	15–23 €

✦ François d' Allaines, La Corvée du Paquier, 71150 Demigny, tel. 03.85.49.90.16, fax 03.85.49.90.19, e-mail francois@dallaines.com ☑
✇ by appt.

GILLES BOUTON

Les Voillenots Dessus 2001

		0.89 ha	3,300	11–15 €

✦ Gilles Bouton, 24, rue de la Fontenotte, Gamay, 21190 Saint-Aubin, tel. 03.80.21.32.63, fax 03.80.21.90.74 ☑
✇ by appt.

C. CHARTON FILS

Cuvée Catherine Bastide 2001

		n.c.	2,100	30–38 €

✦ C. Charton Fils, 38, fg Saint-Nicolas, 21200 Beaune, tel. 03.80.22.53.33, fax 03.80.24.19.73

ALEX GAMBAL

La Maltroie 2000

| | 1er cru | 0.18 ha | 1,118 | | 23–30 € |

☛ Maison Alex Gambal, 4, rue Jacques-Vincent, 21200 Beaune, tel. 03.80.22.75.81, fax 03.80.22.21.66, e-mail alexgambal@wanadoo.fr ☑
Ⓨ by appt.

DOM. LAMY-PILLOT

Morgeot 2001

| | 1er cru | 0.9 ha | 4,700 | | 11–15 € |

☛ Dom. Lamy-Pillot, 31, rte de Santenay, 21190 Chassagne-Montrachet, tel. 03.80.21.30.52, fax 03.80.21.30.02, e-mail contact@lamy.pillot.fr ☑
Ⓨ by appt.

MARCHE AUX VINS 2000

| | | n.c. | 3,600 | | 11–15 € |

☛ Marché aux vins, rue Nicolas-Rolin, 21200 Beaune, tel. 03.80.25.08.20, fax 03.80.25.08.21 ☑
Ⓨ ev.day 9.30am–12noon 2pm–6pm

NAUDIN TIERCIN 2000

| | | n.c. | 1,900 | | 15–23 € |

☛ Naudin Tiercin, av. Charles-de-Gaulle, 21200 Beaune, tel. 03.80.25.91.30, fax 03.80.25.91.29 ☑
Ⓨ ev.day. ex. Sat. Sun. 9am–12noon 2pm–6pm; cl. Aug.

ROPITEAU FRERES 2000

| | | n.c. | 3,000 | | 15–23 € |

☛ Ropiteau Frères, Cour des Hospices, 13, rue du 11–Novembre, 21190 Meursault, tel. 03.80.21.69.20, fax 03.80.21.69.29, e-mail ropiteau@ropiteau.fr ☑
Ⓨ ev.day 9.30am–7pm; cl. Sat. Sun. Nov.–Mar.
☛ J.-Cl. Boisset

Saint-Aubin

Saint-Aubin is topographically the neighbour of the Hautes Côtes, but some of the commune borders Chassagne to the south and Puligny and Blagny to the east. The Murgers des Dents de Chien, Saint-Aubin's Premier Cru, is grown only a very short distance from Chevalier-Montrachet and Les Caillerets and it must be said that the Saint-Aubin Premier Cru is fully their equal in quality. The vineyards have begun to produce a little more red wine – 2,697 hl in 2002 – but the whites – 5,468 hl – reveal St Aubin at its best.

DOM. JEAN CHARTRON

Les Murgers des Dents de Chien 2001★

| | 1er cru | 0.51 ha | 3,600 | | 23–30 € |

Fermented and matured in cask, 30% new, this Saint-Aubin comes from still-young vines. It is pale and brilliant, and its elegant bouquet is quite floral with a touch of vanilla. On the palate it is rounded, fine, delicate and agreeable. Excellent to serve with a sole meunière
☛ Jean Chartron, 13, Grande-Rue, 21190 Puligny-Montrachet, tel. 03.80.21.32.85, fax 03.80.21.36.35 ☑
Ⓨ ev.day 10am–12noon 2pm–6pm; Sat. and Sun. from end Nov. to mid-Mar. by appt.

FRANCOISE AND ET DENIS CLAIR

Les Champlots 2001★

| | 1er cru | 0.3 ha | 1,500 | | 11–15 € |

Coup de cœur last year with a Les Frionnes 2000, this one is a Les Champlots 2001. Golden-straw coloured, this wine has a bouquet shared between hawthorn blossom and lemon. Fleshy and rounded, with a delicate touch of cask and a supple character. One lady taster suggested a gratin of courgettes and tomatoes to accompany it. If you are serving a turbot cooked with dill, choose the white **Les Frionnes Premier Cru 2001 (11–15 €)**, which received a special mention. The **red Saint-Aubin Premier Cru 2001 (8–11 €)** is another that it "worth the detour". Our tasters also took pleasure in it.
☛ Françoise and Denis Clair, 14, rue de la Chapelle, 21590 Santenay, tel. 03.80.20.61.96, fax 03.80.20.65.19 ☑
Ⓨ by appt.

ALEX GAMBAL 2000★

| | 1er cru | 0.32 ha | 2,196 | | 15–23 € |

Alex Gambal is a company set up recently by an avid Burgundy wine-lover; the best way to share his "viticultural philosophy". The result is interesting. Not too much colour, but then, too much is not needed. The nose is perfectly true-to-type: butter, toasted notes, and grapefruit with a very subtle floral note. This attractive, bright, young wine, in which the oak has been completely tamed, could be served from now on with a crayfish gratin.
☛ Maison Alex Gambal, 4, rue Jacques-Vincent, 21200 Beaune, tel. 03.80.22.75.81, fax 03.80.22.21.66, e-mail alexgambal@wanadoo.fr ☑
Ⓨ by appt.

DOM. HUBERT LAMY

Clos de la Chatenière 2001★★

| | 1er cru | 1.3 ha | 8,500 | | 15–23 € |

It is difficult to choose between the wines from this estate which was *coup de cœur* for its 2000, 98 and 96 vintages. This white Chatenière, gold with grey highlights, is close to perfection. No need to bring the nose to the glass: the citrus fruits, toast, hawthorn blossom leap out at you. Weight and power go hand in hand with balance and length. The **red Les Castets Premier Cru 2001** was awarded a star, as was the **white Les Frionnes Premier Cru 2001**, which would go well with a lobster *au beurre blanc*.
☛ Dom. Hubert Lamy, Le Paradis, 21190 Saint-Aubin, tel. 03.80.21.32.55, fax 03.80.21.38.32 ☑
Ⓨ by appt.

DOM. LARUE

Murgers des Dents de Chien 2001★

| | 1er cru | 0.33 ha | 6,000 | | 11–15 € |

More brilliant than golden, but limpid and welcoming, this Premier Cru merits its reputation. It starts on an aromatic complexity which recalls the great enigmas of the Universe. Apricot, dried fruits, vanilla, are all in orbit. Rounded and full, the palate is balanced with a touch of liveliness. It could go on developing for more than five years and would be a good reserve. The construction of a new vat room will allow the estate to improve its equipment and the new cellar will hold 250 barrels.
☛ Dom. Larue, 32, rue de la Chatenière, 21190 Saint-Aubin, tel. 03.80.21.30.74, fax 03.80.21.91.36, e-mail larue.gaec@wanadoo.fr ☑
Ⓨ by appt.

DOM. DES MEIX

Les Murgers des Dents de Chien 2001★

| | 1er cru | 1.1 ha | 7,000 | | 8–11 € |

This Saint-Aubin is a cousin of the Montrachet. Indeed, it is dressed like a courtier and its bouquet contains toasted notes mingled with honey and citrus fruits. Full, long and powerful, very warm, this is a concentrated, lingering wine on floral and oak notes. The estate's new winery awaits you.
☛ Christophe Guillo, Dom. des Meix, 21200 Combertault, tel. 03.80.26.67.05, fax 03.80.26.67.05 ☑
Ⓨ by appt.

DOM. PATRICK MIOLANE
Les Perrières 2001★★

| 1er cru | 0.25 ha | 1,800 | | 8–11 € |

Les Perrières nestles on the edge of the village near Frionnes. Beneath an intense gold colour is an attractive bouquet opening on great prospects for the tasters, who encountered honey, floral notes and mineral too. The touch of acidity is refreshing. This is a singing chatterbox of a wine, complete and with no complexes. Ready to serve in 2004 with a fish cooked with sorrel, as prepared at Les Troisgros, or a terrine of skate with sun-dried tomatoes. Hats off, too, for the true-to-type, successful **Village white 2001**, which received a special mention.
Dom. Patrick Miolane, Derrière chez Edouard, 21190 Saint-Aubin, tel. 03.80.21.31.94, fax 03.80.21.30.62, e-mail domainepatrick.miolane@wanadoo.fr
by appt.

HENRI PRUDHON ET FILS 2000★

| 1er cru | 0.8 ha | 5,300 | | 8–11 € |

Vincent and Philippe are associated with their grandfather, Gérard Prudhon, Mayor of Saint-Aubin, as was their father. Very true-to-type, this wine from the 2000 vintage will not keep for a long time, but it will be excellent served with white meat. The intense ruby-red colour shows some slight highlighting, due to evolution. Black fruits and liquorice notes are there in just measure on a balanced and already opened palate.
Henri Prudhon et Fils, 32, rue des Perrières, 21190 Saint-Aubin, tel. 03.80.21.36.70, fax 03.80.21.91.55
by appt.
Gérard Prudhon

DOM. DE VALLIERE
Les Cortons 2001★

| 1er cru | 0.66 ha | 4,200 | | 15–23 € |

Just as there are Les Echézeaux other than at Flagey, there are Les Cortons elsewhere than at Aloxe. This one, for example, in the Saint-Aubin AOC. There's a good subject for dinner-party conversation! This wine is a charming Chardonnay, as golden as one could wish for, with a rich and fruity bouquet. This 2001 vintage is, nevertheless, very robust and will need a year or two in the cellar to round out, after which it will be a good accompaniment for a herb-flavoured salmon mousse or a dish of moules marinières. From the same *climat*, come the **Domaine de Brully Les Cortons Premier Cru 2001** and the **Domaine Roux Père et Fils Les Pucelles 2001 (11–15 €)**, both of which received a special mention.
Dom. de Vallière, 21190 Saint-Aubin, tel. 03.80.21.32.92, fax 03.80.21.35.00
by appt.

Wines selected but not starred

JEAN-CLAUDE BACHELET
Les Champlots 2000

| 1er cru | 0.39 ha | n.c. | | 8–11 € |

Jean-Claude Bachelet, 1, rue de la Fontaine, 21190 Saint-Aubin, tel. 03.80.21.31.01, fax 03.80.21.91.71, e-mail jcbachelet@aol.com
by appt.

GILLES BOUTON
Les Champlots 2001

| 1er cru | 2 ha | 7,500 | | 8–11 € |

Gilles Bouton, 24, rue de la Fontenotte, Gamay, 21190 Saint-Aubin, tel. 03.80.21.32.63, fax 03.80.21.90.74
by appt.

CH. DE CHASSAGNE-MONTRACHET
Le Charmois 2001

| ■ 1er cru | 2.75 ha | 17,000 | | 11–15 € |

Dom. Michel Picard, Ch. de Chassagne-Montrachet, BP 49, 71150 Chagny, tel. 03.85.87.51.01, fax 03.85.87.51.12
by appt.

DUPERRIER-ADAM
Sur le Sentier du Clou 2001

| 1er cru | 0.66 ha | 1,700 | | 8–11 € |

SCA Duperrier-Adam, 3, pl. des Noyers, 21190 Chassagne-Montrachet, tel. 03.80.21.31.10, fax 03.80.21.31.10
ev.day 9am–12noon 2pm–5pm; Sat. Sun. by appt.; cl. Aug.

SYLVAIN LANGOUREAU
Les Frionnes 2001

| 1er cru | 0.3 ha | 1,900 | | 11–15 € |

Sylvain Langoureau, hameau de Gamay, 20, rue de la Fontenotte, 21190 Saint-Aubin, tel. 03.80.21.39.99, fax 03.80.21.39.99
by appt.

OLIVIER LEFLAIVE
Dents de Chien 2000

| 1er cru | 16.1 ha | 4,000 | | 15–23 € |

Olivier Leflaive Frères, pl. du Monument, 21190 Puligny-Montrachet, tel. 03.80.21.37.65, fax 03.80.21.33.94, e-mail olivier-leflaive@dial.oleane.com
by appt.

DOM. MAROSLAVAC-LEGER
Les Murgers des Dents de Chien 2000

| 1er cru | 0.68 ha | 2,380 | | 15–23 € |

Dom. Maroslavac-Léger, 43, Grande-Rue, 21190 Puligny-Montrachet, tel. 03.80.21.31.23, fax 03.80.21.91.39, e-mail maroslavac-leger@wanadoo.fr
by appt.

DOM. VINCENT PRUNIER
Les Combes 2001

| ■ 1er cru | 0.46 ha | 2,930 | | 8–11 € |

EARL Dom. Vincent Prunier, rte de Beaune, 21190 Auxey-Duresses, tel. 03.80.21.27.77, fax 03.80.21.68.87
by appt.

MICHEL SERVEAU
En l'Ebaupin 2001

| ■ | 0.14 ha | 900 | | 8–11 € |

Michel Serveau, rte de Beaune, 21340 La Rochepot, tel. 03.80.21.70.24, fax 03.80.21.71.87
ev.day 9am–7pm

CHARLES THOMAS 2001

| ■ | n.c. | 8,000 | | 8–11 € |

Charles Thomas, BP 6, 21701 Nuits-Saint-Georges Cedex, tel. 03.80.62.42.00, fax 03.80.61.28.13, e-mail info@thomasfreres.com
ev.day 10am–6pm; cl. Jan.

GERARD THOMAS
Murgers des Dents de Chien 2001

| ■ 1er cru | 1.82 ha | 12,000 | | 11–15 € |

EARL Dom. Gérard Thomas, 6, rue des Perrières, 21190 Saint-Aubin, tel. 03.80.21.32.57, fax 03.80.21.36.51
by appt.

Santenay

The village of Santenay is dominated by the Trois-Croix mountain and, thanks to its salt-water spa which has the most lithium-rich waters in the whole of Europe, it has become a famous spa resort. The village has many attractions, among which are some excellent red wines. Les Gravières, La Comme and Beauregard are the best-known crus. As at Chassagne, the vines of Santenay are often trained in the Cordon de Royat method. The two appellations of Chassagne and Santenay edge over into the Commune de Remigny, in Saône-et-Loire, where we find the appellations of Cheilly, Sampigny and Dezize-lès-Maranges, now included under the Appellation Maranges. In 2002 the AOC Santenay produced 2,190 hl of white wine and 12,995 hl of red wine.

ROGER BELLAND

Commes 2001★

| | 1er cru | 2.21 ha | 11,000 | 🍷 | 11–15 € |

A long-distance beneficiary of the *coup de coeur*, for its Beauregard 96 and 99 vintages. The **red Beauregard 2001** ties for its place with this beautiful ruby-red Commes with attractive highlights for its vintage. Perfumed according to the rules of restraint and good taste, this wine is pleasantly full, with balanced and long tannins. With a very smooth finish, the elegant integration shows an attractive, true-to-type wine that will keep for two years, unless you give yourself the pleasure of drinking it right away.

☛ Dom. Roger Belland, 3, rue de la Chapelle, 21590 Santenay, tel. 03.80.20.60.95, fax 03.80.20.63.93, e-mail belland-roger@wanadoo.fr ☑
☞ by appt.

DOM. DE LA BUISSIERE

Clos des Mouches 2001★

| | 1er cru | 0.92 ha | 5,800 | 🍷 | 15–23 € |

Le Clos de la Mouche is at Beaune. But also at Santenay, and well hidden away. Simone and Jeanne Moreau will be handing over to their grandson after 50 years of work! Their estate covers 9 ha and is installed in the ancient outbuildings of the Chateau Philippe le Hardi. Their 2001 is perfectly true-to-type. The slightly raspberry bouquet remains delicate. The full tannins augur an interesting keeping potential. A balanced wine to lay down for three or four years. The **red Premier Cru Beaurepaire 2001 (11–15 €)** was given a special mention. For drinking in two to four years.

☛ Jean Moreau, Dom. de la Buissière, 4, rue de la Buissière, 21590 Santenay, tel. 03.80.20.61.79, fax 03.80.20.64.76, e-mail moreau.jean@laposte.net ☑
☞ by appt.

DOM. CAPUANO-JOHN

Vieilles Vignes 2001★

| | | n.c. | n.c. | 🍷 | 8–11 € |

Of an intense and slightly evolved ruby-red, the raspberry aromas of this 2001 vintage make you long to taste it. The second nose is firmer. Quite peppered at the start, the velvety palate needs a few seconds to develop. The tannins are restrained but the acidity is there in just measure. A wine to serve with stuffed quail rather than a boeuf Bourguignon.

☛ Dom. Capuano-John, 14, rue Chauchien, 21590 Santenay, tel. 03.80.20.68.80, fax 03.80.20.65.75, e-mail john.capuano@wanadoo.fr ☑
☞ by appt.

CH. DE LA CHARRIERE

La Maladière 2001★

| | 1er cru | 1.17 ha | 6,000 | 🍷 | 11–15 € |

Matured for one year in cask, of which 20% new, this is a characteristic Maladière, elegant and ready to drink in two to three months. Its clear colour is flawless. The bouquet offers currants, prunes, in a fresh and fruity environment. The first impression is also propitious, freshness, then an outline of the body, leaning towards fleshiness and good, quite long tannins.

☛ Yves Girardin, Ch. de La Charrière, 1, rte des Maranges, 21590 Santenay, tel. 03.80.20.64.36, fax 03.80.20.66.32 ☑
☞ by appt.

FRANCOISE AND DENIS CLAIR

Clos Genet 2001★

| | | 1.2 ha | 6,000 | 🍷 | 11–15 € |

The Clos Genet received the *coup de coeur* last year for a 2000 vintage. And the year before that, too. This time once again the wine is entirely in conformity with the spirit of the appellation. Crimson ruby-red, it exhales blackcurrant while showing real charm at the next stage, well-balanced and tending towards delicacy. The pigeon it is to accompany will not fly away.

☛ Françoise and Denis Clair, 14, rue de la Chapelle, 21590 Santenay, tel. 03.80.20.61.96, fax 03.80.20.65.19 ☑
☞ by appt.

DOM. CYROT-BUTHIAU

Clos Rousseau 2001★

| | 1er cru | 0.42 ha | 700 | 🍷 | 11–15 € |

Doctor Lavalle wrote in 1855 that the vineyard at Santenay is one of the best kept of the Côtes, a model of good husbandry. It is still worthy of this reputation. Take the Clos Rousseau, moderate ruby-red colour, with perfumes of rose-petals, sweet spices and oak: the impression is very favourable. The opening is fresh, unctuous. The body is found again in the fine floral notes. The oak is slowly integrating. It will be a most satisfying wine in two or three years' time.

☛ Dom. Cyrot-Buthiau, rte d'Autun, 21630 Pommard, tel. 03.80.22.06.56, fax 03.80.24.00.86, e-mail cyrot.buthiau@wanadoo.fr ☑
☞ by appt.

DOUDET-NAUDIN

Les Crais 2001★

| | | 1 ha | 3,600 | 🍷 | 11–15 € |

A fine wine for a *village*, it came close to receiving two stars, It interested the Jury, which all agreed on the quality of the vinification. It is worth ageing a little. Its acidity is such that it could be laid down for several years. Deep garnet colour, for the moment it is bathed in vanilla-flavoured youthfulness.

☛ Doudet-Naudin, 3, rue Henri-Cyrot, 21420 Savigny-lès-Beaune, tel. 03.80.21.51.74, fax 03.80.21.50.69, e-mail doudet-naudin@wanadoo.fr ☑
☞ by appt.
☛ Yves Doudet

GUY FONTAINE ET JACKY VION 2000★

| | 2 ha | 6,000 | 🍷 | 8–11 € |

This is Don Camillo's wine! It's true; the real Don Camillo de Vallotta, who was the inspiration for the literary series, enjoyed visiting Burgundy and came to taste and lunch at the estate. One could have offered Peppone this red Santenay, burlat cherry in colour, with integrated oak and a powerful, bulky body. Faithful to type and without excessive signs of extraction. A very complex *village* to leave in the cellar for at least two years, then to serve with wild boar.

☛ GAEC des Vignerons, rue du Bourg, 71150 Remigny, tel. 03.85.87.03.35, fax 03.85.87.03.35 ☑
☞ by appt.
☛ Fontaine-Vion

DOM. VINCENT GIRARDIN

Clos du Beauregard 2001★★

| | 1er cru | 1 ha | 7,000 | 🍷 | 11–15 € |

Coup de coeur in the 1995, 2002 and 2003 editions, this estate was again awarded the distinction for this truly superb white Beauregard. It was unanimously admired for its pale-gold colour, its floral mineral quality and its subtle bouquet; and appreciated for its richness, which is all finesse, and its fruity freshness that overwhelms the palate. Vincent Girardin also offered a **red Maladière 2001**, one star. Eighteen months in cask mean it will need to be laid down for three to five years.

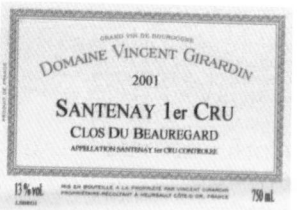

His Santenay 2000 was served at a dinner for French and German parliamentarians in January 2003.

🍇 Caveau des Grands Crus, pl. de la Bascule, 21190 Chassagne-Montrachet, tel. 03.80.21.96.06, fax 03.80.21.96.06 ☑
🍷 ev.day 10am–1pm 2pm–7pm
🍇 Vincent Girardin

DOM. DES HAUTES-CORNIERES 2000★

	3 ha	18,000	🍶	8–11 €

Santenay: from the water-nymph to the god of wine. For this is also a spa. But this wine will not encourage you to go and take the waters; a lively red colour, the Pinot Noir really goes on about ripe red berries, and while it needs to pacify its oak, it seems to have good keeping qualities. A good finish on the palate. It won't be ready for drinking for another three years. The **red Premier Cru Beaurepaire 2000 (11–15 €)** is very much in keeping with the vintage. It received a special mention.
🍇 Ph. Chapelle et Fils, Dom. des Hautes-Cornières, 21590 Santenay, tel. 03.80.20.60.09, fax 03.80.20.61.01, e-mail contact@domainechapelle.com ☑
🍷 ev.day. ex. Sun. 9am–12noon 2pm–5pm; cl. Aug.

LABOURE-ROI 2001★★

	n.c.	n.c.	🍶	11–15 €

The Cottin brothers and their team could serve this wine in the course of a luncheon for the financial press, to discuss the price of their shares on the stock-market. This Santenay has the colour of red fruit and the aromas of black fruit. Stendalian…The mark of the winemaker is very discernible, together with the richness and concentration. A fine future, up to five years at least. "Perhaps a style rather than a terroir," the Jury commented. Quail cooked with grapes would go brilliantly with it.
🍇 Labouré-Roi, rue Lavoisier, 21700 Nuits-Saint-Georges, tel. 03.80.62.64.00, fax 03.80.62.64.10 ☑
🍷 by appt.

LENAIC LEGROS 2001★

	3.5 ha	2,500	🍶	11–15 €

Lénaïc Legros took over the family estate in 1998, after a course of oenological studies. This newcomer offered a wine which should not be drunk too soon (two to three years) and shows excellent qualities. Garnet-red and leaving tears on the glass, it develops aromas of well-ripened cherries. Slightly spicy on the palate, still a touch tannic but full, and long on the fruit. After visiting this estate do go up as far as Les Trois Croix (ten minutes walk) and look at the little 15th century church at the hamlet of Narosse.
🍇 Dom. Lénaïc Legros, 6, rue de la Charrière, 21590 Santenay, tel. 03.80.20.69.21, fax 03.80.20.69.21 ☑
🍷 by appt.

RENE LEQUIN-COLIN

Vieilles Vignes 2000★★

1er cru	1 ha	3,200	🍶	11–15 €

René Lequin-Colin and his wife have just celebrated their tenth harvest in their own winery, after working for 30 years in the family business. This year their recently-married son has joined them, a happy event the Jury's award of the *coup de cœur* will allow them to celebrate. Full and fleshy, produced on 1 ha of *vieilles vignes*, the wine is a very intense red with purple highlights, a generous and concentrated bouquet (red berries, slight oakiness). After a good opening it reveals itself as fleshy, full and rich, with tannins that do not

unbalance it. Its length is promising. The **white Les Hates 2001** was awarded a star.
🍇 René Lequin-Colin, 10, rue de Lavau, 21590 Santenay, tel. 03.80.20.66.71, fax 03.80.20.66.70, e-mail renelequin@aol.com ☑
🍷 by appt.

JEROME MASSON

Beaurepaire 2001★

1er cru	0.8 ha	450	🍶	15–23 €

In 1998, Jérôme Masson took over an ancient farm belonging to the famous Chateau de La Rochepot, an estate nestled in the Hautes Côtes de Beaune and managed by his father, Maurice Masson, then by his mother Nadine. We have come to the Côte to honour this Beaurepaire, an excellent wine in all its aspects. A bluish ruby-red colour, it conforms to the classic norms. Fairly wild aromas of musk and undergrowth; the are tannins present but the wine has depth, is robust and chewy, with good body. Rabbit in a mustard sauce was strongly recommended as its dinner-partner.
🍇 Jérôme Masson, rue Haute, 21340 La Rochepot, tel. 03.80.21.89.72, fax 03.80.21.89.72, e-mail domainemasson@hotmail.com ☑ 🏠
🍷 by appt.

LUCIEN MUZARD ET FILS

Champs Claude Vieilles Vignes 2001★

	2.69 ha	16,500	🍶	11–15 €

There were a great many wines presented for our tasting and the **red Clos Faubard Premier Cru 2001** deserved a star, so characteristic is it of the Santenay wines. This relatively unknown *climat* for Champs Claude offered a wine of a perfect colour. The still delicate bouquet sketches out an evolutionary path on red berries with a barely perceptible oakiness. On the palate it is like biting into cherries. Elegance and substance make up the successful result.
🍇 Lucien Muzard et Fils, 11 bis, rue de la Cour-Verreuil, BP 25, 21590 Santenay, tel. 03.80.20.61.85, fax 03.80.20.66.02, e-mail lucien-muzard-et-fils@wanadoo.fr ☑
🍷 by appt.

NICOLAS PERE ET FILS

Les Charmes Dessous Elevé en fût de chêne 2001★

	0.35 ha	2,000	🍶	8–11 €

A family estate for six generations, with 13 ha in production and of which the head office is at Nolay, stronghold of the Carnot family which provided a President of the French Republic in 1887. The Les Charmes Dessous is the stuff that dreams are made of. Light ruby-red, this clean wine, with its airy kirsch bouquet and supple, full, delicious, welcoming palate, where one has the impression of biting into fruit.
🍇 Dom. Nicolas Père et Fils, 38, rte de Cirey, 21340 Nolay, tel. 03.80.21.82.92, fax 03.80.21.85.47, e-mail nicolas-alain2@wanadoo.fr ☑
🍷 ev.day. 8am–12noon 1.30pm–7pm; cl. 1 week in Feb. and in Aug.
🍇 Alain Nicolas

JEAN-CLAUDE REGNAUDOT ET FILS 2000★

	0.8 ha	1,700	🍶	8–11 €

Deep cherry-red with garnet tinges, this Santenay makes a good impression right from first contact with the bouquet, with frank raspberry notes and oak that is not excessive: the cask is of noble origin and the balance of aromas is pleasant. On the palate, acidity and tannins hold equal sway. Power and suppleness combine without negating the fruit. For serving in two to three years' time with an Epoisse cheese, for example.

➥ Jean-Claude Regnaudot et Fils, Grande-Rue, 71150 Dezize-lès-Maranges, tel. 03.85.91.15.95, fax 03.85.91.16.45 ☑
Ⴑ by appt.

PAUL REITZ 2000★

| | n.c. | 8,500 | ⅠⅢ | 11–15 € |

Jean, known as Dury, Reitz came from the Saar around 1810. He made large wooden barrels and casks, and soon after the family began producing its own wine. We are nearing the bicentenary of this wine-merchant firm, situated on the border of the Côtes de Nuits and of Beaune. Its Santenay 2000 holds well to the road. Its colour is dazzling, very successful. The explosive fruitiness tends towards

cherry-stones and the fresh, straightforward body is a clear indication that one is not wasting one's time.

➥ SA Paul Reitz, 120–122, Grande-Rue, 21700 Corgoloin, tel. 03.80.62.98.24, fax 03.80.62.96.83, e-mail paul.reitz@telepost.fr

ROUX PERE ET FILS

Beauregard 2000★

| ■ 1er cru | 0.76 ha | 3,500 | ⅠⅢ | 15–23 € |

Marcel Roux established his wine-producing estate in 1960. Today it covers 35 ha. This intense ruby-red Beauregard has a delicious, pronounced bouquet of ripe red berries. Elegant throughout the tasting, it evolves on tannins that are fresh and already integrated, giving a most agreeable silkiness. A fine wine for consumption during the next two to three years.

➥ Dom. Roux Père et Fils, 21190 Saint-Aubin, tel. 03.80.21.32.92, fax 03.80.21.35.00 ☑
Ⴑ by appt.

Côte de Beaune (South)

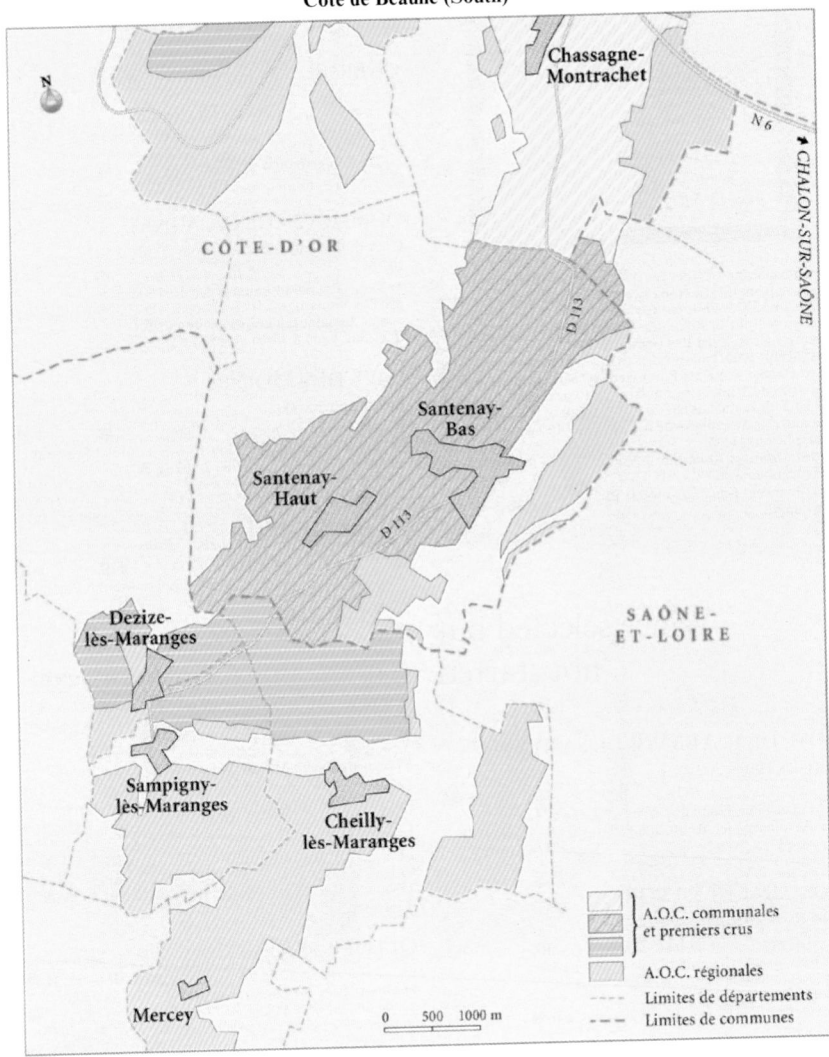

DOM. DES VIGNES DES DEMOISELLES
2001★

| | 1.08 ha | 6,500 | ⅏ | 11–15 € |

A few kilometres to the south of Nolay is Change, home of the Demangeot family who are already well-known to our readers. Their Santenay will take the road to Paradise once it has spent three to four years in the purgatory of the cellar. Clear-cut, with a bouquet tending towards humus and ripe fruit; the wine has more weight than length, at least for the moment. But the tannins are full of promise.
➽ SCE du Dom. Gabriel Demangeot et Fils, rue de Santenay, 21340 Change, tel. 03.85.91.11.10, fax 03.85.91.16.83 ☑
☖ by appt.

JEAN-MARC VINCENT
Beaurepaire 2001★★

| 1er cru | 0.73 ha | 2,000 | ⅏ | 11–15 € |

The revelation of the year! Jean-Marc Vincent (not to mention Anne-Marie) took over the business from his grandfather in 1997. While he took the *coup de coeur* with this well-turned-out Beaurepaire, he also did well with two other Premiers Crus: a **red Les Gravières 2001**, one star, and a **red Passetemps 2000**, two stars. As to this superb dark garnet-red, almost bluish wine, its Pinot element concentrates on musk and crushed fruit before making the "peacock fan" on the palate. Full-bodied, with depth, robustness, presence, and its ripe and elegant tannins are based on well-integrated oak. The future belongs to it.
➽ Jean-Marc et Anne-Marie Vincent, 3, rue Sainte-Agathe, 21590 Santenay, tel. 03.80.20.67.37, fax 03.80.20.67.37, e-mail vincent.j-m@wanadoo.fr ☑
☖ by appt.

Wines selected but not starred

DOM. DE L' ABBAYE DE SANTENAY
Clos des Hâtes 2001

| | 1.76 ha | 2,000 | ⅏ | 11–15 € |

➽ Michel Clair, Dom. de l'Abbaye, 2, rue de Lavau, 21590 Santenay, tel. 03.80.20.62.55, fax 03.80.20.65.37 ☑
☖ by appt.

DOM. BACHEY-LEGROS
Clos Rousseau 2001

| 1er cru | 0.95 ha | 2,150 | ⅏ | 11–15 € |

➽ Dom. Bachey-Legros, 12, rue de la Charrière, 21590 Santenay-le-Haut, tel. 03.80.20.64.14, fax 03.80.20.64.14, e-mail christiane.bachey-legros@wanadoo.fr ☑
☖ by appt.

CLAUDINE CHERRIER 2001

| | 2.2 ha | 7,000 | ▯⅏ | 8–11 € |

➽ Claudine Cherrier, 9–13, rue de la Crêt, 21590 Santenay, tel. 03.80.20.66.90, fax 03.80.20.64.74 ☑
☖ by appt.

DOM. CHEVROT
Clos Rousseau 2001

| | n.c. | 8,000 | ▯⅏⚭ | 11–15 € |

➽ Catherine and Fernand Chevrot, Dom. Chevrot, 19, rte de Couches, 71150 Cheilly-lès-Maranges, tel. 03.85.91.10.55, fax 03.85.91.13.24, e-mail domaine.chevrot@wanadoo.fr ☑ ⌂
☖ ev.day 9am–12noon 1.30pm–6pm; Sun. 9am–12noon

DOM. DE LA CHOUPETTE 2001

| | 11 ha | 15,000 | ⅏ | 8–11 € |

➽ Dom. de La Choupette, 2, pl. de la Mairie, 21590 Santenay, tel. 03.80.20.60.27, fax 03.80.20.65.70 ☑
☖ ev.day. 8am–12noon 2pm–6pm; cl. 10–20 Aug.
➽ Ph. and J.-Ch. Gutrin

GABRIEL AND PAUL JOUARD 2000

| | 1.3 ha | 3,000 | ⅏ | 8–11 € |

➽ Dom. Gabriel and Paul Jouard, 3, rue du Petit-Puits, 21190 Chassagne-Montrachet, tel. 03.80.21.94.73, fax 03.80.21.31.94, e-mail domgetpauljouard@club-internet.fr ☑
☖ by appt.

DOM. RAYMOND LAUNAY
Clos de Gatsulard Monopole 2000

| | 2.95 ha | 12,000 | ⅏ | 8–11 € |

➽ Dom. Raymond Launay, rue des Charmots, 21630 Pommard, tel. 03.80.24.08.03, fax 03.80.24.12.87, e-mail domaine.launay@wanadoo.fr ☑
☖ ev.day. 9am–6.30pm groups by appt.

CAVE DES MOINES
Beauregard 2000

| 1er cru | n.c. | 7,400 | ⅏ | 15–23 € |

➽ Naudin-Varrault, 1, pl. du Jet-d'Eau, 21590 Santenay, tel. 03.80.20.60.40, fax 03.80.20.63.26 ☑
☖ by appt.
➽ R. Fairchild

CH. MOROT-GAUDRY 2000

| | 0.67 ha | 1000 | ▯⅏ | 8–11 € |

➽ Bernard and Chantal Morot-Gaudry, Moulin Pignot, 71150 Paris-l'Hôpital, tel. 03.85.91.11.09, fax 03.85.91.11.09 ☑
☖ by appt.

DOM. JEAN AND GENO MUSSO 2000

| | 0.6 ha | 3,000 | ⅏ | 8–11 € |

➽ Ch. de Sassangy, Le Château, 71390 Sassangy, tel. 03.85.96.18.61, fax 03.85.96.18.62 ☑
☖ by appt.
➽ Jean and Geno Musso

DOM. CLAUDE NOUVEAU
Les Charmes Dessus 2000

| | 0.9 ha | 5,500 | ⅏ | 8–11 € |

➽ EARL Dom. Claude Nouveau, Marchezeuil, 21340 Change, tel. 03.85.91.13.34, fax 03.85.91.10.39 ☑
☖ by appt.

OLIVIER PERE ET FILS 2000

| | 2 ha | 8,000 | ⅏ | 11–15 € |

➽ Olivier Père et Fils, 5, rue Gaudin, 21590 Santenay, tel. 03.80.20.61.35, fax 03.80.20.64.82, e-mail antoine.olivier2@wanadoo.fr ☑
☖ by appt.

DOM. PRIEUR-BRUNET

Maladière 2000

■ 1er cru	5 ha	30,000	〔Ⅱ〕	11–15 €

☛ Dom. Prieur-Brunet, rue de Narosse, 21590 Santenay, tel. 03.80.20.60.56, fax 03.80.20.64.31, e-mail uny-prieur@prieur-santenay.com ☑
☶ by appt.
☛ Dominique Prieur

SORINE ET FILS

Beaurepaire 2001

■ 1er cru	0.9 ha	5,000	〔Ⅱ〕	8–11 €

☛ Dom. Sorine et Fils, 4, rue Petit, Le Haut-Village, 21590 Santenay, tel. 03.80.20.66.27, fax 03.80.20.61.65 ☑
☶ by appt.

ROMUALD VALOT

Clos des Hates Elevé en fût de chêne 2000

■ 1er cru	n.c.	3,600	〔Ⅱ〕	8–11 €

☛ SARL Bourgogne Romuald Valot, 14, rue des Tonneliers, BP 213, 21206 Beaune, tel. 03.80.25.91.30

Maranges

The Maranges vineyard is in Saône-et-Loire (Chailly, Dezize and Sampigny). Since 1989, following a reorganization, it has had its own AOC, which includes six Premiers Crus. Wine production here is predominantly of red, with some white; the reds may also be labelled AOC Côte de Beaune-Villages, which is how they were previously sold. The wines are fruity, full-bodied and well-structured; they can age for between five and ten years. In 2002 AOC Maranges produced 7,585 hl of red wine and 244 hl of white.

DOM. BACHELET

La Fussière Vieilles Vignes 2000★

■ 1er cru	5 ha	20,000	〔Ⅱ〕	8–11 €

One hundred per cent destalked, quite a long period in tank (compared with others), this is a deep red, nicely limpid Pinot Noir. Initially oaky (mocha, vanilla) on the nose, it evolves towards aromas of blackcurrant liqueur. The first impression is amiable, without forcing the pace, then the substance floods the palate. The tannins are well set-up. Not too much weight, but the sort of elegance that is most pleasing and a notable length. As a Premier Cru that is well up to the mark, it will be excellent with a côte de boeuf in two to four years' time.
☛ Dom. Bernard Bachelet et Fils, rue Maranges, 71150 Dezize-lès-Maranges, tel. 03.85.91.16.11, fax 03.85.91.16.48 ☑
☶ by appt.

DOM. MAURICE CHARLEUX ET FILS

Vieilles Vignes 2001★★

■ 1er cru	0.65 ha	2,700	〔Ⅱ〕	8–11 €

Maurice Charleux and his son Vincent work some 13 ha in Les Maranges and at Santenay. Their 2001 Vieilles Vignes is the "Phoenix of the inhabitants of these vines" (to paraphrase La Fontaine). Purplish red in colour, it has a complex bouquet combining cherries, raspberries and stewed prunes. Balanced and compact, this beautiful wine needs several years in the cellar in order to "take its time" and fulfil yours. Apart from that, the **red La Fussière 2001** received one star and the **red Les Clos Roussots 2001** a special mention.
☛ Dom. Maurice Charleux et Fils, Petite-Rue, 71150 Dezize-lès-Maranges, tel. 03.85.91.15.15, fax 03.85.91.11.81 ☑
☶ by appt.

DOM. CHEVROT 2001★

■	0.62 ha	3,500	〔Ⅱ〕	8–11 €

One of the most eminent Burgundy tasters wrote on his card, "Almost perfect," mentioning its fine balance, its colour, finesse, purity, its terroir accent, its floral side, its butter and hazelnut notes and its touch of honey. The Chardonnay has something to say here! This 2001 vintage still needs to age a little before being served with grilled monkfish. This estate also received a special mention for the **red Village 2001**. The country home of seven people, including two qualified oenologist sons, the future of this estate is assured.
☛ Catherine and Fernand Chevrot, Dom. Chevrot, 19, rte de Couches, 71150 Cheilly-lès-Maranges, e-mail domaine.chevrot@wanadoo.fr ☑ ☶
☶ ev.day. 9am–12noon 1.30pm–6pm; Sun. 9am–12noon

DOM. CYROT-BUTHIAU 2001★

■	24 ha	4,500	〔Ⅱ〕	11–15 €

This wine will keep, but should one do so? Limpid and brilliant, showing a slight oakiness on a spicey and raspberry base, this 2001 vintage is already well-balanced. Its tannins are not astringent, the structure is well-made. An elegant wine to drink with eggs poached in red wine.
☛ Dom. Cyrot-Buthiau, rte d'Autun, 21630 Pommard, tel. 03.80.22.06.56, fax 03.80.24.00.86, e-mail cyrot.buthiau@wanadoo.fr ☑
☶ by appt.

DOM. CLAUDE NOUVEAU 2001★

■	1.2 ha	6,000	⬛〔Ⅱ〕◆	5–8 €

Balanced, fully characteristic of its vintage, this is a pleasant and well-made, carefully worked wine which offers a good balance between the lightly-treated body and the cask. A certain firmness on the finish, but the palate is supple and fruity. An excellent wine to serve with a roast fowl.
☛ EARL Dom. Claude Nouveau, Marchezeuil, 21340 Change, tel. 03.85.91.13.34, fax 03.85.91.10.39 ☑
☶ by appt.

DOM. PONSARD-CHEVALIER

Clos Roussot 2000★

■ 1er cru	055 ha	3,500	〔Ⅱ〕	8–11 €

If you are familiar with the wine geography of Burgundy, you will know that this *climat* includes both the Santenay and Maranges AOCs, and that it was divided by the departmental border for no good reason two centuries ago. Intense garnet-red in colour, its bouquet showing a preference for macerated fruit and pepper, this 2000 vintage is fine and silky on the palate, as gentle as an Easter lamb and allowing a little fleshiness to appear beneath its roundness. Pleasant to drink from now on.
☛ Dom. Ponsard-Chevalier, 2, Les Tilles, 21590 Santenay, tel. 03.80.20.60.87, fax 03.80.20.61.10 ☑
☶ by appt.

SERGE PROST ET FILS 2000★

■	1 ha	4,000	⬛ ◆	5–8 €

Founded by the grandfather on his return from the First World War in 1914, the property today covers almost 20 ha. It offered a 2000 vintage which is still somewhat firm, with a structure and acidity that augur well for the future. Bouquet and flavour characteristically blackcurrant. Lively, the palate is not lacking in tonus and an interesting potential shows through. A wine to serve with a highly-seasoned dish.
☛ EARL Serge Prost et Fils, Les Foisons, 71490 Couches, tel. 03.85.49.64.00, fax 03.85.49.64.00 ☑
☶ by appt.

JEAN-CLAUDE REGNAUDOT ET FILS

La Fussière 2000★

■ 1er cru	0.82 ha	2,800	〔Ⅱ〕	8–11 €

This 8 ha estate has not missed its target. Very expressive in its colour and aromas (cherry, a touch of undergrowth), this Pinot Noir is overflowing with substance, tannins, power. It sits comfortably on the palate. The fruit is still very much present, which encourages one to allow it the time to reach its full harmony in the cellar. Leave it there for one to three years then serve it with a leg of lamb. The **Les Clos Roussots red 2001**, full-bodied and spirited, was awarded a star. In two to four years' time it will be excellent with a coq au vin.

🐂 Jean-Claude Regnaudot et Fils, Grande-Rue, 71150 Dezize-lès-Maranges, tel. 03.85.91.15.95, fax 03.85.91.16.45 ☑

✕ by appt.

PAUL REITZ

Clos Roussots 2000★

■ 1er cru	n.c.	7,200	▌ ◖▯	11–15 €

From a *négociant-éleveur* in the Côte de Nuits, this Premier Cru is an attractive, intense brick-red colour. The clean aromas evoke blackcurrants with a hint of aniseed, This wine should soften but it is already full-bodied, rounded and formed in an honest, fruity way. Serve it in two to three years' time with a côte de boeuf.

🐂 SA Paul Reitz, 120–122, Grande-Rue, 21700 Corgoloin, tel. 03.80.62.98.24, fax 03.80.62.96.83, e-mail paul.reitz@telepost.fr

Wines selected but not starred

DOM. DU BEAUREGARD

Les Clos Roussots 2000

■ 1er cru	0.22 ha	1,400	◖▯	8–11 €

🐂 Michel Depernon, Dom. du Beauregard, 9, rue de Mercey, 71510 Saint-Sernin-du-Plain, tel. 03.85.45.55.17, fax 03.85.45.55.17, e-mail michel.depernon@wanadoo.fr ☑

✕ by appt.

DOM. JEAN-CLAUDE BELLAND 2001

■	1.81 ha	6,000	◖▯	8–11 €

🐂 Jean-Claude Belland, 21590 Santenay, tel. 03.80.20.61.90, fax 03.80.20.65.60

DOM. JEAN-FRANCOIS BOUTHENET

Sur le chêne Elevé en fût de chêne 2001

■	0.37 ha	2,500		8–11 €

🐂 Jean-François Bouthenet, Mercey, 4, rue du Four, 71150 Cheilly-lès-Maranges, tel. 03.85.91.14.29, fax 03.85.91.18.24 ☑

✕ by appt.

Y. ET C. CONTAT-GRANGE

Le Clos des Loyères 2001

■ 1er cru	0.28 ha	1,200	◖▯	8–11 €

🐂 EARL Contat-Grangé, Grande-Rue, 71150 Dezize-lès-Maranges, tel. 03.85.91.15.87, fax 03.85.91.12.54, e-mail contat-grange@wanadoo.fr ☑

✕ by appt.

MARINOT-VERDUN

La Fussière 2001

■ 1er cru	n.c.	n.c.	▌	5–8 €

🐂 Marinot-Verdun, Cave de Mazenay, 71510 Saint-Sernin-du-Plain, tel. 03.85.49.67.19, fax 03.85.45.57.21 ☑

✕ ev.day ex. Sun. 8am–12noon 2pm–6pm

DOM. DES ROUGES-QUEUES 2001

■	0.8 ha	2,700	◖▯	8–11 €

🐂 Isabelle and Jean-Yves Vantey, 10, rue Saint-Antoine, 71150 Sampigny-lès-Maranges, tel. 03.85.91.18.69, fax 03.85.91.18.69, e-mail domaine.des.rougesqueues@wanadoo.fr ☑

✕ by appt.

Côte de Beaune-Villages

Not to be confused with the Côte de Nuits-Villages appellation, which has its own special production area, the Côte de Beaune-Villages appellation is not confined to a specific place but may be used by all the red-wine Appellations Communales in the Côte de Beaune, with the exception of Beaune, Aloxe-Corton, Pommard and Volnay. In 2002, 192 hl were declared.

CHANSON PERE ET FILS 2001★

■	n.c.	18,000	▌ ◖▯ ⚬	11–15 €

Deep and frank ruby-red, this wine doesn't hide its colour. The blackcurrant leaf-bud bouquet reminds us that many famous perfumes concocted at Grasse have to thank this leaf-bud for their (Burgundian) charm. Lively but also rounded, this wine comes from a good level in the appellation.

🐂 Dom. Chanson Père et Fils, 10, rue Paul-Chanson, BP 232, 21206 Beaune Cedex, tel. 03.80.25.97.97, fax 03.80.24.17.42, e-mail tmarion@vins-chanson.com

LA TOUR BLONDEAU 2001★

■	n.c.	n.c.	▌ ◖▯ ⚬	11–15 €

Deep purple in colour, this wine was matured in cask, but the light toasted notes of oak against a background of fruit and liquorice in no way detracts from it. It has more weight than power, a certain robustness and is very characteristic of the appellation.

🐂 Grands Vins Forgeot, 15, rue du Château, 21200 Beaune, tel. 03.80.24.80.50, fax 03.80.22.55.88

Wines selected but not starred

ALBERT BICHOT 2000

■	n.c.	20,000	▌ ◖▯ ⚬	8–11 €

🐂 Maison Albert Bichot, 6 bis, bd Jacques-Copeau, 21200 Beaune, tel. 03.80.24.37.37, fax 03.80.24.37.38

Côte Chalonnaise

Bourgogne Côte Chalonnaise

The AOC Bourgogne Côte Chalonnaise was created on 27 February 1990. It produced 20,464 hl of red wine and 7,350 hl of white in 2002. According to the system also applied in the Hautes Côtes, agreements about quality are reached following a second tasting to supplement the compulsory tasting that takes place everywhere.

Located between Chagny and Saint-Gengoux-le-National (Saône et Loire), the Côte Chalonnaise has an individual identity that deserves the recognition it has received.

BLASON DE BOURGOGNE 2001★

| ■ | 15 ha | 80,000 | ◫ | 5–8 € |

A GIE (*Groupe d'Intérêt Economique*, Group with common economic interests) formed by several Burgundy cooperatives, including La Chablisienne. This Blason, whose head-office is in the Chablis, gets its supplies from the cooperative at Buxy. Intense garnet-red, this vintage offers a delicate bouquet of black fruits. Concentrated, the palate is well-made and the tannins are sufficiently fine for the wine to be ready to drink from now on.

☚ GIE Blasons de Bourgogne, rue du Serein, 89800 Chablis, tel. 03.86.42.88.34, fax 03.86.42.83.75, e-mail blasons@blasonsdebourgogne.fr

CH. DE CARY POTET

Vieilles Vignes 2001★

| ■ | 1 ha | 4,500 | ◫ | 5–8 € |

Indispensable at an architects' banquet: Pierre du Besset, co-owner of Cary Potet is in fact one of the most qualified members of that profession in France, and he is not alone in practising wine-growing in Burgundy as a hobby. Light red, this Pinot Noir has a fruity and expressive nose. It needs aerating to open in a fine and light way, without over-playing its hand. Ready to drink now.

☚ Charles and Pierre du Besset, Ch. de Cary Potet, 71390 Buxy, tel. 03.85.92.14.48, fax 03.85.92.11.88 ☑
☓ by appt.

DOM. DU CRAY

Vieilles Vignes 2000★

| ■ | 4 ha | 10,000 | ◫ | 5–8 € |

Les Narjoux have been winemakers in this village since 1640. This 2000 vintage, whose colour shows a few signs of evolution, offers a charming bouquet, well in place, where one finds notes of black fruits, spices and oak. Supported by tannins, the richness shows a well-structured make-up, with plenty of substance. This is a wine which will give pleasure.

☚ Roger and Michèle Narjoux, Dom. du Cray, Cidex 712, 71640 Saint-Martin-sous-Montaigu, tel. 03.85.45.13.17, fax 03.85.45.29.10 ☑
☓ by appt.

DIONYSOS 2001★

| ■ | 1 ha | 3,000 | ◫ | 8–11 € |

A property acquired in 2001 and which, for a beginner, is not doing too badly…as one says in Burgundy. A successful wine, even very successful, one person wrote. Balanced, with a consistant substance, fleshy at the opening, a touch tannic on the middle-palate, it reestablishes itself admirably on the finish. The oak plays its recital against a background of blackcurrant. The colour is fairly intense, like all the 2001 vintage in this appellation

☚ Corinne Tournier and Thierry Gautier, GAEC Dionysos, quartier de la Gare, 71460 Culles-les-Roches, tel. 03.85.44.01.90, fax 03.85.44.08.61 ☑
☓ by appt.

DOM. MICHEL GOUBARD ET FILS

Mont-Avril 2001★★

| ■ | 8 ha | 60,000 | ■ ☙ | 5–8 € |

The illustrious Burgundy historian, the Abbé Courtépée, had pleasant words to say about the Mont-Avril *climat*. The Goubard estate express their gratitude to him on the label of this 2001 vintage, all dressed in episcopal colours. Its aromas? Blackberry jam. The sin of covetousness… Rounded on the palate, highly perfumed, very drinkable, it is a good product. The tannins are fine and very much present, as they should be in a Côte Chalonnaise, which must also show muscle and power.

☚ Dom. Michel Goubard et Fils, 71390 Saint-Désert, tel. 03.85.47.91.06, fax 03.85.47.98.12 ☑
☓ by appt.

DOM. DES PIERRES BLANCHES 2001★

| ■ | 3.1 ha | 18,000 | ◫ | 5–8 € |

The cellars at Buxy house the trifling product of 890 ha of vineyards! It does not, however, sacrifice quality to volume, as is shown by this 2001 vintage red of which the oak and the tannins need more time, but which occupies an honourable place with its bouquet of undergrowth and game. The **red 2001 La Buxynoise** is produced on a vast scale, but still shows finesse and character. It also received one star.

☚ Cave des Vignerons de Buxy, Les Vignes de La Croix, BP 6, 71390 Buxy, tel. 03.85.92.03.03, fax 03.85.92.08.06, e-mail labuxynoise@cave-buxy.fr ☑
☓ ev.day ex. Sun. 9am–12noon 2pm–6.30pm; groups by appt.

VENOT

La Corvée 2001★★

| ■ | 0.67 ha | 2,300 | ◫ | 5–8 € |

Strongly recommended, and not only to lovers of original wine labels! We are dealing with a family GAEC (*Groupement Agricole d'Exploitation en Commun*, a form of cooperative); husband and wife, and the husband's brother. The **red Côte Chalonnaise 2001** is absolutely remarkable. As to its Chardonnay version, it also is very highly ranked in the appellation. Limpid, golden, highly perfumed (aromas of grapes!), this wine is marvellously rounded with just a touch of oakiness, going hand in hand with its tannins. Needs to age for a year or two.

☚ GAEC Venot, La Corvée, 71390 Moroges, tel. 03.85.47.94.02, fax 03.85.47.90.20 ☑
☓ by appt.

Wines selected but not starred

CAVE DE GENOUILLY 2001

| ■ | 6 ha | 20,000 | ◫ | 3–5 € |

☚ Cave des vignerons de Genouilly, 71460 Genouilly, tel. 03.85.49.23.72, fax 03.85.49.23.58 ☑
☓ ev.day ex. Sun. 8am–12noon 2pm–6pm

DOM. GOUFFIER

Clos de Malpertuis 2001

| ■ | 1 ha | n.c. | ■ ☙ | 5–8 € |

☚ Dom. Gouffier, 11, Grande-Rue, 71150 Fontaines, tel. 03.85.91.49.66, fax 03.85.91.46.98, e-mail jerome.gouffier@wanadoo.fr ☑
☓ by appt.

DOM. MICHEL ISAIE 2000

| ■ | 0.8 ha | 5,000 | ■ ◫ ☙ | 5–8 € |

☚ Michel Isaïe, chem. de l'Ouche, 71640 Saint-Jean-de-Vaux, tel. 03.85.45.23.32, fax 03.85.45.29.38 ☑
☓ by appt.

DOM. LE MEIX DE LA CROIX 2001

| ■ | 1.1 ha | 6,000 | ◫ | 5–8 € |

☚ Fabienne and Pierre Saint-Arroman, 71640 Saint-Denis-de-Vaux, tel. 03.85.44.34.33, fax 03.85.44.59.86 ☑
☓ by appt.

LOUIS PICAMELOT 2001

| n.c. | 6,800 | 🍷 | 5–8 € |

☛ Louis Picamelot, 12, pl. de la Croix-Blanche, BP 2, 71150 Rully, tel. 03.85.87.13.60, fax 03.85.87.63.81, e-mail louispicamelot@wanadoo.fr ☑
🍴 ev.day 8am–12noon 1.30pm–6.30pm; Sat. Sun. by appt.

Bouzeron

Bouzeron is a little village between Chagny and Rully, well-known for its wines made from the Aligoté grape, the variety most evident in the commune's vineyard of around 62 ha. Planted on slopes slanting east-southeast, on mainly chalky soil, Aligoté makes lively white wine with lots of character, developing into complex wines of a "sharp roundness". The Appellation Bourgogne Aligoté Bouzeron was created in 1979 and was then promoted to AOC status. In 2002, 2,933 hl were declared from 52.86 ha.

DOM. BORGEOT
Les Tournelles 2001★

| 0.5 ha | 2,500 | 🍷 | 5–8 € |

Better than a simple aperitif wine, here is a Bouzeron which will show astonishing charm with a matured goat's milk cheese. Very successful, it demonstrates its kinship with the grape-variety and the terroir. Bright in colour, its aromas are not easy to discern (apples from the orchards of our youth?) On the palate it offers attractive sensations. It is elegant, well-made and will last for two to three years.
☛ Dom. Borgeot, rte de Chassagne, 71150 Remigny, tel. 03.85.87.19.92, fax 03.85.87.19.95 ☑
🍴 by appt.

DOM. CHANZY
Clos de la Fortune 2001★

| 11.25 ha | 58,000 | 🍷 | 5–8 € |

Clos de la Fortune: "With perseverance and a touch of recklessness," said Daniel Chanzy, "I took it over at the age of 21, there where the vines were long dead." That was in 1974. Since then, what a recovery! Open and fine, the bouquet of this 2001 vintage preceeds a supple and fresh attack. The acidity does not overwhelm the fruit. Excellent vinification of a very true-to-type Bouzeron.
☛ Dom. Chanzy, 1, rue de la Fontaine, 71150 Bouzeron, tel. 03.85.87.23.69, fax 03.85.87.62.12, e-mail daniel.chanzy@wanadoo.fr ☑
🍴 by appt.

A. ET P. DE VILLAINE 2001★

| 10 ha | 50,000 | 🍷 | 8–11 € |

This is the personal domain of the co-manager of the Romanée-Conti estate: his secret garden, shared with his wife Pamela. Aubert de Villaine has made a great contribution to the renaissance of the Bouzeron in his AOC. His 2001 vintage is a clear, intense and brilliant colour; the powerful and very complex bouquet swings between mineral (flint) and ripe fruits. The initial impact is lively, with a just measure of acidity, evolving towards very lingering aromas of citrus fruits. Plenty of depth, to develop and enjoy this year or next. Match it with a goat's milk cheese.
☛ A. et P. de Villaine, 2, rue de la Fontaine, 71150 Bouzeron, tel. 03.85.91.20.50, fax 03.85.87.04.70, e-mail dom.devillaine@wanadoo.fr ☑
🍴 by appt.

Wines selected but not starred

PIERRE COGNY ET DAVID DEPRES 2001

| 3 ha | 7,000 | 🍷 | 5–8 € |

☛ Dom. de la Vieille Fontaine, 71150 Bouzeron, tel. 03.85.87.02.29, fax 03.85.87.02.29 ☑
🍴 ev.day 10am–12noon 1.30pm–7pm; Sun. by appt.

FORGEOT PERE ET FILS 2001

| n.c. | n.c. | 🍷 | 5–8 € |

☛ Grands Vins Forgeot, 15, rue du Château, 21200 Beaune, tel. 03.80.24.80.50, fax 03.80.22.55.88

DOM. FRANCE LECHENAULT 2000

| 3.5 ha | 3,300 | 🍷 | 5–8 € |

☛ Mme Reine Léchenault, 11, rue des Dames, 71150 Bouzeron, tel. 03.85.87.17.56, fax 03.85.91.27.17 ☑
🍴 by appt.

ANDRE LHERITIER 2000

| 0.15 ha | 1000 | 🍷 | 5–8 € |

☛ André Lhéritier, 4, bd de la Liberté, 71150 Chagny, tel. 03.85.87.00.09 ☑
🍴 ev.day 8am–11.30am 2pm–7pm

Rully

The Côte Chalonnaise, or Mercurey region, is the transition point between the Côte d'Or and the Mâconnais. The Appellation Rully extends beyond its original commune into Chagny, which is a local centre of gastronomy. In 2002 more white wine was produced – 11,527 hl – than red – 5,935 hl. Grown on soils originating in the Superior Jurassic era, the wines are appealing and generally keep well. Some of the locations classified as Premiers Crus have already established a good reputation.

DOM. CHRISTIAN BELLEVILLE
Les Chauchoux Monopole 2001★

| 5.57 ha | 45,000 | 🍷 | 8–11 € |

This blood-red 2001 vintage offers a certain complexity on the bouquet, within the mineral quality characteristic of the AOC, with notes of dried fruits. After a good opening, the fruit settles on the middle palate. Dense, but still tannic, this is a well-matured Rully which needs to be laid down in the cellar for two years.
☛ Dom. Christian Belleville, 1, rue des Bordes, 71150 Rully, tel. 03.85.91.06.00, fax 03.85.91.06.01, e-mail dombellevi@aol.com ☑
🍴 by appt.

JEAN-CLAUDE BRELIERE
Les Margotés 2001★

| 1er cru | 2 ha | 9,000 | 🍷 | 11–15 € |

Jean-Claude Brelière first learned English, Spanish and German, then he went through the CFPPA (*Centre de Formation Professionel de Promotion Agricole*, a prestigious agricultural college). His Les Margotés have panache. Golden in colour, its aromas are of humus, spices, undergrowth and mushrooms. Absolutely captivating. The oak is well-integrated and without agression. The balance and length received the unanimous appreciation of our Jurors, who suggested serving this wine with crayfish, or any sauced fish dish.

🍷 Jean-Claude Brelière, 1, pl. de l'Eglise, 71150 Rully, tel. 03.85.91.22.01, fax 03.85.87.20.64, e-mail domainebreliere@wanadoo.fr ☑
🍷 by appt.

DOM. MICHEL BRIDAY 2001★

	3 ha	15,000	🍶🍷🥂	11–15 €

Ready to drink now, this 2001 vintage should nevertheless age well. The touch of green on its gold colour is quite traditional. The bouquet is made up of roses, citrus fruits and mineral, in a word, complex. Lemony at the opening, on the palate it is enticing and long. Undoubtedly this is a very pleasant wine, though perhaps more suitable for serving with fish than with white meat.

🍷 Dom. Michel Briday, 31, Grande-Rue, BP 7, 71150 Rully, tel. 03.85.87.07.90, fax 03.85.91.25.68, e-mail stephane.briday@wanadoo.fr ☑ 🏠
🍷 ev.day 9am–12noon 2pm–6pm; Sat. Sun. by appt.
🍷 Stéphane Briday

DOM. CHANZY

L'Hermitage 2001★

	14.2 ha	n.c.	🍶🍷🥂	8–11 €

This estate was taken over by Daniel Chanzy in 1974 when he was 21 years old. Today it covers 41 ha spread over three Côtes. A fine example of a first generation *vigneron*. This wine should not be taken from the cellar too soon. Very characteristic of the Côte Chalonnaise, ruby-red leaning toward garnet, it has mineral accents, together with a hint of musk. The cask is present but not excessive, the tannins are nicely balanced, the acidity particularly noticeable at the finish, the required slight bitterness is in place and the length very adequate. Some potential for ageing. The **Rully l'Hermitage white 2000** received a special mention. It would go well with veal escaloppes à la crème.

🍷 Dom. Chanzy, 1, rue de la Fontaine, 71150 Bouzeron, tel. 03.85.87.23.69, fax 03.85.87.62.12, e-mail daniel.chanzy@wanadoo.fr ☑
🍷 by appt.

DOM. DE LA CROIX JACQUELET 2000★

	2.49 ha	19,390	🍷	8–11 €

One is undoubtedly aware that this is part of the vast Faively estate in the Côte Chalonnaise. Pale gold with green highlights, very brilliant, this is an excellently-made white Rully which came close to gaining a second star. Liquorice and linden blossom mingle with the cask, where the wine spent eight months. A little firmness on the finish, but especially freshness. Its acidity indicates a possible life of two to three years. A wine to accompany a rabbit terrine or shellfish.

🍷 SBEV Dom. de la Croix Jacquelet, Cidex 892, 71640 Mercurey, tel. 03.85.45.12.23, fax 03.85.45.26.42 ☑
🍷 by appt.

RAYMOND DUREUIL-JANTHIAL 2001★

	1.43 ha	9,000	🍷	11–15 €

Beneath the traditional, rolled-edged parchment label is a much more original and personal wine. A crystal-clear white whose toasty aromas don't overwhelm the fruit. Finesse, richness, length and even a touch of vigour to animate the scene, which will allow it to keep for two to three years. Another good wine was given a special mention: the **Rully Village red 2001**, light but characteristic and pleasant.

🍷 Raymond Dureuil-Janthial, rue de la Buisserolle, 71150 Rully, tel. 03.85.87.02.37, fax 03.85.87.00.24 ☑
🍷 ev.day 9am–12noon 3pm–7pm Sun. by appt.

VINCENT DUREUIL-JANTHIAL

Maizière 2001★

	0.5 ha	2,700	🍷	11–15 €

Coup de coeur in 2001 with its red 98 vintage. This one has no compunction about following in its footsteps. Garnet ruby-red, its aromas are shared between crystallized fruits and the charred notes from the cask. The first impression is frank, the secondary aromas open out on Morello cherries: an

instant pleasure. It is very representative characteristic of its appellation. The **white Rully Village 2001 (8–11 €)** is charming and very satisfying, practically in the same way, and also received one star.

🍷 Vincent Dureuil-Janthial, rue de la Buisserolle, 71150 Rully, tel. 03.85.87.26.32, fax 03.85.87.15.01, e-mail vincent.dureuil@wanadoo.fr ☑
🍷 by appt.

DOM. JACQUES DURY

Le Meix Cadot 2001★

	1er cru	1.78 ha	5,000	🍶🍷	8–11 €

A family estate since 1958, it has extended and modernized (a new winery in 2000). This very densely coloured Meix Cadot starts with floral prospects on the nose. Round and fleshy, its palate is filled with pleasant flavours with renewed woody aromas which don't overwhelm the fruit. Excellent to drink with grilled fish.

🍷 EARL Dom. Jacques Dury, 16, hameau du Château, 71150 Rully, tel. 03.85.87.14.49, fax 03.85.87.37.54 ☑
🍷 ev.day ex. Sun. 8.30am–12noon 2pm–6.30pm

DOM. DE L'ECETTES

Maizières 2000★

	1.2 ha	6,000	🍶🥂	8–11 €

Two equally estimable wines: a **white Rully Village 2000**, the kind of wine one would like to see more often, and this exceptionally well-balanced Maizières. Yellow-gold, a touch over-matured (honey and dried fruits), it unfolds in a pleasant style, unctuous and *moelleux*. The acidity and richness are beyond reproach. A rare example of a winemaker from the Mâconnais who moved in 1983 and installed himself at Rully, now joined by his son Vincent, with a BTS (*Brevet de Technicien Superieur*, an advanced technical qualification) in oenology from Beaune.

🍷 GAEC Jean and Vincent Daux, Dom. de L'Ecette, 21, rue de Geley, 71150 Rully, tel. 03.85.91.21.52, fax 03.85.91.24.33 ☑
🍷 by appt.

DOM. DE LA FOLIE

Clos Saint-Jacques 2000★

	1er cru	1.69 ha	11,000		11–15 €

Among the national occasions for commemoration in 2004 is the anniversary of Etienne-Jules Marey, one of the founding fathers of the cinema ("chronophotography"): he owned this estate and could never be persuaded to attend the Science Academy at harvest time. *Coup de coeur* in 99, this still family-owned estate, situated partly in Chagny, notably offered this pale-gold Clos Saint-Jacques. A good, fruity nose, floral with aromas of citrus fruit. Fine in every way on the palate, in a year or two it will make a very pleasant accompaniment to a chicken pie. The **red Bellecroix Village 2001 (8–11 €)** would be excellent served with pigeons.

🍷 Dom. de la Folie, 71150 Chagny, tel. 03.85.87.18.59, fax 03.85.87.03.53, e-mail domaine.de.la.folie@wanadoo.fr ☑
🍷 ev.day 9am–6pm
🍷 Noël-Bouton

DOM. DES FROMANGES

La Chatalienne 2001★★

	3 ha	12,000	🍶🍷🥂	8–11 €

Martine and Philippe Protheau run the Fromanges estate at the Château d'Etroyes, where there is a commercial concern of the same name, now owned by the J.-B. Béjot company at Meursault. As to this wine, it is still young and shines in the glass, all clad in gold. Its aromas recall honey, fine spices and dried fruits. Its fleshiness sits on a solid base. Remarkable all round and an ideal wine to serve with large fish dishes.

🍷 Dom. des Fromanges, Ch. d'Etroyes, 71640 Mercurey, tel. 03.85.45.10.84, fax 03.85.45.26.05, e-mail martine@domaine-protheau-mercurey.fr ☑
🍷 ev.day 8am–12noon 2pm–6pm; Sun. by appt.
🍷 Martine and Philippe Protheau

Côte Chalonnais and the Mâconnais

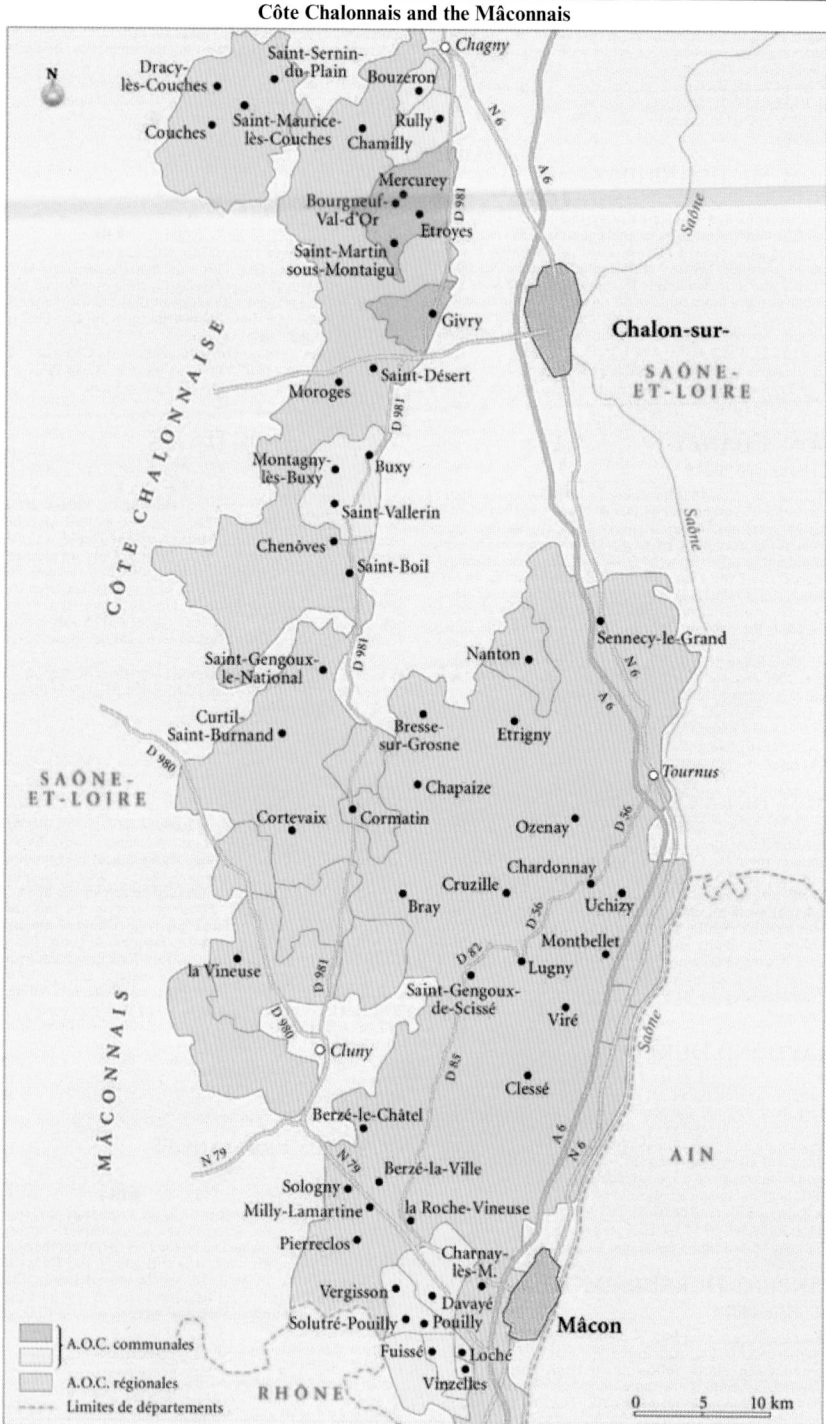

HERITAGE DE NANTOUX

Les Cailloux 2001★

	1.3 ha	4,000	∎⏳♨		5–8 €

Pinot Blanc, they tell us. Really? Pinot Blanc is rare these days. Nevertheless, this straw-gold wine is held in high esteem. It is called Les Cailloux and is very mineral, well suited to its name. Flint? It couldn't be more appropriate: the vineyard is near to the Chassey camp, scene of an important prehistoric culture known as *Chasséenne*. This mineral quality continues on the opening and the whole is fresh, delicious. Not very complex, but characteristic of the appellation.
♄ GAEC Jean Moreteaux et Fils, Nantoux, 71150 Chassey-le-Camp, tel. 03.85.87.19.10, e-mail moreteaux@wanadoo.fr ☑
⏳ by appt.

LES VILLAGES DE JAFFELIN 2001★

	n.c.	n.c.	⏳		11–15 €

Limpid, with gold highlights, this is a great *village*. All one could want on the nose, floral and charming, in an all round atmosphere of freshness. The first impression is delightful, the the palate, well supported by richness, is lined with silk by the already integrated tannins. The vinosity is interesting. Jaffelin is an old Beaune company taken over by Jean-Claude Boisset and sensibly left at Beaune.
♄ Maison Jaffelin, 2, rue Paradis, 21200 Beaune, tel. 03.80.22.12.49, fax 03.80.24.91.87, e-mail jaffelin@maisonjaffelin.com

OLIVIER LEFLAIVE

Rabource 2001★

	1er cru	n.c.	24,000	⏳	11–15 €

A beautiful, not too intense, colour, this is a clear and limpid wine. The bouquet is white pepper, wild herbs, citrus fruit, and a touch mineral. The Jury appreciated its balance and length on nuances of apricot. It will keep for four to five years.
♄ Olivier Leflaive Frères, pl. du Monument, 21190 Puligny-Montrachet, tel. 03.80.21.37.65, fax 03.80.21.33.94, e-mail olivier-leflaive@dial.oleane.com ☑
⏳ by appt.

CH. DE MONTHELIE 2001★

	1er cru	n.c.	5,500	⏳	8–11 €

An authentic old Burgundian family, the Suremains can trace the genealogy of their vine-stock back to 1746. Today they practice organic farming. Worthy of mention is the **red Préaux Premier Cru 2000**: an easy wine to drink. A notch higher is the Premier Cru 2001, white this time. Yellow-gold in colour, it has a complex bouquet which doesn't mask the oak. The floral notes dominate. Supple and mineral, it is balanced on the palate: a truly pleasing wine.
♄ Eric de Suremain, Ch. de Monthélie, 21190 Monthélie, tel. 03.80.21.23.32, fax 03.80.21.66.37 ☑ ✿
⏳ by appt.

DOM. DE LA RENARDE

Varot 2001★

	17,64 ha	15,000	∎⏳♨		8–11 €

Specialist in Crémant-de-Bourgogne, Jean-François Delorme does not for a moment neglect his still wines, as this Varot indicates. Straw-yellow and brilliant, it hints at grapefruit and hazelnut living happily together. Slightly lemony on the follow-up, it maintains its freshness while developing a solid structure. It will be interesting to taste it in magnum in a few years time.
♄ André Delorme, 2, rue de la République, BP 15, 71150 Rully, tel. 03.85.87.10.12, fax 03.85.87.04.60, e-mail andre-delorme@wanadoo.fr ☑
⏳ ev.day ex. Sun. 9am–12noon2pm–6pm; groups by appt.

CH. DE RULLY 2000★★

	19.7 ha	116,716	∎⏳♨		15–23 €

A superb 12th century fortress, this château, belonging to the Compte de Ternay, is today managed by Antonin Rodet. *Coup de cœur* for its 94 and 99 vintages, this estate is not far from repeating the process: this one has the feeling of a great wine. From the colour to the bouquet it is all nuances. Tender, pure, right, clean…read the tasters' cards taken from the table of honour. A delightful wine to drink with a fish terrine, an exotic salad, or even a roast of veal.
♄ Dom. du Ch. de Rully, 71640 Mercurey, tel. 03.85.98.12.12, fax 03.85.45.25.49, e-mail rodet@rodet.com ☑
⏳ by appt. chez Antonin Rodet
♄ Comte R. de Ternay

ALBERT SOUNIT

Grésigny 2001★

	1er cru	1 ha	1,200	⏳	11–15 €

In the 18th century, l'Abbé Courtépée mentioned the excellent Rully *climats* of Varot and Grésigny. This wine is a Grésigny, with that little extra that makes a Premier Cru. An already yellowing gold colour, it is interestingly mineral while paving the way for butter, hazelnut, toast. Supple and heady, it is very expansive on the palate. Also recommended is the **white Saint-Jacques 2001 (8–11 €)**, with one star. Albert Sounit took over the old Janet property in 1930 and sold it in 1993 to his Danish importer, K. Kjellerup. Elsewhere there is another Roland Sounit estate.
♄ Albert Sounit, 5, pl. du Champ-de-Foire, 71150 Rully, tel. 03.85.87.20.71, fax 03.85.87.09.71, e-mail albert.sounit@wanadoo.fr ☑
⏳ ev.day 9am–12noon 2pm–6pm; Sat. Sun. by appt.

Wines selected but not starred

FRANCOIS D' ALLAINES

La Fosse 2001

	1er cru	n.c.	1,800	⏳	11–15 €

♄ François d' Allaines, La Corvée du Paquier, 71150 Demigny, tel. 03.85.49.90.16, fax 03.85.49.90.19, e-mail francois@dallaines.com
⏳ by appt.

CHARTRON ET TREBUCHET 2000

		n.c.	9,000	⏳	11–15 €

♄ Chartron et Trébuchet, 13, Grande-Rue, 21190 Puligny-Montrachet, tel. 03.80.21.32.85, fax 03.80.21.36.35 ☑

DEMESSEY 2001

	1er cru	n.c.	2,970	∎⏳♨	11–15 €

♄ Marc Dumont, Ch. de Messey, 71700 Ozenay, tel. 03.85.51.33.83, fax 03.85.51.33.82, e-mail vin@demessey.com ☑ ✉ ✿
⏳ by appt.

PHILIPPE MILAN ET FILS 2001

	1.65 ha	7,000	∎⏳		8–11 €

♄ Philippe Milan et Fils, 71150 Chassey-le-Camp, tel. 03.85.91.21.38, fax 03.85.87.00.85 ☑
⏳ by appt.

P.M. NINOT

Chaponnières 2000

	0.9 ha	4,500	∎⏳♨		5–8 €

♄ P.M. Ninot, Le Meix Guillaume, 2, rue de Chagny, 71150 Rully, tel. 03.85.87.07.79, fax 03.85.91.28.56, e-mail ninot.domaine@wanadoo.fr ☑
⏳ by appt.

DOM. ROLAND SOUNIT

La Bergerie Elevé et vieilli en fût de chêne 2001

■	1 ha	6,500	❰❙❱	8–11 €

☛ SCEA Dom. Roland Sounit, rte de Monthélie, 21190 Meursault, tel. 03.80.21.22.45, fax 03.80.21.28.05

LA TOUR BLONDEAU 2001

■	n.c.	n.c.	▌❰❙❱	8–11 €

☛ Grands Vins Forgeot, 15, rue du Château, 21200 Beaune, tel. 03.80.24.80.50, fax 03.80.22.55.88

Mercurey

Mercurey is 12 km northwest of Chalon-sur-Saône, on the edge of the Chagny-Cluny road, and borders the Rully vineyard to the south. This appellation communale produces the largest volume of wine on the Côte Chalonnaise: in 2002 24,334 hl of red wine and 3,673 hl of white were produced. It extends into three communes: Mercurey, Saint-Martin-sous-Montaigu and Bourgneuf-Val-d'Or.

Some locations are also classified as Premier Cru. The wines are generally light and pleasant, with some keeping qualities.

DOM. BRINTET

La Charmée 2001★

■	0,47 ha	2,800	❰❙❱	8–11 €

An estate where one can buy with confidence, if one is to believe our Jurors: three of its wines are well up to the mark. The **red Premier Cru La Levrière 2001**, specially mentioned, the **red Cuvée Village Vieilles Vignes 2001 (both at 11–15 €)**, one star, and this delicious Charmée with its fresh and lively ruby-red colour, spicy and musky, which has not yet revealed all its qualities. It opens on ripe fruit and continues without any astringency and an admirable length.
☛ Dom. Luc Brintet, 105, Grande-Rue, 71640 Mercurey, tel. 03.85.45.14.50, fax 03.85.45.28.23, e-mail contact@domaine-brintet.com ☑
☂ by appt.

DOM. CAPUANO-JOHN

Clos du Paradis 2001★

■	1er cru	n.c.	n.c.	❰❙❱	11–15 €

This wine is interesting: attractive, shimmering velvet to look at, the blackcurrant bouquet is all promise, reinforced on the palate by spicy and peppery notes as well as a solid structure (not solely tannic) and a good length. A wine to lay down (three or four years) for a classic, rich, harmonious result.
☛ Dom. Capuano-John, 14, rue Chauchien, 21590 Santenay, tel. 03.80.20.68.80, fax 03.80.20.65.75, e-mail john.capuano@wanadoo.fr ☑
☂ by appt.

CH. DE CHAMIREY 2000★★

■	8.04 ha	69,900		15–23 €

The Château de Chamirey is managed by Bertrand Devillard (Antonin Rodin) and he recalls the memory of his father-in-law, the Marquis de Jouennes d'Herville. This white Mercurey is a pure marvel and will do honour to a fine pike from the Saône river. Brilliant pale-gold, with a floral bouquet, evoking beeswax. Very well turned out, its fresh and fruity palate is also very pleasant. Very characteristic of the *village*, as is the **white Premier Cru La Mission 2000 (23–30 €)**, which was awarded a star. *Coup de coeur* last year for a red 99 vintage.

☛ Dom. du Château de Chamirey, 71640 Mercurey, tel. 03.85.98.12.12, fax 03.85.45.25.49, e-mail rodet@rodet.com ☑
☂ by appt.
☛ Ch. Devillard

CHANSON PERE ET FILS 2001★

■	n.c.	10,100	❰❙❱	11–15 €

This Mercurey has all the colour it needs and red berries to start the conversational ball rolling. Finely oaked, tannins in place, what does it lack for the second star, other than a coating quality on the palate? A wine to lay down and enjoy in three or four years' time with a haunch of venison.
☛ Dom. Chanson Père et Fils, 10, rue Paul-Chanson, BP 232, 21206 Beaune Cedex, tel. 03.80.25.97.97, fax 03.80.24.17.42, e-mail tmarion@vins-chanson.com

JEAN-PIERRE CHARTON

Clos du Roy 2001★

■	1er cru	0.88 ha	5,200	❰❙❱	11–15 €

Seventy-five percent Pinot Noir, stemming from mass selection. A dark, intense colour, this wine is still delicate on the first nose, but a touch of complexity is produced by agitating it in the glass, after which it explodes into spices and a whole basket of fruits. Massive right from the first impression, tannic but also tending to be fleshy, this is a Mercurey which is not very fruity on the palate, but one or two years in the cellar will improve it.
☛ Dom. Jean-Pierre Charton, 29, Grande-Rue, 71640 Mercurey, tel. 03.85.45.22.39, fax 03.85.45.22.39 ☑
☂ by appt.

CH. D' ETROYES

Clos des Corvées 2000★

■	5.81 ha	10,000	▌❰❙❱♣	8–11 €

Since the 2000 and 2001 vintages, the F. Protheau wine-merchant business has belonged to J.-B. Béjot at Meursault. This one is the estate of Maurice Protheay, a family wine-producer, henceforth independent of the business of *négotiant-éleveur* (merchant who also matures wine). This Clos des Corvées is cherry-red, shot through with notes of evolution. With aeration, the bouquet leans towards strawberry. Rounded and fleshy, this wine is ready to drink, but it could just as well wait for three or four years. A fine wine, a **white Ormeaux 2001**, was awarded a star.
☛ Dom. Maurice Protheau et Fils, Ch. d'Etroyes, 71640 Mercurey, tel. 03.85.45.10.84, fax 03.85.45.26.05, e-mail philippe@domaine-protheau-mercurey.fr ☑
☂ ev.day 8am–12noon 2pm–7pm; Sun. by appt.

DOM. DE L' EUROPE

Les Chazeaux 2001★★

■	1.7 ha	4,000	❰❙❱	8–11 €

The Europe of wine! You can see it here. A Belgian artist, wine-grower at Mercurey. Where are they taking us? To a seventh heaven in a hot air balloon: Guy Cinquin was champion of France in 1998. While it does not have an enormous keeping potential (two to three years), this wine, produced by a tiny domain of 2.3 ha was one of the best of the tasting. A red balloon, carried to the heights: an almost black ruby-red colour, stewed red fruit, silky on the tongue, tannins well-enveloped; expressed thus, Europe has much to commend it.
☛ Chantal Côte and Guy Cinquin, Dom. de l'Europe, 5 pl. du Bourg neuf, 71640 Mercurey, tel. 06.08.04.28.12, fax 03.85.45.23.82, e-mail cote-cinquin@wanadoo.fr ☑
☂ by appt.

DOM. PHILIPPE GARREY

La Chassière 2001★

■	1er cru	0.3 ha	1,400	❰❙❱	11–15 €

A deep colour, with black tinges, bouquet marked by small black fruit, this is a quite oaked 2001 vintage. Robust, it is still young, but its structure and length are quality factors. A wine to lay down which, when its tannins have integrated (in five years' time), will be ideal served with red meat.
☛ Dom. Pierre Garrey, 71640 Saint-Martin-sous-Montaigu, tel. 06.30.40.42.21, fax 03.85.45.15.94, e-mail d-pg@wanadoo.fr ☑
☂ by appt.

CH. GENOT-BOULANGER
Les Saumonts 2000★

■ 1er cru	2.01 ha	11,000	⊞	11–15 €

At the centre of the village, this château, with its roof of glazed tiles, has vaulted cellars. Intense garnet-red, with slight amber touches, this Premier Cru offers the nose some vanilla notes followed by undergrowth and a touch of liquorice. The opening is supple, on tannins as rounded as a Roman arch. This Mercurey is very much present on the palate with a good, very aromatic finish. Acidity, alcohol and tannins have an assured balance and the wine's mouth-filling quality is not without charm. An excellent wine to accompany a roast of beef. The **Bacs 2000 en Village white** received a special mention.
↘ SCEV Ch. Génot-Boulanger, 25, rue de Cîteaux, 21190 Meursault, tel. 03.80.21.49.20, fax 03.80.21.49.21, e-mail genot-boulanger@wanadoo.fr ▣
☖ by appt.
↦ Delaby

DOM. EMILE JUILLOT
Les Combins 2001★

■ 1er cru	0.92 ha	5,000	⊞	11–15 €

Either the **red Les Croichots Premier Cru 2001**, which was very pleasing, or this Combins, which is at the same level. Clear garnet-red, this is a wine which is in search of something: it starts with mild spices, adding ripe fruit after aeration (prunes). Warm and tannic, its attack is straightforward. It fills the mouth with substance right to the raspberry finish. The **white Champs Martins Premier Cru 2001** received a special mention.
↘ Nathalie and Jean-Claude Theulot, 4, rue de Mercurey, 71640 Mercurey, tel. 03.85.45.13.87, fax 03.85.45.28.07, e-mail e.juillot.theulot@wanadoo.fr ▣
☖ ev.day 8am–12noon 1.30pm–6pm; Sat. Sun. by appt.; cl. week beginning 15 Aug.

DOM. MICHEL JUILLOT
Clos des Barraults 2001★

■ 1er cru	2.2 ha	10,000	⊞	15–23 €

Several crus were retained by the Jury: the **red Clos Tonnerre Premier Cru 2001**, the **Mercurey Village red 2001** and the **Village white 2000** all received one star (11–15 €), as did this Premier Cru, of an impeccable colour, that launches itself with a superb initial impact. Wild aromas, fruity and slightly roasted. Plenty of body and elegance on the palate, with a nice kirsch sensation. It is everything a Premier Cru should be.
↘ Dom. Michel Juillot, 59, Grande-Rue, BP 10, 71640 Mercurey, tel. 03.85.98.99.89, fax 03.85.98.99.88, e-mail infos@domaine-michel-juillot.fr ▣
☖ ev.day ex. Sun. 9am–12noon 2pm–6.30pm; groups by appt.

DOM. LORENZON 2001★

■	1.5 ha	6,000	⊞	11–15 €

Bruno Lorenzon has still to blow out the candles on the cake at the celebration, in 2007, of his ten years at the head of the estate; years which have not gone unnoticed. Due to his minute labels? Not only that. He offered here a Mercurey that could be decanted now, or kept for a while in the cellar before serving with slightly under-done red meat. The bouquet is of red berries and charred oak. As to the palate, it still has the bite on the opening that is typical of the 2001 vintage, then richness, crystallized cherries, a peaceable finish quickly reached. The few still-young tannins need a little time. The **red Premier Cru Champs Martin Village Cuvée Caroline 2001 (15–23 €)** was awarded one star, as was the **white Premier Cru Champs Martin 2001 (11–15 €)**.
↘ Dom. Bruno Lorenzon, 14, rue du Reu, 71640 Mercurey, tel. 03.85.45.13.51, fax 03.85.45.15.52 ▣
☖ by appt.

DOM. L. MENAND PERE ET FILS
Les Vaux 2001★

■	1 ha	6,000	⊞	5–8 €

You could choose the **red Clos des Combins 2001 Premier Cru (8–11 €)**, which received a special mention. It is a credit to its appellation and there is nothing to be said against it. Even more successful is this *village*, ruby-red with the purple rim

that indicates its extreme youth. The truffle, spice and blackcurrant leaf-bud bouquet opens on a touch of warmth, but the exuberant tannins, delicate oakiness, weight and the potential for ageing, all demand a period of three years in the cellar.
↘ Dom. L. Menand, Chamerose, 71640 Mercurey, tel. 03.85.45.19.19, fax 03.85.45.10.23 ▣
☖ by appt.

FRANCOIS RAQUILLET
Les Naugues 2001★★

■ 1er cru	0.4 ha	23,000	⊞	11–15 €

This wine-grower was awarded one star for each of two different wines: the **red Vieilles Vignes 2001 en Village (8–11 €)** and the **red Premier Cru Les Puillets 2001 (11–15 €)**. More up-market, this wine is a deep and lively garnet-red. The elegant, aromatic palate develops well, and in the mouth it is silky, full flavoured; a thoroughbred in body and spirit. A roast duck would show this Les Nauges off to best advantage.
↘ François Raquillet, 19, rue de Jamproyes, 71640 Mercurey, tel. 03.85.45.14.61, fax 03.85.45.28.05 ▣
☖ by appt.

ALBERT SOUNIT
Clos du Roy 2001★★

▨ 1er cru	0.45 ha	1,500	⊞	11–15 €

They can light the lamps in Copenhagen: taken over by a Danish importer, this estate has produced this excellent Premier Cru which merits its royal name. Clear gold, leaving good legs in the glass, this wine already has an expressive bouquet, without excessive vanilla, making room for pear aromas. Highly flavoured on the palate, where the richness is at its maximum, and with a long and silky finish. It should not be left to age much more; drink it over the next two years with fillets of sole, for example.
↘ Albert Sounit, 5, pl. du Champ-de-Foire, 71150 Rully, tel. 03.85.87.20.71, fax 03.85.87.09.71, e-mail albert.sounit@wanadoo.fr ▣
☖ ev.day 9am–12noon 2pm–6pm; Sat. Sun. by appt.

DOM. ROLAND SOUNIT
Les Varennes Elevé et vieilli en fût de chêne 2001★

■	2.1 ha	14,000	⊞	8–11 €

Burlat cherry, this Les Varennes holds out the promise of richness to the first glance. The cherries, tending towards kirsch, pervade the bouquet. Imagine the senator arriving in the area to celebrate with the Companions of Saint-Vincent and Disciples of the Chanteflûte (a local wine society): the first impression is all amiable roundness. The tannins are of the same mind. The whole is quite concentrated. A few years in the cellar are needed since it will only fully reveal its qualities after two or three years.
↘ SCEA Dom. Roland Sounit, rte de Monthélie, 21190 Meursault, tel. 03.80.21.22.45, fax 03.80.21.28.05

HUGUES ET YVES DE SUREMAIN
La Bondue 1999★

■	2.14 ha	10,000	⊞	11–15 €

A wine from 1999 that sticks close to its vintage and should be laid down for three to four years. Ruby-red with bluish highlights, it needs to be aerated to give up the best of its bouquet. Very fine, after a frank opening it settles for delicacy. On the palate it is balanced and fruity, with good length. Made by an old *coup de coeur* winner.
↘ Hugues et Yves de Suremain, Dom. du Bourgneuf, BP 14, 71640 Mercurey, tel. 03.85.45.20.87, fax 03.85.45.17.88 ▣
☖ by appt.

DOM. TREMEAUX PERE ET FILS
Elevé en fût de chêne 2000★

■ 1er cru	0.5 ha	2,400	⊞	8–11 €

While the Burgundy coat of arms is the wrong way round on the label, this Premier Cru is definitely pointing the right way. Still a very young colour, the bouquet has depth, cherries say it all. The straightforward and charming palate reveals

BURGUNDY

flavours of well-ripened red berries, a touch of spice and an agreeable length, right to the finish. Well above average.
➴ Dom. Trémeaux Père et Fils, rue de Jamproyes, 71640 Mercurey, tel. 03.85.45.23.03, fax 03.85.45.23.03 ☑
☚ by appt.

A. ET P. DE VILLAINE
Les Montots 2001★

■	1.86 ha	11,000	◫	11–15 €

Pamela and Aubert de Villaine in their other wine operations outside their Bouzeron vineyards. The ruby colour of their Mercurey Les Montots is very appealing to the eye. On the bouquet are fruit and violets, like a true child of the Côte de Nuits, but also the earth, stones, the terroir. An appreciable maturation in cask, but there is no lack of fruit to help it develop further in a year or two. This wine has not yet uttered its last word.
➴ A. et P. de Villaine, 2, rue de la Fontaine, 71150 Bouzeron, tel. 03.85.91.20.50, fax 03.85.87.04.70, e-mail dom.devillaine@wanadoo.fr ☑
☚ by appt.

DOM. VOARICK
Clos Paradis 2001★★

■ 1er cru	3.08 ha	18,300	◫	11–15 €

When one is called Clos Paradis, from time to time one raises a glass with Saint Vincent. The velvety colour is very "Moulin Rouge" from the Belle Epoque. Come back down to earth! Powerful, evocative and rich, the bouquet is well-proportioned, On the palate the good, tannic depth is accompanied by blackberries, black fruit. Make a note, too, of the one star **red Clos du Roy Premier Cru 2001 (15–23 €)**.
➴ Dom. Michel Picard, Ch. de Chassagne-Montrachet, BP 49, 71150 Chagny, tel. 03.85.87.51.01, fax 03.85.87.51.12 ☑
☚ by appt.

Wines selected but not starred

FRANCOIS D' ALLAINES
Clos de Touches 2001

■	n.c.	1,200	◫	11–15 €

➴ François d' Allaines, La Corvée du Paquier, 71150 Demigny, tel. 03.85.49.90.16, fax 03.85.49.90.19, e-mail francois@dallaines.com
☚ by appt.

DOM. GERARD BERGER-RIVE ET FILS
Chateaubeau 2001

■	21 ha	12,000	◫	8–11 €

➴ Dom. Gérard Berger-Rive et Fils, Manoir de Mercey, 2, rue Saint-Louis, 71150 Cheilly-lès-Maranges, tel. 03.85.91.13.81, fax 03.85.91.17.06 ☑
☚ by appt.

CH. DE CHAMILLY
Les Puillets 2000

■ 1er cru	1.25 ha	6,900	◫	8–11 €

➴ Véronique Desfontaine, Le Château, 71510 Chamilly, tel. 03.85.87.22.24, fax 03.85.91.23.91, e-mail chateau.chamilly@wanadoo.fr ☑
☚ by appt.

DOM. DE CHARMY
Les Champs Martin 2001

■ 1er cru	n.c.	1,800	◫	15–23 €

➴ Maison P. Misserey, 3, rue des Seuillets, BP 10, 21701 Nuits-Saint-Georges Cedex, tel. 03.80.61.07.74, fax 03.80.61.31.40, e-mail lanvin-sa@worldonline.fr ☑
☚ by appt.

FAIVELEY
La Framboisière 2000

■	11.11 ha	71,000	◫	11–15 €

➴ Bourgognes Faiveley, 8, rue du Tribourg, 21700 Nuits-Saint-Georges, tel. 03.80.61.04.55, fax 03.80.62.33.37, e-mail bourgognes.faiveley@wanadoo.fr ☑

DOM. MICHEL ISAIE
Clos du Paradis 2000

■ 1er cru	0.75 ha	3,600	◫	8–11 €

➴ Michel Isaïe, chem. de l'Ouche, 71640 Saint-Jean-de-Vaux, tel. 03.85.45.23.32, fax 03.85.45.29.38 ☑
☚ by appt.

LUPE-CHOLET 2000

■	n.c.	16,000	◫	11–15 €

➴ Lupé-Cholet, 17, av. du Gal-de-Gaulle, 21700 Nuits-Saint-Georges, tel. 03.80.61.25.02, fax 03.80.24.37.38

DOM. LOUIS MAX
Les Rochelles 2001

■	n.c.	6,000	◫	46–76 €

➴ Louis Max, 6, rue de Chaux, 21700 Nuits-Saint-Georges, tel. 03.80.62.43.01, fax 03.80.62.43.16

CH. DE SANTENAY 2001

■	5.39 ha	36,900	◫	8–11 €

➴ SAS Ch. de Santenay, 1, rue du Château, 21590 Santenay, tel. 03.80.20.61.87, fax 03.80.20.63.66, e-mail chateau.santenay@wanadoo.fr ☑
☚ by appt.

DOM. TUPINIER-BAUTISTA
En Sazenay 2001

■ 1er cru	1.14 ha	6,000	◫	8–11 €

➴ Manuel Bautista, EARL Dom. Tupinier-Bautista, Touches, 71640 Mercurey, tel. 03.85.45.26.38, fax 03.85.45.27.99, e-mail tupinier.bautista@wanadoo.fr ☑
☚ by appt.

Givry

Givry is 6 km south of Mercurey, and is a typical Burgundian village with a wealth of historic monuments. Givry is claimed to have been the favourite wine of Henri IV of France, and mainly red wines are produced – 10,709 hl in 2002). However, the white – 2,107 hl in 2002 – are also of interest. Prices are very affordable. The appellation lies principally in the commune of Givry but spills over slightly into Jambles and Dracy-le-Fort.

DOM. DU CLOS SALOMON

Clos Salomon Monopole 2001★★

| | 1er cru | 1 ha | 35,000 | ◫ | 11–15 € |

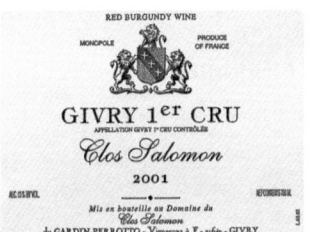

RED BURGUNDY WINE

MONOPOLE   PRODUCE OF FRANCE

GIVRY 1er CRU

APPELLATION GIVRY 1er CRU CONTRÔLÉE

Clos Salomon

2001

Mis en bouteille au Domaine du
Clos Salomon
de GARDIN-PERROTTO - Vignerons à F - 71640 - GIVRY

This is an estate which goes back to the 14th century. This 2001 vintage wine, of a very intense colour, with a rather restrained on the nose (a delicately complex bouquet opening out to blackcurrant and coffee) has been very well matured. It stays well in place on the palate and has enough acidity to reach its peak around 2006. Rich and warming, well made and robust, a perfect wine for laying down.

🕯 Clos Salomon, 16, rue du Clos-Salomon, 71640 Givry, tel. 03.85.44.32.24, fax 03.85.44.49.79 ☑
⍭ by appt.

DANIEL DAVANTURE ET FILS 2001★

| | | 0.48 ha | 500 | ◫ | 5–8 € |

The eighth generation took over this estate in 1996 and its knowledge and ability has already been proved. Apart from the **Givry red 2000**, which received a special mention, the Jury was unanimously seduced by this voluptuous white. All the AOC attributes are present in its colour; the air-filling bouquet opens on notes of almond and citrus fruit. The fresh and lively initial impression is followed by a welcome richness on the palate. A dish of fried queen scallops came to mind among the tasters.

🕯 Daniel Davanture et Fils, rue de la Montée, Cidex 1548, 71390 Saint-Désert, tel. 03.85.47.90.42, fax 03.85.47.95.57 ☑
⍭ by appt.
🕯 GAEC des Murgers

PROPRIETE DESVIGNES

La Grande Berge 2001★★

| | 1er cru | 1.7 ha | 10,000 | ◫ | 8–11 € |

On the wine route from Beaune to Cluny, make a stop at these 17th century cellars. Clean and brilliant, this Premier Cru offers a bouquet that is full of finesse and elegance. Mild spices, blackberries, the pleasure is there. The texture is very noticeable on the supple opening. This promising wine from the 2001 vintage won't remain idle for the next three or four years, on the contrary, it will develop and open out. The year 2004 will commemorate Bossuet (Jacques Bénigne, religious writer, born Dijon, 1627): serve this wine then with a Brie de Meaux, if impatience gets the upper hand.

🕯 Propriété Desvignes, 36, rue de Jambles, Poncey, 71640 Givry, tel. 03.85.44.51.23, fax 03.85.44.43.53 ☑ 🏠
⍭ by appt.

DIDIER ERKER

En Chenèvre 2001★★

| | | 0.64 ha | n.c. | ◫ | 5–8 € |

This wine made a big impression, coming close to a *coup de coeur*. White wines are quite rare at Givry (though increasing) but this one argues solidly in their favour. A clear, limpid gold colour, this is a charming wine with a bouquet of linden-blossom, fern, on a slightly buttery basis, with a very elegant touch of oak. Its finesse and mouth-filling qualities are not contradictory in this case, and immediately bring to mind a sole with beaten butter. Well-matured, this is a 2001 vintage to drink in 2004. A word of advice: open it an hour before serving; it bursts with flavour after aeration.

🕯 Didier Erker, 7 bis, bd Saint-Martin, 71640 Givry, tel. 03.85.44.39.62, fax 03.85.44.39.62,
e-mail erker@givry.net ☑ 🏠
⍭ ev.day 8.30am–8pm

DOM. MICHEL GOUBARD ET FILS

La Grande Berge 2001★

| | 1er cru | 2.64 ha | 15,000 | ▮◫♦ | 5–8 € |

La Grande Berge is on a roll this year. One often encounters it in Givry. It is a wine worthy of serving with a boiled chicken: perfect colour; ripe fruit bouquet, leaning towards kirsch and fruit in alcohol. Full and supple, with a hint of warmth on the palate in the same style as that perceived on the bouquet; powerful, attractive to look at. Could be served with any red meat.

🕯 Dom. Michel Goubard et Fils, 71390 Saint-Désert, tel. 03.85.47.91.06, fax 03.85.47.98.12 ☑
⍭ by appt.

MARINOT-VERDUN 2001★

| | | n.c. | 5,000 | ▮ | 5–8 € |

Cherry-red, with quite good intensity and satisfactory brilliance (generous tears in the glass), this is a *village* 2001 with a bouquet of macerated red berries. Well-supported by tannins, the first impression is straightforward, quite spirited. While the body is not significant, the repeat of the aromas (red-currants) and the creditable length are of a very good level. Lay it down for one or two years.

🕯 Marinot-Verdun, Cave de Mazenay, 71510 Saint-Sernin-du-Plain, tel. 03.85.49.67.19, fax 03.85.45.57.21 ☑
⍭ ev.day ex. Sun. 8am–12noon 2pm–6pm

DOM. MASSE PERE ET FILS

Champ Lalot 2001★

| | | 0.5 ha | 3,200 | ◫ | 8–11 € |

The estate, established in 1918, still uses the label bearing the photograph of the village. It is true that Nicéphore Niépce invented photography a short distance from here. The wine exhales Pinot from the first, starting with its garnet-red colour, with hints of ruby. The bouquet is negligeable for the moment, just a touch of red berries. On the palate? Fleshy and rich, consistent, this Champ Lalot manages a clear round between tannins and acidity. Guaranteed true-to-type, with fine potential.

🕯 Dom. Masse Père et Fils, Theurey, 71640 Barizey, tel. 03.85.44.36.73, fax 03.85.44.36.73 ☑
⍭ ev.day ex. Sun. 9am–7pm

DOM. MOUTON

Les Grands Prétans 2000★

| | 1er cru | 0.32 ha | 2,200 | ▮◫♦ | 8–11 € |

A fine, monastic colour, wrote one of our tasters, no doubt meaning that of a Cardinal. Mossy notes and undergrowth, mixed with musky accents, evoke an early-morning walk in the woods. While this 2000 vintage still has a touch of austerity on the final palate, it is completely constituted on dense tannins. A sound, classic wine that needs two or three more years in the cellar. The **Givry Village 2001 white** was also awarded one star. It would go well with white meat.

🕯 SCEA Dom. Mouton, 6, rue de l'Orcène, Poncey, 71640 Givry, tel. 03.85.44.37.99, fax 03.85.44.48.19, e-mail domaine-mouton@vin-givry.com ☑
⍭ by appt.

MICHEL SARRAZIN ET FILS

Clos de la Putin 2001★

| | | 0.69 ha | 4,800 | ◫ | 8–11 € |

One hardly dares write that this is an easy wine, looking at its name, which could seem hard to bear (Putin is pronounced the same way as *putain*, a prostitute). But no, this wine-grower is proud of it, going as far as indicating that this picturesque place owes its name to the beautiful girls of the 16th century. That doesn't stop the estate (*coup de coeur* for its 90, 95 and 2000 vintages) from sharing with us the joys of a tender, easy to drink wine, with no asperity, though firm and of good length.

🕯 Michel Sarrazin et Fils, Charnailles, 71640 Jambles, tel. 03.85.44.30.57, fax 03.85.44.31.22, e-mail sarrazin2@wanadoo.fr ☑ 🏠
⍭ by appt.

LA SAULERAIE

Champ Nalot 2001★★

	0.3 ha	2,400	Ⅲ		8–11 €

This estate was *coup de cœur* last year and the year before, and again this year, not to mention the year 2000! Better still, our Grand Jury judged two wines worthy of the supreme distinction: the **red Clos Les Grandes Vignes 2001 (11–15 €)** and this one which, like that great lover of the wines from this area, Henry IV, seems to be saying, "Follow my white plume!" Excellent pale-gold colour with deeper-yellow highlights. Very fine oak at the heart of a slightly honeyed, floral bouquet. With great freshness and a pleasant liveliness on the palate, it is all elegance, and worthy of accompanying a fine fish dish. Another wine to buy with the eyes closed is the **red Champ Nalot Cuvée Prestige 2001**, which received one star.
➤ Parize Père et Fils, 18, rue des Faussillons, 71640 Givry, tel. 03.85.44.38.60, fax 03.85.44.43.54,
e-mail laurent.parize@wanadoo.fr ☑
☕ ev.day 9am–7pm

DOM. THENARD

Les Bois Chevaux 2000★

■		7,66 ha	32,000	Ⅲ	5–8 €

Baron Paul Thénard (1819–1884) founded this estate at Givry immediately after his marriage. It was he who discovered the first defence against phylloxera (carbon bisulphide). Light ruby-red, this companionable wine, with a fruity (cherry) bouquet, structured body and good vinosity, is pleasant on the palate. Straightforward and well-balanced, it gives a true picture of its terroir.
➤ Dom. Thénard, 7, rue de l'Hôtel-de-Ville, 71640 Givry, tel. 03.85.44.31.36, fax 03.85.44.47.83 ☑
☕ by appt.

DOM. VOARICK

La Grande Berge 2001★

■ 1er cru	0.16 ha	900	Ⅲ	11–15 €

The Voarick estate was taken over some years ago by Michel Picard. Tender, still a little tannic (and chewy), this wine is of a fine, intense and luminescent colour. Its bouquet is not very articulate, barely opened yet on red berries. It doesn't waste its time on the palate, however: structured and solid, the body is very attractive.
➤ Dom. Michel Picard, Ch. de Chassagne-Montrachet, BP 49, 71150 Chagny, tel. 03.85.87.51.01, fax 03.85.87.51.12 ☑
☕ by appt.

Wines selected but not starred

GUILLEMETTE ET XAVIER BESSON

Les Grands Prétans 2001

■ 1er cru	1.5 ha	9,000	Ⅲ	8–11 €

➤ Guillemette and Xavier Besson, 9, rue des Bois-Chevaux, 71640 Givry, tel. 03.85.44.42.44, fax 03.85.94.88.21 ☑
☕ by appt.

RENE BOURGEON

Clos de la Brûlée 2001

	n.c.	n.c.		8–11 €

➤ GAEC René Bourgeon, 2, rue du Chapitre, 71640 Jambles, tel. 03.85.44.35.85, fax 03.85.44.57.80 ☑
☕ by appt.

PELLETIER-HIBON 2001

	1 ha	4,000	▌Ⅲ	5–8 €

➤ EARL Pelletier-Hibon, chem. de la Vernoise, Poncey, 71640 Givry, tel. 03.85.44.38.82, fax 03.85.44.38.82 ☑
☕ by appt.

DOM. RAGOT

La Grande Berge 2001

■ 1er cru	2.1 ha	13,000	Ⅲ	8–11 €

➤ Dom. Jean-Paul Ragot, 4, rue de l'Ecole, Poncey, 71640 Givry, tel. 03.85.44.38.84, fax 03.85.44.38.84 ☑ ⌂
☕ ev.day ex. Sun.9am–7pm

DOM. JEAN TATRAUX ET FILS

Clos Jus 2001

■ 1er cru	0.25 ha	1,700	Ⅲ	8–11 €

➤ Dom. Jean Tatraux et Fils, 20, rue de l'Orcène, Poncey, 71640 Givry, tel. 03.85.44.36.89, fax 03.85.44.59.43 ☑
☕ by appt.

DOM. BERNARD TATRAUX-JUILLET

Clos Jus 2001

■ 1er cru	0.25 ha	1,800	▌Ⅲ⚲	8–11 €

➤ Dom. Bernard Tatraux-Juillet, 33, rue de la Planchette, Poncey, 71640 Givry, tel. 03.85.44.57.41,
fax 03.85.44.57.20 ☑
☕ by appt.

MARTINE TESSIER 2001

	0.25 ha	1,600		5–8 €

➤ Martine Tessier, 16, rue de l'Ecole, Poncey, 71640 Givry, tel. 03.85.44.40.62, fax 03.85.44.40.62,
e-mail mj.tessei@wanadoo.fr ☑
☕ by appt.

Montagny

Producing only white wines, Montagny, which is the southernmost village of the region, heralds the neighbouring Mâconnais. The appellation can be produced in four communes: Montagny, Buxy, Saint-Vallerin and Jully-lès-Buxy. A climat can only be claimed in the commune of Montagny. Production in 2002 reached 17,165 hl.

BLASON DE BOURGOGNE

Vieilles Vignes 2000★

	n.c.	77,000	▌	5–8 €

The Chablis cooperative is supplied by Alain Pierre, excellent oenologist and cellar-master at the Buxy cellars. With a wide distribution, this Blason is very representative of a Montagny: the attractive bouquet, floral with honey and exotic fruit, introduces the perfect balance of a wine in which acidity and fleshiness join together to ensure it will keep for a short period and be a real pleasure at the table.
➤ GIE Blasons de Bourgogne, rue du Serein, 89800 Chablis, tel. 03.86.42.88.34, fax 03.86.42.83.75,
e-mail blasons@blasonsdebourgogne.fr

LA BUXYNOISE

Les Chagnots 2000★

| | 1er cru | 5 ha | 30,000 | 🍾 ᵭ | | 8–11 € |

With its 890 ha of vineyards, the cooperative at Buxy, founded in 1931, does not lack wine, as is demonstated by this Premier Cru, with its brilliant colour somewhere between pale-gold and straw. Roses and violets on the bouquet make it floral, delicate and full of promise. The first impression is resolute and firm, then richness takes over on citrus fruit. Ready to drink now, with grilled fish, this is a well-made and very characteristic wine. As to the **Cuvée Spéciale Premier Cru 2001 (5–8 €)**, it received a special mention, while the **Villages Les Millières 2000 (5–8 €)** was awarded one star.
☛ Cave des Vignerons de Buxy, Les Vignes de La Croix, BP 6, 71390 Buxy, tel. 03.85.92.03.03, fax 03.85.92.08.06,
e-mail labuxynoise@cave-buxy.fr ☑
☖ ev.day ex. Sun. 9am–12noon 2pm–6.30pm; groups by appt.

CH. DE DAVENAY 2001★

| | 1er cru | 3.48 ha | 27,000 | 🍾 ⑪ ᵭ | | 8–11 € |

According to a local maxim, Le Montagny leaves you with a clear head. Test the theory with this excellent wine produced by Michel Picard. It is a good colour. Its bouquet evokes floral notes and pears and apples. Little acidity but it is fleshy, with length and an appealing character which one can easily associate with a *blanquette de veau* (veal in a white sauce).
☛ Dom. Michel Picard, Ch. de Chassagne-Montrachet, BP 49, 71150 Chagny, tel. 03.85.87.51.01, fax 03.85.87.51.12
☖ by appt.

CH. DE LA SAULE 2001★

| | 1er cru | 5 ha | 35,000 | 🍾 ᵭ | | 11–15 € |

Beneath its limpid colour, this Montagny offers perfumes of green apples, without neglecting its floral aspect. On the palate it is particularly structured and corresponds in every way to a Premier Cru. Honey and quince notes accompany the richness on the middle-palate continuing to the impressive finish. The **Premier Cru 2001, Elevé en Fût de Chêne,** still a little hidden behind the oak, but very well-made, received a special mention.
☛ Alain Roy, La Saule, 71390 Montagny, tel. 03.85.92.11.83, fax 03.85.92.08.12 ☑
☖ by appt.

Wines selected but not starred

CH. DE CARY POTET

Les Burnins 2000

| | | 1.7 ha | 11,000 | ⑪ | | 8–11 € |

☛ Charles et Pierre du Besset, Ch. de Cary Potet, 71390 Buxy, tel. 03.85.92.14.48, fax 03.85.92.11.88 ☑
☖ by appt.

DOM. CHRISTIAN ET BRUNO DENIZOT Les Pidances 2000

| | 1er cru | 1.4 ha | 8,000 | 🍾 ⑪ ᵭ | | 5–8 € |

☛ Dom. Christian et Bruno Denizot, 71390 Bissey-sous-Cruchaud, tel. 03.85.92.13.34, fax 03.85.92.12.87,
e-mail denizot@caves-particulières.com ☑
☖ ev. day ex. Sun. 9am–7pm

DOM. DES MOIROTS

Le Vieux Château 2001

| | 1er cru | 3.59 ha | 6,000 | 🍾 ⑪ ᵭ | | 8–11 € |

☛ Lucien et Christophe Denizot, Dom. des Moirots, 14, rue des Moirots, 71390 Bissey-sous-Cruchaud, tel. 06.83.41.55.24, fax 03.85.92.09.42,

e-mail domainedesmoirots@free.fr ☑
☖ by appt.

JEAN-CLAUDE PIGNERET 2001

| | 1er cru | 1.44 ha | 2,500 | 🍾 ⑪ | | 5–8 € |

☛ Jean-Claude Pigneret, rue de la Pompe, 71390 Saint-Désert, tel. 03.85.47.94.40 ☑
☖ by appt.

ALBERT SOUNIT

Les Jardins 2001

| | 1er cru | 2 ha | 1,800 | ⑪ | | 11–15 € |

☛ Albert Sounit, 5, pl. du Champ-de-Foire, 71150 Rully, tel. 03.85.87.20.71, fax 03.85.87.09.71,
e-mail albert.sounit@wanadoo.fr ☑
☖ ev.day 9am–12noon 2pm–6pm; Sat. Sun. by appt.

VAUCHER PERE ET FILS 2000

| | | n.c. | n.c. | 🍾 | | 5–8 € |

☛ Vaucher Père et Fils, rue Lavoisier, 21700 Nuits-Saint-Georges, tel. 03.80.62.64.00, fax 03.80.62.64.10, e-mail vaucher@axnet.fr

Mâconnais

MACON, MACON SUPERIEUR, MACON-VILLAGES

The appellations Mâcon, Mâcon Supérieur and Mâcon followed by the commune of origin are used for red, white and rosé wines. The white wines can also be called Pinot-Chardonnay-Mâcon and Mâcon-Villages. The vineyard is huge and, from the region of Tournus to the suburbs of Mâcon, the great variety of situations and aspects produces an equally wide range of different wines. In 2002, 206,675 hl of white wine and 42,413 hl of red were produced.

The area of Lugny, Chardonnay, is well-suited to producing the light, pleasant white wines for which it is known. A large number of wine-growers have grouped together in cooperatives to vinify their harvest and market their wines, and production has developed significantly as a result.

Mâcon

RICHARD BENAS

Serrières Les Varennes Vieilles Vignes 2000★

| | | 0.94 ha | 6,000 | 🍾 | | 5–8 € |

Established since 1998 at the heart of the Golden Triangle of Mâcon reds (Bussières, Pierreclos, Serrières), Richard Bénas offered an excellent *cuvée* from the mythical 2000 vintage: a scintillating ruby-red Mâcon. The bouquet opens on smoky, mineral notes, then becomes more intense and fruity. Rich, full and balanced on the palate, it finishes on appetising fruity flavours. "This is an attractive, thouroughbred wine, with character," was the conclusion drawn by one taster.
☛ Dom. Richard Bénas, La Tuilerie, 71960 Serrières, tel. 06.12.95.96.51, fax 03.85.35.73.00 ☑

JEAN-MICHEL COMBIER

Serrières Sélection Vieilles Vignes 2001★★★

■	0.3 ha	2,500	🍷	5–8 €

Jean-Michel Combier has really excelled with this difficult 2001 vintage. He offered two very well-made selections, one of which received a *coup de coeur*. Made from the grapes of *vieilles vignes* planted in the granitic sand of the Serrières slopes, this *cuvée* attracts the eye with its deep garnet-red colour. Warm and powerful, the bouquet offers aromas of red berries and jammed black fruits. Rounded and full, with silky tannins, it is remarkable on the palate. "Superbly elegant, magnificent, velvet," enthused one Juror. Two stars for the **red Mâcon Serrières 2001 (3–5 €)**, grown on younger vines but produced with the same passion.

๑ Jean-Michel Combier, Les Provenchères, 71960 Serrières, tel. 03.85.35.75.80, fax 03.85.35.79.67 **▼**
ϒ by appt.

COMMANDERIE

Des Sarments du Mâconnais 2002★

■	20 ha	100,000	🍷 ◊	3–5 €

Coup de coeur for this Mâcon in 2000, the Thorin company selects wines from Beaujolais and the Mâconnais. This intense ruby-red 2002 vintage, with purple highlights offers an elegant bouquet of cherries and violets. Well-balanced, it is fleshy and aromatic on the palate, with a notable cocoa finish. A wine you can almost crunch; ideal for a snack. The **Mâcon-Villages La Bareille 2002** received a special mention.

๑ Maison Thorin, Le Pont des Samsons, 69430 Quincié-en-Beaujolais, tel. 04.74.69.09.10, fax 04.74.69.09.28, e-mail information@maisonthorin.com

DOM. CORDIER PERE ET FILS

Aux Bois d'Allier 2001★

▨	1.66 ha	9,000	◍	8–11 €

Produced by the Cordier estate, this wine diverted the Jury with its old-gold patina. The bouquet carries the mark of the cask: charred notes, vanilla, roasted. Pleasant on the palate, there, too, it is still under the influence of the wood, for the moment. A simple but surprising Mâcon; one which lovers of oaked wines will rave about.

๑ Dom. Cordier Père et Fils, 71960 Fuissé, tel. 03.85.35.62.89, fax 03.85.35.64.01, e-mail domaine.cordier@wanadoo.fr **▼**
ϒ by appt.

DOM. COTEAUX DES MARGOTS 2001★

■	n.c.	3,000	🍷 ◊	5–8 €

The estate is situated on the magnificent slopes overlooking the Château de Pierreclos. Golden in colour, lightly marked with green tinges, this wine's aromas are floral, with grapefruit notes, while the palate is fresh and unctuous, with good length on the finish. This is a fine Mâcon, ideal to drink with the delicious goat's milk cheeses from Cenves.

๑ Jean-Luc Duroussay, Les Margots, 71960 Pierreclos, tel. 03.85.35.73.91, fax 03.85.35.76.00 **▼** **๑**
ϒ by appt.

DOM. DE LA FEUILLARDE

Prissé 2002★

■	n.c.	14,000	🍷	5–8 €

The intense purple colour of this wine is an instant indication ⁀f its youthful character. The fruity perfumes mingle with notes of cocoa to give an agreeably complex bouquet. With a fine roundedness together with flavours of undergrowth and peonies, this 2002 vintage already has great charm. Very balanced and long, it can hold for another year or to or be served as of now with full-flavoured cold meats.

๑ Lucien Thomas, Dom. de La Feuillarde, 71960 Prissé, tel. 03.85.34.54.45, fax 03.85.34.31.50, e-mail contact@domaine-feuillarde.com **▼**
ϒ ev.day 8am–12noon 1pm–7pm

LES ESSENTIELLES DE MANCEY

Mancey Vieilles Vignes 2001★

■	n.c.	7,000	🍷	3–5 €

This selection, with its evocative name, is bottled under a brick-red label (the colour of its terroir) depicting a knight receiving the accolade. What could be more emblematic for the La Mancey cellars which brings together some 80 winemakers and 140 ha distributed over eight villages? The Mâcon contained in this new and attractive bottle, is not outdone, as the Jurors remarked: "Ravishingly brilliant, intense garnet-red colour," "Powerful bouquet with fruit aromas and musk". Balanced, with good length, it could go on improving for several years.

๑ Cave des vignerons de Mancey, BP 100, RN 6, 71700 Tournus, tel. 03.85.51.00.83, fax 03.85.51.71.20 **▼**
ϒ by appt.

ALAIN NORMAND

La Roche-Vineuse 2001★

■	3 ha	5,000	🍷	3–5 €

The intense garnet-red colour of this wine, and its complex bouquet of well-ripened red berries, slightly spicey, are very eloquent. Clean, balanced and powerful, it is proof of the unremitting work the young Alain Normand puts into the production of his fine *cuvées*. Excellent presentation: this Mâcon has already begun to age and will continue ageing for several more years.

๑ Alain Normand, chem. de la Grange-du-Dîme, 71960 La Roche-Vineuse, tel. 03.85.36.61.69, fax 03.85.51.60.97, e-mail domaine.alain.normand@wanadoo.fr **▼**
ϒ by appt.

PASCAL PAUGET

Prety 2002★

■	0.75 ha	2,500	◍	8–11 €

Pascal Pauget is a regular in the Guide and again this year he confirms his winemaker's talent. Matured 100% in oak casks, this intense ruby-red selection is "worth the detour". Black fruit (blackberries, blackcurrants) and vanilla combine in the most pleasant bouquet. On the palate it is balanced, upright, with flavours of chocolate and vanilla. The oak is present but skillfully measured, and the finish is lingering. A wine to drink in the coming two years. A special mention for the **Mâcon Tournus red 2002 (5–8 €)**, lighter but already pleasant.

๑ Pascal Pauget, La Croisette, 71700 Tournus, tel. 03.85.32.53.15, fax 03.85.51.72.67 **▼**
ϒ by appt.

DOM. DES PITOUX

Bussières 2001★

■	2 ha	5,000	🍷 ◊	3–5 €

The Pitoux estate comprises a dozen or so hectares of vineyards together with a Master-winemaker's house with a Mâconnais gallery and 18th-century cellars, at Bussières. The undulating siliceous-clay soil in this part of the Mâconnais has allowed the vinification of this lively red *cuvée* which gives off intense aromas of red berries and flowers. Very rounded, well-built, this wine lingers long on the palate. Finely-balanced, it is ready to drink now but could wait for a few months. Serve it with white meat.

๑ Jean-Yves Guyard, rue du Grand-Bussières, 71960 Bussières, tel. 03.85.37.74.74, fax 03.85.37.74.74 **▼**
ϒ by appt.

DOM. DES RIOTS

Pierreclos Cuvée Vieilles Vignes 2001★★

| ■ | 1.5 ha | 2,000 | ■ | 5–8 € |

This *cuvée* comes from selected vignes that are more than 60 years old, cultivated by integrated production on the granite slopes of Pierreclos, and hand havested. This Mâcon was vinified in the traditional way, without the addition of chemical yeasts, so as to conserve the characteristics of the terroir. The colour is intense garnet-red; the bouquet is pleasantly complex (black fruit and undergrowth). After a fine first impression come firm tannins, guarantors of quality and longevity. To drink in one to two years' time, with an entrecôte of charolais beef.

☛ Thierry Moreau, Le Pré du Poirier, 71960 Pierreclos, tel. 03.85.35.70.02 ☑
🍷 by appt.
☛ René Moreau

DOM. DE RUERE

Pierreclos Cuvée Prestige Vieilles vignes 2001★★

| ■ | 0.6 ha | 5,000 | ■ | 3–5 € |

Product of the granitic sandy soil at the heart of the Golden Triangle, this limpid, ruby-red selection has good aromas of cherries, redcurrants and strawberries. Its fine, elegant structure is a perfect expression of the Gamay grape. Rounded, fresh, fruity, all these qualities go to make this a thirst-quenching wine which would be the ideal drink with a platter of cold meats, without maskiing a hole in your budget.

☛ Thérèse Eloy, Ruère, 71960 Pierreclos, tel. 03.85.35.70.19, fax 03.85.35.70.19 ☑
🍷 by appt.

JEAN-CLAUDE THEVENET ET FILS

Pierreclos 2001★

| ■ | 6 ha | 13,000 | ■ ♦ | 3–5 € |

Produce of a family vineyard planted on the slopes overlooking the Château de Pierreclos, this ruby-red wine offers a frank bouquet which opens gradually on perfumes of strawberries and undergrowth. Supple and pleasant, it nevertheless has a tannic structure that will allow it to age for a year or two. Judged "appealing" by the tasters, it will seduce you, too, in company with a roast fowl.

☛ Jean-Claude Thévenet et Fils, Le Bourg, 71960 Pierreclos, tel. 03.85.35.72.21, fax 03.85.35.72.03, e-mail vignoblethevenet.jeanclaude@wanadoo.fr ☑
🍷 ev.day ex. Sun. 7.30am–12noon 1.30pm–6pm

DIDIER TRIPOZ

Clos des Tournons 2002★

| ■ | 2 ha | 10,000 | ■ ♦ | 3–5 € |

Les Clos des Tournons, near Charnay-lès-Mâcon, is partly planted with 30–year-old Gamay vines growing in clay-lime soil. Didier Tripoz, who runs it, has chosen to scratch 100% of the grapes and leave them eight days in fermentation. Luck was with him, for this 2002 vintage seduced the Jury. Dark in colour, with purple highlights, the bouquet is still delicate but complex: fruit, liquorice, vanilla and even a few fresh, herbaceous notes. Powerful, vigorous, elegant and robust...after a year or two it will be ready to get together with a coq au vin.

☛ Didier Tripoz, 450, chem. des Tournons, 71850 Charnay-Mâcon, tel. 03.85.34.14.52, fax 03.85.20.24.99, e-mail didier.tripoz@wanadoo.fr ☑
🍷 by appt.

CH. D' UXELLES

Chapaize 2001★

| ■ | 0.3 ha | 2,000 | ■ | 3–5 € |

Along the route of the Burgundy châteaux, stop at Chapaize to admire the highest Roman bell-tower in France and also the fabulous beauty spot, Uxelles, setting for the château which produced this attractive red wine with fruity accents. A fine cherry-red colour, it exudes perfumes of blackberries, raspberries and redcurrants. Fresh, but well-structured, the palate offers the same range of aromatic fruits, augmented by a note of kirsch. This fine, true-to-type wine should be drunk within a year.

☛ Ch. d' Uxelles, 71460 Chapaize, tel. 03.85.50.16.71, fax 03.85.50.15.10, e-mail alfreddelachapelle@wanadoo.fr ☑
🍷 by appt.
☛ De la Chapelle

Wines selected but not starred

JEAN-MARC ET CEDRIC BALANDRAS

Serrières Les Gravières 2001

| ■ | 3 ha | 3,000 | ■ ♦ | 5–8 € |

☛ Jean-Marc and Cédric Balandras, Les Guérins, 71960 Serrières, tel. 03.85.35.72.94, fax 03.85.35.70.82, e-mail jmcbalandras@aol.com ☑ 🏠
🍷 by appt.

DOM. DES CHENEVIERES 2001

| ■ | 0.45 ha | 796 | ■ ♦ | 3–5 € |

☛ Dom. des Chenevières, 71260 Saint-Maurice-de-Satonnay, tel. 03.85.33.31.27, fax 03.85.33.31.71 ☑
🍷 ev.day 9am–12noon 2pm–7pm
☛ Lenoir

CH. DE LA GREFFIERE

La Roche-Vineuse 2001

| ■ | 1.5 ha | 3,000 | ■ | 5–8 € |

☛ Isabelle et Vincent Greuzard, Ch. de La Greffière, 71960 La Roche-Vineuse, tel. 03.85.37.79.11, fax 03.85.36.62.88, e-mail chateaudelagreffiere@free.fr ☑
🍷 ev.day 9am–12noon 2pm–6.30pm

NICOLAS MAILLET

Verzé 2002

| ■ | 0.3 ha | 2,500 | ■ ♦ | 3–5 € |

☛ Nicolas Maillet, Le Clou, 71960 Verzé, tel. 03.85.33.46.76, fax 03.85.33.46.76, e-mail a.rios@free.fr ☑
🍷 by appt.

DOM. MATHIAS 2001

| ■ | 2 ha | 12,000 | ■ ♦ | 5–8 € |

☛ Béatrice and Gilles Mathias, rue Saint-Vincent, 71570 Chaintré, tel. 03.85.27.00.50, fax 03.85.27.00.52, e-mail domaine-mathias@wanadoo.fr ☑ 🏠
🍷 by appt.

DOM. DE MONTERRAIN 2002

| ■ | 5 ha | 40,000 | ■ | 5–8 € |

☛ Patrick and Martine Ferret, Dom. de Monterrain, Les Monterrains, 71960 Serrières, tel. 03.85.35.73.47, fax 03.85.35.75.36 ☑ 🏠 🏠
🍷 by appt.

LES TEPPES MARIUS 2002

| ■ | 18 ha | 144,000 | ■ ♦ | 5–8 € |

☛ Collin-Bourisset Vins Fins, rue de la Gare, 71680 Crèches-sur-Saône, tel. 03.85.36.57.25, fax 03.85.37.15.38, e-mail cbourisset@gofornet.com ☑
🍷 by appt.

Mâcon Supérieur

PAUL BEAUDET
Terres Rouges 2001★★

| | n.c. | 20,000 | ∎ | 3–5 € |

This Terres Rouges selection, bottled by the Beaudet company, is an attractive, intense bigaroon-cherry colour. Its perfumes are fresh and charming and evoke blackberries and raspberries. Following the supple opening, its fleshy substance, wrapped in silky tannins, lingers long on the palate. The tasters described it as "carressing"; this wine has a bright future (three to five years).
➤ Paul Beaudet, rue Paul-Beaudet, 71570 Pontanevaux, tel. 03.85.36.72.76, fax 03.85.36.72.02, e-mail contact@paulbeaudet.com ☑
✠ ev.day ex. Sat. Sun. 8am–12noon 1.30pm–5pm; cl. Aug.

CAVE DU PERE TIENNE 2001★★★

| | 1 ha | 8,000 | ⪫ | 5–8 € |

Product of a calcareous-clay terroir, this selection, vinified by carbonic maceration and matured for eight months in oak and chestnut-wood casks, captivated the Jury. A magnificent, intense, deep-purple colour, it exudes fruity and elegant floral aromas, marked by oaky notes. The tannins are evident but silky, the balance perfect. The aromatic finish lingers on fruity, smoky flavours. Powerful and rich, this wine will accompany a jugged hare. Our congratulations go to Eric Panay, both for this wine and its sibling, the **Mâcon-Villages white 2000**, which was awarded one star.
➤ Cave du Père Tienne, La Place, 71960 Sologny, tel. 03.85.37.78.05, fax 03.85.37.75.95, e-mail caveduperetienne@wanadoo.fr ☑ ☖
✠ ev.day 8am–8pm

VAUCHER PERE ET FILS 2001★

| | n.c. | n.c. | ∎ | 3–5 € |

This wine-merchant located at Nuits-Saint-Georges (the Cottin family) selected this attractive Mâcon, noted first of all for is quite intense, perfectly limpid garnet-red colour. This wine offers, in addition, a very expressive bouquet of red berries and spices. Admirably characteristic, it is fresh and balanced on the palate, and warming on the finish. Drink it this autumn with grilled red meat.
➤ Vaucher Père et Fils, rue Lavoisier, 21700 Nuits-Saint-Georges, tel. 03.80.62.64.00, fax 03.80.62.64.10, e-mail vaucher@axnet.fr

Wines selected but not starred

E. LORON ET FILS 2001

| | n.c. | n.c. | ∎ | 5–8 € |

➤ Ets Loron et Fils, Pontanevaux, 71570 La Chapelle-de-Guinchay, tel. 03.85.36.81.20, fax 03.85.33.83.19, e-mail vinloron@wanadoo.fr

Mâcon-Villages

HERITIERS AUVIGUE
Solutré 2001★

| | 0.19 ha | 1,600 | ⪫ | 5–8 € |

Product of very young vines, organically farmed, this selection was vinified and matured in oak casks. Pale-yellow, it offers a delicate bouquet which needs sustained aeration to deliver a few Chardonnay aromas. On the palate, however, it is well-balanced, fleshy and with a length of several caudalies. Quite harmonious, this wine nevertheless deserves to be laid down until its bouquet develops and opens. Under the marque **André Auvigue**, producer at Solutré-Pouilly (same telephone number), you will fine 2,000 bottles in this appellation which received one star for its 2001 vintage. Under another marque, the wines **Auvigue, Le Moulin du Pont Mâcon-Solutré 2001, Elevé en Fût**, received a special mention.
➤ Héritiers Auvigue, 3131, rte de Davayé, 71850 Charnay-lès-Mâcon, tel. 03.85.34.17.36, fax 03.85.34.75.88 ☑
✠ by appt.

CAVE D' AZE
Azé Cuvée Jules Richard 2001★★

| | 30 ha | 9,600 | ∎ ⚘ | 3–5 € |

This *cuvée*, dedicated to Jules Richard, one of the founders of the d'Azé cellars, carried off the Jurors' votes with great panache! "Superbe attack, this freshness is so magical one wants to dive into it. Once in it, everything is there: floral notes, fresh apples and pears, crystallized fruits, all supported by a fine vigour. And it makes the peacock's tail on the finish. Magnificent!" A great wine at a reasonable price. The **Cuvée Sélection Prestige 2001 (5–8 €)** was awarded one star in Mâcon d'Azé. Matured in cask, it combines roasted and floral notes within an elegant whole.
➤ Cave coop. d' Azé, En Tarroux, 71260 Azé, tel. 03.85.33.30.92, fax 03.85.33.37.21 ☑
✠ by appt.

DOM. DU BICHERON
Péronne 2001★

| | 6 ha | 20,000 | ∎ ⚘ | 5–8 € |

Daniel Rousset started the Bicheron estate in 1984 at Péronne, on a group of predominantly calcareous-clay lots. The bouquet of this pale-gold 2001 vintage with grey highlights is intensely floral (roses, peonies) together with ripe fruit aromas (apricot). Elegant and classy, it will be ready to drink from this autumn onwards as an aperitif wine. Note also, a special mention for the **Mâcon Péronne 2001 Elevé en Fût de Chêne** for 12 months. Still closed at the moment, it has enormous ageing potential. Worth following up.
➤ Daniel Rousset, Dom. du Bicheron, Saint-Pierre-de-Lanques, 71260 Péronne, tel. 03.85.36.94.53, fax 03.85.36.99.80 ☑
✠ by appt.

PAUL BROYER
Solutré 2001★

| | 0.8 ha | 2,600 | ∎ ⚘ | 5–8 € |

Worked and vinified by Paul Broyer, this wine is then bottled and distributed by l'Eventail des Vignerons Producteurs at Corcelles, in Beaujolais. Pale-yellow with green highlights, it exudes the Chardonnay characteristics: floral, with apples and pears enlivened by some notes of citrus fruit on the bouquet. On the palate it is well-balanced with the mineral notes which typify the terroir. Ready to drink this autumn, either as an aperitif or with mixed salads.
➤ Paul Broyer, Le Bourg, 71960 Solutré-Pouilly, tel. 04.74.06.10.10, fax 04.74.66.13.77 ☑
✠ by appt.

DOM. DE CHERVIN

Burgy Cuvée Tradition 2000★

	1.5 ha	5,000	🗌 ♦	8–11 €

The traditional knowledge and skill of Albert Goyard and his son are clearly evident in this wine: the working of the soil, respect for the environment and 18 months maturation. A golden 2000 vintage, it seduced the Jury with its complex bouquet of butter, floral notes and citrus fruit, and its supple and balanced richness on the palate. Nuances of pears and lychees linger a long time on the finish. A wine that is full of finesse, to keep for special occasions.

☛ GAEC Albert Goyard et Fils, Dom. de Chervin, 71260 Burgy, tel. 03.85.33.22.07, fax 03.85.33.00.49 ☑
🍷 ev.day 9am–6pm; Sun. by appt.

CLOS DES RAVIERES

Uchizy Les Ravières 2002★★

	0.9 ha	7,300	🗌🗌	8–11 €

It is no surprise to find Raphaël Sallet on this vintage wine; indeed, the considerable efforts he has made over several years mean that the Arfentière estate now offers wines of character, like this Mâcon Uchizy. The bouquet opens in fruit aromas and toast, signalling its 11 months maturation in cask. Supported by a fine oakiness which harmoniously envelopes well-ripened fruit, the palate shows a good presence and exceptional length. Very promising, it could easily be laid down for three to five years.

☛ EARL Raphaël and Gérard Sallet, L'Arfentière, rte de Chardonnay, 71700 Uchizy, tel. 03.85.40.50.45, fax 03.85.40.59.86, e-mail earlsallet@clubinternet.fr ☑ 🏠
🍷 by appt.

DOM. DE LA COMBE DE BRAY 2000★★

	3 ha	8,000	🗌 ♦	5–8 €

This magnificent *Clunisois* (from Cluny) countryside, land of Roman art, was also blessed by the gods for growing vines. On the fairly steep calcareous-clay slopes, Henri Lafarge has produced a wine from the mythical 2000 vintage. The bouquet of this golden-yellow, slightly amber Mâcon-Villages is unmistakable of the terroir, with largely fruity aromas. On the palate it has a well-balanced robustness and a most appetizing lychee and mandarin finish.

☛ Henri Lafarge, Dom. de La Combe, le Bourg, 71250 Bray, tel. 03.85.50.02.18, fax 03.85.50.05.37, e-mail henri.lafarge@wanadoo.fr ☑
🍷 by appt.

DOM. DES DEUX ROCHES 2001★

	10 ha	60,000	🗌 ♦	5–8 €

This estate has gone through a period of lightning expansion in recent years (purchase and take-over of vineyards, addition of a winery, etcetera). In a continuation of their efforts, the owners have just completed the construction of a magnificent cellar dug out of the rock. Brilliant, tending towards gold, this 2001 vintage offers a delicate bouquet, a subtle mixture of dried fruit and pears together with a hint of marshmallow. The opening is supple, introducing a substance that is fleshy, generous and fruity. This wine leaves a good impression, and will be excellent with a fairly refined goat's milk cheese.

☛ Dom. des Deux Roches, 71960 Davayé, tel. 03.85.35.86.51, fax 03.85.35.86.12 ☑
🍷 by appt.

DOM. FERRAND

Solutré-Pouilly 2001★

	0.4 ha	2,500	🗌	5–8 €

Nadine Ferrand has run this estate since 2000. Grown on 30 year-old vines, this wine is an attractive, limpid pale-yellow colour. Intense and fine, the bouquet evokes confectionery and violets. The opening is supple, full, and develops on floral notes and nuances of citrus fruit rind. Elegant and fresh, this wine is pleasant already but worth laying down for another year or two.

☛ Nadine Ferrand, 71960 Solutré-Pouilly, tel. 03.85.35.86.05, fax 03.85.35.88.01 ☑
🍷 by appt.

MAISON FORGEOT PERE ET FILS 2002★

	n.c.	n.c.	🗌🗌🗌 ♦	5–8 €

Partly matured in oak casks, the *cuvée*, selected by this wine-merchant starts off rich and complex, with perfumes of pineapple, apricot and floral aromas, which develop on the palate, showing a good degree of maturity. The richness is confirmed on the palate, where one finds a pleasant substance and a touch of liveliness, though the finish reveals its extreme youth. A wine to lay down for two to three years and then serve as an aperitif.

☛ Grands Vins Forgeot, 15, rue du Château, 21200 Beaune, tel. 03.80.24.80.50, fax 03.80.22.55.88

DOM. DE FUSSIACUS

Fuissé 2001★

	3 ha	23,000	🗌 ♦	5–8 €

Produced by one of the highly recommended wine concerns of the region, this rich and well-made 2001 vintage is a good gold colour with green highlights. The bouquet offers real complexity: grapes that are fresh and, at the same time, very ripe, citrus fruit, peach stones. After a rather faint opening, the wine is quickly intensified by its smoothness and balance. Still restrained for now, it promises a fine future.

☛ Jean-Paul Paquet, 71960 Fuissé, tel. 03.85.27.01.06, fax 03.85.27.01.07, e-mail fussiacus@wanadoo.fr ☑
🍷 by appt.

DOM. DE LA GARENNE

Azé 2001★

	3 ha	20,000	🗌 ♦	5–8 €

This selection comes from young vines planted 16 years ago on a south-facing hilltop above the famous prehistoric caves at Azé. With a strong personality, due to its mineral and chalky aspect, it nevertheless has agreeable aromas of crystallized fruit. This aromatic theme is confirmed on the lively and firm palate. At its peak in one to two years, this Mâcon will be perfect with a seafood platter.

☛ Renoud-Grappin and Périnet, Dom. de La Garenne, rte de Péronne, 71260 Azé, tel. 04.74.55.06.08, fax 04.74.55.10.08 ☑
🍷 by appt.

DOM. GIROUX

Fuissé 2001★★

	1 ha	6,000	🗌	5–8 €

The Grand Jury for the Mâcon wines approved of this 2001 vintage, coming from the southern part of the appellation. Yves Giroux, a generous man, celebrated his thirty years in the business with this remarkable brilliant straw-yellow wine. The complex bouquet has all the Chardonnay aromas. Well-made, this wine is solid, powerful and well-balanced, and while its roundness and fleshiness make it already harmonious, it will be worthwhile laying it down for two or three years before serving it with a Bresse chicken à la crème.

☛ Yves Giroux, Les Molards, 71960 Fuissé, tel. 03.85.35.63.64, fax 03.85.32.90.08 ☑
🍷 by appt.

DOM. GONON 2001★★

	0.4 ha	3,000	🗌 ♦	5–8 €

This Mâcon-Villages, grown on young vines planted in calcareous-clay soil, came close to being *coup de coeur*. Jean-François Gonon has produced a 2001 that is characteristic of its appellation. Its first appeal? Its fine, limpid pale-gold colour and its already very open bouquet, where one detects notes of citrus fruits, broom and exotic fruits. Well-rounded, supported by a touch of acidity, with impressive richness and balance, it is already harmonious. Serve it with a fricassée of frogs legs.

☛ Dom. Gonon, 71960 Vergisson, tel. 03.85.37.78.42, fax 03.85.37.77.14, e-mail domgonon@aol.com ☑
🍷 by appt.

CAVE DES GRANDS CRUS BLANCS
Loché 2002★★

	16 ha	20,000	🍶 ♦		5–8 €

This group of wine-growers in the heart of the Southern Mâconnais, under the management of Denis Mollard, together vinify the harvest from more than 130 ha. An attractive, diaphanous colour, this Mâcon-Loché is already had a complex and aromatic range: floral, with notes of dried fruit. Supported by a good liveliness, it is subtle and fine on the palate with fruit flavours on the finish (grapes, pineapple and tangerines). This wine has the potential to age and could be laid down for two or three years. The **Mâcon-Vinzelles** from the same vintage received a special mention.

☛ Cave des Grands Crus blancs, 71680 Vinzelles, tel. 03.85.27.05.70, fax 03.85.27.05.71, e-mail contact@cavevinzellesloche.com ☑
🍷 by appt.

DOM. DE LALANDE
Chânes Les Serreudières 2001★★

	1.33 ha	9,000	🍶 ♦		5–8 €

Selected by the Guide for many years, Dominique Cornin is highly recommended in the Mâconnais. Two *cuvées* caught the Jury's attention. This pale-gold Mâcon-Chânes has a fine fruity, floral bouquet. Fleshiness and weight dominate on the palate but the finish is still fruity and fresh. The **Mâcon-Chaintré 2001**, very representative of its region and as fruity as one could wish, was awarded one star.

☛ Dominique Cornin, chem. du Roy-de-Croix, 71570 Chaintré, tel. 03.85.37.43.58, fax 03.85.37.43.58, e-mail dominique@cornin.net ☑
🍷 by appt.

DOM. DE LANQUES
Péronne Les Berthelots 2001★★

	1 ha	2,000	🍶 ♦		5–8 €

This estate, handed on from father to daughter, had an ultra-modern winery built in 2000. The Les Berthelots Cuvée comes from century old vines planted in calcareous-clay soil. Its intense and complex perfumes evoke pineapple, passion-fruit and quince, all that framed in scintillating gold. The body is well-balanced, acid and silky at the same time, the sign of a typical wine to drink with goat's milk cheese.

☛ Papillon, Dom. de Lanques, Saint-Pierre-de-Lanques, 71260 Péronne, tel. 03.85.23.95.70, fax 03.85.23.95.74, e-mail earl.papillon@free.fr ☑ 🏠
🍷 by appt.

DOM. MICHEL LAPIERRE
Solutré-Pouilly 2001★

	0.5 ha	2,000	🍶 ♦		5–8 €

Situated 500 m from the Roche de Solutré, this estate offered a 2001 vintage of a lightly-gilded, yellow colour. The very attractive, Chardonnay bouquet mingles mineral notes and nuances of herbs and fresh butter. The delicate palate is less expressive, but the lemony finish would go very well with grilled fish.

☛ Michel Lapierre, Le Bourg, 71960 Solutré-Pouilly, tel. 03.85.35.80.45, fax 03.85.35.87.61 ☑
🍷 by appt.

DOM. ROGER LUQUET
Les Mulots 2001★

	3.9 ha	26,000	🍶 ♦		5–8 €

A large part of the product of this 24 ha estate is exported around the world; sign of a dynamic wine-grower who is not lacking in projects. His Mâcon-Villages, *coup de coeur* last year, is a good ambassador for the region. Brilliant, with good intensity, the yellow-gold colour of this 2001 vintage is most

attractive. The characteristic and intense bouquet alternates exotic fruit (pineapple, passion-fruit) and dried fruits (almonds, apricots). The palate is smooth, with flavours of Muscat grapes, quite well-balanced and not lacking in presence. This wine, aromatic *par excellence*, could be served next year as an aperitif.

☛ Dom. Roger Luquet, 71960 Fuissé, tel. 03.85.35.60.91, fax 03.85.35.60.12, e-mail domainerogerluquet@club-internet.fr ☑
🍷 ev.day ex. Sun. 9am–7pm

DOM. NICOLAS MAILLET
Verzé Contre le Chemin blanc 2001★

	0.5 ha	4,000	🍶		5–8 €

Harvested by hand on 8 October 2001, this Mâcon-Verzé is vinified with native yeasts and fermented for six months. Its pale-yellow colour is brilliant, its bouquet, restrained at first, opens up on fruity notes followed by nuances of white truffles and marshmallow. The supple and fresh attack gives way to a fine, coated spiciness and a pleasant, lemony finish. A fine and lively wine which should be kept for a while.

☛ Nicolas Maillet, Le Clou, 71960 Verzé, tel. 03.85.33.46.76, fax 03.85.33.46.76, e-mail a.rios@free.fr ☑
🍷 by appt.

DOM. MANCIAT-PONCET
Charnay Les Chênes 2001★

	3.2 ha	25,000	🍶 ♦		5–8 €

These vineyards, situated at a place called Les Chênes, are close to an ancient limestone quarry and produce, as one might expect, a mineral white wine of a limpid pale-gold colour. The bouquet is fresh and elegant, and other than the notes of flint and chalk, one detects ripe fruit aromas (raisins and apricots). While still closed, the palate is fleshy and rests on a firm structure which will guarantee its future.

☛ Dom. Manciat-Poncet, 65, chem. des Gérards, Levigny, 71850 Charnay-lès-Mâcon, tel. 03.85.29.22.93, fax 03.85.29.17.59 ☑
🍷 by appt.
☛ Claude Manciat

DOM. MICHEL
Vieilles Vignes 2001★★

	1 ha	6,000	🍶 ♦		8–11 €

2001

GRAND VIN DE BOURGOGNE

Domaine Michel

à Clessé

MÂCON-VILLAGES
APPELLATION D'ORIGINE CONTRÔLÉE

RENÉ MICHEL ET SES FILS
VITICULTEURS-RÉCOLTANTS "CRAY" À CLESSÉ (SAÔNE-ET-LOIRE)

13.5% vol.   MIS EN BOUTEILLE À LA PROPRIÉTÉ - PRODUIT DE FRANCE   75 cl

The members of the Michel family are passionate about their work and from grapes fully-ripened in their vineyards, produce authentic wines like this Mâcon-Villages which carried off all the Grand Jury's votes. The colour of this poetic wine is a strong, deep yellow-gold. The intense bouquet is a classy mixture of floral notes and exotic fruits. The rounded, powerful palate evokes crystallized fruit. Balanced and perfectly harmonious, this is a highly espressive wine to serve with a creamy chocolate dish.

☛ Dom. René Michel et ses Fils, Cray, 71260 Clessé, tel. 03.85.36.94.27, fax 03.85.36.99.63 ☑
🍷 by appt.

MOMMESSIN
Vieilles Vignes 2002★

	10 ha	60,000	🍶 ♦		5–8 €

It has always been the policy of this wine-merchant, established in 1865, to buy high quality Mâcon wines, and this

Mâcon 2002, while still young, is not the one to refute it. Full of brilliance and golden highlights, this white wine, with a bouquet full of pleasant nuances of ripe fruit, offers an attractive aroma of pears on a balanced and rounded palate. A wine to enjoy this autumn with a pear *clafoutis* (a type of cake).
➥ Mommessin, Le Pont-des-Samsons, 69430 Quincié-en-Beaujolais, tel. 04.74.69.09.30, fax 04.74.69.09.29, e-mail information@mommessin.fr

L' ORIGINEL
Chardonnay 2002★★

	30 ha	150,000	🍶		5–8 €

The Jury was enthusiastic about two selections from the 2002 vintage. This one comes from vineyards situated in the village of Chardonnay, cradle of the famous grape variety. Limpid pale-yellow, with green highlights, its bouquet is fresh and floral, still restrained but elegant. After a clean opening, it reveals a fine balance on the palate and finishes on apple and pear flavours. The **Mâcon-Péronne 2002**, with its golden colour and intense, ripe fruit bouquet (apricots, pineapple), is more exuberant. On the palate it is rich and pulpy, with a very fresh, lemony finish. Two fine wines, produced in good quantity, which could be laid down for one or two years.
➥ SCV Cave de Lugny, rue des Charmes, BP 6, 71260 Lugny, tel. 03.85.33.22.85, fax 03.85.33.26.46, e-mail commercial@cave-lugny.com
🍷 by appt.

LES VINS DES PERSONNETS 2001★

	n.c.	20,000	🍶 ♦		5–8 €

This wine-merchant business was recently established by two wine-growers from the Mâconnais, J.-L. Terrier and C. Collovray, who have a wide knowledge of the sector. They offered an attractive Mâcon-villages, white-gold in colour with silver highlights. The still-restrained bouquet is full of floral notes (acacia blossom, wild roses, honeysuckle, *et cetera*). The structure on the palate is interesting, linking freshness with vitality and good, lemony length. A very appealing aperitif wine.
➥ Les Vins des Personnets, Christian Collovray and Jean-Luc Terrier, 71960 Davayé, tel. 03.85.35.86.51, fax 03.85.35.86.12 🆅
🍷 by appt.

DOM. PASCAL ET MIREILLE RENAUD
Solutré 2002★

	0.52 ha	6,800	🍶 ♦		5–8 €

This Mâcon-Villages, grown on the calcareous-clay soil of the Solutré, is quite a discovery. Its brilliant pale-yellow colour precedes an intense and characteristic bouquet (citronella, floral). The opening on the palate is frank, and roundness combines well with acidic edge of this young wine. Its grapefruit and lemon finish is seductive. It deserves to be laid down for two to three years.
➥ Pascal and Mireille Renaud, Pouilly, 71960 Solutré-Pouilly, tel. 03.85.35.84.62, fax 03.85.35.87.42 🆅
🍷 by appt.

JEAN RIJCKAERT
Montbellet En Pottes Vieilles Vignes 2001★★★

	0.59 ha	3,600	🍾		11–15 €

Jean Rijckaert, from a different background, installed himself in the Mâconnais district in 1998 and since then has never ceased to surprise us. The "Sauternes" colour of this exceptional wine is gold with bronze highlights. The powerful and complex bouquet allies smooth aromas of ripe grapes (quince) with charred wood aromas. Concentrated, rich and classy on the palate, it has perfect balance. A thoroughbred wine which could be laid down for a long period.
➥ Rijckaert, En Correaux, 71570 Leynes, tel. 03.85.35.15.09, fax 03.85.35.15.09, e-mail jeanrijckaert@infonie.fr 🆅
🍷 by appt.

DOM. SAINT-DENIS
Chardonnay 2001★

	2 ha	10,000	🍶 ♦		8–11 €

Hubert Laferrère is one of those passionate people who don't hesitate to get to the bottom of things and see their projects through to the end. This 2001 vintage has a clean approach; brilliant, limpid intense yellow-gold, it is a welcoming wine with its notes of white peaches and honeysuckle. After a supple opening, it gains strength and offers the most pleasant fruity flavours. The finish is long and demands…a second mouthful. Serve it with a Bresse capon à la crème.
➥ Hubert Laferrère, rte de Péronne, 71260 Lugny, tel. 03.85.33.24.33, fax 03.85.33.25.02, e-mail saintdenis@free.fr 🆅
🍷 by appt.

DOM. DE LA SOUFRANDISE
Fuissé le Ronté 2001★

	1 ha	7,500	🍶 ♦		8–11 €

Fifteen years old, the vineyards of the La Soufrandise estate, planted in metamorphic rock, have produced this characteristic and well-balanced Mâcon-Fuissé. Its intense bouquet, fruity (apples and pears) at first, develops towards citrus fruits and flint. Very fresh, it shows roundness on the palate, going on to a stewed-fruit finish. To drink in two years' time with a fairly refined goat's milk cheese.
➥ Françoise and Nicolas Melin, EARL Dom. La Soufrandise, 71960 Fuissé, tel. 03.85.35.64.04, fax 03.85.35.65.57
🍷 by appt.

GERALD ET PHILIBERT TALMARD
Uchizy 2001★

	9.5 ha	88,000	🍶 ♦		3–5 €

Situated in the southern part of the appellation, Uchizy, a charming village, has excellent calcareous-clay, east-facing slopes. Brilliant pale-gold, this Mâcon-Villages develops a delicate bouquet, lemony and lightly spiced. On the palate it is balanced, fine, with a mentholated flavour that gives it good length. Subtle and elegant, this wine is a trifle "mad" and could be served in one to two years' time with a sole meunière.
➥ EARL Gérald and Philibert Talmard, rue des Fosses, 71700 Uchizy, tel. 03.85.40.53.18, fax 03.85.40.53.52, e-mail gerald.talmard@wanadoo.fr 🆅
🍷 by appt.

DIDIER TRIPOZ
Charnay Clos des Tournons 2001★★

	4 ha	30,000	🍶 ♦		5–8 €

Didier Tripoz, who takes great care with the vinification of his wines, presented a well-made 2001 vintage which was much appreciated by the Jury. Yellow with golden highlights, its bouquet is complex, starting with floral (acacia, honeysuckle) then becoming mineral. Supple and wide-awake, it is well-balanced and its flinty finish is "sharp". Should be laid down for two years before being served with an up-market fish.
➥ Didier Tripoz, 450, chem. des Tournons, 71850 Charnay-lès-Mâcon, tel. 03.85.34.14.52, fax 03.85.20.24.99, e-mail didier.tripoz@wanadoo.fr 🆅
🍷 by appt.

BURGUNDY

DOM. DES VALANGES
Davayé 2001★

	2 ha	13,000	▮	5–8 €

In keeping with his reputation, Michel Paquet offered a 2001 vintage which is notable for its aromatic complexity. This wine is redolent of ripe fruit, semolina pudding, confectionery, white truffles, hazelnuts and violets. Very well-constituted, its structure is based on a good acid support which indicates a good potential for ageing.
☛ Michel Paquet, Les Valanges, 71960 Davayé, tel. 03.85.35.85.03, fax 03.85.35.86.67, e-mail domaine-des-valanges@wanadoo.fr ☑
⚥ by appt.

PIERRE VESSIGAUD
Fuissé 2001★

	2.1 ha	19,000	▮	8–11 €

In the Vessigaud family, the *vigneron*'s skills have been handed down through five generations. Despite technical advances, the credo is the same: the search for authenticity. Very characteristic, the bouquet of this 2001 vintage is pleasant, floral, with aromas of almonds and fresh butter. After a supple opening, dried-fruit notes are added to those of the bouquet to give a powerful and elegant whole. An attractive wine that will keep two or three years in the cellar. A special mention, too, for the **Mâcon-Solutré 2001 (5–8 €)**, wine with a William pear nose, with nuances of the characteristic Chardonnay aromas. A fine construction, but to enjoy it at its best needs patience (four to five years).
☛ SCEA Dom. Vessigaud Père et Fils, Hameau de Pouilly, 71960 Solutré-Pouilly, tel. 03.85.35.81.18, fax 03.85.35.84.29 ☑
⚥ by appt.

Wines selected but not starred

FRANCOIS BOURDON 2001

	0.64 ha	2,600	▮	5–8 €

☛ Dom. François and Sylvie Bourdon, Pouilly, 71960 Solutré-Pouilly, tel. 03.85.35.81.44, fax 03.85.35.81.44 ☑
⚥ by appt.

CAVE DE CHAINTRE
Chaintré 2002

	8.07 ha	20,000	▮ ⚥	5–8 €

☛ Cave de Chaintré, 71570 Chaintré, tel. 03.85.35.61.61, fax 03.85.35.61.48 ☑
⚥ by appt.

CH. DE CHARNAY 2001

	n.c.	28,000	▮ ⚥	5–8 €

☛ Caves de Prissé-Sologny-Verzé, Les Grandes-Vignes, 71960 Prissé, tel. 03.85.37.88.06, fax 03.85.37.61.76, e-mail caves.prisse@wanadoo.fr ☑ ▯
⚥ by appt.

CAVE DE CHARNAY
Charnay Vieilles Vignes 2001

	n.c.	n.c.	▮	5–8 €

☛ Cave de Charnay, 71850 Charnay-lès-Mâcon, tel. 03.85.34.54.24, fax 03.85.34.86.84 ☑
⚥ by appt.

CHARTRON ET TREBUCHET 2001

	n.c.	15,000	▮ ⚥	8–11 €

☛ Chartron and Trébuchet, 13, Grande-Rue, 21190 Puligny-Montrachet, tel. 03.80.21.32.85, fax 03.80.21.36.35 ☑

DOM. CHENE
La Roche vineuse Fût de chêne 2001

	1.3 ha	10,000	▮ ▯▯	5–8 €

☛ Dom. Chêne, Ch. Chardon, 71960 Berzé-la-Ville, tel. 03.85.37.65.30, fax 03.85.37.75.39, e-mail gaecchene@aol.com ☑
⚥ by appt.

DOM. CLOS GAILLARD
Solutré 2002

	1.35 ha	6,500	▮	5–8 €

☛ EARL Gérald Favre, Pouilly-le-Bas, 71960 Solutré-Pouilly, tel. 03.85.35.80.14, fax 03.85.35.87.50 ☑
⚥ ev.day 10am–1pm 2pm–8pm

DOM. DE LA CREUZE NOIRE 2001

	1 ha	6,000	▮ ⚥	5–8 €

☛ Dominique et Christine Martin, La Creuze Noire, 71570 Leynes, tel. 03.85.37.46.43, fax 03.85.37.44.17 ☑
⚥ ev.day 8am–12noon 1.30pm–7pm; Sun. 8am–12noon

DOMAINES LANEYRIE
Solutré 2001

	0.5 ha	1,500	▮ ⚥	3–5 €

☛ Domaines Edmond Laneyrie, Le Bourg, 71960 Solutré-Pouilly, tel. 03.85.35.80.67, fax 03.85.35.80.67 ☑
⚥ by appt.

DOM. ALAIN NORMAND
La Roche Vineuse Vieilles Vignes 2000

	1 ha	3,000	▯▯	5–8 €

☛ Alain Normand, chem. de la Grange-du-Dime, 71960 La Roche-Vineuse, tel. 03.85.36.61.69, fax 03.85.51.60.97, e-mail domaine.alain.normand@wanadoo.fr ☑
⚥ by appt.

DOM. JEAN-PIERRE SEVE
Solutré 2001

	0.7 ha	5,600	▮	5–8 €

☛ EARL Dom. Jean-Pierre Sève, Le Bourg, 71960 Solutré-Pouilly, tel. 03.85.35.80.19, fax 03.85.35.80.58, e-mail domaine.jean-pierre_seve@libertysurf.fr ☑
⚥ by appt.

DOM. SIMONIN
Vergisson 2001

	n.c.	n.c.	▮ ▯▯ ⚥	8–11 €

☛ Jacques Simonin, Le Bourg, 71960 Vergisson, tel. 03.85.35.84.72, fax 03.85.35.85.34 ☑
⚥ by appt.

CH. DE LA TOUR PENET 2001

	n.c.	n.c.		5–8 €

☛ Jacques Charlet, 71570 La Chapelle-de-Guinchay, tel. 03.85.36.81.20, fax 03.85.33.83.19

DOM. DE LA TOUR VAYON
Pierreclos Clos de la Condemine 2001

	1 ha	8,666	▮ ⚥	5–8 €

☛ Jean-Marie Pidault, La Condemine, 71960 Pierreclos, tel. 03.85.35.71.78, fax 03.85.35.78.03 ☑
⚥ by appt.

Viré-Clessé

Viré-Clessé is a new appellation, created as recently as 4 November 1998, and has solid ambitions for its white wines. The area of the appellation is 552 ha, four-fifths of which are currently planted with vines, producing 13,340 hl of wine in 2002. The denominations Mâcon-Viré and Mâcon-Clessé disappeared in 2002.

DOM. DES CHAZELLES

Le Creusseromme 2001★

	0.53 ha	2,100	🍶	8–11 €

Situated at the foot of the Viré slope, in the very centre of the appellation, this estate was established in 1860. Jean-Noël Chaland has been applying his wisdom to his work for all of 35 years and has had great success with his pleasant wines. This one stands out for its appealing, soft-fruit bouquet and its elegance and length on the palate. The **La Forétille 2001**, one star, was not matured in cask: still a little austere, it has fine potential and could reach its peak in two or three years' time. Both are wines suitable for drinking with the fresh-water fish of the Saône river.
🌿 Jean-Noël Chaland, En Jean-Large, 71260 Viré, tel. 03.85.33.11.18, fax 03.85.33.15.58, e-mail chazellesdom@aol.com ▼
🍷 by appt.

LE CLOS DU CHATEAU

Cuvée Chartine Vieilles Vignes Elevé en fût de chêne 2001★

	2.5 ha	1,500	🍶	8–11 €

At Clessé there is a Roman church, restored in the 18th century, with an octagonal bell-tower and spire roofed in exceptionally fine Burgundian tiles. At the head of this estate since 1994, Robert Marin offered two selections which were each awarded a star. This one, matured in cask and of a fine, light colour, is delicate, finely oaked and lingering on the palate. The **Le Clos du Château Vieilles Vignes 2001 (5–8 €)**, not matured in cask, is straw-yellow. It opens on perfumes of peaches and hawthorn blossom, and offers an elegant and acidic palate. Two very expressive wines to keep in your cellar.
🌿 Robert and Marielle Marin, rte de la Vigne-Blanche, 71260 Clessé, tel. 03.85.36.95.92, fax 03.85.36.93.07 ▼
🍷 by appt.
🌿 Gilbert Mornand

DOM. DU MORTIER 2000★

	1.45 ha	3,000	🍾 ⚲	8–11 €

Installed as head of this estate only two years ago, Renaud Chandioux makes his entry in the *Guide* with his first vintage, a 2000. A seductive golden colour, this wine has a fresh and complex bouquet of yellow peaches, apricots and fruits bottled in syrup, supported by aniseed notes, The palate, powerful and fine at the same time, is balanced and fruity. With good substance, but remaining utterly elegant, this wine has a large potential for ageing (five years).
🌿 Renaud Chandioux, Le Mortier, 71260 Péronne, tel. 03.85.36.98.93, fax 03.85.36.98.93 ▼
🍷 by appt.

RIJCKAERT

En Thurissey Vieilles Vignes 2001★

	1.2 ha	6,500	🍶	11–15 €

Jean Rijckaert has several strings to his bow: as wine-grower, running 1.3 ha of Viré-Clessé at l'Epinet which produced a pale-yellow **2001 (8–11 €)**, specially mentioned by the Jury for its intense aromas of toast and coffee, and its fullness and length on the palate; as wine-merchant, he buys a part of the production of a young wine-grower at Viré, vinifies it and matures it in oak casks for ten months. His En Thurissey selection, with its pale-gold colour and oaked perfumes and full and rich palate, needs time to achieve its balance. A fine result in both categories.

🌿 Rijckaert, En Correaux, 71570 Leynes, tel. 03.85.35.15.09, fax 03.85.35.15.09, e-mail jeanrijckaert@infonie.fr ▼
🍷 by appt.
🌿 Jean-Marie Chaland

CAVE DE VIRE

Cuvée Prestige Elevée en fût de chêne 2000★

	10 ha	40,000	🍶	5–8 €

This dynamic cooperative challenged its members to develop sustainable farming methods with respect for the environment. Another challenge met is the successful marrying of the oak with the wine of this Viré-Clessé, which is redolent of the ripe harvest. Aromas of yellow fruit, honey, vanilla and toast for a complex and intense bouquet. On the palate, these aromas are augmented by a fine roundness and a balanced oak presence. A very fine wine that will develop well over time. A star shines over the **Cuvée Vieilles Vignes 2001**, judged most pleasant.
🌿 Cave de Viré, En Vercheron, 71260 Viré, tel. 03.85.32.25.50, fax 03.85.32.25.55, e-mail cavedevire@wanadoo.fr ▼
🍷 by appt.

Wines selected but not starred

PAUL BEAUDET 2001

	n.c.	20,000	🍾 ⚲	5–8 €

🌿 Paul Beaudet, rue Paul-Beaudet, 71570 Pontanevaux, tel. 03.85.36.72.76, fax 03.85.36.72.02, e-mail contact@paulbeaudet.com ▼
🍷 ev.day ex. Sat. Sun. 8am–12noon 1.30pm–5pm; cl. Aug.

DOM. ANDRE BONHOMME 2001

	2 ha	25,000		5–8 €

🌿 André Bonhomme, Cidex 2108, rue Jean-Large, 71260 Viré, tel. 03.85.27.93.93, fax 03.85.27.93.94 ▼
🍷 by appt.

DOM. PASCAL BONHOMME

Vieilles vignes 2001

	0.6 ha	3,200	🍾 🍶 ⚲	5–8 €

🌿 Pascal Bonhomme, Le Grand Molard, Cidex 2222, Vérizet, 71260 Viré, tel. 03.85.33.10.27, fax 03.85.33.10.27 ▼
🍷 ev.day 9am–7pm

DOM. SAINTE-BARBE

L'Epinet 2001

	0.4 ha	3,000	🍶	8–11 €

🌿 Jean-Marie Chaland, 71260 Viré, tel. 03.85.33.96.72, fax 03.85.33.15.58 ▼
🍷 by appt.

CAVE DE LA VIGNE BLANCHE 2001

	20 ha	33,000	🍾	5–8 €

🌿 Cave Coop. de Clessé, rte de la Vigne-Blanche, 71260 Clessé, tel. 03.85.36.93.88, fax 03.85.36.97.49, e-mail cavecooperative.vigneblanche@wanadoo.fr ▼
🍷 by appt.

Pouilly-Fuissé

The cliffs of Solutré and Vergisson stretch proudly towards the sky like the prows of two great ships; at their feet lies the most prestigious vineyard of the Mâconnais, Pouilly-Fuissé, stretching over the communes of Fuissé, Solutré-Pouilly, Vergisson and Chaintré. Production reached a total of 43,622 hl in 2002.

The wines from Pouilly have achieved a very substantial reputation, particularly in the export market, and from a price point of view they have always competed with Chablis. The wines are lively, aromatically flavoured and perfumed. Matured in oak barrels, they develop the characteristic flavours of grilled almond or hazelnut as they age.

DOM. ABELANET-LANEYRIE
Le Clos de Monsieur Noly 2001★

| | 0.35 ha | 2,554 | | | 11–15 € |

This is a very successful Pouilly-Fuissé 2001, very characteristic of the appellation, made at an estate with a Mâconnais gallery. A light greenish-gold colour, its bouquet offers floral and mineral scents. Well-balanced on the palate, where dried fruits and toast predominate. To drink during the year with a mature Mâconnais goat's milk cheese. The same mark was received for the **Cuvée Prestige 2000 (15–23 €)**, judged atypical because of its over-ripe aspect, "almost late-harvest," but well-made.
↘ Eric Abélanet, Les Buissonnats, 71570 Chaintré, tel. 03.85.35.61.95, fax 03.85.35.66.43, e-mail ericabel@club-internet.fr ✉
✔ by appt.

AUVIGUE
Cuvée Hors Classe 2001★

| | 0.5 ha | 2,000 | | | 11–15 € |

Severe selection, meticulous maturation and refined presentation are practised by this excellent wine-merchant. The intense gold-yellow of this wine attracts the eye. The well-opened bouquet evokes dried flowers, vanilla and spices. Concentration and balance characterize the structure, with what is needed of oak. This barely acidulated finish calls for a dish of curry. The **Cuvée Vieilles Vignes 2001 (8–11 €)** received a special mention.
↘ Vins Auvigue, Le Moulin-du-Pont, 71850 Charnay-lès-Mâcon, tel. 03.85.34.17.36, fax 03.85.34.75.88, e-mail vins.auvigue@wanadoo.fr ✉
✔ by appt.

CH. DE BEAUREGARD
La Maréchaude 2001★

| | 1 ha | 5,000 | | | 15–23 € |

Acquired in 1883 by the Burrier family, the Château de Beauregard owes its name to its exceptional position: isolated on a plateau among the Fuissé vineyards, it enjoys a unique view over the Solutré and Vergisson rocks. Its Pouilly-Fuissé La Maréchaude, a renowned *climat* of the village of Vergisson, is a beautiful gold colour with silver-grey highlights. The very fine bouquet opens on smooth perfumes of acacia and honey, developing lemony notes. On the palate, fine notes of toast and grilling are succeeded by grapefruit and crystallized orange flavours. Pulpy, the finish is tonic and thirst-quenching. Already an excellent wine, it will keep for two or three years. Serve it with a special fish-dish.
↘ Maison Joseph Burrier, Ch. de Beauregard, 71960 Fuissé, tel. 03.85.35.60.76, fax 03.85.35.66.04, e-mail joseph.burrier@mageos.com ✉
✔ by appt.
↘ F.-M. Burrier

CHANSON PERE ET FILS 2001★

| n.c. | 8,300 | | | 15–23 € |

Selected on the wine-growers' estates, 30 % of this Pouilly-Fuissé from the Chanson company (Bollinger Group) was matured in oak casks. The result is graphic: brilliant gold-yellow colour, a nose of exotic fruit linked with a light oakiness, then a particularly fine floral bouquet. The palate is fruity, confirming the good balance between the richness and acidity. Already quite harmonious, but it could reach perfection in one to two years' time.
↘ Dom. Chanson Père et Fils, 10, rue Paul-Chanson, BP 232, 21206 Beaune Cedex, tel. 03.80.25.97.97, fax 03.80.24.17.42, e-mail tmarion@vins-chanson.com

CLOS DE LA CHAPELLE 2001★★

| | 0.42 ha | 1,600 | | | 15–23 € |

Pascal Rollet is a man with firm beliefs: trained on the job, he has given this estate, of whom he his the tenant, a solid reputation. The Clos de La Chapelle, planted in 1921, is his pride and joy. Cosseted throughout the year, hand-harvested, vinified and matured in oak casks, this wine is a fine straw-gold colour. Its aromas mingle apricot, hazelnut, fresh butter and oaky notes. Its fine and delicate palate has plenty of length. This is a Pouilly-Fuissé that will reach its full potential in a few years. As to the **Domaine de La Chapelle Vieilles Vignes 2001 (11–15 €)**, it is already showing a floral bouquet and gives a sensation of balance on the palate. It received a special mention.
↘ Pascal Rollet, hameau de Pouilly, 71960 Solutré-Pouilly, tel. 03.85.35.81.51, fax 03.85.35.86.43, e-mail rolletp@aol.com ✉
✔ by appt.
↘ Gondard

DOM. CORDIER PERE ET FILS
Fût n° XVI 2001★

| | 0.2 ha | 580 | | | 30–38 € |

From its old-gold colour this wine certainly seemed to be the product of a very ripe harvest. Its aromas, dominated by apples and pears, honey and toast, confirm this impression. On the palate it is warm, concentrated and acidic, but is already showing signs of evolution. Be careful, this is a limited selection and very expensive. The Jury gave a special mention to the **Cuvée Vieilles Vignes 2001 (15–23 €)**, whose oaks will need a few months to integrate.
↘ Dom. Cordier Père et Fils, 71960 Fuissé, tel. 03.85.35.62.89, fax 03.85.35.64.01, e-mail domaine.cordier@wanadoo.fr ✉
✔ by appt.

DOM. CORSIN 2000★

| | 3,5 ha | 19,500 | | | 15–23 € |

This estate, famous for its production of Saint-Véran, also takes care with its Pouilly-Fuissé. Note this wine's shining pale-yellow colour with its green highlights, the lightness of the floral and fruity nuances, the delicate palate, surprising for its oaky notes that were not present on the nose. A fine wine to discover and enjoy.
↘ Dom. Corsin, Les Plantes, 71960 Davayé, tel. 03.85.35.83.69, fax 03.85.35.86.64 ✉
✔ by appt.

DOM. MICHEL DELORME
Vieilles Vignes 2001★

| | 0.9 ha | 4,100 | | | 11–15 € |

Grown on the calcareous-clay Vergisson soil, hand-harvested in crates and partially vinified in cask, this Pouilly-Fuissé is a seductive, pale green-gold colour. Lemon, acacia blossom and nuances of oak make up the fresh bouquet. The opening is prolonged on a mineral quality characteristic of the Vergisson terroir. Well-made, it is a fine, expressive, refreshing wine that one could serve with a Brioche Lyonnaise. With no complexes!
↘ Dom. Michel Delorme, Le Bourg, 71960 Vergisson, tel. 03.85.35.84.50, fax 03.85.35.84.50, e-mail micheldelorme@club-internet.fr ✉
✔ ev.day 10am–12noon 1.30pm–7.30pm

DOM. DENUZILLER

La Frérie 2001★

	1 ha	2,200	⦿	8–11 €

Solutré-Pouilly is rich in cultural and tourist activities, but the village also produces excellent wine, like this pale-gold 2001 vintage, whose pronounced aromas of vanilla, brown sugar and verbena reflect its carefully managed vinification in cask. This wine will have reached its peak in three to four years. The **Le Clos 2001** produced a wine of an attractive gold colour, with green highlights. The bouquet is intense, dominated by citrus fruit (lemon, mandarin oranges) but also a light touch of iris. Floral and silky, the palate finishes on a fresh note recalling the freshness of the citrus fruits. This Pouilly-Fuissé could be served right away with fish with beaten butter, but it will keep for two or three years.
☛ Dom. Denuziller, 71960 Solutré-Pouilly,
tel. 03.85.35.80.77, fax 03.85.35.83.38 ☑
🍷 ev.day. 8am–12.30pm 1pm–7pm

NADINE FERRAND

Prestige 2001★★

	4 ha	2,700	▮ ⦿	11–15 €

At the head of this estate since 2000, Nadine Ferrand, a woman of character and an accomplished winemaker, makes a forceful entry into the Guide with this well-presented Cuvée Prestige. Pleasing, the colour of this wine is intense yellow-gold and in the course of olfaction, it releases aromas of exotic fruit, with floral notes and toast from the cask. On the palate it is full and rich, warm and packed with fruit. Of considerable strength, this wine will develop its full potential if laid down in the cellar for three to four years, before being serve with a Breton lobster. Also notable is the **Pouilly-Fuissé 2001 (8–11 €)**, a very successful, characteristic Chardonnay. This is an estate to watch.
☛ Nadine Ferrand, 71960 Solutré-Pouilly,
tel. 03.85.35.86.05, fax 03.85.35.88.01 ☑
🍷 by appt.

CH. FUISSE 2001★★

	12 ha	50,000	⦿	15–23 €

This château has an 15th century octagonal tower and two 100-year-old yew trees trimmed to the shape of wine-bottles guard the entrance. Jean-Jacques Vincent, renowned winemaker and oenologist, has been at the head of the family business since 1967; he has always bought out the best from his Pouilly and Fuissé terroirs, predominantly calcareous-clay and with a south-south-east exposure. The 2001 vintage is the estate's flagship product: grown on 15 year-old vines, with tempered yield, it combines elegance and structure. Golden to the eye, it has an intense bouquet of dried fruit with nuances of vanilla and oak. On the palate it is fleshy, generous and full-flavoured, giving flavours of white peaches on the finish. Seductive already, it could nevertheless age for two or three more years. The **Vieilles Vignes 2001 (23–30 €)**, 45 years old, was rewarded with a star. Subtle fruity aromas escape from the glass but is largely on the palate that this wine reveals its opulence, richness and balance; it will reach perfection in four to five years.
☛ Jean-Jacques Vincent, Ch. de Fuissé, 71960 Fuissé, tel. 03.85.27.05.90, fax 03.85.35.67.34,
e-mail domaine@chateau-fuisse ☑
🍷 ev.day 8am–12noon 1.30pm–5.30pm; Sat. Sun. by appt.; cl. 1–22 Aug.

DOM. DE FUSSIACUS

Vieilles Vignes 2001★

	3 ha	13,000	⦿	11–15 €

Fifty year-old vines and ten months maturation on fine lees in cask have produced this typical pale-yellow Pouilly-Fuissé, tinged with green. The nose offers an attractive aromatic array: linden-blossom, apricot, iris, fresh butter and toasted hazelnuts. On the palate there is a fine, delicate oakiness, with a little richness and tart lemon notes. A good, aromatic wine, ready to drink as of now.
☛ Jean-Paul Paquet, 71960 Fuissé, tel. 03.85.27.01.06, fax 03.85.27.01.07, e-mail fussiacus@wanadoo.fr ☑
🍷 by appt.

DOM. DES GERBEAUX

Cuvée Jacques Charvet 2001★★

	n.c.	1,500	⦿	15–23 €

An estate that cannot be ignored in this appellation: did its 2000 vintage not take the *coup de cœur*? The 2001, judged a more difficult vintage, came out with honours. This Cuvée Jaques Charvet was vinified and matured in oak casks for 18 months, fact that it has difficulty hiding. The dominant wood aromas on the nose are accompanied by notes of brioche and menthol. Rich and full, the palate is even more marked by the cask, but the structure will permit it to get the upper hand of the oak in two or three years' time. A very fine wine to lay down. One star was awarded to the **Cuvée En Champ Roux 2001 (11–15 €)**, also marked by the wood, but with a good potential for ageing. The **Vieilles Vignes du Terroir de Solutré 2001 (8–11 €)**, with a bouquet of wild-roses, linden-blossom and citrus fruit will be ready to serve a year from now, with a seafood platter. It received a special mention.
☛ Jean-Michel Drouin, Les Gerbeaux, 71960 Solutré-Pouilly, tel. 03.85.35.80.17, fax 03.85.35.87.12 ☑
🍷 by appt.

DOM. DU GRAND PRE

Cuvée Prestige 2001★

	n.c.	1000	⦿	11–15 €

Quietly, industriously, in Pouilly-Fuissé as in Mâcon, Philippe Desroches works his calcareous-clay slopes to produce traditional wines impeccably made. Of a fine, intense gold colour, this Cuvée Prestige exudes harmonious perfumes of toast, vanilla and mocha. Rich and vigorous together, its balance and finesse are seductive. A pleasant wine to drink with white meat.
☛ Philippe Desroches, lot. Le Grand-Pré, 71960 Solutré-Pouilly, tel. 03.85.35.86.94, fax 03.85.35.86.62, e-mail ph.desroches@wanadoo.fr ☑
🍷 by appt.

DOM. JEANDEAU

Terre Jeanduc 2001★★

	0.2 ha	1,200	⦿	15–23 €

Denis Jeandeau, recently returned to the family estate, went back to ploughing with horses in 2001 and now farms organically. Produced on barely 20 ares, the bouquet of this little gleaming golden *cuvée* is made up of powerful floral aromas, ripe grapes and hazelnut. "This has the feel of a great wine," wrote one enthusiast Juror. Fleshy and supple, on the palate it is elegant, rich, supported by a good acidity. The finish is a blaze of glory, with apricot, hazelnut, cinnamon, spice-bread and stewed fruit all putting in an appearance. The **Les Prouges 2001** received a special mention: it is among the most classic wines.
☛ Dom. Jeandeau, Les Prouges, 71960 Fuissé, tel. 03.85.29.20.46, fax 03.85.29.20.46, e-mail madeleine@domainejeandeau.com ☑
🍷 by appt.

DOM. DE LALANDE

Les Chevrières 2001★

	0.75 ha	5,650	⦿	11–15 €

Here in France we like the terroir to determine the character of the wine. Les Chevrières, a *climat* in Chaintré with a southern exposure, produced this Pouilly-Fuissé, made f

hand-harvested grapes and vinified and matured in cask. Fruity notes dominate the powerful bouquet: peaches, apricots, plums, with a few oaky touches. Concentrated, fruity and fresh on the palate, this is a harmonious, balanced, rounded wine and well within the criteria of the AOC. A wine to serve with sea or freshwater fish.
🟏 Dominique Cornin, chem. du Roy-de-Croix, 71570 Chaintré, tel. 03.85.37.43.58, fax 03.85.37.43.58, e-mail dominique@cornin.net ☑
� by appt.

DOM. LAROCHETTE-MANCIAT
Vieilles Vignes 2001★

1 ha	7,000	🍷	11–15 €

An excellent score for these young winemakers from the south of the appellation: three selections came to the attention of the Jury. This old-gold Vieilles Vignes, with a subtle bouquet of roasted hazelnuts and butter-caramel, has a richness and balance on the palate that is worthy of the greatest wines. It will be ready to serve in one to three years' time with frogs' legs. The same mark was given to the **Grande Réserve 2001 (15–23 €)**, matured in cask for 14 months. This one is a limited *cuvée* (2,500 bottles) which will need to be laid down: the oak is very evident in this powerful and aromatic wine with a strong personality. The **Les Grandes Vernes 2001**, more classically made (floral and fruity), was given a special mention.
🟏 Dom. Larochette-Manciat, rue du Lavoir, 71570 Chaintré, tel. 03.85.35.61.50, fax 03.85.35.67.06, e-mail o-larochette@club-internet.fr ☑
� by appt.
🟏 O. and M.-P. Larochette

LES VINS DES PERSONNETS
Rives de Longsault 2001★

n.c.	n.c.	🍷	23–30 €

The Jurors appreciated both the *cuvées* offered by this wine-merchant company founded by Christian Collouray and Jean-Luc Terrier, two talented winemakers from Mâconnais. The **Cuvée La Roche Vieilles Vignes 2001 (15–23 €)**, lively, full-flavoured and rustic, needs time to gain balance. It received a special mention. The Rives de Longsault 2001, perfectly vinified and matured in oak casks, is a luminous yellow-gold colour. The bouquet opens with some remarkable floral perfumes (verbena, linden, elderflower) enhanced by notes of vanilla and brioche. The same aromas recur on the palate, to accompany a dense and velvety substance, Well balanced, this is a wine to serve over the next three or four years with a chicken roasted with herbs.
🟏 Les Vins des Personnets, Christian Collovray et Jean-Luc Terrier, 71960 Davayé, tel. 03.85.35.86.51, fax 03.85.35.86.12 ☑
☲ by appt.

MICHEL REY
Les Vergisson 2001★

3 ha	1,200	🍷	11–15 €

Matured in cask, this golden *cuvée* tinged with aniseed-green, evokes apricots, honey and vanilla. There is fruit on the palate, too, but dried ones (hazelnuts, almonds) against a most agreeable aromatic background. Supple and generous, this wine is rich in substance. It needs a year or two to develop to the full.
🟏 Michel Rey, Le Repostère, 71960 Vergisson, tel. 03.85.35.85.78, fax 03.85.35.87.91, e-mail michel.rey19@wanadoo.fr ☑
☲ by appt.
🟏 Burrier

CH. DES RONTETS
Clos Varambon 2001★

1.7 ha	12,400	🍷 🌢	11–15 €

Uniquely situated, this estate once belonged to a minister of the 3rd Republic, great-grandfather of the present owners who took over in 1995; they are unsparing in their efforts to supply fine, organically-grown grapes to their newly-installed winery. The result is this luminous, shining, green-gold wine. The very intense bouquet is complex, combining the cask aromas (toasted, charred, et cetera) with smoother floral and ̱w-fruit notes. The opening on the palate is marked by

attractive spice and lemon flavours. The great finesse and elegance in the mouth is nevertheless tonic and offers an agreeable finish, salty and mineral. A wine with great personality, to lay down for a few years. The **Cuvée Les Birbettes 2000 (15–23 €)**, specially mentioned for its impressive substance, is still under the influence of the wood.
🟏 Claire et Fabio Gazeau-Montrasi, Ch. des Rontets, 71960 Fuissé, tel. 03.85.32.90.18, fax 03.85.35.66.80, e-mail chateaurontets@compuserve.com ☑
☲ by appt.

DOM. SIMONIN
Vieilles Vignes 2001★

n.c.	n.c.	🍷	11–15 €

Two wines offered by the Simonin estate came to the Jurors' attention. This one, green-gold with an elegant floral and honeyed bouquet, is lively, structured and mineral on the palate, where the maturation in cask was perfectly judged. Typical of its terroir and its vintage, it needs time to finish maturing: drink it at Easter, 2004. The **Cuvée Les Ammonites 2001 (15–23 €)**, with its assertive character, fine and balanced, with an agreeable touch of vanilla, was specially mentioned.
🟏 Jacques Simonin, Le Bourg, 71960 Vergisson, tel. 03.85.35.84.72, fax 03.85.35.85.34 ☑
☲ by appt.

DOM. LA SOUFRANDISE
Vieilles Vignes 2001★

3.5 ha	18,000	🍶 🍷	15–23 €

Working from a house built by one of the heads of Napoleon Bonaparte's Guard, Françoise and Nicholas Melin are known quantities in the appellation and confirmed their reputation once again with this very successful 2001 vintage. Its gold colour is tinged with linden-blossom yellow. Very open, the bouquet combines ripe fruit, hazelnut, floral notes, supported by a fresh hint of mineral. After a frank and clean first impression, the palate evolves pleasantly towards roundness and a certain liveliness, finishing with a lingering pear flavour. A very classy wine, to drink with a cheese flavoured with parsley.
🟏 Françoise and Nicholas Melin, EARL Dom. La Soufrandise, 71960 Fuissé, tel. 03.85.35.64.04, fax 03.85.35.65.57 ☑
☲ by appt.

DOM. THIBERT PERE ET FILS
Vignes de la Côte 2001★★

0.5 ha	3,000	🍷	15–23 €

At Fuissé, one of the leading villages of Pouilly-Fuissé, the Thiberts are acclaimed winemakers. In recent years, this estate had made lightning progress and is now one of the greats in the appellation. It offered this Vignes de la Côte, a superb green-gold wine of excellent origin. The bouquet opens on very pure and distinguished aromas mingling wild-rose and vanilla. After a frank attack, it is balanced, buttery and lemony on the palate. The oak is controlled and the length excellent. Right, true-to-type and elegant, this Pouilly-Fuissé is a benchmark for the appellation. The **Cuvée 2001 non-filtrée** evokes ripe grapes, crystallized pineapple and toast on the nose. Vigorous on the palate, it nevertheless shows depth and body. It finishes on a pleasant vanilla note and was awarded one star.
🟏 GAEC Dom. Thibert Père et Fils, le Bourg, 71960 Fuissé, tel. 03.85.27.02.66, fax 03.85.35.66.21, e-mail domthibe@club-internet.fr ☑ 🏠
☲ by appt.

PIERRE VESSIGAUD
Vieilles Vignes 2001★★★

3 ha	22,000	🍷	11–15 €

Produced by a group of ten different *climats* of the village of Fuissé, this *cuvée* literally captivated the Jury. Matured 11 months in cask, it is a magnificent gold colour with linden-yellow highlights. The bouquet is charming, with floral notes and fresh fruit (apricot) and nuts (almonds and hazelnuts), with a few touches of integrated oak. Equally complex and concentrated, the palate is based on a fine structure and a delicate woodiness, completed by rich flavours of quince and crystallized mandarin oranges. Well-balanced and seductive, this is a Pouilly-Fuissé with character. One star

2001

Pierre
VESSIGAUD
Vigneron

CRU DE BOURGOGNE
POUILLY - FUISSE
Appellation Pouilly Fuissé Contrôlée
"VIEILLES VIGNES"
Mise en bouteille au Domaine Vessigaud
Vigneron à Pouilly 71960 SOLUTRÉ France.

for the **Cuvée Vers Pouilly 2001 (15–23 €)**, remarkable for is
density, but still under the influence of the cask.
☛ SCEA Dom. Vessigaud Père et Fils, Hameau de Pouilly,
71960 Solutré-Pouilly, tel. 03.85.35.81.18,
fax 03.85.35.84.29 ☑
☖ by appt.

Wines selected but not starred

DOM. CHATAIGNERAIE LABORIER
La Roche 2001

	0.5 ha	2,500	⑪	11–15 €

☛ Gilles Morat, Dom. Châtaigneraie-Laborier, Les
Bruyères, 71960 Vergisson, tel. 03.85.35.85.51,
fax 03.85.35.82.42, e-mail gil.morat@wanadoo.fr ☑
☖ by appt.

DOM. DE LA COLLONGE 2001

	2 ha	16,000	▮⑪⚬	11–15 €

☛ Gilles Noblet, Dom. de La Collonge, 71960 Fuissé,
tel. 03.85.35.63.02, fax 03.85.35.67.70,
e-mail gillesnoblet@wanadoo.fr ☑
☖ by appt.

DOM. DE LA CREUZE NOIRE
Le Clos de Monsieur Noly 2001

	2.35 ha	11,000	▮⚬	8–11 €

☛ Dominique and Christine Martin, La Creuze Noire,
71570 Leynes, tel. 03.85.37.46.43, fax 03.85.37.44.17 ☑
☖ ev.day 8am–12noon 1.30pm–7pm; Sun. 8am–12noon

DOM. DE LA DENANTE 2001

	0.25 ha	2,000	▮⑪⚬	8–11 €

☛ Robert Martin, Les Gravières, 71960 Davayé,
tel. 03.85.35.82.88, fax 03.85.35.86.71 ☑
☖ by appt.

CAVE DES GRANDS CRUS BLANCS 2001

	4.33 ha	10,000		11–15 €

☛ Cave des Grands Crus blancs, 71680 Vinzelles,
tel. 03.85.27.05.70, fax 03.85.27.05.71, e-mail contact@
cavevinzellesloche.com ☑
☖ by appt.

DOMAINES EDMOND LANEYRIE 2000

	1 ha	2,500	▮⚬	8–11 €

☛ Domaines Edmond Laneyrie, Le Bourg,
71960 Solutré-Pouilly, tel. 03.85.35.80.67,
fax 03.85.35.80.67 ☑
☖ by appt.

DOM. LAPIERRE
Vieilles Vignes 2001

	2.5 ha	2,000	⑪	11–15 €

☛ Michel Lapierre, Le Bourg, 71960 Solutré-Pouilly,
tel. 03.85.35.80.45, fax 03.85.35.87.61 ☑
☖ by appt.

DOM. DES MAILLETTES
Les Creuzettes 2001

	1 ha	8,000	⑪	8–11 €

☛ Guy Saumaize, Les Maillettes, 71960 Davayé,
tel. 03.85.35.82.65, fax 03.85.35.86.69,
e-mail guy.saumaize.maillette@wanadoo.fr ☑
☖ by appt.

DOM. DU ROURE DE PAULIN
Vignes des Champs 2001

	0.27 ha	1000	▮⑪⚬	11–15 €

☛ Dom. du Roure de Paulin, 71960 Fuissé,
tel. 03.85.35.65.48, fax 03.85.35.68.50,
e-mail domaine.duroure@wanadoo.fr ☑
☖ by appt.

FREDERIC TROUILLET
Les Chailloux 2001

	1.5 ha	5,000	▮⑪⚬	8–11 €

☛ Frédéric Trouillet, Les Concizes, 71960 Solutré-Pouilly,
tel. 03.85.35.80.04, fax 03.85.35.86.03,
e-mail domaine.trouillet@wanadoo.fr ☑
☖ ev.day. 9am–12noon 2pm–7pm

Pouilly-Loché and Pouilly-Vinzelles

These small appellations in the communes of Loché and Vinzelles are much less well-known than their neighbour. They produce wines of the same style as Pouilly-Fuissé, though perhaps with a little less body. Only white wines are produced; in 2002, Loché made 1,759 hl and Vinzelles 2,609 hl.

Pouilly-Loché

ALAIN DELAYE 2001 ★

	0.99 ha	7,700	▮⑪	8–11 €

This family estate, situated half-way up the slope, has a remarkable view over the Pouilly-Loché slopes. Its wine is distinguished by its lovely green-gold colour, its pronounced aromas of flint and hawthorn. Elegant, balanced and flavoursome right up to the citronella and yellow apple finish. Drink it with white meat, preferably a Bresse chicken in a cream sauce.
☛ Alain Delaye, Les Mûres, 429, rte de Fuissé,
71000 Loché, tel. 03.85.35.61.63, fax 03.85.35.61.63 ☑
☖ by appt.

CH. DE LOCHE 2001★★★

n.c. n.c. 15–23 €

"An aristocratic wine," is what one of our lady Jurors concluded, after she had sung the praises and described the qualities of this superb Pouilly-Loché. Golden, leaving generous tears in the glass, it offers a bouquet with multiple perfumes of toast, fresh almonds, fern, linden-blossom and verbena. Very rich and intensely aromatic, it is a sublimely balanced elixir, allying a lively acidity with full fleshiness. Subtle and harmonious, it has all the hallmarks of a great wine, confirming the talents of this wine-merchant who collects the distinctions of the Côte de Nuits in Beaujolais.

Maison Louis Jadot, 21, rue Eugène-Spuller, 21200 Beaune, tel. 03.80.22.10.57, fax 03.80.22.56.03, e-mail contact@louisjadot.com

by appt.

Wines selected but not starred

DOM. CORDIER PERE ET FILS 2001

0.43 ha 2,400 11–15 €

Dom. Cordier Père et Fils, 71960 Fuissé, tel. 03.85.35.62.89, fax 03.85.35.64.01, e-mail domaine.cordier@wanadoo.fr

by appt.

CAVE DES GRANDS CRUS BLANCS 2001

13.83 ha 18,000 8–11 €

Cave des Grands Crus blancs, 71680 Vinzelles, tel. 03.85.27.05.70, fax 03.85.27.05.71, e-mail contact@cavevinzellesloche.com

by appt.

Pouilly-Vinzelles

CAVE DES GRANDS CRUS BLANCS

Les Quarts 2001★

6.88 ha 20,000 8–11 €

Right in the centre of the appellation, the cellar of Les Grand Crus is open seven day a week. This year it offered two very successful wines in this AOC, both of which received the same mark. The **2002**, with its charming aromas of grapefruit and white blossom, is lively and rounded, with attractive floral characteristics. This Cuvée Les Quarts 2001 shines with all its might. Its distinctive bouquet gives off subtle floral perfumes and aromas of fresh fruit. Well-constructed, it is fresh on the palate and its finish on wild-flowers and spices is appetizing.

Cave des Grands Crus blancs, 71680 Vinzelles, tel. 03.85.27.05.70, fax 03.85.27.05.71, e-mail contact@cavevinzellesloche.com

by appt.

LOUIS LATOUR 2000★

10 ha 50,000 8–11 €

Founded in 1797 and established at Beaune since 1867, The Latour company is a family wine-merchant in the Burgundy tradition. Limpid and brilliant yellow-gold, this 2000 offers an elegant bouquet of yellow fruit and spices. Roundness and a lemony liveliness are combined on the palate. The finish is fresh and lingering. A wine to serve with smoked salmon.

Maison Louis Latour, 18, rue des Tonneliers, 21204 Beaune, tel. 03.80.24.81.00, fax 03.80.22.36.21, e-mail louislatour@louislatour.com

by appt.

DOM. MATHIAS 2001★

1.1 ha 8,000 8–11 €

Beatrice and Gilles Mathias are good hosts and able to talk knowledgeably about their winemaking trade. This 2001 vintage seems very pleasant already. Pale-gold in colour, with a restrained bouquet, it comes into its own on the palate: both supple and vigorous, it is also fleshy and rich. Sweet peach and apricot flavours trumpet the finish. A satisfying accompaniment for a rabbit cooked in Pouilly-Vinzelles, a recipe for which is available on demand at the estate. Bon appétit!

Béatrice and Gilles Mathias, rue Saint-Vincent, 71570 Chaintré, tel. 03.85.27.00.50, fax 03.85.27.00.52, e-mail domaine-mathias@wanadoo.fr

by appt.

DOM. DES PERELLES 2001★

0.6 ha 2,000 5–8 €

An estate frequently included in the Guide, two generations of Thiberts work in harmony here making wines in the traditional manner. This pale green-gold 2001 vintage, with its floral perfumes, fills the mouth thanks to its fine texture. Smooth and supple, upheld by a good acidity, it is perfectly balanced on the palate. A splendid representative of its terroir.

Jean-Marc Thibert, Les Pérelles, 71680 Crêches-sur-Saône, tel. 03.85.37.14.56, fax 03.85.37.46.02

by appt.

LA SOUFRANDIERE

Climat Les Quarts Cuvée Millerandée 2001★★

0.7 ha 1,770 15–23 €

Jean-Philippe and Jean-Guillaume Bret, from the new generation of wine-growers, have already shown proof of their talent for producing exceptional wines, and this Cuvée Les Quarts Millerandée does nothing to detract from it. Buttercup-yellow with bronze highlights, it has a complex bouquet going from pear to quince to finely vanilla-tinged oak. The initial impression is unctuous and a multitude of flavours (wood, spices, honey, yellow fruit and floral notes) are combined on the palate. Already very good, this wine will hold for several years and reveal qualities that are not yet apparent. The **Cuvée Climat Les Quarts 2001 (11–15 €)** needs more time; it was awarded one star.

Brothers SARL Bret, La Soufrandière, 71680 Vinzelles, tel. 03.85.35.67.72, fax 03.85.35.67.72, e-mail lasoufrandiere@libertysurf.fr

by appt.

J.-P. and J.-G. Bret

DOM. THIBERT PERE ET FILS 2001★★★

1.1 ha 8,500 8–11 €

In this *cuvée*, the Thibert estate offers a model of its kind, which has everything in hand and in reserve to make a great wine for the future. Its youthful colour is clear and brilliant. The same freshness on the bouquet, where one finds floral aromas, crystallized lemon, vanilla…all characteristic of the Chardonnay grape. On the palate it has a fine robustness contributed by the well-ripened grape. "Suppleness and a lovely body," said one Juror. Tender and fruity, this wine would be the ideal accompaniment for a Bresse chicken à la crème. One star for the **Les Longeays 2001 (11–15 €)**, as floral as one could wish but a wine that needs time to come to its peak. Two fine wines to have in the cellar.

➽ GAEC Dom. Thibert Père et Fils, le Bourg, 71960 Fuissé, tel. 03.85.27.02.66, fax 03.85.35.66.21, e-mail domthibe@club-internet.fr ☑ ⌂

☛ by appt.

Wines selected but not starred

P. FERRAUD ET FILS 2002

n.c.	2,700	▮	8–11 €

➽ Pierre Ferraud et Fils, 31, rue du Mal-Foch, 69220 Belleville-sur-Saône, tel. 04.74.06.47.60, fax 04.74.66.05.50, e-mail ferraud@ferraud.com ☑

☛ ev.day ex. Sun. 8am–12noon 14.15pm–6.15pm

Saint-Véran

Producing only white wines in eight communes in the Saône-et-Loire, Saint-Véran is the last of the Mâcon appellations to be created (1971). In 2002, 39,806 hl were produced, and in quality the wines are somewhere between Pouilly and the Mâcons that are followed by the village name. The wines are light, elegant, fruity and accompany the first courses of meals wonderfully well.

Grown mainly on limestone soil, this appellation marks the southern limit of the Mâconnais.

JEAN BARONNAT 2001★★

n.c.	n.c.	▮ ♦	5–8 €

Gleizé wine-merchant, Jean Baronnat offered a very characteristic Saint-Véran from vines harvested at the peak of maturity. The intense scents of peaches, pears and mangoes go to make a wine with a complex aromatic range. Generous on the palate, this is a rounded and balanced wine; its long, mineral and acidic finish gives it a great freshness, pleasant and true-to-type. It would be excellent with a pike-perch à la crème.

➽ Maison Baronnat, 491, rte de Lacenas, Les Bruyères, 69400 Gleizé, tel. 04.74.68.59.20, fax 04.74.62.19.21, e-mail info@baronnat.com ☑

☛ by appt.

DOM. CORDIER PERE ET FILS

En Faux 2001★★

0.91 ha	6,000	⦀	11–15 €

Regularly placed in the Guide, the Cordier estate produces internationally renowned wines. Vinified and matured in oak casks, according to traditional Burgundian methods, this golden En Fauve Cuvée enchanted the Jury. Honey and acacia-blossom harmonize perfectly with toast and charred notes on the bouquet. Balanced and skilfully combined, the oak blends with richness and fullness on the palate. A wine that merits at least three years in the cellar. The **Les Cras**

2001 Cuvée needs time to assimilate its woodiness. It was awarded one star.

➽ Dom. Cordier Père et Fils, 71960 Fuissé, tel. 03.85.35.62.89, fax 03.85.35.64.01, e-mail domaine.cordier@wanadoo.fr

☛ by appt.

CH. DES CORREAUX

Les Spires 2001★

0.5 ha	4,000	⦀	8–11 €

Members of the Bernard family have been owner wine-growers at Leynes for two centuries. In 2002, having finally acquired the whole of the family property, Jean Bernard went back to the original name of "Château des Correaux". Two selections caught the attention of the Jury. The Les Spires was vinified and matured in oak casks for one year. A brilliant buttercup-gold colour, with an intense bouquet developing aromas of dried apricots, toasted almonds and hazelnuts, this wine is supple and generous initially, then more restrained, leading up to an acidic finish. This is a wine to accompany a veal chop with chanterelle mushrooms. The **Clos des Jullys 2001 (5–8 €)**, judged very successful but on a lighter plane, is well-balanced. It would go well with a *blanquette de veau* (a creamy veal stew).

➽ Jean Bernard, Ch. Les Correaux, 71570 Leynes, tel. 03.85.35.11.59, fax 03.85.35.13.94, e-mail bernardleynes@yahoo.fr ☑

☛ by appt.

DOM. CORSIN 2001★

4.6 ha	38,500	▮ ⦀ ♦	8–11 €

The renown of the Corsin family, established over several generations on the admirable slopes of Davayé, derives from their talent for making great white wines, as is shown by this yellow-gold Saint-Véran 2001, with its green highlights. The intense bouquet releases aromas of vanilla and honey, while on the palate it is rich and balanced. A dried fruit finish prolongs the pleasure of the tasting. The **Tirage Précoce 2001 (5–8 €)** selection, bottled after six months of maturation, is worth a special mention.

➽ Dom. Corsin, Les Plantes, 71960 Davayé, tel. 03.85.35.83.69, fax 03.85.35.86.64 ☑

☛ by appt.

DOM. DES DEUX ROCHES

Les Terres noires 2001★

2.8 ha	18,000	▮ ⦀ ♦	8–11 €

The Les Terres Noires selection, grown on stony soil with a southern exposure, is a golden white wine. Its bouquet evokes brioche, hazelnuts and honeysuckle, aromas that recur on the palate, where it offers a long, elegant finish. The **Saint-Véran 2001, Cuvée Classique**, with a pleasant bouquet of ripe fruit and citron, is rounded and balanced. Its slightly grapefruity finish gives it a certain tonus. It received a special mention.

➽ Dom. des Deux Roches, 71960 Davayé, tel. 03.85.35.86.51, fax 03.85.35.86.12 ☑

☛ by appt.

DOM. DE FUSSIACUS 2001★

1.1 ha	9,800	▮ ⦀ ♦	8–11 €

A great believer in harvesting at full maturity and maturation in oak barrels, Jean-Paul Paquet offered this result of his skills. Olfaction begins with rich notes of almond paste, crystallized fruit, then gives way to fresher aromas, such as mango. After a rich opening, the palate allows an impression of sucrose to penetrate, which contributes to a smooth finish. A good wine to drink with a parsley-flavoured cheese.

➽ Jean-Paul Paquet, 71960 Fuissé, tel. 03.85.27.01.06, fax 03.85.27.01.07, e-mail fussiacus@wanadoo.fr ☑

☛ by appt.

DOM. GUEUGNON-REMOND 2001★★

1 ha	7,000	▮	5–8 €

A top-of-the-range wine which came close to taking the *coup de coeur*, produced by Véronique and Jean-Christophe Rémond, two young winemakers. It cuts a fine figure with its crystalline pale-gold colour. Floral notes, peaches, apricots, brioche and butter make up its superb bouquet. The lively palate, entirely in keeping with the nose, is well-balanced by its richness. A few citrus fruit notes leave a full-flavoured sensation. This Saint-Véran would be ideal with a dish of snails sautéed in garlic-butter.

➶ Dom. Gueugnon-Remond, chem. de la Cave, 71850 Charnay-lès-Mâcon, tel. 03.85.29.23.88, fax 03.85.20.20.72 ☑
✗ by appt.
➶ Remond

PIERRE JANNY 2001★★

10 ha	80,000	🍾 ⬧	5–8 €

Pierre Janny is a wine-merchant and this Saint-Véran is a

Product of France — White Burgundy Wine

SAINT-VÉRAN

Appellation Saint-Véran Contrôlée

Récolté, vinifié et mis en bouteille à la propriété pour

Pierre Janny

Négociant à "La Condemine" 71260 Péronne

Net Contents 75cl — Vin de Bourgogne — alc 13 %by vol

perfect example of his professional skills. Pure white-gold, this wine offers a sublime bouquet mingling such flowers as hawthorn and acacia, and fruit. The attack, rich and full on the palate, is balanced by the freshness of a surrounding mineral quality. A most expressive Saint-Véran to keep for a special occasion.

➶ Sté Janny, La Condemine, Cidex 1556, 71260 Péronne, tel. 03.85.23.96.20, fax 03.85.36.96.58, e-mail pierre-janny@wanadoo.fr

DOM. ROGER LUQUET

Les Grandes Bruyères 2001★

1.4 ha	9,000	🍾 ⬧	5–8 €

This family estate was established in 1966. At that time, Roger Luquet had 4.5 ha; now with his son, his daughter and son-in-law, he has 24 ha. Produced in the traditional way (no yeast, little sulphur dioxide, maturation on the lees), this wine, which develops a pleasant, fruity and floral bouquet, offers a great deal of substance and weight on the palate. At its peak already, it could be served with grilled chicken.

➶ Dom. Roger Luquet, 71960 Fuissé, tel. 03.85.35.60.91, fax 03.85.35.60.12,
e-mail domainerogerluquet@club-internet.fr ☑
✗ ev.day ex. Sun. 9am–7pm

DOM. DES MAILLETTES

En Pommard Grande Réserve 2001★★

0.6 ha	5,000	⬧	8–11 €

A calcareous-clay slope with a north-east exposure at Davayé, En Pommard is one of the great terroirs of the appellation, as is shown by this lovely wine produced from fifty year-old vines. A fine, pale-gold colour, tinged with green, it releases intense perfumes of vanilla, brioche and roasted coffee. On the palate it is frank, remarkably well-balanced, and the combination of oak-wine is particularly successful. Its lemony finish is proof of a good development. Serve it with a Bresse chicken with cream and morels.

➶ Guy Saumaize, Les Maillettes, 71960 Davayé, tel. 03.85.35.82.65, fax 03.85.35.86.69,
e-mail guy.saumaize.maillette@wanadoo.fr ☑
✗ by appt.

DOM. DE MONTAGNY 2001★

n.c.	20,000	🍾 ⬧	8–11 €

The Misserey company was founded by Pierre and Paul Misserey at Nuit-Saint-Georges in 1904. In 1985, Claude and Olivier Lanvin took it over. This Saint-Véran is a brilliant white-gold colour. The intense bouquet recalls a whole basket of fruits, while on the palate lemony flavours and nuances

of flint are awakened. Restrained and elegant, this is an aperitif wine.

➶ Maison P. Misserey, 3, rue des Seuillets, BP 10, 21701 Nuits-Saint-Georges Cedex, tel. 03.80.61.07.74, fax 03.80.61.31.40, e-mail lanvin-sa@worldonline.fr ☑
✗ by appt.

DOM. DES PERELLES 2001★

0,5 ha	4,400	🍾 ⬧	5–8 €

Frequently included in the *Guide*, this estate offered a Saint-Véran which spent six months in oak casks. Its seductive, luminous colour is tinged with gold highlights. The complex nose first releases oaky notes then, after aeration, crytallized fruit and floral aromas come to the fore. Full and powerful on the palate, sustained by a still very noticeable acidity, it finishes on very pleasant notes of bergamot orange. It would make a rich and satisfying combination with a pike-perch cooked with fennel.

➶ Jean-Marc Thibert, Les Pérelles, 71680 Crèches-sur-Saône, tel. 03.85.37.14.56, fax 03.85.37.46.02 ☑
✗ by appt.

DOM. DE LA PIERRE DES DAMES 2001★

1.1 ha	5,300	🍾	5–8 €

Very devoted to the cause of syndicalism in the wine trade, Jean-Michel Aubinel established this estate in 2001 with an associate. Traditional in its presentation, this radiant, elegant, pale-yellow Saint-Véran offers an original mineral quality and a real concentration of aromas (hay, lemon, crushed grapefruit) on both the nose and the palate. Homogenous from first impression to finish, it is worth leaving to age for two or three years, period which will allow it to fulfil its potential.

➶ Dom. de la Pierre des Dames, Mouhy, 71960 Prissé, tel. 03.85.20.21.43, fax 03.85.20.21.43 ☑
✗ by appt.

DOM. DU POETE 2001★

6 ha	12,000	🍾 ⬧	5–8 €

Jojo Lardet, joyous poet at weddings and banquets and indefatigable promoter of the cru, gave his name to this estate. This wine, with its attractive golden highlights, has a delicate bouquet of ripe fruit and vanilla. Powerful and fleshy, it could be laid down for a year or two before being served with white meat.

➶ Paul Beaudet, rue Paul-Beaudet, 71570 Pontanevaux, tel. 03.85.36.72.76, fax 03.85.36.72.02,
e-mail contact@paulbeaudet.com ☑
✗ ev.day ex. Sat. Sun. 8am–12noon 1.30pm–5pm; cl. Aug.

JACQUES SAUMAIZE

Poncetys 2001★

n.c.	n.c.	⬧	8–11 €

Passion, according to Jacques Saumaize, is 8 ha of cherished vineyards, hand-picked harvests, long periods of maturation in barrels with yeast stirring: known as love of a job well done. He offered a limpid 2001 vintage of a white-gold colour, with mingled perfumes of acacia, honey, apples and pears and roasted notes. On a palate remarkable for its volume, it still remains marked by its time in the wood. Fruity and vanilla notes linger a long time. A wine to lay down for several years.

➶ Jacques and Nathalie Saumaize, Les Bruyères, 71960 Vergisson, tel. 03.85.35.82.14, fax 03.85.35.87.00 ☑
✗ by appt.

LA SOLITUDE 2000★

7 ha	60,000	🍾 ⬧ ⬧	8–11 €

This cooperative produced this *cuvée* from the mythical 2000 vintage in honour of Alphonse de Lamartine. Not exactly a limited edition (60,000 bottles), but of very good quality. The colour is straw with golden highlights; the nose spells out notes of crystallized fruits and vanilla. The very fine palate releases flavours of mangoes and toast on a rounded and balanced structure. An honest wine, it would accompany a cooked fish dish.

➶ Caves de Prissé-Sologny-Verzé, Les Grandes-Vignes, 71960 Prissé, tel. 03.85.37.88.06, fax 03.85.37.61.76, e-mail caves.prisse@wanadoo.fr ☑ ⬧
✗ by appt.

DOM. DES VALANGES

Cuvée hors classe Vieilles Vignes 2001★★★

| | 2 ha | 10,000 | 🍷 🎚 ♦ | 8–11 € |

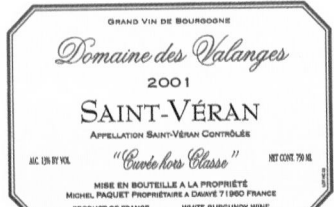

GRAND VIN DE BOURGOGNE

Domaine des Valanges

2001

SAINT-VÉRAN

APPELLATION SAINT-VÉRAN CONTRÔLÉE

ALC. 13% BY VOL.   *"Cuvée hors Classe"*   NET CONT. 750 ML

MISE EN BOUTEILLE À LA PROPRIÉTÉ
MICHEL PAQUET PROPRIÉTAIRE À DAVAYÉ 71960 FRANCE

PRODUCT OF FRANCE   WHITE BURGUNDY WINE

The Valanges estate is inescapable in Saint-Véran. Michel Paquet is at the head of this enterprise, and could it have a better ambassador? Holder of a *coup de cœur* in 99, he does it again with this 2001 vintage, fruit of the estate's *vieilles vignes*. The Jury praised its class. Intense yellow-gold this wine captivates with its aromatic range mingling lemon, peach, apricot, verbena and acacia flowers. The full-flavoured but fine palate has an excellent mineral quality which reflects the great terroir from which it originates. A very seductive balance tending towards the floral, and a remarkable finish make this an exceptional selection. As to the **Cuvée Les Cras 2001**, it was specially mentioned for its fresh fruitiness.
♦⊐ Michel Paquet, Les Valanges, 71960 Davayé, tel. 03.85.35.85.03, fax 03.85.35.86.67, e-mail domaine-des-valanges@wanadoo.fr ☑
🍷 by appt.

Wines selected but not starred

DOM. CHENE

Cuvée Prestige 2001

| | 0.4 ha | 3,300 | 🍷 �🍷 | 5–8 € |

♦⊐ Dom. Chêne, Ch. Chardon, 71960 Berzé-la-Ville, tel. 03.85.37.65.30, fax 03.85.37.75.39, e-mail gaecchene@aol.com ☑
🍷 by appt.

DOM. DES CRAIS 2001

| | 2.2 ha | 10,000 | 🍷 ♦ | 5–8 € |

♦⊐ Jean-Luc Tissier, Les Pasquiers, 71570 Leynes, tel. 03.85.35.10.31, fax 03.85.35.13.04 ☑ 🏠
🍷 ev.day ex. Sun. 8am–12noon 2pm–7pm

DOM. DE LA CROIX SENAILLET

Les Rochats 2001

| | 2 ha | 6,000 | 🍷 ♦ | 5–8 € |

♦⊐ Richard and Stéphane Martin, En Coland, 71960 Davayé, tel. 03.85.35.82.83, fax 03.85.35.87.22 ☑
🍷 by appt.

DOM. DE L' ERMITE DE SAINT-VERAN

Jully Cuvée Vieilles Vignes 2001

| | 0.71 ha | 2,500 | 🍷 | 5–8 € |

♦⊐ Gérard Martin, Les Truges, 71570 Saint-Vérand, tel. 03.85.36.51.09, fax 03.85.37.47.89, e-mail gemartin3@wanadoo.fr ☑
🍷 by appt.

DOM. MARC GREFFET 2001

| | 0.6 ha | 5,000 | ⊐🍷 | 5–8 € |

♦⊐ Marc Greffet, 71960 Solutré-Pouilly, tel. 03.85.35.83.82, fax 03.85.35.84.24 ☑
🍷 by appt.

E. LORON ET FILS 2002

| | n.c. | n.c. | 🍷 ♦ | 5–8 € |

♦⊐ Ets Loron et Fils, Pontanevaux, 71570 La Chapelle-de-Guinchay, tel. 03.85.36.81.20, fax 03.85.33.83.19, e-mail vinloron@wanadoo.fr

DOM. DES PONCETYS

Cuvée Prestige 2001

| | 1.8 ha | 11,000 | ⊐🍷 | 8–11 € |

♦⊐ Lycée viticole de Mâcon-Davayé, Dom. des Poncetys, 71960 Davayé, tel. 03.85.33.56.20, fax 03.85.35.86.34, e-mail domaine-poncetys@macon-davaye.com ☑
🍷 by appt.

DOM. THOMAS 2001

| | n.c. | 12,000 | 🍷 ♦ | 5–8 € |

♦⊐ G. et M. Thomas, Dom. Thomas, 71960 Prissé, tel. 03.85.34.50.56, fax 03.85.34.31.50, e-mail domaine-thomas@wanadoo.fr ☑
🍷 ev.day 8am–12noon 1pm–7pm

DOM. DE LA TOUR VAYON 2001

| | 0.6 ha | 5,094 | 🍷 ♦ | 8–11 € |

♦⊐ Jean-Marie Pidault, La Condemine, 71960 Pierreclos, tel. 03.85.35.71.78, fax 03.85.35.78.03 ☑
🍷 by appt.

DOM. DES VIEILLES PIERRES

Les Pommards 2001

| | 1.3 ha | 5,500 | 🍷⊐🍷 ♦ | 5–8 € |

♦⊐ Jean-Jacques Litaud, Les Nembrets, 71960 Vergisson, tel. 03.85.35.85.69, fax 03.85.35.86.26, e-mail jean-jacques.litaud@wanadoo.fr ☑
🍷 by appt.

CHAMPAGNE

The wine of kings and princes and now the wine for every celebration, champagne is cloaked in glory and prestige and conveys to the world all that is French elegance and seductiveness. Its reputation has as much to do with its history as with its particular characteristics, which means, for many, that only wine from Champagne is *the* champagne; however, it is not as simple as that...

The Champagne region, which is situated less than 200 km northeast of Paris, contains three Appellations d'Origine Contrôlée: Champagne, Coteaux Champenois and Rosé des Riceys, but the last two of these produce only around 100,000 bottles. This northernmost wine-growing region in France extends chiefly over the Marne and the Aube regions, with small areas in the Aisne, Seine-et-Marne and Haute-Marne. The total vineyard area covers 32,710 ha, of which 30,891 ha were in production in 2002.

Between them, Reims and Epernay in the Marne share the role of capital of Champagne. The former has the additional appeal of its monuments and museums, which draw crowds of visitors who, at the same time, can discover the cellars belonging to the "great houses", many of which are very ancient.

The whole of the wine-growing area has similar, undulating countryside, where four main regions are traditionally identified. In the Montagne de Reims (6,814 ha), some of the vineyards face north and are on sandy soil. The Côte des Blancs (3,150 ha), just outside Epernay, benefits from a relatively predictable climate. The Marne valley (1,876 ha) and its two banks (5,152 ha), extend to the vineyards in the Aisne, and the slopes of the Surmelin valley (2,989 ha) are covered in vines. Here, despite what one might expect, the quality of the grapes produced rarely varies, whether the vineyards face north or south. Finally, there is the vineyard of the Aube (7,099 ha) in the extreme southeast of the appellation, and separated from the other areas by a 75-km zone where no vines are grown. The Aube is higher and more susceptible to spring frosts than the other areas, yet it produces wines of no lesser quality. This is where you find the only *appellation communale*: Rosé des Riceys. There are other important geographical regions: Epernay (1,240 ha), the valleys of Vesle (986 ha) and of Ardres (900 ha), the regions of Congy (1,013 ha), Sézanne (1,382 ha) and Vitry-le-François (343 ha).

As the sea retreated some 70 million years ago, upheavals caused by tellurian quakes ensued, forming a chalk base that is permeable and rich in essential minerals and which brings finesse to the wines of Champagne. A shallow layer of clay and limestone covers the subsoil on nearly 60% of the land devoted to vines. In the Aube, the soil composition is marl, which is closer to that found in neighbouring Burgundy.

If frost – and at this latitude, spring frosts are frequent – makes reliable production difficult, the climatic extremes are nevertheless tempered by extensive mountain forests, which balance out the mild Atlantic maritime climate and the harsher continental one, maintaining a certain level of humidity. The lack of extreme heat is also a determining factor in the fine quality of the wines. Naturally enough, the choice of grape variety is made in the context of the wine-growing and climatic conditions. Of the 31,458 ha devoted to vine-growing, Pinot Noir takes up 12,254 ha, Pinot Meunier 10,877 ha and Chardonnay 8,952 ha. Other varieties – Pinot Blanc, Pinot Gris, Petit Meslier and Arbanne (91 ha) – share the remaining area (32,715 ha) under cultivation. The winemaking industry provides 31,000 jobs for the region, including 14,800 wine-growers and producers.

The particular demands of the champagne method, which takes a number of years (three on average and many more for vintage years), requires that over a million bottles be kept in storage at any one time. According to the CFCE (Centre Français du Commerce Extérieur), exportation of champagne (1,574 billion Euros – a rise of +13.2% on 2001 figures) represents an important part of total French wine exports.

Wine has been made in Champagne since at least the time of the Roman invasion. The first wines to be produced were white; later production was of red and then "gris" (grey), which is white or nearly-white wine that comes from pressing black grapes. At an early stage the wine had the irritating habit of fizzing up in the barrels. Systematic bottling of these unstable wines was invented in England, to where, until around 1700, the wine had been delivered in barrels. This had the result of allowing the carbon dioxide to dissolve in the wine, and sparkling wine was born. Dom Pérignon, the procurator of the abbey in Hautvillers and a forward-looking blending technician, produced the best wines at his abbey; he was also able to sell them for the highest prices.

In 1728 the king's council authorized the transportation of wine in bottles; a year later, the first champagne house was founded: Ruinart. Others were to follow, including Moët in 1743, but the majority of the great houses were started or established in the 19th century. In 1804 Madame Clicquot launched the first rosé champagne, and from 1830 the first labels to be stuck on bottles appeared. From 1860 Madame Pommery was famous for her brut wines, while around 1870 the first vintage champagnes began to appear. In 1884 Raymond Abelé invented the first disgorging rack cooled with ice, before phylloxera and two world wars ravaged the vineyards. A great deal of modernization has taken place in the half century since: wooden barrels have for the most part yielded to stainless-steel vats, fining and finishing have been automated and, nowadays, *remuage* or riddling – shifting the angle of the bottle to make the deposit gravitate towards the cork – is being mechanized as well.

A large number of wine-growers in Champagne belong to a category known as grape producers, who "sell by the kilo". They sell all or a proportion of their harvest to the great houses, which vinify, make and sell the wines. This practice has led the champagne makers' trade association to set recommended prices for the grapes and to give each commune a classification depending on the quality of the grapes produced: this is known as the *échelle des crus* (scale of the crus). The wines made in winemaking communes are classified on this descending scale, which first appeared at the end of the 19th century. Wines classified as 100% have the right to be called Grand Cru, those from 90% to 99% may be called Premier Cru; the normal appellation is classified between 80% and 89%. The price of grapes is set according to the percentage allocated to the commune. The maximum amount of grapes produced on each hectare is altered each year, with a maximum of 13,000 kg, while 160 kg of grapes produce more than a hectolitre of must suitable for being vinified as champagne.

Champagne

The uniqueness of champagne is apparent right from the harvest itself. No harvesting machines are permitted, and everything is picked by hand because it is essential that the grapes get to the press in perfect condition. Rather than the hods used elsewhere, pickers carry small baskets to ensure that the grapes are not too crushed. Presses are set up in the heart of the vineyards to shorten the time the grapes are transported. Why is such care taken? Because champagne is a white wine made for the most part from a black grape, the Pinot Noir, and it is essential that the colourless juice should not be stained by contact with the grape skins.

Pressing has to take place as quickly as possible and in such a way as to collect the juice from different concentric parts of each fruit one after the other. This explains the particular shape of the traditional presses in Champagne: to avoid squashing the grapes and to facilitate the circulation of the juice, the grapes are piled over a very wide area but not very deeply. The skins of the harvested grapes must never be damaged.

The pressing itself is strictly regulated. There are 1,929 pressing centres and each must obtain official registration in order to operate. From 4,000 kg of grapes, only 25.5 hl of must, a unit known as a "marc", may be extracted in two pressings. The pressing is done in two phases: the first is known as the *cuvée*, 20.5 hl, and the second as the *taille*, 5 hl. The grapes can be pressed again, but the resulting juice is of no interest and has no appellation. The *rebêche*, or new pressing of the marc, is destined for the distillery. The more you press, the greater the drop in quality. The must is taken from the pressing centres to the wineries by lorry and is then carefully vinified according to the classic white wine method.

At the end of winter, in early spring, the cellarmaster proceeds to "assemble" or mix the *cuvée*. To do so, he tastes all the wines available and blends them in such proportions as to make a wine that reflects the flavour and style of the house. When he makes a non-vintage wine, he may call on wines from the reserve, which were produced in previous years. It is legal in Champagne to add a little red wine to the white wine to make a rosé (although this is forbidden everywhere else). However, some rosé champagnes are obtained by allowing the colour of the skins to "bleed" into the must.

Once the blending is completed, the real work of making the wine begins. This is to change a still wine into a sparkling wine. A *liqueur de tirage*, made of yeasts, old wines and sugar, is added to the wine, which is then bottled: this is called *tirage*. The yeasts will turn the sugar into alcohol and produce carbon dioxide, which dissolves in the wine. This second fermentation in the bottles takes place very slowly, and at low temperatures (11°C), in the famous champagne cellars. After long ageing on the lees (residues left by the second fermentation), which is essential for making small bubbles and producing the aromatic qualities of the wines, the bottles are subjected to *dégorgement*, a process that gradually drains away the lees.

Each bottle is placed in one of the famous *pupitres*, or disgorging racks, so that the deposits will settle in the neck of the bottle, beneath the cork. For two or three months the bottles will be periodically shaken and tilted, neck down, until the wine is perfectly clear (automated riddling in a gyropallet is on the increase). To evacuate the deposit, the neck is frozen in a refrigerating bath and the cork is removed; once the deposit is expelled, the bottle is topped up with a wine that may or may not be sweetened: this is the *dosage*. If pure wine is added, a 100% brut wine is obtained (Brut Sauvage from Piper-Heidsieck, Ultra-Brut from Laurent-Perrier, and champagnes known as *non-dosés*, not sweetened, and now called Brut Nature). If only a very small amount (1%) of sweetened wine is added, the champagne is brut; a content of 2% to 5% produces dry champagne; 5% to 8% produces demi-sec, and 8% to 15% sweet. The bottles are then shaken to blend the wines together and set to rest again to allow the taste of the yeast to disappear. They are then labelled and released onto the market. From then on the champagne is ready to be appreciated at the top of its form. Allowing it to age for too long can only harm it: serious houses flatter themselves that they put their wines on sale only when they have reached their peak.

Some excellent wines made from the first pressing, together with numerous "reserve" wines (for the non-vintages), the talent of the cellar-master, with his finely judged, minimal, undetectable dosing, and the long maturing of the champagne on the lees will combine to produce wines of the highest quality. But it is rare for a buyer to be fully informed about all these issues, and certainly there is no guarantee that the information will be accurate.

Champagne

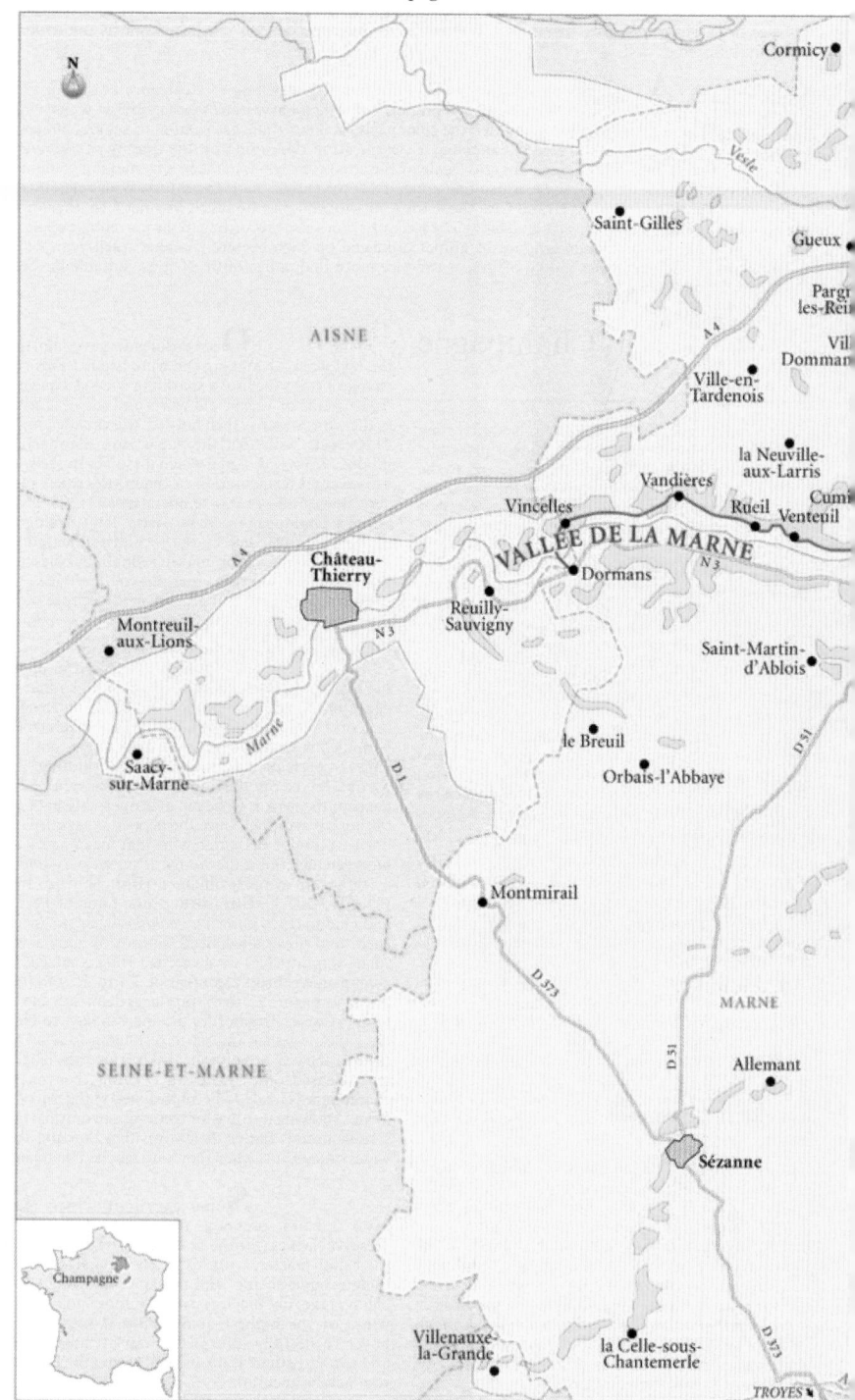

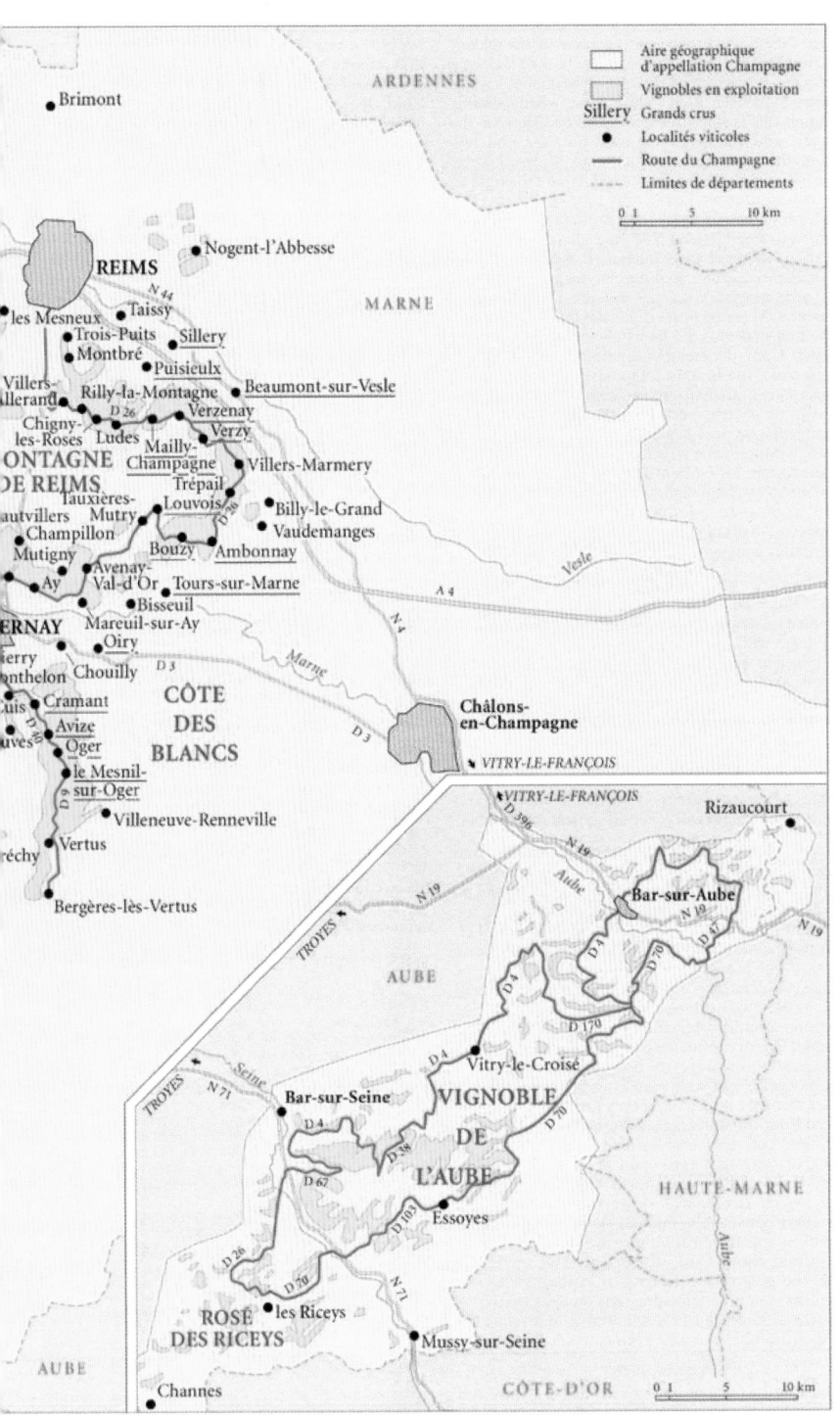

Brimont

ARDENNES

| | Aire géographique d'appellation Champagne |
| | Vignobles en exploitation |
Sillery Grands crus
● Localités viticoles
—— Route du Champagne
---- Limites de départements

0 1   5   10 km

Nogent-l'Abbesse

REIMS

MARNE

N 44

les Mesneux Taissy
Trois-Puits Sillery
Montbré
Villers- Puisieulx
Allerand Rilly-la-Montagne Beaumont-sur-Vesle
D 26 Verzenay
Chigny- Verzy
les-Roses Ludes
MONTAGNE Mailly- Villers-Marmery
DE REIMS Champagne
Trépail
Hautvillers Mutry Louvois Billy-le-Grand
Champillon Vaudemanges
Mutigny Bouzy Ambonnay
Avenay- Tours-sur-Marne
Ay Val-d'Or
Bisseuil
ÉPERNAY Mareuil-sur-Ay
Pierry Oiry
Monthelon Chouilly D 3
Cuis Cramant
Avize CÔTE
Cuves Oger DES
le Mesnil- BLANCS
sur-Oger
Villeneuve-Renneville
Grauves
Vréchy Vertus

Bergères-lès-Vertus

Vesle

A 4

N 4

Marne

D 3

Châlons-
en-Champagne

VITRY-LE-FRANÇOIS

VITRY-LE-FRANÇOIS Rizaucourt

D 396
N 19
Aube
Bar-sur-Aube
N 19 N 10 N 19
N 19 D 1 D 47
TROYES D 1 D 70
AUBE D 170
Seine D 4
TROYES N 71 Vitry-le-Croisé
Bar-sur-Seine VIGNOBLE
D 4 DE
D 38 D 70
L'AUBE
D 62 HAUTE-MARNE
D 105 Essoyes
D 26 Aube
D 70
N 71
ROSÉ les Riceys
DES RICEYS Mussy-sur-Seine
AUBE CÔTE-D'OR
Channes

0 1   5   10 km

519

What can be read on a champagne label? The brand and the name of the maker; the dosage (brut, sec and so on); the year or lack of a year; the phrase blanc de blancs when only white grapes have been used in the wine; when possible (though this is rare), the commune of origin of the grapes, and finally, sometimes, but less and less often, the qualitative classification of the grapes: Grand Cru for the 17 communes that have the right to the description, or Premier Cru for 41 others. The professional standing of the producer must appear, printed in small letters: NM (*négociant-manipulant*), meaning a merchant-winemaker; RM (*récoltant-manipulant*), a grower making champagne from his or her own grapes, with 5% bought in from other sources; CM (*coopérative de manipulation*), a cooperative that makes and sells its own champagne using grapes from its member growers; MA (*marque d'acheteur*), the brand of the buyer; RC (*récoltant-coopérateur*), a small grower who sends his grapes to one or several cooperatives to be made into champagne because he does not have the equipment to do so himself, and who receives the finished champagne to sell; SR (*société de récoltants*), a registered firm set up by champagne growers of the same family who pool their production resources; or ND (*négociant-distributeur*), meaning a merchant who distributes wine bought from others.

What can be gleaned from all this? Simply that the Champenois have deliberately adopted a sales policy that is focused on the brand. A customer will, therefore, order Moët et Chandon, Bollinger or Taittinger because he or she prefers the flavour and style adopted by this or that brand. It is the same for the champagnes produced by the *négociants-manipulants*, the cooperatives and related brands, but not for the *récoltants-manipulants*, who, to qualify as such, make champagne only from their own grapes, generally grouped in a single commune. These champagnes are the so-called Monocrus, and the name of the cru will generally appear on the label.

Although there is only the one appellation, "champagne", a great many different champagnes exist, and the range of characteristics of flavour, scent and appearance can readily satisfy the different needs and varying tastes of every drinker. So, champagne can be blanc de blancs, blanc de noirs (from Pinot Meunier, Pinot Noir or from both) or blends of blanc de blancs and blanc de noirs in any imaginable proportion. It can be from one cru alone or from several, originating from a Grand Cru, a Premier Cru or communes of lesser prestige. It can be vintage or non-vintage (the non-vintage champagnes can be made from young wines or be made up from wines from the reserve, and they are sometimes produced from an assemblage of vintage years). It can be non-dosed or very variably dosed and it can undergo short or long maturation on the lees. It may be disgorged for a longer or shorter time, or be white or rosé (which is obtained either by blending or by bleeding). Then again, most of these options can be combined together in different ways, so there is in fact an infinite number of champagnes. Whatever the type, the general consensus is that the best champagne has matured for a long time on the lees (five to ten years), and is consumed, in France at least, in the six months following disgorgement.

Given all this, it is easy to understand why the price of bottles can vary so widely and

why there are wines at the top of the range or special wines, *cuvées spéciales*. It is unfortunately true that, among the better-known brands, the cheapest champagnes are the least appealing. On the other hand, the big price differences between the upper range (vintage champagnes) and the top-price wines do not always guarantee an equivalent step in quality.

Champagne should be drunk when it is between 7° and 9°C, chilled for the blancs de blancs and young champagnes, not so cold for the vintage and sweeter champagnes. In addition to the classic 75 cl bottle, champagne is also sold in a quarter bottle, a half, a magnum (twice a single bottle), Jeroboam (4 bottles), Methuselah (8 bottles) and Salmanazar (12 bottles). The bottle should be cooled gradually by immersing it in a champagne bucket containing water and ice. To remove the cork, take off the wire cage and foil. If the cork is likely to be pushed out by the pressure, allow it to come out with the cage and foil. If the cork resists, hold it in one hand and turn the bottle with the other. The cork should be removed slowly and noiselessly, avoiding rapid decompression.

Champagne should not be served in goblets but in tall, slender glasses that are completely dry and free from any traces of detergent, which will kill the bubbles and the foam. It can be drunk equally well as an apéritif as with starters and non-oily fish. The richer wines, mostly blanc de noirs, and the great vintages are frequently served with meat dishes with sauce. Drink a demi-sec wine rather than a brut with dessert or sweet dishes, because the sugar in the dish will over-emphasize the palate's sensitivity to the acidity of the brut.

The most recent vintages are 1982, a great vintage everywhere; 1983, straightforward; 1984 was not a vintage, so we can ignore it; 1985, good bottles; 1986, average quality, few wines declared a vintage; 1987, a bad year; 1988, 1989 and 1990, three wonderful years to enjoy; 1991, poor, generally not declared a vintage; 1992, 1993 and 1994, average years; a few important houses declared 1992 and 1993 a vintage; 1995, the best year since 1990; 1996, a great year, declared a vintage in January 2000.

HENRI ABELE 1990★★

	n.c.	n.c.	🍷 👃	38–46 €

Founded in 1757 by a Belgian, this house is among the oldest in Champagne. It is now the property of Freixenet, the number one producer of Spain's traditional-method sparkling wine, cava. The Henri Abelé 1990 is a beautiful wine, made up of two-thirds white grapes, with the remainder Pinot Noir. It earned the same notes at last year's tasting: the Jury admired its youthful pale-yellow colour with hints of green, and its fruitiness and voluptuous length were once again confirmed. They also commended the supple and well-proportioned **Le Sourire de Reims (46–76 €)**, made from the 1990 harvest with 80% Chardonnay, as well as the fruity, lively **Tradition (23–30 €)**, a blend of all three grape varieties in roughly equal measure. (NM)

➤ Henri Abelé, 50, rue de Sillery, 51100 Reims, tel. 03.26.87.79.80, fax 03.26.87.79.81, e-mail mf.lagarde@champagne-abele.com 🇻

ADAM-GARNOTEL

Tradition★

	1er cru	6.17 ha	60,000	🍷 👃	11–15 €

Based in the Montagne de Reims, this 9-ha estate was founded in 1899 by the great-grandfather of the current owner, who took over in 1977. All three Champagne grape varieties play

appreciably equal parts in this *brut* non-vintage, which charmed the Jury with its vinosity and balance. (NM)
☛ Adam-Garnotel, 17, rue de Chigny,
51500 Rilly-la-Montagne, tel. 03.26.03.40.22,
fax 03.26.03.44.47 ◼
✦ by appt.

AGRAPART ET FILS

Blanc de blancs Réserve★

Gd cru	n.c.	20,000	◼ ⏻ ⚲		15–23 €

Arthur Agrapart began making champagne in 1894. His great-grandsons now manage 9.6 ha of vines, and take a particular interest in soil management, having reintroduced the horse-drawn plough for one plot. The estate is in Avize, a grand cru in the Côte des Blancs, with Chardonnay providing the major part of its production. Four of its champagnes were commended by the Jury, all four Grands Crus blancs de blancs. With one star, this Réserve, a blend of 1997 and 1998 wines, is lively and well-balanced, as is the **95 (23–30 €)**, which is at its peak, as is shown by its evolved aromas of stewed fruits and wax, but which remains fresh. Special mentions also go to the unstarred **Brut non-vintage**, made from the harvests of 1998 and 1999, and the **L'Avizoise 96 (30–38 €)**: the first is floral and light, the second lively and long. (RM)
☛ Agrapart et Fils, 57, av. Jean-Jaurès, 51190 Avize,
tel. 03.26.57.51.38, fax 03.26.57.05.06,
e-mail champagne.agrapart@wanadoo.fr ◼
✦ by appt.

ALBERT-BOURDELAT 1996★

	n.c.	n.c.	11–15 €

Edmond Bourdelat's son makes the champagnes at his estate, of which the *cuvée* **Edmond Bourdelat**, a product of the 1998 harvest, has been singled out. Also commended was the limpid and fruity 96 bottled under the estate name (in which the proprietor's name is twinned with his wife's maiden name), an elegant, well-balanced and complex wine. (RM)
☛ Albert-Bourdelat, 13, rue du Château Brugny,
51130 Brugny, tel. 03.26.59.97.95

ALBERT LE BRUN

Vieille France★★

●	n.c.	n.c.	15–23 €

Until not so long ago, this house, founded in 1860, was one of the very few estates in Châlons-en-Champagne. It changed hands recently, and has been relocated to Pargny-lès-Reims. Its celebrated Vieille France *cuvée* comes in an odd-looking, old-fashioned, squat bottle. Sixty per cent Pinot Noir, 30% Chardonnay and 10% red wine give rise to this orange-hued rosé, with its spicy nose and structured, elegant palate of crystallized fruits. (NM)
☛ Albert Le Brun, 19, rte de Dormans,
51390 Pargny-lès-Reims, tel. 03.26.49.28.02,
fax 03.26.49.28.05, e-mail info@champagne-lebrun.com ◼
✦ by appt.
☛ T. Lombard

GILLES ALLAIT★

●	n.c.	n.c.	11–15 €

It is in Passy-Grigny in the Marne valley, within the borders of the Aisne district, that we find this small estate (3.6 ha), established in 1973. The blend of its non-vintage rosé is dominated by Pinot Meunier (70%), accompanied by Chardonnay, with 18% of Meunier red wine bestowing on it its coppery colour. The overall impression is of ripeness, with a flavour of crystallized fruits. The Jury also singled out the estate's **97** vintage, a wine made in barrel, half-Meunier, half-Chardonnay, commended for its balanced roundness. (RM)
☛ Gilles Allait, 2, rue du Château, 51700 Passy-Grigny,
tel. 03.26.52.92.19, fax 03.26.52.97.22 ◼

DE L'ARGENTAINE

Réserve spéciale★

	n.c.	10,000	◼ ⚲	11–15 €

The Vandières cooperative brings together 135 members holding a total of 180 ha of vineyards. Under the Argentaine label, it makes this Réserve Spéciale from two-thirds Pinot

Noir and one-third Chardonnay, from the 1997 harvest. Its lightly developed nose is as intense as its golden colour. On the palate, it displays just the right amount of *dosage*, and a range of spicy, smoky, honeyed flavours. The raspberryish **Brut rosé (11–15 €)**, an identical blend but of 1999 grapes, is fruity, rounded and complex. It would make a fine dessert rosé, to accompany a bavarois. (CM)
☛ Coopérative vinicole l'Union Vandières, Cidex 318,
51700 Vandières, tel. 03.26.58.68.68, fax 03.26.58.68.69,
e-mail delargentaine@wanadoo.fr ◼
✦ by appt.

JEAN-ANTOINE ARISTON

Carte jaune★

	2 ha	20,000	◼	11–15 €

They have been cultivating vines on the Ariston estate for five generations, and making their own champagne since 1975. The vineyard is located in the valley of the Ardre, a river with its source in the Montagne de Reims. The Carte Jaune is a blend of all three champagne grape varieties in appreciably equal shares, from the harvests of 1998, 1999 and 2000. It is a fruity, well-built wine, with a long finish. Another star went to the well-made, balanced and fresh **Carte d'Or**, an identically proportioned blend, but which comes from older wines (1996, 1997, 1998). (RM)
☛ EARL Bruno Ariston, 4, rue Haute, 51170 Brouillet,
tel. 03.26.97.47.02, fax 03.26.97.49.75,
e-mail champagne.ariston@wanadoo.fr ◼
✦ by appt.

MICHEL ARNOULD ET FILS

Grande Cuvée★

Gd cru	1 ha	4,000	◼	15–23 €

At the end of the 19th century, the ancestors of the current producers were wine-growers at Verzenay, a celebrated commune of the Montagne de Reims. The fall in the price of grapes between the two world wars led the family to decide to vinify its own champagne, and the estate continued to be developed up until the late 1960s. Today, it comprises around a dozen hectares. Three grand cru champagnes were selected by the Jury. Made from 70% Pinot Noir and 30% Chardonnay, the Grande Cuvée is the star; although not a vintage, the grapes in it were all harvested in 1996. Like many of the wines of that year, it already appears quite developed on the nose, with notes of dried fruits, and like all the 1996s, it is powerful and well-structured. Also singled out were the soft and fruity **Carte d'Or 97**, made up of half-and-half black and white grapes, and the **rosé (11–15 €)**, a rounded Pinot Noir wine with the flavour of red berries. (RM)
☛ Michel Arnould et Fils, 28, rue de Mailly,
51360 Verzenay, tel. 03.26.49.40.06, fax 03.26.49.44.61,
e-mail info@champagne-michel-arnould.com ◼
✦ ev. day 9am–12 noon 2pm–4.30pm;
Sun. by appt.

L. AUBRY FILS

Blanc de blancs 1996★

1er cru	1.5 ha	5,000 ⚲		15–23 €

Winemakers since the Revolution, the Aubrys today manage a vineyard of 16 ha. They are based in Jouy-lès-Reims, in the north of the Montagne de Reims. Two of their *cuvées* were selected by the Jury. This vintage blanc de blancs was the favourite: a fine 96, powerful on both the nose and palate, with a singular fruitiness that has hints of crystallization. **Le Nombre d'Or 98**, one of the most original champagnes in the *Guide* on account of its use of old grape varieties (Arbanne, Petit Meslier, Pinot Gris), each of which plays its part in the composition of this fine, fresh, lemony, lingering champagne, was also singled out. (RM)
☛ SCEV L. Aubry Fils, 4–6, Grande-Rue,
51390 Jouy-lès-Reims, tel. 03.26.49.20.07,
fax 03.26.49.75.27 ◼
✦ by appt.
☛ Aubry Frères

CH. DE L'AUCHE★

●	n.c.	25,000	◼ ⚲	11–15 €

This group of producers near Reims was founded in 1961, and today owns 120 ha, producing a total of 450,000 bottles. Its Rosé de Noirs (including 85% Pinot Meunier), from the harvests of 1999, 2000 and 2001, is a fruity, soft and lingering wine with overtones of raspberries and wild strawberries. Made from equal parts black and white grapes, the **Château de l'Auche 96** was also given a special mention, not for its developed nose, which is typical of many of the 1996s, but for its freshness and its length on the palate. (CM)

☛ Ch. de l'Auche, Rue de Germigny, 51390 Janvry, tel. 03.26.03.63.40, fax 03.26.03.66.93, e-mail info@champagne-de-lauche.com ▼
⊻ by appt.

AUTREAU DE CHAMPILLON

Réserve★

	1er cru	9.85 ha	30,000	🍶		11–15 €

The village of Champillon, in the south of the Montagne de Reims, is close to Epernay and, on the right bank of the Marne, to Hautvillers, cradle of Champagne. This estate, established in the 1950s, comprises 28 ha of vines. It was distinguished for two equally highly rated *cuvées*. This Réserve, made half of white grapes and half of black, is golden in colour, with scents of brioche and honey, and flavours of white peach and stone fruits. Its balance and its length were both acclaimed. The **Brut Premier Cru** is a blend of the three grape varieties of Champagne (including 22% Chardonnay); its flavours of crystallized fruits seduce, and its sound balance gives the wine character. (NM)

☛ SARL Vignobles Champenois, 15, rue René-Baudet, 51160 Champillon, tel. 03.26.59.46.00, fax 03.26.59.44.85, e-mail champagneautreau@wanadoo.fr ▼
⊻ by appt.

AUTREAU-LASNOT★

		1.5 ha	5,000	🍶 ⅏		11–15 €

In Venteuil, on the slopes of the Vallée de la Marne, the vines are gilded by the midday sun. The present descendants of the Autréau-Lasnot family cultivate 11 ha there. The three champagne grape varieties (60% of the Pinots Noir and Meunier to 40% Chardonnay), from the harvests of 1997, 1998 and 1999, collaborate in this attractive rosé with notes of strawberries and liquorice, to make a rounded, fresh and well-balanced wine. The **Prestige 99**, a half-black, half-white *cuvée*, with discreet citrus fruit flavours on the nose and red berries on the palate, was also commended. (RM)

☛ Autréau-Lasnot, 6, rue du Château, 51480 Venteuil, tel. 03.26.58.49.35, fax 03.26.58.65.44, e-mail info@champagne-autreau-lasnot.com ▼
⊻ ev. day except Sun. 9am–12 noon 1.30pm–6pm; Sun. am and groups by appt.

ARNAUD BAGNOST

Cuvée de réserve★★

	1er cru	0.8 ha	7,000	🍶 ⅃		11–15 €

Fanfares mark the arrival in the *Guide* of Arnaud Bagnost, who has for the first time presented two premier cru *cuvées* to the Hachette tastings; the Jury gave a special mention to one, and two stars to the other. This should provide sufficient encouragement to this young négociant, heir to a line of wine-growers, who launched his brand in 1999. The Cuvée de réserve is a classic blend of 60% Pinot Noir and 40% Chardonnay, from grapes harvested in 2000. Discreet on the nose, it discloses all its qualities on the palate: full-bodied, rounded, fresh, balanced, complex (with spicy, toasty notes of brioche and stewed fruits) and long, it could equally well be served as an aperitif as with white meats. A commendation also went to the **Sélection**, which is made of all three champagne grape varieties (with 60% black grapes), from the year 2000. It is a young and fresh, but structured, wine. (NM)

☛ Arnaud Bagnost, 30, rue du Gal-de-Gaulle, 51530 Pierry, tel. 03.26.54.10.59, fax 03.26.55.67.17 ▼
⊻ by appt.

BANDOCK-MANGIN

Grande Réserve★★

	Gd cru	6.33 ha	4,000	🍶		11–15 €

Two families have united to make up this estate of 6.3 ha at Bouzy. Its Grande Réserve is blended from three times more black grapes than white. The harvests of 1996, 1997 and 1998 contribute to the red fruit flavours and the balance of this champagne, which will make "a good conversation piece," according to one taster. (RC)

☛ Yannick Bandock, 3, rue Victor-Hugo, 51150 Bouzy, tel. 03.26.57.09.09, fax 03.26.51.65.19, e-mail bandock-mangin@wanadoo.fr ▼
⊻ by appt.

PAUL BARA 1997★

	Gd cru	8 ha	10,000	🍶 ⅃		15–23 €

The Bara family has owned vineyards in the Grand Cru village of Bouzy since 1833, today tending 11 ha of vines. Pinot Noir is the star grape variety around these parts, and so it is that this 1997 – a rarely seen and difficult vintage – is only 10% away from being a blanc de noirs. It has an attractively buttery and spicy character, with good presence on the palate, and a vivacity that is typical of this vintage. A blend of 70% Pinot Noir and 30% Chardonnay, the **Spécial Club Grand Cru 98 (23–30 €)** also impressed the Jury: a little short perhaps, it was nonetheless commended for its roundness and fruitiness. (RM)

☛ Paul Bara, 4, rue Yvonnet, 51150 Bouzy, tel. 03.26.57.00.50, fax 03.26.57.81.24 ▼
⊻ by appt.

BARDOUX PERE ET FILS★★

	1er cru	n.c.	9,004	🍶 ⅃		15–23 €

Villedommange is a charming village in the northwest of the Montagne de Reims, where the Bardoux family has been cultivating vines since the time of Louis XIV. Justin and Prudent Bardoux launched the champagne house and, since 1973, Pascal Bardoux has tended its 4 ha. A product of the three champagne grape varieties (with approximately 70% of black grapes), this *brut* non-vintage stood out with its vinosity, fruitiness and complexity, the Jury finding in it notes of ripe fruit, cooked apple, honeysuckle, vanilla and toast. Its notable richness makes it a good wine for drinking with food. Two vintages, also blended from the three varieties, each obtained one star: the **95** is powerful and long, but still young; the **96** is developed in its aromas and yet at the same time still vigorous. (RM)

☛ Pascal Bardoux, 5–7, rue Saint-Vincent, 51390 Villedommange, tel. 03.26.49.25.35, fax 03.26.49.23.15, e-mail contact@champagne-bardoux.com ▼ ⅁
⊻ by appt.

EDMOND BARNAUT

Sélection Ultra-brut★★

	Gd cru	0.5 ha	5,000	🍶 ⅃		15–23 €

The label bears the name of the founder of the house, Edmond Barnaut, who in 1874 established the family vineyard around Bouzy and launched its champagne. His descendant, Philippe Secondé, who has been director of the estate since 1987, has risen superbly to the Hachette challenge. First off is this *coup de coeur*. It is comprised largely of black grapes (90%), in a blend of five- and six-year-old wines. A complex and fine champagne, with its flavours of prunes, mirabelle plums and honey, its multiple nuances attest to the ripeness of the grapes. Other descriptors that figured prominently in tasters' notes were: richness, vinosity, balance, class, length. Two other grands crus each obtained one star: the **Douceur**, a demi-sec, has well-integrated *dosage* and a flavour of passion-fruit; and the vintage **95 (23–30 €)**, made of half and half black and white grapes, is complex, fresh and long. (RM)

☛ Edmond Barnaut, 2, rue Gambetta, BP 19, 51150 Bouzy, tel. 03.26.57.01.54, fax 03.26.57.09.97, e-mail contact@champagne-barnaut.com ▼
⊻ ev. day 10.30am–12.30pm 2pm–5.30pm; Jan. by appt.
☛ P. et E. Secondé

ROGER BARNIER

Cuvée blanche 1997★

	1 ha	4,113	🍾 🎵 ♦	15–23 €

A few small islands of vines survive in the southwest of the Côte des Blancs, towards the Sézannais. One is in Villevenard, where this grower owns 7 ha. We suspect that under cover of this Cuvée Blanche, a blanc de blancs is hiding. The champagne owes its quality and its star award to its finesse, its positive attack and its length. (RM)
♦┑ Roger Barnier, 1, rue Marais-de-Saint-Gond, 51270 Villevenard, tel. 03.26.52.82.77, fax 03.26.52.81.09 ☑ 🏠
☙ by appt.
♦┑ F. Berthelot

BARON ALBERT

Carte d'or★★

	n.c.	30,000	🍾 ♦	11–15 €

The Baron family has been cultivating vines at Charly-sur-Marne in the Aisne district for over three centuries. In 1946, Albert Baron embarked successfully on champagne production, and the vineyard today extends over 30 ha. Dispensing with the malolactic fermentation, the blends produced generally privilege the black grape varieties. That is the case with this Carte d'or (65% black grapes), made from the harvests of 1996, 1997 and 1998. Its fine aromas, both toasty and floral, together with its generosity, its freshness and its length, earn it two stars. The rosé, a blend of the same years but with 45% Chardonnay, impresses for its softness and roundness, and is awarded one star. The same rating goes to the Préférence 96 (15–23 €), which contains three-quarters Chardonnay; fruity, complex, full, fresh and long, it would make a fine aperitif wine. (NM)
♦┑ Baron Albert, 1, rue des Chaillots, Grand-Porteron, BP 12, 02310 Charly-sur-Marne, tel. 03.23.82.02.65, fax 03.23.82.02.44,
e-mail champagnebaronalbert@wanadoo.fr ☑
☙ by appt.

BARON-FUENTE

Esprit★

	4 ha	27,000	🍾	11–15 €

Another branch of the Baron family, still in Charly-sur-Marne, was established when Gabriel Baron married Dolorès Fuentes, who comes from the sherry region of Spain. Their estate, today comprising 50 ha, was created in 1961, with the Baron-Fuenté brand being launched soon afterwards. This house was honoured last year for its 1996 vintage. This year, it is the Esprit that carries the day, a cuvée made from the three grape varieties of Champagne (with 65% black grapes), a slightly liquoricey wine that owes its star to its impressive balance. Two other champagnes crossed the line with commendations: the rosé Dolorès, a blend of all three grape varieties in much the same proportions as the Esprit (from the harvests of 1997, 1998 and 1999), with a scent of redcurrants, followed by strawberries on the palate; and Ampelos, a blanc de noirs of 100% Meunier from the 2000 harvest, a fine, fruity, brioche-like wine with a very attractive finish. (NM)
♦┑ Baron-Fuenté, 21, av. Fernand-Drouet, 02310 Charly-sur-Marne, tel. 03.23.82.01.97, fax 03.23.82.12.00,
e-mail champagne.baron-fuente@wanadoo.fr ☑
☙ by appt.

BAUCHET PERE ET FILS

Saint Nicaise Prestige 1997★

	1er cru	0.5 ha	5,000	15–23 €

Bisseuil, in the Vallée de la Marne, some 10 km upstream of Epernay, is the cradle of this family estate, which has expanded spectacularly since Félicien founded the company with his sons in 1960. It then consisted of just over 3 ha, now grown to 37 ha, including further plantings in the Aube and the Côte des Blancs. The house branched out into wine-making in the 1970s, and is currently headed up by two brothers. Two of its premier cru champagnes passed the mark: with one star is this 1997 vintage, a buttery blanc de blancs with fresh and lively balance; and the commended Sélection (11–15 €), a richly aromatic brut non-vintage made of half black grapes and half white, which has both balance and satisfactory length. (RM)
♦┑ Sté Bauchet Frères, rue de la Crayère, 51150 Bisseuil, tel. 03.26.58.92.12, fax 03.26.58.94.74,
e-mail bauchet.champagne@wanadoo.fr ☑
☙ by appt.

BAUGET-JOUETTE

Blanc de blancs★

	0.35 ha	3,500	🍾 ♦	15–23 €

The Baugets work a vineyard of 14 ha on the outskirts of Epernay. This blanc de blancs non-vintage is in fact made from the harvest of only one year, 1999. The Jury was as one in commending the balance, richness and length of this wine, which can be served as an aperitif, with fish, even with white meat. Made of equal parts black and white grapes, the Jouette (23–30 €) is a young champagne from the harvest of 2001. It was specially mentioned as much for its youthful freshness as for the complexity of its range of flavours, which finish on floral and mineral notes. (NM)
♦┑ Bauget-Jouette, 1, rue Champfleury, 51200 Epernay, tel. 03.26.54.44.05, fax 03.26.55.37.99,
e-mail champagne-bauget@wanadoo.fr ☑

NOEL BAZIN★★

	1er cru	0.6 ha	n.c.	🍾	11–15 €

This is a small family vineyard of 2 ha near Villers-Marmery, where the slopes of the Montagne de Reims look towards the Levant. The proprietors lack nothing in ambition. Hardly has the brand been launched (in 1999) than the red-label cuvée of Noël Bazin achieves a triumph in the champagne chapter of the Guide. It is a blanc de blancs from the harvests of 1999 and 2000. The Jury highlighted the floral (hawthorn) elegance of its bouquet, enlivened with a touch of mint. On the palate, it shows fine flavours of hazelnuts and almonds, as well as richness, stuffing and length, all adding up to a thoroughly refined whole. "A spiritual champagne," was one taster's conclusion. A star was also awarded to the Blanc de Blancs Demi-Sec, a blend of the same two years; the dosage in it, always a tricky issue with this type of wine, has been successfully judged. (RM)
♦┑ Noël and Magali Bazin, 1, rue Perrin, 51380 Villers-Marmery, tel. 03.26.97.97.07, fax 03.26.97.97.07, e-mail noel.bazin@libertysurf.fr ☑
☙ by appt.

ANDRE BEAUFORT

Réserve★★

	Gd cru	1.6 ha	10,000	🍾 🎵	15–23 €

Jacques Beaufort makes the champagnes sold under the André Beaufort label. A notable feature of this estate is that its winemaker was one of the pioneers of radical organic viticulture, as far back as the 1970s. He thus resorts to essential oils and homeopathy to avoid the use of copper sulphate as a pesticide. The method clearly succeeds, since his Réserve, a blend with an 80% majority of black grapes, has carried off a *coup de coeur*. The Jury was filled with enthusiasm for its generous and complex bouquet, whose vanillary, smoky, balsamic notes have been bequeathed by a period in barrel, and for its powerful presence on the palate, where it shows itself harmonious and long, with a discreet woody note. (RM)

� Jacques Beaufort, 1, rue de Vaudemange,
51150 Ambonnay, tel. 03.26.57.01.50, fax 03.26.52.83.50 ☑
☒ by appt.

JACQUES BEAUFORT

Demi-sec 1991★★

| | 2.4 ha | 6,000 | ☷ ⑪ | 15–23 € |

Pinot Noir dominates the plantings at this property, as well as the wines the house produces (it represents, in general, 80% of each blend). Jacques Beaufort is involved with the wood-ageing of the wines, and especially with the demi-sec champagnes, for which he has a particular aptitude. This 1991 vintage thus came very close to achieving a *coup de coeur*. It has everything going for it: lightness, roundness, vinosity, fruit, woodiness, balance and, above all, sheer class. (RM)

➫ Jacques Beaufort, 1, rue de Vaudemange,
51150 Ambonnay, tel. 03.26.57.01.50, fax 03.26.52.83.50 ☑
☒ by appt.

FRANCOISE BEDEL

Extra-brut 1995★

| | 4.55 ha | 13,390 | ☷ ⑪ | 15–23 € |

Françoise Bedel relaunched her father's estate in 1976, converting it to biodynamic methods in 1998. The 1995 vintage is blended from the three grape varieties of Champagne in virtually equal measure. It has subtle aromas of pepper and exotic spices, followed by pronounced citrus-fruit flavours on the palate, with appreciable *dosage*. (RM)

➫ Françoise Bedel, 71, Grande-Rue,
02310 Crouttes-sur-Marne, tel. 03.23.82.15.80,
fax 03.23.82.11.49, e-mail chfbedel@quid-info.fr ☑
☒ by appt.

L. BENARD-PITOIS★

| | 1er cru | n.c. | n.c. | ☷ ⑪ ⬧ | 15–23 € |

Based at Mareuil-sur-A in the south of the Montagne de Reims, on the edge of the Marne, the third generation of the Bénard family have 10 ha of vines on varied terroirs, of which some are grand cru and some premier cru. They make some very distinguished champagnes, such as this woody rosé, which is a blend of 88% Chardonnay with 12% red wine to give it its colour, from the harvest of 1999. It has only one defect, namely its youth. It is a clear-cut, fine, elegant, and discreetly woody champagne. Two other Premier Cru *cuvées* of the estate were singled out, in the lower price range: the Réserve (11–15 €), a blend of 60% Chardonnay with Pinot Noir (from the harvests of 1996, 1998 and 1999), which is pleasant, fresh and light, an aperitif wine; and the Carte Blanche (11–15 €), which is dominated by the two Pinots (56% Pinot Noir to 22% Meunier, from the harvests of 1999 and 2000), and is a powerful and balanced champagne. (RM)

➫ L. Bénard-Pitois, 23, rue Duval, 51160 Mareuil-sur-A,
tel. 03.26.52.60.28, fax 03.26.52.60.12,
e-mail benard-pitois@wanadoo.fr ☑
☒ by appt.

CH. BERTHELOT

Avize Carte noire★

| | Gd cru | n.c. | n.c. | ☷ | 11–15 € |

This brand, launched in 1982, is comprised of a small vineyard of 2 ha. Although the label is black, this champagne is a blanc de blancs, made up of wines from the 1999 and 2000 harvests. The nose is a treat for gourmets, with notes of fruit

syrup, acacia honey and fruits in brandy. Its velvety texture fills the mouth, combining richness and elegance. (RM)

➫ Christian Berthelot, 32, rue Ernest-Valle, 51190 Avize,
tel. 03.26.57.58.99, fax 03.26.51.87.26 ☑
☒ by appt.

BESSERAT DE BELLEFON

Cuvée des Moines★★

| ● | n.c. | n.c. | ☷ ⬧ | 15–23 € |

Founded in 1843 by one Edmond Besserat of Hautvillers, the house became Besserat de Bellefon by marriage in 1927. It has been owned since 1990 by the important cooperative group, Marne et Champagne. Cuvée des Moines is a lightly sparkling champagne, with very fine effervescence. A product of the harvests of 1999 and 2000, it is made up of the three champagne grape varieties in noticeably equal measure (Chardonnay accounting for 35% of the blend), which have not undergone malolactic fermentation. This rosé came very close to a *coup de coeur*: its rich suppleness, its flavours of raspberries and honey and notes of sweet spice, its graceful balance and class, enthused more than one member of the Jury. (NM)

➫ Besserat de Bellefon, 19, av. de Champagne,
51200 Epernay, tel. 03.26.78.50.50, fax 03.26.78.50.99 ☑

BERNARD BIJOTAT★

| | 6 ha | 45,000 | ☷ | 11–15 € |

The Bernard Bijotat brand has been in existence since 1980. It indicates a champagne that is produced only 80 km from Paris, the village of Romeny-sur-Marne being located within the borders of the Aisne and Seine-et-Marne. In this area, Pinot Meunier predominates, as it does in this *brut* non-vintage (82% of the blend, supplemented by 12% Pinot Noir and a dash of Chardonnay), which brings together the harvests of 1999 and 2000. On the nose, which has aromas of nuts and figs, the first suggestion of development manifests itself. As one tastes the wine, one finds oneself assuredly within the company of an honest bourgeois rather than a marquis, but the positive impression is of a wine that satisfyingly fills the mouth with its freshness and length, allowing this champagne a more than honourable inclusion in the *Guide*. (RM)

➫ BBS Bernard Bijotat, 2, rte Nationale,
02310 Romeny-sur-Marne, tel. 03.23.70.12.51,
fax 03.23.70.61.03,
e-mail bbs.champagne.bijotat@wanadoo.fr ☑ ⬧
☒ by appt.

BILLECART-SALMON★

| ● | n.c. | n.c. | ☷ ⬧ | 38–46 € |

A marriage between Nicolas-François Billecart and Elisabeth Salmon, heirs to ancient lineages within Mareuil-sur-Aÿ, stands at the origin of this house, which was founded in 1818. Having remained in the same family ever since, it benefits from an enviable reputation, although it owns no vineyards. Made half of black grapes and half of white (with 10% Pinot Meunier), its *brut* rosé is elegant on the nose, with a touch of peardrop, a fresh and balanced champagne with a long finish. The Cuvée Elisabeth Salmon rosé 97 (more than 76 €), which is half Chardonnay and half Pinot Noir, is vinified in the same manner as the non-vintage rosé, and obtained the same rating. It is complex, lively and light. The Brut Réserve (23–30 €), blended from all three champagne grape varieties (Pinot Meunier 40%, Pinot Noir 25%, Chardonnay 35%), is a rich and well-balanced wine. (NM)

➫ Billecart-Salmon, 40, rue Carnot, 51160 Mareuil-sur-Aÿ,
tel. 03.26.52.60.22, fax 03.26.52.64.88,
e-mail billecart@champagne-billecart.fr ☑
☒ by appt.

BINET 1995★

| | n.c. | n.c. | ☷ ⬧ | 23–30 € |

Created in 1849, this house has always borne the name of its founder, Léon Binet, although it has changed hands with successive relaunches, most recently in 2000 with its acquisition by the Prin group. This 1995 – a fine vintage – is a blend of 60% Chardonnay with Pinot Noir adding suppleness, vinosity and body to what is a pristine wine. The Blanc de Blancs 97 received a star for its good balance, lively attack and rich mouthfeel. The Brut Elite (15–23 €), a blend of 60% of both

Pinots with 40% Chardonnay, was also singled out. It is a champagne with a clean bouquet, which strikes the palate gently and then slowly fades. (NM)

☛ Binet, 31, rue de Reims, 51500 Rilly-la-Montagne, tel. 03.26.88.05.00, fax 03.26.88.05.05, e-mail info@champagne-binet.com ▣

☯ by appt.

R. BLIN ET FILS 1997★

	n.c.	7,000		15–23 €

This grower is based in Trigny, at the heart of the Saint-Thierry vineyards, to the west of Reims. Its 1997 is a blanc de noirs made from Pinot Noir. It impresses for its bouquet of nuts and citrus fruits, which extends on to a full, fresh palate. (RM)

☛ R. Blin et Fils, 11, rue du Point-du-Jour, 51140 Trigny, tel. 03.26.03.10.97, fax 03.26.03.19.63 ▣

☯ by appt.

TH. BLONDEL

Blanc de blancs 1999★

	1er cru	4.5 ha	6,000	▪ ⚬	15–23 €

In 1904, a notary acquired this estate consisting of only one vineyard holding, located at Ludes on the northern slope of the Montagne de Reims. The brand saw the light of day in 1985, when the founder's great-grandchildren reassumed the management of this 9.5-ha domaine. The house has made a very good showing with three premiers crus, thanks in particular to a blanc de blancs: this youthful 99, which is floral, fresh and balanced, a very promising wine. Two further commendations were awarded: to the **Carte d'Or (11–15 €)**, made predominantly of black grapes (70% Pinot Noir) from the harvests of 1999 and 2000, with its subtle bouquet, finesse and freshness; and to the **rosé (11–15 €)**, an attractively fruity rosé de noirs. (NM)

☛ Blondel, Dom. des Monts-Fournois, 51500 Ludes, tel. 03.26.03.43.92, fax 03.26.03.44.10, e-mail contact@champagne-blondel.com ▣

☯ ev. day 9am–12 noon 2pm–7pm

BOIZEL 1996★★

	n.c.	60,000	▪ ⑪ ⚬	23–30 €

Created in 1834, the house has always been headed by the Boizel family, a champagne dynasty in the service of wine since the 17th century. It is now affiliated to the BCC group. This 1996 is made from 60% of both Pinots and 40% Chardonnay, with 7% of the wine having passed through wood. "A coup de coeur was not far away," commented one taster of this developed champagne, in acknowledgement of its "beneficial oxidation". Two further stars were awarded to the **Joyau de France 91 (30–38 €)**, a blend of Pinot Noir (70%) and Chardonnay vinified in the same style as the first wine, which was appreciated for its complexity (nuts, bread crust, smoke, wood, lemon) and its surprising freshness. One star went to the **rosé (15–23 €)**, made from 90% black grapes, a light, fruity wine with a lingering finish. (NM)

☛ Boizel, 46, av. de Champagne, 51200 Epernay, tel. 03.26.55.21.51, fax 03.26.54.31.83, e-mail boizelinfo@boizel.fr

☛ BCC

BOLLINGER

Grande Année 1996★★

	n.c.	n.c.	⑪	46–76 €

Founded in 1829, this grand house at Aÿ is one of the rare family-run companies to have preserved its independence. Succeeding the Grande Année 1995, here is the 96. As always at Bollinger, the blend privileges Pinot Noir (70%, to 30% Chardonnay), and combines wines from 16 crus (75% grands crus, 25% premiers). The champagne is matured in cellars under stopper corks, which ensure better protection against oxidation. It is currently showing no signs of development, but the vintage conditions have bequeathed to it both vigour and fullness of body. Its complexity and its length earn it a coup de coeur. One star was awarded to the **Spécial Cuvée (30–38 €)**, which, despite its name, is the basic cuvée of this house. Made from 60% Pinot Noir and 15% Meunier, supplemented by Chardonnay, it mingles white flowers and white and yellow fruits in its bouquet. Its studied balance makes it the classic model of a brut non-vintage. It only remains to add that the RD 1990, which received a coup de coeur in 2003, is still available. (NM)

☛ Bollinger, 16, rue Jules-Lobet, 51160 Aÿ, tel. 03.26.53.33.66, fax 03.26.54.85.59

BONNAIRE

Tradition★

	20 ha	n.c.	▪ ⚬	11–15 €

Based at Cramant in the Côte des Blancs, this estate has been producing champagne since 1932. To th·ᵗ vineyard have been added 8.5 ha in the Vallée de la Marne,   ᵗcing 22 ha in all. Its Tradition cuvée is a blend of wines fro· 998 and 1999. Full but with evident dosage, it displays aᴜ attractive fruitiness that mixes citrus fruits and mirabelle plums. The same rating was awarded to the **Blanc de Blancs Cramant Grand Cru 95 (15–23 €)**; with notes of butter and brioche on the nose, this champagne combines freshness and toastiness. Finally, a further commendation went to the non-vintage **Blanc de Blancs Grand Cru (15–23 €)**, a product of the harvests of 1998 and 1999, which combines quince and lightly honeyed notes in a balanced and impressive wine. (RM)

☛ Bonnaire, 120, rue d'Epernay, 51530 Cramant, tel. 03.26.57.50.85, fax 03.26.57.59.17, e-mail info@champagne-bonnaire.com ▣ ▤ ◍

☯ by appt.

ALEXANDRE BONNET

Grande Réserve★

	40.44 ha	200,000		11–15 €

This Auboise house was founded in 1932 by the Bonnet family, which sold it in 1998 to the BCC group. Its vineyard extends over more than 40 ha. Dominated by black grapes (90%, including 70% Pinot Noir), this Grande Réserve is a blend of 1999 and 2000 wines. It is so young that it still has aromas of fresh grapes, but its finesse and freshness make it very pleasant to drink. Deriving from the same years, the **Blanc de Noirs** (80% Pinot Noir) was singled out for its floral bouquet and its lightness on the palate. (NM)

☛ Alexandre Bonnet, 138, rue du Gal-de-Gaulle, 10340 Les Riceys, tel. 03.25.29.30.93, fax 03.25.29.38.65, e-mail info@alexandrebonnet.com ▣

☯ by appt.

☛ BCC

BONNET-GILMERT

Blanc de blancs Cuvée de réserve 1993★

	Gd cru	3.75 ha	2,000	▪	11–15 €

Based at Oger on the Côte des Blancs, Denis Bonnet is the descendant of a line of wine-growers dating back to 1800. His family has been making champagne since 1920. Two Grands Crus from this house were commended: the unstarred **Cuvée de Réserve Blanc de Blancs**, from the harvests of 1998 and 1999, with its discreetly floral bouquet; and this single-starred 93, a vintage that is becoming quite rare. With notes of toast and nuts, its aromas are ripe, much like its rounded palate, but the overall impression is of an astonishing freshness that almost leads one to believe the wine will be indestructible. (RM)

☛ Bonnet-Gilmert, 16, rue de la Côte, 51190 Oger, tel. 03.26.59.49.47, fax 03.26.59.00.17, e-mail denisbonnet@free.fr ▣

☯ by appt.

☛ Denis Bonnet

BONNET-PONSON

Cuvée spéciale 1993★

1 ha	5,000	▮ ❑ ⬧	15–23 €

Based at Chamery, on the northern side of the Montagne de Reims, Thierry Bonnet farms around ten hectares of vines. He gives his wines a short period in wood. This Cuvée Spéciale, made from 80% Chardonnay, supplemented by Pinot Noir, comes from the old and rare 1993 vintage. Its full, fine bouquet of white flowers leads on to a rounded and still-lively palate. (RM)
❧ Bonnet-Ponson, 20, rue du Sourd, 51500 Chamery, tel. 03.26.97.65.40, fax 03.26.97.67.11, e-mail champagne.bonnet.ponson@wanadoo.fr ☑
ⵣ by appt.

FRANCK BONVILLE

Blanc de blancs 1998★

Gd cru	15 ha	10,000	▮ ⬧	11–15 €

This estate comprises 15 ha in Avize, a grand cru village in the Côte des Blancs. Franck Bonville launched its champagne in 1945. The house is now led by Gilles Bonville, while Olivier looks after the winemaking. In this blanc de blancs, the Chardonnay is given lively expression by flavours of quince, honey and Viennese biscuits. After a crisp attack, the wine is structured and well-balanced on the palate. (RM)
❧ Franck Bonville, 9, rue Pasteur, 51190 Avize, tel. 03.26.57.52.30, fax 03.26.57.59.90, e-mail franck-bonville@wanadoo.fr ☑
ⵣ by appt.

RAYMOND BOULARD

Tradition★★

2 ha	10,300	▮ ❑	15–23 €

This house has a vineyard of more than 10 ha, distributed among one grand cru in the Montagne de Reims and eight villages in the Vallée de la Marne, in the Vesle district and on the Saint-Thierry massif. Its brand was launched in 1952. Blended from half black grapes and half white, the cuvée Tradition comes from four years (1996–1999). The wines spend three months in wood. Its bouquet of hazelnuts and citrus fruits and its fresh vinosity are the principal assets of this champagne. "A wine of great complexity," wrote one taster at the conclusion of his note. (NM)
❧ Raymond Boulard, 1, rue du Tambour, 51480 La Neuville-aux-Larris, tel. 03.26.58.12.08, fax 03.26.61.54.92, e-mail info@champagne-boulard.fr ☑
ⵣ by appt.

BOULARD-BAUQUAIRE

Blanc de blancs Cuvée Mélanie★★★

0.5 ha	1,500		15–23 €

Their estate does not date back to the 15th century, but to 1969. They do not own a vineyard in some grand cru, but in Cormicy, a village about 15 km north of Reims, towards the Aisne district. They do not possess 50 ha, only a mere seven, and their brand was only founded in 1981. And yet this champagne collects a unanimous three stars from the Jury, an exceedingly rare feat. Tasters were filled with admiration for the complexity of its honeyed, crystallized, exotic aromas, and its crystal-clear palate, which reveals a well-made, warming, elegant wine, with flavours of brioche and great length. A well-kept secret, clearly... As for the **Brut Prestige**

(11–15 €), it is a blanc de blancs made from the 1999 harvest. Its bouquet evolves from mineral notes to crystallized fruits, and it is fresh and long on the palate: one star. A name to follow. (RM)
❧ Boulard-Bauquaire, 30, rue du Petit-Guyencourt, BP 6, 51220 Cormicy, tel. 03.26.61.30.79, fax 03.26.61.34.40, e-mail info@champagne.boulard-bauquaire.fr ☑
ⵣ by appt.

R. BOURDELOIS

Cuvée de réserve★

5.8 ha	20,000		11–15 €

This estate, founded approximately a century ago, is based at Dizy on the right bank of the Marne, facing Epernay. It covers 5.8 ha. Its Cuvée de réserve, made from 60% of both Pinots in equal measure to 40% Chardonnay, comes from the harvests of 1996, 1997 and 1998. It owes its star to a richness of texture lightened by fine acidity, making it a balanced and elegant wine. Good length. (RM)
❧ Bourdelois, 737, av. du Gal-Leclerc, 51530 Dizy, tel. 03.26.55.23.34, fax 03.26.51.29.81 ☑
ⵣ by appt.

BOURGEOIS

Sélection★★

n.c.	n.c.	▮	11–15 €

The Bourgeois family, like many another company of grower-producers, crossed over the line in 1987 when they became négociants, all the while continuing to manage their vineyard of 10 ha in the Vallée de la Marne. This cuvée Sélection is a blend of 80% black grapes (including 60% Pinot Noir) to 20% Chardonnay. The wines do not undergo malolactic fermentation. That makes for a classic champagne, but one that is remarkable in all particulars: perfect development, perfect balance and a perfect finish. In addition, the **Cuvée de l'Ecu 98 (15–23 €)**, a blanc de blancs also without malolactic fermentation, was singled out: it is a vigorous, powerful and long champagne. (NM)
❧ Bourgeois, 43, Grande-Rue, 02310 Crouttes-sur-Marne, tel. 03.23.82.15.71, fax 03.23.82.55.11, e-mail champagne-bourgeois@wanadoo.fr ☑
ⵣ by appt.

CHRISTIAN BOURNAULT

Blanc de blancs Cuvée Grand Eloge★

0.64 ha	1,400	❑	15–23 €

Based at Avize on the Côte des Blancs, the Bournaults have been wine-growers through the generations since 1870, working 6 ha of vines. Their brand is very recent, though, having only been established in 2000. They ferment and mature their base wines in barrel. The Grand Eloge, a blanc de blancs from the harvest of 2000, is a champagne of character. Both on the nose and on the palate, the wood vinification makes its presence felt. The ample structure, and flavours of honey, nuts and crystallized and exotic fruits, help to lengthen its harmonious finish. Also commended was the cuvée **Hermance** (70% Chardonnay, 25% Meunier and a soupçon of Pinot Noir, from 1999 grapes), an interesting wine with toasty aromas, distinguished by its period in wood and by its weight. (RM)
❧ EARL Bournault et Fils, 41, Rempart du Midi, 51190 Avize, tel. 03.26.59.79.41, fax 03.26.58.67.74, e-mail christian.bournault@wanadoo.fr ☑
ⵣ ev. day 10am–12 noon 2pm–6pm; Sun. by appt.

CH. DE BOURSAULT

Blanc de blancs 1994★★

1 ha	1,744	▮ ⬧	23–30 €

The Champagne region numbers only two estates with the Château name: that of Bligny in the Aube, and this one on the left bank of the Marne, to the west of Epernay. Mme Veuve Clicquot had it built in the mid–19th century on an eminence overlooking the valley. The building is surrounded by a vineyard of 15 ha. This 1994 is a blanc de blancs. Toasty on the nose as also on the palate, with nuances of honey and ripe fruit, it has reached its peak but retains a certain freshness. It could successfully be drunk with food. Also singled out was the **Cuvée Prestige**: made of half black grapes and half white, it seems a little short, but its fruity, honeyed flavours, together with its balance, are worth a commendation. (NM)

📍 Ch. de Boursault, 2, rue Maurice-Gilbert, 51480 Boursault, tel. 03.26.58.42.21, fax 03.26.58.66.12, e-mail info@champagnechateau.com ▪

L. ET F. BOYER

Blanc de blancs★

	Gd cru	1.7 ha	6,000		11–15 €

Founded in 1959, this family company has been led since 1994 by Lydie Boyer. She manages a scattered series of vineyards: 2 ha at Chouilly, a Côte des Blancs grand cru, 1.2 ha at Hautvillers and 2 ha at Châtillon-sur-Marne. The base wines are partly wood-aged, as in this blanc de blancs made from the harvests of 1998 and 1999. Brioche-scented, with slightly woody, charred notes, lively and well-balanced, it is a classic champagne. The same rating was awarded to the **Cuvée Jeanne (15–23 €)**, which is predominantly Chardonnay (84% of the blend), and marries the wines of 1997 and 1998; complex, and marked by floral notes, a touch of wood and orchard fruits, it is fine and long. (RM)

📍 L. et F. Boyer, 27, rue Dom-Pérignon, 51530 Chouilly, tel. 03.26.55.41.06, fax 03.26.55.01.78, e-mail francis.boyer@free.fr ▪

⟙ by appt.

BERNARD BREMONT 1996★

	Gd cru	0,61 ha	5,800	▪ ◗	15–23 €

Located at Ambonnay, this estate has 14.5 ha of vines, all of grand cru status. Made from 60% Pinot Noir and 40% Chardonnay, this is one of the most successful 1996s, in that it has managed to avoid the premature development to which certain champagnes of this vintage have fallen victim. Its range of flavours mingles toasty, smoky, bready, honeyed notes with hints of fig, and it has a well-balanced palate of pleasing vigour. (RM)

📍 SCE Bernard Brémont et Fils, 1, rue de Reims, 51150 Ambonnay, tel. 03.26.57.01.65, fax 03.26.57.80.65, e-mail info@champagne-bremont.com ▪

⟙ by appt.

BRETON FILS 1998★

		1.5 ha	10,000	▪ ◗	15–23 €

The Bretons have been making champagne since 1952. Based at Congy, between the Côte des Blancs and the Sézannais, they have considerably increased the size of their estate and now have plots in various sectors of the region (17 ha in all). Their 1998 blanc de blancs is full of good qualities: its range of flavours, which mixes floral and fruity notes with smoky (roasted coffee-bean) and spicy elements, its gentle attack and its long finish. As for the non-vintage **Blanc de Blancs (11–15 €)**, it deserves a special mention for its lemony freshness and its flavours of almonds and hazelnuts. The same rating, finally, went to a **rosé (15–23 €)** made from the three champagne grape varieties (the Pinots making up 56%), which is full of appealing flavours of raspberries, blackcurrants and black cherries. (RM)

📍 SCEV Breton Fils, 12, rue Courte-Pilate, 51270 Congy, tel. 03.26.59.31.03, fax 03.26.59.30.60, e-mail contact@champagne-breton-fils.fr ▪

⟙ ev. day 8.30am–12 noon 1.30pm–5.30pm

BRICE

Cramant★★

	Gd cru	n.c.	n.c.	▪	23–30 €

This house was founded in 1994. It manages 7 ha of its own vineyards at Bouzy and draws from an agglomeration of 27 ha distributed among twenty other crus. Its claim to fame is a range of grand cru champagnes vinified without malolactic fermentation. This one is made from the produce of its vineyard at Cramant on the Côte des Blancs. It comprises wine from the 1999 harvest, together with 20% of reserve wines. From this pale champagne with its fine bubbles escape the most varied fragrances, such as rose-petals, elderflower, a touch of mint, broom and citrus fruits (principally lemon), notes that are echoed on the well-balanced palate with its judicious *dosage*. What would you say to a dish of stuffed crab in Cramant? After this blanc de blancs was commended a near-blanc de noirs (90% Pinot Noir), **A**, made from the harvest of 1998, an original and characterful

champagne combining red berries, blackcurrants and blackberries with a firm edge: it received one star. As for the **Verzenay** (90% Pinot Noir from 1998, with 20% of reserve wines), it is a complex, rich wine of great length, but too young for some tasters. It took a commendation. (NM)

📍 Jean-Paul Brice, 3, rue Yvonnet, 51150 Bouzy, tel. 03.26.52.06.60, fax 03.26.57.05.07, e-mail champagnebrice@wanadoo.fr ▪

⟙ by appt.

BROCHET-HERVIEUX

Brut-extra★

	1er cru	n.c.	90,000		11–15 €

Based at Eceuil, on the northwestern flank of the Montagne de Reims, this estate has succeeded with an attractive Brut-Extra with a majority of black grapes (85%, mainly Pinot Noir), from the harvests of 1997 and 1998. A champagne that is all soft fruits, on the nose as well as the palate, it is "one for the gourmets," or so wrote one taster. (RM)

📍 Brochet-Hervieux, 12, rue de Villers-aux-Noeuds, 51500 Eceuil, tel. 03.26.49.77.44, fax 03.26.49.77.17 ▪

⟙ by appt.

RENE BRUN 1995★

		n.c.	17,000	▪ ◗	15–23 €

This négociant house was founded half a century ago by René Brun, and relaunched in 1995 by René-James Lallier. Its 1995 privileges the Chardonnay grape (85% of the blend, supplemented by Pinot Noir). It has reached its peak and shows beautiful complexity on the nose as well as on the palate. Honey, cooked fruits and dried apricots come together in a harmonious finish. (NM)

📍 René Brun, 4, place de la Libération, 51160 Aÿ, tel. 03.26.55.43.40, fax 03.26.55.79.93, e-mail champagne.renebrun@hexanet.fr ▪

⟙ by appt.

EDOUARD BRUN & CIE

Réserve★★

	1er cru	7 ha	50,000	▪ ▥	11–15 €

Founded more than a century ago, this négociant house has remained within the same family. The wines are fermented in wood and then undergo their malolactic fermentation in tank. Supplemented by Chardonnay, Pinot Noir accounts for three-quarters of this Réserve. The grapes come from the harvests of 1998, 1999 and 2000. Floral on the nose, fruitier on the palate, it offers evidence of roundness, balance and length, attributes that were particularly noticed by the Jury. These qualities also presage good longevity. Barely a notch below, the *cuvée* **L'Elégante Grand Cru (23–30 €)** is predominantly white grapes (80%). The freshness of its bouquet, its flavour of white peaches and its good balance earned it one star. "A tonic and stimulating champagne," according to the tasters. The **1997 (15–23 €)** was also singled out. Made of half black grapes and half white, its roundness is underlined by generous *dosage*. (NM)

📍 Edouard Brun et Cie, 14, rue Marcel-Mailly, BP 11, 51160 Aÿ, tel. 03.26.55.20.11, fax 03.26.51.94.29, e-mail contact@champagne-edouard-brun.com ▪

⟙ by appt.

📍 Delescot

ERIC BUNEL★★

●	4.6 ha	2,000	🄸	11–15 €

On the eastern slope of the Montagne de Reims, Louvois preserves the memory of François Michel Le Tellier, Secretary of State for War under Louis XIV. Eric Bunel established this estate and launched its champagne in 1970, having remained in charge of the vineyard ever since. Predominantly Pinot Noir with a soupçon (15%) of Chardonnay, its clear rosé presents something of a surprise, but a good one. Its aromas of lychees and raspberries, with hints of musk and vanilla, and its flavours of exotic fruits, were strongly admired, as was its overall balance. (RM)
➤ Eric Bunel, 32, rue Michel-Letellier, 51150 Louvois, tel. 03.26.57.03.06, fax 03.26.52.31.66, e-mail champagne.bunel@wanadoo.fr **Ⅴ**
🍷 by appt.

DANIEL CAILLEZ★

●	3.5 ha	5,000	🄸 🄾🄱	11–15 €

Based at Damery, on the right bank of the Marne, Daniel Caillez launched out into champagne production in 1977, and has recently handed over his 5.5 ha of vines to his son Vincent. The two harvests of 1999 and 2000 contributed to this intensely coloured rosé made from Pinot Meunier. This champagne has the violet hue of youth, good vinosity on the nose and fullness on the palate, with a touch of wood. Dominated by black grapes (75%, including 50% Meunier) drawn from the harvests of 1998 and 1999, the **Référence** deserved a commendation for its minerality, roundness, balance and length. (RM)
➤ Daniel Caillez, 19, rue Pierre-Curie, 51480 Damery, tel. 03.26.58.46.02, fax 03.26.52.04.24, e-mail champagnedanielcaillez@club-internet.fr **Ⅴ**
🍷 by appt.

CAILLEZ-LEMAIRE

Grande Réserve★★

●	n.c.	14,242	🄸 ⚲	11–15 €

This estate based in the Vallée de la Marne has a vineyard of 6 ha. Its Grande Réserve, made of half black grapes and half white, is a blend of the harvests of 1999 and 2000. Rather shy on the nose, it moves between flavours of mirabelle plum and greengage on the palate, with a lively attack, fullness and length. Opinions are divided on the **1998 (15–23 €)**, a blend that privileges Chardonnay (60%, to 30% Pinot Noir and 10% Meunier), and on which maturation in barrel has conferred a light woodiness. A fine, toasty, structured wine, this champagne had its ardent supporters, and received a commendation. (RM)
➤ Caillez-Lemaire, rue Pierre-Curie, BP 11, 51480 Damery, tel. 03.26.58.41.85, fax 03.26.52.04.23, e-mail champ-cailllez.lemaire@wanadoo.fr
🍷 by appt.

CANARD-DUCHENE★★

●	n.c.	n.c.	🄸 ⚲	15–23 €

A marriage marked the origin of this brand: that in 1860 of Victor Canard, carpenter and barrel-maker, to Léonie Duchêne, daughter of a winemaking family. The couple lived at Ludes in the Montagne de Reims. Eight years later came the foundation of their negociant house, acquired at the end of the 1970s by Veuve Clicquot, which was incorporated in turn into the LVMH group. Canard-Duchêne today delivers a remarkable *brut* non-vintage, made predominantly from black grapes (80% of both Pinots in equal parts, with 20% Chardonnay). Seductive on the nose, with overtones of brioche and charred notes (coffee, toast), it displays honeyed flavours on the palate, with roundness, freshness and harmony. One star went to the **Grande Cuvée Charles VII**, a blend that gives a slight majority to the Pinots (45% Pinot Noir, 10% Meunier). This is a champagne close in style to the preceding wine, ripe and long. Also singled out was the rare vintage **1993**, combining both Pinots with 28% Chardonnay, a fully developed wine that has reached its peak. (NM)
➤ Canard-Duchêne, 1, rue Edmond-Canard, 51500 Ludes, tel. 03.26.61.11.60, fax 03.26.40.60.17, e-mail info@canard-duchene.fr **Ⅴ**
🍷 ev. day except Sun. 10am–1pm 2pm–5pm; cl. 1st Nov.–30th Mar.

VICOMTE DE CASTELLANE

Croix rouge★★★

●	8 ha	75,000	15–23 €

With its tower resembling the belfry of Lyon railway station – the two buildings were designed by the same architect – the headquarters of this company founded in 1895 by Florens de Castellane is one of the best-known monuments in Epernay. The house was associated with the carefree years of the Belle Epoque as a result of the efforts of a cousin of Florens, a socialite known by the name of Boni, who helped Castellane's champagnes break on to the market. They always shine, thanks to wines such as this salmon-pink rosé, a blend of 70% of both Pinots with Chardonnay. It has an intense nose full of finesse, and a powerful though subtle palate with balance, length and harmony: a *coup de coeur*! The same significant presence of black grapes (70% Pinot Noir) go into the **Cuvée Commodore 91 (23–30 €)**. Made from the harvests of 15 grands crus, this champagne rises to the challenge of creating a top-of-the-range *cuvée* in a minor vintage. It is a curiosity, which has certainly reached its peak, but nonetheless received a special mention, as did the spicy, fruity **1998**. (NM)
➤ de Castellane, 57, rue de Verdun, 51204 Epernay Cedex, tel. 03.26.51.19.19, fax 03.26.54.24.81, e-mail info@castellane.fr **Ⅴ**
🍷 by appt.

CATTIER

Vintage 1996★

🄶	1er cru	18 ha	40,000	🄸 ⚲	15–23 €

Vineyard owners since the 18th century, the Cattiers founded their house in 1921. They manage 18 ha of vines classified as premier cru in the Montagne de Reims, the jewel in the crown of which is the Clos du Moulin, a famous hilltop plot acquired in 1951. Their 1996 is a blend of all three champagne grape varieties (40% Pinot Meunier, 30% Pinot Noir, 30% Chardonnay). It earned its star with its balance, its fruitiness and its length. Made of half black grapes and half white, the **Clos du Moulin (23–30 €)** was singled out for its judicious *dosage* and its honeyed character, while the **Blanc de blancs (11–15 €)** obtained the same rating for its freshness and balance. (NM)
➤ Cattier, 6–11, rue Dom-Pérignon, 51500 Chigny-les-Roses, tel. 03.26.03.42.11, fax 03.26.03.43.13, e-mail champagne@cattier.com **Ⅴ**
🍷 by appt.

CHANOINE

Tsarine★

●	n.c.	n.c.	15–23 €

One of the oldest of all champagne houses (founded in 1730), Chanoine was revived a few years ago by the BCC group. The Tsarine *cuvée* recalls the great days of the 19th century, when the Russian court was one of the principal customers of this house. White grapes and black contribute (40% Pinot Noir, 15% Meunier) to this finely coloured, salmon-pink rosé. It has scents of cherries and strawberries, and is fresh and elegant on the palate. The **Tsarine white 95** is made from equal parts black and white grapes. Aimed, with its developed character, at lovers of ripe champagne, it also obtained a star for its powerful toastiness and stylish length. (NM)
➤ Chanoine Frères, allée du Vignoble, 51100 Reims, tel. 03.26.36.61.60, fax 03.26.36.66.62, e-mail chanoine-freres@wanadoo.fr

CHAPUIS

Blanc de blancs Carte verte★

	Gd cru	6.25 ha	16,000	🍶 ⚲	15–23 €

During the Revolution, one of the Chapuis became mayor of Oger, an achievement imitated recently by one of his descendants. The family vineyard today extends over more than 6 ha. This fine, floral blanc de blancs has developed a fresh, buttery palate. (NM)

☞ SA Chapuy, 8 bis, rue de Flavigny, BP 14, 51190 Oger, tel. 03.26.57.51.30, fax 03.26.57.59.25,
e-mail champagne.chapuy@web-agri.fr ☑
☏ by appt.

JACQUES CHAPUT

Blanc de blancs 1997★

		2 ha	1,800	🍶	15–23 €

The Chaputs have been wine-growers in the district of Bar-sur-Aube over four generations. They founded their house after the Second World War, and today manage 13 ha of vines. Their blanc de blancs 97 delivers complete satisfaction, with its aromas of roasted almonds, its bready, toasty palate, and its balance and freshness. (NM)

☞ Jacques Chaput, La Haie-Vignée, 10200 Arrentières, tel. 03.25.27.00.14, fax 03.25.27.01.75 ☑
☏ ev. day 9am–12 noon 2pm–6pm

ROLAND CHARDIN

Réserve★★

		1.2 ha	6,000	🍶	11–15 €

Near to Riceys, this recently established vineyard, founded in 1970, extends to 6.5 ha, the brand having been launched in 1980. A blend of 80% Pinot Noir and 20% Chardonnay, this Réserve was drawn from the harvests of 1997 and 1998 and had its ardent admirers on the Jury. With its scent of peaches, it is a clean and fresh wine that lingers on the palate. (RM)

☞ Roland Chardin, 25, rue de l'Eglise,
10340 Avirey-Lingey, tel. 03.25.29.33.90,
fax 03.25.29.14.01 ☑
☏ by appt.

CHARDONNET ET FILS

Réserve★

		n.c.	2,000	🍶	11–15 €

With a name like Chardonnet, this family could only be based in the Côte des Blancs, and indeed they have been cultivating 5 ha of vines in the terroirs of Avize, Cramant and Chouilly (and in the Vallée de la Marne) for three generations. The brand was launched in 1970. White grapes, supplemented by Pinot Noir, make up 70% of the blend of this Réserve, which is made from the wines of three years: 1994, 1995 and 1996. It is an expressive champagne that charms by its balance, its generosity and especially its length. (RM)

☞ Michel Chardonnet, 7, rue de l'Abattoir, 51190 Avize, tel. 03.26.57.91.73, fax 03.26.57.84.46 ☑
☏ ev. day 9am–8pm

ROBERT CHARLEMAGNE★

●	0.3 ha	2,500	🍶 ⚲	15–23 €

The Charlemagne of Mesnil-sur-Oger – Robert Charlemagne, that is – launched his champagne in the 1940s. Representing the third generation, Didier Delavier took up the reins of the estate in 1998. He controls 4.3 ha of vines distributed around this famous Côte des Blancs village. Chardonnay forms the great majority of this rosé, made from the harvest of 1998: no less than 85%. It is supplemented by Pinot Noir, which brings a little colour to a clear, fine, elegant champagne, which will please as an aperitif. (RM)

☞ Robert Charlemagne, av. Eugène-Guillaume, 51190 Le Mesnil-sur-Oger, tel. 03.26.57.51.02, fax 03.26.57.58.05, e-mail info@champagne-robert-charlemagne.com ☑
☏ by appt.

CHARLES DU ROY★

	1er cru	n.c.	66,000	🍶 ⚲	11–15 €

This *cuvée* is produced by Champagne Comte de Noiron, which controls a vineyard of 80 ha. A classic blend of 60% Pinot Noir and 40% Chardonnay, this premier cru displays a fruity, vanillary bouquet and a fresh palate with fine floral nuances, evoking hawthorn. (NM)

☞ Comte de Noiron, 17, rue des Créneaux, 51100 Reims, tel. 03.26.82.70.67, fax 03.26.82.19.12 ☑
☏ by appt.

CHARLIER ET FILS 1998★

		14 ha	n.c.	🍶🍶	15–23 €

Charlier's champagnes have been flourishing for many years. The vineyard covers some 14 ha on the right bank of the Vallée de la Marne. Packaged in a screen-printed bottle, this special *cuvée* is a blend of the three champagne grape varieties in nearly equal proportions, and of wines that have been matured for one year in barrel. Its bouquet is intense: toasty, bready and slightly developed. That developed character is confirmed on the palate by flavours of honey and crystallized fruits. From the same estate, the **Rosé de Saignée (11–15 €)** was also singled out. Made from Pinot Noir, it is a rich and vinous champagne. (RM)

☞ Charlier et Fils, 4, rue des Pervenches,
51700 Montigny-sous-Châtillon, tel. 03.26.58.35.18,
fax 03.26.58.02.31,
e-mail champagne.charlier@wanadoo.fr ☑ 🏠
☏ by appt.

J. CHARPENTIER

Réserve★★

		n.c.	40,000	🍶 ⚲	11–15 €

The Charpentiers manage a vineyard of 12 ha on the right bank of the Vallée de la Marne. Their Réserve, a blanc de noirs, blends 80% Pinot Meunier with Pinot Noir. Its scents of crystallized fruits, *pain d'épice* and liquorice lead on to a fresh, well-structured palate that commanded a following among the tasters. The estate also obtained a commendation for its **Cuvée Pierre-Henri (15–23 €)**, a blend of all three champagne grape varieties (including two-thirds black grapes), and a rounded and forceful wine. (RM)

☞ Jacky Charpentier, 88, rue de Reuil,
51700 Villers-sous-Châtillon, tel. 03.26.58.05.78,
fax 03.26.58.36.59,
e-mail champagnejcharpentier@wanadoo.fr ☑ 🏠
☏ by appt.

JEAN-MARC ET CELINE CHARPENTIER Prestige Terre d'émotions★

		1 ha	5,000	🍶 ⚲	15–23 €

In the era when the wines of Champagne had no bubbles, the ancestors of Jean-Marc and Céline Charpentier owned both a vineyard and a postal station, selling their wines to coachmen and passing boatmen. Today the estate, located in the Vallée de la Marne, covers 10 ha. Its *cuvée* Prestige Terre d'Emotions is a blend of all three champagne grape varieties, with the Pinots in a slight majority (60%, including 50% Meunier). Toasty on the nose with a hint of coffee, it is a fresh and complex wine. The same rating was awarded to the **rosé**, which is largely Meunier (80%, supplemented by Chardonnay), and has flavours of soft fruits (strawberries), enhanced by freshness and noticeable *dosage*. A commendation was also given to the **1998** for its fruitiness and vinosity. (RC)

☞ Jean-Marc et Céline Charpentier, 11, rte de Paris,
02310 Charly-sur-Marne, tel. 03.23.82.10.72,
fax 03.23.82.31.80,
e-mail jean-marc@champagne-charpentier.com ☑ 🏠
☏ by appt.

CHARTOGNE-TAILLET
Cuvée Sainte-Anne★★

	n.c.	35,000	🍾 ♦	11–15 €

Merfy, to the northwest of Reims, is close to Saint-Thierry, whose abbey was in the ninth century the cradle of the Champagne vineyard. The Chartognes have been wine-makers here since the 17th century, and now manage 11 ha of vines. Half Pinot Noir and half Chardonnay, their Cuvée Sainte-Anne charmed the Jury with its varied bouquet, which successively evokes buttery brioche, lime blossom, vervain and lemongrass. After a clean attack, the wine's balance and harmony impose themselves on the palate. The **1996 (15–23 €)**, which blends 60% Pinot Noir with Chardonnay, obtained one star. A champagne with the aromas of crystallized fruits and nuts, it is complex, fresh and well-balanced. (RM)
➡ Chartogne-Taillet, 37–39, Grande-Rue, 51220 Merfy, tel. 03.26.03.10.17, fax 03.26.03.19.15, e-mail chartogne.taillet@wanadoo.fr ☑
⚑ by appt.

CHASSENAY D'ARCE
Confidences★

	n.c.	18,650	🍾 ♦	15–23 €

The Arce is a small tributary of the Seine that runs along the foot of the Côte des Bars. It gives its name to this important cooperative, which was founded in 1956. Chassenay d'Arce brings together 130 growers, and vinifies grapes from 310 ha of land. Its Confidences *cuvée* is a blanc de noirs (100% Pinot Noir) from the harvests of 1996 and 1998. With its scents of white flowers and its fine, fresh flavours, its richness, vigour and length, it offers good balance and definite potential. The **Cuvée Sélection (11–15 €)**, blended from the same years as the previous wine, is predominantly black grapes (85% Pinot Noir), and also finds a place in the *Guide*. It is a classic, rounded, balanced and powerful champagne, and receives one star. The **Privilège Cuvée (11–15 €)** combines 60% Pinot Noir with 40% Chardonnay, from the harvests of 1995, 1996 and 1997. It offers strong flavours of *pain d'épice* and of honey, and was commended. (CM)
➡ Chassenay d'Arce, 11, rue du Pressoir, 10110 Ville-sur-Arce, tel. 03.25.38.30.70, fax 03.25.38.79.17, e-mail champagne-chassenay-darce@wanadoo.fr ☑
⚑ by appt.

A. CHAUVET
Cachet vert Blanc de blancs★

	1 ha	8,000	🍾 ♦	15–23 €

Founded in 1848, this négociant house has remained within the same family. It controls a vineyard of 10 ha, most notably at Bouzy. Cachet Vert is the house blanc de blancs, and does not undergo malolactic fermentation. The blend incorporates a majority of wines from 1998, assisted by some 1996 and 1997. Its scents of flowers, honey and citrus fruits are of great finesse, and the palate seems well-balanced, vigorous and long. Two rosés were commended as well: **Le Grand Rosé** and the **1992 (23–30 €)**. Both include in their blend some Bouzy red wine, as well as Pinot Noir and Chardonnay. Both have good vinosity and are fairly developed, particularly the 1992. (NM)
➡ Chauvet, 41, av. de Champagne, 51150 Tours-sur-Marne, tel. 03.26.58.92.37, fax 03.26.58.96.31, e-mail champagnechauvet@yahoo.fr ☑
⚑ by appt.
➡ Famille Paillard-Chauvet

HENRI CHAUVET
Cuvée blanche 1998★

1er cru	0.5 ha	3,000	🍾	15–23 €

The Chauvets established a vineyard of 8 ha around Rilly-la-Montagne, a village on the northern flank of the Montagne de Reims. Damien Chauvet has been at the helm of the estate since 1987. The Cuvée Blanche is a blanc de blancs. It offers a powerful nose of ripe apple and preserved fruits (quince), and a fresh, full and well-balanced palate. Despite its name, the **Cuvée Noire** consists of 26% Chardonnay alongside Pinot Noir. With its fruity nose and its lemony, lively, long finish, it received a commendation. (RM)

➡ Henri Chauvet & Fils, 6, rue de la Liberté, 51500 Rilly-la-Montagne, tel. 03.26.03.42.69, fax 03.26.03.45.14, e-mail contact@champagne-chauvet.com ☑
⚑ by appt.

MARC CHAUVET
Spécial Club 1996★

	n.c.	10,000	🍾 ♦	15–23 €

There is another branch of the Chauvet family in Rilly-la-Montagne. Their Spécial Club 1996 blends 60% Chardonnay with 40% of the two Pinots (with just a dash of Meunier). No malolactic fermentation is undertaken, and the wine is aged for six years on its lees. The bouquet of flowers and citrus fruits (lemon and grapefruit) leads on to a fresh, straightforward palate. Also commended was the **Sélection (11–15 €)**, which is half white grapes and half black, and which also avoids malolactic fermentation. It was singled out for its expressive bouquet, its liveliness and its balance. (RM)
➡ SCEV Marc Chauvet, 1–3, rue de la Liberté, 51500 Rilly-la-Montagne, tel. 03.26.03.42.71, fax 03.26.03.42.38, e-mail chauvet@cder.fr ☑
⚑ by appt.

ARNAUD DE CHEURLIN
Réserve★

	2 ha	15,000	🍾	11–15 €

This Auboise estate of 6.5 ha launched its champagne in 1981. A blend of 75% Pinot Noir and 25% Chardonnay, its Réserve, a brut non-vintage, offers ready proof of the wine's great consistency. Once more faithful to its regular assignation with the *Guide*, it displays an expressive nose, rich and spicy, and a palate of fine vinosity and balance. The **Cuvée Prestige**, made of half black and half white grapes, offer floral scents and a fine palate. It was commended. (RM)
➡ Arnaud de Cheurlin, 58, Grande-Rue, 10110 Celles-sur-Ource, tel. 03.25.38.53.90, fax 03.25.38.58.07, e-mail info@arnaud-de-cheurlin-champagne.com ☑
⚑ by appt.
➡ Eisentrager

RICHARD CHEURLIN
Brut H★

	1.8 ha	8,000	🍾 ♦	11–15 €

Established in the late 1970s from a combination of legacies, plantings and purchases, the vineyard of Richard Cheurlin is located on the Côte des Bars in the Aube. The harvests of 1999 and 2000 contribute to this *brut*, a champagne of equal parts black and white grapes, elegant on both nose and palate, well-balanced and with good length. The same rating was awarded to the **Jeanne 1999 (15–23 €)**. A clean and well-balanced champagne. (RM)
➡ Richard Cheurlin, 16, rue des Huguenots, 10110 Celles-sur-Ource, tel. 03.25.38.55.04, fax 03.25.38.58.33, e-mail richard.cheurlin@wanadoo.fr ☑
⚑ by appt.

GASTON CHIQUET
Tradition★★

1er cru	12 ha	95,000	🍾 ♦	11–15 €

This family of grower-producers is descended from a long line of winemakers going back to the 18th century. They have been making champagne since 1935, and have an attractive vineyard of 22.5 ha, on premier and grand cru land, in the environs of Dizy, Aÿ, Mareuil-sur-Aÿ and Hautvillers. The Tradition *cuvée* brings together the harvests of 1998 and 1999. Black grapes constitute 65% of the blend (with 45% Meunier). A pleasingly fine nose, rounded opening impression, and an elegant, meaty, fruity palate full of fruity, spicy, toasty, mineral flavours, make this one of the most harmonious champagnes of all. One star distinguished the **1997 (15–23 €)**, which blends 60% Pinot Noir with Chardonnay. It has a fine, impressive nose and powerful, vigorous palate of distinctive character. Finally, a commendation went to a curiosity, the **Blanc de Blancs d'Aÿ (15–23 €)**, made from the harvest of 1999 in one of the main redoubts of Pinot Noir. It has subtlety, freshness and finesse. (RM)

☛ Gaston Chiquet, 912, av. du Gal-Leclerc, 51530 Dizy, tel. 03.26.55.22.02, fax 03.26.51.83.81, e-mail info@gaston-chiquet.com ☑

☒ by appt.

☛ Claude Chiquet

CHRISTOPHE
Cuvée Impérial★

	n.c.	10,000	🍾 ⚱	15–23 €

This grower-producer in Colombé-le-Sec launched its brand in 1970, and owns a vineyard of 11 ha. The Cuvée Impérial, a blend of 40% Chardonnay with 60% Pinot Noir, is characterized by flavours of crystallized fruits and honey. It is a rounded and full champagne with good vinosity. (RM)

☛ SCEV Christophe, rue Saint-Antoine, 10200 Colombé-le-Sec, tel. 03.25.27.18.38, fax 03.25.27.27.45 ☑

☒ by appt.

☛ Nicolo

CHARLES CLEMENT★★

	n.c.	n.c.		11–15 €

An Auboise cooperative brand created in 1956 by Charles Clément and several winemaker friends, this group now oversees 155 ha. This is not the first time that it has distinguished itself in the *Guide*, since its **Cuvée Gustave Belon Blanc de Blancs (15–23 €)** won a *coup de coeur* in the 2002 edition. It was singled out again this year for its freshness, while with its floral, honeyed bouquet, the **Cuvée Spéciale (15–23 €)**, which blends both Pinots with 70% Chardonnay, received one star. But the most remarkable wines are the group's brut non-vintages in the lower price range, this one and the **Tradition**. Each receives two stars. Both are blends of the three champagne grape varieties, dominated by the two Pinots (83% in this one, 70% in the Tradition). They possess the same qualities of balance, power and length, and are at their peak. (CM)

☛ SCV Charles Clément, rue Saint-Antoine, 10200 Colombé-le-Sec, tel. 03.25.92.50.71, fax 03.25.92.50.79, e-mail champagne-charles-clement@wanadoo.fr ☑

☒ ev. day except Sun. 8am–12 noon 1.30pm–5.30pm; Sun. open 15 Jun.–1 Sep.

J. CLEMENT
Prestige★★

	0.5 ha	n.c.		11–15 €

Based on the right bank of the Marne, the Cléments have been making champagne all through the postwar years, on an estate comprising 7.5 ha of vines. Made from the harvest of 1997, the Prestige *cuvée* favours Chardonnay (65% of the blend, supplemented by both Pinots). Intense buttery and bready notes are accompanied by more developed touches of crystallized fruits and nuts. Balance, complexity and length characterize this champagne, three qualities that have earned it two stars. It should be drunk with a fish dish. Also commended was the **Vieilles Vignes 97 (15–23 €)**, a blanc de noirs dominated by Meunier (80%), which obtained one star for its floral scents, a whisper of anise, orchard fruits, subtlety and length. (RM)

☛ James Clément, 1, rue de l'Avenir, 51480 Revil, tel. 03.26.58.00.08, fax 03.26.57.10.64, e-mail champj.clement@wanadoo.fr

☒ by appt.

CLERAMBAULT
Cuvée Grande Epoque 1996★

	n.c.	1,204	🍾 ⚱	15–23 €

Clérambault is the brand name of a cooperative on the Côte des Bars, in the Aube district. This year, it presented two highly interesting vintage wines, which each obtained one star. The Grande Epoque is a classic blend of 60% Pinots (40% Pinot Noir) and 40% Chardonnay. Golden yellow in colour, it opens broadly on complex notes of flowers, preserved lemon, honey and mocha coffee. Just as honeyed, with notes of ripe fruits, the palate is rich, sufficiently fresh and rather long. The same rating was achieved by the **Carte Or 93**, a champagne of equal parts black and white grapes, which

displays a developed nose but one of beautiful complexity: honeyed, charred, toasty, with candied fruits and a hint of undergrowth. On the palate, it appears direct, structured, forceful and rich, and has kept its freshness. (CM)

☛ Clérambault, 122, Grande-Rue, 10250 Neuville-sur-Seine, tel. 03.25.38.38.60, fax 03.25.38.24.36, e-mail champagne-clerambault@wanadoo.fr ☑

☒ by appt.

COLIN
Cuvée Alliance★

	1er cru	5 ha	20,000	🍾 ⚱	11–15 €

Established at Vertus on the Côte des Blancs, the house of Colin has been cultivating vines since the beginning of the 19th century, and has accumulated a holding to be proud of: 12 ha of grand and premier cru land. They have been making champagne since 1997. The grapes joined together in this Alliance were harvested in 1999 and 2000. This *cuvée* has all the hallmarks of Chardonnay, present as 80% of the blend (with 15% of Pinot Noir) and a soupçon of Meunier providing the remaining 20%, with its citrus fruit bouquet (grapefruit, lemon) and its fresh, lemony, bready flavours in fine balance. As to the **Blanc de Blancs 98 (15–23 €)**, it was specially mentioned for its roundness and length. (RM)

☛ Colin, 101, av. du Gal-de-Gaulle, 51130 Vertus, tel. 03.26.58.86.32, fax 03.26.51.69.79, e-mail info@champagne-colin.com ☑

☒ by appt.

COLLARD-PICARD
Cuvée Saphir★

	n.c.	2,000	🍾	30–38 €

Based in the Vallée de la Marne, Olivier Collard assumed control of the family house of 6.5 ha in 1996. His champagnes are to be found regularly in the *Guide*. Bottled in a blue carafe, this special *cuvée* is not a vintage, but comes from only one year, 1998. The two Pinots form the majority of the blend (45% Meunier, 15% Pinot Noir, 40% Chardonnay), and the wines spend eight months in wood. The intense nose combines toasted almonds with hints of brioche, while the palate is rich and powerful with flavours of candied fruits. This ripe, seductive wine should be drunk with food (chicken in champagne?). **La Cuvée Prestige (15–23 €)** is drawn from the harvests of 1997, 1998 and 1999, with the Pinots in the majority (75%, including 50% Meunier), and also spends time in wood. It is a well-balanced and long wine, with noticeable *dosage*. (RM)

☛ Collard-Picard, 61, rue du Château, 51700 Villers-sous-Châtillon, tel. 03.26.52.36.93, fax 03.26.59.90.82, e-mail champcp51@aol.com ☑

☒ by appt.

RAOUL COLLET
Grande Réserve Carte rouge★

	70 ha	100,000	🍾 ⚱	11–15 €

Produced by the oldest cooperative in Champagne, based in the grand cru village of A, Carte rouge blends 70% Pinot Noir with 30% Chardonnay. The bouquet combines citrus fruits, vanilla, apples and pears, while the impression of balance on the palate gives one good reason to think that this champagne has reached its peak. (CM)

☛ Raoul Collet, 14, bd Pasteur, 51160 Aÿ-Champagne, tel. 03.26.55.15.88, fax 03.26.54.02.40, e-mail info@champagne-raoul-collet.com ☑

☒ by appt.

CHARLES COLLIN
Cuvée Charles★★

	n.c.	13,600	🍾 ⚱	15–23 €

This Aube cooperative, founded in 1952, makes champagnes from the produce of 255 ha. Located in the extreme south of the region, the village of Fontette actually falls within the *département* of the Côte d'Or. This does not prevent it from making excellent champagnes, such as this top-of-the-range *cuvée* that blends 80% Chardonnay with 20% Pinot Noir. As complex on the nose as it is on the palate, its range of flavours combines honey, brioche, caramel and preserved apple. The palate is powerful, rich, fresh and long. This is a remarkable champagne that would be good with warm entrées and white meats. One star also went to the **Cuvée Tradition (11–15 €)**, a blend of two-thirds Pinot Noir to one-third Chardonnay, a wine of suppleness, fruitiness and length. (CM)

➤ Charles Collin, 27, rue des Pressoirs, 10360 Fontette, tel. 03.25.38.31.00, fax 03.25.29.68.64, e-mail champagne-charles-collin@wanadoo.fr ☑
☼ by appt.

COLLIN-GUILLAUME
Blanc de blancs★

| | 0,5 ha | 1.000 | ■ ♦ | 11–15 € |

Sillery is situated in the Vesle valley, to the southeast of Reims. In spite of the great age of its vineyards, famous since classical times, winemakers are not especially numerous here. One does, however, come across this estate of 6 ha. This blanc de blancs is not a vintage wine, although it is made from only one year, 1998. The bouquet is powerful, buttery and lemony, while the balanced palate has flavours of brioche. (RC)

➤ Collin-Guillaume, 3, rue de la Vesle, 51500 Sillery, tel. 03.26.49.16.75, fax 03.26.49.11.32, e-mail collin-guillaume@clubinternet.fr ☑ 🏠
☼ by appt.

JACQUES COPINET
Blanc de blancs★

| | 1.2 ha | 15.000 | ■ ♦ | 11–15 € |

This property of 7 ha is the work of Jacques Copinet, who established it in 1975. It is a young estate then, located in the Sézannais, in the extreme south of the Marne *département*. That does not stop it from making frequent, well-placed appearances in the Champagne chapter of the *Guide*. Chardonnay thrives on the limestone soils of this southernmost part of the region, and it is often the blancs de blancs that are singled out. Here are three specimens. This non-vintage is fresh, elegant and lively on the attack, its flavours of pink grapefruit surprising and seductive. The **Cuvée Marie-Etienne (15–23 €)** runs it close. It also obtained one star for its floral, anise-like bouquet and its lightness on the palate. The **Blanc de Blancs Sélection (15–23 €)** was commended for its intense, attractive bouquet, its lively palate and its good bready finish. (RM)

➤ Jacques Copinet, 11, rue de l'Ormeau, 51260 Montgenost, tel. 03.26.80.49.14, fax 03.26.80.44.61, e-mail info@champagne-copinet.com ☑
☼ by appt.

CORDEUIL PERE ET FILS★

| | n.c. | 27.200 | ■ ♦ | 11–15 € |

The Cordeuils manage a vineyard of 8 ha on the Côte des Bars, in the Aube district. Black grapes (85% Pinot Noir), supported by Chardonnay, contribute mainly to this *brut* non-vintage, which calls on the harvests of 1999 and 2000. The nose evokes white flowers, while small stone fruits are the order of the day on the supple palate. Altogether an impressive wine. (RM)

➤ Cordeuil Père et Fils, 2, rue de Fontette, 10360 Noé-les-Mallets, tel. 03.25.29.65.37, fax 03.25.29.65.37 ☑ 🏠
☼ by appt.

ROGER COULON
Grande Réserve★

| | 3 ha | 30.000 | ■ ◐ ♦ | 11–15 € |

Eric Coulon has headed the family estate of 9 ha since 1985. It is situated at Vrigny, on the western edge of the Montagne de Reims. The Jury admired his Grande Réserve, a blend of the three champagne grape varieties in almost equal shares. To the harvest of 1998 is added a one-third proportion of reserve wines that have been matured one year in wood. The bouquet recalls buttery brioche, while the middle palate makes a particularly powerful impression. The wine shows evident *dosage*. (RM)

➤ Roger Coulon, 12, rue de la Vigne-du-Roi, 51390 Vrigny, tel. 03.26.03.61.65, fax 03.26.03.43.68, e-mail contact@champagne-coulon.com ☑
☼ by appt.
➤ Eric Coulon

ALAIN COUVREUR
Cuvée de réserve Blanc de blancs★

| | 1 ha | 10.000 | ♦ | 11–15 € |

Located to the west of Reims in the Vesle valley, this estate of 4 ha submitted a non-vintage blanc de blancs, which is in fact made only from the harvest of 1996. It is a ripe champagne, golden-yellow in colour, whose generous range of flavours combines crystallized fruits and buttery brioche. On the palate, there is balance, power and length. "A wine of personality," concluded a taster. As to the rosé, which is made from black grapes (70% Pinot Noir, supplemented by Meunier) from 1998 and 1999, it is dressed in more youthful colours with purple highlights. Its bouquet, however, is more developed than the colour would suggest, and the palate is endowed with good length. It was commended. (RM)

➤ EARL Alain Couvreur, 18, Grande-Rue, 51140 Prouilly, tel. 03.26.48.58.95, fax 03.26.48.26.29, e-mail couvreur.alain@wanadoo.fr
☼ by appt.

DOMINIQUE CRETE ET FILS
Sélection★

| | 1.8 ha | 10.000 | ■ | 11–15 € |

Moussy, to the south of Epernay, is where this 7-ha estate is to be found. Its Sélection is composed of 85% Chardonnay and 15% Pinot Meunier from the harvests of 1999 and 2000. In the glass, it shows fine bubbles, while "the nose is pure Chardonnay," according to one taster. Notes of apple, pear and citrus compete with fruity hazelnuts. "Well-balanced and fresh, this champagne will be delicious with red mullet," noted a *sommelière*. (RM)

➤ Dominique Crété, 99, rue des Prieures, 51530 Moussy, tel. 03.26.54.52.10, fax 03.26.52.79.93 ☑
☼ by appt.

COMTE AUDOIN DE DAMPIERRE★

| | Gd cru | n.c. | 10.000 | 38–46 € |

Dampierre is a négociant brand that was launched in 1986. This *cuvée* has the classic appearance of fine bubbles, and offers a lightly developed bouquet of cooked fruits, followed by a fresh palate that seems astonishing for its age. The **Blanc de Blancs Grand Cru (23–30 €)** was also singled out for its freshness and length. (NM)

➤ Comte Audoin de Dampierre, 3, pl. Boisseau, 51140 Chenay, tel. 03.26.03.11.13, fax 03.26.03.18.05, e-mail champagne.dampierre@wanadoo.fr ☑
☼ by appt.

DEHU PERE ET FILS
Tradition★

| | n.c. | 33.000 | ■ ♦ | 11–15 € |

Based in the Vallée de la Marne, the Déhu family manages a vineyard of 10 ha, and supports methods of sustainable agriculture that respect the environment. The two champagnes selected honour the Pinot Meunier grape, which represents in both cases 75% of the blend, accompanied by Pinot Noir (10%), while white grapes constitute only 15% of their composition. Tradition offers a complex nose of fruit and brioche. Enticing flavours of white peach distinguish a full, fleshy and well-balanced palate. The rosé **Prestige (15–23 €)**, also commended, is another balanced wine that is still full of youth. (RC)

➤ Déhu Père et Fils, 3, rue Saint-Georges, 02650 Fossoy, tel. 03.23.71.90.47, fax 03.23.71.88.91, e-mail varocien@aol.com ☑
☼ by appt.

DELAHAIE★★

| | n.c. | 40.000 | | 11–15 € |

The Delahaie brand denotes champagnes made by Jacques Brochet, of A. This house has given a very good account of itself with two remarkable champagnes. Made from the harvests of 1998 and 1999, the first brut non-vintage favours black grapes (50% Pinot Meunier, 30% Pinot Noir, 20% Chardonnay). The nose is expressive, clean and elegant, with notes of ripe Pinots. The strong presence of those Pinots results in a wine that has good structure and vinosity on the palate. The same rating went to the **Cuvée Sublime (15–23 €)**, which is dominated by contrast by Chardonnay (85%, supplemented by 10% Pinot Noir and 5% Meunier). Buttery notes of Viennese biscuits precede a robust and lengthy palate. (NM)

➽ Jacques Brochet, 22, rue des Rocherets, 51200 Epernay, tel. 03.26.54.08.74, fax 03.26.54.34.45

e-mail champagne.delahaie@wanadoo.fr ☑

☖ by appt.

DELAVENNE PERE ET FILS 1996★

	Gd cru	1.5 ha	12,000	▮ ⚲	15–23 €

Established in the 1920s, this vineyard extends over 8 ha. The house itself is based at Bouzy, a grand cru village in the southeast of the Montagne de Reims. Equal parts black and white grapes, its 1996 shows a touch of development on the nose, like many another champagne of this vintage, but it is especially on the palate that the wine is so seductive. There is ample complexity there, with peach and other fresh fruits in evidence, as well as cooked apple and citrus notes, all combined with freshness and length. The Jury also took an interest in the **Brut non-vintage (11–15 €)**, also half-black, half-white, from the harvests of 1997 and 1998, which earned a commendation. It is a lively champagne of considerable length. (RM)

➽ Delavenne Père et Fils, 6, rue de Tours, 51150 Bouzy, tel. 03.26.57.02.04, fax 03.26.58.82.93 ☑

☖ by appt.

DELBECK

Vintage 1996★★

		n.c.	30,000		23–30 €

At the beginning of the 19th century, one Delbeck, a banker, married the granddaughter of the mayor of Reims, Baron Ponsardin, a union that led to his interest in champagne. The house was founded in 1832. Since then, it has changed hands several times, but the label still proudly displays three fleurs-de-lys in recognition that the house once supplied the court of Louis-Philippe. It has put in a fine performance with its 1996, a model wine in a vintage whose wines have widely suffered from uneven development. Predominantly Pinot Noir (70%), supplemented by Chardonnay, this champagne with its smoky aromas won support for its purity and elegance. It has flavours of preserved fruits, which are rich without being heavy, and the *dosage* is irreproachable. One star went to the **Blanc de Blancs Cramant Grand Cru**, a very lengthy champagne that would go with food. (NM)

➽ Delbeck, 39, rue du Gal-Sarrail, BP 77, 51053 Reims Cedex, tel. 03.26.77.58.00, fax 03.26.77.58.01, e-mail info@delbeck.com ☑

➽ Opson

YVES DELOZANNE 1995★★

	7.5 ha	5,009	▮ ⚲	11–15 €

The village of Serzy-et-Prin is situated to the west of Reims, in the Ardre valley. The Delozannes have been winemakers here for a long time. Today, they manage more than 8.6 ha. This 1995 is recommended to all those who want to know what a good vintage tastes like. Made from the three champagne grape varieties in roughly equal measure, it charmed the Jury with its floral and fruity nose, and especially with its complex palate, which is very well-balanced, with judicious *dosage*, fullness and length. The **1993** (made from the same grape blend), is intense on the nose, and rounded, warming and gentle on the palate, as is the **Tradition**, which strongly favours the black grapes (90%, including 80% Meunier), and shows good vinosity and personality. (RM)

➽ Yves Delozanne, 67, rue de Savigny, 51170 Serzy-et-Prin, tel. 03.26.97.40.18, fax 03.26.97.49.14, e-mail info@champagne-yvesdelozanne.com ☑

☖ by appt.

SERGE DEMIERE

Tradition★★

	2.25 ha	25,000		11–15 €

Based at Ambonnay, Serge Demière has built up a vineyard of 6 ha by means of family inheritance and purchasing. He is a regular entrant in the *Guide* with some very highly rated *cuvées*. Thus, this Tradition non-vintage (but made solely from the 2000 harvest) combines richness and elegance on the nose; on the palate, it is ripely fruity and generous, rounded and well-structured. As for the **Blanc de Blancs Premier Cru**,

which has spent some time in wood, it remained fresh throughout the tasting, and is commended accordingly. (RM)

➽ Serge Demière, 7, rue de la Commanderie, 51150 Ambonnay, tel. 03.26.57.07.79, fax 03.26.57.82.15

☖ by appt.

DEMILLY DE BAERE

Brut zéro★

	0.6 ha	5,000	▮ ⚲	11–15 €

Glassmaking is one of the specialities of Bar-sur-Aube, where this domaine, housed in an old glassworks, is based. The region also of course provides the stuff that goes into those flute glasses, thanks to winemakers like Gérard Demilly, who cultivates 6.5 ha of the three grape varieties of Champagne, as well as Pinot Blanc, which is very rare in the region. Two very similar *cuvées* received the same rating: this Brut Zéro and the **Carte d'Or**. Both derive from the harvests of 1999, 2000 and 2001 and are predominantly black grapes, comprising the same blend (66% Pinot Noir, 5% Meunier, 20% Chardonnay, 9% Pinot Blanc). The difference between them is that the first has received no *dosage*. Discreet on the nose and minerally, it is a fresh, elegant and well-balanced wine. The Carte d'Or bears a strong family resemblance to it, but has been lightly dosed. Either would make a good aperitif champagne. (NM)

➽ Gérard Demilly, Dom. de La Verrerie, rue du Château, 10200 Bligny, tel. 03.25.27.44.81, fax 03.25.27.45.02, e-mail champagne-demilly@barsuraube.net ☑

☖ by appt.

DESBORDES-AMIAUD

Cuvée M'Elodie 1990★★★

	1er cru	n.c.	15,000	▮	15–23 €

This estate of 9 ha is located close to the city of Reims, at the foot of the Montagne. It is managed by a group of women whose skills are demonstrated by their regular inclusion in the *Guide*. Champagnes from this property do not undergo malolactic fermentation. Following on from the 1989, which was awarded a *coup de coeur*, the 1990 has garnered three stars, a rare achievement that points up the excellent development of this fine vintage. A blend of 80% Pinot Noir and 20% Chardonnay, it has reached its quince- and honey-scented peak, and shows rare harmony. "A profound bouquet, dense and ripe, a charmer to whet the appetite. This wine has come into its own. Well done!" one taster declared. One for lovers of fully evolved champagne. Also singled out was the **Premier Cru 95**, a blanc de noirs (from Pinot Noir), soft, rounded, full and ripe, another good one. (RM)

➽ Marie-Christine Desbordes, 2, rue de Villers-aux-Noeuds, 51500 Ecueil, tel. 03.26.49.77.58, fax 03.26.49.27.34 ☑

☖ by appt.

A. DESMOULINS ET CIE

Cuvée Prestige★★

	n.c.	n.c.		15–23 €

It is nearly a century since this négociant house in Epernay was founded. It is distinguished particularly in this edition of the *Guide* with this Cuvée Prestige, which was judged remarkable for its finesse, as evident on the nose as it is on the palate. White flowers, vine blossom, ferns and citrus fruits combine in the bouquet, which, together with a mineral touch on the palate, make for a highly attractive aperitif champagne. "A toothsome wine," wrote one taster. (NM)

➽ A. Desmoulins et Cie, 44, av. Foch, BP 10, 51201 Epernay Cedex, tel. 03.26.54.24.24, fax 03.26.54.26.15, e-mail viboulore@wanadoo.fr ☑

☖ by appt.

DEUTZ

Blanc de blancs 1996★★

	n.c.	40,000	▮ ⚲	46–76 €

Two Germans from Ais-la-Chapelle founded this house in 1838, one of whom gave it his name. This famous A brand was relaunched ten years ago by Roederer, but without affecting its independence. Its blanc de blancs enjoys a justly exalted reputation, which is confirmed by the Hachette Jury (for all that black grapes contributed to its laurels in the last edition). Witness this one, greenish-gold with persistent streams of bubbles. Tasters emphasized the elegant freshness of its floral

nose, with its touch of bergamot, and its sustained power on the palate, allied to rare finesse and beautiful balance. They were also in agreement on the potential of this wine: they recommend leaving it for another two years, and even think that it will still be going strong in 2016! Two stars went to another blanc de blancs, **Amour de Deutz 95 (more than 76 €)**. Similar in style to the previous wine, it has already reached its peak. With notes of hazelnuts, wax and orchard-fruit compote, it is a distinguished, well-balanced wine. (NM)
🍷 Deutz, 16, rue Jeanson, 51160 A-Champagne,
tel. 03.26.56.94.00, fax 03.26.56.94.10,
e-mail france@champagne-deutz.com
🍷 by appt.

PIERRE DOMI
Blanc de blancs★

	1 ha	10,000	🍾	11–15 €

Domi is the brand of a grower-producer in Grauves headed by two brothers. A pair of champagnes each obtained one star, both non-vintage blancs de blancs from the harvest of 1998. The first, which is more developed on the nose than on the palate, is a well-balanced wine with sufficient roundness to allow it to accompany white meats. The second, **Cuvée Spéciale (15–23 €)**, with its bouquet of orchard fruits and acacia, is unctuous and long. (RM)
🍷 Pierre Domi, 8, Grande-Rue, 51190 Grauves,
tel. 03.26.59.71.03, fax 03.26.52.86.91,
e-mail champagnedomipierre@wanadoo.fr ▼
🍷 by appt.

DOM RUINART
Blanc de blancs 1993★★★

	n.c.	n.c.	🍾	+76 €

The senior brand, founded in 1729, roused the Jury to passion. Two *cuvées* each obtained three stars, and were presented with *coups de coeur*: this Blanc de blancs 1993 and the **Dom Ruinart rosé 88**. The Grand Jury unhesitatingly awarded the *coup de coeur* to the 93, a champagne that is the stuff of dreams. Its sensational balance, richness, softness, finesse, and its toasty, floral, mineral flavours add up to a fine champagne of great elegance. As for the 1988 rosé, it has achieved an astonishing level of perfection. Even if the colour has slightly faded, it retains impressive freshness and complexity. "Superb," concluded one taster. The **Ruinart rosé (38–46 €)** was selected by the Jury. Orangey-pink in colour, it offers a fine bouquet of red berries and crystallized fruits, before revealing roundness and balance on the palate. A further star was allotted to the **Blanc de Blancs (38–46 €)** non-vintage, full of finesse with a touch of mint, but with carefully judged *dosage*. The **R de Ruinart (23–30 €)**, which had a note of preserved lemon on both nose and palate, was also commended. (NM)
🍷 Ruinart, 4, rue des Crayères, BP 85, 51053 Reims Cedex,
tel. 03.26.77.51.51, fax 03.26.77.51.00,
e-mail jpmoulin@ruinart.com ▼
🍷 by appt.

DOQUET-JEANMAIRE
Blanc de blancs Coeur de Terroir 1989★★★

	2.1 ha	6,500	🍾	15–23 €

The alliance of two families gave birth, in 1974, to this champagne, which has a vineyard in 15.5 ha. Pascal Doquet, director of the estate since 1995, runs it on the principles of sustainable agriculture. Doquet-Jeanmaire has already distinguished itself in earlier editions with its old vintages. The 1982 was one previous *coup de coeur* winner, as was the 1989. Both were blancs de blancs, Vertus being situated on the Côte des Blancs. Here is another special *cuvée* from 1989. Its complexity captivates: there are notes of toast, spice, chocolate, Viennese biscuits, dried fruits and nuts (notably hazelnuts, dates and figs). On the palate, it is rounded and

honeyed, as rich indeed as it is on the nose. Coeur de Terroir has developed very favourably, and has now hit its peak. It should be drunk with food. (SR)
🍷 Doquet-Jeanmaire, 44, chem. du
Moulin-de-la-Cense-Bizet, 51130 Vertus, tel. 03.26.52.16.50,
fax 03.26.59.36.71,
e-mail info@champagne-doquet-jeanmaire.com ▼
🍷 ev. day 9am–11.45am 2.15pm–6pm;
Sat. and Sun. by appt.

ETIENNE DOUE
Cuvée Sélection★

	3.5 ha	35,000	🍾	11–15 €

There are two Doué vineyards at Montgueux (see below), a small island of vines near Troyes, the grand Champagne city that is worth a detour for its splendid medieval architecture. Planted in the 1970s, the vines here cover a little over 15 ha. Chardonnay is in the majority (60%, supplemented by Pinot Noir) of the Cuvée Sélection, which is a blend of wines from 1998, 1999 and 2000. Tasters appreciated its lively, lemony, floral nose, its positive attack and its balance. (RM)
🍷 Etienne Doué, 11, rte de Troyes, 10300 Montgueux,
tel. 03.25.74.84.41, fax 03.25.79.00.47 ▼
🍷 by appt.

DIDIER DOUE
Blanc de blancs 1996★

	1 ha	4,000	🍾	15–23 €

Based in the Aube, Didier Doué planted his vineyard in the 1970s, now managing 5 ha of vines. He has made frequent appearances in the *Guide* in recent years with *cuvées* that are generally dominated by Chardonnay. This one, a blanc de blancs, comes from the remarkable 1996 vintage. It offers a flattering and complex nose, mingling citrus fruits (lemon), nuts and toasty notes of brioche. Rich, elegant and spicy on the palate, it develops towards a long, fresh finish, a champagne that realizes all the potential of its terroir. (RM)
🍷 Didier Doué, voie des Vignes, 10300 Montgueux,
tel. 03.25.79.44.33, fax 03.25.79.40.04 ▼
🍷 by appt.

DOYARD-MAHE
Blanc de blancs Carte d'or★

	n.c.	n.c.	🍾	11–15 €

A grandson of Maurice Doyard manages this 6-ha vineyard in Vertus, near a small river. Blended from the harvests of 1999, 2000 and 2001, Carte d'or is an elegantly fruity wine full of citrus fruits (lemon), pear and green apple. It is a blanc de blancs of great finesse and freshness. Also singled out was the **rosé**, which is predominantly Chardonnay (88%, supplemented by the 12% Pinot Noir that gives it its colour). Raspberry-pink, its scents and flavours are of boiled sweets, while its length earned it a commendation. (RM)
🍷 Philippe Doyard-Mahé, Moulin d'Argensole,
51130 Vertus, tel. 03.26.52.23.85, fax 03.26.59.36.69,
e-mail champagne.doyard.mahe@hexanet.fr ▼
🍷 ev. day except Sun. 10am–12 noon 2pm–6pm;
cl. 20th Dec.–5th Jan.

DRAPPIER
Blanc de blancs Cuvée signature 1995★★

	n.c.	6,000	🍾	15–23 €

Based in the Côte des Bars, the house of Drappier is proud of its vast twelfth-century cellars, which were probably once part of the nearby monastery of Clairvaux (recalling the involvement of the Cistercians in viticulture in the Middle Ages). It is a fit setting in which to have produced this excellent vintage, the 1995, which the tasters consider will be a long-lasting one. All fell under the charm of this delicately toasty, buttery blanc de blancs, which remains fresh and well-balanced, as fine as it is elegant, as it proceeds towards a harmonious maturity. (NM)
🍷 Drappier, rue des Vignes, 10200 Urville,
tel. 03.25.27.40.15, fax 03.25.27.41.19,
e-mail info@champagne-drappier.com ▼
🍷 ev. day 8am–12 noon 2pm–6pm

DRIANT-VALENTIN★★

● 1er cru	0.8 ha	3,000	🍾 ⚓	15–23 €

Behind Avize, the village of Grauves nestles at the bottom of a small valley. Surrounded by vines, it is overlooked from the north by a wooded plateau and cliffs. In this neighbourhood, Jacques Driant manages the 5.5 ha of the family estate. His rosé de noirs is made by the *saignée* method (involving a direct maceration of the black grapes). Despite its pale-salmon colour, this champagne makes its presence felt but delicately so. After a Pinot nose, the wine shows red berries on the palate (redcurrants in particular), and is full of finesse. It would be good as an aperitif or with a first course. One star was awarded to the **Grande Réserve Extra-Brut Premier Cru**, a blend of 80% Chardonnay and 20% Pinot Noir. It has a pleasant bouquet, a lively, elegant attack and beautiful length. (NM)

➼ Jacques Driant, 4, imp. de la Ferme, 51190 Grauves,
tel. 03.26.59.72.26, fax 03.26.59.76.55,
e-mail champagne.driant-valentin@laposte.net ☑
Ⓣ by appt.

GERARD DUBOIS

Blanc de blancs★

● Gd cru	3,3 ha	2,000	🍾	15–23 €

From Pierry to Avize, the road follows the chalky hillsides of the Côte des Blancs, enough to send the wine-lover into fits of rapture. At the end of the road is a producer who has been making the family champagne for 30 years. This blanc de blancs from the harvests of 1996 and 1997, has limpid golden-yellow colour and a powerful floral bouquet, which extends on to the honeyed palate. (RM)

➼ Gérard Dubois, 67, rue Ernest-Vallé, 51190 Avize,
tel. 03.26.57.58.60, fax 03.26.57.41.94,
e-mail info@champagne-gerard-dubois.com
Ⓣ by appt.

DUMENIL 1998★

●	1.4 ha	23,710	🍾	15–23 €

Chigny-les-Roses sits on the northern flank of the Montagne de Reims. Michel Rebeyrolle manages a vineyard of 10 ha here, which is now nearly a century old. The champagnes are marketed under the Duménil brand. A classic blend of 60% Chardonnay and 40% Pinots (30% Pinot Noir), this 1998 has a fine minerally and fruity bouquet, and is very full on the palate. The **Brut Premier Cru (11–15 €)** was also singled out. It is a product of the 1998 and 1999 harvests, and also blends Pinot and Chardonnay, but in the reverse proportions (40% Chardonnay, 40% Pinot Noir and 20% Meunier). A light aperitif champagne. (RM)

➼ Michel Rebeyrolle, rue des Vignes,
51500 Chigny-les-Roses, tel. 03.26.03.44.48,
fax 03.26.03.45.25,
e-mail info@champagne-dumenil.com ☑
Ⓣ by appt.

DANIEL DUMONT

Grande Réserve★

● 1er cru	n.c.	50,000	🍾	11–15 €

Located on the Montagne de Reims, this family vineyard is now in the hands of the second generation, and extends to 10 ha. Its Grande Réserve blends 60% of Pinots (40% Pinot Noir) with 40% Chardonnay. The expressive nose combines fruity and mineral touches, while the palate is well-balanced, with good vinosity. A further commendation goes to the **Cuvée Excellence 97 (15–23 €)**, a blend made in the opposite proportions: 60% Chardonnay, 40% Pinot Noir. It has the discreet lime-blossom bouquet and light palate of an aperitif champagne. (RM)

➼ SA Daniel Dumont, 11, rue Gambetta,
51500 Rilly-la-Montagne, tel. 03.26.03.40.67,
fax 03.26.03.44.82 ☑
Ⓣ by appt.

PHILIPPE DUMONT

Réserve★

● 1er cru	0.52 ha	4,500	🍾	11–15 €

Based on the Montagne de Reims, Philippe Dumont took up the reins in 1997 of a long line of winemakers, a little

afterwards launching this négociant brand. It makes a triumphant entry into the *Guide* with two non-vintage champagnes that each collected one star. Both are Premiers Crus, and result from almost identical blends of the three champagne grapes, dominated by the black varieties. This Réserve (70% Pinots, 30% Chardonnay) comes from the harvest of 2000. Its aromas are fruity and bready, and it appears quite balanced on the palate, with careful *dosage* and good length. Equally harmonious is the **Brut non-vintage** (80% Pinots, 20% Chardonnay from 2001), which possesses similar qualities. (NM)

➼ Philippe Dumont, 30, rue Sainte-Agathe,
51500 Chigny-les-Roses, tel. 03.26.03.49.48,
fax 03.26.03.53.43,
e-mail champagne.ph.dumont@club-internet.fr ☑
Ⓣ ev. day 9am–1pm 2pm–8pm

R. DUMONT ET FILS 98★★

	3 ha	12,000	🍾 ⚓	11–15 €

Winemakers for two centuries, the Dumonts manage 22 ha in the district of Bar-sur-Aube. In their 1998, Pinot Noir plays the principal part (70%), supplemented by Chardonnay. This vintage wine was fulsomely praised, with some members of the Jury giving it three stars. Expressive on the nose, complex, fine, floral and fruity, it creates a unified impression on the palate with its balance, elegance and a freshness devoid of any aggressiveness. "It's like biting into the flesh of a fruit," wrote one taster. Another star went to the **Brut non-vintage**, a blend of four years (1997–2000), dominated by black grapes (85% Pinot Noir, supported by Chardonnay). It has intense fruitiness, and a well-balanced palate that is soft, rounded and long. (RM)

➼ R. Dumont et Fils, 10200 Champignol-lez-Mondeville,
tel. 03.25.27.45.95, fax 03.25.27.45.97 ☑
Ⓣ by appt.

DUVAL-LEROY

Rosé de saignée★★

●	n.c.	40,000	🍾 ⚓	15–23 €

Founded in 1859, this négociant house based in the Côte des Blancs has remained within the same family ownership. It has made great strides in recent decades, and today owns 160 ha of vines. Since 1991, Carol Duval has run it with brio. This Rosé de Saignée has already received good notices in former editions of the *Guide*. Made from 100% Pinot Noir, it charms with its intense fruitiness, which centres on boiled sweets. A gentle opening impression introduces the well-balanced and long palate, which is shot through with flavours of cherries. It could be drunk as an aperitif, with a main course or with a dessert (the Jury was somewhat divided on this issue), but all are agreed on the main point: this is a very attractive rosé. Also singled out was the **Blanc de Chardonnay 96**, a little short but balanced and lively, which received a commendation. (NM)

➼ Duval-Leroy, 69, av. de Bammental, 51130 Vertus,
tel. 03.26.52.10.75, fax 03.26.52.37.10,
e-mail champagne@duval-leroy.com ☑
Ⓣ by appt.

ALBERIC DUVAT★

	10 ha	n.c.	🍾	11–15 €

Xavier Duvat is based at Fèrebrianges, a village located between the Côte des Blancs and the slopes of the Sézannais. He manages 10 ha of vines. All three champagne grapes – with a predominance of black varieties (40% Pinot Meunier, 20% Pinot Noir) – from 1999 and 2000 are blended in this brut non-vintage with its subtle bouquet, a fresh, well-balanced wine with good structure. A further star was awarded to the **1998 (15–23 €)**, a three-grape blend favouring Chardonnay (60%, to 30% Meunier and 10% Pinot Noir). The base wines spend four months in wood, resulting in an expressive champagne, floral on the nose, vinous and well-structured through to the finish. The barrel maturation lends it a smoky, woody touch. (RM)

➼ Xavier Duvat, 20, Grande-Rue, 51270 Fèrebrianges,
tel. 03.26.59.35.69, fax 03.26.59.34.04 ☑
Ⓣ by appt.

CHRISTIAN ETIENNE

Tradition★

	6 ha	10,000	🍾 ⚬	11–15 €

Situated in the district of Bar-sur-Aube is this property founded in the late 1970s. It has a little over 9 ha of vines, as well as new installations in the winery. The Tradition *cuvée* owes almost all to black grapes (90% Pinot Noir), from 1997, 1998 and 1999. Its aromas are evocative of mirabelle plums and grapes, and on the palate, a certain vinosity does no harm to its lightness or its freshness, for all that the *dosage* is quite evident. A special mention also went to the non-vintage **Prestige** *cuvée*, which is a product exclusively of the 1996 harvest. Equal parts black and white grapes, it is a firm, fresh and balanced champagne. (RM)

🕯 Christian Etienne, rue de la Fontaine, 10200 Meurville, tel. 03.25.27.46.66, fax 03.25.27.45.84 ⊻
⏳ by appt.

FALLET-DART★

●	7 ha	10,039	🍾 ⚬	15–23 €

Based in the Vallée de la Marne, Gérard Fallet manages a significant vineyard holding of 17 ha. Two of his champagnes are honoured, both blends of 1998 and 1999 wines. Of the two, this salmon-pink rosé gets the nod. Its assets are a pleasingly intense bouquet, a suggestion of smokiness, and a palate that is fresh, well-balanced and long. The **Grande Sélection** attracted attention for its impressive bouquet, its freshness, finesse and complexity. (RM)

🕯 Fallet-Dart, Drachy, 2, rue des Clos-du-Mont, 02310 Charly-sur-Marne, tel. 03.23.82.01.73, fax 03.23.82.19.15 ⊻
⏳ by appt.

NICOLAS FEUILLATTE

Palmes d'or 1995★

⚬	n.c.	n.c.	🍾 ⚬	46–76 €

An enormous viticultural centre was created in 1972 under the Nicolas Feuillatte brand. Based at Chouilly, at the foot of the Côte des Blancs, the group gathers together some 4,500 wine-growers, vinifying the harvest of 2,200 ha distributed thoughout the Champagne region. A blanc de blancs 1995 obtained the *coup de coeur* last year. Here is another *cuvée* from this great vintage, but this time blended of equal parts black and white grapes. Fine bubbles ascend through its golden centre, while its complex aromatic range offers cooked fruits, plums, and then notes of vanilla and brioche. On the palate, it proves to be a wine of true beauty and great length. This is a wine that has reached its peak, one for lovers of mature champagne. (CM)

🕯 Nicolas Feuillatte, BP 210, Chouilly, 51206 Epernay, tel. 03.26.59.55.50, fax 03.26.59.55.82 ⊻
⏳ by appt.

BERNARD FIGUET

Cuvée spéciale★★

⚬	6.5 ha	60,000	🍾 ⚬	11–15 €

Eric Figuet heads up a vineyard of 10.5 ha in the Aisne district of the Vallée de la Marne. His family has been making its own champagne here for more than 50 years. The estate is distinguished particularly this year by this Cuvée Spéciale, which accords the better part of its blend to black grapes (90%, including 75% Meunier). It displays pleasingly intense fruit, on the nose as well as on the palate, and shows itself to be well-balanced, fresh and long. Made from half black grapes and half white, the **Cuvée de Réserve** received the same rating. A floral perfume and flavours of toasted brioche distinguish this fresh and lengthy champagne. (RM)

🕯 Bernard Figuet, 144, rte Nationale, 02310 Saulchery, tel. 03.23.70.16.32, fax 03.23.70.17.22 ⊻
⏳ by appt.
🕯 Eric Figuet

FLEURY PÈRE ET FILS 1996★

	6 ha	48,000	🍾 ⚬	15–23 €

At once négociant and wine-grower, Jean-Pierre Fleury manages a vineyard of 13 ha in the Aube. He has made his way by diverging from conventional methods: was he not the first Champenois to devote his vineyard to the biodynamic system

(undergoing a total conversion as early as 1992)? He uses oak barrels, and his champagnes go through their second fermentation under corks, just as was done up until the 1960s. Blending 80% Pinot Noir with 20% Chardonnay, the 1996 is characteristic of the vintage: complex and powerful, but already showing a developed character on the nose. Notwithstanding that, the palate is still very fresh and lively. A special mention also went to the **Tradition Carte Rouge (11–15 €)**, a blanc de noirs with powerful, complex, developed aromas of honey, acacia, wax and toast. (NM)

🕯 Fleury, 43, Grande-Rue, 10250 Courteron, tel. 03.25.38.20.28, fax 03.25.38.24.65, e-mail champagne-fleury@wanadoo.fr
⏳ by appt.

FORGET-CHEMIN

Spécial Club 1998★★

	12 ha	n.c.		15–23 €

Over four generations, the Forgets have built up a vineyard of more than 12 ha around Ludes, in the Montagne de Reims. Their Spécial Club *cuvées*, packaged in distinctive bottles, are always vintage wines. The 1998 is 50% Pinot Noir to 50% Chardonnay. It bowled over the tasters with its elegant scents of buttered brioche, which return on a soft, plump, rich and honeyed palate. It all adds up to a harmonious whole, ripe but still fresh, a wine that has developed well. Drink it now to appreciate all its qualities. (RM)

🕯 Forget-Chemin, 15, rue Victor-Hugo, 51500 Ludes, tel. 03.26.61.12.17, fax 03.26.61.14.51, e-mail champagne.forget-chemin@voila.fr ⊻
⏳ by appt.

FOURNAISE-THIBAUT

Cuvée Prestige★

	1 ha	3,000	🍾	11–15 €

A statue of Pope Urban II, who was born in Châtillon-sur-Marne, dominates the Vallée de la Marne village where this estate is located. Its Cuvée Prestige, made from 1998 wine, is composed of equal parts of the three champagne grape varieties. Golden-yellow in colour, it is a robust, well-balanced wine that would be suitable for drinking with food. Another star was awarded to the **rosé**, a product of the 2000 harvest. Made entirely from Pinot Meunier, it boasts greater complexity than one might have given it credit for. Could this be something to do with the fact that the base wine spends some time in barrel? Its aromatic range plays on ripe, spicy and charred notes, while the palate is in complete harmony: a rosé for gourmets. (RM)

🕯 Daniel Fournaise, 2, rue des Boucheries, 51700 Châtillon-sur-Marne, tel. 03.26.58.06.44, fax 03.26.51.60.91 ⊻
⏳ by appt.

FRANCOIS-BROSSOLETTE

Tradition★★

	8 ha	34,000	🍾 ⚬	11–15 €

This family estate is located a few kilometres upstream of Bar-sur-Seine, in the Aube. It is listed for two highly successful champagnes, blended from the harvests of 1998, 1999 and 2000. Tradition is mostly black grapes (80%, with a preponderance of Pinot Noir). Its very fine nose, rounded palate and good length add up to a well-balanced wine that could accompany a sauced fish dish. As for the **Blanc de Blancs**, it was characterized by one taster as "a young and ambitious wine with a future," and receives one star. (RM)

🕯 François-Brossolette, 42, Grande-Rue, 10110 Polisy, tel. 03.25.38.57.17, fax 03.25.38.51.56, e-mail françois-brossolette@wanadoo.fr ⊻
⏳ by appt.

GABRIEL FRESNE

Brut★

	4.22 ha	20,853	🍾	11–15 €

This estate is situated to the south of Epernay, on the Sézanne road, its buildings having been formerly used as a postal station. It branched out into winemaking at the beginning of the 1970s, and Corinne Fresne has been at its head since 2000. The Brut non-vintage is a blend of wines from 1998 and 1999, with black grapes making up the best part of it (70%, mainly Meunier). It strikes the palate softly, and is full of bewitching finesse. (RM)

☛ EARL Gabriel Fresne, 7, rte Nationale,
51530 Brugny-Vaudancourt, tel. 03.26.59.98.09,
fax 03.26.58.49.02, e-mail gafresne@club-internet.fr ✅
⚑ by appt.

FRESNET-JUILLET
Carte d'or★

	6 ha	64,000	■ ♦	11–15 €

Based at Verzy, a Montagne de Reims village famous for its beech trees, this house created in 1954 owns 8 ha of vines. Carte d'Or blends 75% Pinot Noir with 25% Chardonnay, from the years 1999, 2000 and 2001. Its aromas suggest crystallized fruits and honey, and the palate, after a forthright opening impression, evolves towards ethereal lightness. Another star went to the **Spécial Club Premier Cru 95 (15–25 €)**, which is predominantly Chardonnay (60%, supplemented by Pinot Noir). Very pleasant on the nose, with a floral, buttery bouquet, powerful and long, it has remained beautifully fresh. (NM)

☛ Fresnet-Juillet, 10, rue de Beaumont, 51380 Verzy,
tel. 03.26.97.93.40, fax 03.26.97.92.55,
e-mail info@champagne-fresnetjuillet.fr ✅
⚑ ev. day 9am–12 noon 2pm–5pm; Sat. Sun. by appt.;
cl. 4th–24th Aug.

MICHEL FURDYNA
La loge 1998★

	1 ha	3,000	■	15–23 €

Champagne Michel Furdyna, which controls a vineyard of 8 ha in the Aube, offers a 100% Pinot Noir *cuvée* presented in a screen-printed bottle. It is a white-gold 98 that has the roundness of its vintage, and has now come into balance. (RM)

☛ Michel Furdyna, 13, rue du Trot,
10110 Celles-sur-Ource, tel. 03.25.38.54.20,
fax 03.25.38.25.63,
e-mail champagne.furdyna@wanadoo.fr ✅
⚑ by appt.

G. DE BARFONTARC
Blanc de noirs★

	n.c.	n.c. ♦		11–15 €

Barfontarc, a gentleman of legend, makes a good ambassador for the wine villages of the Côte des Bars (in the Aube), and also for this cooperative group. Its total estate comprises 90 ha of vines, its coat of arms having been designed way back in 1964! It defends its stronghold well with this Blanc de Noirs, a *brut* non-vintage made from the harvest of 1999, deploying its nutty aromas, its finesse, its gentle acidity, and just a touch of what one might call "noble bitterness". It would do well as an aperitif, or with a sauced fish dish. Also successful was the **Cuvée Sainte-Germaine 98**, a blend of Pinot Noir (60%) and Chardonnay. From its fruity aromas comes forth a note of quince jelly, and it has suppleness, vinosity, freshness and elegance. (CM)

☛ G. de Barfontarc, rte de Bar-sur-Aube, 10200 Baroville,
tel. 03.25.27.07.09, fax 03.25.27.23.00 ✅
⚑ ev. day except Sun. 9am–12 noon 1.30pm–5.30pm

LUC GAIDOZ
Tradition★★

	n.c.	n.c.		11–15 €

Luc Gaidoz has been at the helm of a small property of 1.5 ha since 1983. His Tradition *cuvée* is largely composed of black grape varieties: 80% Pinot Meunier and 10% Pinot Noir to 10% Chardonnay. Intense gold in colour, it releases a bouquet of fruit compote, leading on to a rounded and complex palate with impressive vinosity. A wine of excellent overall balance. (RM)

☛ Luc Gaidoz, 4, rue Gambetta, 51500 Ludes,
tel. 03.26.61.13.73, e-mail lgaidoz@wanadoo.fr ✅
⚑ by appt.

GAUTHEROT
Cuvée de réserve★

	7.6 ha	68,239	■ ♦	11–15 €

Celles-sur-Ource in the Côte des Bars tempts the visitor to a voyage of discovery of the vineyards and valleys of the Seine and Ource regions. The point of departure is the town's old laundry. The Gautherots, whose ancestors were first established in this village in the 17th century, submitted this fruity *cuvée*, a well-structured and long wine that could be enjoyed throughout a meal. It is a blend of 75% Pinot Noir and 25% Chardonnay. (RM)

☛ EARL François Gautherot, 29, Grande-Rue,
10110 Celles-sur-Ource, tel. 03.25.38.50.03,
fax 03.25.38.58.14 ✅
⚑ by appt.

GAUTHIER
Demi-sec Grande Réserve★

	n.c.	n.c.		15–23 €

Gaston Burtin of the Marne et Champagne group acquired in 1958 a house that was founded by Charles-Alexandre Gauthier in the mid-19th century. Marne et Champagne's base wines do not undergo malolactic fermentation. This demi-sec made from the harvests of 2000 and 2001 contains a mere 14% Chardonnay. The Jury appreciated its flavours of crystallized fruits and apricot, as well as the properly integrated *dosage*. (NM)

☛ Marne et Champagne, 22, rue Maurice-Cerveaux,
51200 Epernay, tel. 03.26.78.50.50, fax 03.26.78.50.99

MICHEL GENET★★

●	n.c.	3,000	■	15–23 €

Vincent Genet is director of a successful estate of 8 ha of vines, certain of whose plots are in the grands crus of Chouilly and Cramant. His rosé (from the harvests of 1998 and 1999) is coloured with 12% of Pinot Meunier red wine. It is appealingly fresh, owing to its fruity scents of strawberries and blackcurrants, which return on the palate. An elegant champagne and full of youth. The **Blanc de Blancs Grand Cru Prestige de la Cave** was also singled out: tasters were in full agreement over its distinguished character, but advise keeping it for a year or two. (RM)

☛ Michel Genet, 22, rue des Partelaines, 51530 Chouilly,
tel. 03.26.55.40.51, fax 03.26.59.16.92,
e-mail champagne.genet.michel@wanadoo.fr ✅
⚑ by appt.
☛ V. et A. Genet

PIERRE GERBAIS
L'Originale★

	0.5 ha	3,000	■ ♦	15–23 €

Here is a *cuvée* that well deserves its name: where else but in this corner of the Aube could a champagne be born exclusively of Pinot... Blanc? This is a wine that requires one to delve deep for ways of describing it, the more so as the Jury awarded it a star. It has a lively greenish-gold colour and a fine mousse, a shy nose with slight suggestions of preserved citrus fruits combined with a smoky hint, and a fresh, balanced, expressive palate: altogether a pleasing wine. The same rating was accorded to the **Cuvée Prestige**, a classic blend favouring Chardonnay (90%, supplemented by Pinot Noir). Fine bubbles rise in a straw-coloured wine with green highlights, a complex bouquet mixes vanilla, quince and toasty notes, and the palate is attractive, lively, fresh and long. (NM)

☛ Pierre Gerbais, 13, rue du Pont, BP 17,
10110 Celles-sur-Ource, tel. 03.25.38.51.29,
fax 03.25.38.55.17, e-mail champ.gerbais@wanadoo.fr ✅
⚑ by appt.

JEAN GIMONNET
Blanc de blancs 1998★★

1er cru	n.c.	11,550		15–23 €

This 1998 Blanc de Blancs made it all the way to the *coups de coeur* Grand Jury. Tasters were not immune to the charms of its straw-yellow colour, nor its aroma of fresh butter, apples, pears and crystallized fruits. The powerful, rich palate develops elegantly towards a harmonious finish. Was it that note of over-development that just kept this wine from

Champagne

achieving the *coup de cœur*? The **Blanc de Blancs non-vintage** obtained one star for its directness, freshness and youth, while a special mention also went to the fine, floral **Réserve Premier Cru (11–15 €)**, a blend of 90% Chardonnay and 10% Pinot Meunier. (RM)

☛ Jean Gimonnet, 16, rue Jean-Mermoz, 51530 Cuis, tel. 03.26.59.78.39, fax 03.26.51.05.07 ☑

☕ by appt.

PIERRE GIMONNET ET FILS
Chardonnay Spécial Club 1997★

| | 1er cru | n.c. | 25,474 | 🍾 ⚜ | 15–23 € |

Chardonnay occupies the lion's share of this vineyard of 25 ha. Spécial Club 1997 contains 41% of wines from the Cramant grand cru, 34% from the grand cru of Chouilly, and 25% from the premier cru of Cuis. From this pale-yellow champagne with its green highlights emanate floral, honeyed and spicy scents, while the palate has weight and roundness. A fine-laced wine, to be drunk with desserts. The **Fleuron Premier Cru 96** (which contains 50% of Cuis wine, 28% from Cramant and 22% from Chouilly), is rich and balanced, and received a commendation, as did the **Gastronome Premier Cru non-vintage** (made from the harvest of 2000), a fresh, lively wine. Under a different brand, **Larmandier Père et Fils, le Perlé de Larmandier Premier Cru** was awarded one star. It is a blanc de blancs made in the *crémant* style invented by Jules Larmandier. (RM)

☛ SA Pierre Gimonnet et Fils, 1, rue de la République, 51530 Cuis, tel. 03.26.59.78.70, fax 03.26.59.79.84, e-mail info@champagne-gimonnet.com ☑

☕ ev. day except Sun. 8.30am–12 noon 2pm–6pm; Sat. by appt.; cl. 15th Aug.–1st Sep.

☛ Famille Gimonnet

GIMONNET-GONET
Prestige★★

| | | 2 ha | 4,000 | 🍾 | 15–23 € |

This vineyard of 11 ha, led by Philippe Gimonnet, is illustriously situated among the grands crus of the Côte des Blancs, as well as in the Vallée de la Marne. The Prestige *cuvée* (made from 1997 Chardonnay) has floral and mineral tones on the nose, but then butter and lemon flavours take over on the full, fresh palate. The **Cuvée Tradition (11–15 €)**, equal parts Chardonnay and Pinot Noir from the harvests of 1999 and 2000, was commended for its richness and its length. (RM)

☛ Gimonnet-Gonet, 166, rue du Gal-de-Gaulle, 51190 Le Mesnil-sur-Oger, tel. 03.26.57.51.44, fax 03.26.58.00.03 ☑

☕ by appt.

GIMONNET-OGER
Sélection Blanc de blancs★

| | 1er cru | n.c. | 10,000 | 🍾 | 15–23 € |

Having been winemakers in Cuis for three centuries, the Gimonnet clan has become quite numerous. Here, Jean-Luc Gimonnet offers a **Grande Réserve Premier Cru**, made from 90% Chardonnay, supplemented by Pinot Meunier: a straightforward wine that won a commendation. As for this blanc de blancs, it turns out to be an attractive, well-balanced wine, lively and long on the palate. (RM)

☛ Jean-Luc Gimonnet, 7, rue Jean-Mermoz, 51530 Cuis, tel. 03.26.59.86.50, fax 03.26.59.86.53, e-mail chg-o@wanadoo.fr ☑

☕ by appt.

BERNARD GIRARDIN★

| | | 1 ha | 6,000 | 🍾 | 11–15 € |

Sandrine Britès-Girardin seems to have at least two passions: the vine and music. She has also chosen some very pretty labels to decorate her wines. This one is a blend of 65% Chardonnay, 25% Pinot Meunier and 10% Pinot Noir from the harvests of 1995, 1996 and 1997. The bright-gold colour and the fineness of the bubbles captivate, as does the bouquet of fresh fruit. Riper fruits register on the palate – (white peach) – in a wine of good balance. We should also mention that the Vibrato *cuvée* obtained a *coup de cœur* last year. (RM)

☛ Sandrine Britès-Girardin, Champagne Bernard Girardin, 14, Grande-Rue, 51530 Mancy, tel. 03.26.59.70.78, fax 03.26.59.02.02, e-mail info@champagne-bgirardin.com ☑

☕ by appt.

GERVAIS GOBILLARD★

| ● | | 1.5 ha | 15,000 | 🍾 ⚜ | 11–15 € |

The rosé champagnes of Gervais Gobillard represent the house with distinction in this selection. Witness this ebullient Rosé de Noirs with its elegantly raspberryish scents and its fine palate. The **Cuvée Prestige rosé 99 (15–23 €)** uses 60% Chardonnay. Equally evocative of raspberry, it is fresh and long-lasting. These are two fine aperitif wines. (NM)

☛ Gervais Gobillard, 38, rue de l'Eglise, 51160 Hautvillers, tel. 03.26.51.00.24, fax 03.26.51.00.18, e-mail champagne-gobillard@wanadoo.fr ☑

☕ by appt.

PAUL GOBILLARD
Carte blanche★

| | | n.c. | 25,000 | 🍾 ⚜ | 11–15 € |

The Paul Gobillard brand was acquired by Jean-Louis Malard in 2001. Two of its champagnes were honoured by the Jury with a star each. Carte Blanche, a blend of 75% Pinot Noir and 25% Chardonnay, was liked for its floral and fruity character and its freshness. The **Cuvée Réserve (15–23 €)**, which is made from 70% Pinot Noir and 30% Chardonnay, is complex and long. One taster judged it to be "well-made and very clean". (NM)

☛ Paul Gobillard, Ch. de Pierry, BP 1, 51530 Pierry, tel. 03.26.54.05.11, fax 03.26.54.46.03, e-mail paulgobillard@wanadoo.fr ☑

☕ by appt.

☛ Jean-Louis Malard

PIERRE GOBILLARD★

| | 1er cru | 4 ha | 37,000 | 🍾 ⚜ | 11–15 € |

Dominating the Vallée de la Marne, Hervé Gobillard's property enjoys panoramic views over the vines. Thirty per cent Chardonnay and 30% Pinot Noir, supplemented by 40% Pinot Meunier, make up this golden-yellow champagne, whose pronounced vivacity does nothing to undermine the overall roundness of the wine. It is still developing, although already displaying mineral, fruity flavours. Give it more time. The **rosé (15–23 €)**, made from 20% Chardonnay, 40% Pinot Meunier and 27% Pinot Noir, tinted by 13% red wine, fades into delicate floral notes on the palate. It received a commendation. (RM)

☛ Pierre Gobillard, 341, rue des Côtes-de-l'Héry, 51160 Hautvillers, tel. 03.26.59.45.66, fax 03.26.52.04.43, e-mail champagne-pierre.gobillard@wanadoo.fr ☑

☕ by appt.

☛ Hervé Gobillard

J.-M. GOBILLARD ET FILS
Grande Réserve★

| | 1er cru | 10 ha | 90,000 | 🍾 ⚜ | 11–15 € |

Here is a prestigious address: Hautvillers, where Dom Pérignon lived, is considered to be the cradle of Champagne. This house actually faces the abbey. Gobillard has made a champagne with 50% Chardonnay and 50% of Pinots from the harvests of 1999 and 2000. This limpid greenish-yellow wine proves to have great balance, roundness and length. Another star distinguished the **Cuvée Prestige 99 (15–23 €)**, a wine of invigorating freshness, in which Chardonnay (60%) predominates over Pinot Noir. (NM)

☛ J.-M. Gobillard et Fils, 38, rue de l'Eglise, 51160 Hautvillers, tel. 03.26.51.00.24, fax 03.26.51.00.18, e-mail champagne-gobillard@wanadoo.fr ☑

☕ by appt.

GODME PERE ET FILS★★

| ● | Gd cru | 2 ha | 10,000 | 🍾 | 11–15 € |

Over five generations, the Godmé family has built up a vineyard of 12 ha located on three grands crus (Verzenay, Verzy and Beaumont-sur-Vesle) and two premiers crus (Villers-Marmery and Villedommange). This intensely coloured rosé offers a remarkable nose of red berries. Its suppleness on the palate is marked by the same fruit, but without any excessive sharpness. The clean, floral **Blanc de Blancs Premier Cru** is an uncomplicated wine that also received a commendation. (RM)

🕊 Godmé Père et Fils, 10, rue de Verzy, 51360 Verzenay, tel. 03.26.49.48.70, fax 03.26.49.45.30 ☑
🍷 by appt.

PAUL GOERG

Cuvée Lady C. 1996★★

1er cru	90 ha	20,000	▪ 🍷	23–30 €

Lady C. is the top-of-the-range *cuvée* from this cooperative based at Vertus. Mostly Chardonnay (85%, supplemented by 15% Pinot Noir), it has aromas of *pain d'épice* and raisins. Numerous fine bubbles stream through this intensely golden wine with its green highlights, and the palate is well-balanced, complex and long. The **Cuvée Tradition (11–15 €)** was also singled out for its lemony, slightly developed, well-structured character. It is a blend of 40% Pinot Noir and 60% Chardonnay from the years 1997, 1998 and 1999. (CM)

🕊 Paul Goerg, 30, rue du Gal-Leclerc, 51130 Vertus, tel. 03.26.52.15.31, fax 03.26.52.23.96, e-mail info@champagne-goerg.com ☑
🍷 by appt.

MICHEL GONET

Blanc de blancs Prestige 1998★

Gd cru	5 ha	50,000	15–23 €

Michel Gonet is the head of a vast family vineyard of around 40 ha, mainly in the Côte des Blancs. Its blanc de blancs, a grand cru from Oger and Mesnil-sur-Oger, releases a complex, fine bouquet. Structured, rounded and long, the wine has reached its peak. The **Brut Réserve** (70% Chardonnay and 30% Pinot Noir, from the harvests of 2000 and 2001) was also commended. It leaves a memory of exotic fruit flavours and of great freshness. (RM)

🕊 SCEV Michel Gonet, 196, av. Jean-Jaurès, 51190 Avize, tel. 03.26.57.50.56, fax 03.26.57.91.98, e-mail champagne.gonet@wanadoo.fr ☑ 🏠 🏠
🍷 by appt.

PHILIPPE GONET

Réserve★

	8 ha	30,000	▪ 🍷	11–15 €

This Réserve is a blend of all three champagne grape varieties (60% Pinot Noir, 30% Chardonnay and 10% Pinot Meunier). The fruitiness of the Pinots is nicely expressed, and contributes to the impression of roundness in this champagne, which has just reached its peak. (RM)

🕊 Philippe Gonet et Fils, 1, rue de la Brèche-d'Oger, 51190 Le Mesnil-sur-Oger, tel. 03.26.57.53.47, fax 03.26.57.51.03, e-mail info@champagne-philippe-gonet.com ☑
🍷 ev. day except Sat. and Sun. 8am–12 noon 2pm–6pm; Aug. by appt.
🕊 Denise Gonet

GONET-MEDEVILLE

Cuvée Perle noire★

1er cru	2.5 ha	15,000	▪ 🍷	15–23 €

Gonet-Médeville is a new house born in 2000 from the alliance of a reputable Champagne family and a family well-known in the Bordeaux region. It owns a vineyard of 7.5 ha. Perle Noire – a blanc de noirs of course – seduced the tasters with its floral freshness, finesse and softness. Flavours of floral honey contribute to the harmony of a champagne for which one must wait another one or two years. (RM)

🕊 Xavier Gonet, 1, chem. de la Cavotte, 51150 Bisseuil, tel. 03.26.57.75.60, fax 03.56.26.57.60 ☑
🍷 by appt.

GONET-SULCOVA

Spécial Club 1996★

	1 ha	5,000	▥	15–23 €

The Gonet-Sulcova house was created in 1985 from the marriage of a wine-grower of Mesnil-sur-Oger to a young woman of Czech extraction. Based at Epernay, it has a

vineyard of around 15 ha, one parcel of which has gone into this blanc de blancs with its enticing aromas of hazelnuts and toast. Those flavours express themselves with the same intensity on the palate, which is well-balanced and long, with notes of brioche. (RM)

🕊 Gonet-Sulcova, 13, rue Henri-Martin, 51200 Epernay, tel. 03.26.54.37.63, fax 03.26.54.87.73, e-mail gonet-sulcova@wanadoo.fr ☑
🍷 by appt.

GOSSET

Célébris 1998★★

●	n.c.	20,000	▪ ▥ 🍷	46–76 €

The house of Gosset, whose ancestors first established themselves at A in 1584, counts among the oldest in the region. Béatrice Cointreau, owner of Frapin cognac, has been director of it for the last ten years – successfully too, judging by this special *cuvée* in its superb bottle. Made of 61% Chardonnay and 39% Pinot Noir, this wine does not go through a malolactic fermentation. The tasters were enthused by its delicate salmon-pink colour, shot through with fine bubbles, by its elegant range of floral and red fruit notes, and by its complexity and length on the palate, which speaks of perfect harmony between the red and white grape varieties. A lacy champagne to keep for desserts of red fruits. (NM)

🕊 Gosset, 69, rue Jules-Blondeau, BP 7, 51160 A, tel. 03.26.56.99.56, fax 03.26.51.55.88, e-mail info@champagne-gosset.com ☑
🍷 by appt.

GOSSET

Grand Millésime 1996★★

	n.c.	200,000	▪ ▥ 🍷	46–76 €

Gosset goes from strength to strength. In addition to the *coup de coeur* cited above, two other champagnes sparkled with two stars each. The Grand Millésime (62% Chardonnay and 38% Pinot Noir) was judged "sumptuous" by one taster. Rich and vinous, it boasts a robust constitution that amply sustains its flavours of acacia honey. The **Grand rosé (30–38 €)** is a wine of charm, generous and complex, with strong flavours of fruit compote. It is made from 56% Chardonnay, 35% Pinot Noir and 9% of Bouzy and Ambonnay red wine from the harvests of 1996 and 1997. The **Grande Réserve (30–38 €)**, 46% Chardonnay and 54% Pinots of the years 1995–1997, obtained one star for its intensity, its length and its finesse. (NM)

🕊 Gosset, 69, rue Jules-Blondeau, BP 7, 51160 A, tel. 03.26.56.99.56, fax 03.26.51.55.88, e-mail info@champagne-gosset.com ☑
🍷 by appt.

GOSSET-BRABANT

Cuvée Gabriel 1997★

Gd cru	n.c.	n.c.	23–30 €

This special *cuvée* is bottled by the CVC (the Club des Vignerons Champenois), and is made from 70% Pinot Noir and 30% Chardonnay, originating from the grand cru village of Aÿ. Expressive flavours underpin its balanced, mature and long palate. Also commended was the **Tradition Premier Cru (15–23 €)**, which blends 70% Pinot Noir, 20% Chardonnay and 10% Meunier, an original and harmonious champagne. (RM)

🕊 Gosset-Brabant, 23, bd du Mal-de-Lattre-de-Tassigny, 51160 A, tel. 03.26.55.17.42, fax 03.26.54.31.33, e-mail gosset-brabant@wanadoo.fr
🍷 by appt.

GOUSSARD ET DAUPHIN

Prestige★

| | 0.8 ha | 5,600 | 🍶 ⚲ | 11–15 € |

Since 1989, D. Goussard and his brother-in-law J.-C. Dauphin have been making a champagne from part of the harvest of their vineyard of 7 ha in the Riceys district. Their *cuvée* follows classical principles in its composition, which is 60% Chardonnay and 40% Pinot Noir. Its fresh scent of hawthorn and its well-balanced palate offer simple and immediate pleasure. (RM)
🍷 Goussard et Dauphin, GAEC du Val de Sarce, 2, chem. Saint-Vincent, 10340 Avirey-Lingey, tel. 03.25.29.30.03, fax 03.25.29.85.96,
e-mail goussard.dauphin@wanadoo.fr ☑
🍸 by appt.

GOUTORBE-BOUILLOT

Cuvée Prestige Louise B★★

| | n.c. | 5,000 | 🍶 ⚲ | 15–23 € |

This estate not far from Epernay, which owns a vineyard of 8 ha, has produced a straw-yellow champagne with green highlights marked by the character of Chardonnay (70%, against 30% Pinot Noir, harvested in 1998). Scents of bergamot and acacia continue on to the fresh palate, which is full of finesse. The **Réserve (11–15 €)** gathered one star for its liveliness and elegance. It is composed of 80% Pinot Noir and 20% Chardonnay. (RM)
🍷 Goutorbe-Bouillot, 14, rue Anatole-France, 51480 Damery, tel. 03.26.58.40.92, fax 03.26.58.45.36, e-mail goutorbebouillot@verticalwine.com ☑
🍸 by appt.

GRANZANY PERE ET FILS

Cuvée Prestige 1999★

| | 1.5 ha | 150,000 | | 11–15 € |

Distributed among several villages of the Vallée de la Marne, this estate has produced a *cuvée* made of 40% Chardonnay, 30% Pinot Meunier and 30% Pinot Noir, from the harvest of 1999. Its unusual bouquet reminds one of the buds of fir trees, and the palate expresses itself with finesse, balance and length. (RM)
🍷 EARL Granzany Père et Fils, 7, rue de la Poterne, 51480 Venteuil, tel. 03.26.58.60.62, fax 03.26.51.10.21 ☑
🍸 by appt.

J.-M. GREMILLET

Cuvée Elodie★

| | 20 ha | 90,000 | | 8–11 € |

This vineyard of 20 ha overlooks the river Laignes from the top of its hillside. It is responsible for this *cuvée*, made from 65% Pinot Noir and 35% Chardonnay which, together with its pale-gold colour, delights with a fine bouquet of citrus fruits. After a lively attack, it becomes more robust on the palate. Two other champagnes also took one star each: the fruity, minerally **Grande Réserve**, made of equal parts Pinot Noir and Chardonnay, and the **Cuvée des Dames**, a floral-scented blanc de blancs, subtle and long (both 11–15 €). (NM)
🍷 Jean-Michel Gremillet, 10110 Balnot-sur-Laignes, tel. 03.95.29.37.91, fax 03.25.29.30.69, e-mail champagne.jm.gremillet@wanadoo.fr ☑
🍸 ev. day 9am–4pm except Sat. and Sun.

GRONGNET

Blanc de blancs★

| | 1.5 ha | 8,000 | | 11–15 € |

Etoges has a pretty church, parts of which date from the 12th, 15th and 16th centuries. The village is not far from the Côte des Blancs. Two-thirds of the blend of this blanc de blancs have undergone malolactic fermantation, while the remaining third has not. Its old-gold colour announces the perceptible development evident in its aromatic range. On the palate, freshness and roundness are in balance. Also singled out, the **Spécial Club (15–23 €)**, a blend of 60% Chardonnay, 25% Pinot Noir and 15% Meunier, has developed well, its fruity flavours having gained in complexity. (RM)

🍷 Grongnet, 41, Grande-Rue, 51270 Etoges, tel. 03.26.59.30.50, fax 03.26.59.30.98, e-mail champagnegrongnet@wanadoo.fr ☑
🍸 by appt.

ROMAIN GUISTEL

Chardonnay★

| | Gd cru | 1 ha | 8,000 | | 15–23 € |

This blanc de blancs is vinified by Romain and Richard Guistel, whose family has been established in Champagne since the Revolution. They have a vineyard of 5 ha. This champagne is based on the harvest of 1999. The nose is floral, fresh and light, characteristics that one further finds on the palate. This original and elegant brand deserves recognition. (NM)
🍷 Romain Guistel, 1, rue Remparts de l'Ouest, 51480 Damery, tel. 03.26.58.40.40, fax 03.26.52.04.28, e-mail r.guistel@wanadoo.fr ☑
🍸 ev. day 8am–12 noon 2pm–7pm

HAMM

Sélection★

| | n.c. | 40,000 | | 11–15 € |

Michel, Claude and Brigitte Hamm are the descendants of the founder of this négociant house that was created in 1910. Their range includes this blend of three grape varieties (both Pinots in equal shares, plus 20% Chardonnay), a supple, rounded and full wine, which recalls ripe fruits and nuts on the nose, but is more like cinnamon on the finish. Equally successful was their **1996 (15–23 €)**, half black grapes and half white, a fresh, bready champagne. (NM)
🍷 Hamm et Fils, 16, rue N.-Philipponnat, 51160 A-Champagne, tel. 03.26.55.44.19, fax 03.26.51.98.68 ☑
🍸 ev. day 9am–12 noon 2pm–6pm; Sat. Sun. by appt.

HARLIN

Harmonie★★

| | 3 ha | 30,000 | 🍶 ⚲ | 11–15 € |

The Harlins have been established at Tours-sur-Marne for over a century, their vineyard extending to around 10 ha. Blending 35% Chardonnay with Pinot Noir of the harvest of 1999, this fine-bubbled champagne reveals good structure, and is as impressive on the palate as it is on the nose, with fruity and spicy notes predominating. The **Grand Rosé (15–23 €)** comprises 62% Chardonnay, supplemented by Pinot Noir and Bouzy red wine. It attracted one star for its balance and its elegance. (NM)
🍷 Harlin, 41, av. de Champagne, 51150 Tours-sur-Marne, tel. 03.26.51.88.95, fax 03.26.58.96.31, e-mail champagneharlin@yahoo.fr ☑
🍸 by appt.
🍷 Famille Paillard

JEAN-NOEL HATON★

| ● | n.c. | 20,000 | 🍶 ⚲ | 15–23 € |

Jean-Noël Haton heads a house created in 1928, overseeing 13 ha of vines. A blend of 75% black grapes (including 50% Pinot Meunier) with Chardonnay has produced this rosé that is discreetly evocative of redcurrants, at once both rounded and fresh. The fine, persistent mousse on a vivid pink background will look very fetching in the glass when you serve it as an aperitif. (NM)
🍷 Jean-Noël Haton, 5, rue Jean-Mermoz, 51480 Damery, tel. 03.26.58.40.45, fax 03.26.58.63.55 ☑
🍸 by appt.

MARC HEBRART

Spécial Club 1997★★

| | 1er cru | 1 ha | 5,300 | | 15–23 € |

Setting out to visit this vineyard will involve discovering the seven Champagne villages (including the grands crus of Oiry, Chouilly and Aÿ) among which its 66 plots of land are distributed. The estate was created in 1997 from a merger of the holdings of Marc Hébrart and his son Jean-Paul. Fittingly enough, it was a 1997 – a very tricky vintage – that the Jury picked out. More marked by black grapes (60% Pinot Noir) than by white, it conceals beneath its gilded yellow appearance subtle flavours of damp woodland and honey. Its

balance and length on the palate make it a champagne of choice, a worthy accompaniment to a dish of scallops. (RM)
☛ EARL Hébrart, 18, rue du Pont, 51160 Mareuil-sur-Aÿ, tel. 03.26.52.60.75, fax 03.26.52.92.64 ◪
☖ ev. day 9am–12 noon 1.30pm–7pm

CHARLES HEIDSIECK
Blanc des Millénaires 1990★★

	n.c.	25,767	🍾 ♦	46–76 €

This prestigious house, founded in 1851, is noted for its top-of-the-range champagnes, such as this Blanc des Millénaires, one of its blancs de blancs of remarkably regular quality. The 1990, a great vintage, confirms the reputation. Now at its peak, it is soft, rounded and long. From within its golden-yellow depths rise distinct aromas of undergrowth and ripe citrus fruits. the **1995 (38–46 €)**, which contains a greater proportion of Chardonnay (70%) than of Pinot Noir, boasts astonishing youth, as well as fascinating toasty and honeyed notes. It received a commendation. (NM)
☛ Charles Heidsieck, 4, bd Henry-Vasnier, 51100 Reims, tel. 03.26.84.43.50, fax 03.26.84.43.86 ◪
☖ by appt.
☛ Remy-Cointreau

HEIDSIECK & CO MONOPOLE
Blue Top★★

	n.c.	n.c.	🍾 ♦	15–23 €

The whole of Europe, from Prussia, Germany and Britain to Sweden and Russia, has always loved the champagnes of this famous house founded by Florens-Louis Heidsieck in 1785. Now under the aegis of Vranken, Heidsieck & Co Monopole is represented by a fresh, rounded wine of decent length. Blended from 70% Pinot Noir, 20% Chardonnay and 10% Pinot Meunier, it shows a handsome stream of bubbles on a straw-gold background, before releasing scents of ripe fruits, such as apricots, peaches and citrus fruits, beneath a floral top note. A charming aperitif champagne. The **Diamant Bleu 95 (38–46 €)**, half-and-half Chardonnay and Pinot Noir, was singled out for its softness, as well as for its bready, mineral character. (NM)
☛ Heidsieck & Co Monopole, 42, av. de Champagne, 51200 Epernay, tel. 03.26.59.51.32, fax 03.26.59.51.39 ◪
☖ by appt.
☛ Vranken

D. HENRIET-BAZIN★

Gd cru	3 ha	10,000	🍾	15–23 €

In the forest of Verzy, the same place where the Benedictine monks of the abbey of Saint-Basle once cultivated their garden, naturalists will delight in the local beech trees, which are 500 years old. Naturalists and wine-lovers alike will then continue on their way to Villers-Marmery to taste this blanc de noirs (100% Pinot Noir), of which the length alone deserves to be acknowledged. Fine bubbles rise through a pale-yellow wine, releasing delicious aromas of brioche and stewed fruits. A breast of duck with redcurrants would make a fine partner for this rich and well-integrated champagne. (RM)
☛ Henriet-Bazin, 9 bis, rue Dom-Pérignon, 51380 Villers-Marmery, tel. 03.26.97.96.81, fax 03.26.97.97.30, e-mail henriet.bazin@wanadoo.fr ◪
☖ by appt.

HENRIOT
Cuvée des Enchanteleurs 1988★★

	n.c.	n.c.		46–76 €

"Enchanteleurs" is the rather pretty name once given to the workers who handled the barrels. Today, it designates this enchanting champagne, the prestige *cuvée* of a house created in 1808 by the widow Apolline Henriot. Just barely dominated by Chardonnay (56%, against 44% Pinot Noir), this 1988 was described as a wine for meditation by all the tasters: intensely aromatic with notes of mushrooms, hazelnuts and buttered toast, it shows itself to be full, rounded and in a state of complete harmony. One star distinguished the **Blanc Souverain (15–23 €)**, a minerally, soft and balanced blanc de blancs, while commendations were also awarded to the **Brut Souverain (15–23 €)** and to the **1996 (23–30 €)**, both blends containing more Pinot Noir than Chardonnay, and each discreetly floral and well-balanced. (NM)
☛ Henriot, 81, rue Coquebert, 51066 Reims, tel. 03.26.89.53.00, fax 03.26.89.53.10, e-mail contact@champagne-henriot.com
☖ by appt.

PAUL HERARD
Blanc de noirs★

	9 ha	n.c.		11–15 €

This Aube négociant house created in 1925 is today directed by the descendants of its founder, Paul Hérard. It distinguished itself with two beautifully made wines, one of which was this non-vintage blanc de noirs, made from the harvest of 2000. If it seems shy on the nose, the wine discloses good structure on the palate and a pleasantly integrated character. Its abundant mousse serves to emphasize its golden colour. The **Cuvée Paul (15–23 €)** favours Chardonnay (60%, supplemented by Pinot Noir) from the harvest of 1996: its bouquet of acacia honey and vanilla, and its intensely floral freshness, make for a highly successful champagne. (NM)
☛ Paul Hérard, 33, Grande-Rue, 10250 Neuville-sur-Seine, tel. 03.25.38.20.14, fax 03.25.38.25.05 ◪
☖ by appt.

HEUCQ PERE ET FILS★★

	0.35 ha	3,000	🍾 ♦	15–23 €

André Heucq has been at the head of this 5.6-ha vineyard in the Vallée de la Marne for 30 years. His rosé, a blend of Pinot Meunier (70%) and Pinot Noir, harvested in 1999, expresses raspberries all the way through the tasting. A pretty stream of bubbles rises against a background of light ruby, inviting one to savour this pleasantly fresh and lengthy champagne. Two stars also distinguished the elegant **Cuvée Prestige** (60% Chardonnay and 40% Pinot Noir from the years 1997 and 1998), which has scents of flowers, fruit and honey. (RM)
☛ André Heucq, 6, rue Eugène-Moussé, 51700 Cuisles, tel. 03.26.58.10.08, fax 03.26.58.12.00
☖ by appt.

HUGUENOT-TASSIN
Cuvée de réserve★★

	1.5 ha	12,000	🍾	11–15 €

All the Pinot varieties are authorized in Champagne. Benoît Huguenot, who manages 6 ha of vines, thus contributes some Pinot Blanc (35%) to the Pinot Noir (35%) and Chardonnay in this fruity, well-balanced and truly memorable *cuvée*. One taster commented in conclusion the "bouquet evokes the great Chardonnays of Burgundy". And indeed, are we not in Celles-sur-Ource, not far from the Burgundy region? (RM)
☛ Benoît Huguenot, 4, rue du Val-Lune, 10110 Celles-sur-Ource, tel. 03.25.38.54.49, fax 03.25.38.50.40 ◪
☖ by appt.

ROBERT JACOB
Prestige 2000★★

	1.5 ha	6,000	🍾◨ ♦	15–23 €

Having won a *coup de coeur* last year, Daniel Jacob this time offers a remarkable *cuvée* with an oval label, all done in gold just like the colour of this blanc de blancs (which is not, however, described as such on the label). Chardonnay harvested in 2000 has produced a wine with a subtly floral nose (hawthorn), lightly influenced by barrel-ageing (vanilla), and which is fresh, fine and long on the palate. The **Millésimé 96**, a blend of 65% Chardonnay with Pinot Noir, took a commendation. (RM)
☛ Jacob, 14, rue de Morres, 10110 Merrey-sur-Arce, tel. 03.25.29.83.74, fax 03.25.29.34.86, e-mail champagnejacob@wanadoo.fr ◪
☖ ev. day except Sun. 9am–12 noon 2pm–6pm

JACQUART
Mosaïque★

| | n.c. | 1,400,000 | 🗋 ♨ | 15–23 € |

The grapes and wines of about a thousand hectares end up at Jacquart in Reims, seat of this cooperative union whose buildings are decorated with a mosaic of 1896, representing champagne-making. The Brut Mosaïque, made of equal parts black and white grapes of 1997 and 1998, is stimulating, fresh, rounded and well-balanced. Its star award heralds three other champagnes that the Jury took a liking to: **Mosaïque Millésimé 96 (23–30 €)**, an identical blend, has a developed, honeyed nose, and is well-structured, fresh and long; **Mosaïque rosé 98**, made from all three champagne grape varieties, is very powerful and already seems quite evolved; and the **Brut de Nominée (23–30 €)** is a fine, vigorous, spicy wine. (CM)
🖎 Jacquart et Associés Distribution, 6, rue de Mars, 51057 Reims, tel. 03.26.07.88.40, fax 03.26.07.12.07, e-mail jacquart@jad.fr

A. JACQUART ET FILS
Blanc de blancs 1998★

| | Gd cru | 3 ha | 10,000 | 🗋 ♨ | 15–23 € |

Today managing 18 ha of vines, Pierre and Chantal Jacquart use gyropalettes for their *remuage*. Their 1998, a blanc de blancs Grand Cru, is a discreetly floral champagne with a lively attack, which gives way to a well-balanced and perfectly harmonious palate. (RM)
🖎 André Jacquart et Fils, 23, rue des Zalieux, 51190 Le Mesnil-sur-Oger, tel. 03.26.57.52.29, fax 03.26.57.78.14, e-mail info@champagne-a-jacquart-et-fils.com 🆅
⌛ by appt.

YVES JACQUES
Tradition★

| | 1 ha | n.c. | 🗋 ♨ | 11–15 € |

Rémi Jacques joined his father in the business after gaining his oenologist's diploma. The two of them cultivate a vineyard of 14 ha. Their rosé, a blend of 20% Chardonnay and 80% Pinot, including 50% Pinot Meunier, from the harvests of 1999 and 2000, is quite deeply coloured, and offers scents of strawberries, blackcurrants and exotic fruits. It shows good vinosity on the palate. The **Cuvée Sélection** was also singled out. It is a blanc de blancs from the harvests of 1998–2000, floral, fresh and well-balanced. Let us recall that this same *cuvée*, from the years 1996, 1997 and 1998, obtained a *coup de coeur* last year. (RM)
🖎 Yves Jacques, 1, rue de Montpertuis, 51270 Baye, tel. 03.26.52.80.77, fax 03.26.52.83.97 🆅
⌛ by appt.

JACQUES LORENT
Cuvée Tradition★

| | 8 ha | 60,000 | 🗋 | 11–15 € |

This brand belongs to a cooperative that joins together 200 members owning 80 ha of vines around Epernay. Cuvée Tradition comprises 25% Chardonnay and 75% black grapes – including 60% Pinot Meunier – from the vintages of 1998–2000. An intense gold in colour, it displays attractive aromas of white peach and preserved lemon, before showing itself to be structured, meaty and long on the palate. (CM)
🖎 Jacques Lorent, 64, rue de la Liberté, 51530 Mardeuil Cedex, tel. 03.26.55.29.40, fax 03.26.54.26.30 🆅
⌛ by appt.

CAMILLE JACQUET
Blanc de blancs Excellence★

| | Gd cru | 1.5 ha | 10,000 | | 11–15 € |

This brand was launched in 2001 by Champagne Jean Pernet. Its blanc de blancs offers a bouquet of white flowers and grapefruit, followed by a lively attack on the palate, a sign of youth that is confirmed on the finish. Also commended, the **Grande Réserve**, made from the three champagne grape varieties, reveals a discreetly minty nose, as well as a full, well-balanced palate. (NM)

🖎 Camille Jacquet, 3, Le Pont-de-Bois, 51530 Chavot-Courcourt, tel. 03.26.57.54.24, fax 03.26.57.96.98 🆅
⌛ by appt.

JACQUINET-DUMEZ
Agathe★

| | 1er cru | 0.8 ha | 3,000 | 🗋 🌰 ♨ | 15–23 € |

Aline and Olivier Jacquinet cultivate 7 ha of premier cru vineyard. This special *cuvée* is a blanc de noirs matured in wood, an attribute that is not hidden on the complex, toasty nose. Pleasant on the palate, where it is soft and appetizing, fruity and spicy, this is a well-made champagne. The **Grande Réserve (11–15 €)**, also a blanc de noirs but with no wood-ageing, received a commendation. (RM)
🖎 Jacquinet-Dumez, 26, rue de Reims, 51370 Les Mesneux, tel. 03.26.36.25.25, fax 03.26.36.58.92, e-mail jacquinet-dumez@wanadoo.fr 🆅
⌛ by appt.

PH. JANISSON
Cuvée Prestige★★

| | 1er cru | 4 ha | 5,000 | 🗋 ♨ | 11–15 € |

Janisson has built up over several generations a vineyard that now extends to four grands crus and three premiers crus. This rosé is born of a classic blend of Pinot Noir (40%) and Chardonnay (60%). Quite as classical is its style: a lively, elegant bouquet of red berries, and a fresh and well-balanced palate. The **Brut Prestige Premier Cru**, an identical blend to that of the rosé, from the harvests of 1998, 1999 and 2000, presents the same freshness and balance without the colour, but also contains a trace of bitterness. It received one star. It is worth recalling that this *cuvée*, albeit from a very different blend (1998 and 1999) and of all three grape varieties, carried off a *coup de coeur* last year. (NM)
🖎 Philippe Janisson, 17, rue Gougelet, 51500 Chigny-les-Roses, tel. 03.26.03.46.93, fax 03.26.03.49.00, e-mail champagne@janisson.fr 🆅
⌛ by appt.

JEAN DE LA FONTAINE 1996★

| | n.c. | 2,000 | 🗋 ♨ | 11–15 € |

Jean de la Fontaine is a brand of Champagne Baron Albert. Its 1996 is made from 60% white grapes and 40% black. It undergoes no malolactic fermentation, and 20% of the base wines are matured in wood. The seven crus that make up this *cuvée* contribute to its beautiful finesse, its balance and its long, lemony finish. Marinated salmon and other fish would be the appropriate dishes to drink it with. The same rating went to the **rosé** (which contains 45% Chardonnay): the product of a similar style of vinification, it is a non-vintage champagne (from the harvests of 1997, 1998 and 1999) characterized by flavours of red fruits, a wine of richness and length. (NM)
🖎 Jean de la Fontaine, 1, rue des Chaillots, Grand Porteron, BP 12, 02310 Charly-sur-Marne, tel. 03.23.82.02.65, fax 03.23.82.02.44, e-mail champagnebaronalbert@wanadoo.fr 🆅
⌛ by appt.
🖎 Baron Albert

JEANMAIRE
Chardonnay Vintage 1996★

| | n.c. | 22,000 | 🗋 ♨ | 23–30 € |

André Jeanmaire created this house in 1933. In 1981, it was taken over by the Trouillard family. The 1996 is perfectly in conformity with the vintage, with its touch of perceptible development on the nose, and its fresh, fruity complexity on the palate. It should be drunk as an aperitif. The **rosé (15–23 €)**, a blend of 1999 and 2000 wines, composed of 70% Pinot Noir with Pinot Meunier, was singled out for its elegant pale colour and its intense flavours of red berries. (NM)
🖎 Jeanmaire, Ch. Malakoff, 3, rue Malakoff, 51200 Epernay, tel. 03.26.59.50.10, fax 03.26.54.78.52, e-mail contact@chateau-malakoff.com
🖎 J. Trouillard

RENE JOLLY★★

| ● | 3 ha | 6,000 | ▮ | 11–15 € |

CHAMPAGNE
RENÉ JOLLY
BRUT   ROSÉ

The owner of this 10-ha estate lacks nothing in ambition, and his recent investments have reaped their reward in the *coup de coeur* awarded to this deeply coloured rosé, which is virtually red, for all that the *cuvée* includes 80% Chardonnay. Blackcurrants and redcurrants suffuse the nose, while on the palate, "it is as though one were biting into a red fruit," as one taster wrote. Its richness and length won it firm support. A commendation also had to go to the **Blanc de Blancs**, a blend of 1995, 1997 and 1998: with its aromas of butter and passion-fruit, it is a rounded wine of fine vinosity. (RM)
☛ René Jolly, 10, rue de la Gare, 10110 Landreville, tel. 03.25.38.50.91, fax 03.25.38.30.51 ☑
☎ by appt.
☛ Pierre-Eric Jolly

BERTRAND JOREZ

Prestige★

| ● | 1er cru | n.c. | n.c. | 11–15 € |

This estate launched its brand in 1990, and comprises a vineyard of 5 ha on the Montagne de Reims. Its Prestige *cuvée* brings together 40% Chardonnay, the same of Pinot Noir and 20% Pinot Meunier, harvested in 1998. It combines notes of brioche, citrus and crystallized fruits on a well-balanced palate. A champagne to go with first courses. (RC)
☛ EARL Bertrand Jorez, 13, rue de Reims, 51500 Ludes, tel. 03.26.61.14.05, fax 03.26.61.14.96, e-mail bertrand.jorez@wanadoo.fr ☑
☎ by appt.

JEAN JOSSELIN

Cordon Royal★

| ● | 8.83 ha | 5,900 | ▮ | ⚬ | 15–23 € |

Although Josselin's reception area is in a 17th-century house, the wines are made in cellars built in 1998. Three-quarters Pinot Noir and a quarter Chardonnay from the years 1998–2000 are blended in this balanced champagne that one taster wanted to drink alongside turkey with chestnuts. (RM)
☛ Jean-Pierre Josselin, 14, rue des Vannes, 10250 Gyé-sur-Seine, tel. 03.25.38.21.48, fax 03.25.38.25.00, e-mail champagne-josselin@wanadoo.fr ☑
☎ by appt.

KRUG

Clos du Mesnil 1990★★

| | n.c. | 16,417 | ⓘ | +76 € |

This legendary house founded in 1843 by Joseph Krug has always been in the hands of the Krug family, but has been controlled since 1999 by LVMH. The oldest *clos* in Champagne (dating from 1698), Mesnil is planted only with Chardonnay. In an earlier edition of the *Guide*, the 1988 Clos du Mesnil achieved a *coup de coeur*, a distinction accorded this year to the 1990, a wine of such roundness and opulence as one is unaccustomed to finding in a blanc de blancs. A touch of wood contributes to its length. Two stars were decreed for the **Grande Cuvée**, the principal non-vintage blend, made from all three champagne grape varieties, one-third Chardonnay to two-thirds Pinots. It is a full, long, well-balanced wine, made to be served at the table, and well suited to white meats. Another two stars went to the **1988**, a *coup de coeur* in the 2002 *Guide*, and a flawless champagne for drinking over the next twenty years. As to the **Collection 81**, it has not acquired a single wrinkle since it was tasted last year! (NM)
☛ Krug Vins fins de Champagne, 5, rue Coquebert, 51100 Reims, tel. 03.26.84.44.20, fax 03.26.84.44.49, e-mail krug@krug.fr ☑
☎ by appt.

MICHEL LABBE ET FILS

Carte blanche★

| | 1er cru | 8 ha | 18,000 | 11–15 € |

The grandparents of Didier Labbé established this vineyard of 8 ha at the outset of the 20th century. Carte Blanche (which consists of 90% Pinots) charmed the tasters with its bouquet of caramelized fruits and spices, and with its fruity palate and soft finish. The **Brut Prestige (15–23 €)**, Pinot Noir and Chardonnay in equal measure, which shows its development to both eye and nose, is full and well-balanced on the palate. It also obtained one star. (RM)
☛ Michel et Didier Labbé et Fils, 5, chem. du Hasat, 51500 Chamery, tel. 03.26.97.65.45, fax 03.26.97.67.42 ☑
☎ ev. day except Sun. 9am–12 noon 2pm–7pm; cl. 15–31 Aug.

LACROIX★

| ● | 1 ha | 7,000 | ▮ ⓘ | 11–15 € |

Located 1 km from the famous statue of Pope Urban II instituting the Crusades, this estate vinifies part of its wines in large wooden casks. This rosé, of which Chardonnay forms only 20% of the blend, is flattering to the eye. The bouquet is all strawberries, while the palate is well-balanced and youthful. (RM)
☛ Jean Lacroix, 14, rue des Genêts, 51700 Montigny-sous-Châtillon, tel. 03.26.58.35.17, fax 03.26.58.36.39, e-mail champlacroix@wanadoo.fr ☑
☎ by appt.

CHARLES LAFITTE

Grande Cuvée★

| ● | | n.c. | n.c. | 15–23 € |

This brand, created in 1983, belongs to the most dynamic of all those who have made Champagne their home: Paul Vranken. The rosé is a blend of equal parts Chardonnay and Pinot Noir, with 20% Pinot Meunier. Whether it reminds you of wild strawberries or of raspberries, it has in any event reached its peak, as is demonstrated by its intense colour and its structure on the palate. (NM)
☛ Charles Lafitte, 42, av. de Champagne, 51200 Epernay, tel. 03.26.59.51.32, fax 03.26.59.51.39 ☑
☎ by appt.
☛ Vranken

BENOIT LAHAYE★

| | Gd cru | 2 ha | 18,000 | ▮ ⚬ | 11–15 € |

This Bouzy estate is in the process of converting to organic production. Pinot Noir makes up 85% of this *cuvée*, topped up with Chardonnay, and a proportion of the wine (70%) avoids malolactic fermentation. It is a blend of the harvests of 1998 and 1999. With a beautiful white-gold appearance, it has a scent of citrus fruits (lime) and a lively attack. A champagne both powerful and balanced, it has great length. Another brand, **Lahaye-Waroquier, Cuvée Prestige (15–23 €)**, made of Pinot Noir from the same years, was also commended. (RM)
☛ Benoit Lahaye, 33, rue Jeanne-d'Arc, 51150 Bouzy, tel. 03.26.57.03.05, fax 03.26.52.79.94, e-mail lahaye.benoit@wanadoo.fr ☑
☎ by appt.

LANCELOT FILS

Cramant Blanc de blancs Cuvée spéciale 1998★

	Gd cru	0.65 ha	4,158	🍾	15–23 €

Owning 5 ha of vines in the grands crus of Cramant and Avize, this domaine obtained a *coup de coeur* last year for its 1997 vintage of the same *cuvée*. The 1998, a golden wine with green highlights, shot through with impetuous bubbles, turns out to be honeyed, expressive and elegant, though still young. (RM)
➤ Lancelot-Goussard, 30, rue E.-Vallé, 51190 Avize, tel. 03.26.57.94.68, fax 03.26.57.79.02,
e-mail info@champagne-lancelot-goussard.com ☒
🍷 by appt.

LANCELOT-PIENNE Cramant Blanc de

blancs Cuvée Marie Lancelot 1995★★

	Gd cru	1 ha	2,000	🍾	15–23 €

The alliance of two families, that of Albert Lancelot and his wife Brigitte Pienne, gave birth to this domaine, which comprises more than 7 ha of vines. Their son, an oenologist, has since joined them in the business. The Cuvée Marie Lancelot contains only Cramant Chardonnay. It is a powerful, rounded, fleshy, full and well-balanced wine of good length, and could be drunk with fish in creamy sauces. (RM)
➤ Lancelot-Pienne, 1, allée de la Forêt, 51530 Cramant, tel. 03.26.57.55.74, fax 03.26.57.53.02,
e-mail champagne@lancelot.fr ☒
🍷 by appt.

P. LANCELOT-ROYER

Blanc de blancs Cuvée de réserve R.R.★★

		2.2 ha	10,000	🍾	11–15 €

The long history of Champagne Lancelot has been sustained thanks to the relaunch of this vineyard in 1996 by Pierre's daughter, Sylvie, and his son-in-law Michel Chauvet. They keep their reserve wines in large wooden casks. Réserve R.R. is a blend of wines from 1999 and 2000. It is a toasty, soft, rounded, elegant and long champagne. Deserving of one star was the creamy, bready **Cuvée des Chevaliers**, another blanc de blancs, from the vintages of 1998 and 1999. (RM)
➤ EARL P. Lancelot-Royer, 540, rue du Gal-de-Gaulle, 51530 Cramant, tel. 03.26.57.51.41, fax 03.26.57.12.25,
e-mail champagne.lancelot.royer@cder.fr ☒
🍷 by appt.

LANSON

Gold Label 1990★

		45 ha	356,000		30–38 €

The old and well-known house of Lanson, founded in 1760, was relaunched in 1991 by the important cooperative group, Marne et Champagne. As always at Lanson, malolactic fermentation is avoided. This *cuvée* contains practically as much Pinot Noir as Chardonnay. On both nose and palate, it marries honey, caramel and crystallized fruits, with a touch of walnut owing to its stage of development. It would best be enjoyed at the end of a meal. Also commended, the **Gold Label 96 (23–30 €)** amply shows its vintage characteristics, which are accentuated by the absence of "malo". Vigorous, lemony, bready, supplemented by flavours of orchard fruits and nuts, it would accompany a freshwater fish such as trout. (NM)
➤ Lanson, 12, bd Lundy, 51100 Reims, tel. 03.26.78.50.50, fax 03.26.78.50.99 ☒
🍷 by appt.

P. LARDENNOIS

Cuvée Sélection★★

		0.2 ha	1,500	🍾	15–23 €

Eleven generations at the same domaine... They ought to be in the record books. Cuvée Sélection did not quite achieve a unanimous *coup de coeur*, but all the tasters awarded it two stars. Fine and light, its stream of bubbles shoots through a deeply coloured wine. The fruity nose is elegant, with notes of quince on top of grapefruit. Fresh, well-balanced, long, and also powerful, this champagne has been very carefully made. It is a blend of 65% Pinot Noir to 35% Chardonnay, from the years 1993–1996. (RM)

➤ Pierre Lardennois, 33, rue Carnot, 51380 Verzy, tel. 03.26.97.91.23, fax 03.26.97.97.69 ☒
🍷 by appt.

LARMANDIER-BERNIER

Extra-brut Blanc de blancs Spécial Club 1996★

	1er cru	2 ha	6,000	🍾 ⚜ 🥂	23–30 €

Pierre Larmandier, grandson of Jules Larmandier, manages a vineyard of 15 ha. An enthusiastic proponent of biodynamics, he already applies many of its rules. He again submitted his Extra-Brut 1996, a blanc de blancs that has spent six months in oak. This represents a double challenge: an undosed blanc de blancs in a notably acidic vintage. It is after all easier to make an extra-brut with Pinot! The gamble, however, paid off: the champagne is entirely fresh and lively, with notes of roasted almonds and toast. (RM)
➤ Larmandier-Bernier, 43, rue du 28-Août, 51130 Vertus, tel. 03.26.52.13.24, fax 03.26.52.21.00,
e-mail larmandier@terre-net.fr ☒
🍷 by appt.

JACQUES LASSAIGNE★

		1.7 ha	20,000	🍾	11–15 €

With its vineyard of nearly 5 ha, the Jacques Lassaigne brand is about to celebrate its 40th anniversary. Its *brut* non-vintage, which blends Chardonnay and Pinot Noir in equal shares, from the harvests of 1999 and 2000, boasts a clear-straw colour. *Pain d'épice* and toast are discernible on a delicate nose, while the well-structured palate leads on to a refreshing finish. (NM)
➤ Jacques Lassaigne, 7, chem. du Coteau, 10300 Montgueux, tel. 03.25.74.84.83, fax 03.25.78.01.47 ☒

P. LASSALLE-HANIN 1990★★

		0.3 ha	2,500	🍾	15–23 €

This 10-ha family estate has devoted one very small *cuvée* to this vintage wine that filled the tasters with enthusiasm. Equal parts black and white grapes, it presents a colour somewhere between old gold and bright amber. Stewed fruits, brioche, vanilla... "This is a gourmet's wine," wrote one taster, "for lovers of old champagne." The **Cuvée de Réserve (11–15 €)**, made from all three champagne grape varieties (35% Pinot Noir, 20% Pinot Meunier, 25% Chardonnay, and 20% reserve wine), obtained one star. It is lemony, complex, delicious. This is a good address to visit for those who wish to explore the natural park of the Montagne de Reims area. (RM)
➤ P. Lassalle-Hanin, 2, rue des Vignes, 51500 Chigny-les-Roses, tel. 03.26.03.40.96,
fax 03.26.03.42.10,
e-mail gaec.lassalle-hanin@wanadoo.fr ☒
🍷 by appt.

LAURENT-GABRIEL

Cuvée Prestige 1993★★

	1er cru	n.c.	2,400		15–23 €

This grower-producer manages a vineyard of less than 3 ha. It was at the very least bold to submit a 1993 wine to the tasting, but the audacity paid off in the form of two stars and a *coup de coeur*. This *cuvée* is composed of four times more Pinot Noir than Chardonnay. The eye is seduced by it from the start, and the nose evokes fruit jelly and stewed fruits with power and elegance. After a gentle attack, there is a slight balsamic note, along with spices and red fruits. Complexity, length and a perfect balance between maturity and freshness make this a rarity among champagnes. (RM)

➥ EARL Laurent-Gabriel, 2, rue des Remparts,
51160 Avenay-Val-d'Or, tel. 03.26.52.32.69,
fax 03.26.59.92.08,
e-mail champagne.laurent-gabriel@voila.fr ☑
☍ by appt.

LAURENT-PERRIER
Ultra-brut Brut Nature★★

	n.c.	n.c.	🍾 ⚭	30–38 €

The reputation of this great house is owed to the wisdom of Bernard de Nonancourt, who assumed the presidency of it in 1949. Founded in 1812, it did not bear the name of Laurent-Perrier until 1881. Its *cuvées* are always rated highly by the Juries. It is well known that wines without *dosage* are difficult to make. This one, which is minerally and fresh, and full of orchard fruits, finds ideal balance thanks to a blend that is richer in Chardonnay than in the Pinots. One star was awarded to the war-horse of the house, the soft, balanced **Brut LP (23–30€)**, which includes slightly more black grapes than white in the blend, another to the **1995**, equal parts Pinot Noir and Chardonnay, as fresh as it is elegant, and still another to the **Cuvée Grand Siècle (46–76 €)**, a comparable blend and a thoroughly lively wine. (NM)

➥ Laurent-Perrier, Dom. de Tours-sur-Marne,
51150 Tours-sur-Marne, tel. 03.26.58.91.22,
fax 03.26.58.95.10 ☑
☍ by appt.

ALAIN LEBOEUF
Blanc de blancs★

	1 ha	5,000	🍾	8–11 €

Colombé-la-Fosse is situated on the Côte des Bars in the Aube district, within the borders of the Haute-Marne *département* and not far from Colombey-les-Deux-Eglises. Alain Leboeuf manages 6.5 ha of vines there, on a domaine that was created by his grandfather in the 1930s. He submitted a blanc de blancs blended from the harvests of 1999 and 2000, which shows generous fruit and equally generous *dosage*. (RM)

➥ Alain Leboeuf, 1, rue du Moulin,
10200 Colombé-la-Fosse, tel. 03.25.27.11.26,
fax 03.25.27.17.23 ☑
☍ by appt.

PAUL LEBRUN
Blanc de blancs Grande Réserve 1996★

	2.75 ha	25,000	🍾	11–15 €

In 1902, Henri Lebrun of Cramant established a vineyard that, a century on, has reached 16.5 ha, planted entirely with Chardonnay. The two champagnes honoured in the *Guide* are thus all blancs de blancs. The Grande Réserve is a product of the harvest of 1996. If its nose appears delicately lemony, the long and well-balanced palate in turn recalls grapefruit. It should be drunk with chicken dishes in pastry. The **1995 (15–23 €)**, with its perceptible *dosage*, was commended for its toasty aromas and its flavours of citrus fruits. (NM)

➥ SA Vignier-Lebrun, 35, rue Nestor-Gaunel,
51530 Cramant, tel. 03.26.57.54.88, fax 03.26.57.90.02 ☑
☍ by appt.

LECLERC-BRIANT
Divine 1995★

	2 ha	15,000	🍾 ⚭	30–38 €

The Leclercs have been based at A since 1664. One of the ancestors, Louis Leclerc, marketed the estate's first bottle in 1872. Today, Pascal Leclerc-Briant cultivates a biodynamic vineyard of 30 ha. The Divine 1990 was crowned with a *coup de coeur* last year. Its composition – equal parts Pinot Noir and Chardonnay – was the same as this 1995 version, a well-balanced, long, ripe wine that is just as noticeably developed, according to some tasters. (NM)

➥ Leclerc-Briant, 67, rue Chaude-Ruelle, BP 108,
51204 Epernay Cedex, tel. 03.26.54.45.33,
fax 03.26.54.49.59, e-mail plb@leclercbriant.com ☑
☍ ev. day 9am–11.30am 1.30pm–5.30pm;
Sat. Sun. by appt.; cl. 5th–25th Aug.

LE GALLAIS
Cuvée du Manoir★★

	n.c.	n.c.	🍾 ⏚	15–23 €

This wine is made from grapes harvested from the walled estate of Boursault. Two châteaux have been built here, this better-known one in the 19th century, the other, almost hidden now, in the 15th century. Cuvée du Manoir is a *rosé de saignée* (from equal measures of both Pinots). Deeply coloured, it smells strongly of Pinot, and is well-structured on the palate. (RM)

➥ Hervé Le Gallais, 2, rue Maurice Gilbert,
51480 Boursault, tel. 03.26.58.63.15, fax 03.26.58.94.55 ☑
☍ by appt.

LEGOUGE-COPIN
Réserve★

	0.5 ha	5,000	🍾 ⚭	11–15 €

This grower-producer manages a vineyard of 4.5 ha in the Verneuil district of the Vallée de la Marne. Its Brut Réserve, like the **1998 (15–23 €)**, strongly favours Pinot Noir (80%). Both obtained one star: the first soft and toasty with evident *dosage*, the second balanced and full, with good structure. (RM)

➥ Legouge-Copin, 6, rue de l'Abbé-Bernard,
51700 Verneuil, tel. 03.26.52.96.89, fax 03.26.51.85.62,
e-mail legouge-copin@free.fr ☑
☍ by appt.

R. ET L. LEGRAS
Blanc de blancs Saint-Vincent 1990★★

	n.c.	12,000	🍾 ⚭	23–30 €

Over two centuries, the Legras family has accumulated a vineyard of 14 ha in the Chouilly district. In recent times, the Saint-Vincent *cuvée* has been the jewel in its crown. The tasters hailed a great champagne from a great vintage, which has reached its maturity without losing any of its freshness. Its fine, lively effervescence is elegant, just like its colour, which does nothing to betray the age of the wine (13 years old already!). On the other hand, the nose is mature and complex, with notes of nuts, cinnamon (astonishingly) and other spices, as well as honey. Rich and full, the palate plays on flavours of crystallized citrus fruits mixed with honey and raisins. Its honeyed length completely convinced the Jury. One star was awarded to the **Blanc de blancs Cuvée Bernard Loiseau**. One taster wrote, "I'm going to buy this immediately". (NM)

➥ R. et L. Legras, 10, rue des Partelaines, 51530 Chouilly,
tel. 03.26.54.50.79, fax 03.26.54.88.74,
e-mail champagne.r.l.legras@wanadoo.fr ☑
☍ by appt.

LEGRAS ET HAAS
Blanc de blancs 1999★

Gd cru	12 ha	10,000	🍾 ⚭	15–23 €

A family that counts seven generations of growers and three generations of winemakers, and today controls a vineyard of 30 ha, submitted this classically fine, floral, well-balanced blanc de blancs. As for the *cuvée* **Tradition (11–15 €)**, a blend of the three champagne grape varieties, of which 50% is Chardonnay, it is another well-balanced, successful champagne with good length. It would make a fine aperitif. (NM)

➥ Legras et Haas, 7, Grande-Rue, 51530 Chouilly,
tel. 03.26.54.92.90, fax 03.26.55.16.78,
e-mail legras-haas@wanadoo.fr ☑
☍ by appt.

LEGUILLETTE-ROMELOT
Cuvée Harmonie★★

	n.c.	3,000	▮ ⚬	15–23 €

Two families based in Charly-sur-Marne since 1650 were linked in 1968, creating a domaine of 7.6 ha. Cuvée Harmonie comes from the harvest of 1998, and consists of 65% Pinot Meunier, 25% Chardonnay and 10% Pinot Noir. Elegant fizz rises through an intense, clear gold wine, which plays on notes of crystallized fruits while maintaining its freshness. (RC)
➔ Leguillette-Romelot, Le Mont-Dorin, 15, rte de Villiers, 02310 Charly-sur-Marne, tel. 03.23.82.03.79, fax 03.23.82.35.34,
e-mail info@champagne-leguillette-romelot.com ▼

LELARGE-PUGEOT 1996★★

	0.8 ha	5,000	▮	15–23 €

The vineyards of this estate are located in the Reims area. It launched its champagne in 1986. This 1996, made from all three champagne grape varieties, is generous and rich, with good vinosity. "A champagne with heart," wrote one taster. One star each was awarded to the **Cuvée Prestige** and the **rosé (11–15 €)**. The first, full and well-balanced, favours Chardonnay (60%); the second, a rosé de noirs made from both Pinots in 1999, is a fine champagne and, while still fresh, is ready to drink now. (RM)
➔ Dominique Lelarge, 30, rue Saint-Vincent, 51390 Vrigny, tel. 03.26.03.69.43, fax 03.26.03.68.93,
e-mail champagnelelarge-pugeot@wanadoo.fr ▼
☲ by appt.

CLAUDE LEMAIRE
Tradition★★

	n.c.	n.c.		11–15 €

Patrice Lemaire took over his father's estate in 1988, and markets some of the champagnes under his own forename. The three champagne grape varieties, including 50% Pinot Meunier, are blended in this harmonious *cuvée*, which is rich in floral notes and yellow fruits. Under the Patrice Lemaire label, the **1997**, a blanc de blancs that passes through wood and does not undergo a malolactic fermentation, is at once vigorous and woody. It was commended. (RM)
➔ Patrice Lemaire, 9, rue Croix-Saint-Jean, 51480 Boursault, tel. 03.26.58.40.58, fax 03.26.52.30.67 ▼
☲ by appt.

R.C. LEMAIRE
Cuvée Trianon★★

	1er cru	4 ha	40,000	▮ ⚬	11–15 €

Here, the sons-in-law have assumed control of the vineyard of a dozen hectares, located in the Vallée de la Marne and run on organic principles. The wines do not go through malolactic fermentation. Cuvée Trianon, 60% Pinot Noir and 40% Chardonnay, shines for its bouquet of citrus fruits and white flowers, its balance and its great length. A commendation went to the **1997 (23–30 €)**, a blanc de blancs matured for eight months in barrel; it is a woody, spicy, toasty wine, vigorous and woody. (RM)
➔ Gilles Tournant, R.C. Lemaire, rue de la Glacière, 51700 Villers-sous-Châtillon, tel. 03.26.58.36.79, fax 03.26.58.39.28, e-mail tournant@clubinternet.fr ▼
☲ by appt.

LEMAIRE RASSELET
Cuvée Tradition★

	4 ha	10,000	▮ ⚬	11–15 €

Françoise Lemaire made these two champagnes from grapes grown on the slopes of the Vallée de la Marne. Her Cuvée Tradition accords the greater part of its blend to Pinot Meunier (70%), supplemented by equal parts Pinot Noir and Chardonnay: floral, fresh and long, it is intended to be drunk as an aperitif. The **Cuvée Sélection 95**, a blend of all three champagne grape varieties in equal measure, is well-structured and powerful. (RM)

➔ EARL Lemaire-Rasselet, 5, rue de la Croix-Saint-Jean, Villesaint, 51480 Boursault, tel. 03.26.58.44.85, fax 03.26.58.09.47,
e-mail champ.lemaire.rasselet@wanadoo.fr ▼
☲ by appt.

LIEBART-REGNIER
Chardonnay★★

	2 ha	4,000	▮ ▥ ⚬	15–23 €

Laurent Liébart relaunched this estate in 1987. He practises a partial vinification under wood. This blanc de blancs non-vintage comes from the harvest of 1998. Characteristically pale, and full of abundant fizz, it offers a nose of white flowers and toast, complex, fresh and fine. The palate opts for the same register, and is well-balanced, firm and long. (RM)
➔ Liébart-Régnier, 6, rue Saint-Vincent, 51700 Baslieux-sous-Châtillon, tel. 03.26.58.11.60, fax 03.26.52.34.60,
e-mail info@champagne-liebart-regnier.com ▼
☲ by appt.

LOCRET-LACHAUD
Cuvée spéciale★

	1er cru	1 ha	9,716	▮	15–23 €

This estate is based at Hauvillers, Dom Pérignon's village, the great-grandfather of the current owner having marketed its first champagnes in 1920. This rosé is born of the three champagne grape varieties, including 40% Chardonnay, harvested in 1999. It offers a charred, minerally, spicy nose, whereas on the palate, body, roundness and fruit are the main qualities. A champagne for gourmets. (RM)
➔ Locret-Lachaud, 40, rue Saint-Vincent, 51160 Hautvillers, tel. 03.26.59.40.20, fax 03.26.59.40.92, e-mail champagne.locret.lachaud@wanadoo.fr ▼
☲ by appt.

GERARD LORIOT
Tradition★

	5.5 ha	42,000	▮	11–15 €

Two attractive champagnes were submitted by Gérard Loriot, who has been director of this estate since 1981. Tradition, a blanc de noirs from Pinot Meunier, blending the harvests of 1999 and 2000, is all crystallized red fruits on the nose, backed up by hazelnuts. Well-balanced and full, this is a rounded champagne of good length. Another star was obtained by the **Sélection**, which is comprised of 60% Chardonnay and 40% Pinot Meunier from 1999, and offers a fine combination of balance and length. (RM)
➔ Gérard Loriot, rue Saint-Vincent, Le Mesnil-le-Huttier, 51700 Festigny, tel. 03.26.58.35.32, fax 03.26.51.93.71 ▼
☲ by appt.

MICHEL LORIOT★

	n.c.	5,000	▮	11–15 €

Festigny, with its 12th-century church, is 5 km from Châtillon-sur-Marne, where the wine landscapes are superb. The Loriots control 6.4 ha of vines. Their rosé is a rosé de noirs, or would be save for the 10% of Chardonnay that supports its 75% Pinot Meunier, with 15% Pinot Noir for colour. It is a champagne with scents of raspberries, blackcurrants and marshmallow, and a light and ethereal palate. The **Réserve Brut**, a Pinot Meunier blanc de noirs from the years 1999 and 2000, turns out to be fruity all the way through the tasting. It received a commendation. Let us also recall the *coup de coeur* obtained by the Michel Loriot 1996 (in the 2001 *Guide*). (RM)
➔ Michel Loriot, 13, rue de Bel-Air, 51700 Festigny, tel. 03.26.58.34.01, fax 03.26.58.03.98,
e-mail info@champagne-michelloriot.com ▼
☲ by appt.

JOSEPH LORIOT-PAGEL
Carte d'or★

	4 ha	30,000	▮	11–15 €

Gérard Loriot started in winemaking in 1931. His son André then developed the company that, in 1974, his grandson baptized Joseph Loriot-Pagel. The estate has vines in four crus of the Vallée de la Marne, as well as in Avize and

Cramant. Carte d'Or contains 85% black grapes, including 65% Pinot Meunier, from the years 1997–2000. A wine of good vinosity, it displays both balance and length. The **Cuvée de Réserve (15–23 €)**, a similar blend but from 1996, has scents of white flowers and pineapple, which lead on to a well-balanced, fruity palate. It won one star. (RM)

☛ Joseph Loriot, 33, rue de la République, 51700 Festigny, tel. 03.26.58.33.53, fax 03.26.58.05.37 ☑

☖ by appt.

DE LOZEY
Prestige★★

	12 ha	6,000	☖ ⬩	15–23 €

Georges and Philippe Cheurlin run this négociant house at Celles-sur-Ource with panache. Their Brut Prestige, half Pinot Noir and half Chardonnay from 1996, offers aromas of flowers, *pain d'épice* and orange, and expresses itself with freshness and elegance on a well-balanced palate. The **rosé**, which is a rosé de noirs, is fruity, pulpy, unctuous and tender, and received one star. (NM)

☛ de Lozey, 72, Grande-Rue, BP 3, 10110 Celles-sur-Ource, tel. 03.25.38.51.34, fax 03.25.38.54.80, e-mail de.lozey@wanadoo.fr ☑

☖ by appt.

☛ Philippe Cheurlin

MAILLY GRAND CRU
Brut Réserve★★

Gd cru	n.c.	300,000	☖ ⬩	15–23 €

Only two grape varieties enter the blends of this cooperative located in the grand cru village of Mailly: Pinot Noir and Chardonnay. The first constitutes 75% of this *cuvée*; it makes its presence felt on both the nose and palate, its characteristics underpinning the lively robustness of the attack, and contributing to the richness, finesse and length of the wine. The **Blanc de Noirs** and the **rosé (23–30 €)** were both commended. The first is fruity, complex, rich and long, while the second gives the lion's share of its blend over to Pinot Noir (90%), and presents a fresh, youthful profile, with good length. A final commendation goes to the *cuvée* **L'Intemporelle 96 (30–38 €)**, made up of 60% Pinot Noir and 40% Chardonnay: it is a harmonious wine that would accompany refined dishes, such as a steamed turbot with aromatic seasonings. (CM)

☛ Mailly Grand Cru, 28, rue de la Libération, 51500 Mailly-Champagne, tel. 03.26.49.41.10, fax 03.26.49.42.27, e-mail contact@champagne-mailly.com ☑

☖ by appt.

B. MALLOL-GANTOIS
Blanc de blancs Grande Réserve★

Gd cru	6.8 ha	3,500	☖	11–15 €

The 7 ha of vines belonging to this house are distributed between the grand cru villages of Cramant and Chouilly. This blanc de blancs from the harvests of 1996 and 1997 delivers up rich and elegant aromas, which are prolonged on its full-bodied palate. One taster recommended trying it with chocolate. (RM)

☛ Bernard Mallol, 290, rue du Gal-de-Gaulle, 51530 Cramant, tel. 03.26.57.96.14, fax 03.26.59.22.57 ☑

☖ by appt.

HENRI MANDOIS
Cuvée de réserve★★

	20 ha	180,000	☖ ⬩	15–23 €

In the Côte des Blancs, 3 km to the south of Epernay, the village of Pierry was developed by the Benedictine monks who practised viticulture here. In the 17th century, one Brother Oudart, like the more famous Dom Pérignon, was another who contributed to the birth of champagne. This Cuvée de Réserve, a golden-yellow wine with green highlights, is worthy of the prestigious history of the village. Containing as much Chardonnay as Pinot Meunier, supplemented by 20% Pinot Noir, it leaves behind memories of its biscuity, honeyed aromas, while also revealing great balance and complexity. The **Blanc de Blancs 98 Premier Cru** and the **rosé** each obtained one star. The first is rounded, powerful and quite

long; the second is fine and fresh, and mostly Chardonnay (60%). (NM)

☛ Henri Mandois, 66, rue du Gal-de-Gaulle, BP 9, 51130 Pierry, tel. 03.26.54.03.18, fax 03.26.51.53.66, e-mail info@champagne-mandois.fr ☑

☖ by appt.

TRADITION DE MANSARD
Grande Cuvée★

	n.c.	100,000	☖ ⬩	11–15 €

The label is illustrated, like a textbook, with the different stages of champagne production, from the vine-growing up to the cellaring of the wines. It is a book this house has clearly studied well, judging by this half-Pinot Noir half-Chardonnay *cuvée* from the harvests of 1997 and 1998. All flowers and citrus fruits on the nose, it shows a harmonious, creamy character on the palate. The **Brut Premier Cru**, 60% Pinot Noir and 40% Chardonnay from the 1998 harvest, was singled out for its straightforwardness, freshness and balance. (NM)

☛ Mansard-Baillet, 14, rue Chaude-Ruelle, 51200 Epernay, tel. 03.26.54.18.55, fax 03.26.51.99.50 ☑

☖ by appt.

MARGUET-BONNERAVE
Réserve★

Gd cru	4 ha	40,000	☖ ⬙ ⬩	11–15 €

There are two theories as to the origin of the name of the grand cru village of Ambonnay. It could refer to a royal forest (*le bonne haye*), or be homage to a Roman officer named Amboniacus who planted vines on these slopes. Today, the house of Marguet-Bonnerave, which also owns plots in the grands crus of Bouzy and Mailly, flies the Ambonnay flag high with this well-balanced Réserve, fresh and long with flavours of orchard fruits. It is composed of 60% Pinot Noir and 40% Chardonnay. (RM)

☛ Marguet-Bonnerave, 14, rue de Bouzy, 51150 Ambonnay, tel. 03.26.57.01.08, fax 03.26.57.09.98, e-mail benoit@champagne-bonnerave.com ☑

☖ by appt.

MARQUIS DE LA FAYETTE★

1er cru	n.c.	n.c.		15–23 €

This house has been engaged, thanks to the efforts of Hermione La Fayette, in the rebuilding of the *Liberty*, the frigate on which General La Fayette left for America in 1780. Although the label does not mention it, this Premier Cru is a blanc de blancs. It has all the characteristics of such wines: a golden colour with light highlights, floral scents, and a fine palate with balance and length. A champagne for food. (NM)

☛ SA Pierrel et Associés, 26, rue Henri-Dunant, 51200 Epernay, tel. 03.26.51.00.90, fax 03.26.51.69.40, e-mail champagne@pierrel.fr ☑

☖ by appt.

MARQUIS DE POMEREUIL
Cuvée des Fondateurs★

	2 ha	17,392	☖ ⬩	15–23 €

The Riceys cooperative was founded in 1922, and launched its Marquis de Pomereuil brand in 1975. On the nose, this *brut* champagne makes one think of stone fruits such as apricots and white peaches. It develops on the palate with softness and freshness, leaving a lasting impression of complexity. (CM)

☛ Cave coop. des Riceys, 31, rte de Gye, 10340 Les Riceys, tel. 03.25.29.30.08, fax 03.25.38.59.86, e-mail marquis.de.pomereuil@hexanet.fr ☑

☖ ev. day except Sun. 8.30am–12 noon 2pm–6pm

MARQUIS DE SADE
Blanc de blancs★★

	7 ha	n.c.	☖ ⬩	15–23 €

Marquis de Sade is one of the brands of Michel Gonet, who cultivates 40 ha of vines in the Côte des Blancs, the Sézannais and the Aube. This pale gold, floral, brioche-like Blanc de Blancs charmed by its finesse, its complexity and its length. The **rosé**, composed exclusively of Pinot Noir, was also commended: very clear in colour, it has richness on the palate and a vinosity that does nothing to undermine its freshness. (RM)

⌕ SCEV Michel Gonet, 196, av. Jean-Jaurès, 51190 Avize, tel. 03.26.57.50.56, fax 03.26.57.91.98, e-mail champagne.gonet@wanadoo.fr ☑ ▤ ▥
⌕ by appt.

G.H. MARTEL & CO
Prestige★

	20 ha	300,000	▐ ⚲	15–23 €

Another brand of the Rapeneau family, taken over in 1970 when they had just celebrated their 100th anniversary, the Martel house boasts a vineyard of 80 ha. Its Prestige *cuvée* is composed of 70% Pinot Noir and 30% Chardonnay from the years 1998 and 1999. The nose has rather discreet aromas of peach, whereas the palate offers ready proof of roundness, richness and length. The **Premier Cru**, a blend of 60% Pinot Noir and 40% Chardonnay harvested in 1999, has balance and length. It was commended, as was the **Cuvée Victoire** (34% Pinot Noir and 66% Chardonnay, from 1996), a rounded wine still in the course of development. (NM)
⌕ G.H. Martel, 69, av. de Champagne, BP 1011, 51318 Epernay Cedex, tel. 03.26.51.06.33, fax 03.26.54.41.52, e-mail contact@champagnemartel.com ☑
⌕ C. Rapeneau

THIERRY MASSIN 1997★

	n.c.	5,300	▐	15–23 €

This 1997 is predominantly Pinot Noir (75%), assisted by Chardonnay. Its lemony grapefruit bouquet leads on to a palate that is both fresh and creamy, with balance and elegance. The Jury also appreciated its pale-gold, bright appearance. (RM)
⌕ Thierry Massin, 6, rte des Deux-Bar, 10110 Ville-sur-Arce, tel. 03.25.38.74.01, fax 03.25.38.79.10, e-mail champagne.thierry.massin@wanadoo.fr ☑
⌕ ev. day except Sat. Sun. 9am–12 noon 1.30pm–6.30pm

REMY MASSIN ET FILS 1996★★

	1 ha	6,008	▐ ⚲	15–23 €

There is still a beautiful old laundry building at Ville-sur-Arce on the Côte des Bars, which is fully operational again thanks to the efforts of some of the women of the village. There is also a vineyard estate whose wine was decorated with a *coup de coeur* by the tasters. This 1996 is of classic composition (40% Pinot Noir and 60% Chardonnay), but of singular character: a light nose of anise, lemongrass and citrus fruits, perfect balance, notable elegance, and then a lively finish. A wine that will give pleasure both today and tomorrow. (RM)
⌕ Rémy Massin et Fils, 34, Grande-Rue, 10110 Ville-sur-Arce, tel. 03.25.38.74.09, fax 03.25.38.77.67, e-mail remy.massin.fils@wanadoo.fr ☑ ▥
⌕ ev. day 9am–12 noon 2pm–6.30pm; Sat. Sun. by appt.

LOUIS MASSING
Blanc de Blancs★

	Gd cru	3 ha	15,000	▐ ⚲	15–23 €

This Grand Cru comes from the harvest of 1999. Under its golden colour with green highlights, one finds scents of exotic and citrus fruits, then a creamy, brioche-like feel on the palate. A very attractive champagne that will fully reward you in three years' time. (NM)

⌕ SA Deregard-Massing, RD 9, 51190 Avize, tel. 03.26.57.52.92, fax 03.26.57.78.23, e-mail jbmoroy.champagnederegard@wanadoo.fr ☑
⌕ by appt.

MATHIEU-PRINCET★

	1er cru	6 ha	50,000	▐	11–15 €

Not far from Epernay, the village of Grauves is popular with hang-gliders on account of its cliff. Oenophiles know it as a premier cru for champagne. They will find a beautiful illustration of what it can do in this classic *brut*, which combines 60% Chardonnay with 40% Pinot Noir. The mineral and floral bouquet opens gradually, while honeyed, spicy flavours stretch out over the palate. Another star distinguished the rosé **Premier Cru** (50% Chardonnay and 38% Pinot Noir, completed by 12% red wine), because under its black and red fruit accents, it is rich, well-balanced and delicious. (RM)
⌕ SARL Mathieu-Princet, 16, rue Bruyère, 51190 Grauves, tel. 03.26.59.73.72, fax 03.26.59.77.75, e-mail mathieu.princet@cder.fr ☑
⌕ by appt.

PASCAL MAZET 1995★

	1er cru	2 ha	1,400	▐ ▥	11–15 €

Equal shares of Pinot Meunier and Pinot Noir, supplemented by 40% Chardonnay, make up this intensely aromatic champagne with its pale-gold colour, its scents of orchard fruits, and its balanced vinosity. The **Cuvée Tradition** (30% Chardonnay, 50% Pinot Meunier and 20% Pinot Noir, from the harvests of 1997 and 1998) was also singled out: it demonstrates a fine balance between structure and fruitiness. (RM)
⌕ Pascal Mazet, 8, rue des Carrières, 51500 Chigny-les-Roses, tel. 03.26.03.41.13, fax 03.26.03.41.74, e-mail champagne.mazet@free.fr ☑
⌕ by appt.

GUY MEA★★

	1er cru	4 ha	n.c.	▐	11–15 €

Louvois is best known for the château once wished by Mansart for Louis XIV's Chief Minister, but the village also has around 30 ha of vines. This Guy Méa champagne is a blend of the harvests of 1998–2000, 65% Pinot Noir and 35% Chardonnay, which ensures remarkable balance and length. An impression of elegance is given by its golden colour, its very fine nose and its freshness on the palate. To be drunk with grilled fish. (RM)
⌕ Guy Méa, SCE La Voie des loups, 1, rue de l'Eglise, 51150 Louvois, tel. 03.26.57.03.42, fax 03.26.57.66.44 ☑
⌕ by appt.

LE MESNIL
Blanc de blancs Sublime 1997★★

	Gd cru	1 ha	9,160	▐ ⚲	15–23 €

This cooperative only vinifies grapes gathered in the village of Mesnil-sur-Oger, classified as grand cru. Its champagnes are thus solely blancs de blancs. Is this a "sublime" *cuvée*, as its name suggests? It is certainly remarkable. Made from the harvests of southeast-facing plots, it does not undergo malolactic fermentation, which allows it to show all its charming freshness. The compliments accumulate: "Creamy, mineral, complex, fine substance – a delicious wine". Serve it with scallops. A commendation also went to the **Réserve Sélection 98**, a well-balanced, structured and full-bodied wine. (CM)
⌕ Le Mesnil, 19, rue Charpentier-Laurain, BP 17, 51190 Le Mesnil-sur-Oger, tel. 03.26.57.53.23, fax 03.26.57.79.54, e-mail lemesnil@wanadoo.fr ☑
⌕ Mon.-Thu. 8am–12 noon 1.30pm–5pm; Fri., Sat. Sun. by appt.; cl. Aug.

G. MICHEL
Tradition 1989★

		3 ha	25,000	▐ ⚲	15–23 €

Chardonnay and Pinot Meunier comprise equal parts of this champagne which, even if it has reached its peak, has not lost anything of its freshness thanks to a light *dosage*. It has achieved fine balance with notes of honey, crystallized fruits and some nice floral touches. A complex and harmonious wine. The **Brut Réserve (11–15 €)**, from the Guy Michel et Fils brand is born of 50% Pinot Meunier, 30% Chardonnay and 20% Pinot Noir from 1999, and was commended for its appetizing freshness. (RM)

☎ G. Michel, 31, rue du Prieuré, 51530 Moussy,
tel. 03.26.54.03.17, fax 03.26.58.15.84 ☑
⊺ by appt.

J. B. MICHEL
Cuvée blanche★

	7 ha	50,000	▤	11–15 €

This estate comprises 14 ha of vines distributed among 35 plots, including just over one-tenth of a hectare cultivated *en foule* (that is to say, with all the grape varieties blended together). Bruno Michel makes 40% of his wines in barrel. Pinot Meunier (60%) and Chardonnay (40%), from the years 1998 and 1999, are blended in this well-built, densely textured *cuvée* of great length, of which the subtle aromas evoke stone fruits. Another star was awarded to the **Blanc de Blancs Cuvée de la Terre (15–23 €)** from the harvests of 1998 and 1999, which underwent a partial wood maturation of twelve months. This one turns out to be powerful and full, rich and fresh at the same time, and ready to accompany either a crustacean or a white-meat dish with a cream sauce. (RM)

☎ Bruno Michel, 4, allée de la Vieille-Ferme, 51530 Pierry,
tel. 03.26.55.10.54, fax 03.26.54.75.77,
e-mail champagne.j.b.michel@cder.fr ☑
⊺ by appt.

PAUL MICHEL★

● 1er cru	1 ha	7,000	▤	15–23 €

Cuis, on the Côte des Blancs, has a pretty 12th century church that is a classified Historic Monument. In this premier cru village, Philippe and Denis Michel have produced a rosé of onion-skin colour, marked by a scent of kirsch. It is a champagne at once fresh and rounded that you will be able to drink over the course of the next two years. (RM)

☎ Paul Michel, 20, Grande-Rue, 51530 Cuis,
tel. 03.26.59.79.77, fax 03.26.59.72.12 ☑
⊺ ev. day except Sat. Sun. 9am–12 noon 2pm–5pm; cl. Aug.

JOSE MICHEL & FILS
Spécial Club 1996★

	1 ha	7,260	▤	15–23 €

On the hillsides to the south of Epernay, Moussy is surrounded by vines. A small river, the Cubry, runs through it, adding to its charm. This special vintage *cuvée* contains equal shares of Pinot Meunier and Chardonnay, bringing much finesse to a well-balanced and long champagne. From its golden depths emerge pleasant notes of bread and brioche. (RM)

☎ José Michel et Fils, 14, rue Prélot, 51530 Moussy,
tel. 03.26.54.04.69, fax 03.26.55.37.12 ☑
⊺ by appt.

CHARLES MIGNON
Grand Rosé Tête de cuvée★

	n.c.	n.c.	▤ ♦	15–23 €

As an aperitif, certainly, but also with a gratin of red fruits, this Grand Rosé will seduce you with its brilliant colour, somewhere between grey and orange, and with its subtly evocative nose of roses. It is lengthy, distinguished palate is dominated by flavours of red berries. The **Brut Prestige de Pierre Mignon (11–15 €)** was singled out for its aromas of honey and yellow fruits, and for its almondy flavours. The same applies to the **Léon Launois Blue Prestige**, another of this house's brands; it is a blanc de blancs Grand Cru (from Mesnil-sur-Oger), a floral-scented wine of good vinosity, combining roundness and freshness. (NM)

☎ Charles Mignon, 7, rue Joliot-Curie, 51200 Epernay,
tel. 03.26.58.33.33, fax 03.26.51.54.10,
e-mail bmignon@champagne-mignon.fr ☑
⊺ by appt.

MOET ET CHANDON
Dom Pérignon 1995★★

	n.c.	n.c.	▤	+76 €

The house of Moët & Chandon, founded in 1743, proprietor of an immense vineyard of fine quality and member of the

LVMH group, needs no introduction. Its most celebrated special *cuvée* comes in both white and rosé. Both colours shine with two stars in this edition. The Dom Pérignon white, a clear gold sparkling with green highlights, offers an intense nose suggesting grilled toast initially, and then flowers. Its full palate benefits from a beautiful balance of richness and freshness, the flavours stretching lengthily on. A dish of turbot with a sauce will set its qualities off to their best advantage. The **Dom Pérignon rosé 93** is not at all showing its age: it offers up notes of brioche, before extending, on a powerful palate, into its full range of soft fruit flavours. One to be saved for special occasions. (NM)

☎ Moët et Chandon, 20, av. de Champagne,
51200 Epernay, tel. 03.26.51.20.00, fax 03.26.54.84.23 ☑
⊺ ev. day 9.30am–11.30am 2pm–4.30pm; groups by appt.

MOET ET CHANDON
Vintage 1996★★

	n.c.	n.c.	▤	30–38 €

"The 1996 is the 64th vintage from Moët & Chandon. Our first was the 1842", announces the label. The complexity of this pale-gold champagne expresses itself in its intense aromatic range, as well as on the elegant palate, which is both rounded and fresh – complete harmony. The **Brut Impérial (23–30 €)** obtained one star for its flawless balance and its finesse. (NM)

☎ Moët et Chandon, 20, av. de Champagne,
51200 Epernay, tel. 03.26.51.20.00, fax 03.26.54.84.23 ☑
⊺ ev. day 9.30am–11.30am 2pm–4.30pm; groups by appt.

PIERRE MONCUIT
Blanc de blancs Cuvée Hugues de Coulmet★

	4 ha	20,000	▤	11–15 €

The wines of Nicole and Yves Moncuit cross continents and oceans to appear on the most remote tables, as far away as Australia. Will this *cuvée* make the voyage? Powerful and lemony on the nose, it still seems very fresh, full of youth. Let it age a little, and it will gain in harmony. Also singled out was the **Blanc de Blancs Grand Cru 95 (15–23 €)**: its old-gold appearance is a sign of development that is confirmed on both the nose and palate. (RM)

☎ Pierre Moncuit, 11, rue Persault-Maheu, 51190 Le Mesnil-sur-Oger, tel. 03.26.57.52.65, fax 03.26.57.97.89 ☑
⊺ by appt.

MONTAUDON★

	100 ha	750,000	▤ ♦	11–15 €

This house, which is located in the heart of Reims, boasts cellars carved out of the chalk and a grape basket that dates back to the 17th century. Its brut non-vintage, a blend of 50% Pinot Noir, 25% Chardonnay and 25% Pinot Meunier, harvested in 1998, 1999 and 2000, offers up notes of violets and pears. These flavours are prolonged lengthily on the palate, against a background of good vinosity. (NM)

☎ Montaudon, 6, rue Ponsardin, BP 2742, 51100 Reims,
tel. 03.26.79.01.01, fax 03.26.47.88.82,
e-mail info@champagnemontaudon.com ☑
⊺ by appt.

RONALD MOREAU
Blanc de blancs★

	1.14 ha	3,800	▤	11–15 €

Ronald Moreau is based at Chouilly, a Côte des Blancs grand cru. His fresh, floral blanc de blancs shows good balance, and tells the same story from start to finish. A champagne for a pleasant time among friends. (RM)

☎ Ronald Moreau, 14 bis, rue du Moulin, 51530 Chouilly,
tel. 03.26.59.77.28 ☑

MORIZE PERE & FILS 1996★★

	2 ha	9,134	▤	15–23 €

One kilometre from the house of Morize and its 12th century wine cellars, you can make a stop at the château of Ricey-Bas (which dates from the 19th century) and take a walk in its park. You will also be able to taste this 1996, made from 90% Chardonnay. Its aromas of brioche and its fresh, full, well-balanced palate delighted the Jury. One star went to the **Brut rosé (11–15 €)**, which is made solely from Pinot Noir in

CHAMPAGNE

the year 2000. Evocative of crystallized fruits, it is a rounded and long champagne. (RM)
☛ Morize Père et Fils, 122, rue du Gal-de-Gaulle, 10340 Les Riceys, tel. 03.25.29.30.02, fax 03.25.38.20.22 ☑
☉ by appt.

CORINNE MOUTARD
Tradition★★

	3 ha	20,000	☒ ♦	8–11 €

At Polissy in the Aube, the river Laignes mingles with the waters of the Seine in a pretty, vinous landscape. Formerly, a small train ploughed a furrow through the two valleys. The line was built in the late 19th century, to give work to those wine-growers whose livelihoods had been ruined by devastating frosts. Time has passed, and today Corinne Moutard blends 70% of the Pinots Noir and Meunier with 30% Chardonnay to compose this straw-yellow champagne, enlivened by its persistent streams of bubbles. Great finesse emanates from its mineral aromas, and also distinguishes its fine balance of richness and freshness. Save this bottle for a plate of richly dressed seafood. (NM)
☛ Corinne Moutard, 51, Grande-Rue, 10110 Polisy, tel. 03.25.38.52.47, fax 03.25.29.37.46, e-mail champagnecorinnemoutard@wanadoo.fr ☑ ⌂
☉ by appt.

JEAN MOUTARDIER
Carte d'Or★

	23 ha	240,000	☒ ♦	11–15 €

This house was founded in 1926. Elisabeth Moutardier runs it today with her British husband, Jonathan Saxby, one of the rare Englishmen to be involved in the production of champagne. Carte d'Or pays homage to Pinot Meunier (90%), from 1997 to 2000. It has powerful aromas of spiced brioche and citrus fruits, and is full and generous on the palate. Some light development is perceptible. (NM)
☛ Jean Moutardier, chem. des Ruelles, 51210 Le Breuil, tel. 03.26.59.21.09, fax 03.26.59.21.25, e-mail moutardi@ebc.net ☑
☉ by appt.

MOUTARD PERE ET FILS
Extra-brut★★

	2,9 ha	20,000	☒	15–23 €

Buxeuil in the Aube, about 20 km from the Orient forest and its ornithologically rich lake-reservoirs, is dedicated to viticulture. The Moutards control 20 ha of vines there, and produce this half-Chardonnay half-Pinot Noir Extra-Brut, whose pale-gold colour shines with green highlights. Its intense floral aromas carry on through to a long finish on a clean, rounded and elegant palate. The **Grande Réserve (11–15 €)** shines out with one star for its complex aromatic range and its lemony flavours, which would go especially well with a fish dish. Equally successful was the **rosé Prestige** (45% Chardonnay, 40% Pinot Noir and 15% Coteaux-Champenois rouge), which leaves an impression of finesse and balance. (NM)
☛ SARL Moutard-Diligent, 6, rue des Ponts, BP 1, 10110 Buxeuil, tel. 03.25.38.50.73, fax 03.25.38.57.72, e-mail champagne.moutard@wanadoo.fr ☑
☉ by appt.

PH. MOUZON-LEROUX
Prestige★★

Gd cru	n.c.	6,500	☒ ♦	11–15 €

Wines from this house do not go through malolactic fermentation. The Prestige brut is composed of 60% Chardonnay and 40% Pinot Noir, from the years 1996 and 1997. Pale yellow with bright highlights, adorned with a fine mousse, it has developed an elegant bouquet of white flowers and citrus fruits. A pleasing freshness contributes to the harmony of this long-lasting champagne. Quite as remarkable is the **Blanc de Blancs Grand Cru 96 (15–23 €)**, which is powerful, fresh and well-balanced. The **Cuvée Prestige Grand Cru 96 (15–23 €)**, half and half Chardonnay and Pinot Noir, deserved one star for its distinctiveness. (RM)

☛ EARL Mouzon-Leroux, 16, rue Basse-des-Carrières, 51380 Verzy, tel. 03.26.97.96.68, fax 03.26.97.97.67, e-mail champagne-mouzon-leroux@wanadoo.fr ☑
☉ by appt.

G.H. MUMM
Cordon rouge★

	750 ha	5,000,000	☒ ♦	23–30 €

Founded in 1827 by German négociants, Mumm went through several changes of ownership until Allied Domecq acquired it in 2000. Five million bottles of Cordon Rouge are produced each year. Made from 45% Pinot Noir, 30% Chardonnay and 25% Pinot Meunier, this pale-gold wine displays a very fresh bouquet that is echoed well on the long and well-balanced palate. The **Mumm Grand Cru**, richer in Pinot Noir (58%) than Chardonnay, was also singled out. It is distinguished by its structure and its liveliness. (NM)
☛ G.-H. Mumm et Cie, 29, rue du Champ-de-Mars, 51100 Reims, tel. 03.26.49.59.69, fax 03.26.40.46.13, e-mail mumm@mumm.fr ☑
☉ by appt.
☛ Allied Domecq

NAPOLEON 1992★★

	n.c.	n.c.		23–30 €

The house of Ch. and A. Prieur, created in 1825, sells its champagnes under the Napoléon brand. The wines of 1992 were only rarely made into vintage wine, but this limpid, light-gold champagne has reached its peak: balanced, rounded, long, it has gained in complexity and offers flavours of stewed fruits and prunes. The **rosé (15–23 €)** earned a special mention for its spicy aromas, its softness and its vinosity. Serve it with food. (NM)
☛ SARL Ch. et A. Prieur, 2, rue de Villers-aux-Bois, 51130 Vertus, tel. 03.26.52.11.74, fax 03.26.52.29.10, e-mail prieur-napoleon@wanadoo.fr ☑
☉ by appt.

CHARLES ORBAN
Carte blanche★

	5 ha	60,000	☒ ♦	11–15 €

Based at Troissy in the Vallée de la Marne, the house of Charles Orban falls under the aegis of the Rapeneau company. Carte Blanche is in fact a blanc de noirs, favouring the Pinot Meunier grape (80%). An aroma of quince announces some light development, while the palate charms with its roundness and balance. The citrussy **Carte Noire** calls on all three champagne grape varieties (including 50% Pinot Meunier). It was commended alongside the **Blanc de Blancs Carte d'Or**, which is all toasted bread, nuts, honey and brioche. (RM)
☛ Charles Orban, 44, rte de Paris, 51700 Troissy, tel. 03.26.52.70.05, fax 03.26.52.74.66 ☑
☉ ev. day except Sun. Mon. 10.30am–6.30pm
☛ Rapeneau

LUCIEN ORBAN
Cuvée de réserve Carte d'or★

	1 ha	5,000		11–15 €

This Cuvée de Réserve is a blanc de noirs (with 80% Pinot Meunier) from the harvests of 1998 and 1999, which does not undergo malolactic fermentation. It has a fresh, mineral aspect with scents of lime. The **rosé** – a rosé de noirs (80% Pinot Meunier and 20% Pinot Noir) from the years 2000 and 2001 – was commended. Within its deep colour are hidden aromas of blackcurrants and blackberries, and more vanillary fruit flavours are strongly perceptible on the palate. (RM)
☛ Hervé Orban, 8, rue du Gal-de-Gaulle, 51700 Cuisles, tel. 03.26.58.10.51, fax 03.26.52.84.82 ☑ ⌂
☉ by appt.

OUDINOT★

	n.c.	80,000	☒ ♦	15–23 €

The house of Oudinot, founded in 1889, was taken over in the early 1980s by the Trouillard family, also owners of champagnes Jeanmaire and Beaumet. This rosé de noirs (70% Pinot Noir and 30% Pinot Meunier), with its strong orangey-pink colour, offers up scents of raspberries, a sure sign of its youth. Its meaty, fruity palate testifies to its robust constitution. The **Cuvée Blanc de Blancs**, as shy on the nose as it is on the palate, earned a commendation for its balance. (NM)

🐦 Oudinot, Ch. Malakoff, 3, rue Malakoff, 51207 Epernay, tel. 03.26.59.50.10, fax 03.26.54.78.52, e-mail contact@chateau-malakoff.com
🐦 J. Trouillard

BRUNO PAILLARD
Première Cuvée★★

	n.c.	n.c.	🍾 ⊞ ⬥	15–23 €

The talented Bruno Paillard founded this house in 1981, with the intention of making only top-of-the-range champagnes. Each bottle specifies the date of its disgorgement. The results demonstrate the extent of the ambition: the brand's flagship Première Cuvée charmed the tasters with its biscuity roundness, its elegance and its balance. It is made from the three champagne grape varieties in the years 1998 and 1999 (45% Pinot Noir, 33% Chardonnay and 22% Pinot Meunier), supplemented by reserve wines. Another two stars were won by the top wine, **NPU 1990 (+76 €)**, composed of 50% Chardonnay and 50% Pinot Noir from seven grands crus, and vinified in barrel. This one elicited the admiration of the Jury because it has not lost anything of its freshness, despite having reached its peak. Toasty, complex and long, this is a great champagne. One star was awarded to the long and fruity **Première Cuvée rosé (23–30 €)**, which favours Pinot Noir (85%) from the years 1999 and 2000. Lastly, the **Réserve Privée de Chardonnay (23–30 €)** – from the harvest of 1997, bolstered by a proportion of reserve wines – was also judged very successful, on account of its balance and its floral, honeyed character. (NM)

🐦 Bruno Paillard, 1, av. de Champagne, 51100 Reims, tel. 03.26.36.20.22, fax 03.26.36.57.72, e-mail brunopaillard@aol.com ☑
🍷 by appt.

PANNIER 1997★

	n.c.	18,960	🍾 ⬥	15–23 €

Founded in the late 19th century by Louis-Eugène Pannier, this house was taken over in 1971 by a cooperative from Château-Thierry owning 600 ha of vines. Its cellars were dug out in the 12th century during the building of certain monuments in the region. The 1997 vintage, a blend of 45% Chardonnay, 35% Pinot Noir and 20% Pinot Meunier, is characterized by lovely roundness and softness, as well as its yellow hue and green highlights. Its scents of citrus fruits and flowers, sustained by buttery notes, leave a favourable impression. (CM)

🐦 SCVM Covama, 25, rue Roger-Catillon, BP 55, 02403 Château-Thierry Cedex, tel. 03.23.69.51.30, fax 03.23.69.51.31, e-mail champagnepannier@champagnepannier.com ☑
🍷 by appt.

PASCAL-DELETTE
Cuvée Prestige 1997★

	1.67 ha	15,360	🍾	11–15 €

Recently, Yves Pascal has opened guest rooms at the château in Cuisles that he acquired in 2000, 3 km from his cellars and his vineyard of 6 ha. He has succeeded with this difficult vintage by blending as much Pinot Meunier as Chardonnay, supplemented by 20% Pinot Noir. It is a classic champagne, fresh, floral and well-balanced, with a beautiful golden-yellow tint that shows through with green highlights. Drink it as an aperitif or with first courses. Marked by the Pinot Meunier, the **Cuvée de Réserve 99**, a blanc de noirs full of white flowers and citrus fruits, and with appreciable *dosage*, received a commendation. (RM)

🐦 Pascal-Delette, 48, rue Valentine-Régnier, 51700 Baslieux-sous-Châtillon, tel. 03.26.58.11.35, fax 03.26.57.11.93 ☑ ⌂
🍷 ev. day 8am–12.30pm 2pm–7pm

DENIS PATOUX★★

	n.c.	n.c.	🍾 ⬥	11–15 €

Although the estate is more than a century old, it was only in 1945 that the grandfather of the present owner launched out into champagne production. Since that time,

the vineyard has steadily increased. This brut non-vintage is almost a blanc de noirs (80% Pinot Meunier, and only 5% Chardonnay). Its weight, its generosity and its complexity were appreciated by the Jury, as was its intense golden-yellow colour, and its attractive flavour range of ripe citrus fruits, nuts and butter. (RM)

🐦 Denis Patoux, 1, rue Bailly, 51700 Vandières, tel. 03.26.58.36.34, fax 03.26.59.16.10 ☑
🍷 by appt.

PEHU-SIMONET
Cuvée spéciale★★

	Gd cru	0.5 ha	3,000	🍾 ⊞	11–15 €

A cherry clafoutis or strawberry sorbet would be the best accompaniments for this Grand Cru rosé – there are not many of those about – which has not undergone malolactic fermentation. Wines from 1993, 1998, 1999 and 2000 all play their parts in it, in the proportions of 80% Pinot Noir and 20% Chardonnay. Beneath its orangey-pink colour, the marriage of red berries and citrus fruits succeeds perfectly, and is lastingly prolonged on the robustly constituted palate. (RM)

🐦 GAEC Les Grands Terroirs Pehu, 7, rue de la Gare, BP 22, 51360 Verzenay, tel. 03.26.49.43.20, fax 03.26.49.45.06 ☑
🍷 by appt.

JEAN PERNET
Tradition★★

	8 ha	35,000	🍾 ⬥	11–15 €

Frédéric Christophe, director of the house of Jean Pernet in Mesnil-sur-Oger, presents a *brut* non-vintage resulting from 50% Pinot Noir, 40% Chardonnay and 10% Meunier from the years 1999 and 2000. Its nose of honeysuckle, hawthorn, tangerine and acacia honey entices, and the seduction continues on the palate, with a clean attack, pleasant freshness and good length of flavour. (NM)

🐦 Jean Pernet, 6, rue de la Brèche-d'Oger, 51190 Le Mesnil-sur-Oger, tel. 03.26.57.54.24, fax 03.26.57.96.98, e-mail champagne.pernet@wanadoo.fr ☑
🍷 by appt.
🐦 Frédéric Christophe

PERNET-LEBRUN
Cuvée d'Argent-Sol★

	n.c.	5,000	🍾	11–15 €

From the village of Mancy, one can enjoy panoramic views of the Epernay valley. This pale gold *cuvée*, from the harvest of 1999, comprises as much Chardonnay as Pinot Meunier. The nose evokes not just brioche, but also white flowers and acacia honey. Its full, winey, well-balanced palate fits it to sit at the table in the company of a sauced fish dish. The **Blanc de Blancs Grand Cru (15–23 €)**, from the harvest of 1999, also obtained a star, showing itself to be rich, structured and long beneath its spicy accents. (RM)

🐦 Pernet-Lebrun, Ancien-Moulin, 51530 Mancy, tel. 03.26.59.71.63, fax 03.26.57.10.42 ☑
🍷 by appt.

JOSEPH PERRIER
Cuvée royale 1996★

	n.c.	80,000	🍾 ⬥	23–30 €

This house, founded in 1825, was briefly the property of Laurent-Perrier before Alain Thiénot acquired it. The 1996

CHAMPAGNE

(49% Chardonnay, 43% Pinot Noir and 8% Pinot Meunier) is evocative of red berries, has good length and leaves an impression of freshness on the palate. The **Cuvée Joséphine (46–76 €)**, a blend of 45% Chardonnay and 55% Pinot Noir, was also judged very successful: its aromas of fruit compote and beeswax, underpinned by mint, announce a soft and sensual palate. (NM)

➦ SA Joseph Perrier, 69, av. de Paris, BP 31,
51000 Châlons-en-Champagne, tel. 03.26.68.29.51,
fax 03.26.70.57.16, e-mail josephperrier@wanadoo.fr ☑
✸ by appt.

PERRIER-JOUET

Belle Epoque 1997★★

	n.c.	n.c.	🍴 ♦	+76 €

The story of this famous house, founded in Epernay in 1811, is tied up with that of Mumm. The bottle design of the Belle Epoque, created by Emile Gallé in 1904, which was lost and then found again in the cellars at Perrier-Jouët, is often considered to be the most artistic in all of Champagne. That of the 1997 rosé is especially remarkable for the quality of its contents: a fresh, fruity, spicy champagne, whose weight does not at all undermine its lightness, whose meatiness is quite in harmony with its elegance. Its blend is among the most classic, with 40% of Chardonnay and 60% of the two Pinots. (NM)

➦ Perrier-Jouët, 28, av. de Champagne, 51200 Epernay, tel. 03.26.53.38.00, fax 03.26.54.54.55,
e-mail champagne@perrier-jouet.com ☑
✸ ev. day except Sat. Sun. 9am–11.15am 2pm–4.15pm; groups by appt.

DANIEL PERRIN 1996★

	2 ha	13,000	🍴 ♦	15–23 €

Urville, on the Côte des Bars, has a fine example of a kerbstoned well, and typical rural dwellings. The Perrins cultivate around a dozen hectares there. Their 1996, half Pinot Noir and half Chardonnay, releases fine, rich aromas that bear the hallmarks of the vintage. The palate offers evidence of balance and precision. (RM)

➦ EARL Daniel Perrin, rue des Vignes, 10200 Urville, tel. 03.25.27.40.36, fax 03.25.27.74.57 ☑
✸ by appt.

PERTOIS-MORISET

Blanc de blancs Grande Réserve★

Gd cru	10 ha	50,000	🍴	11–15 €

The Pertois family of Cramant, and the Morisets of Mesnil, were affiliated around this brand in 1952, in order to rationalize the production of their 18 ha of vineyards. Deep gold in colour, this blanc de blancs, made from the harvests of 1997 and 1998, offers to the nose and palate complex flavours of patisserie and honey, signs of good development. (RM)

➦ Dominique Pertois, 13, av. de la République, 51190 Le Mesnil-sur-Oger, tel. 03.26.57.52.14, fax 03.26.57.78.98 ☑
✸ by appt.

PIERRE PETERS

Blanc de blancs 1997★

Gd cru	3 ha	16,000		15–23 €

Well-known around Mesnil-sur-Oger on the Côte des Blancs, the Peters family manages a vineyard of 17.5 ha dominated by the Chardonnay grape. 1997 was a difficult vintage. Notwithstanding that, this champagne is of undoubted quality: full and well-balanced, it has a pleasant character of overripe fruits. (RM)

➦ Pierre Peters, 26, rue des Lombards, 51190 Le Mesnil-sur-Oger, tel. 03.26.57.50.32, fax 03.26.57.97.71,
e-mail champagne-peters@wanadoo.fr ☑
✸ by appt.

MAURICE PHILIPPART

Blanc de blancs Tête de cuvée★

1er cru	6 ha	3,206	🍴	11–15 €

This brand was launched before the Second World War by Maurice Philippart. Today, Franck Philippart heads a vineyard of 6 ha in the heart of the Montagne de Reims. His blanc de blancs comes from the harvest of 1999. From its pale core with golden highlights emerges a rather complex nose of

toast, exotic fruits (pineapple, tangerine) and white flowers. The full, fresh palate discloses soft nuances of pipped fruits and quince compote. This is a champagne that will capably see you through a whole meal. (RM)

➦ Maurice Philippart, 16, rue de Rilly,
51500 Chigny-les-Roses, tel. 03.26.03.42.44,
fax 03.26.03.46.05,
e-mail franck.philippart1@libertysurf.fr ☑
✸ by appt.

PHILIPPONNAT

Clos des Goisses 1991★★★

	n.c.	n.c.	🍴 🍴	46–76 €

Pierre Philipponnat, descendant from a line of wine-growers known in Aÿ since 1522, launched this brand before the First World War. Always directed by a member of the Philipponnat family, although it has belonged to the BBC group since 1997, the house consists of a vineyard of 17 ha, most notably the 5.5 ha that constitute the largest *clos* in Champagne, the Clos des Goisses. Grapes from this *clos*, vinified separately, make up a wine that has been declared a *coup de coeur*. 70% Pinot Noir and 30% Chardonnay, partially wood-aged, with no malolactic fermentation. In addition to that, the champagne has been given a long maturation on its lees, and benefits from a very light *dosage* of 5 g. Tasters were astonished to find such aromatic complexity, balance, finesse and power in a 1991, known for being a difficult vintage, but this has all the best qualities of a great champagne, and all those indeed of a great white wine. You could even serve it from a carafe. **La Royale Réserve (15–23 €)**, a blend of the three champagne grapes, with the black varieties in the majority, and including 20% reserve wines, received one star. Its assertive character caused some controversy, with the evaluations of certain tasters tending towards another *coup de coeur*. Also commended was the **Grand Blanc 98 (23–30 €)**, a fine blanc de blancs with a long finish. (NM)

➦ Philipponnat, 13, rue du Pont, 51160 Mareuil-sur-Aÿ, tel. 03.26.56.93.00, fax 03.26.56.93.18,
e-mail info@champagnephilipponnat.com ☑
✸ by appt.
➦ BBC

JACQUES PICARD

Réserve 1997★

	0.6 ha	5,000	🍴	15–23 €

This Réserve, almost entirely composed of Chardonnay (with just 10% Pinot Noir), displays aromas of fruits, *pain d'épice* and butter, and then shows power and structure on the palate, with a mineral finish. The **Prestige 97** comprises 40% Chardonnay and 60% Pinot Noir; it is a floral, lemony, well-balanced champagne, which the Jury commended. (RM)

➦ Jacques Picard, 12, rue de Luxembourg, 51420 Berru, tel. 03.26.03.22.46, fax 03.26.03.26.03 ☑
✸ by appt.

PICARD ET BOYER

Cuvée Tradition★

	2 ha	n.c.	🍴 🍴	11–15 €

This vineyard of 5 ha still has some old vines planted in 1928, the year of its creation. The wines pass through wood before undergoing their secondary fermentation. This blanc de noirs, born of pure Pinot Meunier, appears straw-gold in the glass, animated by a fine mousse. Ripe fruitiness escapes from it, consolidated on the palate by vinosity and roundness, but also a certain freshness. (RM)

•┓ SCEV Picard et Boyer, chem. de Vrilly, 51100 Reims, tel. 03.26.85.11.69, fax 03.26.82.60.88 ☑
⊺ by appt.

PIERREL

Cuvée Tradition★

1er cru	n.c.	n.c.	15–23 €

This Epernay négociant sells some very floridly packaged wines under its Mignon et Pierrel brand, but it tends to be the Cuvée Tradition wines that are the stars. This one is a blanc de blancs, even if that designation does not appear on the label. A bright greenish-gold in colour, it memorably evokes brioche and fruit on the nose, and a touch of spice too, all with great elegance. Its freshness will be as much appreciated served as an aperitif, as alongside a fillet of John Dory with sweet onions. (NM)
•┓ SA Pierrel et Associés, 26, rue Henri-Dunant, 51200 Epernay, tel. 03.26.51.00.90, fax 03.26.51.69.40, e-mail champagne@pierrel.fr ☑
⊺ by appt.

PIERSON-CUVELIER

Cuvée Prestige Carte d'or★★

Gd cru	2.5 ha	5,000	🍾 ♦	11–15 €

The château of Louvois is just a few steps away from this vineyard of 8.5 ha, the creation of which dates back to 1901. The Pierson-Cuvelier brand appeared in 1978, and today attains remarkable heights with this champagne from the harvests of 1994–1996, made exclusively from Pinot Noir. A bright yellow-gold in colour, it exhibits fruity aromas, all the while revealing a balance of power and richness. Try it with a mushroom pie or with turkey. (RM)
•┓ Pierson-Cuvelier, 4, rue de Verzy, 51150 Louvois, tel. 03.26.57.03.72, fax 03.26.51.83.84 ☑
⊺ by appt.

PIPER-HEIDSIECK

Rare★

n.c.	n.c.	🍾 ♦	46–76 €

Of the three Heidsieck houses, Piper-Heidsieck is the oldest, having been founded in 1785. Since 1990, it has been in the hands of Rémy Cointreau. Rare is the name of a top-of-the-range *cuvée* made from all three champagne grape varieties. Aromas of toast and spice, roundness and freshness characterize a lovely golden-coloured wine with tinges of green. Another star was accorded to the long, well-structured **Brut non-vintage (15–23 €)**, which is mostly composed of black grapes (85%). (NM)
•┓ Piper-Heidsieck, 51, bd Henry-Vasnier, 51100 Reims, tel. 03.26.84.43.00, fax 03.26.84.43.49 ☑
⊺ by appt.

GASTON POITTEVIN★★

1er cru	2 ha	14,000	🍾	11–15 €

After disembarking from a short cruise along the Marne at Cumières, your steps may carry you to Gaston Poittevin, who cultivates a vineyard of 6 ha here. His *brut* non-vintage, a blend of the years 1996, 1997 and 1999, bears the pronounced characters of both Pinots (86%, against 14% Chardonnay). From its bright golden core with hints of green emerge intense aromas of preserved citrus fruits, followed by freshness and balance. (RM)
•┓ Gaston Poittevin, 123, rue Louis-Dupont, 51480 Cumières, tel. 03.26.55.38.37, fax 03.26.54.30.89 ☑
⊺ by appt.

POL ROGER 1995★★

n.c.	n.c.	🍾 ♦	38–46 €

"A superb rosé," concluded one taster on his card. This lively, complex champagne, long in its flavours of red berry fruits, comes from a family house led by the descendants of those who founded it in 1849. A blend of 60% Pinot Noir and 40% Chardonnay, coloured with 15% of red wine, it will undoubtedly find its place among the wines the house exports (which amount to 65% of the total production). The **Brut Chardonnay 95**, whose golden core is crossed by fine streams of bubbles, seems already mature, and received a commendation. (NM)

•┓ SA Pol Roger, 1, rue Henri-Lelarge, 51200 Epernay, tel. 03.26.59.58.00, fax 03.26.55.25.70, e-mail polroger@polroger.fr ☑
⊺ by appt.

POMMERY

Royal★

n.c.	n.c.	🍾 ♦	15–23 €

Situated near the cathedral, this prestigious Reims house, created in 1836, invented its Pop label in 1999. It was taken over in 2002 by Paul Vranken. It bears the name of one of those great ladies of Champagne who, left widowed, then devoted themselves to achieving greatness for their companies. In this case, it was Louise Pommery who assumed control in 1858. The Brut Royal is the flagship of this brand: all three champagne grape varieties participate in the blend (38% Chardonnay, 36% Pinot Noir and 26% Pinot Meunier, from the harvests of 1996–1999), giving softness and roundness to the wine. We recall that the Cuvée Louise 1995 received two stars last year. (NM)
•┓ SA Pommery, 5, pl. du Gal-Gouraud, BP 1049, 51100 Reims Cedex 2, tel. 03.26.61.62.56, fax 03.26.61.62.99, e-mail info@pommery.fr ☑
⊺ by appt.
•┓ Vranken

PASCAL PONSON

Grande Réserve★

1er cru	4.17 ha	31,827	🍾 ♦	11–15 €

Pascal Ponson manages a vineyard of nearly 13 ha distributed across five villages. His Grande Réserve comes from all three champagne grape varieties (24% Chardonnay, 35% Pinot Meunier and 11% Pinot Noir), with 30% reserve wines in the blend. It is a well-balanced, robust champagne of good length. (RM)
•┓ Pascal Ponson, 2, rue du Château, 51390 Coulommes-la-Montagne, tel. 03.26.49.20.17, fax 03.26.49.76.48, e-mail ponson@wanadoo.fr ☑
⊺ by appt.

N. POTIE★

5,26 ha	30,000	🍾 ♦	11–15 €

Positioned between the channels of two rivers, Condé-sur-Marne offers not only the spectacle of the lockkeepers, but also that of vines. This champagne (80% Chardonnay and 20% Pinot Noir, from the years 1996 and 2000) captured the attention of the tasters for its combination of roundness and vivacity, complexity, richness and finesse. (RM)
•┓ N. Potié, 6, rue de Reims, 51150 Condé-sur-Marne, tel. 03.26.67.99.08, fax 03.26.64.13.27, e-mail champotie@aol.com ☑
⊺ ev. day except Sun. 9am–12 noon 2pm–6pm; Sat. Sun. by appt.

ROGER POUILLON ET FILS

Le brut Vigneron★

1er cru	n.c.	5,000	🍾	11–15 €

To the east of Aÿ, Mareuil-sur-Aÿ does not lack for charm with its church that dates from the 12th and 13th centuries. Brut Vigneron, equipped with a pretty label depicting a Champenoise woman in traditional costume, is composed of equal parts Chardonnay and Pinot Noir from the years 1997 to 1999. It has a fine mousse, lemony, mineral aromas, and richness and length on the palate. (RM)
•┓ Roger Pouillon et Fils, 3, rue de la Couple, 51160 Mareuil-sur-Aÿ, tel. 03.26.52.60.08, fax 03.26.59.49.83, e-mail contact@champagne-pouillon.com ☑
⊺ by appt.

POUL-JUSTINE

Tradition★★

1er cru	n.c.	17,210	🍾	11–15 €

Avenay-Val d'Or conceals a treasure: the church of Saint-Trézain (12th–16th centuries), which has been classified a Historic Monument. Don't miss its flamboyant Gothic façade and gargoyles. The village also has some remarkable champagnes, like this Tradition from Poul-Justine, which

has seen neither malolactic fermentation nor filtration. Comprised of equal parts Chardonnay and Pinot Noir from the years 1993 to 2000, it captivated with the finesse of its bouquet and the elegance of its bready, well-balanced palate. One star was awarded to the **Blanc de Chardonnay (15–23 €)**, a blend of the harvests of 1993–1999, which leads with citrus fruits and brioche all the way through the tasting. (RM)
🔹 EARL Poul-Justine, 6, rue Gambetta, 51160 Avenay-Val-d'Or, tel. 03.26.52.32.58, fax 03.26.52.65.92, e-mail poul-michel@wanadoo.fr ☑
Ⴏ by appt.

PREVOTEAU-PERRIER

Grande Réserve★

	n.c.	80,000	▮	11–15 €

The village of Damery, not far from Epernay, is well-known to geologists because its subsoil contains many fossils dating from the Tertiary era. You will have to travel in person to the village in order to get a bottle of this champagne, because the house sells only to private individuals. The three grape varieties play equal parts (with some reserve wines) in the production of a yellow-hued wine with green highlights, in which the gentle aromas of crystallized fruits accord well with its balanced development, vinosity and roundness on the palate. (NM)
🔹 Prévoteau-Perrier, 15, rue André-Maginot, 51480 Damery, tel. 03.26.58.41.56, fax 03.26.58.65.88 ☑
Ⴏ by appt.

PRIN PERE ET FILS

Grande Réserve 1995★★

	n.c.	n.c.	▮ ♦	23–30 €

Oenologist Daniel Prin elected to blend 40% Pinot Noir with 60% Chardonnay to compose this brut 1995 with its fresh, concentrated flavours. The smooth palate has crystallized fruits on it, and shows impressive balance. His **Blanc de Blancs Sixième Sens (30–38 €)** is a soft, lemony, well-knit wine that was awarded one star. (NM)
🔹 Prin Père et Fils, 28, rue Ernest-Vallé, 51190 Avize, tel. 03.26.53.54.55, fax 03.26.53.54.56, e-mail info@champagne-prin.com ☑
Ⴏ by appt.

QUENARDEL ET FILS

Cuvée de réserve★

	6 ha	60,000	▮ ♦	11–15 €

Verzenay, in the Montagne de Reims, has a curiosity: a lighthouse built for publicity purposes in 1909 by champagne négociant Joseph Goulet, and now turned into a wine museum. After a visit there, don't forget to look in at the house of Quénardel et Fils (an 8-ha estate), whose Cuvée Millenium 1996 obtained a *coup de coeur* last year. This, the Cuvée de réserve, made from 70% Pinots and 30% Chardonnay from the years 1999 and 2000, offers scents of ripe fruits and dried figs, and then a rounded, complexity and vinous palate. (RM)
🔹 Quénardel et Fils, 1, place de la Mairie, 51360 Verzenay, tel. 03.26.49.40.63, fax 03.26.49.45.21 ☑
Ⴏ by appt.
🔹 Faucomarez

SERGE RAFFLIN

Brut Cuvée★★

	n.c.	n.c.	▮ ♦	11–15 €

The descendant of a wine-growing family going back to 1740, Denis Rafflin took over in 1985 the management of this quality estate of 9.5 ha. The Brut Cuvée, composed of 45% Pinot Noir, 35% Pinot Meunier and 20% Chardonnay, offers a floral nose, whose register continues on the palate in notes of acacia mingled with liquorice. Its abundant mousse, on a golden background with tinges of green, will not fail to charm as an aperitif. The **Cuvée de Prestige 98 (15–23 €)**, with its base of 60% Chardonnay and 40% Pinot Noir, was deservedly commended for its roundness. (RM)

🔹 Denis Rafflin, 10, rue Nationale, BP 25, 51500 Ludes, tel. 03.26.61.12.84, fax 03.26.61.14.07, e-mail denis.rafflin@wanadoo.fr ☑
Ⴏ by appt.

CUVEE DU REDEMPTEUR

Blanc de blancs★

	n.c.	10,000	ⅲ	11–15 €

"Rédempteur" was the nickname given to the grandfather of Claude Dubois at the time of the wine-growers' revolt of 1911. Today, Claude is more concerned with tending his 7 ha of vines in Venteuil, and offers this blanc de blancs from the 1999 harvest, a well-balanced wine but with noticeable *dosage*. The **Champagne du Rédempteur**, made up of equal parts of the three champagne grape varieties, was commended for its fruit compote character and its good finish. The **Cuvée Claude Dubois Demi-Sec**, with only 10% Chardonnay, also deserved a mention for its intensity and overall balance. (RM)
🔹 P. et F. Dubois, EARL du Rédempteur, rte d'Arty, 51480 Venteuil, tel. 03.26.58.48.37, fax 03.26.58.63.46, e-mail redempteur@wanadoo.fr ☑
Ⴏ ev. day 8am–12 noon 2pm–5.30pm; Sat. Sun. by appt.
🔹 Claude Dubois

PASCAL REDON 1996★

	1er cru	0.4 ha	3,600	▮ ♦	15–23 €

Trépail, where Pascal Redon cultivates 4.5 ha and launched his brand in 1982, is known for its Chardonnay. This 1996 is almost a blanc de blancs (containing just 5% Pinot Noir). Rounded and complex, it presents the gentle touch of development typical of this vintage. From its golden-yellow depths arise notes of yellow fruits and white flowers, which would marry well with the flavours of a chicken cooked in honey. The **Cuvée du Hordon Premier Cru**, a blend of the years 1995–1998, from half black grapes and half white, received a commendation: with its evident *dosage*, it is a powerful, honeyed wine. (RM)
🔹 Pascal Redon, 2, rue de la Mairie, 51380 Trépail, tel. 03.26.57.06.02, fax 03.26.58.66.54 ☑
Ⴏ by appt.

LOUIS REGNIER

Grande Réserve★★

	n.c.	n.c.	▮ ♦	23–30 €

This négociant brand, only created in 2002, has made a remarkable debut. It is listed here for its *brut* rosé, blended from the three champagne grape varieties, coloured by red wine. The delicate colour, a pale pink with salmon highlights, envelops scents of fresh red fruits. After a strong attack, its fruitiness is confirmed with finesse and roundness, all the way through to its long finish. A well-balanced champagne to drink on a fine late afternoon in the garden. (NM)
🔹 SAS Louis Régnier, 10, av. de Champagne, 51480 Damery, tel. 03.26.52.39.35, fax 03.26.52.39.35

BERNARD REMY

Prestige★★

	1.1 ha	6,000	▮ ♦	11–15 €

Bernard Rémy has built up a vineyard of more than 8 ha. His Prestige *cuvée* is a classic blend of Pinot (40%) and Chardonnay from the harvests of 1996, 1997 and 2000. Golden-bronze in colour, it greets the taster with a bouquet of quince, pear and mint, before presenting its complex, spicy flavours, which are nicely balanced between liveliness and roundness. One star was awarded to the **Carte Blanche**, made up of equal parts black and white grapes of the years 1998–2000, with its nose of citrus fruits and flowers. Well-balanced and long, it is still in the course of its development. (NM)

☛ Bernard Rémy, 19, rue des Auges, 51120 Allemant, tel. 03.26.80.60.34, fax 03.26.80.37.18, e-mail info@champagnebernardremy.com ☑

⏀ by appt.

ANDRE ROBERT

Blanc de blancs Le Mesnil 1997★

Gd cru	2 ha	10,580	▮	15–23 €

The Roberts have been wine-growers since the beginning of the 20th century. Today, Bertrand Robert cultivates a vineyard of around 10 ha in the Côte des Blancs. Golden-yellow in colour, his concentrated, bready 97 has an invigorating character and good length. (RM)

☛ André Robert, 15, rue de l'Orme, BP 5, 51190 Le Mesnil-sur-Oger, tel. 03.26.57.59.41, fax 03.26.57.54.90 ☑

⏀ by appt.

ERIC RODEZ

Ambonnay Cuvée des Crayères★

Gd cru	6.12 ha	n.c.	▮ ⑪	11–15 €

Eric Rodez, oenologist and owner of just over 6 ha, makes his champagnes with care: blending vatted wines with wood-aged wines, and marrying wines that have undergone their malolactic fermentation with Chardonnay reserve wines that have avoided it. This *cuvée* is composed of equal parts Chardonnay and Pinot Noir from the harvests of 1994–1999 (with a large proportion of that last year). It displays a range of floral scents, fully rounded and harmonious, and with a slight woody note emerging from its pale golden-yellow core. It could accompany a fish served in butter. (RM)

☛ Eric Rodez, 4, rue de Isse, 51150 Ambonnay, tel. 03.26.57.04.93, fax 03.26.57.02.15 ☑

⏀ by appt.

LOUIS ROEDERER

Brut Premier★★

	n.c.	n.c.	▮ ⚲	23–30 €

With its vast domaine of 200 ha, Roederer has remained a family business; today directed by Jean-Claude Rouzaud, it has recently become a patron of the Bibliothèque Nationale de France. Its glory days arose in the 19th century, when it famously supplied the Russian court. It was in 1876 that Louis Roederer conceived the Cristal *cuvée*, so-called because it originally came in crystal bottles, which was reserved for Tsar Alexander II. The 1917 revolution brought about a democratization (relatively speaking) of this prestige champagne, one of the two most widely sold special *cuvées* in the world. Slightly dominated by Pinot Noir (55%, against 45% Chardonnay), the **Cristal 96 (+76 €)** shows itself to be full, concentrated, vigorous and long. A classy wine that one cannot ignore. The Brut Premier blends the harvests of four years, with two-thirds of Pinots and one-third Chardonnay. The reserve wines in it (6–10% of the blend) are matured in large oak casks. Rigorously vinified, it is a champagne of directness and purity. Its great strength is its balance. (NM)

☛ Louis Roederer, 21, bd Lundy, 51100 Reims, tel. 03.26.40.42.11, fax 03.26.47.66.51, e-mail com@champagne-roederer.com

ROGGE CERESER

Cuvée de réserve★★

	7 ha	1,700	▮ ⚲	11–15 €

On the right bank of the Vallée de la Marne, this family estate owns 7 ha of vines, 1 km from the Ferme du Temple, which is the old headquarters of the Knights Templar with its 13th century chapel. This champagne, a blend of the wines of 2000 and 2001, comprises a majority of black grapes: Pinots Noir (19%) and Meunier (70%), topped up with Chardonnay. Its restrained nose of citrus fruits, rising from a pale-gold core, is followed by a fine, fresh palate along the same aromatic lines. (RM)

☛ SCEV Rogge Cereser, 1, imp. des Bergeries, 51700 Passy-Grigny, te. 03.26.52.96.05, fax 03.26.52.07.73, e-mail champagne.rogge.cereser@wanadoo.fr ☑

⏀ by appt.

JACQUES ROUSSEAUX

Cuvée de réserve★

Gd cru	1.2 ha	10,000	▮	11–15 €

Served as an aperitif, this charming champagne could also be drunk to accompany a cold starter. Golden nuances attract the glance, while the fruity, slightly brioche-like aromas delicately unfurl. The palate is fresh and rounded at the same time, and has good length. Eric Rousseaux, whose vineyard of 8 ha is exclusively located in the grands crus of Verzenay and Verzy, has blended 65% Pinot Noir with 35% Chardonnay from the years 1998, 1999 and especially 2000. (RM)

☛ Jacques Rousseaux, 5, rue de Puisieulx, 51360 Verzenay, tel. 03.26.49.42.73, fax 03.26.49.40.72 ☑

⏀ by appt.

ROUSSEAUX-FRESNET★★

	5.55 ha	20,000	▮	11–15 €

This property of 5.55 ha launched its brand in 1983. Twenty years later, it has distinguished itself with a rounded, powerful, vigorous champagne that possesses a remarkable balance of freshness and more developed characters. Scents of ripe red fruits contribute to the charm of a wine derived from 80% Pinot Noir and 20% Chardonnay. The **rosé (15–23 €)** obtained one star for its subtle bouquet of red berries, its balanced vinosity and its length. (RM)

☛ Jean-Brice Rousseaux-Fresnet, 21, rue Chanzy, BP 12, 51360 Verzenay, tel. 03.26.49.45.66, fax 03.26.49.40.09 ☑

⏀ by appt.

LE ROYAL COTEAU 1995★★

	1.2 ha	10,000	▮ ⚲	15–23 €

The Grauves cooperative handles the production of 85 ha of vines. This 1995 comprises as much Chardonnay as Pinot Noir, bolstered by 20% Pinot Meunier. Its intense gold colour indicates its age, but on the nose and the palate, it remains fresh, while undoubtedly having reached its peak. A rounded and well-balanced wine. The **Brut non-vintage (11–15 €)**, an identical blend, obtained one star for its roundness, its vinosity and its simple good balance. (CM)

☛ Le Royal Coteau, 11, rue de la Coopérative, 51190 Grauves, tel. 03.26.59.71.12, fax 03.26.59.77.66 ☑

⏀ by appt.

☛ Lagoutte

RUFFIN ET FILS

Cuvée Chardonnay d'or★

	3 ha	30,000	▮ ⚲	11–15 €

Jean Ruffin created this family house in 1946; he has since been joined by his son Dominique, who became cellarmaster in 1973, and then his grandson Alexandre, head of marketing, in 1995. The vineyard covers 11 ha. It all adds up to a winning team, honoured for this fresh, floral, elegant and long blanc de blancs from 1998 and 1999, in which an abundant mousse manifests itself against a green-tinged golden background. The **rosé**, made of half black grapes and half white, coloured by red wine made from Pinot Noir, was also singled out: it is rich and rounded, with flavours of blackcurrants. (NM)

☛ Ruffin et Fils, 20, Grande-Rue, 51270 Etoges, tel. 03.26.59.30.14, fax 03.26.59.34.96, e-mail champ.ruffin@wanadoo.fr ☑

⏀ by appt.

RENE RUTAT

Blanc de blancs 1996★

1er cru	n.c.	3,500	▮	15–23 €

Vertus in the Vallée de la Marne is a Côte des Blancs village classified as premier cru. Michel Rutat heads a vineyard of 6 ha here, where the fruit of the Chardonnay vine enables him to vinify this impressive blanc de blancs, with its scents of nuts and crystallized fruits. With its clean attack, this intensely coloured straw-gold wine has a warming feel, while remaining well-balanced throughout. A commendation also went to the **Blanc de Blancs non-vintage (11–15 €)**, a blend of

the harvests of 1999 and 2000 in equal measure, which the tasters judged to be straightforward, full and long. (RM)
☞ René Rutat, av. du Gal-de-Gaulle, 51130 Vertus, tel. 03.26.52.14.79, fax 03.26.52.97.36, e-mail champagne-rutat@terre-net.fr Ⓥ
🍷 by appt.

LOUIS DE SACY
Grand Soir★

Gd cru	12 ha	10,000	🗌 🍶 🍶	23–30 €

Two kilometres above the village, the landscape presents an astonishing natural curiosity, the famous ancient beech trees of Verzy that have grown into strange twisted shapes. The Sacy family has been in Champagne since 1633; today, they cultivate 25 ha in all three great regions of the Marne. Grand Soir is a blend of 30% Pinot Noir matured in wood, 40% Pinot Meunier and 30% Chardonnay, harvested in 1996. It is floral and toasty on the nose, while on the palate, it marries roundness, freshness and vigour. (NM)
☞ Louis de Sacy, 6, rue de Verzenay, 51380 Verzy, tel. 03.26.97.91.13, fax 03.26.97.94.25, e-mail contact@champagne-louis-de-sacy.fr Ⓥ
🍷 by appt.

SAINT-CHAMANT
Cuvée de chardonnay 1996★★

	n.c.	12,769	🗌	15–23 €

On the "noble avenue" of champagne houses in Epernay, one finds the headquarters of a grower who is well-known to the readers of this *Guide*. Christian Coquillette is a Chardonnay specialist. His 1996, with its brilliant pale-gold core and fine mousse, offers an elegant nose of butter, brioche and toasted bread. The palate plays on the same notes, and is well-balanced, full and long. Also commended were two non-vintage blancs de blancs, the first **Carte Crème** from 1998, the second **Carte d'Or** from 1999, both lively, fresh, rounded and long champagnes that are still very young. (RM)
☞ Christian Coquillette, Champagne Saint-Chamant, 50, av. Paul-Chandon, 51200 Epernay, tel. 03.26.54.38.09, fax 03.26.54.96.55

DE SAINT-GALL
Blanc de blancs 1998★

1er cru	550 ha	500,000	🗌 🍶	15–23 €

This big cooperative group is one of the major players in Champagne. Under its Saint-Gall brand, it submitted three *cuvées*. This blanc de blancs 1998 has all the characteristics of its grape variety, most notably a touch of minerality. It is fine, light and long, with evident *dosage*. The **Blanc de Blancs Premier Cru non-vintage** was commended. The wines in the blend date from 1998, 1999 and 2000; it expresses itself eloquently enough, but the *dosage* is again rather noticeable. The **Cuvée Orpale 95 (38–46 €)** is a blanc de blancs as imposing as it is long, and deserves its star. (CM)
☞ Union Champagne, 7, rue Pasteur, 51190 Avize, tel. 03.26.57.94.22, fax 03.26.57.57.98, e-mail info@union-champagne.fr Ⓥ

SALON
Blanc de blancs 1995★★

Gd cru	n.c.	45,000		+76 €

Founded in 1906, this is the only house that produces nothing but vintage champagnes. However, not every year is suitable for making vintages. Following the 1990 that was previously honoured by the *Guide*, Salon this year presents its 1995, another fine vintage. Like every champagne Salon has produced since its foundation, it is a blanc de blancs, made of Chardonnay from Mesnil-sur-Oger, a Côte des Blancs grand cru. What is there to say of this thirty-fourth Salon vintage? It is a great blanc de blancs, refined and complete, a wine of handsome weight. Some of those tasting it blind were astonished by its degree of maturity, but this is quite usual in Salon's wines. Indisputably a champagne for food. (NM)
☞ Salon, 5, rue de la Brèche-d'Oger, 51190 Le Mesnil-sur-Oger, tel. 03.26.57.51.65, fax 03.26.57.79.29, e-mail champagne@salondelamotte.com
🍷 by appt.

SANGER
Blanc de blancs★★

Gd cru	n.c.	n.c.	🗌 🍶	11–15 €

The viticultural college at Avize has created its own cooperative whose members are former students. This Grand Cru wine is full of quality, with its floral, liquoricey, minty bouquet, and its smoky, citrussy, minerally flavours, as refined as they are balanced. The Grand Jury of nine tasters elected this wine a *coup de coeur*, whereas the **Blanc de Blancs Grand Cru 97 (15–23 €)**, which does not go through malolactic fermentation, obtained one star. It is a bready, well-balanced champagne, slightly developed in its appearance, as also on the nose and palate. (CM)
☞ Coopérative des Anciens, Lycée viticole, 51190 Avize, tel. 03.26.57.79.79, fax 03.26.57.78.58 Ⓥ
🍷 ev. day except Sat. Sun. 8am–12 noon 2pm–6pm

CAMILLE SAVES 1998★

Gd cru	4.3 ha	11,020		15–23 €

At this family property, founded in 1894, is displayed the first wine press ever used by its ancestors back in the 19th century. Its champagnes are not given a malolactic fermentation, and the reserve wines are aged in *barrique*. The blend of the 1998 contains four times more Pinot Noir than Chardonnay. The nose is buttery and spicy, whereas the smooth palate develops notes of red berries. A champagne of genuine potential, it should be drunk with food (white meats, preferably). The **Cuvée de réserve Grand Cru**, a blend of 1999 and 1998, with 65% Chardonnay, offers an elegant, honeyed bouquet and a fruity palate. It received one star. (RM)
☞ Camille Savès, 4, rue de Condé, 51150 Bouzy, tel. 03.26.57.00.33, fax 03.26.57.03.83, e-mail champagne.saves@hexanet.fr Ⓥ
🍷 by appt.
☞ Hervé Savès

FRANCOIS SECONDE★★

Gd cru	3.3 ha	22,000	🗌	11–15 €

Classified as grand cru, Sillery is home to the vineyards of many of the *grandes marques*. There are some exceptions, such as François Secondé who has had 5 ha of vines here for more than 25 years. His BSA (for which read "Brut Sans Année", or brut non-vintage) is a blend of 70% Pinot Noir and 30% Chardonnay from the harvests of 1997–2000. Gold in the glass, it has a fine, persistent mousse. The harmonious bouquet, which mixes notes of fruit and sweet spice, announces a palate that is well-balanced, with good vinosity, complex, fresh and long. The **Blanc de Blancs Grand Cru 98 (15–23 €)** obtained one star. It is a minerally and distinguished champagne, full of youth. (RM)
☞ François Secondé, 6, rue des Galipes, 51500 Sillery, tel. 03.26.49.16.67, fax 03.26.49.11.55, e-mail francois.seconde@wanadoo.fr Ⓥ
🍷 by appt.

CRISTIAN SENEZ
Carte verte★

	15 ha	n.c.	🗌 🍶	11–15 €

The tenacity of Cristian Senez has been well rewarded. Having started from nothing, with a mere 0.2 ha in 1955, his vineyard has now grown to 30 ha. He launched his brand in 1973, and assumed the status of a négociant in 1985. The Carte Verte, based on Pinot Noir and Chardonnay, has already earned honours in previous editions of the *Guide*. This year, it is a blend of 2000 and 2001. "The small fine bubbles look very merry," noted one taster. This is a floral and fruity champagne, full, meaty and long, for drinking with a sabayon. (NM)

🍷 Cristian Senez, 6, Grande-Rue, 10360 Fontette, tel. 03.25.29.60.62, fax 03.25.29.64.63, e-mail champagne.senez@wanadoo.fr ☑
🍽 by appt.

SIMART-MOREAU

Cuvée des Crayères 1997★

⬤ Gd cru	0,3 ha	2,900	🍾 ♠	15–23 €

One hundred metres from the 15th century church of Chouilly, this cellar dug out of the chalk – hence the reference to chalk pits (*crayères*) in the wine's name – has turned out a blanc de blancs of a success that ought to be saluted in a difficult vintage. Pale gold, balanced, intense, it offers honeyed, lemony peach flavours of fine length. (RM)

🍷 Pascal Simart-Moreau, 9, rue du Moulin, 51530 Chouilly, tel. 03.26.55.42.06, fax 03.26.55.95.92 ☑
🍽 by appt.

A. SOUTIRAN★★

⬤ Gd cru	4.5 ha	40,000	🍾 ♠	15–23 €

Alain Soutiran left his cooperative group in 1986, set up his own winery in 1990 and, seven years later, equipped it with oak barrels. Its success has led him to take on the status of a négociant. Chardonnay (40%) and Pinot Noir are combined in this champagne with its delicate nose of mirabelle plums, which is finely balanced by gently woody reserve wines. The **Blanc de Blancs Grand Cru** was commended for its mature vinosity. (NM)

🍷 A. Soutiran, 12, rue Saint-Vincent, 51150 Ambonnay, tel. 03.26.57.07.87, fax 03.26.57.81.74, e-mail info@soutiran.com ☑
🍽 ev. day except Sun. 9am–12 noon 2pm–6pm; cl. 23rd Dec.–1st Jan and Feb.

PATRICK SOUTIRAN

Blanc de blancs★

⬤ 1er cru	0.75 ha	4,000	🍾 ♠	15–23 €

Established over 50 years in Ambonnay, this family manages a vineyard of 3 ha. Its blanc de blancs from the years 1999 and 2000 offers to the eye a fine, gentle mousse against an intense gold background. Fresh aromas accompany a rounded champagne that is well-balanced, full and long. The **Précieuse d'Argent Grand Cru 95** is a blanc de blancs with the scents of apples and pears, equally smooth and full. It was commended. (RM)

🍷 Patrick Soutiran, 3, rue des Crayères, 51150 Ambonnay, tel. 03.26.57.08.18, fax 03.26.57.81.87, e-mail patrick.soutiran@wanadoo.fr ☑ 🏠
🍽 by appt.

TAITTINGER

Réserve★★

⬤ n.c.	n.c.		23–30 €

Based today in the cellars of the abbey of Saint-Nicaise, built in the 13th century, the house of Taittinger is a powerful group, owning 270 ha of its own vines in Champagne. Established in the United States as well since 1987, with its Domaine Carneros (70 ha in the American appellations of Sonoma and Napa Valley), the company has remained a family concern. The Réserve is the flagship wine. All three grape varieties collaborate in it (20% Pinot Meunier, with 40% Pinot Noir and the same of Chardonnay). The blend comprises a majority of wines from 1999, supplemented by those of 1998 and 1997. Its golden colour seduces from the start, while the nose reveals itself to be complex, mineral, spicy and toasty. On the palate, it is fleshy, creamy, appetising and long. Equally remarkable is the special *cuvée* **Comtes de Champagne Blanc de Blancs 95 (+76 €)**, the great champagne of this house, itself a complex, elegant and fine wine, which inspired one taster to a description to be savoured: "Out of this world". As for the vintage **1998 (30–38 €)**, it obtained one star. (NM)

🍷 Taittinger, 9, pl. Saint-Nicaise, 51100 Reims, tel. 03.26.85.45.35, fax 03.26.50.14.30 ☑
🍽 by appt.

TANNEUX-MAHY

Réserve★

⬤ 3 ha	25,000	🍾 🏠		11–15 €

Based at Mardeuil in the Vallée de la Marne, Jacques Tanneux presents this Réserve which has spent some time in wood and which is mainly made from black grapes (80%, including 60% Pinot Meunier) from the years 1999 and 2000. Its pretty bouquet has scents of acacia honey and white flowers; the palate achieves fine balance, playing off robustness against freshness. One star was allotted to the **Cuvée Vieillie en Fût de Chêne (15–23 €)**, born also of the three champagne grape varieties. Vanillary, honeyed, spicy, fine and well-structured, it is a "great success," as one taster summed it up. (RM)

🍷 Jacques Tanneux, 7, rue Jean-Jaurès, 51530 Mardeuil, tel. 03.26.55.24.57, fax 03.26.52.84.59, e-mail champagne.tanneux@wanadoo.fr ☑
🍽 by appt.

J. DE TELMONT

Grande Réserve★

⬤ 32 ha	1,000,000	🍾 ♠		11–15 €

Founded after the Great War, this family house controls a vast vineyard. Oenologist and engineer Bertrand Lhopital joined his sister at the head of this business in 1996. The Grande Réserve is a blend of equal parts of the three champagne grape varieties, from the years 1998–2000. Its bouquet is elegant, honeyed and toasty, its palate full and robust. One star also went to the *cuvée* **Consécration du Siècle 93 (23–30 €)**: it is a blanc de blancs from the grands crus of Avize and Chouilly, partially fermented and aged in barrel, with toasted, vanillary aromas and flavours of citrus fruits. It seems a young wine for its age. The **Grand Couronnement 96 (15–23 €)**, also a blanc de blancs, was singled out for its elegant structure. (NM)

🍷 J. de Telmont, 1, av. de Champagne, 51480 Damery, tel. 03.26.58.40.33, fax 03.26.58.63.93, e-mail info@champagne-de-telmont.com ☑
🍽 by appt.

THEVENET-DELOUVIN

Prestige du Millénaire★

⬤ 0.25 ha	2,000		11–15 €

Xavier Thévenet took over the family vineyard of 5 ha in 1989. He blends all three champagne grape varieties from the years 1997 to 1999 in this *cuvée*, with its complex aromas of yellow fruits, red berries and brioche. Balanced, full-bodied and long, this champagne bears evidence of well-managed *dosage*. (RM)

🍷 Xavier Thévenet, 28, rue Bruslard, 51700 Passy-Grigny, tel. 03.26.52.91.64, fax 03.26.52.97.63, e-mail xavier.thevenet@wanadoo.fr ☑
🍽 by appt.

ALAIN THIENOT

Grande Cuvée 1995★★

⬤ n.c.	n.c.		46–76 €

Alain Thiénot, who also owns vineyards in Bordeaux, is a busy man. Not content only with directing the champagne houses of Marie Stuart and Joseph Perrier, he created a brand under his own name in 1985. Its top-of-the-range product is the Grande Cuvée, an excellent wine comprising 60% Chardonnay and 40% Pinot Noir. The 1995 has continued developing through the years, and tasters followed the lead of a British member of the panel in admiring its range of flavours, which mingles nuances of preserved fruits, nuts (almonds particularly), apricots and beeswax, as well as smoky and toasty notes. A wine of great harmony. (NM)

🍷 Alain Thiénot, 4, rue Joseph-Cugnot, 51500 Taissy, tel. 03.26.77.50.10, fax 03.26.77.50.19, e-mail infos-vat@alain-thienot.fr ☑
🍽 by appt.

J.M. TISSIER

Apollon 1998★

	4 ha	1,060	▮	15–23 €

J.M. Tissier has a vineyard of nearly 5 ha in the hillsides to the south of Epernay. The Apollon *cuvée*, 60% Chardonnay and 40% Pinots, is distinguished by its roundness – a roundness, however, without undue softness – and by its length. (RM)
☛ Jacques Tissier, 9, rue du Gal-Leclerc, 51530 Chavot-Courcourt, tel. 03.26.54.17.47, fax 03.26.59.01.43 ▼
☖ by appt.

DIOGENE TISSIER ET FILS

Blanc de blancs★

	0.5 ha	5,000	▮	11–15 €

It was in 1931 that the grandfather of the present owner created this brand, setting up his estate a kilometre from the church at Chavot. The golden highlights of the wine show that inimitable green touch imparted by Chardonnay, enlivening a blanc de blancs from the years 1999 and 2000. After a nose of honey, jellied fruits and honeysuckle, the full, long and rich palate offers flavours of almonds and toasted bread. (NM)
☛ Diogène Tissier et fils, 10, rue du Gal-Leclerc, 51530 Chavot-Courcourt, tel. 03.26.54.32.47, fax 03.26.54.32.48, e-mail diogenetissier@hexanet.fr ▼
☖ by appt.

MICHEL TIXIER

Cuvée réservée★

	2 ha	10,000	▮	11–15 €

This brand was launched in 1963 by Michel Tixier, who was succeeded at its helm by Benoît Tixier in 1998. The estate has a vineyard of 4 ha. Its Cuvée Réservée comprises 80% black grapes and 20% white (including 60% Pinot Meunier), harvested in 1998. It offers aromas of crystallized fruits and nuances of toasty maturity. Honeyed and spicy, the wine is as fresh as it is long on the palate. (RM)
☛ Benoît Tixier, 8, rue des Vignes, 51500 Chigny-les-Roses, tel. 03.26.03.42.61, fax 03.26.03.41.80 ▼
☖ by appt.

G. TRIBAUT

Grande Cuvée spéciale★★

	n.c.	5,000	▮	15–23 €

Hautvillers, the village whose abbey is known as the cradle of Champagne, is also remarkable for the 130 wrought-iron signs that line its streets. Gaston Tribaut acquired his first vines here in 1935. The Grande Cuvée spéciale, a brut non-vintage, is a blend of the wines of 1996 and 1998 with as much Chardonnay as Pinot Noir. Its nose mixes flowers and citrus fruits, and it is fresh and long on the palate. It could be served as an aperitif, and then with fish. The **Blanc de Blancs Réserve (11–15 €)**, non-vintage but made from the harvest of 1998, is a long and concentrated champagne that gained one star. (RM)
☛ G. Tribaut, 88, rue d'Eguisheim, BP 5, 51160 Hautvillers, tel. 03.26.59.40.57, fax 03.26.59.43.74, e-mail champagne.tribaut@wanadoo.fr ▼
☖ ev. day 9am–12 noon 2pm–6pm

TRICHET-DIDIER★

Gd cru	0.25 ha	3,500		11–15 €

Pierre Trichet's grandfather planted his first vines in 1951, his father launched the brand in 1970 and he himself took over the vineyard of 3.5 ha in 1989. This Grand Cru is a blanc de noirs (Pinot Noir, to be precise) with a subtle bouquet of quince, rounded, well-balanced and with good length. Drink it with food. (NM)
☛ Pierre Trichet, 11, rue du Petit-Trois-Puits, 51500 Trois-Puits, tel. 03.26.82.64.10, fax 03.26.97.80.99, e-mail trichet-didier@terre-net.fr ▼
☖ ev. day 8am–12 noon 2pm–6pm

JEAN VALENTIN ET FILS

Blanc de blancs Saint-Avertin★

	n.c.	n.c.	▮ ⬥	15–23 €

Sacy, 20 km from Reims, boasts a beautiful 12th century Romanesque church with 16th century wood carvings. Vines are everywhere hereabouts, smothering the slopes of Petite Montagne de Reims. This blanc de blancs, whose fine mousse sparkles against a pale-gold background, has an attractive nose of citrus zests. The palate is fresh, lively and well-balanced, with floral touches on the finish. An aperitif champagne. (RM)
☛ Jean Valentin et fils, 9, rue Saint-Rémi, 51500 Sacy, tel. 03.26.49.21.91, fax 03.26.49.27.68, e-mail givalentin@wanadoo.fr ▼
☖ ev. day except Sun. 8.30am–12 noon 2pm–6pm; Sat. by appt.

VALLOIS-PETRET

Blanc de blancs Cuvée de réserve 1997★★

	0.4 ha	3,500	▮ ⬥	11–15 €

Francis Vallois-Pétret cultivates a vineyard of 3 ha. In 1984, he took over the business from his father, who had himself succeeded his own father, Eugène Pétret, who created the domaine in 1901. It is the classic story of a wine dynasty preserved. The Cuvée de Réserve is a blanc de blancs with a fine and sustained mousse, smoky, expressive, and above all of perfect balance. (RM)
☛ Francis Vallois-Pétret, 8, rue de la Croix-Bleue, 51530 Chouilly, tel. 03.26.55.15.09, fax 03.26.55.15.09 ▼
☖ by appt.

VARNIER-FANNIERE

Blanc de blancs★★

Gd cru	1.5 ha	11,000		11–15 €

Nobody could fail to notice the landscape of vine-covered hillsides on the Côte des Blancs around Avize. Equally, nobody could remain oblivious to this champagne acclaimed by the Grand Jury. Made by Denis Varnier, it is a blend of the years 2000 and 2001. Greenish-gold with a fine, long-lasting mousse, it offers up a superb bouquet of ripe fruits, lightly crystallized apricots, nuts and a remarkable mineral note. It has all the characteristics of a blanc de blancs, together with exceptional roundness and weight. The **rosé** was commended for its elegance, the elegance of a blanc de blancs very slightly tinted by 15% Pinot Noir. (RM)
☛ Varnier-Fannière, 23, rempart du Midi, 51190 Avize, tel. 03.26.57.53.36, fax 03.26.57.17.07, e-mail contact@varnier-fanniere.com ▼
☖ by appt.

VELY-RASSELET

Cuvée Prestige★

	3.3 ha	4,000	▮	15–23 €

Françoise Vély manages a vineyard of just over 3.5 ha in the Vallée de la Marne. This *cuvée* is a cherry-scented blanc de noirs from Pinot Meunier, and is smooth and fleshy on the palate. Also commended, the *cuvée* **Alix 98**, composed of Pinot (30%) and Chardonnay (70%), has a lively attack; its youthful nervousness is balanced by its *dosage*. (RM)
☛ Françoise Vély, 4, rue du Château, 51480 Reuil, tel. 03.26.58.38.60, fax 03.26.57.15.50 ▼
☖ by appt.

DE VENOGE

Blanc de noirs★

	115 ha	n.c.	▮ ◊	23–30 €

Many Germans have founded champagne houses, but only one Swiss has tried his hand at it: Henri-Marc de Venoge, in 1837. This brand belongs today to the young galaxy around Bruno Paillard. The prestige *cuvée*, Grand Vin des Princes, has often won the *coup de coeur*, as did the 1993 last year. Here are two simpler *cuvées*. This one, an alliance of Pinot Noir (80%) and Pinot Meunier, is an elegant dark gold, has a forthcoming bouquet (dominated by ripe black fruits) and lively attack, and is then balanced and quite long. The **Brut Select Cordon Bleu (15–23 €)** obtained the same reward, for its balance and its youth. Chardonnay and Pinot Meunier in equal shares are supplemented by 50% Pinot Noir. (NM)
☛ de Venoge, 46, av. de Champagne, 51200 Epernay, tel. 03.26.53.34.34, fax 03.26.53.34.35 ▼

ALAIN VESSELLE

Cuvée Saint-Eloi★

	Gd cru	n.c.	n.c.	▮ ◊	11–15 €

Bouzy, celebrated for its Coteaux-Champenois rouge, also of course produces champagnes. Eloi Vesselle, who heads this family brand, has fashioned a *cuvée* in which the Pinot Noir and Chardonnay are in equal balance, both coming from the harvest of 1999. The bouquet is fine, slightly aniseedy and floral. On the palate, there is much finesse, the floral aspects supplemented by fruity notes, good balance and the kind of length that will ensure the wine ages well. (RM)
☛ SCEV Alain Vesselle, 8, rue de Louvois, 51150 Bouzy, tel. 03.26.57.00.88, fax 03.26.57.09.77, e-mail champagneavesselle@wanadoo.fr ▼
☱ by appt.

JEAN VESSELLE

Réserve★

		1.5 ha	12,000	▮	11–15 €

Delphine Vesselle honours the memory of her father, whom she lost in 1995, by continuing the long viticultural saga written in the 11 ha of the family vineyard. She presents a Réserve, made from 20% Chardonnay and 80% Pinot Noir. Clear gold in colour, it offers a toasty bouquet, and then a refined palate that is both structured and long. Her **Oeil-de-Perdrix** was also singled out. This salmon-coloured rosé de noirs, with its purple highlights, is discreet on the nose, but fresh and fruity on the palate. (RM)
☛ Jean Vesselle, 4, rue Victor-Hugo, 51150 Bouzy, tel. 03.26.57.01.55, fax 03.26.57.06.95 ▼
☱ by appt.

MAURICE VESSELLE★

	Gd cru	n.c.	n.c.		15–23 €

Maurice Vesselle is a wine-grower at Bouzy. In a previous edition of the *Guide*, his Collection 1985 *cuvée* obtained a *coup de coeur*. His Grand Cru *brut* non-vintage today gains one star for the concentration of its nose of red berries and quince, as well as for its supple palate of considerable vinosity. (RM)
☛ Maurice Vesselle, 2, rue Yvonnet, 51150 Bouzy, tel. 03.26.57.00.81, fax 03.26.57.83.08 ▼
☱ ev. day 10am–12 noon 2pm–6pm

VEUVE A. DEVAUX

Cuvée "D" 1996★★

	20 ha	5,000	▮ ◊	30–38 €

This brand, founded in Epernay in 1846, was taken over in 1967 by the Union Auboise, which has now become its standard-bearer. This 1996 is practically a half-and-half blend of black grapes and white. Fine bubbles rise through its clear-gold core. Toasty and complex on the nose, the wine shows good balance, and its length on the palate encouraged one taster to justify its two stars thus: "A real *grand vin*". The **Grande Réserve (15–23 €)** (two-thirds black grapes and one-third Chardonnay) demands to be commended for its great vivacity. (CM)
☛ Union Auboise, Dom. de Villeneuve, 10110 Bar-sur-Seine, tel. 03.25.38.30.65, fax 03.25.29.73.21, e-mail info@champagne-devaux.fr ▼

VEUVE CLICQUOT PONSARDIN

La Grande Dame 1995★★

	n.c.	n.c.		+76 €

The widow Clicquot, one of the two most famous Frenchwomen of all (the other being Joan of Arc), conferred international renown on the house that bears her name, founded in 1772 and today possessing a fabulous vineyard of 363 ha. At Veuve Clicquot, the standard blend is two-thirds black grapes to one-third white. These are the proportions in the prestige *cuvée* La Grande Dame, which took the *coup de coeur* with its perfect opening impression, all silky-soft and rounded, and its long, gentle finish. The **Carte Jaune (23–30 €)** was commended; it is charming and balanced, if a little short. On the other hand, the **Rich Reserve 96 (38–46 €)** obtained two stars, as did the **Vintage Réserve 96 (38–46 €)**. (NM)
☛ Veuve Clicquot Ponsardin, 12, rue du Temple, 51100 Reims, tel. 03.26.89.54.40, fax 03.26.89.54.46 ▼
☱ by appt.

VEUVE DOUSSOT★

		1 ha	7,000	▮	11–15 €

Owning one of the highest vineyards in Champagne, on the Blu plateau of the Côte des Bars, 340 m above sea-level, the Jolys obtained a *coup de coeur* last year for their Grande Cuvée Extra-brut. Their rosé, a 100% Pinot Noir from the harvests of 1999 and 2000, is dominated on both the nose and palate by morello cherries. Its salmon colour and its fresh, balanced, long palate are most attractive. Blended from the same two years, the full-bodied, refreshing **Grande Cuvée**, composed of 80% Pinot Noir and 20% Chardonnay, was also commended, as was the **1999**, a blend of Pinot and Chardonnay (70%–30%), a wine of both softness and vinosity. (RM)
☛ SCEV des Monts de Noé, 1, rue de Chatet, 10360 Noé-les-Mallets, tel. 03.25.29.60.61, fax 03.25.29.11.78, e-mail champagne.veuve.doussot@wanadoo.fr ▼
☱ by appt.
☛ Joly

VEUVE FOURNY ET FILS

Grande Réserve★

	1er cru	5.5 ha	50,000	▮ ◊	11–15 €

This house founded in 1930 makes sophisticated champagnes, and is very highly regarded. The vineyard includes one of the rare Champagne *clos*, Notre-Dame, which is always vinified separately. This Grande Réserve well deserves its name, since it contains no less than 50% reserve wines, joined by a blend of two-thirds Chardonnay and one-third Pinot Noir. It is a fresh, vigorous and well-structured champagne. Another star went to the **1996 Premier Cru (15–23 €)**, a blanc de blancs champagne, a third of which is matured in wood with stirring of the lees, more elegant than concentrated on the nose, but fresh on the palate, with notes of honey and liquorice. (NM)
☛ Veuve Fourny et Fils, 5, rue du Mesnil, 51130 Vertus, tel. 03.26.52.16.30, fax 03.26.52.20.13, e-mail info@champagne-veuve-fourny.com ▼
☱ ev. day except Sun. 9am–12 noon 2pm–6pm

MARCEL VEZIEN

Brut Sélection★★

	1 ha	10,000	▮	15–23 €

In 1978 Marcel Vézien founded this estate, which is today overseen by one of his sons, Jean-Pierre. The vineyard extends over 15 ha near Celles-sur-Ource in the Aube. The Ource valley offers sumptuous walks, and not far from Celles is the village where the painter Auguste Renoir and his son Pierre, who lived here, are buried. Another reason to visit Celles is to discover this excellent champagne, which comprises four times more Pinot Noir than Chardonnay, from the harvests of 1998 and 1999. An intense gold in colour, it offers up scents of citrus fruits, which presage a fine attack and a generously long palate. (NM)
☛ SCEV Marcel Vézien et Fils, 68, Grande-Rue, 10110 Celles-sur-Ource, tel. 03.25.38.50.22, fax 03.25.38.56.09, e-mail contact@champagne-vezien.com ▼
☱ ev. day 8.30am–6pm; Sat. Sun. by appt.

FLORENT VIARD 1998★

○ 1er cru	0.35 ha	3,000	11–15 €

It was at Vertus that the poet Eustache Deschamps was born in 1340. Florent Viard has also established his vineyard there. His vintage 1998, a blanc de blancs but not labelled as such, has undergone malolactic fermentation. Greenish-gold in the glass, it offers up elegant buttery, biscuity notes before showing itself to be full, complex and long. Its generous palate makes it appropriate for serving with fish in a cream sauce. (RC)

☛ Florent Viard, 35, av. Saint-Vincent, 51130 Vertus, tel. 03.26.51.60.82, e-mail viard.florent@wanadoo.fr ☑
☠ by appt.

VILMART ET CIE

Coeur de cuvée 1997★

○	0.7 ha	5,000	◧	30–38 €

Rilly-la-Montagne in the Montagne de Reims has a church whose choir-stalls depict the life of the wine-grower. Laurent Champs directs this estate of 11 ha, using sophisticated wine-making methods: his wines avoid malolactic fermentation, and spend ten months in wood. This Coeur de cuvée includes 80% Chardonnay. It discloses a powerful bouquet (citrus fruits and nuts), and then a characterful palate (exotic fruits and citrus) that is fresh, well-balanced and long. The **Grande Réserve (15–23 €)**, made from Pinot and Chardonnay in the years 1999 and 2000, was also singled out. (RM)

☛ Vilmart et Cie, 5, rue des Gravières, 51500 Rilly-la-Montagne, tel. 03.26.03.40.01, fax 03.26.03.46.57 ☑
☠ by appt.
☛ Laurent Champs

VINCENT LAMOUREUX

Blanc de blancs Cuvée Saint-Vincent★

○	0.5 ha	2,500	▯	15–23 €

This vineyard was made up of the joining of the two proper-ties of Vincent and Lamoureux. Jean-Michel Lamoureux made this *cuvée* from Chardonnay of the harvests of 1997 and 1998. A bright clear-gold in colour, it displays an elegant bouquet of exotic fruits, toasted almonds and hazelnuts. The well-balanced palate is fresh and lemony. (RM)

☛ Vincent Lamoureux, 2, rue du Sénateur-Lesaché, 10340 Les Riceys, tel. 03.25.29.39.32, fax 03.25.29.80.30 ☑
☠ by appt.

VOIRIN-JUMEL

Tradition★

○	5 ha	40,000	11–15 €

Voirin and Jumel: two names, two families, two vineyards, one at Chouilly, the other at Cramant. The marriage of Gilles Voirin and Françoise Jumel gave birth to this brand and to its estate of 11 ha. The Tradition *cuvée* pays homage to Char-donnay (70%) and to the harvests of 1999 and 2000. Its fruity scents on the nose (peach and pear) are echoed intensely on the palate, and the wine is exceedingly fresh. (RM)

☛ Voirin-Jumel, 555, rue de la Libération, 51530 Cramant, tel. 03.26.57.55.82, fax 03.26.57.56.29, e-mail info@champagne-voirin-jumel.com ☑ ☷
☠ by appt.

VOLLEREAUX

Cuvée Tradition 1997★★

○	2.7 ha	25,000	15–23 €

Champagne Vollereaux is a family négociant company owning a significant vineyard of 40 ha. The Tradition *cuvée* contains 70% Chardonnay. On the nose, one discovers scents of white fruits, ferns and brioche, while the palate is honeyed, vanillary, long and altogether remarkable. One taster wanted to try this bottle more than tart. The **Cuvée Marguerite 94**, with its yellow-gold appearance, is surprisingly youthful on the nose (where it has a mineral freshness), is full, firm and long, and was awarded one star. (NM)

☛ SA Vollereaux, 48, rue Léon-Bourgeois, BP 4, 51530 Pierry, tel. 03.26.54.03.05, fax 03.26.54.88.36, e-mail champagne.vollereauxsa@wanadoo.fr ☑
☠ ev. day 8am–12 noon 3pm–6pm; Sat. 10.30am–12 noon 3pm–6pm; Sun. 10.30–12 noon

VRANKEN

Demoiselle Grande Cuvée★★

○	n.c.	n.c.	15–23 €

Paul Vranken is responsible for Heidsieck Monopole, Pommery and Charles Lafitte, but also this Demoiselle in its elegant bottle. Chardonnay plays the most significant part in it (60%). The bouquet is pure citrus fruits, while on the palate a touch of sweetness balances its youth. Commendations went to two further *cuvées*: the **Demoiselle rosé** and the **Vranken rosé**. The first, which marries red berries and lemon on the nose, owes nearly all to Chardonnay (85%); the second, a blend of all three champagne grape varieties, has good vinosity, structure and balance. (NM)

☛ Vranken, 42, av. de Champagne, 51200 Epernay, tel. 03.26.59.51.32, fax 03.26.59.51.39 ☑
☠ by appt.

WARIS-LARMANDIER★

● 1er cru	0.15 ha	1,000	▯ ⚬	11–15 €

In September 2000, Marie-Hélène Waris was suddenly left with her young children to carry on this estate created in 1991 by the husband whom she had lost too soon. She offers a rosé that owes its finesse and its elegance to 80% Chardonnay, supplemented by 20% Pinot Noir. Its purplish-pink colour clearly indicates the youthfulness of the wines of 1999 and 2000 that are blended in it, and which contribute to the direct-ness of its attack and to the freshness of its grapefruit flavours. An aperitif champagne. (RM)

☛ EARL Waris-Larmandier, 608, rempart du Nord, 51190 Avize, tel. 03.26.57.79.05, fax 03.26.52.79.52 ☑
☠ by appt.

Wines selected but not starred

ARISTON FILS

Carte blanche

○	10.3 ha	10,000	▯	15–23 €

☛ Rémi Ariston, 4 et 8, Grande-Rue, 51170 Brouillet, tel. 03.26.97.43.46, fax 03.26.97.49.34, e-mail contact@champagne-aristonfils.com ☑ ☷
☠ ev. day 9am–12 noon 2pm–6pm; Sun. by appt.; cl. 3rd week Aug.

AYALA

	n.c.	n.c.	15–23 €

☛ Ayala, 2, bd du Nord, BP 6, 51160 Aÿ-Champagne, tel. 03.26.55.15.44, fax 03.26.51.09.04 ☑
☠ by appt.

CHRISTIAN BANNIERE

● Gd cru	n.c.	2,000	▯ ⚬	11–15 €

☛ Christian Bannière, 5, rue Yvonnet, 51150 Bouzy, tel. 03.26.57.08.15, fax 03.26.59.35.02, e-mail contact@christianbanniere.com ☑
☠ by appt.

HERBERT BEAUFORT

Extra-brut Age d'or 1999

○	7 ha	7,500	▯	15–23 €

☛ Herbert Beaufort, 32, rue de Tours-sur-Marne, BP 7, 51150 Bouzy, tel. 03.26.57.01.34, fax 03.26.57.09.08, e-mail beaufort-herbert@wanadoo.fr ☑
☠ ev. day 9am–12 noon 2pm–5pm

BEAUMONT DES CRAYÈRES

Fleur de Rosé 1998

●	3 ha	18,000	🍾 ♦	15–23 €

🍇 Beaumont des Crayères, BP 1030, 51318 Epernay Cedex, tel. 03.26.55.29.40, fax 03.26.54.26.30, e-mail contact@champagne-beaumont.com ☑
🍷 ev. day 10am–12 noon 2pm–5pm; cl. Sat. Sun. from Christmas to Easter

ALAIN BEDEL

●	6.53 ha	2,000	🍾 🕪	11–15 €

🍇 EARL Alain Bédel, 1, rue des Glauriettes, Grand Porteron, 02310 Charly-sur-Marne, tel. 03.23.82.02.74, fax 03.23.82.08.19, e-mail abedel@quid-info.fr ☑
🍷 by appt.

GÉRARD BELIN

Sélection

●	0.7 ha	6,500	🍾 ♦	11–15 €

🍇 Gérard Belin, 30, Aulnois, 02400 Essômes-sur-Marne, tel. 03.23.70.88.43, fax 03.23.83.10.97, e-mail champagne-belin@wanadoo.fr ☑
🍷 by appt.

BÉRÈCHE ET FILS

Blanc de blancs

● 1er cru	0.8 ha	n.c.	🍾	15–23 €

🍇 Bérèche et fils, Le Craon-de-Ludes, BP 18, 51500 Ludes, tel. 03.26.61.13.28, fax 03.26.61.14.14, e-mail info@champagne-bereche-et-fils.com ☑
🍷 by appt.

PIERRE BERTRAND

Cuvée de réserve Sélection

●	2 ha	n.c.	🍾	15–23 €

🍇 Pierre et Thérèse Bertrand, 166, rue Louis-Dupont, 51480 Cumières, tel. 03.26.54.08.24, fax 03.26.55.22.08 ☑

CH. DE BLIGNY

Grande Réserve

●	2.2 ha	21,000	🍾 ♦	11–15 €

🍇 Ch. de Bligny, 10200 Bligny, tel. 03.25.27.40.11, fax 03.25.27.04.52 ☑
🍷 by appt.

H. BLIN ET CIE 1998

●	7 ha	40,000	🍾	15–23 €

🍇 H. Blin et Cie, 5, rue de Verdun, 51700 Vincelles, tel. 03.26.58.20.04, fax 03.26.58.29.67, e-mail contact@champagne-blin.com ☑
🍷 by appt.

JEAN-PAUL BOULONNAIS

Blanc de blancs Réserve

●	5 ha	5,000	🍾	11–15 €

🍇 Jean-Paul Boulonnais, 14, rue de l'Abbaye, 51130 Vertus, tel. 03.26.52.23.41, fax 03.26.52.27.55 ☑
🍷 by appt.

BOURGEOIS-BOULONNAIS

Tradition

● 1er cru	5.5 ha	n.c.	🍾	11–15 €

🍇 Bourgeois-Boulonnais, 8, rue de l'Abbaye, 51130 Vertus, tel. 03.26.52.26.73, fax 03.26.52.06.55, e-mail bourgeoi@hexanet.fr ☑
🍷 by appt.

G. BOUTILLEZ-VIGNON

Cuvée Prestige

● 1er cru	2.5 ha	12,000	🍾 🕪	11–15 €

🍇 G. Boutillez-Vignon, 26, rue Pasteur, 51380 Villers-Marmery, tel. 03.26.97.95.87 ☑
🍷 by appt.

ANDRÉ BROCHOT

Grande Réserve 1997

●	n.c.	4,795	🍾 ♦	15–23 €

🍇 Francis Brochot, 21, rue de Champagne, 51530 Vinay, tel. 03.26.59.91.39, fax 03.26.59.91.39 ☑
🍷 by appt.

BRUGNON

Sélection

●	3 ha	10,000	🍾 ♦	11–15 €

🍇 Alain Brugnon, 1, rue Brûlée, 51500 Ecueil, tel. 03.26.49.25.95, fax 03.26.49.76.56, e-mail brugnon@cder.fr ☑
🍷 by appt.

JACQUES BUSIN

Carte d'or

● Gd cru	5 ha	30,000	🍾 ♦	11–15 €

🍇 Jacques Busin, 17, rue Thiers, 51360 Verzenay, tel. 03.26.49.40.36, fax 03.26.49.81.11, e-mail jacques-busin@wanadoo.fr ☑
🍷 by appt.

GUY CADEL

Carte blanche

●	5 ha	30,000	🍾 🕪 ♦	8–11 €

🍇 Guy Cadel, 13, rue Jean-Jaurès, 51530 Mardeuil, tel. 03.26.55.24.59 e-mail guycadel@terre-net.fr ☑
🍷 by appt.
🍇 M. Thiebault

PIERRE CALLOT

Blanc de blancs Grande Réserve

● Gd cru	0.5 ha	4,000	🍾 🕪	15–23 €

🍇 Pierre Callot et Fils, 100, av. Jean-Jaurès, 51190 Avize, tel. 03.26.57.51.57, fax 03.26.57.99.15 ☑
🍷 by appt.

JEAN-YVES DE CARLINI

Réserve

● Gd cru	3.5 ha	7,000	🍾	11–15 €

🍇 Jean-Yves de Carlini, 13, rue de Mailly, 51360 Verzenay, tel. 03.26.49.43.91, fax 03.26.49.46.46 ☑
🍷 by appt.

CHARLES DE CAZANOVE

Brut Azur

● 1er cru	n.c.	n.c.	🍾	15–23 €

🍇 Charles de Cazanove, 1, rue des Cotelles, 51200 Epernay, tel. 03.26.59.57.40, fax 03.26.54.16.38 ☑

GUY CHARLEMAGNE

Blanc de blancs Cuvée Charlemagne 1998

● Gd cru	1.5 ha	9,000	🍾 ♦	15–23 €

🍇 Guy Charlemagne, 4, rue de La Brèche-d'Oger, BP 15, 51190 Le Mesnil-sur-Oger, tel. 03.26.57.52.98, fax 03.26.57.97.81, e-mail info@champagne-guy-charlemagne.com ☑
🍷 by appt.
🍇 Philippe Charlemagne

COLLARD-CHARDELLE
Cuvée Prestige

| | n.c. | n.c. | 🍶 | 15–23 € |

🍇 Collard-Chardelle, 68, rue de Reuil,
51700 Villers-sous-Châtillon, tel. 03.26.58.00.50,
fax 03.26.58.34.76 ☑
🍷 by appt.

DANIEL COLLIN
Grande Réserve

| | 1 ha | 10,000 | 🍾 ⚲ | 11–15 € |

🍇 Daniel Collin, 3, rue Caye, 21270 Baye,
tel. 03.26.52.80.50, fax 03.26.52.33.62,
e-mail collin@hexanet.fr ☑
🍷 by appt.

S. COQUILLETTE 1998

| | 1 ha | 7,826 | 🍾 | 15–23 € |

🍇 Stéphane Coquillette, 15, rue des Ecoles, 51530 Chouilly,
tel. 03.26.51.74.12, fax 03.26.54.90.97 ☑
🍷 by appt.

LUCIEN DAGONET ET FILS

| | n.c. | 25,000 | 🍾 ⚲ | 11–15 € |

🍇 SCEV Lucien Dagonet et Fils, 7, rue Maurice-Gilbert,
51480 Boursault, tel. 03.26.58.60.38, fax 03.26.58.48.34,
e-mail ldagchamp@wanadoo.fr ☑
🍷 ev. day 9am–6pm

PAUL DANGIN ET FILS
Carte noire

| | n.c. | 68,000 | 🍾 ⚲ | 11–15 € |

🍇 SCEV Paul Dangin et Fils, 11, rue du Pont,
10110 Celles-sur-Ource, tel. 03.25.38.50.27,
fax 03.25.38.58.08 ☑
🍷 by appt.

DEHOURS
Confidentielle

| | 0.4 ha | 4,000 | | 15–23 € |

🍇 Dehours et Fils, 2, rue de la Chapelle, Cerseuil,
51700 Mareuil-le-Port, tel. 03.26.52.71.75,
fax 03.26.52.73.83,
e-mail champagne.dehours@wanadoo.fr ☑
🍷 by appt.

DELABARRE
Tradition

| | 2.5 ha | 20,000 | 🍾 ⚲ | 11–15 € |

🍇 Christiane Delabarre, 26, rue de Châtillon,
51700 Vandières, tel. 03.26.58.02.65, fax 03.26.57.10.94,
e-mail delabarre.christiane@wanadoo.fr ☑
🍷 by appt.

DELAMOTTE

| | n.c. | n.c. | 🍾 | 15–23 € |

🍇 Delamotte, 5, rue de la Brèche-d'Oger,
51190 Le Mesnil-sur-Oger, tel. 03.26.57.51.65,
fax 03.26.57.79.29, e-mail champagne@salondelamotte.com
🍷 by appt.

ANDRE DELAUNOIS
Cuvée sublime

| 1er cru | 3.8 ha | 35,000 | 🍾 | 11–15 € |

🍇 SCEV André Delaunois, 17, rue Roger-Salengro,
51500 Rilly-la-Montagne, tel. 03.26.03.42.87,
fax 03.26.03.45.40,
e-mail champagne.a.delaunois@wanadoo.fr ☑
🍷 by appt.

DELOUVIN NOWACK
Carte d'or

| | 5 ha | 30,000 | 🍾 ⚲ | 11–15 € |

🍇 Delouvin-Nowack, 29, rue Principale, 51700 Vandières,
tel. 03.26.58.02.70, fax 03.26.57.10.11,
e-mail info@champagne-delouvin-nowack.com ☑
🍷 by appt.
🍇 Bertrand Delouvin

MICHEL DEMIERE
Blanc de blancs

| 1er cru | 3 ha | 5,000 | | 11–15 € |

🍇 Michel Demière, 2, allée du Jardinot, 51380 Trépail,
tel. 03.26.57.06.23, fax 03.26.57.83.04 ☑

PAUL DETHUNE

| Gd cru | 5 ha | 30,000 | 🍾 🍶 ⚲ | 11–15 € |

🍇 Déthune, 2, rue du Moulin, 51150 Ambonnay,
tel. 03.26.57.01.88, fax 03.26.57.09.31,
e-mail info@champagne-dethune.com ☑
🍷 by appt.

LOUIS DOUSSET
Blanc de noirs

| | 8 ha | 40,000 ⚲ | | 15–23 € |

🍇 Jean-Roch Floquet, 8, rue Werle, 51360 Verzenay,
tel. 03.26.83.99.08, fax 03.26.83.55.80,
e-mail contact@louis-dousset.com ☑
🍷 by appt.

DOYARD
Blanc de blancs Collection de l'An I 1995

| 1er cru | 2 ha | 7,000 | 🍶 | 23–30 € |

🍇 Robert Doyard et Fils, 61, av. Bammental, 51130 Vertus,
tel. 03.26.52.14.74, fax 03.26.52.24.02,
e-mail champagne.doyard@wanadoo.fr ☑
🍷 by appt.

HERVE DUBOIS
Blanc de blancs Réserve

| Gd cru | 2 ha | 5,000 | 🍾 | 11–15 € |

🍇 Hervé Dubois, 67, rue Ernest-Vallé, 51190 Avize,
tel. 03.26.57.52.45, fax 03.26.57.99.26 ☑
🍷 by appt.

CHARLES ELLNER
Carte d'or

| | n.c. | 230,000 | 🍾 ⚲ | 11–15 € |

🍇 Charles Ellner, 6, rue Côte-Legris, BP 223,
51200 Epernay, tel. 03.26.55.60.25, fax 03.26.51.54.00,
e-mail info@champagne-ellner.com ☑
🍷 by appt.

ESTERLIN
Sélection

| | 120 ha | 100,000 | 🍾 ⚲ | 11–15 € |

🍇 Esterlin, 25, av. de Champagne, BP 342, 51334 Epernay
Cedex, tel. 03.26.59.71.52, fax 03.26.59.77.72,
e-mail contact@champagne-esterlin.fr ☑
🍷 by appt.

JEAN-MARIE ETIENNE 1996

| 1er cru | 0.7 ha | 6,000 | 🍾 | 15–23 € |

🍇 Daniel et Pascal Etienne, 33, rue Louis-Dupont,
51480 Cumières, tel. 03.26.51.66.62, fax 03.26.55.04.65 ☑
🍷 by appt.

EUSTACHE DESCHAMPS

Cuvée de réserve

	n.c.	150,000	▮ ⚬	11–15 €

☛ La Vigneronne, 38, av. Bammental, 51130 Vertus, tel. 03.26.52.18.95, fax 03.26.58.39.47, e-mail coop.lavigneronne@free.fr ☑
⍾ by appt. cl. Aug.

PHILIPPE FAYS

2 ha	19,000	▮	11–15 €

☛ Philippe Fays, 94, Grande-Rue, 10110 Celles-sur-Ource, tel. 03.25.38.51.47, fax 03.25.38.23.04 ☑
⍾ by appt.

FENEUIL-POINTILLART

Cuvée Louis 1996

1er cru	n.c.	2,500	▮	15–23 €

☛ Feneuil-Pointillart, 21, rue du Jard, 51500 Chamery, tel. 03.26.97.62.35, fax 03.26.97.67.70 ☑
⍾ by appt.
☛ Daniel Feneuil

ALEXANDRE FILAINE

Cuvée Confidence

1 ha	3,100	⑪	11–15 €

☛ Fabrice Gass, 17, rue Poincaré, 51480 Damery, tel. 03.26.58.88.39, e-mail fgass@wanadoo.fr ☑
⍾ by appt.

FORGET-BRIMONT

Extra-brut

1er cru	14 ha	20,000	▮ ⚬	15–23 €

☛ Forget-Brimont, 11, rte de Louvois, 51500 Craon-de-Ludes, tel. 03.26.61.10.45, fax 03.26.61.11.58, e-mail contact@champagne-forget-brimont.fr ☑
⍾ by appt.
☛ Michel Forget

PHILIPPE FOURRIER

Cuvée Prestige

3 ha	n.c.	▮	15–23 €

☛ Philippe Fourrier, rte de Bar-sur-Aube, 10200 Baroville, tel. 03.25.27.13.44, fax 03.25.27.12.49, e-mail champagne.fourrier@wanadoo.fr ☑
⍾ by appt.

FRESNET-BAUDOT

Gd cru	2.5 ha	20,000	▮ ⚬	15–23 €

☛ Fresnet-Baudot, 9, rte de Puisieulx, 51500 Sillery, tel. 03.26.49.11.74, fax 03.26.49.10.72, e-mail courrier@champagne-fresnet.fr ☑
⍾ by appt.

FREZIER-ROGELET

Blanc de blancs

Gd cru	1.58 ha	12,650	▮	11–15 €

☛ EARL Frézier-Rogelet, 411, rue Ferdinand-Moret, 51530 Cramant, tel. 03.26.57.57.53, fax 03.26.51.90.25 ☑
⍾ by appt.

GAILLARD-GIROT

Réserve

3.5 ha	25,000	▮ ⑪	11–15 €

☛ EARL Gaillard-Girot, 43, rue Victor-Hugo, 51530 Mardeuil, tel. 03.26.51.64.59, fax 03.26.51.70.59, e-mail champagne-gaillard-girot@wanadoo.fr ☑
⍾ by appt.

GALLIMARD PERE ET FILS

Cuvée de réserve

10 ha	100,000		11–15 €

☛ Gallimard Père et Fils, 18, rue Gaston-Cheq, 10340 Les Riceys, tel. 03.25.29.32.44, fax 03.25.38.55.20 ☑
⍾ by appt.

GAUDINAT-BOIVIN

Tradition

3.75 ha	28,000	▮ ⑪		11–15 €

☛ EARL Gaudinat-Boivin, 6, rue des Vignes, Mesnil-le-Huttier, 51700 Festigny, tel. 03.26.58.01.52, fax 03.26.58.97.46 ☑
⍾ by appt.

RENE GEOFFROY

Cuvée de réserve

6 ha	74,000	▮	11–15 €

☛ René Geoffroy, 150, rue du Bois-des-Jots, 51480 Cumières, tel. 03.26.55.32.31, fax 03.26.54.66.50, e-mail info@champagne-geoffroy.com ☑
⍾ by appt.

HENRI GIRAUD

Réserve

Gd cru	2.7 ha	20,000	▮ ⚬	15–23 €

☛ Henri Giraud, 71, bd Charles-de-Gaulle, 51160 A, tel. 03.26.55.18.55, fax 03.26.55.33.49, e-mail champagne.henri.giraud@wanadoo.fr ☑
⍾ by appt.

FRANCOIS GONET

Blanc de blancs Réserve

1 ha	5,000	▮	11–15 €

☛ Catherine Grivot-Gonet, 5, rue du Stade, 51190 Le Mesnil-sur-Oger, tel. 03.26.58.85.83, fax 03.26.59.37.84 ☑
⍾ by appt.

GRUET 1999

10 ha	132,292	▮ ⚬	11–15 €

☛ SARL Gruet, 48, Grande-Rue, 10110 Buxeuil, tel. 03.25.38.54.94, fax 03.25.38.51.84, e-mail champagne-gruet@wanadoo.fr ☑
⍾ ev. day 8.30am–12 noon 2pm–6pm; Sat. Sun. by appt.; cl. 15th–22nd Aug.

P. GUERRE ET FILS

Réserve

2 ha	19,858		11–15 €

☛ Michel Guerre, 3, rue de Champagne, 51480 Venteuil, tel. 03.26.58.62.72 ☑
⍾ ev. day 9am–11am 2pm–5pm

HATON ET FILS

Blanc de blancs Grande Réserve

1 ha	4,000	▮	11–15 €

☛ Philippe Haton et Fils, 3, rue Jean-Mermoz, 51480 Damery, tel. 03.26.58.41.11, fax 03.26.58.45.98, e-mail champagne.haton.et.fils.philippe@wanadoo.fr ☑
⍾ by appt.

LUDOVIC HATTE

Grande Réserve

5 ha	20,000	▮	11–15 €

☛ Ludovic Hatté, 3, rue Thiers, 51360 Verzenay, tel. 03.26.49.43.94, fax 03.26.49.81.96 ☑
⍾ by appt.

DIDIER HERBERT

| | Gd cru | 2 ha | 7,000 | 🍾 ⚬ | 11–15 € |

� Didier Herbert, 32, rue de Reims,
51500 Rilly-la-Montagne, tel. 03.26.03.41.53,
fax 03.26.03.44.64, e-mail infos@champagneherbert.fr ✅
🍷 by appt.

STEPHANE HERBERT

Réserve Cuvée Véronèse

| | 1er cru | 1.47 ha | n.c. | | 11–15 € |

� Stéphane Herbert, 11, rue Roger-Salengro,
51500 Rilly-la-Montagne, tel. 03.26.03.49.93,
fax 03.26.02.01.39,
e-mail champagneherbert@wanadoo.fr ✅
🍷 by appt.

M. HOSTOMME ET SES FILS

Cuvée Tradition

| | Gd cru | 4 ha | 50,000 | 🍾 🎵 ⚬ | 11–15 € |

➴ Laurent Hostomme, 5, rue de l'Allée, 51530 Chouilly,
tel. 03.26.55.40.79, fax 03.26.55.08.55,
e-mail champagne.hostomme@wanadoo.fr ✅
🍷 by appt.

IVERNEL

Prestige

| | | n.c. | 50,000 | 🍾 ⚬ | 15–23 € |

➴ Ivernel, BP 15, 51160 Aÿ-Champagne,
tel. 03.26.55.21.10, fax 03.26.51.55.88 ✅

PIERRE JAMAIN

Blanc de blancs 1998

| | | 1.5 ha | 11,322 | 🍾 | 11–15 € |

➴ Pierre Jamain, 1, rue des Tuileries, 51260 La
Celle-sous-Chantemerle, tel. 03.26.80.21.64,
fax 03.26.80.29.32 ✅
🍷 by appt.

E. JAMART & CIE

Volupté

| | | n.c. | 5,000 | 🍾 | 15–23 € |

➴ E. Jamart et Cie, 13, rue Marcel-Soyeux,
51530 Saint-Martin-d'Ablois, tel. 03.26.59.92.78,
fax 03.26.59.95.23,
e-mail champagne.jamart@wanadoo.fr ✅
🍷 ev. day except Sun. 9am–12 noon 2pm–5.30pm;
cl. 15th–31st Aug.

CHRISTOPHE JANISSON

Tradition

| | Gd cru | 1 ha | 10,000 | 🍾 | 11–15 € |

➴ Christophe Janisson, 20, rue Kellermann,
51500 Mailly-Champagne, tel. 03.26.49.46.82,
fax 03.26.83.16.54,
e-mail janisson.christophe@libertysurf.fr ✅
🍷 by appt.

JANISSON-BARADON ET FILS

Les Toulettes 1997

| | | 0.8 ha | 2,993 | 🍾 🎵 ⚬ | 30–38 € |

➴ SCEV Janisson-Baradon, 2, rue des Vignerons,
51200 Epernay, tel. 03.26.54.45.85, fax 03.26.54.25.54,
e-mail info@champagne-janisson.com ✅

CUVEE LAHERTE FRERES 1998

| | | 1.3 ha | 9,000 | 🎵 | 15–23 € |

➴ Laherte Frères, 3, rue des Jardins,
51530 Chavot-Courcourt, tel. 03.26.54.32.09,
fax 03.26.51.54.77,
e-mail champagne.laherte.freres@wanadoo.fr ✅ 🌱
🍷 by appt.

RENE-JAMES LALLIER

Blanc de blancs

| | | n.c. | n.c. | 🍾 ⚬ | 15–23 € |

➴ SA René-James Lallier, 4, pl. de la Libération, 51160 A,
tel. 03.26.55.32.87, fax 03.26.55.79.93,
e-mail champagne.lallier@henanet.fr ✅
🍷 by appt.

LAMIABLE

Cuvée Spécial Club 1999

| | Gd cru | 5.8 ha | 3,000 | 🍾 | 15–23 € |

➴ Jean-Pierre Lamiable, 8, rue de Condé,
51150 Tours-sur-Marne, tel. 03.26.58.92.69,
fax 03.26.58.76.67,
e-mail champagne.lamiable@wanadoo.fr ✅
🍷 by appt.

JEAN-JACQUES LAMOUREUX

Réserve

| | | 5 ha | 38,761 | | 11–15 € |

➴ EARL Jean-Jacques Lamoureux, 27, rue du
Gal-de-Gaulle, 10340 Les Riceys, tel. 03.25.29.11.55,
fax 03.25.29.69.22 ✅
🍷 ev. day 9am–12 noon 2pm–6pm

YVES LANCELOT-WANNER

Blanc de blancs 1995

| | Gd cru | 4.25 ha | n.c. | 🍾 🎵 | 15–23 € |

➴ Yves Lancelot-Wanner, 155, rue de la Garenne,
51530 Cramant, tel. 03.26.57.58.95, fax 03.26.57.00.30,
e-mail philippe.lancelot@laposte.net ✅
🍷 by appt.

GUY LARMANDIER

| | 1er cru | 3.8 ha | n.c. | 🍾 ⚬ | 11–15 € |

➴ EARL Guy Larmandier, 30, rue du Gal-Koenig,
51130 Vertus, tel. 03.26.52.12.41, fax 03.26.52.19.38 ✅
🍷 by appt.

LAUNOIS PERE ET FILS

Blanc de blancs Cuvée réservée

| | Gd cru | 10 ha | 100,000 | 🍾 | 11–15 € |

➴ Launois Père et Fils, 2, av. Eugène-Guillaume, 51190 Le
Mesnil-sur-Oger, tel. 03.26.57.50.15, fax 03.26.57.97.82,
e-mail info@champagne-launois.fr ✅
🍷 ev. day 10am–12.30pm 2pm–5.30pm

LE BRUN SERVENAY

| ● | | 0.4 ha | 2,250 | 🍾 ⚬ | 11–15 € |

➴ EARL Le Brun-Servenay, 14, pl. Léon-Bourgeois,
51190 Avize, tel. 03.26.57.52.75, fax 03.26.57.02.71 ✅
🍷 by appt.

LECLERC-MONDET

| | | 6 ha | n.c. | 🍾 | 11–15 € |

➴ Leclerc-Mondet, 5, rue Beethoven,
02850 Trélou-sur-Marne, tel. 03.23.70.23.39,
fax 03.23.70.10.59 ✅
🍷 by appt.

MICHEL LENIQUE

Prestige

| ● | | 1 ha | 2,500 | 🍾 ⚬ | 11–15 € |

➴ SA Lenique et Fils, 20, rue du Gal-de-Gaulle,
51530 Pierry, tel. 03.26.54.03.65, fax 03.26.51.57.14,
e-mail salenique@wanadoo.fr ✅
🍷 by appt.

AR LENOBLE

Blanc de noirs 1998

1er cru	n.c.	25,000	30–38 €

☙ Lenoble, 35, rue Paul-Douce, 51480 Damery,
tel. 03.26.58.42.60, fax 03.26.58.65.57,
e-mail contact@champagne-lenoble.com ☑
🍷 by appt.
☙ Malassagne

LÉTÉ-VAUTRAIN

Traditionnel

	6.2 ha	45,000	11–15 €

☙ Lété-Vautrain, 11, rue de Villers, Hameau de Courteau,
02400 Château-Thierry, tel. 03.23.83.05.38,
fax 03.23.83.87.45, e-mail lete.vautr@quid-info.fr ☑
🍷 ev. day except Sun. 8.30am–12.30pm 1.30pm–6.30pm

M. MAILLART

Cuvée de réserve 1997

1er cru	1.5 ha	14,000	11–15 €

☙ SCEV M. Maillart, 11, rue de Villers, 51500 Ecueil,
tel. 03.26.49.77.89, fax 03.26.49.24.79,
e-mail m.maillart@free.fr ☑
🍷 ev. day except Sat. Sun. 8am–12 noon 1.30pm–6pm;
cl. 15th Aug.–1st Sep.

MALARD

Blanc de blancs Excellence

Gd cru	n.c.	100,000	11–15 €

☙ J.-L. Malard, 65, av. de Champagne, BP 95,
51203 Epernay Cedex, tel. 03.26.57.77.24,
fax 03.26.52.75.54,
e-mail info@champagnemalard.com

DIDIER MARC 1999

	0.5 ha	2,174	15–23 €

☙ Didier Marc, 11, rue Dom-Pérignon,
51480 Fleury-la-Rivière, tel. 03.26.58.60.69,
fax 03.26.52.84.20, e-mail dimadimo@club-internet.fr ☑
🍷 ev. day 8am–7pm

A. MARGAINE

Blanc de blancs Spécial Club 1997

	0.4 ha	3,500	15–23 €

☙ A. Margaine, 3, av. de Champagne,
51380 Villers-Marmery, tel. 03.26.97.92.13,
fax 03.26.97.97.45,
e-mail champagne.margaine@terre-net.fr ☑
🍷 by appt.

MARIE STUART

Cuvée de la Reine

	n.c.	n.c.	23–30 €

☙ Marie Stuart, 8, pl. de la République, 51100 Reims,
tel. 03.26.77.50.50, fax 03.26.77.50.59,
e-mail marie.stuart@wanadoo.fr ☑
🍷 by appt.

JEAN MARNIQUET

Carte blanche

1er cru	6 ha	21,000	11–15 €

☙ EARL Brice Marniquet, 12, rue Pasteur,
51160 Avenay-Val-d'Or, tel. 03.26.52.32.36,
fax 03.26.52.65.89, e-mail marniquet@aol.com ☑

PAUL-LOUIS MARTIN

	3 ha	29,000	11–15 €

☙ Paul-Louis Martin, 3, rue d'Ambonnay, BP 4,
51150 Bouzy, tel. 03.26.57.01.27, fax 03.26.57.83.25 ☑
🍷 by appt.

DENIS MARX

Réserve

	n.c.	30,000	11–15 €

☙ Denis Marx, 31, rue de la Chapelle, 51700 Cerseuil,
tel. 03.26.52.71.96, fax 03.26.52.72.65 ☑
🍷 by appt.

SERGE MATHIEU

Blanc de noirs Cuvée Tradition

	5 ha	40,000	11–15 €

☙ Serge Mathieu, 6, rue des Vignes, 10340 Avirey-Lingey,
tel. 03.25.29.32.58, fax 03.25.29.11.57,
e-mail info@champagne-serge-mathieu.fr ☑
🍷 by appt.

MEDOT

Clos des Chaulins

1er cru	0.61 ha	n.c.	15–23 €

☙ SE Médot, 19, rte de Dormans, 51390 Pargny-lès-Reims,
tel. 03.26.49.28.01, fax 03.26.49.28.04,
e-mail info@champagne-medot.com ☑
🍷 by appt.
☙ T. Lombard

DE MERIC

Grande Réserve sous bois

1er cru	n.c.	50,000	15–23 €

☙ de Méric, 17, rue Gambetta, 51160 Aÿ-Champagne,
tel. 03.26.55.20.72, fax 03.26.55.69.23,
e-mail de-meric@wanadoo.fr ☑
🍷 by appt.

JEAN MICHEL

Carte d'or 1999

	3.5 ha	30,000	11–15 €

☙ Jean Michel, 15, rue Jean-Jaurès, BP 14, 51530 Moussy,
tel. 03.26.54.03.33, fax 03.26.51.62.66 ☑
🍷 by appt.

ALBERT DE MILLY

	15 ha	n.c.	11–15 €

☙ Albert de Milly, lieu-dit La Maladrerie, 51150 Bisseuil,
tel. 03.26.52.33.44, fax 03.26.58.94.00,
e-mail demilly@wanadoo.fr ☑
🍷 by appt.

MONDET

Prestige 1997

	0.5 ha	5,300	15–23 €

☙ Mondet, 2, rue Dom-Pérignon, 51480 Cormoyeux,
tel. 03.26.58.64.15, fax 03.26.58.44.00,
e-mail champagne.mondet@cder.fr ☑
🍷 by appt.

MONMARTHE

Grande Réserve

1er cru	3 ha	25,000	11–15 €

☙ Jean-Guy Monmarthe, 38, rue Victor-Hugo,
51500 Ludes, tel. 03.26.61.10.99, fax 03.26.61.12.67,
e-mail champagne-monmarthe@wanadoo.fr ☑
🍷 by appt.

MOREL PERE ET FILS

Rosé de cuvaison 2000

	2 ha	4,000	11–15 €

☙ Morel Père et Fils, 93, rue du Gal-de-Gaulle, 10340 Les
Riceys, tel. 03.25.29.10.88, fax 03.25.29.66.72,
e-mail morel.pereetfils@wanadoo.fr ☑
🍷 by appt.

PALMER ET CO

	n.c.	n.c.	🍾 ⚲	11–15 €

🍴 Palmer et Co, 67, rue Jacquart, 51100 Reims, tel. 03.26.07.35.07, fax 03.26.07.45.24 ☑
🍷 by appt. cl. Aug.

PAQUES ET FILS

Carte or

1er cru	6 ha	50,000	🍾 ⚲	11–15 €

🍴 Paques et Fils, 1, rue Valmy, 51500 Rilly-la-Montagne, tel. 03.26.03.42.53, fax 03.26.03.40.29, e-mail phil.paques@wanadoo.fr ☑
🍷 by appt.

PERSEVAL-FARGE

Blanc de noirs

1er cru	2 ha	3,000	🍾 ◫ ⚲	15–23 €

🍴 Isabelle et Benoist Perseval, 12, rue du Voisin, 51500 Chamery, tel. 03.26.97.64.70, fax 03.26.97.67.67, e-mail champagne.perseval-farge@wanadoo.fr ☑
🍷 by appt.

PHILIZOT & FILS

Numéro 2

	n.c.	5,000	🍾	11–15 €

🍴 Philizot & Fils, 49, Grande Rue, 51480 Reuil, tel. 03.26.51.02.96, fax 03.26.51.02.96, e-mail sphilizot@hotmail.com ☑
🍷 by appt.

POISSINET-ASCAS

Grande Réserve

	n.c.	12,110	🍾	11–15 €

🍴 Poissinet-Ascas, 8, rue du Pont, 51480 Cuchery, tel. 03.26.58.12.93, fax 03.26.52.03.55, e-mail regis.poissinet@wanadoo.fr ☑
🍷 by appt.

CHARLES POUGEOISE

Blanc de blancs

1er cru	8 ha	n.c.	🍾	11–15 €

🍴 SCEV Charles Pougeoise, 21, bd Paul-Goerg, 51130 Vertus, tel. 03.26.52.26.63, fax 03.26.52.19.66, e-mail charles.pougeoise@wanadoo.fr ☑
🍷 by appt.

YANNICK PREVOTEAU

Cuvée Amandine

	0.6 ha	6,000	🍾	11–15 €

🍴 Gérald et Yannick Prévoteau, 4 bis, av. de Champagne, 51480 Damery, tel. 03.26.58.41.65, fax 03.26.58.61.05, e-mail yannick.prevoteau@wanadoo.fr ☑
🍷 by appt.

DIDIER RAIMOND

Blanc de blancs Cuvée Sublime

Gd cru	0.2 ha	601	🍾	11–15 €

🍴 Didier Raimond, 39, rue des Petits-Prés, 51200 Epernay, tel. 03.26.54.39.05, fax 03.26.54.51.70 ☑
🍷 by appt.

R. RENAUDIN

Réserve

	24 ha	148,000	🍾 ⚲	15–23 €

🍴 SCEV Dom. des Conardins, R. Renaudin, 31, rue de la Liberté, 51530 Moussy, tel. 03.26.54.03.41, fax 03.26.54.31.12, e-mail champagne@r-renaudin.com ☑
🍷 ev. day except Sat. Sun. 9am–12 noon 2pm–5pm
🍴 Tellier

ROUSSEAUX-BATTEUX

●	0.3 ha	3,000	🍾	11–15 €

🍴 Rousseaux-Batteux, 17, rue de Mailly, 51360 Verzenay, tel. 03.26.49.81.81, fax 03.26.49.48.49 ☑
🍷 by appt.

ROYER PERE ET FILS

Cuvée de réserve

	14 ha	130,000	🍾	11–15 €

🍴 Royer Père et Fils, 120, Grande-Rue, BP 6, 10110 Landreville, tel. 03.25.38.52.16, fax 03.25.38.37.17, e-mail infos@champagne-royer.com ☑
🍷 by appt.

SALMON

Réserve

	7 ha	36,718	🍾	11–15 €

🍴 EARL Salmon, 21–23, rue du Capitaine-Chesnais, 51170 Chaumuzy, tel. 03.26.61.82.36, fax 03.26.61.80.24 ☑
🍷 by appt.

DENIS SALOMON

Cuvée Prestige 1999

	1.2 ha	8,900		11–15 €

🍴 Denis Salomon, 5, rue Principale, 51700 Vandières, tel. 03.26.58.05.77, fax 03.26.58.00.25, e-mail info@champagne-salomon.com ☑
🍷 by appt.

SERVEAUX FILS

Carte d'or

	2 ha	15,600	🍾 ⚲	11–15 €

🍴 Pascal Serveaux, 2, rue de Champagne, 02850 Passy-sur-Marne, tel. 03.23.70.35.65, fax 03.23.70.15.99, e-mail serveaux.p@wanadoo.fr ☑
🍷 by appt.

SIMON-SELOSSE

Blanc de blancs

Gd cru	n.c.	n.c.	🍾	11–15 €

🍴 Simon-Selosse, 20, rue d'Oger, 51190 Avize, tel. 03.26.57.52.40, fax 03.26.52.85.16, e-mail champ.simon-selosse@wanadoo.fr ☑
🍷 by appt.

STEPHANE ET FILS

Carte blanche

	6.5 ha	15,000	🍾	11–15 €

🍴 EARL Stéphane et Fils, 1, pl. Berry, 51480 Boursault, tel. 03.26.58.40.81, fax 03.26.51.03.79 ☑
🍷 by appt.
🍴 Xavier Foin

TARLANT

Brut Zéro

	2 ha	14,000	🍾 ◫ ⚲	15–23 €

🍴 Tarlant, 51480 OEuilly, tel. 03.26.58.30.60, fax 03.26.58.37.31, e-mail champagne@tarlant.com ☑
🍷 ev. day except Sun. 10am–12 noon 1.30pm–5.30pm; cl. Jan.

EMMANUEL TASSIN

Cuvée Tradition

	2.5 ha	20,000	🍾	11–15 €

🍴 Emmanuel Tassin, 104, Grande-Rue, 10110 Celles-sur-Ource, tel. 03.25.38.59.44, fax 03.25.29.94.59 ☑
🍷 by appt.

V. TESTULAT

Carte d'or

	13 ha	117,000		11–15 €

🍷 SA V. Testulat, 23, rue Léger-Bertin, BP 21,
51201 Epernay, tel. 03.26.54.10.65, fax 03.26.54.61.18,
e-mail vtestulat@champagne-testulat.com ☑
🍾 by appt.

TRIBAUT-SCHLOESSER

Cuvée René Schloesser

	10.47 ha	20,000		15–23 €

🍷 Tribaut-Schloesser, 21, rue Saint-Vincent, 51480 Romery,
tel. 03.26.58.64.21, fax 03.26.58.44.08,
e-mail tribaut.romery@wanadoo.fr ☑
🍾 by appt.

ALFRED TRITANT

1996

	Gd cru	3 ha	12,000		15–23 €

🍷 Alfred Tritant, 23, rue de Tours, 51150 Bouzy,
tel. 03.26.57.01.16, fax 03.26.58.49.56,
e-mail champagne-tritant@wanadoo.fr ☑
🍾 by appt.

VAZART-COQUART

Blanc de blancs Réserve

	Gd cru	11 ha	40,000		11–15 €

🍷 Vazart-Coquart, 6, rue des Partelaines, 51530 Chouilly,
tel. 03.26.55.40.04, fax 03.26.55.15.94,
e-mail vazart@cder.fr ☑
🍾 by appt.

JEAN VELUT

Tradition

	6 ha	17,000		11–15 €

🍷 EARL Velut, 9, rue du Moulin, 10300 Montgueux,
tel. 03.25.74.83.31, fax 03.25.74.17.25,
e-mail champ.velut@wanadoo.fr ☑
🍾 by appt.

B. VESSELLE

	Gd cru	n.c.	40,000		15–23 €

🍷 Bruno Vesselle, 16, rue des Postes, 51150 Bouzy,
tel. 03.26.57.00.15, fax 03.26.57.09.20,
e-mail contact@champagne-vesselle.fr

VEUVE ELEONORE

Blanc de blancs

	Gd cru	5 ha	30,000		11–15 €

🍷 Bernard Dzieciuck, 11, rue Margot, 51190 Oger,
tel. 03.26.57.50.49, fax 03.26.59.17.72,
e-mail veuve.eleonore@cder.fr ☑
🍾 ev. day 8am–8pm; cl. Aug.

VEUVE MAITRE-GEOFFROY

Grand Rosé

	1er cru	1.5 ha	11,864		11–15 €

🍷 Veuve Maître-Geoffroy, 116, rue Gaston-Poittevin,
51480 Cumières, tel. 03.26.55.29.87, fax 03.26.51.85.77,
e-mail contact@champagne-maitre-geoffroy.com ☑
🍾 by appt.

A. VIOT ET FILS

	3.9 ha	39,000		11–15 €

🍷 A. Viot et fils, 59, Grande-Rue, 10200 Colombé-la-Fosse,
tel. 03.25.27.02.07, fax 03.25.27.77.70 ☑
🍾 by appt.

VOIRIN-DESMOULINS

Tradition

	5 ha	45,000		11–15 €

🍷 Voirin-Desmoulins, 24, rue des Partelaines,
51530 Chouilly, tel. 03.26.54.50.30, fax 03.26.52.87.87 ☑
🍾 by appt.

Coteaux Champenois

Called *Vins Nature de Champagne*, or still wines, they became AOC in 1974 and took the name of Coteaux Champenois. They are white, red or, more rarely, rosé still wines. Drink the whites with respect and a degree of historical curiosity, remembering that they survive from ancient times, before champagne was created. Like champagne itself, Coteaux Champenois can be made from black grapes vinified to make white wine (blanc de noirs), from white grapes (blanc de blancs) or from mixed wines.

The best-known Coteaux Champenois Rouge carries the name of the celebrated commune of Bouzy (a grand cru of the Pinot Noir). In this commune you can admire one of the two strangest vineyards in the world (the other is at Ay). A huge notice proclaims "old, pre-phylloxera French vines"; these would be virtually indistinguishable from the others were they not free-growing, following an ancient technique that has been abandoned everywhere else. All the work is done by hand using old tools. The House of Bollinger maintains this jewel, which is intended for making the most rare and most expensive champagne of all.

The Coteaux Champenois wines are drunk young, at a temperature of 7–8°C for the whites and accompanying dishes that go with very dry wines, and at 9–10°C for the reds, to accompany light dishes (white meats and oysters). In exceptional years, they may be left to age.

HERBERT BEAUFORT

Bouzy 1998 ★

	Gd cru	3 ha	6,000		15–23 €

The red wine of Bouzy, which enjoyed a great vogue after the war, is not as new as some believe it to be, since Beaufort was selling it as early as 1870. This one has been fermented for ten days, then kept in wood (600 l casks) for a year. It has now reached its peak, as is testified by its lightly developed colour and its full, generous fruit, which is quite imposing on the palate. It has a very pleasant, intense bouquet.
🍷 Herbert Beaufort, 32, rue de Tours-sur-Marne, BP 7,
51150 Bouzy, tel. 03.26.57.01.34, fax 03.26.57.09.08,
e-mail beaufort-herbert@wanadoo.fr ☑
🍾 ev. day 9am–12 noon 2pm–5pm

BERNARD BREMONT

Ambonnay 1999 ★

	Gd cru	0.5 ha	991		11–15 €

The first village to the east of Bouzy, Ambonnay has a 12th century church that is worth seeing. On this estate of over 14 ha, half a hectare is devoted to the production of this intensely coloured Grand Cru, with its bouquet of red fruits and vanilla, and a moderately long but balanced palate.
🍷 SCE Bernard Brémont et Fils, 1, rue de Reims,
51150 Ambonnay, tel. 03.26.57.01.65, fax 03.26.57.80.65,
e-mail info@champagne-bremont.com ☑
🍾 by appt.

CAILLEZ-LEMAIRE
Damery★

| ■ | | n.c. | 400 | 〔Ⅱ〕 | 11–15 € |

Damery is interesting for its 13th-century church in which, among many objects and sculptures, there is a beautiful Madonna and Child. Overseeing 6 ha, this grower has produced a Coteaux Champenois made from both Pinots. A dark-garnet colour, its scents of red berries, blackcurrants and leather are underlined by a woodiness that comes from two years' barrel maturation. Its richness contributes to its great length.
☛ Caillez-Lemaire, 14, rue Pierre-Curie, BP 11, 51480 Damery, tel. 03.26.58.41.85, fax 03.26.52.04.23, e-mail champ-cailllez.lemaire@wanadoo.fr ☑
⊥ by appt.

DOYARD-MAHE
Vertus★

| ■ | | 0.6 ha | n.c. | 〔Ⅱ〕 | 11–15 € |

This Vertus thoroughly charmed the Jury. It has cherries all over it: a dark cherry hue, black-cherries on the nose, and on the palate, the richness and smoothness of very ripe cherries. It has been matured for two years in wood, which has given it great structure and length.
☛ Philippe Doyard-Mahé, Moulin d'Argensole, 51130 Vertus, tel. 03.26.52.23.85, fax 03.26.59.36.69, e-mail champagne.doyard.mahe@hexanet.fr ☑
⊥ ev. day except Sun. 10am–12 noon 2pm–6pm; cl. 20th Dec.–5th Jan.

FRESNET-BAUDOT
Sillery★★

| ■ | Gd cru | 0.5 ha | 1,000 | 〔Ⅱ〕 | 15–23 € |

The still wines of Sillery belong to history. If they formerly enjoyed a lofty reputation, today they have become very rare. This one, which tastes like a 1999, is very fine, and full of potential since it has not yet reached its peak. Its intense red colour delights the eye and announces a bouquet of red berries and damp earth, which is as sensual as the smooth, warming palate.
☛ Fresnet-Baudot, 9, rte de Puisieulx, 51500 Sillery, tel. 03.26.49.11.74, fax 03.26.49.10.72, e-mail courrier@champagne-fresnet.fr ☑
⊥ by appt.

RENE GEOFFROY
Cumières 1999★★

| ■ | | 0.6 ha | 2,200 | 〔Ⅱ〕 | 15–23 € |

The village of Cumières profits from a favourable micro-climate, enabling its grapes to be harvested earlier than elsewhere. This red wine from Pinot Noir has been vinified in the Burgundian style, then matured for ten months in large wooden casks. Equipped with intense ruby colour, its bouquet of blackcurrants and redcurrants, with a hint of undergrowth, presages a palate with good tannic structure, lightly woody, where fruit and finesse confer balance and length on the wine. Its *coup de cœur* will be assured if you serve it with white meat.
☛ René Geoffroy, 150, rue du Bois-des-Jots, 51480 Cumières, tel. 03.26.55.32.31, fax 03.26.54.66.50, e-mail info@champagne-geoffroy.com ☑
⊥ by appt.

PIERSON-CUVELIER
Bouzy★★

| ■ | Gd cru | 0.7 ha | n.c. | ■〔Ⅱ〕♦ | 8–11 € |

Created in 1901 by the grandfather of the current owner, this domaine is located 100 m from the château at Louvois. The maturity of this Pinot Noir speaks of the good exposure of the Bouzy hillsides; it is that which confers complexity and richness on the bouquet. A structured wine with ripe tannins, it offers a rounded and harmonious finish.
☛ Pierson-Cuvelier, 4, rue de Verzy, 51150 Louvois, tel. 03.26.57.03.72, fax 03.26.51.83.84 ☑
⊥ by appt.

PATRICK SOUTIRAN
Ambonnay rouge 1996★

| ■ | Gd cru | 0.5 ha | 2,000 | 〔Ⅱ〕 | 15–23 € |

The medieval village of Ambonnay has a depiction of a martyrdom dating from the 13th century. Patrick Soutiran took over the direction of the family estate of 3 ha here in 1975. This is a 1996 to keep, a well-built wine with a rich attack, concentrated aromas of black-cherries and violets, lightly woody from a six-month maturation in barrel, and endowed with great complexity on the finish.
☛ Patrick Soutiran, 3, rue des Crayères, 51150 Ambonnay, tel. 03.26.57.08.18, fax 03.26.57.81.87, e-mail patrick.soutiran@wanadoo.fr ☑ ⌂
⊥ by appt.

TARLANT
Oeuilly 1996★

| ■ | | 0.2 ha | 1,500 | 〔Ⅱ〕 | 15–23 € |

The Tarlants have been wine-growers in Champagne since the beginning of the 17th century; today, four generations work together here – a rare feat. Both Pinots are blended in this wine, 20% Pinot Meunier to 80% Pinot Noir. Given a long maturation in new *barriques* (18 months), this 1996 is now ready to drink. On the nose, it has scents of leather, damp earth, liquorice, even anise, while the palate is generous, tender and enticing. The Jury would have liked to taste this bottle with a pear charlotte.
☛ Tarlant, 51480 OEuilly, tel. 03.26.58.30.60, fax 03.26.58.37.31, e-mail champagne@tarlant.com ☑
⊥ ev. day except Sun. 10am–12 noon 1.30pm–5.30pm; cl. Jan.

EMMANUEL TASSIN
Les Fioles 2000★★

| ■ | | 0.5 ha | 1,200 | 〔Ⅱ〕 | 8–11 € |

The Ource valley is very picturesque; be sure to leave the main roads and discover it. In Celles-sur-Ource, the Tassins offer this very attractive Coteaux Champenois. Pinot Noir is fermented for eight days, and is then matured for 15 months in barrels, a quarter of which are of new wood. It is not filtered, but is fined with egg-white. That new wood is apparent on both the nose and palate, but properly integrated into the perfectly structured body of the wine. Vanilla, cocoa and red fruits contribute to a harmonious finish. An excellent wine for grilled red meats. The **Fioles white 99** obtained one star. It mixes oaky notes (toasted almonds and vanilla) with cooked fruits, and is rich and long on the palate.
☛ Emmanuel Tassin, 104, Grande-Rue, 10110 Celles-sur-Ource, tel. 03.25.38.59.44, fax 03.25.29.94.59 ☑
⊥ by appt.

ALAIN VESSELLE
Bouzy 1997★

| ■ | Gd cru | 3 ha | 10,000 | 〔Ⅱ〕 | 11–15 € |

On the southern slope of the Montagne de Reims, Bouzy has been home since 1885 to the Vesselle family. Their Bouzy 1997, with its brick-red tints, releases a woody, vanillary bouquet derived from six months' maturation in oak. It is rich, structured and long, with flavours of well-ripened fruits. The Jury admired its elegance.
☛ SCEV Alain Vesselle, 8, rue de Louvois, 51150 Bouzy, tel. 03.26.57.00.88, fax 03.26.57.09.77, e-mail champagneavesselle@wanadoo.fr ☑
⊥ by appt.
☛ Eloi Vesselle

JEAN VESSELLE
Bouzy 1997★

| ■ | Gd cru | 1 ha | n.c. | | 11–15 € |

Jean Vesselle's daughter carries on her father's work. Her Bouzy red results from a classic and meticulous vinification, with three days of cold maceration, followed by an alcoholic fermentation lasting ten days. The wine is fined and filtered before bottling. With its nose of berry fruits and under-growth, it has a well-balanced and rounded palate with good vinosity. It can be drunk now.

➟ Jean Vesselle, 4, rue Victor-Hugo, 51150 Bouzy,
tel. 03.26.57.01.55, fax 03.26.57.06.95 ☑
☘ by appt.

Wines selected but not starred

PHILIPPE FOURRIER 1999

| ■ | | 0.5 ha | n.c. | ⬗ | 11–15 € |

➟ Philippe Fourrier, rte de Bar-sur-Aube, 10200 Baroville,
tel. 03.25.27.13.44, fax 03.25.27.12.49,
e-mail champagne.fourrier@wanadoo.fr ☑
☘ by appt.

DOM. LECLERC BRIANT
Cumières 2002

| ■ | | 0.6 ha | 5,000 | ▮ ♦ | 15–23 € |

➟ Leclerc-Briant, 67, rue Chaude-Ruelle, BP 108,
51204 Epernay Cedex, tel. 03.26.54.45.33,
fax 03.26.54.49.59, e-mail plb@leclercbriant.com ☑
☘ ev. day 9am–11.30am 1.30pm–5.30pm;
Sat. Sun. by appt.; cl. 5th–25th Aug.

JEAN MILAN

| ■ | Gd cru | n.c. | n.c. | ⬗ | 11–15 € |

➟ Milan, 6, rue d'Avize, 51190 Oger, tel. 03.26.57.50.09,
fax 03.26.57.78.47, e-mail info@champagne-milan.com ☑
☘ by appt.

Rosé des Riceys

The three villages of Les Riceys (Haut, Haute-Rive and Bas) are located in the extreme south of the Aube, not far from Bar-sur-Seine. The commune of Les Riceys consists of three appellations: Champagne, Coteaux Champenois and Rosé des Riceys. The last is a still wine of great rarity – only 819 hl were harvested in 1999 and 640 hl in 2000 – and of great quality: it is one of the best rosés in France. The wine was already being drunk in the reign of Louis XIV and is said to have been taken to Versailles by the builders who were digging the foundations of the château and who came from Les Riceys.

This rosé is the result of vinification that includes a short maceration of Pinot Noir with a natural alcohol level that cannot be less than 10% . The maceration must be stopped – *saigner la*

cuve, or bleeding the vat – at the precise moment that the unique Riceys flavour appears, otherwise it vanishes. Only the rosés with this special flavour are labelled. The Rosé des Riceys is matured in vat and drunk young, at 8–9°C, as an aperitif or with a first course. Matured in barrels, it can develop over three to ten years and should then be served at 10–12°C throughout the meal.

MARQUIS DE POMEREUIL 2000★★

| ■ | | 0.64 ha | 6,984 | ▮ ⬗ ♦ | 15–23 € |

This old cooperative dating back to 1922 launched its brand in 1975. It handles fruit from 82 ha of vines. This remarkable rosé is partially wood-aged for six months; its colour is intense, its bouquet as enticing as it is distinguished. On the palate, balance, length and harmony come together. A veal escalope would make a good accompaniment to it.

➟ Cave coop. des Riceys, 31, rte de Gye, 10340 Les Riceys,
tel. 03.25.29.30.08, fax 03.25.38.59.86,
e-mail marquis.de.pomereuil@hexanet.fr ☑
☘ ev. day except Sun. 8.30am–12 noon 2pm–6pm

MORIZE PERE ET FILS 1999★

| ■ | | 0.8 ha | 6,412 | ▮ | 11–15 € |

Based a kilometre away from the Château de Ricey-Bas, the Morizes have been in Riceys since 1830, launching their brand in 1964. Their 1999 is a well-coloured, spicy, liquoricey wine with a lively touch of mint. One taster advised serving it with red mullet.

➟ Morize Père et Fils, 122, rue du Gal-de-Gaulle,
10340 Les Riceys, tel. 03.25.29.30.02, fax 03.25.38.20.22 ☑
☘ by appt.

VEUVE A. DEVAUX★

| ■ | | 20 ha | 8,000 | ▮ ⬗ ♦ | 15–23 € |

The Rosé des Riceys of Veuve A. Devaux, which has been one of the brands of the Union Auboise for 34 years, enjoys an excellent reputation, confirmed by this wine from the harvest of 2000 (bottled as a non-vintage). Reddish-pink in colour, it has smoky flavours of macerated fruits, and a long, well-balanced palate.

➟ Union Auboise, Dom. de Villeneuve,
10110 Bar-sur-Seine, tel. 03.25.38.30.65, fax 03.25.29.73.21,
e-mail info@champagne-devaux.fr ☑

Wines selected but not starred

JACQUES DEFRANCE 2000

| ■ | | 2.5 ha | 5,000 | ▮ | 11–15 € |

➟ Jacques Defrance, 28, rue de la Plante, 10340 Les Riceys,
tel. 03.25.29.32.20, fax 03.25.29.77.83 ☑
☘ by appt.

GUY DE FOREZ 2000

| ■ | | 1 ha | 3,500 | ▮ ⬗ | 11–15 € |

➟ SCEA du Val du Cel, rte de Tonnerre, 10340 Les Riceys,
tel. 03.25.29.98.73, fax 03.25.38.23.01 ☑
☘ by appt.

VINCENT LAMOUREUX 2000

| ■ | | 0.5 ha | 2,500 | ▮ ⬗ | 11–15 € |

➟ Vincent Lamoureux, 2, rue du Sénateur-Lesaché,
10340 Les Riceys, tel. 03.25.29.39.32,
fax 03.25.29.80.30 ☑
☘ by appt.

CHAMPAGNE

JURA, SAVOIE AND BUGEY

Jura

A mirror-image of the vineyards of the Haute Bourgogne, on the opposite side of the Saône valley, the Jura vineyards occupy the slopes that descend from the first plateau of the Jura mountains to the plain below. The wine-growing region runs from north to south across the whole department, from the area of Salins-les-Bains in the north to Saint-Amour in the south. Compared with the Côte-d'Or, across the valley, the Jura slopes are scattered and irregular, with many different aspects and exposures. Vines are cultivated only on the most favourably sited slopes, at an altitude of between 250 and 400 m. The vineyard covers about 1,750 ha from which about 82,090 hl were produced in 2002.

The classic continental climate is unusually exaggerated, because of both the general westward orientation of the region and the particular characteristics of its Jurassic contours, especially the boxed-off features known as "blind alleys". Winters are harsh, and the summer weather is unreliable, but there are often many hot days. The harvest takes place over a fairly long period, even extending into November because of the difficulties the grapes have in ripening fully. The soils are in the main sedimentary Triassic deposits, or liassic deposits of Jurassic marl, particularly in the north, and there is also a chalk overlay, mostly found in the south of the department. The local grape varieties are perfectly adapted to the clay soils and produce wines of a remarkably specific regional character. The vines need to be trained quite high to raise the grapes above damaging autumn humidity. They are pruned *en courgées* – that is, in long, arching stems such as can be found on the similar soils of the Mâconnais. If one can believe the writings of Pliny, vine cultivation in the region dates back to at least the beginning of the Christian era; and there is no doubt that the Jura vineyards, particularly appreciated by Henri IV of France, were very much in fashion from the Middle Ages.

The old, peaceful city of Arbois, the wine capital of the region, is full of charm. There are many reminders that the great 19th century scientist Louis Pasteur, who spent his youth in Arbois, frequently returned to it. It was here, using the vines that grew at his family home, that he began his researches into fermentation that were to prove so important to the nascent science of oenology (from the Greek *oinos*, meaning wine) and that led, among other things, to the discovery that harmful micro-organisms could be killed by heat, a technique still known as pasteurization.

Local grape varieties grow alongside later arrivals from Burgundy. One of the native varieties, the Poulsard (or Ploussard), from the lower foothills of the Jura mountains, was apparently only ever cultivated in the Revermont, a geographical area that also includes the Bugey vineyard, where it is known as the Mècle. This very pretty grape, with its large, oblong berries, is deliciously perfumed and has a thin, lightly coloured skin containing little tannin. A typical grape variety for rosé wines, it is more often used here to make red wines. The Trousseau, another local grape variety is, on the other hand, rich in both colour and tannin, and it, too, produces classic red wines that are characteristic of the Appellations d'Origine du Jura. The Pinot Noir, imported from Burgundy, is most frequently added in small quantities in the making of red wines. It also has an important future in the vinification of white wines made from black grapes intended for assembly with blanc de blancs to make high-quality sparkling wines. As in Burgundy, the Chardonnay grows perfectly successfully on the clay soils and gives the white wines their unmatched bouquet. The Savagnin, a local white grape variety, is cultivated on the poorest marly soils and, after six careful years of development on ullage in barrel, produces the magnificent Vin Jaune, or "yellow wine", a Jura classic. Vin de Paille (straw wine) is also produced in small quantities in the Jura.

The region appears to be particularly favourable for obtaining excellent sparkling wine made, as previously mentioned, from blending blanc de noirs (Pinot Noir), white juice from black grapes, with blanc de blancs (Chardonnay), or white juice from white grapes. To achieve their high standards of quality and in order to ensure the necessary freshness, these sparkling wines have to be made from grapes selected at a particular stage of ripeness.

The white and red wines are classic in style, but, apparently because of the appeal of Vin Jaune, growers try to give them a highly developed character that is almost oxidized. Half a century ago, even some red wines were aged for more than a hundred years, but now makers have returned to more normal time frames for the wine's development.

As for the rosé, it is a lightly coloured red wine with low tannin, more frequently resembling red wine than rosés from other vineyards. Because of this, it can be kept for a time. It goes very well with fairly light dishes, the real reds – particularly those made from Trousseau grapes – being kept for more strongly flavoured dishes. The whites accompany the usual dishes, white meats and fish; the older whites partner Comté cheese very well. Vin Jaune excels with Comté and also with Roquefort and some other dishes for which it can be difficult to find an appropriate wine, such as duck with orange or dishes with sauce américaine.

Arbois

This is the best known of the Appellations d'Origine du Jura, and the name applies to all types of wines produced in the 12 communes in the Arbois region, which cover about 842 ha. In 2002 production reached about 37,575 hl, of which 22,521 hl were reds and rosé, 14,516 hl were whites and yellows, 539 hl were Vin de Paille and about 260 hl were sparkling. The Triassic marls of the terroir influence the quite particular character of the rosés made from Poulsard grapes.

FRUITIÈRE VINICOLE D'ARBOIS

Chardonnay 2001★★

	80 ha	115,000	🍷	5–8 €

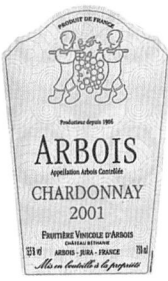

The wine-growers of this active cooperative will soon be able to celebrate its centenary with pride judging by this sappy Arbois. The nose is still restrained, but is quite developed, fresh and with a suggestion of apples. The palate reinforces these impressions, with richness and balance, continuing to a good finish. This wine needs to open out, but it certainly has potential. It will be perfect with fish and shellfish. Also retained with one star was a **Vin Jaune 96 (15–23 €)**, which is expressive and balanced. It will go well with a cream-based dish.
➤ Fruitière vinicole d'Arbois, 2, rue des Fossés, 39600 Arbois, tel. 03.84.66.11.67, fax 03.84.37.48.80 ☑
☎ by appt.

LUCIEN AVIET ET FILS

Trousseau Cuvée des Géologues 2001★

	1 ha	2,500	🍷	8–11 €

Geologists need not worry, this wine is not about to disappear: Bacchus, the little, mischievous Bacchus who raises his cup on the label of this Arbois, is hooked on the Lias soil type that produces this famous "geologist's" *cuvée*. Here is a powerful, intense nose, moving at the same time towards muskiness and cooked red berries. Even with the relatively light structure, there is balance. The flavours remain somewhat weak for the moment (soft red fruits, in particular wild cherry) and should evolve well. A wine that deserves to age for two or three years. The same mark was given to the estate's **Vin Jaune 96 (23–30 €)**, which has a very deep-golden colour, with an intense and complex nose of walnut and mild curry flavours.
➤ Lucien Aviet et Fils, Caveau de Bacchus, 39600 Montigny-lès-Arsures, tel. 03.84.66.11.02 ☑
☎ by appt.

PAUL BENOIT

Pupillin Ploussard 2000★

	1 ha	5,000	🍷	5–8 €

Paul Benoit set up here in 1976 and has created a vineyard that extends today to 8 ha. Now working with his son, Christophe,

he has made an Arbois from pure Ploussard, macerated for five days. The appearance is a light red-brick, typical of this pale-coloured grape variety. The seductive nose is very fruity with a touch of oak. The soft palate does not have much body, but its lightness and fruitiness make this an easy-drinking wine, for example, with *charcuterie*. The estate's **Pupillin Chardonnay 2000** from the same appellation was also judged to be very successful and its freshness would work well with fish.
➤ Paul Benoit et Fils, La Chenevière, rue du Chardonnay, 39600 Pupillin, tel. 03.84.37.43.72, fax 03.84.66.24.61 ☑
☎ ev. day 8am–7.30pm

MARCEL CABELIER 2001★

	2.5 ha	10,000	🍶 🍷 ❅	5–8 €

The nose of this Arbois is quite unusual: "*pâté en croûte*" said one taster, wanting to express that one detects both meaty notes and the nuances of patisserie. The overall effect is pleasant and distinguished. Well structured on the palate and spicy, this wine will go well with grilled meat.
➤ Compagnie des Grands Vins du Jura, rte de Champagnole, 39570 Crançot, tel. 03.84.87.61.30, fax 03.84.48.21.36, e-mail jura@grandschais.fr ☑
☎ by appt.

SYLVAIN FAUDOT

Cuvée Rubis 2001★

	0.45 ha	2,200	🍷	5–8 €

Young wine-grower, Sylvain Faudot established his estate in 1998 in Saint-Cyr, near Arbois. His Rubis is a blend of 70% Trousseau with 30% Ploussard. The powerful nose is dominated by soft red berries, with some gamey notes. Balanced, and marked by good acidity and tannin structure, the palate is no less lively. A "wine to enjoy," which would slip down well with grilled meats, paella or pizza.
➤ Sylvain Faudot, 13, rte de Salins, 39600 Saint-Cyr-Montmalin, tel. 03.84.37.41.03, fax 03.84.37.41.03 ☑
☎ by appt.

Jura

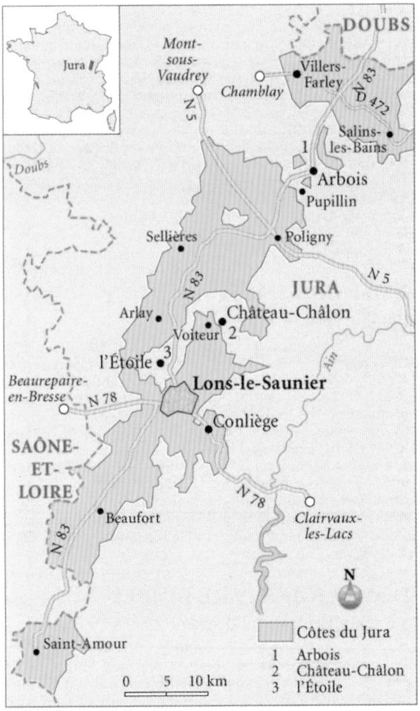

Map of the Jura region showing: DOUBS, Mont-sous-Vaudrey, Villers-Farley, Chambray, Salins-les-Bains, Arbois, Pupillin, Sellières, Poligny, Arlay, Château-Chálon, Voiteur, l'Étoile, JURA, Beaurepaire-en-Bresse, Lons-le-Saunier, Conliège, SAÔNE-ET-LOIRE, Beaufort, Clairvaux-les-Lacs, Saint-Amour.

Legend:
Côtes du Jura
1 Arbois
2 Château-Chálon
3 l'Étoile
0   5   10 km

JURA (vertical side tab)

RAPHAEL FUMEY ET ADELINE
CHATELAIN Cuvée Traditionnelle 1999★★

	0.6 ha	3,000	🍶	8–11 €

This blend of 80% Savagnin alongside 20% Chardonnay has spent three years in cask. Complexity and delicacy show on the very typical Jura nose: hazelnut, walnut, butter and orange blossom. The rounded palate shows a beautiful combination of the best of both grape varieties. The first impression on the palate is of liveliness and freshness, and then the richness emerges with green walnut and hazelnut flavours. The whole effect is warming and well-balanced, integrated, fine and subtle. It was impossible to finish discussing it without reference to a morel mushroom pie! From the same estate, a mention was given to an **Arbois Pinot Noir 2000 (5–8 €)**. This is a pleasant wine, ready to drink from now.
➥ EARL Raphaël Fumey and Adeline Chatelain, 39600 Montigny-lès-Arsures, tel. 03.84.66.27.84, fax 03.84.66.27.84 ☑
☂ by appt.

MICHEL GAHIER
Trousseau Grands Vergers 2000★★

	1.2 ha	5,000	🍶	5–8 €

This *coup de coeur* has arrived at just the right time to celebrate the ten year anniversary of the establishment of Michel Gahier's estate. Aged for 18 months in barrel, this Trousseau selection presents a nose that is both meaty and roasted, powerful with a good potential for development. The tannic palate is a little tough at first, but this austerity simply reflects the robust aspect of the wine. With its strong personality and character, it shows good presence and length too. Two or three years should soften any harshness and reveal a remarkable wine.
➥ Michel Gahier, pl. de l'Eglise, 39600 Montigny-lès-Arsures, tel. 03.84.66.17.63, fax 03.84.66.17.63 ☑
☂ by appt.

EMMANUEL HOUILLON
Pupillin 2001★

	2 ha	6,000	🍶	8–11 €

Emmanuel Houillon took over from Pierre Overnoy on 1 January 2001. Overnoy's wines always demanded an opinion. It should be said that he was a real enthusiast for organic production. His motto? No sulphur. This approach, started by his predecessor in 1968 (almost by chance), is being followed by Emmanuel Houillon. With a golden-yellow colour, his Arbois, made from Chardonnay, is a little developed on the nose, but does not lack depth. The rounded palate shows richness and, in all, it is a promising wine.
➥ Pierre Overnoy Emmanuel Houillon, rue du Ploussard, 39600 Pupillin, tel. 03.84.66.14.60, fax 03.84.66.14.60 ☑
☂ by appt.

DOM. LIGIER PERE ET FILS
Savagnin Elevé en fût de chêne 1999★

	1 ha	4,000	🍶	11–15 €

Two consecutive *coups de coeur*, in previous editions of the *Guide* heralded the opening of the Ligier family's new winery built in Arbois in 2002. It comprises a vat room, barrel ageing room, bottle store and tasting reception for clients. With a golden colour, their Arbois Savagnin already looks most attractive. The nose is open and quite developed with green walnut notes. There is plenty of weight and richness on the palate, but with just the right level of acidity to allow it to last and evolve favourably. There was almost a slight taste of Vin Jaune emerging, but this will not express itself fully until about 2008. Also retained by the jury with one star was a **Trousseau 2001 (5–8 €)**. With an attractive colour of strawberry cordial, this is a rounded wine with masses of fruit.
➥ Dom. Ligier Père et Fils, 7, rte de Poligny, 39380 Mont-sous-Vaudrey, tel. 03.84.71.74.75, fax 03.84.81.59.82, e-mail ligier@netcourrier.com ☑
☂ by appt.

DOM. MARTIN-FAUDOT
Savagnin 2000★★

	0.7 ha	3,000	🍶	11–15 €

The family estate was created in 1879 by Louis Faudot, and in 1998 his great-grandson, Michel Faudot, linked together with Jean-Pierre Martin. With this Arbois, the pair reveals a real savoir faire: this is an estate to watch...Savagnin is often blended with Chardonnay, but here the Savagnin is pure. It offers an attractive nose of green walnuts, fresh and really vivid. This is a distinctive wine. The characteristic palate reveals excellent acidity which really brings out the mid-palate substance. Walnut is present and stays right through to the end. What length! It would be best to leave this wine for two or three years for it to really reach its best, but it is already superb.
➥ Dom. Martin-Faudot, 1, rue Bardenet, 39600 Mesnay, tel. 03.84.66.29.97, fax 03.84.66.29.84 ☑
☂ by appt.

MONTBIEF
Chardonnay 2000★★

	n.c.	40,000	🍶 🔴	11–15 €

Few are not familiar with Henri Maire, the Jura négociant, known for its large sales force. The salesmen will not have too much difficulty in their sales pitch for this golden-yellow Montbief – the write-up is already in the bottle. The nose may appear still closed, but it already reveals a beautiful floral character. Blackcurrants and pineapples emerge on aeration. The first impression on the palate is rich and clean with an attractive weight behind, finishing on a slightly tart and elegant note. The jury found brilliance, charm and elegance in this well-made Chardonnay. Also from Henri Maire, the **Domaine de la Grange Grillard Chardonnay 2001** from the same appellation is given a special mention. It needs time.
➥ Henri Maire, Ch. Boichailles, 39600 Arbois, tel. 03.84.66.12.34, fax 03.84.66.42.42, e-mail info@henri-maire.fr ☑
☂ by appt.

DESIRE PETIT ET FILS
Pupillin Vin de paille 1999★★★

	0.9 ha	4,200	🍶	15–23 €

It is the third year that this estate has been awarded a *coup de coeur* for a Vin de Paille: its 1997 and 1998 received the same distinction. From equal amounts of Poulsard, Chardonnay and Savagnin the wine shows constancy, but also balance. If

the amber colour is a marvel for the eye, the nose is not far behind: quince jelly, apple, dry apricot, prune, walnut...all the fruit kingdom is there, or almost...with superb intensity. The palate confirms all these impressions along with a certain alcoholic richness, but all the while remaining perfectly well balanced. Foie gras is undoubtedly the best choice to go with such a great wine.

➽ Dom. Désiré Petit, rue du Ploussard, 39600 Pupillin,
tel. 03.84.66.01.20, fax 03.84.66.26.59,
e-mail domaine-desire-petit@wanadoo.fr ☑
✗ ev. day 9am–12 noon 2pm–7pm; groups by appt.
➽ Gérard and Marcel Petit

DOM. DE LA PINTE

Terre rouge 2000★★

	2 ha	9,000	⏹	5–8 €

It is now 50 years since Roger Martin created this domaine, directed today by Philippe Chatillon. He made this wine Terre Rouge, from a blend of Trousseau, Poulsard and Pinot Noir grown on red marl from the Triassic era. The persistent nose is distinguished, giving musky and leather aromas, together with notes of black fruits. The intense palate opens cleanly with a firm structure, rounded and full of flavour. Ripe fruits, cherry and a roasted touch complete the symphony of flavours. The wine is powerful, but in complete balance, ready to drink but able to age too.

➽ Dom. de la Pinte, rte de Lyon, 39600 Arbois,
tel. 03.84.66.06.47, fax 03.84.66.24.58,
e-mail accueil@lapinte.fr ☑
✗ by appt.
➽ Martin family

JACQUES PUFFENEY

Savagnin 1999★★

	1.3 ha	7,500	⏹	11–15 €

All wines from Jacques Puffeney are the product of a manual harvest. The nose on this Savagnin is still fresh, though developed. It conceals mineral and toasty notes, with a touch of chocolate that is not unpleasant. Concentrated, the palate still shows lively acidity and is very solid thanks to a concentrated mid-palate. A slight woody note discreetly emphasizes the buttery finish, leaving the taste of a superb wine. It would be best drunk as an aperitif or together with some Comté cheese.

➽ Jacques Puffeney, quartier Saint-Laurent,
39600 Montigny-lès-Arsures, tel. 03.84.66.10.89,
fax 03.84.66.08.36, e-mail jacques.puffeney@wanadoo.fr ☑
✗ by appt.

FRUITIERE VINICOLE DE PUPILLIN

Pupillin Chardonnay Vieilles Vignes 1999★

	1.69 ha	12,000	⏹	8–11 €

Tradition and modernity work together in this wine cellar, where the vat room was modernized in 1998 next door to an 18th century wine cellar. At 58-years old, the vines are not ready to be retired, and at this age they give the best wines! The Pupillin cooperative has produced a special 99 wine here. The nose is full and complex, with notes of butter and vanilla. On the palate it shows richness and, at the same time, sufficient acidity to give it the necessary balance. Hazelnut, butter, cocoa and a delicate touch of oak combine in a beautiful wine, which should still open out. It might go well with veal sweetbreads. Another Arbois wine singled out, was a **Pupillin Pinot Noir 2001 (5–8 €)**, showing the typical colour of that grape variety and good structure.

➽ Fruitière vinicole de Pupillin, rue du Ploussard,
39600 Pupillin, tel. 03.84.66.12.88, fax 03.84.37.47.16,
e-mail fvp39@wanadoo.fr ☑
✗ by appt.

LA CAVE DE LA REINE JEANNE

Chardonnay 2001★

	3 ha	18,000		5–8 €

The Cave de la Reine Jeanne is a négociant created recently by Stéphane and Bénédicte Tissot, also wine-growers in Montigny-lès-Arsures. They buy grapes rather than wine, in order to be able to vinify them according to their house style. The appley nose of this intense 2001 evolves with an oaky vanilla note. Careful vinification is obvious from the balanced palate, which demonstrates an attractive richness. A slight sparkle shows on the finish, whilst a slight dilution reflects the vintage.

➽ Le Cellier des Tiercelines, 54, Grande-Rue,
39600 Arbois, tel. 03.84.66.08.27, fax 03.84.66.25.08 ☑
✗ by appt.
➽ Bénédicte and Stéphane Tissot

DOM. ROLET PERE ET FILS

Vin de paille 1999★★

	3 ha	8,000	⏹	15–23 €

Many novices confuse Vin Jaune and Vin de Paille. There is however nothing in common between these two types of wine, except perhaps the appearance. This Vin de Paille looks superb with a colour of old tarnished gold similar to that of a Vin Jaune. Of beautiful finesse, the nose gives a character of *pain d'épice* and quince jelly. The palate is well balanced, showing crystallized fruits, especially orange rind. Drink as an aperitif, or with foie gras or dessert.

➽ Dom. Rolet Père et Fils, Montesserin, rte de Dole,
39600 Arbois, tel. 03.84.66.00.05, fax 03.84.37.47.14,
e-mail rolet@wanadoo.fr

DOM. DE SAINT-PIERRE

Chardonnay Cuvée Camille 2000★

	1 ha	5,000	∎	5–8 €

A generous nose of beautiful intensity. The ripe and attractively rounded palate is favourably reminiscent of a fully topped-up Savagnin rather than a Chardonnay, and seems as if there was overripeness in the grapes. However, the harvest began on 15 September. This is a well-made wine to drink now or to keep. The **white Domaine de Saint-Pierre Cuvée Renaud 99**, a blend of two-thirds Chardonnay with Savagnin, also obtains one star. Both rounded and fresh, it is dominated by green walnut and is a wine to drink now.

➽ EARL Hubert et Renaud Moyne, Dom. de Saint-Pierre,
39600 Mathenay, tel. 03.84.73.97.23, fax 03.84.37.56.80 ☑
✗ by appt.
➽ Philippe Moyne

JEAN-LOUIS TISSOT
Savagnin 1999★★

1 ha	2,000	◫	8–11 €

One of the members of the Tissot family – there are several in the Arbois area – this 100% Savagnin is a slightly golden yellow with beautiful tinges of green. The nose is mainly walnut and can still develop. The pronounced acidity, weight and structure makes you believe it is a great wine whose potential has not yet been revealed. The estate's **Chardonnay 2000** **(5–8 €)** obtains one star. It can be drunk already, but it should open out with time.

⊶ Jean-Louis Tissot, Vauxelles,
39600 Montigny-lès-Arsures, tel. 03.84.66.13.08,
fax 03.84.66.08.09,
e-mail jeanlouis.tissot.vigneron.arbois@wanadoo.fr ☑

DOM. ANDRÉ ET MIREILLE TISSOT
Savagnin 1998★★

2.5 ha	11,000	◫	11–15 €

Always very entrepreneurial, André, Mireille, Bénédicte and Stéphane Tissot opened a new wine-tasting cellar on the main square in Arbois. Accustomed to *coups de coeur* from Hachette, they have presented for the first time a pure Savagnin wine, aged for three and a half years on its lees, one year with topping up and two and a half years *sous voile* without topping up, This beautiful golden-yellow 98 reveals a fairly powerful but subtle nose, wavering between walnut, oaky aromas and mineral notes. On the palate the walnut and the hazelnut explode to give an astonishing complexity. The wine has already evolved into the style of Vin Jaune. A Bresse chicken or a mature Comté cheese will make a magnificent match. The estate's **Vin Jaune 95 (23–30 €)** obtains one star for its good balance. It will attract the informed wine-lover just as much as the novice.

⊶ André et Mireille Tissot, 39600 Montigny-lès-Arsures,
tel. 03.84.66.08.27, fax 03.84.66.25.08 ☑
Ⱶ by appt.
⊶ Stéphane Tissot

JACQUES TISSOT
Trousseau 2000★★

0.5 ha	1,500	◫	8–11 €

With about 30 ha, Domaine Jacques Tissot is one of the most important wine estates of the Jura. His is the imposing building that one sees in the middle of the vineyards, near the turn-off to Arbois coming from the direction of Besançon. The estate also has two tasting cellars in the town. The colour of this Trousseau is slightly brick-red. The nose is not very intense but is pleasant, fruity with some musky notes showing development. There is a similar expression on the palate, which exudes ripe red berries and crystallized morello cherry within the balanced structure. The wine is ready to drink. The estate's **Vin Jaune 94 (23–30 €)** receives one star for its typical aromas and its powerful palate. It can be drunk immediately but will also keep well.

⊶ Dom. Jacques Tissot, 39, rue de Courcelles,
39600 Arbois, tel. 03.84.66.14.27, fax 03.84.66.24.88,
e-mail courrier@domaine-jacques-tissot.fr ☑ ⌂
Ⱶ by appt.

DOM. DE LA TOURNELLE
Ploussard 1999★

2 ha	2,500	◫	5–8 €

Former technical director for the Jura vineyards, then director of the *Institut des Vins du Jura*, Pascal Clairet became a wine producer in 1991. Unlucky for him, it was the year of a ferocious frost. This Arbois, matured in large wooden casks, has a clear, bright appearance and is quite intense for a pure Ploussard. The complex nose blends spices, red berries and damp woodland characteristics. This is a substantial 99 wine, with much weight, but fortunately plenty of fruit remains. Already opened up, it is ready to drink and will go well with lamb accompanied by ratatouille. The **Domaine de Tournelle Cuvée Curon Chardonnay 2000 (8–11 €)** also impressed the Jury. The fruitiness of its grape variety, and slightly exotic flavours cannot mask the character it obtains from its 24 months ageing in oak casks.

⊶ Pascal Clairet, 5, Petite-Place, 39600 Arbois,
tel. 03.84.66.25.76, fax 03.84.66.27.15,
e-mail domainedelatournelle@wanadoo.fr ☑
Ⱶ ev. day except Sun. 10am–12.30pm 2.30pm–6.30pm

Wines selected but not starred

DANIEL DUGOIS
Trousseau Cuvée Grevillière 2000

1 ha	5,800	◫	8–11 €

⊶ Daniel Dugois, 4, rue de la Mirode, 39600 Les Arsures,
tel. 03.84.66.03.41, fax 03.84.37.44.59 ☑ ⌂
Ⱶ by appt.

DOM. AMÉLIE GUILLOT
Chardonnay Vieilles Vignes 1999

0.4 ha	2,500	◫	8–11 €

⊶ Amélie Guillot, 1, rue du Coin-des-Côtes,
39600 Molamboz, tel. 03.84.66.04.00, fax 03.84.66.04.00,
e-mail amelie.guillot@wanadoo.fr ☑
Ⱶ by appt.

FRÉDÉRIC LORNET
Trousseau des Dames 2001

0.6 ha	2,000	◫	8–11 €

⊶ Frédéric Lornet, L'Abbaye, 39600 Montigny-lès-Arsures,
tel. 03.84.37.44.95, fax 03.84.37.40.17,
e-mail frederic-lornet@club-internet.fr ☑
Ⱶ ev. day 10am–12 noon 1.30pm–7pm

DOM. DE MONTFORT 2001

n.c.	52,000		11–15 €

⊶ SCV des Domaines Henri Maire, 39600 Arbois,
tel. 03.84.66.12.34, fax 03.84.66.42.42

AUGUSTE PIROU
Poulsard 2000

n.c.	41,000	■ ◫ ♦	5–8 €

⊶ Auguste Pirou, Caves royales, 39600 Arbois,
tel. 03.84.66.42.70, fax 03.84.66.42.42,
e-mail info@auguste-pirou.fr

MARCEL POUX
Savagnin Réserve de Curon 2000

n.c.	26,000	◫	5–8 €

⊶ Marcel Poux, 39600 Arbois, tel. 03.84.66.12.34,
fax 03.84.37.42.42

DOM. DE LA RENARDIÈRE
Pupillin Chardonnay 2000

0.8 ha	4,000	◫	8–11 €

⊶ Jean-Michel Petit, rue du Chardonnay, 39600 Pupillin,
tel. 03.84.66.25.10, fax 03.84.66.25.70,
e-mail renardiere@libertysurf.fr ☑
Ⱶ ev. day except Sun. 9am–12 noon 1.30pm–7pm

Château-Chalon

The most prestigious of the Jura wines is exclusively the famous Vin de Voile, produced on 45 ha. This is a Vin Jaune, made according to strict regulations. The grape is harvested in a remarkable landscape of black liassic marl, overlooked by towering cliffs on top of which the old village is perched. Production is limited but in 2002 it reached 1,647 hl. The wine is put on sale precisely six years and three months after the harvest. It is worth noting that the producers themselves, who are constantly concerned to maintain a high level of quality, refused the AOC classification for the harvests of 1974, 1980, 1984 and 2001.

BAUD PERE ET FILS 1995★★

| | 1.9 ha | 1,800 | ◖▯ | 23–30 € |

The Château-Chalon 94 of this important estate received a *coup de cœur* in a previous *Guide*. This remarkable 95 shows a golden-yellow colour, and the attractive and powerful nose reveals brioche and green walnut notes. The palate follows, also powerful at the start, with almost harsh acidity. However, the quality and concentration of fruit will allow further development of the typicity, which is already quite marked. This wine should delight those wine-lovers looking for character.
Baud Père et Fils, rte de Voiteur, 39210 Le Vernois, tel. 03.84.25.31.41, fax 03.84.25.30.09, e-mail abaud@domainebaud.com ☑
⏾ by appt.

DOM. BERTHET-BONDET 1996★★

| | 3 ha | 8,000 | ◖▯ | 23–30 € |

A golden appearance with highlights of green, this beautiful colour is typical of Château-Chalon. The nose breaks through, releasing a subtle and complex character, between almond, lemon and bread dough. The palate is substantial but elegant, with a lemony finish. It can be enjoyed immediately or left for several years in the cellar.
Berthet-Bondet, Chem. de La Tour, 39210 Château-Chalon, tel. 03.84.44.60.48, fax 03.84.44.61.13 ☑
⏾ by appt.

PHILIPPE BUTIN 1996★★

| | 0.16 ha | 950 | ◖▯ | 23–30 € |

This family estate with 40-year-old vines produces a tiny quantity of Château-Chalon, of great quality: a beautiful colour of "yellow vervain liqueur" enhanced by pretty tinges of green. After this delightful start, encountering the nose is even more promising: walnut, almond and dried apples vie with each other. Still hard in acidity, this Château-Chalon provides a full palate which still needs to knit together. It is therefore essential to wait at least three years to open this wine, but if you have the patience to wait 20 years, so much the better.
Philippe Butin, 21, rue de la Combe, 39210 Lavigny, tel. 03.84.25.36.26, fax 03.84.25.39.18 ☑
⏾ by appt.

DOM. DE LA PINTE 1996★

| | 0.4 ha | n.c. | ◖▯ | 30–38 € |

The Domaine de la Pinte has a significant vineyard holding, mainly in the Arbois region. Might it be the way the owners worship the cult of Savagnin that has led them to cultivate it in the place where this grape finds its most suitable terroir? So, even with just 40 ares of vines at Château-Chalon, they have managed to vinify a golden Vin Jaune that already asserts itself strongly on the nose, mingling fresh and dried walnuts together with honey. The palate continues the theme, warm and rich, long and well balanced. Already enjoyable, this wine could last a couple of decades.
Dom. de la Pinte, rte de Lyon, 39600 Arbois, tel. 03.84.66.06.47, fax 03.84.66.24.58, e-mail accueil@lapinte.fr ☑
⏾ by appt.
Famille Martin

Wines selected but not starred

FRUITIERE VINICOLE DE VOITEUR 1994

| | 13 ha | 10,000 | ◖▯ | 23–30 € |

Fruitière vinicole de Voiteur, 60, rue de Nevy-sur-Seille, 39210 Voiteur, tel. 03.84.85.21.29, fax 03.84.85.27.67, e-mail voiteur@fruitiere-vinicole-voiteur.fr ☑
⏾ by appt.

Côtes du Jura

The appellation incorporates the whole area of the vineyard producing fine wines. In 2002 the area of plantation was 503 ha which produced 22,959 hl of all types of wine: 14,725 hl of white wine or Vin Jaune, 7,662 hl of red wine or rosé, 572 hl of Vin de Paille.

CH. D'ARLAY 1998★★★

| | 6 ha | 25,000 | ▮◖▯⚬ | 11–15 € |

This wine is made from Chardonnay and Savagnin with the grapes harvested together, rather than from a blend of the two wines. The wine is matured in fully topped-up casks giving an unusual result that was nevertheless appreciated by the tasters. Both intense and subtle, the nose wavers between toast and exotic fruits, and then finishes on a citronella note. The palate is rounded and balanced. Although atypical for a Jura white wine, especially in this type of blend, the Jury nevertheless found it particularly expressive.
Alain de Laguiche, Ch. d'Arlay, rte de Saint-Germain, 39140 Arlay, tel. 03.84.85.04.22, fax 03.84.48.17.96, e-mail alainlaguiche@aol.com ☑
⏾ ev. day except Sun. 9am–12 noon 2pm–6pm

BERNARD BADOZ
Vin de paille 1999★

| | 1 ha | 4,000 | ◖▯ | 15–23 € |

One of the wine producers based in the heart of the little Jura town of Poligny. The wine has brick-red tints, and the initial impression on the nose is surprising, but it opens up nicely on aeration with delicate notes of dried and crystallized fruits.

This very sweet 99 provides attractive dried fruits and honey on the palate with good flavours on the finish. Ready to drink, the wine will be enjoyed for its great richness.
- ☛ Bernard Badoz, 15, rue du Collège, 39800 Poligny, tel. 03.84.37.11.85, fax 03.84.37.11.18,
e-mail infos@badoz.fr ☑
- ☗ ev. day 8am–12 noon 2pm–7pm

BAUD

Chardonnay 2000★

5.5 ha	6,000	🍶 ⑪ 🍴	5–8 €

Powerful and distinguished on the nose, this golden-yellow, attractive Côtes du Jura shows first vegetal and exotic fruit characteristics, then evolves towards appealing toasty notes. Without being very robust, it is a balanced wine that can be kept: there is sufficient acidity and the finish should soften with ageing. It will be ideal with a freshwater fish in sauce.
- ☛ Baud Père et Fils, rte de Voiteur, 39210 Le Vernois, tel. 03.84.25.31.41, fax 03.84.25.30.09,
e-mail abaud@domainebaud.com ☑
- ☗ by appt.

CELLIER DE BELLEVUE

Pinot 2001★

0.5 ha	2,500	🍶	5–8 €

Since 2002 Daniel Credoz has continued to manage his 5.5-ha estate alone. A beautiful cherry colour adorns this pure Côtes du Jura Pinot Noir. The nose is typical Pinot, commented one of the tasters, and is blackcurrant and gamey at the same time. Identical flavours appear on the palate where one senses a good body but a little rusticity at present; this should round out with ageing. Once it is mature, a dish of wild boar or venison would be the ideal gourmet accompaniment. The **Côtes du Jura Chardonnay 2000** is singled out, but should be kept for a year or two.
- ☛ Daniel Crédoz, Cellier de Bellevue, rte des Granges, 39210 Menétru-le-Vignoble, tel. 03.84.85.26.98, fax 03.84.44.62.41 ☑
- ☗ ev. day 8am–12 noon 1.30pm–7pm; Sun. 8am–12 noon; groups by appt.

PHILIPPE BUTIN

Vin jaune 1996★★

0.3 ha	1,600	⑪	15–23 €

Philippe Butin landed a *coup de coeur* with a Vin Jaune 94, and this is not a bad 96 either! With a colour of old gold, it has a superb appearance. The nose combines finesse and complexity: walnut, hazelnut, mild curry and buttered notes. The palate appears a little hard at first, but very quickly the acid-alcohol balance asserts itself. This structure is made to last: powerful, long and full of flavour, this wine has all its future before it. It will be divine drunk with just a piece of Comté cheese or a square of bitter chocolate.
- ☛ Philippe Butin, 21, rue de la Combe, 39210 Lavigny, tel. 03.84.25.36.26, fax 03.84.25.39.18 ☑
- ☗ by appt.

DANIEL ET PASCAL CHALANDARD

Cuvée Siloé 2000★★

2 ha	10,000	🍶 ⑪	8–11 €

The Cuvée Solène 99 was an enchantment and this Cuvée Siloé is not to be outdone. Matured for six months in tank and 18 months in cask, the wine has a strong golden appearance, even slightly coppered. With notes of mild tobacco and walnut, the nose is already very developed. The palate is initially a little austere, but then evolves agreeably, with an attractive range of flavours of toasty, smoky and spiced tones. Very true to type, this Siloé is incontestably from the Jura.
- ☛ Daniel et Pascal Chalandard, GAEC du Vieux Pressoir, 39210 Le Vernois, tel. 03.84.25.31.15, fax 03.84.25.37.62,
e-mail chalandard.pascal@wanadoo.fr ☑
- ☗ by appt.

CLAUDE CHARBONNIER 2001★★★

1 ha	4,000		5–8 €

A blend of 60% Pinot Noir, 30% Trousseau and 10% Poulsard has created a winner for this deep-red Côtes du Jura. The nose is of condensed fruits: strawberries, raspberries and currants come in waves. The same fruits appear on the palate, where a touch of acidity leads to a rounded structure, with velvety tannins. Here is harmony in its purest form. One taster noted that in a difficult vintage like this one, blends are better than wines made from a single grape variety. Whether this is true or not, this wine is splendid. From the same producer, the pure **Savagnin 98 (11–15 €)** obtains one star. A straightforward wine, it is balanced and fresh, and should be opened two or three hours before serving.
- ☛ Claude Charbonnier, 204, Grande-Rue, 39570 Chillé, tel. 03.84.47.23.78, fax 03.84.47.29.27

DENIS ET MARIE CHEVASSU

Vin de paille 1999★★

n.c.	700	⑪	15–23 €

Equal proportions of Chardonnay, Poulsard and Savagnin bunches were selected and picked mainly by the women of the house. Is this why this Vin de Paille has so much balance, harmony and finesse? The journey through the flavours starts on the nose with apricot, quince and crystallized fruits, and continues on the palate with dried fruits and vanilla. Complex, fruity and lingering, it is a true ode to love. This wine is ideal for a romantic drink in front of the fire.
- ☛ Denis Chevassu, Granges Bernard, 39210 Menétru-le-Vignoble, tel. 03.84.85.23.67, fax 03.84.85.23.67 ☑
- ☗ by appt.

JEAN-MARIE COURBET

Vin de paille 1999★

n.c.	2,000	⑪	11–15 €

The estate is well positioned between the village of Voiteur, dominated by Château-Chalon, and the important tourist village of Baume-les-Messieurs. Jean-Marie Courbet is moreover well known for his professional role as president of the *Société de Viticulture du Jura*, the trade union of the appellation. The nose of his Vin de Paille delivers a really aromatic richness with scents of dried fruits and honey. With firm acidity to begin with, the palate is balanced with a beautiful complexity and is full of flavours particularly dried apricots, figs and bitter oranges. This should be served with chocolate cake.
- ☛ Jean-Marie Courbet, rue du Moulin, 39210 Nevy-sur-Seille, tel. 03.84.85.28.70, fax 03.84.44.68.88 ☑
- ☗ ev. day except Sun. 8am–12 noon 2pm–7pm

DOM. JEAN-CLAUDE CREDOZ

Savagnin 1998★

1 ha	2,000	⑪	8–11 €

Like his brother Daniel, Jean-Claude Credoz works independently. A **Côtes du Jura Chardonnay 2000 (5–8 €)** that was given a special mention by the Jury, he presents this wine, matured in cask for four years, without topping up. Bright, with a deep-gold colour, the nose reveals toasty, almond and spice notes. Pure and angular, this Savagnin has an austerity that will be too much for some, but others will love its strong, nervy character. Accompany it with a freshwater fish in sauce.
- ☛ Dom. Jean-Claude Crédoz, chem. des Vignes, 39210 Menétru-le-Vignoble, tel. 03.84.44.64.91, fax 03.84.44.98.76, e-mail domjccredoz@aol.com ☑
- ☗ by appt.

RICHARD DELAY

Vin de paille 1999★★

0.3 ha	1,200	◗◗	15–23 €

Richard Delay is one of the people that count in this vineyard area in the Sud-Revermont, undeservedly much less known than the Arbois or Poligny environs. This Vin de Paille provides the proof. The very expressive nose remains fresh in spite of its power, showing crystallized fruits, figs and beeswax aromas. The palate remains concentrated but rounded, with a very nice sugar-acid balance. Dried apricot, honey, vanilla and almond are present right through to the very attractive finish. A wine to drink on its own with fried foie gras (but make sure you drink it with a friend...). The perfectly vinified **white Cuvée Paul Delay 2000 (8–11 €)** obtains one star.

🦅 Richard Delay, 37, rue du Château, 39570 Gevingey, tel. 03.84.47.46.78, fax 03.84.43.26.75, e-mail delay@freesurf.fr ☑
⏳ by appt.

FLORIAN FRACHET

La Chapelle 1998★★

0.8 ha	3,500	◗◗	8–11 €

This producer has made a successful first presentation to the *Guide* and is worth visiting as is the fortified church in the village. Fermented in tank and aged in barrel without topping up, this Chardonnay has character: intense and brilliant yellow-gold colour, very open nose with fresh walnuts, ripe apples and almonds. The palate does not disappoint either; it is both lively and mouth-filling. Extremely attractive balance but also a strong personality, it has a spicy finish that lasts and lasts...to drink now or keep.

🦅 Florian Frachet, 39190 Maynal, tel. 03.84.48.97.56, fax 03.84.48.97.56 ☑
⏳ by appt.

DOM. GANEVAT

Cuvée Florine Ganevat Chardonnay 2000★★

0.5 ha	2,000	◗◗	8–11 €

Cellar-master for ten years in the heart of the Côte de Beaune, Jean-François Ganevat undoubtedly practised the Burgundian style of oak ageing and then carried it back to the Jura in his suitcase. Fermented in Burgundy barrels of 228 l, his pure Côtes du Jura Chardonnay remained in barrel for 24 months. Inevitably, that leaves its mark, but here there is balance too. The nose is certainly a little excessively strong, but the citrus and brioche notes are quite pleasing. The palate is supple, rounded and balanced. Very long, it has a most agreeable after-taste. This is a wine for long ageing, to be served with chicken livers.

🦅 Dom. Ganevat, La Combe, 39190 Rotalier, tel. 03.84.25.02.69, fax 03.84.25.02.69 ☑
⏳ by appt.

DOM. GANEVAT

Cuvée Julien Ganevat Pinot noir 2001★★

0.7 ha	2,500	◗◗	8–11 €

This Pinot Noir was barrel-aged for one year including 30% new barrels. The red berry nose is intense and typical Pinot, with a touch of oak. Well-balanced on the palate, it has

good body, some obvious oak and the tannins are almost integrated. This wine is a true success especially in such a difficult vintage for reds.

🦅 Dom. Ganevat, La Combe, 39190 Rotalier, tel. 03.84.25.02.69, fax 03.84.25.02.69 ☑
⏳ by appt.

DOM. GRAND FRERES

Tradition 1999★★★

3 ha	15,000	◗◗	8–11 €

The Grand brothers chose to label this blend of Chardonnay and Savagnin, Tradition. And, the tradition is alive and well, the label carried with pride by this style of wine. Impeccable to look at, it sets the tone with the first sniff: fresh but with character. There is apple, brioche and butter: superb. The palate is just as rich and with a touch of acidity that ensures a remarkable liveliness. The light oaky flavours combine with robust structure and well-balanced fruit: overall it is perfectly made. Underneath this carefully controlled structure, the wine still has great character.

🦅 Dom. Grand Frères, rue du Savagnin, 39230 Passenans, tel. 03.84.85.28.88, fax 03.84.44.67.47, e-mail grandfreres@wanadoo.fr ☑
⏳ ev. day 9am–12 noon 2pm–6pm; cl. Sat. Sun. in Jan. and Feb.

CH. GREA

Vin de paille 1999★★

n.c.	800	◗◗	15–23 €

The Château Gréa estate was first established on 22 September 1679, the date on which Claude Gréa bought a vineyard from the Marquis de Montaigu situated on "the territory of Rotailler, in the Rouchet *lieu-dit*". Orange-yellow, this Vin de Paille looks enticing and the nose brings out the dominant crystallized orange aromas. The structure is interesting, with an attractive balance of flavours: citrus fruits combine with apricot, raisins and quince jelly, all extremely persistent. It is complex and rich, but well balanced too. Sip it slowly otherwise in your eagerness you might miss some subtle note. Nicolas Caire also obtains two stars for his **dry white 2000 (5–8 €)** made from Chardonnay and Savagnin, matured in cask. It would make a good choice to match mushrooms in a cream sauce.

🦅 Nicolas Caire, Ch. Gréa, 14, rue Froideville, 39190 Sainte-Agnès, tel. 06.81.83.67.80, fax 03.84.25.05.47
⏳ by appt.

CAVEAU DES JACOBINS

Rubis 1999★

1 ha	6,500	🍶◗◗	5–8 €

If you can describe a place as out of the ordinary, this is it. Imagine a church built in 1248, and of course nationalized during the Revolution, which houses rows and rows of old, large wooden oak casks. Even if today it is only used for ageing wine, winemaking activities have been carried out here for more than 80 years. This wine is a blend of the three Jura red grape varieties and shows a nose that is both gamey and blackcurrant in aroma. The palate is already quite developed, but follows on with similar flavours. It is still a little astringent, but with rich and promising fruit. The **Côtes du Jura Vin**

Jaune 95 (15–23 €) also obtains one star and should be aged for five years to be at its best.
📞 Caveau des Jacobins, rue Nicolas-Appert, 39800 Poligny, tel. 03.84.37.01.37, fax 03.84.37.30.47, e-mail caveaudesjacobins@free.fr ☑
🍴 ev. day 9.30am–12 noon 2pm–6.30pm

DOM. LABET
Les Varrons Chardonnay 2000★★

	0.4 ha	2,350	〽	11–15 €

The house wine-producing style is the "Labet" method. If you want to know more, you must visit this estate: the wine will make your visit worthwhile! The method really succeeds with Chardonnay wines that in this vintage have already developed superb character on the nose. Vegetal notes dominate with anise in particular. The palate has lively acidity, but the feeling of richness develops towards a supple finish. There is weight, but not to the detriment of finesse. This wine can be drunk immediately but also kept to age.
📞 Alain Labet, pl. du Village, 39190 Rotalier, tel. 03.84.25.11.13, fax 03.84.25.06.75 ☑
🍴 by appt.

DOM. MOREL-THIBAUT
Vin de paille 1999★

	1 ha	3,500	〽	15–23 €

If you go and taste the wines from this estate, you will find a new tasting reception area that was opened in 2002. They even have a parking area for motorhomes. This estate has already landed a *coup de coeur* for its Vin de Paille 98. The nose from this rather fine 99 has nuances of quince jelly and crystallized oranges. The palate is of great richness, long and quite complex. As a contrast, you might like to combine it with a fresh fruit salad. The **Côtes du Jura Vin Jaune 96** obtains the same mark and is a wine of finesse and elegance. Also with one star, the **dry white Tradition 2000 (8–11 €)** is made from equal amounts of Chardonnay and Savagnin and is matured for 24 months in barrel. It needs another three or four years and will then match well with *morillade comtoise* (veal stuffed with morels).
📞 Dom. Morel-Thibaut, 8, rue Coittier, 39800 Poligny, tel. 03.84.37.07.61, fax 03.84.37.07.61 ☑
🍴 by appt.

DOM. PIGNIER
Trousseau 2001★★

	1.2 ha	3,000	〽	8–11 €

Ancestors of the Pignier family acquired this estate in 1794. Since 2002, Antoine Pignier has been converting to organic viticulture. This wine displays a beautiful cherry-red colour with some purplish highlights. The nose is not very intense, undoubtedly still immature, but already one can get attractive hints of strawberry, raspberry and gamey notes mingling together. The same flavoursome tones, very typical of Trousseau, can be found on the palate together with rounded tannins. There is power and richness, but also a beautiful balance. This is a good 2001 to drink now, but it will also be able to age successfully. Under the name of **Cellier des Chartreux, pure Côtes du Jura Chardonnay 2000 (5–8 €)** is also singled out. It needs time for the strong and powerful oaky character to integrate.
📞 Dom. Pignier, Cellier des Chartreux, 39570 Montaigu, tel. 03.84.24.24.30, fax 03.84.47.46.00, e-mail pignier-vignerons@wanadoo.fr ☑
🍴 ev. day except Sun. 8am–12 noon 1.45pm–7pm

JEAN TRESY ET FILS
Vin de paille 1999★

	n.c.	650	〽	15–23 €

There is all that you need in Passenans, a charming little village in the Revermont: a hotel, restaurants, a butcher/delicatessen... there is life here that is extremely pleasurable. Another source of satisfaction is this golden-yellow Vin de Paille. The nose is very clean, recalling crème caramel, dried fruits and vanilla. The structure is balanced with the emergence of full flavours coming through from the nose, augmented by strong citrus fruits on the elegant finish. The **Côtes du Jura Poulsard 2001 (5–8 €)** has a typical attractive

onion-skin colour and is a very good representative of its AOC. It obtains one star.
📞 Jean Trésy et Fils, rte des Longevernes, 39230 Passenans, tel. 03.84.85.22.40, fax 03.84.44.99.73, e-mail tresy.vin@wanadoo.fr ☑
🍴 by appt.

FRUITIERE VINICOLE DE VOITEUR
Chardonnay Vieilli un an en fût de chêne 2000★

	3 ha	20,000	▮〽	5–8 €

Five km from the abbey and caves of Baume-les-Messieurs, you will find the cellar of this cooperative, created in 1957. It presented a tank-matured **Côtes du Jura Chardonnay 2000 (3–5 €)** that the Jury singled out, recommending a match with veal *quenelles*. This second pure Chardonnay is fermented in stainless steel tanks and matured for one year in cask without topping up. The nose shows distinct walnut aromas, but also caramel and spices. It is almost like a blend with Savagnin. Lively, the palate has nevertheless good structure with an excellent substance. It is still somewhat harsh, but there is a beautiful finish revealing bitter almonds and mild curry flavours. This is an attractive wine, very distinctive on the palate, which could improve with time.
📞 Fruitière vinicole de Voiteur, 60, rue de Nevy-sur-Seille, 39210 Voiteur, tel. 03.84.85.21.29, fax 03.84.85.27.67, e-mail voiteur@fruitiere-vinicole-voiteur.fr ☑
🍴 by appt.

Wines selected but not starred

DOM. BERTHET-BONDET
Tradition 2000

	3 ha	10,000	〽	8–11 €

📞 Berthet-Bondet, Chem. de La Tour, 39210 Château-Chalon, tel. 03.84.44.60.48, fax 03.84.44.61.13 ☑
🍴 by appt.

CLAUDE BUCHOT 2000

	1.5 ha	5,800	▮〽	5–8 €

📞 Claude Buchot, 39190 Maynal, tel. 03.84.85.94.27, fax 03.84.85.94.27 ☑
🍴 by appt.

CLAUDE ET CEDRIC JOLY
Pinot noir 2001

	0.9 ha	5,000	〽	5–8 €

📞 EARL Claude et Cédric Joly, chem. des Patarattes, 39190 Rotalier, tel. 03.84.25.04.14, fax 03.84.25.14.48 ☑
🍴 by appt.

LA MAISON DE ROSE
Novelin Savagnin 2001

	0.15 ha	1,000		8–11 €

📞 Dominique Grand, 8, rue de l'Eglise, 39230 Saint-Lothain, tel. 03.84.37.01.32 ☑
🍴 by appt.

PHILIPPE PELTIER
Vin de paille 1999

	0.2 ha	1,200	〽	15–23 €

📞 Philippe Peltier, Caveau du Terroir, 39210 Menétru-le-Vignoble, tel. 03.84.44.90.79, fax 03.84.85.26.67 ☑
🍴 by appt.

DOM. DES VIGNAY

Poulsard 2001

■	1.5 ha	2,500	◗◗	5–8 €

☛ Dom. des Vignay, 19, Grande-Rue, 39190 Grusse,
tel. 03.84.25.15.77, fax 03.84.25.19.63 ☑
𝚼 ev. day except Sun. 9am–12 noon 2pm–6pm
☛ B. Millet M. Rameaux

DOM. VOORHUIS-HENQUET

La Poirière 2000

■	1 ha	6,000	◗◗	11–15 €

☛ Dom. Voorhuis-Henquet, 35–37, rue Neuve,
39570 Conliège, tel. 03.84.24.34.41, fax 03.84.24.36.11,
e-mail jfg.voorhuis@nomade.fr ☑
𝚼 by appt.

Crémant du Jura

The AOC Crémant du Jura was recognized by a decree of 9 October 1995, and it applies to sweet mousseux wines made from grapes harvested within the production area of the AOC Côtes du Jura and vinified according to the strict rules applying to Vins Crémants. The approved red-grape varieties are the Poulsard (or Ploussard), Pinot Noir (known locally as Gros Noirien), Pinot Gris and Trousseau. The white varieties are the Savagnin (known locally as Naturé) and Chardonnay (known as Melon d'Arbois or Gamay Blanc). In 2002, a total of 14,638 hl was declared.

FRUITIERE VINICOLE D'ARBOIS

2000★★★

○	15 ha	n.c.	■ ♦	5–8 €

The professionalism and dynamism of the large Arbois cooperative, founded in 1906, really shows with this *crémant*. Look at the bubbles that radiate through the pale-yellow colour and which form such a fine sparkle. The nose, intense and toasty, explodes with superb freshness. The perfectly balanced palate delivers subtle toasty notes that are only disturbed by the attractive mentholated tones. With a wine like this, alcohol is not the only intoxication.
☛ Fruitière vinicole d'Arbois, 2, rue des Fossés,
39600 Arbois, tel. 03.84.66.11.67, fax 03.84.37.48.80 ☑
𝚼 by appt.

CH. DE L'ETOILE 2000★

○	3 ha	16,000	■	8–11 €

This producer is renowned in particular for its sparkling wines and enjoyed a *coup de coeur* for this appellation in a previous edition of the *Guide*. This *cuvée* from the 2000 vintage has a pretty crown of bubbles with an attractive buttery, lactic nose. It is nervy on the palate, but with fine balance.

☛ G. Vandelle et Fils, GAEC Ch. de L'Etoile, 994, rue Bouillod, 39570 L'Etoile, tel. 03.84.47.33.07,
fax 03.84.24.93.52 ☑
𝚼 by appt.

GRAND FRERES

Prestige★★

○	6 ha	50,000	■ ♦	5–8 €

The fortified château of Fontenay is 1 km from this estate; and just 3 km away is the medieval crypt of Saint-Lothain. There are many reasons to visit here. This Prestige *brut* is worthy of its name. The appearance is clear, almost transparent, with very pretty green tinges. Extremely fresh, the nose is of citrus fruits, but also of acacia and roses. Rounded and with the right amount of *dosage*, the palate is pleasant and would be ideal as an aperitif, with a seafood gratin or with a black forest gateau; it will be a valuable partner to stimulate the gastric juices.
☛ Dom. Grand Frères, rue du Savagnin, 39230 Passenans, tel. 03.84.85.28.88, fax 03.84.44.67.47,
e-mail grandfreres@wanadoo.fr ☑
𝚼 ev. day 9am–12 noon 2pm–6pm;
cl. Sat. Sun. in Jan. and Feb.

CLAUDE JOLY 2001★

○	3 ha	20,000	■ ♦	5–8 €

With a pale-yellow colour, this gives a pretty stream of fine bubbles. The nose is clean and straightforward with an attractive Chardonnay note. This same characteristic also appears on the palate, which is a little closed at present. However this is a quality wine that will be ideal on the dinner table.
☛ EARL Claude et Cédric Joly, chem. des Patarattes, 39190 Rotalier, tel. 03.84.25.04.14, fax 03.84.25.14.48 ☑
𝚼 by appt.

ALAIN LABET 2001★

●	0.5 ha	3,400	◗◗	5–8 €

Here is a rosé that is not commonly found in this appellation. It has been vinified from Pinot Noir. With a very pale-pink colour, tending towards brick-red, the extremely fine bubbles form a pretty stream. The nose is not particularly dramatic but simply gives a beautiful freshness with notes of red berries, such as raspberry. The palate is balanced and still very obviously young. Recommended with strawberry tart.
☛ Alain Labet, pl. du Village, 39190 Rotalier,
tel. 03.84.25.11.13, fax 03.84.25.06.75 ☑
𝚼 by appt.

MARCEL CABELIER 2000★

○	60 ha	300,000	■ ♦	5–8 €

Marketing under this brand, the Compagnie des Grands Vins du Jura is the largest buyer of grapes and young wines in the appellation. It has a very attractive pale-yellow colour with a stream of fine bubbles. The nose is light, but is dominated by elegance and fruit. The palate is light and pleasant with acacia flavours. This is a good, well-made wine.
☛ Compagnie des Grands Vins du Jura, rte de Champagnole, 39570 Crançot, tel. 03.84.87.61.30,
fax 03.84.48.21.36, e-mail jura@grandschais.fr ☑
𝚼 by appt.

DOM. DE MONTBOURGEAU★★

○	1.5 ha	13,000	■ ♦	5–8 €

This estate was bought by the Gros family in 1920 and today Nicole Deriaux, the daughter of Jean Gros runs the business. This *crémant* reveals a fine and intense mousse and a very refreshing nose. The fruit carries it, with citrus fruits, pear and quince. A touch of acidity on the palate maintains this freshness, and it does the trick.
☛ Dom. de Montbourgeau, 39570 L'Etoile,
tel. 03.84.47.32.96, fax 03.84.24.41.44,
e-mail domaine.montbourgeau@wanadoo.fr ☑
𝚼 by appt.

L'Etoile

DOM. DESIRE PETIT
Blanc de blancs Cuvée Désirée 2001★★

| | 1.4 ha | 10,800 | 🍶 ⚘ | 8–11 € |

This *crémant* is not a "loudmouth". It has a reliable character, but one that does not assert itself. With a beautiful yellow colour and green highlights, the bubble is fine, very fine, and the pleasant nose is extremely fresh. The palate plays no false notes, and gives citrus fruit nuances of rare elegance. "A *crémant* to please the ladies," said a male member of the Jury...but the men should enjoy it too.
☛ Dom. Désiré Petit, rue du Ploussard, 39600 Pupillin, tel. 03.84.66.01.20, fax 03.84.66.26.59, e-mail domaine-desire-petit@wanadoo.fr 🆅
🍽 ev. day 9am–12 noon 2pm–7pm; groups by appt.
☛ Gérard and Marcel Petit

DOM. DE LA PINTE★

| | 2 ha | 6,000 | 🍶 ⚘ | 5–8 € |

One cannot really say that it is sparkling when one pours this into the glass, but the bubbles are fine. The nose is elegant and fruity, though this is also not very expansive. This wine reveals much more on the palate, with a pretty fruitiness that leaves an agreeable impression and a delicate, just slightly tart finish. This really is the ideal aperitif wine.
☛ Dom. de la Pinte, rte de Lyon, 39600 Arbois, tel. 03.84.66.06.47, fax 03.84.66.24.58, e-mail accueil@lapinte.fr 🆅
🍽 by appt.
☛ Famille Martin

DOM. ROLET PERE ET FILS
Coeur de chardonnay 2000★

| | 2 ha | 12,000 | 🍶 | 8–11 € |

The selection Coeur de Chardonnay is a very pale yellow, from which emerges a delightful mousse. There are wild flowers, hawthorn and toasty notes on the nose. The palate is quite nervy, but reveals a freshness that will ensure this wine is much enjoyed as an aperitif.
☛ Dom. Rolet Père et Fils, Montesserin, rte de Dole, 39600 Arbois, tel. 03.84.66.00.05, fax 03.84.37.47.14, e-mail rolet@wanadoo.fr 🆅

DOM. DE SAVAGNY★

| | 1.5 ha | 10,000 | 🍶 ⚘ | 5–8 € |

The stream of bubbles is fine, the nose is clean and lemony with fresh fruits. The citrus fruits re-emerge on the palate together with a little green apple. The aromatic tones balance well with the slight tartness behind. Delightfully lively, this might go well with a dessert such as *kugelhopf*.
☛ Dom. de Savagny, rte de Champagnole, 39570 Crançot, tel. 03.84.87.61.30, fax 03.84.48.21.36 🆅 🏠 🏠
🍽 by appt.

JACQUES TISSOT 2000★★

| | 1.5 ha | 9,000 | 🍶 ⚘ | 5–8 € |

Those who are looking for a powerful sparkle might be disappointed, but what finesse this has! The nose is unusual, with a Muscat-grape character and baked apple. The palate starts cleanly with some weight and plenty of fruit. This is a *crémant* with good vinosity that has already developed and can be drunk now with an entrée, such as asparagus quiche.

☛ Dom. Jacques Tissot, 39, rue de Courcelles, 39600 Arbois, tel. 03.84.66.14.27, fax 03.84.66.24.88, e-mail courrier@domaine-jacques-tissot.fr 🆅 🏠
🍽 by appt.

DOM. PHILIPPE VANDELLE 2000★

| | 4 ha | 14,000 | 🍶 ⚘ | 5–8 € |

The vineyard of Château de l'Etoile was split up in 2001 with Philippe and Bernard Vandelle looking after 11.5 ha. This *crémant* of pure Chardonnay has a fine bubble. With slight vanilla on the nose, it has some sweetness on the palate, and a *dosage* that leans to the sugary side. A wine for dessert.
☛ Dom. Philippe Vandelle, 186, rue Bouillod, 39570 L'Etoile, tel. 03.84.86.49.57, fax 03.84.86.49.58, e-mail info@vinsphilippevandelle.com 🆅
🍽 by appt.

Wines selected but not starred

CELLIER DE BELLEVUE 2001

| | 0.4 ha | 3,000 | 🍶 | 5–8 € |

☛ Daniel Crédoz, Cellier de Bellevue, rte des Granges, 39210 Menétru-le-Vignoble, tel. 03.84.85.26.98, fax 03.84.44.62.41 🆅
🍽 ev. day 8am–12 noon 1.30pm–7pm; Sun. 8am–12 noon; groups by appt.

FRUITIERE VINICOLE DE PUPILLIN 2000

| | 2.71 ha | 25,000 | 🍶 | 5–8 € |

☛ Fruitière vinicole de Pupillin, rue du Ploussard, 39600 Pupillin, tel. 03.84.66.12.88, fax 03.84.37.47.16, e-mail fvp39@wanadoo.fr 🆅
🍽 by appt.

XAVIER REVERCHON 2000

| | 1 ha | 3,700 | 🍶 ⚘ | 5–8 € |

☛ Xavier Reverchon, 2, rue du Clos, 39800 Poligny, tel. 03.84.37.02.58, fax 03.84.37.00.58, e-mail reverchon.vinsjura@libertysurf.fr 🆅
🍽 by appt.

L'Etoile

The village owes its name, "The Star", to a certain type of fossilized plant found in the rocks of the area; cross-sections of the plant (a sea lily) form a five-pointed star. In 2002 the vineyards, which cover 55 ha, produced 2,718 hl of white, yellow, straw and sparkling wine.

BAUD PERE ET FILS 1999★★★

| | 3 ha | 8,500 | 🍶 🍶 ⚘ | 5–8 € |

Alain and Jean-Michel Baud cultivate vines in the AOC L'Etoile but they are mainly based in the Côtes du Jura and also at Château-Chalon. The straw colour of this Etoile is already fascinating, but one almost forgets it as soon as one takes one sniff from the glass. Vanilla, butter, oak, toast and

aniseed: the only way to describe this remarkably intense and complex nose. The palate is completely fresh with both vegetal and mineral notes, and no oxidative character appears here. This feeling of freshness does not preclude a rounded, very rich side that expresses itself too. This rather atypical aspect will surprise some wine-lovers, but the force of character and elegance of this wine will overcome any resistance. Recommended with crayfish and lobster.
🕏 Baud Père et Fils, rte de Voiteur, 39210 Le Vernois, tel. 03.84.25.31.41, fax 03.84.25.30.09, e-mail abaud@domainebaud.com ☑
🍷 by appt.

DANIEL ET PASCAL CHALANDARD
Cuvée Axel 2000★

	1.1 ha	8,000	🍶 🍷	5–8 €

Like other estates, the wine cellar of Daniel and Pascal Chalandard is not located in the AOC L'Etoile, but in the area of the Côtes du Jura, in Vernois. This Cuvée Axel has a bright colour, mingling green and yellow. The nose of this Chardonnay-Savagnin blend shows oak, anise and beeswax. On the palate, the Savagnin grape expresses itself only on the finish. Substantial but balanced, it is a rather woody-tasting wine. Admittedly one can drink it now, but the fruit expression will improve in a few years.
🕏 Daniel et Pascal Chalandard, GAEC du Vieux Pressoir, 39210 Le Vernois, tel. 03.84.25.31.15, fax 03.84.25.37.62, e-mail chalandard.pascal@wanadoo.fr ☑
🍷 by appt.

CH. L'ETOILE
Cuvée des Ceps d'or 2000★★

	6 ha	20,000	🍶 🍷 ⚬	8–11 €

The elegant appearance proves that the Cuvée des Ceps d'Or lives up to its name. The Savagnin dominates on the nose, although the Chardonnay makes up the large majority in the blend. It offers a great purity of flavour, with green walnuts dominating. The clarity of the nose is also found on the powerful palate which is both balanced and long. This is an extremely attractive blend combining the roundness of Chardonnay with the finesse of Savagnin, together with green apple and hazelnut. It can be drunk from now, but will not suffer at all from keeping for three to five years.
🕏 G. Vandelle et Fils, GAEC Ch. de L'Etoile, 994, rue Bouillod, 39570 L'Etoile, tel. 03.84.47.33.07, fax 03.84.24.93.52 ☑
🍷 by appt.

CLAUDE ET CEDRIC JOLY
Vin jaune 1995★★

	0.5 ha	1,000	🍷	23–30 €

Together with his son, Claude Joly cultivates almost 8 ha of vines, both in the Côtes du Jura and in the AOC L'Etoile. It is in the Etoile vineyard that he chose to harvest the precious bunches of Savagnin that have allowed him to vinify this pale

Vin Jaune. With lovely tinges of green the colour is as restrained as the nose is powerful, a really pronounced Vin Jaune. Real intensity is also expressed on the palate, coupled with a certain finesse. A touch of walnut and a note of mild curry flavour, this wine is really glorious and has an extremely attractive finish. It is, however, essential to wait until it reaches its best.
🕏 EARL Claude et Cédric Joly, chem. des Patarattes, 39190 Rotalier, tel. 03.84.25.04.14, fax 03.84.25.14.48 ☑
🍷 by appt.

CH. DE PERSANGES 1999★

	0.5 ha	2,500	🍷	11–15 €

At Château de Persanges, certain vineyard work is left for the youngsters from the special-needs institute in Besançon. This Savagnin wine, vinified without topping up the casks, undoubtedly provides a stepping stone for those who want to get to know the mysteries of Vin Jaune, a style that this estate also produces. The nose is pleasing, with notes of hazelnuts, ripe fruits and cut hay. Behind the initial acidity the palate reveals a beautifully fruity mid-palate. This wine should nevertheless stay in the cellar for three or four years before it can reveal its best side.
🕏 Ch. de Persanges, rte de Saint-Didier, 39570 L'Etoile, tel. 03.84.86.03.36, fax 03.84.47.46.56 ☑
🍷 ev. day 9.30am–12 noon 2.30pm–7pm;
Sun. Mon. by appt.
🕏 Lionel-Marie d'Arc

DOM. PHILIPPE VANDELLE
Vin de paille 1999★★

	1 ha	2,500	🍷	11–15 €

This estate results from the division of the vineyard and the wine cellar of Château L'Etoile. A classic *cuvée*, where Chardonnay represents 99% of the blend and is matured six months in tank, six months in cask, **Domaine Philippe Vandelle 2000 (5–8 €)** gains a particular mention and will be enjoyable from this winter with a mushroom dish or a terrine. It was this Vin de Paille that really took the votes: Chardonnay grapes blended with a little Poulsard and Savagnin came together in this wine with amber tinges. Honey is very obvious on the nose, but there is also cocoa, prune and apricot, each appearing in turn. There is just the right level of alcohol and acidity. It has a lovely level of sweetness on the palate, where notes of prune make the first impression followed by cocoa reminiscent of chocolate cake.
🕏 Dom. Philippe Vandelle, 186, rue Bouillod, 39570 L'Etoile, tel. 03.84.86.49.57, fax 03.84.86.49.58, e-mail info@vinsphilippevandelle.com ☑
🍷 by appt.

Wines selected but not starred

DOM. DE MONTBOURGEAU
Vin jaune 1995

	0.5 ha	2,500	🍶 🍷 ⚬	23–30 €

🕏 Dom. de Montbourgeau, 39570 L'Etoile, tel. 03.84.47.32.96, fax 03.84.24.41.44, e-mail domaine.montbourgeau@wanadoo.fr ☑
🍷 by appt.
🕏 Jean Gros

Savoie

From the French shore of Lac Léman to the Isère valley, in the departments of Savoie and Haute-Savoie, the vineyards occupy favourable lower slopes of the Alps. The vineyard is constantly expanding, currently nearly 1,960 ha, and year on year, produces about 130,000 hl. The individual wine-growing areas together form a complex mosaic dictated by the shapes of the various valleys, which are planted in bigger or smaller islets of cultivation. This geographical diversity is echoed in local climatic variations, which are either exaggerated by the relief or tempered by the proximity of Lac Léman and the Lac du Bourget.

Vin de Savoie and Roussette de Savoie are regional appellations, used nearly everywhere; they may be followed by the name of a cru, but apply exclusively to still wines which, for the Roussettes, mean whites only. Wines from Crépy and Seyssel each have a right to their own appellation.

Because of the widely dispersed vineyards, numerous grape varieties are in use but, in fact, many are planted in only limited amounts: this is particularly true of Pinot Noir and Chardonnay. The main varieties are two reds and four whites, alongside others that produce specifically local wines. Gamay, imported from neighbouring Beaujolais post-phylloxera, produces fresh, light red wines to be drunk in the year of production. Mondeuse, a local, quality variety, produces full-bodied red wines, particularly in Arbin, where it is the only variety under cultivation. Pre-phylloxera this was the most widely grown variety in Savoy, and it is to be hoped that it will one day regain its rightful place, because the wines it produces are of good quality with terrific character. Jacquère is the most widely planted white variety; it produces fresh, light white to be drunk young. Altesse, a very delicate variety, typically Savoyard, produces wines sold as Roussette de Savoie. Finally, Roussanne, locally known as Bergeron, also produces white wines of very high quality, especially in Chignin, where it is grown with the cross variety Chignin-Bergeron.

Crépy

Chasselas is the only variety planted in the Crépy vineyard with its 80 ha (of which 59 were used in 2002), as it is along the shores of Lac Léman. It produced about 3,734 hl of light white wine in 2002. This little region obtained its AOC in 1948.

Wines selected but not starred

LA GOUTTE D'OR

Tête de Cuvée 2002

	39 ha	200,000	🍾 ◫ ◈	5-8 €
🕐 Claude Mercier, Dom. de La Grande Cave de Crépy, 74140 Loisin, tel. 04.50.94.01.23, fax 04.50.94.19.86, e-mail clmercier74@aol.com ▼
🍷 by appt.

Vin de Savoie

The vineyard classed as Appellation Vin de Savoie is generally to be found on the ancient glacial moraines (continuous linear deposits of rocks and gravel left by glaciers), or on scree, which because of its geographical dispersal contributes to great diversity in the wines; these are frequently identified by adding a local denomination to the regional appellation. On the French shore of Lac Léman, in Marin, Ripaille and Marignan, Chasselas produces light, white, often slightly fizzy wines, which are best drunk young. Other areas grow different varieties and, depending on the soil types, produce white or red wines. From north to south, from Ayze to the banks of the Arve river, sparkling and fizzy whites give way (south of the Appellation Seyssel) to the red wines of the Lac du Bourget, and La Chautagne, where the reds in particular have a marked character. South of Chambéry, the flanks of Mont Granier produce fresh white wines such as the Apremont and the Cru des Abymes, a vineyard established on a site where the mountain collapsed in 1248, killing thousands of people. Facing it, Monterminod has been smothered by housing developments, but has retained a vineyard which produces remarkable wines; next to it lie the vineyards of Saint-Jeoire-Prieuré, on the far side of Challes-les-Eaux, then Chignin, where the fame of the Bergeron grape is absolutely justified. Going up the Isère on the right bank, the southeast-facing slopes are occupied by the crus of Montmélian, Arbin, Cruet and Saint-Jean-de-la-Porte.

Produced only in limited quantities (around 129,037 hl in 2002), in a region very popular with tourists, the Savoie wines are mainly drunk young, mostly locally, and sold into a market where demand sometimes outstrips supply. The white Savoy wines go well with freshwater and sea fish, while the reds (made from Gamay) are very versatile. It is a shame to drink the Mondeuse reds too young as they need several years to develop and soften: these high-quality wines accompany strongly flavoured dishes such as game, the excellent Tomme de Savoie and the famous Reblochon cheeses.

DOM. BELLUARD FILS

Ayze 2001★★

	10 ha	70,000	🍶 ⬧		5–8 €

This wine is a credit to the Ayze area, traditionally devoted to the production of sparkling wines. From the local Gringet grape variety, it enchanted the Jury from the start with its fine and abundant mousse on a golden-yellow background with green highlights. Its delicate range of flavours moves from floral tones to aromas of mixed nuts, while sweet roasted notes accompany the lively structure of the palate. An extremely pleasant aperitif.
➼ Dom. Belluard, Les Chenevaz, 74130 Ayze,
tel. 04.50.97.05.63 ☑
⏱ ev. day except Sun. 8am–12 noon 2pm–6pm

DOM. GILLES BERLIOZ

Chignin-Bergeron 2002★★

	3.5 ha	4,550	🍶 ⬧		11–15 €

Gilles Berlioz, who has "conducted" his 5-ha property in Chignin since 1990, has made a real success with his Chignin-Bergeron...worthy of a Berlioz symphony. An intense golden-yellow appearance gives way to delicate floral and fruit aromas. The wine shows itself to be full bodied and balanced. Not content with this composition, this producer also presents a **Mondeuse 2002 (8–11 €)**. Aged for four months in barrel, the wine delivers a crimson colour, with an oaky nose and red berry fruit flavours. Once again, the Jury could not just listen to the melody of the wine, they had to award it a star.
➼ Gilles Berlioz, Le Viviers, 73800 Chignin,
tel. 04.79.28.00.51, fax 04.79.71.58.80 ☑

PHILIPPE BETEMPS

Apremont 2002★★

	1.4 ha	13,000	🍶 ⬧		3–5 €

At the foot of the church in Apremont, the 6 ha of vines owned by Philippe Betemps are exclusively planted with Jacquère. The winemaker knew how to bring out the quintessential flavours from this grape variety, grown on a terroir on which it traditionally does well. Enthralled by its delicacy and elegance, the Jury gave their best mark to this Jacquère 2002, which is typical of the appellation. The floral nose is followed by an expressive palate, balanced, with both fruity and mineral characteristics. This wine will be excellent with a seafood platter.
➼ EARL Philippe Betemps, Saint-Pierre, 73190 Apremont,
tel. 04.79.28.33.18 ☑
⏱ ev. day except Sun. 8am–6pm

DOM. G. BLANC ET FILS

Apremont Sélection 2002★

	2 ha	18,000	🍶 ⬧		5–8 €

Gilbert and Willy Blanc have just invested heavily into their customer reception area and their product sales area. They have also updated their press and the vat room. The results have not been slow in coming. This appealing Apremont has intense flavours, as well as roundness and good length. Another style altogether, the **Gamay 2002** is singled out for its fragrance of soft red fruits and long liquorice palate.
➼ Dom. Gilbert Blanc et Fils, 73, chem. de Revaison, 73190 Saint-Baldoph, tel. 04.79.28.36.90, fax 04.79.28.36.90 ☑
⏱ ev. day except Tue. Sun. 9am–12 noon 3pm–7pm

ERIC ET FRANCOIS CARREL

Jongieux Pinot 2002★

	1 ha	6,500	🍶 ⬧		5–8 €

Matured for eight months in tank and eight months in barrel, this brilliant-ruby Pinot supplies a delicate perfume with good intensity, dominated by blackberries and blueberries. A similar subtlety on the palate impresses, even if the tannins do still appear a little austere. One year of ageing will suffice to soften the wine. There is no doubt that the winemaking was well handled. The **Jongieux de Jacquère 2002 (3–5 €)**, was singled out for its range of flavours going from citrus fruits (lemon) to honeysuckle, and on to a buttery note.

➼ François et Eric Carrel, GAEC de la Rosière, 73170 Jongieux, tel. 04.79.44.02.20, fax 04.79.44.03.73 ☑
⏱ by appt.

EUGENE CARREL ET FILS

Jongieux Mondeuse 2002★

	2.05 ha	18,400	🍶 ⬧		5–8 €

The typicity of this Jongieux Mondeuse did not escape the tasters, from its garnet-red colour with bright purplish tinges to its delicate aromas of red berries (perhaps a touch too restrained still), and its rounded, velvety taste. With both personality and authenticity, this wine seems made to drink with game.
➼ Eugène Carrel et Fils, Le Haut, 73170 Jongieux, tel. 04.79.44.00.20, fax 04.79.44.03.06, e-mail carrel-eugene@wanadoo.fr ☑
⏱ by appt.

FREDERIC GIACHINO

Abymes 2002★★

	1.3 ha	10,000	🍶 ⬧		3–5 €

In a previous *Guide*, Frédéric Giachino was singled out for his Abymes 1998. Situated on the Isère side, on land favourable to the Jacquère grape, he has really brought out the typicity of this variety in his 2002, which came close to receiving a *coup de coeur*. Pale yellow with green tinges, the mineral nose is both expressive and attractive. The initial clean, floral character on the palate leads to an intense mineral mid-palate, full and balanced, characteristic of this cru. Another authentic wine.
➼ Frédéric Giachino, La Palud, 38530 Chapareillan, tel. 04.76.45.57.11, fax 04.76.45.57.11 ☑
⏱ by appt.

DOM. JEAN-PIERRE ET PHILIPPE GRISARD Mondeuse Cuvée Prestige et Tradition Elevé en fût 2002★

	1 ha	8,000	🍶🍶		5–8 €

Mondeuse is without doubt the speciality of Jean-Pierre and Philippe Grisard. After receiving a *coup de coeur* for the Saint-Jean-de-la-Porte Mondeuse 2001, these producers present a well-made ruby wine here. Discrete red fruit notes combine well with woody-tasting nuances and pepper to give an overall good balance. A very long wine, which will be more enjoyable after one year of ageing. The **Mondeuse 2002 (3–5 €)**, matured in tank, was also recommended.
➼ Jean-Pierre et Philippe Grisard, Chef-lieu, 73250 Fréterive, tel. 04.79.28.54.09, fax 04.79.71.41.36, e-mail gaecgrisard@aol.com ☑

DOM. DE L'IDYLLE

Mondeuse 2002★★

	5 ha	12,000	🍶 ⬧		5–8 €

Domaine de l'Idylle appears to have produced an idyllic Mondeuse in 2002. Tasters were charmed by this intense ruby-red 2002. Elegantly fruity, it has a velvety structure remarkable for its youth, and the finish does not lack persistence. A delicious wine and typical of its style, it will be delicious with a Savoyarde pork casserole.
➼ Dom. de l'Idylle, Saint-Laurent, 73800 Cruet, tel. 04.79.84.30.58, fax 04.79.65.26.26 ☑
⏱ by appt.
➼ Philippe and François Tiollier

JEAN PERRIER ET FILS Mondeuse Vieilles Vignes Cuvée Gastronomie 2002★★

	n.c.	8,000	🍶 ⬧		5–8 €

Close to the Chartreuse nature reserve, on the banks of Lac Saint-André, the company of Jean Perrier et Fils has made a Mondeuse that is as enjoyable as the local scenery. A ruby colour adorns this fine and complex wine, which has roasted and spicy aromas. The palate begins cleanly and then the supple, silky tannins appear. This is an elegant and well-balanced Mondeuse, which should be aged for a few years before being partnered with game.
➼ Jean Perrier et Fils, Saint-André, 73800 Les Marches, tel. 04.79.28.11.45, fax 04.79.28.09.91, e-mail vperrier@vins-perrier.com ☑
⏱ by appt.

SAVOIE

DOM. J.-PIERRE ET J.-FRANCOIS

QUENARD Chignin-Bergeron Vieilles Vignes 2002★

	0.7 ha	6,000	🍷 ♦	8–11 €

The terroir takes on great importance for this estate, which endeavours to identify each plot in order to vinify its fruit separately. The grapes were harvested in several passes to produce this Chignin-Bergeron. A bright golden-yellow, the wine offers apricot aromas with a good, rich and rounded structure. Already enjoyable now, one should not be reluctant to age it further to improve it even more. **Chignin Cuvée Anne de la Biguerne 2002 (5–8 €)** is especially singled out for its attractive character.
⚫ Dom. J.-Pierre et J.-François Quénard, Le Villard, 73800 Chignin, tel. 04.79.28.08.29, fax 04.79.28.18.92 ☑
☒ by appt.

DOM. RAYMOND QUENARD

Chignin Mondeuse 2002★★

■	0.3 ha	2,500	🍷	5–8 €

Presenting a really classy 2002, it is obvious that Raymond Quénard knew how to draw out the very best from his 30 ares of Chignin Mondeuse. The Jury enjoyed the garnet-red colour with its purple highlights, and the fruity nose, very true-to-type, dominated by blackcurrant and spices. The weight balanced well with seductive tannins giving an overall roundness. Although it has not yet reached its best, this Mondeuse is already impressive. The **Chignin-Bergeron 2002 (8–11 €)** is also recommended.
⚫ Dom. Raymond Quénard, Le Villard, 73800 Chignin, tel. 04.79.28.01.46, fax 04.79.28.16.78, e-mail raymond.quenard@clubinternet.fr ☑
☒ by appt.

PHILIPPE RAVIER

Chignin-Bergeron 2002★★

■	4 ha	25,000	🍷	5–8 €

A double winner for Philippe Ravier. His **Mondeuse 2002 (3–5 €)** obtains one star for its typically spicy aroma and voluptuous weight, leaving you yearning to drink it with a lamb steak. He receives two stars for this rich and elegant Chignin-Bergeron. A perfectly ripe Roussanne indicated by the notes of apricot that streak through the tasting from beginning to end. These are accompanied by crystallized and honeyed nuances that appear on the full and generous palate.
⚫ Philippe Ravier, Léché, 73800 Myans, tel. 04.79.28.17.75, fax 04.79.28.17.75 ☑
☒ by appt.

DOM. DE ROUZAN

Gamay 2002★★

■	0.8 ha	6,500	🍷	5–8 €

The most successful Gamay of the year? You will have to look for it at the estate of Denis Fortin, established since 1991 in a sector traditionally reserved for the production of the white wine of Apremont. This intense ruby-coloured 2002 reveals a complex range of flavours in which fruity notes intermingle with roasted and spicy characteristics. Rounded and balanced, the fruit lasts remarkably well. This is a wine to "cosset" for a little more time in the wine cellar.
⚫ Denis Fortin, 152, chem. de la Mairie, 73190 Saint-Baldoph, tel. 04.79.28.25.58, fax 04.79.28.21.63, e-mail denis.fortin@wanadoo.fr ☑
☒ by appt.

DOM. SAINT-GERMAIN

Mondeuse Le Pied de la Barme 2002★

■	0.45 ha	3,600	🍷 ♦	5–8 €

Behind its intense red colour this wine offers characteristic forest fruit aromas (raspberry, blackcurrant). Typically lively and slightly wild, the palate presents a similar intensity of flavour and good length. It would be best to forget this wine for a few years and then enjoy it with a well-matured Tomme de Savoie cheese.
⚫ Dom. Saint-Germain, rte du Col-du-Frène, 73250 Saint-Pierre-d'Albigny, tel. 04.79.28.61.68, fax 04.79.28.61.68 ☑
☒ by appt.
⚫ Etienne and Raphaël Saint-Germain

CH. LA TOUR DE MARIGNAN

Marignan Perlant 2001★

	2.5 ha	8,000	🍶	8–11 €

Situated on the slopes above Lac Léman, Château La Tour de Marignan produces wines from organically farmed grapes. Its slightly sparkling yellow-gold Chasselas from Marignan reveals an intense and fine nose characterized by crystallized fruits. Rounded and well balanced, the palate is full of hazelnut flavours.
⚫ Bernard Canelli-Suchet, Ch. La Tour de Marignan, 74140 Sciez, tel. 04.50.72.70.30, fax 04.50.72.36.02, e-mail ocanelli@caramail.com ☑
☒ ev. day 9am–12.30pm 2pm–7.30pm; groups by appt.

CHANTAL ET GUY TOURNOUD

Apremont 2002★

	1.87 ha	12,000		5–8 €

Here is a well-made, clear and bright Apremont of pale yellow colour with green tinges. Plenty of aroma nuances, with both floral and fruity notes (citrus in particular), it is characteristic of its terroir. On the palate, it is clean and straightforward, balanced, with a lively touch, characteristic of the appellation. The birthplace of this wine can be spotted with eyes closed.
⚫ Guy Tournoud, Bellecombe, 38530 Chapareillan, tel. 04.76.45.22.05, fax 04.76.45.22.05 ☑
☒ by appt.

LES FILS DE CHARLES TROSSET

Arbin Mondeuse 2002★★

	3.8 ha	20,000	🍷	5–8 €

Regularly mentioned in the *Guide*, and available in all the best places, the Mondeuse Arbin of Charles Trosset wins recognition once again. Made from old vines on average 25 years of age, this will appeal to lovers of lavish red wines. With a promising colour of dark garnet-red, the nose exudes charred flavours. On the palate, these flavours seem to be catalyzed by its significant weight, with attractive peppery notes. This majestic Mondeuse will still improve in the cellar and will be ideal to accompany red meat.
⚫ SCEA Les Fils de Charles Trosset, chem. des Moulins, 73800 Arbin, tel. 04.79.84.30.99, fax 04.79.84.30.99 ☑

ADRIEN VACHER

Abymes La Sasson Cuvée réservée 2002★

	8 ha	n.c.	🍷 ♦	3–5 €

Specialists in marketing the whole range of Savoie wines, the Adrien Vacher company has paid special attention to its selection of white wines including this crystal-clear, pale Abymes. The aromas on the nose are very expressive, showing finesse, and are typical of the appellation. The palate is initially fresh, but fills out to give the taster an impression of weight and length. The company's **Chignin la Sasson Cuvée Réservée 2002** is shorter in length, but deserves singling out for its enjoyable exotic character.
⚫ Maison Adrien Vacher, 2 A, plan Cumin, 73800 Les Marches, tel. 04.79.28.11.48, fax 04.79.28.09.26 ☑
☒ by appt.

DOM. JEAN VULLIEN ET FILS
Chignin-Bergeron 2002★★★

	2.8 ha	25,000	🗍 ⌀	5–8 €

Wine producers who also run a vine nursery, the Vullien family have a dedicated passion for vines and wines. An oak-matured **Mondeuse 2002** with delicate vanilla flavours deserves a mention. But it is this Chignin-Bergeron that appealed especially. The care taken with the harvest is the most important secret of a great wine. Here, the colour is golden; fruity perfumes with apricot to the fore indicate the ripeness of the grapes. The same flavours re-appear on the palate which has a rich and perfectly balanced structure approved by all. Already exceptional, this excellent 2002 will be able to age.
📌 EARL Jean Vullien et Fils, La Grande Roue, 73250 Fréterive, tel. 04.79.28.61.58, fax 04.79.28.69.37, e-mail domaine.jean.vullien.et.fils@wanadoo.fr 📧
🍷 ev. day except Sun. 9am–12 noon 2pm–6.30pm; Sat. 9am–12 noon

Wines selected but not starred

CAVE DE CHAUTAGNE
Chautagne 2002

	65 ha	150,000	🗍 ⌀	5–8 €

📌 Cave de Chautagne, Saumont, 73310 Ruffieux, tel. 04.79.54.27.12, fax 04.79.54.51.37, e-mail info@cave-de-chautagne.com 📧
🍷 by appt.

DOM. LA COMBE DES GRAND 'VIGNES Chignin 2002

	4 ha	32,000	🗍	5–8 €

📌 Denis et Didier Berthollier, Dom. La Combe des Grand'Vignes, Le Viviers, 73800 Chignin, tel. 04.79.28.11.75, fax 04.79.28.16.22, e-mail berthollier@chignin.com 📧
🍷 by appt.

CAVE DELALEX
Marin Cuvée Tradition 2002

	6 ha	30,000	🗍 ⌀	5–8 €

📌 Cave Delalex, EARL La Grappe dorée, Marinel, 74200 Marin, tel. 04.50.71.45.82, fax 04.50.71.06.74 📧
🍷 by appt.

CHARLES GONNET
Chignin 2002

	6 ha	50,000	🗍 ⌀	5–8 €

📌 Charles Gonnet, Chef-lieu, 73800 Chignin, tel. 04.79.28.09.89, fax 04.79.71.55.91, e-mail charles.gonnet@wanadoo.fr 📧

CH. DE LUCEY
Mondeuse 2002

	0.7 ha	4,000	🗍	5–8 €

📌 SCEA de Lucey, Le Château, 73170 Lucey, tel. 04.79.44.01.00, fax 04.79.44.01.00 📧
🍷 by appt.
📌 Defforey

DOM. PERRIER PERE ET FILS
Apremont 2002

	10 ha	30,000	🗍	5–8 €

📌 Dom. Perrier Père et Fils, Saint-André, 73800 Les Marches, tel. 04.79.28.08.28, fax 04.79.28.09.91, e-mail vperrier@vins-perrier.com 📧
🍷 by appt.

LA CAVE DU PRIEURE
Jongieux Mondeuse 2002

	1.5 ha	12,000	🗍 ⌀	5–8 €

📌 Raymond Barlet et Fils, La Cave du Prieuré, 73170 Jongieux, tel. 04.79.44.02.22, fax 04.79.44.03.07, e-mail caveduprieure@wanadoo.fr 📧
🍷 by appt.

LE P'TIOU VIGNERON
Apremont 2002

	7 ha	22,000	🗍 ⌀	3–5 €

📌 Jean-François Maréchal, EARL Le P'Tiou Vigneron, Coteau des Belettes, 73190 Apremont, tel. 04.79.28.33.22, fax 04.79.71.67.10 📧
🍷 ev. day except Sun. 10am–7pm

ANDRE ET MICHEL QUENARD
Chignin-Bergeron Coteau de Torméry Les Terrasses 2002

	2 ha	15,000	🗍 ⌀	8–11 €

📌 André et Michel Quénard, Torméry, 73800 Chignin, tel. 04.79.28.12.75, fax 04.79.28.19.36 📧
🍷 by appt.

BERNARD ET CHRISTOPHE RICHEL
Apremont Vieilles Vignes 2002

	1.58 ha	11,333	🗍 ⌀	5–8 €

📌 Bernard et Christophe Richel, rte de Fontaine-Lamée, 73190 Saint-Baldoph, tel. 04.79.28.36.55, fax 04.79.28.36.55 📧
🍷 by appt.

LE CELLIER DES TOURS
Chignin-Bergeron La Bergeronnelle 2002

	3 ha	25,000	🗍	8–11 €

📌 Les Fils de René Quénard, Les Tours, Cidex 4707, 73800 Chignin, tel. 04.79.28.01.15, fax 04.79.28.18.98 📧
🍷 by appt.

CH. DE LA VIOLETTE
Abymes 2002

	5 ha	40,000	🗍 ⌀	3–5 €

📌 SCEA Ch. de la Violette, 73800 Les Marches, tel. 04.79.28.13.30, fax 04.79.28.09.26 📧
🍷 ev. day except Sun. 9am–12 noon 2pm–6pm; cl.15–30 Aug.

Roussette de Savoie

Made exclusively from the Altesse grape (following a new decree dated 18 March 1998), the Roussette de Savoie is mainly found in Frangy, along the River Usses, in Monthoux and in

SAVOIE

Marestel, on the shore of the Lac du Bourget. The habit of serving the Roussettes too young is a shame since, as they open with age, they are splendid with fish and white meat dishes, and form a perfect accompaniment to the local Beaufort cheese. 2,104 hl were produced in 2002.

VINCENT COURLET
Frangy 2002★

	n.c.	n.c.	🍾 ♦	3–5 €

The Altesse grape variety reaches its best planted on the sunny hillsides of the old glacier moraines of the Usses and the Rhône rivers. Established in 1998, this is Vincent Courlet's first appearance in the *Guide*. His choice to vinify the wine on its lees has given a Roussette with fine and intense floral fragrances. The palate is equally spring-like, with persistent citrus notes, which give the wine freshness. This would be an ideal companion for a local soft cheese.
✆➤ Vincent Courlet, 133, rue Basse, 74270 Frangy,
tel. 04.50.44.75.01, fax 04.50.32.24.10 ☑
⊺ by appt.

CHARLES GONNET 2002★

	1 ha	8,000		5–8 €

Charles Gonnet has drawn out the best from his 1 ha of Altesse that he has reserved for this Roussette. This very pale wine exudes floral and mineral fragrances. Extremely clean on the palate, it shows a lemony freshness that underlines the expression and elegance of this Roussette.
✆➤ Charles Gonnet, Chef-lieu, 73800 Chignin,
tel. 04.79.28.09.89, fax 04.79.71.55.91,
e-mail charles.gonnet@wanadoo.fr ☑

CH. DE MONTERMINOD 2001★

	5.3 ha	10,000	🍾 ♦	5–8 €

The Perrier wine company has taken its business seriously since 1953, as illustrated by this rich wine that displays aromas of quince, wax and honey. It is without doubt characteristic of the style and one would be wrong not to wait patiently for two or three more years before enjoying this promising wine with a white meat dish.

✆➤ Jean Perrier et Fils, Saint-André, 73800 Les Marches,
tel. 04.79.28.11.45, fax 04.79.28.09.91,
e-mail vperrier@vins-perrier.com ☑
⊺ by appt.

DOM. DE ROUZAN 2001★

	0.25 ha	2,000	🍾 ♦	5–8 €

The successful 2000 was noted in a previous *Guide* and the new vintage should be appreciated at least as much. Very intense, dominated by wax and quince, this Roussette has richness and a flavoursome weight leading to an exotic finish. A classic wine, which represents the grape variety well.
✆➤ Denis Fortin, 152, chem. de la Mairie,
73190 Saint-Baldoph, tel. 04.79.28.25.58,
fax 04.79.28.21.63, e-mail denis.fortin@wanadoo.fr
⊺ by appt.

Wines selected but not starred

CH. DE LUCEY
Altesse 2001

	0.6 ha	3,000	🍶	5–8 €

✆➤ SCEA de Lucey, Le Château, 73170 Lucey,
tel. 04.79.44.01.00, fax 04.79.44.01.00 ☑
⊺ by appt.
✆➤ Defforey

BRUNO LUPIN
Frangy Cuvée du Pépé Vieilles Vignes 2001

	0.36 ha	2,800	🍾 ♦	5–8 €

✆➤ Bruno Lupin, rue du Grand-Pont, 74270 Frangy,
tel. 04.50.32.29.12, fax 04.50.32.29.12 ☑ 🏠
⊺ ev. day except Sun. 10am–12 noon 2pm–6.30pm;
cl. 20 Aug.–1 Sept.

Savoie and Bugey

Bugey

Bugey AOVDQS

Located in the Ain department, the Bugey vineyard occupies the lower slopes of the Jura from Bourg-en-Bresse to Ambérieu-en-Bugey (to the extreme south of Revermont), as well as those which run down to the right bank of the Rhône, from Seyssel to Lagnieu. A large vineyard at one time, it is now smaller and more dispersed, with 248 ha. It produced 13,394 hl.

For the most part, it stands on fairly steep slopes of limestone scree. The grape varieties reflect the area's famous neighbours: for reds, the Jura Poulsard – restricted to blending with sparkling wines from Cerdon – is grown alongside Mondeuse from Savoie and Pinot Noir and Gamay from Burgundy. For the whites, Jacquère and Altesse compete with Chardonnay (the most widely grown variety) and Aligoté, as well as Molette, the only truly local variety.

MAISON ANGELOT
Chardonnay Cuvée Maxime 2002★

| | | 2 ha | 13,000 | ∎ ♠ | | 5–8 € |

This pale-yellow Chardonnay with golden tinges from the best hillsides of this 23-ha estate can be described using a broad range of flavours with mineral, vegetal and fruity characteristics. There is also a floral note rendering this wine very immediately attractive. The clean palate blends mineral nuances with grapefruit, all in great harmony. This is a refreshing wine to drink from autumn onwards.
☛ GAEC maison Angelot, 01300 Marignieu, tel. 04.79.42.18.84, fax 04.79.42.13.61 ✓ ⌂
☿ by appt.

DANIEL BOCCARD
Cerdon Demi-sec Méthode ancestrale 2002★★

| ● | | 1.83 ha | 19,100 | ∎ ♠ | 8–11 € |

When Daniel Boccard took over from his father in 1979, he decided to dedicate his estate to vine-growing. He reserves 2 ha for the production of Cerdon, a lightly sparkling sweet rosé, enjoyed as an aperitif. One taster summarizes the impression given by the 2002: "a fresh wine that one wants to drink." One couldn't really ask for more in a wine that combines freshness with sweetness, and with the flavour of red berries behind.
☛ Daniel Boccard, Poncieux, 01640 Boyeux-Saint-Jérome, tel. 04.74.36.84.34, fax 04.74.36.84.34 ✓
☿ ev. day 8am–12 noon 2pm–7.30pm

CHRISTIAN BOLLIET
Cerdon Demi-sec Cuvée spéciale 2002★★

| ● | | 0.5 ha | 3,200 | ∎ ♠ | | 5–8 € |

Accustomed to accolades for his Bugey sparkling wines, Christian Bolliet presents a 2002 based on the Poulsard grape. The nose emits red fruits (strawberry, cherry, raspberry) and these same characteristics can be enjoyed on the palate, which has a refreshing finish of apples. Serve it with an aperitif or with dessert.
☛ Christian Bolliet, Hameau de Bôches, 01450 Saint-Alban, tel. 04.74.37.37.21, fax 04.74.37.37.69 ✓
☿ by appt.

LE CAVEAU BUGISTE
Chardonnay Tradition 2002★

| ■ | | 10 ha | 60,000 | ∎ ♠ | | 3–5 € |

Having previously won a *coup de coeur*, the Chardonnay Tradition also demands attention in the 2002 vintage. A pale yellow with a touch of green, it evokes exotic fruits all through the tasting and shows good balance overall. It would be a wonderful match with *quenelles* in a Nantua sauce. Also gaining one star, the **red Manicle 2002 (8–11 €)**, a barrel-aged Pinot Noir, is really zippy thanks to the flavours of red berries and cherries in *eau-de-vie* that emerge from the toasty flavours behind. The **Mondeuse 2002** is given a special mention.
☛ SARL Le Caveau Bugiste, Chef-Lieu, 01350 Vongnes, tel. 04.79.87.92.32, fax 04.79.87.91.11 ✓ ⌂
☿ ev. day 9am–12 noon 2pm–7pm

DOM. MONIN
Mondeuse Les Griots 2002★★

| ■ | | 1,2 ha | 5,100 | ∎ ⑪ ♠ | | 5–8 € |

The Monin family is closely linked with the history of the wines of the Bugey, and has done particularly well in the 2002 vintage. Note in particular this Mondeuse Les Griots, made using carbonic maceration. The first glance attracts with its reddish-purple colour, and one is enticed further by the intense aromas of fruit, spices and vegetal notes, showing great complexity. Blackcurrant appears on the opulent palate, which is structured by smooth tannins. This is a classy wine, ready to drink from the autumn, but which will also be able to age.
☛ Dom. Monin, 01350 Vongnes, tel. 04.79.87.92.33, fax 04.79.87.93.25 ✓ ⌂
☿ ev. day 9am–12.30pm 3pm–7pm

DOM. MONIN
Mondeuse Les Perrailles 2002★★

| ■ | | 0.6 ha | 3,200 | ⑪ | | 5–8 € |

The Monin estate gains two stars again for another Mondeuse selection. The grapes for Les Perrailles did not go through carbonic maceration. Matured in cask for eight months, oak and spice flavours run through this wine, whilst allowing the fruity characteristics of blackcurrant to emerge clearly on the finish. The tannins are still much in evidence, but promise well for the future. This is a wine to keep for three or four years. The spicy Pinot Noir **Manicle 2002 (8–11 €)** obtains one star and its flavours of cherry in *eau-de-vie* suggest a partnership with fillet of duck.

🕊 Dom. Monin, 01350 Vongnes, tel. 04.79.87.92.33, fax 04.79.87.93.25  🏠
🍷 ev. day 9am–12.30pm 3pm–7pm

FRANCK PEILLOT

Montagnieu 2000★

◯	1 ha	10,000	5–8 €

A blend of Chardonnay (75%) and Altesse, this Montagnieu explodes with perfumes of acacia and lime blossom. The floral theme continues on the palate which shows weight, balance and elegance. Its delicacy would make it enjoyable as an aperitif. The **Mondeuse de Montagnieu 2002** also obtains one star; from whole grapes, not de-stemmed, the wine needs four years ageing for the tannins to soften.

🕊 Franck Peillot, Au village, 01470 Montagnieu, tel. 04.74.36.71.56, fax 04.74.36.14.12, e-mail franckpeillot@aol.com
🍷 by appt.

Wines selected but not starred

CELLIER DE BEL-AIR

Chardonnay 2002

▦	5 ha	20,600	▮ ⚬	5–8 €

🕊 Michelle Férier, Dom. du Cellier de Bel-Air, 01350 Culoz, tel. 04.79.87.04.20, fax 04.79.87.18.23, e-mail cellierbelair@aol.com
🍷 ev. day 9am–12 noon 3pm–7pm ex. Sun. 9am–12 noon

DUPORT DUMAS

Montagnieu 2000

◯	1.31 ha	6,750	▮ ⚬	5–8 €

🕊 SARL Duport-Dumas, Pont-Bancet, 01680 Groslée, tel. 04.74.39.75.19, fax 04.74.39.70.95
🍷 by appt.

MICHEL ET STEPHANE GIRARDI 2000

	0.47 ha	4,900	▮ ⚬	5–8 €

🕊 GAEC Girardi, rue de la Gumarde, 01450 Cerdon, tel. 04.74.39.95.90, fax 04.74.39.93.47
🍷 ev. day 8am–12 noon 1.30pm–8pm

PHILIPPE PERDRIX

Roussette 2002

◯	1.55 ha	13,000	▮ ⚬	3–5 €

🕊 Philippe Perdrix, Villeneuve, 01300 Saint-Benoit, tel. 04.74.39.74.24, fax 04.74.39.74.24
🍷 ev. day except Sun. 9am–12 noon 2pm–7pm

LANGUEDOC AND ROUSSILLON

From the southern edge of the Massif Central to the eastern regions of the Pyrenees, the vineyards of Languedoc and Roussillon stretch over four coastal départements: Gard, Hérault, Aude and Pyrénées-Orientales. This substantial area can be visualized as a ring of hills and mountains running down to the coastal plain. Descending from the heights to sea level there are four successive types of terrain. The highest is a mountainous region, formed mostly from the ancient rocks of the Massif Central; below is a region of rocky out-crops and arid moors (the garrigue), which is the oldest wine-growing area in the region; further down still is the rolling alluvial plain, quite sheltered, with a number of low-lying slopes (200 m); the fourth, the coastal area itself, is a continuous strip of low-lying beaches and lagoons, recently developed into one of Europe's liveliest holiday spots. Greek traders and colonists may have planted vines near their settlements in the region as early as the eighth century BC. Under the Romans, the Languedoc vineyard developed rapidly, competing with Roman vineyards in Italy to such an extent that in AD 92 Emperor Domitian ordered half the area of the vineyards to be grubbed up! For two centuries vine cultivation was limited to the Narbonne area, but in 270 Probus annulled the decrees of 92, giving the vineyards of Languedoc and Roussillon a new start. Production was maintained under the Visigoths, but perished during the Saracen invasions of the ninth century. The beginning of the 11th century marked the rebirth of the vineyard, with monasteries and abbeys playing a significant role. At that time the vines were largely confined to the hillsides, the plains being reserved for food crops.

The wine trade grew considerably during the 14th and 15th centuries as new tech-niques emerged and the number of vineyards increased. Brandy-making became established in the 16th and 17th centuries.

In the 17th and 18th centuries the economic life of the region began to take off: a new port was built at Sète, the Canal des Deux Mers was opened, and the old Roman road was recon-structed.Along with the development of local weaving and silk industries, this economic revival gave a new impetus to vine-growing. A growing export trade of wines and brandies was significantly assisted by the new transport infrastructure.

New vineyards were planted in the plain, utilising the latest ideas about vine-growing terroirs. At that time sweet wines occupied a substantial area. The construction of the railways, between 1850 and 1880, shortened distances and guaranteed the opening of new markets whose needs were to be met by the plentiful production of vineyards that were replanted after the phylloxera crisis.

Taking advantage of propitious soils on the slopes in Gard, Hérault, Minervois, Corbières and Roussillon, a new vineyard, planted with traditional vine varieties, was developed in the 1950s, adjacent to vineyards that had been the glory of Languedoc and Roussillon a century before. A large number of wines were subsequently recategorized as AOVDQS and AOC, part of a general move to produce higher quality wines in the region.

Wine-growing in Languedoc and Roussillon takes place in a range of very different con-ditions as regards altitude, proximity to the sea, growth on terraces or on slopes, soils and terroirs.

The soils and the terroirs include schist from the primary mountains, as at Banyuls and Maury, in Corbières, Minervois and at Saint-Chinian; sandstone from the Liassic or the Triassic periods, which often alternate with marl, as in Corbières and at Saint-Jean-de-Blanquière; gravel terraces and smoothed pebbles from the Quaternary era, an excellent terroir for the vine, to be found at Rivesaltes, Val-d'Orbieu, Caunes-Minervois, in La Méjanelle or Costières de Nîmes. Limestone and stony terrain, occur-ring as slopes or as plateaux, as in Roussillon, Corbières and Minervois contrast with the recent alluvial soils of the Languedoc slopes, as well as with the arenas of granite and gneiss found at Les Fenouillèdes.

The Mediterranean climate, prone as it is to extremes of weather, is a unifying feature throughout Languedoc and Roussillon. It is the hottest region in France (the average annual temperature is close to 14°C, with temperatures that often exceed 30°C in July and August); rainfall is infrequent, unreliable and falls unevenly across the area. The warm season, from 15 May to 15 August, is always significantly dry. In many areas in Languedoc and Roussillon vines or olives are the only crops it is possible to grow. Only 350 mm of rain falls on Barcarès, the driest area in France. However, the quantity of rain can vary by as much as three times depending on the place – 400 mm on the coast, 1,200 mm in the mountains. The winds make the climate even drier when they blow from the land (the Mistral, Cers or Tramontane); on the other hand, winds blowing from the sea temper the effects of the heat and bring a welcome humidity for the vines.

The network of watercourses is particularly dense. There are at least 20 rivers, which may swiftly become torrents after storms or dry up altogether during periods of drought. These rivers have contributed substantially to the formation of the landscape and the terroirs from the Rhône valley as far as the Têt in the Pyrénées-Orientales.

In Languedoc and Roussillon soils and climate combine to create an environment that is exceptionally well suited to vine-growing, which explains why about 40% of France's total annual wine production comes from the area. This totals about 2,700,000 hl of AOC wines and 30,000 hl of AOVDQS per year.

There have been changes in the vine varieties used for table wines since 1950: a significant reduction in the Aramon, a variety making light table wines, widely planted in the 19th century, a corresponding increase in the traditional varieties of Languedoc and Roussillon (Carignan, Cinsault, Grenache Noir, Syrah and Mourvèdre), and the adoption of other, more aromatic varieties (Cabernet Sauvignon, Cabernet Franc, Merlot and Chardonnay).

Languedoc

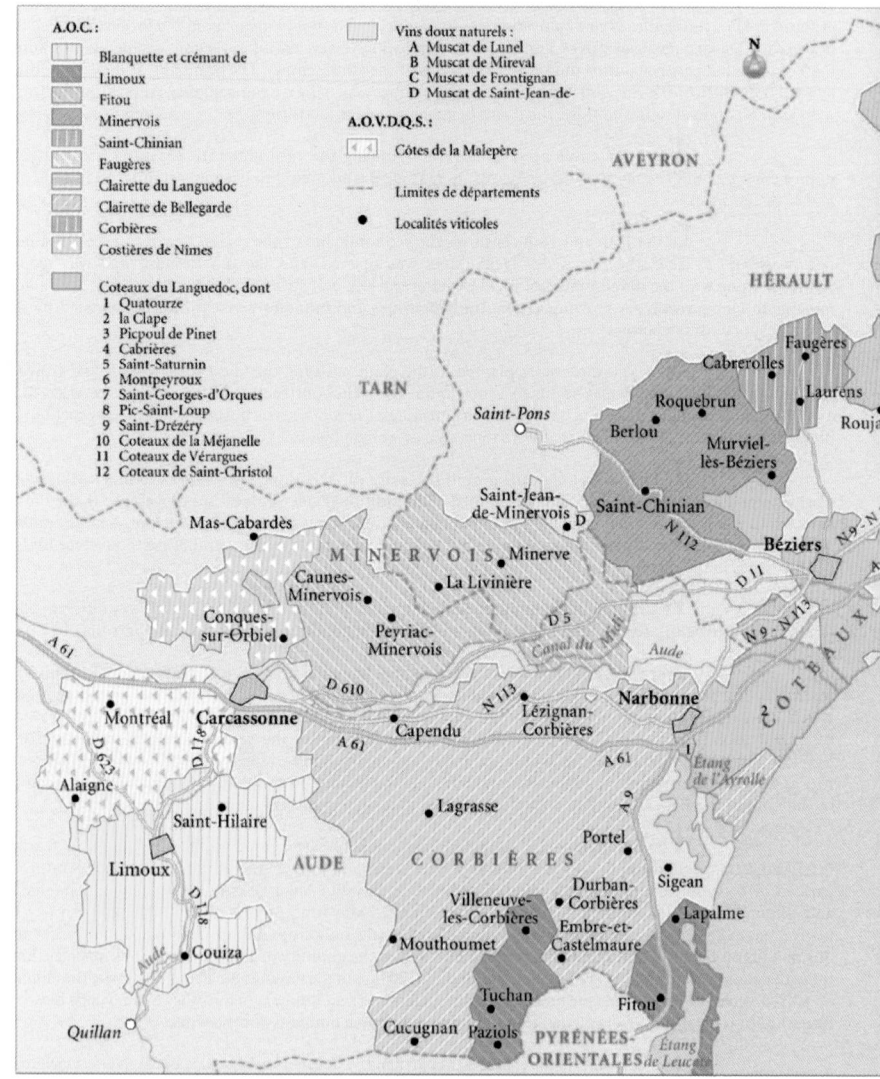

     Among the vineyards producing fine wines, the red varieties are essentially as follows: Carignan, robust and giving the wines structure, strength and colour; Grenache, a variety that, although sensitive to spring rains, gives the wine warmth and bouquet, even though it can oxidize easily when kept too long; Syrah, a fine-quality variety, contributing tannins and a perfume that develops with time; Mourvèdre, which ages well and produces well-bodied wines that have good colour, are rich in tannin and resistant to oxidation; and finally, Cinsault, which grows on poor soil and gives the wines suppleness and a pleasant fruitiness.

     The still white wines are produced mainly from Grenache Blanc, along with Picpoul, Bourboulenc, Macabeu and Clairette – giving wines with a degree of warmth but that maderize quite quickly. In recent years Marsanne, Roussanne and Vermentino have been added to the vine varieties grown. Mauzac, Chardonnay and Chenin are used for sparkling wines.

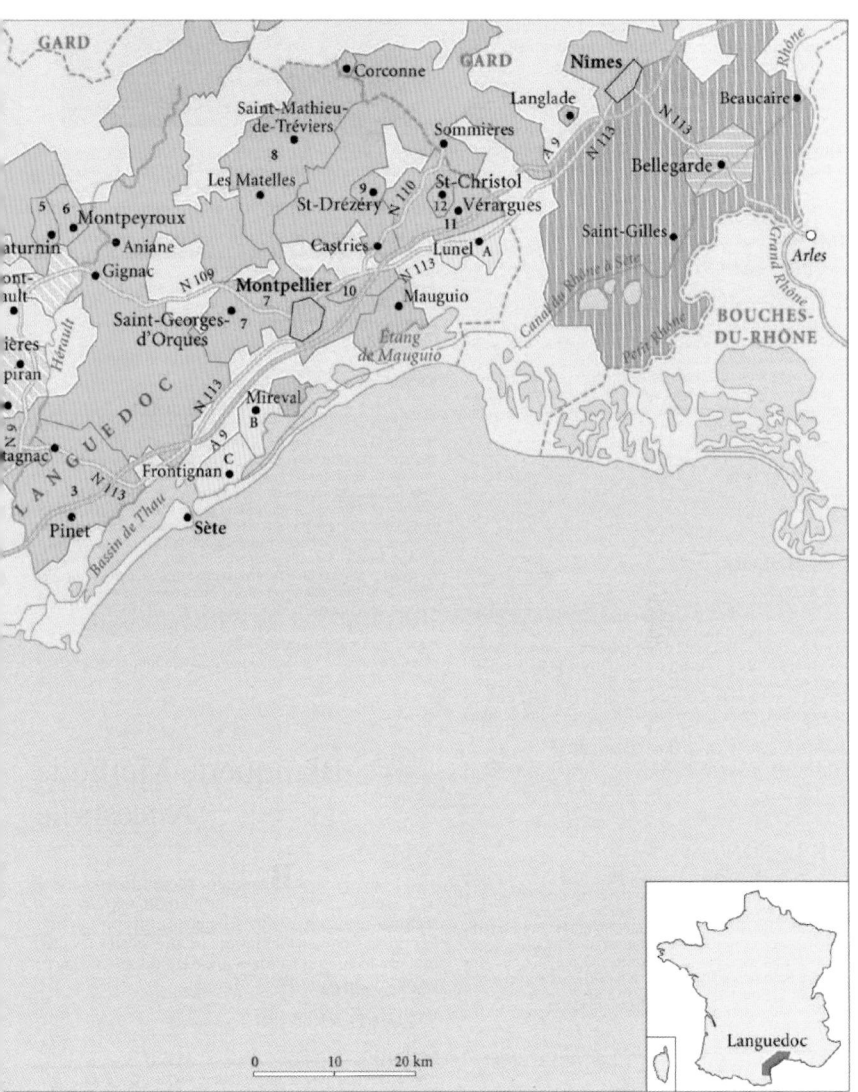

Languedoc

Blanquette de Limoux

The monks of Saint-Hilaire Abbey, which is near Limoux, noticed that their wines went into a second fermentation and were the first people to make Blanquette de Limoux. Three varieties are used to make the wine: Mauzac (90% minimum), Chenin and Chardonnay. The last two of these were introduced in place of Clairette, and they give Blanquette its characteristic acidity and aromatic finesse.

Blanquette de Limoux is made according to the Méthode Traditionelle (Champagne method) in three different styles as brut (dry), demi-sec (medium dry) or doux (sweet).

AIMERY

Cuvée Princesse★★

	n.c.	150,000	5–8 €

This year, the wine technicians of Sieur d'Arques have particularly nurtured this selection, with a view to making it one of their flagship wines. They have indeed succeeded; this elegant offering is the epitome of nobility, offset by its luminous appearance and smooth nose of crystallized orange and garrigue (local scrubland in southern France). Finesse dominates; the *cuvée* mellows nonchalantly, with a light, gentle honeyed sensuality.
➶ Aimery-Sieur d'Arques, av. de Carcassonne, BP 30, 11300 Limoux Cedex, tel. 04.68.74.63.00, fax 04.68.74.63.12 ☑
☂ by appt.

JEAN BABOU

Carte noire★

	n.c.	n.c.	5–8 €

Commented upon in the AOC Limoux section as well, this long-established commercial enterprise has presented us with a *cuvée* that particularly impressed the Jury with its delightful golden appearance, enhanced by fine and long-lasting sparkle. Its full-bodied character would make this wine an ideal mealtime accompaniment. The lingering finish offers hints of honey.
➶ Jean Babou, 5, av. Général-de-Gaulle, BP 15, 11303 Limoux, tel. 04.68.31.00.01, fax 04.68.31.73.40 ☑
☂ by appt.

JEAN LAFON 2001★

	15 ha	100,000	🍾	5–8 €

After business school and a stint in Paris, what better than to return to one's roots and take charge of the family business. This was the case with François Antech who, having modernized the enterprise, introduced a whole raft of exacting specifications for all aspects of harvesting and production. This distinctive Blanquette is complex, full of finesse and exhibits a pleasant bouquet of both floral and fruity overtones; expressive and complex on the palate and sustained, at the finish, by a hint of bitterness.
➶ Georges et Roger Antech, Dom. de Flassian, 11300 Limoux, tel. 04.68.31.15.88, fax 04.68.31.71.61, e-mail courriers@antech-limoux.com
☂ ev. day except Sat. Sun. 8am–12 noon 2pm–6pm

DOM. ROSIER 2001★★

	10 ha	84,000	5–8 €

Michel Rosier features regularly in the *Guide*; his Crémant de Limoux was a *coup de coeur* in 1995 and 2003. This year, his Blanquette de Limoux has received the honour. The lively, sparkling character is reminiscent of the festive mood of a town's annual major celebrations. An intense floral bouquet promises a wine that is well-balanced, full and expressive. The lively finish, enhanced by the Mauzac grape variety, is in true Blanquette tradition.
➶ Dom. Rosier, rue Farman, 11300 Limoux, tel. 04.68.31.48.38, fax 04.68.31.34.16, e-mail domaine-rosier@wanadoo.fr ☑
☂ by appt.

DOM. SAINT-JEAN★

	3 ha	20,000	🍾 🍷 ♦	5–8 €

Probably the oldest enterprise in the region, in view of the fact that the Guinot family has owned the property since the 16th century. It's not surprising, therefore, that the *méthode traditionnelle* endures (namely, riddling and removal of yeast deposits during secondary fermentation, by hand). Made up entirely of Mauzac, a traditional grape variety of the region, this wine has a very attractive appearance, intense floral aromas, and it exhibits a hint of *pain d'épice*, on the finish. Equally singled out, was the **Guinot Cuvée Réservée**, with its powerful aromas and fine balance; a splendid example of the qualitative efforts exerted within this category.
➶ Maison Guinot, 3, av. Chemin-de-Ronde, BP 74, 11304 Limoux, tel. 04.68.31.01.33, fax 04.68.31.60.05, e-mail guinot@blanquette.fr ☑
☂ ev. day except Sat. Sun. 9am–12 noon 2pm–5pm

Blanquette Méthode Ancestrale

Blanquette Méthode Ancestrale is a separate AOC, and the method used is kept secret. The characteristic difference of its production lies in a final fermentation in the bottle. Today, modern techniques allow a low-alcohol sweet wine to be produced from 100% Mauzac.

SIEUR D'ARQUES Tradition★

	50 ha	30,000	5–8 €

This AOC is particularly recommended for those aesthetes who prefer not to put on weight, or who have a penchant for *soft* products, as the alcohol content does not exceed

7%. Pale golden in appearance, with a fine, even shimmer, first impressions of this wine suggest overtones of green apples and crystallized fruits and excellent balance of sweetness and acidity. Recommended to accompany apple tart or fruit dessert.

📞 Aimery-Sieur d'Arques, av. de Carcassonne, BP 30, 11300 Limoux Cedex, tel. 04.68.74.63.00, fax 04.68.74.63.12
🍷 by appt.

Crémant de Limoux

Even though the Crémant de Limoux was officially categorized only as recently as 21 August 1990, it is a tried and tested product. The strict regulations originally laid down for the production of Limoux are very close to those used for Crémant, so there is no difficulty in including the Limouxins in this elite group.

The mature wines have been appearing in wine stores for some time now, and customers are learning to appreciate the subtle blend of the personality and character of Mauzac, the elegance and roundness of Chardonnay and the youth and freshness of Chenin.

ANTECH
Grande Cuvée 2001★

	4.8 ha	32,000	📦	5–8 €

Françoise, daughter of Georges Antech, has returned to the estate after ten years or so working for an international group. This has enabled her to realize her dream and live out her passions: nature, vine and wine. This light, yellow-coloured Crémant offers an intense bouquet, reminiscent of brioche, honey and spices. Its fine structure is fresh and well-balanced; the tasting rounds off with hints of mocha on the finish. Could be drunk with a meal.

📞 Georges et Roger Antech, Dom. de Flassian, 11300 Limoux, tel. 04.68.31.15.88, fax 04.68.31.71.61, e-mail courriers@antech-limoux.com ⊻
🍷 ev. day except Sat. Sun. 8am–12 noon 2pm–6pm

JEAN BABOU
Prestige★

	n.c.	n.c.		5–8 €

This long-established Limouxin concern has recently changed hands. From the outset, this enterprise has been a leader in its field. Here, beyond any shadow of doubt, we have a great, classy sparkler. The light, yellow appearance is accompanied by a fine shimmer. The nose offers intense aromas of freshly mown hay, with overtones of honey and hazelnut. The pleasant palate exhibits hints of ripe fruits, with lightly charred overtones. The **Saint-Vincent** *cuvée* also impressed the Jury.

📞 Jean Babou, 5, av. Général-de-Gaulle, BP 15, 11303 Limoux, tel. 04.68.31.00.01, fax 04.68.31.73.40
🍷 by appt.

DOM. DE MARTINOLLES 1998★★

	5.5 ha	30,000	8–11 €

The monks of Saint-Hilaire, "inventors" of Blanquette were fond of meditating in this small valley, nestling between vines and olive trees. Although this selection was highly rated by the entire Jury, it nevertheless failed to achieve the highest accolade. Beneath the intense golden-yellow appearance, this wine reveals complex aromas of toasted bread, dried fruit, with a slight hint of green apple. The overall effect is extremely pleasing on the palate.

📞 Vignobles Vergnes, Dom. de Martinolles, 11250 Saint-Hilaire, tel. 04.68.69.41.93, fax 04.68.69.45.97, e-mail martinolles@wanadoo.fr ⊻
🍷 ev. day except Sat. Sun. 8am–12 noon 1.30pm–6.30pm

ROBERT 1997★

	4 ha	20,000	8–11 €

After visiting the Abbey of Saint-Hilaire where the production of mousse was discovered, a short journey of 5 km brings you to this estate, which is situated in an area of outstanding natural beauty. You will love this Crémant as well, with its delicate yellow appearance and aromas evocative of springtime flowers. You will discover an abundance of liveliness and freshness on the palate, with a hint of small red berries and length at the finish. Already utterly seductive, this wine could be laid down for a while.

📞 GFA Robert, Dom. de Fourn, 11300 Pieusse, tel. 04.68.31.15.03, fax 04.68.31.77.65 ⊻
🍷 by appt.

SIEUR D'ARQUES
Grande Tradition 1000 Jours★

	n.c.	150,000	8–11 €

In 2002, the Sieur d'Arques wine cellar produced 87% of the AOC Crémant de Limoux, which says as much about its rigorous standards as it does about its contribution to wine production, in general. Here we have a product that sweeps you away with its bouquet of over-mature grapes; a taste of exotic fruits lingers on the palate, and concludes with a liveliness and freshness. Also singled out were the **Sieur d'Arques Cuvée précieuse** and the **Sieur d'Arques 2000**.

📞 Aimery-Sieur d'Arques, av. de Carcassonne, BP 30, 11300 Limoux Cedex, tel. 04.68.74.63.00, fax 04.68.74.63.12
🍷 by appt.

VEUVE TAILHAN 2001★★

	7 ha	60,000	5–8 €

A highly acclaimed specialist in the production of sparkling wines, Michel Rosier is well versed in the rules of the art. This champagne expert, who has been established in the Limoux region for over twenty years, needs no further introduction, as he features regularly in the *Guide*, both in terms of favourably impressing the Jury and in his accumulation of *coups de coeurs*. This year, he has consolidated this fine track record with his choice of Veuve Tailhan, a time-honoured label, dating back to 1885. The pale golden appearance with green tinges exhibits much finesse and is enhanced by a delicate sparkle. The balanced floral and green apple aromas are well developed, with a lingering hint of brioche and dried flowers. This rich and lively wine would make an ideal aperitif and is ready to drink from now on, but could equally be laid down for up to two to three years.

📞 Dom. Rosier, rue Farman, 11300 Limoux, tel. 04.68.31.48.38, fax 04.68.31.34.16, e-mail domaine-rosier@wanadoo.fr ⊻
🍷 by appt.

LANGUEDOC

Limoux

T he Appellation Limoux Nature, recognized in 1938, was in reality a wine used as the base in the making of Appellation Blanquette de Limoux, and all the shippers used to handle a little of it.

In 1981 this AOC regrettably saw the use of the term "Nature" being prohibited, and it became simply Limoux. The wine is still made from 100% Mauzac but has slowly declined, while the wines now used as a base for Blanquette de Limoux are a blend of Chenin, Chardonnay and Mauzac.

This appellation has started up again and was included for the first time at the harvest of 1992. It may now be made from a mixture of Chenin and Chardonnay grapes, but Mauzac must still be present. Unusually, fermentation and development until 1 May must be carried out in oak barrels. The energetic Limouxin team is now starting to reap the benefits of all their hard work.

DOM. D'ANTUGNAC
La Chapelle 2001★

| | 5 ha | 5,000 | 〰 | 11–15 € |

A Burgundy négociant chose, for his initiation into the pleasures of Limoux, the Château d'Antugnac, in the Haute-Vallée region of Aude. All the characteristics exhibited by this bright yellow, delicately oaked wine, with a hint of brioche and a vigorous finish, typify the high terroirs of the Haute-Vallée region. This wine is recommended as an accompaniment for fish and white meat dishes.
☛ Les Vins des Personnets, Christian Collovray et Jean-Luc Terrier, 71960 Davayé, tel. 03.85.35.86.51, fax 03.85.35.86.12
☖ by appt.

JEAN BABOU
Elevé en fût de chêne 2001★★

| | n.c. | n.c. | 〰 | 8–11 € |

This long-established Limouxin winery has recently been bought out by M. Quelin, the current owner, who has soon made a name for himself. If the bright colour of this 2001 is somewhat suspect, the nose makes up for it; the start offers peachy overtones, followed by a delicate mineral-like and toasty finish.
☛ Jean Babou, 5, av. Général-de-Gaulle, BP 15, 11303 Limoux, tel. 04.68.31.00.01, fax 04.68.31.73.40 ☑
☖ by appt.

LES HAUTS CLOCHERS
Elevé en fût de chêne 2001★★

| | 50 ha | 35,000 | 〰 | 8–11 € |

Every year, on Palm Sunday, an auction of selected wines is held at the wine cellars of Sieur d'Arques, in order to raise funds for the restoration of a church steeple in the Limouxin region. Consistent yellow colour, delicately oaked, this intense, full, fleshy wine exudes fine balance between palate and nose; with elegant hints of toast and mocha, this wine offers good length. Also, specially mentioned by the Jury, the **Terroir Autan 2001** exhibits aromas of brioche that mingle pleasantly with hints of vanilla and spices.
☛ Aimery-Sieur d'Arques, av. de Carcassonne, BP 30, 11300 Limoux Cedex, tel. 04.68.74.63.00, fax 04.68.74.63.12 ☑
☖ by appt.

TOQUES ET CLOCHERS
Terroir méditerranéen Elevé en fût de chêne 2001★★

| | 50 ha | 35,000 | 〰 | 8–11 € |

Once in a while, the Terroir Méditerranéen holds greater sway than the Terroir Océanique and the Haute-Vallée. With the national president of oenologists at the helm, the cellar of the Sieur d'Arques wine producers has made a major impact this year on the Limoux AOC. This *cuvée* received a unanimous *coup de coeur* from the Jury. The golden yellow appearance belies the surprising complexity of the intensely aromatic nose, composed of hints of grilled meat, peach and vine; light, toasty overtones, with notes of mango and mocha, the palate displays a broad spectrum of aromatic flavours with plenty of richness and length.
☛ Aimery-Sieur d'Arques, av. de Carcassonne, BP 30, 11300 Limoux Cedex, tel. 04.68.74.63.00, fax 04.68.74.63.12 ☑
☖ by appt.

Clairette de Languedoc

T he vines are cultivated over 112 ha in eight communes in the Hérault valley and produced 4,471 hl in 2002. After vinification at low temperature, with a minimum of oxidation, a generous white wine is produced with an intense yellow robe. It can be dry, medium or sweet. As it ages, it acquires a *rancio*, toasted flavour, that finds its fans. It goes well with bourride sétoise, a local fish stew.

ADISSAN
Moelleux 2002★

| | 20 ha | 30,000 | | 5–8 € |

A traditional Languedoc grape variety, Clairette can be used to produce dry or sweet whites, which have become the speciality of the Adissan Cooperative. This classic sweet white possesses a well developed nose of overripe fruit and honey. Rounded and rich on the palate, the wine offers a delicate balance between the natural sweetness of the grapes and an attractive, mineral freshness.
☛ La Clairette d'Adissan, 34230 Adissan, tel. 04.67.25.01.07, fax 04.67.25.37.76, e-mail clairette-adissan@wanadoo.fr ☑
☖ ev. day except Sun. 9am–12 noon 3pm–6pm

DOM. SAINT ROME
Moelleux 2002★★

| | 10 ha | 22,000 | 〽 | 5–8 € |

A superb achievement both for the Cabrières wine cellar and for its vineyard, perched on shale slopes. A single star for the **Coteaux du Languedoc Prieuré Saint-Martin-des-Crozes red 2001** and the **Château de Cabrières 2000 (11–15 €)** and two stars for this delightful, golden white wine, albeit of somewhat understated colour. The delicate aromas of citrus and exotic fruits are abundantly evident from the first sip. The balanced palate exudes finesse, with its subtle, yet not excessive, sweetness.

🍷 SCA Les Vignerons de Cabrières, Caves de l'Estabel, rte de Roujan, 34800 Cabrières, tel. 04.67.88.91.60, fax 04.67.88.00.15, e-mail sca.cabrieres@wanadoo.fr ☑
🍸 ev. day 9am–12 noon 2pm–6pm

Corbières

Corbières wines, categorized VDQS from 1951, became AOC in 1985. The extent of the appellation covers 87 communes, producing 668,350 hl in 2002 over 14,377 ha (of which 10,240 hl were white). They are powerful wines, ranging between 11% and 13% alcohol, produced from vineyards planted with a maximum of 60% Carignan vines.

Les Corbières is a typical wine-growing area in that it is hardly suitable for any other type of crop. Yet it is a difficult region to classify because, although the Mediterranean influence dominates, there is also a certain degree of maritime Atlantic influence to the west. The great diversity of soil types, the preponderance of Carignan and the partitioning of plots due to the very broken relief contribute to a sense of uniqueness.

CH. AURIS 2002★

■	7 ha	35,000	▮ ♦	3–5 €

The estate is situated close to Fontfroide; this well preserved abbey has been a significant source of revenue and a major wine-producer in its numerous barns, located throughout the area, since the beginning of the 17th century. The Cistercian monks abandoned the monastery nearly a century ago. They were replaced by estates such as this one, which makes its debut in the *Guide* with a 2002 rosé. A light wine with salmon-coloured tinges, delicate, somewhat fruity aromas and fine balance between freshness and fullness.

🍷 Guy et Dominique Martin-Laval, rte de Fontfroide, 11100 Narbonne, tel. 04.68.45.16.85, fax 04.68.45.16.85, e-mail berantel@libertysurf.fr ☑
🍸 ev. day except Sun. 9am–6pm

CH. LE BOUIS
Hélie Elevé en fût de chêne 2000★

■	3 ha	12,000	⬱	8–11 €

Gruissan has become, nowadays, an enclave of Corbières on the southern terraces of the Massif de la Clape. There the Château le Bouïs can be found, offering a combination of music (jazz concerts), conviviality and the opportunity to discover some great wines. This particular wine, a blend of just two grape varieties, Syrah and Mourvèdre, exhibits a distinctly Mediterranean character. It offers fine structure and a complex, vanilla nose.

🍷 SCEA Ch. Le Bouïs, rte Bleue, 11430 Gruissan, tel. 04.68.75.25.25, fax 04.68.75.25.26, e-mail chateau-le-bouis@wanadoo.fr ☑ 🏠
🍸 by appt.
🍷 de Kerouartz

C DE CAMPLONG 2000★

■	7 ha	19,000	⬱	15–23 €

Corbières, Camplong, Cooperative: all begin with a capital C. The C for Camplong implies various other interpretations: C as in crimson, crystalline, complexity of aromas, *coing* (French for quince), *ciste* (a plant native to the garrigue),

cypress, cooked, cocoa, coffee, *chêne* (French for oaky character); and more: *chair* (French for fullness), *corps* (robustness), *charpente* (structure), character, concentration, captivating, complete: a veritable cru.

🍷 Vignerons de Camplong, av. de la Promenade, 11200 Camplong-d'Aude, tel. 04.68.43.60.86, fax 04.68.43.69.21, e-mail vignerons-camplong@wanadoo.fr ☑ 🏠
🍸 ev. day except Sun. 8am–12 noon 2pm–6pm

DOM. DES CHANDELLES 2000★★

■	4 ha	7,000	⬱	11–15 €

An entry in the *Guide*, three years running, for this British-run estate, not to mention a dazzling appearance in the *Guide*, with a 95 *coup de coeur*. The 2000 is a very attractive wine, made up entirely of Grenache and Syrah. A resting period of a year or so has bestowed upon it a deep purple hue, a marked oaky aroma which, moreover, does not dominate the wine; a fine, rounded presence on the palate, a fleshiness and a dash of freshness, with hints of dark fruits. An excellent Corbières.

🍷 Dom. des Chandelles, 5, rte de Narbonne, 11800 Barbaira, tel. 04.68.79.00.10, fax 04.68.79.21.92 ☑
🍸 by appt.
🍷 P. et S. Munday

CLOS CANOS
Les Cocobirous 2001★★

■	1.75 ha	5,860	⬱	15–23 €

The Clos Canos vineyard takes its name from a chapel near Lézignan-Corbières. Only Pierre Galinier, himself, could explain the significance of these *Cocobirous*, a curious designation for this Corbières which is both traditional and modern. This particular wine is a blend, in equal parts, of Carignan, Grenache and Syrah; it delivers more than just toasty aromas; hints of crystallized fruit are also evident; full-bodied, rich, with tannins making their presence felt on the palate, this wine is seductive for its finesse. The **Corbières Château Canos rosé 2002**, also singled out by the Jury, should not be overlooked.

🍷 SCEA Pierre et André Galinier, Dom. de Canos, rue des Etangs, 11200 Luc-sur-Orbieu, tel. 04.68.27.00.06, fax 04.68.27.61.08, e-mail chateaucanos@wanadoo.fr ☑
🍸 by appt.

COURTILLES
Fra vento 2001★

■	2.75 ha	6,000	⬱	23–30 €

To focus attention on a few vineyard plots in the south of the Corbières region, adjoining Fitou territory, an area noted for its high altitude and dry, mineral Massif terroir; such was the risk taken by Bernard Schürr who relied upon the cellar skills of the Embres-et-Castelmaure *vignerons* to develop this selection. The deep coloured Fra Vento is a rich wine, with pronounced oaky flavours and overtones of toast and dark berries. Pleasant, balanced, the *cuvée* gives an impression of genuineness.

🍷 Bernard Schurr, Le Village, 21, bd Jean-Jaurès, 11360 Embres-et-Castelmaure, tel. 04.68.33.57.54, fax 04.68.33.74.54, e-mail b.schurr@courtilles.com

BLANC DE BLANCS DES DEMOISELLES 2002★★★

■	8 ha	25,000	▮ ♦	3–5 €

Blanc de Blancs DES Demoiselles
CORBIÈRES
APPELLATION CORBIÈRES CONTRÔLÉE
2002

The Saint-Laurent-de-la-Cabrerisse cooperative cultivates 780 ha of vines. These Demoiselles have not missed an entry in the *Guide* for five years and this 2002 blend of Grenache Blanc and Macabeu, with a hint of Bourboulenc, has elicited a *coup de coeur*. A pale yet luminous colour, the overall effect is perfect. The aromas? Apple, rose, candy; finesse and richness. The palate may be summed up as follows: soft, mellow, fresh. A true personality of extreme elegance.

➼ SCV Cellier des Demoiselles, 5, rue de la Cave, 11220 Saint-Laurent-de-la-Cabrerisse , tel. 04.68.44.02.73, fax 04.68.44.07.05 ☑
☿ ev. day 8am–12 noon 2pm–6pm

CH. LA DOMEQUE
Cuvée Aimé 2001★★

| ■ | 6.5 ha | 5,800 | ◗ | 15–23 € |

Even though Frédéric Roger inherited the family concern, he is certainly not content to rest on his laurels. Rather than unwavering adherence to traditional production methods, he has explored modern trends and diversified with the Carignan grape variety, which hitherto was poorly adapted to his terrace-style terroir, and has restocked his vineyard with Syrah and Grenache. He chooses to mature his wines in oak, a process that he controls with the utmost skill; testimony to the two vintages retained in the two previous *Guides* and especially this remarkable 2001: full on the palate, with richness and length; freshness accompanies a delicate oak bouquet.

➼ GAEC Roger et Fils, Dom. La Domèque, 11200 Canet-d'Aude, tel. 04.68.43.81.96, fax 04.68.43.86.00 ☑ ☗
☿ by appt.
➼ Frédéric Roger

DOM. DU GRAND ARC
Cuvée des Quarante Elevé en barrique 2001★★

| ■ | 3 ha | 15,000 | ◗ | 5–8 € |

Bruno Schenck has been established for ten years or so in this part of the south, which borders on Les Fenouillèdes, near Cucugnan. He has certainly got the measure of this Corbières, located at the foot of the Citadelles Cathares. Recognized for his rosé, he has now mastered all the subtleties of this high altitude terroir, judging by this **Cuvée des Quarante**, equally as impressive this year as the previous vintage. The 2001 exhibits a range of aromas, with an emphasis on toasted bread, coffee, mocha, chocolate and a hint of vanilla, an indication that it has been nurtured carefully in the wine cellar for several months. This impression is confirmed on the palate, yet the wine exhibits richness, weight and a hint of freshness, all hallmarks of a great wine.

➼ Dom. du Grand Arc, La Fleurine, rue Tranquille, 11350 Padern, tel. 04.68.45.01.03, fax 04.68.45.01.03, e-mail info@grand-arc.com ☑ ▥
☿ by appt.
➼ Bruno Schenck

GRAND OPERA 2001★★

| ■ | 11.5 ha | 68,500 | ◗ | 5–8 € |

Established not far from Sigean and its coastal lagoon, this cooperative owns wine cellars converted from the tunnels of an ancient gypsum quarry; the wine cellars are worth exploring in themselves, as indeed is this particular *cuvée*. One could easily sum up this Grand Opéra as a classic Corbières. Yet, its gracious airs have achieved a repeat performance with the 2001 vintage. Luc Mazot understands full well how to orchestrate the selection of grape varieties (for this 2001, 35% Carignan, 30% Mourvèdre, 20% Grenache Noir and 15% Syrah), the choice of barrels, the maturation period (fourteen months, in this instance). The result is a sunny, garnet-coloured wine, with fading hints of fruits steeped in alcohol, charred and liquorice overtones, lively, full and rich on the palate. Altogether a very pleasant combination.

➼ Caves Rocbère, 11490 Portel-des-Corbières, tel. 04.68.48.28.05, fax 04.68.48.45.92 ☑ ▥ ☗
☿ ev. day 9am–12 noon 2pm–7pm

GRUSSIUS
Elevé en fût de chêne 2001★★★

| ■ | 15 ha | 16,000 | ◗ | 11–15 € |

I bear the signature of a wine cooperative established in south Clape. I have my origins near coastal lagoons, between salt marshes and the Mediterranean, on the gravel slopes of the garrigue (scrubland in southern France). Made up of Mourvèdre (50% of the blend), also Syrah (40%), with a sunny dash of Grenache. The grape harvest has been de-stalked; only the flesh of the grapes has been put into vats: they have waited a few days for this mish-mash to undergo the vinification process; I was then left to rest for a year in oak before revealing to you all my charms: a heady bouquet, aromas of liquorice, blackcurrant, with well integrated oak, crystallized fruits, spices (cinnamon); superb finesse, soft tannins, and exceptionally aromatic length.

➼ SCV La Cave de Gruissan, 11430 Gruissan, tel. 04.68.49.01.17, fax 04.68.49.34.99, e-mail gerardarmangan@wanadoo.fr ☑
☿ by appt.

BERNARD GUIBERT 2001★

| ■ | 4 ha | 11,740 | ▮ ⚶ | 3–5 € |

A rare enough occurrence, worth mentioning: here we have a "Corbière of all Corbières". It is impossible to define its origin with greater accuracy and with good reason. It is the masterpiece of a *négociant-éleveur* – the genuine article, one who researches, protects, cossets the wines in the bottle and promotes the unique brand name of the appellation. A perfect introduction for this 2001; the nose, initially reserved, proceeds to reveal a greater maturity. Powerful, rich, fleshy, dense, warming and long; this is a promising wine. Already pleasant, this wine could be served at table from now on.

➼ Bernard Guibert, Plaine des Astres, 34310 Montady, tel. 05.46.43.11.43, fax 05.46.42.84.12, e-mail bernard.guibert@club-internet.fr ☑

CH. HAUTERIVE LE HAUT 2002★★

| ■ | 1 ha | 5,300 | ▮ ⚶ | 3–5 € |

One cannot go wrong with good terroir, and Boutenac has favoured Jean-Marc Reulet once again. True to form, a slight floral hint for this white Corbières. Agreeable, in the true sense of the word, best describes the palate; remarkable in its intensity and length.

➼ SCEA Reulet, Ch. Hauterive-le-Haut, 11200 Boutenac, tel. 04.68.27.62.00, fax 04.68.27.12.73, e-mail contact@hauterive-le-haut.com ☑
☿ by appt.

CH. HAUT-GLEON
G. de Gléon 2001★

| ■ | 2 ha | 2,700 | ▮ ⚶ | 30–38 € |

Situated in the eastern area of the appellation, around Durban, Haut-Gléon is a long-established domain, part of which was acquired by the Duhamel family in 1991. The operation has presented a special new *cuvée* – produced in limited quantities and an up-market wine – unique in its composition and production: derived from a blend of Grenache (90%) and a *soupçon* of Syrah, it has undergone fermentation, prior to maceration at low temperature; and the wine has not been exposed to oak. This 2001 exhibits genuine character, with its powerful nose of liquorice, toast and warm stone. Finesse and weight, to summarize the tasting.

➼ Ch. Haut-Gléon, Villesèque-des-Corbières, 11360 Durban, tel. 04.68.48.85.95, fax 04.68.48.46.20, e-mail contact@hautgleon.com ☑ ▥ ☗
☿ ev. day 9am–12 noon 1.30pm–5pm
➼ Duhamel

CH. DU LAC SAINT-MARTIN 2001★

| ■ | 3 ha | 16,000 | ▮ ◗ ⚶ | 5–8 € |

Despite its name, this wine does not derive from lakeside terroir, but rather from maritime Corbières, close to the shores of the Mediterranean, a region noted for its excellent Mourvèdre and Grenache. This particular blend is made up of 40% each of both grape varieties, with a balance of traditional Carignan; the blend has been carefully vinified using whole grapes. The result is this deep purple colour, aromas of prune, stewed fruits, with a hint of raspberry. The

wine's fine balance, tannins and intense finish may be fully appreciated on the palate.
🕿 Vignerons Catalans, 1870, av. Julien-Panchot, BP 29000, 66962 Perpignan Cedex 9, tel. 04.68.85.04.51, fax 04.68.55.25.62,
e-mail contact@vignerons-catalans.com ☑
☑ by appt.

CH. DE LASTOURS
Cuvée Simone Descamps 2001★★

■	15 ha	33,000	■ ♦	5–8 €

Between coastal lagoons and the Fontfroide Massif, close to the famous Via Domitiana which historically linked Italy and Spain along the coast, Château de Lastours dates back to the Middle Ages and is nowadays a vast conglomerate, with enterprises extending throughout the domaines: experimental windmills have been set up in the region; as well as rough 4 × 4 driving tracks, a restaurant and a number of establishments offering guest accommodation. Finally, since 1977, a Help Centre has enabled around 60 disabled people to participate in wine production. The resulting wines are good, judging by this elegant *cuvée*, rounded, full-bodied, well-balanced and devoid of artificiality, where overtones of vanilla mingle with hints of fruits and spices.
🕿 C.A.T. Ch. de Lastours, 11490 Portel-des-Corbières, tel. 04.68.48.29.17, fax 04.68.48.29.14,
e-mail chateaudelastours@wanadoo.fr ☑ 🏠
☑ by appt.

DOM. DE LONGUEROCHE 2002★

■	1.2 ha	6,500	■ ♦	5–8 €

The rocky ridge that dominates the village of Saint-André-de-Roquelongue, located between Lézignan and the Mediterranean, inspired the name for this domaine. The rosé is full of appeal: bright, clear and vivid in appearance, straightforward nose, not too lively, yet, thanks to its sheer elegance and finesse, it is impossible to remain indifferent to this wine; glistening on the palate, of good length, without harshness, with a touch of welcome vivacity. A good true Corbières rosé.
🕿 Roger Bertrand, Dom. de Longueroche, 11200 Saint-André-de-Roquelongue, tel. 04.68.41.48.26, fax 04.68.32.22.43,
e-mail domaine-de-longueroche@wanadoo.fr ☑
☑ by appt.

M'11 2001★★

■	10 ha	12,000	❘❙❘	15–23 €

What is this mysterious code that draws your attention to the label? The name of the wine derives from the area in which it was originally produced, Monze (in the north east of the appellation, towards Carcassonne) and from the number of the *département* of Aude (11 – *onze* in French). It was in this village that the wine cellars of Hautes Côtes d'Alaric were established in 1929, the author of this pun and the producer of the *cuvée*, a wine which the Jury, unwittingly, had no problem identifying for its fine qualities: concentrated fruit with an oaky finish, plenty of volume, integrated tannins, vitality, texture and length...
🕿 Cave des Hautes Côtes d'Alaric, 1, rte des Corbières, 11800 Monze, tel. 04.68.78.68.01, fax 04.68.78.78.70 ☑

CH. MANSENOBLE
Réserve 2001★★★

■	13.5 ha	30,000	■❘❙❘♦	11–15 €

Guido Jansegers, formerly an insurance agent in Belgium, has been tending the vine for over a decade in Corbières, to the north of the Montagne d'Alaric. He continues to write wine reviews – his *Violon d'Ingres* – but most notably, he puts into practice what he preaches, for our delectation. A superb 98 is recalled. Here we have a new *coup de cœur*. A discreet start, aromas immediately reveal their finesse and elegance, then, with increasing intensity extend to the complex palate: liquorice, pepper, flowers and soft fruits. Rich, endowed with soft tannins, the palate is enhanced by a welcome freshness, which lends it character and ensures its longevity.
🕿 Guido Jansegers, Ch. Mansenoble, 11700 Moux, tel. 04.68.43.93.39, fax 04.68.43.97.21,
e-mail mansenoble@wanadoo.fr ☑ 🏠
☑ by appt.

CH. MEUNIER SAINT-LOUIS
A Capella 2001★

■	7.5 ha	43,100	❘❙❘	11–15 €

Greatly admired in several previous vintages, this *cuvée* A Capella once again is singled out and is singularly enchanting. Unaccompanied, this wine is sufficient unto itself and already reveals its true character, albeit demurely enveloped in assertive oak overtones. The wine's menthol aspect and its integrated, elegant and refined character are appreciated. A stylish wine.
🕿 Ph. Pasquier-Meunier, Ch. Meunier Saint-Louis, 11200 Boutenac, tel. 04.68.27.09.69, fax 04.68.27.53.34 ☑ 🏠
☑ by appt.

CH. LES OLLIEUX 2000★

■	14 ha	100,000	■ ♦	5–8 €

Not far from Fontfroide, at Montséret, a Cistercian nunnery was founded in the 17th century, which later became the Château des Ollieux. The property owns a domaine of around 50 ha of Boutenac terroir. The estate's 2000 is a blend, in approximately equal parts, of Carignan, Grenache Noir and Syrah, topped up with a dash of Mourvèdre to give it definition. With its straightforward, intense nose of soft fruits, this wine has great depth. Supple, full, balanced, this *cuvée* offers a lingering and assertive finish.
🕿 François-Xavier Surbezy, Ch. Les Ollieux, D 613, 11200 Montséret, tel. 04.68.43.32.61, fax 04.68.43.30.78, e-mail ollieux@free.fr ☑
☑ ev. day 8.30am–8pm; Sat. Sun. 10am–8pm

POINT D'INTERROGATION
Terroir Durban 2001★★

■	5 ha	5,000	❘❙❘	46–76 €

Who will solve the enigma of Embres-et-Castelmaure? Who will answer this question? Maybe you, the lover of originality, the genuine article, sincerity... Suffice it to sample this unusual *cuvée*. The colour may suggest shingle terrain and very low yield; the nose of soft fruits and vanilla, the dominant proportion of Syrah (95% of the blend); the skilful maturation in oak are key to unfolding the secret of this wine. The first sip reveals a charming fullness, enhanced by freshness, expansive, rounded tannins and the discovery of enchanting flavours, on the palate, I rest my case...
🕿 SCV Castelmaure, 4, rte des Cannelles, 11360 Embres-et-Castelmaure, tel. 04.68.45.91.83, fax 04.68.45.83.56, e-mail castelmaure@wanadoo.fr ☑
☑ by appt.

PRIEURE SAINTE-MARIE D'ALBAS
Clos de Cassis Elevé en fût de chêne 2001★

■	3 ha	12,000	❘❙❘	8–11 €

The ancient priory was affiliated to the abbey of Lagrasse. The domaine is situated north of Alaric, a mountain that, according to legend, concealed a Visigoth treasure. Clearly, we have here a more recent treasure, encased in a bottle entitled Clos de Cassis and which is regularly updated in the various editions of the *Guide*. The 2001 exhibits an impeccable hue of deep purple and offers a sensation of clean, natural flavours on the palate, enhanced by spices and an oaky finish. The powerful palate reveals velvety tannins. As with the previous vintage, a wine best left to breathe before serving.
🕿 Gisèle et Jean-Louis Galibert, Prieuré Sainte-Marie-d'Albas, 11700 Moux, tel. 04.68.79.09.64, fax 04.68.79.28.39 ☑
☑ by appt.

CH. DU ROC

Saint-Louis 2001★

| ■ | 5 ha | 20,000 | ■ ⊞ 👌 | 5–8 € |

A domaine handed down through generations, since its foundation at the end of the 18th century, and one of those rare examples in this year's *Guide* of the vineyards on the northern fringes of the appellation, adjoining Minervois. A blend of Carignan (40%), Grenache (30%) and Syrah (30%), this Saint-Louis *cuvée* proudly displays a burlat cherry colour and gives off aromas of spices and mild tobacco, with a distinct presence of strong oaky overtones. After the initial impressions of elegance and balance, a body still undergoing maturation is revealed.

👄 Jacques Bacou, Ch. du Roc, 11700 Montbrun, tel. 04.68.32.84.84, fax 04.68.32.84.85, e-mail jacques-bacou@wanadoo.fr 🅥
🍷 by appt.

CH. DE ROMILHAC

Privilège 2001★★★

| ■ | 2.1 ha | 9,800 | ■ ⊞ 👌 | 15–23 € |

Since taking over this domaine (1992), Elie Bouvier has had to devote almost a decade of unstinting effort, in order to secure a glowing entry in the *Guide* with this wine which borders on perfection: renovations, fitting out a wine cellar and a partially subterranean barrel store; as for the vine, drastic pruning, while unripe, if necessary, harvesting at the peak of maturity, meticulous standards applied to all aspects of the production process. The result? A concentrated, rich Corbières that exhibits generous, varied and then fading aromas on the palate of cocoa, toasted bread, dark fruits, garrigue; a rich wine perfectly balanced on the palate, with a strong, yet velvety tannic presence and unrivalled aromatic length.

👄 Elie Bouvier, Ch. de Romilhac, Chem. des Teyssières, 11100 Narbonne, tel. 04.68.41.59.67, fax 04.68.41.59.67 🅥
🍷 by appt.

ROQUE D'AGNEL

Velours 2001★★

| ■ | n.c. | 6,510 | ⊞ | 3–5 € |

Founded in 1919, this cooperative has realized its true potential: Boutenac terroir, nearby and 600 ha of vines. Harvests that have to be carefully sorted, selected and organized for quality and vinified in separate *cuvées*, matured in oak barrels, as is this Velours (50% Carignan, 20% of both Grenache and Syrah and a touch of Mourvèdre); a wine that may appropriately be described as: rich yet pleasant, elegant, balanced, rounded and fleshy; a *cuvée* that offers a hint of oakiness and a warming, lengthy finish.

👄 SCAV Cellier Roque d'Agnel, 11200 Thézan-des-Corbières, tel. 04.68.43.32.13, fax 04.68.43.35.24, e-mail scav-thezan@tiscali.fr 🅥 🏠
🍷 by appt.

ROQUE SESTIERE

Vieilles Vignes 2002★★

| ■ | 3 ha | 15,000 | ■ 👌 | 5–8 € |

The years roll by, but the old vineyards of Roque Sestière retain their vine stock and their famous white grape varieties. Every year, as usual, Roland Lagarde applies himself to

tending the vine; and this wine has been judged just as remarkable as last year's vintage. Pale-coloured in the glass, crystalline with tinges of silver, the *cuvée* gives off subtle and elegant floral aromas. Balanced, full-bodied, yet, at the same time both rich and fresh, this wine would go well with fish in a sauce or fatted-chicken casserole.

👄 EARL Roland Lagarde, Dom. Roque Sestière, rue des Etangs, 11200 Luc-sur-Orbieu, tel. 04.68.27.18.00, fax 04.68.27.04.18 🅥
🍷 ev. day except Sun. 10am–12 noon 2pm–6pm

DOM. ROUIRE-SEGUR

Vieilles Vignes 2000★★

| ■ | n.c. | 2,500 | ⊞ | 8–11 € |

Geneviève Bourdel's estate is situated near Lagrasse, a Benedictine abbey, dating back to the Middle Ages, an establishment that played an important rôle in the development of the vineyard. Following a very fine rosé that impressed the Jury last year, she has particularly excelled, once again, with this red wine, a blend of Syrah (60%), and equal parts of Carignan and Grenache. The colour is barely developed, the aromas are delicate, yet fine and lingering, with a touch of warm stone, followed by hints of ripe fruit. The remarkable balance heralds a highly subtle wine, with supple, sweet and well-integrated tannins. A fine ambassador for Corbières.

👄 Geneviève Bourdel, Dom. Rouïre-Ségur, 11220 Ribaute, tel. 04.68.27.19.76, fax 04.68.27.62.51 🅥
🍷 by appt.

DOM. SAINTE-MARIE-DES-CROZES

Ecume de Rosée 2002★

| ■ | 0.85 ha | 4,100 | ■ 👌 | 5–8 € |

I originate from the northwest flanks of the Montagne d'Alaric and am composed of Syrah and Grenache. I am not backward in coming forward; my colour is a bright, straightforward pink. I possess aromatic overtones of spring flowers, small soft fruits; lively and seductive, thanks to my Mediterranean temperament, I have the capacity to be fully appreciated as an aperitif, especially if accompanied by tapas.

👄 Bernard Alias, 36, av. des Corbières, 11700 Douzens, tel. 04.68.79.09.00, fax 04.68.79.20.57, e-mail bernard.alias@libertysurf.fr
🍷 by appt.

CH. SAINT-JEAN DE LA GINESTE

Rosée de la Saint-Jean 2002★

| ■ | 3 ha | 15,000 | ■ 👌 | 3–5 € |

Saint-Jean de la Gineste is sometimes singled out as a red, sometimes as a rosé. For the 2002 vintage, it is the turn of the rosé. This wine has a rather intense colour, with purplish tinges; the complex nose exhibits good depth, with fruity and varied herbaceous aromas. The palate seduces with its flattering first impressions, pleasant aromatic progression, weight and its enveloping, rich freshness. Good balance.

👄 Dominique et Marie-Hélène Bacave, Saint-Jean de la Gineste, 11200 Saint-André-de-Roquelongue, tel. 04.68.45.12.58, fax 04.68.45.12.58 🅥
🍷 by appt.

DOM. SAINT-MICHEL LES CLAUSES

Esprit de Grain 2002★★

| ■ | 2.8 ha | 12,600 | ■ | 5–8 € |

Handed down through five generations, the family domaine has, since 1988, been headed by Michel Raynaud, who works from a building that pre-dates the Revolution. His Esprit de Grain is a rosé where Cinsault dominates. Balanced, elegant, fine, it exudes aromatic overtones reminiscent of ferns. Typical of the South of France, this wine would make an ideal accompaniment for cuisine from the African shores of the Mediterranean.

👄 Michel Raynaud, Dom. Saint-Michel, Les Clauses, 11200 Montséret, tel. 04.68.43.36.62, fax 04.68.43.33.70, e-mail domstmichel@aol.com

DOM. SERRES-MAZARD

Cuvée Henri Serres 2001★

| | 5 ha | 16,000 | 🍷 | 11–15 € |

Has Jean-Pierre Mazard made some secret pact with the garrigue? How does he mysteriously, every year, manage to recapture the aromas of wild Corbières? Admittedly, this wine is the product of a passionate soul – of his family (this *cuvée* is dedicated to an uncle), his terroir, his vines and his wine cellar. Fine tannins and subtle texture accompany a festive procession of aromas associated with the South of France: warm stone, black olives, liquorice, mint, thyme, *ciste* (a plant native to the garrigue), rosemary, bay-leaves…
↪ Annie et Jean-Pierre Mazard, Dom. Serres-Mazard, 11220 Talairan, tel. 04.68.44.02.22, fax 04.68.44.08.47 ☑ 🏠
🍴 9am–7pm summer; winter by appt.

CH. SERVIES 2000★★

| | 1 ha | 6,000 | 🍷 ⚭ | 5–8 € |

Founded in 1928, with today around a hundred members, this cooperative has nominated a limited production *cuvée*. The secret of this winning formula: the perfect choice of a plot of Syrah vines (90% of the blend), and vinification of the whole grapes and a maturation process that involves neither barrel nor *barrique*, a fact that should be emphasized. Ripe fruits and liquorice, richness and smoothness, volume and length are all trump cards for this wine that is suitable for laying down.
↪ Cellier Joseph Delteil, 1, rue Joseph-Delteil, 11220 Servies-en-Val, tel. 04.68.24.08.74, fax 04.68.24.01.37,
e-mail cellier.joseph.delteil@wanadoo.fr ☑
🍴 by appt.

SEXTANT 2001★★★

| | 100 ha | 40,000 | 🍷 | 11–15 € |

Typical of the Ornaisons cooperative, a remarkable Corbières, the product of a carefully developed, meticulous, almost laborious original method: the vineyard (chosen specifically for the production of this *cuvée* of Syrah and Carignan in equal proportions), a sense of balance, resulting from part vinification using whole grapes and part crushing the crop, and maturation judiciously carried out in new or mellowed barrels. Dark in appearance with purplish tinges; a nose still subtle, yet of exceptional density mingles fruits with brandy flavours, liquorice and spices. The wine makes a huge impression on the palate, robust, powerful, clearly revealing a sweet fullness enlivened by coffee-cocoa aromas. Superb.
↪ Vignerons du Mont Ténarel d'Octaviana, 53, av. des Corbières, 11200 Ornaisons, tel. 04.68.27.09.76, fax 04.68.27.58.15 ☑
🍴 by appt.

LA TOUR CHATEAU GRAND MOULIN

2002★★

| | 1 ha | 6,500 | 🍷 ⚭ | 5–8 € |

Jean-Noël Bousquet is remarkable for his strength of character; having witnessed his winery devastated by the floods of 1999, he, nevertheless, managed to save some *cuvées*, such as the 99 Corbières, deemed a great success last year. Equally impressing the Jury, in last year's edition, with a white wine, matured in oak barrels, he now proceeds to captivate us with a 2002, of similar hue that has not been oaked. Perfect to the eye, this wine just begs to be uncorked. Long on the palate, with the requisite amount of freshness, the *cuvée* delivers aromas of exotic fruits. Ready to drink at the end of the summer season, it also offers every assurance that it will be equally attractive, in a year or two's time.
↪ Jean-Noël Bousquet, Ch. Grand-Moulin, 6, bd Gallieni, 11200 Lézignan, tel. 04.68.27.40.80, fax 04.68.27.47.61,
e-mail chateaugrandmoulin@wanadoo.fr ☑
🍴 by appt.

CH. TOUR DE MONTREDON

Cuvée Hubert Azam 2000★

| | 8 ha | 20,000 | | 8–11 € |

A highly characteristic red Corbières, dark, with tinges of traditional, red tiles. Attractive depth; the nose has a cooked flavour about it, an assertive oakiness, concentrated, rich,

with hints of undergrowth. In the same aromatic category as sensation of flavour, the palate appears rich, yet supple. The finish is firm, just as Corbières should be.
↪ SCAV de Montredon des Corbières, 16, av. Prof-Vires, 11100 Montredon-des-Corbières, tel. 04.68.42.07.34, fax 04.68.42.37.08 ☑
🍴 by appt.

DOM. DU TRILLOL

Elevé en fût de chêne 2002★★

| | n.c. | 6,600 | 🍷 | 5–8 € |

Discovered last year, this domaine has once again been singled out with a highly praiseworthy 2002. This vintage is the product of a different blend of the Corbières which impressed the Jury last year: Macabeu (40%) plays a major rôle in this year's *cuvée*, along with Roussanne. The skilful *passages* (selection of the best must from the barrels) always adds that Epicurean touch and appeal. Already perfectly balanced, this Corbières will remain so, for another two years or so.
↪ Dom. du Trillol, 11350 Cucugnan, tel. 04.68.45.01.13, fax 04.68.45.00.67, e-mail cave.reverend@wanadoo.fr ☑
🍴 by appt.

DOM. VALMONT

Cuvée Sélection 2000★

| | 3 ha | 7,000 | 🍷 | 5–8 € |

Originally from Belgium, Nancy and Yves Bodson have acclimatized perfectly to Peyriac-de-Mer, a village situated amidst a notably maritime terroir for the Corbières grape variety, between salt marshes and beaches, hills and pine forests: since their first harvest they have attracted the attention of the Jury with a red wine and a strong emphasis on Syrah (70%) and Grenache (30%). This 2000 exudes fruity sensations, with hints of vanilla. Full, it offers plenty of volume and fine length.
↪ Yves et Nancy Bodson, lieu-dit Ferrier, 11440 Peyriac-de-Mer, tel. 04.68.45.22.46, fax 04.68.45.22.71,
e-mail domaine.valmont@wanadoo.fr ☑
🍴 by appt.

CH. DU VIEUX PARC

La Sélection Elevé en fût de chêne 2001★

| | 10 ha | 55,000 | 🍷 | 8–11 € |

A repeat performance for Château du Vieux Parc, situated to the east of Lézignan, and headed by Louis Panis since 1988. This 2001 gives new readers the opportunity to appreciate the professionalism required of the wine producer. Vines cultivated to meticulous standards, a new, carefully rationalized winery that shelters the wine cellar housing the maturation barrels. Carignan (40%) vinified from whole grapes, de-stalking and a lengthy fermentation period for the Syrah (40%), Grenache (15%) and Mourvèdre make up this highly successful wine, which is ready to drink from now on.
↪ Louis Panis, Ch. du Vieux Parc, av. des Vignerons, 11200 Conilhac-Corbières, tel. 04.68.27.47.44, fax 04.68.27.38.29, e-mail louis.panis@wanadoo.fr ☑
🍴 by appt.

CH. LA VOULTE-GASPARETS

Cuvée Romain Pauc 2001★★

| | 13 ha | 37,000 | 🍷 | 15–23 € |

The previous vintage gained a *coup de coeur*. A brilliant performance, since the first editions of the *Guide*, the domaine has particularly excelled thanks to this Cuvée Romain Pauc, produced from old vines: Carignan (60%), Grenache (20%), Syrah and some Mourvèdre. The 2001 displays a deep colour, dark and bright, an indication of a true thoroughbred. Of great finesse, the complex aromatic palate mingles floral and fruity overtones with a hint of leather. Remarkably rich flavours offer tannins that are both full-bodied and supple; a hint of freshness, as well as oaky vanilla. Once you have claimed your treasure, don't hesitate to sample this white 2002 immediately: you won't be disappointed!
↪ Patrick Reverdy, Ch. La Voulte-Gasparets, 11200 Boutenac, tel. 04.68.27.07.86, fax 04.68.27.41.33, e-mail chateau-la-voulte@wanadoo.fr ☑
🍴 ev. day. 9am–12 noon 2pm–6pm

LANGUEDOC

Wines selected but not starred

CH. LA BARONNE

Montagne d'Alaric 2001

■ 20 ha	80,000	■ ⬤	8–11 €

➤ Suzette Lignières, ch. la Baronne, 11700 Fontcouverte,
tel. 04.68.43.90.20, fax 04.68.43.96.73,
e-mail chateaulabaronne@net-up.com ☑
☎ by appt.

DOM. DES DEUX ANES

L'Enclos 2001

■ 7 ha	20,000	■ ⬤ ⬤	8–11 €

➤ Magali et Dominique Terrier, rte de Sainte-Eugénie,
Pech Narbonnais, 11440 Peyriac-de-Mer,
tel. 04.68.41.67.79, fax 04.68.41.61.33,
e-mail mag-terrier@wanadoo.fr ☑
☎ by appt.

CH.DE LUC

Les Murets Elevé en fût de chêne 2001

■ 12 ha	60,000	⬤	5–8 €

➤ GFA Vignoble Louis Fabre, Ch. de Luc, rue du Château,
11200 Luc-sur-Orbieu, tel. 04.68.27.10.80,
fax 04.68.27.38.19, e-mail chateauluc@aol.com ☑ ⌂
☎ by appt.

CH. ROUSSIES

Prestige 2001

■ 5 ha	14,000	■ ⬤ ⬤	5–8 €

➤ Ch. Rioussès, 4, rue Quaranta, 11700 Capendu,
tel. 04.68.79.13.85, fax 04.68.79.13.85 ☑
☎ by appt.
➤ Nouaille

CH. VILLEROUGE LA CREMADE

Evohé 2001

■ 1,5 ha	6,000	⬤	15–23 €

➤ Ch. Villerouge la Crémade, 1, chem. de Thézan,
Villerouge-la-Crémade, 11200 Fabrezan, tel. 04.68.43.59.70,
fax 04.68.43.59.72, e-mail g.miot@cellierbordeaux.com ☑
☎ by appt.
➤ SCI La Crémade

Costières de Nîmes

Some 25,000 ha of land have been classified as AOC of which 12,000 ha are currently planted. Red, rosé or white wines are produced from sunny slopes of smoothed pebbles within a rectangular area bounded by the towns of Maynes, Vauvert, Saint-Gilles and Beaucaire, southeast of Nîmes and north of the Camargue. In 2002, 242,500 hl of wine were sold under the classification of Appellation Costières de Nîmes (of which 9,105 hl were white), produced in an area covered by 24 communes. The rosés go well with the typical charcuterie of the Cévennes, the whites are a natural complement to seafood and Mediterranean fish, and the reds, which are warm and full-bodied, are especially good with grilled meats. An energetic wine society, the Ordre de la Boisson de la Stricte Observance des Costières de Nîmes, has recently revived local wine-related traditions originally established in 1703. A wine route runs through the region, starting from Nîmes.

CH. AMPHOUX

Le Galion des Crêtes Elevé en fût de chêne 2001★★

■ 4 ha	4,000	⬤	8–11 €

Now at its peak, this Galion, with a wonderful purple veil, is distinguished by its maturation in oak barrels for a period of twelve months. The nose exudes hints of cinnamon and vanilla. Excellent length and fullness, on the palate, this wine exhibits complex smoky aromas. Recommended to aficionados of wine that has been prepared in new casks. A star for the **2002 rosé (3–5 €)**, with its light, candy pink appearance and subtle yet pronounced aromas of elderberries and strawberries. A well-balanced wine.
➤ EARL Alain Giran, rue de La Chicanette,
30640 Beauvoisin, tel. 04.66.01.92.57, fax 04.66.01.97.73,
e-mail chateauamphoux@wanadoo.fr ☑
☎ ev. day except Sun. 9am–6pm

CH. DES AVEYLANS

Vieilli en fût de chêne 2002★★

■ 3.12 ha	21,000	⬤	5–8 €

As in the previous edition of the *Guide*, the *cuvée* aged in oak barrels is deemed remarkable by the Jury. The 2002 vintage boasts a deep-coloured appearance, with purple highlights. The complex and elegant nose is promising. The start offers overtones of vanilla and burnt flavours, followed by hints of jammy soft fruits and the sensation of blackcurrant flavours. The palate is full and structured around tannins that have yet to mature. A difficult vintage, successfully accomplished. As this wine has been oaked in new barrels, it would benefit from being kept for a year or two.
➤ EARL Hubert Sendra, Dom. des Aveylans,
30127 Bellegarde, tel. 04.66.70.10.28, fax 04.66.01.01.26 ☑

DOM. BARBE-CAILLETTE

Haut Jovis 2001★★

■ 4.5 ha	4,500	■ ⬤	5–8 €

A totally new estate – set up in 2000 – but already making its third appearance in the *Guide*. A remarkable start, to which this Haut Jovis *cuvée* bears witness. The deep red appearance is characteristic of this wine, with fine, pleasant aromas of violet and blackcurrant and a hint of farmyard. The pleasant, full-bodied and balanced palate exhibits marked yet integrated, supple tannins. The finish has superb length. Recommended with stuffed poultry.
➤ Dom. Barbe-Caillette, Mas Jovis, 30600 Gallician,
tel. 04.66.51.34.97, fax 04.66.51.39.21,
e-mail domaine.barbe-caillette@laposte.net ☑
☎ by appt.
➤ Pelorce

CH. BEAUBOIS

Cuvée Elégance 2001★

■ 3 ha	8,000	■ ⬤	5–8 €

A region of contrasts. The estate is not far from the Camargue, with its coastal lagoons and natural habitat, but here we find vines that are well tended and planted in orderly rows. Roussanne and Grenache Blanc have been used to produce this golden yellow wine with bright highlights. The bouquet of yellow flowers and *pêche de vigne* appears pleasant and complex. Weight and richness mark this warming powerful 2001.
➤ SCEA Ch. Beaubois, 30640 Franquevaux,
tel. 04.66.73.30.59, fax 04.66.73.33.02,
e-mail fannyboyer@chateau-beaubois.com
☎ by appt.
➤ Fanny Boyer

DOM. DE BEAUCHENE
Cuvée Numa 2001★★

| ■ | 0.25 ha | 1,600 | ❙❙ | 8–11 € |

Originally a simple country house, the estate was transformed into a wine-producing domaine in 1850 by an ancestor of the present proprietors, Numa, to whom this *cuvée* pays great tribute. The wine has a deep purple appearance and a somewhat immature nose, distinguished by being freshly matured in oak. Spicy aromas and a hint of leather are, nevertheless, discernible. Weight and firmness, for an up-and-coming wine. The **Cuvée Prestige red 2001 (5–8 €)** receives a star for its richness, almost black colour, concentrated nose and lively, expressive tannins.
➶ Dom. de Beauchêne, rte de Nîmes, 30800 Saint-Gilles, tel. 04.66.87.26.86, fax 04.66.87.01.09, e-mail domainedebeauchene@mageos.com ☑
☕ ev. day 9am–7pm
➶ Anne-Marie Apack et Yves Fumet

CH. DE BELLE-COSTE
Cuvée Saint-Marc 2002★

| ■ | 20 ha | 10,000 | | 5–8 € |

Red, white or rosé, the Château de Belle-Coste Cuvée Saint-Marc is frequently starred in the *Guide*. Today, as in the past, the rosé has succeeded in seducing the Jury. Fresh coloured, it exudes finesse, with hints of strawberry and candy. This is a full and generous wine, where freshness relies upon a slight carbonic sparkle. The finish appears pleasant. Ready to drink now with grills and side-salads.
➶ Bertrand du Tremblay, Ch. de Belle-Coste, 30132 Caissargues, tel. 04.66.20.26.48, fax 04.66.20.16.90, e-mail dutremblay@belle-coste.com ☑
☕ by appt.

DOM. CABANIS
Cuvée Prestige 2001★

| ■ | 2 ha | 6,000 | | 11–15 € |

Make no mistake, the name of this estate, in southern France, that houses the Madagascar domaine, derives from the patois *maii-casca*, which translates as poorly coiffed (or windswept); no resemblance to the island in the Indian Ocean. You will not be disappointed by this Cuvée Prestige that possesses fine aromatic intensity and marries ripe blackcurrant with a hint of vegetation. The wine's suppleness and integrated tannins enamoured the tasters. The domaine is headed by an organic grower.
➶ Jean-Paul Cabanis, Mas Madagascar, Vauvert, 30640 Beauvoisin, tel. 04.66.88.78.33, fax 04.66.88.41.73 ☑
☎
☕ by appt.

DOM. DE CAMPAGNOL 2001★

| ■ | 6.2 ha | 41,300 | | 5–8 € |

Established in 1973, this domaine cultivates 29 hectares. Planted entirely with noble grape varieties, the estate is equally committed to investment in its vineyard as its cellar – efforts that have provided the means to produce this pleasant *cuvée*, with its brilliant, dark appearance and (at the time of tasting) immature nose and aromas of soft fruits. Here we have a pleasant, fruity and balanced wine, with supple and rounded structure.
➶ Marc Jacquet, Dom. de Campagnol, quartier Grès, 30540 Milhaud, tel. 04.66.74.20.44, fax 04.66.74.18.29, e-mail domaine.campagnol@wanadoo.fr ☑
☕ by appt.

CH. DE CAMPUGET
Cuvée Tradition 2002★

| ■ | 9 ha | 50,000 | | 5–8 € |

A firmly established heritage, dating back to 1645, for this château that has been reshaped considerably over the passing centuries. *Firmly established* is a description that applies equally to the estate's reputation. Rarely do the tasters fail to succumb to the charms of this domaine. This year, they have singled out this fine bright cherry-coloured Cuvée Tradition. The flattering nose exhibits aromas of strawberry, raspberry and papaya. A wine that reflects state-of-the art technology and wine-producing know-how.

➶ SCA Ch. de Campuget, 30129 Manduel, tel. 04.66.20.20.15, fax 04.66.20.60.57, e-mail campuget@wanadoo.fr ☑
☕ by appt.

DOM. DES CANTARELLES
Tradition 2002★★

| ■ | 1.18 ha | 2,200 | | 3–5 € |

The label conjures up the landscape of the South. A fine introduction to the tasting of this Tradition. The composition of this bright, yellow-coloured wine typifies all the characteristics of the dominant grape variety, Roussanne. A nose of dried fruits along with a hint of apricot, rounded, fresh palate, balanced, good length and an expressive finish: this is, indeed, a very fine Costières de Nîmes, best appreciated now. With its spicy overtones of leather and smoke, the well-structured **Cuvée Vieilles Vignes red 2001 (5–8 €)** receives a star. The same applies to the **Elevé en Fût de Chêne red 2001** which needs to mature a while before being tasted.
➶ Jean-François Fayel, Dom. des Cantarelles, 30127 Bellegarde, tel. 04.66.01.16.78, fax 04.66.01.01.26 ☑
☕ by appt.

DOM. DES CONSULS
Cuvée Exception 2001★★

| ■ | 1.3 ha | 7,000 | ▮ | 8–11 € |

Cyril Carrière currently manages the 35 ha domaine, originally built by a Consul of Beaucaire. He has nominated a remarkable wine, with an attractive deep red appearance. The aromas are complex: soft fruits, *pain d'épice* and a touch of grilled meats. The pleasant palate exhibits fine, quality tannins, which are well rounded and sweet. The finish is long and the overall effect well balanced.
➶ Vignobles Carrière, 196, chem. du Pont-de-la-République, 30900 Nîmes, tel. 04.66.64.77.92, fax 04.66.64.77.92, e-mail domaine.des.consuls@club-internet.fr ☑
☕ by appt.
➶ Cyril Carrière

CH. FONT BARRIELE 2001★★

| ■ | n.c. | 7,000 | ❙❙ | 8–11 € |

An elegant label adorns the bottle of this deep red-coloured wine, with tinges of black. The initial nose offers aromas of stewed fruits, cool leather and sweet spices. This is followed by flavours of garrigue. Bravo to the wine producers of Jonquières-Saint-Vincent for this powerful and generous wine, a worthy accompaniment for stews and game.
➶ SCEA Les Vignerons de Jonquières, 20, rue de Nîmes, 30300 Jonquières-Saint-Vincent, tel. 04.66.74.50.07, fax 04.66.74.49.40, e-mail cave.jonquieres@wanadoo.fr ☑
☕ ev. day except Sun. 9am–12.30pm 2.30pm–6pm

GARA DE PAILLE 2002★

| ■ | 3.5 ha | 25,000 | ▮ ♦ | 3–5 € |

Enveloped in a fine ruby-red colour, this 2002 first exhibits farmyard aromas, but then develops overtones reminiscent of blackcurrants. The wine is sufficiently rounded on the palate. The lightly herbaceous tannins lend the *cuvée* a distinct air of originality. A well-balanced finish speaks in its favour. Would go well with a beef casserole.
➶ Cellier des Vestiges romains, 30230 Bouillargues, tel. 04.66.20.14.79, fax 04.66.20.13.04, e-mail celvestrom@aol.com ☑
☕ by appt.

CH. GRANDE CASSAGNE 2002★★

| ■ | 12 ha | 80,000 | ▮ ♦ | 3–5 € |

The hard work of the Dardés has paid off with this high achievement. Two stars for two different *cuvées*. The Jury could barely contain their enthusiasm at the tasting of this intensely pink wine. Aromas of strawberry, roundness, freshness and perfect balance, plus a truly enchanting finish. Will give plenty of pleasure, both now and in the future. Pleasure also awaits, with **La Civette red 2002** but, in this instance, in two to three years' time. Overtones of garrigue and of very ripe soft fruits, fine balance, accentuated by hints of blackcurrant and a subtle smell of vegetation; clearly evident

tannins: all the ingredients of a superb Costières de Nîmes are combined in this *cuvée*.
↬ Dardé Fils, Ch. Grande Cassagne, 30800 Saint-Gilles, tel. 04.66.87.32.90, fax 04.66.87.32.90 ☑
🍷 by appt.

CH. GUIOT 2002★

| | 35 ha | 200,000 | ▮ ♦ | | 5–8 € |

If you decide to make a pilgrimage to Saint Jacques de Compostelle, don't forget to stop at Château Guiot; the domaine is en route. Then taste this deep red wine with violet tinges and concentrated, yet immature nose. Following a firm start, the palate reveals good composition, with quality tannins. The **Cuvée Numa red 2000 (8–11 €)** is equally successful. The nose is still immature, but promising. The powerful structure is dominated by tannins and a well-accented oakiness. An improving wine.
↬ GFA Dom. de Guiot, 30800 Saint-Gilles, tel. 04.66.73.30.86, fax 04.66.87.32.09 ☑
🍷 by appt.
↬ Cornut

DOM. HAUT PLATEAU 2002★

| | 5 ha | 12,000 | ▮ ♦ | | 3–5 € |

A fine *cuvée* with a deep red appearance. A complex nose dominated by violet and blackcurrant, followed by flavours of soft fruit, then coffee and garrigue on the palate. Good balance on top of integrated tannins. Interesting length.
↬ Denis Fournier, Dom. Haut Plateau, 30129 Manduel, tel. 04.66.20.31.78, fax 04.66.20.20.53 ☑
🍷 ev. day except Sun. 9am–12 noon 4pm–7pm

CH. LAMARGUE
Cuvée Aegidiane 2001★★

| | 3 ha | 10,000 | ⏷ | | 8–11 € |

The barrel store of this 72 ha estate was completely re-equipped in 2000. This year, the domaine received two stars for the intense red Cuvée Aegidiane. The nose, although still immature, exudes spicy aromas. Well rounded on the palate, with powerful tannins, accompanied by hints of cinnamon. The pleasant, lingering finish augurs well for the future. Most certainly, this Costières has good potential, and is best laid down for up to two years. A star also for the **red 2002 (5–8 €)**. The former is distinguished for its finesse and fruity aromas (peach, apricot, with light lemony overtones); the latter was praised for its complexity, and elegance, on the palate.
↬ Ch. Lamargue, rte de Vauvert, 30800 Saint-Gilles, tel. 04.66.87.31.89, fax 04.66.87.41.87, e-mail domaine-de-lamargue@wanadoo.fr ☑
🍷 by appt.
↬ Campari SPA

MAS CARLOT
Cuvée Tradition 2001★★

| | 12 ha | 80,000 | ▮ ♦ | | 3–5 € |

A unanimous verdict by the Jury of two stars for this high quality, value for money Cuvée Tradition. Everything is perfect: the purple colour, the soft fruit, spicy overtones, roundness, light vegetal tannins. The lingering and interesting aromas suggest a promising future. Ready to drink in two to three years' time.
↬ Nathalie Blanc-Marès, Mas Carlot, rte de Redessan, 30127 Bellegarde, tel. 04.66.01.11.83, fax 04.66.01.62.74, e-mail mascarlot@aol.com ☑
🍷 ev. day 8am–12 noon 2pm–5pm;
Sat. Sun. and holidays by appt.

MAS DES BRESSADES
Cuvée Excellence Elevé en fût de chêne 2002★★

| | 2 ha | 10,000 | | | 8–11 € |

In 1977, peach trees were replaced by vines, on this shingly soil. And, who would succumb the decision, having tasted this well-appointed Cuvée Excellence? Certainly not the Jury, who succumbed both to the glorious appearance of this clear and brilliant golden yellow wine and the fine, delicate bouquet, with distinct hints of vanilla and dried fruits. Exceptional presence on the palate, where freshness and richness lend

fullness. The **Cuvée Tradition white 2002 (5–8 €)** receives a star for its aromatic complexity (dried apricots, pears, exotic fruits, pineapples) and balanced acidity on the palate.
↬ Cyril Marès, Le Grand Plagnol, rte de Bellegarde, 30129 Manduel, tel. 04.66.01.66.00, fax 04.66.01.80.20, e-mail masdesbressades@aol.com ☑
🍷 by appt.

CH. MAS NEUF
Tradition 2001★

| | 24 ha | 200,000 | ▮ ⏷ ♦ | | 5–8 € |

Two hundred thousand bottles: there'll be plenty to go round for everyone! But, don't delay, this purple-coloured wine with a delicate nose of garrigue and bay leaves is ready to drink now. Rounded and pleasant, the *cuvée* just begs to be appreciated.
↬ Ch. Mas Neuf, 30600 Gallician, tel. 04.66.73.33.23, fax 04.66.73.33.49, e-mail lucbaudet@chateaumasneuf.com ☑ ▦
🍷 by appt.
↬ Luc Baudet

DOM. MAS SAINT JOSEPH 2001★

| | 10 ha | 9,000 | ▮ ⏷ ♦ | | 8–11 € |

A sole tenant cultivates this 18 ha domaine, which has nominated this intensely coloured wine that conceals aromas of blackcurrant and spices. A fine start, almost full, distinct tannic presence; aromas of vegetation on the palate present a very pleasant Costières; ready to drink without further delay.
↬ Dom. du Mas Saint Joseph, 30840 Meynes, tel. 04.66.57.51.94, fax 04.66.57.51.94 ☑
🍷 by appt.
↬ P. Béraud et J. Gaveaux

CH. DE NAGES
Réserve 2002★

| | 2.5 ha | 15,000 | ▮ ♦ | | 5–8 € |

A fine achievement of one star for a red and two whites. This Réserve, with its pale, green tinged appearance, offers a fruity (grapefruit) and floral (rose) nose and a lively, balanced palate. A pleasant wine, typical and representative of the vintage. The **Cuvée Vieilles Vignes white 2002 (8–11 €)**, with a rich and complex nose, lightly oaked, appears powerful while, at the same time, still retaining its harmonious balance. Finally, the **Cuvée Vieilles Vignes red 2001 (8–11 €)** is to be recommended to aficionados of wines aged in new oak. Characterized by soft tannins and distinct flavours of vanilla and young wood.
↬ EARL Roger Gassier, 30132 Caissargues, tel. 04.66.38.44.30, fax 04.66.38.44.21, e-mail i.roquelaure@michelgassier.com ☑
🍷 by appt.

DOM. DE LA PATIENCE 2002★

| | 4.8 ha | 32,000 | ▮ | | 3–5 € |

The domaine that received an entry in the 2002 edition of the *Guide*, for the third year running, has achieved a star for a Costières de Nîmes. Enveloped in purple hues, this 2002 exhibits aromas of cherry-stones. Velvety tannins on the palate enhance the distinct blackcurrant flavours. The finish leaves a pleasant impression. A simple, well-made wine.
↬ EARL Dom. de la Patience, chem. du Serre-Plouma, 30210 Ledenon, tel. 04.66.37.40.99, fax 04.66.37.40.99, e-mail aguilar.christophe@libertysurf.fr ☑
🍷 by appt.
↬ Aguilar

PREFERENCE 2002★

| | 25 ha | 200,000 | | | 3–5 € |

Coming from a cooperative, set up in 1993, from the amalgamation of several producers, we have 200,000 bottles of deep red, low-priced Costières. This wine is dominated by aromas reminiscent of imposing garrigue. Supple, highly quaffable, with integrated tannins, a wine ready to drink immediately.
↬ Costières et Soleil, rue Emile-Bilhau, BP 25, 30510 Générac, tel. 04.66.01.31.31, fax 04.66.01.38.85 ☑
🍷 ev. day except Mon. Sun. 9am–12.30pm 3pm–7pm

CH. ROUBAUD

Cuvée Prestige 2002★

■	20 ha	30,000	■ ♦	5–8 €

A vast domaine of 84 ha, cultivated by a sole tenant, who is clearly not on his trial run. He is entitled to pride himself upon more than seventy years of experience. His 2002 appears lively to the eye and nose, with its intense pink colour and flavours of candy and strawberry. The fresh, fruity, palate lives up to the good start, with ripe, mature aromas. A pleasant wine.
➥ SCEA Vignobles Molinier, Ch. Roubaud, Gallician, 30600 Vauvert, tel. 04.66.73.30.64, fax 04.66.73.34.13, e-mail contact@chateau-roubaud.fr ☑
♈ ev. day except Sun. 9am–12 noon 2pm–5.30pm; Sat. by appt.

DOM. DE SAINT-ANTOINE 2002★

■	10 ha	30,000	3–5 €

Salmon-coloured tinges, a floral and fruity nose, with a hint of banana that lingers on the lively palate of this highly successful wine. Recommended with grilled dishes, alfresco.
➥ Jean-Louis Emmanuel, Dom. de Saint-Antoine, 30800 Saint-Gilles, tel. 04.66.01.87.29, fax 04.66.01.87.29 ☑
♈ by appt.

CH. SAINT-CYRGUES

Cuvée Amérique 2001★★

■	4 ha	15,000	◫ 8–11 €

America? A local named it thus, in memory of the departure of a former son of the domaine for the American War of Independence. Today, Château Saint-Cyrgues is run by a Swiss couple, Evelyne and Guy de Mercurio, oenologists, to whose credit we owe this promising wine of deep, purple appearance. The aromatic palate evokes flavours of blackcurrant and raspberry, as well as spices and smoky overtones. Full, balanced, integrated yet distinctly tannic, this *cuvée* possesses a long, warming finish. A star for the **red 2002 (5–8 €)** with an elegant and complex nose. This wine has fine length; best laid down for a year or so. The equally successful **Cuvée Elise-Marie Marquise red 2000**, with its oaked overtones, was also applauded by the Jury.
➥ SCEA de Mercurio, Ch. Saint-Cyrgues, rte de Montpellier, 30800 Saint-Gilles, tel. 04.66.87.31.72, fax 04.66.87.70.76, e-mail saintcyrgues@wanadoo.fr ☑
♈ by appt.

CH. SILEX 2001★

■	4.5 ha	12,000	■ ♦	5–8 €

A pretty red appearance envelops this wine with a fairly complex nose, dominated by flavours of plum and cherry. The fine start continues with a distinctly tannic presence. The finish is warming.
➥ Alliance des Vins Fins, chem. de la Planque, 34800 Ceyras, tel. 04.67.44.90.50, fax 04.67.44.90.51, e-mail vsb.vins@wanadoo.fr

CH. DES SOURCES

Cuvée Vieilles Vignes Elevé en fût de chêne 2001★★

■	1.54 ha	6,000	◫ 5–8 €

The domaine was once the property of Charles Gide, uncle of the writer André Gide and a renowned economist. Today, the estate has nominated a remarkable Syrah-based product, of purple appearance with a nose of cherries in brandy and cinnamon. Powerful, quality tannins, spicy aromas and a long finish augur well for the future.
➥ EARL Ch. des Sources, 30127 Bellegarde, tel. 04.66.01.16.78, fax 04.66.01.01.26 ☑
♈ by appt.
➥ Espinas

CH. LA TOUR DE BERAUD 2001★★

■	30 ha	25,000	■ ♦	3–5 €

The estate, which also organizes jazz concerts and art exhibitions in the wine-tasting cellars is, nevertheless, attentive to its prime function. In the previous edition of the *Guide*, the domaine achieved a *coup de coeur* for the Château Mourgues du Grès and this year, two stars have just been bestowed upon

its Château La Tour de Béraud. This dark red, garnet-coloured wine reveals a complex and elegant bouquet, expands into a palate of spices, pepper, undergrowth and cherry-stones, before evolving with flavours of farmyard, jam and blackcurrant. Richness and fullness combine to produce a warming finish. The **Château La Tour de Béraud Rosé 2002** receives a star: the wine possesses fine substance, with a slight acidity, characteristic of the vintage.
➥ François Collard, Mas des Mourgues du Grès, 30300 Beaucaire, tel. 04.66.59.46.10, fax 04.66.59.34.21, e-mail mourguesdugres@wanadoo.fr ☑
♈ ev. day except Sun. 9am–12 noon 2pm–6pm; Sat. by appt.

CH. DES TOURELLES

La Cour des Glycines 2001★

■	3 ha	12,000	■ ◫ ♦	5–8 €

A superb wisteria, over two centuries old, covers the frontage of the Tourelles farm house and in springtime spreads its scent throughout the property. Pause at the entrance to the estate, to taste this particularly velvety blend of Syrah, Grenache and Mourvèdre, in equal proportions. A dark-coloured wine, with a mature nose and aromas of stewed fruit and cherry brandy; a rounded palate with integrated tannins; balanced finish: the very definition of delectable wine.
➥ Hervé et Guilhem Durand, 4294, rte de Bellegarde, 30300 Beaucaire, tel. 04.66.59.19.72, fax 04.66.59.50.80, e-mail tourelles@tourelles.com ☑
♈ by appt.

CH. DE LA TUILERIE

Carte Blanche 2001★★

■	11 ha	86,700	■ ♦	5–8 €

A regular in the *Guide* that once again presents a remarkable wine. Dark garnet-red, this Carte Blanche exhibits pleasant aromas of soft fruit, quince and *pain d'épice*. This is a well-balanced wine that combines finesse with richness. The finish, on the palate, is lingering and flavoursome. The **Cuvée Eole Elevé en Fût de Chêne red 2000 (15–23 €)** is judged a great success with its interesting aromatic complexity, its finesse and its light oakiness. Also note the **Cuvée Vieilles Vignes white 2002 (8–11 €)**, that will be at its peak in a year or two.
➥ Chantal Comte, Ch. de La Tuilerie, rte de Saint-Gilles, 30900 Nîmes, tel. 04.66.70.07.52, fax 04.66.70.04.36, e-mail vins@chateautuilerie.com ☑
♈ by appt.

CH. DE VALCOMBE

Garance 2001★★★

■	3 ha	3,000	◫	11–15 €

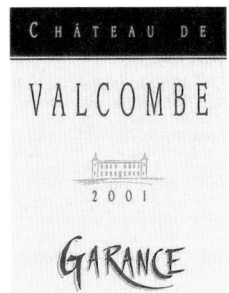

The Jury spared no praise for this Garance *cuvée*, upon which it lavished three stars and a *coup de coeur*. The wine makes an opening statement with its dark, garnet red appearance and deep-coloured highlights. The initial nose unveils rich and complex aromas. Dark fruits dominate, accompanied by smoky hints of vanilla, followed by grilled overtones. Balance merges with roundness and quality tannins. An expressive wine distinguished by successful maturation. The **Cuvée Prestige red 2002 (5–8 €)** was judged remarkable. A successful

LANGUEDOC

wine produced from a particularly difficult year; this *cuvée* possesses true potential for laying down.

☛ Dominique Ricome, Ch. de Valcombe, 30510 Générac, tel. 04.66.01.32.20, fax 04.66.01.92.24, e-mail valcombe@wanadoo.fr ☑
☖ by appt.

Coteaux du Languedoc

These wines are grown in an area of moors and hills stretching from Narbonne to Nîmes. A total of 168 communes, five of which are in the Aude and 19 in the Gard, the remainder in the Hérault, contribute to the appellation, specialising in red and rosé wines. AOC Coteaux du Languedoc has been an Appellation Générale since 1985, added to which are 11 specific denominations of red and rosé wines: La Clape and Quatourze in the Aude, Cabrières, Montpeyroux, Saint-Saturnin, Pic-Saint-Loup, Saint-Georges-d'Orques, Les Coteaux de la Méjanelle, Saint-Drézéry, Saint-Christol and the Coteaux de Vérargues in the Hérault; there are also two white denominations: La Clape and Picpoul de Pinet.

All are descended from wines that have been renowned for centuries. In 2002, the Coteaux du Languedoc produced 65,792 hl of white wine and 424,408 hl of red and rosé wine.

CH. ALTEIRAC

Chantefleur Elevé en fût de chêne 2000★

| ■ | 1.5 ha | 4,000 | ◫ | 8–11 € |

Situated in the hamlet of Terrasses du Larzac, the estate has, since the 17th century, been handed down through generations of the same family. This 2000 does itself proud with its ruby-red appearance and delicate highlights, dried fruit and grilled aromas and supple, mellow palate. It would benefit from being decanted.

☛ Florent Alteirac, 8, rte de Lodève, 34700 Loiras-du-Bosc, tel. 04.67.44.72.77, fax 04.67.44.72.77, e-mail a.florent@tiscali.fr ☑
☖ by appt.

DOM. D'ARCHIMBAUD

La Robe de Pourpre 2001★

| ■ | 3.75 ha | 5,500 | ◫ | 8–11 € |

Although the vineyard itself has been passed down through generations of the same family since 1313, the wine cellar was established as recently as 2001and is only into its second harvest. The domaine's first entry in the *Guide* is welcomed with a dark red garnet-coloured wine and nose of garrigue, stewed fruits and undergrowth. The palate is soft, but not lacking in body, balanced and elegant. Recommended with young rabbit cooked in herbs.

☛ SCEA Dom. d'Archimbaud, 12, av. du Quai, 34725 Saint-Saturnin-de-Lucian, tel. 04.67.96.65.35, fax 04.67.96.65.35 ☑
☖ by appt.
☛ Cabanes

CH. D'ASSAS 2001★

| ■ | n.c. | 12,000 | ◫ | 5–8 € |

If you enjoy listening to the harpsichord, pay a visit to the Château d'Assas. Also, an ideal opportunity to discover this purple-coloured 2001, with a floral and fruity nose. Elegance and well structured body emerge on the palate. The finish of fresh, new wood indicates that this *cuvée* would benefit from being laid down for a while.

☛ SCA Les Vignerons du Pic, 285, av. de Sainte-Croix, 34820 Assas, tel. 04.67.59.62.55, fax 04.67.59.56.39 ☑
☖ by appt.

DOM. HONORE AUDRAN

Cuvée Terroir 2001★

| ■ | 1 ha | 4,000 | ◫ | 5–8 € |

Luc Biscarlet is passionate about his terroir, with its warm, enchanting shades of red. This 2001 is a fine reflection of its origins, with its purple and garnet hues, scents of garrigue, dark fruits, mingled with quince. A full palate, substantial tannins, though well matured, all factors suggest that several years cellaring will not detract from this wine.

☛ GAEC Biscarlet Père et Fils, 8, chem. du Moulin, 34700 Le Bosc, tel. 04.67.44.73.44, fax 04.67.44.73.44 ☑ ⬛
☖ by appt.

A D'AUMIERES 2001★

| ■ | 4.87 ha | 7,000 | ◫ | 15–23 € |

Abandoning his career as a banker, Paul Tori decided, in 2001, to return to the world of the *vigneron*. Here, accordingly, we have his first *cuvée*; deep ruby-coloured with seductive aromas of tobacco, very soft, ripe fruits and spices. Already supple, pleasant and well-integrated, the wine is, nevertheless, sufficiently tannic to lay down.

☛ SCEA Saint-Jean-d'Aumières, Ch. Saint-Jean-d'Aumières, rte de Montpellier, 34150 Gignac, tel. 04.67.57.23.49, fax 04.67.57.46.30, e-mail paul@aumières.com ☑
☖ by appt.
☛ Paul Tori

DOM. D'AUPILHAC

Montpeyroux 2001★★

| ■ | 15 ha | 65,000 | ◫ | 11–15 € |

Everyone is familiar with the passionate personality of Sylvain Fadat. His 2001 is very much in the same mould, with its youthful spirit. Initially, one is struck by the wine's deep, violet-coloured appearance; followed by the intensity of its aromas of cocoa, vanilla, leather and undergrowth; and finally by the richness of the palate, which mingles pleasant substance with delicious fullness. One is tempted to enjoy it immediately, but this wine has been constituted with cellaring in mind.

☛ Sylvain Fadat, 28, rue du Plô, 34150 Montpeyroux, tel. 04.67.96.61.19, fax 04.67.96.67.24, e-mail aupilhac@aupilhac.com ☑
☖ by appt.

DOM. BALLICCIONI 2001★

| ■ | 3 ha | 12,000 | ▮ | 5–8 € |

A very pleasant wine, produced from shale terroir, of dark red, garnet colour and of a fine aromatic complexity that mingles essence of garrigue with truffle, blackcurrant and sweet spices. Full-bodied and rounded on the palate, endowed with fine, tightly knit tannins, this wine would be an excellent match for Couscous Royal.

☛ André Balliccioni, 1, chem. de Ronde, 34480 Autignac, tel. 04.67.90.20.31, fax 04.67.90.20.31, e-mail ballivin@aol.com ☑
☖ ev. day except Sat. Sun. 3pm–7pm

BARON DE SANGONIS 2002★

| ■ | 13 ha | 70,000 | ▮ ⬥ | 3–5 € |

The intensity of the wine's fuchsia-red colour with violet tinges contrasts with the *cuvée*'s finesse and elegance: this selection tempts lovers of sweet wine, and fills the palate with a successful balance between suppleness, sweetness and acidity.

☛ Vignerons de Sangonis, 56, av. de Montpellier, 34725 Saint-André-de-Sangonis, tel. 04.67.57.80.44, fax 04.67.57.94.37, e-mail vigneronsdesangonis@wanadoo.fr ☑
☖ by appt.

DOM. DE BAUBIAC 2000★★

■   2.05 ha   12,248 ▮ ❙❙ ♦   5–8 €

Imagine a landscape of garrigue (scrubland in southern France) with its copses, holm oaks, rosemary shrubs, olive groves and a typical Languedocian house built of stone. You feel it, you breathe it – you are transported there. This 2000 with a deep, dark-coloured appearance, is the product and inspiration of such terroir, mingling spices, garrigue and black olives. The wine should realize its optimum maturity, any time between now and two or three years hence; however, you may appreciate, here and now, the fine blend of flavours of cinnamon and forest berries. The palate exudes perfect balance.

☛ SCEA Dom. de Baubiac, 29, av. du 11-Novembre, 30260 Quissac, tel. 04.66.77.33.45, fax 04.66.77.33.45, e-mail philip@dstu.univ-montp2.fr ⅴ

⊤ by appt.

☛ S. Philip

CH. DE BEAULIEU

Lion d'Azur 2001★

■   3.5 ha   8,000 ▮ ♦   8–11 €

Situated in the heart of the village, this medieval château was renovated by Le Nôtre and the architects of Louis XIV. The 2000's balance and elegance prove that it is well up to the task. The *cuvée*'s dark garnet-red appearance, with delicate tinges, unfolds aromas of tobacco, spices and crystallized fruits. The full, rounded palate is already ripe, with well-integrated tannins.

☛ Georges de Ginestous, baron de La Liquisse, pl. de l'Eglise, 34160 Beaulieu, tel. 04.67.86.45.45, fax 04.67.86.44.44, e-mail contact@chateau-de-beaulieu.com ⅴ

⊤ by appt.

DOM. BELLES PIERRES

Chant des Ames 2001★

■   1 ha   3,000 ❙❙   15–23 €

This village is worth exploring for its Roman fortified hilltop site, which holds no secrets from the Coste family. This white wine immediately attracts attention for its fascinating golden complexion and aromas of very ripe crystallized citrus fruits, smoke and vanilla. The distinctly Mediterranean palate boldly displays its roundedness and fleshy richness.

☛ Damien Coste, Dom. Belles Pierres, 24, rue des Clauzes, 34570 Murviel-lès-Montpellier, tel. 04.67.47.30.43, fax 04.67.47.30.43 ⅴ

⊤ by appt.

BOIS DE CARELLE 2001★

■   5.69 ha   8,000 ▮ ❙❙   5–8 €

The *cuvée* originates from a selection of vine plots, cultivated according to strict agricultural guidelines and production specifications. Derived from the famous clay-flint terroir of Aspères and Sommières, this glistening, deep red-coloured wine was singled out for its fruitiness, liquorice flavours, finesse and elegance. Ready to drink now or suitable for laying down, the palate is so generous, highly aromatic, rounded and pleasant, with enduring body and substance, that there's something in this wine for everyone. Would make a fine companion for the *taureau au riz* (beef and rice) of the herdsmen in the Camargue.

☛ SCA Les Vignerons du Sommiérois, rte de Saussines, 30250 Sommières, tel. 04.66.80.03.31, fax 04.66.77.14.31 ⅴ

⊤ ev. day except Sun. 8am–12noon 3pm–7pm

DOM. CALAS

Révérence Calas 2000★

■   2.03 ha   4,000 ▮ ❙❙ ♦   15–23 €

Some of the vines are planted on basalt, which contributes to the typical characteristics of this wine, a blend of 46% Carignan, Grenache (33%) and Syrah (21%). Deep-coloured, it exhibits intense Mediterranean aromas of tapenade, sweet bay and dark fruits. The palate offers distinct, nice, soft tannins, enhanced by pleasant length. Don't forget to visit the interesting church of Caux, with its Romanesque nave, recast in the 18th century.

☛ Maurice Calas, 7, av. de la Gare, 34720 Caux, tel. 04.67.98.46.83, fax 04.67.98.46.83 ⅴ

⊤ by appt.

CANTAGALS

Elevé en fût de chêne 2001★★

■   1.3 ha   8,900 ❙❙   5–8 €

How enchanting, this terroir that clings tenaciously to the foothills of Larzac, where vines and olive trees grow side by side. Here, the cooperative is long familiar with the choice of appropriate terroir. Captivating, at first glance, with its purple appearance, this wine continues to enchant with its aromas of mocha, stewed, almost caramelized, fruits. Dense, unctuous and integrated, this *cuvée* is excellent now, or in three years' time as an accompaniment for duck.

☛ Les Vignerons de Saint-Jean-de-la-Blaquière, 1, rte de Lodève, 34700 Saint-Jean-de-la-Blaquière, tel. 04.67.44.90.40, fax 04.67.44.90.42, e-mail cave.sjb@wanadoo.fr

⊤ by appt.

CH. DE CAPITOUL

La Clape Les Rocailles 2001★

■   2 ha   8,000 ❙❙   11–15 €

During the 17th century, the estate was owned by the monks of the Cathédrale Saint-Just de Narbonne. Capitoul, moreover, has just built a superb wine cellar. Rigorous standards of continuity, character and consistency prevail, evidence of which is apparaent in this golden-coloured white wine, with its explosive aromas of hazelnut, exotic fruits and honey and its soft, oaked elegance. The somewhat over-discreet palate, is subtle, nevertheless, and manifests itself with finesse and roundedness.

☛ Charles Mock, Ch. de Capitoul, rte de Gruissan, 11100 Narbonne, tel. 04.68.49.23.30, fax 04.68.49.55.71, e-mail chateau.capitoul@wanadoo.fr ⅴ

⊤ ev. day 8.30am–7pm; groups by appt.

DOM. DE CASSAGNOLE 2001★

■   2 ha   5,500 ▮ ♦   5–8 €

Jean-Marie Sabatier set up this domaine in 1988. An advocate of organic growing, he has selected a wine that goes well with game: hare royale or spit-roast stag! The nose exhibits aromas of small berries, elderberries and rose. A very delicate combination, the palate offers supple body, with hints of cocoa and sweet bay. A thoroughbred wine.

☛ Jean-Marie Sabatier, Dom. de Cassagnole, 34820 Assas, tel. 04.67.55.30.02 ⅴ

⊤ ev. day except Sun. 3pm–7pm; Sat. 9am–12.30pm

DOM. CASTAN

Terroir du Lias Elevé en fût de chêne 2000★

■   2 ha   3,000 ❙❙   5–8 €

A combination of clay-limestone terroir and maturation in the barrel for twelve months, lends this wine a brilliant intensity, a pronounced nose of spices (liquorice) and a quality of tannins that envelop the palate, while also leaving an impression of exquisite balance. This wine still has potential, over the next two or three years.

☛ EARL Dom. Castan, av, Jean-Jaurès, 34370 Cazouls-lès-Béziers, tel. 04.67.93.60.77, fax 04.67.93.54.45 ⅴ ⋔

⊤ ev. day except Sun. 10am–12 noon 5.30pm–7.30pm

CH. DE CAZENEUVE

Pic Saint-Loup Les Calcaires 2002★

■   7 ha   20,000 ▮   8–11 €

André Leenhardt has run this domaine since 1987, and has been instrumental in the renovation of Pic Saint-Loup. With 10% Carignan, 20% Mourvèdre and 70% Syrah, planted on clay-limestone slopes, this *cuvée* exhibits clear potential. The dark, very pleasant, intense appearance indicates a winning nose, with hints of soft fruit and violet. Rounded, full, endowed with dense, yet fleshy tannic structure, this wine ought to be laid down for a year or two.

☛ André Leenhardt, Dom. de Cazeneuve, 34270 Lauret, tel. 04.67.59.07.49, fax 04.67.59.06.91 ⅴ ⋔

⊤ by appt.

CH. CHENAIE

Les Douves blanches 2001★★★

■ 1.4 ha	4,500	⏹	11–15 €

A *coup de coeur* last year for the Faugères red, the Chabberts have proved with this white that they certainly have more than one string to their bow. The Jury was dazzled by the wine's golden appearance and its precious aromas: hazelnut, orange blossom, vanilla, honey and quince. The palate, both full and lively, would go well with chicken à la crème. Note, also, that the **Faugères Les Douves red 2001 (8–11 €)** received a star.

➥ EARL André Chabbert et Fils, Ch. Chenaie, 34600 Caussiniojouls, tel. 04.67.95.48.10, fax 04.67.95.44.98 ▼

⊥ by appt.

DOM. LE CLOS DU SERRES

Le Florilège 2001★★

■ 4 ha	3,000	⏹	15–23 €

A debut in the *Guide* with a wine judged remarkable by the Jury, what talent! Talent on the part of the *vigneron*, certainly, but enhanced by the major contribution of the shale and sandstone terroir of Saint Jean de la Blaquière. The inky purple appearance augurs well for the aromatic complexity of this 2001: dried figs, smoke, spices, blackberry and vanilla. After the immediate power, robustness and fullness of this *cuvée*, the liquorice bouquet, on the finish, perfects the seduction. This wine should be laid down in the cellar while you drink the **Les Maros red 2001 (11–15 €)** first, which was awarded a star.

➥ Matthieu Foulquier-Gazagnes, 16, av. du Grand-Chemin, 34700 Saint-Jean-de-la-Blaquière, tel. 04.67.44.78.45, fax 04.67.44.57.65, e-mail leclosduserres@aol.com ▼

⊥ by appt.

CLOS MARIE

Pic Saint-Loup Métairie du Clos 2000★

■ 4 ha	10,000	⏹	23–30 €

Last year, a *coup de coeur*, this year, the domaine has nominated a *cuvée* that has been aged in oak for twenty-five months and is made up of a blend of 60% Grenache, 30% Carignan, topped up with Syrah and Cinsault. Deep garnet-red, but also a sprinkling of bluish, youthful tinges. Gradually, upon breathing, the subtle nose reveals hints of roasting, spices and woodland berries. The palate's balance is captivating; the encouraging weight indicates that this wine could be laid down for at least five years. A fine wine of the South, destined to accompany a shoulder of lamb, slow-roasted in the oven.

➥ Christophe Peyrus et Françoise Julien, Clos Marie, 34270 Lauret, tel. 04.67.59.06.96, fax 04.67.59.08.56, e-mail closmarie@wanadoo.fr

⊥ by appt.

CH. LA CLOTTE-FONTANE

Mouton La Clotte 2001★★

■ 0.8 ha	2,500	⏹	11–15 €

The continuity of excellence is ensured with Maryline Pagès's second vintage! The deep purple colour of this *cuvée* pays tribute to Jean Mouton de La Clotte, the contented proprietor of a domaine that dates back to the 18th century and serves as a reminder of former royal splendour. The flamboyant nose of prunes in brandy and small, soft jammy fruit tempts the taste buds. The same aromas are found on the palate, along with powerful tannins that convey the wine's clay-limestone origins. This full, well-balanced ensemble could happily be laid down for five years. The **Cuvée Crémailh red 2001 (8–11 €)** exudes finesse and elegance and is also awarded two stars.

➥ Maryline Pagès, Ch. La Clotte-Fontane, rte de Lecques, 30250 Salinelles, tel. 04.66.80.06.09, fax 04.66.80.42.60, e-mail clotte@club-internet.fr ▼

⊥ by appt.

COLLECTION VERMEIL

Vermeil du Crès Elevé en fût de chêne 2001★

■ 3.25 ha	15,000	⏹	5–8 €

This wine derives from specially selected vine plots of shingle soil, characteristic of the terroir of the sea-facing Vendres plateau. The bright-coloured appearance still conveys youth, while the nose and palate both confirm the wine's maturity: a delicate mix of stewed fruits, balsamic flavours and pinewood. The tightly knit tannins, still not fully developed, complete the fine balance, underlined by a certain length. The **Rosé Marine Vermeil du Crès 2002 (3–5 €)** should also be specially mentioned for its intense nose and freshness.

➥ SCAV Vignerons de Sérignan, av. Roger-Audoux, 34410 Sérignan, tel. 04.67.32.24.82, fax 04.67.32.59.66 ▼

⊥ ev. day except Sun. 9am–12 noon 3pm–6pm

CONDAMINE BERTRAND

Barrique 2002★

■ 5.25 ha	25,000	⏹	8–11 €

The church of Notre-Dame des Vertus, founded in the 12th century, with its 18th century apse, is not without interest. And, as with this archetypal property, the wine is also a classic of its kind, where Bernard Jany has always produced a Clairette du Languedoc. He has distinguished himself with this Syrah-dominated 2002. The wine is garnet-coloured. The vanilla and spicy nose is sustained by a dense, complex, yet immature palate, which, nevertheless, exhibits real potential. This *cuvée* might be recommended as an accompaniment for hare and mild Lézignan onions.

➥ Jany, Ch. Condamine Bertrand, RN 9, 34230 Paulhan, tel. 04.67.25.27.96, fax 04.67.25.07.55, e-mail chateau.condamineber@wanadoo.fr ▼ ⚲

⊥ ev. day except Sun. 10am–12 noon 2pm–6pm

CONQUETES N° 1 2000★

■ 0.5 ha	2,000	⏹	15–23 €

This Cuvée N° 1 has been nurtured with tender loving care, for more than fifteen months, in oak barrels. The highly discreet and integrated overtones of vanilla and oak are largely attributable to the characteristics of the terroir: mineral, blossom, black olive and coffee notes. Already pleasantly rounded, elegant and lingering, this 2000 could also be laid down for two to three years.

➥ Philippe Ellner, chem. des Conquêtes, 34150 Aniane, tel. 04.67.57.35.99, fax 04.67.57.35.99 ▼

⊥ by appt.

DOM. DE LA COSTE

Saint-Christol Cuvée sélectionnée 2001★★★

■ 11 ha	36,000	▮ ⚬	8–11 €

A *vigneron* of outstanding calibre, grape varieties that are well-adapted to the Villafranchian terraces of Saint-Christol and *voilà*, a *coup de coeur*. Indisputable: this is the Jury's number one. The appearance is truly magnificent, with its inky highlights, followed by a nose that is sumptuous: hints of garrigue mingle with a whole panoply of crystallized fruit and a spicy bouquet. Next, we have a palate with weight, supple richness and exquisite natural sweetness; then, as one recalls, hints of Mediterranean juniper, thyme, eucalyptus and tapenade. An absolute must!

➥ Luc et Elisabeth Moynier, Dom. de La Coste, 34400 Saint-Christol, tel. 04.67.86.02.10, fax 04.67.86.07.71 ▼

⊥ ev. day except Sun. 9am–12.30pm 1.30pm–7pm

CH. DES CRES RICARDS

Les Hauts de Milési 2001★★

| ■ | | 1.35 ha | 7,200 | ⦿ | 8–11 € |

This vintage confirms the quality of the domaine, first discovered last year. The **Cuvée Stécia red** achieves a star, while this deep purple-coloured wine, instantly charmed the Jury with its powerful nose of blackcurrant, vanilla, liquorice and crystallized figs. Supple to the point of being unctuous, robust, yet not lacking in finesse, this wine exudes great affability.

☛ Colette et Gérard Foltran, Dom. des Crès Ricards, 34800 Ceyras, tel. 04.67.44.67.63, fax 04.67.44.67.63, e-mail foltran@cresricards.com ☑
☍ by appt.

DOM. LA CROIX CHAPTAL

Seigneurie de Cambous Elevé en fût de chêne 2001★

| ■ | 1.6 ha | 4,600 | ■⦿⚲ | 15–23 € |

All find expression in the terroir of the Terrasses du Larzac: the old vines, planted on the rolling pebbles and terraces, low yields, carefully selected grapes, painstaking vinification. Here we have, accordingly, this ink-coloured wine, with aromas of crystallized cherry and hints of roasting. Powerful tannins and the sensation of weight on the palate are not mutually exclusive. A wine with great potential and the capacity to develop further.

☛ Pacaud-Chaptal, Dom. La Croix Chaptal, hameau de Cambous, 34725 Saint-André-de-Sangonis, tel. 04.67.70.75.44, fax 04.67.16.09.36, e-mail lacroixchaptal@wanadoo.fr ☑
☍ by appt.

CH. LA CROIX DE RASCAS

Cuvée Edouard 2001★

| ■ | 3 ha | 6,500 | ⦿ | 11–15 € |

A repeat performance for Benoît Touzan, who entered the 2003 *Guide* with his first vintage. Derived largely from shingle terroir, with a strong maritime influence, this wine boasts a deep, yet discreet colour, which only needs to develop slightly. Pause to appreciate fully this *cuvée*, with aromas of kirsch and vanilla; moreover, don't hesitate to drink it from now on with grilled dishes; pleasant first impressions, with discreet hints of softness and maturation, make this wine an ideal accompaniment for rare meats.

☛ Benoît Touzan, 11, av. Paul-Vidal, 34410 Sauvian, tel. 04.67.39.17.85, fax 04.67.39.17.85 ☑
☍ ev. day 10am–1pm 5pm–8pm May–Sep.;
Oct–Apr. by appt.

CH. DAURION

Cuvée Prestige Elevé en fût de chêne 2001★★

| ■ | 1 ha | 2,712 | ⦿ | 11–15 € |

At the heart of the Pézenas terroir, on Villafranche and volcanic soils, this *cuvée* knows how to merge a classic vintage with the deep-rooted characteristics of its terroir. The blend is made up of 10% Carignan, 70% Syrah and 20% Grenache. Aged in oak, and enveloped in a deep red, violet colour, the *cuvée* has developed fragrances of sweet spices, pepper

and garrigue. Balance, on the palate, is superb, very elegant. Richness, combined with finesse allows for immediate drinking or, equally, in four years' time. Pity this wine has been produced in limited quantities!

☛ SCEA Dom. de Daurion, 34720 Caux, tel. 04.67.98.47.36, fax 04.67.98.47.36, e-mail domainedaurion@wanadoo.fr ☑
☍ Henri Collet

DOM. DEVOIS DU CLAUS

Pic Saint-Loup Elevé en fût de chêne 2001★★

| ■ | 1 ha | 3,600 | ■⦿⚲ | 11–15 € |

Between mountain and sea, this family-run vineyard spans four generations. The enterprise was converted into a wine-producing cooperative in 1998, and it was then that André Gely launched his major venture. Following his two stars, last year, for the 2000, he has come up with a remarkable *cuvée* composed, in the main, of Syrah, topped up with 10% Grenache. Harvesting by hand ensures the quality of the grapes. An appealing, dense, ruby colour, overtones of crushed peaches, blackberry and strawberry bestow upon this *cuvée* character to spare. Velvety texture with aromas of garrigue. Here we have the secret of this great wine that enthusiasts would appreciate accompanying a dish of Larzac lamb with thyme.

☛ Dom. Devois du Claus, 38, imp. du Porche, 34270 Saint-Mathieu-de-Tréviers, tel. 04.67.55.29.37, fax 04.67.55.06.86 ☑
☍ by appt.
☍ André Gely

CH. DE L'ENGARRAN Saint-Georges

d'Orques Cuvée Quetton Saint-Georges 2001★★

| ■ | 10 ha | 33,000 | ⦿ | 15–23 € |

The superb caryatids, with their ornate vine branches that adorn the façade of the château, are reproduced on the label of this Cuvée Quetton Saint-Georges. Ensuring the continuity of the 2000, (also two stars), this 2001 displays an even greater concentration than the previous vintage: colour is extremely dark, aromas within a range of smoke, stewed fruit and bitter-sweet liquorice. Fine smoothness, on the palate, tightly knit, integrated tannins, delicately aged in oak and skilfully controlled: all augur well for the future. A wine that would benefit from being decanted.

☛ SCEA du Ch. de l'Engarran, 34880 Laverune, tel. 04.67.47.00.02, fax 04.67.27.87.89, e-mail lengarran@wanadoo.fr ☑
☍ ev. day 10am–7pm
☍ Grill

ERMITAGE DU PIC SAINT-LOUP

Pic Saint-Loup 2001★

| ■ | 15 ha | 70,000 | ■⚲ | 5–8 € |

At the foot of the Château de Montferrand, this domaine has put forward a classic, balanced *cuvée* with fine tannins and good length. The **Cuvée Sainte Agnès red 2000 (11–15 €)** also receives a star.

☛ Ravaille, GAEC Ermitage du Pic Saint-Loup, 34270 Saint-Mathieu-de-Tréviers, tel. 04.67.55.20.15, fax 04.67.55.23.49 ☑
☍ by appt.

CH. L'EUZIERE

Pic Saint-Loup Les Escarbouclès 2001★

| ■ | 12 ha | n.c. | ⦿ | 8–11 € |

Flint terroir, it makes no difference to these Escarbouclès 2001. The appearance is dark, red garnet. An intense nose conveys soft fruit, clove and tapenade aromas. Full-bodied and heady, representative of the vintage, this wine exhibits very concentrated body. The wine could be laid down for at least five years.

☛ Michel and Marcelle Causse, ancien chem. d'Anduze, 34270 Fontanès, tel. 04.67.55.21.41, fax 04.67.55.21.41 ☑
☍ by appt.

DOM. FAURMARIE

Cuvée des Mathilles 2001★

| ■ | 4 ha | 10,000 | ▮ | 5–8 € |

Last year, the Jury was utterly seduced by the intense aromas of the 2000 vintage. The 2001 is in the same category, with its overtones of iris, spices, small red berries and eucalyptus. As for the palate, roundness, suppleness and tannins prevail. A truly fine, Epicurean wine.

☛ Christian Faure, rue du Mistral, 34160 Galargues, tel. 06.16.12.23.95, fax 04.67.86.87.26, e-mail domaine.faurmarie@free.fr ☑
Ⅰ by appt.

DOM. FERRI ARNAUD La Clape Cuvée

Romain Elevé en fût de chêne 2001★★

| ■ | 1.5 ha | 7,000 | ◫ | 11–15 € |

The Romans held sway for many a year over the Clape Massif, a region famous for its vineyards. Here, the Ferri family has nominated a magnificent wine. The powerful nose mingles leather, smoke, crystallized fruit and sweet hints of cinnamon. After a very fine start, the palate evolves with powerful and supple tannins. Perfectly balanced and ready to drink in three to five years' time, this wine ought to be served in a decanter and would go well with a dish of hare royale.

☛ EARL Ferri Arnaud, av. de l'Hérault, 11560 Fleury-d'Aude, tel. 04.68.33.62.43, fax 04.68.33.74.38 ☑
Ⅰ ev. day 9.30am–1pm 3pm–7pm
☛ Richard Ferri

CH. DE FLAUGERGUES

La Méjanelle Cuvée sommelière 2002★

| ■ | 1.5 ha | 8,400 | ▮ ♦ | 5–8 € |

Here we are, entering the first Montpellieran folly, (a residence set amidst greenery), which the Colbert family has generously opened to the public and where 33 ha of vines are located within the confines of the estate, oblivious to the pressures of urbanization. This white is well defined, with its bright, pale appearance, nose of exotic fruits and fine floral, mineral overtones. A wine, noted equally for its rounded palate, as for its delicate character and subtle vivacity.

☛ Henri de Colbert, Ch. de Flaugergues, 1744, av. Albert-Einstein, 34000 Montpellier, tel. 04.99.52.66.37, fax 04.99.52.66.44, e-mail colbert@flaugergues.com ☑ ⌂
Ⅰ by appt.

CAVE DE FLORENSAC

Picpoul de Pinet Cuvée Ressac Prestige 2002★

| ■ | 22 ha | 50,000 | ▮ ♦ | 3–5 € |

The cuvée has an aromatic intensity that enchanted the Jury with its perfumes characteristic of grapefruit, floral hints and the Muscat grape. This is followed by a lively, straight-forward palate and amber nose that lingers with fine bitterness, reminiscent of oysters and shellfish.

☛ Cave coopérative de Florensac, BP 9, 34510 Florensac, tel. 04.67.77.00.20, fax 04.67.77.79.66 ☑

CH. FONT DES PRIEURS

Cuvée des Pères 2001★

| ■ | 4 ha | 15,000 | ▮ ◫ | 11–15 € |

This domaine has dedicated part of its estate, surrounding the medieval priory of Cassan, to the vine. Deep red, this wine is amazing, with its intense nose of aniseed, liquorice, vanilla and rosemary. Remarkable flavours of fruit on the palate, integrated tannins and overall balance. A fine cuvée that could be laid down for another two or three years.

☛ Vignobles Rambier-Tournant, Dom. Haut Bel-Air, rte de Mèze, 34340 Marseillan, tel. 04.67.77.59.17, fax 04.67.77.59.18, e-mail g.rambier@mnet.fr ☑
Ⅰ ev. day except Sun. 10am–12 noon 2pm–7pm (6pm in winter)

CH. FONT-MARS

Picpoul de Pinet 2002★

| ■ | 2 ha | 6,000 | ▮ | 8–11 € |

Located along the ancient Roman road of Queen Juliette, a domaine, where from time immemorial, dinosaurs had laid their eggs. Lemon marmalade, lime and floral overtones make up the expressive nose of this pleasant cuvée with a rounded and balanced palate; lingering vivacity and freshness. An excellent wine to accompany seafood.

☛ GFA Font-Mars, rte de Marseillan, 34140 Mèze, tel. 04.67.43.81.19, fax 04.67.43.79.41, e-mail info@font-mars.com ☑
Ⅰ by appt.
☛ Jean-Baptiste de Clock

DOM. LES GRANDES COSTES

Les Grandes Costes 2000★

| ■ | 2.9 ha | 5,000 | | 11–15 € |

Jean-Christophe Granier has resided, for some time, at the commune of Vacquières, amid the rugged landscape of the foothills of the Cévennes. Lightly developed, the colour exhibits ruby-red and orange highlights. The blackcurrant nose has overtones of garrigue and sweet spices. A spicy start is followed by hints of olive; the palate appears sweet and the finish supple. This full-bodied wine could be served over the next five years.

☛ Jean-Christophe Granier, 2, rte du Moulin-à-Vent, 34270 Vacquières, tel. 04.67.59.27.42, fax 04.67.59.27.42 ☑
Ⅰ by appt.

DOM. DE GRANOUPIAC

Les Cresses 2001★★

| ■ | 3.1 ha | 10,000 | ▮ ◫ ♦ | 8–11 € |

Vintages follow one another and Granoupiac, in the Terrasses du Larzac, is always there to delight the readers. This wine makes an impression with its deep purple and violet colour. The nose offers a whole spectrum of aromas including iris, liquorice, and a waft of ripeness, spices and pepper. A full, supple palate tempers warmth with fine tannic structure; this cuvée could prove a good match for wild boar stew.

☛ Claude et Marie-Claude Flavard, Dom. de Granoupiac, 34725 Saint-André-de-Sangonis, tel. 04.67.57.58.28, fax 04.67.57.95.83, e-mail cflavard@infonie.fr ☑
Ⅰ by appt.

DOM. DES GRECAUX

Montpeyroux Hêméra 2001★★

| ■ | 6 ha | 16,000 | ▮ ◫ | 15–23 € |

Saint-Jean-de-Fos, famous for its glazed roof tiles, is where Alain and Isabelle Caujolle-Gazet vinify the ripe grapes of their Montpeyroux vines. The couple's first vintage was in 1999 and here we already have a coup de coeur. As for this wine? Intensity combined with suppleness: deep colour, fragrances of undergrowth, blackcurrant, vanilla and chocolate; a fine palate, full, sweet and lingering. An instant delight. But, make no mistake, the wine is well capable of being kept for three years, as indeed, is the **Cuvée Terra Solis red 2001 (11–15 €)**.

☛ Caujolle-Gazet, 4, av. du Monument, 34150 Saint-Jean-de-Fos, tel. 04.67.57.38.83, fax 04.67.57.38.83, e-mail caujolle@club-internet.fr ☑
Ⅰ by appt.

CH. GRES SAINT PAUL

Antonin 2001★★

| ■ | 12 ha | 40,000 | ◫ | 11–15 € |

A fourth glorious year for this Cuvée Antonin. Yet again, utterly reliable; the pleasure equally enduring. This wine makes a stage entry with its brilliant ruby colour and then, without hesitating, proceeds to deliver its complex aromas to the audience: ripe fruit, spices, hints of Mediterranean juniper and toasted bread. An explosion of roundness on the palate, is perfectly balanced with tannic finesse. Already expansive, this wine will also bestow beautiful feelings upon those who wait.
✦ GFA Ch. Grès Saint-Paul, rte de Restinclières, 34400 Lunel, tel. 04.67.71.27.90, fax 04.67.71.73.76, e-mail contact@gres-saint-paul.com ☑
⌶ ev. day except Sun. 10am–12.30pm 2pm–7.30pm

DOM. GUINAND

Saint-Christol Elevé en fût 2001★★

| ■ | 2 ha | 10,000 | ◫ | 5–8 € |

A very fine vintage for the Guinand domaine: a star for the **Cuvée Vieilles Vignes red 2001 (3–5 €)** and two stars for this highly attractive *cuvée* with its ruby-red appearance. What a subtle nose of sweet bay, black olive and blackcurrant! As for the palate, lightly oaked and well-balanced, the wine exudes a remarkable unctuousness. Note that all these wines offer excellent quality and value for money.
✦ Dom. Guinand, 36, rue de l'Epargne, 34400 Saint-Christol, tel. 04.67.86.85.55, fax 04.67.86.07.59, e-mail domaineguinand@saint-christol.com ☑
⌶ ev. day except Sun. 10am–12 noon 3pm–6pm

DOM. DE L'HORTUS

Pic Saint-Loup Grande Cuvée 2000★

| ■ | 26.5 ha | 73,045◫ | | 11–15 € |

Hortus was set up in 1978 on garrigue terrain which needed cultivating. The vines, today, have reached a respectable age. Syrah (50%), Mourvèdre (40%) and the balance, Grenache, aged for 13 months in oak barrels, two thirds of which are new, have produced this true-to-type Grande Cuvée, an elegant thoroughbred. The strong, intense colour heralds a complex nose, with hints of undergrowth, menthol and stewed, soft fruits. The elegant, oaked palate mingles with tannic structure, offering a wine of exceptional character. Proprietors since 1998 of another domaine in Saint-Jean-de-Buèges, the Orliacs achieved a star for the **Clos du Prieur red 2000**, a blend of 10% Carignan to 50% Syrah and the balance, Grenache, matured in Bordelaise oak barrels, some new. It is vital to lay down this *cuvée*.
✦ Jean Orliac, Dom. de L'Hortus, 34270 Valflaunès, tel. 04.67.55.31.20, fax 04.67.55.38.03 ☑
⌶ by appt.

CH. HOSPITALET

La Clape Summum Elevé en fût de chêne 2001★

| ■ | 15 ha | 100,000 | ◫ | 8–11 € |

Last year, Gérard Bertrand took over this domaine, which was originally set up by Jacques Ribourel, on fallow garrigue terroir. The wine offers a distinct nose of spices and hints of fruits steeped in brandy. Full and fleshy, the *cuvée* still exhibits pronounced tannins and would benefit from maturing for two to three years. Serve with small game (partridge, thrush). This same **Summum white 2002** *cuvée* also achieves a star: an option to accompany cooked fish or poultry.
✦ Gérard Bertrand, Ch. Hospitalet, rte de Narbonne-Plage, 11100 Narbonne, tel. 04.68.45.36.00, fax 04.68.45.27.17, e-mail vins@gerard-bertrand.com ☑ ♞
⌶ by appt.

CH. ICARD

Saint-Georges d'Orques Elevé en fût de chêne 2001★★

| ■ | 2 ha | 3,200 | ◫ | 11–15 € |

Laurent Icard built his wine cellar, in 1999, on the link road between Saint-Georges d'Orques and the abbey of Vignogoul. This 2001 pays great tribute to its terroir of origin: fine, brilliant ruby colour, with intense highlights and a nose that mingles vanilla, orange zest and cloves. Body and density,

on the palate, but not to excess. With a remarkable finish that fills the mouth, this wine would go well with a leg of venison.
✦ EARL Laurent Icard, rte de Saint-Georges-d'Orques, 34570 Pignan, tel. 04.67.75.31.31, fax 04.67.75.31.63, e-mail laurent.icard@wanadoo.fr ☑
⌶ by appt.

DOM. VIRGILE JOLY

Virgile 2001★★

| ■ | 4.5 ha | 9,000 | ◫ | 23–30 € |

Virgile Joly has achieved success with a flourish for his entry in the *Guide*, with this 2001, his second vintage, where concentration sits comfortably alongside balance. First, the purple appearance, then floral and fruity flavours mingle with a soupçon of vanilla. Finally the palate unfolds with peppery and lightly oaked overtones; tannins are youthful, yet well rounded. Why not choose this wine to accompany a dish of rabbit and prunes?
✦ Dom. Virgile Joly, 22, rue du Portail, 34725 Saint-Saturnin-de-Lucian, tel. 04.67.44.52.21, fax 04.67.44.52.21, e-mail virgilejoly@wanadoo.fr
⌶ by appt.

DOM. LACROIX-VANEL

Clos Fine Amor 2001★

| ■ | 3.2 ha | 8,000 | ▮ | 8–11 € |

On an estate situated in the heart of the old village of Caux, Jean-Pierre Vanel, a passionate *vigneron*, has undertaken the transformation to biodynamic cultivation of the 8 ha which comprise his property. Purple appearance, powerful nose of violet, blackcurrant and liquorice: here we have a delightful and balanced wine, which enthralled the Jury with its texture of the utmost finesse and elegance.
✦ Jean-Pierre Vanel, 46, bd du Puits-Allier, 34720 Caux, tel. 04.67.09.32.39, fax 04.67.09.32.39 ☑
⌶ by appt.

CH. DE LANCYRE

Pic Saint-Loup Vieilles Vignes 2001★★

| ■ | 15 ha | 70,000 | ▮ ♦ | 5–8 € |

Good habits die hard: as one vintage follows another, so do the stars bestowed upon them. The deep red colour is bordering on black. The intense nose has aromas of crystallized fruit, strawberry jam and violet. The wine is rounded, rich, full-bodied with prominent tannic structure. This perfect accompaniment for coq au vin is sure to delight your guests. The **Grande Cuvée red 2001 (11–15 €)** receives a star.
✦ SCEA Ch. de Lancyre, Lancyre, 34270 Valflaunès, tel. 04.67.55.32.74, fax 04.67.55.23.84, e-mail chateaudelancyre@wanadoo.fr ☑ ♞
⌶ by appt.
✦ Durand et Valentin

CH. DE LASCAUX

Les Secrets 2000★★

| ■ | 3 ha | 8,000 | ▮ ◫ ♦ | 15–23 € |

Jean-Benoît Cavalier, President of the Coteaux du Languedoc appellation, proves, once again, that he has not lost his touch as a *vigneron*. This new *cuvée* from Château de Lascaux called "Les Secrets" has turned out to be a great success for the 2000 vintage. The palate unfolds with hints of soft fruit, liquorice, sweet spices and an oakiness that is already well-integrated. The composition of this wine, that is certain to charm with its fresh, fruitiness, complexity and length, makes it a suitable candidate for laying down for three to five years.
✦ Jean-Benoît Cavalier, 34270 Vacquières, tel. 04.67.59.00.08, fax 04.67.59.06.06 ☑
⌶ ev. day 10am–12.30pm 2pm–7pm

DOM. DES LAURIERS

Picpoul de Pinet 2002★★

| ■ | 3.75 ha | 20,000 | ▮ ♦ | 3–5 € |

This domaine certainly offers good value for money, in Picpoul de Pinet. In this region, the wines tend to fill the mouth with abundant richness. And, this is certainly the case with the very fine 2002 *cuvée*. The expressive nose, with aromas of white peach, and banana, is based on

LANGUEDOC

well-balanced structure and a noticeable hint of superb, mineral freshness.

🕊 Dom. des Lauriers, 15, rte de Pézenas,
34120 Castelnau-de-Guers, tel. 04.67.98.18.20,
fax 04.67.98.96.49, e-mail cabrol.marc@wanadoo.fr
⊠ by appt.
🕊 Marc Cabrol

LUCIAN

Saint-Saturnin 2001★★

| ■ | 31 ha | 80,000 | 📗 | 5–8 € |

Following two successive *coups de coeurs*, the Saint-Saturnin wine cellar has perpetuated its star studded performance: a definite star for the **Seigneur des Deux Vierges red 2001 (8–11 €)** *cuvée*, which has the capacity to develop further and two stars for this Lucian, a wine that is already fully developed. First impressions of a dark, violet-coloured wine are followed by a flood of aromas: very ripe fruit, chocolate and spices. Next, a lively, well-rounded melange on the palate, which exudes finesse and elegance.

🕊 Les Vins de Saint-Saturnin, av. Noël-Calmel,
34725 Saint-Saturnin-de-Lucian, tel. 04.67.96.61.52,
fax 04.67.88.60.13,
e-mail contact@vins-saint-saturnin.com ✅ 📧
⊠ by appt.

CH. PAUL MAS

Clos des Mûres Elevé en fût de chêne 2001★

| ■ | 14 ha | 41,000 | 🍷 | 8–11 € |

This 2001 originates from a terroir rich in fossils and history, on the outskirts of Pézenas. Beyond the violet highlights, you will discover aromas of chocolate, spices, inter-mingled with fairly well-developed oaked overtones. It exhibits an accentuated, but fine tannic palate. What would go well with this wine? "Odds and Ends" stew.

🕊 Dom. Paul Mas, Ch. de Conas, 34120 Pézenas,
tel. 04.67.90.16.10, fax 04.67.98.00.60,
e-mail info@paulmas.com
⊠ by appt.

MAS BRUGUIERE

Pic Saint-Loup La Grenadière 2001★

| ■ | 4 ha | 20,000 | 🍷 | 11–15 € |

Established in 1974, Guilhem Bruguière has played an instrumental rôle in the production of Pic Saint-Loup wines. Despite the advent of the new generation, old traditions die hard on the homesteads of the South of France. Renowned for their longevity, Bruguière wines are equally expansive in their first flush of youth. This intense red-coloured La Grenadière *cuvée*, opens out with aromas of soft stewed fruit and toasted bread. The highly delicate tannic structure offers exceptional length. Recommended with an authentic *cassoulet*.

🕊 Guilhem Bruguière, La Plaine, 34270 Valflaunès,
tel. 04.67.55.20.97, fax 04.67.55.20.97 ✅
⊠ ev. day except Sun. 5pm–7pm

MAS DE BAYLE

Grande Cuvée 2001★★

| ■ | 1 ha | 5,500 | 📗 | 5–8 € |

In 2001, Céline Michelon took over the family business and vinified her very first *cuvée*, a real test of one's ability: shimmering, deep purple tinges, a powerful nose (ripeness, cocoa, crystallized fruits, sweet spices), a supple palate, that relies on fine structure. The *cuvée* seduced the Jury with its richness and weight as well as its overtones of highly ripe fruit…as if they were being pulped in a grape crusher.

🕊 EARL Mas de Bayle, 34560 Villeveyrac,
tel. 04.67.78.06.11, fax 04.67.78.06.11,
e-mail celine.michelon@freesbee.fr ✅
⊠ ev. day 10.30am–12.30pm 5pm–7pm; Sun. by appt.;
cl. Oct.–Mar.
🕊 Céline Michelon

MAS DE FOURNEL

Pic Saint-Loup Pierre 2000★

| ■ | 3 ha | 4,600 | 🍷 | 11–15 € |

A family-run business of 26 ha headed by Gérard Jeanjean who received a *coup de coeur* for the 1998 vintage. This 2000 *cuvée* will not disappoint: luminous, dazzling appearance, complex elegant nose, appealing for its soft fruit flavours of raspberry, brioche and caramel. If the rich, powerful palate does not seem very long, it leaves, nevertheless, a lingering memory of soft fruits and balanced tannins.

🕊 Gérard Jeanjean, SCEA Mas de Fournel,
34270 Valflaunès, tel. 04.67.55.22.12, fax 04.67.55.22.12 ✅
⊠ ev. day 9am–7pm

MAS DE LA BARBEN

Les Sabines 2001★

| ■ | 6 ha | 18,000 | 📗🍷♨ | 11–15 € |

On typical clay-limestone terroir in the area surrounding Nîmes, Marcel Hermann pursues the task he embarked upon in 1999, namely, to make a name for the house of Barben. One of his wines has already been awarded a star. Brilliant, dark garnet-coloured, Les Sabines epitomizes the essence of this vineyard. A combination of very ripe fruit, garrigue and spices, in perfect harmony, on both nose and palate. Its richness is bound to mature, if you have the patience to wait for a few years; it will be just as good with game as with quality red meats.

🕊 Mas de la Barben, rte de Sauve, 30900 Nîmes,
tel. 04.66.81.15.88, fax 04.66.63.80.43,
e-mail marcel.hermann@wanadoo.fr ✅
⊠ ev. day except Sun. 10am–12 noon 3pm–7pm
🕊 Marcel Hermann

MAS DE LA SERANNE

Les Griottiers 2001★★

| ■ | 1.5 ha | 6,000 | 📗 | 5–8 € |

We are here on the terroirs of the Terrasses du Larzac, in a recently constructed wine cellar that offers a superb panorama of the foothills of Larzac. Vines nestle on the ancient terraces and lend great character to this garnet-coloured wine that enchants with its fragrances of Mediterranean juniper, cloves and crystallized fruits. The pleasant, powerful, liquorice palate also stands out for its tannic finesse.

🕊 Isabelle et Jean-Pierre Venture, Mas de La Seranne,
34150 Aniane, tel. 04.67.57.37.99, fax 04.67.57.37.99,
e-mail mas.seranne@wanadoo.fr ✅
⊠ ev. day except Sun. 5.15pm–8pm; Sat. and Jul.–Aug.
9am–6pm

MAS DE MARTIN

Cuvée Ultreïa 2001★

| ■ | 6 ha | 21,000 | 🍷 | 11–15 € |

Environmental awareness is high on the agenda of the Mocci family who have lived here since 1990. Low yields contribute to the concentration of this wine, which has not been pressed or filtered: dark, garnet-coloured, sweet aromas of vanilla, soft fruits and liquorice root. A fleshy start, tannic presence, but not excessive, pleasant quaffing, an appropriate wine to drink with loin of lamb.

🕊 Christian Mocci, Dom. Mas de Martin,
34160 Saint-Bauzille-de-Montmel, tel. 04.67.86.80.82,
fax 04.67.86.98.82 ✅ 📧
⊠ by appt.

MAS DE MATHILDE

Picpoul de Pinet 2002★

| ■ | n.c. | n.c. | | 3–5 € |

One of the oldest and most productive cooperatives in Languedoc, La Montagnacoise presents, among others, this pleasant Mas de Mathilde wine, with a lively, pronounced nose of citrus fruit; aromas that confirm an elegant and particularly characteristic palate. A white of exceptional finesse.

🕊 Cave coop. La Montagnacoise, 15, av. d'Aumes,
34530 Montagnac, tel. 04.67.24.03.74, fax 04.67.24.14.78 ✅
⊠ ev. day except sat. Sun. 10am–12 noon 3.30pm–6pm

MAS DES AMOURS 2001★

■	2.6 ha	12,000	■ ⑪	11–15 €

Cal Demoura, the name of this house, translates roughly as "One must stay", in *langue d'Oc* French. Close to the soil, undoubtedly. Just as well for us that Jean-Pierre Jullien decided to do exactly that, for here we have an exquisite *cuvée* steeped in history and memories. Beneath the beautiful, deep purple highlights, this wine exudes aromas of ripe fruit, spices and leather. A rounded start, velvety and lingering palate, the perfect ensemble to try out among friends, with food that has been prepared with tender loving care. The **Mas Cal Demoura L'Infidèle red 2000 (15–23 €)** achieves a star. Best laid down for two or three years.

↬ Jean-Pierre Jullien, Mas Cal Demoura, 34725 Jonquières, tel. 04.67.88.61.51, fax 04.67.88.61.51
⏱ by appt.

MAS DES CIGALES

Campredon 2001★

■	2 ha	10,300	■ ♦	8–11 €

Alain Rasigade left the cooperative winery in 2001 to produce, at last, the wine of his dreams. The outcome, this delightful *cuvée* with a true Mediterranean feel, a blend of 30% Carignan, 32% Grenache, 33% Syrah and 5% Cinsault, exceeds his wildest expectations. Dark garnet-coloured, intense, spicy aromas develop into hints of animal fur and soft fruits. This balanced 2001, with fine, rich, tannins offers generous scents of garrigue. We would also like to point out, that Caux is particularly interesting, not only for its church, but also for its historic houses (15th and 17th century).

↬ EARL Les Mouilhères, 54, bd Anselme-Nougaret, 34720 Caux, tel. 04.67.98.46.18, fax 04.67.98.49.08, e-mail vitiplus@wanadoo.fr ☑
⏱ by appt.
↬ Rasigade

MAS DU POUNTIL 2001★

■	2.8 ha	7,500	■ ⑪ ♦	11–15 €

Discovered last year for their first vintage, the Bautous have notched up a winner with this pleasant, dark-coloured 2001; a nose reminiscent of crystallized fruits in brandy and roasted coffee. Full, firm palate, yet quality tannins; subtle hints of vanilla on the finish. A wine that has several good years ahead of it.

↬ Brice Bautou, 10 bis, rue du Foyer-Communal, 34725 Jonquières, tel. 04.67.44.67.13, fax 04.67.44.67.13 ☑
⏱ by appt.

MAS DU SOLEILLA

La Clape Clot de l'Amandier 2000★

■	3 ha	3,300	⑪	5–8 €

A new entry in the *Guide* worth keeping an eye on: Swiss oenologist, Peter Wildbolz, has bought a vineyard and replaced the existing stock with noble grape varieties. Grenache and Syrah, in equal parts, lend fine typicity to this *cuvée*, which has been aged in oak for a good 18 months. The nose has dominant overtones of toasted bread, blackcurrant and violet. Particularly pleasant on the palate, interesting tannins confirm the wine's good potential for ageing. Best laid down for a while to let the oaky tastes fully assimilate.

↬ Mas du Soleilla, rte de Narbonne-Plage, 11100 Narbonne, tel. 04.68.45.24.80, fax 04.68.45.25.32, e-mail mas-du-soleilla@wanadoo.fr ☑ 🏠
⏱ by appt.
↬ Peter Wildbolz

MAS GOURDOU

Pic Saint-Loup Les Roches blanches 2001★★

■	3 ha	8,500	■	8–11 €

Although this new domaine only went into production recently, the vineyard has been in the family for three generations, passing through the female line. This deep garnet-coloured wine (70% Syrah and 30% Grenache) offers hints of violet, liquorice, and stewed soft fruits. The palate is full, rich and rounded. All this wine needs is the company of a few friends and maybe some duck brochettes. Authentic.

↬ Mas Gourdou, 34270 Valflaunès, tel. 04.67.55.30.45, fax 04.67.55.30.45,
e-mail jtherond@masgourdou.com ☑ 🏠
⏱ ev. day 6pm–8pm; Sat. Sun. 10am–12 noon 4pm–8pm
↬ Jocelyne Thérond

MAS GRANIER

Les Grès 2001★

■	2 ha	13,000	⑪	8–11 €

Every year, without fail, the Granier house makes a reappearance: Aspères terroir coupled with the unstinting efforts of the Granier brothers have gone into producing this exceedingly soft and balanced Les Grès *cuvée*. Intense, garnet colour, scents of spices, cocoa and garrigue whet the appetite. Quality of texture, where skilful maturation in oak barrels enhances the weight of the wine, only adds to the overall Epicurean delight factor.

↬ EARL Granier, Mas Montel, 30250 Aspères, tel. 04.66.80.01.21, fax 04.66.80.01.87, e-mail montel@wanadoo.fr ☑
⏱ ev. day except Sun. 9am–7pm

MAS HAUT-BUIS

Costa Caoude 2001★★

■	6 ha	20,000	⑪	15–23 €

A wine cellar located at an altitude of 750 m, with vines planted above 400 m on the cliffs of Larzac and *voilà*, a wine at the height of the appellation. The *cuvée* is also firmly ensconced on the vinous summits, with its deep purple, highly fragmented appearance, intense bouquet, reminiscent of violet and soft fruits. A certain vivacity adds complexity to the full, structured, yet lingering palate. Don't be afraid to cellar this wine for quite a while.

↬ Olivier Jeantet, rte de Saint-Maurice, 34520 La Vacquerie, tel. 06.13.16.35.47, fax 04.67.44.12.13 ☑
⏱ by appt.

MAS LUMEN

La Sylve 2001★★

■	n.c.	3,373	■ ⑪	15–23 €

Over the years, Pascal Perret has travelled the length and breadth of the wine regions of France as a photographer, before depositing his suitcases in Languedoc in 2001. This deep red-coloured wine is the epitome of *gourmandise*, with its flavours of soft fruit, charred notes, fine, delightful and supple tannins. Full-bodied and concentrated, the palate lingers on spicy overtones, all of which turns ones thoughts to duck *aux morilles*. The **Cuvée Classique Mas Lumen red 2001 (11–15 €)**, from the same stable and composed of 50% Carignan, receives a star.

↬ Pascal Perret, 8, rue François-Oustrin, 34120 Pézenas, tel. 04.67.90.13.66, fax 04.67.90.13.70, e-mail maslumen@wanadoo.fr ☑
⏱ by appt.

MAS MOURIES

M 2001★

■	2.2 ha	10,000		5–8 €

From time immemorial, the site of the Mouriès' dwelling has been cultivated and the vineyard is a designated appellation. The typical clay with limestone fragments terroir has produced this fine garnet-coloured wine, with gloriously elegant aromas of raspberry and grilled meats. The palate is already full-bodied, balanced, with quality tannins. A wine that would go well with roast beef or a leg of lamb.

↬ Eric Bouet, Mas Mouriès, 30260 Vic-le-Fesq, tel. 04.66.77.87.13, fax 04.66.77.87.13 ☑
⏱ by appt.

CH. MIRE L'ETANG

La Clape Cuvée Corail 2002★

■	4 ha	5,000	■ ♦	8–11 €

On the edge of the Clape Massif, Château Mire L'Etang benefits from a maritime climate. The brilliant, redcurrant tinged appearance of this wine mesmerized the Jury, as did its aromas of soft fruits that proceeded to tease the nose.

LANGUEDOC

Roundness, suppleness, fruitiness, with just the right amount of freshness ensure the delightful balance of this *cuvée*.

☛ Ch. Mire L'Etang, 11560 Fleury-d'Aude, tel. 04.68.33.62.84, fax 04.68.33.99.30 ☑
☒ by appt.
☛ P. Chamayrac

MM
Saint-Georges d'Orques 2001★

■				
	0.5 ha	1,700	⬚	8–11 €

Délit d'Initiés is a society that specializes in selling bottled Languedoc wines and is headed by talented oenologists, Michèle Trévoux and José Tastavy. The grapes used by the Murviel-Montarnaud cooperative to produce this *cuvée* originate from the red sandstone terroir of Saint-Georges-d'Orques. This 2001 offers freshness on the palate, floral and sweet spicy aromas, body that asserts itself, without being over-forceful. A star also for the **Les Charmes de Jeanne red 2001 (15–23 €)**, bottled by the *vignerons* de Saint-Jean-de-la-Blaquière.

☛ Délit d'Initiés, Mas de Renard, 34570 Pignan, tel. 06.17.83.03.08, fax 04.67.47.24.83, e-mail michele.tastavy@wanadoo.fr
☒ by appt.
☛ Michèle Trévoux

CH. DE MONTPEZAT
La Pharaonne 2000★★

■				
	0.7 ha	3,000	⬚	15–23 €

Low yields from Villafranchian terroir, technical know-how and the passion of the *vigneron* are some of the key ingredients that give expression to this fine, dark-coloured wine (80% Mourvèdre, 20% Grenache). The fine, complex aromas of menthol and spices envelop both nose and palate. This particular *cuvée* is endowed with rounded and integrated tannins. The vivid, fruity finish is balanced and lingering.

☛ Christophe Blanc, Ch. de Montpezat, rte de Roujan, 34120 Pézenas, tel. 04.67.98.10.84, fax 04.67.98.98.78, e-mail contact@chateau-montpezat.com ☑
☒ ev. day. 10am–12 noon 2pm–7pm; winter by appt.

MORTIÈS
Pic Saint-Loup Que sera sera 2001★★

■				
	5 ha	3,000	⬚	15–23 €

Again, this year, the Mortiès domaine strengthens its position as a successful producer of quality red wines. The 2001 has an inky black appearance; a nose of intense garrigue, cocoa and crystallized fruity aromas. The pleasant, full palate exhibits exceedingly fine substance. The **Mortiès white 2001 (11–15 €)** achieves a star for its lime blossom, apricot and mineral fragrances. Rounded, elegant and lingering, this wine would make an excellent partner for white meat dishes.

☛ Mas de Mortiès, rte de Cazevieille, 34270 Saint-Jean-de-Cuculles, tel. 04.67.55.11.12, fax 04.67.55.11.12, e-mail contact@morties.com ☑
☒ by appt.
☛ Duchemin-Jorcin

CH. MOUJAN
La Clape Cuvée Baronne de Rivières 2001★

■				
	1.85 ha	7,500	⬚	8–11 €

Richness and concentration sum up this 2001. The powerful nose evokes aromas of garrigue, thyme, rosemary and spices (pepper). The equally intense start leaves a pleasant impression of sweetness, followed by tannic density, if somewhat subdued, in comparison with the nose. A wine to uncork in two or three years' time, with a *ragoût* or *cassoulet*.

☛ SCEA Ch. Moujan, rte des Plages, 11100 Narbonne, tel. 04.68.65.24.71, fax 04.68.65.83.31, e-mail contact@chateaumoujan.com ☑ ⌂
☒ by appt.
☛ M. de Braquilanges

CH. DE LA NEGLY
La Clape La Falaise 2001★★

■				
	20 ha	44,000	■ ⬚ ♦	11–15 €

A well-known and indeed widely recognized name in the Coteaux du Languedoc: a name synonymous with serious commitment to maturation and vinification. Grapes harvested at full maturity. This very dark red wine pleasantly mingles liquorice, chocolate and charred overtones. The tasters were impressed by the magnificent tannins and aromatic length. Typical of its appellation, the **La Brise Marine white 2002 (5–8 €)** won a star.

☛ SCEA Ch. de la Négly, 11560 Fleury-d'Aude, tel. 04.68.32.36.28, fax 04.68.32.10.69, e-mail lanegly@wanadoo.fr ☑
☒ by appt.
☛ Jean Paux-Rosset

DOM. DE NIZAS 2001★

■				
	4.5 ha	30,000	⬚	15–23 €

J. Goelet is the proprietor of Clos du Val, in the Napa Valley. In 1998, he invested in this delightful estate, where he applies the rigours of vine cultivation, according to the rules. This substantial 2001 *cuvée* exhibits a purple colour and an aromatic profile of undergrowth, spices and vanilla. The palate is rich and balanced, with powerful fruity overtones. The tannins need to patinate somewhat.

☛ SCEA Dom. Nizas et Salleles, hameau de Salleles, 34720 Caux, tel. 04.69.90.17.92, fax 04.67.90.21.78, e-mail domnizas@wanadoo.fr ☑
☒ by appt.
☛ J. Goelet

DOM. DU NOUVEAU MONDE 2000★

■				
	12 ha	18,600	■	5–8 €

It was one Henri de Monfreid who christened this domaine, long before anyone had heard of New World wines! Jacques Gauch, a pharmacist until 1983, chose to nurture, in tank, this 2000 *cuvée*, for a period of twenty-four months. Today, the wine has realized its full potential: fine, purple appearance, fruity nose – gives the impression of savouring fresh fruit – enveloped in fragrances of cloves, sweet bay; perfect balance, rounded off with an integrated palate and fine length.

☛ Any et Jacques Gauch, Dom. Le Nouveau Monde, 34350 Vendres, tel. 04.67.37.33.68, fax 04.67.37.58.15, e-mail domaine-lenouveaumonde@wanadoo.fr ☑ ⌂
☒ by appt.

DOM. DE L'OCELLE
Saint-Christol Vieilles Vignes 2000★

■				
	10 ha	10,000	⬚	5–8 €

Amid the Villafranchian terraces of Saint-Christol, you might encounter an ocellus, the large green lizard, known locally as the vine crocodile. This dark garnet-coloured 2000, composed of Syrah and Grenache, in equal parts, will add a lovely element of surprise, with its fruity intense aromas of blackcurrant and sweet spices. Supple on the palate, delicate and of exceptional natural sweetness. An absolute delight with lamb in herbs.

☛ EARL Warnery-Da Silva, 28, av. Les Platanes, 34400 Saint-Christol, tel. 04.67.86.04.26, fax 04.67.86.54.18, e-mail domainedelocelle@saint-christol.com ☑
☒ by appt.

CH. PECH-CELEYRAN
La Clape Réserve céleste 2001★

■				
	7 ha	30,000	■ ⬚	8–11 €

Constantly on the lookout for quality enhancements, this vineyard is managed with great care and passion, involving an uphill struggle to remain one step ahead. This 2001 is dark, garnet-coloured, with a nose of small, soft fruits, sweet bay and dried garrigue. With its aromas, a mysterious wine, and a real charmer. The somewhat firm palate by no means fills the mouth, but is certainly lingering. A heavenly wine that will improve with age.

☛ SARL Jacques de Saint-Exupéry, Ch. Pech-Céleyran, 11110 Salles-d'Aude, tel. 04.68.33.50.04, fax 04.68.33.36.12, e-mail saint-exupery@pech-celeyran.com ☑ ⌂ ⌂
☒ ev. day 9am–7.30pm

CH. PECH REDON

La Clape La Centaurée 2000★★

■   5 ha   8,000   ▮ ❚❙   15–23 €

Christophe Bousquet, a member of the new and already great *Vignerons des Coteaux du Languedoc*, is searching for typicity, but also originality and finesse. Protracted and meticulous maturation lend this wine fine, aromatic intensity, with hints of spices, undergrowth and crystallized cherry. A strong, rounded tannic presence on the palate, that possesses very real balance. The aromatic length is exceptional. A perfect match for wild boar stew or jugged (Clape!) hare.
➛ Christophe Bousquet, Ch. Pech Redon, rte de Gruissan, 11100 Narbonne, tel. 04.68.90.41.22, fax 04.68.65.11.48, e-mail bousquet@terre-net.fr ☑ ⌂
⅄ ev. day except Sun. 10am–7pm

DOM. DU PECH ROME

Opulens 2001★

■   1.25 ha   6,500   ▮ ❚❙   11–15 €

Mary and Pascal Blondel's 2001 selection has benefited from their wise move to this village with the interesting 18th century church of Saint-Alban. The upshot is their very first vintage. Two *cuvées*, intense colours, both receive a star: **Concordia red 2001 (5–8 €)**, and this wine with a lightly oaked nose, hints of vanilla and spice and dominant overtones of soft and dark fruits. Body, rich and balanced, with mature, supple and well-integrated tannins.
➛ SCEA de Remparts de Neffies, 17, rue Montée-des-Remparts, 34320 Neffies, tel. 04.67.59.42.05, fax 04.67.59.42.05, e-mail pechromevin@wanadoo.fr ☑
⅄ by appt.
➛ Pascal Blondel

CH. DE PINET

Picpoul de Pinet 2002★

■   4 ha   20,000   ▮   5–8 €

Mme Arnaud-Gaujal, a *vigneronne*, controls the destiny of the Château de Pinet, a property that has remained in the family since the 18th century. The subtle, fine nose heralds a wine of sheer elegance and balance, where richness mingles comfortably with a mineral freshness. Lingering and rounded, with lemony overtones, this wine would go well with grilled bass.
➛ Simone Arnaud-Gaujal, Ch. de Pinet, 34850 Pinet, tel. 04.68.32.16.67, fax 04.68.32.16.39 ☑
⅄ ev. day 10am–1pm 3pm–7pm; Nov.–Apr. by appt.

PLAN DE L'OM

OEillade 2002★

■   18 ha   18,000   ▮ ⚬   8–11 €

After abandoning his career as a pharmacist and seafarer, Joël Foucou planted his first vine, in the locality of Plan de l'Om, in 1988. This is the second vintage vinified in this particular wine cellar: dark red garnet-coloured, aromas of ripe fruit and toasted bread, a full, rounded first impression on the palate. Alongside overtones of Morello cherry, the tannins are fine although, at the time of tasting, still somewhat young. A year in the cellar would ensure that this 2002 achieves its full, fleshy potential.
➛ Joël Foucou, SCEA Plan de l'Om, 34700 Saint-Jean-de-la-Blaquière, tel. 04.67.10.91.25, fax 04.67.10.91.25, e-mail plan-de-lom@wanadoo.fr ☑
⅄ by appt.

PRIEURE DE SAINT-JEAN DE BEBIAN

2001★

■   5 ha   10,000   ❚❙   23–30 €

It is here, on the magnificent lakeside limestone soils, that low yield vines can give full rein to their quintessential character. The Jury admired the beautiful, bright golden appearance, the full, mature aromas of honey, resin and hazelnut, teamed with delicate, oaked overtones. Richness, natural sweetness and strength, tempered by elegance, assert themselves on the palate.

➛ EARL Le Brun-Lecouty, prieuré de Saint-Jean-de-Bébian, rte de Nizas, 34120 Pézenas, tel. 04.67.98.13.60, fax 04.67.98.22.24, e-mail bebian@wanadoo.fr ☑
⅄ ev. day except Sun. 10am–12.30pm 3.30pm–6.30pm; winter by appt.

PRIEURE SAINT-HIPPOLYTE 2002★★

■   30 ha   40,000   ▮ ⚬   3–5 €

The vineyard of Fontès extends around the ruins of Château Mazers, built in the 5th century and part of the Visigoths' kingdom. Here we have a young wine, apparent by its purplish, garnet hue. A nose of stewed dark fruits, bitter-sweet liquorice and leather is followed by a fine, dense palate, well-structured and pleasantly rich. The velvety tannins and fine length make this a suitable *cuvée* for cellaring. Decanting is recommended. The **Prieuré Saint-Hippolyte rosé 2002** and the **Château Mazers red 2001 (5–8 €)** both receive a star.
➛ Cave coop. La Fontesole, bd Jules-Ferry, 34320 Fontès, tel. 04.67.25.14.25, fax 04.67.25.30.66, e-mail la.fontesole@libertysurf.fr ☑
⅄ ev. day except Sun. 8am–12 noon 2pm–6pm

DOM. LES QUATRE PILAS

Saint-Georges d'Orques 2001★★

■   1 ha   3,000   ▮   11–15 €

At Murviel-lès-Montpellier, near the Roman hillside fort, is the spot where these Syrah, Mourvèdre and Grenache grapes attained their full maturity. The powerful nose of this 2001, with hints of coffee, garrigue and dark fruits is truly amazing. Good well-presented structure; fine, tightly knit tannins. The wine would make a good impression with a dish of lamb in herbs.
➛ Joseph Bousquet, chem. de Pignan, 34570 Murviel-lès-Montpellier, tel. 04.67.47.89.32, fax 04.67.47.89.32 ☑
⅄ by appt.

CH. RICARDELLE

La Clape Closablières 2001★

■   4 ha   22,000   ❚❙   5–8 €

Since 1990, Château Ricardelle has adopted a cultivation policy with a view to optimizing the natural qualities of the Clape terroir. Discretion, finesse and elegance leave the tasters with delightful memories. This strong wine has personality; it bears the stamp of its origins, but is also extremely promising. Sweet spices and dark fruits predominate, on both nose and palate. The *cuvée* can be enjoyed in two years' time, but is also delicious now!
➛ Ch. Ricardelle, rte de Gruissan, 11100 Narbonne, tel. 04.68.65.21.00, fax 04.68.32.58.36, e-mail ricardelle@wanadoo.fr ☑ ⌂
⅄ by appt.
➛ Pellegrini

ROCALHAN 2001★★

■   n.c.   2,000   ❚❙   8–11 €

Paul Reder has just taken a big step: following in his father Alain's footsteps, he has taken over the vineyard that nestles in the heart of wild garrigue, a terroir where the soil is dry and exposed (Reder senior is, nowadays, indulging his passion for growing truffles). Summer sea breezes contribute to the fine maturity and balance of this lavish, golden-coloured wine that is so enchanting. Intense aromas of crystallized fruits, spices, apricot and honey are further accentuated on the palate. Rich, pleasant and full. Very Mediterranean.
➛ Paul Reder, Comberousse de Fertalière, 34660 Cournonterral, tel. 04.67.85.05.18, fax 04.67.85.05.18, e-mail rederpaul@yahoo.fr
⅄ by appt.

DOM. DE ROQUEMALE 2001★★

■   1.6 ha   7,000   ▮   11–15 €

In September 2001, at the beginning of the harvest season, the young *vigneron* Dominique Ibanez took over this vineyard. With his first vintage, he has pulled off a master stroke: a wine of true pedigree. The deep purplish colour is very pleasing. The nose is reminiscent of spices, garrigue and woodland berries. A powerful palate, of exceptionally tight and integrated tannins, that does not deny this wine its fine elegance. As with many Languedoc wines, this domaine has created a pleasant label, worthy of featuring on the best of dinner tables.

🍇 Dominique Ibanez, 12, rue des Aires-Basses, 34560 Villeveyrac, tel. 04.67.78.24.10, fax 04.67.78.24.10, e-mail valerie.tabaries@free.fr ☑
☤ by appt.

CH. ROUQUETTE SUR MER
La Clape Cuvée Henry Lapierre 2001★★

| ■ | 4 ha | 6,600 | ◗▯ | 11–15 € |

In the 15th century, it was a freestone country house. In 2003, it is a château, which Jacques Boscary has put to good use as a winery. He receives a star for the **Château Rouquette sur Mer Elevé en Fût de Chêne 2001 red (8–11 €)**. As for this wine, it has a purple appearance and offers a very complex nose (soft fruits, toasted, roasted and liquorice overtones). The structure is sustained by supple tannins and a rounded finish. Of fine extraction, endowed with potential, this very interesting *cuvée* would be better kept for two to four years.

🍇 Jacques Boscary, Ch. Rouquette sur Mer, rte Bleue, 11100 Narbonne-Plage, tel. 04.68.49.90.41, fax 04.68.49.50.49, e-mail chateau.rouquette@libertysurf.fr ☑ ☖
☤ by appt.

DOM. DE ROUVEYROLLES 2001★

| ■ | 0.85 ha | 2,500 | ◗▯ | 15–23 € |

The stones from Château d'Aumelas would have been used to build the walls of this wine cellar, which, today, presents its first vintage. The colour is dark ruby-red. This is followed immediately by aromas of cocoa, fruits steeped in alcohol and a touch of menthol. Tightly packed tannins, the fine, highly oaked structure indicates that this is a wine for keeping.

🍇 Laurent Baudou, 3, rue Croix-des-Barrières, 34230 Vendemian, tel. 04.67.42.75.76, fax 04.67.88.72.26 ☑
☤ by appt.

DOM. SAINT-JEAN DE L'ARBOUSIER
2001★

| ■ | n.c. | 27,000 | ▮ ♦ | 5–8 € |

Located 5 km from Château de Castries and in the middle of the garrigue, is where you will track down this vineyard of 45 ha; an enterprise that understands the benefits of blending the three usual grape varieties with 4% Carignan. Behind its scarlet-ruby hues, elegance and roundness combine. Also, pronounced overtones of garrigue, soft fruits, violet, right up to the pleasant finish.

🍇 EARL Dom. Saint-Jean de l'Arbousier, 34160 Castries, tel. 04.67.87.04.13, fax 04.67.70.15.18, e-mail caviguier@free.fr ☑
☤ by appt.
🍇 Viguier

CH. SAINT MARTIN DE LA GARRIGUE
2001★

| ■ | 3.75 ha | 20,000 | ◗▯ | 11–15 € |

Organized around a Renaissance château, the vines are deeply rooted in red chalky sandstone. This violet-coloured wine introduces a nose with an element of originality: hints of blossom, spices and nuts mingle with refined oak overtones. Straightforward and lingering palate; oaked tannins would benefit from ageing for a while, in order to achieve optimum structural integration. Also singled out was the **white 2002 (8–11 €)**, which was commended for its freshness and aromatic complexity.

🍇 SCEA Saint Martin de la Garrigue, 34530 Montagnac, tel. 04.67.24.00.40, fax 04.67.24.16.15 ☑
☤ ev. day 8am–12 noon 1.30pm–5.30pm; Sat. Sun. by appt.
🍇 Guida

CH. DE SAINT-SERIES 2001★

| ■ | 11 ha | 60,000 | ◗▯ | 8–11 € |

The Roux Père et Fils domaine, a property of 65 ha in Burgundy, has been in business in Languedoc since 1998. The vineyard extends over limestone terraces. Here, undeniably,

the terroir gives full expression to its character in this wine: superb dark garnet colour; nose of spices, leather, tobacco; powerful palate, generous, peppery and vanilla length. All will unfold over the next few years.

🍇 Ch. de Saint-Sériès, 34400 Saint-Sériès, tel. 03.80.21.32.92, fax 03.80.21.35.00, e-mail roux.pere.et.fils@wanadoo.fr ☑
☤ by appt.
🍇 Roux Père et Fils

DOM. DE SERRES CABANIS
Bos de Canna 2001★★

| ■ | 3.47 ha | 12,000 | ▮ ◗▯ ♦ | 8–11 € |

The Jury was won over by the intense and complex aromas of garrigue and stewed prunes, which proudly announced the origins of this wine. The velvety appearance, continued to resound on the full, complex palate; everything is of the utmost finesse, heightened by sweet cinnamon spices. Ready to drink now. The rather more discreet **Cuvée Classique red 2001 (5–8 €)** receives a star.

🍇 André Baniol, chem. de la Pinède, 30260 Vic-le-Fesq, tel. 06.11.50.97.39, fax 04.66.77.93.15

LES SOULS 2001★★★

| ■ | 1 ha | 1,200 | ▮ ◗▯ | 23–30 € |

A real find, this year, the domaine nestling in an amphitheatre, at an altitude of 350 m, on the outskirts of Larzac. Strength from start to finish. Deep purple appearance; intense aromas, (cherry and blackcurrant jam, spices, balsamic notes); full-bodied, well-structured palate. A true thoroughbred, not lacking in refinement. But, don't delay, as there is very little available of this particular *cuvée*.

🍇 Roland Alméras, rue des Fontaines, 34800 Salasc, tel. 04.67.44.21.56, e-mail galmeras@tele2.fr ☑
☤ by appt.

CH. TAURUS-MONTEL Pic Saint-Loup
Prestige Elevé en fût de chêne 2001★★

| ■ | 1 ha | 3,000 | ◗▯ | 11–15 € |

This *cuvée* is made up from vines located in the village of Corconne, on gravel soil. The nose exhibits incredible complexity: hints of cherry, dark fruits, leather, menthol and garrigue. The start is straightforward, clean, with a touch leisurely suppleness. A light-textured wine, with subtle balance.

🍇 SCEA Ch. Montel, 1, rue du Devès, 34820 Teyran, tel. 04.67.70.20.32, fax 04.67.70.92.03, e-mail contact@chateau-montel.com ☑
☤ by appt.

DOM. DE TERRE MEGERE
Les Dolomies 2001★

| ■ | 4 ha | 16,000 | ▮ ♦ | 8–11 € |

Be it the **La Galopine white 2001 (11–15 €)** or these Dolomies, the star is well and truly deserved. First impressions focus on the deep purple colour, then the sheer character of a nose that boldly combines aromas of Morello cherry, cocoa, resin and spices. The roundness was admired, as were the well-integrated tannins. A fine expression of Grès de Montpellier terroir.

🍇 Michel Moreau, Dom. de Terre Mégère, Coeur de Village, 34660 Cournonsec, tel. 04.67.85.42.85, fax 04.67.85.25.12, e-mail terremegere@wanadoo.fr ☑
☤ ev. day except Sun. 3pm–7pm; Sat. 9am–12.30pm

CH. LE THOU
Georges et Clem 2001★

| ■ | 12.5 ha | 65,000 | ▮ ◗▯ | 11–15 € |

This *cuvée* of character pays tribute to the competitive sportsmen, from whom this *cuvée*'s name derives. The deep-coloured, almost black appearance with violet highlights, offers a foretaste of the wine that awaits you: strength and suppleness. After initial impressions of a somewhat restrained nose, the complexity unfolds across a spectrum of stewed fruits and black pepper. Dominant, yet expressive tannins provide good backup for the rounded start and

bestow fine balance upon this wine. Ideal with a *gardianne de taureau* (traditional beef casserole from the Camargue).
☛ SCEA Ch. Le Thou, 34410 Sauvian, tel. 04.67.32.16.42, fax 04.67.32.16.42 ☑
☿ by appt.
☛ Damitio

DOM. DE LA TOUR PENEDESSES
Clos de Magrignan Montée des Schistes 2001★

■	2 ha	6,500	◫	15–23 €

Oenologist in Champagne and a lecturer at the wine university of Suze-la-Rousse, Alexandre Fouque realized his dream in 2000: he became a *vigneron*. He chose Gabian, 1 km from Cassan Priory and a vineyard stocked with twenty-three year old vines. His deep red coloured 2001, with violet tinges, offers an intense, rich nose of leather, garrigue and liquorice. Of remarkable youth, concentrated, this *cuvée* would benefit from being laid down, so that the prominent oakiness has a chance to mellow.
☛ Dom. de La Tour Penedesses, rte de Fouzilhon, 34320 Gabian, tel. 04.67.24.14.41, fax 04.67.24.14.22, e-mail domainedelatourpenedesses@yahoo.fr ☑
☛ Fouque

DOM. DES TREMIERES
Longueur de temps 2001★

■	0.7 ha	2,000	■◫♨	11–15 €

This domaine makes a fine entry in the *Guide* with its velvet, black-garnet coloured wine. The nose has a range of aromas: dried fruits, grilled meats and spices. Then, we have the unleashing of the equally close-knit tannins; this wine fills the mouth; good length. As its name suggests, the *cuvée* will hang on for a while: limited availability.
☛ Bernadette et Alain Rouquette, Dom. des Tremières, 34800 Nébian, tel. 04.67.96.38.05, fax 04.67.96.34.83 ☑
☿ by appt.

CH. DE VALCYRE BENEZECH
Pic Saint-Loup Elevé en fût de chêne 1999★

■	6 ha	n.c.	◫	11–15 €

Since 1995, the domaine has gradually gained increasing recognition, thanks to the efforts of Jacques Gorlier. This *cuvée* aged in oak offers a very pleasant nose, with hints of Morello cherry, clove and liquorice. The palate develops with soft tannins; a wine to be enjoyed straightaway, with beef casserole.
☛ SARL Benezech-Gaffinel, Ch. de Valcyre, 34270 Valflaunès, tel. 04.67.55.28.99, fax 04.67.55.28.99 ☑
☿ by appt.

CH. DE VALFLAUNES
Pic Saint-Loup Hardiesse 2001★

■	2.5 ha	9,400	■◫♨	15–23 €

Established in Valflaunès, home to the famous Grottes de l'Hortus, with evidence of Neanderthal man, Fabien Reboul produces wines to whose charms no one is immune! Aged in oak for fourteen months, this Hardiesse *cuvée* appears young and dark-coloured. The powerful nose exudes black, crushed olives, sweet Viennese breads and fig jam. The palate is supple, velvety, the epitome of delicacy, right up to smooth and luscious finish. Possesses all the fine qualities of a good Mediterranean wine. The **Cuvée Un Peu de Toi red 2001** (eighteen months in oak barrels) also achieves a star and should be aged, in the cellar, for three years.
☛ Ch. de Valflaunès, rue de l'Ancien-Lavoir, 34270 Valflaunès, tel. 04.67.55.76.30, fax 04.67.55.76.30
☿ by appt.
☛ Fabien Reboul

CH. VALOUSSIERE
Elevé en fût de chêne 2000★

■	n.c.	30,000	◫	5–8 €

Here we are, in the wilderness of Aumelas, in the heart of the garrigue, where we come across this large vineyard, with its fine barrel stores, the source of this *cuvée*. A winning formula of oak barrels, terroir and success: ruby-coloured, sweet,

spicy nose, garrigue and liquorice; a well-balanced palate, rich and supple. The pleasure is immediate.
☛ Philippe et Frédéric Jeanjean, Mas de Lunès, Cabrials, 34230 Aumelas, tel. 04.67.88.41.34, fax 04.67.88.41.33

CH. LA VERNEDE
Cuvée Cécilia Elevé en fût de chêne 2001★

■	1 ha	3,000	◫	15–23 €

The site of Vernède, near the hillside fort of Ensérune, was a wine-growing domaine, in Roman times. The exposed, south and southeast facing, clay-limestone hillsides lend this *cuvée* warmth of palate. At first glance, this 2001 brilliant red-coloured wine exhibits a discreet bouquet that combines flavours of Oriental incense, rose-water and spices. Elegance and finesse, as well as a touch of maturation in oak barrels, add up to a wine that is ready to drink with a dish of grilled lamb and herbs, from the publication date of the *Guide* onwards.
☛ Jean-Marc Ribet, GFA De La Vernède, Ch. de La Vernède, 34440 Nissan-lez-Ensérune, tel. 04.67.37.00.30, fax 04.67.37.60.11, e-mail chateaulavernede@infonie.fr ☑
☿ ev. day 9am–1pm 3pm–7pm

Wines selected but not starred

CUVEE JACQUES ARNAL
Elevé en fût de chêne 2000

■	3.5 ha	18,600	◫	8–11 €

☛ SCA Vignerons de Saint-Félix, 21, av. Marcelin-Albert, 34725 Saint-Félix-de-Lodez, tel. 04.67.96.60.61, fax 04.67.88.61.77 ☑
☿ by appt.

DOM. BEAUSEJOUR SAINT-ESPRIT
2001

■	2 ha	10,000	◫	5–8 €

☛ SCEA André Marc, chem. rural 145, 34500 Béziers, tel. 04.67.76.17.71, fax 04.67.76.17.71, e-mail dom.beausejour.st.esprit@wanadoo.fr ☑
☿ by appt.

CHEMIN DE L'ETANG
Picpoul de Pinet 2002

■	16 ha	82,000	■♨	3–5 €

☛ Alliance des Vins Fins, chem. de la Planque, 34800 Ceyras, tel. 04.67.44.90.50, fax 04.67.44.90.51, e-mail vsb.vins@wanadoo.fr

DOM. COUR SAINT VINCENT 2001

■	3 ha	5,000	■♨	5–8 €

☛ Francis Bouys, 1, pl. Saint-Vincent, 34730 Saint-Vincent-de-Barbeyrargues, tel. 04.67.59.60.74, fax 04.99.62.02.06 ☑
☿ by appt.

DIVEM 2000

■	0.55 ha	1,995	◫	23–30 €

☛ Anne Woisard et Gil Morrot, 21, rue des Lions, 34150 Montpeyroux, tel. 04.99.61.22.29 ☑

DOM. LA GRANGETTE
Picpoul de Pinet L'Enfant terrible 2002

| | 5 ha | 8,000 | ■ ↓ | | 3–5 € |

↤ SCEA La Grangette Sainte Rose,
34120 Castelnau-de-Guers, tel. 04.67.98.13.56,
fax 04.67.90.79.36, e-mail michel_moret@yahoo.fr Ⓥ
Ⴕ by appt.
↤ M. et Mme Moret

DOM. HAUT-LIROU
Pic Saint-Loup 2002

| | 2.5 ha | 10,000 | ■ | | 8–11 € |

↤ Rambier, 34270 Saint-Jean-de-Cuculles,
tel. 04.67.55.38.50, fax 04.67.55.38.49,
e-mail domainehaut-lirou@mnet.fr Ⓥ
Ⴕ ev. day except Sun 9am–12.30pm 2pm–6.30pm

CH. LANGLADE
Prestige 2001

| | 1.5 ha | 4,200 | | | 5–8 € |

↤ Ch. Langlade, Cadene Frères, 30980 Langlade,
tel. 04.66.81.30.22, fax 04.67.59.14.50 Ⓥ
Ⴕ by appt.

CH. DE LASCOURS
Pic Saint-Loup L'Ambroisie 2000

| | n.c. | 13,000 | ⑪ | | 8–11 € |

↤ Claude Arlès, Ch. de Lascours, 34270 Sauteyrargues,
tel. 04.67.59.00.58, fax 04.67.59.00.58 Ⓥ ⌂
Ⴕ by appt.

LE LOUP DU PIC
Pic Saint-Loup 2000

| | n.c. | 20,000 | ⑪ | | 8–11 € |

↤ Les Domaines Bru, rte de Teyran, 34160 Saint-Drézéry,
tel. 04.67.86.93.70, fax 04.67.86.94.07 Ⓥ
Ⴕ by appt.

CH. DE MARMORIERES
La Clape 2002

| | 6 ha | 10,000 | ■ ↓ | | 3–5 € |

↤ De Woillemont, Ch. de Marmorières, 11110 Vinassan,
tel. 04.68.45.23.64, fax 04.68.45.59.39,
e-mail marmorières@free.fr Ⓥ
Ⴕ by appt.

MAS BRUNET
Cuvée Prestige Elevé en fût de chêne 2000

| | 1.93 ha | 10,800 | ⑪ | | 8–11 € |

↤ GAEC du Dom. de Brunet, 34380 Causse-de-la-Selle,
tel. 04.67.73.10.57, fax 04.67.73.12.89 Ⓥ
Ⴕ by appt.
↤ Coulet

MAS DOMERGUE
Cuvée de l'Espérance 2001

| | 1.1 ha | 5,000 | ■ ↓ | | 5–8 € |

↤ Olivier Bouis, 12, rue des Aires, 34160 Sussargues,
tel. 04.67.86.61.06, fax 04.67.86.61.06 Ⓥ
Ⴕ Sat. 8am–12 noon 2pm–7pm

LES CAVES MOLIERE
Mirondela dels Arts 2000

| | 25 ha | 10,000 | ■ ⑪ | | 5–8 € |

↤ Les Caves Molière, BP 69, 34120 Caux-Pézenas,
tel. 04.67.98.10.05, fax 04.67.98.35.44 Ⓥ
Ⴕ by appt.

CH. NOTRE-DAME DU QUATOURZE
Nautica 2001

| | 1 ha | 5,800 | ■ ↓ | | 5–8 € |

↤ SCEA Dom. Georges Ortola, Ch. Notre-Dame du
Quatourze, 11100 Narbonne, tel. 04.68.41.58.92,
fax 04.68.42.41.88 Ⓥ
Ⴕ by appt.

L'ORMARINE
Picpoul de Pinet Cuvée Prestige 2002

| | n.c. | 45,000 | ■ | | 3–5 € |

↤ Cave L'Ormarine, 1, av. du Picpoul, 34850 Pinet,
tel. 04.67.77.03.10, fax 04.67.77.76.23,
e-mail ormarine@mnet.fr Ⓥ
Ⴕ ev. day 8am–12 noon 2pm–6pm

DOM. PUECH
Les Grands Devois 2001

| | 3 ha | 6,000 | ■ ↓ | | 5–8 € |

↤ GAEC Dom. Puech, 25, rue du Four,
34980 Saint-Clément-de-Rivière, tel. 04.67.84.12.31,
fax 04.67.66.63.16 Ⓥ
Ⴕ by appt.

SAINT DAUMARY
Pic Saint-Loup Sortilège 2000

| | 2.3 ha | 5,000 | ■ ⑪ ↓ | | 11–15 € |

↤ Julien Chapel, rue des Micolouliers, 34270 Valflaunès,
tel. 04.67.55.21.94, fax 04.67.55.21.94 Ⓥ

DOM. SAINTE MARTHE 2001

| | 9.8 ha | 40,000 | ■ | | 5–8 € |

↤ Cave coopérative La Carignano Gabian, 13, rte de
Pouzolles, 34320 Gabian, tel. 04.67.24.65.64,
fax 04.67.24.80.98 Ⓥ

DOM. DES VIGNES HAUTES
Pic Saint-Loup 2001

| | 5 ha | 15,000 | ⑪ | | 11–15 € |

↤ SCA Cave La Gravette, 30260 Corconne,
tel. 04.66.77.32.75, fax 04.66.77.13.56,
e-mail cavelagravette@wanadoo.fr Ⓥ
Ⴕ by appt.

Faugères

The wines from Faugères have been AOC since 1982, as have those of its neighbour, Saint-Chinian. The region of production covers seven communes north of Pézenas and Béziers and south of Bédarieux, and produced 72,494 hl of wine from 1,872 ha in 2002. The vineyards are planted quite high – 250 m – on steeply sloping hillsides situated on the lower, poorly fertile, schist outcrops of the Cévennes. Faugères is a heady wine with a good purple colour and characteristic perfumes of the garrigue and summer fruits.

ABBAYE SYLVA PLANA
Songe de l'abbé 2000★★

| | 6 ha | 20,000 | ■ ⑪ | | 11–15 € |

This abbot's *Songe* (dream) became a marvellous reality, far removed from the austerity advocated by the Cistercian founders of the abbey, back in 1139. The Jury rated highly this vintage, with its intense aromas of garrigue, smoke and dark fruits. One has the impression that both vinification and maturation, under the guidance of Cédric Guy and Nicolas Bouchard, are of the highest standards. Balance, careful structure; an orderly wine. The **La Closeraie de l'Abbaye 2001 red (8–11 €)** favourably impressed the tasters.

☛ SCEA Bouchard-Guy, 3, rue de Fraisse, 34290 Alignan-du-Vent, tel. 04.67.24.91.67, fax 04.67.24.94.21, e-mail info@vignoblesbouchard.com **☑**
𝖸 ev. day 8am–12 noon 2pm–7pm

DOM. DE L'ANCIENNE MERCERIE

Cuvée Couture 2001★★

■	5 ha	5,000	■ ⑪ ♨	11–15 €

Following a *coup de coeur* for the 2000 vintage, this domaine has excelled itself, once again, with its Cuvée Couture. A fine tribute to the grandmother whose haberdashery shop has since been converted to a wine cellar. The *cuvée* is of a particularly dark appearance; the nose, as yet, immature, but nevertheless, of fine concentration. A superb start enables one to appreciate fully the tannic finesse and aromatic complexity that persist, throughout the tasting. Still relatively young, this is a rich wine, to be laid down.

☛ Nathalie et François Caumette, 6, rue de l'Egalité, 34480 Autignac, tel. 04.67.90.27.02, fax 04.67.90.27.02 **☑**
𝖸 by appt.

CUVEE CECILIA

Vieilli en fût de chêne 2000★

■	20 ha	30,000	⑪	5–8 €

Two wines, a star each, for this négociant: one for the **Domaine de Fenouillet red 2001**, vinified by wine merchant, Jeanjean. The other for this **Cuvée Cécilia**, where the strictly controlled maturation of this 2000 gives elegant expression to its terroir, with hints of mineral, smoke and grilled meats. Despite the severe start, the palate exhibits aromatic length. Clearly, a wine to lay down.

☛ SA Jeanjean, BP 1, 34725 Saint-Félix-de-Lodez, tel. 04.67.88.80.00, fax 04.67.96.65.67

CH. DES ESTANILLES

Cuvée Prestige 2001★★

■	18 ha	50,000	■ ⑪ ♨	8–11 €

The Louisons have certainly not damaged their reputation with this Cuvée Prestige and a **Château des Estanilles Coteaux du Languedoc white 2001**, of the utmost finesse, which receives a star. This Faugères has a purple appearance and offers flavours of dark fruits, spices and smoke. It continues to unfold throughout the tasting. The palate exhibits tannins that require further maturation. However, the power and length indicate an exceptionally promising wine.

☛ Michel Louison, Ch. des Estanilles, 34480 Cabrerolles, tel. 04.67.90.29.25, fax 04.67.90.10.99 **☑**
𝖸 by appt.

DOM. DU FRAISSE 2002★★

■	4.5 ha	22,000	■	5–8 €

For over 30 years, the Pons family has played an active rôle in establishing the fine reputation of this AOC. Their vast domaine (45 ha) is planted on part shale, part marine fossil clay-limestone terroir. This luminous, intense-coloured rosé is showy and elegant, with aromas of soft fruits. A fleshy start is followed by fullness and refreshing graciousness, with fruity flavours that linger to the finish.

☛ Jacques Pons, 1 bis, rue du chemin de Ronde, 34480 Autignac, tel. 04.67.90.23.40, fax 04.67.90.10.20, e-mail domfraisse@aol.com **☑**
𝖸 by appt.

CH. GREZAN

Cuvée Arnaud Lubac 2001★

■	11 ha	40,000	⑪	5–8 €

A vast property of 110 ha, Grézan was once a Roman villa, before being converted to a command-post, in the 12th century. Considerably modified in the 19th century, Grézan is still impressive, with its fortifications. Two *cuvées* received a star each, in the Faugères category: **Les Schistes Dorés red 2001 (15–23 €)** and this wine, both derived from shale

terroir. Roasted overtones and hints of soft fruits, accompany fine, elegant tannins and a fleshy appearance. Wines to uncork among friends, with small game or in the Château's restaurant.

☛ Ch. Grézan, D 909, 34480 Laurens, tel. 04.67.90.27.46, fax 04.67.90.29.01, e-mail chateau-grezan@wanadoo.fr **☑**
𝖸 ev. day 9.30am–12 noon 2pm–6.30pm; Sun. 2pm–6.30pm

HECHT & BANNIER 2001★★

■	n.c.	n.c.	■ ⑪	15–23 €

The 2001 is *négociant-éleveur*, H & B's first vintage. The merchant who matures Languedoc-Roussillon AOC wines has selected this highly promising *cuvée*: first impressions exude charm. Concentration and bouquet: dark fruits, hints of toasted bread and garrigue herald a pleasant wine destined for the cellar. The **H & B Coteaux du Languedoc red 2001** selection achieved a star. A new enterprise to keep an eye on.

☛ H & B Sélection, 42, Grand Rue, 34140 Bouzigues, tel. 04.67.74.66.38, fax 04.67.74.66.45, e-mail contact@hbselection.com **☑**

CH. DE LA LIQUIERE

Cistus 2001★★

■	7 ha	25,000	⑪	11–15 €

A passion handed down from father to son or daughter. A terroir that retains its youth. A typicity to which one cannot remain indifferent. At last, a star for the **Vieilles Vignes 2001 red (8–11 €)** and two for this great wine, named Cistus. Very good reasons for visiting the domaine. Be patient, allow the complexity of this *cuvée* to unfold in due course (five to eight years). This wine fills the mouth with its generosity and emphasis on fine, mature tannins and skilful maturation in barrels; leaves a lingering impression of freshness and roundness. An abundance of charm.

☛ Ch. de La Liquière, La Liquière, 34480 Cabrerolles, tel. 04.67.90.29.20, fax 04.67.90.10.00, e-mail bvidal@terre-net.fr **☑**
𝖸 by appt.
☛ Vidal-Dumoulin

MAS DES CAPITELLES

Vieilles Vignes 2001★

■	3.3 ha	13,000	■ ⑪	5–8 €

Enchanted, one taster claimed that this is a "very Faugères" wine. Sporting deep purple hues, this 2001 exhibits a fine, complex nose, with hints of smoke and garrigue. A pleasant palate is based on good balance between alcohol and acidity. Spices and different types of juniper create a pleasant bouquet. Sheer finesse, this wine is ready to drink, from now on, with a haunch of wild boar.

☛ Mas des Capitelles, rte de Pézenas, 34600 Faugères, tel. 04.67.23.10.20, fax 04.67.95.78.32 **☑**
𝖸 by appt.

MAS GABINELE 2001★★★

■	7.5 ha	20,000	⑪	15–23 €

In charge since 1997, Thierry Rodriguez joins the family of great Faugères with his 2001 vintage. Seduced by the powerful, yet subtle, fine, elegant nose, with hints of chocolate and spices, mingling with dark fruits, the Grand Jury was

LANGUEDOC

unanimous in its decision to award a *coup de coeur*. Exquisite balance, the palate exudes roundness, fine well-integrated and supple tannins; excellent length. The *cuvée* gives perfect expression to the characteristics of its terroir; a superb wine to uncork in two to four years' time.

➤ Thierry Rodriguez, Hameau de Veyran,
34490 Causses-et-Veyran, tel. 04.67.89.71.72,
fax 04.67.89.70.69, e-mail throdriguez@wanadoo.fr ☑
☿ by appt.

DOM. DU METEORE
Réserve Elevé en fût de chêne 2001★

■	4 ha	12,000	◫	8–11 €

A vine planted at the bottom of a crater (220 m diameter and 60 m deep) is yet another curiosity to be found at the Météore domaine. Maturation in oak, for 16 months, has not erased the typicity of the terroir. A bouquet of toasted bread, smoke, spice with a hint of liquorice accompany this highly promising wine, which ought to be laid down, in the cellar, for two or three years before being drunk with large game.

➤ Geneviève Libes, Dom. du Météore, 34480 Cabrerolles,
tel. 04.67.90.21.12, fax 04.67.90.11.92,
e-mail domainedumeteore@wanadoo.fr ☑
☿ ev. day 9.30am–12 noon 3pm–7pm; winter by appt.

MOULIN DE CIFFRE 2001★★

■	5 ha	25,000	◫	8–11 €

In charge of the Moulin de Ciffre since 1998, the Lésineau family came from Pessac-Léognan in Bordelais and have been rapidly adopted into Languedoc. Two stars for this 2001 and one for the **Cuvée Eole 2001 red (11–15 €)**, as well as a commendation for the **Saint Chinian red 2001 (8–11 €)**. All these wines are true to type. This wine offers an explosive nose of fruits and nuts, spices and very ripe, soft fruits. Following a fresh start, the balanced, expressive palate reveals rich, fine, intense body.

➤ Lésineau, SARL Ch. Moulin de Ciffre, 34480 Autignac,
tel. 04.67.90.11.45, fax 04.67.90.12.05,
e-mail info@moulindeciffre.com ☑
☿ by appt.

DOM. OLLIER-TAILLEFER
Castel Fossibus 2001★

■	3 ha	12,000	◫	8–11 €

Françoise returned to work on the domaine with her brother Luc, having been away for eleven years, as director of the Syndicat du Cru. The **Grande Réserve red 2001** was singled out, as was the Castel Fossibus, which notched up a star. Deep red colour, this Faugères mingles flavours of soft, ripe fruits, spices and toasted bread. The wine has plenty of depth, richness and density and develops, remarkably, right up to the lingering finish. The fullness is substantial: needs to be laid down for a year.

➤ Alain Ollier Fils et Fille, rte de Gabian, 34320 Fos,
tel. 04.67.90.24.59, fax 04.67.90.12.15,
e-mail ollier.taillefer@wanadoo.fr ☑
☿ by appt.

DOM. DES PRES-LASSES
Le Castel Viel 2000★

■	7.5 ha	10,000	◫	11–15 €

A fine entry in the *Guide* for these gentlemen, established in Faugères since 1999; they talk about long-term viticulture. Carignan (40%) lends this wine a substantial structure, well patinated by maturation in oak barrels. This 2000, with its glorious purple appearance, gradually unfolds its typical Faugères characteristics (grilled overtones, smoke, mineral). A definite "must" for laying down.

➤ Feigel et Ribeton, 5, rue de L'Amour, 34480 Autignac,
tel. 04.67.90.21.19, fax 04.67.90.21.19 ☑
☿ by appt.

DOM. DE LA REYNARDIERE
Cuvée Prestige 2001★

■	6.8 ha	8,000	▮ ♦	5–8 €

In a medieval village with ramparts, where the church and the château were renovated in the 14th century, this domaine has nominated the Cuvée Prestige and a **Faugères rosé 2002**, which

also receives a star. This 2001, with a deep red-coloured appearance, releases floral fragrances and hints of mineral and liquorice. Powerful and classy, the palate offers fine balance and aromatic length that last for several seconds. Altogether, very elegant.

➤ Dom. de la Reynardière, 7, cours Jean-Moulin,
34480 Saint-Geniès-de-Fontedit, tel. 04.67.36.25.75,
fax 04.67.36.15.80,
e-mail domaine.reynardiere@wanadoo.fr ☑
☿ ev. day except Sun. 10am–12 noon 2pm–7pm
➤ Mégé-Pons

DOM. DU ROUGE GORGE
Cuvée Privilège Elevé en fût de chêne 2000★★★

■	6 ha	30,000	◫	5–8 €

The vine is part of the very fabric of the Bordas existence; and of a family history that perpetuates a life of viticulture. They have put the terroir to good use with this blend of five Faugères grape varieties. Their efforts have been rewarded with this intense, elegant and full-bodied, red wine. The supple texture exhibits hints of ripe fruits, vanilla and liquorice that linger for several seconds. Keep this *cuvée* for the next three years, to accompany game.

➤ Alain Borda, Dom. Les Affanies, 34480 Magalas,
tel. 04.67.36.22.86, fax 04.67.36.61.24,
e-mail borda@terre-net.fr ☑
☿ ev. day 8am–12 noon 2pm–7pm

LE VIEUX FIGUIER 2000★

■	10 ha	58,000	◫	5–8 €

This Le Vieux Figuier *cuvée*, produced by the Laurens cooperative is the choice of the group known as the Vignerons et Passions. Vinified from whole grapes that have undergone a rigorous selection process, the wine is composed of Syrah (60%), Grenache, Carignan (20%) and Mourvèdre. The intense, red colour heralds fruity and grilled overtones. Well-constructed, round, velvety, this vintage still has an oaky taste, due to maturation in oak barrels for 16 months. Tannins, however, are fleshy and should make this wine ready for serving in January 2004.

➤ Vignerons et Passions, BP 1,
34725 Saint-Félix-de-Lodez, tel. 04.67.88.45.75,
fax 04.67.88.45.79, e-mail caveau@vignerons-passions.fr ☑
☿ ev. day except Sun. 10am–12.30pm 1.30pm–6pm

Wines selected but not starred

CH. DES ADOUZES 2002

■	7 ha	26,000	▮ ♦	5–8 €

➤ Jean-Claude Estève, Tras du Castel, 34320 Roquessels,
tel. 04.67.90.24.11, fax 04.67.90.12.74 ☑
☿ by appt.

CH. HAUT-FABREGUES
Cuvée Gaëlle 2000

■	n.c.	n.c.	◫	15–23 €

➤ Saur et Fils, Ch. Haut-Fabrègues, 34480 Cabrerolles,
tel. 04.67.90.28.67, fax 04.67.90.11.17 ☑
☿ by appt.

CH. HAUT LIGNIERES
Romy 2000

■	5 ha	18,000	◫	8–11 €

➤ Elke Kreutzfeldt, lieu-dit Bel-Air, 34600 Faugères,
tel. 04.67.95.38.27, fax 04.67.95.78.51,
e-mail chateau@haut-lignieres.com ☑
☿ by appt.

CH. DES PEYREGRANDES 2002

■	1.5 ha	3,000	◫	3–5 €

❧ SCEA Dom. Bénézech-Boudal, chem. de l'Aire,
34320 Roquessels, tel. 04.67.90.15.00, fax 04.67.90.15.60,
e-mail chateau-des-peyregrandes@wanadoo.fr ✓
⟁ by appt.
❧ Marie Boudal

CH. DE SAUVANES 2001

■	3.5 ha	16,000	■	5–8 €

❧ SCEA Ch. de Sauvanes, 9, av. de la Gare, 34480 Laurens,
tel. 04.67.88.45.75, fax 04.67.88.45.79 ✓
⟁ ev. day except Sun. 10am–12.30pm 1.30pm–6pm

Fitou

The Appellation Fitou, the
oldest AOC for a red wine in Languedoc and
Roussillon (1948), is to be found in the Mediterranean
part of the Corbières region. It covers nine communes,
which are also authorized to produced Vin Doux
Naturel Rivesaltes and Muscat Rivesaltes. In 2002
92,200 hl were produced. The wine is a beautiful deep
ruby colour and has 12% of alcohol; maturation in
casks takes a minimum of nine months.

DOM. BERTRAND BERGE

Cuvée Jean Sirven 2001★★★

■	2 ha	3,000	◫	23–30 €

Coup de coeurs for both the 2000 and 99 vintages, once again
here we have the same *cuvée* topping the bill. Don't change
anything! Moreover, the **Fitou Cuvée Ancestrale 2001 (5–8 €)**
and the **Mégalithes 2001 (8–11 €)** clinch two stars. Deep,
intense colour, this Cuvée Jean Sirven, after swirling, delivers
a bouquet that mingles aromas of undergrowth, violet, blackberry and blackcurrant. The greatest pleasure is reserved for
the palate; this wine has a surprising capacity to fill the mouth
and deliver tannic balance, with fine texture and aromas of
sweetly spiced crystallized fruits and a liquorice finish. The
wine is pleasant now, but will also keep.
❧ Dom. Bertrand-Bergé, av. du Roussillon, 11350 Paziols,
tel. 04.68.45.41.73, fax 04.68.45.41.73,
e-mail bertrand-berge@wanadoo.fr ✓
⟁ ev. day 9am–12 noon 2pm–7pm

DAME DE CEZELLY

Elevé en fût de chêne 2001★

■	n.c.	n.c.	◫	11–15 €

The statue of Françoise de Cezelly graces the marketplace of
Leucate. Following the assassination of her husband, the
town governor, towards the end of the Religious wars of
Henri IV, Françoise was honoured with the keys to the city.
Nobody knows exactly whether she went up on to the plateau
overlooking the cliff to listen to the sound of the waves, but
one thing is certain, that this area was popular for strolling

amid the vines, fig trees, almond trees. It was the Dame de
Cezelly who gave her name to this wine, with pronounced
oaked overtones. Careful maturation has bestowed upon this
cuvée charred hints of vanilla and coffee that merge, to our
utter delight, with fullness, cherry flavours and velvety
tannins, characteristic of the Grenache, Carignan and
Mourvèdre grape varieties.
❧ Cave coop. de Leucate et Quintillan, 2, av. Francis-Vals,
11370 Leucate, tel. 04.68.40.01.31, fax 04.68.40.08.90,
e-mail cave-leucate@wanadoo.fr ✓
⟁ ev. day 9am–1pm 2pm–6pm

CH. DES ERLES 2001★★★

■	40 ha	8,000	◫	23–30 €

The Lurton family was delighted to find this "Fitounie",
amid the shale soils of the Hauts Cantons. The terroir of this
beautiful, rugged landscape has succeeded in yielding a wine
with broad appeal and worldwide distribution potential. This
Fitou, with its intense crimson-red appearance and soft
richness, exudes charred flavours of very ripe fruits and
spices. The palate reveals a power and amazing weight, with
hints of preserved fruit and prominent, yet fine-textured
tannins. A liquorice finish concludes the tasting of this wine
that will achieve its full potential in two to three years time.
Game with cep mushroom dishes will show the *cuvée* off to
best advantage.
❧ SA Jacques et François Lurton, Dom. de Poumeyrade,
33870 Vayres, tel. 05.57.55.12.12, fax 05.57.55.12.13,
e-mail jflurton@jflurton.com

DOM. LERYS

Cuvée Prestige 2001★

■	n.c.	22,500	■ ♦	5–8 €

Villeneuve possesses that indefinable charm associated with
very old, traditional, countryside villages, with its straggling
houses that seem to be listening to each other. Faithful to
its regular rendez-vous with the *Guide*, the Lerys domaine
nominates a wine with hints of very ripe, dark fruits, a touch
of cherry and warm shale mineral flavours. A velvety palate,
rounded and dense colludes with blackcurrants and an
intense tannic, well-structured finish.
❧ EARL Costo Soulano, av. des Hautes-Corbières,
11360 Villeneuve-les-Corbières, tel. 04.68.45.95.47,
fax 04.68.45.86.11, e-mail domlerys@aol.com ✓ ⌂
⟁ by appt.
❧ M. et A. Izard

DOM. MARIA FITA 2001★

■	5 ha	17,000	■ ♦	15–23 €

"Fita" marks the district boundary that gave Fitou its name.
This Maria Fita represents a first vintage in this appellation.
A powerful and carefully researched wine, judging by the very
intense colour, overtones of ripe fruits, verging on leather and
undergrowth. First, violet, on the palate; then one discerns
ripe fruit flavours and tannic structure; all of which indicate
that this is a wine to lay down. After such a fine start, this
domaine is one to watch.
❧ Dom. Maria Fita, 12, rue du Pont-Neuf,
11360 Villeneuve-les-Corbières, tel. 04.68.45.86.12,
fax 04.68.45.86.12 ✓

DOM. MAYNADIER

Elevé en fût de chêne 2001★★

■	3 ha	10,000	◫	5–8 €

In times past, stagecoaches used to travel across this narrow
plain, between hills and coastal lagoon; this domaine was
once a coaching inn. Today, it nominates a traditional Fitou:
aromas of garrigue, with undertones of wild fruit, an expression of ripe fruits unfolds, that develops into flavours of
game, within a substantial overall structure. A wine that fills
the mouth and would make a fine accompaniment for game
and grilled meats.
❧ GAEC Maynadier, RN 9, 11510 Fitou,
tel. 04.68.45.63.11, fax 04.68.45.60.94 ✓
⟁ by appt.

DOM. DE LA ROCHELIERRE
Noblesse du temps 2001★★

| | 1 ha | 4,000 | ⑪ | 15–23 € |

Jean-Marie Fabre is a passionate man, as far as the vine is concerned; in other words, a true *vigneron* and well-respected oenologist. He matured this *cuvée* (and you have not heard the last of it!), in the cool environment of his wine cellar, built right next to Fitou limestone. Purple colour, a reserved nose, reveals finely spiced aromas of dark fruits (blackberry and blackcurrant). On the palate suppleness gives way to freshness; fruits to nuts and cinnamon, accompanied by full-bodied, supple tannins. Pleasant and balanced, this wine will be delicious in two years' time, served with small game, red meats or ripe, mature cheeses.
↖ Jean-Marie Fabre, 17, rue du Vigné, 11510 Fitou, tel. 04.68.45.70.52, fax 04.68.45.70.52 ☑
↧ ev. day 8am–1pm 2pm–7.30pm; cl. am 1 Nov.–1 Apr.

DOM. DE ROLLAND 2000★★

| | 22 ha | 11,000 | ☷ ⚬ | 11–15 € |

At the foot of Mont Tauch, nowadays surrounded by wind-pumps, Tuchan conceals within its alleyways a typical Louis Colomer-style wine cellar. Here we have a *vigneron* renowned for his outstanding performance on the export market: he currently sells 70% of his production abroad. This Domaine de Rolland is a wine in true Fitou tradition, with its dark appearance and bouquet dominated by ripe fruit and flavours of garrigue. Substantial, warming, robust, the *cuvée* evolves with overtones of fruit and spice. Although the wine is pleasant to drink now, its length guarantees its definite potential for laying down. Fully mature, this wine would go well with stews and red meats.
↖ EARL Colomer, imp. Saint-Roch, 11350 Tuchan, tel. 04.68.45.42.47, fax 04.68.45.49.50, e-mail earlcolomer@aol.com ☗
↧ by appt.

SEIGNEUR DE DON NEUVE 2001★★

| | n.c. | 140,000 | ☷ ⚬ | 5–8 € |

The impressive Tuchan wine cellar coordinates production of the neighbouring terroirs of Paziols and Villeneuve. It comes as no surprise, therefore, that the group's 2001 *cuvées* were honoured by the Jury. A relatively young **Prieuré du Château de Ségure 2001**, a **Hommage 2001 (8–11 €)** definitely with a promising future, and a **Domaine Saint-Roch 2001**; three oak aged wines. This Seigneur de Don Neuve, however, steals the show, with its ruby-red appearance. Carbonic maceration adds spiciness and hints of cloves, with undertones of liquorice. This well-balanced Fitou is ready to be served at table, straightaway; equally, it could be laid down.
↖ Les Producteurs du Mont Tauch, 11350 Tuchan, tel. 04.68.45.41.08, fax 04.68.45.45.29, e-mail contact@mont-tauch.com ☑
↧ ev. day except Sat. Sun. 9am–12 noon 2pm–7pm

Wines selected but not starred

LES MAITRES VIGNERONS DE CASCASTEL Carte or 2001

| | 60 ha | 150,000 | ☷ ⑪ ⚬ | 3–5 € |

↖ Les Maîtres Vignerons de Cascastel, Grand-Rue, 11360 Cascastel, tel. 04.68.45.91.74, fax 04.68.45.82.70, e-mail info@cascastel.com ☑
↧ ev. day. except Sat. Sun. 8am–12 noon 2pm–6pm

L'IMPOSSIBLE 2000

| | 15 ha | 33,330 | ⑪ | 5–8 € |

↖ Vignerons et Passions, BP 1, 34725 Saint-Félix-de-Lodez, tel. 04.67.88.45.75, fax 04.67.88.45.79, e-mail caveau@vignerons-passions.fr ☑
↧ ev. day except Sun. 10am–12.30pm 1.30pm–6pm

CH. DE NOUVELLES
Cuvée Gabrielle 2001

| | 10 ha | 9,000 | ⑪ | 11–15 € |

↖ SCEA R. Daurat-Fort, Ch. de Nouvelles, 11350 Tuchan, tel. 04.68.45.40.03, fax 04.68.45.49.21 ☑
↧ by appt.

SAINT-PANCRACE 2001

| | n.c. | 16,000 | ⑪ | 5–8 € |

↖ Cave coop. les Vignerons de La Palme, av. de la Mer, 11480 La Palme, tel. 04.68.48.15.17, fax 04.68.48.56.85 ☑
↧ by appt.

CH. WIALA
Elevé en fût de chêne 2001

| | 15.8 ha | 13,000 | ☷ ⑪ ⚬ | 8–11 € |

↖ SCEA Seubert, rue de la Gare, 11350 Tuchan, tel. 04.68.45.49.49, fax 04.68.45.49.49, e-mail chawiala@hotmail.com ☑
↧ ev. day 9am–12 noon 2pm–6pm

Minervois

Minervois is an AOC wine produced in 61 communes, 45 of which are in Aude and 16 in Hérault. This is a mainly limestone area of low hills with south-facing slopes, protected from the cold winds by the Montagne Noire. It produces white, rosé and red wines; the latter represent 95% of the production. In 2002 a total of 214,584 hl was produced in all three colours from an area of 5,081 ha.

The Minervois vineyard is crossed by many enchanting tourist routes; the local Route des Vins is a signposted itinerary that offers numerous opportunities to visit tasting cellars along the way. The chief tourist attractions of the area include a famous historical site in the ancient city of Minerve, a host of Romanesque chapels and interesting churches in Rieux and Caune. The local wine Confrérie or brotherhood, the Compagnons du Minervois, has its headquarters at Olonzac.

From now on, the commune of La Livinière is brought under the appellation Minervois la Livinière, comprising five communes. Production in 2002 was 8,287 hl from 227 ha.

CH. ARTIX
Terres brûlées 2001★

| | 20 ha | 80,000 | ⑪ | 3–5 € |

This flamboyant wine, the colour of glowing embers, matured in oak for at least 12 months, has scents of quince and blackcurrant, abundantly evident from the start; then, warming and lightly enveloped in toasty tannins. Elegant and lingering, closely packed, this Minervois reminds one of Jacques Brel: "It originates, it would appear, from scorched earth…"
↖ Jérôme Portal, Dom. d'Artix, 34210 Beaufort, tel. 04.68.91.28.28, fax 04.68.91.38.38 ☑
↧ by appt.

DOM. DE BARROUBIO

Cuvée Jean Miquel Vieilles Vignes 2000★

| | 1.5 ha | 5,000 | | 8–11 € |

Barroubio only produces sumptuous Muscats (see chapter on Vin Doux Naturels): this Minervois is sufficient proof thereof; cultivated against all odds, on the clay-limestone area of the vineyard. By dedicating the fruits of his soil to his father, Raymond Miquel has sweated blood and tears to vinify this soft-hearted wine, packed with soft fruits, notably crushed strawberries. Fresh, supple and elegant, the 2000 offers subtle finesse that simply demands appreciation from now on.

Raymond Miquel, Barroubio,
34360 Saint-Jean-de-Minervois, tel. 04.67.38.14.06,
fax 04.67.38.14.06
ev. day 10am–12 noon 2pm–6.30pm

DOM. BORIE DE MAUREL

Cuvée Sylla 2001★★★

| | 2.8 ha | 10,200 | | 15–23 € |

A complete triumph! Indeed, if this Cuvée Sylla is applauded for the umpteenth time, the **white 2002** comes within a hair's breadth of the supreme title, whilst the **Minervois la Livinière La Cuvée Féline 2001** is equally remarkable. Sylla is a consistently soft wine, exuding dark fruits and heady, melt-in-the-mouth flavours of truffle and liquorice. Thick, luscious, full-bodied richness, bursting with sunshine, the *cuvée* could play a winning hand with haute cuisine; alternatively, it could be enjoyed, on its own.

GAEC Michel Escande, Dom. Borie de Maurel,
34210 Félines-Minervois, tel. 04.68.91.68.58,
fax 04.68.91.63.92, e-mail boriedemaurel@wanadoo.fr
by appt.

LES HAUTS DE CHATEAU BORIE NEUVE 2000★

| | 1 ha | 2,000 | | 11–15 € |

Set up by the Marquis of Badens in the 18th century, Borie Neuve proudly boasts that the domaine has remained intact ever since. Today, the property nominates a purple-coloured wine, which enchanted the Jury with its aromas of grilled meats and crystallized fruits. Entrancing warmth, rich tannins emblazoned amidst spices. Complex, powerful, this 2000 catches one unawares with its flavours of prunes that merge on the finish.

SCEA Ch. Borie-Neuve, 11800 Badens,
tel. 04.68.79.28.62, fax 04.68.79.05.06,
e-mail contact@chateauborieneuve.com
by appt.

DOM. LE CAZAL

Le Pas de Zarat 2001★★

| | 8 ha | 26,000 | | 8–11 € |

Zarat was a fearless shepherd, prepared to risk his flock along a narrow, steep path on the precipitous slopes and escarpments of the domaine. This wine with ruby-red tinges, harvested at an altitude of 300m, is packed with flavours of garrigue, mingled with crystallized fruits. The palate is full-bodied, generous, constructed upon velvety tannins of cocoa and cinnamon. The expressive finish echoes with a

resoundingly powerful conclusion…Ready now, or could be laid down.

Claude et Martine Derroja, EARL Dom. Le Cazal,
34210 La Caunette, tel. 04.68.91.62.53, fax 04.68.91.62.53,
e-mail nicolas.rigal@free.fr
by appt.
Pierre Derroja

CH. COUPE ROSES

Cuvée Orience 2000★★

| | 14 ha | 10,000 | | 11–15 € |

Near the Cathar estate of Minerve, nestles La Caunette, a splendid troglodytic village. When you visit this unique location, take time out to visit this cellar. You will appreciate the **Frémillant rosé 2002** and you will fall under the spell of this *cuvée*, bursting with ripe fruit and spices that marry power with finesse, softness with concentration. The full-bodied tannins unfold their full richness, at the flavoursome, fleshy finish.

Françoise Frissant Le Calvez et Pascal Frissant, Ch. Coupe Roses, rue de la Poterie, 34210 La Caunette,
tel. 04.68.91.21.95, fax 04.68.91.11.73,
e-mail coupe-roses@wanadoo.fr
ev. day 8.30am–12.30pm 2pm–6pm; Sat. Sun. by appt.

DOM. CROS

Les Aspres 2001★★

| | 2 ha | 5,000 | | 15–23 € |

With this *cuvée*, derived from superb, sandstone terroir, subtractive vinification techniques become an irrelevance; no harvesting of unripe grapes and, despite the fact that Syrah produces low yields, the grapes are always ripe and of consistently high quality. Add to this a master *vigneron* who cossets his oak barrels and *voilà*, an intense wine that exudes soft fruits, jams, plums and cocoa. The ensemble develops substantial structure and balance, superseded by pleasant, vanilla tannins that give way to length and delicacy. Another fine achievement for Pierre Cros, for whom one has given up counting *coups de coeurs*…

Pierre Cros, 20, rue du Minervois, 11800 Badens,
tel. 04.68.79.21.82, fax 04.68.79.24.03
ev. day 8am–12 noon 2pm–7pm; groups by appt.

CH. DU DONJON

Cuvée Prestige Elevé en fût de chêne 2001★

| | 7 ha | 40,000 | | 8–11 € |

Owned, in olden days, by the monks of Caunes Abbey, the château has remained a family-owned property since the 15th century. Derived from the best *têtes de cuvée* grapes, the wine exhibits aromas of over-ripe soft fruit and smoke. Tannins are patinated by maturation, so as to deliver suppleness and balance to the palate. This Minervois symbolizes the marriage of rich vanilla and elegance. Ideal with roast joints and game

Jean Panis, Ch. du Donjon, 11600 Bagnoles,
tel. 04.68.77.18.33, fax 04.68.72.21.17,
e-mail jean.panis@wanadoo.fr
ev. day 9am–12 noon 2pm–7pm; Sat. Sun. by appt.

LE GRAND PENCHANT 2001★★

| | 2 ha | 5,500 | | 5–8 € |

A great-great-grandfather returning from Zanzibar set up a barrow-gravity-feed harvest reception system here, on this estate. His descendant, who prefers whole-grape vinification, has perfected this demanding process to produce a wine that is full-bodied, lively, and where crystallized cherries flirt with tightly packed dark berries. Of exceptional length, richness and fine origins, this vintage, with fruity, menthol overtones is, in every respect, truly remarkable.

Raymond Julien, Ch. Mirausse, 11800 Badens,
tel. 04.68.79.12.30, fax 04.68.79.12.30
by appt.

LAURAN CABARET 2002★

| | 8 ha | 40,000 | | 3–5 € |

Lauran Cabaret was a Cathar stronghold in the 18th century. The lords would have been proud of this wine, where a blend of Grenache-Marsanne-Roussanne ensures longevity and complexity. A floral bouquet and a panoply of soft fruits lead

LANGUEDOC

the dance upon a fresh, smooth structure. Rounded, warming, elegant, this 2002 is guaranteed not to let down shellfish or seafood dishes.

🍷 Cellier Lauran Cabaret, 11800 Laure-Minervois,
tel. 04.68.78.12.12, fax 04.68.78.17.34,
e-mail laurancabaret@hotmail.com 🆅
☕ ev. day except Sun. 8am–12 noon 2pm–6pm;
open Sun. Jul.–Aug

CH. MALVES-BOUSQUET 2001★

■	20 ha	80,000	■ ♦	5–8 €

When you arrive at the imposing portcullis of this château, two splendid English Setters announce your arrival. You will sample the **rosé 2002**, supple and easy to drink. Then linger over this scented red wine, with sweet spices and green pepper – an invitation to take a stroll in the garrigue – with its fruity overtones that give the impression of munching on soft, velvety peaches. An original, lingering wine. The motto of this domaine "let us limit our chatter and thus drink well" is not surprising, for conviviality does not exist without language!

🍷 SCEA Bousquet, Ch. de Malves,
11600 Malves-Minervois, tel. 04.68.72.25.32,
fax 04.68.72.25.00 🆅
☕ by appt.

LE MOULIN DES NONNES 2002★★

■	3 ha	11,000	⪾	5–8 €

Family-run, for four generations, this enterprise has converted to organic cultivation. If the **Minervois red 2001** achieved a star, then it is the brilliant golden-coloured white, with flavours of garrigue that whips up a fervour and presents the Grand Jury with *coups de coeur*. Full-bodied spiciness, melt-in-the-mouth crystallized fruits, the *cuvée* manages to balance vanilla sweetness with southern French warmth. NB: this domaine, as indeed is the case with several others in this appellation, has come up with extremely eye-catching front and back of bottle wine labels.

🍷 Andrieu Frères, Ch. La Rèze, 11700 Azille,
tel. 04.68.78.10.19, fax 04.68.78.20.42,
e-mail lareze@wanadoo.fr 🆅
☕ ev. day except Sat. Sun. 9am–12 noon 1.30pm–5.30pm
🍷 Louis Andrieu

CH. D'OUPIA

Oppius 2000★★★

■	2 ha	4,000	⪾	15–23 €

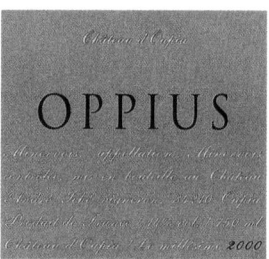

Beyond the pleasant, simple packaging, Oppius offers depth and intensity. One cannot stop praising this wine; it simply flabbergasts the taste buds with its richness and composition. Spices, ripe fruits, cinnamon and blackcurrant merge in an expressive symphony. Concentrated, perfectly balanced with a rich and patinated structure. The refined finish provides a rare and lingering delight. A great amongst greats.

🍷 André Iché, Ch. d'Oupia, 34210 Oupia,
tel. 04.68.91.20.86, fax 04.68.91.18.23,
e-mail oupia@tiscali.fr 🆅 🏠
☕ by appt.

PIQUE-PERLOU

La Sellerie 2000★★

■	3 ha	6,000	⪾	23–30 €

If "*pique-perlou*" in Provençal French translates as "go to the outskirts of the village", then Serge Serris has not been overlooked, as henceforth, he is well-ensconced in the *Guide* as one of the appellation's great classics. This wine, the product of maturation in oak for 24 months, offers vanilla aromas, marked by hints of cocoa and toasted bread. Well-structured, the *cuvée* exhibits an elegant, fruity palate. The finish is truly remarkable.

🍷 Serge Serris, 12, av. des Ecoles, 11200 Roubia,
tel. 04.68.43.22.46, fax 04.68.43.22.46 🆅
☕ by appt.

CH. PLO DU ROY

Le Balcon du Diable Elevé en fût de chêne 2001★★

■	7 ha	33,000	⪾	5–8 €

After languishing, undisturbed for a year or so, this wine has just emerged from its oak barrels; the 99 vintage of this particular *cuvée* received a *coup de coeur*. This crimson-coloured 2001 smacks not of heresy! The wine proceeds to enchant with aromas of prunes, liquorice and toasted bread. Straightforward from the start, this selection seduces the taste buds with velvety soft fruitiness and the warmth of its spices. The rounded, balanced tannins are remarkable as, indeed, is the chocolate-flavoured finish.

🍷 Franck Benazeth, 8, chem. Balti,
11160 Villeneuve-Minervois, tel. 04.67.88.45.75,
fax 04.67.88.45.79 🆅
☕ ev. day except Sun. 10am–12.30pm 1.30pm–6pm

CH. DE POUZOLS

La Gardie 2000★★

■	n.c.	19,950	■ ⪾ ♦	8–11 €

The Château de Pouzols has been in the Fournas family since 1437: a succession of 21 generations! The La Gardie *cuvée*, a great wine of fine pedigree, unfurls with deep, garnet-red hues and opens out with intense flavours of chocolate and ripe fruits. Mourvèdre and Grenache offer warmth and spiciness, while reliable Carignan lends a hint of fruitiness. The powerful, balanced, vanilla tannins are of noble extraction. A lingering finish endorses this wine as a lord among Minervois.

🍷 Ch. de Pouzols, 11120 Pouzols-Minervois,
tel. 04.68.46.13.78, fax 04.68.46.13.78,
e-mail chateaupouzols@aol.com
☕ by appt.
🍷 Baron de Fournas

DOM. DU ROC

Passion 2001★★★

■	2 ha	12,000	⪾	8–11 €

This talented *vigneron*, in charge since the early 1990s, made a favourable impression last year; today, we witness his crowning achievement with a *coup de coeur* for this original *cuvée*. Indeed, the tasters discovered soft flavours of brown tobacco and charcoal, characteristic of maturation in oak, at high temperature. The wine demonstrates strength, warmth and roundness; well-developed and balanced oakiness, with hints of stewed fruits and natural sweetness. The concentrated finish cuts no corners and keeps one in suspense to the very end. Therefore, a trip to Pépieux is called for, where the dolmen of Fades will also be of interest.

🍷 Alain Vies, Dom. du Roc, 15, chem. de Rieux,
11700 Pépieux, tel. 04.68.91.52.14, fax 04.68.91.66.26,
e-mail avies@club-internet.fr 🆅
☕ by appt.

DOM. LA ROUVIOLE

Sélection 2001★

| ■ | 12 ha | 8,200 | ⑪ | 11–15 € |

When faced with the challenge Franck Leonor, assisted by his uncles, set the record straight forthwith, and proceeded to lead the domaine to lofty heights, on two occasions, with three vintages…here, therefore, we have an intense, well-constructed wine, derived from clay-limestone terroir. Supple, spicy and exhibiting straightforward oak overtones, this *cuvée* is powerful, warming and perfectly structured. The wine epitomizes the new wave appellation.

☛ Famille Leonor, Dom. La Rouviole, 34210 Siran, tel. 04.68.91.42.13, fax 04.68.91.42.13, e-mail franck.leonor@wanadoo.fr ☑
☒ ev. day 9am–12 noon 3pm–7pm

CH. RUSSOL GARDEY

Grande Réserve 2000★

| ■ | 4.5 ha | 14,000 | ⑪ | 11–15 € |

In the 16th century, Pontus de La Gardie was in the noble service of King John III of Sweden. Today, the establishment's descendants unreservedly serve the cause of Minervois. This purple wine cuts a fine figure: full-bodied from the start, this wine assails the taste buds with full, spicy flavours. The balanced, powerful body moves briskly on to the palate, while the vanilla tannins, heightened by a distinct fruitiness, proceed to deliver a resounding finish!

☛ Bernard Gardey de Soos, Ch. Russol, 11800 Laure-Minervois, tel. 04.68.78.17.68, fax 04.68.78.13.06, e-mail chateau.russol@wanadoo.fr ☑
☒ ev. day except Sun. 9am–12 noon 2pm–7pm; groups by appt.

DOM. TAILHADES MAYRANNE

A Elise 2001★

| ■ | 1 ha | 1000 | ▮ | 11–15 € |

Within striking distance of Minerve, perching on a craggy peak overlooking the Cesse Valley, lies this little marvel, the newcomer, Elise, daughter of Régis Tailhades, to whom this garnet-coloured *cuvée* is dedicated. Overtones of fruits (raspberry and blackberry) accompany fleshy tannins, wavering between seduction and expressiveness. Carefully matured, well balanced, right up to the supple finish; a highly successful wine.

☛ EARL Dom. Tailhades Mayranne, Dom. de Mayranne, 34210 Minerve, tel. 04.68.91.26.77, fax 04.68.91.11.96, e-mail domaine.tailhades@terre-net.fr ☑ ☗
☒ by appt.

CH. TOUR BOISEE

A Marie-Claude 2001★

| ■ | 9 ha | 40,000 | ⑪ | 8–11 € |

The 80-ha domaine is located 7 km from the abbey of Caunes Minervois. This *cuvée*, dedicated to the *vigneron*'s spouse, is balanced and expressive. The perfect marriage of spices and oaked vanilla flavours develops with a sweet, warming complexity. This pleasant wine is ready to drink, from now on.

☛ Jean-Louis Poudou, Dom. la Tour Boisée, 11800 Laure-Minervois, tel. 04.68.78.10.04, fax 04.68.78.10.98, e-mail info@domainelatourboisee.com ☑
☒ ev. day except Sat. Sun. 10am–12noon 2pm–5pm

CH. TOURRIL 2002★★

| ■ | 1,5 ha | 6,500 | ▮ ♦ | 3–5 € |

"Osmosis" could be the key word for this château because, on this estate, new vinification technologies are practised alongside traditional wine-growing methods. Cinsault (90%) and Syrah deliver a delicate salmon-coloured rosé; soft fruits and slightly sharp sweets develop amid roundness and freshness. This wine exudes the very essence of warmth and fullness and offers an elegant finish.

☛ EARL Ch. Tourril, 11200 Roubia, tel. 04.68.91.36.89, fax 04.68.91.30.24, e-mail chateau.tourril@wanadoo.fr ☑
☒ by appt.

Wines selected but not starred

CH. BELVIZE

Cuvée des Oliviers 2000

| ■ | 5 ha | 25,000 | ⑪ | 5–8 € |

☛ SCEA Ch. Belvize, La Lecugne, 11120 Bize-Minervois, tel. 04.68.46.22.70, fax 04.68.46.35.72, e-mail belvize@terre-net.fr ☑ ☗
☒ ev. day 9am–12 noon 2pm–6pm; cl. 15–31 Dec.
☛ J.-M. Desrues, F. Truyols

DOM. LA CASSAGNE 2000

| ■ | n.c. | 35,000 | | 3–5 € |

☛ Francis Marty, 2, imp. Marcel-Labatut, 11160 Rieux-Minervois, tel. 01.30.98.59.50, fax 01.30.42.02.66

CH. LES DEUX TERRES

Cuvée des Pins 2001

| ■ | 1.05 ha | 4,000 | ▮ ♦ | 11–15 € |

☛ Catherine et Jean-François Prax, Dom. Les Deux Terres, 11700 Azille, tel. 04.68.91.63.28, fax 04.68.91.57.70, e-mail domaine.les.deux.terres@wanadoo.fr ☑
☒ by appt.

DOM. DE GINESTIERES 2001

| ■ | n.c. | 55,000 | | 3–5 € |

☛ Cave coop. de Peyriac, 11160 Peyriac, tel. 04.68.78.11.20, fax 04.68.78.17.93
☛ Joël Venture

DOM. PUJOL

Cuvée Saint-Fructueux 2001

| ■ | 2.5 ha | 12,000 | ⑪ | 11–15 € |

☛ Pujol-Izard, 8 *bis*, av. de l'Europe, 11800 Saint-Frichoux, tel. 04.68.78.15.30, fax 04.68.78.24.58, e-mail jean-claude.pujol3@wanadoo.fr ☑
☒ ev. day except Sun. 8.30am–12 noon 2pm–7pm; Sat. by appt.

DOM. TERRES GEORGES

Quintessence 2001

| ■ | 1.5 ha | 1,200 | ⑪ | 5–8 € |

☛ Anne-Marie et Roland Coustal, 2, rue de la Pinède, 11700 Castelnau-d'Aude, tel. 06.30.49.97.73, fax 04.68.43.79.39 ☑
☒ by appt.

DOM. TOUR TRENCAVEL

Lou Cagarol 2001

| ■ | 2.15 ha | 2,000 | ⑪ | 11–15 € |

☛ GAEC Tour Trencavel, 15, lot de la Clause, 11160 Trausse-Minervois, tel. 04.68.78.34.10, fax 04.68.78.34.10 ☑
☒ by appt.
☛ Fabrie

CH. VILLERAMBERT-MOUREAU

Cuvée des Marbreries Hautes 2001

| ■ | 3 ha | 8,600 | ⑪ | 11–15 € |

☛ Marceau Moureau et Fils, Ch. de Villerambert, 11160 Caunes-Minervois, tel. 04.68.77.16.40, fax 04.68.77.08.14 ☑
☒ ev. day except Sun. 10am–12 noon 2pm–7pm

LANGUEDOC

Minervois la Livinière

DOM. CHABBERT-FAUZAN
Clos la Coquille 2000★

■	2.5 ha	3,000	◀▮▶	8–11 €

If the Jury was impressed by the neighbouring **Minervois white 2002**, it was this Minervois la Livinière wine that made the Jury wax lyrical, derived from the high altitude terroir of Fauzan, bursting with dark fruits and flavours of camphor and vanilla. Well-supported by its substantial, mineral, firm, rich and warming structure, this delightful concentration offers real value; a *cuvée* that will peak in a few months' time.
•┱ Dom. Chabbert-Fauzan, Fauzan, 34210 Cesseras, tel. 04.68.91.23.64, fax 04.68.91.31.17 ☑
⌇ by appt.

CLOS DE L'ESCANDIL 2001★★★

■	5 ha	15,000	◀▮▶	15–23 €

Gilles Chabbert knows how to keep a low profile within the confines of his vineyard, only to reappear at the critical moments! This year, he presents this three-star wine blend of Syrah, Grenache and Mourvèdre. A good 14 months in oak, this 2001 is underlined by superb potential, where woodland fruits and liquorice merge divinely with cocoa and vanilla. The wine is as powerful as a steel fist in a velvet glove: aromas merge right up to the lingering and warming finish, where wine and maturation meet in perfect symbiosis.
•┱ Gilles Chabbert, Dom. des Aires Hautes, 34210 Siran, tel. 04.68.91.54.40, fax 04.68.91.54.40, e-mail gilles.chabbert@wanadoo.fr ☑
⌇ by appt.

LES CRUS DU HAUT-MINERVOIS
Cuvée Gaïa 2001★★

■	10.71 ha	12,000	▮◀▮▶♦	8–11 €

Here, from the time of the "Processions" and throughout the centuries, the faithful have prayed to Saint Abdon for rain. Today, things are looking good for this wine cellar, with its **Vidal la Marquise en Minervois** *cuvée* and especially for this Minervois la Livinière. The glass exudes a concentration of soft fruits, vanilla and spices. On the lips one experiences a delicate and free embrace of toasty aromas, with undertones of velvet tannins. A wine that fills the mouth, tightly packed structure to the breathtaking finish…
•┱ Les Vignerons des Crus du Haut-Minervois, 34210 Azillanet, tel. 04.68.91.22.61, fax 04.68.91.19.46, e-mail les3blasons@wanadoo.fr ☑
⌇ by appt.

CH. FAITEAU 2000★★

■	1.75 ha	8,000	◀▮▶	8–11 €

The vinification area is equipped with four old solidly-built structures, linked to an end station that is said to be cast "in diamonds"; beneath this shelter, Jean-Michel Arnaud offers a gem of a wine, an intense-coloured ruby-red, with refined hints of vanilla, cinnamon and mocha. The palate has a full-bodied start, structured around concentrated spices and soft mouth-watering fruits. Integrated tannins delicately make their presence felt on a finish that sparkles with a thousand lights.
•┱ GAEC Yves et Jean-Michel Arnaud, Ch. Faiteau, rte des Meulières, 34210 La Livinière, tel. 06.15.90.89.48, fax 04.68.91.48.28, e-mail jma-ch-faiteau@wanadoo.fr ☑
⌇ by appt.

Wines selected but not starred

CH. MASSAMIER LA MIGNARDE
Domus Maximus 2000

■	2 ha	10,000	▮◀▮▶♦	11–15 €

•┱ EARL Vènes, Ch. Massamier la Mignarde, 11700 Pépieux, tel. 04.68.91.40.74, fax 04.68.91.44.40 ☑
⌇ ev. day 9am–7pm

PRIMO PALATUM 2000

■	2 ha	2,400	◀▮▶	15–23 €

•┱ Primo Palatum, 1, Cirette, 33190 Morizès, tel. 05.56.71.39.39, fax 05.56.71.39.40, e-mail xavier-copel@primo-palatum.com ☑
⌇ by appt.
•┱ Xavier Copel

Saint-Chinian

Saint-Chinian has been a VDQS from 1945 and became an AOC in 1982. The appellation covers 20 communes spread over 3,204 ha and produces 138,463 hl of red and rosé wines. Located in the Hérault, northwest of Béziers, it lies on seaward-facing hills that rise to 100 and 200 m. The soils are schists, which are mainly in the north, and limestone gravel in the south. The wine has a distinguished tradition, its name having been recorded as early as 1300. A Maison des Vins has been established in Saint-Chinian itself.

BERLOUP
Vignes Royales 2000★★

■	60 ha	66,600	▮	8–11 €

The excellent produce of the Berlou *vignerons*, who cultivate the 600 ha estate, is well known. Three wines were singled out by the Jury: the **Château des Albières Cuvée Georges Darde 2000 (11–15 €)** achieves a star. The **Coteaux du Languedoc Collection white 2001** favourably impressed the tasters. And finally, this Vignes Royales *cuvée*, the third wine to be placed before the Grand Jury. The tasting revealed a dark-coloured appearance, with a powerful, complex nose of soft, crystallized fruits and spices. A pleasant palate emerges, with a soft, delightful tannic presence. A fine work of art, composed of 32% Carignan and 49% Grenache, topped up with Syrah.
•┱ Les Coteaux du Rieu Berlou, av. des Vignerons, 34360 Berlou, tel. 04.67.89.58.58, e-mail pro.berlou@wanadoo.fr ☑ ⚑
⌇ by appt.

BORIE LA VITARELE

Les Schistes 2001★

| ■ | 4 ha | 11,000 | ■ ⑪ ♣ | 11–15 € |

Secluded at the bottom of a valley surrounded by garrigue and Mediterranean forests, Cathy Planes and Jean-François Izarn are in the process of converting their estate to organic vine cultivation. Their sole objective: terroir. This powerful and complex Les Schistes *cuvée* is an unqualified success, with its aromas of toasted bread, smoke and mocha. The full-bodied palate, endowed with fine substance, points to meticulous maturation. This wine has real personality and exceptional potential. Recommended with guinea fowl and saffron. The domaine offers farm-style accommodation.
☞ Jean-François Izarn et Cathy Planes, lieu-dit La Combe, 34490 Causses-et-Veyran, tel. 04.67.89.50.43, fax 04.67.89.70.79, e-mail jf.izarn@libertysurf.fr ☑
☎ by appt.

DOM. DE CANIMALS LE HAUT 2001★★★

| ■ | 1.5 ha | 6,500 | ■ | 5–8 € |

A resounding success for this marvellous 2001 vintage. Jean-Louis and Brigitte Castel present a great, well-balanced and rich Saint-Chinian. Aromas of shale (grilled, smoked), garrigue and spices complement a full, lingering palate, with elegant, fruity undertones. According to one taster, "The pleasures of the flesh". A well-presented wine; to be served with wild boar.
☞ Jean-Louis et Brigitte Castel, Dom. de Canimals Le Haut, 34360 Saint-Chinian, tel. 04.67.38.19.13, fax 04.67.38.19.13 ☑ ☖
☎ by appt.

CH. CAZAL-VIEL

Larmes des Fées 2000★

| ■ | 7 ha | 3,000 | ⑪ | 23–30 € |

Back in the 18th century, the monks of Fontcaude Abbey got it right when it came to cultivating this clay-limestone terroir. Sold off during the Revolution, as indeed were all the clergy's worldly possessions, and later acquired by the Miquels, this vineyard has remained in the same family ever since. Larmes des Fées and **Vieilles Vignes 2001 (5–8 €)** each receive a star, but are not similarly priced. The first shows evidence of pronounced oak maturation that would benefit from further ageing. The second, with very pleasant, integrated tannins would go well with small game and Pardhaillan turnips.
☞ Ch. Cazal-Viel, Dom. de Cazal-Viel, 34460 Cessenon-sur-Orb, tel. 04.67.89.63.15, fax 04.67.89.65.17, e-mail info@cazal-viel.com ☑ ☖
☎ by appt.
☞ Henri Miquel

LE CLOS GOUTINES

Julie Caprice 2001★★

| ■ | 3 ha | 1,400 | ■ ♣ | 8–11 € |

Located between Berlou and Roquebrun, in the regional natural park area of Haut Languedoc, shielded from view, is the Clos Goutines estate. As far as the **Marie Délice 2001 (5–8 €)** is concerned, the Jury highlighting this superb selection. Pleasant appearance, very powerful nose of garrigue and *ciste* blossom (a plant native to the garrigue) herald a pleasant, full-bodied palate, with hints of cocoa. The aromatic length predicts a fine future for this wine.
☞ Christophe Goutines, 5, rue Fontaine-Janaré, 34360 Saint-Chinian, tel. 04.67.38.19.00, fax 04.67.38.19.00 ☑
☎ by appt.

CH. DE COMBEBELLE

Prestige 2000★

| ■ | 2 ha | 5,000 | ⑪ | 11–15 € |

Rigorous selection, care and attention, throughout the production process, ensure that this Prestige *cuvée* is a typical Saint-Chinian wine. Deep colour with tinges of violet; an original and complex nose reveals aromas of fruits steeped in brandy. The unctuous palate pays tribute, from the start, to skilful maturation. Exceedingly fine balance.

☞ EURL Combebelle, Combebelle-le-Haut, 34360 Villespassans, tel. 04.68.91.42.63, fax 04.68.91.62.15, e-mail françois@comtecathare.com

DOM. COMPS

Cuvée de Pénelle 2001★

| ■ | 2 ha | 8,000 | ■ ⑪ ♣ | 3–5 € |

An oenologist marrying a daughter of the vine; surely a winning formula for nurturing very fine, concentrated wines, such as this deep red, garnet-coloured Cuvée de Pénelle 2001 with a floral, spicy nose of blackcurrant, leather and crystallized fruits. The wine exhibits pronounced balance on the palate, with hints of tightly packed tannins and an oaky presence. To be uncorked between 2005 and 2008. Or, maybe you would care to sample the **Cuvée Le Soleiller 2001 (5–8 €)**, from the autumn of 2003 onwards, with its bright-red colour and intense aromas of soft fruits and evident, yet rich, fine structure.
☞ SCEA Martin-Comps, 23, rue Paul-Riquet, 34620 Puisserguier, tel. 04.67.93.73.15 ☑
☎ ev. day 10am–7pm

CH. COUJAN

Cuvée Bois joli 2001★

| ■ | 2,6 ha | 9,500 | ⑪ | 11–15 € |

François Guy is a prominent figure in the history of Languedoc wine. His daughter, Florence, took over the property, in 1990. Derived from sandstone, shingle terroir it reflects the typicity of Saint-Chinian wines. Carefully cultivated, the *cuvée* is powerful, with a fresh and full start. A taster commented upon the wine's fine potential for body and elegance.
☞ SCEA F. Guy et S. Peyre, Ch. Coujan, 34490 Murviel-lès-Béziers, tel. 04.67.37.80.00, fax 04.67.37.86.23, e-mail coujan@mnet.fr ☑
☎ ev. day 9am–12 noon 2.30pm–7pm

DOM. LA CROIX SAINTE-EULALIE

Cuvée Armandélis 2001★

| ■ | 2.6 ha | 12,000 | ■ ♣ | 5–8 € |

At the heart of the village, you will find this domaine, with an emblem of a 16th century cross, situated amidst the vines. Intense colour, still young, the Cuvée Armandélis offers a nose with flavours of fresh, small berries and truffle. Perfectly balanced, this wine develops an impressive concentration that nevertheless exudes ample freshness. Match with wild boar casserole.
☞ Michel Gleizes, av. de Saint-Chinian, hameau de Combejean, 34360 Pierrerue, tel. 04.67.38.08.51, fax 04.67.38.08.51, e-mail michel.gleizes@club-internet.fr ☑
☎ ev. day 9am–12.30pm 1.30pm–7pm

DOM. DESLINES

Delphine Fût de chêne 2000★

| ■ | 2.5 ha | 6,000 | ⑪ | 8–11 € |

A rare occurrence in the world of wine – on this estate a female hand tends the vine. Line Cauquil is a person one ought to meet and her wine certainly warrants a visit. This brilliant intense coloured *cuvée*, opens with characteristic shale-type aromas of spices and garrigue, before revealing its balance and length. Best decanted a few hours before the meal.
☞ Line Cauquil, Dom. Deslines, 34360 Babeau-Bouldoux, tel. 04.67.38.19.95, fax 04.67.38.19.95 ☑
☎ by appt.

CH. LA DOURNIE 2001★★

| ■ | 6 ha | 15,000 | ■ ♣ | 5–8 € |

Continuity is assured with this sixth generation taking the reins at La Dournie, with these magnificent *cuvées*, by way of confirmation. The deep red-coloured Château 2001, with an aromatic nose of soft fruits, cocoa and fine intensity, exhibits fullness and suppleness, on a lingering, well-structured palate. The **Cuvée Elise red 2001 (11–15 €)** is equally subtle, powerful, rich and concentrated, full and fleshy. This *cuvée* receives two stars. The **Rosé 2002 (3–5 €)**

receives a star for the clarity of its appearance, its fruity nose and rounded, soft palate.
❧ EARL Ch. la Dournie, rte de Saint-Pons, 34360 Saint-Chinian, tel. 04.67.38.19.43, fax 04.67.38.00.37, e-mail chateau.ladournie@libertysurf.fr **Ⓥ**
Ⓨ by appt.

DOM. FONTAINE MARCOUSSE
Cuvée Vitorey 2001★★

| ■ | 0,6 ha | 2,500 | 🍾 ♦ | 8–11 € |

Unquestionably a Carignan domaine, dedicated to researching forgotten oxidation methods of maturation. Established since 1999, Myriam and Luc Robert are *vignerons* to follow closely. The Cuvée Vitorey is an unqualified success: brilliant-red appearance, fruit (blackcurrant), with light touches of garrigue vegetation and a hint of menthol. The palate makes a forceful statement with its superb balance. One lingers over a lengthy, fresh finish. The **Cuvée Capellou 2001 (5–8 €)** was singled out by the Jury.
❧ Myriam et Luc Robert, Le Pontil, av. de la Gare, 34620 Puisserguier, tel. 04.67.93.81.37, fax 04.67.62.24.51, e-mail robertmy@wanadoo.fr **Ⓥ 🏠**
Ⓨ by appt.

CH. GUIRAUD BOISSEZON
Cuvée Mélanie 2001★

| ■ | 8 ha | 50,000 | 🍾 ♦ | 5–8 € |

It is impossible to be indifferent to the natural beauty of Roquebrun. In this setting, a wine has been produced that exudes powerful aromas of garrigue, eucalyptus with hints of cherry and cocoa. The soft, supple palate, with tannins that are already well integrated, adds up to a full-bodied, elegant, wine.
❧ Michel Guiraud, Ch. Guiraud Boissezon, 34460 Roquebrun, tel. 04.67.89.68.17, fax 04.67.89.68.17

DOM. DES JOUGLA
Vieilhs Arrasics 2001★★

| ■ | 3 ha | 6,600 | ⦙⦙⦙ | 11–15 € |

Coup de coeur for Alain Jougla's Saint-Chinian – a remarkable reflection both of the characteristics of the terroir and the domaine's fine reputation. Praised by the Jury for its balance, this wine of exceptional concentration gives off the scents of its natural environment, truffle and undergrowth. First impressions, on the palate, of suppleness evolve with weight and very fine tannins. This *cuvée* will be even better, in two to three years' time. A star has also been awarded to the fresh and elegant **Coteaux du Languedoc white 2002 Les Tuileries (5–8 €)**.
❧ Alain Jougla, Le Village, 34360 Prades-sur-Vernazobre, tel. 04.67.38.06.02, fax 04.67.38.17.74 **Ⓥ**
Ⓨ by appt.

DOM. DU LANDEYRAN
Grains de Passion 2001★★

| ■ | 2 ha | 6,500 | 🍾 ♦ | 11–15 € |

The years roll by and the stars continue to rain down on this domaine: a star for the **Cuvée Emilia 2001 (5–8 €)**, where tannins are already evident and two stars for the Grains de Passion. Beyond its purple appearance, a rich and powerful bouquet balances menthol, tapenade and pepper. Rounded

and structured, this wine reveals its power and the influence of terroir. The *cuvée*'s remarkable composition bestows upon it fine potential for laying down (three to five years).
❧ EARL du Landeyran, rue de la Vernière, 34490 Saint-Nazaire-de-Ladarez, tel. 04.67.89.67.63, fax 04.67.89.67.63, e-mail domainedulandeyran@free.fr **Ⓥ**
Ⓨ by appt.

DOM. LA LINQUIERE
Tradition 2002★

| ■ | 7 ha | 36,000 | 🍾 ♦ | 3–5 € |

Almost a quarter of a century of experience for the Linquière estate, where the intense, red-coloured 2002 vintage gives off deep-purple highlights. An aromatic bouquet of prunes, resin, terebinth, is heightened by a touch of leather. The straightforward palate opens with "sharp but charming" tannins and offers rich and full-bodied balance. Singled out by the Jury, the **Le Chant des Cigales 2001 (8–11 €)**, though young, is constantly evolving.
❧ Robert Salvestre et Fils, Dom. La Linquière, 34360 Villespassans, tel. 04.67.38.25.87, fax 04.67.38.04.57 **Ⓥ**
Ⓨ by appt.

DOM. LA MADURA 2001★

| ■ | 7.33 ha | 16,000 | ⦙⦙⦙ | 15–23 € |

Descended from a family of Languedocian viticulturers, Cyril and Nadia Bourgne acquired a Saint-Chinian vineyard, spread across three types of terroir (shale, clay-limestone, sandstone), in 1998. Such diversity is evident in the complexity and typicity of this wine. Once the wine has been allowed to breathe, extremely ripe fruits offer pleasures that continue with the balanced, fleshy, tannic palate. A wine that divulges meticulous care and attention.
❧ Nadia et Cyril Bourgne, Dom. La Madura, 12, rue de la Digue, 34360 Saint-Chinian, tel. 04.67.38.17.85, fax 04.67.38.17.85, e-mail lamadura@wanadoo.fr **Ⓥ**
Ⓨ by appt.

DOM. LA MAURERIE
Vieilles vignes 2001★

| ■ | 3.5 ha | 12,000 | ⦙⦙⦙ | 5–8 € |

The Depaule family has been cultivating the vine on this wonderful shale terroir, since 1788. The clear, ruby-red appearance envelops sweet flavours of bay and blackberry. Pleasant, well-integrated tannins glide over the wine's fruitiness. The ensemble is delicately spiced and would make a fine accompaniment for a three-peppered haunch of venison.
❧ Michel Depaule, Dom. La Maurerie, 34360 Prades-sur-Vernazobre, tel. 04.67.38.22.09, fax 04.67.38.22.09, e-mail michel-depaule@wanadoo.fr **Ⓥ 🏠**
Ⓨ by appt.

CH. MILHAU-LACUGUE 2002★

| ■ | 3.25 ha | 17,000 | 🍾 ♦ | 5–8 € |

Of Roman origins, the Hospitaliers, the Abbey of Fontcaude is only 3 km distance from Château Milhau, an added bonus for both tourism and the palate. Notably, this strong coloured Saint-Chinian rosé, with blue-tinted highlights. The highly intense nose of raspberry, strawberry, blackcurrant and violet aromas announces a full-bodied and rounded palate that is rich and lingering, with a hint of liquorice. The **Saint-Chinian Cuvée des Chevaliers red 2001**, with its concentrated and youthful tannins, also earns a star.
❧ Ch. Milhau-Lacugue, Dom. de Milhau, rte de Cazedarnes, 34620 Puisserguier, tel. 04.67.93.64.79, fax 04.67.93.51.93, e-mail milhau-lacugue@wanadoo.fr **Ⓥ**
Ⓨ ev. day 9.30am–12 noon 1.30pm–5pm; Sat. Sun. by appt.
❧ Lacugue

DOM. MOULIN DU ROCHER 2002★

| ■ | 3.5 ha | 16,000 | ⦙⦙⦙ | 5–8 € |

The mill is real enough and appears to be watching over the vines, deeply rooted in the rocky terrain. Panorama aside, spare a few moments to be tempted by the deep red 2002 vintage, with inky-coloured highlights and heady, caramelized flavours that evolve into aromas of ripe fruit, spices and a dash of cocoa. The palate reveals

concentrated body, fine length and an oakiness that only requires mellowing.
🔑 Luc Frances, 44, av. de Villespassans,
34360 Saint-Chinian, tel. 04.67.38.12.87 ☒
🍷 day 9.30am–12.30pm 3pm–7.30pm

DOM. NAVARRE

Cuvée Olivier Elevé en fût de chêne 2001★★

■ 6 ha 16,000 ▮ ⦀ 11–15 €

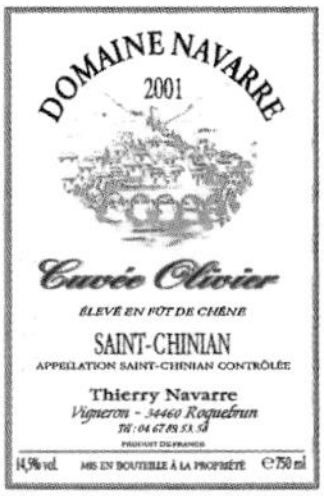

The Grand Jury was unanimous about this marvellous *coup de coeur*. Derived from old Carignan vine stock, Grenache and Syrah, in equal parts, this wine is dominated by the shale terroir of Roquebrun. The complex nose mingles overtones of fruits, toasted bread and prunes steeped in alcohol. Rich and flavoursome, the structure reveals perfectly integrated, supple tannins that point to highly skilful maturation. This wine would be a perfect match for large game, such as wild boar. While waiting, why not sample the one star, oak-aged **Cuvée Le Laouzil 2001 (5–8 €)**?
🔑 Thierry Navarre, av. de Balaussan, 34460 Roquebrun,
tel. 04.67.89.53.58, fax 04.67.89.70.88,
e-mail thierry.navarre@wanadoo.fr ☒
🍷 by appt.

CH. DU PRIEURE DES MOURGUES

2001★

■ 12 ha 41,000 ⦀ 5–8 €

You will not arrive at Pierrerue by chance! A trip to Prieuré des Mourgues involves a detour through rugged countryside, its garrigue and superb terroir. The *cuvée*'s purple colour is in keeping with this wine; a discreet start that develops with charred and chocolate overtones. Roundness dominates the palate, constructed around high quality tannins.
🔑 SARL Vignobles Roger, Ch. du Prieuré des Mourgues,
34360 Pierrerue-Combejean, tel. 04.67.38.18.19,
fax 04.67.38.27.29,
e-mail prieure.des.mourgues@wanadoo.fr ☒
🍷 by appt.

CUVEE ROCHES NOIRES 2002★

■ 25 ha 120,000 ▮ 11–15 €

Close to the botanical garden, on the "penjals" (slopes) of the shale escarpments that engulf the River Orb, the vines reluctantly yield their Cuvée Roches Noires of deep red and violet complexion and a nose of garrigue, pinewood and hints of crystallized fruit. The tannins are still tightly packed, but the balance suggests that this is a wine with fine ageing potential. The **Coteaux du Languedoc Domaine du Mourel 2002 (5–8 €)** is in the same mould (deep colour; powerful nose, rich, floral and spicy; full-bodied, rounded and balanced palate).
🔑 Cave Les Vins de Roquebrun, av. des Orangers,
34460 Roquebrun, tel. 04.67.89.64.35, fax 04.67.89.57.93,
e-mail info@cave-roquebrun.fr ☒
🍷 ev. day except Sun. 8am–12 noon 2pm–6pm

VIGNERONS DE ROUEIRE

Cuvée Saint-Christophe 2002★

■ 10 ha 40,000 3–5 €

The buildings, dating back to the beginning of the 18th century, with signage of a wind *Bollée* (19th century French wind engine, originating in Le Mans), erected in 1898, are classified as historical monuments, now home to the *vignerons* of Roueïre. This 2002 vintage possesses the charm of an intense rosé, with a strong nose that offers the delights of small fruits, underlined by floral hints and a touch of nutmeg. Weight, roundness, richness and length: sheer pleasure on the palate, a feast of flavours. The Jury, was equally impressed by the **white Cuvée Saint Christophe 2002** version, which was singled out for its floral, fruity, fresh, light-heartedness.
🔑 Les Vignerons de Roueïre, Dom. de Roueïre,
34310 Quarante, tel. 04.67.89.40.10, fax 04.67.89.32.20,
e-mail josy@roueire.com ☒
🍷 ev. day except Mon. 10am–12 noon 3pm–6pm

DOM. DU SACRE-COEUR

Cuvée Jean Madoré 2000★

■ 6 ha 3,000 ⦀ 15–23 €

Following a *coup de coeur*, last year, for the Kévin 2000 *cuvée*, Luc Cabaret nominates a wine drawn from the rigorous selection of old Carignans (40%), Syrah and Grenache, in equal proportions, together with 15 months maturation, tailored oak-ageing. This 2000, with a complex and powerful nose reveals strong, very pleasant tannins on the palate. Undoubtedly, this wine will evolve admirably. Cellar for over three years.
🔑 GAEC du Sacré-Coeur, Dom. du Sacré-Coeur, Le Village, 34360 Assignan, tel. 04.67.38.17.97,
fax 04.67.38.24.52, e-mail gaecsacrecoeur@net-up.com ☒
🍷 ev. day except Sun. 9am–12 noon 3pm–6.30pm

DOM. DU TABATAU

Cuvée Lo Tabataïre 2001★

■ 3.15 ha 10,700 ⦀ 8–11 €

Jean-Paul and Bruno Gracia set up this domaine in 1997. After 14 months maturation, in oak barrels, this deep purple *cuvée*, generous to a fault, reveals, upon being allowed to breathe, a freshness, spices and hints of garrigue. The palate appears reasonably firm, yet not devoid of roundness and richness. Decanting is recommended in order to enjoy this wine at its peak, without delaying too long.
🔑 Gracia, Dom. du Tabatau, rue du Bal, 34360 Assignan,
tel. 04.67.38.19.60, fax 04.67.38.19.54,
e-mail domainedutabatau@wanadoo.fr ☒
🍷 by appt.

CH. VEYRAN

Prestige 2000★

■ 2.95 ha 13,000 ▮ 5–8 €

This château houses a Romanesque vaulted wine cellar dating back to the 12th century, as well as an 18th century rib-vaulted cellar. Syrah (90%) imposes its style on this *cuvée*, both in terms of colour (purple) and flavours, dark fruits (blackberry) with hints of spices and garrigue. Overall, this is a typically Languedocian wine, with an already tannic finish that should mellow in two or three years' time.
🔑 Gérard Antoine, Ch. Veyran, 34490 Causses-et-Veyran,
tel. 06.63.85.22.80, fax 04.67.89.67.89,
e-mail antoine@chateau-veyran.com ☒
🍷 by appt.

CH. VILLESPASSANS 2001★★

■ 8 ha 2,500 ▮ ♁ 3–5 €

This Château de Villespassans wine, with its dedicated cellar, has a fine deep-red appearance. Strength and complexity jostle on the nose, with marked overtones of dark fruits, garrigue and liquorice. Fresh, straightforward, full and fine, the velvety palate possesses tannic, yet strong structure. Best laid down for year or two.
🔑 Jean-Christophe Petit, Ch. Villespassans,
34360 Villespassans, tel. 06.12.77.64.80,
e-mail pttjc@aol.com ☒ ⌂
🍷 by appt.

CH. VIRANEL

V de Viranel 2001★

■ 1 ha 4,000 ▮ ♁ 8–11 €

Following the discovery of a Gallo-Roman villa, a Celtic letter V has appeared in the name of this new *cuvée*...Syrah dominates the blend and lends the wine its deep red colour

and a nose, with aromas of violet and soft fruits. The palate is full, supple and velvety, with a finish of the utmost finesse. Easy drinking.
♦�‑ GFA de Viranel, 34460 Cessenon, tel. 04.90.55.85.82, fax 04.90.55.88.97 ☑
☂ by appt.
♦↑ Bergasse-Milhé

Wines selected but not starred

MAS CHAMPART
Causse du Bousquet 2001

■	4.5 ha	15,000	▌ ⦿ ⦿	8–11 €

♦↑ EARL Champart, Bramefan, rte de Villespassans, 34360 Saint-Chinian, tel. 04.67.38.20.09, fax 04.67.38.20.09 ☑
☂ by appt.

MAS DES CERISIERS
Hautes Terres 2001

■	1.56 ha	3,400	⦿	11–15 €

♦↑ Pascal Brunier, Le Pin, 34390 Vieussan, tel. 04.67.97.39.50, fax 04.67.97.39.50, e-mail masdescerisiers@wanadoo.fr ☑
☂ by appt.

PRIEURE SAINT-ANDRE
Cuvée du Capucin 2000

■	1.5 ha	8,000	▌	5–8 €

♦↑ Michel Claparède, Prieuré Saint-André, 34460 Roquebrun, tel. 04.67.89.70.82, fax 04.67.89.71.41 ☑
☂ ev. day 9am–12 noon–6pm

CH. DE SAINT-CELS 2000

■	5 ha	15,000	⦿	5–8 €

♦↑ EARL des Vignobles de Saint-Cels, 34360 Saint-Chinian, tel. 04.67.38.13.32, fax 04.67.38.15.13, e-mail st.cels@wanadoo.fr ☑
☂ by appt.
♦↑ Rouanet

Cabardès

The wines of the Côtes de Cabardès and Obiel come from terroirs north of Carcassonne and west of the Minervois. The vineyard covers 592 ha in 18 communes. In 2002 production was 26,302 hl of both red and rosé wines, which blend vine varieties suited to both the Mediterranean and the Atlantic areas of the appellation. The Atlantic influence in this, the most westerly appellation in the region, make its wines substantially different from other wines in Languedoc and Roussillon.

L'ESPRIT DE LA BASTIDE 2000★★

■	4 ha	20,000	⦿	15–23 €

The history of Rougepeyre takes us back to the 18th century, when this establishment was built. Formerly, however, the house was more or less a village, entrusted with the protection of Lastours's three châteaux. The name "Cabardès" derives from a fortress owned by Roger-Pierre de Cabaret. This concentrated wine, with amazing aromas of juniper is, indeed, a fine achievement. The refined and balanced palate is truly remarkable. Ready to serve now; equally, this *cuvée* could be laid down.
♦↑ SCEA Ch. La Bastide, 11610 Pennautier, tel. 04.68.72.65.29, fax 04.68.72.65.84 ☑
♦↑ Lorgeril

DOM. DE CABROL
Vent d'Est 2001★★★

■	12 ha	10,000	▌ ⦿	8–11 €

The discipline and talent of Claude Carayol who, once again, has achieved a *coup de coeur*, are stamped upon this high-altitude vineyard, that has not reached full maturity. Risk taking is an important factor, but the results are evident in this astonishing wine, with an intense nose of overripe fruits, enhanced by particularly flattering kirsch aromas. Full-bodied, rich, an elegant palate, this wine offers superb balance, with supple, tannic undertones.
♦↑ Claude Carayol, Dom. de Cabrol, D 118, 11600 Aragon, tel. 04.68.77.19.06, fax 04.68.77.54.90 ☑
☂ ev. day except Sun. 11am–12 noon 5pm–7pm

CRISTAL DE GROTTE 2000★★

■	1.2 ha	7,400	▌ ⦿ ⦿	8–11 €

Exceptional originality marks the wine from this cooperative wine cellar; matured in oak barrels for a year, in the caves of Limousis, at a constant temperature of 13°C. The resulting *cuvée*, has been allowed to develop its full finesse, as well as its complexity, at a leisurely pace, as is evident in the nose with overtones of dark, stewed fruits. The concentrated palate offers ample richness and fills the mouth right up to the interesting, prune-flavoured finish.
♦↑ Cellier des Trois Conques, SCV, 11600 Conques-sur-Orbiel, tel. 04.68.77.12.90, fax 04.68.77.14.95, e-mail cellier‑3conques@wanadoo.fr ☑
☂ ev. day except Sat. Sun. 8am–12 noon 2pm–6pm

CH. DE PENNAUTIER
L'Esprit de Pennautier 2000★★

■	6.25 ha	30,000	⦿ ⦿	15–23 €

The château that makes its regular, annual appearance in the *Guide* is just as famous for its wines as its history – what an incentive to explore further! Nicolas and Miren de Lorgeril represent the tenth generation at this château, built in 1620. Finalist, for the *coup de coeur*, this wine is superb, powerful, with liquorice overtones and hints of undergrowth, on the finish. The tannins, on the palate, are well-integrated and lingering. Equally impressing the Jury, the **Pennautier rosé 2002 (3–5 €)** and the **Pennautier red 2001 (3–5 €)**.
♦↑ SCEA Ch. de Pennautier, 11610 Pennautier, tel. 04.68.72.65.29, fax 04.68.72.65.84 ☑
♦↑ Lorgeril

CH. DE RAYSSAC 2001★

| | 7.5 ha | 50,000 | ■ ♦ | 3–5 € |

Château de Rayssac is the sole occupier of a perfectly comfortable sunny hollow, extending over 30 ha. Madame Rigaud is at the helm of this property that has been in the family since 1996. Today, she delivers a highly successful wine. First impressions on the nose are fine and spicy, with hints of garrigue. This particular *cuvée* possesses good body, fine tannins and a very pleasant finish, with flavours of ripe fruits.
☛ SCEA Ch. de Rayssac, 11600 Conques-sur-Orbiel, tel. 04.68.72.65.29, fax 04.68.72.65.84
☛ de Rigaud

CH. SALITIS

Cuvée des Dieux 2001★

| | 4 ha | 14,000 | ■ ♦ | 8–11 € |

Here we have one of the historic domaines of Cabardès that has contributed, for over 20 years, to the fine reputation of this appellation. With its youthful, deep purple appearance, the Cuvée des Dieux offers a powerful nose of very ripe fruits. Perfect balance envelops fine structure. Ready to drink now.
☛ Depaule-Marandon, Ch. Salitis, 11600 Conques-sur-Orbiel, tel. 04.68.77.16.10, fax 04.68.77.05.69, e-mail salitis@wanadoo.fr ☑
☥ by appt.

CH. VENTENAC

Le Carla 2001★★

| | 30 ha | 150,000 | ■ ♦ | 3–5 € |

Featured each year in the *Guide*, Alain Maurel confirms the quality of his wines with this *cuvée*, produced in his new installation that combines innovative technology with old stone surrounds. As well as the **rosé 2002** that was singled out by the Jury, the Le Carla Cuvée, with its beautiful, intense appearance, also receives a special mention. A relatively young nose exudes rich fruitiness. Easy to drink, yet powerful, this 2001 is constructed with elegance.
☛ SARL Vignobles Alain Maurel, 1, pl. du Château, 11610 Ventenac, tel. 04.68.24.93.42, fax 04.68.24.81.16 ☑
☥ ev. day except Sat. Sun. 8am–12 noon 2pm–6pm

Côtes de la Malepère AOVDQS

A total of 42,146 hl of wine was produced in 2002 in this AOVDQS, which covers 31 communes in the Aude. The terroir receives Atlantic influences and is situated in the northwest of the Hauts-de-Corbières, which protect it from Mediterranean aridity. The red and rosé wines, full-bodied and fruity, come not only from Carignan grapes but also from Bordeaux varieties, mainly Cabernet Sauvignon, Cabernet Franc and Merlot, in addition to Grenache and Cot.

CH. DE BARTHE 2000★★

| | n.c. | 12,000 | ◖▮ | 5–8 € |

This new name establishes itself as one of the best buys of the cooperative wine cellar that has just re-equipped its winery with superb new, maturation barrel stores. This 2000 makes an opening statement with its intense colour and a nose of highly ripe fruits, coupled with light hints of vanilla. A powerful start introduces a palate well endowed with fine, yet still prominent tannins and a lingering finish. A wine to lay down, in order to reach its full potential.

☛ Cave la Malepère, av. des Vignerons, 11290 Arzens, tel. 04.68.76.71.71, fax 04.68.76.71.72, e-mail oeno@cavelamalepere.com ☑
☥ ev. day except Sat. Sun. 8am–12 noon 2pm–6pm

CH. DE COINTES 2002★

| | 10 ha | 6,600 | ■ ♦ | 5–8 € |

The origins and name of this family property come from André and Jean Cointes, first Consuls of Carcassonne in the 17th century. Once again, a rosé has been selected. This attractive rosé has an intense, bright, clear-coloured appearance. The nose is dominated by fresh fruits; the palate, accompanied throughout by hints of fruitiness, appears rich and lingering.
☛ Anne Gorostis, Ch. de Cointes, 11290 Roullens, tel. 04.68.26.81.05, fax 04.68.26.84.37, e-mail gorostis@châteaudecointes.com ☑
☥ by appt.

DOM. GIRARD

Cuvée Neri 2001★★

| | n.c. | 2,000 | ◖▮ | 8–11 € |

New *vignerons* embarking upon the adventure of managing this particular wine cellar, André and Philippe Girard have already to their credit some superbly produced wines. The first is as recent as the year 2000; this, their second vintage, is an intense, ruby coloured *cuvée*, with inky-black highlights. A rich nose combines fruits steeped in alcohol with oaked overtones. The powerful palate reveals hints of liquorice and an over-oaked presence. An attractive wine to lay down.
☛ André et Philippe Girard, 5, rue de la Fontaine, 11240 Alaigne, tel. 04.68.69.05.27, fax 04.68.69.05.27 ☑
☥ by appt.

CH. GUILHEM

Cuvée Prestige 2000★★

| | 2 ha | 13,000 | ◖▮ | 5–8 € |

A family property, situated in the ruins of a Gallo-Roman villa. A brilliant repeat performance in the *Guide* endorses the efforts put into both vineyard and wine cellar. The intense nose of dark, ripe fruits is accompanied by hints of grilled meats. A balanced palate, underlined by grilled, oaky flavours offers a lingering finish, with undertones of dark fruits.
☛ Ch. Guilhem, Le Château, 11300 Malviès, tel. 04.68.31.14.41, fax 04.68.31.58.09 ☑
☥ by appt.
☛ B. Gourdou-Guilhem

CH. G. GUIRAUD 2000★★★

| | 18 ha | 120,000 | ◖▮ | 5–8 € |

Once again, the flagship *cuvée* of the Razès cooperative wine cellar was singled out by the Jurors of the *Guide*. This brilliant purple-coloured wine put on a superb performance at the tasting. Spiced nose, with a light touch of vanilla; a fine rounded start, on the palate, offers well-integrated tannins and a lingering finish, accompanied by light oakiness. The tasters were equally impressed by the **Château de Nougayrol red 2001 (3–5 €)** and the **Rosé 2002 (3–5 €)**.
☛ Cave du Razès, 11240 Routier, tel. 04.68.69.02.71, fax 04.68.69.00.49, e-mail info@cave-razes.com ☑
☥ ev. day except Sat. Sun. 9am–12 noon 2pm–6pm

Roussillon

Growing vines in Roussillon may date as far back as the seventh century BC, perhaps instigated by Greek traders, drawn to the Catalan coast by its rich mineral deposits. The trade was well developed by medieval times, and the sweet wines of the region built a solid reputation very early on. After their devastation by phylloxera in the early 20th century, the vineyards were abundantly replanted to flourish once again on the hills of France's southernmost vine-growing area.

Facing the Mediterranean, the Roussillon vineyards are surrounded by three mountain ranges: the Corbières in the north, the Canigou in the west and the Albères, which forms the border with Spain, in the south. The Têt, Tech and Agly rivers have shaped a landscape of gravel terraces where the washed, stony soils are ideally suited to produce wines of quality, particularly Vin Doux Naturels (see relevant section). Also found are soils from different origins made up of black or brown schists and sandy granites as well as hills of Pliocene limestone.

The Roussillon vineyards enjoy a particularly sunny climate, with mild winters and high temperatures in summer. The rainfall – 350–650 mm – is very uneven and often falls in torrential storms that are not beneficial for the vines. Fortunately, a dry, summer period follows, and the heat is intensified by the Tramontane wind, which helps the grapes to ripen.

The vines are trained in the traditional goblet shape and planted 4,000 to the hectare. Tradition still plays a great part in cultivation, which is often only partly mechanized. However, the winemaking equipment in the cellars is being modernized in line with a diversification in vine varieties and vinification techniques. After being carefully checked for ripeness, the harvest is transported in trailers or small trucks without being crushed; some of the grapes are treated by carbonic maceration. Increasingly, temperature during vinification is controlled to protect the delicacy of the aromas: in Roussillon, tradition and modern technology work side by side.

Roussillon

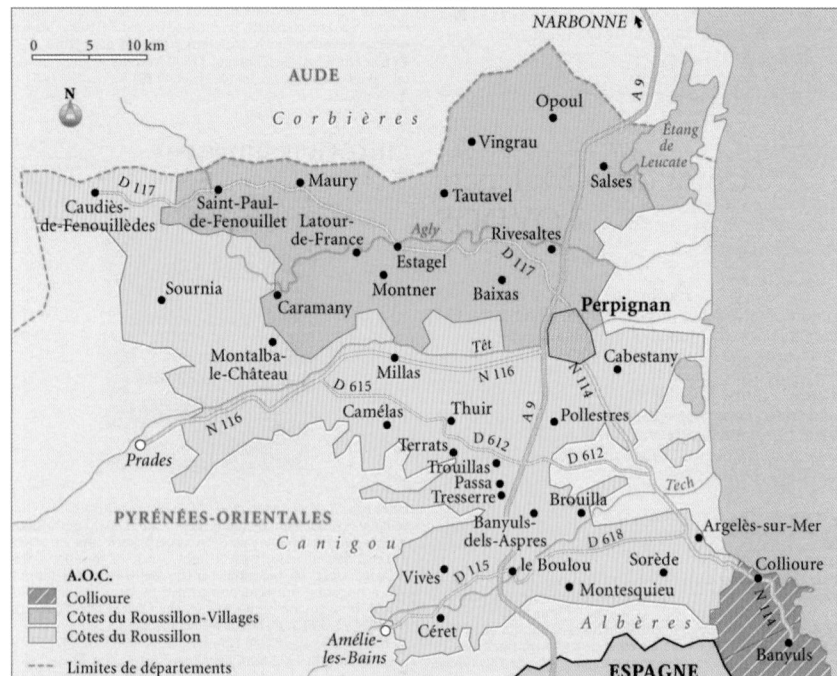

COTES DU ROUSSILLON AND COTES DU ROUSSILLON-VILLAGES

These two appellations are produced from the best soils in the region. The vineyards, about 9,000 ha, produce 310,000 hl across the whole of the appellation. The Côtes du Roussillon-Villages are clustered in the northernmost part of the Pyrénées-Orientales *département*; four communes have an appellation with the village name: Caramany, Lesquerde, Tautavel and Latour-de-France. Gravel terraces, sandy granite and schist give the wines a richness and a qualitative difference that the wine-growers certainly know how to exploit.

The vine varieties used to produce the white wines are mainly Macabeu, Malvoisie du Roussillon and Grenache Blanc, but Marsanne, Roussanne and Rolle are also used and are mainly vinified by direct pressing. The wines themselves are green in type, light and vigorous, with a fine, floral aroma and so go well with seafood, fish and shellfish.

The rosé and red wines are produced using several varieties: Carignan Noir (a maximum of 60%), Grenache Noir, Lladonner Pelut and Cinsault are the main varieties, with Syrah, Mouvèdre and Macabeu (10% maximum in the red wines) as additional varieties; two main varieties are required with another additional variety. All the varieties (except the Syrah) are pruned short down to two buds. Often, a proportion of the harvest is vinified by carbonic maceration: Carignan in particular produces excellent results with this method. The rosé wines are, of necessity, vinified by the *saignée*, or bleeding method.

The rosé wines are fruity, full-bodied and lively; the red wines are fruity, spicy and rich in alcohol, about 12%. The Côtes du Roussillon-Villages are warmer and more full-bodied; some can be drunk young but others can be kept longer and these develop an intense, complex bouquet. Such appeal and individuality make Roussillon wines versatile accompaniments to a wide variety of dishes.

Côtes du Roussillon

DOM. ALQUIER
Cuvée des Filles 2001★★★

	2.5 ha	3,000	🍶	11–15€

"You who pass by, without noticing me...", as sung by the Catalan Charles Trenet, have got it wrong! And many of you pass by the foot of Saint Jean, between Le Boulou and the Col de Perthus, oblivious to its treasures, a mere couple of steps away from the motorway, at the opening to the rugged terrain of the Tech Valley, that is also capable of such clemency, amid the cherry and mimosa trees. Following a remarkable white wine, last year, this Cuvée des Filles is bedecked with stars. Dark, deep, intense appearance; surprising grilled and roasted overtones, intense aromas of

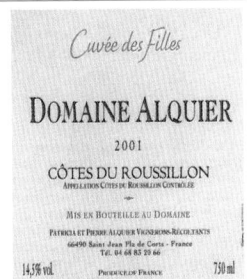

arabica greet the nose and then the palate, before revealing a balanced, full-bodied, fleshy wine with supple tannins and flavours of juniper, crystallized fruit and liquorice. A wine of the utmost finesse; ready to serve now with stews or red meats.

↘ Pierre Alquier, Dom. Alquier,
66490 Saint-Jean-Pla-de-Corts, tel. 04.68.83.20.66,
fax 04.68.83.55.45 ☑
👅 ev. day except Sun. 9am–12 noon 2pm–7pm

ARNAUD DE VILLENEUVE
Vieilles Vignes 2002★

	n.c.	7,000	🍶 🍷	3–5€

The largest vinification unit in the *département* of Pyrénées-Orientales proves, with this white wine, that one can be located in a region famous for its naturally sweet wines and red wines yet also perfect wines produced for a limited audience, such as this white *cuvée*. The 2002, with its pale, greenish appearance, exhibits a delicate nose that mingles floral and rosemary-honey aromas. Suppleness, freshness are accompanied by a welcoming slight sparkle, then a suggestion of fennel and apricot, wavering between flowers and fruits, the finish offers citrus flavours. Pair with bass cooked in fennel?

↘ Les Vignobles du Rivesaltais, 1, rue de la Roussillonnaise, 66602 Rivesaltes, tel. 04.68.64.06.63,
fax 04.68.64.64.69,
e-mail vignobles.rivesaltais@wanadoo.fr ☑
👅 by appt.

CH. BELLOCH 2000★★

	6 ha	6,000	🍶 🍷	3–5€

Throughout its lengthy history, the Têt has deposited, between Perpignan and Canet, a layer of pebbles that has rolled down from the Pyrénées, forming a smooth terrace where vines undulate between sea and coastal lagoons. This terroir has produced for us, today, a wine that is ready to drink now. With its Bordeaux characteristics, the *cuvée* evolves with balsamic aromas and a suggestion of musk and venison. The attractive palate is structured, yet fruity, and accompanied by pleasant hints of smoke and strong tannins. Escalope Cordon Bleu or haunch of wild boar? The choice is immense.

↘ SA Cibaud-Ch. Miraflors et Belloch, rte de Canet, 66000 Perpignan, tel. 04.68.50.24.92, fax 04.68.67.20.02,
e-mail vinscibaud@wanadoo.fr ☑
👅 ev. day 9am–12 noon 3.30pm–6.30pm
↘ Alain Cibaud

CH. DE BLANES
Elevé en fût de chêne 2000★★

	35 ha	n.c.	🍶 🍷 🍷	5–8€

Strolling along the narrow road that leads from Baho to Pézilla, under the shade of the plane trees at the foot of the wine-producing slopes, you encounter the ancient farm of Blanes, with its red-brick towers and shingle pebbles. There you will find this delicate-hued selection, dominated by Syrah (80% of the blend), a pronounced, though well structured oakiness. Fresh, spicy start, elegant and pleasant, this Côtes du Roussillon is ready to drink now.

↘ Les vignerons de Pézilla, 1, av. du Canigou,
66370 Pézilla-la-Rivière, tel. 04.68.92.00.09,
fax 04.68.92.49.91 ☑
👅 by appt.

CH. LA CASENOVE

Cuvée Cdt François Jaubert 2000★★★

■	2 ha	6,000		23–30 €

The profession of the *vigneron* is exacting: one needs to be multi-talented; despite these constraints, certain individuals, such as Etienne Montès are also environmentally aware and do not hesitate to devote time to replenishing old olive groves. The vineyard, in the meantime, is not neglected, as is evident in this *cuvée*, a regular selection in the *Guide* and from where the 2000 vintage derives. The intense, relatively young, ruby-red appearance heralds strong, powerful, rich body and a sun-drenched nose of very ripe fruits, spices and pepper. A wine to lay down. Full, fleshy fruitiness indicate a wine that has been skilfully produced. This *cuvée* would go well with a joint of beef, wild boar or cheese. The Jury was equally impressed by the **Cuvée La Garrigue red 2000 (8–11 €)**.

☛ Etienne Montès, Ch. La Casenove, 66300 Trouillas, tel. 04.68.21.66.33, fax 04.68.21.77.81 ☑
Ⴤ by appt.

VIGNERONS CATALANS

Vica Soleil 2001★★

■	11 ha	60,000	■ ♦	3–5 €

The largest producer of Roussillon dry wines is diversifying its range, with produce from its terroirs or with *cuveés* such as the following: **Côtes du Roussillon Art de Vivre red 2001 (5–8 €)**, singled out by the Jury and certainly destined for the export market, if the label (*The Art of bottling sunshine*) is anything to go by. This attractive ruby-red-coloured wine offers a highly fresh nose that wafts between soft fruits and violet. The palate is dominated by fruity flavours, accompanied by fine tannins; the finish retains freshness and finesse. A balanced wine, ready to drink from now on.

☛ Vignerons Catalans, 1870, av. Julien-Panchot, BP 29000, 66962 Perpignan Cedex 9, tel. 04.68.85.04.51, fax 04.68.55.25.62, e-mail contact@vignerons-catalans.com
Ⴤ by appt.

DOM. DES DEMOISELLES

Le Mas 2001★

■	4 ha	10,000	■	5–8 €

Every autumn, the village of Tresserre celebrates *Les Bruixas* (witches and fairies). For the rest of the year, other young ladies, with magic fingers, cultivate the vine and grapes with equal passion, under the fickle eye of Canigou mountain. Blackcurrant, venison and undergrowth go hand in hand with the cherry-like appearance of this 2001. The palate offers powerful, fleshy, yet unrestrained continuity, within a fine structure. Cellar for a year or two, before serving with game or a thickly cut beef steak.

☛ Isabelle Raoux, Dom. des Demoiselles, Mas Mulès, 66300 Tresserre, tel. 04.68.38.87.10, fax 04.68.38.87.10, e-mail domaine.des.demoiselles@wanadoo.fr ☑ ⌂
Ⴤ ev. day except Mon. 11am–1pm 4pm–8pm; cl. Jan.

DOM. GALY

Prestige 2000★★

■	5 ha	20,000	■ ⏅ ♦	5–8 €

One cannot pass through Bages without noticing the area's emphasis on viticulture. Huge entrances to wine cellars open to the public, wine casks, fine, imposing signage, Catalan colours attract one's attention and draw in the tourists. Here we have the vast Galy domaine, with its remarkable Prestige Cuvée. First impressions offer aromas of soft fruit, vanilla and ripe banana. This is followed by surprising hints of leather and truffle. The start reveals a fresh and fruity wine; rich, aromatic flavours, on the palate, dominated by soft fruits and cinnamon, deftly envelop well-integrated tannins. Such composition should go well with beef or morels.

☛ Dom. Galy, rue du Cinéma, 66670 Bages, tel. 04.68.21.80.49, fax 04.68.21.87.37, e-mail domainegaly.vin@wanadoo.fr ☑
Ⴤ ev.day except Sun. 9.30am–12.30pm 3.30pm–7pm

HELENAE 2001★★

■	3 ha	16,400	■ ♦	3–5 €

A fine selection, this *cuvée* from Elne, a town well known for its romanesque cloisters, for its rich market-gardening terroir

and the *Béa de Roussillon* (a potato variety), as well as the cultivation of Syrah, a grape variety that makes up 80% of this blend. The deep-red-colour of this particular Côtes du Roussillon, is highly characteristic of this grape variety; a well developed nose of overripe fruits, black olive and venison. With its velvety, lightly spiced palate and supple tannins, the wine simply oozes finesse. Serve alongside braised red meats. Also singled out, the very attractive, typically Mediterranean **Château de Castelnou red 99 (5–8 €)**.

☛ SCV Elne pour Méditerroirs, 1870, av. Julien-Panchot, BP 89933, 66962 Perpignan Cedex 09, tel. 04.68.55.88.40, fax 04.68.55.87.67, e-mail mediterroirs@caramail.com

DOM. JOLIETTE

Cuvée André Mercier 2001★★

■	6.09 ha	11,600	■ ⏅ ♦	8–11 €

A pine wood, cicadas, the sea in the distance, beyond the farmhouse a terroir that hovers between dark calcareous marl and red clay soils. In this setting, one cannot help but admire nature and respect it with organic cultivation. The Joliette domaine features regularly in the *Guide*. From the 2001 vintage, the Cuvée André Mercier grabs the spotlight: deep, inky-black colour, a roundness of woodland fruits (blackberry, blackcurrant) frolic around pronounced, charred oak overtones. Key word, on the palate? Balance, with fine structure, fruity fullness and deep, mineral undertones. A measured oak contribution lends suppleness and length. Also specially mentioned by the Jury, the **Cuvée Domaine Joliette Montpins L'Extrait red 2001 (15–23 €)**.

☛ EARL Mercier, Dom. Joliette, rte de Montpins, 66600 Espira-de-l'Agly, tel. 04.68.64.50.60, fax 04.68.64.18.82 ☑
Ⴤ by appt.

DOM. LAFAGE

Cuvée Le Vignon 2000★★

■	1.65 ha	5,500	⏅	15–23 €

The Vignon vineyard specializes in cultivation using short terraces that follow the contours of the land. The domaine extends to an altitude of 300 m, turning its back on the fresh air of Canigou to admire the hills of Aspres, with the sea on the horizon. This environment has produced a garnet-coloured *cuvée*, with a nose that mingles blackcurrant, undergrowth and crystallized fruits; strength, fullness and structure make up the balanced palate, with flavourful tannins and hints of black cherry and vanilla flavoured prunes. Pale and golden, in the glass, the **Domaine Lafage white 2002 (8–11 €)** also impressed the Jury with its fine, oaked overtones and floral aromas of garrigue, as well as its richness and weight.

☛ SCEA Dom. Lafage, Mas Durand, 66140 Canet-en-Roussillon, tel. 04.68.80.35.82, fax 04.68.80.38.90, e-mail domaine.lafage@wanadoo.fr ☑
Ⴤ by appt.

DOM. LAPORTE

Sumeria 2001★

■	n.c.	5,000	⏅	11–15 €

Between Catalan Perpignan and the cosmopolitan seaside resort of Canet, the vine still plays an important role on the terraces of the Têt, dominated by the market gardens of Roussillon. These vines have produced a wine that reflects its maturation in oak and possesses a dark complexion and flavours of spices, blackberry, cherry and patinated leather. The palate follows the same aromatic pattern; powerful, structured, all factors that indicate exceptional balance from now on and up to two or three years hence.

☛ Dom. Laporte, Ch. Roussillon, 66000 Perpignan, tel. 04.68.50.06.53, fax 04.68.66.77.52, e-mail domaine-laporte@wanadoo.fr ☑
Ⴤ by appt.

CH. LAURIGA 2001★

■	15 ha	10,000	■ ♦	8–11 €

Born on the vineyard, René and Jacqueline Clar had to wait until their fifties, before realizing their dream: to become *vignerons*. They converted an old farm house and set up a domaine of around 60 hectares. The fruits of their labour have been bestowed upon this 2001: suppleness, freshness and an engaging, lively red appearance, colluding with blackcurrant berries and undergrowth. The fine, rounded palate reveals well-integrated tannins that give the wine its easy-to-drink qualities and a finish with a hint of menthol. An elegant *cuvée* to uncork with white meat dishes.

☛ Lauriga, traverse de Ponteilla, 66300 Thuir, tel. 04.68.53.26.73, fax 04.68.53.58.37 ☑
🍷 ev. day except Sun. 4pm–8pm; Sat. 10am–7pm
☛ R. et J. Clar

DOM. MARCEVOL

Tradition 2001★

■	6.5 ha	14,500	🍶	5–8 €

To reach Marcevol, one has to ascend the Têt Valley to Les Fenouillèdes. A surprise awaits in the hamlet of Arboussols, for here one comes across a miniature golf course, a priory with a remarkable rose marble portal; magnificent scenery, a Mediterranean backdrop and vines growing to an altitude of 600 m; a well-positioned, south-facing location, with its back to snow-capped Canigou. It is within this setting that Guy Prédal recently set up his enterprise, the produce of which we can sample, in this second vintage. The deep, bright colour reflects the wine's natural habitat. Somewhat lacking in length, the bouquet of soft fruits mingles raspberries, redcurrants with hints of undergrowth. Rounded, full of finesse, integrated, with a touch of scrubland on the finish, all add up to a highly successful wine.

☛ EARL Prédal Verhaeghe, Marcevol, 66320 Arboussols, tel. 04.68.05.74.34, fax 04.68.05.74.34 ☑
🍷 by appt.

DOM. DU MARIDET

Cap de Marra 2001★

■	n.c.	6,300	🍶 ⓲ 🍷	5–8 €

For a long while, making and selling wine was but a dream for Louis Rigaill. In the "madness" of his forties, however, he proceeded, not only to realize his dream but also to promote his produce and the name of his *cuvées*. The upshot is a label with a panther skin design that adorns this deep red-coloured Cap de Marra, a wine that mingles fruity overtones with hints of roasted American coffee. Very pleasant on the palate, lightly spiced, the wine develops flavours ranging between raspberry and redcurrant, before drifting away on a note of violet and bitter liquorice. A tannic, but already pleasant wine.

☛ Dom. du Maridet, 21, bd de la Marine, Mas de L'Alme, 66510 Saint-Hippolyte, tel. 06.86.85.45.95, fax 04.68.59.61.46 ☑
🍷 by appt.
☛ Louis Rigaill

MAS AMIEL

Le Plaisir 2002★

■	10 ha	24,000	🍶 🍷	5–8 €

Renowned for its Maury wines, the Mas Amiel cultivates the characteristic black soil terroir that yields dry, expressive wines such as this **Côtes du Roussillon Hautes Terres red 2001 (8–11 €)** and this extremely attractive rosé. Peony-coloured to the eye, the 2002 is structured around a floral nose that mingles wild flowers with the sweetness of fresh grapes. Pleasant composition, full and rich, this easy-drinking wine would go well with Catalan charcuterie, or white meats.

☛ Dom. Mas Amiel, 66460 Maury, tel. 04.68.29.01.02, fax 04.68.29.17.82 ☑
🍷 ev. day 9am–12 noon 2pm–5pm
☛ Decelle

DOM. DU MAS BECHA

Elevé en fût de chêne 2001★

■	41.74 ha	11,500	🍶 ⓲ 🍷	5–8 €

A great deal of work has been carried out at Mas Bécha in recent years, thanks to the realization of investments in both winery and vines and the unstinting daily commitment of Bernard Bataille, who is in overall charge of the estate. His efforts translate into regular selections in the *Guide* since the 99 vintage. This deep-red-ruby-coloured Côtes du Roussillon presents an intense smoke and vanilla nose structured around aromas of stewed fruits. The start is full-bodied. The wine has a pronounced tannic presence and opens with fruity aromas,

merging, on the finish, with spicy flavours. This fine wine has two or three years ahead of it.

☛ Dom. Mas Bécha, 66300 Nyls-Ponteilla, tel. 04.68.54.52.80, fax 04.68.55.31.89 ☑
🍷 by appt.
☛ Perez

DOM. DU MAS CREMAT 2001★

■	8.5 ha	40,000	🍶 🍷	5–8 €

The black-red volcanic terrain inspired the name of the house of Crémat (smouldering), at Espira-de-l'Agly. C. Jeannin-Mongeard set up the enterprise in 1990, bringing to the Catalan vines this Burgundian look that seems so appropriate. This Côtes du Roussillon has a deep-red-purple-coloured appearance. Once the hesitant nose is allowed to breathe, it exudes aromas of ripe fruit, black-cherry, grapes in brandy and rhubarb. First impressions reveal a rich, balanced palate and substantial tannins; cherry and the fruitiness of the Syrah grape variety are all present. If you cellar this wine for a while you will be surprised by its expressive character.

☛ Jeannin-Mongeard, Mas Crémat, 66600 Espira-de-l'Agly, tel. 04.68.38.92.06, fax 04.68.38.92.23, e-mail mascremat@mascremat.com ☑
🍷 by appt.

MAS D'EN BADIE

Saint-Etienne des vignes 2000★★★

■	4.15 ha	19,914	⓲	11–15 €

What a mountain of achievement by this cooperative in recent years. The *vignerons* of Passa have certainly rolled up their sleeves; new technology equipment has followed and the results are evident. A unanimous verdict for this deep garnet-red 2000, with a ripe nose of cherry jam, venison and undergrowth; the palate endorses the virtues of this wine, warming, full and powerful. Intense, structured tannins evolve with vanilla fruitiness and roasted undertones. A fine wine for today, and tomorrow.

☛ SCA des Vignerons de Passa, rte de Villemolaque, 66300 Passa, tel. 04.68.38.80.74, fax 04.68.38.88.98, e-mail antonin-passa@libertysurf.fr ☑
🍷 by appt.

DOM. DU MAS ROUS

Elevé en fût de chêne 2000★★

■	11 ha	36,000	⓲	5–8 €

Before plunging into the sea, the Pyrénées have had the decency to offer us the Albères. The terraces of the Tech, vine territory, forest, the peak of Neulous (1,100 m), an expanse of blue sky, at all levels…It is in this context that José Pujol set up his enterprise, where the wines are always welcomed by the Jury who awarded a *coup de coeur* for the 1998 vintage. Deep, garnet-red with light tinges, this 2000 mingles fruits in brandy with vanilla. The pleasant palate reveals supple tannins accompanied by hints of charred oak. Pronounced and velvety, this wine is destined for immediate pleasure.

☛ José Pujol, Dom. du Mas Rous, BP 4, 66740 Montesquieu-Albères, tel. 04.68.89.64.91, fax 04.68.89.80.88, e-mail masrous@mas-rous.com ☑
🍷 by appt.

CH. MOSSE

Tradition 2001★★

| ■ | | 15 ha | 20,000 | ■ ♦ | | 5–8 € |

As usual, Jacques Mossé appears on the Côtes du Roussillon section of the *Guide*. This passionate and warm-hearted man has skilfully mastered his art, lavishing extra affection upon his 100 year old Carignans. As in the previous two (superb) years, the **Coume d'Abeille red 2001 (8–11 €)** was singled out by the Jury. A substantial, delicately oaked wine, this deep garnet-coloured Tradition *cuvée* stole the show, as far as the Jury was concerned; bursting with soft fruits and flavours of juniper, warming, fleshy, seductive, with a hint of plum, supple tannic texture and pleasant, exotic finish, with undertones of vanilla, walnut and coconut.

●┐ Jacques Mossé, Ch. Mossé,
66301 Ste-Colombe-de-la-Commanderie,
tel. 04.68.53.08.89, fax 04.68.53.35.13,
e-mail chateau.mosse@worldonline.fr ☑
� by appt.

DOM. PIQUEMAL 2001★★

| ■ | | 20 ha | 50,000 | ■ ♦ | | 5–8 € |

On the face of it, everything is straightforward, but blending the cru's four grape varieties calls for flexible vinification methods and a familiarity with necessary daily routine procedures. That means the exchange of know-how between grandfather Justin Piquemal and Franck, his grandson. This 2001 endorses the domaine's know-how. It nevertheless reflects a remarkable approach. This intense, luminous, red wine mingles spices, garrigue with fruity flavours. A fine, complex palate and a wine that closely resembles its grapes, round, fruity, and already remarkably well integrated. Drink for its sheer fruitiness or cellar for its strength.

●┐ Dom. Piquemal, 1, rue Pierre-Lefranc,
66600 Espira-de-l'Agly, tel. 04.68.64.09.14,
fax 04.68.38.52.94,
e-mail contact@domaine-piquemal.com ☑
� by appt.

CH. PLANERES

La Romanie 2000★★

| ■ | | 8 ha | 10,000 | ⦀ | | 15–23 € |

This domaine cultivates according to traditional methods, throughout the old red-brick building that dominates the plateau of Saint-Jean-Lasseille; the only sop to modernity is a highly functional barrel store. Following a *coup de coeur* for the 2000 white, here we have the same Cuvée La Romanie as a red. Intense, dark garnet-coloured, this wine endorses the talents of the *vigneron*. Discreet, initially, with a pronounced mineral hint of gun flint, followed by expansive flavours of wild fruits and touches of pepper and charred oak. A surprise awaits, on the palate: both supple and pleasant, with velvety tannins, a rare sense of satisfaction is experienced. Blackberry and blackcurrant accompany a touch of Mourvèdre coffee that persists right up to the spicy finish. Is that all? No, the Jury was also impressed by the **Château Planères La Coume d'Ars red 2001 (8–11 €)** and the **Château Planères white Cuvée Prestige 2002 (5–8 €)**.

●┐ Vignobles Jaubert-Noury, Ch. Planères,
66300 Saint-Jean-Lasseille, tel. 04.68.21.74.50,
fax 04.68.21.87.25, e-mail contact@chateauplaneres.com ☑
� ev. day except Sun. 9am–12 noon 2pm–6pm;
winter Sat. by appt.

PRIMO PALATUM 2000★★

| ■ | | 4.5 ha | 2,100 | ⦀ | | 15–23 € |

Singled out by the Jury last year, his Côtes du Roussillon is lined up for high praise once again. Pronounced evidence of oak maturation, the start opens with aromas of spice, liquorice and blackcurrant. Fresh, straightforward first impressions, with undertones of fruit and blackcurrant berries, excellent balance between wine and hints of charred oak, fine length, all add up to a wine that is true to type and that already fills the mouth. Also specially mentioned, a delicately oaked **Primo Palatum white 2001**.

●┐ Primo Palatum, 1, Cirette, 33190 Morizès,
tel. 05.56.71.39.39, fax 05.56.71.39.40,
e-mail xavier-copel@primo-palatum.com ☑
☑ by appt.
●┐ Xavier Copel

PUJOL

La Montadella 2000★★

| ■ | | 1.8 ha | 10,000 | ⦀ | | 8–11 € |

Converting 60 ha to organic growing was a bold move. Mission accomplished! One has to say that Jean-Luc Pujol is not the sort of person to be easily defeated. Highly successful, with his previous vintage, this year's *cuvée* truly seduced the Jury. The particularly lively nose surprised the tasters with its aromas of fruits steeped in brandy and evolving hints of blackcurrant. Following a straightforward, fresh start, one discovers a supple, cheerful, fresh and fruity wine, fine roundness; sampling this *cuvée*'s charms, without further delay, is a must! The more full-bodied style **Pujol 98 red Elevé en Fût (5–8 €)** also impressed the Jury.

●┐ Jean-Luc Pujol, Dom. La Rourède, 66300 Fourques,
tel. 04.68.38.84.44, fax 04.68.38.88.86,
e-mail vins.pujol@wanadoo.fr ☑
☑ ev. day except Sun. 9am–12 noon 3pm–6pm

CH. DE REY

Les Galets roulés 2001★★★

| ■ | | 2.5 ha | 5,300 | ⦀ | | 11–15 € |

The large pebbled terrace that extends towards the Etang de Canet is dominated by the architecture of the Château de Rey, which appears to be emerging from the dreams of Ludwig II of Bavaria. Philippe Sisqueille, great-grandson of the founder of the domaine, has taken over the enterprise. The group has hit the nail on the head with a **Château de Rey white 2001 (3–5 €)** and a **rosé 2001 (3–5 €)**, singled out for their freshness, and this garnet-red Côtes du Roussillon with an attractive nose of soft fruits and hints of spices. This full-bodied wine, with supple tannins, deveops with undertones of ripe fruit and liquorice. A fresh finish concludes the tasting of this exceptionally balanced 2001.

●┐ Philippe et Cathy Sisqueille, Ch. de Rey,
66140 Canet-en-Roussillon, tel. 04.68.73.86.27,
fax 04.68.73.15.03,
e-mail chateau-de-rey@libertysurf.fr ☑ ⌂
☑ by appt.

DOM. RIERE CADENE

Cuvée Jean Rière 2001★

| ■ | | n.c. | 2,300 | | | 8–11 € |

A *vigneron* from Perpignan, Jean-François Rière figures prominently as one of a small number of viticulturists who have managed to resist demands for their land, in order to preserve the pleasures of town and country lovers. This Cuvée Jean Rière wavers between flavours of black-cherry and wild undergrowth. On the palate, we have a typical Syrah-style wine (80% of the blend), uncomplicated but surprisingly fresh and supple, with fine, well-integrated and lightly peppered tannins. Ready to drink from now on, with roasted green peppers or a typical *Boles de Picolat* (meat balls with green olives and mushrooms).

●┐ J.-F. Rière, Dom. Rière Cadène, Mas Bel-Air, chem.
Saint-Génis-de-Tanyères, 66000 Perpignan,
tel. 04.68.63.87.29, fax 04.68.52.30.65,
e-mail riere@wanadoo.fr ☑ ⌂
☑ by appt.

CH. DE SAU

Cuvée réservée 2001★★

| ■ | | n.c. | 19,000 | | | 5–8 € |

Dynamic and passionate is how one would describe Hervé Passama, who is actively involved in the preservation of certain wine cellars. He does not, however, neglect his own terroir, as we can see from a string of *cuvées* that regularly feature in the *Guide*. Derived from Carignan, Grenache and Syrah, in equal proportions, this 2001 was specially mentioned by the Jury. Upon breathing, the ruby-red colour filters through hints of spice and ripe cherry, characteristic of carbonic maceration. The palate reveals a surprising fullness, generous structure, fleshy, grilled flavours. The overall effect

is balanced, rich and full, leaving a lasting impression of fresh fruitiness. A fine wine that should be laid down for a year or two.
🐦 Hervé Passama, Ch. de Sau, 66300 Thuir, tel. 04.68.53.21.74, fax 04.68.53.29.07, e-mail chateaudesau@aol.com ☑
🍷 by appt.

DOM. SOL-PAYRE

Scelerata Ame noire 2001★★★

■	7 ha	25,000	⑾	11–15 €

Grandfather Payré paved the way: a farm worker, turned land-owner in 1903. Generations later, did Jean-Claude Sol feel vaguely melancholic? Did the maze of streets in the old town of Elne (where the wine cellar is located, 200 m from the cathedral and fine cloisters) inspire the unusual, rather Gothic name of this *cuvée*? The deep colour heralds a wine of fine pedigree. Maturation in oak barrels lends a touch of vanilla, mingled with black cherry and blackberry. Powerful and balanced, the wine is rich in tannins and of exceptional finesse, supported by crystallized, spicy fruit flavours. Oak overtones confirm the meticulous standards of maturation and accentuate the wine's fullness and length. The enthusiast will not be disappointed with this Scelerata that should wait to be served with venison stew.
🐦 Jean-Claude Sol, Dom. Sol-Payré, rue de Paris, 66200 Elne, tel. 04.68.22.86.14, fax 04.68.22.50.42, e-mail jeanclaudesold2@wanadoo.fr ☑
🍷 ev. day 9am–12 noon 4pm–7pm; Jan. Feb. Mar. and Sun. mornings

LE ROSE DE TERRASSOUS 2001★

■	4 ha	20,000	▮ ♦	3–5 €

Production of rosés is expanding in Roussillon: this particular wine with its fruitiness and intense colour exhibits typical Mediterranean characteristics. The Terrats cooperative, drawing on a base of Syrah, Grenache and Carignan – a Catalan trilogy – has nominated a remarkable example of this type of wine. The *cuvée* possesses the qualities one has come to expect of a rosé, delicious, welcoming aromas of raspberry, freshness on the palate, a presence that retains its smooth, fruity fullness and vitality. The **Côtes du Rousssillon Villare Juliani red 2001 (5–8 €)** also impressed the Jury.
🐦 SCV Les Vignerons de Terrats, BP 32, 66302 Terrats Cedex, tel. 04.68.53.02.50, fax 04.68.53.23.06, e-mail scv-terrats@wanadoo.fr ☑
🍷 ev. day except Sun. 8am–12 noon 2pm–6pm

Wines selected but not starred

DOM. AMOUROUX

Passion 2000

■	n.c.	2,500	▮ ⑾ ♦	5–8 €

🐦 Dom. Jean Amouroux, 15, rue du Pla-del-Rey, 66300 Tresserre, tel. 04.68.38.87.54, fax 04.68.38.89.90 ☑
🍷 by appt.

CH. DE L'OU 2001

■	1 ha	5,300	▮ ♦	5–8 €

🐦 Ch. de l'Ou, 66200 Montescot, tel. 06.03.13.67.49, fax 04.68.35.50.51, e-mail chateaudelou@wanadoo.fr ☑ 🏠
🍷 by appt.
🐦 Bourrier

DOM. PARCE 2002

■	2 ha	5,200	▮ ♦	5–8 €

🐦 EARL A. Parcé, 21 ter, rue du 14-Juillet, 66670 Bages, tel. 04.68.21.80.45, fax 04.68.21.69.40, e-mail vinsparce@aol.com ☑
🍷 ev. day except Sun. 9.30am–12.15pm 4pm–7.30pm

DOM. DE LA PERDRIX

Cuvée Joseph-Sébastien Pons 2001

■	2 ha	4,500	⑾	8–11 €

🐦 Dom. de la Perdrix, 7, rue des Platanes, 66300 Trouillas, tel. 04.68.53.12.74, fax 04.68.53.52.73, e-mail domaineperdrix@libertysurf.fr ☑
🍷 by appt.
🐦 M. et Mme Gil

CH. LES PINS

Vinifié en barrique 2001

■	8 ha	22,000	⑾	8–11 €

🐦 Cave Les Vignerons de Baixas, 14, av. du Mal-Joffre, 66390 Baixas, tel. 04.68.64.22.37, fax 04.68.64.26.70, e-mail contact@dom-brial.com ☑
🍷 by appt.

DOM. PUIG-PARAHY

Le Fort Saint-Pierre 2001

■	10 ha	16,000	▮ ♦	11–15 €

🐦 Puig-Parahy, Le Fort Saint-Pierre, 66300 Passa, tel. 06.14.55.71.71, fax 04.68.38.88.77, e-mail g.puig-parahy@tiscali.fr ☑ 🏠
🍷 by appt.

CH. ROMBEAU Cuvée Pierre de La Fabrègue

Elevé en fût de chêne 1999

■	14 ha	13,000	⑾	8–11 €

🐦 Pierre-Henri de La Fabrègue, D 12, rte de Perpignan, 66600 Rivesaltes, tel. 04.68.64.35.35, fax 04.68.64.64.66 ☑
🍷 ev. day 10am–7pm

CH. VALFON

Mirabet 2001

■	2 ha	7,000	⑾	8–11 €

🐦 GAEC Dom. Valfon, pl. Gabriel-Péri, 66300 Thuir, tel. 04.68.53.61.66, fax 04.68.53.06.19, e-mail chvalfon@aol.com ☑
🍷 ev. day 9.30am–12.30pm 4.30pm–7.30pm; cl. Thu. am and Sun. pm
🐦 Valette-Fons

CH. VALMY 2001

■	4 ha	23,000	▮ ♦	8–11 €

🐦 Bernard Carbonnell, Ch. de Valmy, Chem. de Valmy, 66700 Argelès-sur-Mer, tel. 04.68.81.25.70, fax 04.68.81.15.18, e-mail chateau.valmy@free.fr ☑
🍷 by appt.

CH. DE VESPEILLES 1999

■	n.c.	11,000	▮ ♦	3–5 €

🐦 SA Destavel, 7 bis, av. du Canigou, 66000 Perpignan, tel. 04.68.68.36.00, fax 04.68.54.03.54, e-mail info@destavel.com
🐦 Gilles Baissas

Côtes du Roussillon-Villages

DOM. DE L'AUSSEIL

Latour de France La Capitelle 2001★★★

■	5 ha	15,000	▮ ♦	8–11 €

An entirely new domaine, set up by a young couple who fell in love with this vineyard, perched on the heights of Latour-de-France. And the first *cuvées* have been particularly success-ful, as illustrated by this dark garnet-red wine with aromas of

ROUSSILLON

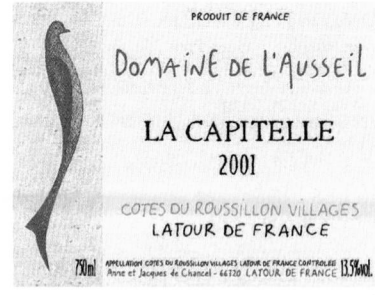

over-ripe red berries. A structure both balanced, substantial and rich give this wine great fullness and remarkable length.
🕭 Dom. de l'Ausseil, bd Gambetta,
66720 Latour-de-France, tel. 04.68.29.18.68,
fax 14.68.29.18.68, e-mail info@lausseil.com ☑
🍷 by appt.
🕭 J. de Chancel

CH. AYMERICH Général Joseph Aymerich
Elevé en fût de chêne 2001★★★

■	5 ha	7,000	⬛	11–15 €

The trilogy: shale; Syrah, the dominant grape variety; and maturation in oak all add up to a winning formula of which this 2001 is sufficient proof. And, as with previous vintages, the wine succeeded in seducing this most exacting of Juries. Fine appearance, with garnet-red highlights. As the tasting progresses, toasted aromas give way to hints of blackcurrant and cherry. Tannin glides over the fleshy, balanced and lingering structure.
🕭 Ch. Aymerich, 52, av. Dr-Torreilles, 66310 Estagel,
tel. 04.68.29.45.45, fax 04.68.29.10.35,
e-mail aymerich-grau-vins@wanadoo.fr ☑
🍷 by appt.
🕭 J.-P., N. et C. Grau-Aymerich

DOM. BILA HAUT
Occultum Lapidem 2000★

■	20 ha	35,000	⬛	5–8 €

It goes without saying that this domaine, purchased by the House of Chapoutier, holds dear the interests of Latour-de-France terroir. Ruby-red appearance, with slight dark-coloured tinges and a nose that introduces distinctly mature characteristics, from the outset. Aromas flit between crystallized fruits, undergrowth and toasted bread. Rounded tannins and full, pronounced flavours still dominate the palate. A fully mature *cuvée*.
🕭 Dom. Bila Haut, Rampe du Sarrat,
66720 Latour-de-France, tel. 04.68.29.31.04,
fax 04.68.29.31.05, e-mail latour@chapoutier.com
🍷 by appt.
🕭 M. Chapoutier

CH. DE CALADROY
Cuvée La Juliane Elevé en fût de chêne 2000★★★

■	12 ha	23,400	⬛	11–15 €

Coup de coeur in last year's *Guide* for the Cuvée La Tour Carrée and this year, Château Caladroy perpetuates the success of its various *cuvées* with this fully-mature oak-aged 2000 vintage. Delicate oak touches dance a panoply of soft crystallized fruits and autumn undergrowth. The tannins are already well patinated; impressions on the taste buds suggest integrated, aromatic length. A perfect companion for sirloin steak.
🕭 SCEA Ch. de Caladroy, 66720 Bélesta,
tel. 04.68.57.10.25, fax 04.68.57.27.76,
e-mail chateau.caladroy@wanadoo.fr ☑
🍷 ev. day except Sat. Sun. 8am–12 noon 1.30pm–5.30pm

LA CARMAGNOLE
Caramany 2001★

■	15 ha	7,000	⬛	5–8 €

This wine cellar practises traditional carbonic maceration, and its gneiss terroir is clearly the source of this wine's typicity. The translucent ruby-red colour envelops aromas of blackcurrant and hints of violet. This *cuvée* offers plenty of suppleness and a palate that develops spicy hints on the finish.
🕭 SCV de Caramany, 66720 Caramany, tel. 04.68.84.51.80,
fax 04.68.84.50.84 ☑
🍷 by appt.

DOM. CAZES
Ego 1998★

■	10 ha	40,000	⬛	8–11 €

It was the aromatic overtones of this already fully matured wine that actually seduced the tasters. Old Russian leather, hints of light tobacco, with toasty undertones and the scent of fruits and nuts that unfold, as soon as one swirls the glass. But it is the tannic structure that holds it together, on the palate, which suggests that we haven't heard the last of this *cuvée*.
🕭 Sté Cazes Frères, 4, rue Francisco-Ferrer, BP 61,
66602 Rivesaltes, tel. 04.68.64.08.26, fax 04.68.64.69.79,
e-mail info@cazes-rivesaltes.com ☑
🍷 by appt.

CLOT DE L'OUM
Saint Bart Vieilles Vignes 2001★★

■	2.5 ha	3,500	⬛	15–23 €

A stroke of genius, as far as this first wine, vinified by a young engineer, who divides his time between La Haye and the slopes of Bélesta, is concerned. These vines are, indeed, 50 years old and cultivated in the most natural way possible. Concentration and elegance go hand in hand with this *cuvée*, composed of old Carignan (33%) and carefully selected Grenache and Syrah. Aromas evoke the grape harvest, at its peak; tannins are powerful. yet already mellow, with a lingering hint of liquorice.
🕭 Eric Monne, Dom. du Clot de l'Oum, 66720 Bélesta,
tel. 06.60.57.69.62, fax 04.68.62.19.78,
e-mail emonne@web.de ☑
🍷 by appt.

LES VIGNERONS DES COTES D'AGLY
Tautavel 2000★★

■	27 ha	20,000	⬛	5–8 €

A wine vinified from the appellation's four main grape varieties, in equal parts. The *cuvée* has an intense ruby red complexion. Overtones of crystallized fruit reveal a harvest at peak maturity. Well-structured tannins, with light hint of vanilla, give an impression of power and warmth on the palate. Roast young wild boar would make a flavoursome match for this wine.
🕭 Les Vignerons des Côtes d'Agly, Cave coopérative,
66310 Estagel, tel. 04.68.29.00.45, fax 04.68.29.19.80,
e-mail agly@tiscali.fr ☑
🍷 ev. day except Sun. 9am–12 noon 2pm–6pm

DOM. FONTANEL
Tautavel Prieuré Vieilli en fût de chêne 2001★★★

■	3.2 ha	9,000	⬛	11–15 €

Always a string of successes for this domaine that clinched a *coup de coeur* last year; the same applies to this *cuvée* or, for that matter, the **Cistes 2001**, which impresses the Jury every year. The dark-red appearance and garnet-coloured highlights indicate substantial structure. On the palate, one discovers tannins that are both fine and fleshy, barely noticeable liquorice flavours, a touch of grilled meats and lingering aromas of sweet bay and garrigue.
🕭 Dom. Fontanel, 25, av. Jean-Jaurès, 66720 Tautavel,
tel. 04.68.29.04.71, fax 04.68.29.19.44,
e-mail domainefontanel@hotmail.com ☑
🍷 ev. day. 10am–12 noon 2pm–7pm
🕭 Fontaneil

LES HAUTS DE FORCA REAL 2000★★

■	5 ha	16,000	⬙	15–23 €

This prestigious *cuvée* was vinified from vine stock that extends down the hilly, shale slopes of Força Réal. The very essence of garrigue is captured in the glass, which reflects garnet red-coloured highlights. Powerful, yet supple tannins; as, indeed, are the hints of smoke that envelop the *cuvée*'s fruitiness, all factors that point to the complexity of this wine with a very fine future.

☛ J.-P. Henriquès, Dom. Força Réal, Mas de la Garrigue, 66170 Millas, tel. 04.68.85.06.07, fax 04.68.85.49.00, e-mail cyril@forcareal.com ☑
☂ by appt.

DOM. GARDIES

Tautavel Vieilles Vignes 2001★★

■	6 ha	n.c.	⬙	15–23 €

The Grotte de Conques, at Vingrau, is historically linked with the settlement of the Magdalenian huntsmen, in the eastern Pyrénées. Today, the estate is given over to viticulture. This *cuvée* favours Grenache, which derives from the glistening limestone terroir that gives the wines their delicate structure. Overtones of garrigue and juniper accompany a weight that fills the mouth. Although young when sampled, indications are that this wine will develop to fine maturity.

☛ Dom. Gardiés, 1, rue Millere, 66600 Vingrau, tel. 04.68.64.61.16, fax 04.68.64.69.36, e-mail domgardies@aol.com ☑
☂ by appt.

HAUTE COUTUME

Schistes de Trémoine 2000★★

■	7 ha	14,300	⬙	8–11 €

Once again, shale terroir takes the credit for this *cuvée*, a blend derived from Rasiguères terroir. Beyond the hints of toasted bread and oaked overtones, this wine exhibits delicate structure that fills the mouth and a balance that verges on sweetness. An impression of oakiness merges with eloquent expression.

☛ Vignerons Catalans, 1870, av. Julien-Panchot, BP 29000, 66962 Perpignan Cedex 9, tel. 04.68.85.04.51, fax 04.68.55.25.62, e-mail contact@vignerons-catalans.com
☂ by appt.

CH. DE JAU

Talon rouge 2001★

■	6 ha	25,000	■ ⬙	15–23 €

The Château de Jau is a magical place. Contemporary art exhibitions, a grill room beneath the mulberry tree, summertime…and wines that are perfectly conducive to this chic, rural idyll. The wine is in keeping with the décor. Refinement, roundness, integrated tannins, a *cuvée* that simply gives pleasure for its own sake.

☛ Ch. de Jau, 66600 Cases-de-Pène, tel. 04.68.38.90.10, fax 04.68.38.91.33, e-mail daure@wanadoo.fr ☑
☂ by appt.
☛ Famille Dauré

MAS DE LAVAIL

Tradition 2001★★★

■	2 ha	n.c.	■	5–8 €

A new domaine on the fringe of the Maury that enjoys the benefits of both superb terroir and old vines, as well as the diversity of grape varieties, cultivated in this region. Not surprising, then, that these first *cuvées* received such high praise. This particular wine is fruit-dominated, with hints of blackcurrant berries, a touch of Morello cherry and slight jammy flavours…An Epicurean delight, that emphasizes elegance and balance.

☛ Nicolas Battle, Mas de Lavail, 66460 Maury, tel. 04.68.59.15.22, fax 04.68.29.08.95 ☑
☂ by appt.

DOM. MATEMALE

Lesquerde 2001★

■	4 ha	21,600	■	5–8 €

The wines of Lesquerde are renowned for the finesse of their terroirs. This selection is a perfect example, with its seductive roundness on the palate and aromas of delicate red berries. Spicy overtones ensure an elegant finish.

☛ SCV Lesquerde pour Méditerroirs, 1870, av. Julien-Panchot, BP 89933, 66962 Perpignan Cedex 9, tel. 04.68.55.88.40, fax 04.68.55.87.67, e-mail mediterroirs@caramail.com

DOM. MOUNIE

Tautavel Expression 2000★★

■	3 ha	11,000	■ ⬙	5–8 €

A domaine of around 20 hectares, established in 1925. Generations have followed one another…to produce wines such as this **Symphonie** *cuvée*, matured in oak, of cherry-red appearance and enveloped in aromas of blackcurrant and blackberry. Elegance is ever present, be it derived from the level of tannins or the aromatic expression.

☛ Dom. Mounié, 1, av. du Verdouble, 66720 Tautavel, tel. 04.68.29.12.31, fax 04.68.29.05.59 ☑
☂ by appt.
☛ Claude Rigaill

CH. LES PINS 2000★

■	25 ha	140,000	■ ⬙	8–11 €

A wine cellar mentioned regularly in the *Guide*, that cultivates 2,100 ha of vines. This year, the Jury has put forward the *vigneron*'s flagship *cuvée*: the Château les Pins. This deep, ruby-coloured wine, with pronounced oakiness, gradually unfolds its spicy overtones. The palate endorses the initial aromas: hints of grilled meats, liquorice flavoured tannins…a lingering finish.

☛ Cave Les Vignerons de Baixas, 14, av. du Mal-Joffre, 66390 Baixas, tel. 04.68.64.22.37, fax 04.68.64.26.70, e-mail contact@dom-brial.com ☑
☂ by appt.

DOM. PIQUEMAL

Les Terres grillées 2001★

■	3 ha	18,000	■ ⬙ ⬙	8–11 €

The fortified church of Sainte-Marie dates back to Roman times. A splendid attraction, worth a visit in itself; Espira-de-l'Agly, however, is also a viticultural village and this domaine has a fine reputation. The vineyard is located on the boundaries between several different types of terroir, including the black shale that gave the *cuvée*, Les Terres Grillées, its name. A dark-coloured appearance exhibits black-cherry highlights. The nose presents aromas of red berries, while a hint of vanilla accompanies the spicy, fleshy palate; balance that is warming and refined.

☛ Dom. Piquemal, 1, rue Pierre-Lefranc, 66600 Espira-de-l'Agly, tel. 04.68.64.09.14, fax 04.68.38.52.94, e-mail contact@domaine-piquemal.com ☑
☂ by appt.

CH. PLANEZES

Elevé en fût de chêne 2000★★

■	5 ha	10,000	⬙	8–11 €

The cooperative wine cellar offers good value, as illustrated by this *cuvée*: aged in oak barrels, but benefiting from a discreet maturation process. This procedure allows the aromas of red

ROUSSILLON

berries and garrigue to be enjoyed to full advantage. Delicate tannins, soft, grilled flavours and seductive length.

🍷 Les Vignerons de Planèzes-Rasiguères, 5, rte de Caramany, 66720 Rasiguères, tel. 04.68.29.11.82, fax 04.68.84.51.93, e-mail contact@rasigueres.com ☑
🍽 ev. day except Sun. 8am–12 noon 2pm–6pm

DOM. POUDEROUX
Terre brune 2001★

■	1.5 ha	4,000	◫	11–15 €

Robert and Cathy Pouderoux express their passion for wine in the *cuvées* of their domaine, perched high above the village of Maury. This wine contains all the typical fruitiness of Grenache, which flourishes, at its best, on this type of terroir. Hints of vanilla surround tannins that have started to patinate, due to maturation in oak barrels.
🍷 Dom. Pouderoux, 2, rue Emile-Zola, 66460 Maury, tel. 04.68.57.22.02, fax 04.68.57.11.63, e-mail 123pou@free.fr ☑
🍽 by appt.

CH. SAINT-ROCH
Le Château 2001★

■	9 ha	30,000	◫ ⚬	8–11 €

"On the edge of the pathway, cherry, carob, apple, holm oak trees and expanses of thyme…" This text, on the rear label of this bottle, sets the scene. This restored 16th century walled town commands a terroir of Maury shale. Francis Guérin and Marc Bournazeau tend vines and wines: no weeding, a selecting table, just careful measurement…for these Les Hauts and Le Château *cuvées*. The latter 2001 vintage has already reached full maturity. The fruit and the fullness of the excellent Grenache and Maury are spot on. An epicurean wine to accompany grills.
🍷 SA Ch. Saint-Roch, Mas Cayrol, 66460 Maury, tel. 04.68.29.07.20, fax 04.68.29.19.15, e-mail mbournazeau@aol.com ☑
🍽 ev. day except Sun. 9am–6pm
🍷 Marc Bournazeau

DOM. DES SCHISTES
Tradition 2001★★

■	14 ha	30,000	◫ ⚬	5–8 €

Physicist, astronomer – but also a man of politics – François Arago was born at Estagel in 1786. The house where he was born is still there. At an altitude of 500 m, you will find this magnificent domaine that has been consistent over the years. This *cuvée*, with a nose of ripe fruits and fruit-stones, reveals its garnet treasures before the tasters and seduces the palate with its stage performance. Tannic finesse is evident at the start, followed by liquorice and fleshy overtones. Fruity hints reappear on the finish.
🍷 Jacques Sire, Dom. des Schistes, 1, av. Jean-Lurçat, 66310 Estagel, tel. 04.68.29.11.25, fax 04.68.29.47.17 ☑
🍽 by appt.

DOM. SEMPER
Lesquerde Voluptas 2001★★

■	2 ha	5,200	◫ ◫ ⚬	8–11 €

A domaine set up by Maury *vignerons* and supported, today, by their 20 and 22-year-old sons. You will find their domaine on the road that links the châteaux of Quéribus and Peyrepertuse. A fine expression of Syrah (50%) grown on granitic sands and perfect oak maturation: this Lesquerde possesses rich, liquorice, tannic structure. Ruby-red appearance, with deep purple highlights surrounding aromas of small, soft fruits steeped in brandy.
🍷 Dom. Paul Semper, 2, chem. du Ree, 66460 Maury, tel. 04.68.59.14.40, fax 04.68.59.14.40, e-mail domaine.semper@club-internet.fr ☑
🍽 by appt.

LES MAITRES VIGNERONS DE TAUTAVEL Tautavel Tradition 2001★★

■	6 ha	30,000	◫ ◫ ⚬	5–8 €

Situated alongside the Museum of Prehistory, which you cannot miss, this wine cellar offers a range of wines

vinified on limestone terraces, which give them their specific characteristics. The Cuvée Tradition 2001 is a good example: deep-coloured appearance, aromas of wild, red berries, hints of garrigue and powerful tannin, fine texture, with light vanilla touches. The recipe for "Lièvre de Tautavel" (Tautavel Hare) must have been dreamt up with a *cuvée* such as this in mind.
🍷 Les Maîtres Vignerons de Tautavel, 24, av. Jean-Badia, 66720 Tautavel, tel. 04.68.29.12.03, fax 04.68.29.41.81, e-mail vignerons.tautavel@wanadoo.fr ☑
🍽 by appt.

CH. DE TRINIAC
Latour de France 2001★

■	6 ha	7,308	◫ ⚬	8–11 €

From its deep colour, with garnet-red tinges, aromas of ripe fruits and light vanilla spices begin to unfold. Fine tannins and lively flavours lend good balance to this wine.
🍷 Les Vignerons de la Tour de France, 2, av. Gal-de-Gaulle, 66720 Latour-de-France, tel. 04.68.29.11.12, fax 04.68.29.14.72, e-mail scv.magasin@la-tour-de-france.com ☑
🍽 ev. day except Sun. 8am–12 noon 2pm–5pm

Wines selected but not starred

DOM. BOUDAU
Tradition Elevé en fût de chêne 2000

■	5 ha	20,000	◫	5–8 €

🍷 Dom. Boudau, 6, rue Marceau, 66600 Rivesaltes, tel. 04.68.64.45.37, fax 04.68.64.46.26 ☑
🍽 ev. day except Sun. 10am–12 noon 3pm–7pm; cl. Sat. in winter

CH. DONA BAISSAS
Les Hauts de Dona Elevé en fût de chêne 2001

■	1.5 ha	4,000	◫	15–23 €

🍷 Ch. Dona Baissas, Ancienne route de Maury, 66310 Estagel, tel. 04.68.29.00.02, fax 04.68.29.09.26, e-mail donabaissas@tiscali.fr ☑
🍽 ev. day except Sat. Sun. 9am–12 noon 2pm–5pm

DOM. JOLIETTE
Cuvée Romain Mercier Elevé en fût de chêne 2001

■	3 ha	17,000	◫	11–15 €

🍷 EARL Mercier, Dom. Joliette, rte de Montpins, 66600 Espira-de-l'Agly, tel. 04.68.64.50.60, fax 04.68.64.18.82 ☑
🍽 by appt.

CH. DE PENA
Elevé en fût de chêne 2000

■	30.78 ha	5,000	◫ ◫ ⚬	8–11 €

🍷 Les Vignerons de Cases-de-Pène, 2, bd Mal-Joffre, 66600 Cases-de-Pène, tel. 04.68.38.93.30, fax 04.68.38.92.41, e-mail chateau-de-pena@wanadoo.fr ☑
🍽 ev. day except Sun. 9am–12 noon 2.30pm–6pm

DOM. DE RANCY 2001

■	2.5 ha	6,500	◫	11–15 €

🍷 Jean-Hubert Verdaguer, Dom. de Rancy, 11, rue Jean-Jaurès, BP 12, 66720 Latour-de-France, tel. 04.68.29.03.47, fax 04.68.29.06.13 ☑
🍽 by appt.

SAVEURS OUBLIEES 2001

| | 160 ha | 800,000 | ▮ ♦ | | 3–5 € |

➹ Vignerons Catalans, 1870, av. Julien-Panchot, BP 29000,
66962 Perpignan Cedex 9, tel. 04.68.85.04.51,
fax 04.68.55.25.62, e-mail contact@vignerons-catalans.com
⚐ by appt.

VILLA ANNES
Caramany Elevé en fût de chêne 2000

| | 5 ha | 19,800 | ◖ | 8–11 € |

➹ SCV Les Vignerons de Cassagnes-Bélesta pour
Méditerroirs, 1870, av. Julien-Panchot, BP 89933,
66962 Perpignan Cedex 9, tel. 04.68.55.88.40,
fax 04.68.55.87.67, e-mail mediterroirs@caramail.com ☑
⚐ by appt.

Collioure

This very small appellation of
480 ha produces about 16,440 hl. The soil is the same
as that found in the Appellation Banyul. The four
communes are Collioure, Port-Bendres, Banyuls-
sur-Mer and Cerbère. The exclusively red or rosé wines are
made at the beginning of the harvest, before the grapes for

The vine varieties grown
are principally Grenache Noir, Carignan and
Mourvèdre, with Syrah and Cinsault as additional
varieties. The exclusively red or rosé wines are made
at the beginning of the harvest, before the grapes for
Banyuls are picked. The small crop produces warm,
full-bodied, highly coloured red wines, with aromas
of well-ripened soft fruits. The rosés are aromatic and
rich, but typically lively.

ABBAYE DE VALBONNE 2001★★

| | n.c. | 145,404 | ◖ | 11–15 € |

A *cuvée* where the contribution of Mourvèdre is evident on
the palate, with its still substantial, tannic structure that
is, nevertheless, enveloped in fullness, with overtones of
liquorice and aromas of soft, crystallized fruits. The
ruby-red-coloured appearance, with garnet tinges, gradually
reveals hints of berries from the garrigue.
➹ Cellier des Templiers, rte du Mas-Reig,
66650 Banyuls-sur-Mer, tel. 04.68.98.36.70,
fax 04.68.98.36.91, e-mail accueil-visite@templers.com ☑
⚐ by appt.

CH. DES ABELLES 2001★★★

| | n.c. | 104,640 | ▮ ♦ | 11–15 € |

This *cuvée* expresses all the complexity of the Grenache,
Carignan and Syrah grape varieties, cultivated on terraces.
Undoubtedly, it is the subtlety of this blend that often comes
to mind, as is the case with this vintage. A brilliant appearance
with ruby-coloured highlights envelops delicate, spicy
tannins. Aromas reminiscent of very ripe cherry, with touches

of toasted bread, melt expressively upon the palate. Catalan
guinea-fowl would make a welcome accompaniment.
➹ Cellier des Templiers, rte du Mas-Reig,
66650 Banyuls-sur-Mer, tel. 04.68.98.36.70,
fax 04.68.98.36.91, e-mail accueil-visite@templers.com ☑
⚐ by appt.

LES DOMINICAINS
Cuvée de la Colline Matisse 2001★

| | 20 ha | n.c. | | 5–8 € |

At the foot of Château royal, stands the ancient 13th century
Dominican convent, which now accommodates this cooperative wine cellar. This bright-red *cuvée* with cherry tinges
presents a bouquet of wild, soft fruits. Full and rounded, the
sweet tannins leave an impression of perfect balance on
the palate.
➹ SCV Le Dominicain, pl. Orfila, 66190 Collioure,
tel. 04.68.82.05.63, fax 04.68.82.43.06,
e-mail le-dominicain@wanadoo.fr
⚐ ev. day 8am–12 noon 2pm–6pm

DOM. DU MAS BLANC
La Llose 2000★

| | 5 ha | 20,000 | ▮ ♦ | 8–11 € |

The renowned Doctor Parcé, who acquainted the rest of the
world with Banyuls (AC area of Grand Roussillon, noted for
the production of sweet, red, fortified wines), would be
proud of this *cuvée*, vinified by his son Jean-Michel. Encased
in ruby-red hues, the bouquet of wild red berries and Mediterranean spices is enchanting. Everything merges perfectly on
the balanced palate around a soft, yet substantial structure.
➹ SCA Parcé et Fils, 9, av. du Gal-de-Gaulle,
66650 Banyuls-sur-Mer, tel. 04.68.88.32.12,
fax 04.68.88.72.24,
e-mail info@domainedu-mas-blanc.com ☑
⚐ ev. day. 9am–12 noon 2pm–6pm; Sat. Sun. by appt.

MAS CORNET 2001★★

| | n.c. | 14,982 | ▮ ♦ | 11–15 € |

A brilliant, ruby-red appearance reveals aromas of crystallized fruits and toasty overtones. The wine offers fine tannins,
lingering and elegant aromas. A wine that exudes refinement.
The **rosé 2002 (11–15 €)**, vinified in wooden casks (600 litres
capacity), achieves a star; the light appearance exhibits
salmon-tinged highlights. The tasting reveals a complex
palate of raspberry brandy and spicy aromas. Also put
forward by the same wine cellar and specially mentioned by
the Jury, the **Domaine de Baillaury 2001 (8–11 €)**.
➹ La Cave de l'Abbé Rous, 56, av. Charles-de-Gaulle,
66650 Banyuls-sur-Mer, tel. 04.68.88.72.72,
fax 04.68.88.30.57, e-mail contact@banyuls.com

DOM. DU ROUMANI 2001★★

| | n.c. | 105,240 | ▮ ♦ | 8–11 € |

Rosemary (*roumani* in Catalan) reminds us that this vineyard
rubs shoulders with Mediterranean garrigue. A *cuvée* that
favours delicate expression on the palate; tannic structure,
with lingering, spicy overtones that become increasingly
flavourful. Aromas of soft, wild berries dominate from
the start.
➹ Cellier des Templiers, rte du Mas-Reig,
66650 Banyuls-sur-Mer, tel. 04.68.98.36.70,
fax 04.68.98.36.91, e-mail accueil-visite@templers.com ☑
⚐ by appt.

CUVEE DE LA SALETTE 2002★

| | n.c. | 142,476 | ▮ ♦ | 8–11 € |

The church in Collioure looks as if it's floating on the Mediterranean on this label that so aptly evokes the maritime world
of this village. A very pale-coloured rosé, with slight salmon
tinges, delivers aromas of soft fruits and spices. Almost
full-bodied on the palate, the wine offers lingering flavours
that might provide a cue for a Mediterranean fish dish of
Zarzuela. The **Cuvée Esperade 2001** was singled out by the
Jury, as was the **Domaine Campi 2001 (11–15 €)**, which
received a star.
➹ Cellier des Templiers, rte du Mas-Reig,
66650 Banyuls-sur-Mer, tel. 04.68.98.36.70,
fax 04.68.98.36.91, e-mail accueil-visite@templers.com ☑
⚐ by appt.

ROUSSILLON

DOM. DE LA TOUR VIEILLE

Puig Oriol 2001★★★

■　　　　　1 ha　　　7,500　　■ ♦　　11–15 €

The years roll by, bearing with them the enthusiasm of the tasters for this domaine, a leading light within the appellation. Overtones of blackcurrant and very ripe cherry seduce the initial nose. The clarity and weight of Grenache strike a perfect note around delicate tannins. The **Cuvée La Pinède 2001** was also singled out for its delightful expressions of Grenache, with more highly pronounced tannins and hints of spices.

● Dom. la Tour Vieille, 12, rte de Madeloc, 66190 Collioure, tel. 04.68.82.44.82, fax 04.68.82.38.42 ☑
꜒ by appt.
● C. Campadieu, V. Cantié

DOM. DU TRAGINER

Cuvée d'Octobre 2000★★★

■　　　4.5 ha　　3,000　　❶❶　　15–23 €

Jean-François Deu's vines are biodynamically cultivated...just like his legendary mule. This oak-aged *cuvée* is a perfect example: aromas of overripe fruits and spicy overtones are enhanced by delicate oaked touches. The wine's balance emphasizes its full and lingering flavours on the palate.

● Jean-François Deu, Dom. du Traginer, 56, av. du Puig-del-Mas, 66650 Banyuls-sur-Mer, tel. 04.68.88.15.11, fax 04.68.88.31.48 ☑
꜒ by appt.

VIAL MAGNERES

Les Espérades 2000★

■　　　1.2 ha　　6,000　　■ ❶❶ ♦　　11–15 €

Bernard Sapéras is father to Banyuls white wine. He also produces a limited number of red *cuvées* that ooze charm, such as this 2000 vintage. With oriental spicy aromas, mingled with slight hints of ripe fruits reflected in the bright-red cherry colour of this *cuvée*, the wine evolves on the balanced, rounded and full-bodied palate.

● Dom. Vial-Magnères, 14, rue Edouard-Herriot, 66650 Banyuls-sur-Mer, tel. 04.68.88.31.04, fax 04.68.88.02.43, e-mail al.tragou@wanadoo.fr ☑
꜒ by appt.
● Olivier Sapéras

Wines selected but not starred

LES CLOS DE PAULILLES 2000

■　　　12 ha　　60,000　　❶❶　　11–15 €

● Jean et Bernard Dauré, Les Clos de Paulilles, Baie de Paulilles, 66660 Port-Vendres, tel. 04.68.38.90.10, fax 04.68.38.91.33, e-mail daure@wanadoo.fr ☑ ⛫
꜒ by appt.

PROVENCE AND CORSICA

Provence

Provence means holidays, a place where "the sun always shines" and where the people, with their melodious accents, take the time to live life as it should be lived... For the wine-growers it is also a place where the sun shines, for 3,000 hours a year! Rain is rare, but violent storms and ferocious winds batter the terrain. When the Phocaean Greeks disembarked at Marseilles around 600 BC, they found vines already growing in the region, and began to cultivate them systematically. Vine-growing continued under the Romans, followed in medieval times by the abbeys and local aristocratic landowners up to and including the wine-grower king, René d'Anjou, Comte de Provence.

Eleanor of Provence, wife of Henry III of England, was the first to give the wines of Provence an international cachet, just as her mother-in-law, Eleanor of Aquitaine, had done for the wines of Gascony. In the centuries which followed, Provençal wines fell out of favour with the international shippers due to difficulties in transport compared with other wine areas. However, in recent decades the development of tourism has brought the wines back to prominence, particularly the rosés, which are fun to drink – perfect companions for summer holidays and delicious Provençal dishes.

The Provençal vineyard is a patchwork of numerous small areas, which helps explain why nearly half of the wine produced is organized though cooperatives: there are no fewer than a hundred in the Var department alone. But the larger "domaines" (which, for the most part, are also bottlers) have retained their influence, and their active presence in marketing and promoting the wines is considered invaluable throughout the region. The annual production reaches between 2 and 3 million hl, of which between 700,000 and 800,000 come from the seven AOCs, and about one million from eight Appellations d'Origine. In the Var department, typical of the region, wine represents 45% of the total agricultural production and vineyards cover 51% of the area.

In common with other southern vineyards, quite a few vine varieties are grown: the Appellation Côtes de Provence allows a total of thirteen. And yet, sadly, the Muscats, the glory of the Provençal terroirs before the phylloxera devastation, have now vanished. The vines are for the most part pruned in the traditional low goblet shape; however, plants trained along cordons are becoming increasingly common. Rosé and white wines (the latter more rare but frequently surprisingly good), are generally drunk young. This might change if it were possible to find conditions for ageing in bottles that were less extreme than those offered by the local climate. The same thought applies to many of the lighter reds. However, the fuller-bodied reds from the Provençal appellations age very well.

The tiny Palette vineyard, at the gates of Aix, incorporates the old enclosure belonging to King René. Its whites, rosés and reds are worthy of attention.

Since Provençal is still spoken in some of the domaines, it is useful to know some of the local terminology: avis is the local word for sarment (wine shoot), a tine is a cuve or vat, and a crotte is a cave or cellar. You may be told that one of the grape varieties is called pecoui-touar or queue tordue (which means "twisted tail"), while ginou d'Agasso means "magpie knee", because of the peculiar shape of the stem of the bunch of grapes.

Côtes de Provence

This appellation has a substantial production (877,555 hl in 2002) and covers a good third of the department of the Var, with extensions into the Bouches-du-Rhone to the edge of Marseilles, and an enclave in the Alpes-Maritimes. The total area under production is more than 20,000 ha. Three terroirs identify it: the crystalline rocks of the Maure mountains in the southeast, bordered to the north by a band of red sand from Toulon to Saint-Raphaël and, beyond, a sizeable massif of hills and limestone plateaux that prefigure the Alps. The charm of these wines lies in their sheer diversity: made from a number of different vine varieties in varying proportions, and grown on equally varied soils with as many different aspects, they share little but the influence of the fierce southern sun. Perhaps this was the charm that the Greek Protis, according to legend, tasted as early as 600 BC when Gyptis, the daughter of a local king, offered him a goblet of wine as a pledge of her love.

The whites from the coast are soft but lively, and are perfectly suited to very fresh seafood; those from a little further north are more "focused" and will go very well with lobster à l'Américaine and tangy cheeses. The rosés can be either soft or lively and, depending on your mood or taste, are best combined with full flavours, such as soup with pesto, anchoïade, aïoli and bouillabaisse, as well as fish and seafood, particularly red mullet, sea urchins and shellfish. The soft reds (which should be drunk slightly chilled) go well with joints of meat, roasts and pot-au-feu and especially with cold pot-au-feu salad. Finally, some of the strong, full-bodied reds are suitable for daubes (rich, slowly cooked stews) and woodcock. And for those who are attracted by unexpected pairings, try cold rosé with mushrooms, red with stewed shellfish, or white with daube of lamb (made with white wine).

DOM. DE L'AMAURIGUE

Cuvée spéciale 2001★

| ■ | 3 ha | 13,800 | ❶❶ | 5–8 € |

This estate was bought in 1999. It has a brand-new cellar, and its 32 ha of vines have been restructured. This dark-garnet wine has a complex bouquet combining stewed

fruits and spices from its time being matured in oak. The first impression is clear-cut, and the palate offers aromas of soft fruits over still youthful tannins. The **rosé 2002** was also awarded one star.

❧ SARL Dom. de l'Amaurigue, rte de Cabasse, 83340 Le Luc-en-Provence, tel. 04.94.50.17.20, fax 04.94.50.17.21 ☑
☖ by appt.
❧ Dick De Groot

CH. DES ANGLADES

Collection privée 2002★★

| ■ | 4 ha | 10,000 | ❚ ❶❶ ♨ | 8–11 € |

Since 2000, the Gautier family has been renovating its 50-ha vineyard in order to make high-quality wines. This one has a pale-salmon colour, and releases aromas of flowers and exotic fruits, then explodes on the palate with not only great body but also freshness. "A superb aperitif," concluded one taster.

Provence

Ch. des Anglades, quartier Couture, 83400 Hyères, tel. 04.94.59.12.40, fax 04.94.59.16.11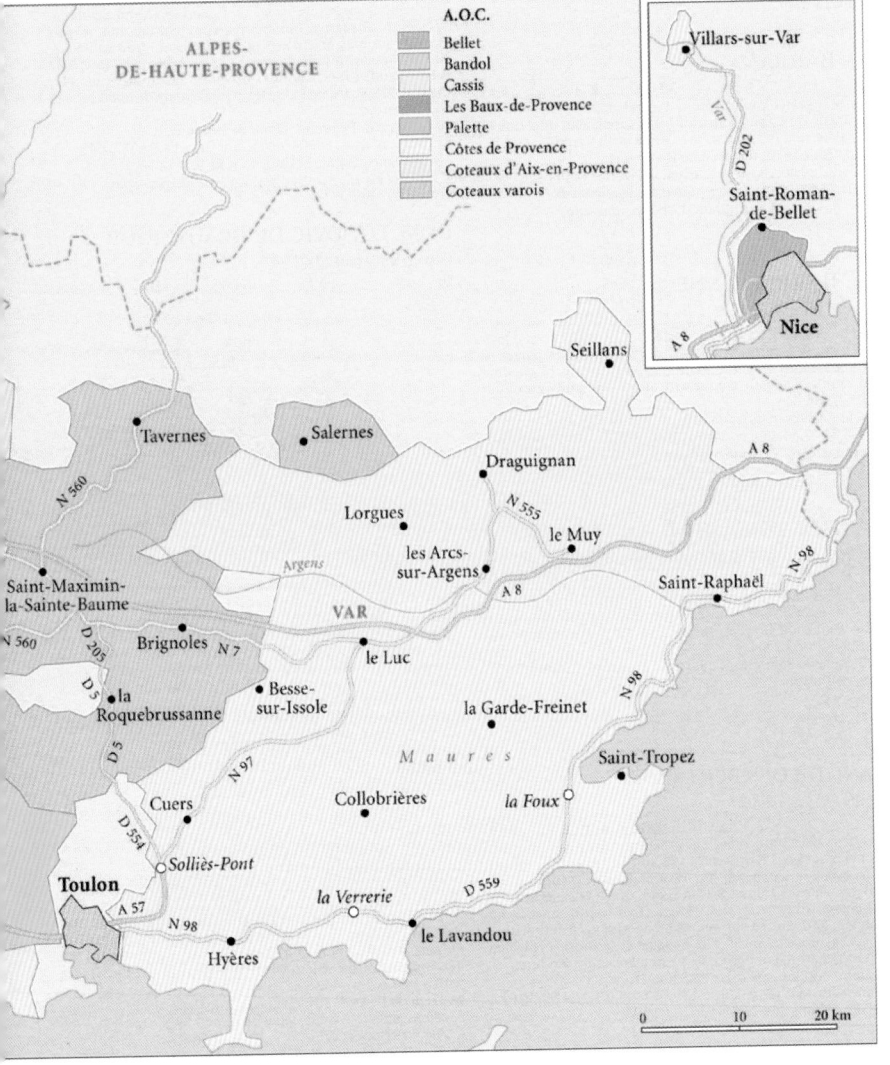
by appt.

DOM. DE L'ANGUEIROUN

Cuvée spéciale 2001★

	2 ha	4,300			8–11 €

The road leading to this 19th century Provençal farm winds through a typically Mediterranean landscape, with the sea in the background. Here you will find this intense-garnet wine full of aromas of small soft fruits (bilberry and blackcurrant). The flavours on the palate reveal themselves slowly and harmoniously with long notes of undergrowth and spices. Although it is ready to drink now, it could be kept for two to three years.

Eric Dumon, 1077, chem. de l'Angueiroun, 83230 Bormes-les-Mimosas, tel. 04.94.71.11.39, fax 04.94.71.75.51
ev. day 8am–12 noon 2pm–6pm

DOM. DES ASPRAS

Cuvée traditionnelle 2002★

	6 ha	25,000		5–8 €

In the centre of Green Provence, at Correns – a village completely given over to organic farming – Michael Latz has a gite on his Piedmontese-style estate, surrounded by 16 ha of vines. He has produced a very lively rosé made from Cinsault and Grenache. This 2002 wine has a pale-salmon colour, and releases lingering and very elegant floral aromas. The **Cuvée Réserve red 1999 (8–11 €)**, matured in barrel for one year, is also awarded one star: flavours of liquorice combine with a powerful structure that will allow it to be kept for two or three years.

Michael Latz, Dom. des Aspras, 83570 Correns, tel. 04.94.59.59.70, fax 04.94.59.53.92, e-mail mlatz@aspras.com
ev. day 9am–12 noon 3pm–7pm
Michael Latz

A.O.C.
Bellet
Bandol
Cassis
Les Baux-de-Provence
Palette
Côtes de Provence
Coteaux d'Aix-en-Provence
Coteaux varois

ALPES-DE-HAUTE-PROVENCE

Villars-sur-Var
Saint-Roman-de-Bellet
Nice

Seillans
Tavernes
Salernes
Draguignan
Lorgues
le Muy
les Arcs-sur-Argens
Saint-Raphaël
Saint-Maximin-la-Sainte-Baume
VAR
Brignoles
le Luc
la Roquebrussanne
Besse-sur-Issole
la Garde-Freinet
Maures
Cuers
Collobrières
la Foux
Saint-Tropez
Solliès-Pont
Toulon
la Verrerie
Hyères
le Lavandou

0 10 20 km

CH. DE L'AUMERADE
Louis Fabre 2002★★

■ Cru clas.	1 ha	4,000	◧	15–23 €

The Château de l'Aumerade has belonged to the Fabre family since 1932. Henri Fabre was one of the founders of the appellation and in 1950, with his son Louis, created one of the best bottles in Provence, inspired by a molten glass by Emile Gallé. There are not many bottles of this wine, but it is richly expressive and will delight lovers of Syrah. It has a complex, though still reserved, nose and a powerful palate, supported by compact tannins, and remains tasty up to the vanilla-flavoured finish. This is a wine to keep (two to five years). The **Château de la Clapière rosé 2002 (8–11 €)** was made by organic methods and was thought very successful, as was the **Château de l'Aumerade Seigneur de Piégros rosé 2002 (8–11 €)**.
☛ SCEA des Domaines Fabre, Ch. de l'Aumerade, 83390 Pierrefeu-du-Var, tel. 04.94.28.20.31, fax 04.94.48.23.09, e-mail info@aumerade.com ▨
☗ ev. day except Sun. 8am–12 noon 2pm–6pm; groups by appt.

CH. BARBANAU 2002★

■	6 ha	30,000	■ ♦	5–8 €

This orangey-coloured rosé is typical of its year, releasing very fresh aromas of soft fruits. It is supple and lingering on the palate, and is a nice wine to drink with friends.
☛ Ch. Barbanau, Hameau de Roquefort, 13830 Roquefort-la-Bédoule, tel. 04.42.73.14.60, fax 04.42.73.17.85, e-mail barbanau@aol.com ▨
☗ ev. day except Sun. 10am–12 noon 3pm–6pm
☛ Cerciello

CH. BARBEIRANNE
Cuvée Camille 2002★

■	2 ha	8,000	◧	5–8 €

This wine is a perfect example of vinification in barrel. It is compact and balanced, with pleasant aromas of coconut and vanilla. The pale colour with shades of sandy grey adds to its originality.
☛ Ch. Barbeiranne, La Pellegrine, 83790 Pignan, tel. 04.94.48.84.46, fax 04.94.33.27.03 ▨
☗ ev. day 9am–12 noon 1pm–6pm
☛ M. Sonniez

BASTIDE DE SAINT JEAN
Cuvée Signature 2002★★

■	3 ha	16,000	■	8–11 €

This rosé is one of the outstanding wines of the year, with its pale colour and sandy glints, elegant nose of pêche de vigne, citrus fruits and flowers, and full, soft and lingering palate. Drink it during 2004.
☛ Bastide de Saint-Jean, quartier Saint-Jean, 83460 Les Arcs-en-Provence, tel. 04.98.10.43.49, fax 04.98.10.43.49 ▨
☗ by appt.
☛ M. Henry

BASTIDE DES BERTRANDS
Vieilles Vignes 2002★

■	2.5 ha	15,000	■ ♦	5–8 €

Between 1968 and 1980, they had to clear the ground, removing rocks as they went, to be able to grow vines on this 90-ha estate in the massif des Maures. This year they offer a brilliant wine the colour of white gold, which releases aromas of banana, strawberry and flowers. This well-balanced and rounded 2002 can be enjoyed as an aperitif or drunk with a Provençal or exotic meal. The **Bouquet de la Bastide red 2000 (8–11 €)**, matured in barrel, was commended by the Jury.
☛ Dom. des Bertrands, rte de Saint-Tropez, 83340 Le Cannet-des-Maures, tel. 04.94.99.79.00, fax 04.94.99.79.09, e-mail info@bastidedesbertrands.com ▨
☗ by appt.
☛ M. Marotzki

DOM. DE LA BASTIDE NEUVE
Cuvée d'Antan 2001★★★

■	3 ha	8,000	◧	11–15 €

The tasters all agreed that the Cuvée d'Antan was a "great wine". You will be attracted by its deep-garnet colour, before enjoying the complexity of the aromas of soft fruits (bilberry and blackberry), liquorice, toast and violet. The palate is compact and balanced. This wine would be great to drink with a tournedos Rossini. Look out also for the **Cuvée Fleur de Rolle white 2002 (8–11 €)**, with its scents of citrus fruits, which is awarded one star.
☛ Dom. de la Bastide Neuve, 83340 Le Cannet-des-Maures, tel. 04.94.50.09.80, fax 04.94.50.09.99, e-mail dnebastideneuve@compuserve.com ▨
☗ ev. day except Sat. Sun. 8am–12 noon 1pm–5pm
☛ Hugo Wiestner

CH. BEAUMET 2002★

■	n.c.	n.c.	■ ♦	5–8 €

This wine is an astute blend of Rolle (80%) and Sémillon. It has an attractive buttercup-yellow colour and reveals pleasant aromas of citrus fruits and broom. You will enjoy its freshness with grilled fish or goat's cheese. The **rosé 2002** is commended for its aromas of spices and stone fruit, as is the **red 1999**, matured in barrel, with flavours of undergrowth and liquorice.
☛ SCEA Ch. Beaumet, Dom. de Beaumet, 83590 Gonfaron, tel. 04.98.05.21.00, fax 04.94.78.27.40, e-mail chateaubeaumet@aol.com ▨ ▨
☗ ev. day except Sat. Sun. 8am–12 noon 1pm–5pm; groups by appt.

DOM. LUDOVIC DE BEAUSEJOUR
Cuvée Bacarras 2001★★★

■	6 ha	6,000	◧	11–15 €

The Cuvée Bacarras is again awarded a *coup de cœur*. It has a deep colour with purplish nuances, and discloses a bouquet rich in truffles and black chocolate. Its mouth-filling qualities, combined with warm accents of coffee and liquorice, are most enjoyable. This is a balanced wine which can be drunk now or allowed to age. The **Cuvée Crystallis white 2001**, matured in oak, is awarded one star for its balance between harmony and freshness.
☛ Dom. Ludovic de Beauséjour, Hameau La Basse-Maure, rte de Salernes, 83510 Lorgues, tel. 04.94.50.91.91, fax 04.94.68.46.53 ▨
☗ by appt.
☛ Ph. Maunier

DOM. LE BERCAIL
Confidence 2001★

■	2 ha	11,000	◧	5–8 €

The Le Bercail estate regularly produces excellent wines, and this 2001 follows in the tradition of previous vintages. Its aromas of small soft fruits and liquorice accompany the development of the palate, which is powerful and full. Serve it with a salmi of woodcock.
☛ Dom. le Bercail, 864, chem. de la Plaine, 83480 Puget-sur-Argens, tel. 04.94.19.54.09, fax 04.94.81.50.80 ▨
☗ ev. day except Sat. Sun. 8am–4.30pm

DOM. DE LA BOUVERIE 2002★

| | 3.5 ha | 13,000 | 🍷 | 5–8 € |

This finely oaked, green-gold wine already reveals good aromas of citrus fruits and marmalade peel. It has been well matured, and is balanced enough to be drunk now with a cassolette of snails, for example. The **rosé 2002**, which tastes of minerals, and the **red 2000**, with its vanilla flavours, were commended.

☛ Jean Laponche, Dom. de la Bouverie, 83520 Roquebrune-sur-Argens, tel. 04.94.44.00.81, fax 04.94.44.04.73 ☑

Ⱡ by appt.

CH. DE BREGANCON
Cuvée Hermann Sabran 2000★

| | Cru clas. | 2.5 ha | n.c. | 🍷 ♦ | 15–23 € |

The Fort of Brégançon, a famous holiday resort where the presidents of the Republic have their summer residence, is also a wine-growing terroir. Jean-François Tézenas has made a wine that has such a supple, blended and lingering structure that it should be tried right away. The flowery **Cuvée Prestige rosé 2002 (8–11 €)** is also commended.

☛ Jean-François Tézenas, Ch. de Brégançon, 639, rte de Léoube, 83230 Bormes-les-Mimosas, tel. 04.94.64.80.73, fax 04.94.64.83.47, e-mail chbregancon@terre-net.fr ☑

Ⱡ ev. day 9am–12 noon 2pm–6pm

LA CADIERENNE 2002★

| | 11.17 ha | 35,000 | 🍷 ♦ | 3–5 € |

The special feature of this Côtes de Provence is its blend of all-Southern grape varieties: Grenache, Cinsault, Carignan, Syrah and Mourvèdre. It has a fresh and fruity tone, resting on soft and integrated tannins that give it good length.

☛ SCV la Cadiérenne, quartier Le Vallon, 83740 La Cadière-d'Azur, tel. 04.94.90.11.06, fax 04.94.90.18.73, e-mail cadierenne@wanadoo.fr ☑

Ⱡ by appt.

CH. CAMP LONG
Cuvée Truchette 2002★★

| | 9.9 ha | 52,330 | 🍷 ♦ | 3–5 € |

This is a family estate run by Patrick and Geneviève Gualtieri and their daughters. At the Pas du Cerf, where in the old days deer roamed the hills, the vineyard planted on schist has produced this pale but luminous wine alive with complex and attractive aromas. The full and lingering palate has a convincing finish. The **Château Pas du Cerf Rocher des Croix white 2002 (5–8 €)**, which is remarkably balanced and fruity, is also awarded two stars, while the **Château Camp long Cuvée Truchette red 2002**, matured in tank, gains one star: its ripe tannins and pleasant freshness make it drinkable now.

☛ Patrick Gualtieri, GFA Camp Long, rte de Collobrières, 83250 La Londe-les-Maures, tel. 04.94.00.48.80, fax 04.94.00.48.81, e-mail info@pasducerf.com ☑

Ⱡ ev. day 9am–12 noon 3pm–6pm

CH. CARPE DIEM Plus 2002★★

| | 3 ha | 10,000 | 🍷 ♦ | 5–8 € |

They have got their growing technique right, and have worked out their aims in terms of quality: Carpe Diem remains faithful to its name. This is a clear and intense ruby-red wine that releases powerful aromas. The palate is full and complex, resting on already integrated tannins that will help it to age well. Keep it for a few years, it can only get better.

☛ Francis Adam, Ch. Carpe Diem, rte de Carces, RD 13, 83570 Cotignac, tel. 04.94.04.72.88, fax 04.94.04.77.50, e-mail chateaucarpediem@libertysurf.fr ☑ 📷 📷

Ⱡ ev. day 9.30am–12.30pm 3pm–7pm; cl. Wed. from 16 Oct. to 14 Mar.

CH. DE LA CASTILLE 2001★

| | 11.73 ha | 15,160 | 🍷 ♦ | 3–5 € |

Formerly a property of the counts of Provence, the Château de La Castille belongs now to the bishopric. The cellars were dug out by convicts from Marseilles around 1730. Today, modern techniques make it possible to produce high-quality wines such as this full and compact 2001, which develops in roundness on spicy and smoky notes. This wine is already

pleasant and can be drunk over the next two years. The **rosé 2002** is balanced and straightforward, though not very aromatic, and is commended.

☛ Fondation la Castille, 83260 La Crau, tel. 04.94.00.80.53, fax 04.94.00.80.51 ☑

Ⱡ ev. day except Mon. Sun. 8am–12 noon 2pm–6pm

CH. CLARETTES
Grande Cuvée Elevage en bois 2001★★

| | n.c. | n.c. | 🍷 | 8–11 € |

Mourvèdre is the main grape variety of this estate, which stands on a Gallo-Roman site. This wine also contains 10% Cabernet Sauvignon. Dark red, almost black in colour, it releases intense and complex aromas of fruit jam with shades of liquorice. After a good first impression, the palate is balanced and long with flavours of fruits and chocolate. Its compact and warm substance promises a good ageing potential of three to five years. The **Grande Cuvée rosé 2002 (5–8 €)**, full of soft fruits, is awarded one star.

☛ Crocé-Spinelli, Dom. des Clarettes, rte des Nouradons, 83460 Les Arcs-sur-Argens, tel. 04.94.47.45.05, fax 04.94.73.30.73, e-mail earlvcs@aol.com ☑

Ⱡ by appt.

DOM. DU CLOS D'ALARI
Cuvée Manon 2001★

| | 0.4 ha | 1,500 | 🍷 | 11–15 € |

The label features a vine leaf, an oak leaf and an olive branch, symbolizing the estate's happy trilogy: wine, truffles and olives. The tasters enjoyed this carefully made wine, produced for a limited number of customers. The intense colour heralds a warm and complex palate that lingers on soft fruits. This wine is ready to drink now.

☛ Anne-Marie et Nathalie Vancoillie, Dom. du Clos d'Alari, 83510 Saint-Antonin-du-Var, tel. 04.94.72.90.49, fax 04.94.72.90.51, e-mail leclosdalari@noos.fr ☑

Ⱡ by appt.

CLOS MIREILLE
L'Insolent 2000★

| | Cru clas. | n.c. | 3,960 | 🍷 | 23–30 € |

This 2000 wine has a very youthful pale-yellow colour. The oak with vanilla and liquorice nuances merges with the full and tasty palate. Drink it with a white meat in a morel sauce or a fish in sauce.

☛ Dom. Ott, Clos Mireille, rte du Fort-de-Brégançon, 83250 La Londe-les-Maures, tel. 04.94.01.53.50, fax 04.94.01.53.51, e-mail closmireille@domaines-ott.com ☑

Ⱡ by appt.

LA CAVE DES VIGNERONS DE COGOLIN Grande Réserve 2002★★

| | 10 ha | 30,000 | 🍷 | 3–5 € |

This wine has a pale-pink colour with grey glints and develops a complex nose of blackberry and yellow peach with shades of citrus fruits. It is rounded and fat, but fresh too, and maintains a good aroma of soft fruits up to the finish.

☛ La Cave des Vignerons de Cogolin, rue Marceau, 83310 Cogolin, tel. 04.94.54.40.54, fax 04.94.54.08.75, e-mail vin–1@wanadoo.fr ☑

Ⱡ by appt.

LES VIGNERONS DE COTIGNAC
Cuvée spéciale 2002★

| | n.c. | 15,000 | 🍷 ♦ | 3–5 € |

The Cotignac cooperative was formed from a merger of two cooperatives in 1967. It offers a wine which is very characteristic of the year, with a brilliant, strong colour, a powerful and complex nose with nuances of capsicum, fairly integrated tannins and good aromatic length.

☛ Coop. Les Vignerons de Cotignac, 83570 Cotignac, tel. 04.94.04.60.04, fax 04.94.04.79.54 ☑

Ⱡ by appt.

PROVENCE

CH. COUSSIN SAINTE VICTOIRE

Cuvée César 2001★★

| ■ | 1 ha | 6,000 | ◫ | 8–11 € |

This wine was made from a selection of Syrah, Mourvèdre and Grenache, and is very true to type. Do not allow yourself to be completely distracted by the original box, designed by the sculptor César, a detail of which features on the collaret of the bottle. The dark colour of the wine, haloed with deep purple, is just as beautiful. The bouquet is full and generous, combining notes of charring, cocoa and brioche. The compact tannins support a powerful substance up to the finish of caramelized fruits and chocolate. This will be great to drink in one or two years. The **Cuvée Cézanne rosé 2002 (3–5 €)** is awarded one star.

↬ Famille Elie Sumeire, Ch. Coussin Sainte-Victoire, 13530 Trets, tel. 04.42.61.20.00, fax 04.42.61.20.01, e-mail sumeire@chateaux-elie-sumeire.fr ☑
⌾ by appt.

DOM. DE LA CRESSONNIERE

Cuvée Prunelle 2002★★

| ■ | 3.7 ha | 14,500 | ■ ⌂ | 5–8 € |

With its image of a typical Provençal country house, this rosé is a worthy representative of Mediterranean wines. It is pale in colour with lively salmon glints and has a delicate floral bouquet. Its fruity balance makes it universally likeable. The **Cuvée Mataro rosé 2001 (11–15 €)**, matured in barrel, is awarded one star for its radiant structure.

↬ Dom. de la Cressonnière, RN 97, 83790 Pignans, tel. 04.94.48.81.22, fax 04.94.48.81.25, e-mail cressonniere@wanadoo.fr ☑
⌾ ev. day except Sun. 10am–12 noon 3pm–6pm
⌾ Depeursinge

CH. DEFFENDS

Cuvée Première 2002★

| ■ | 1.84 ha | 12,000 | ■ ⌂ | 5–8 € |

This wine's bright colour catches the eye, our attention immediately rewarded by a generous range of fruity and amylic notes on the nose. It is a tender and young wine, and has clearly been well made. It would go well with sea bream in an aniseed sauce. The **Cuvées Première white 2002 and red 2002** are also well made and each win one star.

↬ Vergès, EARL Ch. Deffends, 83660 Carnoules, tel. 04.94.28.33.12, fax 04.94.28.33.12 ☑
⌾ ev. day 9am–12 noon 3pm–7pm

DOM. DESACHY

Cuvée Chloé Elevé en barrique 2001★★

| ■ | 1.5 ha | 8,000 | ◫ | 5–8 € |

The dark-garnet colour with purple glints yields a bouquet of soft fruits, cocoa and menthol, underlined by oaky notes. The palate opens with a supple attack, then reveals a compact, structured substance combining fruity and spicy flavours. This wine has remarkable complexity and power, and will need three to five years to mature fully.

↬ GAEC Desachy, Le Bas Pansard, 83250 La Londe-les-Maures, tel. 04.94.66.84.46, fax 04.94.66.84.46 ☑
⌾ ev. day except Sun. 9am–12 noon 3pm–6.30pm

LE DIVIN

Vieilli en fût de chêne 2001★★

| ■ | 0.5 ha | 1,600 | ◫ | 5–8 € |

The cooperative completely renovated its cellar in 2002 and now receives its visitors in a new sales room. There you will find this wine with its superb dark-red, almost black colour and purple glints. Its bouquet of woodland fruits with nuances of vanilla and spices is nicely echoed on the balanced palate, supported by integrated tannins. Clearly, this wine was very skilfully matured in oak.

↬ SCA Cellier Saint-Bernard, av. du Général-de-Gaulle, 83340 Flassans-sur-Issole, tel. 04.94.69.71.01, fax 04.94.69.71.80 ☑
⌾ by appt.

L'ESTANDON

Cuvée bleu mistral 2002★

| ■ | 7 ha | 40,000 | ■ ⌂ | 3–5 € |

A new production plan was started in 2000 to improve the quality of the harvests. The Estandon 2002 is the fruit of these efforts, under its blue label breathing the calm of a late summer in Provence with its balanced and tasty tannins.

↬ Les Vignerons des Caves de Provence, rte de Taradeau, 83460 Les Arcs, tel. 04.94.47.56.56, fax 04.94.47.50.08, e-mail contact@cavesdeprovence.fr

L'ESTELLO 2002★

| ■ | 2.2 ha | 9,000 | ■ ⌂ | 5–8 € |

With the help of his team, Patrick Tordjman continues the work of his father and tries to put soul into the wines from his estate. He has succeeded with this 2002 vintage, which has pretty nuances of peony. Fresh fruits (mango, peach and strawberry) combine with flowers, then recur on the balanced palate.

↬ Dom. de l'Estello, rte de Carces, 83510 Lorgues, tel. 04.94.73.22.22, fax 04.94.73.29.29, e-mail lestello@aol.com ☑
⌾ ev. day except Sun. 9am–12.30pm 2pm–7pm
⌾ R. Tordjman

DOM. DES FERAUD

Cuvée Vieilles Vignes 2002★

| ■ | 6,500 | ■ ⌂ | 8–11 € |

This pale-pink wine with orangey nuances was made from Cinsault (90%) and Grenache (10%) planted in sandy, silty soil. It is rather floral on the nose, then fresh fruits emerge on the palate, followed by a lemony finish. It will do well as an aperitif or drunk with grilled meats.

↬ Dom. des Féraud, rte de La Garde-Freinet, 83550 Vidauban, tel. 04.94.73.03.12, fax 04.94.73.08.58 ☑
⌾ by appt.
⌾ M. Fournier

CH. FERRY LACOMBE

Cuvée Lou Cascaï 2001★★

| ■ | 3 ha | 6,000 | ■ ⌂ | 8–11 € |

The master glass-makers who once owned this estate would have admired the clarity of this straw-yellow wine which releases intense aromas of kiwi and citrus fruits. The fruity palate has notes of grapefruit and shows itself to be rounded, harmonious and long. Drink it as an aperitif or with fish. The **Cuvée Lou Cascaï rosé 2002 (5–8 €)** is awarded one star.

↬ Ch. Ferry-Lacombe, rte de Saint-Maximin, 13530 Trets, tel. 04.42.29.40.04, fax 04.42.61.46.65, e-mail sceaferry@club-internet.fr ☑
⌾ ev. day except Sun. 9am–12 noon 2pm–7pm
⌾ M. Pinot

DOM. DE LA FOUQUETTE

Cuvée Pierres de Moulin 2002★★

| ■ | 3 ha | 8,500 | ■ ⌂ | 5–8 € |

On the first wooded foothills of the Maures, Yves Aquadro cultivates his 15 ha of vines and has rooms for visitors and a table d'hôte. The Jury was unanimous about his Côtes de Provence: a remarkable rosé with a salmon colour and an attractive bouquet with notes of fresh fruits (pêche de vigne). The compact and concentrated palate bears the mark of the Syrah (50% of the blend).

↬ Yves Aquadro, Dom. de la Fouquette, 83340 Les Mayons, tel. 04.94.60.00.69, fax 04.94.60.02.91 ☑ ⌂
⌾ by appt.

CH. DU GALOUPET 2001★

| ■ Cru clas. | 14 ha | n.c. | ◫ | 8–11 € |

The Château du Galoupet has plenty to offer: its vaulted cellar, its open days on the subject of art and wine, held throughout the summer, its nearness to the Iles d'Or... and its Côtes de Provence. Its 2001 vintage is still restrained beneath its deep-ruby colour but offers a powerful and promising palate. The supple tannins give it a lovely structure and make it ready to drink now or to lay down. The **rosé 2002**, made from 90% Tibouren, a typical grape variety on the

Mediterranean coast, has an original nose of stewed fruits and spices. It is commended for its character.
🕿 Ch. du Galoupet, Saint-Nicolas, RN 98, 83250 La Londe-les-Maures, tel. 04.94.66.40.07, fax 04.94.66.42.40, e-mail galoupet@club-internet.fr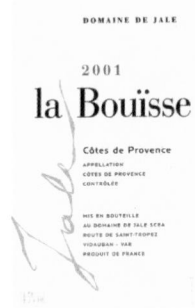
☖ by appt.
🕿 S. Shivdasani

CH. DES GARCINIERES

Cuvée du Prieuré 2002★

■	2 ha	6,600	▮ ♦	5–8 €

This estate dates from the 17th century and contains a chapel dedicated to Saint Philomène. Its Cuvée du Prieuré is very pale to look at, but makes an intense impression of freshness with its aromas of exotic fruits and white flowers. The palate achieves a fine balance between liveliness and roundness, and its fruity charm seems to go on for ever.
🕿 Famille Valentin, Ch. des Garcinières, 83310 Cogolin, tel. 04.94.56.02.85, fax 04.94.56.07.42, e-mail garcinieres@wanadoo.fr ▮
☖ by appt.

DOM. DE GAVAISSON 2002★

■	4 ha	15,000	▮ ♦	11–15 €

Here they are very keen on organic farming, and use it on their 4 ha of vines. This new vintage follows the 2001 version: it is very fresh, has green highlights and releases aromas of citrus fruits followed by elegant fruity notes. It is balanced, and will be delicious as an aperitif or with fillets of mullet in saffron.
🕿 SARL Dom. de Gavaisson, 4033, rte de Saint-Antonin, 83510 Lorgues, tel. 04.94.04.47.96, fax 04.94.72.91.39 ▮
☖ by appt.

DOM. GAVOTY

Cuvée Clarendon 2002★

■	4 ha	22,000	▮ ♦	5–8 €

This property of 53 ha was taken over in 1806 by the Gavoty family, a member of which, Bernard Gavoty, was music critic of the *Figaro* and a member of the Grandes Orgues des Invalides. The estate stands beside the old Roman road, the Via Aurelia. Its Cuvée Clarendon symbolizes a happy marriage between music and wine, winning one star for its red, white and rosé. The rosé is supple and round, and has an elegant colour with salmon highlights. The **Cuvée Clarendon white 2002 (8–11 €)**, is almost transparent with light green highlights, then reveals notes of citrus fruits and white flowers before harmoniously combining liveliness and roundness. The **red 2001 (8–11 €)**, matured in cask, has enough structure to be able to improve over the next two to four years.
🕿 Roselyne et Pierre Gavoty, Le Grand Campdumy, 83340 Cabasse, tel. 04.94.69.72.39, fax 04.94.59.64.04, e-mail domaine.gavoty@wanadoo.fr ▮ 🏠🏠
☖ ev. day except Sun. 8am–12 noon 2pm–6pm

DOM. DE LA GISCLE

Carte noire 2001★

■	2 ha	3,700	◪	8–11 €

The drawing on the label of a flourmill wheel refers to one of the earlier trades on this estate, which started in the 16th century: silkworms were also bred there. Its purplish-ruby wine releases many aromas: macerated soft fruits, spices (pepper and nutmeg), and fine oaky notes. Its full and impressive substance, with nuances of vanilla, is improved by integrated tannins. Although it is still young, this Côtes de Provence will reach its best in two to three years. Also look out for the **Moulin de l'Isle rosé 2002 (5–8 €)**, which was thought very successful.
🕿 EARL Dom. de la Giscle, hameau de l'Amirauté, rte de Collobrières, 83310 Cogolin, tel. 04.94.43.21.26, fax 04.94.43.37.53, e-mail dom.giscle@wanadoo.fr ▮
☖ ev. day except Wed. 9am–12.30pm 2pm–6.30pm; Sun. 9am–12.30pm
🕿 Audemard

DOM. DU GRAND CROS

L'Esprit de Provence 2002★

■	4 ha	21,300	▮ ♦	5–8 €

This attractive rosé with a clear and brilliant colour has a fruity balance and releases fine notes of citrus fruits. Its freshness will make it good as an aperitif and with fish dishes. The **white L'Esprit de Provence 2002** is commended for its pleasantly lemony flavour.
🕿 Dom. du Grand Cros, RD 13, 83660 Carnoules, tel. 04.98.01.80.08, fax 04.98.01.80.09, e-mail info@grandcros.fr ▮
☖ ev. day 9am–12 noon 2pm–7pm
🕿 Famille Faulkner

DOM. DE GRANDPRE

Cuvée spéciale 2001★★

■	3 ha	8,000	▮	5–8 €

The old Carignan grapes of Puget-Ville have an excellent reputation. This winemaker is an expert in carbonic maceration, and this has helped too. The intense spicy nose, the compact substance and evident but good-quality tannins make this a remarkable Côtes de Provence. The **white Clos des Ferrières 2002**, with a straw-yellow colour, is commended for its flavours of yellow fruits.
🕿 Emmanuel Plauchut, Dom. de Grandpré, 83390 Puget-Ville, tel. 04.94.48.32.16, fax 04.94.33.53.49 ▮
☖ ev. day 9am–12 noon 1.30pm–7pm

CH. HERMITAGE SAINT-MARTIN 2002★

■	3.91 ha	13,000	▮ ♦	5–8 €

This organically farmed estate was sold to the Château Sainte-Marguerite. This year it has done particularly well with its lively pink wine with intense aromas and a winey palate. This generous rosé has definite keeping potential.
🕿 Guillaume Fayard, Ch. Hermitage Saint-Martin, BP 1, 83250 La Londe-les-Maures, tel. 04.94.00.44.44, fax 04.94.00.44.45 ▮
☖ by appt.

DOM. DE JALE

La Bouïsse 2001★★★

■	2.1 ha	9,000	◪	11–15 €

After his apprenticeship in the Bordelais, at Château Mayne-Lalande with Bernard Lartigue, François Séminel moved to this region in 1999. This *coup de coeur* is both very encouraging and shows he has settled in well. The wine has a red-madder colour with purple highlights and releases a promising bouquet full of different nuances: fruits in brandy, spices and vanilla. The tasty palate is strengthened by round and integrated tannins which extend the finish of prunes, blackcurrant and liquorice. It will be ready to drink this winter and for several years after.
🕿 Dom. de Jale, rte de Saint-Tropez, chem. des Fenouils, 83550 Vidauban, tel. 04.94.73.51.50, fax 04.94.73.51.50 ▮ 🏠
☖ ev. day except Sun. 9am–12 noon 2.30pm–6.30pm
🕿 François Seminel

CH. DE JASSON

Cuvée Victoria 2002★★★

| ■ | 3.26 ha | 19,400 | ■ ♦ | 8–11 € |

Benjamin Defresne and his wife have made the most of this difficult year by controlling their harvests perfectly. The wine has a strong colour and a complex aromatic range, heralding a powerful wine supported by integrated tannins up to the generous finish. This will be excellent to drink now and for several years more. The **Cuvée Jeanne white 2002** is tasty with lemony and mineral aromas and is awarded one star, as is the **Cuvée Eléonore rosé 2002**.

☛ Benjamin de Fresne, Ch. de Jasson, Les Jassons, RD 88, 83250 La Londe-les-Maures, tel. 04.94.66.81.52, fax 04.94.05.24.84,
e-mail chateau.de.jasson@wanadoo.fr ☑
☒ ev. day 9.30am–12.30pm 2.30pm–7.30pm

DOM. DE LA JEANNETTE

Cuvée du Baguier 2001★

| ■ | 1 ha | 4,400 | ◫ | 5–8 € |

While the Gallo-Roman remains (stone from a wine-press) have come to light to prove the great age of the winemaking here, the recent rebuilding of the vinification cellar demonstrates a wish for modernity as well as respect for tradition. This strong purple 2001 is true to its terroir, with purplish nuances and aromas of soft fruits, sweet spices and even violet. The rounded tannins harmonize well with the alcohol and the oak. This is an open and generous Côtes de Provence. The **Cuvée du Baguier white 2002** was commended.

☛ SCIR du Dom. de la Jeannette, 566, rte des Borrels, 83400 Hyères-les-Palmiers, tel. 04.94.65.68.30, fax 04.94.12.76.07, e-mail domjeannette@aol.com ☑
☒ by appt.
☛ Limon

CH. DES LAUNES

Cuvée spéciale 2002★★

| ■ | 2 ha | 6,900 | ■ ♦ | 5–8 € |

This 2002 is perfect with a meal. It has a charming salmony colour and elegant floral aromas (lilac and carnation). The aromas continue on the structured, sweet palate. The **Château des Launes red 2001 Elevé en Fût (11–15 €)** is awarded one star: it is full, rich and has a subdued oakiness. Drink one bottle this year and keep another one for 2005.

☛ Hans-J. et Brigitte Handtmann, Ch. des Launes, RD 558, 83680 La Garde-Freinet, tel. 04.94.60.01.95, fax 04.94.60.01.43 ☑
☒ by appt.

DOM. DE LA LAUZADE 2002★★

| ■ | 28 ha | 135,000 | ■ ♦ | 5–8 € |

The La Lauzade estate, with its thousand-year-old fountain and 300-year-old plane trees, has an undeniable charm. In 46 BC, it had already caught the eye of the Romans, who built a villa there. Its wines are no less attractive. After winning a *coup de coeur* last year for its Côtes de Provence white 2001, it has this year produced a faultless glittering rosé, which opens with fruity and floral aromas. From the first impression on the palate, its smooth substance is mouth-filling and shows off its flavours all the way to a long finish.

☛ SARL Dom. de la Lauzade, Kinu-Ito, 3423, rte de Toulon, 83340 Le Luc-en-Provence, tel. 04.94.60.72.51, fax 04.94.60.96.26, e-mail contact@lauzade.com ☑
☒ by appt.

CH. MARAVENNE

Collection privée 2002★★★

| ■ | 3 ha | 18,000 | ■ ♦ | 5–8 € |

The Château Maravenne went over to organic farming in 2001, and is a benchmark for the appellation. Here it is rewarded for its rosé whose sweet tender rose colour with fuchsia highlights is matched only by its bouquet with fine floral and fruity notes (raspberry and exotic fruits). The palate is full and round with a similar aromatic intensity, the raspberry lingering into the finish. This is an authentic Mediterranean rosé which will go very well with any number of dishes. The **Collection Privée white 2002** and the **Donum Dei red 2001 (15–23 €)**, matured in barrel, were commended.

☛ EARL Gourjon, Ch. Maravenne, rte du Golf-de-Valcros, 83250 La Londe-les-Maures, tel. 04.94.66.80.20, fax 04.94.66.97.79,
e-mail maraven.gourjon@terre-net.fr ☑ ▥ ▥
☒ ev. day except Sun. 8am–12 noon 1pm–6pm

DOM. DE MARCHANDISE 2002★

| ■ | n.c. | 160,000 | ■ ♦ | 5–8 € |

The label is as sober and elegant as a visiting card, and encloses a rosé which subtly recalls a confectioner's: candyfloss and brioche. Its round and supple palate has a splendid finish of citrus fruits. The **Domaine de Marchandise red 2001**, which was not matured in oak, is commended for its fine-grained substance.

☛ GAEC Chauvier Frères, Dom. de Marchandise, 83520 Roquebrune-sur-Argens, tel. 04.94.45.42.91, fax 04.94.81.62.82 ☑
☒ ev. day 9am–12 noon 2pm–7pm

MAS DES BORRELS 2002★★

| ■ | 3 ha | 17,000 | ■ ♦ | 5–8 € |

Since the beginning of the last century, the Garniers have been wine-growers in the vallée des Borrels. This year, Jeanine and Michel offer a red wine with aromas of ripe fruits (bilberry and blackberry), liquorice and crystallized fruits which emerge when the glass is swirled. The smooth substance, supported by fine tannins, lingers into a tasty finish.

☛ GAEC Garnier, Mas Borrels, Dom. du Cazal, 3ᵉ Borrels, 83400 Hyères, tel. 04.94.65.68.20, fax 04.94.65.68.20
☛ M. Garnier

DOM. DE MATOURNE

Cuvée Prestige 2000★★

| ■ | 0.6 ha | 3,200 | ■ ◫ | 8–11 € |

The commune of Flayosc, long famous for making handmade shoes, now grows olives and vines. The Matourne estate has nearly 6 ha of vines, and used 90% of Cabernets Sauvignons and Syrahs to make this wine which has a lovely garnet-red colour and aromas of fruits in brandy and spices, with a note of capsicum which is typical of Cabernet. The straightforward attack reveals tannins with flavours of vanilla and chocolate, and a rich and powerful substance. Drink it in three to four years with game.

☛ GFA Dom. de Matourne, 235, chem. des Plaines-de-Matourne, 83780 Flayosc, tel. 04.94.70.43.74, fax 04.94.70.40.76,
e-mail jurgen.spaethe@wanadoo.fr ☑ ▥
☒ ev. day 9am–12 noon 2pm–7pm
☛ Jürgen Spaethe

CH. LES MESCLANCES

Cuvée Saint-Honorat 2000★

| ■ | n.c. | n.c. | ◫ | 5–8 € |

Equal shares of Syrah, Mourvèdre and Grenache made up this dark-red wine with a bouquet of spices and chocolate. The complex and intense substance absorbs the tannins well and a touch of menthol leaves a pleasant feeling of freshness in the finish. Drink a bottle of this now, but leave some more to mature.

☛ Xavier de Villeneuve-Bargemon, Les Mesclances, chem. du Moulin-Premier, 83260 La Crau, tel. 04.94.66.75.07, fax 04.94.35.10.03, e-mail mesclances@wanadoo.fr ☑
☒ by appt.

CH. MINUTY

Prestige 2002★★

■ Cru clas.	10 ha	60,000	■ ♦		11–15 €

This Prestige wine can be found up by the château where it was made. It has an extremely elegant pink colour with grey highlights, and an intense bouquet combining an exotic freshness with a floral delicacy. This complex range blossoms further on the full, round and fine palate. Its care-free nature conceals a perfect mastery of the substance. The Grand Jury was not disappointed. The **Cuvée Prestige red 2001**, matured in barrel, is awarded one star, as is the **Cuvée de l'Oratoire rosé 2002**.

↜ Matton-Farnet, Ch. Minuty, 83580 Gassin, tel. 04.94.56.12.09, fax 04.94.56.18.38 ☑
🍷 ev. day 9am–12 noon 2pm–6pm
↜ Matton

CH. MIRAVAL

Natouchka 2001★

■	3 ha	8,000	■ ⑪	23–30 €

In the old Roman village of Val, crossed by the via Aurelia, Joseph Lambot, the inventor of reinforced concrete, built his first structures. Here the Château Miraval grows 30 ha of vines and offers an intense red 2001 with a powerful nose of stewed soft fruits and spicy nuances. The attack is supple, revealing a structure of fine tannins, with both body and lingering flavours of liquorice and spices. It can be drunk now or kept for a few years so that it can mature fully.

↜ SA Ch. Miraval, 83143 Le Val, tel. 04.94.86.39.33, fax 04.94.86.46.79 ☑
🍷 by appt.

DOM. DE MONT REDON

Cuvée Louis Joseph 2002★★

■	3 ha	8,000	■ ♦	5–8 €

The fuchsia colour discloses a deliciously varied bouquet: rose, blackcurrant and strawberry on a base of pepper. The palate is also very tasty and shows real balance, roundness and good length. A taster suggested drinking this wine with a gigot d'agneau à la tapenade. The **Louis Joseph white 2002** is pale yellow and floral, and is awarded one star for its elegance.

↜ Michel Torné, SCEA Dom. Mont Redon, 2496, rte de Pierrefeu, 83260 La Crau, tel. 06.09.53.37.53, fax 04.94.57.82.12, e-mail mont.redon@libertysurf.fr ☑
🍷 by appt.

CH. MOURESSE

Grande Cuvée 2000★

■	1.5 ha	5,000	⑪	8–11 €

This Côtes de Provence has a very intense garnet-red colour and aromas of sweet spices, stone fruits and nuances of garrigue, and leaves a warm impression. Its tannins are certainly powerful, but balanced by the substance which shows good staying power. Drink it with boulettes d'agneau à la créole or a medallion of roe deer in a mustard of soft fruits.

↜ Michaël Horst, Ch. Mouresse, 3353, chem. de Pied-de-Banc, 83550 Vidauban, tel. 04.94.73.12.38, fax 04.94.73.57.04, e-mail info@chateau-mouresse.com ☑
🍷 by appt.

CH. LA MOUTETE

Vieilles Vignes 2002★

■	2.5 ha	13,000	■ ♦	8–11 €

Let your imagination run free when you think of what to eat with this wine. It has a pale-pink colour and releases bold aromas of white flowers and garrigue, while the palate, reserved at first, soon opens out to reveal strong flavours of soft fruits which linger in the memory.

↜ SAS Gérard Duffort, Ch. la Moutète, chem. des Vignes, 83390 Cuers, tel. 04.94.98.71.31, fax 04.94.60.44.87, e-mail contact@domainesduffort.com ☑
🍷 everyday except Sat. Sun. 9am–12 noon 2pm–5pm; open Sat. in summer

DOM. DES MYRTES

Cuvée Le Gaouby Elevé en fût de chêne 2001★

■	n.c.	n.c.	⑪	5–8 €

This garnet-coloured wine with purplish highlights is still reserved but nonetheless releases aromas of soft fruits with oaky nuances. After a pleasant attack, it rests on a prominent tannic structure up to the fruity finish (cherry). Keep it for two to three years. The **Cuvée Spéciale rosé 2002** was commended by the Jury.

↜ GAEC Barbaroux, Dom. des Myrtes, 83250 La Londe-les-Maures, tel. 04.94.66.83.00, fax 04.94.66.65.73 ☑
🍷 by appt.

DOM. DES NIBAS 2002★

■	2.75 ha	5,430	■ ♦	5–8 €

Beneath the massif des Maures, Nicolas Hentz grows 12 ha of vines; he left the cooperative in 1997 to make his own wine from these grapes planted on permian sandstone. His bright-pink wine with fuchsia nuances releases aromas of small soft fruits and citrus fruits which recur on the long and balanced palate.

↜ Nicolas Hentz, Dom. des Nibas, 9130, RD 48, 83550 Vidauban, tel. 04.94.73.67.46, fax 04.94.73.67.46, e-mail alhentz@aol.com ☑
🍷 ev. day 10am–12 noon 2pm–6pm

DOM. PINCHINAT 2001★★

■	5.3 ha	34,000	■ ♦	8–11 €

The Pinchinat estate has become organic for 12 years, and is well known in the *Guide* for its red wines. Syrah is warmly present in this 2001 wine with aromas of very ripe soft fruits. After a powerful attack, the tannins integrate with the fruity substance, leaving an impression of a rich, full wine. Keep this wine for a few years and it will be even more enjoyable.

↜ Alain de Welle, Dom. Pinchinat, 83910 Pourrières, tel. 04.42.29.29.92, fax 04.42.29.29.92, e-mail domainepinchinat@wanadoo.fr ☑
🍷 by appt.

DOM. DE PIQUEROQUE 2001★

■	1.5 ha	10,000	■ ⑪ ♦	5–8 €

As its name suggests, the estate stands on a rocky peak. Pine-woods and Provençal maquis surround the vineyard of 69 ha. Its first vintage last year was commended in the *Guide*, and this year Max Hubbard goes one step further with this solid, firm and powerful 2001 with aromas of wild mint, spices and black-cherry. Be patient for two or three years before you drink this with game or a daube.

↜ SCA Piqueroque, Dom. de Piqueroque, 83340 Flassans-sur-Issole, tel. 04.94.37.30.71, fax 04.94.37.30.72, e-mail piqueroque.isis@wanadoo.fr ☑
🍷 ev. day except Sun. 9am–12 noon 1pm–7pm
↜ M. Hubbard

JEAN-LUC POINSOT

Terroirs des Cuers 2001★

■	1 ha	5,200	⑪	5–8 €

This new firm of négociants makes and distributes its Mediterranean wines. They come from vines planted in the Vallée de Cuers, and the garnet-coloured 2001 offers a lovely bouquet of bigaroon cherry and fresh almond. Although the oak adds to the wine's complexity, it lets the substance come through frankly on notes of blackberry. The finish has

flavours of vanilla and liquorice. This wine is ready now, and will go well with a gigot d'agneau in thyme.
☛ La Badiane, S. Croisette II, RN 154,
83250 La-Londe-les-Maures, tel. 04.78.57.56.21,
fax 04.37.22.05.59, e-mail contact@labadiane.com ☑
🍷 by appt.

CH. DE POURCIEUX
Grand Millésime 1999★

	2 ha	6,500	⑪	11–15 €

Pourcieux is about 30 kilometres from Aix; the château of the same name is a historic monument and overlooks a vineyard of more than 25 ha. This rich wine has a deep colour with rich nuances of tobacco and spices, and is well balanced thanks to its well-coated tannins which last into the vanilla finish. This is a wine for impatient pleasure-seekers.
☛ Michel d'Espagnet, Ch. de Pourcieux, 83470 Pourcieux, tel. 04.94.59.78.90, fax 04.94.59.32.46,
e-mail pourcieux@terre-net.fr ☑
🍷 by appt.

CH. DU PUGET 2002★★

	2.3 ha	4,010	🍾 🍸	5–8 €

It is already six years since Pierre Grimaud invested in renovating his production side. His white 2002 went before the Grand Jury, having made such an impression on the original tasters with its glittering pale colour and complex bouquet of citrus fruits, dried fruits and mineral notes. Its round and tasty substance caresses the palate and leaves a persistent impression of elegance. This is a top-of-the-range wine and difficult to resist. The **Cuvée de Chavette red 2001**, matured in barrel for one year, should develop well and open out in two to three years. It is awarded one star.
☛ SCEA Ch. du Puget, rue Mas-de-Clappier,
83390 Puget-Ville, tel. 04.94.48.31.15, fax 04.94.33.58.55 ☑
🍷 ev. day except Mon. Sun. 9am–12 noon 3pm–6pm
☛ Grimaud

LES CELLIERS DE RAMATUELLE
Cuvée du Navigateur Antiboul 2002★

	8.9 ha	48,000	🍾 🍸	5–8 €

Tibouren is a Provençal grape variety perfectly adapted to the coastal area, and was introduced in the 18th century by a sea captain named Antiboul. This pale-coloured wine has aromas of soft fruits and fresh apricot. It is supple and silky, and altogether seductive.
☛ Les Celliers des Vignerons de Ramatuelle, quartier Les Boutinelles, 83350 Ramatuelle, tel. 04.94.55.59.05,
fax 04.94.55.59.06,
e-mail info@celliers-de-ramatuelle.com ☑
🍷 by appt.

CH. REAL D'OR 2002★

	3 ha	12,000	🍾	5–8 €

The Real d'Or estate is 1 km from the village Les Tortues, and its 21 ha of vines stand on schist soils. Beneath its elegant label, this strong ruby wine offers a sophisticated bouquet and a supple palate with pleasant tannins which are already combining well. The **white 2002** is very fresh and is commended.
☛ SCEA Ch. Réal d'Or, rte des Mayons, 83590 Gonfaron, tel. 04.94.60.00.56, fax 04.94.60.01.05,
e-mail realdor@free.fr ☑
🍷 ev. day 10am–1pm 3pm–7.30pm

CH. REAL MARTIN 2002★

	5 ha	13,300	🍾 🍸	11–15 €

The renovation and additional works at this estate are now finished: the cellar and the inn await you. There you can taste this wine with floral fragrances of hawthorn and fruity ones of citrus fruits. A lemony freshness runs beneath the full body of the balanced and long palate. The **rosé 2002** releases pleasant scents of white flowers and bergamot, and is commended.

☛ Jean-Marie Paul, Ch. Réal Martin, rte de Barjols, 83143 Le Val, tel. 04.94.86.40.90, fax 04.94.86.32.23,
e-mail chateau-real-martin@groupe.score.com ☑
🍷 by appt.

CH. REILLANNE
Grande Réserve 2002★

	85 ha	400,000	🍾 🍸	5–8 €

This rosé has a nice balance, combining freshness and fruity flavours. The notes of citrus fruits and a mineral touch have good length. This same firm produces 600,000 bottles under the brand name **Rose de Satin rosé 2002 (3–5 €)**. This wine is awarded one star. The **Grande Réserve white 2002** should be tasted when young to enjoy its fruity softness. It is commended.
☛ Comte G. de Chevron Villette, Ch. Reillanne, rte de Saint-Tropez, 83340 Le Cannet-des-Maures,
tel. 04.94.50.11.70, fax 04.94.47.92.06 ☑
🍷 ev. day except Sat. Sun. 8am–12 noon 2pm–5pm

DOM. DU REVAOU 2002★

	10 ha	55,000	🍾 🍸	5–8 €

Lou Revaou is a stream which winds through this organically farmed vineyard of about 30 hectares. It gives its name to the estate and to this bright pink wine with aromas of soft fruits and wild mint. It is well structured and has good length, and could be a faithful companion at barbecues during an Indian autumn. The **white 2002 (8–11 €)** has a light aniseed taste and deserves its commendation.
☛ Bernard Scarone, Dom. du Révaou, 3ᵉ Borrels, 83250 La Londe-les-Maures, tel. 04.94.65.68.44, fax 04.94.35.88.54 ☑
🍷 by appt.

RIMAURESQ
R. 2001★★★

Cru clas.	6.1 ha	28,000	⑪	15–23 €

A Scottish family runs this reputable Provençal wine estate. The vines face northwest and are planted on a poor schist soil beneath the massif Notre-Dame-des-Anges, at the end of the massif des Maures, which gives them some shelter from the fierce summer sun. Equal shares of Syrah and Cabernet Sauvignon make up this deep-ruby wine with a rich and intense bouquet combining liquorice, spices and fruits. The palate is powerful and harmonious, revealing integrated oak and a very long finish, the result of efficient growing and vinification. This is a tasty wine to keep for at least two years. Decant it before serving with red meat, game or a daube.
☛ Dom. de Rimauresq, rte de Notre-Dame-des-Anges, 83790 Pignans, tel. 04.94.48.80.45, fax 04.94.33.22.31,
e-mail rimauresq@wanadoo.fr ☑
🍷 by appt.
☛ M. Wemyss

LES VIGNERONS DE ROQUEFORT LA BEDOULE Sur un Air de Mistral 2001★

	6.5 ha	33,000	⑪	5–8 €

This year the Roquefort-la-Bédoule cooperative celebrates its 40th anniversary. Every year they come up with a successful Air de Mistral. The deep-ruby 2001 has an intense nose of soft fruits, and a good and complex substance even though the oak is still dominant. Keep it for two years before drinking it with white meat. The **Cuvée Sur un Air de Mistral rosé 2002**, with its aromas of blackberry, is commended.
☛ Les vignerons de Roquefort-la-Bédoule, rte de Cuges-les-Pins, 13830 Roquefort-la-Bédoule,
tel. 04.42.73.22.80, fax 04.42.73.01.37 ☑
🍷 ev. day except Sun. 8.30am–12 noon 2pm–7pm

LA ROUVEDE
Cuvée Prestige 2001★★★

	2 ha	8,000	⑪	5–8 €

Beneath the massif des Maures, Gonfaron is a pretty village dominated by the Chapelle Saint-Quinis. While it is pleasant to stroll through the narrow streets looking for fountains and old washing places, a detour to the cooperative's cellar is an essential part of the itinerary. Here you will be nicely surprised by a dense wine with aromas of soft fruits, cocoa and sweet spices. Flavours of stewed Morello cherry and

cherry add to the delights of the velvety palate. The **Cuvée Jules César rosé 2002 (3–5 €)** deserves its commendation.
→ Les Maîtres Vignerons de Gonfaron, Cave coopérative, 83590 Gonfaron, tel. 04.94.78.30.02, fax 04.94.78.27.33 ☑
⊤ ev. day 8am–12 noon 2pm–6pm

CH. DE ROUX 2002★

| | 1.2 ha | 7,000 | ■ ♦ | 5–8 € |

This country house surrounded by ancient maritime pines has a typical Provençal charm. The town-hall archives at Cannet-des-Maures show that it dates from the 15th century. Looking ahead to the future, the estate made some new investments in 2000, resulting in this successful wine which leaves in its wake strong and elegant aromas of pear and caramel. The round and lingering substance creates an impression of balance and honesty right up to the final peppery note. Drink it with a simple meal, say a bass grilled in fennel. The **Rosé de Saignée 2002** has a spicy note and will go well with exotic dishes. It is commended.
→ SCEA Ch. de Roux, quartier Roux, 83340 Le Cannet-des-Maures, tel. 04.94.60.73.10, fax 04.94.60.89.79 ☑
⊤ by appt.

DOM. SAINT-ANDRE DE FIGUIERE

Grande Cuvée Vieilles Vignes 2001★★★

| | 2 ha | 8,000 | ⑪ | 8–11 € |

Facing the Îles d'Or de Porquerolles, this estate of 17 ha has been carefully run by Alain Combard for ten years. He has produced this attractive ruby-coloured wine whose aromas and flavours bring out the best in the Mourvèdre. This 2001 vintage has warm touches of liquorice and spices and develops in a smooth and complex way on a subtle oak. The integrated tannins help to create an impression of softness and fullness. This is a good Provençal wine to lay down. The **Grande Cuvée Vieilles Vignes rosé 2002** is awarded one star: it has a classic tasty fruitiness and is nicely fresh.
→ Dom. Saint-André de Figuière, BP 47, 83250 La Londe-les-Maures, tel. 04.94.00.44.70, fax 04.94.35.04.46, e-mail figuiere@figuiere-provence.com ☑
⊤ ev. day except Sun. 9am–12 noon 2pm–6pm
→ Alain Combard

CH. SAINTE MARGUERITE

Cuvée Prestige La Désirade 2002★★

| Cru clas. | 6.12 ha | 16,000 | ■ ♦ | 8–11 € |

In 1977, Brigitte and Jean-Pierre Fayard took over this old wine estate dating back to Antiquity. They have carefully sought to make the most of their clay-siliceous terroir, and in the difficult year of 2002 they produced a remarkable wine. The grapes escaped the bad weather of September which caused so much damage, because the owners started harvesting from 21 August. The wine has harmonious flavours of citrus fruits and acacia, an elegant and balanced structure which extends fluidly to a generous finish. This is a fine representative of the appellation, to be enjoyed over a convivial meal. The **Cuvée Prestige rosé 2002**, with its spring-like colour and fruity flavours, is awarded one star for its honest and tasty nature.
→ Jean-Pierre Fayard, Ch. Sainte-Marguerite, BP 1, 83250 La Londe-les-Maures, tel. 04.94.00.44.44, fax 04.94.00.44.45 ☑
⊤ by appt.

DOM. SAINTE MARIE

Cuvée de la Roche Blanche 2002★★

| | 5 ha | 28,000 | ■ ♦ | 8–11 € |

In the middle of the massif des Maures, a manor house overlooks 270 ha of vines planted on a mica-schist terroir, formerly the property of the chartreuse de la Verne. Henri Vidal has run this estate since 1959, and has carefully cultivated his stock of Syrah, Cinsault and Grenache to produce this very youthful wine with fuchsia highlights and aromas of soft fruits. In the finish, the concentrated and powerful substance forms a harmonious blend of fruitiness and more vegetal nuances. An ideal wine for the autumn and winter of 2003.

→ SA Dom. de Sainte-Marie, rte du Dom, RN 98, 83230 Bormes-les-Mimosas, tel. 04.94.49.57.15, fax 04.94.49.58.57, e-mail domaine.saintemarie@wanadoo.fr ☑
⊤ ev. day except Sun. 9am–1pm 2pm–7pm
→ Henri Vidal

CH. SAINTE-ROSELINE

Cuvée Prieuré 2001★★★

| Cru clas. | 7 ha | 37,000 | ⑪ | 15–23 € |

The chapel next to the estate contains the body of Sainte Roseline, a bas-relief by Giacometti and a mosaic mural by Chagall. It is open to visitors. Afterwards, you can taste this wine which also has great presence. The intense purple colour yields a complex bouquet mingling nuances of vanilla, spices and good oak. The silky palate develops around integrated mature tannins and reveals countless aromas of spices and truffles. This is a Côtes de Provence of character, to be drunk now or kept. The **Cuvée du Prieuré white 2001 (11–15 €)**, matured in barrel, finely absorbs the oak into its rounded style. It is awarded one star.
→ SCEA Ch. Sainte-Roseline, 83460 Les Arcs-sur-Argens, tel. 04.94.99.50.30, fax 04.94.47.53.06, e-mail contact@sainte-roseline.com ☑
⊤ by appt.
→ B. Teillaud

CH. SAINT JEAN 2002★

| | 7.6 ha | 43,200 | ■ ♦ | 3–5 € |

Le Luc is a typical Provençal village with old houses and a hexagonal tower. The Château des Vintimille is worth a stop for its stamp museum. The cooperative has a fresh wine, nicely enhanced by longish fruity and amylic aromas. Its cherry colour with deep-purple highlights is also attractive. A commendation, too, for the **Réserve des Vintimille white 2002**, to be drunk with seafood to bring out its freshness and fragrances of peach and banana.
→ CCV Les Vignerons du Luc, rue de l'Ormeau, 83340 Le Luc-en-Provence, tel. 04.94.60.70.25, fax 04.94.60.81.03

CH. DE SAINT-JULIEN D'AILLE

Triumvir des Rimbauds 2001★

| | 1 ha | 1,600 | ⑪ | 11–15 € |

The clematis, the "white vine" or Vitis alba in Latin, is probably responsible for the name Vidauban, a commune between the plaine des Maures and the vallée de l'Argens, where Yves Robert filmed *Le Château de ma mère*. The Fleury family cultivate 170 ha in this area, and offer a 2001 wine which bears the signs of its maturation for 12 months in oak, both in its straw-yellow colour and its smoky notes. The palate is pleasant and well balanced. The **Triumvir des Rimbaud rosé 2000**, matured in barrel, is also awarded one star for its full character which should soften after a while, and the **Imperator rosé 2002 (5–8 €)** is commended.
→ Ch. Saint-Julien d'Aille, 5480, RD 48, 83550 Vidauban, tel. 04.94.73.02.89, fax 04.94.73.61.31 ☑
⊤ ev. day except Sun. 9am–12.30pm 2pm–6.30pm
→ B. Fleury

DOM. DE SAINT-SER

Les Hauts de Saint-Ser 2000★

| | 2 ha | 9,000 | ⑪ | 15–23 € |

The Pierlot family come from Champagne, and bought this 25-ha estate in 1986. Their deep-ruby wine shows signs of its maturation in oak, and releases strong aromas of soft fruits and liquorice. The palate is structured and powerful, combining the fruity flavours with notes of spices and prune. The **Cuvée Prestige red 2000 (8–11 €)**, matured in large wooden barels, is commended.
→ Dom. de Saint-Ser, RD 17, 13114 Puyloubier, tel. 04.42.66.30.81, fax 04.42.66.37.51, e-mail saintser@wanadoo.fr ☑
⊤ ev. day 11am–12 noon 2pm–6pm
→ Pierlot

PROVENCE

DOM. DE LA SANGLIERE

Cuvée Prestige 2002★

	3 ha	13,300	■ ♦	8–11 €

La Sanglière was created in 1981 from plots belonging to the Léoube estate, since when it has established its own identity and shown great skill in producing rosé wines. This 2002 vintage offers fruity aromas on both nose and palate: soft fruits and pineapple. It shows itself to be frank and persistent, with an old-fashioned air about its strong pink colour with deep-purple highlights.

EARL de la Sanglière, 83230 Bormes-les-Mimosas, tel. 04.94.00.48.58, fax 04.94.00.43.77, e-mail remy@domaine-sangliere.com ▼ ♠
ev. day except Mon. Sat. Sun. 9am–12 noon 3pm–7pm
Conservatoire du littoral

DOM. DE SANT JANET

Elevé en fût de chêne 2001★★

	2 ha	3,200	■ ◑	5–8 €

Located in the Upper Var, the Sant Janet estate cultivates 13 ha of vines surrounded by forest. Three of its wines appear in the *Guide*: the **white 2002**, which is floral and fruity (hawthorn, peach and apricot), and the **Cuvée Aurore rosé 2002** are commended, while the star turn is this Côtes de Provence with a strong and brilliant colour which releases notes of fresh fruits (blackberry and raspberry), before resting on powerful tannins which do not spoil the balance of the substance. The tasters also liked its aromatic length.

Patrick Delmas, Dom. de Sant Janet, 83570 Cotignac, tel. 04.94.04.77.69, fax 04.94.04.76.31, e-mail domaine.st.janet@wanadoo.fr ▼
ev. day 8am–8pm

DOM. DE LA SAUVEUSE 2002★★

	34.76 ha	143,000	■ ♦	5–8 €

This is a light-pink, subtle and aromatic wine. The floral perfumes of the bouquet are succeeded on the palate by a perfectly balanced fruitiness and freshness. This Côtes de Provence has good length and could be drunk throughout a meal. The **red 2001** is recommended for drinking with meat in sauce: its generous, warm bouquet balances with the dense and lastingly tasty substance and the integrated tannins. It also was thought remarkable.

Dom. de la Sauveuse, Grand-Chemin-Vieux, 83390 Puget-Ville, tel. 04.94.28.59.60, fax 04.94.28.59.60, e-mail sauveuse@wanadoo.fr ▼
ev. day except Sun. 8am–12 noon 2pm–6pm
Salinas

DOM. SIOUVETTE

Cuvée Marcel Galfard 2002★

	6 ha	45,000	■ ♦	5–8 €

A baked sea bream would bring the best out of this elegant sand-coloured wine which releases subtle floral notes when the glass is swirled. Although lively, it never loses its essential balance. A good wine to drink next winter.

Sylvaine Sauron, Dom. Siouvette, RN 98, 83310 La Môle, tel. 04.94.49.57.13, fax 04.94.49.59.12, e-mail sylvaine.sauron@wanadoo.fr ▼
by appt.

DOM. SORIN

Cuvée privée 2001★

	3 ha	15,000	◑	11–15 €

In 1994, Luc Sorin, originally from the Auxerrois, moved to this 12-ha estate which is divided between the AOC Côtes de Provence and Bandol. This well-structured and balanced vintage will appeal to lovers of oaky wines. It has an intense colour and is richly aromatic in a rather Burgundian style. It will go very well with various dishes. Try it in two years with game, poultry or white meat.

Dom. Sorin, 1617, rte de La Cadière-d'Azur, 83270 Saint-Cyr-sur-Mer, tel. 04.94.26.62.28, fax 04.94.26.40.06, e-mail luc.sorin@wanadoo.fr ▼ ♠
by appt.
Luc Sorin

DOM. DE TAMARY

Cuvée Vieilles Vignes 2000★

	4 ha	13,000	■ ♦	5–8 €

The vallée du Tamary is unusual in that it is free from any form of urbanization, although it is only a few hundred metres from the coast. Here they grow Grenache, Syrah and Carignan on a schist soil on undulating hillsides. The combination of these grape varieties has produced this wine with a nose of stewed fruits and spices. It is already smooth and fully mature. The **Cuvée Vieilles Vignes rosé 2002** is commended for its good aromatic length and balance.

SCEA Dom. de Tamary, rte de Valcros, 83250 La-Londe-les-Maures, tel. 04.94.66.66.51, fax 04.94.66.95.58 ▼
ev. day except Sun. 10am–12 noon 4pm–7pm
E. Lambert

DOM. DES THERMES 2002★★

	2.3 ha	16,000	■ ♦	3–5 €

Between 1941 and 1998, no wine was made from the grapes at the Domaine des Thermes. Michel Robert then decided to build a modern winery to deal with his vines, planted on an old Roman site. The proof of his abilities lies in this pale-pink wine with sparkling silver highlights and perfumes of ripe strawberry, white peach and citrus fruits. The fresh palate continues these aromas and has excellent length. The **white 2002** is very lively and is commended.

EARL Michel Robert, Dom. des Thermes, RN 7, 83340 Le Cannet-des-Maures, tel. 04.94.60.73.15, fax 04.94.60.73.15 ▼
ev. day 8am–7.30pm

CH. LA TOUR DE L'EVEQUE

Pétale de Rose 2002★

	40 ha	n.c.	■ ♦	8–11 €

The name Pétale de Rose is a good description for this wine's luminous colour. It releases fruity aromas with floral and spicy notes. On the palate it is rounded and balanced, evolving gently to a soft finish with ripe strawberry and brown sugar. This is a very characteristic Provençal wine. The **white 2002 (5–8 €)** is also very bright with flavours of brioche and stewed fruits, and a good balance between body and liveliness. The **Cuvée Noir et or red 2000 (11–15 €)**, matured in barrel, should be kept through this winter. Both were commended.

Régine Sumeire, Ch. La Tour de l'Evêque, La Tour Sainte-Anne, 83390 Pierrefeu-du-Var, tel. 04.94.28.20.17, fax 04.94.48.14.69, e-mail regine.sumeire@toureveque.com ▼
by appt.

DOM. LA TOUR DES VIDAUX

Cuvée Farnoux Elevé en fût de chêne 2001★★

	3.2 ha	8,638	◑	8–11 €

The estate offers not only a table d'hôte but also organizes cultural exhibitions. This includes a stop to taste the Côtes de Provence, particularly this wine whose black-cherry colour heralds the richness of the bouquet: soft fruit jam, spices and leather. The palate reveals strong tannins but retains the fruity promise of the bouquet and adds chocolate-flavoured notes and nuances of truffle. This is wine of character, and should be kept for at least two years. The **Cuvée Farnoux rosé 2002 (5–8 €)** is ethereal and balanced, and is awarded one star.

Volker-Paul Weindel, Dom. La-Tour-des-Vidaux, quartier Les Vidaux, 83390 Pierrefeu-du-Var, tel. 04.94.48.24.01, fax 04.94.48.24.02, e-mail tourdesvidaux@wanadoo.fr ▼ ♠
ev. day except Sun. 8.30am–12 noon 2.30pm–6.30pm

DOM. LA TOURRAQUE 2001★★

	1 ha	2,000	◑	8–11 €

In the middle of the listed site of the Trois Caps (Camarat, Taillat and Lardier), La Tourraque cultivates 40 ha of vines. This wine is a blend of Rolle and 30% Ugni Blanc. It has a brilliant pale-yellow colour and, although marked by oak, also releases good aromas of citrus fruits that continue on the rounded and full-bodied palate.

☛ GAEC Brun-Craveris, Dom. La Tourraque, 83350 Ramatuelle, tel. 04.94.79.25.95, fax 04.94.79.16.08 ☑
⟁ ev. day except Sat. Sun. 9am–12 noon 2pm–6pm

DOM. TURENNE

Cuvée Camille 2002★

| ■ | | 5 ha | 20,000 | ▮ ◊ | | 5–8 € |

Philipe Benezet continues the winemaking work of his grandfather and, three times a year, exhibits the work of young artists in his Provençal farmhouse. You may be able to take in a private viewing when you try this wine with its aromas of strawberry and apricot, followed by lilac. Its jolly freshness would suit a convivial gathering.

☛ Philippe Benezet, Dom. Turenne, 83390 Cuers, tel. 04.94.48.68.77, fax 04.94.28.57.13, e-mail philippebenezet@9online.fr ☑ ▤
⟁ by appt.

DOM. DU VAL DE GILLY Cuvée Alexandre

Castellan Elevé en fût de chêne 2001★

| ■ | | 2 ha | 8,000 | ▮ ⑪ | | 5–8 € |

This wine pays homage to Alexandre Castellan who created the estate in the 1880s. It has a long vatting period and is then matured in oak. It releases generous aromas of soft fruits, spices and liquorice, then on the palate reveals its fruity roundness on evident tannins. You could serve it with a meal now or keep it for one or two years. The **Cuvée Alexandre Castellan rosé 2002 (3–5 €)** is commended; its pleasant fruitiness will add sparkle to the beginning of a meal.

☛ SARL Dom. du Val de Gilly, 83310 Grimaud, tel. 04.94.43.21.25, fax 04.94.43.26.27 ☑
⟁ ev. day except Sun. 9am–12 noon 2pm–7pm; 2pm–7pm Jan. Feb.
☛ Castellan

CH. LES VALENTINES 2002★

| ■ | 1.14 ha | 4,000 | ▮ ◊ | | 8–11 € |

Since 1997, the Château Les Valentines has become a benchmark thanks to the dynamism of Gilles Pons and Pascale Massenot. This Côtes de Provence seems restrained with its pale-yellow colour and slight green highlights and bouquet. However, on the palate it asserts itself well. After a frank and lively attack, it gains in body and rises in a crescendo to a rich and expressive finish. This will go nicely with an autumn meal of feuilleté de Saint-Jacques in ginger or a monkfish in fennel on a bed of potatoes.

☛ SCEA Pons-Massenot, Ch. Les Valentines, lieu-dit Les Jassons, 83250 La Londe-les-Maures, tel. 04.94.15.95.50, fax 04.94.15.95.55, e-mail gilles@lesvalentines.com ☑
⟁ ev. day except Sun. 9am–12.30pm 2.30pm–7pm
☛ Gilles Pons

CH. VEREZ 2002★

| ■ | 20 ha | 20,000 | ▮ ◊ | | 5–8 € |

If you pass through Vidauban, call on Nadine and Serge Rosinoer who will share with you their passion for the region and the wine they produce. Try this rosé with deep-purple highlights, with subtle aromas of medlar and fruits in syrup that show themselves when the glass is swirled. A wine for enjoying with a meal.

☛ Ch. Vérez, 5192, chem. de la Verrerie-Neuve, 83350 Vidauban, tel. 04.94.73.69.90, fax 04.94.73.55.84, e-mail verez@wanadoo.fr ☑
⟁ by appt.
☛ Rosinoer

DOM. DES VINGTINIERES 2002★

| ■ | 8.4 ha | 32,000 | ▮ ◊ | | 5–8 € |

Patrice Moreux offers well-made rosés. Just as his 2001 vintage won one star last year, the Jury was equally impressed with his 2002 wine. It is a very pale-pink in colour with slight orangey highlights, and has a full palate with flavours of summer fruits such as white peach; the balance continues into the elegant and lengthy finish.

☛ Patrice Moreux, Les Vingtinières, rte de Saint-Tropez, 83340 Le Cannet-des-Maures, tel. 04.94.99.81.12, fax 04.94.99.81.12 ☑
⟁ by appt.

VITIS ALBA

Elevé en fût de chêne 2001★★★

| ■ | 4 ha | 5,400 | ⑪ | | 5–8 € |

This wine went before the Grand Jury after its concentration and complexity had impressed the tasters so much. Its almost-black colour veils a bouquet mingling a luxurious oak and soft fruits, leather and cocoa. The compact and structured palate rests on firm tannins but does not mask the flavours of the fruits, spices and truffles in the finish. This wine could undoubtedly be kept for some time. On a more basic aromatic level (fruit drops and strawberry), the **Terroir rosé 2002 (3–5 €)** was liked for its potential as an aperitif, and was commended.

☛ Les Vignerons des Coteaux du Val d'Argens, 89, chem. Sainte-Anne, BP 24, 83550 Vidauban, tel. 04.94.73.00.12, fax 04.94.73.54.67, e-mail administratif@valdargens.com ☑ ⌂
⟁ by appt.

Wines selected but not starred

LOU BAOU 2002

| ■ | n.c. | 15,000 | ▮ | | 3–5 € |

☛ Les Vignerons du Baou, rue Raoul-Blanc, 83470 Pourcieux, tel. 04.94.78.03.06, fax 04.94.78.05.50 ☑
⟁ by appt.

CH. BASTIDIERE 2002

| ■ | 1.05 ha | 7,300 | ▮ ◊ | | 5–8 € |

☛ Dr Thomas Flensberg, Ch. Bastidière, rte de Pierrefeu, 83390 Cuers, tel. 04.94.13.51.28, fax 04.94.13.51.29, e-mail nc-dr.fleth@netcologne.de ☑
⟁ by appt.

CH. DE BERNE

Cuvée spéciale 2002

| ■ | 25 ha | 30,000 | ▮ ◊ | | 8–11 € |

☛ Ch. de Berne, 83510 Lorgues, tel. 04.94.60.43.60, fax 04.94.60.43.58, e-mail vins@chateauberne.com ☑
⟁ ev. day 10am–6pm
☛ Muddyman

CH. DE CABRAN

Cuvée de la Muraille 2001

| ■ | 2 ha | 10,600 | ▮ ◊ | | 5–8 € |

☛ SCEA du Ch. de Cabran, chem. de Cabran, 83480 Puget-sur-Argens, tel. 04.94.40.80.32, fax 04.94.40.75.21, e-mail cabran@libertysurf.fr ☑
⟁ ev. day 10am–12 noon 2pm–7pm (5pm in winter)

CANTA RAINETTE

Grande Réserve Elevé en fût de chêne 2001

| ■ | 2,800 | ⑪ | | 8–11 € |

☛ SCEA Edouard Castellino, Dom. de Canta Rainette, 1144, rte de Bagnols, 83920 La Motte, tel. 04.94.70.28.25, fax 04.94.70.28.25, e-mail canta.rainette@wanadoo.fr ☑
⟁ ev. day except Sun. 9am–12 noon 3pm–6pm

CARBASE 2001

| | 2 ha | 5,000 | ◫ | 8–11 € |

☙ Rabiega Vin, Clos Dière, 83300 Draguignan, tel. 04.94.68.44.22, fax 04.94.47.17.72, e-mail vin@rabiega.com ☑
Ⴤ by appt.

LE CHARME DES DEMOISELLES 2001

| | 2 ha | 4,000 | ▤◫ | 8–11 € |

☙ SEDA les Demoiselles, Dom. Saint-Michel-d'Esclans, 83920 La Motte, tel. 04.94.70.24.60, fax 04.94.84.32.06, e-mail jr.demoiselles@wanadoo.fr ☑
Ⴤ by appt.

CLOS LA NEUVE

Prestige 2000

| | 10 ha | 15,000 | ◫ | 5–8 € |

☙ Pierre Joly, Dom. de La Neuve, 83910 Pourrières, tel. 04.94.78.17.02, fax 04.94.59.86.42 ☑
Ⴤ ev. day 9am–12 noon 2pm–7pm; Sun. 9am–12 noon

CH. COLBERT CANNET 2002

| | 50 ha | 200,000 | ▤ ⚶ | 5–8 € |

☙ SCEA Dom. de Colbert, Causserène, 83340 Le Cannet-des-Maures, tel. 04.94.60.77.66, fax 04.94.60.95.59 ☑
Ⴤ ev. day except Sat. Sun. 8am–12 noon 2pm–5pm

COSTE BRULADE

Réserve 3e millénaire 2001

| | 30 ha | 45,000 | ▤ ⚶ | 8–11 € |

☙ SCA Cellier Saint-Sidoine, rue de la Libération, 83390 Puget-Ville, tel. 04.98.01.80.50, fax 04.98.01.80.59, e-mail courrier@provence-sidoine.com ☑
Ⴤ by appt.

DOM. DE LA COURTADE 2001

| | 3 ha | 12,000 | ◫ | 15–23 € |

☙ SCEA Dom. de La Courtade, 83400 Ile-de-Porquerolles, tel. 04.94.58.31.44, fax 04.94.58.34.12, e-mail la-courtade@terre-net.fr ☑
Ⴤ by appt.

CH. LES CROSTES 2002

| | 33 ha | 100,000 | ▤ ⚶ | 5–8 € |

☙ H.L. Ch. les Crostes, chem. de Saint-Louis, BP 55, 83510 Lorgues, tel. 04.94.73.98.40, fax 04.94.73.97.93, e-mail chateau.les.crostes@wanadoo.fr ☑
Ⴤ ev. day except Sun. 10am–6pm; Jun.–Aug. 9am–8pm

DUPERE BARRERA

Nowat 2001

| | 0.5 ha | 1,500 | ◫ | 23–30 € |

☙ Dupéré Barrera, 122, rue de Dakar, 83100 Toulon, tel. 04.94.23.36.08, fax 04.94.23.36.08, e-mail vinsduperebarrera@hotmail.com ☑
Ⴤ by appt.

CH. DES FERRAGES 2001

| | 1.5 ha | 6,500 | ▤◫ | 8–11 € |

☙ José Garcia, RN 7, 83470 Pourcieux, tel. 04.94.59.45.53, fax 04.94.59.72.49 ☑
Ⴤ by appt.

VIGNOBLE GASPERINI

Cuvée Charlotte 1999

| | 3 ha | 10,000 | ▤ ⚶ | 5–8 € |

☙ Vignoble Gasperini, 42, av. de la Libération, 83260 La Crau, tel. 04.94.66.70.01, fax 04.94.66.10.33, e-mail gasperini.vins@wanadoo.fr ☑
Ⴤ ev. day except Sat. Sun. 8am–12 noon 2pm–6pm

DOM. DE JACOURETTE

Cuvée Tradition 2002

| | 0.8 ha | 5,000 | ▤ ⚶ | 5–8 € |

☙ Dom. de Jacourette, rte de Trets, 83910 Pourrières, tel. 04.94.78.54.60, fax 04.94.78.54.90, e-mail jacourette@club-internet.fr ☑
Ⴤ ev. day except Mon. Sun. 3.30pm–6.30pm
☙ Hélène Dragon

CH. DE LEOUBE 2002

| | n.c. | 13,000 | ▤ ⚶ | 8–11 € |

☙ SCAV Dom. de Léoube, 2387, rte de Léoube, 83230 Bormes-les-Mimosas, tel. 04.94.64.80.03, fax 04.94.71.75.40, e-mail chateauleoube@wanadoo.fr ☑
☙ Sir Bamford

LOU BASSAQUET

Rascailles Cuvée spéciale 2001

| | 12 ha | n.c. | ▤ ⚶ | 3–5 € |

☙ Cellier Lou Bassaquet, chem. du Loup, BP 22, 13530 Trets, tel. 04.42.29.20.20, fax 04.42.29.32.03, e-mail lou.bassaquet@free.fr

CH. MAROUINE 2001

| | 2.8 ha | 12,000 | ◫ | 8–11 € |

☙ Marie-Odile Marty, Ch. Marouïne, 83390 Puget-Ville, tel. 04.94.48.35.74, fax 04.94.48.37.61 ☑
Ⴤ ev. day except Sun. 9am–7pm

MAS DE CADENET 2001

| | 8.5 ha | 30,000 | ◫ | 5–8 € |

☙ Guy Négrel, Mas de Cadenet, 13530 Trets, tel. 04.42.29.21.59, fax 04.42.61.32.09, e-mail mas-de-cadenet@wanadoo.fr ☑
Ⴤ ev. day except Sun. 9am–12 noon 2pm–7pm

CH. DE MAUVANNE 2001

| Cru clas. | 12 ha | 50,000 | ▤ ⚶ | 8–11 € |

☙ SCA Ch. de Mauvanne, 2805, rte de Nice, 83400 Hyères, tel. 04.94.66.40.25, fax 04.94.66.46.29, e-mail chateaudemauvanne@free.fr ☑
Ⴤ by appt.
☙ Rahal Bassim

DOM. DE LA MAYONNETTE

Cuvée Tradition 2002

| | 1 ha | 1,500 | ▤ ⚶ | 5–8 € |

☙ Julian, Dom. de la Mayonnette, rte de Pierrefeu, 83260 La Crau, tel. 04.94.48.28.38, fax 04.94.28.26.66 ☑
Ⴤ ev. day except Sun. 9am–12 noon 1.30pm–6pm

CH. LA MOUTTE 2002

| | 4 ha | 17,900 | ▤ ⚶ | 5–8 € |

☙ La Cave de Saint-Tropez, SCAV Est, av. Paul-Roussel, 83990 Saint-Tropez, tel. 04.94.97.01.60, fax 04.94.97.70.24, e-mail lacavedesttropez@aol.com ☑
Ⴤ by appt.

CH. DE PALAYSON

Grande Cuvée 2001

| | n.c. | n.c. | ◫ | 15–23 € |

☙ SA Dom. de Palayson, Ch. de Palayson, 85320 Roquebrune-sur-Argens, tel. 04.98.11.80.40, fax 04.98.11.80.40, e-mail chateaupalayson@aol.com ☑
Ⴤ by appt.
☙ M. et Mme von Eggers Rudd

DOM. DE LA PARTIDE 2002

| | 4.7 ha | 28,000 | ▤ ⚶ | 3–5 € |

☙ Les Celliers de Saint-Louis, Les Consacs, 83170 Brignoles, tel. 04.94.37.21.00, fax 04.94.59.14.84,

e-mail cellier-saintlouis@wanadoo.fr ☑
☒ by appt.

DOM. DES PEIRECEDES

Cuvée Règue des Botes 2000

■	3 ha	10,000	〗	8–11 €

☞ Alain Baccino, Dom. des Peirecèdes,
83390 Pierrefeu-du-Var, tel. 04.94.48.67.15,
fax 04.94.48.52.30, e-mail alainbaccino@free.fr ☑ ♞
☒ by appt.

CH. DE PEYRASSOL

Cuvée Marie-Estelle 2000

■	1.3 ha	5,700	〗	11–15 €

☞ Françoise Rigord, Commanderie de Peyrassol, RN 7,
83340 Flassans-sur-Issole, tel. 04.94.69.71.02,
fax 04.94.59.69.23, e-mail contact@
commanderie-peyrassol.com ☑
☒ ev. day 8am–12 noon 2pm–6pm;
Sat. Sun. by appt.

LES MAITRES VIGNERONS DE LA PRESQU'ILE DE SAINT-TROPEZ

Carte noire 2002

■	40 ha	150,000	〗 ♦	5–8 €

☞ Les Maîtres vignerons de la Presqu'ile de Saint-Tropez,
83580 Gassin, tel. 04.94.56.32.04, fax 04.94.43.42.57 ☑
☒ ev. day except Sun. 9am–12 noon 3pm–7pm

DOM. RICHEAUME

Cuvée Tradition 2001

■	10 ha	20,000	〗	11–15 €

☞ Sylvain Hoesch, Dom. Richeaume, 13114 Puyloubier,
tel. 04.42.66.31.27, fax 04.42.66.30.59 ☑
☒ by appt.

ROSELINE

Prestige 2002

■	25 ha	120,000	〗	5–8 €

☞ SARL Roseline Diffusion, Ch. Sainte Roseline,
83460 Les Arcs-sur-Argens, tel. 04.94.99.50.30,
fax 04.94.47.53.06, e-mail contact@sainte-roseline.com ☑
☒ by appt.

CH. ROUBINE

Cuvée Philippe Riboud 2001

■	Cru clas.	n.c.	n.c.	〗	8–11 €

☞ Ch. Roubine, RD 562, 83510 Lorgues,
tel. 04.94.85.94.94, fax 04.94.85.94.95, e-mail riboud@
chateau-roubine.com ☑
☒ ev. day except Sun. 9am–6pm
☞ Riboud

DOM. DE LA ROUILLERE

Grande Réserve 2001

■	0.5 ha	3,000	〗	8–11 €

☞ Dom. de la Rouillère, rte de Ramatuelle, 83580 Gassin,
tel. 04.94.55.72.60, fax 04.94.55.72.61, e-mail contact@
domainedelarouillère.com ☑
☒ by appt.
☞ M. Letartre

DOM. SAINT-ALBERT 2002

■	3 ha	12,000	〗 ♦	5–8 €

☞ Olivier Foucou, Dom. Saint-Albert, 3ᵉ Borrels,
83400 Hyères, tel. 04.94.65.68.64, fax 04.94.65.30.66

CH. SAINT-PIERRE

Cuvée Marie 2002

■	2 ha	10,000	〗 ♦	5–8 €

☞ Jean-Philippe Victor, Ch. Saint-Pierre, Les
Quatre-Chemins, 83460 Les Arcs-sur-Argens,
tel. 04.94.47.41.47, fax 04.94.73.34.73 ☑
☒ by appt.

CUVEE CH. TESTAVIN 2001

■	2 ha	5,000	〗 〗 ♦	11–15 €

☞ Dom. du Thouar, 2349, rte d'Aix, 83490 Le Muy,
tel. 04.94.45.10.35, fax 04.94.45.15.44,
e-mail info@domaine-du-thouar.com ☑
☒ ev. day 9am–12 noon 2pm–7pm; (5pm winter);
cl. Sat. Sun. in winter
☞ GFA Testavin

CH. TOUR SAINT HONORE

Cuvée Olivier 2002

■	4 ha	15,000	〗 ♦	5–8 €

☞ Serge Portal, Ch. La Tour Saint-Honoré, RD 559,
83250 La Londe-les-Maures, tel. 04.94.66.98.22,
fax 04.94.66.52.12 ☑
☒ ev. day except Sun. 9am–12 noon 3pm–6.30pm

VAL D'IRIS 2002

■	1.35 ha	2,800	〗 ♦	5–8 €

☞ Anne Dor, Val d'Iris, chem. de la Combe, 83440 Seillans,
tel. 04.94.76.97.66, fax 04.94.76.89.83,
e-mail valdiris@wanadoo.fr ☑
☒ by appt.

Cassis

Accessible only over relatively high passes from Marseilles or Toulon, and tucked away at the foot of the highest cliffs in France, lies Cassis with its inlets, its anchovies and a particular fountain which, the inhabitants claim, makes their town more remarkable than Paris...However, there is also a vineyard over which powerful abbeys disputed ownership in the 11th century, finally calling upon the Pope to arbitrate. Nowadays, the vineyard covers about 184 ha, of which 134 ha are planted with white varieties with an output of 6,646 hl in 2001. The wines are red and rosé but white above all. Mistral said of the whites that he smelled rosemary, heather and myrtle. Don't expect to find important vintages: as soon as they are made they are mostly consumed locally with bouillabaisse, grilled fish and shellfish.

DOM. DU BAGNOL

Marquis de Fesques 2002★★

■	4.42 ha	25,000	〗 ♦	5–8 €

The estate was bought in 1997 by Jean-Louis Genovesi, weary of the bustle of Paris. So the man from Cassis returned to his origins. Last year his cassis white 2001 won a *coup de coeur*, and his 2002 vintage was much praised for its great presence. It opens with an aromatic sequence of acacia, carnation and aniseed, then reveals a full and round palate, supported by a pleasant freshness all the way to the finish. This cassis will delight your guests over a dish of grilled Mediterranean fish or a fresh goat's cheese.
☞ Genovesi, SCEA Dom. du Bagnol, 12, av. de Provence,
13260 Cassis, tel. 04.42.01.78.05, fax 04.42.01.11.22 ☑
☒ by appt.

CLOS VAL BRUYERE 2001★★

| | n.c. | n.c. | 🖓 ♦ | 8–11 € |

The 6 ha of hillside vines facing the sea produce only white wine. The Clos Val Bruyère was made and distributed at the Château Barbanau, at Roquefort-la-Bédoule, where Sophie and Didier Cerciello also make Côtes de Provence in all three colours. This 2001 wine has a fine appearance with its pale-yellow colour. Its range of fine aromas shows a predominance of white flowers and a soft note of brioche. The palate opens in a lively way, then soon becomes more complex with good body and beautiful length, finishing harmoniously. Drink it now with grilled fish or, after a short period in the cellar, with a white meat in sauce.
☛ Ch. Barbanau, Hameau de Roquefort, 13830 Roquefort-la-Bédoule, tel. 04.42.73.14.60, fax 04.42.73.17.85, e-mail barbanau@aol.com ☑
☕ ev. day except Sun. 10am–12 noon 3pm–6pm
☛ Cerciello

DOM. LA FERME BLANCHE
Excellence 2001★

| | 2 ha | 9,000 | 🍶 | 8–11 € |

The vineyard acquired by comte François Garnier in 1714 has stayed in the same family to this day, and their coat of arms appears on the wine labels. This wine was kept for ten months in oak, which gives it rather smoky vanilla-flavoured aromas. After a good attack, it gains in fullness and body, helped by a pleasant touch of freshness. Serve this wine with fish in sauce. It should open out even more in the next two years.
☛ Dom. de la Ferme Blanche, RD 559, 13260 Cassis, tel. 04.42.01.00.74, fax 04.42.01.73.94 ☑
☕ ev. day 9am–7pm
☛ cl. Paret

CH. DE FONTBLANCHE 2002★

| | 12 ha | 50,000 | 🖓 ♦ | 8–11 € |

After the phylloxera crisis, Emile Bodin was one of the first to replant his vineyard in Cassis. It was this winemaker and his friend who were consulted by Frédéric Mistral about the wines of the region: "The bee has no sweeter honey..." This 2002 vintage, made from pure unpressed wine run from the vat, would have pleased the poet: beneath its pale-yellow colour it reveals sweet and warm perfumes of quince, honey and white flowers. Its full palate is helped by a gentle liveliness, leaving a buttery impression at the finish. The rosé 2002 is pale and well balanced, and is commended.
☛ SCEA Bontoux-Bodin Père et Fils, Ch. de Fontblanche, rte de Carnoux, 13260 Cassis, tel. 04.42.01.00.11, fax 04.42.01.32.11, e-mail chateau.fontblanche@terre-net.fr ☑
☕ ev. day 8.30am–12.30pm 2pm–6pm

CH. DE FONTCREUSE
Cuvée "F" 2002★

| | 5.04 ha | 30,000 | 🖓 ♦ | 5–8 € |

The English writer Virginia Woolf is said to have stayed at this estate, which takes its name from the fountain dug out in 1687 to supply it with water. Perhaps she would have liked this bright salmon-coloured rosé with an interesting range of aromas from white flowers to exotic fruits, via peppery menthol and fresh almond. It leaves an attractive impression

up to the aromatic finish. Drink it with a plate of seafood or plainly grilled Mediterranean crayfish. The Cuvée "F" white 2002 is round and lingering on the palate, and is also awarded one star.
☛ J.-F. Brando, Ch. de Fontcreuse, 13, rte Pierre-Imbert, 13260 Cassis, tel. 04.42.01.71.09, fax 04.42.01.32.64, e-mail fontcreuse@wanadoo.fr ☑
☕ ev. day except Sat. Sun. 8.30am–12 noon 2pm–6pm

Wines selected but not starred

CLOS SAINTE-MAGDELEINE 2001

| | n.c. | n.c. | 🖓 ♦ | 8–11 € |

☛ Sack-Zafiropulo, Clos Sainte-Magdeleine, av. du Revestel, 13714 Cassis Cedex, tel. 04.42.01.70.28, fax 04.42.01.15.51 ☑
☕ ev. day except Sat. Sun. 10am–12 noon 3pm–7pm

DOM. COURONNE DE CHARLEMAGNE 2002

| | 4 ha | 20,000 | 🖓 ♦ | 5–8 € |

☛ Bernard Piche, Dom. Couronne de Charlemagne, Les Janots, 13260 Cassis, tel. 04.42.01.15.83, fax 04.42.01.15.83 ☑
☕ ev. day 10am–12 noon 4pm–6pm

DOM. DU PATERNEL
Grande Réserve 2001

| | 2 ha | 5,000 | 🖓 | 8–11 € |

☛ Jean-Pierre Santini, Dom. du Paternel, 11, rte Pierre-Imbert, 13260 Cassis, tel. 04.42.01.76.50, fax 04.42.01.09.54 ☑
☕ ev. day except Sat. Sun. 10am–12 noon 2pm–6pm

Bellet

Only the privileged few know this minute vineyard (44 ha) on the heights above Nice, with a modest production (911 hl in 2002) of wines almost impossible to find anywhere other than in Nice itself. Its original, aromatic whites derive from the high-class Rolle vine variety and the Chardonnay (which is happy this far south when planted facing north and sufficiently high up). The rosés are supple and fresh, the reds sumptuous: two local varieties, the Fuella and the Braquet, give them their highly individual character. They form an entirely appropriate accompaniment to the rich, very distinctive cuisine of Nice, with dishes such as chard pie, baked vegetables, estoficada (a local stew), tripe and pissaladière, and onion tart.

CLOS SAINT-VINCENT
Clos 2001★

| | 3 ha | 4,000 | 🖓 | 15–23 € |

The Clos red 2000 won the *coup de coeur* last year. The 2001 vintage is also full of flavours, mingling blackberry and black-currant with leathery and spicy notes. Its good structure rests on fine and elegant tannins that combine well with the integrated oak. The lingering finish leaves a memory of charring and vanilla. This wine is a good representative of the appellation, and will last you for five to ten years. Another very successful wine is the **Clos Saint-Vincent white 2002 (11–15 €)**, which has a very fine shape and develops warmly; it will soon open out fully.

🐛 Joseph Sergi et Roland Sicardi, Collet des Fourniers, Saint-Roman-de-Bellet, 06200 Nice, tel. 04.92.15.12.69, fax 04.92.15.12.69, e-mail clos.st.vincent@wanadoo.fr ☑
🍷 by appt.

COLLET DE BOVIS 2002★

| | 0.8 ha | 1,300 | ▥ | 11–15 € |

What could be more natural for this university professor, a specialist in Italian theatre and literature, and a wine enthusiast, to put on painting exhibitions and theatrical performances each year in his cellar. His golden-yellow wine has a pleasant character thanks to its floral aromas and warm notes of quince paste, caramel and clove. It remains generous and round, even in the final nuances of liquorice. Although it is ready to drink now, it will certainly keep well.

🐛 Jean Spizzo, Dom. du Fogolar, 370, chem. de Crémat, 06200 Nice, tel. 04.93.37.82.52, fax 04.93.37.82.52 ☑
🍷 ev. day except Sun. 8.30am–12 noon 2pm–7pm

LES COTEAUX DE BELLET 2002★

| | 2,45 ha | 11,000 | ▥ | 11–15 € |

This wine made chiefly from Rolle by a group of producers has aromas of acacia and hawthorn, while lime blossom appears in the glints of its pale colour. This fine, voluptuous wine maintains its floral tone up to the velvety finish.

🐛 SCEA les Coteaux de Bellet, 325, chem. de Saquier, 06200 Nice, tel. 04.93.29.92.99, fax 04.93.18.10.99, e-mail lescoteauxdebellet@wanadoo.fr ☑
🍷 by appt.
🐛 Hélène Calviera

CH. DE CREMAT 2001★

| | 3.1 ha | 11,000 | ▮▥⚥ | 15–23 € |

The Château de Crémat was built at the beginning of the 20th century over ancient castles dating from the Roman period. Its attractive wine has accents of elder and vanilla, and achieves good balance around a coated structure formed by long and integrated tannins. Along with its positive character, it has maintained a youthful freshness. A taster suggested serving it with a velouté of sea urchins.

🐛 Ch. de Crémat, 442, chem. de Crémat, 06200 Nice, tel. 04.92.15.12.15, fax 04.92.15.12.13 ☑
🍷 by appt.
🐛 Cornelis Kamerbeek

MAX GILLI 2001★

| | 0.5 ha | 1,800 | ▮⚥ | 11–15 € |

One of the features of this red wine is that it was not matured in oak. Tasting it makes this clear: its aromas suggest very ripe soft fruits, undergrowth and leather on the nose, evolving towards black soft fruits at the finish of a full and structured palate. This is a fine, rich and lingering wine, which should reach its peak in 2005. Serve it with spicy dishes or game.

🐛 Max Gilli, chem. de Saint-Roman, 06200 Saint-Roman-de-Bellet, tel. 04.93.37.82.71, fax 04.93.37.82.71 ☑ 🏠
🍷 by appt.

DOM. DE TOASC 2002★

| | 0.9 ha | 2,000 | ▮⚥ | 11–15 € |

At the southern edge of the appellation's boundary, this recently created estate has 5 ha of vines; its cellar houses not only wines but also works of art from the Ecole de Nice. There you will find this mouth-filling and rounded pale rosé. Its long aromas of toast, almond and raspberry add to its tasty character at the finish. Serve this elegant wine with farcis niçois. The **red 2001**, matured in barrel, is ready to drink now but if kept for two years it will become more refined. The **Domaine de Toasc white 2002** is simple and enjoyable. Both are commended.

🐛 Dom. de Toasc, 213, chem. de Crémat, 06200 Nice, tel. 04.92.15.14.14, fax 04.92.15.14.00 ☑
🍷 by appt.
🐛 Nicoletti

Wines selected but not starred

DOM. AUGIER 2002

| | 0.4 ha | 1,200 | ▮ | 8–11 € |

🐛 Rose Augier, 680, rte de Bellet, 06200 Nice, tel. 04.93.37.81.47, fax 04.93.37.81.47 ☑
🍷 by appt.

Bandol

A fine wine produced, not in Bandol itself, but on the sun-scorched terraces of the surrounding villages, which cover an area of 1,540 ha and produced 48,356 hl in 2002. Bandol wines are white, rosé or red. The reds are very tannic and full-bodied, qualities contributed by the Mourvèdre variety, which makes up more than half the proportions of grapes used. This powerful wine, with its subtle aromas of pepper, cinnamon, vanilla and black-cherry, is the perfect accompaniment to venison and red meats. It can be kept for a long time.

DOM. BARTHES 2002★

| | 3.3 ha | 16,600 | ▮⚥ | 11–15 € |

Motorists, take care on the picturesque road leading to the Barthès estate in the Val d'Arenc. The newly built cellar is host to a well-made wine, which the Jury admired for its crystal-clear glints and aromas of white fruits. This wine is perfectly balanced, both rounded and slightly acid, with a more vegetal finish. Drink it now with seafood and crustaceans.

🐛 Monique Barthès, chem. du Val-d'Arenc, 83330 Le Beausset, tel. 04.94.98.60.06, fax 04.94.98.65.31 ☑
🍷 by appt.

LA BASTIDE BLANCHE
Cuvée Estagnol 2001★

| | 3 ha | 6,000 | ▥ | 8–11 € |

After a *coup de coeur* last year for the 2000 vintage, the Bastide Blanche offers an intense, warm and full Estagnol with a dark colour. While it still shows signs of youth in its slight final bitterness, the aromas of fruits and jam on an oaky base are very pleasant. This wine has character and a good keeping potential.

🐛 EARL Bronzo, 367, rte des Oratoires, 83330 Le Castellet, tel. 04.94.32.63.20, fax 04.94.32.74.34, e-mail bastide.blanche@libertysurf.fr ☑
🍷 by appt.

CH. DES BAUMELLES 2001★★

| | 2 ha | 8,000 | ▮ | 8–11 € |

Les Baumelles is a 15th century château overlooking a 40-ha vineyard. This 2001 wine is a blend of Mourvèdre and 10%

Bandol

Grenache. It has an impressive structure, suggesting a wine that will keep for a long time. Although the aromas of soft fruits and resin still seem subdued beneath the wine's dark exterior, the palate is mouth-filling and concentrated, with a framework of compact tannins; it leaves a long aftertaste of ripe fruits and liquorice. Keep it carefully in your cellar for at least five years.

↘ EARL Bronzo, 367, rte des Oratoires, 83330 Le Castellet, tel. 04.94.32.63.20, fax 04.94.32.74.34, e-mail bastide.blanche@libertysurf.fr ☑
ℐ by appt.

DOM. CASTELL-REYNOARD 2001★

| | 1 ha | 4,000 | 🍷 | 11–15 € |

The grapes from the clay-limestone terroir at La Cadière are vinified in an old cellar built in 1892, which has been perfectly renovated. After a year and a half of maturation in oak, this Bandol wine releases pleasant aromas of fruits and liquorice. Its well-coated tannins contribute to its balanced and mature character. This wine should not be kept for long, but wants to delight you now.

↘ Castell, Dom. Castell-Reynoard, quartier Thouron, 83740 La Cadière-d'Azur, tel. 04.94.90.10.16, fax 04.94.90.10.16 ☑
ℐ by appt.

CH. DE CASTILLON 2002★

| | 0.45 ha | 2,000 | 🍴 💧 | 5–8 € |

Since the 1970s, René de Saqui de Sannes has run this vine-yard, formerly the property of the lords of Castellet. Equal shares of Clairette and Ugni Blanc have produced this floral wine with scents of iris and jasmine, and a few smoky notes. It is full-bodied and refreshing in the finish, and a good representative of its year, which was particularly tricky. Serve it with a tuna tartare.

↘ René de Saqui de Sannes, Dom. de Castillon, 408, rte des Oratoires, 83330 Le Castellet, tel. 04.94.32.66.74, fax 04.94.32.67.36 ☑
ℐ ev. day except Mon. Sun. 10am–12 noon 2pm–6pm

DUPERE BARRERA

Jade 2000★

| | 1 ha | 1,500 | | 11–15 € |

This new small firm of négociants and winemakers in the Toulon area started producing garage wines in small quanti-ties. This 2000 wine with aromas of soft fruits and roasting shows great maturity in its roundness and well-integrated tannins. This is a wine of character, which conforms perfectly to the requirements of Bandol.

↘ Dupéré Barrera, 122, rue de Dakar, 83100 Toulon, tel. 04.94.23.36.08, fax 04.94.23.36.08, e-mail vinsduperebarrera@hotmail.com ☑
ℐ by appt.

LE GALANTIN 2002★

| | 12 ha | 50,000 | 🍴 💧 | 8–11 € |

Since Le Galantin's first harvest in 1972, things have changed a great deal: the vineyard has progressed and the children of Achille Pascal are gradually making their mark. A rosé made from 50% Mourvèdre wins the estate a new mention in the Guide. Although its colour is extremely pale, the aromas are long-lasting and elegant – citrus fruits and mineral notes – and the high-quality palate is evidence of good maturity.

↘ Famille Achille Pascal, Dom. Le Galantin, 690, chem. du Galantin, 83330 Le Plan-du-Castellet, tel. 04.94.98.75.94, fax 04.94.90.29.55, e-mail domaine-le-galantin@wanadoo.fr ☑ ⌂
ℐ by appt.

DOM. DU GROS'NORE 2000★★

| | 10 ha | 50,000 | | 11–15 € |

The estate was created recently (1996), but Alain Pascal is a seasoned winemaker who follows in the footsteps of his father, Honoré. He is still not able to vinify his own grapes, but that has to be accepted. Following well-made vintages such as the 1998 and 1999 wines, which were mentioned in previous Guides, he now offers a remarkable 2000 with characteristic and elegant aromas, and a dense and integrated substance with notes of roasting. This is an excellent Bandol that should be kept for four to six years.

↘ Alain Pascal, Dom. du Gros'Noré, 675, chem. de l'Argile, 83740 La Cadière-d'Azur, tel. 04.94.90.08.50, fax 04.94.98.20.65 ☑
ℐ ev. day 10am–12 noon 2pm–7pm

LES HAUTS DE SEIGNOL 2002★

| | 1 ha | 3,000 | 🍴 💧 | 8–11 € |

The Val d'Arenc estate owes its name to the terroir that contains a certain amount of sand (arena in Latin). From 1992, its 50 ha of vines have been restructured. Its Bandol white interested the Jury with its complementary aromas of citrus fruits and menthol. Its balance and freshness make it perfect to drink with sea bream in fennel or crustaceans.

↘ SCA Dom. de Val d'Arenc, 997, chem. du Val-d'Arenc, 83330 Le Beausset, tel. 04.94.98.71.89, fax 04.94.98.74.10 ☑
ℐ by appt.

DOM. LAFRAN-VEYROLLES 2001★★

| | 1.5 ha | 6,500 | | 15–23 € |

The Lafran-Veyrolles estate has 10 ha, and is constantly in the Guide. This year it wins another coup de coeur, following those in the 2000 and 2003 editions, for a wine with abundant aromas: soft fruits, clove, cherry, and notes of coffee and cocoa. After a generous attack, the evident but fine tannins support the lingering palate in remarkable fashion. This is an elegant and harmonious Bandol, which will improve further given time.

↘ Mme Jouve-Férec, Dom. Lafran-Veyrolles, 2115, rte de l'Argile, 83740 La Cadière-d'Azur, tel. 04.94.90.13.37, fax 04.94.90.11.18 ☑
ℐ by appt.

DOM. DE LA LAIDIERE 2002★

| | 10 ha | 40,000 | 🍴 💧 | 11–15 € |

La Laidière has produced Bandol wines since 1941, when the appellation was created. It extracts the essence from an original terroir consisting of marls and sands, and makes wines of a very distinctive character. So with this enjoyable rosé which is both powerful and fine. It has a pale colour and releases clean aromas of white peach, pear and other ripe fruits. It shows good balance and could be served in two to three years' time with spicy dishes.

↘ Estienne, Dom. de la Laidière, 426, chem. de Font-Vive; Sainte-Anne-d'Evenos, 83330 Evenos, tel. 04.98.03.65.75, fax 04.94.90.38.05, e-mail info@laidiere.com ☑
ℐ ev. day except Sat. 9am–12 noon 2pm–6pm; Sun. by appt.

DOM. LES LUQUETTES 2002★

| | 4.66 ha | 24,800 | 🍴 💧 | 8–11 € |

Elisabeth Lafourcade has run this family estate of 12 ha since 1996, and has also gone into distributing wine in bottles. For old times' sake, she has kept the vertical Champagne-type press, which dates from 1892. Her pale rosé is made from Cinsault and Mourvèdre, and releases a springlike range of aromas of strawberry, white peach and melon that recur on the pleasant and delicate palate.

↘ Dom. Les Luquettes, 20, chem. des Luquettes, 83740 La Cadière-d'Azur, tel. 04.94.90.02.59, fax 04.94.98.31.95, e-mail les.luquettes@libertysurf.fr ☑
ℐ by appt.
↘ Elisabeth Lafourcade

MOULIN DES COSTES

Charriage 2001★★

| ■ | n.c. | 13,000 | ⑪ | 15–23 € |

The Charriage wine is made from a selection of the property's old Mourvèdre vines. It is very concentrated, and offers such good texture and strength that it feels like chewing fruit. The aromas of soft fruits, vanilla and cocoa linger remarkably on a base of compact but pleasant tannins. This is a powerful, already well-balanced wine.

☞ Bunan, Moulin des Costes, 83740 La Cadière-d'Azur, tel. 04.94.98.58.98, fax 04.94.98.60.05, e-mail bunan@bunan.com ☑
☊ by appt.

CH. DE LA NOBLESSE 2000★

| ■ | 3 ha | 15,000 | ⑪ | 8–11 € |

This wine contains Mourvèdre (95%) and a little bit of Grenache, and is a good representative of the terroir and the year. It releases aromas of coffee, cocoa and spices. It is already mature and supple, despite a slightly austere finish. Serve it with game.

☞ Gaussen, GAEC du Ch. de la Noblesse, 1685, chem. de l'Argile, 83740 La Cadière-d'Azur, tel. 04.94.98.72.07, fax 04.94.98.40.41 ☑
☊ ev. day except Sun. 10am–12 noon 2pm–5.30pm

DOM. DE L'OLIVETTE 2002★

| ■ | 21 ha | 92,000 | ■ ⬦ | 8–11 € |

The pretty country house dating from the 18th century stands among the vines and olive trees and offers a perfect image of a Provençal farmhouse. Here they produce this distinguished and well-made rosé with strong aromas, which leaves a lively aftertaste of ripe fruits. "A true delight," wrote one of the tasters.

☞ SCEA Dumoutier, Dom. de L'Olivette, 83330 Le Castellet, tel. 04.94.98.58.85, fax 04.94.32.68.43, e-mail info@domaine-olivette.com

DOM. DU PEY-NEUF 2002★

| ■ | 2 ha | 5,000 | ■ ⬦ | 8–11 € |

Here the 19th century country house stands proudly among its hundred-year-old olive trees, its alleys of cypress trees and its 36 ha of vines, and overlooks the sea from the small valley ("pey" in Provençal) where it was built. Its Bandol white releases abundant aromas of citrus fruits, almond and menthol that continue on the fresh and well-balanced palate. Drink it as an aperitif with salmon on pieces of toast or during a meal with grilled fish.

☞ Guy Arnaud, 367, rte de Sainte-Anne, 83740 La Cadière-d'Azur, tel. 04.94.90.14.55, fax 04.94.26.13.89, e-mail guyarnaudvigneron5@wanadoo.fr ☑ 🏠 🏠
☊ by appt.

CH. DE PIBARNON 2002★★

| ■ | 12 ha | 50,000 | ■ ⬦ | 11–15 € |

Twenty-five years ago, Pibarnon was created with some 3,5 ha of judiciously cultivated vines. By dint of enthusiastic work, its area has increased to 47 ha and its wines are regularly of high quality. This rosé draws its strength and character from the Mourvèdre, and its flesh and sensuality from the Cinsault. It will be seen at its best with white meats in sauce and as an accompaniment to desserts – strawberries or melon – which will go well with its aromas of vanilla and slightly spicy fruits with white flesh.

☞ Henri et Eric de Saint-Victor, Ch. de Pibarnon, 410, chem. de la Croix-des-Signaux, 83740 La Cadière-d'Azur, tel. 04.94.90.12.73, fax 04.94.90.12.98, e-mail pibarnon@wanadoo.fr ☑
☊ by appt.

LA ROQUE

Les Baumes 2002★

| ■ | 9.24 ha | 29,000 | ■ ⬦ | 5–8 € |

The La Roque cooperative is a major power in the appellation. It was created in 1950, and this year has produced a white wine made chiefly from Clairette. The Jury liked the delicate aromas (acacia, honeysuckle and fresh fruits) and

the harmony of the palate. This is a pleasant and characteristic Bandol.

☞ Coop. de La Roque, quartier Vallon, BP 26, 83740 La Cadière-d'Azur, tel. 04.94.90.10.39, fax 04.94.90.08.11, e-mail cave@laroque-bandol.fr ☑
☊ by appt.

CH. LA ROUVIERE 2001★

| ■ | 6.33 ha | 25,000 | ⑪ | 15–23 € |

The 19th century château was built by an industrialist from Lille and overlooks the vineyard from the top of the hill. It has lent its name to this tasty Bandol, noted for its finesse and the elegance of its perfumes of vanilla and spices. The silky tannins make it pleasant to drink now, but it could be kept for a while. The Mas de La Rouvière rosé 2002 (11–15 €) also wins one star: it releases generous aromas of flowers, orange peel and toast, while growing in roundness and freshness up to a spicy finish.

☞ Bunan, Moulin des Costes, 83740 La Cadière-d'Azur, tel. 04.94.98.58.98, fax 04.94.98.60.05, e-mail bunan@bunan.com ☑
☊ by appt.

CH. SAINTE ANNE

Cuvée Collection 2001★

| ■ | 3 ha | 4,000 | ⑪ | 15–23 € |

Do not be misled by the rather austere look of this château, which has very attractive chambres d'hôte. Its Collection wine is a selection of almost pure Mourvèdre (2% Grenache); it is full and rich and reveals aromas of soft fruits and liquorice, and tannins that are still young but elegant. Let it mature for four to five years.

☞ Dutheil de la Rochère, Ch. Sainte-Anne, 83330 Evenos, tel. 04.94.90.35.40, fax 04.94.90.34.20 ☑ 🏠
☊ ev. day except Sun. 9am–12 noon 2pm–7pm

CH. SALETTES 2002★★

| ■ | 1 ha | 4,500 | ■ ⬦ | 11–15 € |

Although he is kept very busy by his term in office as president of the wine-growers of Bandol, Jean-Pierre Boyer, with efficient help at hand, keeps a watchful eye on the quality of his wines. Here he offers a white wine, made from 60% Clairette, with a likeable freshness and power. You will enjoy its balance, maturity and good length while serving it with a grilled sea bass or fresh cheeses, for example. The Jury also awarded one star to the red 2001 (15–23 €).

☞ EARL Boyer et Fils, Ch. Salettes, 83740 La Cadière-d'Azur, tel. 04.94.90.06.06, fax 04.94.90.04.29, e-mail salettes@salettes.com ☑
☊ by appt.
☞ GFA Ch. Salettes

DOM. SORIN 2000★

| ■ | 2 ha | 10,000 | ⑪ | 15–23 € |

After fermentation in a rotary barrel and maturation for 18 months in barrel, this Bandol wine reveals a broad aromatic range of soft fruits, spices, liquorice and toast. Its tannins are still evident, underlined by oaky notes, but they should soften if kept for four to five years.

☞ Dom. Sorin, 1617, rte de La Cadière-d'Azur, 83270 Saint-Cyr-sur-Mer, tel. 04.94.26.62.28, fax 04.94.26.40.06, e-mail luc.sorin@wanadoo.fr ☑ 🏠
☊ by appt.

DOM. DE SOUVIOU 2002★

| ■ | n.c. | 6,600 | ■ | 8–11 € |

This 22-ha estate can trace its history back to the 16th century, and still has the old juniper-oil oven and beehives. Its Bandol wine will go well with dishes cooked in olive oil. The wine is complex, warm and well balanced, and shows finesse in its original aromas of crystallized lemon, broom and vanilla. It also has good length.

☞ Dom. de Souviou, RN 8, 83330 Le Beausset, tel. 04.94.90.57.63, fax 04.94.96.62.74, e-mail contact@souviou.com ☑
☊ ev. day except Sun. 10am–12 noon 2pm–6pm; ev. day from Easter to Sept.

PROVENCE

DOM. LA SUFFRENE

Cuvée Les Lauves 2001★★★

■	1.5 ha	8,000	◫	11–15 €

The 45 ha of this estate are planted on very varied terroirs, including one clay-limestone plot growing Mourvèdre and Carignan, the basis of this ideal Bandol wine. Complex aromas of soft fruits and spices with slight balsamic notes, which combine harmoniously, pave the way for the mouth-filling and well-balanced palate with its strong and lingering substance, supported by elegant tannins. A great wine for keeping.
�b� GAEC Gravier-Piche, 1066, chem. de Cuges, 83740 La Cadière-d'Azur, tel. 04.94.90.09.23, fax 04.94.90.02.21, e-mail suffrene@wanadoo.fr ✓
⌶ ev. day except Sun. 9am–12 noon 2pm–6pm; Sat. 9am–12 noon

DOM. DE LA VIVONNE 2001★

■	8 ha	23,000	◫	11–15 €

The hills of old Castellet are marvellous for growing Mourvèdre, the grape variety that makes up 100% of this wine. It is still young, with perfumes of blackcurrant, redcurrant and menthol. This is a structured, powerful but tasty wine with a likeable balance. Keeping can only help it to improve.
�b� Walter Gilpin, Dom. de La Vivonne, 3345, montée du Château, 83330 Le Castellet, tel. 04.94.98.70.09, fax 04.94.90.59.98, e-mail infos@vivonne.com ✓
⌶ by appt.

CH. JEAN-PIERRE GAUSSEN 2001

■	4 ha	17,000	◫	15–23 €

�b� Jean-Pierre Gaussen, 1585, chem. de l'Argile, quartier Noblesse, 83740 La Cadière-d'Azur, tel. 04.94.98.75.54, fax 04.94.98.65.34 ✓
⌶ by appt.

JEAN-LUC POINSOT

Cuvée Mourvégué 2001

■	n.c.	3,300	◫	11–15 €

�b� La Badiane, S. Croisette II, RN 154, 83250 La Londe-les-Maures, tel. 04.78.57.56.21, fax 04.37.22.05.59, e-mail contact@labadiane.com ✓
⌶ by appt.

DOM. DE LA RIBOTTE 2002

■	1.8 ha	7,800	■ ⚬	8–11 €

�b� Maurice et Laurence Desblaches, 1072, chem. du Val-d'Arenc, 83330 Le Plan-du-Castellet, tel. 04.94.90.41.40, fax 04.94.90.27.26 ✓
⌶ ev. day except Sun. 3pm–7.30pm; 16 Sept.–30 Jun. by appt.

DOM. DE LA TOUR DU BON 2002

■	8.5 ha	24,000	■ ⚬	8–11 €

�b� SCEA Saint-Vincent, Dom. de La Tour du Bon, 83330 Le Brulat-du-Castellet, tel. 04.98.03.66.22, fax 04.98.03.66.26, e-mail tourdubon@aol.com ✓ ✿
⌶ by appt.
�bꞑ Hocquard

CH. VANNIERES 2001

■	12 ha	30,000	◫	15–23 €

�b� Ch. Vannières, 83740 La Cadière-d'Azur, tel. 04.94.90.08.08, fax 04.94.90.15.98, e-mail info@chateauvannieres.com ✓
⌶ ev. day except Sun. 8am–12 noon 2pm–6pm
�bꞑ Boisseaux

Wines selected but not starred

DOM. DES BAGUIERS 2002

▨	0.38 ha	2,000	■ ⚬	8–11 €

�bꞑ GAEC Jourdan, Dom. des Baguiers, 227, rue des Micocouliers, 83330 Le Castellet, tel. 04.94.90.41.87, fax 04.94.90.41.87 ✓
⌶ by appt.

DOM. DU CAGUELOUP 2001

▨	8.1 ha	40,000	◫	15–23 €

�bꞑ Dom. du Cagueloup, 267, chem. de la Verdelaise, 83270 Saint-Cyr-sur-Mer, tel. 04.94.26.15.70, fax 04.94.26.54.09 ✓
⌶ ev. day except Sun. 8am–12.30pm 3pm–7pm
�bꞑ R. Prebost

DOM. DE FREGATE 2002

▨	1.5 ha	6,500	■ ⚬	8–11 €

�bꞑ Dom. de Frégate, rte de Bandol, 83270 Saint-Cyr-sur-Mer, tel. 04.94.32.57.57, fax 04.94.32.24.22, e-mail domainedefregate@wanadoo.fr ✓
⌶ ev. day 9am–12 noon 2pm–6pm

A tiny vineyard just outside Aix, this includes the old enclosed vineyard that originally belonged to the king, René, Comte de Provence.

W hites, rosés and reds are regularly produced from around 42 ha, amounting to 1,305 hl of wine in 2002. The reds can be kept for a long time, during which they develop scents of violet and pine.

CH. CREMADE 2001★★

▨	1.9 ha	10,000	■ ◫ ⚬	15–23 €

This 18th century Provençal farm was visited by Emile Zola and Cézanne, who painted many pictures there. It was bought in 1998, when its cellar was modernized and equipped with a barrel store. Its tasty wine, with well-controlled oak, releases notes of white fruits. On the palate it is opulent and suave, with an attractive texture and a long, vanilla-flavoured finish. The **rosé 2002 (11–15 €)** is a full-bodied wine with original aromas mingling grapey and oaky notes. It is awarded one star.
�bꞑ Ch. Crémade, rte de Langesse, 13100 Le Tholonet, tel. 04.42.66.76.80, fax 04.42.66.76.81 ✓
⌶ by appt.
�bꞑ Baud

Wines selected but not starred

DOM. DU GRAND COTE 2000

| | 10.45 ha | 64,000 | 𝍫 | 5–8 € |

❧ Cave de Rousset, quartier Saint-Joseph, 13790 Rousset,
tel. 04.42.29.00.09, fax 04.42.29.08.63,
e-mail cave-de-rousset@wanadoo.fr ☒
☙ by appt.

Coteaux d'Aix en Provence

The AOC Coteaux d'Aix en Provence belongs to the western part of the limestone area of Provence, situated between the Durance in the north and the Mediterranean in the south, the Rhodian plains to the west and a region of crystalline rocks from the Triassic period to the east. The relief is formed from a succession of secondary mountain chains running parallel to the sea coast and covered variously with scrub, aromatic moorland vegetation and pine woods: the Nerthe is near the Étang de Berre, and the chain of Costes in the north extends into the Alpilles.

Between these outcrops lie sedimentary basins of different sizes (the Bassin de l'Arc, the Bassin de la Touloubre, and that of the lower Durance) where vine-growing is located. Here limestone and marly structures underlie a matrix of stony, alluvial clays, alternating with structures of molasses and sandstone underlying sandy soils or stony sand and alluvium. The total area of 4,012 ha produced 182,184 hl in 2002, of which 7,911 were white. The production of rosé wines has increased recently. Grenache and Cinsaut are still the mainstays, with Grenache predominant; Syrah and Cabernet Sauvignon are on the increase and are progressively replacing the Carignan.

The rosé wines are light, fruity and pleasant, and have benefited significantly from improved vinification techniques. They should be drunk young with local Provençal dishes: ratatouille, artichokes barigoules (braised with fat bacon), fish grilled with fennel, aïoli...

The reds are balanced, sometimes robust, giving of their best according to terroir and micro-climate. When young, these are fruity, supple wines, excellent with grilled meat and dishes topped with grilled cheese. They reach their peak after two or three years of keeping, when they should be served with meat dishes (particularly those with sauce) and game. These interesting reds are well worth looking out for.

The production of white wines is limited. They seem to do better in the northern part of the vineyard, where they combine the roundness of Grenache Blanc with the finesse of Clairette, Rolle and Bourboulenc.

CH. BARBEBELLE
Grande Réserve 2001★

| | 3 ha | 15,000 | 𝍫 | 11–15 € |

This Aix-style farmhouse, standing at the gates of the city, has belonged to the same family for three generations. Its powerful wine has a smoky nose with a nuance of clove, and reveals good harmony as a whole and notable length. It just needs two years to reach its peak and be served with a delicious dish of truffles. The **Cuvée Madeleine white 2002 (5–8 €)** is commended for its pleasant flavours of citrus fruits (lemon and mandarin).
❧ Brice Herbeau, Ch. Barbebelle, 13840 Rognes,
tel. 04.42.50.22.12, fax 04.42.50.10.20,
e-mail barberelle@aol.com ☒ ⌂
☙ ev. day 9am–12 noon 2pm–6pm

CH. BAS
Cuvée du Temple 2001★

| | 2 ha | 13,000 | 𝍫 | 11–15 € |

The Château Bas was bought in 1981 by a German industrialist and today extends over 80 ha. The vines are planted on a Gallo-Roman site which has remarkable remains: the temple of Vernègues (before 150 BC). This dark-coloured wine makes a good offering. It is balanced, with a well-coated palate revealing a long range of flavours from soft fruits macerated in chocolate to spices. The **Pierres du Sud white 2002** is very full-bodied and the **Pierres du Sud rosé 2002 (5–8 €)** is rich in substance. They too win one star.
❧ EARL Georges de Blanquet, Ch. Bas, 13116 Vernègues,
tel. 04.90.59.13.16, fax 04.90.59.44.35,
e-mail chateaubas@wanadoo.fr ☒
☙ ev. day 9.30am–12.30pm 1.30pm–6.30pm;
Sun. 10am–12.30pm 2.30pm–6.30pm

DOM. DES BEATES 2001★

| | 9 ha | 50,000 | ▮ 𝍫 | 8–11 € |

The estate takes its name from the word *béates*, meaning the morning prayers that the young women made in the old convent. In 1995, the Terrat and Chapoutier families acquired the property, but since 2002 the Terrats have been the sole owners. The 26 ha are farmed organically. This concentrated 2001 releases soft fruits in jam and spices, and shows good balance between the tannins and the alcohol. If kept for one or two years, it will reach its best and be ready for serving with a meal. The **Terra d'Or red 2000 (38–46 €)**, made from a selection from various plots, is commended; it has a very international character.
❧ Dom. des Béates, rte de Caireval, BP 52, 13410 Lambesc,
tel. 04.42.57.07.58, fax 04.42.57.19.70,
e-mail contact@domaine-des-beates.com ☒
☙ ev. day except Sun. 9am–1pm 2pm–7pm
❧ Terrat

CH. BEAUFERAN 2002★

| | n.c. | 6,000 | ▮ | 5–8 € |

The owners of this château have spared no effort to make this 2002 wine. They harvested during the night to shelter the grapes from the heat, de-stemmed all the fruit, and macerated them on the skins for 14 hours at 10°C, before giving them a static clarification and fermenting them at a controlled temperature of 19°C. The result is a very full-bodied wine with restrained floral and mineral aromas.
❧ Ch. Beauferan, 870, chem. de la Degaye, 13880 Velaux,
tel. 04.42.74.73.94, fax 04.42.87.42.96,
e-mail chateau.beauferan@freesurf.fr ☒
☙ ev. day except Sun. 9am–12 noon 2pm–6pm;
Sat. 9am–12.30pm
❧ Sauvage-Veysset

CH. DE CALAVON
Cuvée Tradition 2000★

| | 12 ha | 10,000 | ▮ | 3–5 € |

Michel Audibert cultivates the 47 ha of this estate, on one time the property of the princes of Orange. His wine has a surprising composition – equal shares of Grenache and Carignan – but the taster should not be disappointed because the wine is so full, long and well structured. The aromatic

PROVENCE

range of this pleasant Coteaux d'Aix consists of coffee, vanilla, liquorice, leather and pepper.
🍷 EARL Michel Audibert, Ch. de Calavon, BP 4, 13410 Lambesc, tel. 04.42.57.15.37, fax 04.42.57.15.37, e-mail michel@audibert.fsnet.co.uk
🍷 ev. day except Sun. 9am–12 noon 3pm–6pm

CH. CALISSANNE
Clos Victoire 2002★★

| ◼ | n.c. | n.c. | ◼ | 8–11 € |

In 2001, the CIPM International group acquired the Château Calissanne; a property of 1,000 ha, well protected from the Mistral, and divided between vines (100 ha) and olive trees (50 ha), which for many years has obtained very good results. This powerful rosé has all the qualities of a great wine: it is complex, perfumed with soft fruits such as redcurrant and raspberry, jasmine and violet; it opens generously and leaves an impression of fullness. This is a Coteaux d'Aix en Provence to drink on great occasions, with grilled lamb for example.
🍷 Ch. Calissanne, RD 10, 13680 Lançon-de-Provence, tel. 04.90.42.63.03, fax 04.90.42.40.00, e-mail calissan@club-internet.fr
🍷 by appt.
🍷 CIPM International

CH. CALISSANNE
Cuvée Prestige 2001★★

| ◼ | n.c. | n.c. | ◾ | 5–8 € |

Jean Bonnet has done extremely well, all the wines he offered to the *Guide* attracting the attention of the Jury. He is keen to make the most of this remarkable site facing the hills of l'Estaque and which has remains, in a Roman *oppidum*, of the time when it was a Celto-Ligurian stronghold. This Cuvée Prestige is mouth-filling and concentrated, demonstrating its balance while releasing aromas of undergrowth, spices and very ripe fruits. The **Cuvée Prestige rosé 2002** is powerful and complex, and is awarded one star, like the **Cuvée du Château white 2002**, two harmonious wines which are a testimony to the estate's serious, creative work.
🍷 Ch. Calissanne, RD 10, 13680 Lançon-de-Provence, tel. 04.90.42.63.03, fax 04.90.42.40.00, e-mail calissan@club-internet.fr
🍷 by appt.

DOM. DE CAMAISSETTE
Cuvée Amadeus 2000★★

| ◼ | 3 ha | 15,000 | ◾ | 5–8 € |

Michelle Nasles, whose father was the architect of the Coteaux d'Aix's promotion to an AOC, finds her just reward for efforts put in over more than a quarter of a century. Her 23-ha vineyard has a house typical of rural Provençal architecture in the 17th century. Here she has selected Syrah, Cabernet Sauvignon and Grenache to make a little jewel of a Coteaux d'Aix. It has a garnet-red colour and releases aromas of ripe fruits and spices, joined on the palate by notes of chocolate. Its intense substance, supported by still-evident tannins, finishes with a lingering sensation of roasting, garrigue and pepper. This is a wine to look out for. Its keeping potential makes it suitable for laying down for five to seven years before serving with spicy meats or game. The **rosé 2002 (3–5 €)** has a good balance between body and freshness, and is awarded one star.

🍷 Michelle Nasles, Dom. de la Camaïssette, 13510 Eguilles, tel. 04.42.92.57.55, fax 04.42.28.21.26, e-mail michelle.nasles@wanadoo.fr
🍷 ev. day except Sun. 9.30am–12noon 2.30pm–6.30pm

CH. LA COSTE
Cuvée Lisa 2000★

| ◼ | 15 ha | 80,000 | ◾ ◾ | 5–8 € |

A Provençal daube would go very well with this attractively aromatic wine, whose range includes notes of wild blackberry, spices, pepper and laurel. The tannins are beginning to soften, suggesting it will improve over the next two to three years. The **Cuvée Lisa rosé 2002** is a fine example of the rosé wines of Provence, and is commended.
🍷 GFA du Ch. la Coste, 13610 Le Puy-Sainte-Réparade, tel. 04.42.61.89.98, fax 04.42.61.89.41
🍷 by appt.
🍷 Bordonado

DOM. D'EOLE
Cuvée Léa 2001★

| ◼ | 7.2 ha | 22,000 | ◾ ◾ | 15–23 € |

This estate is committed to organic farming, and offers a garnet-red wine with purplish highlights, made from Syrah, Grenache and 8% of Mourvèdre. It is rich, intense and elegant with aromas of ripe, almost crystallized soft fruits and flowers (violet). Its harmonious and complete nature is charming. On another level, the **Cuvée Principale red 2001 (8–11 €)** from this estate is a wine for instant enjoyment; it is commended.
🍷 EARL Dom. d'Eole, rte de Mouries, D 24, 13810 Eygalières, tel. 04.90.95.93.70, fax 04.90.95.99.85, e-mail domaine@domainedeole.com
🍷 by appt.
🍷 C. Raimont

PETALES DE GLAUGES 2002★

| ◼ | 6 ha | 20,000 | ◾ | 3–5 € |

A *glauge* is small wild yellow iris belonging to the flora of the Alpilles of Upper Provence. It gives its name to this 42-ha estate which was renovated two years ago. A label in braille encloses this supple and soft wine, with notes of raspberry, that you can serve with a grilled sea bass in fennel and olive oil from the Baux.
🍷 SAS Glauges des Alpilles, voie d'Aureille, 13430 Eyguières, tel. 04.90.59.81.45, fax 04.90.57.83.19, e-mail info@glauges.com
🍷 ev. day 9.30am–12.30pm 2.30pm–5.30pm; Sun. 9.30am–12.30pm
🍷 Georges Berrebi

CH. GRAND SEUIL 2001★

| ◼ | 3 ha | 12,000 | ◾ | 11–15 € |

The Château du Seuil was owned by the Michaëlis when Provence was joined to France. In 1970, the Carreau-Gaschereau family moved in and made its first wine four years later. This year, four of its wines attracted the attention of the Jury. This powerful, full-bodied Grand Seuil is still rather oaky but should become more refined in the course of time, when it will go well with a fricassee of poultry in a cream sauce. The **Château du Seuil white 2001 (5–8 €)** was not matured in oak and also wins one star, while the **Château**

Grand red Seuil 2001, which was matured in oak for 12 months, is commended.

☛ Carreau-Gaschereau, Ch. du Seuil, 13540 Puyricard, tel. 04.42.92.15.99, fax 04.42.28.05.00, e-mail contact@chateauduseuil.fr ☑

☙ ev. day 9am–12 noon 2pm–7pm (6pm Nov.-Mar.)

CH. PIGOUDET

La Chapelle 2002★★

	1.3 ha	6,500	🍷 🍶	8–11 €

This wine was "a watercolour," wrote one taster, unaware that the label on the bottle was by a watercolour painter. This rosé is so delicate, it will go well with a skate or coquilles Saint-Jacques. It has a rose-petal colour, an elegant aromatic range of flowers and fruits (fruity fruits) and achieves a good balance. The **Cuvée La Chapelle white 2002** is awarded one star for its aromas and freshness.

☛ SCA Ch. Pigoudet, rte de Jouques, 83560 Rians, tel. 04.94.80.31.78, fax 04.94.80.54.25, e-mail chateau-pigoudet@wanadoo.fr ☑

☙ by appt.
☛ Schmidt-Rabe

CELLIER DES QUATRE TOURS

Cuvée Prestige 2001★

	4 ha	20,000	🍷 🍶	5–8 €

This dynamic producer, firmly anchored in Provençal culture, had its first "Panisse" pneumatic wine press baptised by the widow of Marcel Pagnol. Venelles is the native town of Fernand Charpin, known to film-lovers for his role as maître Panisse in Pagnol's trilogy. The Cuvée Prestige offers a subtle oak which is both toasty and spicy; its lightness means it can be drunk now. Also ready for drinking is the **Cuvée Esprit Sud red 2000 (3–5 €)** which is commended for its tasty fruitiness.

☛ Cellier des Quatre Tours, RN 96, 13770 Venelles, tel. 04.42.54.71.11, fax 04.42.54.11.22

DOM. DE LA REALTIERE

Cuvée Jean-Louis 2001★

	3 ha	6,600	🍶	8–11 €

Two years ago, Pierre Michelland took over this vineyard of 8 ha with his aunt, after his father's death. He pays him a nice homage with this wine which follows the tradition of the estate. It has definite keeping potential behind its structured tannins which will soften in years to come. Also look out for the **Cuvée Spéciale rosé 2002 (5–8 €)**, commended by the Jury.

☛ Pierre Michelland, Dom. de La Réaltière, rte de Jouques, 83560 Rians, tel. 04.94.80.32.56, fax 04.94.80.55.70 ☑ ⚘

☙ ev. day 8am–12 noon 1.30pm–7.30pm

LES VIGNERONS DU ROY RENE

Cuvée Royale 2001★

	15 ha	20,000	🍷 🍶	5–8 €

The Lambesc cooperative merged in 1998 with that of Saint-Cannat to become the most important firm in the Coteaux d'Aix. The village also has one of France's three bells worked by automatons. This elegant and balanced Cuvée Royale is very successful, demonstrating the serious work that went the vinification. The Jury enjoyed its lightness. By contrast, the **Cuvée Jules Reynaud 2001 Elevé en Fût de Chêne** is a solid red wine with very evident tannins; it is commended.

☛ Les Vignerons du Roy René, RN 7, 13410 Lambesc, tel. 04.42.57.00.20, fax 04.42.92.91.52, e-mail lesvigneronsduroyrene@wanadoo.fr ☑

☙ by appt.

CH. VIGNELAURE 2000★

	14.5 ha	54,000	🍶	11–15 €

Vignelaure is "the vineyard of the sacred spring", as the Ancients called this terroir now covering about 60 hectares. Although the wines of Vignelaure have won considerable renown, visitors will also appreciate the architecture of the house and the art gallery which shows the work of fairly famous artists such as César, Arman, Miro, Hartung and Cartier-Bresson. This powerful wine is awarded one star: its oak combines well with the full and structured substance. The tasters discovered its wild and intense aromas of blackberry, leather and spices (vanilla). The **rosé La Source de Vignelaure**

2002 (8–11 €) also wins one star: it has reached maturity and its fruity qualities will go well with Mediterranean dishes.

☛ Ch. Vignelaure, rte de Jouques, 83560 Rians, tel. 04.94.37.21.10, fax 04.94.80.53.39, e-mail vignelaure@wanadoo.fr ☑

☙ ev. day 9.30am–1pm 2pm–6pm
☛ David O'Brien

Wines selected but not starred

JEAN BARONNAT 2001

	n.c.	n.c.	🍷 🍶	3–5 €

☛ Maison Baronnat, 491, rte de Lacenas, Les Bruyères, 69400 Gleizé, tel. 04.74.68.59.20, fax 04.74.62.19.21, e-mail info@baronnat.com ☑

☙ by appt.

CH. DE BEAUPRE

Collection du Château 2000

	3 ha	12,000	🍶	11–15 €

☛ Christian Double, EARL Ch. de Beaupré, RN 7, 13760 Saint-Cannat, tel. 04.42.57.33.59, fax 04.42.57.27.90, e-mail chbeaupre1@aol.com ☑

☙ ev. day 8.30am–12 noon 2pm–6.30pm

CH. LA BOUGERELLE

Vieilli en fût 2001

	2 ha	5,000	🍷 🍶	8–11 €

☛ Nicolas Granier, 1360, rte de Berre, 13090 Aix-en-Provence, tel. 04.42.20.18.95, fax 04.42.20.18.95, e-mail ludi.granier@wanadoo.fr ☑

☙ by appt.

DOM. DE COSTEBONNE 2001

	15 ha	30,000	🍷 🍶	5–8 €

☛ SCIEV Benoît, Cave du Mas de Longchamp, quartier de la Gare, 13940 Mollèges, tel. 04.90.95.19.06, fax 04.90.95.42.00 ☑

☙ ev. day except Sun. 9am–12 noon 2pm–6pm

CH. DES GAVELLES 2002

	4 ha	n.c.	🍷 🍶	3–5 €

☛ SCEA Ch. des Gavelles, 165, chem. de Maliverny, 13540 Puyricard, tel. 04.42.92.06.83, fax 04.42.92.24.12 ☑

☙ ev. day 9.30am–12.30pm 3pm–7pm;
Sun. 9.30am–12.30pm
☛ De Roany

DOM. DES LAVANDES 2001

	10 ha	12,000	🍷 🍶	3–5 €

☛ Cellier Saint-Augustin, quartier de la Gare, 13560 Sénas, tel. 04.90.57.20.25, fax 04.90.59.22.96 ☑

☙ ev. day except Sun. 8am–12 noon 2.15pm–6pm

DOM. DU MAS BLEU 2001

	1.9 ha	12,500	🍷 🍶	3–5 €

☛ EARL du Mas Bleu, 6, av. de la Côte-Bleue, Laure, 13180 Gignac-la-Nerthe, tel. 04.42.30.41.40, fax 04.42.30.32.53 ☑

☙ by appt.
☛ Rougon

PROVENCE

LES VIGNERONS DE MISTRAL
Cuvée Prestige 2002

| ■ | 50 ha | 50,000 | ⓘ ♦ | 3–5 € |

☛ Les Vignerons de Mistral, av. de Sylvanes,
13130 Berre-L'Etang, tel. 04.42.85.40.11,
fax 04.42.74.12.55 ☑
☂ ev. day except Sun. 9am–12 noon 2pm–6pm

DOM. NAIS 2001

| ■ | n.c. | 10,000 | ⓘ ♦ | 3–5 € |

☛ Laurent Bastard et Eric Davin, rte du Puy,
13840 Rognes, tel. 04.42.50.16.73, fax 04.42.50.16.73,
e-mail domainenais@club-internet.fr ☑
☂ ev. day except Sun. 9am–12 noon 2.30pm–6.30pm

DOM. DE L'OPPIDUM DES CAUVINS
2002

| ■ | 4 ha | 32,000 | ⓘ ♦ | 5–8 € |

☛ Rémy et Dominique Ravaute, Dom. de l'Oppidum des
Cauvins, 13840 Rognes, tel. 04.42.50.13.85,
fax 04.42.50.29.40 ☑
☂ ev. day 9am–12 noon 2pm–7pm

CH. PETIT SONNAILLER 2002

| ■ | 1 ha | 6,500 | ⓘ ♦ | 5–8 € |

☛ Dominique Brulat, Ch. Petit Sonnailler, 13121 Aurons,
tel. 04.90.59.34.47, fax 04.90.59.32.30 ☑ 🏠
☂ by appt.

CH. REVELETTE 2002

| ■ | 3 ha | 6,000 | ⓘ ♦ | 5–8 € |

☛ Peter Fischer, Ch. Revelette, 13490 Jouques,
tel. 04.42.63.75.43, fax 04.42.67.62.04,
e-mail chatreve@aol.com ☑
☂ by appt.

LES SANTONS 2001

| ■ | n.c. | n.c. | ⓘ ♦ | 3–5 € |

☛ SA Bréban, BP 47, 83171 Brignoles, tel. 04.94.69.37.55,
fax 04.94.69.03.37

DOM. DE LA VALLONGUE 2002

| ■ | 3 ha | 5,000 | ⓘ ♦ | 8–11 € |

☛ Héritiers Paul-Cavallier, Dom. de La Vallongue, BP 4,
13810 Eygalières, tel. 04.90.95.91.70,
fax 04.90.95.97.76,
e-mail vallongue@wanadoo.fr ☑
☂ by appt.

CH. DE VAUCLAIRE
Grande Réserve Elevé en fût de chêne 2002

| ■ | 0.5 ha | 2,000 | ⓘⓘ | 5–8 € |

☛ Uldaric Sallier, Ch. de Vauclaire, 13650 Meyrargues,
tel. 04.42.57.50.14, fax 04.42.63.47.16,
e-mail chateaudevauclaire@fr.st ☑
☂ ev. day 9am–12 noon 2pm–6pm

CH. VIRANT
Tradition 2002

| ■ | 5 ha | 30,000 | ⓘ ♦ | 3–5 € |

☛ Ch. Virant, 13680 Lançon-de-Provence,
tel. 04.90.42.44.47, fax 04.90.42.54.81,
e-mail rcheylan@aol.com ☑
☂ by appt.
☛ Robert Cheylan

Les Baux de Provence

The Alpilles, the most western secondary chain in the anticlinal mountains of Provence, is an eroded massif with a stunning landscape of crested oblique peaks made of limestone scree and Cretaceous marly limestone. This is paradise for the olive tree, and vines equally flourish on the stony deposits characteristic of the region. The terrace deposits are very thin and the fineness or otherwise of the composition is very important as the water retention ability of the soil depends on it. Here, around the fortified village of Baux-de-Provence, in the heart of the AOC Coteaux d'Aix en Provence, a distinctive micro-climate makes for a highly productive area, 300 ha, that is hot, sunny and rarely subject to frost or rain (650 mm).

More precise production regulations (lower yield, higher density of planting, harder pruning, development for a minimum of 12 months for the red wines, a minimum of 50% for "bleeding" (*saignée*) for the rosés, more clearly defined vine varieties based on the pairing of Grenache and Syrah, sometimes augmented by Mourvèdre, are at the core of the renaissance of this sub-regional appellation nominated in 1995. Only reds (80%) and rosés are produced. Output in 2002 for the area of 332 ha around the citadel in Baux-de-Provence was 8,891 hl.

MAS DE GOURGONNIER
Réserve du Mas 2001★

| ■ | 5 ha | 20,000 | ⓘⓘⓘ | 8–11 € |

The 47 ha of vines are organically farmed, on the lines laid down by Nature et Progrès. This powerful and robust 2001 was made from a very ripe harvest of Syrah (30%), Cabernet Sauvignon (30%) and Grenache (40%). It achieves good balance thanks to the round tannins that combine with flavours of garrigue and spices.
☛ Mme Nicolas Cartier et ses Fils, Mas de Gourgonnier,
13890 Mouriès, tel. 04.90.47.50.45, fax 04.90.47.51.36,
e-mail contact@gourgonnier.fr ☑
☂ by appt.

MAS SAINTE BERTHE
Cuvée Louis David 2001★

| ■ | n.c. | n.c. | ⓘⓘⓘ | 8–11 € |

The Cuvée Louis David is the flagship of this estate, demonstrating its fullness in aromas of spices, garrigue, thyme and chocolate. The oak merges with the full and silky substance, and this makes it pleasant to drink now. The **Passe-Rose rosé 2002 (5–8 €)** also wins one star for its great harmony: the Grenache (50%) gives it its body. The **Cuvée Tradition red 2001 (5–8 €)**, matured in tank, is commended.
☛ GFA Mas Sainte Berthe, 13520 Les Baux-de-Provence,
tel. 04.90.54.39.01, fax 04.90.54.46.17,
e-mail info@mas-sainte-berthe.com ☑
☂ ev. day 9am–12 noon 2pm–6pm;
cl. Sun. 1 Nov.–30 Mar.
☛ Rolland

CH. ROMANIN 2002★

| ■ | 58 ha | 25,000 | ⓘ ♦ | 8–11 € |

No less than seven varieties of grape grown by organic methods make up this powerful and rich rosé, which has the size and freshness of the cathedral-like cellar where it was made. The **Chapelle de Romanin red 2001** and the **Coeur Tertius red 2000 (30–38 €)**, matured in barrel, also win one star.
☛ SCEA Ch. Romanin, 13210 Saint-Rémy-de-Provence, tel. 04.90.92.45.87, fax 04.90.92.24.36,
e-mail contact@romanin.com ☑
☂ by appt.
☛ Peyraud

Wines selected but not starred

MAS DE LA DAME

Rosé du Mas 2002

■ 8 ha 32,000 ■ ♁ 8–11 €

Mas de La Dame, RD 5, 13520 Les Baux-de-Provence, tel. 04.90.54.32.24, fax 04.90.54.40.67, e-mail masdeladame@masdeladame.com ☑

Y ev. day 8.30am–7pm

DOM. DE LA VALLONGUE 2000

■ 35 ha 25,000 ◍ 8–11 €

Dom. de La Vallongue, BP 4, 13810 Eygalières, tel. 04.90.95.91.70, fax 04.90.95.97.76, e-mail vallongue@wanadoo.fr ☑

Y by appt.

Héritiers Paul-Cavalliers

Coteaux Varois

The Coteaux Varois wines are produced in the green, rolling countryside around Brignoles, in the heart of the Var. The wines, best drunk young, are fruity, fun and soft, very much in the image of this pretty little Provençal market town, once the summer residence of the Comtes de Provence. Coteaux Varois became an AOC on 26 March 1993, and the delimited area covers 2,107 ha. In 2002 93,455 hl of rosé, red and white were produced.

DOM. DES ANNIBALS 2002★

■ 10.02 ha 40,000 ■ ♁ 5–8 €

In 2001, Nathalie and Bernard Coquelle took over the estate of 30 ha which they farm organically. A 12th century cellar and a farm from the Louis XIII period add to the charm of the place, as well as the vineyard which was first planted in the 18th century. This attractive-looking and tasty wine sharpens the appetite with its liveliness and powerful aromas of fruits, which linger well. Drink it as an aperitif or with a plate of charcuterie.

Nathalie et Bernard Coquelle, Dom. des Annibals, rte de Bras, 83170 Brignoles, tel. 04.94.69.30.36, fax 04.94.69.50.70 ☑

Y ev. day 9am–7pm

LA BASTIDE DES OLIVIERS

Cuvée Mathieu 2001★

■ 1 ha 3,800 ■ ◍ ♁ 8–11 €

Patrick Mourlan is a determined young winemaker who created his estate on a vineyard of about ten hectares, which he farms organically. He blended Grenache and Syrah to make this intense 2001 with garnet-red highlights, which opens on notes of soft fruits, pepper and roasting. The tannins are still young and cover the palate, followed by a very pleasant return of the spices. This richly expressive wine could be laid down for some time in the cellar.

Patrick Mourlan, Dom. La Bastide des Oliviers, 1011, chem. Louis-Blériot, 83136 Garéoult, tel. 04.94.04.03.11, fax 04.94.04.03.11 ☑

Y by appt.

CH. LA CALISSE 2002★

■ 1.5 ha 5,300 ■ ♁ 8–11 €

Equal shares of Syrah and Grenache make up this wine, which honours the leading light of the place, Patricia Ortelli. It is slightly lively with a lovely aromatic range of cherry, exotic fruits, thyme, garrigue and pepper. This richness is supported by the balanced and harmonious structure. The **Château La Calisse white 2002** is commended, as is the **Cuvée Etoiles red 2002 (15–23 €)** which opts for freshness and lightness in its fruity and peppery tones.

Patricia Ortelli, Ch. La Calisse, RD 560, 83670 Pontevès, tel. 04.94.77.24.71, fax 04.94.77.05.93, e-mail contact@chateau-la-calisse.fr ☑

Y ev. day 9am–8pm

DOM. DE CAMBARET

Cuvée Tradition 2001★

■ 1.5 ha 6,500 ■ 3–5 €

Beneath its intense red colour, this wine with notes of charring and musk reveals a good balance around its fine and round tannins. It is ready to drink now, but could be kept for a good year.

Francis Truc, 4, rue Louis-Cauvin, 83136 Garéoult, tel. 04.94.04.88.81, fax 04.94.04.88.81 ☑

Y by appt.

CH. DES CHABERTS

Cuvée Prestige 2002★★

■ 4 ha 10,000 ■ ♁ 5–8 €

The Château des Chaberts has won many *coups de coeur*, including last year for its Cuvée Prestige white 2001. This year it was this pale-coloured rosé with cherry highlights that appeared before the Grand Jury and was praised for its exotic fruit aromas and complementary peppery flavours, and for its roundness and good length. Drink it at the beginning of a meal. The **Cuvée Prestige red 2001**, matured in barrel, is awarded one star: it is complex and rich in substance, and will develop well in the next two or three years. The **Cuvée Prestige white 2002** is commended.

Ch. des Chaberts, 83136 Garéoult, tel. 04.94.04.92.05, fax 04.94.04.00.97, e-mail chaberts@wanadoo.fr ☑

Y ev. day 9am–12 noon 2pm–6pm; Sun. by appt.

CH. DE CLAPIERS 2002★

□ 1.65 ha 5,000 ■ ♁ 3–5 €

This estate came about after the purchase and conversion of the premises of a former cooperative located in the commune of Bras. Here is a wine with attractive aromas, mainly floral, which has a pleasantly bracing effect. This 2002 wine is faithful to its appellation: a good point in a difficult year.

Pierre Burel, Les Domaines de Provence, rte de Saint-Maximin, 83149 Bras, tel. 04.94.69.99.18, fax 04.98.05.12.06, e-mail clapiers@wanadoo.fr ☑

Y ev. day except Sat. Sun. 2pm–5.30pm

CH. LA CURNIERE 2002★

■ 3.75 ha 6,000 ■ ♁ 5–8 €

La Curnière is a former forestry estate and silkworm farm, and has seen many changes for the better since Michèle and Jacques Pérignon arrived in 1989. Vines were planted, increasing the area to 20 ha, and the cellar was renovated. The couple have made a very successful 2002 rosé, whose crystal-clear colour shows its harmony. On a base of crushed fresh fruits, the round and balanced palate reveals pleasant length. A touch of carbonic gas brings freshness, and this is a good thing. The **Château La Curnière red 1999** should be drunk immediately to make the most of its suppleness and bouquet. It is commended.

Michèle et Jacques Pérignon, Ch. La Curnière, 83670 Tavernes, tel. 04.94.72.39.31, fax 04.94.72.30.06, e-mail curniere@club-internet.fr ☑

Y by appt.

CH. DE L'ESCARELLE
Les Belles Bastilles 2002★

| 4 ha | 16,000 | 🍶 ⚗ | 5–8 € |

The 110 ha of vines are surrounded by 1000 ha of forest. This wine is made from Rolle (90%), with a touch of Ugni Blanc. It has a pale colour and green glints, and was carefully matured on fine lees. It is pleasant from the start, releasing aromas of white peach, iris, moss and broom, then achieves good balance between liveliness and roundness.
➹ Ch. de L'Escarelle, 83170 La Celle, tel. 04.94.69.09.98, fax 04.94.69.55.06, e-mail l.escarelle@free.fr ☑
⚐ by appt.

DOM. DE GARBELLE
Les Barriques de Garbelle 2001★★

| 2 ha | 2,200 | 🍷 | 8–11 € |

This wine won a star last year, and takes the *coup de coeur* for this 2001 vintage made from the estate's oldest vines. The Jury enjoyed the generosity and richness of this deep-garnet wine with purplish highlights. Spicy aromas are first to appear in the bouquet, then are soon joined by notes of soft ripe fruits and a vanilla-flavoured nuance. The tannins are extraordinarily powerful and need to settle down, but they support the long and warm finish well, with its flavours of ginger and pepper. The **Cuvée Principale Domaine de Garbelle red 2001 (5–8 €)**, ready to drink now, has a delightfully complex structure that shows off the wine's flavours of ripe fruits, cocoa and liquorice. It is awarded one star.
➹ Gambini, Dom. de Garbelle, 83136 Garéoult, tel. 04.94.04.86.30, fax 04.94.04.86.30 ☑
⚐ ev. day 8.30am–12 noon 2pm–6pm

CH. LAFOUX 2000★★

| 5 ha | 20,000 | 🍶🍷⚗ | 5–8 € |

With its typical 18th century house and 23-ha vineyard surrounded by an oak forest, the estate has very much the character of Green Provence. Its cheerful wine has likeable aromas of stewed fruits, blackcurrant, then wild mint. It has a supple and full substance that emphasizes flavours of jam, rounded off with notes of undergrowth. Drink it with something simple: grills or kebabs.
➹ Ch. Lafoux, RN 7, 83170 Tourves, tel. 04.94.59.12.40, fax 04.94.59.16.11 ☑
⚐ by appt.

CH. LA LIEUE 2002★

| 2.54 ha | 16,000 | 🍶 ⚗ | 5–8 € |

This authentic 17th century Provençal country house has a long wine-growing tradition and stands on the edge of the Via Aurelia. The grapes were grown organically and harvested during the night to keep them fresh. The result is this bold wine, full of perfumes of citrus fruits and exotic fruits. Its well-balanced liveliness supports the flavours through to a generous finish. This will be good with a grilled fish or a bouillabaisse.
➹ Jean-Louis Vial, Ch. La Lieue, rte de Cabasse, 83170 Brignoles, tel. 04.94.69.00.12, fax 04.94.69.47.68, e-mail chateau.la.lieue@wanadoo.fr ☑
⚐ by appt.

DOM. DU LOOU 2002★

| 7 ha | 7,000 | 🍶 ⚗ | 5–8 € |

An oratory marks the entrance to the estate, which stands near the remains of a Roman villa. In the 2nd century, winemaking was developed at Loou-Sambue. Now 60 ha of vines extend over the commune of La Roquebrussanne, including the Rolle and the Sémillon which make up this brilliant wine with golden glints which evolves on warm notes of quince and apricot. A pleasant liveliness gives way to roundness and lingering aromas of butter and quince paste. This softly autumnal wine will go well with poultry or fish in sauce.
➹ SCEA Di Placido, Dom. du Loou, 83136 La Roquebrussanne, tel. 04.94.86.94.97, fax 04.94.86.80.11 ☑
⚐ by appt.

CH. MIRAVAL 2002★

| 4.5 ha | 20,000 | 🍶 ⚗ | 8–11 € |

Having already won one star for its Côtes de Provence, the Château Miraval was awarded the same distinction for its Coteaux Varois white. This pale-yellow 2002 has an open nose: carnation, iris and exotic fruits. It is tasty, continuing the same aromas on the palate, with added roundness. This is a radiant wine, ready to be drunk with poultry.
➹ SA Ch. Miraval, 83143 Le Val, tel. 04.94.86.39.33, fax 04.94.86.46.79 ☑
⚐ by appt.

DOM. DE RAMATUELLE 2002★★

| 2.7 ha | 17,000 | 🍶 ⚗ | 3–5 € |

The vinification and maturation were certainly carried out well, as can be seen in the wine's fresh, bright colour, and the bouquet with its floral and fruity aromas. The palate is frank, supple and well balanced, with flavours of white fruits. This was one of the best in its class, and was noted by the Grand Jury. The **Domaine de Ramatuelle red 2000 (5–8 €)** is still firm, but enriched by lovely flavours of vanilla, menthol, garrigue and blackcurrant. It is awarded one star.
➹ EARL Bruno Latil, Dom. de Ramatuelle, 83170 Brignoles, tel. 04.94.69.10.61, fax 04.94.69.51.41 ☑
⚐ by appt.

DOM. LA ROSE DES VENTS 2002★

| 9.5 ha | 55,000 | 🍶 ⚗ | 5–8 € |

Gilles Baude, an oenologist, supervises the vinification on this 26.5-ha family estate. His wine has a very bright-pink colour, and leaves a pleasant impression of finesse and balance. The **Domaine La Rose des Vents white 2002** tastes strongly of Rolle, and is supple and showing liveliness. It is commended.
➹ Dom. la Rose des Vents, EARL Bande, rte de Toulon, 83136 La Roquebrussanne, tel. 04.94.86.99.28, fax 04.94.86.91.75, e-mail rose.des.vents@infonie.fr ☑
⚐ ev. day except Mon. Sun. 9am–12 noon 2pm–6pm

CH. ROUTAS
Infernet 2000★

| 4.8 ha | 20,000 | 🍷 | 5–8 € |

The Infernet has an intense cherry-red colour and will appeal to lovers of structured wines. It exudes an attractive bouquet comprising dried fruits, currants, dried fig and prune alongside menthol and liquorice. The finish is nicely expressive, the finish lingering well. A wine to drink with a stew. Also very successful was the **Cuvée Agrippa red 2001 (8–11 €)**, very oaky at present and needing two to three years to settle down.
➹ SARL Rouvière-Plane, Châteauvert, 83149 Bras, tel. 04.98.05.25.80, fax 04.98.05.25.81 ☑
⚐ by appt.
➹ Ph. Bieler

CH. SAINT-BAILLON
Clos Barbaroux 1999★

| 1 ha | 2,900 | 🍷 | 15–23 € |

This wine, produced in limited numbers, is chiefly made from Syrah and has an attractive, complex and intense bouquet of vanilla, spices, cedar and coconut, accentuated by slightly musky notes. It has a generous and supple substance with silky tannins. A good wine for game and meats in sauce.
➹ Hervé Goudard, Ch. Saint-Baillon, 83340 Flassans-sur-Issole, tel. 04.94.69.74.60, fax 04.94.69.80.29 ☑
⚐ ev. day except Sun. 8am–1pm 2pm–7pm

DOM. SAINT JEAN DE VILLECROZE

2002★

| | 1 ha | 3,000 | ∎ | 5–8 € |

In 1993, the Saint-Jean estate, run since 1973 by a Franco-American couple, was taken over by Italian winemakers. They have produced this wine made from Rolle (80%) and white Grenache (20%), though only in a small quantity. Its lively colour with green highlights gives way to a rich and mouth-filling substance with lingering flavours. The oak needs to become more integrated to improve the harmony of this well-made Coteaux-varois, which the Jury termed "original". Drink it in one year with poultry in morel sauce.

↦ SA Dom. Saint-Jean, 83690 Villecroze,
tel. 04.94.70.63.07, fax 04.94.70.67.41 ☑
⊤ ev. day 9.30am–1pm 2pm–6.30pm
↦ F. Caruso

DOM. DE SAINT-JEAN-LE-VIEUX 2001★

| | 2 ha | 12,000 | ∎ ♦ | 3–5 € |

The basilica and royal convent of Saint-Maximin are the Mecca of Provence. Make a stop not only to see the monumental organ from the classical period (1773) but also, on leaving the town, to taste this straightforward wine so typical of its terroir. It has a brilliant red colour and keeps its small soft-fruit aromas fresh on a base of undergrowth. Although the tannins seem a little rigid, they do not mask the flavours of blackcurrant in the finish. This wine is ready to drink now, but is also worth keeping for a year or two.

↦ Dom. Saint-Jean-le-Vieux, 317, rte de Bras,
83470 Saint-Maximin-la-Sainte-Baume, tel. 04.94.59.77.59,
fax 04.94.59.73.35,
e-mail saint-jean-le-vieux@wanadoo.fr ☑
⊤ ev. day except Sun. 8am–12.30pm 2pm–7pm
↦ Pierre Boyer

CH. SAINT-JULIEN

Elevé en fût de chêne 2002★

| | 3 ha | 20,000 | ◑ | 5–8 € |

The Château Saint-Julien won a *coup de coeur* last year for its 2000 wine matured in oak and now offers a 2002 vintage which is typical of the year. Supple and harmonious tannins combine with the light substance, pleasantly accentuated by mineral and liquorice notes in the finish. The **Coteaux Varois white 2002** is commended for its soothing character: green tea, newly mown grass and bitter almond on a very fresh base.

↦ EARL Dom. Saint-Julien, 83170 La Celle,
tel. 04.94.59.26.10, fax 04.94.59.26.10,
e-mail info@domaine-st-julien.com ☑
⊤ ev. day except Mon. Sun. 2pm–6pm
↦ M. Garrassin

CH. THUERRY

Les Abeillons 2000★★

| | 2.3 ha | 13,000 | ∎ ◑ ♦ | 8–11 € |

This property of more than 300 ha has now added contemporary architecture to its rich history. The 12th century country house, surrounded by plane trees many centuries old, now stands beside an ultra-modern barrel store. Tradition is respected in this intensely coloured and aromatic wine. The palate continues in the same spirit: massive tannins add to the feeling of concentration, without ever interrupting the wine's harmony. A taster predicted a great future for this wine and suggested serving it with a wild boar stew. The **rosé 2002 (5–8 €)** has a more contemporary feel. It is complex and expressive, and has such good balance that gourmets will want to drink it with refined dishes such as noix de Saint-Jacques in carpaccio. It deserves its two stars.

↦ Ch. Thuerry, 83690 Villecroze, tel. 04.94.70.63.02,
fax 04.94.70.67.03, e-mail thuerry@aol.com ☑
⊤ ev. day 9am–6.30pm; (7.30pm in summer);
cl. Sun. Apr.–Sept.
↦ Croquet

CH. TRIANS 2000★★

| | 4 ha | 20,000 | ◑ | 8–11 € |

The estate was first an old Gallo-Roman villa, then a silk-worm farm, and was almost dilapidated when it was bought in 1990. Jean-Louis Masurel raised it to the top level of the

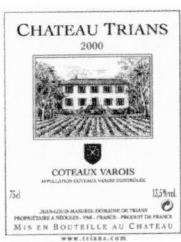

appellation by building a modern vinification cellar, restoring the buildings and producing high-quality wines. He won a *coup de coeur* for his Coteaux Varois red 94, and repeats the feat with this purplish crimson 2000. The bouquet is complex and soft: crystallized and stewed fruits and brioche combine with original notes of precious wood and menthol. After a velvety attack, the substance caresses the palate supported by a good framework of tannins. Then flavours of liquorice and fruits in brandy explode in a remarkable finish. The **white 2001 (5–8 €)** is full and warm, and is commended.

↦ Dom. de Trians, rte de Rocbaron, 83136 Néoules,
tel. 04.94.04.08.22, fax 04.94.04.84.39,
e-mail trians@wanadoo.fr ☑
⊤ ev. day 9am–12 noon 2pm–6pm
↦ J. L. Masurel

Wines selected but not starred

CH. DE CANCERILLES 2002

| | 1.55 ha | 9,400 | ∎ | 3–5 € |

↦ Chantal et Serge Garcia, Ch. de Cancerilles, vallée du Gapeau, 83870 Signes, tel. 04.94.90.83.93,
fax 04.94.90.83.93 ☑ ♠
⊤ ev. day 10am–12 noon 2pm–7pm; cl. Mon. Oct.–Mar.

DOM. DU DEFFENDS

Clos du Bécassier 2001

| | 2 ha | 8,000 | ∎ ♦ | 5–8 € |

↦ J.-S. de Lanversin, Dom. du Deffends,
83470 Saint-Maximin-la-Sainte-Baume, tel. 04.94.78.03.91,
fax 04.94.59.42.69, e-mail domaine@deffends.com ☑ ♠
⊤ ev. day except Sun. 9am–12 noon 3pm–6pm

DOM. DE FONTLADE

Cuvée Saint Quinis 2001

| | 3 ha | 3,600 | ∎ ♦ | 5–8 € |

↦ Baronne Philippe de Montremy, Dom. de Fontlade,
83170 Brignoles, tel. 04.94.59.24.34, fax 04.94.72.02.88,
e-mail fontlade@aol.com ☑
⊤ ev. day except Sun. 9am–1pm 2pm–7pm

LA GRAND'VIGNE 2002

| | 1.15 ha | 8,000 | ∎ ♦ | 3–5 € |

↦ MM Mistre, La Grand'Vigne, rte de Cabasse,
83170 Brignoles, tel. 04.94.69.37.16, fax 04.94.69.15.59,
e-mail rmistre@club-internet.fr ☑
⊤ ev. day 8am–12 noon 2pm–6pm

DOM. DE LA JULIENNE 2002

| | 1.79 ha | 2,250 | ∎ ♦ | 5–8 € |

↦ Marc Sicardi, Dom. La Julienne, Ch. des Plaines,
83170 Tourves, tel. 04.94.78.78.76, fax 04.94.78.81.62 ☑
⊤ ev. day except Sun. 9am–12 noon 1.30pm–7pm

Corsica

"A mountain in the sea": the traditional definition of Corsica is as appropriate when applied to its wines as it is in describing its tourist attractions. The topography of the whole island is folded and buckled to an extreme degree, and even the stretch called the west coast – and which, were it on the Continent, would more properly be described as a coastal area – is far from lacking in elevation and relief. The vine is to be found virtually everywhere on this multiplicity of slopes and hills, normally sun-drenched, but kept relatively damp because of the influence of the sea. Only altitude limits its planting.

The production of wine, mostly Vin de Pays or table wine, is determined by the island's relief and the climatic variations it causes, in association with three main types of soil. The most common soil was originally granite; it covers nearly the whole of the south and west of the island; between this area and the schists of the northeast you find a small deposit of limestone soils.

In addition to the imported vine varieties are highly individual varieties native to Corsica, particularly the Nielluciu which has a dominant tannic characteristic and which excels on limestone. The Sciacarellu produces fruitier wines best appreciated when they are young. For the whites, the Malvasia (Vermentinu or Malvoisie) is capable of producing the best wines grown on the shores of the Mediterranean.

As a general rule, the whites are better when young and this is even more the case for the rosés. Both go well with fish and seafood and with the excellent local goats' cheeses, as well as with brocciou, another local cheese made from goat's or ewe's milk. The reds, depending on bottle age and tannic strength, will complement a variety of different meat dishes and, naturally, all of Corsica's famous sheep's milk cheeses.

Vins de Corse

The vineyards of this appellation cover an area of 1,954 ha. The proportions of grape varieties used, and the different nature of the terroirs, can produce variations in tone and colour from one region to another and between local vineyards. Mostly, these are accounted for by grouping them under the name of a sub-region associated with the appellation (Coteaux du Cap Corse, Calvi, Figari, Porto-Vecchio and Sartène). These wines may be produced virtually anywhere in Corsica except for the Patrimonio region. Most of the 75,561 hl vinified in 2002, of which 67,164 was red and rosé, came from the east coast, where there are a large number of cooperatives.

DOM. AGHJE VECCHIE
Vecchio 2001★

| | n.c. | 12,000 | ■ ⑪ ♦ | 5–8 € |

The estate stands not far from the very fine lighthouse of Alistro. Florence Giudicelli, a friendly winemaker, and her husband Jérôme have run this property since 2000. This year they offer a very pleasant red wine with a bright and brilliant colour. The nose is mineral with notes of soft fruit recalling cherry. The supple and light palate makes this an original wine for the appellation, to be enjoyed for its harmony. Serve it with a côte de charolais.

☛ Jacques Giudicelli, Dom. Aghje Vecchie, 20230 Canale di Verde, tel. 06.03.78.09.96, fax 04.95.38.03.37, e-mail jerome.girard@attglobal.net ☑
Ⴤ by appt.

DOM. ANDRIELLA 2001★★

| | 5.4 ha | n.c. | ■ ♦ | 5–8 € |

For its first presentation to the *Guide*, the Andriella estate, the most southerly vineyard in Corsica, located in the commune of Bonifacio, did not settle for half-measures. This 2001 wine was referred to the Grand Jury which decides the *coups de coeur*. The estate's 5 ha have produced a wine with a lovely deep-ruby colour. The intense bouquet offers a remarkably complex aromatic range combining Morello cherry with liquorice via spicy scents of white pepper. On the palate, the

round and powerful tannins are accentuated by the spicy notes observed in the bouquet. Serve it with a magret au gros sel or a coq au vin.

☛ Jean-Baptiste Grimaldi, rue Sorba, 20170 Levie, tel. 04.95.78.42.59, fax 04.95.71.01.62 ☑
Ⴤ by appt.

DOM. CASABIANCA
Hommage au fondateur 2001★★

| | 8 ha | 37,000 | ■ ♦ | 5–8 € |

This is the largest vineyard in Corsica with 310 ha of vines, 224 of which belong to the AOC. It is located in the commune of Bravone between Cervione and Aléria, and is crossed by the main road, from which you can see a large part of it on either side of the road. The estate is expanding rapidly and also doing a lot of rebuilding. The 2001 vintage has proved a great success for Casabianca with four of its wines attracting the Jury's attention. This Hommage, made in honour of the founder, just missed the *coup de coeur*. It is made from 65% Nielluciu, Syrah and Grenache, has a lovely dark and brilliant colour, an intense bouquet of soft fruits with mineral accents, and a great harmony of taste, balance, power and aromas of ripe fruits. The **Cirnéa 2001 (3–5 €)** is also quite remarkable and was referred to the Grand Jury for *coups de coeur*; it is the colour of blackberry, and a little subdued at the moment, but already offers a complex and fine bouquet with red fruits to the fore. On the palate it has a good structure, concentration and fruity length. The **Cuvée Excellence 2001 (8–11 €)** is very successful (one star), most typical of Syrah: its colour contains purplish highlights, and its intense nose of soft fruits (blackberry) is punctuated by aromas of spices and tar. It is concentrated and long and needs to open out over the next few months. The estate's main wine (126,000 bottles) **Domaine de Casabianca red 2001 (3–5 €)**, also wins one star; it has an intense ruby colour with a mineral and iodized nose with still subdued perfumes of blackberry and cherry. The flavour is fruity, powerful and long; the tannins are still vigorous and need a year to soften.

☛ SCEA Dom. Casabianca, 20230 Bravone, tel. 04.95.38.96.08, fax 04.95.38.81.91, e-mail domainecasabianca@wanadoo.fr

CLOS CULOMBU
Calvi Prestige 2002★★★

| | 17.39 ha | 46,000 | ■ ♦ | 5–8 € |

The owner here is nearly 2m tall, and is known to his friends as "the longest winemaker in Corsica". His rosé is evidence of

Corsica

A.O.C.

Vin de Corse :
1 Coteaux du Cap Corse
2 Calvi
3 Sartène
4 Figari
5 Porto Vecchio

Ajaccio
Patrimonio
Muscat du Cap Corse

---- Limites de départements

the great care he takes with his wines: it was one of the finalists considered by the Grand Jury for *coups de coeur*. Its pink fruit-drop colour arouses the taster's interest. The bouquet is intense and deep, releasing fresh fruits and a small note of fruit drops which makes it seem like a *rosé de saignée*. On the palate the wine gives an impression of softness, with chewy grape flavours along with raspberry and bilberry, all of which are extraordinarily long. Drink it by itself or with a salad of apricots in wild mint. The **Cuvée Prestige white 2002** is commended for its fine appearance and aromas of an exotic nature (pineapple and mango).
☙ Etienne Suzzoni, Clos Culombu, chem. San-Petru, 20260 Lumio, tel. 04.95.60.68.70, fax 04.95.60.63.46 ☑
☥ ev. day 8am–6pm

CLOS D'ORLEA 2002★★

20 ha	30,000	🍾 ✦	3–5 €

The Clos d'Orléa has again delighted wine-lovers this year with a feminine rosé of a clear and bright summery colour, and good aromas of white fruits and spices. The long palate continues the spicy notes and adds floral aromas. This is a delicious rosé which came close to the *coup de coeur*. The **red 2001** is very successful, releasing lovely perfumes of undergrowth. On the palate, the tannins are very evident but already integrated. This wine will go nicely with a hare stew. The

white 2002 is commended for its bright, clear nuances and its liveliness.
☙ François Orsucci, Le Clos d'Orléa, 20270 Aléria, tel. 04.95.57.13.60, fax 04.95.57.09.64 ☑ 🏠
☥ ev. day except Sun. 9am–12 noon 2pm–8pm

CLOS POGGIALE 2001★★

10 ha	61,000	🍾 🎷	11–15 €

The Clos Poggiale is a brand of the Coteaux de Diana cooperative, a 48-ha property in the Skalli group. It is located in the commune of Tallone, not far from the sea, and both vineyard and vinification are very well run by Elise and Christian Costa. This 2001 red was made from Niellucciu (55%) and Syrah, and matured for 11 months in barrel and eight months in tank. Its superb deep-red colour with deep-purple highlights catches the eye. The bouquet is bewitching with an intense red fruitiness, spices and nuts. On the palate it is completely charming: a fruity, very rounded attack supported by a perfect structure and a harmonious balance between fruit tannins and oak. This is a characteristic wine to drink throughout a Corsican meal.
☙ SICA Coteaux de Diana, Terra Vecchia, 20270 Tallone, tel. 04.95.57.20.30, fax 04.95.57.08.98 ☑
☥ by appt.

DOM. DE LA FIGARELLA

Calvi Cuvée Prestige 2002★

7 ha	25,000	🍾 ✦	8–11 €

Calenzana, in the Upper Balagne, about 15 km from Calvi, is overlooked by Monte Grosso (1,937 m) and forms one of the access points to the Parc Naturel. Achille Acquaviva has his estate there, and offers a pleasant and fairly strong raspberry-coloured rosé. The bouquet has nice aromas of flowers (honeysuckle) and apricot. The palate is well structured with good balance between alcohol and acidity, and leaves a pleasant impression of freshness. Try it with a fillet of mullet in olive oil.
☙ Achille Acquaviva, dom. de La Figarella, rte de l'Aéroport, 20214 Calenzana, tel. 04.95.65.07.24, fax 04.95.65.41.58 ☑
☥ Wed. Sat. 4pm–6pm; ev. day 4pm–7pm Jul.–Aug.

DOM. FIUMICICOLI

Sartène 2001★

20 ha	50,000	🍾 ✦	8–11 €

Do not miss the Fiumicicoli estate, which can be found between Propriano and Sartène. The Andréanis, watchful and creative winemakers, will welcome you to their very beautiful tasting cellar and allow you to try an interesting range of wines, including this red 2001 with a ruby colour and a mineral and spicy nose which perfectly reflects the blend of Niellucciu and Sciacarellu grapes. Its smoothness on the palate makes it drinkable by itself or with a dish of regional charcuterie. The **white 2002** is also notable for its aromatic richness (white flowers) and its good shape on the palate, and is awarded one star. Try it with a cream cheese. The **rosé 2002** is commended for its lightly amylic aspect and spicy notes, merging tradition and modernity.
☙ EARL Andréani, Dom. Fiumicicoli, rte de Levie, 20100 Sartène, tel. 04.95.76.14.08, fax 04.95.76.24.24 ☑
☥ by appt.

DOM. MAESTRACCI
Calvi E Prove 2002★★

	5 ha	20,000	▮ ♦	8–11 €

Michel Raoust is a regular in the *Guide*. This year he again shows his talents as a winemaker. His rosé E Prove 2002, made chiefly from Sciacarellu, was presented to the Grand Jury for a *coup de cœur*. This bright and brilliant wine reveals the richness of the grape variety with its typical peppery spices and exceptional length on the palate. It is a traditional rosé to serve with a casserole. The **E Prove red 2000** is commended for its general harmony and the touch of violet on the palate. The other wine from the Maestracci estate, **Clos Réginu rosé 2002 (5–8 €)**, is a cheerful, fruity and chewy wine – an aperitif to be drunk in the cool of early evening. The **Clos Réginu red 2002 (5–8 €)** is very balanced, combining power and length. It is full of soft fruits, enhanced by exotic spices, and will go well with a gigot d'agneau and roasted broad beans. These last two wines each win one star.

☛ Michel Raoust, rte de Santa Reparata, 20225 Feliceto, tel. 04.95.61.72.11, fax 04.95.61.80.16, e-mail clos.reginu@wanadoo.fr ▮
♀ summer: ev. day except Sat. Sun. 9am–12 noon 2pm–7.30pm

DOM. DU MONT SAINT-JEAN 2002★

	3 ha	10,000	▮	5–8 €

Roger Pouyau, wine-grower in the micro-region of Antisanti and a partner in the UVAL group, demonstrates his skills and is awarded one star for each of the wines he presented. His vineyard has a total area of 120 ha, and has produced this very clear white wine made with maceration on the skins, whose bouquet reveals lemony notes typical of the Vermentinu grape, and lime blossom. The **rosé 2002** is pale and chewy with a refreshing touch of acid, and should be drunk with an oriental dish. The **red 2001** is dark and a little closed, but offers fullness and length on the palate. Try it with a Basque chicken.

☛ SCA du Mont Saint-Jean, Campo Quercio, 20270 Aléria, tel. 06.81.05.45.08, fax 04.95.38.50.29, e-mail roger-pouyau@wanadoo.fr ▮
♀ by appt.
☛ Roger Pouyau

DOM. DE MUSOLEU
Cuvée Monte Cristo 2001★★

	2 ha	9,500	▮ ♦	5–8 €

The estate of Charles Morazzani stands beside the main road at the entrance to Folelli, not far from the Tyrrhenian Sea. He is an enthusiastic winemaker who always tries to get the best from his wines, and is prepared to downgrade some of his wines if their quality does not please him. In a very fine year, he has made this Monte Cristo, the name referring to the island opposite his property, formerly inhabited by monks who came several centuries ago to stock up on supplies at the estate. This deep-ruby wine was a finalist before the Grand Jury for *coups de cœur*, and reveals great aromatic power with its scents of undergrowth and soft fruits. The full and very long palate gives the wine its high quality. Serve it with a roasted haunch of wild boar. The **rosé 2002** is bright and fruity, and is commended.

☛ Charles Morazzani, Dom. de Musoleu, 20213 Folelli, tel. 04.95.36.80.12, fax 04.95.36.90.16, e-mail charles.morazzani@wanadoo.fr ▮
♀ ev. day except Sun. 8.30am–12 noon 3pm–7pm

PERAGNOLO 2002★★

	12 ha	30,000	▮ ♦	5–8 €

The Filippi family are regulars in the *Guide*. This year, the rosé Péragnolo won unanimous praise from the tasters. Its colour is bright, and the bouquet has very fruity aromas, evoking the fresh fruit of the Niellucciu and Cinsault grapes. The palate is long, harmonious and quite soft, with a certain liveliness. Drink it as an aperitif or with a dessert such as watermelon with lychees. The **red 2001** was admired for its balance and roundness on the palate, and is commended, as is the **Domaine Filippi Capo di Terra red 2001**, a different wine which has 15% of Mourvèdre in the blend. The wine is ruby-red in colour with some brick-red highlights and an expressive bouquet releasing notes of roasting. The palate is clean with tannins slightly evident in the finish. Drink this in two years' time.

☛ François et Toussaint Filippi, La Ruche Foncière, 20215 Vescovato, tel. 04.95.58.40.80, fax 04.95.36.40.55, e-mail la-ruche-fonciere@wanadoo.fr ▮
♀ by appt.

DOM. DE PETRA BIANCA
Figari Vinti Legna 2001★★★

	n.c.	12,000	▥	8–11 €

Joël Rossi and Jean Curralucci own the very attractive Petra Bianca estate, not far from the village of Figari. They make their wine in a private cellar in the building known as Omu di Cagna. Joël Rossi, keen to get the best out of his grapes, takes an active part in the vinification. Rigorous selection enabled them to present an exceptional 2001. The tasters referred it to the Grand Jury, but at that time the wine's character was masked by too much oak and this prevented them from winning the *coup de cœur*. This is a powerful, brilliant dark-red wine with an intense bouquet of oak, vanilla and chocolate. The vanilla is very evident on the palate along with a very nice structure that is free of harshness. Keep it in your cellar for at least two years, and drink it when the aromas of the wine have settled down. It will go well with a magret de canard in mushroom sauce.

☛ Dom. de Petra Bianca, 20114 Figari, tel. 04.95.71.01.62, fax 04.95.71.01.62, e-mail joel.rossi@worldonline.fr ▮
♀ by appt.

DOM. RENUCCI
Calvi 2002★★

	6.5 ha	23,000	▮ ♦	5–8 €

Since 1991, Bernard Renucci has been doing his best for the vineyard. This year he has surprised us again with this lovely rosé, straightforward and clear to look at, with aromas of summer fruits such as peach and nectarine with a slightly iodized touch characteristic of Sciacarellu, which features heavily in the blend. The freshness on the palate indicates a wine to drink for pleasure. Drink it with a stew or a brochette of Corsican lamb in herbs from the maquis.

☛ Bernard Renucci, 20225 Feliceto, tel. 04.95.61.71.08, fax 04.95.61.71.08 ▮
♀ ev. day 10am–12 noon 4pm–7pm; cl. autumn–winter

RESERVE DU PRESIDENT 2002★★

	45 ha	280,000		3–5 €

We regularly come across serious winemaking from the UVIB group, run by three very good oenological technicians. In a rather difficult year, where talent and technology had to be used to obtain good results, they produced a very pleasant white wine with golden highlights, releasing typical aromas of lemony citrus fruits and several touches of menthol. The palate is full and long, and repeats these fresh notes, finishing with a hint of bitterness so typical of the Vermentinu grape variety. Serve with a roasted dory or simply drink it as an aperitif. The **Réserve du Président rosé 2002**, with its bright-pink colour, delighted the tasters with its fresh notes of summer fruits (peach and apricot) and the rather structured palate with flavours of bigaroon cherry. It also wins two stars.

☛ Union de Vignerons de l'Ile de Beauté, Cave coop. d'Aléria, 20270 Aléria, tel. 04.95.57.02.48, fax 04.95.57.09.59, e-mail barianichaba@aol.com ▮
♀ by appt.

DOM. SAPARALE
Sartène 2002★★

	18 ha	25,000	▮ ♦	3–5 €

Since 1998, Philippe Farinelli has regenerated the wines of Sartène. He is extremely enthusiastic about his work as a winemaker, has a diploma in oenology and knows how to make the most of his terroir. He shows his skills again this year with a lovely, bright rosé made chiefly from Sciacarellu, with aromas of soft spring fruits enhanced by typical notes of citrus fruits. The palate is silky and fairly long. Drink it with a simple salad of tomatoes and mozarella in balsamic vinegar. His very fine **white 2002** is awarded a star for its diaphanous colour, for bringing out the tastes of the Vermentinu grapes and for the slightly mentholated touches which reinforce the

first impression of freshness. In 2002, 1,200 bottles of this wine were produced and are excellent value for money.
☛ Philippe Farinelli, 5, cours Bonaparte, 20100 Sartène, tel. 06.11.89.26.69, fax 04.95.73.43.08, e-mail p.farinelli@libertysurf.fr ☑
🍷 by appt.

DOM. DE TANELLA
Figari Cuvée Alexandra Prestige 2001★★

◼	8 ha	35,000	◼ ◖▯ ◗	8–11 €

The Tanella has appeared several times in the *Guide*. Jean-Baptiste de Peretti Della Rocca is from a very old family of winemakers and is one of those quiet but efficient producers who are ambassadors for Corsican wine. This year, the Grand Jury awarded him a *coup de coeur* for his Alexandra wine. It has a lovely structure and an exceptionally rich nose with spices and undergrowth. The feeling of fullness reappears on the palate, which offers a complex aromatic range running from cinnamon to cedar via toasty and vanilla notes. This wine has great personality and will go well with a stew of roe deer or wild boar. The **Cuvée Alexandra white 2002** has a subdued nose, then becomes more impressive on the palate with its fine balance and lemony, slightly smoky notes. Its complexity means it can be drunk with the first seafoods of autumn. It is awarded one star.
☛ Jean-Baptiste de Peretti della Rocca, Dom. de Tanella, 20114 Figari, tel. 04.95.70.46.23, fax 04.95.70.54.40, e-mail tanella@wanadoo.fr ☑
🍷 by appt.

TERRA NOSTRA 2001★

◼	120 ha	400,000	◼	3–5 €

The Terra Nostra brand has become the flagship AOC of the UVAL group. It promotes nature, tradition and innovation. Each wine is made from a selection from various plots, and is very well vinified; it makes a case for wines made from a single grape variety (which is not traditional). The **rosé 2002**, made from Sciaccarellu, was commended by the Jury. It has a lovely pale-salmon colour and reserved and fine aromas. On the palate, its roundness and elegance give it good balance. The **Cuvée Corsica red 2001 (5–8 €)**, made from 100% Niellucciu, is also commended. The very strong presence of oak (eight months in barrel) cost it one star. This Terra Nostra red 2001, made from 100% Niellucciu, is very successful. Its garnet-red colour and its bouquet of very ripe fruits and liquorice flavours with notes of undergrowth are most attractive. On the palate, these aromas are accentuated by balance, harmony and high quality. Try this immediately.
☛ Uval, Rasignani, 20290 Borgo, tel. 04.95.58.44.00, fax 04.95.38.38.10, e-mail uval.sica@wanadoo.fr

DOM. DE TORRACCIA
Porto-Vecchio Réserve Oriu 2001★

◼	7 ha	35,000	◼	11–15 €

Christian Imbert is a personality among the island's winegrowers. He is fiercely opposed to the globalization of crops and has farmed organically for several years, always seeking to produce wines that are both characteristic and original. His Oriu conforms to his wishes: this is a very lovely bright-ruby wine with a nose releasing notes of redcurrant and blackberry jam. On the palate, it shows a general harmony, good length and a delicious velvetiness. Oriu 2001 will go well with veal in olives.

☛ Christian Imbert, Dom. de Torraccia, Lecci, 20137 Porto Vecchio, tel. 04.95.71.43.50, fax 04.95.71.50.03 ☑
🍷 ev. day except Sun. 8am–12 noon 2pm–6pm

DOM. VICO 2002★

◼	25 ha	80,000		5–8 €

The Vico estate is exceptional in the Vins de Corse appellation, in that it is the only estate located in the region of Ponte Leccia in the centre of the island. It offers a very attractive, strong-coloured rosé with aromas of cherry and peach. The palate is fresh and fairly long, with nice notes of soft fruits. Serve it with a wild trout grilled over a wood fire.
☛ SCEA Dom. Vico, Ponte Leccia, 20218 Morosaglia, tel. 04.95.47.61.35, fax 04.95.36.50.26 ☑
🍷 ev. day 9am–12 noon 2pm–6pm

Wines selected but not starred

CLOS MILLELI 2001

◼	4 ha	25,000	◼ ◗	3–5 €

☛ Cave coop. d'Aghione, Samuletto, 20270 Aghione, tel. 04.95.56.60.20, fax 04.95.56.61.27, e-mail coop.aghionesamuletto@wanadoo.fr ☑
🍷 by appt.

DOM. PERO-LONGO
Sartène 2002

◼	n.c.	6,400	◼ ◗	5–8 €

☛ Pierre Richarme, lieu-dit Navara, rte de Bonifacio, 20100 Sartène, tel. 04.95.77.10.74, fax 04.95.77.10.74 ☑
🍷 by appt.

DOM. PIERETTI
Coteaux du Cap Corse 2001

◼	2 ha	4,800	◼ ◗	8–11 €

☛ Lina Venturi, Santa-Severa, 20228 Luri, tel. 04.95.35.01.03, fax 04.95.35.01.03 ☑
🍷 by appt.

DOM. SAN'ARMETTU
Sartène 2002

◼	10 ha	49,000	◼ ◗	5–8 €

☛ EARL San'Armettu, Les Cannes, 20113 Olmeto, tel. 04.95.76.05.18, fax 04.95.76.24.47 ☑ ⌂
🍷 by appt.
☛ Seroin

SANT'ANTONE 2001

◼	50 ha	200,000	◼	3–5 €

☛ Cave de Saint-Antoine, Saint-Antoine, 20240 Ghisonaccia, tel. 04.95.56.61.00, fax 04.95.56.61.60 ☑
🍷 by appt.

Ajaccio

The vineyards of this appellation occupy 220 ha in a strip several dozen kilometres long running along the hills surrounding the chief town of southern Corsica and its famous gulf. The soils are mostly granitic, and Sciacarello is the main

CORSICA

grape variety. The red wines are suitable for keeping and account for 60.5% of the 2002 production of around 7,370 hl.

DOM. COMTE ABBATUCCI
Cuvée Faustine Abbatucci 2001★

■	10 ha	n.c.	■	8–11 €

Jean-Charles Abbatucci is the president of the Ajaccio AOC, and manages his organic estate with passion and application. This red 2001 is very characteristic. The springlike colour is a bright cherry-red; the perfumes of soft fruits are spicy and fine; the palate is fairly full, resting on very evident tannins that are still a little young. Leave it to mature for at least two years.

↬ Dom. Comte J.-C. Abbatucci, Lieu-dit Chiesale, 20140 Casalabriva, tel. 04.95.74.04.55, fax 04.95.74.26.39 ☑
🍷 by appt.

CLOS D'ALZETO 2002★★

■	4 ha	20,000		5–8 €

This estate stands on a magnificent site at an altitude of 500 m, and has been passed from father to son since it was built in 1820. Pascal Albertini and his son Alexis, an oenologist, continue the tradition in a modern way. The barrel store is worth a visit, as is this white 2002, made from Vermentinu. Its colour is translucent and brilliant, with an intense floral nose of citrus fruits, and a very characteristic, balanced and expressive palate with touch of gunflint, making it a perfect ambassador for the Ajaccio AOC. The **rosé 2002** is very successful. It has a very pretty pink colour, an intense fruity bouquet with fragrances of peach and apricot with notes of maquis, and a very full and generous palate in which the aromas of the bouquet return for a lingering finish.

↬ Pascal Albertini, Clos d'Alzeto, 20151 Sari d'Orcino, tel. 04.95.52.24.67, fax 04.95.52.27.27 ☑
🍷 ev. day except Sun. 8am–12 noon 2pm–6pm (8pm in summer)

DOM. COMTE PERALDI 2002★

■	3.5 ha	16,000	■ ♦	5–8 €

This estate has been owned by the Tyrel de Poix family since 1963, and is one of the largest in the appellation, also one of the best known. It is run by Christophe George, an oenologist originally from the Bordelais, who has real know-how. This white 2002 has good balance; its aromas should open out shortly. The **rosé 2002** is commended. It has a rose-petal colour, a fine and fruity nose, slightly peppery, and on the palate reveals roundness and balance. The **red 2001**, also commended, has a lovely garnet-red colour, and a warm nose with notes of undergrowth; the palate is characteristic, though still firm in the finish. Drink it in a year or two to let the tannins settle down.

↬ Guy Tyrel de Poix, Dom. Peraldi, chem. du Stiletto, 20167 Mezzavia, tel. 04.95.22.37.30, fax 04.95.20.92.91 ☑
🍷 by appt.

DOM. DE PIETRELLA 2002★

■	1 ha	n.c.	■	5–8 €

Toussaint Tirroloni runs this family estate of 38 ha, and this year has been successful with both his white and his rosé. The white has a very bright, pretty colour and reveals a light nose with white flowers. The palate is supple and balanced, giving a very pleasant general impression. The **rosé 2002** is very pale with interestingly intense aromas and smoky and mineral notes. His flavours on the well-balanced and lively palate are reminiscent of soft fruits.

↬ Toussaint Tirroloni, Dom. de Pietrella, 20117 Cauro, tel. 04.95.25.19.19 ☑
🍷 by appt.

DOM. DE PRATAVONE 2002★

■	2.7 ha	16,000	■ ♦	5–8 €

Since 2000, Isabelle Courrèges has run this 31-ha estate by herself, now that her father Jean has retired. This white 2002 is a lovely wine. The very fine and elegant nose clearly indicates the balanced palate with subtle aromas of white flowers and honey. The **red 99**, which is also commended, aroused different views. Its bright brick-red colour prepares the way for sophisticated aromas of prune and brandy with

spicy notes; on the palate the flavours suggest crystallized fruits and fruits macerated in brandy. Drink this immediately.

↬ Isabelle Courrèges, SCEA Dom. de Pratavone, Pila-Canale, 20123 Cognocoli-Monticchi, tel. 04.95.24.34.11, fax 04.95.24.34.74 ☑
🍷 by appt.

Wines selected but not starred

CLOS CAPITORO 2001

■	33 ha	90,000	■ ♦	5–8 €

↬ Jacques Bianchetti, Clos Capitoro, Pisciatella, 20166 Porticcio, tel. 04.95.25.19.61, fax 04.95.25.19.33, e-mail info@closcapitoro.com ☑
🍷 by appt.

CLOS ORNASCA 2001

■	3.48 ha	20,000		5–8 €

↬ Laetitia Tola, Ornasca, Eccica Suarella, 20117 Cauro, tel. 04.95.25.09.07, fax 04.95.25.96.05 ☑
🍷 by appt.

DOM. DE VACCELLI 2002

■	4.4 ha	1,600	⬚	8–11 €

↬ Alain Courrèges, A Cantina, 20123 Cognocoli-Monticchi, tel. 04.95.24.35.54, fax 04.95.24.38.07 ☑
🍷 ev. day except Sun. 9am–12 noon 3pm–7pm

Patrimonio

This small enclave, occupying 420 ha in 2002, is made up of limestone terroirs extending east and mainly south from the Gulf of Saint-Florent. They are remarkably consistent from one to another and can with good management produce high-quality wines. The chief grape varieties are Nielluccio for reds and Malvasia for whites, and these look likely to become the only varieties used. They make very typical wines of excellent quality, especially the sumptuous reds that can be laid down for long maturing. Production was 13,724 hl, of which 1,829 hl were whites.

DOM. ALISO-ROSSI
Cuvée des Seigneurs 1998★★

■	2 ha	n.c.	■ ⬚ ♦	15–23 €

The Aliso-Rossi estate is fairly remote and not easy to find. Fortunately, there is a very nice shop in the middle of Saint-Florent where you can taste and buy the wines you like. This year, Dominique Rossi presented a remarkable 1998 wine. It is dark and strong in colour, with a harmonious and spicy nose and a full, smooth palate of great power and very good balance; this *vin de terroir* will be perfect with wild boar. The **Cuvée des Artistes red 2001 (23–30 €)** is very successful and also worth trying. It is less refined than the previous wine but is powerful and robust with round, liquorice-flavoured tannins, which make it very pleasant. The **Perle de Rosé 2002**

(15–23 €) is commended; it is pleasant with good balance and fruity flavours of the peach-apricot variety.

🕮 Dom. Aliso-Rossi, 20246 Santo-Pietro-di-Tenda, tel. 04.95.37.03.03, fax 04.95.37.71.80 ▼

🍷 by appt.

🕮 Dominique Rossi

DOM. NAPOLEON BRIZI 2002★

| | 3 ha | 8,000 | ∎ ♦ | 3–5 € |

This year, the Brizi estate is represented in the *Guide* by all its wines, produced in an area of 10 ha. Napoléon Brizi is a very friendly winemaker, growing his vines in a traditional manner and respecting organic methods. He is well equipped with Inox material, and combines modernity and ancestral know-how without any problems. This white 2002 has a very aromatic, powerful nose. On the palate there is good balance; the wine is fairly full-bodied and finishes on warm notes, which indicate it should be drunk with fish in a spicy white sauce. The **rosé 2002** is commended, and is elegant and balanced, delivering vegetal notes in the finish. The **red 2001** (5–8 €) is also commended; this has a bouquet of soft fruits and violet, and a light but balanced palate which means it can be drunk now.

🕮 Napoléon Brizi, 20253 Patrimonio, tel. 04.95.37.08.26 ▼

🍷 by appt.

DOM. DE CATARELLI 2001★★

| | 3 ha | 15,000 | ∎ | 8–11 € |

Laurent Le Stunff has been in charge of this family property of 12 ha since 1995. He is a cheerful, friendly young man who regularly makes successful wines. This red 2001 is remarkable for its structure and power. The nose is a little closed but will open out thanks to the pervading fruitiness to be found on the palate. Wait at least two years to avoid disappointment. The **rosé 2002** is awarded one star. This is a modern bright-pink wine with very strong flavours on the palate. It will go very well with a carpaccio of beef in basil. The **white 2002** is commended for its exotic scents; it is light and acid, and well suited to crustaceans.

🕮 EARL Dom. de Catarelli, marine de Farinole, rte de Nonza, 20253 Patrimonio, tel. 04.95.37.02.84, fax 04.95.37.18.72 ▼

🍷 ev. day except Sun. 9am–12 noon 3pm–6pm; cl. Nov.-Mar.

🕮 Laurent Le Stunff

CLOS MARFISI

Vieilles Vignes 2002★

| | 4 ha | 10,000 | ∎ ♦ | 8–11 € |

The Marfisi cooperative, located on the way out of Patrimonio, is old but has been completely modernized to vinify grapes from its 12-ha property in the best possible conditions. The white and the rosé 2002 are very successful and should be tried immediately. The former is made from direct pressing, fermentation for ten days at 18°C and maturation in tank for seven months. This is a very bright and brilliant wine, with a nose that is still closed but will open out in time. On the palate, it is full-bodied and balanced; its finesse comes from its complex aromas. The **rosé 2002**, also made by direct pressing, is a clean-pink colour. Intense aromas of soft fruits linger on the palate, which has harmony and balance.

🕮 Toussaint Marfisi, Clos Marfisi, av. Jules-Ventre, 20253 Patrimonio, tel. 04.95.37.07.49, fax 04.95.37.06.37 ▼

🍷 ev. day 9am–1pm 3pm–8pm; cl. 1 Dec.–1 Mar.

CLOS SIGNADORE 2001★

| | 4 ha | 11,000 | ∎ | 5–8 € |

The Clos Signadore makes its first appearance in the *Guide*. Christophe Ferrandis has been at the commune of Poggiod'Oletta since 2001. Here he demonstrates, if that were needed, that quality does not depend on experience. This intense red 2001 has a powerful bouquet and a well-structured palate. The tannins are still a little youthful and need to become more rounded to show this rich and elegant wine at its best. Keep it for a year or two to let it mature, then it will go perfectly with a hare or wild boar stew.

🕮 Christophe Ferrandis, lieu-dit Morta-Piana, 20232 Poggio-d'Oletta, tel. 06.15.18.29.81, fax 04.95.37.69.68, e-mail christopheferrandis@wanadoo.fr ▼

🍷 by appt.

CLOS TEDDI 2001★★

| | 2 ha | n.c. | ∎ ♦ | 8–11 € |

It is not easy to be a young woman in the winemaking business and make a name for yourself. Well, it is possible, and it can be done in some style, what is more. Marie-Brigitte Poli took over this family estate in difficult conditions and without her own cellar. She is a wilful and determined woman and rose above these difficulties; now she offers three wines that should not be missed. The **white 2002** is remarkable: aromatic, fresh, fruity and well balanced; a delight to drink. The **rosé 2002** has an intense-pink colour and is very successful. It has scents of soft fruits, redcurrant and strawberry, and a full palate, both fruity and balanced with a charming acid finish. This wine will relax even the grumpiest person. And, oh, what a lovely red 2001! Another great surprise. It has a perfect structure, ripe soft fruits, and silky, round tannins... Drink it now or wait a while for it to reach its best.

🕮 Marie-Brigitte Poli-Juillard, Hameau de Casta, sentier des Agriates, 20217 Saint-Florent, tel. 06.10.84.11.73, fax 04.95.37.24.07 ▼

🍷 by appt.

DOM. GENTILE

Sélection noble 2000★★

| | 3.5 ha | 18,000 | ∎ ◆ ♦ | 15–23 € |

The Gentile estate, whose cellar is located on the way in to Saint-Florent coming from Patrimonio, has 30 ha of vines cultivated in a very traditional fashion over three communes in the appellation. The head of the family, Dominique, is basically concerned with the wine-growing, and shares the winemaking part with his son Jean-Paul, an oenologist. This Sélection noble crowns their work together by winning the *coup de coeur* of the Grand Jury. This very powerful wine, which spent 12 months in barrel, has a musky and spicy bouquet with fairly evident oak. On the palate, its structure is excellent, supported by oaky tannins that are still quite long. This 2000 needs to age for two to three years to bring out all its qualities. It will be excellent with wild boar or some other strong-tasting dish. The **Sélection Noble white 2001 (11–15 €)** is commended for its eloquent aromas of nut and its well-shaped palate with honey-flavoured notes. To round off, there is a touch of bitterness in the finish.

🕮 Dom. Gentile, Olzo, 20217 Saint-Florent, tel. 04.95.37.01.54, fax 04.95.37.16.69, e-mail domaine.gentile@wanadoo.fr ▼

🍷 ev. day except Sun. 8.30am–12 noon 2.30pm–7pm; out of season by appt.

DOM. GIACOMETTI

Cru des Agriates 2002★★

| | 6.43 ha | 21,000 | ∎ | 5–8 € |

Christian Giacometti is not a typical wine-grower. His shy, adolescent appearance, long hair and dreamy air of an intellectual do not, however, prevent him from having his feet planted firmly on the ground. Over the years, he has taken complete control of the family business, located in the extreme south of the Patrimonio appellation, on the edge of the Agriates desert. His isolated property is regularly invaded by uncontrollable cattle, and is reached via a track that is a

CORSICA

severe challenge for cars. There he perseveres and is doing very well. The proof lies in this remarkable rosé 2002, selected for the Grand Jury for *coups de coeur*. It has a divine pearl-pink colour, elegant and intense perfumes, and an expressive, balanced and harmonious palate. What more can we say? Also look out for the **white 2002**, which is very successful, grown in an austere granitic terroir and produced, alas, in a very small quantity (3,000 bottles). This unusual wine has a very fine, delicate and elegant bouquet of violet and grapefruit, and a full and round palate, and is very attractive. It is awarded one star.

🖢 Christian Giacometti, Casta, 20217 Saint-Florent, tel. 04.95.37.00.72, fax 04.95.37.00.72 🆅
🍷 by appt.

DOM. LECCIA 2002★★

	3 ha	12,000	🍾 ⬥	11–15 €

Passion is one way to explain the regular and brilliant appearances of the Leccia estate in the *Guide*, but passion alone is not enough when the weather, which controls our vintages, is against us. They say that the professional worth of a wine-grower can be assessed by how well he manages to control his techniques and technology in the difficult years. This remarkable white wine, bursting with authenticity and character, confirms the truth of that saying. After a very expressive and complex bouquet of flowers and fruits, it reveals great finesse on the palate, supported by a very good balance between freshness and length. The **rosé 2002** (*de saignée*), has a very strong colour and was vinified after 12 hours of maceration; it is commended for its intense nose of soft fruits, its balance and character. The **red 2001**, responsible for almost one-third of the vineyard's production (6 ha), is made from 90% Niellucciu and 10% Grenache grown on a clay-limestone terroir. The product of maceration for 15 days at between 25° and 30°C and a blend of free-run and pressed fruit, it is awarded one star. It has a dark, deep colour, and when the glass is swirled releases intense and typical aromas of ripe and spicy soft fruits. The palate is full, round and harmonious, its character already established. It can be drunk now or kept for a while.

🖢 GAEC Dom. Leccia, 20232 Poggio-d'Oletta, tel. 04.95.37.11.35, fax 04.95.37.17.03 🆅
🍷 by appt.

ORENGA DE GAFFORY 2002★★

	13 ha	20,000	🍾 ⬥	8–11 €

The Orenga de Gaffory estate is one of those which, this year, won recognition for all the wines they produced. This white 2002, a very typical wine for Vermentinu de Patrimonio, has a lovely appearance and a charming and very expressive bouquet. The perfect palate is the result of good balance that gives it excellent length. The aromas are complex and enchanting. Drink it with seafood or just as an aperitif to enjoy it for itself. It will be interesting to watch it age. Rosé wine is difficult to make. There is very little time to control the colour and the aromas, and great rosés are rare for that reason. It seems that the **rosé 2002** selected for the Grand Jury may be one of them. This silky wine has an attractive, brilliant rose-petal colour, a harmonious, attractive and very fine floral bouquet, and a subtle, elegant and powerful palate. Drink it by itself or with grilled lamb on a bed of small vegetables. The **red 2001**, although very successful, needs a little time to open out. This full and complex wine with powerful aromas of soft fruits is well structured; its tannins are already rounded and give it a velvety length. It has a promising future. Leave it for a year or two, it can only become even more attractive.

🖢 GFA Orenga de Gaffory, lieu-dit Morta-Majo, 20253 Patrimonio, tel. 04.95.37.45.00, fax 04.95.37.14.25, e-mail orenga.de.gaffory@wanadoo.fr 🆅
🍷 ev. day except Sat. Sun. 9am–12 noon 2pm–6pm

DOM. PASTRICCIOLA 2002★★

	4 ha	16,000	🍾 ⬥	5–8 €

This estate can be found on the way out of Patrimonio, and is inescapable. The vine plots overhanging the cellar are magnificent. The three members of this GAEC have wine in their souls and cosset each grape with their love. The result is a *coup de coeur* for the rosé 2002, brilliant in a difficult year: 16,000 bottles to try out! It has a sublime bright-pink colour, an elegant and expressive bouquet and a harmonious, acid, fruity palate. The **white 2002** is very successful and clearly reflects the Vermentinu grape variety. On the palate it is lively, well-balanced and long, and will be perfect with shellfish. A commendation for the **red 2001**, which is well made and fruity but not very concentrated – just pleasant to drink.

🖢 Dom. Pastricciola, rte de Saint-Florent, 20253 Patrimonio, tel. 04.95.37.18.31, fax 04.95.37.08.83 🆅
🍷 ev. day 9am–7pm; cl. Nov.
🖢 Maestracci-Giovannetti Giormini

DOM. SAN QUILICO 2001★

	14 ha	30,000	🍾 ⬥	5–8 €

The most beautiful pebbles in the world can be found in the area of the Patrimonio appellation, and the San Quilico estate has plenty of them. They come in an infinite range of colours ranging between pale ochre and wine lees, flecked, streaked, hammered, small and large, rounded and slender – and make you want to pick them all up. This should be resisted, however, since it is partly due to them that the terroir produces such beautiful wines. The **rosé 2002** is very successful with a fine appearance. Its modern bouquet is intense and fruity, and its slightly amylic palate caresses the taste buds, charmed by its good balance and harmonious length. It will go well with seafood. This red 2001 has a brilliant ruby colour. The bouquet is very floral with notes of violet, which continue on the palate along with good-quality tannins, which need to soften a little. Keep it for six months and then serve it with braised or grilled red meat.

🖢 EARL Dom. San Quilico, lieu-dit Morta-Majo, 20253 Patrimonio, tel. 04.95.37.45.00, fax 04.95.37.14.25 🆅
🍷 ev. day except Sat. Sun. 9am–12 noon 2pm–6pm

Wines selected but not starred

CLOS MONTEMAGNI 2001

	12 ha	60,000	🍾 ⬥	5–8 €

🖢 SCEA Montemagni, 20253 Patrimonio, tel. 04.95.37.00.80, fax 04.95.37.17.15 🆅 🈺
🍷 ev. day 8am–12 noon 2pm–6pm

THE SOUTH WEST

Grouping appellations as far apart as Irouléguy, on the border with Spain, Bergerac, on the Garonne, and Gaillac, on the Tarn, the wine-growing region of the South West encompasses what the Bordelais call "wines from the high country" and the Adour vineyard. Until the railway was laid, the vineyards of the Garonne and the Dordogne were subject to Bordeaux wine regulations. With the benefit of its strong geographical location and royal support, the port of Lune was in a position to establish laws controlling the wines of Duras, Buzet, Fronton, Cahors, Gaillac and Bergerac. These regions had to wait for the whole of the Bordeaux harvest to be sold, primarily to the English and Dutch, before their wines could be shipped, and they were routinely employed as "dosing" wines to bolster certain clarets. The wines from the foothills of the Pyrenees were not subject to Bordeaux wine law but had to undergo a hazardous journey on the Adour to reach Bayonne. Understandably, their reputation hardly extended beyond their immediate vicinity.

Yet these vineyards, among the oldest in France, represent a living history of the vines of ancient times. In no other area do you find such a range of varieties. The Gascon taste in wine, as in all else, has always been marked by a determined individualism and a preference for the particular. The Manseng, Tannat, Négrette, Duras, Len de l'El (Loin de l'Oeil), Mauzac, Fer Servadou, Arrufiac or Baroque (the Cot), as well as the charmingly named Raffiat de Moncade, are varieties that emerge from the mists of viticultural history and give the local wines their authentic identity, honesty and unmatchable style. Far from despising the term "peasant" wine, these appellations embrace it with pride and give it due nobility. Wine-growing is far from the only agricultural activity in the region, and the wines have always been sold alongside other local produce that they accompany perfectly and naturally, making the South West a region where one can still enjoy the privilege of a traditional gastronomy.

Today, all the vineyards of the region are burgeoning, driven along by the wine cooperative movement and by committed owners. The great efforts being made to raise quality standards, through improved methods of cultivation, by researching cloned varieties better suited to local soils and conditions and by modernizing vinification techniques, mean that the wines are gradually becoming the best value for money in French wine.

The South West

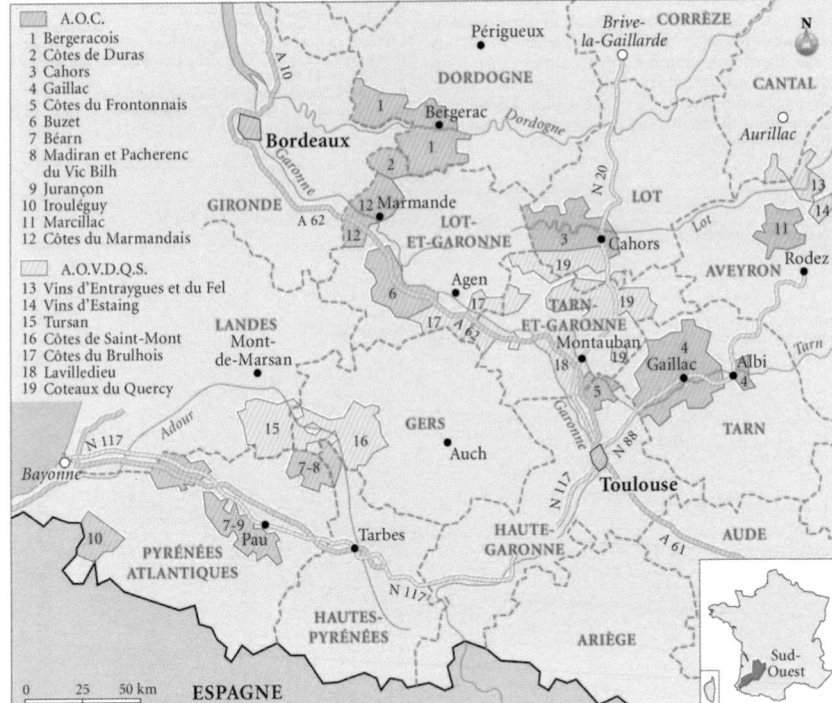

SOUTH WEST

Cahors

The Cahors vineyard (4,448 ha and 212,800 hl in 2002), dating from Roman times, is one of the oldest in France. Jean XXII, the Pope of Avignon, recruited wine makers from Quercy, in Cahors, to cultivate Châteauneuf-du-Pape. François I planted a vine variety from Cadurce in Fontainebleau that the Orthodox Church adopted as the wine for Mass, while the court of the Tsars chose it as a ceremonial wine. Yet the Cahors vineyard has had to come back from the brink. It was totally wiped out by frosts in 1956 and fell back to only 1% of its previous surface area. It was re-established in the meanders of the Lot valley and planted with traditional varieties, mainly Auxerrois, also known as Cot or Malbec, which represents 70% of the plantation along with Tannat (under 2%) and Merlot (about 20%). The terroir of Cahors has now regained the place it deserves among the areas producing wines of quality. In addition, brave attempts are being made to re-establish vineyards on the limestone plateaux that were cultivated in the past.

Cahors wines are powerful and robust, with a deep colour that has given rise to the English term "black wine". These are undoubtedly wines to be kept, yet Cahors wine can also be drunk young: at that stage it is plump and aromatic with good fruit, to be drunk slightly chilled with grilled meat, for example. After two or three years' bottle age it becomes firm and austere, becoming harmonious again after about the same period of time, when it produces aromas of undergrowth and spices. At this stage, its round, mouth-filling qualities make it an ideal wine to accompany charcoal-grilled truffles, cep mushrooms and game of the region. Though the character of the terroir and the varieties planted tend to produce wines capable of being kept, there is also a current trend to produce lighter wines that can be drunk more quickly.

CH. ARMANDIERE 2001★

	10 ha	60,000		5–8 €

This 23-ha vineyard has a crimson wine with black highlights made of Malbec (90%) and Merlot. The bouquet is fairly intense and complex, blending fruits and spices with a touch of violet, while the palate is soft, alcoholic and fruity, with fleshy tannins. This is a well-made Cahors.

➦ Bernard Bouyssou, Port de l'Angle, 46140 Parnac, tel. 05.65.36.75.97, fax 05.65.36.02.23, e-mail armandiere@aol.com ☑
☥ ev. day except Sun. 8am–7pm; cl. 20 Dec.–5 Jan.

DOM. LA BERANGERAIE La Gorgée de Mathis Bacchus Elevé en fût de chêne 2000★

	2 ha	5,000		15–23 €

Bérenger invite their visitors to taste their products on a panoramic terrace overlooking the 22-ha vineyard. Here you will find a dense aubergine-coloured wine. The glass releases strong woody perfumes with toasty and spicy notes, heralding the substantial tannic structure of an impressive palate. The finish is subdued, but the tannins need time to soften. Keep this for three to five years.

➦ Famille Bérenger, Dom. La Bérangeraie, coteaux de Cournou, 46700 Grézels, tel. 05.65.31.94.59, fax 05.65.31.94.64, e-mail berangeraie@wanadoo.fr ☑
☥ ev. day 9am–12 noon 2pm–6pm

CH. BLADINIERES
Préférence 2000★★

	3 ha	24,000		3–5 €

Auxerrois (85%) and Merlot make up this garnet-red wine with purple glints, which releases perfumes of stewed fruits (strawberry) and menthol. The first impression is soft, with a rounded, rich and fairly powerful palate. The tannins are evident, but not overly so, and combine with a good recurring fruity taste in a warm finish. The **Cuvée B 2000 Elevée en Fût de Chêne (8–11 €)** wins one star.

➦ Marie-Claire et Serge Bladinières, Le Bourg, 46220 Pescadoires, tel. 05.65.22.41.85, fax 05.65.36.47.10 ☑
☥ ev. day except Sun. 8am–12 noon 2pm–7pm

Cahors

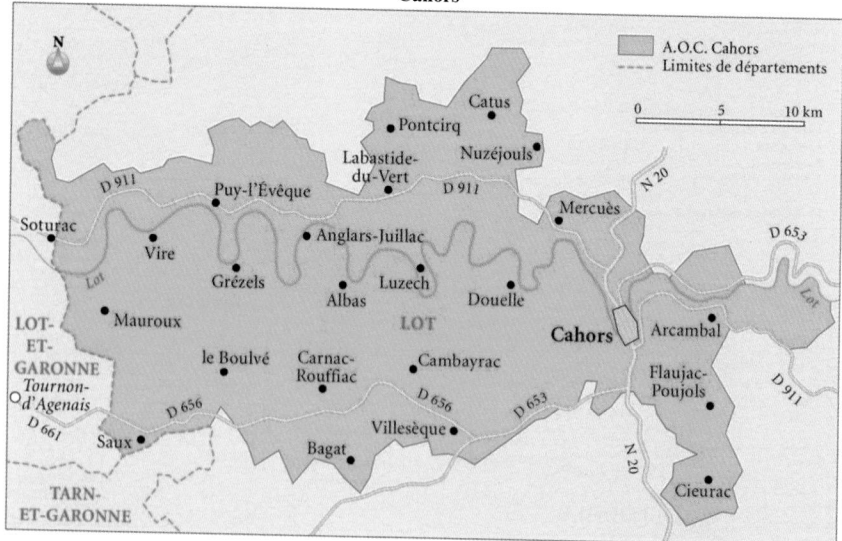

CH. DE CALASSOU 2000★★

■	1 ha	8,000	▮ 3–5 €

This brilliant-black Cahors has plenty of character. The fruit (strawberry) emerges clearly from the aromas and can be tasted fully in the full rich body, which has a remarkable structure. The wine shows all the signs of good extraction.
☛ Michel Souveton, Ch. de Calassou, 46700 Duravel, tel. 05.65.24.62.67, fax 05.65.36.47.22 ☑ ▦
☖ ev. day 8am–8pm

CH. LA CAMINADE
La Commandery 2001★★

■	5.22 ha	28,000	◗◗ 11–15 €

The **Cuvée Esprit 2001 (30–38 €)** offers undeniable potential which is worth one star, but La Commandery steals the show and proves the great skill of its maker. The colour of black-cherry, it offers a complex, still subdued bouquet with musky notes. When the glass is swirled, scents of morello cherry on buttered toast reveal themselves. It develops in a balanced way, combining power and elegance, thanks to the integrated tannins. The woody accents do not disturb the wine's flavours.
☛ M. Resses et Fils, SCEA Ch. La Caminade, 46140 Parnac, tel. 05.65.30.73.05, fax 05.65.20.17.04, e-mail resses@wanadoo.fr ☑
☖ ev. day except Sat. Sun. 9am–11.30am 2pm–6pm

DOM. DE CAUSE
Notre-Dame-des-Champs 2001★

■	2.3 ha	13,000	◗◗ 11–15 €

Between the valleys of the Lot and the Thèze, the estate's 13 ha of vines benefit from a pleasant argilo-siliceous terroir. This Cahors made from pure Cot has a dark-burlat cherry colour. Throughout the tasting it releases relatively complex woody notes, along with spices, liquorice and toast, enclosing firm tannins, which will soften with time. The finish reveals notes of violet under wreaths of smoke.
☛ Serge et Martine Costes, Cavagnac, 46700 Soturac, tel. 05.65.36.41.96, fax 05.65.36.41.95, e-mail domainedecause@wanadoo.fr ☑
☖ ev. day 9.30am–12 noon 2pm–6pm; Sun. by appt.

CH. DU CEDRE
Le Cèdre 2001★★

■	13 ha	48,000	◗◗ 23–30 €

The Verhaeghe brothers rank among the best producers of the appellation, with a long line of selected wines in their 14 years in the *Guide*. The almost black colour of this 2001 wine indicates its strong concentration. The wine opens with perfumes of black fruits in *eau-de vie*, before releasing balsamic accents with clear woody overtones. It acquires its fullest expression with a rich, fleshy and mouth-filling body of good length and remarkable complexity. The finish is enhanced by already silky tannins, which make this wine one to lay down. The **Cuvée GC 2001 (46–76 €)** has an elegant label and is very successful.
☛ Verhaeghe Fils, Bru, 46700 Vire-sur-Lot, tel. 05.65.36.53.87, fax 05.65.24.64.36, e-mail chateauducedre@wanadoo.fr ☑
☖ ev. day except Sun. 9am–12 noon 2pm–6pm

CH. CERINNE 2001★

■	1 ha	6,000	▮ 3–5 €

Jean and Marise Delsériès cultivate only 4 ha, but with great passion. You will soon appreciate their garnet-red Cahors with its perfumes of cherry in *eau-de vie*, truffles and its musky nuances. More developed, rounded and soft aromas come to the fore on the balanced palate.
☛ Jean and Marise Delsériès, Sarlat, 46700 Puy-l'Evêque, tel. 05.65.30.80.68, fax 05.65.30.80.69 ☑
☖ ev. day except Thu. Sun. 10am–12.30pm 3pm–7pm

CH. DE CHAMBERT
Orphée 2000★

■	4 ha	18,000	◗◗ 15–23 €

A vineyard of 58 ha stands today on this historic site, at first a place of retreat in the 15th century and then a château in the 19th. Its Orphée has a dense black-cherry colour, with perfumes of very ripe black fruits, along with notes of spice and balsam (cedar and eucalyptus) in the oak. Its heady palate is both fleshy and ripe, and leaves a warm impression at the finish, in which the oak is still evident. This powerful wine should be laid down for two to six years.
☛ Delgoulet, SCA Ch. de Chambert, Les Hauts Coteaux, 46700 Floressas, tel. 05.65.31.95.75, fax 05.65.31.93.56, e-mail bl@chateaudechambert.com ☑
☖ ev. day 8.30am–12.30pm 1.30pm–6.30pm

LE CLOS D'UN JOUR 2001★★

■	4 ha	12,000	▮ ♦ 5–8 €

In 2000, Véronique and Stéphane Azemar fell in love with this farm dating from the end of the 19th century, and have just finished restoring it while cultivating their 5.5 ha of vines. They offer two attractive Cahors: the **Cuvée Un Jour ... 2001 (11–15 €)**, which wins one star; and this beautifully mature, deep-crimson wine with purple highlights, with its aromas of fruits and in particular blackberry. The tasters enjoyed its rich substance, both fleshy and structured, with its well-coated tannins and persistent fruitiness.
☛ Véronique et Stéphane Azemar, Le Port, 46700 Duravel, tel. 05.65.36.56.01, fax 05.65.36.56.01, e-mail s.azemar@free.fr ☑
☖ by appt.

CLOS TRIGUEDINA 2001★

■	30 ha	150,000	◗◗ 11–15 €

Me trigo de dina. It means "I'm longing for my dinner," and is the source of this famous estate's name. Be patient, though, because you will have to wait four to five years for this wine. It has real potential. At present it has a crimson colour with black highlights, an intense and concentrated bouquet of blackberry jam and smoky, tarry accents. The palate is rich, balanced and mouth filling with a good long structure. The **Balmont 2001 (5–8 €)** is also singled out.
☛ Baldès et Fils, Clos Triguedina, 46700 Puy-l'Evêque, tel. 05.65.21.30.81, fax 05.65.21.39.28, e-mail triguedina@ordi.fr ☑
☖ by appt.
☛ Jean-Luc Baldès

CH. COUAILLAC
Les Dames blanches 2000★

■	2 ha	6,000	▮ ◗◗ ♦ 5–8 €

The White Ladies of Couaillac, owls that call in the night, inspired the producer of this black wine with purplish glints, and fruity and slightly vanilla perfumes. On the palate it is supple, rounded and balanced, with recurring aromas of black fruits and strawberry at the finish.
☛ EARL Pasbeau-Couaillac, La Séoune, 46140 Sauzet, tel. 05.65.36.90.82, fax 05.65.36.96.41, e-mail franck.pasbeau@wanadoo.fr ☑
☖ ev. day except Sun. 8am–12 noon 2pm–6pm

CH. LA COUSTARELLE
L'Eclat 2000★★

■	1 ha	5,000	◗◗ 23–30 €

The "coustarelle" is a small hill facing south and southwest on the right bank of the Lot. Its Malbec has reached perfect maturity, to judge from this crimson wine with purple highlights. It is expressive, with good-quality oak in the accents of toasted, buttered and vanilla bread. It gains power on the palate, which is full bodied and concentrated, and is supported by a long and substantial framework of fleshy tannins. The oak needs to soften and make room for the fruit.
☛ SCEA Michel et Nadine Cassot, Ch. La Coustarelle, 46220 Prayssac, tel. 05.65.22.40.10, fax 05.65.30.62.46 ☑
☖ ev. day except Sun. 9am–12.30pm 2pm–8pm

GRAND COUTALE 2001★★

■	3 ha	10,000	◗◗ 30–38 €

The **Clos La Coutale 2001 (5–8 €)** is very successful and wins one star for its pleasant fruitiness and full-bodied character, which makes it ready to drink now. The Grand Coutale is better still by virtue of its remarkable concentration, already evident in the dark black-cherry colour. Intense jammy perfumes emerge from a gently oaky base, heralding a rich,

soft substance, which combines perfectly with the oak and the fruit. This wine is both powerful and elegant.
➽ Clos la Coutale, 46700 Vire-sur-Lot, tel. 05.65.36.51.47, fax 05.65.24.63.73, e-mail info@coutale.com ☑
⟰ by appt.

CH. LES CROISILLE 2001★

| ■ | 0.8 ha | 2,000 | ⦿ | 11–15 € |

In 2000, the Croisilles planted their 12-ha estate around the family house. However, they have more than 20 years' experience of winemaking. It comes through in this very clear-cut Cahors with its fruity perfumes (blackberry and bilberry), spices (vanilla and cinnamon) and a note of roasting coffee. It has a crimson colour with dark highlights and on the palate it is fairly soft, well balanced, long and full of fruit. You can choose whether to drink it now or wait for three to four years.
➽ B. et C. Croisille, Fages, 46140 Luzech, tel. 05.65.30.53.88, fax 05.65.30.70.33, e-mail contact@chateaulescroisille.fr.st ☑
⟰ ev. day except Sun. 10am–7pm; groups by appt.

CROIX DU MAYNE
Elevé en fût de chêne 2001★★★

| ■ | 16 ha | 120,000 | ⦿ | 5–8 € |

A unanimous *coup de coeur* for this rich and intense black, velvety Cahors that releases scents of blackberry and black-cherry and complex oaky notes: incense, camphor, menthol and a note of roasting coffee. This mouth-filling wine has an elegant structure with excellent aromas and vigour. It has good length on a framework of subtle tannins.
➽ SCEV François Pélissié, 46140 Anglars-Juillac, tel. 05.65.21.45.37, fax 05.65.21.45.38
⟰ by appt.

CH. EUGENIE Cuvée réservée de l'Aïeul Elevé en fût de chêne 2001★★

| ■ | 7 ha | 45,000 | ⦿ | 8–11 € |

This winemaking château is very old, its wines mentioned in archives dating from 1470. They are of high quality, too, and this Cahors was one of those most appreciated by the Grand Jury. Deep fruity perfumes (raspberry and bilberry) emerge from this black wine, accompanied by spices on an oak base. It has a rich and concentrated body, cloaking high-class tannins, which support the liquorice in the finish.
➽ Ch. Eugénie, Rivière-Haute, 46140 Albas, tel. 05.65.30.73.51, fax 05.65.20.19.81, e-mail contact@chateaueugenie.com ☑
⟰ ev. day 9.30am–12.30pm 2pm–7pm; groups by appt.; cl. Sun. except Jul.–Aug.
➽ Couture

CH. FANTOU
L'Elite 2000★

| ■ | 0.9 ha | 4,000 | ⦿ | 11–15 € |

The Cuvée Prestige La Batelière Vieilli en Fût de Chêne 2000 (5–8 €) is singled out for its elegance. This is also a characteristic of this dark-red wine with purplish nuances, its intense aromas of black fruits taking shape on a vanilla base. The palate is rounded and fleshy, and retains the fruity and spicy flavour supported by lingering oak. This Cahors is already pleasant to drink.

➽ B. A. A. Aldhuy, Dom. de Fantou, 46220 Prayssac, tel. 05.65.30.61.85, fax 05.65.22.45.69, e-mail domainedefantou@wanadoo.fr ☑
⟰ ev. day except Sun. 8am–7pm

CH. DE GAUDOU
Renaissance 2001★

| ■ | 3.52 ha | 21,120 | ⦿ | 15–23 € |

Grown on the third terraces of the Lot, this dark, almost black wine releases a varied range of perfumes: soft fruits, pepper, liquorice and menthol. It is rounded, full and winey with good balance and integrated tannins. The oak re-emerges at the finish with liquorice and mineral notes.
➽ Durou et Fils, Gaudou, 46700 Vire-sur-Lot, tel. 05.65.36.52.93, fax 05.65.36.53.60, e-mail info@chateaudegaudou.com
⟰ by appt.

CH. LES GRAUZILS 2001★★

| ■ | 15 ha | 80,000 | 🍶 ♦ | 5–8 € |

This vineyard was established in 1880 and now has 20 ha of vines. Alongside a Cuvée Duc d'Istrie Elevé en Fût de Chêne 2001 (8–11 €), which was judged very successful, the tasters found this purplish Cahors to be well made and full with lasting perfumes of very ripe fruits and liquorice. It combines power, without being hard, and a persistent fruitiness. Its maturity was clear throughout the tasting. This wine could still be kept for a while.
➽ Philippe Pontié, Gamot, 46220 Prayssac, tel. 05.65.30.22.44, fax 05.65.22.46.09, e-mail contact@chateau-les-grauzils.com ☑ 🏠
⟰ ev. day except Sun. 9am–12 noon 2pm–7pm

CH. DE HAUTERIVE 2001★

| ■ | 9.5 ha | 60,000 | 🍶 ♦ | 5–8 € |

A dish of lamb would go well with this already pleasant wine with an elegant structure and a silky framework. This is a balanced wine, fresh and fruity beneath its intense-crimson colour. The Cuvée Elevée en Fût de Chêne 2001 (8–11 €) was also commended.
➽ Filhol et Fils, Le Bourg, 46700 Vire-sur-Lot, tel. 05.65.36.52.84, fax 05.65.24.64.93 ☑
⟰ ev. day except Sun. 8am–12.30pm 2pm–7pm

CH. HAUT MONPLAISIR
Pur Plaisir 2001★★

| ■ | 3.35 ha | 12,000 | ⦿ | 15–23 € |

An elegant label heralding a "Pur Plaisir" leads us to this intense burlat cherry Cahors, which perfectly combines fruity scents (morello cherry and blackcurrant) and oak, with toasty nuances. Its very fine balance results from an alliance of fresh fruitiness and a concentrated, mouth-filling and structured body, in which the oak is not obtrusive. It is elegant and already very good to drink.
➽ Daniel et Cathy Fournié, Ch. Haut Monplaisir, 46700 Lacapelle-Cabanac, tel. 05.65.24.64.78, fax 05.65.24.68.90 ☑
⟰ ev. day except Sun. 9am–12 noon 3pm–7pm

CH. LES HAUTS D'AGLAN
A 2001★★

| ■ | 2.7 ha | 10,600 | 🍶 ♦ | 15–23 € |

In 2000, the owners decided to create an "A" vintage. This new wine has an intense-garnet colour and a powerful bouquet, mainly of ripe fruit (blackcurrant and blackberry). The powerful and distinguished palate has a chewy taste supported by a sturdy structure. The tannins, benefiting from good extraction, help to produce a long finish.
➽ Isabelle Rey-Auriat, Aglan, 46700 Soturac, tel. 05.65.36.52.02, fax 05.65.24.64.27, e-mail isabelle.auriat@terre-net.fr ☑
⟰ ev. day except Sun. 9am–7pm

CH. LES IFS 2001★★

| ■ | 8 ha | 30,000 | 🍶 ♦ | 5–8 € |

This wine has great finesse and won over the tasters from the start with its clear and brilliant-garnet colour. It has perfumes of soft fruits, liquorice and violet. This is a well-structured, natural wine rich in fruit on fine and silky tannins. This harmonious wine is there to be enjoyed. The **Cuvée Prestige 2000** wins one star.

- Buri et Fils, EARL La Laurière, 46220 Pescadoires, tel. 05.65.22.44.53, fax 05.65.30.68.52, e-mail chateau.les.ifs@wanadoo.fr ☑
- ev. day except Sun. 8am–12 noon 2pm–7pm

IMPERNAL

Vieilli en fût de chêne 2001★★

	20 ha	120,000	⊪	8–11 €

There were plenty of prizes for this cooperative from the Côtes d'Olt: **Château Cayrou d'Albas Elevé en Fût de Chêne 2001 (5–8 €)** wins one star, while the **Château Beauvillain-Monpezat 2001 (5–8 €)**, the **Le Paradis Vieilli en Fût de Chêne Neuf 2000 (15–23 €)** and the **Château Les Bouysses 2001** win two stars. To complete the selection, the tasters were also impressed by this dazzling garnet-red Impernal, so heady and expressive with its aromas of spices, soft fruits and burnt wood. The palate is rounded and remains full bodied. The structure is certainly ample, but the tannins are coated with substance. A balanced, beautiful and good wine.

- Cave coop. Côtes d'Olt, 46140 Parnac, tel. 05.65.30.71.86, fax 05.65.30.35.28 ☑
- by appt.

CH. LACAPELLE CABANAC

Cuvée Prestige Elevé en fût de chêne 2001★★

	2 ha	9,000	⊪	5–8 €

Thierry Simon and Philippe Vérax have done well in their first year of winemaking, after taking over the property in August 2001. This very dark, almost black wine clearly bears the signs of 14 months in barrel with its intense charred perfumes and notes of raspberry and clove. It is full, rounded and fleshy, and benefits from supple and integrated tannins to leave a tasty impression. The fruit persists on a base of toast and liquorice. "A good guide for the wines of 2001," was the conclusion of one taster.

- SCEA Ch. de Lacapelle, Thierry Simon et Philippe Vérax, 46700 Lacapelle-Cabanac, tel. 05.65.36.51.92, fax 05.65.36.52.62, e-mail contact@lacapelle-cabanac.com ☑
- by appt.

CH. LAMARTINE

Expression 2000★

	3.5 ha	20,000	⊪	15–23 €

The "Expression" represents a terroir and a grape variety, Cot. It will take some years for this dark-aubergine 2000 to reach its full potential. The bouquet is already powerful and complex with perfumes of morello cherry in *eau-de-vie*, menthol and liquorice, and good support from the oak. The palate has a generous, rich structure, a firm body and fairly lively tannins. The aromatic expression seems more open. This wine has serious potential.

- SCEA Ch. Lamartine, 46700 Soturac, tel. 05.65.36.54.14, fax 05.65.24.65.31, e-mail chateau-lamartine@wanadoo.fr ☑
- ev. day 9.30am–12 noon 2pm–6.30pm; Sun. by appt.
- Alain Gayraud

CH. LATUC 2000★

	3 ha	22,000	ⓘ ♦	5–8 €

This estate seems like a pan-European project. In 1989, some English people created the Domaine Latuc brand, while in 2002 the vineyard, of approximately 19 ha, was taken over by two Belgian agronomists who trained in Alsace. This wine has a ruby colour with brilliant highlights. On aromas of red fruits are clean and intense, it makes a soft first impression on the palate and continues to show roundness as the pleasant fruity taste reappears.

- EARL Dom. de Latuc, Laborie, 46700 Mauroux, tel. 05.65.36.58.63, fax 05.65.24.61.57, e-mail info@latuc.com ☑
- ev. day 9am–11.30am 2pm–7pm
- Famille Meyan

CH. LERET MONPEZAT 2001★

	50 ha	80,000	⊪	8–11 €

Ten years after its first vintage (the 1991), Jean-Baptiste de Monpezat offers a brilliant-ruby Cahors. The powerful scents of plum and bilberry are surrounded by nuances of roasting, while the body appears supple thanks to a structure of fine, slightly sweet tannins. The wine and the oak combine perfectly.

- SCEA Jean-Baptiste de Monpezat, Ch. Leret-Monpezat, BP 159, 46003 Cahors Cedex 9, tel. 05.65.20.80.80, fax 05.65.20.80.81, e-mail vigouroux@g-vigouroux.fr ☑
- by appt.

DOM. DE MAISON NEUVE 2000★

	9.36 ha	19,000	ⓘ ♦	5–8 €

This garnet-red wine with purplish highlights releases subdued notes of soft fruits. The attack is supple, then the wine grows more mouth filling and powerful, though the tannins are still austere. The aromas at the finish are more complex than in the bouquet.

- Delmouly, Maison Neuve, 46800 Le Boulve, tel. 05.65.31.95.76, fax 05.65.31.93.80 ☑
- by appt.

CH. DE MERCUES 2001★

	40 ha	70,000	⊪	8–11 €

The label faithfully reproduces the elegant feudal silhouette of this château, the summer residence of the bishops of Cahors for twelve centuries and today listed in the *Relais et Châteaux*. This 2001 wine has a ruby-garnet colour and releases intense perfumes of soft fruits and sweet spices on a base of charred oak. Although the tannins are still firm, they are enclosed by pleasant oaky notes and a rounded flesh. This is a well-made wine with a powerful finish.

- GFA Georges Vigouroux, Ch. de Mercuès, 46090 Mercuès, tel. 05.65.20.80.80, fax 05.65.20.80.81, e-mail vigouroux@g.vigouroux.fr ☑
- by appt.

METAIRIE GRANDE DU THERON

La Métairie 2001★

	2 ha	6,000	⊪	11–15 €

A vast square court stands in front of this Quercy-style edifice built after the Revolution, which today has 23 ha of vines. The estate's **Cuvée Classique 2001 (5–8 €)**, made from 90% Auxerrois and 10% Merlot, was singled out, but this pure Auxerrois attracted more attention. The intense-ruby colour with garnet highlights gives rise to powerful scents that are both fruity and floral, accompanied by touches of liquorice and smoke. After a fresh first impression, the wine fills the mouth beautifully, and the tannic structure is impressive and oaky with accents of vanilla and roasted coffee. This is a balanced wine that needs laying down.

- Liliane Barat Sigaud, Métairie Grande du Théron, 46220 Prayssac, tel. 05.65.22.41.80, fax 05.65.30.67.32 ☑
- by appt.

CH. NOZIERES 2001★★

	15 ha	100,000	ⓘ ♦	5–8 €

While the **Cuvée L'Elégance 2001 (11–15 €)**, matured in barrel, wins one star for its fruitiness, this crimson 2001 with purple highlights, which was not kept in oak, is already very pleasant to drink now, however it may develop in future. It opens with generous perfumes of blackcurrant and mineral notes, then after a clean attack reveals its fullness and balance, and finishes with agreeably spicy flavours.

- Maradenne-Guitard, Bru, 46700 Vire-sur-Lot, tel. 05.65.36.52.73, fax 05.65.36.50.62 ☑
- ev. day except Sun. 8am–12 noon 2pm–7pm
- Guitard

CH. DE PARNAC

Olympe de Gouges Elevé en fût de chêne 2000★

	4.5 ha	1,500	⊪	15–23 €

In 1793, Olympe de Gouges, after finding refuge in Parnac, was guillotined for having defended the equality of the sexes when defining the rights of Man. This wine pays homage to him. It has an inky colour with crimson highlights, and releases perfumes of black fruits and kirsch, and an intense

SOUTH WEST

oakiness with toasty accents. The powerful and well-structured palate is sufficiently fleshy, then becomes more concentrated in an oaky finish over solid tannins. Let this wine mature for a few years.

➤ Georges Delmas, La Condamine, 46140 Parnac, tel. 05.65.30.73.84, fax 05.65.30.98.21 ☑ ⌂

⌶ by appt.

➤ SCI de Parnac

LE PIGEONNIER 2000★★

■	2 ha	6,300	⑴	46–76 €

LE PIGEONNIER

CAHORS
APPELLATION CAHORS CONTRÔLÉE

While the **Château Lagrézette 2001 (11–15 €)**, matured for 18 months in barrel, is already remarkable and very fruity, full and well structured with integrated tannins, Le Pigeonnier was thought to be a better representative of the 2000 vintage. It is almost opaque, with a black tulip colour, and releases a profusion of spices, ripe black fruits, and liquorice and balsamic notes. Its tasty and elegant body fills the mouth and is evidence of very good extraction. Its maturation for 24 months was carried out with great skill.

➤ Alain-Dominique Perrin, SCEV La Grézette, Dom. de Lagrézette, 46140 Caillac, tel. 05.65.20.07.42, fax 05.65.20.06.95 ☑

⌶ by appt.

CH. DE PONS

L'Eden Vinifié et élevé en fût de chêne 2000★

■	1 ha	3,500	⑴	15–23 €

The burlat cherry colour has brilliant and intense-purple highlights, heralding a powerful bouquet full of perfumes of fruits in spirit and toast. The rich and concentrated body rests on evident but well-coated tannins; the alcoholic finish bears the mark of the oak along with notes of pepper and liquorice. This is a substantial Cahors, which should be laid down.

➤ Pascal et André Semenadisse, Pons, 46800 Fargues, tel. 05.65.36.91.32, fax 05.65.24.97.13, e-mail chateaudepons@wanadoo.fr ☑

⌶ by appt.

PRIMO PALATUM

Classica 2001★★★

■	n.c.	3,600	⑴	15–23 €

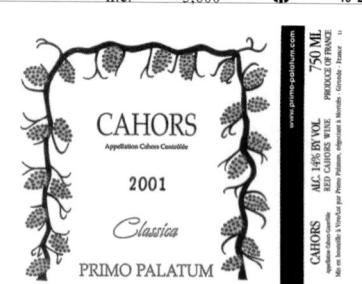

CAHORS
Appellation Cahors Contrôlée

2001

Classica

PRIMO PALATUM

This "Classica" has a beautiful ruby-red colour, which is both expressive and refined. The bouquet judiciously combines complex oaky nuances with notes of butter, mocha coffee and

plenty of fruitiness. The lingering aromas are balanced, supported on an elegant structure with a silky texture. Wine and oak are in perfect harmony. The integrated tannins make it possible to drink this wine now with foie gras, or it could be kept for two or three years.

➤ Primo Palatum, 1, Cirette, 33190 Morizès, tel. 05.56.71.39.39, fax 05.56.71.39.40, e-mail xavier-copel@primo-palatum.com ☑

⌶ by appt.

➤ Xavier Copel

DOM. DU PRINCE

Lou Prince 2000★★

■	0.77 ha	1,800	⑴	15–23 €

This wine was in the front rank of the Cahors tasted by the Grand Jury. Its dense-aubergine colour with black highlights displays a resolutely modern style. It has strong perfumes of macerated fruits and spices with nuances of toast. The grip is firm and alcoholic, with good flesh, supported by a very tasty, notably toasty oak.

➤ Jouves, GAEC de Pauliac, Cournou, 46140 Saint-Vincent-Rive-d'Olt, tel. 05.65.20.14.09, fax 05.65.30.78.94, e-mail domaine.du.prince@libertysurf.fr ☑

⌶ by appt.

CH. LA REYNE

Vent d'Ange 2001★★★

■	0.3 ha	1,600	⑴	30–38 €

This Vent d'Ange was given fourth place by the Grand Jury – no surprise given the concentration of its colour, and the purple tears visible all down the glass. Here is a rich wine, releasing complex scents of fine oak with perfumes of stewed fruits and spices. Its expressive nature is confirmed in the concentrated, rounded and balanced body that lasts all through the tasting. This is a powerful Cahors and yet very integrated and tasty. It is a pity it will only reach a limited public.

➤ Ch. la Reyne, Leygues, 46700 Puy-l'Evêque, tel. 05.65.30.82.53, fax 05.65.21.39.83 ☑

⌶ ev. day except Sun. 9am–12 noon 2pm–6pm

➤ Johan Vidal

CH. DES ROCHES

Vendémiaire 2001★

■	2 ha	10,500	▮	3–5 €

This wine has an intense-garnet colour and a clear-cut, very fruity bouquet (raspberry, fresh blackcurrant and a note of elder), and is not devoid of charm despite its alcoholic character, for it is both mouth filling and has pleasant tannins. The **Le Serment Elevé en Fût de Chêne 2001 (11–15 €)** was also singled out.

➤ Jean Labroue, Les Roches, 46220 Prayssac, tel. 05.65.30.61.49, fax 05.65.30.83.53 ☑

⌶ by appt.

CH. SAINT-DIDIER-PARNAC 2001★

■	37 ha	300,000	⑴	5–8 €

In the 18th century, wines from the château Saint-Didier were sent to Eastern Europe and shipped to the Indies. The old vaulted cellars are still there. This black, velvety Cahors combines a subdued oaky note with spicy nuances and scents of blackcurrant and violet. Thanks to its fairly integrated tannins, it leaves an impression of roundness and balance, finishing on strong toasted notes.

➤ Rigal, Ch. Saint-Didier, 46140 Parnac, tel. 05.65.30.70.10, fax 05.65.20.16.24, e-mail rigal@ordi.fr ☑

⌶ ev. day 8am–12 noon 2pm–6pm

DOM. DU THERON

Cuvée Prestige 2001★

■	5 ha	20,000	⑴	15–23 €

Five years from now, you will be able to enjoy the full development of this intense garnet-red wine which combines fruitiness with toasty and spicy notes deriving from 16 months in oak. This balance and complexity are confirmed in a rounded,

fairly full-bodied palate, although the tannins are firmer at the finish.
- SCEA Dom. du Théron, Le Théron, 46220 Prayssac, tel. 05.65.30.64.51, fax 05.65.30.69.20, e-mail domaine.theron@libertysurf.fr ☑
- ev. day 10am–1pm 2pm–6pm; Sat. Sun. by appt.
- M. Pauwels

DOM. DE VINSSOU 2001★

■	2 ha	8,000	5–8 €

This characteristic Cahors should be drunk young, while it is still has its crimson nuances and fine perfumes of soft fruits, and the fruity freshness of a soft and well-balanced body. A Rocamadour cheese will go well with this wine.
- Louis Delfau, Dom. de Vinssou, rue du Castagnol, 46090 Mercuès, tel. 05.65.30.99.91, fax 05.65.30.99.91 ☑
- ev. day 10am–8pm; groups by appt.

Wines selected but not starred

CH. GAUTOUL
Cuvée Petit Château Gautoul

■	30 ha	40,000	3–5 €

- Ch. Gautoul, 46700 Puy-l'Evêque, tel. 05.65.30.84.17, fax 05.65.30.85.17, e-mail gautoul@gautoul.com ☑
- ev. day 10am–12 noon 2pm–5pm; Sat. Sun. and groups by appt.
- Swenden

Coteaux du Quercy AOVDQS

Located between Cahors and Gaillac, the Quercy wine region is of recent date although, as is common throughout the South West region, vines were grown there in prehistoric times. In between, winemaking suffered several setbacks. In the first century AD, an edict by the Emperor Domitien banned the planting of new vines outside Italy: in the 15th century, the supremacy of Bordeaux spoiled the region's markets, and at the beginning of the 20th century the sheer volume of production in Languedoc and Roussillon had the same effect. Research aimed at improving quality was launched in 1965; hybrid stocks were replaced, and this raised the region to Vin de Pays status in 1976.

Gradually, producers managed to sort out the best grape varieties and the best soils. These improvements in quality culminated in promotion to the AOVDQS category on 28 December 1999. The official territory extends across 33 communes in the departments of Lot and Tarn-et-Garonne.

Appellation wines are limited to reds and rosés. The red wines have a deep-purple colour and are full bodied and hearty, with complex aromas deriving from their Cabernet Franc content,

the main variety which may account for up to 60% of a particular wine, the others being Tannat, Cot, Gamay Noir and Merlot, each up to a limit of 20%. The rosé wines are fruity and lively, and made from the same varieties.

Total production in 2002 amounted to about 14,792 hl from vines covering nearly 385 ha, and comes from about thirty producers, three of which are cooperatives.

BESSEY DE BOISSY
Tradition 2000★

■	15 ha	106,600	3–5 €

Pretty cherry highlights immediately catch the eye, then subtle perfumes of garrigue and overripe fruits blossom forth, with a hint of mentholated herbs. The first impression is supple, and the wine has delightful balance and lasting fruitiness.
- Vignerons du Quercy, RN 20, 82270 Montpezat-de-Quercy, tel. 05.63.02.03.50, fax 05.63.02.00.60, e-mail lesvigneronsduquercy@tiscali.fr ☑
- by appt.

DOM. DE CERROU 2002★

■	5 ha	38,000	3–5 €

This deep-crimson wine with dark-purple glints is a blend of Cabernet, Merlot and Gamay. It is a full-bodied 2002, full of soft fruits and spices, with a note of green pepper. On the palate it is rounded and quite fresh, always fruity and spicy, with a supple structure and a fairly mature body.
- Cave coop. Côtes d'Olt, 46140 Parnac, tel. 05.65.30.71.86, fax 05.65.30.35.28 ☑
- by appt.

DOM. DES GANAPES 2000★

■	4.6 ha	13,333	3–5 €

Jean-Marc Séguy farms just over 11 ha of vines on the hillsides of Mirabel. His Cabernet Franc, Merlot and Tannat grapes have matured well on this terroir to make this 2000 vintage, so much so that one can already taste a complex and original wine combining scents of dried flowers, ripe fruits, musk and mint. It is supple with good aromas, and sufficiently full and balanced to remain pleasant up to the finish.
- Jean-Marc Séguy, Ambayrac, 82440 Realville, tel. 05.63.31.04.81, fax 05.63.31.04.81, e-mail ganapes@wanadoo.fr ☑
- ev. day 8am–12 noon 2pm–7pm

DOM. DE LACOSTE
Vignes du Moulin Elevé en fût de chêne 2000★

■	1 ha	4,800	5–8 €

This estate, established in 1991 on land belonging to the *Lycée Agricole de Cahors-Le-Montat*, exports 15% of its production. This subtle ruby 2000 will no doubt be in demand. It starts out on spicy notes (pepper and cinnamon), then grows more intense as the perfumes of black fruits and oaky notes come through. The body and the oak soften harmoniously after a fresh first impression, and the finish reveals plenty of spices, bringing an original touch to the wine.
- Dom. de Lacoste, LEPA du Montat, 46090 Le Montat, tel. 05.65.21.03.67, fax 05.65.21.00.01, e-mail lpa.cahors@educagri.fr ☑
- by appt.
- Ministère de l'Agriculture

DOM. DE MAZUC 2001★

■	4.5 ha	25,000	3–5 €

With its morello cherry colour, this intense and fine wine opens with good scents of jam on a base of cocoa and mineral notes. The palate is rounded and supple with very good balance: the rich tannins are evident but smooth, and the taste is clean. This wine lacks for nothing.
- Erick Carles, Mazuc, 82240 Puylaroque, tel. 05.63.64.90.91, e-mail domainedemazuc@wanadoo.fr ☑
- by appt.

DOM. DU MERCHIEN 2001★★

■	5 ha	12,000	■	3–5 €

This was a fine performance by David and Sarah Meakin, whose two red Coteaux-du-Quercy 2001 wines were judged to be remarkable: **the label on which the dog motif is in red (5–8 €)** and the gold label, is a blend of Cabernet Franc, Merlot, Cot, Gamay and Tannat. The latter wins a *coup de coeur*. It has a youthful garnet-red colour with purplish nuances, but nevertheless has rich, deep perfumes of black fruits, flowers, pepper and spices. It develops in roundness, becoming full and alcoholic, with a generous and fruity body. The tannins are evident, but well coated in a tasty finish.
✦┓ David et Sarah Meakin, Dom. du Merchien, Penchenier, 46230 Belfort-du-Quercy, tel. 05.63.64.97.21,
fax 05.63.64.97.21, e-mail wine@merchien.net ☑ ✿
𝖸 by appt.

DOM. DE PECH BELY

Cuvée Col rouge 2001★

■	1.33 ha	6,650	■	5–8 €

Montaigu-de-Quercy is very like a dream version of a village in the South West, with its 18th century houses, its dovecote, and its ovens for bread and plums. The Pech Bely 2001 is a very successful wine. Slightly musky at first, it opens with black and red fruits, and spices. This slightly spicy tone recurs in the finish along with fine tannins, which support a rounded, full and fruity body. Make sure you take a walk through the lovely village.
✦┓ Richard et Jooris, Pech Bely,
82150 Montaigu-de-Quercy, tel. 05.63.94.47.28,
fax 05.63.95.31.79 ☑
𝖸 by appt.

DOM. SAINT JULIEN 2001★

■	4.5 ha	8,000	■	3–5 €

It has no more than an averagely red colour with purplish highlights, but don't go by appearances because this is a well-made wine. The bouquet reveals black fruits with spices and pepper, followed on the palate by ripe fruit which adds to the velvety character of this rounded and fresh wine. Well-coated tannins make a long spicy impression at the finish.
✦┓ GAEC Saint-Julien, Au Gros,
46170 Castelnau-Montratier, tel. 05.65.21.95.86,
fax 05.65.21.83.89, e-mail gaecsaintjulien@wanadoo.fr ☑
𝖸 by appt.
✦┓ Jacques Vignals

Wines selected but not starred

DOM. DE LA GARDE

Tradition 2001

■	7 ha	20,000	■ ⬥	5–8 €

✦┓ Jean-Jacques Bousquet, Le Mazut,
46090 Labastide-Marnhac, tel. 05.65.21.06.59,
fax 05.65.21.06.59 ☑
𝖸 ev. day except Sun. 9am–12 noon 2pm–7pm

DOM. DE LAFAGE

Tradition 2000

■	7 ha	40,000	■	5–8 €

✦┓ Bernard Bouyssou, Dom. de Lafage,
82270 Montpezat-du-Quercy, tel. 05.63.02.06.91,
fax 05.63.02.04.55 ☑
𝖸 by appt.

CH. VENT D'AUTAN 2000

■	2.9 ha	15,600	■ ⑪	8–11 €

✦┓ Anne Godin, Moustans-Haut, 46800 Saint-Matre,
tel. 05.65.31.96.75, fax 05.65.31.91.78 ☑
𝖸 by appt.

Gaillac

The origins of the Gaillac vineyard date back to the Roman occupation, as the Roman amphorae (terracotta wine vessels) made in Montels bear witness. In the 13th century, Raymond VII, Count of Toulouse, awarded his domains one of the first equivalents of an Appellation Contrôlée, while the Provençal poet, Auger Gaillard, sang the praises of sparkling Gaillac wine long before champagne had been invented. The vineyard (3,730 ha) is divided into the Premières Côtes (or lower slopes), the Hauts Coteaux, the higher slopes on the right bank of the Tarn, and the plain, the area around Cunac and the district of Cordais. In total the appellation produces 133,417 hl, of red wine and 36,167 hl of white wine.

The limestone slopes are ideal for the cultivation of traditional white vine varieties such as Mauzac, Len de l'El (Loin de l'Oeil), Ondenc, Sauvignon and Muscadelle. The gravel areas are reserved for red wine varieties such as Duras, Braucol or Fer Servadou, Syrah, Gamay, Négrette, Cabernet and Merlot. The range of varieties gives rise to the wide palette of flavours to be found in Gaillac wines.

Among the whites are to be found fresh and aromatic dry and sparkling wines, as well as the soft wines of the lower slopes, which are rich and supple. These wines draw their particular character from the Mauzac grape, historically responsible for the reputation of Gaillac wines. Sparkling Gaillac can be made either by the traditional local method of adding natural grape sugar, producing rather fruity wines, or by the Méthode Champenoise, which European legislation has decreed shall henceforth be known as Méthode Traditionelle. The easy-drinking rosés are produced by the saignée method, which allows the colour of the red skins to bleed into the must, while the red wines, which are said to keep well, have striking character and bouquet.

DOM. BARREAU

Doux Caprice d'Automne 2001★★

■	2.9 ha	9,050	■	11–15 €

Jean-Claude Barreau has been regularly producing good-quality wines since 1987, like this Caprice d'Automne which is continually featured in the *Guide*. His 2001 vintage has a bright colour with golden nuances, and delicate perfumes of dried fruits, crystallized fruits, honey and spices.

Gaillac

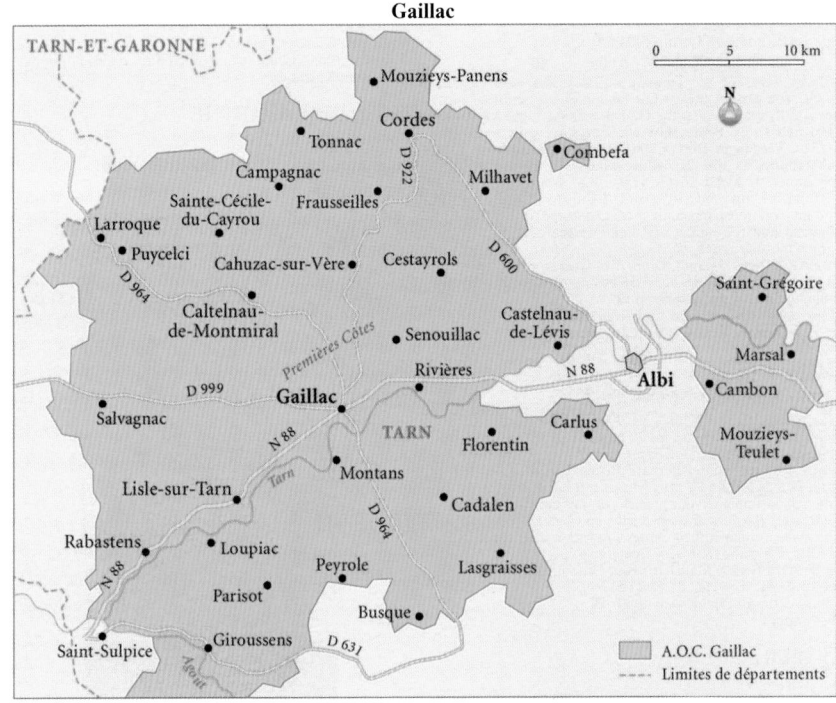

It is light on the palate, rounded and mouth filling, with a perfect balance between sweetness and freshness.
📞 Jean-Claude Barreau, Boissel, 81600 Gaillac, tel. 05.63.57.57.51, fax 05.63.57.66.37 ✅
🍷 by appt.

DOM. DE BONNEFIL
Cuvée L'Authentique 2001★

| ■ | 4 ha | 6,000 | 🍾 🍷 | 5–8 € |

Hints of morello cherry enliven this open and intense wine, grown in a gravel terroir. The bouquet starts on butter and hazelnut, quickly followed by soft fruits that continue on the supple, rounded and fresh palate. This balanced 2001 will go well with charcuterie.
📞 Alain et Martine Lagasse, Bonnefil, 81150 Lagrave, tel. 05.63.41.70.62, fax 05.63.41.70.62, e-mail domaine.de.bonnefil@wanadoo.fr ✅
🍷 ev. day 9.30am–12.30pm 3pm–7pm; Wed. Sun. by appt.

DOM. DE BROUSSE
Haut Cordurier 2001★

| ■ | 1.2 ha | 5,000 | 🍾 🍷 | 5–8 € |

Philippe and Suzanne Boissel grow nearly 7 ha of vines on the lower slopes of the Plateau Cordais. This wine is made from pure Braucol and has a clean and brilliant-red colour, with delicate scents of soft fruits and violet. Although it seems supple and light, it is still nicely balanced and, in particular, full of flavour up to the finish. The opening is the best part. The **Gaillac red Elevé en Fût de Chêne 2001** is also commended.
📞 Philippe et Suzanne Boissel, Dom. de Brousse, 81140 Cahuzac-sur-Vère, tel. 05.63.33.90.14, fax 05.63.33.90.14 ✅ 🏠
🍷 by appt.

BRUMES Doux Rêverie occitane dans les nuées automnales 2001★

| | 0.2 ha | 500 | 🍾 | 11–15 € |

Like its name, this pale-golden Gaillac is a pleasant daydream, dominated by perfumes of crystallized fruits, notes of honey and sweet almond. It is extremely fruity with a balanced softness and good length. Enjoy it as an aperitif.
📞 GAEC Les Salesses, Sainte-Cécile-d'Avès, 81600 Gaillac, tel. 05.63.57.26.89, fax 05.63.57.26.89 ✅ 🏠
🍷 ev. day 8am–12 noon 2pm–7pm
📞 Litré

CH. CANDASTRE
Elevé en fût de chêne 2001★

| ■ | 5.85 ha | 50,705 | 🍾 🍷 | 3–5 € |

The colour is splendid, an intense red, as sparkling as the warm perfumes of spices and cocoa. The tannins have softened to a velvety roundness that continues together with sweet vanilla nuances.
📞 SCEA Ch. Candastre, 81600 Gaillac, tel. 05.63.41.70.88, fax 05.63.57.60.44, e-mail candastre@wanadoo.fr

CH. CHAUMET LAGRANGE 2001★

| ■ | 4.5 ha | 30,000 | 🍾 🍷 | 3–5 € |

Christophe Boizard bought this estate of 34 ha in 2000. On its gravel terroir, he has made two impressive red wines. While the **Cuvée Tradition 2001 (5–8 €)** was singled out, the château's main wine appealed even more to the tasters with its rounded and supple flesh. It has an intense colour with crimson glints and releases pleasant perfumes of soft fruits and blackcurrant.
📞 SCEA Chaumet-Lagrange, Les Fediès, 81600 Gaillac, tel. 05.63.57.07.12, fax 05.63.57.64.12, e-mail chateau.ch.lagrange@wanadoo.fr ✅
🍷 by appt.
📞 Ch. Boizard

DOM. D'ESCAUSSES

Sec La Vigne de l'Oubli 2001★★

	2.5 ha	16,000	⬜	8–11 €

All the wines of the Domaine d'Escausses have elegant labels. You can see them while tasting this selection of four beautifully made wines: the Gaillac reds **La Vigne Mythique 2001** and **Croix Petite 2001** win one star, while the sweet Gaillac **Vendanges Dorées 2001** was thought to be just as outstanding as this dry wine, which is certainly one to remember. It has a lovely crystalline green-gold colour, perfumes of boxwood, citrus fruits, lightly toasted dried fruits and mineral notes. Its palate is well balanced, full of flavour, rounded and refreshing, and lightly reveals its maturation for ten months in oak.

📫 EARL Denis Balaran, Dom. d'Escausses, 81150 Sainte-Croix, tel. 05.63.56.80.52, fax 05.63.56.87.62, e-mail balaran@escausses.com ☑
🍷 ev. day 9am–7pm; Sun. and groups by appt.
📫 Jean-Marc et Roselyne Balaran

DOM. FERRET

Doux Cuvée Saint-Nicolas 2001★

	1.1 ha	2,000	🍶	8–11 €

Bernard Ferret cultivates his 22 ha of vines not far from the château de Mauriac, an impressive 16th century fortress restored by the painter Bernard Bistes. This wine was made from Len de l'El and a little Mauzac, it has a golden colour and rich perfumes of quince paste, orange liqueur and honey. Very sweet flavours of quince jelly, and fig and water melon jam make a concentrated impression with a fresh touch. This Gaillac was made from very ripe grapes.
📫 Bernard Ferret, Mauriac, 81600 Senouillac, tel. 05.63.41.51.94, fax 05.63.41.51.94, e-mail bernard.ferret@wanadoo.fr ☑
🍷 by appt.

GABERLE

Sec Perlé 2002★

	300 ha	2,000,000	🍶	3–5 €

The Labastide cooperative offers two attractive wines: a **red Gaillac Grand Secret 2001 (5–8 €)**, matured in barrel, was singled out by the Jury, and this original slightly sparkling wine, which has retained its quality and this year wins one star. It has a pale colour with very bright-green highlights releasing fine bubbles that convey intense perfumes of flowers, citrus fruit, blackcurrant bud and peach, as well as grapey notes. This is followed by a sweet first impression with gentle bubbles and an elegant, fresh palate with recurring fruit flavours.
📫 Cave de Labastide-de-Lévis, BP 12, 81150 Marssac-sur-Tarn, tel. 05.63.53.73.73, fax 05.63.53.73.74, e-mail info@cave-labastide.com ☑
🍷 by appt.

DOM. DE GINESTE

Sec Cuvée Aurore Fût 2001★★

	2 ha	5,400	⬜	5–8 €

This is a rich Gaillac with a yellow, almost golden colour with soft perfumes of butter, vanilla, fig and exotic fruits on a base of toast. At first the palate is fresh, then develops in roundness, fullness and balance. Although the oak is evident, it is fine and integrated, continuing into a long finish. The **Gaillac Grande Cuvée red 2001 (11–15 €)** wins one star for its fruitiness and good flesh.
📫 EARL Dom. de Gineste, 81150 Técou, tel. 05.63.33.03.18, fax 05.63.81.52.65, e-mail domainedegineste@wanadoo.fr ☑
🍷 ev. day 10am–12.30pm 3.30pm–7pm; Sun. by appt.
📫 Maugeais et Delmotte

CH. DES HOURTETS Sec 2002★

	8 ha	50,000	🍶	3–5 €

In Occitan dialect, a "hourtet" is a small garden. The vineyard owned by Edouard and Anne Kabakian is not remotely small, however, covering 58 ha in a bowl facing south-south-west. Their 2002 has high-spirited with its clear, pale and brilliant-yellow colour. It releases perfumes of boxwood and citronella before settling on a long and fresh palate. The aromas continue along with accents of fruits and flowers.

📫 SCEA Dom. des Hourtets, Laborie, 81600 Gaillac, tel. 05.63.33.19.15, fax 05.63.33.20.49, e-mail kabakian@wanadoo.fr ☑
🍷 ev. day 10am–12 noon 2pm–6pm; Sun. 10am–12 noon
📫 A. et E. Kabakian

DOM. DE LABARTHE

Cuvée Guillaume 2001★

	10 ha	65,000	⬜	5–8 €

This wine was made from Braucol plus 10% Merlot. It has a beautiful brightness, and fine, elegant perfumes of soft fruits and vanilla. The first impression is supple, then the velvety tannins give it a rounded quality which lasts until the very tasty finish. Another wine deserving praise was this very successful **sweet Gaillac Les Grains d'Or 2002 (8–11 €)**.
📫 EARL Albert et Fils, Dom. de Labarthe, 81150 Castanet, tel. 05.63.56.80.14, fax 05.63.56.84.81 ☑
🍷 by appt.
📫 Jean-Paul Albert

DOM. DE LARROQUE

Privilège d'Antan 2001★★

	1.5 ha	7,000	🍶	5–8 €

The Larroque estate is a regular in the *Guide* and this year qualifies with a very well-made red Gaillac. The deep-crimson colour tells us how rich this 2001 wine will be. There are intense perfumes of small soft fruits, liquorice and spices, with a mentholated note adding freshness. The wine is elegantly structured and mouth filling and keeps its fruitiness into the long finish with a further touch of white pepper. This is a remarkably clean-cut wine.
📫 V. et P. Nouvel, Dom. de Larroque, 81150 Cestayrols, tel. 05.63.56.87.63, fax 05.63.56.87.40 ☑
🍷 ev. day except Sun. 9am–12 noon 2pm–7pm

CH. LECUSSE

Cuvée spéciale 2001★★

	3 ha	20,000	🍶	5–8 €

This very pleasant wine was made from Fer Servadou. It has a bright colour with light-purplish highlights, and releases perfumes of soft fruits and spice jams, signs of the grapes' great maturity. The tannic structure rests on a rich and concentrated, mouth-filling palate which is perfectly balanced.
📫 Olesen, Broze, 81600 Gaillac, tel. 05.63.33.90.09, fax 05.63.33.94.36, e-mail post@chateaulecusse.fr ☑
🍷 by appt.

DOM. DE LONG PECH 2001★

		9,000	🍶	5–8 €

The **Méthode Gaillacoise 2002**, singled out by the Jury, will make a good start to a meal thanks to its freshness and its aromas of pear, apple and grape, while the red Gaillac will go well with a meat dish with its notes of fruits in *eau-de-vie* and spices (cinnamon). This 2001 with purple highlights is a warm wine with evident but well-coated tannins and preserves its intense fruitiness. While it is ready to drink now, this wine could also be kept for two or three years.
📫 GAEC Bastide Père et Fille, Lapeyrière, 81310 Lisle-sur-Tarn, tel. 05.63.33.37.22, fax 05.63.40.42.06, e-mail contact@domaine-de-long-pech.com ☑
🍷 ev. day 9am–12 noon 1.30pm–7pm; Sun. by appt.

Gaillac

MANOIR DE L'EMMEILLE
Tradition 2001★★

	8 ha	18,000	🍴 ♦	5–8 €

This medieval manor house once belonged to a monastic community; the tasting cellar is in the former chapel. There you can try this intense garnet-red wine with its very expressive and charming scents of ripe soft fruits, liquorice and spices. Its body is concentrated, full and supple with fine tannins and a long tasty finish
↬ Manoir de l'Emmeillé, 81140 Campagnac, tel. 05.63.33.12.80, fax 05.63.33.20.11, e-mail contact@emmeille.com ☑
𝚈 ev. day except Sun. 9am–12 noon 2pm–7pm
↬ Ch. Poussou

MARQUIS D'ORIAC
Vieilli en fût de chêne 2001★

	16.71 ha	100,000	🍴 🍷 ♦	5–8 €

The **red Gaillac Raimbault Cuvée Magistrale 2001 (3–5 €)**, matured in tank, wins one star for its fruity character. The Marquis d'Oriac is an attractive bright-ruby wine with oaky notes, the result of its maturation for 12 months in barrel, and nuances of fruit creams, though it keeps its freshness. Its slender and balanced palate is charming, with the oak continuing together with vanilla nuances. Keep this wine for two years.
↬ Cave de Rabastens, 33, rte d'Albi, 81800 Rabastens, tel. 05.63.33.73.80, fax 05.63.33.85.82, e-mail rabastens@vins-du-sud-ouest.com ☑
𝚈 by appt.

MAS D'AUREL
Cuvée Alexandra 2000★

	3 ha	20,000	🍴 ♦	5–8 €

This heady, very spicy (pepper) wine has a velvety garnet-red colour. A certain softness enfolds the still evident and rather austere tannins, which support the note of blackcurrant cream at the finish.
↬ Mas d'Aurel, 81170 Donnazac, tel. 05.63.56.06.39, fax 05.63.56.09.21 ☑
𝚈 ev. day except Sun. 8.30am–12 noon 2pm–7pm

DOM. MAS PIGNOU
Cuvée Mélanie 2001★

	3 ha	16,000	🍴 ♦	5–8 €

This wine-growing farm stands on top of a hillside with a fine view over the vineyard. Its garnet-coloured wine with deep-purple glints pays homage to the grandmother of the family, Mélanie. It has a distinguished bouquet of fruits, liquorice and spices. The palate is clean and develops in roundness on silky tannins. The fruit lasts well, along with a spicy touch, emphasizing its well-made, very drinkable character.
↬ Jacques et Bernard Auque, Dom. Mas Pignou, 81600 Gaillac, tel. 05.63.33.18.52, fax 05.63.33.11.58, e-mail maspignou@free.fr ☑
𝚈 ev. day 9am–12 noon 2pm–7pm; Sun. by appt.

DOM. DE MOHUNE
L'Ecuyer de Mohune 2001★

	0.5 ha	3,600	🍴 ♦	5–8 €

Mohune is a 14th century fortified manor house with a vineyard of 18 ha. This wine with purplish glints is a blend of Braucol, Syrah and Duras. Its intense range of flavours includes soft fruits and spices. These same fruits fill the warming palate, which is almost soft and well balanced up to the touch of sweet liquorice at the finish.
↬ EARL Dom. de Mohune, Ch. de Saint-Martial, 81600 Senouillac, tel. 05.63.41.53.92, fax 05.63.41.53.90, e-mail moonajf@wanadoo.fr ☑
𝚈 by appt.
↬ Alistair Moor

CH. MONTELS Doux Les Trois Chênes Elevé en fût de chêne 2000★★

	n.c.	4,000	🍷	8–11 €

After a visit to the medieval city of Cordes, you will enjoy discovering this pretty 19th century white stone family mansion. There you will taste some fine wines: the **red Gaillac 2001**, matured in tank, and the **dry Gaillac 2001**, which was kept in oak. Both are very successful (5–8 €), as is this sweet orange-yellow wine, which reflects the character of its noble grapes with notes of fig and crystallized fruits. These flavours linger on the very rich, fleshy, well-balanced palate.
↬ Bruno Montels, Burgal, 81170 Souel, tel. 05.63.56.01.28, fax 05.63.56.15.46 ☑
𝚈 by appt.

DOM. DU MOULIN
Sec Vieilles Vignes Elevé en fût 2002★

	2 ha	7,500	🍷	8–11 €

This pure Sauvignon is pale yellow with green and silvery highlights. Here the oak prevails over notes of vanilla, cocoa and coconut, which arrive ahead of the aromas of fresh fruits. The first impression is clear-cut and lacks nothing in roundness or freshness, but the fruity flavours are overshadowed by the oak. This is a wine for the future, which will be more rounded in three years. The **red Gaillac Vieilles Vignes 2001** also wins one star.
↬ Nicolas et Jean-Paul Hirissou, Dom. du Moulin, chem. de Bastié, 81600 Gaillac, tel. 05.63.57.20.52, fax 05.63.57.66.67, e-mail domainedumoulin@libertysurf.fr ☑
𝚈 ev. day 9.30am–12 noon 2pm–7pm; Sun. by appt.

LES SECRETS DU CHATEAU PALVIE
Doux 2001★★

	2 ha	7,200	🍷	11–15 €

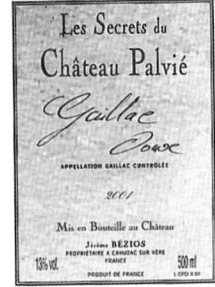

Jérôme Bézios won a *coup de cœur* in the 2003 *Guide* for his sweet Gaillac 2000, and wins another with his 2001 vintage. This brilliant-golden wine leaves pretty tears on the glass that invite you to try its intense, fresh, spicy and crystallized perfumes of pineapple, apricot, ginger and vanilla, the result of maturation for ten months in oak, which blend harmoniously together. It is not only expressive but also lively thanks to its sweet substance, and the flavours seem to go on forever. Its integrated tannins make it ready to drink now.
↬ Jérôme Bézios, Ch. Palvié, 81140 Cahuzac-sur-Vère, tel. 05.63.57.19.71, fax 05.63.57.48.56

DOM. DES PARISES
Doux Loin de l'oeil 2001★

	2 ha	5,000	🍷	5–8 €

Let this perfectly clear yellow-orange Len de l'El surprise you with its perfumes of crystallized fruits, pineapple and a note of resin. The rich substance is accompanied by fruity and spicy notes, and a slightly acid character which makes the taste buds tingle at the finish.
↬ SCEV Jean Arnaud, 25, rue de la Mairie, 81150 Lagrave, tel. 05.63.41.78.63, fax 05.63.41.78.63 ☑ 🐾
𝚈 by appt.

SOUTH

LE PAYSSEL
Sec Tradition 2002★★

| 2 ha | 5,000 | ∎ ⚬ | 3–5 € |

With its necklace of fine bubbles, this Gaillac was made from equal parts of Mauzac and Len de l'El. It unveils a succession of perfumes of peach, apricot and exotic fruits with touches of spice. Its great freshness is balanced by good flesh, and the long finish has a concentrated fruity taste. The **Gaillac rosé 2002** is also commended.
- ✦ EARL Louis Brun et Fils, Vignoble Le Payssel, 81170 Frausseilles, tel. 05.63.56.00.47, fax 05.63.56.09.16 ✓
- ☉ by appt.
- ✦ Eric Brun

PEYRES-COMBE
Doux Flaveurs d'automne 2001★★

| 0.7 ha | 2,300 | ∎ ⚬ | 8–11 € |

The "autumn flavours" mentioned on the label include honey, crystallized fruits, quince, citrus fruit peel, and also a spring-like perfume of lime blossom in flower. Golden tears run down the glass, showing the power of the full, sweet body, which remains full of flavour.
- ✦ Victor Brureau, Dom. de Peyres-Combes, La Combe, 81140 Andillac, tel. 05.63.33.94.67, fax 05.63.33.94.67, e-mail peyres-combe@wanadoo.fr ✓ ⌂
- ☉ by appt.

VIN D'AUTAN DE ROBERT
PLAGEOLES ET FILS Doux Ondenc 2001★★

| 3 ha | 1,866 | ∎ | 30–38 € |

The Vin d'Autan appears regularly before the Grand Jury, and delighted them again this year. One look at its golden colour is enough to captivate the senses. The complex range of flavours includes intense perfumes of fir tree honey, crystallized fruits and quince paste, all heralding a rich *vin liquoreux*. This is a soft and scented Ondenc, which is remarkably persistent. A work of art.
- ✦ EARL Robert et Bernard Plageoles, Dom. des Très-Cantous, 81140 Cahuzac-sur-Vère, tel. 05.63.33.90.40, fax 05.63.33.95.64 ✓
- ☉ by appt.

DOM. RENE RIEUX
Concerto Elevé en fût de chêne 2001★★

| 2 ha | 4,200 | ⊞ | 5–8 € |

The Boissel Centre d'Aide par le Travail has distinguished itself this year with a **sweet Gaillac Concerto 2001 (11–15 €)**, which was singled out by the Jury, and with this dark-red, almost black wine, tasted by the Grand Jury. This has a complex blend of chocolate, vanilla and cinnamon scents, enhanced by wreaths of smokiness. It is supported on a substantial structure and has good flesh and fruitiness with gentle oaky nuances. A lovely Gaillac for laying down.
- ✦ Dom. René Rieux - TRICAT Service, 1495, rte de Cordes, 81600 Gaillac, tel. 05.63.57.29.29, fax 05.63.57.51.71 ✓
- ☉ ev. day except Sun. 9am–12 noon 2pm–5.30pm; groups by appt.

DOM. ROTIER
Doux Renaissance 2001★★

| 3.8 ha | 15,500 | ⊞ | 11–15 € |

From one year to the next, Alain Rotier proves his skill. Here he wins praise for a very successful **Cuvée Renaissance red 2001 (8–11 €)** and a sweet Gaillac on a level with previous vintages. It has a deep and dense-gold colour, well suited to its perfumes of honey, lime blossom, hawthorn, pineapple and vanilla which appear in a subtly fresh tonal range. It has good flesh, fullness, concentration, balance and is full of flavour. A superb wine.
- ✦ Dom. Rotier, Petit Nareye, 81600 Cadalen, tel. 05.63.41.75.14, fax 05.63.41.54.56, e-mail rotier@terre-net.fr ✓ ⌂
- ☉ by appt.
- ✦ Alain Rotier et Francis Marre

CH. DE SALETTES
Sec Premières Côtes 2001★★

| 9 ha | 17,000 | ⊞ | 8–11 € |

This wine was tasted by the Grand Jury, who liked its general harmony. Its bright golden-yellow colour was a good match for the perfumes of dried and crystallized fruits, butter and vanilla, signs of the grapes' maturity and good maturation. The rounded and fleshy palate benefits from a touch of freshness that gives it good balance. The oak gives way fully to the fruit. It can be drunk now or laid down.
- ✦ SCEV Ch. de Salettes, Lieu-dit Salettes, 81140 Cahuzac-sur-Vère, tel. 05.63.33.60.60, fax 05.63.33.60.61, e-mail salettes@chateaudesalettes.com ✓
- ☉ by appt.
- ✦ R. P. Le Net

DOM. SANBATAN
Doux Muscadelle 2001★★

| 1.8 ha | 5,000 | ∎ ⚬ | 8–11 € |

Jacques Grayssac began his career as an agricultural employee in Aveyron before settling in the Gaillac region in 1993. Try a Roquefort, a speciality of his homeland, with this exquisite, sweet wine with its flavours of honey and citrus fruits. The freshness and the flesh are well balanced, and accompanied by elegant aromas.
- ✦ Dom. Sanbatan, Le Lavelanet, 81600 Montans, tel. 05.63.57.25.48, fax 05.63.57.33.42
- ☉ by appt.
- ✦ Jacques Grayssac

CH. DE SAURS 2001★

| 3.5 ha | 21,000 | ∎ ⚬ | 5–8 € |

The château de Saurs is an elegant residence in the Palladian style. It offers a **red Gaillac Réserve Eliézer 2001 Elevé en Fût (8–11 €)** which was commended, and its main wine which was not matured in oak. It has a slightly purplish colour and releases perfumes of fruits and spices. It is rounded and velvety thanks to fine tannins, which do not overwhelm the flavours of ripe fruits and morello cherry. Drink it now or keep it for a while.
- ✦ SCEA Ch. de Saurs, 81310 Lisle-sur-Tarn, tel. 05.63.57.09.79, fax 05.63.57.10.71, e-mail info@chateau-de-saurs.com ✓ ⛁
- ☉ by appt.

DOM. DES TERRISSES
Cuvée Saint-Laurent 2001★★★

| 3 ha | 15,000 | ⊞ | 8–11 € |

This estate was founded in 1750 and has maintained a constantly high standard of production. Its Gaillac, matured for 12 months in barrel, came close to the *coup de cœur*. It has a velvety burlat cherry colour and a complex blend of elegant oak and ripe fruits, liquorice and pepper. The oak is well integrated in the powerful, full and rich palate; well-coated tannins accompany the long finish. The **red Gaillac Cuvée Principale 2001 (5–8 €)**, matured in tank, wins two stars: it is ready to drink now.
- ✦ Brigitte et Alain Cazottes, Les Terrisses, 81600 Gaillac, tel. 05.63.57.16.80, fax 05.63.41.05.87, e-mail domaine.des.terrisses@wanadoo.fr ✓
- ☉ by appt.

BARON THOMIERES
La Réserve du Général 2000★

| ■ | 1 ha | 8,000 | ❶❶ | 8–11€ |

The **Baron Thomières red 2001 (3–5 €)** is rich and mouth filling with soft fruit flavours and wins one star. The same applies to this ruby wine with perfumes of fruits in spirit on a base of vanilla and menthol. The fine tannins and the oak blend in a rounded, supple, well-balanced body that is full of fruit.

☛ Laurent Thomières, La Raffinié,
81150 Castelnau-de-Lévis, tel. 05.63.60.39.03,
fax 05.63.53.11.99,
e-mail laurent.thomieres@wanadoo.fr ☑
�Υ by appt.

CH. TOUNY-LES-ROSES
Cuvée du Poète Elevé en fût de chêne 2000★

| ■ | 2.5 ha | 8,000 | ❶❶ | 8–11€ |

The Gaillac poet Touny-Lérys (1881–1976) lived in this pretty 18th century château. This wine pays homage to him, its crimson colour releasing warm perfumes of cocoa, cherry, plum in *eau-de-vie* and spices, with underlying charred notes. It is very velvety, and increases in roundness all the way to the pleasant finish, thanks to its well-balanced structure.

☛ Ch. Touny-les-Roses, Ch. de Touny, 81150 Lagrave,
tel. 05.63.57.90.90, fax 05.63.57.90.91,
e-mail chateau.touny@wanadoo.fr ☑ ⌂
�Υ by appt.

CH. LA TOUR PLANTADE 2001★★

| ■ | 2 ha | 12,000 | ■ ♦ | 5–8€ |

Syrah, Braucol and Cabernet Sauvignon are harmoniously blended in this deep-red wine with crimson nuances. The complex range of flavours includes fruits, blackcurrant bud, and touches of spice and musk. All the fruit returns on the full, rounded and powerful palate supported by silky tannins.

☛ EARL France et Jaffar Nétanj, La Soucarié,
81150 Labastide-de-Lévis, tel. 05.63.55.47.43,
fax 05.63.53.27.78, e-mail jaffarnetanj@wanadoo.fr ☑ ⌂
�Υ by appt.

DOM. DE VAISSIERE 2001★

| ■ | 1 ha | 5,000 | ■ | 3–5€ |

After visiting the small museum of winemaking equipment, you can taste this garnet-red velvety wine with a strong blackcurrant aroma. It makes a clean first impression, combining a supple and rounded body with a pleasant fruity freshness.

☛ Dom. de Vaissière, 81300 Busque, tel. 05.63.34.59.00 ☑
�Υ ev. day 9.30am–12 noon 3pm–7.30pm

DOM. DE VAYSSETTE
Doux Cuvée Maxime 2001★★

| ■ | 3 ha | 3,000 | ■ ♦ | 11–15€ |

The inevitable Domaine de Vayssette is this year praised for its **Gaillac red Cuvée Léa 2001 Elevé en Fût (8–11 €)**, which was thought very successful, and for this golden wine with orange highlights which promptly delivers its crystallized apricot and honey scents with notes of vanilla and toasty dried fruits. Its intense concentration is confirmed by its remarkable vigour and liqueur taste.

☛ Dom. de Vayssette, Laborie, 81600 Gaillac,
tel. 05.63.57.31.95, fax 05.63.81.56.84 ☑
�Υ ev. day 10am–12 noon 3pm–7pm;
public hols. and groups by appt.

CH. VIGNE-LOURAC
Doux Vieilles Vignes 2001★

| ■ | 6 ha | 30,000 | ■ ♦ | 5–8€ |

Philippe Gayrel offers a range of well-made wines: the dry white **Gaillac Château Vigné-Lourac Vieilles Vignes 2001 (3–5 €)** wins one star, while the **Château Les Méritz Cuvée Prestige red 2001 (3–5 €)**, matured in tank, is singled out. This bright sweet wine with straw-yellow highlights releases subtle notes of acacia and crystallized fruits, then grows in balance, freshness and finesse.

☛ Vignobles Philippe Gayrel, BP 4, 81600 Gaillac,
tel. 05.63.81.21.05, fax 05.63.81.21.09

Wines selected but not starred

DOM. DES ARDURELS
Doux La Muscadelle 2001

| ■ | 1.3 ha | 7,000 | ■ ♦ | 3–5€ |

☛ Sébastien Cabal, Dom. des Ardurels, 81150 Lagrave,
tel. 05.63.33.26.63, fax 05.63.33.26.63 ☑
�Υ ev. day except Sun. 9am–7pm

CH. DE TERRIDE
Elevé en fût de chêne 2001

| ■ | 12 ha | 40,000 | ❶❶ | 5–8€ |

☛ Ch. de Terride, Terride, 81140 Puycelsi,
tel. 05.63.33.26.63, fax 05.63.33.26.63,
e-mail alixdavid@wanadoo.fr ☑
�Υ ev. day except Sun. 9am–12 noon 2pm–7pm
☛ Alix David

Buzet

The Buzet vineyard, sited between Agen and Marmande, has been recognized since the Middle Ages as an integral part of the Haut-Pays Bordelais area. It was originally a monastic domain, which was then developed by the burgers of Agen. Buzet faded into a memory after the devastation of the vineyards by phylloxera but, from 1956, it became a symbol of the renaissance of the vineyards in the Haut-Pays. Two individuals, Jean Mermillod and Jean Combabessouse, presided over the vineyard's revitalization, which also owes a great deal to the Cave Coopérative des Producteurs Réunis, where all the wines are brought on in hogsheads which are regularly renewed. The vineyard now stretches between Damazan and Sainte-Colombe on the lower slopes of the Garonne; it irrigates the tourist towns of Nérac and Barbaste.

The alternating terroirs of alluvial clay, pebbly soils and sandy limestones produce varied wines of striking character. The strong, deeply coloured, fleshy reds are velvety enough to rival some of their Girondin neighbours, and marvellous with local gastronomic dishes such as duck breast, confits (duck or goose preserved in fat), and rabbit cooked with prunes. Buzet wines are traditionally red, but white wines, of which 4,927 hl of the total 104,665 hl from 1,996 ha were produced in 2002, add to a range that is nevertheless dedicated above all to a palette of purples, garnets and vermilions.

BARON D'ALBRET 2000★★

| ■ | 200 ha | 450,000 | ■❶❶♦ | 5–8€ |

This wine was partly matured in barrel to make the tannins more supple. The bouquet is powerful and complex with notes of soft fruits and leather. The intense palate is very integrated, resting on substantial but fresh tannins. The substance, body, fruit and mature tannins are those of a

good terroir. This well-made, genuine and straightforward wine has a good future.
🍷 Les Vignerons de Buzet, BP 17, 47160 Buzet-sur-Baïse, tel. 05.53.84.74.30, fax 05.53.84.74.24,
e-mail buzet@vignerons-buzet.fr
⟁ ev. day except Sun. 9am–12 noon 2pm–6pm
🍇 SEAVA Padere

CH. DU BOUCHET 2001★

| ■ | 18 ha | 80,000 | ■ ◗ ◆ | 5–8 € |

The Château du Bouchet is a successful example of a sound blend of wine and oak. The bouquet has pleasant, fresh, slightly exotic fruits followed by notes of spice and undergrowth. The long and complex structure, with the oak more prominent on the palate, was much liked. This is a fine and distinguished wine of character, particularly well balanced and developing well. The Jury also appreciated the **Cuvée Chantet-Blanet red 2001**. The bouquet is a little closed but very fine. The palate is rounded and soft with well-integrated tannins. The Merlot prevails in this wine, which will be perfect in two years' time with white meat.
🍷 Les Vignerons de Buzet, BP 17, 47160 Buzet-sur-Baïse, tel. 05.53.84.74.30, fax 05.53.84.74.24,
e-mail buzet@vignerons-buzet.fr
⟁ ev. day except Sun. 9am–12 noon 2pm–6pm
🍇 SEAVA Padere

LES VIGNERONS DE BUZET

Cuvée Jean-Marie Hébrard 2000★★

| ■ | 20 ha | 100,000 | ■ ◗ ◆ | 8–11 € |

This wine was made to honour the former director of the cooperative, and is a sound achievement. The bouquet is pleasant and fine, with pronounced notes of toast. The fullness and roundness of the palate show that this is a true Buzet. Although the tannins are a little overwhelmed by the oak, and the finish needs to open out. It is nevertheless an elegant wine that should be kept for two to three years and then served with a tournedos Rossini.
🍷 Les Vignerons de Buzet, BP 17, 47160 Buzet-sur-Baïse, tel. 05.53.84.74.30, fax 05.53.84.74.24,
e-mail buzet@vignerons-buzet.fr
⟁ ev. day except Sun. 9am–12 noon 2pm–6pm

CH. LARCHE 2000★

| ■ | 20 ha | 83,000 | ■ ◆ | 5–8 € |

The name Larché describes a fortified building of a kind no longer found today. The bouquet is a little closed but clearly suggests ripe fruits. The palate is very rounded with nice fruits and a balanced tannic structure. The finish still needs to soften. This pleasant wine can be kept for two to three years. The Jury appreciated the **Marquis du Grez 2000 (8–11 €)** for its well-balanced oak on both nose and palate. It has very good length, with fruity tannins, and the oak is still pronounced at the finish. This is a great wine with a definite future.
🍷 Les Vignerons de Buzet, BP 17, 47160 Buzet-sur-Baïse, tel. 05.53.84.74.30, fax 05.53.84.74.24,
e-mail buzet@vignerons-buzet.fr
⟁ ev. day except Sun. 9am–12 noon 2pm–6pm
🍇 de Tretaigne

CH. PADERE 2000★

| ■ | 45 ha | 125,556 | ■ ◆ | 5–8 € |

The word "padère" describes the first group of houses and meadows after the moorland. This very pleasant wine has a

certain finesse, its bouquet clearly evoking fresh and floral notes. The freshness recurs on the palate with well-balanced tannins. Although rounded and warm, this wine is still immature. Drink it in two years with a navarin of lamb.
🍷 Les Vignerons de Buzet, BP 17, 47160 Buzet-sur-Baïse, tel. 05.53.84.74.30, fax 05.53.84.74.24,
e-mail buzet@vignerons-buzet.fr
⟁ ev. day except Sun. 9am–12 noon 2pm–6pm
🍇 SEAVA Padere

CH. SAUVAGNERES 2001★

| ■ | 7 ha | 43,600 | ■ ◆ | 5–8 € |

This wine made by Bordeaux methods, that is, in a perfectly classical style, won the *coup de coeur* in the 2003 edition of the *Guide*. The intense and complex bouquet of this vintage has lovely notes of soft fruits. After a round and supple attack, the tannins come through, balanced and well structured. This wine should develop well and be very pleasant in two or three years.
🍷 Bernard Thérasse, Sauvagnères,
47310 Sainte-Colombe-en-Bruilhois, tel. 05.53.67.20.23, fax 05.53.67.20.86 ☑
⟁ by appt.
🍇 Jacques Thérasse

DOM. DE LA TUQUE 2000★

| ■ | n.c. | 134,200 | ■ ◆ | 5–8 € |

This is the Château de Gueyze's second wine, which is regularly selected. The bouquet is a little subdued, but suggests perfumes of very pleasant soft fruits. The first impression on the palate confirms this analysis with its ripe fruit and well-rounded tannins. This simple and correct wine is a little short but has a certain finesse, and should be drunk soon.
🍷 Les Vignerons de Buzet, BP 17, 47160 Buzet-sur-Baïse, tel. 05.53.84.74.30, fax 05.53.84.74.24,
e-mail buzet@vignerons-buzet.fr
⟁ ev. day except Sun. 9am–12 noon 2pm–6pm
🍇 SCEA Gueyze

Wines selected but not starred

CH. DU FRANDAT 2001

| ■ | 5 ha | 30,000 | ■ ◗ ◆ | 5–8 € |

🍷 Patrice Sterlin, Ch. du Frandat, 47600 Nérac, tel. 05.53.65.23.83, fax 05.53.97.05.77,
e-mail chateaudufrandat@terre-net.fr ☑
⟁ ev. day except Sun. 10am–12 noon 3pm–6pm; cl. Jan.

CH. TOURNELLES

Cuvée Prestige 2002

| ■ | 15 ha | 10,714 | ■ ◆ | 5–8 € |

🍷 EARL Bertrand Gabriel, Ch. Tournelles,
47600 Calignac, tel. 05.65.20.80.80, fax 05.65.20.80.81,
e-mail vigouroux@vigouroux.fr
🍇 B. Vigouroux

Côtes du Frontonnais

The Côtes du Frontonnais are Toulousain wines from a very old vineyard which was once the property of the Knights of the Order of

Saint-Jean-de-Jérusalem. During the siege of Montauban, Louis XIII and Richelieu were said to have succumbed to comparative tastings...Rebuilt as a result of the establishment of the cooperative cellars of Fronton and Villaudric, the vineyard has stuck to its original varieties including the Négrette, a local variety found in Gaillac, as well as Cot, Cabernet Franc, Cabernet Sauvignon, Syrah, Gamay and Mauzac.

The terroir of silts, clays and pebble layers covers about 2,021 ha of the terraces of the river Tarn. The red wines, with a high proportion of Cabernet, Gamay or Syrah, are light, fruity and aromatic. The wines with the greatest proportion of Négrette are stronger, tannic and have a distinctive flavour of the terroir. The rosés are clean, fresh and pleasantly fruity. Production was 87,658 hl in 2002.

CH. BAUDARE 2002★★

	1 ha	6,000	▮ ♦	3–5 €

At Claude and David Vigouroux's vineyard, a brand-new winery has replaced the one built in 1945. Father and son offer a *rosé de saignée* made from Négrette and Cot, which has a beautiful, brilliant, almost pale-red colour. It has intense floral and mineral notes, heralding a very fresh palate. As the aromas are well integrated in the rounded and full-bodied palate, this 2002 should be served with a grill or a soft fruit tart. Note also the very successful **red Cuvée Tradition 2001**, made from a blend of 70% Négrette and 30% Syrah matured in barrel.
↩ Claude et David Vigouroux, Ch. Baudare, 82370 Labastide-Saint-Pierre, tel. 05.63.30.51.33, fax 05.63.64.07.24, e-mail vigouroux@aol.com ☑
☚ by appt.

CH. BELLEVUE LA FORET

OPTIMUM 2001★

	6 ha	26,600	⬙	8–11 €

The **rosé 2002 (5–8 €)** is very successful, and should be drunk with a soft fruit sorbet or pork in honey, for example. But also try this Optimum, which is warming, rich and structured by firm tannins. Its purplish façade releases a variety of strong perfumes: spices such as pepper, cloves and liquorice, with balsamic notes and, of course, black fruits. This is a lovely wine to keep for three to five years.
↩ Ch. Bellevue la Forêt, 4500, av. de Grisolles, 31620 Fronton, tel. 05.34.27.91.91, fax 05.61.82.39.70, e-mail contact@chateaubellevuelaforet.com ☑
☚ by appt.
↩ Patrick Germain

CH. BONNEVAL 2001★

	3.6 ha	25,000	▮ ♦	3–5 €

In 1998, Jean-Luc Bel, whose family already made wine in the Languedoc, acquired this vineyard of 23 ha. He has produced an attractive wine made mainly from Négrette (50%), plus equal shares of Cabernet Sauvignon and Syrah, with complex and fine perfumes of fruits and spices. Already soft on the palate, this 2001 wine has power, good flesh, great fruitiness and integrated tannins that accompany a finish which is strong on liquorice. Also worth trying is the **rosé 2002**, which is awarded one star.
↩ Jean-Luc Bel, 45, rte d'Auch, 82370 Campsas, tel. 05.63.64.03.31, fax 05.63.30.08.59 ☑
☚ by appt.

CH. BOUISSEL 2001★★

	8 ha	50,000	▮ ♦	5–8 €

Like the **red Haute Expression 2001 (11–15 €)**, which was thought very successful and promising, this wine was not matured in oak. It was made from 50% Négrette, 20% Cabernet Franc, 10% Cot and 20% Syrah, and very well produced. The Jury liked its dense, bright, burlat cherry colour, and its concentrated bouquet offering a vast selection of flowers, black fruits, kirsch and spices. The freshness and the flesh are well balanced, and the well-coated tannins combine with the tasty body.

↩ EARL Pierre Selle, Ch. Bouissel, 82370 Campsas, tel. 05.63.30.10.49, fax 05.63.64.01.22 ☑
☚ ev. day except Sun. 9am–12 noon 2pm–7pm; groups by appt.

CH. CAHUZAC

L'Authentique 2001★

	12 ha	80,000	▮ ♦	5–8 €

A feeling of harmony stems from this full-bodied wine with perfumes of stewed fruits, spices and violet refreshed by a touch of menthol. It has a burlat cherry colour with aubergine highlights, and after a supple and silky first impression reveals its pleasant, unaggressive character, which is both fresh and rich, sufficiently full and always with plenty of flavour.
↩ EARL de Cahuzac, Les Peyronnets, 82170 Fabas, tel. 05.63.64.10.18, fax 05.63.67.36.97 ☑
☚ by appt.
↩ Ferran Père et Fils

CH. CLAMENS

Cuvée Julie 2002★

	1.5 ha	10,600	▮ ♦	3–5 €

Négrette and Syrah make up this pale, bright salmon-coloured rosé with orange nuances. Subdued notes of slightly acid pear-drops are followed by a lively attack with good balance, even though the wine is only moderately full. A warm touch accompanies the fruit at the finish. The **red Cuvée Julie 2001** was singled out.
↩ Jean-Michel Bégué, Ch. Clamens, 720, chem. du Tapas, 31620 Fronton, tel. 05.61.82.45.32, fax 05.62.79.21.73, e-mail begue.clamens@free.fr ☑
☚ by appt.

CH. LA COLOMBIERE

Tradition 2001★

	5.33 ha	34,133	▮ ♦	5–8 €

A 16th century Toulouse-style residence overlooks the 18-ha vineyard planted on siliceous gravel. Négrette plus 20% of the two Cabernets went into the making of this dark wine with crimson glints, which has a good share of spices (pepper and liquorice) on a base of soft fruits. It has a fairly complex balance, leaving an impression of flexibility and sweetness despite some liveliness at the finish.
↩ Diane de Driésen, Ch. la Colombière, 31620 Villaudric, tel. 05.61.82.44.05, fax 05.61.82.57.56, e-mail françois@chateaulacolombiere.com ☑
☚ ev. day except Sun. 9am–12 noon 2pm–6pm

COMTE DE NEGRET 2001★

	110 ha	900,000	▮ ♦	3–5 €

Two wines, the **red Comte de Négret Excellence 2001 Elevé en Fût** and the **rosé 2002** were judged very successful, as well as this Fronton which was not matured in oak. It makes a good start with its bright-aubergine colour and clean perfumes of fruits and spices. Its roundness and warm character are attractive, completing a good-quality wine.
↩ Cave de Fronton, 31620 Fronton, tel. 05.62.79.97.79, fax 05.62.79.97.70 ☑
☚ by appt.

CH. COUTINEL 2002★

	9 ha	70,000	▮ ♦	3–5 €

This château has 46 ha of vines, and from them the Jury selected this deep and brilliant rosé which releases fruit perfumes with a buttery nuance. This is a full, rather rich wine, with a good balance between power and freshness, which accompanies it to a fruity finish.
↩ Jean-Claude Arbeau, 82370 Labastide-Saint-Pierre, tel. 05.63.64.01.80, fax 05.63.30.11.42, e-mail vignobles@arbeau.com ☑
☚ by appt.

DOM. CROIX DE PEYRAT 2001★

	8 ha	12,000	▮ ♦	5–8 €

Denis Dussère blended Négrette (65%) with Cabernet Franc, Syrah and Gamay (5%) to make this well-structured wine, which reveals brick-red nuances in its fairly intense colour.

SOUTH WEST

The perfumes combine a fairly powerful range of ripe fruits, coffee and spices, with a touch of musk. The rich and silky first impression brings a feeling of roundness before the structure takes over with its compact tannins supporting a finish full of flavour.

🕏 Denis Dussère, Dom. Croix de Peyrat, 345, rte de Fabas, 82370 Campsas, tel. 05.63.30.58.50, fax 05.63.30.00.67 ☑
🍷 by appt.

CH. DEVES Allegro 2001★★

■	2 ha	8,000	🍾 ⚬	5–8 €

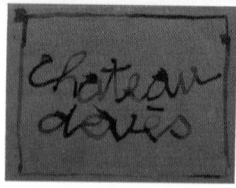

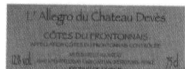

Michel Abart has extracted the fruit extremely well from his Négrette (50%) and Syrah (40%), and produced an authentic and full-bodied Fronton. Enjoy its purplish-crimson colour, which is already very dense. This rich and elegant wine releases scents of ripe fruits and spices with a note of fresh pepper. Then it fills the palate with a lively spice, leaving a warm impression. The flesh coats the ample structure, completing a well-balanced product which is quite simply remarkable.

🕏 Michel Abart, Ch. Devès, 2255, rte de Fronton, 31620 Castelnau-d'Estretefonds, tel. 05.61.35.14.97, fax 05.61.35.14.97 ☑
🍷 by appt.
🕏 André Abart

CH. FERRAN 2002★

■	2 ha	12,000	🍾 ⚬	5–8 €

Nicolas Gélis has run this 27-ha estate since 1994, and sells 50% of his production in Germany, Denmark and Japan. The perfectly limpid dark rosé is very successful, with its intense scents of soft fruits, its roundness and sweetness reminiscent of fruit-drops.

🕏 Nicolas Gélis, Ch. Ferran, 31620 Fronton, tel. 05.61.35.30.58, fax 05.61.35.30.59, e-mail chateau.ferran@wanadoo.fr ☑
🍷 by appt.

CH. FONVIEILLE 2002★

■	2.5 ha	20,000	🍾 ⚬	3–5 €

The Jury found a tasty and comforting fruitiness in this intense rosé with light-purple highlights. Floral notes accompany the rather complex ripe fruits, then the wine develops a slightly acid roundness.

🕏 ABA, 149, av. Charles-de-Gaulle, 82000 Montauban, tel. 05.63.20.23.15, fax 05.63.03.06.64

CH. JOLIET

Symphonie de Joliet Elevé en fût de chêne 2001★

■	1.2 ha	6,500	🍾🍾	8–11 €

The well-made **red Cuvée Fantaisie 2001 (5–8 €)** was singled out by the Jury, who preferred this intense peony-coloured Symphonie which plays on perfumes of black and red fruits, chocolate, flowers and spices, with a light note of brioche. The wine has plenty of suppleness and flavour, revealing its structure gradually all the way to an elegantly oaky finish. It has very good potential.

🕏 François Daubert, Ch. Joliet, 345, chem. de Caillol, 31620 Fronton, tel. 05.61.82.46.02, fax 05.61.82.46.02, e-mail chateau.joliet@wanadoo.fr ☑
🍷 by appt.

CH. LAUROU

Elevé en fût de chêne 2001★★

■	45 ha	10,000	🍾🍾	5–8 €

Négrette and Cabernet Sauvignon share the leading role (40% each), plus 20% of Négrette in this strongly coloured wine with purple highlights which shows a delicate balance between its floral perfumes from the grapes and the spicy notes from the oak. It makes a clear-cut first impression, has a chewy flavour – the result of good extraction – and a substantial structure. This wine has an ambitious and promising style.

🕏 Guy Salmona, Ch. Laurou, 2250, rte de Nohic, 31620 Fronton, tel. 05.61.82.40.88, fax 05.61.82.73.11, e-mail chateau.laurou@wanadoo.fr ☑
🍷 ev. day except Sun. 9am–12 noon 2pm–6pm

CH. MONPLAISIR 2001★

■	3 ha	20,000	🍾	3–5 €

Monplaisir was the first plot cultivated by the Lafforgues, who now have an estate of 18 ha. This Fronton, finely scented with soft fruits and spices, has an intense colour with vermilion glints. The palate is silky and made pleasant by its rich and warming fullness, and solid structure with small compact tannins which accompany a tasty finish.

🕏 Famille Lafforgue, 31340 Vacquiers, tel. 05.63.64.01.80, fax 05.63.30.11.42, e-mail vignobles@arbeau.com ☑

CH. MONTAURIOL

Mons Aureolus 2001★★★

■	6 ha	30,000	🍾🍾	5–8 €

Although the **red Caprice d'Adrien 2001 (15–23 €)**, matured for 18 months in barrel, was thought to be very successful, the Mons Aureolus stole the show. With its splendid black-cherry colour, it combines perfumes of violet, pepper and black fruits in a complex bouquet. Its full and tasty flesh has a fresh quality, because the oak accompanying the substantial structure is softening and letting the aromas burst forth. This is a wine with great personality.

🕏 Nicolas Gélis, Ch. Montauriol, rte des Châteaux, 31340 Villematier, tel. 05.61.35.30.58, fax 05.61.35.30.59, e-mail chateau.montauriol@wanadoo.fr ☑
🍷 by appt.

CH. PLAISANCE 2001★

■	15 ha	80,000	🍾 ⚬	5–8 €

Matured in tank, this fairly intense crimson-red Fronton opens with strong aromas of peony, spices and leather. After a supple attack, it is elegantly rounded and full and develops in finesse and fruitiness, without losing its velvety character. The **red Thibault de Plaisance 2001 (8–11 €)** still bears the mark of its time in barrel, but is no less promising and also wins one star.

🕏 EARL de Plaisance, pl. de la Mairie, 31340 Vacquiers, tel. 05.61.84.97.41, fax 05.61.84.11.26, e-mail chateau-plaisance@wanadoo.fr ☑
🍷 by appt.
🕏 Penavayre

DOM. DES PRADELLES 2001★

■	2.01 ha	16,000	🍾 ⚬	3–5 €

This Fronton made from Négrette (55%), Syrah (35%) and Cabernet (10%) has a beautiful intense-red colour. When the glass is swirled, it releases aromas of ripe fruits accompanied by floral notes. Its frankness emphasizes its good balance and warm flavours of spices and fruits. The tannins are firm but coated as well, and linger in the finish.

🕏 François Prat, chem. de la Bourdette, 31340 Vacquiers, tel. 05.61.84.97.36, fax 05.61.84.97.36 ☑
🍷 ev. day except Sun. 8.30am–7pm

DOM. DE SAINT-GUILHEM

Amadeus 2001★★★

■	1.5 ha	6,900	🍾🍾	5–8 €

This sumptuous Amadeus is crimson with intense highlights. The oak and the wine combine harmoniously in a rich range of aromatic notes. More impressive still is the structured and mouth-filling palate, which reveals judicious extraction of the fruit and well-controlled maturation in barrel. This promising

wine has a fine future. Keep it for four or five years. The **red Cuvée Renaissance 2001**, matured for 14 months in oak, also wins three stars
☛ Philippe Laduguie, 1613, chem. de Saint-Guilhem, 31620 Castelnau-d'Estretefonds, tel. 05.61.82.12.09, fax 05.61.82.65.59 **V**
Ⓣ ev. day 9.30am–12 noon 2pm–7pm; Sun. by appt.

CH. SAINT-LOUIS L'Esprit 2001★

■	2 ha	13,000	❶❶ 5–8 €

This wine's "spirit" evidently comes from the Négrette which makes up 85% of the blend, along with Cabernet Franc. This intense Fronton has a powerful, clean bouquet of spicy black fruits. After a clear-cut attack, it develops in a balanced way with silky tannins; the oak inherited from its 12-month maturation period adds to the fullness of the aromatic expression and the structure which reaches its high point with a pleasant, slightly bitter and nicely spiced flavour. The **red Château Saint-Louis 2001 (3–5 €)** was singled out.
☛ Alain Mahmoudi, SCEA Ch. Saint-Louis, BP 8, 82370 Labastide-Saint-Pierre, tel. 05.63.30.20.20, fax 05.63.30.58.76,
e-mail chateausaintlouis@wanadoo.fr **V**
Ⓣ by appt.

Wines selected but not starred

CH. MARGUERITE
Elevé en fût de chêne 2001

■	50 ha	12,000	❶❶ −3 €

☛ SCEA Ch. Marguerite, 1709, chem. des Cavailles, 82370 Campsas, tel. 05.63.64.08.21, fax 05.63.64.08.21

Lavilledieu AOVDQS

North of the Frontonnais, on the terraces of the Tarn and the Garonne, the little vineyard of Lavilledieu produces red and rosé wines. The production, classified as AOVDQS, is still very little known (2,817 hl in 2002 from 74 ha). The Négrette (30%), Cabernet Franc, Gamay, Syrah and Tannat are the authorized varieties.

CAVE DE LAVILLEDIEU DU TEMPLE
Chevalier du Temple du Christ 2001★★

■	n.c.	200,000	■ ♦ −3 €

The results from the Lavilledieu cooperative are more than satisfactory: the **Maistre des Templiers 2001 (3–5 €)**, aged in tank, is singled out, while the **Le Dôme du Rocher 2001 (5–8 €)**, which was not aged in barrel, wins one star. The best mark went to this fresh red wine with its bouquet of soft fruits and spices. It is supple, cool and fruity, maintaining perfect balance throughout the tasting.
☛ Cave de Lavilledieu-du-Temple, rte de Meauzac, 82290 Lavilledieu-du-Temple, tel. 05.63.31.60.05, fax 05.63.31.69.11, e-mail cave-lavilledieu@wanadoo.fr **V**
Ⓣ ev. day except Sun. 9am–12 noon 2pm–6pm

Côtes du Brulhois
AOVDQS

Since November 1984, these former Vins de Pays have been AOVDQS, and are produced on both banks of the Garonne, in the departments of Lot-et-Garonne and Tarn-et-Garonne, near the small town of Layrac. The appellation covers an area of about 219 ha. Production is mainly of reds from Bordeaux varieties and the local Tannat and Cot and amounted to 10,327 hl in 2002. Two cooperative cellars undertake the majority of the winemaking.

CH. GRAND CHENE
Elevé en fût de chêne 2001★★

■	10 ha	50,000	❶❶ 8–11 €

Under the brand name Château Grand Chêne, the Donzac cooperative offers two remarkable wines. The **Château Grand Chêne Sélection 2001 (5–8 €)**, matured for 18 months in tank, was full and rich. The other wine was aged for a year in barrel, and has seductive aromas of fruits in *eau-de-vie* and a full-bodied oakiness. It is pleasantly mouth filling, gradually increasing in power while revealing its vinosity and tannic structure. Leave it for two or three years to allow the tannins to soften, and serve it with meat in sauce.
☛ Vignerons du Brulhois, 82340 Dunes, tel. 05.63.39.91.92, fax 05.63.39.82.83,
e-mail info@vigneronsdubrulhois.com **V**
Ⓣ ev. day except Sun. Mon. 9am–12 noon 2pm–6pm; groups by appt.

TRADITION 2001★

■	40 ha	200,000	■ ♦ 5–8 €

The Donzac cooperative merged with that of Goulens in 2002, creating the Vignerons du Brulhois. This Tradition, aged for 18 months in tank, has a red colour with brick-red nuances. Intense notes of leather and ripe fruits flavour the warm, well-structured but supple body. This is a well-balanced wine.
☛ Vignerons du Brulhois, 82340 Dunes, tel. 05.63.39.91.92, fax 05.63.39.82.83,
e-mail info@vigneronsdubrulhois.com **V**
Ⓣ ev. day except Sun. Mon. 9am–12 noon 2pm–6pm; groups by appt.

SOUTH WEST

Côtes du Marmandais

Not far from the gravels of Entre-Deux-Mers and the wines of Duras and Buzet, the Côtes du Marmandais wines are mainly produced by the cooperatives in Beaupuy and Cocumont on both banks of the Garonne. The white wines, generally made from Sémillon, Sauvignon, Muscadelle and Ugni Blanc, are dry, lively and fruity. The supple, pleasingly aromatic red wines are made mainly from Bordeaux varieties, along with Abouriou, Syrah, Cot and Gamay. The vineyard covers about 1,635 ha and produced 2,640 hl of white wine and 88,292 hl of red in 2001.

CH. LA BASTIDE
Prestige 2000★

■	2 ha	20,000	◐	5–8 €

This wine embodies its exceptional clay-gravel terroir and its long maturation in barrel. The fruit is a little subdued on the nose, yielding to musky notes. The first impression is very pleasant, both supple and rounded. The tannins are a touch harsh and need two to three years to soften and achieve a better balance. The **La Bastide white 2002 (3–5 €)** was vinified in barrel and the oak is still slightly prominent. The substance is very good; wait until the fruit comes through.
☛ Cave de Cocumont, La Vieille Eglise, 47250 Cocumont, tel. 05.53.94.50.21, fax 05.53.94.52.84,
e-mail accueil@cave-cocumont.fr ☑ ⛁ ⚑
☖ by appt.
☛ GAEC de La Bastide

CH. DE BEAULIEU
Elevé en fût de chêne 2000★

■	26 ha	90,000	◐	5–8 €

Considerable efforts have been made at this vineyard: after high-density replanting with a balanced mix of grape varieties, and controlled yields, they are starting to see the benefits, as can be seen from this wine. Its nose is a little closed at the beginning, but after being swirled in the glass it reveals notes of soft fruits, soon dominated by very toasty and roasted notes. On the palate, where the structure is rich and well balanced, the ripe fruits express themselves immediately, but are slightly masked by a prominent oakiness. This is a concentrated wine which in time will become better balanced.
☛ Robert et Agnès Schulte, Ch. de Beaulieu, 47180 Saint-Sauveur-de-Meilhan, tel. 05.53.94.30.40, fax 05.53.94.81.73,
e-mail chateaudebeaulieu@hotmail.com ☑
☖ ev. day 8am–12 noon 2pm–6pm; Sat. Sun. by appt.

BEROY 2001★★

■	2 ha	10,000	◐	5–8 €

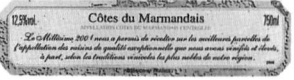

Beroy is a *lieu-dit* in the commune which means "beautiful" in the Gascon dialect. This wine has both a beautiful deep-crimson colour, and a beautiful bouquet combining soft fruits and bilberry on a very fine base of oak and vanilla. The palate too is beautiful, with a very rounded and full-bodied attack of ripe fruits, a touch of liquorice and fine soft tannins. The body has been well controlled and the wine is already pleasant to drink, but could also be laid down for a few years.
☛ Cave de Cocumont, La Vieille Eglise, 47250 Cocumont, tel. 05.53.94.50.21, fax 05.53.94.52.84,
e-mail accueil@cave-cocumont.fr ☑ ⛁ ⚑
☖ by appt.

CHAPELLE SAINT LAURENT 2001★

■	n.c.	200,000	■ ♦	–3 €

This is a traditional wine with a certain charm. Fairly intense fruits and spices combine in the bouquet with great finesse. The attack is pleasing, rounded, and heralds a balanced wine: the fruit is prominent on the palate, accompanied by supple and light tannins. Drink it while young and still full of fruit.
☛ Cave coop. des vignerons de Beaupuy, 47200 Marmande, tel. 05.53.76.05.10, fax 05.53.64.63.90,
e-mail contact@cavedebeaupuy.com ☑
☖ ev. day except Sun. 8.30am–12 noon 2pm–6.30pm

DOM. DES GEAIS 2001★

■	6 ha	45,000	■ ♦	5–8 €

The presence of Syrah is evident in the light, spicy bouquet with its ripe fruits, full of finesse and subtlety. On the palate, the wine is rather easy to drink because its tannins are mature and balanced. This will make it go well with charcuterie or grilled meats.
☛ Vignobles Boissonneau, Cathelicq, 33190 Saint-Michel-de-Lapujade, tel. 05.56.61.72.14, fax 05.56.61.71.01,
e-mail vignobles@boissonneau.fr ☑
☖ by appt.

CH. LA GRAVETTE
Vieilli en fût de chêne 2001★★

■	5 ha	40,000	◐	3–5 €

The nose is complex, very fine and intense. Oaky and grilled notes mingle with small soft fruits and caramel. The first impression is surprisingly fresh but the tannins are rounded, pleasant and well structured. The fruitiness and the oak combine perfectly on the palate. This suggests the wine will be at its best in two to three years. Also enjoyable is Ghislaine Laulan's **Château Lambert**, with its attractive bouquet of overripe fruits and prune. On the palate, the tannin is well balanced with renewed notes of strawberry, bilberry and liquorice. This is a pleasant fruity cocktail.
☛ Cave de Cocumont, La Vieille Eglise, 47250 Cocumont, tel. 05.53.94.50.21, fax 05.53.94.52.84,
e-mail accueil@cave-cocumont.fr ☑ ⛁ ⚑
☖ by appt.
☛ Didier Labeau

LAFON FERRAN 2001★

■	10 ha	80,000	■	3–5 €

Lafon Ferran is not a concentrated wine but, rather, a light and very drinkable product. The bouquet has good fruit and finesse, the attack is rounded revealing soft and smooth tannins and a fruity finish which is very fine. Serve it slightly chilled with a barbecue. The Jury liked this other fruity **Marescot 2001**, which also wins one star. The fruits are very ripe and have a flavour of jam. The tannins are softening and the finish is tasty. Here are two wines to drink now.
☛ Cave de Cocumont, La Vieille Eglise, 47250 Cocumont, tel. 05.53.94.50.21, fax 05.53.94.52.84,
e-mail accueil@cave-cocumont.fr ☑ ⛁ ⚑
☖ by appt.

CH. DE LESCOUR 2001★

■	n.c.	n.c.	■ ♦	3–5 €

After the wine is swirled in the glass, the complex and pleasant bouquet conveys notes of ripe fruits and, in particular, black-currant. These ripe fruit aromas reappear strongly on the palate around a light and supple tannic structure. This wine is balanced and has excellent length. It is already pleasant, and will be perfect in two to three years.
☛ Cave coop. des vignerons de Beaupuy, 47200 Marmande, tel. 05.53.76.05.10, fax 05.53.64.63.90,
e-mail contact@cavedebeaupuy.com ☑
☖ ev. day except Sun. 8.00am–12 noon 2pm–6.30pm
☛ Robert Philippot

CH. SARRAZIERE

Elévé en fût Sélection Vieilles Vignes 2001★

■	2 ha	15,000	❶❶	5–8 €

This wine was obviously matured in barrel, and the wine and the oak combine perfectly in the bouquet. On the palate, the tannic concentration is remarkable, with a good balance between the fruit and the oak. This wine is sufficiently tannic but already supple and rounded, and could be drunk young but will improve with age in a few years. The **Cuvée Classique du Château 2001 (3–5 €)** was not matured in oak; it also wins one star. The tannins are full and fleshy with pleasant notes of blackcurrant. This is a pleasant wine and is very enjoyable to drink.
☛ Cave de Cocumont, La Vieille Eglise, 47250 Cocumont, tel. 05.53.94.50.21, fax 05.53.94.52.84,
e-mail accueil@cave-cocumont.fr ☑ ❷ ❸
☖ by appt.
☛ EARL Duthuron

TAP D'E PERBOS 2001★★

■	5 ha	40,000	❶❶	5–8 €

An extra star this year for a wine that is becoming a safe bet in the Côtes du Marmandais. The nose is both intense and fine with strong fruity aromas of morello cherry and plum pleasantly complemented by the oak. On the palate, the first impression is full bodied. The tannins are beautifully concentrated with notes of prune, liquorice and, of course, vanilla. This is a very attractive wine with good length and complexity. It is advisable to keep it for two to three years.
☛ Cave de Cocumont, La Vieille Eglise, 47250 Cocumont, tel. 05.53.94.50.21, fax 05.53.94.52.84,
e-mail accueil@cave-cocumont.fr ☑ ❷ ❸
☖ by appt.

TERSAC 2001★

■	15 ha	120,000	■ ◆	3–5 €

This Tersac is notable for its pleasant fruitiness. On the nose, the fruits are intense and very fresh. On the palate, the tannins are well integrated and well balanced. The finish is pleasant and persistent, a sign of good grapes well vinified. One star also for the **Château Monplaisir 2001**, with its pronounced oakiness: the bouquet has toasty and vanilla notes, but the tannins are very soft and ripe. Keep it for one or two years so that the oak can soften and reveal the wine.
☛ Cave de Cocumont, La Vieille Eglise, 47250 Cocumont, tel. 05.53.94.50.21, fax 05.53.94.52.84,
e-mail accueil@cave-cocumont.fr ☑ ❷ ❸
☖ by appt.

Vins d'Estaing AOVDQS

The vineyard of Aveyron is surrounded by the limestone plateaux of Aubrac, the Cantal mountains and the Plateau du Lévezou, so it should really be classified with the vineyards of the Massif Central. The little appellations here are very old: their original foundation by the monks of Conques goes back to the 11th century.

The Vins d'Estaing (14 ha) are divided between the fresh, perfumed reds (blackcurrant and raspberry) made from Fer Sevadou and Gamay (444 hl) and the very original whites from mixtures of Chenin, Mauzac and Rousselou (36 hl). The latter are lively, flinty wines with strong terroir character.

Wines selected but not starred

LES VIGNERONS D'OLT

Cuvée Prestige 2002

■	3.5 ha	12,000	■	3–5 €

☛ Les Vignerons d'Olt, Z.A. La Fage, 12190 Estaing, tel. 05.65.44.04.42, fax 05.65.44.04.42,
e-mail cave.vigneronsdolt@wanadoo.fr ☑
☖ by appt.

Vins d'Entraygues et du Fel AOVDQS

The white wines from Entraygues (6 ha producing 151 hl in 2002) are cultivated on schist soils on narrow terracing cut into the steep hillsides. Made from Chenin and Mauzac, they are fresh and fruity: splendid with wild trout and the delicate Cantal cheese. The sturdy, earthy reds, made from Fel (508 hl produced from 15 ha), are good paired with lamb from the Causses and Potée Auvergnate – a substantial soup of vegetables and meat.

Wines selected but not starred

JEAN-MARC VIGUIER 2001

■	2 ha	8,000	■ ◆	5–8 €

☛ Jean-Marc Viguier, Les Buis, 12140 Entraygues, tel. 05.65.44.50.45, fax 05.65.48.62.72 ☑
☖ ev. day 9am–12 noon 2pm–7pm

Marcillac

Cultivated in a natural hollow, the "valley", with a propitious micro-climate, the Mansoi variety (also known as the Fer Servadou) gives the red Marcillac wines their great originality, marked by a tannic simplicity and aromas of raspberries. In 1990, this specialist approach was acknowledged with the award of an AOC, which now covers 158 ha and in 2002 produced 7,415 hl of a highly individual wine that is always instantly recognizable.

DOM. DE LADRECHT 2001★★

■	2 ha	9,500	↑ ♦	3–5 €

While the **Cuvée Réservée 2001** deserves to be singled out, this Domaine de Ladrecht, made from Fer Servadou, made an even greater impression with its garnet-red colour and perfumes of blackcurrant and notes of sweet pepper. After a supple attack, it is mouth filling and rich while remaining fresh and full of flavour. The silky tannins supplement this fresh, fruity and characteristic wine.

↑ Les Vignerons du Vallon, RN 140, 12330 Valady,
tel. 05.65.72.70.21, fax 05.65.72.68.39 ☑
✖ by appt.

Wines selected but not starred

DOM. LAURENS

Cuvée du Château de Flars 2000

■	11 ha	7,600	⑪	8–11 €

↑ Dom. Laurens, 12330 Clairvaux, tel. 05.65.72.69.37,
fax 05.65.72.76.74, e-mail info@domaine-laurens.com ☑
✖ by appt.

Côtes de Millau AOVDQS

The appellation AOVDQS Côtes de Millau was officially recognized on 12 April 1994. The wines are made from Syrah and Gamay Noir and, in a very small proportion, from Cabernet Sauvignon and Fer Servadou. Production reached about 1,854 hl from 47 ha in 2002.

MAITRE DES SAMPETTES 2000★★

■	4.74 ha	20,000	⑪	5–8 €

The Vignerons des Gorges du Tarn have acquired semi-natural caves for their wine cellar, with a constant temperature, and here they mature their red wines. The first wine from this new location is a success. Its intense and complex nose releases notes of sweet spices, cinnamon and stewed fruits. After a supple first impression, the wine is balanced by evident tannins. The flavours on the palate are marked by a very attractive smokiness. This wine is a credit to its appellation.

↑ SCV les Vignerons des Gorges du Tarn, 6, av. des Causses, 12520 Aguessac, tel. 05.65.59.84.11,
fax 05.65.59.17.90 ☑
✖ ev. day except Sun. 8am–12 noon 2pm–6pm

DOM. DU VIEUX NOYER 2002★

■	1.28 ha	5,500	↑ ♦	3–5 €

Bernard Portalier has been running his business since 1994 and is a regular in the *Guide*. This year, he presents a characteristic Côtes de Millau rosé made from Gamay and Syrah. It has a brilliant clear colour, heralding a pleasant nose of soft fruits (strawberry). On the palate it is fresh, vigorous and clear-cut, and will go well with charcuterie.

↑ Dom. du Vieux Noyer, Boyne, 12640 Rivière-sur-Tarn,
tel. 05.65.62.64.57, fax 05.65.62.64.57 ☑ ☎
✖ ev. day 9am–12.30pm 3pm–7pm; cl. Jan.
↑ Bernard Portalier

Béarn

Béarn wines can be produced in three different areas. The first two are the same as for Jurançon and Madiran. The other, Béarn alone, encompasses the communes around Orthez and Salies-de-Béarn, including Bellocq. This AOC covers about 204 ha and produced 8,627 hl of wine in 2002, of which 60 hl was white.

The vineyard was reconstituted after the phylloxera epidemic and occupies the gravels and pre-Pyrenean hills of the Gave region. The red varieties include Tannat, Cabernet Sauvignon and Cabernet Franc (Bouchy), as well as the old varieties of Manseng Noir, Courby Rouge and Fer Servadou. The wines are full bodied and rich, and are good with "garbure" (a local soup), and grilled woodpigeon. The rosés of Béarn, the best wines of the appellation, are lively but delicate with fine aromas from the Cabernet.

DOM. LARRIBERE 2001★

■	6 ha	33,000	↑ ♦	3–5 €

The pretty bigaroon cherry colour heralds fresh aromas of fruits and spices with moderate musky notes. This is a well-made wine, warming and with good tannins which remain agreeably fresh. It does credit to the potential of the Béarn appellation.

↑ Cave des producteurs de Jurançon, 53, av. Henri-IV, 64290 Gan, tel. 05.59.21.57.03, fax 05.59.21.72.06,
e-mail cave@cavejurancon.com ☑
✖ by appt.

Irouléguy

Irouléguy wines are grown on the last remnants of a big Basque vineyard (known as Chacoli on the Spanish side), founded in the 11th century by the monks of Roncevaux abbey, and today's wine-makers are determined to maintain this ancient tradition. The vineyard is laid out on foothills in the communes of Saint-Etienne-de-Baïgorry, Irouléguy and Anhaux, covering some 200 ha. In 2002 it produced 5,539 hl of wine, including 629 hl of white wine.

The older vine varieties have virtually disappeared in favour of Cabernet Sauvignon, Cabernet Franc and Tannat for red wines, and of Courbu and Gros and Petit Manseng for the whites. Practically the whole production is vinified by the cooperative in Irouléguy but new vineyards are now beginning to appear. The Irouléguy red is fragrant and somewhat tannic, worth trying with confits (duck or goose preserved in fat). The cherry-coloured rosé is lively, fragrant and light, and goes well with pipérade (eggs with peppers) and charcuterie.

ANDERENA 2001★

■	5 ha	24,000	↑ ⑪ ♦	5–8 €

In 2002, the cooperative celebrated its 50th anniversary. It has done well with this characteristic wine made from Gros Manseng (85%), Petit Manseng (10%) and Petit Courbu (5%). It is clear with golden highlights and releases elegant floral and fruity perfumes (peels of exotic fruits and citrus fruits). After a fresh attack, it is lively but well balanced with a pleasant sweetness and flavours of honey. The finish is very slightly acid.

⌐ Les Vignerons du Pays Basque, rte de Saint-Jean-Pied-de-Port, 64430 Saint-Etienne-de-Baïgorry, tel. 05.59.37.41.33, fax 05.59.37.47.76, e-mail irouleguy@hotmail.com ▪
☖ by appt.

DOM. ARRETXEA
Cuvée Haitza 2001★★★

| ■ | 1.8 ha | 8,000 | ▮ ◉ ♦ | 11–15 € |

Thérèse and Michel Riouspeyrous arrived in 1989 and run their 6 ha of terraced vines by sustainable agriculture. They use biodynamics on the plot where they grow white grapes. The Tannat is blended with 10% of Cabernet Sauvignon in this almost black wine which is full of aromas. The ripeness of the grapes emerges in crystallized black fruit scents, and again on a full palate perfectly structured by tasty tannins. The oak enhances the wine's complexity. You could keep it for three or four years.

⌐ Thérèse et Michel Riouspeyrous, Dom. Arretxea, 64220 Irouléguy, tel. 05.59.37.33.67, fax 05.59.37.33.67, e-mail domaine.arretxea@free.fr ▪
☖ by appt.

DOM. DE MIGNABERRY 2001★

| ■ | 25 ha | 110,000 | ◉ | 8–11 € |

An expressive wine with good potential. It has an intense black colour and opens strongly with ripe soft fruits. Its structure, well-coated tannins and fruity flavours are all impressive. Although the finish seems a little austere, it should develop well over the next five years. The **Irouléguy red Omenaldi 2001 Elevée en Fût de Chêne (11–15 €)** also wins one star.

⌐ Les Vignerons du Pays Basque, rte de Saint-Jean-Pied-de-Port, 64430 Saint-Etienne-de-Baïgorry, tel. 05.59.37.41.33, fax 05.59.37.47.76, e-mail irouleguy@hotmail.com ▪
☖ by appt.

JURANÇON AND JURANÇON SEC

"**W**hen I was a young woman, I made the acquaintance of a dazzling, imperious prince, as treacherous as any great seducer: Jurançon." So wrote the novelist Colette. Jurançon has been famous since it was served at the baptism of Henri IV and thereafter became the wine of occasion at all royal ceremonies of the House of Navarre. This is the first historical appearance of the notion of Appellation Protégée – since it was forbidden to import foreign wines – as well as the first steps towards Cru and classification, since all the parcels of land were recorded, according to their value, by

the Parliament of Navarre. Like the Béarn wines, those of the Jurançon, then both red and white, were shipped as far as Bayonne via the sometimes hazardous waters of the Gave. Much appreciated by the Dutch and the Americans, Jurançon acquired a star quality which was only extinguished by phylloxera. Under the dynamic leadership of the Cave de Gan and a few committed vineyard owners, the vineyard (100 ha used in 2002) was completely replanted with traditional varieties grown and trained according to the old ways.

Here more than anywhere, year of vintage is extremely important, especially for the sweet Jurançons, for which the grapes must be ripened late on the vine by the passerillage method. The traditional varieties used for Jurançon are whites only, the Gros and Petit Manseng and the Courbu. In cultivation, the vines are trained high to avoid the frosts, and it is not unusual for the harvest to continue until the first snows.

The dry Jurançon, 75% of the production, is a white wine made from white grapes (Blanc de Blancs), noted for its beautiful colour with glints of green, its aromas and its honeyed flavours. It is a good accompaniment to fresh trout and salmon from the river Gave. The sweet Jurançons have a lovely golden colour, and offer complex aromas of exotic fruits (pineapple and guava) and spices (such as nutmeg and cinnamon). Their balance between acidity and sweetness makes them a perfect foil for foie gras. Sweet Jurançons can be kept for a long time to provide big wines for a whole meal from aperitif to dessert, as well as to accompany fish with sauce and ewe's milk cheeses from the Ossau valley. In 2002 production reached 35,516 hl.

Jurançon

DOM. BELLEGARDE
Sélection DB 2001★★

| ■ | 1 ha | 1,500 | ◉ | 46–76 € |

Pascal Labasse produces 80% sweet Jurançons and 20% dry wines. His mastery of these kinds of wine is evident both in the **Cuvée Thibault 2001 (11–15 €)**, which was judged very successful, and in this Sélection with its pronounced coppery-yellow colour. Although the latter's nose seems to be subdued, it is still deep, revealing that the grapes were first dried on the vine, and releases accents of crystallized fruits and a rich oakiness. The full and powerful palate is concentrated and full of sweet flavours. A fine achievement, with an excellent structure.

⌐ Pascal Labasse, quartier Coos, 64360 Monein, tel. 05.59.21.33.17, fax 05.59.21.44.40, e-mail domaine.bellegarde@wanadoo.fr ▪
☖ ev. day except Sun. 10am–12 noon 2pm–7pm

DOM. BORDENAVE
Cuvée Savin 2001★★

| ■ | 5 ha | n.c. | ◉ | 15–23 € |

Gisèle Bordenave has done extremely well. The **sweet Domaine Bordenave Cuvée des Dames 2001 (11–15 €)** was thought remarkable, and the **sweet Jurançon P. Bordenave Harmonie 2001 (8–11 €)** and the **dry Jurançon P. Bordenave Souvenirs d'Enfance 2002 (5–8 €)** win one star. Meanwhile, the Cuvée Savin delighted the Grand Jury with its intense golden appearance. The glass releases a parade of crystallized exotic

fruits with a touch of truffle. The very tasty flavours combine perfectly with the oak, then the fruity finish sees a pleasant return of the freshness. This full wine is already superb and has great potential.
- Gisèle Bordenave, quartier Ucha, 64360 Monein, tel. 05.59.21.34.83, fax 05.59.21.37.32, e-mail domaine.bordenave@wanadoo.fr ☑
- ev. day 9am–7pm

DOM. BRU-BACHE

L'Eminence 2001★★

	n.c.	n.c.	⑪	38–46 €

The **Quintessence 2001 (15–23 €)** features regularly in the *Guide* and wins one star, leaving the place of honour to L'Eminence which this year came very close to the *coup de cœur*. Its old-gold colour with intense coppery highlights releases scents of honey, quince jelly and crystallized exotic fruits which invade the senses, accompanied by a rich oakiness. The very liqueur-like palate is mouth filling, full of flavours and a promising oak. This wine is likely to become exceptional.
- Dom. Bru-Baché, rue Barada, 64360 Monein, tel. 05.59.21.36.34, fax 05.59.21.32.67 ☑
- by appt.
- Claude Loustalot

DOM. DE CABARROUY

Classique 2001★

	1.5 ha	8,000	⋯	8–11 €

This clear straw-coloured wine releases high-quality, fairly complex aromas of flowers with notes of honey and mineral. After a lively first impression, the palate remains fresh and full of flavour while developing a well-balanced roundness. The **Cuvée Sainte-Catherine 2001 (11–15 €)** is also very successful.
- Dom. de Cabarrouy, 64290 Lasseube, tel. 05.59.04.23.08, fax 05.59.04.21.85 ☑
- ev. day 9am–12.30pm 2pm–7pm; Mon. Sun. by appt.
- Patrice Limousin, Freya Skoda

CANCAILLAU

Gourmandise 2001★

	2.5 ha	8,000	⑪	11–15 €

This characteristic Jurançon is very fruity beneath its pale-yellow colour with green highlights. The pure and delicate bouquet offers pineapple, apricot, pear and mango, with nuances of honey and acacia. The flavours increase steadily throughout the tasting.
- EARL Barrère, 64150 Lahourcade, tel. 05.59.60.08.15, fax 05.59.60.07.38 ☑
- ev. day except Sun. 8am–7pm; cl. 8 Oct.–15 Nov.

CLOS BENGUERES

Le Chêne couché 2001★

	1.3 ha	4,000	⑪	11–15 €

This typical Béarn farm has 4.5 ha of vines, and offers this attractive, well-made wine. Butter and pineapple make a strong show throughout the tasting. This is an expressive and lively wine, with a rather intense-yellow colour.
- Thierry Bousquet, Clos Benguères, 64360 Cuqueron, tel. 05.59.21.48.40, fax 05.59.21.43.03, e-mail closbengueres@aol.com ☑
- ev. day 9am–7pm

CLOS CASTET

Cuvée spéciale Vieilli en fût de chêne neuf 2001★

	3 ha	10,000	⑪	11–15 €

This intense golden-yellow Jurançon has plenty of energy with its scents of jam, fruit pastes, mango, medlar and grapefruit. There is a great freshness about the flavours, which remain fruity and very sweet.
- Alain Labourdette, GAEC Labourdette, 64360 Cardesse, tel. 05.59.21.33.09, fax 05.59.21.28.22 ☑
- ev. day 9am–7pm

CLOS GASSIOT

Elégance 2001★

	4 ha	5,000	⋯	11–15 €

Antoine Tavernier has been gradually restoring this estate since 1988; he has just completed the renovation of an old building for maturing his wines. This golden-straw Jurançon has a rather intense, fresh and spicy nose, with nuances of crystallized grapes. It is reasonably sweet and also reveals a certain fruity freshness and a persistent finish. The **Mémoire 2001 (15–23 €)** was singled out.
- Antoine Tavernier, 5, rue du Centre, 64360 Abos, tel. 05.59.60.10.22, fax 05.59.71.58.92 ☑
- ev. day 9am–7pm; Sat. Sun. 10am–1pm 3pm–7pm; cl. 23 Dec.–5 Jan.

CLOS GUIROUILH

Petit Cuyalàa 2001★★

	0.8 ha	1,400	⑪	30–38 €

Petit Cuyalàa is a great Jurançon. It has a splendid golden colour with coppery highlights, and releases a range of rich and fresh flavours combining crystallized fruits, oriental infusions and a beautiful note of truffle. It is dense, perfectly balanced and expressive. A wine of great elegance. The **dry Jurançon Clos Guirouilh 2002 (5–8 €)** wins one star.
- Jean Guirouilh, rte de Belair, 64290 Lasseube, tel. 05.59.04.21.45, fax 05.59.04.22.73 ☑
- by appt.

CLOS MARIE-LOUISE

Elevé en fût de chêne 2001★

	1.5 ha	1,000	⑪	15–23 €

This producer started using sustainable agriculture for his 7 ha of vines in 2000. He offers a wine with a frank golden-yellow colour which releases a vanilla and toasty oak followed by aromas of exotic fruits and apricot. Its full, pleasantly sweet palate reveals buttered and caramelized notes, supported by a welcome freshness.
- Aurisset, 64360 Cardesse, tel. 05.59.21.32.01, fax 05.59.21.32.01 ☑
- by appt.

CLOS THOU

Suprême de Thou 2001★

	2.5 ha	8,000	⑪	11–15 €

A beautiful golden colour welcomes the taster to a wine that releases scents of very mature fruits with exotic accents, liberally honeyed. The palate confirms this impression with a similar intensity, tasting like a mouthful of royal jelly.
- Henri Lapouble-Laplace, chem. Larredya, clos Thou, 64110 Jurançon, tel. 05.59.06.08.60, fax 05.59.06.08.60, e-mail clos.thou@wanadoo.fr ☑
- ev. day except Sun. 9am–12 noon 2pm–6.30pm

CH. LAFITTE

Cuvée Carpen diem 2001★

	0.5 ha	500	⑪	46–76 €

The 14th century château above a hillside covered with vines makes a nice illustration to the label of this intense golden Vin Jaune. The tasters enjoyed its aromas of exotic fruits and scents reminiscent of a honey pot, and the elegant, fresh and fruity flavours which present themselves in abundance. (50 cl bottles)
- Jacques Balent, château Lafitte, 64360 Monein, tel. 05.59.21.49.44, fax 05.59.21.43.01, e-mail j.balent@wanadoo.fr ☑
- by appt.

DOM. LARROUDE

Un Jour d'Automne 2001★★

0.5 ha	1,500	◧	15–23 €

Drink this Jurançon while it is fresh and its golden-yellow colour glitters with coppery highlights, and the subdued but complex bouquet leaves thoughts of *pain d'épice* and fruit cake with crystallized fruits. The attack is sweet and fresh, then rich and mouth-filling, prolonged agreeably with very fruity and slightly acid notes. The **dry Jurançon 2002 du domaine (5–8 €)** wins one star for its finesse.
☛ Julien Estoueigt, EARL du Dom. Larroudé, 64360 Lucq-de-Béarn, tel. 05.59.34.35.92, fax 05.59.34.35.92 ☑
☎ by appt.

DOM. LATAPY 2001★

3 ha	10,000	◧	15–23 €

Irène Guilhendou, together with her mother and three children, cultivates 4.5 ha of vines. Her golden-yellow Jurançon with mineral accents and a bouquet of spices, offers a very sweet, spicy body (cinnamon and saffron), but the wine has an underlying freshness that enlivens the flavours. The **dry Jurançon 2001 (11–15 €)** also wins one star.
☛ Irène Guilhendou, chem. Berdoulou, 64290 Gan, tel. 05.59.21.71.84, fax 05.59.21.71.61 ☑ ☗
☎ by appt.

DOM. DE MALARRODE Cuvée Prestige

Vendanges de novembre Vieilli en fût de chêne 2001★

2.5 ha	6,100	◧	11–15 €

Orange highlights give this wine a coppery colour. The bouquet is surprisingly deep, with aromas of crystallized fruits, notes of medlar and persimmon, spices and honey with oaky accents. The body is full and concentrated, very rich in sugar, and reveals a more pronounced oak, but is always well balanced. This is a true sweet wine.
☛ Gaston Mansanné, quartier Uchaa, 64360 Monein, tel. 05.59.21.44.27, fax 05.59.21.44.27 ☑
☎ by appt.

DOM. MONTAUT

Cuvée Prestige 2001★

3.5 ha	18,700	◧ ♦	8–11 €

This golden Jurançon combines dried fruits and crystallized fruits, honey and acacia, and is full as well as lively. The aromas return in a very lingering finish. A wine with a full range of flavours.
☛ Montaut, quartier Haut-Ucha, 64360 Monein, tel. 05.59.21.38.17, fax 05.59.21.38.17 ☑
☎ ev. day 9am–12 noon 2pm–8pm

DOM. DE MONTESQUIOU

Grappe d'or 2001★★★

2 ha	6,300	◧	11–15 €

Since the 18th century, this estate has been handed down from father to son. The 4.5 ha of vines planted on a hillside facing the Pyrenees were taken over in 2002 by Sébastien Bordenave-Montesquieu. The tasters gave this Jurançon top place. It has a bright golden-yellow colour and an expressive and refined nose combining orange peel, apricot and crystallized pineapple with a praliné aroma. It is full, packed with fruits, and lingering on the palate. Its admirable freshness was the high point of the tasting.
☛ Gérard Bordenave-Montesquieu, Quartier Haut-Ucha, 64360 Monein, tel. 05.59.21.43.49, fax 05.59.21.43.49 ☑
☎ ev. day except Sun. 8am–12 noon 2pm–7pm

DOM. PEYRETTE 2001★★

2 ha	6,000	◧ ♦	8–11 €

Patrick Peyrette has really got the best out of this vintage with this golden straw-yellow wine with intense aromas of exotic fruits (pineapple and mango) and dried fruits (toasted almond). On the palate it is rounded, full and warming, with a perfect balance between the freshness and the sugar. Its body shows great maturity.
☛ Patrick Peyrette, Dom. Peyrette, chem. des Vignes, 64360 Cuqueron, tel. 05.59.21.31.10, fax 05.59.21.31.10 ☑
☎ ev. day 9am–7pm

CH. DE ROUSSE 2001★★

3 ha	12,000	◧	11–15 €

Vines have been grown here since the 15th century. In this old hunting lodge of Henri IV, you will enjoy tasting two beautiful wines from this estate while looking at a panoramic view of the Pyrenees. The **Cuvée Séduction 2001 (11–15 €)** is remarkable and so is this sweet wine. It is rich and dense, reminiscent of roasted grapes and crystallized fruits. Its very concentrated palate offers flavours of honey and jam in a long finish.
☛ Marc Labat, Ch. de Rousse, La Chapelle-de-Rousse, 64110 Jurançon, tel. 05.59.21.75.08, fax 05.59.21.76.54, e-mail marc.labat@wanadoo.fr ☑
☎ by appt.

DOM. DE SOUCH

Cuvée de Marie-Kattalin 2001★

5.5 ha	8,000	◧	15–23 €

Yvonne Hegoburu has run her vineyard of 6.5 ha by biodynamic methods since 1994. She offers a Cuvée de Marie-Kattalin (pronounced "Kattialine") which is well balanced and both warming and fresh. It has an amber-yellow colour and rich aromas of flowers, honey and crystallized apricot plus a mineral note. The **Jurançon dry Domaine de Souch 2001 (8–11 €)** was singled out.
☛ Yvonne Hegoburu, Dom. de Souch, Laroin, 64110 Jurançon, tel. 05.59.06.27.22, fax 05.59.06.51.55 ☑
☎ by appt.

DOM. LES TERRASSES 2001★

5 ha	20,000	◧ ♦	5–8 €

The cooperative has produced a lovely sweet wine, the Domaine Les Terrasses, which has a sparkling golden-yellow colour and opens when the glass is swirled with a cool fruitiness. More expressive is the palate, which is already rounded, balanced and full of flavour, supported by an invigorating freshness. The **Château Les Astous 2001 (8–11 €)** and the **Privilège d'Automne 2001 (11–15 €)** also win one star.
☛ Cave des producteurs de Jurançon, 53, av. Henri-IV, 64290 Gan, tel. 05.59.21.57.03, fax 05.59.21.72.06, e-mail cave@cavejurancon.com ☑
☎ by appt.

Jurançon Sec

DOM. CAPDEVIELLE

Brise Océane 2002★★

1.5 ha	11,000	◧	5–8 €

In 1990, the Capdevielle family concentrated solely on their vines, giving up the maturation process and growing other crops. They find their reward in high-quality wines such as the **sweet Noblesse d'Automne 2001 (8–11 €)**, which is excellent value, and this brilliant Vin Jaune with green highlights. The very promising bouquet seems a little reserved, but is already releasing notes of citrus fruits and pineapple. It is perfectly balanced, and at the same time fresh and rich, with a pleasant impression of roundness and fullness, and promises to open out more with time.

➤ Didier Capdevielle, quartier Coos, 64360 Monein, tel. 05.59.21.30.25, fax 05.59.21.30.25, e-mail domaine.capdevielle@wanadoo.fr ☑
⏳ ev. day 8.30am–12 noon 1pm–7pm; Sun. by appt.

DOM. CASTERA 2002★

	4 ha	19,900	🍾 ♦	5–8 €

The **Jurançon sweet Cuvée Privilège 2001 (11–15 €)** wins one star, like this dry pale-golden wine with green highlights, which opens with notes of grapefruit and dried fruits. The attack is soft and fresh, and the palate follows suit, though with mounting fruitiness, through to the finish.

➤ Christian Lihour, quartier Ucha, 64360 Monein, tel. 05.59.21.34.98, fax 05.59.21.46.34, e-mail christian-lihour@wanadoo.fr ☑
⏳ ev. day except Sun. 9am–12 noon 2pm–7pm

DOM. CAUHAPE

Sève d'Automne 2001★★

	8 ha	32,000	🍾🍾	11–15 €

Henri Ramonteu excels with both sweet and dry wines. He confirms this again with these Jurançons, the **Quintessence du Petit-Manseng 2001 (more than 76 €)**, which is remarkable, and the **Noblesse du Temps 2001 (23–30 €)**, which is very successful, like this dry wine with golden highlights and intense aromas of ripe fruits and flowers with nuances of honey. The well-balanced palate is full, even powerful, and fresh too, and retains its splendid range of flavours. This is high art.

➤ Henri Ramonteu, Dom. Cauhapé, quartier Castet, 64360 Monein, tel. 05.59.21.33.02, fax 05.59.21.41.82, e-mail domainecauhape@wanadoo.fr ☑
⏳ by appt.

DOM. DU CINQUAU 2002★★

	3 ha	12,000	🍾 ♦	5–8 €

This attractive, intense straw-yellow 2002 is a characteristic Jurançon, both fresh and pleasant with complex aromas of exotic fruits (mango and pink grapefruit). Initially fresh on the palate, it soon fills the mouth, and produces concentrated aromas. Also worth trying is the estate's **sweet Jurançon 2001 (11–15 €)**, which wins one star.

➤ Pierre Saubot, Dom. du Cinquau, Cidex 43, 64230 Artiguelouve, tel. 05.59.83.10.41, fax 05.59.83.12.93, e-mail p.saubot@jurancon.com ☑
⏳ by appt.

COLLECTION ROYALE 2002★

	n.c.	n.c.	🍾 ♦	8–11 €

Green nuances enliven the pale-golden colour of this light, fresh wine with perfumes of white peach and brioche, and accents of blackcurrant bud. The palate is both sweet and slightly acid, continuing on a note of grapefruit and a touch of bitterness.

➤ Etienne Brana, 3 bis, av. du Jaï-Alaï, 64220 Saint-Jean-Pied-de-Port, tel. 05.59.37.00.44, fax 05.59.37.14.28, e-mail brana-etienne@wanadoo.fr ☑
⏳ by appt.

GRAIN SAUVAGE 2002★★

	200 ha	100,000	🍾 ♦	3–5 €

The Jurançon producers' cooperative offered a range of very well-made dry Jurançons: the **Château Les Astous 2002 (5–8 €)** and the **Château Roquehort 2002 (5–8 €)** were judged very successful, while this pale, crystalline Grain Sauvage delighted the Jury even more. Its particularly subtle bouquet releases pretty floral notes (acacia and lime blossom), as well as nuances of fresh fruits. The rounded, very fresh palate and intense aromas increase in harmony.

➤ Cave des producteurs de Jurançon, 53, av. Henri-IV, 64290 Gan, tel. 05.59.21.57.03, fax 05.59.21.72.06, e-mail cave@cavejurancon.com ☑
⏳ by appt.

CHARLES HOURS

Cuvée Marie 2001★

	8 ha	50,000	🍾🍾	8–11 €

For 20 years, Charles Hours has belonged to the circle of men who have brought fame to the appellations of the Sud-Ouest. This elegant wine was matured for 11 months in barrel, and confirms the estate's reputation. It is the colour of fresh straw with green highlights, and combines white flowers and exotic fruits with a lemony touch and a vanilla note. Its balanced palate is fresh with good alcoholic support. The aromas continue on the palate up to a slightly bitter finish.

➤ Charles Hours, quartier Trouilh, 64360 Monein, tel. 05.59.21.46.19, fax 05.59.21.46.90 ☑
⏳ by appt.

LAPEYRE 2002★★

	2 ha	n.c.	🍾	5–8 €

This straw-yellow Jurançon attracted the Grand Jury, who noted the skilful maturation evident in its subtle and complex spices, range of ripe-fruit flavours and fresh almond. It is mouth filling, balanced, well structured and has good length. Also worthy of praise is the new **sweet Jurançon, Magendia de Lapeyre 2001 (11–15 €)**, which was very successful.

➤ Jean-Bernard Larrieu, La Chapelle-de-Rousse, 64110 Jurançon, tel. 05.59.21.50.80, fax 05.59.21.51.83, e-mail jean-bernard.larrieu@wanadoo.fr ☑
⏳ ev. day except Sun. 9am–12 noon 2pm–6pm

DOM. LARREDYA 2002★★

	2 ha	12,000	🍾 ♦	5–8 €

This 2002 wine is not just remarkable but one of the best dry Jurançons of the year. With its brilliant golden highlights, it releases intense and fresh floral scents, and spices. After a clear-cut attack, it develops a liveliness which balances its flesh and accompanies the clean aroma. This wine has real presence and is superbly made. The **sweet Jurançon Sélection des Terrasses 2001 (11–15 €)** and the **Simon 2001 (23–30 €)** each win one star.

➤ Jean-Marc Grussaute, La Chapelle-de-Rousse, 64110 Jurançon, tel. 05.59.21.74.42, fax 05.59.21.76.72 ☑
⏳ by appt.

DOM. NIGRI 2002★★

	5 ha	23,000	🍾 ♦	5–8 €

As charming as the landscape it came from, this pretty yellow Jurançon with green highlights releases intense perfumes of fruit drops and white flowers. Its suppleness is immediately evident on the palate, and the rich tannins remain perfectly balanced until the finish. The **sweet Jurançon Réserve du Domaine Nigri 2001 (11–15 €)** is very successful.

➤ Jean-Louis Lacoste, Dom. Nigri, Candeloup, 64360 Monein, tel. 05.59.21.42.01, fax 05.59.21.42.59, e-mail domaine.nigri@wanadoo.fr ☑
⏳ by appt.

PRIMO PALATUM

Classica 2001★★

	1 ha	1,800	ⅷ	15–23 €

This beautifully made Jurançon was in contention for the final round and narrowly missed the *coup de coeur*. With its superb brilliant golden colour, it offers a complex nose with an elegant oak alongside perfumes of ripe fruits and honey. Although the attack is both fresh and sweet at the same time, it gathers fullness and richness to finish with an infinity of flavours. Its composition is quite remarkable.
☛ Primo Palatum, 1, Cirette, 33190 Morizès,
tel. 05.56.71.39.39, fax 05.56.71.39.40,
e-mail xavier-copel@primo-palatum.com ☑
⟡ by appt.
☛ Xavier Copel

Madiran

Madiran has its origins in Roman times and, later, was the wine of pilgrims making the long journey to Santiago de Compostela in Spain. The gastronomy of the Gers region and its popularity in Paris have also helped to promote this Pyrenean wine. Much of the 1,410 ha of the appellation is planted with Tannat, which produces a wine that is tannic in youth, vividly coloured, with preliminary scents of raspberries; it develops after long ageing. Cabernet Sauvignon and Cabernet Franc (or Bouchy) and Fer Servadou (or Pinenc) are blended with it. The vines are trained to half-height. The production was 63,981 hl in 2002.

The Madiran is a supremely virile wine. Its vinification can be adapted so it can be drunk young when its fruitiness and suppleness can be best displayed. It goes well with goose confits (preserved in fat) and duck breasts served rare. The traditional Madiran, with its high proportion of Tannat, ages very well in wooden casks and can mature for a number of years. The mature Madirans are sensual, fleshy and full bodied, with aromas of toasted bread, and go well with game and the ewe's milk cheeses from the high valleys.

CH. D'ARRICAU-BORDES

Grand Vin 2000★★

■	12 ha	2,000	ⅷ	11–15 €

The Tannat variety (50%) plus equal shares of the two Cabernets make up this intense-crimson wine that wins friends with its aromatic fullness. Along with ripe fruits and pronounced notes of roasting on a vanilla base, there is a fine oak. The palate is harmonious, both powerful and full thanks to its coated tannins. This is a Madiran with a future, but it is already drinkable.
☛ SA Ch. d'Arricau-Bordes, 64350 Arricau-Bordes,
tel. 05.62.69.62.87, fax 05.62.69.66.71,
e-mail m.darricau@plaimont.fr ☑
⟡ by appt.

ARTE BENEDICTE

Vieilles Vignes Elevé en fût de chêne 2000★★

■	100 ha	60,000	ⅷ	11–15 €

The Arte Benedicte was singled out in the 2002 *Guide* for its 1998 wine, and this year makes a notable return with an intense purple colour and brick-red highlights. Its maturation in barrel is evident in the toasted notes, chocolate and roasting on a base of blackcurrant and spices. It is certainly well structured, but silky too. Recommended for

patient wine-lovers. Also remarkable is the Madiran **La Mothe Peyran 2000 (5–8 €)** which has beautiful balance and intensity.
☛ Producteurs Plaimont, 32400 Saint-Mont,
tel. 05.62.69.62.87, fax 05.62.69.66.71,
e-mail f.latapy@plaimont.fr ☑ ⌂ ⌂
⟡ by appt.

CH. D'AYDIE 2001★

■	16 ha	80,000	ⅷ	11–15 €

This wine, made of Tannat (95%) and the Cabernets, was harvested on clay-limestone hillsides facing south-south-west and has colossal depth. The intense-black colour clearly reveals its long maturation in barrel. Spicy and toasty aromas re-emerge on a firmly tannic palate which needs to soften. This good-looking Madiran should be kept for three or four years.
☛ GAEC Vignobles Laplace, 64330 Aydie,
tel. 05.59.04.08.00, fax 05.59.04.08.08,
e-mail pierre.laplace@wanadoo.fr ☑
⟡ ev. day 9am–12.30pm 2pm–7pm

DOM. BERNET

Tradition 2001★

■	2 ha	12,000	▮	3–5 €

The pleasure is in the fruit. The dense-purple colour of this Madiran indicates its beautiful substance. The aromas burst forth, in turn evoking raspberry, blackcurrant, strawberry and a touch of pepper. The flavours follow the beautiful tannins of the grape variety. An expressive wine, with a reasonable price.
☛ Yves Doussau, Dom. Bernet, 32400 Viella,
tel. 05.62.69.71.99, fax 05.62.69.75.08 ☑ ⌂
⟡ ev. day except Sun. 8am–12 noon 2pm–7pm

DOM. BERTHOUMIEU

Haute Tradition 2001★★

■	12.3 ha	80,000	▮ ⚬	8–11 €

Didier Barré has won *coups de coeur* and with this Haute Tradition offers one of his classics. The inky, deep-purple colour is a magnificent match for the perfumes of ripe soft fruits and blackcurrant. The wine is very rich on the palate, with refined tannins and an elegant finish. Such are the results of a remarkable piece of winemaking.
☛ EARL Didier Barré, Dutour, 32400 Viella,
tel. 05.62.69.74.05, fax 05.62.69.80.64,
e-mail barre.didier@wanadoo.fr ☑
⟡ ev. day 8.30am–12 noon 2pm–7pm except Sun. 3pm–7pm

CH. BOUSCASSE 2001★

■	80 ha	200,000	ⅷ	8–11 €

Alain Brumont collects stars as well as the local grape varieties making up his Pacherenc-du-Vic-Bilh and his Madiran. This black-cherry coloured wine has a wonderful appearance. Aromas of red fruits are enriched by the oaky notes of the maturation, continuing on a warming palate with accents of fruit in *eau-de-vie*, supplemented by nuances of mocha coffee. The **dry Pacherenc-du-Vic-Bilh Les Jardins de Bouscassé 2002 (5–8 €)**, which was not matured in oak, was singled out, as was the **sweet Brumaire 2001 (11–15 €)** and the **Vendémiaire sweet 2001**, both matured in barrel.
☛ Alain Brumont, Bouscassé, SCEA Montus
Bouscassé, 32400 Maumusson-Laguian, tel. 05.62.69.74.67,
fax 05.62.69.70.46, e-mail brumont.alain@wanadoo.fr ☑
⟡ by appt.

CHAPELLE LENCLOS 2001★

■	6 ha	43,000	■ ⑪ ♦	11–15 €

Patrick Ducournau originated the technique of micro-oxygenation, which consists of introducing oxygen bubbles into the wine in the course of maturation in order to soften the powerful tannins of the Tannat grape variety. This is his version of a Madiran: a purple-coloured wine with a subdued but elegant nose, combining ripe fruits with a fine oak. His 2001 wine is balanced, full and rounded.
➻ Patrick Ducournau, Chapelle Lenclos, Dom. Mouréou, 32400 Maumusson-Laguian, tel. 05.62.69.78.11, fax 05.62.69.75.87 ☑
☚ ev. day 8am–1pm 2pm–6pm; Sat. Sun. and groups by appt.

CLOS FARDET

Moutoué Fardet Elevé en fût de chêne 2001★

■	1.05 ha	4,000	⑪	11–15 €

This is an intense Madiran with a controlled oak and a deep-purple colour. It releases aromas of spices and fruits and with time will gain in complexity, and will be even more mouth filling than it already is.
➻ SCEA Moutoué Fardet, Clos Fardet, 3, chem. de Beller, 65700 Madiran, tel. 05.62.31.91.37, fax 05.62.31.91.37, e-mail closfardet-madiran@libertysurf.fr ☑
☚ by appt.
➻ Pascal Savoret

DOM. DU CRAMPILH

L'Originel 2001★

■	3 ha	20,000	■ ♦	5–8 €

An intense, purplish-red colour clothes this fruity wine dominated by blackcurrant and a touch of pepper. On the palate it is rich and lingering and keeps the same range of flavours, built on coated tannins. It will certainly mature, but it is not a sin to drink it now. The **sweet Pacherenc-du-Vic-Bilh Domaine du Crampilh 2001 (8–11 €)** deserves to be singled out.
➻ Famille Oulié, Dom. du Crampilh, 64350 Aurions-Idernes, tel. 05.59.04.00.63, fax 05.59.04.04.97, e-mail madirancrampilh@aol.com ☑ ⌂
☚ ev. day except Sun. 9am–12.30 2pm–7pm

DOM. DAMIENS 2000★

■	2 ha	11,000	■ ⑪ ♦	8–11 €

Interesting: that was the tasters' verdict on this intense and brilliant-purple wine. The nose is indeed complex and fresh with its notes of soft fruits, kirsch and eucalyptus. The well-structured palate abounds with aromas of black fruits and stewed fruits. What is more, these are lasting pleasures.
➻ André et Pierre-Michel Beheity, Dom. Damiens, 64330 Aydie, tel. 05.59.04.03.13, fax 05.59.04.02.74 ☑
☚ ev. day 9am–12.30pm 2.30pm–6.30pm; Sat. Sun. by appt.

CH. DE DIUSSE

Cuvée Privilège Elevé en fût de chêne 2000★

■	2.5 ha	13,000	⑪	8–11 €

Be patient – in less than four years you will be able to enjoy this wine at its best with a dish of game. It is very complex and promising with its purplish-black colour, indicating its concentration. The aromas of black fruits (blackberry) mingle with toasted notes and touches of musk, while attractive tannins frame the wine as a whole.
➻ Dom. de Diusse, 64330 Diusse, tel. 05.59.04.02.83, fax 05.59.04.05.77 ☑
☚ by appt.

FOLIE DE ROI

Elevé en fût de chêne 2000★

■	20 ha	36,000	⑪	5–8 €

What is this "royal madness"? It is madly elegant with its crimson colour, complex in its evocations of black fruits, of blackberry combined with vanilla and spices, and full too, though somewhat austere, which ageing will have to cure. The cooperative of Crouseilles had some other successes: the Madiran **Château de Crouseilles 2000 Elevé en Fût de Chêne (8–11 €)** and the **C de Crouseilles Grand Vin 2000 (15–23 €)**

win one star, while the **Grande Réserve d'Or 2000 (8–11 €)** is singled out.
➻ Cave de Crouseilles, 64350 Crouseilles, tel. 05.62.69.66.87, fax 05.62.69.66.71, e-mail m.darricau@plaimont.fr ☑
☚ by appt.

DOM. LABRANCHE LAFFONT

Vieilles Vignes 2001★★

■	3.5 ha	20,000	⑪	8–11 €

The 2000 vintage won one star last year, and this one almost reached excellence in 2001. Its dark colour suggests black-cherry, which appears on the nose with aromas of kirsch and fruit in *eau-de-vie*. A touch of liquorice refreshes the palate, while the oak softens into the wine, giving remarkable balance. The **sweet Pacherenc-du-Vic-Bilh 2001** also gains two stars.
➻ EARL Christine Dupuy, 32400 Maumusson, tel. 05.62.69.74.90, fax 05.62.69.76.03 ☑
☚ ev. day 9am–12.30pm 2pm–7pm

DOM. LAFFONT

Hécate 2001★★

■	1 ha	4,900	⑪	15–23 €

Hécate is not only a magical goddess but also a benefactress. She no doubt leant over the barrels during the maturation of this wine, which won the *coup de cœur*. The colour of ink with ruby highlights, it has a fascinating, complex and elegant range of flavours: black fruits with menthol and eucalyptus. It is built round coated tannins, which provide its well-balanced character. A pure Tannat, absolutely marvellous. The sweet **Pacherenc-du-Vic-Bilh 2001 (11–15 €)** receives one star.
➻ Dom. Laffont, 32400 Maumusson, tel. 05.62.69.75.23, fax 05.62.69.80.27 ☑
☚ by appt.
➻ Pierre Speyer

LAPERRE COMBES Grande Réserve Vieilles

Vignes Elevé en fût de chêne 2001★★

■	100 ha	50,000	⑪	11–15 €

The vineyards of Gascogne always have intensely coloured wines. This Madiran follows the rule. It is black with cherry and deep-purple highlights, and once the glass is swirled releases an elegant fruitiness of plum, spices, menthol and cocoa. The palate is long, enclosing rich and rounded tannins. This wine is already pleasant, and can only open out with time. Other wines that satisfied the Jury were the **Château Saint-Bénazit 2000 (5–8 €)**, which wins one star; the **Château Laroche Viella 2000 (8–11 €)** and the **Courtet Laperre Grande Réserve Vieilles Vignes Elevé en Fût de Chêne 2000** were singled out.
➻ Vignoble de Gascogne, 32400 Riscle, tel. 05.62.69.62.87, fax 05.62.69.66.71, e-mail f.latapy@plaimont.fr ☑ ▣ ⌂
☚ by appt.

DOM. DU MOULIE

Cuvée Chiffre 2000★

■	3.5 ha	20,000	■ ⑪	8–11 €

This Madiran made from 40-year-old vines has a crimson colour with purple highlights. The fruitiness is expressed in tones of blackcurrant and redcurrant, with notes of vanilla and pepper. The supple structure is coated with a very ripe fruity substance. To enjoy the fruitiness of the grapes, drink this wine now; for the bouquet, keep it for two or three years. The **Cuvée Principale Domaine du Moulié 2001 (5–8 €)** also wins one star.

🍷 EARL Chiffre-Charrier, Dom. du Moulié,
32400 Cannet, tel. 05.62.69.77.73, fax 05.62.69.83.66 ☑
🍷 ev. day 9am–12.30pm 2pm–7pm
🍷 Charrier

PRIMO PALATUM

Mythologia 2000★★

■	n.c.	1,800	ⱴ	15–23 €

Primo Platum won a *coup de cœur* for the 1999 wine, and now offers a concentrated Mythologia. It was matured for 18 months in barrel, and wine-lovers should resist the temptation to drink it now. It has a black colour flecked with crimson, and aromas of ripe fruits combining with nuances of roasting. The silky and powerful palate allows the black-currant and the blackberry to linger as long as they please.

🍷 Primo Palatum, 1, Cirette, 33190 Morizès,
tel. 05.56.71.39.39, fax 05.56.71.39.40,
e-mail xavier-copel@primo-palatum.com ☑
🍷 by appt.
🍷 Xavier Copel

DOM. SERGENT 2001★

■	5.2 ha	40,000	🍶 ♦	5–8 €

The Sergent estate has done well this year with its **Madiran Cuvée Vieilles Vignes Elevé en Fût de Chêne 2000** winning one star, and this dark-coloured wine with good concentration. The fruitiness is expressed in nuances of blackcurrant and violet throughout the tasting. It has fine tannins, and delightful balance.

🍷 EARL Dousseau, Dom. Sergent, 32400 Maumusson,
tel. 05.62.69.74.93, fax 05.62.69.75.85,
e-mail b.dousseau@32.sideral.fr ☑ ✿
🍷 ev. day except Sun. 8.30am–12 noon 2pm–6.30pm

DOM. TAILLEURGUET 2001★

■	4 ha	25,000	🍶	3–5 €

While the **Domaine Tailleurguet Elevé en Fût de Chêne 2000 (5–8 €)** deserves to be singled out, this Madiran, which was not matured in barrel, is even more interesting. It reflects a serious and respectful example of winemaking. The intense colour with deep-purple highlights heralds a complex range of ripe soft fruits, slightly spiced. The silky tannins are integrated in the full and warming, concentrated body.

🍷 EARL Tailleurguet, 32400 Maumusson,
tel. 05.62.69.73.92, fax 05.62.69.83.69 ☑
🍷 ev. day except Sun. 9am–12.30pm 2pm–7pm
🍷 Bouby

Wines selected but not starred

DOM. D'HECHAC

Le Marquis Vieilli en fût de chêne 2000

■	1 ha	4,000	ⱴ	8–11 €

🍷 GAEC Rémon, Dom. d'Héchac, 65700 Soublecause,
tel. 05.62.96.35.75, fax 05.62.96.00.94 ☑
🍷 ev. day 9am–8pm

DOM. DE LACAVE 2001

■	4 ha	30,000	🍶 ♦	3–5 €

🍷 Patrick Ponsolle, EARL Dom. de Lacave, 32400 Cannet,
tel. 05.62.69.77.38 ☑
🍷 by appt.

DOM. DE MAOURIES

Cailloux de Pyren Vieilles Vignes 2000

■	1.5 ha	8,000	ⱴ	11–15 €

🍷 GAEC Dufau Père et Fils, Dom. de Maouries,
32400 Labarthète, tel. 05.62.69.63.84, fax 05.62.69.65.49,
e-mail domaine.maouries@wanadoo.fr ☑
🍷 by appt.

DOM. RENGOUER 2001

■	1.5 ha	6,000	ⱴ	23–30 €

🍷 SA Producteurs réunis, 65700 Castelnau-Rivière-Basse,
tel. 05.62.31.96.21, fax 05.62.31.71.84 ☑
🍷 by appt.
🍷 Jean Larrouyet-Marcel Castaing

Pacherenc du Vic-Bilh

From the same area as Madiran, this white wine is made from local varieties (Arrufiac, Manseng, Courbu) and others from the Bordelais (Sauvignon, Sémillon); this combination creates a notably rich aromatic palette. According to the climatic conditions of the year concerned, the wines (9,180 hl in 2002 from 277 ha) can be dry and perfumed or medium and lively. Their finesse is quite remarkable; they are fleshy and strong with a nose melding almond, hazelnut and exotic fruits. Pacherenc du Vic-Bilh make excellent aperitif wines and, when medium, are perfect with a terrine of foie gras.

CH. BARREJAT Moelleux Cuvée de la Passion

Elevé en fût de chêne 2001★

■	1 ha	2,000	ⱴ	5–8 €

Denis Capmartin settled in 1992 on this estate of 22 ha. He offers not only a **Madiran Cuvée des Vieux Ceps Elevé en Fût de Chêne 2000**, which was singled out by the Jury, but also this golden-yellow Pacherenc with green highlights, its fruity aromas accompanied by spicy nuances. It is rich, full and very sweet, and releases aromas with an elegant oak. The fairly long finish leaves a sweet impression.

🍷 Denis Capmartin, Ch. Barréjat, 32400 Maumusson,
tel. 05.62.69.74.92, fax 05.62.69.77.54 ☑
🍷 ev. day except Sun. 8am–12 noon 2pm–6pm

COLLECTION PLAIMONT

Moelleux 2001★★

■	15 ha	80,000	ⱴ	5–8 €

It was difficult to separate the two Pacherencs made by the Producteurs Plaimont. The **Saint-Albert Vendanges du 15 Novembre 2001 (11–15 €)** was judged remarkable for its fruity, rounded character, and the perfect balance between softness and freshness. This straw-yellow Collection wine sparkles with golden highlights before releasing intense scents of crystallized fruits, *pain d'épice* and cinnamon. It is immediately supple on the palate, finding real harmony between its sugar and freshness, while overripe flavours continue agreeably, accompanied by toasty notes.

🍷 Producteurs Plaimont, 32400 Saint-Mont,
tel. 05.62.69.62.87, fax 05.62.69.66.71,
e-mail f.latapy@plaimont.fr ☑ ✉ ✿
🍷 by appt.

CH. FITERE
Moelleux 2001★

	1.5 ha	5,000	🔲 👤	8–11 €

An 18th century farm in the Gers with masses of flowers, whose name and style reflect the Spanish origins of the founders. Here they made a brilliant golden 2001 wine, whose palate releases notes of pineapple, flowers of acacia and sweet spices. This Pacherenc offers an intense liqueur-like feeling while remaining pleasantly fresh and scented. Served it as an aperitif.
•🍷 René Castets, 32400 Cannet, tel. 05.62.69.82.36, fax 05.62.69.78.90 ✅
☂ by appt.

HARMONIE
Moelleux 2001★

	73 ha	30,000	🍶	8–11 €

In addition to the **sweet Prélude à l'Hivernal 2001 (11–15 €)**, singled out by the Jury, the Crouseilles cooperative has distinguished itself with this pale-golden 2001 which offers a certain freshness thanks to its blend of accents of citrus fruits and oak. The palate is also very fruity, slightly sweet and supported by a pleasant liveliness. A very tasty bottle.
•🍷 Cave de Crouseilles, 64350 Crouseilles, tel. 05.62.69.66.87, fax 05.62.69.66.71, e-mail m.darricau@plaimont.fr ✅
☂ by appt.

CH. LAFFITTE TESTON
Moelleux Rêve d'Automne 2001★

	5 ha	32,000	🍶	8–11 €

Jean-Marc Laffitte farms 42 ha and his high-quality Pacherencs appear regularly in the *Guide*. This wine tastes like a delicate sugar refinery beneath its old-gold colour with amber highlights. The fine nose releases exotic fruits, while the full palate is rich and very sweet, and continues pleasantly to a honeyed and sweetly oaky finish
•🍷 Jean-Marc Laffitte, 32400 Maumusson, tel. 05.62.69.74.58, fax 05.62.69.76.87, e-mail chateaulaffitteteston@2.sideral.fr ✅
☂ by appt.

DOM. LAOUGUE
Moelleux 2001★

	2 ha	6,000	🍶	11–15 €

This wine has quite a strong golden-yellow colour but its bouquet of ripe fruits and roasting is very restrained, it opens out more generously on the palate. It grows in warmth while releasing its rich flavours of crystallized fruits and oaky nuances, which combine in harmony. The **Madiran Tradition 2001 (8–11 €)** was singled out.
•🍷 Pierre Dabadie, rte de Madiran, 32400 Viella, tel. 05.62.69.90.05, fax 05.62.69.71.41 ✅
☂ ev. day 9am–12 noon 2pm–6pm

CH. DE VIELLA
Moelleux 2001★

	4.5 ha	8,000	🍶	8–11 €

The **Madiran Prestige 2000 (8–11 €)**, matured for 12 months in barrel, will go well with a *magret de canard* thanks to its rounded tannins and blackcurrant aromas. It wins one star. With the next course, you will serve this sweet, well-made and pleasant wine with a blue cheese. Its lively yellow colour will remind tasters of yellow and exotic fruits, with a few hints of smoke. On the palate it is supple, fleshy, with harmonious aromas and good balance.
•🍷 Alain Bortolussi, Ch. de Viella, rte de Maumusson, 32400 Viella, tel. 05.62.69.75.81, fax 05.62.69.79.18, e-mail chateauviella@32.sideral.fr ✅
☂ ev. day except Sun. 8am–12.30pm 2pm–7pm

Wines selected but not starred

DOM. CAPMARTIN Moelleux Cuvée du Couvent Elevé en fût de chêne neuf 2001

	1.2 ha	6,000	🍶	8–11 €

•🍷 Guy Capmartin, Le Couvent, 32400 Maumusson, tel. 05.62.69.87.88, fax 05.62.69.83.07 ✅ 🏠
☂ ev. day except Sun. 9am–1pm 2pm–7pm

Tursan AOVDQS

This vineyard was once the property of Aliénor d'Aquitaine. Nowadays the Tursan terroir covers some 280 ha and produced 11,027 hl of red, rosé and white wines in 2002. The most interesting are the whites made from the original vine variety, the Baroque. Dry, vigorous and inimitably perfumed, Tursan whites go very well with shad, elvers and grilled fish.

BARON DE BACHEN 2001★★

	4 ha	16,440	🔲 👤	11–15 €

The chef Michel Guérard bought the 16th and 18th century Château de Bachen in 1983, along with its vines and its old winery. He continues to cook but now also makes wine. Many years have passed since his first harvests in 1988, and his Tursans are regularly of high quality, as is this well-balanced 2001. It has a straw colour with green and golden highlights, and releases deep aromas combining peach, exotic fruits, vanilla and dried fruits. On the palate it is not rich and full but also pleasantly fresh. The well-proportioned oak elegantly supports a long finish.
•🍷 Michel Guérard, Cie hôtelière et fermière d'Eugénie-les-Bains, 40320 Eugénie-les-Bains, tel. 05.58.71.76.76, fax 05.58.71.77.77, e-mail michel.guerard@wanadoo.fr ✅
☂ by appt.

HAUTE CARTE 2002★★

	80 ha	200,000	🔲 👤	3–5 €

This wine is an intense cherry-red colour and is still subdued but releases attractive scents of spices and soft fruits. It leaves a velvety feeling on the taste buds, thanks to its rounded substance, structured by elegant and long tannins. The Tursan **red Paysage 2002**, matured in tank, and the **Château Bourda Elevé en Fût de Chêne 2002 (5–8 €)** won one star.
•🍷 Les Vignerons Landais, 40320 Geaune, tel. 05.58.44.51.25, fax 05.58.44.40.22, e-mail info@vlandais.com ✅
☂ by appt.

CH. DE PERCHADE 2002★

	4 ha	28,000	🔲 👤	3–5 €

This substantial wine is made from Cabernet Franc (60%) and equal shares of Cabernet Sauvignon and Tannat, origins that account for its intense colour with pronounced purple highlights. The winey bouquet reveals soft fruits, while the very structured palate shows a strong tannic concentration. Keep this wine for at least a year. The **white 2002** and the **rosé 2002** were commended.
•🍷 EARL Dulucq, Château de Perchade, 40320 Payros-Cazautets, tel. 05.58.44.50.68, fax 05.58.44.57.75 ✅
☂ ev. day except Sun. 8am–1pm 2.30pm–7pm

Côtes de Saint-Mont AOVDQS

This is a continuation of the Madiran vineyard. The Côtes de Saint-Mont is the most recent of the Pyrenean appellations (1981), producing wines of superior quality. The vineyard covers about 847 ha, and production in 2002 reached 48,304 hl. The main red grape is the Tannat, the whites being made from Clairette, Arrufiac, Courbu and the two Manseng varieties. Most of the production is managed by the dynamic Union des Caves Coopératives Plaimont. The red wines are vividly coloured and full bodied, rapidly becoming round and pleasant. They are drunk with grilled meats and *Garbure Gasconne*, a local soup. The delicate rosés are appreciated for their fruity bouquet. The whites have a special flavour of the terroir and are dry and lively in character.

COMBES DE BASTZ
Elevé en fût de chêne 2002★

	45 ha	800,000	◫	5–8 €

This blend of Gros Manseng (60%), Arrufiac (20%) and Petit Courbu (20%) has created a very intense wine with aromas of citrus fruits and roasting that last throughout the tasting. Its brilliant colour with green highlights corresponds well with the fresh feeling on the palate, which continues on a slightly acid note.
🍷 Vignoble de Gascogne, 32400 Riscle, tel. 05.62.69.62.87, fax 05.62.69.66.71, e-mail f.latapy@plaimont.fr ☑ ⌂ ⌂
🍷 by appt.

CH. SAINT-GO
Elevé en fût de chêne 2001★★

■	3 ha	130,000	◫	8–11 €

This wine was vinified by the Vignoble de Gascogne cooperative, and immediately delighted with its deep colour and aubergine highlights. Powerful aromas of kirsch and black fruits combine with a spicy, smoky oak, while the body, structured by integrated tannins, continues intensely. The **Château du Bascou 2001 (11–15 €)**, matured in tank, is commended.
🍷 Producteurs Plaimont, 32400 Saint-Mont,
tel. 05.62.69.62.87, fax 05.62.69.66.71,
e-mail f.latapy@plaimont.fr ☑ ⌂ ⌂
🍷 by appt.
🍷 SA du Ch. Saint-Go

LES VIGNES RETROUVEES 2002★

	100 ha	600,000	◫	5–8 €

This pale Vin Jaune with green highlights will be good as an aperitif or with fresh shellfish in pastry. It combines nuances of honey, quince, crystallized dried fruits and citrus fruits, as well as a note of aniseed. Its balance results from its blend of freshness and a body that is full of flavour and shows good length.
🍷 Producteurs Plaimont, 32400 Saint-Mont,
tel. 05.62.69.62.87, fax 05.62.69.66.71,
e-mail f.latapy@plaimont.fr ☑ ⌂ ⌂
🍷 by appt.

The Wines of the Dordogne

The Dordogne vineyard is a natural extension of the Libournais wine-growing area, separated from it only by an administrative boundary. Planted with classic Gironde varieties, the Perigord vineyard is characterized by a very diverse production and a number of appellations. It stretches along slopes on both banks of the Dordogne.

The Appellation Régionale Bergerac comprises whites, rosés and reds. The Côtes de Bergerac offer fuller-bodied white wines with a delicate bouquet, along with reds that are well structured and round, to be drunk with poultry and meat dishes with sauce. The Appellation Saussignac produces excellent fuller-bodied white wines with an ideal balance between freshness and sugar; they are drunk as aperitif wines, tasting somewhere between a Bergerac and a Monbazillac. Montravel, near Castillon, is the vineyard associated with Montaigne; production is divided into dry white Montravel, readily identifiable because of the Sauvignon, and the Côtes de Montravel and Haut-Montravel, fuller bodied, elegant and stylish, which make excellent dessert wines, with a red Montravel being produced from 2003. The Pécharmant is a red wine harvested on the slopes of the right bank where the soil, rich in iron, gives it a very distinctive taste of the terroir. A wine to keep, it has a fine, subtle bouquet and is a perfect accompaniment to the classic dishes of the Perigord. The Rosette is a semi-sweet wine, made from the same varieties as the Bordeaux wines, harvested in an enclave on the right bank of the Dordogne around Bergerac.

Known as early as the 14th century, Monbazillac is one of the most famous "sweet" wines. The vineyard is north facing on limestone interbedded with molassic sands and marl. The localized micro-climate is particularly good for the development of a particular strain of botrytis, the "noble rot". Beautifully golden in colour, Monbazillac wines have scents of wild flowers and honey and a lingering flavour. They can be drunk as an aperitif, or enjoyed with foie gras, Roquefort cheese and chocolate desserts. They are fleshy and strong and, with age, become great sweet wines with a "scorched" flavour.

Bergerac

These wines are produced from the 90 communes of the district of Bergerac; in 2002, 6,876 ha of the vineyard was devoted to red and rosé wines, and 2,960 ha to white. The rosé is fresh and fruity, and is frequently made from Cabernet; the red wine is aromatic and supple, a blend of traditional varieties. In 2002, production reached 149,200 hl of white wine and 311,698 hl of red or rosé wine.

BRENNUS
Vieilli en fût de chêne 2000★

| ■ | 5 ha | 33,000 | ❶❶ | 5–8 € |

The shield of Brennus is the trophy given to the team winning the French rugby championship. The bouquet has the finesse of a line of three-quarters with notes of spices, blackcurrant and an attractive toasty note. The palate has the power of a pack of forwards, with evident and well-integrated tannins and a good aromatic return. It scores a try, but you need to wait for one or two years before converting it.
➦ Closerie d'Estiac, Les Lèves,
33320 Sainte-Foy-la-Grande, tel. 05.57.56.02.02,
fax 05.57.56.02.22, e-mail oeno@univitis.fr ☑
☏ ev. day except Sun. Mon. 9.30am–12.30pm 3.30pm–6pm

CH. LA BRIE
Cuvée Prestige Elevé en fût de chêne 2001★

| ■ | 9.7 ha | 26,000 | ❶❶ | 5–8 € |

When they train tomorrow's technicians, they have to show a good example. And so it was with this Prestige wine, which wins one star like last year. The rather intense nose offers aromas of soft fruits, blackcurrant and redcurrant. The palate is also very fruity with plenty of roundness, flexibility and good flesh. This is a characteristic, balanced Bergerac.
➦ Ch. la Brie, Lycée viticole, Dom. de la Brie,
24240 Monbazillac, tel. 05.53.74.42.42, fax 05.53.58.24.08,
e-mail lpa.bergerac@educagri.fr ☑
☏ ev. day except Sun. 10am–12 noon 1.30pm–7pm; cl. Jan.

CH. BUISSON DE FLOGNY
Carpe Diem 2001★

| ■ | 0.8 ha | 4,000 | ❶❶ | 8–11 € |

Saint-Just probably stayed in this château. The wine estate is much more recent, less than ten years old. But its wine is a delight, even if the nose is austere and a little closed with oaky notes. On the other hand, the palate is silky, very rounded and powerful. The fruits come through well and the tannins are elegant. This is a fruity, concentrated wine that remains balanced. It seems to need four or five years to mature.
➦ Marc Bighetti de Flogny, Le Buisson,
24610 Saint-Méard-de-Gurçon, tel. 05.53.81.00.87,
fax 05.53.80.61.39, e-mail flogny@aol.com ☑
☏ by appt.

CLOS DES CABANES
Prince de Foncalpre 2000★

| ▬ | 1.05 ha | 6,000 | ▆ | 3–5 € |

This old estate, where earlier generations had made wine, has been successfully reconverted. This Bergerac is fresh with perfumes of violet and blackcurrant bud. After a fruity attack, the palate is notably rounded and supple. Drink it with grilled meats.
➦ Georges Lafont, Clos des Cabanes,
24100 Saint-Laurent-des-Vignes, tel. 05.53.24.85.03,
fax 05.53.24.85.03, e-mail clos.des.cabanes@wanadoo.fr ☑
☏ ev. day except Sun. 8am–12 noon 2pm–6pm; cl. Apr.

CLOS DU MAINE-CHEVALIER
Cuvée Prestige 2001★

| ■ | 5.8 ha | 3,800 | ❶❶ | 5–8 € |

This property has been successfully converted. Originally, it was dedicated to the maturation of wines, and now its wine production is recognized and admired. It is located 7 km from the very beautiful medieval village of Issigeac, which is well worth visiting. The very rich perfumes of this wine release notes of soft fruits and breadcrumbs. The attack is superb, rounded and fruity, then the oaky tannins come to the fore. They need some time in the cellar to soften.
➦ GAEC du Maine-Chevalier, Le Maine-Chevalier,
24560 Plaisance, tel. 05.53.58.55.63, fax 05.53.58.55.63 ☑
☏ by appt.
➦ Caillard

Bergerac

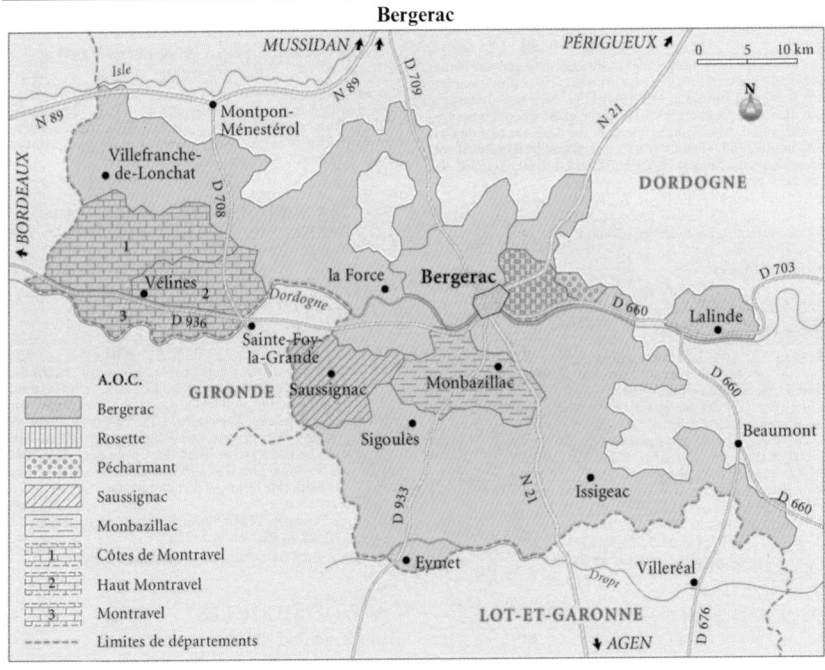

A map showing the Bergerac A.O.C. region with towns including Mussidan, Périgueux, Montpon-Ménestérol, Villefranche-de-Lonchat, Vélines, la Force, Bergerac, Lalinde, Sainte-Foy-la-Grande, Saussignac, Monbazillac, Beaumont, Sigoulès, Issigeac, Eymet, Villeréal, and Agen.

A.O.C.
- Bergerac
- Rosette
- Pécharmant
- Saussignac
- Monbazillac
- 1 Côtes de Montravel
- 2 Haut Montravel
- 3 Montravel
- ----- Limites de départements

CASANOVA DES CONTI 2001★★

| ■ | n.c. | 100,000 | ▮ ▥ ♦ | 3–5 € |

The Conti family's négociant business rigorously selects harvests before buying them, vinifying them and maturing them in barrel for 18 months. The 2001 wine has a bouquet of very ripe black fruits and a cool oakiness. The first impression on the palate is rounded and silky, then the oak makes its presence felt. The substance is beautiful and elegant, and needs three to four years to become more refined.
➴ SARL la Julienne, 24500 Saint-Julien-d'Eymet, tel. 05.53.57.12.43, fax 05.53.58.89.49,
e-mail familledeconti@wanadoo.fr ▨ ✿
⚐ by appt.
➴ Famille de Conti

CH. LA GRANDE PLEYSSADE
Cuvée réservée 2001★

| ■ | 15 ha | 73,500 | ▥ | 3–5 € |

This wine is a good compromise between moderate extraction and well-controlled maturation in barrel. The nose is pleasant with aromas of raspberry, strawberry and a light note of vanilla. The palate is pleasant and full bodied, accompanied by a subtle oak, and rests on well-balanced tannins with no bitterness. A fine example of a Bergerac for a very reasonable price.
➴ SCEA la Grande Pleyssade, 24240 Mescoulès, tel. 05.53.24.27.61, fax 05.53.24.27.61,
e-mail lagrandepleyssade@compuserve.com ▨
⚐ by appt.
➴ Laumond

CH. DE LA JAUBERTIE
Mirabelle 2001★

| ■ | 6 ha | 23,000 | ▥ | 11–15 € |

The Château de la Jaubertie was used as a hunting lodge for King Henri IV. It was acquired in 1973 by Henry Nicolas Ryman, a British citizen whose son studied oenology in Australia. This wine is very oaky, and aromas of toast and roasting predominate. On the palate, it has a lovely concentrated substance which delighted the Jury. A wine for patient wine-lovers to keep. The **dry white Mirabelle 2001** also receives one star. It too has a strongly oaky presence. However, its remarkable concentration will help this to soften. A pleasant Bergerac.
➴ SA Ryman, Ch. de la Jaubertie, 24560 Colombier, tel. 05.53.58.32.11, fax 05.53.57.46.22,
e-mail jaubertie@wanadoo.fr ▨
⚐ by appt.
➴ P. Vien-Graliet

CH. LES JUSTICES 2002★★

| ■ | 7 ha | 54,000 | ▮ | 5–8 € |

This estate has changed from being a family business to a cooperative, and is now a GAEC which vinifies and sells its products direct. This wine has an attractive bouquet of soft fruits and blackcurrant, and powerful, rich, coated tannins from the attack onwards. The structure is well balanced and the finish sees a return of the soft fruits. The **dry Bergerac 2002** is also very fruity and attractive: it shows a good balance between acidity and roundness and wins one star. Here are two wines of excellent quality, very representative of the AOC.
➴ GAEC Vignobles Fruttero, Les Justices, 24500 Sadillac, tel. 05.53.58.41.93, fax 05.53.58.41.93 ▨
⚐ by appt.

CH. LAULERIE
Vieilli en fût de chêne 2001★★

| ■ | 20 ha | 110,000 | ▥ | 5–8 € |

This is a marvellously consistent wine which wins two stars in our selection for 2001 wines, as it also did for its 2000 vintage. The bouquet is remarkable with floral aromas (rose and violet) and a strong spicy presence. The palate is full and perfectly balanced. The oak is well handled and perfectly integrated. This wine has very promising potential, and should be kept for five years at least.
➴ Vignobles Dubard Frère et Soeur, Le Gouyat, 24610 Saint-Méard-de-Gurçon, tel. 05.53.82.48.31, fax 05.53.82.47.64,
e-mail vignobles-dubard@wanadoo.fr ▨ ✿ ✿
⚐ ev. day except Sun. 8am–12 noon 2pm–6pm

CH. MONESTIER LA TOUR 2001★

■ 8 ha 33,000 ❚❙❚ 8–11 €

The buildings have been beautifully restored and the wines have made a remarkable increase in power. This one is complex, with very good substance but still finishes on a slightly rasping note. It will be pleasant in two or three years when the tannins are integrated. Also winning one star, the **Bergerac rosé du Clos de Monestier 2002 (5–8 €)**. It is characterized by its nose of soft fruits, blackcurrant and citrus fruits, and its well balanced and very fresh palate.

✦➔ SCEA Monestier La Tour, 24240 Monestier, tel. 05.53.24.18.43, fax 05.53.24.18.14, e-mail contact@chateaumonestierlatour.com ✓
☿ by appt.
✦➔ Haseth-Moller

CH. LE PAYRAL

Cuvée Héritage 2001★★

■ 1.25 ha 4,000 ❚❙❚ 8–11 €

The 2001 vintage confirms the two stars won by last year's wine. The nose offers intense, very ripe fruits (morello cherry) with a light oak. On the palate, the structure is full bodied, the oak already well integrated. A well-balanced, rounded and rich product. The **dry Bergerac Réserve 2001 (5–8 €)** deserves to be singled out: the nose recalls exotic fruits and also releases grapey and peppery aromas. The palate is initially fresh, then rounded and elegant with fruity notes and finishes with an attractive oakiness. It is ready to drink now.

✦➔ Thierry Daulhiac, 24240 Razac-de-Saussignac, tel. 05.53.22.38.07, fax 05.53.27.99.81, e-mail daulhiac@club-internet.fr ✓ ▥
☿ by appt.

CH. PION 2000★★

■ 4 ha 16,000 ❚❙❚ 8–11 €

This is one of the properties developed by the Monbazillac cooperative. The high percentage of Merlot confers great power on this wine. The bouquet is very intense and complex, releasing notes of almost overripe small soft fruits and a well-integrated oak. After a powerful attack, the tannins prove fine and elegant, accompanied by fruitiness and a remarkable richness. The feature of this great wine is that it lets us choose whether to drink it now, or keep it.

✦➔ Cave coopérative de Monbazillac, rte de Monbazillac, 24240 Monbazillac, tel. 05.53.63.65.00, fax 05.53.63.65.09 ✓
☿ by appt.

CH. ROQUE-PEYRE

Cuvée Ulysse Vallette 2001★

■ 5 ha 30,000 ❚❙❚ 5–8 €

This wine won two stars last year and now offers a complex bouquet of ripe fruits and a very subtle oak. On the palate it is rounded, very fruity and sweet, with very well-balanced, supple tannins. This harmonious wine must be drunk young. The **white Château Roque-Peyre Montravel 2002** also wins one star for its aromas of grapefruit, kiwi fruit and honeysuckle. A pleasant wine.

✦➔ Vallette Frères, GAEC de Roque-Peyre, 33220 Fougueyrolles, tel. 05.53.24.77.98, fax 05.53.61.36.87, e-mail vignobles.vallette@wanadoo.fr ✓ ▥ ▤
☿ by appt.

CH. SEIGNORET LES TOURS

Cuvée Séduction Elevé en fût de chêne 2000★

■ 2 ha 9,000 ❚❙❚ 8–11 €

The 2000 vintage has produced many concentrated wines that were matured in barrel. This is one of them. The bouquet releases aromas of ripe black fruits and, in particular, coffee, with spicy, toasty notes. The palate has a mouth-filling attack and a rich body with compact tannins. The fruit remains evident behind the oak. An attractive wine for laying down so that the oak can soften.

✦➔ Vignobles Serge Gazziola, Ch. Seignoret les Tours, 24240 Saussignac, tel. 05.53.27.01.20, fax 05.53.22.37.79 ✓
☿ by appt.

CAVE DE SIGOULES

Chêne Peyraille 2001★★

■ 42 ha 333,000 ❚❙❚❙ ⬦ 3–5 €

This deep-red wine has a bouquet which is still subtle but elegant with soft fruits and an integrated oak. After a supple and fruity attack, the well-made tannins are compact and concentrated. The long finish allows the ripe fruit to return. This is a fine and elegant wine, rather light, and excellent value for money. The tasters also liked the **Cuvée dry white 2002**, which wins one star. This was well matured on lees, which has given it a remarkable richness that emphasizes the aromas of citrus fruits.

✦➔ Cave de Sigoulès, 24240 Sigoulès, tel. 05.53.61.55.00, fax 05.53.61.55.10 ✓
☿ ev. day except Sun. 9am–12 noon 2pm–5.30pm

CAVE DE SIGOULES

Haute Tradition 2001★

■ 9 ha 66,600 ❚❙❚ 5–8 €

The lovely deep-ruby colour heralds an intense and complex nose in which the prominent oaky and vanilla notes fade before the aromas of fruits and jams. The attack is rounded and supple, then the tannins appear, though still dominated by the oak; the fruits (strawberry and blackcurrant) are a little crushed at the finish. A concentrated wine that will gain in complexity as it ages.

✦➔ Cave de Sigoulès, 24240 Sigoulès, tel. 05.53.61.55.00, fax 05.53.61.55.10
☿ ev. day except Sun. 9am–12 noon 2pm–5.30pm

CH. LE TAP 2002★

■ 3 ha 10,000 ❚ 5–8 €

Gallo-Roman remains are evidence of a significant, much earlier rural activity here. This red Bergerac has a surprising, rather floral nose with a few light notes of menthol. On the other hand, the palate is more classic, with a full and supple first impression. The tannins increase nicely in richness up to the lingering finish, with no bitterness or dryness. Also worth trying is the **Saussignac 2001 Elevé en Fût de Chêne (11–15 €)** which is singled out. This has a very pronounced noble rot, the nose evoking crystallized fruits and honey. The palate is very rich and sweet.

✦➔ Olivier Roches, Ch. Le Tap, 24240 Saussignac, tel. 05.53.27.53.41, fax 05.53.22.07.55, e-mail chateauletap@tiscali.fr ✓
☿ ev. day 9am–1pm 2pm–7pm

CH. VARI 2001★

■ 1.5 ha 9,000 ❚❙❚ 5–8 €

This is a fine example of a restored vineyard which has been planted with high density. This wine was matured for 12 months in barrel. The oak makes its presence felt even though the vanilla and roasted notes are very fine on the nose. The fruit comes through on the palate, revealing an attractive body, then the oak dominates the finish. A supple, charming wine in the New World style, to be drunk young.

✦➔ Vignobles Jestin, Ch. Vari, 24240 Monbazillac, tel. 05.53.24.97.55, fax 05.53.24.97.55 ✓
☿ by appt.
✦➔ Yann Jestin

Wines selected but not starred

impression is balanced, the palate's roundness and fullness combining with tasty fruity aromas. A really enjoyable wine.
🕊 Odile Brichèse, Coutancie, 24130 Prigonrieux, tel. 05.53.58.01.85, fax 05.53.58.52.76, e-mail coutancie@wanadoo.fr ✓ 🛖
𝌠 by appt.

CH. BELINGARD 2002

| | 25 ha | 120,000 | 🍾 🍷 | 5–8 € |

🕊 SCEA Comte de Bosredon, Belingard, 24240 Pomport, tel. 05.53.58.28.03, fax 05.53.58.38.39, e-mail laurent.debosredon@wanadoo.fr ✓
𝌠 ev. day except Sun. 9am–12.30pm 1.30pm–6.30pm

DOM. DES FRETILLERES

Cuvée Vieille Vigne 2000

| | 2 ha | 4,000 | 🍶 | 5–8 € |

🕊 Bernard Rigal, Dom. des Frétillères, 24240 Razac-de-Saussignac, tel. 05.53.27.89.61, fax 05.53.27.99.67, e-mail fretilleres@yahoo.fr ✓
𝌠 by appt.

CH. DES ILLARETS 2000

| | 1.1 ha | 5,270 | 🍾 🍶 | 5–8 € |

🕊 Richard Lacombe, Les Illarets, 24230 Saint-Michel-de-Montaigne, tel. 05.53.58.52.49, fax 05.53.58.52.49 ✓
𝌠 by appt.

CH. DE SANXET

Millenium 2000

| | 8.5 ha | 36,000 | 🍶 | 5–8 € |

🕊 Bertrand de Passemar, Ch. de Sanxet, 24240 Pomport, tel. 05.53.58.37.46, fax 05.53.58.37.46, e-mail sanxet@sanxet.com ✓
𝌠 ev. day 10am–12 noon 2pm–6pm

CH. TOUR MONTBRUN 2000

| | 2 ha | 13,000 | 🍾 | 3–5 € |

🕊 Philippe Poivey, Montravel, 24230 Montcaret, tel. 05.53.58.66.93, fax 05.53.58.66.93, e-mail philippe.poivey@wanadoo.fr ✓
𝌠 by appt.

Bergerac Rosé

DOM. DU CASTELLAT 2002★

| | 4 ha | 8,000 | 🍾 🍷 | 3–5 € |

Le Castellat was an old medieval watchtower, and commands 22 ha. The blend of this rosé is unusual with 80% Cabernet Sauvignon and 20% Cot. The nose is mainly notable for the notes of blackcurrant appropriate to Cabernet Sauvignon. The palate is supple and sweet, giving an impression of lasting richness and a lovely return of the fruits. A rather atypical wine, but original.
🕊 Jean-Luc Lescure, Le Castellat, 24240 Razac-de-Saussignac, tel. 05.53.27.08.83, fax 05.53.27.08.83 ✓ 🛖
𝌠 ev. day except Sun. 9am–7pm

DOM. DE COUTANCIE 2002★

| | 0.35 ha | 2,000 | 🍾 🍷 | 3–5 € |

From this estate, which once belonged to the Fermiers Généraux, there is a remarkable view over the valley of the Dordogne. The colour of this rosé 2002 is strong and fresh, whereas the nose is beautifully intense with an explosion of ripe fruits: redcurrant, raspberry and cherry. The first

CH. FONTAINE DES GRIVES 2002★

| | 3.5 ha | 5,000 | 🍾 🍷 | 5–8 € |

The fuchsia pink of the colour is bright and intense, followed by intense aromas of blackcurrant, boxwood and ivy, indicating the strong presence of Cabernet Sauvignon. The palate is supple and fresh, with a certain sweetness caused by the residual sugars. The finish sees a return of the freshness and acidity. A semi-dry, slightly sweet wine for rosé lovers.
🕊 Mario Zorzetto, Ch. Fontaine des Grives, 24240 Thénac, tel. 05.53.58.46.73, fax 05.53.24.18.49, e-mail jzorzetto@terre-net.fr ✓
𝌠 by appt.

JULIEN DE SAVIGNAC 2002★★★

| | 2.83 ha | 20,000 | 🍾 🍷 | 5–8 € |

Julien de Savignac confirms his position as a leading producer of rosé with this wine. The bouquet is very fruity (lychee and ripe grape). The full-bodied palate is rather mouth filling with a freshness of small wild fruits and a lovely length of flavour. A rosé of great complexity, not to be missed. The **Les Jardins de Cyrano Cuvée Larmandie 2002 (3–5 €)** is made from 70% Cabernet Sauvignon and 30% Merlot. It wins one star. The fullness of the aromatic nuances evokes soft fruits and strawberry. The palate is sweet and soft, finishing on a fairly fresh, crunchy note.
🕊 SA Julien de Savignac, av. de la Libération, 24260 Le Bugue, tel. 05.53.07.10.31, fax 05.53.07.16.41, e-mail julien.de.savignac@wanadoo.fr ✓
𝌠 ev. day 9am–12.30pm 2.30pm–7.30pm; Thu. Fri. Sat. 9am–7.30pm
🕊 Montfort

CH. DE LA NOBLE 2002★

| | 2 ha | 8,000 | 🍾 | 3–5 € |

This family property has been run by Fabien Charron since 1998. The Noble is a rosé matured on lees. It has a constant colour, and a very expressive bouquet with dominant notes of soft fruits. After a fresh, slightly sparkling attack, the palate is structured, full bodied and almost astringent. This is a rosé of character with plenty of body: good for lovers of Clairet.
🕊 Fabien Charron, La Noble, 24240 Puyguilhem, tel. 05.53.58.81.93, fax 05.53.58.81.93 ✓
𝌠 ev. day except Sun. 9am–6pm

LA TUILIERE 2002★

| | 8 ha | 13,000 | 🍾 🍷 | 3–5 € |

This rosé was mainly made from Cabernet Franc, and will accompany your meal from aperitif to cheese. Its lemony aromas give it freshness and length. A pleasant, well-balanced rosé.
🕊 SCEA Moulin de Sanxet, Belingard-Bas, 24240 Pomport, tel. 05.53.58.30.79, fax 05.53.61.71.84 ✓
𝌠 ev. day except Sun. 9am–12 noon 2pm–6.30pm
🕊 Grellier

Bergerac Sec

The mixed soils (limestone, gravel, clay, sand, alluvial deposits and stones) give rise to a range of aromas for these wines. When young, they are fruity and elegant, with a touch of vitality. If they are vinified in wood, it is necessary to wait for a year or two for the flavour of the terroir to become apparent.

ACCENT 2002★★

| | 3 ha | 14,000 | 🔲 ⑪ ↓ | | 5–8 € |

Since it was taken over by the Chemel family in 1999, one senses a real wish to revive and bring the best out of this superb terroir. This wine is still a little closed, with buttered and toasty notes of good intensity. The palate is rich with notes of citrus fruits and very ripe fruits, a well-integrated oak and great freshness. A great Bergerac, the result of a perfect control of both the vine and the winery.
📮 SCEA Ch. Caillevet, Le Caufour, 24240 Thénac,
tel. 05.53.58.80.71, fax 05.53.61.39.94,
e-mail chateaucaillevet@free.fr ☑
🍷 by appt.
📮 Chemel

DOM. DU BOIS DE POURQUIE 2002★★

| | 2 ha | 10,000 | 🔲 ↓ | | 5–8 € |

The nose of this dry white Bergerac is slow to open then discloses floral notes of rose and fruity notes of peach and citrus fruits. The palate is very pleasant, combining flesh and freshness. This is a tasty white full of finesse which should be opened one hour before it is drunk. Also try the **rosé 2002** (one star), which is fruity (wild strawberry and blackcurrant) and fresh with some good flesh and roundness. Along with the Révélation, which won a second *coup de coeur* for Côtes de Bergerac, the demanding wine-lover will find an excellent range in Bois de Pourquié.
📮 Marlène et Alain Mayet, Le Bois de Pourquié,
24560 Conne-de-Labarde, tel. 05.53.58.25.58,
fax 05.53.61.34.59 ☑
🍷 by appt.

DOM. DE LA COMBE 2002★

| | 3 ha | 5,500 | 🔲 ↓ | | 5–8 € |

In 20 years, this estate has gone from 10 to 20 ha of vines. This wine was made by maceration with a short period of skin contact, and is very successful. It is difficult not to recognize the Sauvignon in the rich, almost heady bouquet with its aromas of citrus fruits and lychee. The palate is fleshy and rounded, mouth filling with beautiful length. A classic dry Bergerac.
📮 Sylvie et Claude Sergenton, Dom. de la Combe,
24240 Razac-de-Saussignac, tel. 05.53.27.86.51,
fax 05.53.27.99.87 ☑
🍷 by appt.

CH. GRAND PLACE 2002★

| | 2.5 ha | 6,000 | ⑪ | | 5–8 € |

The property stands quietly in the middle of vines and woods. This wine was made by maceration with a short period of skin contact, and is very successful. The nose reveals the excellent maturity of the grapes. The palate confirms this impression with a liveliness that is a little prominent at the moment. The oak is well integrated at the finish. Drink it young with seafood, or wait for the acidity to fade, when you can serve it with white meats.
📮 SCEA Claude Delmas, Le Prévot Francs, 33570 Lussac,
tel. 05.57.84.38.52 ☑
🍷 by appt.

LES JARDINS DE CYRANO

Quatre Vents 2002★★

| | 1.16 ha | 7,000 | 🔲 ↓ | | 3–5 € |

This firm of négociants offers three more interesting wines. This dry white has complex perfumes of very ripe fruits, of orange and quince. The palate is characterized by its richness and its roundness. A beautiful freshness at the finish emphasizes its fruity qualities. The **red Bergerac Julien de Savignac 2001 (5–8 €)** wins one star. The nose is both fruity and oaky. The palate is pleasant and rounded, with tannins that need two to three years before it is ready. Lastly, to complete the range, the **Clos l'Envège Cuvée Henri IV en Monbazillac (38–46 €)** wins one star. This has a rich and concentrated body which indicates a beautiful future when the wine is more integrated.
📮 SA Julien de Savignac, av. de la Libération, 24260 Le Bugue, tel. 05.53.07.10.31, fax 05.53.07.16.41,
e-mail julien.de.savignac@wanadoo.fr ☑
🍷 ev. day 9am–12.30pm 2.30pm–7.30pm;
Thu. Fri. Sat. 9am–7.30pm

LE TOP DE MAZIERE 2002★★

| | 2.5 ha | 3,000 | ⑪ | | 5–8 € |

This dry Bergerac has a complex bouquet with notes of quince, pineapple and melon. The palate is very fleshy, with ripe fruit, it has a beautifully concentrated body and good acidity. This is an attractive wine which promises to be really tasty. The **red Bergerac 2002 (8–11 €)** wins one star. It reveals aromas of very ripe fruits and prune. The tannins are coated and always integrated, and add to its elegance.
📮 Michel Roche, Dom. de Mazière, 24560 Bouniagues,
tel. 05.53.58.23.57, fax 05.53.58.73.00 ☑
🍷 by appt.

CH. DE PANISSEAU

Cuvée Divin 2001★★

| | 4.16 ha | 12,000 | ⑪ | | 15–23 € |

"Divine" is indeed an appropriate adjective to describe this remarkable wine which does not, however, come cheap. It is particularly intense and complex, with notes of flowers (honeysuckle) and fruits (peach and melon) and a well-integrated oak. On the palate it starts in a lively way, then the feeling of flesh invades the palate. The finish is long with exotic fruits. Very ripe, healthy grapes helped to create this very well-balanced and elegant wine.
📮 Panisseau SA, Ch. de Panisseau, 24240 Thénac,
tel. 05.53.58.40.03, fax 05.53.58.94.46,
e-mail panisseau@ifrance.com ☑
🍷 ev. day except Sun. 9am–12 noon 2pm–6pm

DOM. DE PECOULA 2002★

| | 2 ha | 13,000 | 🔲 ↓ | | 3–5 € |

The nose of this dry Bergerac is not particularly intense, releasing classic aromas of boxwood, blackcurrant leaf and exotic fruits typical of Sauvignon. Its freshness dominates the palate which is enhanced by a slight sparkle. The estate's **Monbazillac Cuvée Prestige 2001 (15–23 €)** was singled out by the Jury; the nose has a strong scent of wax. The palate reveals an enormous sugar concentration. A wine for those who love very sweet wines.
📮 GAEC de Pécoula, 24240 Pomport, tel. 05.53.58.46.48,
fax 05.53.58.82.02 ☑
🍷 by appt.
📮 GFA Labaye

CH. THEULET Prestige de Theulet Elevé en barrique de chêne 2001★

| | 1 ha | 3,000 | ⑪ | | 8–11 € |

This vast property has matured this dry Bergerac by maceration with a short period of skin contact, by fermentation and maturation on lees in oak. It has real complexity. The nose offers floral aromas of boxwood and lime blossom as well as notes of yellow fruits and a subtle oak. The palate is surprisingly lively, then takes on a certain roundness and richness. The Sauvignon is very evident at the long and slightly bitter finish. Serve this with oysters. The **Monbazillac 2000 Cuvée Antoine Alard (30–38 €)** is very rich and well balanced, with the fruit to the fore. It is singled out here, but will certainly win a star in two or three years.
📮 SCEA Alard, Le Theulet, 24240 Monbazillac,
tel. 05.53.57.30.43, fax 05.53.58.88.28,
e-mail alardetfils@wanadoo.fr ☑
🍷 by appt.

CH. TOUR DES GENDRES

Cuvée Anthologia 2001★★

6 ha 6,500 46–76 €

This wine was made in a special way. The grapes were overripened on the vine, then there was fermentation in oak, then maturation in barrel for 14 months with oxygenation. Ripe fruits are prominent on the nose and remarkably intense. The palate is full and powerful, with a multitude of aromas, a light and integrated oak and a very long finish. This is an original wine with a strong personality, but a little atypical, both in character and price.

SCEA De Conti, Ch. Tour des Gendres,
24240 Ribagnac, tel. 05.53.57.12.43, fax 05.53.58.89.49,
e-mail familledeconti@wanadoo.fr
by appt.

CH. TOURMENTINE

Barrique 2001★★

1 ha 5,600 5–8 €

This house of character contains a four-star *gîte* which can sleep 12 people. It is also an excellent wine estate: this dry Bergerac derives its originality from being matured in barrel for a year. The nose is complex and intense, offering notes of citrus fruits (grapefruit) and fine oak. The palate is balanced and powerful up to the finish. The wine's freshness emphasizes its good maturation. A remarkable wine that should be kept for two to three years. The **red Barrique 2001** wins one star. It is very strong on blackcurrant, mouth-filling, rounded and rich; it is still astringent and should be kept for two to three years.

EARL Vignobles Huré, Ch. Tourmentine,
24240 Monestier, tel. 05.53.58.41.41, fax 05.53.63.40.52,
e-mail actjmhure@wanadoo.fr
ev. day except Sun. 9am–12 noon 2pm–6pm

Wines selected but not starred

CH. LE CLOU

Pléiades 2001

0.5 ha 1,800 5–8 €

Ch. Le Clou, 24240 Pomport, tel. 05.53.63.32.76,
e-mail chateau.le.clou@online.fr
ev. day 9am–12 noon 2pm–6pm
Killias

CH. HAUT-FONGRIVE 2002

3.8 ha 32,000 3–5 €

Sylvie et Werner Wichelhaus, Château Haut-Fongrive,
24240 Thénac, tel. 05.53.58.56.29, fax 05.53.24.17.75,
e-mail hautfongrive@worldonline.fr
by appt.

Côtes de Bergerac

This appellation conforms not to a terroir but rather to a set of more restrictive conditions for the harvest, intended to produce rich and well-structured wines. They are sought after for their concentration of flavour and their long-term keeping qualities.

CH. LA BARDE-LES TENDOUX

Vieilli en fût de chêne 2000★

7.5 ha n.c. 11–15 €

This estate was a priory founded in the 11th century, and a large part of it was burned down in the Revolution. The deep-black colour of this wine conveys an early impression of its concentration. The oak is fine and integrated, and the particularly powerful body is well balanced with beautiful length. It will need to be kept for a long time to mature.

SARL de Labarde, Ch. La Barde,
24560 Saint-Cernin-de-Labarde, tel. 05.53.57.63.61,
fax 05.53.58.08.12
by appt.

REVELATION DU BOIS DE POURQUIE

Elevé en fût de chêne 2001★★

1 ha 3,000 15–23 €

A new barrel store was dug out and inaugurated in 2002, and was partly responsible for this wine which, for the second year running, wins a *coup de coeur*. The nose is particularly intense, combining notes of very ripe cherry and roasted coffee. The first impression is supple with a beautiful sweetness, then the tannins show themselves to be silky, integrated and very rich. The fruity finish is remarkably persistent. This powerful, balanced wine needs some time for its aromatic complexity to reach its best.

Marlène et Alain Mayet, Le Bois de Pourquié,
24560 Conne-de-Labarde, tel. 05.53.58.25.58,
fax 05.53.61.34.59
by appt.

CH. COMBRILLAC

Elevé en fût de chêne 2000★

3.41 ha 8,700 11–15 €

This wine bears strong signs of oak and the tannic structure needs time to mature. On the nose, the oak is pleasant, and a little toasty. On the palate, the substance is beautiful and rich but the tannins are very evident. Open it in March 2004 and try it, or give it a little longer.

GFA de Combrillac, Coucombre, 24130 Prigonrieux,
tel. 05.53.57.63.61, fax 05.53.58.08.12

CONSTANT-HERITAGE

Vieilli en fût de chêne 2000★

1 ha 6,000 8–11 €

This special *cuvée* was given a long period of maturation in barrel. The complex nose is dominated by notes of vanilla, toast and roasting. The palate is better balanced, both rounded and rich with a fairly soft oak. Aromas emerge of very ripe soft fruits (blackcurrant and violet). The **red Château Le Terme en Bergerac 2001 (5–8 €)** also wins one star. It is much more supple and drinkable because it was not aged in barrel: fruity and light, it is a wine to drink young.

Steven et Sarah Atkins, Le Terme, 24560 Monsaguel,
tel. 05.53.73.32.12, fax 05.53.73.32.23,
e-mail leterme@club-internet.fr
ev. day except Sun. 12 noon–6pm

CH. HAUT BERNASSE 2001★

■ 5,35 ha   15,000   ⑾   5–8 €

Jacques Blais handed over his property in 2002 to Jules and Marie Villette. This Côtes de Bergerac 2001 has a very beautiful deep colour. The nose is complex, releasing blackcurrant and raspberry. A subtle oak is also present on this promising nose. After a supple and well-balanced first impression, the tannins are well integrated. The finish reveals a powerful return of the fruits. This wine ought to be kept but can be drunk now.

☛ SARL Jules et Marie Villette, Ch. Haut Bernasse, 24240 Monbazillac, tel. 05.53.58.36.22, fax 05.53.61.26.40, e-mail contact@haut-bernasse.com ▩

☥ ev. day 8am–12 noon 1.30pm–6pm; Sat. Sun by appt.

☛ Siebec

K DE KREVEL

Vieilles Vignes Elevé en fût de chêne 2000★

■ 2 ha   8,000   ⑾   5–8 €

Denis Dubourdieu, a teacher at the faculty of oenology in Bordeaux, advises this estate which is already well known to our readers. This dark wine with black highlights was matured for one year in new barrels, and has a particularly intense nose with pleasant perfumes of soft fruits and notes of pepper and liquorice. This balance continues on the palate around tannins that are beginning to soften. The long finish has notes of stewed plums. This is an already attractive wine which will improve with age.

☛ SARL Dom. la Métairie, Ch. Fonfrède, Montpeyroux, 24610 Villefranche-de-Lonchat, tel. 05.53.80.09.85, fax 05.53.80.17.72 ▩

☥ by appt.

LADY MASBUREL 2001★

■ n.c.   14,000   ⑾   8–11 €

The Jury selected two château Masburel wines because of their interesting structures. This Lady Masburel has a bouquet of fine toast and rather musky notes. The rich and silky tannins form a palate with aromas suggesting very ripe fruits and vanilla. The **Château Masburel 2001 (15–23 €)** is much more oaky. It has a strong concentration for a wine which is only just beginning to open. Balance will come but not for two to three years. This 2001 wine was singled out.

☛ SARL Ch. Masburel, Fougueyrolles, 33220 Sainte-Foy-la-Grande, tel. 05.53.24.77.73, fax 05.53.24.27.30, e-mail chateau-masburel@wanadoo.fr ▩

☥ ev. day 9am–12 noon 2pm–6pm; Sat. Sun. by appt.

CH. LE MOULIN Cuvée Haut-Terroir Elevé en fût de chêne 2001★

■ 1.74 ha   6,700   ▮⑾   5–8 €

This wine won two stars for its 2000 vintage: the 2001 wine has promising perfumes full of finesse, both fruity and spicy, with notes of oak and leather. The first impression is powerful and the tannins are ripe and silky. The toasted and vanilla notes at the finish give way to a beautiful return of the fruits. This well-balanced wine will improve with age in two to three years.

☛ Pascal Mahieu, Ch. Le Moulin, 24610 Villefranche-de-Lonchat, tel. 05.53.80.69.86 ▩

☥ by appt.

DOM. DU PETIT PARIS

Cuvée Prestige Elevé en fût de chêne 2001★

■ 1 ha   3,500   ⑾   8–11 €

This wine made from 85% Merlot was matured for 14 months in new barrels. The complex nose has perfumes of cherry, vanilla and violet. The first impression is very supple, and is followed by a pleasant tannic structure which is well coated. The finish is a little austere because of the oak which needs to soften. It can be drunk now or aged for a few years.

☛ EARL Dom. du Petit Paris, RN 21, 24240 Monbazillac, tel. 05.53.58.30.41, fax 05.53.58.30.27, e-mail petit-paris@wanadoo.fr ▩

☥ by appt.

☛ Bénédicte et Patrick Geneste

CH. LA ROBERTIE

La Robertie Haute 2001★

■ 1 ha   4,000   ⑾   8–11 €

A Périgord house, built in 1736, and a vineyard of 19 ha were taken over in 1999 by a family from another universe, who were most concerned about quality. This Robertie is a top-of-the-range wine. The bouquet is attractively fruity, releasing perfumes of raspberry and blackcurrant with a fine and subtle oak. The first impression is warming, then the compact tannins prove to be fruity and austere, but the quality of the wine is evident. Keep it for one to two years to allow the tannins to become more coated and better balanced.

☛ SARL Ch. la Robertie, La Robertie, 24240 Rouffignac-de-Sigoulès, tel. 05.53.61.35.44, fax 05.53.58.53.07, e-mail chateau.larobertie@wanadoo.fr ▩

☥ ev. day 9am–7pm

☛ J.-P. et B. Soulier

CH. THEULET

Cuvée spéciale 2001★★

■ 4.5 ha   20,000   ⑾   5–8 €

This wine is remarkable, as usual, and contested the *coup de coeur* with the Grand Jury. Although dominated by oak, the nose is very fine and elegant with fruity and roasted notes. Well-structured tannins allow fruity aromas to develop. The long finish continues this pattern. This wine should be excellent in four to five years.

☛ SCEA Alard, Le Theulet, 24240 Monbazillac, tel. 05.53.57.30.43, fax 05.53.58.88.28, e-mail alardetfils@wanadoo.fr ▩

☥ by appt.

CH. TOUR DES GENDRES

La Gloire de mon Père 2001★

■ 15 ha   60,000   ⑾   8–11 €

Luc de Conti now farms 46 ha, and is one of the great Bergerac producers. His 2001 La Gloire de mon Père is made from 50% Cabernet Sauvignon, 20% Malbec and 30% Merlot, and was matured for a long time in barrel. The bouquet combines fruits and a toasty oak. This is a powerful, concentrated, structured wine with a great future: the tannins are beginning to soften and combine beautifully with the fruits.

☛ SCEA De Conti, Ch. Tour des Gendres, 24240 Ribagnac, tel. 05.53.57.12.43, fax 05.53.58.89.49, e-mail familledeconti@wanadoo.fr ▩ ⌂

☥ by appt.

CH. LES TOURS DES VERDOTS

Les Verdots selon David Fourtout 2001★★

■ 3.5 ha   14,000   ⑾   15–23 €

A wonderful reception and tasting centre has been installed in the building that houses the barrel store. This was dug out of the rock and is crossed by an underground river. At first the nose of this 2001 wine is fruity (black-cherry and morello cherry), then develops a fine and subtle oak with notes of roasting. After a very supple attack, well-coated tannins come nicely to the fore and continue into the long and warming finish. This wine has a great ageing potential.

☛ EARL David Fourtout, Vignobles des Verdots, 24560 Conne-de-Labarde, tel. 05.53.58.34.31, fax 05.53.57.82.00, e-mail fourtout@terre-net.fr ▩ ⌂

☥ ev. day except Sun. 9.30am–12.30pm 2pm–7pm

CH. DES VIGIERS 2000★

■ 1.75 ha   3,385   ▮⑾♦   11–15 €

This superb 16th century château is now a four-star hotel with an 18-hole golf course. It is also a high-quality vineyard, as this crimson wine shows. The nose is toasty and grilled with vanilla and aromas of soft fruits. The palate is immediately rich and rounded, then the tannins rapidly grow in power.

The oak is very pronounced and needs a few years (three or four) to soften.
☛ SCEA la Font du Roc, Ch. des Vigiers, 24240 Monestier, tel. 05.53.61.50.00, fax 05.53.61.50.20, e-mail vigiers@vigiers.com ☑
☛ Petersson

Côtes de Bergerac Moelleux

These are made from the same varieties as the dry white wines but are harvested when overripe to make popular and supple sweet wines with flavours of preserved fruits.

CH. LES MAILLERIES
Cuvée Dany 2001★★

0.5 ha	1,150	◫	8–11 €

This is not a sweet wine but a true and great *vin liquoreux*. The complex nose combines notes of honeysuckle and peach and also noble rot, accompanied by a well-integrated vanilla. The palate, following the nose, is full and pleasantly balanced, and mouth filling with both floral and fruity aromas and a rather lively finish. This 100% Sémillon is very well made, not heavy but rich with excellent keeping potential. (Bottles of 50 cl.)
☛ Patrice Tevenin, Cauffour, Ch. Les Mailleries, 24240 Thénac, tel. 05.53.57.56.60, fax 05.53.57.56.60 ☑
Ⴤ by appt.

CH. LES MARNIERES 2002★★

6.5 ha	36,000	⏸ ♦	5–8 €

The success of a sweet wine is mainly a matter of balance. This wine has elegant perfumes of fruit (white peach) and honey. The first impression is both supple and fruity with good acidity, then the white fruit gives way to crystallized fruits on a palate which remains light. It is a very harmonious sweet wine. The **red Bergerac 2002** wins one star for its elegance and harmony. Notes of blackcurrant and rich, very well-coated tannins are good signs for the future.
☛ Alain et Christophe Geneste, GAEC des Brandines, 24520 Saint-Nexans, tel. 05.53.58.31.65, fax 05.53.73.20.34, e-mail christophe.geneste2@wanadoo.fr ☑
Ⴤ by appt.

DOM. DU SIORAC
Tradition 2002★

3.12 ha	12,000	⏸ ♦	3–5 €

The nose is particularly fruity, suggesting pear. The first impression is honest and fruity, with a lovely acidity. This well-structured and elegant wine will be perfect as an aperitif.
☛ Dom. du Siorac, 24500 Saint-Aubin-de-Cadelech, tel. 05.53.74.52.90, fax 05.53.58.35.32
Ⴤ ev. day except Sun. 9am–12 noon 2pm–6pm

Wines selected but not starred

CLOS DALMAIN 2001

0.7 ha	1,400	◫	11–15 €

☛ Tim Richardson, Le Bourg, 24500 Saint-Julien-d'Eymet, tel. 05.53.58.09.72, fax 05.53.58.09.72, e-mail tim.richardson@wanadoo.fr ☑
Ⴤ by appt.

LES RAISINS OUBLIES 2001

8 ha	36,000	5–8 €

☛ Vins fins du Périgord, BP 2, 24240 Sigoulès, tel. 05.53.63.78.50, fax 05.53.63.78.59

CH. VIGNAL LA BRIE 2001

34.7 ha	10,000	⏸ ♦	5–8 €

☛ Edgard Gouy, Ch. Vignal la Brie, 24240 Monbazillac, tel. 05.53.24.51.18, fax 05.53.58.89.36 ☑
Ⴤ ev. day 8am–8pm

Monbazillac

Extending over 2,500 ha, of which 1,979 used in 2002 produced 48,935 hl, the Monbazillac vineyard produces rich wines made from grapes with "noble rot". The clay and limestone soils bring intense aromas to the wines as well as a strong and complex structure.

DOM. DE L'ANCIENNE CURE
Cuvée Abbaye 2001★★

5 ha	10,000	◫	15–23 €

A unanimous *coup de coeur*, a reward for the work of both the grower and the vinifier. The nose releases floral notes (white flowers and acacia) which have great finesse and intensity. The palate discloses concentrated crystallized fruits, then a perfect balance between the fruitiness and the oak. The fresh finish is slightly untholated and very long. A superb wine which, despite its great concentration, shows a rare delicacy and remarkable harmony. Great art. (Bottles of 50 cl.)
☛ Christian Roche, Ancienne Cure, 24560 Colombier, tel. 05.53.58.27.90, fax 05.53.24.83.95, e-mail ancienne-cure@wanadoo.fr ☑
Ⴤ ev. day except Sun. 9am–6pm

DORDOGNE

DOM. DE L'ANCIENNE CURE

L'Extase 2001★★

	2 ha	2,000	◫	38–46 €

Another splendid wine from Christian Roche. The nose is still closed but complex with perfumes of crystallized fruits and lime blossom with an elegant oak. The palate is very rich and full, disclosing sweetness and a rather dominating oak. This is definitely a very well-made wine, but it needs keeping. (Bottles of 50 cl.) Two stars also go to the **red Bergerac Cuvée Extase 2001 (15–23 €)**, which at the moment is too oaky but its very concentrated substance shows it will be worth keeping.
☛ Christian Roche, Ancienne Cure, 24560 Colombier, tel. 05.53.58.27.90, fax 05.53.24.83.95,
e-mail ancienne-cure@wanadoo.fr ☑
☨ ev. day except Sun. 9am–6pm

DOM. DE LA BORIE BLANCHE

Elevé en fût de chêne 2001★

	1 ha	1,800	◫	11–15 €

This virtually abandoned property was taken over in 1995 and completely restored. It has a *gîte* and *chambres d'hôte*. This is a traditional blend, vinified in barrel to give the wine a pleasant and intense nose with aromas of fruits and a small floral note. The fresh and rounded palate rests on a beautiful substance which is still a little oaky. Keep it until this has softened. (Bottles of 50 cl.)
☛ Emmanuelle Ojeda, La Borie Blanche, 24240 Pomport, tel. 05.53.73.02.45, fax 05.53.73.02.45 ☑ ⌂ ⌂
☨ ev. day 10.30am–7.30pm; cl. 16 Sept. to 14 Apr.

CH. LA BRIE

Cuvée Prestige Elevé en fût de chêne 2001★

	27.8 ha	13,000	◫	15–23 €

The *Lycée Viticole* is a safe bet in this appellation thanks to its winery where people are trained. This Prestige wine is very classical with its notes of crystallized fruits and dry apricot. The first impression is lively, but the characteristic aromas arrive quickly and a balances is reached. The long finish discloses a subtle oak. A wine to open between 2004 and 2006.
☛ Ch. la Brie, Lycée viticole, Dom. de la Brie, 24240 Monbazillac, tel. 05.53.74.42.42, fax 05.53.58.24.08,
e-mail lpa.bergerac@educagri.fr ☑
☨ ev. day except Sun. 10am–12 noon 1.30pm–7pm; cl. Jan.

CH. CAILLAVEL 2000★★

	20 ha	6,000	◫	11–15 €

Although the oak is very prominent, this wine is remarkably integrated. The nose reveals great power with notes of toast and coffee. The first impression is rather fresh and the palate is rich without any heaviness. The toast and the oak return at the finish, but now in harmony. The **red Côtes-de-Bergerac 2000 (8–11 €)** is also quite oaky. The rich and complex palate offers notes of blackcurrant, but the oak persists. This wine wins one star, and is for informed wine-lovers.
☛ GAEC Ch. Caillavel, 24240 Pomport, tel. 05.53.58.43.30, fax 05.53.58.20.31 ☑
☨ ev. day except Sun. 8am–6.30pm

CH. COMBET 2001★

	19 ha	60,000	◫ ⌂ ⌂	8–11 €

This estate of 30 ha was created in the 1950s on the site of a renovated family farm. The grapes were harvested from 1 October 2001. On the nose, this wine initially releases exotic fruits then a note of oak. Although the substance is rather light, it is nevertheless rounded and quite balanced. The finish is still oaky, so the wine should be kept for a year or two.
☛ EARL de Combet, 24240 Monbazillac, tel. 06.85.33.50.57, fax 05.53.58.33.47,
e-mail combet@oreka.com ☑
☨ ev. day except Sat. Sun. 9.30am–12 noon 2pm–6pm; cl. Jan.

CH. FONMOURGUES 2000★★

	4 ha	3,600	◫ ⌂ ⌂	8–11 €

This is an original wine made with 30% Muscadelle, an excellent grape variety but difficult to cultivate for making sweet wines. The nose is intense and fruity, and discloses grapey notes. The freshness of the attack is a little surprising, then the flesh and the fruits take over. The finish is powerful. This is a very attractive wine which is rather unusual for the appellation.
☛ EARL Dominique Vidal, Ch. Fonmourgues, 24240 Monbazillac, tel. 05.53.63.02.79,
e-mail vidal.dominique@tiscali.fr ☑
☨ by appt.

GRANDE MAISON

Cuvée du Château 2000★★

	2 ha	1,600	◫	30–38 €

This wine was made by sustainable agriculture, and its originality lies in the fact that it consists of white and grey Sauvignon. The nose is rather dominated by oak, and releases aromas of dried apricot. Sugar and honey take over on the palate with some oaky and brioche notes at the finish. A wine of a great concentration and beautiful finesse. But the **Cuvée des Monstres 2000 (more than 76 €)**, winning one star, is both well named and even richer than the other, but fortunately it has both acidity and oak. The sugar is stronger than the alcohol. This is one for lovers of sweet wines to keep.
☛ Thierry Desprès, Grande Maison, 24240 Monbazillac, tel. 05.53.58.26.17, fax 05.53.24.97.36,
e-mail thierry.despres@free.fr ☑
☨ by appt.

CH. LES HAUTS DE CAILLEVEL 2000★

	10 ha	2,500	◫	8–11 €

This estate stands on one of the routes to Santiago de Compostela, and its wines are generally about 60 years old. This wine was fermented and matured in barrel; it has a floral, slightly oaky nose promising good finesse. The first impression is notably fresh, followed by a pleasant palate; the oak enhances the finish. This is a well-balanced wine but needs two to three years to mature. (Bottles of 50 cl.)
☛ Sylvie Chevallier-Ducrocq, Les Hauts de Caillevel, 24240 Monbazillac, tel. 05.53.73.92.72, fax 05.53.73.92.72,
e-mail caillevel@wanadoo.fr ☑
☨ ev. day except Wed. Sun. 10am–12 noon 2pm–6pm

CH. LADESVIGNES

Automne Elevé en fût de chêne 2001★

	5 ha	5,000	◫	15–23 €

This is a classic and particularly pleasant Monbazillac, its nose and palate releasing aromas of ripe fruits and crystallized fruits. The palate is very powerful, enhanced by the well-integrated oak and a long finish full of fruitiness, with a touch of hazelnut. Its freshness will allow this wine to improve in time. The **dry Bergerac 2002 (5–8 €)** wins one star. The Jury liked its fruity character and its concentration. A well-made wine with great finesse.
☛ Ch. Ladesvignes, 24240 Pomport, tel. 05.53.58.30.67, fax 05.53.58.22.64,
e-mail chateau.ladesvignes@wanadoo.fr ☑
☨ by appt.
☛ Michel Monbouché

CH. MONBAZILLAC 2000★

	25 ha	30,000	◫	11–15 €

This wine was made near the 16th century monument that is a symbol of the Bergerac region. It has a fairly expressive nose combining notes of flowers, apricot and cinnamon and a subtle oak. The first impression is very rich in sugar, but not excessively so, and oaky notes reappear at the finish. This wine will be even better in three years.
☛ Cave coopérative de Monbazillac, rte de Monbazillac, 24240 Monbazillac, tel. 05.53.63.65.00, fax 05.53.63.65.09 ☑
☨ by appt.

CH. MONTDOYEN

Cuvée La Part des Anges 2001★★

	2 ha	6,000	◫	15–23 €

The restoration work continues at this property. This wine was fermented and matured in barrel, and on the nose releases exotic fruits and peach. The palate is fruity, and perfectly in

balance with the oak. The finish is long with a beautiful fruity return. A rounded wine of remarkable harmony.
☛ SARL des Vignobles J.-P. Hembise, Ch. Montdoyen, 24240 Monbazillac, tel. 05.53.58.85.85, fax 05.53.61.67.78, e-mail chateaumontdoyen@wanadoo.fr ☑
☘ ev. day 8.30am–12.30pm 1.30pm–6pm; Sat. Sun. by appt.

CH. LA ROUQUETTE 2001★

| | 6 ha | 16,000 | ▮ ↓ | 5–8 € |

This estate exports 80% of its production to Great Britain. Here it offers a very elegant 2001 wine. The nose is particularly fine and complex, with aromas of white fruits, peach and lime blossom. The first impression is supple, rounded and pleasant. Although the sugar content is not exceptional, its well-controlled acidity will give it beautiful balance. An attractive Monbazillac, rather airy and fruity, which avoids heaviness to make it easy to drink. (Bottles of 50 Cl.)
☛ Yvette Lacroix, Les Costes, 24100 Bergerac, tel. 05.53.57.64.49, fax 05.53.61.69.08 ☑
☘ ev. day except Sun. 9am–12 noon 3pm–7pm

CH. TIRECUL LA GRAVIERE 2000★

| | 9,16 ha | 12,900 | ▥ | 23–30 € |

The 2000 harvest made it impossible to produce the Madame wine which, in 1999, won a *coup de coeur*. It is a pity but it shows the rigourousness of the winemakers. The "classic" wine is, however, very successful. The nose is not yet very expressive but releases notes of apricot and almond. After a very elegant first impression marked by a beautiful acidity, the oak does not intrude, even though it is very evident in the toasty notes and brioche. A balanced wine with a long finish which, as usual, will need to be laid down. (Bottles of 50 cl.)
☛ Claudie et Bruno Bilancini, Ch. Tirecul la Gravière, 24240 Monbazillac, tel. 05.53.57.44.75, fax 05.53.24.85.01, e-mail bruno.bilancini@cario.fr ☑
☘ ev. day 9am–12 noon 2pm–5.30pm; Sat. Sun. and other times by appt.

Wines selected but not starred

DOM. DE LA LANDE 2001

| | 2 ha | 700 | ▥ | 5–8 € |

☛ Fabrice Camus, Dom. de La Lande, 24240 Monbazillac, tel. 05.53.73.21.79, fax 05.53.24.27.61 ☑
☘ by appt.

CH. PECH LA CALEVIE 2001

| | 8,5 ha | n.c. | ▮ ↓ | 5–8 € |

☛ GAEC de la Calevie, La Calevie, 24240 Pomport, tel. 05.53.58.43.46, fax 05.53.58.43.46, e-mail calevie@free.fr ☑
☘ ev. day except Sun. 9am–7pm
☛ Tricou

CH. LA TRUFFIERE 2000

| | 3 ha | 6,000 | ▥ | 11–15 € |

☛ SCEA Feytout, La Truffière, 24240 Monbazillac, tel. 05.53.58.30.23, fax 05.53.61.28.63 ☑ ☗
☘ ev. day 10am–12.30pm 2pm–7pm

Montravel

The terroir of Montravel (378 ha), extending over the hills from Port-Sainte-Foy and Ponchapt to Saint-Michel-de-Montaigne, produces dry and sweet wines noted for their elegance. In 2002, the output was 11,832 hl of Montravel, 1,597 hl of Haut-Montravel and 1,825 hl of Côtes de Montravel.

Since the 2001 vintage, AOC Montravel status has also been awarded to red wines, which typically have concentrated and vanilla tannins.

B. BLEUE 2002★

| | 20 ha | 15,000 | | 3–5 € |

This bottle will be easy to find – it is blue; it was also decanted so the tasters would not recognize it. The nose is a subtle blend of fruits revealing the contributions of the Sauvignon and the Muscadelle. The palate is very lively: the Sauvignon comes through in notes of citrus fruits. This will be good with shellfish.
☛ Union de viticulteurs de Port-Sainte-Foy, 78, rte de Bordeaux, 33220 Port-Sainte-Foy, tel. 05.53.27.40.70, fax 05.53.27.40.71, e-mail cavevitipsf@wanadoo.fr ☑ ☗
☘ ev. day 9am–12 noon 2pm–7pm

CH. DU BLOY

Le Bloy 2001★★

| | 0,8 ha | 4,500 | ▥ | 11–15 € |

In 2001, two wine enthusiasts, a lawyer and a consultant in data processing, took over this estate located 5 km from the Château de Montaigne. This first wine offers an intense nose of slightly musky leather, and an attractive grilled and vanilla oak. After a supple first impression, strong tannins appear, it has a concentrated but elegant body. This is a very pleasant, well-balanced wine in which the oak and the fruit combine well.
☛ SCEA Olivier Lambert et Bertrand Lepoittevin-Dubost, Le Blois, 24230 Bonneville, tel. 05.53.22.47.87, fax 05.53.27.56.34, e-mail chateau.du.bloy@wanadoo.fr ☑
☘ by appt.

CH. LAULERIE 2002★★

| | 20 ha | 160,000 | ▮ ↓ | 5–8 € |

Why change a recipe that works well? Once again, the Montravel from Château Laulerie wins two stars. The nose is very powerful and characteristic of Sauvignon, though a little rough. The first impression is quite lively, releasing aromas of ripe grapefruit and crunchy fruits. The finish is a real festival of fruits. An attractive, rich and pleasant wine to drink with a meal.
☛ Vignobles Dubard Frère et Soeur, Le Gouyat, 24610 Saint-Méard-de-Gurçon, tel. 05.53.82.48.31, fax 05.53.82.47.64, e-mail vignobles-dubard@wanadoo.fr ☑ ☗ ☗
☘ ev. day except Sun. 8am–12 noon 2pm–6pm

CH. MASBUREL 2001★

| | n.c. | 26,000 | ▥ | 8–11 € |

The nose of this wine is full of both original and exotic aromas: Muscat, white pepper, lychee, peach and toast. The palate is very fresh and adequately fleshy, with flavours of apricot, spices and Muscat. The finish is more austere and oaky.
☛ SARL Ch. Masburel, Fougueyrolles, 33220 Sainte-Foy-la-Grande, tel. 05.53.24.77.73, fax 05.53.24.27.30, e-mail chateau-masburel@wanadoo.fr ☑
☘ ev. day 9am–12 noon 2pm–6pm; Sat. Sun. by appt.
☛ Olivia Donnan

CH. MASMONTET 2001★

| | 1 ha | 3,200 | ▮▥ ↓ | 11–15 € |

An oven with Gallo-Roman tiles was discovered in the centre of this vineyard taken over by Thibaut Guillermier, son of the founder, in 2001. It has a fruity and elegant nose with enjoyable notes of raspberry and liquorice as well as toasty and cocoa-flavoured notes. The first impression is supple, fresh and fruity, then the tannins appear, overwhelming the palate: the wine must be aged to let them refine. Keep it for two to three years at least.

☛ Thibaut Guillermier, Masmontet, 24230 Vélines, tel. 05.53.74.39.56, fax 05.53.74.39.60 **Ⓥ**
Ⱦ ev. day except Sun. 9am–12 noon 2pm–6pm

CH. MOULIN CARESSE
Cuvée Cent pour 100 2001**★★**

| ■ | 1.5 ha | 6,500 | ◖Ⅱ◗ | 11–15 € |

After many years of trying, the 2001 vintage is the first to see red wines in the AOC. Many words can be used to describe the nose of this wine: oaky, toasted and vanilla-flavoured, and also aromas of liquorice, lemon, bergamot and morello cherry. On the palate, the wine is very open after a powerful, rounded and supple first impression. The tannins are compact but fine grained; the finish appears slightly marked by oak. This fine and elegant 2001 can be drunk now or kept. The **dry white Montravel 2001 Elevé en Fût de Chêne (5–8 €)** is complex and concentrated as well as fruity, rich and fresh: springtime in a glass.

☛ Sylvie et Jean-François Deffarge, Ch. Moulin Caresse, 24230 Saint-Antoine-de-Breuilh, tel. 05.53.27.55.58, fax 05.53.27.07.39,
e-mail moulin.caresse@wanadoo.fr **Ⓥ** **⌂**
Ⱦ ev. day 9am–12 noon 2pm–6pm; Sat. Sun. by appt.

CH. MOULIN DE BEL-AIR 2001**★**

| | 1 ha | 6,500 | ◖Ⅱ◗ | 8–11 € |

This wine was matured in new barrels with stirring of the yeast, and is very oaky, so best for wine-lovers who like that kind of thing. The intense nose offers grilled and toasted notes which admit a few nuances of citrus fruits. On the palate, the first impression is very rich with a strong oaky flavour. Keep it for at least a year, then serve it with fish in sauce.

☛ J.-F. et E. Ley, 24230 Saint-Michel-de-Montaigne, tel. 05.53.58.68.15 **Ⓥ**
Ⱦ ev. day 9am–12 noon 2pm–5pm; cl. Aug.

CH. PAGNON 2002**★★**

| | 3 ha | 5,000 | ■ ⚶ | 5–8 € |

This estate has about 60 ha of which 35 are down to vines. The full range of Sauvignon aromas appears on the bouquet: boxwood, blackcurrant, grapefruit and exotic fruits. The first impression is honest and fresh, then flavours of lemon and grapefruit come to the fore on the palate. This is a very fresh Montravel which can be kept for two or three years.

☛ Dino Moro, SARL Moro Diffusion, Prentygarde, 24230 Vélines, tel. 05.53.27.10.72, fax 05.53.27.56.00, e-mail chateau.pagnon@wanadoo.fr **Ⓥ** **⌂**
Ⱦ by appt.

CH. PIQUE-SEGUE 2001**★★**

| ■ | 3 ha | 14,000 | ◖Ⅱ◗ | 15–23 € |

This wine has the privilege of being the first *coup de coeur* for red Montravels. The nose is particularly intense and complex, with a strong and elegant toasty oak which admits notes of very ripe small soft fruits. The first impression is full and rounded. The tannins are very concentrated but fine and already integrated. A model of complexity and balance that

could be drunk young, but could also be aged for ten years with no problems.

☛ SNC Ch. Pique-Sègue, Ponchapt, 33220 Port-Sainte-Foy, tel. 05.53.58.52.52, fax 05.53.63.44.97,
e-mail chateau-pique-segue@wanadoo.fr **Ⓥ**
Ⱦ by appt.
☛ Mallard

CH. PIQUE-SEGUE 2002**★★★**

| | 25 ha | 130,000 | | 5–8 € |

Two *coups de coeur* for the same estate, in white and red. According to custom, only the label of the red is shown, but the distinction is quite real. The exceptional fruitiness of this 2002 proves that one can good white without yielding to fashionable barrels. A festival of aromas explodes on the nose: raspberry, kiwi, exotic fruits, pineapple and lemon. The palate is supple and very rich, and reveals a power that combines roundness and freshness and a finish of dazzling length. The **Côtes de Montravel 2001** is a sweet, well-balanced wine, neither too fresh nor too sweet, with pleasant grapey aromas. It wins one star.

☛ SNC Ch. Pique-Sègue, Ponchapt, 33220 Port-Sainte-Foy, tel. 05.53.58.52.52, fax 05.53.63.44.97,
e-mail chateau-pique-segue@wanadoo.fr **Ⓥ**
Ⱦ by appt.

LES PORTES DU BONDIEU 2001**★★★**

| | 0.5 ha | 1,500 | ◖Ⅱ◗ | 15–23 € |

This recently created wine wins three stars, and came second with the Grand Jury for *coups de coeur* in white. It has an attractive nose of fresh fruits: peach and cherry with a light oak. After a fresh first impression, the palate is rounded, very flexible and finely oaky. The finish is fruity with a beautiful acidity. This already well-balanced wine can be kept for three to four years.

☛ EARL d'Adrina, Le Bondieu, 24230 Saint-Antoine-de-Breuilh, tel. 05.53.58.30.83, fax 05.53.24.38.21 **Ⓥ**
Ⱦ by appt.
☛ Didier Feytout

CH. PUY-SERVAIN
Cuvée Marjolaine 2001**★★**

| | n.c. | n.c. | ◖Ⅱ◗ | 8–11 € |

This dry white Marjolaine draws its originality from a blend of equal shares of Sémillon and Sauvignon, followed by fermentation and maturation in barrel. The fine and elegant nose offers oaky notes and nuances of toast and citrus fruits. The first impression is fresh, then the palate becomes rounded and full bodied with some flesh and mineral notes. It is a concentrated wine and very crisp on the palate. The **red Cuvée Songe en Montravel (15–23 €)** wins one star. It develops mainly oaky and toasted aromas. The tannins are fine, silky and full of volume, but still a little bitter at the finish. It has very good keeping potential and should improve with time.

☛ SCEA Puy-Servain, Calabre, 33220 Port-Sainte-Foy, tel. 05.53.24.77.27, fax 05.53.58.37.43,
e-mail oenovit.puyservain@wanadoo.fr **Ⓥ**
Ⱦ ev. day except Sat. Sun. 8am–12 noon 2pm–6pm
☛ Hecquet

CH. LE RAZ
Cuvée Grand Chêne 2001**★**

| | 1.4 ha | 5,800 | ◖Ⅱ◗ | 5–8 € |

This top-of-the-range wine, often mentioned in the *Guide*, is most carefully created from the vine to the winery. The nose of this vintage is rather strong on Sauvignon, but there are also aromas of hawthorn and papaw. The palate becomes rounded and powerful and has aromas of exotic fruits. It is an attractive fruity wine with a full-bodied nature. The **Les Filles red 2001 (11–15 €)** wins one star. The oak is fine and elegant, and lets the fruits come through. Open it in two years.

☛ Vignobles Barde, Le Raz, 24610 Saint-Méard-de-Gurçon, tel. 05.53.82.48.41, fax 05.53.80.07.47, e-mail vignobles-barde@le-raz.com **Ⓥ**
Ⱦ ev. day except Sun. 8.30am–12.30pm 2.15pm–7pm; Sat. by appt.

CH. LA RESSAUDIE 2002★

| 4 ha | 18,000 | 🍶 ⚭ | 3–5 € |

This Montravel white has a rather closed bouquet but there are notes of fruits with white flesh and flowers. The first impression is sweet with ripe fruits. A nice acidity comes to support the fruit in mid-palate. It is a tasty, uncomplicated wine, natural and charming. The **red Montravel 2001 (11–15 €)** was singled out by the Jury, and releases aromas of black fruits, cinnamon, truffle, blackcurrant, and, of course, oak. The tannins are not quite integrated. This wine should improve with age.

🔹 Jean et Evelyne Rebeyrolle, Ch. La Ressaudie, 33220 Port-Sainte-Foy, tel. 05.53.24.71.48, fax 05.53.58.52.29, e-mail vinlaressaudie@aol.com ☑ ⚭ ⚭
☗ by appt.

DOM. DE LA ROCHE MAROT 2002★

| 3.4 ha | 6,600 | 🍶 ⚭ | 3–5 € |

Three kilometres from this estate of more than 20 ha, you will find the Gallo-Roman villa of Montcaret. Equal shares of Sauvignon and Sémillon make up this wine which has a fairly open nose marked by very ripe grapes, blackcurrant bud and white peach. The palate is balanced and very fruity. The structure is not very intense but fairly balanced with good freshness. This is a light Montravel, better drunk as an aperitif than with a meal.

🔹 Y. et D. Boyer, GAEC de La Roche Marot, 24230 Lamothe-Montravel, tel. 05.53.58.52.05, fax 05.53.58.52.05 ☑
☗ by appt.

CAVE DE SAINT-VIVIEN 2002★

| 4.5 ha | 33,500 | 🍶 ⚭ | 3–5 € |

On the nose, the Sauvignon is characteristically intense with aromas of boxwood and grapefruit. The palate is very fruity, with grapefruit prominent. It becomes concentrated and full bodied with mineral notes, leading to a very fresh finish which retains the citrus fruits. This is a very attractive fruity wine. The cooperative also produced the **red Château le Pavillon 2000 en Bergerac (5–8 €)** which was singled out by the Jury. It is fruity and supple, with oaky tannins. It should improve with age.

🔹 Viticulteurs réunis de Saint-Vivien-et-Bonneville, 24230 Vélines, tel. 05.53.27.52.22, fax 05.53.22.61.12 ☑
☗ by appt.

Wines selected but not starred

CH. BONIERES

La Dame de Bonières 2002

| 1.3 ha | 8,000 | 🍷 | 11–15 € |

🔹 SCEA Vignobles André Bodin, Ch. Bonières, 33220 Fougueyrolles, tel. 05.53.24.15.16, fax 05.53.22.81.84, e-mail stevalentin@free.fr ☑
☗ by appt.

CH. LES GRIMARD 2002

| 0.95 ha | 6,500 | 🍶 ⚭ | –3 € |

🔹 GAEC des Grimard-Havard, 24230 Montazeau, tel. 05.53.63.09.83, fax 05.53.24.90.14, e-mail ch.lesgrimard@wanadoo.fr ☑
☗ ev. day 8am–7.30pm; Sun. 9am–12 noon
🔹 Jacques Joyeux

Côtes de Montravel

CH. LESPINASSAT

Vieilles Vignes 2002★

| n.c. | 3,000 | | 11–15 € |

To make a *vin liquoreux*, harvests are gathered by selective picking from the old, low and narrow vines. The nose is not very powerful but pleasant thanks to its floral aromas. The palate opens with a fresh attack, then floral notes emerge in mid-palate with a light touch of wax. This is a pleasant wine.

🔹 Agnès Verseau, Les Oliviers, 24230 Montcaret, tel. 05.53.58.34.23, fax 05.53.61.36.57, e-mail chateaulespinassat@hotmail.com ☑
☗ by appt.

Haut-Montravel

CH. FAYOLLE-LUZAC 2001★

| 1 ha | 1,200 | 🍶 ⚭ | 8–11 € |

In 1998, the Van Kempens decide to change professions and settled in the Bergerac region; today they run 23 ha. This wine is not very intense but has a rather fine nose with notes of crystallized fruits and white peach. The first impression is fresh then the palate continues more richly to a very pleasant finish with honey and fruit. Keep this for a few months longer.

🔹 SCEA ch. Fayolle, Fayolle, 33220 Fougueyrolles, tel. 05.53.73.51.68, fax 05.53.73.51.69, e-mail ch.fayolle.luzac@wanadoo.fr ☑
☗ by appt.
🔹 M. et R. Van Kempen

CH. PUY-SERVAIN

Terrement 2001★★

| n.c. | n.c. | 🍷 | 15–23 € |

This is undoubtedly an excellent wine which missed the *coup de cœur* by one vote. It has a very beautiful straw colour. The nose is jammy with aromas of peach and apricot and notes of toast. The palate is mouth filling and remarkably ample; the crystallized fruits explode once again and the finish reveals a very integrated oak. A very attractive wine both in terms of the grapes and the maturation in barrel. It is advisable to keep it for a while.

🔹 SCEA Puy-Servain, Calabre, 33220 Port-Sainte-Foy, tel. 05.53.24.77.27, fax 05.53.58.37.43, e-mail oenovit.puyservain@wanadoo.fr ☑
☗ ev. day except Sat. Sun. 8am–12 noon 2pm–6pm
🔹 Hecquet

Pécharmant

On a slope covered with 409 ha of vines, northeast of Bergerac, the "Pech" produces very rich red wines with good keeping qualities. In 2002 production was 15,113 hl.

CH. BEAUPORTAIL 2001★★★

| 9 ha | 31,000 | 🍷 | 8–11 € |

The avowed aim of this vineyard is to produce the most beautiful grapes, and so they do not hesitate to thin out the leaves and do a green harvest to eliminate 30–50% of the harvest.

The result this time is sumptuous. The nose of this 2001 wine is intense and complex with aromas of ripe fruits, bigaroon cherry and light and well-integrated toasty notes. The first impression is superb and silky, with a cocktail of red and black fruits. The well-integrated and rounded tannins are remarkably long and concentrated. This wine is very pleasant now, and will be even better in two to three years.

🍴 EARL La Truffière Beauportail, 14, rte des Cabernets, 24100 Bergerac, tel. 05.53.24.85.16, fax 05.53.61.28.63, e-mail truffiere@beauportail.com ☑
🍽 ev. day 11am–12.30pm 2pm–7pm
🍷 F. Feytout

CH. DE BIRAN
Cuvée Prestige de Bacchus 2000★★

| ■ | 2 ha | 5,000 | ⑪ | 15–23 € |

This was the preferred choice of the Grand Jury, by a short head: a wine matured for 15 months in barrel with a deep colour and mauve highlights. The nose is powerful with nuances of spices including clove. On the palate, the structure is concentrated with pleasant and integrated tannins. The intense and complex mid-palate offers notes of fruits, chocolate, tobacco and coffee. This wine has the finesse and elegance of a great Pécharmant, and this swayed the decision. The classic **Château de Biran 2001 (8–11 €)** was singled out by the Jury. It needs time to become more refined.

🍴 EARL Vignobles de Biran, 24520 Saint-Sauveur-de-Bergerac, tel. 05.53.22.46.29, fax 05.53.27.54.31, e-mail chbiran@aol.com ☑
🍷 by appt.

DOM. BRISSEAU-BELLOC 2001★

| ■ | 6.23 ha | 40,000 | ⑪ | 5–8 € |

The Union Vinicole in Bergerac-le-Fleix appears in the selection for two Pécharmant estates. The Brisseau-Belloc Domaine is characterized by a certain freshness on the nose and the palate. The tannic structure is not very powerful but is well integrated, with no harsh tannins. This wine is elegant and ready to drink now. The **Château Pech Marty 2001, Elevé en Fût** (one star), has a fairly closed nose. Although the attack is supple and integrated, the tannins assert themselves later and need time to mature.

🍴 SCEA Brisseau-Belloc, 24100 Pécharmant, tel. 05.53.24.64.32, fax 05.53.24.65.46 ☑
🍷 by appt.

CH. CHAMPAREL 2001★★

| ■ | 6.62 ha | 47,500 | ⑪ | 5–8 € |

This vineyard has already celebrated its centenary. Located at the top of the hillside of Pécharmant, it follows a remarkable 2000 vintage with an equally successful 2001. The nose is fairly intense, suggesting fresh fruits with a light oak. The first impression is sweet, without too much oak, and the palate is fruity with silky tannins and, there too, a well-integrated oak. This is a very attractive wine, elegant and balanced, that should be kept for four to five years.

🍴 Françoise Bouché, 24100 Pécharmant, tel. 05.53.57.34.76, fax 05.53.73.24.18 ☑
🍷 by appt.

CH. CORBIAC 2001★

| ■ | 18 ha | 83,000 | ▮ ⑪ ⬦ | 11–15 € |

The whole art is to adapt oneself to the soil and to take account of the *climat* and grow this small wild fruit characteristic of the wines of Corbiac, a *coup de cœur* last year with its 2000. On the nose, this new wine releases perfumes of black fruits then complex oaky and toasty notes. Then powerful, rounded and full-bodied tannins leave the very ripe black fruits to express themselves at the finish. A beautiful wine which should be kept for two years to allow it to reach its potential.

🍴 Bruno de Corbiac, Ch. de Corbiac, rte de Corbiac-Pécharmant, 24100 Bergerac, tel. 05.53.57.20.75, fax 05.53.57.89.98, e-mail corbiac@corbiac.com ☑
🍷 by appt.

DOM. DES COSTES 2001★

| ■ | 10 ha | 50,000 | ▮ ⑪ ⬦ | 8–11 € |

This wine has appeared for many years in the *Guide*. The glass needs to be swirled to release perfumes of ripe fruits, followed by a subtle oak. The first impression is sweet, then the palate is dominated by oak. However, the soft fruits develop well before the supple finish. This wine should be opened in two to three years and will be remarkably fruity.

🍴 Nicole Dournel, Les Costes, 24100 Bergerac, tel. 05.53.57.64.49, fax 05.53.61.69.08 ☑
🍷 by appt.
🍷 Gérard Lacroix

CROS DE LA SAL
Vieilli en fût de chêne 2001★

| ■ | 3 ha | 25,000 | ⑪ | 5–8 € |

Two hundred years ago, the philosopher Maine de Biran liked to meditate among these vines. Today, we are happy to find this wine with its nose of soft fruits and floral. The first impression is reasonably supple and honest, reflecting the same aromatic notes. The tannins are very evident and fine, and suggest an excellent potential for keeping.

🍴 Gérôme et Dolorès Morand-Monteil, Ch. Terre-Vieille, 24520 Saint-Sauveur-de-Bergerac, tel. 05.53.57.35.07, fax 05.53.61.91.77, e-mail gerome-morand-monteil@wanadoo.fr ☑
🍽 ev. day except Sun. 9am–7pm

CH. LES FARCIES DU PECH' 2000★

| ■ | 10 ha | 60,000 | ⑪ | 8–11 € |

A Périgord charterhouse and a park with hundred-year-old trees was for three centuries the property of an old Bergerac family. It was taken over in 2000 by the producers of Château Laulery in Montravel. They offer a wine that is initially rather reserved on the nose, but then smoky and roasted notes arrive, with nuances of cocoa. The first impression is full, supple and beautifully round, with very concentrated but reasonable tannins. A promising wine.

🍴 Dubard-Peytureau, SARL Hameau de Pécharmant, 24100 Bergerac, tel. 05.53.82.48.31, fax 05.53.82.47.64, e-mail vignobles-dubard@wanadoo.fr ☑ 🏠 🏠
🍽 ev. day except Sun. 8am–12 noon 2pm–6pm

DOM. DU GRAND JAURE
Elevé en fût de chêne 2000★

| ■ | 1,5 ha | 8,000 | ⑪ | 8–11 € |

Bertrand and Bernadette Baudry, brother and sister, run this family estate created in 1920. Dark and deep, this wine has an original nose which is strong on soft fruits. Some notes of undergrowth reveal its maturation in barrel. The first impression is tasty, rounded, rather velvety, then the tannins assert themselves. This wine is still very young and should be laid down.

🍴 GAEC Baudry, 16, chem. de Jaure, 24100 Lembras, tel. 05.53.57.35.65, fax 05.53.57.10.13 ☑
🍽 ev. day except Sun. 9am–12 noon 2pm–7pm; Sat. by appt.

DOM. DU HAUT-PECHARMANT

Cuvée Veuve Roches 2001★

| ■ | 4 ha | 21,000 | ❚❙❚ | 8–11 € |

This wine has a special blend dominated by Cabernet Franc (60%), Merlot (20%) and Cabernet Sauvignon. The nose initially evokes roasted coffee before releasing very ripe black fruits (blackberry and blackcurrant). The first impression is a little withdrawn but the progressive increase in power of the tannins is interesting. A lingering return of the black fruits makes an agreeable conclusion to the tasting.

↝ Michel et Didier Roches, Dom. du Haut-Pécharmant, 24100 Bergerac, tel. 05.53.57.29.50, fax 05.53.24.28.05 ☑
𝍬 ev. day except Sun. 8am–12 noon 2pm–7pm

CH. HUGON

Elevé en fût de chêne 2000★★★

| ■ | 1.18 ha | 3,000 | ❙❚❙❚ | 5–8 € |

A small vineyard of 4 ha, cultivated like a garden where each vine is the object of enormous care. The nose of this 2000 is rich and suggests truffle and cherry, with an attractive, well-integrated oak. The palate is full bodied and powerful, with very evident tannins but the oak is well integrated. The finish develops flavours of macerated fruits, tobacco and black chocolate. This wine should be richer in a year or two. Although the Grand Jury only ranked it second, it is exceptional both in terms of quality and value for money.

↝ Bernard Cousy, Haut Pécharmant, 24100 Bergerac, tel. 05.53.63.28.44 ☑
𝍬 ev. day 9am–12 noon 2pm–6pm

CH. DE TIREGAND

Grand Millésime 2001★

| ■ | 4 ha | 11,000 | ❚❙❚ | 15–23 € |

On the right bank of the Dordogne, 4 ha of vines grow on the sandy and gravelly hillsides of Périgord, overlooked by a château listed as a historic monument. The wine has a very dark-carmine colour. The bouquet is rather dominated by vanilla and toast, with aromas of black fruits. The palate is sweet, resting on a high-quality oak which is supported by a good structure. The finish is not obstructed by the tannins and allows a return of the fruit and blackcurrant. A wine with beautiful body, great richness and harmony.

↝ Comtesse F. de Saint-Exupéry, Ch. de Tiregand, 24100 Creysse, tel. 05.53.23.21.08, fax 05.53.22.58.49, e-mail chateautiregand@club-internet.fr ☑
𝍬 ev. day except Sun. 9am–12 noon 2pm–6pm

Wines selected but not starred

LES CHEMINS D'ORIENT

Cuvée Oxus 2001

| ■ | 0.6 ha | 3,000 | ❚❙❚ | 11–15 € |

↝ Régis Lansade, 4, rue Georges-Martin, 24100 Bergerac, tel. 06.75.86.47.54, fax 05.53.22.08.38, e-mail regis.lansade@wanadoo.fr ☑
𝍬 by appt.

DOM. DE LA MÉTAIRIE

Elevé en barrique 2000

| ■ | 3 ha | 20,000 | ❚❙❚ | 11–15 € |

↝ SARL Dom. la Métairie en Pécharmant, Pommier, 24380 Creyssensac-et-Pissot, tel. 05.53.80.09.85, fax 05.53.80.72.14 ☑
𝍬 by appt.

Rosette

Rosette is the least-known appellation and the best-kept secret of the region. It comes from the clay and gravel soils of hills overlooking the town of Bergerac from the north, and in 2002 production was 649 hl.

DOM. DE COUTANCIE

Cuvée Elina 2002★★

| ▨ | 0.38 ha | 2,200 | ❚❙❚ | 5–8 € |

It is unusual to find two wines from the same grower in the selection. The Cuvée Elina reveals its maturation in barrel with a slightly fruity nose and a fine oak. The remarkable, rich and fruity palate ends in a long finish with the oak well integrated. A convivial wine to share with friends. The **Cuvée Classique 2002** wins one star. This is particularly fruity and elegant, with aromas of white fruits. A very successful sweet wine, perfect as an aperitif.

↝ Odile Brichèse, Coutancie, 24130 Prigonrieux, tel. 05.53.58.01.85, fax 05.53.58.52.76, e-mail coutancie@wanadoo.fr ☑ ⌂
𝍬 by appt.

Saussignac

Praised in the 16th century in François Rabelais's *Pantagruel* and located in a superb landscape of plateaus and hills, the terroir produces rich, sweet wines of great quality. In 2002 production was 1,465 hl from 98 ha.

CH. LE CHABRIER

Cuvée Eléna 2001★★

| ▨ | 3.25 ha | 2,900 | ❚❙❚ | 23–30 € |

A small 17th century château, 20 ha of vines grown by organic methods, and this Saussignac whose nose, at first a little closed, opens with perfumes of crystallized fruits and spices. The palate is well balanced, full and rich, with notes of apricot, bitter orange and more spices. A very beautiful, distinguished wine, and very drinkable. The **red Côtes de Bergerac 2001 (5–8 €)** develops a pretty nose of small, rather overripe soft fruits. The structure is powerful. Give it time to mature. This wine was singled out.

↝ Pierre Carle, Ch. Le Chabrier, 24240 Razac-de-Saussignac, tel. 05.53.27.92.73, fax 05.53.23.39.03, e-mail chateau.le.chabrier@libertysurf.fr ☑
𝍬 by appt.

CH. DES EYSSARDS

Cuvée Flavie 2001★★★

| ▨ | 6 ha | 20,000 | ❚❙❚ | 11–15 € |

This Saussignac is one of the rare wines to win three stars, and really is almost perfect. The very complex nose releases notes of flowers, crystallized fruits and citrus fruits. The palate is splendidly fleshy, concentrated, rich and well balanced, long and vigorous with a fine oak. This is an excellent wine which in time will increase in harmony and richness, power and elegance. It can be drunk now but will improve greatly with age. Also worth trying is the **red l'Adagio des Eyssards en Bergerac 2000**, which is still dominated by oak. Its superb potential should be realized in years to come. It wins one star.
🕯 GAEC des Eyssards, 24240 Monestier,
tel. 05.53.24.36.36, fax 05.53.58.63.74,
e-mail eyssards@aquinet-tm.fr 🅥
🍷 by appt.

CH. GRINOU
Vinifié en fût de chêne 2001★★

	1.5 ha	3,700	🍷	15–23 €

Some remains of an old monastery still stand on this property. This Saussignac reveals its concentration caused by noble rot and its time spent in barrel. The nose offers crystallized fruits, roasting and honey with an attractive fine oak, whereas the palate is fleshy, releasing slightly crystallized fruits and notes of apricot. The sugar content is very evident and the oaky finish suggests good potential provided it has time to soften. The **red Le Grand Vin du Château Grinou Bergerac 2001 (8–11 €)** wins one star. Agreeably fruity with vanilla, and well structured, it needs to be kept for two years so the oaky tannins can mature.
🕯 Catherine et Guy Cuisset, Ch. Grinou, 24240 Monestier,
tel. 05.53.58.46.63, fax 05.53.61.05.66,
e-mail chateaugrinou@aol.com 🅥
🍷 by appt.

CH. LESTEVENIE
Elevé en fût de chêne 2001★

	0.5 ha	500	🍷	15–23 €

This estate is located 2 km from the Château de Gageac, and was acquired recently. This is its second year of winemaking. We should also remember that the 2000 wine won a *coup de cœur* last year. The 2001 vintage releases floral, fruity notes and a fine oak. The first impression is superb, disclosing flesh and roundness and the crystallized fruits which continue throughout the tasting. The finish is fresh and long, though the oak is still not integrated. A balanced wine. The **dry Bergerac 2001 (8–11 €)**, is powerful and rounded, and beautifully fresh; the tasters also liked its notes of citrus fruits and its subtle oak.
🕯 Jolaine et Dominique Audoux, Le Gadon,
24240 Gageac-et-Rouillac, tel. 05.53.74.24.48,
fax 05.53.74.24.49, e-mail d.audoux@wanadoo.fr 🅥
🍷 by appt.

CH. LA MAURIGNE
Cuvée La Maurigne 2001★★

	4 ha	7,000	🍷	8–11 €

This château was built in the 17th century on ancient Roman-esque fortifications pulled down in the 8th century by the Moors. It offers a sweet wine with very pure flavours. The notes of roasting and the perfumes of lychee are very powerful. The palate reveals a remarkable concentration of crystallized fruits which has both power and harmony. The oak remains in the background at the finish. A distinguished and balanced sweet wine which could have won the *coup de cœur*. The **red Cuvée spéciale La Maurigne en Côtes-de-Bergerac 2000** wins one star. Notes of cherry mingle with an attractive oak. It is full, rounded and balanced, with a well-integrated oak. Two very nice wines to look out for.
🕯 Chantal et Patrick Gérardin, Ch. La Maurigne,
24240 Razac-de-Saussignac, tel. 05.53.27.25.45,
fax 05.53.27.25.45,
e-mail contact@chateaulamaurigne.com 🅥
🍷 ev. day 9am–7pm

CLOS D'YVIGNE 2000★

	3 ha	n.c.	🍷	23–30 €

To celebrate her ten years in France, Patricia Atkinson made this nice Saussignac. As usual, the Clos d'Yvigne has done well. This wine has an intense and powerful nose, mainly of crystallized fruits and dried apricot. The palate is fairly full but still dominated by the oak. It is a well-balanced wine and very successful for this year. The **dry white Cuvée Nicholas en Bergerac (11–15 €)** was singled out by the Jury. The nose opens with fruits then gives way to notes of spices, cinnamon and white pepper. The fresh palate is fruity. A well-made and promising wine.
🕯 Patricia Atkinson, Clos d'Yvigne , Le Bourg,
24240 Gageac-et-Rouillac, tel. 05.53.22.94.40,
fax 05.53.23.47.67,
e-mail patricia.atkinson@wanadoo.fr 🅥 🏠
🍷 by appt.

Wines selected but not starred

CH. MIAUDOUX 2001

	1.5 ha	5,000	🍷	15–23 €

🕯 N. et G. Cuisset, Les Miaudoux, 24240 Saussignac,
tel. 05.53.27.92.31, fax 05.53.27.96.60,
e-mail gerard.cuisset@terre-net.fr 🅥 🏠
🍷 by appt.

CH. LE PAYRAL
Cuvée Marie-Jeanne 2001

	2 ha	4,000	🍷	11–15 €

🕯 Thierry Daulhiac, 24240 Razac-de-Saussignac,
tel. 05.53.22.38.07, fax 05.53.27.99.81,
e-mail daulhiac@club-internet.fr 🅥 🏠
🍷 by appt.

Côtes de Duras

The Côtes de Duras vineyard, 2,009 ha, is the natural extension of the Plateau de l'Entre-Deux-Mers. There is a local story that, after the Revocation of the Edict of Nantes, exiled Gascon Huguenots used to have Duras wine shipped to them in their Dutch retreats. Tulips were planted at the ends of the rows of vines which they reserved for themselves.

Eroded over the ages by the River Dourdèze and its tributaries, the slopes are made up of sandy-clay and limestone soils naturally suited to the Bordeaux varieties. Sémillon, Sauvignon and Muscadelle are used for the white wines; Cabernet Franc, Cabernet Sauvignon, Merlot and Malbec for the reds. Also found are Chenin, Ondenc and Ugni Blanc. The glory of Duras is, above all, its dry white wine, made mainly from Sauvignon, with 41,282 hl produced in 2002. These are lively wines of pedigree with a specifically identifiable bouquet and are marvellous with seafood and saltwater fish. The red wines, often vinified as varietal wines, are fleshy and round, with a good colour. The region also produces smooth and fruity rosé wines. Reds and rosés together amount to 69,270 hl.

DOM. DES ALLEGRETS
Vieilli en fût de chêne 2001★★

■	3 ha	15,000	Ⅲ		5–8 €

The funny thing was, the Grand Jury for *coups de cœur* hesitated for a long time between this red wine and a *vin liquoreux*, unaware that the sweet wine came from the same estate. This red wine was made from beautiful grapes matured in good oak. The nose releases aromas of prune, crystallized fruits with spices, vanilla and toasted notes. The palate is rich and silky, with deliciously velvety tannins. This is a rounded and tasty wine that can be drunk now or laid down. The sweet wine called **La Cuvée du Grand-Père 2001 (15–23 €)** has a memorably high sugar content on an attractive oaky base. This is for lovers of very sweet wines.
🖐 SCEA Blanchard, Dom. des Allégrets,
47120 Villeneuve-de-Duras, tel. 05.53.94.74.56,
fax 05.53.94.74.56 ☑
🍷 by appt.

DOM. DES ALLEGRETS
Sec Vinifié et élevé en fût de chêne 2002★★

■	0.5 ha	2,000	Ⅲ ↓	5–8 €

This was the only 2002 dry white wine to win two stars. Clearly, the vinification and maturation in barrel were particularly well controlled. On the nose, it is difficult to recognize the Sauvignon with its exotic notes, nuances of grapefruit and a touch of toast. The palate is like the nose, with a very full and fresh first impression. The finish is long, rounded and supple, supported by a beautiful acidity. The Jury also liked the **moelleux 2001** with the aromas of Sauvignon and a subtle and harmonious balance (one star).
🖐 SCEA Blanchard, Dom. des Allégrets,
47120 Villeneuve-de-Duras, tel. 05.53.94.74.56,
fax 05.53.94.74.56 ☑
🍷 by appt.

DOM. AMBLARD
Moelleux 2001★

	7.9 ha	46,800	■ ↓	3–5 €

You might as well enjoy drinking a good sweet wine instead of seeking out one made with noble rot; these are always richer but often heavier too. The nose of this wine is fine and floral, with pronounced notes of Sauvignon. The fresh palate reveals a beautiful balance between the alcohol, the sugar and the acidity. Floral aromas are quite strong. This is a characteristic sweet wine, something which is unfortunately too rare. The **rosé 2002** is slightly sparkling, fresh and rounded on the palate with a well-balanced finish. Two wines from an authentic terroir.
🖐 Guy Pauvert et Fils, Dom. Amblard,
47120 Saint-Sernin-de-Duras, tel. 05.53.94.77.92,
fax 05.53.94.27.12,
e-mail domaine.amblard@wanadoo.fr ☑
🍷 by appt.

DUC DE BERTICOT
Elevé en fût de chêne 2001★★

	8 ha	55,000	■ Ⅲ ↓	5–8 €

Three stars for the 2000 vintage, and two stars for this 2001, should reassure wine-lovers about the quality of Duc de Berticot. The nose is particularly complex with aromas of very ripe fruits on a pleasant vanilla. On the palate, the

integrated tannins are enjoyable; the oak is there, but not excessively so. The finish is particularly tasty and persistent. A balanced wine, attractive and full of finesse. The **Grande Réserve de Berticot red 2001 (3–5 €)** joins the selection with one star. It has lovely concentration, but the oak is very pronounced. Keep it for two or three years.
🖐 SCA Vignerons de Landerrouat-Duras, Berticot,
47120 Duras, tel. 05.53.83.71.12, fax 05.53.83.82.40 ☑
🍷 by appt.

HAUTS DE BERTICOT
Sec Elevé en fût de chêne 2001★

	n.c.	20,000	Ⅲ	3–5 €

This wine's originality comes from its maturation in barrel for 12 months. The nose will not disappoint anyone with its very characteristic notes of exotic fruits, orange and tangerine. After a pleasant first impression, the fruits develop on the palate in a well-balanced manner. The finish is rounded and fresh. An attractive wine to drink now.
🖐 Prodiffu, 17–19, rte des Vignerons, 33790 Landerrouat,
tel. 05.56.61.33.73, fax 05.56.61.40.57,
e-mail prodiffu@prodiffu.com

HONORE DE BERTICOT 2001★

■	n.c.	600,000	■ ↓	3–5 €

Honoré de Berticot is a classic and accessible wine with very prominent fruits. This fruitiness makes itself felt on the nose with aromas revealing great maturity. The body is full, balanced by firm but not excessive tannins. The finish is pleasantly long. This wine is already pleasant to drink but could be kept for two to three years. The **Honoré de Berticot Sauvignon 2002** was also much liked. Complex and floral on the nose, it is beautifully full on the palate and finishes on a touch of acidity. Ideal as an aperitif.
🖐 Prodiffu, 17–19, rte des Vignerons, 33790 Landerrouat,
tel. 05.56.61.33.73, fax 05.56.61.40.57,
e-mail prodiffu@prodiffu.com

CH. CONDOM 2001★

■	2 ha	6,000	■ ↓	5–8 €

The château was built in 1690 by the lord of Condom-Perceval, Master of Horse to the kings of France. The charm of this wine and its classicism undoubtedly come from the fact that it was not matured in oak. The nose is characterized by intense aromas of ripe fruits. The first impression is rounded and full, with fine and tasty tannins. A well-balanced wine with good fruit, which is ready to drink now. The **red Cuvée Delph 2001 (15–23 €)** is very oaky. The tannins are still a little astringent and earn the wine a commendation. Keep it for two or three years.
🖐 SCEA Condom, Ch. Condom-Perceval,
47120 Loubès-Bernac, tel. 05.53.76.05.02,
fax 05.53.76.03.79, e-mail flovones@wanadoo.fr ☑ 🏠
🍷 by appt.

DOM. LA FOND DU LOUP 2000★

	2 ha	6,600	Ⅲ	5–8 €

This 2000 wine is definitely very interesting, and every producer wanted to vinify a top-of-the-range vintage matured in barrel to mark this event. On the nose, the soft fruits are very intense with a beautiful spicy note. On the palate, the flexibility of the tannins and the wine's perfect harmony are memorable. A well-made wine to be enjoyed in the next two or three years.
🖐 Jean-Luc Prévot, Dom. La Fond du Loup,
47120 Saint-Jean-de-Duras, tel. 05.53.89.02.59,
fax 05.53.89.02.59 ☑ 🏠
🍷 ev. day 9am–7pm

DOM. DU GRAND MAYNE
Elevé en fût de chêne 2001★

	5 ha	30,000	Ⅲ	5–8 €

This wine is a safe bet which deserves to appear in the *Guide*. The aromas on the nose are of very ripe fruits, but these are somewhat masked by a prominent oak. The palate confirms this wine's richness and concentration, though the tannins are still a little harsh. It is advisable to wait two or three years for

these to soften. On the other hand, the **rosé 2002** is fresh and light, and should be drunk immediately (singled out).
☛ SARL Andrew Gordon, Le Grand Mayne, 47120 Villeneuve-de-Duras, tel. 05.53.94.74.17, fax 05.53.94.77.02, e-mail agordon@terre-net.fr ☑ ♙
⊤ by appt.

CH. LA GRAVE BECHADE
Cuvée Alexandra Elevé en fût 2001★★

| ■ | 10 ha | 32,000 | ⅏ | 8–11 € |

This Alexandra is becoming a safe bet in the *Guide* after its 2000 vintage won a star last year. The nose offers a pleasant combination of oak and ripe fruits. The first impression is supple, rounded, initially fruity then vanilla. The tannins are very silky and tasty and the fruits make a long return at the finish. This is a well-structured, harmonious wine to be drunk in four or five years. The **red Cuvée traditionelle 2001 (5–8 €)**, not matured in barrel, has a fruitiness and balance that were pleasantly surprising. This very tempting wine will be superb in one or two years; it wins two stars.
☛ Ch. la Grave Béchade, 47120 Baleyssagues, tel. 05.53.83.70.06, fax 05.53.83.82.14, e-mail lagravebechade@wanadoo.fr ☑
⊤ ev. day except Sat. Sun. 8am–6pm

DOM. DE LAPLACE 2001★★

| ■ | 5 ha | 20,000 | ▮ | 3–5 € |

The label is original, combining modernity and tradition, and pays homage to the family's grandfather who created the vineyard in 1924. It releases ripe aromas of soft fruits on the nose, a sure sign of the Merlot. This fruitiness is surprisingly evident on the palate, accompanying tasty, supple tannins, and the finish is a little fresh. A pleasant, authentic wine and unbeatable value for money.
☛ Jean-Luc Carmelli, Laplace, 47120 Saint-Jean-de-Duras, tel. 05.53.83.00.77, fax 05.53.20.85.93, e-mail laplace.carmelli@wanadoo.fr ☑
⊤ by appt.

CH. MOLHIERE
Les Maréchaux 2001★★

| ■ | 2 ha | 14,000 | ⅏ | 5–8 € |

This year, the Maréchaux finished in front of the Pierrot. The Maréchaux has a memorably deep colour, an intense, fruity nose, and an impressive tannic structure. The attack is rounded and fleshy, with tannins remaining prominent until the finish. This authentic wine needs five or six years to mature. The **red Cuvée Pierrot 2000 (11–15 €)** will improve with age. It wins one star.
☛ Patrick Francis Blancheton Frères, La Moulière, 47120 Duras, tel. 05.53.83.70.19, fax 05.53.83.07.30, e-mail patrick.blancheton@wanadoo.fr ☑
⊤ by appt.

CH. LA PETITE BERTRANDE
Vieilli en fût de chêne 2001★★

| ■ | 6 ha | 30,000 | ⅏ | 5–8 € |

Like last year, this wine was very popular with the Jury. The complex nose combines notes of blackcurrant and undergrowth. The palate is supple to begin with, then develops on rich tannins; it is strong both in sugar and body. The finish is tasty with renewed aromas of fruits and undergrowth. This is a powerful, complex wine with an impressive structure which will help it to age well.
☛ Jean-François Thierry, Ch. La Petite Bertrande, 47120 Saint-Astier-de-Duras, tel. 05.53.94.74.03, e-mail vguignard@aol.com ☑
⊤ ev. day except Sun. 10am–12 noon 4pm–7pm
☛ Alain Tingaud

DOM. DU PETIT MALROME
Cuvée Sarah Elevé en fût de chêne 2001★★

| ■ | 1.3 ha | 8,000 | ⅏ | 5–8 € |

The estate has done twice as well as last year with two stars for the Cuvée Sarah and one star for the **Cuvée principale 2001 (3–5 €)**, both made from organically produced grapes. The Cuvée Sarah has a very complex nose combining ripe fruits and vanilla. After a rounded and pleasant first impression,

the enormous but very interesting tannic structure and the beautiful balance between the fruit and the oak are impressive. Keep this for seven to ten years. The other wine, which was not matured in oak, is very drinkable and should be served now.
☛ EARL Geneviève et Alain Lescaut, Dom. du Petit Malromé, 47120 Saint-Jean-de-Duras, tel. 05.53.89.01.44, fax 05.53.89.01.44, e-mail petitmalrome@oreka.com ☑
⊤ by appt.

DOM. DU VIEUX BOURG
Moelleux Cuvée Prestige 2001★

| ■ | 1.5 ha | 4,000 | ⅏ | 11–15 € |

This wine was made from aged vines, harvested very late, and matured in oak to produce a very well-balanced *vin liquoreux*. The old-gold colour is very attractive. Honey and vanilla are largely dominant on the nose. On the palate, the wine reveals complex flavours combining fruit and oak. The first impression is supple, and this is confirmed on the very rich palate which has a beautiful balance between the alcohol and the sugars. The slightly acid finish is also enjoyable. The **dry white 2002 (3–5 €)** also has pleasant fruity flavours of citrus fruits and, in particular, lemon.
☛ Bernard Bireaud, Dom. du Vieux Bourg, 47120 Pardaillan, tel. 05.53.83.02.18, fax 05.53.83.02.37, e-mail vieux-bourg2@wanadoo.fr ☑
⊤ by appt.

Wines selected but not starred

DOM. LES BERTINS
Cuvée Dominique Elevé en fût de chêne 2000

| ■ | 1.5 ha | 12,000 | ⅏ | 8–11 € |

☛ Dom. Les Bertins-Manfé, Les Bertins, 47120 Saint-Astier-de-Duras, tel. 05.53.94.76.26, fax 05.53.94.76.64, e-mail bertins.manfe@wanadoo.fr ☑ ♙
⊤ ev. day 9am–12 noon 2pm–7pm

CH. DES BRUYERES 2000

| ■ | 1.05 ha | 13,300 | ⅏ | 5–8 € |

☛ Piet et Annelies Heide, Ch. des Bruyères, 47120 Loubès-Bernac, tel. 05.53.94.22.61, fax 05.53.94.22.61, e-mail chateaudesbruyeres@wanadoo.fr ☑
⊤ by appt.

DOM. DE LAULAN
Moelleux 2001

| ■ | 1 ha | 3,200 | ▮ ⚶ | 5–8 € |

☛ EARL Geoffroy, Dom. de Laulan, 47120 Duras, tel. 05.53.83.73.69, fax 05.53.83.81.54, e-mail domaine.laulan@wanadoo.fr ☑
⊤ ev. day except Sun. 8am–12 noon 2pm–6pm

CH. LES SAVIGNATTES
Sec sauvignon 2002

| ■ | 1 ha | 6,600 | ▮ ⚶ | 3–5 € |

☛ Maurice Dreux, Les Savignattes, 47120 Esclottes, tel. 05.53.83.72.84, fax 05.53.83.82.97, e-mail bernadette.dreux@wanadoo.fr ☑
⊤ ev. day except Sun. 9am–12 noon 3pm–7pm; Sat. 9am–12 noon

THE LOIRE VALLEY

This enormous area is dominated by a single great waterway, the "royal" Loire. It would justify that epithet on its own merits, though it also became a favoured place of respite for kings and queens, and a cradle of Renaissance arts and culture. The changing countryside of the Loire valley is bathed in a unique light, arising from the subtle marriage of sky and water that enabled the "Garden of France" to burgeon, and the vine to thrive. From the edge of the Massif Central to the estuary, vineyards stud the landscape along the river and a dozen of its tributaries, creating a vast wine-growing region which encompasses much more than the Loire valley itself, and is generally referred to as "The Loire Valley and the Centre". Tourism here is cultural, gastronomic and wine-based, and the roads that follow the river along the heights, or the back roads which run through the vineyards and forests, are unforgettable trails of discovery.

The Loire itself can be narrow and sinuous, or swift-flowing and turbulent, at times imposing and majestic in appearance, at times peaceful. Always the unifying factor in the landscape, it requires attention to its vagaries, particularly when it comes to the wines.

From Roanne or Saint-Pourçain as far as Nantes or Saint-Nazaire, vines grow on the slopes overlooking the banks, braving the nature of the soils and wide differences in climate and local traditions. For some 1,000 km, a vineyard area of more than 70,000 ha produces, with great variations, between 9.5 and 10% of France's total wine production: 1,400,000 hl of AOC white wines and 1,140,000 hl of AOC red and rosé wines. The wines of this vast region share a freshness and delicacy of perfume that are essentially due to the northerly location of most of the producing areas.

All the same, to attempt to group all the different wines produced under the same heading is a little risky, since, even though they are classified as being northern, some vineyards are on a latitude which, in the Rhône valley, enjoys the influence of the Mediterranean climate – Mâcon, for example, shares the same latitude as Saint-Pourçain and Roanne the same as Villefranche-sur-Saône. So it is the topography that works on the climate to limit the influence of the prevailing airflow: the Atlantic winds blow west to east along the corridor eroded by the Loire, weakening little by little as they encounter the hills around Saumur and the Touraine.

The wine areas that form identifiable entities are, thus, the Nantes region, plus Anjou and Touraine. However, we have also included the vineyards of Haut Poitou, the Berry, the Côtes d'Auvergne and the Côtes Roannaises; it is important to attach them to a big region, and this is the closest both geographically and as regards the wines that are produced. In general terms, it is appropriate to identify four big groupings, the first three mentioned plus the Centre.

In the lower Loire valley, the Muscadet area and part of the Anjou are on the Massif Armoricain and made up variously of schists, gneiss and other sedimentary rocks, or of outcrops from the Primary era. The soils that have developed on these underlying structures are very well-suited to the vine and the wines produced are of excellent quality. The first entity, the most westerly area, still called the Nantais, has a gentle landscape in which the hard rocks of the Massif Armoricain have been gouged away into almost vertical valley walls by little rivers. The steep valleys have no cultivable slopes and the vines are planted on hillocks on the plateau. The climate is maritime and fairly uniform throughout the year, and the maritime influence diminishes the seasonal variations. The winters are not particularly harsh and the warm summers are often humid; there is a good deal of sunshine, but spring frosts sometimes disrupt growth.

Anjou is the transitional area between the Nantais region ("le pays Nantais") and the Touraine and, historically speaking, includes Saumur. This wine-growing region lies almost totally within the department of Maine-et-Loire but, geographically, Saumur should more appropriately be attached to western Touraine, with which it has more in common so far as terroir and climate are concerned. The sedimentary soils of the Paris Basin covered the Primary formations of the Massif Armoricain from Brissac-Quincé to Doué-la-Fontaine. Anjou falls into several sub-regions: the north-facing Coteaux de la Loire (an extension of the Nantais region) runs gently down from the edge of the plateau; the Coteaux du Layon, very steep, on schist soils, together with the Coteaux de l'Aubance; finally, a transitional zone between Anjou and Touraine known chiefly for its rosés.

The Saumur terroir is essentially identified by creamy limestone, or tufa, on beds of chalk; underground, wine being aged in bottles competes with the cultivation of Paris mushrooms in galleries and cellars dug out of the chalk. The hills provide shelter from the west winds, helping to create a semi-maritime/semi-continental climate. Across from Saumur, on the right bank of the Loire on the slopes outside Tours, you find the vineyards of Saint-Nicolas-de-Bourgueil. East of Tours, and on the same slopes (an extension of those of Saumur and Vienne), Vouvray and Chinon are the leading wines of the Touraine. Azay le Rideau, Montlouis, Amboise, Mesland and the Coteaux du Cher are other great names to remember from the "Garden of France". The little vineyards of the Coteaux du Loir, the Orléanais, Cheverny, Valençay and the Coteaux du Giennois should be considered with those of the Touraine. It is impossible to decide if you should visit the area for its wines, its châteaux or its goat's cheeses (Saint-Maure, Selles-sur-Cher, Valençay); why not all at once?

The Loire Valley

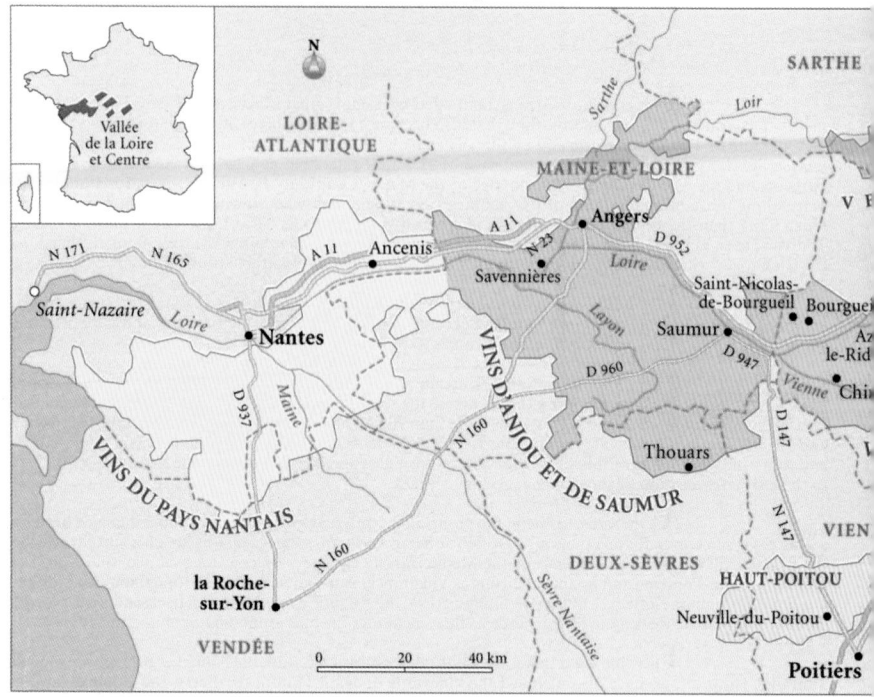

The Berry vineyards make up a fourth region, the Centre, which is quite different in terroir and climate from the other three. Here the soils are essentially Jurassic, as they are in Chablis, Sancerre's neighbour, and in Pouilly-sur-Loire, and the climate semi-continental, with cold winters and hot summers. For ease of presentation, Saint-Pourçain, the Côtes Roannaises and Forez are included in this fourth entity, despite further variations in the soils (primary rock from the Massif Central) and the climate (semi-continental to continental).

This guide follows the same geographic progression to examine the specific wine domains. Starting from the Atlantic coast, Muscadet owes its characteristics to a single grape variety (the Melon) producing a unique, dry, irreplaceable wine. In this area, the Folle Blanche variety is the base for another dry white wine, though of lesser quality, Gros Plant. The region of Ancenis has been "colonized" by Gamay.

In Anjou, Chenin (or Pineau de la Loire) is the main variety for white wines, although Chardonnay and Sauvignon have more recently been introduced. Chenin is the base for the great rich or, depending on how they develop, sweet wines of the area, as well as for excellent dry and sparkling wines. As for the red varieties the Grolleau Noir, once widely planted, traditionally produces semi-dry rosés, while Cabernet Franc (which used to be called "Breton") and Cabernet Sauvignon produce fine, full-bodied red wines with good keeping qualities. The proverbial "sweetness of the Anjou" arises from a combination of depth, due to its strong acidity, and a soft flavour from the presence of the remaining sugars, and this quality is to be found throughout the sometimes confusing multiplicity of wines produced.

West of the Touraine region the main varieties are Chenin, planted in Saumur, Vouvray and Montlouis or on the slopes of the Loir, Cabernet Franc at Chinon, Bourgueil and Saumur, and Grolleau at Azay-le-Rideau. In the eastern region, Gamay for reds and Sauvignon for whites produce light, fruity and pleasant wines. Finally, for the sake of completeness, the Pineau d'Aunis from the Coteaux du Loir, which has peppery flavours, should be mentioned, along with the Gris Meunier in the Orléanais.

In the Centre, Sauvignon (making white wines) reigns supreme in Sancerre, Reuilly, Quincy and Menetou-Salon, as well as in Pouilly, where it is still called Blanc-Fumé. There it shares the slopes with the few remaining vineyards of Chasselas, which produce dry, lively wines. As for the reds, the influence of neighbouring Burgundy in the Pinot Noir wines of Sancerre and Menetou-Salon can already be discerned.

To complete this summary of Loire wines, a few words should be added about Haut Poitou, known for lively, fruity Sauvignons, well-structured Chardonnays, and light, robust reds from Gamay,

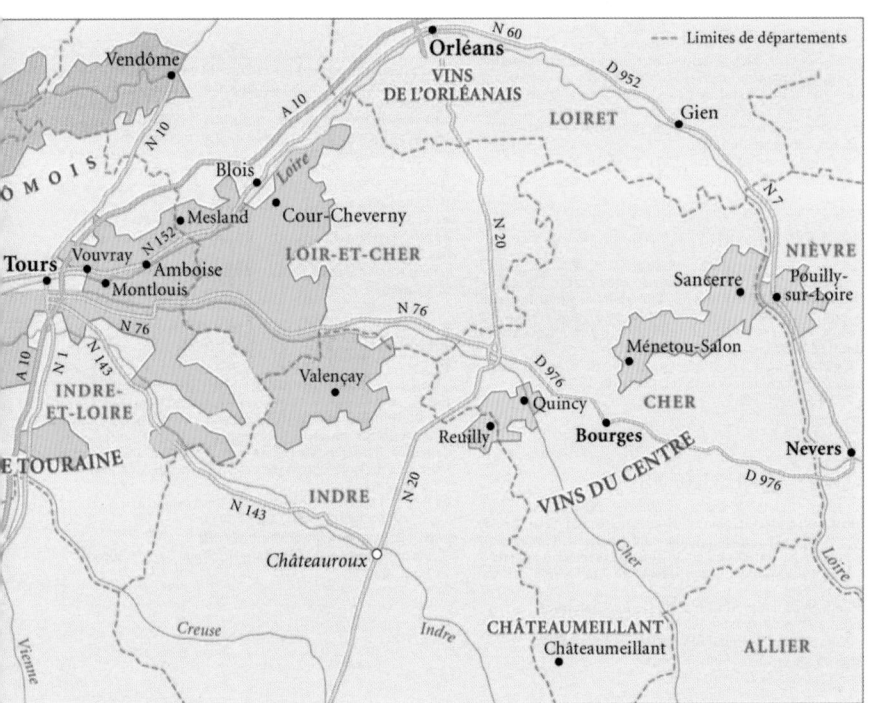

Pinot Noir and Cabernet. Influenced by a semi-maritime climate, Haut Poitou is a zone of transition between the Loire Valley and Bordeaux. Between Anjou and Poitou lies the lesser-known Thouarsais vineyard (AOVDQS). In the Fiefs Vendéens region along the Atlantic coast, an AOVDQS terroir historically known as Vin des Fiefs du Cardinal, the best-known wines are the rosés from Mareuil, made with Gamay and Pinot Noir. The curiosity of the region is the Ragoûtant wine, made from the Négrette variety, but it is difficult to find.

The Loire Valley

Rosé de Loire

These wines from the Appellation Régionale, an AOC since 1974, can be produced within the boundaries of the regional AOCs of Anjou, Saumur and Touraine. Cabernet Franc, Cabernet Sauvignon, Gamay, Pineau d'Aunis and Grolleau are used for making dry rosé wines of which 52,030 hl were produced in 2002.

CH. DE BEAUREGARD 2002★

| | 1,83 ha | 3,000 | ▮ | | 5-8 € |

The château was built in the 19th century on part of a building dating from the 17th century, and its 13th century porch was part of the fortified wall. This particularly delicate Rosé de Loire is very representative of its appellation. It has a light pink colour. Boiled sweets and red berries define the palate, which is simple, but fresh and well-balanced. Here is a wine that can be served throughout a meal.

↰ SCEA Alain Gourdon, Ch. de Beauregard, 4, rue Saint-Julien, 49260 Le Puy-Notre-Dame, tel. 02.41.52.25.33, fax 02.41.52.29.62, e-mail christinegourdon@wanadoo.fr ☑
☖ by appt.

CH. DE BROSSAY 2002★

| ▮ | 5 ha | 30,000 | ▮ | ♦ | 5-8 € |

Located in the village where the Layon River has its source, very close to the *département* of Deux-Sèvres, this 40-hectare estate presents a Rosé de Loire which does not express all its potential yet. The aromas emerge with aeration and are reminiscent of fresh fruits and flowers. The attractive palate is long, balanced and generous. This is a rosé to enjoy with a meal.

↰ Raymond et Hubert Deffois, Ch. de Brossay, 49560 Cléré-sur-Layon, tel. 02.41.59.59.95, fax 02.41.59.58.81, e-mail chateau.brossay@wanadoo.fr ☑
☖ ev. day except Sun. 8am–12 noon 2pm–7pm

LOIRE

CH. DE CHAMPTELOUP 2002★★

■   30 ha   120,000   ▐ ♦   3–5 €

The wine from this 80-hectare property has been vinified by a *négociant-éleveur*. This Rosé de Loire is a great representative of its appellation, characterized by its salmon-pink colour with light purplish tinges and by its aromas of exotic fruits, grapefruit and roses. The refreshing palate is rounded and well balanced, and signals a remarkably successful wine overall.
☛ SCEA Champteloup,
49700 Brigné-sur-Layon, tel. 02.41.59.65.10,
fax 02.41.59.63.60

LE CLOS DES MOTELES 2002★

■   2.11 ha   4,800   ▐   –3 €

The vineyard of Clos des Motèles is located near to Thouars in the *département* of Deux-Sèvres. The fresh flavour of this wine is astonishing. The palate provides a particularly enjoyable sensation of slightly tart red fruits giving a thirst-quenching and refreshing wine.
☛ Basset-Baron, 42, rue de la Garde, GAEC Le Clos des Motèles, 79100 Sainte-Verge, tel. 05.49.66.05.37, fax 05.49.66.37.14 ▼
🍷 by appt.

DOM. DU FRESCHE 2002★

■   1.2 ha   3,000   ▐ ♦   3–5 €

From a well-known Coteaux de la Loire estate, this Rosé de Loire tastes like a treat; a delicate pink, with a nose of bananas, strawberries and small soft red berries, the palate is refreshing and well balanced. Here is an Anjou wine that is a real tasty treat.
☛ Alain Boré, Dom. du Fresche, rte de Chalonnes,
49620 La Pommeraye, tel. 02.41.77.74.63,
fax 02.41.77.79.39, e-mail alainbore@aol.com ▼
🍷 ev. day except Sun. 8am–12.30pm 2pm–7pm

SELECTION LACHETEAU 2002★★

■   20 ha   120,000   ▐ ♦   3–5 €

Lacheteau SA is a négociant specializing in the production of sparkling wines and rosés. This Rosé de Loire delighted the tasting Jury with its light pink appearance with hints of crimson and its delicate strawberry and raspberry flavours. Refreshing and thirst-quenching, it gives an impression of biting into ripe fruits.
☛ SAS Lacheteau, ZI de la Saulaie,
49700 Doué-la-Fontaine, tel. 02.41.59.26.26,
fax 02.41.59.01.94, e-mail contact@lacheteau.fr

DOM. DES MATINES 2000★

■   3 ha   5,000   ▐ ♦   3–5 €

Grandfather Mallard was one of the pioneers of red wine production in the Saumur area. A touch of carbon dioxide delicately entices the palate and leaves an enjoyable feeling of freshness. Delicate red fruit flavours recall cherries and strawberries to give an easy-drinking Rosé de Loire.
☛ Dom. des Matines, 31, rue de la Mairie, 49700 Brossay, tel. 02.41.52.25.36, fax 02.41.52.25.50, e-mail domainedesmatines@wanadoo.fr ▼
🍷 by appt.
☛ Etchegaray

DOM. OGEREAU 2002★

■   1,35 ha   8,400   ▐ ♦   5–8 €

Domaine Ogereau is one of the benchmark estates in Anjou. One can no longer count its *coups de cœur* and its Rosé de Loire surprised the tasting Jury with its richness and its long palate. Nevertheless, it is a delicate wine that will make a perfect accompaniment to mixed salads and country buffets.
☛ Vincent Ogereau, 44, rue de la Belle-Angevine,
49750 Saint-Lambert-du-Lattay, tel. 02.41.78.30.53,
fax 02.41.78.43.55 ▼
🍷 by appt.

DOM. DU REGAIN

Pop Wine 2002★

■   1 ha   4,000   ▐ ♦   3–5 €

This estate was created in 2002 by the former director of the Institut Technique du Vin (technical wine institute) in Angers, who chose to pay homage to the writer Jean Giono by baptizing his estate after his novel *Regain*. This is the result of his first winemaking attempt, which gives a most encouraging result. The grenadine-pink appearance is delicate. The aromas emerge with aeration and are reminiscent of flowers, especially violets. Pleasant and well balanced, here is a true Rosé de Loire.
☛ F. et F. Etienne, Dom. du Regain, Le Pied de Fer,
49540 Martigné-Briand, tel. 02.41.40.28.20,
fax 02.41.40.28.21,
e-mail domaine.regain@wanadoo.fr ▼
🍷 by appt.

DOM. DES TROTTIERES 2002★

■   22.95 ha   128,000   ▐ ♦   3–5 €

The person that set up this estate was one of the pioneers of the introduction of phylloxera-resistant American rootstocks. Built in colonial style, the winery is topped by a tower that overlooks the whole vineyard. This Rosé de Loire is really delicious. The delicate palate provides a sensation of fresh fruit, and the nose is light with red berry aromas. Overall it is a refreshing wine.
☛ SCEA Dom. des Trottières, 49380 Thouarcé,
tel. 02.41.54.14.10, fax 02.41.54.09.00,
e-mail lestrottieres@worldonline.fr ▼
🍷 ev. day except Sat. Sun. 8am–12.30pm 2pm–6.30pm
☛ Lamotte

Wines selected but not starred

DOM. DE GAGNEBERT 2002

■   10 ha   20,000   ▐ ♦   3–5 €

☛ GAEC Moron, Dom. de Gagnebert, 2, chem. de la Naurivet, 49610 Juigné-sur-Loire, tel. 02.41.91.92.86, fax 02.41.91.95.50,
e-mail moron@domaine-de-gagnebert.com ▼
🍷 ev. day except Sun. 9am–12 noon 3pm–7pm

DOM. DE GATINES 2002

■   1.7 ha   8,000   ▐ ♦   3–5 €

☛ Vignoble Dessèvre, 12, rue de la Boulaie, 49540 Tigné, tel. 02.41.59.41.48, fax 02.41.59.94.44 ▼
🍷 ev. day except Sun. 8am–12 noon 2pm–6pm

DOM. D'ORGIGNE 2002

■   9 ha   50,000   ▐ ♦   3–5 €

☛ Delaunay, Dom. d'Orgigné,
49320 Saint-Saturnin-sur-Loire, tel. 02.41.54.21.96,
fax 02.41.91.72.25 ▼
🍷 by appt.

DOM. DE TERREBRUNE 2002

■   5.3 ha   45,000   ▐ ♦   3–5 €

☛ SCA Dom. de Terrebrune, La Motte,
49380 Notre-Dame-d'Allençon, tel. 02.41.54.01.99,
fax 02.41.54.09.06,
e-mail domaine-de-terrebrune@wanadoo.fr ▼
🍷 by appt.

Crémant de Loire

Here again, the Appellation Régionale can be applied to sparkling wines produced within the boundaries of Anjou, Saumur, Touraine and Cheverny. The Traditional méthod or Champagne method works wonders here; production of these celebration wines was up to around 34,852 hl in 2002. A number of grape varieties are grown: Chenin or Pineau de Loire, Cabernet Sauvignon and Cabernet Franc, Pinot Noir, Chardonnay, etc. Even though production is largely of white wines, some rosés are also made.

DOM. DE L'ANGELIERE 2000★

	2 ha	12,000	🍾 ⚐	5–8 €

The Angelière estate owns approximately 45 ha of vineyards in the heart of the Coteaux du Layon area and produces wines from ten appellations. The effervescence is intense, almost exuberant. Once it has settled down, this Crémant de Loire shows a different side: light fruit and delicate wild flowers, with a well-balanced, refreshing palate, which leaves a sensation of freshly chopped fruit.

�often GAEC Boret, Dom. de L'Angelière, 49380 Champ-sur-Layon, tel. 02.41.78.85.09, fax 02.41.78.67.10 ☑
🍷 by appt.

DOM. BENASTRE 2001★★

	0.75 ha	7,000		5–8 €

Above an imposing entrance gate is an 18th century stone carved by the old estate workers. It represents a star and the moon, and gives its name to the estate since "Bénastré" means "beneath a good star" in old French. Here is a Crémant de Loire to reserve for high days and holidays – a delicate effervescence that persists across the appearance of pale yellow and light golden highlights. The aromas conjure up fresh white peaches and dried apricots. The fine and well-balanced palate allies the feeling of freshness and of softness remarkably well.

↱ EARL Bruno Roux, 33, imp. Painlevé, 49260 Montreuil-Bellay, tel. 02.41.52.43.47, fax 02.41.52.42.91, e-mail roux@domaine-benastre.com ☑
🍷 ev. day except Sun. 8am–12.30pm 1.30pm–7pm

CHESNEAU ET FILS 2001★

	0.8 ha	6,700		5–8 €

A charming wine whose bubbles tantalize the palate, you can serve this *crémant* not only as an aperitif, but also during a meal.

↱ EARL Chesneau et Fils, 26, rue Sainte-Néomoise, 41120 Sambin, tel. 02.54.20.20.15, fax 02.54.33.21.91, e-mail contact@chesneauetfils.fr ☑
🍷 by appt.

DOM. COCTEAUX★★

	3.56 ha	12,000		5–8 €

Produced exclusively from Chardonnay, this pale-coloured *crémant* appeals greatly with its lightness and elegance. The first impression is soft and the palate is of an extremely high standard, with good fruitiness on the finish.

↱ M. et Mme Franck Cocteaux, Dom. de Fleuray, 37530 Cangey, tel. 02.47.30.01.44, fax 02.47.30.05.09 ☑
🍷 ev. day except Sun. 8am–7pm

DOM. DE LA DESOUCHERIE 2000★★

	1 ha	9,000		8–11 €

With a beautiful yellow-gold colour, the very fine bubbles form a delicate and persistent necklace. The first impression on the palate is soft and its perfect balance makes it a quality aperitif.

↱ GAEC Christian Tessier et Fils, 47, voie de la Charmoise, 41700 Cour-Cheverny, tel. 02.54.79.98.90, fax 02.54.79.22.48, e-mail tessier.christian@libertysurf.fr ☑ 🏠
🍷 ev. day 8am–12 noon 2pm–6pm; groups and Sun. by appt.

GARNIER 2000★

	1 ha	6,500		8–11 €

Before he established the Domaine des Noëls in 1994, J.-M. Garnier was the oenologist at Rémy Pannier and primarily made sparkling wines. This early experience could be only beneficial. Delicate and persistent effervescence, a pleasant nose of fruits and ripe grapes, the palate is light, giving a sensation of freshness and balance: this *crémant* has what it takes to satisfy a sparkling wine-lover.

↱ SCEA Dom. des Noëls, Les Noëls, 49380 Faye-d'Anjou, tel. 02.41.54.18.01, fax 02.41.54.30.76, e-mail domaine-des-noels@terre-net.fr ☑
🍷 by appt.

DOM. DE LA GERFAUDRIE 2001★★

	1.2 ha	10,000		5–8 €

This estate is situated on the steep cliffs above the Anjou corniche, which is also the territory of the Gerfaut falcon. To be served as an aperitif or with dessert – at any time, this pale yellow *crémant* has beautiful, fine and persistent bubbles, with aromas giving nuances of wild flowers and ripe fruits. On the palate it is refreshing and light, finishing on notes of ripe fruits. Overall, this is a remarkably successful wine.

↱ SCEV J.-P. et P. Bourreau, 25, rue de l'Onglée, 49290 Chalonnes-sur-Loire, tel. 02.41.78.02.28, fax 02.41.78.03.07, e-mail domaine-gerfaudrie@wanadoo.fr ☑
🍷 by appt.

LEON LEROI★

	7 ha	43,000		5–8 €

This négociant house makes primarily rosés and sparkling wines. This one offers particularly good, expressive aromas with notes reminiscent of golden grapes, ripe and crystallized fruits, as well as flowers. The palate is equally good giving a feeling of great richness.

↱ SAS Lacheteau, 22, rue de la Saulaie, 49700 Doué-la-Fontaine, tel. 02.41.59.26.26, fax 02.41.59.01.94, e-mail contact@lacheteau.fr

DOM. DE MONTGILET 2001★★

	1.5 ha	7,500		5–8 €

The vineyard is situated on slate schist used since the 12th century as a slate quarry. The estate is well-known to lovers of white wines, in particular for its sweet Coteaux de l'Aubance wines. This brightly-coloured *crémant* looks very inviting. Both the aromas and the yellow colour are intense. The palate is powerful, rounded and well balanced, providing a particularly pleasant feeling of ripe fruit.

↱ Victor et Vincent Lebreton, Dom. de Montgilet, 49610 Juigné-sur-Loire, tel. 02.41.91.90.48, fax 02.41.54.64.25, e-mail montgilet@terre-net.fr ☑
🍷 ev. day except Sun. 9am–12 noon 2pm–6pm; cl. Sat. Jan. and Feb.

CH. DE PASSAVANT 2001★

	3 ha	20,000		8–11 €

The fortified castle of Passavant was built in the 10th and 11th centuries by Foulques Nerra. It overhangs a vast water reservoir. This *crémant* has an extremely attractive effervescence with delicate and persistent strings of bubbles running through the yellow colour whose depth indicates slight development. The toasty and floral aromas are characteristic of this type of wine. Here is a wine that can be served as an aperitif or throughout a meal.

↱ SCEA David Lecomte, Ch. de Passavant, 49560 Passavant-sur-Layon, tel. 02.41.59.53.96, fax 02.41.59.57.91, e-mail passavant@wanadoo.fr ☑
🍷 ev. day except Sun. 8am–12 noon 2pm–7pm; Sat. by appt.

DOM. DU PETIT VAL 2001★

| | 1 ha | 5,000 | 🍷 ♦ | 5–8 € |

This estate was created in 1950 with 4 ha of vines, and today has 50 ha with a small section in the famous cru Bonnezeaux. Here is a Crémant de Loire to relish. Its beautiful pale yellow colour and light, delicate aromas are very representative of the appellation; the palate is well balanced with a broad range of flavours emerging right through the tasting.
☛ EARL Denis Goizil, Dom. du Petit Val, 49380 Chavagnes, tel. 02.41.54.31.14, fax 02.41.54.03.48, e-mail denisgoizil@tiscali.fr 🅥
🍷 by appt.

PRINCE DE PIEGUE 2000★★

| | 1 ha | n.c. | 🍷 ♦ | 5–8 € |

In 1920, Grandfather Van der Hecht left Cairo and purchased the Piégué property comprising 7 ha of vines that were rather neglected. Today the estate includes 25 ha of vines in the village of Rochefort-sur-Loire. Delicacy reigns in this Crémant de Loire: the yellow colour has slight tinges of gold, flavours recall floral and honey notes. The palate associates a sensation of freshness with some softness. This can be served all through a meal or with a fish in sauce.
☛ Ch. Piégué, Piégué, 49190 Rochefort-sur-Loire, tel. 02.41.78.71.26, fax 02.41.78.75.03, e-mail antoine-van-der-hecht@wanadoo.fr 🅥 🏠
🍷 by appt.
🍷 Van der Hecht

CH. DE PUTILLE 2000★★★

| | 5 ha | 35,000 | 🍷 ♦ | 5–8 € |

The Château de Putille is a benchmark for Anjou wine-lovers. This *coup de coeur* confirms once again the excellence of this estate. The effervescence is both delicate and persistent. The yellow colour appeals with its tinges of gold. Aromas of ripe fruits, golden grapes and brioche herald a great wine. The palate is full, concentrated, and delicate putting the finishing touches to an overall exceptional wine.
☛ EARL Ch. de Putille, 49620 La Pommeraye, tel. 02.41.39.02.91, fax 02.41.39.03.45 🅥
🍷 ev. day except Sun. 8.30am–12.30pm 2pm–7pm
🍷 Pascal Delaunay

DOM. DE ROCHAMBEAU 2000★

| | 0.5 ha | n.c. | 🍷 | 8–11 € |

Maurice Forest is the new chairman of the Coteaux de l'Aubance growers' syndicate. His *crémant* appealed from the start. With great finesse, the bubbles evolve in long streams with an intense yellow appearance tinged with light golden-green. On the other hand, the nose is powerful, with ripe fruit dominating. The attractive palate appears almost restrained taking into account the exuberance of the nose.
☛ EARL Forest, Dom. de Rochambeau, 49610 Soulaines-sur-Aubance, tel. 02.41.57.82.26, fax 02.41.57.82.26 🅥
🍷 by appt.

DOM. DES VARINELLES 1999★

| | 3 ha | 25,000 | 🍷 ♦ | 5–8 € |

The Domaine des Varinelles is an old family property located in the heart of the Saumur-Champigny wine area. Claude and

Laurent Daheuiller are grower-producers and supervise the whole wine production process. This Crémant de Loire has matured for three years on its lees. Overall of great finesse, the aromas have nuances of wild flowers, ripe fruits, patisserie and green apples. The palate is very attractive and links the sensations of freshness and softness perfectly.
☛ SCA Daheuiller et Fils, 28, rue du Ruau, 49400 Varrains, tel. 02.41.52.90.94, fax 02.41.52.94.63 🅥
🍷 ev. day except Sun. 8am–12 noon 2pm–6.30pm; Sat. by appt.

Wines selected but not starred

DOM. DE LA BESNERIE

| | 0.6 ha | 4,000 | 🍷 ♦ | 8–11 € |

☛ François Pironneau, Dom. de la Besnerie, 41, rte de Mesland, 41150 Monteaux, tel. 02.54.70.23.75 🅥
🍷 by appt.

CH. DE LA DURANDIERE 2000

| | 2.62 ha | 12,000 | 🍷 ♦ | 5–8 € |

☛ SCEA Antoine Bodet, Ch. de La Durandière, 51, rue des Fusillés, 49260 Montreuil-Bellay, tel. 02.41.40.35.30, fax 02.41.40.35.31, e-mail durandiere.chateau@libertysurf.fr 🅥
🍷 ev. day 8am–7pm; Sat. Sun. by appt.

FRANCIS ET PATRICK HUGUET 2000

| | n.c. | 4,000 | | 5–8 € |

☛ GAEC Patrick Huguet, 11–12, rue de la Franchetière, 41350 Saint-Claude-de-Diray, tel. 02.54.20.57.36, fax 02.54.20.58.57 🅥
🍷 by appt.

DOM. MICHAUD

| | 1.4 ha | 13,000 | 🍷 ♦ | 5–8 € |

☛ EARL Michaud, 20, rue Les Martinières, 41140 Noyers-sur-Cher, tel. 02.54.32.47.23, fax 02.54.75.39.19 🅥
🍷 ev. day except Sun. 8.30am–12.30pm 2pm–7pm

MURANO

| | 5 ha | 30,000 | 🍷 ♦ | 5–8 € |

☛ SCEA Dom. d'Artois, La Morandière, 41150 Mesland, tel. 02.54.70.24.72, fax 02.54.70.24.72 🅥
🍷 by appt.
🍷 J.-L. Saget

VEUVE AMIOT

| | 35 ha | 281,000 | | 5–8 € |

☛ Veuve Amiot, BP 67, 49400 Saint-Hilaire-Saint-Florent, tel. 02.41.83.14.14, fax 02.41.50.17.66 🅥
🍷 ev. day 10am–6pm; cl. Oct.-Apr.

The Nantes Region

Some two thousand years ago the Roman legions introduced the vine to the Nantes area, at the crossroads of Brittany, the Vendée, the Loire and the Atlantic coast. After a terrible winter in 1709 when the sea froze solid along the shore and the vines were completely destroyed, the vineyards were replanted, mainly with the Melon variety from Burgundy.

The Pays Nantais vineyard area now covers 16,000 ha south and east of Nantes, extending slightly over the borders of the Loire-Atlantique into the Vendée and the Maine-et-Loire. The vines grow on sunny slopes exposed to maritime influences. The soils are rather light and stony, composed of both ancient and volcanic rocks. The region produces 960,000 hl of four AOC wines: Muscadet, Muscadet des Coteaux de Loire, Muscadet de Sèvre-et-Maine and Muscadet Côtes de Grand-Lieu, as well as the AOVDQS Gros Plant du Pays Nantais, Coteaux d'Ancenis et Fiefs Vendéens.

THE MUSCADET AOCS AND GROS PLANT FROM THE PAYS NANTAIS

Muscadet is a white wine that has been an AOC since 1936. It is made from a single grape variety: the Melon. The vineyard area covers 12,908 ha. There are four Appellations d'Origine Contrôlée, identified according to their geographical location, which produced a total of 773,700 hl of wine in 2002: Muscadet de Sèvre-et-Maine, which alone represents 9,958 ha and 579,978 hl; Muscadet Côtes de Grand-Lieu with 315 ha, 18,197 hl, Muscadet des Coteaux de la Loire with 287 ha, 15,761 hl and Muscadet: 2,404 ha, 159,764 hl.

Gros Plant du Pays Nantais, classified AOVDQS in 1954, is also a dry white wine, but made from a different grape variety, the Folle Blanche. In 2002, 152,970 hl were produced from an area of 2,084 ha.

Bottling on the lees (*sur lie*) is a traditional technique in the region, subject to precise regulations which were made more stringent in 1994. In order to qualify for the *sur lie* suffix, the wines must spend no more than one winter in tanks or casks, having been matured on the lees and kept in the wine store where they were made until bottling. The wine bottling can take place only during precisely defined periods and in no circumstances before 1 March, and sales are permitted only after the third Thursday in March. These regulations are designed to maximize freshness, finesse and bouquet. Muscadet is a white wine, dry but not acid, with a generous bouquet, a wine for any occasion. It is the perfect accompaniment for fish, shellfish and seafood and also makes an excellent aperitif. It should be served chilled, but not ice-cold (8–9°C). Gros Plant is the ideal wine to drink with oysters.

The Nantes Region

LOIRE

Muscadet

Wines selected but not starred

LE MOULIN DE LA TOUCHE
Sur lie 2002

0.81 ha	6,000	🍴 🍷	3–5 €

☛ Joël Hérissé, Le Moulin de la Touche, 44580 Bourgneuf-en-Retz, tel. 02.40.21.21.79, fax 02.40.21.47.89 ☑
☍ by appt.

DOM. DE LA NOE 2002

7 ha	55,000	🍴 🍷	–3 €

☛ Dom. de la Noë, 44690 Château-Thébaud, tel. 02.40.06.50.57, fax 02.40.06.50.57, e-mail domainelanoe@wanadoo.fr ☑
☍ ev. day except Sun. 8am–12.30pm 2pm–7pm
☛ Drouard Frères

DOM. DES QUATRE ROUTES 2002

12 ha	20,000	🍴 🍷	3–5 €

☛ Dom. Henri Poiron et Fils, Les Quatre Routes, 44690 Maisdon-sur-Sèvre, tel. 02.40.54.60.58, fax 02.40.54.62.05, e-mail poiron.henri@wanadoo.fr ☑
☍ by appt.

Muscadet-Sèvre et Maine

ABBAYE DE SAINTE-RADEGONDE
Sur lie 2002★★

21 ha	154,930	🍴 🍷	3–5 €

To the north of Loroux-Bothereau, the abbey of Sainte-Radegonde is worth a visit for its museum devoted to the vine and wine. The tasters awarded a *coup de coeur* to this *cuvée*, with its complex scents of cut hay and wild flowers, and whose supple palate ends with a note of plump fruits. This is a wine that one could readily keep and drink with zander cooked in butter.
☛ SCEA Abbaye de Sainte-Radegonde, 44330 Le Loroux-Bottereau, tel. 02.40.03.74.78, fax 02.40.03.79.91 ☑

DOM. AUDOUIN
Sur lie 2002★

8 ha	15,000	🍴 🍷	3–5 €

From a *momenière* (a small hill) on the road from Landreau towards Vallet, Joseph Audouin has produced a pretty pale-coloured wine with light tinges of green allowing a few fine bubbles to appear on the rim. The rather restrained nose is on the fruity side: citrus fruits and passion-fruit. The softness and roundness of the palate are accompanied by a slightly acidic touch. From the same estate, the **Gros Plant du Pays Nantais Sur Lie 2002** obtains a star.
☛ EARL Audouin, La Momenière, 44430 Le Landreau, tel. 02.40.06.43.04, fax 02.40.06.47.89 ☑
☍ ev. day 9am–6pm

CAROLINE BARRE
Sur lie Cuvée du Moulin neuf 2002★

3 ha	10,000	🍴 🍷	3–5 €

This *cuvée* still offers youthful aromas of fresh apple, and then on the palate an intense fruitiness appears accompanied by a slightly acid note which adds to the impression of freshness. The light astringency on the finish is a sign of an unquestionable future. This wine will make a pleasant accompaniment to filet of sole with a rich cream sauce.
☛ Caroline Barré, Montifault, 44330 Le Pallet, tel. 02.40.80.40.62, fax 02.40.80.43.17, e-mail montifault@wanadoo.fr ☑
☍ by appt.

DOMAINES A. BARRE
Sur lie 2002★★

10 ha	50,000	🍴 🍷	3–5 €

The firm of Barré is an old négociant in the Nantes area. It presents a wine that is marked by intense white fruits (peach and apricot). With good length, rich and soft, this wine is worth drinking as of now. "Perfect", wrote one of the tasters in conclusion. Very successful, the **Muscadet de Sèvre et Maine Sur Lie Barré Frères Célébration 2002 (5–8 €)** was enjoyed for its slightly iodized nose and complex, well-balanced palate. It also obtains two stars.
☛ Auguste Barré, Beau-Soleil, BP 10, 44190 Gorges, tel. 02.40.06.90.70, fax 02.40.06.96.52 ☑
☍ by appt.

DOM. DE BEAUREPAIRE
Sur lie 2002★

2.76 ha	22,000	🍴 🍷	5–8 €

This 18.5-ha estate can be found at the far end of Mouzillon. Jean-Paul Bouin-Baumard has vinified an intensely coloured wine, whose attractive and fine nose is reminiscent of fresh mint. The lightly sparkling touch results from the *sur lie* wine-making process; it emphasizes the roundness and the softness of the palate which finishes well on floral notes.
☛ Jean-Paul Bouin-Boumard, 5, La Recivière, 44330 Mouzillon, tel. 02.40.36.35.97, fax 02.40.36.35.97 ☑
☍ ev. day 10am–7pm; Sun. by appt.

LE DOM. BEDOUET
Sur lie 2002★★

13 ha	100,000	🍴 🍷	3–5 €

Michel Bedouet blended grapes harvested on early maturing plots of mica-schist with biotite (black mica) and from gneiss with two mica plots to vinify this lively wine, which shows good intensity. Well balanced and powerful, it has a pleasantly long finish and shows evidence of excellent potential: it will improve in the cellar for between two and five years.
☛ Michel Bedouet, 28, Le Pé-de-Sèvre, 44330 Le Pallet, tel. 02.40.80.97.30, fax 02.40.80.40.68, e-mail michel@bedouet-vigneron.com ☑
☍ by appt.

DOM. DE BEGROLLE
Sur lie 2002★

16 ha	124,000	🍴 🍷	3–5 €

Leaving La Haye-Fouassière, on the road to Vertou, you cannot miss the Domaine de Bégrolle. There you will discover

a well-made Muscadet, showing good typicity: this one reveals not only lemon aromas, but also a mineral character accentuated by a light sparkle on the finish. This wine, revealing its terroir of otho-gneiss, has great potential and could be drunk, for example, with grilled bass with fennel.
☛ Jean-Pierre Méchineau, Bégrolle, 44690 La Haye-Fouassière, tel. 02.40.54.80.95, fax 02.40.54.80.95 ☑

DOM. DE LA BERNARDIERE

Sur lie 2002★

10 ha	15,000	🍷 ♦	3–5 €

Bernardière is a small village close to an old lime kiln and to a landing stage from where visitors can board a boat to visit the Goulaine marshes. Dominique Coraleau has produced a fresh and fine wine here, with scents of hawthorn. The palate is not bad either, even if it is worth leaving for some time to open out.
☛ Dominique Coraleau, 14, rue des Châteaux, La Bernardière, 44330 La Chapelle-Heulin, tel. 02.40.06.76.21, fax 02.40.06.76.21 ☑
Ⴇ by appt.

CH. DE LA BLANCHETIERE

Sur lie 2002★

7.24 ha	57,000	🍷 ♦	3–5 €

The history of the Château de la Blanchetière is linked with that of the Vendée wars; it was burnt down in 1793. Since then, it has rediscovered its serenity and offers a wine with delicate yellow highlights. The powerful nose merges fruit with mineral notes, while the fresh palate opens out showing good balance before concluding on a lively touch.
☛ Joël Dugast, Ch. De La Blanchetière, 44330 Vallet, tel. 02.40.06.73.76 ☑

DOM. DE LA BODINIERE

Sur lie 2002★

14 ha	112,800	🍷 ♦	3–5 €

Here is a clear-cut wine that is full of flavour. Soft at first, its floral character, especially of broom, is accompanied by some citrus fruit notes that accentuate its freshness. The wine is the result of impeccable winemaking.
☛ SCEA Orpale, 3, rue d'Anjou, 44330 La Regrippière
Ⴇ by appt.
☛ Luc Terrier

DOM. GILBERT BOSSARD

Sur lie 2002★

11 ha	50,000	🍷 ♦	3–5 €

This estate is noted for its use of a particular winemaking technique known as malolactic fermentation, used for part of the wines. This gives this Muscadet a quite distinct character: aromas of butter and brioche and a full palate. Here is a 2002 wine of great richness and good appearance, which will match pike in butter sauce.
☛ GAEC Gilbert Bossard, La Basse-Ville, 44330 La Chapelle-Heulin, tel. 02.40.06.74.33, fax 02.40.06.77.48, e-mail gilbert.bossard@wanadoo.fr ☑
Ⴇ ev. day 8.30am–12 noon 2pm–6.30pm

CH. DE LA BOTINIERE

Sur lie 2002★

45 ha	330,000	🍷 ♦	3–5 €

Situated at the boundary between Vallet and Mouzillon, the Château de la Botinière has been completely restored and its vineyard was replanted with Melon around 20 years ago. Produced on a relatively late-ripening terroir with a gabbro (dark, volcanic rock) subsoil, this Muscadet-Sèvre et Maine was enjoyed for its powerful nose of citrus fruits, peach and apricot. Well balanced, it is rich and round, and the palate is sustained until a lively touch on the finish, typical for wines from a late-ripening terroir.
☛ SE Ch. de la Botinière, 44330 Vallet, tel. 02.40.06.73.83, fax 02.40.06.76.49
☛ Jean Beauquin

DOM. DE LA BRAUDIERE

Sur lie 2002★★

11 ha	10,000	🍷 ▥ ♦	3–5 €

This small 15-hectare vineyard, located to the southeast of Vallet, is famous for its Muscadet- Sèvre et Maine from old vintages. However, this year the Jury awarded the *coup de coeur* to a pale 2002 tinged with green, and with a restrained but complex nose blending mineral and floral characters with a croissant note. Balanced and rounded, the palate is long with ripe fruits and a touch of minerality; it should form an exquisite alliance with sea bass baked in salt. This wine can also be cellared for two or three years.
☛ Guy Breteaudeau, Braudière, 44330 Vallet, tel. 02.40.36.20.62 ☑
Ⴇ by appt.

MICHEL BREGEON 1996★★

8 ha	63,000	🍷	5–8 €

Recognized several times in the *Guide* (with a *coup de coeur* for the 1997 vintage), Michel Brégeon makes his unusual wines from a small ten-hectare vineyard. He keeps back numerous old vintages for enlightened wine-lovers, like this bright yellow 1996, which explodes with a range of fruity and flowery flavours. Despite its eight years of age, the wine has retained great freshness and could be cellared for another few years. Decant it before serving.
☛ André et Michel Brégeon, 5, Les Guisseaux, 44190 Gorges, tel. 02.40.06.93.19, fax 02.40.06.95.91 ☑
Ⴇ ev. day except Sun. 10am–7pm

DOM. DE LA BRETONNIERE

Sur lie Cuvée sélectionnée 2002★★

4 ha	21,000	🍷 ♦	3–5 €

Bretonnière is one of the many wine villages attached to the *commune* of Landreau. Two brothers joined together to farm this 34-ha vineyard: they have produced a very fresh wine with floral aromas, and a palate with appealing roundness.
☛ GAEC Charpentier-Fleurance, La Bretonnière, 44430 Le Landreau, tel. 02.40.06.43.39, fax 02.40.06.44.05 ☑
Ⴇ by appt.

DOM. DU CENSY Sur lie Cuvée du

Haut-Censy Vinifié en fût de chêne 1999★★

n.c.	1,200	▥	3–5 €

From a manual harvest, this *cuvée* benefited from fermentation in cask. The Jury noted its great structure and intense flavours of white fruits, citrus fruits and slight notes of nuttiness. The first impression on the palate is fresh and then it opens up showing good balance, though with a certain level of acidity that should soften out given a little time. Keep this wine to allow it to open out fully.
☛ François Rivière, 14, Le Gast, 44690 Maisdon-sur-Sèvre, tel. 02.40.03.86.28, fax 02.40.33.56.91 ☑
Ⴇ by appt.

VIGNOBLE DU CHATEAU DES ROIS

Sur lie 1995★★★

	6 ha	2,000	🍾 🍷	5–8 €

Some of the terroir of Mouzillon is well known for producing wines suitable for ageing such as this perfect 1995 selection; it was also entered for the Grand Jury of "old" vintages. This has retained a yellow straw colour with delicate green highlights and it reveals a very intense nose of ripe fruits, hazelnuts and grilled almonds. Tasting the wine shows beautiful balance and great complexity right the way through. This wine can still be kept for a few years. From the same producer, the **Domaine du Haut-Coudray Sur Lie 2002 (3–5 €)** is also well made.
🍷 Gilbert Ganichaud et Fils, 9, rte d'Ancenis, 44330 Mouzillon, tel. 02.40.33.93.40, fax 02.40.36.38.79, e-mail ganichaud@wanadoo.fr 🗑
🍷 ev. day 8am–12.30pm 2pm–7pm; Sun. by appt.

DOM. DE LA CHAUVINIERE 1997★★★

	1 ha	4,000	🍾 🍷	5–8 €

The granite terroir of Château-Thébaud has the reputation of producing early maturing wines. Yet, the *coup de coeur* is well and truly allotted to a golden-tinged 97. This selection is very expressive, with a complex toasty nose, followed up beautifully by a rounded palate that also shows very attractive power. It could be kept for two or three years. Note the **Domaine de la Chauvinière Sur Lie 2002 (3–5 €)** that gains a star.
🍷 Yves et Jérémie Huchet, La Chauvinière, 44690 Château-Thébaud, tel. 02.40.06.51.90, fax 02.40.06.57.13,
e-mail domaine-de-la-chauviniere@wanadoo.fr 🗑
🍷 by appt.

CH. LA CHEVILLARDIERE

Sur lie 2002★

	10 ha	78,660	🍾 🍷	3–5 €

La Chevillardière is an 18th century property, an old dependence of the feudal Château des Mouty. Today it produces an expressive Muscadet-Sèvre et Maine, mixing flowers and fruits: rose and peach. The same peachy flavours are revealed on the palate, which shows good length too.
🍷 Raymond Pichon, La Chevillardière, 44330 Vallet, tel. 02.40.06.74.29, fax 02.40.06.74.29 🗑
🍷 ev. day 8am–12.30pm 2pm–7pm

CLOS DES ROSIERS

Sur lie Vieilles Vignes 2002★

	10 ha	25,000	🍾 🍷	3–5 €

Produced from schistous terroir located at the edge of Vallet, on the road to Corbeillières, this fruity wine appears to have attractive balance. It could be enjoyed from now with seafood.
🍷 Philippe Laure, Les Rosiers, 44330 Vallet, tel. 02.40.33.91.83, fax 02.40.36.39.28 🗑
🍷 by appt.

CLOS DU GAUFFRIAUD

Sur lie 2002★

	1 ha	7,800	🍾	3–5 €

Typical of the appellation's style, this wine is full of flavour with pear dominant. There is good evidence of balance and

nice roundness. Fruit emerges on the finish together with a characteristic touch of minerality.
🍷 Jean-Luc Viaud, La Renouère, 44430 Le Landreau, tel. 02.40.06.40.65, fax 02.40.06.45.43 🗑
🍷 ev. day except Sun. 9am–12.30pm 2pm–7pm

DOM. DE LA COGNARDIERE

Sur lie Cuvée Bella verte 2002★

	7 ha	40,000	🍾 🍷	5–8 €

If you visit the winery of the Domaine de la Cognardière, you will be surprised by the original decor conceived by the owner. This *cuvée* seems a little backward still, but it has all the requirements for ageing well: a clear-cut nose, both floral and mineral, and balanced acidity. Leave it to open out for a year.
🍷 Fabienne Richard de Tournay, La Cognardière, 44330 Le Pallet, tel. 02.40.80.42.30, fax 02.40.80.44.37,
e-mail f.richard-de-tournay@wanadoo.fr 🗑
🍷 by appt.
🍷 Dominique Richard

DOM. DE LA CORNULIERE

Sur lie Excellence Vieilles Vignes 2002★

	1.5 ha	11,000	🍾 🍷	5–8 €

Marked by its late-ripening gabbro (dark, volcanic rock) terroir, this wine only emerges bit by bit, but provides real typicity. The light acidity will soften with time. This should be laid down, to consume in two or three years.
🍷 Jean-Michel Barreau, La Cornulière, 44190 Gorges, tel. 02.40.03.95.06, fax 02.40.54.23.13 🗑
🍷 by appt.

DOM. DE LA COUR DU CHATEAU DE LAPOMMERAIE Sur lie 2002★★

	15 ha	80,000	🍾 🍷	3–5 €

In the north of Vallet, on the road to Ancenis, the Château de La Pommeraie is home to a centre for vocational training. Its wine is distributed by an old négociant house. This refreshing 2002 provides flavours of white fruits (passion-fruit and citrus fruits). The slightly lemony palate gives a remarkable impression of finesse thanks to the good balance between acidity and body.
🍷 SARL Gilbert Chon et Fils, Le Bois Malinge, 44450 Saint-Julien-de-Concelles, tel. 02.40.54.11.08, fax 02.40.54.19.90
🍷 Albert Poilane

DOM. MICHEL DAVID

Sur lie Clos du Ferré 2002★

	13.25 ha	60,000	🍾 🍷	3–5 €

One of the most famous *clos* in the village of Vallet is without question the Clos du Ferré. The mica-schist terroir gives the character to this wine: a powerful fruity nose of peaches, great length of flavour, roundness on the palate and balanced, it is ideal for fish in sauce.
🍷 EARL David, Le Landreau-Village, 44330 Vallet, tel. 02.40.36.42.88, fax 02.40.33.96.94 🗑
🍷 ev. day except Sun. 8.30am–12 noon 2.15pm–7pm

MICHEL DELHOMMEAU

Sur lie Cuvée Harmonie 2002★★

	4 ha	25,000	🍾 🍷	3–5 €

The Cuvée Harmonie releases very pleasant and quite distinctive flavours, characteristic of wines from the gabbro (dark, volcanic rock) sector of La Huperie. The acidity is well developed, with good balance and a dominant mineral flavour.
🍷 Michel Delhommeau, La Huperie, 44690 Monnières, tel. 02.40.54.60.37, fax 02.40.54.64.51,
e-mail michel.delhommeau@wanadoo.fr 🗑
🍷 by appt.

DOM. DES DORICES

Sur lie Grande Garde 2000★★

	8 ha	20,000	🍾 🍷	5–8 €

At the start of the 20th century this 40-ha wine estate belonged to the Marquis de Rochechouart. He sold it in 1930

to the great-grandfather of the Boullault brothers, who today produce this exceptional Muscadet-Sèvre et Maine, made from 40-year-old vines planted on mica-schist. The first flavour that comes through reveals a great terroir: delicate and complex flavours of ripe fruits emerge. On the palate there is perfect balance, with a touch of acidity that provides good backbone to the wine.
☛ Boullault Frères, rte du Puiset-Doré, 44330 Vallet, tel. 02.40.33.95.30, fax 02.40.36.26.85 ☑
🍷 by appt.

ECLAT DE MER 2002★

15.2 ha	112,000	🍾 ♦		–3 €

This old Nantes négociant house presents its Eclat de Mer with a powerful floral nose and a fine, delicate palate. The tasters would have appreciated a little more weight on the palate, but the quality–price ratio of this wine should be stressed. The cuvée **Eric Tabarly Sur Lie 2002 (3–5 €)** also obtains a star for its character and its intense range of pepper and citrus fruit flavours.
☛ SA Marcel Sautejean, Dom. de L'Hyvernière, 44330 Le Pallet, tel. 02.40.06.73.83, fax 02.40.06.76.49
🍷 by appt.

CH. ELGET

Sur lie Cuvée Prestige 2002★

12 ha	50,000	🍾 ♦	3–5 €

Behind its gold colour, this Muscadet reveals a nose of great intensity, with dominant floral notes of broom. Balanced, slightly sparkling and fruity on the palate, it should gain in length after a little time.
☛ Gilles Luneau, Ch. Elget, Les Forges, 44190 Gorges, tel. 02.40.54.05.09, fax 02.40.54.05.67,
e-mail chateau.elget@wanadoo.fr ☑
🍷 ev. day 8am–12.30pm 2pm–7pm; Sat. Sun. by appt.

DOM. DE L'EPINAY

Sur lie 2002★

6 ha	35,000	🍾 ♦	3–5 €

The Domaine de l'Epinay was a Spanish seigniory in the 16th century and bore the name of Espinose. Today, it cultivates 30 ha of vines and presents a 2002 wine with a subtle, somewhat mineral, nose. Rounded and balanced, and with good length, this wine shows elegance. Also very successful, the *cuvée* **L'Espinose Vieilles Vignes Vinifié en Fût de Chêne 2000** has an oaky nose, a rich and refreshing palate, and a pleasant finish of hazelnut.
☛ EARL Paquereau, 20, rte de la Sablette, L'Epinay, 44190 Clisson, tel. 02.40.36.13.57, fax 02.40.36.13.57 ☑
🍷 ev. day 8am–7pm

CH. DE LA FAUBRETIERE

Sur lie 2002★

10 ha	6,000	🍾 ♦	3–5 €

This 2002 is distinguished by a pale yellow colour and, on the nose, a slightly buttery note. After a good fresh start, the light body is balanced by a slight sparkle and light acidity. It can be drunk from the autumn.
☛ Patrick Suteau, 2, rue des Iris, 44690 La Haye-Fouassière, tel. 02.40.54.81.53, fax 02.40.54.81.53 ☑
🍷 ev. day except Sun. 8.30am–8pm

DOM. DE LA FOLIETTE

Sur lie Clos de La Fontaine Vieilles Vignes 2002★

5 ha	40,000	🍾 ♦	5–8 €

A *foliette* means a place of festivity or folly, and the Nantais built this one outside the city of Nantes. The residence itself, which is attached to the 34-ha vineyard, dates from the 14th century. It is shown on the label of this expressive wine which has complex aromas of toast and brioche. The powerful palate evolves towards ripe and crystallized fruits then concludes on a peppery note. One star was also allotted to the *cuvée* **Tradition Vinifié Sur Lie Fine en Fût de Chêne 2001**, a balanced and unusual wine with acacia and toasty notes on the nose.

☛ Dom. de la Foliette, 35, rue de la Fontaine, La Foliette, 44690 La Haye-Fouassière, tel. 02.40.36.92.28, fax 02.40.36.98.16,
e-mail domaine.de.la.foliette@wanadoo.fr ☑
🍷 by appt.

CH. DE FROMENTEAU

Sur lie 2002★

14 ha	7,000	🍾 ♦	3–5 €

The Château de Fromenteau already existed in 1260 and, before the Revolution, mass was celebrated in its chapel. Nowadays, in July and August, visitors to the 18-ha estate can attend an educational session on the topic of the vine and wine. They will also discover this yellow-tinged wine, which is quite fruity, with an underlying mineral touch. Soft and rounded, it gives a pleasant refreshing character and will be a good accompaniment for sautéed scallops and baby vegetables.
☛ EARL Anne et Christian Braud, Fromenteau, 44330 Vallet, tel. 02.40.36.23.75, fax 02.40.36.23.75,
e-mail labyrinthe-des-vignes@wanadoo.fr ☑
🍷 by appt.

CH. DES GAUTRONNIERES

Sur lie 2002★

12.86 ha	60,781	🍾 ♦	3–5 €

Originally built in the 15th century, the Château des Gautronnières was destroyed during the Revolution, and then rebuilt in the 18th century. Today the large country house is surrounded by the vineyard. Partly made from old vines planted on the clay-siliceous soil typical of the area, this limpid and very expressive wine demonstrates beautiful balance on the palate, with freshness and intense fruit flavours.
☛ Claude Fleurance, Ch. des Gautronnières, 44330 La Chapelle-Heulin, tel. 02.40.06.74.06, fax 02.40.06.74.06 ☑

DOM. DU GRAND-AIR

Sur lie 2002★

11 ha	10,000	🍾	–3 €

Behind its limpid colour, this wine reveals a clean nose in which notes of flowers are underlined by a mineral, flinty note and touches of spice. Refreshing from the start, the palate shows a touch of attractive bitterness on the finish. It can be drunk from this December.
☛ Maurice Loiret, 6, rue du Grand-Air, Bournigal, 44190 Clisson, tel. 02.40.54.31.03, fax 02.28.06.00.29 ☑
🍷 by appt.

CH. DE LA GUIPIERE

Sur lie Cuvée Excellence Vieilles Vignes 2002★

3 ha	30,000	🍾 ♦	3–5 €

The winery of the Château de la Guipière has been tastefully restored allowing for modernisation for the sake of the winemaking process. From a terroir of mica-schist, this light green-tinged 2002 reveals a predominant floral character. Its straightforward palate, with a touch of acidity, has weight and structure, and offers evidence of good length of flavour indicating that it can last. Also very successful, the **Gros Plant du Pays Nantais Sur Lie 2002 (–3 €)** provides a fruity nose, with richness and a light, but welcome touch of bitterness on the finish.
☛ GAEC Charpentier Père et Fils, Ch. de La Guipière, 44330 Vallet, tel. 02.40.36.23.30, fax 02.40.36.38.14 ☑
🍷 by appt.

DOM. LA HAUTE FEVRIE Sur lie Le Clos

Joubert Vinifié en fût de chêne 1999★

1 ha	3,500	🍾🍾	5–8 €

Established on the hillsides of the Sèvre River, between Saint-Fiacre and Monnières, the Domaine La Haute Févrie is in the heart of the appellation area. Its Clos Joubert comes from a plot dominating the Sèvre, in which the vines are hand harvested. It releases attractive flavours of nutty vanilla, and then softness on the palate with a good balance between sweetness and acidity, even if the evident wood tannins need three or four years of ageing to tone them down. The finish is prolonged and with predominant fruity notes. Guy Branger

LOIRE

also presented his **Domaine des Févries Sur Lie 2002 (3–5 €)**, which was rounded and fruity, very well made.
☛ Claude Branger, Dom. la Haute Févrie, 109, La Févrie, 44690 Maisdon-sur-Sèvre, tel. 02.40.36.94.08, fax 02.40.36.96.69, e-mail haute-fevrie@netcourrier.com ▼
🍷 by appt.

DOM. DE L'HERMINE

Sur lie 2002★★

	7.44 ha	58,533	🍾 ♦		3–5 €

This small property has a delightful label and the 2001 obtained three stars. Its little brother, the 2002 follows on. Pale yellow with tinges of green, its colour encourages you to continue the tasting. The nose was attractive, developed, powerful, floral and fruity. The very expressive palate is full, balanced and rounded; its notes of ripe fruits accompanying the long finish. One taster would have liked to have tried this wine with grilled lobster.
☛ Luc Terrien, Ch. Plessis-Brezot, 44690 Monnières, tel. 06.85.70.24.05
🍷 by appt.

DOM. DE LA HOUSSAIS

Sur lie Elevé en fût de chêne 2001★

	0.3 ha	1,500	🍾🍾		5–8 €

On the border between the villages of Loroux-Bottereau and La Chapelle-Heulin, the Domaine de la Houssais presents an oak-matured 2001, very clear-coloured with a vast range of dried fruits and nuts including hazelnuts, grapes and figs. Very well balanced, the wine is long with a mineral finish, underlined by a touch of violet. It would make a happy marriage with *Coquille Saint-Jacques*.
☛ Bernard Gratas, Dom. de La Houssais, 44430 Le Landreau, tel. 02.40.06.46.27, fax 02.40.06.47.25 ▼
🍷 by appt.

DOM. DE LA JOCONDE

Sur lie 2002★

	10 ha	80,000	🍾 ♦		3–5 €

Le Pé-de-Sèvre is a small, picturesque, old stone-built village dominating the River Sèvre. The Domaine de la Joconde has made a green-tinged wine, enlivened with a light sparkle. One notices much finesse in the flavours of white fruits and considerable freshness on the palate, which shows no aggressiveness.
☛ Yves Maillard, Le Pé-de-Sèvre, 44330 Le Pallet, tel. 02.40.80.43.29, fax 02.40.80.43.29 ▼
🍷 by appt.

CH. DE LA JOUSSELINIERE

Sur lie 2002★

	12 ha	70,000	🍾 ♦		3–5 €

On the road from Vertou to Loroux-Bottereau, in this pretty 17th century château, which was re-built in 19th century, you can admire the neo-Norman styled wine cellar and appreciate this characteristic Muscadet, with its dominant mineral flavours. Sufficiently long, structured and balanced, the palate offers a beautiful touch of flavour. The wine will improve on keeping for a year or two.
☛ GAEC de la Jousselinière, La Jousselinière, 44450 Saint-Julien-de-Concelles, tel. 02.40.54.11.08, fax 02.40.54.19.90, e-mail muscadetchm@aol.com ▼
🍷 ev. day except Sun. 10am–12 noon 2pm–6pm
☛ GFA du Parc

CHRISTOPHE MAILLARD

Sur lie La Maison vieille 2002★

	0.75 ha	5,000	🍾 ♦		5–8 €

In Pé-de-Sèvre, on the banks of the River Sèvre, Christophe Maillard cultivates 16 ha of vines. He has produced this flavourful wine, which without revealing a particularly pronounced personality has a very pleasant softness and good length.
☛ Christophe Maillard, Le Pé-de-Sèvre, 44330 Le Pallet, tel. 02.40.80.44.92 ▼
🍷 by appt.

MARQUIS DE GOULAINE

Sur lie Cuvée du Millénaire 2002★

	15 ha	56,000	🍾 ♦		3–5 €

Distributed by a major négociant in the Nantes area, the Cuvée du Millénaire is a wine of elegant appearance, with a characteristic floral nose. Rounded and rich, the finish reveals some exotic fruit notes.
☛ SARL Vinival, La Sablette, 44330 Mouzillon, tel. 02.40.36.66.00, fax 02.40.33.95.81

DOM. DE LA MARTINIERE

Sur lie 2002★

	15 ha	40,000	🍾 ♦		3–5 €

Dominating the Goulaine marshes, the Domaine de la Martinière has vinified a pale yellow wine with hints of green, which blends harmoniously intense floral and mineral characteristics. The balanced palate is pleasantly developed with ripe fruits including peaches and apricots. A touch of acidity and a light astringency ensures that it can keep. From the same producer, the fresh and elegant **Domaine du Montru Sur Lie 2002** also obtains a star.
☛ EARL Catherine et Gerard Baron, 8, rue de La Martinière, 44330 La Chapelle-Heulin, tel. 02.40.06.75.11, fax 02.40.06.76.23 ▼
🍷 by appt.

CH. DE LA MERCREDIERE

Sur lie 1999★★

	35 ha	40,000	🍾 ♦		5–8 €

In the Gallo-Roman era, worship of the god Mercury was celebrated here, and it is to this that the château owes its name. This wine has an expressive mineral nose which leads to smoky notes on the palate before finishing on a touch of bitterness which should tone down with time.
☛ Futeul Frères, Ch. de La Mercredière, 44330 Le Pallet, tel. 02.40.54.80.10, fax 02.40.54.89.79 ▼
🍷 ev. day except Sat. Sun. 9am–12 noon 2pm–6pm; cl. 1–20 Aug.

DOM. MOREAU

Sur lie Prestige de l'Hermitage 2002★

	2 ha	13,000	🍾 ♦		3–5 €

On the main road to La Rochelle, before Aigrefeuille, the Moreau establishment is one of the last estates at the western end of the Muscadet-Sèvre and Maine appellation. This wine has been made by C. Moreau, first president of the new inter-professional organisation for the Nantes area. With a lemon-yellow colour, it is characterized by an unusual nose of honey and citrus fruits. Following on, there is a fresh start to the palate and good balance suggesting a match with filet of sole in cream sauce, for example.
☛ GAEC Moreau, La Petite Jaunaie, 44690 Château-Thébaud, tel. 02.40.06.61.42, fax 02.40.06.69.45, e-mail gaecmoreau@wanadoo.fr ▼
🍷 ev. day except Sun. 8am–7pm

DOM. DE MOTTE-CHARETTE

Sur lie 2002★

	8 ha	60,800	🍾 ♦		3–5 €

Still restrained, fruit flavours, especially citrus fruits mix with wild flower notes and make a pleasant impression. This wine already appears very rich, but an extra few months will benefit it even more.
☛ GAEC Motte-Charette, La Simplerie, 44190 Gorges ▼
☛ Mabit

DOM. DES MOULINS D'ASTREE

Sur lie Vieilles Vignes 2002★

	4.5 ha	25,000	🍾 ♦		3–5 €

With its simple range of flavours, slightly floral (with note of broom), this Muscadet-Sèvre et Maine has no pretensions but is pleasant to drink especially as an aperitif.
☛ Jean-Daniel Bretaudeau, 28, rue de la Poste, 44690 Monnières, tel. 02.40.54.60.04, fax 02.40.54.66.38 ▼
🍷 by appt.

CH. L'OISELINIERE DE LA RAMEE

Sur lie 2002★

	10 ha	70,000	🍾	5–8 €

Dominating the River Sèvre within a few hundred metres of the mouth of the River Maine, the Château L'Oiselinière de la Ramée was a holiday spot for families from Nantes. This wine, produced from an ortho-gneiss subsoil, reveals a fruity nose and a well-balanced body. It is perfect to drink right away. From the same producer, the **Château de Chasseloir Comte Leloup Cuvée des Ceps Centenaires Sur Lie 2002** is especially singled out for its range of floral aromas and its balanced palate that shows a touch of acidity.
🍾 Bernard Chéreau, 2, imp. Port-de-la-Ramée, Ch. de L'Oiselinière, 44120 Vertou, tel. 02.40.54.81.15, fax 02.40.03.19.32, e-mail bernard.chereau@wanadoo.fr 🆅
🍷 by appt.

DIANA ET ALAIN OLIVIER

Le Tradition 1995★★

	2.7 ha	7,000	🍾 🍷	5–8 €

This *cuvée* is from the fruit of a manual harvest, a practice that is now rare in the Nantes region. The wine reveals a highly developed colour and, after a good grip at first, retains quite pronounced nutty flavours, a typical sign of development. This well structured 95 is ready to drink from now on.
🍾 Alain Olivier, La Moucletière, 44330 Vallet, tel. 02.40.36.24.69, fax 02.40.36.24.69 🆅
🍷 by appt.

CH. LA PERRIERE

Sur lie 2002★

	6 ha	40,000	🍾 🍷	3–5 €

Not far from the wine museum in Le Pallet, the Château La Perrière has made an intense and complex wine blending floral touches with apricot scents. The rich and powerful palate also provides excellent freshness. Leave this 2002 a little longer.
🍾 Vincent Loiret, Ch. La Perrière, 44330 Le Pallet, tel. 02.40.80.43.24, fax 02.40.80.46.99, e-mail viloiret@wanadoo.fr 🆅
🍷 ev. day except Sun. 8am–12 noon 2pm–6pm; cl. 10–20 Aug.

DOM. DES PERRIERES

Sur lie 2002★

	17 ha	30,000	🍾 🍷	3–5 €

The terroir of the eastern sector of Mouzillon generally produces late-ripening wines which need to be left until Easter – implying they need to remain on their fermentation lees until this time. True to the style, this averagely intense 2002 shows aromas with floral characteristics and provides quite a fresh and lively palate right through to the slightly acidic finish. The wine needs a little time before being served.
🍾 Philippe Augusseau, Les Perrières, 44330 Mouzillon, tel. 02.40.03.92.14, fax 02.40.03.92.14 🆅
🍷 by appt.

DOM. DES PERRIERES

Sur lie 2002★★

	4.8 ha	36,000	🍾 🍷	–3 €

Near the famous ridge of Roche du Loroux-Bottereau which dominates the marshes and the Château de Goulaine, the Domaine des Perrières has produced a Muscadet of good intensity that mixes white fruits (peach) and flowers. The expressive and balanced palate has roundness, making it a perfect match for a meal of fish in sauce.
🍾 Daniel Pineau, La Martelière, 44430 Le Loroux-Bottereau, tel. 02.40.33.81.82, fax 02.40.33.81.82 🆅
🍷 by appt.

DOM. DES PETITES COSSARDIERES

Sur lie Cuvée Vieilles Vignes 2002★

	5 ha	34,600	🍾 🍷	3–5 €

The Domaine des Petites Cossardières has already been honoured in the *Guide: coup de coeur* for its Gros Plant 94 and its Muscadet-Sèvre et Maine Sur Lie 97. This lively-coloured 2002 selection offers a restrained nose, followed on by a palate showing the freshness of aniseed to start with and overall good balance. It will express its potential better in a few months.
🍾 Jean-Claude Couillaud, 17, rue de la Loire, 44430 Le Landreau, tel. 02.40.06.42.81, fax 02.40.06.49.14, e-mail jeanclaude.couillaud@wanadoo.fr 🆅
🍷 by appt.

DOM. DES PIERRES BLANCHES

Sur lie 2002★★

	7.67 ha	60,400	🍾 🍷	3–5 €

The powerful aromas of fresh fruits evolve towards ripe fruits, presaging the round and soft palate. This wine is worth trying today accompanied by a dish of guinea fowl with cabbage.
🍾 EARL Albert, 18, rue des Ouches, 44120 Vertou, tel. 02.40.34.81.27, fax 02.40.34.81.27 🆅
🍷 by appt.
🍾 Pierrick Albert

CH. DE LA PINGOSSIERE

Sur lie Tête de cuvée 2002★★

	6 ha	30,000	🍾 🍷	5–8 €

Located in the middle of the vineyards to the northeast of Vallet, it is not easy to find the Château de la Pingossière, however this wine is worth the detour. With a powerful aroma, the wine is rich and gives an enjoyable fruity impression, at the same time showing the typicity of its terroir of origin. To enjoy it at its best, it will be necessary to wait a while. **Cuvée Grand Or Sur Lie 2002 (3–5 €)** from the Guilbaud brothers also obtains two stars for its elegant fruity and floral range of flavours, and its fine middle palate.
🍾 SCEA Guilbaud-Moulin, 1, rue de la Planche, 44330 Mouzillon, tel. 02.40.06.90.69, fax 02.40.06.90.69 🆅
🍷 by appt.

DOM. DE LA POULFRIERE

Sur lie 2002★

	4.05 ha	10,000	🍾 🍷	5–8 €

The name of Poulfrière is that of a registered plot on the estate. This quite intense and bright-coloured wine is reminiscent of yellow flowers and ripe fruits. The palate continues in the same vein with peach and apricot, showing a good balance between richness and acidity. This expressive 2002 is the quintessence of good Muscadet.
🍾 Bernard et Christophe Paquereau, 8, La Poulfrière, 44330 Mouzillon, tel. 02.40.54.02.96, fax 02.40.54.08.57, e-mail paquereau.gaec@free.fr 🆅
🍷 ev. day except Sun. 8am–12.30pm 2pm–6.30pm

DOM. DE LA PROUTIERE

Sur lie Cuvée royale 2002★

	4.5 ha	12,000	🍾 🍷	3–5 €

From a gabbro (dark, volcanic rock) terroir, this beautifully limpid wine arouses interest with its developed and powerful aromas. The supple and very long palate confirms the quality of this wine.
🍾 GAEC Blanchard, 4, Le Quarteron, 44190 Gorges, tel. 02.40.54.07.82, fax 02.40.36.01.76 🆅
🍷 by appt.

DOM. DE LA PYRONNIERE

Sur lie 2002★

	2 ha	8,000	🍾 🍷	3–5 €

The Domaine de la Pyronnière vinifies its wines traditionally, while controlling temperatures. Its pale coloured 2002 is very typical of the appellation with a finely floral nose. The first impression on the palate remains lively, with pronounced freshness and structure from its terroir. Keep this wine for another two or three years.
🍾 EARL Stéphane et Henri Drouet, La Pyronnière, 44190 Gorges, tel. 06.80.10.06.38, fax 02.40.06.98.98 🆅
🍷 ev. day except Sun. 8.30am–7pm; Sat. 8.30am–12 noon; cl. 15–30 Aug.

LOIRE

DOM. DU RAFOU

Sur lie Clos de Béjarry 2002★

	8 ha	40,000	🍾 ♦		3–5€

Dominating Sanguèze, the Domaine du Rafou is one of the best estates of Tillières. Characterised by its terroir, its wine is powerfully full of flavour, balanced with an enjoyable roundness right from the start. It can be kept for another two years to enable it to express itself fully.

🍷 EARL Marc et Jean Luneau, Dom. du Rafou de Béjarry, 49230 Tillières, tel. 02.41.70.68.78, fax 02.41.70.68.78 ☑
🍷 by appt.

DOM. DES ROUAUDIERES

Sur lie 2002★★

	n.c.	10,000	🍾 ♦		3–5€

Still restrained, this wine comes from the late-ripening vines of Mouzillon. A nose of apple and grapefruit opens up gradually and gives an impression of freshness. The flavours build in power on the well-made palate. Leave this in your cellar for a while.

🍷 Jacky Bordet, La Rouaudière, 44330 Mouzillon, tel. 02.40.36.22.46, fax 02.40.36.39.84 ☑
🍷 ev. day 8am–12 noon 2pm–7pm

DOM. PATRICK SAILLANT

Sur lie 2002★

	2.25 ha	11,000	🍾 ♦		3–5€

On the border of Maisdon and Château-Thébaud, La Grenaudière overlooks the River Maine. This Muscadet is a little restrained on the nose, but is full of character and structured on the palate. A sensation of freshness is released with a middle palate of great finesse.

🍷 EARL Saillant-Esneu, 8, La Grenaudière, 44690 Maisdon-sur-Sèvre, tel. 02.40.03.80.10, fax 02.40.03.80.10 ☑
🍷 by appt.
🍷 Patrick Saillant

DOMINIQUE SALMON

Sur lie Réserve du fief Cognard 2002★

	20 ha	140,000	🍾 ♦		3–5€

Elegant with pale yellow highlights and an expressive nose leaning towards mineral notes, this wine asserts itself on the palate from the first impression with a straightforward and slightly acid touch. The roundness and light sparkle balance together harmoniously.

🍷 Dominique Salmon, Les Landes de Vin, 44690 Château-Thébaud, tel. 02.40.06.53.66, fax 02.40.06.55.42 ☑
🍷 by appt.

DOM. DE LA SAULZAIE

Sur lie 2002★★

	1.18 ha	8,900	🍾 ♦		3–5€

The terroir of the Chapelle-Basse-Mer produces rather early maturing wines. The Domaine de la Saulzaie 2002 is no exception to the rule. Its aromas of wild flowers and lemon lean towards grapefruit on the rich and full palate that finishes on a slightly acid touch. Ready to drink, this wine could be served with salmon cooked with dill, for example.

🍷 EARL Luc Pétard, 60, rte de la Loire, 44450 La Chapelle-Basse-Mer, tel. 02.40.33.30.92, fax 02.40.33.30.92 ☑
🍷 by appt.

LA SEIGNEURIE DE LA BARILLIERE

Sur lie Vieilles Vignes 2002★★

	1.5 ha	7,500	🍾 ♦		3–5€

Perfectly balanced, this yellow and straw-tinged Muscadet-Sèvre et Maine develops intense aromas of honey and *pain d'épice*, and on the palate provides an impression of great weight. This perfect harmony is worthy of a match with grilled lobster with *fines herbes*.

🍷 Xavier Gouraud, 1, Le Pin, 44330 Mouzillon, tel. 02.40.36.62.85, fax 02.40.36.39.95, e-mail xavier.gouraud@worldonline.fr ☑
🍷 by appt.

DOM. DE LA SENSIVE

Sur lie Grande Réserve 2002★

	10 ha	70,000	🍾 ♦		5–8€

The Domaine de la Sensive, at the gateway to the vineyard of Haute-Goulaine, is distinguished by being directed by two women. It produced a quite flavourful wine with fruit, especially peaches, dominating. A delicate start on the palate prolongs these tones and it goes on to a long finish. In general, the balance is excellent.

🍷 GFA Dom. de La Sensive, Le Landreau-Village, 44330 Vallet, tel. 02.40.33.90.23, fax 02.40.33.90.23 ☑
🍷 by appt.
🍷 Drouet-Bonhomme

ANTOINE SUBILEAU

Sur lie Marie-Louise 2002★

	117 ha	920,000	🍾 ♦		–3€

In 1998 this old Nantais négociant house built a very modern vinification plant. This selection gives a mixture of apple and lime scents on the nose. Well balanced, slightly sparkling and fruity, the wine is easy to drink and will not disappoint.

🍷 SA Antoine Subileau, 6, rue Saint-Vincent, 44330 Vallet, tel. 02.40.36.69.70, fax 02.40.36.63.99, e-mail antoine-subileau@wanadoo.fr

DOM. DE LA THEBAUDIERE

Sur lie 2002★★

	1.17 ha	9,000	🍾 ♦		3–5€

La Thébaudière continues on from the hill of La Roche from where there is a splendid panorama on to the Goulaine marshes. The wine from this estate has character, an intense range of aromas, pronounced by its terroir. Quite balanced, it has the imprint of freshness and exudes floral notes on the finish.

🍷 EARL Philippe Pétard, La Thébaudière, 44430 Le Loroux-Bottereau, tel. 02.40.33.81.81, fax 02.40.33.81.81 ☑
🍷 ev. day except Sun. 8am–12.30pm 2.30pm–7pm

LA TOUR DU FERRE

Sur lie 2002★

	4.5 ha	33,000	🍾 ♦		5–8€

Close to Clos du Ferré, a famous terroir of the Nantes area, this estate has produced a characteristic wine, managing to be both powerful and fresh at the same time, with the nose delicately underlined with honeysuckle. It is ready to drink now. From the same estate, the **Muscadet-Sèvre et Maine 2001 (8–11 €)** is peppery and full, it also obtains a star.

🍷 Philippe Douillard, La Champinière, 44330 Vallet, tel. 02.40.36.61.77, fax 02.40.36.38.30, e-mail fdouillard@terre-net.fr ☑
🍷 by appt.

DOM. DE LA TOURLAUDIERE

Sur lie Vieilles Vignes 2002★

	6 ha	22,000	🍾 ♦		5–8€

Behind its gold colour adorned with fine beads of bubbles, this old vine selection shows a nose of good intensity, with dominant apple and pear fruits. Rich, full and slightly sparkling, it finishes on a touch of bitterness which will tone down in time.

🍷 EARL Petiteau-Gaubert, Dom. de La Tourlaudière, 174, Bonne-Fontaine, 44330 Vallet, tel. 02.40.36.24.86, fax 02.40.36.29.72, e-mail tourlaudiere2@wanadoo.fr ☑
🍷 by appt.
🍷 R. et J. Petiteau

DOM. DES TROIS VERSANTS

Sur lie La Févrie 2002★

	10 ha	60,000	🍾 ♦		3–5€

A pretty winemaker's village bordering the River Sèvre, Févrie is famous for its young vine plants selected by generations of nurseries and wine-growers. The nose on this wine is restrained at first, but then opens up to complex stony flavours with gun-flint. On the palate it reveals some mineral flavours.

🔹 Yves Bretonnière, La Févrie, 44690 Maisdon-sur-Sèvre, tel. 02.40.54.89.27, fax 02.40.54.86.08 ☑
Ⴤ by appt.

DOM. DU VIEUX FRENE
Sur lie 2002★

	2 ha	14,000	🍾 ⚜	5–8 €

This typical Nantais estate moved in the 1960s from mixed farming to dedicated vine growing. The wines, from the late-ripening sectors of this eastern part of the vineyard, have a pronounced character. This bright-coloured 2002 has an intense nose and a fresh palate thanks to the presence of a slight sparkle. It shows good balance but needs to mature to develop richness.

🔹 EARL Baudrit, La Récivière, 44330 Mouzillon, tel. 02.40.36.47.70, fax 02.40.36.47.70 ☑
Ⴤ ev. day except Sun. 8am–12 noon 2pm–8pm

DANIEL ET GERARD VINET
Sur lie Le Muscadet 1999★★

	n.c.	n.c.	🍾 ⚜	5–8 €

Generally La Haye-Fouassière produces very fine wines, such as this subtle, fruity 99 with flavours of melon, white fruits and nuts. Thanks to its softness and remarkable balance, this wine can still be left for another two years.

🔹 Daniel et Gérard Vinet, La Quilla, 44690 La Haye-Fouassière, tel. 02.40.54.88.96, fax 02.40.54.89.84, e-mail gerard.vinet@wanadoo.fr ☑
Ⴤ by appt.

Wines selected but not starred

DOM. DE LA CHENAIE
Sur lie Cuvée Prestige 2002

	16.5 ha	50,000	🍾 ⚜	3–5 €

🔹 EARL Katia et Dominique Martin, Dom. de la Chenaie, Les Sauvionnières, 44330 Vallet, tel. 02.40.36.23.04, fax 02.40.36.23.04 ☑
Ⴤ by appt.

LES FRERES COUILLAUD
Collection privée M 1999

	2 ha	15,000	🍾 ⚜	8–11 €

🔹 GAEC Ragotière, Couillaud Frères, Ch. Ragotière, 44330 La Regrippière, tel. 02.40.33.60.56, fax 02.40.33.61.89 ☑
Ⴤ ev. day 8am–12 noon 2pm–6pm

JOEL FORGEAU
Sur lie Le Coin des Evêques 2002

	6 ha	30,000	🍾 ⚜	5–8 €

🔹 Florence et Joël Forgeau, La Rouaudière, 44330 Mouzillon, tel. 02.40.33.95.37, fax 02.40.36.47.33, e-mail joel-forgeau@wanadoo.fr ☑
Ⴤ by appt.

DOM. DES HAUTES NOELLES
Sur lie Vieilles Vignes 2002

	12 ha	60,000	🍾 🍶 ⚜	3–5 €

🔹 Pierre Bertin, Dom. des Hautes Noëlles, 44430 Le Landreau, tel. 02.40.06.44.06, fax 02.40.06.47.90, e-mail pierre.bertin.dhn@wanadoo.fr ☑
Ⴤ by appt.

DOM. DE LA RENOUERE
Sur lie 2002

	4.2 ha	26,000	🍾 ⚜	3–5 €

🔹 Vincent Viaud, La Renouère, 44430 Le Landreau, tel. 02.40.06.43.05, fax 02.40.06.46.01, e-mail viaudv@club-internet.fr ☑
Ⴤ by appt.

Muscadet Côtes de Grand-Lieu

LE DEMI-BOEUF
Sur lie 2002★

	n.c.	n.c.	🍾 ⚜	3–5 €

The name "Demi-Boeuf" originates from a legend dating back to the wars of the Vendée. *Les Blancs* (the Royalists) would have eaten half an ox before being driven out by the revolutionist armies. This vineyard is located on green rocks, which give very characteristic and complex wines with aromas reminiscent of broom with a nuance of mango. On tasting the wine, there follows an impression of finesse and lightness. The **Gros Plant Sur Lie 2002** was singled out, too.

🔹 EARL Michel Malidain, Le Demi-Boeuf, 44310 La Limouzinière, tel. 02.40.05.82.29, fax 02.40.05.95.97, e-mail m.malidain@free.fr ☑
Ⴤ by appt.

DOM. DU FIEF GUERIN
Sur lie 2002★★★

	17 ha	130,000	🍾 ⚜	3–5 €

By taking the old route from Nantes to Pornic, on your right you will find an old 16th century residence, and then a pretty vineyard which extends along the road up to a large umbrella pine. This is the estate and vineyard of Fief Guérin, amounting to approximately 17 ha. The vines, clinging on to this gun-flint soil, produce a well-structured wine that expresses all the minerality of a good terroir. After an intense nose, rich and floral, the palate responds by being rounded, long and very expressive; absolutely an interesting wine.

🔹 Jérôme Choblet, Les Herbauges, 44830 Bouaye, tel. 02.40.65.44.92, fax 02.40.65.58.02, e-mail choblet@domaine-des-herbauges.com ☑
Ⴤ by appt.

CH. DE LA GRANGE
Sur lie 2002★

	15 ha	50,000	🍾 ⚜	3–5 €

The Château de la Grange belongs to an old Nantes family, the Goulaines. This significant property, located primarily on

green rocks, presents a brilliant yellow Muscadet Côtes de Grand-Lieu, with a very fine, floral and concentrated nose. On the palate, it also reveals a great concentration of exotic fruits. The château also produces a very characteristic **Gros Plant Sur Lie 2002 (–3 €)** which was singled out.
Comte Baudouin de Goulaine, Ch. de la Grange, 44650 Corcoué-sur-Logne, tel. 02.40.26.68.66, fax 02.40.26.61.89
by appt.

DOM. DE LA GUILLAUDIERE
Sur lie 2002★★

4.39 ha 34,000 –3 €

The Domaine de la Guillaudière was put together ten years ago in the village of Corcoué-sur-Logne. Driving from Corcoué towards Roche-Servière, you will not be able to miss this entirely new estate. From a terroir of "green rocks", this Muscadet Côtes du Grand-Lieu offers a nose that has great intensity while being very elegant, too. On the palate, it is well balanced, with a certain personality that promises a good future. **Gros Plant Sur Lie Château de la Gillières 2002** from the Sèvre et Maine area also has obtained a star.
Dominique Régnier, SAS des Gillières, 44690 La Haye-Fouassière, tel. 02.40.54.80.05, fax 02.40.54.89.56
by appt.

DOM. DU HAUT BOURG
Sur lie Cuvée Le Pavillon 2002★★

4 ha 20,000 3–5 €

The Domaine du Haut Bourg has been given a special mention in the *Guide* several times. This 40-ha property is established on a terroir which has been protected from the intense urbanization of the village of Bouaye. Its Muscadet Côtes du Grand-Lieu Sur Lie has a sustained colour with tinges of green. On the nose, it shows very intense flavours of exotic fruits. Very rich on the palate, but with a touch of attractive bitterness, this leads us to predict that this wine can be aged.
SCA Dom. du Haut Bourg, 11, rue de Nantes, 44830 Bouaye, tel. 02.40.65.47.69, fax 02.40.32.64.01
ev. day except Sun. 9am–12 noon 2pm–7pm

DOM. DU PARC
Sur lie 2002★★

6.6 ha 40,000 5–8 €

By taking the road from Corcoué-sur-Logne to Roche-Servière, you can find the Domaine du Parc. Produced from a hillside of amphibolite rock, its Muscadet Côtes du Grand-Lieu has a very lively nose, and shows beautiful length on the palate; perhaps a little closed at present, but this is a wine for ageing, and one can expect good development in the long term, characteristic of wines produced on this type of soil.
EARL Pierre Dahéron, Dom. du Parc, 44650 Corcoué-sur-Logne, tel. 02.40.05.86.11, fax 02.40.05.94.98
by appt.

LES VIGNERONS DES TERROIRS DE LA NOELLE Sur lie Lieu-dit Grandville 2002★

n.c. 45,000 3–5 €

The cooperative of Noëlle vinifies wines from 783 ha of vines. The Grandville *lieu-dit* draws its name from a château built in the 1820s, which dominates Achneau. Clear and bright, this Muscadet Côtes du Grand-Lieu is cut through with a tinge of green and offers an excellent menthol nose. It retains great freshness on the palate, very good balance and a long length.
Les Vignerons des Terroirs de la Noëlle, bd des Alliés, BP 155, 44154 Ancenis Cedex, tel. 02.40.98.92.72, fax 02.40.98.96.70, e-mail vignerons-noelle@cana.fr
by appt.

Gros Plant AOVDQS

Gros Plant du Pays Nantais is a dry, white wine, AOVDQS since 1954, made from a single grape variety, Folle Blanche, originally from the Charente, and here called Gros Plant. Like Muscadet, Gros Plant can be bottled on the lees and is perfect for seafood in general and shellfish in particular. It should also be served chilled, but not ice-cold at 8–9°C.

DOM. DE BEAU-LIEU
Sur lie 2002★

1.08 ha 10,000 3–5 €

To the east of the village of Vallet, the Domaine de Beau-Lieu has part of its vines located in the catchment area of Saugeze, one of the most famous terroirs of this village. This estate produces a lively, clear-coloured Gros Plant, with a very characteristic palate, good grip and a slight tartness.
GAEC Travers Fils, Dom. de Beau-Lieu, La Fosse, 44330 Vallet, tel. 02.40.33.91.58, fax 02.40.33.91.58
by appt.

DOM. DE BEAUREPAIRE
Sur lie 2002★

2.72 ha 5,000 5–8 €

The village of Mouzillon, famous for its Gallo-Roman bridge, harvests its grapes quite late due to its geographical position and geological make-up with many outcrops of "green rocks". This elegant wine shows great finesse and good length on the palate. It would be ideal with a dozen Brittany oysters.
Jean-Paul Bouin-Boumard, 5, La Recivière, 44330 Mouzillon, tel. 02.40.36.35.97, fax 02.40.36.35.97
ev. day 10am–7pm; Sun. by appt.

DOM. DE LA BLANCHETIERE
Sur lie 2002★★

1.5 ha 7,000 –3 €

Located by the boundary between the villages of Loroux-Bottereau and Landreau, this 25-ha estate is owned by the Luneau family which has cultivated the vine there since the 15th century. Established on mica-schist, the Folle Blanche produces a very fresh Gros Plant with a floral note, a light sparkle, characteristic of wines matured on their fine lees, and good length.
Christophe Luneau, Dom. de La Blanchetière, 44430 Le Loroux-Bottereau, tel. 02.40.06.43.18, fax 02.40.06.43.18
by appt.

DOM. DE LA BOITAUDIERE
Sur lie 2002★★★

8.85 ha 41,300 –3 €

Selected unanimously by all the tasters, this Gros Plant is the work of Serge Sauvêtre. Remarkably powerful and balanced, it exudes intense aromas derived from wild hawthorn flowers. With very great richness on the palate, this lively wine has no

trace of aggressiveness. Currently at its peak, it will provide great satisfaction to connoisseurs.
➽ EARL Ch. de la Boitaudière, 44430 Le Landreau, tel. 02.40.06.42.69, fax 02.40.06.42.69 ☑

DOM. DE LA BRETONNIERE
Sur lie 2002★★

▪	4 ha	20,800	▪ ⚗	3–5 €

Located near the Château de Briacé, the village of La Bretonnière is completely dedicated to Gros Plant. This one has an intense and complex nose of quince, lemon and green apple. It ends with a full and long finish.
➽ GAEC Charpentier-Fleurance, La Bretonnière, 44430 Le Landreau, tel. 02.40.06.43.39, fax 02.40.06.44.05 ☑
⚗ by appt.

CH. DE BRIACE
Sur lie 2002★

▪	1.5 ha	16,000	▪ ⚗	3–5 €

The home of an important wine college for the Nantes area, the Château de Briacé burnt down during the period of the Revolution. The college trains a large number of local wine-growers in wine production and cultivates its own vines using sustainable agriculture linked with the Terra Vitis organization. The nose of this wine is very attractive, and the palate reveals a perfect balance between fruit and acidity.
➽ AFG Ch. de Briacé, Lycée agricole, 44430 Le Landreau, tel. 02.40.06.49.16, fax 02.40.06.46.15 ☑
⚗ by appt.

LA CHATELIERE
Sur lie 2002★★

▪	39.42 ha	410,000	▪ ⚗	–3 €

This Gros Plant has been made by the Rolandeau winemaking firm, the largest wine production cellar in the Nantes area that acts for producers to vinify grapes from neighbouring properties. This wine offers quite a fruity nose. With good length on the palate, it is well balanced.
➽ Les Vendangeoirs du Val de Loire, La Frémonderie, 49230 Tillières, tel. 02.41.70.45.93, fax 02.41.70.43.74, e-mail vvl@rolandeau.fr

DOM. LES COINS
Sur lie 2002★

▪	5 ha	18,000	▪ ⚗	3–5 €

The Domaine Les Coins is situated in the village of Corcoué-sur-Logne which has three churches (Saint-Jean, Saint-Etienne and Benate). The 90-ha property vinifies its wines in a traditional way. This *cuvée* recalls floral and lemony notes, and is fresh and lively on the palate with good weight. Also worth noting with one star is the **Muscadet Côtes de Grand-Lieu 2002** which has a very expressive, citrus fruit nose supported by excellent balance on the palate.
➽ Jean-Claude Malidain, Le Petit-Coin, 25 bis, rue du Stade, 44650 Corcoué-sur-Logne, tel. 02.40.05.95.95, fax 02.40.05.80.99, e-mail jeanclaude.malidain@free.fr ☑
⚗ by appt.

DOM. LE FAY D'HOMME
Sur lie 2002★★

▪	3.2 ha	14,000	▪ ⚗	–3 €

Based at this 36-ha domaine since 1986, Vincent Caillé has vinified a beautiful **Muscadet-Sèvre et Maine Sur Lie 2002 (3–5 €)**, and, more beautiful still, this bright Gros Plant with a crystalline appearance and a very powerful nose. Very supple and rich on the palate, it demonstrates real balance, which makes it worth discovering.
➽ Vincent Caillé, Les Coteaux, 44690 Monnières, tel. 02.40.54.62.06, fax 02.40.54.64.20, e-mail lefaydhomme@wanadoo.fr ☑
⚗ by appt.

LA GARNAUDIERE
Sur lie 2002★

▪	5 ha	2,000	▪ ⚗	3–5 €

The property of La Garnaudière is located on the site of an old 17th century manor. The unusual feature of the village of Limouzinière is the existence of a tower in the middle of the vineyards. This Gros Plant is a little closed at present but is fresh and delicate. It shows a certain elegance.
➽ Henri Denis, La Garnaudière, 44310 La Limouzinière, tel. 02.40.05.82.28, fax 02.40.05.99.43 ☑
⚗ by appt.

HAUTE-COUR DE LA DEBAUDIERE
Sur lie 2002★

▪	2.46 ha	13,000	▪ ⚗	–3 €

Located on a steep hillside on the border between Vallet and Monzillon, the estate of Débaudière obtained approval from the Terra Vitis association for its environmental vineyard practices for the 2002 vintage. With a fairly pale appearance, marked by a delicate golden reflection, this wine shows subtle aromas, full of finesse and delicacy. It is well balanced on the palate.
➽ Chantal et Yves Goislot, La Débaudière, 44330 Vallet, tel. 02.40.36.30.73, fax 02.40.36.20.23, e-mail ycgoislot@aol.fr ☑
⚗ by appt.

LA HAUTE-VRIGNAIS
Sur lie 2002★★★

▪	12.8 ha	61,045	▪ ⚗	–3 €

Sainte-Radegonde also owns a property in the Sèvre et Maine area in Loroux-Bottereau. The Gros Plant made from the Haut-Vrignais property at Saint-Philbert-de-Bonaine is very well balanced with a floral and expressive nose, as well as good balance on the palate. It is, in a word, a wine to enjoy.
➽ SCEA Abbaye de Sainte-Radegonde, 44430 Le Loroux-Bottereau, tel. 02.40.03.74.78, fax 02.40.03.79.91 ☑
⚗ by appt.
➽ Elzinga

DOM. DE LA PAPINIERE
Sur lie 2002★

▪	3.6 ha	5,000	▪	3–5 €

Tillières is one of the last vineyard villages before you arrive at the Mauges area. Lemony and mineral on the nose, this wine is full-bodied on the palate with substantial structure. It reveals complex flavours of pineapple and crystallized fruits with good length.
➽ GAEC Cousseau Frères, Dom. de La Papinière, 49230 Tillières. tel. 02.41.70.46.31, fax 02.41.58.61.51 ☑
⚗ by appt.

VINCENT ET STEPHANE PERRAUD
2002★

▪	1.5 ha	8,000	▪ ⚗	–3 €

This property is located 3 km from Clisson, a very attractive medieval town. The Gros Plant produced by this estate is a wine to drink soon: quite floral, it is reminiscent of acacia flowers. The citrus fruit finish, and more specifically grape-fruit, will make it a good match with shellfish.
➽ Stéphane et Vincent Perraud, Bournigal, 44190 Clisson, tel. 02.40.54.45.62, fax 02.40.54.45.62 ☑
⚗ ev. day except Sun. 8am–12.30pm 2pm–7pm

CH. LA PERRIERE
Sur lie 2002★

▪	3 ha	25,000	▪	–3 €

Located in the village of Pallet, famous for its chapel of Héloïse and Abélard, this 31-ha property produces quite a rich dry white wine, supported by good length on the palate. It is for current drinking.
➽ Vincent Loiret, Ch. La Perrière, 44330 Le Pallet, tel. 02.40.80.43.24, fax 02.40.80.46.99, e-mail viloiret@wanadoo.fr ☑
⚗ ev. day except Sun. 8am–12 noon 2pm–6pm; cl. 10–20 Aug.

DOM. DE LA ROCHERIE

Sur lie 2002★

	2 ha	8,000	🍴 🍷	–3 €

On a rather early-maturing terroir, the Domaine de la Rocherie produces quite a distinctive wine due to the hydromorphic and clay sands. The character is more pronounced on the palate than on the nose, and the wine has very good balance. It is so marked by its terroir that it is recommended for real lovers of Gros Plant.

➤ Daniel Gratas, La Rocherie, 44430 Le Landreau, tel. 02.40.06.41.55, fax 02.40.06.48.92 🆅
🍷 ev. day except Sun. 8am–8pm

CH. DE LA ROULIERE

Sur lie 2002★

	0.95 ha	5,000	🍴 🍷	3–5 €

Located a few kilometres from the Lac du Grand-Lieu, the Château de la Roulière produces a Gros Plant on a very unusual terroir of sand and *galets* (large pebbles). The wines resulting from this type of soil are full of flavour, fresh and delicious. After a good fresh start to the palate, this wine reveals good balance though a little firm. It seems ideal for connoisseurs, especially oyster lovers.

➤ René Erraud, Ch. de La Roulière, 44310 Saint-Colomban, tel. 02.40.05.80.24, fax 02.40.05.53.89 🆅
🍷 by appt.

YVONNICK ET THIERRY SAUVETRE

Sur lie 2002★

	1.8 ha	18,800	🍴 🍷	–3 €

Located at the exit of the village of Loroux-Botbereau on the road to Nantes, the estate produces a Gros Plant from schistous terroir. This wine has good intensity on the nose and attractive balance on the palate, with a slightly acid touch on the finish. It is very true-to-type.

➤ Sauvêtre et Fils, La Landelle, 44430 Le Loroux-Botbereau, tel. 02.40.33.81.48, fax 02.40.33.87.67 🆅
🍷 by appt.

DOM. DU VIEUX PRESSOIR 2002★★

	0.5 ha	5,200	🍴 🍷	–3 €

In the village of Saint-Lumine-de-Clisson, among the various farms, one comes across a few islands of vineyards from which wine-producers are making some good wines. This Gros Plant vinified on its fine lees is very pleasant to drink. It exudes floral and fruity flavours, more specifically quince.

➤ Bernard Maillard, Les Défois, 44190 Saint-Lumine-de-Clisson, tel. 02.40.54.74.37, fax 02.40.54.71.29, e-mail bernard.maillard5@wanadoo.fr 🆅
🍷 by appt.

Fiefs Vendéens
AOVDQS

Historically these domains were the property of Cardinal Richelieu. The name of this appellation is evocative of the history of these wines, replanted in the Middle Ages, as so often at the instigation of the monks, and later enjoyed by the Cardinal. The denomination AOVDQS was awarded in 1984 in recognition of the efforts made to improve quality and these continue on the 453 ha planted with vines, which, in 2002 produced 22,114 hl of red and rosé wine and 3,068 of white.

The Mareuil region produces rosés and fine reds with good bouquet and fruit from Gamay, Cabernet and Pinot Noir; the whites are little known. The Brem vineyard, not far from the sea, produces dry whites from Chenin and Grolleau Gris, but also some rosé and red wines. In the area round Fontenay-le-Comte, dry whites are made (from Chenin, Colombard, Melon and Sauvignon), while rosés and reds (Gamay and Cabernet) come from the regions of Pissotte and Vix. These wines should be drunk young, partnering the appropriate dishes.

DOM. DE LA CAMBAUDIERE 2002★

	3 ha	13,000	🍴 🍷	3–5 €

Pinot Noir (60%, as against 40% Gamay) dominates in this pale pink *cuvée* with orange tinges. Delicate flavours highlight raspberry in particular, while the palate, soft to start with, moves on towards a slightly tart finish. The **red Fiefs Vendéens 2002**, with Cabernet dominating is given a special mention.

➤ Michel Arnaud, La Cambaudière, 85320 Rosnay, tel. 02.51.30.55.12, fax 02.51.28.21.02 🆅
🍷 by appt.

COIRIER

Pissotte Sélection 2002★

	8 ha	50,000	🍴 🍷	5–8 €

Located at the far east of the Fiefs Vendéens area, near the forest of Morvent, the village of Pissotte is famous for its wines. This deep raspberry pink wine charms with its delicate flavours and rich body. Powerful and persistent, it will go well with grilled eels.

➤ GAEC Coirier, La Petite Groie, 15, rue des Gélinières, 85200 Pissotte, tel. 02.51.69.40.98, fax 02.51.69.74.15 🆅
🍷 by appt.

DOM. DES DAMES

Les Aigues Marines 2002★★

	7 ha	15,000	🍴 🍷	3–5 €

Here is a superb wine with an intense nose of soft red berries, especially raspberry. Delicate and balanced, notes of Morello cherry can be picked out on the long palate, and these support its acidity very nicely. From the same producer, the **white Mareuil Les Pierres Blanches 2002** and the **Mareuil Les Agates red 2002** are given a special mention.

➤ GAEC Vignoble Daniel Gentreau, Follet, 85320 Rosnay, tel. 02.51.30.55.39, fax 02.51.28.22.36, e-mail domaine.des.dames@oreka.com 🆅
🍷 by appt.

DOM. DU LUX EN ROC

Brem Rosé d'une nuit 2002★

	n.c.	6,500	🍴 🍷	3–5 €

Brem-sur-Mer has maintained its exceptional terroir that looks over the sea. There this estate has produced a deep orange-coloured rosé. A nuance of ripe fruit appears on the palate and this adds to an impression of sweetness. Also interesting is the **red Brem 2001**, with a base of 38% Négrette, a grape variety from the Frontonnais called "Ragoutant" in the Vendée. Slightly musky on the nose, fruity on the palate and reasonably tannic, it is also singled out.

☛ Jean-Pierre Richard, 5, imp. Richelieu, 85470 Brem-sur-Mer, tel. 02.51.90.56.84 ☑
☒ ev. day except Sun. 9.30am–12.30pm 3pm–7.30pm

CH. MARIE DU FOU

Mareuil 2002★

| ■ | 25.57 ha | 210,000 | ■ ↓ | 3–5€ |

In the Middle Ages the Château Marie du Fou was the famous impregnable fortress of the ducs de Mareuil. Today, its vineyard produces this blend of Cabernets (60%) and Pinot Noir (40%). Bright and slightly purple, the wine exudes a subtle blackcurrant aroma, and then discovers power on the long palate. Also given a special mention was the **white Château Marie du Fou Mareuil 2002**.
☛ J. Mourat Père et Fils, 5, rue de la Trémoille, 85320 Mareuil-sur-Lay, tel. 02.51.97.20.10, fax 02.51.97.21.58, e-mail chateau.marie.du.fou@wanadoo.fr ☑
☒ ev. day except Mon. Sun. 9am–12.30pm 2.30pm–7pm

CH. DE ROSNAY

Mareuil Vieilles Vignes 2002★

| ■ | 9 ha | 45,000 | ■ ↓ | 3–5€ |

The Château de Rosnay, located in the heart of the village of the same name, has made a rosé with an expressive bouquet, on the fruity side. Soft on the palate, this very harmonious and balanced 2002 keeps going until a long and intense finish. From the same producer, the **white Mareuil Elegance 2002** has ripe citrus fruits and obtains a star, while the **red Mareuil Vieilles Vignes 2002** is also singled out.
☛ Christian Jard, EARL Ch. de Rosnay, 85320 Rosnay, tel. 02.51.30.59.06, fax 02.51.28.21.01, e-mail christianjard@tiscali.fr ☑
☒ ev. day 9am–12 noon 2pm–6pm

DOM. SAINT NICOLAS

Brem Reflets 2002★★

| ■ | 4 ha | 16,000 | ■ ↓ | 5–8€ |

The Domaine Saint Nicolas, which is working towards biodynamic wine production, presents a slightly raspberry-coloured rosé, with attractive red berry fruit aromas. Rounded to begin with, the power of this wine builds up nicely on the palate and would go with a local ham. **Brem Les Clous 2002 white (8–11 €)**, based on Chenin and Chardonnay is given a special mention.
☛ M.-J. Michon et Fils, 11, rue des Vallées, 85470 Brem-sur-Mer, tel. 02.51.33.13.04, fax 02.51.33.18.42, e-mail contact@domaine-saint-nicolas.com ☑
☒ by appt.

DOM. DE LA VIEILLE RIBOULERIE

Mareuil Cuvée des Moulins Brûlés 2002★

| ■ | 4 ha | 8,000 | ■ ↓ | 3–5€ |

Cardinal Richelieu appreciated the wines from these Vendée soils. At the edge of the River Yon, this 17-ha estate has produced an intensely flavourful 2002, a blend of 60% Gamay with Cabernet Franc. The tannins seem already integrated and supple, but the slight astringency on the finish suggests that this wine can be kept a few months. Also very successful, the **white Mareuil 2002**, really fresh with notes of grapefruit, and the **Mareuil Cuvée de Rêves Yon 2002 rosé** is scented and rich.
☛ Hubert Macquigneau, Le Plessis, 85320 Rosnay, tel. 02.51.30.59.54, fax 02.51.28.21.80 ☑
☒ ev. day 8am–12 noon 2pm–7pm; Sun. by appt.

Coteaux d'Ancenis AOVDQS

The Coteaux d'Ancenis wine region has been classified AOVDQS since 1954. Four single-variety wines are produced: from Gamay (80% of production), Cabernet, Chenin and Malvoisie. The area under vines is 130 ha and in 2002 production was 15,509 hl, of which about 504 hl was white wine.

EGLISE SAINT-PIERRE

Gamay 2002★★

| ■ | 19 ha | 100,000 | ■ ↓ | 3–5€ |

Vinified exclusively from Gamay by the wine cooperative at Noëlle, this Coteaux d'Ancenis is of an elegant cherry-red appearance. On the nose, it reveals a rich cocktail of fruits, notably blackcurrant and blueberry. Its round and soft structure means that it can be drunk right away. A special mention is given to **La Pierre Couvretière 2002**, which is slightly spicy on the nose, refreshing and fruity, with fairly soft tannins.
☛ Les Vignerons des Terroirs de la Noëlle, bd des Alliés, BP 155, 44154 Ancenis Cedex, tel. 02.40.98.92.72, fax 02.40.98.96.70, e-mail vignerons-noelle@cana.fr ☑
☒ by appt.

DOM. DES GALLOIRES

Gamay 2002★

| ■ | 1.28 ha | 10,000 | ■ | –3€ |

The Domaine des Galloires is based in the grounds of an old manor founded in the 11th century, which belonged to the lords of Tourlandry, ancestors of Joachim du Bellay. This bright-coloured Gamay has a raspberry nose with a freshness about it. Drink it with a barbecue before Christmas. Also very successful, is a soft and elegant **red Gamay 2002 Cuvée Sélection (3–5 €)** with a slightly peppery finish. Similarly noted is the **Muscadet des Coteaux de la Loire, Cuvée Terroir 2002 (3–5 €)**, which was singled out by the Jury.
☛ GAEC des Galloires, Dom. des Galloires, 49530 Drain, tel. 02.40.98.20.10, fax 02.40.98.22.06, e-mail contact@galloires.com ☑
☒ by appt.

DOM. DES GENAUDIERES

Malvoisie 2002★★

| ■ | 1.5 ha | 10,000 | ■ ↓ | 5–8€ |

Located on an exceptional site, the Domaine des Génaudières enjoys a panoramic view over the Loire. This sweet Coteaux d'Ancenis is a pure Malvoisie, a very rare grape variety in this area. Everything about it suggests finesse and harmony. The delicate flavours recall white and crystallized fruits of peach and apricot; the elegant palate has nuances of fruit. Given a special mention is the **Muscadet des Coteaux de la Loire Sur Lie 2002 white (3–5 €)**, with an intense floral nose, it is soft and balanced.
☛ EARL Athimon et ses Enfants, Dom. des Génaudières, 44850 Le Cellier, tel. 02.40.25.40.27, fax 02.40.25.35.61 ☑
☒ ev. day except Sun. 9am–12 noon 2pm–7pm

DOM. DU HAUT FRESNE

Pineau 2002★★

| ■ | 0.5 ha | 2,000 | ▥ | 3–5€ |

Overlooking the Loire, the Domaine du Haut Fresne makes the visitor wonder whether it is still within the Nantes area or actually in Anjou. This is due not only to the make-up of its soil but also to the grape varieties cultivated here. The yellow-golden Chenin or Pineau, which has been replanted on this estate offers most attractive flavours characteristic of very ripe late-harvested grapes, and also provides a vanilla note from its maturation in cask. It can be drunk in four or five years. A special mention is given to the **Muscadet des**

Coteaux de la Loire Sur Lie 2002 which has an attractive citrus fruit note.
❧ Renou Frères, Dom. du Haut Fresne, 49530 Drain, tel. 02.40.98.26.79, fax 02.40.98.27.86 ☑
� ev. day except Sun. 9am–12 noon 2pm–6pm

❧ EARL Allard-Redureau, La Tranchaie, 49530 Liré, tel. 02.40.09.06.88, fax 02.40.09.03.04 ☑
� ev. day except Tue. Sun. 8am–8pm

CH. DE LA VARENNE
Sur lie 2002★★

	4 ha	30,660	🍶 🥄	-3 €

With its imposing château dominating the Loire, Varenne is the largest village in the Maine-et-Loire registered for the appellation Muscadet des Coteaux de la Loire. Pascal Pauvert has produced a bright yellow-tinged wine there, which reveals floral aromas. Fine and lingering on the palate, and quite firm, this is certain of a great future. It might suit drinking with a terrine of monkfish with *fines herbes*.
❧ Pascal Pauvert, Le Marais, 49270 La Varenne, tel. 02.40.98.55.58

Muscadet Coteaux de la Loire Sur Lie

DOM. DE LA CAMBUSE
Sur lie 2002★★

	5 ha	1,500	🍶	-3 €

The Domaine de la Cambuse is a small vineyard of 5 ha in Muscadet, whose wine has been singled out by the tasters. Very typical of a Muscadet des Coteaux de la Loire, on the palate this lively 2002 reveals a really clean and mouth-filling mineral quality. However, this wine needs to be aerated before tasting at its best. **Coteaux d'Ancenis Gamay 2002 red** from the same property obtains two stars: it is fresh and delicious, fruity and soft.
❧ Dom. de la Cambuse, 49530 Drain, tel. 02.40.83.91.63 ☑
� ev. day except Sun. 9am–12.30pm 2pm–7pm
❧ Toublanc

DOM. DU MOULIN GIRON
Sur lie 2002★★

	1.5 ha	4,000	🍶 🥄	3-5 €

The Domaine du Moulin Giron is a regular in the *Guide*: it was *coup de cœur* in 2003. Overlooking the Loire, this property is located in the village of Liré, on the border between the Nantes and Anjou areas. Very typical of the appellation, this powerful 2002 exhibits a mineral nose, powerful and intense, underlined by notes of white fruits. It is characterized by good length on the palate, by finesse and by balance.
❧ EARL Dom. du Moulin Giron, Le Bois Prieur, 49530 Liré, tel. 02.40.09.03.15, fax 02.40.09.07.39 ☑
� by appt.
❧ Allard Père et Fille

DOM. DE SAINT MEEN
Sur lie 2002★

	5 ha	30,000	🍶 🥄	3-5 €

Originating in Landreau, Sèvre et Maine, the Luneau-Papin family was one of the first to cross the Loire to take on a vineyard in the Coteaux de la Loire region. The Domaine de Saint Méen dominates the river on an impressive hillside on the north bank. It offers a wine with a rather subtle nose, but showing quality. On the palate, this very rich 2002 has notes of liquorice and good weight. It needs a few months to open out completely. The same producer is given a special mention for **Muscadet-Sèvre et Maine Sur Lie Clos des Allées Vieilles Vignes 2002**.
❧ Pierre Luneau-Papin, Dom. Pierre de La Grange, 44430 Le Landreau, tel. 02.40.06.45.27, fax 02.40.06.46.62 ☑
� by appt.

DOM. DE LA VALLEE
Sur lie 2002★

	1.15 ha	7,800	🍶 🥄	3-5 €

In the village of Liré, the Domaine de la Vallée offers a golden-yellow-tinged Muscadet des Coteaux de la Loire with intense and unusual scents of hawthorn. On the palate, this soft 2002 reveals a light touch of bitterness on the finish. It needs to age a little to reach its peak. Also retained and given a special mention by the Jury was the **Coteaux d'Ancenis Gamay 2001 red**.

Wines selected but not starred

LES FOLIES SIFFAIT
Sur lie 2002

	20 ha	70,000	🍶 🥄	3-5 €

❧ Les Vignerons des Terroirs de la Noëlle, bd des Alliés, BP 155, 44154 Ancenis Cedex, tel. 02.40.98.92.72, fax 02.40.98.96.70, e-mail vignerons-noelle@cana.fr ☑
� by appt.

DOM. DE LA PLEIADE
Sur lie 2002

	2 ha	14,000	🍶 🥄	-3 €

❧ Bernard Crespin, rue de la Pléiade, 49530 Liré, tel. 02.40.09.01.39, fax 02.40.09.07.42 ☑
� ev. day except Sun. 8.30am–12.30pm 2pm–7pm

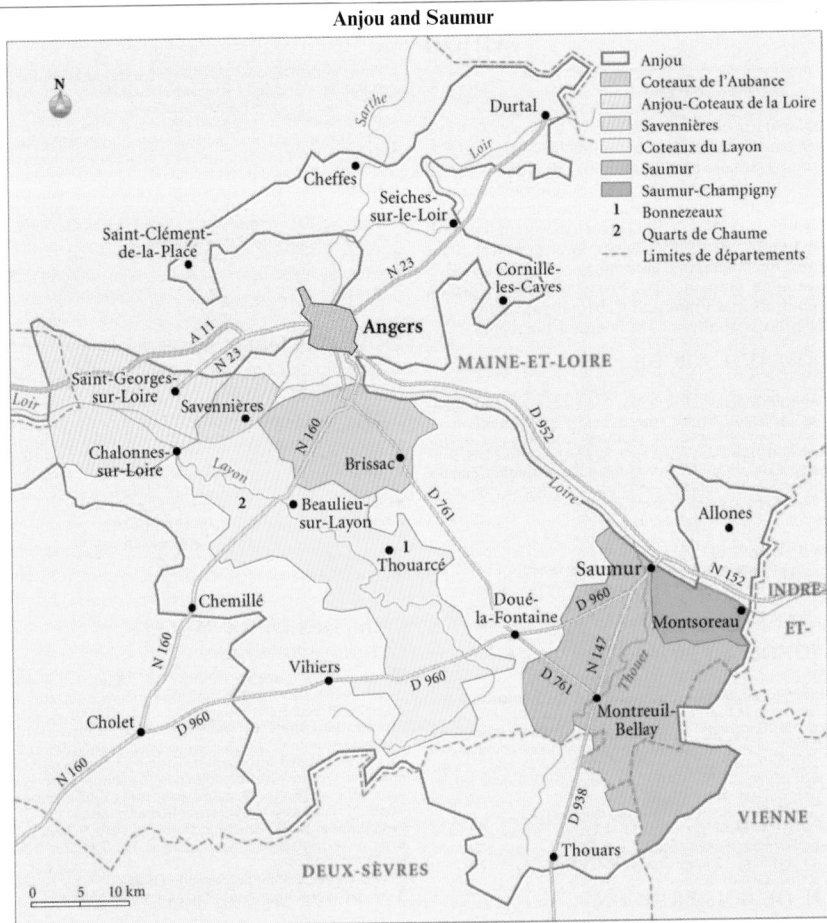

Anjou and Saumur

Anjou
Coteaux de l'Aubance
Anjou-Coteaux de la Loire
Savennières
Coteaux du Layon
Saumur
Saumur-Champigny
1 Bonnezeaux
2 Quarts de Chaume
--- Limites de départements

Anjou and Saumur

The Anjou and Saumur vineyards occupy Maine-et-Loire, extending a little into the north of the Vienne and the Deux-Sèvres. This undulating landscape, criss-crossed with numerous watercourses, lies at the northern limits of vine cultivation, under the influence of an Atlantic climate.

Vines have always been grown on the slopes of the Loire, the Layon, the Aubance, the Loir and the Thouet. At the end of the 19th century, the vineyard was at its most extensive. Dr Guyot, in a survey for the Minister of Agriculture, reported 31,000 ha under vines in Maine-et-Loire. Phylloxera was to decimate the vineyard, as everywhere else in France. Replanting took place at the beginning of the 20th century, with further efforts in the 1950s and 1960s, though it fell back thereafter. Today, the vineyard covers about 14,500 ha and produces from 800,000 to 1 million hl, depending on the weather.

As always, the combination of terroir and climate determines the character of the local wines. However, it is important to identify the clear difference between those grown on "Anjou Black" soils of schists and other primary rocks from the Massif Armorican, and those produced on "Anjou White", or Saumurois, the sedimentary soils of the Paris Basin, where white, chalky limestone is most in evidence. The rivers and streams of the region have also played an important role in the wine trade: one can still find ruins of the little loading ports on the Layon. Planting density is between 4,500 and 5,000 plants per hectare; pruning, which used mainly to be in goblet or fan shapes, is now more usually in cordons.

Anjou has always been best known for its sweet white wines, those from the Coteaux du Layon being the most highly rated. However, wine styles are changing, moving more towards semi-dry or dry white wines and to red wines. In Saumur, the reds are the most highly regarded, alongside the sparkling wines that have seen a significant increase, particularly the AOC Saumur-Mousseux and Crémant de Loire.

Anjou

The geographical area of this regional appellation, made up of a group of nearly 200 communes, incorporates all the Anjou AOCs. White wines are produced (51,070 hl in 2002) and so are reds (255,454 hl). For many, Anjou wine is synonymous with sweet or medium white wines made with Chenin or Pineau de la Loire. However, in line with the trend towards drier wines, local producers have opted for mixing in Chardonnay or Sauvignon, to a maximum limit of 20%. Production of red wines, from Cabernet Franc and Cabernet Sauvignon, is in the process of altering the image of the region.

DOM. DE L'ARCHE 2002★

| | 2.5 ha | 15,000 | ▮ ⬧ | 5–8 € |

Originally founded in 1920, this 20-ha estate has been taken over by Benoît Proffit (the company Proffit-Longuet of Domaine des Bleuces that produces red and sweet wines). Here it offers a lively red Anjou, in which intense black fruit flavours are indicative of a very ripe harvest. Youthful tannins are sufficiently supple to contribute to the overall good balance. The wine is extremely attractive.
↦ Proffit-Longuet, Les Bleuces,
49700 Concourson-sur-Layon, tel. 02.41.59.11.74,
fax 02.41.59.97.64,
e-mail domainedesbleuces@coteaux-layon.com
⟁ ev. day except Sun. 9am–12 noon 1.30pm–5.30pm;
Sat. by appt.
↦ Benoît Proffit

VIGNOBLE DE L'ARCISON 2002★

| | 10 ha | 15,000 | ▮ ⬧ | 3–5 € |

This 26-ha estate is situated in the village of Thouarcé, in the Layon area, but more than half of its vineyards are planted with the Cabernets. It offers a typical and well-balanced Anjou with a deep red, almost black colour. Powerful yet lively, the nose exudes characteristic notes of black fruits, which follow on to the rich, full-bodied and complex palate. This is a classy wine.
↦ Damien Reulier, Le Mesnil, 49380 Thouarcé,
tel. 02.41.54.16.81, fax 02.41.54.31.12,
e-mail damien.reulier@wanadoo.fr ▾
⟁ ev. day 8am–12 noon 2pm–6pm; cl. Oct.

CH. DE BOIS-BRINCON

Le Clos Bertin 1999★

| | 2 ha | 9,000 | ◖▯ | 8–11 € |

Regularly mentioned in the *Guide* for its red or sweet wines, this 27-ha property is probably one of oldest in the Anjou area. Eighty-year-old vines from the Clos Bertin and 18 months maturation in wood are behind this intense red 99 which displays purplish highlights. The oaky vanilla aromas on the nose re-appear on the palate showing attractive length, with tannins that are still harsh, but which will round out quickly.
↦ Xavier Cailleau, Ch. de Bois-Brinçon,
49320 Blaison-Gohier, tel. 02.41.57.19.62,
fax 02.41.57.10.46 ▾ ♞
⟁ by appt.

DOM. DES CHESNAIES

La Potardière 2001★

| | n.c. | 3,000 | ◖▯ | 5–8 € |

Olivier de Cenival has taken over this 17-ha estate. The 16th century buildings include *chambres d'hôte* (bed and breakfast accommodation) and open out on to a romantic garden. At the domaine one can taste a white Anjou in which freshness and strength link together well. Pale yellow with golden tinges, this lively 2001 shows citrus fruit and floral aromas. Attractive, balanced and warming on the finish, this wine can be drunk from the end of 2003.
↦ Olivier de Cenival, Dom. des Chesnaies, La Noue,
49190 Denée, tel. 02.41.78.79.80, fax 02.41.68.05.61,
e-mail odecenival@free.fr ▾ ♙
⟁ by appt.

LE CLOS DES MOTELES 2002★

| | 8 ha | 25,000 | ▮ | –3 € |

Located in the Deux-Sèvres *département* in the south of the appellation, this family vineyard is established on gravelly soil. It produces wines in all three colours, still and sparkling, but it is above all its rosés and reds that are described in the *Guide*. However the Jury did appreciate a lively **white Anjou 2002**, simple, but pleasant with pear-drop flavours characteristic of low-temperature fermentation – a wine to drink now. Better still was this deep-coloured red Anjou, crossed through with ruby highlights, with an expressive, slightly spicy red berry nose. The flavourful palate is supported by silky tannins that give it an easy-drinking character.
↦ GAEC Le Clos des Motèles, 42, rue de la Garde,
79100 Sainte-Verge, tel. 05.49.66.05.37, fax 05.49.66.37.14 ▾
⟁ by appt.

DOM. DES DEUX ARCS 2002★

| | 2 ha | 10,000 | | 3–5 € |

Having taken over from four successive generations of farmers, Michel Gazeau became a full-time wine-grower in 1975. The 35-ha estate has often been featured in the *Guide* for its red, but shows its red wine expertise with this Anjou. An intense red colour with garnet hints, the nose is delicate dominated by scents of redcurrants and blackcurrants. Pleasant, fresh, long and only lightly tannic, this is a wine to enjoy as of now.
↦ Dom. des Deux Arcs, 11, rue du 8-Mai-1945,
49540 Martigné-Briand, tel. 02.41.59.47.37,
fax 02.41.59.49.72, e-mail do2arc@wanadoo.fr ▾
⟁ by appt.
↦ Michel Gazeau

DOM. DES DEUX VALLEES

Le Tirchaud 2002★

| | n.c. | n.c. | ▮ ⬧ | 5–8 € |

A new name, new owners and new premises for the old Domaine Branchereau, bought out in April 2001. Located between the Loire and Layon, around Rochefort-sur-Loire and Saint-Aubin-de-Luigné, more than two-thirds of the vineyard is planted with Chenin. The red vines have given an intense red Anjou with a complex nose, combining red berries with some more vegetal notes. Full, fruity and with good length, this is a wine to appreciate from now on.
↦ Philippe et René Socheleau, Dom. des Deux Vallées,
Bellevue, 49190 Saint-Aubin-de-Luigné, tel. 02.41.78.33.24,
fax 02.41.78.66.58,
e-mail socheleau.philippe@wanadoo.fr ▾
⟁ ev. day except Sun. 9am–12 noon 1.30pm–7pm

DOM. DITTIERE 2002★

| | 2 ha | 8,000 | ▮ ⬧ | 5–8 € |

Based near Brissac on sandy-gravel terroir, and made from 40-year-old vines, this 35-ha estate has vinified a dark ruby Anjou. The elegant nose displays much fruit and freshness. The first impression on the palate is expressive, with good structure and body, which together with a fine tannic finish combine in a distinguished wine, which one can begin to drink now or leave in the wine cellar for a year or two.
↦ Dom. Dittière, 1, chem. de la Grouas,
49320 Vauchrétien, tel. 02.41.91.23.78, fax 02.41.54.28.00,
e-mail domaine.dittiere@wanadoo.fr ▾ ♞
⟁ by appt.

DOM. DE L'ENCHANTOIR 2002★

| | 6 ha | 10,000 | ▮ ⬧ | 5–8 € |

The establishment of this estate goes back to 1850, but the vines were already cultivated on these lands in the 16th century. With 19 ha today, Didier Wieder took over the property in 2001. Exhibiting a deep colour with ruby highlights, his red Anjou exudes pleasant flavours of soft red berries that appear again on the balanced and powerful palate, expressive on the finish.
↦ EARL Didier Wieder, 4, rue l'Arguray, Chavannes,
49260 Le Puy-Notre-Dame, tel. 02.41.52.26.33,
fax 02.41.52.23.34 ▾
⟁ by appt.

Anjou

VIGNOBLE DES ESSARTS 2002★

| | 2 ha | 6,000 | ∎ | | 3–5 € |

Chaudefonds-sur-Layon is located in the lower part of the Layon, where the valley widens. Olivier Fardeau farms around 15 hectares in the area; having taken over the family estate in 1994, he built a modern winery between Chalonnes and Chemillé. His red Anjou is not short of assets: a ruby appearance with purple tinges, powerful scents of very ripe soft red and black berries, especially blackcurrants, and a supple palate that is well structured and long. In all, this is a characteristic and nicely-balanced wine.
↬ Olivier Fardeau, Dom. des Essarts,
49290 Chaudefonds-sur-Layon, tel. 02.41.78.27.69,
fax 02.41.74.04.39 ☑
⏳ by appt.

CH. DE FESLES

Vieilles Vignes 2002★

| | 8 ha | 60,000 | ∎ ⬧ | | 5–8 € |

Owned by Bernard Germain since 1996, the Château de Fesles is closely linked with the Bonnezeaux appellation. A red Anjou was selected because of this dark-coloured 2002 with purple highlights. The intense smell reveals notes of blackcurrant and redcurrant. A clean first impression on the palate is followed by full body on the middle palate with silky tannins.
↬ Vignobles Germain et Associés Loire, Ch. de Fesles,
49380 Thouarcé, tel. 02.41.68.94.00, fax 02.41.68.94.01,
e-mail loire@vgas.com ☑
⏳ by appt.
↬ Bernard Germain

DOM. DE GATINES 2002★

| | 2 ha | 10,000 | ∎ ⬧ | | 3–5 € |

A Domaine de Gatines is shown on a map dated 1769. The current owner, in charge of the estate since 1996, farms 44 ha of vines on established schist and *faluns* (fossil-rich sand). It appears more and more regularly in the *Guide* for its red wines. This example, intense red with purplish highlights, shows an expressive nose of red berries, which reappear on the supple palate, exhibiting most attractive weight.
↬ Vignoble Dessèvre, 12, rue de la Boulaie, 49540 Tigné,
tel. 02.41.59.41.48, fax 02.41.59.94.44 ☑
⏳ ev. day except Sun. 8am–12 noon 2pm–6pm

DOM. GROSSET

Harmonie 2001★

| | n.c. | 900 | ⬙ | | 8–11 € |

Located in the heart of the Layon area, this family estate with around 15 hectares presents a wine that has spent one year in cask. With a deep red colour, almost black and very bright, this complex 2001 has a powerful nose with more than its fair share of very ripe, almost cooked red fruit. Soft to start with, the rich palate evolves and has good length, with the emphasis on fruit. It is a very well-balanced wine that can be kept for at least three years in a good wine cellar.
↬ Serge Grosset, 60, rue René-Gasnier,
49190 Rochefort-sur-Loire, tel. 02.41.78.78.67,
fax 02.41.78.79.79,
e-mail serge.grosset@libertysurf.fr ☑
⏳ by appt.

CH. DE LA GUIMONIERE

La Haie Fruitière 2002★★

| | 3.5 ha | 12,000 | ∎ ⬧ | | 5–8 € |

One of the Anjou estates owned by Bernard Germain, the 15th century château dominates a vineyard of around 20 hectares in the Coteaux du Layon and Anjou appellations. After a superb barrel-aged wine selected last year, here is an unoaked, but very satisfactory 2002. It has a very star-bright and attractive ruby appearance. Powerful and complex, the nose combines red and black fruits, especially blackberries, redcurrants and raspberries with a slight walnut note evident. A supple tannic structure makes the wine easy to drink. Fruit accompanies a superb finish indicating a wine suitable for a few years ageing.
↬ Vignobles Germain et Associés Loire, Ch. de Fesles,
49380 Thouarcé, tel. 02.41.68.94.00, fax 02.41.68.94.01,
e-mail loire@vgas.com ☑
⏳ by appt.

DOM. DES HAUTES OUCHES 2002★

| | 10 ha | 20,000 | ∎ ⬧ | | 3–5 € |

This estate has developed rapidly from year to year. Real savoir-faire and 52 ha of vines have meant that its wines, of all of the Anjou colours, have often appeared in the *Guide*. Its red 2002 captures the attention with its deep appearance. Notes of capsicum come through on the complex nose. The palate does not disappoint, with its structure of rounded tannins and its long finish showing herbaceous and liquorice notes. One star is also given to a medium dry **white Anjou 2001 (5–8 €)** vinified in oak (residual sugar: 14 g/l). The nose combines ripe fruits with vanilla and spices; the medium sweet palate provides good acidity on the finish.
↬ EARL Joël et Jean-Louis Lhumeau, 9, rue
Saint-Vincent, 49700 Brigné-sur-Layon, tel. 02.41.59.30.51,
fax 02.41.59.31.75 ☑ ⬕
⏳ by appt.

DOM. DES IRIS 2002★★

| | 8 ha | 63,000 | ∎ ⬧ | | 3–5 € |

For five years Monsieur Petit has worked in partnership with the firm of J. Verdier for winemaking consultancy and marketing. Deep ruby, his red Anjou offers a nose of soft red berries and a hint of vanilla. The tannins are obvious but integrated and the long finish ensures an excellent balance.
↬ EARL Dom. des Iris, La Roche Coutant, 49540 Tigné,
tel. 02.41.40.22.50, fax 02.41.40.22.60,
e-mail j.verdier@wanadoo.fr

DOM. LEDUC-FROUIN

La Seigneurie 2001★★

| | 1 ha | 2,500 | ⬙ | | 5–8 € |

A vineyard established in Sousigné, a village where one can find many wine cellars as well as troglodytic caves dug into the *faluns* (fossil-rich sand). The estate is one to trust: it appears regularly in the *Guide*. Matured for 18 months in barrel, this white Anjou selection was judged as superb with rich and complex, overripe grape, almost botrytized aromas, and a rich palate which is astonishingly full-bodied. It can be drunk at the end of the year. Exhibiting a red-purple tinge, the tank-matured **red Anjou 2002 (3–5 €)** obtains the same mark for its bouquet of spicy red berries and its well-balanced, long palate. It can be drunk right away.
↬ Dom. Antoine et Nathalie Leduc-Frouin, La Seigneurie,
Sousigné, 49540 Martigné-Briand, tel. 02.41.59.42.83,
fax 02.41.59.47.90,
e-mail domaine-leduc-frouin@wanadoo.fr ☑
⏳ by appt.

LE LOGIS DU PRIEURE 2002★★

| | 4 ha | 25,000 | ∎ ⬧ | | 3–5 € |

Established in the upper Layon, this 30-ha estate produces a great variety of wines, sweet whites, reds and rosés, and has made a remarkably successful red Anjou 2002. The extremely bright and deep appearance leans towards garnet. Rich and yet delicate, the nose delivers extremely fine black fruit scents. The rounded and balanced palate has a silky tannin backbone giving an excellent overall make-up.
↬ SCEA Jousset et Fils, Le Logis du Prieuré,
49700 Concourson-sur-Layon, tel. 02.41.59.11.22,
fax 02.41.59.38.18 ☑
⏳ ev. day except Sun. 9am–12.30pm 2pm–7pm

DOM. MATIGNON 2002★

| | 4 ha | 15,000 | ∎ ⬧ | | 3–5 € |

From this property, one can see the ruins of the château of Martigné-Briand, which was burnt down in 1793, during the war of the Vendée. The red Anjou 2002 from this estate is adorned with a deep garnet-red colour and purplish highlights. The complex nose offers notes of very ripe red berries. The palate is at first full and soft, but soon the tannins come into play and these need a little time to round out.
↬ EARL Yves Matignon, 21, av. du Château,
49540 Martigné-Briand, tel. 02.41.59.43.71,
fax 02.41.59.92.34,
e-mail domaine.matignon@wanadoo.fr ☑ ⬕
⏳ by appt.

CH. DE LA MULONNIERE 2001★

| | n.c. | 6,000 | ▐ | 5–8 € |

The Château de la Mulonnière is located in Beaulieu-sur-Layon, at the foot of a south-facing hill. Yellow with gold tinges, its white Anjou 2001 lacks the richness of other wines of the appellation, but gives an impression of elegance and of lightness. The range of aromas combines floral fragrances (floral, acacia) with slightly vegetal notes. Fresh and well-balanced on the palate, it is a wine to open towards the end of 2003.

➼ SCEA Ch. de la Mulonnière, Les Mulonnières,
49750 Beaulieu-sur-Layon, tel. 02.41.78.47.52,
fax 02.41.78.63.63 ▮
Ⱦ by appt.

DOM. OGEREAU

Cuvée Prestige 2001★

| | 2.42 ha | 8,000 | ▐ ▐▐ ⚬ | 8–11 € |

This well-known estate is considered to be a benchmark for Anjou. Their Cuvée Prestige gained a *coup de coeur* in the previous vintage. The 2001 displays intense aromas of over-ripe grapes and crystallized fruits. Powerful, with a strong ripe fruit and nutty character, the palate finishes on a warming note. Of great quality, the weight of this wine needs time to tone down: it should be left in the cellar for a year to allow it to express its full potential.

➼ Vincent Ogereau, 44, rue de la Belle-Angevine,
49750 Saint-Lambert-du-Lattay, tel. 02.41.78.30.53,
fax 02.41.78.43.55 ▮
Ⱦ by appt.

DOM. D'ORGIGNE 2002★★★

| | 1 ha | 6,000 | ▐ ⚬ | 3–5 € |

Managed by two brothers, this is a young domaine – the vine-yard was planted in 1989. It is an estate to follow, because its red Anjou 2002 filled the Jury with enthusiasm. Intense and deep, the red colour with a nuance of purple is superb. The powerful flavours of very ripe red fruit was accompanied by spicy notes, and are expressed both on the nose and on the palate. The weight and structure promise real potential. This is a classy wine to age.

➼ Delaunay, Dom. d'Origné,
49320 Saint-Saturnin-sur-Loire, tel. 02.41.54.21.96,
fax 02.41.91.72.25 ▮
Ⱦ by appt.

DOM. DE PAIMPARE 2002★

| | 1.5 ha | 7,000 | ▐ ⚬ | 3–5 € |

Saint-Lambert-du-Lattay, in the Layon area, is the village that is the most immersed in wine in Anjou. One can visit a museum there dedicated to the vines and wine of Anjou, located within 500 m of this property. Michel Tessier has produced a characteristic 2002. With a red colour, tinged with purple and a complex, pleasant nose dominated by soft red fruit, it is as fresh to the eye as to the nose. The palate is structured by rounded tannins that are already well integrated giving overall a very well-balanced wine.

➼ SCEA Michel Tessier, 32, rue Rabelais,
49750 Saint-Lambert-du-Lattay, tel. 02.41.78.43.18,
fax 02.41.78.41.73 ▮
Ⱦ by appt.

CH. DE PASSAVANT

Jarret de Montchenin 2001★★

| | 2 ha | 3,000 | ▐▐ | 11–15 € |

This white Anjou is a good representative of "The Loire Renaissance" group that unites wine producers dedicated to vinifying wines of substance. The grapes were selectively picked by hand, and both fermentation and maturation were in oak over 14 months. Intense, the aromas single out honey, vanilla and nuts. The palate leaves this feeling of opulence, of lusciousness, but also of elegance, the mark of a top-class wine. This is a superb wine to drink with chicken or grilled fish.

➼ SCEA David-Lecomte, Ch. de Passavant, rte de Tancoigne, 49560 Passavant-sur-Layon, tel. 02.41.59.53.96,
fax 02.41.59.57.91, e-mail passavant@wanadoo.fr ▮
Ⱦ ev. day 8am–12 noon 2pm–7pm; Sat. Sun. by appt.

DOM. DU PETIT CLOCHER 2002★

| | 22 ha | 30,000 | ▐ ⚬ | 3–5 € |

Founded in 1930 this estate acquired a most engaging spectacular extension of a new 12-ha vineyard in 2002: the property now makes up 67 ha of vines. We have rediscovered its red Anjou. The vintage 2002 exhibits a most engaging appearance, deep red with purple tinges. The light and complex nose combines fruitiness with slightly smoky notes. Supple and full, the palate reveals tannins that need some time to soften but which promise an attractive future for this wine.

➼ A. et J-N. Denis, GAEC du Petit Clocher, 3, rue du Layon, 49560 Cléré-sur-Layon, tel. 02.41.59.54.51,
fax 02.41.59.59.70, e-mail petit.clocher@wanadoo.fr ▮
Ⱦ by appt.

DOM. DES PETITES GROUAS 2002★

| | 2 ha | 10,000 | ▐ ⚬ | 3–5 € |

Made up of many different vineyard plots, this property was taken over in 1989 by Philippe Léger. It is often singled out from this appellation and this red Anjou follows on from two equally successful vintages. The intense red colour with brilliant purple highlights makes it "mouth-watering", said one taster. A basket of soft red berries is offered on the nose, with some herbaceous nuances. Complex flavours of rasp-berry and cherry fill the powerful palate that has some silky tannins. This is a beautiful wine which still has more to reveal.

➼ EARL Philippe Léger, Cornu, Les Petites Grouas,
49540 Martigné-Briand, tel. 02.41.59.67.22,
fax 02.41.59.69.32 ▮
Ⱦ by appt.

DOM. DES PIECES MADAME 2002★

| | 2.3 ha | 18,000 | ▐ ⚬ | 3–5 € |

Six years ago, the Domaine de la Gaubretière formed a partnership with the house of Joseph Verdier for the wine-making and marketing of its wines. This one presents a limpid appearance of light, but intense red. Still restrained, with agitation, it releases a perfume full of finesse and elegance. The very enjoyable palate is balanced and sufficiently full-bodied.

➼ EARL Dom. de la Gaubretière, 8, rue Gaubretière,
49540 Martigné-Briand, tel. 02.41.40.22.50,
fax 02.41.40.22.60, e-mail josephverdier@wanadoo.fr

DOM. PIED FLOND 2002★

| | 5.5 ha | 20,000 | ▐ ⚬ | 3–5 € |

Franck Gourdon represents the seventh generation on this estate, which was acquired by his ancestors in 1864. From 45-year-old vines, he has vinified a deep garnet-coloured Anjou that has a complex, fruity nose with a vegetal nuance. The first impression is rich with a full structure and length on the palate. The tannins have not yet fully rounded out, but one could approach this wine by the end of the year 2003.

➼ Franck Gourdon, Dom. Pied Flond,
49540 Martigné-Briand, tel. 02.41.59.92.36,
fax 02.41.59.92.36 ▮
Ⱦ by appt.

CH. PIEGUE

La Croix des Gardes 2001★

| | 1 ha | 3,000 | ▐▐ | 5–8 € |

Built in 1840 on the top of a hillside, the château dominates an estate of 25 ha. It offers dry white Anjou vinified in barrels of 400 l. This pale yellow, bright 2001 offers delicate aromas of wild flowers, hazelnut and crystallized fruit. Full and balanced on the palate, it combines a feeling of freshness with some oaky notes. It can be drunk as of now or kept for a few years. Also successful, the **red Anjou Vielles Vignes 2001** gives aromas of red berries and a rounded, well-balanced palate, it should be drunk soon.

➼ Ch. Piéguë, Piéguë, 49190 Rochefort-sur-Loire,
tel. 02.41.78.71.26, fax 02.41.78.75.03,
e-mail antoine-van-der-hecht@wanadoo.fr ▮ ▨
Ⱦ by appt.
➼ Van der Hecht

DOM. DU PRIEURE

Les Hauts du Moulin 2000★

| | 0.3 ha | 800 | 🍷 | 8–11 € |

Here is one of the first wines released by Franck Brossaud, who set up in 2000 after having completed a doctoral thesis. Previously the *Guide* had already given a special mention to a Cuvée Promesses Coteaux de l'Aubance 2000. The promises seem to have been born out. To succeed in such a difficult vintage was far from certain, and yet he managed extremely well. With its golden-yellow appearance and its range of flavours mixing buttery notes, nuances of toast, patisserie and caramel, this white Anjou gives an excellent impression. The finish may be a little transient, but generally the rich and complex palate gives complete satisfaction.

🍷 Franck Brossaud, 1 bis, pl. du Prieuré, 49610 Mozé-sur-Louet, tel. 02.41.45.30.74, fax 02.41.45.30.74, e-mail franck.brossaud@wanadoo.fr ☑
🍽 by appt.

DOM. DU REGAIN 2002★★

| | 3 ha | 8,000 | 🍷🍂 | 5–8 € |

A second career has begun for Frédéric Etienne, who became a wine producer after being director of the Institut Technique du Vin (technical wine institute) in Angers. His first year is most encouraging, since several wines have been selected. The white Anjou is outstanding: with a pale gold colour and subtle aromas of lime blossom and crystallized fruits, its palate is full-bodied, intense and complex, combining strength and delicacy. As for the full and fleshy **red Anjou Vieilles Vignes 2002**, it still remains restrained, but promises well and receives a mention.

🍷 F. et F. Etienne, Dom. du Regain, Le Pied de Fer, 49540 Martigné-Briand, tel. 02.41.40.28.20, fax 02.41.40.28.21, e-mail domaine.regain@wanadoo.fr ☑
🍽 by appt.

DOM. RICHOU

Les Rogeries 2001★★★

| | n.c. | n.c. | 🍷🍷 | 8–11 € |

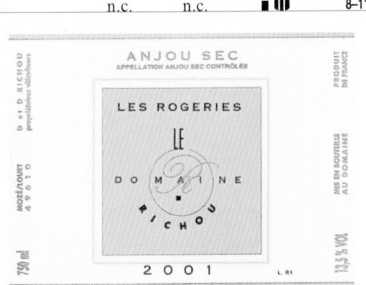

For several years, Cuvée Les Rogeries has been one of the very best examples of dry white Anjou wines. Grown on the rhyolites of the Massif Armoricain, it comes from a rigorous manual selective picking. The wine is adorned with a pale yellow appearance and gold highlights. With notes of caramelized apples, the flavours conjure up *tarte tatin* (apple tart). The palate is powerful, rounded and fresh, leaving a sensation of ripe grapes, signing off a high-class wine.

🍷 Dom. Richou, Chauvigné, 49610 Mozé-sur-Louet, tel. 02.41.78.72.13, fax 02.41.78.76.05 ☑
🍽 by appt.

DOM. ROBINEAU CHRISLOU 2002★

| | 4.09 ha | 5,000 | 🍷🍂 | 3–5 € |

An important wine village of the Layon area, Saint-Lambert-du-Lattay is home to many wine producers who, like Louis Robineau and his wife, produce the whole range of Anjou wines, especially sweet wines and red wines. The estate appears again in the *Guide* in this appellation thanks to a very well-made red Anjou. A vivid red colour with purple tinges, on swirling this still-restrained 2002, it releases delicious fruity aromas. This attractive fruitiness appears again on the

fresh and balanced palate, where the tannins are still harsh, needing time to soften.
🍷 Louis Robineau, 14, rue Rabelais, 49750 Saint-Lambert-du-Lattay, tel. 02.41.78.36.04, fax 02.41.78.36.04 ☑
🍽 by appt.

CH. DE LA ROCHE BOUSSEAU 2002★

| | 2 ha | 12,000 | 🍷🍂 | 3–5 € |

A 15th century château burnt down during the Revolution, with the land acquired by the family in August 1796 (*8 fructidor an IV* in the revolutionary calendar): this estate summarizes part of the animated history of the area. The vineyard produced a very attractive red Anjou 2002, from its light, bright colour to its long and generous finish, passing through delicate fruity flavours, present on both the nose and the palate, and incorporating beautiful balance, with well-integrated obvious tannins.

🍷 SCEV F. Regnard de la Ville-Fromoit, Petite Roche, 49310 Trémont, tel. 02.41.59.43.03, fax 02.41.59.69.43 ☑
🍽 ev. day 8am–8pm

CH. DES ROCHETTES 2002★★

| | 10 ha | 20,000 | 🍷 | 5–8 € |

Owned by Jean Douet's family since the 18th century, this 25-ha vineyard, located in the upper Layon, has become known for its sweet wines, and preceding editions of the *Guide* have described an anthology of several vintages. It also shows real expertise in red winemaking, as demonstrated with this deep-coloured, almost black 2002, which displays a powerful and attractive nose of red berries. Well balanced on the palate, it reveals dense structure and quite integrated tannins, which indicate very good ageing potential. It can easily be left for two years in the cellar.

🍷 Jean Douet, Ch. des Rochettes, 49700 Concourson-sur-Layon, tel. 02.41.59.11.51, fax 02.41.59.37.73 ☑
🍽 by appt.

DOM. DU ROY RENE

Les Pierres 2001★

| | 0.9 ha | 850 | 🍷 | 8–11 € |

This estate in Chanzeaux was established on the borders between Layon and the woodland of the Mauges. Between 1793 and 1795, the village was the theatre of bloody confrontations between the royalist peasants and *les Bleus* (the revolutionaries). You might prefer to evoke the memory of the chivalrous King René, the last sovereign of Anjou. Antoine Chéreau took over the estate in 2000, after his studies amongst the Burgundian wine-growers. His white Anjou has been vinified and matured for one year in barrel. A pale yellow colour with golden highlights, it shows a full range of aromas mixing floral (acacia notes), with wax and honey. The palate is balanced and fresh with notes of citrus fruits, especially grapefruit making an unusual but very attractive wine.

🍷 Antoine Chéreau, Le Bon René, 49750 Chanzeaux, tel. 02.41.78.32.32, fax 02.41.78.38.34, e-mail domaine.roy.rene@wanadoo.fr ☑
🍽 by appt.

DOM. SAINT-ARNOUL 2002★★

| | 4 ha | 5,500 | 🍷🍂 | 3–5 € |

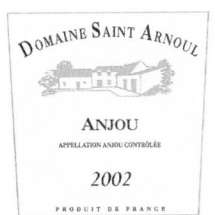

This vineyard was created in 1963 by Georges Poupard, who was joined by his son Alain in 1986. In April 2000 Alain Poupard linked up with the oenologist Xavier Maury, a profitable collaboration judging by this dark ruby red Anjou, shimmering with purple reflections. The attractive nose of very ripe fruits reveals a wine of great concentration, confirmed on the rich and smooth palate, supported by excellent tannic structure to back up the flavours. Here is a substantial, balanced wine to age, and an estate to follow.
↰ GAEC Poupard et Maury, Sousigné,
49540 Martigné-Briand, tel. 02.41.59.43.62,
fax 02.41.59.69.23, e-mail saint-arnoul@wanadoo.fr ☑
☒ by appt.

CH. SOUCHERIE

Champ aux Loups Elevé en fût de chêne 2001★★

■				
	2 ha	10,000	⬗	5–8€

Bought in 1952 by Paul Tijou from the marquise de Brissac, the property is established on a schistous hillside facing south and dominating the hillside of Chaume. Run today by Pierre-Yves Tijou, joined recently by Vincent, it was renovated in 2000. This 2001 was the first to be in the new barrel cellar. Its garnet-red appearance is animated with tinges of crimson and purple, its complex nose mixes aromas conferred by the maturation, vanilla, cocoa and oak notes. Full, rounded and rich, the palate presents an attractive concentrated fruitiness and an exuberant finish of red berry fruit. This is a wine of remarkable balance, to age. As for the **Anjou Les Mouchis 2001 white**, also matured in wood, it reveals a welcome freshness. With aromas of acacia flowers and nuts, a slightly sparkling palate and a finish of ripe fruits, it is singled out for a mention.
↰ Pierre-Yves Tijou et Fils, EARL Ch. Soucherie,
49750 Beaulieu-sur-Layon, tel. 02.41.78.31.18,
fax 02.41.78.48.29, e-mail chateausoucherie@yahoo.fr ☑
☒ by appt.

DOM. DE TERREBRUNE 2002★

■				
	7 ha	50,000	■ ⚬	3–5€

The colour of deep and clear ruby is immediately attractive. The intense nose reels off all the soft red berries, very ripe and even jammy. Very balanced and elegant, the palate is supported by a strand of silky tannins which fill the palate. This wine really gives pleasure. It can be drunk now or kept for two years.
↰ SCA Dom. de Terrebrune, La Motte,
49380 Notre-Dame-d'Allençon, tel. 02.41.54.01.99,
fax 02.41.54.09.06,
e-mail domaine-de-terrebrune@wanadoo.fr ☑
☒ by appt.

LES VIGNERONS DES TERROIRS DE LA NOELLE Les Marillais 2002★

■				
	10.6 ha	80,000	■ ⚬	3–5€

Created in 1955, this cooperative vinifies the grapes from 800 ha in the appellations of the Nantes area, Coteaux d'Ancenis and even Anjou. It presents a deep-coloured red Anjou tinged with garnet. The intense nose has the freshness of red berries. With quite obvious tannins, the palate remains supple and rounded. A beautiful freshness of flavour confers this wine with a lively side and it should be served cool to emphasize this fruitiness.
↰ Les Vignerons des Terroirs de la Noëlle, bd des Alliés,
BP 155, 44154 Ancenis Cedex, tel. 02.40.98.92.72,
fax 02.40.98.96.70, e-mail vignerons-noelle@cana.fr ☑
☒ by appt.

DOM. VERDIER 2002★

■				
	1 ha	6,000	■ ⚬	3–5€

Founded in the 1970s, this family estate in the Layon area is very often singled out for its Anjou. A deep red colour veering to black, this exhibits a nose that manages to be both intense and subtle, and moves from red berry fruit towards black-currant and liquorice. The palate is balanced, structured and fresh. Its substantial tannic backbone, richness and flavours contribute to the pleasure of this wine. One can serve it as from now with meat stews, or let it age.
↰ EARL Verdier Père et Fils, 7, rue des Varennes,
49750 Saint-Lambert-du-Lattay, tel. 02.41.78.35.67,
fax 02.41.78.35.67 ☑
☒ by appt.

DOM. DU VIGNEAU 2002★

■				
	2.5 ha	5,500	■ ⚬	3–5€

Patrick Robichon has been established for ten years in Passavant-sur-Layon. He presents a limpid 2002, with powerful aromas of red berries that reappear attractively on the palate. This is honest, lively and with an astonishing length, a real "wine for pleasure" to drink now.
↰ Patrick Robichon, pl. de l'Eglise,
49560 Passavant-sur-Layon, tel. 02.41.59.51.04,
fax 02.41.59.51.04 ☑
☒ by appt.

LES VIGNES DE L'ALMA

Cuvée Prestige 2001★

■				
	0.75 ha	4,000	■ ⚬	5–8€

This domaine, with one sole owner, is made up of 10 ha of vineyards surrounding the estate buildings. It is located on a plateau from where one can see a panorama over Saint-Florent-le-Vieil and the Loire Valley. Its Cuvée Prestige emerges from a very deep purplish colour. Pleasant and slightly musky, the nose is dominated by red berries. Equally fruity, the structured palate is rounded and mouth-filling, and should develop well with time. This red Anjou can be kept for two or three years.
↰ Roland Chevalier, L'Alma, 49410 Saint-Florent-le-Vieil,
tel. 02.41.72.71.09, fax 02.41.72.63.77,
e-mail chevalier.roland@wanadoo.fr ☑
☒ ev. day except Sun. 8.30am–12.30pm 2pm–7pm

Wines selected but not starred

CH. DE CHAMBOUREAU

Cuvée d'Avant 2001

■				
	3.5 ha	21,000	⬗	5–8€

↰ EARL Pierre Soulez, Ch. de Chamboureau,
49170 Savennières, tel. 02.41.77.20.04, fax 02.41.77.27.78 ☑
☒ by appt.

DOM. DE LA COUCHETIERE

Elevé en fût de chêne 2001

■				
	0.9 ha	6,000	⬗	3–5€

↰ GAEC Brault, Dom. de la Couchetière,
49380 Notre-Dame-d'Allençon, tel. 02.41.54.30.26,
fax 02.41.54.40.98 ☑
☒ ev. day except Sun. 8.30am–12.30pm 2pm–7pm

DOM. DES HARDIERES

Valentin Fleur 2002

■				
	1 ha	4,000	■ ⬗ ⚬	5–8€

↰ Aubert Frères, Les Hardières,
49750 Saint-Lambert-du-Lattay, tel. 02.40.98.50.02,
fax 02.40.98.50.44 ☑
☒ by appt.

DOM. DE MIHOUDY 2002

■				
	5 ha	20,000	■	5–8€

↰ EARL Cochard et Fils, Dom. de Mihoudy,
49540 Aubigné-sur-Layon, tel. 02.41.59.46.52,
fax 02.41.59.68.77, e-mail mihoudy@wanadoo.fr ☑
☒ by appt.

CH. DE PIMPEAN

Cuvée du Festival 2002

| | 9.5 ha | 53,000 | ▮ ⚬ | | 3–5 € |

● SCA Dom. de Pimpéan, Ch. de Pimpéan, 49320 Grézillé,
tel. 02.41.68.95.96, fax 02.41.45.51.93,
e-mail maryset@pimpean.com ▼
☿ ev. day 8am–12 noon 1.30pm–5.30pm
● Gilles et Maryse Tugendhat

DOM. DE PUTILLE 2002

| | 2.34 ha | 7,000 | ▮ ⚬ | | 3–5 € |

● Isabelle Sécher et Stève Roulier, Dom. de Putille,
49620 La Pommeraye, tel. 02.41.39.80.43,
fax 02.41.39.81.91 ▼
☿ by appt.

SAUVEROY

Cuvée Iris 2001

| | 4.63 ha | 30,000 | ▮ ⚬ | | 3–5 € |

● Pascal Cailleau, Dom. Sauveroy,
49750 Saint-Lambert-du-Lattay, tel. 02.41.78.30.59,
fax 02.41.78.46.43, e-mail domainesauveroy@terre-net.fr ▼
☿ by appt.

DOM. DE LA VILLAINE

Cuvée spéciale Elevé en fût de chêne 2001

| | n.c. | 2,500 | ▥ | | 5–8 € |

● GAEC des Villains, La Villaine, 49540 Martigné-Briand,
tel. 02.41.59.75.21, fax 02.41.59.75.21
☿ by appt.

Anjou-Gamay

A red wine made from the Gamay Noir grape. On the area's more schisty soils, when well-vinified, it can produce an excellent carafe wine. Several growers have specialized in this type of wine, which has no ambition other than seeking to please in its year of harvest. In 2002, production was 13,315 hl.

DOM. DE L'ANGELIERE 2002★

| | 3 ha | 4,000 | ▮ ⚬ | | 3–5 € |

With 45 ha of vines, this estate produces wines from ten different Anjou appellations. With its deep red colour and purplish highlights, its Anjou-Gamay is visually attractive. The bouquet is still restrained, but the fruit is revealed on tasting. Rounded, supple and light, it is a balanced wine that will not let you down.
● GAEC Boret, Dom. de L'Angelière,
49380 Champ-sur-Layon, tel. 02.41.78.85.09,
fax 02.41.78.67.10 ▼
☿ by appt.

DOM. PIED FLOND 2002★

| | 0.4 ha | 3,500 | ▮ ⚬ | | 3–5 € |

This estate of monastic origins entered into the family of Franck Gourdon in 1864. A deep ruby with purple tinges, its Anjou-Gamay opens up gradually to reveal complex aromas. After a sumptuous start, the palate appears full of flavour and richness, with the flavours lasting right through the tasting. This is a wine to really relish.
● Franck Gourdon, Dom. Pied Flond,
49540 Martigné-Briand, tel. 02.41.59.92.36,
fax 02.41.59.92.36 ▼
☿ by appt.

LES VIGNES DE L'ALMA 2002★

| | 3 ha | 15,000 | ▮ ⚬ | | 3–5 € |

This 10-ha estate, all in one plot, is established on a plateau from where one can look over Saint-Florent-le-Vieil and the Loire Valley. Adorned with a deep red colour, its Anjou-Gamay develops a beautiful complexity of flavour. Unambiguous, pleasing and balanced, it can be drunk right away, but its length promises the ability to age for up to two years.
● Roland Chevalier, L'ALMA, 49410 Saint-Florent-le-Vieil,
tel. 02.41.72.71.09, fax 02.41.72.63.77,
e-mail chevalier.roland@wanadoo.fr ▼
☿ ev. day except Sun. 8.30am–12.30pm 2pm–7pm

Wines selected but not starred

DOM. DU FRESCHE 2002

| | 1.2 ha | 6,000 | ▮ ⚬ | | 3–5 € |

● Alain Boré, Dom. du Fresche, rte de Chalonnes,
49620 La Pommeraye, tel. 02.41.77.74.63,
fax 02.41.77.79.39, e-mail alainbore@aol.com ▼
☿ ev. day except Sun. 8am–12.30pm 2pm–7pm

DOM. DE MONTGILET 2002

| | 1.48 ha | 5,000 | ▮ ⚬ | | 3–5 € |

● Victor et Vincent Lebreton, Dom. de Montgilet,
49610 Juigné-sur-Loire, tel. 02.41.91.90.48,
fax 02.41.54.64.25, e-mail montgilet@terre-net.fr ▼
☿ ev. day except Sun. 9am–12 noon 2pm–6pm;
cl. Sat. Jan. and Feb.

DOM. DU REGAIN 2002

| | 4 ha | 12,000 | ▮ ⚬ | | 3–5 € |

● F. et F. Etienne, Dom. du Regain, Le Pied de Fer,
49540 Martigné-Briand, tel. 02.41.40.28.20,
fax 02.41.40.28.21, e-mail domaine.regain@wanadoo.fr ▼
☿ by appt.

Anjou-Villages

The terroir of this AOC is drawn from a selection of regions within the Anjou appellation. To qualify, soils must be healthy, early-flowering and well-exposed. They mainly lie on schists, whether altered or not. The ten communes making up the geographical area of the AOC Anjou-Village-Brissac, recognized in 1998, occupy a plateau sloping gently down to the Loire, bordered to the north by the river and to the south by the steep hillsides of Layon. The soils are deep, and the special nature of the terroir is also influenced by the proximity of the Loire, which guards against extreme variations in temperature. In 2002 the harvest produced 13,077 hl of Anjou-Villages and 6,590 hl of Brissac.

DOM. D'AMBINOS 2001★

| | 1.15 ha | 7,000 | ▮ | | 5–8 € |

This estate based at Beaulieu-sur-Layon devotes itself particularly to sweet wines, but it does have a few hectares planted with the Cabernets. Bright red with brown tinges, its

LOIRE

Anjou-Villages delivers restrained scents of black fruits. The palate is structured, supported by very obvious tannins that promise an attractive future. Overall, this is a very well balanced wine.

☛ Jean-Pierre Chéné, 3, imp. des Jardins,
49750 Beaulieu-sur-Layon, tel. 02.41.78.48.09,
fax 02.41.78.61.72,
e-mail domainelambinos@libertysurf.fr ☑
☿ by appt.

CHARLES BÉDUNEAU 2001★

| | 1.5 ha | 5,000 | ▮ ♦ | 3–5 € |

Created in 1958 with 4 ha of vines, this estate has quintupled its vineyard area and produces a diverse range of Anjou wines in all three colours. It presents a ruby Anjou-Villages, with a red-berry nose and a well-balanced palate. The overall impression is extremely pleasant, even if the tannins need time to integrate. A short period of ageing for a year or two will improve it.

☛ EARL Charles Béduneau, 18, rue Rabelais,
49750 Saint-Lambert-du-Lattay, tel. 02.41.78.30.86,
fax 02.41.74.01.46,
e-mail charles.beduneau@caramail.com ☑
☿ by appt.

DOM. DE LA BERGERIE

Le Chant du Bois 2001★★

| | 2 ha | 12,000 | ▮ ♦ | 5–8 € |

Regular readers of the *Guide* will know the white wines of Yves Guégniard well, in particular his sweet wines (Quarts de Chaume and Coteaux du Layon) which have made the reputation of the estate. With this Anjou-Villages the producer shows that he can also draw the best from Cabernet. This deep-coloured 2001 reveals very attractive ruby tinges and an intense nose of red berries with a touch of liquorice. Supple with si cy tannins, the palate continues this flavourful aspect. "I cou d really drink plenty of this wine," concluded one taster.

☛ Yves Gué iard, Dom. de la Bergerie,
49380 Cham ur-Layon, tel. 02.41.78.85.43,
fax 02.41.78. .13,
e-mail domainede.la.bergerie@wanadoo.fr ☑
☿ by appt.

DOM. DES BLEUCES 2001★★★

| | 1,33 ha | 3,500 | ▥ | 5–8 € |

Benoît Proffit has run this estate, which amounts to about 30 hectares, since 1994. This deep-garnet Anjou-Villages stands out. The intensity of its aromas of stewed black fruits is impressive. Rich and mouth-filling, powerful and rounded, the palate is structured by attractive tannins which create superb balance. Don't hesitate to search this out.

☛ Proffit-Longuet, Les Bleuces,
49700 Concourson-sur-Layon, tel. 02.41.59.11.74,
fax 02.41.59.97.64,
e-mail domainedesbleuces@coteaux-layon.com ☑
☿ ev. day except Sun. 9am–12 noon 1.30pm–5.30pm;
Sat. by appt.
☛ Benoît Proffit

DOM. MICHEL BLOUIN 2001★

| | 1,31 ha | 6,000 | ▮ | 3–5 € |

Founded in 1870, the estate has around 20 hectares of vines and is often featured in the *Guide* for Coteaux du Layon or for its reds. Its Anjou-Villages 2001 creates a very good impression with an appearance of deep and brilliant ruby, and a complex nose combining very ripe black fruits with nuances of leather and spices. The palate does not disappoint: a supple first impression with good structure, the flavours are powerful but attractive with beautiful balance overall.

☛ Dom. Michel Blouin, 53, rue du Canal-de-Monsieur,
49190 Saint-Aubin-de-Luigné, tel. 02.41.78.33.53,
fax 02.41.78.67.61 ☑
☿ by appt.

DOM. FARDEAU

Elevé en fût de chêne 2001★★

| | 0.7 ha | 4,400 | ▮ ▥ ♦ | 5–8 € |

This estate in the lower Layon produces sweet wines too. Its Anjou-Villages is particularly distinguished in the year 2001. An intense, limpid garnet-red colour; delicate woodland fruits aroma, with a touch of oak; balanced palate with well-integrated tannins, noticeable length; these all contribute to the overall harmony of the wine.

☛ Dom. Chantal Fardeau, Les Hauts Perrays,
49290 Chaudefonds-sur-Layon, tel. 02.41.78.67.57,
fax 02.41.78.68.78 ☑
☿ by appt.

DOM. DE LA GERFAUDRIE

Cuvée Prestige 2001★

| | 1.3 ha | 9,000 | ▥ | 3–5 € |

As in a previous *Guide*, the Domaine de la Gerfaudrie has been selected for its red and its sweet white wines. Intense red with purplish tinges, its Anjou-Villages delivers an aroma that manages to be powerful and to show delicate black fruits that reappear on the palate through to the finish. Full-bodied and soft, with well-integrated tannins, it has a long finish.

☛ SCEV J.-P. et P. Bourreau, 25, rue de l'Onglée,
49290 Chalonnes-sur-Loire, tel. 02.41.78.02.28,
fax 02.41.78.03.07,
e-mail domaine-gerfaudrie@wanadoo.fr ☑
☿ by appt.

LUC ET FABRICE MARTIN 2001★★

| | 1 ha | 5,000 | ▥ | 5–8 € |

This 23-ha property is dedicated mainly to growing Chenin, from which it produces excellent sweet wines. It is no less worthy with its reds, judging by this Anjou-Villages. With a deep and most engagingly crystal-clear red, it shows an attractive, complex nose mixing scents recalling red berries with a light oaky note. Both supple and structured, it should come together by the end of 2003.

☛ GAEC Luc et Fabrice Martin, 2 bis, rue du Stade,
49290 Chaudefonds-sur-Layon, tel. 02.41.78.19.91,
fax 02.41.78.98.25 ☑
☿ by appt.

DOM. DE LA MOTTE 2001★

| | 2 ha | n.c. | ▮ ▥ | 5–8 € |

Running the family estate (20 ha of vines planted on the southern bank of the Loire), Gilles Sorin vinifies wines that are regularly selected by the *Guide*, especially reds. Again he has presented two very well made Anjou-Villages. Beautifully deep to look at, the classic *cuvée* is powerful on the nose, where the soft red berries are accompanied by slightly spicy notes. Full, balanced and structured by silky tannins, it shows an expressive finish. The same mark is given to the **Cuvée La Garde 2001 (8–11 €)**. It has been 100% barrel-aged for 12 months, as revealed by its deep colour and smell, where although wood dominates the red fruit character, it remains rounded and balanced.

☛ Gilles Sorin, Dom. de la Motte, 31–35, av. d'Angers,
49190 Rochefort-sur-Loire, tel. 02.41.78.72.96,
fax 02.41.78.75.49, e-mail sorin.dommotte@wanadoo.fr ☑
☿ by appt.

DOM. OGEREAU

Côte de La Houssaye 2001★

| | 1.1 ha | 4,700 | ▥ | 11–15 € |

One can buy from this estate in complete confidence as it is a collector of stars and *coups de coeur* from the *Guide*, both for reds and for sweet white wines. In a somewhat low-key vintage, Vincent Ogereau has drawn out the best with this Anjou-Villages, which has been matured for 18 months in wood. With a deep colour, it exudes pleasant aromas of soft red berries that reappear on the rounded, powerful and long palate.

☛ Vincent Ogereau, 44, rue de la Belle-Angevine,
49750 Saint-Lambert-du-Lattay, tel. 02.41.78.30.53,
fax 02.41.78.43.55 ☑
☿ by appt.

DOM. DU PETIT CLOCHER 2001★

■ 2 ha 6,500 ⭘ 5–8 €

When it was founded in 1930, the estate had just 6 ha of vines; in 2003 it owned more than 67 ha, including 12 purchased this year. It attracted the attention of the Jury with this garnet-red Anjou-Villages, mixing delicate perfumes of red fruits with notes of liquorice. The palate is just as good, tannic but without aggressiveness. This wine will give pleasure before the end of the year.

●➔ A. et J.-N. Denis, GAEC du Petit Clocher, 3, rue du Layon, 49560 Cléré-sur-Layon, tel. 02.41.59.54.51, fax 02.41.59.59.70, e-mail petit.clocher@wanadoo.fr 🆅
Ⴏ by appt.

DOM. DU PETIT VAL 2001★

■ 1 ha 4,000 ■ ♦ 3–5 €

Created in 1950 by Vincent Goizil, the father of Denis, this estate has expanded its vineyard area considerably, rising from 4 to 50 ha. Whether reds or sweet whites, its wines find their place in this Guide. After swirling a glass of this extremely attractive, deep red 2001 it releases powerful aromas of very ripe soft red fruits. Full and rich, the palate is balanced, with integrated tannins.

●➔ EARL Denis Goizil, Dom. du Petit Val, 49380 Chavagnes, tel. 02.41.54.31.14, fax 02.41.54.03.48, e-mail denisgoizil@tiscali.fr 🆅
Ⴏ by appt.

CH. PIERRE-BISE

Sur Schistes 2001★

■ 2.5 ha 13,000 ■ ♦ 5–8 €

Here is an Anjou-Villages made by one of the virtuosos of sweet white wines, based in the Layon area. On the nose, this dark ruby 2001 reveals a well-handled, rich harvest of quality. The first impression on the palate is rich, rounded, and really soft, indicative of great balance.

●➔ Claude Papin, Ch. Pierre-Bise, 49750 Beaulieu-sur-Layon, tel. 02.41.78.31.44, fax 02.41.78.41.24 🆅
Ⴏ by appt.

DOM. DE LA POTERIE 2001★★

■ 4 ha 3,000 ■ 5–8 €

Son of a farmer in the north of France, Guillaume Mordacq became a wine producer in 1996. Based in Thouarcé, he farms 12 ha of vines using sustainable agriculture. His wines are regularly present in the Guide and this year, he was particularly singled out for his Anjou-Villages 2001. The ruby colour is intense and so are the fruity and jammy aromas. The palate begins by showing finesse and continues to a long finish. This is a fine ambassador for the appellation.

●➔ Guillaume Mordacq, La Chevalerie, 16, av. des Trois-Ponts, 49380 Thouarcé, tel. 02.41.54.12.29, e-mail mordacq@club-internet.fr 🆅
Ⴏ by appt.

CH. DE PUTILLE 2001★★

■ 5 ha 15,000 ■ ♦ 5–8 €

Very well known for its white wines, the 40-ha Château de Putille is also associated with the revival of the red wines of Anjou. The Anjou-Villages 98 obtained a *coup de coeur*. This

wine appealed because of its complexity and overall balance. With an intense garnet colour, it develops a fine smell of very ripe, almost stewed soft red fruits. The palate starts on a luscious note and the same fruits fill the palate, joined by spicy notes. It has weight and fruit.

●➔ Pascal Delaunay, EARL Ch. de Putille, 49620 La Pommeraye, tel. 02.41.39.02.91, fax 02.41.39.03.45 🆅
Ⴏ ev. day except Sun. 8.10am–12.30pm 2pm–7pm

DOM. DE PUTILLE 2001★

■ 1.4 ha 4,980 ■ ♦ 5–8 €

Situated 30 km from Angers, on the hillsides of the Loire River, this 15-ha estate offers a wide range of wines made from Chenin, Gamay and Cabernet. It obtained a *coup de coeur* for the Anjou-Villages 99. The 2001 vintage looks inviting, with a deep colour and a straightforward nose of attractive red berries. The palate confirms this good impression, full, well structured and balanced. The tannins require time to integrate but promise that it will age. It needs another three years.

●➔ Isabelle Sécher et Stève Roulier, Dom. de Putille, 49620 La Pommeraye, tel. 02.41.39.80.43, fax 02.41.39.81.91 🆅
Ⴏ by appt.

DOM. DES QUARRES

Métis 2001★★

■ 1 ha 4,500 ⭘ 5–8 €

A part of this vineyard covers a terraced hillside on the right bank of the Layon. The estate has its office in a large vine-grower's house on three levels, dating back to 1900. It offers an Anjou-Villages that is enjoyable right through the tasting: a deep colour of a lively, jolly ruby colour; a straightforward fruity bouquet, simple but charming; a supple start to the palate and an elegant, long finish with notes of Morello cherries and wild strawberries.

●➔ Dom. des Quarres, 66, Grande-Rue, 49750 Rablay-sur-Layon, tel. 02.41.78.36.00, fax 02.41.78.62.58 🆅 🜹
Ⴏ ev. day 9.30am–12 noon 2.30pm–6pm; Sat. Sun. by appt.

DOM. DES QUATRE ROUTES 2001★★

■ 0.75 ha 5,300 ■⭘♦ 5–8 €

Now that their son has joined the estate, having returned from Australia, they can display their ambitions: the winery was renovated in 2001, and an old barn has been restored and fitted out to receive groups. Anjou wine-lovers will be able to call in there to taste this excellent, well-made Anjou-Villages. A deep ruby 2001, it releases perfumes of soft red berries accompanied by oaky notes. Rounded and well-balanced with integrated tannins, the palate invites opening a bottle right away.

●➔ Poupard et Fils, Dom. des Quatre Routes, 49540 Aubigné-sur-Layon, tel. 02.41.59.44.44, fax 02.41.59.49.70, e-mail domainedes4routes@wanadoo.fr 🆅
Ⴏ ev. day 9am–7pm; Sat. Sun. by appt.

DOM. JEAN-LOUIS ROBIN-DIOT

Le Haut du Cochet 2001★

■ 2 ha 5,000 ⭘ 8–11 €

Established for more than 30 years, Jean-Louis Robin-Diot has devoted himself to the protection of the Anjou appellations, in particular Coteaux du Layon and Anjou-Villages. We have discovered his *cuvée* Le Haut du Cochet, noteworthy in the two previous vintages. A really pretty 2001: an intense bright red colour; a nose that is equally intense with red fruit accompanied by slightly burnt notes; and a full-bodied palate with obvious, promising tannins that are already supple and rounded. In all, it has beautiful balance.

●➔ Dom. Jean-Louis Robin-Diot, Les Hauts Perrays, 49290 Chaudefonds-sur-Layon, tel. 02.41.78.68.29, fax 02.41.78.67.62 🆅 🜹
Ⴏ by appt.

MICHEL ROBINEAU 2001★★

■ 0.64 ha 3,000 ■⭘ 3–5 €

This estate has only existed for 13 years. It is not immense (9 ha) but enjoys a very good reputation, confirmed by the number of stars and *coups de coeur* in the *Guide*. Garnet-red with purple tinges, its Anjou-Villages 2001 has much charm. Its red fruit aromas are slightly spicy and continue on the very well-balanced palate, with obvious but softened tannins. This wine can be enjoyed as of now.

•ᴚ Michel Robineau, 3, chem. du Moulin, Les Grandes Tailles, 49750 Saint-Lambert-du-Lattay, tel. 02.41.78.34.67 **▼**

I by appt.

DOM. DES SAULAIES 2001★★

| ■ | 1.21 ha | 8,885 | ▌ ♦ | 5–8 € |

A baby, Gabin Leblanc, arrived in 2003. Will he be a wine producer like his father and his ancestors before him since the time of the Sun King? The estate made some beautiful wines in the 2001 vintage. This Anjou-Villages exhibits a dark red appearance and intense black fruit aromas. Dense and full of flavour, it has velvety tannins and outstanding balance.

•ᴚ EARL Philippe et Pascal Leblanc, Dom. des Saulaies, 49380 Faye-d'Anjou, tel. 02.41.54.30.66, fax 02.41.54.17.21 **▼**

I by appt.

DOM. DE TERREBRUNE 2001★

| ■ | 2.77 ha | 20,000 | ▌❙▮❙ ♦ | 5–8 € |

This 45-ha estate is often selected for its Bonnezeaux, and also produces well-made rosés, as proved by the *coup de coeur* it received for a Cabernet d'Anjou 2001. Here, it also shows its know-how in red winemaking. This Anjou-Villages displays a deep colour with tinges of ruby. The nose is quite restrained but after swirling releases some hints of red berry fruit. There is no lack of character on the balanced palate thanks to some very obvious tannins. It provides a pleasant finish and is a promising wine.

•ᴚ SCA Dom. de Terrebrune, La Motte, 49380 Notre-Dame-d'Allençon, tel. 02.41.54.01.99, fax 02.41.54.09.06, e-mail domaine-de-terrebrune@wanadoo.fr **▼**

I by appt.

Anjou-Villages-Brissac

DOM. DE BABLUT 2001★★

| ■ | n.c. | n.c. | | 5–8 € |

Established for a very long time in the Anjou vineyard area, the estate took a new direction with the arrival of the oenologist Christophe Daviau. After a long fermentation, this 2001 was meticulously matured on its fine lees and the result is astonishing. No feeling of hardness or astringency, but on the contrary, the first impression is of an almost delicate wine, which offers lightly fruity notes, in particular of cherry, with nuances of dried fruits and flowers. This is a wine for connoisseurs.

•ᴚ SCEA Daviau, Dom. de Bablut, 49320 Brissac-Quincé, tel. 02.41.91.22.59, fax 02.41.91.24.77, e-mail daviau@refsa.fr **▩**

I ev. day except Sun. 9am–12 noon 2pm–6.30pm

CH. DE BRISSAC 2001★

| ■ | n.c. | n.c. | | 5–8 € |

The Château de Brissac is emblematic of the Anjou-Villages-Brissac appellation; every year at the Salon des Vins de Loire (Loire Valley wine show) it welcomes the press and the gourmets who come to taste the new vintage. This delicate ruby-coloured 2001 shows aromas of ripe fruits that appear to be quite delicate. The palate is well balanced and reels off sensations of red and black berry fruits through to its delicate and long finish. Here is a wine that is very representative of the schistous soils from which it was produced and the expertise of the winemaker, who has been able to express the full quality of the grapes.

•ᴚ SCEA Daviau, Dom. de Bablut, 49320 Brissac-Quincé, tel. 02.41.91.22.59, fax 02.41.91.24.77, e-mail daviau@refsa.fr **▩**

I ev. day except Sun. 9am–12 noon 2pm–6.30pm

•ᴚ Duc de Brissac

DOM. DE HAUTE-PERCHE 2001★★

| ■ | 5 ha | 20,000 | ▌ ♦ | 5–8 € |

This estate has been considerably expanded and re-planted by Christian Papin. Now primarily planted with the noble grape varieties, Cabernet and Chenin, it covers 30 ha. Its Brissac is mentioned very often in the *Guide* and, marked highly, like this deep red 2001. This wine offers a complex nose exuding very ripe cherries. Supple, rounded and powerful, the palate reveals tannins which will integrate with time. The finish is warming, long and well-balanced.

•ᴚ EARL Agnès et Christian Papin, Dom. de Haute Perche, 7, chem. de la Godelière, 49610 Saint-Melaine-sur-Aubance, tel. 02.41.57.75.65, fax 02.41.57.75.42 **▼**

I ev. day except Sun. 8.30am–12 noon 2pm–6pm; Sat. by appt.; cl. 15–31 Aug.

DOM. DU PRIEURE 2001★★★

| ■ | 0.6 ha | 3,000 | ▌ ♦ | 5–8 € |

Domaine du Prieuré

Anjou-Villages Brissac
Appellation Anjou-Villages Brissac Contrôlée

2001
MIS EN BOUTEILLE AU DOMAINE

par Franck Brossaud, vigneron
49610 MOZE SUR LOUET - 02 41 45 30 74

13% vol.   Produit de France   750 ml

After pursuing a doctoral thesis at INRA (the national agricultural research institute) in Angers, Franck Brossaud established a property of 13 ha. His first wine, from the 2000 vintage, has been selected in the *Guide*, and this *coup de coeur* confirms the expertise of this new wine producer. From behind the clear ruby colour emerge powerful and fine perfumes of red fruit. This intense fruitiness runs through the tasting, filling the soft, elegant and clean palate, and leaving a most attractive impression. This wine is an excellent ambassador for the appellation.

•ᴚ Franck Brossaud, 1 bis, pl. du Prieuré, 49610 Mozé-sur-Louet, tel. 02.41.45.30.74, fax 02.41.45.30.74, e-mail franck.brossaud@wanadoo.fr **▼**

I by appt.

DOM. RICHOU
Les Vieilles Vignes 2001★

| ■ | n.c. | n.c. | | 5–8 € |

Really only developed since 1970, one could say that it was H. Richou who put the production of the red Anjou wines into orbit. He belongs to a family of astonishing wine producers, distinguished by two *coups de coeur* in the *Guide*, one for white Anjou and another for Coteaux de l'Aubance. A very beautiful intense ruby colour with crimson highlights, this Brissac needs to be aerated to reveal its flavours recalling concentrated black and red fruits. The luscious palate is full and fruity through to the end.

•ᴚ Dom. Richou, Chauvigné, 49610 Mozé-sur-Louet, tel. 02.41.78.72.13, fax 02.41.78.76.05

I by appt.

DOM. DES ROCHELLES
La Croix de Mission 2001★★

| ■ | n.c. | n.c. | | 8–11 € |

Jean-Yves Lebreton is one of the masters when considering the red wines of Anjou. His *cuvée* La Croix de Mission can henceforth be regarded as a benchmark amongst the wines of the northern Loire Valley. Once again in 2001 it is characterized by elegance from the start and provides an incredible impression of lightness: complex aromas of damp woodlands, peat, liquorice and black fruits; intense and supple palate with a long finish that brings out stewed fruits and again, liquorice. The **Cuvée Principale 2001 (5–8 €)**, of a similar intensity remains simpler with primarily fruity flavours.

↬ J.-Y. A. Lebreton, Dom. des Rochelles,
49320 Saint-Jean-de-Mauvrets, tel. 02.41.91.92.07,
fax 02.41.54.62.63, e-mail jy.a.lebreton@wanadoo.fr
⚑ by appt.

CH. LA VARIERE
Grande Chevalerie 2001★

				11–15 €
	n.c.	n.c.	🍶	

Château La Varière makes the greatest sweet wine appellations of Anjou, especially Bonnezeaux and Quarts de Chaume. When it comes to red wines, the route taken is to vinify the best wines in oak barrels. When they age, the wines are astonishing, linking feelings of power, roundness and spicy flavours with stewed and vanilla characters. These are wines that leave no-one indifferent and which can either fill a taster with enthusiasm or disorientate him. The vintage 2001 does not go against the rule. It impresses with its strength, but at present remains dominated by wood.

↬ Jacques Beaujeau, Ch. la Varière, 49320 Brissac-Quincé, tel. 02.41.91.22.64, fax 02.41.91.23.44,
e-mail chateau.la.variere@wanadoo.fr
⚑ by appt.

Wines selected but not starred

CH. D'AVRILLE
Elevé en fût de chêne 2001

				3–5 €
10 ha	50,000	🍶🍶		

↬ Biotteau Frères, Dom. d'Avrillé,
49320 Saint-Jean-de-Mauvrets, tel. 02.41.91.22.46,
fax 02.41.91.25.80,
e-mail chateau.avrille@wanadoo.fr ✅ 🏠
⚑ by appt.

DOM. DE MONTGILET 2001

			5–8 €
n.c.	n.c.		

↬ Victor et Vincent Lebreton, Dom. de Montgilet,
49610 Juigné-sur-Loire, tel. 02.41.91.90.48,
fax 02.41.54.64.25, e-mail montgilet@terre-net.fr
⚑ ev. day except Sun. 9am–12 noon 2pm–6pm;
cl. Sat. Jan. and Feb.

Rosé d'Anjou

Although very successful in export markets, nowadays this medium-dry wine is hard to sell. The principal variety is Grolleau, which used to be trained in the goblet shape, when it produced light rosé wines called "rougets". It is increasingly being vinified as light red table wine or Vin de Pays.

DE PREVILLE 2002★

				3–5 €
20 ha	130,000	🍶		

This is a négociant house vinifying primarily rosés and sparkling wines. Here, the flavours emerge slowly with aeration and their finesse is attractive. Notes of roses, boiled sweets and strawberry build up little by little throughout the tasting of this particularly delicate rosé.

↬ SAS Lacheteau, ZI de la Saulaie,
49700 Doué-la-Fontaine, tel. 02.41.59.26.26,
fax 02.41.59.01.94, e-mail contact@lacheteau.fr

ELYSIS 2002★★★

				3–5 €
60 ha	400,000	🍶		

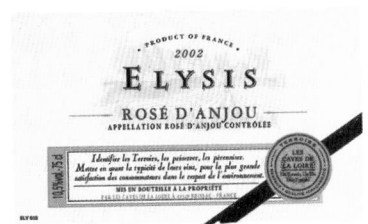

Les Caves de la Loire was created in 1951 and primarily produces rosé wines. A style of wine that is little-known and often underestimated, rosés are one of the traditional wines of Anjou and deserve greater attention as can be seen with this wine. A pale, delicate pink appearance; aromas of acacia flowers, soft red berries and mixed nuts, especially toasted almonds; the palate is subtle, harmoniously marrying a sensation of freshness and sweetness. This is, quite simply, a great wine.

↬ Les Caves de la Loire, rte de Vauchrétien,
49320 Brissac-Quincé, tel. 02.41.91.22.71,
fax 02.41.54.20.36, e-mail loire-wines@vapl.fr ✅
⚑ ev. day except Sun. 8.30am–12.30pm 2pm–6.30pm

CHANTAL FARDEAU
Rosé lumineux 2002★

				5–8 €
0.89 ha	8,000	🍶		

This estate is located at the foot of the Anjou corniche, within a few kilometres of the confluence of the Layon with the Loire. It is a simple rosé that offers attractive flavours throughout. Flavours of blackcurrants and strawberries run right through the palate and leave a particularly pleasant sensation of fresh fruits.

↬ Dom. Chantal Fardeau, Les Hauts Perrays,
49290 Chaudefonds-sur-Layon, tel. 02.41.78.67.57,
fax 02.41.78.68.78 ✅
⚑ by appt.

DOM. DE LA PETITE CROIX 2002★

				3–5 €
7 ha	10,000	🍶		

The Domaine de la Petite Croix is located on the left bank of the Layon at Thouarcé, just opposite the famous Bonnezeaux cru. The grapes were macerated for 24 hours in order to extract the colour and the flavours. The appearance is of an intense pink and the nose emerges on aeration with notes highlighting grenadine and flowers. The palate harmoniously blends sensations of freshness and sweetness and overall the wine is very well made.

↬ A. Denéchère et F. Geffard, Dom. de la Petite Croix,
49380 Thouarcé, tel. 02.41.54.06.99, fax 02.41.54.30.05,
e-mail scea@lapetitecroix.com ✅
⚑ by appt.

CH. PRINCE 2002★

				3–5 €
1.37 ha	6,000	🍶		

This vineyard was taken over by a new, young wine producer just before the 2002 harvest. It is his first attempt at winemaking and his first successful wine! Everything about this Rosé d'Anjou indicates the ripeness of the grapes: the deep pink colour with almost red highlights; the delicate aromas of

spices and blackcurrant; and the rounded, powerful and sweet palate. This wine is a success.
🖙 SCEA Levron-Vincenot, Princé,
49610 Saint-Melaine-sur-Aubance, tel. 02.41.57.82.28, fax 02.41.57.73.78,
e-mail scea.levron.vincenot@wanadoo.fr 🆅
🍷 ev. day except Sun. 9am–12 noon 2pm–6.30pm

Wines selected but not starred

CH. DE MONTGUERET 2002

| ■ | 4.69 ha | 40,000 | 🍾 ⚘ | | 3–5 € |

🖙 SCEA Ch. de Montguéret, BP 07,
49560 Nueil-sur-Layon, tel. 02.41.59.26.26, fax 02.41.59.59.02 🆅
🍷 by appt.
🍷 Lacheteau

DOM. ROBINEAU CHRISLOU 2002

| ■ | 1.74 ha | 1,800 | 🍾 ⚘ | | 3–5 € |

🖙 Louis Robineau, 14, rue Rabelais,
49750 Saint-Lambert-du-Lattay, tel. 02.41.78.36.04, fax 02.41.78.36.04 🆅
🍷 by appt.

Cabernet d'Anjou

There are some excellent medium-dry rosés made from the Cabernet Franc and Cabernet Sauvignon varieties in this appellation. Served chilled, they go well with melon as a starter or with desserts that are not too sweet. As they age, the wines take on a tile-red colour and can be drunk as an apéritif. Production was 197,325 hl in 2002. The best examples come from the fossiliferous sands of the Tigné region and the Layon.

VIGNOBLE DE L'ARCISON 2002★

| ■ | 5 ha | 6,000 | 🍾 ⚘ | | 3–5 € |

This estate markets approximately 70% of its production at the cellar door and makes giving its customers a good welcome a priority. At its peak towards the end of this year, this wine is characterized by a brilliant pale pink colour, aromas of delicate fresh fruits and red berries, and a palate that marries sweetness with acidity.
🖙 Damien Reulier, Le Mesnil, 49380 Thouarcé, tel. 02.41.54.16.81, fax 02.41.54.31.12,
e-mail damien.reulier@wanadoo.fr 🆅
🍷 ev. day 8am–12 noon 2pm–6pm; cl. Oct.

DOM. DE BOIS MOZE 2002★

| ■ | 2.5 ha | 20,000 | 🍾 ⚘ | | 5–8 € |

This old 18th century manor used to belong to the Aubigné family, but since the 1920s, the Boury family have cultivated the vines and made the wine. With an orangey-pink colour, and pleasant flavours of soft red and black fruits this wine is lively and full-bodied with very persistent blackcurrant notes, characteristic of the Cabernet Sauvignon grape variety. Overall it is fresh and well balanced, and can be drunk on its own.

🖙 Boury Frères, Dom. de Bois-Mozé, 49320 Coutures, tel. 02.41.57.91.28, fax 02.41.57.93.71 🆅
🍷 by appt.
🍷 Lancien

DOM. CADY 2002★

| ■ | 1 ha | 5,000 | 🍾 ⚘ | | 3–5 € |

This is an estate whose sweet wines are really brilliant and which deserves attention for the rest of its range. With a delicate, light salmon-pink colour, this wine offers complex aromas of red fruits, including raspberries, and of spices. The fresh and full-bodied palate displays a sensation of ripe fruits. This Cabernet d'Anjou will be perfect with eastern, spicy dishes.
🖙 EARL Dom. Philippe Cady, Valette,
49190 Saint-Aubin-de-Luigné, tel. 02.41.78.33.69, fax 02.41.78.67.79, e-mail cadyph@wanadoo.fr 🆅
🍷 by appt.

CH. DE CHAMPTELOUP 2002★

| ■ | 25 ha | 120,000 | 🍾 ⚘ | | –3 € |

The négociant, Champteloup also farms their own 80-ha vineyard. Linked with its very pale colour, this delicate Cabernet d'Anjou gives a rather restrained first impression. The palate, however, surprises with its richness and the fruity notes on the finish. It should be drunk right away.
🖙 SCEA Champteloup, 49700 Brigné-sur-Layon, tel. 02.41.59.65.10, fax 02.41.59.63.60 🆅

DOM. LA CROIX DES LOGES 2002★★

| ■ | 7 ha | 10,000 | 🍾 ⚘ | | 3–5 € |

The 2002 gives this estate a third *coup de coeur* in this appellation. It has vinified its Cabernet d'Anjou with 48 hours of skin contact followed by vinification at an ideal temperature of 15°C. Very flavoursome with notes of strawberry, spices and citrus fruits, it gives a particularly pleasant velvety feeling on the palate. The richness builds through the tasting and ends in an explosion of fruit with blackcurrants, redcurrants and raspberries.
🖙 SCEA Bonnin et Fils, Dom. La Croix des Loges, 49540 Martigné-Briand, tel. 02.41.59.43.58,
fax 02.41.59.41.11, e-mail bonninlesloges@aol.com 🆅
🍷 by appt.

DE PREVILLE 2002★★

| ■ | 30 ha | 200,000 | | | 3–5 € |

This négociant is based in Doué-la-Fontaine and has produced a string of successes with its 2002 rosés. The palate of this Cabernet d'Anjou reminds one of biting into soft red fruits, in particular wild strawberries. The finish is all freshness and delicacy. This is a tasty wine, ideal for a meal on a fine autumn day.
🖙 SAS Lacheteau, ZI de la Saulaie,
49700 Doué-la-Fontaine, tel. 02.41.59.26.26, fax 02.41.59.01.94, e-mail contact@lacheteau.fr

DOM. DES DEUX ARCS 2002★

| ■ | 1 ha | 4,500 | 🍾 ⚘ | | –3 € |

This estate is very representative of the village of Martigné which is primarily directed towards the production of rosé and red wines. The presence of a touch of carbon dioxide lightens this Cabernet d'Anjou. It emphasizes the aromatic notes of fruit salad and contributes to a feeling of freshness that is particularly pleasant on the palate. This is a very attractive aperitif wine.

🔹 Dom. des Deux Arcs, 11, rue du 8-Mai-1945, 49540 Martigné-Briand, tel. 02.41.59.47.37, fax 02.41.59.49.72, e-mail do2arc@wanadoo.fr 🆅

🍷 by appt.

🔹 Michel Gazeau

ELYSIS 2002★★

| | 50 ha | 400,000 | 🍾 🍷 | 3–5 € |

Les Caves de la Loire was founded in 1951 primarily to produce rosé wines. Overall in the 2002 vintage it shows a remarkable level of quality for the whole of this category (its Rosé d'Anjou was marked as noteworthy by the tasting Jury). This fresh and lively wine is characterized by a very beautiful expression on the nose with nuances of ripe and soft red fruits including redcurrants, with the same fruit emerging on the palate. With good colour, it can be served all through a meal.

🔹 Les Caves de la Loire, rte de Vauchrétien, 49320 Brissac-Quincé, tel. 02.41.91.22.71, fax 02.41.54.20.36, e-mail loire-wines@vapl.fr 🆅

🍷 ev. day except Sun. 8.30am–12.30pm 2pm–6.30pm

DOM. DE FIERVAUX

Elevé en fût de chêne 2002★

| | 3 ha | 5,000 | | 5–8 € |

The vineyard of Fiervaux is located in the Saumur region, at Oiré, a small hamlet built out of the tuffeau rock. The colour is so deep it is reminiscent of blood orange juice. The aromas conjure up flowers and citrus fruits. The palate shows great character with impressive richness. This Cabernet d'Anjou could be drunk with spicy or eastern dishes.

🔹 SCEA Cousin-Maitreau, 235, rue des Caves, 49260 Vaudelnay, tel. 02.41.52.34.63, fax 02.41.38.89.23, e-mail christ-cousin@wanadoo.fr 🆅 🏠

🍷 by appt.

DOM. GAUDARD 2002★★

| | 4.33 ha | 13,000 | | 3–5 € |

Pierre Aguilas, the important chairman of the Fédération viticole d'Anjou et Saumur (Anjou and Saumur wine federation), has a weakness for the appellation Cabernet d'Anjou, which he considers one of the most interesting of the Anjou wine area. The orangey-pink appearance is superb. On aeration the aromas suggest delicate notes of peach, nectarine and orange marmalade. The palate is delicate with a remarkable potential overall: a very good wine, it will open out into a thousand nuances on ageing.

🔹 Pierre Aguilas, Dom. Gaudard, rte de Saint-Aubin, 49290 Chaudefonds-sur-Layon, tel. 02.41.78.10.68, fax 02.41.78.67.72 🆅

🍷 ev. day 9am–12 noon 2pm–6pm; Sun. and public holidays by appt.

DOM. DES HAUTES OUCHES 2002★★

| | 9 ha | 10,000 | 🍾 🍷 | 3–5 € |

The Domaine des Hautes Ouches picks up rewards in all the categories of Anjou wines. Naturally, this wine is part of the estate's success story: a brilliant pink appearance, with light, yet intense aromas of flowers and soft red berries, the powerful palate is well balanced with a lively finish showing notes of blackcurrant.

🔹 EARL Joël and Jean-Louis Lhumeau, 9, rue Saint-Vincent, 49700 Brigné-sur-Layon, tel. 02.41.59.30.51, fax 02.41.59.31.75 🆅 🏠

🍷 by appt.

DOM. DES MAURIERES 2002★

| | 5.4 ha | 5,000 | 🍾 🍷 | 5–8 € |

The estate has a few acres in the famous cru of Quarts de Chaume. Its Cabernet d'Anjou appears drier than most of the wines of the appellation: it will accompany chicken in aspic and cold fish dishes. The terracotta colour is austere, whereas its perfume recalls spring flowers such as hyacinth. It is well balanced and very fruity with red berry notes.

🔹 EARL Moron, Dom. des Maurières, 8, rue de Perinelle, 49750 Saint-Lambert-du-Lattay, tel. 02.41.78.30.21, fax 02.41.78.40.26 🆅

🍷 by appt.

DOM. DES NOELS 2002★★

| | 2 ha | 8,000 | 🍾 🍷 | 3–5 € |

Having been the oenologist for a Saumur company specializing in the production of sparkling wines, J.-M. Garnier created the Domaine des Noëls in 1994. Here he has produced a great wine that seduced the tasting Jury with its delicate orangey-pink appearance and its complex fruit aromas with blackberry, blackcurrant and raspberry notes. The rich and well-balanced palate shows a long finish of black fruits. This is a superb wine.

🔹 SCEA Dom. des Noëls, Les Noëls, 49380 Faye-d'Anjou, tel. 02.41.54.18.01, fax 02.41.54.30.76, e-mail domaine-des-noels@terre-net.fr 🆅

🍷 by appt.

🔹 J.-M. Garnier

CH. DE PASSAVANT 2002★

| | 2.5 ha | 10,000 | 🍾 🍷 | 5–8 € |

This estate has always been in the forefront of technical wine advances: weed-killing in 1960, grassing down and pruning to a short cane in 1975, sustainable agriculture in 1999 and organic farming in 2000. This rosé has been produced from a short maceration over one night. It provides a particularly enjoyable feeling of richness and power: with ripe and stewed fruit flavours, the palate is soft and rounded, finishing with toasty notes mixed with fruit salad.

🔹 SCEA David-Lecomte, Ch. de Passavant, rte de Tancoigne, 49560 Passavant-sur-Layon, tel. 02.41.59.53.96, fax 02.41.59.57.91, e-mail passavant@wanadoo.fr 🆅

🍷 ev. day 8am–12 noon 2pm–7pm; Sat. Sun. by appt.

DOM. DES PETITES GROUAS 2002★★★

| | 1 ha | 5,000 | 🍾 🍷 | 3–5 € |

Located in Martigné-Briand, capital of Anjou rosé wines, this is an estate of 13 ha. The wine received all the votes of the Grand Jury: an intense pink with orange highlights, the appearance is perfectly true to type. Its aromas are to be applauded, bursting through on the nose evoking plum blossom, broom, citrus fruits, red fruits and pears too. The palate is full, fresh and long, all the way through confirming the formidable first impression. This wine is superb.

🔹 EARL Philippe Léger, Cornu, Les Petites Grouas, 49540 Martigné-Briand, tel. 02.41.59.67.22, fax 02.41.59.69.32 🆅

🍷 by appt.

DOM. SAINT ARNOUL 2002★

| | 5 ha | 15,000 | 🍾 🍷 | 3–5 € |

The name of the estate comes from the 13th century chapel of Saint-Arnoul located a few hundred metres away and a classified monument. The terroir on which this Cabernet d'Anjou was produced is a sandy limestone or *falun* (fossil-rich sand) particularly favourable for this type of wine and which is a hallmark of the village of Martigné-Briand, capital of the rosé wines of Anjou. It has a dazzling pink colour with fruity and floral aromas very representative of the appellation. The palate is balanced and fruity, with a very attractive sensation of freshness.

🔹 GAEC Poupard et Maury, Sousigné, 49540 Martigné-Briand, tel. 02.41.59.43.62, fax 02.41.59.69.23, e-mail saint-arnoul@wanadoo.fr 🆅

🍷 by appt.

LOIRE

DOM. DES TOUCHES 2002★

| ■ | 3 ha | 5,000 | | 3–5 € |

This estate is located in an old troglodytic village. Its Cabernet d'Anjou is elegant and generous. A salmon pink, it offers fruity and floral aromas that are very typical for the appellation. Full-bodied yet at the same time delicate, this is a versatile wine for many occasions: aperitif, desserts (fruit salads with red berries in particular) or with starters (mixed salads, charcuterie, etc.).
☛ Daniel Belin, Dom. des Touches, 49320 Coutures, tel. 02.41.57.90.06, fax 02.41.57.90.56 ☒
☒ by appt.

DOM. DES TROTTIERES 2002★

| ■ | 24.78 ha | 158,000 | ▮ ▲ | 3–5 € |

This estate was founded in 1906 with a vineyard area of 60 ha in a single plot, at that time the largest single plot in the Loire Valley. Its Cabernet d'Anjou was produced from a cold skin maceration for 90% of the grapes and a *saignée* for the remaining 10%. Restrained aromas open out with aeration and evoke fresh fruits. The palate is both lively and supple.
☛ SCEA Dom. des Trottières, 49380 Thouarcé, tel. 02.41.54.14.10, fax 02.41.54.09.00, e-mail lestrottieres@worldonline.fr ☒
☒ ev. day except Sat. Sun. 8am–12.30pm 2pm–6.30pm
☛ Lamotte

DOM. DU VIGNEAU 2002★

| ■ | 1.5 ha | 3,000 | ▮ ▲ | 3–5 € |

This estate is located in the vineyards of the upper Layon a few kilometres from the source of the Layon. A particularly good balance marks out this Cabernet d'Anjou, which harmoniously combines the sensations of freshness and sweetness. Flavours recall crystallized fruits and exotic fruits. The salmon-pink colour is also delicate and overall this is a very attractive wine.
☛ Patrick Robichon, pl. de l'Eglise, 49560 Passavant-sur-Layon, tel. 02.41.59.51.04, fax 02.41.59.51.04 ☒
☒ by appt.

Wines selected but not starred

DOM. DES EPINAUDIERES 2002

| ■ | 4.2 ha | 13,000 | ▮ ▲ | 3–5 € |

☛ SCEA Fardeau, Sainte-Foy, 49750 Saint-Lambert-du-Lattay, tel. 02.41.78.35.68, fax 02.41.78.35.50, e-mail fardeau.paul@club-internet.fr ☒
☒ by appt.

DOM. DES GRANDES BROSSES 2002

| ■ | 1.7 ha | 10,500 | ▮ ▲ | 3–5 € |

☛ EARL Longépé, Les Grandes Brosses, 49380 Champ-sur-Layon, tel. 02.41.54.16.16, fax 02.41.54.02.99 ☒
☒ by appt.

DOM. DES QUATRE ROUTES 2002

| ■ | 0.4 ha | 3,400 | ▮ ▲ | 3–5 € |

☛ Poupard et Fils, Dom. des Quatre Routes, 49540 Aubigné-sur-Layon, tel. 02.41.59.44.44, fax 02.41.59.49.70, e-mail domainede4routes@wanadoo.fr ☒
☒ ev. day 9am–7pm; Sat. Sun. by appt.

DOM. DE TERREBRUNE 2002

| ■ | 9 ha | 78,000 | ▮ ▲ | 3–5 € |

☛ SCA Dom. de Terrebrune, La Motte, 49380 Notre-Dame-d'Allençon, tel. 02.41.54.01.99, fax 02.41.54.09.06, e-mail domaine-de-terrebrune@wanadoo.fr ☒
☒ by appt.

Coteaux de l'Aubance

T he banks of the little Aubance river are schist slopes planted with old Chenin vines, giving a sweet wine which improves with age. Production was 4,714 hl in 2002. This appellation imposes strict limits on production.

S ince 2002, the phrase "Sélection de Grains Nobles" has been authorized for wines made from grapes giving a minimum natural sugar content of 234 g/l, or 17.5% potential alcohol without any chaptalization. They can only be sold 18 months after the harvest.

DOM. DE BABLUT
Vin Noble 2001★

| ■ | n.c. | 3,000 | ▮▮ | 15–23 € |

From a family based in Brissac, where they already owned vines and mills in the 16th century, this is one of the estates appearing regularly in the *Guide* in this appellation. They converted their vineyard to organic farming a few years ago. Matured for 18 months in barrel, their Vin Noble is a Sélection de Grains Nobles, in fact this 2001 is characteristic of wines from botrytized grapes. The aromas conjure up orange rind, tangerine and spices, especially nutmeg. Giving an impression of lightness despite its great richness, it is a very delicate wine, sold in 50 cl bottles. Also matured for the same length of time in wood, the **Grandpierre 2001** also releases aromas indicative of overripeness: ripe fruits, crystallized fruits and dried figs. Delicate, yet powerful, it has a most attractive balance and obtains the same mark.
☛ SCEA Daviau, Dom. de Bablut, 49320 Brissac-Quincé, tel. 02.41.91.22.59, fax 02.41.91.24.77, e-mail daviau@refsa.fr ☒ ▦
☒ ev. day except Sun. 9am–12 noon 2pm–6.30pm

DOM. DES DEUX MOULINS
Cuvée Exception 2001★

| ■ | 4 ha | 4,000 | ▮▮ | 8–11 € |

In the previous two editions this won the *coup de coeur* for the appellation. Vinified and matured in oak for ten months, the 2001 wine is a golden yellow. Delicate, even after aeration, the aromas suggest ripe fruits, flowers, vanilla and spices. Pleasant and balanced, the palate is accentuated on the finish by oaky notes. This wine could be drunk from the end 2003 but it will keep for a decade or more. (50 cl bottles.)
☛ Daniel Macault, Dom. des Deux Moulins, 20, rte de Martigneau, 49610 Juigné-sur-Loire, tel. 02.41.54.65.14, fax 02.41.54.67.94, e-mail lesdeuxmoulins@wanadoo.fr ☒
☒ by appt.

DOM. DITTIERE
Les Boujets 2002★★

| ■ | 5 ha | 5,000 | ▮ ▲ | 8–11 € |

Located a few kilometres from Brissac, this estate owns 35 ha of vines, including three in the Coteaux de l'Aubance. It offers a remarkably harmonious 2002. A golden yellow colour; delicate flavours of crystallized and dried fruits, characteristic of the appellation; and a structured, opulent palate that conjures

up particularly attractive notes of dried apricot and mango on the finish, it all makes a really excellent impression.
↘ Dom. Dittière, 1, chem. de la Grouas, 49320 Vauchrétien, tel. 02.41.91.23.78, fax 02.41.54.28.00, e-mail domaine.dittiere@wanadoo.fr ☑ ⌂
☿ by appt.

ELYSIS

Excellence 2001★

8 ha	12,000	▮ ⌘		5–8 €

Les Caves de la Loire was founded in 1951. Although specializing in the production of rosés, on occasion they demonstrate their expertise in making sweet wines, such as this one that tastes like a special treat. After aeration, the nose releases youthful aromas of fresh fruits and flowers. Just as fresh, the palate is lively on the finish. In all, this is a rather simple wine, but particularly enjoyable.
↘ Les Caves de la Loire, rte de Vauchrétien, 49320 Brissac-Quincé, tel. 02.41.91.22.71, fax 02.41.54.20.36, e-mail loire-wines@vapl.fr ☑
☿ ev. day except Sun. 8.30am–12.30pm 2pm–6.30pm

DOM. DE HAUTE PERCHE

Les Fontenelles 2001★

10 ha	12,000	▮⏅⌘		8–11 €

This estate is often noted for its wines from this appellation, in particular Les Fontenelles, which was served to French and German ministers at an important lunch in January 2003 arranged to celebrate the 40th anniversary of the Elysée Treaty. The 2001 demonstrates the terroir of the Coteaux de l'Aubance really well, an appellation that was unknown a decade ago. Delicate aromas recall ripe fruits and herbs with some toasty notes. The balanced palate finishes with nuances of crystallized fruits, dried fruits and flowers, in all, most harmonious.
↘ EARL Agnès et Christian Papin, Dom. de Haute Perche, 7, chem. de la Godelière, 49610 Saint-Melaine-sur-Aubance, tel. 02.41.57.75.65, fax 02.41.57.75.42 ☑
☿ ev. day except Sun. 8.30am–12 noon 2pm–6pm; Sat. by appt.; cl. 15–31 Aug.

DOM. DE MONTGILET

Clos Prieur 2001★★

1.14 ha	1,200	⏅		23–30 €

CLOS PRIEUR

COTEAUX DE L'AUBANCE
APPELLATION COTEAUX DE L'AUBANCE CONTROLÉE

DOMAINE DE MONTGILET
VICTOR & VINCENT LEBRETON

The labels from this estate illustrate the schistose slate – which was mined from the 12th century – on which the vineyard is established. It has a solid reputation as a producer of sweet wines and counts among the rare properties regularly awarded *coups de coeur*. The Clos Prieur obtained this distinction in the 95 vintage and the 2001 joins the club. A deep yellow colour with copper highlights, it has powerful flavours of fruit jelly and ripe fruits, with the palate being rich, opulent and elegant too. The finish reveals jam, honey, crystallized and dried fruits, all attesting to the richness of the grapes. (50 cl bottles.) **Les Trois Schistes 2001 (11–15 €)** also earned two stars.
↘ Victor et Vincent Lebreton, Dom. de Montgilet, 49610 Juigné-sur-Loire, tel. 02.41.91.90.48, fax 02.41.54.64.25, e-mail montgilet@terre-net.fr ☑
☿ ev. day except Sun. 9am–12 noon 2pm–6pm; cl. Sat. Jan. and Feb.

DOM. RICHOU

Les Trois Demoiselles 2001★★

3 ha	n.c.	⏅		15–23 €

Les Trois Demoiselles conquered many hearts... This Coteaux de l'Aubance has reached the summit more than once, and the 2001 vintage did well with the Grand Jury. The white Anjou from Richou obtained a *coup de coeur* as well: this is an estate that cannot be ignored in this area, especially for its white wines. With astonishing aromas of flowers, ripe and crystallized fruits, citrus fruits, honey and exotic fruits, the harmonious palate mixes sensations of freshness and richness: the wine has an inexplicable magic and should be shared with real friends. (50 cl bottles.) Lighter but still a great treat, the *cuvée* **Le Pavillon 2001 (11–15 €)** obtained a star.
↘ Dom. Richou, Chauvigné, 49610 Mozé-sur-Louet, tel. 02.41.78.72.13, fax 02.41.78.76.05 ☑
☿ by appt.

Wines selected but not starred

DOM. DE GAGNEBERT 2001

12 ha	10,000		5–8 €

↘ GAEC Moron, Dom. de Gagnebert, 2, chem. de la Naurivet, 49610 Juigné-sur-Loire, tel. 02.41.91.92.86, fax 02.41.91.95.50, e-mail moron@domaine-de-gagnebert.com ☑
☿ ev. day except Sun. 9am–12 noon 3pm–7pm

CH. PRINCE 2002

3.5 ha	4,700	▮ ⌘		5–8 €

↘ SCEA Levron-Vincenot, Princé, 49610 Saint-Melaine-sur-Aubance, tel. 02.41.57.82.28, fax 02.41.57.73.78, e-mail scea.levron.vincenot@wanadoo.fr ☑
☿ ev. day except Sun. 9am–12 noon 2pm–6.30pm

LOIRE

Anjou-Coteaux de la Loire

This appellation is limited to white wines made from Chenin, known here as Pineau de la Loire. Production, which was 1,079 hl in 2002, is limited by the size of the area, a dozen commenes situated exclusively on schists and lime-stone at Montjean. Careful picking encourages the grapes to reach over-ripeness, giving the generally medium-dry wines a greener colour than those of Coteaux de Layon. In this region, as elsewhere in Anjou, there is an increasing shift towards the production of red wines.

CH. DE PUTILLE
Cuvée Pierre Carrée 2001★

	5.3 ha	4,000	🍴 🍷	8–11 €

The Château de Putille is worth discovering for all of its range and it has undoubtedly contributed to the reputation of this small appellation. Taking its name from the volcanic rocks which are broken down into small parallelepipeds, this *cuvée* obtained a *coup de coeur* in the last two vintages. Resulting from a thorough selection at the vine, it displays a deep straw colour and releases flavours of crystallized fruits and honey, characteristic of wines from botrytized grapes. The palate is of an extreme richness and provides an astonishing sensation of sweetness. (50 cl bottles.) From the same appellation, the **Château de Putille Clos du Pirouet 2002 (5–8 €)** also obtained a star for its notes of overripe crystallized and dried fruits, and of fresh pear, and for its rich palate that finishes with a touch of acidity typical for the sweet wines of the Loire.
🍷 EARL Ch. de Putille, 49620 La Pommeraye,
tel. 02.41.39.02.91, fax 02.41.39.03.45 ☑
🍴 ev. day except Sun. 8.30am–12.30pm 2pm–7pm
🍷 Pascal Delaunay

Wines selected but not starred

DOM. DE PUTILLE
Cuvée des Hautes Blanches 2001

	n.c.	1,980	🍴 🍷	11–15 €

🍷 Isabelle Sécher et Stève Roulier, Dom. de Putille,
49620 La Pommeraye, tel. 02.41.39.80.43,
fax 02.41.39.81.91 ☑
🍴 by appt.

Savennières

These are dry white wines made from Chenin, mainly produced in the commune of Savennières. The schists and purple sandstone of the area give the wines a particular character which has led them in the past to be defined as part of the Coteaux de la Loire, but they deserve a place in their own right. The wines are a little firm, but full of aromatic flavour, excellent with cooked fish. The production of Savennières and the growths Coulée de Serrant and Roche aux Moines was 4,447 hl in 2002.

DOM. DES BARRES
Les Bastes 2002★

	1.2 ha	3,500	🍷	5–8 €

Based in Saint-Aubin-de-Luigné, the "pearl of the Coteaux du Layon", Patrice Achard also farms vines on the right bank of the Loire, in the Savennières appellation. Well-known to readers of the *Guide*, his selection Les Bastes 2002 offers a promising, yellow colour with golden tinges and mixes characteristic aromas of the appellation (floral and quince) with oaky notes coming from barrel-fermentation. Fresh, well balanced and long, it finishes on some spicy notes. Endowed with good ageing potential, it will acquire depth with time.
🍷 Patrice Achard, Dom. des Barres,
49190 Saint-Aubin-de-Luigné, tel. 02.41.78.98.24,
fax 02.41.78.68.37 ☑ 🏠
🍴 by appt.

DOM. DES BAUMARD
Clos de Saint Yves 2000★

	9.5 ha	35,000	🍴 🍷	11–15 €

Florent Baumard is based in Rochefort-sur-Loire, and on the other side of the river farms the Clos de Saint Yves vineyard, located just above the town of Savennières. The year 2000 gave a fresh wine with exuberant aromas of Williams pear, exotic fruits and wild flowers. Delicate and elegant, the palate offers a warming and long finish. A fine fish dish would be an ideal accompaniment, but should it be sole or bass?
🍷 Florent Baumard, SCEA Dom. des Baumard, 8, rue de l'Abbaye, 49190 Rochefort-sur-Loire, tel. 02.41.78.70.03, fax 02.41.78.83.82, e-mail contact@baumard.fr ☑
🍴 by appt.

CH. DE BELLEVUE
La Croix Picot 2002★

	0.6 ha	3,600	🍴 🍸 🍷	8–11 €

Built in the 19th century, the Château de Bellevue has 28 ha of vines split between the two banks of the Loire. La Croix Picot is a south-facing hillside overlooking the river. The grapes from this vineyard were harvested with a natural alcohol potential close to 14%. The wine releases intense aromas of quince, indicative of the great ripeness of the grapes. The wine has great potential, which should reveal itself fully by the end of the year 2003.
🍷 EARL Tijou et Fils, Ch. de Bellevue,
49190 Saint-Aubin-de-Luigné, tel. 02.41.78.33.11,
fax 02.41.78.67.84 ☑
🍴 by appt.

DOM. EMILE BENON
Clos du Grand Hamé Elevé en fût de chêne 2001★

	4.5 ha	6,000	🍴 🍸 🍷	8–11 €

Located in the hamlet of Epiré, this estate is regularly selected by the *Guide* Juries in this appellation, with this Clos du Grand Hamé selected for the sixth time. The 2001 stayed in wood for four months. Simple, almost varietal on the first sniff, with scents of broom and boxwood, it then reveals more delicate notes of toasted almonds, apricot and white peach. The light palate is particularly pleasant and there is a feeling of balance.
🍷 Dom. Emile Benon, rte de la Lande, Epiré,
49170 Savennières, tel. 02.41.77.10.76, fax 02.41.77.10.76,
e-mail earl.benon@wanadoo.fr ☑
🍴 by appt.

CH. DE LA BIZOLIERE 2001★

	32 ha	15,000	🍸	8–11 €

Pierre Soulez is a lover of old buildings. The head office of the estate, the Château de Chamboureau, is a 15th century manor with an overhanging octagonal tower forming the staircase. **Savennières Château de Chamboureau Cuvée d'Avant 2001** is given a special mention. It needs time, just like this Château de la Bizolière, vinified in two-year-old barrels with maturation on the lees and lees stirring. Its appearance is limpid, yellow with gold tinges; wild flowers, ripe fruits and honey aromas are typical of the appellation; the rich and full palate finishes on a touch of bitterness. This wine can be drunk from the end of 2003.
🍷 EARL Pierre Soulez, Ch. de Chamboureau,
49170 Savennières, tel. 02.41.77.20.04, fax 02.41.77.27.78 ☑
🍴 by appt.

DOM. DU CLOSEL

Les Coteaux 2001★★

| | 1 ha | 4,710 | 🍶 ⚬ | 15–23 € |

The Château de Vaults is the head office of this property. All the hallmarks of the 19th century adorn this residence, including high-roofed wings and a vast landscaped garden, but the estate and vineyard go back to the Middle Ages. The terroir of Les Coteaux is made up of volcanic rocks. The very ripe grapes measured a natural potential alcohol of 14%; the fermentation did not go right through and left a few grammes of sugar. The first sniff gives mineral notes, then white peach, apricot and toasted almonds, typical aromas of the appellation. On the palate, one finds roundness and delicacy. It can be served with foie gras or grilled fish. **Clos du Papillon (11–15 €)** which draws its name from the shape of this *lieu-dit* obtains a star. Its complex nose releases mineral nuances, and then delicate fragrances of citrus fruits, lychees, ripe fruits and walnuts. Rounded, fine and elegant, the palate finishes on a warming note. It is a wine for fine food, to match with monkfish or lobster, for example. From the same estate, the simpler **Cuvée des Caillardières 2001 (11–15 €)** is given a special mention.

☛ EARL Dom. du Closel, Ch. des Vaults, 1, pl. du Mail, 49170 Savennières, tel. 02.41.72.81.00, fax 02.41.72.86.00, e-mail closel@savennieres-closel.com 🅥

☕ ev. day except Sat. Sun. 9am–12.30pm 2pm–7pm

☛ Mmes de Jessey

DOM. DES FORGES

Moulin du Gué 2001★

| | 1.5 ha | 6,000 | 🍷 | 8–11 € |

Claude Branchereau has committed himself passionately to gaining recognition for the Coteaux du Layon vineyards and was behind the very recent recognition of the AOC Chaume. However, he has not neglected his Savennières, which this year has been most successful. Pale yellow colour with tinges of green, it has delicate aromas of buttercups and ripe fruits together with vanilla notes and spice from the maturation in oak vats. The palate is balanced and expressive with a finish showing nuances of honey and crystallized fruit, characteristic of a top-class wine: it has an attractive future and will open out fully by the end of 2003.

☛ Vignoble Branchereau, Dom. des Forges, rte de la Haie-Longue, 49190 Saint-Aubin-de-Luigné, tel. 02.41.78.33.56, fax 02.41.78.67.51, e-mail vitiforge@wanadoo.fr 🅥

☕ by appt.

NICOLAS JOLY 2001★

| | n.c. | n.c. | 🍷 | 11–15 € |

Nicolas Joly is an enthusiastic supporter of biodynamic farming whose objective is to bring back all the goodness to the land. This wine certainly gives a beautiful representation of its appellation, combining mineral flavours with the sweetened notes of ripe fruits. **Clos de la Bergerie Roche-aux-Moines 2001** is also given a mention.

☛ EARL Nicolas Joly, Ch. de la Roche aux Moines, 49170 Savennières, tel. 02.41.72.22.32, fax 02.41.72.28.68, e-mail coulee-de-serrant@wanadoo.fr

☕ ev. day except Sun. 8.30am–12 noon 2pm–5.45pm

MOULIN DE CHAUVIGNE 2002★

| | 3 ha | 15,000 | 🍶 ⚬ | 5–8 € |

Created in 1992 this recent estate, based in an old mill dating from 1750, has expanded it vineyard fast, going from 3 to 11 ha. Its Savennières 2002 is certainly still restrained on the nose, but seduced the Jury with its weight and elegance. The finish on crystallized fruit and quince seemed very promising. This wine should be more expressive by the end of 2003.

☛ Sylvie Termeau, Le Moulin de Chauvigné, 49190 Rochefort-sur-Loire, tel. 02.41.78.86.50, fax 02.41.78.86.56, e-mail lemoulindechauvigne@wanadoo.fr 🅥

☕ by appt.

DOM. DU PETIT METRIS

Clos de la Marche 2002★

| | 2 ha | 12,000 | 🍷 | 8–11 € |

In the family since 1742, this estate covers all the great white wine appellations in Anjou. Still young, its Clos de la Marche will express its character given time. For now it shows aromas reminiscent of raisins and grapes dried on the vine and a well-balanced palate with a fruity finish full of promise.

☛ GAEC Joseph Renou et Fils, Le Grand Beauvais, 49190 Saint-Aubin-de-Luigné, tel. 02.41.78.33.33, fax 02.41.78.67.77 🅥

☕ by appt.

CH. DE PLAISANCE

Le Clos 2001★

| | 1 ha | 4,000 | 🍶 🍷 | 11–15 € |

The vineyard belonging to the president of the new AOC Chaume is mainly established on the left bank of the Loire. That does not prevent Guy Rochais from successfully championing wines from the right bank, as proved by his two Savennières, both judged very successful and starred. **Château de Plaisance Cuvée Principale 2001 (8–11 €)**, matured in tank, and this Le Clos which had some oak. Both offer the same delicate mineral notes, nuances of wild flowers and ripe fruits, to which are added, in Le Clos flavours of nuts and toast from the well-handled maturation in oak. The ideal food accompaniment might be shellfish or fish, in particular the classic zander cooked in butter.

☛ Guy Rochais, Ch. de Plaisance, Chaume, 49190 Rochefort-sur-Loire, tel. 02.41.78.33.01, fax 02.41.78.67.52 🅥

☕ by appt.

Wines selected but not starred

CLOS DU PAPILLON

Cuvée d'Avant 2001

| | 2 ha | 5,900 | 🍷 | 15–23 € |

☛ EARL Pierre Soulez, Ch. de Chamboureau, 49170 Savennières, tel. 02.41.77.20.04, fax 02.41.77.27.78 🅥

☕ by appt.

CH. D'EPIRE

Cuvée spéciale 2002

| | 1 ha | 4,500 | 🍶 ⚬ | 8–11 € |

☛ SCEA Bizard-Litzow, Chais du château d'Epiré, 49170 Savennières, tel. 02.41.77.15.01, fax 02.41.77.16.23, e-mail luc.bizard@wanadoo.fr 🅥

☕ by appt.

DOM. LAUREAU

Cuvée des Genêts 2001

| | 5.6 ha | 14,000 | 🍶 | 8–11 € |

☛ Dom. Laureau du Clos Frémur, La Bénétrie, Butte de Frémur, 49000 Angers, tel. 02.41.72.25.54, fax 02.41.72.87.39 🅥

☛ Damien Laureau

CH. DE VARENNES 2001

| | 7 ha | 48,000 | 🍷 | 11–15 € |

☛ Vignobles Germain et Associés Loire, Ch. de Fesles, 49380 Thouarcé, tel. 02.41.68.94.00, fax 02.41.68.94.01, e-mail loire@vgas.com 🅥

☕ by appt.

☛ Bernard Germain

SAVENNIERES-ROCHE AUX MOINES, SAVENNIERES-COULEE DE SERRANT

damp woodlands and peat; thereafter emerge fragrances of white fruits, especially apple and plums macerated in alcohol. Warming and powerful the palate provides a remarkable finish of toast and spices.
⤚ EARL Nicolas Joly, Ch. de la Roche aux Moines,
49170 Savennières, tel. 02.41.72.22.32, fax 02.41.72.28.68,
e-mail coulee-de-serrant@wanadoo.fr ☑
☤ ev. day except Sun. 8.30am–12 noon
2pm–5.45pm

Savennières

It is difficult to distinguish between two growths so similar to each other in character and quality. The Coulée de Serrant is grown on a smaller area (7 ha), sited on both sides of the valley of the little Serrant river, but mainly on a steep slope with a southwesterly exposure. Totally owned by the Joly family, this appellation has attained the highest reputation at national level for its quality and value for money. It takes five or ten years for the wines to reach their peak. Roche aux Moines is owned by several growers and covers a declared area of 19 ha (though not all planted), producing an average of 600 hl. Even though quality is not as consistent, you can find certain vintages of which its namesake would not be ashamed.

Savennières-Roche aux Moines

DOM. AUX MOINES 2000★

| | 8 ha | 27,000 | 🍶 🍷 | 8–11 € |

One of the many monastic vineyards sold as a state-owned property during the Revolution. Pale yellow with hints of bronze, its Savennières opens up slowly, but with aeration provides evidence of finesse and elegance, characteristics of wines from a great terroir. The full range of flavours mixes flowers with ripe fruits, granny smith apples and citrus fruits. The overall balance is particularly successful. Classic of the appellation, it should be served with zander in butter.
⤚ SCI Mme Laroche, La Roche aux Moines,
49170 Savennières, tel. 02.41.72.21.33, fax 02.41.72.55.86 ☑
☤ by appt.

Savennières-Coulée de Serrant

NICOLAS JOLY 2001★★

| | 7 ha | 15,000 | 🍷🍷 | 38–46 € |

According to Curnonsky, the "Gastronome Prince", the vineyard of Coulée de Serrant appears amongst the most important of France, together with Château d'Yquem, Le Montrachet, Château-Chalon, etc. An eloquent supporter of biodynamics, Nicolas Joly has offered a wine that lives up to its reputation. The nose is at first austere, reminiscent of

Coteaux du Layon

These are medium-dry, medium-sweet and sweet white wines, of which 55,630 hl were produced in 2002, from the slopes of 25 communes on the banks of the Layon, from Nueil to Chalonnes. Chenin is the only variety grown. Several villages have a reputation for quality: the best known is Chaume, producing from 78 ha. Six other names can also be added to the appellation: Rochefort-sur-Loire, Saint-Aubin-de-Luigné, Saint-Lambert-du-Lattay, Beaulieu-sur-Layon, Rablay-sur-Layon and Faye-d'Anjou. Since 2002 the phrase "Sélection de Grains Nobles" has been authorized for wines made from grapes giving a minimum natural sugar content of 234 g/l or 17.5% potential alcohol without any chaptalization. They can only be sold 18 months after the harvest. They are subtle wines, golden green at Concourson, yellower and stronger downstream, with aromas of honey and acacia from the overripe grapes. Their ability to keep is exceptional.

DOM. DES BARRES
Saint-Aubin Les Paradis 2002★★

| | 2 ha | 4,000 | 🍶 🍷 | 8–11 € |

This estate is a previous winner of a *coup de coeur* and one of those featured in the *Guide* to rely on. Les Paradis originates from a soil of pudding stone of the Carboniferous era, cemented gravel, the typical terroir of Saint-Aubin-de-Luigné, the 'pearl of the Layon'. This 2002 wine has great promise! Aromas of ripe fruits, wax, honey, and raisins; freshness and power combine harmoniously on the palate, there are plenty of signs for a great future. A touch of bitterness on the finish will integrate with time. Two stars are also awarded to the **Coteaux du Layon Cuvée François 2001 (15–23 € for a 50 cl bottle)** which has spent one year in wood. Its assets include delicate aromas of ripe or even concentrated fruits characteristic of grapes harvested very ripe; a full, long palate; and very attractive balance. As for its ageing potential, it should last several decades.
⤚ Patrice Achard, Dom. des Barres,
49190 Saint-Aubin-de-Luigné, tel. 02.41.78.98.24,
fax 02.41.78.68.37 ☑ 🏠
☤ by appt.

CH. DE BOIS-BRINCON
Faye Cuvée Matisse 2001★★

| | 5.5 ha | 3,000 | 🍷🍷 | 11–15 € |

The Bois-Brinçon estate goes back to medieval times. Xavier Cailleau arrived there in 1991 and since then the sweet wines made by the estate have taken off. This one offers a very beautiful expression of flavour with notes of apricot, grapefruit and almond. There is evidence of remarkable balance on the palate, in particular on the finish where finesse and richness combine. This wine provides an expressive feel, characteristic of the great sweet wines of the Loire Valley.
⤚ Xavier Cailleau, Ch. de Bois-Brinçon,
49320 Blaison-Gohier, tel. 02.41.57.19.62,
fax 02.41.57.10.46 ☑ 🏠
☤ by appt.

CH. DU BREUIL

Beaulieu Vieilles Vignes 2001★★

| | 8 ha | 3,000 | 🍶 | 11–15 € |

From Normandy to Bordeaux, in France there are many Châteaux du Breuil, a place name of Gallic origin. This one is located at Beaulieu-sur-Layon. Its Coteaux du Layons have been mentioned in the *Guide* since the first edition. With a light yellow-straw colour, the 2001 wine has great delicacy, with fresh aromas indicating acacia and stewed or crystallized fruits. The palate is generous and balanced finishing on notes of honey and apricot. Also interesting and given a mention is the **Cuvée Orantium 2001 (23–30 € for a 50 cl bottle)** which remained in barrel for 16 months. More powerful, it reveals some oaky notes that need time to integrate.

➽ Ch. du Breuil, 49750 Beaulieu-sur-Layon,
tel. 02.41.78.32.54, fax 02.41.78.30.03,
e-mail ch.breuil@wanadoo.fr 🟦
☿ by appt.
➽ Marc Morgat

DOM. CADY

Saint-Aubin Les Varennes 2002★

| | 3 ha | 6,500 | 🍶 ♦ | 8–11 € |

Saint-Aubin-de-Luigné is a small, pretty village on the banks of the Layon. The visitor can stroll there contemplating its old residences, unless he prefers to make an excursion on to the steep hillsides or take a boat down the river. He must not miss tasting the Coteaux du Layon wines from the village and can call in with complete confidence at Domaine Cady, whose wines have been selected in the *Guide* since the first edition, often with very good marks. A famous *lieu-dit* based on green schist above the carboniferous layer; Les Varennes has a hillside position. The vine there is ripened by the midday sun and gives rise to wines which combine austere notes with opulence. This is the case with this elegant 2002 that offers mineral aromas on the first sniff, and then reveals ripe and concentrated fruits, with notes of rhubarb. Fresh, both delicate and concentrated, the palate is marked by its great terroir.

➽ EARL Dom. Philippe Cady, Valette,
49190 Saint-Aubin-de-Luigné, tel. 02.41.78.33.69,
fax 02.41.78.67.79, e-mail cadyph@wanadoo.fr 🟦
☿ by appt.

DOM. DELAUNAY

Saint-Aubin 2002★

| | 3.75 ha | 15,000 | 🍶 ♦ | 3–5 € |

The little town of Montjean-sur-Loire has an ecological museum that traces life all along the river. This family property amounts to 40 hectares of vines covering the hillsides bordering the Loire. It presents a Saint-Aubin whose delicacy is attractive: this wine does not tire the palate with its richness. Aromas of citrus fruits and lemon are simple and refreshing; honey appears behind. The touch of bitterness on the finish will tone down with time.

➽ Dom. Delaunay Père et Fils, Daudet, rte de Chalonnes,
49570 Montjean-sur-Loire, tel. 02.41.39.08.39,
fax 02.41.39.00.20, e-mail delaunay.anjou@wanadoo.fr 🟦
☿ ev. day 8am–12 noon 2pm–6.30pm; Sat. Sun. by appt.

PHILIPPE DELESVAUX

Sélection de grains nobles 2000★★★

| | 8 ha | 2,500 | 🍶 | 15–23 € |

Philippe Delesvaux is a great supporter of Sélections de Grains Nobles. For the third year running, he presents a superb example. Here one finds the finesse and delicacy of an Impressionist painting. The complex flavours are restrained: orange and other citrus fruits, fruit jelly, liquorice and medicinal plants (verbena, lime blossom, etc.). The palate also shows all these nuances and, in spite of its concentration, remains ethereal, refined and of great class. (50 cl bottles.)

➽ Philippe Delesvaux, La Haie Longue,
49190 Saint-Aubin-de-Luigné, tel. 02.41.78.18.71,
fax 02.41.78.68.06,
e-mail dom.delesvaux.philippe@wanadoo.fr 🟦
☿ by appt.

DOM. DHOMME

Sélection de grains nobles 2001★★

| | 4 ha | 2,400 | 🍶 | 11–15 € |

One is always interested to taste the latest wines from this estate since it obtained a *coup de coeur* in this appellation with a memorable 99. The grapes behind this 2001 wine were affected 100% by noble rot and had a natural potential alcohol of 22%. Richness is the distinguishing mark in tasting this *cuvée*: rich perfumes favour liquorice, stewed fruits, and caramelized apple; the palate evokes crystallized grapes and there are plenty of signs of a great future. This wine will still improve with time, to reveal a multitude of different flavours.

➽ Dom. Dhommé, Le Petit Port-Girault,
49290 Chalonnes-sur-Loire, tel. 02.41.78.24.27,
fax 02.41.74.94.91 🟦
☿ ev. day except Sun. 9am–12 noon 2pm–7pm

DOM. DULOQUET

Cuvée Quintessence 2001★

| | 6 ha | n.c. | 🍶 | 23–30 € |

Hervé Duloquet took over the family estate 12 years ago and has specialized in making and champ ioning great sweet wines. Some spectacular successes have made the reputation of the estate. This year, it presented two *cuvées* which each obtain a star. Vinified from grapes with a natural potential alcohol of more than 20%, Cuvée Quintessence exhibits an intense nose where quince appears alongside honey, almonds and other nuts. One finds honey, combined with crystallized fruits on a full-bodied palate with a great length of flavour, finishing on an impression of sweetness. (50 cl bottles.) More accessible, the **Cuvée Prestige 2002 (8–11 €)** appears lighter and fresher.

➽ Hervé Duloquet, Les Mousseaux, 4, rte du Coteau,
49700 Les Verchers-sur-Layon, tel. 02.41.59.17.62,
fax 02.41.59.37.53 🟦
☿ by appt.

DOM. DES EPINAUDIERES

Saint-Lambert Cuvée Prestige Juliette 2001★

| | 0.6 ha | 2,300 | 🍶 | 11–15 € |

Twelve years ago Paul Fardeau joined the estate of his father, Roger, who established the property in 1966. The latest generation is also associated with the future of the vineyard: after Cuvée Clement comes this one dedicated to Juliette, born in the year 2001. The wine combines finesse with richness. Of an intense golden yellow, it offers aromas of honey and of grapes affected by noble rot. Fresh and rich, on the middle palate is honey with crystallized fruits and quince.

➽ SCEA Fardeau, Sainte-Foy,
49750 Saint-Lambert-du-Lattay, tel. 02.41.78.35.68,
fax 02.41.78.35.50, e-mail fardeau.paul@club-internet.fr 🟦
☿ by appt.

DOM. FARDEAU

Vieilles Vignes 2002★

| | 1.8 ha | 7,000 | 🍶 ♦ | 8–11 € |

This estate is opposite the Anjou corniche and offers a pretty panorama of the Coteaux du Layon vineyard area. Here is his *cuvée* Vieilles Vignes. Even if it is not yet fully expressive, the 2002 reveals concentrated aromas indicating a harvest of very ripe grapes. Powerful and rich, the palate shows notes of honey and crystallized fruit characteristic of noble rot. It can be drunk from the end of the year 2003.

➽ Dom. Chantal Fardeau, Les Hauts Perrays,
49290 Chaudefonds-sur-Layon, tel. 02.41.78.67.57,
fax 02.41.78.68.78 🟦
☿ by appt.

DOM. DES FORGES

Chaume Les Onnis 2001★★

| | 4 ha | 6,000 | 🍶 | 11–15 € |

Chaume was recognized as AOC (from the 2002 vintage), together with the very coveted mention "Premier Cru des Coteaux du Layon". Claude Branchereau, who presents a remarkable wine here, is no stranger to this term. The *Guide* discovered his wine Les Onnis 2001 that shows an astonishing power yet gives a sensation of freshness characteristic of the great sweet wines of Anjou. Its intense aromas evoke crystallized fruit, dried apricot, fig and tangerine. Already in balance, this wine can be drunk from the end of 2003, but is capable of ageing for several decades.

☛ Vignoble Branchereau, Dom. des Forges, rte de la Haie-Longue, 49190 Saint-Aubin-de-Luigné, tel. 02.41.78.33.56, fax 02.41.78.67.51, e-mail vitiforge@wanadoo.fr ☑
☖ by appt.

VIGNOBLE DE LA FRESNAYE

Vieilles Vignes Rossignolet 2002★

	1.2 ha	3,200	▮ ♦	5–8 €

Established in Saint-Aubin-de-Luigné, the "pearl of the Layon", this estate amounts to approximately 17 ha. From vines that are half a century old, its Vieilles Vignes selection is dominated by notes of ripe fruits (quince, pear, peach) and of honey which runs through the tasting. Elegant, fresh and full, the palate shows a very beautiful balance of alcohol, sugar and acidity. It is a simple, enjoyable Coteaux du Layon that is very representative of its appellation.

☛ Joseph Halbert, Villeneuve, 49190 Saint-Aubin-de-Luigné, tel. 02.41.78.38.21, fax 02.41.78.66.44 ☑
☖ by appt.

CH. DU FRESNE

Faye Clos des Cocus 1998★★

	1.15 ha	1,500	▮ ⦿ ♦	15–23 €

The result of a partnership between two great wine-growing families, this estate amounts to more than 76 ha of vineyard, among them the small but famous Clos des Cocus (meaning cuckold). Evocations of ripe apricot made golden by the sun, runs through the tasting; the palate is sweet, balanced, and dominated on the finish by dried fruits: this charming 98 will give back a taste for life to those disappointed in love, and to others! It should be drunk right away. Also notable is the **Coteaux du Layon Faye Butte de Chevriottes 2001 (8–11 €)**, which is singled out.

☛ Vignoble Robin-Bretault, Ch. du Fresne, 49380 Faye-d'Anjou, tel. 02.41.54.30.88, fax 02.41.54.17.52, e-mail fresne@voila.fr ☑
☖ by appt.

DOM. GAUDARD

Saint-Aubin-de-Luigné Cuvée Claire 2002★

	4 ha	3,000		15–23 €

For a decade Pierre Aguilas has worked relentlessly to return greatness to the Anjou wine area. Domaine la Gaudard has produced two Coteaux du Layon that were both so successful they have both been retained by the Jury: this Cuvée Claire, a Saint-Aubin, is a full-bodied wine which nevertheless gives a pleasant feeling of freshness, much enjoyed for its fruit and finish of accents of ripe pears and exotic fruits; and, more accessible, a straw-yellow **Coteaux du Layon Les Varennes 2002 (5–8 €)** with tinges of gold that has aromas of ripe fruits, grapes turned golden by the sun and a delicate finish marked by stewed fruits and quince; an unambiguous wine, which on the palate gives a most attractive impression of lightness.

☛ Pierre Aguilas, Dom. Gaudard, rte de Saint-Aubin, 49290 Chaudefonds-sur-Layon, tel. 02.41.78.10.68, fax 02.41.78.67.72
☖ ev. day 9am–12 noon 2pm–6pm;
Sun. and public holidays by appt.

DOM. DE LA GERFAUDRIE

Les Hauts de la Gerfaudrie 2002★★

	2.7 ha	12,000	▮	5–8 €

An estate close to the confluence of the Loire and Layon, the *gerfaut* (falcon) takes flight here with Les Hauts de Gerfaudrie, which almost reached a *coup de coeur*! Captivating and varied, the aromas express ripe and exotic fruits (passion-fruit, lychee), citrus fruits and wax. On the palate, without being very powerful, this wine leaves a feeling of balance and astonishing finesse. It has personality, delicacy, and tasted like a real treat.

☛ SCEV J.-P. et P. Bourreau, 25, rue de l'Onglée, 49290 Chalonnes-sur-Loire, tel. 02.41.78.02.28, fax 02.41.78.03.07, e-mail domaine-gerfaudrie@wanadoo.fr ☑
☖ by appt.

DOM. LES GRANDES VIGNES 2002★

	5.72 ha	9,300	⦿	5–8 €

Here is an estate you can trust for reds and for sweet whites, you only have to look at previous editions of the *Guide* over the years. In spite of its youth which has not allowed this wine to express itself fully, this appealing 2002 shows lively notes of lemon and apricot, and on the palate provides an impression of lightness despite its concentration. This is a very great wine in the making.

☛ GAEC Vaillant, Dom. Les Grandes Vignes, La Roche Aubry, 49380 Thouarcé, tel. 02.41.54.05.06, fax 02.41.54.08.21, e-mail vaillant@domainelesgrandesvignes.com ☑
☖ by appt.

DOM. GROSSET

Rochefort Acacia 2001★

	1 ha	500	⦿	23–30 €

Domaine Grosset works in an old-fashioned way and looks after its vineyards particularly well. Its barrel cellar deserves a visit. This year the property has produced a wine of astonishing richness. Noble rot has given characteristic flavours of dried fruits, overripe fruits, and quince jelly. This is a wine that can be kept for several years. (50 cl bottles.)

☛ Serge Grosset, 60, rue René-Gasnier, 49190 Rochefort-sur-Loire, tel. 02.41.78.78.67, fax 02.41.78.79.79, e-mail serge.grosset@libertysurf.fr ☑
☖ by appt.

CH. DE LA GUIMONIERE

Chaume 2001★★

	10 ha	10,000	⦿	23–30 €

Owned by Vignobles Germain since 1996, the Château de la Guimonière has taken the best grapes of the 2001 vintage for this wine, which typically blends freshness and austerity (through a touch of bitterness of the finish) with richness and even opulence. Intense, the range of flavours lists dried fruits and currants side by side with notes from the maturation: subtle roasted coffee nuances, spices and vanilla. The impatient can open this wine right away, but it will keep for a decade.

☛ Vignobles Germain et Associés Loire, Ch. de Fesles, 49380 Thouarcé, tel. 02.41.68.94.00, fax 02.41.68.94.01, e-mail loire@vgas.com ☑
☖ by appt.
☛ Bernard Germain

LE LOGIS DU PRIEURE

Le Clos des Aunis 2002★

	1.5 ha	6,000	▮	8–11 €

Concourson, in the upper Layon, was formerly a port. From this village, the river was canalised in the 18th century to transport wines and coal. The mines of the area declined from the 19th century, but the wines have a good market, thanks to estates like this one. The *Guide* rediscovered Le Clos des Aunis, which was very successful in previous years. Even if the aromas of the 2002 are not yet fully revealed, the ripe fruits, quince and apple emerge on the middle palate which is already full and powerful. This is overall a promising wine that should be ready by the end of the year.

☛ SCEA Jousset et Fils, Le Logis du Prieuré, 49700 Concourson-sur-Layon, tel. 02.41.59.11.22, fax 02.41.59.38.18 ☑
☖ ev. day except Sun. 9am–12.30pm 2pm–7pm

LUC ET FABRICE MARTIN

Sélection de grains nobles 2001★★★

	1.5 ha	2,000	⦿	15–23 €

"An Anjou wine with the colour of gold and a fine bouquet is the wine of angels": this 15th century homage to the white wines of the area applies wonderfully to this scintillating golden yellow Sélection de Grains Nobles, which in the

previous vintage obtained a *coup de coeur*. Smoky notes, toasted almonds, crystallized fruit, dried banana and ginger jostle together on the nose. Fresh to start with, the palate builds up in power and deploys a profusion of flavours: crystallized orange, truffle, spices (clove). Already exceptional, this 2001 will still improve with time. (50 cl bottles.) From the same property, the **Coteaux du Layon Cuvée Prestige (8–11 €)**, matured for 12 months in barrel, obtained one star for its delicate nose mixing stewed apple, quince and crystallized fruit with a rich palate showing a very attractive balance between alcohol and sugar and a honeyed finish. Here is an estate whose sweet wines are definitely impossible to ignore.
➺ GAEC Luc et Fabrice Martin, 2 bis, rue du Stade, 49290 Chaudefonds-sur-Layon, tel. 02.41.78.19.91, fax 02.41.78.98.25 ☑
☂ by appt.

DOM. DE LA MOTTE

Rochefort Cuvée La Garde 2002★★

	1 ha	2,000	⑪	11–15 €

Located at the eastern end of the Anjou corniche, the little town of Rochefort-sur-Loire is worth visiting not least for this estate whose winery is at the entrance to the village. There one will find this very unusual Coteaux du Layon Rochefort that displays remarkable lightness. The palate reveals a freshness of citrus fruits; the range of flavours link delicate lemony notes with light touches of oak notes. (50 cl bottles.)
➺ Gilles Sorin, Dom. de la Motte, 31–35, av. d'Angers, 49190 Rochefort-sur-Loire, tel. 02.41.78.72.96, fax 02.41.78.75.49, e-mail sorin.dommotte@wanadoo.fr ☑
☂ by appt.

CH. DES NOYERS

Réserve Vieilles Vignes 2001★

	5.5 ha	5,000	⑪	11–15 €

Classic and austere, the Château des Noyers controls a vineyard of around 20 hectares. The grapes for its Réserve Vieilles Vignes required eight successive selected pickings. It offers beautiful weight and mixes crystallized fruits and flowers with oak notes. Rich and powerful, the palate finishes on flavours of honey, characteristic of wines from grapes affected by noble rot. This wine has real potential and will improve with time. (50 cl bottles.)
➺ Ch. des Noyers, 49540 Martigné-Briand, tel. 02.41.54.03.71, fax 02.41.54.27.63, e-mail webmaster@chateaudesnoyers.fr ☑
☂ by appt.
➺ J.-P. Besnard

DOM. OGEREAU

Saint-Lambert Clos des Bonnes Blanches 2001★★

	2 ha	2,000	⑪	15–23 €

The Domaine Ogereau harvests *Hachette coups de coeur* each autumn, or very nearly; as for stars, it collects them in pairs, at the very least. When two great names in the Anjou wine area cross each others' path, Domaine Ogereau and Clos des Bonnes Blanches, the result can be only amazing! The 99 obtained a *coup de coeur*, this 2001 came very close to one. A golden yellow appearance with orange tinges; aromas made up of floral notes, stewed fruits, honey and quince evocative of botrytized grapes; and a rich and powerful palate with a multitude of flavours come together to make a wine of great quality. (50 cl bottles.)

➺ Vincent Ogereau, 44, rue de la Belle-Angevine, 49750 Saint-Lambert-du-Lattay, tel. 02.41.78.30.53, fax 02.41.78.43.55 ☑
☂ by appt.

DOM. DES PETITES GROUAS 2001★

	1 ha	1,400	⑪	15–23 €

With its clay-limestone soil, the village of Martigné-Briand is the rosé wine capital of Anjou. Locally, however, there are small hillside areas that give interesting sweet wines. Hence why this estate, generally selected for its red or rosé, figures in the Coteaux du Layon section. From very rich grapes and vinified for 16 months in barrel, this 2001 releases flavours of overripe grapes. Powerful on the palate, impressions of surprising richness and sweetness are around to dominate. It will last decades. (50 cl bottles.)
➺ EARL Philippe Léger, Cornu, Les Petites Grouas, 49540 Martigné-Briand, tel. 02.41.59.67.22, fax 02.41.59.69.32 ☑
☂ by appt.

DOM. DU PETIT VAL

Cuvée Simon 2002★★

	2 ha	6,000	▮ ♦	8–11 €

Created in 1950, this property originally had just 4 ha of vines: today it owns 50 ha. Its Cuvée Simon has been discovered and is most welcome in this vintage. The dried and crystallized fruits and apricot indicate that the harvest was of extremely ripe grapes. The palate is pleasant, powerful and rich, "an ambassador for its appellation", according to the tasters. Some tasters would have liked to have given it a *coup de coeur*.
➺ EARL Denis Goizil, Dom. du Petit Val, 49380 Chavagnes, tel. 02.41.54.31.14, fax 02.41.54.03.48, e-mail denisgoizil@tiscali.fr ☑
☂ by appt.

CH. PIERRE-BISE

L'Anclaie 2001★★

	6 ha	9,000	⑪	11–15 €

Claude Papin collects *coups de coeur*. Dedicated to his various terroirs, he brings out the characteristics of each *lieu-dit* with loving care. This year, the *cuvée* L'Anclaie has astonishing richness and harmony. An intense yellow with gold highlights, it delivers aromas of crystallized fruits, quince and honey. With remarkable finesse, the palate comes back on the finish with honey and quince again, to which is added caramel. This is a wine of very great personality. (50 cl bottles.)
➺ Claude Papin, Ch. Pierre-Bise, 49750 Beaulieu-sur-Layon, tel. 02.41.78.31.44, fax 02.41.78.41.24 ☑
☂ by appt.

CH. DE PLAISANCE

Chaume Les Zerzilles 2001★

	13 ha	5,000	⑪	15–23 €

Located right in the middle of Chaume, the Château de Plaisance seems to be the guardian of this great terroir. Les Zerzilles is the flagship wine of the estate. The seductive 2001 expresses a mixture of honey, acacia, almond and bruised apple aromas on the nose. Full-bodied, rich and generous, on the finish it reveals a delicate freshness that brings out the floral and mineral flavours. This has real character.
➺ Guy Rochais, Ch. de Plaisance, Chaume, 49190 Rochefort-sur-Loire, tel. 02.41.78.33.01, fax 02.41.78.67.52 ☑
☂ by appt.

DOM. DU PORTAILLE

Planche Mallet 2002★★

	5 ha	n.c.	⑪	5–8 €

This estate is situated on the little hill of Millé that appears in a number of the *lieux-dits* of vineyards documented in the 18th century. The new generation took over the reins here in 1998 and excelled particularly with this Coteaux du Layon. Delicate aromas of honey, *pain d'épice* and dried fruits are characteristic of a harvest of very ripe grapes. Both powerful and fresh, the palate has remarkable harmony and finesse.

Coteaux du Layon

This *cuvée* was not far from gaining a *coup de coeur*. It has a life expectancy of several decades.
➤ EARL Tisserond, Dom. du Portaille, 18, rue de Jarzé, Millé, 49380 Chavagnes, tel. 02.41.54.31.63☑
⏳ by appt.

DOM. DU REGAIN
Le Paradis 2002★★

| 1.2 ha | 2,000 | ⑪ | 11–15 € |

Here is a new name in the *Guide*! Frédéric Etienne, having been the director of the Institut Technique du Vin (technical wine institute) in Angers, has started a second career by taking over a vineyard in 2002. The name of the estate evokes a novel by Giono and his return to difficult lands. The wine from 2002, the first from the estate, had not yet expressed all its potential on the day of the tasting. But already, there were only positive signs! Aromas of crystallized fruits and of grapes dried in the sun, with a rich, complex and balanced palate: perhaps it will taste like paradise next year? (50 cl bottles.)
➤ F. et F. Etienne, Dom. du Regain, Le Pied de Fer, 49540 Martigné-Briand, tel. 02.41.40.28.20, fax 02.41.40.28.21, e-mail domaine.regain@wanadoo.fr ☑
⏳ by appt.

VIGNOBLE MICHEL ROBINEAU
Saint-Lambert-du-Lattay Sélection de Grains Nobles 2001★

| 2 ha | 2,500 | ⑪ | 11–15 € |

Michel Robineau started his estate in 1990 with 2 ha. Thirteen years later, the estate has increased to 9 ha and enjoys an excellent reputation. The 2001 has been vinified from grapes of more than 20% natural potential alcohol. On the first sniff, the aromas are slightly iodized and then evolve with aeration towards liquorice and tangerine. Concentrated and powerful, the palate finishes with a note of acidity and a delicious sensation of overripe grapes. The wine needs to be left for one to two years.
➤ Michel Robineau, 3, chem. du Moulin, Les Grandes Tailles, 49750 Saint-Lambert-du-Lattay, tel. 02.41.78.34.67 ☑
⏳ by appt.

DOM. DE LA ROCHE MOREAU
Saint-Aubin 2001★★

| n.c. | 2,500 | ▮ ◊ | 8–11 € |

The tasting cellar offers a panoramic view over the Loire Valley and the Coteaux du Layon vineyards. Nearby is a monument dedicated to Anjou-born René Gasnier, one of the first people to fly with a "heavier-than-air" machine. Like the biplane of this aviation pioneer, this Coteaux du Layon reaches great heights. Rather closed at first, it slowly releases delicate floral aromas on the nose along with fresh fruits and honey. As for the palate, it reveals both richness and delicacy.
➤ André Davy, Dom. de la Roche Moreau, La Haie Longue, 49190 Saint-Aubin-de-Luigné, tel. 02.41.78.34.55, fax 02.41.78.17.70, e-mail davy.larochemoreau@wanadoo.fr ☑
⏳ by appt.

DOM. DU ROY RENE
Saint-Lambert Les Cartelles 2001★

| 3 ha | 1,500 | ⑪ | 15–23 € |

After working for two and a half years in the vineyards of Burgundy, Antoine Chéreau took over this Anjou estate in the year 2000. Although the Chablis and Côte d'Or areas do not produce sweet wines, he still shows a sure hand concerning the grapes, to judge by this Saint-Lambert Coteaux du Layon. The grapes for this wine basked in the sun and had an impressive potential alcohol; that can be guessed from the intense golden yellow appearance and aromas of ripe and crystallized fruits, accompanied by oxidative notes of old alcohol. More proof comes from the powerful palate that finishes with a feeling of sweetness similar to that of fruit jelly. (50 cl bottles.)
➤ Antoine Chéreau, Le Bon René, 49750 Chanzeaux, tel. 02.41.78.32.32, fax 02.41.78.38.34, e-mail domaine.roy.rene@wanadoo.fr ☑
⏳ by appt.

DOM. DES SABLONNETTES
La Bohème 2001★★★

| 1 ha | 1,500 | ⑪ | 23–30 € |

Joel Ménard has an approach that cannot go unnoticed: he runs his vineyard on organic lines and vinifies his Coteaux du Layon without sulphur and, of course, without any chaptalization. Already noteworthy last year, its selection La Bohème was approved unanimously this year. Quince, honey, mint and spices make up the delicate and complex range of flavours. Powerful, the palate appears light and balanced with a thousand nuances to be found. This is a great sweet Anjou wine. (50 cl bottles.)
➤ Joël et Christine Ménard, EARL Dom. des Sablonnettes, Lieu-dit l'Espérance, 49750 Rablay-sur-Layon, tel. 02.41.78.40.49, fax 02.41.78.61.15, e-mail domainedessablonnettes@wanadoo.fr ☑
⏳ by appt.

DOM. DES SAULAIES
Faye Les Tremellières 2001★

| 0.33 ha | 1,350 | ⑪ | 15–23 € |

Here, one cultivates family trees: that of this wine-growing family goes back to 1622 and has just been added to with a new line. However, the vineyards are not forgotten. They gave a Coteaux du Layon Faye with a very beautifully expressive flavour: one finds acacia flowers, crystallized fruits, almonds and figs. The palate provides a pleasant feeling of freshness and on the finish delivers flavours of ripe fruits, both typical characteristics of grapes dried on the vine.
➤ EARL Philippe et Pascal Leblanc, Dom. des Saulaies, 49380 Faye-d'Anjou, tel. 02.41.54.30.66, fax 02.41.54.17.21 ☑
⏳ by appt.

SAUVEROY
Saint-Lambert-du-Lattay Cuvée Nectar 2001★

| 0.8 ha | 3,200 | ⑪ | 15–23 € |

Created in 1947 by the father of Pascal Cailleau, the estate has grown from 1–27 ha of vines. It is one of the most representative estates in the Anjou wine area, and has received a number of stars and several *coups de coeur* in the *Guide*. Vinified and matured in oak for one year, this Cuvée Nectar marries a delicate crystallized fruit character with the charred, spiced and vanilla notes from its maturation. Rich and full, the palate finishes on particularly pleasant flavours of currants, citrus fruits and quince.
➤ Pascal Cailleau, Dom. Sauveroy, 49750 Saint-Lambert-du-Lattay, tel. 02.41.78.30.59, fax 02.41.78.46.43, e-mail domainesauveroy@terre-net.fr ☑
⏳ by appt.

DOM. DES TROTTIERES 2002★

| 2.57 ha | 6,800 | ▮ | 5–8 € |

This vast estate was founded in 1906. Regularly present in the *Guide* for its reds and rosés, here it appears with a Coteaux du Layon. This 2002 presents an image of simplicity and delicacy. Fresh aromas of wild flowers, broom and slightly acid fruits, with a light palate, full of vitality and a touch of acidity

on the finish, make it a dapper wine that is easy to drink and suitable for all occasions.
➤ SCEA Dom. des Trottières, 49380 Thouarcé, tel. 02.41.54.14.10, fax 02.41.54.09.00, e-mail lestrottieres@worldonline.fr ☑
𝐘 ev. day except Sat. Sun. 8am–12.30pm 2pm–6.30pm
➤ Lamotte

DOM. VERDIER

Saint-Lambert 2002★

▨	0.6 ha	2,500	▮ ♦	5–8 €

Based at Saint-Lambert-de-Lattay for four generations, the Verdier family farm approximately 25 ha of vineyards. Even if still immature on the nose, their Coteaux du Layon Saint-Lambert gained attention due to its very beautiful balance between alcohol, sugar and acidity, and its promising finish with notes of ripe fruits, raisins, honey and crystallized fruits.
➤ EARL Verdier Père et Fils, 7, rue des Varennes, 49750 Saint-Lambert-du-Lattay, tel. 02.41.78.35.67, fax 02.41.78.35.67 ☑
𝐘 by appt.

Wines selected but not starred

DOM. DE LA BELLE ANGEVINE

Saint-Lambert Les Bonnes Blanches 2001

▨	1.5 ha	5,500	▮ ♦	5–8 €

➤ Florence Dufour, Dom. de la Belle Angevine, La Motte, 49750 Beaulieu-sur-Layon, tel. 02.41.78.34.86, fax 02.41.72.81.58, e-mail fldufour@club-internet.fr ☑
𝐘 by appt.

CH. DE BELLEVUE 2002

▨	6.5 ha	12,000	▮ ⑪ ♦	5–8 €

➤ EARL Tijou et Fils, Ch. de Bellevue, 49190 Saint-Aubin-de-Luigné, tel. 02.41.78.33.11, fax 02.41.78.67.84 ☑
𝐘 by appt.

DOM. DES CLOSSERONS

Faye Elevé en fût de chêne 2001

▨	2.7 ha	3,400	⑪	15–23 €

➤ EARL Jean-Claude Leblanc et Fils, Dom. des Closserons, 49380 Faye-d'Anjou, tel. 02.41.54.30.78, fax 02.41.54.12.02 ☑
𝐘 by appt.

DOM. DE L'ETE

Cuvée Soleil 2001

▨	3 ha	20,000	▮ ♦	8–11 €

➤ SCEA Dom. de l'Eté, 49700 Concourson-sur-Layon, tel. 02.41.59.11.63, fax 02.41.59.95.16, e-mail domainedelete@wanadoo.fr ☑
𝐘 ev. day except Sat. Sun. 9am–12 noon 2pm–6pm
➤ Catherine Nolot

DOM. DE PAIMPARE

Saint-Lambert Réserve du Domaine 2002

▨	3 ha	1000	▮ ♦	8–11 €

➤ SCEA Michel Tessier, 32, rue Rabelais, 49750 Saint-Lambert-du-Lattay, tel. 02.41.78.43.18, fax 02.41.78.41.73 ☑
𝐘 by appt.

DOM. DU PETIT METRIS

Saint-Aubin Clos des Treize Vents 2001

▨	2 ha	3,500	⑪	8–11 €

➤ GAEC Joseph Renou et Fils, Le Grand Beauvais, 49190 Saint-Aubin-de-Luigné, tel. 02.41.78.33.33, fax 02.41.78.67.77 ☑
𝐘 by appt.

DOM. DES PETITS QUARTS

Faye 2002

▨	1.5 ha	2,000	▮ ⑪ ♦	8–11 €

➤ Godineau Père et Fils, Dom. des Petits Quarts, 49380 Faye-d'Anjou, tel. 02.41.54.03.00, fax 02.41.54.25.36 ☑
𝐘 ev. day except Sun. 8am–12 noon 2pm–5.30pm

DOM. DES QUARRES

Faye La Magdelaine Prestige 2001

▨	6 ha	4,500	⑪	11–15 €

➤ Dom. des Quarres, 66, Grande-Rue, 49750 Rablay-sur-Layon, tel. 02.41.78.36.00, fax 02.41.78.62.58 ☑ ⛺
𝐘 ev. day 9.30am–12 noon 2.30pm–6pm; Sat. Sun. by appt.

DOM. DES QUATRE ROUTES

Champfleury 2001

▨	1 ha	1,600	⑪	15–23 €

➤ Poupard et Fils, Dom. des Quatre Routes, 49540 Aubigné-sur-Layon, tel. 02.41.59.44.44, fax 02.41.59.49.70, e-mail domainedes4routes@wanadoo.fr ☑
𝐘 ev. day 9am–7pm; Sat. Sun. by appt.

DOM. JEAN-LOUIS ROBIN-DIOT

Rochefort Clos du Cochet 2001

▨	2 ha	4,000	⑪	8–11 €

➤ Dom. Jean-Louis Robin-Diot, Les Hauts Perrays, 49290 Chaudefonds-sur-Layon, tel. 02.41.78.68.29, fax 02.41.78.67.62 ☑ ⛺
𝐘 by appt.

DOM. SAINT-ARNOUL 2002

▨	n.c.	3,600	▮ ♦	3–5 €

➤ GAEC Poupard et Maury, Sousigné, 49540 Martigné-Briand, tel. 02.41.59.43.62, fax 02.41.59.69.23, e-mail saint-arnoul@wanadoo.fr
𝐘 by appt.

Bonnezeaux

Dr Maisonneuve said in 1925 that this wine was "inimitable" as an accompaniment for desserts. At the time it was the custom to consume great sweet wines either with dessert, or in the afternoon, socially amongst friends. Nowadays, this very perfumed and vigorous Grand Cru is more generally appreciated as an aperitif. It owes its qualities to an exceptional terroir: the three steep little slopes of schists (La Montagne, Beauregard and Fesles) above the village of Thouarcé.

In 2002, the volume of production reached 1,874 hl. The area of production includes 130 ha of plantable land. This is a good value, consistently reliable wine that will keep a long time.

DOM. DES COQUERIES

Cuvée Prestige 2002★

	2.5 ha	2,000	⑪	15–23 €

The estate was established in about 1900, and the fourth generation still has a vineyard in Bonnezeaux dating back to this time. As for the vines used for this Cuvée Prestige, they are not less than 80 years old. The 2002 wine, on the other hand, is very young and needs to be kept. However, the Jury found on the palate ripe fruit flavours, citrus fruits, pineapples and other exotic fruits characteristic for the appellation. This should be tasted again at the end 2003.

☛ EARL Philippe Gilardeau, Les Noues, 49380 Thouarcé, tel. 02.41.54.39.11, fax 02.41.54.38.84 ◪
🍷 by appt.

DOM. LES GRANDES VIGNES 2001★

	2.1 ha	5,600	⑪	11–15 €

Two brothers, a sister and about 50 hectares of vineyards, this is an estate that is well-known to wine-lovers and regularly mentioned in the *Guide*. The Bonnezeaux 2001 divided opinions: too much oak showing for some, for others, the fruit character was brought out by the oak maturation. In any case, the perfume of ripe fruits, dried fruits and citrus fruits are very obvious, side by side with vanilla and spicy notes, and this complexity of flavours is to be welcomed. It needs at least another year of ageing.

☛ GAEC Vaillant, Dom. Les Grandes Vignes, La Roche Aubry, 49380 Thouarcé, tel. 02.41.54.05.06, fax 02.41.54.08.21, e-mail vaillant@domainelesgrandesvignes.com ◪
🍷 by appt.

DOM. DE MIHOUDY 2002★

	1 ha	1,500	⑪	23–30 €

A *coup de coeur* and a *Grappe de bronze* in a previous *Guide* for a red Anjou 1995, this estate collects stars from the Jurors. Its Bonnezeaux 2002 appears full of promise: a brilliant gold in the glass, it mixes ripe fruits, *pêche de vigne* and crystallized fruits with vanilla and spices. The palate builds with aeration showing finesse and elegance. It needs to be left in the cellar for a year.

☛ EARL Cochard et Fils, Dom. de Mihoudy, 49540 Aubigné-sur-Layon, tel. 02.41.59.46.52, fax 02.41.59.68.77, e-mail mihoudy@wanadoo.fr ◪
🍷 by appt.

DOM. DES PETITS QUARTS 2001★★

	2 ha	1000	⑪	15–23 €

To take account of the length of maturation time the *Guide* gave permission for the same vintage to be presented for tasting as last year in this appellation. It is worth noting here the remarkable performance in front of the Grand Jury who, tasting blind, once again voted for this wine from grapes harvested berry by berry. The Jury emphasized the exceptional work carried out in the grape selection. What richness and what sweetness this wine has! All jam and fruit jelly, the exuberant palate continues to a long finish of various crystallized fruits. "Nectar, not to be missed!" the members of the Jury concluded in unison. Two other *cuvées* have collected a star: **Beauregard 2002** and **Le Malabé 2002** (both 11–15 €). They should be kept for at least a year and drunk as an aperitif or with sautéed foie gras.

☛ Godineau Père et Fils, Dom. des Petits Quarts, 49380 Faye-d'Anjou, tel. 02.41.54.03.00, fax 02.41.54.25.36 ◪
🍷 ev. day except Sun. 8am–12 noon 2pm–5.30pm

LOUIS ET CLAUDE ROBIN

Cuvée Floriane 2001★★

	2 ha	2,000	⑪	15–23 €

This estate, run by the second and the third generation, is brilliantly represented by the Cuvée Floriane, made from grapes harvested very selectively from vines more than 70 years old. The range of aromas is extremely refined and made up of flowers, fresh and crystallized fruits, lemons and others citrus fruits. The palate combines opulence with freshness and the wine will offer great pleasure in the future.

☛ EARL Louis et Claude Robin, Dom. le Mont, 49380 Faye-d'Anjou, tel. 02.41.54.31.41, fax 02.41.54.17.98 ◪
🍷 by appt.

Wines selected but not starred

DOM. DES CLOSSERONS 2002

	1.69 ha	5,460	▮ ▮	11–15 €

☛ EARL Jean-Claude Leblanc et Fils, Dom. des Closserons, 49380 Faye-d'Anjou, tel. 02.41.54.30.78, fax 02.41.54.12.02 ◪
🍷 by appt.

DOM. DES FONTAINES

Cuvée Prestige 2001

	5.5 ha	10,000	▮ ▮	11–15 €

☛ Alain Rousseau, Les Noues, 49380 Thouarcé, tel. 02.41.54.32.30, fax 02.41.54.34.44 ◪
🍷 ev. day except Sun. 8am–12 noon 2pm–7pm; cl. 2nd fortnight Aug.

DOM. DES GAGNERIES

Cuvée Benoît 2001

	2.5 ha	5,000	▮ ⑪ ▮	11–15 €

☛ EARL Christian et Anne Rousseau, Dom. des Gagneries, 49380 Thouarcé, tel. 02.41.54.00.71, fax 02.41.54.02.62 ◪
🍷 by appt.

DOM. RENE RENOU

Cuvée Zénith 2001

	8 ha	3,600	⑪	30–38 €

☛ Dom. René Renou, pl. du Champ-de-Foire, 49380 Thouarcé, tel. 02.41.54.11.33, fax 02.41.54.11.34, e-mail domaine.rene.renou@wanadoo.fr ◪
🍷 by appt.

Quarts de Chaume

The original nobleman owner kept a quarter ("*quart*") of the production for himself; naturally, he kept the best, meaning the wine produced on the best soil. The appellation, which covers 40 ha, is located on a hump of a hill, facing due south, at Rochefort-sur-Loire. A total of 562 hl was produced in 2002.

The combination of old plants, the southerly exposure and the capabilities of the Chenin variety means that only a limited amount of wine is produced, although of very high quality. Selective picking during harvest encourages over-ripening of the grapes, giving a sweet white wine that is firm and full of flavour, and ages well.

CH. BELLERIVE

Quintessence 2001★

	12 ha	n.c.		30–38 €

The residence is covered with Anjou slates, but holm oaks and shrubs, lavender and rosemary give its park a slightly southern feel. Two wines from the estate caught the attention of the Jury. The best mark was given to this Quintessence, vinified partly from the richest selected grapes from the vineyard. Concentrated fruits and richness summarize this wine in two words. With a deep gold colour; a range of aromas that mix austere mineral notes with more opulent nuances (stewed and crystallized fruits and fruit jelly); and a palate that combines freshness with equally good structure, this wine offers everything that one should expect from a great terroir. Another **Château Bellerive 2001 (15–23 €)** was specially mentioned. Still closed at present, it will fully open up in a year or two.

🕿 SARL Ch. Bellerive, Chaume,
49190 Rochefort-sur-Loire, tel. 02.41.78.33.66,
fax 02.41.78.68.47, e-mail chateau.bellerive@wanadoo.fr ☑
🍴 ev. day 10am–12 noon 2pm–6pm; Sat. Sun. by appt.
🕿 Serge Malinge

DOM. DE LA BERGERIE

Cuvée de Décembre 2000★★

	1.25 ha	1,400		15–23 €

The grapes for this wine were harvested on 15 December: the grapes were fully affected by noble rot. This provides an intense golden colour with amber tinges, delicate aromas of dried fruits, toast, crystallized fruits and fresh lemony notes, with a powerful and concentrated palate that, however, gives an astonishing feeling of lightness. It is a wine of real class. (50 cl. bottles.) Also interesting is the **Quarts de Chaume 2001 (23–30 €)**: aromas of sun-dried grapes; a rich and opulent middle palate; the finish leaving a trail of ripe pear, crystallized citrus fruit and currants; and its ageing potential of several decades make the wine most worthy of a star.

🕿 Yves Guégniard, Dom. de la Bergerie,
49380 Champ-sur-Layon, tel. 02.41.78.85.43,
fax 02.41.78.60.13,
e-mail domainede.la.bergerie@wanadoo.fr ☑
🍴 by appt.

CH. DE L'ECHARDERIE

Clos Paradis 2001★★

	1.2 ha	3,000		30–38 €

The Clos Paradis is one of the historical *lieu-dits* of the appellation. It gave a wine which charmed with its elegance and delicacy. Ripe and crystallized fruits, citrus fruits and spices come together on the complex nose which gives an impression of lightness. Freshness and richness join harmoniously on the palate. Here is, in every sense, a real Quarts de Chaume, which can be enjoyed from the end 2003. The 99 vintage obtained a *coup de coeur*. (50 cl. bottles.)

🕿 Vignobles Laffourcade, Ch. de l'Echarderie,
49190 Rochefort-sur-Loire, tel. 02.41.54.16.54,
fax 02.41.54.00.10,
e-mail laffourcade@wanadoo.fr ☑

DOM. DES FORGES 2001★

	1 ha	2,200		23–30 €

This was a *coup de coeur* in a previous edition and is a benchmark wine for the Coteaux du Layon. The 2001 wine is very concentrated, and still needs time to express its true potential. The aromas are characteristic of a botrytized harvest and mix with spicy, vanilla and smoky notes, from a period of maturation in oak. Rich, even opulent, the palate demonstrates a feeling of freshness all the way through. This wine will be at its peak in a few years.

🕿 Vignoble Branchereau, Dom. des Forges, rte de la Haie-Longue, 49190 Saint-Aubin-de-Luigné,
tel. 02.41.78.33.56, fax 02.41.78.67.51,
e-mail vitiforge@wanadoo.fr ☑
🍴 by appt.

CH. PIERRE-BISE 2001★★★

	3 ha	3,300		15–23 €

Claude Papin is passionate about his work as a wine producer. His approach to wine is one of great sensitivity and an exemplary rigour. His Quarts de Chaume gained unanimous votes. From behind the amber-gold colour, aromas emerge that signal a harvest of grapes affected by noble rot. Dry and crystallized fruits (especially pineapple) make up the wide range of flavours. Powerful, immense even, the palate has extraordinary length. It should be savoured at length and can be served as an aperitif. (50 cl. bottles.)

🕿 Claude Papin, Ch. Pierre-Bise,
49750 Beaulieu-sur-Layon, tel. 02.41.78.31.44,
fax 02.41.78.41.24 ☑
🍴 by appt.

DOM. DE LA ROCHE MOREAU 2001★★

	n.c.	n.c.		23–30 €

Here is an anecdote that the master of the house likes to relate: the wine cellar, dug into an old mining tunnel, was walled up during the last war to conceal its contents from the eyes of the occupying forces. It could be said that it was a cache of gold! Gold oozes from this Quarts de Chaume, from one of the very best parts of this appellation's remarkable terroir. Lemon-yellow appearance; complex aromas of citrus fruits and crystallized fruit; and a full palate, delicately fresh and keeping the theme of crystallized fruit flavours: it is elegant throughout.

🕿 André Davy, Dom. de la Roche Moreau, La Haie Longue, 49190 Saint-Aubin-de-Luigné, tel. 02.41.78.34.55,
fax 02.41.78.17.70,
e-mail davy.larochemoreau@wanadoo.fr ☑
🍴 by appt.

Wines selected but not starred

DOM. DU PETIT METRIS
Les Guerches 2001

	1 ha	1,300	◐◍◑	23–30 €

🍷 GAEC Joseph Renou et Fils, Le Grand Beauvais, 49190 Saint-Aubin-de-Luigné, tel. 02.41.78.33.33, fax 02.41.78.67.77 ☑
🍸 by appt.

Saumur

The area of production, 2,735 ha covers 36 communes. In 2002, a total of 138,914 hl of red and white (both dry and lively) wine was produced. This included 61,932 hl of sparkling wines, from the same grape varieties as the AOC Anjou wines. All keep well.

The vineyards stretch along the Loire and the Thouet. The white Turquant and Brézé wines were well thought of in the past; the red wines of Puy-Notre-Dame, Montreuil-Bellay and Tourtenay, among others, have acquired a good reputation. However, the appellation is best known for its sparkling wines, and it is worth stressing how much these have improved in quality. The makers, all of whom are based in Saumur, own cellars hollowed out of the tufa that are well worth a visit.

CH. DE BEAUREGARD
Méthode traditionnelle 2001★★

	6 ha	50,000	◧ ⚬	5–8 €

Everything about this *brut* Saumur, a blend of 70% Chenin with 30% Chardonnay, builds to a crescendo. The pale yellow appearance offers tinges of green with a delicate and persistent effervescence. The notes of wild flowers mix with nuances of butter reminiscent of the smells of patisserie. The finish provides remarkable feeling of balance and richness. The Château de Beauregard also obtains two mentions for red Saumur: one for **Cuvée Nathalie 2001**, supple, fruity and delicious and the other for **Cuvée Louis Léon Vieilles Vignes 2000**, which has been barrel-aged.
🍷 SCEA Alain Gourdon, Ch. de Beauregard, 4, rue Saint-Julien, 49260 Le Puy-Notre-Dame, tel. 02.41.52.25.33, fax 02.41.52.29.62, e-mail christinegourdon@wanadoo.fr ☑
🍸 by appt.

DOM. BENASTRE 2002★

	2 ha	16,000	◧ ⚬	3–5 €

"Beneath a good star", is the translation of "Benastré" from the old French, and above the immense gate to the estate, a carved stone in the tufa represents the moon and a star. It is a lucky wine, indeed. Exhibiting a very deep colour with beautiful purplish tinges, after swirling the glass it goes on to express quite complex fruitiness, and an overripened character, that one finds on the middle palate. Supple, there is also enough tannin and overall it is a pleasant wine.
🍷 EARL Bruno Roux, 33, imp. Painlevé, 49260 Montreuil-Bellay, tel. 02.41.52.43.47, fax 02.41.52.42.91, e-mail roux@domaine-benastre.com ☑
🍸 ev. day except Sun. 8am–12.30pm 1.30pm–7pm

DOM. DE LA BESSIERE
Méthode traditionnelle 1996★★

	0.5 ha	3,000	◧ ⚬	5–8 €

This Méthode Traditionnelle is from an estate located on the Turonien side of the Saumur-Champigny vineyards. "An elegance that takes your breath away!" Delicate aromas of lime blossom, peach and ripe fruits are in line with the well-structured palate that reveals a whole range of fresh fruit characters. This is a very vivid wine that provides a superb example of the sparkling wines of Saumur.
🍷 Thierry Dézé, SCEV Dom. de La Bessière, rte de Champigny, 49400 Souzay-Champigny, tel. 02.41.52.42.69, fax 02.41.38.75.41 ☑
🍸 by appt.

DOM. DU BOIS MIGNON
La Belle Cave 2002★★

	n.c.	15,000	◧ ◍◑ ⚬	3–5 €

This estate often appears in the *Guide* with its red Saumur. In fact, two-thirds of this 24-ha property, located in the south of the appellation, in the Vienne *département*, are planted with Cabernet Franc. The 2002 displays a most engaging appearance, an intense ruby with garnet tinges, after agitation it releases beautiful perfumes of red berries. Dense, full, rich, soft and silky, it should improve over the years.
🍷 SCEA Charier Barillot, Dom. du Bois Mignon, 86120 Saix, tel. 05.49.22.94.59, fax 05.49.22.91.54, e-mail p.barillot@wanadoo.fr ☑
🍸 by appt.

DOM. LA BONNELIERE 2002★

	1 ha	6,500	◧ ⚬	5–8 €

Created in 1972 by André Bonneau and his wife, the estate is now run by their two sons and consists of more than 22 ha of vineyards. Its red Saumur 2002 presents a very attractive, deep ruby colour. Still restrained on the nose, it appears very fruity on the palate. Rounded and well balanced, it offers, moreover, good length promising an excellent ageing potential.
🍷 EARL Bonneau et Fils, Dom. La Bonnelière, 45, rue du Bourg-Neuf, 49400 Varrains, tel. 02.41.52.92.38, fax 02.41.67.35.48 ☑
🍸 by appt.

DOM. DE LA CHENARDIERE 2002★

	5 ha	42,000	◧ ⚬	3–5 €

This white Saumur is marketed by the Domaine du Cléray, a négociant house with 100 hectares. It results from of a period of skin contact, low-temperature fermentation and six months maturation on its fine lees. Its expresses mixed flavours of white fruits, flowers (broom) and citrus fruits, leaving a feeling of freshness. Showing a similar character, the palate finishes on a touch of freshness, characteristic of white wines produced on chalky soil. Also notable is the **red Domaine de la Chenardière 2002**, specially singled out for its fruity nose and its balanced, full and rich palate. It is a wine suitable for ageing.
🍷 SCEA Dom. du Cléray, Le Bourg, 49700 Les-Verchers-sur-Layon, tel. 02.40.33.93.46, fax 02.40.36.26.26

DOM. LA CROIX DES LOGES
Méthode traditionnelle Eden 2000★

	1 ha	7,000		5–8 €

The *cuvée* Eden is a new product from the Domaine La Croix des Loges and has benefited from a maturation on lees for two years. The Jury particularly appreciated the delicacy of its range of aromas, where there was a blend of ripe fruits, patisserie, mixed nuts and cut hay notes. The same elegance reigns on the palate where a feeling of freshness was found to be very attractive.
🍷 SCEA Bonnin et Fils, Dom. La Croix des Loges, 49540 Martigné-Briand, tel. 02.41.59.43.58, fax 02.41.59.41.11, e-mail bonninlesloges@aol.com ☑
🍸 by appt.

CH. DE LA DURANDIERE

Méthode traditionnelle 2001★

| ● | 5.5 ha | 24,000 | ▮ ♦ | 5–8 € |

The appearance and aromas of this Méthode Traditionnelle show astonishing delicacy; really light notes recall small red berries. The long palate is fruity and well balanced. This sparkling wine can be served as an aperitif or with salmon in cream sauce. From the same estate, the **still white Saumur 2002 (3–5 €)** has been given a special mention. A characteristic, simple and light wine it has pleasant fruity (citrus fruits) and floral perfumes and a rounded palate with a touch of acidity on the finish. It should be drunk within the year.

➥ SCEA Antoine Bodet, Ch. de La Durandière, 51, rue des Fusillés, 49260 Montreuil-Bellay, tel. 02.41.40.35.30, fax 02.41.40.35.31, e-mail durandiere.chateau@libertysurf.fr ☑
☒ ev. day 8am–7pm; Sat. Sun. by appt.

CH. D'ETERNES 2000★★

| ■ | 11 ha | 50,000 | ⦿ | 11–15 € |

Situated in the *département* of Vienne, on the border with Poitou, the Château d'Eternes is an old ecclesiastical estate, mentioned at the end of the ninth century in a paper on King Eudes, an ancestor of the Capétiens. It was taken over in 1994 by the Marteling family who are endeavouring to restore the vineyard, planted on the southern slopes of a hillside. Even if the owners are currently interested in expanding the white grape varieties, it is Cabernet that dominates the grape varieties grown. It has provided some outstanding Saumur reds which have been hailed in the *Guide* for the past two years. This year, the preference is for Château d'Eternes, aged for 18 months in cask: a brilliant appearance; an elegant, intense nose, with vanilla and restrained oak notes; and quite a dense middle palate but with very well-integrated tannins. It is a well-balanced wine that is capable of ageing. The **red Saumur Eternes 2002 (5–8 €)** received a star for its opulent weight reflecting the very ripe grapes. It also needs time.

➥ SCEV Ch. d'Eternes, 86120 Saix, tel. 05.49.22.34.77, fax 05.49.22.34.77, e-mail lea.scherina@libertysurf.fr ☑ ⌂
☒ by appt.
➥ Marteling

DOM. DE FIERVAUX

Elevé en fût de chêne 2001★★

| ■ | 4 ha | 5,000 | ⦿ | 5–8 € |

Large wooden casks are lined up in the estate cellar that dates back to the 12th century. This 2001 vintage remained there for a year. It is packaged with an attractive, deep ruby colour. With notes of toast and nuances evocative of the garrigue of the south, the nose indicates beautifully ripe grapes. The first impression on the palate is rounded, revealing good structure and balance, along with well-formed and integrated tannins. From the same property, the **red Saumur Cuvée Summum 2001**, which has been aged for six months in barrel, obtained a star for its balance, potential and intense flavourful expression reminiscent of black fruits.

➥ SCEA Cousin-Maitreau, 235, rue des Caves, 49260 Vaudelnay, tel. 02.41.52.34.63, fax 02.41.38.89.23, e-mail christ-cousin@wanadoo.fr ☑ ▦
☒ by appt.

DOM. FILLIATREAU

Château Fouquet 2002★

| ■ | 6.05 ha | 20,000 | ▮ ♦ | 5–8 € |

Known for their Saumur-Champigny, Paul Filliatreau and his son also have vines in the Saumur appellation. Château Fouquet is a small vineyard which they farm organically. The 2002 has turned out extremely well: with a ruby colour, tinged with purple and a beautiful perfume of red berries, these recur on the full, soft palate that has rounded tannins. It is a very balanced wine.

➥ Paul Filliatreau, Chaintres, 49400 Dampierre-sur-Loire, tel. 02.41.52.90.84, fax 02.41.52.49.92, e-mail domaine@filliatreau.fr ☑
☒ ev. day 8am–12 noon 1.30pm–5.30pm; Sat. Sun. by appt.

FOUCHER-LEBRUN

Les Hirondelles 2002★

| ◐ | n.c. | n.c. | ▮ | 3–5 € |

This négociant house was founded in 1921 by Paul Lebrun who, trained as a cooper, easily forged connections with the wine-growers of the Loire Valley. Today, his grandson, Jack Foucher, heads up the business. Les Hirondelles is garnet with purplish highlights, exhibiting quite a complex nose where red berries combine with a spicy touch. On the palate one discovers fruitiness along with silky tannins and good length.

➥ Foucher-Lebrun, 29, rte de Bouhy, 58200 Alligny-Cosne, tel. 03.86.26.87.27, fax 03.86.26.87.20, e-mail foucher.lebrun@wanadoo.fr ☑
☒ ev. day except Sun. Mon. 8am–12 noon 2pm–6pm

DOM. GERON

Méthode traditionnelle Clos de la Tronnière★★

| ◐ | 0.25 ha | 1,500 | | 5–8 € |

The Clos de la Tronnière vineyard is located in the northern end of the Deux-Sèvres *département*, a few kilometres from Thouars, a town known for its art and history. This Saumur *brut* shows a remarkably high quality of flavours, with notes of wild flowers and broom, stewed fruits and fruit jelly. The wine will be at its peak at the end of 2003 and should not be left to age longer. It can be drunk throughout a meal and could even work with grilled red meat.

➥ EARL Dom. Géron, 14, rte de Thouars, 79290 Brion-près-Thouet, tel. 05.49.67.73.43, fax 05.49.67.80.89 ☑
☒ by appt.

GRATIEN ET MEYER

Cuvée Flamme★★

| ◐ | n.c. | 25,000 | | 8–11 € |

Founded in 1864 by Alfred Gratien when he was only 23 years old, this house was taken over by Albert Meyer in 1885. The Cuvée Flamme rosé comes from a blend of grape varieties with 68% Cabernet Franc combined with Grolleau. The wine is really thrilling. The very attractive mousse is revealed in long strands of fine bubbles that cut through the light pink colour. The aromas are based on fresh fruits; the palate is pleasant, well balanced and on the finish provides an impression of chewing red berries. The **Saumur Brut Cuvée Principale white (5–8 €)** obtains a star.

➥ Gratien Meyer, rte de Montsoreau, BP 22, 49401 Saumur Cedex, tel. 02.41.83.13.30, fax 02.41.83.13.49, e-mail contact@gratienmeyer.com ☑
☒ ev. day 10am–12 noon 2pm–6pm

DE GRENELLE

Montmorency Méthode traditionnelle★

| ◐ | n.c. | n.c. | | 5–8 € |

The Louis de Grenelle company was founded in 1859 and has remained a family firm. The four wines presented were all selected by the Jury and judged very successful. The Montmorency selection was particularly appreciated for its elegance and finesse. Its aromas subtly suggest ripe fruits, flowers and patisserie. Well made, the palate is agreeably fresh. **Grande Cuvée Louis de Grenelle white (8–11 €)**, as well as the **Louis de Grenelle Cuvée Principale white** and **rosé** both obtain the same mark.

➥ Caves de Grenelle, 20, rue Marceau, BP 206, 49415 Saumur, tel. 02.41.50.17.63, fax 02.41.50.83.65, e-mail grenelle@caves-de-grenelle.fr ☑
☒ ev. day 9am–12 noon 1.30pm–6pm; cl. Sat. Sun. 1 Oct.–30 Apr.

DOM. GUIBERTEAU EGGERTON 2002★★

| ■ | 4 ha | 15,000 | ▮ ⦿ | 5–8 € |

A Frenchman and an Englishman are partners in this estate, run along organic lines. The results are outstanding. The main wine is presented in a flattering light with a bright, pure ruby colour. The fruit conjures up small woodland fruits, especially strawberries, and this lasts through to the finish of the attractive, elegant palate. The **red Les Motelles 2002 (11–15 €)** has been aged for 18 months in barrel, but this does not stop the emergence of an attractive fruitiness. The quality of its

flavours, its weight and the elegance of its tannins make the wine worthy of the same mark.
☛ Dom. Guiberteau Eggerton, 3, imp. du Cabernet, Mollay, 49260 Saint-Just-sur-Dive, tel. 02.41.38.78.94, fax 02.41.38.56.46,
e-mail domaine.guiberteaueggerton@wanadoo.fr ☑
♈ by appt.

DOM. DE LA GUILLOTERIE 2002★

| ■ | 10 ha | 25,000 | ▮ ♦ | 5–8 € |

Owned by the Duveau family for several generations, this estate has vinified red Saumur that provides much pleasure: visually attractive, with a ruby colour of perfect clarity; on the nose, nice flavours of small red berries, and these re-occur on the supple palate which has a balanced structure.
☛ SCEA Duveau Frères, 63, rue Foucault, 49260 Saint-Cyr-en-Bourg, tel. 02.41.51.62.78, fax 02.41.51.63.14, e-mail dom.guilloterie@wanadoo.fr ☑
♈ by appt.

CH. DU HUREAU 2001★★

| ■ | 2 ha | 7,000 | ⑪ | 8–11 € |

Saumur-Champigny, Saumur; Cabernet, Chenin; all have been awarded *coups de cœur* and stars by the *Guide*: the Château du Hureau has become impossible to ignore by anyone who really loves the best wines of this area. What is astonishing in this white Saumur is the constant finesse which is expressed on the remarkably structured and powerful palate, and which translates into both good weight and character. On the nose are delicate perfumes of wild flowers and spices, but also of stronger honey and ripe fruit notes. The palate is rich, with a subtle and lemony finish. It is superb.
☛ Philippe Vatan, Ch. du Hureau, 49400 Dampierre-sur-Loire, tel. 02.41.67.60.40, fax 02.41.50.43.35,
e-mail philippe.vatan@wanadoo.fr ☑
♈ ev. day except Sat. Sun. 8am–12 noon 2pm–5pm; cl. 1–15 Aug.

MLLE LADUBAY

Eclat 2000★★★

| | n.c. | 30,000 | ▮⑪♦ | 8–11 € |

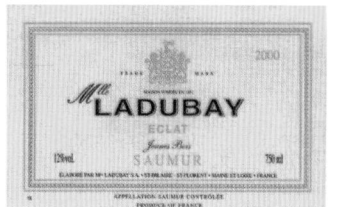

For seven years, the firm Bouvet-Ladubay, founded in 1851, has organized a national event, the *Journées du Livre et du Vin* (days of books and wine), bringing together writers, actors and politicians. The *cuvée* Mlle Ladubay has exceptional elegance and delicacy. The pale yellow colour has delicate tinges of green; the subtle aromas mix notes of cut hay with vanilla (the base wine was partly aged in oak) and ripe fruits. Rich yet, at the same time light, the palate is no less seductive. It can be drunk throughout the meal. The **white Trésor Elevée en fût de chêne 2000 (11–15 €)** receives two stars, and the **white Le Grand Saumur de Chapin et Landais 2000 (5–8 €)**, another brand from Bouvet-Ladubay, one star. All the wines are at a very high level.
☛ Bouvet-Ladubay, 1, rue de l'Abbaye, 49400 Saint-Hilaire-Saint-Florent, tel. 02.41.83.83.83, fax 02.41.50.24.32, e-mail contact@bouvet-ladubay.fr ☑
♈ ev. day 9am–12 noon 2pm–5.30pm

DOM. LANGLOIS-CHATEAU 2002★★

| ■ | 16 ha | 90,000 | ▮ ♦ | 5–8 € |

Originally specializing in sparkling wines, this property widened its range to still wines and expanded its acquisition of vineyards, while still retaining its character of a family firm. Today it has real scope with vineyards throughout the

Loire Valley, from the Nantais area to the Sancerre region. This expansion has not been at the expense of quality, as proved by two consecutive *coups de cœur*. This year the main *cuvée* of red Saumur receives this honour. With a scintillating appearance, ruby with touches of garnet and a fine, complex nose: the presentation is excellent. The wine has everything, very ripe grapes, a perfect extraction of colour and tannins, and a beautiful structure. It is a model of opulence and sophistication.
☛ Langlois-Château, 3, rue Léopold-Palustre, 49400 Saint-Hilaire-Saint-Florent, tel. 02.41.40.21.40, fax 02.41.40.21.49, e-mail contact@langlois.chateau.fr ☑
♈ ev. day 10am–12.30pm 2.30pm–6.30pm; cl. Jan.

DOM. LANGLOIS-CHATEAU

Vieilles Vignes 2002★

| ■ | 7.5 ha | 40,000 | ⑪ | 11–15 € |

This Saumur white received a *coup de cœur* for the previous vintage. It is the result of grapes whose natural richness was greater than 13% and was vinified and matured for a year in barrel. The intense nose mixes aromas of overripe grapes with mixed nuts. The palate is balanced and still slightly woody-tasting. This promising wine should be enjoyed with much pleasure at the end of the year. Given a special mention by the Jury, the **red Saumur Vieilles Vignes 2001** was also aged in oak. It expresses cocoa, plum and fig flavours both on the nose and on the palate. Mouth-filling, generous and rich, this wine reveals austere tannins that need two or three years to soften.
☛ Langlois-Château, 3, rue Léopold-Palustre, 49400 Saint-Hilaire-Saint-Florent, tel. 02.41.40.21.40, fax 02.41.40.21.49, e-mail contact@langlois.chateau.fr ☑
♈ ev. day 10am–12.30pm 2.30pm–6.30pm; cl. Jan.

DOM. DES MATINES

Cuvée la Falaiserie 2001★

| ■ | 1 ha | 1,500 | ⑪ | 8–11 € |

Created in 1950 this estate extends to 53 ha of vineyards. The barrel-aged Cuvée La Falaiserie 2001 is awarded a star. It exhibits a dark crimson colour and a seductive, powerful nose of slightly woody, soft red fruits. The maturation also shows through on the palate, where the oak and fruit integrate well in a pleasant middle palate. It needs to age for at least two years.
☛ Dom. des Matines, 31, rue de la Mairie, 49700 Brossay, tel. 02.41.52.25.36, fax 02.41.52.25.50,
e-mail domainedesmatines@wanadoo.fr ☑
♈ by appt.
☛ Etchegaray Mallard

CH. MONTREUIL-BELLAY 2002★

| ■ | 4 ha | 20,000 | ▮ ♦ | 3–5 € |

Here is a real Loire château, dating back to the Renaissance, which is also a wine château, complete with a Gothic wine cellar. The colour of this Saumur is of an intense ruby red. The nose is just as intense, with strawberry notes mixing with raspberry. After a rich start, one discovers a powerful and long palate, with flavours of soft red and black fruits. Integrated and velvety tannins ensure a very attractive finish.
☛ M. de Thuy, Ch. de Montreuil-Bellay, 49260 Montreuil-Bellay, tel. 02.41.52.33.06, fax 02.41.52.37.70 ☑
♈ by appt.

LYCEE VITICOLE DE MONTREUIL-BELLAY 2002★

| | 1.29 ha | 5,400 | ■ ♦ | | 3–5 € |

Created in 1967 to train the wine-growers and the wine-technicians of the Loire Valley, for practical studies the *lycée* (college) of Montreuil-Bellay works a 10-ha estate, which has to be financially self-supporting. From a manual harvest, this 2002 offers a very beautiful expression full of white fruit and floral flavours. Supple, balanced and harmonious on the palate, floral notes reappear on the finish, combined with nuances of honey. This very pleasant wine would work well with shellfish or fish.

☛ Lycée prof. agricole de Montreuil-Bellay, rte de Méron, 49260 Montreuil-Bellay, tel. 02.41.40.19.27, fax 02.41.38.72.86, e-mail expl.lpa.montreuil-bellay@educagri.fr ☑
⚎ ev. day except Sat. Sun. 9am–12 noon 2pm–5pm; groups by appt.

DOM. DU PAS SAINT MARTIN
Vieilles Vignes 2001★

| | 0.7 ha | 2,000 | ■ ♦ | | 5–8 € |

Located 40 km south of Angers, the village of Doué-la-Fontaine was built on the site of the old "*mer des faluns*" ("sea of fossil-rich sands") that covered the area in the Tertiary Era. The waters left behind a sandy and chalky rock that was friable and easy to dig. This explains the number of troglodytic buildings in the town. This organically-run estate was built near an old church, whose basement is currently used as the barrel store. From 80-year-old vines, its *cuvée* Vieilles Vignes gives a feeling of opulence with aromas indicative of very ripe grapes, a powerful and rounded palate and a warming finish. Also of interest is the estate's **white Saumur Méthode Traditionnelle Brut 1999** which was singled out: its light perfume evokes wild flowers and pear-drops, and the structured finish gives it weight.

☛ GAEC Charrier-Massoteau, Douces, 49700 Doué-la-Fontaine, tel. 02.41.59.14.35, fax 02.41.59.14.35, e-mail pas.saint.martin@wanadoo.fr ☑
⚎ by appt.

DOM. DES RAYNIERES 2002★★

| | 3.7 ha | 25,000 | ■ ♦ | | 3–5 € |

In charge of 28 ha of vineyards, Jean-Pierre Rébeilleau presents an attractive 2002 wine. Its crimson colour with touches of garnet and scarlet is extremely attractive, and its intense and very ripe red fruit scents encourage one to continue the tasting. Soft at first, the full-bodied palate reveals itself to be rounded and opulent. A ripe wine, the winemaker has extracted the very best from the grapes.

☛ Jean-Pierre Rébeilleau, SCEA Dom. des Raynières, 33, rue du Ruau, 49400 Varrains, tel. 02.41.52.95.17, fax 02.41.52.48.40 ☑
⚎ by appt.

DOM. DES SABLONNIERES
Méthode traditionnelle★

| | 4 ha | 14,000 | | | 8–11 € |

Taken over in 1990, today this estate includes 17 ha of vines. It is established at Doué-la-Fontaine, a city that is full of troglodytic sites built into the *faluns* (fossil-rich sand). It offers simple, pleasant Saumur *brut* with very beautiful, fine and persistent bubbles. The delicate aromas appear little by little with aeration, and the palate leaves an attractive impression of lightness. This wine can be been drunk with starters or with white meats.

☛ GAEC Bébin-Raboin, 365, rue Jean-Gaschet, 49700 Doué-la-Fontaine, tel. 02.41.59.00.41, fax 02.41.59.99.27, e-mail lessablonnieres@wanadoo.fr ☑
⚎ by appt.

ANTOINE SANZAY
Les Salles Martins 2002★

| | 0.4 ha | 1,600 | ⦷ | | 8–11 € |

The estate has been passed down from father to son for six generations, and this 2002 wine is the first made by Antoine Sanzay. It has been a successful baptism of fire, with many plus points to start with: a manual harvest with two selective pickings, natural ripeness of the grapes at 14% potential alcohol, and fermentation and maturation in oak for 12 months. The oaky notes are still very obvious, but the potential is good. The wine should be re-tasted at the end of the year.

☛ Antoine Sanzay, 19, rue des Roches-Neuves, 49400 Varrains, tel. 02.41.52.90.08, fax 02.41.50.27.39, e-mail antoine-sanzay@wanadoo.fr ☑
⚎ by appt.

DOM. DE LA SEIGNEURIE DES TOURELLES 2002★

| | 8.3 ha | 66,000 | ■ ♦ | | 3–5 € |

For six years this estate has worked in partnership with the négociant Joseph Verdier. It presents an intense ruby red Saumur, with a delicate red berry fruit nose. The fruitiness asserts itself with intensity on the powerful palate. Here is a "wine for enjoyment" to drink as of now. The **Domaine de la Seigneurie des Tourelles 2002 white** was singled out. Its fresh flavours of citrus fruits (grapefruit) and wild flowers, which come back on the palate, are characteristic of low-temperature fermentation. The lively finish lifts the palate agreeably.

☛ SCEA Dubé Père et Fils, 49260 Le Vaudelnay, tel. 02.41.40.22.50, fax 02.41.40.22.60, e-mail j.verdier@wanadoo.fr

CH. DE TARGE
Blanc de Targé 2001★★

| | 1 ha | 3,900 | ■ ⦷ ♦ | | 11–15 € |

The Château de Targé was the hunting residence of the private secretaries of the Kings Louis XIV and Louis XV. Some of their descendants, including Edgard Pisani, worked for the Republic. The current owner, Edouard Pisani-Ferry, comes from the same family. A trained agronomist, he farms a 25 ha vineyard. This Blanc de Targé reflects through and through the great ripeness of the grapes. A pale yellow with green-gold tinges, it releases complex aromas of flowers, nuts and ripe fruits; the delicate palate gives the feeling of biting into very ripe Chenin grapes. Overall it has superb balance.

☛ SCEA Edouard Pisani-Ferry, Ch. de Targé, 49730 Parnay, tel. 02.41.38.11.50, fax 02.41.38.16.19, e-mail edouard@chateaudetarge.fr ☑
⚎ ev. day except Sun. 8.30am–12.30pm 2pm–6pm; Sat. by appt.

VEUVE AMIOT
Méthode traditionnelle Cuvée réservée 1999★★

| | 1 ha | 8,500 | | | 5–8 € |

This 1999 vintage wine is classic of its appellation. Its pale yellow appearance with green-gold highlights is suffused with long streams of delicate bubbles. It has ethereal aromas of fruits, flowers and brioche. With great freshness, balanced, fruity and persistent, it is an elegant wine that would go well with starters. The **rosé Méthode Traditionnelle**, from pure Cabernet Franc, obtains a star.

☛ Veuve Amiot, BP 67, 49400 Saint-Hilaire-Saint-Florent, tel. 02.41.83.14.14, fax 02.41.50.17.66 ☑
⚎ ev. day 10am–6pm; cl. Oct.-Apr.

DOM. DU VIEUX PRESSOIR
Les Silices 2002★★

| | 10 ha | 50,000 | ■ ♦ | | 3–5 € |

A very typical Saumur estate, whose vineyard is mainly located on the Jurassic plateau of Vaudelnay, this is one of the names to trust in the region. It offers a remarkable red wine. The scarlet colour evokes very ripe cherries. The nose is initially closed but promises great richness; after swirling the glass it reveals a ripe fruity character. Heady, rounded, mouth-filling and with beautiful length, the palate just needs time to open up. Overall this is a promising wine for the future. The **Méthode Traditionnelle Brut 2001 (5–8 €)** is classic: fine and abundant bubbles, ethereal notes of ripe fruits and wild flowers, the palate is well balanced, fresh and complex, typical of sparkling Saumur. Obtaining a star, this wine can be

LOIRE

recommended for those who want to try this appellation for the first time.

☛ EARL B. et J. Albert, 205, rue du Château-d'Oiré, 49260 Vaudelnay, tel. 02.41.52.21.78, fax 02.41.38.85.83, e-mail vieuxpressoir@wanadoo.fr ▼
🍷 by appt.

CH. DE VILLENEUVE

Les Cormiers 2001★★

	2 ha	8,000	⦀	11–15 €

Here is an estate that is impossible to ignore in Saumur, as proved by the many *coups de cœur* and stars awarded to its wines in the *Guide*. Vinified only in years that give a degree of natural potential alcohol higher than 13%, the *cuvée* Les Cormiers is a great example of top-class white wine from this appellation. The 2001 reveals itself slowly and with great delicacy. Its subtle aromas are reminiscent of ripe fruits, nuts (walnut) and apples. In spite of its richness, the palate remains delicate with mineral and lemony touches. This is a wine of great complexity to enjoy at leisure.

☛ SCA Chevallier, Ch. de Villeneuve, 3, rue Jean-Brevet, 49400 Souzay-Champigny, tel. 02.41.51.14.04, fax 02.41.50.58.24 ▼

Wines selected but not starred

DOM. DE BRIZE

Méthode traditionnelle 2001

	4 ha	31,000		5–8 €

☛ Marc et Luc Delhumeau, Dom. de Brizé, 49540 Martigné-Briand, tel. 02.41.59.93.35, fax 02.41.59.66.90, e-mail delhumeau.scea@free.fr ▼
🍷 by appt.

DOM. DES CHAUFFAUX

Méthode traditionnelle 2000

	1 ha	5,000		5–8 €

☛ Ligaud et Fils, Dom. des Chauffaux, 2, rue de l'Eglise, 49400 Distré, tel. 02.41.59.96.84, fax 02.41.59.96.84, e-mail ligaud@club-internet.fr ▼ 🏠
🍷 by appt.

DOM. DES CLOS MAURICE 2002

	0.5 ha	4,000	🍾 ♦	3–5 €

☛ Maurice et Fils Hardouin, Dom. des Clos Maurice, 18, rue de la Mairie, 49400 Varrains, tel. 02.41.52.93.76, fax 02.41.52.44.32, e-mail clos.maurice@wanadoo.fr ▼
🍷 ev. day 8am–12 noon 2pm–6pm

COMTE DE COLBERT

Méthode traditionnelle Cuvée spéciale 2001

	2.2 ha	20,984		8–11 €

☛ Comte Bernard de Colbert, Ch. de Brézé, BP 3, 49260 Brézé, tel. 02.41.51.62.06, fax 02.41.51.63.92 ▼
🍷 ev. day 10am–6.30pm

YVES DROUINEAU

Les Beaumiers 2002

	5 ha	9,000	🍾 ♦	3–5 €

☛ EARL Yves Drouineau, 3, rue Morains, 49400 Dampierre-sur-Loire, tel. 02.41.51.14.02, fax 02.41.50.32.00, e-mail yves.drouineau@wanadoo.fr ▼
🍷 by appt.

DOM. DUBOIS 2002

	0.8 ha	6,000	🍾	3–5 €

☛ Dom. Dubois, 8, rte de Chacé, 49260 Saint-Cyr-en-Bourg, tel. 02.41.51.61.32, fax 02.41.51.95.29 ▼
🍷 by appt.

DOM. DE L'ENCHANTOIR 2002

	2.5 ha	10,000	🍾 ♦	5–8 €

☛ EARL Didier Wieder, 4, rue l'Arguray, Chavannes, 49260 Le Puy-Notre-Dame, tel. 02.41.52.26.33, fax 02.41.52.23.34 ▼
🍷 by appt.

DOM. DE L'EPINAY

Cuvée du Haut Clos 2002

	5 ha	10,000	🍾 ♦	5–8 €

☛ Laurent Menestreau, Dom. de l'Epinay, 86120 Pouançay, tel. 05.49.22.98.08, fax 05.49.22.39.98 ▼
🍷 by appt.

DOM. DE LA FUYE 2002

	6 ha	30,000	🍾	5–8 €

☛ Philippe Elliau, 527, rue du Château, Sanziers, 49260 Vaudelnay, tel. 02.41.38.87.31, fax 02.41.38.87.31 ▼
🍷 by appt.

DOM. DU MOULIN 2002

	1.4 ha	8,000	🍾	3–5 €

☛ SCEA Marcel Biguet, 5, pl. la Paleine, 49260 Le Puy-Notre-Dame, tel. 02.41.52.26.68, fax 02.41.38.85.64, e-mail sbiguet@terre-net.fr ▼ 🏠
🍷 by appt.

CAVE DES VIGNERONS DE SAUMUR

Réserve des Vignerons 2002

	120 ha	1000,000	🍾 ♦	3–5 €

☛ Cave des Vignerons de Saumur, rte de Saumoussay, 49260 Saint-Cyr-en-Bourg, tel. 02.41.53.06.06, fax 02.41.53.09.04 ▼
🍷 ev. day 9am–12 noon 2pm–6pm

DOM. DES VIGNES BICHES

Vieilles Vignes La Sicardière 2002

	8 ha	40,000	🍾 ♦	3–5 €

☛ SARL Vinival, La Sablette, 44330 Mouzillon, tel. 02.40.36.66.00, fax 02.40.33.95.81

Coteaux de Saumur

They received their patents of nobility long ago: Coteaux de Saumur, the Saumurois equivalent of Anjou's Coteaux du Layon, is made exclusively from Chenin grapes grown on the chalky tufa. In 2002, only 505 hl were produced.

DOM. DE NERLEUX 2002★

	1 ha	1000	⦀	11–15 €

An old seigniorial estate going back to the 16th century, the property inherited buildings of the 17th and 18th centuries, which have been rejuvenated by restoration work carried out in 2002. Its Coteaux de Saumur is very characteristic of sweet wines from limestone soil, giving a sensation of freshness right through tasting. Its delicate aromas evoke ripe fruits and citrus fruits, and the palate appears light and on the

finish gives notes of mixed nuts and vanilla. Overall, it is an easy-drinking wine.
☛ Régis Neau, Dom. de Nerleux, 4, rue de la Paleine, 49260 Saint-Cyr-en-Bourg, tel. 02.41.51.61.04, fax 02.41.51.65.34, e-mail contact@domaine-de-nerleux.fr
♈ ev. day except Sun. 8am–12.30pm 2pm–6pm; Sat. 8am–12.30pm

☛ SCEA Dom du Bois de la Croix, 49400 Souzay-Champigny, tel. 02.41.40.22.50, fax 02.41.40.22.60

DOM. DU BOIS MOZE PASQUIER
Vieilles Vignes 2002★★

	0.5 ha	4,000		5–8 €

In 1994 Patrick Pasquier took over the small 6-ha property started by his parents in 1955 and is maintaining his inheritance with talent, judging by this outstanding wine. The vines are of a really respectable age: almost a half-century old. The colour of this garnet-red 2002 is intense and so is the nose which evokes concentrated aromas of red fruit jam. Balanced and fresh, the palate manages to be both dense and silky. Already appealing, this wine will be at its peak in two or three years' time. Two stars is also given to the **Cuvée Clos du Bois Mozé 2002 (3–5 €)**, aged in tank, which has an intense fruitiness with a rounded, full, powerful and well-balanced palate.
☛ Patrick Pasquier, 7, rue du Bois-Mozé, 49400 Chacé, tel. 02.41.52.42.50, fax 02.41.52.59.73
♈ by appt.

Wines selected but not starred

DOM. DES MATINES 2002

	0.9 ha	3,200		8–11 €

☛ Dom. des Matines, 31, rue de la Mairie, 49700 Brossay, tel. 02.41.52.25.36, fax 02.41.52.25.50, e-mail domainedesmatines@wanadoo.fr
♈ by appt.
☛ Etchegaray-Mallard

Saumur-Champigny

Touring the narrow streets of Saumurois villages, you will find yourself in heaven among the tufa cellars, which shelter many aged bottles. Even though this vineyard, which covers 1,497 ha, has only recently expanded, the red wines from Champigny have been renowned for many centuries. Production comes from nine villages, using Cabernet Franc (or Breton) grapes, and the wines are light, fruity and agreeable. In 2002, output was 85,747 hl. The Winemakers' Cellar in Saint-Cyr-en-Bourg has been influential in the development of the vineyard.

DOM. DE LA BESSIERE
Clos de la Croix 2002★

	1.8 ha	13,000		3–5 €

Established in 1987 with a vineyard area of 7 ha, today Thierry Dézé farms around 15 ha. His *cuvée* Clos de la Croix is eye-catching with its deep and bright garnet-red colour, enlivened with vivid bluish hints. The very attractive nose made up of slightly tart red berries reflects the good ripeness of the grapes. Full-bodied and structured by well-extracted tannins, this wine already gives pleasure but will not be at its peak for another three years.
☛ Thierry Dézé, SCEV Dom. de La Bessière, rte de Champigny, 49400 Souzay-Champigny, tel. 02.41.52.42.69, fax 02.41.38.75.41
♈ by appt.

DOM.DU BOIS DE LA CROIX 2002★

	5 ha	40,000		5–8 €

This estate, which for six years has worked in partnership with the négociant house Joseph Verdier, offers a light cherry-coloured wine. The nose combines red berries with slightly smoky notes. Fresh and soft, fruity and long, this Saumur-Champigny provides a "style reminiscent of spring-time", according to one taster. It can be drunk from now on.

DOM. LA BONNELIERE
Cuvée des Poyeux 2002★★

	2 ha	15,000		5–8 €

A descendent of several generations of wine-growers, André Bonneau created this estate, renamed Domaine La Bonnelière in 1995 with a few hectares of old vines. His two sons, Anthony and Cédric, have joined the estate which today has more than 22 ha. This year, the property is particularly distinguished in this appellation, as three wines have been selected by the Jury. The one they preferred was this Cuvée des Poyeux, which comes from the oldest vines: a deep colour; very open nose of cherries and blackberries; an attractive acidity on the rich palate; and a silkiness disclosing a marriage of wood and fruit, it is not far from a *coup de coeur*. The two other wines each obtain a star: **Cuvée Symphonie 2002**, also matured partially in barrel with beautiful fruit indicating ripe grapes, and the **Cuvée Principale 2002** which had no oak, but was enjoyed for its lively character.
☛ EARL Bonneau et Fils, Dom. La Bonnelière, 45, rue du Bourg-Neuf, 49400 Varrains, tel. 02.41.52.92.38, fax 02.41.67.35.48
♈ by appt.

DOM. DES BONNEVEAUX
Cuvée Nicolas 2002★

	1,25 ha	10,000		3–5 €

This estate, which takes its name from a *lieu-dit* in the Saumur-Champigny appellation, was created in 1985 and has a vineyard of 15 ha. Its Cuvée Nicolas catches the eye with its deep garnet-red appearance. Expressive, the nose evokes ripe Morello cherries and provides great pleasure. Even if it appears less intense on the palate, the wine discloses good balance and length.
☛ Camille et Nicolas Bourdoux, 79, Grand-Rue, 49400 Varrains, tel. 02.41.52.94.91, fax 02.41.52.99.24
♈ by appt.

Saumur-Champigny

DOM. DES CHAMPS FLEURIS
Les Tufolies 2002★★

| | 28 ha | 100,000 | ▮ ♦ | 5–8 € |

Denis Rétiveau, his sister Catherine and brother-in-law Patrice Rétif run this 33-ha estate. The vineyards are located in the Saumur-Champigny area and, in particular, on the hillside that overlooks the Loire, which was a major white wine-producing area before being colonized by the Cabernet variety. The latter dominates the mix of grape varieties on the estate and is also often retained for use in some of its white wines. A discovery this year is the *cuvée* Les Tufolies and the 2002 wine really has the edge. The deep red, bright colour reveals a touch of amber. On swirling the glass, scents of a ripe harvest are revealed. There is good acidity on first tasting and the palate is well balanced with rounded tannins. Very ripe red berries accompany the soft finish and show a most attractive continuity from the nose to the palate.
➤ EARL Rétiveau-Rétif, 54, rue des Martyrs,
49730 Turquant, tel. 02.41.38.10.92, fax 02.41.51.75.33,
e-mail domainechamps-fleuris@wanadoo.fr ☑
☖ by appt.

BRUNO DUBOIS
Cuvée d'Automne 2002★

| | 0.7 ha | 6,000 | ▮ | 5–8 € |

This Cuvée d'Automne is the first vintage made by Bruno Dubois, who in 2002 took over the reins of this small 6.5-ha estate. It shows the serious work that has been done both in the vineyards and in the winery. With a beautiful garnet-red colour, on the nose it expresses the freshness of the soft red berries. Equally full of flavour, the palate is light and pleasant.
➤ Bruno Dubois, 8, rue de La Judée,
49260 Saint-Cyr-en-Bourg, tel. 06.07.70.95.20,
e-mail b-d@wanadoo.fr ☑
☖ ev. day except Sun. 8am–12 noon 2pm–6pm

DOM. DUBOIS
Vieilles Vignes 2002★

| | 0.7 ha | 5,000 | ◖◗ | 8–11 € |

Very often mentioned in the *Guide*, this vineyard extends to more than 18 ha. Made from 40-year-old vines, its *cuvée* Vieilles Vignes was matured for one year in cask. This has given a deep red appearance with tinges of brown and a fruity nose with a touch of liquorice. Full, elegant and long, the palate has attractive overall balance. It is an extremely oaky wine, that is rather atypical in this appellation, but it will find its supporters.
➤ Dom. Dubois, 8, rte de Chacé,
49260 Saint-Cyr-en-Bourg, tel. 02.41.51.61.32,
fax 02.41.51.95.29 ☑
☖ by appt.

DOM. FILLIATREAU 2002★★

| | 25 ha | 140,000 | ▮ ♦ | 5–8 € |

In 1967, Paul Filliatreau set up his estate with 8 ha of vineyards bequeathed to him by his father. He became interested in making red wines at a time when rosés dominated the local production and has considerably extended the estate to 35 ha today. His son Fredrik has been working with him since 1990. The young vines gave a scintillating ruby wine that is most attractive due to a nose that suggests subtle and bright scents of black fruits, and a palate that has a good, quite silky tannic structure and an elegant finish. With almost the same mark the **Cuvée Vieilles Vignes 2002 (8–11 €)** has character; it exhibits a deep red colour, a very expressive nose suggesting attractive, very ripe grapes and offers a flavourful palate that is structured and long. Lastly, the Saumur-Champigny **Lena Filliatreau 2002 (5–8 €)** also obtains a star: full of flavour and balanced, it is classic and well made.
➤ Paul Filliatreau, Chaintres, 49400 Dampierre-sur-Loire, tel. 02.41.52.90.84, fax 02.41.52.49.92,
e-mail domaine@filliatreau.fr ☑
☖ ev. day 8am–12 noon 1.30pm–5.30pm; Sat. Sun. by appt.

CH. DU HUREAU
Cuvée Lisagathe 2002★

| | 2 ha | 10,000 | ▮ ◖◗ ♦ | 11–15 € |

Philippe Vatan has run this 20-ha estate with talent since 1987, witness the numerous *coups de coeur* that he has obtained: no less than eight in 16 years, all in this appellation! This Cuvée Lisagathe has, moreover, been honoured in previous editions. This vintage, not quite so lucky, has given a wine of an unambiguous, intense ruby. It is full of soft red berries on the nose, a sign of well-handled extraction. Soft and delicious, the palate is filled with beautiful strawberry-raspberry fruit. It is wine to drink right away.
➤ Philippe Vatan, Ch. du Hureau,
49400 Dampierre-sur-Loire, tel. 02.41.67.60.40,
fax 02.41.50.43.35, e-mail philippe.vatan@wanadoo.fr ☑
☖ ev. day except Sat. Sun. 8am–12 noon 2pm–5pm;
cl. 1–15 Aug.

RENE LEGRAND
Les Lizières 2002★

| | 4 ha | 15,000 | | 5–8 € |

René Noël Legrand farms 15 hectares in the large wine-growing village of Varrains, between the Loire River and Thouet. This beautiful deep garnet-red Saumur-Champigny has an intense nose of red and black fruit. This power reappears on the well-constructed, rich palate, which has a well-balanced middle palate. Already pleasant, it should improve with time.
➤ René-Noël Legrand, 13, rue des Rogelins,
49400 Varrains, tel. 02.41.52.94.11, fax 02.41.52.49.78 ☑
☖ by appt.

DOM. DE LA PERRUCHE
Clos de Chaumont 2002★

| | 5 ha | 10,000 | ▮ ◖◗ ♦ | 8–11 € |

Recently restored, the Château de Montsoreau, rebuilt in the 15th century, overlooks the confluence of the Rivers Vienne and Loire, on the border between Anjou and Touraine. The estate is situated in a very beautiful village and has a vineyard of 38 ha. The Clos de Chaumont comes from a late harvest, 25 October for this vintage. It gives a very attractive appearance of deep crimson. The fruitiness appears attractive from the start, reflecting the ripeness of the grapes. It is toned down by liquorice notes at the start and oaky notes on the finish, which emphasize the tannic structure. Overall it has beautiful balance.
➤ SCEV Dom. de la Perruche, 29, rue de la Maumenière, 49730 Montsoreau, tel. 02.41.51.73.36, fax 02.41.38.18.70,
e-mail domainedelaperruche@terre-net.fr ☑
☖ ev. day except Sun. 9am–7pm

LE PETIT SAINT VINCENT 2002★★

| | 6 ha | 20,000 | ▮ ◖◗ ♦ | 5–8 € |

Dominique Joseph is based on a hillside overlooking the Loire Valley. He named his estate after the patron saint of wine-growers. Could he produce bad wine with that name? This dark ruby 2002 exhibits a fruitiness that is both delicate and intense with stewed black fruits, and liquorice notes. The palate has the silky tannins of a great wine. "What length and what pleasure!" concluded one taster. It is the result of outstanding winemaking.
➤ EARL Dominique Joseph, 10, rue des Rogelins,
49400 Varrains, tel. 02.41.52.99.95, fax 02.41.38.75.76,
e-mail d-joseph@terre-net.fr ☑
☖ by appt.

DOM. DES RAYNIERES 2002★

| | 4 ha | 30,000 | ▮ ♦ | 5–8 € |

Jean-Pierre Rébeilleau owns 28 ha around the wine village of Varrains. He presents a wine that is very typical of the appellation: a colour of spring-time with beautiful, very ripe fruitiness suggesting red berries and woodland fruits, appearing both on the nose and on the palate. It is a most elegant wine.
➤ Jean-Pierre Rébeilleau, SCEA Dom. des Raynières, 33, rue du Ruau, 49400 Varrains, tel. 02.41.52.95.17,
fax 02.41.52.48.40 ☑
☖ by appt.

DOM. DE ROCFONTAINE
Vieilles Vignes 2002★★

	3 ha	20,000	🟦 ♦	8–11 €

Parnay is one of the villages that are dotted along the Loire, between Saumur and Montsoreau. On the river, a small, sandy island stretches out and provides a home for large colonies of marine birds, whilst the wine cellars stretch along the tufa cliffs on its border. Philippe Bougreau has done extremely well in the year 2002, since his two Saumur-Champignys have been selected by the Jury: **Cuvée Tradition (5–8 €)** received one star: balanced and fruity, it is a very good representative of its appellation. As for this *cuvée* Vieilles Vignes, it was the favourite: intense crimson with bluish tinges, it delivers engaging black fruit scents of ripe blueberries. Soft at first and velvety, the palate reflects grapes of good ripeness. Fruitiness asserts itself on the finish giving a very pleasant wine.
🐦 Philippe Bougreau, Dom. de Rocfontaine, 7, ruelle des Bideaux, 49730 Parnay, tel. 02.41.51.46.89, fax 02.41.38.18.61 ☑ ♠
🍷 by appt.

DOM. DES ROCHES NEUVES
Terres Chaudes 2002★★

	5 ha	20,000	🍶	11–15 €

This estate forms part of the Anjou galaxy of vineyards owned by Germain et Associés. Thierry Germain took excellent advantage of the year 2002, judging by his Saumur-Champigny. The Terres Chaudes received unanimous votes, with its deep, attractive garnet-red colour; accents of liquorice and smoke that emerge on the nose; and fine extraction of tannins shown on the well-balanced structure. Drawn from grapes harvested at optimum maturity, it is an outstanding wine to lay down. **Cuvée Domaine 2002 (5–8 €)**, aged in tank, offers complex flavours of overripe red berries that reappear on the full-bodied palate together with liquorice notes. Also for ageing, it obtained two stars.
🐦 Thierry Germain, 56, bd Saint-Vincent, 49400 Varrains, tel. 02.41.52.94.02, fax 02.41.52.49.30, e-mail thierry-germain@wanadoo.fr ☑
🍷 by appt.

DOM. DES SABLES VERTS
Cuvée Ligerienne 2002★

	2 ha	10,000	🟦 ♦	5–8 €

The estate takes its name from the sands deposited in the Secondary era, including greater or lesser amounts of limestone and rich in glauconite, with minerals contained within the tufa, which give the soils a greenish colour. With 15 ha of vineyards, it was taken over in 1985 by Alain and Dominique Duveau who farm it using sustainable agriculture with grassing down between the vine rows. Of a rather intense garnet, this Cuvée Ligérienne reveals itself to be still restrained, but on aeration releases perfumes of red berries, indicating good ripeness. The palate confirms these first impressions; unctuous, it discloses good structure and guarantees real ageing potential.
🐦 GAEC Dominique et Alain Duveau, 66, Grand-Rue, 49400 Varrains, tel. 02.41.52.91.52, fax 02.41.38.75.32, e-mail duveau@domaine-sables-verts.com ☑
🍷 by appt.

DOM. DE SAINT-JUST
La Montée des Roches 2002★

	5 ha	10,000	🟦🍶♦	8–11 €

He moved from being a financial specialist to a wine producer, though it is true that the giant insurance company where Yves Lambert worked owned a great wine estate and that his wife's family work in the Saumur wine business. Yves Lambert established his estate definitively in 1996 and, advised by Denis Duveau, a master when considering the Saumur-Champigny appellation, he quickly made his name. La Montée des Roches, produced from a clay-limestone terroir, has already obtained two *coups de coeur* for the 97 and 98 vintages. Matured partly in barrel, this intense red wine releases aromas of nuts with nuances of liquorice and vanilla. A mouth-filling wine, the flavours on the middle palate should develop with time.
🐦 Yves Lambert, Dom. de Saint-Just, 12, rue de la Prée, 49260 Saint-Just-sur-Dive, tel. 02.41.51.62.01, fax 02.41.67.94.51, e-mail info@st-just.net ☑ ♠
🍷 by appt.

DOM. SAINT VINCENT
Les Adrialys 2002★

	3 ha	10,000	🟦🍶♦	5–8 €

Patrick Vadé took over the family estate in 1984. He farms some 25 ha of vines on the hillsides which overlook the Loire (in geological terms, these are the high grounds of the turonien cuesta that makes up the vineyards of the Saumur-Champigny appellation). Selected several times by the Hachette Juries, Les Adrialys presents an attractive appearance, of a deep red colour. After agitation, it releases superb black fruit scents of ripe blackcurrants. Well structured, fine, elegant, full, rich and balanced, it is a real success for the vintage. The unoaked *cuvée* **Les Trézellières 2002** is given a special mention. Still immature, it needs time.
🐦 Patrick Vadé, Dom. Saint-Vincent, 49400 Saumur, tel. 02.41.67.43.19, fax 02.41.50.23.28, e-mail pvade@st-vincent.com ☑
🍷 by appt.

DOM. DES SANZAY
Vieilles Vignes 2002★

	1.5 ha	7,500	🍶	5–8 €

Just less than 30 hectares make up the property and the majority is planted to red vines intended for Saumur-Champigny. Fifty-year-old vines are behind this deep garnet-red wine. Still restrained, on swirling the glass, the nose exudes most attractive scents of black fruit. Pleasant, and quite balanced, there is beautiful length on the palate, even if the austere tannins make their presence felt for the moment.
🐦 Didier Sanzay, Dom. des Sanzay, 93, Grand-Rue, 49400 Varrains, tel. 02.41.52.91.30, fax 02.41.52.45.93, e-mail didier-sanzay@domaine-sanzay.com ☑
🍷 by appt.

ANTOINE SANZAY 2002★

	1 ha	7,000	🟦	5–8 €

They have cultivated the vine here for six generations, but this 2002 is the first vintage made by Antoine Sanzay. The barrel cellar has also been too renovated this year. The result is most encouraging looking at this Saumur-Champigny. An intense red colour; soft red berry aromas accompanied by slightly smoky notes; the palate is fruity and elegant with integrated tannins making the wine particularly pleasant all in all.
🐦 Antoine Sanzay, 19, rue des Roches-Neuves, 49400 Varrains, tel. 02.41.52.90.08, fax 02.41.50.27.39, e-mail antoine-sanzay@wanadoo.fr ☑
🍷 by appt.

DOM. DES VARINELLES
Vieilles Vignes 2001★

	6 ha	30,000	🍶	8–11 €

The property is richly endowed with 42 ha planted to Cabernet Franc, Chenin and Chardonnay. The average age of the vines is quite high. Those which were used for this wine are of a minimum of 70 years old. This 2001 remained in two-year-old barrels for 13 months. Of an intense ruby with delicate purplish tinges, it offers a restrained nose that on agitation reveals soft red fruit scents along with liquorice notes. On the palate, it shows beautiful weight, richness and good structure made up of obvious but integrated and silky tannins. A long finish concludes the tasting.

➤ SCA Daheuiller et Fils, 28, rue du Ruau, 49400 Varrains, tel. 02.41.52.90.94, fax 02.41.52.94.63 ☑
🍷 ev. day except Sun. 8am–12 noon 2pm–6.30pm; Sat. by appt.

Wines selected but not starred

LE CLOS DES CORDELIERS
Cuvée Tradition 2002

| ■ | 12 ha | 80,000 | ■ ♦ | 5–8 € |

➤ Michel et Sébastien Ratron, Clos des Cordeliers, 49400 Champigny, tel. 02.41.52.95.48, fax 02.41.52.99.50, e-mail ratron@clos-des-cordeliers.com ☑
🍷 ev. day except Sun. 8am–12 noon 2pm–6pm

DOM. DES CLOS MAURICE 2002

| ■ | 13 ha | 70,000 | ■ ♦ | 5–8 € |

➤ Maurice et Fils Hardouin, Dom. des Clos Maurice, 18, rue de la Mairie, 49400 Varrains, tel. 02.41.52.93.76, fax 02.41.52.44.32, e-mail clos.maurice@wanadoo.fr ☑
🍷 ev. day 8am–12 noon 2pm–6pm

DOM. FOUET La Rouge et Noire Cuvée
VieillesVignes Elevée en fût de chêne 2002

| ■ | 1 ha | 6,000 | ⅠⅠⅠ | 8–11 € |

➤ Fouet, 3, rue de la Judée, 49260 Saint-Cyr-en-Bourg, tel. 02.41.51.60.52, fax 02.41.67.01.79, e-mail j-fouet@domaine-fouet.com ☑
🍷 ev. day except Sun. 10am–2pm

CH. MARCONNAY Cuvée Théophile Vieilles
Vignes Elevé en fût de chêne 1999

| ■ | 1.1 ha | 4,700 | ⅠⅠⅠ | 11–15 € |

➤ Hervé Goumain, Ch. du Marconnay, 49400 Souzay-Champigny, tel. 02.41.50.08.21, fax 02.41.50.23.04, e-mail marconnay@wanadoo.fr ☑ ⌂
🍷 ev. day 10am–12 noon 2pm–6pm;
1 Oct.–31 Mar. by appt.

VIGNOBLE PATRICK VADE
Cuvée les Baunelles 2002

| ■ | 7 ha | 40,000 | | 3–5 € |

➤ SARL Vinival, La Sablette, 44330 Mouzillon, tel. 02.40.36.66.00, fax 02.40.33.95.81

Touraine

The interesting collections housed in the Musée des Vins de Touraine (Touraine Wine Museum) in Tours exhibit the history of the advances made in vine-growing and wine in the region. It relates semi-mythical accounts of the life of Saint Martin, the bishop of Tours in 380, and illuminates the "Golden Legend" with images relating to vine cultivation and wines. By the year 1000, the Abbey at Bourgueil was already cultivating the Breton (Cabernet Franc) variety in its famous enclosed vineyard and, years later, Rabelais, the great French writer, was eloquently singing its praises during the 16th century. History is still much in evidence today along the tourist routes from Mesland to Bourgueil on the right bank (through Vouvray, Tours, Luynes, Langeais), and from Chaumont to Chinon on the left bank (through Amboise and Chenonceaux, the Cher valley, Saché, Azay le Rideau and the forest of Chinon).

The Touraine vineyard has been famous for a considerable time, but underwent its most significant expansion at the end of the 19th century. Its present-day area, which is about 13,000 ha, is actually less than it was before the phylloxera disaster; it lies mainly within the departments of Indre-et-Loire and Loir-et-Cher but, in the north, encroaches into the Sarthe. Tasting very old wines from 1921, 1893, 1874 or even 1858, for example at Vouvray, Bourgueil or Chinon, reveals characteristics fairly close to the wines of today. Thus, despite developments in cultivation techniques and the science of winemaking, the "style" of Touraine wines remains relatively unchanged, probably because each of the appellations is founded upon a single grape variety. The climate also plays its part: maritime and continental influences find expression in the wines, the slopes forming a screen from the north winds. In addition, the east-west valleys of the Loir, the Loire, the Cher, the Indre and the Vienne create a multitude of tufa slopes propitious for vine-growing, enjoying a local climate that shows little variation and maintains a healthy level of humidity. The tufa, a soft, creamy-yellow limestone, is hollowed out into innumerable subterranean caves. In the valleys, clay is mixed with limestone or sand and sometimes silica, while down on the banks of the Loire and the Vienne gravelly soils predominate.

These local variations are reflected in the wines. Each valley corresponds to an appellation, and each year the wines have different individual characteristics depending on the weather. The association of the year of bottling with the description of the cru is thus essential.

Classification varies between the tannic reds of Chinon or Bourgueil (softer when they are grown on gravelly soils, better structured when they come from the slopes), and the lighter growths from the Appellation Touraine, sometimes sold en primeur. There are also variations in the rosés, which are drier or not so dry depending on the amount of sunshine; the same is true of the whites of Azay le Rideau or Amboise, and of those from Vouvray and Montlouis, where the styles range from dry to sweet and include sparkling wines. Specific local vinification techniques also play their part. The tufa caves provide an excellent storage environment at a constant temperature of around 12°C, ideal for ageing; in addition, the vinification of the white wines is carried out at a controlled temperature, fermentation sometimes lasting several weeks, or even several months for the sweet wines. The light Touraine reds are produced from short periods of fermentation; with Bourgueil and Chinon, however, fermentation is longer: two to four weeks. While the reds undergo malolactic fermentation, the whites and rosés owe their freshness, conversely, to the presence of malic acid.

Touraine

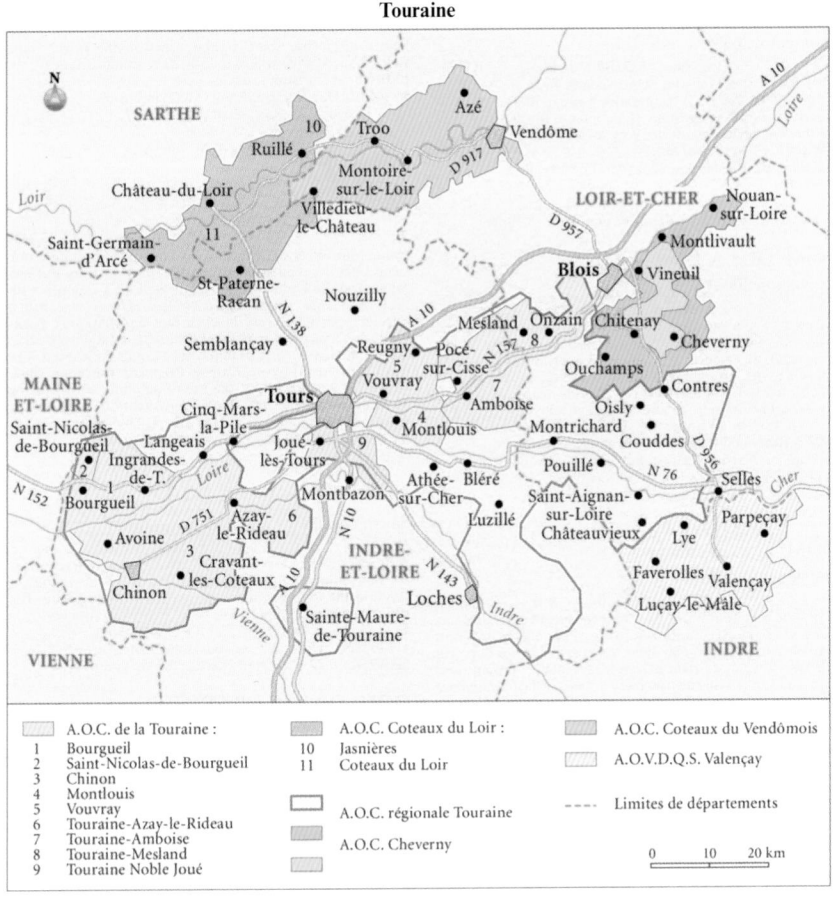

A.O.C. de la Touraine :
1 Bourgueil
2 Saint-Nicolas-de-Bourgueil
3 Chinon
4 Montlouis
5 Vouvray
6 Touraine-Azay-le-Rideau
7 Touraine-Amboise
8 Touraine-Mesland
9 Touraine Noble Joué

A.O.C. Coteaux du Loir :
10 Jasnières
11 Coteaux du Loir

A.O.C. régionale Touraine

A.O.C. Cheverny

A.O.C. Coteaux du Vendômois

A.O.V.D.Q.S. Valençay

– – – – Limites de départements

0   10   20 km

Touraine

The Appellation Régionale Touraine covers 5,438.71 ha, stretching from the outskirts of Montsoreau in the west as far as Blois and Selles-sur-Cher in the east. It is located principally in the valleys of the Loire, the Indre and the Cher. Tufa emerges rarely; the soils most often overlie clay with silica. The main variety for red wines is Gamay, alongside more tannic varieties such as Cabernet Franc and Côt, depending on the terrain. The majority of red wines, including the light and fruity *vins primeurs*, are made exclusively with Gamay. Reds made from a mixture of two or three of the main varieties keep well in bottle. The dry white wines are made with the Sauvignon, which in the last forty years has replaced all other varieties. A proportion of the white wines is made as sparkling wines by the Traditional, or Champagne method. Finally, the rosés are always dry, fresh and fruity, made with the red wine grape varieties of the region. Production in 2002 amounted to 285,100 hl.

DANIELLE DE L'ANSÉE
Sauvignon 2002★

	n.c.	35,000	🍾 ♦	3–5 €

This golden-yellow wine has beautiful presentation. Wild flowers, peaches and honey jostle for position around a balanced structure. One can really smell the ripeness of the grapes.
🍾 Danielle de l'Ansée, Les Martinières, 15, rue des Vignes, 41140 Noyers-sur-Cher, tel. 02.54.71.09.95, fax 02.54.75.29.79, e-mail danielle-de-lansee@wanadoo.fr
🍷 ev. day except Sun. 10am–12 noon 2.30pm–6pm
🍷 Pascal Gibault

DOM. DE L'AUMONIER
Sauvignon 2002★

	29 ha	106,000	🍾 ♦	3–5 €

This beautiful wine was much appreciated by the Jury for its intense expression of exotic fruits. Very full, it discloses a light smokiness coming without doubt from the numerous flinty soils in Couffy, and which brings a touch of freshness with this very ripe wine.
🍷 Thierry Chardon, Villequemoy, 41110 Couffy, tel. 02.54.75.21.83, fax 02.54.75.21.56, e-mail domaine.aumoniertchardon@wanadoo.fr 🅥
🍷 by appt.

CELLIER DU BEAUJARDIN

Sauvignon 2002★

| | 20 ha | 20,000 | ▮ ♦ | 3–5€ |

Here is an attractive wine which comes from the range of Cellier du Beaujardin, a cooperative based in Bléré. This wine presents a faultless harmony in its intense floral aromas, its full-bodied structure and its very long finish. The **Touraine Cot 2001** is also singled out.

↬ Cellier du Beaujardin, 32, av. du 11-Novembre, 37150 Bléré, tel. 02.47.57.91.04, fax 02.47.23.51.27, e-mail cellier.beaujardin@wanadoo.fr ▌
✝ ev. day except Sun. 8.30am–12 noon 2pm–6.30pm

DOM. DE LA BERGERIE

Sauvignon 2002★

| | 6 ha | 26,000 | ▮ ♦ | 3–5€ |

Located on the southern hillside of the Cher River in the *lieu-dit* Tesnière on a soil of *perruche* (sandy-clay with underlying clay), this vineyard makes up 18 ha. It is a classic white Touraine with an intense nose of boxwood and pineapple. Unctuous at first, the freshness builds with exotic fruit flavours. The finish is suitable for its age and it can be drunk with seafood or Asian dishes. The estate's **Touraine Gamay 2002** is fruity and fresh, and gains a special mention.

↬ François Cartier, La Tesnière, 13, rue de la Bergerie, 41110 Pouillé, tel. 02.54.71.51.54, fax 02.54.71.74.09 ▌
✝ ev. day except Sun. 9am–12 noon 2pm–6pm;
cl. 3rd week Aug.

DOM. DES BESSONS

Sauvignon 2002★★

| | 0.8 ha | 3,300 | ▮ ♦ | 3–5€ |

A producer in Touraine-Amboise, François Péquier also has some vines in AC Touraine, from where this Sauvignon derives. The terroir of clay-limestone with siliceous covering produces a wine of bright pale gold, revealing a peachy nose with some underlying mentholated notes. The tasters appreciated the well-handled freshness and fullness on the palate.

↬ François Péquin, Dom. des Bessons, 113, rue de Blois, 37530 Limeray, tel. 02.47.30.09.10, fax 02.47.30.02.25 ▌
✝ by appt.

VIGNOBLES DES BOIS VAUDONS

Cot Le Cent Visages 2001★

| | 2.5 ha | 11,000 | ▮ | 5–8€ |

This Cent Visages bears its name well. It immediately explodes with fruity flavours and musky notes. The soft palate, of unusual length, evokes well-ripened grapes with its spicy flavours and red fruit (Morello cherry). The **red L'Alliance des Générations 2001 Elevé en Fût**, presents blackcurrant and blackberry fruit underneath the still very evident wood influences. This wine deserves a special mention.

↬ GAEC Jean-François et Jacky Mérieau, 38, rte de Saint-Aignan, 41400 Saint-Julien-de-Chédon, tel. 02.54.32.14.23, fax 02.54.32.84.03, e-mail merieau2@wanadoo.fr ▌
✝ by appt.

PAUL BUISSE

Tradition 2001★★

| | n.c. | 20,000 | ▮ | 3–5€ |

Reputed for the quality of his work and enthusiasm, Paul Buisse presents this structured but supple 2001. The fruity nose (blackcurrant) follows through with persistent jammy flavours and a supple, full body.

↬ SA Paul Buisse, 69, rte de Vierzon, BP 112, 41402 Montrichard Cedex, tel. 02.54.32.00.01, fax 02.54.32.09.78, e-mail contact@paul-buisse.com ▌
✝ ev. day except Sat. Sun. 8am–12 noon 2pm–6pm

DOM. DES CAILLOTS

Cabernet 2001★

| | 2 ha | 10,000 | ▮ ♦ | 3–5€ |

A very old wine estate dating from the18th century, whose area has doubled since 1983, the year when Dominique Girault arrived. This wine with its deep garnet colour

emanates musky and floral (carnation) notes that produce a beautiful effect. The soft, rich palate presents supple tannins before disclosing some smoky notes on the finish. This well-balanced wine will make a perfect accompaniment to a pheasant at Christmas lunch.

↬ EARL Dominique Girault, Le Grand Mont, 41140 Noyers-sur-Cher, tel. 02.54.32.27.07, fax 02.54.75.27.87 ▌
✝ ev. day 8.30am–12 noon 2pm–7pm; Sun. am by appt.

DOM. DE LA CHARMOISE

Gamay 2002★

| | 28 ha | 150,000 | ▮ ♦ | 5–8€ |

Henri Marionnet has directed his famous 52-hectare estate since 1969. Its reputation has continued to grow in Europe, Japan and the United States. Cultivated on a clay soil with flint, this Gamay has produced a well-structured wine, with a purple appearance. Very blackcurrant on a liquorice background, it is very powerful yet also shows finesse and elegance. One would like to taste a Gamay such as this more often. The fine textured Touraine **Gamay Première Vendange 2002**, which was made without the use of sulphur, as well as the Touraine **Sauvignon 2002 (both 5–8 €)**, are also successful.

↬ Henry Marionnet, La Charmoise, 41230 Soings, tel. 02.54.98.70.73, fax 02.54.98.75.66 ▌
✝ by appt.

DOM. DE LA COLLINE

Sauvignon 2002★

| | 4.3 ha | 37,300 | | 3–5€ |

A curiosity for the Jury, this 2002 has intense flavours combining both mineral and floral notes. Fresh for the vintage, it stays on the notes of gun-flint and flint on the palate. The wine finishes with suppleness, while remaining lively.

↬ GAEC Guy et Rémy Colin, Le Grand Mont, 41140 Noyers-sur-Cher, tel. 02.41.40.22.50, fax 02.41.40.22.60, e-mail j.verdier@wanadoo.fr

DOM. DE LA GIRARDIERE

Sauvignon 2002★

| | 6.85 ha | 15,000 | ▮ ♦ | 3–5€ |

In 1988, Patrick Léger took over the family estate, created after the Second World War by his grandfather, from his father. He presents this fine 2002 with pronounced citrus fruit flavours, which the Jury appreciated for its progressive development and complexity on the palate. Its balance and mineral note finish will enchant the wine amateurs of Touraine. The Touraine **Gamay 2002**, lively with humus tones, is singled out.

↬ Patrick Léger, La Girardière, 41110 Saint-Aignan, tel. 02.54.75.42.44, fax 02.54.75.21.14, e-mail leger.patrick@wanadoo.fr ▌
✝ by appt.

LES MAITRES VIGNERONS DE LA GOURMANDIERE

Gamay 2002★★

| | 180 ha | 21,742 | ▮ ♦ | 3–5€ |

The wine cellar of Gourmandière changed its president at the 2002 harvest, but has adhered to the same level of quality. This is perceptible in this remarkable rosé with its intense pink colour. Full flavoured on the attack, with a light peppery note, it reveals a slender body, then elegant length. The Jury also awarded two stars to **La Reine Blanche 2001 (5–8 €)**, a typical *méthode traditionelle* of the appellation, its mousse is as fine as its flavours.

↬ Les Maîtres Vignerons de la Gourmandière, 24, rue de Chenonceaux, 37150 Francueil, tel. 02.47.23.91.22, fax 02.47.23.82.50, e-mail info@vignerons-gourmandiere.com ▌
✝ by appt.

CAVE DE LA GRANDE BROSSE

Sauvignon 2002★

| | 7 ha | 13,000 | ▮ ♦ | 3–5€ |

In this tenth century wine cellar carved into the tufa take your time to appreciate this white wine with its floral notes of lily and fruity apricot tones. From a direct attack the palate develops a great freshness that time will be able to moderate. To accompany a *blanquette de veau* in 2004.

📞 Cave de la Grande Brosse, 41700 Chémery, tel. 02.54.71.81.03, fax 02.54.71.76.67, e-mail cave-grande-brosse@wanadoo.fr 🔲
🍷 by appt.
📞 Philippe Oudin

DOM. GUENAULT 2002★

	n.c.	42,933	–3 €

A négociant involved in the promotion of *vins de pays* within the ANIVIT, Jean-Claude Bougrier is also a producer in the heart of the Cher valley. His 2002 was appreciated for its mature flavour (citrus fruit) and round finish. It will be a good accompaniment to fresh salmon in puff pastry.

📞 J.-C. Bougrier, SCEA Dom. des Hauts-Lieux, 41400 Saint-Georges-sur-Cher, tel. 02.54.32.31.36, fax 02.54.71.09.61
🍷 by appt.

DOM. DU HAUT-PERRON

Le Cerf joli 2002★★

5 ha	40,000	🍾 ♦	3–5 €

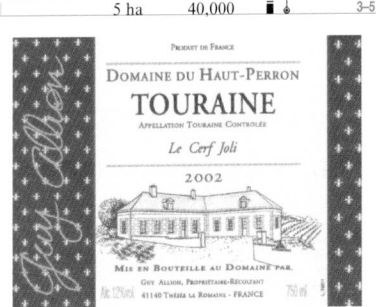

The domaine of Haut-Perron, with its beautiful Touraine-style house of tufa surrounded by Sauvignon vines, astonished and enchanted the Jury with this wine made from vines grown on *perruche* soil (sandy clay) and produced in a winery that was renovated in 2001. The pale-gold colour with green highlights is already inviting. Its nose is expressive with tropical flowers and blackcurrant buds. The palate exhibits a strong personality combining freshness and fullness. Real richness.

📞 Guy Allion, 15, rue du Haut-Perron, 41140 Thésée, tel. 02.54.71.48.01, fax 02.54.71.48.51, e-mail contact@guyallion.com 🔲 🔲
🍷 by appt.

DOM. LEVEQUE

Tradition 2001★★

	n.c.	4,000	🍾 ♦	3–5 €

Located at the eastern end of the Cher hills, the Lévêque domaine farms 23.6 ha as AOC Touraine. The Cuvée Tradition, well-made with its deep garnet-red colour, seduced the Jury with its intense musky notes combined with red berries. Full bodied and full flavoured, already a fine wine to

accompany food. Remarkable also, the Touraine **Cabernet rosé 2002** is round and fruity.

📞 Luc Lévêque, Le Grand Mont, 41140 Noyers-sur-Cher, tel. 02.54.71.52.06, fax 02.54.75.47.65 🔲
🍷 by appt.

DOM. DE MARCE

Sauvignon 2002★★

10 ha	40,000	🍾 ♦	3–5 €

Established in the heart of the Sologne wine region this estate wants to be recognized for its particular characteristics within AOC Touraine by requesting a classification Cru Oisly. Daniel Godet presented a 2002 which enchanted the Jury with its expressive floral and aniseed aromas, uplifted by a touch of liquorice. Flowers dominate on a palate, which is full and well made with a long, round finish packed with ripe fruit.

📞 GAEC Godet, Dom. de Marcé, 41700 Oisly, tel. 02.54.79.54.04, fax 02.54.79.54.45 🔲
🍷 ev. day 8am–12 noon 2pm–7pm

DOM. JACKY MARTEAU

Gamay 2002★

8.6 ha	20,000	🍾 ♦	3–5 €

Silence around the tasting table! What a treat to inhale the lovely fruit jelly aromas (if only time would stop to permit full enjoyment of the headiness of this wine). The 2002 is a reminder that the contents of the glass are as important as the food on the plate. The **red Cuvée Harmonie 2001 (5–8 €)** beautifully expresses the Touraine terroir, and deserves a special mention.

📞 Jacky Marteau, 36, rue de La Tesnière, 41110 Pouillé, tel. 02.54.71.50.00, fax 02.54.71.75.83 🔲
🍷 by appt.

DOM. MICHAUD

Cuvée Ad Vitam Vieilles Vignes 2001★

2.3 ha	14,000	🍾	5–8 €

Awarded a *coup de coeur* in the last edition of the *Guide* for his 2000, Thierry Michaud has succeeded well with this 2001, a vintage that Mother Nature did not spare. An intense ripe blackcurrant nose, a silky body and a lingering fruitiness (cherry) on the finish make this a very pleasurable wine.

📞 EARL Michaud, 20, rue Les Martinières, 41140 Noyers-sur-Cher, tel. 02.54.32.47.23, fax 02.54.75.39.19 🔲
🍷 ev. day except Sun. 8.30am–12.30pm 2pm–7pm

J.-M. MONMOUSSEAU

Les Drageonnières 2001★

2 ha	11,400	🍾 ♦	3–5 €

Monmousseau cellars, created in 1886, are today a subsidiary company of the Luxembourg group, Bernard-Massard. They present this deep crimson wine, balanced and supple with good length that will benefit from two years in the cellar, even if it is pleasant to drink now.

📞 SA Monmousseau, 71, rte de Vierzon, BP 25, 41401 Montrichard, tel. 02.54.71.66.66, fax 02.54.32.56.09, e-mail monmousseau@monmousseau.com 🔲
🍷 ev. day 10am–6pm; groups by appt.; cl. 1 Nov.–31 Mar.
📞 Bernard Massard

Touraine

DOM. DE MONTIGNY
Cuvée Prestige 2001★

| | 2 ha | 6,700 | | | 3–5 € |

Cultivated according to the specifications of Terra Vitis, this family vineyard of 22.5 ha is the source of two very successful Touraine wines. This purple-coloured wine does not lack elegance with its classic style. It releases Morello cherry aromas on the nose, then proclaims its varietal characteristics on the palate, still austere but with a promising finish. Wait another year to taste it at its peak. The Touraine **Sauvignon 2002** shines out equally with its rounded balance and distinctive notes of broom, boxwood and blackcurrant buds.
➦ Annabelle Michaud, Dom. de Montigny, 41700 Sassay, tel. 02.54.79.60.82, fax 02.54.79.07.51 ☑
☉ by appt.

DOMINIQUE PERCEREAU 2002★★

| | 2 ha | 2,000 | | | 3–5 € |

In his wine cellar carved into the tufa, Dominique Percereau perpetuates the Touraine winemaking spirit. This 2002 is seductive with wonderful floral notes of acacia and hawthorn combined with passion-fruit. Its soft palate is rich and full. A wine with undeniable charm.
➦ Dominique Percereau, 85, rue de Blois, 37530 Limeray, tel. 02.47.30.17.86, fax 02.47.30.16.51 ☑
☉ ev. day except Sun. 8am–12.30pm 2pm–7pm

CAVES DU PERE AUGUSTE
Cuvée des Marreux 2001★

| | 7 ha | 18,000 | | | 3–5 € |

Alain Godeau is involved in defending the Touraine AOC within the wine-growers syndicate which he directs. At the same time he develops his vineyards and produces wines of quality like this Marreux selection. A member of the Jury wrote, "beautifully expressive wine from hillsides bathed in the sun". What more can be said?
➦ Famille Godeau, GAEC Caves du Père Auguste, 14, rue des Caves, 37150 Civray-de-Touraine, tel. 02.47.23.93.04, fax 02.47.23.99.58,
e-mail caves-du-pere-auguste@wanadoo.fr ☑
☉ ev. day 8.30am–12.30pm 2pm–7pm; Sun. 10am–12 noon

DOM. DU PRE BARON
L'Elégante 2002★

| | 4 ha | 13,000 | | | 5–8 € |

Jean-Luc Mardon presents a balanced wine, grown on the sandy-gravel terroir of Sologne. A golden appearance, this wine hides ripe citrus fruit flavours (orange, grapefruit), then reveals a suppleness and frankness before finishing elegantly on a ripe lemon note. In a more classic style, the **white Cuvée Principale 2002 (3–5 €)** could also be appreciated now. It merits a special mention.
➦ Guy et Jean-Luc Mardon, Dom. du Pré Baron, 41700 Oisly, tel. 02.54.79.52.87, fax 02.54.79.00.45 ☑
☉ ev. day except Sun. 8.30am–12 noon 2pm–6.30pm

CH. DE LA PRESLE
Sauvignon 2002★

| | 23 ha | 160,000 | | | 3–5 € |

A large 18th century manor house, acquired in 1885 by the ancestors of Penet. The Jury appreciated the maturity of this wine with its discreet grapefruit and buttery notes. Its fruitiness lingers through to the finish. The mineral finish is typical of this particular Sologne terroir at the heart of the AOC Touraine.
➦ Dom. Jean-Marie Penet, Ch. de la Presle, 41700 Oisly, tel. 02.54.79.52.65, fax 02.54.79.08.50,
e-mail domaine-jean-marie-penet@wanadoo.fr ☑
☉ ev. day except Sun. 9am–12 noon 2pm–7pm; groups by appt.
➦ F. et A.-S. Meurgey-Penet

CH. DE QUINCAY
Cot 2001★

| | 5 ha | 13,000 | | | 3–5 € |

A traditional Touraine grape variety, unfortunately forsaken for other varieties more in vogue, the Cot reveals its noble background. Fresh and fruity with notes of Morello cherry, elegant with plump tannins, the finish shows some warmth. Taste – it's an original. Also awarded one star, the **red Cuvée Principale 2001 (5–8 €)**, made up of 50% Cot and 50% Cabernet, is well made; it can be drunk now or in two or three years. The **Sauvignon Vieilles Vignes 2002** is also a success. With its floral range of flavours and roundness it would be a perfect accompaniment to grilled fish.
➦ GAEC Ch. de Quinçay, 41130 Meusnes, tel. 02.54.71.00.11, fax 02.54.71.77.72 ☑ ☎
☉ by appt.

DOM. DE LA RENAUDIE
Sauvignon 2002★

| | 8 ha | 55,000 | | | 3–5 € |

Approachable with a beautiful presentation, this pale-coloured Touraine with green glints releases discreet exotic fruit flavours of honey and apricot. It opens out to a memorable finish. A special mention goes to the **Cuvée Tradition red 2001** that has sweet pepper notes typical of the Cabernet.
➦ Patricia et Bruno Denis, Dom. de La Renaudie, 115, rte de Saint-Aignan, 41110 Mareuil-sur-Cher, tel. 02.54.75.18.72, fax 02.54.75.27.65,
e-mail domaine.renaudie@wanadoo.fr ☑
☉ by appt.

DOM. DU RIN DU BOIS
Gamay 2002★

| | 12 ha | 60,000 | | | 5–8 € |

This Sologne property, Rin du Bois, presents a pretty wine which is a perfect image of the art of Touraine living and the beauty of its gardens. Its stewed fruit aromas flatter from the start and, in the same way, the finish testifies to the concentrated body. The softness and elegance will prove pleasing.
➦ Pascal Jousselin, Dom. du Rin du Bois, 41230 Soings-en-Sologne, tel. 02.54.98.71.87, fax 02.54.98.75.09, e-mail jousselin@netcourrier.com ☑
☉ by appt.

DOM. DE RIS
Seigneur Clément 2001★

| | 3.3 ha | 8,000 | | | 5–8 € |

Just outside the heart of the vineyard region, the Ris domaine is not unworthy of representing the appellation. Seigneur Clément sets high standards, with this wine that invades the palate with raspberry and blackberry flavours. It has strong but soft tannins that give volume and define the structure. To accompany game or rib of beef.
➦ SCEV Dom. de Ris, 37290 Bossay-sur-Claise, tel. 02.47.94.64.43, fax 02.47.94.68.46 ☑
☉ ev. day except Sun. 5.30pm–7pm; Sat. 10am–7pm

CH. DE LA ROCHE
Sauvignon 2002★

| | 9 ha | 51,760 | | | 3–5 € |

The historic Château de la Roche is a beautiful residence with ivy-clad walls. It is within this setting that Pierre Chainier, also a négociant, produces a well-balanced wine, perfumed with slightly honeyed apricot and passion-fruit aromas. This well-made, well-structured wine can be enjoyed today or equally kept in the cellar. The rich, fruity **rosé 2002**, also obtains a star.
➦ SCA Dom. Chainier, Ch. de La Roche, 37530 Chargé, tel. 02.47.30.73.07, fax 02.47.30.73.09
☉ by appt.

DOM. DE LA ROCHETTE
Pineau d'Aunis 2002★★

| | 3 ha | 20,000 | | | 3–5 € |

A beautiful property (46 ha) on the best Cher hillside whose vines are planted on *perruche* (sandy clay) soil. Pale and

778

slightly orange, this rosé is typical of the local Pineau d'Aunis with its finely peppered notes. It is particularly elegant and well balanced with a combination of roundness and freshness. Imagine you are sitting beside the Cher in the shade of the acacias. The **Sauvignon 2002** obtains one star: pale gold, it is full and fresh, with grapefruit and spring flower notes.
☛ François Leclair, 79, rte de Montrichard, 41110 Pouillé, tel. 02.54.71.44.02, fax 02.54.71.10.94, e-mail info@vin-rochette-leclair.com ☑
🍷 ev. day 8am–11.30am 2pm–5.30pm; Sat. Sun. by appt.

DOM. SAUVETE

Les Gravouilles 2002★★

	4 ha	20,000	🍾 ⚲	5–8 €

On the siliceous hillsides bordering the Cher, the grapes, cultivated organically since 2001, have been carefully collected so as not to damage them. From these Jérôme and Dominique Sauvète have made this ruby-coloured 2002, with a Morello cherry nose and robust body. A true pleasure. Also keep in mind the **Cuvée Passion red 2002**, a very good wine.
☛ Dom. Sauvète, 9, chem. de La Bocagerie, 41400 Monthou-sur-Cher, tel. 02.54.71.48.68, fax 02.54.71.75.31, e-mail domaine-sauvete@wanadoo.fr ☑
🍷 ev. day except Sun. 9am–12 noon 2pm–7pm; cl. 15–31 Aug.

LES VAUCORNEILLES

Gamay 2002★★

	1 ha	3,500	🍾 ⚲	5–8 €

A producer in AOC Touraine-Mesland, the estate of Vaucorneilles also produces Touraine from pure Gamay. This lovely 2002 with its shimmering, purple-highlighted appearance has an intense nose of blackcurrants and jam. The powerful palate has obvious tannins and a long, full finish. A beautiful wine, which will benefit from some time in your wine cellar.
☛ GAEC Les Vaucorneilles, 10, rue de l'Egalité, 41150 Onzain, tel. 02.54.20.72.91, fax 02.54.20.74.26, e-mail les.vaucorneilles@wanadoo.fr ☑
🍷 by appt.

Wines selected but not starred

DOM. JEAN-PIERRE BARON

Vieilles Vignes 2001

	0.3 ha	2,200	⚲	3–5 €

☛ Jean-Pierre Baron, 6, rue Jean-Pinaut, 41140 Thésée, tel. 02.54.71.58.67, fax 02.54.71.41.30, e-mail vignoblebaron@aol.com ☑
🍷 by appt.

DOM. BEAUSEJOUR

L'Excellence 2001

	5 ha	40,000	🍾 ⚲	3–5 €

☛ Philippe Trotignon, Dom. Beauséjour, 14, rue des Bruyères, 41140 Noyers-sur-Cher, tel. 02.54.71.34.17, fax 02.54.71.77.61, e-mail philippe.trotignon@wanadoo.fr ☑ 🏠

DOM. DE BEAUVAL

Sauvignon 2002

	3 ha	18,700	🍾 ⚲	3–5 €

☛ Dominique Simonnet, Dom. de Beauval, 41110 Saint-Aignan, tel. 02.41.40.22.50, e-mail j.verdier@wanadoo.fr
☛ Joseph Verdier

DOM. BELLEVUE

Sauvignon 2002

	11 ha	70,000	🍾 ⚲	3–5 €

☛ EARL Patrick Vauvy, Les Martinières, 41140 Noyers-sur-Cher, tel. 02.54.71.42.73, fax 02.54.75.21.89, e-mail domainebellevue@terre-net.fr ☑
🍷 by appt.

DOM. DE LA BLINIERE

Cuvée Prestige 2001

	1,5 .	2,000	🍾 ⓐ ⚲	3–5 €

☛ Denis Marinier, Dom. de la Blinière, 41140 Saint-Romain-sur-Cher, tel. 02.54.71.48.60, fax 02.54.71.56.45 ☑
🍷 by appt.

DOM. DES CORBILLIERES 2001

	5 ha	n.c.	🍾 ⚲	5–8 €

☛ EARL Barbou, Dom. des Corbillières, 41700 Oisly, tel. 02.54.79.52.75, fax 02.54.79.64.89 ☑
🍷 by appt.

CH. DES COULDRAIES

Sauvignon 2002

	0,36 ha	2,400	🍾 ⚲	3–5 €

☛ Ch. des Couldraies, Les Couldraies, 41400 Saint-Georges-sur-Cher, tel. 02.54.32.27.42, fax 02.54.32.40.03, e-mail courrier@couldraies.com ☑ 🏠 🏠
🍷 by appt.

DOM. DE LA CROIX BOUQUIE

Sauvignon 2002

	6 ha	25,000	🍾 ⚲	3–5 €

☛ Christian et Annie Girard, 1, chem. de la Chaussée, Phages, 41400 Thenay, tel. 02.54.32.50.67, fax 02.54.32.50.67 ☑
🍷 ev. day 9am–12 noon 2pm–7pm

THIERRY ET JOEL DELAUNAY

Saveurs 2001

	3 ha	1,700	⚲	5–8 €

☛ EARL Dom. Thierry et Joël Delaunay, 48, rue de la Tesnière, 41110 Pouillé, tel. 02.54.71.45.69, fax 02.54.71.55.97, e-mail joeldelaunay@terre-net.fr ☑
🍷 ev. day except Sun. 9am–12 noon 2pm–6pm

VIGNOBLE DUBREUIL

Sauvignon 2002

	5 ha	5,000	🍾 ⚲	3–5 €

☛ Rémi Dubreuil, La Touche, 41700 Couddes, tel. 02.54.71.34.46, fax 02.54.71.09.64, e-mail dubreuil.remi@wanadoo.fr ☑
🍷 by appt.

JACQUELINE LOUET
Cuvée Prestige 2001

	3 ha	12,000	▪ ⚱	5–8 €

✦┐ Jacqueline Louet, Cave Pierre Louet, Le Marchais, 41120 Monthou-sur-Bièvre, tel. 02.54.44.01.56, fax 02.54.44.01.18 ☑
☊ by appt.

JEAN-CHRISTOPHE MANDARD
Tradition 2001

	1 ha	6,000	▪ ⚱	5–8 €

✦┐ Jean-Christophe Mandard, 14, rue du Bas-Guéret, 41110 Mareuil-sur-Cher, tel. 02.54.75.19.73, fax 02.54.75.16.70, e-mail mandard.jc@wanadoo.fr ☑
☊ by appt.

DOM. DE LA MECHINIERE
Sauvignon 2002

	7 ha	30,000	▪ ⚱	3–5 €

✦┐ Valérie Forgues, La Méchinière, 22, rte de Saint-Aignan, 41110 Mareuil-sur-Cher, tel. 02.54.75.15.80, fax 02.54.75.27.61, e-mail domaine-mechiniere@wanadoo.fr ☑
☊ by appt.

MAISON MIRAULT

	n.c.	4,000	▪ ⑪ ⚱	3–5 €

✦┐ Maison Mirault, 15, av. Brûlé, 37210 Vouvray, tel. 02.47.52.71.62, fax 02.47.52.60.90, e-mail maisonmirault@wanadoo.fr ☑
☊ ev. day except Sun. 8am–12 noon 2pm–6pm; Sun. by appt.

CH. DE NITRAY
Sauvignon 2002

	2 ha	10,000	▪ ⚱	3–5 €

✦┐ Ch. de Nitray, 37270 Athée-sur-Cher, tel. 02.47.50.29.74, fax 02.47.50.29.61 ☑
☊ ev. day 9am–12 noon 2pm–7pm
✦┐ de l'Espinay

DOM. OCTAVIE
Sauvignon 2002

	11 ha	50,000	▪ ⚱	5–8 €

✦┐ Noë Rouballay, Dom. Octavie, Marcé, 41700 Oisly, tel. 02.54.79.54.57, fax 02.54.79.65.20, e-mail octavie@netcourrier.com ☑
☊ ev. day 9am–12.30pm 2pm–6.30pm; Sun. by appt.

JAMES PAGET
Cuvée Tradition 2001

	1.25	7,500		3–5 €

✦┐ EARL James et Nicolas Paget, 13, rue d'Armentières, 37190 Rivarennes, tel. 02.47.95.54.02, fax 02.47.95.45.90 ☑
☊ ev. day except Sun. Mon. 9am–12.30pm 2.30pm–7pm

PERONNE

	3 ha	10,000	⑪	3–5 €

✦┐ Les Vignerons des Coteaux Romanais, 50, rue Principale, 41140 Saint-Romain-sur-Cher, tel. 02.54.71.70.74, fax 02.54.71.41.75 ☑
☊ by appt.

PASCAL PIBALEAU
L'Héritage d'Aziaum 2001

	0.4 ha	2,000	⑪	5–8 €

✦┐ EARL Pascal Pibaleau, 68, rte de Langeais, Lure, 37190 Azay-le-Rideau, tel. 02.47.45.27.58, fax 02.47.45.26.18, e-mail pascal.pibaleau@wanadoo.fr ☑
☊ ev. day except Sun. 8am–12.30pm 1.30pm–7pm

DOM. DU PRIEURE
Sauvignon 2002

	3 ha	4,000	▪ ⚱	3–5 €

✦┐ Jean-Marc Gallou, Dom. du Prieuré, 41120 Valaire, tel. 02.54.44.11.62, fax 02.54.44.16.92, e-mail jean-marc.gallou@wanadoo.fr ☑ 🏠
☊ by appt.

DOM. DES TABOURELLES
Sauvignon Clos du Menais 2002

	0.65 ha	4,500		3–5 €

✦┐ EARL Les Tabourelles, 9, rte de Vierzon, 41400 Bourre, tel. 02.54.32.07.58, fax 02.54.32.07.58, e-mail domainedestabourelles@cario.fr ☑
✦┐ J.-P. Germain

DOM. DU VIEUX PRESSOIR
Cuvée des Sourdes Vieilli en fût de chêne 2001

	5 ha	8,000	⑪	5–8 €

✦┐ Joël Lecoffre, 27, rte de Vallières, 41150 Rilly-sur-Loire, tel. 02.54.20.90.84, fax 02.54.20.99.66, e-mail joel.lecoffre@wanadoo.fr ☑
☊ by appt.

Touraine-Noble-Joué

Known at the court of Louis XI, this wine's reputation was at its peak during the 19th century. The vineyard nearly disappeared, nibbled away by the urbanization of Tours, but has been reborn due to the efforts of winegrowers who reconstituted it. This *vin gris*, made from a blend of Meunier, Pinot Gris and Pinot Noir, now regains its historic place thanks to its recognition as a new AOC. In 2002 production amounted to 1,130 hl over an area of 21 ha.

BERNARD BLONDEAU 2002★★

	1 ha	n.c.	▪	3–5 €

Established at Saint-Avertin, Bernard Blondeau, located at the gates of Tours, resists galloping urbanism by cultivating his vines between houses on the plateau skirting the Cher. After a successful 2001, this 2002 enchanted the Jury with its intense nose mixing smoky notes with dried flowers. The terroir, rich in flint, is expressed on the palate by a slight mineral touch. This wine guarantees success at dinner.
✦┐ Bernard Blondeau, 42, rue de la Castellerie, 37550 Saint-Avertin, tel. 02.47.27.88.29, fax 02.47.27.88.29 ☑

CLOS DE LA DOREE 2002★

| ■ | 1.5 ha | n.c. | ■ ♠ | 3–5 € |

With its lovely pale pink colour, this slightly smoky rosé does not lack appeal. Balanced and round, it will be appreciated on any occasion.
•┐ GAEC Clos de La Dorée, La Guérinière,
37320 Esvres-sur-Indre, tel. 02.47.26.50.65,
fax 02.47.26.46.46 ☑

JEAN-JACQUES SARD 2002★

| ■ | 3.5 ha | 17,000 | ■ ♠ | 3–5 € |

Owner of 3.5 ha of vines at Esvres, Jean-Jacques Sard knew how to recreate the harmony of the Touraine landscape in this clear, salmon-coloured wine with mineral notes and fruitiness: an invitation to discover the beautiful Indre valley.
•┐ Jean-Jacques Sard, La Chambrière,
37320 Esvres-sur-Indre, tel. 02.47.26.42.89,
fax 02.47.26.57.59 ☑
ⵏ by appt.

Wines selected but not starred

REMI COSSON 2002

| ■ | 2.5 ha | 5,000 | ■ ♠ | 3–5 € |

•┐ Rémi Cosson, La Hardellière, 37320 Esvres-sur-Indre,
tel. 02.47.65.70.63, fax 02.47.34.80.13,
e-mail remi.cosson@libertysurf.fr ☑
ⵏ by appt.

ANTOINE DUPUY 2002

| ■ | | n.c. | 20,000 | ■ ♠ | 3–5 € |

•┐ EARL Antoine Dupuy, Le Vau, 37320 Esvres-sur-Indre,
tel. 02.47.26.44.46 ☑

ROUSSEAU FRERES 2002

| ■ | 11 ha | 40,000 | ■ ♠ | 3–5 € |

•┐ Rousseau Frères, Le Vau, 37320 Esvres-sur-Indre,
tel. 02.47.26.44.45, fax 02.47.26.53.12,
e-mail rousseau-freres@libertysurf.fr ☑
ⵏ ev. day except Sun. 9am–12.30pm 2pm–7pm

Touraine-Amboise

Sited on both banks of the Loire and dominated by the 15th and 16th century Château d'Amboise, the vineyard of the Appellation Touraine-Amboise (161 ha), which is between 150 and 200 ha is not far from the Manoir Clos-Lucé, where Leonardo de Vinci spent his last days. Production is mainly of red wines (8,519 hl in 2002) from Gamay, Côt and Cabernet Franc. These are full wines with only a little tannin; when the Côt and Cabernet are dominant, the wines have some keeping potential. The same varieties also produce dry, charming rosés that are fruity and well defined. The whites, 1,792 hl in 2002, are dry or medium-dry, depending on the year, and they, too, may be kept.

GUY DURAND
Les Grands Riages des Monceux 2001★

| ■ | 0.25 ha | 950 | ■ ♠ | 5–8 € |

This white medium-dry 2001 illustrates one of the styles of the Touraine-Amboise appellation. It has a beautiful golden-yellow colour and the nose releases intense notes of fruit (apricot) and honey. The well-balanced palate results in a harmonious wine, worthy of the high quality white wines of the Loire.
•┐ Guy Durand, 11, Chemin-Neuf, 37530 Mosnes,
tel. 02.47.30.43.14, fax 02.47.30.43.14 ☑
ⵏ by appt.

DOM. DE LA GABILLIERE
Cuvée François I er 2001★

| ■ | 3 ha | 15,600 | ■ ♠ | 3–5 € |

An experimental estate belonging to the Lycée Viticole d'Amboise, Gabillière regularly presents elegant cuvées. After an intense garnet-red appearance, this wine stirs up curiosity with its complex flavours of jammy red fruit uplifted by a peppered note. Appealing body and structure. To drink now or keep, according to your mood.
•┐ Dom. de la Gabillière, Lycée viticole, 46, av.
Emile-Gounin, 37400 Amboise, tel. 02.47.23.35.51,
fax 02.47.57.01.76, e-mail expl.lpa.amboise@educagri.fr ☑
ⵏ ev. day except Sat. Sun. 8am–12 noon 1.30pm–5.30pm

DOM. DE LA PERDRIELLE 2001★

| ■ | 2 ha | 4,200 | ■ ♠ | 3–5 € |

A very pleasing pale-gold 2001 with green highlights, which reveals the perfume of spring flowers, then the supple palate impresses with its lingering pêche de vigne flavours on the finish. A beautiful wine that merits being served at your dinner table. Light and fresh, the Cuvée François I red 2001 is singled out by the Jury.
•┐ EARL Jacques et Vincent Gandon, Dom. de La Perdrielle, 24, vallon de Vauriflé, 37530 Nazelles-Négron,
tel. 02.47.57.31.19, fax 02.47.57.77.28,
e-mail vgandon@club-internet.fr ☑
ⵏ ev. day 9am–12.30pm 2pm–7pm; Sun. by appt.

DOM. DE LA PREVOTE
Cuvée de la Prévôté 2001★

| ■ | 10 ha | 16,000 | ■ ⑪ | 5–8 € |

Serge and Pascal Bonnigal present two well-made cuvées. The Prévôté, spicy and oaky, has elegant tannins but it needs to be kept for three or four years to achieve perfect harmony. The red Cuvée François I 2001 (3–5 €), matured in tank, light and full flavoured, will also keep in your wine cellar.
•┐ Dom. de la Prévôté, GAEC Bonnigal, 17, rue d'Enfer,
37530 Limeray, tel. 02.47.30.11.02, fax 02.47.30.11.09 ☑
ⵏ ev. day except Sun. 9am–12 noon 2pm–7pm

Wines selected but not starred

DOM. DES BESSONS
Cuvée François I er 2001

| ■ | 1.8 ha | 3,200 | ■ ⑪ ♠ | 3–5 € |

•┐ François Péquin, Dom. des Bessons, 113, rue de Blois,
37530 Limeray, tel. 02.47.30.09.10, fax 02.47.30.02.25 ☑
ⵏ by appt.

XAVIER FRISSANT
L'Orée des Frênes 2001

| ■ | 1.2 ha | 7,000 | ⑪ | 5–8 € |

•┐ Xavier Frissant, 1, chem. Neuf, 37530 Mosnes,
tel. 02.47.57.23.18, fax 02.47.57.23.25,
e-mail xavier.frissant@wanadoo.fr ☑

DOM. DE LA GRANDE FOUCAUDIERE
Clos du Vau 2001

■	0.8 ha	4,000	❶❶	5–8 €

☙ Lionel Truet, La Grande Foucaudière,
37530 Saint-Ouen-les-Vignes, tel. 02.47.30.04.82,
fax 02.47.30.03.55, e-mail lioneltruet@aol.com ☑ 🏠
⏳ ev. day 8am–8pm

DOM. LA GRANGE TIPHAINE
Cuvée François Ier 2001

■	1.5 ha	10,000	🍾	3–5 €

☙ Jackie Delecheneau, 1353, rue du Clos-Chauffour,
37400 Amboise, tel. 02.47.57.64.17, fax 02.47.57.39.49,
e-mail lagrangetiphaine@ifrance.com ☑
⏳ ev. day 9am–12 noon 2pm–7pm

DOM. MESLIAND 2001

■	0.6 ha	4,000	❶❶	5–8 €

☙ Dom. Mesliand, 15 bis, rue d'Enfer, 37530 Limeray,
tel. 02.47.30.11.15, fax 02.47.30.02.89 ☑ 🏠
⏳ ev. day 8am–9pm; groups by appt.

ROLAND PLOU ET SES FILS
Prestige 2001

■	2 ha	10,000	🍾 ♦	3–5 €

☙ EARL Plou et Fils, 26, rue du Gal-de-Gaulle,
37530 Chargé, tel. 02.47.30.55.17, fax 02.47.23.17.02 ☑
⏳ ev. day 9am–1pm 3pm–7.30pm

Touraine-Azay le Rideau

Grown on 150 ha along both banks of the Indre, the wines here are as elegant as the riverside château of Azay le Rideau after which they are named. Half are particularly fine whites – 945 hl in 2002 – from Chenin Blanc (Pineau de la Loire), which range from dry to soft, and age well. Grolleau (60% minimum of a mixed wine), Gamay and Côt (with a maximum 10% of Cabernets) make very fresh, dry, fruity rosés – 1,418 hl in 2002.

PASCAL PIBALEAU
La Noblesse d'Aziaum 2001★

■	0.4 ha	1,900	❶❶	5–8 €

Awarded a *coup de coeur* in the previous edition of the *Guide*, Pascal Pibaleau presented this very attractive and well-made Touraine-Azay le Rideau. It has a yellow-green colour with golden highlights, and an elegant nose both floral and fruity. Quality flavours – peach and apricot – with a well-balanced body and a rich finish. The Jury also has awarded one star to the **rosé 2002 (3–5 €)**, which is supple and lively and appreciated for the finesse of its flavours.

☙ EARL Pascal Pibaleau, 69, rte de Langeais, Lure,
37190 Azay-le-Rideau, tel. 02.47.45.27.58,
fax 02.47.45.26.18,
e-mail pascal.pibaleau@wanadoo.fr ☑
⏳ ev. day except Sun. 8am–12.30pm 1.30pm–7pm

Wines selected but not starred

JAMES ET NICOLAS PAGET 2001

■	1.2 ha	6,500	🍾 ♦	3–5 €

☙ EARL James et Nicolas Paget, 13, rue d'Armentières,
37190 Rivarennes, tel. 02.47.95.54.02, fax 02.47.95.45.90 ☑
⏳ ev. day except Sun. Mon. 9am–12.30pm 2.30pm–7pm

CH. DE LA ROCHE 2002

■	2 ha	6,000	🍾 ♦	8–11 €

☙ Ch. de La Roche, 37190 Cheillé, tel. 02.47.45.46.05,
fax 02.47.45.29.60,
e-mail louis.jean.sylvos@wanadoo.fr ☑ 🏠
⏳ ev. day 10am–12 noon 3pm–8pm
☙ Louis-Jean Sylvos

LA CAVE DES VALLEES 2002

■	3.35 ha	5,000	🍾 ♦	3–5 €

☙ Marc Badiller, 29, Le Bourg, 37190 Cheillé,
tel. 02.47.45.24.37, fax 02.47.45.29.66 ☑
⏳ ev. day except Sun. 9am–12 noon 3pm–7pm

Touraine-Mesland

The vineyard of this appellation covers 200 ha on the right bank of the Loire, north of Chaumont and downstream from Blois. In 2002, 4,261 hl of wine were produced, including 724 hl of white. The soils are a mixture of flinty clays covered here and there with Eocene sands and gravel. Production is mostly of red wines, from Gamay mixed with Cabernet or Côt, with good structure and character. Dry whites (mainly from Chenin) and rosés are also produced.

DOM. DES CAILLOUX
Petits Cailloux 2002★

■	6 ha	25,000	🍾 ♦	3–5 €

Established in the village of Onzain, opposite the Château de Chaumont-sur-Loire, Jean-François Gabillet works a score of hectares on sand and quartz-rich gravel soils on the hills bordering the Loire. He presented the Jury with two characteristic wines from the Mesland terroir. The red, intense through to the finish, presents a good balance, but it will be advisable to let it age for some time. The oak-matured **white Touraine-Mesland Marnières 2002 Elevé en Fut de Chêne**, with citrus fruit aromas and an underlying mineral note, has much freshness. It obtains one star.

☙ Dom. des Cailloux, 17, rue d'Asnières, 41150 Onzain,
tel. 02.54.20.78.77, fax 02.54.33.79.63 ☑
⏳ by appt.

DOM. DE RABELAIS 2002★

■	0.3 ha	2,000	🍾 ♦	5–8 €

Produced on the terroir where small round gravel stones dominate, this salmon-coloured rosé 2002 is well made. The delicate nose of fresh fruit is followed by an explosive palate of red berries. The **red Domaine de Rabelais 2002** also gains a star for its intensity, red berry flavours, balance and perfect maturity.

☙ GAEC Chollet, 23, chem. de Rabelais, 41150 Onzain,
tel. 02.54.20.79.50, fax 02.54.20.79.50 ☑
⏳ by appt.

Wines selected but not starred

DOM. D'ARTOIS 2002

▨	3.8 ha	22,000	∎ ⚲ 3–5 €

➤ SCEA Dom. d'Artois, La Morandière, 41150 Mesland,
tel. 02.54.70.24.72, fax 02.54.70.24.72 ☑
🍷 by appt.
➤ J.-L. Saget

CLOS DE LA BRIDERIE 2002

■	7 ha	30,000	∎ ⚲ 5–8 €

➤ SCEA Clos de La Briderie, 70, rue de la Briderie,
41150 Monteaux, tel. 02.54.70.28.89, fax 02.54.70.28.70 ☑
🍷 by appt.
➤ Girault

CH. GAILLARD 2001

■	9 ha	20,000	∎ ⚲ 3–5 €

➤ Vincent Girault, Clos Ch. Gaillard, 41150 Mesland,
tel. 02.54.70.25.47, fax 02.54.70.28.70 ☑
🍷 by appt.

DOM. DES TERRES NOIRES 2002

▨	0.4	1,300	∎ ⚲ 3–5 €

➤ GAEC des Terres Noires, 81, rue de Meuves,
41150 Onzain, tel. 02.54.20.72.87, fax 02.54.20.85.12 ☑
🍷 by appt.

LES VAUCORNEILLES 2002

▨	1.2 ha	5,500	∎ ⦿ ⚲ 5–8 €

➤ GAEC Les Vaucorneilles, 10, rue de l'Egalité,
41150 Onzain, tel. 02.54.20.72.91, fax 02.54.20.74.26,
e-mail les.vaucorneilles@wanadoo.fr ☑
🍷 by appt.
➤ Chelin

Bourgueil

The Appellation Contrôlée Bourgueil area, which covers 1,368 ha, lies on the right bank of the Loire, west of the Touraine and on the borders of Anjou. In 2002 69,503 hl of the distinctive Bourgueil red wines were produced from the Cabernet Franc variety, also known as Breton. These are thoroughbred wines, graced with elegant tannins, which have undergone a long period of fermentation; those from the yellow tufa slopes have great keeping qualities. The best vintages (1976, 1989 or 1990, for example) will continue to develop for decades. Those from the terraces of gravelly and sandy soil are smoother and fruitier in character. A few hundred hectolitres are vinified as dry rosés. It is worth pointing out that the members of the Coopérative de Restignée (a quarter of the Bourgueil growers) often age their wines in their own cellars.

YANNICK AMIRAULT

Les Quartiers Vieilles Vignes 2001★★★

▨	1.5 ha	8,000	⦿ 8–11 €

It was only to be expected: Yannick Amirault obtained a *coup de coeur*. Her reputation increases and her skill is confirmed

once again. This wine has a constant colour and opens with a powerful nose with a touch of vanilla. The straightforward attack is followed by a tannic structure that is already integrated, balanced between the oak and the fruit. An impression of roundness and elegance prevails, a testimony of exceptional know-how.
➤ Yannick Amirault, 5, pavillon du Grand-Clos,
37140 Bourgueil, tel. 02.47.97.78.07, fax 02.47.97.94.78 ☑
🍷 by appt.

HUBERT AUDEBERT

Vieilles Vignes 2001★★

■	2 ha	10,000	∎ ⚲ 5–8 €

Hubert Audebert is someone who knows how to be welcoming and says what he thinks. It is always interesting to pay him a visit, especially when he suggests that you taste the Cuvée Vieilles Vignes, which has an intense garnet colour and a nose that reveals ripe fruit, with hints of violet. The round attack is followed by a touch of freshness and rather strong tannic presence, but without aggressiveness. Overall it is full and well balanced right through to the finish. A good wine to lay down.
➤ Hubert Audebert, 5, rue Croix-des-Pierres,
37140 Restigné, tel. 02.47.97.42.10, fax 02.47.97.77.53 ☑
🍷 by appt.

DOM. AUDEBERT ET FILS

Les Marquises 2001★★

■	1.5 ha	10,000	∎ ⦿ ⚲ 5–8 €

Both a merchant and wine-grower at the same time, the Audebert business contributed, through the quality of its wines and their diffusion in the CHR, to the notoriety of the appellation. The estate includes 21 ha on the old alluvial terraces of the Loire. Those located near the hillside have sometimes been altered by the addition of clay: these stronger soils rest on top of the limestone as at the *lieu-dit* Marquises. Firmly-structured wines are produced here, such as this 2001, the tannins of which are very evident but are well balanced with body and fruit. A beautiful Bourgueil worth waiting for. The **red Domaine du Grand Clos 2001**, round, fruity and elegant, obtains one star, while the **Bourgueil rosé 2002**, with its redcurrant flavours, and the **red Les Grands Rangs 2001** are singled out.
➤ Dom. Audebert et Fils, av. Jean-Causeret,
37140 Bourgueil, tel. 02.47.97.70.06, fax 02.47.97.72.07 ☑
🍷 ev. day 8.30am–12 noon 2pm–6pm; Sat. Sun. by appt.

HENRI BOURDIN 2001★★

■	3 ha	n.c.	∎ ⚲ 3–5 €

2001 was a difficult year, but this experienced wine producer knew how to handle the vintage. This Bourgueil, with its brilliant dark-ruby colour opens out with small berry fruit. A smooth attack is followed by a full body and good tannic structure that continues through to the long spicy finish. This wine is probably one to keep.
➤ Henri Bourdin, 7, rue du Bourg-de-Paille,
37140 Bourgueil, tel. 02.47.97.96.69, fax 02.47.97.96.69 ☑
🍷 by appt.

BRESSON-PENET 2001★

■	2.5 ha	3,000	∎ ⦿ 5–8 €

One doesn't question the traditional wine-growing methods or winemaking at Bresson-Penet. There is a vine of more than 100 years old still in production. This lovely 2001 comes from 30-year-old vine stock. After the supple attack it develops freshness with good tannic structure that is present, yet integrated. A pretty wine that could be kept for a while, true to type.

➤ Bresson-Penet, 2, rte des Caves-Saint-Martin, 37140 Restigné, tel. 02.47.97.88.47, fax 02.47.97.88.47 ☑
☧ by appt.

CATHERINE ET PIERRE BRETON
Clos Sénéchal 2001★★

| ■ | 2 ha | 6,000 | ▮ | 11–15 € |

"Drink good fresh wine, because in wine there is strength and power" – a Bourgueil proverb adopted by this young couple of wine producers, who have cultivated their 11 ha of vines organically for more than ten years. This is perhaps the key to this well-made wine's success. Deep red almost violet, this wine releases on the nose scents of red berries, violet and undergrowth. The palate is round, full, and has rich tannins that persist at the long finish.

➤ Catherine et Pierre Breton, 8, rue du Peu-Muleau, Les Galichets, 37140 Restigné, tel. 02.47.97.30.41, fax 02.47.97.46.49,
e-mail catherineetpierre.breton@libertysurf.fr ☑
☧ by appt.

DOM. DE LA CHANTELEUSERIE
Cuvée Alouettes 2001★

| ■ | 4 ha | 18,000 | ▮ ⚜ | 5–8 € |

Chanteleuserie is the place where larks sing (a bird is depicted on the label). The Cuvée Alouettes comes in first this year, with well-developed red berry flavours. It shows flexibility and strength, proving that it can go far. Its long finish is also promising. The **Cuvée Vieilles Vignes 2001**, another successful wine, could go just as far with its light oakiness.

➤ Thierry Boucard, La Chanteleuserie, 37140 Benais, tel. 02.47.97.30.20, fax 02.47.97.46.73,
e-mail tboucard@terre-net.fr ☑
☧ ev. day except Sun. 9am–12 noon 2pm–7pm

DOM. DU CHENE ARRAULT
Cuvée Vieilles Vignes 2001★

| ■ | 1.33 ha | n.c. | ▮ ⚜ | 5–8 € |

Christophe Deschamps represents the eighth generation of wine producers from the same family that originally set up the domaine. More than 13 ha are planted over different terroirs, with the majority consisting of clay-limestone soils. This *cuvée* deserves time. On the nose there are strong aromas of cooked prune, which are reproduced on the full palate that has also richness and tannins. A rustic wine? Certainly a wine which will develop in time, with tertiary flavours which are not lacking in finesse.

➤ Christophe Deschamps, 4, Le Chêne-Arrault, 37140 Benais, tel. 02.47.97.46.71, fax 02.47.97.82.90,
e-mail domaine.du.chene.arrault@wanadoo.fr ☑
☧ by appt.

DOM. DES CHESNAIES
Cuvée Prestige 2001★★

| ■ | 9 ha | 64,500 | ▮▮ | 5–8 € |

If Lucien Lamé, founder of the Chesnaies estate, was still of this world he would be proud of the work of his two grandchildren, Philippe and Stéphanie Boucard, both graduates. An alliance of modern techniques and traditional know-how

is certainly the origin of this superb *cuvée* that receives a *coup de cœur*. An elegant bouquet of plum, cherry and ripe blackcurrants constitutes an opening to the full body. This wine is a success with a supple attack, good volume, freshness and perfectly blended tannins. A wine waiting to be enjoyed. **Cuvée Vieilles Vignes 2001** is singled out.

➤ Lamé-Delisle-Boucard, Dom. des Chesnaies, 21, rue de la Galottière, 37140 Restigné, tel. 02.47.96.98.54, fax 02.47.96.92.31,
e-mail lame.delisle.boucard@wanadoo.fr ☑
☧ ev. day except Sun. 9am–12 noon 1.30pm–5.30pm; Sat. 9am–12 noon
➤ Boucard

DOM. DE LA CLOSERIE
Vieilles Vignes 2001★

| ■ | 5 ha | 15,000 | ▮ ▮▮ ⚜ | 5–8 € |

One is very vigilant about the use of manure and pesticides at the Closerie estate because sustainable agriculture is practised. Respect for the earth is perhaps the origin of this wine's character. The first impression is supple and emerges from a framework of quality tannins: this predicts a wine for ageing, equipped with strength and promising richness. Notes of fruit and liquorice dominate the palate.

➤ Jean-François Mabileau, La Closerie, 28, rte de Bourgueil, 37140 Restigné, tel. 02.47.97.36.29, fax 02.47.97.48.33 ☑
☧ by appt.

COGNARD
Les Tuffes 2001★

| ■ | 1.6 ha | 9,500 | ▮ ⚜ | 5–8 € |

From the start of the ripening period, Max Cognard, persuaded that good wine can only be made with good grapes, strips around the bunches by hand and eliminates the grapes that are behind in maturation. This ensures that a homogeneous and fully ripe harvest arrives in the tanks. The 2001 is a balanced wine, whose black fruit scents hint at menthol. Supple at the first impression, the palate shows a good wealth of tannins that will not fail to integrate in time. The length of flavour is an added bonus.

➤ Max Cognard, Chevrette, 37140 Saint-Nicolas-de-Bourgueil, tel. 02.47.97.76.88, fax 02.47.97.97.83, e-mail max.cognard@wanadoo.fr ☑
☧ by appt.

LE COUDRAY LA LANDE
Vieilles Vignes 2001★

| ■ | 4 ha | 20,000 | ▮ ▮▮ ⚜ | 5–8 € |

This estate was created after dismantling an old Bourgueil property which, in the middle of the 19th century, was classified along the lines of the Bordeaux crus. One imagines that during this époque it counted among the best. Is it the terroir or is it man's intervention that is responsible for this *cuvée*. Well-ripened red berry fruit and blackberry on the nose, the attack is soft, tannins not very exuberant and on the finish, which returns in full force, there are fruit flavours and touches of menthol and spice.

➤ Jean-Paul Morin, 30, rue de La Lande, 37140 Bourgueil, tel. 02.47.97.76.92, fax 02.47.97.98.20,
e-mail morinjpwine@wanadoo.fr ☑
☧ by appt.

FOUCHER-LEBRUN
Les Grands Jardins 2001★

| ■ | n.c. | 15,000 | ▮ | 3–5 € |

Created in 1921, the Foucher-Lebrun business was originally a cooperage. Driven by his passion for wine and the bonds he maintained with the wine producers, its founder undertook to market a complete range of Loire wines. Here is a light yet well-made Bourgueil, still fruity. Red berry fruit and prune appear throughout the palate. Enjoy now.

➤ Foucher-Lebrun, 29, rte de Bouhy, 58200 Alligny-Cosne, tel. 03.86.26.87.27, fax 03.86.26.87.20,
e-mail foucher.lebrun@wanadoo.fr ☑
☧ ev. day except Sun. Mon. 8am–12 noon 2pm–6pm

DOM. DES GELERIES

Tradition Vieilles Vignes 2001★★

| ■ | 2 ha | 8,900 | ■ ⑪ ⚬ | 5–8 € |

Located in the heart of the appellation, near the abbey where the Bourgueil vineyard was created more than 1000 years ago, this domaine of 17 ha has a jewel of a terroir. The wines reflect this, such as this Cuvée Vieilles Vignes that sags under an avalanche of compliments: a ruby colour is followed by aromas of caramel, soft fruits, liquorice with a touch of vanilla; a soft attack is followed by an elegant tannic structure, rich and full bodied, with a long and well-blended finish. A characteristic Bourgueil wine to keep in the cellar. **Cuvée Les Sablons 2001**, matured in tank, is singled out as a very good wine.
•┐ Jean-Marie Rouzier, Les Géléries, 37140 Bourgueil, tel. 02.47.97.74.83, fax 02.47.97.48.73,
e-mail jean-marie.rouzier@wanadoo.fr ☑
♈ ev. day except Sun. 9am–12.30pm 2.30pm–7pm; cl. 25 Sep. until 10 Oct.

VIGNOBLE DE LA GRIOCHE

Cuvée Santenay 2001★★

| ■ | 0.8 ha | 3,000 | ■ | 5–8 € |

Awarded a *coup de coeur* last year, Jean-Marc Breton and his son Stéphane were ready to renew the exploit with this selection which is neither lacking colour (purple with violet touches) nor a powerful nose (very ripe fruit and a little undergrowth). After a soft opening there is a substantial tannic structure, already showing signs of development. The omnipresent richness softens the finish. This Bourgueil will evolve well. The **Cuvée Prestige 2001**, matured five months in barrel, gains a star with its generous body and velvety tannins.
•┐ Jean-Marc Breton, 19, rue des Marais, 37140 Restigné, tel. 02.47.97.31.64, fax 02.47.97.92.39 ☑ ☗
♈ by appt.

DOM. HUBERT 2001★

| ■ | 4 ha | 30,000 | ⑪ | 3–5 € |

It is already two years since Franck Caslot went back to work at the family vineyard, and this Domaine Hubert selection carries his signature. The vintage compels; this wine is fruity, light, and reminiscent of spring. Full flavoured, it is ready to be drunk now. A good wine to have in the cellar whilst waiting for the other vintages to mature.
•┐ EARL Franck Caslot, La Hurolaie, 37140 Benais, tel. 02.47.97.30.59, fax 02.47.97.45.46 ☑
♈ by appt.

DOM. DE LA LANDE

Cuvée des Pins 2001★

| ■ | 2 ha | 10,000 | ■ ⑪ ⚬ | 5–8 € |

Followers of new oak, the Delaunays? That's nothing. They remain faithful to the ancient processes: this *cuvée* is therefore more classic. An intense red colour with violet, almost black, glints is followed by powerful aromas that oscillate between smoky and musky notes. Full-bodied with promising tannic structure. Do not open for three or four years: you will be highly rewarded.
•┐ EARL Delaunay Père et Fils, Dom. de La Lande, 20, rte du Vignoble, 37140 Bourgueil, tel. 02.47.97.80.73, fax 02.47.97.95.65 ☑
♈ by appt.

HERVE MENARD

Cuvée Vieilles Vignes 2001★

| ■ | 1.1 ha | 6,000 | ■ | 8–11 € |

A rare thing in the wine world, this estate is born from the fusion of two vineyards. Christophe Chasle and Herve Ménard aimed to reduce costs and share work. The regrouping wasn't in place for the 2001 vintage, but Herve Ménard now presents his *cuvée* that is fruity, supple and full. The tannins are already round and remain rather discreet, while the palate develops with an elegant finish. Flavourful nuances of small berry fruit are revealed throughout.
•┐ SCEA Christophe Chasle et Hervé Ménard, 16, rue des Roches, 37130 Saint-Patrice, tel. 02.47.96.95.95, fax 02.47.96.99.23, e-mail christophe.chasle@wanadoo.fr ☑
♈ by appt.

NAU FRERES

Les Blottières 2001★

| ■ | 6 ha | 22,000 | ■ ⚬ | 5–8 € |

Work at the Nau vineyard carries on as in the past: respect for the grape, punching down by foot, (pushing down the cap of skins manually, not mechanically) long fermentation and racking to avoid filtering. The wines are authentic, such as this winey and well-made *cuvée*, whose tannins indicate that it will keep well. Powerful blackcurrant flavours have great presence. **Cuvée Vieilles Vignes 2001** is also highly praised.
•┐ Nau Frères, 52, rue de Touraine, 37140 Ingrandes-de-Touraine, tel. 02.47.96.98.57, fax 02.47.96.90.34,
e-mail naufreres@wanadoo.fr ☑
♈ by appt.

DOM. DE LA NOIRAIE

Cuvée Prestige 2001★

| ■ | 6 ha | 40,000 | ■ ⚬ | 5–8 € |

Vincent Delanoue, still at wine college, prepares to join the estate managed by his father and uncle. To cultivate 23 ha of vines on the clay-limestone hills of Benais is a tricky business, and all the help available is welcome. A family portrait then, this *cuvée* of intense purple, which reveals a range of red berry flavours. With its soft attack, roundness and elegant tannins, it can be drunk now or kept in the wine cellar. The **Cuvée Saint-Vincent 2001** is worth noting.
•┐ GAEC Delanoue Frères, 19, rue du Fort-Hudeau, 37140 Benais, tel. 02.47.97.30.40, fax 02.47.97.46.95, e-mail delanoue@terre-net.fr ☑
♈ ev. day 8.30am–12.30pm 2pm–7.30pm

BERNARD OMASSON 2001★

| ■ | 2 ha | 2,000 | ■ ⑪ ⚬ | 5–8 € |

The first impression is soft but the tannins jump out and ambush the palate. They are not aggressive, however, being held ready to play their role in the maturation of the wine. Leave this *cuvée* to age, especially since the flavours promise to evolve.
•┐ Bernard Omasson, La Perrée, 54, rue de Touraine, 37140 Ingrandes-de-Touraine, tel. 02.47.96.98.20 ☑
♈ by appt.

DOM. DES OUCHES

Clos Prince 2001★

| ■ | 3.5 ha | 16,000 | ⑪ | 5–8 € |

A substantial team handles this domaine of 14 ha: Paul, the father, wise and experienced, and Thomas, the son, dynamic and entrepreneurial. One or the other will welcome you with open arms and share their wine knowledge. They present an intense crimson-coloured selection, which opens gradually with ripe soft fruit flavours and light oaky tones. The rich palate with powerful tannins, makes it difficult to appreciate today, but promises a beautiful future. The **Sélection Vieilles Vignes 2001**, matured in barrel, is also awarded one star.
•┐ Paul Gambier et Fils, 3, rue des Ouches, 37140 Ingrandes-de-Touraine, tel. 02.47.96.98.77, fax 02.47.96.93.08,
e-mail domaine.des.ouches@wanadoo.fr ☑
♈ by appt.

ANNICK PENET 2001★

| ■ | 0.79 ha | 2,000 | ■ ⑪ | 5–8 € |

With more than 45 years of experience on this small family vineyard, this female wine-grower must know not only all the vines, but also the best method of winemaking for the harvest. This is a classic ruby *cuvée*, with slightly oaky fruit. Supple on the attack, it is quickly garnished with pleasant tannins, accompanied by a good full-flavoured freshness. To lay down for two years.
•┐ Annick Penet, 29, rue Basse, 37140 Restigné, tel. 02.47.97.33.68 ☑
♈ by appt.

DOM. DU PETIT BONDIEU

Le Petit Mont 2001★★

■	2 ha	12,000	▌▮▌ ⚭	5–8 €

At Petit Bondieu the cultivation, the winery equipment and winemaking all remain classic. A successful concept that explains his regular appearance in the *Guide*. In 2001 he distinguished himself in exuberant manner with this supple wine, whose rich body has already well-integrated tannins. To complement this there is a wonderful powerful nose with black and red fruits, spices and lasting charred notes. **Cuvée Les Couplets 2001** is singled out.

➶ EARL Jean-Marc et Thomas Pichet, Le Petit Bondieu, 30, rte de Tours, 37140 Restigné, tel. 02.47.97.33.18, fax 02.47.97.46.57, e-mail jean-marcpichet@wanadoo.fr ☑
⟙ ev. day except Sun. 9am–12 noon 2.30pm–7pm; cl. in Oct.

CH. DE LA PHILBERDIERE 2001★

■	6.5	43,000	▌ ⚭	5–8 €

This elegant 15th and 17th century residence, with its imposing dovecote and park where deer and llama roam, is located in the heart of the wine region. There are 6.5 ha of vines grown on gravel and limestone soil, the origin of this unique *cuvée* that will delight fans of light, fruity, fresh wines that "satisfy the soul".

➶ SCV Aubry et Fils, La Philberdière, 37140 Restigné, tel. 01.42.83.70.62, fax 01.48.85.91.14 ☑
⟙ by appt.

DOM. LES PINS

Vieilles Vignes 2001★

■	2.5 ha	15,000	▌ ⚭	5–8 €

A pretty 17th century building symbolizes this 19-hectare estate. This Vielles Vignes selection is also a symbol often classified as one of the best Bourgueil wines. Some musky notes appear on airing. The tannins are quite present, but their effect is moderated by great richness and pretty fruit. Without question, this is a wine to lay down. The very good **Cuvée Clos les Pins 2001** needs time to mature.

➶ EARL Pitault-Landry et Fils, Dom. les Pins, 8, rte du Vignoble, 37140 Bourgueil, tel. 02.47.97.47.91, fax 02.47.97.98.69 ☑
⟙ by appt.

DOM. PONTONNIER-CASLOT

Vieilles Vignes 2001★

■	1.3 ha	9,000	▌▮▌ ⚭	8–11 €

Situated on hillside slopes, this domaine includes 15 ha of vines. The soils, mostly clay-limestone, sit directly on the tufa. The wines are generally fleshy and ample. Such is the case with this *cuvée*, with its nose of tobacco and black fruits. The palate opens with suppleness then fills out with an abundant, almost creamy body. A well-balanced wine that is both ready now and will keep for the future.

➶ Dom. Pontonnier-Caslot, 4, chem. de L'Epaisse, 37140 Saint-Nicolas-de-Bourgueil, tel. 02.47.97.84.69, fax 02.47.97.48.55 ☑
⟙ ev. day except Sun. 9am–12 noon 2pm–6pm; Sat. by appt.; cl. 15 Aug.–1 Sep.
➶ Caslot

DOM. DU PRESSOIR FLANIERE

Vieilles Vignes 2001★

■	2 ha	10,000	▌ ⚭	5–8 €

The vineyard of 16 ha covers the hillsides of Ingrandes, dominating the Loire; the soils, clay-limestone towards the summit and more gravelly at the bottom of the slope, benefit from exposure at midday. An exceptional situation, which created this *cuvée* with its pronounced finesse and elegance. The structure is light, sufficiently enriched and endowed with a lovely fruitiness. A delicious wine, alert and fresh.

➶ GAEC Galteau, 44–48, rue de Touraine, 37140 Ingrandes-de-Touraine, tel. 02.47.96.98.95, fax 02.47.96.90.91 ☑ ▥ ⚭
⟙ ev. day except Sun. 8am–12 noon 2pm–7pm; cl. 1–15 Oct.

DOM. DES RAGUENIERES

Cuvée Clos de la Cure 2001★

■	1.1 ha	6,000	▌▮▌ ⚭	5–8 €

Passion and know-how animate this couple of wine-growers on their domaine of nearly 19 ha, allowing them to obtain convincing results like this *cuvée* of great richness and fine tannins, qualities that indicate that it is a wine to lay down. In a few years it will be more approachable and the oak will have mellowed.

➶ SCEA Dom. des Raguenières, 11, rue du Machet, 37140 Benais, tel. 02.47.97.30.16, fax 02.47.97.46.78 ☑
⟙ by appt.
➶ Viemont

VIGNOBLE DES ROBINIERES

Cuvée Vieilles Vignes 2001★★

■	3 ha	9,000	▌ ⚭	5–8 €

Created in 1965, then inherited by the son and now managed by the grandson: such is the destiny of many family vineyards of Bourgueil. The 15 ha of clay-limestone soils of Robinières ensure the production of rich wines such as this well-balanced 2001, endowed with a nose of red berry fruit, and soft, elegant tannins. A well-handled maturation is perceived on behalf of this young wine producer.

➶ EARL Marchesseau Fils, 16, rue de l'Humelaye, 37140 Bourgueil, tel. 02.47.97.47.72, fax 02.47.97.46.36, e-mail earl.marchesseau@libertysurf.fr ☑
⟙ ev. day except Sun. 9am–12 noon 2pm–7pm

DOM. DU ROCHOUARD

Cuvée Coteau 2001★

■	2 ha	4,000	▌ ⚭	5–8 €

Restoration of the winery and installation of a reception room are now finished. A compelling reason to stop in Rochouard, where the welcome is always warm. Taste this round and fruity wine dominated by blackcurrant – it is ready to drink. The **Cuvée Prestige 2001 (8–11 €)** is also very good.

➶ GAEC Duveau-Coulon et Fils, 1, rue des Géléries, 37140 Bourgueil, tel. 02.47.97.85.91, fax 02.47.97.99.13 ☑
⟙ ev. day 8.30am–12.30pm 2pm–6.30pm

GUY SAGET

L'Echellerie 2001★★

■	n.c.	20,000	▌ ⚭	5–8 €

Guy Saget, *négociant-éleveur* at Pouilly-sur-Loire and specialist in wines of the Central vineyards, diversifies his production with a well-made Bourgueil. On the nose there is blackcurrant and smoke characteristic of the grape variety, the powerful, winey palate reveals a good structure with strong tannins that are ready to soften out. The flavours persist, and there is some freshness on the finish. A wine able to age.

➶ SA Guy Saget, La Castille, BP 26, 58150 Pouilly-sur-Loire, tel. 03.86.39.57.75, fax 03.86.39.08.30 ☑
⟙ by appt.
➶ J.-L. Saget

DOM. DES VALLETTES

Vieilles Vignes 2001★

■	2 ha	11,000	▌▮▌ ⚭	5–8 €

The domaine of Vallettes is established at Saint-Nicolas-de-Bourgueil. Recently, it was associated by inheritance to vines at Bourgueil. Moreover, the son, François Jamet, has just joined his father at the domaine. This *cuvée* still carries the imprint of the latter. In the mouth it is light and fresh and the tannins make an appearance on the finish. The fruit is present, as is the balance. No reproaches for this wine, which will develop further in the cellar.

➶ Francis et François Jamet, Dom. des Vallettes, 37140 Saint-Nicolas-de-Bourgueil, tel. 02.41.52.05.99, fax 02.41.52.87.52, e-mail francis.jamet@les-vallettes.com ☑
⟙ by appt.

Wines selected but not starred

VIGNOBLE AUGER 2001

■　　　　15 ha　　30,000　　◍　　　3–5 €

❧ Vignoble Auger, 58, rte de Bourgueil, 37140 Restigné,
tel. 02.47.97.41.37, fax 02.47.97.49.78 ☑
Ⴤ ev. day except Sun. 9am–12 noon 2pm–7pm

DOM. DE LA CHEVALERIE
Cuvée du Peu-Muleau 2001

■　　　　2 ha　　10,000　❚◍⬧　　5–8 €

❧ Pierre Caslot, Dom. de La Chevalerie, 37140 Restigné,
tel. 02.47.97.37.18, fax 02.47.97.45.87 ☑
Ⴤ ev. day 9am–12 noon 2pm–6pm; Sun. by appt.

SERGE DUBOIS
Cuvée Prestige 2001

■　　　　2 ha　　11,000　　◍　　5–8 €

❧ Dom. Serge Dubois, 49, rue de Lossay, 37140 Restigné,
tel. 02.47.97.31.60, fax 02.47.97.43.33,
e-mail domaine.sergedubois@wanadoo.fr ☑ ⌂
Ⴤ by appt.

DOM. BRUNO DUFEU
Cuvée Clémence 2001

■　　　　n.c.　　4,000　❚◍⬧　　3–5 €

❧ Bruno Dufeu, Les Neusaies, 37140 Benais,
tel. 02.47.97.76.53, fax 02.47.97.76.53 ☑ ⌂
Ⴤ by appt.

LAURENT FAUVY
Vieilles Vignes 2001

■　　　2.5 ha　　2,800　　❚　　5–8 €

❧ EARL Laurent Fauvy, 14, rte de Saint-Gilles,
37140 Benais, tel. 02.47.97.46.67, fax 02.47.97.95.45 ☑
Ⴤ by appt.

DOM. DES MAILLOCHES
Cuvée Samuel 2001

■　　　1 ha　　5,000　　◍　　5–8 €

❧ Jean-François et Samuel Demont, Dom. des Mailloches,
40, rue de Lossay, 37140 Restigné, tel. 02.47.97.33.10,
fax 02.47.97.43.43,
e-mail infos@domaine-mailloches.fr ☑ ⌂
Ⴤ by appt.

CH. DE MINIERE 2001

■　　　7 ha　　15,000　❚⬧　　5–8 €

❧ Ch. de Minière, 37140 Ingrandes-de-Touraine,
tel. 02.47.97.32.87, fax 02.47.97.46.47
Ⴤ by appt.
❧ B. de Mascarel

DOMINIQUE MOREAU
Cuvée du Clos Sénéchal 2001

■　　　1 ha　　7,000　❚⬧　　3–5 €

❧ EARL Dominique Moreau, L'Ouche Saint-André,
37140 Restigné, tel. 02.47.97.31.93, fax 02.47.96.83.30 ☑
Ⴤ by appt.

DOM. LE PONT DU GUE 2001

■　　　1 ha　　6,900　❚⬧　　5–8 €

❧ EARL Eric Ploquin, Le Pont du Gué, 37140 Bourgueil,
tel. 02.47.97.90.82, fax 02.47.97.95.68 ☑
Ⴤ ev. day 8am–12 noon 2pm–6pm

DOM. DE LA VERNELLERIE 2001

■　　　2 ha　　7,000　❚⬧　　3–5 €

❧ Camille et Marie-Thérèse Petit, EARL Dom. de La
Vernellerie, 37140 Benais, tel. 02.47.97.31.18,
fax 02.47.97.31.18 ☑
Ⴤ by appt.

Saint-Nicolas-de-Bourgueil

T he commune of Saint-
Nicolas-de-Bourgueil (a single parish that was
detached from Bourgueil in the 18th century) has its
own appellation, even though the terroir is similar to
the neighbouring area of Bourgueil.

A t least two-thirds of the slopes
are made up of the sandy, gravel terraces of the Loire.
At the top, the hill is protected from the north wind
by forest and a covering of sand overlies the tufa outcrops. Saint-Nicolas-de-Bourgueil wines are made
from a mixture of varieties, and are generally
regarded as being lighter than the Bourgueils
(not always the case with wine grown on the heights).
In 2002, they produced 59,232 hl.

YANNICK AMIRAULT
Les Graviers Vieilles Vignes 2001★★

■　　　2.5 ha　　13,000　　◍　　8–11 €

It would have been a lovely duo. Awarded a *coup de coeur* in
Bourgueil, Yannick Amirault just missed it in Saint-
Nicolas-de-Bourgueil. He has produced a wine where the fruit
and structure play an equal part, whereas, in this appellation
of gravelly soil, the fruit generally dominates. Undoubtedly a
search for maximum maturity is the key to his success. Very
open with soft fruit and musky notes, with an underlying light
oakiness, this 2001 is remarkable for the balance of its components. The Jury advises laying it down to develop.
❧ Yannick Amirault, 5, pavillon du Grand-Clos,
37140 Bourgueil, tel. 02.47.97.78.07, fax 02.47.97.94.78
Ⴤ by appt.

DOM. DU BOURG
Cuvée Prestige 2001★

■　　　n.c.　　12,000　　◍　　5–8 €

The headquarters of the estate is in the centre of the village.
The major part of the vineyard, which covers 15 ha, is
established on gravel, the remainder being located on the
clay-limestone hillside. This Cuvée Prestige is dominated by
wood, hardly leaving room for the fruit at the moment, whilst
the youthful tannins start to soften. Time will enable it to
achieve harmony. The **Cuvée Les Graviers 2001** is singled out.
❧ EARL Jean-Paul Mabileau, 6, rue du Pressoir,
37140 Saint-Nicolas-de-Bourgueil, tel. 02.47.97.82.02,
fax 02.47.97.70.92 ☑
Ⴤ ev. day 9am–12 noon 2pm–7pm

LE CLOS DES QUARTERONS
Vieilles Vignes 2001★★

■　　　2.42 ha　　13,800　❚◍⬧　　5–8 €

This large manor house in the centre of Saint-Nicolas village,
dating from the end of the 19th century, presents two remarkable wines. The first has an intense nose of ripe fruit,
combined with vanilla and mint. The round, fresh attack precedes a well-balanced, supple structure, which develops and
finishes with great length and an uplifting freshness. The

LOIRE

second, **Les Quarterons 2001**, also with two stars, reveals both fresh fruitiness and strength.

↘ Thierry Amirault, Clos des Quarterons,
37140 Saint-Nicolas-de-Bourgueil, tel. 02.47.97.75.25,
fax 02.47.97.97.97 ☑
☨ ev. day except Sun. 8am–12 noon 2pm–6pm

CLOS DU VIGNEAU
Les Dames du Temps Jadis 2001★

■	2 ha	7,500	◫	5–8 €

Since the acquisition by Pierre Jamet, in 1820, of Clos du Vigneau, six generations have succeeded one another on the estate that today comprises 23 ha and that produced a very interesting wine in 2001. This wine has an attractive full-flavoured nose and a pleasant palate, well balanced with just a hint of oak. **Clos du Vigneau 2001** (principal *cuvée* of the estate) is also very good: it can be appreciated now, while the first wine must age a little.

↘ EARL Clos du Vigneau, BP 6,
37140 Saint-Nicolas-de-Bourgueil, tel. 02.47.97.75.10,
fax 02.47.97.98.98, e-mail clos.du.vigneau@wanadoo.fr ☑
☨ ev. day except Sun. 8.30am–12 noon 2pm–7pm
↘ GFA Dom. du Vigneau

DOM. DE LA CLOSERIE
Vieilles Vignes 2001★

■	3 ha	13,000	▮◫⚲	5–8 €

This Vieilles Vignes selection presents itself at its best. With its profile of a supple, fruity, light, easy-to-drink wine, it enters the register of classic Saint-Nicolas wines. It will be appreciated drunk fresh (14° C).

↘ Jean-François Mabileau, La Closerie, 28, rte de Bourgueil, 37140 Restigné, tel. 02.47.97.36.29,
fax 02.47.97.48.33 ☑
☨ by appt.

LYDIE ET MAX COGNARD-TALUAU
Cuvée Estelle 2001★★

■	6.6 ha	50,000	▮⚲	5–8 €

One star for the Bourgueil, two stars for this Saint-Nicolas – Max and Lydie Cognard-Taluau definitely knew how to take advantage of the 2001 vintage. Their *cuvée*, certainly the result of a good harvest, has very expressive aromas of ripe fruit and jam. This full-flavoured character reappears on the palate in the form of passion-fruit. There are also elegant tannins rounded by a rich body, which leads to a velvet texture on the finish. A wine with great potential.

↘ Max Cognard, Chevrette,
37140 Saint-Nicolas-de-Bourgueil, tel. 02.47.97.76.88,
fax 02.47.97.97.83, e-mail max.cognard@wanadoo.fr ☑
☨ by appt.

VIGNOBLE DE LA CONTRIE 2001★

■	0.89 ha	6,000	▮◫⚲	5–8 €

The Audebert business is renowned as much in Bourgueil as in Saint-Nicolas. This deep-red selection remains discreet, with notes of muskiness. It opens out agreeably with roundness, in spite of a still austere finish. It will improve with laying down for a short while. The **Vignobles Audebert et Fils, les Graviers 2001** was commended.

↘ Maison Audebert et Fils, 20, av. Jean-Causeret,
37140 Bourgueil, tel. 02.47.97.70.06, fax 02.47.97.72.07,
e-mail maison@audebert.fr ☑
☨ ev. day 8.30am–12 noon 2pm–6pm; Sat. Sun. by appt.

LE VIGNOBLE DU FRESNE 2001★

■	0.8 ha	5,000	▮◫⚲	3–5 €

Classic for the appellation, with its ruby colour and open nose, elegant and fruity. A supple attack with round tannins, good length: the type of Saint-Nicolas that comes from gravelly soil. This wine will benefit from a little patience, but it is also pleasant now.

↘ Patrick Guenescheau, 1, Le Fresne,
37140 Saint-Nicolas-de-Bourgueil, tel. 02.47.97.86.60,
fax 02.47.97.42.53 ☑
☨ by appt.

VIGNOBLE DE LA JARNOTERIE
Cuvée Concerto Vieilles Vignes 2001★★

■	2.2 ha	n.c.	▮◫⚲	8–11 €

A fairly deep colour with a rich nose of ripe soft fruits and hints of menthol, this fruity impression combines well with the body. If some undisciplined tannins appear, they will return quickly to their place after a short stay in the cellar, unless you prefer to rebel and enjoy some now. The well-structured **Cuvée MR 2001 (5–8 €)** is singled out.

↘ Jean-Claude Mabileau et Didier Rezé, La Jarnoterie,
37140 Saint-Nicolas-de-Bourgueil, tel. 02.47.97.75.49,
fax 02.47.97.79.98 ☑
☨ by appt.

FREDERIC MABILEAU
Eclipse 2001★★

■	1 ha	5,000	◫	11–15 €

Frédéric Mabileau produced two remarkable *cuvées*. A *coup de coeur* last year, it just missed the same award this year. An impressive crimson colour, it reveals a nose of stewed fruits, combined with pleasant oak. The attack returns to fruit and wood but a beautiful structure emerges, enveloped with richness and evolving into a long finish. A powerful wine that needs time for the imprint of the oak maturation to integrate better. The second, **Les Coutures 2001 (8–11 €)**, also awarded two stars and matured 12 months in barrel, has the same capacity for development.

↘ Frédéric Mabileau, 17, rue de la Treille,
37140 Saint-Nicolas-de-Bourgueil, tel. 02.47.97.79.58,
fax 02.47.97.45.19,
e-mail mabileau.frederic@wanadoo.fr ☑
☨ by appt.

JACQUES ET VINCENT MABILEAU
La Gardière Vieilles Vignes 2001★★

■	2.5 ha	15,000	▮	8–11 €

Jacques and Vincent Mabileau know how to draw wines with richness and expression from the south-facing clay-limestone soils. This *cuvée*, evocative of very ripe fruit, is round and full thanks to already mellow tannins that lead to a silky finish. It is the result of well-handled maturation. A special mention is given to, **La Gardière 2001 (5–8 €)**, matured in tank, which needs time to develop.

↘ EARL Jacques et Vincent Mabileau, La Gardière,
37140 Saint-Nicolas-de-Bourgueil, tel. 02.47.97.75.85,
fax 02.47.97.98.03 ☑
☨ by appt.

DOM. LAURENT MABILEAU 2001★

■	10 ha	65,000	◫	8–11 €

This *cuvée* will attract wine amateurs who like oak. The oak maturation is perceptible throughout the palate, side by side with the fruit, body and expressive tannins. It needs a long time in the cellar before a fine overall harmony is achieved.

↘ Dom. Laurent Mabileau, La Croix du Moulin-Neuf,
37140 Saint-Nicolas-de-Bourgueil, tel. 02.47.97.74.75,
fax 02.47.97.99.81, e-mail domaine@mabileau.fr ☑
☨ ev. day except Sun. 10am–12.30pm 2pm–7pm

LYSIANE ET GUY MABILEAU
Vieilles Vignes 2001★

■	0.5 ha	4,000	▮⚲	5–8 €

This Vieilles Vignes selection comes from a small part of the 12-hectare vineyard that is planted on gravelly soil. Pleasant fruit on the nose and aromas of cocoa appear when the wine is swirled in the glass. The opening is round, followed by an impression of great suppleness that stays through to the finish. An agreeable wine to drink now, but which is not without potential.

↘ GAEC Lysiane et Guy Mabileau, 17, rue du Vieux-Chêne, 37140 Saint-Nicolas-de-Bourgueil,
tel. 02.47.97.70.43, fax 02.47.97.70.43 ☑
☨ ev. day except Sun. 9am–7pm

DOM. DU MORTIER

Cuvée Dionysos 2001★

| ■ | 1.7 ha | 8,000 | 💷 | 5–8 € |

This *cuvée* is produced from grapes from the oldest plots of the vineyard. Attractive, with oaky notes, the wine has a frank attack, followed by a well-made structure and good length. The maturation in cask was well handled. Matured in tank, the **Gaïa 2001** selection, which symbolizes Earth (and the terroir, of course), is singled out especially for its generous fruit.

🔸 Boisard Fils, Dom. du Mortier,
37140 Saint-Nicolas-de-Bourgueil, tel. 02.47.97.98.32,
fax 02.47.97.94.68, e-mail info@boisard-fils.com ☑
🍷 by appt.

DOM. OLIVIER

Cuvée du Mont des Olivier 2001★

| ■ | 3 ha | 18,000 | ■ ▲ | 5–8 € |

This wine has a garnet-red colour, which is followed by intense and elegant fruit flavours. At the start it is round and fruity, then the palate discloses its weight and suppleness before disappearing slowly on the long finish. The tannins are controlled from beginning to end. A well-balanced Saint-Nicolas that will continue to develop. The principal selection **Domaine Olivier 2001** is singled out.

🔸 Dom. Olivier, La Forcine,
37140 Saint-Nicolas-de-Bourgueil, tel. 02.47.97.75.32,
fax 02.47.97.48.18, e-mail patrick.olivier14@wanadoo.fr ☑
🍷 by appt.

LES CAVES DU PLESSIS

Sélection Vieilles Vignes 2001★★

| ■ | 4.3 ha | 33,000 | ■ ▲ | 5–8 € |

The name of this wine cellar, dug into the tufa and bought in 1912, has been chosen to designate the estate. The latter is positioned on the clay-limestone hillside. If the wine seems a little timid on the nose, it does not, however, lack potential: charming at the first impression, it opens out to become full-bodied and well structured. Without question, a *cuvée* to lay down.

🔸 Claude Renou, 17, La Martellière,
37140 Saint-Nicolas-de-Bourgueil, tel. 02.47.97.85.67,
fax 02.47.97.45.55 ☑
🍷 ev. day except Sun. 9am–12 noon 2pm–6.30am

DOM. PONTONNIER

Cuvée Prestige 2001★

| ■ | 3 ha | 13,000 | ■ 💷 | 8–11 € |

A recent installation (2001) in a family environment and the first wines on this 15-hectare estate are encouraging. This *cuvée*, soft right through to its lovely finish, finds a good balance between the fruit, tannins and body. It is an attractive fruity wine which will please the amateurs of classic Saint-Nicolas.

🔸 Dom. Pontonnier-Caslot, 4, chem. de L'Epaisse,
37140 Saint-Nicolas-de-Bourgueil, tel. 02.47.97.84.69,
fax 02.47.97.48.55 ☑
🍷 ev. day except Sun. 9am–12 noon 2pm–6pm;
Sat. by appt.; cl. 15 Aug.–1 Sep.

DOM. CHRISTIAN PROVIN

Cuvée Coteau Vieilles Vignes 2001★

| ■ | 16 ha | n.c. | ■ ▲ | 11–15 € |

The estate is located north of Saint-Nicolas, on the hillside. A good part of the vineyard that covers 17 ha is situated on clay-limestone soil. The Coteau selection, made from this terroir, exhibits an intense red berry nose, indicating a good mature harvest. There is good balance between body, freshness and tannins. The latter, very discreet, support a fruity finish, which has an added touch of balsamic. To drink now.

🔸 Christian Provin, L'Epaisse,
37140 Saint-Nicolas-de-Bourgueil, tel. 02.47.97.85.14,
fax 02.47.97.47.75 ☑
🍷 by appt.

DOM. DU ROCHOUARD

Cuvée de la Pierre du Lane 2001★★

| ■ | 2 ha | 3,600 | ■ ▲ | 5–8 € |

Created at Bourgueil, the domaine of Rochouard only extended into AOC Saint-Nicolas-de-Bourgueil in 1986. The Pierre du Lane selection comes from a small appellation where the terroir is composed of clay with flint. It carries the trait of its birthplace in the fruity expressive nose and the perfect structure of the palate: a supple attack, full, well-integrated, silky tannins, lovely length. "A perfect wine for the appellation," exclaimed the Jury. And the Grand Jury show their approval by awarding it a *coup de cœur*. The principal *cuvée* **Domaine du Rochouard 2001** deserves noting. These two wines are ready to drink now.

🔸 GAEC Duveau-Coulon et Fils, 1, rue des Géléries,
37140 Bourgueil, tel. 02.47.97.85.91, fax 02.47.97.99.13 ☑
🍷 ev. day 8.30am–12.30pm 2pm–6.30pm

JOEL TALUAU

Le Vau Jaumier 2001★★

| ■ | 6 ha | 33,000 | ■ | 5–8 € |

Here are two beautiful wines that we owe to the talent of two wine producers: Joël Taluau who, by his work and tenacity, has already brought fame to this domaine of 23 ha at the foot of the hillside; and his son-in-law. Dominated by blackcurrant, the Vau Jaumier opens on roundness and suppleness before developing over quite ripe, integrated tannins. Its balance makes it an agreeable wine already. The **Cuvée Vieilles Vignes 2001 (8–11 €)**, which is more of a wine to lay down, is singled out as "very successful".

🔸 EARL Taluau-Foltzenlogel, Chevrette,
37140 Saint-Nicolas-de-Bourgueil, tel. 02.47.97.78.79,
fax 02.47.97.95.60, e-mail joel.taluau@wanadoo.fr ☑
🍷 ev. day except Sat. Sun. 9am–11.30am 2pm–6pm
🔸 Joël Taluau

GERALD VALLEE

Le Vau Jaumier 2001★★

| ■ | 4 ha | 13,300 | 💷 | 8–11 € |

The ancestor of Gérald Vallée, representative of the king, was thrown into the Loire by the republicans and saved *in extremis* by mariners. Without him this Vau Jaumier selection wouldn't exist – and that would be too bad. The nose subtly blends blackcurrant and raspberry with light oak. After a first impression of roundness, the palate reveals fullness, supported by supple tannins that will ensure the wine will keep.

🔸 EARL Gérald Vallée, La Cotelleraie,
37140 Saint-Nicolas-de-Bourgueil, tel. 02.47.97.75.53,
fax 02.47.97.85.90, e-mail gerald.vallee@wanadoo.fr ☑
🍷 ev. day except Sun. 9am–6.30pm

DOM. DES VALLETTES 2001★

| ■ | 18 ha | 90,000 | ■ ▲ | 5–8 € |

In conjunction with his father, Francis Jamet produced this Saint-Nicolas that opens gradually on scents of crystallized and stewed fruit. The tannins are still very present and have not finished evolving. It will therefore be necessary to wait at least two years to appreciate this wine.

🔸 Francis et François Jamet, Dom. des Vallettes,
37140 Saint-Nicolas-de-Bourgueil, tel. 02.41.52.05.99,
fax 02.41.52.87.52, e-mail francis.jamet@les-vallettes.com ☑
🍷 by appt.

Wines selected but not starred

DOM. DE BEAU PUY
Vieilles Vignes 2001

| ■ | 2.5 ha | 11,000 | ▮ ⅢⅡ ↓ | 5–8 € |

♠ Jean-Paul Morin, 30, rue de La Lande, 37140 Bourgueil, tel. 02.47.97.76.92, fax 02.47.97.98.20, e-mail morinjpwine@wanadoo.fr ☑
☏ by appt.

DOM. DES BERGEONNIERES 2001

| ■ | 14 ha | 50,000 | ▮ ↓ | 5–8 € |

♠ André Delagouttière, Les Bergeonnières, 37140 Saint-Nicolas-de-Bourgueil, tel. 02.47.97.75.87, fax 02.47.97.48.47, e-mail andre.delagouttiere@laposte.net ☑
☏ ev. day except Sun. 8.30am–12 noon 2pm–6pm

CAVE BRUNEAU DUPUY
Vieilles Vignes 2001

| ■ | 6 ha | 30,000 | ⅢⅡ | 5–8 € |

♠ Sylvain Bruneau, La Martellière, 37140 Saint-Nicolas-de-Bourgueil, tel. 02.47.97.75.81, fax 02.47.97.43.25, e-mail cave-bruneau-dupuy@netcourrier.com ☑
☏ by appt.
♠ Jean Bruneau

FOUCHER-LEBRUN
Les Grands Jardins 2001

| ■ | n.c. | 15,000 | ▮ ↓ | 5–8 € |

♠ Foucher-Lebrun, 29, rte de Bouhy, 58200 Alligny-Cosne, tel. 03.86.26.87.27, fax 03.86.26.87.20, e-mail foucher.lebrun@wanadoo.fr ☑
☏ ev. day except Sun. Mon. 8am–12 noon 2pm–6pm

DOM. DES GESLETS
La Contrie 2001

| ■ | 2 ha | 10,000 | ▮ ↓ | 5–8 € |

♠ EARL Vincent Grégoire, Dom. des Geslets, 37140 Bourgueil, tel. 02.47.97.97.06, fax 02.47.97.73.95, e-mail domainedesgeslets@oreka.com ☑
☏ ev. day except Sun. 10am–6pm

DOM. GUY HERSARD
Vieilles Vignes 2001

| ■ | 5 ha | 25,000 | ▮ ↓ | 5–8 € |

♠ Guy Hersard, 5–7, Le Fondis, 37140 Saint-Nicolas-de-Bourgueil, tel. 02.47.97.76.13, fax 02.47.97.92.06, e-mail guy.hersard@wanadoo.fr ☑
☏ by appt.

Chinon

The AOC Chinon, which covers 2,200 ha, surrounding the old medieval fort from which it takes its name, lies amid countryside made famous by Rabelais in his epics *Gargantua* and *Pantagruel* (1534). The various terroirs include the ancient gravel terraces of the Véron (a triangle formed by the confluence of the Vienne and the Loire), the low, sandy terraces of the Vienne (Cravant) valley, the higher slopes on both sides of the valley (Sazilly) and chalk (Chinon). Cabernet Franc, also known as Breton, made 108,609 hl of delicious red wines in 2002, plus a few thousand hectolitres of dry rosé which equal Bourgueil in quality: they have pedigree, elegant tannins and keep well, for several decades in the case of some exceptional vintages! Less known outside the area, but very original, is white Chinon, of which 1,110 hl were produced in 2002, a rather dry wine that softens with bottle age.

DOM. DE L'ABBAYE
Vieilles Vignes 2001★

| ■ | 10 ha | 35,000 | ⅢⅡ | 5–8 € |

Starting with 1.5 ha in 1975, Michel Fontaine now has 55 ha thanks to the regrouping of small vineyards that have been cultivating vines since the 11th century. It presents an attractive, light, fruity *cuvée* which has a violet nose, which has all the assets to be appreciated now. The rather oaky **Clos de la Collarderie Cuvée Unique red 2001 (8–11 €)** is singled out for its beautiful structure.
♠ Michel Fontaine, Le Repos Saint-Martin, 37500 Chinon, tel. 02.47.93.35.96, fax 02.47.98.36.76 ☑
☏ by appt.

CHRISTOPHE BAUDRY
Grande Cuvée 2001★

| ■ | 1 ha | 3,000 | ⅢⅡ | 11–15 € |

Christophe Baudry, who manages a vineyard located between gravel and clay-limestone soils on the slopes of Cravant, presents two *cuvées*, both equally appreciated. The Grande Cuvée, matured partly in new oak, reveals oakiness and balanced tannins. On the intense blackcurrant and raspberry nose, it relegates the oakiness to the background. The well-handled maturation in barrel gives undoubtedly good results. The **red Cuvée Vieilles Vignes 2001 (5–8 €)** has also seen wood, but its character is not yet well integrated; a little time will remedy that.
♠ Dom. de la Perrière, Cravant-les-Coteaux, 37500 Chinon, tel. 02.47.93.15.99, fax 02.47.98.34.57 ☑ ⌂
☏ by appt.

DOM. DE BEAUSEJOUR 2002★

| ■ | 4 ha | 7,000 | ▮ ↓ | 3–5 € |

Followers of Chinon rosé seek out this type of wine with its frank attack and robustness, but with sufficient liveliness and fruitiness right through to the finish. Balanced but refreshing, this substantial 2002 will accompany many dishes beautifully.
♠ Earl Gérard et David Chauveau, Dom. de Beauséjour, 37220 Panzoult, tel. 02.47.58.64.64, fax 02.47.95.27.13, e-mail info@domdebeausejour.com ☑ ⌂ ⌂
☏ by appt.

DOM. DE BEL AIR
Pauline 2002★★

| ■ | 0.6 ha | 2,000 | ▮ | 3–5 € |

Jean-Louis Loup took over this estate of nearly 14 ha in 1997. He has got to grips with it, and it is natural that he should now present this remarkable rosé. It has a brilliant clear-salmon colour and emanates delicate scents of white fruits. Fresh and thirst-quenching, the wine exudes youth and invites you to a barbecue. The **red La Croix Boissée 2000 (11–15 €)**, matured in barrel, is awarded one star.
♠ Jean-Louis Loup, Dom. de Bel Air, 37500 Cravant-les-Coteaux, tel. 02.47.98.42.75, fax 02.47.93.98.30, e-mail jean-louis.loup@wanadoo.fr ☑
☏ by appt.

VINCENT BELLIVIER 2001★

| ■ | 1.3 ha | 5,800 | ▮ ↓ | 3–5 € |

On his property of 3.5 ha close to the forest of Chinon, Vincent Bellivier works according to ancient tradition, without addition of yeast, or filtering: the wine is created naturally. The result is an intense red Chinon, which releases aromas of Morello cherry with touches of vanilla. At the same time round and fresh, it needs just to integrate its modest tannins. It will keep.

➦ Vincent Bellivier, 12, rue de la Tourette, 37420 Huismes, tel. 02.47.95.54.26, fax 02.47.95.54.26 ✓ ☷
ℐ by appt.

PHILIPPE BROCOURT

Vieilles Vignes 2001★

■	n.c.	7,000	■ ◗	5–8 €

Forty-year-old vines, established on clay-limestone soils dominating the Vienne, have produced this Chinon, matured in oak barrels in the tufa wine cellar. Supple, rich and built around fine tannins, it evokes the maturity of the harvest. A well-handled light oakiness is welcome. One can predict a long life for this wine.

➦ Philippe Brocourt, 3, chem. des Caves, 37500 Rivière, tel. 02.47.93.34.49, fax 02.47.93.97.40 ✓
ℐ by appt.

DOM. CAMILLE

Cuvée Prestige 2001★

■	2 ha	2,500	■	5–8 €

Alain Camille is not looking to expand. He cultivates 6 ha of vines on the gravelly soils of Vienne and concentrates all his efforts towards quality. He practises sustained agriculture and adheres to the environmental quality charter of APIVIS, respecting rigorous regulations. He achieves convincing results, such as this deep-ruby wine, exuding jammy fruit and chocolate. A soft attack is followed by fruitiness of good quality, quickly joined by tannins of character. Attractive length, but needs to mature.

➦ Alain Camille, 14, rue Grande, 37220 Tavant, tel. 02.47.95.26.67, fax 02.47.95.26.67 ✓
ℐ by appt.

DOM. DE LA CHAPELLE

Vieilles Vignes 2001★

■	4 ha	10,000	◗◗	8–11 €

The old chapel on the domaine does not exist anymore, but left its name to this vineyard divided between two terroirs: one gravelly, coming from the old alluvia from Vienne, the other, clay-limestone resting on the tufa of the slopes of Cravant. The Cuvée Vieilles Vignes results from a selection of more than 30-year-old vines planted on the two terroirs. It has a brilliant-ruby colour, and on the nose emanates banana, coconut and a distinctive oaky note. The discreet body hides behind the wood. One guesses however at a certain roundness and ripe fruit flavours. A wine intended to be laid down for better harmony.

➦ Philippe Pichard, 9, rue Malvault, 37500 Cravant-les-Coteaux, tel. 02.47.93.42.35, fax 02.47.98.33.76 ✓
ℐ by appt.

DOM. DANIEL CHAUVEAU

Cuvée Domaine 2001★★

■	4 ha	17,000	■ ◗◗	5–8 €

Daniel and Christophe Chauveau have a lovely collection of corkscrews. This year they present this well-made and elegant wine. The complex flavours are outlined by a certain oakiness that is confirmed on the palate by burnt notes. The tannins are imposing on the opening, but soon find their right place, while letting the body develop. Keep for three or four years.

➦ Dom. Daniel Chauveau, Pallus, 37500 Cravant-les-Coteaux, tel. 02.47.93.06.12, fax 02.47.93.93.06, e-mail domaine.daniel.chauveau@wanadoo.fr ✓
ℐ by appt.

CLOS GUILLOT

Vieilles Vignes 2000★

■	1 ha	4,500	■ ◗◗	5–8 €

Thierry Landry has matured this wine 14 months in barrel in his 15th century wine cellar. This has given a wine of supple character, round and full of flavour (intense notes of red and black fruits). The substantial tannins are lying in wait, ready

to support a rich body over the long wait in the cellar. The woody note on the finish will integrate gradually.

➦ Thierry Landry, 39, rue de Turpenay, Les Closeaux, 37500 Chinon, tel. 06.68.46.86.49 ✓
ℐ by appt.

DOM. DU COLOMBIER 2001★

■	3.5 ha	13,000	■ ◗	5–8 €

The commmune of Beaumont-en-Véron occupies a high position in the Chinon region, and its clay-limestone soils sit directly on the tufa: in fact warm soils, drained well often produce wines that are not only full, but also fruity and fresh. Such is the case with this selection: enlivened by scents of cherry and rose, it dons a perceptible tannic screen, which doesn't show any suppleness. Pleasant today, it will also keep a year or two. The red Cuvée Vieilles Vignes 2001, which is ready to drink, is singled out.

➦ EARL Loiseau-Jouvault, Dom. du Colombier, 37420 Beaumont-en-Véron, tel. 02.47.58.43.07, fax 02.47.58.93.99, e-mail chinon.colombier@club-internet.fr ✓
ℐ ev. day except Sun. 8am–12 noon 2pm–6.30pm

DOM. COTON 2001★

■	n.c.	27,000	◗◗	3–5 €

Like many Chinon vineyards of the past, the Coton domaine was directed towards mixed farming and cattle rearing. It wasn't until the 1960s that the terroir again found its viticultural vocation, somewhat forsaken during the war. Today, only wine is thought of at Crouzilles, and rightly so, given the success obtained. This slightly spicy, bright-ruby wine with aromas of small berry fruit benefits from a supple, elegant body; the quality shows with great length on the finish. It has potential that needs to be exploited. The lively rosé 2002 is singled out.

➦ EARL Dom. Coton, La Perrière, 37220 Crouzilles, tel. 02.47.58.55.10, fax 02.47.58.55.69 ✓
ℐ by appt.

CH. DE COULAINE

Bonnaventure 2001★

■	4 ha	15,000	■	11–15 €

The Château de Coulaine has been in the Bonnaventure family since the year 1300. Its medieval architecture is still perceptible in spite of the slight Italian influence. Etienne de Bonnaventure, who came here in 1988, tried to revive the vineyard which had been reduced to only 1.5 ha after the phylloxera crisis. Today, master of 12 ha, he has produced two interesting wines. With its purple colour, the first, Bonnaventure, opens on discreet soft fruit and wild woodland fruit notes. On the palate, it is the structure that takes the stage, a structure that is rigid and round at the same time, guaranteeing good keeping potential. The second, the red La Diablesse 2001 (15–23 €), is singled out; it has seen wood.

➦ Ch. de Coulaine, 2, rue de Coulaine, 37420 Beaumont-en-Véron, tel. 02.47.98.44.51, fax 02.47.93.49.15, e-mail chateaudecoulaine@club.internet.fr ✓ ☷
ℐ by appt.
➦ E. et P. de Bonnaventure

JEAN-PIERRE CRESPIN

Artissimo Le Vin des Humanistes 2001★

■	1.15 ha	4,500	◗◗	15–23 €

Jean-Pierre Crespin is in charge of a company owning the "Le Vin des Humanistes" brand. This one has vineyards, but also has contracted with Chinon wine-growers, whose harvests they process with rigour. Their production is subjected to regulations, which control cultivation and especially vine yields. The first cuvée, Artissimo, is known as an "artist's wine", free from middle-class constraints, free of all conventions". It benefits from this freedom and expresses fine woody, vanilla aromas, accompanied by musky nuances, and presents a rich and powerful body. The oakiness inherited from a maturation of 18 months in barrel needs time to integrate. The Cuvée Arlequin red 2001 (11–15 €) also obtains one star.

➦ SARL Jean-Pierre Crespin, Ch. de l'Aulée, 37190 Azay-le-Rideau, tel. 02.47.45.44.24, fax 02.47.45.44.24, e-mail jean-pierre.crespin@mageos.com ✓
ℐ by appt.

RENAUD DESBOURDES

Réserve de la Marinière 2001★★

| ■ | n.c. | 4,500 | ❚❙❙ | 5–8 € |

Four oak trees more than 100 years old welcome you to this ancient smallholding of the Lords of Roncé. The cellars, carved into the tufa as and when the vineyards expanded, are an invaluable tool for maturing the wine. This Réserve de la Marinière cannot deny its origin, so strongly does the Cabernet show in its character: purple glints, rich nose of stewed fruit, imposing tannic structure and rich body. A characteristic wine from the appellation that deserves to wait because the oak is not yet integrated. The **Cuvée La Galippe red 2001** is singled out.

☞ Renaud Desbourdes, La Marinière, 37220 Panzoult, tel. 02.47.95.24.75, fax 02.47.95.24.75 **☑**
☕ by appt.

FRANCIS & FRANCOISE DESBOURDES

Cuvée Prestige 2001★

| ■ | 2.5 ha | n.c. | ■ ♦ | 5–8 € |

Located at the edge of a small picturesque valley renowned for its calm and appreciated by tourists, the property of L'Arpenty is a haven of peace where each person works with serenity to make expressive wines. This limpid, garnet-coloured wine has a restrained nose but opens out quickly with fullness and richness embellished with red berries; the substantial tannins indicate good evolution.

☞ EARL Francis et Françoise Desbourdes, 11, rue de la Forêt, L'Arpenty, 37220 Panzoult, tel. 02.47.95.22.86, fax 02.47.95.22.86 **☑ ⌂**
☕ by appt.

FOUCHER-LEBRUN

Elevé en fût de chêne 2001★★

| ■ | n.c. | n.c. | ❚❙❙ | 5–8 € |

Created in 1921, the Foucher-Lebrun company was originally a cooperage. Driven by his passion for wine and the bonds that he maintained with the wine producers, its founder undertook to market a full range of Loire wines. Here is a superb Chinon, at first the nose opens on vanilla but soon develops flowery and white fleshed peach aromas. The palate is rather lively on the attack and then opens out with elegant oak that is well balanced with the richness. The discreet tannins add length to the finish. A wine with a future, which can also be drunk now.

☞ Foucher-Lebrun, 29, rte de Bouhy, 58200 Alligny-Cosne, tel. 03.86.26.87.27, fax 03.86.26.87.20, e-mail foucher.lebrun@wanadoo.fr **☑**
☕ ev. day except Sun. Mon. 8am–12 noon 2pm–6pm

DOM. DES GALUCHES 2001★

| ■ | 8.8 ha | 3,000 | | 3–5 € |

Having taken over this small estate of 10 ha from their parents, Laurence and Christian Millerand have upgraded the winery and the winemaking equipment. The name of Galuches reflects the rich gravelly soils and large round stones found on the banks of the Loire River. The terroir has, without doubt, given this selection its suppleness, its flattering fruitiness, of blackcurrant, liquorice and red berry fruit, in short, its fresh and fruity character. Drink now in order to benefit from fruitiness in full bloom.

☞ Millerand, 2 bis, imp. des Galuches, 37420 Savigny-en-Véron, tel. 02.47.58.45.38, fax 02.47.58.08.52 **☑**
☕ by appt.

FABRICE GASNIER

Cuvée Prestige 2001★★

| ■ | 3 ha | 12,000 | ❚❙❙ | 8–11 € |

Meticulous care and attention has been given to the vine right through to the winery. They started stripping the vines in the summer to limit yields and to achieve better ripening of the grapes. This was followed, at harvest time, by sorting and selecting the grape clusters and strict control during fermentation; maturation in oak for one year completed the procedure. This *cuvée*, with its pronounced Cabernet flavours

of sweet pepper, opens out to reveal a touch of oakiness. After a supple attack, it develops roundness, sustained by richness. The tannins appear on the finish indicating its potential. Fabrice Gasnier's classic **red Chinon 2001** is especially singled out for its qualities of liveliness and balance.

☞ Fabrice Gasnier, Chézelet, 37500 Cravant-les-Coteaux, tel. 02.47.93.11.60, fax 02.47.93.44.83, e-mail fabricegasnier@wanadoo.fr **☑**
☕ by appt.

DOM. DES GELERIES

Le Puy Blanc 2001★

| ■ | 2 ha | 7,000 | ■ | 5–8 € |

Jean-Marie Rouzier is a Bourgueil wine producer who is interested in the Chinon wines. Starting with two hectares in 1981, he now has nearly eight, while still continuing his activities in Bourgueil. This selection has all the characteristics of an attractive wine, ready to adapt to all circumstances. The first impression is supple, the body is full and fruity and has agreeable tannins. A very pleasant wine. The **red Vieilles Vignes 2001**, which requires ageing, is singled out.

☞ Jean-Marie Rouzier, Les Géléries, 37140 Bourgueil, tel. 02.47.97.74.83, fax 02.47.97.48.73, e-mail jean-Marie.rouzier@wanadoo.fr **☑**
☕ ev. day except Sun. 9am–12.30pm 2.30pm–7pm; cl. 25 Sep. until 10 Oct.

DOM. GOURON

Vieilles Vignes 2001★

| ■ | 3 ha | 12,000 | ■ ❚❙❙ | 5–8 € |

The vine enjoys a favourable position on the heights of Cravant – a little paradise for wines. This one, of an intense red, is rather discreet, giving out a light oakiness perceptible both on the nose and on the palate. But it is round, full and enhanced with prune flavours right through to the vanilla finish. Leave to age so that the integration of the oak improves.

☞ GAEC Gouron, 2, La Croix de Bois, 37500 Cravant-les-Coteaux, tel. 02.47.93.15.33, fax 02.47.93.96.73, e-mail info@domaine-gouron.com **☑**
☕ ev. day except Sun. 8am–12 noon 1.30pm–6pm

CH. DE LA GRILLE 2001★

| ■ | 27 ha | 10,000 | ❚❙❙ | 11–15 € |

One of the rare château wines from the Loire valley, La Grille dates from 15th century, but was greatly altered in 1855. Its wines are marketed in bottles originating from the style of 18th century champagne bottles. Sylvie and Laurent Gosset, the current owners and winemakers, present a rich and elegant wine with evident yet mellow tannins. It will not be on sale before 2005. The **rosé 2002 (8–11 €)** is singled out for its freshness and fruitiness. Note that Château de la Grille received the *Grappe d'argent* for its Chinon 2000 during the launching of the French 2003 edition of the *Guide*.

☞ Laurent et Sylvie Gosset, Ch. de La Grille, BP 205, rte de Huismes & Ussé, 37500 Chinon, tel. 02.47.93.01.95, fax 02.47.93.45.91 **☑**
☕ by appt.

VIGNOBLE GROSBOIS

Cuvée Printemps 2001★

| ■ | 7 ha | 15,000 | ■ | 3–5 € |

Jacques Grosbois works 8 ha of vines on limestone soils situated on the south-facing hillsides of Panzoult. He presents a wine with a frank attack, round, long on the finish, with a lovely freshness. A pleasant wine which will accompany many dishes well.

☞ Jacques Grosbois, Le Pressoir, 37220 Panzoult, tel. 02.47.58.66.87, fax 02.47.95.26.52 **☑**
☕ by appt.

DOM. DE LA HAUTE OLIVE 2002★

| ■ | 0.32 | 2,000 | ❚❙❙ | 5–8 € |

A *cuvée* created from Pineau grapes such as those coveted in the Picrochole War and of which Rabelais spoke in praise. Here the compliments flow: a nose rich with lemon and crystallized apricot aromas, a round palate with toasty and almond notes on a background of oak. This all indicates that the wine is the product of a harvest of well-ripened fruit.

☛ EARL Dom. de la Haute Olive, 38, rue de la Haute-Olive, 37500 Chinon, tel. 02.47.93.04.08, fax 02.47.93.99.28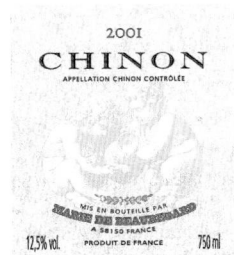

Ⓣ by appt.

DOM. HERAULT

Vieilles Vignes 2001 ★

■	2.63 ha	19,000	▮ ⌕	3–5 €

This estate consisted of merely 50 ares at its creation in 1964, but today covers 21 ha. Meanwhile, a modern winery has been built and a wine cellar installed in the galleries of an 18th century quarry, discovered by chance. Here is a wine tempting with its suppleness, fullness and uplifting finish of spices and red berry fruit. These same aromas that identify Cabernet appeared on the palate of this shimmering coloured wine.

☛ EARL Eric Hérault, Le Château, 37220 Panzoult, tel. 02.47.58.56.11, fax 02.47.58.69.47 ▮

Ⓣ by appt.

DOM. CHARLES JOGUET

Clos de la Dioterie 2001 ★

■	2.5 ha	10,000	◫	15–23 €

This vineyard, today covering 40 ha, became one of the pioneers of quality. Its history seems to go back several centuries, and certain *clos* were already known during the Renaissance. La Dioterie, on the left bank of the Vienne, is planted today with 80-year-old vines. One expects this terroir to give wines of character, complexity and keeping qualities. This 2001 doesn't disappoint: a dense colour and a nose that reveals a range of ripe soft fruit aromas; full-bodied and rich; structured with elegant tannins; a long finish which predicts longevity. A beautiful future also for the **red Cuvée Les Varennes du Grand Clos 2001 (11–15 €)**, judged to be a very successful wine.

☛ Dom. Charles Joguet, La Dioterie, 37220 Sazilly, tel. 02.47.58.55.53, fax 02.47.58.52.22, e-mail joguet@charlesjoguet.com ▮

Ⓣ by appt.

BEATRICE ET PASCAL LAMBERT

Cuvée Marie 2001 ★★

■	2 ha	9,000	◫	11–15 €

Owning only 4 ha in 1986, Béatrice and Pascal Lambert today cultivate 13 ha and are well equipped for making and storing wines and receiving visitors. Their wines are very successful and regularly gain places of honour. The very oaky Marie selection still hides its assets, but one can foretell its richness supported by an elegant tannic structure. Give it time. Made from Pineau and also with pronounced oak, the **Chinon Cuvée Antoine white 2001 (15–23 €)** is awarded one star.

☛ Béatrice et Pascal Lambert, Les Chesnaies, 37500 Cravant-les-Coteaux, tel. 02.47.93.13.79, fax 02.47.93.40.97, e-mail lambert-chesnaies@wanadoo.fr ▮

Ⓣ by appt.

PATRICK LAMBERT

Vieilles Vignes 2001 ★

■	2 ha	5,000	▮ ◫	5–8 €

Patrick Lambert took over part of his parents' estate in 1990. Since then he has expanded and now farms nearly 9 ha. Two hectares of, on average, 45-year-old vines have been used to produce this characteristic *cuvée*. The nose is full and fruity, the palate well balanced, powerful and with firmly anchored tannins. The wine shows class and just needs to develop. The **Cuvée Tradition red 2001 (3–5 €)** that is singled out due to its length and freshness can be kept in the cellar for a little time.

☛ Earl Patrick Lambert, 6, Coteau de Sonnay, 37500 Cravant-les-Coteaux, tel. 02.47.93.92.39, fax 02.47.93.92.39 ▮

Ⓣ by appt.

JACQUELINE ET PIERRE LEON 2001 ★

■	0.8 ha	4,000	▮ ◫	5–8 €

Jacqueline and Pierre Leon have spent 25 years in the service of this small estate of 5 ha planted on sand and gravel soils of

---

the Loire. They stand down for their daughter Angélique who will continue in the same spirit of tradition and achievement that has always sustained her parents. This therefore is their last *cuvée*. Supple, it evokes soft fruits, with a refreshing note of violet. A considerable tannic structure indicates good potential.

☛ Jacqueline Léon, 2, rue des Capelets, 37420 Savigny-en-Véron, tel. 02.47.58.93.37, fax 02.47.58.93.37 ▮

Ⓣ by appt.

CH. DE LIGRE 2002 ★

■	3.3 ha	20,000	▮ ⌕	5–8 €

Pierre and Fabienne Ferrand invite us to "enter the secret of the terroirs and *cuvées*". Here is a white Chinon made from Pineau: a clear bright-yellow, it develops gradually – floral before opening out with honeyed notes, while also hinting at citrus fruits. The first impression is soft and then develops a pleasant freshness. White fruit flavours crown the whole. A pleasing well-balanced wine.

☛ Pierre Ferrand, Ch. de Ligré, 1, rue Saint-Martin, 37500 Ligré, tel. 02.47.93.16.70, fax 02.47.93.43.29, e-mail pierre.ferrand4@wanadoo.fr ▮

Ⓣ ev. day 9am–12 noon 2pm–6pm; Sat. Sun. by appt.

MARIE DE BEAUREGARD 2001 ★★

■	1 ha	6,800	◫	8–11 €

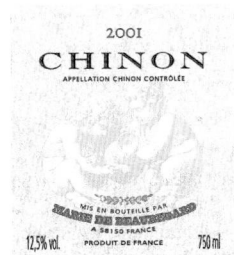

Guy Saget, *négociant-éleveur* at Pouilly-sur-Loire and specialists in wine from the Central vineyards, diversifies its activities. Here is its Chinon from a small vineyard proving the quality of its work. Good techniques and rigorous care enabled it to produce two beautiful *cuvées*, the first, Marie de Beauregard, obtains, almost unanimously, a *coup de coeur* from the Grand Jury. Deep-red, this wine opens on intense blackcurrant and blackberry aromas, then the palate impresses with its length, fullness and soft tannins. It will be even better in four to five years. The **red Les Tenonceaux 2001 (5–8 €)** obtains one star.

☛ SA Guy Saget, La Castille, BP 26, 58150 Pouilly-sur-Loire, tel. 03.86.39.57.75, fax 03.86.39.08.30 ▮

Ⓣ by appt.

VINCENT NAULET

Vieilles Vignes 2001 ★

■	0.86 ha	5,000	◫	3–5 €

The first wine for a very young wine-grower who has only just started up. For a first attempt, it is a masterstroke. Fairly intense garnet-red colour with bright highlights. The bouquet is an attractive combination of small berry fruit and under-growth. The tannins appear in the middle of the palate, but are not overpowering. The overall impression is roundness with a light oak touch. An encouraging result.

☛ Vincent Naulet, 22, rue des Rabottes, 37420 Beaumont-en-Véron, tel. 02.47.58.80.40, fax 02.47.58.84.60 ▮

Ⓣ by appt.

DOM. DE LA NOBLAIE 2002 ★

■	11 ha	6,000	▮ ⌕	5–8 €

This year the Jury proposes a well-made rosé, whose perfumes form a fruit basket. Explosive flavours that reappear on the elegant and lengthy palate. Fish or cured meats would

accompany it well. The Chinon **red 2001** and **white 2002** are also singled out.
☞ SCEA Manzagol-Billard, 2, rue des Hautes Cours, 37500 Ligré, tel. 02.47.93.10.96, fax 02.47.93.26.13 ▣
�། by appt.

J.-L. PAGE

Sélection Clément Martin 2001★★

■	1 ha	5,000	▥	5–8 €

Jean-Louis Page, who runs a vineyard of 6.5 ha inherited from his grandfather, gave the name of his children to this *cuvée*. This very successful wine presents a bouquet of soft fruit, which evolves gently towards undergrowth. Round, with a balanced tannic structure, it is appealing through to the finish. A wine to enjoy in its youth, like children, who grow up too quickly. The **red Cuvée Vielles Vignes 2001** receives a recommendation.
☞ Jean-Louis Page, 12, rte de Candes, 37420 Savigny-en-Véron, tel. 02.47.58.96.92, fax 02.47.58.86.65 ▣
☍ by appt.

DOM. JAMES ET NICOLAS PAGET

Vieilles Vignes 2001★

■	1.5 ha	n.c.	▥	5–8 €

The event of 2001 was the arrival of Nicolas, the son, at the heart of the vineyard. Now continuation of the estate is assured. This wine could not fail to be a success with such good news. The nose, initially discreet, reveals on opening notes of jam, Morello cherry and bilberry. Full-bodied, the tannins affirm their presence and suggest that this wine needs keeping so that the touch of oak integrates.
☞ EARL James et Nicolas Paget, 13, rue d'Armentières, 37190 Rivarennes, tel. 02.47.95.54.02, fax 02.47.95.45.90 ▣
☍ ev. day except Sun. Mon. 9am–12.30pm 2.30pm–7pm

DOM. CHARLES PAIN

Cuvée Prestige 2001★★

■	12 ha	35,000	▤▥♦	5–8 €

The Charles Pain estate covers 26 ha over the three villages situated at the eastern edge of the appellation. As usual, the Prestige selection is placed in the first rank. On the nose, red berry fruit dominates followed by a light grilled note. On the palate, all is harmony: body, tannins and finish. The empyreumatic (charred) aftertaste, however, is charming. Without question a wine with a future. The **Rosé de Saignée 2002 (3–5 €)** is also singled out
☞ EARL Dom. Charles Pain, Chezelet, 37220 Panzoult, tel. 02.47.93.06.14, fax 02.47.93.04.43, e-mail charles.pain@wanadoo.fr ▣
☍ by appt.

VIGNOBLE DE LA POELERIE 2002★

■	20 ha	3,000		3–5 €

The property of Poëlerie has been in the Caillé family for 200 years. Made up of 20 ha of established vines on the gravelly terraces of the Vienne, it is now managed by the son, François. Already picked out last year for a rosé, it astonishes again with this type of wine. Fresh, elegant and fruity, the 2002 has sufficient character to animate a whole meal. The Chinon **red Vieilles Vignes 2001 (5–8 €)** is singled out.
☞ François Caillé, Le Grand Marais, 37220 Panzoult, tel. 02.47.95.26.37, fax 02.47.58.56.67 ▣
☍ by appt.

DOM. DU PUY RIGAULT

Vieilles Vignes 2001★

■	1 ha	4,000	▥	5–8 €

Very soft with lots of finesse, such is this 2001 produced by Michel Page at his winery on the banks of the Vienne. A pleasant opening on the palate reveals smooth tannins and evident fruit present through to the finish. A lively wine, impatient to join us at the table.
☞ EARL Dom. du Puy Rigault, 6, rue de la Fontaine-Rigault, 37420 Savigny-en-Véron, tel. 02.47.58.44.46, fax 02.47.58.99.50 ▣
☍ by appt.
☞ Michel Page

JEAN-MAURICE RAFFAULT

Le Puy 2001★★

■	1 ha	4,000	▥	11–15 €

The 17th century wine cellars of Jean-Maurice Raffault and their impressive alignment of more than 700 barrels testify to the attachment to tradition of this family. It is Rodolphe, the son, who officiates in the vines and the winery, while treading in the footsteps of his father to maintain the reputation of the business. The selection Le Puy, thanks to its development, its measured oakiness and the flavours that range from raspberry to blackcurrant, has been classified amongst the best Chinons. Well-structured, it will improve over time as the oak integrates into the rich body. The **red Clos des Capucins 2001** obtains one star; it will also improve from keeping.
☞ EARL Jean-Maurice Raffault, La Croix, 37420 Savigny-en-Véron, tel. 02.47.58.42.50, fax 02.47.58.83.73, e-mail rodolphe-raffault@wanadoo.fr ▣
☍ by appt.

DOM. DE LA ROCHE HONNEUR

Cuvée Rubis 2001★

■	5 ha	23,000	▥	5–8 €

Of course, one will stop at Stéphane Mureau's to taste his wines always faithful to the terroir, and also to visit the immense wine cellar artistically carved into the tufa. The Rubis impressed the Jury that, in one voice, exclaimed: "beautiful palate, beautiful tannins, good length". There is nothing to add to that. The oaky **red Diamant Prestige 2001** is singled out, so is the lively **rosé 2002**.
☞ Dom. de la Roche Honneur, 1, rue de la Berthelonnière, 37420 Savigny-en-Véron, tel. 02.47.58.42.10, fax 02.47.58.45.36, e-mail roche.honneur@libertysurf.fr ▣
☍ by appt.
☞ Stéphane Mureau

DOM. DU RONCEE

Clos des Marronniers 2001★

■	7.05 ha	25,000	▥	8–11 €

Fruit from different *clos* of this old stronghold of Châtellerie de l'Ile-Bouchard (12th century) is produced separately. The Clos des Marronniers produced this fruity, full-bodied wine that liberally exudes raspberry and blackcurrant notes. Its caressing richness has great length because the tannins remain discreet. A wine with to keep hold of. The estate's **red Chinon 2001 (5–8 €)** is singled out.
☞ Dom. du Roncée, La Morandière, 37220 Panzoult, tel. 02.47.58.53.01, fax 02.47.58.64.06, e-mail info@roncee.com ▣
☍ by appt.

CH. DE SAINT-LOUAND

Réserve de Trompegueux 2001★★

■	n.c.	12,300	▥	5–8 €

This nice domaine of 6.5 ha, bought in 1987 by Charles Walther, president of l'Académie de Médecine, is managed today by his grandchildren. This Réserve de Trompegueux just missed a *coup de coeur*. The origin of the name goes back to the Middle Ages, when the "gueux" (beggars) climbed the hillsides with heavy shoes called "trompes" on their feet.

Today, this wine will not mislead anybody since the qualities on the palate are remarkable: a soft opening, abundant body and long finish. It will have a good career.
➡ Bonnet-Walther, Ch. de Saint-Louand, 37500 Chinon, tel. 02.47.93.48.60, fax 02.47.98.48.54 ☑
🍷 ev. day 9am–12 noon 2pm–6pm; Sat. Sun. by appt.

CAVES DE LA SALLE
Vieilles Vignes 2001★

■	4 ha	12,000	🍾	5–8 €

An 18th century house but above all a well-equipped winery and wine cellar where these classic Chinons are produced in good conditions. Remi Desbourdes holds the secret. This wine, characterized by the terroir, fruity and structured, already expresses itself well, but should improve if one gives it time.
➡ Rémi Desbourdes, La Salle, 37220 Avon-les-Roches, tel. 02.47.95.24.30, fax 02.47.95.24.83 ☑
🍷 ev. day except Sun. 8am–12 noon 2pm–6.30pm

SUBLIME
Prestige 2001★

■	6.8 ha	50,000	🍾	5–8 €

This important négociant, specialist in the wines of the Loire, runs its business near Saumur. Its products are widely diffused in France and abroad, and are already well known. It was guaranteed success with its Chinon since it was highly appreciated by the Jury: intense-ruby colour, open on the nose, elegant and evoking ripe fruit, it has a lively attack prolonged by an impression of suppleness and fullness, with fleshy tannins and meritable length. A wine that will improve after three years.
➡ Sté Albert Besombes-Moc-Baril, 24, rue Jules Amiot, 49404 Saint-Hilaire-Saint-Florent, tel. 02.41.50.23.23, fax 02.41.50.30.45
🍷 by appt.

Wines selected but not starred

DOM. DES BEGUINERIES
Cuvée du Terroir 2001

■	3 ha	13,500	🍾	5–8 €

➡ Jean-Christophe Pelletier, 52, Clos de la Rue Braie, Saint-Louans, 37500 Chinon, tel. 06.08.92.88.17, fax 02.47.93.37.16 ☑
🍷 by appt.

DOM. DES BOUQUERRIES
Cuvée Royale Vieilles Vignes 2001

■	5.5 ha	30,000	🍾🍷	5–8 €

➡ GAEC des Bouquerries, 4, Les Bouquerries, 37500 Cravant-les-Coteaux, tel. 02.47.93.10.50, fax 02.47.93.41.94 ☑
🍷 by appt.
➡ Guillaume et Jérôme Sourdais

DOM. PASCAL BRUNET
Cuvée Tradition 2001

■	8 ha	10,000	🍾🍷	3–5 €

➡ Dom. Pascal Brunet, 11, Etilly, 37220 Panzoult, tel. 02.47.58.62.80, fax 02.47.58.62.80 ☑
🍷 by appt.

DOM. DU CARROI PORTIER 2002

■	0.73 ha	5,200	🍾	3–5 €

➡ Dom. Spelty, Le Carroi Portier, 37500 Cravant-les-Coteaux, tel. 02.47.93.08.38, fax 02.47.93.93.50, e-mail spelty@free.fr ☑
🍷 by appt.

DOM. DES CHAMPS VIGNONS
La Jolirie Elevé en fût de chêne 2001

■	3 ha	13,000	🍷	8–11 €

➡ EARL Les Champs Vignons, 2, rue Saint-Martin, 37500 Ligré, tel. 02.47.93.18.48, fax 02.47.98.41.64 ☑
🍷 ev. day 9am–7pm
➡ Nicolas Reau

CLOS DE LA CROIX MARIE
Vieilles Vignes 2001

■	3.67 ha	20,000	🍾🍷	5–8 €

➡ EARL Barc Père et Fils, Clos de La Croix Marie, 37500 Rivière, tel. 02.47.93.02.24, fax 02.47.93.99.45 ☑
🍷 by appt.

CLOS DE L'ECHO 2001

■	17 ha	75,000	🍷	11–15 €

➡ Couly-Dutheil, 12, rue Diderot, 37500 Chinon, tel. 02.47.97.20.20, fax 02.47.97.20.25, e-mail webmaster@coulydutheil-chinon.com ☑
🍷 by appt.

DOM. DE LA COMMANDERIE
Sélection 2001

■	8.2 ha	20,000	🍾🍷	5–8 €

➡ Philippe Pain, Dom. de La Commanderie, 37220 Panzoult, tel. 02.47.93.39.32, fax 02.47.98.41.26, e-mail philippepain@wanadoo.fr ☑
🍷 by appt.

LE LOGIS DE LA BOUCHARDIERE
Les Clos Vieilles Vignes 2001

■	6.61 ha	44,000	🍷	5–8 €

➡ Serge et Bruno Sourdais, Le Logis de la Bouchardière, 37500 Cravant-les-Coteaux, tel. 02.47.93.04.27, fax 02.47.93.38.52 ☑
🍷 by appt.

MANOIR DE LA BELLONNIERE
Vieilles Vignes 2001

■	5 ha	15,000	🍾🍷	3–5 €

➡ Béatrice et Patrice Moreau, La Bellonnière, 37500 Cravant-les-Coteaux, tel. 02.47.93.45.14, fax 02.47.93.93.65 ☑

LES MENILLES 2001

■	9 ha	66,000	🍾	3–5 €

➡ SICA des Caves des Vins de Rabelais, Les Aubuis, Saint-Louans, 37500 Chinon, tel. 02.47.93.42.70, fax 02.47.98.35.40 ☑
🍷 by appt.

DOM. DES MILLARGES
Les Trotte-Loups 2001

■	5 ha	25,000	🍾🍷🍷	5–8 €

➡ Dom. des Millardes, Les Fontenils, 37500 Chinon, tel. 02.47.93.36.89, fax 02.47.93.96.20 ☑
🍷 by appt.
➡ Lycée agricole Tours-Fondettes

VIGNOBLE DU PARADIS
Clos de la Niverdière 2001

■	3 ha	15,000	🍾🍷	5–8 €

➡ Vignoble du Paradis, 57, rue du Véron, 37420 Beaumont-en-Véron, tel. 02.47.95.81.57, fax 02.47.95.86.78 ☑
🍷 by appt.

DOM. DES QUATRE VENTS 2002

■	n.c.	9,000	🍾	3–5 €

➡ Philippe Pion, La Bâtisse, 37500 Cravant-les-Coteaux, tel. 02.47.93.46.79, fax 02.47.93.99.59 ☑
🍷 by appt.

MARIE-PIERRE ET NICOLE RAFFAULT Les Loges Vieilles Vignes 2001

| ■ | 3 ha | 10,000 | 🍶 | | 5–8 € |

🍷 Marie-Pierre Raffault, Les Loges, 37500 Chinon,
tel. 02.47.93.17.89, fax 02.47.93.92.60,
e-mail marie-pierre.raffault@wanadoo.fr ✅
🍽 by appt.

DOM. OLGA RAFFAULT

Les Barnabés 2001

| ■ | 11 ha | 70,000 | 🍶🍶 | | 5–8 € |

🍷 Olga Raffault, 1, rue des Caillis,
37420 Savigny-en-Véron, tel. 02.47.58.42.16,
fax 02.47.58.83.61, e-mail eric-delavigerie@wanadoo.fr ✅
🍽 by appt.

DOM. DU RAIFAULT

Les Allets Cuvée Prestige 2001

| ■ | 4.5 ha | 24,000 | 🍶🍶🍶🍶 | | 5–8 € |

🍷 Julien Raffault, 23–25, rte de Candes,
37420 Savigny-en-Véron, tel. 02.47.58.44.01,
fax 02.47.58.92.02,
e-mail domaineduraifault@wanadoo.fr ✅
🍽 ev. day 8am–7pm; Sun. by appt.

DOM. WILFRID ROUSSE

Cuvée Terroir 2001

| ■ | 5 ha | 5,000 | 🍶🍶🍶🍶 | | 5–8 € |

🍷 Wilfrid Rousse, La Halbardière, 21, rte de Candes,
37420 Savigny-en-Véron, tel. 02.47.58.84.02,
fax 02.47.58.92.66, e-mail wilfrid.rousse@wanadoo.fr ✅
🍽 ev. day 9am–12 noon 2pm–7pm; Sun. by appt.;
cl. 15–31 Aug.

DOM. DE LA SEMELLERIE

Cuvée Déborah Elevé en fût de chêne 2001

| ■ | 2.5 ha | 10,000 | 🍶🍶🍶 | | 8–11 € |

🍷 Fabrice Delalande, La Semellerie,
37500 Cravant-les-Coteaux, tel. 02.47.93.18.70,
fax 02.47.93.94.00
🍽 by appt.

PIERRE SOURDAIS

Réserve Stanislas 2001

| ■ | 4 ha | 20,000 | 🍶🍶🍶 | | 5–8 € |

🍷 Pierre Sourdais, Le Moulin à Tan,
37500 Cravant-les-Coteaux, tel. 02.47.93.31.13,
fax 02.47.98.30.48 ✅ 🏠
🍽 by appt.

DOM. DE LA TOUR

Cuvée Vieilles Vignes 2001

| ■ | 6 ha | n.c. | 🍶🍶🍶 | | 8–11 € |

🍷 Guy Jamet, Dom. de La Tour, 25, rue de la Buissonière,
37420 Beaumont-en-Véron, tel. 02.47.58.47.61,
fax 02.47.58.40.24 ✅
🍽 by appt.

Coteaux du Loir

This AOC and its cru, Jasnières, the only two vineyards in the Sarthe, occupy the slopes of the Loir valley. About 25 years ago, Coteaux du Loir was on the verge of extinction, but is now fully revived. The vines are planted on silicious clays over tufa. The wines have great appeal, and in 2002 included 1,873 hl of light, fruity reds (Pineau d'Aunis, mixed with Cabernet, Gamay or Côt) and rosés, together with 1,217 hl of dry white (Chenin, known here as Pineau Blanc de la Loire).

BERNARD CROISARD 2002★

| ■ | 2.5 ha | 7,000 | 🍶🍶🍶 | | 5–8 € |

For amateurs of authentic, structured medium-dry wines. The nose reveals flowers and ripe grapefruit, a persistent freshness through to the refreshing finish make this a wine to discover now.
🍷 Bernard Croisard, La Pommeraie, 72340 Chahaignes,
tel. 02.43.44.47.12 ✅
🍽 by appt.

JEAN-JACQUES MAILLET

Réserve d'Automne 2002★★

| ■ | 0.6 ha | 3,000 | 🍶 | | 5–8 € |

The Loir valley does honour to this lovely 2002 that confirms the excellent aptitude of Chenin in this northern region. Here's the splendid Coteaux du Loir from Jean-Jacques Maillet. The silvery white appearance already heralds a pleasant wine. Elegant with its floral notes of acacia and hawthorn, and well balanced on the palate, where jasmine appears, the wine explodes on the finish.
🍷 Jean-Jacques Maillet, La Pâquerie,
72340 Ruillé-sur-Loir, tel. 02.43.44.47.45,
fax 02.43.44.35.30 ✅
🍽 by appt.

LES MAISONS ROUGES 2001★

| ■ | 1.4 ha | 2,700 | 🍶 🍶 | | 3–5 € |

This wine with a light-ruby colour surprises with its spicy notes, typical of the local grape variety, Pineau d'Aunis. The mellow tannins coat the palate. Ready to drink with grilled meat.
🍷 Elisabeth et Benoît Jardin, Les Maisons Rouges, Les Chaudières, 72340 Ruillé-sur-Loir, tel. 02.43.79.50.09,
e-mail maisons.rouges@tiscali.fr ✅
🍽 by appt.

Wines selected but not starred

DOM. BELLEVUE 2002

| ■ | 2 ha | 5,350 | 🍶 | | 3–5 € |

🍷 Thierry Leloup, 1, rue Percheron,
72340 La-Chartre-sur-le-Loir, tel. 02.43.44.57.88,
fax 02.43.44.57.88 ✅
🍽 by appt.

DOM. DE CEZIN 2002

	4 ha	10,000	▮ ♦	3–5 €

➤ François Fresneau, Dom. de Cézin, rue de Cézin,
72340 Marçon, tel. 02.43.44.13.70, fax 02.43.44.13.70,
e-mail earl.francois.fresneau@wanadoo.fr ▨
☗ by appt.

CHRISTOPHE CROISARD

Rasné 2002

	3 ha	8,000	▮	5–8 €

➤ Christophe Croisard, La Pommeraie, 72340 Chahaignes,
tel. 02.43.79.14.90, fax 02.43.79.14.90 ▨
☗ by appt.

DOM. DE LA GAUDINIERE 2001

	1 ha	6,000	▮ ⑪	3–5 €

➤ EARL Claude et Danielle Cartereau, La Gaudinière,
72340 Lhomme, tel. 02.43.44.55.38 ▨
☗ by appt.

PASCAL JANVIER 2002

	1 ha	n.c.	▮	5–8 €

➤ Pascal Janvier, La Minée, 72340 Ruillé-sur-Loir,
tel. 02.43.44.29.65, fax 02.43.79.25.25 ▨
☗ by appt.

Jasnières

This cru within Coteaux du Loir
is precisely delimited on a single south-facing slope, 4
km long and only a few hundred metres wide. In 2002
it produced 2,240 hl of single-variety white Chenin
which can be quite sublime in great years. As one
authority wrote: "Three times in a century, Jasnières
is the best white wine in the world." Experts recommend it as an elegant accompaniment for *marmite
Sarthoise*, a local speciality, as well as for other
delicacies of the region, such as chicken and rabbit
dishes with steamed vegetables. A rare wine in every
sense – a discovery waiting to be made.

DOM. DE CEZIN 2002★

	1.8 ha	8,000	▮ ♦	5–8 €

Actively engaged in the wine syndicate to energize the vineyards of Jasnières, François Fresneau produces wines that are
fairly representative of the AOC. His silvery yellow-grey 2002
has a complex range of flavours. Harmony and balance reign in
this dry wine suitable for ageing, but which can be drunk now.
➤ François Fresneau, Dom. de Cézin, rue de Cézin,
72340 Marçon, tel. 02.43.44.13.70, fax 02.43.44.13.70,
e-mail earl.francois.fresneau@wanadoo.fr ▨
☗ by appt.

DOM. DE LA GAUDINIERE 2002★

	4 ha	10,000	▮	5–8 €

At the origin of the creation of AOC Jasnières in 1937, the
Cartereau family presents a beautiful wine with brioche
aromas and a harmonious body. The long, fresh finish is typical
of the local style.
➤ EARL Claude et Danielle Cartereau, La Gaudinière,
72340 Lhomme, tel. 02.43.44.55.38 ▨
☗ by appt.

DOM. DES GAULETTERIES 2002★

	12 ha	40,000	▮	5–8 €

The Loir valley sometimes resembles a piece of Gruyere, with
so many wine cellars and tunnels burrowing into the hillsides.
Francine and Raynald Lelais will surely take you to discover
their splendid galleries dug out for wine. The Jury found this
same passion in this straw-yellow Jasnières, with its lovely
nose of peach and apricot, perfumes which one finds only in
high-class white wines. Overall there is beautiful balance with
a mineral touch on the finish.
➤ Francine et Raynald Lelais, Les Gauletteries,
72340 Ruillé-sur-Loir, tel. 02.43.79.09.59,
fax 02.43.79.09.59, e-mail vins@domainelelais.com ▨
☗ by appt.

LES MAISONS ROUGES

Les Mollières 2002★

	1.1 ha	3,750	▮ ⑪	5–8 €

Since the creation of this vineyard in 1994, Elisabeth and
Benoît Jardin have continued planting. Today they cultivate
5 ha using sustainable agricultural methods. This attractive 2002 is a typical dry Jasnières. Both floral and lively, it
is enchanting.
➤ Elisabeth et Benoît Jardin, Les Maisons Rouges, Les
Chaudières, 72340 Ruillé-sur-Loir, tel. 02.43.79.50.09,
e-mail maisons.rouges@tiscali.fr ▨
☗ by appt.

DOM. J. MARTELLIERE

Cuvée du Poète 2002★★

	0.21 ha	1,100	⑪	8–11 €

Already appreciated in the *Guide* 2003, the Poète de Joel
Martellière selection achieves success with this new vintage. A
pale-straw colour with silver glints, the nose emanates hazelnut and other mixed nuts, indicating a fine white wine.
Mineral notes and apricot combine well on the full palate. A
rich wine, well made, that needs to be kept for at least five
years and which you could even keep for your child's 20th
birthday. Also particularly commended, in a more classic
style, is the **Cuvée du Vert Galant 2002 (5–8 €)**.
➤ SCEA du Dom. J. Martellière, 46, rue de Fosse,
41800 Montoire-sur-le-Loir, tel. 02.54.85.16.91 ▨
☗ by appt.

BENEDICTE DE RYCKE

Cuvée Louise 2002★

	1.5 ha	7,000	▮ ♦	8–11 €

Pale in colour, the nose is agreeably surprising with its aromas
of grapefruit. The fairly supple palate returns to these ripe
citrus fruit flavours right through to the refreshing finish. This
2002 is irreproachable.
➤ Bénédicte de Rycke, La Pointe, 72340 Marçon,
tel. 02.43.44.46.43, fax 02.43.79.63.54 ▨
☗ by appt.

Wines selected but
not starred

PASCAL JANVIER 2002

	4 ha	7,300	▮	5–8 €

➤ Pascal Janvier, La Minée, 72340 Ruillé-sur-Loir,
tel. 02.43.44.29.65, fax 02.43.79.25.25 ▨
☗ by appt.

LOIRE

JEAN-JACQUES MAILLET 2002

	4 ha	17,000	∎		5–8 €

➤ Jean-Jacques Maillet, La Pâquerie,
72340 Ruillé-sur-Loir, tel. 02.43.44.47.45,
fax 02.43.44.35.30 ✓
⟁ by appt.

JEAN-MARIE RENVOISE 2002

	4 ha	12,000	∎		5–8 €

➤ Jean-Marie Renvoisé, Le Vaugermain,
72340 Chahaignes, tel. 02.43.44.89.37, fax 02.43.44.89.37 ✓
⟁ by appt.

PHILIPPE SEVAULT 2002

	3 ha	12,500	∎		5–8 €

➤ Philippe Sevault, 72340 Poncé-sur-le-Loir,
tel. 02.43.79.07.75, fax 02.43.79.07.75 ✓
⟁ by appt.

Montlouis-sur-Loire

This appellation of 1,000 ha of vines including 400 in the AOC Montlouis-sur-Loire, is bounded by the Loire to the north, the forest of Amboise to the east and the Cher to the south. The flinty clay soils, with sandy overlays in places, are planted with Chenin (Pineau de la Loire) and produce lively white wines of considerable finesse; they can be dry or sweet, still or sparkling. In 2002, 17,870 hl, were produced. The dry wines are aged in bottle in tufa cellars, and can be kept for a good ten years.

ALEX MATHUR
Demi-sec Dionys 2001 ★★

	0.95 ha	3,800	◗◖		5–8 €

Two years ago Eric Gougeat took control of the estate of Claude Levasseur. A big challenge when one remembers the quality of the wines that were produced there. With this attractive medium-dry, It can be said that it was a complete success: beautiful intense colour with yellow-green highlights, well-integrated oak which manifests itself as vanilla, round and full. The richness, sugar and acidity cohabit harmoniously, it is a superb wine. This *coup de coeur* is very encouraging for a newcomer in the appellation.
➤ Dom. Levasseur-Alex Mathur, 38, rue des Bouvineries, Husseau, 37270 Montlouis-sur-Loire, tel. 02.47.50.97.06, fax 02.47.50.96.80 ✓
⟁ by appt.
➤ Eric Gougeat

DOM. AURORE DE BEAUFORT
Moelleux 2001 ★

	1.5 ha	6,000	∎		5–8 €

The Scourion de Beaufort were Jean-Marie Moyer's ancestors and it is Aurore who gave her name to the domaine. Here there is a pretty 19th century manor surrounded by 6 ha of vines and wine cellars dug out of tufa. Two beautiful wines are credited to this young wine producer. The first is sweet with 72 g/l residual sugar, concentrated, with astonishing length and an impression of perfect balance. The second, the **Demi-Sec 2001**, is singled out for its typicity.
➤ Jean-Marie Moyer, 23, rue des Caves, 37270 Saint-Martin-le-Beau, tel. 02.47.50.61.51, fax 02.47.50.27.56,
e-mail aurore-de-beaufort@wanadoo.fr ✓
⟁ ev. day except Sun. 8am–8pm

CLAUDE BOUREAU
Sec Coulée des Muids 2001 ★

	0.5 ha	1000	◗◖		8–11 €

Claude Boureau has done well this year! Two very successful wines. The first, a dry wine, has body and freshness in a range of flavours where flowers and fruits jostle together. A wine destined for seafood. Secondly, the **Méthode Traditionnelle (5–8 €)**, will be very popular at aperitif time.
➤ Claude Boureau, 1, rue de la Résistance, 37270 Saint-Martin-le-Beau, tel. 02.47.50.61.39 ✓
⟁ by appt.

LA CHAPELLE DE CRAY
Méthode traditionnelle Brut 2000 ★

	5.1 ha	48,266	∎ ◊		3–5 €

An English négociant and a Touraine wine producer combined together to handle this significant estate of 65 ha which extends over the hills of Lussault, above the Loire. Their *méthode traditionelle* will please amateurs all over Europe. Its generous mousse, fine bubbles, perfumes of acacia and, especially, its vinosity balanced by a long fresh finish, place it at the forefront of wines of this type.
➤ SARL La Chapelle de Cray, rte de l'Aquarium, 37400 Lussault-sur-Loire, tel. 02.47.57.17.74, fax 02.47.57.11.97,
e-mail chapelledecray@wanadoo.fr
⟁ by appt.
➤ M. Boutinot

LAURENT CHATENAY
Sec Les Maisonnettes 2001 ★★

	1.15 ha	5,000	◗◖		8–11 €

The draftsman Laurent Chatenay didn't know that his fate was to become a winemaker. He arrived here in 1996 after a BTA in viticulture and winemaking, in 1999 he enlarged the estate to 12 ha and, this year, made a crashing entry into the elite of Montlouis wine producers. A *coup de coeur* for this dry Montlouis with touches of oak, but it is full-bodied and fresh. It's not clear whether it should be drunk now or kept. The golden appearance is followed by ripe fruit aromas that transport you to the vineyards, and the overall harmony enchants. But that is not all, the **Moelleux Le Clos Michet 2001 (23–30 € per 50 cl bottle)** is remarkable. And again, the **Demi-Sec La Vallée 2001** receives one star. What a success for this well-launched wine producer who has plenty more surprises in store for us.
➤ Laurent Chatenay, 41, rte de Montlouis, Nouy, 37270 Saint-Martin-le-Beau, tel. 02.47.50.65.58, fax 02.47.50.29.90,
e-mail laurent.chatenay@wanadoo.fr ✓
⟁ by appt.

FRANCOIS CHIDAINE
Méthode traditionnelle★

	n.c.	n.c.	◧	5–8 €

Well-equipped in winemaking material and with deep wine cellars dug into the hillsides of Husseau, François Chidaine achieves good results every year. The *méthode traditionelle* with its generous effervescence has a lasting fruitiness and vinosity. Flavours of biscuit, almond and citrus fruits are present. An attractive, light and well-balanced wine. The lightly oaked **Demi-Sec Clos Habert 2001 (8–11 €)** was singled out.
🕿 GAEC François Chidaine, 5, Grande-Rue,
37270 Montlouis-sur-Loire, tel. 02.47.45.19.14,
fax 02.47.45.19.08, e-mail francois.chidaine@wanadoo.fr ☑
☌ by appt.

FREDERIC COURTEMANCHE
Demi-sec 2001★

	1 ha	3,000	▐	5–8 €

Frédéric Courtemanche in the 2004 *Guide*? Not really a surprise, since this young winemaker regularly produces wines of quality. He presents a medium-dry with a full, silky palate. Delicate minerality and remarkable length make it "a Chenin at its most beautiful," according to the Jury.
🕿 Frédéric Courtemanche, 12, rue d'Amboise,
37270 Saint-Martin-le-Beau, tel. 06.83.07.82.89 ☑
☌ by appt.

DOM. DE LA CROIX MELIER
Moelleux 2000★★

	1 ha	10,000	◧	5–8 €

A late 16th century house, located within a typically Touraine village, continues to use ancient methods in the vineyards and the wine cellar: it is tradition which counts in La Croix Melier. This Moelleux, full of volume, tasty and full bodied, evokes intense flavours of brioche, exotic fruit, apple and lemon. The palate endorses this with apricot, fig and rhubarb, and this fruitiness is lasting. The **Demi-Sec 2001 (3–5 €)** is especially commended.
🕿 Pascal Berthelot, Dom. de La Croix Mélier, 2, chem. Ste-Catherine, 37270 Montlouis-sur-Loire,
tel. 02.47.45.12.14, fax 02.47.50.77.85 ☑
☌ by appt.

SEBASTIEN DELAHAYE
Méthode traditionnelle★

	2 ha	7,000	▐	5–8 €

Sébastien Delahaye updated his winery to enable him to work effectively and receive visitors. In fact he's playing the tourism card. The wine cellar is located near the Aquarium of Touraine, currently in restoration. The Méthode Traditionelle, with its beautiful sparkle, emits scents of apricot and almond. Full of volume and rich, it will go well with a piece of tart. The **Demi-Sec 2001 (3–5 €)** is singled out.
🕿 Sébastien Delahaye, 4, rte d'Amboise,
37400 Lussault-sur-Loire, tel. 02.47.57.66.81,
fax 02.47.57.15.20 ☑
☌ ev. day 9am–7pm

DANIEL FISSELLE
Moelleux 2001★

	1 ha	2,500	▐ ♦	5–8 €

Daniel Fisselle has just built a tasting room for visitors. He will undoubtedly make you taste this Moelleux with 45 g/l residual sugar. Clothed in gold, the wine develops perfumes of pineapple, honey and warm straw, leaving an impression of overripe harvests. The palate, powerful and rich, finishes on a sugary-acid note that will integrate with time.
🕿 Daniel Fisselle, Les Caves du Verger, 74, rte de Saint-Aignan, 37270 Montlouis-sur-Loire,
tel. 02.47.50.93.59, fax 02.47.50.93.59 ☑
☌ ev. day 10am–8pm

ALAIN JOULIN
Demi-sec 2001★

	1 ha	3,500	▐	3–5 €

A well-made, pale yellow medium-dry, coming from the hillsides of the Cher which have made a reputation for the wines of Saint-Martin-le-Beau. This wine is packed with flavours of quince jam, apples and apricots. Rich from the start, it acquires finesse with a good balance between softness and freshness. Well balanced and with some length, it is a typical wine of the appellation.
🕿 Alain Joulin, 58, rue de Chenonceaux,
37270 Saint-Martin-le-Beau, tel. 02.47.50.28.49,
fax 02.47.50.69.73 ☑
☌ ev. day 9am–12 noon 2pm–7pm

DOM. DES LIARDS Moelleux La Montée des Liards Vieilles Vignes 2001★

	n.c.	11,000	▐ ♦	5–8 €

Five generations have succeeded one another on this domaine, which today covers nearly 20 ha on the Cher hillsides. The younger generation still rely on their parents, the two Berger brothers have made a name for the business and have everything in hand; the proof shows in this Moelleux that opens on honey and fruit, with the right balance between roundness and freshness. A return to the fruit on the finish, it is a true pleasure.
🕿 EARL Berger Frères, 33, rue de Chenonceaux,
37270 Saint-Martin-le-Beau, tel. 02.47.50.67.36,
fax 02.47.50.21.13 ☑
☌ by appt.

DOM. SAINT-GEROME
Moelleux Cuvée Saint-Gérôme 2001★

	3 ha	1,500	▐ ♦	11–15 €

Jacky Supligeau managed this estate of 10 ha, located on the hillsides of the Loire, for 25 years (a situation favourable for overripening and the production of high-class sweet wines. Here is an attractive wine with a brilliant gold colour, hinting at honey, crystallized fruit and ripe grapes. From the first impression it is well balanced, and this is confirmed by signs of a perfect maturity and a finish without excessive sweetness. A rich wine that will always be drunk too early.
🕿 Jacky Supligeau, 7, quai Albert-Baillet,
37270 Montlouis-sur-Loire, tel. 02.47.45.07.75,
fax 02.47.45.07.75 ☑
☌ by appt.

DOM. DE LA TAILLE AUX LOUPS
Sec Cuvée Rémus 2001★

	8 ha	15,000	◧	8–11 €

Here is Rémus, which achieved success with the 2000 vintage. The 2001 exudes wood, admittedly, but with some reserve, and with sweet spices, dried fruits and vanilla. The oaky attack quickly rounds off in the full, rich body, while the finish is long and fresh. The components of this wine must integrate to achieve harmony. The **Montlouis Sec Dix Arpents 2001 (5–8 €)** is also singled out.
🕿 Dom. de la Taille aux Loups, 8, rue des Aitres,
37270 Montlouis-sur-Loire, tel. 02.47.45.11.11,
fax 02.47.45.11.14,
e-mail la-taille-aux-loups@wanadoo.fr ☑
☌ ev. day 9am–6pm; cl. Sun. Nov.–Mar.
🕿 Jacky Blot

DOM. DES TOURTERELLES
Méthode traditionnelle★

	2 ha	4,000	▐	5–8 €

The clay-limestone and siliceous slopes of the Cher hillsides can be alluded to as the heart of the appellation. This Méthode Traditionelle with its abundant mousse and flowery, fruity nose with hints of coffee derives from here. The palate starts with freshness but quickly opens out to reveal suppleness and good balance. Almond and lemon on the finish, very surprising. The **Méthode Traditional Demi-Sec** is singled out.
🕿 Jean-Pierre Trouvé, 1, rue de la Gare,
37270 Saint-Martin-le-Beau, tel. 02.47.50.63.62,
fax 02.47.50.63.62 ☑
☌ by appt.

LOIRE

Wines selected but not starred

Vouvray

PATRICE BENOIT
Demi-sec 2001

	1 ha	2,500	⬛	3–5 €
☛ Patrice Benoît, 3, rue des Jardins, Nouy,
37270 Saint-Martin-le-Beau, tel. 02.47.50.62.46,
fax 02.47.50.63.93 ☑
☥ by appt.

THIERRY CHAPUT
Demi-sec 2000

	1.25 ha	5,000	⬛⬛⬥	5–8 €
☛ Thierry Chaput, 21, rue des Rocheroux, Husseau,
37270 Montlouis-sur-Loire, tel. 02.47.50.80.70,
fax 02.47.50.71.46 ☑
☥ by appt.

DOM. DES CHARDONNERETS
Méthode traditionnelle 2000

	2.5 ha	16,000	⬛⬥	5–8 €
☛ GAEC Daniel et Thierry Mosny, 6, rue des Vignes,
37270 Saint-Martin-le-Beau, tel. 02.47.50.61.84,
fax 02.47.50.61.84 ☑ ☗
☥ ev. day 8am–7pm

DOM. DE L'ENTRE-COEURS
Méthode traditionnelle 2001

	1.3 ha	9,000	⬛⬥	5–8 €
☛ Alain Lelarge, 10, rue d'Amboise,
37270 Saint-Martin-le-Beau, tel. 02.47.50.61.70,
fax 02.47.50.68.92 ☑
☥ by appt.

JEAN-PAUL HABERT
Méthode traditionnelle

	2.5 ha	10,000	⬛⬥	5–8 €
☛ Jean-Paul Habert, Le Gros Buisson, 3, imp. des Noyers,
37270 Saint-Martin-le-Beau, tel. 02.47.50.26.47,
fax 02.47.50.26.47 ☑
☥ by appt.

CAVE DE MONTLOUIS-SUR-LOIRE
Cuvée Réservée Méthode traditionnelle 2000

	5 ha	30,000	⬛⬥	5–8 €
☛ Cave Coop. des Producteurs de Montlouis-sur-Loire, 2,
rte de Saint-Aignan, 37270 Montlouis-sur-Loire,
tel. 02.47.50.80.98, fax 02.47.50.81.34,
e-mail cave-montlouis@france-vin.com ☑
☥ by appt.

CH. DE PINTRAY
Sec Elevé en fût de chêne 2001

	5 ha	1000	⬛	5–8 €
☛ Marius Rault, Ch. de Pintray, 37400 Lussault-sur-Loire,
tel. 02.47.23.22.84, fax 02.47.57.64.27,
e-mail marius.rault@wanadoo.fr ☑ ☗
☥ ev. day 9am–8pm

DOM. DE LA ROCHEPINAL
Sec 2001

	0.85 ha	5,000	⬛⬥	5–8 €
☛ Hervé Denis, 4, rue de la Barre,
37270 Montlouis-sur-Loire, tel. 02.47.45.16.65,
fax 02.47.50.71.70 ☑
☥ by appt.

Vouvray

Vouvray's full qualities become apparent only after a long time in cellar and in bottle. These whites come from an appellation of 2,000 ha in the north of the Loire, stretching across the wide valley of the river Brenne, with the A10 motorway cutting through its northern tip (though the TGV express train goes through a tunnel). Here Chenin (Pineau de la Loire) and Sauvignon are used in the production of still wines, dry or sweet depending on the year, of very high quality. Fizzy or sparkling wines with a high alcohol content, are also produced. The sparkling wines should be drunk young, while the still wines can be kept for a long time, giving them time to develop aromatic complexity. Fish and goat's cheese go well with some, delicate dishes or light desserts with others, and the wines also make excellent aperitifs. In 2002, 115,903 hl were produced.

JEAN-CLAUDE ET DIDIER AUBERT
Demi-sec 2000★

	6 ha	30,000	⬛⬥	5–8 €
Father and son complement one another on this 25-hectare estate. The winery, situated just two paces away from the Loire, is well equipped to control the fermentation process. This medium-dry *méthode traditionnelle* has an intense-yellow straw colour and fine bubbles. On the nose it is slightly floral while the palate is delicate, dominated by orchard fruits, and successfully combines together both sugar and acidity; the finish leaves an impression of sweetness. The **Vouvray Sec 2001**, matured for seven months in tank and seven months in barrel, is commended.
☛ Jean-Claude et Didier Aubert, 10, rue de la Vallée-Coquette, 37210 Vouvray, tel. 02.47.52.71.03, fax 02.47.52.68.38 ☑
☥ ev. day 8.30am–12.30pm 2pm–7pm

DOM. DU BAS-ROCHER
Brut 2001★

	1.5 ha	6,000	⬛	5–8 €
In this part of Vouvray, the tufa forms a cliff; the vines dominate the bed of the Loire, receiving the sun's rays and maritime influences. After the death of his father, Christophe Boutet-Saulnier and his mother, Monique, created a GAEC to handle this estate of almost 8 ha. They form a solid and experienced team. Their *méthode traditionnelle* is very characteristic and could accompany a whole meal, provided that the principal dish is white meat. Mineral notes hide behind citrus fruit aromas. The palate is both soft and agreeably lively. The **Vouvray Sec 2001** is singled out for its touch of bitter.
☛ GAEC Boutet-Saulnier, 17, rue de la Vallée-Chartier, 37210 Vouvray, tel. 02.47.52.73.61, fax 02.47.52.63.27 ☑
☥ by appt.

PASCAL BERTEAU ET VINCENT MABILLE Demi-sec★

	14 ha	5,000	⬛⬥	3–5 €
Two young entrepreneurial winemakers took over this estate of 18 ha from their parents. There are not many good medium-dry Vouvrays, but here is one that deserves a mention. Behind its abundant and persistent mousse, with fine and delicate bubbles, it presents an attractive nose with characteristic and subtle aromas. The balance between softness and freshness is almost perfect.
☛ GAEC BM P. Berteau - V. Mabille, Vaugondy, 37210 Vernou-sur-Brenne, tel. 02.47.52.03.43, fax 02.47.52.03.43 ☑
☥ by appt.
☛ P. Berteau et V. Mabille

DOM. DE LA BLOTIERE

Brut 2000★

	2 ha	13,000	🍷	5–8 €

Blotière is a typical Touraine house made from white tufa. Surrounded by 11 ha of vines, it is located at the top of the Vouvray hills. The grapes mature well there, giving beautiful results: a *méthode traditionnelle* with lovely Chenin characteristics. Richness, freshness, good length: a sparkling wine which will improve with a little time. The **Vouvray Sec 2001** (3–5 €) is commended – a good and well-balanced wine.
➤ Jean-Michel Fortineau, La Blotière, 37210 Vouvray, tel. 02.47.52.74.24, fax 02.47.52.65.11 Ⓥ
☓ by appt.

BONGARS

Moelleux Cuvée Marine 2001★

	1 ha	5,000	🍷 ◊	5–8 €

After her father retired in 1996, Denise Bongars energetically took over the vineyard with her mother's help and Lucette and Denise form an efficient team. Marine, Denise's daughter, gave her name to this beautiful *moelleux* wine with 47 g/l residual sugar. An intense citrus fruit nose, which evolves to reveal vanilla and flowers, a fairly rich and complex palate with a good sugar-acid balance already make this a wine of some interest that will also develop with time.
➤ Denise et Lucette Bongars, 232, coteau de Venise, 37210 Noizay, tel. 02.47.52.11.64, fax 02.47.52.05.73 Ⓥ
☓ by appt.

MARC BREDIF

Brut★★

	10 ha	50,000	🍷 ◊	5–8 €

The Brédif company is the flagship of the Vouvray terroir. Created in 1893, it has an immense wine cellar dug into the rock which visitors admire: long galleries where oak barrels are aligned, a circular wine tasting room, old wooden wine-presses from centuries past. The art of blending and a modern winery produce the quality sparkling wines that remain the speciality of the house. This *méthode traditionnelle* received nothing but compliments. The nose is packed with gingerbread and caramel; the round palate has a richness evoking brioche and a very long finish. A wine that is not far from achieving a *coup de cœur*. Also remarkable, the **Vouvray Sec Vigne Blanche 2001** will accompany grilled lobster perfectly.
➤ Marc Brédif, 87, quai de la Loire, 37210 Rochecorbon, tel. 02.47.52.50.07, fax 02.47.52.53.41, e-mail bredif.loire@wanadoo.fr Ⓥ
☓ by appt.

YVES BREUSSIN

Brut★

	4 ha	15,000	🍷 ◊	3–5 €

Yves and Denis Breussin will receive you in a room dug into the rock which was formerly the winemaker's dwelling; in front of a good fire, they will speak to you about the country and discuss their wines, such as this *méthode traditionnelle brut*. The nose is fine, floral, with subtly lactic notes and caramel. The palate has a touch of brioche and smoky and toasty tones, with good length finishing on an attractive note of apricot.
➤ EARL Yves et Denis Breussin, Vaugondy, 37210 Vernou-sur-Brenne, tel. 02.47.52.18.75, fax 02.47.52.13.66, e-mail breussindenis@aol.com Ⓥ
☓ by appt.

DOM. GEORGES BRUNET

Demi-sec 2001★

	2 ha	3,000	🍷	5–8 €

This 13-hectare vineyard is situated on *aubuis* (clay-limestone) soils at the top of the slopes of the Vallée Coquette, where the exposure and the flint are major assets. This medium-dry is well made and very open, evoking vanilla, custard cream with underlying honey notes, quince and acacia. The palate takes over with crystallized fruit, rose jam and exotic touches that persist through to the finish. A wine which will go well with dessert.

➤ Georges Brunet, 12, rue de la Croix-Mariotte, 37210 Vouvray, tel. 02.47.52.60.36, fax 02.47.52.75.38, e-mail info@vouvray-brunet.com Ⓥ
☓ ev. day 9am–8pm

OLIVIER CAREME

Brut 2000★

	n.c.	n.c.		5–8 €

Finesse and delicacy are the characteristics of this *méthode traditionnelle*. A bright colour, some flowers on the nose and ripe fruits on the palate: a wine to enjoy amongst friends
➤ Olivier Carême, 14, rue de la Vallée-Chartier, 37210 Vouvray, tel. 02.47.52.69.69, fax 02.47.62.69.79 Ⓥ
☓ by appt.

JEAN-CHARLES CATHELINEAU

Pétillant 1998★

	n.c.	9,000	🍷 ◊	3–5 €

The property of Jean-Charles Cathelineau, Les Devants in the Vau valley, dates from the 18th century. For over six generations the domaine has been enlarged, improved and refurbished. One can visit the troglodyte house of their ancestors and a small wine museum. This year, two sparkling wines were awarded one star: the **Demi-Sec**, very soft and subtle, will drink well with a tart, and this delicately sparkling wine, which is nicely fruity and round. This type of wine is less and less frequent in Vouvray, with the pressure in the bottle half that of a classic *méthode traditionnelle*.
➤ Jean-Charles Cathelineau, 24, rue des Violettes, 37210 Chançay, tel. 02.47.52.20.61, fax 02.47.52.20.61 Ⓥ
☓ by appt.

DOM. CHAMPION

Brut★★

	5 ha	5,000	🍷 ◊	5–8 €

Take a walk in the Cousse de Vernou valley, kitted out with your rucksack. Along the picturesque walk you should stop at Pierre Champion to taste this well-made *méthode traditionnelle*: brioche and mixed nuts on the nose, a full-bodied palate that reflects the terroir, and a round finish. You will also appreciate the **Demi-Sec 2001**, awarded one star, and the **Sec 2001**, which is commended.
➤ EARL Pierre Champion, 57, Vallée-de-Cousse, 37210 Vernou-sur-Brenne, tel. 02.47.52.02.38, fax 02.47.52.05.69 Ⓥ
☓ ev. day except Sun. 8am–12.30pm 2pm–7pm

CLOS DE NOUYS

Sec 2001★★

	4 ha	20,000	🍶	8–11 €

Success has come to this property of 15 ha located on the slopes of the appellation that counts amongst the oldest in Vouvrillon. Firstly, there is this dry Vouvray with its intense golden-yellow colour enlivened with bright green glints. It discloses intense ripe fruit and spring flower aromas enhanced with a little oak. It opens with suppleness and then moves on to reveal a well-balanced body and just the right amount of freshness. A well-blended oaky note does not harm the elegance and finesse found on the finish. The **Moelleux 2001** also obtains two stars for its full-flavoured richness and balance. Cheers to this winemaker!
➤ Clos de Nouys, 46, rue de la Vallée-de-Nouys, 37210 Vouvray, tel. 02.47.52.73.35, fax 02.47.52.06.09 Ⓥ
➤ F. Chainier

DOM. DU CLOS DES AUMONES

Brut 2000★

	3 ha	27,000	🍷 ◊	8–11 €

A district of Vouvrillon where the wine is famous for its character. This *méthode traditionnelle* brilliant with gold highlights, seems a little timid at first but then releases perfumes of flowers and ripe fruit. Lively but not aggressive, well balanced with good length of citrus fruit flavours.
➤ Philippe Gaultier, 10, rue Vaufoynard, 37210 Rochecorbon, tel. 02.47.54.69.82, fax 02.47.42.62.01, e-mail domaine-du-clos-des-aumones@nomade.fr Ⓥ
☓ by appt.

LOIRE

LE CLOS DU PORTAIL
Sec 2001★★

	12 ha	2,400	⑪	11–15 €

Didier and Catherine Champalou have place of honor in the *Guide* with three beautiful wines. The first, a dry Vouvray Le Clos du Portail, impresses with its structure, full body and near-perfect balance. Still with strong oak character, it must stay in the wine cellar until this softens out. The **Champalou Sec 2001 (5–8 €)** has admittedly less personality, but seems smoother at present; it obtains one star. The **Moelleux 2001**, with intense quince and acacia flavours enriched with grilled notes, was also singled out by the Jury.
↬ Catherine et Didier Champalou, Le Portail, 7, rue du Grand-Ormeau, 37210 Vouvray, tel. 02.47.52.64.49, fax 02.47.52.67.99, e-mail champalou@wanadoo.fr ☒
🍷 by appt.

JEAN-PAUL COUAMAIS
Moelleux 2001★

	3 ha	20,000	🍶 ♠	3–5 €

It needs a quick swirl in the glass to reveal the floral (acacia) aromas on a honey background. A pale-yellow colour and promising flavours are joined on the palate by richness and a lovely balance. However, the whole needs to integrate. A wine for ageing.
↬ Jean-Paul Couamais, 8, rue du Haut-Cousse, 37210 Vernou-sur-Brenne, tel. 02.47.52.18.93, fax 02.47.52.04.91 ☒
🍷 by appt.

MAISON DARRAGON
Brut Cuvée antique 2000★★

	n.c.	n.c.		5–8 €

Cuvée antique: should this *méthode traditionelle* be presented in an amphora? Not at all. If they make an allusion to the past at the Darragons it is merely with respect for tradition. Due to limited yields and meticulous winemaking, this wine expresses Chenin perfectly. The fine and dynamic bubbles on a background of yellow straw seem to support the richness. The palate is very powerful, full-flavoured, rich and very long. It is rare to find such definition of the grape variety in a sparkling wine. The characteristic, **Demi-Sec Les Hauts des Ruettes 2001** is singled out.
↬ SCA Maison Darragon, 34, rue de Sanzelle, 37210 Vouvray, tel. 02.47.52.74.49, fax 02.47.52.64.96
🍷 by appt.

REGIS FORTINEAU
Brut 2000★

	1 ha	5,000	🍶	5–8 €

The 11 ha of Régis Fortineau's vines are well placed in the heart of the Vouvrillon and Coquette valleys, on stony *aubuis* (clay-limestone) soils, south-facing and close to the Loire. The winery is well equipped. All that remains for the winemaker to do is show his talent. This *méthode traditionelle*, pale-yellow with green highlights, has a delicate citrus fruit aroma. After a rather lively start, the palate reveals good balance, with an attractive touch of breadcrumbs on the finish. The commended **Méthode Traditionnelle Demi-Sec 2000** needs a little time in the cellar.
↬ Régis Fortineau, 4, rue de la Croix-Mariotte, 37210 Vouvray, tel. 02.47.52.63.62, fax 02.47.52.69.97 ☒
🍷 by appt.

DOM. FRESLIER
Brut★

	5 ha	13,000	⑪	5–8 €

Jean-Pierre and Christine Freslier are a friendly couple of wine producers, who enjoy entertaining. They present a *méthode traditionelle* that one would like to find more often from this terroir: it has agreeably surprising finesse and elegance. Delightful aromas of gingerbread, ripe fruit and citrus fruits reappear on the palate. A delicately rich wine that will be appreciated by everyone as an aperitif.
↬ Dom. Jean-Pierre and Christine Freslier, 92, rue de la Vallée-Coquette, 37210 Vouvray, tel. 02.47.52.76.61, fax 02.47.52.78.65 ☒ ☎
🍷 ev. day except Sun. 8am–12 noon 2pm–7pm

CH. GAUDRELLE
Sec 2001★

	2 ha	6,000	⑪	8–11 €

This country house is mentioned in departmental records since the 16th century. This admirably situated 14-hectare vineyard dominates the village of Vouvray. Alexandre Monmousseau manages everything with dynamism and enthusiasm. His dry Vouvray explodes with ripe fruit and almonds, whereas the wood remains discreet and takes some time to make an appearance. The soft opening is followed by some freshness that adds balance. The oak influence reappears. Allow this pretty wine to evolve so that the stamp of maturation mellows.
↬ EARL A. Monmousseau, 87, rte de Monnaie, 37210 Vouvray, tel. 02.47.52.67.50, fax 02.47.52.67.98, e-mail gaudrelle1@libertysurf.fr ☒
🍷 ev. day 8am–12 noon 2pm–6pm

DOM. SYLVAIN GAUDRON
Brut★★

	6 ha	40,000	🍶 ♠	5–8 €

Vernou, a village where one finds the good life, with its shaded square, its charming 12th century church and, especially, its rue Neuve along which Jeanne d' Arc rode on the way to Orléans; today, both sides of the road are lined with nothing but wine cellars and wineries. Gilles Gaudron, who succeeded his father Sylvain, presents three beautiful wines this year. The *methode traditionelle* with its yellow colour and characteristic nose suggests moderate notes of caramel and pear. The supple palate, long and winey with good vinosity, returns to the pear and caramel tones. A wine to drink as an aperitif. The **Vouvray Sec 2001** and the **Demi-Sec 2001** (both 3–5 €) each obtain one star.
↬ EARL Dom. Sylvain Gaudron, 59, rue Neuve, 37210 Vernou-sur-Brenne, tel. 02.47.52.12.27, fax 02.47.52.05.05 ☒
🍷 by appt.
↬ Gilles Gaudron

DOM. GENDRON
Brut Cuvée Extra Réserve 1997★★

	1 ha	5,500	🍶 ⑪ ♠	5–8 €

Leaving the wines on the lees for several years contributes to the quality. This attractive 97 proclaims its date of birth with a bright-gold colour and assertive aromas evocative of old Vouvray. The first impression is remarkable, with an imposing effervescence accompanied by flavours of sweet chestnut. The finish is long with a little roundness that confirms the mature character of the wine and that will please delicate palates. The **Brut 2000 (3–5 €)** is awarded one star.
↬ EARL Dom. Philippe Gendron, 10, rue de la Fuye, 37210 Vouvray, tel. 02.47.52.63.98, fax 02.47.52.74.71 ☒
🍷 ev. day except Sun. 8.30am–12.30pm 2pm–8pm; cl. 1–15 Aug.

DOM. DE LA HAUTE BORNE
Tendre 2001★

	1 ha	3,000	⑪	8–11 €

Vincent Carême has been running this 7-hectare estate with the help of his father since 1999. While waiting to be able expand, he is refining his vineyards and wines. He says that his dry Vouvray is "slightly sweet" because it has a little residual sugar. This type of wine accompanies white sauces very well. Rich and lengthy, this 2001 has plenty of flavours: pear, Mirabelle plum, vanilla – nearly atypical, but a very good wine.
↬ Vincent Carême, 6, allée de la Vallée-Chartier, 37210 Vouvray, tel. 02.47.52.71.28 ☒
🍷 by appt.

DANIEL JARRY
Demi-sec 2001★

	0.25 ha	2,000	⑪	3–5 €

Nearing retirement, Daniel Jarry is a little less active now but still looks after the wine production and does it very well. Look at this structured, lively wine, made for keeping. Already full-flavoured (acacia, notes of overripening), it will open out and reveal a more nicely-balanced profile in three or four years.

☛ Daniel Jarry, 99, rue de la Vallée-Coquette, 37210 Vouvray, tel. 02.47.52.78.75, fax 02.47.52.67.36 ☑
⟜ ev. day 8am–7pm

DOM. LE CAPITAINE 2000★

	10 ha	25,000	⬛ ⬗		5–8 €

Two brothers, Alain and Christophe Le Capitaine, began as farm labourers ten years ago, before building up this estate of 18 ha on the best slopes of the appellation. One will not be astonished to see them often mentioned in the *Guide*. Their *méthode traditionelle* catches the eye. Surprising with its roundness on the attack, it discloses a typical Vouvray character. A long finish on this wine reflects its terroir beautifully.

☛ Alain et Christophe Le Capitaine, 23, rue du Cdt-Mathieu, 37210 Rochecorbon, tel. 02.47.52.53.86, fax 02.47.52.85.23, e-mail lecapitainealain@aol.com ☑
⟜ by appt.

DOM. DES LOCQUETS

Demi-sec★

	3 ha	20,000	⬛ ⬗		5–8 €

Stéphane Deniau took over this property of 12 ha, which belonged formerly to the abbey of Marmoutier. However the wine presented was made by his father, Michel, an important figure in the wine world of Vouvray. Gentle, with a delicate finish and harmony, which is just how this type of wine should be, this medium-dry wine opens out with floral, slightly spicy notes. Ideal with a tart or marzipan cake.

☛ Michel Deniau, 27, rue des Locquets, 37210 Parçay-Meslay, tel. 02.47.29.15.29, fax 02.47.29.15.29, e-mail stephanedeniau2@wanadoo.fr ☑
⟜ by appt.

FRANCIS MABILLE

Brut 2000★

	1.7 ha	14,700	⬛ ⬗		5–8 €

This *méthode traditionelle brut* is attractive with a fine mousse on a clear and bright background. The first impression is fruity, especially of white-fleshed peach, which then opens out to give an impression of lightness. The length is good. An aperitif wine and a wine of honour – both custom made.

☛ EARL Francis Mabille, 17, Vallée-de-Vaugondy, 37210 Vernou-sur-Brenne, tel. 02.47.52.01.87, fax 02.47.52.19.41 ☑
⟜ by appt.

DOM. DE LA MABILLIERE

Demi-sec 2001★

	1.8 ha	2,500			8–11 €

At La Mabillière they follow the trend by presenting organic wines. Consumers who are trying to go back to nature will appreciate two pretty wines. The first, a bright straw-yellow medium-dry wine, combines aromas of citrus fruit, over-ripened fruit and honey. The palate, round and rich, enlivened by a touch of freshness, is true to type. Drink now. The second, a **Méthode Traditionelle Brut**, which was commended, has a mineral character.

☛ Dom. de la Mabillière, 16, rue Anatole-France, 37210 Vernou-sur-Brenne, tel. 02.47.52.10.03, fax 02.47.52.14.98 ☑
⟜ by appt.

GILLES MADRELLE

Moelleux 2001★★

	0.3 ha	1000	⬛		5–8 €

Considerable scientific know-how and effort were necessary to produce *moelleux* wines in 2001. Here is one which is extraordinary: clear appearance, subtle floral nose, full bodied and rich on the palate where honey, exotic fruit and toasty notes appear in equal quantities, and with a superb length predicting a promising future. Congratulations to Gilles Madrelle who has played a masterstroke.

☛ EARL Gilles Madrelle, 24, rue de la Vallée-Chartier, 37210 Vouvray, tel. 02.47.52.78.59, fax 02.47.52.78.59 ☑ ⌂
⟜ by appt.

LAURENT ET FABRICE MAILLET

Brut 1999★★

	4.3 ha	25,000	⬛ ⬗⬗		5–8 €

Marc Maillet retired after 45 years of hard work; his two sons, Laurent and Fabrice, gradually took over these 22 ha bordering the Vallée Coquette. Two young, open-minded and hard-working people, who find in this *coup de coeur* the reward for their efforts. "It is a still wine that would have bubbles," said a member of the Jury. The abundant mousse persists a long time before it diminishes to a light sparkle. The nose sways between honey and apricot with a citrus fruit touch. On the palate there is roundness, fruit and harmony. A fine representative of the appellation which will drink well during the entire meal. The **Moelleux Vouvray Coulée d'Or 2001 (8–11 €)** gains one star.

☛ EARL Laurent et Fabrice Maillet, 101, rue de la Vallée-Coquette, 37210 Vouvray, tel. 02.47.52.76.46, fax 02.47.52.63.06 ☑
⟜ ev. day 9am–7pm; groups by appt.

DOM. DU MARGALLEAU

Demi-sec 2001★

	n.c.	n.c.	⬛ ⬗		5–8 €

A fine success for Bruno and Jean-Michel Pieaux this year: three wines have been selected. The medium-dry is very typical of the appellation: a bouquet exploding with honey, where acacia and overripe grapes herald a long, rich palate and where softness and freshness are perfectly combined. The **Vouvray Sec 2001** and the **Méthode Traditionelle Brut** are singled out.

☛ GAEC Bruno et Jean-Michel Pieaux, Vallée de Vaux, rue du Clos-Baglin, 37210 Chançay, tel. 02.47.52.25.51, fax 02.47.52.27.59 ☑
⟜ by appt.

DOM. DE LA POULTIERE

Demi-sec 2000★

	2 ha	10,000	⬛ ⬗		3–5 €

Damien Pinon joined his father Michel on the domaine two years ago. The medium-dry sparkling wine has a palate invaded with finesse and a lengthy soft finish with hints of apple, honey and acacia. Perfect aperitif wine as an accompaniment to delicious biscuits.

☛ Michel et Damien Pinon, 29, rte de Châteaurenault, 37210 Vernou-sur-Brenne, tel. 02.47.52.15.16, fax 02.47.52.07.07 ☑
⟜ by appt.

DOM. DE POUVRAY

Demi-sec 2000★

	3.3 ha	26,630	⬛ ⬗		5–8 €

In the heart of the Vernou terroir, from Cousse to Vaugondy, the Pouvray estate vineyards cover more than 20 ha. Gilbert Vincendeau, who produces wines using traditional methods, presents a medium-dry wine of character, with substantial structure. Rich on the nose with aromas such as apple, acacia and breadcrumbs, the palate is balanced right through to the finish where one finds a touch of sweetness. A nicely-balanced wine. The **Méthode Traditionelle Brut** is singled out.

☛ Gilbert Vincendeau, Dom. de Pouvray, 37210 Vernou-sur-Brenne, tel. 02.47.52.02.36, fax 02.47.52.09.82, e-mail gilbert.vincendeau@terre-net.fr ☑
⟜ by appt.

LOIRE

Vouvray

DOM. DE LA RACAUDERIE
Demi-sec 2001★

| | 1 ha | 2,000 | 🍾 ⚭ | 5–8 € |

A small wine village now threatened by urbanization; Parçay-Meslay still keeps its position in Vouvrillon because of its quality terroir recognized since the fourth century, when the abbey of Marmoutier added its vineyard to it. This well-made medium-dry wine, with a floral and honeyed nose and slight Muscat grape character, presents freshness, balance, length and typicity. It is to drink now. From the same terroir, the **Méthode Traditionelle Brut 2000** is awarded one star.
🍷 Jean-Michel Gautier, La Racauderie,
37210 Parçay-Meslay, tel. 02.47.29.12.82,
fax 02.47.29.12.82 ☑
🍾 by appt.

VINCENT RAIMBAULT
Demi-sec 2001★

| | 1,2 | 7,000 | 🍾 ⚭ | 5–8 € |

The Atlantic influences that have allowed the Chenin grape, a late-ripening variety, to adapt to the Touraine climate pass through the Brenne, a tributary of the Loire. The estate belonging to Vincent Raimbault covers the hillsides that skirt this river, and the grapes easily attain their full maturity. This medium-dry wine develops a beautiful aromatic composition; the first impression is a little lively but balance is soon restored. Powerful and lengthy, this characteristic wine is suited to laying down. The equally characteristic **Méthode Traditionelle Brut 2000** is commended.
🍷 Vincent Raimbault, 9, rue des Violettes, 37210 Chançay, tel. 02.47.52.92.13, fax 02.47.52.24.90 ☑
🍾 ev. day except Sun. 9.30am–12.30pm 2pm–7pm; cl. 10–20 Aug.

VIGNOBLE ALAIN ROBERT ET FILS
Sec Cuvée La Sablonnière 2001★★

| | 0.6 ha | 4,200 | 🍾 ⚭ | 3–5 € |

Alain Robert's vineyard is well established on the slopes of the left bank of the Brenne, a tributary of the Loire. With its southwesterly exposition, it receives the maritime air that goes up the valley, coming from the river, which is beneficial for the maturation of the grapes. This privileged situation is the reason for the high quality of this dry wine, but don't forget that it is attributed also to the meticulous care during the harvest and the practice of a *maceration pelliculaire* (five hours before pressing). Fairly intense gold, this 2001 presents a powerful, rich nose that covers the range of flavours of *moelleux* wines. Freshness and richness create a balance on the palate and eventually integrate on the finish. A Vouvray which will have more to offer in a few years.
🍷 Vignoble Alain Robert et Fils, Charmigny, 37210 Chançay, tel. 02.47.52.97.95, fax 02.47.52.27.24, e-mail vignoblerobert@wanadoo.fr ☑
🍾 by appt.

DOM. DE LA ROCHE FLEURIE
Moelleux 2001★

| | 1 ha | 3,000 | 🍾 | 5–8 € |

Michel Brunet started in 1974, by renting a patch of vines. Due to his hard work and tenacity, the estate has expanded and today consists of nearly 13 ha. His son has worked with him for three years. Their bright-yellow *moelleux* with green

tinges, seems a little timid at first but it opens gradually with exotic fruits and hot apple. The apple flavour returns on the palate, adding an overall lightness and balance. The finish is a bit short but that doesn't diminish the qualities of this wine. The **Méthode Traditionelle Demi-Sec 2000 (3–5 €)** also gains one star.
🍷 Michel Brunet, 6, rue Roche-Fleurie, 37210 Chancay, tel. 02.47.52.90.72 ☑
🍾 ev. day except Sun. 8am–12.30pm 2pm–7pm; cl. from 15–31 Aug

DOM. DE LA ROULETIERE
Brut★

| | 9 ha | 30,000 | 🍾 ⚭ | 5–8 € |

A long time ago, the abbey of Marmoutier established a vineyard at Parçay-Meslay. It was also in this village, at the La Rouletière estate, that Gilet produced the first *méthode traditionelle* in the 1950s. Their experience explains the quality of this wine with its fine and abundant mousse, evocative of brioche and acacia. Having good potential, this wine will be able to evolve well. The characteristic **Vouvray Sec 2001 (3–5 €)** is awarded one star.
🍷 SCEA Gilet, Dom. de La Rouletière, 20, rue de la Mairie, 37210 Parçay-Meslay, tel. 02.47.29.14.88, fax 02.47.29.08.50, e-mail scea.gilet@wanadoo.fr ☑
🍾 ev. day 10am–12 noon 3pm–7pm; Sun. by appt.

ERIC ET YVES THOMAS
Demi-sec★

| | 4 ha | 20,000 | | 3–5 € |

Two cousins joined up to work this small vineyard of 8.5 ha which they run for their parents. They are renowned for producing medium-dry *méthode traditionelle*. This wine presents a beautiful mousse and a persistent stream of bubbles. The nose remains discreet, but on the palate the grape variety is to the fore. An elegant finish of apple and pear leaves its signature on the wine.
🍷 GAEC Yves et Eric Thomas, 10, rue des Boissières, 37210 Parçay-Meslay, tel. 02.47.29.09.13, fax 02.47.29.09.13 ☑
🍾 by appt.

DOM. DU VIEUX BUIS
Brut Cuvée Fin de Siècle★

| | 0.5 ha | 4,000 | 🍾 | 8–11 € |

A generous mousse gradually abates to permit the appearance of a gold-yellow colour with fine beads. If the nose is spicy, this doesn't reappear on the palate. This wine is dominated by Chenin grown on tufa, a perfect expression of the terroir. It all hamonizes beautifully on the finish for this authentic *méthode traditionelle*.
🍷 Alain Rohart, 85 bis, rte de Monnaie, La Loge, 37210 Vouvray, tel. 02.47.52.63.70, fax 02.47.52.76.55, e-mail alain.rohart@caramail.com ☑
🍾 by appt.

DOM. VIGNEAU-CHEVREAU
Sec 2001★

| | 4 ha | 20,000 | 🍾🍾 | 5–8 € |

Five generations have participated in the development of this 26-hectare vineyard. This pale-yellow dry Vouvray, grown on siliceous-clay soil, does not lack personality. It develops white fruit aromas which are embellished by slightly spicy floral notes. Supple on the opening, it develops a balance between sugars and acidity, while keeping a certain roundness through to the fruity and mentholated finish. It is given one star for the full-bodied **Demi-Sec 2001** while the **Moelleux 2001 (8–11 €)** is commended.
🍷 Dom. Vigneau-Chevreau, 4, rue du Clos-Baglin, 37210 Chançay, tel. 02.47.52.93.22, fax 02.47.52.23.04, e-mail contact@vigneau-chevreau.com ☑
🍾 by appt.

ANTOINETTE VIGNON
Brut Tête de cuvée★

	n.c.	60,000	🍾 ♦	5–8 €

The Roger Félicien Brou company, created in 1969, has a vast wine cellar for sparkling wine production in Rochecorbon, on the banks of the Loire. Antoinette Vignon is an attractive wine, interesting for its lightness and elegance. Far from being boring on the palate, it has a lovely freshness on the finish. Two other brands, **Désiré Soudrille Brut** and **Roger Félicien Brou Brut**, are singled out; they will do well as aperitifs.
➦ SA Roger Félicien Brou, 10, rue Vauvert, 37210 Rochecorbon, tel. 02.47.52.54.85, fax 02.47.52.82.05, e-mail rf.brou@wanadoo.fr

DOM. DU VIKING
Brut 1999★

	3 ha	5,000	🍾	5–8 €

Lionel Gauthier is favoured by the terroir and he knows that leaving the wine to age on the lees will bring forth its best qualities. The intense yellow-coloured 99 has light, fine bubbles. The nose is rich in aromas of ripe fruit and undergrowth and it is slightly peppery. The suppleness, balance and typicity of his Vouvray flatter the senses, especially on the finish that echoes the undergrowth notes. The **Sec 2001** also obtains one star, while the non-vintage **Méthode Traditionelle** is singled out.
➦ Lionel Gauthier, 1300, rte de Monnaie, Melotin, 37380 Reugny, tel. 02.47.52.96.41, fax 02.47.52.24.84, e-mail viking@france-vin.com ☑
♈ by appt.

CAVE DES PRODUCTEURS DE VOUVRAY Moelleux 2001★

	n.c.	13,966	🍾 ♦	5–8 €

The vast cellars of this cooperative in the Coquette valley, on Vouvray terroir, must be visited. Its immense wine cellar has produced this limpid, yellow-gold sweet wine. The intense nose presents aromas of linden flowers, honey and acacia, and in the mouth the wine is airy and round, with good length and a perfect balance. A success for this vintage.
➦ Cave des producteurs de Vouvray, 38, la Vallée-Coquette, 37210 Vouvray, tel. 02.47.52.75.03, fax 02.47.52.66.41, e-mail cavedesproducteurs@cp.vouvray.com ☑
♈ ev. day 9am–12 noon 2pm–7pm

Wines selected but not starred

JEAN-PIERRE BOISTARD
Sec 2001

	0.5	3,000	🍾	5–8 €

➦ Jean-Pierre Boistard, 216, rue Neuve, 37210 Vernou-sur-Brenne, tel. 02.47.52.18.73, fax 02.47.52.19.95 ☑
♈ by appt.

VIGNOBLES BRISEBARRE
Brut

	10 ha	15,000	🍾 ♦	5–8 €

➦ EARL Philippe Brisebarre, La Vallée-Chartier, 37210 Vouvray, tel. 02.47.52.63.07, fax 02.47.52.65.59 ☑
♈ by appt.

CLOS BAUDOIN
Sec Aigle-blanc 2001

	1.3 ha	4,460	🍾🍾	8–11 €

➦ Philippe Edmond Poniatowski, EAV SARL Clos Baudoin, vallée de Nouys, 37210 Vouvray, tel. 02.47.52.71.02, fax 02.47.52.60.94, e-mail pep@magic.fr ☑
♈ by appt.

DOM. DU CLOS DE L'EPINAY
Brut Cuvée du Tricentenaire 2000

	0.72 ha	6,300	🍾 ♦	8–11 €

➦ Luc Dumange, Dom. du Clos de L'Epinay, L'Epinay, 37210 Vouvray, tel. 02.47.52.61.90, fax 02.47.52.71.31, e-mail ldumange@terre-net.fr ☑
♈ ev. day except Sun. 2pm–5.30pm; cl. 15 Feb.–4 Mar

CLOS DU PETIT MONT
Moelleux Sélection Balzac 2001

	2 ha	3,000	🍾🍾	8–11 €

➦ GAEC Allias Père et Fils, 106, rue Vallée-Coquette, 37210 Vouvray, tel. 02.47.52.74.95, fax 02.47.52.66.38, e-mail domaine.allias.@wanadoo.fr ☑
♈ ev. day except Sun. 8am–12 noon 2pm–7pm

DOM. THIERRY COSME
Demi-sec 2001

	0.5 ha	1,500	🍾	5–8 €

➦ Thierry Cosme, 1127, rte de Nazelles, 37210 Noizay, tel. 02.47.52.05.87, fax 02.47.52.11.36 ☑
♈ by appt.

DOM. DE LA FONTAINERIE
Sec Coteau Les Brûlés 2001

	1.7 ha	2,500	🍾🍾	8–11 €

➦ Catherine Dhoye-Déruet, Dom. de La Fontainerie, 64, Vallée-Coquette, 37210 Vouvray, tel. 02.47.52.67.92, fax 02.47.52.79.41, e-mail lafontainerie@oreka.com ☑
♈ by appt.

DOM. DE LA FUIE
Brut 2000

	4 ha	10,000	🍾 ♦	3–5 €

➦ GAEC Dom. de La Fuie, 1679, rte de Nazelles, 37210 Noizay, tel. 02.47.52.14.95, fax 02.47.52.08.79 ☑
♈ ev. day 8.30am–8.30pm
➦ L. Gatineau et A. Delorme

DOM. DE LA GALINIERE
Brut Cuvée Clément 1999

	5 ha	35,000	🍾	5–8 €

➦ Dom. de la Galinière, La Galinière, 37210 Vernou-sur-Brenne, tel. 02.47.52.15.92, fax 02.47.52.15.92 ☑
♈ by appt.

DOM. GANGNEUX
Sec 2001

	1 ha	5,500	🍾🍾	5–8 €

➦ Gérard Gangneux, 1, rte de Monnaie, 37210 Vouvray, tel. 02.47.52.60.93, fax 02.47.52.67.66 ☑
♈ ev. day except Sun. 8am–12 noon 2pm–7pm

GAUTIER
Brut Antique 2000

	5 ha	10,000	🍾 ♦	5–8 €

➦ Benoit Gautier, Dom. de La Châtaigneraie, 37210 Rochecorbon, tel. 02.47.52.84.63, fax 02.47.52.84.65, e-mail info@vouvraygautier.com ☑
♈ by appt.

C. GREFFE
Brut Carte noire

| | | n.c. | 64,000 | | 5–8 € |

•⌐ C. Greffe, 35, rue Neuve, 37210 Vernou-sur-Brenne,
tel. 02.47.52.12.24, fax 02.47.52.09.56,
e-mail savardja@club-internet.fr ☑
🍷 by appt.
•⌐ Jacques Savard

DOM. DES LAURIERS
Demi-sec 2001

| | | 2 ha | 8,000 | ⅰ | 5–8 € |

•⌐ Laurent Kraft, Dom. des Lauriers, 29–31, rue du
Petit-Coteau, 37210 Vouvray, tel. 02.47.52.61.82,
fax 02.47.52.61.82, e-mail flkraft@wanadoo.fr ☑
🍷 ev. day 8am–12 noon 2pm–7pm

METIVIER
Demi-sec 2001

| | | 0.18 ha | 1,320 | ⅰ ♦ | 3–5 € |

•⌐ GAEC Métivier, 51, rue Neuve,
37210 Vernou-sur-Brenne, tel. 02.47.52.01.95,
fax 02.47.52.06.01 ☑
🍷 by appt.

CH. MONCONTOUR Brut Cuvée Prédilection
Grande Réserve du domaine 1999

| | | 5 ha | 40,000 | ⅰ ♦ | 5–8 € |

•⌐ Ch. Moncontour, 37210 Vouvray, tel. 02.47.52.60.77,
fax 02.47.52.65.50, e-mail info@moncontour.com ☑
🍷 by appt.
•⌐ M. et Mme Feray

MONMOUSSEAU
Moelleux 2001

| | | 25.9 ha | 172,666 | ⅰ | 5–8 € |

•⌐ SA Monmousseau, 71, rte de Vierzon, BP 25,
41401 Montrichard, tel. 02.54.71.66.66, fax 02.54.32.56.09,
e-mail monmousseau@monmousseau.com ☑
🍷 ev. day 10am–6pm; groups by appt.; cl. 1 Nov.–31 Mar.
•⌐ Bernard Massard

DOM. D'ORFEUILLES
Brut 1999

| | | 5 ha | 25,000 | ⅰ ♦ | 5–8 € |

•⌐ EARL Bernard Hérivault, La Croix-Blanche,
37380 Reugny, tel. 02.47.52.91.85, fax 02.47.52.25.01,
e-mail earl.herivault@france-vin.com ☑
🍷 by appt.

VINCENT PELTIER
Brut 2001

| | | 1.5 ha | 10,000 | ⅰ ♦ | 5–8 € |

•⌐ Vincent Peltier, 41 bis, rue de la Mairie, 37210 Chançay,
tel. 02.47.52.93.34, fax 02.47.52.96.98 ☑
🍷 by appt.

DOM. DES RAISINS DORES
Sec 2001

| | | 1 ha | n.c. | ⅰ | 5–8 € |

•⌐ Jacqueline Benoist, 36, rue du Pr-Debré,
37210 Vernou-sur-Brenne, tel. 02.47.52.00.54,
fax 02.47.52.00.54 ☑
🍷 by appt.

DOM. RONSARD Brut

| | | 16.69 ha | 60,000 | ⅰ ♦ | 5–8 € |

•⌐ Eve Dumange, Dom. Ronsard, la Vallée-Chartier,
37210 Vouvray, tel. 02.47.52.80.85, fax 02.47.52.82.05

DOM. DE VAUGONDY
Demi-sec 2001

| | | 3 ha | 10,000 | ⅰ ♦ | 5–8 € |

•⌐ EARL Perdriaux, 3, Les Glandiers,
37210 Vernou-sur-Brenne, tel. 02.47.52.02.26,
fax 02.47.52.04.81 ☑
🍷 by appt.

Cheverny

Classified as VDQS in 1973,
Cheverny proceeded to AOC in 1993. The appellation
area extends a considerable way along the left
bank of the Loire, from Sologne, in the Blésois, to the
outskirts of Orléans. Numerous grape varieties are
planted in this appellation of 488 ha of vineyards in
an area of more than 2,000 ha, where the terroir is
predominantly sandy (sand on Sologne clay and the
terraces of the Loire). The producers have managed
to establish a Cheverny "style" from a mixture of
varieties in proportions that vary slightly depending
on the terroir. In 2002 12,033 hl of red wine were produced, mainly from Gamay and Pinot Noir. They are
fruity in youth, later developing an animal muskiness
in harmony with the hunting traditions of the region.
The Gamay rosés are dry and perfumed. The whites,
of which 8,979 hl were produced in 1999, and for
which a little Chardonnay is added to Sauvignon, are
floral and finely made.

DOM. DU CROC DU MERLE 2002★

| | | 3 ha | 10,000 | ⅰ ♦ | 3–5 € |

Floral perfumes and blackcurrant bud notes mix together
with elegance in this brilliant pale-yellow wine. Just as harmonious, the palate has good length, indicating a ripe harvest
with its roundness and complex notes of fruits and mineral.
The red Cheverny 2002 is singled out: still young, it needs to
evolve to express itself fully.
•⌐ Patrice et Anne-Marie Hahusseau, Dom. du Croc du
Merle, 38, rue de La Chaumette, 41500 Muides-sur-Loire,
tel. 02.54.87.58.65, fax 02.54.87.02.85,
e-mail patricehahusseau@aol.com ☑
🍷 ev. day 9am–12.30pm 2pm–7pm; Sun. 9am–12 noon;
cl. 25–31 Aug.

BENOIT DARIDAN 2002★

| | | 3 ha | 6,000 | ⅰ ♦ | 3–5 € |

The Pinot Noir (60%) makes a pact with the Gamay, but it is
the character of the Pinot grape that one can see in the
orange-toned colour, in the roundness and solidity on the
lengthy palate. The Jury singled out Benoit Daridan's
Cour-Cheverny 2001 for its freshness.
•⌐ Benoît Daridan, La Marigonnerie,
41700 Cour-Cheverny, tel. 02.54.79.94.53,
fax 02.54.79.94.53 ☑
🍷 by appt.

DOM. DE LA DESOUCHERIE 2002★

| | | 10 ha | 50,000 | ⅰ ♦ | 8–11 € |

Since 2001, Christian Tessier has been able to count on his son
to help cultivate the 25.5 ha of vines planted on the highest
point of Cour-Cheverny. Good, mature grapes have made it
possible to produce a wine with a good extraction of colour,
and an elegant nose evoking Morello cherry. The palate is
round and well structured with good balance. The Cuvée Christian Tessier white 2002 is singled out, as is Cour-Cheverny 2001.
•⌐ GAEC Christian Tessier et Fils, 47, voie de la Charmoise,
41700 Cour-Cheverny, tel. 02.54.79.98.90, fax 02.54.79.22.48,
e-mail tessier.christian@libertysurf.fr ☑ ⌂
🍷 ev. day 8am–12 noon 2pm–6pm;
groups and Sun. by appt.

DOM. DE LA GAUDRONNIERE

Cuvée Tradition 2002★

| ■ | 10.68 ha | 18,000 | ■ ⏳ | 5–8 € |

Since 1985 Christian Dorléans has worked on this domaine of a little more than 17 ha. This is a blend of 50% Gamay (carbonic maceration vinification), 40% Pinot Noir and 10% Cot which produces an orange-red wine, attractive with a fresh fruitiness denoting Morello cherry. The balance is pleasant, nicely sustained by the Pinot flavours right through to the long finish. The **white Cuvée Laetitia 2002**, which is full of character, also gains one star, while the **Cour-Cheverny Le Mûr de La Gaudronnière 2002 (8–11 €)** is singled out.

➴ Christian Dorléans, Dom. de La Gaudronnière, 41120 Cellettes, tel. 02.54.70.40.41, fax 02.54.70.38.83 **V**
⏳ by appt.

MAISON PERE ET FILS 2002★

| ■ | 25 ha | 50,000 | ■ ⏳ | 5–8 € |

An attractive ruby Cheverny. The timidity on the nose is forgotten when the elegance, balance and supple tannins are revealed. The floral, honeyed and round **2002 white** is commended.

➴ EARL Maison Père et Fils, 22, rue de la Roche, 41120 Sambin, tel. 02.54.20.22.87, fax 02.54.20.22.91 **V**
⏳ ev. day 8am–7pm
➴ Jean-François Maison

LE PETIT CHAMBORD 2002★

| ■ | 5 ha | 17,000 | ■ ⏳ | 5–8 € |

Straw-yellow in colour, this wine offers delicate perfumes of very ripe fruit. A finesse that is also present on the palate which is round and long, with apricot and peach notes. The **2002 red** also obtains one star: full-flavoured with soft fruits, it is supple and silky.

➴ François Cazin, Le Petit Chambord, 41700 Cheverny, tel. 02.54.79.93.75, fax 02.54.79.27.89 **V**
⏳ by appt.

DOM. DU SALVARD 2002★

| ■ | 8 ha | 45,000 | ■ ⏳ | 5–8 € |

The current owner's grandfather bought this typical Sologne estate in 1920. Today there are 33 ha, renowned for Cheverny white and red. This complex coloured wine lets the Sauvignon speak out for itself (85% of the blend) with a nose that passes through the range of delicate smoky notes. The Chardonnay (15%) takes over on the palate, bringing good balance and length. A goat's cheese will go well with this wine. Also very successful, the **red Domaine du Salvard 2002** is a rounded wine, with a mineral finish. The **white Cuvée L'Héritière 2002 (8–11 €)** is singled out for its varietal character (85% Sauvignon).

➴ EARL Delaille, Dom. du Salvard, 41120 Fougères-sur-Bièvre, tel. 02.54.20.28.21, fax 02.54.20.22.54, e-mail delaille@libertysurf.fr **V**
⏳ by appt.

DOM. SAUGER 2002★

| ■ | 6 ha | 20,000 | ■ ⏳ | 5–8 € |

Practising sustainable agriculture (Terra Vitis) on their 22 ha of vines, Sauger knew how to draw the best from the appellation in 2002. This intensely coloured Cheverny red, flatters the senses with its scents of ripe soft fruits as well as the silky tannins which make it ready to drink now. The **white Domaine Sauger 2002** testifies to a well-handled wine vinification: its harmony and finish of citrus fruits earn it one star. The **white Domaine Sauger Vieilles Vignes 2002 (8–11 €)** was also judged to be a fine wine due to the finesse of its aromas of fruit and vegetation (boxwood), and it is rich, well-balanced palate.

➴ EARL Dom. Sauger, Les Touches, 41700 Fresnes, tel. 02.54.79.58.45, fax 02.54.79.03.35, e-mail domaine.sauger@terre-net.fr **V**
⏳ ev. day except Sun. 9am–12 noon 2pm–6pm; by appt. from 1 Sep. until 31 Mar.

DOM. PHILIPPE TESSIER

Le Point du Jour 2002★

| ■ | 4.8 | 12,000 | ■ | 5–8 € |

Philippe Tessier practises organic farming on his 20 ha. His lovely ruby Cheverny liberally expresses soft fruits and the palate has surprising richness and fine tannins. The

Cour-Cheverny Cuvée de la Porte Dorée 2001 is singled out: true to type but still very lively, it is worth waiting one or two years.

➴ EARL Philippe Tessier, 3, voie de la rue Colin, 41700 Cheverny, tel. 02.54.44.23.82, fax 02.54.44.21.71, e-mail domaine.ph.tessier@wanadoo.fr **V**
⏳ by appt.

Wines selected but not starred

PASCAL BELLIER

Sélection 2002

| ■ | n.c. | 19,600 | ■ ⏳ | 5–8 € |

➴ Pascal Bellier, 3, rue Reculée, 41350 Vineuil, tel. 02.54.20.64.31, fax 02.54.20.58.19 **V** ♨
⏳ ev. day except Tue. Thu. Sun. 2pm–7pm

ERIC CHAPUZET

Cuvée Mont-Crochet 2002

| ■ | 4 ha | 25,000 | ■ ⏳ | 3–5 € |

➴ Eric Chapuzet, La Gardette, 41120 Fougères-sur-Bièvre, tel. 02.54.20.27.21, fax 02.54.20.28.34, e-mail e.chapuzet@wanadoo.fr **V**
⏳ by appt.

CHESNEAU ET FILS 2002

| ■ | 2.7 ha | 10,000 | ■ | 3–5 € |

➴ EARL Chesneau et Fils, 26, rue Sainte-Néomoise, 41120 Sambin, tel. 02.54.20.20.15, fax 02.54.33.21.91, e-mail contact@chesneauetfils.fr **V**
⏳ by appt.

MICHEL CONTOUR 2002

| ■ | 1.3 ha | 3,000 | ■ | 3–5 € |

➴ Michel Contour, 7, rue La Boissière, 41120 Cellettes, tel. 02.54.70.43.07, fax 02.54.70.36.68, e-mail m.contour@wanadoo.fr **V**
⏳ ev. day 8am–12.30pm 2pm–7pm

JEAN-MICHEL COURTIOUX 2002

| ■ | 5 ha | 3,000 | | 3–5 € |

➴ Jean-Michel Courtioux, 41120 Chitenay, tel. 02.54.70.42.18 **V**
⏳ by appt.

MICHEL GENDRIER

Le Pressoir 2002

| ■ | 3 ha | 18,000 | ■ ⏳ | 5–8 € |

➴ Jocelyne et Michel Gendrier, Les Huards, 41700 Cour-Cheverny, tel. 02.54.79.97.90, fax 02.54.79.26.82, e-mail info@gendrier.com **V**
⏳ ev. day 9am–12 noon 2pm–7pm; Sun. by appt.

HUGUET 2002

| ■ | 1 ha | 6,000 | ■ ⏳ | 3–5 € |

➴ GAEC Patrick Huguet, 11–12, rue de la Franchetière, 41350 Saint-Claude-de-Diray, tel. 02.54.20.57.36, fax 02.54.20.58.57 **V**
⏳ by appt.

LOIRE

JEROME MARCADET

Cuvée de l'Orme 2002

| | 2.5 ha | 8,000 | ∎ ♦ | | 3–5 € |

➤ Jérôme Marcadet, L'Orme Favras, 41120 Feings,
tel. 02.54.20.28.42, fax 02.54.20.28.42 ☑
⏱ ev. day except Sun. 8am–12.30pm 2pm–6.30pm

MARQUIS DE LA PLANTE D'OR 2002

| | 3 ha | 14,000 | ∎ ♦ | 5–8 € |

➤ Philippe Loquineau, La Demalerie, 41700 Cheverny,
tel. 02.54.44.23.09, fax 02.54.44.22.16 ☑ ⛪
⏱ by appt.

DOM. DE MONTCY

Cuvée Louis de La Saussaye 2002

| | 3.7 ha | 21,000 | ∎ ♦ | 5–8 € |

➤ R. et S. Simon, La Porte dorée, 32, rte de Fougères,
41700 Cheverny, tel. 02.54.44.20.00, fax 02.54.44.21.00,
e-mail domaine-de-montcy@wanadoo.fr ☑
⏱ ev. day except Sun. 10am–12 noon 2pm–6pm;
Sat. by appt.; cl. 25 Aug.–7 Sep. 24 Dec.–4 Jan.

LES VIGNERONS DE MONT-PRES-CHAMBORD 2002

| | 30 ha | 200,000 | ∎ ♦ | 5–8 € |

➤ Les Vignerons de Mont-près-Chambord, 816, la
Petite-Rue, 41250 Mont-près-Chambord,
tel. 02.54.70.71.15, fax 02.54.70.70.65,
e-mail cavemont@club-internet.fr ☑
⏱ ev. day except Sun. 9am–12 noon 2pm–6pm;
Mon. 2pm–6pm

LA CONFRERIE DES VIGNERONS DE OISLY ET THESEE 2002

| | 10 ha | 70,000 | ∎ ♦ | 5–8 € |

➤ Confrérie des Vignerons de Oisly et Thésée, 41700 Oisly,
tel. 02.54.79.75.20, fax 02.54.79.75.29,
e-mail oisly.thesee@wanadoo.fr ☑
⏱ ev. day 9am–12 noon 2pm–5.30pm; groups by appt.

PIERRE PARENT 2002

| | 1.24 ha | 6,400 | ∎ | 5–8 € |

➤ Pierre Parent, 201, rue de Chancelée,
41250 Mont-près-Chambord, tel. 02.54.70.73.57,
fax 02.54.70.89.72 ☑
⏱ by appt.

DOM. LE PORTAIL 2002

| | 10 ha | 30,000 | ∎ ♦ | 5–8 € |

➤ Michel Cadoux, Le Portail, 41700 Cheverny,
tel. 02.54.79.91.25, fax 02.54.79.28.03 ☑
⏱ by appt.

DANIEL TEVENOT 2002

| | 2 ha | 14,000 | ∎ ♦ | 5–8 € |

➤ Daniel Tévenot, 4, rue du Moulin-à-Vent, Madon,
41120 Candé-sur-Beuvron, tel. 02.54.79.44.24,
fax 02.54.79.44.24 ☑
⏱ by appt.

DOM. DU VIVIER

Jean-François Deniau et Fils 2002

| | 3.15 | 18,000 | ∎ ♦ | 5–8 € |

➤ Jocelyne et Michel Gendrier, Les Huards,
41700 Cour-Cheverny, tel. 02.54.79.97.90,
fax 02.54.79.26.82, e-mail info@gendrier.com ☑
⏱ ev. day 9am–12 noon 2pm–7pm; Sun. by appt.

Cour-Cheverny

A decree dated 24 March 1993
recognized Cour-Cheverny as a separate AOC, limited
to white wines made using only the Romorantin
variety. The area of production comprises the former
AOS Cour-Cheverny Mont-Près-Chambord and a
few surrounding communes where the variety was
maintained. The terroir is typical of the Sologne (sand
on clay). Production in 2002 totalled 2,095 hl.

DOM. DE L'AUMONIERE 2002★

| | 2.98 | 10,000 | ∎ ♦ | 3–5 € |

Gérard Givierge cultivates more than 18 ha on this domaine
created in 1836. Its Cour-Cheverny attracted the Jury with
its beautiful pale-yellow colour with green highlights that
indicates a well-handled fermentation. The nose is still closed
but has fine fruit in harmony with the balanced palate. The
estate's **Cheverny rosé 2002** is singled out for its roundness.
➤ Gérard Givierge, Dom. de l'Aumonière,
41700 Cour-Cheverny, tel. 02.54.79.25.49,
fax 02.54.79.27.06 ☑
⏱ ev. day 8am–12 noon 2pm–8pm; groups by appt.

LE PETIT CHAMBORD 2001★

| | 4 ha | 16,000 | ∎ ⦿ ♦ | 5–8 € |

One discovers a Petit Chambord packed with honey and
yellow flowers hiding under a pale-yellow colour. The attack
is soft and opens to reveal perfect balance. Open a bottle
today, but keep some for the two next years.
➤ François Cazin, Le Petit Chambord, 41700 Cheverny,
tel. 02.54.79.93.75, fax 02.54.79.27.89 ☑
⏱ by appt.

Wines selected but not starred

MICHEL ET CHRISTOPHE BADIN 2002

| | 0.56 ha | 2,000 | ∎ ♦ | 3–5 € |

➤ GAEC Michel et Christophe Badin, L'Aubras,
41120 Cormeray, tel. 02.54.44.32.98, fax 02.54.44.23.43 ☑
⏱ by appt.

DOM. DE LA GRANGE 2001

| | n.c. | 4,500 | ∎ ♦ | 3–5 € |

➤ Jean-Michel et Guy Genty, La Grange,
41350 Huisseau-sur-Cosson, tel. 02.54.20.31.31,
fax 02.54.20.31.17 ☑
⏱ by appt.

DOM. DES HUARDS 2001

| | 5.75 ha | 16,000 | ∎ | 5–8 € |

➤ Jocelyne et Michel Gendrier, Les Huards,
41700 Cour-Cheverny, tel. 02.54.79.97.90,
fax 02.54.79.26.82, e-mail info@gendrier.com ☑
⏱ ev. day 9am–12 noon 2pm–7pm; Sun. by appt.

Orléans AOVDQS

The wines of Orléanais AOVDQS have had a change of name as a result of the INAO recognizing two distinctly different appellations: Orléans and Orléans-Cléry.

Among the "French wines" the wines of Orléans had their moment of glory in medieval times, but the vine still prospers on about 132 ha among the gardens, nurseries and famous orchards of the Orléanais. Since the 10th century, the winemakers have adapted the following varieties, which it is claimed were imported from the Auvergne, but which are identical to the ones in Burgundy: Auvernat Rouge (Pinot Noir), Auvernat Blanc (Chardonnay) and Gris Meunier, to which was added Cabernet (or Breton) with its aromas of red- and blackcurrants.

The tradition was kept going mainly on the sandy, gravelly terraces of the south bank of the Loire, where the INAO recognized the Orléans-Cléry appellation, reserved for red wines made from Cabernet Franc. This new area (11.78 ha) produced 478 hl in 2002. The Orléans appellation extends on both sides of the Loire. It is reserved for white wines made from Chardonnay and for very original red and rosé wines made from Pinot Meunier. Production of red Orléans wines amounted to 2,934 hl in 2002. Only a small amount of white was produced (745 hl).

The wines should be drunk with partridge and roast pheasant, game pâtés from neighbouring Sologne and ash cheeses from the Gâtinais.

VIGNOBLE DU CHANT D'OISEAUX
Gris meunier 2002★

	2 ha	10,000	▮ ♦	3–5 €

The Chant d' Oiseaux vineyard was created more than 20 years ago. Its name reappears regularly in the *Guide* thanks to characteristic Orléans wines like this charming 2002 with its ruby appearance. A lovely fruitiness appears on the palate balanced by evident tannins that will not take long to soften. Ideal with poultry in a sauce. The **white 2002** is commended.
↬ Jacky Legroux, 315, rue des Muids,
45370 Mareau-aux-Prés, tel. 02.38.45.60.31,
fax 02.38.45.62.35 ☑
♈ by appt.

CLOS SAINT-FIACRE 2002★★★

	6.41 ha	29,000		3–5 €

Hubert and Bénédicte Piel have carried out the family business on this 20-hectare vineyard since 2003. They have achieved huge success this year, both with Orléans-Cléry, the new appellation and with Orléans. The *coup de cœur* is awarded to this ruby wine which releases intense-red berry fruit aromas. Well-balanced with evident but rich tannins, supporting a long finish. The **white Clos Saint-Fiacre 2002** obtains two stars: its lovely yellow-straw colour indicates well-matured grapes, the same goes for the elegant notes of exotic fruit. On the palate, it is soft, velvety and balanced. And to supplement the range, the **rosé 2002**, which is all soft fruits, achieves one star.
↬ Montigny-Piel, Clos Saint-Fiacre, 560, rue de Saint-Fiacre, 45370 Mareau-aux-Prés, tel. 02.38.45.61.55, fax 02.38.45.66.58, e-mail clos.saintfiacre@wanadoo.fr ☑
♈ by appt.

SAINT AVIT 2002★

	2.25 ha	4,000	▮ ♦	3–5 €

A beautiful yellow colour with green tinges, this wine reveals all the generosity of the floral and fruity Chardonnay, underlined with a mineral touch. The same white fruit flavours returns on a palate that is well balanced and has good length. The **rosé 2002** is singled out.
↬ Javoy Père et Fils, 450, rue du Buisson,
45370 Mézières-lez-Cléry, tel. 02.38.45.66.95,
fax 02.38.45.69.77 ☑
♈ ev. day except Sun. 8.30am–12 noon 2pm–7pm
↬ Pascal Javoy

Wines selected but not starred

LES VIGNERONS DE LA GRAND'MAISON 2002

	9.89 ha	34,933	▮ ♦	3–5 €

↬ Les Vignerons de la Grand'Maison, 550, rte des Muids,
45370 Mareau-aux-Prés, tel. 02.38.45.61.08,
fax 02.38.45.65.70,
e-mail vignerons.orleans@free.fr ☑
♈ by appt.

Orléans-Cléry

VIGNOBLE DU CHANT D'OISEAUX
2002★

	2.8 ha	12,000	▮ ♦	3–5 €

At the *lieu-dit* Chant d'Oiseaux, Jacky Legroux cultivates nearly 10 ha, using sustainable agricultural methods. A well-matured harvest in 2002 enabled him to produce a rich, fruity wine, whose tannins reveal a certain velvety quality. Wait just under two years to enjoy it even more
↬ Jacky Legroux, 315, rue des Muids,
45370 Mareau-aux-Prés, tel. 02.38.45.60.31,
fax 02.38.45.62.35 ☑
♈ by appt.

CLOS SAINT-FIACRE 2002★

	2.83 ha	18,000	▮ ♦	3–5 €

The Clos Saint-Fiacre has found its place in this new appellation, obtaining a *coup de cœur* as AOVDQS Orléans. The 2002 shows how well the vinification has been handled with its intense-red colour and nose that tends towards black fruits. This elegant Orléans-Cléry is promising.
↬ Montigny-Piel, Clos Saint-Fiacre, 560, rue de Saint-Fiacre, 45370 Mareau-aux-Prés, tel. 02.38.45.61.55, fax 02.38.45.66.58, e-mail clos.saintfiacre@wanadoo.fr ☑
♈ by appt.

LOIRE

Wines selected but not starred

SAINT AVIT 2002

	4.5 ha	20,000	⬛ ⚱		3–5 €

☛ Javoy Père et Fils, 450, rue du Buisson,
45370 Mézières-lez-Cléry, tel. 02.38.45.66.95,
fax 02.38.45.69.77 ☑
Ⴗ ev. day except Sun. 8.30am–12 noon 2pm–7pm
☛ Pascal Javoy

Coteaux du Vendômois

Coteaux du Vendômois was recognized as an AOC in 2001. This unique appellation, between Vendôme and Montoire, produces the highly distinctive *vin gris* Pineau d'Aunis, noted for its very pale colour and peppery aromas. The whites, made from Chenin, resemble those from the neighbouring AOC Coteaux de Loire and Jasnières, which are grown on similar soils.

The range of red wines is a newer development, in response to consumer demand. The delicately spicy liveliness of the Pineau d'Aunis is combined with Gamay for smoothness, and either improved in finesse by including Pinot Noir or in tannin by using Cabernet.

In 2002 production was 7,771 hl. Visitors can enjoy walking by the Loire and exploring the surrounding hillsides with their "troglodyte" cave dwellings and cellars carved out of the tufa.

DOM. DU CARROIR 2002★

	4 ha	10,000		3–5 €

Jean and Benoît Brazilier regrouped as a GAEC seven years ago in order to work their 24-hectare estate. They produced a pale-yellow wine that readily emits floral notes of acacia. Its elegant suppleness makes it particularly pleasant. The **Vin Gris 2002** also merits one star because it offers all the spicy aromas of the Pineau d'Aunis grape variety.
☛ GAEC Jean et Benoit Brazilier, 17, rue des Ecoles, 41100 Thoré-la-Rochette, tel. 02.54.72.81.72, fax 02.54.72.77.13 ☑ ⬛
Ⴗ by appt.

PATRICE COLIN

Moelleux Pente des Coutis 2002★

	n.c.	4,000		5–8 €

This sweet Chenin created lively interest amongst the tasters with the finesse of its flavours, roundness and balance. Enjoy it today or lay it down. The **red Cuvée Pierre François 2002 (3–5 €)** is singled out for the fullness of its flavours; it needs to age a little.
☛ Patrice Colin, Dom. de la Gaudetterie, 41100 Thoré-la-Rochette, tel. 02.54.72.80.73, fax 02.54.72.75.54 ☑
Ⴗ by appt.

DOM. DU FOUR A CHAUX 2002★★

	3 ha	6,000	⬛ ⚱		3–5 €

The Jury members could not all agree on awarding a *coup de coeur*, but this wine still represents the Pineau d'Aunis of Vendômois beautifully. It has a salmon colour and an intense

nose with peppery nuances, then it opens to reveal a supple body, tasty and long. The **red Coteaux du Vendômois 2001** obtains one star for its promising structure and balance.
☛ EARL Dominique Norguet, Berger, 41100 Thoré-la-Rochette, tel. 02.54.77.12.52, fax 02.54.80.23.22 ☑
Ⴗ ev. day except Sun. 8am–12 noon 2pm–7.30pm

DOM. J. MARTELLIERE

Gris Cuvée Jasmine 2002★

	1.3 ha	4,000		3–5 €

The troglodyte wine cellar of this domaine of 10 ha produced this typical *vin gris* selection from Vendômois. The elegant nose is perfectly matched by a refreshing, balanced palate.
☛ SCEA du Dom. J. Martellière, 46, rue de Fosse, 41800 Montoire-sur-le-Loir, tel. 02.54.85.16.91 ☑
Ⴗ by appt.

LES VIGNERONS DU VENDOMOIS

2002★

	4.5 ha	32,000	⬛ ⚱		3–5 €

Created in 1929, the cooperative shines out in the appellation with three starred wines. This one is an elegant white wine with a pale-yellow appearance, long and well balanced. There is a **Lieu-dit Cocagne rosé 2002** fresh and full flavoured, which is a very good wine. And again a **Vin Gris 2002**, awarded one star, which is all citrus and exotic fruits sustained with a touch of pepper.
☛ Cave des Vignerons du Vendômois, 60, av. Dupetit-Thouars, 41100 Villiers-sur-Loir, tel. 02.54.72.90.69, fax 02.54.72.75.09, e-mail caveduvendomois@wanadoo.fr ☑
Ⴗ ev. day except Sun. Mon. 9am–12 noon 2pm–6pm

Wines selected but not starred

DOM. DE LA CHARLOTTERIE

Tradition 2002

	1.5 ha	10,000	⬛ ⚱		3–5 €

☛ Dominique Houdebert, Dom. de la Charlotterie, 2, rue du Bas-Bourg, 41100 Villieresfaux, tel. 02.54.80.29.79, fax 02.54.73.10.01, e-mail dominique.houdebert@wanadoo.fr ☑
Ⴗ by appt.

CHARLES JUMERT

Moelleux La Douceur de Saint-François 2002

	n.c.	800	⬛⬛	8–11 €

☛ EARL Jumert, 4, rue de la Berthelotière, 41100 Villiers-sur-Loir, tel. 02.54.72.94.09, fax 02.54.72.94.09 ☑ ⬛
Ⴗ by appt.

DOM. MINIER 2002

	n.c.	n.c.	⬛ ⚱		3–5 €

☛ GAEC Claude et Gisèle Minier, Les Monts, 41360 Lunay, tel. 02.54.72.02.36, fax 02.54.72.18.52 ☑ ⬛
Ⴗ by appt.

DOM. JACQUES NOURY

Gris 2002

	1.11 ha	4,000	⬛		3–5 €

☛ Dom. Jacques Noury, Montpot, 41800 Houssay, tel. 02.54.85.36.04 ☑
Ⴗ by appt.

Valençay AOVDQS

Bordering Berry, Sologne and the Touraine is an area of mixed agriculture, forestry and husbandry (particularly goat-rearing) in which the vine plays its part. The soils are mainly clay and silica or alluvial clay. There are more than 300 ha under vines, half of which is declared as Valençay (128 ha in 2002), offering wines for early drinking from the classic varieties of this part of the Loire. Sauvignon produces aromatic wines with notes of blackcurrant or broom, and an added fullness when mixed with Chardonnay. The red wines are assembled from Gamay, Cabernet, Côt and Pinot Noir in various proportions. Production in 2002 was 1,588 hl of white wine and 2,024 hl of red.

The same appellation is also famous for its goat's cheese, awarded an AOC in 1998. Depending on how mature they are, the little pyramids of goat's cheese will accompany any of Valençay's red and white wines.

CHANTAL ET PATRICK GIBAULT 2002★

| | 2.9 ha | 15,000 | ∎ ♦ | 3–5€ |

Pinot Noir, Gamay, Cot on clay soil with flint: one does not change a winning combination and it's the 2002 vintage that wins the star for this Valençay red made by Chantal and Patrick Gibault. A beautiful ruby colour, the nose opens with abundant soft fruit notes and presents a balanced, supple body. A reference wine for the appellation.
●➊ EARL Chantal et Patrick Gibault, 183, rue Gambetta, 41130 Meusnes, tel. 02.54.71.02.63, fax 02.54.71.58.92, e-mail gibault.earl@wanadoo.fr ☑
⏸ ev. day except Sun. 9am–12 noon 2pm–7pm

DOM. JACKY PREYS ET FILS
Cuvée Prestige 2002★

| | n.c. | n.c. | ∎ ♦ | 3–5€ |

Grown on a clay soil with flint, the Gamay and Pinot Noir are in equal prortions (40% each) in this blend, with Cot making up the rest. It results in an intense-red wine, red berry fruit (raspberry) aromas, rounded thanks to the supple tannins.
●➊ Dom. Jacky Preys et Fils, Bois Pontois, 41130 Meusnes, tel. 02.54.71.00.34, fax 02.54.71.34.91 ☑
⏸ by appt.

JEAN-FRANCOIS ROY 2001★★

| | 7.1 ha | 20,000 | ∎ ♦ | 3–5€ |

This Valençay, a very good example of the appellation, is the result of the *perruche* terroir (sandy clay). Admire the intense colour, appreciate the complex nose that combines the subtle flavours of three grape varieties: Gamay, Pinot Noir and Cot. The integrated tannins support the finish well. The **white Valençay 2002** is singled out for its attractive citrus fruit flavours.
●➊ Jean-François Roy, 3, rue des Acacias, 36600 Lye, tel. 02.54.41.00.39, fax 02.54.41.06.89 ☑
⏸ by appt.

CAVE DES VIGNERONS REUNIS DE VALENCAY Tradition 2002★

| | 3 ha | 22,000 | ∎ ♦ | 3–5€ |

All Sauvignon, this wine attracted the Jury with its pale-yellow colour with green highlights, along with its elegant, generous nose of fruit. Its suppleness and balance have agreeable length on the finish. Shellfish or cheeses from Valençay will go well with this wine. Another star is allotted to the **red Cuvée Terroir 2002**, which combines soft fruits and spices, then goes on to develop body supported by good tannins.
●➊ Cave des Vignerons réunis de Valençay, 36600 Fontguenand, tel. 02.54.00.16.11, fax 02.54.00.05.55, e-mail vigneronvalençay@aol.com ☑
⏸ ev. day except Sun. 9am–12 noon 2pm–6pm; groups by appt.

Wines selected but not starred

JACKY ET PHILIPPE AUGIS 2002

| | 3 ha | 10,000 | ∎ ♦ | 3–5€ |

●➊ Dom. Jacky Augis, Le Musa, 1465, rue des Vignes, 41130 Meusnes, tel. 02.54.71.01.89, fax 02.54.71.74.15 ☑
⏸ ev. day except Sun. 8am–12 noon 2pm–7pm; cl. 15–31 Aug.
●➊ Philippe Augis

DOM. FRANCK CHUET 2001

| | 0.48 ha | 4,000 | ∎ | 3–5€ |

●➊ Franck Chuet, rue Claude-Debussy, 41130 Meusnes, tel. 02.54.71.01.06, fax 02.54.71.46.82 ☑
⏸ ev. day except Sat. Sun. 8am–12 noon 2pm–7pm

DOM. GARNIER 2002

| | 1.5 ha | 12,000 | ∎ ♦ | 3–5€ |

●➊ Dom. Garnier, 81, rue Eugène-Delacroix, 41130 Meusnes, tel. 02.54.00.10.06, fax 02.54.05.13.36, e-mail garnier@terre-net.fr ☑
⏸ by appt.

FRANCIS JOURDAIN
Cuvée Chèvrefeuille 2002

| | 2 ha | 10,000 | ∎ ♦ | 3–5€ |

●➊ Francis Jourdain, Les Moreaux, 36600 Lye, tel. 02.54.41.01.45, fax 02.54.41.07.56 ☑
⏸ by appt.

HUBERT SINSON ET FILS 2001

| | 2.76 ha | 10,000 | ∎ | 3–5€ |

●➊ GAEC Hubert Sinson et Fils, 1397, rue des Vignes, Le Musa, 41130 Meusnes, tel. 02.54.71.00.26, fax 02.54.71.50.93 ☑
⏸ by appt.

GERARD TOYER 2002

| | 1.5 ha | 10,500 | ∎ | 3–5€ |

●➊ Gérard Toyer, 63, Grande-Rue, Champcol, 36600 Selles-sur-Cher, tel. 02.54.97.49.23, fax 02.54.97.46.25 ☑
⏸ by appt.

Poitou

Haut-Poitou AOVDQS

In 1865 Dr Guyot reported that the Vienne vineyard covered 33,560 ha. Nowadays, apart from the vineyard attached to the Saumur area in the north of the department, wine-growing is reduced to the area around the cantons of Neuville and Mirebeau. Marigny-Brizay is the commune with the largest number of individual growers. The others grouped together to set up the Cave de Neuville-de-Poitou. The wines of Haut-Poitou produced 28,309 hl in 2002, 12,946 of which were whites in a declared area of 506 ha.

The soils of the Neuville plateau, a mixture of limestone and Marigny clay as well as marl, are well suited to the different varieties of this appellation; the best known of them is Sauvignon (for white wines).

DOM. DU CENTAURE

Gamay 2002★★

	0.46 ha	2,200		3–5€

This 7-hectare domaine is located on clay-limestone terroir that is very representative of the Haut-Poitou vineyards. This lengthy and balanced wine has both fleshy and fresh qualities at the same time. The clear-ruby colour has violet-pink highlights; its charred, smoky aromas complement the delicate notes of wild strawberry on the fresh, supple palate. A remarkable wine.

↪ Gérard Marsault, 4, rue du Poirier, 86380 Chabournay, tel. 05.49.51.19.39, fax 05.49.51.14.25 ☑
☿ ev. day except Sat. 9am–1pm 2pm–7pm

CAVE DU HAUT-POITOU

Sauvignon 2002★

	120 ha	400,000		3–5€

The Sauvignon is the traditional grape variety of these vineyards. The minerals and blackcurrant bud aromas are characteristic to this grape variety. The fresh palate refreshes, with touches of lime flowers and boxwood. A harmonious wine that will go well with a carpaccio of salmon.

↪ SA Cave du Haut-Poitou, 32, rue Alphonse-Plault, 86170 Neuville-de-Poitou, tel. 05.49.51.21.65, fax 05.49.51.16.07, e-mail c-h.p@wanadoo.fr ☑
☿ by appt.

CAVE DU HAUT-POITOU

Gamay 2002★

	92 ha	600,000		3–5€

The Cave du Haut-Poitou was created in 1948 well before the VDQS Haut-Poitou was recognized (1970). The Gamay is the principal red grape variety of the appellation. Here it has produced this bright ruby-coloured wine. The aromas of soft fruits (cherry, strawberry) and vegetal notes are characteristic of the grape variety and precede a pleasant, fresh palate. Overall, simple, supple and very well balanced, this wine will accompany a plate of cold cured meats.

↪ SA Cave du Haut-Poitou, 32, rue Alphonse-Plault, 86170 Neuville-de-Poitou, tel. 05.49.51.21.65, fax 05.49.51.16.07, e-mail c-h.p@wanadoo.fr ☑
☿ by appt.

DOM. DES LISES

Sauvignon 2002★

	1 ha	2,500		3–5€

The Domaine des Lises winery is situated at the entrance to the medieval city of Mirebeau, by the château. Here's a nervous, delicate Sauvignon true to type with its boxwood, spring flowers and blackcurrant bud nose. To be served with another speciality from Poitou, goat's cheese – in particular Poitou *chabis* (AOC goat's cheese).

↪ Pascale Bonneau, 21, rue Nationale, 86110 Mirebeau, tel. 05.49.50.53.66, fax 05.49.50.90.50, e-mail pascale.bonneau@libertysurf.fr ☑
☿ ev. day except Sun. 10am–7pm; winter 6pm–7pm and Sat. 10am–6pm

DOM. LA TOUR BEAUMONT

Chardonnay Tradition 2001★

	0.3 ha	1,500		5–8€

This Domaine is regularly mentioned in the *Guide*. Vinification took place in two-year-old barrels and this has realized the potential of this Chardonnay. The colour is pale yellow. On the nose white and ripe fruits marry delicately with vanilla and toastiness deriving from the maturation. The palate is full and generous. An original wine which will not be far from its peak now.

↪ Gilles et Brigitte Morgeau, 2, av. de Bordeaux, 86490 Beaumont, tel. 05.49.85.50.37, fax 05.49.85.58.13 ☑
☿ ev. day except Sun. 2pm–6pm

DOM. DE LA TOUR SIGNY

Sauvignon 2002★

	6 ha	30,000		3–5€

A domaine located on the chalky hillock of Marigny-Brisay, within 7 km of Futuroscope. The intense aromas of blackcurrant bud, linden flowers and boxwood give an impression of freshness and delicacy. The palate reflects the same finish on particularly pleasant notes of citrus fruits (lemon dominating). Perfect with snails in pastry.

↪ Christophe Croux, 2 rue de Tue-Loup, 86380 Marigny-Brizay, tel. 05.49.55.31.21, fax 05.49.62.36.82 ☑
☿ by appt.

Wines selected but not starred

DOM. DE LA ROTISSERIE

Sauvignon 2002

	1.8 ha	6,500		3–5€

↪ Jacques Baudon, 35, rue de l'Habit-d'Or, 86380 Marigny-Brizay, tel. 05.49.52.09.02, fax 05.49.37.11.44 ☑
☿ ev. day 8am–12 noon 1.30pm–7pm

DOM. DE VILLEMONT

Sauvignon 2002

	1.93 ha	5,000		3–5€

↪ Alain Bourdier, Dom. de Villemont, Seuilly, 86110 Mirebeau, tel. 05.49.50.51.31, fax 05.49.50.96.71, e-mail domaine-de-villemont@wanadoo.fr ☑
☿ ev. day except Sun. 9.30am–12.30pm 2pm–7pm

Wines from Central France

From the hills of Forez to the Orléans area, the main wine-growing sectors of the Centre are located on the best exposed sites of hills and plateaux eroded through successive geological eras by the Loire and its tributaries, the Allier and the Cher. These areas, on the hillsides of the Côtes d'Auvergne, in parts of Saint-Pourçain and Châteaumeillant, are located on the eastern and northern flanks of the Massif Central, and yet still open on to the Loire basin.

The vine-growing soils are either silica or limestone, always well situated and exposed, sustaining a limited number of varieties of which the most common are Gamay for red and rosé wines and Sauvignon for white wines. A few special local varieties are grown here and there: the Tressallier at Saint-Pourçain and the Chasselas at Pouilly-sur-Loire for whites; Pinot Noir at Sancerre, Menetou-Salon and Reuilly for reds and rosés, plus the delicate Pinot Gris, again in the latter vineyard; finally, the Meunier which, near Orléans, makes the original Gris Meunier. When all is said and done, it is a notably rich selection.

Whatever the terroir, all the wines made from these varieties share a light, fresh and fruity character which makes them particularly appealing, pleasant and drinkable, especially when matched with the gastronomic specialities of the region. The green, peaceful countryside of the Auvergne, the Bourbonnais, the Nivernais, the Berry or the Orléanais encompasses a region of wide horizons and varied landscapes. The wines are grown in vineyards that are often family-owned and run in traditional ways, and, secure in their roots and traditions, the winemakers are expert in showing off their worthy wines to best advantage.

Châteaumeillant AOVDQS

Here, the Gamay is raised on terroirs of volcanic soils, in an old established wine region. In 2002 this covered 92 ha with an output of 4,351 hl.

The reputation of Château-meillant was founded on its famous *gris*, a wine made from the first pressing of Gamay grapes, and notable for its remarkable texture, freshness and fruitiness. The reds (which should be drunk young and chilled), combine bouquet, smoothness and sheer drinkability.

VALERIE ET FREDERIC DALLOT
Tradition 2001★

■	3 ha	9,500	▮ ◆	5–8 €

Regularly selected in the *Guide*, the Cuvée Tradition once more caught the attention of the Jury. The colour is particularly youthful (mauve-ruby). On the nose it shows strong character (crushed strawberry, spices and pepper). The tannins, discreet on the attack, increase in strength, becoming fresh and tight. The terroir is well represented. Needs time.

➐ Frédéric et Valérie Dallot, La Bidoire, 18370 Châteaumeillant, tel. 02.48.56.31.84, fax 02.48.61.35.14 ✉
☖ ev. day 9am–12 noon 2pm–6pm

DOM. GEOFFRENET-MORVAL
Cuvée Jeanne Vieilles Vignes 2002★

■	1.07 ha	4,800	▮ ◆	5–8 €

Fabien Geoffrenet continues to enlarge his small vineyard that started out as a plot of 0.5 ha. Violet-ruby, this red wine expresses typical notes of wormwood after airing. The fleshy, good-quality tannins will become more refined in the coming months.

➐ EARL Geoffrenet-Morval, 2, rue de La Fontaine, 18190 Venesmes, tel. 02.48.60.50.15, fax 02.48.24.62.91,

Wines from Central France

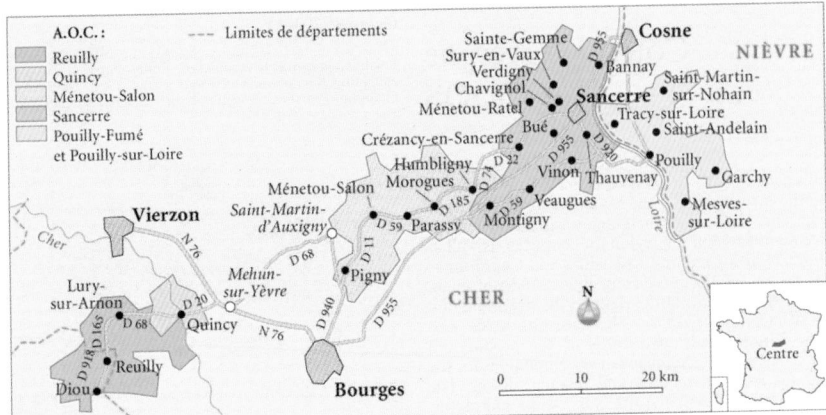

e-mail fabien.geoffrenet@wanadoo.fr
Ⓣ by appt.

DOM. LE PAVILLON 2002★★

	1.66 ha	8,000	🍴 ♦	5–8 €

José-Marc Da Costa was looking for a holiday home. He found this splendid dovecote, the start of his dream: to become a wine producer. A deep violety-purple, this Châteaumeillant exhales complex flavours: blackberry, blackcurrant, spices and a touch of resin. Well structured and well balanced it has excellent potential. The commended **Vin Gris 2002** is proof of finesse and freshness.
🕙 José-Marc Da Costa, 31, av. Antoine-Meillet, 18370 Châteaumeillant, tel. 02.48.61.43.12, fax 02.48.61.43.12, e-mail lepavillon18@aol.com ☑
Ⓣ ev. day 9.30am–12.30pm 2.30pm–7.30pm

PRESTIGE DES GARENNES

Vin gris 2002★

	5 ha	50,000	🍴 ♦	5–8 €

Salmon-grey to the eye, it opens out with fruitiness and floral notes. From the freshness at the start it goes on to develop weight on the mid-palate, proceding to an interesting finish. It should go well with an osso-bucco of turkey, according to a member of the Jury. The **Légier de la Chassaigne rosé 2002** and **red 2001** are mentioned but are unstarred.
🕙 Cave du Tivoli, rte de Culan, 18370 Châteaumeillant, tel. 02.48.61.33.55, fax 02.48.61.44.92, e-mail cave@chateaumeillant.com ☑
Ⓣ ev. day except Sun. 8am–12 noon 1.30pm–5.30pm; Sun. May–Aug.

Wines selected but not starred

DOM. DU CHAILLOT 2002

	0.75 ha	5,600	🍴 ♦	5–8 €

🕙 Dom. du Chaillot, pl. de la Tournoise, 18130 Dun-sur-Auron, tel. 02.48.59.57.69, fax 02.48.59.58.78, e-mail pierre.picot@wanadoo.fr ☑
Ⓣ by appt.
🕙 Pierre Picot

Côtes d'Auvergne AOVDQS

Whether grown on the volcanic hills called puys, in Limagne, or on the hills (dômes) on the eastern edge of the Massif Central, Auvergne wines are made with the Gamay variety, which has been cultivated in the region for centuries, as well as Pinot Noir for red and rosé wines and Chardonnay for the whites. Produced from about 370 ha of vines, these wines have had the right to the denomination AOVDQS since 1977. The unusual rosés and easy-drinking reds (two-thirds of the production) are particularly recommended as companions for the famous local charcuterie and regional dishes. The best growths can acquire surprising character,

fullness and personality. In 2002, 15,695 hl were produced, including 913 hl of white wine.

VIGNOBLE DE L'ARBRE BLANC

Gamay Vieilles Vignes 2001★★

	0.5 ha	900	⑪	11–15 €

Frédéric Gounan started out just three years ago at the entrance to the Parc des Volcans with the desire to produce quality Côtes d'Auvergne. Today he has achieved that. But

hurry to buy this 2001 (the vineyard consists of only 1.6 ha). A bright-garnet colour, the wine offers intense scents of red berries, uplifted by a touch of vanilla. Long legs in the glass indicate unctuousity on the palate. The silky finish is long.
🕙 Frédéric Gounan, rue de l'Arbre-Blanc, 63450 Saint-Sandoux, tel. 04.73.39.40.91 ☑
Ⓣ by appt.

CHARMENSAT

Boudes 2002★

	7.15 ha	35,000	🍴 ♦	5–8 €

Annie Charmensat took charge of the family estate in 1999. Here they practise sustainable agriculture and grassing down on little more than 9 ha of vines, aged from ten to 100 years and planted in terraces facing south. She should be satisfied with the 2002 harvest, which has earned her three mentions in the *Guide*. The bright ruby-red Boudes has a fairly discreet nose but it opens out on the palate with a lovely freshness. The tannins seem round, in spite of a little austerity on the finish that will disappear in a few months. The **Boudes rosé 2002** will accompany cold meats well, while the **Boudes Chardonnay 2002** only needs fish to bring out its freshness. Both are singled out.
🕙 GAEC Charmensat, rue du Coufin, 63340 Boudes, tel. 04.73.96.44.75, fax 04.73.96.58.04, e-mail charmensat@wanadoo.fr ☑
Ⓣ ev. day except Sun. 9am–12 noon 2pm–6pm

GILLES PERSILIER

Gergovia 2001★★

	1 ha	4,000	⑪	5–8 €

Former agricultural technician, Gilles Persilier has been cultivating 8 ha of vines at Gergovie since 1995. The Jury was unanimous in its comments about the golden Chardonnay,

with its delicate exotic fruits complemented with honey and

mint. The well-balanced palate has a lovely oakiness that adds richness to the finish. A good representative Côtes d'Auvergne.
🐦 Gilles Persilier, 27, rue Jean-Jaurès, 63670 Gergovie, tel. 04.73.79.44.42, fax 04.73.87.56.95 ✓
🍷 by appt.

JEAN-PIERRE ET MARC PRADIER
Tradition 2002★

| ■ | 2.7 ha | 14,000 | ■ ♦ | 3–5 € |

Don't forget that the red Tradition 2000 was elected a *coup de coeur* in the 2002 edition of the *Guide*. This agreeable 2002, a blend of Gamay (95%) and Pinot, is very pleasing with its ruby colour with orange highlights and its perfumes of soft fruits with a touch of pear-drops. Its supple tannins make it lively. The **Corent rosé 2002** also deserves one star: rich with red berries blended with vegetal nuances, soft and round. The **Chardonnay 2001 (5–8 €)**, matured one year in barrel, is commended.
🐦 Jean-Pierre et Marc Pradier, 9, rue Saint-Jean-Baptiste, 63730 Les Martres-de-Veyre, tel. 04.73.39.86.41, fax 04.73.39.88.17, e-mail jpmpradier@wanadoo.fr ✓
🍷 by appt.

CAVE SAINT-VERNY
Première Cuvée 2002★

| ■ | 40 ha | 40,000 | ■ ♦ | 5–8 € |

The harvests that undergo vinification at the cooperative come from vineyards scattered over 53 villages. This Première Cuvée is pure Gamay. The colour is garnet-red with purple highlights, the nose entirely minerally. After a clean first impression, it shows great length and suppleness due to the silky tannins. A Saint-Nectaire cheese will suit it well. The **Première Cuvée white 2002**, a Chardonnay, and the **Corent rosé 2002** also each obtain one star: one for its fresh fruitiness, the other for its elegant roundness.
🐦 Cave Saint-Verny, rte d'Issoire, 63960 Veyre-Monton, tel. 04.73.69.60.11, fax 04.73.69.65.22, e-mail saint.verny@limagrain.com ✓
🍷 by appt.

SAUVAT
Boudes Gamay Prestige Elevage bois 2001★

| ■ | 0.7 ha | 4,000 | ⦀ | 8–11 € |

Sauvat concentrated this year on Gamay. Matured 12 months in wood, presenting a dark-garnet colour, dominated by aromas of vanilla and toast. The fairly lively opening precedes a well-balanced mid-palate, sustained by integrated tannins that reappear on the finish. Matured in tank, the **Boudes Demoiselles Oubliées du Donazat Sélection 2002 (5–8 €)** is singled out. It is very open with black fruits and suppleness. As a result of direct pressing, the Gamay goes to make up this discreet but rounded **Boudes Les Charmeuses de la Côte Sélection rosé 2002 (5–8 €)**. Commended.
🐦 Claude et Annie Sauvat, 63340 Boudes, tel. 04.73.96.41.42, fax 04.73.96.58.34, e-mail sauvat@terre-net.fr ✓
🍷 ev. day except Sun. 9am–12 noon 2pm–7pm; Sun. 2pm–7pm Apr.until Jun.
🐦 Annie Blot

DOM. SOUS-TOURNOEL 2002★

| ■ | 1.9 ha | 4,500 | ⦀ | 3–5 € |

Alain Gaudet cultivates his vines in Volvic country – nothing surprising about that since the vine has grown here since the fifth century. The violet-hued rosé is pleasant due to its roundness and subtle fruitiness that enhances the fresh finish. The **red 2002**, a blend of Gamay (90%) and Pinot matured one year in cask, is singled out: its profile is that of a light fruity wine, in the style of a *primeur*.
🐦 Alain Gaudet, Dom. Sous-Tournoël, 63530 Volvic, tel. 04.73.33.52.12, fax 04.73.33.62.71 ✓
🍷 by appt.

Wines selected but not starred

JACQUES ABONNAT
Boudes 2002

| ■ | 1 ha | 3,000 | ■ | 5–8 € |

🐦 Jacques Abonnat, 63340 Chalus, tel. 04.73.96.45.95, fax 04.73.96.45.95 ✓
🍷 by appt.

YVAN BERNARD
Corent Gamay 2002

| ■ | 0.65 ha | 2,860 | ■ ⦀ | 3–5 € |

🐦 Yvan Bernard, chem. des Pales, 63114 Authezat, tel. 04.73.71.60.28 ✓
🍷 by appt.

HENRI BOURCHEIX
Chanturgue Gamay 2002

| ■ | 1.31 ha | 8,900 | ■ ♦ | 5–8 € |

🐦 Henri Bourcheix, 4, rue Saint-Marc, 63170 Aubière, tel. 04.73.26.04.52, fax 04.73.27.96.46, e-mail vins-henri-bourcheix@wanadoo.fr ✓
🍷 by appt.

ODETTE ET GILLES MIOLANNE
Volcane rouge 2002

| ■ | 3.5 ha | 19,000 | ■ | 3–5 € |

🐦 Odette et Gilles Miolanne, EARL de la Sardissère, 17, rte de Coudes, 63320 Neschers, tel. 04.73.96.72.45, fax 04.73.96.25.79 ✓
🍷 by appt.

DOM. MONTEL-CAILLOT
Châteaugay 2002

| ■ | 1.23 ha | 8,100 | ■ | 3–5 € |

🐦 GAEC de Bourrassol, 33, Grande-Rue, 63200 Ménétrol, tel. 04.73.38.24.12, fax 04.73.38.89.90 ✓
🍷 by appt.

Côtes du Forez

Great efforts have gone into maintaining this smart and spectacular vineyard, covering 175 ha in 21 communes around Boën-sur-Lignon (Loire).

Nearly all the excellent dry, robust rosé and red wines, made exclusively from Gamay, are grown on Tertiary terrains in the north and Primary soils in the south. Production comes mainly from a splendid Cave Coopérative. These wines which received an AOC in the year 2002, when production amounted to 6,405 hl, are best drunk young.

GILLES BONNEFOY
La Madone 2002★★

| ■ | 0.7 ha | 4,000 | ■ ♦ | 3–5 € |

Gilles Bonnefoy has built a wine cellar of 250 m³. Last year, La Madone 2001 red received a *coup de coeur*, this 2002 rosé *cuvée* is no less remarkable. The colour of quince jelly with rose tinges, limpid and bright, it evokes with cleaness ripe

LOIRE

grapes, yellow-fleshed peaches, grapefruit and passion-fruit. Fruity and rich, the palate discloses fullness and roundness, and on the finish, a good structure of tannins. A harmoniously structured rosé, fresh and long, to enjoy with a pear charlotte. The **red Gamay Madone 2002** is singled out.

☞ Gilles Bonnefoy, Le Pizet, 42600 Champdieu, tel. 04.77.97.07.33, fax 04.77.97.79.38, e-mail g.bonnefoy@42.sideral.fr ☑
☏ by appt.

CLOS DE CHOZIEUX
Vieilles Vignes 2002★

| ■ | n.c. | 5,000 | ◫ | 3–5 € |

A winemaker's house built in 1840 commands over the 55-year-old vines of this estate. This dark red *cuvée* opens on characteristic notes of gun-flint, allied with light oak inherited from a maturation of four months. The palate opens on soft fruits, then evolves to show elegant tannins, with peppery and woody flavours. A *vin de terroir* to drink or keep in the wine cellar for one to two years.

☞ EARL Clos de Chozieux, 42130 Leigneux, tel. 04.77.24.38.54, fax 04.77.24.39.75 ☑
☏ ev. day 9am–12 noon 2pm–7pm
☞ J.-L. et Y. Gaumon

LES VIGNERONS FOREZIENS
Tradition 2002★

| ■ | 13 ha | 80,000 | ▮ ♦ | 3–5 € |

The cooperative who vinifies most of the appellation made this dark, limpid, garnet-red wine, where peppery aromas underline mineral nuances and kirsch flavours. This range of flavours continues throughout the round palate, ready to drink. The **Cuvée Pierre Dellenbach red 2002 (5–8 €)** is singled out.

☞ Les Vignerons Foréziens, Le Pont-Rompu, 42130 Trelins, tel. 04.77.24.00.12, fax 04.77.24.01.76, e-mail vigneronsforeziens@wanadoo.fr ☑
☏ by appt.

DOM. DU POYET
Cuvée des Vieux Ceps 2002★

| ■ | 1.5 ha | 7,000 | ▮ | 3–5 € |

Located within 1 km of a château where there are hawk demonstrations, the domaine produced this garnet-red wine from old vines, the oldest being 60 years old. It is very dark and limpid, opening on gun-flint mixed with blackcurrant and liquorice. The round, fleshy palate opens to reveal pleasant notes of sweet chestnut, and spices balance well with the blackcurrant on the finish. Equipped with a fine tannic structure, this *cuvée* is ready to drink, but can still wait one to two years. The **rosé 2002** is singled out.

☞ Jean-François Arnaud, Dom. du Poyet, au Bourg, 42130 Marcilly-le-Châtel, tel. 04.77.97.48.54, fax 04.77.97.48.71 ☑
☏ ev. day 8am–8pm; groups by appt.

O. VERDIER ET J. LOGEL
Amasis 2002★★

| ■ | 2 ha | 8,000 | ▮ ♦ | 3–5 € |

Odile and Jacky Logel took over the family vines in 1992 and today work the vineyards employing organic farming

methods. After ten years of activity, they at last receive a *coup de coeur* for this intense garnet-red wine which opens out with quite pronounced mineral notes, hinting at pepper and a touch of soft fruits. A well-balanced structure of integrated tannins follows a round attack, and there is no lack of freshness. A wine ready to drink, but which can wait one or two years. The **red Cuvée des Gourmets 2002** receives one star.

☞ Odile Verdier et Jacky Logel, La Côte, 42130 Marcilly-le-Châtel, tel. 04.77.97.41.95, fax 04.77.97.48.80,
e-mail cave.verdierlogel@wanadoo.fr ☑ ☖
☏ ev. day 9am–12 noon 2pm–7pm; Sun. by appt.

Wines selected but not starred

DOM. DE LA PIERRE NOIRE
Cuvée spéciale 2001

| ■ | 1 ha | 4,000 | ▮ ♦ | 3–5 € |

☞ Hélène et Christian Gachet, Dom. de la Pierre Noire, chem. de l'Abreuvoir, 42610 Saint-Georges-Hauteville, tel. 04.77.76.08.54 ☑
☏ ev. day 8am–7pm

Coteaux du Giennois

This appellation, classified as AOC in 1998, covers silicious or limestone soils stretching along the hills of the upper Loire into the Nièvre and the Loiret. In 2002, three traditional varieties, Gamay, Pinot Noir and Sauvignon, produced 7,727 hl, including 2,960 hl of light, fruity white wines with little tannin, expressing the highly distinctive terroir. They can be drunk for up to five years and can be drunk with all meat dishes.

Planting is progressing appreciably in the Nièvre and also increasing somewhat in the Loiret, promising continuing good health for this vineyard, which covers 153 ha.

EMILE BALLAND 2002★★

| ■ | 0.3 ha | 1,200 | ◫ | 11–15 € |

Established since 2000 on the Coteaux du Giennois, Emile Balland produced a remarkable red wine, presented for a *coup de coeur* and made from vines of about 30 years old. The maturation in cask lasted four months. Somewhere between garnet and crimson, the deep colour encourages you to discover the complex nose of stewed fruit and jamminess, with a touch of liquorice. The tannins coat the palate, providing a background for the round, supple body. Be patient for two or three years to fully appreciate the potential of this well-balanced and lengthy 2002. The **white 2002** is awarded one star: it appears fresh and fruity followed by toasty, vanilla notes.

☞ Emile Balland, RN 7, BP 9, 45420 Bonny-sur-Loire, tel. 03.86.39.26.51, fax 03.86.39.26.51, e-mail emile.balland@infonie.fr ☑
☏ by appt.

JOSEPH BALLAND-CHAPUIS

Cuvée Marguerite Marceau 2001★

	1 ha	6,000	🔳 ⬭	5–8 €

The Marguerite Marceau selection is made from vines of more than 30 years old. Very mature grapes were harvested at the end of October. Dark fruits (*pêche de vigne* and quince) dominate on the nose, moderated by a little honey. Part of the maturation was spent in cask resulting in this well-made palate: opening beautifully with roundness, richness and length. The Jury singles out the **Joseph Balland-Chapuis white 2002** for its length and **red 2001** for fruitiness.
•¬ SCEA Dom. Balland-Chapuis, 6, allée des Soupirs, 45420 Bonny-sur-Loire, tel. 02.48.54.06.67, fax 02.48.54.07.97 🔳
•¬ Jean-Louis Saget

DOM. DES BEAUROIS 2002★★

	2 ha	12,000	🔳	5–8 €

Anne-Marie and Bernard Marty have been working in Beaulieu-sur-Loire since 1998, their vineyard made up of small plots on gravelly-type soils of the Loire. Situated in an old barn, their winery sheltered this remarkably characteristic wine, which releases intense exotic fruit notes: pineapple and passion-fruit. The consistent palate is rich with persistent length. Awarded a *coup de coeur*.
•¬ Anne-Marie Marty, Dom. des Beaurois, 89170 Lavau, tel. 03.86.74.16.09, fax 03.86.74.16.09 🔳 ⬛
🍷 ev. day except Sun. 11am–12.30pm 4pm–7pm

MICHEL LANGLOIS 2002★

	1,2	10,000	🔳 ⬩	5–8 €

The winery was built in 2001, the barrel store restored in 2002, a new reception area built in 2003: Michel Langlois has the means to work in the best conditions. After a *coup de coeur* last year for Champ de La Croix 2000 red, he presents a 2002 clear rosé with salmon, almost grey highlights. On the nose there is a subtle mix of aromas, floral, fruity and spicy, while the palate is lively and well structured. The **white Coteaux du Giennois 2002** and **red Cuvée Champ de La Croix 2002** are singled out: one for its length, the other for its lively character.
•¬ Michel Langlois, Le Bourg, 58200 Pougny, tel. 03.86.28.47.08, fax 03.86.28.59.29 🔳
🍷 ev. day except Sun. 9am–1pm 3pm–7pm

POUPAT ET FILS

Le Trocadéro 2002★

	1,1 ha	9,600	🔳 ⬩	5–8 €

The presentation of this Poupat wine, which is the issue of the local clay-siliceous soil, gives great pleasure. The power and strength of the structure are in perfect balance with the spicy and fruity character. Still fresh, the mineral finish predicts a good keeping potential of three or four years.
•¬ Poupat et Fils, Rivotte, 45250 Briare, tel. 02.38.31.39.76, fax 02.38.31.39.76 🔳
🍷 by appt.

LES TUILERIES 2002★

	6 ha	13,300	🔳 ⬩	5–8 €

The Caves de Pouilly-sur-Loire have been making Coteaux du Giennois since 1970. Their Tuileries selection honours the cooperative as much as the appellation. Its has a purple colour with violet tinges, the nose is still reserved but has some soft

fruits and spices that testify to youth. After the round first impression the palate quickly opens out with great freshness and fairly pronounced tannins. To drink now or wait for two to four years.
•¬ Caves de Pouilly-sur-Loire, Les Moulins à Vent, 39, av. de la Tuilerie, BP 9, 58150 Pouilly-sur-Loire, tel. 03.86.39.10.99, fax 03.86.39.02.28, e-mail caves.pouilly.loire@wanadoo.fr 🔳
🍷 by appt.

DOM. DE VILLEGEAI

Terres des Violettes 2002★★

	3.03 ha	12,000	🔳 ⬭ ⬩	5–8 €

François and Michel Quintin took the vine and wine route in 1991. Today they receive a *coup de coeur* for this intense-crimson Coteaux du Giennois, which, after a fleeting scent of violet, opens quickly with stone fruits, enhanced by floral and honeyed touches. The palate develops suppleness and freshness, and reveals grilled flavours (this wine is finely oaked). A fruity finish concludes the tasting of this *cuvée* of charm and elegance.
•¬ SCEA Quintin Frères, Villegeai, 58200 Cosne-sur-Loire, tel. 03.86.28.31.77, fax 03.86.28.20.77, e-mail quintin.francois@wanadoo.fr 🔳
🍷 by appt.

Wines selected but not starred

LYCEE AGRICOLE DE COSNE-SUR-LOIRE 2002

	1.2 ha	6,000	🔳 ⬩	3–5 €

•¬ Lycée agricole de Cosne-sur-Loire, 66, rue Jean-Monnet, Les Cottereaux, BP 132, 58206 Cosne-sur-Loire, tel. 03.86.26.99.84, fax 03.86.26.99.84 🔳
🍷 ev. day 8.30am–12.30pm 1.30pm–5.30pm
•¬ Conseil régional Bourgogne

DOM. DE MONTBENOIT 2002

	2.3 ha	18,000	🔳	3–5 €

•¬ Jean-Marie Berthier, Dom. des Claireaux, 18240 Sainte-Gemme-en-Sancerrois, tel. 02.48.79.40.97, fax 02.48.79.39.55 🔳 ⬛ ⬦
🍷 by appt.

DOM. DE VILLARGEAU 2002

	2 ha	10,500	🔳	5–8 €

•¬ GAEC Thibault, Villargeau, 58200 Pougny, tel. 03.86.28.23.24, fax 03.86.28.47.00, e-mail fthibault@wanadoo.fr 🔳
🍷 by appt.
•¬ Thibault Frères

Saint-Pourçain AOVDQS

Gentle, fertile Bourbonnais boasts a lovely vineyard, in nineteen communes, stretching over 535 ha southwest of Moulins. In 2002, production amounted to 24,489 hl of wine.

Limestone or gravelly slopes and plateaux, skirting the banks of the charming Sioule river, grow Gamay and Pinot Noir which combine to give the red and rosé wines their fruity appeal.

In the past, the native Tressallier variety made remarkable white wines that established Saint-Pourçain's reputation. Today, the original Tressallier is assembled with Chardonnay and Sauvignon to make distinctively aromatic wine worthy of more than a passing comment.

DOM. DE BELLEVUE

Grande Réserve 2002★★

	5.5 ha	40,000			3–5 €

Jean-Louis Pétillat cultivates 18 ha of vines, half of which surround the typically Bourbonnais house. Although he modernized the estate in 1995, he still wants to preserve the traditional spirit of the terroir. Objective achieved in this Réserve with green highlights that did not leave the Jury unmoved. The complex range of flavours combines fruits and flowers, however on the palate there is a developing roundness. Ideal with trout. The **white Domaine de Bellevue Reflets 1999** is singled out: both its attractive flavours of honey uplifted by mint and the balance will impress as an aperitif.
☎ Jean-Louis Pétillat, Bellevue, 03500 Meillard, tel. 04.70.42.05.56, fax 04.70.42.09.75, e-mail jean-louis-petillat1@wanadoo.fr ▮

BERNARD GARDIEN ET FILS

La Réserve des Grands Jours 2001★

	3 ha	20,000			5–8 €

Worked from father to son since 1924, this estate today covers 20 hectares. Its star *cuvée* was singled out by the Jury: **Nectar des Fées 2002 (3–5 €)** stands down to let this Réserve des Grands Jours take first place. A pretty red with orange tones, this is intense on the nose with spicy red berries, typical of the Pinot Noir of which there is 70% in the blend. The supple attack opens out to richness on the palate complemented by supple tannins. The **white Réserve des Grands Jours 2001** is singled out.
☎ Dom. Gardien, Chassignolles, 03210 Besson, tel. 04.70.42.80.11, fax 04.70.42.80.99, e-mail c.gardien@03.sideral.fr ▮
✠ ev. day except Sun. 8am–12 noon 2pm–7pm

CAVE JALLET

Les Ceps centenaires 2002★

	1.5 ha	5,000			3–5 €

The Jallet family is proud of their vineyard where some of the vine stock is up to 100 years old. The Gamay Noir, combined with 10% Pinot Noir, produces this wine which at first is supple and then opens out to reveal freshness on the palate where the balance carries through to the finish. Enjoy it as of today.
☎ Cave Jallet, Les Cailles, 03500 Saulcet, tel. 04.70.45.33.78 ▮
✠ ev. day 8am–12 noon 2pm–7pm

NEBOUT

Tradition 2002★

	3.5 ha	22,000			3–5 €

The unforgettable Odile and Serge Nebout regularly appear in the *Guide*. They present this intensely-red 2002 that presents generous characteristic aromas of the Pinot Noir (20% of

the blend). The integrated tannins accompany the persistent fruit flavours on the finish. The **red Cuvée de La Malgarnie 2002 (5–8 €)**, an agreeable wine full of cherry flavours, and the **white Cuvée des Gravières 2002** are singled out.
☎ Serge et Odile Nebout, rte de Montluçon, 03500 Saint-Pourçain-sur-Sioule, tel. 04.70.45.31.70, fax 04.70.45.12.54 ▮
✠ ev. day except Sun. 8am–12 noon 2pm–7pm

LES VIGNERONS DE SAINT-POURCAIN

Cuvée Réservée 2002★

	n.c.	50,000			3–5 €

The Cave de Saint-Pourçain presents two very good wines. This pale rosé, discreet both in colour and on the nose, regains ground on the palate with a beautiful balance and suppleness, with a slightly refreshing acid note on the finish. The **white Cuvée Réservée 2002** also obtains one star. This blend of Chardonnay, Tressallier and Sauvignon releases grapefruit aromas before opening out with suppleness that finishes on a lemony note.
☎ Union des vignerons de Saint-Pourçain, 3, rue Ronde, 03500 Saint-Pourçain-sur-Sioule, tel. 04.70.45.42.82, fax 04.70.45.99.34, e-mail udv.stpourcain@wanadoo.fr ▮
✠ ev. day except Sun. 8am–12 noon 2pm–6pm

CAVE TOUZAIN

Feuille pourpre 2002★★

	2 ha	9,800			3–5 €

For a first wine, Yannick Touzain has played a masterstroke. A lovely Saint-Pourçain, garnet with purple tinges. The Jury was unanimous thanks to its soft attack and full, well-balanced palate. The tannins sheath their claws and the very long finish recalls the ripeness and spicy flavours offered liberally by the nose. The range doesn't stop there: the floral and fresh **white Cave Touzain 2002** is singled out, as is the **rosé 2002**.
☎ Yannick Touzain, 9, rte de Moulins, 03500 Lontigny, tel. 04.70.45.95.05, fax 04.70.45.95.05 ▮
✠ by appt.

Wines selected but not starred

DOM. GROSBOT-BARBARA

Le Vin d'Alon 2002

	1.6 ha	10,000			3–5 €

☎ Dom. Grosbot-Barbara, Montjournal, rte de Montluçon, 03500 Cesset, tel. 04.70.45.26.66, fax 04.70.45.54.95 ▮
✠ ev. day 9am–12 noon 2pm–7pm

FRANCOIS RAY 2002

	3 ha	15,000			5–8 €

☎ Cave François Ray, Venteuil, 03500 Saulcet, tel. 04.70.45.35.46, fax 04.70.45.64.96 ▮
✠ ev. day except Sun. 9am–12 noon 2pm–7pm; groups by appt.

Côte Roannaise

Volcanic soils on valley slopes in the east, south and southwest create a terroir in which the Gamay is very much at home.

Fourteen communes, covering 192 ha situated on the left bank of the river produce excellent red wines and rather unusual, fresh rosés. Vinification, which totalled 7,826 hl in 2002, takes place on the growers' own properties; they create original wines of character appealing to the most prestigious chefs in the region. The area's wine-growing traditions are on show at the Musée Forézien in Ambierle.

ALAIN BAILLON 2002★★

■	0.8 ha	5,000	■ ♦	3–5 €

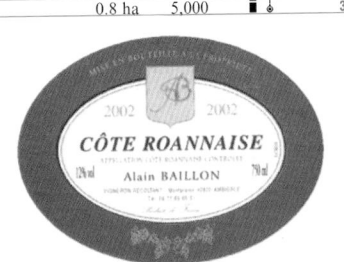

Created in 1989, Alain Baillon's vineyard today has a holding of 6.2 ha of vines. The Jury was attracted by this very pale pink wine, limpid and brilliant. Its elegant currant and raspberry flavours, joined by a mineral note, complement the roundness of the first impression. This fresh and fruity rosé, balanced and with fine tannins, will be appreciated within the year accompanied by plum tart or a crème brûlée. The **red Montplaisir 2002 (5–8 €)** receives two stars for its richness, strength and ripe fruit flavours.
➤ Alain Baillon, Montplaisir, 42820 Ambierle, tel. 04.77.65.65.51, fax 04.77.65.65.65 ☑
☾ by appt.

PAUL ET JEAN-PIERRE BENETIERE

Vieilles Vignes 2002★★

■	1.4 ha	9,000	■ ♦	5–8 €

Some 60-year-old vines have gone to produce this intense-crimson wine which exhales elegant perfumes of blackberry, red berries and flowers. Full bodied and powerful it opens with suppleness and volume. This structured and rich 2002 can be drunk during the next two years with cured meats. The **red Cuvée Fruitée 2002 (3–5 €)** obtains one star.
➤ Jean-Pierre and Paul Benetière, pl. de la Mairie, 42155 Villemontais, tel. 04.77.63.18.29, fax 04.77.63.18.29 ☑
☾ by appt.

CH. DE CHAMPAGNY

Grande Réserve 2002★

■	1.5 ha	10,000	■ ♦	3–5 €

After the *coup de coeur* of last year, Grande Réserve returns clothed in garnet-red, brilliant and limpid, the nose packed with soft fruits (strawberry, cherry) and charred notes. The first, fleshy impression develops beautiful length with mellow tannins, fruity notes and coffee flavours. Structured and rather long, this *cuvée* is ready, but can still keep for two years. The **red Domaine de Champagny 2002** is singled out.
➤ André et Frédéric Villeneuve, Champagny, 42370 Saint-Haon-le-Vieux, tel. 04.77.64.42.88, fax 04.77.62.12.55 ☑
☾ by appt.

DOM. DES POTHIERS 2002★★

■	0.75 ha	5,000	■ ♦	5–8 €

This old galleried farm (with a balcony skirting the first floor) has kept the name of its former owners although it was taken over in 1981 by Denise and George Paire; they will soon be joined by their son who is studying for a BTS in viticulture and winemaking. A winning team, judging by this characteristic, balanced and elegant 2002. Crimson in colour, the wine reveals rich, winey aromas: spices and mature soft fruits (strawberry and blackcurrant). The rich, fleshy palate finishes with a slight freshness. Lay this wine down for two years. The **red Côte Roannaise George Paire 2002 (3–5 €)** is singled out.
➤ Georges et Denise Paire, Les Pothiers, 42155 Villemontais, tel. 04.77.63.15.84, fax 04.77.63.19.24 ☑ ☗
☾ by appt.

DOM. DE LA ROCHETTE

Vieilles Vignes 2002★★★

■	1.5 ha	8,000	◫	5–8 €

This *coup de coeur* rewards a family whose wine-producing ties go back to 1630. The product of 60-year-old vines, this *cuvée* has a dark-crimson colour with purple highlights, and the straightforward, powerful nose reveals rich black fruit with nuances of vanilla and liquorice. It is full bodied and supple, its well-structured tannins lightly touched with elegant vanilla and oak, the palate round and harmonious. With such potential, this 2002 will be appreciated after two or three years with red meat or a game. The **red Domaine de La Rochette Bératard 2002 (3–5 €)**, matured in tank, receives two stars in reward for its complex fruit and great structure.
➤ Antoine Néron, La Rochette, 42155 Villemontais, tel. 04.77.63.10.62, fax 04.77.63.35.54, e-mail antoine.neron@wanadoo.fr ☑ ☗
☾ ev. day except Sun. 8am–7pm

ROBERT SEROL ET FILS

Les Vieilles Vignes 2002★

■	6 ha	40,000	■ ♦	3–5 €

Some 40-year-old vines, cultivated on sandy-granite soils and farmed according to the Terra Vitis protocol, are the source of this intensely garnet-red wine, bright with beautiful purple tinges. Rather intense and distinguished perfumes evoke woodland fruits, rose and peony, then the full and fleshy palate with its good vinosity opens out with sufficient length. A well-made and balanced *cuvée* to drink now or to lay down for one to two years. The **red Les Millerands 2002 (5–8 €)** is commended for laying down.
➤ EARL Robert Sérol et Fils, Les Estinaudes, 42370 Renaison, tel. 04.77.64.44.04, fax 04.77.62.10.87, e-mail domaine.serol@wanadoo.fr ☑
☾ ev. day 9am–12.30pm 2pm–7pm; Sun. by appt.

PHILIPPE ET JEAN-MARIE VIAL

Découverte 2002★

■	6 ha	35,000	■ ♦	5–8 €

The 2002 is the first production respecting the Terra Vitis charter. Here is this crimson-coloured Côte Roannaise with an intense nose of raspberry and strawberry aromas and hints of spice. If it reveals light tannins, it does not lose anything of

its roundness and has pleasant stewed fruit on the palate. A well-balanced wine, drinking in two years with red meat.
� Philippe et Jean-Marie Vial, Bel-Air, 42370 Saint-André-d'Apchon, tel. 04.77.65.81.04, fax 04.77.65.91.99 ▼
🍷 by appt.

Wines selected but not starred

FRANCOIS CHABRE
Cuvée Tradition 2001

■	1.5 ha	7,000	▮	5–8 €

↝ François Chabré, La Martinière, 42820 Ambierle, tel. 04.77.65.69.43, fax 04.77.65.63.98 ▼
🍷 by appt.

MICHEL ET ERIC DESORMIERE
Tradition 2002

■	3.25 ha	12,000	▮	3–5 €

↝ Michel et Eric Desormière, Le Perron, 42370 Renaison, tel. 04.77.64.48.55, fax 04.77.62.12.73 ▼
🍷 ev. day 8am–12.30pm 1.30pm–7pm; Sun. by appt.

FRANCOIS LASSEIGNE
Malème 2002

■	0.5 ha	730	▮	3–5 €

↝ François Lasseigne, Le Bourg, 42640 Saint-Romain-la-Motte, tel. 04.77.64.54.72, fax 04.77.64.54.72 ▼
🍷 by appt.

MICHEL ET LIONEL MONTROUSSIER
Bouthéran 2002

■	1.7 ha	8,000	▮ 🍷	3–5 €

↝ GAEC Michel et Lionel Montroussier, La Baude, 42370 Saint-André-d'Apchon, tel. 04.77.65.80.86, fax 04.77.65.92.76 ▼ 🏠 🏡
🍷 ev. day 8am–7pm; Sun. by appt.

DOM. DE LA PAROISSE
Cuvée à l'ancienne 2002

■	2 ha	7,000	◫	5–8 €

↝ Jean-Claude Chaucesse, La Paroisse, 42370 Renaison, tel. 04.77.64.26.10, fax 04.77.62.13.84 ▼
🍷 by appt.

Menetou-Salon

Menetou-Salon owes its vinous beginnings to the proximity of the medieval metropolis of Bourges. Unlike many other once-famous wine regions this one has remained a wine-growing area; the present vineyard is of high quality and covers 400 ha.

Menetou-Salon's favoured slopes share the same soils as its prestigious neighbour, Sancerre, and grow the same varieties, Sauvignon Blanc and Pinot Noir. From these, the appellation produces fresh, spicy white wines,

delicate, fruity rosés, and harmonious, scented reds, all of which should be drunk young. They are the pride of viticulture in Berry and splendidly accompany full-flavoured classic dishes (as an aperitif or with hot starters for the whites; with fish, rabbit or charcuterie for the reds, which should be served slightly chilled). Production reached 24,038 hl in 2002, of which 14,650 hl were white wines.

DOM. DE CHATENOY 2002★★

	35 ha	300,000		8–11 €

A stainless steel vat room for white wines, a barrel store with *barriques* for the red: Isabelle and Pierre Clément have a real concern for quality, concern that shows in this bright Menetou-Salon bursting with complexity. Still reserved, the nose opens with citrus fruits, blackcurrant, lychee and rose. Full and fleshy like a fruit with white flesh, the wine is long and predicts a good evolution. The **white Dame de Châtenoy 2001** is awarded one star for its flavours of overripe fruits and well-preserved freshness; with its good tannic concentration the **red Domaine de Châtenoy 2002** is also very successful.
↝ Isabelle et Pierre Clément, Dom. de Châtenoy, 18510 Menetou-Salon, tel. 02.48.66.68.70, fax 02.48.66.68.71 ▼
🍷 ev. day except Sat. Sun. 8.30am–12 noon 1.30pm–5.30pm; cl; 15 Aug.–1 Sep.

G. CHAVET ET FILS 2002★

	9.88 ha	83,000	▮ 🍷	5–8 €

The Chavet family are wine producers of reputation, their history goes back to 1710. It demonstrates its competence by presenting this floral and herbaceous wine (boxwood), the palate offering roundness and a discreetly mentholated pineapple fruitiness, all at the same time. To drink with a goat's cheese. The **red 2002** also receives one star for its fruitiness and harmony, while the supple **rosé 2002** is singled out.
↝ G. Chavet et Fils, GAEC des Brangers, 18510 Menetou-Salon, tel. 02.48.64.80.87, fax 02.48.64.84.78, e-mail contact@chavet-vins.com ▼ 🏡
🍷 ev. day except Sun. 8am–12 noon 2pm–6pm

DOM. GILBERT 2002★

■	n.c.	108,000	▮ 🍷	8–11 €

The main building of the estate – a beautiful manor house – appears on the label of this 2002 which has good concentration. Firstly there are aromas of cocoa and graphite on the nose, then they become more classic (strawberry and pepper). Round on the first impression, the wine discloses richness before finishing on tannins that need to be tamed since they still the mask the flavours. Leave it time to mature. The **red Les Renardières 2001 (11–15 €)**, matured in cask for 13 months, is singled out.
↝ Dom. Gilbert, Les Faucards, 18510 Menetou-Salon, tel. 02.48.66.65.90, fax 02.48.66.65.99, e-mail gilbert.p@wanadoo.fr ▼
🍷 by appt.

DOM. DE LOYE 2002★

■	3.2 ha	19,430	▮ 🍷	8–11 €

The Domaine de Loye, near Morogues, covers 12 ha on clay-limestone soils. The 2002 harvest of Pinot Noir is converted into this dark purple-ruby wine, with its dominant ripe aromas on a fruity nose. Round and supple at first, when open it reveals a slightly acid freshness and a sharp finish. It will improve in a few months. Also very good, the **white Domaine de Loye 2002 (5–8 €)** has elegant minerality.
↝ Dom. de Loye, 18220 Morogues, tel. 02.48.64.35.17, fax 02.48.64.41.29 ▼
🍷 by appt.
↝ Moindrot

DOM. HENRY PELLE
Clos de Ratier 2002★★

	5 ha	25,000	▮ ◫ 🍷	11–15 €

The village of Morogues is well preserved, in particular its church constructed from black sandstone. Henry Pellé set up

here as a wine-grower and a négociant. His white Menetou-Salon requires only a little airing to disclose its complex fruitiness, pronounced by the smell of herbs and elderflower. A vanilla character derived from an oak maturation of 15 months blends in on the palate with notes of honey and almond paste. An original personality which leaves a good impression. The **white Morogues 2002 (8–11 €)** obtains one star, while the selection **red Les Gris 2001** is singled out.
• Dom. Henry Pellé, 18220 Morogues, tel. 02.48.64.42.48, fax 02.48.64.36.88, e-mail info@henry.pelle.com ☑
🍷 ev. day except Sun. 8.30am–12 noon 1.30pm–5.30pm; Sat. by appt.; cl. 15–31 Aug.
• Anne Pellé

LE PRIEURE DE SAINT-CEOLS 2002★★

	2.5 ha	15,000	🍶 🍷	5–8 €

At Saint-Céols, located halfway between Bourges and Sancerre, Pierre Jacolin welcomes visitors in an old Benedictine priory. He produced this ruby wine which affirms its aromas of raspberry and blackberry on airing. The tannins develop powerfully to finish with a certain severity. The aftertaste of soft fruits is very satisfying. A wine with excellent potential that needs laying down for three to five years. The **white Le Prieuré de Saint-Céols 2002** obtains one star, while the **white Cuvée des Bénédictins 2001** is singled out.
• Pierre Jacolin, Le Prieuré de Saint-Céols, 18220 Saint-Céols, tel. 02.48.64.40.75, fax 02.48.64.41.15, e-mail sarl-jacolin@libertysurf.fr ☑
🍷 ev. day 8am–7pm; Sun. by appt.

DOM. JEAN TEILLER 2002★

	5.85 ha	36,000	🍶 🍷	5–8 €

In July 2002, Patricia Teiller, an oenologist trained at Bordeaux, and her friend Olivier joined Jean-Jacques Teiller on this estate of 15 ha. All three produced this concentrated wine. The purple-ruby colour is dense, the nose is packed with matured grape flavours (cherry, incense, spices), the palate has a good body supported by tannins that at first remain discreet, but become more austere on the finish. This Menetou-Salon will be able to accompany red meat in a little while.
• Dom. Jean Teiller, 13, rte de la Gare, 18510 Menetou-Salon, tel. 02.48.64.80.71, fax 02.48.64.86.92, e-mail domaine-teiller@wanadoo.fr ☑
🍷 ev. day except Sun. 8.30am–12 noon 2pm–6pm
• Jean-Jacques Teiller

LA TOUR SAINT-MARTIN

Morogues 2002★★

	8 ha	55,000	🍶 🍷	8–11 €

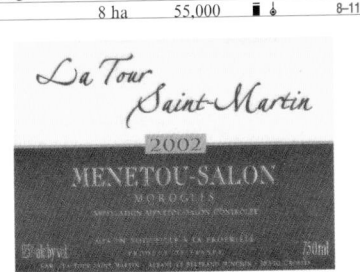

There is no need to introduce Bertrand Minchin since this passionate winemaker regularly obtains stars and *coups de c*[...] in the *Guide*. Here awarded a *coup de coeur* for a white wine [...] knows how to combine notes of vegetation (boxwood) [...] matured fruitiness (pear, citrus fruits) with elegance. Its richness, structure and great finesse ensure a remarkably well-balanced wine. A perfectly typical Menetou-Salon from this terroir. None the less remarkable is the **red Morogues 2002**, also awarded a *coup de coeur*. The aromas are astonishingly rich: very ripe fruit, almost jammy (plum, raspberry), pepper and spices. Good length. A splendid wine for ageing.
• Albane et Bertrand Minchin, EARL La Tour Saint-Martin, 18340 Crosses, tel. 02.48.25.02.95, fax 02.48.25.05.03, e-mail tour.saint.martin@wanadoo.fr ☑
🍷 by appt.

Wines selected but not starred

DOM. DE BEAUREPAIRE 2002

	7 ha	55,000	🍶 🍷	5–8 €

• Cave Gilbon, Dom. de Beaurepaire, 18220 Soulangis, tel. 02.48.64.41.09, fax 02.48.64.39.89, e-mail jf.gilbon@wanadoo.fr ☑
🍷 ev. day except Sun. 9am–12 noon 2pm–6.30pm; cl. 15–30 Aug.

DOM. DE COQUIN 2002

	4.7 ha	37,000	🍶 🍷	5–8 €

• Francis Audiot, Dom. de Coquin, 18510 Menetou-Salon, tel. 02.48.64.80.46, fax 02.48.64.84.51 ☑
🍷 ev. day except Sun. 9am–12 noon 1.30pm–6.30pm

CHRISTOPHE ET GUY TURPIN

Morogues 2002

	4.5 ha	30,000	🍶 🎯 🍷	5–8 €

• EARL Christophe Turpin, 11, pl. de l'Eglise, 18220 Morogues, tel. 02.48.64.32.24, fax 02.48.64.32.24, e-mail christopheturpin@wanadoo.fr ☑
🍷 by appt.

POUILLY-FUME AND POUILLY-SUR-LOIRE

The delightful vineyard of Pouilly-sur-Loire was first established by Benedictine monks. The Loire pounds against a limestone promontory as it turns northeast, and the soil, less chalky than at Sancerre, provides excellent growing conditions for the south-southeast facing slopes. The main variety is Sauvignon Blanc Fumé, which will shortly have entirely supplanted the traditional Chasselas, previously the source of appealing white wines when cultivated on silica soils. Pouilly-sur-Loire covers 40 ha while Pouilly-Fumé represents 1,070 ha. Total production was 64,247 hl of a wine that has all the qualities associated with a limestone terroir, marked by a freshness which does not lack a certain structure, and a full array of varietal aromas. It is matured within the area where it is grown according to certain conditions under which the must is fermented.

Pouilly-Fumé

CH. DE L'ABBAYE 2002★

	2.5	18,000	🍶 🎯 🍷	5–8 €

The 16th century Château de l'Abbaye, has been in the Morlat family since 1850, but the vineyard was only really developed in the 1970s and today there are 12 ha. This lovely 2002 vintage,

with its heady perfume, evokes fruit salad, apricots in syrup, crystallized apricots, William pears and pineapple. A lemon-peel flavour skips along the palate right through to the explosive finish. One taster suggested an alliance with a trout terrine.
- Pierre Morlat et Fils, GAEC de l'Abbaye,
58150 Saint-Laurent-l'Abbaye, tel. 03.86.26.11.96,
fax 03.86.26.19.78 ☑
- ev. day 8am–6pm

MICHEL BAILLY 2002★

14 ha	20,000	■ ♦	5–8 €

Michel Bailly and his son David have recently refitted their wine cellar, where you will discover this wine with its powerful citrus fruit scents, followed by touches of undergrowth. The slightly acid attack doesn't bother the palate, opening out to finish with a pleasant freshness and good length. To be served with shellfish or seafood.
- Michel Bailly et Fils, 3, rue Saint-Vincent, Les Loges,
58150 Pouilly-sur-Loire, tel. 03.86.39.04.78,
fax 03.86.39.05.25,
e-mail domaine.michel.bailly@wanadoo.fr ☑
- by appt.

JEAN-PIERRE BAILLY 2002★

11 ha	50,000	■ ♦	5–8 €

Jean-Pierre Bailly is an active member of the *Confrérie des Baillis de Pouilly*, recognizable by their black and gold clothing. His Pouilly-Fumé is a pleasantly impulsive wine, to drink by itself as an aperitif. It presents intense ripe fruit married with floral (privet and honeysuckle) flavours and leaves an impression of roundness and richness on the finish.
- Jean-Pierre Bailly, Les Girarmes, 11, rue des Coteaux,
58150 Tracy-sur-Loire, tel. 03.86.26.14.32,
fax 03.86.26.16.13 ☑
- by appt.

DOM. BOUCHIE-CHATELLIER
Premier Millésimé 2002★★

1 ha	6,000	■ ♦	11–15 €

Established on the hillock of Saint-Andelain, the estate of Bernard Bouchié (15 ha) is characterized by the high proportion of clay-flint terroirs. Rewarded several times in the *Guide*, the Cuvée Premier Millésimé, made from a selection of parcels of land, achieves a *coup de coeur*. It exudes a symphony of intense flavours: white peach, blackcurrant and gooseberry. Its roundness seems engraved with minerals and spices. With such finesse, elegance and complexity, this wine deserves to be tasted with interest and patience. It will keep for two years.
- EARL Bouchié-Chatellier, La Renardière,
58150 Saint-Andelain, tel. 03.86.39.14.01,
fax 03.86.39.05.18,
e-mail pouilly-fume.bouchie.chatellier@wanadoo.fr ☑
- by appt.

DOM. BOUCHIE-CHATELLIER
La Chatellière 2002★★

1,9	10,000	■ ♦	8–11 €

A ripe wine, a complex bouquet of white fruits and spring flowers, with a pretty hint of iris. A pleasant first impression opens out on the palate, which becomes invaded by an elegant roundness, marked by notes of toast and mineral touches. Subtle and already attractive, this 2002 will be able to accompany duck with orange. The **Cuvée La Renardière 2002** is awarded one star for fullness and suppleness.

- EARL Bouchié-Chatellier, La Renardière,
58150 Saint-Andelain, tel. 03.86.39.14.01,
fax 03.86.39.05.18,
e-mail pouilly-fume.bouchie.chatellier@wanadoo.fr
- by appt.

DOM. DU BOUCHOT 2002★

7,5	60,000	■ ♦	8–11 €

The domaine derives its name from the wine village of Bouchot, located nearby. It is also a close relation to the Château de Nozet. Regularly present in the *Guide*, with a *coup de coeur* for the 2000 vintage, this year it presents a young wine that should develop well. The finesse is already showing on the nose, revealing meringue, grenadine and syringa, while, after a firm attack, the palate returns agreeably to iris. The fresh **Cuvée Regain 2002** is singled out.
- EARL Dom. du Bouchot, BP 31, 58150 Saint-Andelain,
tel. 03.86.39.13.95, fax 03.86.39.05.92 ☑
- by appt.
- Kerbiquet

A. CAILBOURDIN
Triptyque 2001★

1 ha	5,000	⦀	15–23 €

To the north of Pouilly-sur-Loire, Maltaverne is situated at the exit of the new Paris-Nevers motorway. Alain Cailbourdin cultivates 16 ha of vines there. The Cuvée Triptych, produced on clay-limestone soil, has been matured half in barrel for eight months and half in tank. Well-balanced, it has an assertive structure and smoky flavour while keeping a pleasant freshness. It will be a good accompaniment to poultry with morel mushrooms.
- Dom. Alain Cailbourdin, Maltaverne,
58150 Tracy-sur-Loire, tel. 03.86.26.17.73,
fax 03.86.26.14.73 ☑
- by appt.

DOM. CHAMPEAU
Sélection Vieilles Vignes 2001★★

n.c.	n.c.	⦀	11–15 €

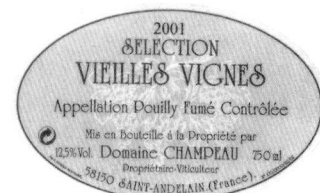

At the top of the hillock of Saint-Andelain, near the church which can be seen from several kilometres away, is the wine cellar of Franck and Guy Champeau. Both know how to combine the expression of flint terroir with maturation in wood in this intensely fruity wine (grape and *pêche de vigne*), all integrated into a finely engraved vanillary wood base. Firmness, richness and a long finish leave a pleasant memory. The **Pouilly-Fumé 2002 (5–8 €)** is singled out.
- SCEA Dom. Champeau, Le Bourg,
58150 Saint-Andelain, tel. 03.86.39.15.61,
fax 03.86.39.19.44,
e-mail domaine-champeau@wanadoo.fr ☑
- ev. day except Tue. am Sun. 9am–12 noon 2pm–6pm

LES CHANTALOUETTES 2002★

2.27	20,500	■ ♦	8–11 €

Taken over in 2001, this estate has not taken long to achieve success. This is quantified in this strong, promising wine, which expels fully-ripened grape aromas. It evokes fruit salad, ripe yellow peaches, apricots and exotic fruits. Its fleshy and full character make it an ideal accompaniment to fish or white meat.
- EARL Les Chantalouettes, 16, rue René-Couard,
58150 Pouilly-sur-Loire, tel. 03.86.39.56.60,
fax 03.86.39.08.30

LES CHARMES CHATELAIN 2002★

	2 ha	16,000	∎ ⑪ ⏚	8–11 €

Vincent, who handles the winery, is a 12th generation Chatelain wine producer at Saint-Andelain. He chose maturation of eight months in tank and five months in cask, which shows here in the perceptible vanilla and mocha coffee aromas. This 2002 is bursting with energy right through to the lengthy finish, impetuosity being a trait of youth. A wine to put aside for a few years. The principal *cuvée* of the estate, the **Chatelain 2002 (5–8 €)**, is commended.
↜ SA Dom. Chatelain, Les Berthiers,
58150 Saint-Andelain, tel. 03.86.39.17.46,
fax 03.86.39.01.13,
e-mail jean-claude.chatelain@wanadoo.fr ☑
�⌁ ev. day except Sun. 8am–12 noon 1.30pm–6pm;
Sat. by appt.; cl. Sun.

PATRICK COULBOIS

Les Cocques 2002★★

	7.5 ha	25,000	∎ ⏚	5–8 €

One can enjoy a splendid panoramic view of the Loire valley from the Patrick Coulbois' wine cellar. It will be pleasant to associate this visual pleasure with this intense and complex wine, with its perfect maturity: fruits, flowers, refreshing with a subtle aniseed note. This 2002 develops with richness, regularity and length on the palate. Its character is quite strong.
↜ Patrick Coulbois, Les Berthiers, 58150 Saint-Andelain, tel. 03.86.39.15.69, fax 03.86.39.12.14 ☑
�⌁ by appt.

DIDIER DAGUENEAU

En Chailloux 2001★

	2 ha	20,000	⑪	23–30 €

The beautiful golden brightness belies the youthfulness of this wine, which bursts with powerful aromas of exotic fruit, clementine and pineapple, sustained by a mellow vanilla touch. The maturation in barrel is evident, this robust 2001 is ready to sustain at least three years in the cellar. The **Pur Sang 2001 (30–38 €)** is also awarded one star for its concentration and full flavour.
↜ EARL Didier Dagueneau, rue de l'Ecole, 58150 Saint-Andelain, tel. 03.86.39.15.62, fax 03.86.39.07.61, e-mail silex@wanadoo.fr ☑
⏛ by appt.

MARC DESCHAMPS

Tradition des Loges 2002★

	3.9	20,000	∎ ⏚	8–11 €

There is no doubt about the regularity of production of Marc Deschamps, after judging the three *cuvées* presented and retained in the *Guide*, as last year. This Tradition des Loges opens with a fresh and straightforward note of cut apple. The palate starts off with discreet charm but concludes with an explosive, yet refined, finish. The **Les Porcheronnes 2002** gains one star for the elegant flower and citrus fruit flavours, while the **Cuvée Vielles Vignes 2002** is singled out.
↜ Marc Deschamps, Les Loges, 58150 Pouilly-sur-Loire, tel. 03.86.69.16.43, fax 03.86.39.06.90 ☑
⏛ by appt.
↜ Colette Figeat

ANDRE DEZAT ET FILS 2002★★

	14 ha	100,000	∎ ⏚	8–11 €

In 1980, André Dezat and his sons decided to take a risk and begin their adventure in the Pouilly vineyards. The 2002 vintage earned their reward. A beautiful floral and fruity touch (white peach) finds expression in this fresh, fine, straightforward and full-bodied wine. The round finish outlines the richness. A classy Pouilly-Fumé with good potential.
↜ SCEV André Dezat et Fils, rue des Tonneliers, Chaudoux, 18300 Verdigny, tel. 02.48.79.38.82, fax 02.48.79.38.24 ☑
⏛ by appt.

JEAN-PAUL MOLLET

Les Sables 2002★

	1.5	12,000	∎ ⏚	8–11 €

Boisgibault is a winemaking village where Jean-Paul Mollet cultivates some 5 ha of the old family estate. This very pale gold, almost platinum wine is attractive with its blackcurrant nuances (fruit and bud) being particularly evident. It successfully combines strength and finesse, which stays through to the round, elegant and long finish, persistent and elegant.
↜ Jean-Paul Mollet, 11, rue des Ecoles, Boisgibault, 58150 Tracy-sur-Loire, tel. 02.48.54.13.88, fax 02.48.54.09.28, e-mail jeanpaulmollet@wanadoo.fr ☑
⏛ ev. day 8am–12 noon 2pm–7pm

F. TINEL-BLONDELET

L'Arrêt Buffatte 2002★

	3 ha	24,000	∎ ⏚	8–11 €

L'Arrêt Buffatte joins the range of vines from the 2000 vintage at Tinel-Blondelet. Fresh aromas of spring flowers gradually open out on airing. But the wine, of an agreeable character, is balanced and quite characteristic. The Jury also singled out the fresh and floral **Cuvée Genetin 2002**.
↜ Dom. Tinel-Blondelet, La Croix-Canat, 58150 Pouilly-sur-Loire, tel. 03.86.39.13.83, fax 03.86.39.02.94, e-mail tinel-blondelet@wanadoo.fr ☑
⏛ by appt.
↜ Annick Tinel

Wines selected but not starred

CEDRICK BARDIN 2002

	5.6 ha	45,000	∎ ⏚	5–8 €

↜ Cédrick Bardin, 12, rue Waldeck-Rousseau, 58150 Pouilly-sur-Loire, tel. 03.86.39.11.24, fax 03.86.39.16.50, e-mail cedrick.bardin@terre-net.fr ☑
⏛ by appt.

DOM. DE BEL AIR 2002

	13 ha	40,000	∎ ⏚	5–8 €

↜ Mauroy-Gauliez, Le Bouchot, 6, rue Waldeck-Rousseau, 58150 Pouilly-sur-Loire, tel. 03.86.39.15.85, fax 03.86.39.19.52, e-mail mauroygauliez@aol.com ☑
⏛ ev. day 9am–12 noon 2pm–7pm
↜ Mauroy

DOM. DES BERTHIERS 2002

	12.5 ha	85,000	∎ ⏚	8–11 €

↜ SCEA Dom. des Berthiers, Les Berthiers, BP 30, 58150 Saint-Andelain, tel. 03.86.39.12.85, fax 03.86.39.12.94, e-mail claude@fournier-pere-fils.fr ☑
⏛ ev. day 10am–5pm; Sat. Sun. by appt.
↜ Jean-Claude Dagueneau

HENRI BOURGEOIS

La Demoiselle de Bourgeois 2001

| | 3.8 | 31,952 | | | 11–15 € |

➹ SA Dom. Henri Bourgeois, Chavignol, 18300 Sancerre, tel. 02.48.78.53.20, fax 02.48.54.14.24, e-mail domaine@bourgeois-sancerre.com ☑
🍷 by appt.

HENRY BROCHARD

Sélection 2002

| | n.c. | 40,000 | | | 8–11 € |

➹ Henry Brochard, Chavignol, 18300 Sancerre, tel. 02.48.78.20.10, fax 02.48.78.20.19, e-mail lesvins-henrybrochard@wanadoo.fr ☑
🍷 by appt.

DOM. CHAUVEAU

La Charmette 2002

| | 7.5 ha | 68,000 | | | 8–11 € |

➹ EARL Dom. Chauveau, Les Cassiers, 58150 Saint-Andelain, tel. 03.86.39.15.42, fax 03.86.39.19.46, e-mail pouillychauveau@aol.com ☑
🍷 ev. day 9am–12 noon 2pm–7pm

DOM. DE CONGY

Cuvée Les Galfins 2002

| | 1.7 ha | 10,000 | | | 5–8 € |

➹ SCEA Bonnard Père et Fils, Dom. de Congy, 58150 Saint-Andelain, tel. 03.86.39.14.20, fax 03.86.39.10.79 ☑ 🏠
🍷 by appt.

DOM. PAUL CORNEAU

Cuvée Sélection 2002

| | 7 ha | 35,000 | | | 5–8 € |

➹ Paul Corneau, Le Bouchot, 58150 Pouilly-sur-Loire, tel. 03.86.39.17.95, fax 03.86.39.16.32, e-mail domainecorneau@wanadoo.fr ☑
🍷 by appt.

JEAN DUMONT

Le Grand Plateau 2002

| | 8.15 ha | 70,000 | | | 8–11 € |

➹ Jean Dumont, RN 7, La Castille, 58150 Pouilly-sur-Loire, tel. 03.86.39.57.75, fax 03.86.39.08.30, e-mail wanadoo-saget@guy-saget.com
🍷 ev. day except Sat. Sun. 8am–12 noon 2pm–5.30pm
➹ J.-L. Saget

CH. FAVRAY 2002

| | 14 ha | 105,000 | | | 8–11 € |

➹ Ch. Favray, 58150 Saint-Martin-sur-Nohain, tel. 03.86.26.19.05, fax 03.86.26.11.59, e-mail favray@cario.fr ☑
🍷 by appt.
➹ Quentin David

ANDRE ET EDMOND FIGEAT

Côte du Nozet 2002

| | 4 ha | 25,000 | | | 11–15 € |

➹ André et Edmond Figeat, Côte du Nozet, 58150 Tracy-sur-Loire, tel. 03.86.39.19.39, fax 03.86.39.19.00 ☑
🍷 by appt.

DOM. DES FINES CAILLOTTES 2002

| | 17 ha | 150,000 | | | 8–11 € |

➹ Jean Pabiot et Fils, 9, rue de la Treille, Les Loges, 58150 Pouilly-sur-Loire, tel. 03.86.39.10.25, fax 03.86.39.10.12, e-mail jean.pabiot@terre-net.fr ☑
🍷 ev. day 8am–12 noon 2pm–6pm

FOURNIER

Grande Cuvée Vieilles Vignes 2001

| | 2.5 ha | 14,500 | | | 15–23 € |

➹ SA Fournier Père et Fils, Chaudoux, BP 7, 18300 Verdigny, tel. 02.48.79.35.24, fax 02.48.79.30.41, e-mail claude@fournier-pere-fils.fr ☑
🍷 ev. day 8am–12 noon 1.30pm–6.30pm; Sat. Sun. by appt.

DOM. DES MARINIERS 2002

| | 12.6 ha | 40,000 | | | 11–15 € |

➹ SARL Jacques Marchand, rue des Francs-Bourgeois, Les Loges, 58150 Pouilly-sur-Loire, tel. 02.48.78.54.53, fax 02.48.78.54.55 ☑
🍷 by appt.
➹ Alexandre Mellot

DOM. MASSON-BLONDELET

Les Angelots 2002

| | 6 ha | 40,000 | | | 8–11 € |

➹ Jean-Michel Masson, 1, rue de Paris, 58150 Pouilly-sur-Loire, tel. 03.86.39.00.34, fax 03.86.39.04.61, e-mail masson.blondelet@wanadoo.fr ☑
🍷 by appt.

DOMINIQUE PABIOT

Les Vieilles Terres 2002

| | 7 ha | 50,000 | | | 8–11 € |

➹ Dominique Pabiot, pl. des Mariniers, Les Loges, 58150 Pouilly-sur-Loire, tel. 03.86.39.19.09, fax 03.86.39.09.91, e-mail dominique.pabiot@cario.fr ☑
🍷 by appt.

DOM. DIDIER PABIOT 2002

| | 13 ha | 100,000 | | | 5–8 € |

➹ EARL Didier Pabiot, Les Loges, BP 5, 58150 Pouilly-sur-Loire, tel. 03.86.39.01.32, fax 03.86.39.03.27 ☑
🍷 by appt.

CAVES DE POUILLY-SUR-LOIRE

Les Vieillottes 2002

| | 6 ha | 40,000 | | | 11–15 € |

➹ Caves de Pouilly-sur-Loire, Les Moulins à Vent, 39, av. de la Tuilerie, BP 9, 58150 Pouilly-sur-Loire, tel. 03.86.39.10.99, fax 03.86.39.02.28, e-mail caves.pouilly.loire@wanadoo.fr ☑
🍷 by appt.

DOM. SAGET 2002

| | 2.92 ha | 25,000 | | | 8–11 € |

➹ SCEA Dom. Saget, 4, rue René-Couard, 58150 Pouilly-sur-Loire, tel. 03.86.39.57.75, fax 03.86.39.08.30 ☑
🍷 ev. day except Sat. Sun. 8am–12 noon 2pm–6.30pm
➹ J.-L. Saget

OLIVIER SCHLATTER 2002

| | n.c. | 5,300 | | | 5–8 € |

➹ Olivier Schlatter, 41, rue des Mardrelles, Boisgibault, 58150 Tracy-sur-Loire, tel. 03.86.26.19.31, e-mail olivier.schlatter@wanadoo.fr ☑
🍷 by appt.

DOM. HERVE SEGUIN 2002

| | 13.3 ha | 100,000 | | | 8–11 € |

➹ EARL Dom. Hervé Seguin, Le Bouchot, 58150 Pouilly-sur-Loire, tel. 03.86.39.10.75, fax 03.86.39.10.26, e-mail herveseguin@wanadoo.fr ☑ 🏠
🍷 by appt.

SEBASTIEN TREUILLET 2002

| | 2 ha | 16,000 | 🍶 🔖 | 5–8 € |

☛ Sébastien Treuillet, Fontenille, 58150 Tracy-sur-Loire,
tel. 03.86.26.17.06, fax 03.86.26.17.06 ☑
🍷 ev. day 8am–12 noon 2pm–7pm

REMY VINCENT 2002

| | n.c. | 30,000 | 🍶 🔖 | 8–11 € |

☛ Rémy Vincent, Chavignol, 18300 Sancerre,
tel. 02.48.78.20.10, fax 02.48.78.20.19,
e-mail lesvins-remyvincent@wanadoo.fr ☑

Pouilly-sur-Loire

DOM. DE BEL AIR 2002★

| | 0.6 ha | 3,000 | 🍶 🔖 | 3–5 € |

Pale gold, bright with many green highlights, this wine initially
reveals breadcrumb flavours before moving on to citrus fruits,
with subtle hints of Mirabelle plum. On the palate it is nervous
but full, and develops on a ripe lemon note at the finish. This
Pouilly-sur-Loire deserves to accompany a rustic dish.
☛ Mauroy-Gauliez, Le Bouchot, 6, rue Waldeck-Rousseau,
58150 Pouilly-sur-Loire, tel. 03.86.39.15.85,
fax 03.86.39.19.52, e-mail mauroygauliez@aol.com ☑
🍷 ev. day 9am–12 noon 2pm–7pm

GILLES BLANCHET 2002★★

| | 0.76 ha | 6,000 | 🍶 🔖 | 3–5 € |

The Jury was struck by the originality of the aromas of this
2002: fresh hazelnut and apricot are certainly classic notes,
but toasty and buttery notes are rarer in Pouilly-sur-Loire.
Round and lively, the palate has lengthy grapefruit flavours. A
remarkable personality.
☛ Gilles Blanchet, Le Bourg, 58150 Saint-Andelain,
tel. 03.86.39.14.03, fax 03.86.39.00.54 ☑
🍷 by appt.

JEAN DUMONT
Les Genièvres 2002★★

| | 6 ha | 26,000 | 🍶 🔖 | 5–8 € |

Flavours are surprisingly expressive for a Pouilly-sur-Loire.
They confirm complexity: floral and fruity, enhanced by mentholated notes and aniseed. Round, with richness, and
mouthfilling. The fullness and structure predict a good future.
☛ Jean Dumont, RN 7, La Castille,
58150 Pouilly-sur-Loire, tel. 03.86.39.57.75,
fax 03.86.39.08.30, e-mail wanadoo-saget@guy-saget.com
🍷 ev. day except Sat. Sun. 8am–12 noon 2pm–5.30pm
☛ J.-L. Saget

DOM. DE RIAUX 2002★

| | 0.4 ha | 3,000 | 🍶 🔖 | 5–8 € |

Already very good last year, the Pouilly-sur-Loire of the
Domaine de Riaux remains a sure bet in 2002. After smoky
notes, it develops fullness on the palate which is frank and
fresh. The lively finish is long with touches of yellow peach
and gentian.
☛ GAEC Jeannot Père et Fils, Dom. de Riaux,
58150 Saint-Andelain, tel. 03.86.39.11.37,
fax 03.86.39.06.21 ☑
🍷 by appt.

GUY SAGET
La Castille 2002★★

| | 6 ha | 45,000 | 🍶 🔖 | 5–8 € |

It would be a shame to drink this wine now since it is destined
for laying down. Youthful with pleasant floral perfumes combined with a touch of fennel. Full and fresh, it leaves a lasting
note of marzipan and a touch of iodine.

☛ SA Guy Saget, La Castille, BP 26,
58150 Pouilly-sur-Loire, tel. 03.86.39.57.75,
fax 03.86.39.08.30 ☑
🍷 by appt.

Wines selected but not starred

BARILLOT PERE ET FILS 2002

| | 0.35 ha | 2,300 | 🍶 🔖 | 3–5 € |

☛ Barillot Père et Fils, Le Bouchot,
58150 Pouilly-sur-Loire, tel. 03.86.39.15.29,
fax 03.86.39.09.52 ☑
🍷 ev. day 9am–12 noon 1.30pm–7pm; groups by appt.

DOM. CHAMPEAU 2002

| | n.c. | n.c. | 🍶 | 5–8 € |

☛ SCEA Dom. Champeau, Le Bourg,
58150 Saint-Andelain, tel. 03.86.39.15.61,
fax 03.86.39.19.44,
e-mail domaine-champeau@wanadoo.fr ☑
🍷 ev. day except Tues. am. Sun. 9am–12 noon 2pm–6pm

DOM. LANDRAT-GUYOLLOT
La Roselière 2002

| | 1 ha | 8,000 | 🍶 🔖 | 5–8 € |

☛ Dom. Landrat-Guyollot, Les Berthiers,
58150 Saint-Andelain, tel. 03.86.39.11.83,
fax 03.86.39.11.65 ☑
🍷 by appt.

Quincy

The vineyards of Quincy and
Brinay cover 174 ha on plateaux covered with sand
and ancient gravels along the banks of the Cher, not
far from Bourges and Mehun-sur-Yèvre, in an area
rich in the history of the 16th century.

Quincy wines, of which 7,576 hl
were produced in 2002, are made only from Sauvignon, and are fresh, fruity and extremely drinkable,
with real finesse and personality.

If, as the French wine authority
Doctor Guyot wrote, variety determines character,
Quincy also provides evidence that the same variety
can provide different wines in the same region
depending on the structure of the soils. The
wine-lover will find this one of the most elegant of
the Loire wines, to be drunk with fish and seafood, as
well as with the goat's cheeses of the region.

DOM. BAILLY
Beaucharme La Croix Saint-Ursin 2002★★

| | n.c. | 22,000 | 🍶 🔖 | 5–8 € |

Jacques Bailly, who has been running the vineyard since 1991,
is a Sancerrois in Quincy. This wine delighted tasters by the
intensity of its flavours of pineapple, passion-fruit and
acacia. Fresh and lively, it shows richness and has lengthy

LOIRE

fruity and spicy notes. The **Cuvée Les Grands Cœurs 2001** is also singled out.

☛ Dom. Sylvain Bailly, la Croix Saint-Ursin, 71, rue de Venoize, 18300 Bué, tel. 02.48.54.02.75, fax 02.48.54.28.41, e-mail jacquesbailly3@wanadoo.fr

☖ ev. day 8am–12 noon 1.30pm–6pm; Sun. by appt.

☛ Jacques Bailly

DOM. DES BALLANDORS 2002★★

	8 ha	47,000			5–8 €

The Ballandors domaine chose for its symbol the grape treader, reproduced on the Roman frescos in the 12th century church at Brinay, illustrating the month of September in the country calendar. An elegant label for a rich and well-balanced Quincy. Even though it is reserved, the nose promises a great complexity combining mineral, fruity, spicy notes with a subtle vegetal touch. The palate is remarkable with softness and length.

☛ Chantal Wilk et Jean Tatin, Le Tremblay, 18120 Brinay, tel. 02.48.75.20.09, fax 02.48.75.70.50, e-mail jeantatin@wanadoo.fr

☖ by appt.

DOM. PIERRE DURET 2002★

	10.11 ha	60,000			5–8 €

Alexandre Mellot, owner of this domaine since 1995, built a new wine cellar and created a marketing website in 2002. This vintage is very pleasant with its peach, apricot and smoky flavours. Though discreet, the wine has appreciable balance and a piquant finish, tending towards the spicy. The wine is well balanced.

☛ SARL Pierre Duret, rte de Quincy, 18120 Brinay, tel. 02.48.51.30.17, fax 02.48.51.35.47

☖ by appt.

☛ Alexandre Mellot

DOM. MARDON 2002★

	11 ha	60,000			5–8 €

On 1st January 2003, Hélène Mardon joined her family on this domaine. The 2002 vintage produced this balanced, agreeable wine. With some complexity, the nose reveals pear-drops and nougat sustained by citrus fruits. The palate opens with precision and carries on with frankness. To drink with shellfish or seafood.

☛ Dom. Mardon, 40, rte de Reuilly, 18120 Quincy, tel. 02.48.51.31.60, fax 02.48.51.35.55, e-mail domaine.mardon@libertysurf.fr

☖ ev. day 9am–12 noon 2pm–6.30pm; Sat. Sun. by appt.

DOM. DE PUY-FERRAND 2002★★

	2 ha	n.c.			5–8 €

Becoming a wine-grower in 1995, Jean-Claude Roux presents this wine made on siliceous-clay soil. An intense Sauvignon nose develops on notes of orange juice, boxwood, spring flowers. The mineral freshness contributes to the elegance and complexity of this Quincy that one can appreciate from now. Poultry would form a perfect culinary match.

☛ Jean-Claude Roux, Puy-Ferrand, 18340 Arcay, tel. 02.48.64.76.10, fax 02.48.64.75.69

☖ by appt.

RASSAT
Cuvée Prestige 2002★

	1 ha	6,000			5–8 €

The Sauvignon underwent a short period of skin contact, then the wine was matured on lees for approximately eight months in order to obtain this *cuvée* with its attractive aromatic range: fennel, green pepper, citrus fruits and almond. Freshness brings liveliness to a rich palate. Without any doubt, this Quincy has potential and deserves to be kept some time.

☛ Didier Rassat, Champ-Martin, 18120 Cerbois, tel. 02.48.51.70.19, fax 02.48.51.79.27

☖ ev. day 9am–12.15pm 3pm–6.30pm

DOM. JACQUES ROUZE
Vignes d'antan 2002★

	3.5 ha	12,000			5–8 €

A pretty traditional maisonnette opens its doors to you in the middle of the vines. Here you will discover this wine with its

fine notes of fresh mint and lime, still reserved on the nose. The firm, one-dimensional palate is long with citrus fruits and mineral notes. The **Cuvée Tradition 2002** is also singled out for its pleasant freshness.

☛ Jacques Rouzé, chem. des Vignes, 18120 Quincy, tel. 02.48.51.35.61, fax 02.48.51.05.00, e-mail rouze@terrenet.fr

☖ by appt.

DOM. DU TREMBLAY
Cuvée Vieilles Vignes 2002★

	2 ha	12,000			5–8 €

Vines of about 30 years old cultivated on sand and gravel soil have produced this wine which combines vegetal notes and fruitiness with intensity. Richness shows itself from the start, then freshness appears and even a touch of bitterness which time will blur.

☛ Jean Tatin, Le Tremblay, 18120 Brinay, tel. 02.48.75.20.09, fax 02.48.75.70.50, e-mail jeantatin@wanadoo.fr

☖ by appt.

DOM. DE VILLALIN 2002★★

	3 ha	16,000			5–8 €

These young wine-growers established here since 1999, adopted a traditional procedure: they work their vineyard with the assistance of a donkey. Their pretty label has the silhouette of the faithful beast. You will have time to appreciate it while tasting this wine with its superb fruity (apple, pear, peach) and floral (acacia) nose. Direct on the attack, it fills the palate with freshness and richness. This pleasant Quincy that has not yet delivered all its qualities should continue to develop in strength because it already expresses the richness of the vintage.

☛ Marchand-Smith, Le Grand Villalin, 18120 Quincy, tel. 02.48.51.34.98, fax 02.48.51.09.74, e-mail vquincy@club.internet.fr

☖ by appt.

Wines selected but not starred

HENRI BOURGEOIS
Haute Victoire 2002

	7 ha	48,933			5–8 €

☛ SA Dom. Henri Bourgeois, Chavignol, 18300 Sancerre, tel. 02.48.78.53.20, fax 02.48.54.14.24, e-mail domaine@bourgeois-sancerre.com

☖ by appt.

DOM. DES CAVES 2002

	4 ha	30,000			5–8 €

☛ Bruno Lecomte, 105, rue Saint-Exupéry, 18520 Avord, tel. 02.48.69.27.14, fax 02.48.69.16.42, e-mail quincy.lecomte@wanadoo.fr

☖ by appt.

DOM. DES CROIX 2002

| | 2 ha | 14,000 | 🍷 🍶 | 5–8 € |

🍷 Sylvie Lavault-Rouzé, Chem. des vignes, 18120 Quincy,
tel. 02.48.51.35.61, fax 02.48.51.05.00,
e-mail rouze@terrenet.fr 🆅
🍷 by appt.

DOM. DU GRAND ROSIERES 2002

| | 2 ha | 15,000 | 🍷 🍶 | 5–8 € |

🍷 Jacques Siret, Dom. du Grand Rosières, 18400 Lunery,
tel. 02.48.68.90.34, fax 02.48.68.03.71,
e-mail jac.siret@wanadoo.fr 🆅
🍷 by appt.

DOM. ANDRE PIGEAT 2002

| | 3 ha | 9,000 | 🍷 🍶 | 3–5 € |

🍷 Dom. André Pigeat, 18, rte de Cerbois, 18120 Quincy,
tel. 02.48.51.31.90, fax 02.48.51.03.12,
e-mail gaec.pigeat-viticulteur@wanadoo.fr 🆅
🍷 ev. day 8.30am–12.30pm 1.30pm–8pm
🍷 Philippe Pigeat

PHILIPPE PORTIER 2002

| | 8.5 ha | 70,000 | 🍷 🍶 | 8–11 € |

🍷 EARL Philippe Portier, Dom. de la Brosse,
18120 Brinay, tel. 02.48.51.04.47, fax 02.48.51.00.96 🆅
🍷 by appt.

DOM. VALERY RENAUDAT 2002

| | 1.9 ha | 13,000 | 🍷 🍶 | 5–8 € |

🍷 Dom. Valéry Renaudat, 3, pl. des Ecoles, 36260 Reuilly,
tel. 02.54.49.38.12, fax 02.48.51.03.12,
e-mail domainevaleryrenaudat@wanadoo.fr 🆅
🍷 by appt.

DOM. DU TONKIN 2002

| | 3.24 ha | 22,000 | 🍷 🍶 | 5–8 € |

🍷 EARL du Tonkin, Le Tonkin, 18120 Brinay,
tel. 02.48.51.09.72, fax 02.48.51.11.67 🆅
🍷 by appt.
🍷 Jacques Masson

Reuilly

Steep, sunny hills and remarkable soils make Reuilly a natural environment for the vine.

The appellation covers 158 ha ranging over seven communes in the Indre and the Cher, a charming region crossed by the green valleys of the rivers Cher, Arnon and Théols. It produced 8,255 hl of wine in 2002.

Reuilly white wines are dry, fruity Sauvignons, which can achieve notable fullness; production was 4,121 hl in 2002. Pinot Gris provides a rosé from direct pressing that is as delicate and distinguished as one might wish. However, the more versatile Pinot Noir, producing fresh, smooth, lustrous rosés and, more particularly, full, complex, fruity reds, is rapidly supplanting this local favourite.

BERNARD AUJARD 2002★★★

| ■ | 0.68 ha | 3,800 | 🍷 🍶 | 5–8 € |

Bernard Aujard's vineyard is located partly in the village of Lazenay, in Cher, and partly in Reuilly, in Indre. Already a *coup de coeur* for the rosé 1999 and red 2000 in the preceding edition of the *Guide*, it finds the supreme reward with this rosé 2002. A very pale characteristic colour, the nose is intense, rich and has great purity: ripe fruits, aniseed and liquorice. The palate, with great richness and finesse, is perfectly balanced; its length is "incredible," according to one of the tasters. Bernard Aujard's **red Reuilly 2002** is awarded one star for its soft fruit flavours, well-balanced roundness and freshness.
🍷 EARL Bernard Aujard, 2, rue du Bas-Bourg,
18120 Lazenay, tel. 02.48.51.73.69, fax 02.48.51.79.74 🆅
🍷 by appt.

GERARD BIGONNEAU
Les Bouchauds 2002★

| ■ | 4 ha | 25,000 | 🍷 🍶 | 5–8 € |

Three wines presented, three wines gain a mention: Gérard Bigonneau produced a beautiful 2002 vintage. This white wine with citrus fruit scents (lemon, grapefruit) has a subtle richness. Warming and without harshness, it develops sufficiently, following in the style of the gravely sand of Reuilly. The subtly aromatic and balanced **Les Bouchauds rosé 2002** also obtains one star, while the **red Les Bouchauds 2002** is singled out.
🍷 Gérard Bigonneau, La Chagnat, 18120 Brinay,
tel. 02.48.52.80.22, fax 02.48.52.83.41 🆅 🏠
🍷 by appt.

CHANTAL ET MICHEL CORDAILLAT
2002★

| ■ | 1.5 ha | 12,000 | 🍷 🍶 | 5–8 € |

The Cordaillat estate is established on the clay-limestone terroirs of Chéry and Reuilly. Its 2002 vintage evokes mixed nuts (hazelnut) and after airing reveals an added citrus fruit touch. It is supple on the attack and then opens out to disclose a ripeness, already mature, round and rich. It exhibits a certain complexity and finesse. The **Reuilly rosé 2002** deserves to be singled out.
🍷 EARL Dom. Cordaillat, Le Montet, 18120 Méreau,
tel. 02.48.52.83.48, fax 02.48.52.83.09 🆅
🍷 ev. day except Sun. 2pm–7pm

PASCAL DESROCHES
Les Varennes 2002★★

| ■ | 3.8 ha | 34,400 | 🍷 🍶 | 5–8 € |

Regularly mentioned in the *Guide*, Pascal Desroches should be satisfied with the 2002 vintage. The white Reuilly attracted the Jury with its pronounced citrus fruit flavours and even more with its flavoursome qualities: freshness and pleasant finesse. This well-balanced *cuvée* has good potential. The easy-drinking **Les Lignis rosé 2002** is very good and the **red La Sablière 2002** was singled out.
🍷 Pascal Desroches, 13, rte de Charost, 18120 Lazenay,
tel. 02.48.51.71.60, fax 02.48.51.71.60 🆅
🍷 by appt.

LOIRE

CLAUDE LAFOND
La Raie 2002★★

	9 ha	60,000		5–8 €

Created by André Lafond in the 1960s, the domaine was taken over by Claude in 1977 and has not stopped progressing in size and fame since. A *coup de coeur* for the 2000 vintage, Cuvée La Raie renewed the reputation. This wine tends towards fine floral fragrances, jellied fruits, grapefruit and barley-sugar. The velvety attack is followed by just the right amount of freshness. The finish has a hint of minerality that adds balance to this lovely wine. Claude Lafond's **La Grande Pièce rosé 2002** is so supple and full of flavour that it deserves one star, while **Les Grandes Vignes red 2002** is singled out.
➤ Claude Lafond, Le Bois Saint-Denis, rte de Graçay, 36260 Reuilly, tel. 02.54.49.22.17, fax 02.54.49.26.64, e-mail claude.lafond@wanadoo.fr ☑
☒ by appt.

ALAIN MABILLOT 2002★

	n.c.	n.c.		5–8 €

The deep crimson colour with purple tinges, is a good omen. This wine is packed with fruit: black-cherry and black-currant. The ripe tannins that are very evident provide structure for these flavours, guaranteeing fine development over the next year.
➤ Alain Mabillot, Villiers-les-Roses, 36260 Sainte-Lizaigne, tel. 02.54.04.02.09, fax 02.54.04.01.33 ☑
☒ by appt.

VALERY RENAUDAT 2002★★

	0.7 ha	5,000		5–8 €

When passing Diou, notice the church's leaning bell-tower: according to legend, an impure woman married in this church, invoking the wrath of God. No reproach could be made of this crimson Reuilly with purple highlights, already open and complex with notes of red berries. The tannins are round and mellow, adding richness and length to the wine.
➤ Dom. Valéry Renaudat, 3, pl. des Ecoles, 36260 Reuilly, tel. 02.54.49.38.12, fax 02.54.49.38.26, e-mail domainevaleryrenaudat@wanadoo.fr ☑
☒ by appt.

DOM. DE REUILLY 2002★

	3.7 ha	25,000		5–8 €

Even though the vines were planted here a long time ago, these vineyards remained abandoned after the phylloxera crisis at the end of the 19th century. It wasn't until 1986 that Denis Jamain came along and replanted them. Today it produces pretty wines such as this ruby 2002, which fully expresses the Pinot with kirsch and Morello cherry flavours. Fresh, fruity and attractive, this wine is ready for a barbecue. The **rosé 2002** is singled out for its fullness, enabling it to accompany spicy nibbles.
➤ SCE Dom. de Reuilly, chem. des Petites-Fontaines, 36260 Reuilly, tel. 02.38.66.16.74, fax 02.38.66.74.69, e-mail denis.jamain@wanadoo.fr ☑
☒ ev. day 8am–6pm
➤ Jamain

DOM. DE SERESNES 2002★★

	3.78 ha	21,000		5–8 €

It is not surprising to find Jacques Renaudat at this level: he is a red wine specialist and boasts many *coups de coeur*. This rich and characteristic 2002 evokes raspberry and blackcurrant coulis. Its rich character has a good round structure to support it and the finish is uplifted with notes of prune and spices. Elegant and attractive, it can be drunk immediately or kept a year or two. The **rosé 2002** is a very good wine: round and agreeable, with a floral nose then fruit on the finish, it would marry well with a rich poultry dish. The **white 2002** is singled out.
➤ Jacques Renaudat, Seresnes, 36260 Diou, tel. 02.54.49.21.44, fax 02.54.49.30.42 ☑
☒ ev. day 8.30am–12 noon 1.30pm–6.30pm; Sun. by appt.

DOM. JEAN-MICHEL SORBE 2002★

	1.54 ha	11,000		5–8 €

Jean-Michel Sorbe's estate was taken over by Alexandre Mellot, négociant-winemaker of Sancerre. This rosé impressed the tasters with its intense flower and fruit flavours (strawberry, pear). Despite the lively attack, the wine remains agreeably balanced. With such finesse this wine would go well with seared calves liver. The **white Reuilly La Commanderie 2002** is singled out as representative of the vintage.
➤ SARL Jean-Michel Sorbe, Le Buisson Long, rte de Quincy, 18120 Brinay, tel. 02.48.51.30.17, fax 02.48.51.35.47, e-mail jeanmichelsorbe@jeanmichelsorbe.com ☑
☒ by appt.
➤ Alexandre Mellot

JACQUES VINCENT 2002★

	3 ha	16,000		5–8 €

The village of Lazenay is located at the edge of the Champagne Berrichonne area. Jacques Vincent, established here since 1984, has produced this rosé of quality. Orange highlights give a pretty tonality to this intensely fruity wine (strawberry and apricot), with some floral scents of peony. Its roundness and its richness would go well with Far Eastern dishes.
➤ Jacques Vincent, 11, chem. des Caves, 18120 Lazenay, tel. 02.48.51.73.55, fax 02.48.51.14.96 ☑
☒ ev. day 9am–12 noon 2pm–7pm; Sun. by appt.

Wines selected but not starred

ANDRE BARBIER 2002

	0.37 ha	3,000		5–8 €

➤ André Barbier, Le Crot-au-Loup, 18120 Chéry, tel. 02.48.51.75.81, fax 02.48.51.72.47 ☑
☒ by appt.

LES BERRYCURIENS
Les Chatillons 2002

| | 0.5 ha | 2,600 | ▮ ⚭ | 5–8 € |

● SCEV Les BerryCuriens, Le Buisson Long, rte de Quincy, 18120 Brinay, tel. 02.48.51.30.17, fax 02.48.51.35.47 ☑
☉ by appt.

DOM. HENRI BEURDIN ET FILS 2002

| | 1.1 ha | 8,000 | ▮ ⚭ | 5–8 € |

● SCEV Dom. Henri Beurdin et Fils, 14, Le Carroir, 18120 Preuilly, tel. 02.48.51.30.78, fax 02.48.51.34.81, e-mail domaine.beurdin@terre-net.fr ☑
☉ ev. day 8am–12 noon 1.45pm–6.30pm; Sun. by appt.

JEAN-SYLVAIN GUILLEMAIN 2002

| | 0.79 ha | 6,400 | ▮ ⚭ | 5–8 € |

● Jean-Sylvain Guillemain, Palleau, 18120 Lury-sur-Arnon, tel. 02.48.52.99.01, fax 02.48.52.99.09 ☑
☉ by appt.

Sancerre

The hilltop village of Sancerre, overlooking the Loire, commands a magnificent panorama of well-exposed, sheltered slopes, perfect for winegrowing, stretching over 11 communes. The terroir is composed variously of limestone and chalky marl, which suit the vine and contribute to the quality of the wines. About 2,570 ha are planted, and produced 158,810 hl in 2002, of which 126,099 hl were white wine.

Two varieties reign supreme in Sancerre: Sauvignon and Pinot Noir, both uniquely capable of expressing the spirit of the terroir to the full. This is amply demonstrated in the wines: fresh, young, fruity whites (the most numerous wines); supple, subtle rosés, and light, perfumed, complex reds.

In addition to this, Sancerre represents, in a unique way, the contribution of wine-growers and winemakers. It requires great skill and dedication to produce a great wine from Sauvignon, which is a late-ripening variety, so near to the northern limit of vine-growing, and at heights of 200 and 300 metres. Add to these challenges the vagaries of the local climate, slopes that are among the steepest in the country, and the fact that fermentation takes place at a critical moment at the end of a late season!

White Sancerre is particularly to be appreciated with dry goat's cheeses, such as the famous Crottin de Chavignol, from a village which itself produces wines. It also goes well with hot starters or fish that are not too strongly seasoned. The reds go well with poultry and the meat dishes of the region.

DOM. AUCHERE 2002★

| | 6 ha | 40,000 | ▮ | 8–11 € |

Jean-Jacques Auchère, wine-grower at Bué, has more than 8 ha of vines in AOC Sancerre, with 6 ha of Sauvignon, on clay-limestone soil. This *cuvée* exhales fruit aromas such as citrus fruits, pineapple and mango. On the palate, the first impression is soft but the flavours open out to a crescendo. An elegant wine, full-flavoured with length.
● Jean-Jacques Auchère, 18, rue de l'Abbaye, 18300 Bué, tel. 02.48.54.15.77, fax 02.48.78.03.46 ☑
☉ by appt.

SYLVAIN BAILLY
Prestige 2002★

| | n.c. | 8,000 | ▮ ◍ ⚭ | 11–15 € |

The Sylvain Bailly estate produces AOC Sancerre and Quincy. This vintage seems to be a success for this estate. Appreciate Cuvée Prestige for its handpicked harvest, slow fermentation and maturation for eight months on fine lees. It is elegant with fruity and floral notes that linger to the finish. To drink with a fish dish. Discover also the **red Sancerre La Louée 2002 (8–11 €)** and the **white Terroirs 2002 (8–11 €)**, singled out by the Jury.
● Dom. Sylvain Bailly, la Croix Saint-Ursin, 71, rue de Venoize, 18300 Bué, tel. 02.48.54.02.75, fax 02.48.54.28.41, e-mail jacquesbailly3@wanadoo.fr ☑
☉ ev. day 8am–12 noon 1.30pm–6pm; Sun. by appt.
● Jacques Bailly

DOM. JEAN-PAUL BALLAND 2002★★

| | 15.5 ha | 100,000 | ▮ ⚭ | 8–11 € |

Successor to a long line of wine producers, Jean-Paul Balland works 24 ha of vines on the hillsides of Bué, along with his wife, Magali. He can pride himself this year on three selected wines. The maturation on lees has added roundness and richness to this white Sancerre. The flavours, initially mineral, evolve towards fruitiness and finish on a mentholated note. The Jury recommended the **rosé 2002**, with its clear salmon colour and spicy-fruity nose, as well as the **red 2001**, matured in barrel, which seems round and balanced.
● Dom. Jean-Paul Balland, 10, chem. de Marloup, 18300 Bué, tel. 02.48.54.07.29, fax 02.48.54.20.94, e-mail balland.jeanpaul@wanadoo.fr ☑
☉ by appt.

JOSEPH BALLAND-CHAPUIS
Chêne Marchand 2001★

| | 0.65 ha | 5,000 | ▮ ◍ ⚭ | 11–15 € |

This regular to the *Guide* once again succeeds with its Cuvée Chêne Marchand, whose grapes come from a 30-year-old plot of Sauvignon on limestone terroir. The grapes, harvested manually, and carefully selected, then underwent a slow pressing which made it possible to extract the best. The golden-coloured 2001 presents an intense nose, blending fruit (peach, citrus fruits) with vanilla notes inherited from partial maturation in barrel. The palate, both lively and round at the same time, completes the harmony. Singled out, the **white Sancerre Le Vallon 2002 (8–11 €)** shows mineral notes and fruitiness. Fresh, it should open out with time.
● SARL Joseph Balland-Chapuis, La Croix-Saint-Laurent, 18300 Bué, tel. 02.48.54.06.67, fax 02.48.54.07.97 ☑
☉ by appt.
● J.-L. Saget

CEDRICK BARDIN 2002★

| | 3.2 ha | 25,000 | ▮ ⚭ | 5–8 € |

Set up at Pouilly-sur-Loire, Cédrick Bardin owns 3 ha in Sancerre, the inheritance of the union of a grandfather from Pouilly and a grandmother from Sancerre. This wine discloses the flint terroir well with its mineral edge and floral notes. Dominated by citrus fruits, the lively opening is followed by roundness and fruitiness. The mineral notes are found on the finish.
● Cédrick Bardin, 12, rue Waldeck-Rousseau, 58150 Pouilly-sur-Loire, tel. 03.86.39.11.24, fax 03.86.39.16.50, e-mail cedrick.bardin@terre-net.fr ☑
☉ by appt.

GERARD BOULAY 2002★

| | 6 ha | 12,000 | ▮ ⚭ | 8–11 € |

Cultivated on limestone soil, according to sustainable agricultural methods, 40-year-old vines have produced a bright Sancerre with golden tinges. A taster notes that this 2002 recalls springtime. Indeed, violet and lilac dominate the citrus fruit flavours, and the well-balanced, floral palate finishes with a lengthy freshness. A typical Sancerre.

� Gérard Boulay, Chavignol, 18300 Sancerre,
tel. 02.48.54.36.37, fax 02.48.54.36.37,
e-mail gerardboulay@chavignol.net ✓
Υ by appt.

HUBERT BROCHARD

Aujourd'hui comme autrefois 2002★★

	3 ha	16,000	▮ ♦	8–11 €

This is traditional winemaking, the same for 400 years. Tell your friends about this Sancerre already recommended last year for the 2001. Made from old vines grown on limestone, the grapes have been handpicked; the wine is neither fined nor filtered. This *cuvée* represents the grape variety well with its flavours of boxwood and blackcurrant bud. It has richness and good structure. The **red Cuvée Classique 2002 (11–15 €)**, matured 12 months in cask and the floral **white Vieilles Vignes 2002 (15–23 €)** are also singled out.

➱ Hubert Brochard, Dom. du Moulin-Grauger, Chavignol, 18300 Sancerre, tel. 02.48.78.20.10, fax 02.48.78.20.19, e-mail domaine-hubertbrochard@wanadoo.fr ✓
Υ by appt.

DOM. MICHEL BROCK

Le Coteau 2002★

	2.25 ha	19,300		8–11 €

Michel Brock created this estate in 1968, taking over the vineyard of his father-in-law. He then developed its markets: 90% of the wines are exported. The Coteau is a wine partially fermented in barrel that releases mineral and vegetal notes. The pleasant palate finishes on ripe fruit. Discover this floral **white Sancerre Domaine de Sarry 2002** to enliven your meat dishes, and the **red Domaine de Sarry 2000**, with flavours of prune, black-cherry, spices and vanilla. Both are singled out.

➱ Dom. Michel Brock, Le Briou, rte de Bourges, 18300 Sancerre, tel. 02.48.79.07.92, fax 02.48.79.05.28 ✓
Υ ev. day except Sat. Sun. 8am–12 noon 1.30pm–5.30pm

DOM. DES CAVES DU PRIEURE 2002★

	10 ha	70,000	▮ ♦	5–8 €

This family estate respects the terroir and the grape, carefully controlling the alcoholic fermentation with indigenous yeast. Drink this round, balanced wine with seafood. It has length, is floral with flavours of citrus fruits. The **Tradition red 2001 (8–11 €)** is singled out as an accompaniment to game. This is supple and fruity.

➱ Jacques Guillerault, Dom. des Caves du Prieuré, Reigny, 18300 Crézancy-en-Sancerre, tel. 02.48.79.02.84, fax 02.48.79.01.02, e-mail caves.prieure@wanadoo.fr ✓
Υ ev. day except Sun. 8.30am–12.15pm 1.30pm–7pm

ROGER CHAMPAULT

Les Pierris 2002★

	6 ha	40,000	▮ ♦	8–11 €

The vineyard is located both in AOC Sancerre (20 ha) and Menetou-Salon (1 ha). The wine tasting room is housed in a 16th century belfry, once part of the Champtin seigniory. You will have the choice between three wines very much admired by the Jury. This red Sancerre, fruity, soft and balanced should open out in time. The **Perle de Rosée rosé 2001**, very pale pink with golden hints, has fine peach and citrus fruit flavours, and roundness too. Lastly, the **white Le Roy Clos du 2001**, with its mineral and floral (acacia) tones, is fresh, balanced and richly structured.

➱ Roger Champault et Fils, Champtin, 18300 Crézancy-en-Sancerre, tel. 02.48.79.00.03, fax 02.48.79.09.17 ✓
Υ by appt.

DOM. DE LA CHEZATTE 2001★

	23.68 ha	205,000	▮ ♦	5–8 €

Domaine de La Chézatte is within 2 km of the market town of Sainte-Gemme, at the foot of a vast southeast facing hillside where the majority of its vines (30 ha) are planted. This 2001 has preserved all its freshness: vegetal notes, such as boxwood, dominate equally on the nose and the palate. After

a frank attack it opens with freshness. It will go well with a dish of fried fish from the Loire.

➱ SARL Dom. de La Chézatte, 18240 Sainte-Gemme-en-Sancerrois, tel. 02.48.79.37.14, fax 02.48.79.32.76, e-mail chezatte@domaine-chezatte.fr ✓
Υ by appt.
➱ GFA de La Chézatte

DANIEL CROCHET 2002★

	2.5 ha	20,000	▮ ♦	5–8 €

Daniel Crochet has done well this year with a pretty wine trio from two vintages, proof of his serious, consistent work. The first was recommended not only for its rich nose, which has a lot of finesse (orange, grapefruit, rose), but also for its freshness and harmony. The floral notes emerge on the palate. To drink with fish in sauce. The second to be singled out is the **red Sancerre 2002**, very full-flavoured (matured soft fruits, spices) and structured. The subtle and balanced **red Cuvée Prestige 2001 (8–11 €)** is also commended.

➱ Daniel Crochet, 61, rue de Venoize, 18300 Bué, tel. 02.48.54.07.83, fax 02.48.54.27.36 ✓
Υ ev. day 9am–12 noon 2pm–7pm

DOM. DAULNY

Le Clos de Chaudenay 2001★

	0.9 ha	7,000	▮ ❚❙ ♦	8–11 €

Regularly appearing in the *Guide*, the Daulny estate presents a beautiful duo. This Clos de Chaudenay has fruity (apricot, peach) and mentholated notes, while enriching the palate with fullness, roundness and mellow oak. Also very good is the **white Sancerre Domaine Daulny 2002 (5–8 €)**, matured in tank. Its black label decribes the terroir: the grapes come from 90% clay-limestone soil and 10% on limestone. Both fresh and round, with fruitiness, minerals and slightly spicy, it has good potential for the future (40,000 bottles available).

➱ Etienne Daulny, Chaudenay, 18300 Verdigny, tel. 02.48.79.33.96, fax 02.48.79.33.39 ✓
Υ by appt.

DOM. VINCENT DELAPORTE 2002★

	16.5 ha	140,000	▮	5–8 €

A very successful vintage here: all of the three colours of Sancerre were selected, a reward for meticulous work. The white, the result of a ripe harvest, seems round, balanced, elegant and attractive with exotic fruits. The **red 2002**, balanced and fruity with charred notes, will be a success at a barbecue. It is singled out along with the rosé **2002**.

➱ SCEV Vincent Delaporte et Fils, Chavignol, 18300 Sancerre, tel. 02.48.78.03.32, fax 02.48.78.02.62 ✓
Υ by appt.

DOM. DE LA GARENNE 2002★★

	5 ha	40,000	▮ ♦	8–11 €

Domaine de la Garenne is established at Verdigny with 11 ha of vines. This wine, the product of the terroirs of pebbles or little stones and *terres blanches* (white earth), delighted the tasters. Flavours are very intense and persistent: fruitiness, floral and mineral. The full, rich palate continues in the same vein as the nose. A very representative AOC Sancerre.

➱ Bernard-Noël Reverdy, Dom. de la Garenne, 18300 Verdigny, tel. 02.48.79.35.79, fax 02.48.79.32.82 ✓
Υ by appt.

SERGE LALOUE 2002★★

8 ha	65,000	▮ ⚬	8–11 €

Serge Laloue cultivates 18 ha of vines planted mainly on clay-siliceous soil. Its Sancerre deserves to be served from a decanter to enhance its fruitiness and vegetal flavours. On the palate it reveals suppleness and freshness through to the citrus fruit finish. Wait a year to see it to open out completely. The **white Silex 2002** is also very good. It is powerful and fruity and will accompany pike in a cream sauce or be drunk as an aperitif.
➤ Serge Laloue, Thauvenay, 18300 Sancerre,
tel. 02.48.79.94.10, fax 02.48.79.92.48,
e-mail laloue@terre-net.fr ▼
�178 by appt.

LAPORTE

Le Grand Rochoy Vieilles Vignes 2000★

n.c.	6,000	▮ ⦿ ⚬	11–15 €

Le Grand Rochoy comes from a plot of old vines at the heart of a 9-hectare vineyard planted on siliceous soil. The terroir character is retained using traditional winemaking techniques, maturation on lees and partial maturation in oak. The result is a pleasant, long and round wine with fruity notes (citrus fruits) and vanilla. This 2000 knew how to retain its youth. The fine and fairly lively **Domaine du Rochoy 2001 white (8–11 €)** is also awarded one star.
➤ SARL Dom. Laporte, Cave de La Cresle, rte de Sury-en-Vaux, 18300 Saint-Satur, tel. 02.48.78.54.20, fax 02.48.54.34.33, e-mail info@domaine-laporte.com ▼
�178 by appt.

PHILIPPE LEMAIN-POUILLOT 2002★

3.5 ha	10,000	▮	5–8 €

Formerly a butcher, this successful producer took over his father-in-law's vineyard in 1990. He presents a wine made from Sauvignon, cultivated on clay-limestone soil, which explodes with floral aromas (acacia, broom), boxwood and citrus fruits. Initially lively, this 2002 develops balance and structure through to the rather long finish. An authentic Sancerre.
➤ Philippe Lemain-Pouillot, 18300 Bué, tel. 02.48.54.11.09, fax 02.48.54.06.75 ▼
�178 ev. day 9am–7pm; cl. 15–30 Aug.

JOSEPH MELLOT

Les Vignes du Rocher 2002★

0.75 ha	5,000	▮ ⚬	11–15 €

In 1991, the Joseph Mellot company set up its buildings in the heart of the vineyard, in Sancerre. It has grown well, mainly due to the production of several appellations from the Val de Loire under his négociant label. This *cuvée* has noticeable mineral notes that express the flint terroir well, on a background of citrus fruits. After a direct attack, it develops suppleness and roundness, sustained by discreet freshness.
➤ SA Joseph Mellot, rte de Ménétréol, BP 13, 18300 Sancerre, tel. 02.48.78.54.54, fax 02.48.78.54.55, e-mail alexandremellot@josephmellot.com ▼
�178 ev. day 8am–12 noon 1.30pm–5pm; Sat. Sun. by appt.

THIERRY MERLIN-CHERRIER 2001★

0.18 ha	1,900	⦿	11–15 €

From the top of the Bué hillsides there is a beautiful view of Sancerre. Thierry Merlin-Cherrier looks after his wines and their labelling, refined and elegant. This Sancerre has a pretty colour for the vintage. The intense and complex nose concentrates on fruit and vanilla, as well as well-dosed oaky and toasty notes. The quality of the harvest shows in the well-balanced body with length, and charred touches from the barrel. The **white Sancerre 2002 (5–8 €)** obtains one star for its harmony and full-flavoured complexity: ripe fruit, citrus fruit, apricot and honey.
➤ Thierry Merlin-Cherrier, 43, rue Saint-Vincent, 18300 Bué, tel. 02.48.54.06.31, fax 02.48.54.01.78 ▼
�178 by appt.

DOM. FRANCK MILLET 2002★

2 ha	15,000	▮ ⦿ ⚬	8–11 €

The cherry-red colour with purple highlights denotes the youth of this wine, the intense nose of which evokes game and

charred flavours, then flowers after airing. A fruitiness takes over on the supple and balanced palate. One taster suggested that it would to go well with rabbit. The **white Sancerre 2002**, product of limestone soils, is singled out: tending towards citrus and exotic fruits, it starts off fresh before offering a certain roundness.
➤ Franck Millet, 68, rue Saint-Vincent, 18300 Bué,
tel. 02.48.54.25.26, fax 02.48.54.39.85 ▼
�178 by appt.

DOM. GERARD MILLET 2002★★

13.29 ha	114,985	▮ ⚬	8–11 €

Since 1979, the year when Gerard Millet took over from his grandfather, the vineyard has expanded gradually over the *caillottes* (pebbles). This attractive and elegant wine has good keeping qualities. The product of handpicking and harvesting at perfect maturity, it reveals a floral bouquet, then invades the palate with its fresh, round and finely-balanced body.
➤ Gérard Millet, rte de Bourges, 18300 Bué,
tel. 02.48.54.38.62, fax 02.48.54.13.50,
e-mail gmillet@terre-net.fr ▼
�178 by appt.

DOM. DU NOZAY 2002★

10 ha	84,000	▮ ⚬	8–11 €

Philippe de Benoist set up at the Château du Nozay in 1970. At the time, there was neither water, electricity, vines, nor a winery. With courage and hard work, this producer planted a vineyard that now covers an area of 22.5 ha. This Sancerre, from a clay-limestone terroir, has an intense nose focussing on ripe grapes and lychee. Rather soft on the attack and fairly round, it seems an ideal wine for desserts.
➤ Dom. du Nozay, Ch. du Nozay,
18240 Sainte-Gemme-en-Sancerrois, tel. 02.48.79.30.23,
fax 02.48.79.36.64, e-mail nozays@aol.com ▼
�178 by appt.
➤ de Benoist

DOM. HENRY PELLE

La Croix au Garde 2002★

4 ha	25,000	▮ ⚬	8–11 €

Grower and négociant, Henri Pellé is certainly an enthusiastic defender of AOC Menetou-Salon, but he also presents Sancerres. On airing, this wine delivers powerful and varied perfumes: gooseberry, broom, lemon and minerals. On the palate there is a feeling of freshness and roundness. The **red La Croix au Garde 2001** deserves a mention for its flexibility and notes of wild woodland fruits.
➤ Dom. Henry Pellé, 18220 Morogues, tel. 02.48.64.42.48, fax 02.48.64.36.88,
e-mail info@henry.pelle.com ▼
�178 ev. day except Sun. 8.30am–12 noon 1.30pm–5.30pm; Sat. by appt.; cl. 15–31 Aug.
➤ Anne Pellé

DOM. DE LA PERRIERE 2002★

20 ha	160,000	▮ ⚬	8–11 €

A *coup de coeur* last year for the white Sancerre 2001, the Perrière estate is recommended again this year. This 2002, made from various terroirs – *caillottes* (pebbles), flint and clay-limestone – blends mint, peach and citrus fruits. If it is balanced, it could still open out in the months to come. The well-balanced **red Domaine de La Perrière 2002 (11–15 €)**, which is true to type, also gains one star, while the **white Pierre Archambault 2002**, which is very concentrated on white fruits, is commended.
➤ SCEA Dom. de la Perrière, Cave de la Perrière, 18300 Verdigny, tel. 02.48.54.16.93, fax 02.48.54.11.54 ▼
�178 ev. day 8am–12 noon 2pm–6pm;
cl. Sat. Sun. from 20 Dec. until 15 Mar.
➤ J.-L. Saget

DOM. DU P'TIT ROY 2002★★

6.45 ha	40,000	▮ ⚬	8–11 €

It is worth turning off the main road to discover Sury's beautiful church, charming fountain and little lanes. Then go towards Mainbray and you will find the wine hamlet of Sury, where Pierre and Alain Dezat cultivate a little less than 10 ha. Pale gold, this Sancerre is still discreet but already complex and develops with elegance and balance. The fruit will open out shortly. While waiting, enjoy the floral and vegetal **rosé 2002** with its freshness; it is singled out.

📣 Pierre et Alain Dezat, Maimbray, 18300 Sury-en-Vaux, tel. 02.48.79.34.16, fax 02.48.79.35.81 **V**

📅 by appt.

NOEL ET JEAN-LUC RAIMBAULT

Les Moulins à vent 2002★

	4.5 ha	40,000	🍾 🍷	5–8 €

Produced on clay-limestone soils, this bright wine is subtly mineral, herbaceous, floral (acacia) and fruity (lychee). These attractive flavours reappear on the palate that is initially fresh, then round and always balanced.

📣 Noël et Jean-Luc Raimbault, Lieu-dit Chambre, 18300 Sury-en-Vaux, tel. 02.48.79.36.56, fax 02.48.79.36.56 **V**

📅 by appt.

PHILIPPE RAIMBAULT

Les Godons 2002★

	3.1 ha	24,000	🍾 🍷	8–11 €

Philippe Raimbault exhibits his collection of fossils (sea urchins, ammonites), all found in the Sancerre subsoil. You must also taste his wine, especially Les Godons, fruit of his fifth solo wine production. This *cuvée* with its intense notes of broom, exotic fruits and *pêche de vigne* reveals a full and rich body. The **white Sancerre Apud Sariacum 2002** has roundness as well but its floral flavours are more discreet: it is singled out.

📣 Philippe Raimbault, rte de Maimbray, 18300 Sury-en-Vaux, tel. 02.48.79.29.54, fax 02.48.79.29.51 **V**

📅 by appt.

ROGER ET DIDIER RAIMBAULT 2002★

	10.5 ha	55,000	🍾 🍷	8–11 €

After the *coup de coeur* of last year for the red Sancerre 2001, the tasters enjoyed this pleasant white wine, whose keeping potential is interesting. A pale-yellow colour with a complex nose: mineral and vegetal nuances, ripe grapes, peach and flowers. The first impression of freshness is soon overtaken by roundness and a lengthy fruitiness. Serve this wine with fish.

📣 Roger et Didier Raimbault, Chaudenay, 18300 Verdigny, tel. 02.48.79.32.87, fax 02.48.79.39.08 **V**

📅 ev. day 9am–12 noon 2pm–6pm; Sun. by appt.

DOM. HIPPOLYTE REVERDY 2002★

	1 ha	6,000	🍾 🍷	8–11 €

This wine comes from 1 ha of vines planted on limestone. Bright old-rose, it presents rich fruity and spicy perfumes, then a beautifully balanced freshness and richness. The finish leaves a memory of crystallized citrus fruits and white peach. It would be pleasant to drink as an aperitif. The **red Sancerre 2002** is singled out for its flavours of soft fruits and flowers; it simply needs to fill out with time.

📣 Dom. Hippolyte Reverdy, rue de la Croix-Michaud, Chaudoux, 18300 Verdigny, tel. 02.48.79.36.16, fax 02.48.79.36.65 **V**

📅 by appt.

PASCAL ET NICOLAS REVERDY

Terre de Maimbray 2002★★

	9 ha	65,000	🍾 🍷	8–11 €

These regulars in the *Guide*, awarded a *coup de coeur* in the 2002 edition, today present their white Sancerres, which are flagships for the appellation. The Terre de Maimbray has finesse: its bouquet of floral, grapefruit and gunflint is indeed elegant. And its palate opens out richly with the same flavours, to which are added nuances of menthol and liquorice. The **Vieilles Vignes 2002 (11–15 €)** shines with one star; produced in cask, it delicately combines the fruit of the grape with the vanilla of the wood. The **red Cuvée Evolution 2002 (11–15 €)**, matured 12 months in wood, is commended.

📣 Pascal et Nicolas Reverdy, Maimbray, 18300 Sury-en-Vaux, tel. 02.48.79.37.31, fax 02.48.79.41.48 **V**

📅 by appt.

ROGER REVERDY CADET ET FILS

Cuvée des Cadet 2002★

	0.4 ha	3,000	🍾 🍷	11–15 €

The Cuvée des Cadet is only made in years when the grapes reach the desired quality, and is only sold to private individuals. Its delicate and pure fragrances combine mineral notes, passion-fruit and flowers, while on the palate a lemony touch brings freshness right through to the long finish. The powerful **red Domaine des Trois Noyers 2002 (8–11 €)**, which is also very successful, only needs to open out. The **white Domaine des Trois Noyers 2002 (8–11 €)** is singled out for its balance.

📣 Reverdy-Cadet et Fils, rte de la Perrière, Chaudoux, 18300 Verdigny, tel. 02.48.79.38.54, fax 02.48.79.35.25 **V**

📅 by appt.

DOM. REVERDY-DUCROUX

Beau Roy 2002★★

	n.c.	50,000	🍾 🍷	8–11 €

Reverdy-Ducroux practises sustainable agriculture in their vineyards. Made from limestone terroir (the famous *caillotes*), their *cuvée* enchanted the Jury from the first glance – its pale colour with its green highlights, testifying to youth. Attractive aromas: lemon, grapefruit, fruit (Mirabelle plum) and breadcrumbs. Then the balance of roundness and freshness, and the complexity of fruity-floral flavours are really appealing.

📣 Dom. Reverdy-Ducroux, rue du Pressoir, 18300 Verdigny, tel. 02.48.79.31.33, fax 02.48.79.36.19, e-mail reverdy.ducroux-sancerre@wanadoo.fr **V**

📅 by appt.

DOM. BERNARD REVERDY ET FILS

2002★

	1.2	7,000	🍾 🍷	8–11 €

An agreeable rosé with bright salmon tones that combines rose, *pêche de vigne* and other fruits with finesse. Clean on the opening, it then gains roundness and has good length with soft fruits. A prune tart would suit it well. The **red Sancerre 2001** from the estate is singled out.

📣 Bernard Reverdy et Fils, rte des Petites-Perrières, Chaudoux, 18300 Verdigny, tel. 02.48.79.33.08, fax 02.48.79.37.93 **V**

📅 by appt.

CLAUDE RIFFAULT

Les Boucauds 2002★★

	5.2 ha	40,000	🍾 🍷	8–11 €

A regular in the *Guide*, Claude Riffault is recommended again for this full-flavoured wine: notes of exotic fruits are found throughout, with some citrus fruit. The balance is superb: fresh attack, finesse and roundness on the middle palate, then a long fruity finish. Real harmony. The **red La Noue 2002**, which is perfumed with soft fruits, is awarded one star and will be at its peak within two years.

📣 SCEV Claude Riffault, Maison-Sallé, 18300 Sury-en-Vaux, tel. 02.48.79.38.22, fax 02.48.79.36.22 **V**

📅 ev. day 8am–12 noon 2pm–7pm; Sun. by appt.

DOMINIQUE ROGER
La Jouline Vieilles Vignes 2001★★

0.8 ha	4,000	🍾 ❚❙❘ ⬧	11–15 €

Is it necessary to prove that the Sancerre can age well? This 2001, from a terroir of *caillottes* (little stones), will bring you the ultimate proof. 70% of the wine has been produced in tank, 30% in barrel. The result is a fine and complex character (menthol, exotic fruits, dried fruits and honey) which is round and delicate. One of the tasters concluded that it was like "a mature woman in the guise of a young girl".
☛ Dominique Roger, 7, pl. du Carrou, 18300 Bué, tel. 02.48.54.10.65, fax 02.48.54.38.77, e-mail dominique.roger11@wanadoo.fr ☑
🍷 ev. day 8.30am–12 noon 1.30pm–7pm; Sun. by appt.

DOM. DE SAINT-PIERRE
Cuvée Maréchal Prieur 2001★★

n.c.	2,000	❚❙❘	11–15 €

Pierre Prieur and his sons, Thierry and Bruno, perpetuate a family tradition with brilliance: three recommended wines, one of which achieves a *coup de coeur*. The Cuvée Maréchal Prieur pays homage to an ancestor who, in 1887, started exporting wines to Great Britain. Clothed in cherry-red tinged with brown – a sign of development – it releases pleasant, complex and intense aromas: a delicate oakiness, vanilla, charred notes, red and black fruits. It appears soft because of its well-integrated tannins and concludes on a vanilla note. The **white Domaine de Saint-Pierre 2002 (8–11 €)** also obtains two stars; it is well-balanced, rounded (due to maturation in barrel), with dominant floral and fruity flavours. Tasters could imagine it with grilled lobster. The commended **red Domaine de Saint-Pierre 2001 (8–11 €)**, which is fruity and spicy, but a little short, will go well with grilled meats.
☛ Pierre Prieur et Fils, Dom. de Saint-Pierre, 18300 Verdigny, tel. 02.48.79.31.70, fax 02.48.79.38.87, e-mail prieur.pierre@netcourrier.com ☑
🍷 ev. day except Sun. 8.30am–12 noon 2pm–6pm

DOM. DE SAINT ROMBLE
Grande Cuvée Vieilles Vignes 2001★★

1.8 ha	11,500	🍾 ⬧	8–11 €

In January 1996, the Fournier family took over the vineyard of this 12.5-hectare estate, regularly mentioned in the *Guide*. This Grande Cuvée received unanimous praise: "a remarkable wine from a difficult year," comments one of the tasters. The nose evolves between mineral, floral and fruity notes. Freshness is found on the palate, which is full, balanced and long. The **red Domaine de Saint-Romble 2001** and the **white 2002** are singled out. One is fruity (cherry, prune), lively and long, to drink from now; the other is rich and full, and will keep a few years.
☛ SARL Paul Vattan, Dom. de Saint Romble, BP 45, Maimbray, 18300 Sury-en-Vaux, tel. 02.48.79.30.36, fax 02.48.79.30.41, e-mail claude@fournier-pere-fils.fr ☑
🍷 by appt.

LES CELLIERS SAINT-ROMBLE 2002★

15 ha	110,000	🍾 ⬧	8–11 €

André Dezat is a well-known figure in the Sancerre vineyards. Today, it is his sons who carry the torch. Served as an aperitif, this white Sancerre will titillate the palate with its exotic fruits, citrus fruits and floral flavours, which also show balance and

finesse. Ripe grapes have produced this supple and long **red Sancerre 2002**, with aromas of overripe soft fruits and spices. The Jury highly recommends it.
☛ SCEV André Dezat et Fils, rue des Tonneliers, Chaudoux, 18300 Verdigny, tel. 02.48.79.38.82, fax 02.48.79.38.24 ☑
🍷 by appt.

CH. DE SANCERRE 2002★

4 ha	30,000	🍾 ❚❙❘ ⬧	8–11 €

The château, bought in 1920 by the founder of the famous Grand-Marnier liqueur company, dominates Sancerre and the Loire valley. The Tour de Fiefs, represented on the wine label, is the only remaining part of the fortified 13th century château. This deep-red 2002 needs to open soon; at the moment it is floral, aniseedy, then fruity on the palate. Balanced and long, it indicates a ripe harvest.
☛ Sté Marnier-Lapostolle, Ch. de Sancerre, 18300 Sancerre, tel. 02.48.78.51.52, fax 02.48.78.51.56 ☑

DOM. THOMAS ET FILS
Le Pierrier 2002★

11 ha	75,000	🍾 ⬧	8–11 €

This estate, created at Verdigny by one of the family ancestors in the 17th century, now has 12 ha spread over six villages within the area of the appellation. A vast range of flavours (cut hay, mineral, toast, citrus fruits and apple) is echoed on the palate with its lively attack that develops suppleness and harmony. Ideal with trout in a cream sauce.
☛ Dom. Thomas et Fils, Verdigny, 18300 Sancerre, tel. 02.48.79.38.71, fax 02.48.79.38.14 ☑
🍷 ev. day 8am–12 noon 2pm–6pm

CLAUDE ET FLORENCE THOMAS-LABAILLE La Fleur de Galifard 2002★

0.5 ha	1000	❚❙❘	15–23 €

Claude and Florence Thomas-Labaille took over from their grandfather in 1994 and now run this Chavignol estate. The vines are located on the sloping hillsides of Chavignol with its famous hill, the Monts Damnés, at the top of which the panoramic view of Sancerre is admirable. This top-of-the-range *cuvée* comes from the oldest vines (75 years) on the Galifard *lieu-dit*. Fruit and vanilla dominate this fresh wine, fine and round, very elegant. Two other Sancerre whites were also singled out by the Jury: **Les Aristides 2002 (8–11 €)**, which is more concentrated on exotic fruits, and **L' Authentique 2002 (5–8 €)**, all flowers.
☛ Claude et Florence Thomas-Labaille, Chavignol, 18300 Sancerre, tel. 02.48.54.06.95, fax 02.48.54.07.80 ☑
🍷 ev. day 10am–12 .30pm 2pm–6pm

ROLAND TISSIER ET FILS 2002★★

1 ha	5,000	🍾	5–8 €

With his two sons, Rodolphe and Florent, Roland Tissier cultivates 10 ha planted with 85% Sauvignon and 15% Pinot Noir. He has an inn at Chavignol, *La Bonne Auberge*. His ruby Sancerre reveals notes of red berry fruit, underscored by coffee and toastiness. It opens with roundness and balance. The very successful **white Sancerre 2002** has length on fruity, floral and mineral flavours. With its richness and body, it will go well with scallops.
☛ Roland Tissier et Fils, 5, rue Saint-Jean, 18300 Sancerre, tel. 02.48.54.12.31, fax 02.48.78.04.32, e-mail sancerretissier@aol.com ☑
🍷 by appt.

DOM. VACHERON
Belle Dame 2001★★

1.6 ha	8,106	❚❙❘	23–30 €

Located in old Sancerre, the domaine is housed in buildings dating from the 15th, 16th and 17th centuries. Jean-Louis, Jean-Dominique, Denis and Jean-Laurent Vacheron work the 38 ha of vines using organic methods and manual harvests. The result is this rich wine, with lots of character, which reveals ripe grapes at their best. The intense and complex nose evokes red and black berries, liquorice, and vanilla. The palate

LOIRE

is balanced and supple with well-integrated oak. On the finish, there is touch of chocolate.
•๑ Dom. Vacheron, 1, rue du Puits-Poulton, 18300 Sancerre, tel. 02.48.54.09.93, fax 02.48.54.01.74, e-mail vacheron.sa@wanadoo.fr ☑
⚊ by appt.

DOM. DU VIEUX PRECHE 2002★

▩	1.19 ha	9,000	🔳	8–11 €

Don't hesitate to climb the Sancerre peak to enjoy an unspoilt view of the Loire valley and the narrow lanes of the village. At Robert Planchon's vineyard, taste this ruby wine with its pronounced black fruits (blackcurrant), cherry and charred notes. The palate at first opens with suppleness and then evolves to present a structure of fine tannins. Good keeping potential.
•๑ SCEV Robert Planchon et Fils, Dom. du Vieux-Prêche, 3, rue Porte-Serrure, 18300 Sancerre, tel. 02.48.54.22.22, fax 02.48.54.09.31, e-mail robert-planchon@terre-net.fr ☑
⚊ by appt.

DOM. DES VIEUX PRUNIERS 2002★★

▩	1.9 ha	16,600	🔳 🍷	5–8 €

Originally established in 1984 on a small area, in 1986 Christian Thirot-Fournier and his wife created The Domaine des Vieux Pruniers. They now farm 9 ha of vines on a clay-limestone hillside. This wine enchanted tasters by the typicity of its nose with lemon, floral and boxwood aromas, by its fresh attack that is followed by a round, well-balanced body. An ideal Sancerre to introduce you to the appellation.
•๑ Christian Thirot-Fournier, 1, chem. de Marcigoi, 18300 Bué, tel. 02.48.54.09.40, fax 02.48.78.02.72 ☑
⚊ by appt.

DOM. DE LA VILLAUDIERE 2002★★

▩	14 ha	120,000	🔳 🍷	8–11 €

The domaine covers 15 ha planted with 75% Sauvignon and 25% Pinot Noir. Jean-Marie Reverdy works in well-equipped buildings (an air-conditioned winery and a temperature-controlled vat room) while respecting the typicity of Sancerre. The results are convincing. The pale-gold 2002 reveals intense mineral and vegetal notes, with fruit. It does not lack personality: supple on the first opening, the body gains in freshness as it opens out. Throughout the palate it has mineral and exotic fruit flavours.
•๑ Jean-Marie Reverdy, rte de Chaudenay, 18300 Verdigny, tel. 02.48.79.30.84, fax 02.48.79.38.16 ☑
⚊ by appt.

DOM. LA VOLTONNERIE 2002★

▩	1.72 ha	3,000	🔳 🍷	8–11 €

Jack Pinson reaps the reward for meticulous work in this selection. His Sancerres of all three colours obtain a star. The fine, well-balanced rosé reveals freshness uplifted by a touch of carbon dioxide. Pleasant floral and fruity notes (apricot) appear on the palate. The **white Domaine La Voltonnerie 2002**, which is still discreet on the nose, pleases with its balance, while the dark-ruby **red 2002** promises a beautiful future thanks to its quality structure.
•๑ Jack Pinson, Le Bourg, 18300 Crézancy-en-Sancerre, tel. 02.48.79.00.94, fax 02.48.79.00.11, e-mail j.pinson@terre-net.fr ☑
⚊ by appt.

Wines selected but not starred

PASCAL BALLAND 2002

▩	7.5 ha	55,000	🔳 🍷	5–8 €

•๑ EARL Pascal Balland, rue Saint-Vincent, 18300 Bué, tel. 02.48.54.22.19, fax 02.48.78.08.59 ☑
⚊ by appt.

DOM. DES BUISSONNES 2002

▩	1.99 ha	15,000	🔳	11–15 €

•๑ Cave Roger Naudet, SCEA des Buissonnes, Maison Sallé, 18300 Sury-en-Vaux, tel. 02.48.79.34.68, fax 02.48.79.34.68 ☑
⚊ ev. day 9am–12 noon 2pm–7pm

DOM. DES CLAIRNEAUX 2002

▩	6.56 ha	45,000	🔳 🍷	5–8 €

•๑ Jean-Marie Berthier, Dom. des Clairneaux, 18240 Sainte-Gemme-en-Sancerrois, tel. 02.48.79.40.97, fax 02.48.79.39.55 ☑ 🏠 🏠
⚊ by appt.

DOM. DOMINIQUE ET JANINE CROCHET 2002

▩	0.5 ha	4,000	🔳 🍷	5–8 €

•๑ Dom. Dominique et Janine Crochet, 64, rue de Venoize, 18300 Bué, tel. 02.48.54.19.56, fax 02.48.54.12.61 ☑
⚊ by appt.

DOM. ROBERT ET FRANCOIS CROCHET 2002

▩	0.6 ha	3,700	🔳 🍷	8–11 €

•๑ Robert et François Crochet, Marcigoué, 18300 Bué, tel. 02.48.54.21.77, fax 02.48.54.25.10 ☑
⚊ ev. day 9am–7pm; Sun. by appt.

PAUL DOUCET 2002

▩	1 ha	2,000	🔳 🍷	5–8 €

•๑ EARL Paul Doucet, Les Plessis, 18300 Sury-en-Vaux, tel. 02.48.79.33.40, fax 02.48.79.28.14 ☑
⚊ by appt.

DOM. DOUDEAU-LEGER 2002

▩	6.36 ha	49,000	🔳 🍷	5–8 €

•๑ Dom. Doudeau-Léger, Les Giraults, 18300 Sury-en-Vaux, tel. 02.48.79.32.26, fax 02.48.79.29.80 ☑ 🏠
⚊ by appt.
•๑ Pascal Doudeau

DUC DE TARENTE 2002

▩	n.c.	13,000	🔳 🍷	11–15 €

•๑ Cave des vins de Sancerre, av. de Verdun, 18300 Sancerre, tel. 02.48.54.19.24, fax 02.48.54.16.44, e-mail infos@vins-sancerre.com ☑

GERARD FIOU 2002

▩	0.45 ha	3,400	🔳 🍷	8–11 €

•๑ Gérard Fiou, 15, rue Hilaire-Amagat, 18300 Saint-Satur, tel. 02.48.54.16.17, fax 02.48.54.36.89 ☑
⚊ ev. day 8am–12 noon 2pm–7pm; Sat. Sun. from 10am

FOUCHER-LEBRUN

Elevé en fût de chêne 2001

	n.c.	n.c.	▮ ❶❷	8–11€

☛ Foucher-Lebrun, 29, rte de Bouhy, 58200 Alligny-Cosne, tel. 03.86.26.87.27, fax 03.86.26.87.20, e-mail foucher.lebrun@wanadoo.fr ☑
☫ ev. day except Sun. Mon. 8am–12 noon 2pm–6pm

CHRISTIAN LAUVERJAT

Perle blanche 2002

	1.5 ha	8,000	▮ ⚬	5–8€

☛ Christian Lauverjat, SCEA des Vrillères, Moulin des Vrillères, 18300 Sury-en-Vaux, tel. 02.48.79.38.28, fax 02.48.79.39.49, e-mail lauverjat.christian@wanadoo.fr ☑
☫ by appt.

DOM. RENE MALLERON 2002

	0.76 ha	7,441		11–15€

☛ Dom. René Malleron, Champtin, 18300 Crézancy-en-Sancerre, tel. 02.48.79.06.90, fax 02.48.79.42.18 ☑
☫ by appt.

FLORIAN MOLLET

Roc de l'Abbaye 2002

	1 ha	32,000	▮ ⚬	8–11€

☛ Florian Mollet, 84, av. de Fontenay, 18300 Saint-Satur, tel. 02.48.54.13.88, fax 02.48.54.09.28, e-mail mollet.jean-paul@wanadoo.fr ☑
☫ ev. day 8am–12 noon 2pm–7pm

ROGER NEVEU ET FILS

Clos des Bouffants 2002

	11 ha	75,000	▮ ⚬	8–11€

☛ Dom. Neveu et Fils, 18300 Verdigny, tel. 02.48.79.40.34, fax 02.48.79.32.93, e-mail neveu@terre-net.fr ☑
☫ by appt.
☛ Roger Neveu

PAUL PRIEUR ET FILS 2002

	1.06 ha	8,500	▮ ⚬	8–11€

☛ Dom. Paul Prieur et Fils, rte des Monts-Damnés, 18300 Verdigny, tel. 02.48.79.35.86, fax 02.48.79.36.85, e-mail paulprieurfils@wanadoo.fr ☑
☫ ev. day 9am–12 noon 2pm–7pm; Sun. by appt.

JEAN REVERDY ET FILS

Les Villots 2002

	1 ha	6,000	▮ ⚬	8–11€

☛ Jean Reverdy et Fils, 18300 Verdigny, tel. 02.48.79.31.48, fax 02.48.79.32.44 ☑
☫ by appt.

GUY SAGET

Sélection première 2002

	7.5 ha	50,000	▮ ⚬	5–8€

☛ SA Guy Saget, La Castille, BP 26, 58150 Pouilly-sur-Loire, tel. 03.86.39.57.75, fax 03.86.39.08.30 ☑
☫ by appt.

DOM. CHRISTIAN SALMON 2001

	4.5 ha	25,000	▮ ❶❷ ⚬	8–11€

☛ Christian Salmon, Le Carroir, 18300 Bué, tel. 02.48.54.20.54, fax 02.48.54.30.36 ☑
☫ by appt.

DOM. MICHEL THOMAS 2002

	9 ha	70,000	▮ ⚬	8–11€

☛ SCEV Michel Thomas et Fils, Les Egrots, 18300 Sury-en-Vaux, tel. 02.48.79.35.46, fax 02.48.79.37.60, e-mail thomas.mld@wanadoo.fr ☑
☫ ev. day except Sun. 8am–12 noon 2.30pm–7.30pm

DOM. ANDRE VATAN

Maulin Bèle 2002

	0.45 ha	3,900	▮ ⚬	8–11€

☛ André Vatan, rte des Petites-Perrières, 18300 Verdigny, tel. 02.48.79.33.07, fax 02.48.79.36.30 ☑
☫ by appt.

LOIRE

THE RHONE VALLEY

As the mighty Rhône races south towards the Midi and the sun, it unites rather than divides the great tracts of country either side of it. Along both its banks stretch vineyards that are among the oldest in France, prestigious in some places, yet unknown in others. In terms of producing fine wines, the Rhône valley is the second largest viticultural area in France, after Bordeaux. In terms of quality it can compete at the highest level with some of the Bordeaux crus and can excite the interest of connoisseurs just as much as some of the most highly prized Bordeaux and Burgundies.

For a long time, however, Côte du Rhône wine was underestimated: it was considered to be a nice, popular little bar wine and, as such, appeared only rarely on dinner tables. It was known as a vin d'une nuit (a one-night wine), because its fleeting stay in the vat made it light, fruity and a little tannic, quite at home alongside Beaujolais in the Lyonnais bouchons (bars). Nonetheless, true wine-lovers had always appreciated the Grands Crus, tasting a Hermitage with the respect reserved for great bottles. Nowadays, thanks to the efforts of the 12,000 Rhône winegrowers and their professional organizations, along with a constant improvement in quality, the image of the Côte du Rhône wines has improved. While they still flow joyously in bars and bistros, they are also taking their place at the best tables and, while their true richness remains in their diversity, they have reclaimed the success they enjoyed in times past.

Few wine regions are able to lay claim to so glorious a past and from Vienne to Avignon there is no single village that is not recorded in some of the most memorable pages of French history. The oldest vineyard in the country is said to be on the banks of the Vienne, originally created by Phocaean Greeks who journeyed up from Marseille and further developed by the Romans. By the 4th century BC, vineyards are recorded in the areas now famous as Hermitage and Côte-Rôtie, while those in the region of Die appeared at the very beginning of the Christian era. The Templars, in the 12th century, planted the first vines at Châteauneuf-du-Pape and the work was continued by Pope John XXII two centuries later. As for the Côte du Rhône wines in the Gard, they used to be very fashionable in the 17th and 18th centuries.

Today, in the southern sector, on the left bank of the river, the medieval château of Suze-la-Rousse has been reconverted to serve the wine industry: the Université du Vin has its headquarters there and organizes courses, professional training and various events.

Looking at the valley as a whole, some commentators make a distinction between the wines of the left bank as being heavier and more heady and the wines on the right bank which are lighter. More generally they distinguish between two main sectors which are clearly differentiated: the sector of the northern Côtes du Rhône, north of Valence and that of the southern Côtes du Rhône, south of Montélimar, divided from each other by an area about 50 km deep where no vines are grown.

The neighbouring appellations of the Rhône valley should not be left out. Even though they are less well known to the general public, they nonetheless produce original wines of quality. These are the Coteaux du Tricastin in the north, the Côtes du Ventoux and the Côtes du Luberon in the east and the Côtes du Vivarais in the northwest. There are three further appellations that are geographically more distant still from the valley proper: the Clairette de Die and the Châtillon-en-Diois in the Drôme valley, on the edge of the Vercors and the Coteaux de Pierrevert, produced in the *département* of the Alpes-de-Haute-Provence. Finally, it is worth noting the two appellations of Vins Doux Naturels (naturally sweet wines) of the Vaucluse: Muscat de Beaumes-de-Venise and Rasteau (see the chapter on Vins Doux Naturels).

Looking at the variations of soils and climate, it is still possible to identify three sub-groupings within the vast region of the Rhône valley. North of Valence, the climate is temperate with a continental influence, the soils are mostly granites or schists, deposited on hills with very steep slopes; the red wines come from a single variety, Syrah and the whites from Marsanne and Roussanne, while the Viognier variety is used to make Château-Grillet and Condrieu. In the Diois, the climate is influenced by the mountain relief and the limestone soils are made up of screes at the foot of the slopes, good conditions for the Clairette and Muscat varieties. South of Montélimar the climate becomes Mediterranean and the very varied soils are spread out on a limestone stratum (terraces of rolled pebbles, red clay and sand soils, molasses and sands). Grenache is the main variety here, but the extremes of climate force the wine-growers to use a number of varieties to obtain perfectly balanced wines: these include Syrah, Mourvèdre, Cinsault, Clairette, Bourboulenc and Roussanne.

After a considerable reduction in the planted area in the 19th century, the vineyard of the Rhône valley was extended again and today it is still expanding. In general terms it covers 59,000 ha producing on average 2.9 million hl a year; nearly 50% of the wine produced in the northern area is sold by shippers and 70% is sold by cooperatives in the southern area.

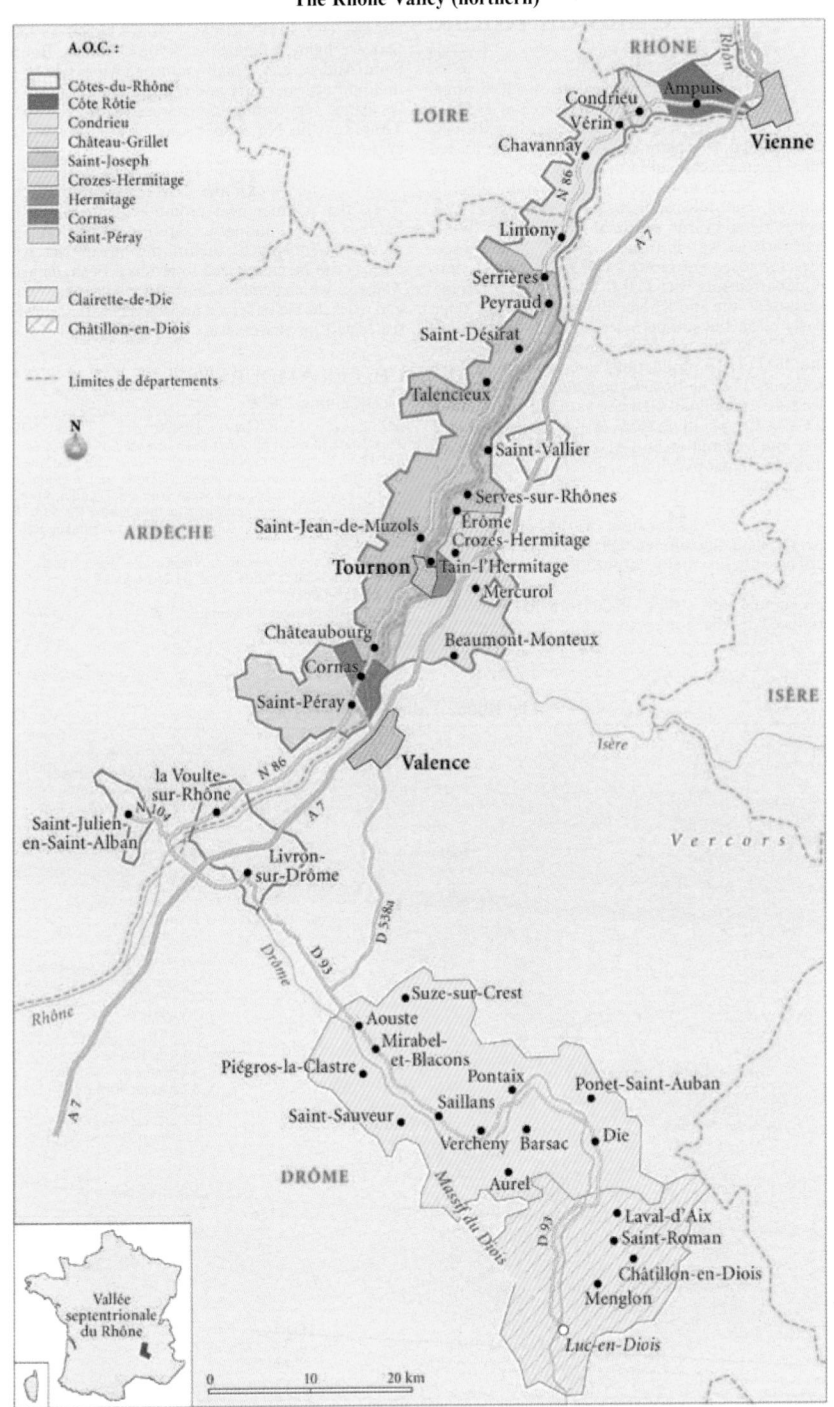

Côtes du Rhône

The Appellation Régionale Côtes du Rhône was defined by decree in 1937. In 1996, a new decree set conditions regarding the vine types planted, to be implemented from 2004: for red wines, Grenache should form a minimum proportion of 40%, Syrah and Mourvèdre should also be included. Naturally enough, this arrangement only applies to vineyards south of Montélimar. White wine varieties will, in future, only be allowed where vines for rosés are grown. The AOC extends into six départements: the Gard, the Ardèche, Drôme, Vaucluse, Loire and Gard. Produced on 43,170 ha, nearly all in the southern sector, these wines make 2,053,170 hl, the red wines having the lion's share with 96% of the production, rosés and whites each producing 2%. The 10,000 winemakers are divided up into 1,610 individual cellars (35% of the volume) and 70 Caves Coopératives (65% of the volume). Out of three hundred million bottles sold each year, 40% are consumed in people's homes, 30% in restaurants and 30% are exported.

Because of the variations in microclimate, the differences in the soil and the vine varieties, these vineyards produce wines that can satisfy every palate. Long-keeping red wines that are rich, tannic and strong, ideal with red meat, are produced in the hotter areas and on the diluvial alpine soils (Domazan, Estézargues, Courthézon, Orange, etc). Fruity, firmer reds are grown on soils that are lighter (Puyméras, Nyons, Sabran, Bourt-Saint-Andéol, etc). Finally, nouveau wines (about 15 million bottles), fruity and smooth and designed to be drunk very young, are released from the third Thursday in November and are enjoying an ever-growing success.

In the case of the whites and rosés, the summer heat promotes a characteristic balance and roundness. Careful cultivation and modern oenological techniques mean that the aromas can be maximized to produce fresh, delicate wines for which demand continually increases. White and rosés should be served respectively with saltwater fish, salads and charcuterie.

CH. LES AMOUREUSES
La Byzantine 2001★

| | 3.5 ha | 10,000 | 8–11 € |

This estate has several times been awarded a *coup de coeur*, notably in the previous edition of the *Guide*. This year, the La Byzantine *cuvée* has rich, intense colour and a powerful, complex nose with notes of fresh fruit and vanilla. On the palate it is full-bodied and presents those same flavours. An approachable wine that testifies to a skilled winemaker. Ready to drink now.

Alain Grangaud, chem. de Vinsas,
07700 Bourg-Saint-Andéol, tel. 04.75.54.51.85,
fax 04.75.54.66.38,
e-mail alain.grangaud@wanadoo.fr
by appt.

The Rhône Valley (southern)

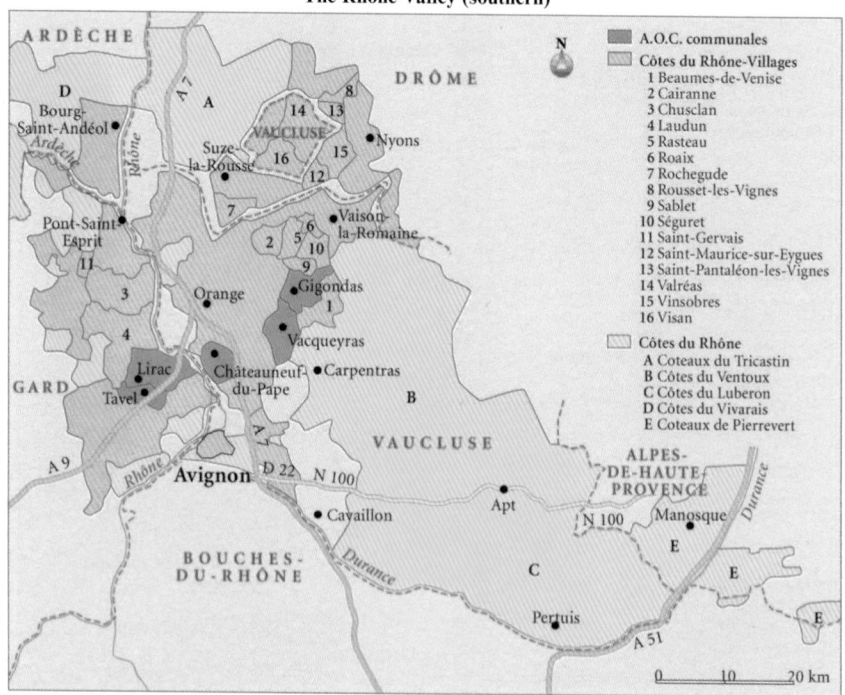

- A.O.C. communales
- Côtes du Rhône-Villages
  1 Beaumes-de-Venise
  2 Cairanne
  3 Chusclan
  4 Laudun
  5 Rasteau
  6 Roaix
  7 Rochegude
  8 Rousset-les-Vignes
  9 Sablet
  10 Séguret
  11 Saint-Gervais
  12 Saint-Maurice-sur-Eygues
  13 Saint-Pantaléon-les-Vignes
  14 Valréas
  15 Vinsobres
  16 Visan

- Côtes du Rhône
  A Coteaux du Tricastin
  B Côtes du Ventoux
  C Côtes du Luberon
  D Côtes du Vivarais
  E Coteaux de Pierrevert

DOM. DES BACCHANTES 2001★★

■　　　10 ha　　20,000　■ ◦　　3–5 €

Three new *cuvées* in the range of the Estézargues cellar where, ideally, one should take the time to taste all its high-level wines. Domaine des Bacchantes, owned by Didier Kupke, has a dark colour edged with violet and a nose marked by fruit and peppery notes. These flavours reappear on the palate, together with spices. A well-balanced wine that some might serve with duck in bilberry sauce and others might keep for the cheese board. One star for the **red Domaine d'Andézon 2001**, unfiltered, which should be drunk young to make the most of its fruit. But you should wait two or three years before serving it with game. This estate belongs to Thierry Lampietro and Serge Paneboeuf. The **red Domaine de Pierredon 2001**, from Christian Granier, gets one star for its supple attack and roundness.

☛ Cave des Vignerons d'Estézargues, rte du Grès, 30390 Estézargues, tel. 04.66.57.03.64, fax 04.66.57.04.83, e-mail les.vignerons.estezargues@wanadoo.fr ▣
☖ ev. day except Sun. 8am–12 noon 2pm–6pm; Sat. 2pm–5pm

LA BASTIDE SAINT VINCENT 2002★

■　　　1 ha　　5,500　■ ◦　　5–8 €

Laurent Daniel, who heads this attractive 21 ha family-run estate, is a *Guide* regular. His *rosé de saignée* is a great success. It is open on the nose with floral notes predominating. Long and fleshy, this wine is nevertheless pleasantly fresh.

☛ Laurent Daniel, La Bastide Saint Vincent, rte de Vaison-la-Romaine, 84150 Violès, tel. 04.90.70.94.13, fax 04.90.70.96.13, e-mail bastide.vincent@free.fr ▣
☖ ev. day except Sun. 9am–12 noon 2pm–6pm; cl. 10 Sep.–10 Oct.
☛ Guy Daniel

CH. DE BEAULIEU
Cuvée Prestige 2001★

■　　　1.7 ha　　10,000　■　　5–8 €

The earliest written references to this estate date back to 1399. Today, it produces two highly regarded wines. One is Cuvée Prestige, which is 80% Syrah, well concentrated, with very pleasing liquorice notes breaking through. It should be kept for two or three years before being enjoyed with some good game. The other is **red Cuvée Sélection 2001**, from a traditional blend, which is pleasantly full of flavour and well balanced – a typical Côtes du Rhône.

☛ SCEA Merle et Fils, Ch. de Beaulieu, rte de Sérignan, 84100 Orange, tel. 04.90.34.07.11, fax 04.90.34.07.11, e-mail chateau.de.beaulieu.orange@wanadoo.fr ▣
☖ by appt.

DOM. DE BEAURENARD 2002★

■　　　14 ha　　60,000　■ ◦　　5–8 €

Two wines are presented and both are judged very good. The red, with its purple colour, delivers what it promises: silky, fruity and heightened by very fine tannins, it is ready to drink now. The **rosé 2002**, in keeping with its vintage, is a little fresher but still delicious thanks to its velvety character. Its tannins are there, but are not excessive. Ready to drink now and for the next two years.

☛ SCEA Paul Coulon et Fils, Dom. de Beaurenard, 84230 Châteauneuf-du-Pape, tel. 04.90.83.71.79, fax 04.90.83.78.06, e-mail paulcoulon@beaurenard.fr ▣
☖ ev. day except Sun. 9am–12 noon 1.30pm–5.30pm; groups by appt.

LOUIS BERNARD
Grande Réserve 2001★★

■　　　n.c.　　40,000　　8–11 €

As in the last edition of the *Guide*, the Grande Réserve presented by this négociant from Orange gets two stars. A consistent performer! The 2001 vintage has an intense, deep ruby colour. It is open on the nose, pleasing and rich, with notes of flowers and ripe fruit. On the palate it is full-bodied and generous, with more ripe fruit over tannins that are already very fine. Ready to drink.

☛ Salavert-Les Domaines Bernard, rte de Sérignan, 84100 Orange, tel. 04.90.11.86.86, fax 04.90.34.87.30, e-mail sldb@sldb.fr

CH. DU BOIS DE LA GARDE 2002★

■　　　65 ha　　33,000　■　　5–8 €

Napoleon's troops no longer stand guard over this estate; instead, Robert Barrot keeps an eye on the winemaking. Twelve hours' maceration, pressing and traditional vinification produce a highly satisfying result. It is rich on the palate, firmly orientated towards soft fruits enhanced with spices. Rounded and fleshy, this 2002 vintage is most enjoyable.

☛ Robert Barrot, 1, av. du Baron-Leroy, 84230 Châteauneuf-du-Pape, tel. 04.90.83.51.73, fax 04.90.83.52.77, e-mail chateaux@vmb.fr ▣
☖ by appt.

DOM. DU BOIS DE SAINT-JEAN
Cuvée de Voulongue Réserve 2001★★

■　　　2 ha　　6,000　■ ◦　　5–8 €

Cuvée de Voulongue is made from 100% Grenache grown on rolled shingle and gravelly soil and is judged remarkable for its power and balance. Its dark colour indicates excellent maturity and soft stewed fruit is present on the nose. The estate's **2001 red (3–5 €)**, with very dark colouring, is extremely good. With good structure and strong character, it gives off lovely notes of stewed fruit and is good for laying down.

☛ EARL Vincent et Xavier Anglès, 126, av. de la République, 84450 Jonquerettes, tel. 04.90.22.53.22, fax 04.90.22.53.22 ▣
☖ ev. day 8am–12 noon 2pm–8pm

CH. LA BORIE 2001★

■　　　n.c.　　9,300　■ ◦　　5–8 €

This estate exports its wine all over the world, even to Africa and Asia. What will be the fate of these 9,300 bottles, which the Jury found remarkable? Tasters found zesty soft fruit, a strong gamey edge and a note of liquorice. They enjoyed the wine's good structure and length on the palate. They suggest the 2001 vintage be drunk within two or three years. Its **Côtes du Rhône-Villages, Château La Borie 2000 (8–11 €)** gets one star. It can be kept for five to six years.

☛ Ch. La Borie, 26790 Suze-la-Rousse, tel. 04.75.04.81.92, fax 04.96.16.02.65, e-mail jerome.margnat@chateau-la-borie.fr ▣
☖ by appt.
☛ Jérôme Margnat

DOM. BOUDINAUD 2001★★

■　　　9.1 ha　　6,000　■ ◦　　8–11 €

This 9.10 ha estate was formed by the breakup of a large estate in 2001. Véronique Boudinaud has ably managed the transition to a single cellar and offers a wine that narrowly misses a *coup de coeur*. This 2001 vintage thoroughly deserves its two stars, being clean on the nose, rich and full of very ripe, stewed, soft fruit. On the palate it remains initially fresh and fruity, almost majestic in its elegance. Ready to drink now, but equally suitable for laying down.

☛ Vignobles Boudinaud, Grand-Rue, 30210 Fournes, tel. 04.66.37.27.23, fax 04.66.37.03.56, e-mail boudinaud@infonie.fr ▣
☖ by appt.
☛ Véronique Boudinaud

CH. DE BOURDINES 2001★

■　　　15 ha　　4,000　■　　5–8 €

The popes of Avignon, who came here to rest and escape the heat, no doubt appreciated this wine, which encapsulates the best tradition has to offer. Its 20% Mourvèdre content brings complexity to the Grenache and Syrah blend and the wine offers soft fruit with balance, body, robustness and well rounded tannins.

☛ EARL Baroux, Ch. de Bourdines, 84700 Sorgues, tel. 04.90.83.36.77, fax 04.90.83.00.20 ▣
☖ ev. day except Sun. 2pm–7pm

LA BOUVAUDE
Signature Elevé en fût de chêne 2000★★

■　　　1 ha　　1,500　◫▯　　23–30 €

Cuvée Signature, which is 100% Syrah, spends two years in barrel, with remarkable results. Dark in colour, this powerful wine develops burnt, baked and fruity flavours. On the palate it is still quite oaky but this should develop and give way to unusually complex fruit. Worth waiting for.

•ₐ Stéphane Barnaud, Dom. La Bouvaude, 26770 Rousset-les-Vignes, tel. 04.75.27.90.32, fax 04.75.27.98.72, e-mail stephane.barnaud@wanadoo.fr ☑
ᚷ ev. day 10am–7pm

DOM. CASTAN 2001★★★

| ◼ | 4 ha | 10,000 | ◼ ♦ | 3–5 € |

DOMAINE CASTAN

CÔTES DU RHÔNE

13% Vol   APPELLATION CÔTES DU RHÔNE CONTRÔLÉE   750 ml
MIS EN BOUTEILLE AU DOMAINE
D. et G. CASTAN - VIGNERONS - GAEC DE CHANTECLER - DOMAZAN - F30390
PRODUCE OF FRANCE

The Jury were full of praise, with "magnificent" and "exceptional" appearing on the tasting notes for this *coup de cœur*. Ruby colour suffused with violet indicates astonishing youth for this high-quality wine. Its leathery nose tends towards blackcurrant and cherry and its supple tannins show flavours of lightly spiced stewed fruit. To do justice to this great wine, it should be served in a few years' time, with a roast young chicken stuffed with herbes de Provence. The **Côtes du Rhône-Villages 2001 (5–8 €)** gets one star.

•ₐ SCEA Chantecler, mas Chantecler, 30390 Domazan, tel. 04.66.57.00.56, fax 04.66.57.07.57 ☑ ♠
ᚷ ev. day 8am–12 noon 2pm–7pm
•ₐ Damien Castan

LES VIGNERONS DU CASTELAS

Les Mésanges 2002★★

| ◼ | n.c. | 6,000 | ◼ ♦ | 3–5 € |

The starred wines of the Castelas cellar always offer excellent value for money and this remarkable Mésanges is no exception. It is a veritable firework display of lemony, citrus and flowery flavours, already showing great class and elegance. The **red Castelas 2000**, already very jammy, gets one star. Its tannic structure is noticeable but very rounded and the finish is rather soft.

•ₐ Les Vignerons du Castelas, 30650 Rochefort-du-Gard, tel. 04.90.31.72.10, fax 04.90.26.62.64, e-mail vcastelas@hotmail.com ☑

DOM. DE CHANABAS

Séduction 2001★

| ◼ | 2 ha | 2,000 | ◼ | 5–8 € |

Robert Champ has had work done to make his cellar more efficient. However, he has not for all that neglected his winemaking, as the 2001 vintage demonstrates: it is supple and robust and needs to be aerated to take full advantage of its flavours. On the palate, very ripe fruit combines with spices, making this wine entirely worthy of being drunk with wild boar, venison, or hare.

•ₐ Robert Champ, Dom. de Chanabas, 84420 Piolenc, tel. 04.90.29.63.59, fax 04.90.29.55.67, e-mail domaine-chanabas@wanadoo.fr ☑ ♠
ᚷ by appt.

CHANTECOTES

Collection or 2002★

| ◼ | 1.5 ha | 8,000 | | 3–5 € |

The Chantecôtes cellar has been extended, notably by increasing its number of oak casks. Its wines were appreciated by the Jury, which has singled out two of them: Cuvée Collection Or, which is perfectly vinified and whose flavours are fully brought out. Fruit is present from the nose to the finish. This rosé is an aperitif for very hot days. The **red Cuvée Cécilia 2001** was singled out by the Jury, with its surprising notes of fruits

and undergrowth. A powerful wine which cannot fail to impress.

•ₐ Chantecôtes, cours Maurice-Trintignant, 84290 Sainte-Cécile-les-Vignes, tel. 04.90.30.83.25, fax 04.90.30.74.53, e-mail chantecotes@wanadoo.fr ☑
ᚷ ev. day 8.30am–12.15pm 2.30pm–7pm

DOM. CHAPOTON 2001★

| ◼ | 3 ha | 8,000 | | 11–15 € |

The land covered by this estate was under cultivation as early as the 17th century. Today, it produces some very good wines, such as this 2001 vintage. Strongly Viognier in character (95%), it offers a very exotic experience, with notes of citrus fruit and peaches to the fore. On the palate it is well balanced and rounded. This rich wine will perfectly accompany an entire fish menu.

•ₐ Remusan, Dom. Chapoton, rte du Moulin, 26790 Rochegude, tel. 04.75.98.22.46, fax 04.75.98.22.46 ☑
ᚷ by appt.

DOM. LA CHARADE 2001★

| ◼ | 22 ha | n.c. | ◼ ♦ | 3–5 € |

Elegant and floral, the **white from the same domaine 2002 (5–8 €)** has a strong fruit character. Fruit on the nose and fruit on the palate: fruit is a speciality of this estate. The warming red also gives of soft and stewed fruit flavours.

•ₐ M. et L. Jullien, Dom. La Charade, 30760 Saint-Julien-de-Peyrolas, tel. 04.66.82.18.21, fax 04.66.82.33.03
ᚷ ev. day except Sun. 9am–12 noon 2pm–7pm

CELLIER DES CHARTREUX 2002★

| ◼ | 6.18 ha | 42,800 | ◼ ♦ | 3–5 € |

As delicate as angels' tears, citrus fruit notes mingle with floral ones in this ocean of exotic flavours. It is round on the palate, full of freshness and hope – just like the winemakers of this cellar, who were among those in the Gard *département* worst affected by the floods of the autumn of 2002.

•ₐ Cellier des Chartreux, RN 580, 30131 Pujaut, tel. 04.90.26.39.40, fax 04.90.26.46.83 ☑
ᚷ by appt.

CLOS CHANTEDUC 2001★

| ◼ | 2.34 ha | 8,000 | ◼ ♦ | 5–8 € |

Walter Wells, senior editor of the *International Herald Tribune* and his wife Patricia, a food writer, own Clos Chanteduc. They can be justly proud of its wines. This handsome, purple-coloured 2001 freely gives off toasted and coffee notes both on the nose and the palate. An enjoyable, well-balanced wine.

•ₐ Ludovic Cornillon, Le Gas du Rossignol, 26790 La Baume-de-Transit, tel. 04.75.98.11.51, fax 04.75.98.19.22, e-mail domainesaintluc@wanadoo.fr ☑ ♠ ♠
ᚷ ev. day except Sun. 9am–12 noon 2pm–6pm

CLOS DE LA MAGNANERAIE 2000★★

| ◼ | 0.74 ha | 3,600 | ◼ ▥ ♦ | 5–8 € |

Clos de La Magnaneraie takes its name from a small plot on the edge of Nyons, whose vines produce this remarkable wine. "More than an ordinary Côtes du Rhône!", wrote one member of the Jury. A 2000 vintage to lay down. Rich, complex, powerful and well balanced with tannins melting into delicate oak, it is highly promising.

•ₐ François Vallot, Dom. du Coriançon, 26110 Vinsobres, tel. 04.75.26.03.24, fax 04.75.26.44.67, e-mail françois.vallot@wanadoo.fr ☑
ᚷ ev. day except Sun. 9am–12 noon 2pm–7pm

CLOS DE L'HERMITAGE 2001★★★

| ◼ | 4 ha | 20,000 | ▥ | 11–15 € |

This vineyard, owned by the racing driver Jean Alesi, is the last remaining one within the boundary of Villeneuve-lès-Avignon and produces a sensational wine. From cellar to vine, Henri de Lanzac has nurtured this veritable nectar. Its intense flavours are seductive, with notes of jam and fruit. The attack is rich and the sensation lingers long afterwards. A truly great wine with game or chocolate – and, at all events, for keeping (three to five years).

CÔTES DU RHÔNE
APPELLATION CÔTES DU RHÔNE CONTRÔLÉE

2001 2001

Clos de l'Hermitage

NON FILTRÉ

AC 14% VOL   MIS EN BOUTEILLE A LA PROPRIÉTÉ   750ML
HENRI de LANZAC • PROPRIÉTAIRE · RÉCOLTANT • 30126 LIRAC · FRANCE
PRODUCE OF FRANCE

☛ SCEA Henri de Lanzac, Ch. de Ségriès, chem. de la
Grange, 30126 Lirac,
tel. 04.66.50.22.97, fax 04.66.50.17.02 **V**
✗ by appt.

CLOS MARTIN 2000★★

■	2 ha	6,000	◖▮	8–11 €

The 2000 vintage narrowly missed a *coup de coeur*, surprising
the Jury with its strong spice and smoky notes. The flavours
are noble, with red berries pleasantly covering the palate. The
lasting impression is one of richness, depth and elegance. Wait
at least three years before opening and enjoy with red meats or
cheese.
☛ François Martin, Dom. Martin de Grangeneuve,
84150 Jonquières, tel. 04.90.70.62.62, fax 04.90.70.38.08,
e-mail martin@grangeneuve.com **V**
✗ by appt.

COSTEBELLE 2002★

■	30 ha	8,000	▮ ♦	3–5 €

Despite poor weather in the autumn of 2002, the Costebelle
cellar offers two very fine wines from that year. Certainly,
good grapes lie at their heart, but the winemaker's skill also
played its part. The white is fine, floral, warming and well balanced. The **2002 rosé** is very fresh and fruity, with pronounced
good balance.
☛ Cave Costebelle, 26790 Tulette, tel. 04.75.98.32.53,
fax 04.75.98.38.70, e-mail cave.costebelle@wanadoo.fr **V**
✗ ev. day 8.30am–12 noon 2pm–6.30pm

CAVE COSTES ROUSSES
Cuvée réservée 2002★

■	6 ha	10,000	▮ ♦	3–5 €

An absolutely typical Côtes du Rhône, with intense
colour and a nose giving off red berries and combining power,
elegance and freshness. It lingers on the palate, which makes
it suitable for drinking with Asian food. A very fine Cuvée
Réservée.
☛ SCA Cave Costes Rousses, 2, av. des Alpes,
26790 Tulette, tel. 04.75.97.23.10, fax 04.75.98.38.61 **V**
✗ by appt.

LES VIGNERONS DES COTEAUX
D'AVIGNON Réserve des armoiries 2001★

■	50 ha	70,000	▮ ♦	3–5 €

J.-F. Pasturel, cellar master, offers this fine wine, worthy of
being served with grills or dishes with sauce. The light ruby
colour heralds a captivating, enjoyable and well balanced
Côtes du Rhône with hints of fruit. A pleasing, approachable
wine. In **Côtes du Rhône-Villages, La Réserve de la Grande
Audience 2000 (5–8 €)** impressed the Jury.
☛ SCA Les Vignerons des Coteaux d'Avignon, 457, av.
Aristide-Briand, 84310 Morières-lès-Avignon,
tel. 04.90.22.65.65, fax 04.90.33.43.31,
e-mail lescoteauxdavignon@wanadoo.fr **V**
✗ by appt.

DOM. DE CRISTIA 2001★

■	3.5 ha	10,000	▮ ♦	5–8 €

When the present owner's grandfather began to make wine on
this estate, in 1942, it covered just 2 ha. Today it covers 20 ha
and, since 1999, Baptiste Grangeon has been in charge of bottling. He offers a delicate Côtes du Rhône with attractive,
bright, intense and limpid fruit colouring. Stewed fruit and
liquorice flavours resurface on the palate during tasting. With
its well-integrated tannins, it bears all the hallmarks of
Grenache.
☛ Baptiste Grangeon, 33, fg Saint-Georges,
84350 Courthézon, tel. 04.90.70.24.09, fax 04.90.70.25.38,
e-mail domainedecristia@hotmail.com **V**
✗ ev. day 8am–1pm 2pm–7pm

CUILLERON-GAILLARD-VILLARD
Les Cranilles 2001★★★

■	n.c.	4,000	◖▮	11–15 €

Les Cranilles is not a *coup de coeur*, but it was a close-run
thing. This wine is exceptional to look at, on the nose and on
the palate and it captivated the Jury. Its intense colour
promises a pleasant tasting experience and its complex peach,
apricot and prune bouquet confirms this. It is harmonious on
the palate, with strong structure which contains partly developed stewed fruit flavours. Plenty of length confirms all these
qualities. Enjoy in two or three years' time. This team of three
winemakers also offers **Cairanne La Perdendaille 2001** (two
stars), with great complexity combining fruit and woody
notes, as well as **Visan La Tine 2001** (one star).
☛ SARL Les Vins de Vienne, Bas-Seyssuel, 38200 Seyssuel,
tel. 04.74.85.04.52, fax 04.74.31.97.55,
e-mail vinsdevienne@terre-net.fr **V**
✗ by appt.

DOM. DEPEYRE-CLEMENT 2002★

■	2.6 ha	10,000	▮	5–8 €

La Chapelle Notre-Dame-des-Vignes stands near the estate
and overlooks the vineyard that makes this elegant, dark-coloured rosé. It is a robust Côtes du Rhône, with blackcurrant
notes on the nose and on the palate, where it proves powerful
but not aggressive. A well-made wine; serve with salad.
☛ Depeyre, SCEA Notre-Dame-des-Vignes, Clos du Père
Clément, rte de Vaison, 84820 Visan, tel. 04.90.41.93.68,
fax 04.90.41.97.04,
e-mail info@clos-pere-clement.com **V**
✗ by appt.

DOM. DES FILLES DURMA
La Galance 2001★★

■	n.c.	n.c.		8–11 €

A remarkable terroir and a remarkable wine. Vinsobres will
soon be a local appellation and produces a very classy Côtes
du Rhône. La Galance, with its intense colour with violet
overtones, has a rare fruitiness with toasted notes – a happy
combination. A very fine wine, to be drunk in four years' time.
The estate's **red Cuvée Principale 2000 (5–8 €)**, which is
slightly more developed, reveals soft fruit flavours in a most
pleasing combination.
☛ EARL Durma Soeurs, quartier Hautes-Rives,
26110 Vinsobres, tel. 04.75.27.64.71, fax 04.75.27.64.50 **V**
✗ by appt.

DOM. DE L'ESPIGOUETTE 2001★

■	7 ha	35,000	▮◖▮ ♦	3–5 €

Since 1973, Bernard Latour has run this 27 ha estate. Ten per
cent Carignan goes into the classic blend of this fruity, floral
wine with supple structure, which six months in oak casks
have not harmed, only mellowed. It has good potential for
ageing.
☛ Bernard Latour, L'Espigouette, BP 6, 84150 Violès,
tel. 04.90.70.95.48,
fax 04.90.70.96.06 **V**
✗ by appt.

CH. DE L'ESTAGNOL 2001★

■	n.c.	15,660	▮ ♦	3–5 €

Before you walk up to the château, it is worth stopping at La
Suzienne cellar to taste this red with a complex, very lively

RHONE

nose. Let yourself be seduced by the ripe fruit and spice flavours. A well-balanced bottle, typical of this appellation.
🕿 EURL Caveau La Suzienne, 26790 Suze-la-Rousse, tel. 04.75.04.80.04, fax 04.75.98.23.77 **V**
⚲ by appt.

CUVEE DES EVEQUES
Les Grandes Cuvées 2001★★

■	5 ha	20,000	■ ▥ ♦	5–8 €

Evêques has a very intense colour. This wine, for which the Syrah has been partly matured in barrel, is both rich and complex. Its tannins are well integrated and its depth is as intense as its colour. Ready to drink now. Gabriel Meffre also offers the **red Laurus 2001 (8–11 €)**, which is powerful and clean and gets one star. It coats the palate with its richness and can be drunk now thanks to its short time in barrel, though it also has good ageing potential. The **white Laurus 2002 (8–11 €)**, which is fine and delicate, gives off some floral notes. It is fresh and harmonious on the palate: a well-balanced wine well worth savouring and which impressed the Jury.
🕿 Maison Gabriel Meffre, Le Village, 84190 Gigondas, tel. 04.90.12.32.42, fax 04.90.12.32.49

DOM. LA FAVETTE 2001★

■	4 ha	24,000	■	3–5 €

This wine is 50% Grenache and 50% Syrah, grown on an exceptional terroir on the Ardèche Côtes du Rhône. Pleasant red fruit (cherry) flavours precede tantalizing sensations on the palate. It is powerful and warming, yet with the balance typical of an elegant Côtes du Rhône.
🕿 Philippe Faure, Dom. La Favette, rte des Gorges, 07700 Saint-Just-d'Ardèche, tel. 04.75.04.61.14, fax 04.75.98.74.56 **V**
⚲ ev. day 8am–8pm
(15 Sep.–31 May 9am–12.30pm except Sun.)

DOM. DE FERRAND
Cuvée antique Vieilles Vignes 2001★

■	6 ha	10,000	■ ♦	5–8 €

Is Cuvée Antique a tribute to the ancient town of Orange, where this estate lies? Perhaps. This wine's rich and complex appearance bodes well – an impression confirmed by its refined, soft spices on the nose. Silky, rounded tannins and flavours of cherry, pepper and spices combine to make this a very fine Côtes du Rhône.
🕿 EARL Charles Bravay, chem. de Saint-Jean, 84100 Orange, tel. 04.90.34.26.06, fax 04.90.34.26.06 **V**
⚲ by appt.

DOM. FOND CROZE 2001★★

■	6 ha	30,000	■ ♦	3–5 €

This estate has not rested on its laurels. Having secured a *coup de coeur* in the *Guide*'s last edition, it has again been singled out by the Jury and narrowly missed out on a *coup de coeur* a second time. It bursts with soft fruit (blackcurrant) and spicy, slightly vanilla notes, before a supple attack, followed by rare richness on the palate. Unusually fine tannins indicate great potential: this is undeniably a wine with a future. The more impatient will drink it now; the rest of us will wait three years.
🕿 Bruno et Daniel Long, Dom. Fond Croze, Le Village, 84290 Saint-Roman-de-Malegarde, tel. 04.90.28.97.07, fax 04.90.28.97.07, e-mail fondcroze@hotmail.com **V**
⚲ by appt.

DOM. DE FONTAVIN 2002★★

■	0.6 ha	4,000	■ ♦	5–8 €

The Fontavin estate produces a salmon-pink rosé that leaves a most agreeable sensation of freshness, with plenty of well-rounded fruit all the way to the lingering finish.
🕿 EARL Hélène et Michel Chouvet, Dom. de Fontavin, 1468, rte de la Plaine, 84350 Courthézon, tel. 04.90.70.72.14, fax 04.90.70.79.39, e-mail helene-chouvet@fontavin.com **V**
⚲ ev. day except Sun. 9am–12 noon 2pm–6pm; summer 9am–7pm

CH. DE FONTSEGUGNE
Santo Estello 2001★★★

■	2.5 ha	15,000		5–8 €

The vinification cellar was built recently, in 2001, but already it produces wonderful wines, such as this 2001 vintage, which delighted the Jury. Richness, structure, plenty of length and a lingering finish for this Santo Estello. Its assertive red fruit flavours clearly place it within this appellation. Spicy and silky, this wine would make a good accompaniment to meat dishes with sauce. The **red Cuvée Tradition 2001 (3–5 €)**, equally representative of the appellation, earns one star. It is attractively powerful and should be drunk with game.
🕿 GAEC Fontségugne, 976, rte de Saint-Saturnin, le Vieux Moulin, 84470 Châteauneuf-de-Gadagne, tel. 04.90.22.58.91, fax 04.90.22.42.40, e-mail gerenjm@aol.com **V**
⚲ ev. day 10am–7pm
🕿 Famille Geren

DOM. GALEVAN 2000★

■	1.5 ha	8,000	■	5–8 €

This wine speaks for itself. Deep colour with purple glints, intensity and ripe fruit on the nose. On the palate it does not disappoint: supple and with plenty of depth, is gives of lovely notes of fruit and cocoa.
🕿 Coralie et Jean-Pierre Goumarre, 127, rte de Vaison, 84350 Courthézon, tel. 04.90.70.84.26, fax 04.90.70.28.70, e-mail domaine.galevan@planetis.com **V**
⚲ ev. day except Sun. 8.30am–12.30pm 1pm–7.30pm

DOM. LA GARRIGUE
Cuvée romaine 2001★

■	30.84 ha	21,300	■ ♦	5–8 €

A Roman amphora adorns the label of this attractive Cuvée Romaine, made from equal proportions of Grenache and Syrah. Its bouquet cleverly combines jammy and redcurrant flavours with toasty notes, giving a balanced, robust and fleshy wine.
🕿 SCEA A. Bernard et Fils, Dom. La Garrigue, 84190 Vacqueyras, tel. 04.90.65.84.60, fax 04.90.65.80.79 **V**
⚲ ev. day 8am–12 noon 2pm–7.30pm; Sun. by appt.

DOM. DES GIRASOLS
Cuvée gracieuse 2000★★

■	3.4 ha	20,000	■	5–8 €

A suggested accompaniment to ossobuco, Cuvée Gracieuse has slightly minty fruit flavours and plenty of substance on the palate. Its tannins are perfectly rounded, giving a lingering, almost velvety finish.
🕿 Famille Paul Joyet, Dom. des Girasols, 84110 Rasteau, tel. 04.90.46.11.70, fax 04.90.46.16.82, e-mail domaine@girasols.com **V**
⚲ ev. day except Sun. 9am–12 noon 2pm–6pm

DOM. DES GRANDS DEVERS
La Syranne 2000★★

■	4 ha	20,800	■	5–8 €

A few years ago the four Bouchard brothers decided to pool their various skills and write a new chapter in the family's 300-year-old history. They offer La Syranne, which is 100% Syrah and rather atypical. Power and elegance come together and the fruit flavours are largely eclipsed by peppery spices and a pleasing, complex smokiness. "I'll buy it!" one juror wrote on the tasting notes. A wine to savour with a truffle omelette – the truffles being produced on the estate.
🕿 Paul-Henri Bouchard ses et Frères, Dom. des Grands-Devers, rte de Saint-Maur-par-la-Montagne, 84600 Valréas, tel. 04.90.35.15.98, fax 04.90.34.49.56, e-mail phbouchard@grandsdevers.com **V** 🏠
⚲ by appt.

DOM. GRAND VENEUR

Blanc de viognier 2002★★

	n.c.	3,000		8–11 €

A *Guide* regular in different appellations which, this year, achieves a fine double with two wines the Jury thought were remarkable. The white Côtes du Rhône, with its damp woodland notes and peach flavours, is exemplary – the very essence of well-matured Viognier. It has plenty of fleshiness and impressive length. Sadly, production is limited to 3,000 bottles. If you miss out, you can drown your sorrows with the **red Réserve Grand Veneur 2001 (5–8 €)**, whose production runs to 120,000 bottles. It is a powerful, expressive wine with red fruit flavours and real potential.

➐ SARL Alain Jaume, Dom. Grand Veneur, rte de Châteauneuf-du-Pape, 84100 Orange, tel. 04.90.34.68.70, fax 04.90.34.43.71,
e-mail jaume@domaine-grand-veneur.com ☑
☉ by appt.

DOM. DU GROS PATA

Vieilli en fût de chêne 2001★

	1.54 ha	10,666	▮ ⬛ ⬥	5–8 €

This estate offers a symphony of different grape varieties with this oak-aged wine made from Mourvèdre (20%), Grenache (60%) and Syrah (20%). The last of these develops floral flavours initially, ending with liquorice. A fleshy, full wine, a classic of this appellation.

➐ Gérald Garagnon, Dom. du Gros Pata, 84110 Vaison-la-Romaine, tel. 04.90.36.23.75, fax 04.90.28.77.05,
e-mail sabine.garagnon@free.fr ☑ ☖
☉ by appt.

DOM. DE LA JANASSE 2002★

	1.5 ha	5,000	▮ ⬥	3–5 €

With 55 ha divided up between very fragmented plots, this estate figures in the *Guide* almost every year. Our sole reservation is that production is often very limited. Yet again, there won't be enough to go round, with just 5,000 bottles of rosé and 6,000 of white. These hand-harvested wines were popular with the Jury for their frank character. The rosé is floral, not very acid and warming on the palate. The **2002 white (5–8 €)**, which impressed the Jury with its fresh citrus notes, has a lively, balanced attack, making it a good aperitif.

➐ Aimé Sabon, Dom. de La Janasse, 27, chem. du Moulin, 84350 Courthézon, tel. 04.90.70.86.29, fax 04.90.70.75.93,
e-mail lajanasse@free.fr ☑
☉ ev. day 8am–12 noon 2pm–7pm; Sat. Sun. by appt.

CH. JOANNY 2002★★

	10 ha	20,000	▮ ⬥	3–5 €

This large family-run estate, covering 125 ha, was founded in 1880 by a forebear, a négociant in the Beaujolais. Is that his portrait on the label? At all events, he would have been proud of this remarkable wine, which bears witness to the perfect mastery of the vinification process by this reputable estate. A floral bouquet is followed by a full, generous palate supported by excellent balance in this rosé de saignée, Provençal in its quality and seductive in its appeal.

➐ Ch. Joanny, rte de Piolenc, 84830 Sérignan-du-Comtat, tel. 04.90.70.00.10, fax 04.90.70.09.21 ☑
☉ ev. day except Mar. 8am–12 noon 2pm–6pm
➐ Famille Dupond

DOM. LAFOND ROC-EPINE 2001★★

	20 ha	12,000	▮ ⬥	5–8 €

We have lost count of the times this estate has been in the *Guide*. With its rather intense ruby colour, this wine unleashes stewed fruit and prune flavours that blend with toasted notes. Rich and smooth, this elegant wine is a fine accompaniment to a good roast.

➐ Dom. Lafond Roc-Epine, rte des Vignobles, 30126 Tavel, tel. 04.66.50.24.59, fax 04.66.50.12.42,
e-mail lafond@roc-epine.com ☑
☉ ev. day except Sat. Sun. 8am–12 noon 1.30pm–5.30pm

DOM. DE LASCAMP

Le Sieur d'Ornac 2001★

	10 ha	3,000	⬛	5–8 €

New labels of elegant and simple design have adorned all bottles produced by the Imbert family since January 2003. Le Sieur d'Ornac has a dark, slightly violet hue and combines red berries and musky notes on the nose. Some vanilla flavour appears when swirled in the glass, suggesting oak ageing. The palate is powerful and the tannins fine. Wait three years before opening.

➐ EARL Clos de Lascamp, Cadignac, 30200 Sabran, tel. 04.66.89.69.28, fax 04.66.89.62.44 ☑
☉ by appt.
➐ Imbert

DOM. LE MALAVEN 2001★★

	6.21 ha	15,300	▮ ⬥	5–8 €

No visit to Tavel is complete without a stop at this estate, to visit its cellars built in 2002 and to taste this 2001 Côtes du Rhône, which is remarkable for its powerful structure characterized by stewed soft fruit. Rich and full-bodied, it is perfect already, but could also be laid down for two years before being served with stuffed tomatoes.

➐ Dominique Roudil, rte de la Commanderie, BP 28, 30126 Tavel, tel. 04.66.50.20.02, fax 04.66.50.90.42,
e-mail dominique.roudil@terre-net.fr ☑
☉ ev. day 8am–12 noon 2pm–6pm

CH. DE MARJOLET 2002★

	2 ha	13,000	▮	3–5 €

Just 2 ha of this estate's 48 ha produce this blend of Roussanne (60%), Grenache (30%) and Viognier (10%). This powerful 2002 has citrus flavours and is both rich and subtle, with honeyed notes on the palate. A most rewarding wine. The **2001 red** impressed the Jury. With dominant red berries, it is lively and attractive – a real pleasure.

➐ Bernard Pontaud, Dom. de Marjolet, 30330 Gaujac, tel. 04.66.82.00.93, fax 04.66.82.92.58,
e-mail chateau.marjolet@wanadoo.fr ☑

DOM. MARTIN 2000★

	16 ha	60,000	⬛	5–8 €

Although too late to celebrate the cellar's 50th anniversary in 1999, this 2000 vintage is not too young to drink now – but it can be laid down too. Born of a stony, clay-limestone soil and the result of classic vinification, it is a pure Côtes du Rhône, enhanced by woody notes due to ageing in large wooden casks. The nose is of medium intensity and lightly floral.

➐ SCEA Dom. Martin, Plan de Dieu, 84850 Travaillan, tel. 04.90.37.23.20, fax 04.90.37.78.87 ☑
☉ ev. day except Sun. 8.30am–12 noon 1.30pm–7pm; groups by appt.

CH. MAUCOIL 2002★

	0.5 ha	3,300	▮ ⬥	5–8 €

Which would you rather quench your thirst with: spring water from a cave on this estate, or this 2002 rosé? The Jury only tasted this fresh Côtes du Rhône. With its delicious strawberry flavours and especially silky palate, this bottle can be drunk throughout a meal. In short, a fine wine.

➐ Ch. Maucoil, BP 7, 84231 Châteauneuf-du-Pape Cedex, tel. 04.90.34.14.86, fax 04.90.34.71.88,
e-mail contact@chateau-maucoil.com ☑
☉ ev. day except Sat. Sun. 8am–12 noon 2pm–6pm
➐ Arnaud

LES MOIRETS

Elevé en fût de chêne 2001★

	n.c.	300,000	⬛	3–5 €

The Jury were captivated by this very well-made wine which allies power with fruity and woody notes. The **red Héritage des Caves des Papes 2001 Elevé en Foudre de Chêne**, which has a slightly higher concentration of Syrah, will reach its best in a few years. Nevertheless, it is already supple, though with strong structure. The **Côtes du Rhône-Villages, Les Moirets Elevé en Fût 2001 (5–8 €)** gains one star, as does the **Le Monastère 2002.**

☛ Ogier-Caves des Papes, 10, av. Louis-Pasteur, BP 75, 84232 Châteauneuf-du-Pape Cedex, tel. 04.90.39.32.32, fax 04.90.83.72.51, e-mail ogiercavesdespapes@ogier.fr ☑
✆ by appt.

CH. DE MONTFAUCON
Baron Louis 2001★★★

	10 ha	67,000	■ ◫ ◆	11–15 €

A clear *coup de coeur* for this exceptional Baron Louis, thanks to its intense, deep colour, powerful, spicy, vanilla nose and its rich palate where well-rounded, silky tannins coat red berry, soft fruit and spice flavours. While Baron Louis turns his attention to restoring the château, Rodolphe de Pins, his great-nephew, is restoring the image of his Côtes du Rhône through rigorously competent winemaking.

☛ Rodolphe de Pins, Ch. de Montfaucon, 30150 Montfaucon, tel. 04.66.50.37.19, fax 04.66.50.62.19, e-mail chateau.montfaucon@wanadoo.fr ☑
✆ ev. day except Sat. Sun. 2pm–6pm; groups by appt.

CH. MONT-REDON 2002★★

	1 ha	3,800	■ ◆	5–8 €

The Château de Mont-Redon, one of the famous estates of Châteauneuf-du-Pape, devotes just 1 ha to this 2002 blend of 60% Grenache and 40% Cinsault – a little-used combination today since the Côtes du Rhône regulations stipulate a maximum of 30% Cinsault from 2004. In the meantime, though, what a remarkable wine! Excellent grapes produced this charming 2002, rich, supple and fine, with toasted notes. The fruity **white Mont-Redon 2002**, made with the same attention to quality, impressed the Jury, as did the **white Viognier 2002 (11–15 €)**. It is a fleshy, complex, fruity and floral wine of great unctuousness.

☛ Ch. Mont-Redon, BP 10, 84231 Châteauneuf-du-Pape, tel. 04.90.83.72.75, fax 04.90.83.77.20, e-mail contact@chateaumontredon.fr ☑
✆ by appt.

NOTRE-DAME D'ARGELIER
Réserve 2001★

	n.c.	15,000	■ ◆	3–5 €

An extremely well-made wine. Bursting with sunshine, it gives off intense ripe fruit flavours; the palate is fresh, with supple tannins.

☛ Cave la Vigneronne, 84110 Villedieu, tel. 04.90.28.92.37, fax 04.90.28.93.00 ☑
✆ by appt.

DOM. DE L'ORATOIRE SAINT-MARTIN
2001★

	2 ha	10,000	■ ◆	5–8 €

This estate, which comprises 26 ha of vines on the Cairanne hills, needs no introduction since it appears regularly in the *Guide* and won a *coup de coeur* last year with a Cairanne 1999. Frédéric and François Alary produce a Côtes du Rhône in the finest Grenache tradition. The nose has undertones of damp woodland and leaf mould, as well as macerated red berries. Supporting tannins are supple and full of character. A fine blend, worthy of the house of Alary.

☛ Frédéric et François Alary, rte de Saint-Roman, 84290 Cairanne, tel. 04.90.30.82.07, fax 04.90.30.74.27 ☑
✆ ev. day except Sun. 8am–12 noon 2pm–7pm

CH. DE PANERY
Tradition 2001★★

	5 ha	25,000	■ ◆	5–8 €

Wheat, sunflowers, truffles and vines – all these are grown on the Panery estate. This diversity seems to bring it luck, for two of its wines are awarded two stars. The colour of the Tradition *cuvée* is simply magnificent; the remarkably intense nose recalls stewed Morello cherries, covered in spices. Liquorice and spices counterbalance a slight astringency on the palate. A bottle that can wait two or three years, as can **Cuvée Henry red 2001**, which offers essentially the same qualities as the Tradition but with some woody notes, which in no way reduce the wine's density.

☛ Ch. de Panery, 30210 Pouzilhac, tel. 04.66.37.04.44, fax 04.66.37.62.38,
e-mail chateaudepanery@wanadoo.fr ☑ ☗
✆ by appt.
☛ R. Gry Seels

DOM. DU PARC SAINT CHARLES
Cuvée Saint-Charles 2001★

	3 ha	15,000	■ ◆	5–8 €

During the 17th and 18th centuries this estate was home to the artillery park of the marquis Charles de Monteynard, hence its name. Today, vines have replaced weaponry. Planted on clay and sandy soil covered with shingle, they produce this charming wine, which has lovely stewed fruit notes on the nose. The fresh attack bodes well for ageing. However, this wine is so full that it can be enjoyed now.

☛ SCEA du Parc Saint-Charles, 30490 Montfrin, tel. 04.66.57.22.82, fax 04.66.57.54.41,
e-mail florent.combe@wanadoo.fr ☑
✆ by appt.

DOM. DE PONT LE VOY 2000★

	3 ha	10,000	◫	5–8 €

This Côtes du Rhône, dark purple in colour with violet glints, is dominated by stewed fruit, nut and spice flavours. It is supple on the attack and balanced on the palate, with hints of vanilla rounding off this excellent blend.

☛ Dom. de Pont Le Voy, 30330 Saint-Paul-les-Fonts, tel. 06.08.24.44.29, fax 04.66.82.08.29
✆ by appt.
☛ Xavier Dumas

DOM. DE LA PRESIDENTE
Grands Classiques 2002★★

	4 ha	10,000		5–8 €

This lovely and extensive (180 ha) estate at Sainte-Cécile-les-Vignes dates from 1701. It has regularly appeared in the *Guide* and organizes an annual festival of vines and wine. A good opportunity to taste some interesting vintages? The Grands Classiques *cuvée* is ready to drink. Its very softened attack surprises with its notes of dried fruit, which are then followed by roundness and a delicious finish. A very straightforward wine. **Au Coeur du Village Confidences white 2001 (46–76 €)** also earns two stars and is very marked by oakiness to the detriment of the alcohol-acidity balance. But it still deserves a mention, for the grape variety's character will certainly intensify to produce a very great wine. Be warned: production is extremely limited at just 600 bottles and the price reflects this.

☛ Famille Max Aubert, Dom. de La Présidente, rte de Cairanne, 84290 Sainte-Cécile-les-Vignes, tel. 04.90.30.80.34, fax 04.90.30.72.93,
e-mail aubert@presidente.fr ☑
✆ ev. day except Sun. 9am–12 noon 2pm–6pm; Jan.-Mar. 2pm–6pm
☛ Famille Aubert

CAVE DE RASTEAU
Grande Cuvée 2001★★

■	30 ha	130,000		3–5 €

The Rasteau winemakers' cellar and its director, M. Paollucci, offer three wines that were singled out by the Jury. **Les Viguiers rosé 2002**, clear with bright glints, has lovely floral notes and fine balance. Equally good is **Les Viguiers red 2001**, a powerful, warming wine with hints of *pain d'épice* and rosemary. The Grande Cuvée is aptly named, with its powerful jammy and kirsch flavours, producing a silky wine of remarkable length.
☛ Cave des Vignerons de Rasteau et de Tain-l'Hermitage, rte des Princes-d'Orange, 84110 Rasteau, tel. 04.90.10.90.10, fax 04.90.46.16.65, e-mail vrt@rasteau.com

DOM. DES RELAGNES
Vieilles Vignes 2001★

■	5 ha	10,000	■	5–8 €

Equal proportions of Syrah and Grenache produce a well-structured 2001 with a ruby red colour. On being swirled in the glass it gives off lovely notes of red berries followed by dried fruit. On the palate these fruits reappear, followed by some hints of herbs. A warming, robust wine that cries out to be laid down.
☛ SCEA Dom. des Relagnes, rte de Bédarrides, 84230 Châteauneuf-du-Pape, tel. 04.90.83.73.37, fax 04.90.83.52.16, e-mail domaine-des-relagnes@wanadoo.fr ☑
☒ by appt.
☛ Hillaire

DOM. LA REMEJEANNE
Les Chèvrefeuilles 2002★

■	9 ha	57,000	■ ◆	5–8 €

This wine comes with a unique recommendation, in a year that was almost under a curse, such was the difficulty of keeping the grapes in good condition as far as the cellar. Only selective picking on plots that already produced low yields allowed Rémy Klein to produce a quality Côtes du Rhône that year. An attractive dark colour, nose with soft fruit and blackcurrant notes and great suppleness in the mouth despite pronounced structure: one of the few 2002 wines for laying down. **Les Arbousiers red 2002** was singled out by the Jury. Soft fruit on the nose gives way to a full palate with enough tannins to ensure good development.
☛ EARL Ouahi et Rémy Klein, Cadignac, 30200 Sabran, tel. 04.66.89.44.51, fax 04.66.89.64.22, e-mail remejeanne@wanadoo.fr ☑
☒ by appt.

CH. LA RENJARDIERE 2001★

■	115 ha	500,000	■ ◆	5–8 €

A fine late 19th century house – whose architecture, with its external colonnaded galleries, recalls the most beautiful villas of southern Italy – overlooks this estate's 135 ha of vines. Of these, 115 ha have been devoted to this floral 2001, marked by blackcurrant and lightly peppery on the palate. It is pleasantly long. One star, too, for the **2001 rosé**, floral, fresh and elegant thanks to faint violet notes. A very classic Côtes du Rhône rosé.
☛ Pierre Dupond, 235, rue de Thizy, 69653 Villefranche-sur-Saône, tel. 04.74.65.24.32, fax 04.74.68.04.14, e-mail p.dupond.cvc@wanadoo.fr
☛ Hervé Dupond

DOM. RIGOT
Prestige des garrigues 2001★★★

■	10.5 ha	30,000	■	5–8 €

Could you be tempted to linger a while in the gîte that Camille Rigot runs, in the heart of the vineyard? You will not be able to resist exploring the Rigot estate and tasting the Cuvée Prestige des Garrigues, a thoroughly Provençal *coup de cœur*. This blend of 80% Grenache and Syrah is the result of a classic, gimmick-free vinification process. The nose is lightly toasty, with notes of slightly spicy ripe fruit. The palate is supple with a lusty, lasting finish. Drink over the next two years. The **red Cuvée Jean-Baptiste Rigot 2001** is fruity and very well made.

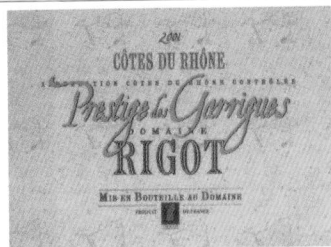

☛ Dom. Camille Rigot, Les Hauts Débats, 84150 Jonquières, tel. 04.90.37.25.19, fax 04.90.37.25.19, e-mail contact@domaine-rigot.fr ☑ ☗
☒ ev. day 8am–12 noon 3pm–8pm; Sun. by appt.

DOM. ROCHE-AUDRAN
César 2001★★

■	5 ha	5,000	⫿	8–11 €

This wine was placed under the aegis of the Roman emperor, which proved to be a good omen. The Jury were captivated. Concentration, structure, depth and flavours of leather, ripe fruit and light oakiness combine to produce a remarkable wine. All these qualities mingle to form an exceptionally harmonious whole, which will reach its best within two years.
☛ Vincent Rochette, Dom. Roche-Audran, rte de Saint-Roman, 84110 Buisson, tel. 04.90.28.96.49, fax 04.90.28.90.96, e-mail vincent.rochette@mnet.fr ☑
☒ by appt.

CH. ROCHECOLOMBE 2001★

■	11.5 ha	53,000	■ ◆	3–5 €

A handsome Renaissance château towers over the heart of this vineyard, which produces a wine of remarkably intense colour that tickles the taster's curiosity. The flavours, initially restrained, later open up, with stewed fruit. On the palate it is initially velvety, but jammy notes then appear. A perfect accompaniment to a traditional filet mignon.
☛ EARL G. Herberigs, Ch. Rochecolombe, 07700 Bourg-Saint-Andéol, tel. 04.75.54.50.47, fax 04.75.54.80.03, e-mail rochecolombe@aol.com ☑
☒ ev. day 9am–12 noon 2pm–7pm; groups by appt.

CAVE DES VIGNERONS DE ROCHEGUDE 2002★

■	8 ha	16,000	■ ◆	3–5 €

This technologically advanced cellar produces interesting wines that regularly figure in the *Guide*. The 2002 white, which has very intense flavours of roses and apricot, is well balanced and will be popular among those who love warming, rich wines. **Cuvée du Docteur Barbe 2001 red** was singled out by the Jury for its fruity, elegant character. Enjoy with grilled meat.
☛ Cave des Vignerons de Rochegude, 26790 Rochegude, tel. 04.75.04.81.84, fax 04.75.04.84.80 ☑
☒ by appt.

DOM. DE ROCHEMOND
Elevé en fût de chêne 2001★

■	n.c.	25,000	⫿	5–8 €

As its name suggests, this oak-aged *cuvée* is delicately woody on the nose, with ripe fruit and a touch of vanilla. On the palate it is very harmonious and attractive; perfect with ragout of roasted woodcock. The **2002 white**, which earns one star, is made from 100% Viognier, producing the sort of wine this royal grape variety is capable of in skilled hands. It has many subtle nuances, both fruity and floral and would go well with fish cooked in sauce or – and why not? – Banon cheese.
☛ Eric Philip, 1, chem. des Cyprès, Cadignac-sud, 30200 Sabran, tel. 04.66.79.04.42, fax 04.66.79.04.42 ☑
☒ by appt.

RHONE

DOM. DES ROCHES FORTES

Prestige 2001★★

	n.c.	4,000	🏆 Ⅲ ♦	5–8 €

Coup de cœur in 97, two stars in the last edition of the *Guide* and two stars this year: Prestige has pulled out a trump card once again. Its blend of 80% Syrah with Grenache has been remarkably well aged: its time in barrel has allowed the red berries to be rounded off with subtle vanilla notes. With its good length of flavour, this very fine wine will reach its best within four or five years. One star for **Les Andiolles 2000 red**, whose strong structure gives it very good balance.

☛ EARL Brunel et Fils, quartier Le Château,
84110 Vaison-la-Romaine, tel. 04.90.36.03.03,
fax 04.90.28.77.14 ⓥ 🏠
🍷 ev. day except Sun. 10.30am–12 noon 1.30pm–6.30pm

CH. DE ROUANNE 2001★

	0.86 ha	6,000	🏆	3–5 €

Facing due south, this estate favours full ripening of the grapes, which is fully apparent in this wine. Very lively after swirling in the glass, its attack of red berries rapidly develops into notes of spices and liquorice. This wine's structure means it has good potential.

☛ Ferrentino, Ch. de Rouanne, 26110 Vinsobres,
tel. 06.83.57.26.61, fax 04.90.46.90.07 ⓥ
🍷 ev. day except Sat. Sun. 10am–12 noon
3pm–5pm; cl. 15–31 Aug.
☛ Lambert-Ferrentino

DOM. SAINT-AMANT

Les Clapas 2001★

	1.5 ha	7,000	🏆 ♦	5–8 €

This estate at Suzette occupies terraced hillsides facing due south, at 500 metres altitude. The Les Clapas *cuvée* bears the name of the plot where the grapes are grown to make this typically Syrah wine. Bright red and long on the palate, it shows good power and develops lovely stewed fruit notes. Balanced and harmonious, it is well worth laying down.

☛ Dom. Saint-Amant, 84190 Suzette, tel. 04.90.62.99.25,
fax 04.90.65.03.56, e-mail saintamant@wanadoo.fr ⓥ
🍷 by appt.

DOM. SAINT-ANTHELME 2001★★

	20 ha	100,000	🏆	5–8 €

A Côtes du Rhône typical of the Gard *département*, with deep colour and violet glints. Its intense nose conjures up the scents of the garrigue, with red berries to the fore. Gentle and delicious tannins give fine balance to this wine which fruit, once again and a tinge of chocolate render irresistible. Try it with beef stew in one or two years' time.

☛ Morad Layouni, Dom. la Genestière, chem. de
Cravailleux, 30126 Tavel, tel. 04.66.50.07.03,
fax 04.66.50.27.03,
e-mail garcin-layouri@domaine-genestiere.com ⓥ
🍷 ev. day 9am–12.30pm 1.30pm–5.30pm;
Sat. Sun. by appt.

CAVE DES VIGNERONS REUNIS DE SAINTE-CECILE-LES-VIGNES

Elevé en barrique 2002★★

	n.c.	5,000	Ⅲ	8–11 €

One hundred per cent Viognier, aged in oak. Fashionable perhaps, but one taster wrote: "I like this a lot." Why not, then? A rich and complex wine with great intensity of flavour, tending towards citrus fruit and lightly woody. Real ageing potential: up to five years.

☛ Cave des Vignerons réunis de Sainte-Cécile-les-Vignes,
35, rte de Valréas, BP 21, 84290 Sainte-Cécile-les-Vignes,
tel. 04.90.30.79.30, fax 04.90.30.79.39,
e-mail cave@vignerons-saintececile.fr ⓥ
🍷 by appt.

LES VIGNERONS DE SAINT-HILAIRE-D'OZILHAN Rive droite 2001★

	37.5 ha	260,000	🏆 ♦	3–5 €

The label on this bottle shows the Pont du Gard, a reminder that this architectural wonder is just 5 kilometres from Saint-Hilaire-d'Ozilhan. Rive Droite (right bank – of the Gard certainly) has pretty ruby glints in its colour. The rich bouquet unveils notes of Morello cherries and damp woodland. The palate is fine, well-rounded and warming, also evoking fruity, woodland scents. A delicate wine.

☛ Les Vignerons de Saint-Hilaire-d'Ozilhan, av.
Paul-Blisson, 30210 Saint-Hilaire-d'Ozilhan,
tel. 04.66.37.16.47, fax 04.66.37.35.12,
e-mail contact@cotes-du-rhone-wine.com
🍷 ev. day except Sun. 10am–12 noon
2.30pm–6.30pm; Mon. 2.30pm–6.30pm;
groups by appt.

CH. SAINT-JEAN 2002★★

	n.c.	40,000	🏆 ♦	5–8 €

This vineyard, covering a single block of land on the Plan de Dieu plateau, has a good reputation. In 2002 it produced a wine that was praised for its red berry and bilberry flavours. Very harmonious and slightly amylic on the palate, with good intensity, it is a typical Côtes du Rhône. Distributed by Gabriel Meffre.

☛ SCA Ch. Saint-Jean, Le Plan-de-Dieu, 84850 Travaillan,
tel. 04.90.12.32.42, fax 04.90.12.32.49

SEIGNEUR DE LAURIS 2001★

	10 ha	60,000	🏆 Ⅲ ♦	5–8 €

A négociant wine of quality becomes a reality with this Seigneur de Lauris. A slightly closed nose gives hints of raspberry notes and the gently oaked palate gradually grows in power to leave a warming, supple sensation. "An honest wine," wrote one taster.

☛ Arnoux et Fils, Portail Neuf, 84190 Vacqueyras,
tel. 04.90.65.84.18, fax 04.90.65.80.07 ⓥ 🏠 🏠
🍷 ev. day except Sun. 8am–12 noon 2pm–6pm

CH. SIMIAN 2001★★

	8.4 ha	42,000	🏆 ♦	5–8 €

The N 7 main road which takes you there is the subject of a museum on this estate. This fine wine is heady and powerful. The nose, with scents of violet and stewed red berries, is perfectly complemented by the palate, where well-rounded tannins support the ever-present fruit. Rustic and strong, this Côtes du Rhône is a good accompaniment to meat dishes with sauce.

☛ Jean-Pierre Serguier, Ch. Simian, 84420 Piolenc,
tel. 04.90.29.50.67, fax 04.90.29.62.33,
e-mail chateau.simian@wanadoo.fr ⓥ
🍷 ev. day 8.30am–12.30pm 1.30pm–7.30pm

CH. SOUFFLES DE COSTERELLE 2001★

	19 ha	130,000	🏆 ♦	5–8 €

Louis Pasteur, who lived for a time in Bollène, where he studied epizootic diseases, would surely have enjoyed this lovely wine, which is very drinkable and immediately striking with its bright garnet-red colour. It has strong flavours, marked on the nose by hints of fresh strawberry and raspberry. The palate, which has a similar character, has a finish that is both strong and supple.

☛ Ch. des Souffles de Costerelle, quartier Guffiages,
84500 Bollène, tel. 04.90.51.75.87, fax 04.90.51.73.36,
e-mail chateaubeauchene@worldonline.fr
☛ Bernard

DOM. TENON

Cuvée Fiston 2000★

	1.5 ha	5,000	🏆	5–8 €

Father and son work together on this estate, which offers a wine highly typical of this appellation, made from vines planted on a marvellous clay-limestone terroir. Rich flavours are dominated by raspberry, with light floral notes. Balance – though still tannic – is pleasant. Perfect with poultry.

☛ GAEC Dom. Tenon, rte d'Avignon, 84150 Violès,
tel. 04.90.70.93.29, fax 04.90.70.92.90 ⓥ
🍷 by appt.
☛ Ph. et P. Combe

DOM. LES TEYSSONNIERES 2001★

| ■ | 1.06 ha | 7,000 | ▮ ♦ | 3–5 € |

This old cellar, dating from 1838, whose vines did not succumb to phylloxera, offers a classic blend of equal parts of Grenache and Syrah. With its bright garnet-red colour, this wine offers an intense nose with notes of stewed fruit and violet. The palate is fleshy and dense, an early sign of its quality. Drink in two years' time, with shoulder of lamb.
☙ Franck Alexandre, Dom. Les Teyssonnières, 84190 Gigondas, tel. 04.90.12.31.31, fax 04.90.12.31.32, e-mail domaine.lesteyssonnieres@wanadoo.fr ☑
🍷 ev. day except Sun. 8am–1pm 2pm–7pm

CH. DU TRIGNON
Cuvée du Bois des Dames 2001★

| ■ | 8 ha | 15,000 | ▮ ♦ | 5–8 € |

Both the white and the red are wines for laying down. Bois des Dames 2001 is well structured, generous and balanced. Red berries predominate over marked chocolate notes. **Cuvée Roussanne 2002 white (8–11 €)** is dominated by floral flavours. Both are promising for laying down over the next two to three years. **Rasteau 2001 (8–11 €)**, which was singled out by the Jury, is powerful and should be laid down.
☙ Ch. du Trignon, 84190 Gigondas, tel. 04.90.46.90.27, fax 04.90.46.98.63, e-mail trignon@chateau-du-trignon.com ☑
🍷 ev. day 9am–12 noon 2pm–7pm
☙ Pascal Roux

DOM. DU VAL DES ROIS
Enclave des Papes 2001★

| ■ | 1 ha | 5,000 | ◫ | 8–11 € |

This estate was one of the first papal vineyards. Generation after generation, the Bouchard family has continued to produce some lovely wines, such as this Enclave des Papes 2001, which is most pleasing with its slightly oaky nose of red berries. The palate shows all the signs of oak ageing with its suppleness and vanilla notes on a structure of fine tannins. The **Cuvée Signature Côtes du Rhône-Villages 2000 (5–8 €)** impressed the Jury.
☙ Emmanuel Bouchard, Dom. du Val des Rois, 84600 Valréas, tel. 04.90.35.04.35, fax 04.90.35.24.14, e-mail info@valdesrois.com
🍷 by appt.

DOM. VALMEYRANE 2001★

| ■ | 18 ha | 100,000 | ▮ ♦ | 3–5 € |

Montfrin is a village in the Gard *département*, halfway between Nîmes and Avignon, which Molière is said to have visited and where, the story goes, he had his first assignation with Madeleine Béjart. Today, the cellar at Montfrin awaits you, with its two wines that are a fine example of their vintage. Domaine Valmeyrane is awarded its star thanks to a smooth palate where toasted and smoky notes round of the fruit. It is still developing, so best to wait a while before drinking.
☙ Cave des Vignerons de Montfrin, rte de la Gare, 30490 Montfrin, tel. 04.66.57.53.63, fax 04.66.57.55.50 ☑
🍷 by appt.

DOM. DE LA VERDE 2000★

| ■ | 10 ha | 60,000 | | 5–8 € |

Fine colour and well brought out fruit, notably thanks to a system of concrete, hourglass-shaped tanks used to make this subtle wine. Perfectly balanced and with good length on the palate, it is still rather young for its vintage. It is worth waiting one or two years.
☙ Dom. de la Verde, 84190 Vacqueyras, tel. 04.90.65.85.91, fax 04.90.65.89.23 ☑
🍷 by appt.
☙ Camallonga

DOM. DU VIEUX COLOMBIER 2001★

| ■ | 6 ha | 36,000 | ▮ ♦ | 3–5 € |

A royal estate until 1518, this is where the monarchist writer Rivarol grew up. Today, the only kind of politics discussed here is wine politics! This cherry-coloured, vat-aged 2001, is

mischievously springlike and could make some formidable enemies. Very clean and young, with a well-balanced palate full of ripe grapes. Drink with a leg of lamb.
☙ Jacques Barrière et Fils, Dom. du Vieux Colombier, 485, chem. du Pigeonnier, 30200 Sabran, tel. 04.66.89.98.94, fax 04.66.89.98.94 ☑
🍷 by appt.

XAVIER VIGNON
Povidis 2001★★★

| ■ | 3.5 ha | 15,000 | ▮ ♦ | 5–8 € |

In 1999 Xavier Vignon, a winemaking consultant in the Rhône valley, decided to make his own selection of wines. For the 2004 edition of the *Guide*, they were assessed by the Jury, in various appellations. Povidis is an exceptional *cuvée*, with a magnificent pure red colour, that exhales a palette of intense aromas. From the moment it touches the palate it gives off spices, rounded with chocolate and some musky notes. A bottle is to be savoured with duckling cooked with rosemary. The **red Cuvée Xavier 2001 (8–11 €)**, extremely well made, offers lovely concentrated red berries.
☙ Xavier Vignon, chem. de Caromb, 84330 Le Barroux, tel. 04.90.62.33.44, fax 04.90.62.33.45, e-mail povidis@wanadoo.fr ☑ 🏠
🍷 by appt.

DOM. VILLESECHE 2001★★

| ■ | 13 ha | 86,000 | ▮ ♦ | –3 € |

A remarkable wine for not much money? That's what the Compagnie Rhodanienne offers, with Domaine de Villesèche. Its intoxicating bouquet is bursting with blackcurrant and violet aromas. The Syrah, which is very noticeable in this blend, must have been of perfect quality judging by the results it has produced. A complete, well-balanced wine with a delicious finish and good ageing potential. Equally remarkable is **Domaine André Brémond 2001 red (3–5 €)**. A nose of red berries and soft fruit (redcurrant and blackcurrant) heightened by spices and a soft, deep, concentrated palate make this a most enjoyable wine. Also by the Compagnie Rhodanienne, **red Domaine du Farlet 2001** impressed the Jury. A warming wine, full of sun, to be enjoyed with Mediterranean cooking.
☙ La Compagnie Rhodanienne, Chemin-Neuf, 30210 Castillon-du-Gard, tel. 04.66.37.49.50, fax 04.66.37.49.51, e-mail cie.rhodanienne@wanadoo.fr
🍷 by appt.

Wines selected but not starred

CH. DE BASTET 2001

| ■ | 21 ha | 100,000 | ▮ ♦ | 5–8 € |

☙ Jean-Charles Aubert, Ch. de Bastet, 30200 Sabran, tel. 04.66.39.33.36, fax 04.66.39.92.01, e-mail chateau.bastet@wanadoo.fr ☑ 🏠
🍷 ev. day except Sat. Sun. 8.30am–12 noon 1.30pm–6.30pm

CH. DE BOUSSARGUES 2002

| ■ | 1 ha | 4,600 | ▮ ♦ | 3–5 € |

☙ Chantal Malabre, Ch. de Boussargues, 30200 Sabran, tel. 04.66.89.32.20, fax 04.66.79.81.64 ☑ 🏠
🍷 ev. day 8am–7pm

DOM. DE LA CHARITE 2001

| | 30 ha | 100,000 | 🍶 🥄 | | 3–5 € |

🍷 Vignobles Coste, 5, chem. des Issarts, 30650 Saze,
tel. 04.90.31.73.55, fax 04.90.26.92.50,
e-mail earlvc@club-internet.fr ☑
🍴 ev. day except Sun. Mon. 5pm–7pm; Sat. 2pm–7pm

DOM. DE LA CHARTREUSE DE

VALBONNE Cuvée de la Font des Dames 2001

| | 3.5 ha | 14,850 | 🍶 | | 5–8 € |

🍷 ASVMT Chartreuse de Valbonne, CAT Ph.-Delord,
30130 Saint-Paulet-de-Caisson, tel. 04.66.90.41.21,
fax 04.66.90.41.36,
e-mail domaine@chartreusedevalbonne.com ☑
🍴 by appt.

CH. CHEVALIER BRIGAND 2001

| | 6 ha | 40,000 | 🍶 | | 5–8 € |

🍷 SCEA Vignobles Jean-Marie Saut, Ch. de Codolet,
caveau Chevalier Brigand, 30200 Codolet,
tel. 04.66.90.18.64, fax 04.66.90.11.57,
e-mail chevalierbrigand@aol.com ☑
🍴 ev. day except Sat. Sun. 9am–12.30pm 2pm–6.30pm

DOM. DEFORGE 2000

| | 2 ha | 12,000 | 🍶 🍷 | | 5–8 € |

🍷 Mireille Deforge, rte de Jonquerettes,
84470 Châteauneuf-de-Gadagne, tel. 04.90.22.42.75,
fax 04.90.22.18.29, e-mail dom.deforge@infonie.fr ☑
🍴 ev. day except Sun. 9h30–12 noon 3pm–6.30pm

MAS GRANGE BLANCHE 2001

| | 2.1 ha | 10,000 | 🍶 🥄 | | 5–8 € |

🍷 EARL Cyril et Jacques Mousset, Ch. des Fines-Roches,
84230 Châteauneuf-du-Pape, tel. 04.90.83.73.10,
fax 04.90.83.50.78, e-mail contac@mousset.com ☑
🍴 by appt.

DOM. ROGER PERRIN

Prestige Blanc 2002

| | 1.5 ha | 10,000 | 🥄 | | 5–8 € |

🍷 EARL Dom. Roger Perrin, La Berthaude, rte de
Châteauneuf-du-Pape, 84100 Orange, tel. 04.90.34.25.64,
fax 04.90.34.88.37 ☑
🍴 by appt.
🍷 Luc Perrin

DOM. DES ROMARINS 2001

| | 10 ha | 15,000 | 🍶 🥄 | | 3–5 € |

🍷 SARL Dom. des Romarins, rte d'Estézargues,
30390 Domazan, tel. 04.66.57.05.84, fax 04.66.57.14.87,
e-mail domromarin@aol.com ☑
🍴 Wed. Fri. Sat. 3pm–7pm; groups by appt.
🍷 Fabre

CH. DE RUTH

Cuvée Françoise de Soissans 2001

| | 1.5 ha | 6,500 | 🍷 | | 5–8 € |

🍷 Christian Meffre, Ch. de Ruth,
84290 Sainte-Cécile-les-Vignes, tel. 04.90.65.88.93,
fax 04.90.65.88.96,
e-mail chateau.raspail@wanadoo.fr ☑
🍴 ev. day except Sat. Sun. 8am–12 noon 1.30pm–5.30pm

SAINT COSME 2002

| | 3.5 ha | 21,000 | 🍶 🍷 🥄 | | 5–8 € |

🍷 SARL Barruol, Ch. de Saint Cosme, 84190 Gigondas,
tel. 04.90.65.80.80, fax 04.90.65.81.05,
e-mail louis@chateau-st-cosme.com ☑ 🏠
🍴 ev. day except Sun. 9am–12 noon 1.30pm–5.30pm

Côtes du Rhône-Villages

Within the Côtes du Rhône
area, some communes have terroirs that produce
wines with characteristics and qualities that are
unanimously acknowledged and appreciated. The
conditions of production for these wines, which is
about 287,853 hl are more restrictive than for the
Côtes du Rhône, especially with regard to boundaries, yield and alcohol content. A small amount
(5,008 hl in 2002) of white wine goes to make up the
significant volume of Côtes du Rhône-Villages.

There are two categories of
Côtes du Rhône-Villages wines. On the one hand,
there are those entitled to include the name of a
commune; the 16 names that have been recognized
historically are: Chusclan, Laudun and Saint-
Gervais in the Gard; Beaumes-de-Venise, Cairanne,
Sablet-Séguret, Rasteau, Roaix, Valréas and Visan in
the Vaucluse; Rochegude, Rousset-les-Vignes,
Saint-Maurice, Saint-Pantaléon-les-Vignes and
Vinsobres in the Drôme.

On the other hand, there are the
Côtes du Rhône-Villages where no commune name is
specified, their territory covering the remainder of all
the communes in the Gard, the Vaucluse and the
Drôme within the area of the Côtes du Rhône.
Seventy communes have been included. The purpose
of defining the territory had the primary objective of
making it possible to produce wines that would keep.

DOM. D'AERIA

Cairanne Cuvée Prestige 2000 ★★

| | 2 ha | 6,000 | 🍷 | | 11–15 € |

Remains discovered on the estate testify to the presence of the
Romans at this site, which has panoramic views over to the
Dentelles de Montmirail, the Mont Ventoux and the Aigue
valley. A *cuvée* assessed several times by the Jury, notably in
the 1998 edition, when it was pronounced exceptional and
last year, when it was awarded a *coup de coeur*. The 2000
vintage again perfectly expresses the character of the terroir
and appellation. Intense, dark red colour, with a powerful,
aromatic nose marked by spices and red berries, it has fine
tannins and good structure, with a long finish ending on notes
of stewed fruit and spices. Keep in the cellar for at least five
years. **Cuvée Tradition 2000 red (8–11 €)**, which is just as
remarkable, can be drunk in four years' time with game. The
red Côtes du Rhône 2000 Domaine d'Aéria (5–8 €) is awarded
one star.
🍷 SARL Dom. d'Aéria, rte de Rasteau, 84290 Cairanne,
tel. 04.90.30.88.78, fax 04.90.30.78.38,
e-mail domaine.aeria@wanadoo.fr ☑ 🏠
🍴 by appt.
🍷 Rolland Gap

DOM. DANIEL ET DENIS ALARY

Cairanne La Font d'Estévenas 2001 ★★

| | 2 ha | 10,000 | | | 8–11 € |

The Alary family have lived here for ten generations, since
1692. Every year, the estate run by Daniel and Denis Alary
has a date with the *Guide*, run by Daniel and Denis Alary
this year. La Font d'Estévenas is a fine wine! Grenache is
king here, complemented by Syrah. The colour is intense and
dark. Macerated fruit mingles with spices, garrigue and
musky notes to give a complex bouquet. Such potential on
the palate! Silky tannins, fruit and spices, with elegance and
balance to make a truly great bottle. The same number of
stars for **Cuvée Cairanne 2001 red**, which charmed the Jury

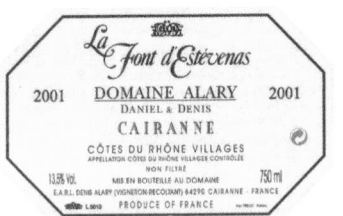

with its complex nose and remarkable harmony. Drink one or two years from now.
☛ Dom. Daniel et Denis Alary, La Font d'Estévenas, 84290 Cairanne, tel. 04.90.30.82.32, fax 04.90.30.74.71, e-mail alary.denis@wanadoo.fr ☑
⚲ ev. day except Sun. 8am–12 noon 2pm–6pm

DOM. DES AMADIEU
Cairanne Cuvée Vieilles Vignes 2001★

▪	1.25 ha	6,480	▮ ♠	5–8 €

In 2000 Michel and Marylène Achiary gave up their careers in medicine and teaching to devote themselves to their 7 ha family estate near the Dentelles de Montmirail and Mont Ventoux. No doubt they do not regret doing so, for two of their wines have kept their places in the *Guide*. Their Cuvée Vieilles Vignes, with its dark colour and garnet red glints, is well made. The nose demands to be opened up, to give off red berry flavours. The palate is concentrated, giving flavours of liquorice and vigorous tannins. **Cuvée Vitalis 2001 red**, with red berries on the nose, impressed the Jury.
☛ Michel Achiary, quartier Beauregard, 84290 Cairanne, tel. 04.90.66.01.28, fax 04.90.66.17.41, e-mail maryachiary@yahoo.fr ☑
⚲ by appt.

CH. BEAUCHENE
Les Charmes 2001★

▪	7.5 ha	40,000	⦿	5–8 €

This family have been growing vines since 1794. In 1971 Michel Bernard once again took over the estate, which is 5 km from Orange. Brilliant carmine colour, a fresh nose dominated by red berries, full palate with plenty of length on well-integrated tannins, the freshness of cherries and raspberries. A most appealing bottle, which can wait three years.
☛ Ch. Beauchêne, rte de Beauchêne, 84420 Piolenc, tel. 04.90.51.75.87, fax 04.90.51.73.36, e-mail chateaubeauchene@worldonline.fr ☑
⚲ ev. day except Sat. Sun. 8am–12 noon 1.30pm–5.30pm
☛ M. Bernard

DOM. DE BEAUMALRIC
Beaumes-de-Venise 2001★

▪	5 ha	n.c.	▮ ♠	5–8 €

A Grenache base (75%) complemented by Syrah (25%), three weeks' vatting and 18 months' ageing in tank have given this wine an excellent alcohol-acidity ratio over elegant tannins. On the palate, fruit and spices are to the fore. The nose has very ripe red berries. A fine bottle, to serve with leg of lamb cooked with rosemary.
☛ Isabelle et Daniel Begouaussel, Saint-Roche, Dom. de Beaumalric, BP 15, 84190 Beaumes-de-Venise, tel. 04.90.65.01.77, fax 04.90.62.97.28 ☑
⚲ by appt.

DOM. DE BEAURENARD
Rasteau 2001★

▪	8 ha	50,000	⦿	8–11 €

After visiting the winemaking museum at Rastau, you can savour this wine that has been seven generations in the family. The years are consistent at the Beaurenard estate. Once again the Jury awarded one star to Rasteau, which will be ready to drink in three years' time. Tannins are strongly present. The

nose is intense and elegant, with soft fruit aromas. A lively, warming wine on the palate, where woody notes mingle with stewed fruit. A most promising bottle.
☛ SCEA Paul Coulon et Fils, Dom. de Beaurenard, 84230 Châteauneuf-du-Pape, tel. 04.90.83.71.79, fax 04.90.83.78.06, e-mail paulcoulon@beaurenard.fr ☑
⚲ ev. day except Sun. 9am–12 noon 1.30pm–5.30pm; groups by appt.

DOM. DE LA BERTHETE 2002★

▪	1.2 ha	6,000	▮	5–8 €

Made from 100% white Grenache, this wine is typical of the appellation, with its handsome brilliant yellow colour and greenish glints. The floral nose is both fine and intense and there is a firm attack from this pleasant, fresh wine. It has floral flavours and plenty of length. A bottle that promises much drinking pleasure.
☛ Pascal Maillet, Dom. de la Berthète, rte de Jonquières, 84850 Camaret-sur-Aigues, tel. 04.90.37.22.41, fax 04.90.37.74.55, e-mail la.berthete@wanadoo.fr ☑

DOM. DE BOISSAN
Sablet Cuvée Clémence 2001★

▪	5 ha	10,000	▮ ⦿	5–8 €

This wine's dark red colour is probably the result of its generous maceration period. A rich nose, where red berries and truffle marvellously complement light oakiness. Alcohol and tannins combine happily with stewed red berries. A powerful wine.
☛ Christian Bonfils, Dom. de Boissan, 84110 Sablet, tel. 04.90.46.93.30, fax 04.90.46.99.46, e-mail c.bonfils@wanadoo.fr ☑
⚲ by appt.

CH. DE BORD
Laudun 2002★

▪	2 ha	6,000	▮ ⦿	5–8 €

The château, some of which survives, dates from the 11th century, when it belonged to the bishops of Uzès and later to the count of Toulouse. Today it belongs to the Brotte family, who have 22 ha of vines. This pale yellow wine with greenish glints has a pleasant nose where honey and flowers are very present. The palate, which is full and well-rounded, is rich in flavours. This bottle will be ready to drink for the festive season. **Cuvée Bord Laudun 2001 red** was singled out by the Jury. It should be laid down for two or three years.
☛ Laurent-Charles Brotte, Le Clos, BP 1, 84230 Châteauneuf-du-Pape, tel. 04.90.83.70.07, fax 04.90.83.74.34, e-mail brotte@brotte.com ☑
⚲ ev. day 9am–12 noon 2pm–6pm

DOM. BOUCHE
La Grappe d'Or 2002★★

▪	2 ha	4,666	▮ ♠	8–11 €

This estate, which suffered badly from flooding, nevertheless offers this remarkable wine, La Grappe d'Or. With a pale yellow colour and greenish glints, it has a superbly intense nose, developing intense aromas of white flowers and honey. The attack is pleasant and the palate reveals plenty of substance, ending with notes of honey and lilies. A masterpiece of winemaking. Drink as an aperitif. The **red Côtes du Rhône La Truffière 2001** was awarded one star.
☛ Dominique Bouche, chem. d'Avignon, 84850 Camaret-sur-Aigues, tel. 06.62.09.27.19, fax 04.90.37.74.17 ☑
⚲ by appt.

DOM. BRESSY-MASSON
Rasteau A la Gloire de mon Père 2001★

▪	1 ha	3,700	⦿	15–23 €

This wine's name is a reference to the title of a novel by Marcel Pagnol, who spent his childhood in the nearby Lubéron. Go and try it, in this former stables converted into a cellar. It is very rich in spices both on the nose and on the palate, with red berry and liquorice notes, fine balance and plenty of length. It is made from Grenache and

RHONE

Syrah planted on stony hillsides. **Cuvée Paul Emile 2001 red (11–15 €)** is a fine wine for ageing.

☎ Marie-France Masson, Dom. Bressy-Masson, rte d'Orange, 84110 Rasteau, tel. 04.90.46.10.45, fax 04.90.46.17.78, e-mail marie-francemasson@terre-net.fr
⌐ ev. day except Sun. 9am–12 noon 2pm–7pm

DOM. BRUSSET

Cairanne Coteaux des Travers 2002★

■	3 ha	8,000	▮	5–8 €

This is not the first time that Coteaux des Travers from the Brusset estate figures in the *Guide*. In the previous edition it had charmed the Jury in its white incarnation. Now, it is the rosé that gets one star. It is orange, brilliant and with an amber glint and the nose gives off lovely fruity notes. Finesse and harmony characterize a palate where alcohol and acidity are well balanced. The long flavours are full of fruit. A total of 100,000 bottles of **Coteaux des Travers 2001 red**, which impressed the jury, were produced.

☎ SA Dom. Brusset, Le Village, 84290 Cairanne, tel. 04.90.30.82.16, fax 04.90.30.73.31
⌐ by appt.

CASTEL-MIREIO

Cuvée Tradition 2001★

■		n.c.	25,000	▮ ◖	5–8 €

Syrah, Grenache and Mourvèdre make up this very pleasant, well-made wine, which has a deep red colour. The nose is very open, with fruit and cocoa. The palate is well balanced and dominated by red berries, cocoa and liquorice on a good alcohol base. Save for drinking with a Provençal stew.

☎ Michel et André Berthet-Rayne, rte d'Orange, 84290 Cairanne, tel. 04.90.30.88.15, fax 04.90.30.83.17
⌐ by appt.

LA CHAPELLE NOTRE DAME D'AUBUNE Beaumes-de-Venise 2001★★

■	120 ha	660,000	▮	5–8 €

The Cave des Vignerons de Beaumes-de-Venise, founded in 1956 by the pharmacist in the village, has a place in the *Guide* thanks to its La Chapelle Notre Dame d'Aubune, in red, white and rosé. The red gets the most stars. Harvesting by hand and traditional vinification take us back to the basic values of *villages*. The nose is very pleasant with its palette of red fruit. The palate, too, is most agreeable, giving off flavours of fresh fruit (cherries, blackcurrant, redcurrant), well sustained by alcohol and tannins. **Chapelle Notre Dame d'Aubune 2002 white** is rich, thanks to the maturity of the white Grenache and elegant thanks to the roundness of the Viognier and the floral character of Clairette. It was judged a great success, as was the same wine in **2002 rosé**: fine *saignée* and excellent vinification technique.

☎ Vignerons de Beaumes-de-Venise, quartier Ravel, 84190 Beaumes-de-Venise, tel. 04.90.12.41.00, fax 04.90.65.02.05, e-mail vignerons@beaumes-de-venise.com
⌐ by appt.

DOM. CHAUME-ARNAUD

Vinsobres 2001★

■	8.5 ha	45,000	▮	5–8 €

Until 1956 there were more olive trees than vines on this estate. But a particularly harsh winter changed that and since then the vine has ruled over a total of 37 ha. Grenache, Syrah, Mourvèdre, Vieux Carignan and Cinsault make up this wine with its deep violet colour and soft fruit nose with hints of spice. Tasting reveals a full wine with concentrated stewed fruit flavours and vanilla notes. A most elegant *cuvée*.

☎ EARL Chaume-Arnaud, Les Paluds, 26110 Vinsobres, tel. 04.75.27.66.85, fax 04.75.27.69.66, e-mail chaume-arnaud@wanadoo.fr
⌐ by appt.

DOM. CLAVEL

Saint Gervais Cuvée L'Etoile du Berger 2001★

■	2.38 ha	13,000	▮ ◖	8–11 €

Several of this winemaker's wines have been judged worthy of representing their appellation, but L'Etoile du Berger was the undisputed favourite. Red berries and soft fruit mingle with spices. Syrah leaves its mark on the palate of flavours, whose length lasts several *caudalies*. This wine's very harmonious balance should last for many years. **Chusclan 2001 red (5–8 €)** impressed the jury.

☎ Denis Clavel, rue du Pigeonnier, 30200 Saint-Gervais, tel. 04.66.82.78.90, fax 04.66.82.74.30, e-mail clavel@domaineclavel.com  ◧
⌐ by appt.

LE CLOS DU CAILLOU 2001★★

■	7.6 ha	34,000	◖◗	11–15 €

Elie Dussaud, architect of the bridge at Suez and the port of Marseille, built this estate's cellar in 1867. It produces a wine with garnet red/violet colouring and a sumptuous bouquet of ripe fruit, prunes, spices and truffles. The palate is concentrated, with alcohol dominant. The tannins are silky, against a background of spices, prune and cherry. Is it ready to drink? Certainly, but if you keep it in your cellar a while it will give you even more pleasure, for it will have reached its best. The **Côtes du Rhône Le Bouquet des Garrigues 2001 red** gets one star and the **2002 white (8–11 €)** was singled out by the Jury. Ageing is carried out very competently.

☎ Jean-Denis et Sylvie Vacheron, Clos du Caillou, 84350 Courthézon, tel. 04.90.70.73.05, fax 04.90.70.76.47
⌐ ev. day except Sun. 9am–12 noon 1.30pm–5.30pm

CLOS PETITE BELLANE

Valréas Les Echalas 2001★

■	2.7 ha	13,000	◖◗	11–15 €

When you visit this estate, admire the panoramic view over the Mont Ventoux and Dentelles de Montmirail. Les Echalas is characterized by a fine tannin base and eight months in oak casks. With its spice, roasted and red berry flavours this wine, which is long in the mouth, is still immature. It has the potential to age well, reaching its best in two or three years.

☎ SARL sté nouvelle Petite Bellane, rte de Vinsobres, chem. de Sainte-Croix, 84600 Valréas, tel. 04.90.35.22.64, fax 04.90.35.19.27, e-mail info@clos-petite-bellane.com
⌐ ev. day 9am–12 noon 2pm–6pm; cl. 20 Dec.–2 Jan.
☎ Olivier Peuchot

CAVE LA COMTADINE

Cuvée Le Chasseur 2001★

■	n.c.	26,078	▮	5–8 €

The cooperative of Puyméras, a village a few kilometres from Vaison-la-Romaine, offers two Côtes du Rhône-Villages. Cuvée Le Chasseur is aptly named, with gamey and tobacco notes on the nose. On the palate it has good length and unleashes pleasant flavours of fruits in brandy, blackcurrant, spices and subtle tannins. **La Comtadine 2000** also receives one star for its good balance. The **Côtes du Rhône La Comtadine 2000 red** wins one star for its suppleness and rounded character.

☎ Cave La Comtadine, 84110 Puyméras, tel. 04.90.46.40.78, fax 04.90.46.43.32, e-mail cave-lacomtadine@wanadoo.fr
⌐ ev. day 8am–12 noon 2pm–6pm (Jul.-Aug. 7pm)

DOM. DU CORIANCON

Vinsobres 2001★★

	10 ha	11,000	▇ ♦	5–8 €

Two stars once again this year for this 55-ha estate. Careful choice of plots, harvesting at full maturity and 25 to 40 days' maceration produced this well-structured wine with strong, lively tannins. It has ample flavours of very ripe red berries and a dark colour with purple glints. A wine for ageing; serve with venison stew. **Le Haut des Côtes 2000 (11–15 €)**, fruity and woody, impressed the Jury. It needs time to reach its best.
☛ François Vallot, Dom. du Coriançon, 26110 Vinsobres, tel. 04.75.26.03.24, fax 04.75.26.44.67, e-mail françois.vallot@wanadoo.fr ▼
☖ ev. day except Sun. 9am–12 noon 2pm–7pm

DOM. DES COTEAUX DES TRAVERS

Rasteau Cuvée Prestige 2001★

	n.c.	13,000	▥	8–11 €

A rewarding wine that gives off aromas of red berries and blackberries followed by roasted, spicy and fig notes. It has a good alcohol base and woodiness, as well as hints of fruit. Drink with a red meat dish.
☛ Robert Charavin, Dom. des Coteaux des Travers, BP 5, 84110 Rasteau, tel. 04.90.46.13.69, fax 04.90.46.15.81, e-mail robert.charavin@wanadoo.fr ▼
☖ by appt.

CH. COURAC

Laudun 2001★

	3.57 ha	20,000	▇	5–8 €

Syrah and Grenache harvested at full ripeness have produced this wine with a brilliant, intense, carmine colour. On the nose it has aromas of coffee, cocoa and red berries that develop musky notes and on the palate it has well-integrated tannins. Good balance and length; ready to drink now, with game stew.
☛ SCEA Frédéric Arnaud, Ch. Courac, 30330 Tresques, tel. 04.66.82.90.51, fax 04.66.82.94.27 ▼
☖ by appt.

CH. LA COURANCONNE

Rasteau Magnificat 2001★★

	1.52 ha	8,500	▥	8–11 €

A great wine, which merits a church service! Such panache in its carmine colour! Good ripeness on the nose, where blackcurrant and Morello cherry are rounded with strong muskiness. Tannins give a good base for the fruit and toasted notes in an elegant, fresh palate. One taster suggested this be enjoyed with roast beef cooked with garlic.
☛ Ch. La Courançonne, Le Plan de Dieu, 84150 Violès, tel. 04.90.70.92.16, fax 04.90.70.90.54, e-mail info@lacouranconne.com ▼

CH. LA DECELLE

Cuvée Saint-Paul 2001★

	3 ha	10,000	▇ ♦	8–11 €

Saint-Paul-Trois-Châteaux is worth visiting for its Romanesque cathedral and its truffle museum. Afterwards, you can go and try the wines of Château La Décelle. Saint-Paul is very good: you can smell the terroir, its ripeness, red berries and herbs of Provence and very fine tannins. Vat ageing has allowed this wine to retain all its freshness. Drink with a red meat dish.
☛ Ch. la Décelle, rte de Pierrelatte, D 59, 26130 Saint-Paul-Trois-Châteaux, tel. 04.75.04.71.33, fax 04.75.04.56.98, e-mail ladecelle@wanadoo.fr ▼
☖ ev. day except Sun. 9am–12 noon 2.30pm–6.30pm; groups by appt.
☛ Seroin

DOM. DURIEU 2001★

	31 ha	15,000		5–8 €

This is the former estate of Jean Avril. A surprisingly musky nose ends on floral notes and a complex palate develops stewed fruit. A well-structured wine with good length – typical of the region and well made.

☛ Paul Durieu, 27, av. Pasteur, 84850 Camaret-sur-Aigues, tel. 04.90.37.28.14, fax 04.90.37.76.05 ▼
☖ by appt.

DOM. DES ESCARAVAILLES

Rasteau La Ponce 2000★

	5.5 ha	29,000	▇ ▥ ♦	11–15 €

This 65 ha estate in the heart of the Rasteau vineyards enjoys magnificent views over the surrounding villages, a setting that lends itself well to enjoying La Ponce. Made from 80% Grenache complemented by Syrah, it reflects its AOC status with good acidity-alcohol balance over well integrated, silky tannins. Stewed strawberry flavours give it good length. The nose is intense and floral. Drink with grilled thrushes. The **Côtes du Rhône 2002 white (8–11 €)** impressed the Jury.
☛ Ferran et Fils, Dom. des Escaravailles, 84110 Rasteau, tel. 04.90.46.14.20, fax 04.90.46.11.45 ▼
☖ by appt.

ESPRIT DE TERROIR

Chusclan Excellence 2001★★

	4 ha	20,000	▇ ♦	11–15 €

A fine result for this team of winemakers and oenologists, who have captured the spirit of this terroir well. Both the nose and the palate have strong fruit: first fresh red berries, then stewed fruit and finally fruit in brandy. The tannin base is well rounded, the structure harmonious with intriguing length. A fine bottle.
☛ Cave des Vignerons de Chusclan, rte d'Orsan, 30200 Chusclan, tel. 04.66.90.11.03, fax 04.66.90.16.52, e-mail cave.chusclan@wanadoo.fr ▼
☖ by appt.

DOM. DE FENOUILLET

Beaumes-de-Venise Cuvée Tradition 2001★

	7 ha	20,000	▇ ♦	5–8 €

The Fenouillet estate is 2 km from the Dentelles de Montmirail and 20 km from Mont Ventoux. The Soard family cellars secrete some old bottles, some dating from as long ago as 1953! The very good 2001 has a lovely colour with violet glints. The nose has fruit and leathery aromas with a musky note. A wine of character, whose tannic structure is complemented by spicy flavours. It has a good future ahead of it.
☛ GAEC Patrick et Vincent Soard, Dom. de Fenouillet, allée Saint-Roch, 84190 Beaumes-de-Venise, tel. 04.90.62.95.61, fax 04.90.62.90.67, e-mail pv.soard@freesbee.fr ▼
☖ by appt.

FERAUD-BRUNEL

Rasteau 2000★

	20 ha	20,000	▇ ▥	8–11 €

This négociant at Châteauneuf-du-Pape exports 95% of his wines. You might be lucky enough to taste this wine with its intense, amber colour. Very fresh on the nose, which develops raspberry aromas. The palate is pleasantly balanced and well structured, with plenty of substance. Spice and peppery notes are rounded with glycerol.
☛ Féraud-Brunel, chem. du Bois-de-la-Ville, 84230 Châteauneuf-du-Pape, tel. 04.90.83.72.62, fax 04.90.83.51.07, e-mail pegau@pegau.com

DOM. DE LA FERME SAINT-MARTIN

Beaumes-de-Venise Cuvée Saint-Martin 2000★

	4 ha	12,000	▇ ♦	8–11 €

A trip through the lovely Dentelles de Montmirail takes you to the estate of Ferme Saint-Martin, which went organic in 2000. This blend of 80% Grenache and 20% Syrah has concentrated fruit and spice aromas. Good balance, complexity and robust tannins combine to make a fine, typical wine.
☛ Guy Jullien, Dom. de la Ferme Saint-Martin, 84190 Suzette, tel. 04.90.62.96.40, fax 04.90.62.90.84, e-mail guy.jullien@tiscali.fr ▼ ☖
☖ ev. day except Sun. 10am–12.30pm 1.30pm–6pm; Jan.– Feb. by appt.

DOM. LES GRANDS BOIS

Cairanne Cuvée Mireille 2001★★

| ■ | 1.2 ha | 6,000 | 🍾 ⑪ 🍷 | 8–11 € |

In the last edition of the *Guide*, the Jury were charmed by Eloïse. This time they were seduced by Mireille, a name redolent of Provence. A fine, full wine whose intense colour has violet glints. A rich palette of aromas on the nose: leather, kirsch, damp woodland, smoke and menthol. The complex palate has good length with notes of garrigue and spices over robust, well-rounded tannins.

🐤 Dom. Les Grands Bois, 55, av. Jean-Jaurès, 84290 Sainte-Cécile-les-Vignes, tel. 04.90.30.81.86, fax 04.90.30.87.94, e-mail mbesnardeau@grands-bois.com
⚍ by appt.
🐤 Besnardeau

DOM. DES GRAVENNES 2000★

| ■ | 8 ha | 15,000 | | 5–8 € |

In 1996, Bernadette Bayon de Noyer decided to take over part of the family estate, thus creating the estate of Gravennes, which takes its name from the limestone plateau on which its vines are planted. In 2001, she was joined by her oenologist husband. The 2000 vintage, with intense red colour, gives off very ripe aromas where fruit in alcohol dominates over notes of blackcurrant and damp woodland. A balanced, well-structured wine with fruit flavours and good tannins on the finish.

🐤 Bayon de Noyer, Dom. des Gravennes, chem. d'Empaulet, 84810 Aubignan, tel. 04.90.62.71.49, fax 04.90.62.70.31,
e-mail domaine.des.gravennes@wanadoo.fr
⚍ by appt.

DOM. GRES SAINT VINCENT 2001★

| ■ | 10 ha | 30,000 | 🍾 🍷 | 3–5 € |

Just 5 km from Pont du Gard, the Vignerons d'Estézargues cellar offers three lovely wines, each with its original label. Domaine Grès Saint Vincent, made from grapes ripened on red clay terraces with shingle, is most agreeable with its nose of stewed fruit and spicy notes. An elegant wine on the finish, with good length where cherry predominates. **Domaine Les Genestas 2001 red** (drink with lamb *en croûte*) by Michel Trébillon, impressed the Jury, as did the woody **Domaine d'Andezon 2001 red (5–8 €)**, belonging to Iampietro-Paneboeuf.

🐤 Cave des Vignerons d'Estézargues, rte du Grès, 30390 Estézargues, tel. 04.66.57.03.64, fax 04.66.57.04.83, e-mail les.vignerons.estezargues@wanadoo.fr
⚍ ev. day except Sun. 8am–12 noon 2pm–6pm;
Sat. 2pm–5pm
🐤 Vincent Maria

DOM.LES HAUTES CANCES

Cairanne Cuvée Tradition 2000★★★

| ■ | 0.5 ha | 3,200 | 🍾 ⑪ 🍷 | 5–8 € |

Anne-Marie and Jean-Marie Astart thought long and hard before leaving their careers in medicine to devote themselves to the family vines. They probably do not regret it, given the rewards showered upon them. Two of these wines were judged exceptional and the grand Jury settled matters by awarding *coup de coeur* to Cairanne Cuvée Tradition. The secret of this wine's success lies in organic methods, or in the traditional vinification without the addition of cultured yeast or filtration and with 12 months in French casks – as well as,

undeniably, in the winemaker's skill. This *coup de coeur* has a very deep black-red colour. Its bouquet, full of nuances, runs from red berries to spices. It is a powerful, rounded wine: balanced, harmonious, warming and full, with plenty of length of spicy flavour. It offers excellent quality for the price and should be carefully aged in the cellar for eight years. If you miss out on the Cuvée Tradition – only 3,200 bottles were made – you can console yourself with **Cairanne Cuvée Vieilles Vignes**, which is ready to drink now and just as exceptional (10,500 bottles produced). Its intense colour contains violet glints. On the nose, red berries precede a lightly oaky palate, which is powerful with good length. A most harmonious wine.

🐤 SCEA Achiary-Astart, quartier Les Travers, 84290 Cairanne, tel. 04.90.30.76.14, fax 04.90.38.65.02, e-mail contact@hautescances.com
⚍ by appt.

CH. D'HUGUES

L'Orée des Collines Vieilli en fût de chêne 2000★

| ■ | 1.49 ha | 8,200 | ⑪ | 11–15 € |

The château of Hugues has belonged to the Pradier family since 1869. In 1988, Sylviane and Bernard were awarded a *coup de coeur* for their first vintage. The first impression this 2000 vintage makes is promising and confirmed throughout tasting. Power, warmth, maturity, balance, structure and length: this most enjoyable wine has them all, starting with a nose that opens out in ripe fruit. Wait three years before drinking, with a red meat dish. The **red Côtes du Rhône Grande Réserve 2001** impressed the Jury.

🐤 Sylviane et Bernard Pradier, Ch. d'Hugues, 84100 Uchaux, tel. 04.90.70.06.27, fax 04.90.70.10.28, e-mail chateau.dhugues@terre-net.fr
⚍ ev. day 9am–12 noon 2pm–7pm;
Sat. Sun. by appt.

DOM. JAUME

Vinsobres 2001★

| ■ | 8 ha | 35,000 | 🍾 ⑪ 🍷 | 8–11 € |

Just a few kilometres from Nyons, a mecca for olives, in a scenically beautiful wine-growing area, the charming village of Vinsobres is home to the Jaume estate which, every year, impresses the *Guide*'s Jury. This time, they were charmed by the *villages*, with its cherry colour with dark red glints. The nose is fine, with spice and damp woodland aromas. The mouth unleashes tannins, fine structure and a concentration of red berry flavours. A wine for ageing, before serving with leg of lamb in puff pastry with truffle sauce.

🐤 Dom. Jaume, 24, rue Reynarde, 26110 Vinsobres, tel. 04.75.27.61.01, fax 04.75.27.68.40,
e-mail cave.jaume@libertysurf.fr
⚍ by appt.

DOM. DES LAUSES

Cuvée Maëva 2001★

| ■ | 1 ha | 5,700 | 🍾 ⑪ 🍷 | 5–8 € |

In 1994 Gilbert Raoux decided to leave the cooperative cellar to set up the family-run Lauses estate. Now he has a place in the *Guide* with Cuvée Maëva, named after his eldest daughter. An honest cherry colouring, leathery nose with red berries, spices and liquorice and very fine tannins – all make a very fine wine. A most convivial bottle, ready to drink, that can be enjoyed throughout a meal.

🐤 Dom. des Lauses, quartier des Pessades, 84830 Sérignan-du-Comtat, tel. 04.90.70.09.13, fax 04.90.70.09.13
⚍ by appt.
🐤 Gilbert Raoux

LOUIS BERNARD

Grande Réserve 2001★

| ■ | n.c. | 27,000 | | 8–11 € |

A fruitful partnership between the négociant and the winemaker produced this Grande Réserve, which is still two or three years from its best. It has an intense, dark colour and unleashes flavours of fruit, tobacco and spices both on the nose and on the palate.

🐤 Salavert-Les domaines Bernard, rte de Sérignan, 84100 Orange, tel. 04.90.11.86.86, fax 04.90.34.87.30, e-mail sldb@sldb.fr

DOM. MARIE BLANCHE

Cuvée du Solitaire 2001★

	2 ha	10,000	■ ◫ ↓	8–11 €

The name of this wine is a reference to an episode that took place on the estate in December 2001, when a *solitaire* (wild boar) attacked two dogs belonging to the Delorme family. It is a story of animals and a musky wine with a very open nose that gives of blackcurrant aromas. It is well-balanced on the palate, with integrated tannins and red berry flavours. A *villages* that is entirely typical of its appellation.
● Jean-Jacques Delorme, Dom. Marie-Blanche, 30650 Saze, tel. 04.90.31.77.26, fax 04.90.26.94.48 ☑
☓ ev. day except Sun. 10.30am–12.30pm 4pm–7.30pm

MAS DE LIBIAN

La Calade 2001★★

	1 ha	1,900	◫	11–15 €

Mas de Libian, which covers 17 ha in the Ardèche gorges, produces some remarkable results. It is an organic estate and two of its wines have been awarded two stars. The Jury seems to have had a weakness for La Calade, a blend of Mourvèdre (75%) and Grenache (25%). It has intense, deep colour with violet glints, a powerful nose of stewed fruit and prunes, followed by a full, rich, structured and fruity palate that ranges from blackberries to blackcurrants. Hurry – before it sells out! You may have more luck with the estate's **Cuvée Principale Mas de Libian 2001 (5–8 €)**, of which 16,000 bottles were made. It is a most attractive wine, powerful and rounded, typical of the appellation. There are also 35,000 bottles of **red Côtes du Rhône Mas de Libian 2001 (5–8 €)**, which was awarded one star; it is powerful and promising.
● Thibon, Mas de Libian, 07700 Saint-Marcel-d'Ardèche, tel. 04.75.04.66.22, fax 04.75.98.66.38, e-mail h.thibon@wanadoo.fr ☑
☓ by appt.

DOM. DE LA MAVETTE 2001★

	1.5 ha	8,000	■	5–8 €

Warmth and maturity are the main features of this wine, with ripe fruit, leather and spice flavours. Tannins are present on notes of pepper and liquorice and stewed flavours appear on the finish. A worthy representative of its appellation; wait two years before drinking.
● EARL Lambert et Fils, Dom. de La Mavette, 84190 Gigondas, tel. 04.90.65.85.29, fax 04.90.65.87.41, e-mail mavette@club-internet.fr ☑
☓ ev. day except Mon. 8am–12 noon 2pm–6pm

CH. MONGIN 2001★★★

	2 ha	10,000	◫	5–8 €

José Carballar and his pupils at the Orange winemaking college have succeeded in producing an exceptional wine with intense black colour: an example of fine work and dedication for all aspiring winemakers. This *villages* deploys a fine palette of very southern aromas: garrigue plants concentrated on spices and ending with prunes. It is structured with silky tannins, which are a good foundation for stewed fruit, blackcurrant, spices and the long finish with its liquorice flavour. Enjoy with stewed hare.
● Lycée viticole d'Orange, Ch. Mongin, 2260, rte du Grès, 84100 Orange, tel. 04.90.51.48.04, fax 04.90.51.11.92, e-mail chateau.mongin@educagri.fr ☑
☓ by appt.

DOM. LA MONTAGNE D'OR

Séguret 2001★

	3 ha	20,000	■ ↓	5–8 €

Alain Mahinc's estate is in the town of Vaison-la-Romaine, which attracts many visitors to its cathedral, château and medieval village. Grenache, the sole grape variety used here, brings structure, balance and roundness to this deep garnet-red wine. Red berry notes are dominated by blackcurrant, which appears intensely on the nose as well as on the palate. Ready to drink in three years.
● Alain Mahinc, La Combe, 84110 Vaison-la-Romaine, tel. 04.90.36.22.42, fax 04.90.36.22.42, e-mail lamontagnedor@yahoo.fr ☑
☓ by appt.

DOM. DU MOULIN

Vinsobres Cuvée Charles Joseph 2000★

	1.5 ha	6,000	◫	11–15 €

The Vinsons, who were awarded a *coup de coeur* last year, are passionate winemakers, as we can see from the fine Cuvée Charles Joseph, which shows the signs of careful barrel ageing. It is fresh and balanced, with good overall harmony: elegant, pleasant, with a long fruity finish. The **Côtes du Rhône 2001 red (5–8 €)** impressed the Jury.
● Denis Vinson, Dom. du Moulin, 26110 Vinsobres, tel. 04.75.27.65.59, fax 04.75.27.63.92 ☑
☓ ev. day except Sun. 8am–12 noon 1.30pm–7pm

DOM. DE MOURCHON

Séguret Grande Réserve 2001★★

	8 ha	20,000	■ ◫ ↓	11–15 €

This estate, in a village that has been dubbed "the most beautiful in France," is run by Scots who have skilfully combined traditional and modern winemaking techniques. They offer this remarkable Grande Réserve, with dark colour showing garnet-red glints. Spice, vanilla and red berry aromas mingle on the nose. The palate is balanced and structured, developing a very fine, integrated oakiness. Grenache contributes red berry flavours and ageing adds vanilla notes. A fine wine: open in two years.
● SCEA Dom. de Mourchon, La Grande Montagne, 84110 Séguret, tel. 04.90.46.70.30, fax 04.90.46.70.31, e-mail info@domainedemourchon.com ☑
☓ ev. day except Sun. 10am–12 noon 2pm–6pm
● McKinlay

DOM. GUY MOUSSET

Les Garrigues 2000★

	3 ha	15,000	◫	8–11 €

This 2000 vintage is Franck and Olivier Mousset's first Côtes du Rhône-Villages. Les Garrigues is aptly named, with its nose that exhales all the aromas of the garrigue, together with a touch of liquorice. Stewed fruit and roasted flavours develop over well-integrated tannins. A well-made and pleasing wine. The **red Côtes du Rhône, Cuvée des Elégants 2001 (3–5 €)** gets one star. Drink with a white meat dish, from this autumn onwards.
● Vignobles Guy Mousset et Fils, Le Clos Saint Michel, rte de Châteauneuf, 84700 Sorgues, tel. 04.90.83.56.05, fax 04.90.83.56.06, e-mail mousset@clos-saint-michel.com ☑
☓ ev. day 10am–12 noon 2pm–6pm

DOM. DE L'OLIVIER

Vieilli en fût de chêne 2001★

	3.4 ha	17,000	◫	5–8 €

The Olivier estate is 3 km from the Pont du Gard. This well-made *villages* consists of 50% Grenache and 50% Syrah that have undergone traditional vinification and 12 months in cask. Very ripe grapes have produced soft fruit, toasted and kirsch flavours over very present tannins. The oakiness needs a little time to acquire roundness. "A wine very worthy of AOC," concluded one taster. In **Côtes du Rhône, Domaine de l'Olivier 2001 red** impressed the Jury, as did the **2002 white**.
● Eric Bastide, EARL Dom. de L'Olivier, 1, rue de la Clastre, 30210 Saint-Hilaire-d'Ozilhan, tel. 04.66.37.08.04, fax 04.66.37.00.46 ☑
☓ by appt.

DOM. DE L'ORATOIRE SAINT-MARTIN

Cairanne Cuvée Prestige 2001★★

	7 ha	25,000	■ ↓	11–15 €

Once again the Oratoire Saint-Martin estate has carried off a *coup de coeur*. What a fine terroir this Cairanne is! This remarkable wine comes from 60% Grenache and 40% Mourvèdre, giving fine ripeness where kirsch, prunes and dried figs indulge the nose. Substance, body and warmth round off the tannins over notes of fruit. The flavours linger well. Wait five years before enjoying with roasted leg of wild boar. **Cuvée Haut-Coustias 2000 red (15–23 €)**, which was a *coup de coeur* in the last edition, gets two stars this year too. A

RHONE

harmonious wine with a long finish, but which needs a little time. Serve with roasted woodcock..
➥ Frédéric et François Alary, rte de Saint-Roman, 84290 Cairanne, tel. 04.90.30.82.07, fax 04.90.30.74.27 ☑
🍷 ev. day except Sun. 8am–12 noon 2pm–7pm

DOM. DES PASQUIERS

Sablet 2001★

| | 6 ha | 2,000 | 🍶 | 5–8 € |

Sablet is 2 km from Gigondas, on the road to Vaison-la-Romaine. This is the first wine Jean-Claude and Philippe Lambert have made since the family estate was divided in 1998. The colour is crimson with violet glints. On the nose, damp woodland, game and quince form a good structure above well-integrated tannins. This wine needs two or three years for the fruit to develop fully.
➥ SCEA Vignobles des Pasquiers, rte d'Orange, 84110 Sablet, tel. 04.90.46.83.97,
fax 04.90.46.83.97 ☑
🍷 by appt.
➥ Lambert

DOM. PELAQUIE 2001★

| | 20 ha | 60,000 | 🍶 ♦ | 5–8 € |

Saint-Victor-la-Coste boasts a 13th century castle – and this estate, which is listed because of three of its wines. Domaine la Pélaquié is very pleasant, offering well-integrated tannins, depth and balance with spicy structure. Red berries and cherries on the nose and a fine, well-developed garnet red colour. The **2002 white** gets a mention for its good balance, as does the **Côtes du Rhône 2002 white**, which is Clairette-based, fine and floral.
➥ SCEA Dom. Pélaquié, 7, rue du Vernet, 30290 Saint-Victor-la-Coste, tel. 04.66.50.06.04, fax 04.66.50.33.32,
e-mail contact@domaine-pelaquie.com ☑
🍷 ev. day except Sun. 9am–12 noon 2pm–6pm
➥ GFA du Grand Vernet

DOM. DU PETIT-BARBARAS

Le Chemin de Barbaras Sélection 2001★★

| | 3 ha | 13,000 | 🍶 🍷 ♦ | 5–8 € |

The Jury spent a long time tasting this wine. Some members called it out of this world. And what a nose! Very ripe fruit, jam and chocolate aromas with notes of blackcurrant and spices. The palate is rich too, with elegant, velvety tannins, red berry flavours and cocoa notes too. Balance and roundness help to make this a remarkable bottle. **Cuvée Tradition 2001 red** gets one star for its overall harmony.
➥ SCEA Feschet Père et Fils, Dom. du Petit-Barbaras, 26790 Bouchet, tel. 04.75.04.80.02, fax 04.75.04.84.70 ☑
🍷 ev. day except Sun. 9am–12 noon 2pm–7pm

DOM. DE PIAUGIER

Sablet Montmartel 2000★★

| | n.c. | 7,600 | 🍶 🍷 | 8–11 € |

With its streets in concentric circles around its very old church, Sablet is a pretty spot for the wine-loving tourist to explore. Do be patient to allow this wine to reach its full potential. For the moment it is still immature, but its tannic structure is clear. It is aromatic and oaky but not excessively so and has good length. One for the cellar.
➥ Jean-Marc Autran, Dom. de Piaugier, 3, rte de Gigondas, 84110 Sablet, tel. 04.90.46.96.49, fax 04.90.46.99.48, e-mail piaugier@wanadoo.fr ☑ 🏠
🍷 by appt.

DOM. LE PUY DU MAUPAS 2001★

| | 3.5 ha | 5,900 | | 8–11 € |

Just 5 km from the Roman ruins of Vaison-la-Romaine, this estate has doubled its area and tripled its cellar's capacity in 15 years. Grenache (60%), Syrah (30%), Mourvèdre (5%) and Carignan (5%), planted on clay-limestone soils, have given this wine its attractive intense colour with garnet-red glints. The nose, of violet on red berries, is very pleasant. The palate is well structured, tannic and full of flavour. **Domaine Le Puy du Maupas Vinsobres 2000 red**, with good fruit, impressed the Jury.
➥ Christian Sauvayre, Dom. Le Puy du Maupas, rte de Nyons, 84110 Puyméras, tel. 04.90.46.47.43, fax 04.90.46.48.51,
e-mail sauvayre@puy-du-maupas.com ☑ 🏠 🏠
🍷 ev. day 9am–12 noon 2pm–7pm

CH. LES QUATRE FILLES

Cairanne 2001★

| | 5 ha | 7,636 | 🍷 | 8–11 € |

The cellar of this estate, which converted to organic agriculture a few years ago, celebrated its 20th anniversary in 2002. Perhaps by drinking some of this dark red 2001 wine? However, it would be wiser to let it age in the cellar, so that its woody, aromatic tannic potential can be fulfilled. Stewed fruit flavours mingle with cocoa and spice notes. Its bouquet has vanilla aromas.
➥ Roger Flesia, Ch. Les Quatre-Filles, rte de Lagarde-Paréol, 84290 Sainte-Cécile-les-Vignes, tel. 04.90.30.84.12, fax 04.90.30.86.15,
e-mail contact@chateau–4filles.com ☑
🍷 ev. day 8am–7pm

ROUGE GARANCE 2001★

| | 5 ha | 20,000 | 🍶 ♦ | 8–11 € |

The fame of the actor Jean-Louis Trintignant (who with the Cortellini couple owns this estate) and that of Enki Bilal, who designed its first label, may well have contributed to its reputation. Nevertheless, this would be meaningless without quality wines such as this traditional Côtes du Rhône-Villages, with its fruity character, good alcohol-acidity balance, well-integrated tannins and garrigue and truffle notes. The colour and flavours are perfectly brought out. A fine wine to enjoy after a stroll to the Pont du Gard.
➥ SCEA Dom. Rouge Garance, chem. de Massacan, 30210 Saint-Hilaire-d'Ozilhan, tel. 04.66.37.06.92, fax 04.66.37.06.92, e-mail rougegarance@wanadoo.fr ☑
🍷 by appt.
➥ Cortellini-Trintignant

DOM. SAINTE-ANNE

Saint-Gervais 2000★★

| | 3 ha | 10,000 | 🍶 ♦ | 11–15 € |

The 34 ha Sainte-Anne estate is a *coup de coeur* champion, having shown astonishing consistency. This year the Steinmaiers have not disappointed, earning two stars for the Saint-Gervais, made from 50% Mourvèdre with equal parts of Grenache and Syrah. Ten months in tank have given this wine a lovely dark colour and an elegant, fine and open nose with violet and red berries. The well-structured palate, typical of the appellation, has finesse and elegance with fruity length. **Les Mourillons 2000 red**, with all the hallmarks of cask ageing, gets one star.
➥ EARL Dom. Sainte-Anne, Les Cellettes, 30200 Saint-Gervais, tel. 04.66.82.77.41, fax 04.66.82.74.57 ☑
🍷 ev. day except Sun. 9am–11am 2pm–6pm
➥ Steinmaier

CH. SAINT ESTEVE D'UCHAUX

Vieilles Vignes 2000★★

| | 6 ha | 25,000 | 🍶 🍷 ♦ | 11–15 € |

The Château Saint Estève at Uchaux organizes an annual piano festival every August – a chance for music lovers and wine lovers to mingle and enjoy this remarkable Vieilles Vignes, where Syrah and Grenache give of their best. It is dark red in colour, with powerful red berry flavours in a well-structured palate and does not disappoint, with plenty of length in its tannins and flavours. This virtuoso has perfected his technique.

☎ Ch. Saint Estève d'Uchaux, rte de Sérignan, D 172, 84100 Uchaux, tel. 04.90.40.62.38, fax 04.90.40.63.49, e-mail info@chateau-saint-esteve-d-uchaux.com ☑
🍷 by appt.

DOM. SAINT ETIENNE

Les Molières 2000★

■	n.c.	n.c.			5–8 €

This estate, on gravel terraces, offers Les Molières, which has an astonishing range of spicy aromas and flavours, dominated by black pepper, both on the nose and on the palate. Tannins are fine and silky. Balanced, aromatic and very enjoyable, this wine has stewed red berries on the finish.

☎ Michel Coullomb, Dom. Saint Etienne, 26, fg du Pont, 30490 Montfrin, tel. 04.66.57.50.20, fax 04.66.57.22.78 ☑
🍷 by appt.

CAVE DES VIGNERONS DE SAINT-GERVAIS Saint-Gervais Prestige 2001★★

■	n.c.	15,000	■	♦	5–8 €

This is the Saint-Gervais cellar's most prestigious wine. The Jury liked the attractive blackcurrant red and violet colour and the elegant nose with good concentration of soft fruit (blackcurrant and bilberry) on lovely spicy and leathery notes. The amylic, well-structured palate has good depth and freshness. A remarkable wine, to age two or three years before enjoying with a game stew. **Cuvée Spéciale 2001 red** was judged a great success. It is a seductive wine that will reach its best within three years.

☎ Cave des Vignerons de Saint-Gervais, Le Village, 30200 Saint-Gervais, tel. 04.66.82.77.05, fax 04.66.82.78.85, e-mail contact@cavesaintgervais.com. ☑
🍷 by appt.

CH. SAINT-MAURICE

Laudun Cuvée Vieilles Vignes 2001★

■	3.5 ha	13,000	■ ◫ ♦		11–15 €

Historians say that it was from L'Ardoise that Hannibal crossed the Rhône. Be that as it may, this estate offers Laudun – aged 24 months, 12 of them in cask, which have allowed it to develop very ripe fruit, crushed blackcurrant and liqueur notes. The palate is structured, rich and mature and the tannins well-integrated. The fruit carries good length.

☎ SCA Ch. Saint-Maurice, RN 580, L'Ardoise, 30290 Laudun, tel. 04.66.50.29.31, fax 04.66.50.40.91, e-mail chateau.saint.maurice@wanadoo.fr ☑ ☗
🍷 ev. day except Sun. 8am–12 noon 2pm–6pm
☎ Valat

CH. SAINT-NABOR

Cuvée Prestige 2000★

■	2 ha	10,000	◫		5–8 €

Gérard Castor's estate is in Cornillon, a village listed for its architectural heritage. With its 25 days' maceration and nine months' ageing in barrel, this 2000 vintage needs to age some more. It is still young and has strong tannins that will become integrated with time. And here's a secret: Gérard Castor has fallen in love with Martinique and will talk endlessly about this little corner of paradise to anyone who will listen.

☎ Gérard Castor, Vignobles Saint-Nabor, 30630 Cornillon, tel. 04.66.82.24.26 ☑
🍷 ev. day except Sun. 9am–12 noon 2pm–6pm

LES SALYENS

Cairanne 2000★

■	45 ha	200,000	■ ◫		8–11 €

The Cairanne cellar has set up a sensory itinerary to allow newcomers to appreciate its wines – a playful and friendly entry into the world of wine, that ends with an initiation into tasting. Armed with what you have learned there, you can try this lovely Les Salyens, noted for the finesse of its tannins, which give it excellent balance. The palate combines red berry, bilberry, toasted and pepper notes, while the nose opens with redcurrant. There is plenty of length. **Grande Réserve 2002 white (5–8 €)**, as easy on the eye as in the mouth, gets the same

rating. **Grande Réserve 2002 rosé (5–8 €)** impressed with its fruit and freshness.

☎ Cave de Cairanne, 84290 Cairanne, tel. 04.90.30.82.05, fax 04.90.30.74.03, e-mail info@cave-cairanne.fr ☑
🍷 by appt.

SAVEURS DU TEMPS 2001★★

■	33 ha	54,000	■	♦	5–8 €

Same estate, same blend, same exposure to the sun, same ageing – and same rating for Saveurs du Temps and **Domaine Les Aulières 2001**. The first is a *coup de coeur*. Both wines have intense garnet red colour and a highly developed nose marked by stewed red berries and a hint of blackcurrant. The palate is superb: balanced, with very present tannins and good length of fruit flavour. In two or three years these wines will have reached their best.

☎ Les Vignerons de Saint-Hilaire-d'Ozilhan, av. Paul-Blisson, 30210 Saint-Hilaire-d'Ozilhan, tel. 04.66.37.16.47, fax 04.66.37.35.12, e-mail contact@cotes-du-rhone-wine.com
🍷 ev. day except Sun. 10am–12 noon 2.30pm–6.30pm; Mon. 2.30pm–6.30pm; groups by appt.

CH. SIGNAC

Cuvée Tradition 2001★★

■	37 ha	32,000			5–8 €

This estate has already featured in the *Guide* several times, often earning a star. It completes its collection of awards with two stars for a wine of dark garnet-red colour, with a powerful, complex stewed fruit nose that still needs to develop. Good concentration on the palate, where red berry, truffle and damp woodland flavours are unleashed over well-integrated tannins. A harmonious wine, which should be aged in the cellar at least two years. **Cuvée Terra Amata 2001 red (8–11 €)**, impressed for its fruit.

☎ SCA Ch. Signac, rte d'Orsan, 30200 Bagnols-sur-Cèze, tel. 04.90.83.59.02, fax 04.90.83.79.69, e-mail chateausignac@wanadoo.fr ☑
🍷 by appt.

DOM. DU SOLEIL ROMAIN

Séguret Harmonie 2001★

■	4.5 ha	1,500	■	♦	5–8 €

A golden label on a black background for this very well-made Soleil Romain, whose colour shows purplish glints. Fruit, gamey notes and garrigue aromas make up a pleasingly intense bouquet. The palate has good length, substance, fruit and integrated tannins.

☎ Bernard Giely, Dom. du Soleil Romain, quartier Saint-Martin, 84110 Vaison-la-Romaine, tel. 04.90.36.12.69, fax 04.90.28.71.89, e-mail soleilromain@cario.fr ☑
🍷 by appt.

DOM. DE LA VALERIANE 2001★

■	5 ha	6,000	■ ◫ ♦		5–8 €

Domazan, on the right bank of the Rhône, has a lovely terroir of pebbly soil, which produces this wine of intense colour with garnet-red glints. The subtle nose is dominated by red berries. Good structure, with well-integrated tannins, spice and well-developed fruit flavours, with a point of alcohol on the finish. Ready to drink now. Following in his parents' footsteps, the oenologist Valérie Castan also offers three wines of his own: **Côtes du Rhône 2001 red**, **2002 rosé**, and **2002 white**. The first two earn a star each and the third was singled out by the Jury.

🍴 Mesmin et Maryse Castan, rte d'Estézargues, 30390 Domazan, tel. 04.66.57.04.84, fax 04.66.57.04.84, e-mail valeriane.mc@terre-net.fr ☑
Ⴒ by appt.

CH. DU VIEUX TINEL 2001 ★

■	25.7 ha	120,000	🍶	3–5 €

The négociant who followed this *cuvée* from harvest to vinification did a good job. Initial impressions are of very ripe grapes, soon followed by cherry jam and spicy (pepper) flavours, sustained by well-structured tannins. A traditional Côtes du Rhône-Villages in a fine bottle. Excellent value for money, as is **Cuvée Donjon des Dames 2001 red**, which the Jury singled out for its fruit and spicy notes.

🍴 La Compagnie Rhodanienne, Chemin-Neuf, 30210 Castillon-du-Gard, tel. 04.66.37.49.50, fax 04.66.37.49.51, e-mail cie.rhodanienne@wanadoo.fr
Ⴒ by appt.

CAVE LA VINSOBRAISE

Cuvée Therapius 2001 ★★

■	n.c.	4,000	🍶	8–11 €

Four thousand bottles of nectar. This Cuvée Therapius is marvellous, with its deep, dark, garnet-red colour. The intense red berry and blackcurrant nose is dominated by raspberries. Structure and balance on the palate sustain a fine concentration of red berries and very present tannins. Wait at least three years before drinking. **Sélection Terroir 2001 red (3–5 €)** gets one star for its fruit and freshness. Keep for two or three years.

🍴 Cave La Vinsobraise, 26110 Vinsobres, tel. 04.75.27.64.22, fax 04.75.27.66.59 ☑
Ⴒ ev. day 8am–12 noon 2pm–6pm

DOM. VIRET

Emergence 2001 ★★

■	2.5 ha	10,000	🍶	15–23 €

It is thoroughly worth making a detour to visit this estate's cellar and hear its owners explain their growing and vinification methods – and, of course, to taste the remarkable Emergence, ripened on this lovely terroir. Its colour is an intense red and its nose opens with red berries and blackcurrant. The palate is rounded and balanced, with silky tannins. There is plenty of length in the intense red berry flavours.

🍴 Dom. Philippe Viret, EARL Clos du Paradis, Les Escoulenches, Dom. Viret, 26110 Saint-Maurice-sur-Eygues, tel. 04.75.27.62.77, fax 04.75.27.62.31, e-mail viretwine@aol.com ☑
Ⴒ by appt.

Wines selected but not starred

DOM. DES BOUZONS

Cuvée Beauchamp 2001

■	1.15 ha	6,600	🍶🍶	5–8 €

🍴 Dom. des Bouzons, 194, chem. des Manjo-Rassado, 30150 Sauveterre, tel. 04.66.82.52.43, fax 04.66.82.52.43 ☑
Ⴒ by appt.
🍴 Marc Serguier

LA CABOTTE

Elevé en fût de chêne 2001

■	3 ha	5,000	🍶	8–11 €

🍴 Marie-Pierre Plumet, La Cabotte, 84430 Mondragon, tel. 04.90.40.60.29, fax 04.90.40.60.62, e-mail lacabotte@netcourrier.com ☑
Ⴒ by appt.

LA DOMELIERE 2001

■	n.c.	150,000 🍶	5–8 €

🍴 Cave des Vignerons de Rasteau et de Tain-l'Hermitage, rte des Princes-d'Orange, 84110 Rasteau, tel. 04.90.10.90.10, fax 04.90.46.16.65, e-mail vrt@rasteau.com

LA GARDE DES LIONS 2000

■	16 ha	80,000	🍶🍶	3–5 €

🍴 Cave Les Coteaux de Visan, BP 12, 84820 Visan, tel. 04.90.28.50.80, fax 04.90.28.50.81, e-mail cave@coteaux-de-visan.fr ☑
Ⴒ by appt.

CH. DE LA GARDINE 2000

■	35 ha	160,000	🍶	8–11 €

🍴 Brunel, Ch. La Gardine, rte de Roquemaure, 84350 Châteauneuf-du-Pape, tel. 04.90.83.73.20, fax 04.90.83.77.24, e-mail direction@gardine.com ☑
Ⴒ by appt.

DOM. GRAND NICOLET 2001

■	5 ha	22,000	🍶🍶	5–8 €

🍴 Jean-Pierre Bertrand, rte de Violès, 84110 Rasteau, tel. 04.90.46.12.40, fax 04.90.46.11.37, e-mail cave-nicolet-leyraud@wanadoo.fr ☑ ⬥
Ⴒ by appt.
🍴 Nicolet-Leyraud

LE GRAVILLAS

Sablet 2001

■	53 ha	280,000	🍶🍶	3–5 €

🍴 Cave Le Gravillas, 84110 Sablet, tel. 04.90.46.90.20, fax 04.90.46.96.71 ☑
Ⴒ by appt.

LES QUERADIERES

Sablet 2001

■	43.5 ha	20,000	🍶🍶	3–5 €

🍴 Cellier de l'Enclave des Papes, rte d'Orange, BP 51, 84602 Valréas Cedex, tel. 04.90.41.91.42, fax 04.90.41.90.21, e-mail france@enclavedespapes.com ☑

DOM. DE LA RENJARDE 2001

■	48 ha	220,000 🍶🍶 🍶	5–8 €

🍴 Guillaume Dugas, Dom. de la Renjarde, rte d'Uchaux, 84830 Sérignan-du-Comtat, tel. 04.90.70.00.15, fax 04.90.70.12.66, e-mail renjarde@wanadoo.fr ☑
Ⴒ by appt.
🍴 P. Richard

CAVE DES VIGNERONS DE SAINTE-CECILE-LES-VIGNES 2000

■	n.c.	14,000	🍶🍶	3–5 €

🍴 Cave des Vignerons réunis de Sainte-Cécile-les-Vignes, 35, rte de Valréas, BP 21, 84290 Sainte-Cécile-les-Vignes, tel. 04.90.30.79.30, fax 04.90.30.79.39, e-mail cave@vignerons-saintececile.fr ☑
Ⴒ by appt.

SAINT-PANTALEON-LES-VIGNES

Cuvée Prestige 2001

| | n.c. | 16,000 | 🔲 🌡 | 5–8 € |

Cave coop. de Saint-Pantaléon-les-Vignes, rte de Nyons, 26770 Saint-Pantaléon-les-Vignes, tel. 04.75.27.90.44, fax 04.75.27.96.43 ☑
🍷 by appt.

Côte-Rôtie

Situated at Vienne, on the right bank of the river, this is the oldest vineyard of the Rhône Valley. In 2002, its output was 7,638 hl from a production area of 210 ha, spread through the communes of Ampuis, Saint-Cyr-sur-Rhône and Tupins-Sémons. The vines are cultivated on hills that are so steep as to be almost vertiginous. If the Côte Blonde has a separate identity from the Côte Brune it could, according to one story, be in memory of a Maugiron noble who, in his will, divided his lands between his two daughters, a blond and a brunette. It is perhaps worth observing that the wines of the Côte Brune are more full-bodied while the Côte Blonde wines are more delicate.

The soils are the richest in schist in the region. Only red wines are produced, made from the Syrah variety and a proportion of Viognier, which may be added to a maximum of 20%. The Côte-Rôtie wine is deep red in colour, its delicate, fine bouquet dominated by aromas of raspberry and spices, with a touch of violet. Well-structured, tannic and richly flavoured, it holds an unchallenged position at the top of the range of Rhône wines, a perfect accompaniment to all dishes that deserve great red wines.

CH. D'AMPUIS 1999★

| | n.c. | n.c. | | 46–76 € |

Marcel Guigal, the owner of Château d'Ampuis, has expanded considerably by acquiring the estates of Jean-Louis Grippat and Vallouit. This wine, which bears the Château's label, strikes you as powerful, rich in ripe fruit aromas and vanilla. It is well concentrated on the palate, resting on integrated, silky tannins accompanied by stewed fruit notes. A fully rounded wine. **E. Guigal, Brune et Blonde 2000 (23–30 €)** is an accessible wine that will be enjoyable to drink in a few years.
🍷 E. Guigal, Ch. d'Ampuis, 69420 Ampuis, tel. 04.74.56.10.22, fax 04.74.56.18.76, e-mail contact@guigal.com
🍷 by appt.

DOM. DE BONSERINE

La Sarrasine 2001★

| | n.c. | 30,000 | 🍷 | 23–30 € |

This wine is constantly improving and gets one star again this year. It is fine and classy and should be kept for five years to allow it to achieve "complete harmony," one taster wrote. It already has much finesse in the structure, with silky tannins and a long, spicy finish.
🍷 Dom. de Bonserine, 2, chem. de la Viallière, 69420 Ampuis, tel. 04.74.56.14.27, fax 04.74.56.18.13, e-mail bonserine@aol.com ☑
🍷 ev. day except Sun. 9am–5.30pm

YVES CUILLERON

Terres Sombres 2000★

| | n.c. | 9,000 | 🍷 | 30–38 € |

Since 1987 Yves Cuilleron has made a name for his 32 ha estate – we have lost count of the number of stars his 32 ha achieved in the Hachette *Guides*. His Côte-Rôtie is surprising for a 2000 vintage, for it has remained very young. Combining power with finesse, it is silky and retains all its freshness. The balance of oaky fruit is finely tuned, giving an impression of lusciousness and heralding great potential.
🍷 Yves Cuilleron, 58 RN, Verlieu, 42410 Chavanay, tel. 04.74.87.02.37, fax 04.74.87.05.62, e-mail ycuiller@terre-net.fr ☑
🍷 by appt.

CUILLERON-GAILLARD-VILLARD

Les Essartailles 2001★★

| | n.c. | 14,000 | 🍷 | 30–38 € |

There is strength in numbers, it is said. These three estate owners struck out as négociants in 1998, each offering fine wines from their own estates. But it is this wine that they have made together that wins the *coup de cœur*, such is its substance that is a sophisticated reflection of the terroir. It bears witness to great skill and professionalism. Its sumptuous colour is edged with violet and the nose is rich and complex: oakiness gives way to fruit and spices, an impression repeated on the palate, which is silky and long. Serve in four or five years, with beef rib in black pepper.
🍷 SARL Les Vins de Vienne, Bas Seyssuel, 38200 Seyssuel, tel. 04.74.85.04.52, fax 04.74.31.97.55, e-mail vinsdevienne@terre-net.fr ☑
🍷 by appt.

PIERRE GAILLARD

Rose pourpre 2001★

| | 0.8 ha | 4,000 | 🍷 | 38–46 € |

If you go up the Malleval gorge you come upon this pretty village, where this wine – more red than pink, but certainly deep purple – is made. The Jury were unanimous in pronouncing it skilfully aged. It is rewarding with its vanilla aromas, supple on the attack with silky tannins and quickly asserts itself as firm and substantial. Its flavours should develop with time and balance is guaranteed.
🍷 EARL Pierre Gaillard, lieu-dit Chez Favier, 42520 Malleval, tel. 04.74.87.13.10, fax 04.74.87.17.66, e-mail vinsp.gaillard@wanadoo.fr ☑
🍷 by appt.

JEAN-MICHEL GERIN

Champin le Seigneur 2001★★

| | 5 ha | 20,000 | 🍷 | 23–30 € |

In 1987 Jean-Michel Gerin took the reins of this 9 ha family estate. Using 10% Viognier, he produces a very oaky wine that is still closed. When the effect of the cask is attenuated, this will be a good wine. Very ripe fruit (blackcurrant), musky notes and spices will happily combine, as will the tannins, which are very present on the finish. A classy, stylish wine.
🍷 Jean-Michel Gerin, 19, rue de Montmain, BP 7, 69420 Ampuis, tel. 04.74.56.16.56, fax 04.74.56.11.37, e-mail gerin.jm@wanadoo.fr ☑
🍷 by appt.

RHONE

LA LANDONNE 1999★★

■	n.c.	n.c.		+76 €

The Côte-Rôtie AOC indisputably belongs to the aristocracy of French wine and Marcel Guigal occupies its best terroirs. La Landonne is a remarkable wine: its colour is perfect, as is that of its two siblings, La Mouline and La Turque. On the nose, it speaks of macerated cherries, soft fruit and cocoa. The palate is highly structured, resting on present but elegant tannins, ripe fruit and power. All this points to a great future.
✆ E. Guigal, Ch. d'Ampuis, 69420 Ampuis,
tel. 04.74.56.10.22, fax 04.74.56.18.76,
e-mail contact@guigal.com
☘ by appt.

VIGNOBLES DU MONTEILLET

Fortis 2001★

■	0.4 ha	1,800	⑪	30–38 €

A *coup de coeur* last year (2000 vintage), this estate offers the same wine, Fortis, in 2001. Thanks to ageing in new casks, stacked with their bungs on the side, this wine is clearly strongly oaked, but good body is already discernible, with hints of liquorice and vanilla. A fine result, which will be most rewarding in three to five years with wild duck ragout.
✆ Vignobles Antoine et Stéphane Montez, Dom. du Monteillet, 42410 Chavanay, tel. 04.74.87.24.57,
fax 04.74.87.06.89 ▼
☘ by appt.

LA MOULINE

Côte Blonde 1999★★★

■	n.c.	n.c.		+76 €

The reputation of this wine, La Turque's neighbour, is far from overrated. And, though produced in rather limited quantities, it is of superb quality. "What a treat!" exclaimed one taster. Dark, almost black in colour, it gives off vanilla but also game, menthol and garrigue aromas. The palate is impressive, combining finesse and delicacy with fullness and power. This supremely elegant bottle should be opened in ten years' time for a great occasion.
✆ E. Guigal, Ch. d'Ampuis, 69420 Ampuis,
tel. 04.74.56.10.22, fax 04.74.56.18.76,
e-mail contact@guigal.com
☘ by appt.

MOUTON PERE ET FILS 2001★

■	0.6 ha	2,500	⑪	15–23 €

"It will reach its best in five years' time," pronounced one expert. The tannins are clearly very present and need to become integrated, but there is finesse and elegance in the attack followed by well-integrated oakiness, spice and finally assertive red berries. Keep for two years.
✆ André et Jean-Claude Mouton, Le Rozay,
69420 Condrieu, tel. 04.74.87.82.36, fax 04.74.87.84.55 ▼
☘ ev. day 9am–12 noon 2pm–6.30pm; groups by appt.

DOM. DE ROSIERS 2001★

■	7 ha	33,000	⑪	23–30 €

Winning a *coup de coeur* last year with the 2000 vintage – the latest of many awards – this is one of the most reliable AOC estates. Syrah, with 3% Viognier, produces a wine of intense

colour, with finesse making itself felt followed by power. Silky and full, it bursts out on the nose with aromas of blackcurrant, cocoa and prunes in brandy. It is well-balanced and can wait two to five years, to allow the oakiness to become integrated..
✆ Louis Drevon, 3, rue des Moutonnes, 69420 Ampuis,
tel. 04.74.56.11.38, fax 04.74.56.13.00,
e-mail ldrevon@terre-net.fr ▼
☘ by appt.

SAINT COSME 2001★

■	2 ha	7,500	⑪	15–23 €

"A négociant with the attitude of a winemaker" is the self-proclaimed role of Louis Barruol, who set up in business in 1997. Made from 100% Syrah, this wine of garnet-red colour was appreciated for its well-integrated tannins but also for its bouquet – and explosion of blackcurrant, clove and cocoa aromas. Skilfully aged, this wine leaves no one indifferent, even though one taster thought it was more typical of a Syrah than of a Côte-Rôtie.
✆ SARL Barruol, Ch. de Saint Cosme, 84190 Gigondas,
tel. 04.90.65.80.80, fax 04.90.65.81.05,
e-mail louis@chateau-st-cosme.com ▼ ♖
☘ ev. day except Sun. 9am–12 noon 1.30pm–5.30pm

LA TURQUE

Côte Brune 1999★★

■	n.c.	n.c.	⑪	+76 €

An extraordinary label by Moretti for this legendary, highly sought-after wine. We still remember the *coup de coeur* of the 1990 vintage. It is a superb terroir, perfectly orientated, for it receives the sun's rays all day long. This 1999 Côte Brune displays its typical slightly austere character, with spice and subtle fruit. It is powerful and ready to drink now, but its full complexity will be reached after several years' ageing.
✆ E. Guigal, Ch. d'Ampuis, 69420 Ampuis,
tel. 04.74.56.10.22, fax 04.74.56.18.76,
e-mail contact@guigal.com
☘ by appt.

DOM. GEORGES VERNAY

Maison Rouge 2000★

■	1.3 ha	4,000	ⓘ⑪♦	30–38 €

Since 1996 Christine Vernay has been the right-hand woman of her father, who took this estate to fame. She is responsible for **Blonde du Seigneur 2000 (23–30 €)**, which won the same rating as Maison Rouge. It has a lovely, complex nose (soft fruit, liquorice and damp woodland) but we expected the structure to be stronger and more rounded. It will take two or three years for the tannins to develop fully.
✆ Dom. Georges Vernay, 1, rte Nationale, 69420 Condrieu,
tel. 04.74.56.81.81, fax 04.74.56.60.98,
e-mail pa@georges-vernay.fr ▼
☘ by appt.

FRANCOIS VILLARD

La Brocarde 2000★★

■	0.22 ha	1,200	⑪	38–46 €

Created in 1989, this 10 ha estate practises sustainable agriculture and is autonomously run, while at the same time being part of a company set up by two winemaking friends and which wins a *coup de coeur* in this AOC. The Jury stressed that this wine should not be drunk for four years. Not surprisingly, then, it does not yet burst out and remains closed – hence a certain austerity. However, it fills the mouth and has a present though not aggressive structure. It has remarkable body – full, almost voluminous and offers intense flavours with musky notes mingled with blackcurrant, liquorice and vanilla.
✆ Dom. François Villard, Montjoux,
42410 Saint-Michel-sur-Rhône, tel. 04.74.56.83.60,
fax 04.74.56.87.78, e-mail vinsvillard@aol.com ▼
☘ by appt.

Wines selected but not starred

DOM. GILLES BARGE

Côte Brune 2000

| | 1.08 ha | 5,000 |  | 23–30 € |

🕿 Gilles Barge, 8, bd des Allées, 69420 Ampuis,
tel. 04.74.56.13.90, fax 04.74.56.10.98 ☑
🍷 by appt.

DE BOISSEYT-CHOL

Côte Blonde 2001

| | 0.8 ha | 3,000 | | 23–30 € |

🕿 De Boisseyt-Chol, 178 RN 86, 42410 Chavanay,
tel. 04.74.87.23.45, fax 04.74.87.07.36,
e-mail infos@deboisseyt-chol.com ☑
🍷 ev. day except Sun. 9am–12 noon 2pm–6pm;
cl. 15 Aug.–10 Sep.
🕿 Didier Chol

PATRICK ET CHRISTOPHE BONNEFOND 2001

| | 4 ha | 16,000 | | 15–23 € |

🕿 Patrick et Christophe Bonnefond, Mornas,
69420 Ampuis, tel. 04.74.56.12.30, fax 04.74.56.17.93 ☑
🍷 by appt.

EDMOND ET DAVID DUCLAUX 2001

| | 4.5 ha | 20,000 | | 23–30 € |

🕿 GAEC Edmond et David Duclaux, RN 86,
69420 Tupin-Semons, tel. 04.74.59.56.30,
fax 04.74.56.64.09 ☑
🍷 by appt.

LES HAUTS DES CHEYS 2001

| | 2.1 ha | 11,000 | | 15–23 € |

🕿 Cave des Vignerons de Rasteau et de Tain-l'Hermitage,
rte des Princes-d'Orange, 84110 Rasteau,
tel. 04.90.10.90.10, fax 04.90.46.16.65,
e-mail vrt@rasteau.com

DOM. JAMET 2000

| | 6 ha | 25,000 | | 23–30 € |

🕿 Dom. Jean-Paul et Jean-Luc Jamet, Le Vallin,
69420 Ampuis, tel. 04.74.56.12.57, fax 04.74.56.02.15 ☑
🍷 by appt.

Condrieu

The vineyard is on granite soils, 11 km south of Vienne, on the right bank of the Rhône. Only wines made exclusively from the Viognier variety are entitled to the appellation which, in seven communes and three *départements*, covers a mere 110 ha. All its characteristics contribute to Condrieu's image as a white wine of very rare quality since it only produced 3,985 hl in 2002. Rich in alcohol, fleshy and supple but at the same time fresh, it is highly perfumed, releasing floral aromas – the scent of violets dominates – and notes of apricot. This is a unique wine, exceptional and unforgettable and while it can be drunk young (with all fish dishes),

it can also develop with bottle age. In recent years wines from late harvesting have appeared which are made from successive pickings (sometimes as many as eight times in a harvest).

LAURENT BETTON 2001★★

| | 1.7 ha | 1,900 | | | 15–23 € |

A small estate of just 3.4 ha, of which 1.3 ha is Saint-Joseph and 1.7 ha Condrieu. A third of the vinification takes place in new casks, a third in two-year-old casks and a third in tank with 10 days' fermentation. This wine underwent its malolactic fermentation in May 2002. The nose is full of white flowers, followed by violets and peaches. The Jury appreciated the balance between delicate oakiness and fruit. On the palate, acacia makes itself felt. It has substance, so can be enjoyed with foie gras.
🕿 Laurent Betton, La Côte, 42410 Chavanay,
tel. 04.74.87.08.23, fax 04.74.87.08.23 ☑
🍷 by appt.

YVES CUILLERON

Les Ayguets 2001★★

| | 1.5 ha | 4,000 | | 30–38 € |

The Jury did not stint on superlatives: "a very great wine"; "superb"; "exceptional". This wine was greeted by a thunder of applause. A sunny overture, dark golden yellow, followed by a first movement of powerful dried fruit and toasted notes and a second movement that sings the praises of the balance of sugar and acidity. The finale is endless. **Les Chaillets 2001 (23–30 €)** gets one star.
🕿 Yves Cuilleron, 58 RN, Verlieu, 42410 Chavanay,
tel. 04.74.87.02.37, fax 04.74.87.05.62,
e-mail ycuiller@terre-net.fr ☑
🍷 by appt.

CUILLERON-GAILLARD-VILLARD

La Chambée 2001★

| | n.c. | 3,500 | | 23–30 € |

Tasting this wine was a true pleasure; it guarantees conviviality. Good ripeness and aromas of lime-blossom tea and mint. Honey and peach share the palate in a most effective balance. There is plenty of length and this wine can be aged for four or five years.
🕿 SARL Les Vins de Vienne, Bas-Seyssuel, 38200 Seyssuel,
tel. 04.74.85.04.52, fax 04.74.31.97.55,
e-mail vinsdevienne@terre-net.fr ☑
🍷 by appt.

DELAS

La Galopine 2001★

| | n.c. | 13,000 | | 23–30 € |

The must is fermented at low temperature (16°C) to make the most of the complexity of the Viognier grape. The wine is then aged on fine lees, to develop body and structure. There is violet and apricot amid unctuous richness, which is not excessive, with restraint and great class.
🕿 Delas Frères, ZA de l'Olivet,
07300 Saint-Jean-de-Muzols, tel. 04.75.08.60.30,
fax 04.75.08.53.67, e-mail f-mathis@delas.com ☑
🍷 by appt.

Condrieu

DOM. FARJON 2001★

| | 0.6 ha | 2,000 | ◫ | 15–23 € |

In 2002 Thierry Farjon celebrated 10 years on this estate. His pale yellow, brilliant Condrieu is rather floral but still restrained. In compensation, on the palate expresses all its exotic fruit and vanilla. It is full-bodied and fleshy with an intriguing finish. Wait a few years before opening.
➼ Thierry Farjon, Morzelas, 42520 Malleval,
tel. 04.74.87.16.84, fax 04.74.87.95.30 ☑
⚍ by appt.

PHILIPPE FAURY 2001★

| | 1.7 ha | 8,000 | ▮◫⚭ | 15–23 € |

Philippe Faury has run this 13 ha estate for almost 25 years, from his village of granite houses. Brilliant, pale yellow colour immediately sets this wine's tone: restraint on the nose, a mingling of white flowers and almonds and great gentleness in the fleshiness that envelopes the whole. Its balance is better than its fullness: it is simple and effective. Same rating for **Cuvée La Berne 2001 (23–30 €)**.
➼ EARL Philippe Faury, La Ribaudy, 42410 Chavanay,
tel. 04.74.87.26.00, fax 04.74.87.05.01,
e-mail p.faury@42.sideral.fr ☑ ⌂
⚍ by appt.

PIERRE GAILLARD

Fleurs d'automne 2002★★

| | 0.5 ha | n.c. | ◫ | 23–30 € |

Not all Condrieu wines are dry! Viognier lends itself remarkably well to making sweet wines too, such as this one, which has 191 g/l. of residual sugar. It is surprising for a 2002 vintage. A fine golden colour, it asserts its sweet nature with a nose of stewed fruit (apricot and orange) with some dried fruit. It has body and is full and balanced, with excellent harmony. An unusual wine, full of interest and charm. **Condrieu Sec 2002 (15–23 €)**, aged six months in wood, will become a great wine. It gets one star.
➼ EARL Pierre Gaillard, lieu-dit Chez Favier,
42520 Malleval, tel. 04.74.87.13.10, fax 04.74.87.17.66,
e-mail vinsp.gaillard@wanadoo.fr ☑
⚍ by appt.

JEAN-MICHEL GERIN

La Loye 2002★

| | n.c. | n.c. | ◫ | 15–23 € |

Very young – yet already brilliant. White flowers and ripe apricot and the Jury commented on its mouth-filling qualities, which should increase in a year or two. It already has fine balance, which can only get better.
➼ Jean-Michel Gerin, 19, rue de Montmain, BP 7,
69420 Ampuis, tel. 04.74.56.16.56, fax 04.74.56.11.37,
e-mail gerin.jm@wanadoo.fr ☑
⚍ by appt.

E. GUIGAL

La Doriane 2001★

| | n.c. | n.c. | ▮◫⚭ | 30–38 € |

This wine, presented by Maison Guigal, is old-gold in colour with greenish glints and iris and grapefruit on the nose. Combining liveliness and fleshiness in a perfect balance, it has a fresh finish where bitter almonds answer toasted almonds. Enjoy with foie gras.
➼ E. Guigal, Ch. d'Ampuis, 69420 Ampuis,
tel. 04.74.56.10.22, fax 04.74.56.18.76,
e-mail contact@guigal.com ☑
⚍ by appt.

FRANCOIS MERLIN 2001★

| | 1 ha | 5,000 | ▮◫⚭ | 15–23 € |

François Merlin, who is self-taught, has opted to use sustainable methods and traditional vinification, ageing this wine half in cask, half in tank. This gives very pleasant results. It can be enjoyed as an aperitif: fresh, mineral, slightly violet-flavoured and well balanced, it asks no questions.
➼ François Merlin, Le Bardoux,
42410 Saint-Michel-sur-Rhône, tel. 04.74.56.61.90,
fax 04.74.56.61.90 ☑
⚍ by appt.

VIGNOBLES DU MONTEILLET

Les Grandes Chaillées 2001★★

| | 1 ha | 5,000 | ◫ | 15–23 € |

The year 2001 was exceptional on this estate. *Coup de coeur* in Saint-Joseph, two wines in Condrieu (Domaine du Monteillet and Les Grandes Chaillées) earning two stars and both narrowly missing out on a *coup de coeur*. Both have good volume and concentration, where oak is well-integrated. The Jury pronounced Les Grandes Chaillées to be the better of the two, by a narrow margin; they appreciated its style, with buttery, roasted and dried fruit (apricot) notes and a very long finish. **Domaine du Monteillet 2001 (23–30 €)** is equally remarkable, but needs to wait longer.
➼ Vignobles Antoine et Stéphane Montez, Dom. du Monteillet, 42410 Chavanay, tel. 04.74.87.24.57,
fax 04.74.87.06.89 ☑
⚍ by appt.

MOUTON PERE ET FILS

Côte Châtillon 2002★

| | 0.7 ha | 3,000 | ▮◫⚭ | 15–23 € |

Father and son run this estate, whose terraces face due south in the heart of the village of Condrieu. It is aged without added yeast and 60% of it has the yeast stirred in barrel on the lees. This wine is powerful and lively, with very present fruit. It is full of promise and should be enjoyed with a fine fish dish.
➼ André et Jean-Claude Mouton, Le Rozay,
69420 Condrieu, tel. 04.74.87.82.36, fax 04.74.87.84.55 ☑
⚍ ev. day 9am–12 noon 2pm–6.30pm;
groups by appt.

ALAIN PARET

Lys de Volan 2001★★

| | 2.5 ha | 3,900 | ◫ | 23–30 € |

South-facing and sheltered from the wind, this terraced vineyard has been run by Alain Paret since 1972. This wine is remarkable and has plenty of power. It has a thumping attack with violet and iris that will intoxicate you. But you must have the patience to wait a long time: once opened, this bottle brings forth seductive fleshiness and notes of stewed apricots. A true, great Condrieu!
➼ Alain Paret, pl. de l'Eglise, 42520 Saint-Pierre-de-Boeuf, tel. 04.74.87.12.09, fax 04.74.87.17.34 ☑
⚍ by appt.

ANDRE PERRET

Clos Chanson 2001★★

| | 0.5 ha | 2,000 | ◫ | 15–23 € |

André Perret, a biologist, took over the family estate in 1985. He has since extended it and won it an international reputation to which this wine does full justice. Produced in a true walled vineyard, from vines about 40 years old, it is remarkably intense both in appearance, with its brilliant golden colour and nose, a riot of ripe fruit (apricot and peach) with violet and elegant spice. The well-integrated oakiness does not hide the wine's typical character and long finish, for which the Jury had no hesitation in awarding a *coup de coeur*.
➼ André Perret, Verlieu, 42410 Chavanay,
tel. 04.74.87.24.74, fax 04.74.87.05.26 ☑
⚍ by appt.

CHRISTOPHE PICHON

Patience 2000★

| 0.4 ha | 1,400 | 🍶 | 30–38 € |

A new, elegant label for Patience, a very sweet wine (225 g/l. of residual sugar), aged 24 months in cask. It is a must, with its nose of prunes in brandy and palate evoking beeswax and exotic fruits with fleshiness and roundness. A wine worthy of a Roquefort. Also worth noting is **Condrieu Sec 2001 (15–23 €)**, which was given one star.

➥ Christophe Pichon, Le Grand Val, Verlieu,
42410 Chavanay, tel. 04.74.87.06.78, fax 04.74.87.07.27 ✓
✗ by appt.

SAINT COSME 2001★

| 1 ha | 2,700 | 🍶 | 15–23 € |

The emblem of this young firm is the 12th century chapel of Saint Cosme. It offers a rather complex wine that unleashes a blend of stewed fruit, honey, buttery notes and a hint of cinnamon. Rounded and fleshy, it has a touch of acidity on the finish which retains its freshness.

➥ SARL Barruol, Ch. de Saint Cosme, 84190 Gigondas,
tel. 04.90.65.80.80, fax 04.90.65.81.05,
e-mail louis@chateau-st-cosme.com ✓ ⌂
✗ ev. day except Sun. 9am–12 noon 1.30pm–5.30pm

GEORGES VERNAY

Coteau de Vernon 2001★

| 1.69 ha | 5,000 | 🍶 | 38–46 € |

Readers will not need reminding of the eminent part Georges Vernay has played in Rhône wine. His successes are legion. This wine, the most highly regarded, is elegant: brilliant gold with honey, white flowers, white peaches and hazelnuts on the nose. Perfect oakiness, roundness and length complete its charms. There are two other starred wines from this estate: **Les Terrasses de l'Empire 2001 (23–30 €)** unleashes – without being explosive – the appellation's classic aromas of apricot, white flowers and violets. The attack is fine and the acidity clean. It is warming, with violets on the finish. **Les Chaillées de l'Enfer 2001 (30–38 €)** was appreciated as a well-meaning wine.

➥ Dom. Georges Vernay, 1, rte Nationale, 69420 Condrieu,
tel. 04.74.56.81.81, fax 04.74.56.60.98,
e-mail pa@georges-vernay.fr ✓
✗ by appt.

FRANÇOIS VILLARD

Le Grand Vallon 2001★★

| 1.25 ha | 5,000 | 🍶 | 23–30 € |

Three wines were presented and all were rated by the Jury. Le Grand Vallon displays a well-developed personality, leading one member of the Jury to exclaim: "Open it without hesitation to discover a true Condrieu." An elegant wine, full of finesse, with floral, mineral and fruit (apricot, peach) hints. **Deponcins 2001** received one star; it is very fleshy. **Les Terrasses du Palat 2001** also got one star for its class. François Villard has demonstrated his skill.

➥ Dom. François Villard, Montjoux,
42410 Saint-Michel-sur-Rhône, tel. 04.74.56.83.60,
fax 04.74.56.87.78, e-mail vinsvillard@aol.com ✓
✗ by appt.

Wines selected but not starred

DOM. BOISSONNET 2001

| | n.c. | 1,980 | 🍶 | 15–23 € |

➥ Frédéric Boissonnet, rue de la Voûte, 07340 Serrières,
tel. 04.75.34.07.99, fax 04.75.34.04.55 ✓
✗ by appt.

CAVE DE CHANTE-PERDRIX 2001

| 1.3 ha | 6,000 | 🍴🍶🥄 | 15–23 € |

➥ Philippe Verzier, Izeras, La Madone, 42410 Chavanay,
tel. 04.74.87.06.36, fax 04.74.87.07.77,
e-mail chanteperdrixverzier@wanadoo.fr ✓
✗ by appt.

GILLES FLACHER 2001

| 0.8 ha | 2,000 | 🍶 | 15–23 € |

➥ Gilles Flacher, 07340 Charnas, tel. 04.75.34.09.97,
fax 04.75.34.09.96 ✓
✗ by appt.

FRANÇOIS GÉRARD

Côte Chatillon 2001

| 1 ha | 4,000 | 🍴🍶🥄 | 15–23 € |

➥ François Gérard, Côte Chatillon, 69420 Condrieu,
tel. 04.74.87.88.64, fax 04.74.87.88.64 ✓
✗ by appt.

DIDIER MORION 2001

| 0.8 ha | 3,000 | 🍶 | 15–23 € |

➥ Didier Morion, Epitaillon, 42410 Chavanay,
tel. 04.74.87.26.33, fax 04.74.48.23.57 ✓
✗ by appt.

DOM. RICHARD

L'Amaraze 2001

| 1.8 ha | 8,500 | 🍴🍶🥄 | 15–23 € |

➥ Hervé et Marie-Thérèse Richard, RN 86, Verlieu,
42410 Chavanay, tel. 04.74.87.07.75, fax 04.74.87.05.09,
e-mail earl.caverichard@42.sideral.fr ✓
✗ by appt.

Château Grillet

An unusual situation in French wine regions, this appellation is made only by one single domaine. With just 4 ha and 78 hl produced in 2002 in two communes, it is one of the smallest appellations d'origine contrôlée. The vines are established on well-exposed granite terraces, sheltered from the wind, protected by an amphitheatre towering above the Rhône Valley. This terroir brings its unique qualities to this white wine, which like Condrieu, is made from the Viognier grape variety. It can be drunk young, but on ageing it develops flavour and class, making it an ideal wine to drink with fish.

CHATEAU-GRILLET 2001★

| 3.5 ha | n.c. | 🍴🍶🥄 | 38–46 € |

81 82 85 (86) 88 |89| |90| 92 |93| 94 |95| 98 00 01

A Château-Grillet in the best tradition. Warming and very fleshy, it needs to be well aerated to develop its full palette of flavours. Apricot and peach are the first to make themselves known, followed by a hint of lily-of-the-valley and white flowers, the whole rounded with buttery notes. The finish has green lemon. A wine that will grow in a few years.

➥ Neyret-Gachet, Château-Grillet, 42410 Vérin,
tel. 04.74.59.51.56, fax 04.78.92.96.10 ✓
✗ by appt.
➥ Famille Canet

Saint-Joseph

The appellation stretches over about 900 ha along the right bank of the Rhône, in the Ardèche and Loire *départements*, on steep gravel slopes with beautiful views of the Alps, Mount Pilat and the Doux gorges. Saint-Joseph reds (28,751 hl in 2002) are made from Syrah grapes and are elegant, relatively light and soft, with subtle aromas of raspberry, pepper and blackcurrant, which open when accompanying grilled chicken and certain cheeses. The white wines (2,522 hl), made from the Roussanne and Marsanne varieties, are reminiscent of the Hermitage whites. They are fleshy with a delicate perfume of flowers, fruit and honey and are best drunk fairly young.

M. CHAPOUTIER
Les Granits 2001★★

| ■ | n.c. | 6,000 | | 46–76 € |

This wine is as solid as granite: a sound but still rounded and well-integrated structure gives it character. But that's not all: it gives off ripe fruit (raspberry, crushed strawberries), leather and finally aniseed and vanilla notes, which complete the palate.
☛ Maison M. Chapoutier, 18, av. du Dr-Paul-Durand, BP 38, 26601 Tain-l'Hermitage Cedex, tel. 04.75.08.28.65, fax 04.75.08.81.70, e-mail chapoutier@chapoutier.com ☑
♟ by appt.

DOM. COURBIS
Les Royes 2001★

| | 1 ha | 3,000 | ◫ | 15–23 € |

The Courbis family started making wine here in the 16th century. They have 26 ha of vines, of which 22 are on steep slopes. This wine has volume and a warming finish. Oakiness is well-integrated and gives off delicate toasted and vanilla notes. The rather complex nose offers floral aromas reminiscent of white peaches. **Les Royes 2001 red** impressed the Jury, as did the **the traditional white of the same vintage (11–15 €)**.
☛ Dom. Courbis, rte de Saint-Romain, 07130 Châteaubourg, tel. 04.75.81.81.60, fax 04.75.40.25.39, e-mail domaine-courbis@wanadoo.fr ☑
♟ by appt.

DOM. COURSODON
Le Paradis Saint-Pierre 2001★★

| ■ | 0.8 ha | 3,000 | ◫ | 15–23 € |

Can you go to heaven twice? Well, this cellar did with this wine, which already won a *coup de cœur* last year with the 2000 vintage. A very fine wine, whose dark colour is shot through with glints of light, it has a complex nose where ripe fruit and oaky notes combine pleasantly. Balanced and well-integrated, yet concentrated too, the palate has plenty of length, is well structured. You can seriously consider ageing for 10 years. Note that Paradis Saint-Pierre comes from 70-year-old vines. **Domaine Coursodon 2001 white (11–15 €)**

gets one star. It has finesse on the nose and notes of white peach and grapefruit with fleshiness on the palate, all with a lively finish. The same ratings were awarded to **La Sensonne 2001 red (15–23 €)**, which is too oaky at present and **L'Olivaie 2001 red (15–23 €)**, a wine of character which has yet to develop.
☛ EARL Pierre Coursodon, pl. du Marché, 07300 Mauves, tel. 04.75.08.29.27, fax 04.75.08.75.72 ☑
♟ by appt.

YVES CUILLERON
Saint-Pierre 2001★

| | 1.5 ha | 5,000 | ◫ | 15–23 € |

Yves Cuilleron works as a négociant with two winemaker friends, but has not abandoned his own estate. Using Roussanne alone, he has produced this Saint-Joseph, which the Jury unanimously judged to be rounded and fleshy with good length. The nose opens delicately on roasted aromas but also with floral and herbaceous notes.
☛ Yves Cuilleron, 58 RN, Verlieu, 42410 Chavanay, tel. 04.74.87.02.37, fax 04.74.87.05.62, e-mail ycuiller@terre-net.fr ☑
♟ by appt.

DELAS
Les Challeys 2001★

| ■ | n.c. | 60,000 | ▮ ◫ ↓ | 11–15 € |

A large wine merchant, now linked to the champagne company Roederer, Delas has produced a wine full of fruit and freshness, ready to drink now because it is already well integrated.
☛ Delas Frères, ZA de l'Olivet, 07300 Saint-Jean-de-Muzols, tel. 04.75.08.60.30, fax 04.75.08.53.67, e-mail f-mathis@delas.com ☑
♟ by appt.

LES FAGOTTES 2001★

| | 4 ha | 11,000 | ▮ ↓ | 8–11 € |

This is a fine-looking bottle, containing a wine with mineral and floral notes. Good acidity brings balance and freshness. **Cuvée Champtenaud 2000 red (11–15 €)** impressed the Jury. It has been aged 12 months in cask.
☛ SCA Cave de Sarras, pl. Jean-Moulin, 07370 Sarras, tel. 04.75.23.14.81, fax 04.75.23.38.36, e-mail contact@cavedesarras.fr ☑
♟ by appt.

PHILIPPE FAURY
La Gloriette Vieilles Vignes 2001★

| ■ | 1 ha | 4,000 | ◫ | 11–15 € |

Destined to be served with game birds in two or three years' time, this complex, subtle wine does not completely show its hand yet. It is very young on the nose, which reveals aromas of strawberry and ripe soft fruit (blackcurrant) over toasted and vanilla notes. The palate is concentrated, with plenty of body, tannins that are present but already aromatic with fine length and good structure.
☛ EARL Philippe Faury, La Ribaudy, 42410 Chavanay, tel. 04.74.87.26.00, fax 04.74.87.05.01, e-mail p.faury@42.sideral.fr ☑ ♞
♟ by appt.

PIERRE FINON
Les Rocailles 2001★

| ■ | 2.5 ha | 6,000 | ◫ | 8–11 € |

This estate offers two well-made wines of the same vintage, the difference lying in the age of the vines from which they are made. Both receive one star. Les Rocailles, made from vines 25 years old or older, is balanced, full and well rounded. It comes in an old-style bottle. The main wine, **Pierre Finon 2001 red**, comes from 12-year-old vines.
☛ Pierre Finon, Picardel, 07340 Charnas, tel. 04.75.34.08.75, fax 04.75.34.06.78 ☑
♟ by appt.

PIERRE GAILLARD

Les Pierres 2001★★

| | 1 ha | 5,000 | | 15–23 € |

Proclaimed in 1974, the Pilat regional nature park is a protected area covering almost 65,000 ha. When it was set up a rural development policy was already in place, based on tourism but also on agriculture. Pierre Gaillard has set up his estate on the edge of this park. In AOC Saint-Joseph, he offers the remarkable Les Pierres. Even though its nose is still closed on tasting, this wine already reveals good complexity of flavour on the palate (pepper, red berries, blackberries) with an oaky, elegant finish. Its great ageing potential means you can keep it for at least five years before opening, by which time it will have reached its best. **Clos de Cuminaille 2001 red** gets the same rating for its elegance; one taster would like to drink it with duck with olives! The classic **2001 red (8–11 €)** impressed the Jury.

☛ EARL Pierre Gaillard, lieu-dit Chez Favier, 42520 Malleval, tel. 04.74.87.13.10, fax 04.74.87.17.66, e-mail vinsp.gaillard@wanadoo.fr ☑
⟁ by appt.

PIERRE GONON

Les Oliviers 2001★★

| | 2 ha | 5,000 | | 15–23 € |

A very professional estate, which is always in the *Guide* and which has distinguished itself with its 2001 white. This wine gives an impression of freshness and finesse (acacia flowers, dried apricots). It is full and the palate fresh with a note of apricot on the finish, accompanied by toasted impressions coming from the cask. It has great length and should age well. The **Cuvée Principale 2001 red (11–15 €)**, which is more robust and rustic, gets one star. Perfect with game.

☛ Pierre Gonon, 34, av. Ozier, 07300 Mauves, tel. 04.75.08.45.27, fax 04.75.08.65.21 ☑
⟁ by appt.

DOM. BERNARD GRIPA 2001★

| | 6 ha | 25,000 | | 11–15 € |

A most impressive estate, which offers four wines in Saint-Joseph, all of which were highly rated. The chief one is this ruby-coloured wine with violet glints, which is very open on notes of strawberry and blackberry. Oak ageing has been to good effect, for the toasted notes are not dominant but well-integrated. The palate is very complex, with supple, silky tannins. Note that **Le Berceau 2001 red (15–23 €)**, made from vines more than 80 years old, receives the same rating and is a good wine for ageing. The **2001 white of the same** *cuvee* receives one star while the **Cuvée Principale du Domaine 2001** impressed the Jury.

☛ Dom. Bernard Gripa, 5, av. Ozier, 07300 Mauves, tel. 04.75.08.14.96, fax 04.75.07.06.81 ☑
⟁ by appt.

DOM. LES MONTAGNONS 2001★

| | 2.5 ha | 10,000 | | 8–11 € |

Grape selection at the picking stage and vinification in small containers (15–20 hectolitres): every care is taken to produce a wine that is elegant on the nose and powerful on the palate. There is still a slight imbalance between the finesse of the nose and the power of the palate, which could be explained by the fact the grapes are not de-stalked on picking, but time will smooth over this clash. Distributed and bottled by the Gabriel Meffre company.

☛ Jean-Yves Lombard, 07300 Mauves, tel. 04.90.12.32.42, fax 04.90.12.32.49

VIGNOBLES DU MONTEILLET

Fortior 2001★★

| | 1.4 ha | 7,000 | | 15–23 € |

This estate deserves the highest praise: a *coup de coeur* for both white and red wines in the same year and same appellation! You cannot have too much of a good thing. Complexity, finesse and fleshiness on peach and apricot notes for **Domaine Monteillet 2001 white (11–15 €)** were enthusiastically received by the Jury. But first prize went to the red, which testified to great skill in ageing a very ripe grape harvest, producing spice, roasted, blackberry and bilberry notes: a full, fleshy wine with

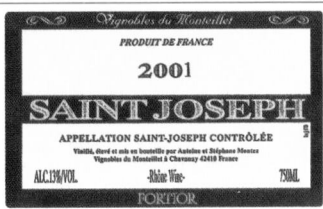

plenty of freshness. **Cuvée du Papy 2001 red (11–15 €)** was given one star: it should age well. For it has good structure.

☛ Vignobles Antoine et Stéphane Montez, Dom. du Monteillet, 42410 Chavanay, tel. 04.74.87.24.57, fax 04.74.87.06.89 ☑
⟁ by appt.

DIDIER MORION

Les Echets 2001★

| | 0.6 ha | 3,000 | | 8–11 € |

In the Pilat regional nature park, which is famous for its biodiversity, this young 7.5 ha estate ages this wine for 15 months in cask, producing results that will please lovers of oakiness. An attractive violet, almost purple colour, it has a deep nose where oakiness mingles with floral and fruit notes (stewed red berries), spiced with plenty of character. Well structured, fleshy and rounded, the palate bears the marks of ageing; this wine needs to be laid down for two or three years. The **Cuvée Principale 2001 red**, which impressed the Jury, is supple and harmonious: drink while waiting for Les Echets to reach its best.

☛ Didier Morion, Epitaillon, 42410 Chavanay, tel. 04.74.87.26.33, fax 04.74.48.23.57 ☑
⟁ by appt.

CAVE DE SAINT-DESIRAT

Cuvée Côte-Diane Elevé en fût de chêne 2001★

| | 6 ha | 25,000 | | 8–11 € |

Made from 80% Marsanne and 20% Roussanne, this 2001 white underwent maceration on the skins. It is floral and fruity. Roasted notes are a sign of the 12 months it has spent in cask. Balanced, rounded and elegant, it should be enjoyed with poultry and white meats. There are two wines from this cellar that impressed the Jury, **Cuvée Côte-Diane 2001 red** and **Cuvée des Mariniers 2001 red**, which all label-collectors should hasten to buy.

☛ Cave de Saint-Désirat, 07340 Saint-Désirat, tel. 04.75.34.22.05, fax 04.75.34.30.10, e-mail cave.saint.desirat@wanadoo.fr ☑
⟁ by appt.

FRANCOIS VILLARD

Reflet 2000★

| | 1.8 ha | 8,500 | | 23–30 € |

This wine was made from young vines – just 10 years old. Dark colouring with violet glints and a nose that gives glimpses of the wine's concentration, with musky notes mingled with stewed soft fruit (notably cherries). Fine body, also bearing the marks of oak ageing. This 2000 vintage should be aged between three and 10 years.

☛ Dom. François Villard, Montjoux, 42410 Saint-Michel-sur-Rhône, tel. 04.74.56.83.60, fax 04.74.56.87.78, e-mail vinsvillard@aol.com ☑
⟁ by appt.

Wines selected but not starred

BOIS DES BLACHES 2001

| | ■ | 3.75 ha | 20,000 | ⅏ | | 5–8 € |

� La Compagnie Rhodanienne, Chemin-Neuf,
30210 Castillon-du-Gard, tel. 04.66.37.49.50,
fax 04.66.37.49.51, e-mail cie.rhodanienne@wanadoo.fr
⅄ by appt.

DE BOISSEYT-CHOL 2001

| ■ | 3 ha | 20,000 | ⅏ | 11–15 € |

☛ De Boisseyt-Chol, 178 RN 86, 42410 Chavanay,
tel. 04.74.87.23.45, fax 04.74.87.07.36, e-mail infos@
deboisseyt-chol.com ☑
⅄ ev. day except Sun. 9am–12 noon 2pm–6pm;
cl. 15 Aug.–10 Sep.

DOM. BOISSONNET 2001

| ■ | n.c. | 6,050 | ⅏ | 8–11 € |

☛ Frédéric Boissonnet, rue de la Voûte, 07340 Serrières,
tel. 04.75.34.07.99, fax 04.75.34.04.55 ☑
⅄ by appt.

MAISON BOUACHON

Roquebrussane 2000

| ■ | n.c. | n.c. | | 11–15 € |

☛ Maison Bouachon, av. Pierre-de-Luxembourg,
84230 Châteauneuf-du-Pape, tel. 04.90.83.58.37,
fax 04.90.83.77.23 ☑
⅄ ev. day 9am–12 noon 2pm–7pm; cl. 15 Jan.–15 Feb.

CALVET 2000

| ■ | n.c. | n.c. | | 11–15 € |

☛ Calvet, 75, cours du Médoc, BP 11, 33028 Bordeaux
Cedex, tel. 05.56.43.59.00, fax 05.56.43.17.78,
e-mail calvet@calvet.com

CAVE DE CHANTE-PERDRIX

La Madone 2001

| ■ | 2 ha | 7,000 | ⅏ | 11–15 € |

☛ Philippe Verzier, Izeras, La Madone, 42410 Chavanay,
tel. 04.74.87.06.36, fax 04.74.87.07.77,
e-mail chanteperdrixverzier@wanadoo.fr ☑
⅄ by appt.

CUILLERON-GAILLARD-VILLARD 2001

| ■ | n.c. | 12,000 | ⅏ | 11–15 € |

☛ SARL Les Vins de Vienne, Bas-Seyssuel, 38200 Seyssuel,
tel. 04.74.85.04.52, fax 04.74.31.97.55,
e-mail vinsdevienne@terre-net.fr ☑
⅄ by appt.

DOM. FARJON 2001

| ■ | 4 ha | 13,000 | ⅏ | 8–11 € |

☛ Thierry Farjon, Morzelas, 42520 Malleval,
tel. 04.74.87.16.84, fax 04.74.87.95.30 ☑
⅄ by appt.

DOM. DE LA FAVIERE

Cuvée La Favière 2001

| ■ | 1 ha | 5,000 | ⅏ | 8–11 € |

☛ Pierre Boucher, Dom. de la Favière, 42520 Malleval,
tel. 04.74.87.15.25, fax 04.74.87.15.25,
e-mail domainedelafaviere@hotmail.com ☑
⅄ by appt.

GUYOT

Grande Réserve 2000

| | n.c. | 30,000 | ⅏ | 11–15 € |

☛ SA Guyot, 60, montée de l'Eglise, 69440 Taluyers,
tel. 04.78.48.70.54, fax 04.78.48.77.31,
e-mail contact@vins-guyot.com ☑
⅄ ev. day except Sun. Mon. 9am–12 noon 1.30pm–6pm

PASCAL JAMET 2001

| | 0.5 ha | 1,500 | ⅏ | 8–11 € |

☛ Pascal Jamet, RN 86, 07370 Arras-sur-Rhône,
tel. 04.75.07.09.61, fax 04.75.07.09.61,
e-mail jametpascal@aol.com ☑
⅄ by appt.

J. MARSANNE ET FILS 2000

| ■ | 5 ha | 5,000 | ⅏ | 11–15 € |

☛ Jean Marsanne et Fils, 25, av. Ozier, 07300 Mauves,
tel. 04.75.08.86.26, fax 04.75.08.49.37 ☑
⅄ by appt.

ALAIN PARET

420 Nuits 2001

| ■ | 4 ha | 15,400 | ⅏ | 15–23 € |

☛ Alain Paret, pl. de l'Eglise, 42520 Saint-Pierre-de-Boeuf,
tel. 04.74.87.12.09, fax 04.74.87.17.34 ☑
⅄ by appt.

CUVEE PARSIFAL 2001

| ■ | n.c. | n.c. | | 8–11 € |

☛ Cave des Vignerons de Rasteau et de Tain-l'Hermitage,
rte des Princes-d'Orange, 84110 Rasteau,
tel. 04.90.10.90.10, fax 04.90.46.16.65,
e-mail vrt@rasteau.com

Crozes-Hermitage

This appellation, which is on land that is easier to cultivate than Hermitage, extends over 11 communes around Tain-l'Hermitage. It is the largest vineyard of the northern appellations: the area of production is 1,317 ha and produced 55,025 hl. The soils, which are richer than those of the Hermitage appellation, produce less powerful, fruity wines that are better drunk young. The red wines are fairly supple and aromatic; the whites are dry and fresh, light in colour, with a floral aroma. Like the Hermitage whites, they go splendidly with freshwater fish.

DOM. BERNARD ANGE 2001★

| ■ | n.c. | 15,000 | ⅏ | 8–11 € |

This cellar was founded in 1998 on a former beach hotel on the banks of a river. It has an old-fashioned kiosk, which today is used for tastings. This was formerly the ticket office for people who used to come here by tram from Romans to dance at weekends. Times change and it is no longer cheap refreshment-stall wine that is tasted here, but instead a fine Crozes, clear and brilliant, harmonious and fleshy, that makes the taste buds dance. Rêve d'Ange 2000 red (11–15 €) also deserves its star.

☛ Bernard Ange, Pont-de-l'Herbasse, 26260 Clérieux,
tel. 04.75.71.62.42, fax 04.75.71.62.42 ☑
⅄ ev. day except Sun. 9am–7pm

M. CHAPOUTIER
Les Varonniers 2001★

■	n.c.	4,000		38–46 €

Chapoutier is constantly in search of the structure that lies at a wine's heart. This one has great ageing potential, with tannins that are still harsh on the finish. But all is as it should be: liquorice, vanilla, soft fruit (blackcurrant) and fullness in the mouth. A symphony of flavours in three or four years' time.

⚛ Maison M. Chapoutier, 18, av. du Dr-Paul-Durand, BP 38, 26601 Tain-l'Hermitage Cedex, tel. 04.75.08.28.65, fax 04.75.08.81.70, e-mail chapoutier@chapoutier.com ☑
☕ by appt.

YANN CHAVE
Tête de Cuvée 2001★★

■	4 ha	18,000	⊞	11–15 €

This estate has changed its first name. That's life: the son is now carrying the torch and has lit up the 2001 vintage with this deep garnet-red wine. Soft fruit, liquorice and leather signal good ageing. The Jury liked this wine's generosity, well-integrated woodiness and fine tannins. **Cuvée Traditionnelle 2001 red (8–11 €)** gets one star; it is well made and has plenty of length. The family can be proud of its son.

⚛ Yann Chave, La Burge, 26600 Mercurol, tel. 04.75.07.42.11, fax 04.75.07.47.34

DOM. LES CHENETS 2000★★

■	6 ha	37,000	⊞	5–8 €

A very good wine, offering very good value for money! Not too much ageing in new casks (15%) to allow room for the ripe fruit (blackcurrant, blackberry). Its spicy side comes out on the palate, which is very fleshy and has a long, harmonious finish. **Mont Rousset 2001 white (8–11 €)** is made from 100% Marsanne, chosen from old vines more than 40 years old, aged in oak casks (a third new, a third having held one wine and a third having held two). It has finesse, with floral and honeyed notes; one star.

⚛ Dom. les Chenêts, Cave Fonfrède et Berthoin, 26600 Mercurol, tel. 04.75.07.48.28, fax 04.75.07.45.60 ☑
☕ ev. day 8.30am–12 noon 2pm–6pm

CAVE DES CLAIRMONTS
Cuvée des Pionniers 2000★★

■	5 ha	14,760	⊞	8–11 €

This cellar's founding fathers, Joseph Borja and Léon Defrance, would be proud of Cuvée des Pionniers, created in 1992 to celebrate the cellar's 20th anniversary. It is a fitting tribute: a harmonious, balanced wine with plenty of length, fleshy and balanced. Ready to drink now, but it could also wait up to two years. The **Cuvée Traditionnelle 2001 red**, vat aged, impressed the Jury.

⚛ SCA Cave des Clairmonts, Vignes-Vieilles, 26600 Beaumont-Monteux, tel. 04.75.84.61.91, fax 04.75.84.56.98 ☑
☕ ev. day except Sun. 9am–12 noon 2pm–6pm; groups by appt.

CLOS LES CORNIRETS
Vieilles Vignes 2001★

■	0.83 ha	5,000	⊞	8–11 €

The Fayolle family have lived on the hills of the village of Crozes-Hermitage since 1830. Adding to the family's skills by training as an oenologist, Laurent Fayolle has had the vineyard classed as a *clos* for it is surrounded by walls. This deep ruby wine has an intense nose of red berries and the harmonious structure. Clos Les Cornirets was *coup de coeur* last year with the 2000 vintage. From the same producer, **Les Pontaix 2001 red** impressed the Jury. A fine, typical wine from which, according to the Jury, the flavours have been wrung a little too much, to the detriment of the grapes' intrinsic qualities. Wait a year to enjoy it.

⚛ Cave Fayolle Fils et Fille, 9, rue du Ruisseau, 26600 Gervans, tel. 04.75.03.33.74, fax 04.75.03.32.52, e-mail laurent@cave-fayolle.com ☑
☕ by appt.

DOM. DU COLOMBIER
Cuvée Gaby 2001★★★

■	4 ha	20,000	⊞	11–15 €

This wine is very handsome, rich and fills the mouth; it has good ageing potential. Leave it in the cellar for the time being. It is remarkably balanced, with mineral, peppery and charred hints – and what length! The main wines, **Domaine du Colombier 2001 red** and **2001 white** each receive one star. A good year for this 15 ha estate, well known to wine-lovers.

⚛ Dom. du Colombier, SCEA Viale, Mercurol, 26600 Tain-l'Hermitage, tel. 04.75.07.44.07, fax 04.75.07.41.43 ☑
☕ by appt.

DOM. COMBIER
Clos des Grives 2001★★★

■	1 ha	3,500	⊞	15–23 €

A *coup de coeur* for sure. Both red and white were presented to the grand Jury and the white received the accolade. This organic estate offers two exceptional wines: the lovely **Clos des Grives 2001 red**, powerful and remarkably well aged with well-integrated oak and this admirably well-made white. "Exemplary," one taster said. Restrained oakiness, with freshness and toasted notes blending with floral and exotic fruit hints. Few estates can claim to have been awarded three stars twice! Readers are guaranteed good quality here.

⚛ Dom. Combier, RN 7, 26600 Pont-de-l'Isère, tel. 04.75.84.61.56, fax 04.75.84.53.43 ☑
☕ by appt.

CUILLERON-GAILLARD-VILLARD
Les Palignons 2001★

■	n.c.	3,000	⊞	15–23 €

These three winemakers decided to set up as négociants together. They are interested in organic methods but also practise sustainable agriculture. In this case, grape buying. For the moment, oakiness still masks the nuances of flavours, but this wine has everything still to come: its good substance and structure promise a fine work in the making. The Jury betted it would fulfil its potential. Wait two years at least before opening.

⚛ SARL Les Vins de Vienne, Bas-Seyssuel, 38200 Seyssuel, tel. 04.74.85.04.52, fax 04.74.31.97.55, e-mail vinsdevienne@terre-net.fr ☑
☕ by appt.

DELAS

Les Launes 2001★

| ■ | n.c. | 150,000 | ▮ ⑪ | 8–11 € |

This wine has everything it takes for ageing: good acidity and substance. The fruity nose (blackcurrant) is very elegant and the oakiness well developed, for 30% of the wine is barrel aged but this is not at all overpowering. **Les Launes 2001 white** impressed the Jury.
🕿 Delas Frères, ZA de l'Olivet,
07300 Saint-Jean-de-Muzols, tel. 04.75.08.60.30,
fax 04.75.08.53.67, e-mail f-mathis@delas.com ☑
𝕀 by appt.

DOM. DES ENTREFAUX 2001★

| ■ | 15 ha | 72,000 | ▮ ⑪ ⌖ | 8–11 € |

A new and most attractive, label adorns this bottle and we know how much pleasure this gives the estate's owners. This wine has most agreeable fruit – "Moreish" said one taster – which does not however mask the present and well-rounded tannins, or a finish that is still a little austere but which will acquire refinement with ageing. This estate was awarded *coup de coeur* last year for its 2000 vintage.
🕿 Dom. des Entrefaux, quartier de la Beaume,
26600 Chanos-Curson, tel. 04.75.07.33.38,
fax 04.75.07.35.27 ☑
𝕀 by appt.
🕿 Charles et François Tardy

LES HIRONDELLES 2000★

| ■ | 4 ha | 15,000 | ⑪ | 8–11 € |

A 26-ha estate, 23-year-old Syrah vines and ageing in large oak casks for 15 months: although a 2000 vintage, this wine is still immature, but it is rounded and supple, with good length and a leathery side to it associated with stewed ripe fruit and quality tannins. The Jury believed it has good ageing potential.
🕿 GAEC Pradelle, 26600 Chanos-Curson,
tel. 04.75.07.31.00, fax 04.75.07.35.34 ☑
𝕀 ev. day except Sun. 8am–12 noon 1.30pm–6pm

DOM. DU MURINAIS

Vieilles Vignes 2001★

| ■ | 3.5 ha | 18,000 | ⑪ | 8–11 € |

A fine Dauphiné-style house on an estate of a dozen hectares. This wine is made using five days of low-temperature pre-fermentation maceration followed by three weeks of warm maceration using only native yeast. This produces a very clean wine, with good fruit and charming roundness. **Les Amandiers 2001 red** needs to wait until the tannins have become integrated. It too gets one star.
🕿 Luc Tardy, Dom. du Murinais, quartier Champ-Bernard, 26600 Beaumont-Monteux, tel. 04.75.07.34.76,
fax 04.75.07.35.91 ☑
𝕀 by appt.

DOM. DES REMIZIERES

Cuvée Christophe 2001★★

| ■ | 1.5 ha | 8,000 | ⑪ | 8–11 € |

The grand Jury were unanimous awarding this wine *coup de coeur*. "An expressive wine of typical character," was their verdict. White flowers, mineral notes, juniper and lovely complexity on the nose, roundness and finesse in the mouth and great respect for the terroir. The **Cuvée Particulière 2001 white (5–8 €)**, also made using maceration on the skins, gets one star. **Christophe 2001 red (11–15 €)** was singled out by the Jury, but they felt it was too strongly oaked.
🕿 Cave Philippe Desmeure, rte de Romans,
26600 Mercurol, tel. 04.75.07.44.28, fax 04.75.07.45.87,
e-mail desmeure.philippe@wanadoo.fr ☑
𝕀 by appt.

DOM. DES SEPT CHEMINS 2001★

| ■ | 8 ha | 25,000 | ⑪ | 5–8 € |

Ravaged by phylloxera at the beginning of the 20th century, this large estate replanted some of its vines and also diversified into growing peach and apricot trees. Vines remain the mainstay, however. This wine is aged 12 months in cask. The palate is rounded and pleasing: it is an enjoyable wine, lacking in any aggression. Macerated red berries, damp woodland and spices give it a certain complexity and oak is well integrated. Drink as soon as the *Guide* comes out, or in a year's time.
🕿 Jean-Louis Buffière, Dom. des Sept-Chemins,
26600 Pont-de-l'Isère, tel. 04.75.84.75.55,
fax 04.75.84.62.94 ☑
𝕀 by appt.

DOM. DE THALABERT 2000★★

| ■ | 35 ha | 22,500 | ⑪ | 11–15 € |

Founded in 1834, this is a very professional concern, as this wine again demonstrates: it is brilliant, clear and ruby in colour. Ready to drink now thanks to its balance and roundness, but there is nothing to stop you keeping it for a festive season meal with a venison terrine, for example. Its quality in the nose is remarkable, with ripe red berries (blackcurrant, raspberry) heightened with a hint of spice. A treat! **Domaine Raymond Roure 2000 red (15–23 €)** was singled out by the Jury. It needs to age in the cellar.
🕿 Paul Jaboulet Aîné, Les Jalets, RN 7, 26600 La Roche-de-Glun, tel. 04.75.84.68.93, fax 04.75.84.56.14,
e-mail info@jaboulet.com
𝕀 by appt.

Wines selected but not starred

EMMANUEL DARNAUD

Mise en Bouche 2001

| ■ | 1.3 ha | 2,000 | ⑪ | 5–8 € |

🕿 Emmanuel Darnaud, 21, rue du Stade, 26600 La Roche-de-Glun, tel. 04.75.84.81.64, fax 04.75.84.81.64 ☑
𝕀 by appt.

GUYOT

Le Millepertuis 2001

| ■ | n.c. | 55,000 | ⑪ | 8–11 € |

🕿 SA Guyot, 60, montée de l'Eglise, 69440 Taluyers,
tel. 04.78.48.70.54, fax 04.78.48.77.31,
e-mail contact@vins-guyot.com ☑
𝕀 ev. day except Sun. Mon. 9am–12 noon 1.30pm–6pm

ORATORIO 2001

| ■ | n.c. | 10,000 | ▮ ⌖ | 11–15 € |

🕿 Ogier-Caves des Papes, 10, av. Louis-Pasteur, BP 75, 84232 Châteauneuf-du-Pape Cedex, tel. 04.90.39.32.32, fax 04.90.83.72.51, e-mail ogiercavesdespapes@ogier.fr ☑
𝕀 by appt.

CAVE DE TAIN L'HERMITAGE

Les Hauts du Fief 2000

| ■ | 2.8 ha | 15,000 | ⑪ | 8–11 € |

🕿 Cave de Tain-l'Hermitage, 22, rte de Larnage, BP 3, 26601 Tain-l'Hermitage Cedex, tel. 04.75.08.20.87,
fax 04.75.07.15.16,
e-mail commercial.france@cave-tain-hermitage.co ☑
𝕀 by appt.

Hermitage

The Hermitage slope is located northeast of Tain-l'Hermitage, with an excellent southerly aspect. Vine cultivation there goes back to the 4th century BC, but the origin of the appellation's name is attributed to the knight Gaspard de Sterimberg who, on his return from the Albigensian crusade in 1224, decided to withdraw from the world. He built a hermitage, cleared the land and planted vines.

The appellation covers about 135 ha. To the west, the granite soils of the Tain mountain provide an ideal terrain for producing red wines (Les Bessards). In the southeast, the soils of broken stones and loess (deposits of fine-grained, wind-blown silt and sand) are suited to producing white wines (Les Rocoules, Les Muerts).

The Hermitage red (4,238 hl in 2002) is a very big, tannic wine that is extremely aromatic and needs to be aged from five to ten years and even up to 20 years, before it develops its bouquet, which is of rare richness and quality. After so long in the bottle, it should be opened well in advance and served at between 16–18°C with game and tasty red meat. The Hermitage white (1,073 hl) (made from the Roussanne and particularly the Marsanne varieties) is a very fine wine that lacks acidity, but is supple, fleshy and very perfumed. It can be enjoyed from the first year but reaches its full expression after between five and ten years' bottle age. However, for both white and red wines, the great years can be kept for as long as 30 or 40 years.

M. CHAPOUTIER
De L'Orée 2001★★

	n.c.	8,000	▥	+76 €

Michel Chapoutier achieves excellence in Hermitage, offering three remarkable wines of which this one carried off the *coup de coeur*. It is a worthy standard-bearer for this house, whose coat of arms consists of three barrels. One Jury member called this "an adolescent wine". Its ample tannins are still very present but they do not mask the fleshiness, nor the flavours of stewed fruit, apricot, peach, spices and of honey on the finish. The Jury were unanimous that it will take 10 years for this 2001 to reach adulthood. Then, its full richness of substance will have developed.
☛ Maison M. Chapoutier, 18, av. du Dr-Paul-Durand, BP 38, 26601 Tain-l'Hermitage Cedex, tel. 04.75.08.28.65, fax 04.75.08.81.70, e-mail chapoutier@chapoutier.com ☑ ▼ by appt.

M. CHAPOUTIER
Chante-Alouette 2001★★

	n.c.	27,000	▥	30–38 €

Behind these famous labels, which bear Braille lettering, hide two very well-made wines. **Cuvée Le Pavillon 2001 red (+76 €)** was presented to the Grand Jury for a *coup de coeur*. It received two stars for its rich body and for its power which in no way masks its elegance, as did Chante-Alouette, which is unctuous on the palate and develops floral but also spicy, toasted and roasted flavours.
☛ Maison M. Chapoutier, 18, av. du Dr-Paul-Durand, BP 38, 26601 Tain-l'Hermitage Cedex, tel. 04.75.08.28.65, fax 04.75.08.81.70, e-mail chapoutier@chapoutier.com ☑ ▼ by appt.

DOM. JEAN-LOUIS CHAVE 2000★★★

	10 ha	30,333	▥	+76 €

PRODUCT OF FRANCE

Hermitage

APPELLATION HERMITAGE CONTRÔLÉE

ALC. 13% BY VOL. 750 ML

DOMAINE JEAN-LOUIS CHAVE

MISE EN BOUTEILLES A LA PROPRIÉTÉ
PROPRIÉTAIRE-VITICULTEUR · MAUVES EN ARDÈCHE · FRANCE

The Rhône can be proud of growers such as these, for they are truly world-class winemaking stars. This one is, without doubt, one of the greatest. Happy are those that can taste this wine. Sumptuously presented, it has a nose that, after aeration, gives off aromas of ripe grape harvest and intense red berries. The palate is more of a "palace," such is its richness, endowed with remarkable tannins: it manages to combine the wine's power with the finesse of its flavours. If you really want to spoil yourself, wait five years.
☛ Dom. Jean-Louis Chave, 37, av. du Saint-Joseph, 07300 Mauves, tel. 04.75.08.24.63, fax 04.75.07.14.21

DOM. JEAN-LOUIS CHAVE 2000★★

	5 ha	17,283	▥	+76 €

This wine deserves the utmost respect. The very moment it is poured into the glass, it gives of fine aromas (floral notes, lime-blossom tea and camomile). After a time, a powerful evocation of beeswax appears. Fleshy and remarkably well-structured, while remaining harmonious, warming and increasingly powerful, this Hermitage keeps on growing into its long finish. Decant and serve with fattened Bresse chicken with mushrooms.
☛ Dom. Jean-Louis Chave, 37, av. du Saint-Joseph, 07300 Mauves, tel. 04.75.08.24.63, fax 04.75.07.14.21

YANN CHAVE 2001★

	n.c.	6,300	▥	38–46 €

This estate has featured in the *Guide* for many years under the name of Bernard Chave, but from now on is known as Yann Chave. With remarkable, intense dark colour, this finely oaked wine on the nose gives off red berry notes. Do not shrink from enjoying it: embrace its generous, rounded and silky side. It should age well.
☛ Yann Chave, La Burge, 26600 Mercurol, tel. 04.75.07.42.11, fax 04.75.07.47.34

GAMBERT DE LOCHE 2000★

	2 ha	6,000	▥	30–38 €

Coup de coeur last year for the 1999 vintage, this excellent cooperative in Tain carries out malolactic fermentation in new casks. Certainly, this wine bears strong marks of oakiness, even appearing slightly astringent for a moment. But the harmony of the flavours that develop in the mouth,

passing from soft fruit to leather, is most intriguing. Wait before drinking.
🕯 Cave de Tain-l'Hermitage, 22, rte de Larnage, BP 3, 26601 Tain-l'Hermitage Cedex, tel. 04.75.08.20.87, fax 04.75.07.15.16,
e-mail commercial.france@cave-tain-hermitage.co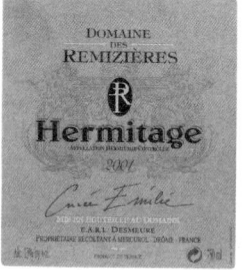
Ⴤ by appt.

PAUL JABOULET AINE
Le Chevalier de Sterimberg 2001★

	5 ha	25,900	🍷	38–46 €

A knight returning from the Crusades settled down in a hermitage in the heart of a vineyard. This label, emblematic of the AOC, could also be seen as a testament to the futility of religious wars. But that's not the point! This wine's only armour is an intense yellow colour with green glints and aromas of minerals and slightly honeyed dried grapes. The terroir is felt on the palate, but in a restrained fashion. It will take two or three years to reach its best.
🕯 Paul Jaboulet Aîné, Les Jalets, RN 7, 26600 La Roche-de-Glun, tel. 04.75.84.68.93, fax 04.75.84.56.14,
e-mail info@jaboulet.com
Ⴤ by appt.

PAUL JABOULET AINE
La Chapelle 2000★

	21 ha	87,300	🍷	46–76 €

The famous Chapelle, sought after the world over, is a wine for keeping. The 2000 vintage is no exception. It does not reveal its true face, for the moment. You must be very patient. The nose is still very immature and spices and stewed fruits (prunes, bilberries, Morello cherries) are barely perceptible. The tannins from the cask where it has spent 15 months still mask a great many things, but they raise hopes of a fine development to come.
🕯 Paul Jaboulet Aîné, Les Jalets, RN 7, 26600 La Roche-de-Glun, tel. 04.75.84.68.93, fax 04.75.84.56.14,
e-mail info@jaboulet.com
Ⴤ by appt.

ORATORIO 2001★

	n.c.	3,500	🍷	23–30 €

An oratorio that could be played on the great organs of Notre-Dame. Deep, very gamey and well concentrated, it needs aeration to release its very ripe red berries and, on the palate, a very pleasant velvety smoothness.
🕯 Ogier-Caves des Papes, 10, av. Louis-Pasteur, BP 75, 84232 Châteauneuf-du-Pape Cedex, tel. 04.90.39.32.32, fax 04.90.83.72.51,
e-mail ogiercavesdespapes@ogier.fr
Ⴤ by appt.

DOM. DES REMIZIERES
Cuvée Emilie 2001★★

	0.5 ha	3,000	🍷	23–30 €

A *coup de cœur* rewards the excellent wine produced by this estate in Hermitage. Vinified in cask (50% in new casks, 50% in one-year-old casks), it is certainly a wine for ageing. It already has intriguing complexity of flavours: white flowers, lemon, almonds, hazelnuts, roasted notes. But what is equally impressive about this wine is its length, against a supple,

unctuous background. Wait five years to allow the full bouquet of this firework display to develop.
🕯 Cave Philippe Desmeure, rte de Romans, 26600 Mercurol, tel. 04.75.07.44.28, fax 04.75.07.45.87, e-mail desmeure.philippe@wanadoo.fr
Ⴤ by appt.

DOM. DES REMIZIERES
Cuvée Emilie 2001★★

	2 ha	11,000	🍷	23–30 €

This Hermitage will be a fine wine until at least 2013. Already showing strong red berries and spices, it is perfectly balanced, powerful and elegant at the same time. The Jury noted the good ripeness of the grapes that produced this wine, which has been remarkably well aged in cask for 15 months.
🕯 Cave Philippe Desmeure, rte de Romans, 26600 Mercurol, tel. 04.75.07.44.28, fax 04.75.07.45.87,
e-mail desmeure.philippe@wanadoo.fr
Ⴤ by appt.

Lying across the river from Valence, the appellation (97.20 ha declared in 2002) covers the commune of Cornas. The granite soils, on fairly steep ground, are held in place by low walls. Cornas (3,225 hl) is a virile, well-structured wine that must be aged for at least three years (but can often wait a good deal longer) to allow it to express its fruity, spicy aromas. Serve it with red meats and game.

LOUIS BERNARD 2001★

	n.c.	3,600		15–23 €

Jean-François Ranvier, the oenologue at this négociant, is an advocate of long maceration. Here, after four weeks in vat and a time in cask, he offers a wine that is ready to drink now but which could also wait between two and four years. It has been very well made, with fine, supple, well-integrated tannins. Its bouquet is typical of Cornas, with red berries and spices.
🕯 Salavert-Les Domaines Bernard, rte de Sérignan, 84100 Orange, tel. 04.90.11.86.86, fax 04.90.34.87.30, e-mail sldb@sldb.fr

M. CHAPOUTIER 2000★

	n.c.	29,000		15–23 €

Michel Chapoutier is a passionate supporter of organic agriculture, espousing its most complete strand, known as biodynamic agriculture – while at the same time expounding anthroposophy. This might appear dauntingly complex, but it has done nothing to hinder the international development of his concern. This wine is garnet red in colour. Medium in concentration, it has blackcurrant and cherry on the attack, which then give way to gamey notes. Tannins are still pronounced, but it has plenty of body. This wine till take three years to develop fully.
🕯 Maison M. Chapoutier, 18, av. du Dr-Paul-Durand, BP 38, 26601 Tain-l'Hermitage Cedex, tel. 04.75.08.28.65, fax 04.75.08.81.70, e-mail chapoutier@chapoutier.com
Ⴤ by appt.

A. CLAPE 2001★★

	4 ha	18,000	🍷	30–38 €
76 78 85 88 **89 |90| |91| 95** 96 97 **98 99** 00 01				

Family-owned for almost 250 years, this estate is one of the beacons of French viticulture and this wine testifies to a great concern for elegance. Its time in large oak casks has given it a well-integrated quality which its still austere structure – which will mellow with time – does nothing to change. It took 12 days in tank to produce this delicious wine. This is not

Cornas

APPELLATION CORNAS CONTROLÉE

13% alc./vol.   750 ml

MIS EN BOUTEILLE A LA PROPRIÉTÉ

A. CLAPE, S.C.E.A Propriétaire-Viticulteur à CORNAS, FRANCE

excessive: the winemaker simply wanted to extract the grapes' full essence. The well-ripened grapes appear on the nose with blackberry aromas where a hint of raspberry is also discernible. This wine confirms the idea that Cornas need five to 10 years' ageing before drinking.

➥ SCEA Dom. Clape, 146, rte Nationale, 07130 Cornas, tel. 04.75.40.33.64, fax 04.75.81.01.98

⌶ by appt.

➥ Auguste et Pierre Clape

DOM. COURBIS
Les Eygats 2001★★

■	1.5 ha	7,000	⑪	30–38 €

Founded in the 16th century, this family estate has 26 ha of vines, of which 22 are on the steep hillsides that give the Rhône landscape its characteristic beauty. Perfectly put together, this wine has excellent ageing potential, being very rich and very modern. Given that the endless battle between traditionalists and modernizers shows no sigh of abating, purists of this appellation might consider it atypical; but all tasters will acknowledge its dark, sumptuous colour and powerful nose where spices, damp woodland and underlying fruit all mingle. The palate is concentrated but fleshy, well-structured and dense.

➥ Dom. Courbis, rte de Saint-Romain, 07130 Châteaubourg, tel. 04.75.81.81.60, fax 04.75.40.25.39, e-mail domaine-courbis@wanadoo.fr Ⓥ

⌶ by appt.

CUILLERON-GAILLARD-VILLARD
Les Barcillants 2001★

■	n.c.	8,000	⑪	23–30 €

Three excellent winemakers joined forces to found this négociant, buying the grapes but vinifying their own *cuvées*. Balanced structure, with good acidity and very present tannins (grapes and cask), promises good ageing over the next four or five years. The nose is already fine and intense, being spicy and lightly toasted, with red berries (redcurrant, bilberry). A dead cert!

➥ SARL Les Vins de Vienne, Bas-Seyssuel, 38200 Seyssuel, tel. 04.74.85.04.52, fax 04.74.31.97.55, e-mail vinsdevienne@terre-net.fr Ⓥ

⌶ by appt.

DELAS
Chante-Perdrix 2000★

■	n.c.	10,000	■⑪♦	15–23 €

The technical director of the Delas firm, which was founded in 1835, is from Burgundy and the firm itself is owned by the Deutz champagne house, which belongs to the Roederer group. But the wine is a true Rhône. Very elegant, its attack is instant, with blackcurrant that you can chew. But be patient: it takes time for the notes of liquorice and pepper to develop. The Jury liked this wine for its finesse.

➥ Delas Frères, ZA de l'Olivet, 07300 Saint-Jean-de-Muzols, tel. 04.75.08.60.30, fax 04.75.08.53.67, e-mail f-mathis@delas.com Ⓥ

⌶ by appt.

DUMIEN-SERRETTE
Patou Cuvée Vieilles Vignes 2001★

■	1.8 ha	5,000	⑪	11–15 €

A very small estate, but a fine wine already – and it is the cheapest of the Cornas listed here. It is typical of the appellation, both for its young colour, with violet glints and for its rich flavours where ripe fruit mingles with spice (vanilla, liquorice). It has good complexity over a fleshy, well-structured body.

➥ Dumien-Serrette, 18, rue du Ruisseau, 07130 Cornas, tel. 04.75.40.41.91, fax 04.75.40.41.91, e-mail contact@serrette.com Ⓥ

⌶ by appt.

ERIC ET JOEL DURAND 2001★★

■	2.5 ha	11,500	⑪	15–23 €

Châteaubourg is on the right bank of the Rhône, between Saint-Péray and Tournon. The grapes – de-stemmed and aged 12 months in cask after 25 days' fermentation – have produced a typically Cornas wine, even if for the moment it appears very oaked. Powerful and fleshy, it has balance and harmony. It has a fine nose, where oaky touches are present without being overbearing and are accompanied by a blend of red berries and gamey notes. It will age for a long time.

➥ Eric et Joël Durand, 6, imp. de la Fontaine, 07130 Châteaubourg, tel. 04.75.40.46.78, fax 04.75.40.29.77 Ⓥ

⌶ by appt.

Wines selected but not starred

DOM. J. DESPESSE
Les Côtes 2001

■	0.25 ha	1,800	⑪	11–15 €

➥ Dom. J. Despesse, 10, Basses-Rues, 07130 Cornas, tel. 04.75.80.03.54, fax 04.75.80.03.26 Ⓥ

⌶ by appt.

DOM. DU TUNNEL
Cuvée Prestige 2001

■	1.5 ha	2,800	⑪	15–23 €

➥ Stéphane Robert, 20, rue de la République, 07130 Saint-Péray, tel. 04.75.80.04.66 Ⓥ

⌶ ev. day except Sun. 2pm–8pm

Saint-Péray

Situated on the opposite bank of the river from Valence, the vineyard of Saint-Péray (59 ha, 2,110 hl in 2002) is dominated by the ruined Château de Crussol. Saint-Péray has a relatively cooler micro-climate and richer soils than elsewhere in the region, producing white wines that are more acid, drier and lower in alcohol, but ideal for making sparkling blanc de blancs by the *méthode traditionelle*, or champagne method. This, the main type of wine made under this appellation, is one of the best sparkling wines in France.

RHONE

DOM. DARONA PERE ET FILS

Demi-sec 1997★

	1 ha	5,000	■	8–11 €

Lovely fine bubbles appear in this yellow wine with golden glints. What is surprising is the palate, which is more expressive than the nose. But the customer is unlikely to complain. The palate has a sweet side to it (this is nominally a medium-dry wine) and presents floral flavours with dried fruit notes. The finish gives the impression of fruit-flavoured sweets. Serve with tarte Tatin, for example.

🍷 Dom. Darona Père et Fils, Les Faures, 07130 Saint-Péray, tel. 04.75.40.34.11, fax 04.75.81.05.70 ■
🍸 by appt.
🍷 Guy Darona

DOM. BERNARD GRIPA

Les Figuiers 2001★★

	0.8 ha	3,000	◫	11–15 €

A blend of Roussanne (60%) and Marsanne (40%) gives a fine balance to this pale yellow with golden, straw-coloured glints. Roasted aromas (roasted coffee) testify to its time in cask. The palate then develops notes of white fruit (peach), stewed quince and caramel. A good wine from this grower, which has also had success with its Saint-Joseph wines.

🍷 Dom. Bernard Gripa, 5, av. Ozier, 07300 Mauves, tel. 04.75.08.14.96, fax 04.75.07.06.81 ■
🍸 by appt.

PAUL JABOULET AINE

Les Sauvagères 2001★

	1.27 ha	n.c.		8–11 €

Pure, de-stemmed Marsanne is vinified in new oak casks. The colour is brilliant pale yellow with green glints. The nose is not yet completely open, but the Jury were struck by the balance and fleshiness of this wine with its toasted aromas.

🍷 Paul Jaboulet Aîné, Les Jalets, RN 7, 26600 La Roche-de-Glun, tel. 04.75.84.68.93, fax 04.75.84.56.14, e-mail info@jaboulet.com ■
🍸 by appt.

Wines selected but not starred

LES VIGNERONS REUNIS DE TAIN-L'HERMITAGE Brut

	n.c.	n.c.	■ ♦	5–8 €

🍷 Cave des Vignerons de Rasteau et de Tain-l'Hermitage, rte des Princes-d'Orange, 84110 Rasteau, tel. 04.90.10.90.10, fax 04.90.46.16.65, e-mail vrt@rasteau.com

Gigondas

The famous Gigondas vineyard, at the foot of the breath-taking Dentelles de Montmirail mountains, covers a series of slopes and valleys within the commune of Gigondas itself. Winemaking here is a very ancient tradition, but its real development dates from the 19th century (the vineyards of le Colombier and les Bosquets), greatly assisted by Eugène Raspail. Gigondas was originally classed as a Côtes du Rhône, then in 1966 a Côtes du Rhône-Villages, until it finally obtained its "letters patent" in 1971, when it became a specific appellation. Today it covers 1,244 ha, of which 1,217 were declared in 2002 with a production of 33,912 hl.

Soil and climate combine to make Gigondas red wines (41,310 hl in 2001), very rich in alcohol, powerful, well-structured and well-balanced, with fine aromas of liquorice, spices and stone fruits. The wines develop slowly in the bottle and can retain their qualities for many years, making a very suitable accompaniment to game dishes. Gigondas rosés are powerful and heady in character.

LA BASTIDE SAINT VINCENT 2001★

	6 ha	14,000	■ ♦	8–11 €

This estate is one of the Rhône valley's landmarks and very rarely fails to make it into the *Guide*. Its 2001 wine is light and fresh, with red berry aromas – particularly pleasant and well structured. The colour is pleasing and the whole appetizing.

🍷 Laurent Daniel, La Bastide Saint Vincent, rte de Vaison-la-Romaine, 84150 Violès, tel. 04.90.70.94.13, fax 04.90.70.96.13, e-mail bastide.vincent@free.fr ■
🍸 ev. day except Sun. 9am–12 noon 2pm–6pm; cl. 10 Sep.–10 Oct.

DOM. DE BOISSAN

Vieilles Vignes 2001★

	4 ha	40,000	■ ◫	8–11 €

Though seductive with its deep, limpid colour, this wine is timid on the nose at first, before swirling in the glass reveals good complexity with aromas of liquorice, red berries, cocoa and wild strawberries. The perfect harmony between tannins and red berries produces balance and power. A most harmonious bottle.

🍷 Christian Bonfils, Dom. de Boissan, 84110 Sablet, tel. 04.90.46.93.30, fax 04.90.46.99.46, e-mail c.bonfils@wanadoo.fr ■
🍸 by appt.

DOM. DES BOSQUETS

Préférence 2001★★★

	2 ha	6,500	■	23–30 €

This aptly-named wine was certainly the preference of the Jury. The eye is struck by the very deep purple colour. The nose is open and complex, giving off aromas of soft fruit, vanilla and liquorice. The palate is powerful and balanced, with fine tannins and good harmony, bearing witness to skilled harvesting. This wine has fine potential and can be aged five to eight years in the cellar. The estate's **Cuvée Principale 2001 red (11–15 €)** impressed with its roundness. An attractive, rewarding wine: drink with the cheese board.

🍷 Dom. des Bosquets, 84190 Gigondas, tel. 04.90.65.80.45 ■
🍸 by appt.
🍷 Famille Bréchet

DOM. BRUSSET

Tradition Le Grand Montmirail 2001★★

	12 ha	38,000	■ ◫	11–15 €

Two wines have been selected from this 87 ha estate at Cairanne. Le Grand Montmirail, a solidly-built wine with excellently integrated oak, was particularly appreciated by the Jury. On the palate, tannins are present but silky and pleasantly integrated. A refined wine typical of its type; serve with wild boar. **Les Hauts de Montmirail red 2001 Elevé en Fût de Chêne (15–23 €)**, powerful and expressive, gets one star. Wait a few years before opening.

🍷 SA Dom. Brusset, Le Village, 84290 Cairanne, tel. 04.90.30.82.16, fax 04.90.30.73.31 ■
🍸 by appt.

DOM. DU CAYRON 2001★

	16 ha	65,000	🍷	11–15 €

This wine has a dark colour and a nose of stewed soft fruit where notes of damp woodland and liquorice mingle. Syrah seems to have the upper hand, then Grenache appears on the palate, with very ripe fruit and truffle flavours. Cinsault (5% of the blend) makes itself known discreetly. There is complexity and finesse wins the day. A very harmonious bottle, which is best kept before opening.
↝ Michel Faraud, Dom. du Cayron, 84190 Gigondas, tel. 04.90.65.87.46, fax 04.90.65.88.81 ☑
☐ by appt.

CUILLERON-GAILLARD-VILLARD

Les Pimpignoles 2001★

	n.c.	5,300	🍷	15–23 €

A lovely négociant wine, to be forgotten in the cellar for three years. On the nose it initially displays the intensity and power characteristic of this kind of wine. Very persistent oakiness is perfectly controlled. Fullness on the palate bodes very well for this wine's future development.
↝ SARL Les Vins de Vienne, Bas-Seyssuel, 38200 Seyssuel, tel. 04.74.85.04.52, fax 04.74.31.97.55, e-mail vinsdevienne@terre-net.fr ☑
☐ by appt.

CUVEE DES CARIATIDES

Les Grandes Cuvées 2001★

	8 ha	30,000	🍷 ⚖	11–15 €

Botticelli's *Allegory of Spring* adorns the label of this wine, one of Gabriel Meffre's range of Grandes Cuvées which, once again, is aptly named. The highly complex bouquet immediately makes itself known, with red berries, spices and gamey notes. A robust wine whose rich tannins will take time to achieve harmony.
↝ Christian Meffre, Le Village, 84190 Gigondas, tel. 04.90.12.32.42, fax 04.90.12.32.49

GIGONDAS LA CAVE

Signature Accords en sol majeur 2000★★

	34 ha	200,000	🍷	8–11 €

G major chords? Well, perhaps. At all events this wine's aromas (liquorice, cocoa, spices, pepper, peaches and apricots) are all in harmony. The palate, slightly astringent on the attack, then reveals roundness and fine unctuousness with agreeable tannins. A good combination of softness and structure that is well worthy of a signature.
↝ Gigondas La Cave, Les Blaches, 84190 Gigondas, tel. 04.90.65.86.27, fax 04.90.65.80.13, e-mail gigondas.lacave@wanadoo.fr ☑
☐ by appt.

DOM. GIROUSSE 2001★

	1.36 ha	4,900	🍷	11–15 €

This estate's small area (1.36 ha) allows its owner, Benoît Girousse, to carry out all the tasks of viticulture himself, by hand. Judging by this typically Gigondas wine, he does it well. Intense red berry, vanilla and liquorice aromas mingle harmoniously with well-integrated oakiness. The careful oak-ageing is noticeable on the nose as on the palate. Tannins are present and silky. The whole displays a powerful balance. Serve with leg of lamb.
↝ Girousse, Le Cours, 84410 Bedoin, tel. 04.90.12.81.47 ☑
☐ by appt.

DOM. DU GRAND BOURJASSOT

Cuvée Cécile 2001★★

	1 ha	4,500	🍷 🍷	8–11 €

Just 1 ha is devoted to making Cuvée Cécile, a classic blend from old Syrah and Grenache vines. Ripe soft fruit, spices, vanilla and charred notes give off pleasant aromas. The palate is a treat: long and full, it rests on silky tannins and skilfully controlled oakiness. A harmonious, complex wine, to bring up from the cellar in five to eight years' time.

↝ Pierre Varenne, Dom. du Grand Bourjassot, quartier Les Parties, 84190 Gigondas, tel. 04.90.65.88.80, fax 04.90.65.89.38 ☑
☐ ev. day except Sun. 10am–12 noon 2.30pm–6.30pm

DOM. GRAND ROMANE 2001★

	40 ha	85,000	🍷	8–11 €

Long maceration after partial de-stemming, followed by ageing in cask and large barrels, produce a nose which is intensely oaky at first and then gives way to fruit aromas (blackcurrant, bilberry). Tannins are fine and overall balance asserts itself over sound length. A few years' ageing will do the rest.
↝ SCEA de Gigondas, Dom. Grand Romane, 84190 Gigondas, tel. 04.90.65.85.90, fax 04.90.65.82.14, e-mail grand.romane@pierre-amadieu.com ☑
☐ by appt.
↝ Claude Amadieu

DOM. DU GRAPILLON D'OR

Elevé en vieux foudre 2001★★★

	14 ha	60,000	🍾 🍷 ⚖	11–15 €

An aptly-named wine, for it wins three stars and a *coup de cœur* from a delighted Jury. The secret of its success lies in the skill of picking grapes at the right degree of ripeness. The intense, complex and refined bouquet gives off fresh fruit and liquorice, which mingle harmoniously. But it was the palate that won over the Jury: intense and balanced, with well-integrated oakiness, it was universally judged to be superb. This dazzling, noble, Gigondas has remarkable density. In six years' time it can be enjoyed with woodcock brochettes or stewed woodpigeons.
↝ Bernard Chauvet, Le Péage, 84190 Gigondas, tel. 04.90.65.86.37, fax 04.90.65.82.99 ☑
☐ ev. day 9am–12 noon 2pm–5.30pm

DOM. NOTRE DAME DES PALLIERES

Cuvée Fût neuf 2000★

	4 ha	10,000	🍷	11–15 €

Two wines from this Gigondas estate are listed. The intense, charming bouquet of the 2000 vintage gives off red berries and spices, with some subtle smoky and oaky notes (from new casks). The structure on the palate is up to the nose: fleshiness, unctuousness and length promise good quality (five years). The **2002 rosé (5–8 €)** impressed the Jury. It was very fresh strawberry and raspberry notes, with fleshiness and roundness.
↝ Jean-Pierre et Claude Roux, chem. des Tuileries, 84190 Gigondas, tel. 04.90.65.83.03, fax 04.90.65.83.03, e-mail n.d-pallieres@wanadoo.fr ☑
☐ by appt.

L'OUSTAU FAUQUET

Cuvée Cigaloun 2001★★

	4 ha	14,000	🍾 ⚖	8–11 €

Cuvée Cigaloun was *coup de cœur* in the 2002 *Guide*, with a 99! The 2001 vintage is no less deserving. Blackcurrant and cherry develop their aromas in a powerful, complex, full nose. The palate confirms these sensations with even more depth, warmth and roundness. A fine representative of Gigondas. "This wine is a pleasure to drink," wrote one taster.

🕿 Roger Combe et Filles, Dom. La Fourmone, rte de Bollène, 84190 Vacqueyras, tel. 04.90.65.86.05, fax 04.90.65.87.84, e-mail domaine.fourmone@wanadoo.fr ⚅

☕ ev. day except Sun. 9.30am–12 noon 2pm–6pm; cl. Feb.

DOM. LE PEAGE 2001★

| | 15 ha | 70,000 | ▮ | 11–15 € |

In 1989 Sabine Saurel, who worked in a bank, decided to take over at the helm of her grandfather's estate. Today, she devotes her talents to it, producing lovely wines such as this one, with its deep red colour. The gamey nose, with its hints of chocolate, liquorice, laurel, thyme, red berries and leather, shows signs of development. Its powerful, even slightly rustic, structure produces a result endowed with some finesse nevertheless. A wine typical of the appellation; wait a few years before drinking.

🕿 Sabine Saurel, La Beaumette, 84190 Gigondas, tel. 04.90.70.96.80, fax 04.90.70.96.80, e-mail saurelchauvet@wanadoo.fr ⚅

☕ by appt.

DOM. DU PRADAS 2001★★

| | 4.5 ha | 20,000 | | 8–11 € |

A small estate (4.5 ha) certainly, but a wine of great potential. This 2001 vintage plays powerfully on a spicy theme. Fruit brings a note of freshness. The complexity and strength of the tannins combine perfectly to give immediate pleasure – but this will be greater if you can wait – longer than it takes to cook a good game dish.

🕿 Dom. du Pradas, 84190 Gigondas, tel. 04.90.62.94.28 ⚅

🕿 Sylvie Cottet

JEROME QUIOT 2001★

| | n.c. | 12,000 | ▮ ⚬ | 11–15 € |

Jérôme Quiot, négociant and grower in Châteauneuf-du-Pape, offers a wine with a garnet-red colour, that has an interesting personal note on the nose because of the ripeness of the Grenache and the presence of several secondary varieties (Mourvèdre, Syrah, Clairette and Cinsault). Length on the palate prolongs balanced tannin structure. This wine is a good representative of its year. "Serve, in a few years' time, with fillet of beef cooked with Roquefort," suggested one taster.

🕿 Sélection Jérôme Quiot, av. Baron-Le-Roy, BP 38, 84231 Châteauneuf-du-Pape Cedex, tel. 04.90.83.73.55, fax 04.90.83.78.48, e-mail vignobles@jeromequiot.com

DOM. RASPAIL-AY 2001★

| | 16.2 ha | 50,000 | ⬤ | 8–11 € |

After a moment's hesitation the aromas are released: spices, truffle, stewed fruit, very ripe fruit, peaches and apricots. They reappear on the palate against a background of blackcurrant and pepper, which lingers long. This wine's balance is founded on power and complexity. A fine example of the Gigondas terroir.

🕿 Dominique Ay, Dom. Raspail-Ay, 84190 Gigondas, tel. 04.90.65.83.01, fax 04.90.65.89.55 ⚅ 🏠

☕ by appt.

CH. REDORTIER 2001★★

| | 5 ha | 20,000 | ▮ | 11–15 € |

Climb up to Suzette, a hill village that overlooks Beaumes-de-Venise and its vineyards and make a detour to Château Redortier, whose Gigondas impressed the Jury. The nose is expressive, marked by red berries, stewed fruit, cinnamon and mushroom. The palate is full, rounded and with good length, with fruit hints and well-rounded tannins that contribute to the harmony of the whole. A wine to drink in 10 years' time. With it, would you choose thrushes or venison steak?

🕿 EARL Ch. Redortier, 84190 Suzette, tel. 04.90.62.96.43, fax 04.90.65.03.38 ⚅

☕ ev. day 10am–12 noon 2pm–7pm

🕿 S. et I. de Menthon

DOM. DU ROUCAS DE SAINT-PIERRE

Le Coteau de mon rêve 2001★

| | n.c. | 21,000 | | 8–11 € |

At just over 20 years old, this estate is in the prime of life. It offers prettily-named wine Le Coteau de Mon Rêve (Hill of my Dreams). It has a nose of great richness: fine, almost refined, with mineral, spice (cinnamon), roasted, *pain d'épice* and wild plum notes. Volume, warmth, balance and elegance produce a charming wine, to enjoy with fine cooking. Why not a trotter with morel mushrooms, or a boletus mushroom fricassée?

🕿 Dom. du Roucas de Saint-Pierre, 84190 Gigondas, tel. 06.10.44.02.98, fax 04.90.65.89.23 ⚅

☕ by appt.

🕿 Yves Chéron

SAINT-DAMIEN

Cuvée Les Souteyrades 2001★★

| | 3.5 ha | 7,000 | ▮ ⬤ | 11–15 € |

Quality and consistency seem to be the motto of this estate which, as last year, was awarded a *coup de coeur* by the Jury. This blend of Grenache (80%) and Mourvèdre (20%), with its long, powerful finish, shows the signs of technical skill. A magnificent red colour and deep tar on the nose suggest this fine-textured wine should be aged for five years. The **Cuvée Principale 2001 red (8–11 €)** gets one star for its intense fruit dominated by cherry and raspberry. The good attack is backed up by a clean, rounded, spicy palate. The **Cuvée Classique 2001 red (8–11 €)**, which is aptly named, recalls the traditional wines of former times. It impressed the Jury. Three wines bearing the name of St Damien, patron saint of physicians and surgeons – but to be drunk in moderation nevertheless!

🕿 Joël Saurel, Dom. Saint-Damien, 84190 Gigondas, tel. 04.90.70.96.42, fax 04.90.70.96.42 ⚅

☕ by appt.

DOM. SAINT-GAYAN

Fontmaria 2001★★

| | 1 ha | 2,000 | ⬤ | 15–23 € |

Coup de coeur in the last edition of the *Guide*, Fontmaria retains its position with the 2001 vintage, which was judged to be remarkable. The bouquet shows signs of very mature grapes and develops a palette of aromas that includes cherry jam, garrigue and spices. Some find this wine still a little austere, but the oak is well integrated and the structure well put together. A very fine wine, to be enjoyed with a beef stew. The **Cuvée Traditionnelle 2001 red (11–15 €)**, more floral on the nose, has finesse, even though tasters described it as robust. It was awarded one star.

🕿 SCEA Jean-Pierre et Martine Meffre, Dom. Saint-Gayan 84190 Gigondas, tel. 04.90.65.86.33, fax 04.90.65.85.10, e-mail martine@saintgayan.com ⚅

☕ by appt.

DOM. LES TEYSSONNIERES 2001★

| | 8.5 ha | 35,000 | ▮ ⬤ ⚬ | 8–11 € |

A few of the vines on this estate founded in 1838 did not succumb to phylloxera. Those used to make this wine are 80 years old. It offers a magnificent bouquet of prunes, kirsch and spices, which reveals strong Grenache character. It is

harmonious and has good length. The terroir's personality comes through particularly well.
☛ Franck Alexandre, Dom. Les Teyssonnières, 84190 Gigondas, tel. 04.90.12.31.31, fax 04.90.12.31.32, e-mail domaine.lesteyssonnieres@wanadoo.fr ✅
Ⓣ ev. day except Sun. 8am–1pm 2pm–7pm

CH. DU TRIGNON 2001★

| ■ | 24 ha | 85,000 | 🍶 ⑪ | 11–15 € |

A family estate for the last five generations, this became part of the Gigondas appellation in the 1960s. The grapes are harvested by hand and sorted, showing great care is taken with the raw material for this wine. The result is a very effective expression of the garrigue, with rosemary, cyste and sage aromas. The palate is mineral and balsamic, but red berries have the last word. This wine shows great personality and could be enjoyed with pheasant or quail, according to taste.
☛ Ch. du Trignon, 84190 Gigondas, tel. 04.90.46.90.27, fax 04.90.46.98.63, e-mail trignon@chateau-du-trignon.com
Ⓣ ev. day 9am–12 noon 2pm–7pm
☛ Pascal Roux

DOM. VARENNE

Vieux fût 2001★★

| ■ | 1.4 ha | 6,500 | ⑪ | 11–15 € |

Old casks make the best wine, or so one is tempted to conclude on tasting Vieux Fût. Tasters were charmed by the bouquet's highly original mineral character. A powerful but fine and complex nose with well-integrated oakiness. On the palate, the oak gives way after a time to a refined structure and remarkable length of flavour.
☛ Dom. Varenne, Le Petit Chemin, 84190 Gigondas, tel. 04.90.65.85.55, fax 04.90.12.39.28 ✅

VIEUX CLOCHER 2000★

| ■ | 3 ha | 13,000 | 🍶 ⑪ ♦ | 8–11 € |

This négociant in Vacqueyras offers rooms, gîte and of course wine – notably one with deep colour heightened by shades of mahogany. A trio of aromas – spices, musk and fruit – is given off on the nose. The palate is fresh on the attack, already showing itself to be almost fully developed. There is fleshiness, roundness and remarkable power.
☛ Arnoux et Fils, Portail Neuf, 84190 Vacqueyras, tel. 04.90.65.84.18, fax 04.90.65.80.07 ✅ 🏠 🏠
Ⓣ ev. day except Sun. 8am–12 noon 2pm–6pm

Wines selected but not starred

DOM. DE LA BOUISSIERE

Cuvée Tradition 2001

| ■ | 5 ha | 20,000 | 🍶 ⑪ | 11–15 € |

☛ EARL Faravel, rue du Portail, 84190 Gigondas, tel. 04.90.65.87.91, fax 04.90.65.82.16, e-mail labouissiere@aol.com ✅
Ⓣ ev. day 9am–12 noon 3pm–7pm

DOM. DE CABASSE 2000

| ■ | 3 ha | 12,000 | ⑪ | 11–15 € |

☛ Dom. de Cabasse, 84110 Séguret, tel. 04.90.46.91.12, fax 04.90.46.94.01, e-mail info@domaine-de-cabasse.fr ✅
Ⓣ by appt.
☛ Alfred Haeni

DOM. DE LA DAYSSE 2001

| ■ | 15 ha | 60,000 | 🍶 ♦ | 11–15 € |

☛ SCEA Domaines Jack Meffre et Fils, 84190 Gigondas, tel. 04.90.12.32.42, fax 04.90.12.32.49

DUC DE MAYREUIL 2000

| ■ | n.c. | 70,000 | ⑪ | 8–11 € |

☛ Ogier-Caves des Papes, 10, av. Louis-Pasteur, BP 75, 84232 Châteauneuf-du-Pape Cedex, tel. 04.90.39.32.32, fax 04.90.83.72.51, e-mail ogiercavesdespapes@ogier.fr ✅

DUC DE MONTFORT 2000

| ■ | n.c. | n.c. | ⑪ | 11–15 € |

☛ Maison Bouachon, av. Pierre-de-Luxembourg, 84230 Châteauneuf-du-Pape, tel. 04.90.83.58.37, fax 04.90.83.77.23 ✅
Ⓣ ev. day 9am–12 noon 2pm–7pm; cl. 15 Jan.–15 Feb.

DOM. GONDRAN 2001

| ■ | n.c. | 8,000 | 🍶 ♦ | 8–11 € |

☛ Cellier de l'Enclave des Papes, rte d'Orange, BP 51, 84602 Valréas Cedex, tel. 04.90.41.91.42, fax 04.90.41.90.21, e-mail france@enclavedespapes.com

DOM. DU GRAND MONTMIRAIL

Cuvée Vieilles Vignes 2001

| ■ | 10 ha | 40,000 | | 8–11 € |

☛ Dom. du Grand Montmirail, 84190 Gigondas, tel. 04.90.62.94.28, fax 04.90.65.89.23 ✅
Ⓣ by appt.
☛ Denis Chéron

DOM. DU POURRA 2002

| ■ | 8.5 ha | 6,000 | | 8–11 € |

☛ J.-C. Mayordome, Dom. du Pourra, rte de Vaison, 84110 Sablet, tel. 04.90.46.93.59, fax 04.90.46.98.71, e-mail domaine.du.pourra@wanadoo.fr ✅
Ⓣ by appt.

CH. RASPAIL 2001

| ■ | 42 ha | 30,000 | 🍶 | 8–11 € |

☛ Christian Meffre, Ch. Raspail, 84190 Gigondas, tel. 04.90.65.88.93, fax 04.90.65.88.96, e-mail chateau.raspail@wanadoo.fr ✅ 🏠
Ⓣ by appt.

DOM. DU TERME 2000

| ■ | 10 ha | 40,000 | 🍶 ⑪ ♦ | 8–11 € |

☛ Rolland Gaudin, Dom. du Terme, 84190 Gigondas, tel. 04.90.65.86.75, fax 04.90.65.80.29, e-mail domaine.terme@free.fr ✅ 🏠
Ⓣ ev. day 10am–12 noon 2pm–6pm; Jan. Feb. by appt.

DOM. DE LA TOURADE

Cuvée Morgan 2000

| ■ | 1.14 ha | 5,300 | ⑪ | 15–23 € |

☛ EARL André Richard, Dom. de La Tourade, 84190 Gigondas, tel. 04.90.70.91.09, fax 04.90.70.96.31, e-mail tourade@aol.com ✅
Ⓣ ev. day 9am–7pm

DOM. DES TOURELLES 2001

| ■ | 9 ha | 29,000 | 🍶 ⑪ | 11–15 € |

☛ Roger Cuillerat, Dom. des Tourelles, 84190 Gigondas, tel. 04.90.65.86.98, fax 04.90.65.89.47, e-mail domaine-des-tourelles@wanadoo.fr ✅
Ⓣ by appt.

Vacqueyras

The Appellation d'Origine Contrôlée Vacqueyras, made according to conditions of production defined in the decree of 9 August 1990, is the 13th and most recent of the local AOCs of the Côtes du Rhône.

It competes with Gigondas and Châteauneuf-du-Pape in the hierarchy of the Vaucluse *département*. Lying between Gigondas to the north and Beaumes-de-Venise to the southeast, the territory it covers stretches over the two communes of Vacqueyras and Sarrians. The 1,298 ha of vines produced a little more than 43,948 hl of wine in 2002, including 542 hl of white wine.

Twenty-three bottlers, a Cave Coopérative and three merchant growers sell 1.5 million bottles of Vacqueyras annually.

The red wines (95% of production), made mainly from Grenache, Syrah, Mourvèdre and Cinsault, are capable of ageing (three to ten years). The rosés (4% of production) are from the same varieties. The whites remain less well known (varieties: Clairette, Grenache Blanc, Bourboulenc, Rousanne).

DOM. DES AMOURIERS
Les Genestes 2001★★

	3 ha	10,000	▮ ♦		11–15 €

A family of Polish origin runs this 22 ha estate, chosen for its Les Genestes wine. Already subtle and fine, it will soon be especially rich. Initially, floral, vanilla and liquorice notes mingle with garrigue and gentle spices. Roundness and fleshiness then come to the fore, powerfully yet elegantly. Its development will be impressive.
☛ Indivision Chudzikiewicz, Les Garrigues, Dom. des Amouriers, 84260 Sarrians, tel. 04.90.65.83.22, fax 04.90.65.84.13 ▼
ꝏ by appt.

DOM. LA BOUISSIERE 2001★

	2 ha	5,600	ⅢⅠ		11–15 €

For their first wine in this appellation, this is a success. Concentration is the watchword of this 2001 vintage. The nose is intense, oaky and floral, preparing the taster for an impressive palate. Full, fleshy and substantial, this wine should be aged for a few years to give the tannins time to become more rounded.
☛ EARL Faravel, rue du Portail, 84190 Gigondas, tel. 04.90.65.87.91, fax 04.90.65.82.16,
e-mail labouissiere@aol.com ▼
ꝏ ev. day 9am–12 noon 3pm–7pm

DOM. DE LA BRUNELY
Elevé en fût de chêne 2001★★

	n.c.	14,000	▮ⅢⅠ♦		5–8 €

A silver unicorn on a blue background is the coat of arms of this estate, whose oak-aged wine charmed the Jury. Before tasting, admire the magnificent colour with deep glints. Red berries, soft fruit and oaky notes alternate pleasantly on the nose. Tannins are velvety but very present. The palate is powerful, but not ostentatiously so. Length of flavour is that of a great wine, as is its fine overall harmony.
☛ Anne et Charles Carichon, Dom. de La Brunély, 84260 Sarrians, tel. 04.90.65.41.24, fax 04.90.65.30.60,
e-mail charles-carichon@terre-net.fr ▼
ꝏ ev. day except Sun. 8am–12 noon 2pm–5pm

CALVET 2001★

	n.c.	n.c.	▮ ♦		5–8 €

A highly classic colour is followed by an elegant nose. Soft fruit mingles with marshmallow and some gamey notes. Although charmingly rounded, this wine is not very long – but its balance and fleshiness are fully worthy of Vacqueyras.
☛ Calvet, 75, cours du Médoc, BP 11, 33028 Bordeaux Cedex, tel. 05.56.43.59.00, fax 05.56.43.17.78,
e-mail calvet@calvet.com ▼

DOM. DE LA CHARBONNIERE 2001★★

	4.33 ha	20,000	▮ⅢⅠ♦		11–15 €

For the fifth year running the Vacqueyras of the Charbonnière estate has been listed by the Jury. With two stars, it is out in front. Soft fruit and spice aromas mingle with gamey notes to give off an expressive bouquet. But it is the velvetiness of the tannins that wins the day over this wine's other qualities. Warmth, alcohol and the smoothness of glycerol blend elegantly.
☛ Michel Maret, Dom. de La Charbonnière, 26, rte de Courthézon, 84230 Châteauneuf-du-Pape, tel. 04.90.83.74.59, fax 04.90.83.53.46,
e-mail maret-charbonnière@club-internet.fr ▼
ꝏ by appt.

DOM. LE CLOS DES CAZAUX
Réserve 2001★

	3.5 ha	15,000	▮ ♦		5–8 €

Coup de coeur notably in the last edition of the *Guide*, this estate, which has been organic since 1989, returns this year with a strongly structured but nevertheless silky and unctuous wine. The traditional aromas of fruit are accompanied by attractive notes of new leather. Grenache, the region's ruling grape variety, expresses its full character in its favoured terroir, making this wine an absolutely typical Vacqueyras.
☛ EARL Archimbaud-Vache, Dom. Le Clos des Cazaux, 84190 Vacqueyras, tel. 04.90.65.85.83, fax 04.90.65.83.94,
e-mail closdescazaux@wanadoo.fr ▼
ꝏ ev. day except Sun. 9am–11.30am 2pm–5.30pm
☛ Maurice Vache

DOM. DE L'ESPIGOUETTE 2000★

	1.8 ha	9,000	▮ⅢⅠ♦		5–8 €

A blend of Grenache and Syrah, the latter being very noticeable. Gamey and violet aromas mix pleasantly with toasted notes due to 12 months in cask. gentle spices and silky tannins produce a palate full of finesse. A balanced wine, ready to drink now.
☛ Bernard Latour, L'Espigouette, BP 6, 84150 Violès, tel. 04.90.70.95.48,
fax 04.90.70.96.06 ▼
ꝏ by appt.

DOM. LA FOURMONE
Sélection Maître de Chais 2001★

	9 ha	33,000	▮ ♦		8–11 €

Three interesting wines from this estate, which was awarded *coup de coeur* in the last edition of the *Guide*. Sélection Maître de Chais gives off pleasant spicy aromas heightened by a base of peach and apricot. Tannins are present but velvety, with balance, power and length of flavour, giving an elegant and very typical wine. One star, too, for **Fleurantine 2002 white**, a classic blend of Grenache and Clairette, which gives off a lovely bouquet of aromas (white flowers, lime-blossom tea, quince and menthol) which lingers on the palate. A fresh, aromatic delight to be drunk now. **Cuvée des Ceps d'Or 2001 red** impressed the Jury. Ready to drink now.
☛ Roger Combe et Filles, Dom. La Fourmone, rte de Bollène, 84190 Vacqueyras, tel. 04.90.65.86.05, fax 04.90.65.87.84,
e-mail domaine.fourmone@wanadoo.fr ▼
ꝏ ev. day except Sun. 9.30am–12 noon 2pm–6pm; cl. Feb.

LES GRANDS CYPRES 2001★★★

| ■ | 6.5 ha | 30,000 | ■ ♦ | 8–11 € |

LES GRANDS CYPRÈS

2001

VACQUEYRAS

APPELLATION VACQUEYRAS CONTRÔLÉE
Mis en bouteille par Gabriel Meffre, Négociant-Éleveur à Gigondas (Vse) France

13,5% vol   *GABRIEL MEFFRE*   750 ml

The Dentelles de Montmirail and hedges of cypress shelter plots of Grenache, Syrah and Cinsault from the Mistral. These produce an exceptional wine, distributed by Gabriel Meffre. The colour is intense, brilliant, garnet red. The nose is powerful and rich, with floral (violet), fruit (blackcurrant) and spice notes. Elegance, structure, power and harmony for a wine of great class, chorused the tasters. Wait two years before opening.
↠ Maison Gabriel Meffre, Le Village, 84190 Gigondas, tel. 04.90.12.32.42, fax 04.90.12.32.49

DOM. DES LAMBERTINS 2001★

| ■ | 13.99 ha | 45,000 | ■ ♦ | 8–11 € |

A regular in the *Guide* and *coup de coeur* in 1995 for a 92 wine. The 2001 struck the Jury for its expressive nose with fresh red berries. It has length and very present tannins, whose length of flavour ends on attractive notes. Drink in three years' time with red meats.
↠ EARL Dom. des Lambertins, La Grande Fontaine, 84190 Vacqueyras, tel. 04.90.65.85.54, fax 04.90.65.83.38 ☑
Ⱦ ev. day except Sun. 9.30am–12.30pm 2pm–6.30pm
↠ Gilles Lambert

LOUIS BERNARD 2001★

| ■ | n.c. | 150,000 | | 5–8 € |

This big Rhône valley négociant needs no introduction. Rigorous quality once again earns it a place in the *Guide* with this very well-made 2001 wine. The appellation's classic blend is tempered by 5% Cinsault. Spices spring out from a subtle, pleasant whole. Good tannic structure and balance guarantee this wine a choice place on the best tables.
↠ Salavert-Les domaines Bernard, rte de Sérignan, 84100 Orange, tel. 04.90.11.86.86, fax 04.90.34.87.30, e-mail sldb@sldb.fr

DOM. MAS DU BOUQUET 2001★

| ■ | 17 ha | 50,000 | | 5–8 € |

The nose gradually develops, revealing fruit, liquorice, then floral and finally spice notes. Good power on the palate, an unctuous attack and present, harmonious tannins for a wine with a future. Serve in three years' time.
↠ Cave des Vignerons de Vacqueyras, rte de Vaison, BP 1, 84190 Vacqueyras, tel. 04.90.65.84.54, fax 04.90.65.81.32, e-mail vacqueyras@vinsdutroubadour.t.m.fr ☑
Ⱦ by appt.

DOM. LA MONARDIERE

Vieilles Vignes 2001★

| ■ | 4 ha | 13,000 | | 11–15 € |

Gentle aeration is advisable to take full advantage of the spicy, particularly vanilla, notes as well as the stewed red berries of this complex aromatic palette. Full and voluptuous from the attack, this wine has well-integrated oakiness. Concentration and suppleness combine – a sign of highly skilled winemaking.
↠ Dom. la Monardière, Les Grès, 84190 Vacqueyras, tel. 04.90.65.87.20, fax 04.90.65.82.01, e-mail monardiere@wanadoo.fr ☑
Ⱦ ev. day except Sun. 10am–12 noon 2pm–6pm
↠ Christian Vache

MONTIRIUS 2001★

| ■ | 22 ha | 50,000 | ■ ♦ | 8–11 € |

This estate, which has been organic since 1996, opened a new cellar in 2002. It offers Montirius, a clever contraction of the names Manon, Justine and Marius, the children of the Saurels. This 2001 wine has been made from well-ripened, slightly overripe, grapes. Spice and truffle aromas are beginning to appear. This richness and complexity on the nose then produce a concentrated, long and particularly harmonious palate. A wine that needs to wait a few years. **Montirius 2001 red** impressed the Jury. Though more substantial, it will nevertheless please the most demanding palates.
↠ Christine et Eric Saurel, Le Deves, 84260 Sarrians, tel. 04.90.65.38.28, fax 04.90.65.48.72, e-mail montirius@wanadoo.fr ☑
Ⱦ by appt.

CH. DE MONTMIRAIL

Cuvée de l'Ermite 2001★

| ■ | 3 ha | 10,000 | ■ ♦ | 8–11 € |

This hermit does not seem to mind the company of other wines, for it is regularly listed in the *Guide*. As in the previous edition, it is made from equal parts of Syrah and Grenache and is awarded one star. It makes up for weakness on the nose by the good length of its fruit flavours (blackcurrant, raspberry, cherries in brandy). With its present tannins and warming finish, this Vacqueyras is highly representative of its appellation.
↠ SCEV Archimbaud-Bouteiller, Ch. de Montmirail, cours Stassart, BP 12, 84190 Vacqueyras, tel. 04.90.65.86.72, fax 04.90.65.81.31, e-mail archimbaud@chateau-de-montmirail.com ☑
Ⱦ ev. day except Sun. 9am–12 noon 2pm–6pm
↠ M. Archimbaud

DOM. LE SANG DES CAILLOUX

Cuvée Floureto 2001★★

| ■ | 12 ha | 30,000 | ■ ⊞ | 15–23 € |

This is one of the Rhône valley estates to be reckoned with. In the first edition of the *Guide*, in 1986, it was awarded a *coup de coeur*. Since then it has received plenty more, including one last year. With two stars, Cuvée Floureto follows this tradition of quality. It has an intense, gamey nose, dominated by Syrah (20% of the blend). This animal character resurfaces in its rounded, balanced palate. This 2001 vintage will go well with venison, preferably in two years' time.
↠ Dom. le Sang des Cailloux, rte de Vacqueyras, 84260 Sarrians, tel. 04.90.65.88.64, fax 04.90.65.88.75, e-mail le-sang-des-cailloux@wanadoo.fr ☑
Ⱦ ev. day except Sun. 2pm–6pm; mornings by appt.

DOM. DE LA VERDE 2001★

| ■ | 10 ha | 50,000 | ■ ♦ | 11–15 € |

A well-made blend of Grenache, Syrah and Mourvèdre. Tannins agreeably coat the palate. Full and balanced, the finish is clean and natural. Stewed fruit and spices reveal their flavours on the attack and last until the finish. A wine that still needs to develop, for about three years.
↠ Dom. de la Verde, 84190 Vacqueyras, tel. 04.90.65.85.91, fax 04.90.65.89.23 ☑
Ⱦ by appt.
↠ Camallonga

XAVIER VIGNON

Povidis 2000★★

| ■ | 5 ha | 15,000 | ■ ♦ | 11–15 € |

After appreciating Xavier Vignon's Povidis in Côtes du Rhône, the tasters thoroughly enjoyed it in Vacqueyras. The nose is still closed, but nevertheless hints at the power that it will produce in a few years' time. Already, kirsch, liquorice and cocoa combine happily. The palate is a paradox, both supple and tannic, fine and powerful. This wine has a robust style and needs to wait three or four years. **Xavier 2001** was also singled out by the Jury, who enjoyed the balance of its tannins and its good finish. Here's a tip: check out the Côtes-du-Ventoux section!

🦅 Xavier Vignon, chem. de Caromb, 84330 Le Barroux, tel. 04.90.62.33.44, fax 04.90.62.33.45, e-mail povidis@wanadoo.fr ☑ 🏚
🍷 by appt.

Wines selected but not starred

LA BASTIDE SAINT VINCENT

Pavane 2001

■	5.5 ha	17,000	🍶 ⚬	5–8 €

🦅 Laurent Daniel, La Bastide Saint Vincent, rte de Vaison-la-Romaine, 84150 Violès, tel. 04.90.70.94.13, fax 04.90.70.96.13, e-mail bastide.vincent@free.fr ☑
🍷 ev. day except Sun. 9am–12 noon 2pm–6pm; cl. 10 Sep.–10 Oct.
🦅 Guy Daniel

BOUVENCOURT 2001

■	4 ha	16,000	◨	8–11 €

🦅 Laurent-Charles Brotte, Le Clos, BP 1, 84230 Châteauneuf-du-Pape, tel. 04.90.83.70.07, fax 04.90.83.74.34, e-mail brotte@brotte.com ☑
🍷 ev. day 9am–12 noon 2pm–6pm

CECILE CHASSAGNE 2000

■	n.c.	10,000	🍶	8–11 €

🦅 Dom. Cécile Chassagne, SARL Le Camassot, 16, rte de Vaison, BP 13, 84110 Sablet, tel. 04.90.46.84.19, fax 04.90.46.84.19 ☑
🍷 by appt.

DOM. LE COLOMBIER

Cuvée Tradition 2001

■	3.6 ha	18,260	🍶 ⚬	5–8 €

🦅 Jean-Louis Mourre, Dom. Le Colombier, 84190 Vacqueyras, tel. 04.90.12.39.71, fax 04.90.65.85.71 ☑
🍷 by appt.

DOM. LE COUROULU

Cuvée Classique 2000

■	10 ha	32,000	🍶 ◨ ⚬	5–8 €

🦅 EARL Le Couroulu, La Pousterle, 84190 Vacqueyras, tel. 04.90.65.84.83, fax 04.90.65.81.25 ☑
🍷 ev. day except Sun. 9am–12 noon 2pm–6pm
🦅 Guy Ricard

DOM. GONDRAN 2000

■	5.8 ha	27,000	🍶 ⚬	5–8 €

🦅 Cellier de l'Enclave des Papes, rte d'Orange, BP 51, 84602 Valréas Cedex, tel. 04.90.41.91.42, fax 04.90.41.90.21, e-mail france@enclavedespapes.com

DOM. DU GRAND MONTMIRAIL 2001

■	2.4 ha	12,000		8–11 €

🦅 Dom. du Grand Montmirail, 84190 Gigondas, tel. 04.90.62.94.28, fax 04.90.65.89.23
🍷 by appt.
🦅 Denis Chéron

Châteauneuf-du-Pape

This appellation, which was the first legally to define its conditions of production in 1931, covers nearly the whole commune from which it derives its name, together with similar terroirs in the neighbouring communes of Orange, Courthézon, Bédarrides and Sorgues (3,178 ha declared in 2002). The vineyard is located on the left bank of the Rhône, 15 km north of Avignon. The unique character of its wines comes from a terroir largely composed of vast terraces at different heights, covered with layers of pebbly red clay. The vine varieties are very varied with a predominance of Grenache, Syrah, Mourvèdre and Cinsault. The yield is not greater than 35 hl/ha.

The Châteauneuf-du-Pape wines are noted for their intense colour and good keeping qualities, although the time they can be kept varies with the vintage. They are expansive, well-structured, full-bodied wines with a strong, complex bouquet, excellent companions to red meat, game and fermented cheeses. The whites, produced in small quantities (5,994 hl), counterbalance their strength with flavour and the finesse of their aromas. The appellation's total annual production was 82,687 hl in 2002.

DOM. DE L'ARNESQUE 2001 ★

■	5 ha	16,000	🍶 ◨	23–30 €

Les Grandes Serres is a négociant that specializes in ageing and distributing Rhône valley wines and which, for the past year, has also produced olive oil. It offers a Châteauneuf-du-Pape 2001 which is very warming at first tasting, before abundant, well-integrated tannins assert themselves. Still fruity, this wine can be kept for five or six years.

🦅 Les Grandes Serres, BP 17, 84231 Châteauneuf-du-Pape Cedex, tel. 04.90.83.72.22, fax 04.90.83.78.77, e-mail les-grandes-serres@wanadoo.fr ☑
🍷 by appt.

DOM. BARVILLE 2001 ★★★

■	9 ha	40,000	🍶 ◨	15–23 €

The Jury was enthusiastic and did not hesitate to award this exceptional wine three stars and *coup de cœur*. It has a remarkable palette of flavours, from leather to spices and chocolate. It has fine complexity and its harmony should be dazzling in five to ten years' time. We pay tribute to the winemaker's great skill. One taster even suggested it should be "drunk on its own, without any contrivance".

🦅 Laurent-Charles Brotte, Le Clos, BP 1, 84230 Châteauneuf-du-Pape, tel. 04.90.83.70.07, fax 04.90.83.74.34, e-mail brotte@brotte.com ☑
🍷 ev. day 9am–12 noon 2pm–6pm

LA BASTIDE SAINT DOMINIQUE 2001★

■   8 ha   30,000   ▮ ⬩   11–15 €

A fine, fresh attack from this wine with abundant fruit. It is long and very harmonious on the palate. A very well-made wine that can be drunk now or kept for two or three years. Enjoy with game.
•┓ Gérard Bonnet, La Bastide Saint Dominique, 84350 Courthézon, tel. 04.90.70.85.32, fax 04.90.70.76.64, e-mail contact@bastide-st-dominique.com ☑ ⌂
⌶ by appt.

CH. DE BEAUCASTEL 2001★

■   60 ha   200,000   38–46 €

What freshness from this 2001 wine, made from organically grown grapes! It has a clear red colour with violet nuances. The nose is young, with fresh fruit and leather aromas that combine well. Fruit (strawberry, cherries) reappears on the palate over a very attractive tannic base. Good balance, warmth and a hint of vanilla make this a wine to keep for a decade.
•┓ Pierre Perrin, Société fermière des vignobles, Ch. de Beaucastel, 84350 Courthézon, tel. 04.90.70.41.00, fax 04.90.70.41.19, e-mail perrin@vinsperrin.com ☑
⌶ by appt.

CH. BEAUCHENE

Grande Réserve 2001★

■   3.5 ha   15,000   ⑪   15–23 €

A year's maceration and a year in cask have produced this attractive wine, with dark colour and a fresh, floral nose with red berries. The palate is well balanced, rounded and fleshy over well present but integrated tannins. A wine with fine length that ends on a note of liquorice.
•┓ Ch. Beauchêne, rte de Beauchêne, 84420 Piolenc, tel. 04.90.51.75.87, fax 04.90.51.73.36, e-mail chateaubeauchene@worldonline.fr ☑
⌶ ev. day except Sat. Sun. 8am–12 noon 1.30pm–5.30pm
•┓ Michel Bernard

DOM. DE BEAURENARD 2001★★

■   23.73 ha   80,000   ⑪   15–23 €

The deep colour already promises a solid structure. The palette of flavours invites you into a world that ranges from red berries to spices. Tannic structure is very marked, demanding five or six years' ageing. On the other hand, you could forget it in your cellar for 10 to 15 years and then rediscover it.
•┓ SCEA Paul Coulon et Fils, Dom. de Beaurenard, 84230 Châteauneuf-du-Pape, tel. 04.90.83.71.79, fax 04.90.83.78.06, e-mail paulcoulon@beaurenard.fr ☑
⌶ ev. day except Sun. 9am–12 noon 1.30pm–5.30pm; groups by appt.

MAISON BENEDETTI 2001★★

■   0.5 ha   1,500   ▮ ⬩   15–23 €

This wine has great complexity, with a wealth of flowers and fruit. A well-balanced 2001 with good ageing potential (six or seven years), which will seduce lovers of more developed notes of wax and honey. Sadly, production is rather limited at just 1,500 bottles.
•┓ Dom. Benedetti, quartier Roquette, 84370 Bédarrides, tel. 04.90.33.24.77, fax 04.90.33.24.97, e-mail vins-mb@free.fr ☑
⌶ by appt.

LOUIS BERNARD 2001★

■   n.c.   150,000   11–15 €

The Bernard estates are known for their high standards when buying grapes, as well as for their partnerships. This policy has, once again, reaped rewards. Louis Bernard has great finesse, with complex, well-rounded tannins. Notably, has a strong liquorice finish. Wait two or three years before drinking.
•┓ Salavert-Les domaines Bernard, rte de Sérignan, 84100 Orange, tel. 04.90.11.86.86, fax 04.90.34.87.30, e-mail sldb@sldb.fr

DOM. BERTHET-RAYNE

Cuvée Cadiac 2001★

■   1.5 ha   5,000   ⑪   15–23 €

This attractive Cuvée Cadiac, with its dark red colour, allows you to discover the full richness of spices and soft fruit. It is a long, well-structured wine which should wait five years. A further five would allow it to develop to the full. Enjoy with a red meat dish of equivalent calibre.
•┓ Dom. Berthet-Rayne, 2334, rte de Caderousse, 84350 Courthézon, tel. 04.90.70.74.14, fax 04.90.70.77.85, e-mail christian.berthet-rayne@wanadoo.fr ☑
⌶ ev. day except Sat. Sun. 8am–12 noon 1.30pm–6.30pm; cl. 10–20 Aug.

BOSQUET DES PAPES

Chante Le Merle Vieilles Vignes 2001★

■   3 ha   10,000   ▮ ⑪ ⬩   30–38 €

A pretty name for this wine, which has only been produced in great vintages since 1990. It is made from traditional grape varieties (Grenache, Syrah, Mourvèdre and Cinsault), complemented by small quantities of Counoise and Vaccarèse. It has an expressive nose dominated by red berries and a full, generous palate. A silky wine with good tannin structure, which should be aged in the cellar for at least five years.
•┓ Maurice et Nicolas Boiron, Dom. Bosquet des Papes, 18, rte d'Orange, BP 50, 84232 Châteauneuf-du-Pape Cedex, tel. 04.90.83.72.33, fax 04.90.83.50.52, e-mail bosquet.des.papes@club-internet.fr ☑
⌶ by appt.

DOM. LA BOUTINIERE 2001★★

■   8.5 ha   15,000   ⑪   11–15 €

This winemaker has produced a great wine thanks to the care with which the blend has been put together: 70% Grenache with equal parts of Syrah, Cinsault and Mourvèdre. The character of the former comes through remarkably well. "A moreish wine," wrote one taster. It is ready to drink but gives a glimpse of intriguing ageing potential (five to eight years).
•┓ Gilbert Boutin, Dom. La Boutinière, 17, rte de Bédarrides, 84230 Châteauneuf-du-Pape, tel. 04.90.83.75.78, fax 04.90.83.76.29, e-mail frederic.boutin1@libertysurf.fr ☑
⌶ by appt.

DOM. DU CAILLOU 2001★

■   1.42 ha   9,500   ⑪   15–23 €

This estate deserves a visit for its fine cellar – which was dug in 1867 and consists of a series of vaulted galleries – and of course for its wines. For example, this 2001 wine, which contains many treasures. Its fine tannins need to become more supple. Forget it for five or six years in the cellar, to allow it to develop to its full potential. Then get a bottle out and enjoy it with game or poultry. The **2001 white (23–30 €)** gains the same rating. Serve in two years' time with fish in sauce.
•┓ Jean-Denis et Sylvie Vacheron, Clos du Caillou, 84350 Courthézon, tel. 04.90.70.73.05, fax 04.90.70.76.47 ☑
⌶ ev. day except Sun. 9am–12 noon 1.30pm–5.30pm

DOM. CHANTE PERDRIX 2001★

■   18 ha   60,000   ⑪   11–15 €

This estate, more than a century old, has regularly featured in the *Guide*. In the 2001 vintage it offers a wine with ripe fruit and exotic wood, with balance and roundness. A solid wine, that should be kept for at least five years and enjoyed with a good cheese board rather than with the partridge its name suggests.
•┓ Guy et Frédéric Nicolet, Dom. Chante Perdrix, BP 6, 84231 Châteauneuf-du-Pape Cedex, tel. 04.90.83.71.86, fax 04.90.83.53.14, e-mail chante-perdrix@wanadoo.fr ☑
⌶ by appt.

DOM. DE LA CHARBONNIERE

Les Hautes Brusquières Cuvée Spéciale 2000★

■ 2.65 ha 12,000 ▮ⅠⅡ♨ 23–30 €

The Jury has selected two wines. Les Hautes Brusquières is rich, with a fine palette of soft fruit and red berry flavours. Well-integrated tannins give good structure to this wine, which has considerable ageing potential (about six years). **Cuvée Mourre des Perdrix 2000 red** was singled out by the Jury for its harmony.

☛ Michel Maret, Dom. de La Charbonnière, 26, rte de Courthézon, 84230 Châteauneuf-du-Pape, tel. 04.90.83.74.59, fax 04.90.83.53.46, e-mail maret-charbonniere@club-internet.fr ☑
⟙ by appt.

CLOS SAINT MICHEL 2002★

■ 2 ha 8,000 ▮ ♨ 15–23 €

A straightforward wine, with notes of stewed fruit and honey. Well-rounded, it can hold its own with a fish dish in sauce. **Cuvée Réservée 2000 red (23–30 €)**, with its dark ruby colour, was equally popular with the Jury, notably because of its finesse. It should be kept for three years.

☛ Vignobles Guy Mousset et Fils, Le Clos Saint Michel, rte de Châteauneuf, 84700 Sorgues, tel. 04.90.83.56.05, fax 04.90.83.56.06, e-mail mousset@clos-saint-michel.com ☑
⟙ ev. day 10am–12 noon 2pm–6pm

DIFFONTY

Cuvée du Vatican Réserve Sixtine 2001★

■ 6 ha 22,000 ▮ⅠⅡ♨ 23–30 €

Papal patronage seems to have benefited this estate, which has appeared in the *Guide* countless times! Sixtine (Sistine), named after the Vatican chapel decorated by Michelangelo, among others, found favour with the Jury. Leave this wine in the cellar for four or five years to allow the tannins to become integrated. Then they can reveal their full finesse. That gives you plenty of time to visit Rome.

☛ SCEA Félicien Diffonty et Fils, 10, rte de Courthézon, BP 33, 84231 Châteauneuf-du-Pape Cedex, tel. 04.90.83.70.51, fax 04.90.83.50.36, e-mail cuvée_du_vatican@mnet.fr ☑
⟙ ev. day except Sun. 10am–12 noon 2pm–6pm; cl. 21 Dec.–4 Jan.

DOM. DUCLAUX 2000★

■ 10 ha 40,000 ▮ⅠⅡ♨ 15–23 €

The Duclaux, this estate's former owners, were consuls at Châteauneuf-du-Pape between 1627 and 1832. Jérôme Quiot, who now owns part of the vineyard, has done justice to the reputation established by this old family with a very rewarding wine, which has well-controlled power and great length. Serve with stewed hare, but only in four or five years' time.

☛ Sélection Jérôme Quiot, av. Baron-Le-Roy, BP 38, 84231 Châteauneuf-du-Pape Cedex, tel. 04.90.83.73.55, fax 04.90.83.78.48, e-mail vignobles@jeromequiot.com ☑

LA FAGOTIERE 2001★

■ 18 ha 18,000 ⅠⅡ 11–15 €

This wine comes from 18 ha of vines and is aged in large barrels for 18 months. Its sumptuous colour, which is dark, almost black, heralds a very rich nose with charred notes but also red berries. Well-structured, concentrated and tannic, this wine should be kept for four or five years.

☛ SCEA Pierry Chastan, La Fagotière, 84100 Orange, tel. 04.90.34.51.81, fax 04.90.51.04.44, e-mail lafagotiere@wanadoo.fr ☑
⟙ by appt.

CH. DES FINES ROCHES

Fines Roches 2001★

■ 1.4 ha 6,600 ⅠⅡ 23–30 €

Coup de coeur in the last edition of the *Guide* with its 2000 wine, the château of Fines Roches is famous for looking like a medieval fortress, though in fact it was built in the 19th century. This year it features with two wines. **Château des**

Fines Roches 2002 white (11–15 €) has white flower and peach notes. Pleasant and fine, it should not be kept too long and served chilled as an aperitif. Fines Roches has a deep colour and a gamey, warm, powerful nose. On the palate is fruity, spicy and rounded over well present tannins. Its laurel-flavoured finish is highly recommended to be enjoyed with sucking pig, in five or six years' time.

☛ Robert Barrot, 1, av. du Baron-Leroy, 84230 Châteauneuf-du-Pape, tel. 04.90.83.51.73, fax 04.90.83.52.77, e-mail chateaux@vmb.fr ☑
⟙ by appt.

DOM. FONT DE MICHELLE

Cuvée Traditionnelle 2001★

■ 24 ha 70,000 ⅠⅡ 15–23 €

The oldest plots on this 30 ha estate are a century old and this wine was made from 60-year-old vines. Grenache (70%), Syrah (10%) and Mourvèdre (10%) complemented by Cinsault and others, produce a substantial wine, which has been patiently aged in cask for 15 months. The ruby colour contains some orange glints. Rich and silky, mingling gamey and fruity notes, it will not disappoint. It should accompany red meats or coq au vin.

☛ SCEA Etienne Gonnet, 14, imp. des Vignerons, 84370 Bédarrides, tel. 04.90.33.00.22, fax 04.90.33.20.27, e-mail egonnet@terre-net.fr ☑
⟙ ev. day except Sat. Sun. 9am–12 noon 2pm–5.30pm; cl. 24 Dec.–3 Jan.

DOM. DE LA FONT DU ROI 2001★

■ 16 ha 60,000 ▮ ♨ 15–23 €

This wine contains 5% Muscardin, a grape variety found only in Châteauneuf-du-Pape and 70% Grenache which gives all its finesse. The slightly developed colour heralds notes of macerated berries and prunes. A balanced wine with plenty of finish, to be enjoyed with a good cheese board.

☛ EARL Cyril et Jacques Mousset, Ch. des Fines-Roches, 84230 Châteauneuf-du-Pape, tel. 04.90.83.73.10, fax 04.90.83.50.78, e-mail contac@mousset.com ☑
⟙ by appt.

DOM. GALEVAN 2000★

■ 0.71 ha 3,000 ⅠⅡ 11–15 €

The nose, which has toasted and coffee notes, is still closed. The attack is supple, with a most enjoyable sensation of freshness, no doubt produced by the 5% Mourvèdre in the blend. This wine is gradually developing and needs time to reveal its full palette of flavours. Wait at least three years.

☛ Coralie and Jean-Pierre Goumarre, 127, rte de Vaison, 84350 Courthézon, tel. 04.90.70.84.26, fax 04.90.70.28.70, e-mail domaine.galevan@planetis.com ☑
⟙ ev. day except Sun. 8.30am–12.30pm 1pm–7.30pm

CH. DE LA GARDINE

Cuvée Tradition 2001★

▨ 5 ha n.c. ▮ⅠⅡ♨ 23–30 €

This estate is a benchmark of the region and unmissable thanks to its 22-metre tower. Two of its wines are extremely good. This Châteauneuf-du-Pape white delights the eye with its pale yellow hue. Rich in floral and citrus fruit notes, it is harmonious and will keep between four and six years. The **Cuvée Tradition 2001 red** is also a great, powerful and complete wine. It needs five or six years to develop its full potential.

☛ Brunel, SCA Ch. de La Gardine, rte de Roquemaure, 84230 Châteauneuf-du-Pape, tel. 04.90.83.73.20, fax 04.90.83.77.24, e-mail direction@gardine.com ☑
⟙ by appt.

DOM. GRAND VENEUR

Les Origines 2001★★

■ 15 ha 33,000 ▮ⅠⅡ♨ 15–23 €

This estate in Orange, a town famous for the Chorégies festival held every year in its ancient theatre, offers Les Origines, a veritable symphony of red berries, spices and cocoa. There is perfect harmony between the intensity of flavour and the structure. A superb wine, with deep colour and intense bouquet. It can be drunk in four or five years, but can be kept up to eight.

•⊓ SARL Alain Jaume, Dom. Grand Veneur, rte de Châteauneuf-du-Pape, 84100 Orange, tel. 04.90.34.68.70, fax 04.90.34.43.71, e-mail jaume@domaine-grand-veneur.com ☑

⊥ by appt.

DOM. DE LA JANASSE 2001★★★

| ■ | 5 ha | 12,000 | ⬛ | 15–23 € |

This 55-ha estate, founded in 1973 by Aimé Sabon and now part of the Rhône Vignobles group, has featured in the *Guide* before. This year it reaches new heights with two exceptional wines. This *cuvée* wins a *coup de coeur*: roundness and complexity combine well with elegance and the quintessence of the Grenache grape appears in all its majesty. The Jury were unanimous on its qualities, disagreeing on just one point: should it be drunk now, or kept in the cellar for ten years? The tasters were almost as enthusiastic for the **Cuvée Vieilles Vignes 2001 red (38–46 €)**, which also gets a *coup de coeur* and was described as "pure self-indulgence" by one. To round off this remarkable trophy haul, the **red Cuvée Chaupin 2001 (30–38 €)** was singled out for its harmony.

•⊓ Aimé Sabon, Dom. de La Janasse, 27, chem. du Moulin, 84350 Courthézon, tel. 04.90.70.86.29, fax 04.90.70.75.93, e-mail lajanasse@free.fr ☑

⊥ ev. day 8am–12 noon 2pm–7pm; Sat. Sun. by appt.

LAFOND ROC-EPINE 2001★★★

| ■ | 0.87 ha | 4,000 | ⬛ ⬥ | 15–23 € |

Don't look for this estate at Châteauneuf-du-Pape: it is actually at Tavel, a few kilometres away on the opposite side of the Rhône. It has just 87 ares of Châteauneuf-du-Pape vines, but this does not stop it regularly featuring in the *Guide*. This exceptional 2001 was unanimously praised by the Jury. They never tired of admiring its sumptuous dark red colour. And such finesse on the nose! The palate reveals flavours of vanilla, very ripe fruit and spices, with plenty of length from a wine that will carry high the reputation of this appellation. It will hold pride of place at the table, now, or in 15 years' time.

•⊓ SCEA Lafond Roc-Epine, rte des Vignobles, 30126 Tavel, tel. 04.66.50.24.59, fax 04.66.50.12.42, e-mail lafond@roc-epine.com ☑

⊥ by appt.
•⊓ Lafond

CH. MONGIN 2001★

| ■ | 2 ha | 5,000 | ⬛ | 11–15 € |

Château Mongin is the estate of the Orange wine college. For an apprentice's work, this shows the master's touch: the wine has a lovely purple colour, good balance and roundness. It has good ageing potential (ten years) but can be enjoyed now.

•⊓ Lycée viticole d'Orange, Ch. Mongin, 2260, rte du Grès, 84100 Orange, tel. 04.90.51.48.04, fax 04.90.51.11.92, e-mail chateau.mongin@educagri.fr ☑

⊥ by appt.

DOM. MONPERTUIS 2001★★★

| ■ | 3 ha | 12,000 | ⬛ ⬥ | 11–15 € |

The Jury were unanimous in giving this very harmonious 2001 the top mark, for its finesse and floral notes. The palate is full and rich in flavour and should reach its best in five or six years'

time. Keep to enjoy with a bouillabaisse. It would be a pity not to taste the estate's **Cuvée Principale 2001 red**. It was singled out by the Jury, being full of fruit and rounded, though its tannins need to soften. Serve in three or four years' time with a beef roast with boletus mushrooms.

•⊓ Vignobles Paul Jeune, 14, chem. des Garrigues, BP 48, 84232 Châteauneuf-du-Pape Cedex, tel. 04.90.83.73.87, fax 04.90.83.51.13, e-mail vignoblespauljeune@wanadoo.fr ☑

⊥ by appt.

CH. MONT-REDON 2002★

| ■ | 16 ha | 65,000 | ⬛ ⬥ | 15–23 € |

This terroir has been under cultivation for six centuries and continues to produce some excellent wines such as this fine 2002 with a lovely pale colour and nose of white flowers and peach. This aromatic wine, full of finesse, is ready to drink now. The **2001 red** is also well made, with good structure and long ageing potential (five to ten years).

•⊓ Ch. Mont-Redon, BP 10, 84231 Châteauneuf-du-Pape, tel. 04.90.83.72.75, fax 04.90.83.77.20, e-mail contact@chateaumontredon.fr ☑

⊥ by appt.

DOM. DE LA MORDOREE
Cuvée de la Reine des Bois 2001★★

| ■ | 3.2 ha | 12,000 | ⬛ ⬛ | 30–38 € |

Do this estate and its Cuvée de la Reine des Bois need any introduction? Each year it finds its place in the *Guide* and no one is complaining. In 2001, it again reaches great heights! It has elegant, intense colour, powerful balance and intense oakiness. This wine has all the requisite qualities and a great future before it. Readers should not be put off by its price.

•⊓ Dom. de la Mordorée, chem. des Oliviers, 30126 Tavel, tel. 04.66.50.00.75, fax 04.66.50.47.39 ☑

⊥ ev. day except Sun. 8am–12 noon 1.30pm–5.30pm
•⊓ Delorme

DOM. FABRICE MOUSSET 2001★

| ■ | 2 ha | 8,000 | ⬛ | 11–15 € |

A very well made wine with a lovely, complex nose and clean attack. Well-rounded, it will keep five or six years and can be enjoyed with a fish dish with sauce or white meat.

•⊓ Fabrice Mousset, Ch. des Fines Roches, BP 15, 84231 Châteauneuf-du-Pape Cedex, tel. 04.90.83.50.05, fax 04.90.83.50.78, e-mail contact@mousset.com ☑

⊥ by appt.

DOM. DE NALYS 2001★★

| ■ | 40 ha | 196,000 | ⬛ | 11–15 € |

The Nalys estate is known for its remarkable wines, offering consistent quality at reasonable prices. Don't expect any limited production wines here – only one is produced. The 13 grape varieties of the appellation all go to make up this wine, which is full of finesse and has ample length with notes of liquorice, figs and coffee. It can be drunk now, to enjoy its fruit, or be left to develop.

•⊓ Dom. de Nalys, rte de Courthézon, 84230 Châteauneuf-du-Pape, tel. 04.90.83.72.52, fax 04.90.83.51.15 ☑

⊥ ev. day except Sun. 8am–12 noon 1pm–6pm; Sat. by appt.

CH. LA NERTHE 2002★

| ■ | 9 ha | 40,000 | ⬛ ⬛ ⬥ | 23–30 € |

"When the wine of La Nerthe vibrates and laughs in the glass …" The wines of this château and Provence, inspired Frédéric Mistral, who would certainly have appreciated this fine *cuvée* with green glints, great finesse and rounded, full palate. It can be drunk on its own, now and for the next two or three years, or with a meal with a fish dish in sauce. **Cuvée des Cadettes 2000 red (38–46 €)** is very well made, consisting of almost equal proportions of Grenache, Syrah and Mourvèdre. It bears strong signs – too strong for one taster – of 12 months' ageing in cask. Give it time: eight or ten years from now it will be perfect.

•⊓ SCA Ch. La Nerthe, rte de Sorgues, 84230 Châteauneuf-du-Pape, tel. 04.90.83.70.11, fax 04.90.83.79.69, e-mail la.nerthe@wanadoo.fr ☑

⊥ ev. day 9am–12 noon 2pm–6pm
•⊓ Pierre Richard

ORATORIO 2001★

| ■ | n.c. | 25,000 | ⑪ | 15–23 € |

A skilfully orchestrated oratorio from this large Rhône valley négociant. Let us raise the curtain on this wine, with its dark purple colour, very ripe nose of stewed fruit and prunes in brandy and full palate where notes of truffle and vanilla linger. Cask ageing has been skilfully done. **Les Closiers 2001 red (11–15 €)**, singled out by the Jury, has also been aged in cask. Tannins are present and the palate gives off a certain warmth, with plenty of length.

➼ Ogier-Caves des Papes, 10, av. Louis-Pasteur, BP 75, 84232 Châteauneuf-du-Pape Cedex, tel. 04.90.39.32.32, fax 04.90.83.72.51, e-mail ogiercavesdespapes@ogier.fr ☒
☿ by appt.

PARC DES PAPES 2000★

| ■ | 1 ha | 2,000 | ▮⑪♨ | 11–15 € |

This estate, now owned by the Arnauds, formerly belonged to La Pise, a lord and archivist of the house of Orange Nassau. It now offers an attractive wine, whose lovely colour gives off cherry glints and which asserts itself from the attack. Soft fruit, controlled tannins, well-dosed oakiness and a chocolate finish are the features of this very successful Parc des Papes. It will keep two or three years.

➼ Ch. Maucoil, BP 7, 84231 Châteauneuf-du-Pape Cedex, tel. 04.90.34.14.86, fax 04.90.34.71.88, e-mail contact@chateau-maucoil.com ☒
☿ ev. day except Sat. Sun. 8am–12 noon 2pm–6pm
➼ Arnaud

DOM. DU PEGAU

Cuvée Réservée 2001★

| ■ | 18 ha | 60,000 | ⑪ | 23–30 € |

Pepper and liquorice dominate this wine, whose colour is very young. It is balanced, full and long. Serve with red meats, from now until three or four years' time.

➼ Dom. du Pegau, 15, av. Impériale, 84230 Châteauneuf-du-Pape, tel. 04.90.83.72.70, fax 04.90.83.53.02, e-mail pegau@pegau.com ☒
☿ by appt.

DOM. DU PERE CABOCHE 2002★

| ■ | 2.85 ha | 12,000 | | 11–15 € |

The Boisson family have been blacksmiths and winemakers for generations, so much so that they are nicknamed *caboche*, a term denoting the nails used to attach the horseshoe to the hoof and which has given this estate its name. It is now run by Jean-Pierre Boisson who, unlike his forebears, devotes himself to viticulture and offers a harmonious 2002 that combines freshness with fruit, with plenty of roundness and warmth on the palate. Open within two years and serve, for example, with goat's cheese.

➼ SCEA Jean-Pierre Boisson, rte de Courthézon, 84230 Châteauneuf-du-Pape, tel. 04.90.83.71.44, fax 04.90.83.50.46, e-mail boisson@jpboisson.com ☒
☿ by appt.

DOM. DU PERE PAPE 2001★

| ■ | 9 ha | 35,000 | ▮⑪♨ | 15–23 € |

This 44-ha estate has a 17th century building with a vaulted cellar containing 50 hl casks. In these, a third of this very good 2001 has been aged, the rest being vat-aged. The violet red colour recalls velvet. It is a spicy wine, whose tannins need to become more rounded. Wait a while before enjoying with game birds. The same producer offers **Domaine du Grand Coulet 2001 red (11–15 €)**, which is just as good. Harmonious and very aromatic, it gives off blackberry, cherry and liquorice notes. It has good structure and needs to be aged for four or five years.

➼ Dom. du Père Pape, 24, av. Baron-le-Roy, 84230 Châteauneuf-du-Pape, tel. 04.90.83.70.16, fax 04.90.83.50.47, e-mail beatrice.mayard@wanadoo.fr ☒
☿ by appt.
➼ Mayard

DOM. DES PERES DE L'EGLISE

Le Calice de Saint Pierre 2001★

| ■ | 1.5 ha | 5,000 | ⑪ | 8–11 € |

Ageing in 20-40-hl casks has developed traditional flavours of fruit in alcohol and spices. This wine, structured with fine tannins, will reach its best in two or three years. Do yourself a favour and enjoy it with game rather than with a John Dory (Saint-Pierre)!

➼ SCEA Paulette Gradassi & Fils, Dom. des Pères de l'Eglise, 2, av. Impériale, 84230 Châteauneuf-du-Pape, tel. 04.90.83.71.37, fax 04.90.83.71.37 ☒
☿ by appt.

DOM. ROGER PERRIN 2001★

| ■ | 15 ha | 50,000 | ▮⑪♨ | 11–15 € |

A long, 21-day, fermentation has realised the raw material's potential to the full. Spicy and fruit notes are the features of this rich, rounded wine which has a base of fine tannins. Enjoy it in two to five years with some fine game.

➼ EARL Dom. Roger Perrin, La Berthaude, rte de Châteauneuf-du-Pape, 84100 Orange, tel. 04.90.34.25.64, fax 04.90.34.88.37 ☒
☿ by appt.
➼ Luc Perrin

DOM. DE LA PINEDE 2001★

| ■ | n.c. | 6,000 | ⑪ | 15–23 € |

This very harmonious wine has a handsome deep colour with intense glints. Leather, spices, peaches and apricots make up the palette of flavours. Can easily age two to four years in a good cellar.

➼ Georges-Pierre Coulon, SCEA du Dom. de la Pinède, 84230 Châteauneuf-du-Pape, tel. 04.90.83.71.50, fax 04.90.83.52.20 ☒
☿ by appt.

DOM. DES RELAGNES

La Cuvée Vigneronne 2001★

| ■ | 2 ha | 12,000 | ⑪ | 15–23 € |

This 18 ha estate has been owned by the same family since the 18th century. Coffee and cocoa on the nose from this Cuvée Vigneronne, which bears the marks of long cask-ageing (minimum ten months). It also has vanilla and tar notes. Full and complex, the palate is deep and harmonious. A wine for modest ageing – four to five years – but which can be enjoyed now.

➼ SCEA Dom. des Relagnes, rte de Bédarrides, 84230 Châteauneuf-du-Pape, tel. 04.90.83.73.37, fax 04.90.83.52.16, e-mail domaine-des-relagnes@wanadoo.fr ☒
☿ by appt.

SAINT COSME 2001★

| ■ | 1.5 ha | 4,500 | ⑪ | 15–23 € |

This powerful 2001 releases countless aromas, while retaining its freshness and finesse. It has excellent overall harmony and should be opened within two years to enjoy its fruity character. Ten years from now, it can accompany a good game dish.

➼ SARL Barruol, Ch. de Saint Cosme, 84190 Gigondas, tel. 04.90.65.80.80, fax 04.90.65.81.05, e-mail louis@chateau-st-cosme.com ☒ ♙
☿ ev. day except Sun. 9am–12 noon 1.30pm–5.30pm

CH. SAINT-ROCH 2000★

| ■ | 2 ha | 9,000 | ▮⑪♨ | 15–23 € |

Château Saint-Roch and Château de la Gardine, both owned by Maxime and Patrick Brunel, face each other across the River Rhône. The first offers an attractive wine with a robust red colour, subtle, silky nose and fleshy palate. How can you resist all that? This wine should be kept for four or five years to appreciate it to the full.

➼ Maxime et Patrick Brunel, Ch. Saint-Roch, chem. de Lirac, 30150 Roquemaure, tel. 04.66.82.82.59, fax 04.66.82.83.00, e-mail brunel@chateau-saint-roch.com ☒
☿ ev. day except Sat. Sun. 8am–12 noon 2pm–5pm; cl. 1–15 Aug.

DOM. DE SAINT SIFFREIN 2000★

■   12 ha   20,000   �**Ⅲ**   11–15 €

A skilfully made wine, which is gently approaching maturity. Very elegant, it does not impose itself but can hold its own with a meat dish in sauce, for example. The more impatient drinker can open it now, but it would be better to wait at least five or six years.

↬ EARL Claude Chastan, Dom. de Saint-Siffrein, rte de Châteauneuf, 84100 Orange, tel. 04.90.34.49.85, fax 04.90.51.05.20, e-mail domainesaintsiffrein@wanadoo.fr ☑
☖ by appt.

DOM. DES SAUMADES 2001★

■   2 ha   6,000   �**Ⅲ**   11–15 €

A very small estate, with just 2.2 ha of vines. Would that it were bigger, so enjoyable are these 6,000 bottles of Châteauneuf-du-Pape. Rich in red berry and damp woodland flavours, this very rounded wine can be kept in the cellar for ten years.

↬ Franck et Murielle Mousset, 20, fg Saint-Georges, 84350 Courthézon, tel. 04.90.70.83.04, fax 04.90.70.83.04 ☑
☖ by appt.

DOM. SERGUIER 2001★

■   5 ha   8,000   �**Ⅲ**   11–15 €

The estate's cellar is built on the walls of Châteauneuf-du-Pape itself. When visiting the town, make sure you stop there to buy some of this wine, whose sunny hints beautifully evoke the terroir of Châteauneuf. This wine will keep for ten years: save it for red meat with sauce.

↬ Daniel Nury, 13, rue Alphonse-Daudet, 84230 Châteauneuf-du-Pape, tel. 04.90.83.73.42, fax 04.90.83.73.42 ☑
☖ by appt.

DOM. DE LA SOLITUDE

Cuvée Barberini 2001★

■   1 ha   2,400   �**Ⅲ**   38–46 €

The name Cuvée Barberini pays homage to the Italian family and this wine's label bears three bees, from the family's coast of arms. The tribute is all the more pertinent since the wine has notes of beeswax and honey. Its oakiness needs two or three years to become more rounded. Enjoy with truffle brouillade.

↬ SCEA Dom. Pierre Lançon, Dom. de La Solitude, BP 21, 84231 Châteauneuf-du-Pape Cedex, tel. 04.90.83.71.45, fax 04.90.83.51.34, e-mail solitude@mnet.fr ☑
☖ ev. day except Sat. Sun. 8am–12 noon 2pm–6pm

TERRES DES PONTIFES 2001★

■   9 ha   35,000   ▯ ♦   15–23 €

From the 14th century onwards the papacy contributed to the fame of the remarkable terroir of Châteauneuf, a fact recalled by the name of this wine. It has a fine deep colour with violet glints and its nose combines red berries with the smoky notes typical of Syrah. A very attractive palette of flavours from this full, long wine, which already displays very good harmony but which will keep six to eight years. The **Cuvée Les Consuls 2001 red en Lirac (8–11 €)** gets one star.

↬ Maison Gabriel Meffre, Le Village, 84190 Gigondas, tel. 04.90.12.32.42, fax 04.90.12.32.49

DOM. PIERRE USSEGLIO ET FILS

Cuvée de mon Aïeul 2001★

■   3 ha   10,000   ▯ �**Ⅲ** ♦   30–38 €

The label shows an old photograph of a man riding a horse, that is pulling a cart. Perhaps this is a forefather of Pierre Usseglio, to whom this wine is dedicated? This is a wine to buy for a family celebration that is still a long way off. It has potential, but the tannins need time to become more rounded: ageing for at least five years will allow it to gain finesse and complexity. It is a pity that this wine is so expensive.

↬ Dom. Pierre Usseglio et Fils, 10, rte d'Orange, 84230 Châteauneuf-du-Pape, tel. 04.90.83.72.98, fax 04.90.83.56.70 ☑
☖ by appt.

CH. DE VAUDIEU 2001★

■   60 ha   77,000   ▯ ♦   15–23 €

A large (70 ha) Châteauneuf-du-Pape estate and one not to be missed. It offers a fine 2001 with a deep colour with violet glints. The palate is very rounded, with remarkably fine tannins. Good substance, for which we can thank the estate's oenologist and plenty of harmony too. Enjoy with game, but not before five years.

↬ Ch. de Vaudieu, SARL Giaconda, rte de Courthézon, 84230 Châteauneuf-du-Pape, tel. 04.90.83.70.31, fax 04.90.83.51.97 ☑
☖ by appt.
↬ Brechet

Wines selected but not starred

ANCIEN DOMAINE DES PONTIFES

Cuvée Elise 2002

■   0.4 ha   1,000   �**Ⅲ**   15–23 €

↬ Françoise Granier, 13, rue de l'Escatillon, 30150 Roquemaure, tel. 04.66.82.56.73, fax 04.66.90.23.90, e-mail croze-garnier@wanadoo.fr ☑
☖ by appt.

DOM. PAUL AUTARD

Cuvée La Côte Ronde 2000

■   12 ha   46,000   �**Ⅲ**   30–38 €

↬ Dom. Paul Autard, rte de Châteauneuf-du-Pape, 84350 Courthézon, tel. 04.90.70.73.15, fax 04.90.70.29.59, e-mail jeanpaul.autard@wanadoo.fr ☑
☖ ev. day except Sat. Sun. 9am–12.30pm 3pm–6.30pm

PAUL DURIEU

Réserve Lucile Avril 2001

■   n.c.   6,500   15–23 €

↬ Paul Durieu, 27, av. Pasteur, 84850 Camaret-sur-Aigues, tel. 04.90.37.28.14, fax 04.90.37.76.05 ☑
☖ by appt.

FERAUD-BRUNEL 2000

■   n.c.   12,000   ▯   15–23 €

↬ Féraud-Brunel, chem. du Bois-de-la-Ville, 84230 Châteauneuf-du-Pape, tel. 04.90.83.72.62, fax 04.90.83.51.07, e-mail pegau@pegau.com

DOM. DE FERRAND 2001

■   5 ha   15,000   ▯ �**Ⅲ** ♦   11–15 €

↬ EARL Charles Bravay, chem. de Saint-Jean, 84100 Orange, tel. 04.90.34.26.06, fax 04.90.34.26.06 ☑
☖ by appt.

LAURUS 2001

■   3 ha   12,000   �**Ⅲ**   15–23 €

↬ Gabriel Meffre, Le Village, 84190 Gigondas, tel. 04.90.12.30.22, fax 04.90.12.30.29, e-mail gabriel-meffre@meffre.com ☑
☖ by appt.

MARQUIS ANSELME MATHIEU

Vignes Centenaires 2001

■   2.5 ha   11,500   ▯ ♦   15–23 €

↬ SCEA du Dom. Mathieu, rte de Courthézon, BP 32, 84231 Châteauneuf-du-Pape Cedex, tel. 04.90.83.72.09, fax 04.90.83.50.55, e-mail dnemathieu@aol.com ☑
☖ by appt.

DOM. DE PANISSE

Confidence Vigneronne 2001

| ■ | 2 ha | 12,000 | ⅢⅡ | 15–23 € |

� Jean-Marie Olivier, Dom. de Panisse, 161, chem. de Panisse, 84350 Courthézon, tel. 04.90.70.78.93, fax 04.90.70.81.83 ☑
Ⓣ ev. day except Wed. Fri. Sun. 9am–11.15am 2pm–6pm; cl. Feb.

DOM. SAINT BENOIT

La Truffière 2000

| ■ | 3.43 ha | 16,000 | ■ ⚬ | 23–30 € |

� Marc Cellier, rte de Sorgues, BP 72, 84232 Châteauneuf-du-Pape Cedex, tel. 04.90.83.51.36, fax 04.90.83.51.37, e-mail saint.benoit@wanadoo.fr ☑
Ⓣ ev. day except Sat. Sun. 10am–12 noon 2pm–6pm

DOM. DES SENECHAUX 2002

| ■ | 3 ha | 11,500 | | 11–15 € |

� Pascal Roux, Dom. des Sénéchaux, 3, rue de la Nouvelle-Poste, 84230 Châteauneuf-du-Pape, tel. 04.90.83.73.52, fax 04.90.83.52.88 ☑
Ⓣ by appt.

CH. SIMIAN 2001

| ■ | 3 ha | 14,000 | ■Ⅲ⚬ | 11–15 € |

� Jean-Pierre Serguier, Ch. Simian, 84420 Piolenc, tel. 04.90.29.50.67, fax 04.90.29.62.33, e-mail chateau.simian@wanadoo.fr ☑
Ⓣ ev. day 8.30am–12.30pm 1.30pm–7.30pm

Lirac

Lirac has produced quality wines since the 16th century, when the magistrates of Roquemaure authenticated them by burning the letters "C d R" into the barrels with a red-hot iron. The climate and terroir are nearly the same here, in an area between Lirac, Saint-Laurent-des-Arbres, Saint-Geniès-de-Comolas and Roquemaure, as at Tavel, further north. Since Vacqueyras became an AOC, Lirac is no longer the only southern cru to make three colours of wine. Lirac rosés and whites are full of grace and perfume; they go pleasantly with fish from the Mediterranean nearby and should be drunk young and cool. The reds are strong, with a pronounced terroir character and offer an ideal accompaniment to red meat. In 2002, Lirac produced 22,253 hl from nearly 642 ha.

DOM. AMIDO 2001★

| ■ | 5.98 ha | 15,000 | ■Ⅲ⚬ | 5–8 € |

Christian Amido has been at the head of this estate since 1987. This wine, made with 10% Mourvèdre complementing Syrah (30%) and Grenache, is ready to drink and delighted the Jury. The nose is well developed with red berries, vanilla and pepper; the attack is fine, with tannins and alcohol forming the structure; and the finish is spicy. A very well-produced Lirac.
➡item Christian Amido, Le Palais-Nord, rte de la Commanderie, 30126 Tavel, tel. 04.66.50.04.41, fax 04.66.50.04.41 ☑
Ⓣ by appt.

L'HERITAGE D'AQUERIA 2000★★

| ■ | 3 ha | 10,000 | ■Ⅲ | 15–23 € |

Three brothers, Bez, Vincent and Bruno, run the Château d'Aquéria, which won a *coup de coeur* last year with an exceptional Tavel 2001. Now they offer a wine with intense purple colouring and a nose that has developed remarkably with coffee, cocoa and orange peel. This tannic, oaky wine develops chocolate, prune and spice notes. It has style and length of eight to nine caudalies. Rich flavours, good structure and a complex nose earn **Château d'Aquéria Lirac 2001 red (5–8 €)** two stars.
➡item SCA Jean Olivier, Ch. d'Aquéria, 30126 Tavel, tel. 04.66.50.04.56, fax 04.66.50.18.46, e-mail contact@aqueria.com ☑
Ⓣ ev. day except Sat. Sun. 8am–12 noon 2pm–6pm

LOUIS BERNARD

Grande Réserve 2001★★

| ■ | n.c. | 9,300 | | 8–11 € |

The Bernard estates have made a good acquisition with this Grande Réserve, which has intense colour with violet glints. It is a most attractive wine, with blackcurrant aromas with liquorice notes and a full palate given structure by present, well-integrated tannins.
➡item Salavert-Les Domaines Bernard, rte de Sérignan, 84100 Orange, tel. 04.90.11.86.86, fax 04.90.34.87.30, e-mail sldb@sldb.fr

DOM. DES CARABINIERS 2001★★

| ■ | 18 ha | 20,000 | | 8–11 € |

The richness of Grenache, the aromas of Syrah and the structure of Mourvèdre combine to produce a particularly pleasant, typical wine. Ready to drink now. Since 1997 the estate has been organic.
➡item Christian Leperchois, Dom. des Carabiniers, 30150 Roquemaure, tel. 04.66.82.62.94, fax 04.66.82.82.15, e-mail carabinier@wanadoo.fr ☑
Ⓣ by appt.

DOM. DUSEIGNEUR 2000★

| ■ | 12 ha | 60,000 | ■Ⅲ⚬ | 5–8 € |

Since 1970, this estate has been reclaimed from the garrigue, its vines being planted on the hillsides. Delicate red berry, spice and garrigue aromas, plenty of fullness on the palate and very present tannins add up to a very balanced wine. The Jury suggests this wine can be enjoyed now, with beef with mushrooms and parsley.
➡item Frédéric Duseigneur, rte de Saint-Victor, 30126 Saint-Laurent-des-Arbres, tel. 04.66.50.02.57, fax 04.66.50.43.57, e-mail freduseigneur@infonie.fr ☑
Ⓣ by appt.

DOM. DE LA GENESTIERE

Cuvée Eliott 2001★★

| ■ | 1.5 ha | 6,000 | Ⅲ | 11–15 € |

A large (50 ha) estate bought in 1994 by the Garcin family. This wine has spent 11 months in new oak casks and will be popular with those who love wine with vanilla notes. The attack is clean, with present tannins over ripe fruit, the nose complex, spicy and jammy. A remarkable bottle, which should be kept three or four years.
➡item Jean-Claude Garcin, Dom. de La Genestière, chem. de Cravailleux, 30126 Tavel, tel. 04.66.50.07.03, fax 04.66.50.27.03 ☑
Ⓣ ev. day 9am–12.30pm 1.30pm–5.30pm; Sat. Sun. by appt.

DOM. DE LA GRIVELIERE

Mont-Pegueirol 2001★

| ■ | 2 ha | 10,000 | Ⅲ | 5–8 € |

This négociant has aged this wine in large barrels for 12 months. It has light oakiness, with leather, spice and garrigue aromas. Tasting reveals the presence of tannins, good structure and length with fruits in alcohol.
➡item Laurent-Charles Brotte, Le Clos, BP 1, 84230 Châteauneuf-du-Pape, tel. 04.90.83.70.07, fax 04.90.83.74.34, e-mail brotte@brotte.com ☑
Ⓣ ev. day 9am–12 noon 2pm–6pm

DOM. LAFOND ROC-EPINE

La Ferme romaine 2001★★

| ■ | 2 ha | 8,000 | ⑪ | 11–15 € |

How can we count the *coups de coeur* earned by this 75 ha estate in successive editions of the *Guide*? This wine has an intense red, almost black colour. Aromas of ripe fruit and cocoa mingle with gamey notes. A complex, long and balanced wine where fruit blends happily with smoky and coffee notes. **Domaine Lafond Roc-Epine 2001 red (8–11 €)** gains one star for its body, power and liquorice finish. Finally, **Domaine Lafond Roc-Epine 2002 white (8–11 €)** was singled out by the Jury for its toasted dried fruit and citrus fruit aromas.
☛ Dom. Lafond Roc-Epine, rte des Vignobles, 30126 Tavel, tel. 04.66.50.24.59, fax 04.66.50.12.42, e-mail lafond@roc-epine.com ☑
Ⴤ ev. day except Sat. Sun. 8am–12 noon 1.30pm–5.30pm

DOM. MABY

La Fermade Cuvée Prestige 2000★★★

| ■ | 0.5 ha | 1,500 | ⑪ | 8–11 € |

A miniature *cuvée* (1,500 bottles), but what a great wine! A long time in cast has allowed the oakiness to achieve wonderful harmony with the soft fruit notes. The palate is clean, powerful and oaky, with tannins out in force sustained by stewed fruit and spices and vanilla and liquorice notes on the finish.
☛ Dom. Roger Maby, rue Saint-Vincent, 30126 Tavel, tel. 04.66.50.03.40, fax 04.66.50.43.12, e-mail domaine-maby@wanadoo.fr ☑
Ⴤ by appt.

DOM. DE LA MORDOREE

Cuvée de la Reine des bois 2001★★

| ■ | 22 ha | 30,000 | ∎ ⑪ | 11–15 € |

Another shower of stars for La Mordorée, *coup de coeur* in the last edition of the *Guide* and this year in Tavel (see below). This 2001 wine has intense deep red colour. Its nose tends towards ripe fruit, musk and gamey notes. Tasting reveals good roundness, vigorous tannins and intriguing structure. In short, a fine wine.
☛ Dom. de la Mordorée, chem. des Oliviers, 30126 Tavel, tel. 04.66.50.00.75, fax 04.66.50.47.39 ☑
Ⴤ ev. day except Sun. 8am–12 noon 1.30pm–5.30pm
☛ Delorme

DOM. DES RAMIERES 2001★

| ■ | 9 ha | 15,000 | ⑪ | 5–8 € |

Grenache (75%), Syrah (20%) and Mourvèdre, the three main varieties of this AOC, make up this wine aged in large barrels, which has dark, intense colour and a nose marked by damp woodland and prune flavours. The palate, full of finesse, is fresh and harmonious.
☛ Morad Layouni, Dom. la Genestière, chem. de Cravailleux, 30126 Tavel, tel. 04.66.50.07.03, fax 04.66.50.27.03, e-mail garcin-layouri@domaine-genestiere.com ☑
Ⴤ ev. day 9am–12.30pm 1.30pm–5.30pm; Sat. Sun. by appt.

DOM. LA ROCALIERE 2001★★

| ■ | 1.2 ha | 5,000 | | 8–11 € |

This 55 ha estate enjoys an excellent reputation, which this wine confirms. This 2001 vintage has intense colour and a gamey nose with almond and fig aromas. It is a powerful, complex, balanced wine, with plenty of length.
☛ Dom. la Rocalière, Le Palais-Nord, BP 21, 30126 Tavel, tel. 04.66.50.12.60, fax 04.66.50.23.45, e-mail rocaliere@wanadoo.fr ☑
Ⴤ ev. day except Sat. Sun. 8am–12 noon 2pm–6pm
☛ Borrelly-Maby

CH. SAINT-ROCH

Cuvée Confidentielle 2001★

| ■ | 3 ha | 10,000 | ⑪ | 11–15 € |

Equal parts of Grenache, Mourvèdre and Syrah give a harmonious wine, with garnet-red colour giving off violet glints. The nose is complex, with red berries and ripe fruit. Despite 11 months in cask, tannins are silky, with good length of flavour. **Cuvée Saint-Roch Tradition 2001 red (8–11 €)** gets one star for its elegance and ripe fruit flavours.
☛ Maxime et Patrick Brunel, Ch. Saint-Roch, chem. de Lirac, 30150 Roquemaure, tel. 04.66.82.82.59, fax 04.66.82.83.00, e-mail brunel@chateau-saint-roch.com ☑
Ⴤ ev. day except Sat. Sun. 8am–12 noon 2pm–5pm; cl. 1–15 Aug.

CH. DE SEGRIES 2002★

| ■ | 1.5 ha | 3,000 | ∎ | 5–8 € |

Skilful fermentation has produced this pale yellow wine. The palette is floral, with toasted fruit mingling with aniseed and white flowers. Good structure, roundness and intriguing length of flavour all add up to a very well made wine. Drink as an aperitif or with grilled peppers.
☛ SCEA Henri de Lanzac, Ch. de Ségriès, chem. de la Grange, 30126 Lirac, tel. 04.66.50.22.97, fax 04.66.50.17.02 ☑
Ⴤ by appt.

DOM. TOUR DES CHENES 2001★★

| ■ | 2.5 ha | 10,000 | ⑪ | 8–11 € |

This wine won two stars in the last edition of the *Guide* in its rosé version. Now it is the turn of the red to stand out for its fullness and balance. Integrated tannins and eight months in cask leave it a liquorice and stewed fruit character. This wine is for ageing and possesses plenty of freshness and youth.
☛ Tour des Chênes, 30126 Saint-Laurent-des- Arbres, tel. 04.66.50.01.19, fax 04.66.50.34.69, e-mail tour-des-chenes@wanadoo.fr ☑
Ⴤ ev. day except Sat. Sun. 9am–12 noon 3pm–7pm; cl. Dec.

DOM. LE VIEUX MOULIN 2000★

| ■ | 3.19 ha | 17,000 | ⑪ | 5–8 € |

Tasting reveals plenty of potential for developing flavour with a few years' ageing. The attack is intriguing, with fruit flavours (Morello cherry, blackcurrant) and liquorice notes. The nose is elegant, fine, pleasant and fruity. Enjoy with leg of lamb.
☛ SCEA Henri Roudil, rte de la Commanderie, Le Palais Nord, 30126 Tavel, tel. 04.66.50.05.64, fax 04.66.79.36.89 ☑
Ⴤ ev. day except Sat. Sun. 8am–12 noon 1.30pm–5.30pm

Wines selected but not starred

CH. BOUCARUT 2001

■	6 ha	25,000	📖 ⊞ 8–11€

☛ Christophe Valat, Ch. Boucarut, BP 76,
30150 Roquemaure, tel. 04.66.50.26.84, fax 04.66.50.40.91 ☑
🍷 by appt.

CH. DE BOUCHASSY 2002

■	2 ha	5,000	📖 🍷 5–8€

☛ Gérard Degoul, Ch. de Bouchassy, rte de Nîmes,
30150 Roquemaure, tel. 04.66.82.82.49, fax 04.66.82.87.80 ☑
🍷 ev. day except Sun. 8am–12 noon 2pm–7pm

DOM. LE MALAVEN 2000

■	2.99 ha	10,600	📖 🍷 5–8€

☛ Dominique Roudil, rte de la Commanderie, BP 28,
30126 Tavel, tel. 04.66.50.20.02, fax 04.66.50.90.42,
e-mail dominique.roudil@terre-net.fr ☑
🍷 ev. day 8am–12 noon 2pm–6pm

DOM. PELAQUIE

Cuvée Prestige 2000

■	3 ha	8,000	⊞ 8–11€

☛ SCEA Dom. Pélaquié, 7, rue du Vernet,
30290 Saint-Victor-la-Coste, tel. 04.66.50.06.04,
fax 04.66.50.33.32,
e-mail contact@domaine-pelaquie.com ☑
🍷 ev. day except Sun. 9am–12 noon 2pm–6pm
☛ GFA du Grand Vernet

CUVEE SAINT VALENTIN 2001

■	3.04 ha	n.c.	📖 ⊞ 🍷 5–8€

☛ Les Vignerons de Roquemaure, 1, rue des Vignerons,
30150 Roquemaure, tel. 04.66.82.82.01, fax 04.66.82.67.28 ☑
🍷 by appt.

Tavel

Considered by many to be the finest rosé in France, this great wine from the Côtes du Rhône comes from a vineyard situated in the *département* of the Gard, on the right bank of the river. The vines are grown on land around Tavel, together with a few parcels in the commune of Roquemaure, on 948 ha of sand, alluvial clay or smoothed pebbles. Tavel is the only Rhône appellation to produce rosé wines; production was 40,396 hl in 2002. A wine of great character, with a floral, then fruity bouquet, Tavel should be served as an accompaniment for fish dishes with sauce, charcuterie and white meats.

DOM. AMIDO

Les Baussières 2002★

■	7 ha	30,000	📖 🍷 5–8€

The Jury listed two wines from this estate, run by Gabriel Meffre. Les Baussières, with its light colouring, has a floral nose with stewed fruit aromas (Morello cherry, raspberry), which reappear on the palate. Just as elegant is **Domaine des Oiseaux 2002 de Christian Leperchois**, which is awarded the same rating.

☛ Maison Gabriel Meffre, Le Village, 84190 Gigondas,
tel. 04.90.12.32.42, fax 04.90.12.32.49
☛ Christian Amido

CH. D'AQUERIA 2002★★

■	45.38 ha	60,000	📖 🍷 5–8€

The first vines were planted on this estate in the 16th century. The Olivier family, which bought it in 1920, still runs it successfully today. Château d'Aquéria, which has already been awarded a *coup de coeur* several times, is remarkable in the 2002 vintage. Like its illustrious predecessor, the 2001 vintage, it has fresh red berries (redcurrant and cherry). The delightful nose gives off aromas of peach and honey. A wine with fine length, which can be drunk throughout a meal.
☛ SCA Jean Olivier, Ch. d'Aqueria, 30126 Tavel,
tel. 04.66.50.04.56, fax 04.66.50.18.46,
e-mail contact@aqueria.com ☑
🍷 ev. day except Sat. Sun. 8am–12 noon 2pm–6pm

COMBE DES RIEU 2002★★

■	3.89 ha	2,380	📖 🍷 5–8€

Combe des Rieu, made by Mireille Petit-Roudil, narrowly missed a *coup de coeur*. With its lovely, brilliant peony colour, it has a powerful, lively, floral, complex and clean nose. The attack has great finesse and freshness. A very harmonious wine, which has good structure and particularly pleasing length of flavour. **Domaine Moulin-la-Vignerie, Cuvée Réservée 2002** gained one star – a well-made wine.
☛ SCEA les Vignobles Mireille Petit-Roudil, rue de la Combe, BP 16, 30126 Tavel, tel. 04.66.50.06.55,
fax 04.66.79.37.07 ☑
🍷 by appt.

DOM. LAFOND ROC-EPINE

Cuvée Jean-Baptiste 2002★

■	5 ha	15,000	📖 🍷 8–11€

This estate won a *coup de coeur* in Lirac (see above). Cuvée Jean-Baptiste seduces with its colour, which has beautiful deep, brilliant red glints, as well as with its intense nose. This wine has strong red berries, balance, power and freshness. It is typical of the AOC. The **Cuvée Principale du Domaine Lafond Roc-Epine 2002** (120,000 bottles) gets the same rating.
☛ SCEA Lafond Roc-Epine, rte des Vignobles,
30126 Tavel, tel. 04.66.50.24.59, fax 04.66.50.12.42,
e-mail lafond@roc-epine.com ☑
🍷 by appt.
☛ Lafond

DOM. DE LA MORDOREE

La Dame Rousse 2002★★

■	8 ha	50,000	📖 8–11€

Christophe Delorme likes giving his wines very poetic names, such as Reine des Bois (Queen of the Woods) or Dame Rousse, which have figured in successive editions of the *Guide*. This Tavel, which was awarded a *coup de coeur* by the Grand Jury, has a wonderful intense colour with red and violet glints. The nose is clean and intense, with red berry and peach notes. The very fine palate combines power, balance, fleshiness, length and red berries.
☛ Dom. de la Mordorée, des Oliviers, 30126 Tavel,
tel. 04.66.50.00.75, fax 04.66.50.47.39 ☑
🍷 ev. day except Sun. 8am–12 noon 1.30pm–5.30pm
☛ Delorme

DOM. VERDA 2002★

| ■ | 2 ha | 10,600 | ▮ | 5–8 € |

This wine is made from 60% de Grenache Noir with Cinsault, completely de-stemmed. Fifteen hours' maceration are followed by *saignée*. This Tavel, with its lively, brilliant colour and good acidity, is pleasant on the palate, with peach and flint flavours. The nose has floral and peach aromas, with great finesse. Serve as an aperitif or with Basque-style chicken.
🖙 EARL Dom. Verda, 2749, chem. de la Barotte, 30150 Roquemaure, tel. 04.66.82.87.28, fax 04.66.82.87.28 ☑
⏲ ev. day except Sun. 8am–12 noon 2pm–6.30pm

DOM. DU VIEUX RELAIS 2002★

| ■ | n.c. | 5,600 | ▮ | 8–11 € |

This estate, whose history dates back to the 19th century, is in the heart of the village. Deep pink colour with red glints heralds a wine with a powerful, spicy nose marked by redcurrant and ripe fruit. It has good structure and balance to which acidity brings plenty of freshness. Drink with grilled fish or bouillabaisse.
🖙 GAEC Dom. du Vieux Relais, rte de la Commanderie, 30126 Tavel, tel. 04.66.50.36.52, fax 04.66.50.36.52 ☑
⏲ by appt.
🖙 Bastide

Wines selected but not starred

LES LAUZERAIES 2002

| ■ | 13 ha | 80,000 | ▮ ♦ | 5–8 € |

🖙 Les Vignerons de Tavel, rte de la Commanderie, 30126 Tavel, tel. 04.66.50.03.57, fax 04.66.50.46.57, e-mail tavel.cave@wanadoo.fr ☑
⏲ ev. day 9am–12 noon 2pm–6pm

DOM. ROC DE L'OLIVET 2002

| ■ | 2 ha | 7,000 | ▮ | 5–8 € |

🖙 Dom. Thierry Valente, Roc de l'Olivet, chem. de la Vaussière, 30126 Tavel, tel. 04.66.50.37.87, fax 04.66.50.37.87 ☑
⏲ by appt.

Clairette de Die

Clairette de Die is one of the oldest known wines in the world. The vineyard occupies the hillsides of the middle valley of the Drôme, between Luc-en-Diois and Aouste-sur-Sye. A sparkling wine is produced mainly from the Muscat variety (75% minimum). The fermentation stops naturally in the bottle, according to ancient Die practice. No "liqueur de tirage" (a mixture of yeasts, old wine and sugar) is added. Production was 66,771 hl in 2002.

CAROD 2001★

| ○ | 35 ha | n.c. | ▮ ♦ | 5–8 € |

In 1993 this estate built a museum devoted to Clairette-de-Die. Displays with a soundtrack take visitors through the winemaking process and describe the region's traditions in the early part of the 20th century. And you can also buy this fine, elegant, pale yellow wine, whose Muscat aromas are very marked.
🖙 GAEC Carod Frères, 26340 Vercheny, tel. 04.75.21.73.77, fax 04.75.21.75.22, e-mail info@caves-carod.com ☑
⏲ ev. day 8am–12 noon 2pm–6pm

JAILLANCE

Cuvée impériale✦✦

| ○ | n.c. | 780,000 | | 5–8 € |

A well-established cooperative with more than 1,000 ha under cultivation. This wine has fine, elegant mousse and plenty of richness. It gives off very complex aromas: white fruit (pear), exotic fruit (lychee), flowers (roses) and a peppery, musky quality that wraps up the whole in a harmonious length. Try it with a fruit salad – maybe of exotic fruit. The **Cuvée Tradition** gets one star.
🖙 La Cave de Die Jaillance, av. de la Clairette, BP 79, 26150 Die, tel. 04.75.22.30.00, fax 04.75.22.21.06 ☑
⏲ by appt.

SALABELLE

Tradition Cuvée Adline 2001★

| ○ | 1 ha | 3,000 | | 5–8 € |

Founded in 1845, this estate presented **Tradition 2001** (90% Muscat and 10% Clairette), which impressed the Jury, as well as Tradition Cuvée Adline. Made from pure Muscat, the latter appears a cut above, with more power and harmony. It has lychee and peach flavours, which give it real complexity.
🖙 GAEC Salabelle et Fils, 26150 Barsac, tel. 04.75.21.70.78, fax 04.75.21.70.78 ☑
⏲ by appt.

Wines selected but not starred

CHAMBERAN 2001

| ○ | 20 ha | 150,000 | | 5–8 € |

🖙 Union des Jeunes Viticulteurs Récoltants, rte de Die, 26340 Vercheny, tel. 04.75.21.70.88, fax 04.75.21.73.73, e-mail ujvr@terre-net.fr ☑
⏲ ev. day 9am–12 noon 2pm–6.30pm

JACQUES FAURE 2001

| ○ | 3 ha | n.c. | ▮ ♦ | 5–8 € |

🖙 Jacques Faure, RD 93, 26340 Vercheny, tel. 04.75.21.72.22, fax 04.75.21.71.14 ☑
⏲ ev. day 9am–12 noon 2pm–7pm

Crémant de Die

The AOC Crémant de Die was recognized by decree on 26 March 1993. It is made solely from the Clairette variety by the "Champagne" method involving secondary fermentation in the bottle.

CAROD 1998★

| ○ | 5 ha | 15,000 | ▮ ♦ | 5–8 € |

Would you like to try this lovely *crémant*, ideal as an aperitif to start off a good meal? It is fine and elegant, combining white fruit (pear) and white flowers. It has a good attack,

titillating the taste buds, which are then ready to savour some fine cooking.
🍴 GAEC Carod Frères, 26340 Vercheny, tel. 04.75.21.73.77, fax 04.75.21.75.22, e-mail info@caves-carod.com ☑
🍷 ev. day 8am–12 noon 2pm–6pm

JAILLANCE

Grande Réserve 1997★★

	5 ha	30,000		5–8 €

A very great *crémant*, which can be drunk throughout a meal. It is all there: a good attack, balance, liveliness, perfect control of flavours. There is fleshiness everywhere and the palate is remarkably long. "A perfect wine," wrote one taster. The **Jaillance** made from organically grown grapes also gets two stars. It is an elegant, balanced, fresh and fruity wine.
🍴 La Cave de Die Jaillance, av. de la Clairette, BP 79, 26150 Die, tel. 04.75.22.30.00, fax 04.75.22.21.06 ☑
🍷 by appt.

MARCEL MAILLEFAUD ET FILS 2000★

◯	1 ha	7,000	8–11 €

During the 2002 grape harvest this estate hosted the filming of the series *Un Gars et une Fille* (Boy and Girl), which was broadcast on France 2. Did the film crew take advantage of the location to enjoy this *crémant*, which foams so enticingly in the glass? The bubbles are fine and clear-cut and the colour is pale gold with green glints. Tasting reveals flavours of white flowers mingled with citrus notes and the finish is peppery. However, the Jury would have liked to see a little more length.
🍴 Marcel Maillefaud et Fils, GAEC des Adrets, 26150 Barsac, tel. 04.75.21.71.77, fax 04.75.21.75.24 ☑
🍷 ev. day 8am–12 noon 2pm–7pm

Wines selected but not starred

CHAMBERAN 1998

◯	0.67 ha	5,000	5–8 €

🍴 Union des Jeunes Viticulteurs Récoltants, rte de Die, 26340 Vercheny, tel. 04.75.21.70.88, fax 04.75.21.73.73, e-mail ujvr@terre-net.fr ☑
🍷 ev. day 9am–12 noon 2pm–6.30pm

JEAN-CLAUDE RASPAIL

Cuvée Flavien Brut extra 1999

◯	1.5 ha	9,000	▮ ◈		8–11 €

🍴 Jean-Claude Raspail et Fils, Dom. de la Mûre, 26340 Saillans, tel. 04.75.21.55.99, fax 04.75.21.57.57, e-mail jc.raspail@wanadoo.fr ☑
🍷 ev. day 9am–12 noon 2pm–6.30pm; cl. 5–31 Jan.

Châtillon-en-Diois

The vineyard of Châtillon-en-Diois covers 50 ha on the slopes of the high valley of the Drôme, between Luc-en-Diois, at 550 m altitude and Pont-de-Quart, 465 m. The appellation produces light and fruity reds (from the Gamay variety), to be drunk young and whites (from the Aligoté and Chardonnay varieties) that are pleasant and firm. Total production was 2,455 hl in 2002.

CLOS DE BEYLIERE 2001★

▮	0.5 ha	2,500	⊞	5–8 €

Seasoned readers of the *Guide* will already know Didier Cornillon and especially his Clos de Beylière, which has regularly been featured. This year, three colours are listed. The **Clos de Beylière 2001 red** impressed the Jury with its freshness and the **2001 rosé (3–5 €)** wins one star. However, it was Clos de Beylière that was the most attractive: made from pure Chardonnay grapes and aged one year in cask, it is well balanced, with good freshness and hazelnuts on the attack.
🍴 Didier Cornillon, 26410 Saint-Roman, tel. 04.75.21.81.79, fax 04.75.21.84.44 ☑
🍷 ev. day 10am–12.30pm 2.30pm–7pm; Oct.-Mar by appt.

Wines selected but not starred

DOM. DE LA CHAPELLE 2002

▮	1.1 ha	6,600	5–8 €

🍴 La Cave de Die Jaillance, av. de la Clairette, BP 79, 26150 Die, tel. 04.75.22.30.00, fax 04.75.22.21.06 ☑
🍷 by appt.

Coteaux du Tricastin

This appellation covers 2,000 ha, in 22 communes on the right bank of the Rhône, from La Baume-de-Transit in the south, through Saint-Paul-Trois-Châteaux, to Granges-Gontardes in the north. The very pebbly ancient alluvial soils and the sandy slopes situated at the limit of the Mediterranean climate produced about 115,434 hl of wine in 2002. The boundaries of this appellation have recently been redrawn.

DOM. DES AGATES

Le Privilège de Montagut 2001★

▮	1.07 ha	5,000	▮ ⊞ ◈		8–11 €

After 40 years working in the cooperative, Olivier Chabanis's parents handed the estate over to him. With Jean-Claude Riffard, he set up this cellar and the two decided to make and sell wine on their own account. Their first year has already produced different *cuvées*. This year, they offer a special wine, aged 16 months in cask. The nose of red berries and well-integrated vanilla oak extends on to the palate, where balance and length promise good ageing. In the meantime, try **Plaisir des Bruyères 2002 rosé (3–5 €)**, an aperitif wine par excellence, which recalls fields of spring flowers in the Drôme *département* of Provence. A simple but most enjoyable wine.
🍴 SCEA Vignerons Chabanis Riffard, Dom. des Agates, chem. de l'Etang, 26780 Châteauneuf-du-Rhône, tel. 04.75.90.80.03, fax 04.75.90.75.59, e-mail info@domainedesagates.com ☑
🍷 Mon-Fri.5pm–8pm; Sat. Sun. 9am–7pm

DOM. ALMORIC 2001★

▮	18.3 ha	30,000	▮	3–5 €

At this family-run estate amid the vines, they like to remember the time when wine was taken to Montélimar by horse-drawn wagon, but they also use modern winemaking techniques. This wine's concentrated, almost black, colour heralds great maturity. On the palate, gamey flavours nevertheless let through notes of raspberry, blackcurrant, peach and apricot.

Concentration in no way upsets the silkiness of the tannins. This substantial wine will go well with game stew.
↦ Jean-Pierre Almoric, 3, rte de Montélimar, 26780 Allan, tel. 04.75.46.65.23, fax 04.75.46.65.23 ☑
🍷 by appt.

CH. DES ESTUBIERS 2000★★

■	n.c.	13,000	◖▮	8–11 €

This estate belongs to the Chapoutier company (Tain-l'Hermitage) and grows grapes organically. With strong Syrah aromas, the already well-developed bouquet integrates notes from all the families of aroma (leather, fruit, game, coffee), which are joined on the palate by liquorice and vanilla. None of this detracts from the wine's fleshiness and roundness, or from its remarkable length.
↦ Ch. des Estubiers, 26290 Les Granges-Gontardes, tel. 04.75.98.54.78, fax 04.75.98.54.81
🍷 by appt.
↦ M. Chapoutier

DOM. DE GRANGENEUVE
Cuvée de la Truffière 2001★

■	7.5 ha	24,000	◖▮	8–11 €

Built on the ruins of a 1st century Roman villa, this estate was founded by Odette and Henri Bour in 1964. They cleared land and planted vines and played a leading role in gaining recognition for the wines of Tricastin. Dark colour and gamey aromas contrast with the velvetiness of particularly agreeable tannins. Time will put the finishing touches on this work. The **Cuvée Tradition 2001 red (5–8 €)**, aged in stainless steel vats, is full of fruit, with length, roundness and great finesse. A proportion of Cinsault and a minimal amount of Syrah give this wine a different but nevertheless very effective style.
↦ SARL Domaines Bour, Dom. de Grangeneuve, 26230 Roussas, tel. 04.75.98.50.22, fax 04.75.98.51.09, e-mail domaines.bour@wanadoo.fr ☑
🍷 ev. day 9am–12 noon 2pm–7pm

DOM. DE MONTINE
Emotion 2001★

■	10 ha	15,000	◖▮	5–8 €

Famous for its château and organs of its collegiate church, Grignan is also a town with a great interest in literature, hosting a letter-writing festival in honour of Madame de Sévigné. This estate offers a wine made from equal quantities of Syrah and Grenache, aged 12 months in cask. With its toasted and smoky notes, this wine undeniably has good potential. Flavours are complex and harmony will reach its best in a year's time.
↦ Monteillet, Dom. de Montine, GAEC de la Grande Tuilière, 26230 Grignan, tel. 04.75.46.54.21, fax 04.75.46.93.26, e-mail domainedemontine@wanadoo.fr ☑ 🏠
🍷 ev. day 9am–12 noon 2pm–7pm

Wines selected but not starred

CH. LA CROIX CHABRIERE
Florilège de Colette 2002

■	1 ha	3,000	▮ ♦	5–8 €

↦ Ch. la Croix Chabrière, rte de Saint-Restitut, 84500 Bollène, tel. 04.90.40.00.89, fax 04.90.40.19.93 ☑
🍷 ev. day 9am–12 noon 2pm–6pm;
Sun. 9am–12 noon; groups by appt.

DOM. DU VIEUX MICOCOULIER 2001

■	100 ha	100,000	▮ ♦	5–8 €

↦ SCGEA Cave Vergobbi, Le Logis de Berre, 26290 Les Granges-Gontardes, tel. 04.75.04.02.72, fax 04.75.04.41.81 ☑
🍷 ev. day 9.30am–12 noon 2.30pm–6.30pm;
Sun. and holidays by appt.

Côtes du Ventoux

This vineyard is at the foot of the limestone Massif du Ventoux, the "giant of the Vaucluse" (1,912 m), on soil composed of tertiary sediments and stretches over 51 communes (7,450 ha) between Vaison-la-Romaine in the north and Apt in the south. The wines produced are essentially reds and rosés. The climate, cooler than that of the Côtes du Rhône, causes the grapes to ripen later. The red wines have a lesser alcoholic content, but are fresh and elegant when young; they are better structured in the more westerly communes (Caromb, Bédoin, Mormoiron). The rosé wines are pleasant and need to be drunk young. Total production reached 311,102 hl in 2002.

DOM. DES ANGES 2002★

■	3.84 ha	21,000	▮ ♦	5–8 €

For the second year running, the white wine made by the Irish winemaker Ciaran Rooney on behalf of this estate's Irish owner, Gabriel MacGuiness, wins a star. With its colour giving off green glints, it has a flowery, slightly exotic bouquet and good harmony; enjoy with seafood. **L'Archange 2000 red (11–15 €)**, which is very well made, is the result of traditional vinification and long vat ageing. Soft fruit, cherry and kirsch on the nose and prune flavours sustained by oaky vanilla, add up to a lovely rich, powerful wine that has still to develop. Drink with Provençal stew.
↦ Dom. des Anges, 84570 Mormoiron, tel. 04.90.61.88.78, fax 04.90.61.98.05, e-mail ciaranr@club-internet.fr ☑
🍷 ev. day 9am–12 noon 2pm–6pm; 1 Oct.–1 Apr. by appt.

DOM. AYMARD 2002★

■	2 ha	12,000	▮ ♦	5–8 €

Plenty of freshness and fruit in this *rosé de saignée*, which is most alluring. It is well balanced and rewarding, leaving an impression of suppleness and roundness. Drink as an apéritif or with a grill.
↦ Dom. Aymard, Les Galères, Serres, 84200 Carpentras, tel. 04.90.63.35.32, fax 04.90.67.02.79, e-mail jeanmarie.aymard@free.fr ☑
🍷 by appt.

DOM. DE LA BASTIDONNE 2002★

■	2.5 ha	10,000	▮ ♦	5–8 €

Two wines from this estate are listed this year. Is this a gift for the Marreau family, who celebrate their centenary in 2003? The rosé has a limpid, brilliant colour with violet glints. The bouquet is dominated by red berries (forest fruits) and blackcurrant aromas with amylic hints are very elegant. A balanced, harmonious, delicious wine that makes a perfect aperitif. Just as well made is **Les Coutilles 2001 red (11–15 €)** which has a powerful nose of ripe fruit and prunes in brandy, as well as fine, though still rather fiery, tannins. Enjoy with fillet of beef or leg of lamb in two or three years.
↦ SCEA Dom. de la Bastidonne, 84220 Cabrières-d'Avignon, tel. 04.90.76.70.00, fax 04.90.76.74.34 ☑
🍷 ev. day except Sun. 9am–12 noon 2pm–6pm
↦ Gérard Marreau

CAVE BEAUMONT DU VENTOUX

Elevé en fût de chêne 2000★

| | n.c. | 26,658 | 🍶 | 5–8 € |

The management of this cooperative plan to develop vine growing on terraces, with the aim of producing first-class wines from low yields. For the moment the cellar offers a lovely wine with a very beautiful, intense red colour. Ripe red berries and fairly dense oakiness predominate, but harmony will be achieved with time. It will go perfectly with game or meat dishes with taste.
🍷 Cave coop. Beaumont-du-Ventoux, rte de Carpentras, 84340 Beaumont-du-Ventoux, tel. 04.90.65.11.78, fax 04.90.12.69.88, e-mail jacod.michel@fr ✓
🍾 ev. day 9am–12 noon 2pm–6pm

LOUIS BERNARD

Grande Réserve 2001★★

| | n.c. | 14,000 | 🍶 | 5–8 € |

This Rhône valley négociant offers three Côtes du Ventoux in different styles, all equally well-made. The **Domaine des Herbes Blanches 2002 red (3–5 €)**, with its notes of slightly acid red berries, wins one star. But the Grande Réserve wins the jackpot with two stars and high praise: it is powerful and well integrated. This wine, made by long vat fermentation and aged in oak casks, is completely balanced.
🍷 Salavert-Les domaines Bernard, rte de Sérignan, 84100 Orange, tel. 04.90.11.86.86, fax 04.90.34.87.30, e-mail sldb@sldb.fr

DOM. DU BON REMEDE

Secret de Vincent Elevé en fût de chêne 2001★★

| | 2 ha | 5,000 | 🍶 | 5–8 € |

After building a new winery in 2001, this estate doubled its acreage in 2002: it now covers 15 ha. A long fermentation period (three weeks) has given this wine a complex bouquet of figs, stewed fruit and raspberry. The palate is rich, powerful and with good length. It can age three to four years. The **Cuvée Vieilles Vignes 2001 red (3–5 €)**, with its attractive dark colour with bluish glints, is very well made and will also keep well.
🍷 Lucile et Frédéric Delay, 1248, rte de Malemort, 84380 Mazan, tel. 04.90.69.69.76, fax 04.90.69.69.76 ✓
🍾 by appt.

CANTEPERDRIX 2002★

| | 6 ha | 40,000 | 🍶 | 3–5 € |

A clay-limestone terroir and a predominance of Clairette complemented by Bourboulenc have produced this brilliantly coloured 2002 with green glints. This wine is dominated by a bouquet of exotic fruit (lemon, grapefruit), to which floral aromas give added finesse.
🍷 Cave Canteperdrix, rte de Caromb, BP 15, 84380 Mazan, tel. 04.90.69.70.31, fax 04.90.69.87.41 ✓
🍾 ev. day 8am–12 noon 2.30pm–6.30pm

DOM. DE CHAMP-LONG 2002★

| | 2.5 ha | 12,000 | 🍶 | 3–5 € |

The Champ-Long estate is a family concern. In 1964 Maurice Gély founded the cellar. In 1994 his son Christian, who has run the estate since, renovated it. In 2003, three of the estate's wines have been listed in the *Guide*. First, this brilliantly-coloured 2002 with green glints, made from a blend of several grape varieties: Grenache Blanc, Clairette, Roussanne and Bourboulenc. Its nose is fine and complex. Tasting reveals lively, fresh flavours. Enjoy with a tray of seafood. Two other wines impressed the Jury: the **2001 red (5–8 €)** is promising and the **Cuvée Spéciale 2000 red (5–8 €)** needs a little time to polish its tannins.
🍷 Christian Gély, Dom. de Champ-Long, 84340 Entrechaux, tel. 04.90.46.01.58, fax 04.90.46.04.40, e-mail domaine@champlong.fr ✓
🍾 ev. day except Sun. 9am–12.30pm 2pm–7pm

DOM. CHAUMARD

Cuvée des Campagnolles 2001★

| | 2 ha | 12,000 | | 3–5 € |

The oenologist Christine Chaumard, who has been at the head of this estate since it was founded more than ten years

ago, offers another lovely wine of attractive appearance. Dark colour with bluish tints, a very fruity bouquet, soft spice notes and intense red berry flavours with a few hints of liquorice, add up to, in the words of one Jury member, "an easy-drinking wine for an informed enthusiast".
🍷 Dom. Chaumard, rte d'Aubignan, 84330 Caromb, tel. 04.90.62.43.38, fax 04.90.62.35.84 ✓
🍾 ev. day except Sun. 8am–12 noon 2pm–6pm

CH. CRILLON 2000★

| | 12 ha | 80,000 | 🍶 🥂 | 3–5 € |

This highly typical Château Crillon has an attractive garnet-red colour. It is a warm wine, southern in character and very good of its type. It has real potential, but needs to acquire roundness with time. Two other wines by the Vignerons du Mont Ventoux impressed the Jury: the **Altitude 400 2001 red**, which achieves good balance between aromas and flavours and the classic **Chais du Grillon 2001 red**.
🍷 SCA Les Vignerons du Mont-Ventoux, quartier de la Salle, 84410 Bedoin, tel. 04.90.12.88.00, fax 04.90.65.64.43, e-mail bvieubled@bedouin.com ✓
🍾 by appt.

DU PELOUX 2000★

| | n.c. | n.c. | | 3–5 € |

A Côtes-du-Ventoux of strong Grenache character, well-integrated with freshness in a fine balance. It is a credit to the appellation.
🍷 Vignobles Du Peloux, rte d'Orange, 84350 Courthézon, tel. 04.90.70.42.00, fax 04.90.70.42.15, e-mail dupeloux@vignoblesdupeloux.com
🍾 by appt.

DOM. DE LA FERME SAINT-MARTIN

Clos des Estaillades 2001★

| | 1.5 ha | 6,000 | 🍶 🥂 | 5–8 € |

As in the preceding edition of the *Guide*, Clos des Estaillades is awarded one star. It is made from Grenache, with 10% Cinsault, vinified by traditional methods. The nose is still a little closed in fruit (raspberry, redcurrant), but the palate gives full rein to red berries and has pleasant herbaceous notes. It should reach its best in two or three years.
🍷 Guy Jullien, Dom. de la Ferme Saint-Martin, 84190 Suzette, tel. 04.90.62.96.40, fax 04.90.62.90.84, e-mail guy.jullien@tiscali.fr ✓ 🏠
🍾 ev. day except Sun. 10am–12.30pm 1.30pm–6pm; Jan.-Feb. by appt.

LA FERME SAINT PIERRE

Roi Fainéant 2001★★

| | 6 ha | 25,000 | 🍶 🥂 | 8–11 € |

The idle king (roi fainéant) certainly isn't the oenologist who made this wine! A great deal of work and care have gone into producing it. The beautiful deep colour, limpid and brilliant, invites you to taste it. The complex bouquet reveals soft fruit, cherry and spice aromas with subtle oak notes. A superb attack announces good substance which develops over supple, well present tannins. An attractive wine that can be drunk now but has good ageing potential. Serve with game. Paul Vendran gets one star for **Cuvée Juliette 2002 rosé (5–8 €)**, which bears the name of his daughter, who was also born in 2002. A wine full of freshness, with exotic fruit.
🍷 La Ferme Saint Pierre, 84410 Flassan, tel. 04.90.61.90.88, fax 04.90.61.89.96, e-mail paulvendran@free.fr ✓
🍾 by appt.
🍷 Paul Vendran

DOM. DE FONDRECHE 2002★

| | 4 ha | 15,000 | 🍶 | 5–8 € |

A lot of care has been taken over the vines on this estate in recent years (high trellising, de-budding, a green harvest, leaf-thinning) in the interests of quality. And once again, M. Vincenti has made a complete success of his winemaking. This limpid-coloured 2002 with green glints reveals very rich vanilla, cocoa and roasted coffee aromas that the Jury thoroughly enjoyed. The **red Cuvée Persia 2001 (11–15 €)**, which was awarded a *coup de coeur* for the 97 and 99 vintages, was considered very good. It has a pleasant bouquet of red forest fruits, aromas of vanilla and liquorice and subtle oak. One taster felt this wine was "in line with current trends and the latest tastes". Drink with stewed hare or wild boar.

☛ Dom. de Fondrèche, quartier Fondrèche, 84380 Mazan, tel. 04.90.69.61.42, fax 04.90.69.61.18 ☑
⚲ by appt.
☛ Mme Barthélemy et M. Vincenti

DOM. GRANDJACQUET

Le Rabassier 2001★

| ■ | 3 ha | 13,000 | 🍶 ô | 5–8 € |

Patricia and Joël Jacquet's second year of winemaking is also their second appearance in the *Guide*. They favour working by hand and have started converting to organic methods. Rabassier 2001 has very dark colour and a bouquet of stewed red berries. Fruit flavours and gamey notes have plenty of length. This wine has good overall harmony and is ready to drink. To eat: woodpigeon wing with boletus mushrooms. The **Cuvée Aymard Savinas 2002 white**, which was singled out by the Jury, has a pretty label in the warm colours of Provence.

☛ Dom. GrandJacquet, 2869, La Venue de Carpentras, 84380 Mazan, tel. 04.90.63.24.87, fax 04.90.63.24.87 ☑
⚲ by appt.
☛ Joël Jacquet

DOM. LES HAUTES-BRIGUIERES

Cuvée Prestige Elevé en fût de chêne 2001★

| ■ | 2 ha | 8,200 | ⑪ | 5–8 € |

In 2000 the new generation, mindful of quality as well as of ecology, adopted sustainable methods. Cuvée Prestige has been made according to these principles. Cold maceration followed by long fermentation (a month) has given it its lovely purplish-red colour, complex bouquet of menthol, chlorophyll and garrigue and finely oaked flavours. A very well-made wine that goes with a highly-seasoned or spicy dish. The **Cuvée Quintessence 2001 Elevée en Fût de Chêne red (8–11 €)** impressed the Jury. It has good length of flavour (fruit, spices and leather).

☛ François-Xavier Rimbert, Dom. Les Hautes-Briguières, 84570 Mormoiron, tel. 04.90.61.71.97, fax 04.90.61.85.80, e-mail fxrimbert@aol.com ☑
⚲ ev. day 3pm–8pm; Sat. Sun. 10am–7pm

CH. JUVENAL 2002★

| ■ | 4.3 ha | 28,400 | 🍶 | 3–5 € |

Excellent value for money from this very attractive wine with plenty of fruit. It is made from well-ripened, healthy Grenache (80%) and the result is extremely worthwhile. Despite its youth, this wine already displays roundness and unctuousness. Another star for the Vignerons de Beaumes-de-Venise with **Domaine Alban 2002 red (5–8 €)**. The vintage's difficulties notwithstanding, here is plenty of power, thanks to the part played by Mont Ventoux and to M. Alban's dedication. Drink with young guinea-fowl with peaches, duck with bitter orange, or black pudding with apples.

☛ Vignerons de Beaumes-de-Venise, quartier Ravel, 84190 Beaumes-de-Venise, tel. 04.90.12.41.00, fax 04.90.65.02.05, e-mail vignerons@beaumes-de-venise.com ☑
⚲ by appt.

DOM. LE MURMURIUM

Carpe Diem 2001★★

| ■ | 5 ha | 15,000 | 🍶⑪ ô | 11–15 € |

This estate covered only 8 ha when it was founded, but now boasts almost 20. Better still, it occupies a distinguished place in the *Guide*, gaining two stars for two of its wines. There is plenty of substance and finesse in Carpe Diem, which has lovely harmony with its subtle aromas of prune accompanied by roasted notes. A remarkable bottle in every sense, to be enjoyed with a meat dish in sauce, a game dish, or blue cheese. The concert programme of the **Cuvée Opéra 2001 red (15–23 €)**, which was also awarded two stars, are: garrigue aromas (thyme and sage), ripe fruit flavours, Virginia tobacco and vanilla notes and above all, lots of drinking pleasure. Serve with thrushes.

☛ SCEA Marot-Metzler, Dom. Le Murmurium, rte de Flassan, 84570 Mormoiron, tel. 04.90.61.73.74, fax 04.90.61.74.51 ☑
⚲ ev. day except Sat. Sun. 9am–12 noon 3pm–6pm

LA QUINTESSENCE DU CH. PESQUIE

2001★

| ■ | 14 ha | 70,000 | ⑪ | 11–15 € |

The site of Château Pesquié (Vivier in Provençal) has been inhabited since the Middle Ages, because there are numerous springs nearby. Water was at a premium in this warm region. But was it as sought-after as the very dark-coloured Quintessence? It has red berry flavours at first, then spices take over and the warm, gentle finish reveals well-made tannins that still need to become rounded.

☛ SCEA Ch. Pesquié, rte de Flassan, BP 6, 84570 Mormoiron, tel. 04.90.61.94.08, fax 04.90.61.94.13, e-mail chateaupesquie@yahoo.fr ☑ 🎪
⚲ ev. day 9am–12 noon 2pm–6pm;
cl. Sat. Sun. Oct.-Easter
☛ Familles Chaudière Bastide

DOM. DU PUY MARQUIS

Vieilli en fût de chêne 2001★

| ■ | 3.5 ha | 13,600 | ⑪ | 5–8 € |

A few kilometres from Rustrel and from the Colorado of Provence (an ochre quarry), Claude Leclercq, a former professional cyclist, offers a very harmonious 2001. The combination of wine and oak is perfect and the length of flavour remarkable. Wait about two years.

☛ Claude Leclercq, Dom. du Puy Marquis, rte de Rustrel, 84400 Apt, tel. 04.90.74.51.87, fax 04.90.04.69.80 ☑ 🎪
⚲ ev. day except Sun. 10.15am–12 noon 3pm–6.30pm

CAVE SAINT MARC 2001★

| ■ | 80 ha | 100,000 | 🍶 ô | 8–11 € |

This cellar bears the name of the patron saint of the winemakers of Provence: a good start for this wine, born of a clay-limestone terroir. It has a purple colour and hints of red berries on the nose. Suppleness and roundness dominate the palate, over very silky tannins. Ready for drink now on. The **Cuvée Le Clocher 2002 rosé (5–8 €)** was mentioned for its salmon-pink colour and fruity redcurrant and raspberry flavours.

☛ Cave coopérative Saint Marc, av. de l'Europe, BP 16, 84330 Caromb, tel. 04.90.62.40.24, fax 04.90.62.48.83, e-mail saint-marc@mageos.com ☑
⚲ ev. day 8am–12 noon 2pm–6pm

SAINT MIRAT 2001★

| ■ | 5.8 ha | 46,400 | ⑪ | 3–5 € |

A most fruitful result of the collaboration between the Compagnie Rhodanienne and the producers of Saint Mirat, which looks attractive and is bottled by Jean Berteau. On the nose and palate, little red berries dominate over fine tannins. Plenty of freshness and length of flavour, with a note of liquorice on the finish. Ready to drink.

☛ La Compagnie Rhodanienne, Chemin-Neuf, 30210 Castillon-du-Gard, tel. 04.66.37.49.50, fax 04.66.37.49.51, e-mail cie.rhodanienne@wanadoo.fr
⚲ by appt.

CH. TALAUD 2001★★

| ■ | 12.5 ha | 40,000 | 🍶 | 3–5 € |

RHONE

Towering over a breathtaking région, now classed as a world biosphere reserve because of its unique flora and fauna, Mont Ventoux rises to 1,909 m. The Giant of Provence overlooks Château Talaud, granted a *coup de cœur* by a unanimous Jury. This elegant wine has a cherry red colour with dark tints and a very intense bouquet dominated by stewed red berries with mineral, leather and violet notes. A well-structured, powerful wine with plenty of fleshiness. Do be patient and keep it for two years before enjoying it with a Provençal dish.
🕏 SCEA Ch. Talaud, 84870 Loriol-du-Comtat, tel. 04.90.65.71.00, fax 04.90.65.77.93, e-mail chateautalaud@infonic.fr ☑ ⑪ ⬧
🍷 by appt.
🕏 Henricus Deiters

DOM. DE TARA

Hautes Pierres 2001★

	1 ha	3,700	⑪	11–15 €

A ten-ha estate, two kilometres from the ochre cliffs of Roussillon. Hautes Pierres allows Syrah to come through loud and clear, while developing vanilla and fresh red berry hints. The palate, a little too oaky, is dominated by roasted flavours, which mingle pleasantly with the structure. Give the oak time to become integrated.
🕏 Dom. de Tara, Les Rossignols, 84220 Roussillon, tel. 04.90.05.74.87, fax 04.90.05.71.35 ☑
🍷 ev. day except Sun. 2pm–6pm
🕏 Droux

DOM. LES TERRASSES D'EOLE

Lou Mistrau 2000★★

	2 ha	12,900	▮⑪⬥	8–11 €

When Stéphane Saurel took the helm of the family estate he decided to leave the cooperative and built his own winery. In 1999 he signed off his first wine. His second, this Côtes du Ventoux 2000, was judged remarkable. Lou Mistrau is a blend of Grenache and Syrah that has partly undergone classic maceration and partly semi-carbonic maceration. The nose is astonishing, with aromas of soft fruit (blackcurrant predominating), truffle, garrigue, eucalyptus and more. A powerful wine with cocoa and prune notes and rich, silky tannins. Enjoy with game or meat in sauce.
🕏 Claude et Stéphane Saurel, Dom. Terrasses d'Eole, chem. des Rossignols, 84380 Mazan, tel. 04.90.69.84.82, fax 04.90.69.84.90, e-mail stephane@terrasses-eole.fr ☑ ⬧
🍷 ev. day except Sun. 9am–12 noon 2pm–6.30pm

TERRE D'ANTAN 2001★★

	2 ha	3,000	⑪	11–15 €

Bonnieux is one of France's most beautiful hill villages. Since 1920 its cooperative has produced good wines, such as this remarkable Terre d'Antan. It has dark red colour with blue tints. Oak notes break through only to be quickly covered by fruit. Tasting brings home the richness of this wine: volume, fullness, good tannic support and a finish of oak with roasted and vanilla notes. Tasters were liberal with their adjectives: very generous, complex, harmonious and so forth. Two other wines impressed the Jury: the **2001 red Elevé en Fût de Chêne (5–8 €)**, strictly for lovers of oak and **Les Roussins 2002 rosé (3–4 €)**, which is typical of its appellation and vintage.
🕏 Cave de Bonnieux, quartier de la Gare, 84480 Bonnieux, tel. 04.90.75.80.03, fax 04.90.75.98.30, e-mail webmaster@cave-bonnieux.com ☑

CH. VALCOMBE

Les Griottes 2001★★

	3 ha	12,000	▮	5–8 €

In 2000, the Paul Jeune vineyards were extended by the acquisition of the former estate of Claude Fonquerle. Now they offer Les Griottes, made from equal parts of Grenache and Syrah, which has intense ruby colouring with violet glints. The complex nose of Morello cherry, spices and blackberry is followed by flavours of soft fruit in brandy. An elegant wine that is still young and has real ageing potential (three or four years). The elegance and fresh flavour of the **Cuvée Signature 2001 red** earned it one star.

🕏 Vignobles Paul Jeune, Ch. Valcombe, 84330 Saint-Pierre-de-Vassols, tel. 04.90.83.73.87, fax 04.90.83.51.13, e-mail vignoblespauljeune@wanadoo.fr ☑
🍷 by appt.

DOM. DE LA VERRIERE 2001★★

	4 ha	21,300	▮⬥	3–5 €

This former estate of King René of Provence, run since 1988 by Jacques Maubert, is a regular in the *Guide*. In the previous edition, le Haut de Jacotte received two stars; now it is the turn of this deep red 2001 with violet glints. It is dominated by soft fruit and liquorice and its robust structure offers an especially pleasant, long finish. A superb wine that is very representative of its appellation. The Jury were equally besotted by the limited-production (1,100 bottles) **Cuvée Saint-Michel 2001 red (11–15 €)**, whose complex bouquet has spices and liquorice with cocoa. To round off this collection of awards, the **2002 rosé** impressed the Jury for its fruit flavours and pleasant hints of honey.
🕏 Jacques Maubert, Dom. de La Verrière, 84220 Goult, tel. 04.90.72.20.88, fax 04.90.72.40.33, e-mail laverriere2@wanadoo.fr ☑
🍷 ev. day except Sun. 9am–12 noon 2pm–6pm

XAVIER VIGNON

Xavier 2001★★★

	4 ha	20,000	▮⑪⬥	8–11 €

This new winemaker, an oenologist, works in partnership with the cellars and estates of the region. This yields results, witness his many wines listed in this *Guide* and this *coup de cœur* awarded unanimously by the Jury! This superbly-presented 2001, ruby with black tints, gives off aromas of fruit and garrigue. Its rich palette of flavours mingles fruit, spices, liquorice, leather and more. An exceptional wine, which should improve with time. Save for white meat with truffles.
🕏 Xavier Vignon, chem. de Caromb, 84330 Le Barroux, tel. 04.90.62.33.44, fax 04.90.62.33.45, e-mail povidis@wanadoo.fr ☑ ⑪
🍷 by appt.

Wines selected but not starred

APTA JULIA 2001

	3 ha	7,000	▮⬥	5–8 €

🕏 SCA les Vins de Sylla, 178, quartier du Viaduc, BP 141, 84405 Apt Cedex, tel. 04.90.74.05.39, fax 04.90.04.72.06 ☑
🍷 by appt.

DOM. LES AUMETTES 2001

	6 ha	40,000	▮⬥	5–8 €

🕏 Cave Terraventoux, La Rode, 84570 Mormoiron, tel. 04.90.61.80.07, fax 04.90.61.97.23, e-mail infos@cave-terraventoux.com ☑
🍷 ev. day except Sun. 8am–12 noon 2pm–6pm

PIERRE CHANAU 2002

| ■ | 27.2 ha | 200,000 | ■ ♦ | –3 € |

🕯 Cellier de Marrenon, rue Amédée-Giniès, BP 13, 84240 La Tour-d'Aigues, tel. 04.90.07.40.65, fax 04.90.07.30.77, e-mail marrenon@marrenon.com
⊺ ev. day 8am–12 noon 2pm–6pm (summer 8am–12 noon 3pm–7pm); Sun. 8am–12 noon

DOM. L'ESTAGNOL

Hommage à Louis Fayard 2001

| ■ | 1.5 ha | 4,000 | ⦀ | 8–11 € |

🕯 SCEA Dom. L'Estagnol, 135, rte de Caromb, 84380 Mazan, tel. 04.90.69.68.88, fax 04.90.69.68.88, e-mail domaine@estagnol.fr **☑**
⊺ ev. day except Sun. 10am–12 noon 3pm–7pm
🕯 Laurent Favier

DOM. LES GRAND'TERRES

Cuvée spéciale 2001

| ■ | 5 ha | 10,000 | ⦀ | 5–8 € |

🕯 Comte O. d'Ollone, Dom. Les Grandes Terres, 84330 Le Barroux, tel. 04.90.62.43.09, fax 04.90.62.48.50 **☑ ♙**
⊺ ev. day except Sun. 8am–12 noon 2pm–6pm; cl. 15 Jan.–15 Feb.

DOM. PELISSON

Réserves 2002

| ■ | n.c. | 8,000 | | 5–8 € |

🕯 Patrick Pelisson, 84220 Gordes, tel. 04.90.72.28.49, fax 04.90.72.28.49 **☑**
⊺ by appt.

Côtes du Luberon

T he Appellation Côtes du Luberon was created on 26 February 1988.

T he 36 communes included in this appellation extend over the northern and southern slopes of the limestone mountains of the Luberon and the vineyard covers nearly 4,013 ha and in 2002 170,427 hl were produced. Côtes du Luberon produce good red wines with a marked character from the quality of the varieties used (Grenache, Syrah) and the distinctive terroir on which they grow. The climate is cooler than in the Rhône valley and the late harvests explain the large proportion of white wines (25%) and the acknowledged quality for which they are sought.

DOM. DE LA BASTIDE DE RHODARES 2000★★★

| ■ | 2 ha | 8,500 | ⦀ | 11–15 € |

Treat yourself to a short jaunt to Lourmarin, a pretty Provençal village steeped in associations with Albert Camus, who won the Nobel Prize for literature. Take the opportunity to stop off at the cooperative cellar. This also produced the **Hau Coulobre 2002 rosé (3–5 €)**, which gets one star, as do **Hau Coulobre 2002 white**, with its aromas of honey and honeysuckle and **Domaine de Gerbaud 2001 red (5–8 €)**. The tasters were ecstatic before the magnificent intense, almost black, colour of this wine. They were not disappointed by its remarkably intense bouquet, with its toasted, spicy and oaky notes. And what can we say about the flavours of highly concentrated soft fruit and hints of citrus fruit! "A lovely personality; a wine of character that I recommend," wrote one member of the Jury. **Domaine Rhodarès 2001 Elevé en Fût de Chêne red (5–8 €)** gets one star. The nose has hints of leather

and red berries but is still a little closed; in two or three years, however, this wine should have fulfilled its potential.
🕯 SCA Cave de Lourmarin-Cadenet, montée du Galinier, 84160 Lourmarin, tel. 04.90.68.06.21, fax 04.90.68.25.84 **☑**

CH. LA CANORGUE 2002★★

| ■ | 9 ha | 36,000 | ■ ♦ | 5–8 € |

A magnificent 17th century château is the headquarters of this estate, run on organic principles for more than 15 years by Jean-Pierre and Martine Margan. The care lavished on the vines has borne fruit – witness this rosé, which won high praise from the Jury. Its salmon-pink colour, quite pale, is unusual for a Côtes du Lubéron. The honeyed nose gives off nuances of white flowers, while the palate reveals well-rounded fruit flavours. Balanced, tempting and seductive, this wine can be drunk from now on, as an aperitif, with poultry, or with a grill. The **2001 red (8–11 €)** impressed the Jury with its elegant nose and fine fullness.
🕯 EARL Jean-Pierre et Martine Margan, Ch. La Canorgue, 84480 Bonnieux, tel. 04.90.75.81.01, fax 04.90.75.82.98, e-mail chateaucanorgue.margan@wanadoo.fr **☑**
⊺ by appt.

DOM. CHASSON 2001★

| ■ | 6.87 ha | 40,000 | ⦀ | 5–8 € |

At the foot of the cliffs of Roussillon, the Chasson estate enjoys exceptional sunshine, which allows it to produce some lovely wines, such as this 1999 vintage. Although it is difficult to assess now, wrote one taster, for its tannins are very marked, its wood and spice flavours are nevertheless intriguing. This wine needs to be kept for two or three years before being enjoyed with game or meat in sauce. **Cuvée Guillaume de Cabestan 2000 red (8–11 €)** impressed the Jury. Dominated by oakiness, it needs to acquire suppleness. It can then accompany Provençal cooking.
🕯 Jean-Claude Chasson, SCEA Ch. Blanc, quartier Grimaud, 84220 Roussillon, tel. 04.90.05.64.56, fax 04.90.05.72.79 **☑**
⊺ ev. day 8am–12 noon 1.30pm–7pm

DOM. DE LA CITADELLE 2000★★

| ■ | 10 ha | 54,843 | ■ ⦀ ♦ | 5–8 € |

In 1989, Yves Rousset-Rouard bought an old Provençal farmhouse and eight ha of vines. Now his vineyard covers 40 ha in the communes of Ménerbes and Oppède. Of these, ten ha are devoted to producing this remarkable 2000, with intense garnet-red colour and a nose of fruit and soft spices. The palate is balanced, dominated by concentrated soft fruits and rather tannic on the finish. It is pleasantly harmonious and has good concentration: a fine representative of its appellation. The **2002 white** is very well made, with nuances of aroma with citrus fruit. Serve as an aperitif. Finally, the **2002 rosé** impressed the Jury.
🕯 Rousset-Rouard, Dom. de la Citadelle, rte de Cavaillon, 84560 Ménerbes, tel. 04.90.72.41.58, fax 04.90.72.41.59, e-mail domainedelacitadelle@wanadoo.fr **☑**
⊺ ev. day 10am–12 noon 2pm–6pm except Sun. from Nov. to Mar.; groups by appt.

CH. CONSTANTIN-CHEVALIER

Cuvée des Fondateurs 2000★★

| ■ | 12 ha | 40,000 | ■ ⦀ ♦ | 5–8 € |

This estate has undergone substantial modernization since 1991, both in its winery and in its vine-growing. It makes quality wines and 80% of its production is for export. Cuvée des Fondateurs, whose 1998 vintage was awarded *coup de cœur*, delighted the Jury. With deep-red colour and an intense nose of ripe fruit with peppery and charred notes, it shows good harmony. Tannins are present but integrated. A remarkably powerful 2000 that will satisfy lovers of southern Rhône wines. Enjoy with game or other meat stew – Provençal style, naturally. The **white Cuvée des Fondateurs 2002**, a harmonious wine dominated by citrus fruit, impressed the Jury.
🕯 EARL Constantin-Chevalier et Filles, Ch. de Constantin, 84160 Lourmarin, tel. 04.90.68.38.99, fax 04.90.68.37.37 **☑**
⊺ ev. day except Sun. 10am–12 noon 3pm–6pm
🕯 Allen Chevalier

RHONE

Côtes du Luberon

CH. EDEM

Seigneurie du Lubéron 2002★

| ■ | 1.63 ha | 10,100 | ■ ♦ | 5–8 € |

In 2001, Emmanuelle and Eduard Van Wely, who have owned Château Edem since 1985, decided to set up their own cellar. This rosé comes from their ultra-modern winery and has a very pleasant pale pink colour, an amylic nose with fruit notes and a supple, harmonious palate. It could be served as an aperitif, with an exotic dish, or with chicken.
•┐ Eduard et Emmanuelle Van Wely, Ch. Edem, lieu-dit Saint-Véran, 84220 Goult, tel. 04.90.72.36.02, fax 04.90.72.34.71, e-mail chateau.edem@wanadoo.fr ☑
☎ by appt.

DOM. FAVEROT

Cuvée du Général Elevé en fût de chêne 2001★★

| ■ | 2 ha | 6,000 | ■ ❙❙ ♦ | 11–15 € |

This wine is named in honour of General Faverot de Kerbrech, assistant to the Master of the Horse of Napoléon III and ancestor of the estate's present owners. This wine has an oaky, vanilla nose with red berry aromas (cherry, Morello cherry). A very fruity, powerful, well-structured wine which needs to wait four or five years before being enjoyed with pheasant with chestnuts, or other game.
•┐ Dom. Faverot, L'Allée, BP 9, 84660 Maubec, tel. 04.90.76.65.16, fax 04.90.76.65.16, e-mail domainefaverot@wanadoo.fr ☑ ☎
☎ by appt.

DOM. FONDACCI

Vieilli en fût de chêne 2001★

| ■ | 1.5 ha | 6,000 | ❙❙ | 8–11 € |

A new estate, founded in 2000 – and already appearing in the *Guide* for the second time. Its 2001 wine, made from 80% Syrah and vinified by traditional methods, has an intense ruby colour and a pleasant nose of ripe berries. The palate is well structured, rounded and with good length. This wine will go well with meat in sauce, game, or stew. The vat-aged **2001 red (3–5 €)** impressed the Jury with its fresh fruit and liquorice nose.
•┐ Dom. Guy Fondacci, quartier La Sablière, 84580 Oppède, tel. 04.90.76.95.91, fax 04.90.71.40.38, e-mail guyfondacci@aol.com ☑
☎ ev. day 10.30am–12 noon 2.30pm–6pm

DOM. DE FONTENILLE

Cuvée Prestige Vieilli en fût de chêne 2001★★

| ■ | 5 ha | 2,000 | ❙❙ | 11–15 € |

This estate has fine 16th century vaulted cellars and stone vats more than 300 years old. But its Cuvée Prestige has been aged in cask and delighted the Jury with its beautiful, intense, dark, almost black colour, bouquet of very ripe fruit and pastry (almond purée) and flavours of cherries in brandy and coffee. There is plenty of substance in this wine, which should preferably be served in three to five years' time, with red meat, game, or a dish with sauce.
•┐ EARL Lévêque et Fils, Dom. de Fontenille, 84360 Lauris, tel. 04.90.08.23.36, fax 04.90.08.45.05, e-mail domaine.fontenille@wanadoo.fr ☑ ☎
☎ ev. day except Sun. 9am–12.30pm 2pm–7pm

DOM. DE LA GARELLE 2001★★

| ■ | 4 ha | 20,000 | | 3–5 € |

A remarkable wine with dark garnet-red colour, a nose of red berries (redcurrant, cherry) and plenty of weight – a typical Syrah. It is ready to drink, but could also be aged two years in the cellar.
•┐ Cave des Vignerons de Rasteau et de Tain-l'Hermitage, rte des Princes-d'Orange, 84110 Rasteau, tel. 04.90.10.90.10, fax 04.90.46.16.65, e-mail vrt@rasteau.com ☑

GRAND LUBERON

Elevé en fût de chêne 2001★★★

| ■ | 35 ha | 150,000 | ❙❙❙ | 5–8 € |

The Marrenon estate practises plot selection and has put together a handbook of viticulture. In 2000 it built a winery for producing top-end wines – an effort that was rewarded with this *coup de cœur* awarded to Grand Luberon, which is a very great Luberon indeed. Magnificent in appearance, with its violet colour and dark tints, powerful, elegant nose (cinnamon, bilberry) and concentrated, balanced palate with exceptional flavours (liquorice, violets, red flowers), it should be enjoyed in four or five years with roast shoulder of lamb. The **Grande Toque 2002 rosé (3–5 €)**, vinified by low-temperature *saignée*, gains one star. It is fruity and amylic.
•┐ Cellier de Marrenon, rue Amédée-Giniès, BP 13, 84240 La Tour-d'Aigues, tel. 04.90.07.40.65, fax 04.90.07.30.77, e-mail marrenon@marrenon.com ☑
☎ ev. day 8am–12 noon 2pm–6pm (summer 8am–12 noon 3pm–7pm); Sun. 8am–12 noon

CH. DE L'ISOLETTE 2002★

| | 5 ha | 20,000 | ■ ♦ | 8–11 € |

This estate covers more than 100 ha, of which 43 were entirely planted with noble grape varieties between 1965 and 1970. It has also won a large number of stars in the *Guide*! This year, it adds to its collection with Château de l'Isolette white, which wins one star for its fine, elegant nose dominated by honey and citrus fruit. This harmonious wine will go well with simple dishes such as pizza or salad. One star, too, for **Château La Sable 2002 white (5–8 €)**, which has a bouquet of honeysuckle and citrus fruit. The palate is well balanced, supple, slightly acidic and with good length. Drink as an aperitif or at the beginning of a meal.
•┐ EARL Luc Pinatel, Ch. de l'Isolette, rte de Bonnieux, 84400 Apt-en-Provence, tel. 04.90.74.16.70, fax 04.90.04.70.73, e-mail pinatel@chateau-isolette.com ☑
☎ ev. day except Sun. 8am–11.30am 2pm–5.30pm

DOM. DE MAYOL 2001★★

| | 10 ha | 60,000 | ■ ♦ | 5–8 € |

Bernard Viguier spares no efforts in his winemaking. Having won a *coup de cœur* in the previous edition of the *Guide* with his Cuvée Tradition, he wins two stars for this brilliant red 2001 with violet glints. The elegant nose, with notes of liquorice and soft fruit, is followed by flavours of spices and cherries in kirsch. Enjoy in three or four years with leg of lamb.
•┐ Bernard Viguier, Dom. de Mayol, rte de Bonnieux, 84400 Apt, tel. 04.90.74.12.80, fax 04.90.04.85.64 ☑ ☎
☎ by appt.

DOM. DE LA ROYERE

Vieilles Vignes Elevé en fût de chêne 2000★★

| ■ | 4.5 ha | 16,600 | ❙❙❙ | 8–11 € |

A woman, Anne Hugues, runs this estate. This year, it offers two remarkable wines. Vieilles Vignes has a red and black label, an attractive colour and a nose with good intensity, whose fruit aromas reappear on the palate. It is a well-balanced wine, with good harmony and silky tannins. "A classic, well-made, a benchmark," noted a delighted taster. Enjoy in three to five years. The **Cuvée Quercus 2001 red (15–23 €)** is more limited in production (1,300 bottles) and gains the same rating. It has noticeable oak, which gives way to blackcurrant notes on the finish. With good harmony and length, it has a tannic structure that will allow it to age two or three years in the cellar before being enjoyed with game. **L'Oppidum Cuvée Spéciale 2001 red (5–8 €)**, deserves a mention for the intensity of its bouquet dominated by red berries with liquorice notes.

☞ Anne Hugues, Dom. de La Royère, 84580 Oppède, tel. 04.90.76.87.76, fax 04.90.76.79.50, e-mail info@royere.com ☑
☖ ev. day except Sun. 9am–12 noon 2pm–6.30pm; 9am–12 noon in winter

CH. THOURAMME 2001★★

■	n.c.	13,000		5–8 €

A very fine result from the Lumières cellar, which narrowly misses a *coup de cœur* with this remarkable 2001. It has an attractive cherry colour with mauve glints. Its complex nose mingles floral and raspberry aromas with spice notes. Tasting reveals perfect balance between superb chocolate and spice (black pepper, cumin) flavours and tannins, which produce a silky, rounded structure.

☞ Cave de Lumières, 84220 Goult, tel. 04.90.72.20.04, fax 04.90.72.42.52 ☑
☖ ev. day except Sun. 9am–12 noon 2pm–4pm

CH. VAL JOANIS

Réserve Les Griottes 2000★★★

■	14 ha	60,000	⑪	11–15 €

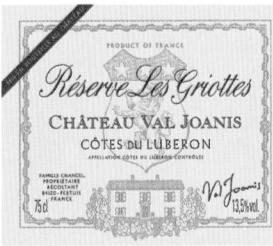

Château Val Joanis is one of France's few estates to have lived through history and revolutions without seeing its acreage diminish. Faithful to tradition, it produces lovely wines, which regularly appear in the *Guide*. Its Griottes 2000 reaches great heights. This wine enchanted the Jury with its intense ripe fruit and spice bouquet, its concentrated aromas (roasted, vanilla, spices and berries) and its very present tannins. Pleasantly integrated oak adds to this wine, which should be aged three or four years and will then be perfect with Provençal stew. The **Cuvée Principale 2000 red (5–8 €)** gains one star for its pleasant fruit, elegance, suppleness and attractive, silky tannins. **Vigne du Chanoine Trouillet 2001 red (30–38 €)** is just as good, but very expensive.

☞ SC du Ch. Val Joanis, 84120 Pertuis, tel. 04.90.79.20.77, fax 04.90.09.69.52, e-mail info.visites@val-joanis.com ☑
☖ ev. day 10am–7pm
☞ Chancel

LA VIEILLE FERME 2002★

■	25 ha	50,000	■ ♦	5–8 €

Making fine wines is an old tradition in the Perrin family. The story begins in 1909, when Gabriel Tramier bought the Château de Beaucastel. His son-in-law Pierre Perrin later took over the estate, cautiously introducing new techniques. The company, now run by the fifth generation of the family, presents a 2002 white with a delightful, intense nose, both floral and fruity. It is a wine with a strong personality, fleshy on the palate; the Jury were struck by its elegance.

☞ Perrin, La Ferrière, rte de Jonquières, 84100 Orange, tel. 04.90.11.12.00, fax 04.90.11.12.19, e-mail perrin@vinsperrin.com ☑
☖ by appt.

Wines selected but not starred

CAVE DE BONNIEUX

Elevé en fût de chêne 2001

■	n.c.	12,000	⑪	5–8 €

☞ Cave de Bonnieux, quartier de la Gare, 84480 Bonnieux, tel. 04.90.75.80.03, fax 04.90.75.98.30, e-mail webmaster@cave-bonnieux.com ☑

CH. LA DORGONNE

L'expression du Terroir 2001

■	3 ha	8,000	⑪	8–11 €

☞ SCEA Ch. la Dorgonne, rte de Mirabeau, 84240 La Tour-d'Aigues, tel. 04.90.07.50.18, fax 04.90.07.56.55 ☑
☖ ev. day 8am–8pm

DOM. DE FONTPOURQUIERE

Cuvée Peyrefiot Elevé en fût de chêne 2000

■	2.5 ha	5,200	■ ⑪ ♦	5–8 €

☞ Yves Ronchi et Fille, rte de Lumière, CD 106, 84480 Lacoste, tel. 04.90.75.80.02, fax 04.90.75.80.02 ☑
☖ ev. day 10am–12 noon 2pm–6pm

DOM. DE PERPETUS 2001

■	8.5 ha	60,000		5–8 €

☞ François Paquet, Le Pont des Samsons, 69430 Quincié-en-Beaujolais, tel. 04.74.69.09.10, fax 04.74.69.09.28

CH. SAINT-PIERRE DE MEJANS 2002

■	3.5 ha	5,733	■ ♦	5–8 €

☞ Laurence Doan de Champassak, Ch. Saint-Pierre de Mejans, 84160 Puyvert, tel. 04.90.08.40.51, fax 04.90.08.41.96, e-mail bricedoan@yahoo.fr ☑
☖ ev. day except Mar. 9.30am–12 noon 2.30pm–7pm

Coteaux de Pierrevert

Located in the Alpes-de-Haute-Provence *département*, the appellation lies mostly on the slopes of the right bank of the Durance (Corbières, Saint-Tulle, Perrevert, Manosque, etc), on about 296 ha. Climatic conditions restrict cultivation to about ten communes of the 42 legally included in the area of the AOC. The red, rosé and white wines (11,867 hl in 2002) are fairly low in alcohol, but lively enough and are enjoyed by the many who travel through this tourist region. The Coteaux de Pierrevert were recognized as an Appellation d'Origine Contrôlée by the National Committee of the INAO in 1998.

BASTIDE DES OLIVIERS 2001★★

■	10 ha	20,000	■ ♦	5–8 €

Made from organically grown grapes, this wine has an intense colour with violet glints. A very clean nose of soft fruit (blackberries), spices, musk and cinnamon delighted the Jury, as did the power on the palate, finesse of the tannins and length of finish. This wine has fine ageing potential and will go well with game in sauce. The **Château Régusse 2002 rosé de saignée** wins one star.

↝ Dieudonné, SARL Cave et Vignobles de Régusse, rte de la Bastide-des-Jourdans, 04860 Pierrevert, tel. 04.92.72.30.44, fax 04.92.72.69.08, e-mail domaine-de-regusse@wanadoo.fr ☑
⊼ by appt.

DOM. LA BLAQUE 2001★

■	17 ha	70,000	■ ↯	5–8 €

The **Réserve 2000 red (8–11 €)** – a blend of Syrah and Grenache aged in cask – is awarded one star for its red berry, liquorice and spice flavours. The more classic 2001 impressed the Jury with its pleasant bouquet of spices, garrigue and leather. Its tannins are still young and it needs to wait two years before being enjoyed with grilled meat or stew.

↝ Gilles Delsuc, Dom. Châteauneuf-La Blaque, 04860 Pierrevert, tel. 04.92.72.39.71, fax 04.92.72.81.26, e-mail domaine.lablaque@wanadoo.fr
⊼ by appt.

CAVE DES VIGNERONS DE PIERREVERT Cuvée du Village d'or 2002★

■	20 ha	20,000	■ ↯	3–5 €

Lovers of beautiful landscapes, visiting the Alpes-de-Haute-Provence, a land of a thousand different kinds of light, may want to stop off at the Coteaux-de-Pierrevert cellar. M. Silvestre, the jovial cellarmaster, will let you taste his 2002 vintage, which has an expressive nose of citrus fruit, honey and white flowers. A very fresh wine, lively but balanced, which is ready to drink with shellfish, bouillabaisse, or goat's cheese.

↝ Cave des Vignerons de Pierrevert, 1, av. Auguste-Bastide, 04860 Pierrevert, tel. 04.92.72.19.06, fax 04.92.72.85.36 ☑
⊼ ev. day except Sun. 8am–12 noon 2pm–6pm

Wines selected but not starred

CH. DE ROUSSET

Grand Jas 2000

■	n.c.	10,000	▥	8–11 €

↝ Hubert et Roseline Emery, SCEV Ch. de Rousset, 04800 Gréoux-les-Bains, tel. 04.92.72.62.49, fax 04.92.72.66.50 ☑
⊼ by appt.

Côtes du Vivarais

At the northwestern limit of the southern Côtes du Rhône, the Côtes du Vivarais straddle the *départements* of the Ardèche and the Gard, covering 647 ha. These wines, produced on limestone soils, are mainly made from Grenache (30% minimum) and Syrah (30% minimum), with some typically fresh rosés, which should be drunk young. This former VDQS, which was recognized as an AOC in May 1999, produced 33,892 hl of wine in 2002.

DOM. DU BELVEZET 2001★

■	3 ha	7,000		3–5 €

If you follow the Ardèche Gorges tourist route, you will pass Domaine du Belvezet, which offers a wine whose rich nose matches its intense colour. Grape selection has produced fine results, as might be expected. There is good balance, with integrated tannins and remarkable length. Length of flavour makes itself known by notes of soft fruit, damp woodland and mushroom, which explode in the finish.

↝ René Brunel, rte de Vallon-Pont-d'Arc, 07700 Saint-Remèze, tel. 04.75.04.05.87, fax 04.75.04.05.87, e-mail belvezet.brunel@wanadoo.fr ☑
⊼ ev. day except Mon. Sun. 9am–12 noon 3pm–7pm; cl. 31 Dec.–15 Mar.

CLOS DE L'ABBE DUBOIS 2002★

■	1.5 ha	6,000	■	5–8 €

The Abbé Dubois, who came from Saint-Remèze, studied the habits and customs of the Indians between 1790 and 1820. He paid an allowance to his nephew, which allowed him to build the present cellar where you can try this remarkable wine. A strawberry colour, aromas of ripe and dried fruit, particularly good balance between fleshiness and liveliness all go to make up a wine that you want to taste again and again! With game, choose **Cuvée Simone 2001 red**, named in honour of Simone, a Belgian painter who created the labels of Clos de l'Abbé Dubois. This red Côtes du Vivarais is very well made, with integrated tannins. Its bouquet bursts out with soft fruit charred notes hints, developing gamey notes.

↝ Claude Dumarcher, Clos de l'Abbé Dubois, 07700 Saint-Remèze, tel. 04.75.98.98.44, fax 04.75.98.98.44 ☑ ♠
⊼ by appt.

UNION DES PRODUCTEUR D'ORGNAC-L'AVEN Réserve 2001★★

■	n.c.	100,000		3–5 €

What character this Côtes du Vivarais has! It will flatter game and strong-flavoured meats in sauce. The complex nose of soft fruit, damp woodland and spices is very promising. The attack is clean and complexity of flavours on the palate is every bit as good as that on the nose. Good balance in a wine that is typical of its terroir yet also elegant. The **2002 rosé**, fruity and fresh, was singled out by the Jury.

↝ Union des Producteurs d'Orgnac-l'Aven, 07150 Orgnac-l'Aven, tel. 04.75.38.60.08, fax 04.75.38.65.90 ☑
⊼ ev. day except Sat. Sun. 8am–12 noon 2pm–6pm; cl. 5 Sep.–5 Oct.

DOM. DE VIGIER

Cuvée Prestige 2001★★

■	3 ha	n.c.	■ ▥	5–8 €

Concentration is already clearly visible in the intense garnet-red colour of this wine. The nose conveys all the wildness of the Ibie valley through gamey, fruit (blackcurrant) and spicy notes, acompanied by hints of damp woodland. Structure is not yet very developed but can be enjoyed with relish. Have a little patience and this wine's already remarkable balance will reach its best. While you are waiting, the **2002 rosé (3–5 €)**, which gets one star, offers a rich nose and is very pleasant from the attack to the finish.

↝ Dupré et Fils, Dom. de Vigier, 07150 Lagorce, tel. 04.75.88.01.18, fax 04.75.37.18.79 ☑
⊼ ev. day 9am–12 noon 2.30pm–6.30pm; groups by appt.

Wines selected but not starred

DOM. DE LA BOISSERELLE 2001

▦   3 ha   15,000   **3–5 €**

🕯 Richard Vigne, Dom. de La Boisserelle, rte des Gorges, 07700 Saint-Remèze, tel. 04.75.04.24.37, fax 04.75.04.24.37, e-mail domainedelaboisserelle@wanadoo.fr **V**
🍸 by appt.

BERNARD VIGNE 2002

▦   2 ha   5,000   **3–5 €**

🕯 Bernard Vigne, Dom. Vigne, vallée de l'Ibie, 07150 Lagorce, tel. 04.75.37.19.00 **V**
🍸 by appt.

LES CHAIS DU VIVARAIS 2002

▦   n.c.   5,000   🍷   **3–5 €**

🕯 SCA Les Chais du Vivarais, 07700 Saint-Remèze, tel. 04.75.04.08.56, fax 04.75.98.47.40, e-mail cave.stremeze@wanadoo.fr **V**
🍸 by appt.

RHONE

VINS DOUX NATURELS
(NATURALLY SWEET WINES)

The winemakers of Roussillon have made highly regarded sweet wines since the 13th century, when Arnaud de Villeneuve perfected the principle of "mutage". This involves adding brandy to the must of red or white wines at the moment of full fermentation, a process that prevents further fermentation but preserves a certain quantity of sugar.

The AOC of these sweet wines stretches discontinuously through various parts of southern France: Pyrénées-Orientales, Aude, Hérault, Vaucluse and Corsica – but never too far from the Mediterranean. The principal grape varieties used are the Grenaches (Blanc, Gris and Noir), Macabeu, Malvoisie du Roussillon, also called Tourbat, Muscat à Petit Grains and Muscat d'Alexandrie. Compulsory regulations govern the way the vines are grown and pruned.

The yields are low and, at harvest, the must is required to have a minimum 252 g of sugar per litre. The sugar released at harvest varies depending on the region. Individual wines are accepted only after meeting rather stringent criteria: they must have reached between 15% and 18% alcohol by volume, have a minimum 45 g of sugar per litre (up to more than 100 g per litre for the Muscats), and have a total alcohol level (alcohol content plus strength of alcohol) of at least 21.5%. Some are sold only after three years' ageing in wooden barrels, the traditional method. The level is maintained by topping up with younger wines. Wines aged in this way acquire the particular flavour described as "*rancio*", which is a legal definition in wine law. Current total production of these wines was 393,670 hl.

BANYULS AND BANYULS GRAND CRU

This exceptional terroir is on the extreme east of the Pyrénées, with steeply sloping hills overlooking the Mediterranean. Only the four communes of Collioure, Port-Vendres, Banyuls-sur-Mer and Cerbère are entitled to the appellation. The terraced vineyards (roughly 1,200 ha) are on schistous soils with a rocky substratum which, when not immediately visible, is often covered with a thin layer of topsoil. Thus the terroir is poor, often acid, and supports only very ordinary vine varieties, such as Grenache, producing a very low yield, often less than about 20 hl per ha. In 2002 production of Banyuls was 24,000 hl.

On the other hand, the amount of sunshine is maximized by the terraced cultivation (the wine-growers have to maintain the terraces by hand to protect the soil, which can be washed away by the slightest storm). With the additional benefit of proximity to the Mediterranean, the grapes become gorged with sugar and aromatic qualities.

Old Grenache vines predominate. Vinification involves macerating the bunches of grapes; "mutage" (the addition of brandy) may be carried out at this stage, allowing substantial maceration lasting more than ten days, a method known as maceration in alcohol.

The way in which the wine is brought on plays an essential part. In general, it tends to favour the oxydative development of the wine, either in wood (large barrels of 200–300 hectolitres or wooden casks of 600 litres) or in *bonbonnes* (glass demijohns) exposed to the warmth of the sun under the roofs of the cellars. The different vintages brought on in this way are blended with the greatest care by the cellar-master to create the numerous types of wine that we know. In some contrary cases, the wine is brought on in a way specifically designed to maintain its youthful fruitiness and prevent oxidization: thus, different wines are obtained with highly specific characteristics; these are called the *rimages* or "varieties". To earn the Appellation Grand Cru, wines must be brought on in wooden casks for 30 months.

The wines range in colour from ruby to mahogany, and have a characteristic bouquet of dried grapes, cooked fruit, grilled almonds, coffee and prune brandy. The *rimages* retain their aromas of soft fruit, cherry and cherry brandy. Banyuls wines should be served at temperatures from 12–17°C, according to their age. They may be drunk as an aperitif, with dessert (some consider Banyuls the only wine to drink with a chocolate dessert, for example), with coffee and a cigar, but equally with foie gras, duck with cherries or figs and also with certain cheeses.

Banyuls

LES CLOS DE PAULILLES
Rimage mise tardive 2000★

■	3 ha	8,000	⦀	11–15 €

Hidden from view behind stone walls only a few paces away from the beaches of the sheltered bay of Paulilles, a summer mecca for holidaymakers and yachtsmen, stand squat barrels of precious young Banyuls maturing over a period of months to yield late *rimages*. This honest deep-ruby 2000 emerges as a successful permutation of red fruits and spicy oak, a happy blend which persists on the palate with flavours of cherry, ripe fruit and a hint of pepper combined with velvety tannins.
☛ Les Clos de Paulilles, Baie de Paulilles, 66660 Port-Vendres, tel. 04.68.38.90.10, fax 04.68.38.91.33, e-mail daure@wanadoo.fr ☑ ☗
☏ by appt.
☛ Famille Daure

Vins Doux Naturels

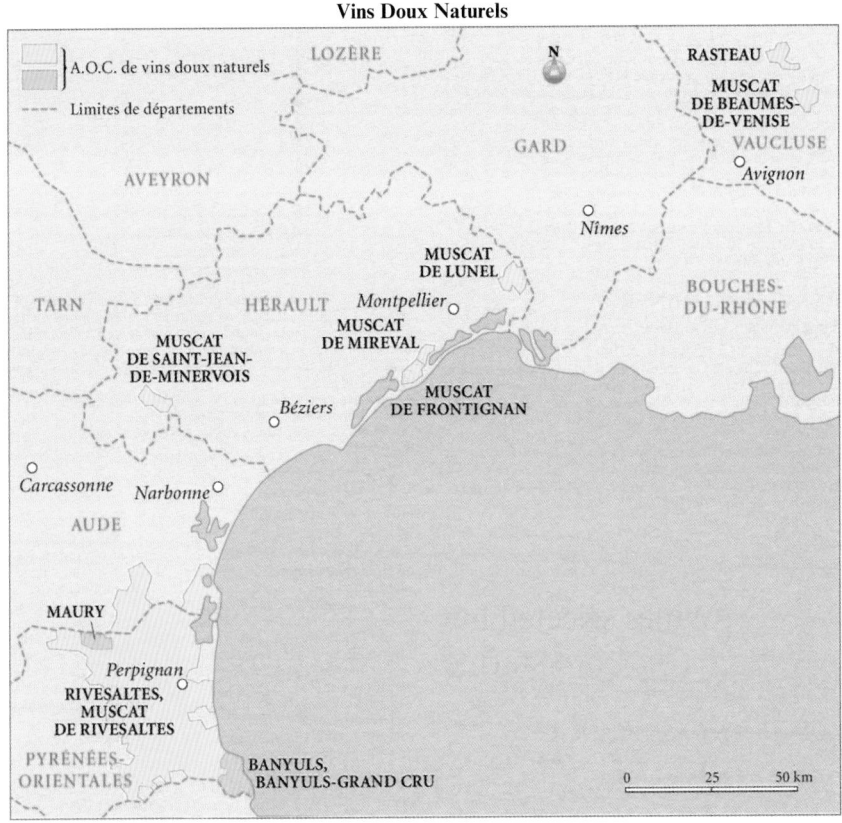

A.O.C. de vins doux naturels

--- Limites de départements

LOZÈRE

N

RASTEAU

MUSCAT
DE BEAUMES-
DE-VENISE

GARD

VAUCLUSE

Avignon

AVEYRON

Nîmes

MUSCAT
DE LUNEL

TARN

HÉRAULT Montpellier

BOUCHES-
DU-RHÔNE

MUSCAT
DE SAINT-JEAN-
DE-MINERVOIS

MUSCAT
DE MIREVAL

Béziers

MUSCAT
DE FRONTIGNAN

Carcassonne Narbonne

AUDE

MAURY

Perpignan

RIVESALTES,
MUSCAT
DE RIVESALTES

PYRÉNÉES-
ORIENTALES

BANYULS,
BANYULS-GRAND CRU

0   25   50 km

LE DOMINICAIN

Cuvée Hanicotte Hors d'âge★★★

| ■ | 10 ha | 4,000 | ◖▮▮ | 15–23 € |

Barrel-matured Banyuls are housed in this 13th century Dominican convent resplendent with exposed ceiling beams and a delightful interplay of light and shade. This Hors-d'Age has taken on a distinctive bouquet of *rancio* and coffee that complements the intense and complex flavours of figs, dried bananas and hazelnuts. A pleasantly full and well-integrated wine that opens on a spicy note, with full-bodied fruit flavours gradually yielding pride of place to roasted coffee and nuts, cocoa, chocolate, coffee and Havana tobacco.

●�‐ SCV Le Dominicain, pl. Orfila, 66190 Collioure, tel. 04.68.82.05.63, fax 04.68.82.43.06, e-mail le-dominicain@wanadoo.fr ☑
♈ ev. day 8am–12 noon 2pm–6pm

L'ETOILE

Extra-Vieux 1991★★

| ■ | 10 ha | 20,000 | ◖▮▮ | 15–23 € |

What could be more pleasant than strolling under a Banyuls sun and exploring, glass in hand, this maze of casks replete with mature Banyuls? Here, the **Macéré Tuilé 93 (11–15 €)**, the **Cuvée 75ᵉ Anniversaire (23–30 €)** and a host of other superb wines await one's pleasure, among them this timeless tawny with its notes of blond tobacco, honeyed mature wood, cocoa and roasted almonds. A fine, elegant and remarkably well-balanced wine overlaid with flavours of candied fruit coated in chocolate.

●← Sté coopérative de l'Etoile, 26, av. du Puig-del-Mas, 66650 Banyuls-sur-Mer, tel. 04.68.88.00.10, fax 04.68.88.15.10, e-mail cave.letoile@tiscali.fr ☑
♈ ev. day 8am–12 noon 2pm–6pm

DOM. PIETRI-GERAUD 2001★

| | 1.1 ha | 2,500 | ◖▮▮ | 11–15 € |

Banyuls is a wine that never ceases to surprise, none more so than this white produced by two female laureates of 2000. This 2001 boasts an attractive amber robe and hints at vanilla, roasted coffee and honeyed flowers, opening confidently on full and fleshy accents of exotic fruits and apricot and finishing on a toasted note. An ideal accompaniment to an aperitif or a summer fruit dessert. Also worthy of mention is a **Rimage 2000 Mademoiselle O (8–11 €)**.

●← Maguy et Laetitia Piétri-Géraud, 22, rue Pasteur, 66190 Collioure, tel. 04.68.82.07.42, fax 04.68.98.02.58, e-mail domaine.pietri- geraud@wanadoo.fr ☑
♈ ev. day 10am–12.30pm 3.30pm–6.30pm; cl. Sun. Mon. from Nov. to Jun. and during school holidays

VDN

DOM. LA TOUR VIEILLE 2001★★

| ■ | 1 ha | 6,500 | ■ ◆ | 11–15 € |

It is a privilege to live all year round in Collioure, where the vines are cosseted by gentle sea breezes, their leaves caressed by the *tramontane* under the blue skies so loved by Matisse. A privilege indeed to settle down in the evening to a glass of this Banyuls with its brick-red robe and intense flavours of over-ripe grapes and fresh figs which opens full and fleshy on a spicy note and delivers velvety and well-balanced tannins. (50 cl bottles)
➥ Dom. la Tour Vieille, 12, rte de Madeloc, 66190 Collioure, tel. 04.68.82.44.82, fax 04.68.82.38.42 ☑
☒ ev. day 10.30am–12.30pm 4.30pm–7.30pm; from 1 Oct. to 30 Mar. by appt.
➥ C. Campadieu et V. Cantié

DOM. DU TRAGINER
Rimage mise tardive 1999★★

| ■ | 4.5 ha | 2,700 | ◉ | 11–15 € |

Two pairs of hands and a mule are *de rigueur* when working this steeply-sloping narrow-terraced organically-cultivated vineyard. The mahogany robe of this Rimage is tinted pastel. The intense and complex nose is of brandied fruits, cocoa and roasted coffee, resolving into honest fleshy accents of fig, nuts and cocoa. A wine to be enjoyed perhaps as an accompaniment to a blue cheese? (50 cl bottles)
➥ J.-F. Deu, Dom. du Traginer, 56, av. du Puig-del-Mas, 66650 Banyuls-sur-Mer, tel. 04.68.88.15.11, fax 04.68.88.31.48 ☑
☒ by appt.

Wines selected but not starred

DOM. DE LA CASA BLANCA

| ▬ | 0.5 ha | 2,000 | ■ ◆ | 5–8 € |

➥ Dom. de la Casa Blanca, rte des Mas, 66650 Banyuls-sur-Mer, tel. 04.68.88.12.85, fax 04.68.88.04.08 ☑
☒ by appt.
➥ Soufflet et Escapa

DOM. DE LA GALLINE 1998

| ■ | | n.c. | 11,970 | ◉ | 5–8 € |

➥ SIVIR, rte des Crêtes, 66652 Banyuls-sur-Mer, tel. 04.68.88.03.22, fax 04.68.98.36.97, e-mail sivir@templers.com

VIAL-MAGNÈRES Vintage 2000

| ■ | 2.5 ha | 4,000 | | 11–15 € |

➥ Dom. Vial-Magnères, 14, rue Edouard-Herriot, 66650 Banyuls-sur-Mer, tel. 04.68.88.31.04, fax 04.68.88.02.43, e-mail al.tragou@wanadoo.fr ☑
☒ by appt.
➥ Olivier Saperas

Banyuls Grand Cru

LA CAVE DE L'ABBE ROUS
Cuvée Christian Reynal 1994★★★

| ■ | | n.c. | 19,866 | ◉ | 30–38 € |

The impeccably-kept Abbé Rous cellar lies within a stone's throw of the beach and boasts ancient casks containing grands crus, among them this Christian Reynal of exceptional consistency. The robe resolves over time into mahogany, musk

and sienna. What follows is a pure delight: opening accents of brandied plum, nuts, charred coffee and meadow mingle with greengages and plums in the presence of velvety tannins, the whole finishing on a note of *rancio*. A superb wine to accompany foie gras, dark chocolate, orange cake, coffee and much more besides…
➥ La Cave de l'Abbé Rous, 56, av. Charles-de-Gaulle, 66650 Banyuls-sur-Mer, tel. 04.68.88.72.72, fax 04.68.88.30.57, e-mail contact@banyuls.com
☒ by appt.

L'ETOILE
Cuvée réservée 1988★★★

| ■ | | 10 ha | n.c. | ◉ | 15–23 € |

Much may have changed in Banyuls over the last four decades, but this cellar remains a feature at the heart of the village, surrounded by the hustle and bustle of the summer months and coming into its own as autumn draws closer, the beaches start to empty and the grape harvest enters full swing. This Grand Cru harvested 15 years ago caught the attention of the Jury on account of its mahogany robe with hints of red and its flavours of coffee, cocoa, plum and orange peel. Long maturation in oak barrels has imparted a fleshy roundness and strength, together with aromas of stewed orange, cocoa and roasted notes. Uncommonly long tannins ensure that this vintage is resilient over time. Ideal with mocha, chocolate or a fine cigar…
➥ Sté coopérative de l'Etoile, 26, av. du Puig-del-Mas, 66650 Banyuls-sur-Mer, tel. 04.68.88.00.10, fax 04.68.88.15.10, e-mail cave.letoile@tiscali.fr ☑
☒ ev. day 8am–12 noon 2pm–6pm

CELLIER DES TEMPLIERS
Mas de la Serra 1995★★

| ■ | | n.c. | 234,000 | ◉ | 15–23 € |

The "Templars' Cellar" is a shrine to vintage Banyuls, justly celebrated for the quality and consistency of its wines, each of which asserts its own individuality in terms of origin, year, age, type and content. The Jury singled out a **Viviane Le Roy Type Sec 91 (23–30 €)**, a **Président Henry Vidal 93 (30–38 €)** (barrel-matured for eight years), an **Amiral François Vilarem 95 (30–38 €)**, very well-integrated after 30 months in the cask, and this **Mas de la Serra 95**, selected not only on account of its aromatic complexity (stewed fruit and roasted coffee) but also in acknowledgment of its exceptional equilibrium and its sensuous notes of tobacco and cocoa. Open and ready for drinking now or in a few years.
➥ Cellier des Templiers, rte du Mas-Reig, 66650 Banyuls-sur-Mer, tel. 04.68.98.36.70, fax 04.68.98.36.91, e-mail accueil-visite@templers.com ☑
☒ by appt.

Rivesaltes

In terms of area this is the biggest appellation of Vins Doux Naturels, with 14,000 ha producing 264,000 hl in 1995. In 1996 the Rivesaltes Plan was introduced to re-organize the vineyard, now in economic difficulties, but in 2000 production was 131,000 hl. It reached 126,180 hl in 2002 but it was overtaken in volume by Muscat de Rivesaltes with 150,488 hl. The terroir of Rivesaltes lies in Roussillon and in a very small part of Corbières, on poor, dry, hot soils that produce well-ripened grapes. Four varieties are permitted: Grenache, Maccabeu, Malvoisie and Muscat, although only small proportions of Malvoisie and Muscat are included. White wines are generally vinified normally, but maceration is also used, especially for the Grenache Noir, to achieve a maximum in colour and tannin.

How the Rivesaltes wines are brought on is crucial in determining quality. Whether brought on in the vat or in wooden casks, they develop very different bouquets. (In difficult years, there is also an option for the wines to be downgraded as Appellation Grand Roussillon.)

The wines range in colour from amber to tile-red, with a bouquet, at its most expressive, recalling roasting coffee, dry fruit or the nutty flavour of *rancio*. When young, red Rivesaltes have aromas of soft fruit: cherry, blackcurrant or blackberry. They may be drunk as an aperitif or with dessert, and should be served at a temperature from 11–15°C, depending on their age.

ARNAUD DE VILLENEUVE

Ambré Hors d'âge 1982★★★

	n.c.	6,000	◉	15–23 €

Remembered for a splendid 77 Hors d'Age (23–30 €) and an unforgettable 82, the rolled-pebbled terroir between the fortress of Salses and the commune of Rivesaltes is again in the spotlight with its judicious blend of white Grenache and Muscat grapes masterminded from harvesting to point-of-sale by F. Baixas, whose experience and acumen are without peer. The wine in question is reddish-amber in colour and both limpid and luminous, giving off accents of wet hay, verbena and a hint of orange-pekoe tea. On the palate, the wine is rounded and fleshy, with notes of apricot and other dried fruit, nuts and a surprising touch of orange. It remains superbly balanced through to a long finish punctuated by citrus fruits.
➥ Les Vignobles du Rivesaltais, 1, rue de la Roussillonnaise, 66602 Rivesaltes, tel. 04.68.64.06.63, fax 04.68.64.64.69,
e-mail vignobles.rivesaltais@wanadoo.fr 🆅
🍷 by appt.

DOM. CAZES

Ambré 1993★★★

	3.8 ha	15,000	◉	11–15 €

Cazes, inevitably Cazes: an exceptional Aimé Cazes 76 (46–76 €), an unctuous yet delicate Rivesaltes Tuilé 86 (15–23 €) and, not least, this Ambré 93, each a tribute to the know-how of this talented family. Citrus fruits, stewed fruits, quince, roasted nuts and a limpid amber-mahogany colour.

The bouquet reveals honey, blond tobacco, dried hay, citrus fruits and roasted almonds, soft, suave and sustained flavours that tease the taste buds. It should be added that this vast 160 ha estate (a part of which once belonged to Maréchal Foch) is cultivated along biodynamic lines.
➥ Sté Cazes Frères, 4, rue Francisco-Ferrer, BP 61, 66602 Rivesaltes, tel. 04.68.64.08.26, fax 04.68.64.69.79, e-mail info@cazes-rivesaltes.com 🆅
🍷 by appt.
➥ André et Bernard Cazes

DOM. DES CHENES

Tuilé 1998★

	1.4 ha	3,000	◉	11–15 €

This small estate nestling at the foot of the Cirque de Vingrau offers a point of departure for splendid sightseeing walks between clifftops and vineyards. This Tuilé, characterized by aromas of fig, leather and cask, makes its mark by virtue of its roundness and its notes of cooked plums and stewed fruit. Rounded, silky tannins ensure a harmonious balance. A wine to be enjoyed with foie gras. Also noted: a well-made Ambré 99 (8–11 €).
➥ SCEA Dom. des Chênes, 7, rue du Mal-Joffre, 66600 Vingrau, tel. 04.68.29.40.21, fax 04.68.29.10.91, e-mail domainedeschenes@wanadoo.fr 🆅
🍷 ev. day except Sun. 9am–12 noon 2pm–6pm; Sat. by appt. from Oct. to May.

LES VIGNERONS DES COTES D'AGLY

Cuvée François AragoTuilé Hors d'âge Vieilli en fût de chêne 1994★

	15 ha	n.c.	🍶◉◆	8–11 €

The cellar is a major wine-growing centre in the Vallée de l'Agly and a focal point and economic force in the village of Estagel. Rigorous attention to detail may come at a price, but it is the touchstone of success. Arago, a native of the region, deserves credit for this Tuilé that hovers between stewed fruit and the honey flavours of old casks. The wine tastes pleasantly roasted on the palate, the finish is redolent of figs. An ideal aperitif served with nuts and dried fruit.
➥ Les Vignerons des Côtes d'Agly, Cave coopérative, 66310 Estagel, tel. 04.68.29.00.45, fax 04.68.29.19.80, e-mail agly@tiscali.fr 🆅
🍷 ev. day except Sun. 9am–12 noon 2pm–6pm

DOM. DEPRADE-JORDA

Ambré Vieilli en fût de chêne 1997★★

	1 ha	1,600	🍶◉	11–15 €

The Deprade family cultivates some 60 ha at the foot of the Albères but has only recently started to market wines by the bottle – successfully, as this first-ever entry in the *Guide* reveals. The Ambré Vieilli 97 is sustained with some accents of *rancio*. The nose suggests dried fruit, freshly mown hay and barrel-maturation. On the palate, the wine offers sustained notes of roasted coffee and dried apricot. The whole is full and remarkably well rounded.
➥ Jacques Deprade, 98, rte Nationale, 66700 Argelès-sur-Mer, tel. 04.68.81.10.29, fax 04.68.89.04.64 🆅
🍷 by appt.

CH. DONA BAISSAS

Grenat 2001★

	10 ha	3,000		8–11 €

From Estagel, follow the narrow winding road between Agly and Têt to a vineyard set on the schist slopes of the Col de la Dona where grenache grapes yield this very fresh and pleasant Grenat, with its intense flavours of brandy-macerated cherries. Fruit flavours predominate in a wine that is smooth and richly tannic on the palate. Also of note is a fine Ambré Hors d'Age Château Dona Baissas (5–8 €).
➥ Cellier de la Dona, Ch. Dona Baissas, ancienne rte de Maury, 66310 Estagel, tel. 04.68.29.00.02, fax 04.68.29.09.26, e-mail donabaissas@tiscali.fr 🆅
🍷 ev. day except Sat. Sun. 9am–12 noon 2pm–5pm
➥ Baissas

VDN

DOM. DU MAS ALART

Ambré Hors d'âge 1992★★

| | 6 ha | 600 | | 11–15 € |

This old *mas* with its shingle roof and typical Roussillon bricks has been in the same family for several generations and has only recently – some five years ago – started producing Côtes du Roussillon appellation wines, having developed over a hundred years' expertise in the production of naturally sweet wines. This russet-coloured Ambré has matured in the cask for the best part of ten years in order to acquire its honeyed barrel-matured notes of plum, a hint of roasted nuts and an embryonic *rancio*. The wine is warm and balanced, sustained on the palate with pronounced *rancio*, nut and dried fruit flavours. In short, a genuine *rancio* to go with chocolate or blue cheese. Also noted: a classic and fruitier **Ambré 98 (8–11 €)**.
☛ EARL Dom. du Mas Alart, RD 22, 66280 Saleilles, tel. 04.68.50.51.89, fax 04.68.50.87.29, e-mail mas.alart@wanadoo.fr
☛ ev. day except Sun. 11am–7pm
☛ Belmas

DOM. NIDOLERES

Grenat 2000★

| | 4 ha | 4,000 | | 8–11 € |

After their visit to his estate, Pierre Escudié will in all likelihood regale guests with helpings of Catalan culture and cuisine: drawing on the experience of eight generations of wine-growers, Escudié himself is as adept in the kitchen as he is in the vineyard. The red robe of this Grenat 2000 vintage is pronounced, with flavours of ripe black cherries persisting on the palate. The whole is balanced, robust and highly typical. Tannins augur well for the future, but the wine can be drunk as of now, possibly to accompany a dessert of wild fruits.
☛ Pierre Escudié, Dom. de Nidolères, 66300 Tresserre, tel. 04.68.83.15.14, fax 04.68.83.31.26
☛ by appt.

CH. DE NOUVELLES

Tuilé 2000★★★

| | n.c. | 7,000 | | 8–11 € |

"Nouvelle," perhaps, but a Corbières estate with a long history nonetheless, set well back from the sea across wild and sinuous scrubland extending towards the Col d'Extrême. The setting merits a detour, as does this still very young Tuilé 2000 with its flavours of freshly picked grapes and spicy black-cherries. The cherry flavour persists and intensifies on the ample and well-balanced palate and is complemented by pronounced tannins that combine to make this a wine that will age and develop well.
☛ SCEA R. Daurat-Fort, Ch. de Nouvelles, 11350 Tuchan, tel. 04.68.45.40.03, fax 04.68.45.49.21
☛ by appt.

LES VIGNERONS DE PEZILLA

Ambré 1994★★

| | 166 ha | 10,000 | | 5–8 € |

The Pézilla winery features regularly in the present *Guide*, offering a happy mix of dry wines, VDN Tuilé and Ambré. This year, the Jury applauded an expressive and progressively successful wine grown from vines on the high terraces: a russet Ambré with aromas of stewed orange and apricot with a

suggestion of old Armagnac. This is a well-balanced fruity wine that is full on the palate, with notes of spicy dried fruit, hay and a honeyed hint of blond tobacco. A wine destined to be enjoyed as an aperitif or to accompany plain cake.
☛ Les vignerons de Pézilla, 1, av. du Canigou, 66370 Pézilla-la-Rivière, tel. 04.68.92.00.09, fax 04.68.92.49.91
☛ by appt.

CH. LES PINS

Ambré 1995★★

| | 6 ha | 20,000 | | 11–15 € |

Baixas is an archetypical Catalan village with a maze of narrow streets leading to an impressive church with a remarkable retable whose burnished golden amber is reflected in the colour of this Ambré 1995. Bitter orange and lime are juxtaposed with the vanilla flavour from the cask. On the palate, the wine tastes of stewed oranges, dried apricots and roasted almonds which complement the smoke and spices of the wood.. The whole is rounded, rich, superbly balanced and ready to drink. The **Dom Brial Ambré 89** is equally pleasurable and more fully developed.
☛ Cave Les Vignerons de Baixas, 14, av. du Mal-Joffre, 66390 Baixas, tel. 04.68.64.22.37, fax 04.68.64.26.70, e-mail contact@dom-brial.com
☛ by appt.

DOM. ROZES

Tuilé 1992★★

| | 3.43 ha | 10,000 | | 8–11 € |

The black Grenache grape is a superb variety which contributes not only to the production of young or mature Côtes du Roussillon wines but also to young and fruity naturally sweet wines of the Grenat variety or the rarer Rivesaltes Tuilés Hors d'Age such as this ten year old wine. Over time, the robe has faded to somewhere between amber and orange. The nose betrays flavours of stewed fruit, plum and a hint of leather from cask-maturation, while the rounded palate offers some hints of chocolate. An exceptional Tuilé to accompany chocolate or *clafoutis*.
☛ SCEA Tarquin-Dom. Rozès, 3, rue de Lorraine, 66600 Espira-de-l'Agly, tel. 04.68.38.52.11, fax 04.68.38.51.38, e-mail rozes.domaine@wanadoo.fr
☛ by appt.
☛ Antoine Rozès

CH. DE SAU

Ambré Hors d'âge★★★

| | 2 ha | 3,950 | | 15–23 € |

An exceptional wine that derives its unique personality from extended in-cask maturation and a grape variety seldom found outside Roussillon, the Grenache Gris. Time and care are needed to produce this beautifully clear amber wine with its complex mix of overripe fruit, quince and freshly-mown hay These flavours persist on the palate, where they commingle with hints of milk caramel and dried bananas and apricots against a background of gentle oak.
☛ Hervé Passama, Ch. de Sau, 66300 Thuir, tel. 04.68.53.21.74, fax 04.68.53.29.07, e-mail chateaudesau@aol.com
☛ by appt.

DOM. SINGLA

Mas Passe Temps Ambré Hors d'âge 1990★

| | 2 ha | 2,600 | | 8–11 € |

The estate owners are direct descendants of a family of wine-shippers from the Cévennes region that settled in the Montpin and Opoul vineyard areas of Roussillon some two and a half centuries ago. This La Singla 1990 boasts a reddish-amber robe as a result of time spent in the barrel and yields notes of scrubland and dried fruit. This is a forceful wine – full-bodied and unctuous, with notes of plum brandy and, above all, of roasted nuts; the smoky finish is a blend of dark tobacco and a hint of nut. (37.5 cl bottles)
☛ Laurent de Besombes, Dom. Singla, 4, rue de Rivoli, 66250 Saint-Laurent-de-la-Salanque, tel. 04.68.28.30.68, fax 04.68.28.30.68, e-mail laurent.debesombes@free.fr
☛ by appt.

TERRASSOUS

Ambré Vinifié en fût de chêne 1998★★★

	3 ha	5,000	🍶	5–8 €

Quality wine is a function of terroir, grape variety and human expertise, all of which are present in the case of this two-starred red **Tuilé 95**, all suppleness and fruit, and a white Ambré 98, with its clear amber robe and a nose that vacillates between hazelnut, apricot and scrub. On the palate, the fruit takes on a stewed flavour, with roasted nuts commingling with dried fruit and a honeyed blond tobacco. The wine exhibits silky tannins and is ideal both as an aperitif and as a dessert accompaniment.
☛ SCV Les Vignerons de Terrats, BP 32, 66302 Terrats Cedex, tel. 04.68.53.02.50, fax 04.68.53.23.06,
e-mail scv-terrats@wanadoo.fr ☑
🍷 ev. day except Sun. 8am–12 noon 2pm–6pm

CH. DE VILLARGEIL

Ambré Réserve Xavier Girves 1995★

	10 ha	3,000	🍶🍶🍶	5–8 €

Irrespective of whether the wine in question is red or white, cask, barrel or *bonbonne* maturation may result over time in the wine taking on a colour somewhere between amber and *tuilé*, as is the case with this selection, which opens with a suggestion of *rancio* complemented by nuts, dark tobacco and dried grass. This 95 is ample and full-bodied on the palate, with notes of plums, dried grass and roasted nuts combining to develop an excellent and unusually smooth and velvety *rancio*.
☛ Laurent Viguier, Ch. Villargeil,
66490 Saint-Jean-Pla-de-Corts, tel. 04.68.83.20.62,
fax 04.68.83.51.31 ☑
🍷 by appt.

Wines selected but not starred

CH. DE CANTERRANE

Hors d'âge 1976

	58 ha	6,000	🍶🍶	11–15 €

☛ Jacques Conte, Dom. de Canterrane, 66300 Trouillas, tel. 04.68.53.47.24, fax 04.68.53.28.15 ☑
🍷 ev. day except Sun. 8am–12 noon 2pm–6pm;
Sat. 8am–12 noon

HENRI DESBOEUFS

Grenat 2000

	0.6 ha	2,000	🍶🍶	8–11 €

☛ Henri Desboeufs, 39, rue du
4–Septembre, 66600 Espira-de-l'Agly, tel. 04.68.64.11.73,
fax 04.68.38.56.34 ☑
🍷 by appt.

DOM. FONTANEL

Ambré 1996

	4 ha	7,000	🍶🍶🍶	8–11 €

☛ Dom. Fontanel, 25, av. Jean-Jaurès, 66720 Tautavel, tel. 04.68.29.04.71, fax 04.68.29.19.44,
e-mail domainefontanel@hotmail.com ☑
🍷 ev. day 10am–12.30pm 2pm–7pm
☛ Fontaneil

LES VIGNERONS DE FOURQUES

Ambré Hors d'âge

	90 ha	4,000	🍶🍶🍶	8–11 €

☛ SCV Les Vignerons de Fourques, 1, rue des Taste-Vin, 66300 Fourques, tel. 04.68.38.80.51, fax 04.68.38.89.65, e-mail les.vignerons.de.fourques@wanadoo.fr ☑
🍷 ev. day except Sun. 9.30am–12 noon 2pm–6pm

MAS CRISTINE

Ambré 1999

	6 ha	15,000	🍶🍶🍶	11–15 €

☛ Famille Dauré, Mas Cristine, 66700 Argelès-sur-Mer, tel. 04.68.38.90.10, fax 04.68.38.91.33,
e-mail daure@wanadoo.fr ☑

DOM. DE LA PERDRIX

Grenat 2001

	n.c.	1,800	🍶🍶	8–11 €

☛ Dom. de la Perdrix, 7, rue des Platanes, 66300 Trouillas, tel. 04.68.53.12.74, fax 04.68.53.52.73,
e-mail domaineperdrix@libertysurf.fr ☑
🍷 by appt.

CH. PRADAL

Tuilé Cuvée Aurélien Hors d'âge 1995

	1.5 ha	3,000	🍶🍶🍶	8–11 €

☛ André Coll-Escluse, Ch. Pradal, 58, rue Pépinière-Robin, 66000 Perpignan, tel. 04.68.85.04.73, fax 04.68.56.80.49 ☑
🍷 by appt.

PUIG-PARAHY 1977

	35 ha	5,000	🍶🍶🍶	15–23 €

☛ Puig-Parahy, Le Fort Saint-Pierre, 66300 Passa, tel. 06.14.55.71.71, fax 04.68.38.88.77,
e-mail g.puig-parahy@tiscali.fr ☑ 🏠
🍷 by appt.

DOM. DE RANCY

Ambré Elevé en fût de chêne 1991

	16 ha	n.c.	🍶🍶🍶	15–23 €

☛ Jean-Hubert Verdaguer, Dom. de Rancy, 11, rue Jean-Jaurès, 66720 Latour-de-France, tel. 04.68.29.03.47, fax 04.68.29.06.13 ☑
🍷 by appt.

DOM. SARDA-MALET

La Carbasse 2000

	3 ha	4,800	🍶🍶	15–23 €

☛ Dom. Sarda-Malet, Mas Saint-Michel, chem. de Sainte-Barbe, 66000 Perpignan, tel. 04.68.56.72.38, fax 04.68.56.47.60,
e-mail jerome.malet@sarda-malet.com ☑
🍷 ev. day 8am–12.30pm 1.30pm–6pm; Sat. Sun. by appt.
☛ Jérôme Malet

Maury

The terroir (1,700 ha) covers the commune of Maury, north of Agly, together with some of the bordering communes. The vines (Grenache Noir) grow on steep schistous slopes, producing about 33,000 hl of wine in 2002.

Vinification is often achieved through long maceration, and the way in which the wine is brought on encourages the production of some remarkable vintages.

When young, the wines are garnet in colour, later turning mahogany. The bouquet is initially of soft fruit, developing aromas of cocoa, cooked fruit and coffee with age. Maury wines can be enjoyed as an aperitif or with desserts and sweet foods, but also with spicy dishes.

CAVE JEAN-LOUIS LAFAGE
Prestige Vieilli en fût de chêne 1992★★

| | 0.4 ha | 1,200 | ▮ ⅋ | 11–15 € |

An excellently-produced Maury which aspires to perfection in terms of purity. This beautiful Tuilé has a remarkable nose of old leather, orange peel, stewed fruits and coffee. On the palate, it is equally complex, with a roasted taste allied to brandied fruit. Overall, a wine that is both elegant and forceful, ideally suited as an accompaniment to a chocolate pudding.
📞 Jean-Louis Lafage, 13, rue Dr-F.-Pougault ou, 29, av. Jean-Jaurès, 66460 Maury, tel. 04.68.59.12.66, fax 04.68.59.13.14, e-mail dernierbastion@aol.com ☑
🍷 ev. day except Sun. 9.30am–12.30pm 3pm–6pm; cl. from 1 Oct. to 1 Apr.

MAS AMIEL
Prestige 15 ans d'âge★★★

| | 10 ha | 25,000 | ⅋ | 23–30 € |

The Mas Amiel came up trumps yet again. The Jury selected and tasted several wines, including a surprising and original **Maury Blanc 2001 (15–23 €)** and two remarkable vintages, a **Cuvée Charles Dupuy 2001 red (30–38 €)** – in homage to the erstwhile proprietor – and a **2001 (11–15 €)**. To cap it all came this superb intensely-brown Prestige with its flavours of patinated cask, leather, coffee and brandied fruit: a powerful, rich, fleshy thoroughbred that achieves impeccable balance. The palate detects cocoa, figs, tobacco, dried fruit, and the wine finishes on a characteristic and splendid *rancio* of roasted nuts.
📞 Dom. Mas Amiel, 66460 Maury, tel. 04.68.29.01.02, fax 04.68.29.17.82 ☑
🍷 ev. day except Sun. 9am–12 noon 2pm–5pm

MAS DE LAVAIL
Expression 2001★★

| | 1 ha | 5,000 | ▮ ⅋ | 8–11 € |

An impressive début for this newcomer to the Maury stable. Nicolas Battle is the scion of a long line of vineyard proprietors who, ably assisted by his father, has opted to move into wine production. His decision has paid off: anticipating the advent of mature Maury, this deep-red Expression 2001 already hints at scrub and ripe fruit and achieves a delicate balance that imparts a spicy note. The presence of excellent tannins ensures that this wine holds on the palate. Ideal with duck in cherry sauce, perhaps, or with a chocolate-coated blackcurrant sorbet.
📞 Nicolas Battle, Mas de Lavail, 66460 Maury, tel. 04.68.59.15.22, fax 04.68.29.08.95 ☑
🍷 by appt.

LES VIGNERONS DE MAURY
Trésor Rouge 2001★★

| | n.c. | 28,000 | ▮ ⅋ | 5–8 € |

A substantial area under cultivation – albeit one whose inventory represents a considerable financial burden on this cooperative – and an area which admits technical experimentation with an extensive selection of grape varieties and products. An excellent value-for-money **Grande Réserve 1992 (8–11 €)** was selected alongside this Trésor Rouge 2001, where wild fruit and spices combine well. The wine is supple on the palate, with a seductive note of cherry underpinned by elegant velvety tannin. Best with a fruit salad with a touch of cinnamon.

📞 SCV Les Vignerons de Maury, 128, av. Jean-Jaurès, 66460 Maury, tel. 04.68.59.00.95, fax 04.68.59.02.88 ☑
🍷 by appt.

DOM. POUDEROUX 2001★★★

| | 4 ha | 16,000 | | 11–15 € |

The wide variety of terroirs between Agly and Têt attests to the potential of this estate which, over the years, has proved eminently successful in fully exploiting and adapting the individuality and complexity of each. The **La Grande Réserve (8–11 €)** is hogshead cask-matured or exposed to the sun in *bonbonnes* over a period of five years. The Jury was captivated by the freshness of this 2001, with its deep, dark robe and its intense opening redolent of undergrowth, violets and blackcurrant, with the merest suggestion of cocoa. The wine exhibits a rounded fruitiness that combines with pronounced tannins to yield an imposing wine that can be laid down with confidence.
📞 Dom. Pouderoux, 2, rue Emile-Zola, 66460 Maury, tel. 04.68.57.22.02, fax 04.68.57.11.63, e-mail 123pou@free.fr ☑
🍷 by appt.

DOM. DES SCHISTES
La Cerisaie 2001★

| | 3 ha | 7,000 | ▮ ⅋ ⚬ | 11–15 € |

Mature vines, low yields and an excellent elevation combine with passion, commitment and a sense of respect for the terroir to produce wines of the highest quality. Cask-maturation occasionally blunts the intensity of the fruit but, in exchange, imparts more aggressive notes of leather, truffle and blond tobacco. A mix of already very pronounced tannins and ripe fruit and a finish segueing into cocoa make this Cerisaie 2001 an ideal accompaniment to chocolate gateau.
📞 Jacques Sire, Dom. des Schistes, 1, av. Jean-Lurçat, 66310 Estagel, tél. 04.68.29.11.25, fax 04.68.29.47.17 ☑
🍷 by appt.

Wine selected but not starred

DOM. DE LA COUME DU ROY 2000

| | 16 ha | 2,500 | ▮ ⚬ | 11–15 € |

📞 A. de Volontat-Bachelet, Dom. de la Coume du Roy, 5, rue Emile-Zola, 66460 Maury, tel. 04.68.59.67.58, fax 04.68.59.67.58, e-mail de.volontat.bachelet@wanadoo.fr ☑
🍷 by appt.

Muscat de Rivesaltes

This sweet 100% Muscat can be made anywhere in Rivesaltes, Maury and Banyuls provided the blend is composed exclusively of Muscat varieties. The area of this vineyard covers more than 5,595 ha and produced 150,488 hl in 2002. The two varieties permitted are Muscat à Petits Grains and Muscat d'Alexandrie. The first, frequently called Muscat Blanc or Muscat de Rivesaltes, ripens early and is happy in relatively cool soils, preferably limestone. The second, also known as Muscat Romain, is a later-ripening variety which is very resistant to dry conditions.

Vinification is either by direct pressing, or by maceration for a shorter or longer time, according to the winemaker's judgement. The must is kept in a closed container, to prevent the first aromas released from being oxidized.

The wines are required to have a minimum of 100 g of sugar per litre. They should be drunk young, served at 9–10°C, with desserts such as lemon, apple or strawberry tarts, sorbets, ice creams, fruit, touron and marzipan. They are also good with Roquefort cheese.

DOM. DES AMANDIERS 2002★★

	n.c.	5,000	🍶 ♦	5–8 €

With its sustained golden yellow robe tinged green and a highly original nose reminiscent of boxwood, blackcurrant, mint and fresh lemon, this perfumed and invigorating wine tastes fleshy on the palate and is distinguished by its length and overall liveliness.
•┓ SIVIR, rte des Crêtes, 66652 Banyuls-sur-Mer, tel. 04.68.88.03.22, fax 04.68.98.36.97, e-mail sivir@templers.com

ARNAUD DE VILLENEUVE 2002★★

	n.c.	20,000	🍶 ♦	8–11 €

The 1993 merger of Salses-le-Château and Rivesaltes, two of the most important cellars of this appellation, offers the wine-lover a broad range of top quality wines, such as this 2002 Muscat, with its panoply of exotic fruits (passion fruit, mangoes and bananas), flowers (honeysuckle and broom) and spices (ginger, mace and turmeric). On the palate, this selection exhibits perfect strength, complexity and balance; as such, an excellent representative of the appellation as a whole.
•┓ Les Vignobles du Rivesaltais, 1, rue de la Roussillonnaise, 66602 Rivesaltes, tel. 04.68.64.06.63, fax 04.68.64.64.69, e-mail vignobles.rivesaltais@wanadoo.fr ☑
🍷 by appt.

DOM. BOUDAU 2002★★

	10 ha	20,000	🍶 ♦	8–11 €

The Muscat d'Alexandrie grape variety finds its fullest aromatic expression in the red soils of Rivesaltes. This estate's Boudau 2002 is intense and highly redolent of exotic fruits, pears, roses and acacia blossom. The wine is rounded, fresh and fruity and delicious on the palate. Compliments are in order to Pierre and Véronique Boudau for their continuing success; a *coup de coeur* also for their **Rivesaltes 2000**.
•┓ Dom. Véronique et Pierre Boudau, 6, rue Marceau, 66600 Rivesaltes, tel. 04.68.64.45.37, fax 04.68.64.46.26 ☑
🍷 ev. day except Sun. 10am–12 noon 3pm–7pm; cl. 16 Sep. to 31 May

CH. DE CANTERRANE 2002★

	23 ha	4,800	🍶 ♦	8–11 €

This 2002 Muscat from an estate clinging to the shingle terraces of the eponymous Canterrane boasts an excellent gold-studded yellow robe, a nose that is fresh and intense with hints of mango, beeswax, resin and acacia blossom, and a palate that develops aromas of stewed fruit and quince.
•┓ Jacques Conte, Dom. de Canterrane, 66300 Trouillas, tel. 04.68.53.47.24, fax 04.68.53.28.15 ☑
🍷 ev. day except Sun. 8am–12 noon 2 pm–6pm; Sat. 8am–12 noon
•┓ Jacques Conte

DOM. CAZES 2001★

	37 ha	100,000	🍶 ♦	11–15 €

It is now several years since the Cazes family opted for biodynamic cultivation. While the techniques employed may have changed, the Muscat they produce continues to be of the blue-chip variety. This 2001 combines notes of stewed lemon, verbena and mimosa in a wine that is superbly balanced and elegant on the palate.

•┓ Sté Cazes Frères, 4, rue Francisco-Ferrer, BP 61, 66602 Rivesaltes, tel. 04.68.64.08.26, fax 04.68.64.69.79, e-mail info@cazes-rivesaltes.com ☑
🍷 by appt.

DOM. DES CHENES 2001★★

	1.7 ha	2,500		8–11 €

Virtually omnipresent in the present *Guide* since it was first published, this estate is particularly well represented by a pale yellow and green highlight Chênes 2001, which gives off decidedly ethereal aromas of lemon-grass, pear, lychee and roses. The wine is ample and elegant on the palate and finishes superbly long on notes of stewed fruit. One member of the Jury was disposed to award it a *coup de coeur* (only awarded in the event of Jury unanimity, however) on the grounds that it would provide an excellent accompaniment to a fruit trifle or a *zabaglione*.
•┓ SCEA Dom. des Chênes, 7, rue du Mal-Joffre, 66600 Vingrau, tel. 04.68.29.40.21, fax 04.68.29.10.91, e-mail domainedeschenes@wanadoo.fr ☑
🍷 ev. day except Sun. 9am–12 noon 2pm–6pm; Sat. by appt. from Oct. to May
•┓ Razungles

CH. LAS COLLAS

Elevé en fût de chêne 1999★

	1,5 ha	3,000	🍶🍶	11–15 €

A highly individualistic Muscat 99 matured in oak casks to yield an intense robe with amber highlights. The flavours have developed a pleasing complexity, permutating resin, cedar essence, stewed fruit, bitter orange and coffee. An unusual but extremely attractive example of the appellation.
•┓ Jacques Bailbé, Ch. Las Collas, 66300 Thuir, tel. 04.68.53.40.05, fax 04.68.53.40.05 ☑ ✿
🍷 by appt.

CH. CORNELIANUM 2000★★

	1.6 ha	1,500	🍶🍶	8–11 €

Château Cornelianum 2000 is a prestigious wine matured in wood, offering a sumptuous robe of shimmering gold with the merest suggestion of orange. A powerful wine, giving off aromas of stewed grapefruit, dried apricot, quince, beeswax and vanilla, it opens on the palate to yield nuances of spices and dried fruit. A very attractive and decidedly original wine. (50 cl bottles)
•┓ Cellier Cassell Réal, 152, rte Nationale, 66550 Corneilla-la-Rivière, tel. 04.68.57.38.93, fax 04.68.57.23.36, e-mail cassell-real-com@wanadoo.fr ☑
🍷 ev. day except Sun. 9.30–12 noon 2.30pm–6pm (or 7pm from Jul. until Sep.)

DOM. DES DEMOISELLES

Dona del Sol 2001★

	1.09 ha	4,700	🍶 ♦	8–11 €

The Demoiselles estate has been handed down from mother to daughter over several generations. This "Lady of the Sun" is most attractive in her clear golden robe with green highlights and with her very fresh perfume that combines notes of white flowers and fruit. A young lady who shows both poise and promise…
•┓ Isabelle Raoux, Dom. des Demoiselles, Mas Mulès, 66300 Tresserre, tel. 04.68.38.87.10, fax 04.68.38.87.10, e-mail domaine.des.demoiselles@wanadoo.fr ☑ ✿
🍷 ev. day except Mon. 11am–1pm 4pm–8pm; cl. Jan.

DOM. GARDIES

Flor 2001★

	9 ha	10,000	🍶 ♦	11–15 €

The robe is a brilliant pale yellow with tinges of green, while the nose yields fresh fruit, gentle spices and mint. The first impression is rounded, developing into a very fresh and spicy taste on the palate. The whole is extremely well balanced.
•┓ Dom. Gardiés, 1, rue Millere, 66600 Vingrau, tel. 04.68.64.61.16, fax 04.68.64.69.36, e-mail domgardies@aol.com ☑
🍷 by appt.

VDN

JEAN D'ESTAVEL
Prestige 2002★★

	n.c.	12,000	🍶 🥄		5–8 €

This Muscat 2000 from a specialist merchant attests to the latter's expertise and knowhow. Powerful and complex aromas predominate: orange blossom, roses, citrus fruits, beeswax and exotic fruit. A perfect balance is achieved between amplitude and liveliness.
↬ SA Destavel, 7 bis, av. du Canigou, 66000 Perpignan, tel. 04.68.68.36.00, fax 04.68.54.03.54, e-mail info@destavel.com
↬ Gilles Baissas

DOM. LAFAGE 2001★★

	3.05 ha	9,000	🍶 🥄		8–11 €

This estate has for many years served as a benchmark for various types of wine listed in this *Guide*. The Jury was captivated by this Lafage 2001 and awarded it a *coup de cœur* in acknowledgment of its fresh fruit, rose, lychee and surmature grape aromas allied to discreet suggestions of mint. The wine is powerful and harmonious on the palate, perfectly poised between sweetness and freshness. An excellent aperitif to be shared with close friends...
↬ SCEA Dom. Lafage, Mas Durand, 66140 Canet-en-Roussillon, tel. 04.68.80.35.82, fax 04.68.80.38.90, e-mail domaine.lafage@wanadoo.fr 🆅
☧ by appt.
↬ J.-Marc Lafage

DOM. LAPORTE 2002★★★

	n.c.	10,000	🍶 🥄		8–11 €

The estate extends across the shingle terraces of the Têt near the former site of Ruscino and is directed authoritatively by Raymond Laporte, whose Laporte 2002 emerges as a fresh jewel of a wine, with its dominant aromas of pear, grapefruit zest and lime accented by hints of exotic blossoms. The wine is perfectly balanced on the palate. A superb *coup de cœur*!
↬ Dom. Laporte, Ch. Roussillon, 66000 Perpignan, tel. 04.68.50.06.53, fax 04.68.66.77.52, e-mail domaine-laporte@wanadoo.fr 🆅
☧ by appt.

DOM. DU MAS ALART 2000★

	14,16 ha	6,600	🍶 🥄		5–8 €

The Mas Alart is an old Catalan farmhouse surrounded by some 30 ha of vines. The colour of this 2000 is a clear gold with points of green. The strong yet elegant nose has accents of smoke, minerals, grapefruit zest and a slight suggestion of mint, culminating in a wine that is delicate and well balanced.
↬ EARL Dom. du Mas Alart, RD 22, 66280 Saleilles, tel. 04.68.50.51.89, fax 04.68.50.87.29, e-mail mas.alart@wanadoo.fr 🆅
☧ ev. day except Sun. 11am–7pm
↬ Belmas

LES VIGNERONS DE MAURY 2002★

	57 ha	21,000	🍶 🥄		5–8 €

The label draws inspiration from the "Sun cloths," the most recent generation of traditional Catalan textiles, and the wine itself has similar pale gold luminosity with points of green. The flavours recall ripe grapes, yellow peaches and exotic fruits. The Maury 2002 is smooth and slightly fresh on the palate, with a hint of stewed apricot.
↬ SCV Les Vignerons de Maury, 128, av. Jean-Jaurès, 66460 Maury, tel. 04.68.59.00.95, fax 04.68.59.02.88 🆅
☧ by appt.

CH. DE NOUVELLES
Cuvée Prestige 2002★

	3 ha	7,000	🍶 🥄		8–11 €

This superb estate, once the property of the man destined to become Pope Benoît XII in 1334, nestles in the Corbières region and has been in the Daurat-Fort family for six generations. The robe of this Cuvée Prestige is elegant, with a gentle gold suffused by touches of green. The nose presents a distinctive muscat flavour, combining notes of lime, almond and exotic fruit. This elegant and delicately perfumed wine is fresh and invigorating on the palate thanks to its delicious aromas of lime zest and mint.
↬ SCEA R. Daurat-Fort, Ch. de Nouvelles, 11350 Tuchan, tel. 04.68.45.40.03, fax 04.68.45.49.21 🆅
☧ by appt.

CH. DE PENA 2002★

	34.35 ha	15,000	🍶 🥄		5–8 €

This Pena 2002 from the black soil of the Vallée de l'Agly boasts a variety of flavours ranging from freshly-cut Virginian tulip branches (as one member of the Jury insisted at length), lemon-grass, honeysuckle, stewed lemon and verbena. The robe is an attractively clear almond colour and the wine as a whole is an exceptionally well-balanced and vivacious example of the appellation.
↬ Les Vignerons de Cases-de-Pène, 2, bd Mal-Joffre, 66600 Cases-de-Pène, tel. 04.68.38.93.30, fax 04.68.38.92.41, e-mail chateau-de-pena@wanadoo.fr 🆅
☧ ev. day except Sun. 9am–12 noon 2.30pm–6pm

DOM. DES SCHISTES 2001★★

	7 ha	10,000	🍶 🥄		5–8 €

Estagel has played a central role in the history of Roussillon dating back to the Magdalenian culture of the upper palaeolithic. This Schistes 2001 boasts an attractive pale gold robe, together with strong aromas of white fruit and citrus fruit, lemon grass and ripe grapes. The wine is elegant on the palate and very well balanced. In sum, a genuine treat and a credit to the dynamic and enthusiastic couple who produce it.
↬ Jacques Sire, Dom. des Schistes, 1, av. Jean-Lurçat, 66310 Estagel, tel. 04.68.29.11.25, fax 04.68.29.47.17 🆅
☧ by appt.

Wines selected but not starred

DOM. CELLER D'AL MOULI 2002

	4.7 ha	6,700	🍷 ⚬	5–8 €

🍇 Pierre Pelou, 9, rue de la République, 66720 Tautavel,
tel. 04.68.29.02.21, fax 04.68.29.02.21,
e-mail ppelou@aol.com 📹 🏠
🍷 by appt.

CH. LES FENALS 2002

	5.26 ha	8,000	🍷 ⚬	8–11 €

🍇 Mme Roustan Fontanel et sa Fille, Les Fenals,
11510 Fitou, tel. 04.68.45.71.94, fax 04.68.45.60.57,
e-mail les.fenals@wanadoo.fr 📹
🍷 by appt.

DOM. GALY
Réserve 2002

	2.5 ha	7,000	🍷 ⚬	5–8 €

🍇 Dom. Galy, rue du Cinéma, 66670 Bages,
tel. 04.68.21.80.49, fax 04.68.21.87.37,
e-mail domainegaly.vin@wanadoo.fr 📹
🍷 ev. day except Sun. 9.30am–12.30pm 3.30pm–7pm

CH. DE JAU 2002

	16 ha	40,000	🍷 ⚬	8–11 €

🍇 Ch. de Jau, 66600 Cases-de-Pène, tel. 04.68.38.90.10,
fax 04.68.38.91.33, e-mail daure@wanadoo.fr 📹
🍷 by appt.
🍇 Dauré

CAVE DE LESQUERDE 2002

	8.25 ha	25,000	🍷 ⚬	5–8 €

🍇 SCV Lesquerde, rue du Grand-Capitoul,
66220 Lesquerde, tel. 04.68.59.02.62, fax 04.68.59.08.17,
e-mail lesquerde@wanadoo.fr 📹
🍷 ev. day except Sun. 9am–12 noon 2pm–6pm

DOM. DU MAS ROUS 2002

	4.9 ha	5,300	🍷 ⚬	5–8 €

🍇 José Pujol, Dom. du Mas Rous, BP 4,
66740 Montesquieu Albères, tel. 04.68.89.64.91,
fax 04.68.89.80.88, e-mail masrous@mas-rous.com 📹
🍷 by appt.

CH. MONTNER 2001

	15 ha	20,000	🍷 ⚬	5–8 €

🍇 Les Vignerons des Côtes d'Agly, Cave coopérative,
66310 Estagel, tel. 04.68.29.00.45, fax 04.68.29.19.80,
e-mail agly@tiscali.fr 📹
🍷 ev. day except Sun. 9am–12 noon 2pm–6pm

LES PRODUCTEURS DU MONT
TAUCH Cuvée Prestige 2001

	30 ha	70,000	🍷 ⚬	5–8 €

🍇 Les Producteurs du Mont Tauch, 11350 Tuchan,
tel. 04.68.45.41.08, fax 04.68.45.45.29,
e-mail contact@mont-tauch.com 📹
🍷 ev. day except Sat. Sun. 9am–12 noon 2pm–7pm

DOM. MOUNIE 2002

	3 ha	7,000	🍷 ⚬	8–11 €

🍇 Dom. Mounié, 1, av. du Verdouble, 66720 Tautavel,
tel. 04.68.29.12.31, fax 04.68.29.05.59 📹
🍷 by appt.
🍇 Rigaill

CH. PLANERES
Excellence 2002

	8 ha	12,000	🍷 ⚬	5–8 €

🍇 Ch. Planères, Vignobles Jaubert et Noury,
66300 Saint-Jean-Lasseille, tel. 04.68.21.74.50,
fax 04.68.21.87.25, e-mail contact@chateauplaneres.com 📹
🍷 ev. day except Sun. 9am–12 noon 2pm–6pm

CH. PRADAL 2002

	8 ha	12,000	🍷 ⚬	5–8 €

🍇 André Coll-Escluse, Ch. Pradal, 58, rue Pépinière-Robin,
66000 Perpignan, tel. 04.68.85.04.73, fax 04.68.56.80.49 📹
🍷 by appt.

DOM. DE ROMBEAU 2002

	15 ha	20,000	🍷 ⚬	8–11 €

🍇 Pierre-Henri de La Fabrègue, Dom. de Rombeau, RD
12, rte de Perpignan, 66600 Rivesaltes, tel. 04.68.64.35.35,
fax 04.68.64.64.66 📹
🍷 by appt.

CH. VALFON 2002

	1.5 ha	6,000	🍷 ⚬	8–11 €

🍇 GAEC Dom. Valfon, pl. Gabriel Péri, 66300 Thuir,
tel. 04.68.53.61.66, fax 04.68.53.06.19,
e-mail chvalfon@aol.com 📹
🍷 ev. day 9.30am–12.30pm 4.30pm–7.30pm;
cl. Thu. am and Sun. pm.
🍇 Valette-Fons

CH. VALMY
Cachet d'Or 2001

	2.13 ha	13,014	🍷 ⚬	8–11 €

🍇 Ch. Valmy, chem. de Valmy, 66700 Argelès-sur-Mer,
tel. 04.68.81.25.70, fax 04.68.81.15.18,
e-mail chateau.valmy@free.fr 📹
🍷 by appt.
🍇 Bernard et Martine Carbonnell

VAQUER 2001

	3 ha	3,400	🍷 ⚬	8–11 €

🍇 Dom. Vaquer, 1–2, rue des Ecoles, 66300 Tresserre,
tel. 04.68.38.89.53, fax 04.68.38.84.42,
e-mail domaine.vaquer@terre-net.fr 📹
🍷 by appt.

Muscat de Frontignan

Frontignan was the first Muscat to be awarded Appellation d'Origine Contrôlée in 1936. This was a judgement from the Montpellier tribunal, dated 4 July 1935, which specified the type of terroir suitable to produce these wines. Muscat de Frontignan may only be produced from generally dry, stony and rocky ground, originally from ancient Jurassic strata with molasse and alluvial deposits, giving soil on which nothing else will grow. The wines are made only from the variety Muscat à Petits Grains (which used to be called "Muscat de Frontignan"). They must have at least 125 g of residual sugar. Although powerful, these wines are always elegant.

VDN

CH. DES ARESQUIERS 2001★★

	1.6 ha	7,000	∎	5–8 €

Elisabeth and Brigitte Jeanjean have featured regularly in this *Guide* over the years. Their Aresquiers 2001 is firmly in line with the winemaking tradition of the château of that name and merits a *coup de coeur* for its permutation of elegance and expressiveness. A pale gold robe and aromas of lychee, fresh muscat grapes, dried fruit and stewed lemons presages a wine that is rounded, fresh and full of character on the palate, with the sustained and sumptuous finish that comes only with outstanding knowhow. To be drunk as an aperitif *par excellence*.
↪ Elisabeth et Brigitte Jeanjean, Dom. du Mas Neuf des Aresquiers, 34110 Vic-la-Gardiole, tel. 04.67.78.37.44, fax 04.67.78.37.46

CAVE DE FRONTIGNAN 20 Ans★★★

	n.c.	3,500	⬭	15–23 €

The cooperative cellars routinely offer a "forgotten wine" in the guise of a wine matured in 25 hl oak barrels and reserved for lovers of great *rancios*. This example made its mark with the Jury on account of its superbly brilliant amber robe, coupled with a nose that is intensely powerful, elegant and complex, with successive aromas of dried fig, honey, stewed orange and roasted coffee. The wine is full and elegant on the palate; tart yet mellow at one and the same time, it exhibits the exceptional finesse that is only achieved in the wake of protracted and patient maturation. A wine to be enjoyed on its own and on any occasion.
↪ SCA Coop. de Frontignan, 14, av. du Muscat, 34110 Frontignan, tel. 04.67.48.12.26, fax 04.67.43.07.17 ☑
𝖄 ev. day 9.30am–12.30pm 2.30pm–6.30pm; groups by appt.

CH. DE LA PEYRADE
Sol Invictus 2002★★

	n.c.	7,000	∎	8–11 €

Frontignan wines from this estate have been awarded no fewer than six *coups de coeur* since the first edition of the present *Guide*. This time around, the Pastourel family offers two muscats that are securely in the tradition of their illustrious predecessors. Aromas abound of white flowers, white peaches and eucalyptus leaves, and the wine is rounded and fleshy on the palate, with that suggestion of freshness and youth that is a *sine qua non* of great muscats. The **Cuvée Prestige 2002** is perhaps less aromatic than its predecessor, but it offers an unusual range of complex stewed fruit flavours. On the palate, this wine does full justice to the terms "balance" and "finesse".
↪ Yves Pastourel et Fils, Ch. de La Peyrade, 34110 Frontignan, tel. 04.67.48.61.19, fax 04.67.43.03.31, e-mail info@chateaulapeyrade.com ☑
𝖄 by appt.

CH. SIX TERRES 2002★

	20 ha	37,000	∎	5–8 €

The Frontignan Wine Cooperative was established in 1907 and today processes close on 80% of Frontignan grape variety production from 275 members cultivating a total of some 615 ha. The cooperative has successfully embraced new winemaking techniques and technology over the last century without sacrificing its commitment to the muscat tradition. This Six Terres 2002 exhibits a clear pale gold robe and a fresh nose with nuances of stewed apricot, ripe pears and quince; it

is soft and mellow on the palate. A perceptible hint of carbon dioxide enables the wine to preserve the requisite freshness and vitality. Overall, a true-to-type Frontignan, with all the implicit virtues of the appellation.
↪ SCA Coop. de Frontignan, 14, av. du Muscat, 34110 Frontignan, tel. 04.67.48.12.26, fax 04.67.43.07.17 ☑
𝖄 ev. day 9.30am–12.30pm 2.30pm–6.30pm; groups by appt.

CH. DE STONY
Sélection de Vendanges 2001★

	6,3 ha	32,000	∎ ♦	8–11 €

A beautiful golden yellow wine that is still slightly closed at first tasting but ultimately reveals its complex nature as flavours of verbena, fruit paste and a hint of honey successively emerge. The wine is rounded and elegant on the palate and finishes long and harmoniously; as such, it is ready to be drunk now.
↪ Frédéric et Henri Nodet, GAEC Ch. de Stony, rte de Balaruc, 34110 Frontignan, tel. 04.67.18.80.30, fax 04.67.43.24.96 ☑
𝖄 by appt.

Muscat de Beaumes-de-Venise

Located north of Carpentras, beneath the impressive mountains of the Dentelles de Montmirail, the landscape is one of grey limestones and red marls. The terroir is partly composed of sands, marls and sandstone together with weathered, faulted terrain dating from the Triassic and Jurassic eras. Here again, the only grape variety used is the Muscat à Petits Grains, although, on some parcels of land, a mutation has led to pink or red grapes. Muscat de Beaumes-de-Venise wines, of which 11,845 hl were produced in 2002, are required to contain a minimum of 110 g of sugar per litre of must; aromatic, fruity and elegant, they are perfect as an aperitif or with cheese.

DOM. DE DURBAN 2002★

	n.c.		∎	8–11 €

The estate stands out against a pine-clad hill-top, its vines overlooking the village of Beaumes, an area of natural beauty that deserves to be better known. The Durban 2002 is a Muscat with an attractive robe of pale gold with points of green. The nose is expressive, with hints of iris and hyacinth. The wine is fine and unctuous, with a very sustained finish. Ideal served chilled as an aperitif. Ready to drink now, but can be laid down for three to four years.
↪ SCEA Leydier et Fils, Dom. de Durban, 84190 Beaumes-de-Venise, tel. 04.90.62.94.26, fax 04.90.65.01.85 ☑
𝖄 ev. day except Sun. 9am–12 noon 2pm–6pm

LAURUS 2001★★

	3 ha	8,000	∎ ♦	15–23 €

A quality wine with a nose of fresh fruit developing into stewed fruit. Equal subtlety characterises the perfectly balanced and sustained taste on the palate. The care and attention lavished on this Laurus 2001 have been amply rewarded. To be drunk on its own or as an accompaniment to foie gras.
↪ Gabriel Meffre, Le Village, 84190 Gigondas, tel. 04.90.12.30.22, fax 04.90.12.30.29, e-mail lionel-chol@meffre.com ☑
𝖄 by appt.

CH. SAINT-SAUVEUR 2000★

	6.5 ha	25,700	🛢 ♦	8–11 €

This 58 ha estate lies off the D 55 some 1.4 km from Aubignan; its cellars are housed in an ancient chapel. The Saint-Saveur 2000 boasts a magnificent robe of nuanced gold. Aromas include dried fruit, apricot, fig and nuts. A wine that brings out the best in foie gras or a mature Roquefort cheese.
☛ EARL les Héritiers de Marcel Rey, Ch. Saint-Sauveur, rte de Caromb, BP 2, 84810 Aubignan, tel. 04.90.62.60.39, fax 04.90.62.60.46 ☑
👤 ev. day except Sun. 9am–12.15pm 2.15pm–7pm
☛ Guy Rey

Wines selected but not starred

VIGNERONS DE BEAUMES-DE-VENISE

Carte or 2002

	100 ha	40,000	🛢 ♦	8–11 €

☛ Cave des Vignerons de Beaumes-de-Venise, quartier Ravel, 84190 Beaumes-de-Venise, tel. 04.90.12.41.00, fax 04.90.65.02.05, e-mail vignerons@ beaumes-de-venise.com ☑
👤 by appt.

DOM. BOULETIN 2002

	6 ha	20,000	🛢 ♦	8–11 €

☛ Dom. Bouletin et Fils, quartier La Plantade, 84190 Beaumes-de-Venise, tel. 04.90.62.95.10, fax 04.90.62.98.23 ☑
👤 by appt.

DOM. DE FENOUILLET 2002

	7.79 ha	27,000	🛢 ♦	8–11 €

☛ GAEC Patrick et Vincent Soard, Dom. de Fenouillet, allée Saint-Roch, 84190 Beaumes-de-Venise, tel. 04.90.62.95.61, fax 04.90.62.90.67, e-mail pv.soard@freesbee.fr ☑
👤 by appt.

DOM. DE FONTAVIN 2002

	2.6 ha	7,000	🛢 ♦	8–11 €

☛ EARL Hélène et Michel Chouvet, Dom. de Fontavin, 1468, rte de la Plaine, 84350 Courthézon, tel. 04.90.70.72.14, fax 04.90.70.79.39, e-mail helene-chouvet@fontavin.com ☑
👤 ev. day except Sun. 9am–12 noon 2pm–6pm; summer 9am–7pm; groups by appt.

Muscat de Lunel

A sweet (minimum 125 g of sugar per litre) wine made only from Muscat à Petits Grains. Located around Lunel, the hilltop vineyards sit amid a typical landscape of rolled stones on red clay earth over alluvial folds. A total of 10,300 hl was declared in 2002.

CLOS BELLEVUE

Cuvée Vieilles Vignes 2002★

	4 ha	13,000	🛢 ♦	11–15 €

Every year, Francis Lacoste offers a Muscat de Lunel which stands out on account of its delicate aromas redolent of a basket of freshly-picked citrus fruits. His Cuvée Vieilles Vignes 2002, with its aromas of fresh grapes, exhibits a particular elegance and freshness that found immediate favour with the Jury. Mention should also be made of a **Cuvée Tradition 2002 (8–11 €)**, whose organoleptic qualities are very similar to those of the Vieilles Vignes 2002. Le Clos Bellevue must rank as a blue-chip example of the appellation.
☛ Francis Lacoste, Dom. de Bellevue, rte de Sommières, 34400 Lunel, tel. 04.67.83.24.83, fax 04.67.71.48.23, e-mail muscatlacoste@wanadoo.fr ☑
👤 ev. day except Sun. 9am–7pm; winter 9am–6pm; groups by appt.

CH. DE LA DEVEZE 2001★

	15.5 ha	52,000	🛢 ♦	5–8 €

The wine presents very well, with a clear golden yellow robe and a complex nose of dried flowers and raisins complemented by a note of coffee. The Devèze 2001 is smooth on the palate, revealing a perfect balance of alcohol, sweetness and freshness. It finishes long and sustained. The cooperative also offers a **Château de la Tour de Farges 2001** distinguished by very fresh aromas and interlaced Muscat flavours.
☛ Les Vignerons du Muscat de Lunel, rte de Lunel-Viel, 34400 Vérargues, tel. 04.67.86.00.09, fax 04.67.86.07.52, e-mail info@muscat-lunel.com ☑
👤 by appt.

CH. GRES SAINT-PAUL

Sévillane 2001★

	2.73 ha	8,386	🛢 ♦	8–11 €

Monsieur Servière, known also as a producer of AOC Coteaux du Languedoc, has recently opened a public sales outlet whose particularly immaculate décor is no more than a reflection of his entire operation. His Sévillane 2001 presents a golden robe with intense highlights and a nose that the Jury found complex to the extent that it gives off aromas not only of dried flowers but also of an intricate mix of dried fruits and a mint fragrance. To all intents and purposes, a most successful wine.
☛ GFA Ch. Grès Saint-Paul, rte de Restinclières, 34400 Lunel, tel. 04.67.71.27.90, fax 04.67.71.73.76 ☑
👤 ev. day except Sun. 9.30am–12 noon 2.30pm–7pm
☛ Servière

LES VIGNERONS DU MUSCAT DE LUNEL Cuvée Prestige 2001★★

	19 ha	65,000	🛢 ♦	5–8 €

This cooperative was established in 1965 and today encompasses in excess of 350 ha of vine stocks. This Cuvée Prestige lives up to its designation: an attractive, delicately golden robe and a complex nose which combines overripe fruit and stewed citrus aromas complemented by a roasted note. The attack is precise and clear, giving way to an elegant and discreet sweetness. The wine finishes long and fresh. In all, a *coup de cœur* for a wine that is remarkable in every respect.
☛ Les Vignerons du Muscat de Lunel, rte de Lunel-Viel, 34400 Vérargues, tel. 04.67.86.00.09, fax 04.67.86.07.52, e-mail info@muscat-lunel.com ☑
👤 by appt.

DOM. SAINT-PIERRE DE PARADIS
Vendange d'Automne 2000★★

3 ha	5,000	🍾 ⑪ ⚲	8–11 €

This Saint-Pierre de Paradis 2000 is distinguished by an attractively clean amber robe and a rich and pungent nose that associates multiple-nuanced aromas of dried fruit, dark chocolate and roasted notes. It is perfectly balanced on the palate and finishes on an unusually sustained roasted note. Excellent with a chocolate fondant or, in years to come, as a stand-alone aperitif.

🍷 Les Vignerons du Muscat de Lunel, rte de Lunel-Viel, 34400 Vérargues, tel. 04.67.86.00.09, fax 04.67.86.07.52, e-mail info@muscat-lunel.com ☑
☨ by appt.

Muscat de Mireval

This vineyard is bordered by the Etang de Vic, and stretches between Sète and Montpellier on the south-facing slope of the Massif de la Gardiole. The soils are of ancient Jurassic alluvium, smoothed stones and the predominant limestone. The single grape variety is Muscat à Petits Grains; in 2002, 5,753 hl of Vins Doux Naturels were produced.

Mutage is carried out fairly early, because the wines must reach a minimum of 125 g of sugar per litre; they are sweet, fruity and rich.

DOM. DE LA CAPELLE
Parcelle n° 8 2001★

12 ha	20,000	🍾 ⚲	15–23 €

Alexandre Maraval's family has worked since 1880 to clear the *garrigue* (scrubland) and plant new vines. This Parcelle No 8 of 2001 boasts an attractive yellow robe with points of green. The wine is initially somewhat closed, but gradually opens to yield aromas of citrus fruits and green buds. On the palate, these aromas develop as flavours of stewed fruit. This 2001 Muscat is balanced and fluent, with good length and a distinctive personality.

🍷 Alexandre Maraval, Dom. de La Capelle, 34110 Mireval, tel. 04.67.78.15.14, fax 04.67.78.58.96, e-mail domainecapelle@hotmail.com ☑
☨ by appt.

DOM. DE LA CAPELLE
Maguelonne 1995★★

6 ha	17,000	⑪	23–30 €

A Muscat of venerable age and maturity sure to please lovers of *rancio*, the Maguelonne 1995 is distinguished by a mahogany robe which reveals characteristic oxidization and notes of dried almonds, nuts and dried fruit. The wine is fresh and elegant on the palate, its freshness complemented by notes of flowers and dried fruit. The finish is light but elegant. An extremely interesting wine that can age a further ten years.

🍷 Alexandre Maraval, Dom. de La Capelle, 34110 Mireval, tel. 04.67.78.15.14, fax 04.67.78.58.96, e-mail domainecapelle@hotmail.com ☑
☨ by appt.

CH. D'EXINDRE
Vent d'Anges 2001★★

2.51 ha	3,500	🍾 ⚲	8–11 €

The 2003 edition of the *Guide* awarded a *coup de coeur* to this estate's Magdalaine 2000, and Madame Sicard-Géroudet's Cuvée Vent d'Anges 2001, with its gold highlight robe and pungent nose commingling aromas of honey, stewed fruit and

a hint of quince, has once again won over the Jury. The stewed fruit flavours persist on the palate and gradually predominate. This is an extremely well-rounded and fleshy wine that is both powerful and expressive. The finish is sustained, not to say infinite. This "angels' breath" provides an excellent companion to chocolate desserts when not served on its own as an aperitif.

🍷 Catherine Sicard-Géroudet, La Magdelaine d'Exindre, 34750 Villeneuve-lès-Maguelonne, tel. 04.67.69.49.77, fax 04.67.69.49.77 ☑ ☏
☨ by appt.

DOM. DU MAS NEUF 2002★★

62 ha	60,000	🍾	5–8 €

Bernard-Pierre Jeanjean routinely produces blue-chip Muscat de Mireval and this 2002 from his Mas Neuf estate is certainly no exception to the rule. The Jury was impressed by its brilliant robe of pale yellow with points of green and its richly-intense and elegant nose that presents agreeably surprising notes of flowers, oranges and grapefruit. The 2002 is light and elegant on the palate without prejudice to an underlying strength and expressiveness. A wine only a hair's breadth away from a *coup de coeur*. Recommended to be served chilled as an accompaniment to foie gras.

🍷 Bernard-Pierre Jeanjean, Dom. du Mas Neuf des Aresquiers, 34110 Vic-la-Gardiole, tel. 04.67.78.37.44, fax 04.67.78.37.46

Muscat de Saint-Jean de Minervois

This Muscat is produced on parcels of land amid the garrigue, the classic high (average 200 m) stony moorland of southwest France. It follows that the harvest is late, about three weeks after the other Muscat appellations. Some vines are on primary schist terrain but most grow on limestone interspersed with red clays. Muscat à Petits Grains is the single variety planted; the wines must have a minimum sugar content of 125 g per litre. They are very aromatic with great finesse and characteristic floral notes. This is the smallest Muscat AOC, producing 4,912 hl in 2002.

DOM. DE BARROUBIO
Cuvée bleue 2001★★★

16 ha	6,000	🍾 ⚲	5–8 €

Yet another exceptional wine from the Barroubio estate: an attractive pale gold robe and an intense nose evocative of

fresh citrus fruits complemented by an astute suggestion of mint. On the middle palate, accents of mango seem to issue from a basket of overripe fruit; on the palate proper, there is a strength and an elegance that attest to a wine of the highest quality. What more is there to say? Recommended with a crème brûlée?

☛ Raymond Miquel, Barroubio,
34360 Saint-Jean-de-Minervois, tel. 04.67.38.14.06,
fax 04.67.38.14.06 ☑ ⌂
☋ ev. day 10am–12 noon 2pm–6.30pm

DOM. DE BARROUBIO

Classique 2001★★

	16 ha	46,000	🍾 ♦	8–11 €

This Classique 2001 boasts a pale gold robe with green-gold highlights and a panoply of delightfully complex aromas that includes mint, fresh figs and orange zest. The wine is balanced and pungent on the palate, yet with a freshness that must rank this as one of the most successful vintages of the appellation. One member of the tasting panel even suggested it as an accompaniment to chicken curry…

☛ Raymond Miquel, Barroubio,
34360 Saint-Jean-de-Minervois, tel. 04.67.38.14.06,
fax 04.67.38.14.06 ☑ ⌂
☋ ev. day 10am–12 noon 2pm–6.30pm

LE MUSCAT

Petit Grain 2001★★

	n.c.	48,000	🍾 ♦	8–11 €

An attractive yellow robe with copper highlights and a nose that opens progressively on aromas of fruit, fresh apricots and peach skins. This Petit Grain 2001 opens still further on the middle palate, suggesting a cocktail of exotic fruits. Balance and freshness predominate on the palate, combining to yield a Saint-Jean-de-Minervois that is in every respect remarkable.

☛ SCA Le Muscat, 34360 Saint-Jean-de-Minervois,
tel. 04.67.38.03.24, fax 04.67.38.23.38 ☑
☋ ev. day except Sat. Sun. 8am–12 noon 2pm–4pm;
groups by appt.

DOM. DU SACRE-COEUR

Cuvée Kevin 2002★

	2 ha	8,000		8–11 €

Marc Cabaret comes from a marketing background. He decided in 1991 to try his hand at wine-growing and, in 1995, was joined on the estate by his son Luc, who had recently completed his studies at the excellent agricultural college of La Tour Blanche in the Sauternes region. This Cuvée Kevin 2002 offers a very pale robe and a highly-defined nose redolent of white peaches, heightened on the middle palate by accents of citrus fruits and mint. On the palate proper, the wine combines elegance and youthfulness to yield a muscat that is unequivocally elegant. To be drunk as an aperitif.

☛ GAEC du Sacré-Coeur, Dom. du Sacré-Coeur,
34360 Assignan, tel. 04.67.38.17.97, fax 04.67.38.24.52,
e-mail gaecsacrecoeur@net-up.com ☑
☋ ev. day 8.30am–12.30pm 2pm–7pm
☛ Marc et Luc Cabaret

Rasteau

Located in the very north of the Vaucluse department, this vineyard is spread over two distinct geological formations: sand, marl and pebbles in the north, and ancient alluvial terraces left by the Rhône (from the Quaternary era) with smoothed pebbles in the south. The Grenache varieties are responsible for all the wines here. A limited quantity is produced: 380 hl in 2002.

DOM. DES ESCARAVAILLES 2000★★

	1.27 ha	5,400	🍾 ⦿ ♦	11–15 €

Two very attractive wines from the 2000 vintage – one white, the other red, both based on the grenache grape variety. The Rasteau Rouge carries the day by virtue of its pronounced elegance and its aromas of cocoa. The wine is firm on the palate, with notes of red fruits, Morello cherries and cocoa, and promises to become more interesting with age. Ready to drink now, but also appropriate to lay down. The **Rasteau Blanc 2000** is awarded one star and, in the opinion of one member of the tasting jury, would go well with fresh melon.

☛ Ferran et Fils, SCEA des Escaravailles, 84110 Rasteau,
tel. 04.90.46.14.20, fax 04.90.46.11.45 ☑
☋ by appt.

CAVE DE RASTEAU

Signature 1998★

	n.c.	n.c.		8–11 €

A clear red robe with points of mahogany distinguishes this festive wine whose powerful palate and aromas of spices and cocoa would constitute an exquisite accompaniment to a candlelit dinner. The Signature 1998 exhibits considerable potential for delicious Yuletide desserts in years to come, not least those featuring oranges and chocolate…

☛ Cave de Rasteau, rte des Princes-d'Orange,
84110 Rasteau, tel. 04.90.10.90.10, fax 04.90.46.16.65,
e-mail rasteau@rasteau.com ☑
☋ by appt.

Wines selected but not starred

DOM. DIDIER CHARAVIN 2001

	1 ha	n.c.	🍾	8–11 €

☛ Didier Charavin, rte de Vaison, 84110 Rasteau,
tel. 04.90.46.15.63, fax 04.90.46.16.22 ☑
☋ ev. day 9am–12 noon 2pm–6pm

DOM. DES COTEAUX DES TRAVERS 2000

	n.c.	n.c.		8–11 €

☛ EARL Robert Charavin, Dom. des Coteaux des Travers,
BP 5, 84110 Rasteau, tel. 04.90.46.13.69,
fax 04.90.46.15.81,
e-mail robert.charavin@wanadoo.fr ☑
☋ by appt.

VDN

Muscat du Cap Corse

The Appellation Muscat du Cap Corse was officially recognized on 26 March 1993, the culmination of lengthy efforts made by a handful of winemakers working on the limestone soils of Patrimonio and the schist soils of the AOC Vin de Corse-Coteaux du Cap Corse. The AOC is located in 17 communes in the extreme north of the islands. Production is limited and amounted to 2,080 hl in 2002.

Since 1993, AOC wines have been limited to Muscat Blanc à Petits Grains and have had to fulfil the stipulated production conditions of Vin Doux Naturels, which require at least 95 grams of residual sugar per litre.

↱ GAEC Dom. Leccia, 20232 Poggio-d'Oletta,
tel. 04.95.37.11.35, fax 04.95.37.17.03 ☑
☥ by appt.

DOM. DE CATARELLI 2002★

	2 ha	5,000	🍴 ⚲	11–15 €

Inveterate wine-grower Laurent Le Stunff offers this seductive and harmonious muscat whose extreme clarity and freshness are perhaps inspired by the waters of the nearby Saint-Florent creek which borders on his small estate. Comparatively intense aromas of flowers and apricots fill the nose and flood the palate from a wine that finishes long and balanced with overtones of honey. A wine to be enjoyed with foie gras.
↱ EARL Dom. de Catarelli, marine de Farinole, rte de Nonza, 20253 Patrimonio, tel. 04.95.37.02.84,
fax 04.95.37.18.72 ☑
☥ ev. day except Sun. 9am–12 noon 3pm–6pm;
cl. Nov. to Mar.
↱ Laurent Le Stunff

CLOS DE BERNARDI 2002★

	1 ha	4,000	🍴 ⚲	11–15 €

Jean-Laurent de Bernardi and his younger brother work out of one of the most attractive cellars in the region, constantly renovated in the traditional Patrimonio style. Their Clos de Bernardi 2001 is an accomplished muscat with a yellow robe with points of gold and green highlights and aromas of mixed spring and summer blossoms that persist on the palate to yield a well-balanced sweetness. Little by little, new flavours of stewed apricot and exotic fruit emerge from this idiosyncratic vintage.
↱ Jean-Laurent de Bernardi, 20253 Patrimonio,
tel. 04.95.37.01.09, fax 04.95.32.07.66 ☑
☥ ev. day 9am–12 noon

DOM. LECCIA 2002★★

	3.2 ha	12,000	🍴 ⚲	15–23 €

This property, located in the heart of the Nebbiu in the commune of Poggio d'Oletta, extends over 20 ha, of which 3.2 ha are planted with Muscat à Petits Grains. Yves Leccia is an oenologist by profession but a Corsican *vigneron* at heart, a skilled wine-grower versed in the art of producing wines highly typical of the region. This excellent Leccia 2002 is a judicious blend of the old and the new: very ripe grapes grown on a clay-limestone substrate are subjected to 48 hours of pre-fermentation maceration at a temperature of 15°C. Yves Leccia does not disclose all his secrets; suffice it to say that one is captivated by the golden colour of this quality wine with its typical aromas of muscat and spices which deliver an unforgettable complexity and strength to the palate.

ORENGA DE GAFFORY 2002★

	10 ha	20,000	🍴 ⚲	8–11 €

With its 10 ha of Muscat à Petits Grains, the Orenga de Gaffory property surely ranks among the best in Corsica as a producer of the Patrimonio appellation. Masterminded by Henri Orenga de Gaffory, the estate applies state-of-the-art maturation technology to produce wines such as this very successful 2002, with its clear pale yellow robe and a nose albeit still closed but nonetheless developing subtle aromas of exotic fruit and muscat grapes. The attack is gentle and well balanced, with an elegance that extends into a sustained and invigorating finish.
↱ GFA Orenga de Gaffory, Lieu-dit Morta-Majo,
20253 Patrimonio, tel. 04.95.37.45.00, fax 04.95.37.14.25,
e-mail orenga.de.gaffory@wanadoo.fr ☑
☥ ev. day except Sat. Sun. 9am–12 noon 1.30pm–6pm;
groups by appt.
↱ H. Orenga et P. de Gaffory

Wines selected but not starred

NAPOLEON BRIZI 2002

	2.5 ha	10,000	🍴 ⚲	8–11 €

↱ Napoléon Brizi, 20253 Patrimonio, tel. 04.95.37.08.26 ☑
☥ by appt.

CLOS MARFISI 2002

	3.5 ha	10,000	🍴 ⚲	11–15 €

↱ Toussaint Marfisi, Clos Marfisi, av. Jules-Ventre,
20253 Patrimonio, tel. 04.95.37.07.49, fax 04.95.37.06.37 ☑
☥ ev. day 9am–1pm 3pm–8pm;
cl. from 1 Dec. to 1 Mar.

VINS DE LIQUEUR

This type of wine is the result of blending must with grape brandy during fermentation. In all cases, wines described as Vins de Liqueur must have between 16% and 22% of alcohol by volume. The addition of brandy to the musts is called mutage; both brandy and must should originate from the same vineyard. The AOC (the equivalent of the EU designation VLQPRD) used to apply only to Pineau des Charentes (apart, in rare instances, from a few Frontignans). However, Floc de Gascogne (classified 27 November 1990) and Macvin du Jura (classified 14 November 1991) have now also joined the Appellation Contrôlée Vin de Liqueur.

Pineau des Charentes

Pineau des Charentes is produced in the Cognac region on an extensive plain sloping gently westwards from a maximum altitude of 180 m towards the Atlantic Ocean. The climate, maritime in character, is typified by a remarkable amount of sunshine and very even temperatures, factors that promote the slow ripening of the grapes.

More than 80,000 ha of vines are planted on limestone slopes in a hinterland watered by the Charente river. The grapes are intended mainly for the production of Cognac. Pineau des Charentes is produced by mixing Cognac with partially fermented grape must.

According to legend, a somewhat distracted winemaker once made the mistake of filling a hogshead that still contained some Cognac with grape must. Noticing that the barrel did not ferment, he left it in the back of the cellar. A few years later, when he was preparing to empty the hogshead, he discovered a clear, delicate liquid with a sweet, fruity flavour: this is said to be the origin of Pineau des Charentes. The legend dates from the 16th century, but the blend is still current today, as is the traditional method of production, because Pineau des Charentes may only be made by wine-growers. Its reputation remained localized for a long time before gradually achieving first national, then international recognition.

The grape musts for white Pineau des Charentes come mainly from Ugni Blanc, Colombard, Montils and Sémillon, while Cabernet Franc, Cabernet Sauvignon and Merlot are used for the rosé. The vines are trained low and cultivated without nitrogenous fertilizers. The grapes have to produce a must of over 170 g/l of sugar. After the blending process, Pineau des Charentes is aged in oak casks for a minimum of one year before bottling.

As is the case with Cognac, it is not the practice to show the vintage. On the other hand, the age of the wine is frequently indicated. The term Vieux Pineau is reserved for Pineau that is more than five years old and Très Vieux Pineau for Pineau that is more than ten years old. In both cases, it must be aged exclusively in the hogshead, and the quality of this ageing process has to be checked by the Commission de Dégustation (the tasting panel). Alcoholic strength must be between 17% and 18% by volume and the content of non-fermented sugar from 125–150 g/l; the rosé is typically sweeter and fruitier than the white, which is firmer and drier. The annual production exceeds 58,491 hl of white and 32,219 hl of rosé.

This is a nectar of honey and fire, its marvellous sweetness camouflaging real power. Pineau des Charentes can be drunk young (after two years) when all its fruit aromas (even fuller in the rosé) are on show. With age, these aromas take on a nutty *rancio* character. Traditionally, Pineau des Charentes is drunk as an aperitif or with desserts; however, its roundness also perfectly accompanies foie gras and Roquefort. Its sweet flavour intensifies the natural flavour and sweetness of some kinds of fruit, particularly melon (Charentais melon), strawberries and raspberries. Pineau des Charentes is also used as an ingredient in traditional regional dishes such as mussel stew.

C. AUDEBERT Vieux★

	6 ha	4,000	⦿	15–23 €

This traditional Charentais estate, worked by a father and his two sons, lies in the vicinity of romanesque churches and a Gallo-Roman theatre. Their old Pineau Blanc has an elegant old-gold colour with bright amber glints. The nose is dominated by hints of dried fruits and a *rancio* of great finesse. The palate is full and round, with oaky notes that add to the wine's expressive character.
☛ Claude Audebert, Les Villairs, 16170 Rouillac, tel. 05.45.21.76.86, fax 05.45.96.81.36, e-mail erclaude@wanadoo.fr ☑
☚ ev. day 7.30am–1pm 2pm–8pm; groups by appt.

BARBEAU
Très Vieux Rosé Grande Réserve★★★

	1 ha	2,000	⦿	11–15 €

The Barbeau family has worked this estate for more than a century, and began direct-selling of its products in 1970. This Pineau Rosé is made wholly from Merlot grapes. Its lovely crimson colour has slightly orangey highlights conferred by the ageing in oak. The nose will be appreciated for its fine yet powerful quality; it is very aromatic with notes of orange marmalade, toast, and spices. The palate begins well, then opens to reveal a supple, full, round character, with notes of oakiness that integrate well to form a exceptional whole. In this case, the classic combination with chocolate cake will be really delicious.
☛ Maison Barbeau et Fils, Les Vignes, 17160 Sonnac, tel. 05.46.58.55.85, fax 05.46.58.53.62 ☑
☚ by appt.

VEUVE BARON ET FILS★★

| | 3 ha | 18,000 | 🍶 | 8–11 € |

Last year this concern, based since 1851 in a former hunting-lodge dating from François I's reign, obtained a *coup de coeur* for its old Pineau Blanc. The estate lies within the Borderies wine area. This year's version is a lovely, bright straw colour, with golden highlights – very attractive. The nose has highly individual aromas of dried fruits and figs, with notes of *pain d'épice* (a sweetish spice loaf). It is powerful on the palate, where its *rancio* will be appreciated together with the vanilla tones resulting from its maturation in oak.
🍷 Jean-Michel Baron, Logis du Coudret,
16370 Cherves-Richemont, tel. 05.45.83.16.27,
fax 05.45.83.18.67 ☑
🍽 by appt.

JOAN BRISSON★

| | 2.3 ha | 5,700 | 🍶 | 8–11 € |

This wine-grower has a bamboo collection, exhibits old tools, and holds a public open-day during the second weekend in August. Her attractive Pineau Blanc, which is a brilliant golden-yellow colour, has a pleasant, if somewhat subtle nose. The palate is well balanced, has good aromatic length, and provides an impression of freshness.
🍷 Joan Brisson, 7, rue Saint-Hérie, 17160 Matha, tel. 05.46.58.25.07, fax 05.46.58.26.40,
e-mail joan.brisson@cognac.fr ☑
🍽 by appt.

FREDDY BRUN★

| | 1 ha | 2,000 | 🍶 | 8–11 € |

The Brun family have been wine-growers for several generations, and began producing Pineau in 1984. This is a dark rosé with brick-red glints and orange-coloured highlights. The nose is highly aromatic with notes of crystallized soft fruits. The palate is full and fresh, with a slight acidity that emphasizes the wine's successful fruitiness.
🍷 Freddy Brun, chez Baboeuf, 16300 Barret, tel. 05.45.78.00.73, fax 05.45.78.98.81 ☑
🍽 by appt.

CHAI DU ROUISSOIR★★

| | 0.5 ha | 1,500 | 🍶 | 8–11 € |

A wine-grower since 1972, Didier Chapon, joined by Hugues, works a vineyard whose Pineau and Cognac production he has marketed only since 2000. This Pineau has a sumptuous purple colour and a highly fruity nose with developing aromas of blackcurrant and raspberry, much appreciated by the Jury. The palate's excellent balance is accompanied by sensations of crystallized fruits. A remarkably well-integrated wine.
🍷 Chai du Rouissoir, Roussillon, 17500 Ozillac, tel. 05.46.48.14.76, fax 05.46.48.14.76,
e-mail chaidurouissoir@hotmail.com ☑
🍽 ev. day except Sun. 10am–8pm
🍷 Chapon

PASCAL CHAIGNIER★

| | 1.2 ha | 3,000 | | 8–11 € |

Located close to a spa, this family wine estate has marketed its production for over twenty years with a degree of success that owes nothing to chance. Their well-crafted Pineau Rosé is ruby in colour with brick-red highlights and has a very distinguished nose particularly suggestive of cherry aromas. The well-balanced palate similarly expresses notes of soft fruits, and these continue into the lightly acid finish.
🍷 Pascal Chaignier, Chez Bellot, 17500 Lussac, tel. 05.46.48.31.63, fax 05.46.48.31.63 ☑ 🏠
🍽 by appt.

DOM. DU CHENE Vieux★★

| | 1 ha | 3,000 | 🍶 | 15–23 € |

In the heart of romanesque Saintonge, the Chêne estate, which is family-owned, is entirely devoted to the production of Pineau des Charentes and Cognac. The colour of their old Pineau is a brilliant and intense dark amber with copper highlights. Similar testimony to the wine's lengthy maturation is afforded by its enduring aromas of dried fruits, fruit kernels and almonds, creating a highly individual *rancio*. The palate is round and long-lasting with notes of apricot and acacia honey. Magnificent.

🍷 Doussoux-Baillif, 20, rue des Chênes,
17800 Saint-Palais-de-Phiolin, tel. 05.46.70.92.29,
fax 05.46.70.91.70, e-mail baillif.jm@wanadoo.fr ☑
🍽 ev. day 8.30am–10am 2.30pm–7pm;
Sun. by appt.

PASCAL CLAIR★

| | 0.5 ha | 4,000 | 🍶 | 8–11 € |

This family concern is located in Petite Champagne, the great terroir for Cognac. Merlot and Cabernet Sauvignon have combined to make this Pineau Rosé. The colour is a clean ruby red with brick-red highlights, and the bouquet releases gorgeous berry-fruit aromas. The flavours are mouth-fillingly large and long-lasting, with a finish evocative of crystallized berry fruit.
🍷 EARL Pascal Clair, La Genébrière, 17520 Neuillac, tel. 05.46.70.22.01, fax 05.46.48.06.77,
e-mail pascal.clair@free.fr ☑
🍽 by appt.

FELIX-MARIE DE LA VILLIERE★★

| | n.c. | 3,500 | | 5–8 € |

The vineyard belonging to this family concern, founded in 1934, is located on limestone hillsides in Petite Champagne. It has produced this beautiful straw-yellow Pineau Blanc with slightly amber highlights. This fine Pineau is developing fairly intense aromas of cherry-stones. The wine's good length confirms its excellent balance. The **Pineau Rosé**, with its intense colour and strong bouquet of berry fruits, is awarded one star.
🍷 Distillerie Vinet, 3, imp. Félix-Chartier,
17520 Brie-sous-Archiac, tel. 05.46.70.04.66,
fax 05.46.70.25.30, e-mail distillerie@aol.com ☑
🍽 ev. day except Sat. Sun. 8am–12 noon 2pm–5pm

HENRI GEFFARD Vieux★★

| | 1 ha | n.c. | 🍶 | 11–15 € |

Located in the vicinity of the Né valley, where the film *Va Savoir* was made with Gérard Klein, this family estate has produced a old-gold Pineau with tawny highlights that is well worth discovering. The intense *rancio* blends with aromas of dried fruits and a predominance of walnuts. The palate has great length and suppleness; it stays light, with a pleasing acidity that integrates well with the delicate *rancio*.
🍷 Henri Geffard, La Chambre, 16130 Verrières, tel. 05.45.83.02.74, fax 05.45.83.01.82,
e-mail cognac.geffard@freesbee.fr ☑ 🏠
🍽 ev. day 8am–12 noon 1.30pm–6.30pm

GOUSSELAND Vieux★

| | 10 ha | 7,000 | 🍶 | 15–23 € |

The family have cultivated vines here on their estate since 1711. In the Revolution of 1789, the village's château was destroyed, and legend has it that Saint Rémy took refuge in a treasure trove – the one in its barrel store, perhaps? In any event, this old Pineau is magnificent old-gold in colour with plenty of highlights. The nose is very perfumed and redolent of walnut and figs. The palate is pleasantly round, revealing a developing *rancio*, and there is a hint of acidity in the long-lasting finish.
🍷 Alain Gousseland, Saint-Rémy, 17120 Chénac, tel. 05.46.90.64.14, fax 05.46.90.65.58,
e-mail agousseland@cer17.cernet.fr ☑
🍽 by appt.

GUILLON-PAINTURAUD★★

| | 2 ha | 16,000 | ⑪ | 8–11 € |

This family vineyard dates from 1610, and its site includes a shop that sells locally-made furniture and pottery. A third reason to visit Segonzac is this gleaming straw-yellow Pineau, which has old-gold glints and a truly fine bouquet of honey and linden blossom. The palate is very supple, with great length and an unexpected roundness; it leaves an excellent impression. A very elegant product.
↝ Guillon-Painturaud, Biard, 16130 Segonzac,
tel. 05.45.83.41.95, fax 05.45.83.34.42,
e-mail infos@guillon-painturaud.com ☑
� ev. day except Sun. 9am–12 noon 2pm–6pm

LOGIS DE MONTIFAUD★

| | 2 ha | 8,000 | ⑪ | 8–11 € |

The 18th century Logis de Montifaud nestles beside a charming stream, the Né. They have been wine-growers down the generations here, and C. and J. Landreau take great pains to produce high-quality products. This is a bright, clear, golden wine that offers an intense floral bouquet. On the palate, it creates an impression of good balance and a very agreeable freshness.
↝ Christian Landreau, Logis de Montifaud,
16130 Salles-d'Angles, tel. 05.45.83.67.45,
fax 05.45.83.63.99 ☑
☯ by appt.

MAINE LAURE★

| | 7.5 ha | 5,000 | ⑪ | 8–11 € |

The owners' ancestors were potters before they became interested in Cognac. Located on three Cognac crus, worked from father to son over several generations, the estate has marketed its Pineau since 1998 under the name Maine Laure. The appearance is clear and bright, deep pink in colour with ruby highlights, and there is a bouquet of very evident blackcurrant and raspberry aromas. The palate is round and unctuous, confirming the wine's harmonious character.
↝ SARL Maine Laure, Le Maine Laure, 16360 Le Tatre,
tel. 05.45.78.54.14, fax 05.45.78.53.66,
e-mail sca.r.sauvaitre@wanadoo.fr ☑
☯ by appt.

J.-Y. ET F. MOINE
Très vieux★★

| | n.c. | 800 | | 15–23 € |

Members of the *Bienvenue à la Ferme* network, the Moine brothers established in 1992 the *Circuit du Chêne*, which has highlighted the importance of oak barrels. Coming here, one learns about the work of the cooper. Even so, this very old Pineau is enough reason for your interest. It is a sumptuous old-gold colour with plenty of highlights and has a bouquet of intense aromas of walnut and a delightful *rancio*. The palate is well balanced, rich, and long-lasting. The *rancio* makes its presence felt amid oaky, spicy notes of great complexity. This would be an excellent accompaniment to foie gras. A **Vieux Pineau Rosé** was also greatly appreciated by the Jury.
↝ SNC Jean-Yves et François Moine, Villeneuve,
16200 Chassors, tel. 05.45.80.98.91, fax 05.45.80.96.01,
e-mail lesfreres.moine@wanadoo.fr ☑
☯ by appt.

CH. DE L'OISELLERIE
Gerfaut Ambré★

| | 5 ha | 10,000 | ⑪ | 5–8 € |

Bred and trained for hunting in the 15th century, the falcon (or gerfalcon), that symbol of power and majesty, is the emblem of the Domaine de l'Oisellerie, located at the gates of Angoulême. These days, the Domaine is an agricultural college presided over by M. Jausserand. With its golden-yellow colour and amber highlights, this very characteristic Pineau has aromas of honey and dried fruits. After first impressions of suppleness, the palate broadens out to confirm these same flavours, finishing with a warm oakiness and a well-balanced, lively sweetness.
↝ Lycée agricole l'Oisellerie, 16400 La Couronne,
tel. 05.45.67.36.89, fax 05.45.67.16.51,
e-mail exploitation.oisellerie@wanadoo.fr ☑
☯ by appt.

LE PATOISAN★

| ▪ | 2 ha | 4,500 | ⑪ | 8–11 € |

The Morandière family runs a vineyard on slopes close to the Gironde estuary. The clay-limestone soil is planted with Merlot, Cabernet Franc and Cabernet Sauvignon. Garnet in colour, with plenty of highlights, this Pineau has a delicate nose of redcurrant, blackberry and cherry. The palate is lively and fruity yet well integrated. There is a perfect balance of flavours.
↝ Vignobles Morandière, Le Breuil,
17150 Saint-Georges-des-Agouts, tel. 05.46.86.02.76,
fax 05.46.70.63.11 ☑
☯ ev. day 9am–12 noon 2pm–6.30pm

DOM. DE LA PETITE FONT VIEILLE★

| | 1.2 ha | 6,000 | ⑪ | 8–11 € |

Jarnac has many attractions, including a romanesque church, and this estate is located on a typically Charentais farm. The musts from which this Pineau is derived come from old vines (50 years old) planted on clay-limestone slopes. This particular wine has a really lovely straw-yellow colour with lots of highlights. The nose has complex and elegant aromas of dried fig and banana, and these flavours are also found on the palate in combination with apricot, all sustained by fine oak tannins. A well-balanced wine with excellent length.
↝ Eric et Carole Aiguillon, EARL Grimard, 10, rue Grimard, 17520 Jarnac-Champagne, tel. 05.46.49.55.54,
fax 05.46.49.55.54,
e-mail la.petitefontvieille@wanadoo.fr ☑
☯ by appt.

PRINCE DE DIDONNE★

| | n.c. | 20,353 | ⑪ | 5–8 € |

This cooperative vinifies the harvests from some excellent terroirs. A bright golden yellow with amber glints, this Pineau Blanc is redolent of honey and apricot with elegant hints of hazelnut. Well balanced, round and immensely supple, the palate reveals a well-blended, agreeable fruitiness.
↝ SA Unicognac, 30, av. Foch, BP 102, 17503 Jonzac Cedex, tel. 05.46.48.10.99, fax 05.46.48.47.70,
e-mail info@unicognac.com ☑
☯ by appt.

DOM. DU PUITS FAUCON★

| ▪ | 1 ha | 2,500 | ⑪ | 8–11 € |

This vineyard in the Borderies district has been cultivated by Daniel Bouillard's family since 1886. With its lively pink colour and cherry perfumes, his Pineau Rosé is very nice indeed. The palate is well structured and has a certain roundness, with elegant notes of berry fruits (Morello cherry, raspberry and cherry).
↝ Daniel Bouillard, 8, rte de Chez Gaillard, 17770 Burie,
tel. 05.46.94.92.40, fax 05.46.94.67.72,
e-mail puits.faucon@wanadoo.fr ☑
☯ by appt.

DOM. DE LA RAMBAUDERIE★★

| | 3 ha | 9,000 | ▪⑪ | 5–8 € |

The Domaine de la Rambauderie, at the heart of a vineyard of 18 ha, has been worked for several generations by the same family. The lovely, clear golden-yellow colour, with its many glints, is not the least of this Pineau's attractions. The nose has intense aromas of wild flowers, peach and apricot. The palate is perfumed and very pleasurable, offering both a remarkable balance of flavours and great length. This wine is a superb representative of the appellation.
↝ SCEA Suzette Boucher et Fils, Dom. de La Rambauderie, 78, rue des Ajoncs,
17150 Saint-Sorlin-de-Conac, tel. 05.46.86.00.72,
fax 05.46.49.06.58 ☑
☯ by appt.

REYNAC★

| | 19 ha | 264,000 | ⑪ | 5–8 € |

Established in 1967 by a cooperative of wine-growers, this label is now in the hands of H. Mounier. A lovely, bright straw-yellow colour, this Reynac has an expressive, intense nose of hazelnut and almond, with notes of citrus fruit. The palate of this pleasing, well-integrated Pineau has plenty of roundness and suppleness.

☛ H. Mounier, 49, rue Lohmeyer, BP 35, 16102 Cognac Cedex, tel. 05.45.82.45.77, fax 05.45.82.83.04, e-mail hmounier@hmounier.fr ▪
Ⓣ by appt.

ROUSSILLE★★

| | n.c. | 7,000 | Ⅲ | 8–11 € |

Linars is 6 km from Angoulême. Founded in 1928, this firm has acquired a solid reputation justified by its numerous appearances in the *Guide*. Its Pineau Blanc is a very attractive amber colour with coppery glints, and has scents of honey and linden blossom, with enduring notes of fine-quality walnuts. The same flavours are present on the palate, which is round and full-bodied, with spicy overtones. This is a well-integrated wine. The **Pineau Rosé**, with its berry-fruit aromas, also impressed the Jury.

☛ SCA Pineau Roussille, Libourdeau, 16730 Linars, tel. 05.45.91.05.18, fax 05.45.91.13.83 ▪
Ⓣ by appt.

CH. SAINT-SORLIN

Vieux★

| | 4.25 ha | n.c. | Ⅲ | 11–15 € |

In the hands of the same family for seven generations, this vineyard is cultivated in a way that respects nature; harvesting is by hand. Visitors are received by the owner, who is well versed on the terroir's advantages. Here is an old Pineau Rosé with a lovely intense colour and brick-red highlights. Fine, elegant and complex, the nose mixes aromas of walnut and cherry-stones. After a powerful attack, the palate reveals a soft, supple complexity with a long, pleasing finish. This Pineau would go well with strawberries or could be drunk on its own.

☛ Ch. Saint-Sorlin, 17150 Saint-Sorlin-de-Conac, tel. 05.46.86.01.27, fax 05.46.70.65.59, e-mail chateau-saintsorlin@eurodial-com.fr ▪
Ⓣ ev. day 8am–1pm 2pm–8pm; Sun. by appt.

ANDRE THORIN Extra★★

| | 4 ha | n.c. | Ⅲ | 11–15 € |

This family vineyard, on clay-limestone soil in Grande Champagne, has produced a very classy Pineau Blanc which is a lovely straw-yellow colour with green glints. There is an intense bouquet of dried fruit aromas and a well-developed *rancio*. The round palate has great presence and finishes on a slight vanilla oakiness that confirms the wine's balance and quality.

☛ Claude Thorin, chez Boujut, 16200 Mainxe, tel. 05.45.83.33.46, fax 05.45.83.38.93, e-mail claudethorin@cognac-thorin.com ▪ 🏠
Ⓣ by appt.

DOM. DE LA VILLE★

| | n.c. | 2,000 | ⅢⅢ | 5–8 € |

This estate, established in 1947, produces only Pineau. The grapes are grown on a clay-limestone hillside overlooking the Gironde estuary. This old-gold Vin de Liqueur has strong and complex notes of walnut, honey, wild flowers and oak. The supple, long-lasting palate leaves a most agreeable impression.

☛ Dom. de la Ville, La Ville, 17150 Saint-Thomas-de-Conac, tel. 05.46.86.03.33, fax 05.46.70.67.00, e-mail excaillet@caramail.com ▪ 🏠🏠
Ⓣ by appt.
☛ Jacques Caillet

Wines selected but not starred

FIEF DE RASSINOUX

| | 5 ha | 6,000 | | 8–11 € |

☛ SCEA des Piniers, Le Pinier, 17130 Courpignac, tel. 05.46.49.44.22, fax 05.46.49.17.73 ▪
Ⓣ ev. day 9am–7pm
☛ Chotard

ILRHEA

| | 50 ha | 200,000 | ⅢⅢ | 5–8 € |

☛ Coop. des Vignerons de l'Ile de Ré, 17580 Le Bois-Plage-en-Ré, tel. 05.46.09.23.09, fax 05.46.09.09.26 ▪
Ⓣ by appt.

DOM. DU PERAT

| | 1 ha | 15,000 | ⅢⅢ | 8–11 € |

☛ Dominique Barribaud, 30, rue de la Petite-Champagne, Le Perat, 17520 Saint-Martial-sur-Né, tel. 05.46.49.50.20, fax 05.46.04.37.14, e-mail domaineduperat@free.fr ▪
Ⓣ by appt.

Floc de Gascogne

Floc de Gascogne is produced in the same geographical area as the Appellation Bas Armagnac, Ténarèze and Haut Armagnac, as well as in all the communes within the Appellation Armagnac. This wine-growing region is part of the Pyrenean foothills and extends into three *départements*: the Gers, the Landes and Lot-et-Garonne. To give themselves extra power, the winemakers of Floc de Gascogne established a new principle. Instead of describing and defining specific growing areas, as is the case for wines, or a simple geographical area, as for brandies, they propose an annual list of growing areas for approval by the INAO.

The whites (3,185 hl) are produced from Colombard, Gros Manseng and Ugni Blanc, which together must make up at least 70% of the range of varieties planted. Since 1996, no individual variety can exceed 50%; other varieties included are Baroque, Folle Blanche, Petit Manseng, Mauzac, Sauvignon and Semillon. Rosés (4,000 hl) are produced from Cabernet Franc and Cabernet Sauvignon, as well as from Cot, Fer Servadou, Merlot and Tannat, of which the latter may not exceed 50% of the varieties planted.

The regulations laid down by the producers are highly restrictive: a maximum of 3,300 plants per hectare, trained *en guyot* or in cordons, the number of buds to the hectare to be fewer than 60,000. Artificial irrigation of the vines is strictly forbidden in any season, and the basic yield from the parcels of land must be less than or equal to 60 hl/ha.

Every year, each wine-grower must submit a declaration of intent to make the wines and send it to the INAO, so that the organization may actually inspect the conditions of production on the ground. The musts harvested may not have less than 170 g/l of must sugar. Once the grapes have been stripped from the stalks and separated from the sediment, they are placed in a receptacle where the must undergoes the beginnings of fermentation. No addition of external products is permitted. The mutage of the must takes place with *eau de vie* d'Armagnac at a minimum of 52% alcohol by volume. The result is left to rest for at least nine months. It may be brought out of the vat room only after 1 September of the year following the harvest. All the lots of wine are tasted and analyzed. Given the variations that arise in this type of product, the best of the wine emerges only after ageing in the bottle.

BORDENEUVE-ENTRAS★

	0.8 ha	10,300	🍷	8–11 €

The brand-new president of the *Comité Interprofessionel du Floc de Gascogne* confirms his credentials by offering your palate this Floc Rosé made from Merlot and Cabernet Sauvignon blended with quality Armagnac. The wine is a bright, deep black-cherry colour with an intense nose of ripe fruit (plum and prune). The powerful palate is rich with flavours of crystallized fruits and is exceedingly long-lasting. It would go well with a charlotte dessert.
🍇 GAEC Bordeneuve-Entras, 32410 Ayguetinte,
tel. 05.62.68.11.41, fax 05.62.68.15.32,
e-mail mbrmaestrojuan@wanadoo.fr ▼
🍷 ev. day 9am–12.30pm 2pm–6pm;
summer (8pm); groups by appt.
🍇 Maestrojuan

DOM. DES CASSAGNOLES★★

	5 ha	9,100	🍷 ♦	5–8 €

The Baumann family are used to awards and are known for their professionalism, modesty and commitment to quality. This Floc Rosé received a unanimous *coup de coeur*. The colour is deep and intense, the nose powerful and complex, with notes of raspberry, cherry and blackcurrant. The palate offers a basket of ripe fruits, which slowly diffuse until they reach a broad, mouth-filling, supple finish. Enjoy with a chocolate dessert. The Jury also commended the **Floc de Gascogne Blanc** for its pale colour with green highlights, its nose of hawthorn flowers and linden blossom, and the slightly Armagnac-flavoured palate.
🍇 J. et G. Baumann, Dom. des Cassagnoles, EARL de la Ténarèze, 32330 Gondrin, tel. 05.62.28.40.57,
fax 05.62.28.42.42,
e-mail j.baumann@domainedescassagnoles.com ▼
🍷 by appt.

DE CASTELFORT★

	8 ha	53,000	🍷 ♦	5–8 €

At Nogaro, apart from the famous automobile circuit, there is a cooperative founded in 1962. Technical improvements and a special Floc de Gascogne barrel store have helped create two Flocs of equal quality. The white is a limpid yellow, with surprising aromas of tobacco and roasting coffee. The palate has good sugar balance, flavours reminiscent of the bouquet, and

a note of vanilla, all making this a pleasing Floc. The **Rosé** is a deep, lively red, with a fine, delicate, subtle bouquet of crystallized fruits, a deep, intense and well-balanced palate. A lovely duo.
🍇 Cave des Producteurs réunis de Nogaro, Les Hauts de Montrouge, 32110 Nogaro, tel. 05.62.09.01.79,
fax 05.62.09.10.99 ▼
🍷 by appt.

CAVE DE CONDOM★

	20 ha	20,000	🍷 ♦	8–11 €

The cooperative at Condom, capital of the Ténarèze district, dates from 1952 and is located half-way between the fortified village of Larressingle and the château at Cassaigne (5 km). Its brilliant pale-yellow Floc, with its floral, fruity bouquet influenced by good-quality Armagnac, is a fine, intense wine. The palate is rich, aromatic and well balanced. This very successful Floc provides a sensation of freshness. The **Rosé** is a light red colour and is commended for its bouquet of ripe fruits, warm attack and spicy finish.
🍇 Les Producteurs de la Cave de Condom-en-Armagnac, 59, av. des Mousquetaires, 32100 Condom,
tel. 05.46.49.96.78, fax 05.62.68.39.62,
e-mail tdg.cave-condom@wanadoo.fr ▼

DOM. D'EYSSAC★

	1.4 ha	8,000		5–8 €

Gilles Lhoste has presided over this estate for 30 years and has given it an added extra by restoring an old windmill for conversion into a *gîte*. His white Floc de Gascogne, with its beautiful golden colour, has an intense bouquet of quince. Pleasantly sweet, it has excellent plummy length. A very traditional estate-made Floc.
🍇 Gilles Lhoste, Dom. d'Eyssac, 32290 Averon-Bergelle,
tel. 05.62.08.52.57, fax 05.62.61.84.86 ▼ 🏠
🍷 ev. day except Sun. 8am–12 noon 2pm–6pm

FERME DE GAGNET★★

	1.5 ha	4,000	🍷	8–11 €

In southwestern Lot-et-Garonne, the village of Mézin, with its 12th century church and national cork museum, has been home to three generations of the Tadieu family, also producers of Armagnac and foie gras. In charge since 1995, Madame Lorenzon, the daughter of the house, presented the Jury with a ruby-red Floc Rosé with bright highlights. The fine, subtle nose has red berry aromas and is supported by a palate whose first impressions are straightforward, round and slightly winey, with a pleasant cherry fruitiness that is powerful and long-lasting. A wine to drink in company.
🍇 Lorenzon, Dom. de Gagnet, 47170 Mézin,
tel. 05.53.65.73.76, fax 05.53.97.22.04,
e-mail fermedegagnet@wanadoo.fr ▼ 🏠
🍷 ev. day 8am–12 noon 3pm–8pm

DOM. DE LAGUILLE★

	15 ha	5,000		11–15 €

The Vignoli family, which has been producing Floc de Gascogne for just three years, has scored a try in this rugby-loving region by having two Flocs commended by the Jury. The gorgeous light-yellow Floc Blanc has an intense, classy bouquet of flowers and stone fruits (peach). The wine's attack and development are supple, with fruit flavours (pear), good length and well-blended Armagnac producing a Floc to be tasted with eyes closed for sheer pleasure. The complex, elegant Floc **Rosé** is brick-red with tawny highlights, has a fruity (strawberry, raspberry) and floral (honey) nose and a supple, round, long-lasting palate.
🍇 Dom. de Laguille, 32800 Eauze, tel. 05.62.09.77.05,
fax 05.62.09.84.77, e-mail laguille@wanadoo.fr ▼
🍷 by appt.
🍇 Guy Vignoli

DOM. DE LAUROUX★

	0.6 ha	5,300	🍷	5–8 €

On alluvial slopes in the heart of Lower Armagnac, Rémy Fraisse produces Côtes de Gascogne country wine, Armagnac and, of course, Floc de Gascogne. He often appears in the *Guide*, and this time offers a small quantity of white Floc de Gascogne, which is a pretty straw colour with silvery highlights. It has a fairly intense bouquet of flowers and fruits

(Morello cherry). The palate has matching flavours, together with good balance and harmony.

☛ Rémy Fraisse, EARL de Laroux, 32370 Manciet, tel. 05.62.08.56.76, fax 05.62.08.57.44 **V**
⊤ by appt.

CH. DE MILLET★

| | n.c. | n.c. | ■ | 8–11€ |

The Dèche family, here for five generations, has converted an outbuilding into a reception and tasting hall in line with the "Excellence Gers" charter (Quality, Welcome, Environment); they have also transformed an 18th century pigeon loft into a *gîte* (with a three star rating). They presented a white Floc de Gascogne with a bright straw-yellow colour and an attractively complex bouquet of white flowers, caramel and vanilla. After a soft beginning, the palate has flavours of apples and pears, leading to a honeyed finish. This is a very successful Floc.

☛ Francis Dèche, Ch. de Millet, 32800 Eauze, tel. 05.62.09.87.91, fax 05.62.09.78.53, e-mail chateaudemillet@wanadoo.fr **V** 🏠
⊤ ev. day 9am–12 noon 2pm–6pm

CH. DE MONLUC★★

| | 1.5 ha | 5,000 | | 8–11€ |

This château, rich in Gascony's history, first built in 950, then destroyed and reconstructed several times over, is the birthplace of Blaise de Monluc, marshal of France in the 16th century. M. Lassus is new to production of Floc de Gascogne, but has been stunningly successful with these two wines. The white, a pale straw yellow with an aromatic nose of floral notes (hyacinth, jasmine), vanilla, and fruit (apricot), is a perfect marriage of grapes and Armagnac; the palate is very pleasant because of its good sucrosity. A thoroughbred wine, this. The **Rosé** is dark red, redolent of kirsch and Morello cherry, with a palate similarly influenced by quality Armagnac (prune); it is complex, well balanced, and long-lasting.

☛ Dom. de Monluc, Ch. de Monluc, 32310 Saint-Puy, tel. 05.62.28.94.00, fax 05.62.28.55.70, e-mail monluc-sa-office@wanadoo.fr **V**
⊤ by appt.

DOM. DE MONS★

| | 2 ha | 6,000 | ■ ⚲ | 8–11€ |

Dating from the late 13th century and acquired by the Gers Chamber of Agriculture in 1963, this château is today a satellite of the Institut Technique du Vin (ITV). No wonder it was able to produce this very successful Floc Blanc. The colour is a pale yellow with bright highlights, and the nose is highly floral yet slightly musky. The palate is well balanced and intense.

☛ Dom. de Mons, Chambre d'agriculture du Gers, 32100 Caussens, tel. 05.62.68.30.30, fax 05.62.68.30.35, e-mail chateau.mons.cda.32@wanadoo.fr **V**
⊤ by appt.

DOM. DE POLIGNAC★★

| | 3 ha | 10,000 | | 8–11€ |

Situated on top of a stony clay-limestone slope with a view of the Pyrenees when the weather is fine, the Polignac estate makes quality products, not least this Floc Rosé with its intense, lively red colour and fine, complex nose of ripe red fruits with cherry overtones. The excellent balance of sugar, alcohol and fruit on the palate, plus its intensity and length, make for a well-integrated, authentic wine. Just as noteworthy is the straw-yellow **Blanc**, which has fine floral (lavender) and fruit (pear) aromas. It is a lively, airy wine and very easy to drink. Excellent with foie gras – from the Gers, needless to say!

☛ EARL Gratian, Dom. de Polignac, 32330 Gondrin, tel. 05.62.28.54.74, fax 05.62.28.54.86 **V**
⊤ ev. day 10am–1pm 3pm–8pm

LES VIGNOBLES DE LA TENAREZE★★

| | n.c. | 6,660 | ▥ | 8–11€ |

The cooperative at Vic-Fezensac has produced two excellent Flocs on clay-limestone soil. This white, a light yellow colour with green highlights, has a complex bouquet of floral (white flowers) and fruit (quince, plum) aromas, which satisfy the palate with power, good balance, fullness and well-blended fruit. A remarkable combination. Also highly successful is the

Rosé, which is a cherry-red wine with ruby highlights; both the nose and palate have power, balance, and fruitiness (blackcurrant). The presence of Armagnac lends to the finish a warm sensation that is quite special.

☛ Les Vignerons de la Ténarèze, rte de Mouchan, 32190 Vic-Fezensac, tel. 05.62.58.05.25, fax 05.62.06.34.21 **V**
⊤ by appt.

Wines selected but not starred

DOM. DE CASSAGNAOUS

| | 0.7 ha | 3,000 | ■ ▥ | 8–11€ |

☛ EARL de Cassagnaous, Au Cassagnaous, 32250 Montréal-du-Gers, tel. 05.62.29.44.81, fax 05.62.29.44.81 **V** 🏠
⊤ by appt.
☛ Isabelle Zago

CH. DE LAGRANGERIE

| | 0.2 ha | 2,600 | | 5–8€ |

☛ GAEC de Lagrangerie, 47170 Lannes, tel. 05.53.65.70.97, fax 05.53.65.88.97, e-mail lagrangerie@wanadoo.fr **V**
⊤ ev. day 9am–12 noon 2pm–7pm
☛ de Langalerie

DOM. DE LARTIGUE 2000

| | 1 ha | 3,333 | ■ | 8–11€ |

☛ Francis Lacave, Au Village, 32800 Bretagne-d'Armagnac, tel. 05.62.09.90.09, fax 05.62.09.79.60 **V**
⊤ ev. day 8am–12.30 1.30pm–7pm

DOM. DE PAGUY

| | 3 ha | 3,600 | ■ | 8–11€ |

☛ Albert Darzacq, Dom. de Paguy, 40240 Betbezer-d'Armagnac, tel. 05.58.44.81.57, fax 05.58.44.68.09, e-mail albert-darzacq@wanadoo.fr 📆 🏠
⊤ ev. day 9am–12 noon 2pm–7pm

CH. DE SALLES

| | 0.5 ha | 3,500 | ■ | 8–11€ |

☛ Benoît Hébert, Ch. de Salles, Lagarde, 32330 Salles-d'Armagnac, tel. 05.62.69.03.11, fax 05.62.69.07.18, e-mail chsalle@club-internet.fr **V** 🏠
⊤ by appt.

DOM. SAN DE GUILHEM

| | 1.74 ha | 16,000 | ■ ⚲ | 5–8€ |

☛ Alain Lalanne, Dom. San de Guilhem, 32800 Ramouzens, tel. 05.62.06.57.02, fax 05.62.06.44.99 **V**
⊤ ev. day except Sat. Sun. 8am–12 noon 2pm–7pm

Macvin du Jura

This highly distinctive wine could equally well have been called Galant, the name by which it was known in the 14th century, when Marguerite de France, duchess of Burgundy and wife of Philippe le Hardi, declared it her favourite wine.

The Macvin – historically Maquevin or Marc-vin – was probably first made in the medieval abbey of Château-Chalon. It was recognized as an AOC under the name of Macvin du Jura by decree on 14 November 1991. The Société de Viticulture began the procedures for AOC recognition in 1976. The inquiry took a long time because agreement had to be reached on a definitive approach to making the wine. Macvin began as a "cooked" wine, with herbs and spices added to it; it then became *mistelle*, a fortified wine made from musts that were concentrated by heating (cooking them), then a Vin de Liqueur muted with *eau-de-vie* from the Franche-Comté. The last method was the one ultimately agreed upon; for the AOC, this means using a Vin de Liqueur with must that has undergone a very slight initial fermentation, muted with *eau-de-vie de marc* made from wines from the AOC Franche-Comté, which have to come from the same property as the musts. The must should come from vine varieties and a production area with the right to the AOC. The *eau-de-vie* should be aged in an oak cask for a minimum of 18 months.

After this final mixing, the Macvin should rest for a year, without being filtered, in oak casks, since it cannot be sold before 1 October of the year following its harvest.

Production, which is growing, is about 2,413 hl in 2002 (from 57 ha). Macvin du Jura is enjoying an appreciable development since it is greatly enjoyed, particularly locally, as the aperitif of choice for connoisseurs of Jura wines. It completes the range of appellations in the Comté area and is perfect served with local specialities.

CLAUDE BUCHOT★

| | 0.3 ha | n.c. | | 11–15 € |

The yellow colour and orange highlights make for an old-fashioned look, and the nose evokes the sort of caramels some of us had as children. The palate is a mouth-filling mixture in which honey and caramel predominate with just the right amount of acidity to tickle the taste-buds. A very authentic Macvin representative of the Jura school.
✦ Claude Buchot, 39190 Maynal, tel. 03.84.85.94.27, fax 03.84.85.94.27
☖ by appt.

ELISABETH ET BERNARD CLERC★

| | n.c. | 1000 | | 11–15 € |

Elisabeth and Bernard Clerc have kept to their time-honoured custom by again making their Macvin with Savagnin must. What a bouquet! Beeswax, apricots, honey and crystallized fruits all emerge from its aromatic strength. The alcohol is a quiet presence on the palate, which makes this a light, subtle yet fine and elegant Macvin. The finish evokes maple syrup and is very attractive. To be recommended with an ice-cream dessert.
✦ Elisabeth et Bernard Clerc, rue de Recanoz, 39230 Mantry, tel. 03.84.85.58.37 ☑
☖ by appt.

DOM. JEAN-CLAUDE CREDOZ★

| | 0.3 ha | 1,400 | | 11–15 € |

Founded in 1855, the estate runs to 4 ha and vinification now takes place at Château-Chalon in an old wine-producing establishment. An attractive wine with an engaging brilliance, it has a bouquet in which alcohol dominates and yet blends well with the ripe grapes. The palate has good alcohol-sugar-acidity balance and dried fruit flavours that make this a classy, elegant Macvin.
✦ Dom. Jean-Claude Crédoz, chem. des Vignes, 39210 Menétru-le-Vignoble, tel. 03.84.44.64.91, fax 03.84.44.98.76, e-mail domjccredoz@aol.com ☑
☖ by appt.

RICHARD DELAY★★

| | 0.5 ha | 3,000 | | 11–15 € |

Eighteen months in a 228-litre oak cask have produced this amber colour and an intense bouquet in which honey, dried apricot, almond and toast are powerfully and spicily present. The palate is equally aromatic with hints of raisin that gather in intensity. It is evocative of a Vin de Paille. There is beautiful balance here, with power and richness, and a noteworthy finish. Don't waste any time before sampling with a chocolate dessert or a walnut ice-cream!
✦ Richard Delay, 37, rue du Château, 39570 Gevingey, tel. 03.84.47.46.78, fax 03.84.43.26.75, e-mail delay@freesurf.fr ☑
☖ by appt.

RAPHAEL FUMEY ET ADELINE CHATELAIN★

| | 0.15 ha | n.c. | | 11–15 € |

Four years' maturing in oak has yielded a Macvin fortified with pure Savagnin must. It is a lovely golden yellow with a bouquet of herbs and walnut. The palate is quite lively, owing to a measure of acidity, but this feature gives this Macvin a kind of freshness that is quite agreeable. A thoroughbred wine that could pep up the occasional winter evening spent by the fireside with chocolates or a cigar.
✦ EARL Raphaël Fumey et Adeline Chatelain, 39600 Montigny-lès-Arsures, tel. 03.84.66.27.84, fax 03.84.66.27.84 ☑
☖ by appt.

DOM. DE MONTBOURGEAU★

| | 0.5 ha | n.c. | | 11–15 € |

Three years' maturing in oak has produced a Macvin that does not deny its "alcoholic" origins: the marc spirit makes its presence felt, though with finesse. The palate is well balanced, with tones of walnut and hazelnut. Nothing will be gained by storing this wine – it is at its best now. A good aperitif.
✦ Dom. de Montbourgeau, 39570 L'Etoile, tel. 03.84.47.32.96, fax 03.84.24.41.44, e-mail domaine.montbourgeau@wanadoo.fr ☑
☖ by appt.

DOM. DESIRE PETIT★★

| | 0.48 ha | 5,600 | | 11–15 € |

This is gold to the eyes and speaks aromatic volumes of crystallized fruits, *pain d'épice* (a sweet, spiced loaf), caramel and mandarin orange. It is almost enough just to inhale it. But the taste does not disappoint, for it explodes with a power and complexity that are equalled only by its finesse. Crystallized fruits, honey, and notes of toast and roasting coffee charm their way through a long finish. This is a really authentic AOC Macvin du Jura.
✦ Dom. Désiré Petit, rue du Ploussard, 39600 Pupillin, tel. 03.84.66.01.20, fax 03.84.66.26.59, e-mail domaine-desire-petit@wanadoo.fr ☑
☖ ev. day 9am–12 noon 2pm–7pm; groups by appt.
✦ Gérard et Marcel Petit

DOM. DE LA PINTE★

| | 2 ha | 3,000 | | 11–15 € |

The must used to make this Macvin comes from organic Savagnin and Chardonnay grapes. The golden-yellow colour is

slightly amber, and the nose, though perfumed with dried fruits and honey, has yet to evolve. There is plenty of alcohol on the palate, but it does not over-dominate. Odd notes of crystallized fruits and honey emerge from this well-balanced wine.
- Dom. de la Pinte, rte de Lyon, 39600 Arbois, tel. 03.84.66.06.47, fax 03.84.66.24.58, e-mail accueil@lapinte.fr ☑
- ⊥ by appt.
- Famille Martin

LES VINS AUGUSTE PIROU★

	n.c.	22,600	⑪	8–11 €

The Macvin of famous wine-merchant Henri Maire, widely marketed under the Auguste Pirou label, is made using must from a blend of Savagnin (majority), Chardonnay, Poulsard and Trousseau variety grapes. The colour is a bright golden yellow, and although the bouquet is quite alcoholic, the spirit harmonizes well with the aromas of dried fruits and honey. Notes of walnut, hazelnut and cocoa produce a well-balanced, classy palate. Beautifully put together.
- Auguste Pirou, Caves royales, 39600 Arbois, tel. 03.84.66.42.70, fax 03.84.66.42.42, e-mail info@auguste-pirou.fr

LA CAVE DE LA REINE JEANNE★

	0.5 ha	3,000	⑪	11–15 €

This small wine-merchants belongs to Bénédicte and Stéphane Tissot, who are also wine-growers at Montigny-lès-Arsures. Made using single-variety Savagnin must, this Macvin is an appetizing golden colour. The bouquet is a charming mix of floral and fruity aromas. A fine acidity contributes the supplementary freshness required. There is good length of fruity flavour.
- Le Cellier des Tiercelines, 54, Grande-Rue, 39600 Arbois, tel. 03.84.66.08.27, fax 03.84.66.25.08 ☑
- ⊥ by appt.
- Bénédicte et Stéphane Tissot

DOM. DE SAVAGNY★

	1.2 ha	6,300	⑪	11–15 €

This wine estate, which used to belong to Claude Rousselot Pailley, has been given over to the Compagnie des Grands Vins du Jura, a Crançot wine-merchant. The very bright golden-yellow colour is a joy to the eye, and the wine's attack is fruity, mellow, and slightly acid; the alcohol is quite restrained. Roundness and sweetness dominate, giving the palate a lovely suppleness that is complex and generous in aromatic notes, with engaging exotic fruit overtones.
- Dom. de Savagny, rte de Champagnole, 39570 Crançot, tel. 03.84.87.61.30, fax 03.84.48.21.36 ☑ ⛩ ⛩
- ⊥ by appt.

JEAN-LOUIS TISSOT★★

	0.2 ha	2,000	⑪	11–15 €

There have been innumerable generations of wine-growers in the Tissot family, one of whom founded the Fruitière Vinicole d'Arbois. This Macvin has a nose of real intensity and a lovely complexity that is essentially floral but also mineral. The attack is good without too much sweetness, and there is beautiful freshness. Vanilla, dried fruits and crystallized fruits follow. The grape sugar has definitively succumbed to the marc to provide a well-blended balance. This delicate wine would go well with melon.
- Jean-Louis Tissot, Vauxelles, 39600 Montigny-lès-Arsures, tel. 03.84.66.13.08, fax 03.84.66.08.09, e-mail jeanlouis.tissot.vigneron.arbois@wanadoo.fr ☑

JEAN-YVES VAPILLON★

	0.3 ha	900	⑪	8–11 €

In 1995, Jean-Yves Vapillon settled near the prefecture of the Jura *département* after studying at Beaune and Montpellier. His Macvin has an immensely powerful bouquet of hazelnuts, dried fruits, stewed fruit, and *marc* (needless to say), with a hint of roasting coffee. The palate has corresponding flavours with a development characterized by honey. A welcome touch of acidity peps up this very full-bodied wine.

- Jean-Yves Vapillon, 120, rte de Macornay, 39000 Lons-le-Saunier, tel. 03.84.47.45.65, fax 03.84.43.21.88 ☑
- ⊥ by appt.

FRUITIERE VITICOLE DE VOITEUR
Vin galant★★

	2 ha	10,000	⑪	11–15 €

This cooperative began in 1957 below the famous Château-Chalon vineyard. It offers a beautifully golden, slightly amber Macvin whose nose is evocative of the south and summer with its fresh and fruity notes of canteloupe and water-melon. The palate is completely non-aggressive and has finesse and elegance, with flavours hinting of jam that correspond to the bouquet's aromas.
- Fruitière vinicole de Voiteur, 60, rue de Nevy-sur-Seille, 39210 Voiteur, tel. 03.84.85.21.29, fax 03.84.85.27.67, e-mail voiteur@fruitiere-vinicole-voiteur.fr ☑
- ⊥ by appt.

Wines selected but not starred

CELLIER DE BELLEVUE

	0.25 ha	1,600	⑪	11–15 €

- Daniel Crédoz, Cellier de Bellevue, rte des Granges, 39210 Menétru-le-Vignoble, tel. 03.84.85.26.98, fax 03.84.44.62.41 ☑
- ⊥ ev. day 8am–12 noon 1.30pm–7pm; Sun. 8am–12 noon; groups by appt.

CAVEAU DES BYARDS

	1 ha	8,000	⑪	11–15 €

- Caveau des Byards, 39210 Le Vernois, tel. 03.84.25.33.52, fax 03.84.25.38.02, e-mail info@caveau-des-byards.fr ☑
- ⊥ by appt.

JEAN-MARIE COURBET

	n.c.	n.c.		11–15 €

- Jean-Marie Courbet, rue du Moulin, 39210 Nevy-sur-Seille, tel. 03.84.85.28.70, fax 03.84.44.68.88
- ⊥ ev. day except Sun. 8am–12 noon 2pm–7pm

DANIEL DUGOIS 2001

	0.25 ha	2,400	⑪	11–15 €

- Daniel Dugois, 4, rue de la Mirode, 39600 Les Arsures, tel. 03.84.66.03.41, fax 03.84.37.44.59 ☑ ⛩
- ⊥ by appt.

CH. GREA

	n.c.	1,500	⑪	11–15 €

- Nicolas Caire, Ch. Gréa, 14, rue Froideville, 39190 Sainte-Agnès, tel. 06.81.83.67.80, fax 03.84.25.05.47 ☑
- ⊥ by appt.

DOM. MARTIN-FAUDOT

	0.6 ha	4,000	⑪	11–15 €

- Dom. Martin-Faudot, 1, rue Bardenet, 39600 Mesnay, tel. 03.84.66.29.97, fax 03.84.66.29.84 ☑
- ⊥ by appt.
- J.-P. Martin et M. Faudot

DOM. DE LA RENARDIERE

0.5 ha   2,300   ◗◖   11–15 €

➴ Jean-Michel Petit, rue du Chardonnay, 39600 Pupillin,
tel. 03.84.66.25.10, fax 03.84.66.25.70,
e-mail renardiere@libertysurf.fr ☑
☖ ev. day except Sun. 9am–12 noon 1.30pm–7pm

DOM. ROLET

2 ha   12,000   ◗◖   11–15 €

➴ Dom. Rolet Père et Fils, Montesserin, rte de Dole,
39600 Arbois, tel. 03.84.66.00.05, fax 03.84.37.47.41,
e-mail rolet@wanadoo.fr

ANDRE ET MIREILLE TISSOT

1 ha   5,000   ◗◖   11–15 €

➴ André et Mireille Tissot, 39600 Montigny-lès-Arsures,
tel. 03.84.66.08.27, fax 03.84.66.25.08 ☑
☖ by appt.
➴ Stéphane Tissot

JEAN TRESY ET FILS

0.45 ha   3,000   ◗◖   11–15 €

➴ Jean Trésy et Fils, rte des Longevernes, 39230 Passenans,
tel. 03.84.85.22.40, fax 03.84.44.99.73,
e-mail tresy.vin@wanadoo.fr ☑
☖ by appt.

VINS DE PAYS

Although the term "*vin de pays*" has been widely applied since 1930, it is only comparatively recently that it has been used as a formal designation to denote "a table wine representative of the geographical sector, *département* or region from which it originates". A directive issued on 1 September 2000 repealed an earlier directive of 4 September 1979 (as amended) and made specific provision for *vin de pays* production guidelines, recommended preferred grape varieties and maximum yields. The 2000 directive also established specific parameters for analytical standards such as alcohol content, admissible degree of acidity and the presence of permitted additives in a bid to regulate *vins de pays* in the best interests of the consumer public and to ensure that these wines attain a quality level that ranks them among the best table wines produced in France.

Like any appellation wine, a *vin de pays* is subject to strict monitoring and compliance procedures complemented by adjudication by a tasting panel. Unlike an AOC wine, a *vin de pays* is not subject to INAO regulation but, instead, to supervision by the ONIVINS (Office National Interprofessional des Vins), a body comprised of accredited wine professionals and trade associations charged with maintaining the regional character of each *vin de pays*. ONIVINS also supervises domestic and foreign marketing of *vins de pays*. Its efforts to date have resulted in *vins de pays* emerging as a relatively important component of France's wine exports.

There are three *vin de pays* categories, each reflecting the geographical area in which the wine is produced and its specific denomination. The first category comprises those *vins de pays* named after their *département* of origin, albeit to the exclusion of *departements* which are themselves the name of an AOC (i.e., Jura, Savoie and Corsica). The second category comprises wines named after a designated zone. And the third category contains those *vins de pays* which are designated "regional", which is to say, produced in one of five large zones, each of which in turn is made up of several *départements*. These "regional" *vins de pays* may be blended in order to guarantee wines of a consistent quality and style. For the record, the individual regions are as follows: Jardin de la France (Val de Loire); Comté Tolosan; Pays d'Oc; Comtés Rhodaniens; and Portes de Méditerranée. Each *vin de pays* category is subject to the provisions of the 1 September 2000 directive; over and above this, each zone and region imposes its own, typically more stringent regulations.

The bulk of the current 11 million hectolitre annual production of *vins de pays* is produced by cooperatives. Between 1980 and 2000, designated *vin de pays* production virtually trebled, rising from 4 to 11 million hectolitres annually. Of the latter amount, some 200,000 to 250,000 hl annually are classed as "vins primeurs" or "vins nouveaux". Varietal wines represent a substantial percentage of *vin de pays* production: most (85%) are from the vineyards of the Midi. These are simple and unpretentious *ordinaires* for everyday drinking and, as such, provide an insight into winemaking typology and consumption in the various regions of the country. In the following, *vin de pays* production zones are listed by reference to regions as defined in the new legislation. It should be noted that those regions do not correspond to AOC and AOVDQS wine regions, and that a directive of 4 May 1995 specified the exclusion of certain zones from *vin de pays* production, namely the *départements* of the Rhône, Bas-Rhin, Haut-Rhin, Gironde, Côte d'Or and Marne.

Calvados   The Loire Valley

Wines selected but not starred

ARPENTS DU SOLEIL
Pinot 2002

	0.15 ha	1,400		5–8 €

☛ Gérard Samson, 3, rue d'Harmonville,
14170 Saint-Pierre-sur-Dives, tel. 02.31.20.80.41,
fax 02.31.20.29.70 ☑

The wines of the Jardin de la France, a regional classification, currently make up 95% of *vin de pays* production in the Loire Valley, a vast territory comprising no fewer than thirteen *départements*: Maine-et-Loire, Indre-et-Loire, Loiret, Loire-Atlantique, Loir-et-Cher, Indre, Allier, Deux-Sèvres, Sarthe, Vendée, Vienne, Cher and Nièvre. Additionally, the classification includes *vins de pays* from *départements* and other localities such as the *vins de pays* of Retz (south of the Loire Estuary), the Marches de Bretagne (southeast of Nantes) and the Coteaux Charitois (around Charité-sur-Loire).

Total production in the region is currently running at some 617,000 hl, for the greatest part comprising traditional Loire grape varieties. Whites represent around 45% and are typically dry, fresh and fruity, made from Chardonnay, Sauvignon Blanc and Grolleau Gris grapes. Reds and rosés are made from Gamay, Cabernet and Grolleau Noir grape varieties.

Generally speaking, these *vins de pays* should be drunk young, although the occasional Cabernet vintage may benefit from cellaring.

Cher

Wines selected but not starred

VENESMES
Sauvignon 2002

	2.2 ha	6,000	■ ᵠ	3–5 €

➤ SCEV de Venesmes, 18190 Venesmes, tel. 06.08.23.59.04, fax 02.48.60.68.01 ☑
⌷ by appt.

Coteaux Charitois

DOM. DU PUITS DE COMPOSTELLE
Pinot noir Elevé en fût de chêne 2002★

	1 ha	3,000	■ ⅰⅱ ᵠ	5–8 €

This estate opened for business in 1999 on the initiative of a number of oenologist friends who acquired a small vineyard on the pilgrim's route to Santiago de Compostela. The still-young Pinot Noir grape variety yields a typical black-berry nose and taste accompanied by distinct tannins which will develop over time to produce a balanced wine.
➤ Dom. du Puits de Compostelle, 11, bis Cours du Château, 58400 La Charité-sur-Loire, tel. 03.86.70.03.29, fax 03.86.70.06.74, e-mail puitsdecompostelle@st.fr ☑
⌷ by appt.

DOM.DE LA VERNIERE
Pinot Noir 2002★

	1.4 ha	8,500	■ ⅰⅱ ᵠ	5–8 €

Denis Beaulieu cultivates this 6-ha vineyard surrounding an 18th and 19th century château. The Pinot Noir grape variety used has resulted in a manifestly young wine whose aromas have yet to emerge fully but which augur well. This is a struc-tured wine that should reveal its full potential a few years from now. The harmonious **Chardonnay 2002** was also noted.
➤ Dom. de la Vernière, La Vernière, 58350 Chasnay, tel. 03.86.70.06.74, fax 03.86.70.06.74 ☑
⌷ by appt.
➤ Simon Beaulieu

Jardin de la France

ADEA CONSULES
Ligéria 2000★★

	0.8 ha	3,000	ⅰⅱ	30–38 €

Cabernet Franc, Cabernet Sauvignon, Merlot and Cot varieties are blended and stored in-cask for 19 months to yield this dark and intense wine with an expressive nose of wood notes and pleasant spices. The wine is rich on the palate, with still a merest hint of cask which will soon give way to other aromas.
➤ Adéa Consulès, 3, rue Saint-Martin, 49540 Martigné-Briand, tel. 02.41.59.19.51, fax 02.41.59.16.86, e-mail bpaumard@ansf.net ☑
⌷ by appt.
➤ B. Paumard

DOM. DES CHEVRIERES
Gamay 2002★★

	5 ha	18,000	■ ᵠ	3–5 €

Martine and Christophe Réthoré have produced a richly-coloured wine with luminous highlights which develops pronounced aromas of ripe fruit. On the palate, the wine is rich and well-balanced and capable of ageing well. This estate also received a mention for its **Cabernet 2002** and its **Pinot Noir 2002**.
➤ Vignoble Réthoré, Les Vignes, 49110 Saint-Rémy-en-Mauges, tel. 02.41.30.12.58, fax 02.41.46.35.44 ☑
⌷ by appt.

DOM. DE LA COCHE
Cabernet 2002★

	2 ha	6,000	■ ᵠ	3–5 €

Two young winemakers joined forces some 12 years ago to set up this 21-ha estate planted with eight different grape varieties. Their purple Cabernet 2002 has aromas of black-currant and is well-structured. It achieves a mix of freshness, roundness and balanced structure and would go well with roast beef.
➤ Emmanuel Guitteny, Dom. de la Coche, 44680 Sainte-Pazanne, tel. 02.40.02.44.43, fax 02.40.02.43.55, e-mail eguitteny@aol.com ☑
⌷ by appt.

COMTE DE LAUDONNIERE
Chardonnay 2002★

	20 ha	70,000	■ ᵠ	–3 €

Wine-merchants Vinival offer this pale yellow Chardonnay 2002 with its wide range of aromas. Fresh and balanced on the palate and pleasantly flavourful.
➤ SARL Vinival, La Sablette, 44330 Mouzillon, tel. 02.40.36.66.00, fax 02.40.33.95.81 ☑

DOM. BRUNO CORMERAIS
Elevé en fût de chêne 2001★★

	0.8 ha	3,000	ⅰⅱ	5–8 €

A wine assembled from Cabernet Franc, Sauvignon and Abouriou grape varieties and developed in-cask over nine months. The last-named grape variety, from the southwest, is reputed to yield well-balanced wines; this 2001 is a fine example, not least by virtue of its deep-red colour and spicy aromas. The attack is smooth and accompanied by toasted notes, leading to a harmonious and balanced finish.
➤ EARL Bruno et Marie-Françoise Cormerais, La Chambaudière, 44190 Saint-Lumine-de-Clisson, tel. 02.40.03.85.84, fax 02.40.06.68.74 ☑
⌷ by appt.

DOM. DE LA COUCHETIERE
Grolleau 2002★

	1.5 ha	18,000	■ ⅰⅱ ᵠ	–3 €

The De la Couchetière estate at Notre-Dame-d'Allençon boasts a range of agricultural produce, but viticulture started to predominate as of the 1980s. An attractive cellar reveals a seductive Grolleau with intense aromas of red fruit, notably cherries. Fresh and slightly tart, this 2002 boasts ample tannins and could benefit from cellaring for a further year before being served as an accompaniment to red meat.
➤ GAEC Brault, Dom. de la Couchetière, 49380 Notre-Dame-d'Allençon, tel. 02.41.54.30.26, fax 02.41.54.40.98 ☑
⌷ ev. day except Sun. 8.30am–12.30pm 2pm–7pm

Vins de Pays

1 Vin de pays des Coteaux de Coiffy
2 Vin de pays de Franche-Comté
3 Vin de pays des Coteaux de l'Auxois
4 Vin de pays de Sainte-Marie-la-Blanche
5 Vin de pays des Coteaux du Cher et de l'Arnon
6 Vin de pays des Coteaux charitois
7 Vin de pays des Coteaux de Tannay
8 Vin de pays du Bourbonnais
9 Vin de pays d'Allobrogie
10 Vin de pays d'Urfé
11 Vin de pays des Balmes dauphinoises
12 Vin de pays des Coteaux du Grésivaudan
13 Vin de pays des Coteaux de l'Ardèche
14 Vin de pays des Collines rhodaniennes
15 Vin de pays des Coteaux des Baronnies
16 Vin de pays du Comté de Grignan
17 Vin de pays des Coteaux du Verdon
18 Vin de pays de Mont-Caume
19 Vin de pays des Maures
20 Vin de pays d'Argens
21 Vin de pays de la Petite Crau
22 Vin de pays d'Aigues

23 Vin de pays de la Principauté d'Orange
24 Vin de pays des Sables du Golfe du Lion
25 Vin de pays du Duché d'Uzès
26 Vin de pays des Cévennes
27 Vin de pays de la Vistrenque
28 Vin de pays des Côtes du Vidourle
29 Vin de pays de la Vaunage
30 Vin de pays de Cèze
31 Vin de pays des Coteaux du Pont du Gard
32 Vin de pays des Coteaux flaviens
33 Vin de pays du Val de Montferrand
34 Vin de pays du Mont Baudile
35 Vin de pays des Côtes du Ceressou
36 Vin de pays des Monts de la Grage
37 Vin de pays des Coteaux d'Enserune
38 Vin de pays des Coteaux du Libron
39 Vin de pays des Coteaux de Murviel
40 Vin de pays des Coteaux de Laurens
41 Vin de pays des Côtes de Thongue
42 Vin de pays de la Bénovie
43 Vin de pays de Cassan
44 Vin de pays de la Haute Vallée de l'Orb
45 Vin de pays de Saint-Guilhem-le-Désert
46 Vin de pays des Coteaux de Bessilles
47 Vin de pays de l'Ardailhou
48 Vin de pays des Côtes du Brian
49 Vin de pays de Cessenon
50 Vin de pays des Coteaux du Salagou
51 Vin de pays de la Vicomté d'Aumelas
52 Vin de pays des Collines de la Moure
53 Vin de pays de Caux
54 Vin de pays des Coteaux de Fontcaude
55 Vin de pays de Bessan
56 Vin de pays du Bérange
57 Vin de pays des Côtes de Thau
58 Vin de pays des Coteaux de Peyriac
59 Vin de pays de la Haute Vallée de l'Aude
60 Vin de pays des Coteaux de Narbonne
61 Vin de pays des Côtes de Prouilhe
62 Vin de pays de la Cité de Carcassonne
63 Vin de pays de Cucugnan
64 Vin de pays du Val de Dagne
65 Vin de pays des Coteaux du Littoral audois
66 Vin de pays des Côtes de Pérignan
67 Vin de pays des Coteaux de la Cabrerisse
68 Vin de pays des Hauts de Badens
69 Vin de pays du Torgan
70 Vin de pays des Côtes de Lastours
71 Vin de pays du Val de Cesse
72 Vin de pays de la Vallée du Paradis
73 Vin de pays des Coteaux de Miramont
74 Vin de pays d'Hauterive
75 Vin de pays cathare
76 Vin de pays des Côtes catalanes
77 Vin de pays de la Côte Vermeille
78 Vin de pays charentais

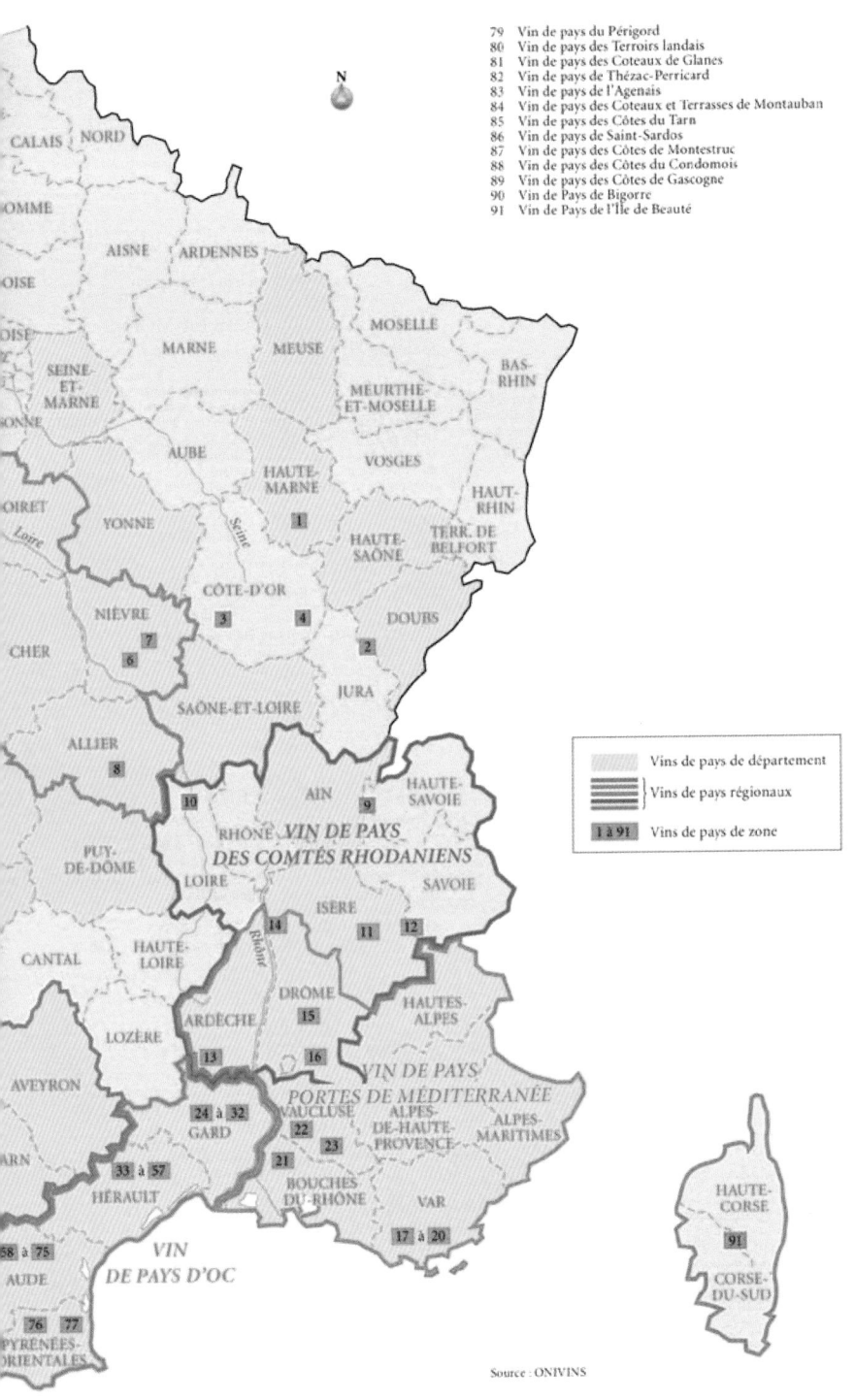

79 Vin de pays du Périgord
80 Vin de pays des Terroirs landais
81 Vin de pays des Coteaux de Glanes
82 Vin de pays de Thézac-Perricard
83 Vin de pays de l'Agenais
84 Vin de pays des Coteaux et Terrasses de Montauban
85 Vin de pays des Côtes du Tarn
86 Vin de pays de Saint-Sardos
87 Vin de pays des Côtes de Montestruc
88 Vin de pays des Côtes du Condomois
89 Vin de pays des Côtes de Gascogne
90 Vin de Pays de Bigorre
91 Vin de Pays de l'Île de Beauté

Vins de pays de département

} Vins de pays régionaux

1 à 91 Vins de pays de zone

Source : ONIVINS

VINS DE PAYS

VDP

DOM. DE LA COUPERIE Cuvée Clyan
Cabernet Elevé en fût de chêne 2001★★

■	2 ha	6,000	🍾	3–5 €

The care that has gone into the production of this 2001 is evident from the very first sip. Impeccable cask maturation has spawned a subtle mix of vanilla, cinnamon and even cocoa aromas. The wine is harmonious on the palate, with silky tannins.
➦ EARL Claude Cogné, La Couperie,
49270 Saint-Christophe-la-Couperie, tel. 02.40.83.73.16,
fax 02.40.83.76.71 ☑
🍷 by appt.

LA COUR DE BLOIS
Cabernet Vieilli en fût de chêne 2001★

■	1 ha	5,300	🍾	5–8 €

This estate was totally revamped in 1985 with the planting of noble grape varieties, and Christine and Thierry Brangeon go to great lengths to produce premium-quality wine. The dark-red robe of this Cabernet 2001 presages a wine that has a fruity nose and works well on the palate. Wood aromas are still evident, but the wine is equal to being laid down over several years. The aromatic **Gamay rosé (3–5 €)** also held the Jury's interest.
➦ Christelle et Thierry Brangeon, La Cour de Blois,
49270 Saint-Christophe-la-Couperie, tel. 02.40.83.77.04,
fax 02.40.83.77.05 ☑
🍷 ev. day except Sun. 3pm–7pm

DOM. DE L'ERRIERE
Cabernet 2002★

■	2,26 ha	10,000	🍾 ♦	3 €

This 32-ha estate is located in the commune of Landreau in the Loire Atlantique. Two Cabernets contribute to a wine that deserves to be cellared for a period of years: an intensely flowery nose, sustained balance and pronounced aromas of red fruit combine to make this a most successful vintage.
➦ GAEC Madeleineau Père et Fils, Dom. de L'Errière,
44430 Le Landreau, tel. 02.40.06.43.94,
fax 02.40.06.48.82 ☑
🍷 by appt.

DOM. DE FLINES
Grolleau 2002★

■	1,88 ha	20,000	🍾 ♦	3–5 €

The Chantal Motheron family came originally from Touraine and has been involved in winemaking since the 18th century. As of the end of the 1960s, it has now extended its operations in the Anjou region. Forty-year-old Grolleau vines underpin this attractive and sprightly wine with its complex nose and intense aromas of spicy red fruit. Full and well-balanced, this should prove an ideal accompaniment to grilled meat.
➦ C. Motheron, Dom. de Flines, 102, rue d'Anjou,
49540 Martigné-Briand, tel. 02.41.59.42.78,
fax 02.41.59.45.60 ☑
🍷 by appt.

DOM. DU FOUR A CHAUX
L'Anthocyane 2000★

■	5 ha	13,000	🍾	3–5 €

Visitors to the estate can admire the newly-renovated eponymous whitewashed oven; they will also admire this Anthocyane 2000 comprising 60% of Cabernet Sauvignon and 40% of Cot grape varieties, with its intensely-red robe with mauve highlights and its notes of peony. Fruit flavours flood the palate, together with softened tannins. This is a balanced wine which can be drunk now or laid down for one to two years.
➦ EARL Dominique Norguet, Berger,
41100 Thoré-la-Rochette, tel. 02.54.77.12.52,
fax 02.54.80.23.22 ☑
🍷 ev. day except Sun. 8am–12pm 2pm–7.30pm

DOM. LA FRAIRIE DE LA MOINE
Gamay 2002★

■	1 ha	2,300	🍾 ♦	3 €

This 18.5-ha vineyard extends along the banks of the Moine only a few kilometres from the medieval city of Clisson. The Gamay grape variety yields a pale rosé 2002 which develops notes of fruit, notably raspberry and cherry. The clean attack builds towards a wine that is balanced and pleasant.
➦ Hubert Chapeleau, La Garnière,
49230 Saint-Crespin-sur-Moine, tel. 02.41.70.41.55,
fax 02.41.70.49.44 ☑
🍷 ev. day except Sun. 9am–12 noon 2pm–7pm

DOM. DES GILLIERES
Pays de Retz Grolleau 2002★

■	9,02 ha	100,000	🍾	3 €

This Pays de Retz Grolleau 2002 is macerated briefly on the skin; it comes into its own in the glass, where it gives off delicate notes of very ripe red fruit (cherry, gooseberry) that are echoed on a smooth and delicate palate, where hints of peach and apricot intrude. Best served with cold cuts.
➦ Dominique Régnier, SAS des Gillières, 44690 La Haye-Fouassière, tel. 02.40.54.80.05, fax 02.40.54.89.56 ☑
🍷 by appt.

DOM. DU GRAND FIEF
Cuvée Prestige Chardonnay 2002★★

■	3,2 ha	15,000	🍾 🍾 ♦	5–8 €

This straw-yellow Chardonnay 2002 exudes fruit aromas underpinned by floral notes. A voluminous and elegantly-fresh wine with flavours of mango and peach: quite simply, an aperitif for all seasons.
➦ EARL Dominique Guérin, Les Corbeillères,
44330 Vallet, tel. 02.40.36.27.37, fax 02.40.36.27.16 ☑
🍷 ev. day except Sun. 8am–8pm

DOM. DU GRAND LOGIS
Sauvignon 2002★

■	2 ha	4,000	🍾 ♦	3 €

In the 17th century, a seigneurial domaine stood on the site of this 35-ha estate. The Sauvignon grape variety yields this archtypical 2002 with notes of boxwood and supple and lingering flavours on the palate that make it an obvious and ideal companion to seafood.
➦ EARL Lebrin, L'Aujardière, 44430 La Remaudière,
tel. 02.40.33.72.72, fax 02.40.33.74.18,
e-mail earl.lebrin@wanadoo.fr ☑
🍷 by appt.

DOM. LES HAUTES NOELLES
Grolleau 2002★

■	1,5 ha	10,000	🍾	3–5 €

This expressive Grolleau 2002 comes from a small vineyard some ten kilometres from the Lac de Grand-Lieu. Its lively red robe with violet highlights opens on a nose of aromas of very ripe red berries (cherry) and a slightly amylic note. The fruitiness persists on the palate, where blackcurrant flavours

predominate against a backdrop of soft tannins. A fresh and fruity wine which deserves to be drunk as of now.
☛ Serge Batard, La Haute Galerie,
44710 Saint-Léger-les-Vignes, tel. 02.40.31.53.49,
fax 02.40.04.87.80, e-mail sb.lhn@free.fr ☑
⊥ by appt.

DOM. DE LA HOUSSAIS

Marches de Bretagne Cabernet 2001★

■	1.5 ha	9,000	■ ⑪ ♦	3–5 €

Characteristic pepper notes blend with spice and smoked aromas in this 2001 Marches de Bretagne Cabernet. Good tannins and overall balance suggest this typical wine may need two more years to express its full potential.
☛ Bernard Gratas, Dom. de La Houssais, 44430 Le Landreau, tel. 02.40.06.46.27, fax 02.40.06.47.25 ☑
⊥ by appt.

DOM. DE L'IMBARDIERE

Cabernet 2002★

■	3.2 ha	10,000	–3 €

A deep-red wine with violet highlights typical of the Cabernet grape variety. The nose gives off ripe fruit and the whole opens rich and harmonious on the palate.
☛ Joseph Abline, L'Imbardière,
49270 Saint-Christophe-la-Couperie, tel. 02.40.83.90.62, fax 02.40.83.74.02, e-mail abline49vins@aol.com ☑
⊥ by appt.

MANOIR DE L'HOMMELAIS

Gamay 2002★★

■	1.5 ha	16,000	■ ♦	3–5 €

A weekend in the Nantes region is incomplete without a visit to Dominique Brossard's remarkable manor house, where he will tempt you with this Gamay rosé 2002 that exudes remarkable aromas of melon, pear and boiled sweets. The wine is fresh and delicate on the palate, with overtones of mixed and citrus fruits. A wine to be savoured in the company of close friends. His blackcurrant-perfumed **2002 red Cabernet** is a full and powerful wine which deserves to be laid down.
☛ Dominique Brossard, Manoir de l'Hommelais,
44310 Saint-Philbert-de-Grand-Lieu, tel. 02.40.78.96.75, fax 02.40.78.76.91 ☑
⊥ by appt.

DOM. DU MOULIN

Chardonnay 2002★

■	2.6 ha	2,000	–3 €

This 21 ha family-run estate near the Lac de Grand-Lieu boasts the remains of an 18th century mill that features on the label of this typically clear yellow Chardonnay with its persistant fruit aromas developing into a slightly tart yet charming finish.
☛ Michel Figureau, Dom. du Moulin, 5, rue du Plessis, 44860 Pont-Saint-Martin, tel. 02.40.32.70.56, fax 02.40.02.12.26, e-mail figureau-michel@wanadoo.fr ☑
⊥ by appt.

LE MOULIN DE LA TOUCHE

Pays de Retz Grolleau 2002★

■	2 ha	8,000	■ ♦	–3 €

Centres of local interest fringe this estate – the Museum of Retz two kilometres away, a vantage point from which to look over the salt marshes and the sea, an 18th century windmill perched on a hillside, and – not least – this attractively rounded rosé Grolleau 2002, all fruit and citrus flavours. Drunk with cold cuts or grilled meat, it will bring back pleasant memories of summer vacation days.
☛ Joël Hérissé, Le Moulin de la Touche,
44580 Bourgneuf-en-Retz, tel. 02.40.21.47.89, fax 02.40.21.47.89 ☑
⊥ by appt.

PANNIER

Chardonnay 2002★

■	71.46 ha	857,600	–3 €

This Chardonnay 2002 is distinguished by its golden robe and its flavours of almond and dried fruit and nuts. A fleshy and well-balanced palate makes it a most attractive table companion. A star also goes to the estate's **Chenin 2002**, with its green highlights, nuanced aromas of white flowers and full-bodied long finish.
☛ Rémy Pannier, rue Léopold-Palustre,
49426 Saint-Hilaire-saint-Florent, tel. 02.41.53.03.10, fax 02.41.53.03.19, e-mail contact@remy-pannier.com
⊥ ev. day 9am–12 noon 2pm–6pm

DOM. DU PARC

Pays de Retz Grolleau 2002★★

■	5 ha	40,000	■	5–8 €

An attractive pink tinges the light and lustrous robe of this Grolleau 2002 with its citrus fruit (lemon) aromas which mingle on the palate in a mix that is both fresh and fully-rounded. Can be drunk as of now with fish or grilled meat. The estate's **Vin de Pays du Jardin de la France Chardonnay 2002** was also noted.
☛ EARL Pierre Dahéron, Dom. du Parc,
44650 Corcoué-sur-Logne, tel. 02.40.05.86.11, fax 02.40.05.94.98 ☑
⊥ by appt.

LA PERRIERE

Chardonnay 2002★

■	3 ha	15,000	■ ♦	3–5 €

The La Perrière estate is situated in Pallet, a commune that also has a reputation for quality muscadets. The Chardonnay 2002 is golden in colour and exudes very delicate aromas. Fleshy, fruity and fresh, it can be confidently predicted to age into an elegant wine.
☛ Vincent Loiret, Ch. La Perrière, 44330 Le Pallet, tel. 02.40.80.43.24, fax 02.40.80.46.99,
e-mail viloiret@wanadoo.fr ☑
⊥ ev. day except Sun. 8am–12 noon 2pm–6pm; cl. 10–20 Aug.

DOM. PETIT CHATEAU

Chardonnay 2002★★

■	7 ha	80,000	■ ♦	5–8 €

A pre-Revolution château at La Ragotière lends its name to this 67-ha vineyard with its bourgeois manor. The tasting panel found this light Chardonnay 2002 typically supple and rounded, with a pleasantly fresh finish. The Couillaud brothers also showed two further chardonnays which were noted by the Jury, a **Domaine Couillaud 2002** and their **Domaine la Morinière 2002**.
☛ Couillaud Frères, Ch. Ragotière, La Regrippière,
44330 Vallet, tel. 02.40.33.60.56, fax 02.40.33.61.89,
e-mail frères.couillaud@wanadoo.fr ☑
⊥ ev. day except Sat. Sun. 8am–12 noon 2pm–6pm

DOM. DE PIERRE BLANCHE

Sauvignon 2002★

■	1.4 ha	6,000	■	5–8 €

This pale yellow Sauvignon 2002 with green highlights comes from a 40-ha vineyard. It has a delicate and elegant nose which translates on the palate to an attack that is lively and persistent. A fine example of this vintage.

☛ EARL Vignoble Lecointre, Ch. La Tomaze, 6, rue du Pineau, 49380 Champ-sur-Layon, tel. 02.41.78.86.34, fax 02.41.78.61.60 ☑ ☗
⟟ by appt.

DOM. DES PRIES

Pays de Retz Grolleau 2002★

	2.5 ha	8,000	▮ ↓	3–5 €

Exposure to the spray coming off the Atlantic Ocean and the presence of a sand and gravel soil contribute to the pleasant character of this Grolleau 2002. This is a fruity wine (raspberry, gooseberry and strawberry) which has a lively and slightly tart taste. The **Chardonnay 2002 du Pays de Retz (5–8 €)** was also noted.

☛ Gérard Padiou, Les Priés, 44580 Bourgneuf-en-Retz, tel. 02.40.21.45.16, fax 02.40.21.47.48 ☑
⟟ by appt.

DOM. DES QUATRE ROUTES

Gamay 2002★

	0.69 ha	8,000	▮ ↓	3–5 €

A relatively sustained salmon-pink robe is a feature of this Gamay 2002, as is its delicate perfume of spring flowers and citrus fruits underpinned by mineral notes. The wine continues fruity on the palate (strawberries) and has an appealing freshness. A wine to quench one's thirst and to accompany smoked salmon, salads and cold cuts.

☛ Dom. Henri Poiron et Fils, Les Quatre Routes, 44690 Maisdon-sur-Sèvre, tel. 02.40.54.60.58, fax 02.40.54.62.05, e-mail poiron.henri@wanadoo.fr ☑
⟟ by appt.

MICHEL ROBINEAU

Sauvignon 2002★★

	0.32 ha	1,600	▮	3–5 €

Citrus fruits and touches of blackcurrant announce a Sauvignon 2002 that opens cleanly and continues to taste fresh and fruity on the palate. The domaine's **2002 red Grolleau (–3 €)** also attracted the Jury's attention.

☛ Michel Robineau, 3, chem. du Moulin, Les Grandes Tailles, 49750 Saint-Lambert-du-Lattay, tel. 02.41.78.34.67 ☑
⟟ by appt.

DOM. DE ROCHANVIGNE

Sauvignon 2002★

	1.28 ha	10,000	▮ ↓	5–8 €

In days gone by it was quite common in the area between the Loire-Atlantique and the Vendée to come upon small farm vineyards where wine was produced exclusively for family consumption. The tradition has been maintained in this instance with the development of an honest and fruity Sauvignon 2002, redolent of peaches and ripe pears, that would go well with a fillet of pikeperch in a white butter sauce.

☛ Yann Corcessin, Le Plessis, 44116 Vieillevigne, tel. 02.51.43.92.95, fax 02.51.43.92.95 ☑
⟟ by appt.

DOM. DE LA ROCHERIE

Cabernet Vieilli en fût de chêne 2001★

	2 ha	10,000	▥	–3 €

This very typical Cabernet offers excellent value for money. The merest hint of wood precedes aromas of red berries against a background of relatively supple tannins. Good with red meat and cheese.

☛ Daniel Gratas, La Rocherie, 44430 Le Landreau, tel. 02.40.06.41.55, fax 02.40.06.48.92 ☑
⟟ ev. day except Sun. 8am–8pm

CAVE DE LA ROUILLERE

Chardonnay 2002★

	16 ha	150,000	▮ ↓	–3 €

A typical Chardonnay: pale-yellow robe with green highlights and a powerful nose with exotic nuances. This is a wine that is

---

not only supple but also fresh and sufficiently aromatic as to provide an excellent companion to grilled fish or fish served with a sauce. The **Chardonnay Cuvée Gaston Rolandeau 2002** is also recommended.

☛ Les Vendangeoirs du Val de Loire, La Frémonderie, 49230 Tillières, tel. 02.41.70.45.93, fax 02.41.70.43.74, e-mail vvl@rolandeau.fr

DOM. DE LA VIAUDIERE

Sauvignon 2002★

	1.5 ha	8,000	▮ ↓	3–5 €

A family-run vineyard which has been handed down from father to son over four centuries. The label on this pale-yellow Sauvignon 2002 shows a statue at the Domaine de la Viaudière replicating that on the *fronton* wall of Angers cathedral dating from the 16th century. The wine itself has a distinct hint of blackcurrant; it develops well on the palate into a most agreeable finish worthy of a first-rate representative of this vintage.

☛ Giovannoni, EARL Vignoble Gélineau, la Viaudière, 49380 Champ-sur-Layon, tel. 02.41.78.60.27, fax 02.41.78.60.45, e-mail gelineau@wanadoo.fr ☑
⟟ ev. day except Sun. 9am–12.30pm 2pm–6pm

Wines selected but not starred

DESTINEA

Sauvignon 2002

	n.c.	110,000	▮ ↓	5–8 €

☛ SA Joseph Mellot, rte de Ménétréol, BP 13, 18300 Sancerre, tel. 02.48.78.54.54, fax 02.48.78.54.55, e-mail alexandremellot@josephmellot.com ☑
⟟ ev. day 8am–12 noon 1.30pm–5pm; Sat. Sun. by appt.

DOM. DE LA HALLOPIERE

Chardonnay 2002

	20 ha	100,000	▮ ↓	3–5 €

☛ Vignerons des Terroirs de la Noëlle, Bd des Alliers, BP 155, 44154 Ancenis Cedex, tel. 02.40.98.92.72, fax 02.40.98.96.70, e-mail vignerons-noelle@cana.fr ☑
⟟ by appt.

Aquitaine et Charentes

The Aquitaine and Charentes region virtually encircles the city of Bordeaux and comprises the *départements* of Charente and Charente-Maritime, Gironde, Landes, Dordogne and Lot-et-Garonne. The majority of the wines are supple, aromatic reds produced in the Aquitaine using Bordeaux grape varieties complemented by a few somewhat rustic local grapes such as Tannat, Abouriou, Bouchalès and Fer. Charente, Charente-Maritime and Dordogne produce in the main white *vins de pays* which may be fine and light (Ugni Blanc, Colombard), rounded (Sémillon blends) or robust (Baroque). Charentais, Agenais, Terroirs Landais and Thézac-Perricard are sub-regional designations, whereas Dordogne, Gironde and Landes are *département*-based denominations.

Agenais

DOM. DE BORDES

Moelleux 2002★

	1 ha	6,600	▮ ⚬	5–8€

Christian Morel, who also produces his own brand of armagnac, inherited this traditional family estate some 20 years ago. His Moelleux 2002 is a clear straw-yellow wine distinguished by a strong attack. Complex aromas of citrus fruits underpin a liveliness that tempers the pronounced overall sweetness.
• Christian Morel, Dom. de Bordes,
47170 Sainte-Maure-de-Peyriac, tel. 05.53.65.62.16,
fax 05.53.65.21.63 ▣
▼ ev. day 8.30am–7pm except Sun. by appt.

DOM. DE CAZEAUX

Cuvée Tradition 2001★★

	8 ha	4,000	▮ ⦿ ⚬	5–8€

An elegant label for a clear garnet-coloured wine which has been cask-matured to develop attractive aromatic notes without eclipsing the flavours of pepper and violets. The aromas continue on the palate and remain delightful through to a long finish on persistent notes of undergrowth.
• Eric Kauffer, Dom. de Cazeaux, 47170 Lannes,
tel. 05.53.65.73.03, fax 05.53.65.88.95,
e-mail domainecazeaux@free.fr ▣
▼ by appt.

INSTANT CHOISI

Merlot-cabernet Fruit rouge★

	10 ha	30,000	▮ ⚬	–3€

Excellent value for money from this Merlot-Cabernet Fruit red. A clear and lively robe discloses on the palate a mix of small red berries. The wine opens strongly, reveals a balanced structure together with flavours of brandied fruits, and closes on a persistently smokey finish.
• Cave des Sept Monts, ZAC de Mondésir,
47150 Monflanquin, tel. 05.53.36.33.40,
fax 05.53.36.44.11 ▣
▼ ev. day 9am–12.30pm 3pm–6.30pm

DOM. LOU GAILLOT

Merlot Excellence 2001★

	1 ha	6,000	⦿	5–8€

Gilles Pons is an oenologist who has directed this 15-ha family-operated business since 1999. His Merlot Excellence 2001 is a lustrous ruby wine whose principal appeal lies in its bold attack and its full and fleshy impact on the palate. Gentle tannins blend smoothly with well-integrated wood notes and traces of caramel.
• Gilles Pons, Les Gaillots, 47440 Casseneuil,
tel. 05.53.41.04.66, fax 05.53.01.13.89 ▣
▼ ev. day except Sun. 9am–12.30pm 2pm–7.30pm

Wines selected but not starred

DOM. DE CAMPET

Grain d'automne Gros manseng 2001

2.4 ha	2,600	▮ ⚬	5–8€

• Carole et Joël Buisson, SCEA de Campet, 47170 Sos,
tel. 05.53.65.63.60, fax 05.53.65.36.79 ▣
▼ by appt. cl. Feb.

Charentais

BRARD BLANCHARD 2002★

	1.6 ha	16,600	▮	3–5€

Merlot, Cabernet Franc, Sauvignon and Malbec come together in this vineyard which has operated along organic lines for some 30 years. This 2002 has a fruity nose and opens round, subtle and well balanced on the palate, providing an excellent accompaniment to cold cuts and meat.
• GAEC Brard Blanchard, 1, chem. de Routreau, Boutiers,
16100 Cognac, tel. 05.45.32.19.58, fax 05.45.36.53.21 ▣ ⌂
▼ ev. day except Sun. 9am–12 noon 2pm–6pm;
Sat. 9am–12 noon

DOM. BRUNEAU

Sauvignon 2002★

	1 ha	8,000	▮ ⚬	3–5€

The hills and valleys of Rouffignac are a rambler's paradise. Alain Pillet's small domaine in Rouffignac produces a well-balanced Sauvignon which gives off fresh aromas that will perfectly complement seafood platters and even poultry.
• Alain Pillet, chez Bruneau, 17130 Rouffignac,
tel. 05.46.49.04.82, fax 05.46.70.07.95 ▣
▼ by appt.

CHAI DU ROUISSOIR

Cabernet Terroir de Fossiles 2002★

	1 ha	1,500	▮ ⚬	3–5€

Didier Chapon and his son Hugues have been producing *vins de pays* since 1996. Together, they have developed this attractive and elegant rosé which appeals both to the eye and to the palate. Recommended to be served on its own as an aperitif or as an accompaniment to cold cuts.
• Chapon, Roussillon, Chai du Rouissoir, 17500 Ozillac,
tel. 05.46.48.14.76, fax 05.46.48.14.76,
e-mail chaidurouissoir@hotmail.com ▣
▼ ev. day except Sun. 10am–12 noon 5pm–7pm

DOM. DE LA CHAUVILLIERE

Chardonnay 2002★★

	10 ha	40,000	▮ ⚬	5–8€

A Chardonnay 2002 that opens on intense aromas of citrus fruits and sustains flavours through to a persistent finish. Should be drunk with fish dishes and seafood – all the more so since the oyster beds of the Marennes lie only some 20 kilometres away.
• EARL Hauselmann et Fils, Dom. de La Chauvillière,
17600 Sablonceaux, tel. 05.46.94.44.40,
fax 05.46.94.44.63 ▣ ⌂
▼ by appt.

DOM. GARDRAT

Colombard 2002★★

	4.8 ha	47,000	▮ ⚬	3–5€

Jean-Pierre Gardat tends to this 28-ha vineyard on the slopes of the Gironde, carrying on a family tradition dating back to the end of the 18th century. His Colombard 2002 gives off aromas of mango and passion fruit which pre-empt an elegant and balanced palate. Can be taken as an aperitif or drunk throughout the meal.
• Jean-Pierre Gardrat, La Touche, 17120 Cozes,
tel. 05.46.90.86.94, fax 05.46.90.95.22,
e-mail lionel.gardrat@wanadoo.fr ▣
▼ by appt.

DOM. DU GROLLET

Merlot cabernet-sauvignon 2001★

	20.1 ha	30,000	▮ ⦿ ⚬	3–5€

The celebrated cognac producer Rémy-Martin has converted some 20 ha of this 200-ha estate to the production of *vins de pays*. This 2002 is a harmonious wine which will mature into an agreeable accompaniment to meat dishes.
• SA Les Dom. Rémy-Martin, 29, rue de la
Société-Vinicole, BP 37, 16100 Cognac, tel. 05.45.35.76.00,
fax 05.45.35.77.94

VINS DE PAYS

VDP

MOINE FRERES

Chenin 2002★

1.92 ha	1,700	▪ ♦	−3€

Jean-Yves et François Moine offer a conducted tour of Chêne that enables visitors to the estate to learn something of the skills that go into oak-splitting and barrel-making. Their lively Chenin 2002 boasts pleasant notes of refreshing citrus and goes best with seafood.
☛ SNC Jean-Yves et François Moine, Villeneuve, 16200 Chassors, tel. 05.45.80.98.91, fax 05.45.80.96.01, e-mail lesfreres.moine@wanadoo.fr ☑
Ⴎ by appt.

LE ROYAL

Ile de Ré 2002★

25 ha	240,000	▪ ♦	−3€

Fish dishes and seafood platters are the order of the day in the case of this likeable Chardonnay – typical of the Ile de Ré – which comprises roughly equal parts of Sauvignon, Chardonnay and Colombard grape varieties.
☛ Coop. des Vignerons de l'Ile de Ré, 17580 Le Bois-Plage-en-Ré, tel. 05.46.09.23.09, fax 05.46.09.09.26 ☑
Ⴎ by appt.

SORNIN Cabernet-sauvignon merlot Cuvée

Privilège Elévé en fût 2001★

3.7 ha	29,000	◫	3–5€

Eight-month maturation in oak barrels yields this well-rounded and very aromatic Cuvée Privilège which deserves a regular place at the family table.
☛ SCA Cave de Saint-Sornin, Les Combes, 16220 Saint-Sornin, tel. 05.45.23.92.22, fax 05.45.23.11.61, e-mail contact@cavesaintsornin.com ☑
Ⴎ ev. day except Sun. 8am–12 noon 2pm–6pm

ST A.

Merlot 2001★

5 ha	13,000	▪ ◫♦	5–8€

From cooperative cellars dating from 1999 comes this fruity and well-rounded Merlot 2001. A wine that is ready to be drunk with meat dishes and specialties of the Charentes region.
☛ Cave coop. ACV, ZI du Malestier, 16130 Ségonzac, tel. 05.45.36.48.38, fax 05.45.36.48.36, e-mail cave.acv@wanadoo.fr ☑
Ⴎ by appt.

TERRA SANA 2002★★

17 ha	130,000	▪ ♦	5–8€

Jacques and François Lurton export some 90% of this *vin de pays* produced from organically-cultivated grape varieties (as the label clearly indicates). Fruit flavours assail the nose and the wine is fine and subtle on the palate, persuading the tasting panel of the inherent charms of this blend of Ugni Blanc, Sauvignon and Colombard grapes. To be drunk with seafood.
☛ SA Jacques et François Lurton, Dom. de Poumeyrade, 33870 Vayres, tel. 05.57.55.12.12, fax 05.57.55.12.13, e-mail jflurton@jflurton.com

Landes

FLEUR DES LANDES

Cabernet-tannat 2002★

6 ha	50,000	▪ ♦	3–5€

This supple, rounded and fully open blend of 60% Cabernet and 40% Tannat yields a wine that is deep in colour and pleasant to the nose. An added attraction is its colourful floral label.

☛ Vins Duprat Frères, quai Pièce-Noyée, chem. Saint-Bernard, 64100 Bayonne, tel. 05.59.55.65.65, fax 05.59.55.41.52, e-mail vins.duprat@wanadoo.fr
Ⴎ ev. day except Sat. Sun. 8am–12 noon 2pm–5pm

Wines selected but not starred

DOM. D'ESPERANCE

Cuvée d'or 2002

12 ha	16,000	▪ ♦	3–5€

☛ Claire de Montesquiou, Dom. d'Espérance, 40240 Mauvezin-d'Armagnac, tel. 05.58.44.85.93, fax 05.58.44.85.93, e-mail info@espérance.com.fr ☑ ♨
Ⴎ by appt.

Périgord

VIN DE DOMME

Tradition 2002★

5 ha	22,000	▪ ♦	5–8€

This cooperative has emerged as a proactive force in the rebirth of Périgord Noir winemaking following the decimation of vineyards in the region by phylloxera. A walk through the countryside offers visitors an opportunity to see the original wine-worker cabins of dry stone and with their cone-shaped *lauze*-tiled roofs. The Domme Tradition 2002 is distinguished by a richly-red robe and pungent aromas of preserved red fruit with pronounced mineral notes – the distinctive signature, as it were, of this type of wine. On the palate, the wine lives up to expectations both in terms of volume and robustness. That said, the tasting panel would have appreciated a longer finish. An interesting wine that is well worth discovering.
☛ Les Vignerons des Coteaux du Céou, Moncalou, 24200 Florimont-Gaumier, tel. 05.53.28.14.47, fax 05.53.28.32.48, e-mail vignerons-du-ceou@wanadoo.fr ☑
Ⴎ by appt.

Terroirs Landais

ROUGE DE BACHEN 2001★★

10 ha	15,500	▪ ◫♦	11–15€

928

Starred chefs regularly feel the temptation to try their hand at winemaking: Blanc, Meneau, Lorain have done so and now so too Michel Guérard with this 80% Merlot and 20% Tannat 2001 blend produced on 10 ha of a 20-ha estate. He is to be complimented on a wine that boasts a shimmering robe, and a fine and full wood-flavoured nose, and a full and fruity palate – suitable in short to grace the best of tables.

🍴 Michel Guérard, Cie hôtelière et fermière d'Eugénie-les-Bains, Ch. de Bachen, 40800 Duhort-Bachen, tel. 05.58.71.76.76, fax 05.58.71.77.77, e-mail michel.guerard@wanadoo.fr ☑
🍷 by appt.

COTEAUX DE CHALOSSE 2002★

| ■ | 6 ha | 50,000 | ■ ♦ | 3–5 € |

Cabernet (70%) and Tannat (30%) varieties go into the making of this attractively-coloured wine whose nose is discreet but unambiguous. This 2002 is rounded on the palate and leaves a distinct impression of fullness. The Jury also awarded a star each to the estate's **Vins de Pays des Landes red Gailande 2002** and a **rosé 2002 (–3 €)**.

🍴 Les Vignerons Landais, 40320 Geaune, tel. 05.58.44.51.25, fax 05.58.44.40.22, e-mail info@vlandais.com ☑
🍷 ev. day except Sun. 9am–12 noon 2pm–5.30pm

DOM. DE LABALLE

Sables fauves 2002★

| ■ | 12 ha | 40,000 | ■ ♦ | 3–5 € |

Dominique Laudet was a Gascon gentleman who spent some time in America before acquiring this estate in 1820. The estate has remained in the family ever since, producing armagnac (of course) and, as of 1982, also wine. Colombard, Gros Manseng and Ugni Blanc (60, 30 and 10% respectively) go into this pale-gold 2002 with its pungent aromas of confectionery and acacia blossom. Alcohol content and acidity are well-balanced and there is a hint of residual sugar which is by no means unpleasant. A wine made for foie gras perhaps? The Jury also selected a **Chardonnay des Landes 2002 (5–8 €)**.

🍴 SCEA Noël et Christian Laudet, Le Moulin de Laballe, 40310 Parleboscq, tel. 05.58.44.33.39, fax 05.58.44.92.61, e-mail n.laudet@wanadoo.fr ☑
🍷 ev. day except Sat. Sun. 8am–5pm

DOM. DU TASTET

Coteaux de Chalosse 2002★

| ■ | n.c. | 5,000 | ■ ♦ | –3 € |

A Coteaux de Chalosse developed from a blend of Cabernet Franc (80%) and Tannat grape varieties, this liquorice-tasting red develops aromas of red fruit accompanied by elegant tannins. The tasting Jury also selected the estate's moderately-priced **Gros Manseng Moelleux 2002 (3–5 €)**.

🍴 EARL J.-C. Romain et Fils, Dom. du Tastet, 2350, chem. d'Aymont, 40350 Pouillon, tel. 05.58.98.28.27, fax 05.58.98.27.63, e-mail domaine-tastet@voila.fr ☑
🍷 by appt.

Wines selected but not starred

DOM. D'AUGERON

Sables fauves 2002

| ■ | 7 ha | 4,200 | ■ ♦ | 3–5 € |

🍴 Régine Bubola, Dom. d'Augeron, 40190 Le Frèche, tel. 05.58.45.82.30, fax 05.58.03.13.81, e-mail domaine.augeron@wanadoo.fr ☑
🍷 ev. day except Sun. 8am–12 noon 2pm–6pm

DOM. DE CAMENTRON

Sables de l'océan Cabernet franc 2002

| ■ | 1 ha | 6,000 | ■ ♦ | 5–8 € |

🍴 Bouyrie-Dutirou, SCEA Les vignes de Camentron, chem. de Camentron, 40660 Messanges, tel. 05.58.48.83.81, fax 05.58.48.92.30 ☑
🍷 by appt.
🍴 Bouyrie-Dutirou

Thézac-Perricard

VIN DU TSAR

Le Bouquet 2001★

| ■ | 2.5 ha | 20,000 | ■ ♦ | 3–5 € |

An aroma of red fruits complemented by hints of game exudes from this ruby-red wine with violet highlights. The Bouquet 2001 derives its balance from soft and fleshy tannins which accompany a persistent and musky finish. The **Vin du Tsar Tradition 2001** was also selected.

🍴 Les Vignerons de Thézac-Perricard, Plaisance, 47370 Thézac, tel. 05.53.40.72.76, fax 05.53.40.78.76, e-mail info@vin-du-tsar.tm.fr ☑
🍷 ev. day 9.15am–12.15pm 2pm–6pm; Sun. 2pm–6pm

Pays de la Garonne

To the extent that Toulouse lies at its heart, this region embraces the designation "*vin de pays* du Comté tolosan" which includes the following *départéments*: Ariège, Aveyron, Haute-Garonne, Gers, Lot, Lot-et-Garonne, Pyrénées-Atlantiques, Hautes-Pyrénées, Tarn and Tarn-et-Garonne. Sub-regional or local designations are Côtes du Tarn; Coteaux de Glanes (Haut-Quercy, to the north of Lot – reds worth ageing); Coteaux du Quercy (south of Cahors – structured reds); Saint-Sardos (left bank of the Garonne river); Coteaux et Terrasses de Montauban (light reds); Côtes de Gascogne, Côtes du Condomois and Côtes de Montestruc (the armagnac-producing areas of Gers; mainly whites); and Bigorre. Haute-Garonne, Tarn-et-Garonne, Pyrénées-Atlantiques, Lot, Aveyron and Gers are designations that correspond to *départements*. Overall, this highly-diversified region produces a total of some 200,000 hl of red and rosé wine and around 400,000 hl of whites (in the Gers and Tarn). Soil and climatic variations in this region and along the Atlantic seaboard south of the Massif Central combine with an uncommonly wide range of grape varieties; accordingly, there is every incentive to develop wines made to a consistent standard which, as of 1982, have been labelled Vin de Pays du Comté Tolosan; at the time of writing, however, the volume of production remains comparatively low at around a mere 40,000 hl out of a total production some 15 times greater for the region as a whole.

Comté Tolosan

FRANCOIS DAUBERT
Madrigal sur le Mauzac 2001★★

0.6 ha	1,500	ⅠⅡ	8–11 €

Frontonnais vineyards are known above all for their output of red wines. That said, certain winemakers – and François Daubert is a case in point – have the expertise and knowhow to produce viable whites. This Mauzac 2001, for example, has a vanilla nose, is perfectly balanced on the palate with rich aromas of pear, quince and honey, and has a hint of wood that allows it to finish long and full-bodied.
☞ François Daubert, Ch. Joliet, 345, chem. de Caillol, 31620 Fronton, tel. 05.61.82.46.02, fax 05.61.82.34.56, e-mail chateau.joliet@wanadoo.fr ☑
𝕏 by appt.

DOM. DE RIBONNET
Chardonnay sauvignon 2001★★

n.c.	6,500	ⅠⅡ ↓	5–8 €

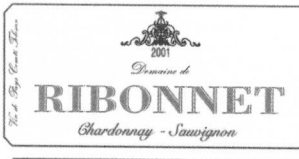

Christian Gerber's Domaine de Ribonnet offers a wide range of *vins de pays*, each with its own forceful personality. The Jury was particularly attracted to this Chardonnay-Sauvignon with its delicate yet complex and distinctive nose and discreet hints of wood. The wine finishes long, full and spicy on the palate. Top-of-the-range is the watchword in this instance – a truly epicurean pleasure.
☞ SARL Vallées et Terroirs, Dom. de Ribonnet, 31870 Beaumont-sur-Lèze, tel. 05.61.08.71.02, fax 05.61.08.08.06 ☑
𝕏 by appt.

VIN DE FLEUR 2002★

15 ha	100,000	↓	–3 €

The Vin de Fleur range in white, rosé and red from the Crouseilles cellars has long been synonymous with wines that are pleasingly full and that make for easy drinking. This predominantly Colombard-based 2002 literally glides across the tongue; its citrus fruit nose is pungent, and it is finely-balanced and nuanced on the palate.
☞ Cave de Crouseilles, 64350 Crouseilles, tel. 05.62.69.66.87, fax 05.62.69.62.71, e-mail m.darricau@plaimont.fr ☑
𝕏 by appt.

Corrèze

Wines selected but not starred

MILLE ET UNE PIERRES
Elevé en fût de chêne 2001

15 ha	100,000	ⅠⅡ	5–8 €

☞ Cave viticole de Branceilles, Le Bourg, 19500 Branceilles, tel. 05.55.84.09.01, fax 05.55.25.33.01, e-mail cave-viticole-de-branceilles@wanadoo.fr ☑
𝕏 ev. day except Sun. 10am–12 noon 3pm–6pm

Coteaux et Terrasses de Montauban

DOM. DE MONTELS
Louise 2001★★

2 ha	10,000	↓	5–8 €

Philippe et Thierry Romain offer a complete range of top-quality wines, among which the Jury selected a Louise 2001 with a pungent nose of red berries and violets. The wine opens strongly; the evolving tannins are as yet delicate, full and well balanced, with notes of spice and quince. Lady Louise promises to be a delight.
☞ Philippe et Thierry Romain, Dom. de Montels, 82350 Albias, tel. 05.63.31.02.82, fax 05.63.31.07.94 ☑
𝕏 ev. day except Sun. 8am–12 noon 2pm–7pm

Côtes du Condomois

PRESTIGE DU CONDOMOIS 2002★

n.c.	100,000	↓	3–5 €

Les Terres de Gascogne yield red or rosé *vins de pays* that deserve to be better known on account of their dominant aromas of peach and apricots and fresh, fruity and well-balanced impact on the palate.
☞ Vignoble de Gascogne, Cave de Condom, 32400 Riscle, tel. 05.62.69.62.87, fax 05.62.69.66.71, e-mail f.latapy@plaimont.fr ☑ 🏠 ⌂
𝕏 by appt.

Côtes de Gascogne

DOM. LES ACACIAS
Petit manseng 2002★

1.5 ha	6,700	↓	8–11 €

This Petit Manseng 2002 perfectly illustrates a typical Gascon vintage which expresses a wide assortment of exotic fruit aromas, notably mango, together with some hints of white blossoms. The wine is fine and well-balanced on the palate. A wine to be discovered and enjoyed.

☞ Dom. les Acacias, GAEC Camp du Haut, 32310 Bezolles, tel. 05.62.28.57.16, fax 05.62.28.57.16, e-mail gersmoutarde@aol.com ☑

☖ ev. day 10.30am–12.30pm 4pm–7pm; Mon. Sun. by appt.

☞ I. Dupouy et M. Delaère

DOM. LE BOUSCAS

Merlot 2001★

| | 1 ha | 6,000 | ☖ ☖ | 8–11 € |

An exquisite ruby-robed Merlot with a rounded yet delicate aroma of ripe red fruit (notably strawberries) that comes into its own on the palate.

☞ Floréal Romero, Dom. le Bouscas, 32330 Gondrin, tel. 05.62.29.11.87, fax 05.62.29.11.87, e-mail fromero@free.fr ☑

☖ by appt.

CAPRICE DE COLOMBELLE 2002★

| | n.c. | 250,000 | ☖ ☖ | 3–5 € |

Plaimont is known for its range of white and particularly aromatic Côtes de Gascogne; this Caprice de Colombelle 2002 does justice to that tradition. The robe is a beautiful yellow with hints of green highlights, the nose intense and bursting with aromas of boxwood and exotic fruits, the palate well-defined and balanced, the finish long. A most accomplished wine.

☞ Producteurs Plaimont, 32400 Saint-Mont, tel. 05.62.69.62.87, fax 05.62.69.61.68, e-mail f.latapy@plaimont.fr ☑ ☖ ☖

☖ by appt.

DOM. DES CASSAGNOLES

Gros manseng Sélection 2002★★

| | 6 ha | 40,000 | ☖ ☖ | –3 € |

J. and G. Baumann have contrived to bring out the best in Gascon grape varieties in their comprehensive range of *vins de pays*. The Jury opted for this Gros Manseng 2002 with its sustained yellow-to-gold colour and green highlights. The delicate mint aromas are complemented by hints of preserved fruit, toast and pear. The wine tastes of citrus fruits and finishes long and structured.

☞ J. et G. Baumann, Dom. des Cassagnoles, EARL de la Ténarèze, 32330 Gondrin, tel. 05.62.28.40.57, fax 05.62.28.42.42, e-mail j.baumann@domainedescassagnoles.com ☑

☖ ev. day except Sun. 9am–5.30pm

DOM. D'EMPEYRON 2001★

| | 10 ha | 5,000 | | 3–5 € |

The winemakers of Ténarèze may produce principally Côtes de Gascogne whites, but they also offer a not inconsiderable range of reds, including this Domaine d'Empeyron 2001 with its intense fruit aromas, notably of slightly spicy strawberry and plum, and gentle yet full and well-structured tannins which round out on the palate.

☞ Les Vignerons de la Ténarèze, rte de Mouchan, 32190 Vic-Fezensac, tel. 05.62.58.05.25, fax 05.62.06.34.21 ☑

☖ by appt.

DOM. DE JOY

Sauvignon gros manseng 2002★★★

| | 3 ha | 20,000 | ☖ | 3–5 € |

A perfect balance is achieved between the Sauvignon and Gros Manseng grape varieties in this 2002 where the hint of boxwood from the former is overlaid by the more complex citrus aromas of the latter variety. On the palate, this first impression is sustained, with boxwood flavours giving way to the more exotic and fleshy taste of the Gros Manseng to ensure both length and body. Olivier and Roland Gessler are to be applauded for this skilful blend which brings out the best features of both grape varieties. This is a very, *very* good wine.

☞ Olivier et Roland Gessler, Dom. de Joy, 32110 Panjas, tel. 05.62.09.03.20, fax 05.62.69.04.46, e-mail contact@domaine-joy.com ☑ ☖

☖ ev. day except Sun. 9am–12.30pm 2pm–7pm

DOM. DE LARTIGUE 2001★★

| | 3 ha | 6,600 | ☖ | 3–5 € |

This Côte de Gascogne 2001 exhibits a deep-red robe and is uncommonly rich in strong and complex aromas and floral, fruit and vegetable notes. The palate detects red fruits and nuances of fig, and is honest and balanced. The wine finishes full-bodied and long as a complete red should.

☞ Francis Lacave, Au Village, 32800 Bretagne-d'Armagnac, tel. 05.62.09.90.09, fax 05.62.09.79.60 ☑

☖ ev. day 8am–12.30pm 2pm–7pm

DOM. DES PERSENADES

Gros manseng Moelleux 2002★

| | 1.1 ha | 10,000 | ☖ ☖ | 3–5 € |

This 2002 boasts a clear yellow robe with beautiful green highlights. The nose is strong, exuding smells of white blossoms and citrus, notably grapefruit, but it is on the palate that this wine genuinely comes into its own, thanks to the surprising persistence of lightly vanilla-scented peach and apricot flavours. A wine that runs the full gamut of freshness, body and perfect balance.

☞ Christian Marou, Dom. des Persenades, 32800 Cazeneuve, tel. 05.62.09.99.30, fax 05.62.09.84.64, e-mail marou@terre-net.fr ☑

☖ ev. day 8am–8pm

DOM. DU TARIQUET

Les Premières Grives 2002★★

| | 85 ha | 1000,000 | ☖ ☖ | 5–8 € |

The Domaine du Tariquet needs no introduction to wine-lovers who have long delighted in its comprehensive range of dry and sweet whites, cask-matured and other reds, accomplished blends and judiciously-selected single grape or double-grape varieties. This Premières Grives 2002 with its straw-coloured robe and golden highlights is distinguished by powerful yet elegant aromas of mandarine orange, apricot and vanilla. The wine tastes full, lively and balanced on the palate, with commingling flavours of honey, dried fruit and prune. A must – as always.

☞ SCV Ch. du Tariquet, 32800 Eauze, tel. 05.62.09.87.82, fax 05.62.09.89.49, e-mail contact@tariquet.com ☑

☞ Famille Grassa

Wines selected but not starred

COLLIER DE LA TOISON D'OR 2002

| | 32.5 ha | 350,000 | ☖ ☖ | –3 € |

☞ La Fiée des Lois, 21, rue Montgolfier, BP 90022, 79232 Prahecq Cedex, tel. 05.49.32.15.15, fax 05.49.32.16.05, e-mail selection@fdlois.fr

VDP

DOM. DE LA HIGUERE
Cabernet-sauvignon merlot Cuvée boisée 2001

■ 17 ha	20,000	◫	3–5 €

☛ Paul et David Esquiro, Dom. de la Higuère,
32390 Mirepoix, tel. 05.62.65.18.05, fax 05.62.65.13.80,
e-mail esquiro@free.fr ☑

DOM. D'UBY
Colombard-ugni blanc 2002

■ 20 ha	20,000	■ ♦	3–5 €

☛ EARL Jean-Charles Morel, Uby, 32150 Cazaubon,
tel. 05.62.09.51.93, fax 05.62.09.58.94,
e-mail domaineuby@wanadoo.fr ☑
⟟ by appt.

Côtes du Tarn

DOM. SARRABELLE
Chardonnay 2001★★

■ 1 ha	6,000	■ ♦	3–5 €

The Jury singled out this Chardonnay 2001 from the range of
single-grape Côtes du Tarn on offer from Laurent and Fabien
Caussé. A slight but distinctive sparkle confers a freshness
that is particularly well balanced and harmonious.
☛ Laurent et Fabien Caussé, Les Fortis,
81310 Lisle-sur-Tarn, tel. 05.63.40.47.78,
fax 05.63.40.47.78, e-mail domaine-sarrabelle@free.fr ☑
⟟ ev. day except Sun. 8am–7pm

DOM. VIGNE LOURAC
Sauvignon Prestige 2002★

■ 3 ha	30,000	■ ♦	–3 €

For a long time now, Alain Gayrel has produced excellent
Sauvignons – and this 2002 is no exception to the rule: a
powerfully floral nose and intense fruit flavours impart a
pleasing freshness.
☛ Vignobles Philippe Gayrel, BP 4, 81600 Gaillac,
tel. 05.63.81.21.05, fax 05.63.81.21.09

LES VIGNES DES GARBASSES
Syrah 2002★★

■ 0.5 ha	2,000	■	5–8 €

A number of Tarn winemakers produce single-variety *vins de
pays*, among them Guy Fontaine, who has successfully developed this garnet-coloured Syrah 2002 of unusual brilliance
and intensity. The elegant nose is dominated by aromas of
flowers, and the wine builds volume and structure thanks to
the presence of forceful tannins. A wine that should age well.
☛ Guy Fontaine, Le Bousquet, 81500 Cabanes,
tel. 05.63.42.02.05 ☑
⟟ by appt.

Wine selected but not starred

DOM. D'EN SEGUR
Cuvée Germain Elevé en fût de chêne 2000

■ n.c.	43,694	◫	5–8 €

☛ SCEA En Gourau-En Ségur, rte de Saint-Sulpice,
81500 Lavaur, tel. 05.63.58.09.45, fax 05.63.58.09.45,
e-mail ensegur@terre-net.fr ☑
⟟ by appt.
☛ Pierre Fabre

Lot

DOM. DES ARDAILLOUX
Chardonnay Cuvée Tradition 2002★★★

■ 4.8 ha	24,130	■ ♦	8–11 €

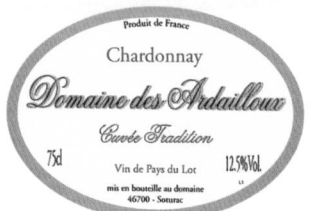

This Chardonnay Tradition 2002 from the Domaine des
Ardailloux, little more than a stone's throw from the magnificent castle of Bonnaguil, attests to the fact that the vintners of
the Lot region produce some remarkable white *vins de pays*.
This 2002 is brimming with individuality, from its pungent
floral nose to its fullness on the palate and long finish.
☛ SCEA Ch. des Ardailloux, Les Ardailloux,
46700 Soturac, tel. 05.53.71.30.45, fax 05.53.71.19.05,
e-mail ardailloux@aol.com ☑
⟟ ev. day 10am–6pm except Sat. Sun. Oct.-Apr.

Lot-et-Garonne

COTEAUX DU MEZINAIS
Gros manseng Moelleux 2002★

■ 0.9 ha	8,000	◫	3–5 €

A clear and luminous straw-yellow robe pre-empts aromas of
ripe fruit and honey. Wood flavours assault the palate and
rapidly convey a sense of roundness leading to a full-bodied
and long finish which ends on toasted notes.
☛ Cave des Coteaux du Mézinais, 1, bd du Colome,
47170 Mézin, tel. 05.53.65.53.55, fax 05.53.97.16.73,
e-mail cave.mezinais@wanadoo.fr ☑
⟟ by appt.

Saint-Sardos

GILLES DE MORBAN 1999★

■ 90 ha	120,000	■ ♦	3–5 €

The small vineyard of Saint-Sardos yields wines that are
decidedly robust and this Gilles de Morban is no exception. If
the tannins are fine and soft, the wine is certainly tannic, although
the tannins are fine and soft, contributing to an overall fleshiness and amplitude.
☛ Cave des vignerons de Saint-Sardos, Le Bourg,
82600 Saint-Sardos, tel. 05.63.02.52.44, fax 05.63.02.62.19,
e-mail cave.saintsardos@free.fr
⟟ by appt.

Languedoc and Roussillon

T he Languedoc-Roussillon region, shaped like some vast amphitheatre opening onto the Mediterranean, is home to vineyards that extend from the Rhône down to the eastern Pyrenees. This region, the largest wine-growing area in all of France, produces close on 80% of all *vins de pays*. Aude, Gard, Hérault and Pyrénées-Orientales, the four designations that take their name from *départements*, yield a total of some 3.1 million hectolitres annually. Within each of these *départements*, *vins de pays* produced in more closely delineated zones (of which there are no fewer than 57) total around 1 million hl. "Vin de Pays d'Oc", the regional designation, produces some 80% of the total annual 3.5 million hl yield from the six principal grape varieties (Cabernet Sauvignon, Merlot and Syrah reds and Chardonnay, Sauvignon and Viognier whites)

V ins de pays from Languedoc and Roussillon are produced by individually fermenting selected harvests of traditional grape varieties (Carignan, Cinsault, Grenache and Syrah for the reds and rosés, and Clairette, Grenache Blanc, Macabeu, Muscat and Terret for the whites), together with varieties from other regions, notably Merlot, Cabernet Sauvignon, Cabernet Franc, Cot, Petit Verdot and Pinot Noir for the reds and, for the whites, Chardonnay, Sauvignon and Viognier.

Aude

DOM. DE LA BOUYSSE

Merlot 2001★

| ■ | 1.5 ha | 4,730 | ▮ ♦ | 5–8 € |

Martine Pagès and Christophe Molinier have taken charge of the domaine once operated by their grandfather and have trebled the planted surface area (50 ha) and reconfigured it along biodynamic lines. This Merlot 2001 has a cherry robe with violet highlights; it opens very gently, giving off aromas of vanilla. The tannins are distinctly rounded in a wine full of character.

🏷 Dom. de la Bouysse, rue des Ecoles, 11200 Saint-André-de-Roquelongue, tel. 04.68.45.50.34, fax 04.68.45.09.86 ☑ 🏠
☗ by appt.

DOM. DE FONTENELLES

Cuvée du Poète Renaissance 2002★

| ■ | 11 ha | 20,000 | ▮ ♦ | 5–8 € |

The Fontenelles domaine has been in the same family for five generations and runs to 40 ha in total. Meeting Thierry Tastu, Renaissance Man personified, is an experience not to be missed. A composer-poet who conjures up rare harmonies of Merlot and Grenache and Syrah and Vieux Carignan. His luminous, darkly-brooding Cuvée du Poète Renaissance, produced on 11 ha, is a delight to the eye, to the nose – a complex mix of ripe fruit and chocolate – and to the palate, where it opens full and fleshy. A good wine.

🏷 Thierry Tastu, 78, av. des Corbières, 11700 DOUZENS, tel. 04.67.58.15.27, fax 04.67.58.15.27, e-mail t.tastu@montpellier.cci.fr ☑
☗ by appt.

Bénovie

DOM. DES HOSPITALIERS

Merlot 2001★

| ■ | n.c. | 6,000 | ▥ | 5–8 € |

The eponymous "hospitallers" of the domaine name date back to the 12th century Foundation of the Order of Hospitaliers of St. John of Jerualem. Today, the domaine boasts some 40 ha in total. This Merlot 2001 is irreproachable in terms of colour, with a powerful nose redolent of gooseberries and with a hint of vanilla from the cask. The tannins are well-structured and the finish packs a punch.

🏷 Martin-Pierrat, Dom. des Hospitaliers, 34400 Saint-Christol, tel. 04.67.86.01.15, fax 04.67.86.00.19 ☑
☗ ev. day 8am–8pm

Cassan

DOM. SAINTE MARTHE

Syrah 2002★

| ■ | 10 ha | 120,000 | ▮ ♦ | 3–5 € |

An attractively deep colour for this Syrah 2002, which develops delicate aromas of fruit. The wine shows balance and density. This is a serious Syrah which, provided it lives up to its early promise, deserves a "most honourable mention".

🏷 Olivier Bonfils, Dom. de Sainte-Marthe, 34320 Roujan, tel. 04.67.93.10.10, fax 04.67.93.10.05

DOM. DE LA TOUR PENEDESSES

Tempranillo Mas de Couy Elevé en fût de chêne 2001★★

| ■ | 3 ha | 8,000 | ▮ ♦ | 8–11 € |

Alexandre Fouque describes himself as an "artisan-vigneron" on the label of this 2001. An oenologist by profession, Fouque learned his craft in Champagne and Suze-la-Rousse. His vat room is furnished with equipment from Burgundy. A truly ecumenical winemaker, then, whose Temperanillo brings tears to the eyes. This is a version of the celebrated *oeil-de-lièvre* ("eye of the hare") Rioja successfully transposed to the Languedoc. Bouquet and body are full, warm and welcoming, with aromas of mature fruit. A wine to be served at room temperature as an accompaniment to small game paté or a Tarte Tatin.

🏷 Dom. de La Tour Penedesses, rte de Fouzilhon, 34320 Gabian, tel. 04.67.24.14.41, fax 04.67.24.14.22, e-mail domainedelatourpenedesses@yahoo.fr ☑
☗ by appt.

Catalan

MAS BAUX

Grenache noir Velours rouge 2001★★

| ■ | 3.71 ha | 4,517 | ▮ ♦ | 11–15 € |

These alluvial terraces bordering the *Via Domitia* have been planted with vines since time immemorial and the Catalan farmhouse by the roadside has been here since the 16th century. This Grenache Noir 2001 vintage, with its attractive fuchsia highlights, gives off aromas of minerals and ripe fruit

VDP

in equal proportions. It is full-bodied, supple and velvet-like on the palate. Two stars each are also awarded to a **Mas Baux red Gorge 2001** and a **Mas Baux red Baux 2001**.

➼ EARL Mas des Baux, Chem. du Mas Durand, 66140 Canet-en-Roussillon, tel. 04.68.80.25.04, fax 04.68.80.25.04, e-mail mariepierre.baux@libertysurf.fr
Ⴈ by appt.

DOM. MOSSE

Le Carignan 2001★★

■	3 ha	3,500	⬗ 15–23 €

An excellent example of the Carignan grape variety from century-old vine stock, this 2001 boasts a purple robe with even deeper purple highlights and a nose that is laced with spices, liquorice and preserved fruit. The wine opens strongly on the palate but maintains its essentially rounded character.

➼ Jacques Mossé, Ch. Mossé, BP 8, 66301 Ste-Colombe-de-la-Commanderie, tel. 04.68.53.08.89, fax 04.68.53.35.13, e-mail chateau.mosse@worldonline.fr ⛊
Ⴈ by appt.

Cathare

DOM. DE SAUTES

Signature Cathare 2002★

■	3 ha	30,000	▮ 3–5 €

This 2002 is a torch-bearer blend of Merlot (50%), Caladoc and Syrah and, as such, is a near-perfect wine: deep purple robe, a pungent and well-developed nose, and supple and voluminous on the palate.

➼ Guy et Emmanuel Giva, Dom. de Sautes, RN 113, 11000 Carcassonne, tel. 04.68.78.77.98, fax 04.68.78.51.66, e-mail domainedesautes@libertysurf.fr ⛊
Ⴈ ev. day except Sun. 10am–12 noon 2pm–6pm

Caux

CAUSSES DE NIZAS

Carignan Vieilles Vignes 2002★

■	2 ha	6,000	▮ ⚭ 11–15 €

John Goelet acquired this vineyard in 1998, adding to his collection of estates that includes the illustrious Clos du Val in California, Clover Mill in Tasmania, and Taltarni in Australia. This Carignan Vieilles Vignes 2002 has a dark purple robe and gives off flavours of toast and preserved fruit. It is firm and decisive on the palate. Overall, a well-structured wine.

➼ John Goelet, SCEA Dom. Nizas et Salleles, hameau de Salleles, 34720 Caux, tel. 04.67.90.17.92, fax 04.67.90.21.78, e-mail domnizas@wanadoo.fr ⛊
Ⴈ by appt.

Cévennes

CLOS DE LA ROQUE

Pinot noir 2001★

■	1 ha	4,000	⬗ 8–11 €

This is Huguenot territory and the winery's sales office is housed in the former temple building. This Pinot Noir 2001 offers a sustained cherry robe and flavours of cherry and strawberry with a hint of liquorice. It is ample on the palate.

➼ Yves et Anne-Marie Simon, 589, Le Ranquet, 30500 Saint-Ambroix, tel. 04.66.24.12.00, fax 04.66.24.12.00 ⛊
Ⴈ by appt.

Collines de la Moure

MAS DE MANTE

Vertige de la Moure 2001★★

■	1.5 ha	7,000	⬗ 11–15 €

The 60-ha Mas de Mante estate at the foot of La Gardiole Massif was acquired by the Lahoz and Boutennet families in 2001 and has since been given new life. This 2001 Syrah variety has an impeccable robe and tastes of red berries and liquorice. The estate's **Domaine de Mujolan white 2002** receives one star.

➼ Dom. de Mujolan, Mas de Mante, RN 113, 34690 Fabrègues, tel. 04.67.85.11.06, fax 04.67.85.47.71, e-mail contact@mujolan.com ⛊
Ⴈ ev. day except Sun. 9am–12 noon 3pm–7pm

Coteaux des Fenouillèdes

DOM. SALVAT

Fenouil 2002★★

■	15 ha	48,000	▮ ⚭ 3–5 €

As of the 2003 vintage, Coteaux des Fenouillèdes wines will come under the Vin de Pays des Côtes Catalanes denomination. The Jury acknowledged a **Vin de Pays des Côtes Catalanes Fenouil white 2002**, but preferred this blend of Merlot, Syrah and Grenache with its bright purple robe, flavours of red and black berries, its impressive silkiness on the palate and its persistently aromatic finish. A wine that is elegance personnified.

➼ Dom. Salvat, 8, av. Jean-Moulin, 66220 Saint-Paul-de-Fenouillet, tel. 04.68.59.29.00, fax 04.68.59.20.44, e-mail salvat.jp@wanadoo.fr ⛊
Ⴈ by appt.

Coteaux du Libron

DOM. DE LA COLOMBETTE Chardonnay
Demi-muid Vinifié en fût de chêne 2001★★

■ 6.6 ha	n.c.	◫	8–11 €

This innovative domaine lies to the north of Béziers, open to the Mediterranean and, for a century or so, has struggled to cope with all the uncertainties and ups and downs that characterise wine-growing in southern France. This Chardonnay 2001 – a Chardonnay in these parts? – has typical green highlights. On the palate, it has a rare and subtle elegance and is extremely aromatic, with hints of toasted bread. The jury also acknowledged a most successful **Cabernet Sauvignon 2001**.
✆ François Pugibet, Dom. de la Colombette, anc. rte de Bédarieux, 34500 Béziers, tel. 04.67.31.05.53, fax 04.67.30.46.65, e-mail lacolombette@freesurf.fr ☑
⌇ by appt.

DOM. DE PIERRE-BELLE
Réserve 2001★★★

■ 0.9 ha	5,600	◫	8–11 €

This Réserve 2001 from Syrah grapes has the ruby-red robe and touches of violet that constitute the very essence of the Midi, the Pays d'Oc. Blackberries and blackcurrant aromas vie with each other, with a hint of cocoa and a suggestion of wood from cask maturation. A full, fleshy wine with tannins so silky that one seems to be drinking pure velvet.
✆ Michel Laguna, Dom. de Pierre-Belle, 34290 Lieuran-lès-Béziers, tel. 04.67.36.15.58, fax 04.67.36.15.58, e-mail pierrebelle@chez.com ☑
⌇ ev. day 9.30am–12 noon 3.30pm–7pm

Coteaux de Murviel

DOM. DE CIFFRE
Val Taurou 2001★★

■ 3 ha	12,000	◫	8–11 €

This 2001 derives from a happy marriage of Cabernet Sauvignon (50%), Syrah and a touch of Grenache varieties and is a signature wine from this domaine acquired in 1998. The robe is a very dark red and the flavours evidence a pleasing blend of red berries and roasted coffee compounded by 12-month in-cask maturation. On the palate, the wine is agreeably round and friendly, with a suggestion of butter which does not detract from the underlying pungency of the fruit.
✆ Ch. Moulin de Ciffre, 34480 Autignac, tel. 04.67.90.11.45, fax 04.67.90.12.05, e-mail info@moulindeciffre.com ☑
⌇ by appt.

DOM. DE COUJAN
Rolle 2002★

■ 5 ha	26,600	⫶ ⌕	3–5 €

Rolle is not exclusive to the AOC Bellet. In this instance, it has resulted in a light and luminous straw-coloured wine with a nose that is redolent of a florist's shop. It is sprightly on the palate and should prove excellent with smoked salmon.
✆ SCEA F. Guy et S. Peyre, Ch. Coujan, 34490 Murviel-lès-Béziers, tel. 04.67.37.80.00, fax 04.67.37.86.23, e-mail coujan@mnet.fr
⌇ ev. day 9am–12 noon 2.30pm–7pm

DOM. DE RAVANES
Les Gravières du Taurou Grande Réserve 2000★★

■ 3.2 ha	13,000	◫	15–23 €

Equal parts of Merlot and Petit Verdot have gone into this unusual and strikingly-coloured 2000 with its rich, lively hint of balsam, phenomenally empyreumatic (charred) nose, and its appealingly dense and solidly-structured palate. The wine finishes on an aromatic note, with the silkiness of the Merlot balanced by the liveliness of the Petit Verdot.
✆ Guy et Marc Benin, Dom. de Ravanès, 34490 Thézan-lès-Béziers, tel. 04.67.36.00.02, fax 04.67.36.35.64, e-mail ravanes@wanadoo.fr ☑
⌇ by appt.

Côtes Catalanes

ARNAUD DE VILLENEUVE
Muscat Moelleux 2002★

■ 15 ha	3,000	⫶ ⌕	3–5 €

The cooperative cellars of Salses and Rivesaltes pooled resources some ten years ago to represent 3,000 ha planted with 20 or so different grape varieties. This Muscat 2002 is made predominantly (80%) from the Alexandrie grape with a small quantity of Muscat *à petits grains* added to yield a sweet wine with emerald highlights. The wine is distinctively fresh on the palate and the finish is refined and sustained. The hand is perhaps not iron, but the glove is decidedly velvet.
✆ Les Vignobles du Rivesaltais, 1, rue de la Roussillonnaise, BP 56, 66600 Rivesaltes, tel. 04.68.64.06.63, fax 04.68.64.64.69, e-mail vignobles.rivesaltais@wanadoo.fr ☑
⌇ by appt.

DOM. BOUDAU
Le Petit Clos 2002★

■ 4 ha	18,000	⫶ ⌕	3–5 €

Brother and sister Pierre and Véronique Boudau took over at the helm of this 80-ha family estate some ten years ago. Grenache, Syrah and Cinsault grape varieties combine in this forthright rosé with its gooseberry-colour robe shading to a bouquet of violets and white peach. The Petit Close 2002 is lively on the palate and exhibits remarkable length for a rosé. The estate's **Muscat Sec 2002** was also awarded a star.
✆ Dom. Boudau, 6, rue Marceau, 66600 Rivesaltes, tel. 04.68.64.45.37, fax 04.68.64.46.26, e-mail domaineboudau@wanadoo.fr ☑
⌇ ev. day except Sun. 10am–12 noon 3pm–7pm; cl. Sat. in winter

DOM. LAFAGE
Côté Est 2002★

■ 2.8 ha	30,000	⫶ ◫ ⌕	8–11 €

This family-owned estate was taken over in 1995 and has since been renovated; it draws largely on the experience of Jean-Marc Lafarge, who previously worked as a wine-grower overseas. This individualistic 2002 is a blend of Sauvignon (45%), Chardonnay (30%), Grenache Blanc (20%) and

Muscat (5%) grape varieties. It is straw-coloured with green highlights and has a nose redolent of fruit flavours which persist on the palate.
🡒 SCEA Dom. Lafage, Mas Durand,
66140 Canet-en-Roussillon, tel. 04.68.80.35.82,
fax 04.68.80.38.90, e-mail domaine.lafage@wanadoo.fr ☑
🍷 by appt.

Côtes de Pérignan

J.-M. HORTALA

Les Coustades Elevé en fût de chêne 2000★

■	1.5 ha	6,000	🍾 🍶 🥄	8–11 €

This family-owned estate goes back to 1893 and produces wines in the Languedoc tradition, including this Coustades 2000 with its attractive robe and its unusual mix of aromas vacillating between musk and smoke. The wine is lively and decidedly interesting on the palate.
🡒 Jean-Marie Hortala, 20, rue Diderot,
11560 Fleury-d'Aude, tel. 04.68.33.37.74,
fax 04.68.33.37.75, e-mail vins-hortala@wanadoo.fr ☑
🍷 by appt.

CH. DE LA NEGLY

Palazy 2002★

■	1.5 ha	7,500	🍾 🥄	3–5 €

This family château stands facing the sea in the Massif de La Clape. The 2002 rosé has a clear salmon-pink robe and boasts a fresh and floral nose, finishing round and deliciously fruity. A wine to be drunk among friends, possibly to accompany a mixed grill.
🡒 Jean Paux-Rosset, SCEA Ch. de la Négly,
11560 Fleury-d'Aude, tel. 04.68.32.36.28,
fax 04.68.32.10.69, e-mail lanegly@wanadoo.fr ☑
🍷 by appt.

Côtes de Thau

HUGUES DE BEAUVIGNAC

Sauvignon 2002★

■	40 ha	150,000	🍾 🥄	3–5 €

A top-of-the-range Sauvignon 2002 from this cooperative: a very light-coloured robe presages a range of elegant flavours of citrus fruits and white flowers. The wine leaves a highly commendable freshness on the palate. The cooperative's **Rosé de Syrah 2002** is also awarded a star.
🡒 Cave les Costières de Pomérols, 34810 Pomérols,
tel. 04.67.77.01.59, fax 04.67.77.77.21 ☑
🍷 by appt.

DOM. DE MARIE-ANAIS

Syrano 2001★

■	1.1 ha	6,900	🍾 🍶 🥄	5–8 €

The cellars of this family-owned domaine are housed in a converted barn and the domaine itself takes its name from that of the family's only daughter. Merlot and Syrah varieties are assembled into an attractive dark purple wine with a distinctive and persistent nose of red berries and a well-structured and comparatively rounded palate.
🡒 André Garcia, Dom. de Marie-Anaïs, 16, rue Basassac,
34510 Florensac, tel. 04.67.77.04.18, fax 04.67.77.04.18 ☑
🍷 by appt.

Côtes de Thongue

DOM. DE L'ARJOLLE

Merlot Synthèse 2001★

■	8 ha	70,000	🍷	11–15 €

"Synthesis" is an apt choice of name for this Merlot 2001 from the Domaine de l'Arjolle. The robe is garnet-red with a hint of brick-red, the nose slightly vanilla-flavoured, and the whole aromatic and full-bodied on the palate. A well-balanced wine. The Arjolle **Sauvignon 2002** is also awarded a star.
🡒 Dom. de L'Arjolle, 6, rue de la Côte, 34480 Pouzolles,
tel. 04.67.24.81.18, fax 04.67.24.81.90,
e-mail domaine@arjolle.com ☑
🍷 ev. day except Sun. 8am–12 noon 2pm–6pm

DOM. DE LA CROIX BELLE

Cascaïllou 2001★★

■	1,07 ha	4,000	🍾 🥄	11–15 €

Made predominantly from Grenache Noir grapes with added Syrah and Mourvèdre varieties, this 2001 boasts a pronounced robe and a nose that is nuanced, with a hint of fruit. An elegant and well-structured blend that might best accompany a veal roast.
🡒 Jacques et Françoise Boyer, Dom. La Croix-Belle,
34480 Puissalicon, tel. 04.67.36.27.23, fax 04.67.36.60.45,
e-mail information@croix.belle.com ☑
🍷 ev. day 8am–12 noon 2pm–6pm; Sun. by appt.

MONTARELS

Sauvignon 2002★

	60 ha	60,000	🍾 🥄	–3 €

Vins de pays have the singular and appealing merit of refreshing our knowledge of geography. Côtes de Thongue? Where exactly is that? At all events, this clear and lustrous Sauvignon 2002 simply explodes with fruit flavours and proves to be an excellent ambassador for the area. The aromas are well-defined and the wine has a vivacity that earmarks it as an excellent aperitif, possibly even with crème de cassis or a dash of blackberry liqueur. The Jury also singled out a **Vent des Collines red 2001** as being most accomplished.
🡒 Cave Coopérative Alignan-du-Vent, rue Lissac,
34290 Alignan-du-Vent, tel. 04.67.24.91.31,
fax 04.67.24.96.22, e-mail info@cavecooperative.com ☑
🍷 ev. day except Sat. Sun. 8am–12 noon 1.30pm–5.30pm

DOM. DE MONT D'HORTES

Sauvignon 2002★★★

	2.2 ha	16,000	🍾 🥄	5–8 €

Some *vins de pays* are fit to be up there with the best wines, as witness this Sauvignon 2002 from a domaine along the *Via Domitia* where a Roman villa once stood. A brilliantly clear golden-straw colour presages a nose that takes off like a rocket but, for all its dynamism, retains its dignity and its intense fruit flavours. Equal vivacity persists on the palate, where the wine emerges as pungent and full-bodied, impressively replete with flavour.
🡒 Jacques Anglade et Fils, Dom. de Mont d'Hortes,
34630 Saint-Thibéry, tel. 04.67.77.88.08,
fax 04.67.30.17.57 ☑
🍷 ev. day 9am–12 noon 2pm–6pm

DOM. MONTPLEZY

Félicité 2001★★

■	0.42 ha	1,700	◗┓	11–15 €

This 2001 from the Domaine Montplézy near Pézenas is felicitous indeed: an *assemblage* where the Carignan grape variety predominates, with the addition of some Grenache. The robe is distinguished less by its colour than by its luminosity. The gentle finesse of the bouquet carries over onto the palate, where it is difficult to conceive of a more subtle sensation. A rack of lamb with rosemary would undoubtedly bring out the best in this aptly-named Félicité 2001.

◗┓ Anne Sutra de Germa et Christian Gil, Dom. Monplézy, 34120 Pézenas, tel. 04.67.98.27.81, fax 04.67.98.27.81, e-mail domainemonplezy@free.fr ▼
Ⴑ by appt.

TARRAL

Sauvignon 2002★

■	11.57 ha	45,000	■ ♦	3–5 €

Tarral came into being following the 1995 merger of the cooperative cellars of Valros and Pouzolles in the windswept area known as the Côtes de Thongue. This clear golden Sauvignon 2002 has a nose full of fruit and an elegant structure lifted by the merest hint of sparkle. A wine ideally suited to accompany prawns, oysters au gratin, or mussels in a white Sauvignon sauce.

◗┓ UCA le Tarral, Site de Valros, av. de la Montagne, 34290 Valros, tel. 04.67.98.52.65, fax 04.67.98.59.54, e-mail info@tarral.com ▼
Ⴑ ev. day except Sat. Sun. 9am–12 noon 2pm–4pm

Gard

MAS DE FORTON 2001★★

■	30 ha	100,000	■ ♦	3–5 €

The Durand family specialises in the production of "Roman" wines, marketing the celebrated Orpailleur label from Quebec and, not least, making *vins de pays* like this blend of Syrah and Merlot grape varieties. The 2001 is a luminous ruby-red, with a nose that carries pronounced aromas of cherry and raspberry. Its tannins have already softened to produce a wine that is delicate yet well-balanced on the palate.

◗┓ Hervé et Guilhem Durand, 4294, rte de Bellegarde, 30300 Beaucaire, tel. 04.66.59.19.72, fax 04.66.59.50.80, e-mail contact@tourelles.com ▼
Ⴑ by appt.

LEYRIS MAZIERE 2001★★

■	1.2 ha	1,500	◗┓	15–23 €

This tiny property amounting to no more than ten hectares produces an interesting blend of Carignan (30%) and Alicante grape varieties. The 2001 in question is dark violet in colour, with a nose that is redolent of the nearby garrigue scrubland, together with balsamic undertones. On the palate, it develops a distinctly velvet feel.

◗┓ Leyris Mazière, chem. des Pouges, 30260 Cannes-et-Clairan, tel. 04.66.93.05.98, fax 04.66.93.05.98, e-mail gilles.leyris@libertysurf.fr ▼
Ⴑ by appt.

DOM. DE MOLINES

Vieilles Vignes 2000★

■	4 ha	40,000	◗┓	5–8 €

Four hectares of this 100-ha domaine are given over to Cabernet Sauvignon vines. This Vieilles Vignes 2000 is intensely dark in colour, with a nose rich in spices and red berries. It opens cleanly and develops quite generously on the palate.

◗┓ EARL Roger Gassier, Ch. de Nages, 30132 Caissargues, tel. 04.66.38.44.30, fax 04.66.38.44.21, e-mail i.roquelaure@michelgassier.com ▼
Ⴑ by appt.

Hérault

MAS DE DAUMAS GASSAC 2002★★

■	12 ha	n.c.		30–38 €

Tiny patches of vines are dotted around clearings in this vast forest, for all the world like an enchanted wood in a fairy tale. It is a matter of historical record that the monk St. Benoît d'Aniane declared his preference for Languedoc over his native Burgundy and settled here to work the land. Viognier, Chardonnay, Petit Manseng and some thirty other grape varieties in miniscule quantities go into this golden 2002 whose bouquet recalls that of white flowers with a hint of vanilla. A wine that is fresh and balanced on the palate. Equally remarkable is the **Mas Daumas Gassac red 2001**.

◗┓ Famille Guibert, SAS Moulin de Gassac, Mas Daumas Gassac, 34150 Aniane, tel. 04.67.57.71.28, fax 04.67.57.41.03, e-mail contact@daumas-gassac.com ▼
Ⴑ ev. day 10am–12.30pm 2pm–6.30pm; groups by appt.

DOM. DE JONQUIERES 2001★

■	2 ha	6,000	◗┓	11–15 €

Wines from Jonquières have been exported since as far back as 1870, notably to Canada. The dry 2001 white from this historic family-owned château permutates grape varieties planted on a limestone gravel soil: Chenin (40%), Grenache Blanc (45%), Roussane and Viognier. The robe is a clear straw colour, while the nose suggests nine months of in-cask maturation in addition to floral overtones. The wine has body and roundness – a highly successful vintage.

◗┓ François de Cabissole, Ch. de Jonquières, 34725 Jonquières, tel. 04.67.96.62.58, fax 04.67.88.61.92, e-mail chateau.de.jonquieres@wanadoo.fr ▼
Ⴑ by appt.

DOM. JORDY

Marselan 2001★★

■	1 ha	n.c.	◗┓	15–23 €

This Marselan 2001, grown on a tiny corner of the domaine, is a blend of Cabernet Sauvignon and Grenache Noir grape varieties. The robe is dark and intense; the subsequent flavours evoke blackberry and blackcurrant with an acceptable hint of wood. Overall, a silk-bodied wine that deserves to be drunk in the company of one's best friends.

◗┓ Frédéric Jordy, Loiras, 9, rte de Salelles, 34700 Le Bosc, tel. 04.67.44.70.30, fax 04.67.44.76.54 ▼
Ⴑ ev. day except Sun. 8am–8pm

MAS DE JANINY

Cabernet-sauvignon 2001★★

■	1.8 ha	5,000	■ ◗┓	5–8 €

A bottle that one might purchase for no other reason than on account of its most attractive label. That said, the contents of this 2001 are on a par with its aesthetic presentation: intensely deep-red in colour, it develops a strong personality building on pungent aromas of undergrowth and ripe fruit. The body exhibits good and unctuous tannins and the long finish is a panoply of aromas.

◗┓ Julien Frères, Mas de Janiny, 21, pl. de la Pradette, 34230 Saint-Bazille-de-la-Sylve, tel. 04.67.57.96.70, fax 04.67.57.96.77, e-mail julien-thierry@wanadoo.fr ▼
Ⴑ by appt.

Oc

DOM. DE MOULINES

Merlot 2002★

	20 ha	210,000	■		3–5 €

28 ha under cultivation when the domaine was acquired in 1914 and 55 ha today: an evident tribute to the work of three generations. This Merlot 2002 has good, sustained colour and elegant and complex aromas of overripe fruit. It is well-structured and agreeably full-bodied. A wine that is faithful to its heritage. The **Cuvée Prestige 2001**, is also awarded one star.
➦ Michel Saumade, GFA Mas de Moulines,
34130 Mudaison, tel. 04.67.70.20.48, fax 04.67.87.50.05 ☑
🍴 ev. day except Sun. 9am–12 noon 2pm–7pm

DOM. LES QUATRE PILAS

Cuvée de la Mouchère 2001★★★

	1.3 ha	5,000	■	8–11 €

Cleared garrigue scrubland makes a positive contribution to this harmonious blend of Cabernet Franc, Cabernet Sauvignon and Marselan grape varieties. The robe of this 2001 is a very dark red. Mint-flavour notes form a counterpoint to strong aromas of blackcurrant. The wine has body and texture, combining in perfect harmony yet still retaining its individuality. By any standards, an exceptional *coup de coeur*.
➦ Joseph Bousquet, chem. de Pignan,
34570 Murviel-lès-Montpellier, tel. 04.67.47.89.32,
fax 04.67.47.89.32 ☑
🍴 by appt.

Monts de la Grage

DOM. DES SOULIE

Merlot 2000★★

	2 ha	5,000	⑪	3–5 €

The Domaine des Soulié has been in the same family for many, many years. Today, it occupies some 30 ha of organically-cultivated vines. This garnet-red Merlot 2000 has distinctive amber highlights which attest to 15 months of in-cask maturation. Full-bodied and warm fruit flavours delight the palate. A wine that is ready to be drunk as of now.
➦ Aurore et Rémy Soulié, Dom. des Soulié, Carriera de la Teuliera, 34360 Assignan, tel. 04.67.38.11.78,
fax 04.67.38.19.31, e-mail remy.soulie@wanadoo.fr ☑
🍴 by appt.

DOM. D'AIGUES BELLES

Cuvée lombarde 2001★

	1.85 ha	5,884	■ ⑪ ⚬	8–11 €

Bon coq gaulois ne boit que vin ("a real Frenchman drinks only wine") was the dogmatic slogan once appended to this domaine established in 1870 by Eugène Bosc. Some years ago now, the 20-ha estate was revamped and replanted with a selection of noble grape varieties, best illustrated perhaps by this Cuvée Lombarde 2001, a mix of Grenache, Merlot and Cabernet varieties. The wine shows early signs of ageing well. It has traces of vanilla and of floral notes introduced by the Grenache. The 2001 opens aimiably, with tannins gradually becoming more pronounced.
➦ Nicole Palatan, Dom. d'Aigues Belles,
30260 Brouzet-lès-Quissac, tel. 06.07.48.74.65,
fax 01.46.43.86.96 ☑
🍴 by appt.

DOM. DE BAUBIAC

Merlot 2001★

	1.37 ha	9,000	■ ⚬	5–8 €

Voltaire once suggested that "to win is not enough, it is essential to seduce". This frank Merlot 2001 would appear to heed his admonition to the letter. The robe is a distinctive garnet-red, the nose a complex amalgam of very ripe fruit and charred wood, the palate rich in well-established tannins. A wine with winning *and* seductive ways.
➦ SCEA Dom. de Baubiac, 29, av. du 11-Novembre,
30260 Quissac, tel. 04.66.77.33.45, fax 04.66.77.33.45,
e-mail philip@dstu.univ-montp2.fr ☑
🍴 by appt.

DOM. DE LA BAUME 2000★

	1.97 ha	2,500	■	15–23 €

This 2000 is a Cabernet Sauvignon through and through, with a colour that hints at red brick, a maturing nose with aromas of pepper, and a long finish that is full and robust with a suggestion of wood.
➦ Dom. de la Baume, rte de Pezenas, RN 9, 34290 Servian, tel. 04.67.39.29.49, fax 04.67.39.29.40 ☑
🍴 by appt.

DOM. DE BEAUSEJOUR JUDELL

Impatience Cabernet merlot 2001★

	3.6 ha	20,000	■ ⑪ ⚬	8–11 €

Adelaide-born Australian Graeme Judell and his French wife Catherine fell in love with this domaine in 1998 and decided to settle here and restore it to its former glory. Their impatience to do so, reflected perhaps in the name of this Merlot 2001, is readily understood. The wine itself, a 50–50 mix of Merlot and Cabernet Sauvignon grape varieties, is a clear ruby-red with an expressive bouquet that suggests vegetal matter. It is a robust wine with modulated tannins, and can be laid down with impunity until being brought out and served with game.
➦ Graeme Judell, TM 14, RN 9, 34800 Nébian,
tel. 04.67.96.27.80, fax 04.67.96.39.57,
e-mail contact@beausejour-judell.com ☑ ⌂
🍴 ev. day except Sat. Sun. 9am–6pm

DOM. DE LA BERGERIE D'AMILHAC

Syrah 2001★★

	1.2 ha	10,000	■	3–5 €

Never let it be said that the winemakers of Chablis have no taste for adventure. Christian Adine is a case in point, one of numerous Burgundian winemakers who have upped stakes and come to work in the Midi. He opted to settle on this 20-ha estate with a characteristic farmhouse at its hub, wild boar and partridges on his doorstep, and Syrah and Chardonnay vines all around. His Syrah 2001 is as purple as it gets, with violet highlights and aromas of wild strawberries all the way through to a glorious finish. It could be added that his **Cabernet Sauvignon 2001** could also tempt the pillars of the

Chablis establishment to drop by for dinner when they are in the vicinity.
↖ EARL Christian Adine, 2, allée du Château, 89800 Courgis, tel. 03.86.41.40.28, fax 03.86.41.45.75, e-mail nicole.adine@free.fr ☑

LE BOSC

Syrah 2002★★

■	7 ha	50,000		3–5 €

Warm, luminous, aromatic – a typical Pays d'Oc Syrah with all the vitality of a flamenco dancer. This Syrah 2000 is a delight on the palate. A treat with small game.
↖ SICA Delta Domaines, Dom. du BÀ2sc, 34450 Vias, tel. 04.67.21.73.54, fax 04.67.21.68.38 ☑
♈ by appt.

DOM. LE BOUIS

Zoé 2001★

■	6 ha	12,000	■ ♦	5–8 €

This vintage is dedicated to the owners' eldest daughter Zoé. Made 100% from Carignan grapes, this 2001 exhibits a deep purple robe with commensurate highlights. Aromas of spices and red berries gradually develop and become increasingly pronounced. This spiciness is again apparent on the palate, adding up to a wine that is supple and eminently drinkable.
↖ De Keroualtz, SCEA CH. Le Bouïs, rte Bleue, 11430 Gruissan, tel. 04.68.75.25.25, fax 04.68.75.25.26, e-mail chateau-le-bouis@wanadoo.fr ☷
♈ by appt.

CALVET DE CALVET

Chardonnay 2002★

■	n.c.	65,000	■ ⦿ ♦	3–5 €

Calvet de Calvet – almost the name of a chic perfume but, in the case of this Chardonnay 2002, a blend of Cabernet Sauvignon, Merlot and Syrah grape varieties with a beautiful golden robe and a nose redolent of honeysuckle. On the palate, this 2002 achieves a pleasing roundness without sacrificing a certain vivacity which in no way detracts from the overall harmony.
↖ Calvet, 75, cours du Médoc, BP 11, 33028 Bordeaux Cedex, tel. 05.56.43.59.00, fax 05.56.43.17.78, e-mail calvet@calvet.com

CAMAS

Pinot noir 2001★

■	20 ha	15,000	■ ⦿	5–8 €

An attractively luminous cherry-red Pinot Noir that succeeds in far-from-easy conditions a long way from home. This 2001 makes the grade, however, subtly and optimally permutating flavours of black fruit. Good with chicken – of the free-range variety, naturally.
↖ Cave Anne de Joyeuse, 41, av. Charles-de-Gaulle, 11300 Limoux, tel. 04.68.74.79.40, fax 04.68.74.79.49, e-mail fabre.adj@wanadoo.fr ☑
♈ by appt.

DOM. CAMP-GALHAN

Liqueyrol 2001★

■	4 ha	10,300	⦿	11–15 €

Alain and Lionel Pourquier exemplify a phenomenon observed quite frequently of late: in 2000, they left the bosom of the cooperative to grow and commercialise their own output. This go-it-alone decision was underpinned by their acquisition of the Camp-Galhan domaine, a *terroir* comprised of rolled shingle deposits left by the Gardon. Merlot and Cabernet Sauvignon have been combined to impart a deep colour to this Liqueyrol 2001 with hints of toasted bread complementing aromas of gooseberry and raspberry. The palate still detects a suggestion of wood resulting from 12-month in-cask maturation, but the overall effect remains unimpaired and balanced.
↖ GAEC de la Roque, 1, rue des Aires, 30720 Ribautes-Les-Tavernes, tel. 04.66.83.48.47, fax 04.66.83.56.92, e-mail colioaires@worldonline.fr ☑
♈ Mon. Wed. Fri. 2pm–6.30pm; Sat. 9.30am–12 noon 2pm–6.30pm

DOM. DE CHAMBERT

Chardonnay 2002★

■	n.c.	100,000	⦿	–3 €

Chardonnay would appear to be as much at home in the Pays d'Oc as it seems to be anywhere else in the world. This straw-yellow 2002 has the now-familiar bouquet of acacia and hawthorn blossom, but opens unusually pleasantly on the palate and sustains well. It is also moderately-priced – which, as they say, never hurts.
↖ SA Chantovent, Quai du Port-au-Vin, BP 7, 78270 Bonnières-sur-Seine, tel. 01.30.98.59.01, fax 01.30.98.59.19, e-mail adv.france@chantovent.com

DOM. LES CHARMETTES

La Magdelaine 2001★

■	2 ha	5,000	⦿	8–11 €

Viognier, Grenache Blanc, Sauvignon, Terret, Chardonnay: the list goes on and on in the case of this Magdelaine 2001. Pale gold in colour and with familiar aromas of hawthorn and acacia blossom, it goes on to develop strong flavours of lemon and grapefruit. A pleasurable wine produced at Les Carmettes, a property acquired in 1987 by a family that already operates another 40-ha domaine.
↖ Famille Alcon, Dom. Les Charmettes, Rte de Florensac, 34340 Marseillan, tel. 04.67.77.66.16, fax 04.67.77.66.16, e-mail alcon.nicolas@laposte.net ☑
♈ by appt.

DOM. DU CHATEAU D'EAU

Cabernet-sauvignon 2001★

■	4.5 ha	40,000	■ ⦿ ♦	3–5 €

From the aptly-named Domaine du Château d'Eau, whose square tower overlooks the sea, the Montagnes Noires and on occasion, the Pyrenees, comes this Cabernet Sauvignon 2001 that also occupies a dominant position. Blood-red in colour and with pronounced aromas of very ripe red berries and peppers, this 2001 persists on the palate, combining distinctive flavours with non-obtrusive tannins. The producer? None other that Moillard from Nuits-Saint-Georges, one of numerous vintners attracted to the Languedoc where Moillard now operates a far-from-modest 84-ha estate.
↖ Dom. du Château d'Eau, c/o B. Montariol, 34290 Lieuran-Les-Béziers, tel. 03.80.62.42.22, e-mail nuicave@wanadoo.fr ☑
↖ Moillard

CIGALUS 2000★

■	15 ha	26,000	⦿	23–30 €

Gérard Betrand, who already owns *inter alia* the Domaine Villemajou in Corbières and the Château Hospitalet at La Clape, acquired this property in 1997. In the main, this 2000 combines Merlot and Cabernet Sauvignon grape varieties to yield a robe with red-tile highlights and complex aromas of leather and cherry brandy. A full-bodied wine with discreet wood notes and a good finish.
↖ Gérard Bertrand, Ch. Hospitalet, rte de Narbonne-Plage, 11100 Narbonne, tel. 04.68.45.36.00, fax 04.68.45.27.17, e-mail vins@gerard-bertrand.com ☑
♈ by appt.

DOM. DE LA CLAPIERE

Jalade 2002★

■	0.84 ha	4,300	■ ♦	5–8 €

This manor house dates back to the 17th century and was built by one François Clapier who left France shortly after the repeal of the Edict of Nantes. The local population commonly referred to the manor as "La Clapière" and the name has stuck until today. The Jalade 2000 is a delightful and discreetly-coloured rosé, unequivocally fresh and fruity from first to last. This is an extraordinarily vivacious wine that, above all, bears witness to the successful textural marriage between the Cinsault and Syrah grape varieties.
↖ Dom. de la Clapière, 34530 Montagnac, tel. 04.67.34.07.52, fax 04.67.24.06.16, e-mail laclapierewines@wanadoo.fr ☑
♈ by appt.

CLOS DEL REY

Grenache – carignan 2001★

| | 10 ha | 5,000 | ◫ | 23–30 € |

After 26 years spent working in a cooperative wine cellar, Jacques Montagné elected to take matters into his own hands. His 20-ha *clos* nestles in the shadow of the Château de Queribus in the heart of garrigue scrubland. Carignan and Grenache grape varieties are teamed in this instance to yield a deep garnet wine with a residual hint of wood from 12 months of in-cask maturation. This 2001 is a complex wine with unobtrusive tannins. It has already reached maturity.

➼ Jacques Montagné, 7, rue Barbusse, 66460 Maury, tel. 04.68.59.15.08, fax 04.68.59.15.08 ☑

CONDAMINE BERTRAND

Petit verdot Gourmandise 2001★★

| | 1 ha | 6,000 | ◫ | 23–30 € |

This Petit Verdot from a splendid 18th century château domaine has not only a magnificent cardinal's robe but all the other hallmarks of a great wine. Its mint bouquet is as delightful as its elegant structure and quality of its tannins are admirable. A perfect accompaniment perhaps to braised beef – albeit not quite yet: this 2001 is still improving and will benefit from being laid down for some years.

➼ B. Jany, Ch. Condamine Bertrand, RN 9, 34230 Paulhan, tel. 04.67.25.27.96, fax 04.67.25.07.55, e-mail chateau.condamineber@wanadoo.fr ☑ ⌂
☖ ev. day except Sun. 10am–12 noon 2pm–6pm

LA CROIX DU PIN

Cinsault Cuvée Prestige 2002★

| | 8 ha | 70,000 | ☖ ↓ | –3 € |

A very moderately-priced Cinsault rosé that has the added attraction of being, quite simply, a good wine. The robe is salmon-pink, the nose is lively, and the wine performs well on the palate. An easy-drinking wine in the best sense of the term.

➼ La Fiée des Lois, 21, rue Montgolfier, BP 90022, 79232 Prahecq Cedex, tel. 05.49.32.15.15, fax 05.49.32.16.05, e-mail selection@fdlois.fr

GEORGES DUBOEUF

Merlot Cuvée Prestige 2001★

| | n.c. | 60,000 | ☖ ◫ ↓ | 3–5 € |

Georges Duboeuf may well rule the roost in Beaujolais, but he is also to be found elsewhere – in Poitou, for example, and here in the Languedoc. His Merlot Prestige 2001 is rosy-cheeked and fresh-complexioned, with overripe fruit predominating. The palate is silky, rounded and full-bodied. Duboeuf has emerged as an important négociant intermediary between wine-growers and the marketplace.

➼ SA Les Vins Georges Duboeuf, La Gare, BP 12, 71570 Romanèche-Thorins, tel. 03.85.35.34.20, fax 03.85.35.34.25, e-mail gduboeuf@duboeuf.com ☑
☖ ev. day 9am–6pm at Hameau-en-Beaujolais; cl. 1–15 Jan.

DOM. ELLUL-FERRIERES

Vieilles Vignes 2000★

| | n.c. | 5,000 | ☖ ◫ | 8–11 € |

A "boutique winery", as they say in California: a 3-ha property planted with Grenache acquired in 1997 that has been expanded into a small (7 ha) domaine. This Vieilles Vignes 2000 has a pleasing colour with brick-red highlights commensurate with its age. Nose and palate are promisingly fruity and sustained. A supple wine available only in limited quantity, so it's best to order now.

➼ Dom. Ellul-Ferrières, Fontmagne, RN 110, 34160 Castries, tel. 06.15.38.45.01, fax 04.67.16.04.49, e-mail ellulferrieres@aol.com ☑
☖ ev. day 5pm–7pm

LOUIS FABRE

Chardonnay 2002★

| | 10 ha | 80,000 | ☖ ↓ | 3–5 € |

The shade of the Viscount de la Courtade, a vassal in the service of the Bishop of Béziers, hangs over this 16th century manor house surrounded by the 70-ha domaine that has yielded this Chardonnay 2002 with an impeccably-coloured robe. Classic aromas of acacia and hawthorn blossom presage a wine that has body and character. Excellent with fish prepared in a sauce.

➼ Louis Fabre, rue du Château, 11200 Luc-sur-Orbieu, tel. 04.68.27.10.80, fax 04.68.27.38.19, e-mail chateauluc@aol.com ☑ ⌂
☖ by appt.

DOM. DE LA FADEZE

Merlot Elevé en fût de chêne 2000★★

| | 4 ha | 15,000 | ◫ | 8–11 € |

The 2000 is a pure Merlot whose robe already shows early indications of ageing. The bouquet has a certain vigour, with wood notes complementing aromas of fruit. The wine is quite well-structured with unobtrusive tannins.

➼ Lenthéric, Dom. La Fadèze, 34340 Marseillan, tel. 04.67.77.26.42, fax 04.67.77.20.92 ☑
☖ ev. day except Sun. 9am–12 noon 2pm–6pm

DOM. FAURE

Cinsault 2002★

| | 0.29 ha | 1,734 | ☖ ↓ | 3–5 € |

A peach-coloured Cinsault rosé that is made-to-measure from a domaine that extends a warm welcome to visitors and artists alike. The wine boasts delicately-balanced aromas of flowers and fruit. It opens perhaps over-modestly but finishes honourably. The domaine's **Merlot 2002** also receives a star.

➼ Denis Faure, 1, av. de la Liberté, 11300 La Digne-d'Aval, tel. 04.68.31.72.66, fax 04.68.31.72.66 ☑
☖ by appt.

DOM. DE LA FERRANDIERE

Grenache gris 2002★

| | 6 ha | 60,000 | ☖ ↓ | 3–5 € |

Jacques Gau and his co-workers currently cultivate some 70 ha of vines together with 25 ha of apple trees. The domaine is situated at Aigues-Vives, where the salt air represents a clear disadvantage, but Gau and his team are fighting back, as witnesses this Grenache Gris 2002 with its lustrous peach-blossom robe and its sprightly flavours on the palate that are not without a certain elegance. A refined wine suitable perhaps for an exotic cuisine.

➼ SARL Les Ferrandières, Dom. de la Ferrandière, 11800 Aigues-Vives, tel. 04.68.79.29.30, fax 04.68.79.29.39, e-mail info@ferrandiere.com ☑
☖ ev. day except Sat. Sun. 8am–12 noon 2pm–6pm
➼ Jacques Gau

DOM. FONT-MARS

Mourvèdre syrah 2001★

| | 3.8 ha | 15,000 | ◫ | 8–11 € |

Wine has been produced on this Gallo-Roman domaine since 1878. This 2001 blends Mourvèdre and Syrah varieties in the ratio of 60:40 to develop a dark red *cuvée* with overtones of ripe fruit and dried nuts. The wine is handsomely structured, with harmonious tannins. Good with cheese, even better with a soft cheese.

➼ GFA Font-Mars, rte de Marseillan, 34140 Mèze, tel. 04.67.43.81.19, fax 04.67.43.79.41, e-mail info@font-mars.com ☑
☖ by appt.
➼ Jean-Baptiste de Clock

GRANGE DES ROUQUETTE

Agrippa 2001★★

| | 2 ha | 6,000 | ☖ ◫ ↓ | 5–8 € |

A 2001 dedicated to the Emperor Agrippa who is credited with building the watercourses that serve this region. As it happens, the vineyard is crossed by the conduits of the Pont de Gard, a mere five minutes' walk away. This Agrippa 2001 is a blend of Syrah (70%) and Mourvèdre grape varieties. It sports a robe of imperial purple and a bouquet redolent of pungent fruit and spices that seems to last forever. In all, a genuinely rounded wine.

🔸 Vignobles Boudinaud, Grand-Rue, 30210 Fournes, tel. 04.66.37.27.23, fax 04.66.37.03.56, e-mail boudinaud@infonie.fr ☑
🍷 by appt.

DOM. LAMARGUE

Syrah 2001★

■	2.5 ha	13,000	◧	5–8 €

This 72-ha domaine was recently acquired by Campari and has been restored and renovated from top to bottom. The Syrah 2001 reveals a ruby robe with dark purple highlights. The nose is ample and rich in fruit aromas. Anjou may be proverbially sweet and gentle, but this supple and persistent Pays d'Oc rosé is no less so. 90% of current production is currently earmarked for export.

🔸 Ch. Lamargue, rte de Vauvert, 30800 Saint-Gilles, tel. 04.66.87.31.89, fax 04.66.87.41.87, e-mail domaine-de-lamargue@wanadoo.fr ☑
🍷 by appt.

DOM. LAUGE

Cuvée Saint-Joly 2002★

■	1.3 ha	n.c.	■	5–8 €

A 50:50 blend of Syrah and Carignan grape varieties underpins this well-made and individualistic wine with its robe of deep-garnet velvet. The nose detects aromas of musk and the wine opens in determined fashion with, so to speak, a double helping of flavours. Its finish is long and straightforward, with an unmistakable suggestion of liquorice.

🔸 GAEC Les Carretals, rue du Minervois, 34210 Aigne, tel. 06.79.70.71.53, fax 04.68.91.13.42 ☑
🍷 by appt.

DOM. DES LAURIERS

Syrah-grenache 2001★★

■	2 ha	5,000	■ ◊	3–5 €

The domaine was established in 1969 (although the cellars date back to 1900) and has gradually expanded to its present 42 hectares. The blackcurrant tinge that marks the robe of this wine, made from Syrah and Grenache, is echoed subsequently on the palate, together with floral and mineral notes. The wine is supple, balanced and amply-rounded.

🔸 Marc Chabrol, Dom. des Lauriers, 15, rte de Pézenas, 34120 Castelnau-de-Guers, tel. 04.67.98.18.20, fax 04.67.98.96.49, e-mail cabrol.marc@wanadoo.fr ☑
🍷 by appt.

DOM. DE MAIRAN

Chardonnay Les Hauts de Mairan 2001★★

▨	n.c.	n.c.		5–8 €

The eponymous Monsieur de Mairan was a dedicated physicist ennobled by Louis XV in recognition of his contributions to science. This time around, the honour goes to a gold-green Chardonnay 2001 which exudes discreet mineral aromas, notably flint (silex). On the palate, the wine achieves a balance between strength and subtlety. From the same domaine come a most accomplished **Cabernet Franc 2002** and a remarkable **Cabernet Sauvignon 99**.

🔸 Jean Peitavy, Dom. de Mairan, 34620 Puisserguier, tel. 04.67.93.74.20, fax 04.67.93.83.05 ☑
🍷 ev. day 8am–8pm

DOM. DE MALAVIEILLE

Charmille 2002★

■	2.2 ha	4,900	■ ◊	5–8 €

The soil of Salagou still carries the footprints of the dinosaurs but it is now given over to Sauvignon, Viognier and Chardonnay grape varieties which impart to this Charmille 2002 its radiant, albeit somewhat pale colour, its delicately fresh floral aromas, and its flavours on the palate that are lively and expressive if rather short on finish.

🔸 Mireille Bertrand, Malavieille, 34800 Mérifons, tel. 04.67.96.34.67, fax 04.67.96.32.21 ☑
🍷 by appt.

DOM. DE MALLEMORT

Cuvée Alexandre 2000★★

■	1 ha	3,600	■ ◧ ◊	11–15 €

Back in the Middle Ages, Mallemort was certainly not a place to be: it was here that capital punishment was meted out and the streets were typically festooned with bodies suspended from the hangman's noose. Times have changed, however, and there is today no reason to miss out on an *in situ* opportunity to taste this ruby-red Cuvée Alexandre 2000, a marriage of Cabernet Sauvignon (65%) and Merlot grape varieties which has been matured for 12 months in the vat and a further year in cask. The wine gives off intense aromas of preserved fruit underpinned by delicate spices, yielding to a silky finish devoid of harsh tannins.

🔸 Luc Peitavy, Dom. de Mallemort, 34620 Puisserguier, tel. 04.67.93.74.20, fax 04.67.93.83.05 ☑
🍷 by appt.

MAS MONTEL

Jéricho 2001★★

■	3 ha	20,000	◧	5–8 €

The Jéricho 2001 is the offspring of a marriage of Syrah (80%) and Grenache varieties. The wine boasts a robe of imperial purple, with aromas of musk and spices, and flavours heightened by excellent tannins. A compact, elegantly-textured and well-structured wine that would go well with thrushes and juniper berries.

🔸 EARL Granier, Mas Montel, 30250 Aspères, tel. 04.66.80.01.21, fax 04.66.80.01.87, e-mail montel@wanadoo.fr ☑
🍷 ev. day except Sun. 9am–7pm

DOM. DE MONTLOBRE

Tête de Cuvée 2000★★

■	20 ha	6,000	◧	15–23 €

The two domaines known as La Jasse and Montlobre were acquired a couple of years ago by a négociant from The Netherlands. Accordingly, this Tête de Cuvée 2000 from the latter estate may fly a Dutch flag, but its *lingua franca* is decidedly that of the Midi. The wine is assembled from Merlot and Cabernet Sauvignon grape varieties, with a touch of Syrah for good measure. Its robe is deepest red with amber highlights and its bouquet attests to a long period of successful in-cask maturation which has not, however, deprived the wine of its musky aroma. Well-proportioned tannins are such that this wine can be cellared for a further one or two years, The domaine's **L'Ermitage Domaine des Deux Soleils Tête de Cuvée 2000** proved equally remarkable in the eyes of the tasting panel.

🔸 SCEA Mas de La Jasse, La Jasse, 34980 Combaillaux, tel. 04.67.67.04.04, fax 04.67.67.92.20, e-mail f.quermel@jasse.fr ☑
🍷 by appt.
🔸 Walraven

CELLIERS DES NEUF FIEFS

Sauvignon 2002★★

▨	n.c.	30,000	■ ◊	3–5 €

An accomplished golden Sauvignon that is clearly earmarked as an accompaiment to a seafood platter. The nose is rich and redolent of floral and plant notes, and this 2002 is lively, balanced and undeniably elegant.

🔸 Les Coteaux de Neffiès, av. de la Gare, 34320 Neffiès, tel. 04.67.24.61.98, fax 04.67.24.62.12, e-mail cavecoop.neffies@wanadoo.fr ☑
🍷 by appt.

DOM. DE L'ORVIEL

Sauvignon 2002★

▨	1.5 ha	6,400	■ ◊	5–8 €

This Sauvignon 2000 is the first wine to emanate from a privately-owned cellar that was entirely renovated when the Cabane brothers left the cooperative. Judging by this wine, the brothers are off to a good start: a sun-drenched robe gives way to a cocktail of mildly exotic floral and citrus aromas, followed by aromatic flavours that persist on the palate through to a long and balanced finish.

☛ SCEA Cabane frères, Mas Flavard,
30350 Saint-Jean-de-Serres, tel. 04.66.83.45.96,
fax 04.66.83.45.96 ☑
☂ by appt.

DOM. PREIGNES LE VIEUX

Cuvée Preixanum 2002★

▣	4.5 ha	10,000	▤ ⑪ ♨	3–5 €

This domaine is situated on agricultural land going back 1,000 years. The Vic family – the current proprietors – will celebrate their century as owners in 2005. Viognier and Vermentino grapes share the honours in this Cuvée Preixanum 2002. The robe is golden with green highlights, and the wine opens cleanly with notes of toast and honey that anticipate a well-structured whole. The domaine's rosé 2002 Cuvée Bérenger was also adjudged to be most accomplished.

☛ SCEA Preignes le Vieux, 34450 Vias, tel. 04.67.21.67.82, fax 04.67.21.76.46, e-mail preigneslevieux@aol.com ☑
☂ ev. day except Sun. 8am–12 noon 1pm–6pm
☛ Vic

DOM. DE SAINT-LOUIS 2001★★

▣	14 ha	30,000	⑪	5–8 €

The Domaine de Saint-Louis has its place in history by virtue of a dispute between Louis Pasteur, who visited in 1863, and the Privat family, who had recently developed a process to preserve wine by heating it; Pasteur went on to develop his pasteurisation technique a short year later. This lively 2001 with its wild fruit aromas and sustained bouquet is a blend of Cabernet Sauvignon and Merlot with an added touch of Syrah varieties.

☛ Philippe Captier, Dom. de Saint-Louis, 34140 Loupian, tel. 04.67.43.92.62, fax 04.67.43.70.80 ☑
☂ by appt.

LA SAUVAGEONNE 2001★

▣	3.6 ha	12,000	⑪	11–15 €

This 31-ha domaine, acquired by new owners in 2001, is given over to Merlot and the two Cabernet grape varieties, all three of which are present in this 2001, albeit with the lion's share going to Merlot. The red robe and aromas of preserved fig, spices and liquorice anticipate flavours that are full and generous, with tannins clearly present but kept firmly in their place and never allowed to dominate.

☛ Dom. de La Sauvageonne, rte de Saint-Privat,
34700 Saint-Jean-de-la-Blaquière, tel. 04.67.44.71.74,
fax 04.67.44.71.02, e-mail la-sauvageonne@wanadoo.fr ☑
☂ by appt.

ROBERT SKALLI

Merlot 2001★

▣	17 ha	120,000	▤ ⑪ ♨	5–8 €

Robert Skalli is recognised as having played a crucial role in developing the wines of southern France and his output always merits attention. This Merlot 2001 boasts a sustained garnet colour with amber highlights and a pungent nose redolent of spices and ripe fruit. The wine has softened somewhat but not so as to traduce its intrinsically solid structure.

☛ Les vins Skalli, 278, av. du Mal.-Jun., BP 376, 34204 Sète Cedex, tel. 04.67.46.70.00, fax 04.67.46.71.99,
e-mail info@vinskalli.com

SOLSTICE

Merlot Réserve Barrique 2001★★

▣	2 ha	13,000	▤ ⑪ ♨	5–8 €

The Réserve Barrique 2001 is a youthful and sprightly garnet-coloured Merlot matured for ten months in both cask and vat. Its aromas suggest mild spices and mint, and its flavours on the palate are elegant and graceful, underpinned by unctuous tannins and sustained aromas.

☛ Domaines du Soleil, Ch. Canet, 11800 Rustiques,
tel. 04.90.12.30.22, fax 04.90.12.30.29 ☑

CELLIER DU TERRAL

Cabernet-sauvignon 2001★

▣	5 ha	5,000	▮	3–5 €

The Cellier du Terral is a cellar cooperative that accommodates grape yields from some 600 ha, 5 ha of which are given over to this deep-purple-to-mauve Cabernet Sauvignon 2001, whose spicy aromas emanate from vat rather than an in-cask maturation. Mature and elegant tannins complement a wine that opens very strongly and develops well on the palate. If one is so inclined, this 2001 can be allowed to age a little before being served as an accompaniment to red meat.

☛ Cellier du Terral, 34660 Cournonterral ☑
☂ ev. day except Sat. Sun. 9am–12 noon 1.30pm–5pm

DOM. TERRE GEORGES

Merlot 2001★

▣	1.06 ha	7,500	⑪	5–8 €

Roland Coustal opened for business some three years ago when he took charge of this family-owned domaine whose grapes had previously been processed by a cellar cooperative. The "Georges" featuring on the label of this Merlot 2001 is in honour of the fater of his wife, Anne-Marie. Genealogies apart, the wine is good, very good even. Although rather dark in colour (it is, when all is said and done, a Merlot), the wine is replete with blackcurrant aromas. It opens forcefully, with pronounced and well-defined flavours and finishes on a positive note of cherry.

☛ Anne-Marie et Roland Coustal, 2, rue de la Pinède,
11700 Castelnau-d'Aude, tel. 06.30.49.97.73,
fax 04.68.43.79.39 ☑
☂ by appt.

DOM. DE TERRE MEGERE

Cabernet-sauvignon 2002★★

▣	2 ha	20,000	▤ ♨	5–8 €

A deep-purple Cabernet Sauvignon with violet highlights, a pronounced nose and an opening that is full of character – in short, a good wine in its category. This 2002 is vat-matured and remarkably straightforward, with a flavourful fleshiness that enhances the tasting pleasure. It remains to be said that the "mégère" (shrew) that features in the domaine name has been well and truly tamed...

☛ Michel Moreau, Dom. de Terre Mégère, Coeur de Village, 34660 Cournonsec, tel. 04.67.85.42.85,
fax 04.67.85.25.12, e-mail terremegere@wanadoo.fr ☑
☂ ev. day except Sun. 3pm–7pm; Sat. 9am–12.30pm

TERRES NOIRES

Sauvignon 2002★

▣	3 ha	30,000	▤ ♨	3–5 €

This Sauvignon 2002 boasts a clear pale straw-coloured robe and a nose typical of the breed, together with aromatic properties that are lively and sustained. The tasting Jury also awarded a star to the domaine's Colombard 2002 des Terres Noires.

☛ Dominique Castillon, Dom. Les Terres Noires,
34450 Vias, tel. 04.67.21.73.55, fax 04.67.21.68.38 ☑
☂ ev. day except Sat. Sun. 8am–12 noon 2pm–5pm

VERMEIL DU CRES

Muscat sec 2002★

▣	4.68 ha	26,000	▤ ♨	3–5 €

A dry Muscat with a soft robe and familiar fresh flavours on the palate. The same cooperative also produced a decidedly accomplished Vermeil du Crès Chardonnay 2002.

☛ SCAV Vignerons de Sérignan, av. Roger-Audoux,
34410 Sérignan, tel. 04.67.32.24.82, fax 04.67.32.59.66 ☑
☂ ev. day except Sun. 9am–12 noon 3pm–6pm

DOM. DE LA VERNEDE Merlot Les Artistes

Création n° 2 Fût de chêne 2001★

▣	5.18 ha	2,400	⑪	3–5 €

The ecosystem of the Aude estuary plays host to a number of rare birds and this is surely one of them – a fiery purple Merlot 2001 that has been matured in oak casks for six months. Notes of leather and very ripe fruit – notably of unpicked

cherries – stand out amid a host of flavours present in this well-structured, full and balanced wine.
☙ Jean-Marc Ribet, GAF de La Vernède, 34440 Nissan-lez-Ensérune, tel. 04.67.37.00.30, fax 04.67.37.60.11, e-mail chateaulavernede@infonie.fr ☑
☖ ev. day 9am–1pm 3pm–7pm

DOM. VIGNE BLANCHE
Cabernet-sauvignon 2001★★

	3 ha	16,000	⬛	5–8 €

A highly-coloured Cabernet Sauvignon 2001 from this domaine on the limestone-flecked flanks of the irascible Orbieu river very close by the Abbaye de Frontfroide. Pungent and complex aromas are the order of the day, notably vanilla-flavoured spices and mature red fruit. Good tannins contribute to an elegant and full-bodied structure. The domaine's **Domaine des Combes red 2001** received one star.
☙ Vignerons de la Méditerranée, 12, rue du Rec-de-Veyret, ZI Plaisance, BP 414, 11104 Narbonne Cedex, tel. 04.68.42.75.00, fax 04.68.42.75.01, e-mail rhirtz@listel.fr
☙ E. Barsalou

WINTER HILL RESERVE
Chardonnay 2002★

	n.c.	n.c.		–3 €

From the name on the label – *Winter Hill Reserve* – one might almost be in Australia and, as it happens, this cellar adopts Australian methodology: harvesting the grapes at night, rapid chilling, and so on. This very pale and very clear Chardonnay 2002 represents good value. White flowers and fresh fruit aromas dominate throughout. A light and delicate wine that lives up to its provenance.
☙ UC Foncalieu, Dom. de Corneille, 11290 Arzens, tel. 04.68.76.21.68, fax 04.68.76.32.01, e-mail mkt@foncalieuvignobles.com
☙ Cave des Coteaux de Saint-Cyr

DOM. LES YEUSES
Syrah Les Epices 2001★

	2.8 ha	13,000	⬛	5–8 €

The domaine name "Yeuses" is somewhat deceptive in that the word is commonly applied to a particular species of oak known variously as "holm" or "evergreen" oak (*Quercus ilex*), whereas the 80-ha property cultivated today by Jean-Paul and Michel Dardé is a tract of land lying between the foreshore and garrigue scrubland. This Syrah 2001 is distinguished by a purple-violet robe and by a relatively complex structure that is aromatic and sustained, hinting at flowers and leather. Overall, a pleasing combination.
☙ Jean-Paul et Michel Dardé, Dom. Les Yeuses, rte de Marseillan, 34140 Mèze, tel. 04.67.43.80.20, fax 04.67.43.59.32, e-mail jp.darde@worldonline.fr ☑
☖ ev. day except Sun. 9am–12 noon 3pm–7pm

Sables du Golfe du Lion

DOM. DE JARRAS
Gris de gris 2002★

	40 ha	400,000	⬛	3–5 €

Grenache, Carignan and Cinsault grape varieties contribute in that order to this Gris de Gris 2002 which confidently lives up to expectations. A pale robe with copper highlights precedes a nose and palate that are consistently fresh, aromatic and sustained.

☙ Domaines Listel, Ch. de Villeroy, BP 126, 34202 Sète Cedex, tel. 04.67.46.84.00, fax 04.67.46.84.55, e-mail jbonnardel@listel.fr ☑
☖ ev. day 10am–5pm; cl. Sat. Sun. in winter

DOM. DU PETIT CHAUMONT
Chardonnay 2002★★

	8 ha	10,000	⬛	5–8 €

Camargue bulls roam free about this domaine where vines are dotted among the seashore sand dunes and a number of inland ponds – a clear illustration, perhaps, of the onerous circumstances under which this Chardonnay 2002 is produced. The vines appear to thrive under these conditions, however, yielding a wine that is refined and redolent of exotic fruits, with full and persistent flavours on the palate.
☙ GAEC Bruel, Dom. du Petit Chaumont, 30220 Aigues-Mortes, tel. 04.66.53.60.63, fax 04.66.53.64.31, e-mail petitchaumont@netcourrier.com
☖ ev. day except Sun. 9am–12.30pm 3pm–7pm; groups by appt.

Provence, Basse Vallée du Rhône, Corsica

Provence

T he great majority of wines produced in this vast zone are reds, which amount to some 60% of the 900,000-hl yield from the *départements* in the Provence-Alpes-Côte d'Azur (PACA) administrative region. Rosés (30%) are made mostly in Var, and whites come from Vaucluse and the area that lies to the north of the Bouches-du-Rhône. A broad range of southern grape varieties is grown here and is rarely utilised singly; depending on soil and climatic conditions, they are typically blended in varying proportions with grape varieties from other wine-growing regions, such as Chardonnay, Sauvignon, Cabernet Sauvignon or Merlot from around Bordeaux or Syrah grapes from the Rhône valley. Designations based on *départements* apply to Vaucluse, Bouches-du-Rhône, Var, Alpes-de-Haute-Provence, Alpes-Maritimes and Hautes-Alpes; sub-regional designations apply to the Principality of Orange, Petite Crau (southeast of Avignon), Mont Caumes (west of Toulon), Argens (between Brignoles and Draguignan, in Var), Maures, Coteaux du Verdon (Var), the recently-recognized Aigues (Vaucluse), and Corsica's Ile de Beauté. As of the 1999 grape harvest, wine denominated "Vin de Pays Portes de Méditerranée à vocation régionale" completes this overview. Its production extends across the PACA region to the exclusion of the Bouches-du-Rhône, Drôme and Ardèche in the Rhône-Alpes.

LA MADELEINE
Cabernet-sauvignon 2002★★

	8 ha	15,000	⬛	3–5 €

A deep red nose and aromas of leather, dark berries and smoked notes characterise this Cabernet Sauvignon 2002. The finish reveals soft, well-rounded tannins complemented

by a persistent flavour of red and black berries. This is an excellent wine to accompany a leg of lamb *à la Provençale*. The Jury's attention was also drawn to a remarkable **Marselan 2002** (a cross between Cabernet Sauvignon and Grenache Noir grapes) which, it was agreed, would be most appropriate with game.

➤ Pierre Bousquet, Cave la Madeleine, 04130 Volx, tel. 04.92.72.13.91, fax 00.00.00.00.00 ☑
Ⅰ ev. day except Sun. 9am–12 noon 2pm–6.30pm

DOM. DE REGUSSE
Pinot noir Elevé en fût de chêne 2001★

| | n.c. | n.c. | 🍷⊞♦ | 5–8 € |

A handsome Pinot Noir with an elegant vanilla nose and distinct wood notes that will attenuate over time, given the excellent overall balance and quality of this 2001. Raspberry aromas and subtle hints of vanilla add to one's tasting pleasure. The Jury also spoke well of the estate's oak-cask-matured **Syrah 2002 Elevé en Fût de Chêne** and its **Muscat Moelleux 2002**.

➤ Dieudonné, SARL Cave et Vignobles de Régusse, rte de la Bastide-des-Jourdans, 04860 Pierrevert, tel. 04.92.72.30.44, fax 04.92.72.69.08, e-mail domaine-de-regusse@wanadoo.fr ☑
Ⅰ by appt.

DOM. DE ROUSSET
Viognier 2001★

| | 1 ha | 2,000 | 🍷♦ | 5–8 € |

From Hubert and Roseline Emery comes this expressive Viognier with flower (violet) notes and aromas of dried fruit (apricot) that are clearly present on the palate. This appealing wine is best allowed to breathe for a time before being served either alone as an aperitif or with sweet and savoury dishes.

➤ Hubert et Roseline Emery, SCEV Ch. de Rousset, 04800 Gréoux-les-Bains, tel. 04.92.72.62.49, fax 04.92.72.66.50 ☑
Ⅰ by appt.

DOM. DE SAINT-JEAN 2002★

| | 10 ha | 5,000 | 🍷♦ | 3–5 € |

The 2002 is a blend of Merlot and Cabernet Sauvignon grape varieties. It gives off intense aromas of stewed fruit and is silky on the palate, with flavours of red and dark fruit (blackberries). The sound overall structure is an indication that the grapes were harvested at optimal maturity. Recommended as a wine to be served with a rack of lamb with Provençal herbs and spices.

➤ Dom. de Saint-Jean, Chem. des Vannades, 04100 Manosque, tel. 04.92.72.50.20, fax 04.92.87.84.01 ☑
➤ d'Herbès

Alpes-Maritimes

LOU VIN D'AQUI 2002★★

| | 0.4 ha | 3,900 | | 5–8 € |

The tasting panel was seduced by this white made from the Provençal Rolle (or Vermentino) grape variety. The robe is clear and pale with green highlights and the wine opens on extremely delicate aromas of mild spices, fennel and passion fruit. The wine is ample on the palate and sustains spice and fruit notes through to an elegant finish. A wine that will hold its own remarkably well in the company of a blanquette of veal.

➤ Dom. de Toasc, 213, chem. de Crémat, 06200 Nice, tel. 04.92.15.14.14, fax 04.92.15.14.00 ☑
Ⅰ by appt.

Argens

TERROIR DU VAR
Gris★

| | 87.5 ha | 700,000 | 🍷♦ | –3 € |

A well-made and moderately-priced light rosé which typically finds its way to supermarket shelves. This *vin gris* has an attractive colour and a nose that gives off notes of citrus fruits, notably grapefruit, which are sustained on the fresh and clean palate. A wine to be served with impunity to accompany a cold buffet.

➤ Les Celliers de Saint-Louis, Les Consacs, 83170 Brignoles, tel. 04.94.37.21.00, fax 04.94.59.14.84, e-mail cellier-saintlouis@wanadoo.fr ☑
Ⅰ by appt.

Bouches-du-Rhône

DOM. DE L'ATTILON 2002★

| | 10 ha | 12,000 | 🍷♦ | 3–5 € |

This 2001 is a pleasantly clear and luminous rosé with intense aromas of pulped wild strawberry and hints of boiled sweets. In short, a straightforward and refreshing wine that can be drunk either alone as an aperitif or as an accompaniment to a fish terrine or Provençal-style starter.

➤ Comte de Roux, Dom. de L'Attilon, 13200 Arles, tel. 04.90.98.70.04, fax 04.90.98.72.30, e-mail de.roux.renaud@wanadoo.fr ☑
Ⅰ by appt.

VIOGNIER DE LA GALINIERE
Viognier 2001★★

| | 3.3 ha | 1,500 | ⊞ | 15–23 € |

The finesse, power and excellent balance of this Viognier 2001 found immediate favour with the tasting panel, not least because the apricot and toasted flavours imparted by the Viognier grape came through very strongly. A delightful prospect when served with duck foie gras.

🐦 Amédée-Laurent Musso, Ch. de la Galinière,
13790 Châteauneuf-le-Rouge, tel. 04.42.29.09.84,
fax 04.42.29.09.82,
e-mail chateaudelagaliniere@wanadoo.fr ▼
🍷 ev. day 9am–7pm

DOM. DE L'ILE SAINT-PIERRE
Chardonnay 2002★

▪	30 ha	50,000	▮ ♦		3–5 €

A most successful Chardonnay distinguished by a brilliant
robe with green highlights, aromatic intensity with some
honey notes, and a perfect balance on the palate. The wine
finishes long on floral (honeysuckle) notes and the whole is a
model of harmony. Best perhaps with fish in a white sauce.
🐦 Marie-Cécile et Patrick Henry, Dom. de
Boisviel-Saint-Pierre, 13104 Mas-Thibert,
tel. 04.90.98.70.30, fax 04.90.98.74.93 ▼
🍷 by appt.

DOM. LA MICHELLE 2002★★

▪	2 ha	12,000	▮ ♦		5–8 €

This rosé from the Vignerons du Garlaban is remarkable for
its finesse and balanced structure. The wine is aromatic to a
fault, with notes of fruit, hawthorn and broom which extend
to a silk-like palate. The **Caladoc rosé 2002 des Vignerons du
Garlaban (3–5 €)** also impressed the Jury. Both wines are
suggested as an ideal accompaniment to roast rabbit.
🐦 Dom. La Michelle, 13390 Auriol, tel. 04.42.04.40.63,
fax 04.42.04.40.63,
e-mail domainelamichelle@club-internet.fr ▼
🍷 ev. day except Sun. Mon. 9am–12 noon 2pm–6pm

MINNA VINEYARD 2000★★

▪	2 ha	5,900	⦿		11–15 €

This remarkable blend of Cabernet Sauvignon and
Syrah grape varieties attests to a complete mastery of the
vinification process and subsequent in-cask maturation.
The nose is complex (undergrowth) and sophisticated, with
notes of vanilla. A wine to be enjoyed as of early 2004. A
genuine delight.
🐦 Villa Minna Vineyard, Roque Pessade CD 17,
13760 Saint-Cannat, tel. 04.42.57.23.19, fax 04.42.57.27.69,
e-mail villa.minna@wanadoo.fr ▼
🍷 ev. day except Sun. 9am–6pm Sat. 9am–1pm; cl. Aug.

DOM. SAINT-VINCENT
Merlot Cabernet 2002★

▪	3 ha	12,000	▮ ♦		3–5 €

With this Merlot Cabernet 2001, the Michel brothers have
blended Merlot and Cabernet Sauvignon grape varieties to
make an attractive rosé rather than the red one might typically
expect. The robe is a deep colour and the nose is nothing short
of explosive, with aromas of ripe fruit and blackcurrant. The
wine is well-rounded on the palate, with sustained blackcurrant
flavours which attest to the optimal maturity of the grapes
when harvested. A bottle destined to prove a delicious accompaniment to a starter of aubergine caviar or a *pissaladière*.
🐦 P. et J.-P. Michel, GAEC Mas de Valériole, 13200 Arles,
tel. 04.90.97.00.38, fax 04.90.97.01.78,
e-mail phmichel@wanadoo.fr ▼
🍷 by appt.

DOM. DE VALDITION
Cuvée Ludovic Dacla 2001★

▪	1.1 ha	3,276	▮ ⦿ ♦		15–23 €

This 2001 is a well-made wine distinguished by maturation in
new casks and, as such, an example of a modern approach to
winemaking where wood flavours quickly fall away, enabling
a wine to mature more quickly. This approach is, of course, a
matter of taste. The Jury also appreciated an intensely floral
and well-rounded **Cuvée des Filles white 2002 (8–11 €)** made
from Chasan grapes.
🐦 Francine et Alain Godard, Dom. de Valdition, rte
d'Eygalières, 13660 Orgon, tel. 04.90.73.08.12,
fax 04.90.73.05.95 ▼
🍷 ev. day 9am–7pm

DOM. VIRANT
Chardonnay 2002★★

▪	3 ha	6,000	▮ ♦		3–5 €

A powerful Chardonnay with nonetheless distinct and delicate
notes of grapefruit and lychee. This 2002 opens unambiguously, then rounds out on the palate to an agreeable balance of
citrus flavours which persist through the finish. The domaine's
Cabernet Sauvignon 2002 was awarded one star.
🐦 Robert Cheylan, Ch. Virant, CD 10,
13680 Lançon-de-Provence, tel. 04.90.42.44.47,
fax 04.90.42.54.81, e-mail rcheylan@aol.com ▼
🍷 by appt.

Wines selected but not starred

DOM. DES MASQUES Chardonnay Philippe
Cézanne Elevé en fût de chêne 2000

▪	5 ha	5,000	⦿		11–15 €

🐦 Didier et Magali Garçon, Dom. des Masques,
13100 Saint-Antonin-sur-Bayon, tel. 04.42.12.38.50,
fax 04.42.12.38.50 ▼
🍷 by appt.

DOM. DE SURIANE 2002

| ■ | 17.64 ha | 600 | ⬗ | 3–5 € |

🕿 Marie-Laure Merlin, SCEA Dom. de Suriane, CD 10, 13250 Saint-Chamas, tel. 04.90.50.91.19, fax 04.90.50.92.80, e-mail mlmerlin@hotmail.com ☑
🍷 ev. day except Sun. 9.30am–12.30pm 2pm–7.30pm

Coteaux du Verdon

LA COLLINE DE VIGNELAURE
Merlot Cabernet-sauvignon 1999★★

| ■ | 2 ha | 4,000 | ⬗ | 15–23 € |

The Jury responded with enthusiasm to this vintage, noting that in-cask maturation has not detracted from the wine's overall amplitude and roundness. Notes of vanilla and dark fruits are still distinctly present and seem likely to intensify and become more complex with time. Excellent with a fillet of beef *en croûte*. A cask-matured **l'Esprit de Vignelaure Élevé en Fût Cabernet Sauvignon 2000 (5–8 €)** was also commended on account of its classic structure and spicy aromas.
🕿 David O'Brien, Dom. Vignelaure, rte de Jouques, 83560 Rians, tel. 04.94.37.21.10, fax 04.94.80.53.39, e-mail vignelaure@wanadoo.fr ☑
🍷 ev. day 9.30am–1pm 2pm–6pm

Hautes-Alpes

DOM. ALLEMAND 2002★

| ■ | 2 ha | 9,000 | ⬗ | 3–5 € |

This clear pale white from the Allemand estate met with approval on account of its aromatic intensity (citrus fruits, notably grapefruit) and its fresh and lively lemon notes on the palate. A most agreeable wine to accompany grilled fish. The tasting panel also singled out a **rosé 2002** and a cask-matured **Cuvée Vieilles Vignes red 2001** made from a local grape variety (Mollard).
🕿 EARL L. Allemand et Fils, La Plaine de Théus, 05190 Théus, tel. 04.92.54.40.20, fax 04.92.54.41.50 ☑
🍷 ev. day except Sun. 9am–12 noon 2pm–6pm

DOM. DE TRESBAUDON 2001★

| ■ | 2.3 ha | 10,000 | ⬗ | 5–8 € |

This 2001 is made exclusively from Merlot grapes, although the label does not specify the particular variety in question but merely identifies the vintage by its estate name only. The wine has a relatively intense nose, with notes of liquorice, mint and vanilla, and a fullness on the palate attributable to

flavours of preserved fruit, pepper and spices which combine most agreeably.
🕿 Olivier Ricard, Les Lauzes, 05130 Tallard, tel. 04.92.54.19.28, fax 04.92.54.17.67, e-mail tresbaudon@wanadoo.fr ☑
🍷 by appt.

Ile de Beauté

DOM. AGHJE VECCHIE
Vecchio Pinot noir 2001★

| ■ | 1 ha | 4,000 | ⬗ | 5–8 € |

In 2000, Florence Giudicelli started to work alongside her father at this estate which was established in 1962 and now runs to close on 8 ha. The 2001 Pinot Noir deserves a mention if for no other reason than its lustrous and clear ruby-red robe. That said, it has the added merits of powerful aromas typical of this grape variety and a balance and roundness accompanied by rich tannins. Suggestion: open one bottle now and save the others for later.
🕿 Jacques Giudicelli, Dom. Aghje Vecchie, 20230 Canale-di-Verde, tel. 06.03.78.09.96, fax 04.95.38.03.37, e-mail jerome.girard@attglobal.net ☑
🍷 by appt.

CORSAIRE BLANC
Chardonnay 2002★

| ■ | 80 ha | 500,000 | ⬗ | –3 € |

An elegant freebooter of a wine with a yellow robe and green highlights, this 2002 exudes sustained aromas typical of the Chardonnay grape variety and achieves a balanced overall structure. A wine that can be enjoyed as of now. The **Marestagno rosé 2002**, a blend of Grenache and Niellucciu varieties, was also awarded one star in recognition of its freshness and subtle aromas. A **Les Polyphonies de Cépages Cabernet Sauvignon 2002** was also selected.
🕿 Union des Vignerons de l'Ile de Beauté, Cave coop. d'Aléria, 20270 Aléria, tel. 04.95.57.02.48, fax 04.95.57.09.59, e-mail barianichaba@aol.com ☑
🍷 by appt.

DOM. DON PAOLU 2002★

| ■ | 3.5 ha | 32,400 | ⬗ | 3–5 € |

This 2002 is a yellow Vermentino with points of green. It evokes flowers and a hint of aniseed which are pronounced on the palate but quickly fade. A wine ready to be drunk now.
🕿 Cave coop. d'Aghione, Samuletto, 20270 Aghione, tel. 04.95.56.60.20, fax 04.95.56.61.27, e-mail coop.aghionesamuletto@wanadoo.fr ☑
🍷 ev. day except Sat. Sun. 8.30am–12 noon 1.30pm–5.30pm

MODERATO
Nectar d'Automne 2002★★

| ■ | 16.5 ha | 20,000 | ⬗ | 8–11 € |

The 310 hectares of the Casabianca Estate constitute the largest family-owned domaine on the island. The estate's sweet Moderato, a *moelleux* made from Muscat *à petits grains*, found favour with the Jury by virtue of its crystalline robe with gold highlights. Intense citrus and preserved fruit aromas sustain on the palate and an almost imperceptible sparkle lifts the wine and imparts remarkable balance. A wine to be enjoyed now or in a year's time. Another sweet Muscat from this estate, a **Cantabilé Nectar d'Automne 2002**, was awarded one star.

🍷 SCEA du Dom. Casabianca, 20230 Bravone, tel. 04.95.38.96.08, fax 04.95.38.81.91, e-mail domainecasabianca@wanadoo.fr

MONTE E MARE 2002★

■	25 ha	200,000	■	–3 €

The cooperative cellars of Saint-Antoine date from the mid-1970s. The Jury awarded a star to a supple **red Gaspa Mora 2002** with aromas of liquorice as well as to this unctuous and fruity Monte e Mare which should go well with meats with gravy.

🍷 Cave de Saint-Antoine, Saint-Antoine, 20240 Ghisonaccia, tel. 04.95.56.61.00, fax 04.95.56.61.60 ▮
🍽 by appt.

DOM. DU MONT SAINT-JEAN

Pinot Noir 2002★★

■	4.5 ha	10,000	■ ♦	–3 €

The Domaine du Mont Saint-Jean was set up in 1961 and extends over 95 hectares situated close to the very beautiful village of Antisanti. The domaine offers an already most agreeable Pinot Noir which will beyond doubt improve over time. A dark-red robe opens up on generous and predominantly floral aromas which emerge on the palate as flavours of spicy red fuit (cherries). Soft tannins contribute to a subtle overall balance. The commended **Aleatico 2002** boasts a deep-red robe and aromas typical of the Muscat grape variety; it is a wine that deserves to be better known. The tannic and persistent **Merlot 2002** was also selected.

🍷 Roger Pouyau, Dom. du Mont Saint-Jean, Campo Quercio, BP 19 Antisanti, 20270 Aléria, tel. 06.81.05.45.08, fax 04.95.38.50.29, e-mail roger-pouyau@wanadoo.fr ▮
🍽 by appt.

DOM. DE PETRAPIANA

Nielluciu 2002★★★

■	5 ha	15,000	■ ♦	–3 €

Ten out of ten and a *coup de coeur* for this superb deep-red Niellucciu with its complex aromas of lightly-spiced red fruit which tantalise the nose and delight the palate. This subtle and impeccably structured wine can be enjoyed now or laid down with impunity. Also worth noting is the estate's vat-matured **Merlot 2002**, which is awarded one star. A typical example of this grape variety, it will benefit from ageing for one to three years.

🍷 Eric Poli, Linguizzetta, 20230 San-Nicolao, tel. 04.95.38.86.38, fax 04.95.38.94.71 ▮
🍽 by appt.

DOM. DE SALINE

Pinot noir 2001★★

■	n.c.	n.c.	■	3–5 €

The Marana Cooperative has literally stopped counting the number of stars it has received over the years for this Pinot Noir from the Saline Estate. A dark garnet-red robe opens on intense aromas typical of this grape variety, and the wine boasts good tannic structure which ensures length and balance both now and in years to come, not least as an accompaniment to game and red meat. The **Domaine de Terrazza Merlot 2002** was awarded one star in acknowledgment of its violet aromas and its overall suppleness, and the **Domaine de Lischetto Chardonnay 2002 (5–8 €)**, a decidedly fleshy wine with a plethora of fruit aromas and flavours, was also selected.

🍷 Cave coop. de la Marana, Rasignani, 20290 Borgo, tel. 04.95.58.44.00, fax 04.95.38.38.10, e-mail uval.sica@corsicanwines.com ▮
🍽 by appt.

DOM. TERRA VECCHIA 2002★★

■	n.c.	n.c.		5–8 €

The Terra Vecchia Estate garnered a *coup de coeur* last year for its white *vin de pays* 2001 made from Chardonnay and Vermentino grape varieties. This year, the estate returns in triumph with a red 2002 assembled from Merlot, Cabernet Sauvignon and Grenache grapes. This is a clear ruby-red wine which exudes intense aromas of red fruit attenuated by a hint of iodine, combining to evoke a splendid array of pungent and sustained flavours on the palate. A wine that already exhibits excellent balance and harmony, but which will benefit from cellaring.

🍷 Coteaux de Diana, Dom. Terra Vecchia, Aléria, 20270 Tallone, tel. 04.95.57.20.30, fax 04.95.57.08.98 ▮
🍽 ev. day except Sat. Sun. 9am–1pm 2pm–6pm

Wine selected but not starred

TERRA MARIANA

Merlot 2002

	50 ha	3,000,000	■	3–5 €

🍷 Uval, Rasignani, 20290 Borgo, tel. 04.95.58.44.00, fax 04.95.38.38.10, e-mail uval.sica@wanadoo.fr ▮

Maures

DOM. DE L'ANGLADE

Merlot 2002★

■	2 ha	13,500	■ ♦	5–8 €

A well-balanced Merlot which the Jury appreciated as an archetypal example of the genre. Suffice it to say that the nose is expressive, with attractive floral notes, and that the overall impression is of a rounded and supple wine full of character. Would be excellent in the company of a *daube Provençale*. The state's rosé 2002, made from Grenache and Cinsault grapes, also found favour with the Jury.

☛ Bernard Van Doren, Dom. de l'Anglade, av. Vincent-Auriol, 83980 Le Lavandou, tel. 04.94.71.10.89, fax 04.94.15.15.88, e-mail dom.langlade@wanadoo.fr ▼
☖ by appt.

LE GRAND CROS

Chardonnay L'Esprit de Provence 2002★

	1 ha	n.c.	⑪	5–8 €

A delightful Chardonnay with a nose redolent of spices, brioche and white-flesh fruit; open and straightforward on the palate, with a judicious balance of peach and citrus fruit flavours. Although the finish is on the short side, this is a wine to be enjoyed, for example, with white fish baked in an almond and honey crust.

☛ Famille Faulkner, Dom. du Grand Cros, D 13, 83660 Carnoules, tel. 04.98.01.80.08, fax 04.98.01.80.09, e-mail info@grandcros.fr ▼
☖ ev. day 9am–12 noon 2pm–7pm

MAROUINE

Carignan Vieilles Vignes 2001★★

	0.9 ha	3,800		3–5 €

The substantive overall harmony exhibited by the Carignan Vieilles Vignes 2001 was a decisive factor in its being awarded a *coup de coeur*. The nose gives off distinct and already complex aromas of red fruit, while the wine's roundness and suppleness on the palate are nothing short of remarkable. A very attractive wine which will possibly age well, assuming one has the patience to allow it to do so.

☛ Marie-Odile Marty, Ch. Marouïne, 83390 Puget-Ville, tel. 04.94.48.35.74, fax 04.94.48.37.61 ▼
☖ ev. day except Sun. 9am–7pm

PASTOURETTE

Cabernet-sauvignon 2002★

	0.2 ha	1,300		–3 €

There is not enough of this to go around, but those fortunate enough to lay their hands on this cherry-red-robe 2002 rosé will not be disappointed. Nose and palate reveal aromas and flavours of red fruit. A most successful wine that tastes fresh, fully rounded and balanced.

☛ SCA Cellier Saint-Bernard, av. du Général-de-Gaulle, 83340 Flassans-sur-Issole, tel. 04.94.69.71.01, fax 04.94.69.71.80 ▼
☖ by appt.

Wine selected but not starred

LONGUE TUBI

Cabernet-sauvignon 2002

	0.6 ha	5,000		5–8 €

☛ Buisine, Dom. de Longue Tubi, 25, bd du Mas, 83700 Saint-Raphaël, tel. 04.94.82.37.09, fax 04.94.19.27.03, e-mail cfb.viti@wanadoo.fr

Mont-Caume

DOM. DU PEY-NEUF 2002★

	2.5 ha	20,000		3–5 €

The Domaine du Pey-Neuf can take pride in the fact that the tasting panel singled out not only its cask-matured Vin de Pays du Mont-Caume red 2001 but also this 2002 white. The former is an accomplished red with distinct *garrigue* overtones, the latter an attractive white with clear floral notes and an unctuous, "more-ish" impact on the palate, coupled with an agreeable sensation of length. An ideal accompaniment to grilled fish or a seafood platter.

☛ Guy Arnaud, 367, rte de Sainte-Anne, 83740 La Cadière-d'Azur, tel. 04.94.90.14.55, fax 04.94.26.13.89, e-mail guyarnaudvigneron5@wanadoo.fr ▼ ⊞ ⌂
☖ by appt.

Petite Crau

CELLIER DE LAURE

Cabernet Cuvée Pétrarque et Laure 2002★

	5.89 ha	12,296		3–5 €

An excellent rosé obtained from a blend of robust red grape varieties, where the overall structure does not prejudice appreciation of the notes of fruit and nuanced spices. To be drunk with grilled chicken or a plate of pasta garnished with basil. Equally excellent is the cellar's Cuvée Prestige red 2001 (5–8 €), which should appeal to lovers of cask-matured wines.

☛ SCA Cellier de Laure, 1, av. Agricol-Viala, 13550 Noves, tel. 04.90.94.01.30, fax 04.90.92.94.85, e-mail cellierdelaure@free.fr ▼
☖ ev. day except Sun. 8am–12 noon 2pm–6.30pm

Portes de Méditerranée

DOM. LA BLAQUE

Pinot noir 2001★★

	9 ha	48,000	⑪	5–8 €

A clear, dark-red Pinot Noir that gives off subtle aromas of wood. A well-made wine with a certain finesse and elegance. Considerable expertise has clearly gone into in-cask maturation.

☛ Gilles Delsuc, Dom. Châteauneuf-La Blaque, 04860 Pierrevert, tel. 04.92.72.39.71, fax 04.92.72.81.26, e-mail domaine.lablaque@wanadoo.fr ▼
☖ by appt.

Wine selected but not starred

CHARDONNAY DU PESQUIE 2002

	3.86 ha	6,000	⊞	5–8 €

➡ SCEA Ch. Pesquié, rte de Flassan, BP 6,
84570 Mormoiron, tel. 04.90.61.94.08, fax 04.90.61.94.13,
e-mail chateaupesquie@yahoo.fr ☑ ⌂
🍷 ev. day 9am–12 noon 2pm–6pm; cl. Sat. Sun. Oct.-Easter

Principauté d'Orange

DYONYSOS

Viognier 2002★

	2.8 ha	3,000	▮ ⧫	5–8 €

This Viognier 2002 makes its presence felt initially by dint of its attractively clean and brilliant robe, then goes on to impress by virtue of its pungent nose redolent of floral (violet) and liquorice notes. The wine opens forcefully, with straightforward flavours of fruit which gradually soften into a well-rounded finish. A persuasively harmonious wine.
➡ EARL Dionysos, Chez M. Farjon, chem. du Marquis, 84100 Orange, tel. 04.90.34.46.31, fax 00.00.00.00.00 ☑
🍷 by appt.

FONT SIMIAN 2002★

	2 ha	12,000	▮ ⧫	3–5 €

This beautifully-balanced Font Simian 2000 is assembled from Rolle, Chardonnay, Sauvignon and Marsanne grape varieties. It opens in lively yet restrained fashion, and the sensation of freshness intensifies with hints of lemon. The whole shows considerable finesse. The nose deserves special mention on account of its pronounced and generous floral attributes. Also worthy of mention is **Jean-Pierre Serguier's Numéro 2 Version 2003 (5–8 €), Vins de Pays du Vaucluse red**, which is a tribute to this winemaker's knowledge and skill.
➡ Jean-Pierre Serguier, Ch. Simian, 84420 Piolenc, tel. 04.90.29.50.67, fax 04.90.29.62.33,
e-mail chateau.simian@wanadoo.fr ☑
🍷 ev. day 8.30am–12.30pm 1.30pm–7.30pm

Var

DOM. DE GARBELLE

Vermentino 2002★★

	0.75 ha	1,500	▮ ⧫	5–8 €

A typical Provençal assembly of Rolle or Vermentino, distinguished by its pale, clear and very brilliant colour and a nose that presents aromas of pineapple, citrus fruit skins and a suggestion of iodine. A well-balanced wine that persists on the palate. Strongly recommended as an accompaniment to scallops or grilled sea bass.
➡ Mathieu Gambini, Dom. de Garbelle, 83136 Garéoult, tel. 04.94.04.86.30, fax 04.94.04.86.30 ☑
🍷 ev. day 8.30am–12 noon 2pm–6pm

THUERRY

Les Templiers de Villecroze 2000★

	1 ha	6,000	▮ ⧫	5–8 €

An attractive 2000 with a very deep-red robe inherited no doubt from the principal grape variety used (Cabernet Sauvignon). The mature grapes that went into this vintage have imparted a roundness that sustains through a long finish. The nose is fully open to reveal a variety of fruits. Perhaps best with a leg of Provençal lamb.
➡ Ch. Thuerry, 83690 Villecroze, tel. 04.94.70.63.02, fax 04.94.70.67.03, e-mail thuerry@aol.com ☑
🍷 ev. day 9am–6.30pm (7.30pm in summer);
cl. Sun. from Apr. to Sep.
🍴 Croquet

Wine selected but not starred

TRIENNES

Saint-Auguste 1999

	15 ha	50,000	▮ ⊞ ⧫	5–8 €

➡ Dom. de Triennes, RN 560, 83860 Nans-les-Pins, tel. 04.94.78.91.46, fax 04.94.78.65.04,
e-mail triennes@wanadoo.com ☑
🍷 ev. day except Sun. 9am–12pm 1pm–6pm;
groups by appt.

Vaucluse

DOM. DES ANGES

Chardonnay 2001★

	2.8 ha	6,600	⊞	5–8 €

This sustained yellow Chardonnay develops subtle floral aromas (white blossom) and unusual hints of broom and caramel cream. Wood flavours remain decidedly pronounced. The Jury also selected the estate's **Cabernet Sauvignon (8–11 €)**, a wine matured in oak for 11 months and distinguished by a complex nose and ample, woody palate.
➡ Dom. des Anges, 84570 Mormoiron, tel. 04.90.61.88.78, fax 04.90.61.98.05, e-mail ciaranr@club-internet.fr ☑
🍷 ev. day 9am–12pm 2pm–6pm; 1 Oct.–1 Apr. by appt.

DOM. DE LA BASTIDONNE

Chardonnay 2002★

	1.17 ha	2,000	▮ ⧫	5–8 €

This fresh and, for want of a better word, pleasant Chardonnay 2000 is consistently light on the nose and palate, yet develops aromas of acacia blossom. The attack opens straightforward and convincing and the whole finishes round and long. Excellent as a stand-alone aperitif but also recommended with a grilled sole or sea bream.
➡ Gérard Marreau, SCEA Dom. de La Bastidonne, 84220 Cabrières-d'Avignon, tel. 04.90.76.70.00, fax 04.90.76.74.34 ☑
🍷 ev. day except Sun. 9am–12 noon 2pm–6pm

DOM. BOUCHE

Sauvignon 2002★

	0.65 ha	2,666	▮ ⧫	5–8 €

This light-gold Sauvignon 2000 with delicate floral aromas (white blossom) won over the Jury; the tasting panel unanimously awarded it one star on discovering its freshness, balance, roundness on the palate and extended finish on flowers and peach notes. An archetypically harmonious Sauvignon that will go well with all manner of fish and seafood.
➡ Dominique Bouche, chem. d'Avignon, 84850 Camaret-sur-Aigues, tel. 06.62.09.27.19, fax 04.90.37.74.17 ☑
🍷 by appt.

DOM. DE LA CITADELLE
Cabernet-sauvignon 2002★★

	4 ha	16,000	∎ ↓	3–5 €

A dark, almost-black robe with brilliant violet highlights presages a complex panoply of blackberry, liquorice, pepper and spice aromas which are beautifully sustained on the palate through to a rounded and well-structured finish. This 2002 is a credit to the winemaker and a rare delight to the wine-lover as an accompaniment to grilled sirloin – now or at any time up to 2005.

🡒 Rousset-Rouard, Dom. de la Citadelle, rte de Cavaillon, 84560 Ménerbes, tel. 04.90.72.41.58, fax 04.90.72.41.59, e-mail domainedelacitadelle@wanadoo.fr ☑
☿ ev. day 10am–12 noon 2pm–6pm; cl. Sun. from Nov. to Mar.; groups by appt.

DOM. FONDACCI
Chasan 2002★★

	2.5 ha	10,000	∎ ↓	3–5 €

It proved necessary to choose between two Chasan grape-based wines presented by Guy Fondacci. The oak cask-matured **2001 Elevé en Fût de Chêne** was adjudged remarkable, but the 2002 stole the show and earned a *coup de coeur* on the strength of the exceptional level of quality, expertise and commitment demonstrated by a winemaker confronted by what, after all, tended to be a problematic vintage. Suffice it to say that the splendid aromas of exotic fruits persist through to a protracted finish. This wine is a delight, even more so when enjoyed as an accompaniment to sweet and savoury dishes.

🡒 Dom. Guy Fondacci, quartier La Sablière, 84580 Oppède, tel. 04.90.76.95.91, fax 04.90.71.40.38, e-mail guyfondacci@aol.com ☑
☿ ev. day 10.30am–12 noon 2.30pm–6pm

DOM. FONTAINE DU CLOS
Chardonnay 2002★★

	4 ha	5,000	∎ ↓	3–5 €

A Chardonnay 2002 whose remarkable qualities captivated the Jury: an intense nose redolent of white-flesh fruit and peaches, a structured roundness on the palate with distinct flavours of peaches in syrup, and a sustained and protracted finish. In short, unadulterated pleasure from beginning to end.

🡒 EARL Jean Barnier, Dom. Fontaine du Clos, 84260 Sarrians, tel. 04.90.65.42.73, fax 04.90.65.30.69, e-mail cave@fontaineduclos.com ☑
☿ ev. day except Sun. 9am–12 noon 3pm–7pm

DOM. GRAND CALLAMAND
Merlot 2000★

	1 ha	6,000	◗	5–8 €

A very interesting and expressive Merlot 2000 with a deep-red, virtually-black robe, a nose that permutates generous aromas of coffee, cocoa, toast and liquorice, and a sustained fullness on the palate (albeit with a pronounced and sustained undertone of wood). A wine that is destined to be served with game.

🡒 M. et Mme Österlöf, Dom. Grand Callamand, Rte de la Loubière, 84120 Pertuis, tel. 04.90.09.61.40, fax 04.90.09.64.00, e-mail chateau-grandcallamand@wanadoo.fr ☑ ☗
☿ by appt.

DOM. DE MAROTTE
Viognier 2002★★★

	2 ha	4,000	∎ ↓	5–8 €

This 2002 from the Domaine de Marotte is a quite exceptional Viognier from a difficult year, an expressive wine that makes its point marvellously and unequivocally in the glass. The astonishing nose exudes aromas of apricot blossom and quince. The wine performs remarkably on the palate, recapturing and sustaining the apricot and quince flavours. The long finish is a delightful bonus. The tasting panel also recommended the **Vin de Pays de Vaucluse rosé 2002 (3–5 €)**, a wine based on the Mourvèdre grape variety.

🡒 EARL la Reynarde, Dom. de Marotte, petit chemin de Serres, 84200 Carpentras, tel. 04.90.63.43.27, fax 04.90.67.15.28, e-mail marotte@wanadoo.fr ☑
☿ ev. day except Mon. 8.30am–12 noon 2.30pm–6.30pm; cl. Jan. Feb.

DOM. MEILLAN-PAGES
Sauvignon 2002★

	1.57 ha	6,000	∎ ↓	3–5 €

Jean-Pierre Pagès offers this fruity and harmonious Sauvignon 2002 whose only flaw is a certain lack of length. This notwithstanding, the Jury also singled out the supple structure of the same domaine's **Cabernet Sauvignon red 2001.**

🡒 Jean-Pierre Pagès, Dom. Meillan-Pagès, quartier La Garrigue, 84580 Oppède, tel. 04.32.52.17.50, fax 04.90.76.94.78, e-mail meillan@terre-net.fr ☑
☿ ev. day 10am–8pm

Wines selected but not starred

DOM. DU COULET ROUGE
Cabernet 2002

	2 ha	8,000	∎ ↓	5–8 €

🡒 Bonnelly & Fils, Dom. du Coulet Rouge, Les Bâtiments Neufs, 84220 Roussillon, tel. 04.90.05.61.40, fax 04.90.05.61.40 ☑
☿ ev. day 8am–12 noon 1.30pm–7pm

LASKAR 2001

	4 ha	15,114	∎ ↓	3–5 €

🡒 SCA les Vins de Sylla, 178, quartier du Viaduc, BP 141, 84405 Apt Cedex, tel. 04.90.74.05.39, fax 04.90.04.72.06 ☑
☿ by appt.

DOM. DE LA VERRIERE
Viognier Elevé en fût de chêne 2002

	1.25 ha	5,300	◗	5–8 €

🡒 Jacques Maubert, Dom. de La Verrière, 84220 Goult, tel. 04.90.72.20.88, fax 04.90.72.40.33, e-mail laverriere2@wanadoo.fr ☑
☿ ev. day except Sun. 9am–12 noon 2pm–6pm

Alpes et Pays Rhodaniens

This region extends from Auvergne to the Alps and includes the eight *départements* of the Rhône-Alpes and the Puy-de-Dôme. The terroir is thus exceptionally disparate, a factor which in itself results in a wide range of regional wines. Burgundy grape varieties (Pinot, Gamay, Chardonnay) grow side-by-side with southern varieties such as Grenache, Cinsault and Clairette, not to mention other regional varieties such as Syrah, Roussanne and Marsanne in the Rhône Valley, together with Mondeuse, Jacquère or Chasselas in Savoie, and Etraire de la Dui and Verdesse (oddball varieties from the Val d'Isère). Bordeaux grape varieties have also entered the region, notably Merlot, Cabernets and Sauvignons, further expanding and enriching the range of vines now present.

Production is on the increase and is approaching 400,000 hl, whereby Ardèche and Drôme produce the majority of the reds. The five departmental designations are those of Ain, Ardèche, Drôme, Isère and Puy-de-Dôme; the eight further regional denominations are Allobrogie (Savoie and Ain, 7,000 hl of predominantly white wines), Coteaux du Grésivaudan (central Isère, 1,500 hl), Balmes Dauphinoises (Isère, 1,000 hl), Urfé (Loire Valley between Forez and Roannais, 2,000 hl), Collines Rhodaniennes (20,000 hl, mostly reds), Comté de Grignan (southwest of Drôme, 25,000 hl, principally reds), Coteaux des Baronnies (southeast of Drôme, 25,000 hl, reds only) and Coteaux de l'Ardèche (300,000 hl of reds, whites and rosés).

In addition to the above come two regional *vin de pays* designations: Vin de Pays des Comtés Rhodaniens (about 5,000 hl) – which can perhaps also be produced in the eight Rhône-Alpes *départements* (Ain, Ardèche, Drôme, Isère, Loire, Rhône, Savoie, Haute-Savoie); and a Vin de Pays Portes de Méditerranée, which applies to the Provence-Alpes-Côte d'Azur (PACA) region and to Drôme and Ardèche.

The Jury awarded its *coup de coeur* to this remarkable and beautifully pale-yellow Jacquère 2002 elaborated by the Demeure-Pinet estate. The wine exudes delicate and subtle aromas of white flowers, honey, apricot and lime. It is fresh, lively and slightly sparkling on the palate, with a broad palette of flavours ranging from citrus fruits to new-mown grass. This is a highly-accomplished and true-to-type Jacquère that will do full justice to freshwater fish. From this estate also, the Jury selected a **Chardonnay 2002 (3–5 €)** which proved to be a very well-balanced and attractively rounded wine that holds on the palate with flavours of ripe white fruit.

🕿 Le cellier de Joudin, Dom. Demeure-Pinet-Joudin, 73240 Saint-Genix-sur-Guiers, tel. 04.76.31.61.74, fax 04.76.31.61.74 ☑

🍽 ev. day except Sun. pm

Ardèche

DOM. DE CHAMPAL
Viognier Arzelle 2002★★

	3.7 ha	8,000	⬛ 🍸	8–11 €

The Domaine de Champal has produced this most promising of Viogniers, an Arzelle 2002 with a pale-white robe and points of silver. This harmonious wine gives off aromas of flowers and white fruit. It is still young however, and will benefit from a year in the cellar before being enjoyed with a spring salad.

🕿 Eric Rocher, Dom. de Champal, quartier Champal, 07370 Sarras, tel. 04.78.34.21.21, fax 04.78.34.30.60, e-mail vignobles-rocher@wanadoo.fr ☑

🍽 by appt.

DOM. DU CHATEAU VIEUX 2001★

	0.09 ha	900	⬛⬛	5–8 €

This estate has been a standard-bearer of winemaking in the Drôme for no less than five generations. This 2001 from the cellars of the 18th century Domaine Château Vieux comes in the guise of a most handsome Syrah matured in oak casks, a decidedly individualistic wine with a dark-red robe and a nose that exudes aromas of ripe fruit. On the palate, flavours of spice and hints of vanilla make their presence felt against a backdrop of fine, elegant and softening tannins. A wine to be discovered in conjunction with poultry – *poularde à la vanille* perhaps?

🕿 Fabrice Rousset, Le Château Vieux, 26750 Triors, tel. 04.75.45.31.65, fax 04.75.71.45.35, e-mail domainechateauvieux@chez.com ☑

🍽 by appt.

Allobrogie

DOM. DEMEURE-PINET
Jacquère 2002★★

	3.5 ha	30,000	⬛ 🍸	–3 €

Collines Rhodaniennes

Wines selected but not starred

CAVE DE TAIN L'HERMITAGE
Marsanne Nobles Rives 2002

	n.c.	105,000	⬛ 🍸	3–5 €

🕿 Cave de Tain-l'Hermitage, 22, rte de Larnage, BP 3, 26601 Tain-l'Hermitage Cedex, tel. 04.75.08.20.87, fax 04.75.07.15.16, e-mail commercial.france@cave-tain-hermitage.com ☑

🍽 by appt.

Comté de Grignan

Wine selected but not starred

CAVE DE LA VALDAINE
Cabernet-Sauvignon 2002

■	36.32 ha	6,600	■ ↓	–3 €

↩ SCA Cave de la Valdaine, av. Max-Dormoy, 26160 Saint-Gervais-sur-Roubion, tel. 04.75.53.80.08, fax 04.75.53.93.90, e-mail cave.valdaine@free.fr ☑
⏳ by appt.

Coteaux de l'Ardèche

CAVE COOPERATIVE D'ALBA
Pinot noir Sélection 2001★

■	2 ha	10,000	■ ⬛ ↓	5–8 €

This cellar cooperative is one of 27 in the Ardèche, whose winemakers have an undisputed reputation for quality. This carefully thought-out Pinot Noir Sélection 2001 comes with a ruby robe with points of violet, and a pungent nose commingling kirsch, cherry, gingerbread and vanilla aromas. The wine retains these flavours on the palate, which is supple yet robust, with closed tannins. This is a wine that will come into its own in the company of cold-cut specialties from the Ardèche region.
↩ Cave coop. d'Alba, La Planchette, 07400 Alba-la-Romaine, tel. 04.75.52.40.23, fax 04.75.52.48.76, e-mail cave.alba@free.fr ☑
⏳ ev. day except Sun. 9am–12 noon 1.30pm–6pm; summer 2pm–7pm

LES VIGNERONS ARDECHOIS
Viognier Prestige 2001★★

■	n.c.	n.c.	3–5 €

CUVÉE PRESTIGE

VIOGNIER

VIN DE PAYS DES COTEAUX DE L'ARDÈCHE

2001

14% vol. MIS EN BOUTEILLE PAR LES VIGNERONS ARDECHOIS 75 cl
VIGNERONS RÉCOLTANTS - RUOMS ARDECHE, FRANCE
ET 6025 PRODUIT DE FRANCE

The Vignerons Ardéchois unite under their banner 25 cooperatives in the Ardèche region and can confidently claim to have met the challenge first thrown down some 30 years ago, namely to put quality wines from the region firmly on the map. This Viognier Prestige 2001 demonstrates clearly and yet again that their confidence is not misplaced. This remarkable wine fully merits the Jury's *coup de coeur*: pungent, balanced and full of pedigree, it gives off delightful aromas of peach and apricot, and exhibits excellent length and body on the palate. One star was awarded to the **Merlot Prestige 2001**, which the Jury adjudged to be harmonious, elegantly

powerful and with an attractive nose permutating red fruit aromas with floral and balsamic notes.
↩ Les Vignerons Ardéchois, quartier Chaussy, 07120 Ruoms, tel. 04.75.39.98.00, fax 04.75.39.69.48, e-mail uvica@uvica.fr
⏳ by appt.

DOM. DE BOURNET
Cuvée Chris 2000★★

■	6 ha	12,000	⬛	8–11 €

A magnificent 17th century *mas* situated among the gorges of the Ardèche lies at the hub of the family-owned domaine which routinely turns out highly original wines full of character. The Cuvée Chris 2000 is a blend of Cabernet Sauvignon and Merlot matured in oak cask for 12 months, a seductive wine with a deep-red robe, an expressive nose of spices and mineral notes, and a perfect overall balance and power. This is a wine that can be laid down almost indefinitely.
↩ GAEC Dom. de Bournet, 07120 Grospierres, tel. 04.75.39.68.20, fax 04.75.39.06.96, e-mail domaine.debournet@advalvas.be ☑
⏳ ev. day 9am–12 noon 2pm–6pm

GRAND ARDECHE
Chardonnay 2001★★

■	50 ha	250,000	⬛	8–11 €

The celebrated Burgundy house of Louis Latour opted in 1979 for the Ardèche as an appropriate area in which to produce top-of-the-range Chardonnay *vins de pays*. The gamble has paid off, due in no small part to redoubtable Latour expertise and knowhow. This Chardonnay 2001 is a shining example: an inordinately rich wine matured for ten months in oak casks to yield a pungent yet elegant nose, with subtle notes of spice, vanilla, exotic fruits and honey. A thoroughbred in every sense, powerful and fleshy, which should be cellared for at least two years before being enjoyed with a fillet of turbot or grilled fowl.
↩ Maison Louis Latour, La Téoule, 07400 Alba-la-Romaine, tel. 04.75.52.45.66, fax 04.75.52.87.99 ☑

DOM. DES LOUANES
L'Encre de Sy 2002★★

■	1.23 ha	800	■ ⬛ ↓	5–8 €

This family-owned estate in the commune of Balazuc is run on organic lines. The Encre de Sy 2002 is a Syrah grape variety that boasts a dark-red, virtually black robe with points of violet and a nose bursting with aromas of ripe fruit. A powerful and well-balanced wine that promises to age well over the next one to three years before being served to accompany game dishes.
↩ Jérôme Poudevigne, Les Louanes, 07120 Balazuc, tel. 04.75.37.75.09, fax 04.75.37.75.09, e-mail claforet@netcourrier.com ☑
⏳ by appt.

MAS DE BAGNOLS
Chardonnay 2002★

■	0.66 ha	2,500	⬛	5–8 €

This golden-yellow Chardonnay 2002 comes from the family-owned Mas de Bagnols estate situated near the medieval village of Vinezac. The nose is pleasant and well-advanced, with mineral notes and aromas of fruit and spices. On the palate, the wine reveals its true aromatic complexity, juxtaposing nuances of dried fruit, spices and ripe fruit. A fresh and rounded wine that will go well with, for example, grilled fish.
↩ Pierre Mollier, Mas de Bagnols, 07110 Vinezac, tel. 04.75.36.83.10, fax 04.75.36.98.04 ☑
⏳ ev. day except Sun. 8am–12 noon 2pm–6pm

MAS D'INTRAS
Cabernet-sauvignon 2000★★

■	1.6 ha	13,000	■	5–8 €

"Powerful", "robust" and "expressive" are the epithets that spring to mind in the case of this Cabernet Sauvignon 2000 with its concentrated aromas of spices and musk. A wine to be enjoyed with a boar stew. The Jury also selected the estate's

Syrah 2001, which delivers aromas of stewed red fruit and tastes full and fleshy on the palate. It is awarded a star, as is the Grenache-based **Cuvée Trace Nègre**.
➤ Denis and Emmanuel Robert, Mas d'Intras, 07400 Valvignères, tel. 04.75.52.75.36, fax 04.75.52.51.62, e-mail contact@masdintras.fr ☑
🍷 ev. day 9.30am–12 noon 1.30pm–6.30pm; Sun. 1.30pm–6.30pm

Wines selected but not starred

CAVE COOPERATIVE DE MONTFLEURY Syrah 2002

■	30 ha	58,000	▮	–3 €

➤ Cave coop. de Montfleury, quartier gare, 07170 Villeneuve-de-Berg, tel. 04.75.94.82.76, fax 04.75.94.89.45 ☑
🍷 by appt.

CAVE COOP. DE VALVIGNERES

Viognier 2002

■	50 ha	10,000	▮ ♦	–3 €

➤ Cave coop. de Valvignères, quartier Auvergne, 07400 Valvignères, tel. 04.75.52.60.60, fax 04.75.52.60.33, e-mail cave.valvigneres@free.fr ☑
🍷 by appt.

Coteaux des Baronnies

DOM. DU RIEU FRAIS

Cabernet-sauvignon Cuvée Alexandre 2000★★

■	3 ha	19,000	▥	5–8 €

From his vantage in this magnificent Provençal domaine, Jean-Yves Liotaud brings 20 years of experience to bear in this distinguished Cabernet Sauvignon-based Cuvée Alexandre 2000. The robe is dark red with points of blue, the nose both discreet and complex, with aromas of peppers and spices, and the palate detects elegant soft tannins which commingle with spice and ripe-fruit flavours. This balanced and elegant vintage goes perfectly with game dishes or a strong cheese.
➤ Jean-Yves Liotaud, quartier du Rieux-Frais, 26110 Sainte-Jalle, tel. 04.75.27.31.54, fax 04.75.27.34.47, e-mail jean-yves.liotaud@wanadoo.fr ☑
🍷 ev. day 9am–12 noon 2pm–6pm; cl. Sun. Nov.-Feb.

DOM. LA ROSIERE

Merlot 2001★★

■	5 ha	20,000	▮ ♦	3–5 €

This dark-garnet Merlot 2001 from the Domaine La Rosière near the feudal village of Rochebrune was enthusiastically received by the Jury on account of its excellent pedigree and structure, together with its plethora of concentrated aromas ranging from blueberries to blackcurrants by way of mineral notes and spices. The wine tastes round and fleshy on the palate, with flavours of black fruit and musk. Balanced and exceptionally harmonious, this is a wine to be enjoyed with a serving of grilled beef.
➤ EARL Serge Liotaud et Fils, Dom. La Rosière, 26110 Sainte-Jalle, tel. 04.75.27.30.36, fax 04.75.27.33.69, e-mail vliotaud@yahoo.fr ☑ 🏠
🍷 ev. day 9am–7pm

DOM. DE ROUSTILLAN

Cuvée fruitée 2001★

■	15 ha	n.c.	▮	3–5 €

The Domaine de Roustillan can boast of 25 years' experience of organic cultivation. The deep garnet-red 2001, made from an assembly of Grenache, Merlot, Gamay and Syrah grape varieties, is aromatically complex, commingling red fruits with traces of vanilla. The wine opens on a note of fresh fruit. Balanced and robust, it is perhaps best suited to being drunk as an accompaniment to game dishes.
➤ Frédéric Alaïmo, Dom. de Roustillan, 26170 La Penne-sur-Ouréze, tel. 04.75.28.09.58, fax 04.75.28.12.49, e-mail domaine.de.roustillan@wanadoo.fr ☑
🍷 ev. day 10am–2pm 3pm–7pm; Sun. 3pm–7pm

Drôme

DOM. LE PLAN 2001★

■	1.77 ha	16,000	▮	5–8 €

Dirk Vermeersch works from an 18th century Provençal farmhouse to produce this intense 2001 red with its pronounced aromas of ripe red fruit and spices. The wine emerges balanced and rounded on the palate, with flavours of stewed red fruit against a background of softened tannins. A wine to be reserved for grilled meat dishes.
➤ Dom. Le Plan-Vermeersch, Le Plan, 26790 Tulette, tel. 04.75.98.36.84, e-mail dva@domaine-leplan.com ☑ 🏠 🏠
🍷 ev. day 10am–12 noon 3pm–6pm; cl. 11 Nov.–31 Mar.

The East

Т he modest remnants of vines decimated by phylloxera in the 19th century are to be found in this area of France. These are vines that had their hour of glory – or glory reflected, as it happens, from their prestigious neighbours in Burgundy and in Champagne. Grape varieties from those two regions are still cultivated here, together with vines originating in Alsace and the Jura. For the most part, these are vinified singly and, as a result, generally reflect the individual character of their provenance: Auxerrois, Chardonnay, Pinot Noir, Gamay or Pinot Gris.

V ins de pays from Franche-Comté, Meuse, Saône-et-Loire, Haute-Marne or Yonne are all, virtually without exception, light, fresh and aromatic; although yields are increasing, notably in respect of white wine varieties, total annual production still stands at around a mere 9,000 hl, of which whites represent 5,000 hl and reds 3,000 hl.

Coteaux de l'Auxois

VIGNOBLE DE FLAVIGNY
Chardonnay Fût de chêne 2001★★

	2.5 ha	5,000	🍷	5–8 €

It is only ten years since the first stocks were planted here in this 15-ha vineyard at Flavigny in the Côte d'Or where, once upon a time, the slopes bristled with vines. What better way to celebrate this renaissance then, than with this Chardonnay 2001, an unctuous buttered-toast of a wine which opens fresh and subsequently releases flavours of honey and almonds? Also recommended is an **Auxerrois 2002 (3–5 €)** with attractive notes of quince and a rounded body.
🔻 Ida Nel, SCEA Vignoble de Flavigny, Dom. du Pont Laizan, 21150 Flavigny-sur-Ozerain, tel. 03.80.96.25.63, fax 03.80.96.25.63,
e-mail vignoble-de-flavigny@wanadoo.fr ☑
♈ by appt.

VILLAINES-LES-PRÉVOTES-VISERNY
Cuvée Tradition 2002★

	n.c.	n.c.	🍷	3–5 €

Intrepid pioneering winemakers settled here between Semur and Montbard in the Côte d'Or and planted speculative vines that are now starting to yield good results as this yellow-robed and modestly aromatic blend of Chardonnay (60%), Pinot Gris (25%) and Auxerrois (15%) demonstrates. Suggestions of fruit emerge on the palate as the different grape varieties gradually release their respective flavours. A full and well-structured wine.
🔻 SA des coteaux de Villaines-les-Prévôtes-Viserny, 21500 Villaines-les-Prévôtes, tel. 03.80.96.71.95, fax 03.80.96.71.95,
e-mail vins.villainesviserny@wanadoo.fr ☑
♈ by appt.

Coteaux de Coiffy

LES COTEAUX DE COIFFY
Auxerrois 2002★

	4 ha	15,000	🍷	3–5 €

These vines grow in Haute-Marne, not far from the thermal baths of Bourbonne-les-Bains. After half a century of enforced hibernation, this 15-ha vineyard has re-emerged and is gradually starting to make its mark. The golden-yellow Auxerrois 2002 appeals to the eye, nose and palate. Fruit aromas predominate, together with a hint of mint, and sustain on the palate in a wine that opens lively and rounds out well. The vineyard's **Pinot Gris 2002** was also selected on the strength of its ripe fruit flavours.
🔻 Renaut-Camus, SCEA les Coteaux de Coiffy, 52400 Coiffy-le-Haut, tel. 03.25.84.80.12, fax 03.25.90.18.84, e-mail renautlaurent@aol.com ☑
♈ ev. day 2.30pm–6pm

Franche-Comté

VIGNOBLE GUILLAUME
Chardonnay Collection Réservée 2001★★

	1 ha	5,000	🍷	15–23 €

Back in the Middle Ages, this vineyard in the Haute-Saône belonged to the archbishops of Besançon. The Guillaume family – in the wine business since the 18th century – now cultivates this 33-ha property and also grows vinestocks for export to the four corners of the world. The Jury enjoyed a cask-matured **Pinot Noir Collection Réservée** and felt it worthy of a star, but waxed eloquent over this Chardonnay 2001 with its brilliantly clear and consistent colour and bouquet of honey and brioche. Wood flavours are still present after time spent in the cask, but toasted notes assert themselves on the palate and a hint of sparkle lifts this mature, well-rounded and concentrated vintage.
🔻 Vignoble Guillaume, rte de Gy, 70700 Charcenne, tel. 03.84.32.80.55, fax 03.84.32.84.06,
e-mail vignoble.guillaume@wanadoo.fr ☑
♈ by appt.

PASCAL HENRIOT

Auxerrois Coteaux de Champlitte 2001★

| ■ | 1.5 ha | 3,300 | ■ | 3–5 € |

Champlitte in the Haute-Saône near the Côte d'Or is a monument to rural tradition, exemplified by its most attractive museum of country life and, not least, by the vines that were replanted here some 30 years ago by Pascal Henriot, a wine-grower who works organically under the watchful eye of Ecocert. Pascal is to be congratulated on this excellent light-gold Auxerrois 2001 with an expressive nose of ripe fruit and subtle suggestions of honey. In short, an attractively-textured wine with pronounced aromatic qualities.

↦ Pascal Henriot, 5, rue des Capucins, 70600 Champlitte, tel. 03.84.67.68.85, e-mail pascal.henriot2@wanadoo.fr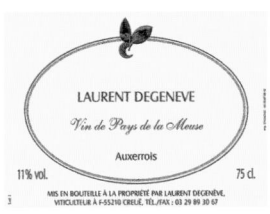
⟟ by appt.

Haute-Marne

LE MUID MONTSAUGEONNAIS

Pinot noir Elevé en fût de chêne 2001★★★

| ■ | 1.9 ha | 14,200 | ◫ | 5–8 € |

Vaux-sous-Aubigny nestles on the plateau of Langres in the south of the Haute-Marne not far from the Côte d'Or. The townspeople of Vaux and neighbouring Montsaugeon pooled resources in 1988 in a bid to breathe new life into this former vineyard: 12 hectares of vines now under cultivation yield excellent results, never more so than in the case of this absolutely marvellous Pinot Noir 2001. With its impeccable garnet-red robe and complex and refined nose redolent of Morello cherries and myrtilles, this 2001 tastes full, concentrated and pungent on the palate, building to an irreproachably solid structure with perceptible yet restrained tannins. The estate's vat-matured **Pinot Noir 2002 Elevé en Cuve**, boasts a robustness that augurs well.

↦ Le Muid Montsaugeonnais, 23, av. de Bourgogne, 52190 Vaux-sous-Aubigny, tel. 03.25.90.04.65, fax 03.25.90.04.65, e-mail muidmontsaugeonnais@wanadoo.fr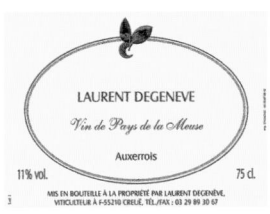
⟟ by appt.

Meuse

L'AUMONIERE

Vin gris 2002★

| ■ | n.c. | 4,600 | ■ | –3 € |

Auxerrois, Chardonnay and Pinot Noir grape varieties make up this *ménage à trois* from a 5.6-ha property near Lac de Madine. The light salmon-pink robe of this Vin Gris 2002 gives little away, but the wine emerges as both aromatic and flavourful, soft and fruity on the palate and with a sustained finish. The vineyard itself was established as recently as 1984; on the strength of this 2002, however, it is already making its mark.

↦ L'Aumonière, Viéville-sous-les-Côtes, 55210 Vigneulles-les-Hattonchâtel, tel. 03.29.89.31.64, fax 03.29.90.00.92

DOM. DE COUSTILLE

Gris 2002★★

| ■ | 1 ha | 5,200 | ■ | 3–5 € |

From the 7-ha Domaine de Coustille comes this blend of Gamay, Pinot Noir and Auxerrois grape varieties (in decreasing order of importance) which has yielded a dark-pink Gris 2002 which is admirably round from robe to aftertaste. This is a very agreeable wine indeed – well-structured, fruity and uncommonly persistent on the palate.

↦ N. Philippe, SCEA de Coustille, 23, Grand-Rue, 55300 Buxerulles, tel. 03.29.89.33.81, fax 03.29.90.01.88, e-mail n.philippe@domaine-de-coustille.com
⟟ by appt.

LAURENT DEGENEVE

Auxerrois 2002★★

| ■ | 0.5 ha | 3,800 | ■ ⬥ | 3–5 € |

Two wines were selected – a typically limpid, salmon-pink **Gris 2002** with good aromas and a convincing structure on the palate, and this Auxerrois 2002, a white wine with a pale-yellow robe with points of green, that is richly aromatic and tastes somewhat exotic on the palate, where flavours of grapefruit and lime sustain through to a long and balanced finish.

↦ Laurent Degenève, 7, rue des Lavoirs, 55210 Creuë, tel. 03.29.89.30.67, fax 03.29.89.30.67, e-mail laurent.degeneve@wanadoo.fr
⟟ by appt.

DOM. DE LA GOULOTTE

Gris 2002★

| ■ | 1 ha | 7,000 | ■ | 3–5 € |

A slice of quiche Lorraine would probably go down well in the company of this pink-tinged Gris 2002 from the Meuse. Red fruit aromas reflect the wine's blend of Gamay (80%) and Auxerrois grape varieties. This selection boasts a liveliness on the palate, extending into a most creditable finish. The 5-ha Goulotte domaine has, over the years, passed through more winemaking hands than the present family cares to count.

↦ Philippe Antoine, EARL Dom. de la Goulotte, 6, rue de l'Eglise, 55210 Saint-Maurice, tel. 03.29.89.38.31, fax 03.29.90.01.80
⟟ by appt.

DOM. DE MUZY

Pinot Noir 2001★

| ■ | 2 ha | 8,000 | ◫ | 3–5 € |

This Pinot Noir 2001 comes from a village that was totally destroyed during the Second World War and subsequently had to be rebuilt in its entirety. Jean-Marc Liénhard has followed in his grandfather's footsteps as a vintner and distiller (of mirabelle, naturally). His **Auxerrois 2002** was awarded one star in recognition of its fresh citrus flavours and overall structure and roundness, and his **Vin Gris 2002** was also selected. That said, the Jury came out in favour of this rich ruby-red Pinot with a peppery nose and pleasing wood notes. An ample, fleshy wine with soft tannins, seemingly predestined to be served with jugged hare.

↦ Véronique et Jean-Marc Liénard, Dom. de Muzy, 3, rue de Muzy, 55160 Combres-sous-les-Côtes, tel. 03.29.87.37.81, fax 03.29.87.35.00, e-mail muzylienard@wanadoo.fr
⟟ by appt.

Sainte-Marie-la-Blanche

Wine selected but not starred

Yonne

Wine selected but not starred

BLANCHE
Chardonnay 2001

| | 2.5 ha | 26,000 | ▮ ⚬ | 3–5 € |

🔑 Les Caves des Hautes-Côtes, rte de Pommard,
21200 Beaune, tel. 03.80.25.01.00, fax 03.80.22.87.05,
e-mail vinchc@wanadoo.fr ☑
🍷 by appt.

DOM. LA FONTAINE AUX MUSES
Pinot noir 2002

| | 0.5 ha | 3,000 | ▮ | 5–8 € |

🔑 Vincent Pointeau-Langevin, La Fontaine aux Muses,
89116 La Celle-Saint-Cyr, tel. 03.86.73.40.22,
fax 03.86.73.48.66, e-mail fontaineauxmuses@aol.com ☑
🍷 by appt.

GLOSSARY

1er Cru. See "Premier Cru".

Acerbic. Describes a wine made tart and sour from having far too much tannin and acidity. A very serious defect.

Acidity. In moderation, acidity helps the balance of a wine, giving it freshness and vigour. But if there is too much, it is a defect, making the wine biting and sour. Too little, however, and the wine will be flabby and lacking in grip.

Aggressive. A wine that is too strong (usually in tannins) and attacks the palate in an unpleasant way.

Agreeable. A pleasant, nicely balanced wine in every respect.

Alcohol. The next largest component of wine after water, ethyl alcohol gives wine its warming character. But if there is too much, the wine is said to be hot.

Alcoholic strength. This is generally expressed in degrees or per cent corresponding to the alcoholic content of the wine by volume.

Aligoté. White grape variety used for making Bourgogne Aligoté, an everyday wine to be drunk young.

Altesse. White grape variety used to make very fine Roussette de Savoie.

Amber. If white wines are aged for a long time or are oxidised prematurely, they sometimes take on an amber colour.

Amigne. Traditional white grape variety grown in tiny quantities in the Valais, Switzerland, making dry and sweet wines of high quality.

Ampelography. The study of vine varieties, especially grape vines.

Ample. Term for a harmonious wine which appears to fill the mouth well.

Amylic. Smell of amyl acetate, similar to pear-drops, banana or bubble-gum. Usually detected on young white or rosé wines that are made using cool fermentation, or on reds made with carbonic maceration.

Animal. Smells evoking the animal kingdom: musk, venison, leather. Mostly found in old red wines.

AOC. Appellation d'Origine Contrôlée. A regulatory system which guarantees the authenticity of a wine made in a particular area. Almost all the great wines come from AOC regions.

Aroma. In the technical language of wine-tasting, this term is used for olfactory sensations perceived in the nose and, sometimes, on the palate. It is particularly used for the simple fruit smells of young wines to differentiate from "bouquet", which is used for smells of more mature wines. The adjective "aromatic" may describe a generally pleasant smell. See also "Bouquet".

Arvine. See "Petite Arvine".

Assemblage. A blending of several lots of wine from the same area to obtain the desired final blend. Term used in particular in Champagne for the blending of the base wine *cuvées*, and in Bordeaux for the final blending for the Grand Vin or main Château wine.

Astringency. A rather rough, rasping taste or, technically, a tactile sensation around the gums and on the roof of the mouth. It is often found in young red wines having more tannin than fruit.

Auxerrois. White grape variety used to make Alsace Klevner; the name is also a synonym for the red Malbec variety in Cahors.

Balanced. Describes a wine with a good balance of acidity and sweetness in whites, or tannin and fruit in red wines.

Balsamic. Used to describe smells evoking the world of perfume, including, among others, vanilla, incense, resin and benzine.

Balthasar. Very large bottle containing the equivalent of 16 ordinary bottles (12 litres).

Barrique. Barrel or cask, usually made of oak; it generally refers to a barrel of around 225 l as traditionally used in Bordeaux, and now increasingly elsewhere.

Bâtonnage. Stirring the yeast in a barrel with a pole or baton. Particularly used for fine barrel-fermented whites.

Bitartrate deposit. Technical term for the deposit of tartaric acid crystals, often known simply as tartrates and sometimes found in bottled wines.

Bitterness. Caused by tannins overwhelming the fruit. Bitterness can be an advance warning of astringency, which can soften out, while bitterness is an abiding fault.

Blanc Fumé. Name given to Sauvignon at Pouilly-sur-Loire, where the Pouilly-Fumé appellation comes from (not to be confused with Pouilly-Fuissé from Burgundy, which is made from the Chardonnay grape).

Blend. May refer to a wine made from more than one grape variety, or a wine from grapes sourced in different vineyards, or in Champagne, for example, wine produced from different vintages. It may also be used simply to refer to a selected wine from a producer or estate that may make more than one wine. See also "cuvée".

Blending. The mixing together of different lots of wines; see also "Assemblage" and "Blend".

Body. Characteristic of a well-structured, warming and fleshy wine.

Botrytis cinerea. A fungus which attacks the skins of grapes. Although detrimental to red grape varieties, it can be beneficial for certain whites given certain climatic conditions. In such cases it concentrates the sugars and flavours of the grape enabling the great sweet wines to be made. See also "Noble rot".

Botrytised. Grapes that have been affected by *botrytis cinerea* or noble rot.

Bouquet. Smells sensed by the nose while sniffing wine in the glass. Technically used to refer to the smells in more mature wines that emerge as the wine ages. This differentiates it from "aroma", which is used for smells in younger wines. See also "Aroma".

Bourboulenc. Medium-quality white grape variety from the Rhône Valley and southern France.

Breton. Name given to Cabernet Franc in the Loire Valley.

Brilliant. Said of wine having a very bright or brilliant colour which glints strongly in the light.

Burning. Describes a wine containing too much or an excessive balance of alcohol, leaving a burning sensation in the mouth.

Burnt. Sometimes ambiguous term for smells ranging from caramel to burnt wood, usually associated with ageing in oak.

Brut. Term for dry sparkling wines and champagnes containing very little sweetness (just enough to temper the wine's acidity); "Extra Brut" or, in French, *brut zéro* means there is virtually no added sugar, giving a very dry sparkling wine.

Cabernet Franc. Red grape variety blended with Cabernet Sauvignon and/or Merlot in Bordeaux, also the main quality red grape in the Loire Valley. It is capable of producing a very fine wine for long-term keeping.

Cabernet Sauvignon. Noble red grape variety predominant in the Médoc and Graves regions of Bordeaux, also used elsewhere in South West and southern France and producing wines for long-term keeping.

Carbonic maceration. Method of vinifying red wine by macerating whole grapes in vats saturated with carbon dioxide. It is used mainly to produce wines to be drunk very young (Vins de Primeur) and is widely used in Beaujolais.

Carignan. Red grape variety from southern France producing very well-structured, robust wines.

Casse. Fault in wine caused by oxidation or chemical reduction which makes wine lose its clarity.

Chai. Winery located on the ground floor in regions where they do not dig out underground cellars, especially in the Médoc region of Bordeaux.

Chaptalization. The addition of sugar to fermenting must to obtain a more robust wine by increasing its richness in alcohol when this is too weak; this process is subject to legal controls.

Chardonnay. Noble white grape variety from Burgundy, also grown in other regions such as Jura. It produces fine wines likely to age well. It is also a key grape variety for champagne and other sparkling wines.

Chasselas. White grape variety grown chiefly as a table grape but also used for making dry wine (in Switzerland, Alsace and Savoie).

Château. Term often used to describe a wine estate even though – sometimes – it does not contain a real château.

Chenin or Chenin Blanc. White grape variety very common in the Loire Valley, producing fine, balanced wines likely to keep well.

Cinsaut or Cinsault. Red grape variety from the Rhône Valley and South of France which makes very fruity wines.

Clairet. Light, fruity red wine, or dark rosé wine produced in Bordeaux.

Clairette. White grape variety from the Rhône Valley and South of France producing fairly fine dry and sparkling wines.

Claret. English term for red wine from Bordeaux.

Clarification. Separating the sediment from grape juice or wine; see also "Filtration" and "Fining".

Clavelin. Unusually shaped bottle holding 62 cl and used for the Vins Jaunes or yellow wines of the Jura.

Climat. In Burgundy, refers to an area characterized by soil type and micro-climate.

Clonal selection (of vines). A contemporary method of selection and propagating vines from the strongest or most disease-resistant plants in a vineyard. New plantings are increasingly with clonally selected vines.

Clone. Group of vinestocks grown from cuttings that have been multiplied from a single parent stock.

Clos. Term used in some regions, especially Burgundy, to describe an enclosed vineyard usually surrounded by walls (e.g. Clos de Vougeot).

Colombard. White grape variety from the South West of France, producing fairly ordinary, everyday wines.

Cornalin. Obscure red grape variety grown in the Valais, Switzerland.

Cot or Côt. Name given to the Malbec grape variety in the Loire Valley.

Coulure. Poor fruit set following wet or windy weather resulting in the fruit (as small, unformed berries) falling off after flowering.

Corked. A wine suffering from a tainted smell and taste from a faulty cork. The typical smell is musty, mousy or corky.

Crémant. Sparkling AOC wine.

Cru. French term for a vineyard, often translated as "growth". The meaning of this term varies from region to region and may be linked to a quality system. See also "Premier Cru" and "Grand Cru". It may be used to denote certain superior areas of vineyards, e.g., the Beaujolais crus such as Juliénas or Fleurie. May also be used loosely to mean a particular wine.

Cru Bourgeois. Classification for châteaux in the Médoc region of Bordeaux which is below that of the 1855 classification.

Crushing. The process of breaking up the grape skins to extract the juice.

Cuve. Vat, tun or tank used for the fermentation and storage of wine.

Cuvée. Literally, the produce from one vat but is generally a very loose French term to imply a selected wine from a producer or estate that may make more than one wine.

Decant. To transfer a wine from its bottle into a carafe or decanter to separate the wine from its sediment and allow the wine to breathe.

Dégorgement. See disgorgement.

Demi-sec. Medium dry, for still wines. For a sparkling wine, the term means medium-sweet.

De-stemming. Removing the stems or stalks from the grapes. If grapes are not de-stemmed, they can give wine a certain astringency.

Deposit. Solid particles in a wine, particularly in old wines, which are removed by decanting before the wine is served.

Diolinoir. Red grape crossing giving deep-coloured wines and grown in Switzerland, mainly in the canton of Vaud. Sometimes used in a blend.

Disgorgement. The act of expelling the sediment caused by the secondary fermentation in the bottle of sparkling wine. This is followed immediately by topping up and insertion of the final cork.

Dosage. French term for the sweetened wine added to a sparkling wine or champagne after the yeast deposit has been removed. The level of dosage determines the final style, e.g., Doux, Demi-sec or Brut.

Doux. Term applied to sweet wines rich in sugar and to highly dosed wines in Champagne.

Dry. In still wines, describes a wine with virtually no residual sweetness (less than 4g/l); on the sweetness scale of sparkling wines, it means having little sugar (between 17 and 35g/l), which gives a medium-dry taste.

Duras. Red grape variety mainly produced in Gaillac in South West France. (Not to be confused with the appellation of the same name.)

Eau-de-vie. Brandy i.e. distilled product from grapes or other fruit.

Echelle des crus. Term used in Champagne for the classification or grading of Premier and Grand Cru vineyards.

Empyreumatic. Term for smells recalling things burnt, cooked or smoked.

Espalier. Rare method of training vines.

Fat. Synonym for mellow or unctuous.

Feminine. Said of wines suggesting tenderness and lightness.

Fer or Fer Servadou. Red grape variety used to make wines for long-term keeping in South West France.

Fermentation. Process by which grape juice becomes wine through the action of yeasts which turn the grape sugar into alcohol.

Fillette. Small bottle holding 35 cl, used in the Loire Valley.

Filtration. The process of filtering out deposits from must or wine to clarify it.

Finesse. Term for a wine that is delicate and elegant.

Fining. Process for clarifying wine by adding a coagulant (e.g. egg white, isinglass) which draws off particles still in suspension. These are subsequently filtered out.

Flavour. Overall sensation in the mouth imparted by a wine's taste and its aromas.

Flesh, fleshy. Said of a wine that gives an impression of fullness and density in the mouth, without any roughness.

Folle Blanche. White grape variety producing very fresh, lively wine (Gros Plant).

Foudre. Large oak barrel or cask of indeterminate size.

Foxy. Term for a smell given off by wine made from certain hybrid grape varieties.

Free-run juice. The juice of fermenting wine that runs freely from the vat, as opposed to the juice obtained by pressing the skins. (Only applies to red wines.)

Fresh. Said of a wine that is lightly but not excessively acid, and imparts a feeling of freshness or liveliness.

Full. Said of a wine which has the requisite qualities of a good wine and leaves a feeling of fullness in the mouth.

Fût. Small barrel, usually of new oak.

GAEC Family estate (this is a legal status for small, usually family-owned estates).

Gamay. Red grape variety, the only one permitted in Beaujolais, also grown widely in the Loire Valley. Makes a very fruity, lively wine.

Gamey. Tasting term used in a positive way for the smell of red wines that is reminiscent of the smell of various game birds or animals.

Garanoir. Red grape crossing grown in Switzerland, mainly in the cantons of Geneva and Vaud. Similar parentage to Gamaret.

Garrigue. Scrub or scrubland in southern France that is usually full of wild herbs such as thyme, mint and rosemary. When used as a tasting term, describes a particular flavour reminiscent of the smell of the garrigue and often found in red wines from the Rhône Valley or southern France.

Generic. Term having several applications but often describing a brand-name wine rather than a Cru or Château wine, sometimes directed in a derogatory way at regional appellations such as Bordeaux, Burgundy, etc.

Generous. Said of a wine that is ripe and strong in alcohol but not tiresomely so, as in a heady wine.

Gewurztraminer. Very aromatic white grape variety from Alsace.

Glycerol. A higher alcohol and by-product of fermentation. Present in most wines, it is found in greater concentration in botrytized wines. It adds to the sweetness and oiliness of a wine.

Goût de terroir. Literally the taste from (not of) the soil. The notion of terroir includes soil, climate and exposure. In modern terms, a *goût de terroir* refers to a wine that tastes of where it comes from. See also "Terroir".

Grafting. Method used since the phylloxera disaster whereby a vine is grafted onto a root-stock (usually American) resistant to the phylloxera plant louse.

Grains nobles. Grapes that have been affected by noble rot or *botrytis cinerea* and usually used to make a sweet wine. See also *Sélection de Grains Nobles*.

Grand Cru. Literally "Great Growth", usually left untranslated. Generally refers to the best category in the AOC classification systems that exist in Alsace and in Burgundy. Vineyards may be classified as Grand Cru (also in Champagne) and the wine made from grapes harvested in those vineyards may subsequently be called Grand Cru. The term is also used in various individual classification systems that exist in Bordeaux, and is incorporated into the AOC Saint-Emilion Grand Cru.

Grand Vin. Term used by the Crus Classés châteaux of Bordeaux to describe the first wine of the château, e.g. in Margaux, Château Margaux is the Grand Vin of that château and Le Pavillon Rouge de Château Margaux is the second wine.

Gravel. Soil consisting of rounded pebbles and gravel, giving very good drainage. Very suitable for making high-quality red wines and found particularly in the Médoc and Graves areas of Bordeaux.

Green. Said of a wine that is too acidic.

Grenache. Red grape variety grown principally in the Rhône Valley and in some regions of the South such as Banyuls and Languedoc-Roussillon, giving a fruity and very alcoholic wine.

Gris, Vin. Pale rosé wine usually made by direct pressing of red grapes which results in a slightly coloured white wine.

Grolleau. Red grape variety from the Loire Valley used mainly in the production of rosé wines.

Gros Plant. Name given to the Folle Blanche grape variety in the Nantes area of the Loire Valley.

Hard. Said of wine that is too astringent and acid, with too much tannin.

Harmonious. Describes a wine, usually a mature wine, in which the different characteristics are balanced and make a well-rounded whole.

Harshness. A rough, rather biting feeling, caused by far too much tannin.

Heady. Term for a wine that is very high in alcohol and possibly unbalanced.

Heavy. Said of an excessively rich wine.

Heida. White aromatic grape variety grown in some of the highest vineyards of the Valais, Switzerland and thought to be related to the Savagnin of Jura.

Herbaceous. Term (often used pejoratively) for aromas recalling grass or vegetation.

Hogshead. Barrel.

Humagne. Traditional red grape variety giving rustic wines in the Valais, Switzerland. There is also a white Humagne Blanche.

Hybrid. Term for grape varieties created from two different species of vine, as distinct from a grape crossing. Hybrids are rarely grown in France today and may only be used for table wines.

INAO. Institut National des Appellations d'Origine. Public body established to administer AOC and AOVDQS wines and regulate their production conditions.

Jacquère. White grape variety found in Savoie which makes a wine to be drunk fairly young.

Jeroboam. Large bottle holding the equivalent of four bottles (three litres) in Champagne and six bottles (4.5 litres) in Bordeaux.

Johannisberg. Wines made from the Sylvaner grape are named Johannisberg in the Valais canton of Switzerland.

Jurançon. Little-used white grape variety still found in Charente; also a red variety from the South East used to make fairly ordinary wine. It is also the name for a dry or sweet white AOC wine made from the Gros et Petit Manseng and Courbu varieties in South West France around the Jurançon commune.

Lactic acid. Acid obtained during malolactic fermentation (q.v.).

Lees. The natural precipitation of yeast cells and colouring matter that forms as a wine matures in a vat or barrel. When this happens in the bottle, it is called sediment.

Len de l'el. An obscure grape variety grown in the appellation of Gaillac in South West France.

Lie, sur. A white wine may be referred to as having matured *sur lie* when it has been left in vat or barrel in contact with the lees or dead yeast cells and other deposits. This may impart more flavour to the wine and is particularly used in Muscadet in the Loire Valley where the term *sur lie* when used on labels means the wine is subject to certain stringent production rules.

Lieu-dit. Literally means a named place. Usually refers to a small part of a hamlet or village and is widely used in Burgundy to refer to wines coming from a particular small area.

Light. Said of a light-coloured wine with little body, but well-balanced and pleasant. In general, a wine to be drunk fairly young.

Limpid. Said of a clear, brightly coloured wine having no sediment.

Liquoreux. Particularly sweet and rich in sugar, the Vins Liquoreux are made from grapes allowed to develop noble rot and have a generally honeyed bouquet.

Lively. Said of a fresh, light wine, a little bit acid but still pleasant.

Long. Tasting term used when the flavours of a wine make a pleasing and persistent impression in the mouth after tasting; wine is also said to have "length" or "good length".

Macabeu. White grape variety from the Roussillon that makes a pleasant wine to be drunk young.

Maceration. When the must and the grapes' solid matter (skins, pips, etc) are still in contact during fermentation.

Maderised. Said of a white wine which is slightly oxidized, taking on an amber colour while ageing and a taste like madeira.

Magnum. Bottle holding the equivalent of two bottles (1.5 litres).

Malbec. Name given in Bordeaux to the Cot grape variety.

Malic acid. Acid naturally present in all wines and which may be turned into lactic acid by malolactic fermentation.

Malolactic fermentation. The transformation, through the action of lactic bacteria, of malic acid into lactic acid and carbon dioxide. It is considered essential for stability in red wines and is sometimes used for whites. Its effect is partly to make the wine less acid, and for whites to develop a generally softer or creamier character.

Malvoisie. Synonym used in the Valais, Switzerland for the Pinot Gris grape.

Manseng. Gros Manseng and Petit Manseng are two of the white grape varieties used to make Jurançon.

Marc. Solid material left over after pressing; also the popular name of the marc brandy made from it.

Marsanne. White grape variety grown in Hermitage and elsewhere in the Rhône Valley and the South.

Mass selection (of vines). A method of propagating new vines from cuttings in the vineyard. The traditional alternative to clonal selection.

Maturation. The period of time the wine spends between the end of the vinification or winemaking process and it being drunk. Maturation may take place in vats or oak barrels, or later in the bottle. The French word *maturation* refers to the ripening process of the grapes, which in English is simply called ripening.

Mauzac. White grape variety cultivated in southern and South West France, making a fine wine for early drinking; it is also used as the base for sparkling wines.

Melon de Bourgogne. Originally from Burgundy, Melon is a synonym for the white Muscadet grape grown in the Nantes area of the Loire Valley.

Merlot. Main red grape variety in the Pomerol and Saint-Emilion districts of Bordeaux and blended with the Cabernets.

Methuselah. Name used in Champagne for a large bottle equivalent to eight ordinary bottles (six litres). In Bordeaux, this is also called the imperial bottle.

Mildew. Vine disease caused by a parasitic fungus which attacks the stems and leaves.

Millerandange. A condition that causes bunches of grapes to have uneven sizes of berries following poor setting of the fruit. It often follows *coulure*. Not always viewed badly as the condition leads to a reduction in yield that may even improve quality.

Mistelle. Sweet mixture of grape must and alcohol. The fermentation of the must of fresh grapes is stopped by the addition of alcohol. See also "VDN" and "VDL".

Moelleux. Term generally used for medium to sweet white wines.

Mondeuse. Red grape variety from Savoie which makes a high-quality wine for long-term keeping.

Mourvèdre. Red grape variety from Provence and the Rhône Valley producing fine wines which keep very well.

Mousse. Sparkle or fizziness as seen and tasted in champagne and other sparkling wines.

Mousseux. French word for sparkling which can be applied to sparkling wines made using all methods.

Muscadelle. White grape variety from Bordeaux which is blended with Sémillon and Sauvignon.

Muscadet. White grape variety grown in the Loire Valley which makes a very fresh wine generally made to be drunk young.

Muscat. A family of grape varieties which all have a similar grapey or floral aroma. The word is also used for wines made from Muscat grapes.

Musky. Said of a smell that recalls musk.

Must. The sugary juice extracted from grapes.

Musty. Describes a wine that has lost some or all of its bouquet through partial oxidation or other faults.

Mutage. Process of stopping the must's alcoholic fermentation by adding wine-based spirit. Mistelle, Vins de Liqueurs and Vins Doux Naturels are made this way.

Nebuchadnezzar. Giant bottle in Champagne, equivalent to 20 ordinary bottles (15 litres).

Négociant, négociant-éleveur. See "Wine-merchants".

Négrette. Red grape variety in South West France giving a rich, strongly coloured wine with little acidity.

Nervy. Said of a lively wine which leaves pronounced flavours and some acidity on the palate, but not too much.

Niellucciu. Red grape variety planted in Corsica, giving high-quality wines for long-term keeping (particularly Patrimonio).

Noble rot. Name given to the action of the *Botrytis cinerea* on white grapes to make the finest sweet white wines.

Nouveau. Wine from the latest harvest to be drunk young. See also "Primeur".

Oenologist. Trained, professional wine taster or winemaker.

Oenology. The scientific study of wine.

Oïdium. Powdery mildew, a fungal disease of the vine which can attack stalks, leaves or grape bunches and leaves a powdery grey residue which severely affects yields; can be treated with sulphur.

OIV. Office International de la Vigne et du Vin. Based in France, this is the inter-governmental body which supervises technical, scientific and economic matters related to growing vines and making wine.

Old. Term with several applications, usually describing a wine which is several years old and has aged in the bottle after its period in the barrel; but may also be said of a wine that is simply past its best.

Onivins. The French Interprofessional Office for Wines. This body succeeded Onivit in its mission to direct and regulate the wine market.

Organoleptic. Describes the qualities and properties noted by the senses during wine tasting, e.g. colour, smell or taste.

Ouvrée. Measurement of land area. 23 ouvrées = 1 hectare.

Oxidation. The action of oxygen (air) on wine. If there is too much, the colour fades and both the smell and taste of the wine are affected.

Pasteurization. Heat-sterilizing process perfected by Louis Pasteur.

Pêche de vigne. Small, fairly sour peach used mainly in cooking and traditionally found in vineyards. The aroma of certain white wines are likened to that of *pêche de vigne*.

Persistence. Length of time that the flavours of a wine remain in the mouth after swallowing. Good persistence, or length, is a positive sign.

Pétillant. A Vin Pétillant is a lightly sparkling wine, less fizzy than Vin Mousseux.

Petite Arvine. Traditional white grape variety grown in the Valais, Switzerland and producing wines of high quality.

Petit Verdot. In the Médoc district of Bordeaux, a minor red grape variety which may be blended in small quantities with the Cabernets and Merlot.

Phylloxera. Plant louse which between 1860 and 1890 ravaged French vineyards by eating vine roots and thus killing the vines. It is controlled today by grafting vines onto phylloxera-resistant rootstocks. See also "Grafting".

Pineau d'Aunis. Minor red grape variety grown in some regions of the Loire Valley and producing a pale-coloured wine.

Pinot Blanc. White grape variety grown mainly in Alsace.

Pinot Gris. High-quality white grape variety grown mainly in Alsace, where it used to be known as Tokay.

Pinot Meunier. Red grape variety which is mainly used in Champagne as part of the blend. It is a hardier and earlier-ripening grape than Pinot Noir, to which it is related.

Pinot Noir. The main red grape variety in Burgundy, where it gives wines with immediate fruitiness which nevertheless keep well. It is also an important part of the blend for champagne, where it is pressed quickly so as not to extract colour. It is the only permitted red grape in Alsace, and small quantities are grown in the South.

Piquant. Said of a wine with a sharp, acid taste.

Poulsard. Red grape variety grown mainly in the Jura and producing pale-coloured wines sold as rosé or red.

Powerful. Said of a wine which combines a full body with generosity and a rich bouquet.

Premier Cru. Literally First Growth, usually left untranslated. In Burgundy it refers to the second best category in the AOC classification systems. Vineyards may be classified as Premier Cru (also in Champagne) and the wine made from grapes harvested in those vineyards may subsequently be called Premier Cru. In Bordeaux the term may be used for certain châteaux that are classified as Premier Cru Classés.

Pressing. Process of pressing the grapes to extract juice or wine, leaving the skins and other solid matter behind.

Pricked. Property of a wine suffering from acescency, which gives it a sour, vinegary smell.

Primeur. A Vin de Primeur is from the latest harvest and is made to be drunk very young. See also "Nouveau".

Racking. Process of transferring a wine from one barrel or vat to another to separate it from the lees or sediment.

Rancio. Originally Spanish, this tasting term is applied to some wines, especially VDN, which, when they age, may take on a vaguely nutty, almost maderized character.

Rasping. Said of a rough, astringent wine.

Ratafia. Vin de Liqueur made in Champagne by mixing grape spirit and fermenting must.

Remuage. Riddling. During the secondary fermentation in the bottle in the Traditional (Champagne) method, this is the shaking and turning process by which the remaining sediment is brought down to rest on the cork so that it can be disgorged. Formerly done by hand, it can now be done mechanically with rotating pallets.

Rich. Said of a well-balanced, generous, powerful wine with good colour.

Riesling. White grape variety grown in Alsace and making wines of great distinction.

Rimage. Term used in some areas, especially Banyuls and Beaujolais to denote a higher quality selection of wine.

Roasted. Characteristic taste and aromas of crystallized fruits in sweet wines made from grapes affected by noble rot. Also refers to red wines made from grapes that have been literally "roasted" by the sun.

Robust. Said of a wine having body.

Rolle. White grape variety from Provence which makes very fine wines.

Romorantin. Rare white grape variety grown in some parts of the Loire Valley.

Rootstock. The part of the vine that is not visible, i.e. which is below ground. Most European grape varieties are grafted onto American rootstocks, since these are resistant to phylloxera.

Rough. Describes a very astringent, rasping wine.

Round, rounded. Said of a supple, ripe and fleshy wine which leaves a pleasant, harmonious feeling in the mouth.

Roussanne. White grape variety grown mainly in the northern Rhône Valley, a little in the southern Rhône and in small quantities in Savoie, giving a very fine wine for long-term keeping.

Saignée, Rosé de. Rosé wine run off the skins of red grapes after a very short maceration period.

Salmanazar. Very large bottle in Champagne containing the equivalent of 12 ordinary bottles (nine litres).

Sauvignon. White grape variety grown in many regions, but especially in the Loire Valley and Bordeaux, and making a fine wine which keeps well and has a characteristic smoky aroma.

Savagnin. Grape variety from the Jura giving the famous Vin Jaune or yellow wine and making up part of the blend for other Jura white wines. It may be related to the Klevner and Gewurztraminer from Alsace.

Scent. Another word for smell, indicating something scented or perfumed, or delicately aromatic.

Sciacarellu. Red grape variety grown in Corsica and giving a fleshy, fruity wine.

Sediment. Solid particles held in suspension in must or wine.

Sélection de Grains Nobles. Term used traditionally in Alsace, but increasingly adopted elsewhere for a wine made from grapes affected by noble rot or *botrytis cinerea*.

Sémillon. Noble white grape variety grown mainly in Bordeaux and making sweet wines such as Sauternes as well as fine dry wines.

Sensory analysis. Technical term for wine tasting.

Short. Said of a wine having little length in the mouth after tasting; "short in the mouth" is also used.

Silky. Said of a supple, mellow, velvety, pleasantly harmonious and elegant wine.

Smoky. Term for a smell like that of smoked foods, characteristic of, among others, the Sauvignon grape variety (hence the name Blanc Fumé or "smoky white").

Smooth. A smooth or supple, pleasant wine, easy to drink and which "slips down well".

Solid. Said of a well-constituted, well-structured wine.

Sour. Having a highly acid character, accompanied by a smell very like that of vinegar.

Sparkling. Term for wines that have dissolved carbon dioxide, usually the result of a second fermentation.

Stabilization. All the processes, such as filtration and fining, used before bottling to ensure a wine is kept in good condition. Especially refers to the process of removing tartaric acid crystals before bottling.

Stale. A wine that has lost some or all of its bouquet, usually through oxidation.

Stemming. Alternative term sometimes used for de-stemming (q.v.).

Still wine. Non-sparkling wine.

Straightforward. Said of a frank wine with a well-defined character.

Structure. Describes the general form and constitution of a wine, especially its acidity and tannin.

Substantial. Said of a wine that has a strong colour and in the mouth feels rather heavy and thick.

Sulphur. A sulphur solution may be added to must or wine to protect it from faults such as oxidation, or, at the point of fermentation, to kill off certain unwanted yeast strains. Sulphuring refers to the treatment of the vine by spraying with copper sulphate, to prevent fungal diseases.

Supple. A smooth wine, its mellowness prevailing over its astringency.

Sylvaner. White grape variety from Alsace which generally makes straightforward wine for early drinking.

Syrah. High-quality red grape variety mainly planted in the Rhône Valley and Languedoc-Roussillon.

Tannat. Red grape variety grown in the South West and producing very well-structured fine wines which keep well.

Tannic. A rough, astringent sensation in a wine caused by tannin.

Tannin. Substance found in grape skins, pips and stems which helps wine to keep for a long time and forms part of its structure. Particularly noticeable in young reds.

Tartrates. Tartaric crystals that form in the cask, vat or bottle if the wine has been subjected to intense cold.

Tastevinage. Seal awarded by the Confrérie des Chevaliers du Tastevin to certain Burgundy wines.

Tears. Term for the traces of wine on the glass, sometimes also called "legs".

Temperature regulation. Technique for checking and adjusting the temperature in the vat during fermentation and storage.

Terroir. A place where wine is grown. Each terroir has its own physical characteristics (soil, subsoil, exposure, etc) which influence the kind and quality of the wine produced there. See also "*Goût de terroir*".

Thermovinification. A method of fermentation employing heat, used mainly for red wines. It may result in soft, fruity, early-drinking red wines.

Tired. Term for a wine that has lost some of its quality. This may be temporary (for example after being transported) and it may just need time to recover.

Tokay. Term used in Alsace for wines made from the Pinot Gris grape variety. Because of the confusion with Hungarian Tokay, to which it is not related, the EU now forbids its use on labels without the additional reference to Pinot Gris, as in Tokay Pinot Gris. However, in the region the wines are often referred to simply as Tokay.

Topping up. Process of adding wine to the barrel to keep it full and prevent the wine from coming into contact with air.

Traditional method. Method of making sparkling wines which includes a secondary fermentation in the bottle, as is done for champagne. Identical to the "Champagne method".

Trousseau. Red grape variety from the Jura, producing wine with a darker colour than the Poulsard or Pinot Noir.

Ugni Blanc. White grape variety grown in the South (and in Charente to make Cognac under the name of Saint-Emilion) and giving a fairly acid wine which does not keep well.

Ullage. Space left at the top of a closed bottle. If there is too much ullage, the wine will oxidise. Also refers to the space left in the top of a barrel. See also "Topping up".

Unctuous. Said of a wine that is pleasantly mellow, fleshy and full-bodied in the mouth.

VDL. Vin de Liqueur. A sweet wine made by mixing must and alcohol (e.g. Pineau des Charentes). These sweet wines do not conform to the legal norms for the VDNs.

VDN. Vin Doux Naturel. A sweet wine made from Muscat, Grenache, Macabeu or Malvoisie grapes. The wine is obtained by stopping the fermentation of the must with the addition of grape spirit, in line with strict conditions about the wine's sweetness and how it is made.

VDP. Vin de Pays. A wine legally belonging to the table wines group, ie below that of AOC and AOVDQS wines, but which carries a mention on the label of the geographical region it comes from. Some VDP may be of high quality.

VDQS. Now AOVDQS: Appellation d'Origine Vin Délimité de Qualité Supérieure. The regional wines in this group are made according to strict regulations.

Vegetal. Said of the bouquet or aromas of a wine (generally a young one), which recall grasses or vegetation.

Véraison. The period in the vine's growth cycle when colour changes in the grapes and they start to soften, marking the beginning of the ripening period.

Vermentino. White grape variety grown particularly in Corsica where it is known sometimes as Malvoisie. It may be the same as Rolle in Provence.

Vigneron. Loose term that may refer to a person who simply owns and/or farms a vineyard, or to a producer, who also makes the wine from the grapes of his own vineyard. May be translated as wine-grower.

Village. As well as the normal usage of the word, this term may be used in Burgundy to denote a wine that has the simple *village* appellation rather than the grander Premier or Grand Cru appellation e.g. Volnay as opposed to Volnay Premier Cru.

Villages. Term used in some regions to single out a superior area within a larger appellation (Beaujolais, Côtes du Rhône, Mâcon).

Vin de glace. Term used in Luxembourg for very sweet "ice wine" produced from frozen grapes harvested in early winter after the first heavy frost.

Vin de Paille. Term used mainly in Jura for sweet wine made from grapes that have been harvested and then left for several months to dry and for the natural sugars and flavours to concentrate. Traditionally the grapes were laid out on straw (*paille*), but today they are often simply left in wooden crates or suspended from the rafters in a well-ventilated room.

Vin de Table. Table wine. The lowest quality category in the hierarchy of French wines. The designation is not regionally specific, beyond the country of production. Labels for Vin de Table may not state any geographic reference (apart from country), nor a grape variety, method of production or vintage. The term may also be used in a looser, derogatory way to describe a wine of low quality.

Vin de Terroir. A wine that shows clearly the *terroir* that it comes from.

Vin Jaune. Unusual "yellow wine" produced in Jura from the Savagnin variety. The wine is stored for over six years in old oak casks that are not topped up. A "*voile*" or film of yeast forms on the surface protecting the wine from extreme oxidation and imparting a special flavour.

Vinous. Said of a wine fairly rich in alcohol which seems to sum up neatly the differences between wine and other alcoholic drinks.

Vintage. The year in which the wine was harvested.

Viognier. White grape variety grown in the Rhône Valley and the South and producing a fine, high-quality wine.

Virile. Said of a well-structured, full-bodied and powerful wine.

Voile, sous. Literally "beneath a veil". Refers to the ageing of Vin Jaune in the Jura.

VQPRD. Vin de Qualité Produit dans une Région Déterminée. This category includes the French AOC and VDQS wines and sets them apart from the table wines category in the European Union.

Warming. Said of a wine conveying an impression of warmth, usually because of its alcoholic strength.

Well structured. Said of a well-constituted wine with plenty of acidity and tannin that will probably age well.

Wine-merchants. In the French wine business, there are straightforward wine-merchants and shippers (négociants), but also others (*négociants éleveurs*) who, especially in the big appellation regions, not only buy and sell wine but take over the maturation of young wine and see it through every stage up to bottling. In Champagne, the *négociant-manipulateur* buys grapes to make his own champagne wine.

Yeasts. Microscopic single-celled organisms which convert sugar to alcohol during fermentation.

Young. Very relative term, used for a wine in its first year as well as for the taste of an older wine that has not yet developed to its full potential.

963

INDEX OF APPELLATIONS

APPELLATIONS

965   INDEX OF APPELLATIONS

INDEX OF COMMUNES

968

INDEX OF COMMUNES

COMMUNES

COMMUNES

971

INDEX OF PRODUCERS

INDEX OF PRODUCERS

978

INDEX OF PRODUCERS

980

986

990

992

INDEX OF WINES

996

1002

INDEX OF WINES

WINES

1008

INDEX OF WINES

DOM. DE LA **REALTIERE**, 663
MICHEL **REBOURGEON**, 459, 463
DOM. **REBOURGEON-MURE**, 459, 463
DOM. HENRI **REBOURSEAU**, 404-405, 409, 420
CH. **RECOUGNE**, 187
CUVEE DU **REDEMPTEUR**, 554
PASCAL **REDON**, 554
CH. **REDORTIER**, 872
DOM. DU **REGAIN**, 724, 745, 747, 762
A. **REGIN**, 99
REGNARD, 381, 393
JEAN-CLAUDE **REGNAUDOT ET FILS**, 484, 487
LOUIS **REGNIER**, 554
DOM. DE **REGUSSE**, 944
CH. **REILLANNE**, 650
LA CAVE DE LA **REINE JEANNE**, 573, 918
REINE PEDAUQUE, 462
VIGNOBLES **REINHART**, 105
PAUL **REITZ**, 485, 488
DOM. DES **RELAGNES**, 845, 880
CH. **RELEOU**, 181
CH. LES **RELIGIEUSES**, 253
DOM. LA **REMEJEANNE**, 845
DOM. DES **REMIZIERES**, 866, 868
HENRI ET GILLES **REMORIQUET**, 371, 430
DOM. DU **REMPART**, 224
DOM. DES **REMPARTS**, 394
BERNARD **REMY**, 554
DOM. LOUIS **REMY**, 412
ROGER ET JOEL **REMY**, 361, 450, 454
REMY-BREQUE, 199
CUVEE **RENAISSANCE**, 257, 262
DOM. JACKY **RENARD**, 394
JACKY **RENARD**, 361
CH. **RENARD MONDESIR**, 219
DOM. DE LA **RENARDE**, 493
DOM. DE LA **RENARDIERE**, 574, 919
LA CAVE DES **RENARDS**, 99
DOM. PASCAL ET MIREILLE **RENAUD**, 505
DOM. VALERY **RENAUDAT**, 827
VALERY **RENAUDAT**, 828
DOM. DE LA **RENAUDIE**, 778
R. **RENAUDIN**, 566
RAYMOND **RENCK**, 125
DOM. **RENGOUER**, 701
DOM. DE LA **RENJARDE**, 856
CH. LA **RENJARDIERE**, 845
DOM. RENE **RENOU**, 764
DOM. DE LA **RENOUERE**, 735
EDMOND **RENTZ**, 99
DOM. **RENUCCI**, 670
JEAN-MARIE **RENVOISE**, 798
CH. **REPIMPLET**, 211
RESERVE DU PRESIDENT, 670
CH. DE **RESPIDE**, 287
CH. **RESPIDE-MEDEVILLE**, 288
CH. LA **RESSAUDIE**, 715
CH. DU **RETOUT**, 314
DOM. DE **REUILLY**, 828
DOM. DU **REVAOU**, 650
CH. **REVELETTE**, 664
XAVIER **REVERCHON**, 580
CH. **REVERDI**, 319
DOM. HIPPOLYTE **REVERDY**, 832
PASCAL ET NICOLAS **REVERDY**, 832
ROGER **REVERDY CADET ET FILS**, 832

DOM. BERNARD **REVERDY ET FILS**, 832
JEAN **REVERDY ET FILS**, 835
DOM. **REVERDY-DUCROUX**, 832
CH. DE **REY**, 634
MICHEL **REY**, 159, 510
REYNAC, 913
DOM. DE LA **REYNARDIERE**, 618
CH. LA **REYNE**, 680
CH. **REYNIER**, 181, 273
DOM. **REYNON**, 279
CH. LE **REYSSE**, 304
CH. **REYSSON**, 314
DOM. DE **RIAUX**, 825
CAVE VINICOLE DE **RIBEAUVILLE**, 125
DOM. DE **RIBONNET**, 930
DOM. DE LA **RIBOTTE**, 660
CH. LES **RICARD**, 204
CH. **RICARDELLE**, 613
DOM. DE **RICAUD**, 271
DOM. **RICHARD**, 861
DOM. HENRI **RICHARD**, 404, 407
DOM. **RICHEAUME**, 655
BERNARD ET CHRISTOPHE **RICHEL**, 585
DOM. **RICHOU**, 745, 750, 755
THIERRY **RICHOUX**, 394
RIEFFEL, 85
LUCAS ET ANDRE **RIEFFEL**, 129
RIEFLE, 99
DOM. **RIERE CADENE**, 634
PIERRE ET JEAN-PIERRE **RIETSCH**, 129
DOM. DU **RIEU FRAIS**, 953
CH. **RIEUSSEC**, 348
DOM. RENE **RIEUX**, 686
CLAUDE **RIFFAULT**, 832
DOM. **RIGAUD**, 262
DOM. **RIGOT**, 845
DOM. **RIGOUTAT**, 361
RIJCKAERT, 374, 507
JEAN **RIJCKAERT**, 505
RIMAURESQ, 650
CH. LE **RIMENSAC**, 205
DOM. DU **RIN DU BOIS**, 778
ARMELLE ET BERNARD **RION**, 361, 416, 420
DOM. MICHELE ET PATRICE **RION**, 361, 367
PATRICE **RION**, 417
DOM. DANIEL **RION ET FILS**, 425, 430, 433
DOM. DES **RIOTS**, 501
DOM. DE **RIS**, 778
CH. LA **RIVALERIE**, 189, 205
CH. DE **RIVEREAU**, 213
CH. DE LA **RIVIERE**, 218
CH. LA **RIVIERE**, 348
CH. **ROBERPEROTS**, 275
ROBERT, 593
ANDRE **ROBERT**, 555
VIGNOBLE ALAIN **ROBERT ET FILS**, 804
CH. LA **ROBERTIE**, 710
CH. **ROBIN**, 266
LOUIS ET CLAUDE **ROBIN**, 764
THIERRY ET CECILE **ROBIN**, 168
DOM. JEAN-LOUIS **ROBIN-DIOT**, 749, 763
MICHEL **ROBINEAU**, 749
MICHEL **ROBINEAU**, 926
VIGNOBLE MICHEL **ROBINEAU**, 762
DOM. **ROBINEAU CHRISLOU**, 745, 752
VIGNOBLE DES **ROBINIERES**, 786
CH. DU **ROC**, 598

DOM. DU **ROC**, 622
CH. **ROC DE BOISSAC**, 262
CH. **ROC DE BOISSEAUX**, 254
CH. **ROC DE CALON**, 259
CH. **ROC DE JOANIN**, 267
DOM. **ROC DE L'OLIVET**, 885
CH. **ROC DE TIFAYNE**, 268
CH. **ROC PLANTIER**, 213
ROCALHAN, 613
DOM. LA **ROCALIERE**, 883
DOM. DE **ROCFONTAINE**, 773
DOM. DE **ROCHAMBEAU**, 726
DOM. DE **ROCHANVIGNE**, 926
CH. DE LA **ROCHE**, 778, 782
DOM. DE LA **ROCHE**, 146
DOM. DE LA **ROCHE AIGUE**, 467, 469
AMAVINUM DU CH. LA **ROCHE BEAULIEU**, 266
CH. DE LA **ROCHE BOUSSEAU**, 745
DOM. DE LA **ROCHE FLEURIE**, 804
DOM. DE LA **ROCHE HONNEUR**, 794
DOM. DE LA **ROCHE MAROT**, 715
DOM. DE LA **ROCHE MERE**, 164
DOM. DE LA **ROCHE MOREAU**, 762, 765
DOM. DE LA **ROCHE PILEE**, 161
CH. LA **ROCHE SAINT JEAN**, 181
DOM. DE **ROCHE SAINT JEAN**, 161
DOM. DE LA **ROCHE SAINT MARTIN**, 148
DOM. **ROCHE-AUDRAN**, 845
CH. **ROCHEBELLE**, 254
DOM DE **ROCHEBONNE**, 142
DOM. DE **ROCHEBRUNE**, 146
CH. **ROCHECOLOMBE**, 845
CAVE DES VIGNERONS DE **ROCHEGUDE**, 845
DOM. DE **ROCHE-GUILLON**, 156
DOM. DE LA **ROCHELIERRE**, 620
DOM. DE LA **ROCHELLE**, 165
DOM. DES **ROCHELLES**, 750
DOM. DE **ROCHEMOND**, 845
CH. DE **ROCHEMORIN**, 296
DOM. DE LA **ROCHEPINAL**, 800
CH. LA **ROCHE-PRESSAC**, 266
CH. **ROCHER CORBIN**, 259
CH. **ROCHER-BONREGARD**, 226
DOM. DE LA **ROCHERIE**, 738, 926
CH. DES **ROCHERS**, 256, 266
CH. DES **ROCHES**, 680
DOM. **ROCHES BLANCHES**, 266
LES **ROCHES BLEUES**, 149
CH. LES **ROCHES DE FERRAND**, 218
DOM. LES **ROCHES DES GARANTS**, 155
DOM. DES **ROCHES DU PY**, 162
DOM. DES **ROCHES FORTES**, 846
DOM. DES **ROCHES NEUVES**, 773
CUVEE **ROCHES NOIRES**, 627
DOM. DE LA **ROCHETTE**, 778, 819

DOM. JOEL **ROCHETTE**, 167
CH. DES **ROCHETTES**, 745
DOM. DU **ROCHOUARD**, 786, 789
CH. LES **ROCQUES**, 211
ANTONIN **RODET**, 420, 430
ERIC **RODEZ**, 555
LOUIS **ROEDERER**, 555
DOMINIQUE **ROGER**, 833
ROGGE CERESER, 555
LA CAVE DU **ROI DAGOBERT**, 112
CH. **ROL VALENTIN**, 247
CH. **ROLAND LA GARDE**, 205
DOM. **ROLET**, 919
DOM. **ROLET PERE ET FILS**, 573, 580
CH. **ROLLAN DE BY**, 304
DOM. **ROLLAND**, 151
DOM. DE **ROLLAND**, 620
CH. **ROLLAND-MAILLET**, 247
WILLY **ROLLI-EDEL**, 99, 105
DOM. **ROLLIN PERE ET FILS**, 440
ROLLY GASSMANN, 106
DOM. DE LA **ROMANEE-CONTI**, 421-422, 426-427, 476
DOM. **ROMANESCA**, 165
CH. **ROMANIN**, 664
DOM. DES **ROMARINS**, 848
CH. **ROMBEAU**, 635
DOM. DE **ROMBEAU**, 905
CH. **ROMER DU HAYOT**, 348
CH. **ROMFORT**, 205
CH. DE **ROMILHAC**, 598
ERIC **ROMINGER**, 128
DOM. DU **RONCEE**, 794
DOM. **RONSARD**, 806
CH. DES **RONTETS**, 510
DOM. DE LA **RONZE**, 167
DOM. DES **RONZE**, 162
ROPITEAU FRERES, 481
LA **ROQUE**, 659
ROQUE D'AGNEL, 598
CH. **ROQUE LE MAYNE**, 266
ROQUE SESTIERE, 598
CH. **ROQUEBERT**, 279
CH. **ROQUEFORT**, 181
LES VIGNERONS DE **ROQUEFORT LA BEDOULE**, 650
DOM. DE **ROQUEMALE**, 613
CH. **ROQUE-PEYRE**, 706
CH. LES **ROQUES**, 342
CH. **ROQUETAILLADE LA GRANGE**, 288
CUVEE **ROSARIO**, 234
CH. LA **ROSE BELLEVUE**, 207
LA **ROSE BOISSIERE**, 195
CH. LA **ROSE COTES ROL**, 254
DOM. LA **ROSE DES VENTS**, 666
CH. LA **ROSE DU PIN**, 181
CH. LA **ROSE FIGEAC**, 226
LA **ROSE PAUILLAC**, 332

WINES

1016

WINES

1017

NOTES